The Peruvian Experiment Reconsidered

The Peruvian Experiment
Reconsidered

---

edited by Cynthia McClintock and
Abraham F. Lowenthal

Princeton University Press
Princeton, New Jersey

Copyright © 1983 by Princeton University Press
Published by Princeton University Press,
41 William Street, Princeton, New Jersey
In the United Kingdom: Princeton University Press,
Guildford, Surrey

All Rights Reserved
Library of Congress Cataloging in Publication Data will be
found on the last printed page of this book

This book has been composed in CRT Baskerville
Clothbound editions of Princeton University Press books
are printed on acid-free paper, and binding materials are
chosen for strength and durability.
Paperbacks, although satisfactory for personal collections,
are not usually suitable for library rebinding.

Printed in the United States of America by Princeton
University Press, Princeton, New Jersey

To All the Peruvian Experiments

Contents

List of Tables

Appendices to Chapter 5

Preface

On October 3, 1968, units of the Peruvian armed forces surrounded Lima's National Palace, hustled President Fernando Belaúnde Terry to the airport (and exile), and proclaimed the formation of a "Revolutionary Government of the Armed Forces." The new government, headed by General Juan Velasco Alvarado—then Peru's top-ranking general—immediately announced a series of ambitious goals. Through various statements, the new government declared its aims to transform Peru's basic economic and social structures; to end external dependence, especially on the United States; to force foreign investors to be more responsive to Peru's needs; to seek a third path to development that was "neither capitalist nor communist" through such innovative measures as worker-managed enterprises; and even to alter national values in order to create a "new Peruvian man," one dedicated to "solidarity not individualism."

Skeptics who considered the Peruvian military's earnest rhetoric as just another empty *pronunciamiento* were soon severely jolted. Within a week, Peru had expropriated the International Petroleum Company, an Exxon subsidiary long prominent in the country's politics. Within less than a year, the regime had decreed a sweeping agrarian reform and had begun its implementation of the reform dramatically by seizing the rich coastal sugar estates.

With a burst of laws and regulations, the Peruvian military undertook to reform production and distribution, labor-management relations, the role of foreign enterprise in Peru's economy, the state's role in the economy and the media, and the nation's international relationships. An "industrial community" was created in privately owned firms, a reform that gave workers an increased stake in corporate profits and a say in management. It was announced that a new "special property" sector of worker-managed firms would become the predominant mode of economic organization. An ambitious educational reform was designed to attack class and ethnic divisions in a country where more than half the population in six highland provinces still did not speak Spanish when the 1961 census was taken.

The educational reform and the state-controlled media were to promote the country's new social values: cooperation, not competition; social conscience, not selfishness; and renewed national pride. With full fanfare, the military government launched a new agency—the National System to Support Social Mobilization (SINAMOS)—to mobilize the previously nonparticipatory sectors of Peru's fragmented society, to raise popular consciousness, and to channel the resulting energies into the national political process. Various other institutions—in the rural areas, in urban shantytowns, in the labor movement—were organized, avowedly to spur social transformation. And Peru became a major participant in various international fora, taking a leading role particularly on new international economic order issues. All in all, Peru's experiment seemed to many (including us co-editors) in the early 1970s an auspicious effort to break Peru's cycle of underdevelopment. Political leaders from Fidel Castro to Juan Perón praised the Peruvian undertaking, military officers in several other countries followed it closely, and scholars swooped down on Peru to chronicle its attempt.

By 1980, perspectives on the Peruvian experiment had changed remarkably. On May 18, 1980—just twelve and a half years after the military coup—over 5 million Peruvians went to the polls, for the first time since 1963, to choose from among fifteen candidates for Peru's presidency. An overwhelming 45.4 percent supported the return to power of former president Belaúnde, enough to elect him without a run-off in Congress.

By returning President Belaúnde to the National Palace so decisively, the Peruvian electorate wrote an eloquent epitaph to the "Peruvian experiment." The electorate's support also for APRA (historically the army's enemy), for rightist Luis Bedoya Reyes, and for a motley assortment of far-left parties reflected how widespread was the public repudiation of Peru's military government. Only two parties—the Unidad de Izquierda (UI), headed by General Leonidas Rodríguez Figueroa, and the Organización Política de la Revolución (OPRP), led by General Javier Tantaleán—were linked to the military government's program; together they obtained less than 5 percent of the vote. Peru's population—from all regions of the country, all sectors, and all classes—had repudiated the military regime.

The Peruvian experiment did not really end in 1980 by electoral mandate and the triumphant return of Belaúnde, however; it ended back in August 1975 when General Velasco was ousted by General Francisco Morales Bermúdez. Velasco had been unable to sustain support for his programs from either military officers or civilian groups. Although in 1975 Morales and his colleagues in khaki verbally emphasized the continuity of the military regime's program, in practice, "Phase Two" of the Peruvian experiment under Morales saw a systematic dismantling of many reforms of the Velasco era.

Did the Peruvian revolution thus "fail"? Most of us contributing to this volume agree that, if the revolution's performance is measured by its goals, it did. Having sought to end external dependence, Peru found itself so deeply in debt in the late 1970s that the International Monetary Fund became the country's principal economic policy maker. For most Peruvians, the government's proclaimed goal of a "fully participatory social democracy" seemed largely rhetorical. Among the regime's programs, only the agrarian reform and the expansion of the state's economic role endured into 1980. Even the innovative property and management reforms in the industrial sector did not survive.

To conclude that the Peruvian Revolution was a total failure, however, would be too broad and sweeping a judgment, as Abraham Lowenthal emphasizes in greater detail in the final chapter. Perhaps the revolution should be assessed not by the standards it set for itself but by what most Latin American revolutions have achieved. The concluding chapters by Susan Eckstein and John Sheahan point out that these other revolutions did not fare so well either. Examining land reform, health care, nutrition, and income distribution as measures of social welfare, Eckstein finds that improvements in social welfare were limited not only in Peru's "revolution from above" but also in the "revolutions from below" in Mexico, Bolivia, and Cuba. She suggests that the redistributive capacity of all the revolutions was limited by the weak and peripheral position of these (and most) Third World countries in the capitalist world economy. John Sheahan compares economic strategies in Velasco's Peru to those in other "populist-reformist" regimes in Latin America, particularly Perón's Argentina and Allende's Chile, and perceives very similar economic errors in the strategies of all three governments.

Moreover, it may still be too early to draw general conclusions of "failure." As Julio Cotler and Luis Pásara emphasize, the military's reform measures dramatically increased political awareness in Peru—even if, as these authors believe, the military did not intend this result. Although Belaúnde, more or less a centrist in the political spectrum, won at the polls in 1980, leftist parties did much better than in the 1960s. The long-term consequences in the growth of support for the left are still impossible to foresee. Further, although most of the military's programs were scuttled, its agrarian reform and its expansion of the state role in the economy endured the second phase under Morales, and it is not yet clear whether or not Belaúnde will, or can, dismantle these reforms completely. The changes in land tenure and in state economic power, perhaps the most important reforms of the Velasco government, set in motion political and economic dynamics with long-term consequences that also cannot yet be fully discerned.

The central question for most authors in the volume, however, is why Peru's revolution did not achieve more. Were the problems beyond any government's control? Or were there relatively clear paths to the government's "third way" goals that it did not take? The authors in this volume provide many different answers to these questions.

The book begins with the pessimistic perspective of Julio Cotler, who believes that the centuries-old abyss between state and citizen in Peru makes it very difficult for any government—either the pre-1968 oligarchical regimes, the Velasco government, or the current Belaúnde administration—to legitimize a dominant order and institutionalize popular participation. Social contradictions are now extremely severe, in Cotler's view. Dramatic redistributive programs are necessary, but the potential for such programs is limited as Peru is integrated into the new model of capitalist accumulation on a world scale at a time of world economic crisis.

More optimistic are two of the contributions by economists, the chapter by Daniel Schydlowsky and Juan Wicht and the chapter by John Sheahan. Schydlowsky and Wicht are confident of the economic and social advantages of export-based growth *in industry* (in contrast to the conventional Latin American approach of the primary sector as the key export sector, with industry developing primarily through an import substitution policy). They focus upon the full utilization of already existing capital as a key means to a more competitive industry with a greater employment potential and contend that promotion of industrial exports could have been a viable strategy for the achievement of growth with equity.

Comparing economic strategies in Velasco's Peru, Perón's Argentina, and Allende's Chile, Sheahan concludes that some "paths not taken" were available for these governments. Both egalitarian reform and economic growth could have been attained, Sheahan believes, if the government had turned from the unsuccessful policy packages of the past, which neglected market criteria. Market criteria apparently seemed immoral to Latin America's populist-reformist regimes because they are based on selfish, individual choices rather than social goals. Sheahan hopes that in the future market criteria will be perceived as potential policy instruments for the enhancement of social justice. He recommends effective taxation, restraint on urban consumption of industrial products, and (along with Schydlowsky and Wicht) industrial export promotion.

Rosemary Thorp and E.V.K. FitzGerald, also economists, believe that the economic difficulties facing Peru in 1968 were more serious and the solutions more difficult than Schydlowsky and Wicht or Sheahan suggest but also believe that some (at least partial) ways out were possible. Thorp highlights the mounting economic vicissitudes facing Peru in the 1960s as the supply of traditional agricultural exports declined in an economy that had always been based on traditional exports (and also long suffered from a traditional "boom and bust" export cycle). To overcome this crisis, Peru required "a sophisticated dynamic local entrepreneurial group and a competent experienced state," in Thorp's words, "yet precisely because of the historical process leading to 1968, neither existed." Thorp sees a growth in technical expertise by the end of the military government, yet also an economy that remains perilously dependent on traditional exports.

Like Thorp, FitzGerald perceives a serious economic crisis in Peru by 1968 and an attempted solution via a new governmental role in the ownership and promotion of industry. FitzGerald believes that the initiatives of the Velasco government were sufficiently coherent and purposeful to constitute a "state capitalist" model of development in the country. In his view, state capitalism is the only known route to development for smaller, late-developing nations without strong entrepreneurial groups, except further penetration by multinational corporations or socialist transition. It had a reasonable chance to work in Velasco's Peru but did not. The approach was undermined primarily by the regime's failure to gain access to profits in the economy, its neglect of the capital needs of agriculture, and its failure to rationalize the use of foreign exchange.

Were international economic contraints also important to the failure of the military's economic policies? Barbara Stallings believes that external opposition was not significant. She contends that the government's policies were in fact favorable to foreign capital, at least over the long run, and that the reaction of foreign capital was not particularly hostile, expecially if this reaction is contrasted to the pressures imposed upon neighboring Chile during the Allende government. Stallings emphasizes the willingness of international banks to loan to Peru.

Laura Guasti disagrees. She argues that international corporations, particularly extractive enterprises (mining and petroleum) and manufacturing enterprises, responded to the military's policies by abandoning the country. As a result, the government unexpectedly had to assume a vastly expanded entrepreneurial role in the key mining/petroleum sector. The new role was very costly, requiring additional funds to compensate the firms and to increase production. Further, as manufacturing firms declined to invest, the Velasco government also had to borrow to maintain industrial investment. Guasti concludes that Peru, like other Third World nations, cannot successfully challenge international corporate interests and seek industrialization based on capital-intensive advanced techlology at the same time.

Part Three of the volume turns to the political character and strategy of the military government. Why did it appear so "strong"—rapidly initiating an array of reforms—only to ultimately fail to institutionalize most of these reforms? How important was the military character of the regime to both its successes and failures? Was the military united behind a clear reform plan, or not—and did the degree of unit and clarity vary over time?

The chapters by Peter Cleaves and Henry Pease García and by Cynthia McClintock highlight certain political resources of the military government, and suggest that the government's limitations were related to the dilemmas of reform processes in Latin America more than to the military character of the regime. Cleaves and Pease García believe that, due to the disarray of the Peruvian elite and the cohesion of the military in 1968, the Velasco government enjoyed relatively high autonomy from social forces between 1968 and 1972. Thus, the government was able to implement significant reforms sounding the death knell to "oligarchical" social groups—the agricultural exporters, traditional highlands landowners, and traditional bankers. By 1973, however, the most dynamic sectors of Peru's dominant class had regrouped; they began to challenge the government. The regime's autonomy was gradually reduced as these sectors took advantage of the military's inherent anticommunism and the increasing heterogeneity of political positions within the armed forces. McClintock highlights serious dilemmas of reform-mongering that she believes confront military and civilian regimes alike. She points to a Catch-22 for reform-mongering governments: success for the reform programs seems to require stealthy, closed tactics that confuse the opposition; but these same tactics confuse and alienate other citizens, too. McClintock examines the Velasco government's agrarian, industrial, and participation policies to illustrate the tension between carrying out reforms and gaining popular support.

In contrast to Cleaves and Pease and McClintock, Luis Pásara believes that the military character of the regime was a key element in its breakdown and that the chances for almost any political successes by a regime such as Velasco's were slim indeed. Petty bourgeois as well as military in nature, the regime's program was "utopian and conciliatory, authoritarian and arbitrary, and could not be taken by anyone as his own." The regime's political strategies were its selective use of concession and repression mechanisms and its attempt to "enclose" or "co-opt" citizens in government organizations. Such a "plan" conducted by such a government was unlikely to attain meaningful reform, Pásara believes, and he supports his argument through a description of the largely ineffective judicial reform.

Liisa North is the first scholar to explore with any methodological rigor the ideological orientations of Peru's military rulers. She analyzes selected public statements by fifty-nine officers who occupied ministerial-level positions between October 1968 and August 1976, with special attention to their attitudes toward mass mobilization and their favored solutions for Peru's economic development problems. North identifies some important points of consensus among the officers, especially a concern for mass welfare goals during the time they came to power, but explores in greatest detail the nature of the ideological divisions that emerged after the extent of social conflict resulting from some of the regime's reforms had become apparent.

In sum, this volume aims to illuminate a significant chapter in Peru's history, to help us better understand the meaning of this period in Peru's national context as well as the likely comparative significance of Peru's experiment. It does not pretend to be exhaustive— many important elements of Peru's experience during these years are treated lightly or not at all. Nor does it claim to be definitive; many aspects of the period are still difficult to learn about, and the eventual results of some aspects of Peru's experience may not become evident for years.

One topic, for example, that we would have liked very much to include in the book is the impact of the military government's policy on the Peruvian people. We wanted an analysis of which groups gained, which lost, and in what ways. Solid information is available only for the peasantry, however, and we reluctantly decided that the book could not encompass this issue.

We do believe, however, that this volume goes farther than any yet available toward presenting a diverse, balanced, and nuanced set of intermediate perspectives on Peru's experience since 1968. Fifteen authors—five from Peru, seven from the United States, two from the United Kingdom, and one from Canada—have collaborated closely in constructing this book. We differ on many issues—methodological, political, and epistemological—but we are all social scientists intent on using our training to help clarify a major social phenomenon.

In closing, we wish to acknowledge the debt that we and all the authors in this volume owe to the other participants in the workshop on "The Peruvian Experiment Reconsidered," held in November 1978 at the Woodrow Wilson International Center for Scholars in Washington, D.C. Most of the chapters in this book are based on early drafts presented for discussion to the seminar; in the spirited exchange of ideas at the workshop, many new insights were gained. Thus, all thirty-two participants in the workshop have contributed to this volume.

We are also grateful to the Wilson Center and its sources of financial support for making the workshop possible, and to the Inter-American Foundation for underwriting some of the costs of preparing the manuscript for publication.

June 7, 1982   Cynthia McClintock and
Abraham F. Lowenthal

The participants included Roberto Abusada-Salah, Catholic University of Peru; Susan Bourque, Smith College; Kay Warrent, Mount Holyoke College; José María Caballero, Catholic University of Peru; Peter S. Cleaves, Ford Foundation; Julio Cotler, Instituto de Estudios Peruanos; Susan Eckstein, Boston University; E.V.K. FitzGerald, University of Cambridge, U.K.; Henry Pease García, DESCO; Laura Guasti, Purdue University; Shane Hunt, Boston University; Peter Knight, World Bank; James Kurth, Swarthmore College; Ricardo Letts, Lima, Peru; Abraham F. Lowenthal, Latin American Program, Wilson Center; Cynthia McClintock, George Washington University; Kevin J. Middlebrook, Harvard University; Liisa L. North, York University; Felipe Ortiz de Zevallos, *Peru Economico;* Luis Pásara, CEDES; David Scott Palmer, Foreign Service Institute; Amos Perlmutter, American University; José Salaverry, Inter-American Development Bank; John Sheahan, Williams College; Daniel M. Schydlowsky, Boston University; Barbara Stallings, University of Wisconsin; Alfred C. Stepan, Yale University; Rosemary Thorp, University of Oxford, U.K.; Ellen Kay Trimberger, California State College; Richard C. Webb, International Bank of Reconstruction & Development; Robert White, *Minneapolis Tribune;* Laurence Whitehead, El Colegio de Mexico; Juan J. Wicht, Boston University.

Contributors

Peter S. Cleaves (Ph.D. University of California, Berkeley 1972) was Ford Foundation representative in Mexico from 1977 to 1982. His writings include *Bureaucratic Politics and Administration in Chile* (California: University of California Press, 1974), *Agriculture, Bureaucracy, and Military Government in Peru* (Ithaca, N.Y.: Cornell University Press, 1980), and "The Professions and the State in Mexico" (1982).

Julio Cotler (Ph.D. University of Burdeos 1960) is a professor at the Universidad de San Marcos in Lima, Peru. He is also a research sociologist at the Instituto de Estudios Peruanos in Lima and has been a member of the Joint Committee on Latin American Studies of the Social Science Research Council. He has published many books and articles, in Spanish and English, on Peruvian society and politics.

Susan Eckstein (Ph.D. Columbia 1972) is an associate professor of sociology at Boston University. Her publications include *The Poverty of Revolution: The State and Urban Poor in Mexico* (Princeton: Princeton University Press, 1977), *The Impact of Revolution: A Comparative Analysis of Mexico and Bolivia* (Sage Professional Papers, 1976), and numerous articles on Latin America. She is currently writing a book on Latin American twentieth-century revolutions.

E.V.K. FitzGerald (Ph.D. Cambridge 1973) is professor of development economics at the Institute of Social Studies, The Hague. He worked as adviser to the Peruvian government between 1972 and 1976. His published work includes *The Political Economy of Peru 1956–1978: Economic Development and the Restructuring of Capital* (Cambridge: Cambridge University Press, 1979) and articles on Peru, Mexico, and Central America. His current research is on the relation between capital accumulation and income distribution in semi-industrialized economies.

Laura Guasti (Ph.D. Wisconsin 1977) is an assistant professor of political science at Purdue University. She carried out research in Peru during 1974–1976. Her publications include "Industrialización y Revolución en el Perú: 1968–1976," *Estudios Andinos* (1981) and "Clientelism in Decline: A Peruvian Regional

Study," in S. N. Eisenstadt and René Lemarchand, eds., *Political Clientelism, Patronage, and Development* (Sage Publications, 1981).

Abraham F. Lowenthal (Ph.D. Harvard 1971) directs the Latin American Program at the Woodrow Wilson International Center for Scholars in Washington, D.C. He has worked previously at the Ford Foundation in Latin America (including Peru), at Princeton University, and at the Council on Foreign Relations. He edited and contributed to *The Peruvian Experiment* (Princeton: Princeton University Press, 1975) and has authored various other books and articles.

Cynthia McClintock (Ph.D. Massachusetts Institute of Technology 1976) is associate professor of political science at The George Washington University. She is the author of *Peasant Cooperatives and Political Change in Peru* (Princeton: Princeton University Press, 1981) and a variety of articles on Peruvian society and politics.

Liisa L. North (Ph.D. Berkeley 1973) is an associate professor of political science and acting director of the Centre for Research on Latin America and the Caribbean (CERLAC) at York University in Toronto. She conducted research in Peru in 1968–1969 and 1976. She is co-author of *The Peruvian Revolution: Reform Policies and Ideological Orientations of the Officers in Power, 1968–1976* (Montreal: McGill University Developing Area Centre, 1981) and co-author of *Bitter Grounds: The Roots of Revolt in El Salvador* (Toronto: Between-the-Lines Press, 1981), among other publications.

Luis Pásara (Ph.D. Catholic University of Peru 1978) is currently the director of the Center for Studies of Law and Society (CEDYS) in Lima. A sociologist with a specialty in legal studies, he has focussed his most recent work on judicial administration. At the same time, he has been writing a large number of journalistic works, primarily in the area of political analysis, for various Peruvian publications.

Henry Pease García (M.S. Catholic University of Peru 1975) is currently the director of Center for the Study and Promotion of Development (DESCO) in Lima. He is also a professor at the Catholic University of Peru. He has written various books on the Peruvian military government, including *El Ocaso del Poder Oligárquico: Lucha Política en la Escena Oficial 1968–1975* (Lima: DESCO, 1977) and *Los Caminos del Poder: Tres Años de Crisis en la Escena Política* (Lima: DESCO, 1979) as well as numerous articles.

Daniel M. Schydlowsky (Ph.D. Harvard 1966) is a professor of economics and senior research associate at the Center for Latin American Development Studies and Center for Asian Development Studies, Boston University. He has written extensively on the industrialization, international trade, and macroeconomic policy of Latin American countries and has conducted original research on the under-utilization of installed capacity in Latin America.

John Sheahan (Ph.D. Harvard 1954) is a professor of economics at Williams College. He worked with the Department of Planning in Colombia during 1963–1965 and at El Colegio de Mexico during 1969–1971. He did research in Peru in 1978 and returned to follow new developments in each of the three following years. He has published articles on economic change in Colombia and Mexico, and on the relationships between economic and political developments in Latin America.

Barbara Stallings (Ph.D. Stanford 1975, Cambridge 1982) is an associate professor of political science at the University of Wisconsin at Madison. Her publications include *Class Conflict and Economic Development in Chile* (Stanford: Stanford University Press, 1978) and various articles on international finance in Peru, Latin America, and Europe.

Rosemary Thorp (M.A. Oxford 1962) is a lecturer in Latin American economics at the University of Oxford and a fellow at St. Antony's College. She is co-author with Geoffrey Bertram of *Peru 1890–1977: Growth and Policy in an Open Economy* (London: Macmillan & Co., 1978) and has written on current problems of inflation in Latin America and on the economic history of Peru and Colombia.

Juan J. Wicht (M.A. Harvard 1972) is a research associate at the Center for Latin American Development Studies, Boston University. From 1972 to 1976, he worked at the Instituto Nacional de Planificación in Lima. His fields of major interest are population, employment, and international economics.

I

The Peruvian Experiment in
Historical Perspective

1

Democracy and National Integration in Peru

Julio Cotler

From its very first days in 1968, Peru's government of the armed forces persisted in asserting its "revolutionary" character. The political-military command declared, repeatedly, that its abundant legislation was intended to eradicate "the traditional structures" responsible for the overall backwardness of the country and for its subordination to imperial centers. These problems, which reinforced each other, underlay not only the divisions among the nation's social classes but also the divisions within them. The political-military command believed that these tensions were constantly growing sharper, and threatening the existence of the society and the state. In its view, these tensions blocked the collective efforts necessary to confront the problems of underdevelopment and dependency and to thwart the expansionist geopolitical designs of neighboring countries.

In its zeal to cut the gordian knot that was stifling national development, the high military command proclaimed an original project of historic dimensions. Developed with the help of ideologues, propagandists, and technicians, this project "would preserve its complete conceptual autonomy" with respect to other processes of social transformation. The military leadership thus underlined the singular and experimental character of its revolution.

It is now evident that the military failed to resolve the problem of integrating Peruvian society. This chapter seeks to explain the origins and development of this revolution as well as the factors that contributed to its denouement. The chapter begins by describing some of the most serious aspects of the problem of Peru's integration—the national and political aspects. It considers how this problem came to be the center of attention in Peru and how it was viewed by different social sectors, particularly the military. In subsequent sections, the chapter traces the development of the process initiated by the military, the reactions stirred, and the results obtained.

THE STATE AND OLIGARCHICAL SOCIETY

Elsewhere, I advanced the thesis that Peru's central historical problem may be defined, in summary form, as the absence of a leadership group capable of sustaining the process of Peru's national and political integration.[1] Specifically, throughout its history, Peru has not had a leading class with the capacity and will to realize the following tasks: (1) acceleration of capitalist development, both extending it throughout the country and deepening it, in order to permit a homogenization of the productive structure and of the organization and relations among social classes (this process should have culminated in an integrated national market); (2) incorporation of progressively popular demands into the daily operation of the state, thereby developing consensus between rulers and ruled concerning the legitimacy of the state and establishing the limits and institutional procedures of political participation; and (3) unification of the population and the territory through effective governmental centralization, with the objective of ending the cultural fragmentation prevailing among classes and their ethnic correlates and enabling the establishment of a collective identity, the Peruvian nation.

In other words, throughout the history of the republic, Peru's dominant classes did not succeed in organizing the population around the principles of the state. Thus, they did not achieve objectives common to the society, nor did they create the image of a state representative of collective interests. In brief, these classes were not capable of incorporating and accommodating popular demands into state activity and thus realizing a process of relative democratization of Peruvian society and politics. On the contrary, the dominant classes and the state answered popular demands with scorn and repression, stirring violence and desperation. For that reason, the Peruvian state came to be most appropriately defined as an oligarchical one, raising popular alienation, mistrust, and opposition, which—for fifty years—accounted for the country's chronic political instability.

Capitalist Penetration of Peru

Although the fission between the state and the popular classes is extremely longstanding, as a result of the jealous protection by the propertied classes of their "colonial heritage," we must consider other

[1] Julio Cotler, *Clases, Estado, y Nación en el Perú* (Lima: Instituto de Estudios Peruanos, 1978).

factors that exacerbated the problem. At the end of the nineteenth century, with the expansion of the international market, capitalism began slowly to *penetrate* Peru. A weak commercial and agrarian "bourgeoisie" emerged and rose to participate, with difficulty, in the feeble and limited state apparatus. Peruvian capitalism was thus a response to external factors rather than a result of the contradictions created by internal dynamics. For that reason, the rise of this bourgeoisie did not bring about a class with landowning interests; in fact, there was a mutual, though unstable, accommodation. The shape of Peruvian society continued to be cast in a definitively precapitalist mold: social relations were characterized by exploitation of the peasantry, in a clearly colonial pattern. The new group, which for lack of a better term we have called the "bourgeoisie," was neither "creator" nor "conqueror"; on the contrary, following the best colonial tradition, it developed via governmental grants and sinecures. Glossing Pareto, we may say that this bourgeoisie dominated due to the political favors it knew how to reap, rather than to the iron it knew how to produce.

In these circumstances, foreign capital entered the country, establishing the model of export-led growth based on mining and agriculture.[2] The propertied classes and the state neither intervened nor had the capacity to negotiate the terms of this entry. Thus a handful of foreign enterprises easily and rapidly achieved monopoly in the capitalist productive system. These enterprises expanded to include finance, international commerce, and transportation, without creating linkages with nascent industry and the non-export-oriented agarian sector. In other words, foreign capital penetrated the country without furthering domestic capitalism: it did not facilitate an increase in productivity nor the transformation of social relations in different economic sectors that would have extended and integrated the market. In this sense, and *only in this sense,* the capitalism established in Peru had the characteristics of an enclave. It could not be otherwise, because the objective of foreign capital was to obtain raw materials at low costs and to realize, in the original countries, the reproduction of capital. Thus the cycle of capital *begun* in Peru was completed elsewhere.

The advantage for foreign enterprises resulted from the low salaries demanded by the Peruvian worker ("the cheap *cholo*") in comparison with those demanded in metropole countries. Salaries were kept

---

[2] Rosemary Thorp and Geoffrey Bertram, *Peru 1890–1977: Growth and Policy in an Open Economy* (London: Macmillan & Co., 1978).

down because opportunities for salaried employment in Peru were scarce. Precapitalist conditions thus became a reservoir of cheap and abundant labor and food supply that facilitated the maintenance of relatively low wages. In this way, under the dynamic advanced by capitalism, a mutually reinforcing articulation was established with precapitalist interests.

In the entry of foreign capital, the Peruvian bourgeoisie found new opportunities for enrichment that did not require transformation of the existing social structure. The bourgeois enlisted as lawyers, political representatives, and junior partners—becoming clients—to these new patrons. In return, the bourgeois attained a new type of prebends, reinforcing their "señorial" status and severing them more sharply from the general population. The penetration of capitalism into Peru also generated social dislocation. In some regions, peasant communities, landholders, small property owners, artisans, and merchants were eliminated, while proletarianization began and labor mobility increased. At the same time, in other regions the process of peasant feudalization was restored and reinforced. These social dislocations provoked the beginning of popular political mobilization at the end of the 1920s.[3]

The fission within the propertied class also culminated at this time. One faction drew behind it a limited segment of the politically mobilized urban class to stand against another faction that sought to restrict penetration of foreign capital. The struggle ended in the exclusion of this second faction from political life. The coalition between the triumphant group of property owners, led by President Augusto B. Leguía, and the mobilized popular classes, seemed likely to initiate their political incorporation into the state. But such incorporation required measures that would alter the nature of Peruvian society, and it was quickly thwarted. Leguía tended to favor the expansion of capitalism without modifying the social bases of feudal domination, on which the export-led economic model was based. In this way, the *Oncenio*—Leguía's dictatorial eleven-year rule—was a prolongation of the Civilist party's nineteenth-century programs.[4]

Under these circumstances, the newly mobilized popular groups broke free from their subordinate role in the movement led by Leguía and embraced the thought and action of Víctor Raúl Haya de la

---

[3] Peter Klarén, *Modernization, Dislocation, and Aprismo* (Austin: University of Texas Press, 1973).

[4] Howard L. Karno, "Augusto B. Leguía: The Oligarchy and the Modernization of Peru 1870–1930" (Doctoral dissertation, University of California, Los Angeles, 1970).

Torre and José Carlos Mariátegui. When the economic crisis of 1930 hit Peru, political mobilization among the popular and middle classes rose sharply. A political explosion occurred in the cities, as well as in agricultural and mining centers, with a considerable proletarian concentration. The contradiction between the interests of the dominant classes represented in the state and the interests of the popular groups, gradually organizing amid the turbulence of capitalist penetration, became ever more clear.[5]

Given their social characteristics and subordination to foreign capital, the bourgeoisie and the state were neither able nor willing to accommodate the new popular interests with the dominant ones. Such an accommodation would have required the recognition of the popular classes—Indians in majority—as citizens. For the white, "foreign-Peruvians," this possibility was out of the question. Besides, at a time of world recession, this would have implied the reduction of the benefits of capital. As the state was incapable of institutionally channeling the popular movement, repression marked the subsequent development of Peruvian society.

The unequivocally oligarchical nature of the state was evident in its complete exclusion of popular demands and consideration of only the dominant interests, foremost among which was foreign capital. In 1932, when the popular movement led by the American Popular Revolutionary Alliance party (APRA) confronted the government's violent repression, the United States ambassador to Peru wrote Washington that:

> A personal friend who saw Lanatta [minister of finance] late yesterday afternoon told me that he was again trying to obtain from foreign companies the money necessary to pay the expenses of the prisoners the government had been taking, on the theory that law and order were for the benefit of those companies and that the government should be assisted by them for that reason.[6]

APRA and the Oligarchical State, 1930–1948

The organizational development of the popular and middle classes gave rise to the crisis of the oligarchical system in 1930, which did not really end until 1968 with the establishment of self-proclaimed Revolutionary Government of the Armed Forces. This prolonged decline

[5] Cotler, *Clases, Estado, y Nación,* chapters 4 and 5.
[6] U.S., State Department, Decimal file on Peru 1929–1937, Roll no. 1, Washington, D.C.

of the oligarchical system was marked by the development of the popular forces, organized around two classical figures, Haya de la Torre and Mariátegui.

Haya de la Torre and his APRA party represented the radicalized views of the urban petty bourgeoisie, which sought the transformation of the country. Seeing the basic contradiction as that between the masses and the oligarchical state, Haya proposed a program that would favor the national, and therefore, democratic development of the economy, society, and polity. The state would assume new and vigorous productive functions that, under technical management by professionals, would enable the establishment of state capitalism. In other words, the state would come to carry out the functions that in other countries has been fulfilled by the "conquering bourgeoisie." Subject to government regulations, the middle classes would emerge as capitalists and would support the action of the government to enlarge and integrate the internal market. Thus, as a result of the hegemony of a state directed by the petty bourgeoisie, a national bourgeoisie would be formed.

Politically, the incorporation of the "national" classes and their concerns would provide the necessary legitimacy to the state for forging new institutions of a corporatist character, enabling it to arbitrate among social classes. Ultimately, the integration of the interests of the society into the concerns of the state would establish the basis for achieving a national identity, subsuming the particular social and ethnic differences and conflicts of the population. Only then, when the state had been strengthened by social consensus and the ensuing legitimacy, would it be in a position to "contract," or make arrangements with, foreign capital, so that it would serve to complement efforts now truly national in character.[7]

Mariátegui, in contrast, insisted that the primary problem of Peru, and of Latin America in general, did not lie in the oligarchical character of the state but rather in its domination by imperialist capital, which led him to classify the Latin American societies as "semicolonial." He supported a democratic and nationalist revolution only because he perceived it as a step in the eventual transition toward socialism. Mariátegui anticipated that the "national" capitalism resulting from a merely anti-oligarchical revolution would be rapidly submerged by the dynamics of imperialist capitalism; he saw Mexico as an example of this tendency. In that sense, he sought unsuccessfully

[7] Víctor Raúl Haya de la Torre, *El Antimperialismo y el Apra. Obras Completas,* vol. 4 (Lima: Editorial Juan Mejía Baca, 1976).

to orient popular mobilization toward the eradication of class exploitation and the establishment of national and political integration along socialist principles.[8] For various reasons, including the undifferentiated nature of the popular classes, Haya's concrete proposals and his organizational capacity advanced much farther than the ideas of Mariátegui. The difference between the two became more marked when Mariátegui's political heirs aligned themselves with the directives of the Communist International.

Unable to assimilate institutionally the popular challenge organized by APRA, the oligarchical state resorted to the army for its defense. The confrontation between the oligarchical state via the army and the popular classes continued until 1945, at the end of World War II. During this muffled civil war, APRA (also called the Aprista party) gained hegemony among the popular classes and important middle sectors, including groups of officialdom. The APRA leadership was essentially middle class, intellectual, urban, and coastal; the popular classes organized by the party were largely in the coastal urban centers. Shaped by its long period underground, APRA adopted a very hierarchical structure, evident in the sustained personality cult of Haya de la Torre. Haya was able to dictate and modify the party's ideological principles and lines of action according to the needs of the moment as well as to arbitrate rifts within the organization. APRA's exceptional capacity for organization and mobilization, rivaling that of the army, reinforced the refusal by the dominant class to incorporate the popular classes politically (at least as they were led by the party). Between 1930 and 1945 the various governments attempted through timid "welfare" programs and extensive anti-APRA propaganda to divorce the masses from their political leadership, but they never succeeded.[9]

In 1945, the democratic climate brought about by the defeat of fascism in Europe and the popular mobilization led by APRA forced the oligarchical coalition to recognize APRA legally and incorporate it into the political scene. As the most prominent representatives of the oligarchy had foreseen, this plunged the country into social, economic, and political upheaval. The political system became relatively more open to popular representation. The number of worker, peasant, and student organizations multiplied; the number of magazines and daily papers suddenly expanded; conferences and meetings dis-

[8] José Carlos Mariátegui, *Siete Ensayos de Interpretación de la Realidad Peruana* (Lima: Editorial Amauta, 1965), and *Ideología y Política* (Lima: Editorial Amauta, 1972).

[9] Cotler, *Clases, Etado, y Nación*, chapter 5.

cussing the problems of the popular and middle strata were held with unusual frequency. Although the interests of the propertied classes were still expressed from the pulpit, the university, and the newspapers, a new public opinion, opposed to these interests, emerged. A succession of workers' strikes occurred in the cities and the countryside; workers sought wage increases, better living conditions, and greater respect from employers. Peasant invasions of haciendas also occurred, as peasants sought landownership. Students launched strikes, pursuing the democratization of education.

Class struggle grew to be part of the country's daily life, becoming a permanent challenge to a state without the resources to satisfy these social demands. Haya de la Torre unsuccessfully sought formulas for political mediation with the propertied classes. He hoped to preserve parliamentary procedures, which he assumed would allow a smooth "transfer" of state power to APRA. The APRA leadership feared that the interruption of parliamentary procedures would bring on, once again, long periods of military dictatorship; in the future, this concern became a fundamental basis for the leadership's political activity.

In order to preserve parliamentary procedures and mollify the established interests, APRA postponed *sine die* the pursuit of its nationalistic and anti-oligarchical program. The inevitable social confrontation was deferred. And by 1948, the Aprista masses, formerly awaiting the call to battle, were demoralized and demobilized. The propertied classes rallied around General Manuel Odría, and the democratic experience ended with a new coup.[10]

The defeat of the popular movement stirred new thinking by the radical sectors of APRA. They concluded that the dominant coalition and the oligarchical state would never cede their power willingly and that, therefore, the only remaining alternative was to destroy them through popular revolt. Disillusioned by the APRA leadership, they left the party in the middle 1950s, becoming the first to split the party. They joined the new reformist organizations emerging at the time and the embryonic groups of the revolutionary left that sought new alternatives to transform the society and the state.

*The 1950s and 1960s: A New Economic Model and
New Social Contradictions*

During the 1950s and 1960s, Peru underwent a new and accelerated capitalist penetration, and old and new contradictions in the so-

[10] Ibid.

cial political order were joined. In unforeseen ways, these contradictions ultimately led to the collapse of the oligarchical regime.

Due to the requirements of foreign capital, in the early 1950s Odría's dictatorship decreed a series of laws favoring important investments that increased exports from extractive enterprises.[11] At mid-decade, the production of fishmeal became a new and lucrative export, which also received considerable support from foreign capital. This surge in exports augmented the state's fiscal resources, which were used to increase current and investment spending. Through these expenditures, the state sought to satisfy popular urban demands, to expand the number of consumers of industrial items, to neutralize Aprista mobilization, and to increase the number of prebends among clients of the dictatorship, thus enlarging the established bourgeoisie.

Toward the end of the 1950s, the government ordered the first measures for industrialization via import substitution. This was due to the limited investment opportunities in traditional exports, to the pressures of foreign and native capital and the pressures of the new professional groups eager for the industrialization of the country, and to the demands for employment of the growing urban population. Since import permits were distributed in the traditional way, as "favors," and since new industries were overprotected and the size of the market was small, a few enterprises gained control of each branch of industrial production.[12] Moreover, given that the export sector was already controlled by foreign capitalist enterprises, industrial activity emphasized the manufacture of nondurable consumer goods. Subsidiaries of North American firms were quickly established in Peru through credit granted by branches of North American banks (which soon captured a significant proportion of Peruvian national savings); they imported machinery, intermediate goods, and inputs from their home offices, at oligopoly prices and at technological standards that they set themselves. Around the subsidiaries, the Peruvian bourgeoisie developed satellite firms. Jointly they produced goods for people at the highest income levels, generating a new lifestyle, which was promoted by the media.

In contrast to the results of capitalist development based on agricultural and mining exports, the realization of capital in the Peruvian

[11] Thorp and Bertram, *Peru 1890–1977;* Charles Goodsell, *American Corporations and Peruvian Politics* (Cambridge: Harvard University Press, 1974); Michael Roemer, *Fishing for Growth* (Cambridge: Harvard University Press, 1970).

[12] Jorge A. Torres, *Estructura Económica de la Industria en el Peru* (Lima: Editorial Horizonte, 1975).

market entailed a new process of concentration of the industrial and financial apparatus in the hands of transnational monopoly capital. Once again, and in a very significant way, the participation of the Peruvian bourgeoisie and of the state in the process of capitalist accumulation was severely limited. In addition, given the nature of capitalist expansion, the classic heterogeneity and fragmentation of the productive system and of society in general were exacerbated. This new model of capitalist growth assumed relatively stable real wages and an expanding middle sector capable of purchasing durable consumer goods. To these ends, after 1950, successive governments controlled food prices, subsidizing food imports. This policy further impoverished both peasants and landowners, leaving Peru's provinces in an even more serious state of deprivation. In short, the new model of development severely punished the precapitalist sector of society.

Faced with this situation, highlands landowners pursued various strategies. They transferred the income produced by renting rural land to dynamic urban centers; or, disposing of their lands, they moved to the cities where they became professionals, bureaucrats, or small merchants. The majority of small landowners could not avail themselves of these alternatives, however; they tried to place more demands upon their peasants but could no longer rely on the state's firm political support for these efforts, for the state's major concern was to assure urban development.

To the decline in rural income in the highlands was added the progressive exhaustion of the land, demographic pressure, and the new demands by landowners. As a result, a wave of peasant revolts shook this highlands region, where the precapitalist sector of the country was concentrated. These revolts aimed to recover land that had originally belonged to peasant communities but had been taken over by haciendas and to eliminate the servile tributes and services demanded by the *hacendados* from the peasants.[13] Simultaneously, migration sharply increased from the highlands to the coast, and from the countryside to the city. The strata of workers in the city were consequently restructured, and an important new urban sector of underemployment was formed.

These changes were accompanied by the reemergence and strengthening of the professional middle classes, ever more diverse, as

[13] Giorgio Alberti and Rodrigo Sanchez, *Poder y Conflicto Social en el Valle del Mantaro* (Lima: Instituto de Estudios Peruanos, 1974); Hugo Blanco, *Tierra o Muerte. Las Luchas Campesinas en el Peru* (Mexico: Siglo xxi, 1972); Hugo Neira, *Los Andes, Tierra o Muerte* (Madrid: Editorial XYZ, 1968); Aníbal Quijano, *Problemas Agrarios y Movimientos Campesinos* (Lima: Mosca Azul Editores, 1979).

well as by the emergence of a new sector of small and medium-sized industrialists. These sectors sought to expand their "social space," which had been reserved for them in the traditional oligarchical system but which they felt had been narrowing due to the increasing financial and industrial concentration.

The Political Crisis of the 1950s and 1960s

As a result of this type of capitalist development and the new contradictions it produced, various social groups burst onto the political scene with unusual force in the mid-1950s. These groups included the peasants, especially highlands peasants; the expanded working class; the subproletariat of migrants; and the new middle sectors, who assumed the leadership of the protests by the popular groups. This phenomenon was entirely new in the history of Peru; the crisis of 1930 had been marked by the participation of limited sectors of the popular classes, but from the 1950s on, political participation spread throughout all regions of the country and to all social levels. This growing popular participation—anti-oligarchical, democratic, and nationalist—threatened the oligarchical political order. Thus, the experience of 1930 was repeated with greater intensity.

Substantive modifications of the political order resulted. Until then the oligarchical system had been able to contain and control popular mobilization for the most part through the armed forces' repression of pockets of social resistance. Coercion was not the only instrument of domination, however. An extended and relatively complex system of political clientelism delegated to rural and urban patrons at diverse political, social, and administrative levels the power to duplicate oligarchical modes of domination. Still, in the new circumstances, neither coercion nor clientelism was sufficient to maintain the exclusive, elitist order. It was essential that the state *directly* assume distributive functions of a clearly welfare variety. The aim would be to achieve the legitimacy and social consensus that would enable the institutionalization of popular participation in established channels. The new political channels would have to accept popular demands and process them at the state level if new types of political control were to be established.

It was for this purpose that the dominant class incorporated APRA into the state in 1956, with the establishment of the administration dubbed the "Convivencia" ("living together," in reference to the unlikely political alliance between Haya de la Torre and the conservative president Manuel Prado). Such incorporation assumed that the party would gather, moderate, and organize the growing demands and adapt them to the "real possibilities" of the state (that is, of the dominant interests). Special support would be given to the popular urban groups with a greater capacity for political pressure. APRA apparently hoped to gain through the "Convivencia" the political space and power it had unsuccessfully sought in 1945. But the decision to enter the government in the "Convivencia" arrangement cost APRA a new group of radical leaders, who abandoned the party, as well as the bulk of the population newly entering the political life of the country, who felt betrayed by APRA. This population joined the new reformist forces that were being organized.

During this challenge to the dominant order, Pedro Beltrán emerged as the oligarchical system's ideologue, proclaiming the need to assimilate the popular classes into the state through a "market economy." In the pages of the daily newspaper *La Prensa,* which the principal national property owners had bought in the mid-1940s with the explicit purpose of defending their interests, Beltrán presented a program intended to resolve the problem of political incorporation of the popular classes. The program sought, first, the consolidation of the constitutional state, institutionalizing citizens' control over their political representatives. (At the time, over half the adult population did not have the franchise, and property was highly concentrated in a small number of enterprises.) To develop the constitutional state, Beltrán proposed unrestricted freedom for the market, arguing that only in this way could the nation's scarce resources be efficiently allocated and entrepreneurial initiatives encouraged. By providing the most profit to the boldest and most capable, the market would encourage investment and, thus, workers' employment—improving the distribution of income over the long run. Moreover, foreign investment would be stimulated, thereby speeding the dynamic that would lead to political democracy and economic development. Beltrán's proposal assumed that the state's functions would be reduced to a minimum—to the maintenance of order—so that the market could develop and expand. The state would not intervene in the market, as such intervention would involve bureaucratization, political corruption, and production inefficiencies—and ultimately totalitarian, communist tendencies.[14]

This program, aiming to replicate the "German miracle" in Peru,

---

[14] Roberto Miro Quesada, "Contradicciones al Interior de la Burguesía Peruana a Través del Análisis de los Diarios *El Comercio* y *La Prensa*" (Bachelor's thesis, Universidad de San Marcos, Lima, 1975).

had no political significance, even within Beltrán's own
its taste for sinecures, Beltrán's group did not want to los
tion and favors bestowed by the government and foreign
Moreover, the exclusive political regime, dating from th
of the century and now supported by APRA, was crum
the onslaught of the popular movement, which was bein
reformists.

Against Beltrán's liberalism, the popular movement demanded a
substantial redistributive policy that would break down the oligarchy's wall. The movement insisted that the state and national capital
must be present in the realms of policy making and production if the
country were to develop and the integration of state and society were
to be achieved. Further, agrarian reform was proposed to improve
production and peasant incomes, which in turn would increase industrial demand. Control of the industrial and financial systems by the
state and by national capital would check the flow of capital out of
the country and spur domestic reinvestment, thereby also expanding
and integrating the market. The overall diagnosis of the reasons for
the country's underdevelopment was its dependence on *foreign* capital,
and the basic remedy proposed was "structural change" to nationalize the economy and establish the state as an effective social arbiter.
In other words, this "new" proposal resurrected the Aprista program
at a time when it had been abandoned by APRA itself for tactical
reasons pertaining to the attainment of the "transfer of power."

Impulse was given to this reformist program of the new middle sectors by popular struggles, and the program was adopted by the daily
paper *El Comercio*. Engaging in a polemic with *La Presna*, *El Comercio*
gained the support of the new reformist political forces, and also of
important sectors of the church and the army. Transnational enterprises and their publicity agents, however, became hostile. Thus the
split within the dominant group became evident.

El Comercio, the church, and the army adopted the reformist program because they believed that the changing social situation required structural change "from above," via technocratic measures
that would maintain the "principle of authority." They understood
that otherwise the masses, led by the evolving revolutionary sector,
might realize these transformations and end not only the oligarchical
character of society but also its capitalist foundations.[15] The "lessons"

[15] See the weekly journal "Libertad," of the Movimiento Social Progresista
that was published between 1958 and 1961. See also Hector Cornejo Chavez,
Nuevos Principios para un Nuevo Peru (Lima, 1960); Peruvian Church, *Exigencias Sociales del Catolicismo en el Perú* (Lima, 1959).

of the Cuban Revolution were salient, and they had been emphasized in the doctrines of the Economic Commission for Latin America (ECLA) and the Alliance for Progress. In this context, the "theory" of national security emerged in the army. In its view, social reform encouraging development and popular welfare would be the only bulwark against institutional decay, the autonomous political development of the popular classes, and intensified class struggle. Only an integral body of social reforms could bring Peruvians together and enable Peru's defense to stand against external dangers: atheistic Communism, the geopolitical expansion of the country's neighbors, and the imperialist governments and enterprises.[16]

The 1960s opened, therefore, with a reformist mandate, widespread among diverse social groups and manifest in open criticism of the political order. The realization of APRA's 1930s proposals was now squarely on the country's political agenda. The presidential election of Fernando Belaúnde Terry in 1963 seemed to herald the realization of the new anti-oligarchical and nationalistic measures. These hopes were quickly frustrated, however. The American government gave a conditional support to Belaúnde: the loans of the Alliance for Progress and the private investment were held on a stand-by basis because Belaúnde had promised to solve the longstanding problem with the International Petroleum Company (IPC). Second, the Belaúnde government was steadfastly opposed by the "Coalition"— the alliance between APRA and General Odría. This alliance continued the political tradition of the "Convivencia" and, for the third time in twenty years, spurred APRA cadres to abandon the party and become militants in the new reformist and revolutionary organizations.[17] A third obstacle to the government's reformist ambitions was its rejection of popular mobilization as an alternative to oppose the coalition. The allies of the reformist government—*El Comercio,* the church, and the army—opposed popular mobilization that would upset technocratic norms and thereby endanger the principle of authority.

With the rapid end of the government's reformist impulse came

[16] General José del Carmen Marin, "Preparación para el Alto Mando," *Revista Militar del Peru,* vols. 1-2, 1956; General Edgardo Mercado Jarrin, "La Política y la Estrategia Militar en la Guerra Contrasubversiva en America Latina," *Revista Miltar del Peru,* no. 67075, 1967; Coronel Enrique Gallegos, "Debe Preocuparnos la Guerra Subversiva?" *Revista de la Escuela Superior de Guerra,* enero-mayo, 1960; Coronel Carlos Bobbio, "Qué Ejercito Necesita el Perú?" *Revista Militar del Peru,* no. 675, 1963; Victor Villanueva, *El CAEM y la Revolución de la Fuerza Armada* (Lima: Instituto de Estudios Peruanos, 1972).

[17] Cotler, *Clases, Estado, y Nación,* chapter 7.

various political changes. First, professional groups felt t
became convinced that it was impossible to realize the
forms in the prevailing political context. A radical per:
emerged among this group. The failure of reform also sp
popular movements of peasants, workers, and white-colla
conspicuous in these movements were groups who now re
mist principles and were trying to define their own alternative basis
on class analysis. Moreover, and critically significant, APRA lost its
hegemony in the universities and the emerging revolutionary left
gained a place in these educational centers. The failure of the new
government to enact the reforms demanded by the society thus gave
rise to the development of radical ideologies among university and
intellectual groups and, added to the successful Cuban experience,
ended in guerrilla movements, first in 1963 and then in 1965.

Although rapidly crushed, these outbreaks and the simultaneous
peasant movements increased the importance of the military intelligence branch in the armed forces, bearing out its technocratic-refor-
mist position as a way to prevent popular uprising. The neglect of
these problems by the "political class" convinced the military intelligence that a democratic government could not resolve the critical national security issues. The military saw a need to consider the "global
interests of the state," which they thought tended to be ignored by the
"particular" interests of the parties.

Meanwhile, the contradictions of capitalist development based on
import substitution were leading to a new economic crisis. This crisis
was evident in the stagnation of traditional exports and the simultaneous increase of both industrial and food imports. The economic
difficulties were exacerbated by increases in government spending, financed by external indebtedness (the poorly orchestrated response of
the government and the opposition to the rising social demands). The
result was balance-of-payments problems, monetary devaluation, and
yet greater impoverishment of the population, with its political consequences.[18]

By 1967–1968, these contradictions had led to two important political changes. First, the revolutionary left began to organize and important new groups of the working class formed a central union independent of APRA control—the General Confederation of Workers of
Peru (CGTP). Second, APRA and the modern capitalist sector for-

[18] Pedro-Pablo Kuczynski, *Peruvian Democracy under Economic Stress: An Account of the Belaúnde Administration, 1963–1968* (Princeton: Princeton University Press, 1977).

mulated a political agreement. This agreement sought to remove landowners and the nationalistic middle classes from the political scene simultaneously, beginning a process of capital modernization that would give a greater room for maneuvering to domestic propertied classes in the context of a massive penetration by foreign capital.

Before either of these alternatives got very far, however, a small number of army officers—occupying strategic positions in the military command—ousted the shaky and discredited government. Claiming to represent the entire military institution, they established the Revolutionary Government of the Armed Forces (GRFA). These officers hoped to waylay the left and prevent any restructuring of capitalism in Peru that would subordinate the national businessman to international capital, a restructuring they thought would exacerbate the already sharp sociopolitical tensions. The officers also felt a need to block the alliance of APRA and the modern capitalists from power; they feared that this alliance would underestimate Peru's national security problem and would try to subordinate the armed forces to civilian power and priorities.

Summary

Peru's development in the twentieth century has been marked by various rhythms of capitalist penetration, entailing successive processes of social dislocation and growing political participation by the middle sectors and popular classes, committed to the assertion and exercise of their previously denied rights as citizens. Subordinate to foreign monopoly capital and allied with the landowners, the state had neither the resources nor the institutional means to confront and resolve citizens' nationalistic and democratic aspirations. The popular political groups, directed by the middle sectors, were also unable to resolve the nation's dilemmas. The mechanisms established to assist certain segments of society were always ultimately insufficient to satisfy the massive and diverse popular demands.

These various political failures facilitated the emergence of a new revolutionary tendency, oriented toward the political independence of the popular classes from the middle class and the development of a political alternative appropriate to their interests. Thus, a new variant of political thought and social interest began to be sketched out, responding to the tortuous trajectory of capitalism in Peru and to its class differentiations. This released the forces that brought the oligarchical regime to an end. It shaped the institutional development of the armed forces and its reformist bent.

THE MILITARY GOVERNMENT, 1968–1980

A small group of army officers, disillusioned by the utter ineffectiveness of the oligarchical system, overthrew the government to establish the Revolutionary Government of the Armed Forces. To justify its action, this group of officers cited the immorality of the "politicians" and their inability to resolve the contradictions and problems made evident by the popular mobilization. The officers also cited the will and the ability of the armed forces to resolve "once and for all" the problem of the national and political integration of the Peruvian people. It was contended that, in contrast to politicians, military officers identified not with the particular interests of any one group or social class, but with the "general interests of the country."

The officers who established the GRFA claimed to represent the whole of the armed forces. The military institution was thus hypothetically the inspiration and the guide of their actions, and the only entity to which they had to answer. In other words, it became judge and plaintiff. The integration and political will of the armed forces contrasted sharply with the weakness of the oligarchical regime and of the politically concerned middle sectors, which allowed the military command to begin its leadership with a considerable degree of autonomy in relation to Peruvian society. Thus the command was able to establish—without opposition, but also without significant support—a number of the programs that had been proposed in the last decade by the reformist political forces. The military command assumed the functions and characteristics of a ruling social class that sought to reorder the state and society to fit its own purposes and aspirations. If the government was reduced to being the administrative arm of the armed forces, the armed forces also tried to absorb and monopolize the state, enclosing within its ranks all political life.

The GRFA and Its "Aims"

In general terms, the "military's objective" was to realize the promises left unfulfilled by the political parties, as a way of eliminating "external dependence and internal domination," causes of "national disunity" and of the hostility between the people and the armed forces. To this end, a series of dramatic structural changes were executed rapidly and suddenly by the administrative apparatus, under the strict direction and surveillance of the military. As the GRFA manifested its reformist and nationalistic intentions in action, it increasingly won the support of disillusioned professionals and militants of various political tendencies and of radicalized sectors of the church. In spite of subordination to distinct military heads, these "assistants" fulfilled decisive administrative and technical functions as well as creating and disseminating an ideology that emphasized the anti-oligarchical orientation of the military government.

As professionals, officers, and ecclesiastics moved into the vanguard of the reformist movements during the 1960s, they made possible what was radical in the GRFA's measures. For this same reason, however, the government's program combined aims of a middle-class nature with aims specifically military and Catholic. I have thus characterized the GRFA's political scheme as populist and military.[19]

The middle-class character of the military government was evident in the government's diagnosis of the Peruvian problem as rooted in the penetration by foreign capital, which subordinated the country to foreign interests (just as APRA, and then subsequent reformist organizations, had emphasized). On the basis of this analysis, the government committed itself to "domestically focused development" via the eradication of the enclaves. But whereas in 1930 capitalism was concentrated in agricultural and mineral production destined for export, since 1950, a pattern of accumulation had been superimposed that favored industrial development and urban consumption, weakening the social and political basis of the oligarchical order. Thus, to seek the end of the hegemonic order and industrial development without modifying the pattern of accumulation meant also to encourage new forms of penetration by monopoly and foreign capital.[20]

The GRFA pursued "autonomous development" that would establish a "society of solidarity" (a fundamental term of official discourse) among social classes, under the tutelage of the military state. It denied representing the exclusive interests of any one class and identified itself as "neither capitalist nor communist." Thus, too, the military government came to be defined as "Third World-ist." Similarly, the government sought harmony among social classes through the establishment of corporatist institutions. Said General Velasco, the head of state: "We'll all pull the same end of the rope"; "We'll all play on the same team." The ingredient of Catholic thought that assumed the construction of the City of God through "communitarian" entities enabled the GRFA to try to legitimize its actions through the new social message in church encyclicals. For this reason, too, the

[19] Julio Cotler, "Crisis Política y Populismo Militar," *Peru Hoy* (Mexico City: Siglo xxi, 1971).

[20] Aníbal Quijano, *Nationalism and Capitalism in Peru* (New York: Monthly Review Press, 1971).

GRFA won the political endorsement of the religious authorities and was able to deflect accusations of communist inspirations in the government.

The political scheme fit not only petty bourgeois interests but strictly military objectives as well. Class harmony was to assure national security on the domestic front, by eliminating social frictions. The Peruvian Revolution was to eliminate the obstacles to a strong, united defense of the national territory in face of neighbors' threats. For this purpose, the GRFA emphasized infrastructure, beginning a series of grandly ambitious works requiring effort over a long period of time, which often met geopolitical concerns (such as the Majes irrigation and the northern Peru oil pipeline).

These nationalistic and anti-oligarchical measures, which were enacted in what is euphemistically referred to today as the "Phase One" of the revolution, signified an important change in the country's society and economy. The landowning structure, the traditional agrarian and commercial bourgeoisie, and the foreign enclaves were excised from the productive system. The state, which had had a very limited participation in production by Latin American criteria, was transformed into a most significant economic factor: whereas in 1965 the state's share of total investment was 16 percent, ten years later, it reached 50 percent.[21]

The explicit purpose of these measures was to redistribute property and income and to stimulate the horizontal and vertical integration of economic sectors, developing linkages forward and backwards to extend, deepen, and consolidate the domestic market. This action would be directed by the state in collaboration with the industrial bourgeoisie, no longer weighed down by the oligarchy. Because of this bourgeoisie's social origins and its weak position in the productive structure, however, it would be made subject to "national" interests, as defined by military officers and technical experts. Development would also be attained through properly regulated foreign investment in industry, which would contribute the necessary capital and technology. Meanwhile, agreements would be established with international capital interested in joint mineral production with the state, in order to enhance international economic ties and the balance of trade.

Just as this body of measures would improve the social and regional distribution of income and social resources generally, it would effect social and cultural democratization. The society would pivot

[21] Oficina Nacional de Estadística: Cuentas Nacionales.

upon its own internal dynamic and would not revolve like a satellite around foreign interests. Ultimately, as a result of these activities, the state would be recognized by the people as the embodiment of their hopes and the core of their national and collective identity.

Simultaneously with the economic measures came an unusual turn in Peru's international policy. The Peruvian foreign ministry, which previously never lost an opportunity to support the United States government in any international forum, advocated the development of a Third World and Non-Aligned block of nations, to seek jointly the establishment of a "new international order" ending domination by the developed countries. In accordance with this policy, Peru established relations with Eastern European countries and with China (months before President Nixon's trip). The United States blockade against Cuba was no longer upheld by Peru. Further, Peru strongly supported the Andean pact, which promised not only economies of scale and economic integration among its members but also the reduction of political and military tensions among these countries. The new international policy would create various political alliances that could counteract a potential blockade by the United States government or companies and that could provide access to alternative economic and military resources to advance the GRFA's national objectives.

In sum, the overall purpose of the military scheme was to combine capitalist accumulation by the state and by the private sector in order to enlarge and deepen the internal market, and also to make it more homogeneous—and thereby attain national economic and social integration. To the extent that such integration could be achieved and the society and economy made more democratic, cultural unity would be forged. Educational reform and the nationalization of the mass media were especially important instruments to achieve this goal. These steps, it was thought, would bring spontaneous popular support to the government, consummating the union between "the people" and the armed forces. Meanwhile, a set of international political alliances would be shaped that would neutralize potential aggressions by "enemies of the revolution," inside and outside the country. Thus, the military's program aimed to assure the national and political integration of Peruvian society under military leadership and to bring the struggles made since 1930 by the middle sectors to their culmination and resolution.[22]

[22] See, for example, the *Plan Nacional de Desarrollo, 1971–1975* (Lima: Instituto Nacional de Planificación); *Velasco: La Voz de la Revolución,* 2 vols. (Lima: Ediciones Participación, Oficina Nacional de Difusión del Sinamos, 1972).

The Economic Policies of the Military Government

The GRFA's nationalist and reformist measures were immediately opposed by the affected foreign enterprises, predominantly in the United States, and by the United States government. From the very first, Peru tried to reduce the tensions and eliminate the possibility of confrontation, trying to negotiate payment for the nationalized enterprises through the White House and the State Department. In their intermediary roles, these branches of the United States executive sought to block the possibility of the Peruvian Revolution's being "cubanized" and allying itself with the governments of Allende in Chile and Torres in Bolivia (thus potentially threatening North American "national security," supposedly the crux of United States foreign policy concerns). In contrast to its relations with Cuba, the United States government attempted to prevent radicalization of the military's nationalism. General Velasco hinted at the possibility of socialist policies, perhaps as a way of blackmail, and the United States government worked with American firms to forge an agreement that would end the conflict over Peru's expropriations. In this agreement, signed in 1974, the United States government granted a loan to the Peruvian government to enable it to pay the costs of compensation.

Until 1974, however, while the GRFA was nationalizing enterprises and seeking an "honorable" settlement with the United States government, Peru suffered a visible blockade by the grant and loan agencies of the United States government. After 1972 and the refinancing of the Peruvian government's debt, however, Peru borrowed in the Eurodollar market, sparking a dizzy spiral of debt,[23] which, as Manuel Moreyra, then president of the Central Bank, said recently, financed the Peruvian Revolution.

It was not only the negotiations and the subsequent Peruvian–United States agreement that allowed Peru to gain the confidence of international financial capital; also important was the prediction by the creditors that Peru was entering a cycle of prosperity and would be able to repay the loans. Copper prices were high, and it seemed certain that important oil depostis would be found in the jungle—and the value of these had multiplied thanks to OPEC's new policy. Moreover, the GRFA repeatedly showed that it did not aspire to modify the model of dependent capitalist development.

[23] Barbara Stallings, "Peru and the U.S. Banks: Privatization of Financial Relations," in Richard R. Fagen, ed., *Capitalism and the State in U.S.–Latin American Relations* (Stanford: Stanford University Press, 1979); Oscar Ugarteche, *La Banca Transnacional, la Deuda externa y el Estado, Peru 1968–1978* (Lima: Instituto de Estudios Peruanos, 1980).

The GRFA's policies changed the property structure in favor of the state and of those small segments of the urban and rural population who were incorporated into the labor communities and the more profitable agrarian cooperatives, respectively. The reforms selectively incorporated popular social segments and, particularly, the middle classes, into state concerns; some analysts thus categorized the measures as a revolution *by* and *for* the middle class. These reforms were insufficient to meet the vital needs of the rural and urban majorities, however, despite reiterated official statements to the contrary.

Although in the new property structure the relative weight of distinct groups appropriating the economic surplus was changed, for the most part the use of this surplus was not. The major structural reforms, agrarian and industrial, redistributed income in favor of those strata of peasants and workers with considerably higher incomes already.[24] The reforms also reinforced the system of production based on import substitution aimed at the consumption by higher-income classes. The state bureaucracy was greatly expanded and diversified. Nearly 150 public enterprises were created. Whereas in 1970 the number of state employees, inclusive of public enterprises, was about 300,000, in 1977, this figure rose to approximately 670,000.[25] Public spending and investment increased. A considerable proportion of these expenditures favored international capital enterprises, which retained much power to affect the structure of production and employment, the personal and regional distribution of income, and consumption patterns—all of which benefited the high-income groups and punished the popular strata.[26] Thus the high degree of concentration of industrial production and its oligopolistic character and the diversification of consumer durable goods continued, in spite of the industrial law.[27]

The military's policies entailed various ramifications and results. High-income groups, living in Lima, were subsidized;[28] the regressive

[24] Adolfo Figueroa and Richard C. Webb, *La Distribución del Ingreso en el Perú* (Lima: Instituto de Estudios Peruanos, 1975).

[25] Information taken from various sources: National Institute of Public Administration, National Office of Statistics, and the Annual Files of Public Enterprises.

[26] Alberto Couriel, *Peru, Estrategia de Desarrollo y Grados de Satisfacción de las Necesidades Básicas* (Santiago de Chile: PREALC, International Labor Organization, 1978).

[27] Jaime Gianella and Andres González, "Análisis de la Concentración en el Sector Industrial, 1972" (Manuscript, Lima, 1975).

[28] Carlos Amat, León Chavez, Hector León Hinostroza, *Estructura y Niveles de Ingreso Familiar en el Peru* (Lima: Ministry of Economy and Finance, 1977).

tax system continued unchanged;[29] subsidies to capitalists from public enterprises were available, and exemptions and concessions to private capital increased;[30] agricultural prices were controlled, keeping them low, while food imports were subsidized,[31] thus reducing rural incomes; credit policy hurt agriculture and favored industry, as interest rates and exchange rates were frozen, which made the real value of the currency drop to half its 1968 value.[32] Imports increased at a dizzying rate, with a high incidence of "over-invoicing."[33] Finally, commercial facilities and urban services centered in Lima were expanded, to add impulse to the dynamic of new commercial capital.

Thus, the military acted under the shield of an ideology and of administrative activity that sought simultaneously income redistribution favoring the popular sectors, the development of a domestic bourgeoisie, and the establishment of an effective state. These were the conditions necessary for an accumulation process via the activities of multinational enterprises associated with the state. Mariátegui's theory relevant to the future of APRA's policy of national capitalism in the period of imperialist development was borne out in practice.

The government's economic policy was plagued by the contradictions inherent in populist regimes. As already noted, the military's structural reforms had a distributive effect for small segments of the popular classes but failed to satisfy the needs of the vast popular majority for a truly democratic and national program. The reforms were constrained by a general context that favored multinational capital, with a secondary role for the Peruvian bourgeoisie, through state subsidy and support.

Yet, on the other hand, the statist and reformist measures prevented a smooth, regular, legitimate flow of profits to capital. The labor community, the restrictions upon the dismissal of personnel, the control of prices and of exchange, and some government support for union demands supposedly upset "the authority principle" of the enterprises and sometimes narrowed profit margins. Moreover, the state

[29] Ugarteche, *La Banca Transnacional.*

[30] German de la Melena, *La Reforma Financiera, Octubre 1978–Octubre 1973* (Lima: Ministry of Economy and Finance, 1973), p. 178.

[31] Elena Alvarez, *Política Agraria y Estancamiento de la Agricultura, 1969–1977* (Lima: Instituto de Estudios Peruanos, 1980).

[32] Roberto Abusada-Salah, "Reformas Estructurales y Crisis Económica en el Sector Industrial Peruano," The Woodrow Wilson Center's Latin American Program, working paper no. 29.

[33] Ugarteche, *La Banca Transnacional.*

penetrated some productive spheres, restricting the activity of the bourgeoisie; gave priority to the new area of "social property"; and enlarged and strengthened state supervision and fiscal control, with nuisance and administrative inefficiency as a consequence. A climate of great insecurity for the dominant class emerged. Moreover, much of the media had been nationalized and frequently denounced enterprise "abuses." An ambitious educational reform was also established. These measures were perceived by the dominant economic class as attempts to destroy its last political and ideological bulwarks and begin a transition to communism "Yugoslav-style." Capital and capitalists left the country, considering useless the various economic measures in their favor.

This trend became evident in 1974 when General Velasco—who now personally controlled the military apparatus and from it the state—indignantly refused the timid request of experts from the National Planning Institute for measures to alleviate the immediate fiscal crisis. Various government policies had brought on a balance of payments crisis. The overvaluation of the currency sharply stimulated imports and consumption, despite high international prices, while at the same moment exports were stagnating. Second, increasing government subsidies for food and fuel imports weighed more and more heavily on the balance of payments and discouraged agrarian production. Third, the public enterprises were obliged to continue both subsidies to private capital and sale prices below the cost of production, leaving them underfinanced and adding a burden to the state budget. As if all this were not enough, from the end of 1973, because of military fears of war with Chile (discussed in detail in the next subsection), the GRFA began a frantic arms purchasing campaign.

The budget deficits, like previous deficits, were made up mainly by internal borrowing until 1972. After 1972, however, the deficit and growth of imports were covered by external borrowing. In 1974, due to the economic and political factors previously cited, private investment came to a halt; the government's recourse was a dramatic increase in loans from the Eurodollar market, which financed 45 percent of that year's budget. In 1974, more agreements were also signed with international banks to enable arms imports. Economic chaos was imminent.

In the context of such economic difficulties, popular unrest flared up again and attacks by the bourgeoisie became more frequent. In the face of the "egoism" and "incomprehension" of the bourgeoisie, repudiating Velasco's constant appeals that they join his political design, Velasco decided to expropriate the major news media, Lima's daily papers. This expropriation sealed the divorce between the bourgeoisie and the military, but it also made increasingly obvious the deepening divisions existing within the military command.[34] Thus, the economic crisis of military populism hastened the bankruptcy of the "peculiar" experiment of military revolution.

The Failure of the Military's Program

Some analysts explain the GRFA's economic policy as a series of follies born of the ignorance of the military officers and their advisers, and exacerbated by the arbitrary nature of the political regime. The "revolution" failed, it is agreed, because officers in charge of the economy refused to listen to the suggestions and criticisms of those who were presumably experts in this field. This argument cites "technical" reasons, remote from the interests of social classes, their representatives, and of the state, which are considered "political" factors, "external" to the economic order.[35]

It is important to understand, however, the rationale of the apparently chaotic economic policy of the military government. At the risk of repetition, the GRFA sought to solve the problem of the national security of the country through mandating integration of the society into the state; in turn the state would respond to the military command's design, modernizing and thus strengthening the external capacity of the country. The petty bourgeois, radically reformist, and military government shaped a program to eliminate the anachronistic elements of society and to promote import substitution industrialization through the association of the state with multinational capital and the weak national bourgeoisie. The program was founded on the expectation of massive state revenues from huge petroleum and mineral exports. These revenues were to compensate for the debt contracted by the military government, especially in the context of high international prices for these goods. This strategy was frustrated, however, by various factors.

After Chile's Popular Unity government fell and military dictatorship was established in 1973, the Peruvian government began the systematic purchase of a considerable amount of arms: defense expenditures rose (in 1970 prices) from an annual increase of 7.2 percent between 1970 and 1974 to an annual increase of 22 percent between

---

[34] Henry Pease García, *El Ocaso del Poder Oligárquico: Lucha Política en la Escena Oficial, 1968–1975* (Lima: DESCO, 1977).

[35] Daniel M. Schydlowsky and Juan Wicht, "The Anatomy of an Economic Failure," Chapter 4 of this volume.

1974 and 1977. In the first period, these expenditures constituted an annual average of 3.5 percent of the GNP, but in 1975–1978 they signified 5.6 percent.[36] In 1967, Colonel Enrique Gallegos (who was to have a future in the military government) had said: "Chile is like a tube, and when it has too much internal pressure, its cork flies off," and this attitude was once again prevalent among the military leaders. Peruvian strategists perceived imminent conflict threatening, simultaneously, on the southern, northern, and eastern frontiers. Thus, the government cast aside all other considerations and decided to equip the military quickly as well, in order to discourage Chile's bellicose proclivities. Soon after this decision, various events did threaten war between Chile and Peru.

Under these circumstances, the GRFA was particularly concerned to maintain a sort of equilibrium among different social classes to assure the military rearguard and prevent a repetition of 1879. In 1879 Chile defeated the Peruvian army in the War of the Pacific, a defeat that became the nightmare of the Peruvian army. The government's actions were guided by a new "hypothesis of war"—but Peruvian society was kept ignorant of this assessment.

It was for these reasons that, when the experts urged policy readjustments to confront the gathering economic storm—readjustments that assumed austerity and rationalization of public expenditure and debt—the top officers rejected their recommendations. The generals and admirals opted to continue military equipment purchases and deficit spending, at least until its ambitious public works were completed and increased exports thereby forthcoming. Simultaneously, state organizations would be developed to check the increasingly autonomous popular movement and to quiet the protests of the bourgeoisie.

Contrary to its hopes, however, the GRFA became tangled up in the hostile actions its policies unleashed. The contradiction between the government's words and its acts prevented its winning the support of any significant sector of the society. On the contrary, opposition of the various social forces to the state increased. Moreover, the various political tendencies in the government, which had tolerated each other until then, ruptured. The rupture culminated in the ousting of Velasco, and the beginning of the very distinct "second phase of the Peruvian Revolution."

This failure did not belong only to the military. The various political schemes elaborated by different radical sectors of the petty bour-

[36] Manual Moreyra (in a presentation on January 25, 1979 at IPAE, in Lima).

geoisie over the last fifty years had also aimed to integrate state and society through "communitarian, humanist, Christian, libertarian, socialist, pluralist, and anti-imperialist" measures—and they had also failed.

Quis Custodium Custodiet?

The search for a "new man" identified with the needs of the national community, took concrete form in the development of a society "neither capitalist nor communist," through an accumulation model based on the state, multinational capital, and the national bourgeoisie. This *menage à trois* was conditional upon the government's capacity to enclose social classes within the state apparatus. In other words, along the conceptual lines elaborated by Haya de la Torre in the 1930s, the state would achieve hegemony over the society through the expertise of technocrats and military officers.

The GRFA's reforms, elaborated independently of the interests, perspectives, and organizations of Peru's social classes, provoked opposition in many and varied quarters. The government tried to overcome it, using carrots and sticks first with one group and then another, but eventually alienating everyone. The final outcome was profound economic and social conflict. The government insisted upon maintaining its autonomy from society, however. The gap between society and the military government was widened by the mobilization of different social sectors against the government's policies. Thus, the government did not gain the authority and legitimacy to recruit the social classes into corporatist formulas, nor did "Ideological Bases of the Peruvian Revolution," a major official publication, ever achieve national acceptance.

The unpopularity and political inefficiency of the government, rooted in its petty bourgeois character, suggested a definition of its nature as "Bonapartist." The government seemed Bonapartist because it sought to maintain itself above and equidistant from social classes, assuming that it represented the whole, while in reality it represented only itself. But the Bonapartist character of the GRFA also reflected its institutional military nature. Given its hierarchical and authoritarian structure (a faithful copy of the class and ethnic stratification of Peruvian society), the military could not tolerate an order in which superiors' commands were not fully respected by subordinates, or the popular classes (the two were the same to the military). General Tantaleán, once minister of fisheries, told me that the principal defect of the revolution was its fear of the people.

State and Society during "Phase One" of the Military Government

The GRFA was relatively autonomous from social sectors in its actions. Its measures were authoritarian and technocratic. The source of all legislative initiative was the executive and the Council of Official Assistants to the President (COAP); the interests of social classes were not represented in state activity. The top level of the armed forces made itself the leadership responsible for government, without permitting citizens to examine and check its activities.

The government also adopted the organizing principles of the armed forces—hierarchy and segmentation. Important posts were assigned to officials from the distinct branches of the armed forces, who worked only with their "assistants" and were responsible only to their own bosses, strictly following the military line of command. The intelligence services were given additional responsibilities: to assure that development plans remained "state secrets," to detect "infiltrators" into the government, and to silence criticism. The government repudiated public opinion and social conflict, thus reinforcing the traditional system of politics.

Although one of the government's most marked general traits was its distance from society, it neither sought nor achieved social support, despite its claims to harmonize opposing social interests. There were bridges across the chasm, however. Officers and assistants in the government denied that they were political intermediaries, but in fact they were, and they represented the major interests of opposed social classes. These classes were represented to different degrees in the government, establishing permanent tensions within it. Under the pretext of a need for secrecy, the government tried to hide these tensions and maintain the fiction of monolithic government unity.

The military government silenced the political parties APRA and Acción Popular, which, along with the oligarchy and imperialism, it blamed for the country's underdevelopment and dependency. It anticipated that the transfer of property, with the "concomitant transfer of political power," would bring it widespread, spontaneous popular support and that political parties would waste away in a context of public indifference. According to Haya de la Torre, APRA, faced with repeated government attacks against its leaders, had to "do what the English recommend: wait and see"—avoid confrontation and await events that would require the military to recognize the political parties. On the rare occasions when Haya made public declarations, however, as on his birthday (Apristas' "Brotherhood Day"), he suggested support for the economic reforms, underlining that he had been proposing them since 1930, and requested dialogue between the government and "the civilians"—i.e., himself. Acción Popular was more seriously affected. Its leaders, former president Belaúnde, and a small group of other top leaders were deported and a systematic government campaign aimed to discredit the party and its recent government. The party disappeared completely (albeit temporarily) from the public political scene.

The national bourgeoisie was also unable to assert its perceived interests. In the official ideology, this class had played a negative role in the country's development and was to be required to fulfill new functions in the future. These principles were embodied in abundant legislation, but the national bourgeoisie had no influence over its elaboration.

As the reforms easily destroyed the hypothetical might of the oligarchy, and as the criticisms made by other propertied sectors were rudely rejected, and bourgeoisie sought to infiltrate the state by establishing individual ties to civilian and military officials. They hoped in this way to adapt to the new situation and enable themselves to take advantage of the model of industrial accumulation. Although the political weakness of the bourgeoisie reinforced its taste for personal favors, these contacts permitted an association between the state and private capital, and an incorporation of both military officers and technical experts in the operation of enterprises. Perceptions of massive corruption at the highest levels of the public administration became widespread.

Thus, the GRFA successfully undermined the traditional petty bourgeois political organizations without resorting to repression. It also immobilized the organizations of the bourgeoisie; when it nationalized the newspapers, it took away the bourgeoisie's last means of political pressure. A political vacuum was created that demonstrated once again the political precariousness of the dominant class.

Although the GRFA brought the bourgeoisie and the political parties to their knees, it could not do the same to the popular classes and the new political forces of the revolutionary left. As mentioned previously, the government granted a series of concessions to the popular sectors—"presents that the revolution is giving the Peruvian people," according to Velasco's personal secretary, Augusto Zimmerman.

The Communist party (PC) supported the GRFA, perceiving it to be carrying out an antifeudal, anti-imperialist, and nationalist revolution, and ultimately even gaining classification as a national liberation movement. The PC did not interrupt its support for the military government, establishing a *quid pro quo* with the military. One factor in this was the government's establishment of diplomatic relations with Cuba and the Soviet Union. Whereas the government attacked APRA, virtually paralyzing its workers' federation—the Confederación de Trabajadores del Perú (CTP)—it allowed the Communist party to agitate among working sectors, and the Confederación General de Trabajadores del Perú (CGTP) (the workers' federation of the PC) took over the role previously played by the CTP.

This tie between the PC and the government did not enable the state to win over the working class, however. If the relative income distribution policy of the government was generally contradictory to its model of capitalist accumulation, in the circumstances of Peru's development, the limited potential of both policies was clear. Trying to play both sides of the game, the government was immediately outflanked by intense popular mobilizations. Moreover, over the last two decades, a tendency toward political independence had developed among the popular classes. After the Cuban revolution and the Sino-Soviet split, this tendency was reinforced by the development of a "new left."

When popular mobilization escaped the control of the PC and the military, however—as it did in the cases of the miners and the teachers—the government attacked it. As a result, important groups of workers left the CGTP, and the rank and file became hostile to its leadership. Simultaneously, the embryonic revolutionary left laid down significant political roots among the popular classes, as active participants and leaders in peasant, urban, and regional mobilizations that spread throughout the country after 1971. The revolutionary left's leaders became national figures. The government and the PC aligned to denounce the new left, classifying it as "extremist," "an agent of imperialism," "anti-revolutionary," and "destabilizing." These condemnations did not weaken the ties between the left and the large popular sectors, however. The intensification of the class struggle and the growing opposition to the state challenged the ideological imagination of the government. The leadership believed that significant sectors of society would soon recognize the value of the government's programs and transfer their allegiance to the official "process." When this did not happen, the regime's ideologues proposed the gradual creation of a "fully participatory social democracy," encompassing all social classes into a "socially harmonious" framework on corporatist terms; the interests of each class would be represented by military officers. In the official ideological design, the property structure was to be modified and the class structure eliminated; and for the first time in Peru's history, a consensus between rulers and ruled was to be established. The consensus was to be evident in the way citizens would willingly accept, without seeking to influence, the policy and orders of the leaders of the revolution.[37]

It was soon evident, however, that "property transfer" would not be enough to achieve the political integration, on subordinate terms, of the population into the military government. Thus, in spite of resistance from important military sectors, the government decided to create institutional mechanisms to "guide popular participation" and "support social mobilization," on the assumption that Peruvian society was simply apathetic and not hostile. (It very rapidly became clear that what the officers and their experts understood by "participation" was a military parade.) Together with the institutional reforms decreed by the military government, their propagandists simultaneously began an inflammatory attack upon the core ideologies of the oligarchy, of the APRA and AP parties, and of the revolutionary left. They insisted on the "originality" of the revolutionary process and on its "humanistic, Christian, gradualistic, socialist, libertarian" characteristics, aimed at achieving Peru's "second independence."

It was under these circumstance that the organized popular sectors, transferring their loyalties from the populist parties to the left, became more intensely active politically. They pursued economic demands, intervened in the administration of agrarian cooperatives and "reformed" industrial enterprises, and sought an autonomous national organization that would coordinate and radicalize the operation of the "industrial community." Moreover, peasants increasingly invaded lands and took them over, to bring about their own agrarian reform. Thus—both thanks to and in spite of the military government—the popular sectors increased their autonomy and organizational capacity.

In response, the government established a set of organizations to contain popular pressures, to channel demands through the military hierarchy, and to divide and control popular mobilization generally. The National System for the Support of Social Mobilization (SINAMOS), the Confederation of Workers of the Peruvian Revolution (CTRP), and other union federations were created under the aegis of the Ministry of the Interior and other official departments. Inaugurated with substantial official support, SINAMOS was quickly

[37] Carlos Delgado, *Revolución Peruana, Autonomía y Deslindes* (Lima: Editorial Universo, 1975); Carlos Franco, *La Revolución Participatoria* (Lima, 1974); Hector Béjar: *La Revolución en la Trampa* (Lima: Ediciones Socialismo y Participación, 1977).

wracked by the contradiction between the political development of the society and the authoritarian tendencies of the military. From the start, SINAMOS was to fulfill clearly contradictory tasks. On the one hand, it was to organize the population to hasten the government's reforms, thus stimulating the hostility of the dominant classes, of the technocratically oriented public institutions, and especially of the intelligence services, which never ceased to suspect that the directors of SINAMOS sought political autonomy. On the other hand, SINAMOS aspired to supplant popular organizations, and thus stirred their opposition. SINAMOS was caught in cross-fire between the basic classes in the society, and the ambivalence of the military government was revealed. For these reasons, SINAMOS was gradually paralyzed and ultimately "deactivated."

The rapid failure of SINAMOS demonstrated the urgency of the need to resolve the problem of popular "participation." In 1974, when economic and political crisis was evident, government interest in a proposal for a party of the Peruvian Revolution revived. One official sector supported the establishment of a party with the hope of building a popular front that would pressure the government and radicalize it. A second sector, in opposition to the first, hoped that the party would completely regiment the population and destroy the popular autonomous organizations. Yet a third group opposed both these positions, maintaining the "no-party thesis," on the grounds that the political party was inherently antidemocratic, since in the end it would always adhere to the "iron rule of oligarchy." These ideologues (who, without knowing it, were repeating old European theories) used this argument to insist upon the "spontaneous" development of rank-and-file organizations; "supported" by SINAMOS, these organizations would work to resolve the immediate problems of citizens in their work places and communities and would ultimately stir support for the military government.

But these intellectual fancies hid the central issue. As Ismael Frias, one government propagandist lucidly said, the creation of the party would undermine the makers of the Peruvian Revolution—the armed forces. The presence of a mass party on the political scene was diametrically opposed to the military predilection for exclusive leadership of the "revolutionary process." Organizing popular support might encourage impingements upon government decisions and offer openings into the political system for different social groups, a possibility ferociously rejected by the government's ideologues.

Beginning in 1973, the open confrontation between the popular classes and the state led General Velasco to say "Enough!" After the failure of SINAMOS and other state institutions with similar aims, the Revolutionary Labor Movement (MLR) was created. The MLR, which had been projected in the first years of the GRFA, aimed to repress the popular strata politically. It immediately provoked the tenacious opposition of workers and political organizations affiliated with the revolutionary left. Their successful resistance, at the culmination of the series of government failures, brought the armed forces and Velasco to political collapse. A day after the official press had called him "the undisputable and indisputed head of the Peruvian Revolution," President Velasco was deposed by the military command. Only about a dozen people were present to witness his departure to his personal residence.

Phase Two

Phase One of the Peruvian Revolution (1968–1975) eliminated the oligarchical-imperialist structure, implemented nationalist-populist structures designed to incorporate, on subordinate terms, the citizenry into the state, and proclaimed a new model of capital accumulation based on the alliance of state capital, private bourgeois capital, and multinational capital. Through these measures, the aspirations developed during the last four decades were to have been realized. The second phase, a result of the political crisis that undid Velasco's government, signified the gradual eradication of the nationalist-populist features of the first phase. It attempted to end the contradictions that blocked the new social pact between the state and capital. As the nationalist-populist measures were eradicated, the military government became increasingly isolated. The popular classes, especially the proletariat and the salaried middle classes, assailed the government for its antipopular policies, while the bourgeoisie and multinational capital continued to oppose the government for its unwillingness to discard entirely the populist legacy—and for not incorporating their own interests into those of the government.

Under these circumstances, the government saw itself obliged to devise a strategy of political withdrawal. Only through such a withdrawal could it avoid compromising military integrity and authority and destroying any legitimacy for future involvement in the political scene. The government called elections for the Constituent Assembly to begin to institutionalize the class struggle and legitimize repression of the dominated classes. The gates of political activity were opened once again to the traditional reformist political parties and, for the first time in Peruvian history, organizations of the revolutionary left emerged on the official scene. After the effective realization of the Constituent Assembly, the government felt obligated to maintain its commitment to call general elections in 1980, and eventually to accept the results.[38]

LEGACY OF THE PAST AND PERSPECTIVES OF THE FUTURE

The relative democratization that the GRFA formulated to integrate the society nationally and politically was a failure. The centuries-old problems of Peru remained pending. The military government's attempt to conciliate conflicting social interests and create a collaborative society failed because it sought to impose distributive policies in the context of a development model based on the concentration of income and capital. This development model undermined the distributive measures—which, in turn, prevented the smooth development of capital. This economic design was affected, and the entire political and economic framework complicated, by the military's own preoccupations with national security.

The overall outcome was the opposite of what the military government had proposed. A new level of social contradictions were provoked and became evident in the intensification of the class struggle and the widespread opposition to the GRFA. As the politically autonomous organizations for peasants, workers, and the salaried middle class grew, the government was unable to contain them through corporatist measures. The government's military nature rendered it incapable of promoting organized political participation and assimilating it into the interests of the state. These social contradictions intersected economic policy in such a way that Peru bordered on economic bankruptcy, and the social contradictions intensified further.

At this time, the military government decided to call elections for the Constituent Assembly and to promise a transfer of power to civilians in 1980. It also delegated to technical experts the direction of an economic policy of stabilization and repression. In other words, the military cadres correctly anticipated that the traditional political parties would take the responsibility for channeling popular demands within a legal framework appropriate to the capitalist accumulation model. The need for such institutional enclosure of popular participation was shown to be especially urgent when, in the elections for the

[38] Julio Cotler, "Intervenciones Militares y Transferencia del Poder a la Civilidad en el Peru," The Woodrow Wilson Center's Latin American Program, working paper no. 84.

Constituent Assembly, about one third of the population, centered in Lima and the south, voted for organizations of the left.

It is unlikely that institutionalization of popular participation and its absorption into a new political order can be achieved. Political fragmentation prevails and the capacity of the government to legitimize itself is very restricted, given its inability to satisfy the minimum needs of the society. Political fragmentation will not be overcome, despite the efforts by the government and the traditional rightist parties to forge "pacts" that would assure future political stability. First, an organic integration of the distinct interests of the dominant classes and political groupings is lacking; thus, none of the political groups can establish itself as the exact political representative of the dominant class. Second, each of the parties has its own interests to defend and political clients to protect. Thus, the current political scene reflects the precarious political character of Peru's dominant class.

The government's capacity for distribution and legitimation is limited for other important reasons, too: the integration of the society into the new model of capitalist accumulation on a world scale; the strengthening of the bourgeoisie; the requirements of the international financial centers; and the world economic crisis. Popular mobilization is increasingly widespread given the massive cut in citizens' incomes and opportunities, while the market continues to encourage aspirations for greater consumption.

The failure of the military's scheme demonstrated the profound limitations of a populist-nationalist regime, even a radical one. Many observers, however, persist in attributing the failure to the *military* character of the government. The reformist parties are trying to take advantage of this widespread assessment to propose various populist models to unite the population politically. Thus, in 1980, the new government was subjected, on the one hand, to multitudinous demands by peasants, workers, the salaried middle class, and that half of the population unemployed or underemployed and, on the other hand, to the pressures of capital for the consolidation of its predominance, now that the obligarchical groups have been eliminated. This last proposition must be qualified. It is probable that the new government will achieve support from the middle and popular sectors, thanks to a welfare policy, albeit a very limited one. But such a welfare policy will not be sufficient, given the extent of popular mobilization; history will be repeated.

Any effort to go beyond the reformist parameters of economic policy—by creating a million new jobs, for example—would assure colossal inflation. The idea of a "social-democratic" program based on the Swedish or Israeli model is literary license in bad taste. It is entirely beyond the realm of possibility to place upon international capital and the Peruvian bourgeoisie a tax burden similar to that in these societies (a burden necessary to increase public spending and state investment without promoting inflation). Thus, any "civilian" government will have to seek support from the armed forces, constituting a "mixed" government in which party and military organizations compete for the use of state resources.

The 1980s will culminate a long and slow process of dependent-capitalist development and of growing popular mobilization, increasingly autonomous from directives not representing its own interests. The state has shown itself unable to create bases for political legitimacy to channel this popular mobilization. In this way, Peru presents the same contradictions observed in other nations at the periphery of monopolistic capitalism: the contradiction between the democratic and national concerns brandished by the popular organizations and the weak capacity of the traditional parties and the state to legitimize the dominant order and institutionalize popular participation.

To what point in the coming years will the government and the reformist parties be able to repress and mediate these conflicts, directing the society toward a new institutionality? Will the remilitarization of the state be the only recourse of the system of domination for crushing popular organizations and demands? To what degree will the popular classes, in their confrontation with the dominant interests, achieve their political independence? Will there be evidence to support Mariátegui's proposition that only socialism can fulfill the democratic and national demands of the Peruvian people? All these are open questions.

The Evolution of Peru's Economy

Rosemary Thorp

This essay attempts to shed light on the relationship between the difficulties of the experimental regime that took power in Peru in 1968 and long-run trends of Peruvian economic development in the twentieth century. The first section summarizes Peru's twentieth-century experience, drawing on a detailed analysis made elsewhere.[1] The following sections discuss the first and second phases of the military government and explore how closely the economic problems faced by each were linked to the historical pattern discerned.

LONG-RUN TRENDS IN PERUVIAN DEVELOPMENT

Peru's twentieth-century economic history is characterized by a succession of export booms based on the country's plentiful and diverse natural resources. Sugar, cotton, and mining expanded in the 1890s; oil and copper exports dominated the first decades of this century. Soon after the economic collapse of 1929, cotton production once more emerged as a buoyant sector, as did small-scale mining of gold, lead, and zinc. Mining—and eventually fishmeal—provided the impetus in the 1950s and 1960s.

Peru's resources allowed it to be tightly integrated into the international economy as a primary producer. The strength of the forces pushing the economy to an export-led focus, however, retarded industrial development compared to other Latin American countries.[2] In certain periods of strong export growth, the income and linkage effects were fairly powerful, particularly from cotton, yet they failed to compensate for the relative absence of government policies to pro-

---

[1] I would like to acknowledge the contribution of Geoff Bertram, who co-authored with me the book on which the first and some of the second sections of the paper draw: Rosemary Thorp and Geoffrey Bertram, *Peru 1890–1977: Growth and Policy in an Open Economy* (London: Macmillan & Co., 1978).

[2] Industrial production in 1950 was only 14 percent of the gross domestic product in Peru, compared to 17 percent in Colombia and 22 percent in Chile.

mote industrial diversification (the more typical Latin American experience was that such policies developed originally in response to foreign exchange shortage and subsequently found a base in class interests that sustained them). The weakness of forces leading to diversification was consolidated by the manner in which foreign capital was built into the process. Although this foreign capital was a crucial element, it consistently allowed a fruitful symbiotic relationship with domestic capital, because it never dominated all export sectors and, more important, because, in mining in particular, the large foreign companies preferred to do business with a number of Peruvian producers rather than buy out an entire sector.[3] The symbiotic relationship, and its corollary of significant opportunities for profits within the export sector for the Peruvian elite, further weakened forces that in other countries led to the development of "nationalist" groups, protectionist pressures, an interventionist style of policy making, and ultimately the growth of administrative capabilities and structures.

Peru's entirely logical pattern of development, then, had produced by the 1960s a distinctive situation in which export-led growth created a rather undeveloped state, a weak industrial base, and comparatively weak industrial groups closely integrated with foreign capital. The nature of the bond between domestic industrialists and foreign businessmen has been discussed and documented elsewhere;[4] it can perhaps be seen most vividly in the response of domestic elite groups to opportunities in the booming fishmeal business in the early 1960s as opportunities in the export sector in general were for almost the first time becoming considerably less attractive. Much Peruvian capital entered the sector, but most of it entered indirectly via the banking system and always in conjunction with foreign capital. An illustrative quote came from a member of the Peruvian business elite when he finally decided in 1964 to enter the fishmeal trade in partner-

---

[3] This is the key reason, for example, why "returned value" in Peruvian copper mining was historically relatively high: over 50 percent on average for the major firm, Cerro de Pasco. For the years 1922–1937, this return compared with 17 percent for the International Petroleum Company and 30–40 percent for the Chilean Gran Minería, as reported by Clark Reynolds. (The estimates are taken from I. G. Bertram, "Development Problems in an Export Economy: A Study of Domestic Capitalists, Foreign Firms and Government in Peru, 1919–1930" [Doctoral dissertation, Oxford University, 1974], chapter 5).

[4] E.V.K. FitzGerald, "Peru: The Political Economy of an Intermediate Regime," *Journal of Latin American Studies* 8, no. 1 (1976): 1–21; A. Ferner, "The Industrial Bourgeoisie in the Peruvian Development Model" (Doctoral dissertation, University of Sussex, June 1977); Thorp and Bertram, Peru 1890–1977, chapter 13.

TABLE 2.1
Quantum Index of Exports, 1960–1977

1960	76	1968	112	1973	81
1964	100	1969	101	1974	81
1965	97	1970	109	1975	76
1966	96	1971	102	1976	74
1967	100	1972	110	1977	93

Sources: 1960–1969, Rosemary Thorp and Geoffrey Bertram, *Peru 1890–1977: Growth and Policy in an Open Economy* (London: Macmillan & Co., 1978); 1970–1977, Banco Central de Reserva, *Memoria* (Lima: annual), and unpublished data.

ship with a Texan oilman: "This whole fishmeal business has always smelled highly to me. But if Mr. Mecom is interested, why then, it smells like a rose."[5]

This is only part of the significance of the historical pattern; by the 1960s the old export-led model was running into a deep-rooted crisis stemming from inconsistencies between the needs of resource development and a changing socio-political context. The crisis manifested itself in increasing stagnation of exports and investment.

Peru's slowdown of export supply in the 1960s (Table 2.1) was unique in her economic history, since it was for once not related to external markets. In Table 2.2, production figures for the period since 1955 reveal steady deceleration during the 1960s. (Mining is the one exception, which I discuss below.) The slowdown was in part the result of natural resource constraints. This was the case, for example, in fishing (though such constraints were exacerbated by poor resource management). The dramatic fall in the anchovy catch after 1971 is reflected in the drop in fishmeal exports (Table 2.2). Oil production was similarly limited; despite great hopes and large investment by the multinationals, little was found.

In other cases, the projects necessary to reverse the slowdown were of such a scale and complexity that they apparently required a more dynamic and developmental state than existed in Peru. In agriculture, for example, major irrigation projects on the coast were necessary to relieve the supply constraints on cotton and sugar. Table 2.2 shows that both products had reached their limit by the mid-1960s.

Copper presented yet another problem. Business conditions that the multinational companies had come to expect in Peru—extreme liberality and security—were becoming inconsistent with new social and political trends. The increasing awareness of the implications of foreign economic penetration stirred nationalistic sentiments and a

[5] *Peruvian Times* (Lima, March 1965), quoting Augusto Wiese.

TABLE 2.2

The Volume of Production of Major Export Products, 1975–1976

(Annual Averages, Indices, 1965–69 = 100)

	Cotton	Sugar	Fishmeal	Copper	Iron Ore	Silver	Lead	Zinc	Petroleum
1945–49	60.9	57.8	0	12.7	0	31.5	34.0	21.2	58.3
1950–54	81.6	69.6	0.6	16.8	20.9[a]	48.7	59.2	42.8	64.1
1955–59	101.7	92.3	7.2	25.4	38.0	70.0	80.0	53.9	72.9
1960–64	127.4	109.7	64.5	91.7	71.2	94.4	88.7	65.9	83.3
1965–69	100.0	100.0	100.0	100.0	100.0	100.0	100.0	100.0	100.0
1970–74	79.9	108.8	78.4	110.8	87.9	113.1	113.2	137.7	100.8
1975–76	59.5	111.5	42.6	108.2	48.8	103.4	115.5	157.4	108.0

Sources: Thorp and Bertram, *Peru 1890–1977*, tables 11.9, 12.2, 12.3, 12.5; Banco Central; *Memoria*, selected yearbooks.
[a] Production began only in 1953.

suspicion that the traditional oligarchy had betrayed its responsibilities. We are familiar with the manner in which these changes were to culminate in pressures for radical ownership reforms after 1968; in the meantime, they interacted with other factors to aggravate the structural crisis. The multinationals, which controlled the major deposits, responded by withholding investment in the mining sector during the 1960s (although the copper supply was abundant) in the hope of pressuring the government to return to its former liberal attitude. (There were other motives for withhlding investment also, but this hope played a major role.) The full import of this went unnoticed for a time because supply rose sharply after the Toquepala copper mine and the Marcona iron ore project went into production in 1959–1960. In the 1960s, the role of nontraditional exports was miniscule. Peru was moving into import substitution at this point and almost nothing was as yet being done toward export promotion. "Other products" amounted consistently to some 5 percent of total exports during the decade.

The problems in the export sector in turn explain the decline in the investment coefficient (Table 2.3), although it is also related to rural unrest and the prospect of land reform, which led to a decline in agricultural investment. Expansion of state spending to compensate for the decline in private investment and the drop in exports, without adequate financing, increased foreign debt under Belaúnde, while the slowdown in other sectors led to the promotion of industry through high import content and foreign technology, thus further upsetting the balance of payments.

TABLE 2.3
Investment as a Percent of GDP,
1955–1976

	Private	Public
1955–58	17.5%	4.8%
1959–63	15.3	3.3
1964–68	10.8	4.6
1969–73	7.9	4.8
1974–76	6.5	8.8

Source: E.V.K. FitzGerald, *The Political Economy of Peru, 1956–78: Economic Development and the Restructuring of Capital* (Cambridge: Cambridge University Press, 1979).

It is clear that whatever else contributed to the October 1968 coup, it was in some measure a response to the emerging crisis as we have here described it. The military regime faced an enormous development task: it not only had to revive the economy and break the export supply bottleneck but also had to respond to mounting pressure for a somewhat wider and more nationally oriented distribution of benefits in a country that lacked a strong domestic industrial class and a well-developed and experienced state.

The previous chapter has demonstrated the unusual degree of political autonomy that characterized the early years of the Velasco regime. This was complemented by an unusual degree of autonomy in economic management provided by rising world commodity prices, by the tax reform eventually achieved by the Belaúnde government too late for its own rescue, and by the relatively low level of economic activity between 1968 and 1970. Such autonomy allowed the new government to respond to radical-nationalist trends among military officers and technocrats; the result was the so-called Peruvian experiment. The next two sections of this chapter discuss the difficulties experienced under the Velasco regime and during the *segunda fase*, in the light of Peru's historical experience.

VELASCO'S ECONOMIC STRATEGY

The Velasco policies need no description here: their content, their implicit assumptions, and their remarkable effect on the ownership structure have all been fully documented. It is also clear from various works that at first there was not a very coherent strategy; policy evolved as short-run pressures pushed the government first in one direction, then another. The regime's strategy[6] assumed that the structural and distributional aspects of the economy were strongly related, and in a rather straightforward fashion. The military claimed that the monopolization and misallocation of economic resources by the oligarchy and by foreign investors were responsible for the economic slowdown, for the growing disequilibrium, and for the failure of benefits to filter adequately through the system. It followed, therefore, that ownership reform was the crucial element necessary to restructure the economy. The goal, as reflected in the first development plan, was "new-style" export-led growth with higher value added in the export sector and increased integration into the local economy. Cen-

---

[6] For accounts, see Abraham F. Lowenthal, ed., *The Peruvian Experiment: Continuity and Change under Military Rule* (Princeton: Princeton University Press, 1975), chapter 1; E.V.K. FitzGerald, *The State and Economic Development: Peru since 1968* (Cambridge: Cambridge University Press, 1976); Thorp and Bertram, *Peru 1890–1977*. FitzGerald (p. 36) shows how the government's share of the GNP rose from 11 to 26 percent, whereas foreign capital fell from 21 to 8 percent and domestic private capital from 30 to 22 percent.

tral to government planning with respect to the balance of payments was the implementation of major mining projects in the newly expanded state sector. Gains would also come from import substitution in intermediate products and reduced outflows of profits and capital (e.g., for technology) once the role of foreign firms was limited and/or their activities more stringently regulated. Nontraditional exports were to be seriously promoted. Ownership reforms and increased protection would permit the domestic private sector to again play its part, and the appropriation of profitable export sectors would help to provide a source of funds.

Unfortunately, four major inconsistencies and false assumptions underlay this striking effort at reform. First, it was believed that the Peruvian private sector would respond to nationalistic reforms with a surge of investment. Second, nationalization was presumed to give access not only to potential but also to actual surplus. Third, a continued role for foreign investment on new terms was thought to be compatible with the government's plans. Finally, these assumptions had implications for a fourth: that in various, though rather unclear ways, the reforms would have a significant and rapid effect on the various disequilibria within the economy.

The government was soon to be disillusioned on all fronts. First, the Peruvian private sector—not noted for its dynamism after years of foreign domination—was badly shaken by the industrial community legislation and by the increased level of economic intervention. The result was that in the early years of the experiment private investment grew slowly; as Table 2.4 shows, the total growth between 1970 and 1972 was only 8 percent (despite the low level in 1970). There was some reinvestment of profits in order to avoid distribution of profits to the industrial community, but the best strategy was to make no apparent profit at all, using techniques such as overpricing to remove capital from the firm and the country.[7] As a result, until 1974, private investment fell steadily as a percentage of GDP in spite of the almost total protection available.[8]

Second, the facile expectation that nationalization of a profitable foreign firm would give ready access to surplus proved false. It was discovered that many enterprises had been run down (if not decapitalized) and desperately needed funds.[9]

[7] An interesting hypothesis to explore would be whether reinvestment of profits was negatively associated with the practicality of capital flight.

[8] The Industrial Register forbade imports of goods that could be produced locally and was in practice administered in a very protectionist fashion.

[9] This was true—not surprisingly—of both the International Petroleum Company and Cerro.

TABLE 2.4
Gross Domestic Product by Expenditure, 1970–1979
(1973 prices)

	1970	1971	1972	1973	1974	1975	1976	1977	1978	1979
	bil. soles				Indices 1970 = 100					
Private consumption	240	106	111	117	122	126	½131	132	127	128
Public consumption	40	107	114	121	132	151	159	181	162	158
Gross fixed investment:	45	115	80	147	207	197	172	128	113	122
Central goverment	78	103	117	103	157	135	103	112	84	97
Public enterprises	40	88	134	249	528	508	415	271	199	239
Private	31	113	108	138	144	172	153	130	112	122
Exports	76	95	102	69	71	71	73	81	90	109
Minus imports	49	103	101	113	145	136	123	124	85	98
Gross domestic product	353	105	107	111	120	125	128	128	127	131

Source: Instituto Nacional de Planificacion, Oficina Nacional de Estadistica, *Cuentas Nacionales del Perú, 1950–1979* (Lima, 1980).

Third, it proved decidedly difficult to persuade foreign firms to invest on the scale required by government planners, given the uncertainty generated by nationalizations and by new regulations on worker participation and technology transfer. Troublesome negotiations caused disastrous delays; eventually, the government was forced to modify its position.

Fourth, there is no evidence, for example, that nationalization did much to improve the balance of payments. This was so partly because such questions as the cost implied by dependence on foreign firms and on foreign technology were not seriously tackled by the military government. Presumably there was some reduction of profit outflow with nationalization, but in contrast to Chile, the Peruvians were willing to pay compensation, and outflows due to technology and capital goods continued unabated.[10] The only serious attempt to deal with the question of foreign currency outflow came in 1974. An import control system had existed since the early years of the regime in name only. In 1974, the Junta de Transacciones Externas (at that time an organ of the Ministry of Economy and Finance) was reformed to create an effective system of planned import control through import permits and regulation of financing. But apart from grave difficulties arising from a lack of information, the experiment conflicted with the private sector and the government was soon halted.

The problem was not only one of false assumptions; it has to be admitted—even by those most sympathetic to the goals of the Velasco regime—that there was also considerable misallocation of limited resources and a failure to develop adequate budgeting and control techniques to monitor the spending of the ministries and the mushrooming public agencies. Misallocation was particularly conspicuous in regard to the food supply bottleneck. The complex infrastructure required to support the land reforms begun under Belaúnde was almost entirely lacking. And the major irrigation project aimed at food supplies—"Majes"—is widely regarded as a grave error in economic terms, and only comprehensible in geopolitical terms, given the historical role of southern Peru.

Nontraditional exports represented the only area in which results were somewhat more promising. An export promotion scheme ("Certex") was introduced in 1968, involving rebate of certain duties and

[10] ITINTEC was the agency created by the General Industrial Law to further the development of local technology and to supervise foreign contracts. It had very little impact, however, and suffered from institutional factors as well as the long-term nature of the problem.

TABLE 2.5

Nontraditional Exports and Export Incentives, 1970–1977

(Nontraditional Exports as Percent of Total Exports)

	Total	Under Certex Scheme	Manufactures Only	Rebates and Exemptions as Percent of Value of Certex Export
1970	5.4%	1.2%	2.3%	22.0%
1971	5.0	1.8	2.3	22.0
1972	6.7	3.4	4.1	25.5
1973	9.6	7.0	8.2	24.3
1974	10.4	8.1	8.2	23.9
1975	8.2	5.7	5.2	23.8
1976	9.8	7.1	6.9	31.5
1977	12.8	9.6	8.9	32.4

Sources: H. Gonzales Cano, "Evaluación de las Incentivos Tributarios a las Exportaciones no Tradicionales en Perú," mimeograph (Buenos Aires, OEA, 1978), and data provided by the secretariat of the Ministry of Commerce.

taxes and exemption from others according to a product-ranking based on a number of criteria. The application of the scheme was gradually widened between 1970 and 1974, thus counteracting the effect of the frozen exchange rate. Table 2.5 shows that the rebates and exemptions represented an average subsidy of between 22 and 25 percent (this was increased with the 1976 reforms).[11]

The rise in nontraditional exports was certainly significant up to 1974; afterwards, the rise in internal prices and the constant exchange rate discouraged exports. It should be noted, however, that by 1974 the figure was still only 10 percent of exports, including many products with relatively low value added. A 1977 World Bank report on Latin American exports of manufactures found that in per capita terms Peru had the lowest figure of any country except Ecuador and a 1972–1974 growth rate that was far below the average.[12]

The result of all these factors was that while, on the one hand, the government was forced to do more than it had originally intended (given the failure of the private sector), on the other hand, the resources available to finance its increased role were less than anticipated. The problem became worse as the modern sector labor force, its expectations aroused by government propaganda surrounding the

[11] A fund for granting subsidized loans was also introduced. See H. Gonzales Cano, "Evaluación de las Incentivos Tributarios a las Exportaciones no Tradicionales en Perú," mimeograph, Programa del Sector Público de las OEA (Buenos Aires, 1978).

[12] International Bank for Reconstruction and Development, "Tendencias Recientes en las Exportaciones Manufactureras y Totales de Paises en Vías de Desarrollo," mimeograph (Washington, D.C., June 1977).

TABLE 2.6
Real Wages and Salaries in Lima,
1970–1977
(Indices, 1973 = 100)

	Wages	Salaries
1970	76	86
1971	84	92
1972	92	96
1973	100	100
1974	94	92
1975	94	88
1976	98	77
1977	79	65

Source: Universidad Católica, La Economía Peruana en 1977, mimeograph (Lima).

These are the figures published by the Ministry of Labor for enterprises with ten or more employees. Unofficial estimates exist giving a large fall in real terms 1973–76—for example, figures cited in B. Stallings, "Peru and the U.S. Banks: Who Has the Upper Hand?" (Madison, Wis.: University of Wisconsin, mimeograph, 1978), show a fall of 30 percent in wages 1973–1976, where the ministry data show only 23 percent. Recent unofficial estimates give the change in real wages in 1977 as −21 percent, and in 1978 as −18 percent (BOLSA Review, March 1979, p. 192).

creation of industrial communities, began to press for a larger share of the pie, thereby cutting further into state enterprise profits. Real wage and salary figures are shown in Table 2.6.

The regime faced a final and important inconsistency between its redistributive goals, which prescribed controlled prices for basic products, and the lack of a base for a solution to the resulting financial problem, once costs began to rise. The logical solution was tax reform. But the military officers were unprepared to bite either into profits or the living standards of the middle classes.[13] Their unwillingness was reinforced by the coincidence of acute financial need with surplus world liquidity—and a moment of peak optimism, internally and externally, about Peru's credit worthiness. This was the period not only of the commodity price boom but also of the first oil strikes in the Peruvian Selva. Unfortunately, the nature of the early strikes provided at least some ground for the assumption that they represented a single source and led to Petroperu's commitment to production of 200,000

[13] The middle classes, of course, included themselves. See Richard C. Webb, Government Policy and the Distribution of Income in Peru, 1963–1973 (Cambridge: Harvard University Press, 1977), chapter 4, for an analysis of the tax policies of the Velasco regime.

TABLE 2.7
Export Figures for 1977: Projections and Reality

	1977 Projection as of 1974	1977 Actual	Degree over or under Estimation
Fishmeal			
Value[a]	420	179	+135%
Volume (1000 tons)	1,400	430	+226
Price ($/ton)	300	416	−28
Cotton			
Value	84	50	+68
Volume (1000 quintales)	1,020	485	+210
Price (US ¢/lb.)	83	104	−20
Sugar			
Value	254	81	+214
Volume (1000 tons)	450	413	+9
Price (US ¢/lb.)	26	9	+187
Coffee			
Value	69	196	−65
Volume (1000 tons)	52	43	+21
Price (US ¢/lb.)	61	210	−71
Wool			
Value	12	18	−33
Volume (1000 tons)	3	3	0
Price ($/ton)	3,820	5,749	−34
Copper			
Value	737	392	+88
Volume (million tons)	418	331	+26
Price (US ¢/lb.)	80	54	+48
Iron ore			
Value	85	97	−12
Volume (million tons)	9	6	+50
Price ($/ton)	9	15	−40
Silver			
Value	144	179	−20
Volume (million oz.)	42	41	+2
Price (US ¢/oz.)	347	434	−20
Lead			
Value	82	87	−6
Volume (1000 tons)	247	172	+44
Price (US ¢/lb.)	15	23	−35
Zinc			
Value	172	155	+11
Volume (1000 tons)	460	422	+9
Price (US ¢/lb.)	17	17	0
Petroleum			
Value	396	43	+821
Volume (million bbls.)		3	
Other products			
Value	400	221	+81
Total Value	2,855	1,735	+65

Source: Estimates made by Peruvian officials for 1974 Paris Club negotiations. Actual data: Banco Central de la Reserva.

[a] All values in thousands of dollars.

TABLE 2.8
External Public Debt, 1968–1977
(In Millions of Dollars)

	1968	1970	1971	1972	1973	1974	1975	1976	1977
Gross inflow	199	190	183	286	673	1,035	1,077	846	993
Servicing	140	167	213	219	433	456	474	533	635
Net inflow	143	23	−30	67	239	579	603	313	358
Outstanding debt	797	945	997	1,121	1,491	2,182	3,066	3,641	4,243
DEBT SERVICES AS PERCENT OF EXPORTS									
Debt services	15%	16%	24%	23%	39%	30%	37%	39%	37%

Sources: Banco Central, *Memoria* (1976), p. 169, and unpublished figures.

This is debt of more than one year. If short-term debt and private sector debt is included, the figure for outstanding debt as of 1978 is estimated at around $9 billion.

barrels a day.[14] Once the oil price rose late in 1973, it seemed entirely rational to borrow abroad.

Perhaps the most vivid commentary on this period is given in Table 2.7, which compares 1974 export projections with actual 1977 exports. These are Peruvian estimates made for the Paris Club negotiations of 1974. What is remarkable is the extent to which the optimism is universal: apart from the fact that they did not foresee the effect of the Brazilian frost on coffee prices, and while the beneficial effects of the 1976 exchange reforms and other measures on small and medium mining (i.e., zinc, lead, and silver) make the overestimation somewhat less than in other cases, the phenomenon is widespread, and in volume more than in price.[15]

This moment of optimism concerning credit worthiness *also* coincided, as we have mentioned, with the boom in international lending following the growth in world liquidity in the early 1970s and the appearance of the Eurodollar market. These events are particularly significant when combined with the recession in the industrialized countries following the oil price increase; as "first-class" borrowers dropped out of the market, the banks sought clients among countries normally ranked as "second-class" borrowers. The new source of borrowing available to Third World countries was more expensive than official loans but attractive nonetheless because the loans came on exclusively commercial terms and free of all strings. By 1974 Peru was the fourth largest LDC borrower in the Eurodollar market.

The results of external borrowing are shown in Tables 2.8 and 2.9.

[14] Based on the report of a United States firm that assessed the prospects for the government.
[15] Note that the margin of error in making projections is no greater than that frequently found even in those made by more developed countries.

TABLE 2.9
New Contracted Debt by Use, 1968–1976
(In Millions of Dollars)

	1968	1970	1971	1972	1973	1974	1975	1976
Primary	5	1	76	28	153	340	30	30
Secondary	31	15	6	188	114	34	85	192
Tertiary	30	31	103	142	135	406	446	373
Refinanc-ing	93	50	3	115	293	135	160	15
Other[a]	17	130	32	28	330	380	263	773
Total	176	227	220	501	1,025	1,295	984	1,383

Source: Oficina de Credito Público, Ministerio de Economía y Finanzas.

[a] Generally understood to comprise principally defense.

This borrowing was supported and approved by the external agencies: the World Bank reported in October 1974 that "the level of non-project borrowing appears justified as a means for bridging Peru's resource gap until mineral and possible petroleum exports expand substantially starting in 1977–78" (IBRD, 1974). Predictably enough, however, given the hostility of the World Bank and the United States government to the radical nationalism displayed by Peru after 1968, ready access to the international capital market could be obtained only by moderating various elements of the military's policies.[16] In February 1974, Peru signed the Greene Agreement with the United States government, which called for a payment by Peru of $150 million as settlement of all outstanding disputes[17] with United States businesses in exchange for withdrawal of United States opposition to loans to Peru.

New contracted debt, having risen by 100 percent in 1973, subsequently rose a further 26 percent in 1974. The item "other" accounted for 26 percent of the new debt contracted in that year (Table 2.9), reflecting growing concern about a possible armed conflict with Chile.[18]

What is *not* shown in these tables, however, is extremely important, namely the rise in short-term borrowing. This was in large part due to the inadequate financial arrangements made for the wide range of new state enterprises. Without proper provision for their working

[16] See Chapter 5 of this volume, by Barbara Stallings.

[17] Officially, no compensation was paid for IPC. A lump sum was paid for the United States to allocate as it saw fit, however.

[18] It is generally accepted that the item "other" is comprised very largely of defense items.

capital needs and limited by law as to local borrowing, such enterprises were often unable to generate their own resources through pricing policy, either because they lacked market or political power, or because, as we have mentioned, the distributional policies of the Velasco regime stressed low prices of basic products. The notorious case is Petroperú, whose external debt began to rise at an alarming rate. Extensive borrowing abroad in 1974, however, increased international reserves by $282 million, in spite of the fact that the current account deficit was $807 million (Table 2.10). These credits financed the rise in imports that now began to occur: it is beyond doubt that the effect of the credits was also to encourage imports by providing an incentive to higher import content.[19]

The implicit logic of the strategy followed since 1968 held that greater command of the economic surplus would allow investments designed to reduce the vulnerability of the economy by (1) increasing export supply; (2) increasing value added in the export sector; (3) expanding domestic food supplies; (4) substituting imports at intermediate levels; (5) hardening the terms on which foreign capital entered; and (6) moving into exports of manufactures. Unfortunately, not only were the financial aspects of the plan based on fatally mistaken assumptions that led to a major increase in debt, as we have explained, but the gestation period of crucial investments also proved lengthy. (One reason for the delay was the unexpected difficulties in organizing external cooperation.) Moreover, at times the net foreign exchange effect was less dramatic than hoped. The favorable balance-of-payments effect was reduced in part because of the financial aspect, which necessitated borrowing abroad for all major projects. The net result: stagnation of export volume (a crucial long-run problem) continued up to and included 1976 (Table 2.10). The financial constraints and the political importance of urban food prices led to a disastrous policy for internal terms of trade, which, aided by misdirected investments, contributed to continued stagnation of rural production and increased external debt. By mid-1975 all these factors had combined to create a situation of acute external imbalance.

[19] The fact that this phenomenon is unmeasurable does not make it any the less important. Conversations with officials involved in the import program in 1974 confirm that the fact that finance was sought abroad did increase import content. This was not only for the usual reasons but also because it was administratively easier to obtain funds for an entire project from one source, tied to the purchasing of imports, rather than disaggregate a project and be forced to find separate financing for locally purchased components. (This was reinforced by the sheer difficulty of obtaining local finance.)

TABLE 2.10
Balance-of-Payments Summary, 1969-1976
(In Millions of Dollars)

	1969	1970	1971	1972	1973	1974	1975	1976	1977	1978	1979
Exports	880	1,034	889	945	1,112	1,503	1,291	1,359	1,726	194	3,474
Imports	−659	−700	−730	−812	−1,033	−1,909	−2,390	−2,100	−2,164	−1,600	−2,090
Visible trade balance	221	334	159	133	79	−406	−1,099	−741	−438	340	1,384
Financial services:											
Public	−37	−31	−48	−51	−66	−104	−193	−275	−300	−420	−462
Private[a]	−147	−117	−78	−70	−115	−114	−47	−91	−127	−158	−483
Non-financial services and transfers	−37	−2	−67	−44	−90	−183	−199	−85	−62	46	174
Current account balance	0	184	−34	−32	−192	−807	−1,538	−1,192	−926	−192	618
Long-term capital:											
Public	124	101	15	116	314	693	793	479	674	421	892
Private	20	−77	−43	−2	70	202	342	196			
Basic balance	144	208	−62	82	192	88	−403	−517	−252	230	1,510
Short-term capital	−56	21	−80	24	−125	244	−173[b]	−351[b]	−114[b]	−76[b]	84[b]
Monetary movements, errors, and omissions	−88	−229	142	−106	−67	−332	576[b]	867[b]	367[b]	−154[b]	−1,594[b]

Sources: Banco Central, *Memoria*, *Cuentas Nacionales del Perú* (Lima: annual); Oficina Nacional de Estadística, *Cuentas Nacionales del Perú, 1950–1979*.

[a] Undistributed profits for foreign firms are here treated as outflows on current account and inflows on capital account in accordance with present Peruvian practice. If undistributed profits are excluded, the current-account deficit is reduced to $7.2 million for 1971 and $18.8 million for 1972, with a correspondingly greater net outflow of long-term capital.

[b] Errors and omissions are included with short-term capital in this year.

PHASE TWO: THE ADJUSTMENT PROCESS[20]

Initially after Velasco was replaced by Morales Bermúdez, an attempt was made to maintain the myth of the continuation of Velasquista policies. Under pressure of the worsening crisis, however, it rapidly became clear that aid was needed from the international financial community and that internal stabilization measures were necessary, both in their own right and as the price of foreign aid. It took until mid-1976 to prepare and launch a policy. Its intensity varied over the following months according to the international options open and the degree of resistance at home, but its basic "shape" conformed to the general pattern of "orthodox" stabilization policy: demand restraint and exchange rate manipulation to improve the balance of payments by placing strict ceilings on internal credit to the public and private sectors and directly limiting imports via limiting credit.

As with earlier policies of the military, this policy too was based on false assumptions—reducible to two principal points. First, it presupposed that a drop in demand would occur by cutting public and private consumption, not investment, thus achieving compatibility between short-term and long-term goals. Second, it assumed that contraction of demand and exchange rate adjustment would improve the balance of payments in three ways. First, exports would be stimulated through adjustment of the price of tradables and increased supply following the compression of internal demand; second, a decrease of imports would result from the same two mechanisms. Third, the removal of distortions—especially in the exchange rate—would have a beneficial effect on both long- and short-term foreign capital flows.

Even a brief glance at the figures is sufficient to show that there was something radically wrong with at least some of these assumptions. Table 2.10 reveals that the balance-of-payments crisis initially worsened in 1976 and improved in 1977, due to long-awaited dividends from new copper mines, the effect of the exchange rate on nontraditional exports, falling investments which slowed imports, and fuel substitution. But the improvement was not enough to prevent an increase in debt from $3 billion in 1975 to $3.6 billion in 1976 and $4.2 billion in 1977 (Table 2.8). And the debt service/exports ratio hovered close to 40 percent. In the newly contracted debt of 1976 (Table

---

[20] Adjustment policies in this period are discussed more fully in Rosemary Thorp and Laurence Whitehead, eds., *Inflation and Stabilization in Latin America* (London: Macmillan & Co., 1979), chapter 4.

TABLE 2.11
Public Sector Revenue and Expenditure, 1974–1977
(Percent of GDP)

	1974	1975	1st half 1976	2nd half 1976	1977
Central Government					
Current expenditure:					
Wages and salaries	5.3%	5.9%	5.7%	5.3%	5.3%
Military outlays	3.5	4.6	4.4	5.5	7.3
Other	5.1	6.0	4.8	5.7	5.9
Total	13.9	16.5	14.9	16.5	18.5
Investment	4.5	5.1	4.0	5.5	3.8
Total expenditure	18.4	21.6	18.9	21.9	22.2
Revenue	15.2	16.0	14.4	14.2	14.3
State Enterprises					
Current expenditure	12.7	15.4	17.9	15.8	19.8
Investment	4.7	5.3	5.3	4.7	3.6
Revenue	13.1	14.5	17.3	20.2	22.0
Total Public Sector					
Current expenditure	28.7	33.6	34.0	33.7	38.3[a]
Investment	9.1	9.5	8.7	9.8	7.4
Revenue	31.6	32.7	33.2	35.8	36.3
Overall deficit	−6.2	−10.4	−9.4	−7.7	−9.4[a]

Source: Banco Central, unpublished data.

[a] The total public sector figure for 1977 does not include local government and municipal budgets. The weight of these in the total is tiny, as will be seen by comparing central government and state enterprises with the totals given for earlier years.

2.9) and 1977 (no figures available), defence played an overwhelming role, accounting for more than half in 1976.

The problem was augmented by rising short-term debt, primarily due to a failure to raise gasoline prices to a level that put Petroperú's financing on an adequate basis. Suppliers' credits for imports of crude petroleum sent the agency's short-term debt soaring from $195 million in 1974 to $228 million in 1975, $357 million in 1976 and $421 million by the end of 1977.[21] By 1978, therefore, the external problem remained acute, even though investment had fallen heavily, as had real wages (Tables 2.4 and 2.6). In 1977 overall growth was negative, and unemployment and underemployment was almost 60 percent of the working population.

Why so little adjustment? One important element in the explanation is that fiscal restraint was not in fact practiced. Table 2.11 makes it very clear that whatever the intentions of the Central Bank nothing was done to curb public spending. Current expenditure rose steadily

[21] Ministerio de Economía y Finanzas, "El Problema de Caja de Petroperú en 1978" (Lima: February 1978).

as a percentage of GDP throughout the supposed "adjustment" period; most of the increases were in military outlays.[22] Cuts were made in real terms in the public sector wage and salary bill, but these caused it to fall only slightly as a percentage of GDP.[23] (In fact, several categories of expenditure showed signs of leveling off in the second half of 1976; it was the 1977 failures, on top of the defense rise, that led to expenditure reaching an all-time high of 38 percent of GDP by 1977.) By 1977, the regime resorted to compression of investment spending; it fell more in the early months of 1978 but not enough to offset the effect of the depression of tax revenue.[24] The only serious gains came from increases in public enterprise prices, which reduced the overall public sector deficit in the second half of 1976. Even these increases were not enough, however, to prevent the continued build-up of foreign debt, even at short term.

The failure to attain balance led directly to continuing increases in external debt and, consequently, to drastic cuts in private sector credit and real wages and salaries. The private sector bore the brunt of credit restraint and was pushed increasingly into the informal credit market, where the higher rates formed another reason for rising unit costs with depression.

The squeeze on the private sector obviously meant that the second part of the assumption that cuts would fall on consumption, not investment, was invalid not only in regard to the public sector but even here. Private investment fell even further—despite a desperate attempt to woo the private investor by changing in 1976–1977 the Industrial Community and Social Property legislation—to the point that by 1977 it was generally agreed that the last traces of the novel elements of the "revolutionary" government had disappeared.

The gradual abandonment of all pretense at redistributive goals was also involved. The area of demand easiest to compress was real earnings and as the corrective inflation "bit," the fall in real wages and salaries was drastic (Table 2.6). The response was, for Peru, an exceptional degree of political mobilization and grassroots reaction

[22] In the case of military spending, purchases of equipment appear under "current expenditure."

[23] About 73 percent of public sector wages and salaries are comprised by the ministries of Education, Interior, and Defense. In this period, it is inconceivable that the last two could have been cut, and the extremely influential left-wing teachers' union, SUTEP, would certainly have strongly resisted more compression in education.

[24] For example, income tax was 4.9 percent of GDP in 1974 but only 2.8 percent in 1976.

TABLE 2.12
Manufacturing: Volume of Production,
1975–1978
(Percent of Change)

1975	1976	1977	1978
4.1%	4.0%	−4.3%	−3.5%

Source: Oficina Nacional de Estadística, *Cuentas Nacionales del Perú, 1950–1979* (Lima, 1980).
    Calculations include an estimate for artisan production.

(beginning with the provincial riots of June 1977) that contributed to the incoherent policy that characterized the following months.[25]

The uneven compression of demand was reflected in a drop in industrial production (Table 2.12) and in growing unemployment. Meanwhile inflation accelerated, due to the public sector price increases, the exchange rate movement, and rising unit costs as output fell. By mid-1978, the official consumer price index (CPI) was estimated to be rising at an annual rate of nearly 60 percent; in 1975 the rate was 23 percent.[26] Of the 34 percent increase in CPI in 1976, 23 points were estimated to represent "corrective" inflation resulting from policy measures; in 1977, 27 points of 38.[27]

The question why so little adjustment was actually achieved in public spending derives in part, but only in part, from the composition of the spending. Massive dismissals would be necessary to make a significant difference in the wage and salary figures; since it is inconceivable that the police, the military, or teachers, who account for over 70 percent of the wage and salary bill, could be seriously reduced in number, only ridiculous cuts in other ministries would be of any avail.[28]

Nevertheless, perhaps more economies might have been achieved, especially in public enterprises were it not for the lack of solidarity behind the stabilization policy. It is clear that even in the most coherent period of policy making (June 1976–March 1977), the impetus came from one point, the Central Bank team, unevenly supported by the minister of economy. And the objective of every other element of

[25] The regional commanders who had to handle the troubles were very influential in achieving the policy reversals of July 1977. In that month, it was obvious that internal tensions within the military were extremely high.

[26] Instituto Nacional de Estadística.

[27] Estimates made by Carlos Amat, Ministry of Economy and Finance.

[28] In mid-1978 large numbers of dismissals were in fact decreed in certain ministries—but the measure was eventually rescinded after considerable protest and a number of strikes.

the public sector was to evade restrictions as far as possible.[29] This suggests that in addition to the obvious political preconditions for adjustment, a widely based team that controls and/or speaks for diverse elements of the public sector may also be necessary.[30]

The difficulties of this type of adjustment policy sprang not only from a lack of political preconditions, however, but also from the inherent difficulties in the Peruvian economy. The strategy assumes that adjustment of relative prices and demand will secure adjustment of the external disequilibrium, with, in the Peruvian case, particular attention paid to the relationship between internal fiscal disequilibrium and external debt. But Peruvian exports are barely consumed at home. Domestic demand contraction did not increase supply—and the problem *was* a supply constraint, not lack of competitiveness. Only nontraditional exports and possibly small mining might potentially benefit, but in a period of world recession significant gains were not likely.[31]

As to debt items, many went unaffected (e.g., royalty payments), while even within visible imports relative prices had virtually no effect. The impact of demand contraction was limited by the concentration of imported industrial inputs in a few sectors.[32] A contraction in this area large enough to be significant requires a disproportionate degree of recession in the industrial sector if all sectors are contracted uniformly. This explains the limited success regarding imports: leaving defense aside, a depression of the size indicated by a fall of over 10 percent in industrial production in two years and a drop in real wages of well over 25 percent had very little effect on imports. Economies were achieved by cutting investment and by import substitution in fuel. Even in 1978 when imports were at last estimated to be signifi-

[29] This resulted, for example, in practices such as making sure that when the budget was exhausted before December, the element left uncovered was wages and salaries. Another example is the rash of advertisements for new posts that appeared when a freeze on public appointments was known to be coming in May 1977.

[30] This was one of the chief conclusions of a report written at the government's request by Duisenberg, a Dutch economist and ex-minister of finance, in May 1978.

[31] There was in fact a strong expansion in this area: exports of manufactures rose from 5 percent of total exports in 1975 to 7 percent in 1976 and 9 percent in 1977 (Table 2.5) under the impact of the exchange reform of 1976 and the increase in subsidies. The contribution on this front was important, although it involved a sharp increase in subsidies to achieve it; even so, the quantitative effect was not very great.

[32] Sixty percent of imported industrial inputs go to only three sectors, comprising a mere 22 percent of industrial value added. (Calculated from unpublished data of the Ministry of Industries.)

cantly reduced, 49 percent of the reduction was from fuel, 44 percent from defense, and only 4 percent each from consumer goods and intermediate inputs, the two elements directly sensitive to the level of demand.[33]

The remaining important element in the balance of payments is the capital account. The International Monetary Fund's negotiations with Peru have tended to emphasize the relationship between exchange rate confidence and short-term capital; the IMF's underlying assumption is clearly that a healthy, undistorted economy will attract long-term capital.[34] Unfortunately, it appears that in Peru, capital movements, both long- and short-term, are related closely to more intangible variables of confidence in internal policy making and issues such as the Industrial Community. The atmosphere of strikes and political uncertainty partly associated with stabilization ensured that private capital flows would not be favorable.

CONCLUSION

I have reviewed here two sharply different phases of the Peruvian experiment. Many different factors contributed to its failure, including a number of instances of bad luck and unfortunate timing on the international scene, such as rising import prices in 1973–1974 and optimism based on oil. What I have tried to show in the preceding pages is the extent to which the solution that was opted for required—and presupposed—a sophisticated, dynamic local entrepreneurial group and a competent, experienced state. Yet precisely because of the historical process leading to 1968, neither existed. The ensuing problems of mismanagement and lack of response and/or of resources all culminated in acute internal and external disequilibrium in 1975.

The route chosen to handle that disequilibrium generated high social and economic costs and small, if any, gains. In practice, investment bore the brunt of the cuts, given the lack of political and institutional preconditions needed to reduce government consumption and the effect of the depression on tax revenue. Decreased investment expenditure, however, was not enough to prevent a continuing rise in external debt, and sharp cuts in wages and industrial output had minimal beneficial effects on the external imbalance.

Much of my analysis suggests that a different type of policy, con-

[33] Estimated from preliminary figures supplied by the Banco Central.

[34] See, for example, E. Spitzer, chapter 20, in N. de Vries et al., *The International Monetary Fund, 1945–65,* vol. 3 (Washington, D.C.: International Monetary Fund, 1969).

centrating on *selective* cuts and restrictions and working to create new export openings, would have been more effective. But the point of this analysis is that there was an absence of the necessary capacity to apply the type of sophisticated policy necessary, in light of the small room left for maneuvering once the crisis became acute. There were no groups ready to respond in the private sector, either. Further, a history of export-led growth closes certain options—for example, by creating dependence on imported foodstuffs, it makes a moratorium on external debt virtually impossible.

When one adds to these elements the inflexibility of the international financial communities,[35] it is small wonder that the government made no serious effort to pursue a nonorthodox line. Instead it committed itself increasingly to orthodox policies, even though this meant the gradual abandonment of important elements of the original "revolutionary" policies. And it is not surprising that in due course the economic problems encountered so sharpened divisions within the military that the regime decided to relinquish power altogether by 1980, so finally ending the Peruvian experiment.

What do we learn, then, from that ten-year experiment? Could it have succeeded with less bad luck and more flexibility from the international community? The long-run perspective I have tried to sketch here strongly suggests that the obstacles were of such magnitude that it would have taken much more than a little luck to allow the original policies to work. The inconsistencies of the policies and the institutional weaknesses required a substantial learning period, but neither political nor economic breathing space can be expected to last more than three or four years in an economy dependent on international primary product prices. In addition, breathing space tends to weaken the instinct for reform.

Were there nevertheless significant changes? Chapter 1 depicts the increase in political mobilization; in economic terms, it is the increased role of the state that is more striking, and there are indications that questions of control and coordination within the state system began to be tackled toward the end of the period. In the crucial areas of distribution and the ability to withstand international economic fluctuations, however, we can record no progress. There may have been a certain expansion of nontraditional exports, but it is nevertheless true that Peru's economic health remains perilously dependent on the price of copper and on limited supplies of oil.

[35] The degree of flexibility is always a matter of the bargaining strength of the two sides as well as a question of confidence in the capacity of government to handle different types of policy. Peru had recently been in a relatively poor position on both counts.

II

The Experiment from Economic Perspectives

State Capitalism in Peru: A Model of Economic Development and Its Limitations

E.V.K. FitzGerald

The year 1978 may be taken to mark the end of the Peruvian experiment in a double sense: it saw the election of the Constituent Assembly, charged with drawing up the first constitution in nearly fifty years, and the abandonment of the economic expansion of the "Peruvian model," upon which the military regime had based its hopes of overcoming dependency and underdevelopment. In 1980 the military permitted the very man they had replaced over a decade before, Fernando Belaúnde Terry, to return to the presidency; and in the same year the economy was finally stabilized by recourse to two traditional Peruvian remedies—favorable changes in international prices and draconian wage restrictions. This leap back to the political and economic past was motivated to a considerable extent by the limitations of the state capitalist model established between 1968 and 1975, although the problems encountered in the implementation of this model will continue into the 1980s.

An analysis of the economic model pursued by the Revolutionary Government of the Armed Forces serves as a key element in the understanding of the political economy of the 1970s in Peru; but it should also—insofar as the model reflected the explicit beliefs of many Latin American reformist intellectuals concerning the obstacles to be overcome (such as land tenure, foreign ownership, and insufficient infrastructure) and their implicit reliance on state capitalism as a means of achieving a new model of accumulation—shed light upon both the adequacy of the intellectuals' diagnosis and the validity of the original prognosis:

> The academic tendency . . . was to believe that the anti-imperialist struggle could lead to the reorganization of the economy and nationalist policy. It was thought that, under the impulse of large state enterprises and an agriculture stimulated by land reform, it

would be possible to achieve industrialization, strengthening the national entrepreneurs and increasing popular participation[1]

The economic problems that beset the GRFA sprang from the intrinsic nature of the state capitalist model in general and from the particularly unbalanced form in which it was instituted in Peru. They were not just a matter of inept economic management or of exogenous circumstances, although there are examples of both. On the one hand, the decision to press forward with anchovy fishing in 1970–1971 despite evidence of overfishing, the almost willful neglect of food production between 1969 and 1974, and the lack of control over foreign borrowing between 1973 and 1976 can only be described as policy errors; on the other, the discovery that there was only a limited amount of oil in the Amazon basin after all, the halving of the world price of copper in 1974, and the impact of transfer pricing by the multinationals were factors neither under the control of the planners nor easily anticipated. These problems can not be understood merely as the result of inconsistent policy measures adopted by a government experiencing internal dissent and a changing power balance, either; as we shall attempt to show, there was an overall logic to the strategy, limited as it was by its own contradictions. In retrospect, the relative stability of the regime between 1968 and 1979, despite the conservative shift in 1975 and the attempts to stabilize the economy after 1976, stands out clearly.

The state capitalist model was adopted for particular historical reasons related to the breakdown of the traditional Peruvian growth model and a "vacuum" in the political structure. Such a model contains specific political inconsistencies derived from the "relative autonomy" of the regime that institutes it, a relative autonomy that is reduced to the extent that the state becomes a capitalist itself and develops new relationships with various groups and classes. In the Peruvian case, however, it would seem that the model was mortally weakened by the economic difficulties caused by the transfer of the burden of investment from the private to the public sector without the latter having access to the former's profits. To understand this problem, it is necessary to examine economic strategy during the 1968–1979 period in relation to the essential economic features of the model and, in

---

[1] Fernando Henrique Cardoso, "El Estado Actual de los Estudios sobre Dependencia," in José Serra, ed., *Desarrollo Latino-Americano: Ensayos Críticos* (Mexico: Fondo de Cultura Económica, 1974), p. 329 (my translation). See also Cardoso, "The Originality of the Copy: ECLA and the Idea of Development," *Working Papers Series,* No. 27 (Cambridge: Centre for Latin American Studies, 1977).

turn, to Peru's social and political structure. It is not the purpose of this chapter, therefore, to discuss detailed aspects of topics such as production, sectoral policy, economic structure, or negotiations with foreign banks; rather, it is to attempt to grasp the economic essence of the Peruvian model itself.

The State Capitalist Model

Historically, the process of transforming an export-led economy based on natural resources to one based on industry serving domestic markets requires an extensive restructuring of capital, involving change not only in the pattern of production (sectoral balance, input use, and so on) but also in the ownership of assets on the one hand and in the relationship between capital and labor on the other. This restructuring, which is an essential part of economic development, implies the establishment of a new model of accumulation, that is, new investment and savings patterns, a different distribution of income, and the creation of capital in fresh forms. There is a familiar argument to the effect that, in view of the weakness of the "national industrial" groups in underdeveloped countries, unless restructuring is undertaken by foreign enterprises, the state will have to perform this task itself. This belief arises for two reasons: first, because restructuring requires massive amounts of investment, close coordination, and little profitability in the short term; second, because it involves action against the immediate interests of ownership groups that dominate the economy—particularly "traditional" landowning, trading, and financial groups and foreign interests. This "historical task" is held to explain the occurrence of state capitalism in developing countries.[2]

By "state capitalism" in this context[3] we mean that the state takes responsibility for organizing production and accumulation in the modern sector of the economy and that public ownership replaces private ownership in key branches. This concept should be clearly distinguished from the concept of "state monopoly capitalism" as used by Marxist economists to describe mature capitalist economies in which giant corporations enjoy a symbiotic relationship with a

[2] James Petras, "State Capitalism and the Third World," *Development and Change* 8 (1977):1. The classic argument to this effect is, of course, Alexander Gerschenkron, *Economic Backwardness in Historical Perspective* (Cambridge: Harvard University Press, Belknap Press, 1962).

[3] Tamás Szentes, *The Political Economy of Underdevelopment* (Budapest: Akademiai Kiado, 1973), pp. 311–321.

large welfare state—a case that does not apply to a developing country because domestic business is weaker and the welfare function less significant. Moreover, it should not be confused with the purely formal jurisdiction that all governments have over business in any mixed economy through instruments such as labor laws, investment permits, and credit control. Although the relationship between capital and labor is similar to that obtaining under private capitalism, state capitalism should be capable of investing more rapidly, in a more coherent manner, and in productive rather than profitable projects of more concern to national objectives (such as the balance of payments) than the individual private investor. In other words, it should be able to take a wider and longer view of economic development.

In order to achieve the required restructuring of capital, the state must possess—or more accurately, the political conditions must be such that there exists—a considerable degree of "relative autonomy" from the various ownership groups or "fractions of capital" that are to be affected.[4] In fact, the normal management of a semi-industrialized economy requires such relative autonomy in order to make effective alterations in, say, exchange rates without a prolonged process of political bargaining and in the interest of capital accumulation as a whole rather than the profits of a particular group. The restructuring of a whole production system requires, inevitably, extensive state intervention from a long-term viewpoint. The classic example of this type of "exceptional state" is found in a nation at war, but the history of the push toward industrialization in peace time has also involved significant cases, for example, Japan and Germany in the last century, Brazil and South Korea in this. On the periphery of the world economy, however, the combination of a weak domestic elite with the naturally strong national resistance to control of the economy by foreign investors in postcolonial nations seems to be an ideal situation for the emergence of so-called intermediate regimes that attempt to tread the familiar path of *ni capitalista ni comunista*.[5] In Latin America, even though the postcolonial experience is hardly relevant today, the impact of foreign investment upon the domestic elite and the nationalism of the emergent "professional middle class" (which includes the

---

[4] Alfred Stepan, *The State and Society: Peru in Comparative Perspective* (Princeton: Princeton University Press, 1978), and Thomas Bamat, "Relative State Autonomy and Capitalism in Brazil and Peru," *The Insurgent Sociologist* 7 (1977):2, have discussions of the concept of "relative autonomy" in general and its application to Peru in particular.

[5] "Social and Economic Aspects of Intermediate Regimes," in Michal Kalecki, *Essays on the Economic Growth of the Socialist and Mixed Economy* (Cambridge: Cambridge University Press, 1972).

military) has at times created the conditions of relative autonomy—domestically if not internationally—for the establishment of an intermediate regime.[6] Such a regime naturally relies on state accumulation to provide the growth dynamic and attempts to reduce dependency by nationalizing foreign assets and pursuing import substitution; but its popular base is fragile and it does not involve mass mobilization.

For a state capitalist model to be coherent, it must not only invest but also mobilize sufficient resources. In macroeconomic terms, it must shift the surplus away from the private sector (affecting profits and wages) and toward itself. In financial terms this implies both high profitability for state enterprises and a surplus on fiscal account so that the public sector can generate savings commensurate with its investment burden; otherwise, the treasury will create too much demand pressure through budget deficits or engage in excessive foreign borrowing. Heavy taxes, high enterprise profits, and wage control, however, will weaken the position of the state on a domestic political plane, while its role as a capitalist will inevitably force it into direct conflict with its own labor force on a social one. Finally, if foreign technology is used in the industrialization process, the state will continue much the same relationship with the multinationals that weakened the domestic elite, particularly if its bargaining position is further compromised by reliance on external finance for its investment program. There are good reasons, therefore, to believe that the relative autonomy upon which state capitalism rests—in the absence of a strong political base beyond the interests of the bureaucracy and the military—will be eroded by the very dynamic of the accumulation model itself. Specifically, it may well be that a state capitalist model will of itself move toward an accommodation with foreign business and confrontation with organized labor (compromising thereby any nationalist and populist basis of its domestic support) because the transition to socialism would require popular mobilization on a scale incompatible with an intermediate regime—particularly of the military variety.

STATE CAPITALISM IN PERU

The economic problems of Peru in the decade leading up to October 1978 were far from temporary. They did not merely reflect the trade

[6] E.V.K. FitzGerald, "On State Accumulation in Latin America," in E.V.K. FitzGerald, Edgardo Floto, and A. David Lehmann, eds., *The State and Economic Development in Latin America,* conference series no. 1 (Cambridge: Centre for Latin American Studies, 1977).

cycle or policy mismanagement, although these were contributory factors. Rather, the decade was one in which the domestic elite's political control broke down, along with the traditional model of growth and investment. This breakdown created a political vacuum and at the same time demonstrated the need for a new model of accumulation if economic development were to be achieved; the military was willing to occupy the "political space" and progressive technocrats were ready to implement new development schemes.[7]

The very considerable changes that did take place in the economy between 1968 and 1975 can easily be overlooked if the social impact of the self-styled Peruvian Revolution on the work force alone is observed rather than the changes in ownership and control over the economy. If we assume that control over gross domestic product in the corporate sector is the appropriate indicator,[8] then in 1950, about 72 percent was controlled by domestic private business, 17 percent by foreign enterprise, and 11 percent by the public sector—mainly central government wages. The expansion of foreign mining interests (Toquepala and Marcona), the arrival of manufacturing multinationals, and the establishment of public enterprises changed these proportions by 1968 to 51 percent private, 33 percent foreign, and 16 percent public. Indeed, one of the main reasons given by the new regime for the military intervention of that year was precisely this increase in foreign penetration and the continued "oligarchic" control of much of export agriculture, banking, and heavy industry—large multisectoral ownership groups may have accounted for as much as 25 percent of corporate production in 1968. The nationalization of mining, fishing, and heavy industry, the agrarian reform, and the expansion of public enterprise after 1968 did, therefore, result in a considerable shift in the pattern of ownership: by 1975, 31 percent of corporate sector output was controlled by the public sector, 17 percent was still in the hands of foreign firms, only 40 percent was accounted for by domestic private business, and 12 percent by the new coopera-

---

[7] E.V.K. FitzGerald, "Peru: the Political Economy of an Intermediate Regime," *Journal of Latin American Studies* 8 (1976):1. The argument is further developed in E.V.K. FitzGerald, *The Political Economy of Peru, 1956–78: Economic Development and the Restructuring of Capital* (Cambridge: Cambridge University Press, 1979), chapter 3. See also the references in footnote 4, this chapter, and Julio Cotler, "The New Mode of Political Domination in Peru," in Abraham F. Lowenthal, ed., *The Peruvian Experiment: Continuity and Change under Military Rule* (Princeton: Princeton University Press, 1975).

[8] See appendix to E.V.K. FitzGerald, *The State and Economic Development: Peru since 1968*, Cambridge University Department of Applied Economics occasional paper no. 49 (Cambridge: Cambridge University Press, 1976). Also see FitzGerald, *The Political Economy of Peru, 1956–78*, chapter 4.

tive sector (mainly as the result of the agrarian reform). In addition, the state became responsible for three quarters of exports, one half of imports, more than half of fixed investment, two thirds of bank credit, and a third of all employment in the corporate sector. These changes were achieved with remarkably little resistance, mainly because of the very breakdown in the political order that had permitted the new regime to exist.

This new ownership pattern was part of the restructuring of capital that the regime thought necessary for development. A new relationship between capital and labor was another key element. But the attempt to introduce worker participation in enterprise management and ameliorate social conflicts between labor and capital was overridden by the logic of the market economy. The agrarian reform created a form of cooperative in the countryside,[9] essentially as an adjunct to the public sector, but one that conflicted with both free labor and the state itself. Labor participation in state enterprise management or profits was ruled out at a very early stage, and the "social property" experiment quickly foundered because there was no room for new firms in highly concentrated manufacturing branches. Even the industrial communities eventually served to strengthen the political cohesion of the labor movement and deter private investment rather than foster harmony between the two. Although the intentions of some of the more progressive members of the Velasco government (particularly the civilians) may have included a real change in the social relations of production, the major important change in ownership between 1968 and 1975 was not "worker participation" at all but the establishment of the bases of state capitalism in Peru,[10] the effect of which was precisely to limit popular control of the means of production and create conflict between the government and trade unions. It is in terms of its capacity to raise and sustain the rate of productive investment that the Peruvian model must be judged, therefore.

INVESTMENT

The central economic aim of the Peruvian experiment was the recovery of the system of investment and the shift of the structure of capital

[9] See José María Caballero, *Agricultura, Reforma Agraria y Pobreza Campesina* (Lima: IEP Ediciones, 1980); also Caballero and Enrique Alvarez, *Aspectos Cuantitativos de la Reforma Agraria 1969–79* (Lima: IEP Ediciones, 1980).

[10] This term did cause some problems in Peru: the author was criticized by a Peruvian general for using it in an internal planning document on the grounds that "eso es lo que tienen en Rusia, no?"

toward industry. The rate of private investment had tended to decline over the long run, and moreover, productive investment had shifted toward profitable activities such as real estate development (see tables 3.1 and 3.2). In the 1960s, the state had already begun to increase its infrastructure provision and development loans on an in-

TABLE 3.1

Aggregate Investment, 1959–1979

(Percent of GDP)

	1959–63	1964–68	1969–73	1974–76	1977–78	1979
Gross fixed capital formation:						
Private	15.3%	10.8%	7.9%	8.1%	8.3%	8.3%
Public	3.3	4.6	4.8	8.4	5.7	5.5
	18.6	15.4	12.7	16.5	14.0	13.8
Stock-building	2.5	2.8	1.5	2.3	0.5	0.2
Gross capital formation	21.1	18.2	14.2	18.8	14.5	14.0
"Productive investment":[a]						
Private	10.1	4.6	3.9	5.1	4.8	5.5
Public	1.7	2.4	3.1	7.2	5.7	4.5
	12.1	8.0	7.0	12.3	10.5	10.0

Source: E.V.K. FitzGerald, *The Political Economy of Peru, 1956–1978: Economic Development and the Restructuring of Capital* (Cambridge: Cambridge University Press, 1979), Table 6.1, p. 150. This and the succeeding tables on Peru are calculated from the official national accounts and budgetary figures, discussion of which can be found in FitzGerald, op. cit. Estimates for 1979 and correction of the 1978 figures are based on the following sources: ONEC, *Cuentas Nacionales del Perú, 1970–1979* (Lima, 1980); J. Iguiñez and I. Rivera, "La Economía Peruana en 1979," *Economía* 3 (1980):5; G. Saberbein, ed., *Informe de la Economía Peruana, 1979* (Lima: Editorial Universo, 1980).

[a] Investment in the primary, secondary, and economic infrastructure sectors.

TABLE 3.2

Composition of Gross Fixed Capital Formation, 1960–1976

(Percent of GDP)

	1960–1968			1969–1976		
	Private	Public	Total	Private	Public	Total
Agriculture	0.4%	0.3%	0.7%	0.2%	0.6%	0.8%
Mining, oil	0.3	—	0.3	1.5	1.1	2.6
Fishing	1.0	—	1.0	—	—	—
Industry	3.6	0.5	4.1	2.1	1.6	3.7
Production	5.3	0.8	6.1	3.8	3.3	7.1
Transport	2.1	1.2	3.3	0.4	0.9	1.3
Other sectors	5.6 [a]	1.9	7.5	3.9 [a]	2.3	6.2
Total	13.0	3.9	16.9	8.1	6.5	14.6

Source: FitzGerald, *The Political Economy of Peru, 1956–1978*, Table 6.1, p. 150.

[a] Mainly housing.

sufficient savings base, leading to inflationary budget deficits and considerable foreign borrowing. After 1968 this imbalance assumed far more significance because the state became the center of accumulation—accounting for two thirds of productive investment by the 1974–1976 period—while the private sector (apart from foreign oil and mining ventures in conjunction with the state) was investing only enough to cover replacement requirements. The state failed to acquire a significant proportion of the profits previously earned by the private sector, however; although private profits (Table 3.3) and private domestic savings (Table 3.4) continued to *rise* as a proportion of

TABLE 3.3
Aggregate Savings, 1959–1979
(Percent of GDP)

	1959–63	1964–68	1969–73	1974–76	1977–78	1979
Personal savings	8.0%	3.0%	1.4%	11.4%	13.9%	16.2%
Company savings	10.3	13.4	12.2			
Current government surplus	1.7	−0.5	1.0	0.3	−1.5	2.9
Internal savings	20.0	15.9	14.6	11.7	12.3	19.1
Foreign finance	1.1	2.3	−0.4	7.1	2.2	−4.3
Total savings	21.1	18.2	14.2	18.8	14.5	14.8
Private funds:						
Own	18.2	16.4	13.0	11.6	12.6	15.2
Foreign	1.8	.0	−2.2	1.5	−1.9	−4.0
	20.0	16.4	10.8	13.1	10.7	11.2
Public funds:						
Own	1.8	−0.5	1.6	−1.0	−3.2	3.9
Foreign	−0.7	2.3	1.8	5.6	4.1	−0.3
	1.1	1.8	3.4	5.7	4.1	3.6

Source: FitzGerald, *The Political Economy of Peru, 1956–1978,* Table 6.4, p. 157; updated as in footnote to Table 3.1, this volume.

TABLE 3.4
Composition of National Expenditure, 1960–1979
(Percent of GDP)

	1960	1965	1970	1975	1979
Consumption:					
Government	8.4%	10.8%	10.1%	11.6%	10.8%
Other	67.4	71.9	72.8	78.5	64.9
	75.8	82.7	82.9	90.1	75.9
Gross capital formation	21.6	18.6	12.9	19.7	14.0
Plus exports	23.7	18.0	20.1	12.4	29.7
Minus imports	21.1	19.3	15.9	22.1	19.4
Gross domestic product	100.0	100.0	100.0	100.0	100.0

Source: FitzGerald, *The Political Economy of Peru, 1956–1978,* Table 6.9, p. 169; updated as in footnote to Table 3.1, this volume.

national income, dividend distribution increased and capital flight worsened (Table 3.5), while the rate of private investment fell. This was the basic imbalance in the Peruvian version of the state capitalist model: an imbalance expressed as inflationary budget deficits covered by illusory treasury funding from the state banks, large-scale borrowing on the North American and European money markets, and an excessive level of private consumption out of profits.

Just why private investment should have fallen off so sharply—from 13 percent of the gross domestic product (GDP) between 1964 and 1968 to 9 percent between 1974 and 1976 and 8 percent between 1977 and 1979—is not entirely clear. Attributing it to a "lack of business confidence" after 1968 doubtless contains more than a grain of truth but is too facile a solution. First, the trend had been downward for some time, declining from 22 percent of GDP between 1955 and 1968 to 18 percent in 1959–1963 and 13 percent between 1964 and 1968. Further, the rate of *productive* nonmining investment had already fallen by half between 1959–1963 and 1964–1968; in fact, it remained at that level in the 1969–1973 period. Second, the decline cannot be attributed to a shortage of funds resulting from govern-

TABLE 3.5
Public Sector Accumulation, 1959–1979
(Percent of GDP)

	1959–63	1964–68	1969–73	1974–76	1977–78	1979
General government:						
Current income	15.3%	17.7%	18.7%	17.1%	17.9%	19.7%
Current expenditure	13.6	18.2	17.7	17.9	22.6	16.8
	1.7	−0.5	1.0	−0.8	−4.7	2.9
Public enterprise						
surplus	—	—	0.6	−0.2	1.5	1.0
	1.7	−0.5	1.6	−1.0	−3.2	3.9
Gross fixed capital						
formation:						
General government	1.6	2.4	2.6	2.8	3.6	2.2
State enterprise	1.7	2.2	2.2	5.6	3.0	2.5
Total	3.3	4.6	4.8	8.4	6.6	4.7
Economic deficit	1.6	5.1	3.2	9.4	9.8	0.8
Public financial						
investment	0.6	1.2	1.3	2.7	2.0	n.a.
Financial deficit	2.2	6.3	4.5	12.1	11.8	n.a.
Public sector borrowing						
requirement:						
Domestic	2.9	4.0	2.7	6.5	7.6	—
Foreign	−0.7	2.3	1.8	5.6	4.2	−0.3
	2.2	6.3	4.5	12.1	18.8	n.a.

Source: FitzGerald, *The Political Economy of Peru, 1956–1978,* Table 7.7, p. 207; updated as in footnote to Table 3.1, this volume.

TABLE 3.6
Functional Distribution of Income, 1960–1979
(Percent of Net Disposable Income)

	1960	1965	1970	1973	1976	1979
Earned income:						
Empleados	22.2%	23.8%	24.2%	24.4%	23.9%	41.0%
Obreros	22.7	23.4	21.6	23.9	22.1	
Independents:						
Agricultores	13.3	11.5	11.8	7.9	8.9	23.3
Other	15.3	15.8	15.1	15.7	15.6	
Property:						
Local profits	14.9	16.1	19.5	22.0	24.5	24.7
Expatriated profits	2.8	1.9	1.7	1.3	0.8	7.3
Rents and interest	8.8	7.5	6.0	4.7	4.2	3.7
	100.0	100.0	100.0	100.0	100.0	100.0

Source: FitzGerald, *The Political Economy of Peru, 1956–1978,* Table 5.5, p. 129; updated as in footnote to Table 3.1, this volume. The effect of land reform on income distribution would not show up here, because both estate agriculture and cooperatives would come under "profits," although the effect was small (not more than 2 percent of GDP); the effect of the industrial community should be to lower profits in favor of wages.

ment borrowing ("crowding out"), because the profit rate remained high and unused credits were always available from development banks, although the consequent inflation did make speculation in stocks (inventories rose sharply, see Table 3.6) and against the sol (i.e., capital flight) a very attractive proposition. Third, although there was considerable excess manufacturing capacity for output expansion without further investment in 1968, it had been almost used up by 1974 and further private investment was urgently needed; only the sharp demand inflation from 1976 onwards prevented a severe underproduction crisis. The military regime *wanted* "independent" industrialists to invest, and considerable fiscal incentives were offered under the General Industrial Law—against which the Industrial Community was hardly an insurmountable obstacle. This strategy was apparently based upon the ECLA belief that the "independent industrialists" had been blocked by traditional oligarchies and multinationals;[11] the removal (or at least the hampering) of the oligarchical and multinational restraints should allow the independents to spring forward as investors. But this the independents did not do. The reason, in retrospect, was not just that they lacked confidence in the future but also that the structure of ownership in industry deter-

[11] See footnote 1, this chapter. Anthony M. Ferner, "The Dominant Class and Industrial Development in Peru," *Journal of Development Studies* 15, no. 4 (1979) has an interesting analysis of the political role of these industrialists in the events of 1968–1975, although he tends to overestimate their economic role.

mined that the two groups badly hit by other reforms—the oligarchy and the multinationals—were in fact responsible for most industrial assets.[12] The major multisectoral ownership groups were in organizational disarray by the 1960s and were effectively dismembered by the post-1968 reforms, while the nonmining multinationals clearly regarded government policy in general—and the enforcement of Andean Pact provisions in particular—as inimicable to their interests.

Throughout the 1968–1979 period, private domestic investment net of replacements and housing was almost negligible. Foreign investment was confined to mining and oil; only two special projects of any size were undertaken in other sectors (the Bayer chemical plant for the Andean Common Market and the Lima Sheraton to use up blocked compensation funds). In effect, all these projects could be classed as "joint ventures," along with the technology contracts for tractors in Trujillo and copper refining in Ica, because they depended on highly specific government concessions. Private domestic investment in the 1973–1977 period was only 21 percent of the national total, compared to 34 percent by the foreign companies and 45 percent by the public sector.[13]

Because private investment did not recover, the state became the center of accumulation, accounting for half of fixed investment, financing much of the rest, and responsible for the negotiation of the two major foreign investment projects of the period—Amazon oil and Cuajone copper. This is not the place to dwell on these negotiations, except to note that in both cases the regime's strong nationalist position involved considerable costs—the trans-Andean oil pipeline instead of Amazon tankerage or an Ecuadorian spur and the two-year delay over copper marketing arrangements—and that the result was to integrate the economy more firmly than ever into the international division of labor as a virtual mono-exporter. More important for our argument, the expansion of public investment and the decline of public sector savings rates expanded the public sector borrowing requirement from 2 percent of GDP in 1969 to 13 percent in 1976; shifts of this magnitude involved, between 1974 and 1976, the transfer of over a quarter of private savings to the public sector and external official borrowing at a rate of 5 percent of GDP to cover nearly a half of public investment. The effects of this imbalance upon any economy,

[12] Roughly one half of production was in the hands of foreign firms and a further sixth in those of the "oligarchy," plus ten percent in those of state enterprise in 1968, leaving no more than a quarter to the independent industrialists. For source, see footnote 8, this chapter.

[13] Emilio Zuñiga, "The Process of Capital Formation in the Peruvian Economy, 1968–78" (M.Phil. dissertation, Cambridge University, 1979).

TABLE 3.7
Private Company Profits, 1958–1976
(Percent of GDP)

	1958–63	1964–68	1969–73	1974–76
Company savings:				
Depreciation funds	5.6%	6.0%	5.0%	5.0%
Retained profits	4.8	7.3	6.3	6.5
	10.3	13.3	11.3	11.5
Distributed profits:				
Domestically	3.3	2.8	6.1	8.1
Abroad	2.3	2.1	1.3	0.9
Profit taxes	3.9	3.1	3.7	3.9
Gross company profits	19.9	21.3	22.4	24.4

Source: FitzGerald, *The Political Economy of Peru, 1956–1978,* Table 6.5, p. 158.

let alone one with an inelastic supply structure, was bound to be destabilizing, to say the least. This problem can be characterized as a "fiscal crisis of the Peruvian state,"[14] a crisis that represented a fundamental contradiction in a model of accumulation and not just a problem of excess demand pressure on the parity stemming from too high a money supply. The sharp reversal of the public sector savings position in 1979, after the continued deficits of 1977–1978 despite stabilization policies, was mainly due to cuts in investment and automatic recovery of tax income from mineral exports; in other words, the fiscal crisis as such was not resolved.

FINANCE

As Table 3.7 indicates, the principal feature of the general government account was the stability in current income as a percentage of GDP. Despite efforts to improve direct tax collection, rationalize consumption taxes, and raise import tariffs,[15] there was no real improvement in government savings, even though current expenditure was kept within reasonable limits up to 1976. This had already caused severe difficulties under President Belaúnde, but he had faced insurmountable congressional opposition to his tax proposals.[16] It is very

[14] The term stems from James O'Connor, *The Fiscal Crisis of the State* (New York: St. Martin's Press, 1973). O'Connor's model is rather more relevant to Latin America than it is to the United States, where his application of it is somewhat simplistic; see E.V.K. FitzGerald, "The Fiscal Crisis of the Latin American State," in J.F.J. Toye, ed., *Taxation and Economic Development* (London: Cass, 1978).

[15] In fact, collection efforts just about compensated for the decline in tariff income due to import substitution.

[16] For an excellent "insider" account of this period, see Pedro-Pablo Kuczynski, *Peruvian Democracy under Economic Stress: An Account of the Belaúnde Administration* (Princeton: Princeton University Press, 1977).

TABLE 3.8
Balance-of-Payments Summary, 1965–1979
(In Millions of Dollars)

	1965–67	1968–73	1974–76	1977–78	1979
Exports f.o.b.	739	950	1,384	1,930	3,467
Imports f.o.b.	−760	−768	−2,133	−2,035	−2,060
Trade balance	−22	182	−749	−105	1,407
Profit and interest	−119	−149	−229	−511	−819
Other services (net)	−75	−49	−202		
	−216	−16	−1,180	−616	588
Long-term capital (net):					
Public	122	129	655	483	855
Private	28	−17	247	66	30
Short-term capital[a]	52	−53	−298	−92	13
	193	60	604	457	898
Reserves, etc.	23	44	576	−159	1,486

Source: FitzGerald, *The Political Economy of Peru, 1956–1978,* Table 4.8, p. 86; updated as in Table 3.1, this volume.

[a] Includes "errors and omissions"; attributable mainly to the private sector.

difficult to understand why a substantial tax reform was not implemented after 1968: the 1971–1975 National Development Plan did include direct tax increases that would have raised general government current income from 19 percent of GDP in 1970 to 22 percent in 1975, but these were never carried out; with hindsight, it is clear (see Table 3.8) that the increased rate of profit in the private sector would have left "room" enough to raise company taxes or even urban land taxes, and would probably have had less effect on private investment than the imposition of the Industrial Community legislation.

Clearly, the desire to avoid antagonizing either business or upper-middle-class interests (including those of the military and senior bureaucrats themselves) was important in this decision, but there seem to have been some positive reasons for inaction. First, tax increases did not seem to be critical at the time: if the output and export projections of the 1971–1975 plan had materialized, the fiscal deficit would have been much less serious; the slight effect of the ownership reforms on private profits was not understood, either. By 1975, when these problems were understood, it was too late to take further radical moves. Second, there was a widespread but mistaken belief that indirect taxation was regressive and should be limited in order to improve income distribution,[17] even though a politically feasible tax reform might have been based on luxury consumer goods. Third, a

[17] Richard C. Webb, *Government Policy and the Distribution of Income in Peru, 1963–1973* (Cambridge: Harvard University Press, 1977).

squeeze on nonessential consumption through such a reform, though it would have left wages and profits untouched, would have reduced demand for the products of precisely those "dynamic" manufacturing branches (i.e., *electrodomesticos*) upon which the industrialization strategy depended.

Meanwhile, the public enterprise sector was not generating a surplus primarily because, first, many public enterprises (such as Centromín, Pescaperú, and the railways) were virtually bankrupt before their takeover;[18] second, the regime was reluctant to raise key product prices, ostensibly to protect real wages; and third, sales of imported foodstuffs were subsidized. Petroperú was a crucial case. Despite the need for an increased cash flow to finance exploration and the concentration of gasoline demand among the relatively well-off consumers, the domestic price of fuels was virtually frozen until 1975, while import prices rose rapidly, apparently because it was felt that fuel price rises would act as a "signal" for generalized price increases in the private sector. Only in 1976, by Decree-Law 21532, were public enterprises given the flexibility to set their own equilibrium prices: their aggregate current savings rate rose from a loss of 1.8 percent on sales in 1976 to a gain of 7.9 percent in 1978. Overall, the public sector was not generating anything close to enough resources for its own investment, while private consumption was allowed to rise as a proportion of national income—the algebraic consequence being the expansion of "external savings," that is, the current account deficit on the balance of payments. The crucial point is that the public sector continued to subsidize the private sector in general and profits in particular, even though it had taken over the burden of investment that previously justified such subsidies.

The worsening external situation and the eventual success of the efforts of the International Monetary Fund (IMF) to get United States private banks to support its intervention in Peruvian economic policy forced a retraction of the model in 1977–1978.[19] Despite the

---

[18] This is one reason why they were relatively easy to take over.

[19] Rosemary Thorp, "Stabilization Policies in Peru, 1959–77," in Thorp and Laurence Whitehead, eds., *Inflation and Stabilization in Latin America* (London: Macmillan & Co., 1979) contains a good account and critique of this imposition of stabilization policy on monetarist principles. Barbara Stallings, "Peru and the U.S. Banks: Privatization of Financial Relations," in Richard R. Fagen, ed., *Latin America and United States Foreign Policy* (Stanford: Stanford University Press, 1979) throws light on the role of the United States private banks. Some of the relevant IMF documentation is included in Hugo Cabieses and Carlos Otero, *Economía Peruana: Un Ensayo de Interpretación* (Lima: DESCO, 1977).

increases in public enterprise prices that restored the nongovernment public sector to some sort of equilibrium, however,[20] the central government budget (which had not been a major problem in previous years) entered into a serious deficit due to the weakness of tax revenue during a depression and the higher cost of foreign debt service under the devalued sol. The economic deficit of the public sector in 1977–1978 was 7 percent of GDP, a reduction from the 9 percent of the 1974–1976 period, but still far more than the 4 percent of the 1969–1973 period. In consequence, the required suppression of aggregate demand had to be achieved by the time-honored means of real wage cuts.[21] The alternative possibility of cutting military expenditure was resisted, not only from self-interest, but also because of the growing threat of invasion from Chile. The effect was to drive down real GDP growth, already decelerating because of export stagnation, from the 6 percent per annum average of the 1971–1974 period to 3.2 percent in 1975–1976 and −1.5 percent in 1977 and 1978. Industrial output *fell* by 6 percent in 1977 and 5 percent in 1978, and average income per head dropped by about 4 percent in both years. By 1978 real wages had returned to the level of ten years before.

Finally, in 1979, public sector finance was brought into balance: tax pressure rose to nearly 20 percent of GDP as mineral export prices rose (adding the traditional source of Peruvian fiscal income once again to the new indirect tax base); current expenditure on welfare was cut back; the subsidies were eliminated; and cancellation of new public investment projects finally had some effect as "old" projects worked their way through the system. The model had been abandoned, and no attempt was made to acquire the private sector surplus.

THE EXTERNAL BALANCE

The relationship between the balance of payments and the fiscal crisis in Peru was not quite the simple matter of governmental incontinence that the "monetary approach to the balance of payments" would have us believe. It is true, nonetheless, that this is where the in-

[20] The net effect of devaluation was probably to increase their surplus, too, for the parastatal enterprises exported more than they imported.

[21] Lima real wages fell by 27 percent between mid-1976 and mid-1977 and by another 14 percent in the following 12 months; by 1979, they were to stand at only 51 percent of the 1973 level (from the official *Informe Estadístico ONE-INP* for January-December 1979).

TABLE 3.9
External Trade, 1965–1979

	1965	1968	1970	1973	1976	1979
	TRADE VOLUME, IN MILLIONS OF DOLLARS					
Exports f.o.b.	118.6	151.4	186.3	200.4	244.9	624.7
Imports f.o.b.	127.4	129.9	135.1	199.4	405.4	397.6
	TRADE INDICES, 1963 = 100					
Export volume	108.9	123.7	124.9	105.9	109.9	166.8
Import volume	123.2	145.4	149.5	167.5	208.0	145.1
Export unit value	91.8	81.7	149.2	189.2	222.8	374.5
Import unit value	103.4	89.3	99.8	119.0	194.9	274.0
Barter terms of trade	88.8	91.5	149.5	159.0	114.3	136.7
Income terms of trade	114.7	169.5	186.7	168.4	125.6	227.8

Source: FitzGerald, *The Political Economy of Peru, 1956–78,* Table 4.7, p. 83; updated as in footnote to Table 3.1, this volume.

consistency in the Peruvian state capitalist model was exposed. On the export side, the gradual exhaustion of natural resource projects and the need to use more coastal land for domestic food supplies had made new "steps" in export more difficult to achieve as well as more urgent.[22] By 1970, fishing was clearly in crisis, and there had been no new mining projects for over ten years. In fact, most of the growth in export revenue had been from improvement in the terms of trade rather than increased volume (Table 3.9). The disappointing search for oil was a severe blow to the planners, and the extreme difficulty of securing agreement on Cuajone while Mineroperú insisted upon control over marketing held up the copper increment until the real price of copper had fallen to half of its 1970 level. Meanwhile, the purchasing power of exports (dollar revenue deflated by the import price index) had declined by 1976 to a level almost identical to that of ten years before, when real demand in the economy had been about 60 percent of its 1976 level. In addition, price rises of Peruvian imports seem to have been excessive,[23] owing to the transfer pricing practices of both multinational and national firms; this can be seen as a reaction to government policy, perceived as inimicable to business inter-

[22] This is a central argument in Rosemary Thorp and Geoffrey Bertram, *Peru 1890–1977: Growth and Policy in an Open Economy* (London: Macmillan & Co., 1978); see also Chapter 2 in this volume.

[23] Between 1973 and 1976, Peruvian import prices rose by 98 percent, while the IMF world import price index rose by only 57 percent. There are problems of weighting here, of course, but the virtual absence of oil in the Peruvian import price index would tend to make it lower than the world value, whatever the other composition differences.

ests, of course, but this merely serves to underline the problem of relying on the private sector to support structural transformation, even if it is in its own interest.

In other words, there were considerable "exogenous" forces that added to a deterioration of the balance of trade. The sharp improvement in the trade balance in 1979 came about largely for the same reason: a reversal in the trend in the external terms of trade. In addition, the regime had engaged in a massive investment program without cutting back on private consumption (and so imported inputs to industry), a program that was financed by long-term borrowing but that placed enormous pressure on the balance of trade between 1974 and 1976. The planners, moreover, had not backed up the long-term investment program (which could not hope to produce results before the end of the decade) with appropriate short-term productive projects. A tax reform might have covered the budget deficit but would not of itself have provided more foreign exchange, unless domestic demand had been cut proportionately or import substitution had been pursued more aggressively. But the combination of little new net investment in private manufacturing and the insistence by public enterprises that they use the "best" (i.e., foreign) technology made aggressive import substitution impossible. Direct foreign exchange rationing was only introduced in 1976 when it was already too late to curb imports significantly without directly controlling whole branches of industry.[24]

Meanwhile, on capital account of the balance of payments—and this has generally been overlooked—the private sector was generating a massive *outflow* of funds. Despite the inflow of capital for the oil and mining projects, the amortization of previous investments in other sectors and the smuggling of currency on a vast scale (revealed under "errors and omissions" in Table 3.5) meant that nearly half of public long-term borrowing in both the 1968–1973 and 1974–1976 periods was needed just to cover this outflow. It related to speculation against an overvalued currency, but clearly it was more a matter of "sovereign risk" than of "forward arbitrage," as the bankers put it. The exponential growth of external indebtedness that resulted is well known: total official long-term debt rose from a mere $875 million at the end of 1970 to $3.641 billion at the end of 1976, while the debt service ratio rose from 13 to 30 percent between these two years. The

---

[24] Direct foreign exchange rationing is potentially an extremely effective means of rationalizing private sector economic activity, but the political conditions by that time prevented it from being used except as a general restriction.

continued availability of credit from the North American and European money markets—due initially to their excess liquidity, rather than Peru's credit-worthiness, and subsequently to their fear of a Peruvian moratorium—allowed the disequilibrium to continue for a time, but it seems reasonable to suggest that sooner or later the Peruvian authorities would have acted dramatically to cut imports, even had credit still been fairly available.

The IMF had been pressing for devaluation to a parity of 100 soles to the dollar since 1974, not apparently from a belief in the "elasticities" effect upon export supply or import demand, but rather in an attempt to cut domestic demand through the inflationary impact on real wages.[25] In the case of Peru, the fact that exports are resource-constrained while imports are linked to industrial output means that the only solution appeared to be to reduce investment and consumption demand. The choice of public investment and workers' consumption as the targets was not only pressed by the IMF but also reflected the political shifts within the military and the increasing influence of financial and civilian influences within the state as the cohesion of the military declined. In the case of Peru, imports in 1978 were cut right back to the 1968 level in real terms by the depression we have already noted; meanwhile, exports began to rise as the Cuajone production came on stream—with faint echoes of the stabilization policies of 1958 and 1967. Even though exports slightly exceeded imports in 1978, however, the debt service ratio was 49 percent, requiring continued massive borrowing; the total outstanding was $5.346 billion at the end of that year. The Peruvian model had clearly demonstrated its external as well as its internal incoherence.

The year 1979 saw a dramatic reversal of fortune on external account, for with import volume held down to its new level equivalent to that of the mid-1960s (see Table 3.9), the increase in export volume and prices could be completely reflected in a current account surplus, itself used to pay off a large amount of short-term external debt contracted in 1977–1978. The increase in export prices was entirely the result of higher world mineral prices; the volume was mostly minerals, too, the result of so much investment in previous years. The contribution of nontraditional exports was significant (about a third of the increase) but based on the surplus of textiles and fish products

[25] Curiously, this corresponds to a classical as opposed to a neoclassical position on the effects of devaluation; that is, the dominance of the income effect over the price effect.

from domestic demand depression rather than new industrial developments.

INCOME DISTRIBUTION

In sum, the twin failures to gain access to the domestically realized surplus (i.e., profits) and to rationalize foreign exchange use became the Achilles' heel of the new model of accumulation. The ownership changes that accompanied the model were insufficient to gain control over profits and foreign-exchange use directly; company taxation and industrial licensing were inadequate to achieve it indirectly. As Table 3.8 indicates, neither wage nor salary increases were very large in real terms: employees' and workers' share of national income remained at levels remarkably similar to those before 1968. It was the share of local profits—increasingly distributed and consumed by shareholders as the reinvestment of company earnings declined—that rose.

Ownership reforms did not lead to a massive downward redistribution of income.[26] Leaving aside the problem that after 1976 the stabilization policy itself provoked a substantial decline in real corporate wages and presumably urban slum earnings (although what happened in the countryside with the improvement in the internal terms of trade is uncertain), there are two points that seem to have led to some confusion in discussions of this "failure." The first arises from the dual structure of the economy.[27] The dichotomy between the corporate, modern element (using capital, organizing wage labor, generating profits, and engaging in external trade) and the noncorporate, informal element in each production sector of the Peruvian economy dictates that only one-third of the work force is employed in organized jobs (little more than a quarter when government employees are separated out). As a result, any system of profit redistribution at

[26] Adolfo Figueroa, "The Impact of Current Reforms on Income Distribution in Peru," in Alejandro Foxley, ed., *Income Distribution in Latin America* (London: Cambridge University Press, 1976); and Webb, *Government Policy and the Distribution of Income in Peru 1963–1973.*

[27] Here, the term "dual" does not mean the neoclassical separation of "modern" and "traditional" sectors. Rather, it refers to the incomplete articulation of capitalist relations of production within a social formation characterized by the capitalist mode of production; the dynamic of accumulation takes in the "corporate" sector, but the noncorporate sector supplies food and petty urban services to it, deriving therefrom its own limited dynamic and absorbing the remainder of the work force not needed by the technologically advanced corporate sector. See Szentes, *The Political Economy of Underdevelopment,* chapter 3.

the firm level was bound to be limited in its effect, and limited to the better-paid quartile of the labor force at that. In fact, the increase in the incomes of those affected was probably quite considerable, but dualism in the economy is rooted in the flinty soil of uneven capitalist growth and cannot be pulled up that easily.

Just how income could have been redistributed to the noncorporate sector is not at all clear. The post-1975 food price increases were officially defended as improvements in peasant incomes, and the national accounts do show some gains between 1973 and 1976. But they also depressed *barriada* real incomes and almost certainly those of rural laborers who controlled sub-subsistence landholdings. It is true that the determined use of more labor-intensive technologies in industry (particularly in food, drink, and textiles) and public works and a major agricultural drive might have improved the situation in the long term—and would also have benefited foreign exchange use—but not in the short run; it is regrettable that the social property venture was not seen in this context. Above all, the nature of the state capitalist model requires high rates of accumulation financed from profits based on wage restraint and involves industry rather than agriculture, high rather than low technologies. It is, after all, a capitalist model. Indeed, a combination of high investment and savings rates with higher consumption for the poor would require a form of socialism; the political preconditions for this certainly did not exist in Peru. As we have noted above, this is one of the intrinsic contradictions of state capitalism. And it leads to a natural confrontation with organized labor, a confrontation that might have been ameliorated or postponed in other cases by an effective populist party—for which the SINAMOS was little more than an apology.

The redistribution required for the model's internal stability would not be from profits to wages but rather the reallocation of profit from the private to the public sector. In the longer term, an internally balanced model of state capitalism might have generated the resources necessary to reduce the dualism,[28] but few funds were in fact allocated to agriculture between 1968 and 1978: just 6 percent of total national investment went to that sector between 1969 and 1976, as opposed to 4 percent between 1960 and 1968. The redistribution problem was not only connected to agriculture through employment creation; insufficient food supplies contributed to lower real wages

---

[28] It could be argued, however, that the model could not achieve this because of the entrenched political position of those that benefited from the dual economy.

and thus to a deterioration in income distribution,[29] which in Peru could only be halted by massive food imports. Food output had risen by 46 percent between 1960 and 1967, but only by 27 percent between 1967 and 1975. Foodcrops output per head of population, when measured against the average for the 1946–1950 period, stood at only 102 in 1969–1970 and fell to 97 in the 1971–1975 period; the aggregate increase was from livestock output, which was not accessible to most Peruvians. Neither the creation of a specific ministry for food supply nor the substantial improvement in the internal terms of trade after 1975 appear to have stimulated greater production. Average agricultural output growth in between 1975 and 1979 was only 0.7 percent, compared with an average of 2.1 percent between 1970 and 1974, itself well below the population growth rate of 2.8 percent in the 1970s.

Low and inflexible rates of growth in food output and taxation are considered by Kalecki to be the "gist" of the problem:

> In other words, the rate of increase of supply of necessities, as fixed by institutional barriers to the development of agriculture, determines the rate of growth of national income r which is warranted without infringing our basic postulates (i.e., that there should be no deterioration in the income distribution). Next is determined the rate of growth of total consumption c which makes sufficient allowance for investment required for the expansion of the national income at a rate r. In order to restrain the increase in total consumption to the rate c appropriate taxation of higher income groups and non-essentials must be devised. This seems to me to be the gist of the problem of financing development in a mixed economy.[30]

This simple (or perhaps difficult) lesson appears to have been overlooked by the Peruvian planners; it certainly was not considered explicitly in the 1971–1975 or 1975–1978 development plans.

THE ALTERNATIVES

One way of resolving the inconsistency in the model would have been to extend the scope of state control to make comprehensive planning of the modern sector possible. The capacity to program the existing

[29] A point well made for Peru in the 1960s by Rosemary Thorp, "A Note on Food Supplies, the Distribution of Income, and National Income Accounting in Peru," *Bulletin of the Oxford University Institute of Economics and Statistics* 31, no. 4 (1969).

[30] "Problems of Financing Economic Development in a Mixed Economy," in Kalecki, *Essays on the Economic Growth of the Socialist and Mixed Economy*, p. 152.

public sector effectively was not demonstrated, however, and the potentialities of the banking system were not fully realized; the state used the banking system as a source of finance for its fiscal deficits and of working capital for its enterprises rather than for the mobilization of fresh savings for use by the public sector or the use of credit as a means of obliging the private sector to conform to the plans.[31] An initiative from within the public sector to take over the two hundred largest firms in order to make industrial planning more effective was seriously considered in 1975, but the change in presidency and the increasing leverage of the foreign creditors ruled out this option. Without moves of this sort, it is difficult to see how planning could have been made more effective, even if the technical weaknesses of the National Planning Institute could have been overcome.[32] The problem was not technical; it was an issue of control over the surplus. Insofar as a transition to state socialism was never a political option, central planning was never an economic one, even though it could have resolved many of the inconsistencies we have observed. Yet, external markets and the informal sector would have remained outside state control, severely limiting the scope for effective programming of the economy.

Another solution, it has been argued, might have been to adopt a more "open" economic policy, particularly with respect to manufactured exports. This would have implied more than export promotion *within* the existing model, as in 1977–1979, involving the reduction of import barriers and the reduction of restrictions on foreign enterprises, because only they could have secured the external markets,[33] particularly as these began to stagnate in the mid-1970s. The use of industrial excess capacity as a source of supply at low marginal cost required severe reductions in real wages across the board to make exports profitable for a few branches. The fact that this did contribute to external balance in 1979 hardly makes it a desirable development strategy. Manufactured exports *can* be combined with improved income distribution, but this requires a degree of industrial rationalization tantamount to centralized programming,[34] and industrial plan-

---

[31] Oscar Ugarteche, *Apuntes para una Interpretación del Sistema Financiero Peruano 1965–75* (Lima: INP-OIP, 1978).

[32] See FitzGerald, *The Political Economy of Peru,* chapter 8.

[33] Rys O. Jenkins, "Manufactured Exports: Development Strategy or Internationalization of Capital," *Bulletin of the Society for Latin American Studies,* no. 28 (1978).

[34] A point conceded in Daniel M. Schydlowsky, "Capital Utilization, Growth, Employment, Balance of Payments and Price Stabilization," in Jere Behrman and James A. Hanson, eds., *Short Term Macroeconomic Policy in Latin America* (Cambridge, Mass.: Ballinger, 1979).

ning had long since been abandoned as an objective. As we have seen, this was even less of an option for sustained accumulation than allowing the multinationals to restructure Peruvian industry. The unwillingness of domestic industrialists to invest in order to meet domestic demand, moreover, throws doubt upon their potential to expand exports by more than the margin of immediate excess capacity created by deflation, as the experience of Chile and Colombia indicates.

The purpose of this discussion is not to examine alternatives that were not adopted (still less has it been to exculpate the government from its numerous policy errors[35]), but rather to assess the viability of the chosen model. Insofar as we have concluded that it was inherently unstable, the question remains: why did the GRFA adopt it? It might be argued that this model simply emerged as an accumulation of decisions made in reaction to circumstances,[36] but this seems to underestimate the Peruvian military in particular and the current of Peruvian history in general.[37] We have already suggested that the model was the only real alternative remaining after the failure of the Prado and Belaúnde strategies of *laissez-faire* and gradualist reformism; it also responded to the widespread Latin American belief in the capacity of a reformist state to overcome the barriers to industrialization presented by dependent dualism. Further, with the benefit of hindsight, it is easy to forget that at the outset of the period the prospects for the model were favorable: optimism about mining exports was widely shared, land reform was expected to stimulate agricultural output, the industrialists supported the regime, and it was felt that planning could achieve rationality without overcentralization.

It may well be, however, that the strongest justification for the model was national security.[38] This rationale had two facets. On the one hand, worker participation, income redistribution, and land reform would reduce popular unrest and the internal threat of communism along the lines suggested during the five years before 1968 by the Alliance for Progress. On the other hand, rapid industrialization, reduced foreign ownership of resources, and a strong state would

[35] See FitzGerald, *The Political Economy of Peru*, chapter 8.

[36] George D. E. Philip, "The Soldier as Radical: the Peruvian Military Government 1965–75," *Journal of Latin American Studies*, vol. 8 (1976).

[37] Victor Villanueva, *El CAEM y la Revolución de la Fuerza Armada* (Lima: Instituto de Estudios Peruanos, 1972) makes the first point, Thorp and Bertram, *Peru 1890–1977*, the second.

[38] Villanueva, *El CAEM y la Revolución Peruana*, and Stepan, *The State and Society*, both make this point.

strengthen the capacity of the nation to resist external aggression along the lines established in the hundred years before 1968. That these two aims were incompatible in the context of the mixed economy was not understood by orthodox development economists at the time. Finally, although it might seem trite to say so, it should be remembered that to most Peruvian leaders in 1968, state capitalism seemed the obvious course to adopt; by 1974, when its inconsistencies were distinguishable from temporary difficulties, it was too late to change course. Whether there was any other realistic option at the time had not been demonstrated.

PERU IN COMPARATIVE PERSPECTIVE

At first sight, Chile would appear to be the most relevant parallel to Peru. The economic impasse reached under the Frei administration was not dissimilar to that faced by Belaúnde, and it can be argued that the problems of economic management under Allende were also centered on the fiscal crisis and the food supply. But the differences implied by the far greater degree of popular mobilization in Chile on the one hand and by the fact that the Peruvian problem was caused by investment rather than redistribution on the other make economic comparison difficult. Moreover, the swings in economic policy in Chile's attempted transition to socialism and its return to the nineteenth century far exceeded the radicalism of the Peruvian administration.

If size of public sector is the basis for comparison, Brazil and Mexico might be more suitable because in both countries the state accounts for over half of fixed investment and finances a considerable proportion of the rest. It should be borne in mind, of course, that both of these economies are far more developed than Peru's, have a longer history of industrialization, enjoy far wider domestic markets, and possess a domestic technological capacity. Nonetheless, there are some points that merit discussion even though a direct comparison of the state capitalist model is not possible because neither Mexico nor Brazil has undergone widespread ownership changes. From their respective reactions to the problem of financing public investment and securing adequate food supplies, Brazil and Mexico do present interesting contrasts and parallels to Peru.

The process of postwar industrialization led naturally to greater intervention by Latin American states in support of private investors. Such intervention not only required greater expenditures for infrastructure and welfare but also reduced tax receipts due to the fiscal incentives extended to investors and low tariff revenues as import substitution took hold.[39] As a result, in most countries, the budget deficit became a structural problem that generated steadily greater external debt and required successively greater pressure on real wages to control aggregate demand. The imposition of stabilization policies has, in recent years, involved a number of attempts to reduce state involvement and return to open economies based on primary exports and imported technology.

The major economy that does not fit into this pattern is, however, Brazil's. Severe public sector deficits were experienced in the early 1960s as state savings accounted for only a fifth of the national total while public investment approached one half. The deficits were exacerbated by the operating losses of public enterprises and led to inflationary domestic borrowing and external debt. Although fiscal pressure was increased in the late 1950s by raising consumption taxes, much of the impact of the taxes was lost by the virtual elimination of export duties (equivalent to profit taxes on agro-exporters), and the new revenue failed to balance new expenditure commitments established under Kubitschek. A major step was taken in the mid-1960s: the income tax system was reorganized in 1964 to bear more heavily on personal income and less so on profits (the effective rate of corporation tax fell), and regional sales taxes were reformed in 1967 on the basis of a value-added tax. Total tax pressure rose from 16 percent of GDP in 1950 to 20 percent in 1960 and 27 percent in 1970, finally reaching the extraordinarily high level of 31 percent in 1975. In addition, public enterprise pricing policy was set to maintain an overall public sector surplus of on the order of 5 percent of GDP, and social security funds were tapped as the main source of local currency finance. Although this system did not prevent a large external Brazilian debt, it does seem to have given the state much greater financial stability than in Peru, despite the disbursements of subsidized funds to the private sector through the state banking system. The feasibility of achieving tax reform based on extracting the income of labor rather than capital, however, was predicated upon political coercion. Moreover, it was because the state was not regarded as a threat to domestic or foreign business that private investment rates could be maintained as public intervention increased.[40]

[39] See FitzGerald, "The Fiscal Crisis of the Latin American State," in Toye, ed., *Taxation and Economic Development,* and "On State Accumulation in Latin America," in FitzGerald, Floto, and Lehmann, eds. *The State and Economic Development in Latin America.*

[40] Unfortunately, national accounts in Brazil are not presented in such a way as to allow a separation of the public sector and thus a comparative table; but see

TABLE 3.10

Mexico: Aggregate Accumulation Account, 1947–1976

(Percent of GDP)

	1947–56	1957–66	1967–71	1972–76
Public sector saving	4.3%	3.8%	4.7%	1.8%
Private sector saving	9.6	11.3	12.3	15.9
	13.9	15.1	17.0	17.7
External finance to:				
Public sector	0.6	1.5	0.9	2.1
Private sector	0.1	0.3	1.3	1.2
	0.7	1.8	2.2	3.3
Total savings	14.6	16.9	19.2	21.0
Public sector investment	5.4	6.1	7.4	9.0
Private sector investment	9.2	10.8	11.8	12.0
Total investment	14.6	16.9	19.2	21.0

Source: E.V.K. FitzGerald, "The State and Capital Accumulation in Mexico," *Journal of Latin American Studies* 10, no. 2.

In contrast, the Mexican case appears to have more in common with the Peruvian experience. After two decades of rapid growth and industrialization (sustained in part by the success of postwar agricultural investment by the state and the activities of development banks), it had become apparent by the end of the 1960s that large-scale public investment in oil, agriculture, heavy industry, and social services was required if growth were to continue. Again, as in Peru, private investment in productive sectors had been slackening and the trade deficit widening, and it proved politically impossible to carry through a projected direct tax reform. As a result, the rapidly expanding state sector under Echeverría began to generate a vast resource deficit that even the sophisticated Mexican banking system could not handle, as Tables 3.10 and 3.11 indicate. With open exchanges, an enormous amount of private capital was exported—for security as much as speculation—effectively financed (as in Peru) by large-scale government borrowing on North American and European money markets. A drastic stabilization policy based on devaluation and real wage cuts was implemented in 1976–1977 under IMF supervision, but it proved very difficult indeed to reduce the essentially structural budget deficit significantly. It is only the prospect of imminent oil revenues that prevents further foreign (and domestic banking) pressure for renewed demand restraint after 1978. The Mexican state had encountered many of the same inconsistencies and many of the same external pressures as it attempted to curtail the penetration

J. R. Wells, "State Expenditures and the Brazilian Economic Miracle," in Fitz-Gerald, Floto, and Lehmann, *The State and Economic Development in Latin America.*

TABLE 3.11
Mexico: Public Sector Accumulation, 1950–1976
(Percent of GDP)

	1950–59	1960–68	1969–72	1973–76
Federal government:				
Current income	7.7%	7.5%	8.2%	9.8%
Current expenditure	4.5	6.1	6.5	8.9
Current surplus	3.2	1.3	1.6	0.9
Other public sector saving	0.9	1.4	2.6	0.3
Total	4.1	3.7	4.2	1.2
Public sector investment:				
Federal government	2.1	2.0	2.2	3.2
Other public sector	3.3	4.9	5.1	6.0
	5.4	6.9	7.3	9.2
Public sector borrowing:				
Internal	0.5	2.1	2.5	5.4
External	0.8	1.1	0.6	2.6
	1.3	3.2	3.1	8.0

Source: FitzGerald, "The State and Capital Accumulation in Mexico."

of foreign companies. But the crucial parallel seems to have been the assumption of responsibility for the bulk of capital accumulation by the state, which, in the face of a commitment to maintain real wages, was incapable of restraining consumption and balancing the budget by fiscal access to profits.

Underlying the problem of sustaining a high rate of industrial accumulation is the real wage, and underpinning that, food production. Brazil, during its period of rapid growth between 1964 and 1974, restrained real wages through coercion but also successfully encouraged a dynamic capitalist agriculture that could both feed the work force and earn foreign exchange. In Mexico between 1940 and 1965, the mechanism was different, involving strong control over trade unions by an official party and extensive public investment in agricultural infrastructure before the main import-substitution drive. In consequence, state expansion in both countries took place within a stable surplus-generating system; it seemed that they had, so to speak, grasped Kalecki's "gist of the problem of financing economic development in a mixed economy." In sharp contrast, the Peruvian military faced a weak agricultural sector that urgently required capitalization, yet it had no politically acceptable means of controlling the labor force. Here again the parallel with the Echeverría administration is striking; the trade unions escaped the control of the Institutionalized Revolutionary Party (PRI), and food output growth rates fell below population rates. In the long run, of course, the Peruvian agrarian reform may have unexpected results in terms of both production (and thus the real urban wage) and the political structure itself. But unless the Peruvian state is able to allocate substantial resources to agriculture (with further strain on the budget), it is difficult to envision much success in the foreseeable future.

CONCLUSION

An economic evaluation of the 1968–1978 period will ultimately depend upon events in the 1980s, because the reforms may turn out to have been "necessary preconditions" for an economic strategy as yet unforeseen. What this analysis has attempted to do is to increase our understanding of the nature of state intervention in economic development and our knowledge of a particular period in Peruvian history.[41]

It seems that if the state is to take on the burden of accumulation, then it must achieve commensurate access to the economic surplus. The inability to attain this in a mixed economy is the inherent contradiction of state capitalism as a "middle road" between capitalism and socialism on the economic plane and it undermines the stability of intermediate regimes on the political plane. But for the smaller, late-developing countries without strong entrepreneurial groups, such a course seems to be the only alternative to further penetration by the multinational corporations, and if state capitalism cannot achieve development in Latin America without arrangements equivalent to a transition to socialism, then the prospects for independent industrialization may be bleak indeed for all but the largest economies, i.e., Brazil and Mexico.

As for Peru itself, it is difficult to see how a democratic government, constrained electorally and institutionally from moving too far to the right or to the left, can make the economy work, reestablish a balanced rate of growth, and construct a stable accumulation model (involving a high rate of productive investment and a reasonable income distribution) any better than the military. The Peruvian solution to this problem will doubtless be as significant as the Peruvian experiment itself.

[41] For a Marxist critique of my approach, condemned as "neo-Keynesian," see Armando Pillado, *Acumulación, Crisis, Estado, y Socialismo* (Lima: DESCO, 1978), pp. 55–61.

The Anatomy of an Economic Failure

Daniel M. Schydlowsky and
Juan J. Wicht

Since October 1968, and the beginning of the Peruvian experiment, much has happened in Peru. But even more has failed to happen; the promising Peruvian vision of structural reform ended in the worst economic, social, and political crisis that the country has seen in the twentieth century. Some people believe that the Peruvian experiment failed because it was not, or could not be, truly revolutionary, that Third World development requires a socialist revolution, which would eliminate private property and sharply reduce the influence of international capital. Others hold the opposite view: development requires freedom for private enterprise, open economic frontiers, and little or no state intervention. According to them, the failure of the Peruvian experiment was due to the obstacles it introduced or reinforced against the capitalist system in Peru.

This chapter adopts another view altogether. It focuses on certain types of economic disequilibria induced by wrong economic policies that can emerge, whatever the political system, and suggests that these policies were the primary reasons for the failure of the experiment. The technical requirements of production, and capital utilization in particular, are emphasized. In our view, the 1975–1978 crisis was not inexorably determined; it was not a result of class interests, nor of a particular political system, but of serious mistakes and incorrect economic policies, policies that were not grounded in a coherent, consistently applied economic model. The chapter has four sections: a

Both authors share responsibility for the whole chapter; Daniel M. Schydlowsky undertook primary drafting of the second and third sections, and Juan J. Wicht of the first and fourth. The views expressed are those of both authors, but not necessarily those of their institutions. The authors wish to thank the Center for Latin American Development Studies (CLADS) of Boston University and the National Bureau of Economic Research at Stanford University for logistic support, as well as their colleague Shane Hunt for extensive comments that did much to improve the product.

description of the performance record of the military government; an assessment of the causes of Peru's economic crisis; a consideration of the alternatives that were available to the military government in a "rerun" of history; and an analysis of the alternatives available for the future.

THE RECORD

The Government's Heritage in 1968

Peru was just beginning to pull out of an economic crisis in October 1968.[1] Prior to the 1967–1968 downturn, however, the country had achieved a very respectable growth rate—5.4 percent per year from 1945 to 1966, somewhat higher than the Latin American average of 5.2 percent.[2] All the same, Peruvian production per capita in 1968 was still 18 percent below the Latin American average, and its distribution has been described as one of the most uneven on the South American continent.[3] Within the rather satisfactory aggregate growth performance, a number of economic disequilibria—sectoral differences in output, prices, cost, and labor productivity—had begun to appear.

Through 1968, agriculture was the largest employer in the economy (57 percent of all Peruvian workers in 1950 and 47 percent in 1968, with an absolute increase of more than 370,000 workers during the eighteen-year interval[4]) and provided the largest share of the domestic consumption basket (50 percent for the vast majority of the population). The rural area and agriculture, however, with the exception of the key export crops sugar and cotton in the 1950s, had been systematically neglected. Starting in 1959, industry received top priority for investment incentives and tariff protection. Domestic price controls were consistently biased against agriculture. Although during his political campaign Belaúnde had promised that "the last

[1] Real product per capita was declining for the second consecutive year; inflation was at an all-time high of 19 percent per annum; the balance of payments on current account was not quite in balance after having been strongly negative the previous year; and the fiscal deficit was 3.4 percent of GNP. See Banco Central de Reserva, *Cuentas Nacionales del Perú, 1960–1969* (Lima).

[2] U.N. Cuadernos de la CEPAL, "Series Históricas del Crecimiento de América Latina" (Santiago, 1978).

[3] Richard C. Webb, *Government Policy and the Distribution of Income in Peru, 1963–1973* (Cambridge: Harvard University Press, 1977), p. 7.

[4] See Banco Central de Reserva, *Cuentas Nacionales del Perú, 1950–1965,* and *1960–1969,* Table 11.

would be the first," in fact, he tightened price controls on many basic foodstuffs (e.g. flour, meat, milk, rice, sugar), aggravating price-cost differentials that diminished opportunities for food supply growth and improvement of rural incomes, the lowest in the economy. Shortages in domestic food production forced the country to import $150 million worth of food in 1968—21.8 percent of total imports that year.[5] Industrial protection allowed manufacturing production to grow quickly but weakened this sector's competitiveness and capacity to generate foreign exchange (anti-export bias) and led toward over-capitalization (antilabor bias) as the price of capital was systematically lowered in relation to labor. It should be noted that part of the increase in the recorded value of industrial output was due to artificially high prices.

Table 4.1 shows the declining growth rate of the primary foreign exchange producing sectors, although most agricultural output was consumed domestically. Manufacturing, which required foreign exchange for imported machinery and inputs (although initially it saved some foreign exchange by substituting domestic production for goods previously imported), represented almost one fifth of the gross national product by the mid-1960s and was growing much more rapidly than the primary sectors.

While unbalanced output growth occurred in different sectors of the economy, employment problems were becoming ever more serious. The labor supply in the cities was growing at 5.3 percent a year in the late 1960s, due to the reduced infant mortality in the 1940s and 1950s, to massive migratory movements from the rural areas, and to increasing participation of women in the labor force.[6]

The economy was characterized by a new duality:[7] the backward sector was originally in the rural areas, where the high labor/land coefficient made it difficult to raise average labor productivity; migration to the cities increased the urban labor force, but jobs were insufficient in the modern-formal (capital-intensive) sector. Therefore, the traditional-informal urban sector (independent, occasional, marginal activities) grew extraordinarily in the 1960s and lowered the annual urban labor productivity growth rate from 2 percent in the previous decade to .5 percent. The transfer of thousands of landless low-paid peasants to marginal urban jobs was an improvement; the

[5] See "Exposición del Ministro de Hacienda," Nov. 25, 1968.
[6] See Instituto Nacional de Planificación, *El Problema del Empleo y los Desequilibrios de la Economía Peruana* (Lima, October 1977).
[7] On this point see also E.V.K. FitzGerald, *The State and Economic Development, Peru since 1968* (Cambridge: Cambridge University Press, 1976), p. 9.

TABLE 4.1
GNP by Sectors, 1950–1968

| | IN MILLIONS OF SOLES, AT CONSTANT 1963 PRICES | | | | | ANNUAL RATES OF GROWTH (IN %) | | | |
	1950	1955	1960	1965	1968	1950–55	1955–60	1960–65	1965–68
Agriculture	8,790	11,190	13,386	14,875	14,350	4.9%	3.6%	2.1%	−1.2%
Fishing	160	333	1,041	1,513	2,074	15.8	25.6	7.8	11.1
Mining	1,768	2,667	4,585	5,325	5,701	8.6	11.4	3.0	2.3
Total primary	10,718	14,190	19,012	21,713	22,125	5.8	6.0	2.7	0.7
Manufacturing	5,286	7,681	10,642	16,330	19,284	7.8	6.7	8.9	5.7
Other sectors	22,952	30,194	34,521	50,103	53,944	5.7	2.7	7.7	2.5
Total GNP	38,956	52,065	64,175	88,146	95,353	6.0	4.3	6.6	2.7

Source: Banco Central de Reserva, *Cuentas Nacionales del Perú, 1950–1965* and *1960–1969*.

national average of labor productivity was still rising, but it was due to geographical migration rather than to increased efficiency. By the mid-1960s, the challenge was not only to alleviate the poverty in the rural area but also to decrease urban underemployment.[8]

During the 1950s, Peru had essentially a liberal economy based on a free-trade ideology and characterized by moderate state intervention.[9] In the 1960s, new and growing social pressures from urban sectors demanded a different approach from Belaúnde. The underlying model was akin to the guidelines of the Economic Commission for Latin America (ECLA) in the late 1950s: in a "peripheral" economy below full employment, the cause of its problems could be found in structural insufficiency of demand; the government should adopt an import-substitution strategy with fixed exchange rates and trade restrictions to reduce dependence on the rest of the world and foster domestic industrialization. As consumption and investment fall short of the level required to absorb unemployed labor, it is necessary to increase public expenditure, which, through the multiplier effect, will push the economy toward full employment equilibrium. Inflation is a lesser evil; it will not be caused by excess demand (as long as there is unemployed labor), but rather by structural rigidities, which will gradually disappear through controls and planned public expenditure.[10] Two characteristic and related features of the ECLA mentality were a distrust of market mechanisms and a disregard for the foreign trade balance. These views prevailed in many academic circles and certainly were not ignored at the Centro de Altos Estudios Militares (CAEM), where military officers paid growing attention to the problems of national security and development.

Although Belaúnde did not adopt the entire ECLA doctrine, industrialization was promoted by tariff protection with little concern

[8] See full version in Spanish of the present study, *Anatomía de un Fracaso Económico: Peru 1968–1978* (Lima: Universidad del Pacífico, June 1979), Table 2: "Tendencias del Producto, del Empleo y de la Productividad en el Perú, 1950–1968," p. 22. (English version: Discussion Paper Series, no. 32, February 1979, Center for Latin American Development Studies, Boston University).

[9] To some, this situation meant a privatization of power, e.g., Frits Wils, *Industrialists, Industrialization, and the Nation State in Peru* (Lima: CISEPA, 1975); Carlos Malpica, *Los Dueños del Perú,* ed. Ensayos Sociales, 1968; and writings of Cotler, Quijano, and Bourricaud. Others regarded such a policy as eminently desirable, e.g., Rómulo A. Ferrero, "Economic Development of Peru," in *Economic Development Issues, Latin America* (New York: Committee for Economic Development, 1967).

[10] See Celso Furtado, *Economic Development of Latin America,* 2nd ed. (New York: Cambridge University Press, 1976), Chapter 22.

for inflationary pressures, fiscal deficits, or balance-of-payments developments. These problems eventually became uncontrollable, especially as Belaúnde did not have the backing of an opposition-dominated Congress. The result was the 1967–1968 crisis and the replacement of traditional democracy by the military government in 1968.[11]

The Peruvian Experiment, Phase One (1968–1975)

The explicit economic objective of the Revolutionary Government of the Armed Forces was clearly stated in their Estatuto of October 3, 1968: "To promote to superior living standards, compatible with human personal dignity, the least favored sectors of the population, changing the economic social and cultural structures of the country."[12] If by "revolution" we mean a deep and lasting change in favor of those who have less, the explicit goal was revolutionary. The military officers announced their firm determination to transform Peru's structure and their intention to stay in power until the revolutionary process had become "irreversible." After only six days in power, they seized the International Petroleum Company installations, and shortly thereafter, they introduced a series of reforms affecting almost all spheres of society: agrarian reform (1969), reorganization of public administration and creation of new public enterprises (since 1969), new banking and financial regulations with increased government ownership (1970), industrial reform (1970), educational reform (1971). From 1969 to 1974, the military enjoyed strong political power, and the old political parties, including Acción Popular and the APRA, were discredited as derechistas (right-wingers) and widely viewed as incapable of carrying out the reforms their leaders had promised for so many years.

The intentions of the revolutionary government may be found in several official documents[13] and in the considerandos (prefaces of each reform law); the means to achieving its intentions are expressed in the articles (articulos or parte dispositiva) of the reform laws. Matching one

[11] See Pedro-Pablo Kuczynski, *Peruvian Democracy under Economic Stress: An Account of the Belaúnde Administration* (Princeton: Princeton University Press, 1977).

[12] *Estatuto del Gobierno Revolucionario de la Fuerza Armada*, Decree-Law no. 17063.

[13] For basic political documents, see: *Manifiesto, Estatuto*, and *Bases Ideológicas* (October 1968 and March 1975), as well as official speeches of President Velasco. On economic and social issues see "Lineamientos de la Política Economico-Social del Gobierno Revolucionario" (Lima, July 1969), and *Plan Nacional de Desarrollo, 1971–1975* (Lima: Instituto Nacional de Planificación, 1971).

with the other, however, it is difficult to see what the economic model of the revolutionary military government was; the officers did not seem to clearly understand some of the economy's basic mechanisms.[14] Hardly able to perceive the economic structures of the country, they were certainly unable to transform them. Politics and political insight prevailed over economic knowledge.

Table 4.2 shows the sectoral growth pattern during "Phase One" of the military government. The same sectoral trends that prevailed in the 1960s are observed from 1970 to 1975: stagnation or decline in the primary sectors, augmented by the anchovy crisis; continued industrial growth, at a slightly lower rate; and further expansion of the tertiary sectors, which were obliged to absorb most of the increases in the urban labor force.

From 1968 to 1975, total national product increased by 55 percent in real terms; industrial production grew by 75 percent. But the stagnation of the primary sectors, which the development strategy had identified as providers of foreign exchange, caused an export quantum *decline* of 21 percent. The necessary foreign exchange had to be obtained through favorable international prices for primary products or from foreign loans. In 1975, Peru's external dependence was more marked than ever.[15] In 1973 and 1974, export prices rose extraordinarily; they fell sharply in 1975. Simultaneously, investment and the prices of imports caught up, and Peru had its most serious current account deficit on record. Long-run capital inflows prevented a more serious drain on reserves.

Consumption maintained a high expansion rate (6.6 percent) through 1975, and investment grew in real terms by 66 percent from 1972 to 1975 through capital-intensive projects that had high import component and employed few workers. The high consumption and the external deficit stand out clearly as proportions of each year's GNP (Table 4.3). In 1970, the investment coefficient was very low— 13 percent of GNP—and there was a surplus of exported goods and

[14] This lack of a coherent scheme is also obvious in many chapters of the Plan Inca, allegedly written by Velasco and his closest companions in 1968 before the coup, but published only on July 30, 1974. Each brief chapter has only three parts: "Situation" (a very sharp, precise description), "Objective" (highly idealistic), and "Actions" (that offer little assurance of reaching the "objective"). All of the economic problems seem to be due to the lack of control by the state; therefore the "action" most commonly found in the Plan Inca is "to create the necessary public institutions." See, for instance, the chapters on industry, commerce, and housing. The latter has, as Action Three, "eliminate shepherd's hovels." The Plan Inca, of course, does not say how.

[15] See Schydlowsky and Wicht, *Anatomía de un Fracaso Económico,* pp. 28 and 29.

TABLE 4.2
GDP by Sectors, 1970–1975

	IN BILLIONS OF SOLES, AT CONSTANT 1970 PRICES						ANNUAL RATES OF GROWTH (IN %)		
	1970	1971	1972	1973	1974	1975	1950–60	1960–70	1970–75
Agriculture	36.2	37.3	37.6	38.5	39.4	39.8	4.3%	2.0%	1.9%
Fishing	6.6	5.7	3.0	2.3	3.1	2.6	16.3	9.3	−17.0
Mining	19.8	19.0	20.4	20.3	21.0	18.7	10.0	4.0	−1.1
Total primary	62.6	62.0	61.0	61.1	63.5	61.1	5.9	3.8	−0.5
Manufacturing	57.2	62.1	66.7	71.6	77.0	80.6	7.2	7.5	7.1
Other sectors	120.9	128.9	140.1	151.7	163.4	172.3	4.2	6.3	5.5
Total GDP	240.7	253.0	267.8	284.4	303.9	314.0	5.3	5.6	5.5

Source: Banco Central de Reserva, *Memoria, 1973* and *1976*, Appendix 38

TABLE 4.3
GDP by Type of Expenditure, 1970–1975
(At Constant 1970 Prices)

	Annual Rates of Growth (in %)			Composition (%)		
	1950–60	1960–70	1970–75	1960	1970	1975
Consumption	4.8%	7.4%	6.6%	71%	83%	88%
Investment	6.0	3.2	16.0	11	13	21
Exports	9.3	4.3	−5.6	23	20	11
Imports	10.5	10.5	11.0	11	16	20
Total GDP	5.3	5.6	5.5	100	100	100

Source: Banco Central de Reserva, *Memoria,* 1976, Anexo 36.

services over imports; five years later, investment (largely public investment) represented one fifth of GNP, but consumption accounted for nine tenths of GNP. The foreign trade gap, consequently, was practically one tenth of the national product. Foreign public debt increased from $2.2 billion in 1974 to $3.1 billion in 1975, but these figures were not public at the time.

In 1969, 243,000 workers were unemployed and 1,901,000 underemployed; in 1975, the unemployed were 248,000 and the underemployed 2,142,000. Unemployment rose, in part because the government perceived it not as a problem in itself that could be solved, but as an inevitable component of the larger problem of underdevelopment. There is no chapter on "employment" among the thirty-one chapters of the Plan Inca, and the few pages that deal with it in the 1971–1975 National Development Plan were included at the last minute upon the insistence of government economists (who were by no means always at one with the top policy makers in the military during this period).

At least during Phase One, the military government sincerely wanted to change and develop the country, to make Peru a more unified nation less dependent on foreign pressures, and to help the poorest groups of the population. Politically, several ambiguities both in theory and practice were hidden in the slogan "neither capitalism nor communism" and in the gradualism of the revolutionary process (see Part III of this volume). At the economic level, however, there was a complete vacuum instead of a consistent, theoretical model.

Four sectors of property (five, if we add the cooperatives' sector) were established, with differing ownership systems and differing, often conflicting, rules of behavior. The state sector was to grow stronger and be the controller and the leader; the reformed private sector, still the largest sector in 1975, was to remain dynamic in industry; the new social property sector was supposed to be "hegemonic";

and the small private property sector was also to be developed because it had the largest share of the labor force. No thought was given to the macroeconomic total of all this, particularly in balance-of-payments terms, nor was attention paid to intersectoral coordination problems and their implications for the work effort of laborers and entrepreneurs, quality of management, allocation of resources, employment, output, and prices.

The lack of understanding of economics among the top military leaders and their political advisors allowed them to believe that they were changing Peru's economic structures. When the economic crisis erupted in 1975, they could not understand it; they thought it was political sabotage. (At first, the generals imprisoned or exiled those who wrote about the crisis; then when the crisis could not be denied, the military's official explanation was that it was part of a worldwide crisis of international capitalism.) Political leaders, however, rarely understand economics; it is perhaps more surprising that many social scientists, including more than one economist, claimed in 1975 that the Peruvian economy had really changed, and changed for the better. They believed that, in fact, the military government "had unquestionably closed one chapter of Peru's history and opened another, [because it had] brought profound transformations to the economic, political and social life of Peru";[16] "the progress so far [June 1975], for all its shortcomings, does represent an important example of how a small dependent export economy can achieve a substantially greater degree of autonomous economic development by determined state intervention in the economy."[17]

The military's reforms put spectacular emphasis on the redistribution of property (although not necessarily on the redistribution of income, for property and wealth generate income in direct proportion to the efficiency with which resources are used), left empty-handed the poorest 60 percent of the population, and did not change the economy's essential rules of behavior. They represented a transitory political success and an economic failure that was unavoidable as long as the government did not see—and thus, of course, did not solve—the economy's structural disequilibria that had been accumulating since before 1968.

The agrarian reform distributed 10 million hectares (1 hectare = 2.5 acres) of latifundia to 340,000 families. But Peruvian peasant fam-

---

[16] Julio Cotler, "The New Mode of Political Domination in Peru," in Abraham F. Lowenthal, ed., *The Peruvian Experiment: Continuity and Change under Military Rule* (Princeton: Princeton University Press, 1975), p. 44.

[17] FitzGerald, *The State and Economic Development*, p. 2.

ilies totaled 1,200,000; 72 percent of the peasants (860,000 families), with the poorest of all among them, received nothing. Furthermore, the price policy, urban-biased in the 1960s, became even more so after 1972, when very tight price controls were imposed on all food production and marketing. Although the sharp increase in fertilizer prices in late 1973 made higher domestic prices for foodstuffs imperative, and government economists so advised Velasco, the general rejected the advice angrily, saying that the peasants now had land and should not get more advantages. Velasco's adamant decision not to raise food prices for urban consumers forced the government to pay subsidies on imported foods in the face of rising world food prices, adding severe pressures to the external and fiscal balances. The agrarian reform was undertaken explicitly to establish social justice and increase production and productivity in the countryside. This was not achieved. Only the sugar cooperatives' beneficiaries prospered, moving up from the fourth to the second decile in income distribution. Although the large estates disappeared, there was no lasting qualitative change in the rural power structure. Moreover, agricultural output grew at 1.9 percent a year from 1970 to 1975, hardly an improvement from the 2 percent of the 1960s.

The industrial reform was perhaps the most dramatic economic mistake from the social-revolutionary point of view.[18] To achieve its goal—"permanent, self-sustained, national independent industrial development"—industrial priorities were defined, not in terms of any dynamic comparative advantage or economic consideration, but primarily in terms of the physical sequence of elaborating industrial products, with the state to be given all the "basic" industries. Generous tax incentives were accorded even those industries of third priority to encourage reinvestment and importation of capital goods and inputs.

Minister of Industries Jorge Dellepiane was considered one of the most "leftist" in the government in 1970, and he sharply criticized the capitalistic mentality of entrepreneurs. Businessmen were frightened by Dellepiane's socialistic rhetoric and by the Industrial Community Law;[19] but this law and its regulations gave them more tax exemptions and higher protection, including a total ban on the importation of any good that was produced domestically, than any of the traditional governments' programs. In addition, they were allowed

[18] See "Ley General de Industrias," Decree-Law no. 18350, July 27, 1970.

[19] *Comunidades Laborales* were established in the industry, fishing, mining, and telecommunications sectors. In 1975, the total number of workers who belonged to the *comunidades* was less than 6 percent of the total labor force.

"cheap" dollars (at a fixed, overvalued exchange rate) and flexible output price ceilings in soles. If they submitted to the new, complex bureaucratic regulations, they could easily obtain high short-run profits, and many did. The industrial growth pattern of the 1970s is similar to that of the 1960s, but with more serious disequilibria:[20] a higher incidence of oligopoly, greater overcapitalization, even more limited labor absorption, and constrained output due to a severe shortage of foreign exchange. The word "export" does not appear even once in the thirty-nine-page Industrial Reform Law.

One of the essential features of the Peruvian experiment was the new role of the state in the economy. According to the 1971–1975 Development Plan: "The overcoming [*superación*] of the dependent capitalist model and underdevelopment requires the state to promote and lead national development, through its direct and indirect intervention in economic, sociocultural and political activity."[21] New ministries were created, such as Industry, Commerce, Transports and Communications, Housing, and Food; and new controls and regulations were established. At the same time, public enterprises were created or reorganized as a result of nationalization of foreign firms—Petroperú, Centromin, Hierroperú, Entelperú, Enafer, etc.— or takeovers of whole subsectors of economic activity—Pescaperú, Electroperú, Induperú, Epsa, etc.

The new role of the state in the economy was undertaken without regard to the most basic principles of economics. From the beginning, as the 1971–1975 Development Plan was being prepared, serious blunders and miscalculations were made in almost every ministry. For instance, it was stated that the agrarian reform would increase labor productivity and would slow migration to the cities; in fact, the opposite occurred, and easily could have been foreseen through a simple calculation of agricultural resources, prices, and incomes. Ministry of Industry officials insisted that industrial production would grow at 12 percent per year, although imported inputs could not be paid for at that rate of growth, because, they said, industrial growth could be "self-sustained" (*autosostenido*). Meanwhile, at the top of the planning system, the government never had a macroeconomic understanding of Peru's development problems, much less a clear and consistent view of the economic goals of the Peruvian Revolution.

[20] See Roberto Abusada-Salah, "Capital Utilization: A Study of Peruvian Manufacturing" (Doctoral dissertation, Cornell University, 1976), and "Políticas de Industrialización en el Perú, 1970–1976," in *Economía* (Universidad Católica) no. 1 (Lima, 1978).

[21] *Plan Nacional de Desarrollo, 1971–1975*, pp. 76 and 77.

Public officials believed that by establishing "controls" they could effectively direct the country's economic activity; in fact, controls complicated and slowed the economy and made businessmen more inclined than ever to bypass regulations. Public investment grew to offset sluggishness in the private sector and, because the government was unwilling to raise taxes, the treasury deficit shot up from 382 million soles in 1969 to 30,591 million in 1975.[22] Moreover, public enterprises paid little attention to efficient economic management; government policies set very low sales prices for their products, and financial support was guaranteed by the Banco de la Nación. Petroperú provides one of the most dramatic examples: in May 1975, gasoline prices were below September 1968 levels, despite the fact that one third of the oil was imported at international prices that had more than tripled since the end of 1973. Shane Hunt, sympathetic to the new role of the public sector in Peru, had, however, warned in 1974: "In the next decade the Peruvian economy will prosper or atrophy according to the effectiveness with which the new public enterprises are managed."[23] Whereas prior to takeover these enterprises made profits and paid taxes, after takeover they did not; some did not even cover their own costs. Moreover, the enterprises did not care to integrate their activities into the planning system. In 1967, the public sector in Peru was small and weak; in 1975, it was big and bankrupt.

The Peruvian Experiment, Phase Two (1976–1978)

On August 29, 1975, General Velasco was removed, General Morales Bermúdez became president, and important changes were made in several cabinet posts. Political analysts find 1975 a tumultuous year, from the riots of early February, to the repressive measures of May to July, the fall of Velasco in August, the renewed "socialist" stance of Morales, and the fall of Graham and Leonidas Rodriguez at the end of the year. In terms of changes in economic policy, however, "Phase Two" started only in 1976.

The country was facing serious problems on every economic front: foreign imbalance, fiscal deficit, inflationary pressures, and growing unemployment. Without an economic model and under pressure from the international banking community, the military had to accept not only the sad reality of an unexpected crisis but also a whole new set of ideas and explanations: the economic gospel according to

---

[22] For a year-by-year account of the central government budget, see Schydlowsky and Wicht, *Anatomía de un Fracaso Económico*, p. 37.

[23] Shane J. Hunt, "Direct Foregin Investment in Peru: New Rules for an Old Game," in Lowenthal, ed., *The Peruvian Experiment.*

the International Monetary Fund. The essence of this message is that closing the gaps in the balance of payments, in the fiscal budget, and in the price level may be painful, but it is necessary and healthy. According to the IMF, the Peruvian economy was suffering from "excess demand," and therefore, it was necessary to reduce public and private expenditures; financial disorder had been introduced by state intervention, and therefore, it was necessary to return to free market mechanisms, especially in the foreign sector. In sharp contrast to the previous strategy (1963–1975), which had assumed "insufficient demand" and encouraged protectionism, a fixed exchange rate, price controls, and increased public expenditures, the new policies required: (1) devaluation to reduce imports (and to some extent increase exports) and thus eliminate the external deficit and save enough foreign exchange to pay the heavy debt service; (2) reduction of the money supply growth rate to reduce the inflation rate and dampen the pressure on the balance of payments; (3) reduction of public expenditure (and increase of fiscal revenues) to cover the fiscal deficit and restrain total demand; (4) elimination of subsidies and controls on prices and wages to allow the economy to function "properly" (i.e., freely) and all markets to be cleared. Unemployment would certainly increase, but only until the economy returned to its "equilibrium" point.

The Peruvian government was not quick to accept either the diagnosis or the medicine provided by the IMF but finally accepted both. The rate of exchange was devalued 350 percent over 30 months; severe restraints were placed on the expansion of the money supply and the budget was readjusted downward; since 1977, controls have been repeatedly relaxed and almost all subsidies on consumption goods have been eliminated.

The results of these policies are shown in Table 4.4: a severe recession, with a drop in per capita income (.2 percent rate of growth in 1976, −4 percent in 1977, −4.4 percent in 1978); a balance-of-payments deficit (and therefore continued drain of net reserves, at −$1.3 billion in 1978), although the current account deficit was reversed, mostly because imports were sharply reduced;[24] a continued deficit in the public budget, with lower public expenditure in real terms, but lower public revenues as well; and galloping inflation estimated at 73 percent in 1978, due not to expansionary monetary policies, but to devaluation.

The most dramatic result, however, was massive and growing un-

---

[24] For the external debt situation at the end of 1977, see Schydlowsky and Wicht, *Anatomía de un Fracaso Económico*, p. 42.

TABLE 4.4
Gross Domestic Product, 1975–1978

	1975	1976	1977	1978	1976	1977	1978
	IN BILLIONS OF SOLES, AT CONSTANT 1970 PRICES				ANNUAL RATES OF GROWTH (IN %)		
Agriculture	39.8	41.1	41.1	39.9	3.3%	0.0%	−3.0%
Fishing	2.6	3.1	3.0	3.9	19.9	−5.5	30.1
Mining	18.7	20.4	26.0	29.5	8.4	27.2	13.5
Manufactures	80.6	84.0	78.5	76.9	4.2	−6.5	−2.1
Construction	18.6	18.1	16.7	14.0	−2.8	−7.7	−16.1
Services	153.7	156.8	154.4	149.8	2.1	−1.5	−3.0
Total GDP	314.0	323.6	319.7	314.0	3.0	−1.2	−1.8
Consumption	275.9	281.6	281.7	261.3	2.1	−0.0	−7.2
Investment	65.3	57.9	45.0	39.2	−11.2	−22.3	−12.9
Exports	36.5	37.1	42.2	48.8	1.6	13.7	15.6
Imports	63.6	53.1	49.1	35.4	−16.5	−7.5	−27.9
	AS PERCENT OF GDP						
Consumption	87.9%	87.0%	88.1%	83.2%			
Investment	20.8	17.9	14.1	12.5			
	IN SOLES, AT CONSTANT 1970 PRICES						
GDP per capita	20,297	20,342	19,532	18,675	0.2	−4.0	−4.4

Source: Banco Central de Reserva, *Memoria*, 1979.

employment, even in the industrial sector, where installed capital was being used well below its normal level.[25] In 1978, 57.4 percent of the labor force was unemployed or underemployed, an increase of 10.2 percentage points since 1975. When the reduction in participation rates is taken into account, the deterioration rises to 12.9 percentage points—805,000 additional people without adequate employment opportunities.

The Structural Disequilibria of the Peruvian Economy

During 1976, many civilian political advisers and supporters of phase one were gradually removed from their jobs. Many of them had worked hard to build the most promising Latin American experiment in the 1970s and certainly deserved more success for their efforts; but their economic oversights and mistakes proved fatal. Without a coherent economic model, the government was not able to see the distortions of the economy or to reorient the development strategy.

The annual growth rate of the national average productivity per

[25] For the statistics on open, disguised and hidden unemployment, see ibid., p. 44.

worker dropped from 2 percent in the 1960–1968 period to only 1.7 percent during Phase One, and to −2.1 percent during Phase Two. If we consider the situation by regions, we note that in the rural area the actual rate was 1.1 percent in Phase One and 0.0 percent in Phase Two, whereas in the urban area, labor productivity grew only 0.4 percent in Phase One and dropped to −2.7 percent in Phase Two. The countryside, always economically neglected, fell into total stagnation, but the crisis hit the cities, where the number of workers had increased by more than one million (from 2,320,000 to 3,350,000) during Phase One alone, particularly hard.

The distortions in employment and productivity are particularly noticeable on a sectorally disaggregated basis. More than two thirds of the agricultural workers did not benefit from any of the structural reforms of the Peruvian experiment, nor from any significant income redistribution policy, such as new infrastructure or new social services in health or education. Migration increased in absolute and relative numbers. In the cities, meanwhile, the traditional informal sector (production units of less than five workers, such as artisan workshops, masonry, petty commerce, and services) exploded from 1968 to 1975. It was not touched by any of the structural reforms or by mandated salary increases, because most of the workers in this sector were "independent" (self-employed). This sector was aided indirectly, however, by the urban consumption subsidies and the demand expansion policies of Phase One. Its labor force grew by 8.4 percent per year, in an eruption of ambulatory commerce, unregistered and temporary squatter manufacturing activities, and all kinds of marginal services that reduced the average productivity of this sector below the 1950 level in real terms, although in 1975 it still had twice the average income level of the rural area. In the second half of the decade, however, this urban-marginal sector was the most severely hit by the "stabilizing" policies of Phase Two; these workers and their families had little or no defense against price increases and overall demand contraction.

The urban formal sectors depend heavily upon the public budget, the availability of foreign exchange, and domestic credit expansion. They expanded their output and, to a lesser extent, their labor force form 1968 to 1975. These sectors, the most favored by the structural reforms and the overall development strategy, became the most distorted of the economy as the foreign exchange generating subsectors (agricultural exports, fisheries, and mining) stagnated and the foreign exchange demanding subsectors (industry and transportation) increased steadily (see Table 4.2). Manufacturing, which had expanded at an annual average rate of 7.1 percent during 1970–1975, slowed to 4.2 percent in 1976 and then contracted by −6.5 percent in 1977 and −2.1 percent in 1978. The only sectors with positive growth rates between 1975 and 1978 were fishing and mining, but they employed less than 4 percent of the labor force. The foreign exchange they generated was not enough to reestablish balance to the trade account and certainly not enough to close the deficit in the balance of payments when the capital account is also considered. The urban modern sectors were paralyzed by a shortage of foreign exchange and by a lack of liquidity and domestic demand in the internal market.

As a result of these disequilibria, the number of unemployed and underemployed workers did not diminish during Phase One and dramatically increased during Phase Two, in absolute terms and also as a percentage of a rapidly growing labor force. In 1969, there were 250,-000 unemployed and 1,900,000 underemployed (1,000,000 in the rural areas and 900,000 in the cities). By 1978, the number of unemployed were 380,000 and the underemployed had become 2,500,000 (of which 1,400,000 were in the cities). At the same time, installed industrial capital in the cities increased by over $1 billion, but it remained idle in ever higher proportions.

A most severe recession was accompanied by record inflation induced by drastic global devaluations, which did not solve the foreign imbalance because preexisting domestic price distortions in many cases remained and the recession was aggravated as tight monetary policies were applied to reduce "excessive demand."

The economic disequilibria reduced considerably the total national product achieved in the last two decades and made income distribution more skewed. The Peruvian experiment in Phase One neglected economics and emphasized redistribution and reform rather than growth; a bit of income redistribution occurred, as well as some "growth" at the cost of public sector and foreign balance deficits. In Phase Two, economics could no longer be neglected, but painful and inefficient policies were applied in an attempt to eliminate deficits without solving the structural imbalances that tied up the supply side of the economy.

CAUSES OF THE ECONOMIC CRISIS

Because the economic crisis came at the end of phase one, it is tempting to conclude *post hoc ergo propter hoc* that phase one was its cause. Causality, as usual, is more complex, however.

The Velasco government is by no means the only one that has

adopted import-substitution industrialization policies, nor did it initiate them in Peru. Thus it should not bear the responsibility for the disastrous results of these policies alone. If the Velasco government had implemented only the same import-substitution measures that the Belaúnde administration had, a crisis would have occurred also. Argentina, Brazil, Uruguay, Brazil before 1964, and Colombia before 1957 all pursued import-substitution policies, and all suffered economic crises as a result. However, because the Velasco government pursued this strategy in a most vigorous, extreme and steadfast manner—as only an autocratic government could—the crisis was more severe and more rapid.

The policies of Phase One should not bear full responsibility for the economic crisis for other reasons as well. The economic legacies of the pre-1968 era were significant to the crisis in various ways. Further, the severity of the crisis was at least in part due to the successful effort to postpone it with an aggressive foreign debt policy. Last but not least, substantial misdiagnosis of the nature of the crisis led to the adoption of counterproductive remedies during Phase Two, which made the crisis much worse than it needed to be.

Yet various Phase One policies did accelerate and exacerbate the crisis that would have eventually occurred in any case due to the import-substitution strategy. These policies of the military government directly caused problems that culminated in the destruction of part of the managerial system of the country and disorganization of the remainder; reduction of the growth rate of the primary, foreign-exchange-producing sectors; increases in capital and foreign exchange intensity of investment, current production, and final demand; elimination of most of the flexibility in the import bill; and inflation of the balance-of-payments problem through excessive borrowing.

The Development Strategy: Industrialization for the Domestic Market

The Peruvian Revolution inherited from Belaúnde a development strategy based on industrial growth under a protective umbrella of ever-higher tariffs. The policy had been successful during the 1960s: industrial growth was substantial, imports of goods Peru could produce decreased, and the import bill changed in composition, with a smaller share for finished goods and a much larger one for raw materials and intermediate goods. The industrialization strategy adopted by Belaúnde was, moreover, very congenial to the military. Industry signified modernity and would generate employment. Import-substituting industrialization, however, may exacerbate balance-of-payments problems.[26] Instead of importing consumption goods, which can be done without, countries import raw materials and intermediate goods, which cannot be dispensed with if part of the domestic industrial system is not to be paralyzed. Import-substituting industrialization does not solve the employment problem, nor does it counter any secular deterioration that may occur in the terms of trade. Rather, any loss of purchasing power has more severe consequences because domestic economic activities are now dependent on imported inputs. But above all, industrialization for the domestic market contains an inherent inconsistency that leads inexorably to serious difficulties.

The central tenet of import-substituting industrialization is that industry must grow at a faster rate than the primary sectors of the economy. Because industry requires imported raw materials, its rapid growth means that the demand for imported inputs—and hence for foreign exchange—will also grow very rapidly. The supply of foreign exchange, however, is provided by the primary sectors, which by design grow more slowly. The divergence in growth rates of the demand and supply of foreign exchange is sustainable for a time because industry grows from a much smaller base than the primary sectors and because import substitution generates some foreign exchange savings. The time comes, however, when industry's growth rate outstrips the ability of the primary sectors to supply the necessary foreign exchange. At that point, a balance-of-payments crisis arises.

The inherent limitations of the import-substituting strategy are also, unfortunately, self-perpetuating. Because a central policy in the strategy is protection, the prices of industrial products are above those on the international market. When only final goods are involved, no serious structural consequences result. As industrialization proceeds, however, and intermediate goods begin to be produced domestically under protective barriers, the cost of production rises at successive stages of transformation. As a result, when the import-substitution process matures, industrial cost levels are pushed above world cost levels. When the balance-of-payments crisis occurs, the country cannot easily earn foreign exchange through industrial exports because costs are too high. In consequence, it turns to further import substitution. This, however, begets more of the same—further increases in the

[26] See, for example, Ian M. D. Little, Tibor Scitovsky, and Maurice F. C. Scott, *Industry and Trade in Some Developing Countries: A Comparative Study* (New York: Oxford University Press, 1970).

industrial cost structure and reductions of investment productivity and foreign exchange savings—until complete paralysis ensues.[27]

At the policy level, the successive phases of import-substitution policy are reinforced by an illusion that industry is even more inefficient than it is in reality. This "industrial inefficiency illusion" arises from a simple-minded comparison of domestic cost of production with world prices by dividing the former by the exchange rate. Such an exercise, however, ignores the fact that the industrial producers do not buy their inputs at costs comparable with world prices. Rather, the exchange rate affecting their inputs is supplemented by the cost-raising effect of import duties or other import restrictions. When the industrial costs are translated into dollars at exchange rates that incorporate the import regime, the dollar cost of domestic industrial production appears much lower. Although some real inefficiency remains, it is by no means as great as the simplistic calculation makes it appear. The industrial inefficiency illusion affects policy making because nobody wishes to support the export efforts of a hopelessly inefficient industry. Without export support, however, Peruvian industrial producers are hard put to sell abroad, precisely because of the (largely policy caused) high costs of inputs. But as long as industry does not export, the absence of exports appears to confirm industrial inefficiency, thereby strengthening the position of those who claim that industry does not deserve support for export. Naturally, in the absence of industrial export growth, import substitution is the only alternative and thus is the policy that must be adopted.[28] The development strategy of the revolution, then, was one that inexorably leads to balance-of-payments crisis and, while it was a strategy inherited from the previous regime, it was pursued with gusto and full conviction by the revolutionary government.

Reform of Management and Decision Making

The revolutionary government prided itself on a major reform of the nation's economic decision making. The government would be-

[27] See Marcelo Diamond, *Doctrinas Económicas, Desarrollo e Independencia*, ed. Paidós (Buenos Aires, 1973); Daniel M. Schydlowsky, "International Trade Policy in the Economic Growth in Latin America," in S. E. Guisinger, ed., *Trade and Investment Policies in the Americas* (Dallas: Southern Methodist University Press, 1973).

[28] Daniel M. Schydlowsky, "Policy Making for National Economic Growth in Latin America," in Luigi Einaudi, ed., *Beyond Cuba: Latin America Takes Charge of the Future* (New York: Crane, Russak & Co., 1974).

come the principal motor of development. It would set up investment in infrastructure and productive facilities. For the latter purpose, a large government-owned production sector was created, partly by nationalizing existing enterprises. Inevitable management learning costs ensued, but there was also a widespread lack of concern for cost control and microeconomic efficiency, both in the public enterprises themselves and in the ministries that supposedly supervised them. Moreover, consistent macroeconomic planning of the sector was lacking as well. The result was chaotic growth, the evaporation of the annual profits made previously, and the bankrolling of ambitious investment programs through deficit financing, primarily foreign debt.

The revolution also created a "reformed private sector" in which workers were to acquire an increasing share of the equity through their "industrial community." The industrial community hamstrung entrepreneurs' day-to-day operations but preserved their discretion in matters of investment and purchasing. Businessmen made investments only to defend existing property. (The reinvestment provision of the industrial community legislation made it possible to postpone the day when workers would have 50 percent ownership.) Businessmen also imported new equipment as a way to export capital through over-invoicing. Government incentives and government desires were clearly operating at cross-purposes: while the goal was to improve equity, expand industry, and police the undesirable actions of entrepreneurs, the result was to consolidate an aristocracy of workers, encourage entrepreneurial efforts to find ways around the system, spark capital flight, and inhibit new job creation.

The agrarian reform created a new group of owners, but it also resulted in extensive decapitalization of existing agricultural enterprises, because many new owners believed that these good times would not last and proceeded to consume as quickly as possible. (It is ironic to note that they were right.) Although output did not decline in the large agricultural enterprises, investment, even for replacement of old capital stock, did. The government, for its part, invested in costly, long-run irrigation projects such as Chira-Piura and Majes, but overall, the sector was decapitalized for the short and medium term, and output potential consequently shrank.

The social property sector also represented a major innovation but was too small to affect the immediate economic situation to a significant degree, although it did have a major negative impact on the business climate.

Concurrent with these reforms at the firm level, unlimited protection of all import-competing economic activities was established and administered through import licensing and import restrictions. Food, however, was excepted from import restrictions, for the policy was to keep prices down, importing whatever volume was needed and selling through the government food corporation at ever more subsidized prices.

The reforms of ownership and decision making not only did little to create a "noncapitalist" economic system but also had three undesirable effects. First, enormous inefficiency resulted. The economy performed with a vast under-utilization of labor and capital and misused the foreign exchange it had. Entrepreneurs paid little attention to the efficient operation of industrial plants; private and public investment resources were systematically misallocated. Second, government spending grew dangerously large. A larger state role required larger staffs; and the number of government employees about doubled. Investment on government account was slated to rise as well. The tax base had shrunk, however, due to nationalization, and the government's enterprises yielded large losses. Thus, government revenues could not cover government expenditure. The inevitable fiscal deficit was covered in the "easy" way—foreign borrowing. Third, demand for foreign exchange increased, both to pay for imported inputs, imported food, and imported capital equipment and also to cover over-invoicing. At the same time, the growth of the foreign exchange supply was reduced as the less efficient producing units could not maintain export levels, or operated poorly in world markets as a result of little marketing expertise.

The impact of the management reforms significantly aggravated the balance-of-payment crisis already gathering momentum as a result of the development strategy. Equally important, however, these reforms also sharply reduced the quality of management in all sectors and impaired the economy's ability to respond to *any* economic policy, thus setting the stage for the economic disorganization in Phase Two, when the crisis really hit.

Side Effects of the Reform

The elements of the development strategy and management reforms that propelled Peru into a balance-of-payments crisis were exacerbated by various side effects of these policies. The overall result was that the supply of foreign exchange grew slowly while demand for it grew rapidly, and economic production became more rigidly tied to export purchases.

One important side effect was a fall in the output growth of the primary sector. Agriculture suffered from the systematic bias in price policy and from new, inexperienced management; a greater percentage of the nation's food had to be imported. Two of the three large metals mines became government enterprises and did not expand output significantly; iron exports, in fact, decreased. Foreign private investors, with one notable exception—Cuajone—did not participate in major new ventures. Domestic private investment slowed, particularly in the small mining sector, where price and new bureaucratic regulations made investment unattractive. In oil, a number of companies were initially drawn in despite the tough-sounding terms of the "Peru-model" contract (actually an adaptation of the Indonesian model), but little commercially exportable oil was found. Eventually, only Occidental remained in Peru, but on terms alleged to be much better than those of the initial Peru model.

Second, investment and current production became more capital intensive. In the private reformed sector, this was the natural result of the incentives provided in the industrial law. Owners who wished to postpone the day when workers would own half of the enterprise had to invest; to keep their labor problem to a minimum, such investment was concentrated on automated equipment. Workers had exactly the same interests—the more the entrepreneur invested, the greater the absolute size of the profits available for distribution; the more capital intensive (i.e., automated) the investment, the larger the share for each employed worker. Rarely has legislation generated such congruence between the interests of labor and capital to the detriment of the society as a whole.

In the government sector, capital-intensive projects were the natural outcome of three elements: the size of the enterprises; the desire to have "modern," automatic, large-scale production plants; and the decision to develop "basic" industry, which is almost always capital intensive (e.g., petrochemicals, steel, metal refineries). But higher capital intensity in Peru meant increased demand for imported machinery and often increased demand for particular kinds of imported raw materials and intermediate goods on a sustained basis. The additional import requirements raised foreign exchange demand even further beyond supply.

Third, the complementarity of imports to domestic production was dramatically increased. The import system implemented early by the military government telescoped import substitution into a few years by simply prohibiting imports of any goods the country was producing. Almost overnight, all imports became things that the economy could not do without. At the same time, the infinite protection available generated inordinately inefficient production activities because cost increases could easily be passed on to the public. As a consequence, import needs became almost totally inflexible. By policy and legislation, the reduction in imports had to come about through decreased domestic industrial output, or through reduced food consumption, or through lower investment. The rigidities it took other countries numerous years to achieve, were put in place in Peru quite rapidly.

Fourth, although the revolutionary government wanted to redistribute income in favor of the poor, in fact it redistributed income from the top 5 percent to the next 15 percent. The result was a marked increase in Peru's middle class, which in turn increased the demand for industrial goods; as a result, the level of industrial output and demand for imports grew. The divergence between the demand and supply of foreign exchange became yet greater.

Together, these side effects exacerbated the elements of the development strategy that were propelling the country into a balance-of-payments crisis. The growth of the provision of foreign exchange was slowed down, the growth of the demand for foreign exchange was speeded up, and the rigidities that tied the output of the economy to its import bill were strengthened.

Foreign Debt Policy

After 1971, Peru's foreign debt policy was to borrow to the hilt. The Peruvian government clearly was ready to borrow to finance all projects for which someone was willing to lend. The justification was often the importance, not the quality, of the investment projects. Many times, however, borrowing was necessary, first to cover growing fiscal deficits arising either in the central government or in the public enterprises and eventually to cover a balance-of-payments gap.

Concurrently with the will to borrow, the government gained the means. It acquired enterprises with established credit lines and foreign banking connections; it took over a number of banks that had correspondent relationships; and, of course, it had its traditional lines for development indebtedness. Moreover, banks and others were willing to lend freely to Peru. This resulted in part from an aura of fiscal responsibility and order that the military government cultivated in its first years, in part from temporarily rising export prices, and in part from the government's forecasts of large future increases in foreign exchange earnings due to oil allegedly available in the Amazon region. World lenders also wanted an outlet for funds coming from the large growth in inflows to the Eurodollar market.

As a result of willingness by both borrower and lenders, Peru increased its public foreign debt to more than $3.5 billion by 1975. Evidently the debt increase made it possible to finance the foreign exchange using development "strategy" in its accelerated form, thus delaying the inevitable crisis implicit in that strategy by three or four years. At the same time, however, it also made the crisis much worse when it finally arrived. In the absence of extensive borrowing, all that would have caused the crisis was the current account deficit; but with the acquired debt, the country was faced with an abrupt turnaround of capital flow and had to finance a capital account movement several times the magnitude of the current account deficit.

Exogenous Factors

Some elements in the economic crisis were partially or totally beyond the control of the Peruvian authorities. One such element was national defense spending. While the amount of foreign exchange required for armaments is not definitively documented, available estimates indicate that it was between $1.5 billion and $2 billion. The extent to which any government would have increased defense spending in light of international tensions and arms build-ups in almost all neighboring countries, particularly Chile, is difficult to assess. Some money would probably have been spent on armaments regardless of the nature of the Peruvian government.

World prices constituted a second exogenous factor. Excepting fishmeal, Peru has virtually no control over the prices at which its exports sell. Export prices went up strongly from 1968 to 1974 and then started to fall, just as the worldwide oil price increase was pushing up the cost of Peru's imports. The timing of the turnaround of Peru's terms of trade could not have been worse.

A third and very important exogenous element was the drop in the fishmeal harvest. Probably because of both climatic changes and previous overfishing, the anchovy catch fell drastically during 1972. As a result, export revenues from fishmeal fell from $331 million in 1970 to $136 million in 1973.

Phase One Causality in a Nutshell

The development strategy adopted by the Peruvian Revolution would have by itself carried the country into economic crisis. This has been the experience of every country that has followed a similar import-substituting industrialization strategy; Argentina, Chile, Uruguay, Brazil before 1964, and Colombia before 1967 provide ample evidence of this. If the Peruvian revolutionary govenment had followed this strategy with only the intensity of the previous government, the crisis would still have occurred. To some extent, therefore, the crisis was independent of the revolutionary character to this government. It took a revolutionary and autocratic government, however, to follow the chosen line with such "purity" and steadfastness. To this extent the crisis is due to the nature of the government. An administration less convinced of its rightness and righteousness and/or more diffuse in its power structure would have strayed from the path leading to the crisis much earlier. Moreover, the mere choice of development strategy was obviously not the whole story.

The revolutionary government's policies, whatever their other merits, accelerated the speed and increased the intensity with which the development strategy was accumulating its basic inconsistency. Destruction of part of the managerial system of the country and disorganization of the remainder; reduction in growth of the primary, foreign-exchange-producing sectors; increase in capital and foreign exchange intensity of investment, current production, and final demand; elimination of most of the flexibility in the import bill; inflation of the balance-of-payments problem through excessive borrowing; all these elements were ascribable directly to the nature of the Peruvian experiment and aggravated the situation considerably. So did the exogenous factors at work.

Compounding the Problem: Counterproductive Stabilization Policies

If Phase One of the revolutionary government in one way or another caused the economic crisis, Phase Two multiplied its pain by its choice of remedies. Consider the situation. Here was a crisis due basically to imbalance in the productive capacities of primary and secondary sectors: to operate industry at a normal level of capacity use required more imports of raw materials and intermediate goods than could be purchased with agricultural and mining exports while maintaining investment. As a result, the foreign debt had been run up. True, the problem was exacerbated by managerial disorganization and government red tape. There was no generalized excess demand, however. Indeed, not much of a dent had been made in the chronic under-utilization of capacity in industry[29] and services. Nor was lack of savings the problem; after all, to install new capital

[29] See Roberto Abusada-Salah, "Utilización de Capital Instalado en el Sector Industrial Peruano" (Boston, August 1975, mimeograph).

equipment when the existing stock is under-utilized is a questionable proposition. The simple fact is that in 1975 Peru's foreign lenders were no longer willing to watch the country's debt grow exponentially—they wanted to see at least some loans paid off.

A net reduction in foreign debt required either spending less foreign exchange or earning more, or some of both. The first alternative (i.e. a fall in imports) implies a reduction of investment, industrial output, and possibly, food consumption. In other words, lower imports imply deflation. The second alternative, earning more foreign exchange, requires a greater volume of exports, particularly in the short run. Yet an increase in Peru's traditional exports was not likely in the short term: (1) mining projects have a gestation period of several years and require a large initial investment; and (2) agriculture requires a degree of managerial capability that was scarce after the agrarian reform. Only industry was capable of a rapid response, and in industry, excess capacity coexisted with underemployed and unemployed labor. Thus, a potential source of supply *was* available. Industry had high money costs, however, due in part to the high costs of inputs (recall the inefficiency illusion discussed previously), which would have to be compensated if at least part of Peruvian industrial production were to be competitive on world markets.

To solve the balance-of-payments crisis at a minimum social and economic cost, the foreign exchange constraint had to be overcome primarily from the supply side, by exporting industrial goods. The potential of such a policy is described in the next section. Deflation should constitute only a complementary line of defense, temporarily countering the shortfall of foreign exchange that is only gradually covered by new and growing export revenue and the debt roll-over backed by that new revenue.

The government failed to undertake an export promotion policy, however; and Phase Two officials instead adopted a mix of Phase One and IMF strategies to deal with the situation. From Phase One they took tighter import controls. The damage to potential exporters did not seem to occur to them; any such side effect, they reasoned, would only demonstrate the need for even better and tighter foreign exchange rationing. From the IMF they took an aggregate diagnosis of the problem as excessive demand accompanied by too little saving (particularly in the public sector).

The specific policies adopted were devaluation, tighter import controls, and tight money. Recession ensued, as did massive inflation and increased government deficits. None of this should have been surprising. A general devaluation would not promote exports of manufactures because costs of inputs go up with the exchange rate. Besides, the exchange licensing system ensured that export producers were starved for foreign inputs quite as much as everyone else. Moreover, devaluation had little effect on traditional exports because supply elasticity was very low in the short run.

On the import side, price responsiveness was also low. Prices for imported food and all other food rose with the exchange rate; import volume fell as consumers' real income fell and not because people switched from imported foodstuffs to domestically produced ones. Industrial raw materials were so tightly rationed that a higher price could not reduce their demand, but a drop in economic activity could and did. Capital goods imports depended on government expenditure and could be cut directly, albeit at the loss of some foreign aid disbursements. Thus, imports could fall as a result of devaluation only insofar as a recession was thereby induced. Lower real spending, however, could occur only as a result of reduced purchasing power caused by price increases. "Fortunately," the devaluation did push up the prices of imported and domestic food, all imported inputs, and all goods whose sellers did not wish to lose by virtue of the higher prices of their purchases. In short, all prices rose and everyone's real income fell. Income receivers did attempt to reestablish their purchasing power, however, and thereby set off an inflationary spiral between incomes and the exchange rate. Balance-of-payments improvement thus depended on the exchange rate staying ahead of nominal incomes to keep aggregate demand down. Inflation and depression were the essential ingredients in gaining control over the external accounts.

The government deficit did not narrow significantly during this process because depression reduced tax revenue. The ever larger nominal deficits fed inflationary expectations, thus aggravating the price spiral. At the same time, the progressive tightening of credit to the private sector deepened the depression, further reducing tax revenue.

As this policy took hold, the country sank into a morass of depression with inflation and of public unrest and government perplexity at the crisis that it did not know how to handle. Yet in the final analysis, the failure of the stabilization policy was rooted in a false diagnosis: there was no shortfall of productive capacity compared to demand, nor was there excess consumption compared to income. There *was* a shortfall in the provision of foreign exchange, which throttled production and caused a reduction in output, taxes, and savings. The correct cure was, evidently, to expand the supply of foreign exchange.

The policy adopted had an additional and very grave drawback insofar as it reestablished external equilibrium and credit-worthiness: it laid the groundwork for the next crisis, for as long as the sectoral imbalance of foreign exchange production and usage persisted, normal growth would entail a balance-of-payments crisis. Recession only masks the symptoms; a cure requires that industry earn its own foreign exchange through exports.

The faulty diagnosis and the counterproductive policy of Phase Two converted a balance-of-payments crisis into a full-fledged economic crisis and into a *crise de regime*. In 1978, the result that one could already see was an abandonment of the social objectives of the revolution and a move of the military back to their barracks. Whether under a constitutional administration there would also be an economic reorganization destined to put the economy on a vigorous and balanced growth path remained to be seen.

RERUNNING HISTORY

Criticizing what was done is not enough. Could the objectives of the revolution have been more successfully pursued by other means? How difficult would it have been? A complete answer is not possible but available alternatives may be identified and their consequences simulated. To do so is essential; otherwise, a suspicion remains that history, bad as it was, may have represented the only option available.

This section presents two possible scenarios for Peru in the last decade. The first one, set in 1969, develops a growth strategy that would have explicitly countered the inherent limitations of import-substituting industrialization by making industry a foreign-exchange-earning sector alongside agriculture, mining, and fishing. Industrial development would have been independent from the growth of the primary sectors, and the basic contradiction in Peru's development strategy would have been eliminated. We will analyze specifically the employment and income distribution consequences of such a strategy, the necessary correlated economic policy, and how this policy would have fit revolutionary objectives. The second scenario deals with the stabilization problem as of 1975. Our purpose is to show that the costs of stabilization could have been greatly reduced and that an effective recovery of the economy could have been achieved by 1980.

Capacity Utilizing Export-Led Growth

In addition to a development strategy, the revolutionary government inherited about a quarter of a million unemployed, almost two million underemployed laborers, and, what is more remarkable, a substantial stock of under-utilized capacity. On average, the industrial sector worked about one and a quarter shifts per day in 1968. Moreover, the average factory was closed 20 percent of the days of the year.[30]

Such capital waste in the midst of capital scarcity had numerous causes. One fundamental cause was relative factor costs. Capital had been kept cheap through controls on interest rates and through the liberal availability and low cost of imported capital goods. On the other hand, labor had been made expensive through extensive social legislation.

Tax policy was a second cause of under-utilization. Tax write-offs were provided for reinvested profits that were used to buy machinery and equipment. Moreover, depreciation rates were independent of capacity utilization. Thus, second- and third-shift profits were taxed at a higher rate than first-shift profits. These measures amounted to a reduction in the cost of investment, if in the form of fixed assets.

Foreign exchange policy was also a factor. While tariffs were the main import-restricting device, capital goods were subject to lower tariffs or were frequently exempt from them. When, under the military government, quotas became the rule, investment goods enjoyed preferential access to foreign exchange. Furthermore, the amount of capacity installed was obviously an important consideration when import licenses for current imports were assigned.

Entrepreneurial imitation also played a role. Peruvian industrialists adopted the "tried and true" production procedures of the countries from whence the capital goods came. These countries, however, were typically economies in which plentiful capital and scarce labor justified single shifts and many machines. These same techniques and organizational forms yield disappointing results in an economy with radically different resource endowments.[31]

Greater utilization of capital represented a major resource for increasing the welfare of the Peruvian population. If the existing excess labor were put to work on the existing excess capital, a large amount

[30] See Abusada-Salah, "Utilización del Capital Instalado en el Sector Industrial Peruano."

[31] On causality of under-utilization of capacity, see Roger Betancourt and Christopher Clague, "An Economic Analysis of Capital Utilization," *Southern Economic Journal* (July 1975); Patricio Millan, "The Intensive Use of Capital in Industrial Plants: Multiple Shifts as an Economic Option" (Doctoral dissertation, Harvard University, 1975); Daniel M. Schydlowsky, "On Determining the Causality of Underutilization of Capacity: A Working Note" (May 1973, mimeograph); Roberto Abusada-Salah, "A Statistical Shift-Choice Model of Capital Utilization," Discussion Paper Series no. 15, Center for Latin American Development Studies, Boston University, 1975.

of output could be generated. Naturally, it would be necessary to find a market for the output, to obtain the necessary imported inputs, and to finance the working capital to get the factories going.

In part, an extensive capacity utilization program would generate its own market, because, concurrently with the manufacture of additional product, wages and profit would be distributed that would boost the buying power of the population. While the increased buying power would match the increased supply of goods in the aggregate, no such equality would obtain at the sectoral level. In particular, increased demand would occur for agricultural goods, the supply of which would not have expanded concurrently.[32] Additional import demand would therefore arise. Simultaneously, some of the industrial supply could not be placed in the domestic market, precisely because people do not spend all their income on industrial products. A foreign market therefore would be needed for industrial production, backed by the support measures essential to make their prices competitive. On the import side, demand would increase for intermediate goods and raw materials to support greater industrial production, as would the demand for agricultural imports mentioned above. These would all have to be paid for with the foreign exchange earned from the export of industrial products not absorbed in the domestic market. Finally, the working capital needed could be financed out of the savings generated by the additional output, although some temporary credit resources might be necessary.[33]

While the output effects of capacity utilization export-led growth are clear, the equity effects are more mixed. Such a strategy would undoubtedly create very significant increases in employment and the wage bill. It would also, however, make existing industry more profitable and increase the return to capital. Thus, while workers' income would definitely increase, whether they would also gain in relative terms would depend on the growth of aggregate wage income as compared to profit income and on the distribution of each of these between income strata.

Using existing installed capacity with existing idle labor provides a

[32] This is not to say that a supply response from agriculture would be entirely absent; only that in the short run not all the new demand could be satisfied from increased domestic production.

[33] For an algebraic formulation of these interactions, see P. Millan and Daniel M. Schydlowsky, "Macroeconomic Consequences of Multiple Shifting," presented to the Fourth Conference on Utilization of Capacity in Industry, Caracas, January 1973 (mimeograph). Also, Daniel M. Schydlowsky, "Capital Utilization, Growth, Employment and Balance of Payments and Price Stabilization," in Jere Behrman and James A. Hanson, eds., *Planning and Short-Term Macroeconomic Policy in Latin America* (Cambridge, Mass.: Ballinger, 1979).

one-time gain, albeit a considerable one. In addition, however, a growth effect arises if new investment is also used henceforth on a multiple-shift basis. Then not only is the per capita income raised once and for all, but growth proceeds at a higher rate from a higher base.

Some Figures

The conceptual analysis described in the previous section only represents a real and interesting alternative if the empirical magnitudes are of an appropriate size and sign. The data presented below are drawn largely from work by Luis Valdivieso, based on earlier work by Roberto Abusada-Salah, Patricio Millan, and Daniel Schydlowsky.[34]

Information on capacity utilization is available in Peruvian industrial statistics and has been tabulated for 1971. We have reason to believe that the situation in 1969 was no better. It is astonishing to note that, on average, twelve out of twenty industrial sectors were idle more than 42 percent of the day. Almost no sector worked more than 80 percent of the year.[35]

About 65 percent of the plants worked single shifts and some 20 percent triple shifts. Single-shift firms employed about 45 percent of the labor force and triple-shift firms only 36 percent, despite the fact that by triple shifting, each plant employs proportionately more workers. In production terms, however, the triple-shift firms produced about 50 percent of industrial output while the single-shift firms produced only about one third,[36] indicating that the multiple-shift firms were more capital intensive than those running single shifts. By the same token, multiple shifting could have a more than proportionate impact on employment, since it is the labor-intensive firms that would move to more shifts. On a more disaggregated basis, one can see that virtually all sectors have single-, double-, and triple-shift firms.[37] Thus, the shifting decision is not industry specific but reflects more basic considerations.

A utilization policy affects output in two ways. Industrial output

[34] We attempt here to give only an overview of some of the magnitudes. For more detailed information, see Schydlowsky and Wicht, *Anatomía de un Fracaso Económico,* and the earlier works by Luis Valdivieso, "The Distributive Effect of Alternative Policies to Increase the Use of Existing Industrial Capacity" (Doctoral dissertation, Boston University, 1978); Millan and Schydlowsky, "Macroeconomic Consequences of Multiple Shifting"; Abusada-Salah, "A Statistical Shift-Choice Model."

[35] Schydlowsky and Wicht, *Anatomía de un Fracaso Económico,* p. 77.

[36] Ibid., p. 78.

[37] Ibid., pp. 79–80.

TABLE 4.5

Total Impact of Multiple Shiftwork on the Functional
Distribution of Income of the Nonprimary[a] Sectors, 1969
(In Millions of Soles)

Basic Model with Depreciation	1969	%	Generalized 2 Shifts			Generalized 3 Shifts		
			1969	%	% Increase	1969	%	% Increase
Value added	129,525	100%	161,303	100%	24.5%	198,871	100%	53.5%
Wages	50,482	39	65,657	41	30.2	82,600	42	63.6
Profits & depreciation	59,628	46	71,161	44	19.3	85,500	43	43.4
Taxes	19,415	15	24,485	15	26.1	30,771	15	58.5

Source: L. Valdivieso, "The Distributive Effect of Alternative Policies," p. 180, Table 19.

[a] Includes sectors 10–40 of INP input-output table for 1969. Assumption: 35 percent marginal tax on gross profits.

increases directly because of multiple shifting. And services increase output as the derived demand from industrial income has a multiplier effect in that sector. Thus, the combined output effect will be greater than the direct impact on industrial output. Table 4.5 shows the increased value added obtainable in 1969 by moving to generalized two and three shifts, assuming that the pattern of utilization was the same in 1969 as in 1971. Also shown are the major elements of the functional income distribution, i.e., wages, profits and depreciation, and tax revenues. Of particular note are the percentage increases involved:[38] value added increases by 25 percent at two shifts and 54 percent at three shifts; wages increase by 30 percent and 64 percent. Note that wages and taxes increase proportionately more than returns on capital.

A utilization policy also benefits the balance of payments, as a result of increased export revenues from the new industrial exports, less the increased imports of competitive goods (food, as well as those industrial products for which increase in demand exceeds the increase in supply) and complementary imports (raw materials and intermediate goods). The net balance is strongly positive, by about $120 million for generalized second shift and about $210 million for generalized third shift.[39]

Moreover, the fiscal effects of a utilization policy are positive for both levels of shifting: 4,485 million soles (at 1969 prices) and 8,272 million, respectively.[40] These positive effects result from additional

[38] Measured against the base of observed magnitudes in the nonprimary sectors in 1969.

[39] See Schydlowsky and Wicht, *Anatomía de un Fracaso Económico*, p. 84.

[40] Ibid.

TABLE 4.6
Total Impact of Multiple Shiftwork on
the Distribution of Labor Income, 1969
(In Percent)

Quantiles of 20% (From Poorest to Richest)	1969		Generalized 2 Shifts		Generalized 3 Shifts	
CASE I: UNEMPLOYED LABOR HAS VIRTUALLY NO INCOME						
I.	.74% ⎫		.6% ⎫		3.7% ⎫	
II.	.77 ⎬ 10.5		5.1 ⎬ 21.4		11.0 ⎬ 30.2	
III.	9.0 ⎭		15.7 ⎭		15.5 ⎭	
IV.	25.6		23.4		21.1	
V.	64.3		55.3		48.7	
Total	100		100		100	
Top 5%	31.2		26.3		22.8	
Top 1%	12.0		9.6		8.0	
CASE II: UNEMPLOYED HAVE INCOME EQUAL TO THE AVERAGE OF THE RURAL INCOME EARNERS						
I.	6.28 ⎫		5.19 ⎫		5.22 ⎫	
II.	6.67 ⎬ 12.95		6.89 ⎬ 26.6		10.78 ⎬ 31.2	
III.	9.80 ⎭		14.6 ⎭		15.26 ⎭	
IV.	21.8		21.8		20.79	
V.	55.4		51.5		47.94	
Total I to V	100		100		100	
Top 5%	26.93		24.51		22.38	
Top 1%	10.32		8.96		7.87	

Source: Valdivieso, "The Distributive Effect of Alternative Policies," pp. 188, 189, tables 25, 26.

tax collections on imports and on the additional incomes generated, less the additional expenditure necessary to make exports for industrial goods competitive on the world market.

Finally, the multiple-shift policy also increases employment substantially. The supervisory, skilled, and semiskilled categories show the largest gains. This is due to expansion of sectors more intensive in these kinds of labor because they have lower capacity utilization. Employment increases for unskilled labor, however, are as much as those for directors and managers and more than those for white-collar groups. The total increase in employment is 295,843 workers and 622,600 workers for two shifts and three shifts, respectively; in relative amounts, an increase of 33.7 percent and 70.1 percent over the number employed in 1969.[41]

Table 4.6 shows the impact of multiple shifting on labor income when it is assumed that the unemployed have either an income of practically zero (Case I) or an income equal to the average rural in-

[41] Ibid., p. 86.

come earner (Case II), who made 10,000 soles in 1969 (about $300). The latter amount represents the upper bound of income that the underemployed laborer may plausibly have earned. The changes in the distribution of labor incomes are very impressive. The shares of the second and third quintiles increase markedly under both alternatives, while those of the top 1 percent and 5 percent decrease quite significantly.

Labor income is only part of the total picture, however; combining labor income and capital income for the total distribution, we find strong shifts from the lowest stratum to the second lowest, with the third stratum gaining somewhat as well.[42] These gains are achieved at the expense of the top of the distribution if one assumes that unemployed labor has virtually no income, as in Case I; in Case II, there are increases in the top segment.[43] Moreover, the shifts in distribution are not merely redistributing the same size pie; rather, as noted before, income has risen markedly in the process. These increases are the result of very strong changes in the marginal distribution of income that are large enough to affect the average observed after the utilization policy.

A reasonable estimate is that generalized second shifting on new investment would add .9 percent to the annual per capita growth rate;[44] generalized triple shifting would add 3.8 percent. By the year 2000, these higher growth rates would push Peru's per capita income one-third higher under double shifting and three times higher under triple shifting. The combinations of a higher one-time increase in base, a lower capital/output ratio, and compound interest is a powerful one indeed.

Policies for Capacity Utilizing Export-Led Growth

Because the reasons for under-utilization of capacity are many and interact in complex ways, achieving a higher level of utilization also requires a complex policy package. Moreover, changing utilization patterns involves crossing a threshold. Incentives to utilization that

---

[42] Ibid., p. 89.

[43] Note that when rural underemployed are absorbed within the industrial labor force as in Case II, the remaining rural workers experience an increase in employment, income and welfare. This improvement has not been included in our measurement.

[44] See Schydlowsky, "Capital Utilization, Growth, Employment, Balance of Payments and Price Stabilization," in Behrman and Hanson, eds. *Planning and Short-Term Macroeconomic Policy.*

fall just short of changing behavior are equivalent to no incentives at all. This section describes how capital utilizing export-led growth could be promoted by policy measures in five major areas.

With respect to trade policy, industrial exports must be made competitive on the world market. Exports must be supported through compensation for the high cost of domestic production arising from import regulations, labor laws, and taxes. Moreover, the red tape restricting exports must be removed. Such support can be provided by compensatory export subsidies for individual goods or through compensated devaluation in which exchange-rate and import restrictions are modified concurrently in offsetting directions.[45] Both measures keep import prices virtually unchanged and thus create minimal internal cost-push effects.

On the import side, trade policy must assure the automatic availability of raw materials: inputs must not be subjected to discretionary import licensing because uncertain supplies of inputs would discourage entering into export commitments. In other words, any existing quota systems must be replaced by tariffs or by an automatic licensing system for imported inputs required for export production.

In the domestic tax policy sphere, the incentives usually available only for expansion of capital stock should be extended to its utilization. In particular, depreciation rates can be made proportional to the number of shifts worked, and the tax exemption available for reinvestment in capital goods can be extended to increased output due to intensive use of existing capital or it can be replaced by an allowance for greater capacity utilization. Furthermore, the tax system can be used to offset high labor costs on second and third shifts by allowing an additional credit for multiple-shift labor expenses. Finally, the corporate tax rate can be raised for single-shift firms and lowered for double- and triple-shift firms.

New credit and monetary policies are also necessary. Expansion of output through shift work requires additional working capital, but the fixed capital available as security for loans remains unchanged. Therefore, loans must be made against the cash flow of future earnings from expanded output rather than against the security of the chattel mortgage. Thus, banking customs must evolve and/or credit

[45] For details, see Schydlowsky, "International Trade Policy in the Economic Growth of Latin America," in Guisinger, ed., *Trade and Investment Policies in the Americas;* also Daniel M. Schydlowsky, "From Import Substitution to Export Promotion for Semi-Grown-Up Industries: A Policy Proposal," *Journal of Development Studies* (July 1967), and "Short-Run Policy in Semi-Industrialized Economies," *Economic Development and Cultural Change* (April 1971).

policy must make specific allowance for lending to capacity utilizers. Correspondingly, the monetary program must incorporate credit expansion for increased capacity utilization.

With respect to labor policy, it is important that higher shift-labor costs be made the same as first-shift costs and that tenure regulations on higher shifts be flexible. Legislated shift premia discourage employment of additional labor on second and third shifts; given market wages above the marginal social cost of labor, higher afternoon or night wages aggravate an already undesirable situation. Tenure regulations are also significant; if workers cannot be fired once they have been hired, expanding the labor force involves a major risk for the entrepreneur.

Entrepreneurs' willingness to innovate must be encouraged and rewarded. Rules should be flexible. An atmosphere should be created in which dynamic entrepreneurs (just as efficient workers) feel appreciated and undynamic ones are motivated to become dynamic.

Some new policies with respect to foreign private investment are also necessary. Export marketing channels are often in the hands of multinational enterprises that become very interested in sourcing from countries in which they have subsidiaries. Hence, investment on the part of enterprises which may source in Peru is an important complementary policy. Support for the export endeavors of foreign investors already in the country is obviously of equal importance.

*Capacity Utilizing Export-Led Growth
and the Peruvian Revolution, Phase One*

Let us return now to our starting point. How would the export-led growth strategy have fit the revolution's economic purposes?

The export-led growth strategy would have allowed the revolution to achieve dynamic and self-sustained industrial development. This goal can be achieved only in this way by a small country. This strategy has succeeded in nations with different resource endowments, development levels, and labor union strength; Taiwan, Korea, Singapore, Israel, and, more recently, some Latin American countries are examples. Even Brazil, comprising half a continent, found itself unable to grow only inwardly.

Equity would also be enhanced by the export-led growth strategy. Although such an approach may appear superficially to be pro-entrepreneurial and to encourage profits, in fact it merely distributes a share of the increased output as a fee to the managers who propel the system onward and upward. In the process, the poor grow rich faster than the wealthy (Table 4.6). Agriculture, and hence the interior of the country, also benefit through withdrawal of surplus workers and through an enlarged domestic market. Recall, in contrast, the dismal outcome of Peru's import substituting path, in which distribution and per capita income both worsened.

Such a strategy would also increase independence. The essence of independence is freedom of choice. Such freedom requires flexibility, which is assured only by participating in many markets and dealing through many channels. An export-oriented economy suffers less if one export price falls or one market becomes inaccessible. The large number of options reduce vulnerability. Export diversification affords independence equally vis-à-vis a foreign country, a multinational enterprise, or an international agency.

A strong and determined government is also necessary to implement an export-led growth policy, for such a policy is difficult to implement. It involves a major break with past policy and with management traditions; a virtual revolution in the labor market as the possibility of full employment drastically affects union power; and a major confrontation with the General Agreement on Tariffs and Trade (GATT) and individual countries over export supports.

Turning an industry accustomed to easy sales behind tariffs into an industry actively competing in world markets is no easy task, even with financial export supports. Imitative firms must be converted into innovative, export-oriented, multiple-shift firms. The drive and demands of a doubled industrial labor force must be integrated into the overall welfare dictates of the nation. The GATT and the importing nations must be persuaded to accept the country's export supports. All these tasks would be difficult even for a determined government.

But what of the revolution's major reforms? Centralized economic decision making via exchange control and sectoral laws would not have been consistent with export-led growth. Such measures, however, would also have been unnecessary. Worker participation in management would also have made the success of this strategy difficult; for in its Peruvian form, at least, worker participation meant capital intensity, labor and management sloth, risk aversion, and pressure for government patents of monopoly via the exchange control rules. Agrarian reform was more consistent with export-led growth. Systematic nationalization of foreign enterprises, however, would not have been feasible, although the government could have worked to make foreign investors' and national interests compatible—as Phase One officials did to some extent. The International Petroleum Company could have been taken over as an isolated case, but other transnational companies would have been welcome to contribute to Peru's export-led growth.

Peru did try timidly to promote exports through the CERTEX (Certificate for the Reimbursement of Taxes upon Export), established in January 1969. Unfortunately, the minister who initiated the CERTEX, General Angel Valdivia, was fired shortly thereafter, and it languished despite the best efforts of the officials responsible for it in the Ministry of Industry. In the face of a fixed, overvalued exchange rate and increasing price distortions due to the quota system, CERTEX rates were usually too low. Its regulations made specialized commercial exporters ineligible for the incentive and thus disconnected the commercialization channels from producers. In addition, it was not coordinated with the rest of commercial policy. Thus, the import licensing system was not tied into export promotion at all, and a producer with an export market could well obtain a competitive CERTEX but be denied the import licenses to buy the raw materials to produce the goods. Coordination with the credit system was also lacking; producers often had import licenses, but not the credit to finance working capital, and vice versa.

Export support was wrongly regarded as a fiscal drag, an unnecessary transfer of income to capitalists, rather than a tool that would activate the economy and generate larger and more equitably distributed incomes. Furthermore, the narrow fiscal view maintained by Phase One officials emphasized the cost of export support and failed to consider that the higher level of output generated by exports would add sorely needed income to the treasury.

Stabilizing and Activating the Economy in 1975

Would it still have been possible to save the situation in 1975 by a radical reorientation of policy? This subsection cannot provide a definitive answer, but it does suggest the potential of an industrial export-based stabilization strategy.

The scope for action. In 1975, the current account deficit stood at $1.5 billion and the fiscal deficit was 30.6 billion soles (10 percent of GNP). Previously, we showed that a three-shift strategy in 1969 could have added some 70 billion soles to GNP, some $750 million to exports, and some 17 billion soles to fiscal revenue. Such economic expansion would also have increased imports, however, and would have required export support from the treasury. On a net basis, a three-shift strategy would have meant a balance-of-payments surplus of $220 million and a fiscal surplus of 8 billion soles. At first sight, these figures seem to fall short of the yawning deficits of 1975. But in the intervening years, there were two crucial events: prices rose, and the economy grew. The 1969 estimates have to be readjusted to 1975 prices.[46] Also, from 1969 to 1975, installed capacity approximately doubled, but output grew only by about half, which means that unutilized capacity grew to a level three times that present in 1969.[47] Incorporating the intervening price changes and growth, we show the three-shift mobilization economic potential in 1975 and compare it to the size of the economic crisis. The figures suggest that if three-shift output had been put into effect immediately, Peru's 1975 crisis could have been resolved without any deflation at all. In fact, however, the change to three-shift production would have required more time:

Three-Shift Mobilizable Economic Potential in 1975 (1975 Prices)

GDP	S/.	400 billion
Exports	$	3.1 billion
BOP surplus	$	1 billion
Tax revenue	S/.	100 billion
Fiscal surplus	S/.	36 billion

Dimensions of the Crisis

BOP deficit:	$	1.5 billion
Fiscal deficit:	S/.	30.6 billion

It should be mentioned at this point that there are three sources of underestimation in our calculation of the mobilizable economic potential. First, in excess capacity, we did not consider the days on

---

[46] Adjusting the 1969 figures for price changes is not simple, for the appropriately disaggregated price indices are not readily available. The cost of living in 1975 stood some 90 percent above that in 1969, while world prices of industrial goods went up only about half as much. It would seem appropriate therefore to revalue all soles projections by 90 percent and all foreign trade accounts by 45 percent. See Schydlowsky and Wicht, *Anatomía de un Fracaso Económico*, pp. 97–103, for further discussion of adjustments in the calculation and for the results of the operations with respect to 1969 three-shift mobilizable economic potential at 1975 prices.

[47] The calculation is simple enough. In 1969, capacity was 100 units, utilized capacity was 66 units, and unutilized capacity was 34 units. In 1975, capacity was 200 (growth of 100 percent), utilized capacity was 100 (growth of 50 percent), and unutilized capacity was the remainder, 100. Unused capacity thus grew by 200 percent when compared to the base of 34 in 1969.

which factories are closed (more than 20 percent of the year). On this score alone, our estimates of the economic potential of capacity utilization is low by 25 percent (20 percent not worked equals 25 percent of the 80 percent of days worked). Second, we did not consider all of the increases in output that arise from better and more effective use of capital as output rises, i.e., from under-utilization *within* shifts. Surely this would add another 10 to 20 percent. Third, we ignored the increases in the demand for money and in other financial assets resulting from the rise in GNP. Hence, overall, our estimated economic stabilization potential for 1975 represents an underestimation of the true figure by 40 percent to 60 percent. Moreover, a further cushion remains: elimination of food subsidies and changes in tariff policy would have positive effects.

Let us look now at the phasing of output increases over time. The crux of the problem lies in marketing $3.1 billion worth of industrial exports annually. We estimate that five years would have been required to reach this goal. Such growth would have been fast, but not as fast as some other countries (e.g., Korea). The resulting balance-of-payments and fiscal surpluses would have been the following, in millions of dollars and billions of soles, respectively:

	1975	1976	1977	1978	1979
Exports	$ 500	1,000	1,800	2,500	3,100
BOP surplus	$ 160	320	580	800	1,000
Fiscal surplus	S/. 6	12	21	29	36

It is clear that with this phasing the 1975–1979 period would have shown current account deficits despite the new industrial export policy. Reducing these deficits would have required a number of policy measures (some of which were implemented during Phase Two but in a very different context from that proposed here). One measure would have been a moratorium on investment. Such a moratorium, an inexpensive stop-gap because capital was under-utilized in any case, could have saved between $500 and $600 million a year. Arms import moderation would have been a second measure. It could have saved from $200 million on a declining scale per year. The relative prices of food and fuel should also have been corrected: removal of subsidies on a *gradual* basis could have yielded from $150 million upwards.

Considering these savings, the annual deficit (surplus in parentheses) would have been the following, in billions:

	1975	1976	1977	1978	1979
Initial deficit[48]	$1.5	$1.5	$1.5	$1.5	$1.5
3-shift surplus	.2	.3	.6	.8	1.0
Moratorium on investment	.5	.5	.5	.5	.5
Arms moderation	.2	.1	.1	—	—
Relative prices	.1	.3	.5	.7	.8
Final deficit (surplus)	.5	.3	(.2)	(.5)	(.8)

Thus, with these measures, a surplus would have appeared by 1977, and only $800 million would have been needed in new debt over the two intervening years. As of 1977, surpluses would have been available to repay debt and phase out the investment moratorium. Also, throughout this period, GNP would have been rising due to increasing capacity utilization; employment would have been growing for the same reason. Price increases for subsidized items (food and fuel) would have occurred against the backdrop of an improving private economy and rising employment. Furthermore, the government could have released some of its estimated 400,000 employees to the export-oriented growth sectors, providing relief to the exchequer.

In sum, a successful stabilization from the supply side appeared to be economically possible in 1975. It would have brought the economy onto an even keel by 1979 or 1980 through a process of growth toward equilibrium, rather than through contraction of output and employment toward balanced external accounts and greater overall disequilibrium.

Stabilization policies from the supply side. A synchronized macroeconomic and microeconomic policy was necessary for industrial export-led stabilization in 1975. At the macroeconomic level, it was necessary to ensure that Peruvian export prices were competitive, that the demand for imported inputs was met without delay or bureaucratic obstacles, and that financing for working capital was available. In turn, policy at the microeconomic level should have assured the entrepreneur of control over his plant, minimized the fixed costs for new output to reduce risk, and focused entrepreneurial attention on production and sales, not upon protection of property and "form of regime."

The macroeconomic policy changes were significant and difficult. The CERTEX had to be revitalized and rates greatly increased (in order to avoid a large and inefficient across-the-board devaluation);

---

[48] The deficit does not grow from year to year due to the investment moratorium.

the exchange control regulations had to include automatic mechanisms for transferring inputs into export production expeditiously, and the priorities for credit allocation had to be reordered away from the public sector. If all these changes proved too difficult, then CERTEX could have been replaced by a Certificate for Import and Export (CERTIMPEX), a transferable import entitlement given to the exporter.[49]

At the microeconomic level, even greater changes were necessary. If the entrepreneur were to control the work process in his plant, the industrial community legislation would have to be modified and the employer's power to fire workers restored. The latter measure was necessary to minimize fixed cost (and risk) and absorb more employment. Reorientation of entrepreneurial attention to business concerns required that the regime's rhetoric shift from anti-business to pro-business.

If legal modifications to the industrial community and labor tenure regulations had applied only to *new* output and employment, the desired incentive effect might still have been achieved. The response of entrepreneurs would probably have depended in good measure on their perception of the general attitude of the government toward business. The labor movement, on the other hand, would have accepted this change in strategy as soon as the positive results in employment and income distribution became evident.

The meaning of supply-based stabilization for phase two. The policy followed during Phase Two of the military government, stabilization-cum-recession (or stabilization from the demand side), has had exceedingly high social costs in terms of unemployment and inflation. Along the way, Phase Two undid many of the reform measures instituted by Phase One: the industrial community and labor tenure laws were amended beyond recognition; public enterprises were returned to private hands; the social property sector was quietly stripped of funds and personnel. All these changes did not produce any positive results, however.

[49] The premium that the CERTIMPEX would have commanded for the importation of very scarce goods would have provided the exporter with the bonus to make his prices competitive; the flexibility inherent in being able to import license-free would have allowed exporters to use their own or others' CERTIMPEX to bring in whatever inputs they needed. In addition to the CERTIMPEX, it would probably have been desirable to start on a slow exchange rate crawl to prevent further overvaluation and eventually to reduce the overvaluation existing in 1975.

If Phase Two had been based on a capacity-using export drive in industry, a completely different chapter in Peruvian history would have been written. Rather than a 10 percent per capita decline in GNP, there would have been growth. Rather than 30–50 percent fall in real wages with increasing unemployment and underemployment, there would have been an increase in individual earnings (despite a small fall in average real wages)[50] and a large expansion of employment. The balance of payments would have been brought into equilibrium at a much higher export level, and the debt service ratio would have been brought down considerably. Perhaps more fundamental, however, is that the economy's illness—manifested in the balance-of-payments deficit, but really originating in the imbalance among sectors—would have been cured rather than just repressed.

CONCLUSION

In this final part of the chapter, we summarize the key economic lessons of the Peruvian experiment and consider the paths open to the Peruvian economy in the short and long runs. We also respond to various common criticisms of our argument.

The Economic Lessons of the Past

Throughout the 1950s, liberal free-trade policies with successive booms in primary exports produced economic growth but little apparent social development. Then a new approach was adopted that emphasized greater governmental intervention and import-substituting industrialization. Intersectoral disequilibria in prices and resource allocation since the mid-1960s slowed the economic growth rate, worsened income distribution, and created increasingly serious unemployment.

The Peruvian experiment during Phase One had ambitious social objectives and strong political power, but it exacerbated economic problems. Most fundamentally, there was no recognition of basic economic interrelations at both the micro and macro levels. A partial shuffle of fixed assets ownership did not change the old unbalanced trends of sectoral growth; interventionist rhetoric and controls hindered but did not transform the behavior of the economy (instead,

[50] Pay for any given job would have fallen, but the tighter labor market would have produced extensive promotion up the job ladder, thus raising individuals' incomes.

they reinforced preexisting intersectoral disequilibria); public sector expansion was artificial because it was not built upon sound economic grounds; and intensive, inward looking industrialization and heavy borrowing from abroad led to the widest foreign exchange gap in recent Peruvian history.

Phase Two of the revolutionary government began with a broken economy and applied, reluctantly and piece by piece, conventional (à la IMF) cures that proved to be worse than the disease. After almost three years of across-the-board devaluations and monetary restrictions, the foreign exchange and the fiscal gaps began to be painfully closed "downwards," that is, with a real income below the 1975 level. Inflation and recession in 1978 were much worse than in 1975. Social goals were put aside as the military government tried desperately to solve a crisis that they did not foresee and never understood. Compared to the 1975–1978 crisis, the 1967–1968 troubles seem very minor indeed. The payments deficit on current account in 1967 was $125 million; in 1975, it was $1.5 billion; the foreign public debt in 1968 was $742 million; in 1978, it stood at $6.1 billion; inflation was 19 percent in 1968; in 1978, it exceeded 70 percent.

Peru's economic experience in the last ten years is a particularly salient example of a phenomenon that is by no means exclusively Peruvian. Under slightly different circumstances, this same "stop and go" macroeconomic pattern appears in many other countries, particularly in Latin America.[51] The basic problems of these economies cannot be solved as long as intersectoral disequilibria are ignored and global, restrictive policies from the demand side applied.

There was an alternative: directly restoring the balance among the different productive sectors, and thus breaking down the bottlenecks that asphyxiate the supply side of the economy. This alternative obtains not only higher output but also better income distribution, as it leads toward full employment of the labor force, which requires increasing the utilization rate (and not only the amount) of Peru's scarcest and most wasted resource, capital. Keeping more than one half of the installed capital capacity idle while more than 57 percent of the labor force is unemployed or underemployed is absurd.

The valiant nationalistic spirit, the merits of latifundia redistribution, and the educational reforms of the Peruvian Revolution pale into insignificance beside the soaring inflation and the deep recession that the country has now suffered. The economic policy of Phase One

[51] Particularly instructive on the Argentine case is Diamand, *Doctrinas Economicas, Desarrollo e Independencia.*

failed not because it emphasized state intervention but because it applied the wrong, and inefficient, controls, ignored the importance of the foreign sector (i.e., both the possibilities of foreign demand and the requirements of foreign supply), and neglected the most basic principles of economics and management regarding prices, productivity, and income. Phase Two failed not because it gave special attention to the foreign sector and tried to reintroduce some free market mechanisms, but because it diagnosed the basic illness to be "excessive demand" and applied global, restrictive, monetary measures. In fact, the Peruvian economy in 1975–1978 suffered from constrained supply and massive unemployment caused by a lack of foreign exchange that could not be overcome without the adoption of specific sectoral policies to correct the distortions in Peruvian trade policy and to absorb the excess capacity in industry.

Projecting the Future (1979–1990)

In 1990, Peru will be a country of approximately 23,320,000 people with a labor force of 8 million workers (working or looking actively for a job).[52] In contrast to trends elsewhere, the rural population will grow to approximately 6.4 million. The urban population, which is 12 million now, will then be close to 17 million, of which 8,180,000 will be in Lima (35 percent of the population). Given these population parameters, two alternative development strategies will be considered.

If Peru pursues the "old" strategy of the 1960s and 1970s, more incentives for investment in industry will be given, although a great proportion of the installed capital will not be fully utilized; higher tariffs and quotas will be established, because industry will still be in an "infant" stage in 1990; and huge mining projects will be mounted with direct foreign investment (although the oligopolistic power of transnational corporations in mining is stronger than in industry) in order to obtain, with increasing difficulty, the foreign exchange the country will need.

[52] According to the preparatory documents for the Long-Run National Development Plan (1978–1990), Instituto Nacional de Estadística (INE), and Instituto Nacional de Planificación (INP). Other population statistics in this paragraph are also drawn from these sources. Note that in August 1976 the Peruvian government approved the "Lineamientos de la Política de Población en el Perú," which established excellent guidelines in education and health services for free, responsible parenthood of families in a context of social and structural change. The success of this population policy will affect (and will depend upon) the overall development of the Peruvian society.

The investment, output, and employment performance of the economy under the old strategy has been estimated by the National Planning Institute in its preparation of the 1978–1990 National Development Plan.[53] By these estimates, the annual growth rate of GNP from 1978 to 1990 will be 4 percent (in contrast to 4.2 percent from 1960 to 1978), but the annual growth rate of labor productivity will be a dismal .5 percent (in contrast to 1.2 percent from 1960 to 1978); annual export growth will be only 4 percent. Deep socioeconomic disequilibria will continue.[54] Although the economy will experience short periods of relief when new mining or oil projects come into operation, it will live with a severe foreign exchange shortage—which will force large and inefficient devaluations, which will generate increasing internal inflation each time—and a structural employment problem that worsens annually.

A new development strategy, along the lines presented in the third section of this chapter, would correct the structural disequilibria of the Peruvian economy. As opposed to the traditional views (structuralist and monetarist) that have been applied in the past, what is needed is a model with these three characteristics: 1) disaggregation by sectors, to see the disequilibria that arise within the economy; 2) full integration of the foreign sector within the framework of analysis; 3) special attention to the employment problem and its consequences on productivity levels and income distribution. The urban modern sector would also be the key sector, but with two essential modifications: full use of installed capital and openness to the world market so that industry will be able to compete abroad and produce foreign exchange.

The third section of this chapter showed that a full use of installed industrial capacity (generalized triple shift) obtained in three or four years would yield a 50 percent increase in nonprimary national product as compared with the old strategy. If we assume a less optimistic utilization of capital and export of manufactures (i.e., generalized second shift),[55] the Peruvian economy would achieve in 1990 an out-

[53] For detailed information on the results of these studies, see Schydlowsky and Wicht, *Anatomía de un Fracaso Económico*, pp. 114–117.

[54] Consider, for example, these National Planning Institute projections for 1970–1990 under this strategy. Labor productivity in the modern sectors, constrained by the external bottleneck, will rise by only 1.4 percent per year; modern-sector workers will grow from 970,000 (in 1978) to 1,370,000 (in 1990), but the proportion of the urban labor force in the modern sector will diminish from 27 percent today to 22 percent in 1990. Rural income per capita in 1990 will still be less than one-third of the average urban income of forty years before.

[55] We are also assuming, however, special efforts on agriculture and regional development, as well as added investment for medium- and long-range projects.

put 47 percent higher than under the old strategy and 135 percent higher than its 1978 level, with an annual average growth rate of 7.4 percent over twelve years.

From 1979 to 1990, the labor force in the modern sectors would grow at 7.5 percent per year, instead of 2.9 percent under the old strategy. Industrial output would be 29.6 percent of GNP, instead of only 20.1 percent of a much smaller GNP with the old strategy; industrial exports would reach $1.3 billion in 1963 prices, and industrial production for the domestic market would be 65 billion soles, compared with only 40 billion under the old strategy.[56] Even traditional exports would be 14 percent higher because several mining projects postponed for lack of public funds could, with a balanced and growing public budget, be undertaken before 1990.

The most important feature of the new strategy, however, is that the modern sector *labor force* would be 2,310,000 workers, instead of only the 1,370,000 who could be accommodated under the old strategy. The traditional but formal service sectors would absorb an additional one-half million workers, and underemployment in the cities would be much less extreme. Greater, and more productive, rural-to-urban migration would become possible.

Since 1978, when the National Planning Institute made these forecasts, what policies has Peru's government pursued? The military have passed a law to promote nontraditional exports and partially reorganized the import regime. Due to these policies, and also due to refinancing of the foreign debt and high international prices for Peru's primary products, Peru's export earnings in 1979 and 1980 have been much greater than those in 1978. The crisis is not over, however. Inflation is still high, and unemployment has not decreased. Income per capita did not grow for a third straight year in 1979, while credit and budgetary restrictions were still in force to counteract inflation. Moreover, the price increase for traditional exports is cyclical; it will not last too long. Although there is temporarily no acute shortage of foreign exchange, the internal disequilibria in resource allocation and the sectoral distortions on the supply side of the economy have not changed substantially. The export promotion law is a good start, but it is still only an isolated measure. A much more comprehensive policy is still necessary, especially with regard to employment of labor and fixed capital utilization, in order to restore the

[56] This projection indicates the fallacy of the argument "if we exported shoes, we would have to go barefoot." See, for instance, *Actualidad Económica*, year 1, no. 9 (Lima, October 1978). A 63 percent higher domestic consumption of manufactured goods would be obtained, in spite of (or rather thanks to) exporting 30 percent of industrial production.

loss of real income of the labor force and reduce inflationary pressures through higher levels of real supply.

Now Peru has a civilian government. Yet, remembering the 1960s, we know that civilian government is no guarantee of a sound development strategy. The military officers do not hold exclusive rights to faulty economics; they were helped neither by the ideologues of Phase One nor by the financial experts who pressured them in Phase Two. A new generation of economists and social scientists must convince political leaders to adopt sounder development strategies.

Capacity Utilization Policies in Critical Perspective

Some social scientists and political leaders argue that Peru and all Third World countries should not follow the "outward looking orientation" sketched in this chapter, but rather "inward looking policies" (*crecimiento hacia adentro*). If "inward-looking policies" means to emphasize the development of the interior of the country and to avoid mechanical imitations of development paths and consumption patterns, we agree. If, however, it means to reduce foreign trade because "it is not good for underdeveloped countries to produce what developed countries consume, nor to consume what developed countries produce," then we disagree; for all the reasons discussed in this chapter, an external bottleneck is inevitable under such a policy.

Other scholars and political leaders consider the new strategy desirable, but difficult to achieve because of the protectionist policies of the rich, importing countries. This obstacle is real, but it can be faced by diversifying industrial exports. Nevertheless, a trade-oriented development policy, if adopted by all LDCs, might not be feasible under the prevailing international economic order. A small country like Peru, however, can take advantage of her size and verify the importance of being unimportant.

Another objection sometimes raised is that the strategy would deliver the economy of the country into the hands of transnational corporations. It is a fact that today almost every product, from chemicals and electronics to soaps and light beverages, is produced by corporations that do not know national borders. Although we cannot eliminate their influence, we should not easily yield to them. A powerful and efficient national planning system, with real labor and management representation, is necessary to design policies that will make the transnationals' behavior and interests compatible with a country's own social and economic goals.

Are we proposing a development policy that could be labeled *Taiwanizar el Peru* ("Make Peru into Taiwan," a phrase used to discredit outward looking policies)? Would the only solution to Peruvian problems be the export of products based on cheap labor, i.e. *cholo barato?* Such criticisms suggest that labor-intensive exports are degrading. Yet the only alternative is a minority of *cholo caro* (expensive labor) and plenty of *cholo desempleado* (unemployed labor). Moreover, Peru's manufactures have not been competitive in the world market *not* because its labor has had higher salaries and better living standards than foreign workers, but because its misguided exchange and trade policies make its industry "expensive" abroad and distort the whole economy.

If we compare developed and underdeveloped countries, we will not find any substantial difference in their capital/output ratios, but we will certainly find a large and increasing difference in their capital/labor ratios. Over the next forty years, industrialized and developed countries (the "North") will increase their labor force by 20 percent; the underdeveloped ("Southern") countries, already facing a serious unemployment and underemployment situation, will increase their labor force by approximately 200 percent. In other words, "Southern" countries will *triple* their number of workers in the next four decades.[57] The relative gap in the capital/labor ratios will begin to decrease only after the populations of the Third World countries have reached their demographic stationary state, probably in the middle of the twenty-first century. Thus it is imperative that developing countries give maximum attention not only to the increase of installed capital, but also to the full use of that capacity. Although almost all development textbooks correctly insist upon the importance of investment, very few speak about the effective utilization of the capital stock. An essential point of Peru's experience is to demonstrate the tragedy of high labor unemployment coexisting with considerable idle capital.

The Peruvian Revolution was certainly inspired by humanistic principles. It set high social goals for the country, specifically to favor those who until 1968 had been *marginados.* Unfortunately, there are still *marginados* because, on top of political shortcomings and weaknesses, there came a vacuum of economic strategy and a series of economic mistakes in both Phase One and Phase Two. The Peruvian experiment, however, will not have been a complete failure if we reestablish the fundamental social objectives and develop a way to reach them, having understood what went wrong and why.

[57] Further details and figures may be found in the study "Proyecciones a Largo Plazo (1975–2005) de la Población y de la Economía del Peru," *Instituto Nacional de Planificación,* January 1977.

International Capitalism and the
Peruvian Military Government

Barbara Stallings

The influence of external forces is obviously a crucial aspect of any analysis of the Peruvian military government during the 1968–1978 period. In spite of, or perhaps because of, the importance of the actions by foreign corporations and foreign governments, there is little consensus on how to interpret them. Were they a key determinant in the downfall of Velasco and the increasingly conservative policies of his successor or was foreign impact marginal, of little consequence in shaping the course of events in Peru? Did the military government's policies complement or contradict the interests of foreign capital?

At the risk of oversimplification, three major positions on these questions can be described: (1) government reforms were positive for international capitalists, and the capitalist response to the reforms was positive or at least neutral; (2) the reforms were negative, and the response was negative; and (3) the foreign sector was not particularly relevant—domestic factors provided the key to understanding the process. This essay will review these various approaches and suggest that they confuse a number of issues crucial to interpreting the foreign role, including timing, level of abstraction, structures versus participants, types of participants, and objective versus subjective views. In an interpretation based on these distinctions, I will argue that the main influence of foreign capital on Peru came through the historical structuring of the socioeconomic system; short-term influences were of minimal importance. With respect to the effects of Peru's reforms on foreign capital, I see them as beneficial for maintaining a capitalist mode of production in the long run though harming various individual firms in the process.

The author wishes to thank the following people for help and comments on earlier drafts of this essay: Heraclio Bonilla, Julio Cotler, Abraham Lowenthal, and Cynthia McClintock.

Various Approaches to International Influence

Aníbal Quijano's early and influential study, *Nationalism and Capitalism in Peru,* directly challenged the widely held view that the Peruvian generals were initiating a process that contradicted the interests of imperialism. Writing in 1970, Quijano argued that the reforms being made represented a change in the *form* of imperialist control rather than its elimination:

> Without prejudging the Junta's undeclared intentions, what it has done to date with regard to economic policy can be satisfactorily placed within the process that we have called the redefinition of the relations of imperialist domination in Latin America. If this policy follows the same lines in the future, the result may well bring Peru a new mode of operating within the imperialist system, and an economic structure that is dependent in a new way. Such dependency will doubtless be less offensive to national sensibilities of the intermediate sectors of society if it is without enclaves, and is more organic, more complex—in short, more "modern."[1]

A year later, after Velasco had more clearly declared his intentions, Quijano reaffirmed his earlier view, saying, "It is perfectly obvious . . . that there is absolutely no question here of eliminating imperialist investment. . . . Under the formal limits established by the law, the margins of imperialist participation are sufficient to assure it a dominant position in the country's economy, even though it may be subject to state supervision."[2]

The new form of dependency involved changes in several different aspects of the imperialist system, according to Quijano. One was a change in the sectors where imperialist control was concentrated, especially the move out of the agricultural export sector and into industry. Another was the elimination of the enclave nature of foreign investment, with particular emphasis on mining and petroleum (although it also involved such industrial sectors as automobiles). Foreign investment in the future would be much more closely integrated into the national economy. A third important characteristic of the new dependency was the diversification away from clear United States domination toward a greater role for European and Japanese capital in Peru. Even the newly established relationships with Eastern

[1] Aníbal Quijano, *Nationalism and Capitalism in Peru: A Study in Neo-Imperialism* (New York: Monthly Review Press, 1971), p. 47.

[2] Ibid., p. 73.

Europe were seen as complementary to capitalist investment. A final characteristic was the new role for the state as intermediary between domestic and foreign capital, as partner of foreign capital, and as regulator of the economy.

Quijano saw these changes as favorable to imperialism in general and believed that the imperialist powers were not opposed to them. Both in 1970 and 1971, he wrote of the mild United States reaction and the enthusiastic European/Japanese reaction. With respect to the former, he said, "In general, it can be said that the conduct of U.S. imperialism in its relations with the Military Junta, both from the point of view of the imperialist state and the bourgeoisie, has been characterized by a flexible combination of cautious diplomacy and hesitant financial blockade."[3] On the one hand, he pointed to the failure of the United States government to implement the Hickenlooper Amendment (stopping United States aid) although the international organizations did cut credits. (Later, however, he stressed the thaw on the part of the latter as well.) On the other hand, Quijano cited numerous instances of European and Japanese capitalists rushing to invest in Peru.

A quite different approach is offered by Laura Guasti in Chapter 6 of this volume. Guasti emphasizes the negative aspects of the military government's policies toward foreign corporations. In her view, at the same time the corporations' interests were being challenged, the government was also pursuing an industrialization policy that required their help:

> Therefore the military government was challenging the basic motivations and interest of international corporations at the same time that it created a large requirement for precisely those resources most concentrated in the hands of international corporate groups—capital and advanced technologies. International corporations, particularly manufacturers, and international banks thereby were placed in strong positions to affect the achievement of industrialization goals in response to autonomy-promoting policies that affected their activities. And when an international recession seriously weakened the government's economic position, they were able to directly, intensively pressure against the autonomy-promoting policies.[4]

[3] Ibid., p. 41.

[4] Laura Guasti, "The Peruvian Military Government and International Corporations," Chapter 6 of this volume, pp. 204–205.

Guasti sees the negative implications mainly with respect to extractive corporations, but she extends the analysis to some effects of the policies on industry as well. Concerning mining, Guasti focuses on policies that reserved refining activities to the government, gave the government the right to set production and investment targets for private concessionaires, and limited concessions to five years (although they were renewable). The response of most of the corporations, she says, was to abandon their mining activities in Peru. The challenge to industry was less formidable, principally contained in the Industrial Community legislation and the fade-out joint venture (the requirement that multinationals reduce ownership in corporations to 49 percent within 15 years). The corporations' response in this case was an investment boycott that forced the government to expand its role beyond its original intentions and led to a burgeoning foreign debt that put the government at the banks' mercy. Guasti sees the banks as opposing industrialization that would benefit and strengthen domestic entrepreneurs (an important part of the military's strategy), thus making it "very difficult for a Peruvian government to again promote economic autonomy in the foreseeable future."[5] In conclusion, Guasti warns that "a Third World nation that intends to challenge international corporations cannot simultaneously place itself in the position of requiring the resources that have given the international corporations their greatest strength."[6]

A third position tends implicitly to relegate the foreign sector to a minor role by virtually ignoring it in discussions of the origins of Peru's political-economic crisis. Overwhelming emphasis is placed on internal factors as determinants of the process. The "technocratic" version of this argument stresses mismanagement and faulty economic strategy; a clear example of this position is embodied in Chapter 4 of this volume, "The Anatomy of an Economic Failure," by Daniel Schydlowsky and Juan Wicht.[7] Schydlowsky and Wicht emphasize two failings in the government's handling of the economic situation. First, the military's reliance on import-substitution industrialization rather than export promotion led inevitably to a crisis (in other countries as well as in Peru). Because of its high import content,

[5] Ibid., p. 206
[6] Idem.
[7] Daniel M. Schydlowsky and Juan Wicht, "The Anatomy of an Economic Failure," Chapter 4 of this volume. For an economic approach that concentrates on structural contradictions of the Peruvian model, see E.V.K. FitzGerald, "State Capitalism in Peru: A Model of Economic Development and Its Limitations," Chapter 3 of this volume.

import substitution eventually outruns the primary export sector's capacity to supply foreign exchange. Second, mismanagement exacerbated elements of the development strategy that had led to the balance-of-payments crisis:

> Enormous inefficiency resulted. The economy performed with a vast under-utilization of labor and capital and misused the foreign exchange it had. Entrepreneurs paid little attention to the efficient operation of industrial plants; private and public investment resources were systematically misallocated. . . .
>
> The impact of the management reforms significantly aggravated the balance-of-payments crisis already gathering momentum as a result of the development strategy. Equally important, however, these reforms also sharply reduced the quality of management in all sectors and impaired the economy's ability to respond to *any* economic policy, thus setting the stage for the economic disorganization [later] when the crisis really hit.[8]

Occasionally, Schydlowsky and Wicht mention certain "exogenous factors," including the need to purchase arms for national defense, the fluctuations in world commodity prices, and the disappearance of the anchovies, but these are clearly not seen as key explanatory factors.

Another version of this third approach can be seen in James Petras' and Eugene Havens' article, "Peru: Economic Crisis and Class Confrontations."[9] Petras and Havens pay more attention than Schydlowsky and Wicht to the role of international factors in determining the course of events in Peru but again place primary emphasis on domestic forces. In their analysis, however, the crucial domestic factors are political and social rather than strictly economic. They are mainly interested in the increasing mobilization of the working class under Marxist leadership and the ways this new movement limited the options available to the military regime.

One set of constraints upon the government derived from conflicts between workers and bureaucrats over control of political and economic decisions. Further, the regime's need to acquire a base of popular support gave rise to populist policies that limited the government's ability to finance the crucial industrialization drive. These domestic problems then led to reliance on foreign loans. Such con-

---

[8] Schydlowsky and Wicht, "Economic Failure," p. 115. The effects of mismanagement play a lesser role in the present version of the Schydlowsky-Wicht analysis than they did in earlier drafts. There they were the dominant factor.

[9] James Petras and A. Eugene Havens, "Peru: Economic Crises and Class Confrontations," *Monthly Review* 30, no. 9 (February 1979), pp. 25–41.

flicts culminated in the change from Velasco to Morales Bermúdez in August 1975:

> The military became disenchanted with Velasco's incapacity to form a populist base compatible with the state capitalist nature of the regime, the increasingly independent mobilization of workers and peasants, the growing conflicts between the industrial proletariat and state managers in the state firms over control of the nationalized enterprises, and the emerging economic crisis. The coalition which Velasco had tried to hold together, and which included capitalists and workers, bureaucrats and peasants, foreign investors and nationalist petty bourgeoisie, disintegrated. That sector of the military more closely allied with foreign and local big business emerged as the dominant group.[10]

After the change in leadership, the role of foreign capital and the international agencies, especially the IMF, increased substantially. Nevertheless, the new policies are seen as arising from demands by the domestic as well as the international bourgeoisie, and working-class mobilization continued to play a crucial role in shaping the regime's actions.

A CRITIQUE

Aspects of each of these three positions are useful in trying to analyze the role of international capitalist forces vis-à-vis the Peruvian regime, but none of the three alone is satisfactory. In this section, I briefly critique each of the three approaches and suggest the factors that I think need to be considered to provide a more satisfactory interpretation.

Quijano's underlying premise is sound—that is, the reforms undertaken by the Velasco regime were not harmful to capitalism per se. In fact, they were positive in the sense that they encouraged and stimulated the development of a more modern version of capitalism, a version that was more flexible and therefore had more chance of surviving in the long run. Nevertheless, I find two important problems with Quijano's analysis. First, he fails to take into sufficient account the imperialist actors' perceptions of the reforms and how their businesses would be affected. Even though, *in objective terms,* the reforms may have been beneficial to capitalism, the companies involved did not necessarily understand this in the short term. Because individuals act on the basis of their perceptions, these must be taken into account. A

[10] Ibid., p. 31.

second and related problem is that Quijano seems to mix up various levels of analysis. When he says that the Velasco reforms were beneficial to capitalism in the long run, the focus is on the capitalist *system* or mode of production. This can be true, and at the same time, the reforms can also harm certain individual firms and/or sectors. Quijano does distinguish between European/Japanese and United States capital and occasionally refers to sectoral differences, but he too often sees imperialism as a unit.

Laura Guasti, by contrast, makes the sectoral distinction within capitalism—extractive, industrial, and banking capital—the key to her analysis. This is a very useful approach that shows the different interests of corporations in various structural positions. Nevertheless, in her more general statements, she seems to discard the categories she has defined. She implies a unity between banking and industrial capital, whereas the Peruvian case actually provides a good example of important conflicts between the two (industry, even the multinationals, being squeezed in order that sufficient foreign exchange may be available to pay off the banks). More broadly, she sees all kinds of foreign capital being "directly challenged" because the government was tampering with the "basic motivating dynamics" of international accumulation. As I will argue subsequently, and as Quijano has argued, I do not think this can be established.

Finally, although the position of those who posit the irrelevance of foreign capital's response, who believe that domestic forces are sufficient to account for events, may serve as a useful antidote to recent tendencies to see the United States as responsible for almost all events in Latin America, nevertheless the crucial part of any analysis must be the *interrelationship* between domestic and international forces. Furthermore, it is not sufficient to simply look at the current period to determine the influence of foreign actors. Peru has been a part of the international capitalist system for almost two centuries, and its historical legacy—economic, political, and ideological—must be taken into account as well.

These criticisms point to several considerations that must inform our evaluation of the role of foreign actors including timing, structure versus participants, differences among participants, level of analysis, and viewpoint.

First, the long-term historical impact of foreign capital must be distinguished from such capital's immediate influence in any recent period (such as the post-1968 period in Peru). With respect to the former, attention should be focused on the extent to which foreign investment has structured the economy—made it reliant on primary exports, limited its industrial base, accentuated the gap between city and countryside, shaped the class structure and the organizational capacity of different classes, and molded perceptions of what is possible and/or desirable. Regarding the more immediate impact of foreign corporations and governments, political decisions and their effects must be examined, especially concerning the granting or withholding of political support and financial resources. A second timing issue in the Peruvian case is the distinction between the Velasco and the Morales periods. It is possible that the foreign impact was different between 1968 and 1975 than between 1975 and 1978.

It is also important to distinguish between the effects created by simply being part of the international capitalist system and those effects (positive or negative) that are deliberately planned by foreign powers. Thus, for example, price fluctuations will affect growth patterns, the balance of payments, government revenue, and income distribution without any individual participants trying to manipulate anything. Likewise, an international recession will affect the volume of goods that can be sold on international markets and new inventions can affect export markets. In addition to these "anonymous" market forces, however, foreign influence can also spring from specific decisions by international corporations, foreign governments, and multilateral agencies (or sometimes all three acting in concert). Diplomatic pressure, credit blockades, and participation in coup attempts are examples of this variety of foreign influence.

Among capitalist powers, three distinctions must be made: (1) Quijano's distinction between firms and governments from Europe and Japan and those from the United States; (2) Guasti's distinctions among industrial, extractive, and banking sectors; and (3) the distinction between private and public response, since bilateral and multilateral reactions are not always identical to those of private corporations. Moreover, we must consider not only capitalist participants but also the governments of the socialist countries. Under certain circumstances, these governments may provide an alternative source of economic aid and political support, thus giving more "space" to Third World governments desiring to increase their independence from the capitalist system.[11]

The term "capitalism" must also be used with explicit reference to the level of analysis. Three possible levels can be suggested: one is the

---

[11] A different set of distinctions is presented by Alfred Stepan. Among the most important distinctions Stepan makes are those related to stages of the foreign investment process (ranging from uncommitted to sunken) and the importance that the state attaches to attracting foreign investment. See Alfred Stepan, *The State and Society: Peru in Comparative Perspective* (Princeton: Princeton University Press, 1978), chapter 7.

capitalist mode of production ("capital as a whole"), which consists of a set of institutions and rules whereby economic control and appropriation of surplus rest with those who own the means of production. A second level is fractions of capital, which groups firms by size, sector, and national origin. A final level is individual firms. These levels must be distinguished because their interests may be contradictory. For example, survival of individual firms, and even certain fractions of capital, that are especially weak or exploitative, may endanger the system as a whole.

Finally, it is crucial to differentiate between objective reality and subjective views of a government's policies and their effects. For example, certain reforms may be enacted in the objective interests of capitalism (greater stability, larger markets, etc.), but individual corporations may not perceive them this way. Over the long run, one might reasonably expect objective reality and subjective perceptions to converge; but in the short run, there is no reason that this should be so. Therefore, since individuals act on the basis of their subjective views, these must be seriously considered.

Taking these five distinctions into account, we can begin a more balanced analysis of foreign influence in Peru.

THE IMPACT OF PERUVIAN REFORMS ON FOREIGN CAPITAL

The Velasco government's attitude toward foreign capital was grounded in two principles: foreign investment was to be sought since it was considered essential for economic development, but a new set of rules was to be established to increase the power of the government vis-à-vis foreign capital.

First, foreign investment would be banned from the natural resource sector and basic industries; these would be reserved for state enterprises. Second, in those areas where foreign investment was allowed, it would be either through joint ventures or private companies that would revert to state control after the principal had been covered and an "acceptable rate of return" attained. Third, foreign companies would be subject to profit sharing and worker participation requirements of the General Industrial Law. Other regulations on access to credit, profit repatriation, and so on were spelled out in Decision 24 of the Andean Pact, which the Peruvians were influential in drafting.[12]

---

[12] Analysis of foreign investment rules in Peru can be found in Quijano, *Nationalism and Capitalism;* Guasti, "Peruvian Military Government"; Stepan, *State and Society;* Shane Hunt, "Direct Foreign Investment in Peru: New Rules for an Old Game," in Abraham F. Lowenthal, ed., *The Peruvian Experiment: Continuity and*

Considering capital as a whole, the Velasco reforms were favorable to foreign and domestic capital alike. The principal interest of capital as a whole is the preservation of the capitalist mode of production; the reforms aided this goal. The old form of capitalism in Peru—enclaves, domination by the oligarchy, small market, lack of social mobility, lack of national integration—had become a liability. A continuation of this inflexible, traditional form threatened capitalism per se. The wide gap between the privileges of the few and the poverty of the majority would provoke attacks on the system that produced this discrepancy, once the majority had any kind of organizational capacity and consciousness of its own potential power. Peru, for example, had the most unequal land tenure structure of major Latin American countries—large farms represented only 1 percent of the total number of farms, but over 82 percent of agricultural land.[13] In terms of personal distribution of income, the bottom 40 percent of the income structure had only 7 percent of total income, again the most regressive distribution of major Latin American countries.[14] Moreover, the rigidity and closed nature of the system prevented it from absorbing and co-opting those who wanted to bring about reforms. Thus, an attack on certain practices became necessarily an attack on the system. The peasant revolts of the 1960s constituted a symbol of the potential crisis, even if they were effectively put down at the time.

The Belaúnde government was an attempt by certain civilian sectors to modernize and reform the Peruvian socioeconomic system, but for reasons that will not be elaborated here, it did not succeed.[15] The task of reform was thus left to the military officers who viewed the traditional system as a threat to national security as well as to capital-

---

Change under Military Rule (Princeton: Princeton University Press, 1975), pp. 302–349; Charles Goodsell, *American Corporations and Peruvian Politics* (Cambridge: Harvard University Press, 1974); and Andrew Nickson, *Las Empresas Transnacionales de los Estados Unidos de Norteamérica en el Perú, 1966–74* (Lima: Instituto Nacional de Planificación, 1977).

[13] Data are from studies by the Inter-American Committee for Agricultural Development as presented in Solon Barraclough and Arthur Domike, "Agrarian Structure in Seven Latin American Countries," in Rodolfo Stavenhagen, ed., *Agrarian Problems and Peasant Movements in Latin America* (Garden City, N.Y.: Anchor Books, 1970), pp. 41–94.

[14] E.V.K. FitzGerald, *The Political Economy of Peru, 1956–78: Economic Development and the Restructuring of Capital* (Cambridge: Cambridge University Press, 1979), p. 140.

[15] The most complete studies of the Belaúnde period are Jane S. Jaquette, *The Politics of Development in Peru*, Latin American Dissertation Series, no. 33 (Ithaca, N.Y.: Cornell University, 1971); and Pedro-Pablo Kuczynski, *Peruvian Democracy under Economic Stress: An Account of the Belaúnde Administration, 1963–1968* (Princeton: Princeton University Press, 1977).

ism.[16] What role was foreign capital to play in the military strategy for modernizing Peruvian capitalism? As one expert said, "This question [was] surely answered by the Greene compensation agreement if it was not answered earlier by the Cuajone contract. The Peruvian Revolution [had] no intention of severing economic relations with Western capitalism. On the contrary, it desire[d] to normalize and thus strengthen those relations."[17]

Two items controlled by foreign capital were crucial for the economic development of the Velasco regime: technology and finance. In order to gain access to these items, the government was willing to offer various incentives: the attractions of the Andean market; joint ownership of corporations, with a consequently privileged relationship with the state; and imaginative (and lucrative) types of contractual arrangements. This does not mean that the new regulations failed to restrict the privileges that foreign capital had previously enjoyed in Peru. They did—but not so much as to eliminate the attractiveness of investment in those sectors in which foreign participation was desired. The regulations did not threaten capital accumulation. Lack of profits was not a complaint of foreign business, and the multiple ways of indirectly remitting profits made the 14-percent limit no great hindrance.[18] Exemptions were often given in order to attract foreign investment. For example, the local content and taxation requirements for the reorganized automotive sector were repeatedly relaxed, and the industrial community requirement for Bayer was eliminated. The situation was summarized by one foreign economist as follows: "Nearly all new investors coming into the country do so through special contracts, as in the cases of petroleum, tractors, and diesels. Being partly owned by the government and judged important in government development plans, such firms can be more confident of entering a facilitating environment. The government wants them to succeed."[19] This success, in turn, would strengthen the long-run prospects of the capitalist system.

Nevertheless, not all sectors of capital or all individual corporations benefited from the Velasco reforms. Some foreign firms were treated

[16] For an analysis of the relationship between national security problems, economics, and the 1968 military takeover, see Luigi Einaudi, *Latin American Institutional Development: Changing Military Perspectives in Peru and Brazil* (Santa Monica: Rand Corporation, 1971).

[17] Hunt, "Direct Foreign Investment," pp. 343–344.

[18] See discussion of transfer pricing in FitzGerald, *Political Economy*, pp. 130–131.

[19] Hunt, "Direct Foreign Investment," p. 341.

handsomely, either in terms of compensation paid or incentives offered; others were ousted unceremoniously. Treatment often varied according to sector. In line with the stronger state role in the economy, portfolio investment was preferred over direct investment, and foreign banks received favorable treatment. This tendency was highlighted by the terms offered Chase Manhattan when its Banco Continental was taken over in the government's move to control the domestic banking system. Chase was paid three times the book value and almost six times the market value of its property.[20] Two years later, it returned the favor, agreeing to lead the syndicate to finance the Cuajone copper project. The other important sectoral difference concerned types of direct investment. Firms in natural resources and utilities were thrown out, although compensation varied according to the past history of the corporations in Peru. Thus, the International Petroleum Company and the Peruvian Corporation were treated poorly, while Cerro and Marcona fared better. One company, Southern Peru Copper Corporation (SPCC), was even invited to stay and enlarge its holdings. Firms that could be useful in the industrialization drive were welcomed and given important incentives; Bayer, Massey-Ferguson, and Volvo are examples.[21]

In international terms, European and Japanese companies fared better than American firms. In part, this was because most of the antiforeign feeling was directed against the United States for historical reasons; in part, it was because European—and especially Japanese—firms tended to be more flexible than American businesses and more willing to enter joint ventures and contract arrangements. The oil barter deal with the Japanese, pursued in order to obtain capital to build the trans-Andean pipeline, was a good example.[22] Even the opening of relations with the socialist countries was not a challenge to capitalist prerogatives. As Quijano says:

> Given the present structure of economic domination in Latin America, these new commercial relations with Eastern Europe, while widening the margin of maneuver of states with nationalist

[20] Ibid., p. 316.

[21] For case studies of the treatment of different foreign corporations, see Jessica Einhorn, *Expropriation Politics* (Lexington, Mass.: Lexington Books, 1974) (on IPC); Hunt, "Direct Foreign Investment," (on the Peruvian Corporation, Standard Oil of California, and Chase Manhattan); and César Germana, "Si es Bayer . . . es bueno?" in *Sociedad y Política,* no. 2 (October 1972) (on Bayer).

[22] For an analysis of Japanese investment in Peru, see C. Harvey Gardiner, *The Japanese and Peru, 1873–1973* (Albuquerque: University of New Mexico Press, 1975), especially chapter 8.

pretensions, cannot help but also favor imperialist companies. Since these companies control the majority of the resources and the mechanisms of foreign trade in their products, they can obtain effective advantages in the course of this broadening of commercial relations.[23]

Even those firms that were potential beneficiaries of the reforms, however, did not always react positively to the government programs. This had to do with different interpretations of the risk factor involved. Some companies reacted negatively to the reforms, stressing the high risk of the new investment rules. As one American businessman put it, these rules constituted "a legal structure so precarious that any company putting its faith in it is just putting its head into a trap."[24] Others were more aggressive, and for them, the advantages of the Andean market outweighed the uncertainty involved. Even among the banks, which were not greatly affected by the new rules, there were important differences in perception of risk. Some of the larger banks were more conservative, while the smaller international banks, including the consortium banks, considered Peru an opportunity to establish an important foothold in Latin America.[25]

The Industrial Community legislation was perhaps the key to the objective-subjective dichotomy. The basic intent of this law was to harmonize relations between capital and labor and thus to increase productivity and output. This view was openly expressed by the then director of SINAMOS:

> The irreducible opposition between "bourgeoisie" and "proletariat" will no longer exist, not because the interests of the two classes will have been "conciliated" but because the absolute polarity between total property on the one hand and lack of property on the other will have ceased to exist. In sum, the proletariat as well as the bourgeoisie will have ceased to exist as social classes.[26]

Similar types of experiments to reduce conflict between capital and labor have been tried quite successfully in such advanced capitalist

[23] Quijano, *Nationalism and Capitalism*, p. 46.

[24] Hunt, "Direct Foreign Investment," p. 342.

[25] See Robert Devlin, *Los Bancos Transnacionales y el Financiamiento Externo de América Latina: La Experiencia del Perú, 1965–1976* (Santiago: Naciones Unidas, 1980).

[26] Cited in Julio Cotler, "Bases del corporativismo en el Perú," *Sociedad y Política*, no. 2 (October 1972). See also the debate among ex-government officials in "Autogestión y empresas autogestionarias" (Lima: CIDIAG, June–August 1979).

countries as West Germany and Sweden; the co-opting of workers into the system has benefited capitalism. Nevertheless, many foreign (and domestic) investors in Peru saw the Industrial Community as a major threat and failed to recognize the potential stabilizing effect of the scheme and the benefits with which it could provide them. Their response was based on subjective impressions, which, in turn, limited the number of foreign firms that Peru could attract.

To summarize, the Velasco reforms were enacted in the long-term interests of capital as a whole. This was recognized by some foreign firms, principally European and Japanese companies, but other firms perceived only the short-term aspects and therefore felt threatened. Furthermore, some firms were indeed hurt by the reforms. It is essential, however, not to confuse the problems of individual firms, nor the perceptions of individuals, with the consequences of these reforms for the preservation of the capitalist mode of production (albeit in a modified form) and therefore the long-run interests of capital as a whole.

THE IMPACT OF FOREIGN CAPITAL IN PERU

Historical Influence

The most important way in which foreign capital influenced the Peruvian military government was through its historical role in shaping Peruvian economic and social structures. Some of these structures date back to the colonial period, beginning with the Spanish conquest in 1532,[27] while others are associated with the years of British hegemony in the nineteenth century.[28] Some fairly minor

---

[27] It should be stressed here that the argument being made is not that foreign powers were the only force that shaped Peruvian history, merely that they were an important one. Further information on external influence during the colonial period can be sought in the following works and in references cited therein: Pablo Macera, "Feudalismo Colonial Americano: El Caso de las Haciendas Peruanas," in his *Trabajos de Historia* 3 (Lima: Instituto Nacional de Cultura, 1977): 139–228; John Fisher, *Government and Society in Colonial Peru* (London: University of London, 1970); Karen Spalding, *De Indio a Campesino: Cambios en la Estructura del Perú Colonial* (Lima: Instituto de Estudios Peruanos, 1974); Guillermo Cespedes del Castillo, *Lima y Buenos Aires* (Seville, Spain, 1947); and José Carlos Mariátegui, *Seite Ensayos de Interpretación de la Realidad Peruana* (Lima: Editorial Amauta, 1965). A more general work on the same theme is Stanley and Barbara Stein, *The Colonial Heritage of Latin America* (New York: Oxford, 1970).

[28] On the British period, see Heraclio Bonilla, *Guano y Burguesía en el Perú* (Lima: Instituto de Estudios Peruanos, 1972); Shane Hunt, "Growth and Guano in

modifications occurred under United States domination after World War I.[29]

Probably the most significant legacy of the colonial period was Peru's incorporation into the international market (together with other Latin American countries) as an exporter of primary products and an importer of industrial goods. This subordinate position has led to great economic vulnerability. Export products have been replaced by synthetic substitutes, violent price fluctuations have made long-range planning impossible, and waiting for price changes (rather than improving the productive process) has tended to become the customary manner of resolving crises. In general, the stimulus for growth and structural change has come from outside rather than from domestic decision making.

Peruvian exports changed over time as resources were exhausted or displaced by substitutes. In the colonial era, silver was produced under the system of forced labor known as the *mita*. One fifth of the silver (the *quinto*) went directly to the Spanish Treasury, and most of the balance went to Spain via the private sector to help finance European development. After independence, guano became the major export commodity. Although the fields were owned and operated by the Peruvian state, British merchants monopolized the trade in guano, which was sent to Britain to improve agricultural productivity there. Sugar and cotton were also developed as export sectors during this period. As copper became the dominant product in the twentieth century, foreign capital moved into direct ownership as well as trade. The United States-owned Cerro de Pasco mining complex (including smelters and refineries) produced the majority of Peruvian copper. By 1968, three American firms (Cerro, Southern Peru Copper Corpora-

---

Nineteenth-Century Peru," discussion paper 34, Woodrow Wilson School, Princeton University, 1973; William Wynne, *State Insolvency and Foreign Bondholders* 2 (New Haven: Yale University Press, 1951): 109–181; D.C.M. Platt, ed., *Business Imperialism 1840–1930: An Inquiry Based on British Experience in Latin America* (London: Oxford University Press, 1977), especially chapters 9 and 10.

[29] On the twentieth century and United States influence, see Heraclio Bonilla, "The Emergence of U.S. Control of the Peruvian Economy: 1850–1930," in Joseph Tulchin, ed., *Hemispheric Perspectives on the United States* (Westport, Conn.: Greenwood Press, 1978), pp. 325–351; James Carey, *Peru and the United States, 1900–1962* (Notre Dame, Ind.: University of Notre Dame Press, 1964); Rosemary Thorp and Geoffrey Bertram, *Peru 1890–1977: Growth and Policy in an Open Economy* (London: Macmillan & Co., 1978); Julio Cotler, *Clases, Estado, y Nación en el Perú* (Lima: Instituto de Estudios Peruanos, 1978); Aníbal Quijano, *Imperialismo, Clases Sociales, y Estado en el Perú, 1890–1930* (Lima: Mosca Azul, 1978); FitzGerald, *Political Economy;* and Einhorn, *Expropriation Politics.*

tion, and Marcona) controlled about three-fourths of mining output in Peru, and 85 percent of production was processed and marketed through them.[30] Because direct rather than portfolio investment was involved, these foreign firms came to play a crucial role in the investment process. Thus their decisions in the 1960s to cut back investment—due in part to political trends in Peru and some changes in government policies toward these firms—had extremely damaging effects on productive capacity.

The other aspect of Peru's role in the international division of labor was the lack of an industrial sector. During the colonial period, Spain attempted to prevent the development of industry by issuing legal prohibitions against the production of competing goods. In spite of this, important advances in textiles and wine production were made by local businessmen, although the economic-political power relations that were fashioned in this period—and that were maintained into the twentieth century—favored mercantile capital and agricultural landowners over industrial capital.

The creation of the British "informal empire" in the nineteenth century exacerbated the problem of industry. Britain had an enormous industrial capacity but lacked an adequate domestic market. Peru and other Latin American countries played an important role in absorbing the massive exports of British textiles. Since these exports, mass produced, had costs so low that local artisans could not compete, the latter were driven out of business; the result was the elimination of the base on which a domestic industrial sector might have been built. The maintenance of an open economy throughout the nineteenth and the first half of the twentieth centuries, partly induced by British commercial and ideological influence, perpetuated the unequal competition in the local market. Thus, *potential* Peruvian industrialists decided that it made better business sense to invest in export agriculture or to make loans to the government at high interest rates.

It was only during the 1960s, after the election of the reformist Belaúnde government, that this pattern finally began to change. Specifically, the process of import-substitution industrialization, which had been initiated in other major Latin American countries in the 1930s, was established in Peru. Under the control of foreign capital, which, as always, was looking for quick ways to make profits, industrialization was oriented toward the production of luxury goods for the higher income groups and relied on capital-intensive technology that

[30] FitzGerald, *Political Economy*, p. 111.

further prejudiced the interests of the majority of the population by limiting jobs.

These economic structures had their social and political counterparts. In social terms, the colonial division of society—originally based on the *mita* and the *encomienda*—established the basic opposition between *blancos* and *indios,* in spite of the later appearance of a substantial mestizo community. This division led to a highly unequal division of income and wealth among classes in Peru, but it also contributed to important inequalities in geographical terms. Wealth tended to be concentrated in the coastal area where the white population predominated, while the Indian population in the sierra lived under semifeudal conditions outside the money economy.

The colonial and neocolonial heritage also had important consequences for the social class structure. The traditional absence of industry, coupled with its later promotion under the aegis of foreign capital, blocked the development of a strong domestic bourgeoisie. The one opportunity for the emergence of such a class—the guano boom of 1844–1879—was a failure. Merchants, financiers, and agroexporters, all of whom benefited from the export of guano, preferred to invest their resources in export agriculture and loans to the state rather than take the risk of trying to develop an internal market. Instead of a national bourgeoisie, then, the Peruvian upper class was dominated by a *comprador* bourgeoisie and a group of rentiers, collectively known as the oligarchy.

Similarly, there was no large urban proletariat. As late as 1960, 55 percent of the labor force (synonymous with the Indian portion of the population) still worked in the primary sector, while only 13 percent was in manufacturing. Furthermore, about two thirds of the manufacturing workers were in firms employing fewer than five workers.[31] This social structure, of course, had important economic implications; since the majority of the population was outside the market economy, the domestic market was too small to support a large industrial sector.

The social structure also had implications in the political sphere. The Indian population was effectively excluded from political life as well as from the market. The state in Peru had traditionally been the state of a small group, the oligarchy of mine owners, agro-exporters, and financiers referred to above. With the support of the armed forces, the oligarchy used the state to promote its interests, including freedom from taxes, favorable exchange rate policy, easy access to credit, and control of the working class. In the twentieth century, the

[31] Ibid., p. 87.

entry of the Aprista party brought certain middle-sector groups into politics, but the state continued to serve the interests of a small minority of the population.

This oligarchical state tended to rely heavily on foreign capital rather than creating its own domestic resource base through taxation. One of the important roles of the British in the nineteenth century, in fact, was that of providing loans to the Peruvian state. In the 1920s, this function was taken over by United States investment banks and later by United States government agencies and commercial banks. As a result of relying on foreign funds, however, Peru was vulnerable to foreign influence. The most dramatic example was the negotiations between the Peruvian government and British bondholders in the 1890s and the eventual formation of the Peruvian Corporation, which came to control the country's railroads as well as certain other resources. Such action continued in the twentieth century through the influence of the International Monetary Fund and the United States Agency for International Development (AID) in economic decision making in Peru. A final example before the military took over in 1968 was the United States government's financial blockade of the Belaúnde regime in an attempt to influence government policy. Aid was withheld to try to force a favorable resolution of Peru's long-standing dispute with IPC, Standard Oil's subsidiary. When the policy did not seem to be working, aid funds were restored, only to be cut again over the issue of Peru's purchase of Mirage jets from France. This blockade led the Peruvians to the private capital markets and greatly enlarged the foreign debt, the service of which furthered the vicious cycle of debt and foreign influence.

The Velasco Period

Upon taking power in October 1968, the Velasco government thus inherited a socioeconomic structure partially shaped by the actions of foreign governments and corporations. This structure proved crucial in at least two senses. On the one hand, it suggested the goals of the new government—industrialization, redistribution, national integration, and increased national autonomy. On the other hand, it also accounted for many of the constraints the regime would face—inelastic supply of exports coupled with strong price fluctuations, a growing need for imports coupled with generally rising prices, and the consequent reliance on foreign borrowing with the accompanying debt problems. In all of these areas, the foreign sector would play an important role; indeed, in the short run, foreign influence was concentrated in the financial sector as reflected in the balance of payments.

The government's potential financial problems can be quantified, at least in approximate terms. An examination of the import content of proposed investment projects and certain assumptions about other foreign exchange requirements suggest that the following would be the likely annual demands for foreign exchange between 1971 and 1975:[32]

Investment projects	$750 million
Other imports	850
Debt service	216
Budget deficit	29
Total	$1.845 billion

Given expected current annual account revenues of $1.37 billion,[33] the government was forced to seek about $480 million a year in long-term public and private capital flows.

With this background on Peru's likely demand for foreign capital, we can now examine how external forces influenced the supply of capital. Two interrelated aspects of "structural" or market impact of foreign capital are especially important: international price fluctuations and changes in the level of economic activity in the advanced industrial countries. These variations were reflected primarily in the trade balance.[34]

Much has been written about export stagnation in Peru, which arose in large part from the lack of investment in the 1960s. Nevertheless, it must be recognized that, in spite of their relatively slow growth, exports actually performed better than expected during the 1971–1975 National Development Plan, growing at an average rate of 11.8 percent rather than the projected 4.1 percent.[35] The only sector that significantly declined in value was fish products, owing to the oft-discussed disappearance of anchovies. Although the export situa-

[32] The methodology for arriving at these estimates is explained in an earlier version of this paper. See Barbara Stallings, "International Capitalism and the Peruvian Military Government, 1968–78," The Woodrow Wilson Center's Latin American Program, working paper 20, pp. 4–6.

[33] *Plan Nacional de Desarrollo, 1971–1975* (Lima: Instituto Nacional de Planificación, 1971), 1:22.

[34] The association of market forces with the trade balance and policy decisions with capital flows is not a wholly satisfactory one. Thus, for example, trade flows can be influenced by boycotts or dumping; likewise capital flows are also affected by market factors. See the discussion in the next section on private bank loans to Peru stimulated by excess liquidity in the international markets.

[35] Expected exports are calculated from figures in *Plan Nacional de Desarrollo, 1971–1975* 1:22. Actual increases are calculated from Appendix 5.1.

tion would obviously have been better were it not for the anchovies, the fishmeal drop was more than compensated for by increased revenue from minerals and agricultural products (see Appendix 5.1, p. 174). An analysis of price and volume tends, however, shows that most of the increase in export value was due to price rather than volume increases.[36]

In spite of the disappearance of the anchovies and the price fluctuations for other products, the blame for the trade balance cannot be laid primarily on exports (especially when compared with the Peruvians' own projections). The problems are more readily attributable to overruns in import costs. Imports of merchandise and services were supposed to increase by 10 percent per year during the 1971–1975 Development Plan; they actually increased by 23 percent.[37]

With respect to merchandise imports, we must also consider the relative importance of price versus volume changes. The most spectacular price change was for oil imports, but Peru suffered less from this jump than most other Third World countries because much of its oil was supplied from domestic sources. Prices of food and raw materials imports and manufactured goods also rose, but the chief source of the increase in import value was what had been expected from the beginning. From 1973 to 1975, the *volume* of capital equipment imports and intermediate goods for the industrialization drive increased greatly.[38]

If Peru's trade problems can be attributed largely to anonymous market forces, the same cannot be said of capital flows. Here the scene changes to the realm of conscious manipulations by those trying to in-

[36] Statistics on price and volume are most readily available in IMF, *International Financial Statistics* (monthly publication). Probably the biggest blow in terms of export volume was a "non-event" (in the sense that it never showed up directly in the balance of payments). The reference is to the petroleum exports that were scheduled to begin in 1978. Growing emphasis was put on oil by Peruvians and foreigner alike, from the time Petroperú struck oil in 1971 until most of the companies left in 1976. Now, of course, earlier expectations are being realized.

[37] Expected imports are calculated from figures in *Plan Nacional de Desarrollo 1971–1975* 1:22. Actual increases are calculated from Appendix 5.1.

[38] It can even by hypothesized that insofar as there was a major problem with the current account of the balance of payments (trade and services balances), it did not concern absolute amounts. That is, the average deficit over the 1971–1975 period was only slightly over $500 million—or very close to the estimate made on p. 162 of this chapter. Rather, the problem was one of timing. First, the deficits were not spread out over the period, but concentrated at the end, creating the impression of growing crisis. Second, there was the coincidence of increase in world prices and volume increases in Peruvian imports for industry. Third, the need to finance large deficits on the current account coincided with the disillusionment about Peruvian oil reserves, so that borrowing became more difficult. These timing items, more than the failure of exports or even the overrun in imports, set the stage for the 1976–1978 crisis.

fluence a regime whose policies they regarded as unacceptable. The most inflexible participants in this game were the United States government and the multilateral agencies. Private investors, and especially the banks, took a more flexible approach.

The focal point of the United States-Peruvian controversy between the fall of 1968 and the spring of 1974 was the Peruvian government's nationalization without compensation of the International Petroleum Company. In response to this nationalization, Washington imposed an informal economic blockade on Peru; the Hickenlooper Amendment was not invoked, but a policy of "non-overt economic pressure" was applied. As explained by one analyst, non-overt economic pressure means that disbursements of previously authorized loans continue, but no new authorizations are made. Public debt renegotiations are made very difficult, and signals are sent to the private sector encouraging slowdowns in investment and credit flows. Economic—rather than political—justifications are offered if such policies are questioned, with heavy emphasis on credit-worthiness.[39]

The result of this non-overt economic pressure was that Peru received almost no new loans from AID or the Export-Import Bank between 1969 and 1974. Total disbursements amounted to $72 million from previous authorizations (see Appendix 5.2). Money lost through AID was not very significant because AID's Latin American allocations in general began to dry up about this time. More important were the Eximbank's actions, because some corporations tied large investments to Exim participation. Nevertheless, the United States government did not try to exert major pressure on private corporations and banks. This meant that Peru was able to get the funds it needed although, as will be seen, at a higher cost.

In February 1974, the United States and Peru formally resolved the controversy over nationalization without compensation with the signing of the so-called Greene Agreement, negotiated by James Greene, then senior vice-president of Manufacturers Hanover. In a feat of economic diplomacy, it provided a lump sum as compensation for *all* companies nationalized by Peru. The United States government distributed this money among all companies, including IPC, while the Peruvians saved face by establishing a separate list of companies they considered to be eligible for compensation. The latter list excluded IPC.[40]

[39] Einhorn, *Expropriation Politics,* pp. 28–29.
[40] For details, see *Latin America Economic Report,* vol. 2, no. 9 (March 1, 1974).

In spite of the economic pressure the United States government put on Peru, it must be recognized that the military government was still allowed breathing space. This is brought out most clearly by comparing Peru to Allende's Chile. In Chile, not only was a much tighter financial blockade imposed but United States government funds were authorized to "destabilize" the country and the Central Intelligence Agency was encouraged to cause as much trouble as possible. The goal in Chile was to oust the Allende government; in Peru Washington's aims were much more limited.[41]

Peru's relations with the multilateral agencies were in large part shaped by the United States-Peruvian conflict. The World Bank did have its own policy against giving loans to governments that nationalized foreign property without compensation, but the United States later threatened the Inter-American Development Bank (IDB), implying that the absence of a similar nationalization policy might make it difficult for the United States to continue its association with the IDB.[42] Between 1968 and 1971, United States pressure on the multilaterals was of the "non-overt" type; then in January 1972, President Nixon's statement on expropriations made the policy an open one.[43] As a result of these pressures, the flow of multilateral funds was slowed but never stopped entirely. The World Bank provided only $79 million during the 1969–1974 period, while the IDB authorized $109 million (see Appendices 5.3 and 5.4).

Private direct investment, especially by United States corporations, paralleled the position of the United States government, although it would be a misleading oversimplification to see a direct cause and effect relationship between the two. Two of the three main United States mining corporations—Cerro de Pasco and Marcona—decided to sell their Peruvian holdings to the government rather than comply with the new investment requirements.[44] The third company, Southern Peru Copper Corporation, maintained its Peruvian interests, but its big investments in the Cuajone mine were linked to Eximbank participation and thus were delayed until the signing of the Greene Agreement in February 1974. In contrast to the United States firms, the European and Japanese firms proved willing to negotiate with the Velasco government, and a number of medium-sized projects (e.g.,

[41] See comparisons between Peru and Chile in James Petras and Morris Morley, *The United States and Chile* (New York: Monthly Review Press, 1975), chapter 4 and *passim*.

[42] Einhorn, *Expropriation Politics,* p. 80.

[43] *New York Times,* January 22, 1972.

[44] Guasti, "Peruvian Military Government," p. 189.

Bayer, Volvo, Massey-Ferguson) were established.[45] Nevertheless, direct foreign investment did not become a significant source of foreign exchange until 1974 (see Appendix 5.5).

The banking sector behaved quite differently from its industrial and mining counterparts.[46] Although they limited themselves to refinancing Peruvian loans between 1969 and 1971, by 1972 the private banks began pouring money into the Peruvian economy. So massive was this inflow, in fact, that it more than replaced the funds lost from the public sector, thus cancelling the effect of the blockade. Flush with excess liquidity because of a lack of demand from advanced industrial countries, the banks began looking for Third World clients, and Peru's mineral resources made it appear a good risk in spite of its government's rhetoric. In February 1972, the military government obtained its first loan, and by the end of the year, it had raised $160 million (see Appendix 5.6). Urged on by Wells Fargo, which reportedly hired a Peruvian banker to build up Peruvian business, the government raised $628 million in Eurocurrency loans in 1973, becoming the fifth largest Third World borrower. Between 1974 and 1976, annual loan totals averaged around $400 million and involved all of the major United States, European, and Japanese banks.

The effect of this borrowing spree was a dramatic change in the size and structure of Peru's public sector foreign debt. The debt leapt from $1.1 billion in 1968 to $2.5 billion in 1973; and by 1976, it had soared to $5.5 billion (see Appendix 5.7). Moreover, whereas the banks held 24 percent of Peru's debt in 1968, they accounted for 49 percent by 1976.[47] The increasing size of the debt, of course, meant increasing service payments. By 1971, Peru was already using almost 20 percent of its export for revenues for debt service. Including some prepayments made in 1973 and 1974, the country was paying over $400 million in interest and amortization, or approximately the same amount being borrowed on the international markets.

The switch to private capital was part of the reason for the squeeze. As can be seen by comparing information in Appendices 5.2, 5.3, 5.4,

[45] Ibid., p. 196.

[46] For studies on private bank loans to Peru, see Barbara Stallings, "Peru and the U.S. Banks: The Privatization of Financial Relations," in Richard R. Fagen, ed., *State and Capitalism in U.S.–Latin American Relations* (Stanford: Stanford University Press, 1979); Oscar Ugarteche, *La Banca Transnacional, La Deuda Externa y el Estado, Perú 1968–1978* (Lima: Instituto de Estudios Peruanos, 1980); and Devlin, *Los Bancos Transnacionales.*

[47] World Bank, *World Debt Tables,* October 26, 1977, supplement.

and 5.6, the maturity for private loans is significantly shorter than for public capital. The majority of private loans had terms of five to ten years, whereas loans from the IDB and the World Bank had fifteen- to twenty-year terms, or up to thirty years for Fund for Special Operations (FSO) credits. There was also likely to be a longer grace period on public loans so that repayment would not begin so soon. The shorter terms, together with repayment burdens of the rescheduled debt inherited by the military government, led to a payments squeeze at precisely the time the trade balance crunch began to bite. Thus the stage was set for the 1976–1978 crisis.

Before turning to the crisis, however, it is important to clarify the question of timing—that is, why the financial constraints were not crippling during the Velasco, or radical, phase of the Peruvian process. The effective years of the United States-led credit blockade were 1969, the first half of 1970, and 1971 (the "humanitarian" aid following the serious earthquake that rocked Peru in mid-1970 neutralized the squeeze during the second half of 1970). There was no great need for foreign capital during this period, however, for at least two reasons: (1) the government's projects were still in the planning stages and could not have absorbed large amounts of foreign capital even if they had been available, and (2) Peru enjoyed a positive trade balance. In fact, in 1970, Peru achieved that rarity in Latin America—a positive balance on the current account. In 1969, the trade and service/transfer balance exactly cancelled each other out; only in 1971 was there a current account deficit, and this was small ($34 million). By 1972, Peru and the private capital markets had discovered each other, and these funds more than compensated the public capital squeeze. The fact that the private credits were given on relatively disadvantageous terms (i.e., shorter maturities than public loans) did not become significant until 1975–1976. Thus, it is hard to argue that the Velasco model itself was seriously constrained by international capital.

The Morales Period

The foreign sector was more heavily involved in Peru under Morales Bermúdez than under Velasco. In fact, one of the chief factors differentiating the two regimes was precisely the changed evaluation of the role of foreign capital. Both saw foreign capital as necessary for Peruvian development, but the Morales economic team did not have the same reservations about its negative side effects.

Foreign influence during the Morales period derived from a bal-

ance-of-payments crisis and was exerted by two groups of participants—the private banks in 1976 and the IMF in 1977–1978. The crisis was entering its critical phase as Morales assumed the presidency
in August 1975. That year saw the largest current account deficit of
the military period—$1.5 billion—and the first significant overall
deficit—$580 million (Appendix 5.5). Reserves were drawn down to
cover the deficit while domestic economic policy was manipulated to
try to reduce the external disequilibrium. The exchange rate was devalued and demand restricted, which led to recession, reconcentra-
tion of income, and political protest. The external problems were not
resolved, however, and the Morales government had to take additional steps. The traditional solution would have been to sign a Letter
of Intent with the IMF. This would give access to IMF funds and,
more important, would open further doors to multilateral, bilateral,
and private banking sources that wanted an IMF "seal of approval"
before lending. The problem was that the IMF would demand a
drastic stabilization program, which would increase the government's
political problems; consequently, it was decided to approach the
major international banks in hopes of getting help on less onerous
terms.[48]

The bankers reluctantly agreed to make a $400 million balance-of-
payments loan on two conditions: (1) institution of an orthodox stabilization program, though of a milder sort than the IMF would have
imposed, involving a 44 percent devaluation, price increases, and
minor budget cuts; and (2) better treatment of foreign investment,
including favorable agreements with Marcona on a price to be paid
for its mine and with SPCC on payments due.[49]

The most controversial aspect of the program was that the banks
were to monitor the Peruvian economy to ensure that the agreed-
upon inflation, budget, and other targets were met. Not since the
1920s had private banks become so involved in the domestic affairs of
a foreign government. The loan was divided into two equal parts; the
first was drawn immediately, and the second was held for several
months. Release of the second part was contingent upon agreement
among 75 percent of the lenders (by dollar participation) that Peru
was making satisfactory economic progress. Even the bankers admitted the weakness of the arrangement in comparison with the more
detailed IMF monitoring. As one banker stated: "We won't be seeing

[48] Stallings, "Peru and the U.S. Banks," pp. 237–238. For a discussion of why
the bankers agreed to give the loan, see pp. 238–239; for their reasons for pulling
out in 1977, see pp. 242–244.

[49] Interviews with former Central Bank officials.

any major changes. This second drawdown is just something to keep *some* sort of control."[50]

The package was put together by Citibank with the participation of Bank of America, Chase Manhattan, Manufacturers Hanover, Morgan Guaranty, and Wells Fargo. Thus six banks comprised the "steering committee" for the loan, because no bank was willing to take total responsibility as lead manager. The banks agreed to provide $200 million, contingent on a further $200 million to be raised from private banks in Western Europe, Canada, and Japan. Above and beyond the special conditions described above, the terms of the loan itself were quite stiff. The interest rate was 2.25 percent above the London Inter-Bank rate (the cost of funds to the banks themselves), and the maturity was only five years.

The effects of the stabilization program were swift and negative. Production dropped, unemployment increased, and real wages and salaries returned to their 1968 level.[51] In addition, private enterprise in general, and foreign capital in particular, began to regain much of the economic and political power lost during the Velasco years.

The second phase of foreign involvement under Morales was dominated by the International Monetary Fund. Though the 1977 balance of payments was expected to improve, a huge trade deficit still threatened and service payments on the debt remained oppressive. Peru had to look for foreign financing again. This time, however, the banks refused to provide loans without IMF participation. Negotiations over the exact nature and stringency of the stabilization program lasted over eighteen months while the government verged on bankruptcy. The key issue was the budget deficit, specifically arms purchases and government subsidies for basic consumer goods.[52] An agreement with the IMF was signed in the fall of 1977, but it proved politically impossible to implement. In February 1978, the IMF cancelled payments, declaring Peru in massive violation of the agreement. The banks, in turn, called off a $260 million loan under negotiation; the United States government also refused further assistance. Thus, the budget deficit was cut, paving the way for a new IMF agreement and a complete rescheduling of the foreign debt.[53]

The role of foreign capital was clearly apparent between 1975 and

[50] Nancy Belliveau, "What the Peruvian Experiment Means," *Institutional Investor* (October 1976).

[51] Stallings, "Peru and the U.S. Banks," pp. 241–242.

[52] Ugarteche, *La Banca Transnacional*, chapter 7.

[53] *New York Times*, November 20 and December 30, 1978.

1978. The question, however, is how to interpret that role. Was the stabilization program "imposed" from outside, or was it the result of a coincidence of interests between external and internal forces? The evidence appears to support the latter interpretation.

By 1975, the limitations of Velasco's "third way" model had become evident. Greater state participation in the economy without obtaining control of the necessary resources created huge financial—and political—disequilibria. These were compounded by the attempt to satisfy all constituencies—workers with wage increases, the bourgeoisie with subsidies and incentives, the military with arms purchases. Two broad types of responses were possible: (1) a move toward greater state control of the economy, or (2) a move toward greater reliance on market mechanisms. The former would probably have implied, among other measures, a debt moratorium, greater controls on foreign trade and foreign exchange movements, tax increases, and perhaps even worker control of factories and farms. The latter required increased reliance on the private sector (domestic and foreign), and on the reduced controls and increased incentives necessary to create an environment of "business confidence."

Morales Bermúdez and the civilian and military groups that supported him had no interest in a state-run economy;[54] reforming capitalism was one thing, socialism was quite another. Socialism had never been part of the military plans. The decision to move toward greater reliance on market mechanisms was made independently of pressures by the private banks in 1976 and the IMF in 1977–1978. Evidence of this can be found in policy steps taken by the Morales government *before* the negotiations with the banks in mid-1976. One such example was the stabilization measures introduced in June 1975 and January 1976.[55] Another was the greater reliance on private capital—the social property area was deemphasized, state enterprises were sold off, and many small and medium-sized firms were exempted from the *comunidad laboral* in an attempt to boost private investment. In institutional terms, the National Planning Institute lost

[54] In his recent book on the Peruvian military, *The Rise and Fall of the Peruvian Military Radicals, 1968–76* (London: University of London, 1978), George Philip reports that Morales had always been identified with what he labels the "developmentalist" wing of the military, as opposed to the "radicals" or "conservatives." "Thus, whereas the military radicals would later call themselves socialists (although of the Christian rather than the Marxist kind), the 'developmentalists' ... were fundamentally pro-capitalist even though they wished to carry out a number of pressing structural reforms" (p. 96).

[55] See *Latin America Economic Report*, vol. 3, no. 27 (July 11, 1975); and *Andean Report*, January 1977.

importance to the more conservative Ministry of Finance.[56] Politically, Morales and his supporters began maneuvering out leftist military officers and other Velasco appointees well before the crunch when the Fernández Maldonado/de la Flor/Gallegos trio was forced to resign in July 1976. Prominent among earlier casualties were generals Leonidas Rodríguez Figueroa and José Graham Hurtado and the editors of all the state-controlled newspapers.[57]

All of these tendencies were reinforced by the 1976 negotiations with the banks and, more important, by the 1977–1978 negotiations with the IMF. Evidence indicates that the military's anger with the IMF was genuine, but it did not center on IMF demands for wage cuts or the lowering of tariff barriers or greater entree for foreign capital. Instead, this anger focused on the demand for a cut in arms purchases, which may or may not have been linked with another kind of foreign influence on the Peruvian process: the perceived threat from neighboring Chile.[58] Although foreign capitalists and their public sector allies were undoubtedly pleased with the new directions taken by the Morales government, it would nevertheless be a misinterpretation to argue that these policies were imposed on an unwilling government.

CONCLUSIONS

A narrow focus on the decade of military rule indicates that the foreign sector played a relatively minor role in determining the fate of the military regime. Because the United States government's attempt to impose economic sanctions against Peru was only half-hearted, it was cancelled out by the activities of the private banks. In the medium run, these bank loans contributed heavily to the balance-of-payments crisis that engulfed Peru in 1976, but in the short run (i.e., the Velasco period), the foreign exchange impact was positive. Likewise, the structural impact of the international capitalist system, as manifested through international trade, was not of major importance.

[56] Analysis of these various policy changes can be found in *Latin America Political Report,* vol. 10, no. 10 (March 5, 1976) and vol. 10, no. 18a (May 7, 1976); and *Latin America Economic Report,* vol. 4, no. 15 (April 9, 1976).

[57] *Latin America Political Report,* vol. 9, no. 44 (November 7, 1975).

[58] Interviews with military officers as reported to author by Julio Cotler and Oscar Ugarteche. The perception of a threat arose from the large build-up of the Chilean military after the coup in 1973, coupled with anti-Peruvian rhetoric on the part of the new Chilean government. Rumors of war between the two countries filled the local and international press during much of 1974 and returned later in connection with negotiations for Bolivia's "opening to the sea."

Explanations for the demise of the Velasco regime are better sought domestically. Similarly, the Morales policies cannot be directly attributed to foreign influence. These policies began before the banks and the IMF entered the picture in mid-1976 and were rooted in domestic interests in both military and civilian sectors.

The foreign sector was not, however, irrelevant in the determination of events in Peru. Rather, the importance of foreign influence must be understood in terms of the historical impact of foreign capital and governments. This impact was exercised in the shaping of economic, social, and political structures that, in turn, put severe limits on possible government initiatives. These long-term structural factors, at least in the case under study, were much more important than short-term events—whether credit blockades or the disappearance of anchovies—during the military period itself.

What effect did the Velasco reforms have on these structural conditions? Obviously it did not remove them; the only question is to what extent it successfully modified them. I would suggest the following points as the most important in evaluating the degree of success. First, Peru remains a primary product exporter, still subject to all the vagaries that this implies. The dramatic financial recovery period 1979—owing largely to international price changes—is the latest reminder of the economy's dependence on international market conditions. The export sector, however, is now in better shape with regard to capacity, and the change in ownership means that the state, rather than foreign corporations, can now make decisions (albeit constrained) about investment rates, type of technology, and so on. Second, Peru has taken major steps toward creating an industrial base, although the sector is currently in severe straits because of the years of austerity programs. Some argue that the way in which industry was developed (via import substitution) has created more problems than it has solved, but progress has been made in increasing the country's self-sufficiency and its capacity to provide jobs. Third, the reforms concentrated a great deal of economic power in the hands of the state, at the expense of both domestic and foreign capital. State ownership of the basic sectors of the economy and a greater state role in regulating the private sector provide the necessary preconditions, the potential, for Peru to deal on a more equal basis with the foreign sector. Fourth, as a result of the above-mentioned three factors, Peru has accumulated a very large debt to foreign government agencies, international organizations, and private banks and suppliers. Since a repudiation of this debt, or even a moratorium on payments, is not a viable alternative unless Peru is prepared to turn to autarchy, this debt gives foreign capital increased potential to exert influence over Peru. Finally, the most important, the Velasco period created a new political consciousness vis-à-vis foreign capital, which makes it impossible to return to the status quo ante. The Velasco years showed that even a small, poor country need not simply grovel before foreign powers; it can affect, even if not totally determine, its own destiny. What has occurred in Peru is a type of political "rachet effect"— many individual reforms may be reversed, but even a right-wing government cannot return to the subservient relationships Peru has with foreign capital before 1968.

In summary, then, the Velasco reforms modified the political-economic structure that the regime inherited in order to provide future governments with more room to maneuver in their international dealings. At the same time, they also created new problems via import substitution and the foreign debt. The relative weight of these various factors will be determined by the future decisions and strategies of Peruvians and foreigners alike. The military decade clearly suggests the extreme difficulty in "resolving" the problem of economic dependency, especially for a government without a popular political base of support. It does not, however, provide a definitive case of confrontation between foreign capital and a radical regime— the showdown did not come until after the Velasco (or radical) period was over. The question of whether participation of international capital is incompatible with a noncapitalist (as opposed to an anticapitalist) project remains open. The Peruvian experience provides a useful place to begin such an analysis, but it does not provide the answer.

APPENDIX 5.1
Exports and Imports of Peru, 1968–1978
(In Millions of Dollars)

	1968	1969	1970	1971	1972	1973	1974	1975	1976	1977	1978
Exports											
Fish products[a]	233.5	219.6	346.3	327.7	265.9	157.2	261.5	208.1	200.7	242.0	281.2
Mineral products[b]	418.0	474.0	471.8	365.2	427.3	631.2	753.0	590.9	744.0	969.2	1,091.9
Agricultural products[c]	159.1	146.3	160.0	152.1	188.1	216.7	322.5	386.7	281.8	355.5	281.2
Others	56.0	39.6	55.8	44.4	63.7	106.6	156.6	105.2	132.9	201.4	330.1
Total	866.1	879.5	1,034.3	889.4	945.0	1,111.8	1,503.9	1,290.9	1,359.4	1,768.1	1,940.7
Imports											
Consumer goods	97.1	90.4	88.3	97.2	109.2	154.4	185.9	238.7	n.a.	n.a.	n.a.
Fuel & lubricants	23.3	18.9	12.2	24.8	44.8	56.6	244.5	317.7	n.a.	n.a.	n.a.
Raw materials and Intermediate goods	301.9	288.7	296.5	399.1	401.5	407.5	879.0	1,088.3	n.a.	n.a.	n.a.
Capital goods	206.9	204.3	224.2	226.8	236.8	381.2	733.0	936.8	n.a.	n.a.	n.a.
Others	2.1	1.1	0.9	3.8	4.2	18.8	6.2	3.4	n.a.	n.a.	n.a.
Total	631.4	603.3	622.1	751.7	796.2	1,018.5	2,028.7	2,584.8	2,100.0	2,095.0	1,600.5

Source: Banco Central de Reserva.

[a] Fish meal and fish oil.

[b] Copper, iron and iron ore, silver, zinc, lead, petroleum.

[c] Cotton, sugar, coffee, and wool.

APPENDIX 5.2
United States Government Loans and Grants to Peru, 1968–1978
(In Millions of Dollars)

	Agency for International Development				Export-Import Bank
	Loans	Grants	Total		Credits
1968	0.1	5.4	5.5	1968	4.7
1969	0	4.0	4.0	1969	9.8
1970	0	11.3	11.3	1970	0
1971	3.0	3.9	6.9	1971	4.3
1972	27.6	4.1	31.7	1972	0
1973	0	3.8	3.8	1973	0
1974	0	12.1	12.1	1974	55.3
1975	7.0	1.9	8.9	1975	16.3
1976	11.0	1.7	12.7	1976	34.0
1977	15.0	2.4	17.4	1977	2.2
1978	19.0	3.0	22.0	1978	0.7

Source: Agency for International Development, *U.S. Overseas Loans and Grants*, 1979.

APPENDIX 5.3
World Bank Loans to Peru, 1968–1978
(All loans are from the IBRD; Peru received no loans from the IDA.)

	Purpose	Amount ($ Millions)	Interest Rate (%)	Term (Years)
1968		0	n.a.	n.a.
1969		0	n.a.	n.a.
1970	Roads	30.0	7.25%	30
1971		0	n.a.	n.a.
1972		0	n.a.	n.a.
1973	Agriculture	25.0	7.25	18
	Education	24.0	7.25	18
1974	Roads	26.0	7.25	24
1975	Highways	76.5	8.5	25
1976	Electricity	36.0	8.5	30
	Mining	40.0	8.5	15
	Urbanization Development Corporation	21.6	8.85	20
		35.0	8.7	17
1977	Irrigation	25.0	8.5	17
1978[a]		0	n.a.	n.a.

Source: IBRD, *Statement of Loans*, 1978.

[a] Through June 30.

APPENDIX 5.4
Inter-American Development Bank Loans to Peru, 1968–1978

	Purpose	Amount ($ millions)	Interest Rate (%)	Term (Years)
		ORDINARY CAPITAL RESOURCES		
1968		0	n.a.	n.a.
1969	Electric Power	9.0	8%	15
1970		0	n.a.	n.a.
1971		0	n.a.	n.a.
1972		0	n.a.	n.a.
1973	Mining	6.0	8	15
1974	Tourism	26.5	8	20
1975	Industry[a]	15.0	8	15
1976	Electricity	32.3	8	20
	Mining[b]	33.4	8.6	15
	Pre-investment study[b]	2.0	8.6	20
1977	Industry[b]	20.0	n.a.	n.a.
1978	Mining	6.0	n.a.	n.a.
		FUND FOR SPECIAL OPERATIONS		
1968		0	n.a.	n.a.
1969		0	n.a.	n.a.
1970	Earthquake aid	35.0	2.25	25
	Irrigation	23.3	2.24	20
1971	Highways	11.8	3.25	15
	Agriculture	12.0	2.25	20
1972			0	0
1973	Agriculture	6.0	2	30
	Health	6.3	2	30
1974	Tourism	2.8	2	30
	Water	4.7	2	30
1975	Water	30.5	2	30
1976	Highways	37.6	2	25
	Agriculture	30.0	2	30
	Pre-investment study	8.0	2	20
1977		0	n.a.	n.a.
1978	Mining	1.0	n.a.	n.a.
	Industry	0	n.a.	n.a.

Source: Inter-American Development Bank, *Annual Report,* 1969–1978.

[a] Venezuelan Trust Fund.

[b] Interregional Capital.

APPENDIX 5.5
Peruvian Balance of Payments, 1968–1978
(In Millions of Dollars)

	1968	1969	1970	1971	1972	1973	1974	1975	1976	1977	1978
Exports, f.o.b.	840	880	1,034	889	945	1,112	1,503	1,290	1,359	1,768	1,941
Imports, f.o.b.	−673	−659	−700	−730	−812	−1,033	−1,909	−2,390	−2,100	−2,095	−1,601
Trade balance	167	221	334	159	133	79	−406	−1,099	−741	−327	340
Services	−57	−36	−1	−68	−44	−89	−149	−275	−80	−48	46
Profits, interest	−151	−185	−149	−125	−121	−181	−219	−240	−371	−436	−578
Balance	−208	−221	−150	−193	−165	−252	−322	−456	−451	−484	−532
Current account	−41	0	185	−34	−32	−191	−807	−1,538	−1,192	−811	−192
Long-term public capital	81	124	101	15	119	375	710	764	480	596	383
Long-term private capital											
Direct investment	n.a.	19	−79	−50	24	49	144	316	171	54	25
Loans	n.a.	1	2	7	−29	20	58	26	25	15	14
	−13	20	−77	−43	−5	69	202	342	196	69	39
Short-term capital, Errors & omissions	−42	−109	49	−14	−33	−240	178	−145	−351	−189	−149
Capital account	26	35	73	−42	81	204	1,090	961	325	476	274
Deficit/surplus	−15	35	258	−76	49	13	282	−577	−867	−335	82
Net reserves	130.6	165.8	423.2	347.0	397.3	410.6	692.5	115.8	−751.8	−1,086.8	−1,024.9

Source: Banco Central de Reserva.

APPENDIX 5.6
Eurocurrency Credits to Peru, 1972–1978

Date	Lead Bank	Borrower	Interest Rate (% over LIBOR)	Amount ($ Millions)	Term (Years)
2/72	Manufacturers Hanover	Central Government	1.250%	$30.0	5
8/72	Williams & Glyn	Mineroperú[a]	n.a.	12.7	5
8/72	Williams & Glyn	Mineroperú[a]	n.a.	21.2	10
10/72	Dresdner Bank	Central Government	n.a.	30.0	7
11/72	Manufacturers Hanover	Banco de la Nación	2.000	14.0	7
12/72	Wells Fargo	Banco de la Nación	n.a.	40.0	7
12/72	Williams & Glyn	Corp. Financiera de Desarrollo[b]	n.a.	12.0	n.a.
Total 1972				159.9	
4/73	Wells Fargo	Central Government[c]	n.a.	100.0	8
4/73	Wells Fargo	Central Government	n.a.	35.4	7
4/73	Crocker National Bank	Central Government	n.a.	40.0	7
6/73	Bank of Tokyo	Corp. Financiera de Desarrollo[d]	n.a.	40.0	9
6/73	Bank of Tokyo	Corp. Financiera de Desarrollo[d]	n.a.	2.6	n.a.
9/73	Citicorp	Banco de la Nación[e]	1.600	130.0	10
12/73	Wells Fargo	Central Government	1.250	80.0	10
12/73	Chase Manhattan	S. Peru Copper Corp.[f]	1.875	200.0	10
Total 1973				628.0	
2/74	Morgan Guaranty Trust Co.	Central Government[g]	1.000	76.0	10
6/74	Wells Fargo	Central Government[h]	1.125	80.0	10
4/74	Bank of Tokyo	Banco de la Nación[i]	1.150	50.0	10
7/74	Commerzbank	Central Government[j]	n.a.	10.0	10
7/74	Dresdner Bank	Central Government[k]	1.375	82.0	10
12/74	Rabomerica International Bank	Central Government	1.500	10.5	7
12/74	Lloyds Bank International	Southern Peru Copper Corp.[l]	n.a.	32.5	12.5
/74	Crocker National Bank	Banco de la Nación	1.250	30.0	4
Total 1974				371.0	

1/75	Credit Industrial et Commercial	Banco de la Nación	n.a.	10.0	7
3/75	Amex International	Central Government[m]	2.125	20.0	7
3/75	Amex International	Central Government	1.491	20.0	7
3/75	Wells Fargo	Petroperú[n]	1.750	50.0	7
4/75	Wells Fargo	Petroperú[n]	1.750	50.0	7
7/75	Dresdner Bank	Corp. Financiera de Desarrollo	2.000	24.3	5
10/75	Manufacturers Hanover	Central Government[o]	1.875	150.0	5
10/75	First Chicago	Banco de la Nación[p]	1.875	50.0	3.5
11/75	First Chicago	Central Government[p]	1.875	60.0	3.5
Total 1975				434.3	
4/76	Wells Fargo	Emp. Minera del Centro[q]	n.a.	50.0	n.a.
12/76	Credit Lyonnais	Banco Central de Reserva[r]	2.250	90.0	5
12/76	Citicorp	Central Government[r]	2.250	210.0	5
Total 1976				350.0	
3/77	Svenska Handels Banken	Central Government[r]	n.a.	91.0	n.a.
12/77	Chase Manhattan	Southern Peru Copper Corp.	n.a.	53.4	n.a.
Total 1977				144.4	
Total 1978				0.0	

Source: Barbara Stallings, "Latin America and the U.S. Capital Markets, 1900–1980" (Ph.D. dissertation, Cambridge University, 1982).

[a] Purpose: Finance Cerro Verde copper mine.
[b] Purpose: State petroleum, mining, and other.
[c] Purpose: Finance public investments and current external obligations.
[d] Purpose: Finance industrial projects.
[e] Purpose: Finance economic development projects.
[f] Purpose: Finance Cuajone copper mining project.
[g] Purpose: Finance nationalizations (in conjunction with Green Agreement).
[h] Purpose: Prepay portion of external debt.
[i] Purpose: Finance public sector debt.
[j] Purpose: Finance irrigation project.
[k] Purpose: Finance government operations.
[l] Purpose: Finance operations in Cuajone mine.
[m] Purpose: Finance regional and rural hospitals.
[n] Purpose: Finance construction of North Peruvian pipeline.
[o] Purpose: Finance oil imports.
[p] Purpose: Finance major development projects.
[q] Purpose: Finance pre-export of mineral shipments.
[r] Purpose: Finance balance of payments deficit.

APPENDIX 5.7
Peruvian Debt and Debt Service, 1968–1978
(In Millions of Dollars)

	Public Debt[a]	Service Payments[b]	Service Ratio[c]
1968	1,100	146	14.6%
1969	1,132	126	11.8
1970	1,196	168	13.7
1971	1,309	209	19.6
1972	1,538	182	15.8
1973	2,542	398	29.6[d]
1974	3,545	432	23.5[d]
1975	3,990	436	25.8
1976	5,545	454	26.0
1977	6,406	652	30.5
1978	7,177	798 (1,048)[e]	42.0 (55.0)[e]

Sources: IDB, *Economic and Social Progress in Latin America, 1977* (1968–1971), *1979* (1972–1978); IMF, "Peru—Recent Economic Developments," August 30, 1978 (service payments and ratio for 1978 before and after refinancing).

[a] Disbursed and undisbursed public and publicly guaranteed debt.

[b] Interest plus amortization.

[c] Service payments/exports of goods and services.

[d] Includes prepayments.

[e] Figures in parentheses are those that would have been paid without the refinancing.

The Peruvian Military Government and the International Corporations

Laura Guasti

A major goal of Juan Velasco Alvarado's regime was to initiate autonomous economic development in Peru by placing greater control of economic activities and resources in the hands of national actors while promoting full-scale industrialization. Although the regime aimed to reduce the influence of international corporations on the economy, it only succeeded in changing which international corporate groups would have the most impact. The influence of extractive corporations with enclave orientations was reduced, but that of international manufacturers was maintained. The interactions between the government and international corporations also expanded the government's entrepreneurial role and its capital needs much further than the regime originally intended. As a result, international banks acquired direct influence on government policy, the economy, and the direction of future industrial growth.

Most chapters in this volume that discuss the economic aspects of the Peruvian experiment focus on broad structural constraints that impinged upon Peru before the military government as well as during it. Although these chapters each emphasize distinct restrictions, they share the general view that broader structural factors are the most important in explaining the outcomes of the military government's policies. In contrast, I maintain that specific constraints imposed on the military government by international actors in response to the regime's programs are as important as the broader structural elements. They limited the implementation of the regime's policies and thereby prevented the regime from achieving its goals of industrialization and autonomy. When the military government tried to counter the actions of the international corporations, the efforts brought the regime new difficulties.

THE VELASCO REGIME'S INDUSTRIALIZATION PROGRAM

Within its first year, the Velasco government initiated a series of policies that came to comprise a broad economic program. The goal of fully industrializing the economy required removal of structural obstacles to industrialization that had existed until 1968, and national economic autonomy meant that Peruvian manufacturers would have to be the chief beneficiaries of industrial growth in order to strengthen them as an industrial class.

The mining/petroleum sector was the key to the government's industrialization plans. Rapid growth in the production of raw materials and processed goods was of primary importance for two purposes: first, to provide increasing inputs for Peruvian manufacturing in the medium to long run; and second, to provide a rapidly growing volume of exports that, in the short to medium run, would earn the large amounts of capital and foreign exchange needed to pay for imported inputs as industry's rapid growth was achieved. A broad agrarian reform would redistribute income from landowners to the agrarian labor population in order to establish a wider, growing domestic market for industrial goods. The creation of the Andean regional market would provide a rapidly expanding market in the short to medium run to stimulate industrial expansion. While higher foreign exchange earnings and larger markets were being provided, industrial expansion into real intermediate and capital goods production and progressively higher domestic content in industrial production would be stimulated to establish linkages within industry and with mineral extraction. For all these changes to occur, however, the economic strength of international corporations in Peru, as well as their orientations and practices, had to be confronted and changed.

International corporations had established oligopolistic positions in Peru by 1968, particularly in two key sectors—mining/petroleum and manufacturing—thereby acquiring control over a significant proportion of the production in the two sectors. Foreign mining companies controlled 72 percent of Peruvian mining/metallurgic production, 90 percent of mineral refining, and 80 percent of mineral exports.[1] International oil corporations produced over 65 percent of Peruvian crude oil and accounted for over two thirds of existing refining capacity. In manufacturing, international corporations con-

[1] Two international mining corporations, the Southern Peru Copper Corporation and the Cerro de Pasco Company, accounted for over one third of all Peruvian exports.

trolled only 14 percent of the enterprises but accounted for 40 percent of the fixed assets and 44 percent of the value of production. Foreign firms, however, controlled over 50 percent of the production in fifteen manufacturing sectors, ten of which were intermediate and capital goods producing industries.[2] In addition, international banks, through branches and minority or majority ownership of Peruvian commercial banks, controlled over 70 percent of commercial banking.

The activities of international corporate subsidiaries in mining (the most important extractive activity) had traditionally posed two problems for industrial growth. First, as a result of the enclave focus of extraction, linkages between mining and manufacturing were absent. International companies supplied inputs to their subsidiaries from abroad and exported most of their mineral production.[3] This reduced the domestic market for manufacturing and because local primary materials were scarce, required industrial businesses to import them.[4]

Second, Peruvian industrial stability and growth had become directly tied to the performance of the major exports, especially mineral products, due to the high import content of manufactured goods. The foreign exchange that export products could earn was comparatively low, however, because minerals were exported chiefly as ore concentrates rather than refined metals. The reduced foreign exchange earnings from mining limited both imports of industrial inputs and capital available locally to expand mining production or related industries.[5]

---

[2] Eduardo Anaya Franco, *Imperialismo Industrialización y Transferencia de Tecnología en el Perú* (Lima: Editorial Horizonte, 1974), pp. 51–52. There were a total of sixty-two manufacturing sectors.

[3] The enclave focus in extraction is the production of raw materials primarily for export. It is characterized by integration with economic activities located overseas rather than with local economic activities. When carried out by international corporations, raw material production is integrated into the transnational corporate economy rather than the local economy.

Evidence indicates that at least one major international mining subsidiary, the Cerro de Pasco Company, purchased less than 50 percent of its inputs locally before 1968. See Janet C. Ballantyne, *The Political Economy of Peruvian Gran Minería,* Dissertation Series, no. 60 (Ithaca, N.Y.: Latin American Studies Program, Cornell University, 1975), p. 76.

[4] Domestic industrial consumption of total mining production was approximately 5 to 8 percent. Ibid., p. 163.

[5] Eighteen percent of copper exports were refined copper, 13 percent were ore concentrates, and 60 percent were blister copper. Fifty-four percent of lead exports and 76 percent of zinc exports were ored concentrates. The majority of iron

International corporate manufacturing subsidiaries operating in Peru's limited, slow-growing market also presented problems for continued industrial growth. Most were assemblage plants whose products had a high import content.[6] The subsidiaries' important position within the manufacturing sector had contributed to a high import content for Peruvian industry as a whole.[7] Moreover, the corporations established their strongest oligopoly positions in what are classified as intermediate and capital goods sectors.[8] Much of the production in these sectors, however, was in fact of consumer goods.[9] These characteristics contributed to the absence of linkages within industry.

In addition, the transfer of capital through royalties and services payments, overpricing of imports, and profit remissions channeled profits overseas to the parent corporations,[10] leaving relatively little

---

exports were in pellet form which, like blister copper and ore concentrates, was a semirefined stage of mineral processing. Ibid., pp. 78–79.

With the exception of iron, most of the ore concentrate production for export was connected to the overseas smelting and refining operations of parent corporations. Profits from refined metals were earned overseas by the parent corporations. In the case of iron, the exports from the subsidiary of the United States-based parent corporation were directed largely to firms in Japan that had helped finance the development of the mine and pelletizing plant in Peru. Thus, while profits from refining were not earned by the parent corporation, they were earned overseas.

[6] This was the result of operating within a limited Peruvian market and using relatively more advanced, frequently more capital-intensive technology.

[7] By 1968, the manufacturing sectors in which over half the production was controlled by international corporations had the highest imports of intermediate and capital goods inputs. See Anaya, *Imperialismo*, p. 94.

[8] The intermediate sector included paper, rubber products, chemical products, and basic metals. The capital goods sector included electrical and non-electrical machinery, metal products, and transport equipment. Sixty percent of international corporations active in Peruvian industry were located in these two sectors. Ibid., p. 36.

[9] In 1969, for example, foreign capital accounted for 73 percent of the fixed assets in the "diverse chemicals" sector, which is classified as an intermediate goods sector (sector 319 in the Standard International Industrial Classification system). In that year, the six products with the highest gross value of production were candles, toothpaste, detergents, bar soaps, phonographic goods, and pharmaceutical goods, all nondurable final consumer goods. For further detail, see Marie Beaulne, *Industrialización por Sustitución de Importaciones, Perú 1958–1969* (Lima: ESAN/Campodónico, 1975), particularly pp. 141–144. For details on the distribution of foreign capital by industrial sectors, see Anaya, *Imperialismo*.

[10] See Anaya, *Imperialismo*, p. 64, and Ronald Muller, "The Multinational Corporation and the Third World," in Charles K. Wilber, ed., *The Political Economy of Development and Underdevelopment* (New York: Random House, 1973), p. 133. It should be clear that the parent corporations transferred capital overseas because they perceived that investment in Peru's small and slow-growing market

available for reinvestment or new investment in Peruvian industry. The transfer of capital also increased pressures on the Peruvian balance of payments. Finally, the international corporations' oligopolistic market positions within the manufacturing sector would make them, rather than Peruvian industrialists, the beneficiaries of industrial growth, particularly with the expansion of the industrial base into intermediate and capital goods production.

Adequate information on international bank practices in Peru before 1968 has not appeared. From what is known generally about international bank practices overseas, however, it could be inferred that the credit controlled by international banks was directed preferentially to the international corporate clients of the parent banks, rather than to Peruvian manufacturers.[11] This would also imply that credit for industry was directed largely to financing production of final consumer goods.

To promote rapid and more balanced industrialization, the military government had to reorient the enclave focus of extraction and the concentration of industrial production in final consumer goods as well as redirect credit toward new manufacturing activities. To do this, and enable Peruvian manufacturers to benefit preferentially from the structural changes, the orientations or oligopolistic positions of the international corporations had to be changed. That the government did not intend to eliminate international corporate activities in the key sectors was clear not only in its original policies but also in its first National Development Plan, for 1971–1975, which called for $700 million in new investments from international firms in manufacturing and extraction. The regime instead sought to subordinate

---

would yield lower rates of return than investment opportunities outside Peru that were available to the parent corporations, though not to Peruvian-owned enterprises.

[11] International banks expanded overseas to follow their major corporate clients. The tendency has been for overseas international bank branches and affiliates to lend preferentially to the overseas subsidiaries of their major clients. One reason for this is that international corporations are perceived as better lending risks compared with local enterprises, particularly in less-developed countries. A second reason is that the local bank affiliates or branches prefer to continue servicing the local subsidiaries of major corporate clients rather than competitor local enterprises in order to retain the global business of the parent banks' clients. See Julien-Pierre Koszul, "American Banks in Europe," in Charles Kindleberger, ed., *The International Corporation* (Cambridge: MIT Press, 1970), pp. 273–289; Ronald Muller, "Poverty is the Product," *Foreign Policy,* no. 13 (Winter 1973–1974), pp. 71–102; and Muller, "The Multinational Corporation," pp. 129–130. When international banks were in partnership with Peruvian bankers, credit also would be directed to the manifold activities of the Peruvian agroexporters.

international corporate activities to the national goal of rapid autonomous industrialization.

Specifically, the Velasco government chose to modify international corporate practices by: (1) supervising or taking over important managerial functions of international mining/petroleum corporations; (2) limiting the growth of international manufacturing corporations, transferring control of managerial functions and half of subsidiary ownership to Peruvian entrepreneurs, and controlling technology contract practices; and (3) reducing and limiting international banks' access to domestic savings and their control over the distribution of credit.

There are several indications that the government did not see that these policies would have major negative consequences for international corporations or would seriously impair cooperation between the government and the corporations. In 1969, Velasco said: "Latin American development needs foreign capital. . . . It also is advantageous to them [the foreign investors] to come. There is, in consequence, reciprocal accommodation that should be clearly and justly altered for the benefit of both sides."[12] A year later, he said: "it will be equally important to accord treatment to possible foreign investment that, without ignoring their rights, subordinates them to the interests of the member countries so that they constitute a factor of support to independent development."[13] Moreover, the regime considered it feasible to plan for $700 million in additional foreign investments during the first five years that the policies were in force.

The route chosen by the government represented, however, a direct challenge to major prerogatives and motivations of the international corporations; it was an attempt to take over managerial control, limit the corporations' economic strength and market positions, and reduce the benefits the corporations accrued from their activities. The corporations developed various responses to this challenge, according to the type of economic activity each engaged in and its corporate orientations and needs.

DIFFERENCES IN INTERNATIONAL CORPORATE ORIENTATIONS

The interests and requirements of international corporations involved in manufacturing are different from those involved in extraction. In-

[12] General Juan Velasco Alvarado, Independence Day speech, July 28, 1969, in *Velasco: La Voz de la Revolución,* 2 vols. (Lima: Ediciones Participación, Oficina Nacional de Difusión de Sinamos, 1972), 1:64–65.

[13] Velasco, Independence Day speech, July 28, 1970. Ibid., 1:233.

ternational extractive corporations are interested in Third World nations as raw material sources, but not as major markets for their refined products. International manufacturing firms, in contrast, do seek markets in the Third World. Their continued worldwide expansion is directly connected to the growth of industries and markets in countries in which the corporations already manufacture or plan to enter to acquire new markets.

As a result, international extractive companies are more likely to resist changes in a Third World economy that aim to remove obstacles to industrialization created by the existing structure of export extraction. The prospect of industrialization presents uncertain and indirect future corporate benefits but direct immediate costs. International manufacturing corporations, on the other hand, are more likely to support structural changes in the economy because of the benefits that industrialization and the creation of larger markets could provide. Foreign manufacturing firms are apt to oppose efforts to achieve *autonomous* industrialization or to create a strong, indigenous industrial class, however. Such industrialization would reduce the benefits of industrial and market growth available to foreign manufacturers and create new competitors in the local market.

International banks are in a pivotal position with regard to the two types of international corporations, because the banks provide financing to both. There is a direct connection between the global growth of international corporations and that of international banks. Moreover, through interlocking directorates and holdings of corporate stock, international banks can influence corporate policies. The role of the international banks, therefore, can become critical when differences of interest between the two types of international corporation are aggravated by industrialization efforts in a Third World nation. In addition, international banks can play an independent role in industrialization by lending directly to governments.[14]

Policy and Corporate Response in the Mining/Petroleum Sector

The original policies of the Velasco regime established an important entrepreneurial role for the government in mining and petroleum. Service contracts with international oil companies required the corporations to cover the costs of exploration and development of de-

[14] The direct role of the banks was facilitated in the 1970s by several factors, including the growing availability of petrodollars to the banks for recycling to Third World nations. For further detail, see Chapter 5 in this volume, by Barbara Stallings.

posits and to divide the petroleum extracted with the state enterprise, Petroperú, according to sharing formulas that ranged from 50/50 to 44/56. Petroperú was responsible for the marketing of its share of the petroleum and for the exploration and development of the deposits it retained.

Eighteen oil corporations agreed to operate in Peru under the service contracts. In December 1975, however, thirteen of the companies claimed they had failed to find oil, terminated their contracts, and abandoned their concessions. At the time, the government was facing an increasingly serious balance-of-payments deficit and an approaching foreign exchange reserve deficit. The government needed renewed inflows of investment capital and increased oil production to provide higher foreign exchange earnings (as well as to satisfy more of the domestic demand for oil in the face of rising world prices). Within six months after the oil corporations left, the government announced that new, less-restrictive oil exploration contracts would be issued.[15]

Under the Mining Law of April 1970 (amplified in 1971 by the General Mining Law), the right to refine copper and market all minerals was reserved exclusively for the new state enterprise, Mineroperú. The rights to refine other minerals were to be issued as government concessions. Mining rights were to be granted under five-year concession contracts, and the government retained the option to take control of the mines at the expiration of the contracts. The government also had the responsibility to set rapid exploration and development schedules for mineral deposit concessions and mandatory investment and production levels for all mining activities. In addition, the existing mineral depletion allowance was replaced by a reinvestment allowance that set an upper limit to the amount of tax-free reinvestment capital available to mining enterprises.

The legislation thus authorized the government to assume central managerial functions that previously had enabled parent corporations to control and coordinate corporate activities, including the optimal distribution of production levels among various mineral sources. The reinvestment allowance made it necessary for subsidiaries that wanted to carry out major expansion programs to borrow from their parent corporations or from other external sources, rather than rely solely on capital earned in Peru. The five-year concession limit threatened the long-term security of investment benefits. And most important, the new terms of operation meant that the government would determine the rate of corporate growth.

[15] *Washington Post,* August 29, 1976.

The international mining corporations responded to the government's policies in three ways, two of which were essentially to abandon mining in Peru. First, in the face of government deadlines in 1970 to begin the exploration and development of deposits, three of the five international corporations that held unworked mineral concessions relinquished them to the government.[16]

Second, two of the three largest international mining corporations, the Cerro de Pasco Company and the Marcona Mining Company, chose to abandon their mining and processing activities. Within three years of the issuance of the original policies, both began negotiations to sell their subsidiaries to the government because of the specific impact the Velasco policies had on their operations. Cerro used less-advanced mining technology than the other major international mining corporations in Peru; during the 1960s, its profits had fallen by 50 percent. From about 1968 onward, it did not make replacement investments in its mining facilities or new investments, and its fixed assets depreciated rapidly.[17] By the end of the decade, Cerro's remaining major advantage in mining was its ownership of the sole Peruvian copper refinery. The government's obligatory investment schedules were directly contrary to Cerro's investment decisions, and the government's monopolization of copper refining threatened Cerro's only advantage in extraction. Marcona, on the other hand, had by 1968 diversified its activities into the more profitable area of shipping, while in 1971 it experienced losses in its iron mining activities. Marcona initially accepted the government's policies in 1970 in order to carry out a previously planned expansion of iron production, but within three years, it decided that further investment in iron mining was not warranted. In both cases, the government's policies to promote rapid growth in mining would force the corporations to invest in the activities they considered less profitable.

It should be pointed out that during the first five years of the Velasco regime only one international extractive enterprise, the International Petroleum Company, had been expropriated. Statements by Velasco and the original policies for the mining sector indicated that the government did not intend to jeopardize the ownership of international mining subsidiaries. During the protracted negotiations

[16] The American Smelting and Refining Company relinquished the Michiquillay concession, Anaconda the Cerro Verde deposit, and Cerro de Pasco gave up four concessions. Homestead Mining retained the Madrigal concession and Southern kept Cuajone but relinquished Quellaveco.

[17] Felipe Portocarrero, "El Gobierno Militar y el Capital Imperialista," *Cuadernos de Sociedad y Política* 1, no. 1 (1976), pp. 28–29.

for the sale of the subsidiaries, however, Cerro and the government could not reach agreement on the form of ownership transfer or the purchase price, while Marcona engaged in illegal behavior perceived as a direct challenge to the government's legal sovereignty.[18] This led the military government to choose to expropriate them, indicating in the Cerro case reluctance, and in the Marcona case, refusal to pay compensation. Two state enterprises were created to operate the expropriated businesses.

The third response to the regime's mining policies was made by the remaining major international mining corporation in Peru, the Southern Peru Copper Corporation. It chose to retain its existing mine and one of its mineral concessions but successfully pressured for exemptions from important aspects of the government's program. Unlike the other mining corporations, Southern had neither diversified nor experienced losses in its mining activities. As one of the most technologically advanced of the international mining companies, its mining activities had proved very profitable. Even prior to 1968, it had expressed interest in developing another Peruvian mineral concession. Southern, however, wished to operate under the old terms. Aided by pressure from international lending agencies and banks (applied during the renegotiation of the external debt in 1969[19]), Southern obtained a contract that freed its concession from some of the new government measures issued four months later, including the reinvestment allowance.[20]

[18] At the time of the Marcona expropriation the government charged the company with tax evasion, hidden profits, and other violations. On the Cerro negotiations, see Elizabeth Dasso, "Sector Minero," in Henry Pease García, et al., *Realidad Social Peruana* (Lima: Universidad Católica, Estudios Generales, Letras, 1974), pp. 31–33.

[19] See the account by Shane Hunt, "Direct Foreign Investment in Peru: New Rules for an Old Game," in Abraham F. Lowenthal, ed., *The Peruvian Experiment: Continuity and Change under Military Rule* (Princeton: Princeton University Press, 1975), p. 327.

[20] It is clear that when the Cuajone contract was signed with Southern at the end of 1969, the major outlines of the changes for the mining sector had already been established. Within the contract, the government anticipated some of the changes that would be made with the promulgation of the Ley Normativa de la Industria Minera in April 1970. The stipulation that the government would control the marketing and refining of Cuajone copper, and a mandatory investment and development schedule were included in the contract. Southern would continue to use the depreciation allowance rather than the reinvestment deduction, however, and there was no provision for the possible reversion of the mine to the government after recovery of the initial investment. When the Ley Normativa was issued, the government simultaneously issued a resolution that exempted the Cuajone contract from the requirement to adopt the reinvestment deduction. See

The cumulative effect of the international corporations' responses to the Velasco regime's policies and the government's countermeasures was that the government expanded its entrepreneurial role considerably beyond the level originally planned and became the primary mining/petroleum entrepreneur. The government took over most of the investment and managerial responsibilities of the international extractive corporations, especially in mining, and the operation of a number of major mines, most existing oil fields, and all mineral and oil refineries. Through state enterprises, the government also took control of basic industries, allowing it to directly provide inputs to manufacturing. Once it assumed entrepreneurial control, the government initiated several projects in mining and basic industry in an attempt to achieve the desired growth in production.[21]

Dolph W. Zink, *The Political Risks for Multinational Enterprises in Developing Countries with a Case Study of Peru* (New York: Praeger Publishers, 1973), p. 88. It should also be noted that the Cerro Corporation, parent of the Cerro de Pasco Company, was a minority owner of Southern with 22.3 percent of the stock. (The majority owner, the American Smelting and Refining Company, held 51.5 percent, while Phelps Dodge and the Newmont Mining Corporation held 16 percent and 10.2 percent, respectively.) The fact that the Cerro Corporation held an interest in the international mining subsidiary that was the most technologically advanced and profitable in Peru, with plans for expansion, may help explain Cerro's willingness to give up its wholly-owned Peruvian subsidiary. The circumstance may also throw some light on the Peruvian government's ultimate willingness to pay Cerro compensation for its expropriated subsidiary. On the latter, see footnote 50, this chapter.

[21] The major basic industries under state control were steel, under the control of Siderperú, the state enterprise created prior to the military government; paper and pulp, which the government acquired through the expropriation of the W. R. Grace holdings under the agrarian reform; and cement. The state also owned enterprises that produced chemicals, industrial alcohol, fertilizer, and salt.

Mineroperú and Petroperú developed projects or initiated production in basic industry as well as in raw material production and refining. Mineroperú developed the Cerro Verde copper deposit and had thirteen other copper projects in various stages of planning. In addition to a new zinc refinery that was in the planning stages, Mineroperú constructed the Ilo copper refinery, which began operations in 1975, to process the raw materials from Southern's Toquepala mine and the Cuajone and Cerro Verde mines when they came on stream. Ilo was planned as the base for a copper complex to be constructed in conjunction with Induperú, the state industrial management corporation. The complex would involve basic industries producing copper inputs for the manufacturing sector. Mineroperú also had a carbon project underway and was carrying out feasibility studies for the development of a synthetic fertilizer complex at Bayovar based on phosphates and potassium salts.

Petroperú initiated the construction of an oil pipeline from the Amazon oil zone to Bayovar, where the enterprise intended to build a refinery as the base for

The increased entrepreneurial role of the state proved costly, how-ever. Expansion of mining production was delayed as the government negotiated to acquire technical and other expertise and as it experienced difficulty in acquiring financing.[22] The delays greatly slowed the achievement of the regime's industrialization goals and hampered its ability to earn the larger amounts of foreign exchange anticipated for this period. The economy was left vulnerable to the impact of the 1973 oil price rises and, more importantly, to the price inflation and volume increase in other imports. The expansion of the state entrepreneurial role also demanded larger amounts of capital, much more than originally planned, and the regime was forced to resort to external borrowing for this additional capital.[23] This meant that the regime had to maintain a favorable relationship with international lending agencies and international banks.[24] As will be seen, this was to make the military government's national policy vulnerable to the pressures and influence of international banks.

Policy and Corporate Response in the Manufacturing Sector

In contrast to the mining/petroleum policies, the policies for the manufacturing sector, established in the late 1960s and early 1970s, did not create an important entrepreneurial role for the government. The goal was to limit the growth of international corporations in the

---

a petrochemicals complex that was in the planning stages. In basic industry, Petroperú also built and operated three plants producing carbon black, solvents, and urea. Siderperú initiated a project to quintuple steel production at its existing plant and to construct a second steel plan at Nazca.

[22] Cerro Verde, the first and to date only state-developed mine to begin production, came on stream three years later than the government originally planned.

[23] The government had some success in attracting corporations and consulting firms that had not previously been active in the sector through contract arrangements. It was able to initiate the development of the Cerro Verde copper deposit under Mineroperú's control via a British/Canadian consortium. With the projects initiated in steel production, copper and zinc refining, and the development of a petrochemicals industry, the government operated via consulting arrangements or by contracting out projects. In no case through 1976, however, did the government succeed in getting an international corporation or investment group to enter as a partner in a mining/metallurgy venture in order to share the investment burden. All financial assistance received for the government's projects was in the form of external credits and loans that would have to be repaid.

[24] International credits to the Peruvian government had been restricted soon after the military took control in 1968 and expropriated the International Petroleum Company.

Peruvian and Andean markets in order to direct the benefits of industrial expansion to Peruvian industrialists. The government sought to do this by creating the fade-out joint venture, which required all international corporations manufacturing in Peru to reduce ownership in their Peruvian subsidiaries to 49 percent or less within fifteen years.[25] The government also established measures to control transfer prices, royalty rates, and technology contract practices between parent corporations and their subsidiaries or Peruvian manufacturers.[26] Further, all industrial enterprises, including corporate subsidiaries, were required to create an industrial community that would receive 25 percent of net profits annually. Fifteen percent of net profits were to be reinvested in the enterprise until the industrial community owned half the firm's stock.[27]

The Velasco regime, therefore, did not challenge international manufacturing corporations in the same way in which it challenged international extractive corporations. International manufacturers were allowed to exercise basic management prerogatives for the time being; the government did not seek to replace international manufacturers within industry. Nevertheless, the policies did threaten corporate managerial control and long-term growth. Moreover, they directly threatened corporate ownership. The most important means the government employed for limiting international manufacturers' influence in Peru was the fade-out joint venture.

[25] Through pressure from the Peruvian government, the fade-out joint venture also was included in the code governing the Andean regional market.

[26] These measures, which were quite vague, were included in the General Industrial Law. Transfer pricing, left to parent corporation determination, is an important means to shift capital out of subsidiaries in the form of undeclared profits. Overpricing of subsidiary imports serves to lessen tax payments to host governments and by-pass profit remission restrictions, in addition to raising the final cost of subsidiary products to the consumer. Technology contracts with subsidiaries and licensing contracts with local manufacturers frequently contain clauses requiring the purchase (import) of intermediate and capital goods inputs from the parent corporation. Many also specifically prohibit, limit, or control the use of locally produced inputs. In addition, it is common for such contracts to prohibit or limit export of the products manufactured by the subsidiaries or local license holders. On the overpricing of imports, see Constantine Vaitsos, "Comercialización de Tecnología en el Pacto Andino," *América-Problema* 6 (Lima: Instituto de Estudios Peruanos, 1973):65–68; and Muller, "The Multinational Corporation," p. 133. On technology contracts, see Vaitsos, "Comercialización," especially pp. 60–78.

[27] The industrial community was composed of all permanent workers in an enterprise, including white-collar employees and management. The remaining 10 percent of net profits were to be distributed annually to the industrial community members.

Through forced divestiture, the fade-out venture would undermine the corporations' control over internal decision making and would deny them the long-term benefits of their investments. It would restrict the corporations' future growth in the Peruvian and Andean markets and force them to cede half their market positions and, ostensibly, their managerial control to Peruvian industrialists. At the same time, controls on technology contracts and other activities would challenge corporate growth strategies and decision-making prerogatives, including the freedom to invest capital in areas of rapid growth within the corporate network.

The industrial community presented a somewhat different problem. The obligatory transfer of half ownership to the industrial community and mandatory 51 percent divestment in fifteen years appeared to require the international corporations to divest to a single partner. This in turn, might make retention of managerial control under 49 percent ownership more difficult.[28] And the industrial community was a more immediate problem. Most fade-out contracts were signed by 1974, but some 2,900 industrial communities were in existence by 1971. The majority of these were located in medium- and large-sized enterprises, which included the international corporate subsidiaries.[29] Nevertheless, international manufacturing corporations could avoid the potential difficulties of enterprise co-ownership with their workers by various means, including the reduction of declared net profits.

In the long run, the fade-out venture was the more serious threat to corporate prerogatives and activities. If the fade-out policies were implemented, there would be no obvious ways to circumvent forced divestiture and its attendant consequences (with the possible exception of transferring ownership to a large number of Peruvian entrepreneurs). Yet in contrast to the international extractive corporations, which were not originally threatened with loss of ownership, the international manufacturers did not respond to the government's policies by abandoning their Peruvian activities. Their response was to effect a holding action until the strength of the government's challenges could be ascertained or diminished.

Following the promulgation of the General Industrial Law in 1970,

[28] Alfred Stepan argues that this was the important difficulty for international corporations created by the two policies in conjunction. See Alfred Stepan, *The State and Society: Peru in Comparative Perspective* (Princeton: Princeton University Press, 1978), pp. 275–276.

[29] Ministerio de Industria y Turismo, Oficina de Comunidades Laborales, *Estadística de Comunidades Industriales* (Lima: n.d.), pp. 9, 88.

TABLE 6.1
Foreign Capital Invested in the Peruvian Industrial Sector[a]

	1971	1972	1973	% change 1971–72	% change 1972–73
		In Thousands of Soles			
Consumer goods industries	3,861,990	3,862,141	3,968,742	.0039%	2.76%
Intermediate goods industries	6,936,060	7,193,070	7,347,146	3.7	2.1
Capital goods industries	1,294,251	1,400,860	1,509,260	8.2	7.7
Total	12,092,301	12,456,071	12,825,148	3.0	2.96

Source: Ministerio de Industria y Turismo, Oficina de Estadística, *El Capital Extranjero en el Sector Industrial* (Lima, n.d.).

[a] Excludes the fishmeal industry.

international manufacturing corporations maintained generally low levels of new investment in Peru and limited themselves to reinvestment in existing plant and stock (see Table 6.1).[30] This occurred in the face of the strong incentives to invest in priority industrial areas offered by the government. Most of the international corporate investment was directed to the lower or nonpriority industrial areas of the government's program.[31]

The Velasco regime continued to want international corporate investment in priority industrial areas, however, and attempted to attract new international corporations to Peruvian industry within the

[30] The higher growth rate of foreign capital invested in the capital goods industries might have indicated that international corporations were responding favorably to government policies and incentives by investing in "first priority" industries. The capital goods classification included the production of many durable consumer goods, however; this was especially characteristic of the capital goods industries in which international corporations predominated. FitzGerald has observed that most of the rapid growth in the Peruvian capital goods industries between 1969 and 1973 appears to have been the growth in production of household equipment. E.V.K. FitzGerald, *The State and Economic Development: Peru since 1968* (Cambridge: Cambridge University Press, 1976), p. 63.

[31] In 1972, 29 percent of the increase in international manufacturing investment went into the capital goods sector, while 70 percent went into the intermediate goods sector and 1 percent into the consumer goods sector. In 1973, again only 29 percent of the increase went into capital goods, while 42 percent went into intermediate goods and 29 percent into consumer goods. As a result, the distribution of international manufacturing investments in Peruvian industry was 12 percent in capital goods in 1973, versus 11 percent in 1971, 57.2 percent in intermediate goods versus 57.4 percent in 1971, and 31 percent in consumer goods versus 32 percent in 1971. Ministerio de Industria y Turismo, Oficina de Estadística, *El Capital Extranjero en el Sector Industrial* (Lima: n.d.), p. 31. See also FitzGerald, *The State and Economic Development: Peru since 1968*, p. 74.

context of mandatory divestment in fifteen years. The resolution of this inconsistency between government policy and corporate motivations and interests was sought through special joint ventures involving the government and international firms. It was largely within the special advantages of this type of enterprise that new international corporations entered Peruvian industry in high priority areas.

Three special joint ventures were formed between the government and international corporations from 1968 to 1976: Bayer Industrial with Bayer, Tractores Andinos with Massey Ferguson, and Motores Diesel with Volvo-Perkins. In all three cases, the special joint-venture status gave the international corporate partners: (1) access to the fast-growing, newly opening Andean regional market on a monopolistic or quasi-monopolistic basis; (2) the most generous tax and financial terms available under the government's industrial policies, thus yielding higher returns on investment; and (3) a long-term guarantee that the ventures' high priority status and special benefits would continue, because state participation gave the government a direct stake in the success and growth of these enterprises. All were special advantages not provided to international corporations already manufacturing within Peru or to Peruvian industrialists. Nevertheless, of the sixteen joint-venture projects the regime outlined between 1972 and 1976, only three new corporate investments in high priority areas were acquired.[32]

Consequently, the Velasco regime increasingly assumed direct responsibility for industrial investment through the state enterprises that controlled basic industries as well as through the creation of state businesses and special joint ventures to establish new areas of industrial activity. These expanded state activities also added to the government's capital requirements within the industrialization program. In addition, the fade-out ventures were not implemented rapidly

---

[32] The other important area of government policy that involved international manufacturing corporations was the government's reorganization of the automotive industry. The first round of the reorganization resulted in the closing down of eight of the thirteen international subsidiaries that operated in the industry. The second round sought to separate auto, light truck, and heavy truck production and apportion each on a monopoly or semimonopoly basis among four of the remaining five international subsidiaries. As of mid-1975, this policy had not been implemented successfully. The international subsidiary chosen to have most of the passenger car market (Toyota) only held 21 percent of the market, while the subsidiary that continued with the largest market share (Chrysler, with 31 percent) officially had been eliminated from that market. In addition, the original policies for a one-year fade-out venture and the rapid substitution of domestic content in the industry were repeatedly lowered and/or postponed. On the distribution of the passenger car market, see La Prensa, August 2, 1975, pp. 10, 13.

during this period, and estimates vary on the extent to which transfer prices, royalty rates, and technology contracts were effectively regulated.[33] As a result, the government did not succeed in changing the ownership pattern in the industrial sector, controlling or changing international corporate practices, or achieving rapid real growth by privately owned industry in high priority areas.

In sum, international corporations in extraction and manufacturing had different responses to the military government's challenges to their production orientations and interests. Whereas most of the foreign extractive corporations in Peru, particularly the mining companies, abandoned their Peruvian raw material sources, the international manufacturing corporations did not leave their Peruvian and Andean markets. Rather than leave Peru, the manufacturers reduced their investments to minimum levels until more advantageous new policies were forthcoming. As a result of the different responses, the government acquired direct control of Peruvian mining/metallurgic output and direction of growth, but not direct control over final industrial output or the direction of industrial growth. Peruvian manufacturers also did not acquire predominant control within industry. The international extractors' and manufacturers' responses in combination, however, resulted in the state gaining a much wider entrepreneurial role and, with it, higher capital requirements to carry out the industrialization policies than it had originally anticipated. The evolution of the industrialization policies greatly increased the public external debt, which gave international banks important and direct impact on major government policies, on the condition of the economy, and on the shape of further industrial growth.

The Industrial Program and International Banks

The regime sought to base its ability to direct Peruvian industrialization upon the financial sector. By displacing the international banks as controlling shareholders in the major Peruvian banks and placing

[33] It was not until four and a half years after the policy was issued that most international corporations had signed the fade-out contracts. It is not clear what difficulties within the government itself led to the delay in issuing the guidelines and deadlines for the contracts. Stanley F. Rose, *Business Operations in Peru* (Washington, D.C.: Bureau of National Affairs, Tax Management Foreign Income, #329, 1975), pp. 26–27, cited in Stepan, *The State and Society*, p. 272.

The more detailed analyses available indicate that few changes in or limitations on corporate practices in transfer pricing, royalty rates, and technology contracts occurred. See the studies cited in Anaya, *Imperialismo*, pp. 58, 68, 94, and the contradictory accounts in Anaya, pp. 94–95, and FitzGerald, *The State and Economic Development: Peru since 1968*, p. 297.

sharp restrictions on the growth of local branches, the government became the major controller of credit distribution in Peru.[34] The original capital requirements set by the industrialization policies were high, however, and were increased by international corporate responses to the policies. The result was a new and greatly expanded role of international banks as major direct lenders to the government.

The 1971–1975 National Development Plan, issued in 1970, before the impact of international corporate responses was felt, called for the government's share of domestic investment to increase 56 percent by 1975.[35] Industrialization goals stated in the plan required $1.1 billion in international financing between 1971 and 1975, due to the government's narrow resource base.[36] International financing also was necessary to avoid deterioration in the balance of payments by offsetting the $7.5 billion in imports that the plan required over the five-year period.[37]

One of the most important effects of the industrialization program's high external financing requirement was the change in the way international capital was to enter the economy. The larger portion of international capital was to enter via international credits and loans rather than via direct corporate investment. The anticipated amount of international financing was nearly twice that of new international investment capital to be acquired between 1971 and 1975. As a result, the government would become an intermediary between international capital and Peruvian economic activites, enabling it to direct the major portion of external capital into priority production areas and to select Peruvian recipients.

[34] A government banking network centered in the Banco de la Nación was created and given control over more than half of domestic credit. International bank branches' access to domestic savings was restricted and limits were set on the amount branches could borrow from Peruvian banks. The creation of new branches was prohibited. Jane S. Jacquette, "Revolution by Fiat: The Context of Policy-Making in Peru," *Western Political Quarterly* 25, no. 4 (December 1972), p. 655.

[35] Investment by state enterprises was to increase sixfold. Public investment was slated particularly for the expansion projects in mining and basic industry. In addition, the government would have to bear the costs of carrying out the agrarian reform and acquiring basic industries. Instituto Nacional de Planificación, *Plan Nacional de Desarrollo, 1971–1975* (Lima, 1970), p. 23.

[36] In mining alone, the government required $421 million in international loans to provide 36 percent of forecasted investment. For further discussion of the government's narrow resource base, see E.V.K. FitzGerald, "The Political Economy of State Capitalism," Chapter 3 of this volume.

[37] Robert E. Klitgaard, "Observations on the Peruvian National Plan for Development, 1971–1975," *Inter-American Economic Affairs* 25, no. 3 (Winter 1971), p. 18.

TABLE 6.2
Movement of Foreign Private Capital, 1971–1974
(In Millions of Dollars)

	1971	1972	1973	1974	1971–74
Financial services[a]	−78	−70	−115	−114	−377
Long-term capital[b]	−43	−5	70	202	224
Net movement	−121	−75	−45	88	−153

Source: Banco Central de Reserva, *Cuentas Nacionales del Perú, 1960–1974*.

[a] Includes interest, profit remissions, dividends, and undistributed profits.

[b] Includes direct investment and private loans. Undistributed profits were counted as an outflow in the financial services account and an inflow in the long-term capital account.

The negative responses of the international corporations to the regime's industrialization program, however, greatly increased the importance of international financing. The extensive new investments by foreign corporations anticipated in the development plan failed to materialize; instead, there was a net outflow of capital from the economy in the first four years of the plan (see Table 6.2). Government investment had to increase substantially to offset the loss and stagnation of corporate investment.[38]

The failure of international corporations to make new investments accelerated the switch to international banks as the predominant source of capital. By 1974, the government was providing nearly seven times the net capital inflows into the economy that international corporations were providing (see Table 6.3). Of equal importance, the regime's unwillingness to abandon its industrialization goals, despite the failure of international firms to provide needed external capital in the government-designated economic areas, led to an increase in the external debt between 1971 and 1975 that was more than twice as high as originally intended ($2.9 billion instead of $1.1 billion). The overextension in public sector debt was one of the two preconditions for an important shift in government bargaining power vis-à-vis international banks. The second precondition was that during the same period the government assumed a central position within the economy.

By 1976, state enterprises accounted for 52 percent of the added value of production in the major economic sectors and over a quarter of all domestic production. The government was responsible for nine

[38] This also occurred to a lesser extent as a result of the generally low level of new investment by Peruvian entrepreneurs. For a discussion of the interaction between the Velasco government and Peruvian entrepreneurs, see Laura Guasti, "State-Capital Relationships in the Context of Industrialization, Peru 1968–1976" (Doctoral dissertation, University of Wisconsin, 1977), chapters 5, 8, and 9.

TABLE 6.3
External Capital Movements, 1969–1974
(In Millions of Dollars)

	1969	1970	1971	1972	1973	1974
Foreign private capital						
Financial services[a]	−147	−117	−78	−70	−115	−114
Long-term capital[b]	20	−77	−43	−5	70	202
Net movement	−127	−194	−121	−75	−45	88
State capital						
Financial services[c]	−37	−31	−48	−51	−66	−104
Long-term capital	124	101	15	116	314	693
Net movement	87	70	−33	65	248	589

Source: Banco Central de Reserva, *Cuentas Nacionales del Perú, 1960–1974.*

[a] See Table 6.2.

[b] See Table 6.2.

[c] Includes interest on public external loans.

tenths of the exports, half of the imports, and more than half of the investments. It was the major entrepreneur in mining, fishing, basic industry, and the international marketing of essential products, including food.[39] In addition, the state was responsible for the most important new investments in mineral extraction and manufacturing.

The government's great need for international financing made it directly reliant on international banks. By 1973, a rapidly rising government deficit was 56 percent financed by international financial sources.[40] During 1974 and 1975, after the Greene Agreement fully reestablished Peru's credit standing, the government nearly doubled its debt to international lending institutions (both multilateral agencies and private banks).[41] The public external debt grew from $2.4 billion in 1973 to $4.0 billion at the end of 1975. The larger result of this situation, in combination with the government's important entrepreneurial role and its greatly expanded control over the economy, was that the Peruvian economy, as well as the direction, quality, and pace of industrial growth, came to rely significantly on international banks.

This was a major qualitative change in the reliance of the government and economy on international actors. Within the new context, the recession that struck Peru with such severity in 1975–1976 caused

[39] FitzGerald, *The State and Economic Development: Peru since 1968,* pp. 35, 95, 117; and Dr. Luis Barúa Castaneda, Ministro de Economía y Finanzas, televised speech, January 17, 1976.

[40] InterAmerican Development Bank, *Economic and Social Progress in Latin America,* Annual Report (Washington, D.C., 1974), p. 395.

[41] For details of the agreement, see footnote 50, this chapter.

a quantitative change, greatly magnifying the degree to which the government and economy relied on international banks' willingness to provide capital. In these first two years of the recession, during which the economy needed increasingly higher inflows of capital, international banks, with their direct and indirect ties to international corporations in both mineral extraction and manufacturing, took advantage of the opportunity to modify industrialization policies that had sought to restructure international corporate positions within the Peruvian economy.

In 1973, Peru began to experience the effects of the inflation occurring in the industrialized economies from which it imported industrial inputs and food. Prices for imported goods increased 16 percent that year, resulting in a 23 percent increase in the import account, despite an increase in real terms of less than 7 percent.[42] The price increase was reflected in the domestic inflation rate, which reached 13.4 percent in 1973, compared with an annual average rate of 5.1 percent between 1970 and 1972. Exports, however, were growing more slowly. In 1973, they increased in value by 18 percent. The following year, imports exceeded exports by $403 million; imports rose 85 percent, exports only 35 percent. In 1975, the trade deficit reached $1.1 billion, as imports grew by 35 percent and exports fell 7 percent in value.[43]

By the end of 1975, foreign exchange reserves were reduced to $100 million, down from more than $600 million in 1974. By July 1976, the reserves reached a $500 million deficit, undermining Peru's ability to pay for its industrial and food imports. The means perceived to resolve the crisis in the balance of payments and in the recessionary economy was to gain major new inflows of international capital through loans and direct investments.

At the beginning of 1976, when the foreign exchange reserves still had a small positive balance but were rapidly heading toward deficit, the government began to negotiate with an international bank consortium for a major loan to cover the anticipated deficit and meet the government's external debt obligations. Negotiations continued until the foreign exchange reserves reached the $500 million deficit. At that

[42] The sharp rise in the import account was almost three times the average annual growth rate of imports between 1970 and 1972. InterAmerican Development Bank, *Economic and Social Progress,* pp. 390, 398.

[43] *Marka,* January 8, 1976. At this time, oil imports did not account for a large proportion of the total value of imports. In 1974, oil imports came to $175 million and accounted for only 7 percent of the import bill. The growth in total imports occurred despite the import quotas established by the government in 1974.

point, the consortium "bailed out" the government by agreeing to a $240 million loan.

The bank consortium made the loan contingent, however, on the settlement of a compensation agreement with the Marcona Mining Company for its iron mines expropriated a year earlier by the Velasco regime.[44] At that time, the regime had indicated it would not pay compensation because of backlogs of unpaid taxes and tax fraud. Marcona had wanted to divest itself of the iron mines but retain control of a marketing and transportation monopoly for Peruvian iron ore exports.[45] As part of the loan provisions, the government agreed to a $68 million payment to Marcona and recognized the company's exclusive right to market and transport Peruvian iron ore exports.[46]

Additionally, changes in government policies were required by the consortium, giving the banks the role of overseeing a stabilization program for the Peruvian economy. The changes included a devaluation of the Peruvian currency, a reduction in the growth of the state's entrepreneurial role, and a relaxation of the rules for international corporate investment in Peruvian manufacturing.[47] In mid-1976, the military government announced that: it had devalued the Peruvian currency by 44 percent; it would reduce the activities of state enterprises by $149 million, including a 25 percent reduction in capital goods expenditures; and it would support the easing of the Andean Code restrictions on international corporate investments in manufacturing within Peru and the Andean market.[48] Simultaneously, the remaining members of the Velasco government, who had been major promoters of the industrialization program, were maneuvered out of the cabinet and into retirement.[49]

The $240 million loan was formally agreed to a month later. Part of the loan was to be disbursed immediately and the remainder at the end of the year, in order for the banks to ascertain if policy changes were being carried out. In November, the Industrial Community Law also was changed to reduce the maximum ownership share of the in-

[44] See *Marka*, May 27, 1976; and *Washington Post*, August 29, 1976.

[45] For an extended discussion of this conflict, see Guasti, "State-Capital Relationships," chapter 4.

[46] The $68 million payment in part would come out of the $240 million loan from the international banks. *Washington Post*, August 29, 1976; and *New York Times*, October 18, 1976.

[47] *Marka*, May 27 and June 17, 1976.

[48] *La Prensa*, June 30, July 1, and July 26, 1976. The Andean Pact restrictions included the fade-out joint venture and limitations on profit remissions.

[49] Velasco had been ousted in a coup in August 1975 and part of his cabinet had been replaced by the end of that year.

dustrial community to 33 percent, distribute the shares to individuals (rather than to the industrial community as a single entity), and permit transfer of individual shares to persons outside the community, thus eliminating the possibility that managerial control would be transferred to workers in all medium- and large-sized industrial enterprises, including international corporate subsidiaries.

By attaching such requirements to a loan, the international banks demonstrated their willingness to support (in a negative way) the interest of international extractive companies by ensuring that funds were provided not for enclave export activities, but for investment in more dynamic areas of growth.[50] More importantly, the banks positively supported the interests of international manufacturers, by using their influence to pressure against locally created obstacles to international corporate growth, motivations, and prerogatives in industry.

CONCLUSIONS

The means that the military government chose to use in restructuring the Peruvian economy succeeded in lessening the power of international extractive corporations but not that of international manufacturing firms, and they *increased* the direct impact of international banks on the government, on the economy, and on the future of Peruvian industrialization. Rather than diminish the effects of international corporate dynamics on Peru, the government only changed

---

[50] This was the second demonstration of the international banks' willingness to support the interests of international extractive corporations in a negative way. When the Southern Peru Copper Corporation was negotiating with an international bank consortium for a major loan to develop the Cuajone concession, the consortium required a loan guarantee in the form of a United States Export-Import Bank loan. The Exim Bank refused to lend until the Peruvian government paid compensation for the expropriated holdings of North American-based extractive corporations. The impasse was resolved in February 1974 by the Greene Agreement between the United States and Peruvian governments, in which the Peruvian government agreed to make a $76 million payment to the United States government, which would distribute the money to the expropriated corporations. The Peruvian government also agreed to allow an additional $74 million in profit remissions to the parent corporations. With the signing of the agreement, the Exim bank quickly made a small loan to Southern and the bank consortium loan followed in a few days. Thus, with one exception (Southern's mining activities), international banks again did not promote the continuation of international extractive corporations' enclave export activities, but pressured the Peruvian government to pay compensation to these corporations, which was then available for investment in newer areas of growth.

which international corporate groups would have the most domestic impact. The recession only augmented the influence of international banks on national policy; it did not cause it. The causal relationship had been established prior to the recession by the industrialization policies chosen by the regime, the responses of international manufacturing and extractive corporations to the policies, and subsequent government actions to counteract the impact of the responses.

One of the prime elements in the government's industrialization program to which the state-corporate interplay can be traced was the emphasis on the use of capital-intensive advanced technology.[51] In order to gain, in the short to medium run, the greater amounts of capital and foreign exchange needed to procure foreign technology and repay the finance capital acquired from international sources to initiate capital-intensive industrial projects, the regime emphasized the expansion of the mining/petroleum sector and, to a lesser extent, export agriculture. As a result, the government directed the greatest portion of its internally and externally acquired capital to the export extraction and manufacturing sectors and failed to invest substantial resources in the near-subsistence level agricultural labor population. In consequence, the industrialization program was unable to fulfill a major requirement for an autonomous indigenous industry—the development of a viable internal market.

The larger result was that the government required increased foreign investment in extraction and manufacturing and extensive borrowing from international sources to obtain advanced technology and capital for industrialization. Thus, basic choices made by the regime established the importance of the resources held by international corporations and banks within the industrialization program. Because the military government emphasized industrialization achieved autonomously, however, it also sought to change the character of international corporate activities within Peru.

Therefore the military government was challenging basic motivations and interests of international corporations at the same time that it created a requirement for precisely those resources most concentrated in the hands of international corporate groups—capital and advanced technologies. International corporations, particularly manufacturers, and international banks thereby were placed in strong positions to affect the achievement of industrialization goals in response

---

[51] For further discussion of the emphasis on capital-intensive technology see Chapter 3 of this volume by E.V.K. FitzGerald and Chapter 4 by Daniel Schydlowsky and Juan Wicht.

to autonomy-promoting policies that interfered with their activities. And when an international recession seriously weakened the government's economic position, they were able to directly, intensively pressure against the autonomy-promoting policies.

A number of implications for Peruvian industrialization can be derived from the new role of international banks as direct lenders to the government. The international banks' actions signal that they will not oppose further industrialization efforts in Peru over the long run if these efforts serve to benefit international manufacturing corporations' worldwide growth. International banks, however, will not support further industrialization efforts in Peru aimed primarily at consolidating Peruvian manufacturers into an industrialist class. And it is clear that it will be very difficult for a Peruvian government to again promote economic autonomy in the foreseeable future.

The experience of the military government's industrialization program also highlights a possible dilemma for Third World nations with relative capital scarcity that pursue economic autonomy as well as industrialization: they can seek autonomous industrialization, thereby challenging international corporate dynamics, or they can seek industrialization based on capital-intensive advanced technology, but they are unlikely to successfully do both. Perhaps the simplest, and the hardest lesson of the Peruvian experiment is that a Third World nation that intends to challenge international corporations cannot simultaneously place itself in the position of requiring the resources that have given the international corporations their greatest strength.

III

The Experiment from
Political Perspectives

State Autonomy and Military Policy Making

Peter S. Cleaves and Henry Pease García

Policy making in military regimes compared with that in institutional democracies generally takes place within a smaller circle of governing elites and amid greater secrecy. Nevertheless, all leaders, the military executive included, must abide by similar rules when designing policy: they must maintain the governing coalition and mediate pressures from relevant social groups. Military leaders may find it to their advantage to open up the policy-making process, either by calling upon the expertise of state bureaucrats or by soliciting the advice of class spokesmen. These tactics help improve the policies' technical features before promulgation and enhance their chances for popular acceptance afterwards. This chapter examines President Juan Velasco Alvarado's skillful management of a polity that defied the usual limits on state autonomy and produced important changes in Peruvian society. The Velasco regime (1968–1975) utilized an image of unified armed forces and the policy-making process itself to advance social reforms that weakened the dominant class and significantly increased the power of the state apparatus. At the same time, the regime suffered politically from internal disunity, incoherent economic policies, and a lack of popular support. Opposition forces in the society eventually regrouped and succeeded in reducing the regime's autonomy.

To maintain a high degree of policy-making discretion, Velasco sought to insulate the governing elite from interfering pressures. The regime propagated the myth of the unity of the armed forces, repressed unruly groups and radical spokesmen of the dominant class, and co-opted many of Peru's intellectual and technical specialists, while keeping them at a prudent distance from decision centers. After experiencing early defeats, many economic elites, fearful of further

This chapter is based on separate papers prepared for the November 1978 symposium entitled "A Decade of Military Policymaking in Peru" (Cleaves) and "Sobre el Proceso de Toma de Decisiones en el Gobierno de la Fuerza Armada, 1968–1975" (Pease). The authors are listed here in alphabetic order.

change, tried to penetrate the governing group by means of family contacts, well-placed bureaucrats, and editorials and advertisements in the national newspapers. They also advised against international loans and engaged in economic noncooperation locally. Eventually, they succeeded in gaining at least partial representation for their interests, and consequently, a silent political struggle broke out at the summit of power between military leaders committed to reform and their more conservative colleagues. Toward 1974 the unity of the government started to crumble. The regime of Francisco Morales Bermúdez, taking power in August 1975, gave full access to spokesmen from the dominant classes, shifted the ideology of government to the right, and restored government unity after expelling military radicals. State autonomy was notably reduced during "Phase Two" of the military government (1975–1980). The generals prepared to return government to traditional civilian parties after fulfilling their purpose of "reforming the reforms" in order to render them inoffensive to the then most powerful groups in society.

The first section of this chapter presents background on the crisis that preceded the emergence of the Velasco regime. The military's position in the correlation of forces at the time helps explain the degree of autonomy it achieved. Subsequent sections describe the policy-making styles of the Velasco and Morales Bermúdez governments and provide empirical information on the changes in several variables: state power, state unity, the unity of the dominant class, and its relation with other social forces. By way of conclusion, we put forth various observations on the political implications of this overall experience.

The Capitalist State and Relative Autonomy

The relationship between class and state differentiates among theories of the modern state. Some theories have not dismissed simplistic propositions that consider the state a servile instrument of the economic interests of the dominant class. Other theories persist in conceiving the state as an entity that exists *above* social classes or a juridical abstraction that is somehow separate from class interests. Policy-making studies, however, depart from a prior analysis of the function and role of the state in a given social formation. Their value lies not just in understanding the process of policy formulation and decision making but also in clarifying the relationship between the state and dominant classes at certain historical moments.

Recent contributions to Marxist theory have elaborated on the classical works of Marx, Engels, and Gramsci by describing the capitalist state as a cohesive element in the unity of a social formation.[1] The capitalist state distinguishes itself from other types of states (based on the divine right of kings or a hierarchical distinction between citizens and noncitizens) because specific class domination is absent or obscured in the workings of formal institutions. The capitalist state is thus a complex web of class relations, not only ideological but also political. Therefore, the administration of power requires a combination of mechanisms to achieve consensus or apply coercion, joined together in distinct ways depending on each social formation. Gramsci's main contribution was the concept of hegemony, which stressed the importance of the governing class's ideological predominance over subsidiary or allied classes; he also showed how this relationship is maintained by means of coercion.[2] Hegemony (consensus) and coercion (dictatorship) combine to lend consistency to the capitalist state. When the state relies mainly on coercion (such as in typical dictatorships), it is usually entering or leaving a crisis that has brought into question the state's ability to unify the interests of the dominant classes, their fractions, and allies.

As Poulantzas writes, the way to avoid conceiving of the state as a simple instrument of the dominant class is to stress the "self-unity" or the "relative autonomy" of institutionalized political power.[3] This cohesive factor impedes competitive relations among subgroups in the power bloc from leading to extreme fragmentation or repartition of institutionalized power. To achieve this level of cohesion, the state needs and attains a "relative autonomy from the classes or fractions of the power bloc and, by extension, of its allies or support groups."[4]

This theoretical elaboration reaffirms the class character of the modern state but discards the idea of a state totally subject to a dominant class. It also assumes that part of the unifying function allows

[1] For Marx's and Engels' major statements on the concept, see Karl Marx, *Capital: A Critique of Political Economy* (New York: Random House, 1906), "The Working Day," pp. 255–330; *Grundisse: Foundations of the Critique of Political Economy* (rough draft), trans. by Martin Nicolaus (Harmondsworth, England: Penguin Books, 1973); Marx, *The Eighteenth Brumaire of Louis Bonaparte* (New York: International Publishers, 1963); and Karl Marx and Friedrich Engels, *Correspondence 1846–1895*, trans. by Dona Torr (London: Lawrence and Wishart, 1936), "Letter to Conrad Schmidt," p. 480.

[2] See Antonio Gramsci, *Notas sobre Maquiavelo, sobre la Política y sobre el Estado Moderno* (Mexico City: Juan Pablos Editores, 1975).

[3] Nicos Poulantzas, *Clases Sociales y Poder Político en el Estado Capitalista* (Mexico City: Siglo XXI, 1969).

[4] Ibid., pp. 331–333.

the state at times to confront directly the interests of bourgeois groups.[5] The political writings of Marx, especially *The Eighteenth Brumaire of Louis Bonaparte*, suggest that the dominant class can be fragmented, particularly when it intervenes in politics. Marx (as well as Gramsci), however, referred to relative autonomy only in certain situations, such as in an equilibrium of social forces or a tumultuous political upheaval, when an impasse in the power bloc leads to extreme cases of state autonomy.[6] Poulantzas goes one step further by proposing that relative autonomy is a characteristic of capitalist states in general, without which they could not achieve self-unity in their institutionalized political power. From this perspective, relative autonomy is understood to be present in all situations, not just in times of equilibrium or impasse. The margin of autonomy varies according to the correlation of social forces and their weight in the political arena. Specific instances of relative autonomy are thus best analyzed in the context of the traits of each social formation, the organization of the state, and the orientations and interplay of its various subunits, including, as in Peru, the armed forces.[7]

An important consideration in studying state autonomy in authoritarian systems is the unity of the state apparatus. A state riddled by disputes over doctrine, policy options, or personal loyalties cannot enjoy high autonomy for two reasons. First, these divisions prevent a consolidation of institutional objectives because the state becomes little more than an amalgam of factions. Second, a fragmented state increases the number of entry points for private sector representatives who can exploit the state's internal disharmony to their own advantage. If these representatives are able to gain allies throughout the state apparatus, the margin of autonomy declines noticeably. Both tendencies were evident in Peru after the midpoint of the Velasco regime.

In normal instances, policy-making styles vary depending upon the degree of state autonomy, the peculiar mixture of formal state insti-

[5] Ibid., pp. 394–395. By its nature, Poulantzas argues, the capitalist state is led by a hegemonic class, but this does not deny the state's relative autonomy vis-à-vis the power bloc, or the hegemonic class or fraction within it.

[6] Gramsci does not limit high relative autonomy (Caesarism) only to a situation of equilibrium of "fundamental" social forces but urges the analyst to examine the relations between principal groups (socioeconomic and sociotechnical) of the dominant classes and the auxiliary elements that are guided by or subordinated to their hegemonic influence, paying particular attention to peasants and military groups. See Gramsci, *Notas,* p. 88.

[7] Poulantzas, *Clases Sociales,* pp. 331–332. (Poulantzas concedes that this notion is not sufficiently developed analytically but argues that it nonetheless has value.)

tutions that may exist, such as a parliament and a judiciary, and the nature of the crisis that gave rise to the regime. When high relative autonomy exists, the state should be able to formulate and execute measures that are different from, indeed contrary to, those proposed by classes or fractions in the power bloc.[8] Under conditions of low autonomy, state officials would remain accessible to forces from all corners; policy options might spring from any of a number of groups interested in the issue area. Normally, economic interest groups work out their differences in the private arena and join forces to pressure the government toward a specific policy. The situation is reversed when state autonomy is high and the governing nucleus can maintain its distance from other power groups. Leadership makes judgments on the nature of the problem, checks its observations with sympathetic technocrats and ideologues, and dictates orders from the top. To carry out its policies, the state uses the support it has from one of the pillars of the executive branch of government (in Peru's case, the armed forces) and proceeds with the passive acceptance of subordinated groups.

Two interesting aspects of the Velasco government were its high autonomy and its efforts to use that autonomy to increase state power. It is important not to confuse relative autonomy with the power of the state, however, particularly in the economic sphere. The two are obviously interrelated, but the distinction is necessary, because high degrees of autonomy do not always correspond to high degrees of power. Thus, the Brazilian state in 1964 could be powerful and nonetheless display little autonomy. And the Chilean state under Allende could be weak and highly autonomous. In the Peruvian case, the autonomy achieved by Velasco in 1968 was sufficiently high to force a partial reshuffling of the power bloc. At the same time, the state's economic power was quite weak and it strengthened itself, at least in relative terms, through the expropriation of property belonging to the oligarchy. In the context of a new correlation of forces, both nationally and internationally, state autonomy had declined considerably by 1975, despite the fact that the state was manifestly more powerful in the economy.

In considering the Peruvian experiment, it is important to remember that Peru's social formation is peripheral capitalism, and in 1968, neither the state nor civil society was highly institutionalized, which

[8] A complete study of relative autonomy should include a qualitative examination of favorable opinion of policies by fractions of the dominant class, the policies' effect on their objective interests, and the policies' impact on the interests of the bourgeoisie in general.

indicates that noncapitalist traits were to be found at the time. The armed services, which throughout the republican period had frequently headed governments, were by far the most stable and consolidated organizations. The prevalence of authoritarianism in the society, the past frequency of dictatorships, and the exclusion of vast sectors of the population from the political system facilitated a high degree of relative autonomy for the state when the power bloc lacked unity of command. Thus, the political characteristics of the pre-1968 state and the situation in which the military regime came to power help explain its possibilities for action.

THE REVOLUTIONARY GOVERNMENT OF THE ARMED FORCES

The 1968 military coup was the culmination of the crisis of Peru's so-called oligarchic state, a form of domination that traces its origins to the nineteenth century and reached its peak in the 1950s.[9] Members of the power bloc during this period were social classes and fractions controlling large plantations on the coast, *latifundistas* in the middle and high sierra (whose local power was based on the persistence of noncapitalist relations of production), and large banking and insurance concerns. These fractions, together with large merchandizers, tended to resist capitalist modernization, although they had begun to diversify into industry. Important foreign investors, particularly from the United States, controlled such natural resources as mining and petroleum, and transnational industries had penetrated the local economy after the Second World War (see Chapter 2, this volume, by Rosemary Thorp). The hegemonic fraction of the power bloc, however, was made up of the agricultural exporters (denominated "sugar barons" by the APRA in the 1930s). After 1950, the growth and dynamism of modern industrial sectors and the demands of the middle classes posed serious challenges to this hegemony. The crisis of the oligarchic state was characterized by a decline in the cohesiveness of the power bloc and was reflected in successive compromise regimes incapable of articulating a consistent polity.

Tensions in the system also occurred outside the power bloc. Mod-

[9] Concerning political regimes prior to 1968, see Henry Pease García, *El Ocaso del Poder Oligárquico: Lucha Política en la Escena Oficial, 1968–1975* (Lima: DESCO, 1977), chapters 1 and 5; Julio Cotler, *Clases, Estado, y Nación en el Perú* (Lima: Instituto de Estudios Peruanos, 1978); and Laura Madalengoitia, *Burguesía y Estado Liberal* (Lima: DESCO, 1979). The political regimes from 1930 to 1950 had as one of their primary purposes the control of anti-oligarchic forces, namely, the APRA.

ernization in manufacturing, construction, fishing, and mining concerns increased the size and weight of the working class and generated important sectors of small and middle-sized enterprises. After 1960, the oligarchy was less able to control the working class movement. The decline of the semifeudal latifundia led to a rupture in the rural economy and provoked out-migration, rapid urbanization, and an end to traditional rural isolation. In the 1950s, peasants had a significant impact on the political scene by invading land, forming unions, and demanding more humane working conditions; in response, the state provided social services to divert lower-class pressures. From 1930, faced with the growth of APRA and the socialists, the oligarchy had reverted to repressive military dictatorships to maintain itself in power. Later, it attempted to achieve national consensus among the lower and middle classes through the construction of public works and the provision of social services. By the 1960s, such techniques were no longer sufficient to maintain its dominant position.

Great national enthusiasm accompanied the inauguration of President Fernando Belaúnde Terry in 1963. The political alliance between the Acción Popular and Christian Democratic parties was a new attempt to satisfy the most pressing demands of the popular sectors. Agrarian and industrial reform, reorganization of the state bureaucracy, educational reform, and defense of democratic liberties also appealed broadly to the middle classes and were espoused by their political parties. Spokesmen for the modern wing of the dominant class also proposed economic measures favoring its interests, such as a halt to devaluations that prejudiced industry and favored those oligarchic sectors dealing in exports. The emergent industrial bourgeoisie also urged the creation of an activist state that would nurture industrialization. The challenge to oligarchic domination transformed itself into an overt threat when a guerrilla movement appeared in 1965. These insurgents, however, were rapidly eliminated by the armed forces, thus restoring the belief of the dominant class that it could avoid change. Moreover, the ability of the lower class to mobilize was hampered by the state's willingness to make partial concessions to its demands and by close military monitoring of organizing activities of the Aprista party.

Consequently, during the Belaúnde presidency, the oligarchic sectors firmly and systematically resisted reform. In alliance with the old Aprista party and supporters of ex-dictator Manuel Odría, they controlled parliament and were able to turn back Belaúnde's reformist initiatives. By the end of his presidential administration, Belaúnde no longer represented a force for change but sought instead to execute public works projects, a superannuated means of obtaining consensus in light of the seriousness of national problems. In the last months of his government, widespread public discontent was generated by the suspicion that the president had caved in to United States pressure and came to an agreement that favored the International Petroleum Company. The weakness of the political party system impeded a resolution of the crisis through the parliament or judiciary.

Into this scene marched the Revolutionary Government of the Armed Forces, led by General Juan Velasco Alvarado. On October 3, 1968, the event seemed like just another *golpe,* but the regime legitimized itself soon afterward by nationalizing the IPC oil wells, installations, and refinery. Encouraged by acclaim for this move, the government confronted and rapidly displaced those oligarchic fractions occupying the most important seats of power. It undertook a serious agrarian reform, which had been frustrated during the previous regime, and expropriated in one act the large sugar-exporting plantations. Gradually, the government nationalized major components of the banking and commercial sectors and took over the traditional latifundia of the sierra. Their owners, by being "masters of lives and haciendas," had been the local constables for the system of oligarchic domination by controlling the peasant masses. The regime also strengthened the power of the state in the economy by nationalizing many Peruvian and foreign firms involved in natural resource extraction, basic industry, and the provision of services.

The content of Velasco's policies emerged from an interpretation of Peru's socioeconomic problems prevalent in the political community in the 1960s. The analysis, molded by middle-class civilian intellectuals and technocrats who were influenced by dependency theory, was picked up by the military and propagated in part through academic courses at the CAEM. The underlying principles were that Peru's underdevelopment stemmed from disproportionate economic and political power in the hands of an anachronistic upper class, lack of national integration, a weak state, and inordinate dependence on the international market. Moreover, the major reforms undertaken later (in agriculture, industry, education, natural resources, public administration, etc.) had been central elements of the political party platforms on the left, including the Communist party. Some military men adopted these points of view after fighting the 1965 guerrilla movement and observing at close quarters the defects of the traditional order they were supposed to defend. Broader segments of the military justified their new role on the principle of national defense and on the thesis, which gained ascendancy during the Vietnam War, that internal security was precarious as long as a country was under-developed.[10] The post-1968 reforms thus derived from an ideological framework that included concepts of national defense and class conciliation, significantly influenced by the middle sectors who made their presence felt in this regime as they had over the previous decades in molding this way of thinking.

The main support for the military regime came from the armed forces themselves. In the beginning, the regime took advantage of the general passiveness of the society, which was a by-product of the longevity of the oligarchic state, and the disenchantment of the majority of the population with Belaúnde's reform program. The 1968 coup, however, cannot be described as a concerted effort by the military as an institution. The initiative for the takeover came from Velasco, who at the time was ranking head of the army and of the joint chiefs of staff, and from a group of colonels who made up the nucleus of the new government. The formal summit of power also consisted of the revolutionary junta, made up of the commanding officers of the three branches of the armed services, who were supposedly endowed with governing authority over regime initiatives.

The military reforms brought about an accelerated reshuffling of the classes and fractions in the power bloc, within a framework of class reconciliation of the groups deemed to have legitimate roles in national development. The result was virtually to exclude the oligarchy (agricultural exporters, traditional landowners and bankers, and large merchants) from power and enhance the relative status of modern industrialists. These changes, however, came about not under the direction of the industrial bourgeoisie, but under military leaders who forged a state that could intervene significantly in the economy. Because of the degree of autonomy achieved during the initial period, the state was able to impose its will on various sectors of the industrial class. By 1975, the state sector controlled agriculture (in that the peasant cooperatives were under the strong influence of state officials and a great number of middle-sized properties had also been expropriated), important manufacturing industries, a large proportion of

---

[10] This point is discussed in the contributions by Julio Cotler (Chapter 1) and Luis Pásara (Chapter 10) to this volume and thus is not elaborated upon here. The importance of national defense to military ideology is fundamental but does not displace the other elements mentioned. It served as a factor to join the heterogeneous elements of the armed forces faced with the ideological implications of the socioeconomic reforms. Alfred Stepan also discusses the maturation of the military's outlook in *The State and Society: Peru in Comparative Perspective* (Princeton: Princeton University Press, 1978), pp. 127–147.

the country's natural resources in copper (Cerro de Pasco) and iron (Marcona), and the whole of the oil industry (Petroperú). State agencies also managed all essential public services (such as electrical power, telephones, and railroad transport), and the state acted as the principal intermediary for Peruvian exports. The result was a new form of Peruvian state that implied significant changes in the relationship between economics and politics and a different configuration of forces in the power bloc.

Nationalization and property reform were ideological catchwords of the 1960s and were at the core of Velasco's plan to transform Peruvian society. The government expected to move toward a system of modern, state-directed capitalism that reconciled the interests of new economic classes with those of the popular sectors. The regime was not, however, able to devise a program that was acceptable to both groups, for the orthodox economic policies pursued by Velasco's finance minister, Francisco Morales Bermúdez, worked at cross-purposes. The government substantially increased public investment while attempting to provide tax incentives, but private investors were wary. The industrialization policy corresponded to the import-substitution model and was expected to garner support from national and foreign entrepreneurs, but they too were less than cooperative. Although the regime's rhetoric implied a rejection of capitalism, its economic decisions did not replace the prevailing productive structure or alter substantially the logic of capital accumulation. A form of state capitalism was consolidated during "Phase One" of the military regime, but conditions did not exist to assure its stability, as E.V.K. FitzGerald argues in Chapter 3 of this volume. Although many observers felt that the economic measures were the next step in a continuing process of capitalist modernization, the Velasco government soon became engaged in serious conflicts with modern fractions of the bourgeoisie that needed to be resolved prior to the inception of a stable form of political domination.

Velasco demonstrated a high degree of state autonomy during his confrontations with modern industrial sectors. At the beginning, the groups most negatively affected by the regime's policies were members of the traditional oligarchy. Later the reforms impinged on the rest of the agrarian bourgeoisie, including middle-sized landowners, and industrial sectors that, although not expropriated, clashed with the regime over the Industrial Community, restrictions on firing of workers, and measures to increase the state's role in the economy. The government offered industrialists a series of generous short-term economic incentives while it continued its reform program, ignored industrialists' complaints, and even deported some outspoken businessmen. From 1970 to 1975, these sectors engaged the government in a succession of tense confrontations that reverberated in the armed forces and eventually eroded the regime's main base of support.[11] The attacks were not carried out in unison because some industrialists appeared to accept concilatory overtures from the government. The fact was, however, that the protests of the industrial sectors did not cease until the end of Phase One of the military government and the ouster of Velasco. Under Morales, the situation was reversed. These fractions in the power bloc gained ascendancy and were able to obtain considerable satisfaction for their demands during the second phase.

The Velasco government was not an accidental detour in the evolution of Peruvian politics, however, but rather a crucial link between one period and another. It was a natural consequence of a long history of gradual though significant changes in the economy that had not yet had their impact on the make-up of the power bloc. The military reform program reassembled the country's main power contenders and stimulated the emergence of a new dominant class. That the industrial bourgeoisie had no program of its own helps explain the wide autonomy that the Velasco regime enjoyed once it liquidated the traditional agricultural exporters. As we discuss later, the conflicts within the military government after 1972 were suggestive of the contradictory aims of different fractions of this emerging dominant class.

In summary, the Velasco government enjoyed relatively high autonomy soon after its inception, and by 1973 the oligarchic purge was almost complete. Its unity, however, eroded concurrently with the reconstitution of a power bloc that allowed the country's bourgeoisie to take the initiative in designing a new form of political domination. Industrial, commercial, middle-sized agricultural, and professional groups and the Aprista, Acción Popular, and Christian Popular political parties never completely buckled under the military; even popular groups participated in strikes and showed growing opposition to the regime. Velasco's refusal to admit the existence of an impending economic crisis and his reckless disregard of a threatening international situation involving Peru, Chile, and Bolivia contributed to the creation of a new coalition of forces that agreed at least on the need for his overthrow. In Phase Two, faced with pressure from powerful civilian groups, the military government saw its relative autonomy decline as it tried to stay on top of a deteriorating economic situation

[11] See Pease, *El Ocaso,* for a periodization of the political struggle at the summit of power between 1968 and 1975.

TABLE 7.1
Group Interests and Public Policy, 1968–1980

	Powerful Groups							Weak Groups		
	Importers-Exporters	*Industrialists*	*Military*	*Church*	*Foreign Capitalists*	*Bureaucracy*	*Medium-Sized Farmers*	*Peasants*	*Workers*	*Shantytown Dwellers*
VELASCO PERIOD										
Industrial policies	—	N	—	—	N	Y	—	—	Y	—
Foreign policy	N	N	—	—	N	—	—	—	—	—
Agrarian policies	N	Y	Y	—	N	—	N	Y	Y	Y
Education policy	—	N	—	N	—	—	—	—	Y	Y
SINAMOS activities	N	N	N	—	N	—	N	—	N	Y
State growth	N	N	Y	—	N	Y	—	—	—	—
Press reform	N	N	—	—	N	Y	N	Y	Y	—
Social property	N	N	—	—	N	Y	—	—	Y	Y
Urban land	—	N	—	—	—	—	N	Y	—	Y
MORALES BERMÚDEZ PERIOD										
Devaluations	—	N	—	—	Y	—	N	N	N	N
Foreign policy	Y	Y	—	—	Y	—	—	—	—	—
Social property	—	Y	—	—	Y	N	Y	—	N	N
Industrial policies	Y	Y	—	—	Y	N	—	—	N	—
Labor policies	Y	Y	—	—	—	—	Y	N	N	N
Withdrawal of food subsidies	—	N	—	N	—	—	Y	Y	N	N
Military hardware	N	N	Y	—	—	—	—	—	—	—

Y = group interests generally consistent with policy goals
N = group interests generally inconsistent with policy goals
— = policy goals are irrelevant or ambiguous for group interests

and a severely split governing elite. To satisfy the insistent demands of the dominant class (particularly local industrialists and foreign capital), the Morales Bermúdez government shifted to the right in 1976 and tried to squash the political protests of popular sectors.[12]

Table 7.1 illustrates the degree of overlap between state policies and the interests of powerful and weak civilian groups during the two phases of the military government.[13] Many of the policies included in

[12] The turn to the right is analyzed in Henry Pease García, *Los Caminos del Poder: Tres Años de Crisis en la Escena Política* (Lima: DESCO, 1979).

[13] A caution on the methodology utilized in constructing Table 7.1 is appropriate. Only those policies considered to represent major changes in the respective policy arenas are included in the left-hand column. The indication of whether they were in the interests of the various social and economic groups is judgmental, worked out in consultation with analysts of Peruvian politics of this period. In addition, it should be clear that these are public laws that touched broad seg-

the table are discussed in other chapters of this book and will not be elaborated upon here. This table is meant to serve two purposes: it points out the basic positions of groups that participated in the debate over various state initiatives; and it provides an idea of the degree of conflict between powerful groups and Velasco and the more harmonious relationship between these groups and Morales Bermúdez. The table suggests that the state under Velasco was considerably more autonomous than under Morales. Many more of Velasco's policies were detrimental to the dominant class than corresponded to its interests. Under Morales, policies were more likely to benefit the powerful than to counter their interests; only one clearly favored a lower-class group. The table helps clarify why traditional power holders, although not totally enchanted with Morales Bermúdez, were considerably more at ease with him in the presidential chair than with his predecessor. In line with the definitions presented earlier in this chapter, we conclude that the state under Velasco enjoyed relatively high autonomy, whereas under Morales Bermúdez it was characterized by moderate autonomy.

AUTONOMY AND POLICY MAKING

Between 1968 and 1977, Peruvian governments passed more than 4,000 laws. The content of these decrees and the style used to formulate them were generally different under Velasco and Morales Bermúdez. Major policy initiatives under Velasco were in the spheres of foreign affairs, agriculture (agrarian reform), economic growth, industrialization, natural resources (including fishing and forestry), the mass media, and property reform. Under Morales Bermúdez, important decrees involved devaluations, economic measures pertaining to wages and prices (the stabilization package), weakening the industrial community requirement, rescinding workers' job security, and military hardware purchases.[14] Despite this multitude of cases, few

---

ments of the political community. A considerable number of decisions were formulated that influenced the political scene but do not appear here, such as military promotions, the selection of individuals for deportations, the appointment of ministers and military investigative commissions, and so forth. The reader should consider that this figure is intended for illustrative purposes only.

[14] For several in-depth articles on programs of the Velasco regime, see Abraham F. Lowenthal, ed., *The Peruvian Experiment: Continuity and Change Under Military Rule* (Princeton: Princeton University Press, 1975). The compendium edited by Henry Pease García and Olga Verve, *Perú, 1968–1976: Cronología Política* (Lima: DESCO, 1974, 1977), contains rich data culled from newspaper files on the progression of events after the military seized power. First-person reports of the

studies exist of the policy-making process, partially because, in the absence of a parliament, most decisions were taken behind closed doors.

Decision making in Peru at this time was centralized in a governing elite. Under Velasco, this elite was comprised of the president, the revolutionary junta, and the heads of ministries, who were grouped together in the cabinet. This governing elite was dependent on a broad consensus within the military establishment, which needed to feel it had a voice in the system. Each of the ministries was designated to one of the three branches of the armed services. All ministers were either generals (including the air force) or admirals in active service appointed by the president from a list of three names provided by the commander of the respective service branch. Until 1975, the cabinet encompassed both the president and the members of the junta and was empowered to debate and vote on all laws, a responsibility that diluted the authority of the junta. Under Morales Bermúdez an important change occurred at the summit of power—the junta was separated from the cabinet and awarded authority over the most important political and military decisions. This move placed the three heads of the armed services on an equal footing at a moment when divisions among military leaders were prevalent. The new distinction between the cabinet and the junta was also a principal cause of the stagnation in the decision-making process during the first months of phase two, and it marked the beginning of the turn to the right. Morales acted more like the president of the junta in this context, as opposed to Velasco, who was clearly the head of the cabinet.

The summit of power retained maximum formal and real power over the direction of government and the state administration. The principal policy-making parties under Velasco were the Comité de Asesoramiento de la Presidencia (COAP), the sectoral ministries within their own domains, ministries advising on the policies in other sectors, and "miscellaneous consultants." The most influential of these consultative groups were the general staffs and intelligence services of each branch of the armed forces. The COAP was made up of

---

Velasco regime are Francisco Moncloa, *Perú: ¿Qué Pasó?* (Lima: Editorial Horizonte, 1977); and Hector Béjar, *La Revolución en la Trampa* (Lima: Ediciones Socialismo y Participación, 1977). For more details on the property reforms, see Peter T. Knight, *Perú, ¿Hacia la Autogestión?* (Buenos Aires: Editorial Proyección, 1974); and on the educational reform, Peter S. Cleaves, "Implementation of the Agrarian and Educational Reforms in Peru," *Technical Papers Series*, no. 8 (Institute of Latin American Studies, University of Texas at Austin, 1977).

about thirteen colonels under the direction of an army general who had the rank of a state minister and the authority to request the floor (but not to vote) in cabinet meetings. COAP acted as the president's staff and was the functional equivalent of a parliamentary commission that coordinated laws before presenting them for a final vote.

Reshaping the state in its own image, the military split the public bureaucracy into a large number of sectoral ministries. In the cabinet meetings, each minister was recognized as the virtual authority in his field and his wishes were generally accepted. When a minister was successfully challenged (mainly by the president, and sometimes by the COAP), he generally resigned and was often replaced by a more malleable personality. The various ministries and principal public offices were permanently assigned to the three armed services, ensuring a certain continuity in the sectoral split but giving the internal conflicts wider effects. The ministry with the greatest influence on policy originating elsewhere was the Economy and Finance (because of the tax, budgetary, and foreign currency implications of each policy). Over time, intersectoral coordination became a problem and new "horizontal" agencies were created, whose directors had the right to attend cabinet meetings. Despite their integrating functions, these agencies did not substantively alter the inertia of sectoral prerogatives.

Miscellaneous individuals were often consulted during policy formulation, especially on complex or momentous issues. These outside individuals helped advise the COAP (which called together ad hoc task forces whose members often served *ad honorem*), ministers, and sometimes the president directly. They were generally professionals in various fields, technocrats, high-level public servants, and, less frequently, class spokesmen, either from the unions or interest groups. It is important to remember that because the regime defined itself strictly as the government of the armed forces (the strength of this sentiment was one of its main props) the government elite always kept these civilian consultants at arm's length.

Behind the scenes, various elements of the armed forces intervened both subtly and more overtly in policy formulation. Out of the public eye, officers made known their preferences on policy alternatives to their comrades-in-arms holding political posts. Ranking military officers on the general staffs and intelligence services participated formally in the policy-making process by submitting their opinions on particular issues or joining special investigative commissions. Each ministry had its own version of a mini-COAP to advise the minister, the most important of which were in the Ministry of Agriculture, the National Planning Institute, and SINAMOS. The civilians appointed to these groups had little independent power and needed to rely on well-placed military officers to exert influence. The appointment of civilian ministers of state under Morales Bermúdez did not substantively alter this power balance, except in the economic sphere and during the last few months of the military government. Class spokesmen and the large newspapers also contributed to the tone and content of policy debate.

The regimes displayed not one, but four main policy-making patterns; these can be classified from the most closed to the most open. In the first, policy decisions originated in COAP on instructions from the president and his closest advisors, and after a cabinet session, the legislation was promulgated as a *fait accompli*. This procedure was characteristic primarily of Velasco; for example, the parties affected by the 1969 press law were not privy to the legislative deliberations and became aware of the government's intentions virtually upon publication of the law.

In the second pattern, policy suggestions originated in the ministries and were submitted to COAP and the president for approval, without consultation with representatives of other governmental and nongovernmental jurisdictions. The laws governing currency and the banks, devaluation, the 1974 press expropriation, urban land reform, and the industrial sector were enacted in this manner. Again, Velasco was more prone than Morales Bermúdez to utilize this more restricted policy-making procedure.

The third pattern of policy making saw initial drafts originate in the ministry and the COAP "coordinate" their circulation among other governmental agencies for suggestions, invite the reserved comments of preselected miscellaneous individuals, and draw up the final legislation. The coordination procedure—described in Directive 3B of 1969—was recognized as the model policy-making formula, for the large majority of laws abided by it. Most of the Velasco administration's coordinated legislation was of little import, however, with the exception of the Industrial Community Law, the nationalization of the fishing industry, and the founding of SINAMOS.

The fourth method of policy making involved submitting a measure to broader public or private scrutiny. Under Velasco, civic-minded individuals sent written observations to the local press (which published some of them), discussing the native communities' jungle law and social property; these critiques appeared in print before the laws were promulgated. The educational reform was also debated more openly, and a constituent assembly was democratically elected to draw up university statutes (which, subsequently, were not ratified by the regime).

These policy-making patterns refer to formal decisions that became public decrees. Often, however, events manipulated prior to the issuance of a decree were equally important. The forced resignation of a leading political figure might pave the way for a new law, as did the departures of Minister José Benavides prior to the Agrarian Reform Law, Minister Luis Vargas Caballero prior to the expropriation of the press, and ministers Jorge Fernández Maldonado, Miguel de la Flor, and Enrique Gallegos just prior to the government's turn to the right. In these cases, powerful members at the summit of power were able to exert their influence on the direction of government without participating in the nuts and bolts of drafting precise legislation. The most significant example of this informal policy-making process took place in the period preceding the overthrow of President Velasco on August 29, 1975. Fervent activity by class spokesmen and other pressure groups set the stage for Velasco's ouster.

High autonomy was most characteristic of the policy-making process during the early years of the Velasco government and was concomitant with closed policy making, the absence of challengers to regime authority, and the success of initial reform measures—the expropriation of IPC and the large sugar plantations, for example, which required secrecy to be effective. When the Velasco regime was sufficiently confident of the passivity of potential opposition and quick action was necessary, policy continued to be made in the inner circles of government and implemented rapidly. When legislative initiatives required a great deal of technical expertise and were the exclusive domain of one ministry, they were drafted in the sector and approved by the president on the advice of COAP. The regime followed Directive 3B when potential opposition was of such magnitude that countervailing opinions had to be completely aired, or when the law required the collaboration of a number of ministries or groups for its implementation. By ostensibly sharing authority, the directive allowed the regime to co-opt both bureaucratic representatives and civilian elements whose support (or neutrality) it needed to proceed with its overall plan. Many observers, however, have commented on the hollow nature of this participation. Over time, the policy-making style moved perceptibly from secrecy toward fuller public debate. The regime showed a trend toward airing its structural reforms more widely before instituting them when it sensed its power and unity were on the decline or when the reform's impact lay far in the future and the regime could score ideological points while minimizing the antagonism of opposing groups.[15]

The early period of the Morales Bermúdez government, dubbed "spring politics," was characterized by a broadside attack by spokesmen of the dominant class on the armed forces and governing elite. This attack placed the government on the defensive and reduced its leeway for negotiation. Morales Bermúdez did not resist the attempt by local and foreign private interests to penetrate decision-making circles. During this second phase of military government, the COAP and the National Planning Insitute were downgraded. Although the military retained the prerogative of making and announcing decisions, Morales conferred extensively with industrialists, officials of the International Monetary Fund and World Bank, executives of transnational corporations, and political party leaders, who were much better organized than they had been during Phase One. Government policy soon resembled their list of priorities: for economic elites, the priorities were to repress strikes, permit the firing of workers, enervate the industrial community, and undercut social property; for political leaders of the bourgeoisie, they were the promise of elections and the forced retirement of military radicals; and for the International Monetary Fund, implement an austerity plan or face national bankruptcy. Meanwhile, the government met head-on the organized popular sectors that were angered by regressive economic policies. The state was powerful in the economy, in its repressive capabilities, in its control of almost all forms of mass communication (newspapers, radio, and television), but the relative autonomy of this government vis-à-vis the newly reconstituted dominant classes was clearly reduced. Earlier, state power had helped buffer the regime from the interests of these groups, but eventually, in the absence of popular support, it exacerbated the regime's general isolation, which was fully manifest by 1977.[16]

STATE UNITY

We can now address in more detail the subjects of unity, relative power, state autonomy, and policy making. The first issue, state unity, involves that of the governing elite, the cabinet—which retained legislative and executive functions—the leadership of the

[15] For information on which of these four styles the military government used for major policy initiatives, see Peter S. Cleaves and Martin J. Scurrah, *Agriculture, Bureaucracy, and Military Government in Peru* (Ithaca, N.Y.: Cornell University Press, 1980), p. 92.

[16] This political juncture is treated in Pease, *Los Caminos*, pp. 103–332.

armed forces, and the bureaucratic apparatus. The October 1968 coup was promoted by a nucleus of officers close to Velasco that collaborated in the planning and execution of the overthrow of Belaúnde. This nucleus was not a full-fledged government faithfully representing the three service branches, but a team of like-minded army officers who surrounded the president and gradually moved into important jobs in the government.[17]

It soon became apparent, however, that there was no substantive agreement among military officers about the policies the government would undertake. The summit of power was heterogeneous, and most of its members had been weaned on the militant anticommunism of the 1950s; these officers were prepared to be the protectors of the established order and not the promoters of social change. As Liisa North points out in Chapter 8 of this volume, over time, it was possible to differentiate between those military officers who participated actively in the coup, or accorded the revolution unquestioning loyalty, and those who adjusted to the new situation and sought a position of influence within it. Some members of the armed forces wished to mend fences with the oligarchy and the IPC; others were intransigent about ending their dominant role in the economy. Some military men wished to promote industrial development through a strong state, and others were more attracted to a liberal economic model. A few officers totally rejected capitalism and spoke freely of socialism, whereas officers sympathetic to the private sector beat their breasts furiously whenever investors complained about insufficient guarantees for capital. Some officers, inculcated with elitist and hierarchical principles, were repelled by government rhetoric that exalted the popular sectors. Others, flattered by crowd applause but fearful of lower-class power, preferred to supervise and manipulate popular participation through state-controlled organizations. Over time, some officers sought ways to facilitate popular participation (within the limits posed by the regime's ideology and military base), which would stymie their colleagues' corporatist advances through a rear-guard action. Thus self-management styles of development were widely heralded while the government was imposing bureaucratic, vertical controls on increasingly mobilized popular classes.

The typical behavior of individual state ministers, generals, or ad-

[17] The best known members of the military nucleus in 1968 were Colonels Jorge Fernández Maldonado, Leonidas Rodríguez Figueroa, Enrique Gallegos, and Rafael Hoyos. Later they were joined by Colonels José Graham Hurtado, Miguel de la Flor, Raúl Meneses, Javier Tantaleán, Pedro Richter, and several others. With time, the concept of the nucleus loses its utility because of political differentiation in the governing elite.

mirals included a clear commitment to change, conformism, militant anticommunism, or protection of the established order, all of which existed simultaneously in a swirl of nuances, concealed prejudices, and ideological confusion. These crosscurrents were evident in the society as a whole and also penetrated the summit of power. Although the generals at first tried to keep their disputes hidden, gradually these differences were transformed into definable political tendencies that reared up in moments of crisis.[18] They cannot be considered minor nuances because they help explain the range of government policies and the contradictions that plagued them, especially when military men became spokesmen for class positions while trying to maintain institutional loyalty.

Divisions in the unity of the armed forces were present from the beginning and subtly manifested themselves as early as the IPC nationalization and the agrarian reform. The regime managed the situation fairly easily during the first years of government, however, and outsiders had difficulty identifying the membership of different tendencies. The discrepancies were mitigated by the ministers' or generals' common adherence to military norms, which inhibited them from rushing to join cliques, political parties, or military lodges that would have revealed these splits more clearly. Velasco continually emphasized the regime's military nature. As a result, civilians were not permitted entry into the governing elite. They could advise, support, or implement policies, but they could not claim full membership in the military government. This exclusiveness increased the military's identification with the process.

The original basic nucleus needed to be broadened if only to attract competent officers to fill government positions. The COAP was the primary testing ground for assaying the capabilities and loyalties of military officers who wished to be generals and ministers. These newly recruited military men were used to displace the conservative and liberal officers who participated in the government in the first

---

[18] It is not possible to predict military political behavior simply from the class origins of the military personnel, given the organization and doctrines of the military institutions and the way they are formed in society. The military is clearly part of the capitalist system, but one cannot extrapolate mechanically from that fact the behavior, interests, or objectives of individuals or fractions of the armed services. Nor can the contradictions, conflicts, or public declaration of the period be explained solely on the basis of the ideological beliefs of different generals or their frequent references to issues of national defense. Rather, these outcomes must be analyzed in relation to the ability of dominant social forces to regroup politically and the range of options that were available to economic groups and military officers after each successive crisis.

two years. But as the size of the nucleus grew, so did the resentment and/or ambitions of officers with differing views. Slowly but surely, spokesmen for powerful classes began to map out the contours of political opinion within the regime and achieve representation for their views. More than one military minister became a spokesman for narrow economic interests. Consequently, the defeat of oligarchic sectors during the first years of government also forced the departure of several ministers in uniform. Likewise, when the regime later collided with liberal members of the industrial bourgeoisie, another group of military men left the government. This jostling eventually broke the unity not only of the regime but also of the armed forces.

By the midpoint of the Velasco regime, the state apparatus was also pervaded by internal conflicts among ministries, agencies, and the newspapers (which the government had expropriated and placed under its control). These splits hindered the coherence and effectiveness of the state. For example, the Agriculture Ministry expropriated farms for the agrarian reform; then the Housing Ministry cancelled the expropriations on the excuse that the lands were needed for urban growth. State functionaries carrying out their duties embargoed rural properties; then the navy courts, under pressure from middle-sized farmers, arrested and tried the officials for "sabotaging the agrarian reform." In the economic sphere, food subsidies and price controls impoverished the countryside at the same time that agrarian reform was supposed to be a priority. In social mobilization, SINAMOS struggled initially for influence over popular and union organizations created by the Ministries of Fisheries, Industries, and Education, with the connivance of military intelligence. The battle raged until SINAMOS was reorganized and handed over to the corporatist faction of the army. Other divisions in the state included frequent bureaucratic conflicts between the central government ministries and the public enterprises.

Although at any one time only about three hundred officers served in the civilian bureaucracy, military presence was pervasive among ministerial advisors, vice-ministers, agency heads, heads of state enterprises, and regional directors of SINAMOS. Many generals and colonels, skillful in generating consensus within the ranks for the government program, counted on later appointments to high positions in ministries or public enterprises. The placement of military officers in those posts complicated the political crosscurrents in the regime, because it permitted bureaucratic cleavages to disrupt the armed forces. The divisions were reflected in tense personal relationships between officers, favoritism in promotions and transfers, aspirations to obtain lucrative public sector posts, and a sensation that those who remained in strictly military affairs were not getting ahead.

Those spokesmen of the dominant class who raised the specter of communism and warned about the dangers of "politization and divisions in the armed forces" found fertile ground to cultivate among resentful military officers. The conflict between the group known as "La Misión," which was corporatist-leaning, and the so-called progressive military leaders intensified in the last years of the Velasco regime. "La Misión" had followers among the modern industrialists organized in the Exporters' Association (ADEX), but not in the larger National Industrial Society (SNI), and was opposed by the more radical military men. The dispute involved principally the relationship between the regime and popular groups but was complicated by the fact that only a minority of industrialists felt "La Misión" could serve their interests, for it promised stability even at the cost of repressive measures.[19] An intense ideological struggle ensued, spurred by the fervid anticommunism of "La Misión," whose McCarthyite tactics against the progressive generals caused consternation in military circles. The dispute over policy positions at the summit of power led to political rigidity, an increasing use of authoritarian methods to quiet civilian critics, and an inability to articulate a new form of political domination. This *immobilisme* aggravated the regime's isolation, gave a free hand to "La Misión" in its intimidation tactics, and finally gave rise to the alliances that resulted in the overthrow of Velasco and the installation of Morales Bermúdez.

Morales Bermúdez moved against Velasco on the basis of widespread adverse opinion to the president and the ministers forming "La Misión." Even the progressive generals who had supported Velasco since 1968 felt that he needed to be removed from office in order to thwart the aspirations of "La Misión," whose leader, General Javier Tantaleán, saw himself as the next president. Subsequently, the progressive generals failed to gain influence in the new government, and they too were gradually displaced, victims of the antagonism of the dominant class, its international allies, generals who wished to return the army to its original functions, and conservative admirals who wanted to reverse Velasco's policies. Morales Bermúdez sought to strengthen military unity in several ways. The most important change was to upgrade the role of the junta by restoring its ascendancy over the cabinet. Another important change was to invite rank-

[19] The "La Misión" group promoted the Movimiento Laboral Revolucionario from the Ministry of Fishing, headed by Javier Tantaleán, to splinter unions.

ing military generals (for example, heads of regional military districts) to take part in crucial political deliberations, particularly during the regime's weakest period (1976–1978). Meeting in the army staff headquarters or in the National Palace, these generals played a decisive role in purging radicals from the government and mapped a strategy for dealing with international tensions.

STATE POWER

In 1968, the public bureaucracy was ripe for reform. The absence of modern budgeting and planning mechanisms, the existence of multifunctional ministries, and disruptive antagonism between the executive and legislative branches made the Peruvian bureaucracy during the last months of Belaúnde's regime perhaps the most chaotic in Latin America. The executive was impotent and faced an irresponsible Congress; the constitutional framework facilitated corruption and blocked policy innovation. The bureaucracy was characterized by overlapping functions, reduced size and economic activity, little executive control (except over the forces of repression), and rampant penetration of private parties into public decision making. The national budget, considered by many specialists the key to rational public policy making, had become a bad joke.[20] After the coup, the military rulers—with strong support from civilian *técnicos*—initiated a series of reforms that transformed the public sector. Practically overnight, the regime implemented a number of administrative measures, widely practiced elsewhere in Latin America, only nascent in Peru, to strengthen the state. Under Velasco, the state reflected relatively high sectoral definition, centralized administrative processes, dynamic growth, and absorption of an ever greater percentage of the GNP.

To facilitate the coordination of the industrial, agrarian, and national resource sectors, the regime considered it absolutely necessary to break up the unwieldy Ministry of Development and Public Works. The structural reform of 1969 initiated a movement toward functional specialization broken only by the creation of SINAMOS. The number of ministries grew from eleven in 1968 to seventeen in early 1975, with several national systems with ministerial rank under

[20] See Pedro-Pablo Kuczynski, *Peruvian Democracy under Economic Stress: An Account of the Belaúnde Administration, 1963–1968* (Princeton: Princeton University Press, 1977); Jane S. Jaquette, *The Politics of Development in Peru,* Latin American Dissertation Series, no. 33 (Ithaca, N.Y.: Cornell University, 1971); and Naomi J. Caiden and Aaron Wildavsky, *Planning and Budgeting in Poor Countries* (New York: John Wiley, 1973).

the presidency. The administrative reform coincided with the state's assumption of new functions. By 1975, little remained of the image of the state apparatus led by President Belaúnde. The state controlled the greater part of the banking system, important enterprises in the natural resource sector (mining, petroleum, and fishing), and manufacturing industries (paper, cement, steel, naval construction), as well as a large number of public services formerly in private hands.[21] With the disappearance of the large landowners, the state regulated the agrarian cooperatives and foreign commerce and, although with difficulty, began to intervene in internal food marketing.

Simultaneously, the influence of the National Planning Institute (INP) rose significantly. Before 1968, the INP was politically crippled in the cross fire between Belaúnde and the National Congress. Belaúnde had considerable confidence in his own grand design for the country; the Congress, unable to censure the INP director because he was not a cabinet minister, chose instead to reduce the INP's powers and budget. In 1966, many professional planners, completely demoralized, left the institute and were replaced by nonspecialists. With the military government, however, the situation turned around dramatically and the INP became one of the most important agencies in the Peruvian public sector. From 1969 to 1971, its budget increased by a quarter in real terms. It hired staff members with new technical skills, and it established sectoral planning offices in all the large investment ministries. Each year's Annual Operating Plan gave the INP authority to pass on budgetary entries, an important requisite for effective short-term planning. INP officials helped set original budgetary ceilings (in association with the budget bureau), ordered sectoral projects by priority (both at the ministerial level and with Finance's Department of Economic Affairs), and approved all modifications in sectoral investment.

The growth of the state apparatus coincided with the displacement of traditional power groups, the nationalization of foreign enterprises, and the implementation of new industrial legislation. Although the proportion of the gross national product controlled by the state was significant, the regime found that it was enormously difficult to supervise and coordinate all of the activities it absorbed. These changes occurred in such a short period of time that in most cases formal state

---

[21] Actually, a state steel company and shipyards existed previously, but they were relatively small enterprises. For the growth of the state's presence in the economy, see E.V.K. FitzGerald, *The State and Economic Development: Peru since 1968* (Cambridge: Cambridge University Press, 1976), and his contribution to this volume (Chapter 3).

authority was subject to extensive interference by domestic and international economic forces. The state's learning process in the marketing of minerals and fishmeal was painful and costly, leading to management errors that were picked up by groups in the governing elite skeptical of full state control. The INP, despite its political power, never succeeded in completely overcoming sectoral competition, reinforced by divisions in the summit of power. The development plans proved difficult to execute, and many of the large public sector enterprises operated without paying much attention to INP directives.

Although funds from international lending agencies dried up soon after Velasco's ascension to the presidency, after renegotiating the public debt and reaching agreements on partial indemnization for nationalizations, the government was able to obtain large loans from private international banks. These loans were oriented toward long-term development projects in irrigation, mines, and petroleum and toward the expansion of public enterprises. Based on 1970 trends, military and civilian planners projected that from 1971 to 1975 exports of fishmeal, minerals, and sugar would reap $6.8 billion and imports would total $7.5 billion or less. By increasing its foreign debt by $564 million, the government could maintain its balance of payments at a reasonable level while creating the necessary infrastructure in the extractive industries to finance, into the late 1970s and beyond, such other aspects of the polity as educational reform, social property, and gearing up the agrarian cooperatives to full production.[22]

A short period of economic expansion took place until 1973, at which time the first indications appeared that Peru was entering one of the worst periods of economic crisis in its history. By 1973, the government had achieved a modest increase in real wages, but this indicator declined steadily thereafter. The government attempted to compensate for inflation through a policy of food subsidies until 1975; their withdrawal alienated popular groups. The regime refused to recognize the existence of an economic crisis in 1974 and early 1975. The fact was that the Velasco regime was trying to implement a national industrial plan based on import substitution and an agrarian reform that did not increase food productivity, without attempting to modify the rate of population growth and without breaking the country's economic dependency on the international system. These con-

---

[22] See *Plan Nacional de Desarrollo, 1971–1975* (Lima: Instituto Nacional de Planificación, 1971).

tradictions eventually undermined the viability of any specific reform and exacerbated differences within the governing elite.

Morales Bermúdez, the principal architect and promoter of Velasco's economic policies, led the transition from crisis to stabilization as prime minister in the months prior to the coup. The government confronted the economic crisis of 1975 to 1978 with successive attempts at stabilizing policies, reaching agreements first with United States banks and later with the International Monetary Fund, but found itself incapable of sufficient discipline to apply their provisions. The regime reached its nadir in 1977 and 1978, when it was almost totally isolated, internationally and at home. State power, although objectively much greater than in 1968, was still insufficient to restore the economy or resist international and domestic pressures. Unable to attract a minimum amount of popular support, the government accepted one by one the claims of local entrepreneurial groups and foreign capitalists to cancel social reforms, discard some state industries, eliminate members of the governing elite, repress the unions, and drastically alter the regime's ideological principles. The aimless acquiescence to these political demands, together with the draconian measures imposed by the International Monetary Fund, led to depression and turmoil that, for the military, could be resolved only through incentives for the private sector and a return to electoral politics.

UNITY OF THE DOMINANT CLASS

The high relative autonomy of the state in 1968 was due to the lack of unity in the dominant classes and a favorable international situation. When these factors changed, so did the regime's freedom of action. The initial reforms of the Velasco period sounded the death knell for those social groups that were considered oligarchical—the agricultural exporters, traditional sierra landowners, and traditional bankers. Industrial and agrarian bourgeoisies could not be called "oligarchic" because of their clear rejection of the governing model since the late 1950s. But the inability of the military to strike an accord with modern industrialists, which were at the same time the most dynamic element of the dominant class, placed the industrial class in the opposition to the regime and induced it to seek alliances with middle-sized farmers, disenchanted journalists unemployed after the expropriation of the press, and leaders of middle-class political parties. In 1973, entrepreneurs belonging to the National Industrial Society recognized that their error to date was their failure to coordinate their actions with other economically powerful groups that opposed the regime; this alliance set the stage for the eventual redefinition of the power bloc.[23]

Beginning with the General Industrial Law in 1970, the industrialists confronted the government on several fronts, simultaneously negotiating, obstructing, and obtaining short-term benefits. They utilized import privileges (designed to spur industrial growth) to increase the capital base of their industries and freeze the size of the labor force. They took advantage of loopholes in the Industrial Communities Law and the complicity of the minister of industries to slow movement toward worker ownership to a snail's pace. They declined to invest handsome short-term profits to increase productive capacity, preferring to buy government bonds or transfer their monies abroad. They used their contacts with military officers to try to block reform initiatives and sharpened divisions at the summit of power by mounting a consistent ideological campaign, including McCarthyite attacks on progressive military officers, to defend what they called "Western and Christian civilization."

Small and middle-sized farmers, under the leadership of agrarian bourgeoisie, whose interests were threatened by the agrarian reform, became effective allies of the industrialists.[24] After trying to evade the agrarian reform by parcelling large farms, the bourgeoisie waged a consistent newspaper campaign against the government and succeeded in expanding its numbers through the addition of many small landowners who, although not under threat of expropriation, were fearful of the government's intentions. In the end, the land of many middle-sized property owners was expropriated, and the government worked hard to regain the support of small property owners; but the impact of this political mobilization was unsettling to the armed forces.[25]

Industrialists and farmers perceived that the Achilles' heel of the government was the heterogeneity of political positions in the armed forces and the military's inherent anticommunism. Campaigns were

[23] See the declarations of the president of the SNI on July 19, 1973, in response to a homage to him by industrialists, farmers, the College of Lawyers, and other interest associations, cited in Pease, *El Ocaso,* p. 112.

[24] See Henry Pease García, "La Reforma Agraria en la Crisis del Estado Oligárquico," in Pease, et al., *Estado y Política Agraria* (Lima: DESCO, 1977).

[25] For a broad treatment of agrarian policies during this period, see Cleaves and Scurrah, *Agriculture, Bureaucracy, and Military Government in Peru.* Also, Cynthia McClintock, *Peasant Cooperatives and Political Change in Peru, 1969–1977* (Princeton: Princeton University Press, 1981); and Mariano Valderrama, *Siete Años de Reforma Agraria* (Lima: Pontificia Universidad Católica, 1975).

thus designed to spread confusion about the government's objectives and portray the country as nearing a social transformation led by communist infiltrators. The major daily newspapers, which remained in the hands of private owners until July 1974, perpetuated these campaigns on a massive scale. An analysis of *La Prensa* and *El Comercio* between 1973 and 1975 indicates a high degree of coordination in the actions of the SNI, small and middle-sized farmers, traditional political spokesmen, and such interest groups as the College of Lawyers. These newspapers' editorials, written principally for a military audience, had their desired effect of sowing uncertainty in the upper levels of the armed forces.

In summary, the deep divisions at the summit of power and throughout the government must be analyzed in the context of systematic opposition by the modern fractions of the dominant class that were not part of the oligarchy. Ironically, because the regime nurtured hopes for eventual reconciliation, the dominant class was gradually able to regroup and gain the strength to undermine state unity. The struggle was not just between the regime and its adversaries but rather permeated all levels of the government and the armed forces. Although the liberal bourgeoisie lost several of its leaders through deportations and its spokesmen inside the regime through forced resignations (such as that of Admiral Vargas Caballero in May 1974), it never lost touch with decision-making circles. Indeed, new spokesmen, such as "La Misión," even won access to the summit of power. The political struggle, therefore, was characterized by the progressive recomposition of the dominant class, which was melded in its opposition to the military government. This two-sided game of shifting alliances had its effect on governmental unity, and on the final definition of the regime.

The world political situation also increased the isolation and rate of decay of the Velasco government. In 1968, the international scene favored the regime. Velasco's confrontation with the United States over the nationalization of the IPC took place at a time when American eyes were turned toward Asia. By 1970, Velasco was hardly the only problem for the American State Department in Latin America and perhaps not even the most important. Salvador Allende was confirmed as the first Marxist president elected in the hemisphere. In Bolivia, a leftist general, J. J. Torres, became head of state. In Argentina, Juan Perón returned from a long exile abroad in the midst of widespread uncertainty about his intentions. In Ecuador, Guillermo Rodríguez Lara deposed José María Velasco Ibarra and promised social reforms *a la peruana*. This series of events bolstered Peru's feelings of military security vis-à-vis her traditional rivals, Chile and Ecuador, which appeared to have like-minded governments, and for three years Velasco was not distracted by issues of national defense.

By 1973, however, the tables had turned. Allende and Torres had been toppled and the Pinochet and Banzer dictatorships were using geopolitical rivalries to distract and unite their repressed citizenries. With the support of some exiled Peruvians, the Inter-American Press Society focused on the expropriation of the daily newspapers, and its members published sensational articles on repression in Peru. After receiving a negative reply from Washington, the Velasco government purchased armaments from the Soviet Union, thus straining relations with the United States, a country that had provided arms to Chile even under the Allende regime. International and geopolitical issues had special relevance for the armed forces, which were, in the last analysis, responsible for national security. Velasco's opponents aggravated worries on this front by claiming that the regime, given its isolation in Latin America and its poor relations with the United States, could even lead Peru to military defeat should hostilities break out with Chile.

The correlation of forces at the summit of power proved to be progressively unfavorable for the continuation of the Velasco government. Until now, we have analyzed the regime's relative autonomy with regard to the dominant class and their international support. The recomposition of the dominant groups and the breakdown of military unity cannot be fully explained, however, without making reference to the popular sectors. The latter have to be included to understand the isolation of the regime, its inability to broaden its social base, and the absence of popular protest when it was finally toppled.

THE REGIME'S ISOLATION FROM POPULAR GROUPS

Despite its setbacks in the 1950s, the oligarchic state had retained its ability to fragment and demobilize popular organizations, either through official repression or the inertia of the traditional landholding structure. Although by the end of the 1960s, peasant unions had gained some strength and were able to challenge prevailing patterns of domination, there was no centralization in the peasant movement. Moreover, the Belaúnde government, alarmed by the guerrilla insurgency of 1965, strove to neutralize those peasant unions that existed. At the time, there was only one officially recognized workers' confederation, the Confederación de Trabajadores del Perú, which was controlled by the APRA and which lost influence during the Belaúnde period because of membership dissatisfaction with the leadership and because of APRA's connivance with the oligarchy in opposing Belaúnde's reforms.

The political parties were weak in 1968, partially as a consequence of the general disillusionment with the country's democratic institutions and the abstract content of most political discourse. The leftist parties were certainly weaker. Upon the disappearance of the parliament, Velasco found the parties so inoffensive that his regime did not bother to outlaw them. The APRA, the only mass party, did not even attempt to challenge the strength of the military government in 1968.

The government took advantage of the passive consensus of the majority of the population to move forward with the initial reforms. But over time, its actions helped mobilize these groups, often in opposition to the government. In the countryside, the struggle for land took place both inside and outside the limits of the Agrarian Reform Law and crystallized political consciousness in existing peasant unions. The Velasco regime witnessed the first serious attempts to centralize the peasant movement in the Confederación de Campesinos del Perú (led by leftist forces) and the Confederación Nacional Agraria (a creation of government in 1974). In the city, workers' organizations multiplied. The Confederación General de Trabajadores del Perú (CGTP), controlled by the Communist party, obtained legal recognition from the government and became the most influential labor organization. The regime promoted its own central coordinating body for the working class, without much success, but the creation of the industrial communities greatly affected the workers' movement. The campaign by labor leaders against the entrepreneurs' attempt to evade the profit- and ownership-sharing law raised the workers' political consciousness. Other sectors of the popular classes became organized through their participation in social property cooperative enterprises or neighborhood groups in the shantytowns (*pueblos jóvenes*). From incipient levels in 1968, regional and sectoral popular mobilization increased considerably. Although lacking central coordination, this movement succeeded in socializing a new generation of opposition leaders who would become prominent during the second phase of the military government.

A political plan derived from the ideology of the middle sectors was unlikely to spur mass mobilization. Moreover, the impact of government policy toward popular organizations prevented the regime from gaining any consistent support. Flushed by its early successes, the government felt it could ignore many existing labor leaders and generate its own backing. It recognized that the left was sharply divided between those affiliated with popular groups, those in opposition to the regime at the national level, and those supporting the government. But in trying to take advantage of the situation, the regime overplayed its hand. It created parallel organs of "representation" in industries and in modern plantations, tried to displace traditional union militants, and was stalemated by a prolonged adversary relationship with skillful labor organizers that sapped its energy. Although Velasco's reforms provided many material benefits for workers, its labor policies split the workers into numerous factions. The regime's "representative" organs were received differently. The Confederación Nacional Agraria (CNA), promoted by SINAMOS, managed to win a considerable measure of popular support, while the Sindicato de Educadores de la Revolución Peruana (SERP) and the Central de los Trabajadores de la Revolución Peruana (CTRP) remained bureaucratic. All, however, became targets of opportunity for the progressives and "La Misión" adherents. Government agents became increasingly manipulative in managing these groups and actually dampened their members' enthusiasm for the regime.

The absence of popular support stemmed from the fundamental contradiction between the concept of mass mobilization and the norms of military hierarchy. The regime's ideas on popular participation were authored by civilians close to the regime rather than by the military leaders themselves. Nevertheless, the original members of the basic nucleus were receptive to these innovations and helped give them form and substance in the creation of SINAMOS. SINAMOS was instituted only after two previous attempts to link government with the people (the Committees for the Defense of the Agrarian Reform and the Committees for the Defense of the Revolution) had been accused of communist infiltration. From 1972 onward, SINAMOS was continuously in the eye of the hurricane. Led first by Leonidas Rodríguez Figueroa, who felt perfectly at ease with progressive civilian collaborators, it was later headed by two generals (Rudecindo Zavaleta and Pedro Sala Orosco) who were sympathetic to principles of vertical command and, toward the end of the Velasco regime, actually opposed the progressive officers. As part of "La Misión," and assisted by intelligence operatives, Zavaleta and Sala Orosco took on the responsibility of breaking the back of incipient popular organizations, creating parallel entities, and selectively repressing those they could not control. Even during its heyday, SINAMOS was interpreted by popular groups as an attempt to manage their affairs from the "top down." Its behavior was relatively benign, however, compared with the clandestine operations of the Interior

Ministry, the complicity of the ministries of Labor and Industry and the intelligence services in reorganizing the National Confederation of Industrial Communities, and the not-so-subtle police suppression of striking miners and school teachers. SINAMOS' ultimate fate demonstrated that for this regime popular mobilization needed to be accompanied by vertical and bureaucratic controls.

Although the "top down" label was resented by committed civilians in the regime, the interpretation was, on the whole, accurate. In designing a program for participation, the regime could achieve military consensus only by incorporating popular groups under the institutionalized tutelage of the armed forces. The progressive officers could not propose an alliance with popular organizations that the military did not directly control. This aspect of the process represented the ultimate gordian knot, because civilian mobilization created anxieties in the military and Velasco was unwilling to sever his relationship with the armed forces. The government avoided the main issue by choosing to engage in dialogue with only those groups that provided overt support, such as the CGTP, a tactic that failed to secure stable props for its rule. The Velasco regime's inability to deal adequately with the question of participation was perhaps its most significant failing.

This analysis of the regime and its contradictions points out the recurring elusiveness of an alliance between the military and popular organizations. This miscarriage is symptomatic of a regime that by definition is *of* the armed forces. Even Velasco did not foresee that, as the political competition intensified, the regime could not break ranks with the military. Nor could it mount an effective campaign against a capitalist system which had given life to these very same military institutions. The coup of August 29, 1975, which was greeted with applause from the right and absolute silence from the popular sectors, was simply a military act that confirmed the internal bankruptcy of the regime.[26]

The decline of real salaries, which began in 1973, accelerated with the implementation of stabilization policies under the Morales Bermúdez government. The popular sectors joined forces to protest

---

[26] The deterioration in the health of the regime and of Velasco himself led to a consensus among military leaders that Velasco needed to be replaced. The original recommendation to force his voluntary retirement was overruled by Morales Bermúdez. The ouster is treated in Pease, *Los Caminos,* pp. 55–76, and in Carlos Urrutia, et al., *Autogestión en el Perú, 1968–1979* (Lima: CIDIAG, 1980), which also includes comments by General Arturo Valdéz, who was subdirector of the COAP and secretary of the cabinet, on political events at the time.

their deteriorating economic situation; the repression by the government simply strengthened their resolve. A general strike in July 1977 paralyzed the country, further isolating the military regime, and helped convince the armed forces to return to an electoral system of government.

CONCLUSIONS

Exceptional state autonomy between 1968 and 1972 appeared to coincide with an impasse at the summit of power caused by the collapse of the oligarchic state, the inability of potentially powerful bourgeois groups to act politically to serve their interests, and the institutional coherence of the armed forces (which filled the vacuum). Taking advantage of the crisis, Velasco utilized this high relative autonomy during the first phase of the military government to exclude the traditional classes and fractions from the power bloc and strengthen the state economically. A closed policy-making style prolonged the initial thrust, kept traditional politicians, entrepreneurs, and spokesmen of the dominant class off balance, and postponed their ability to reconsolidate in effective opposition to the regime. Although the class character of the state was inferred from its continuing tolerance of capitalism, the political regime did not express the interests of classes and fractions dominant in the society at large. While Velasco did not institute socialism and promulgated many policies that were in the long-term interests of the industrial class, the regime relied for its support on the military institutions and did not enter into partnership with modern bourgeois groups.

The lack of such an alliance under Velasco can be explained by the liberal ideology of the industrial bourgeoisie (which wished to subordinate the oligarchic classes rather than eliminate them); by the industrial bourgeoisie's relative inexperience in trying to protect its interests through political means; and by the progressive radicalization of key members of the governing military elite, who personally were not at ease with the values of the entrepreneurial class. Although the military government essentially was offering the industrial bourgeoisie a set of reforms based on class reconciliation and state backing for private industrialization, these modern sectors interpreted the government's intentions as an all-out attack on the capitalist order.

The military regime faced the prospect that although they were temporarily scattered, the most dynamic sectors of the dominant class would eventually regroup. Velasco's early political victories contributed to the radicalization of the polity at the summit of power, but they also helped to solidify the coordinated opposition of the industrial interest groups. In 1973, these opponents began to retake the offensive, which together with setbacks on the geopolitical and international economic fronts and a lack of support from the popular classes led to increased internal struggle, receptivity to opposition demands by members of the governing group, and the gradual reduction of the state's initial high relative autonomy.

The second phase of the military government, headed by Morales Bermúdez, displayed less relative autonomy until decisions were made to transfer power back to civilians in 1979. In 1976 and 1977, the bourgeoisie appeared to be united in its attempt to substitute civilians for the military rulers. Nonetheless, Morales was able to control the pace and direction of the turn to the right, including the repression of some bourgeoisie spokesmen in 1976, the imposition of a timetable that included a constituent assembly to precede general elections (against the wishes of important segments of the bourgeoisie), and a contradictory economic plan that gave priority to the demands of international capital and negatively affected companies that produced for the internal market. These events were consistent with a normal level of relative autonomy of the state; the regime could maneuver between fractions of the dominant class and even make concessions to popular pressures. It could not, however, end its isolation until it determined to transfer power from military hands.

Although the return to civilian rule was the principal demand of the dominant class, the position was not accompanied by a definable political program that would bridge the considerable gaps between the bourgeois political parties. For this reason, the Morales Bermúdez government was able to retain some negotiating room in the armed forces and the political community at large.[27] The new civilian president was installed in a situation much different from that in 1963 or 1968, because now the dominant class was relatively homogeneous and there was a military class that was battle-tested during the Velasco period and watchful of the political direction the government would take.

Policy-making styles over this long period appear to be correlated with levels of autonomy and state power. High autonomy is feasible only temporarily and is usually accompanied by a secretive policy-

[27] The best example was the economic policy of Minister Javier Silva Ruete, which provided tangible benefits to entrepreneurs and helped assure approval of the government's approach to transferring power to civilians. At the time, these measures increased the level of state autonomy, which was nonetheless quantitatively much less than the extraordinary situation in 1968.

making style. The Velasco regime displayed characteristics of high power and autonomy during the 1968–1972 period, and its policy-making style followed suit. The early years of the regimes of Kemal Ataturk in Turkey and Fidel Castro in Cuba are comparable examples. The state that is weak, whether as a result of severe internal divisions or a low resource base, is susceptible to the bullying of powerful economic or political interests; its low autonomy is manifest in public policies that favor those interests. The first years of the state under Morales Bermúdez had features that were consistent with this description. The state was divided, power was scattered, and representatives of powerful interests had a predominant say in shaping policy. The constraints on each regime, however, are not understood simply through the success or failure of its reforms, but in terms of the social groups which accorded it support, and its evolving relations with the dominant classes and rising popular sectors.

What final evaluation can be made of the unusually high autonomy of the Velasco period? It is evident that closed policy making helped—though it was not essential—to force the decline of the agricultural and financial oligarchy and in a way to assist the regrouping of the power bloc. The hermetic style of the governing elite was essential for designing a polity that could paralyze, momentarily, those economic power holders who, Velasco felt, prevented the popular sectors from improving their social condition.

It appears that the Velasco government did not recognize the inherently temporary nature of high autonomy, especially when it repeatedly claimed in its speeches that the reforms were "irreversible." Disregarding the fundamental interests of powerful economic and institutional participants is a viable strategy as long as those elements are in disarray. Misrepresentation of one's ultimate objectives and high autonomy itself have their own half-life.[28] Velasco and his entourage can claim little credit for the disarray of the upper class and the degree of cohesion of the military in 1968. Notwithstanding, his administration forcefully took advantage of the high state autonomy prevailing at the time to advance several reforms that would have been dead letter in other historical circumstances.

In summary, the Velasco government tried to keep the dominant classes off balance and its military cohorts in line, and it made overtures to the popular sectors. The effort fell short, but it reaffirms the importance of relative autonomy as one means of changing the com-

[28] For further discussion of this point, see the chapter by Cynthia McClintock in this volume.

position of the governing group. The Velasco experience is also reminder of several other principles. First, social and economic reforms derived from an ideology of the middle sectors are unlikely to appeal to the authentic interests of popular sectors. Second, a military establishment that owes its existence to the capitalist system will not easily destroy its source. Third, institutions based on the norms of vertical command and discipline—such as the armed forces—are intolerant of spontaneous and autonomous organization of labor unions and popular groups. Fourth, high relative autonomy is a temporary phenomenon; over time, dominant classes will regroup or a new power bloc will emerge. Finally, the armed forces, even when they appear to be leftist leaning and enter government in a situation of high relative autonomy, are, in the last analysis, unreliable leaders of revolutionary movements.

8

Ideological Orientations of Peru's Military Rulers

Liisa L. North

To what extent did the military men who ruled Peru from 1968 to 1976 share ideological orientations and goals concerning economic development and citizen participation in the reformed society they proposed to create? And how did the social conflicts generated by the attempt to carry out specific reforms affect the degree of consensus among the officers in power? I will address these questions here by first analyzing the political role of the Peruvian military from the Great Depression to the late 1960s in order to identify the nature and degree of institutional consensus and cohesion at the moment of the regime's ascension to power. The second and major part of the paper examines the ideological debate that emerged among the officers in the course of reform implementation and the impact of the right-wing opposition campaign on that debate. Selected public statements by fifty-nine officers who occupied ministerial-level positions between October 1968 and August 1976 are analyzed to characterize the variety of attitudes toward mass mobilization and to identify differences in the central concepts that determined these officers' proposed solutions to the problems of economic underdevelopment. The explanation for the turn to the right in August 1975 will then be sought in the degree of ideological congruence between the majority of the officers and the major parties and associations that led the right-wing opposition to the Velasco reforms. A brief concluding section will attempt to place the Peruvian experiment into comparative context,

The original research and field work for this essay was generously supported by Canada Council; the York University Centre for Research on Latin America and the Caribbean later provided funds for a research assistant. I owe special thanks to José Nun, with whom I began work on this essay, especially for our discussions of mass mobilization. My perceptions of the development process are, to a large extent, the outgrowth of discussions with Louis Lefeber. I must also thank David Scott Palmer and Javier Iguiñez, who criticized earlier versions of this essay, and Victor Villanueva and his family, who provided me with an ideal home and intellectual environment during my stay in Lima (from May to August 1976). Finally, I would like to thank the archive staff of *La Prensa*.

examining the extent to which its political-ideological dynamics and choice of economic policies parallel other prominent post-depression efforts to implement fundamental structural reforms in Latin America.

THE HISTORICAL CONTEXT: THE MILITARY AS CRISIS MANAGER

The Peruvian armed forces have played a central role in the maintenance of the country's sociopolitical system since the hegemony of the export oligarchy and its alliance with foreign capital were first challenged by an organized national mass movement, the Alianza Popular Revolucionaria Americana (APRA), during the Great Depression. The frequency and length of military governments since the 1930s provides proof enough of the significance of the institution in the political process.[1] In fact, the armed forces substituted for the party the oligarchy was incapable of generating. That is, governments fundamentally based on military power and headed by military figures provided the protective bulwarks behind which the conflicting interests of dominant classes could be reconciled with their "enlightened" common interests (characterized by minimal responses to popular demands). While the repressive role of the military, particularly in the rural highlands and against APRA, is well known, less stress has been placed on the fact that conservative military dictators like Oscar Benavides (1933–1939) and Manuel Odría (1948–1956) cultivated popular support, for example, by providing employment through public works programs and enforcing labor legislation among strategic sectors of the urban working class.[2] They also consciously strove to foster and accentuate divisions among popular organizations, favoring political groups and unions too weak to pose a serious threat to the stability of the system of military cum oligarchic domination. Thus,

> [m]ost of Peru's very progressive labor and welfare legislation was enacted by military dictators. Their objective was clearly to bypass the union by linking the individual worker directly to the government. So far as unions were concerned, the dictator's policy was to

[1] Presidents Luís M. Sanchez Cerro (1931–1933), Oscar Benavides (1933–1939), and Manuel A. Odría (1948–1956) were all military figures. The civilian government of Manuel Prado (1939–1945) relied heavily on military support. After the interim military government of 1962–1963, Fernando Belaúnde's (1963–1968) ascension to the presidency was greatly facilitated by military backing.

[2] See, for example, Baltazar Caravedo Molinari, *Burguesía e Industria en el Perú* (Lima: Instituto de Estudios Peruanos, 1976), pp. 127–131.

suppress reformists—the APRA, in Peru—favoring instead Communist infiltration of the union movement.[3]

By the late 1950s, APRA was of course "tamed." It no longer represented a security problem; APRA had been incorporated into the system through the partial satisfaction of the material claims of its clientele groups, a process facilitated by the generally good performance of Peru's diversified export economy. Moreover, much of the party's mass base resided in the areas of export expansion. But the systemic crisis dating back to the depression was not resolved. On the contrary, Peru had not even found its way to planned import-substituting industrialization or a modernization of the state apparatus, the near ubiquitous policy responses of postdepression Latin American governments. The unified military rejection of APRA and support for the established power of the export oligarchy had in fact proscribed these policies in Peru.[4] Shorn of its radical rhetoric, the APRA project for transformation, even in the 1930s, added up to moderately nationalistic policies to regulate foreign capital and promote industrialization through a strengthened and modernized state. The "bankruptcy of the old [oligarchically sponsored] socioeconomic model" reflected in "the increasingly profound stagnation of exports and of investment"[5] and the arrogant behavior of foreign corporations accustomed to the traditionally liberal investment laws of Peruvian governments increasingly concerned some military figures in the 1960s. It was a new wave of mass protests and mobilizations, however, that turned the structural crisis of the socioeconomic order into a question of national political/military emergency and led the armed forces to a general examination of the society and their role in it.

[3] David Chaplin, "Blue-Collar Workers in Peru," in David Chaplin, ed., *Peruvian Nationalism: A Corporatist Revolution* (New Brunswick: Transaction Books, 1976), p. 207.

[4] Elsewhere in Latin America, the reformist, middle-class-led parties that emerged during the depression, or earlier in some cases, provoked serious divisions within the armed forces and obtained their support to attain political power. In Peru, APRA also attempted to gain military support. The radical militancy of the party's middle-level leadership and cadres, however, led to a series of violent confrontations between APRA and the armed forces. These ranged from the Trujillo Rebellion of 1932 and its "massacre of officers" to the Callao Revolt of 1948. The armed forces were thus effectively alienated from the party. See, for example, Victor Villanueva, *Ejército Peruano: Del Caudillaje Anárquico al Militarismo Reformista* (Lima: Librería Editorial Juan Mejía Baca, 1973), pp. 185–264.

[5] See "The Evolution of Peru's Economy," Chapter 2 of this volume, by Rosemary Thorp. See also Julio Cotler, "Democracy and National Integration in Peru," Chapter 1 of this volume, for an analysis of the broader structural/historical context of crisis in which the Peruvian experiment emerged.

While APRA's constituency acted according to the logic and the rules of the system of oligarchic domination that the military had maintained, newly mobilized workers and peasants did not. The army was again called in to play a public and central "crisis management" role during the last years of the second presidency of Manuel Prado by suppressing the peasant movements of La Convención and Lares (1959–1963). More dramatically, and traumatically for the officers, the army later put down a wave of largely spontaneous peasant land invasions that spread through the highlands during 1963–1964 and defeated several guerrilla groups in 1965.[6] Meanwhile, the urban labor movement was beginning to manifest signs of a new militancy.[7] All of this, moreover, was taking place in the new international context created by the success of the Cuban Revolution and the dramatic failure of the most powerful state in the world to repress a peasant-based liberation movement in Vietnam. Obviously, it was not only the military organizations that were rudely awakened by these national events and a new global situation. By the 1960s, an anti-oligarchic and nationalist ideology, which included an awareness of the urgency of agrarian reform, had permeated sectors of all political organizations; the popular consensus on the necessity of reforms was further reinforced by the new social philosophy of the Catholic Church as the progressive ideas of Vatican II struck roots among perhaps even a majority of the clergy. Yet the leadership of the parties with power to influence national policy making equivocated and compromised[8]—inaction on the major issues and politicking for short-term advantages distinguished the behavior of the executive and parliamentarians.

In short, the military in 1968 responded to an accumulation of national problems and proposed solutions dating back to the depression, which were brought to the center of the political stage in an acute form in the 1960s. But the fact that a certain type of progressive consensus was expressed in the formation of the Revolutionary Government of the Armed Forces was not only the product of the context of the 1960s and the historical centrality of the armed forces in the polit-

[6] See Howard Handelman, *Struggle in the Andes* (Austin: University of Texas Press, 1975); and Hector Béjar, *Peru 1965* (New York: Monthly Review Press, 1970).

[7] See Denis Sulmont, *Dínamica Actual del Movimiento Obrero Peruano* (Lima: Pontoficia Universidad Católica, Taller de Estudios Urbano Industrialies, 1972).

[8] See, for example, Abraham F. Lowenthal, "Peru's Ambiguous Revolution," in Abraham F. Lowenthal, ed., *The Peruvian Experiment: Continuity and Change under Military Rule* (Princeton: Princeton University Press, 1975), pp. 3–43.

ical process. It was also related to the military's institutional characteristics as the modern repressive arm of a backward state. The military's solid opposition to APRA and traditional support for the "law and order" of the export oligarchy had made it relatively impermeable to factionalization by civilian political interests, facilitating the development of a strong bureaucratic structure built on merit criteria, internal cohesion and discipline, and esprit de corps.[9] Therefore, as the crisis of the 1960s unfolded, the officer corps was able to address social and economic issues and question the very rationality of the order they had so effectively supported, while maintaining a degree of institutional cohesion and "distance" from civilian political organizations with few parallels in Latin America.

The officers' critique of the existing order found its point of departure in military problems—questions of national security and internal war. However, in the course of addressing those problems in the Centro de Altos Estudios Militares (CAEM) as well as the Escuela Superior de Guerra (war school) they were necessarily led into an examination of the country's outstanding economic, social, and political conflicts, a practice encouraged by United States military missions and training programs.

> The "latent insurgency" dilemma appeared to convince many officers that Peru needed agrarian reform combined with industrialization, or in the more abstract language of the Ministry of War, a "General Policy of Economic and Social Development." According to this view, similar to the McNamara-Rostow thesis that violence springs from economic backwardness, conditions of injustice in the countryside needed to be removed, so that the absentee landlord and his local henchmen no longer would exploit and oppress the rural-peasant masses, whose marginal living conditions were making them political recruits for future subversion.[10]

Already during the interim military government of 1962–1963, "a few younger elements in the military . . . would have liked more deliber-

---

[9] See Liisa North, *Civil Military Relations in Argentina, Chile and Peru* (Berkeley: University of California Press, Institute of International Studies, 1966).

[10] Luigi R. Einaudi, "Revolution from Within? Military Rule in Peru since 1968," in David Chaplin, *Peruvian Nationalism*, p. 410. See also Frederick M. Nunn, "Professional Militarism in Twentieth Century Peru: Historical and Theoretical Background to the *Golpe de Estado* of 1968," *Hispanic American Historical Review* (August 1979). This extremely thorough and useful piece of work was brought to my attention recently and consequently has not been integrated into the text in the manner it deserves.

ate action in such areas as land reform."[11] General José Graham Hurtado, head of Velasco's presidential advisory committee from 1969 to 1975, was among the many officers who frankly admitted the impact of peasant insurgency and the guerrilla movements of 1965 on military thinking.

> "It was the guerrillas who rang the bell that awakened the military to the reality of the country. . . ." He added that at the moment that the guerrilla *focos* appeared, it was the Army that said that this problem was not going to be resolved with bullets. And that is why it presented the development plan for La Convención Valley.[12]

Thus, a military institutional response developed independently of any one civilian political position on reform, although it was a product of the military's historical function in the civilian political process.

In summary, a complex of mutually reinforcing determinants related both to the historical process and the evolution of the military qua institution converged in the formation of the Revolutionary Government of the Armed Forces. By 1968, a significantly large group of officers was convinced that Peru's dominant classes and major political parties had disgracefully failed to resolve the accumulated social conflicts and economic problems and were unlikely to do so in the future. The last civilian failure in this respect had been Belaúnde, whose weakness in dealing with the IPC and the APRA-Odría coalition in parliament (viz., the watered-down agrarian reform law) represented a particular source of frustration to nationalist and reform-minded officers. They understood the necessity of widespread structural transformations in contrast to the old-style neutralization of popular demands through limited palliative measures. In addition, these officers were convinced that their modern and cohesive military institutions could tackle and resolve Peru's basic problems by forcefully addressing the issues of foreign investment, agrarian reform, and industrialization in a pragmatic, task-oriented, objective fashion; to do this, moreover, the pitfalls of ideological politics and alliances with civilian political groups (which had repeatedly demonstrated their willingness to sacrifice long-term national interests to short-term political advantage) had to be avoided.

The components of the military institutional consensus in 1968 in-

[11] Pedro-Pablo Kuczynski, *Peruvian Democracy under Economic Stress: An Account of the Belaúnde Administration, 1963–1968* (Princeton: Princeton University Press, 1977), p. 48.

[12] *Expreso,* August 22, 1972.

cluded: (1) distrust of civilian politicians and the traditionally dominant sectors due to their mismanagement of national affairs; (2) a technocratic/managerial orientation toward economic development and social change; (3) a perception of the necessity of agrarian reform and the expansion of state social and economic planning to guarantee internal security through a mix of developmental and distributive policies; and (4) a nationalism fundamentally based on military patriotism. There was nothing particularly radical in this consensus, but it was broadly and firmly enough held to overrule the claims of a minority of traditionally conservative officers and to provide institutional support for another minority—the moralistically radical group led by General Juan Velasco Alvarado.

The officers most closely identified with Velasco shared strongly held convictions concerning social justice and the dignity of the common man and an optimistic self-assurance concerning their capacity to carry out a fundamental transformation of Peruvian society. Just as had their comrades in arms, they held voluntaristic and often simplistic notions of social, political, and economic change. The depth and naiveté of these convictions made the officers objects of ridicule in the gossip circuits and the local press. But the expressions of moral indignation by Velasco and others must be taken seriously, for they formed the basis for a phase of radicalization that was not fully halted until the consolidation of the Morales Bermúdez presidency.[13]

IDEOLOGICAL ORIENTATIONS AND DIVISIONS
AMONG THE OFFICERS IN POWER, 1968–1976

The agrarian and industrial reforms of the first years of the Velasco regime accentuated class conflicts and provoked extensive mobilizations of peasants and workers, which were opposed by rural and urban entrepreneurial associations, the traditional parties, and, until its nationalization in July 1974, the national press.[14] These class and

[13] For example, General Mesa Cuadra stated: "I have seen how the sweat of labor and the tears of misery have been paid with coca and alcohol. I have seen how the greatest exploitation of man by man has taken place. And this has left a mark in our souls that no one can erase," *El Peruano,* July 4, 1969. A somewhat different message but with a similar moral tone is a statement by Vargaz Prieto: "The values of unlimited profit seeking, the irresponsible exploitation of natural resources of the planet and the aspirations of the great transnational giants have thrown them into an economic and financial crisis," *Expreso,* November 5, 1975.

[14] See especially Henry Pease García, *El Ocaso del Poder Oligárquico: Lucha Política en la Escena Oficial, 1968–1975* (Lima: Centro de Estudios y Promoción del Desarrollo, 1977); Jorge Alberti, Jorge Santistevan, and Luis Pásara, *Estado y Clase: La*

TABLE 8.1
The Distribution of Officers by Political Tendency

	Army	Air Force	Navy	Total	Total %
Progressives	6	0	1	7	12%
Center left	5	2	1	8	14
Center	12	6	2	20	34
Center right	8	2	8	18	30
Extreme right	4	1	1	6	10
Total	35	11	13	59	

sectoral conflicts had profound repercussions in the officer corps, provoking a process of ideological differentiation which left the Velasquistas of the early years in sharply divergent positions: the "progressives," primarily identified with General Jorge Fernandez Maldonado and General Leonidas Rodríguez Figueroa on the left; and General Javier Tantaleán Vanini's proto-fascist Movimiento Laboral Revolucionario (MLR) on the extreme right. The majority of officers continued to occupy a centrist position, shading off into tendencies more or less sympathetic toward the military left or right.

How can these groups be characterized and what was the range of ideological diversity that emerged as reform implementation provoked widespread social conflict? The analysis of the divergent tendencies shown in Table 8.1 is based on speeches, public statements, and interviews given by fifty-nine officers who occupied ministerial-level positions between October 1968 and August 1976.[15] The number, quality, and length of the statements reviewed for each officer varied considerably, and the placement of specific officers in one or another political tendency was more frequently than not troublesome.[16] *It is on the identification of general patterns and tendencies rather than*

Comunidad Industrial en el Peru (Lima: Instituto de Estudios Peruanos, 1977); and Henry Pease García, Diego Gardía-Sayán, Fernando Eguren Lopez, and Marcial Rubio Correa, *Estado y Política Agraria* (Lima: Centro de Estudios y Promoción del Desarrollo, 1977).

[15] Velasco, as arbiter among the conflicting tendencies, is not included in the analysis.

[16] It must be pointed out that very few officers made statements that clearly refer to all the issues raised below. Consequently, the assignment of an officer to one or another group is based on "partial responses." Off-the-cuff remarks, statements made in interviews, and responses to journalist's probes were considered more reliable indicators of attitudes than prepared speeches. Many speeches, after all, were prepared by civilian advisers. The military minister, however, also put in his views and he could choose his advisers. Thus speeches should not be dismissed; but they have to be treated with a certain amount of care, case by case. In a few instances, the disparity between speeches and remarks delivered in re-

the "correct" placement of any one officer within a particular category that the argument rests.

It was difficult to characterize the different tendencies, because all of the officers adopted a "regime language" that created the appearance of ideological unity. This language included rejection of political parties as instruments of manipulation and dismissal of the traditional economic elite as selfish exploiters; the characterization of the Peruvian Revolution as unique, neither capitalist nor communist; a constant stress on "economic pluralism," humanism, and the "full participation" of the people in all aspects of the reform process; reiteration of themes of fairness to all sectors, social harmony, peace, and order; the characterization of opponents as antipatriotic, selfish, immature, and lacking knowledge; and the necessity of patience and sacrifice. Rather than attempting to identify ideological tendencies by focusing on conjunctural choices or on the frequency of particular words, phrases, and themes in the public utterances of officers, I have

---

sponse to questions is so great that the speeches were given very little weight in determining the officer's position. In the case of General de la Flor Valle, his well-known progressive role was taken into consideration in the analysis of his statements, which, given his portfolio, focused on foreign rather than internal policy. As a general rule, however, officers were placed into the different tendencies on the basis of what they said; i.e., there was a conscious effort not to be biased by existing journalistic and academic works that had already "labeled" some officers on the basis of both their words and actions.

The analysis was also conducted in the light of field experiences. I traveled to Lima in May 1976 to interview members of the government on their attitudes toward mass mobilization and socioeconomic development, on their perceptions of the military institution, and to acquire information on their social backgrounds and career experiences. I prepared the interview schedule jointly with José Nun. The conflicts within the government made it impossible to interview a large enough number of officers for analyzing the ideological tendencies within the regime in general. I did, however, obtain lengthy interviews with six officers; the entire interview schedule was completed with five officers and only partly completed with the sixth. In addition, I had the opportunity to converse at length with two other officers concerning general social and economic problems. Of the eight officers, one was a major, three were lieutenant colonels, and four were generals. With reference to ideological tendencies described here, three fit in with the progressives, four with the center, and one with the center-right. In addition, I interviewed and/or conversed informally with numerous civilians who had had direct experiences with the military government. These interviews are not utilized directly here; they form part of the general data base on which the analysis was constructed, however. For a complete relation of the sources used for this essay, as well as the interview schedule prepared with José Nun, see Liisa North and Tanya Korovkin, *The Peruvian Revolution: Reform Policies and Ideological Orientations of the Officers in Power, 1968–1976* (Montreal: McGill University Centre for Developing Area Studies, 1981).

attempted to analyze the internal logic and articulation of each officer's discourse taken as a whole in order to reconstruct his vision of (1) the process of economic development (the fundamental problems, the necessary forms of the organization of production and its goals) and (2) mass mobilization (its desirability as such and appropriate forms it should take).

It must be emphasized that the ideological tendencies identified here cannot be equated with actual or effective political alliances among the officers in each category. My concern is twofold: identification of the range of reform options discussed within the officer corps during the course of the Peruvian experiment; and the degree of congruence between such options and the ideological positions of organized civilian political groups.

The Progressives: A Socialist Option?

As the reform policies of the Velasco years catalyzed the mobilization and organization of masses of workers and peasants, the bourgeoisie was haunted by the specter of socialist revolution. For the propertied classes, the government's apparent willingness to respond to mass pressures for accelerated reforms and the radical militancy of popular organizations associated with the government—the Confederación Nacional Agraria (CNA), the Confederación Nacional de Comunidades Industriales (CONACI), and even groups within SIN-AMOS—became much more frightening phenomena than the non-government left-wing opposition. The potential leaders of the socialist revolution were identified by some in the bourgeoisie as General Rodríguez Figueroa and General Fernandez Maldonado, the commander of the most important military region of the country and the minister of energy and mines, respectively, during the critical July 1974–August 1975 period of acute internal government conflict.[17] These and other officers were raising issues that so far had been left off the regime's agenda; they were identified as the military figures who could unite sectors of the left inside and outside the government.

Fundamentally, the progressives' position called for the eradication of the worst forms of mass poverty through income redistribution pol-

---

[17] Whether or not this perception of a possible socialist revolution with a military leadership was "correct" as a real possibility, it was firmly believed. Even though the possibility of its success, a prominent businessman maintained in an interview in June of 1976, was one in a hundred, the same could be said for that small group of guerrillas in the Cuban Sierra Maestra. Referring to General Leonidas Rodríguez, he concluded: "I'm just glad that Leonidas wasn't a lion."

icies, including reduction of the concentration of resources in the urban sector, modification of the content of production in response to mass needs, and promotion of full employment.[18] Their position was grounded in the necessity of reform to meet popular needs and in an awareness of the social and economic structural factors that perpetuate mass poverty. Officers whose point of departure for economic policy making was the eradication of mass poverty manifested an open-minded and questioning attitude concerning the appropriate organizational means for achieving their goals; and in that sense, they were not committed to a capitalist system. Of the seven officers here identified as progressives on socio-economic policy, three also explicitly approved autonomous mass mobilization and organization, even arguing that political participation began with a critical examination of society and government policies.

According to General Marco del Pont, head of the National Planning Institute from April 1969 to January 1974, and General Enrique Gallegos Venero, one of the original group of "radical colonels" and minister of agriculture from November 1974 to July 1976, the fundamental social and economic problems of the country were rooted in the uneven distribution of income and resources between the urban and the rural areas. Gallegos argued that rural development was the essential first step to national development and that the basis for development planning had to be the reversal of the mechanisms through which the rural surplus was extracted by the urban sector. In a more political tone, Gallegos added that the *campesinado,* or peasantry, constituted the "vanguard" of the new society being created by the revolutionary government.[19] On another occasion, he concluded that "the farmer is the man who works outside the city but for the city. The peasant is doubly exploited: when he buys and when he sells."[20]

In a similar manner, Marco del Pont argued that the structural cri-

---

[18] For an analysis of these issues focused around the role of the agricultural sector in the development of third world economies, see Louis Lefeber, "On the Paradigm for Economic Development," *World Development,* vol. 2, no. 1 (1974), and "Spatial Population Distribution: Urban and Rural Development," in Louis Lefeber and Liisa North, eds., *Democracy and Development in Latin America* (Toronto: CERLAC-LARU Studies in the Political Economy and Culture of Latin America and the Caribbean Number 1, 1981). For documentation on income distribution and the concentration of resources in the modern sector, see Richard C. Webb, "Government Policy and the Dist 1963–1973," in Lowenthal, ed., *The Peruvian Experiment.*

[19] *El Peruano,* June 25, 1975.

[20] *Expreso,* November 29, 1975.

sis of the Peruvian economy circa 1968 arose from the way in which its pattern of development "favored the more modern urban sector, creating profits for the very few and reinforcing the power and consumption patterns of these minorities; in this manner, the vicious circle of opulence was closed, around which and without being able to break it, the vicious circle of poverty and underemployment continued to extend itself."[21] Growth of a certain type had taken place, but if poverty and underemployment became the central concerns of development planning, "there are more important issues than maximizing the possible growth rate, such as asking: growth for what and for whom?" He concluded by quoting Velasco: "As much and more than economic development as such, we are interested in how the wealth produced is distributed."[22] Fernandez Maldonado's statements on economic planning and sectoral conflicts raised the same concerns; in addition, he emphasized Peru's subordination within the world capitalist system in the growth and maintenance of structural imbalance.

Without specifically addressing the relationships between urban and rural sectors, Rear Admiral Dellepiane, minister of industries and tourism from October 1969 to April 1971, reiterated the importance of examining the content and distribution of production in order to respond to the needs of the majority. In a magnificently quixotic and often confused discourse, which nevertheless displayed a certain intuitive sense of distributive economics, Dellepiane railed against "fictitious industries" that contributed to growth rates but not to real development, observed that automobile production involved "a problem of luxury production that the country can't afford," and proposed the creation of "a really democratic market for the majorities."[23]

Although generals Rodríguez, Meneses, and de la Flor Valle did not address economic issues as specifically, their political discourse and identification of the revolution's objectives had definite implications for economic policy making. For Rodríguez, "the central, profound, permanent, and substantive goal" of revolutionary reform was raising mass living standards.[24] Meneses' reasons for rejecting communism left open the possibility of a socialist organization of the economy. In an interview, he emphasized that his rejection was based only on the excessive concentration of power in a state bureaucracy

[21] Guillermo Marco del Pont, "Desarrollo Revolucionario—1968–1973," *Oiga,* January 11, 1974.

[22] Ibid.

[23] *Oiga,* December 19, 1969.

[24] *Expreso,* May 21, 1972.

and then turned the journalist's question, which would have provoked a broad anticommunist response from many another officer, into an attack on anticommunists: communism, he said, is not "a system that one should fear as *criollo* political bigotry and McCarthyism argue through the reactionary press."[25] Accordingly, when asked to identify the most important measure enacted by the government, Meneses chose the priority given to the social property sector, a response with strong if unrealized potential for the reorganization of the productive apparatus.[26] Finally, within both Rodríguez's and de la Flor Valle's endorsement of the Cuban Revolution lay the implication that a similar process was relevant to Peru and Latin America generally. Rodríguez declared that the leaders of Peru's government-supported mass organizations should learn about Cuba directly and "bring the experience of this brother revolutionary people . . . to Peru and transmit it to their bases," a remark that, as might be expected, provoked a major scandal in the press.[27]

In fact, General Rodríguez, one of the "radical colonels" of the 1968 coup and head of SINAMOS from July 1971 to January 1974, was the principal spokesman for mass mobilization in the GRFA. Although Rodríguez (and others who supported mass mobilization) defended the government's "no-party of the revolution" line as well as the government-created participatory organizations, his attitude toward popular organizations was genuinely democratic. It bore little relationship to the notions of proper channels for action or participation on the job and in community work programs that dominated the discourse of the center, and none at all to the authoritarian law-and-order themes of the center right. Rodríguez argued that mobilization began with a critical "questioning" by the powerless masses of their role in the society and continued on to "a substantive alteration of the structure of power."[28] The goal of mobilization was the "assumption of economic, political, and social power" by the poor; it had to "be generated and conducted by the men and women of the people itself."[29] And because the participant citizen was a critical and responsible individual, Rodríguez asked him to view the government in that spirit: "participation is not the submissive and uncritical acceptance of what the Revolutionary Government says and does."[30] This attitude toward the government was particularly important for Rod-

---

[25] *Expreso*, October 3, 1973.
[26] *La Crónica*, February 17, 1973.
[27] *La Crónica*, April 15, 1973.
[28] *Correo*, July 25, 1971.
[29] Ibid.
[30] *El Peruano*, December 16, 1972.

ríguez. Quoting Velasco, he argued that because "a great sector of the counterrevolution is in the hands of bad government functionaries,"[31] it was imperative for the people to denounce these individuals[32] and thereby control—not simply accept—the conduct of the representatives of the state.

Fernandez Maldonado was perhaps even more controversial in his defense of popular action and struggle when he linked nineteenth-century guerrilla movements and the armed forces in an article that appeared to be primarily addressed to military personnel: "the vitality of our brave guerrillas beneficially nourished the ranks of our army. . . . A vital and direct point of contact was thus established between the people and its armed forces in every definitive instance of crisis."[33] In a similar vein, Meneses stated that "all grades of leftism are respectable" to the extent that they are based on "realistic criteria" but associated the notion of the absolute necessity of violence with a "pseudo-left."[34] From this perspective, it followed that official government action would not be sufficient to maintain the momentum of reform and that the people would have to check reactionary opposition. Thus Rodríguez argued: "I believe that the counterrevolutionary press is condemned to disappear. . . . It is condemned to disappear through the actions of the Peruvian people itself."[35]

Issues of poverty, redistribution, and unemployment rooted in the organization and content of production dominate the progressive officers' discourse. In addition, the political vision of some of the progressives favored autonomous action of the masses; the officers were aware (or quickly developed an awareness) that the major socioeconomic transformations being attempted by the government also involved major shifts in the social, political, and economic power of all classes and class sectors, and that a transformation of such dimensions had to enjoy the onergy and support of the masses. It was for these types of progressive tendencies that Velasco provided a clear and vocal leadership during the early years of reform. Their popularity accentuated the opposition of the entrepreneurial associations and middle-class parties to the military government and heightened their fears of encroaching socialism. Such fears were not ungrounded even though the progressive officers only outlined the basic problems and asked the dangerous questions. They never proposed a coherent polit-

---

[31] *La Crónica,* November 5, 1972.

[32] *La Crónica,* June 12, 1972.

[33] Jorge Fernandez Maldonado, "Fuerza Armada, Cristianismo, y Revolución en el Peru," *Oiga,* September 7, 1973.

[34] *Expreso,* October 3, 1973.

[35] *La Crónica,* April 15, 1973.

ico-economic project that might have constituted an alternative to the policies already pursued. Moreover, these officers never constituted a unified political action group within the government[36] and, similar to officers who held different beliefs, they tended to place a premium on the maintenance of the institutional integrity of the armed forces.

The Center: The Technocratic Planner's Utopia?

To the extent that there was a coherence to the reform policies of the Peruvian experiment, it was based by default on the vision of the military center; officers on the left and right partially shared its logic.

[36] In the case of General Marco del Pont, for example, the progressive position on economic policy apparently was not coupled with a favorable attitude toward mass mobilization. In practice, this meant that Marco del Pont did not form part of the progressive "alliances" of officers identified by, among others, Pease (*El Ocaso del Poder Oligárquico*) and Guillermo Thorndike (*No Mi General!* [Lima: Mosca Azul Editores, 1976]). His position on economic policy, however, was nevertheless significant for the conduct of the regime, giving it a progressive thrust. On the basis of the analysis being advanced in this paper, the alliances that Pease and Thorndike identify were in fact ideologically heterogeneous—that is, officers placed in a centrist position in practice allied themselves with Velasco when he was clearly in charge of orienting the more radical tendencies. This should not be surprising, for real political alliances, even among small groups, are always the product of a multiplicity of factors and not solely based on a shared "ideological purity."

The classification of Marco del Pont among the progressives on the basis of his socioeconomic policy position raises general methodological issues that can only be briefly addressed here. As it was indicated earlier, most officers were placed into categories on the basis of partial responses, for depending on their role in the government as well as factors related to personal prestige, they tended to speak on a narrow or a broad set of issues. If an officer's discourse even on a limited set of issues clearly articulated a mode of thinking representative of one or another tendency, he was placed with that tendency despite his lack of reference to other issues on which the abstracted identification of the tendency as a whole was constructed.

Despite these difficulties, I am convinced of the *approximate weight and nature of each tendency* presented here, although specific officers may be misidentified. It should also be noted that especially during their first years in power, the officers' self-confidence in their roles permitted them to be quite frank in their public statements. Their political inexperience, in fact, often led them into stating opinions and responding to journalists' questions that an experienced politician would have avoided. In this respect, for thirty-one of the fifty-nine officers considered here (53 percent), extensive interviews with journalists were found in the archive of *La Prensa*. Finally, the interview schedule prepared with José Nun (see footnote 16), as well as the economic analyses of Lefeber and ul Haq, were used as general guides to abstract the material from the secondary sources for constructing the portraits of the officers and the tendencies.

The center's point of departure for social transformation and development planning was rooted in what World Bank economist Mahbub ul Haq identifies as the generally accepted (though erroneous) wisdom among development economists: "the pursuit of certain high levels of per capita income" without sufficient regard to " 'what [is] produced and how it [is] distributed.' "[37] This position presumes that the existing system of production is essentially sound and can be expanded to solve the fundamental problems of development. In concrete terms, the centrists wound up supporting an accelerated policy of import-substitution industrialization on a national and regional (Andean Pact) level and promoted nontraditional exports. Because it did not rely on an understanding of sectoral and class power relationships, their vision of economic development made political mobilization irrelevant. Rather, the center's agenda demanded participation in civic action programs and on the job, under the rational guidance of the government's *técnicos,* to ensure increasing production.

Twenty officers, 34 percent of the total sample, occupy the center, including such prominent revolutionary figures as General Ernesto Montagne Sánchez, minister of war from October 1968 to January 1973, General José Graham Hurtado, head of the Presidential Advisory Committee for six years, General Rafael Hoyos Rubio, one of the "radical colonels" in the 1968 coup, and the head of state from 1975 to 1980, General Francisco Morales Bermúdez. Also included is a majority of the air force officers—six out of the eleven in the total. They proposed reforms to counter an often vaguely defined situation of underdevelopment and dependency in which only the oligarchy and a few prominent foreign corporations were identified as the central blocks to progress. Rather than questioning the content of production and the system of distribution, they tended to simply reiterate calls for growth and increased production. In sharp contrast to the statements made by Gallegos within the same month and concerning similar problems in the rural sector, according to Hoyos, "the only thing we can know for certain concerning the agrarian sector is that we must produce; that's where the essential problem lies and I hope that our people will attend to it. If there are obstacles to be vanquished, let's vanquish them."[38]

The centrist officers' notions of economic development can be reduced at times to simplified ECLA-school propositions concerning in-

[37] Mahbub ul Haq, "Employment in the 1970s: A New Perspective," in Charles K. Wilbur, ed., *The Political Economy of Development and Underdevelopment* (New York: Random House, 1973), p. 269.

[38] *7 Días,* November 21, 1975.

dustrialization and state intervention in the economy, filtered through the "general welfare" and "national security" vocabulary of the CAEM. In fact, the Peruvian military had "sent some of its military [school] faculty . . . to training programs . . . administered by] the United Nations Economic Commission for Latin America and the Institute for Social and Economic Planning in Chile."[39] A preoccupation with efficiency, productivity, and technological advance—often implicitly associated with the private sector and explicitly related to improving Peru's competitive position in the Andean Pact—was coupled with a naive faith in the expert and the technician. Thus the minister of labor, Air Force General Luis Galinado Chapman, could assert: "it is the truth that everything in life depends on *técnicos*."[40] It was this orientation toward economic development, rather than any concrete system of alliance, that made the centrist officers *de facto* defenders of local private capital and, despite their nationalist rhetoric, foreign capital.

A voluntaristic notion of social and economic transformation was inherent in this centrist perspective. It was a logical component of both the faith in technology and rational planning and of the incapacity to perceive the sectoral and class power at stake in a process of fundamental reform. Instead of identifying issues of social and political power, the centrists concentrated on the egotistical and misled actions of small groups. Montagne was probably the most eloquent exponent of these views, convinced that reform within enterprises, particularly the industrial community, "eliminates social differences and ends the profound class separation of other epochs whose formal manifestation was always the motivation for conflicts and resentments."[41] Thus the revolution was creating an "industrial society with dignity, which consolidates human values";[42] it would become an irreversible process when people understood the harmonizing and national welfare goals of the government, when a "new mentality" and a spirit of cooperation had permeated the entire population—workers, peasants, and capitalists.

Because in the centrists' view of the socioeconomic development process there were no fundamental class- and sector-determined sources of conflict and inequality that could not be resolved by tinkering with the distribution of profits within enterprises, promoting

[39] Alfred Stepan, *The Military in Politics: Changing Patterns in Brazil* (Princeton: Princeton University Press, 1971), p. 175.

[40] *La Prensa,* July 13, 1976.

[41] *El Peruano,* November 13, 1970.

[42] Ibid.

rapid per capita growth rates, and instituting rational planning, the revolution was essentially finished for them after enactment of the agrarian reform and industrial community laws and the nationalization and state management of strategic economic sectors. Consequently, organized popular action was not seen as necessary for the achievement of the revolution's goals: after all, fundamental issues of power were not included in their set of perceptions on socioeconomic transformation. The centrists emphasized voluntaristic and moralistic notions, a "new mental outlook," and shifted the discourse on participation away from collective sociopolitical action to individual ethics and personal will, from the social organizational level to the psychological. Thus the minister of health, Air Force General Jorge Tamayo de la Flor, could maintain that "all is possible when there is a will to work, sincerity, effort, and honesty."[43] In a similar vein, General Fernando Miro Quesada Bahamonde, another air force officer who had headed the same ministry from 1971 to 1975, announced that the first of his ministerial actions would be "the operation change of mentality."[44] Although government slogans of "full participation" and "autonomous popular action" punctuated the statements of centrists as well as progressives, among the former the meaning given to these slogans was divorced from structurally determined political power relationships. Accordingly, Montagne asked the people "to participate with consciousness in the acts of the government,"[45] that is, to support the reforms determined by the technocrats and planners rather than participate actively and critically in the determination of the goals themselves.[46]

It is difficult to identify the point at which these centrist perspectives of socioeconomic development and popular participation diverge from the main body of technocratic civilian planning wisdom of the 1960s. In fact, civilian technocratic and military values reinforced one another, with one or the other dominating the discourse and actions of particular officers at particular moments. There can be litte question about the origins of General Artemio García Vargas's response to journalists' probes concerning civilian opposition calls for the military's return to the barracks: "In the armed forces, we will not

[43] *La Prensa,* March 20, 1976.

[44] *La Crónica,* December 2, 1972.

[45] *Correo,* February 3, 1973.

[46] The same attitude was reflected in a somewhat premature statement by the minister of education, General Alfredo Carpio Becerra: "We are carrying out the postulates of the Revolution, and the people have already understood that everything we do is for their benefit." *La Prensa,* August 22, 1971.

accept any retreat; on the contrary, our objective is victory, which entails forging ahead with the fundamental principles which gave origin to the present revolutionary process."[47]

Military style manifested itself at least equally strongly among most of the eighteen officers who populated the center right. Without entering into an extensive analysis of either the center right (30 percent of the total), or the center left (13 percent), suffice it to note that the rightist variation from the center carries technocratic logic, stress on increasing production, and an emphasis on "law and order" to the point of disagreement with the redistributive and participatory concerns of the progressives and at least some of their partners on the center left.[48] The center leftists combined the typical logic of the center with the moralism of Velasco and some forceful stands on structural cum redistributive issues. While moralism and concern for social justice provided the élan for the revolutionary government, however, the centrist military technocratic position provided the unity. The centrist development project was, finally, utopian, divorcing production from distribution, relying on "will" (voluntad) separated from social power, and positing an abstract national interest above class and sectoral interests.

The Extreme Right: A Fascist Option?

The extreme right exhibited two sharply diverging tendencies. On the one hand, there is Admiral Luis Vargas Caballero. Minister of housing and construction from April 1969 to January 1972 and minister of the navy from January 1972 to May 1974, he was the regime's most forceful and daring advocate of limiting the state's economic

[47] La Crónica, June 27, 1976. The same military spirit is also clearly present in the earlier cited statements of Hoyos and Miro Quesada, i.e., "vanquishing" obstacles on the path of increasing agricultural production and the "operation" change of mentality in the Ministry of Public Health.

[48] There are two variations in the center right position. One is the strong statist technocratic position; the other involves an explicit defense of free enterprise capitalism (identified with efficiency, productivity, innovation, etc.) within the parameters of state planning and control. With reference to this second group, we have Air Force General Rolando Caro Constantini who, referring to health services, rhetorically asked: "and who can do this great work of solving the country's major problems? The Revolutionary Government? No. No, the Revolutionary Government promotes, but it is private activity that has to do it." La Prensa, March 16, 1970. In addition to the law and order themes mentioned above, the common elements in the two variations of the center right involve the absence of expressed concern for even the functional forms of participation and the issues of social welfare that are characteristic of the center.

role; at one point, he argued that "without private activity, without private initiative, without private investment, there is no efficient country."[49] When Vargas Caballero was sacked from the government and from his military position by Velasco on May 30, 1974, the leadership of the extreme right passed to General Javier Tantaleán Vanini, who championed the other tendency of the right wing—the mobilizational and statist project. According to Tantaleán,

> at times the people fail to understand this important necessity [of fortifying the power of the state] and attack when the state strengthens itself. "Don't you see that the bureaucracy is growing?" The bureaucracy! Certainly it has to grow, because it performs functions of control, vigilance, technological advance, rational and accelerated development of the country so that the rich won't rob our reserves.[50]

Among the mobilization rightists, the glorification of state control was tied to a demand for mass participation, but in a manner that contrasted sharply with the progresssive position. Their discourse, punctuated by a compulsive antileftist rhetoric, consisted of agitational and insistent demands for participation to support the revolutionary government through the appropriate hierarchically organized channels. At times, the mobilizational rightists could sound like progressives. This was particularly evident in the speeches of General Rudecino Zavaleta, who succeeded Rodríguez as the head of SINAMOS in 1974. Most likely, Zavaleta was also constrained by the traditions of the institution he inherited when he stated: "The work of liberating the workers has to be their own work; in Peru, the armed forces have only given the initial impulse—nothing and no one can replace the effort, skill, and responsibility of the worker."[51] But even in his speeches, the adjectives that qualify leftist opposition tended to be different from the progressives' careful distinctions among types of left-wing opposition. Zavaleta, moreover, never appealed to the peoples' critical consciousness à la Rodríguez, nor did he ask for their organized action to control the representatives of the state. Instead, he emphasized "dialogue" between government and the people—the favorite phrase of all ministers of the post-Velasco period.

With none of Zavaleta's equivocations, respect for hierarchy was

[49] *La Crónica*, May 28, 1973. Vargas Caballero had provided inspiration and leadership to that sector of the center right which proposed primary reliance on the private sector. His position, in this respect, was so strongly and explicitly advocated that he was placed with the extreme right.

[50] *Oiga*, June 28, 1974.

[51] *El Peruano*, December 14, 1974.

the transparent articulating principle on participation in the statements of Tantaleán and Air Force General Pedro Sala Orosco, minister of labor from October 1970 to December 1974. According to Tantaleán, in the new, just society being created by the revolution, the worker could struggle to compete in the hierarchy of natural inequality:

> One must not look with envy on him who is theoretically above . . . and no one should envy the boss, because you have to struggle to make sure that all your sons can be bosses. Unfortunately, life is not like that; there's a natural selection that takes place little by little but everyone has to have the same opportunity and the same justice.[52]

It is in this context that Tantaleán advised Peru to "learn from other countries by making workers who are capable of increasing production into heroes";[53] similarly, Sala Orosco complained of "infiltrated agents" in labor federations and argued that "traditional slogans like class struggle"[54] would have to disappear in the "new," "responsibly" organized labor movement.[55]

While the workers were the "bulwark of the Revolution," "its vanguard and shaft point," they had to "accept the Revolution with all its rights and wrongs and criticize through proper channels."[56] They must be protected against infiltrators in the lower levels of government organizations such as SINAMOS. In a remarkably aggressive statement of modern authoritarian paternalism, Tantaleán described his own success with the masses in his capacity as minister of fisheries:

> We have struggled together with the fishermen. And no one to this date has heard a complaint from these workers. That is why I love them; that's why I get along with them. And they get along with me because they know for sure that we are struggling together. And they now work at all levels in the ministry and in Pescaperú, participating actively.[57]

Finally, genuinely perplexed, Tataleán could not understand why the people welcomed into his MLR "should be called fascists."[58]

---

[52] *Oiga,* November 26, 1971.
[53] Ibid.
[54] *La Crónica,* May 1, 1973. See also *La Crónica,* August 5, 1972.
[55] Tantaleán, *La Crónica,* August 20, 1975.
[56] Sala Orosco, *Ultima Hora,* December 31, 1974.
[57] *Oiga,* June 28, 1974.
[58] *La Crónica,* January 31, 1975.

Changing Ideological Orientations: The Temporal
Sequence and Civilian Opposition

The ideological differences described above emerged in the social and political conflicts generated by the attempt to implement, in particular, the agrarian and industrial reform laws. Precisely because the military government was not tied to any one set of class or sectoral interests and was oriented toward national and popular interests, its reform measures, considered one by one, satisfied no organized interest, and its policies appeared inconsistent, indefinite, and contradictory. As a result, the traditional party organizations, the associations of urban and rural propertied classes, old and newly created workers' and peasants' organizations—in short all factions of civil society— began to struggle and maneuver to impose their definition of desirable goals on the regime. The extent of ideological variety among the officers in power reflected the acuteness of the class conflicts generated by the reforms and the indeterminacy of the process; even the military managers were aware of this. The mobilizational right within the military, for example, was a response to a left-wing mobilization outside the government, which appeared to be increasingly allied with progressive officers. It was the centrists, however, who played the pivotal role in both the initial phase of radicalization and the subsequent conservative regime of Morales Bermúdez.

The centrists' moderate and technocratic vision of socio-economic change included a deep-seated concern for popular welfare—"general welfare" and "the welfare of all Peruvians" were the current phrases. As has been argued, however, they did not recognize the fundamental class and sectoral conflicts that stood in the way of achieving welfare goals. Nevertheless, their genuine concern for improving living standards permitted the centrists to recognize some merit in the questions raised by more progressive officers and the critique of the reforms made by worker and peasant leaders as well as the civilian left. In practical terms, they supported, or at least tolerated, the radicalization of the agrarian reform process, defended collective forms of ownership in agriculture, and sponsored the industrial community. Their concern with "general welfare" and their conviction that opponents to their eminently rational proposals were selfish, egotistical, and antipatriotic, caused the Sociedad Nacional de Industrias' aggressive attack on the Industrial Community legislation to momentarily back-fire, weakening the industrialists' capacity to influence the government directly.[59] The vociferous opposition of landowners' and in-

[59] See, for example, Jorge Alberti, et al., *Estado y Clase.*

dustrialists' associations to reforms initially confirmed these officers' views that the dominant classes were corrupt and lacked national vision. The concern with welfare, coupled with the nature of the opposition from the propertied sectors, formed the ideological basis for radicalization. Montagne's pleas to the entrepreneurs synthesize this position, with all its contradictions and good intentions:

> we want people to understand [the reforms], because we know that these measures are not of a taxing character, they do not contain anything restrictive or menacing. Rather, they are measures for the benefit of the great majorities.
>
> All these transformations, which are designed for the welfare of the national majorities, undoubtedly, in one form or another, affect the interests of small groups; and they affect them, I would say, in a form which is not very serious. They exaggerate the consequences of such measures because they have been accustomed to not lose anything and to get everything they want. . . . We haven't taken anyone's fortune away. There are still rich men in Peru.[60]

The centrists began to turn against peasant and worker demands, blaming them for their lack of understanding, good will, patriotism, and patience, and class conflicts became increasingly bitter and widespread during phase one of the military government—the intended reform beneficiaries struck for higher wages in nationalized enterprises, demonstrated for strict enforcement of the new laws, and even demanded a role in the determination of future measures. By 1973, Montagne was arguing that "strikes without a reason" represented the most serious problem confronting the government.[61] Similarly, minister of energy and mines, General Luis La Vera Velarde, with the righteousness of a man convinced that he and his government have intended and acted well, asked a group of labor leaders from the Communist-party-affiliated Confederación General de Trabajadores del Peru (CGTP): "Has any labor organization offered an extra hour of work for this revolution up to date?"[62]

As peasant and labor militancy increased and possibilities of rapprochement between progressive officers and sectors of the civilian left appeared, the propaganda offensive of the civilian right—including APRA, the Belaúndista sector of Acción Popular, the conservative Bedoyista sector of Christian Democracy, the entrepreneurial

[60] *La Crónica*, November 4, 1972.

[61] *Correo*, February 3, 1973.

[62] *El Comercio*, September 21, 1975. It should be recalled that the CGTP was officially recognized, and for the first time in its history, by the military government.

and landowners' associations, and the country's major newspapers—reached hysterical proportions. Largely intended for the officer corps, it aimed to isolate and eventually remove the progressives from the government and critical military command positions and to convince the institutional center that only an alliance with national capital could achieve economic development goals. The impact of the propaganda was certainly facilitated by the officers' social origins in sectors of the middle class, which headed the right-wing opposition to the government's reform program.[63]

The influence of the right-wing campaign on the middle class and on the officers in power should not be underestimated, for in the arena of political ideological debate, the right dominated, alternatively provoking fear (e.g., the specter of totalitarian communism) and arguing "reasonably" (e.g., the economic irrationality of certain policies).[64] The left-wing was never able to match it, due to its defense of proletarian and/or peasant vanguardism, its organizational and geographical fragmentation, and its inability to formulate a national leftist alternative, a political-economic project to attract allies among the officers. The military government itself could not match the right-wing political offensive, paying for failing to organize a political support base, torn between conflicting tendencies, and beset by 1974 with acute economic problems largely induced by its policies—all adding up to a loss of confidence in its own capacities.

[63] One indicator of middle-class family background can be deduced from family names, that is, immigrant background. Peru received a considerable number of European immigrants in the late nineteenth and twentieth centuries, and these immigrant families were successfully mobile in the modern professions and played an important entrepreneurial role in urban commerce and industry. Examining the family names of the fifty-nine officers whose statements were analyzed, 23 percent in the navy, 31 percent in the army, and an amazing 64 percent in the air force have either one or two foreign names. Moreover, these percentages underrepresent the extent of immigrant origin since the data for separating Peruvian Spanish names from more recent Spanish families are not available.

For a discussion of immigration to Peru, see Janet E. Worral, "Italian Immigration to Peru: 1860–1914" (Doctoral dissertation, University of Indiana, 1972). The dissertation includes a discussion of immigrant communities of other nationalities and an analysis of their role in Peruvian society after the First World War turned away new arrivals in substantial numbers. Much of the right-wing propaganda may be found summarized in Alfonso Baella Tuesta, *El Poder Invisible* (Lima: private publication, 1976); Guidi Chirinos Lizares and Enrique Chirinos Soto, *El Septenato: 1968–1975* (Lima: Editorial 'Alfa,' 1977); and Pedro G. Beltrán, *La Verdadera Realidad Peruana* (Madrid: Librería Editorial San Martin, 1976).

[64] For a more detailed analysis of the right's propaganda offensive and the social backgrounds/contacts of officers, see North and Korovkin, *The Peruvian Revolution*.

In short, the outcome of the Peruvian experiment during the Morales presidency, and everything it has signified, was certainly determined in part by factors within the military—the strength of the moderately reformist and technocratic center and the remarkable tenacity of institutional loyalties and values based on order and hierarchy. No officer was willing to push internal disputes to the point of provoking a rupture within the armed forces. But it was also a product of the interaction between the military and society, the relative strengths and capacities of organized socio-political forces that entered into the class and ideological struggles provoked by the reforms of the early Velasco years. In those struggles, the social origins of the officers certainly predisposed them toward a more sympathetic hearing of entrepreneurial logic. Class cannot by iteslf, however, explain the formation of political alliances. The real differences, *en fin*, between the centrists' vision of a harmonious national community based on general welfare and the consequences of unfettered capitalist development should not be minimized.

If the position of the progressive officers and the center left was anathema to the propertied classes, and the centrists displayed unfortunate proclivities toward experimentation with the structure of ownership and profits, why didn't the entrepreneurial associations jump on Tantaleán's bandwagon? In fact, Tantaleán was also an unreliable partner, in word and action, due precisely to the fascist logic of his supremely statist and mobilizational option. The Tantaleán-supported state takeover of the fishing industry, as far as the private sector was concerned, was a direct attack on national capital; the general's arguments concerning other opportunities for private investment[65] were simply beside the point if the industrial bourgeoisie were not permitted to decide when, where, how, and with what degree of security they could invest. Moreover, the mobilizational militancy of the extreme right and its identification with the claims of workers was double edged: while MLR action was directed against left-wing workers' organizations, "bad entrepreneurs" were also on its list of enemies, and it consequently possessed a dynamic logic of its own that could become uncontrollable and "slip towards an effective anticapitalism."[66] The MLR, as an embryonic fascist movement, shared the radical ideological elements of fascism; Laclau argues that "fascism, far from being the typical ideological expression of the most

[65] See *Caretas,* May 21, 1973.

[66] Ernesto Laclau, *Politics and Ideology in Marxist Theory: Capitalism—Fascism—Populism* (London: New Left Books, 1977), p. 121.

conservative and reactionary sectors of the dominant classes was, on the contrary, one of the possible ways of articulating the popular-democratic interpellations into political discourse."[67]

The potential for coordination of progressive officers supporting the more autonomous government-sponsored popular organizations with sectors of the left-wing opposition appeared grave to the civilian and military right. The extreme right within the military understood that the incipient revolutionary left had to be contested in the mass arena; their counterrevolution, whether or not it is called fascist *tout court*, consequently had to incorporate popular demands, borrowing "its central ideas, objectives, styles and methods from the revolution"[68] potentially in the making. It was "mimetic," and precisely because it necessarily had to be that, "the counterrevolution acquire[d] a project and thrust that transcend[ed] the mere restoration of order and the *status quo ante.*"[69] The MLR's counterrevolution was a potentially dangerous option for the civilian right-wing opposition because it did not promise a return to 1968. Its will to monopolize the political arena was not perceived favorably by the traditional parties. (Its statist economic project had already been discussed.) The civilian political right and the propertied classes, correctly, preferred to count on the "good sense" of the military center.

SOME COMPARATIVE NOTES

The Peruvian experiment invites a number of different interrelated comparisons with post-depression socio-economic and political transformations in Latin America. It can be viewed as a headlong, "catch up" effort at import-substituting industrialization (ISI), which accentuated all the attendant problems of that set of policies experienced elsewhere in Latin America by condensing the process into seven years.[70] It can also be viewed as a radical reform process that attempted to go *beyond* the standard set of ISI policies favoring the national bourgeoisie and the urban sector in order to accomplish a significant redistribution of income and expansion of the national market; as such, it quickly confronted the opposition of all vested in-

[67] Ibid., p. 111.

[68] Arno J. Mayer, *Dynamics of Counterrevolution in Europe, 1870–1956: An Analytic Framework* (New York: Harper & Row, 1971), p. 45.

[69] Ibid. The term "mimetic" is also Mayer's.

[70] See Werner Baer, "Import Substitution and Industrialization in Latin America: Experiences and Interpretations," *Latin America Research Review*, vol. 7, no. 1 (Spring 1972). See also Daniel M. Schydlowsky and Juan Wicht, "The Anatomy of an Economic Failure," Chapter 4 in this volume; I agree with their general critique but not with the alternatives recommended.

terests and, *mutatis mutandis,* repeated the sequence of radicalization/conservatization and intra-regime division characteristic of Latin American populist movements in general. Finally, it may be viewed as a typical military government, characteristically incapable of generating a political formula to maintain mass support and constrained—by its reliance on the military establishment—from flexible policy making.

As far as ISI is concerned, once a socialist option was rejected, the approach for rapid economic development was based, *faut de mieux,* on the examples of the industrialization and planning of the more prosperous Latin American countries and on the dominant planning wisdom of the epoch.[71] A not atypical example of the generals' faith in the technocrats and planning experts of international organizations was provided by the minister of labor, General Sala Orozco; confronted by journalists on the issue of increasing unemployment, he responded that he was waiting for the arrival of a mission from the International Labor Organization (ILO) to help "formulate a plan for resolving this problem."[72] In more general terms, the centrist officers' orientations toward economic development (as indicated earlier) were embedded in the thought of the ECLA school. Peruvian officers had attended courses at the ECLA-administered Institute for Social and Economic Planning. Moreover, institutional forces tied to the predominance of the modern urban and export sectors and the evolution of the Peruvian economy and the policies of the Belaúnde administration[73] pushed policy in the same direction. In vain, the military government attempted to use industrial and export promotion policies to increase employment and living standards across the board. In fact, the basic economic policy choices undermined expanded employment, general welfare, and redistributive goals.

[71] See ul Haq, "Employment in the 1970s":
We development economists persuaded the developing countries that life begins at $1,000 [per capita income] and thereby we did them no service. They chased elusive per capita income levels, they fussed about high growth rates in GNP, they constantly worried about "how much was produced and how fast," they cared much less about "what was produced and how it was distributed."

Besides a constant preoccupation with GNP growth, another direction we went wrong was assuming that income distribution policies could be divorced from growth policies. . . . We [now] also know that once production has been so organized as to leave a fairly large number of people unemployed, it becomes almost impossible to redistribute incomes to those who are not even participating in the production stream.

For a critique of the excesses of ISI from a surprising source, see Raúl Prebisch, "Crítica al Capitalismo Periférico," *Revista de la Cepal* (Primer semestre de 1976).

[72] *La Nueva Crónica,* April 27, 1974.

[73] See Kuczynski, *Peruvian Democracy,* passim.

In this respect, Peru is not unique. For example, even in an apparently successful Latin American development effort, Mexico's post-World War II industrialization policies, as of 1963–1964, had left "40 percent of the population in the lowest income brackets . . . totally excluded from the benefits of development."[74] Today, even with tremendous petroleum resources to finance ambitious industrialization projects and with anticipated 8 to 10 percent GNP growth rates, many Mexican economists express no hope of solving "the most serious social problem: full or partial unemployment of half the 18 million labor force. Capital-intensive industrial projects create few jobs. . . . With 800,000 entering the job market every year, Mexico's huge challenge is to stop the continued *growth* of unemployment and eventually reduce it."[75]

Nevertheless, the seriousness of the Peruvian generals' commitment to welfare goals led them to question the adequacy of the traditional mix of ISI policies and, as a consequence, led them to the experiments in reorganizing the property structure. It also led to the expression of the dangerous alternatives concerning the content and distribution of production posed by the progressive officers (and by some officers here classified as holding centrist/mainstream positions). The willingness to experiment and the belief that the capitalist features of the economy would have to be progressively eliminated to come to grips with the problems of mass welfare[76] roused the opposition of all the entrepreneurial and related political groups discussed earlier. This is where comparison with other Latin American reformist regimes becomes relevant. Typically, reformist coalitions whose political-economic policy mandates are based on a vague national popular ideology, and hence ill defined, begin to fragment during the institution of reforms. They do so in relation to the politically organized strength and unity of the social support and opposition they encounter. *Mutatis mutandis,* after a moment of initial unity and a drive toward radical transformation that attempts to integrate all sectors of national society, different tendencies favoring one or another set of more clearly

[74] Celso Furtado, *Economic Development of Latin America: A Survey from Colonial Times to the Cuban Revolution* (Cambridge: Cambridge University Press, 1970), p. 63. For a discussion and data on increasing income inequality in Latin America with specific reference to Peru, see Richard Weiskoff and Adolfo Figueroa, "Traversing the Social Pyramid: A Comparative Review of Economic Distribution in Latin America" (New Haven: Yale University Economic Growth Center, paper no. 246, 1977).

[75] *New York Times,* February 18, 1979. Italics in the original.

[76] See the statements of Rodríguez, *La Crónica,* February 24, 1973.

defined class and sectoral interests emerge. This was the pattern of Cardenismo in Mexico between 1934 and 1940,[77] the Movimiento Nacional Revolucionario in Bolivia between 1952 and 1964,[78] Varguismo in Brazil, and Peronismo in Argentina. For example, Peronist populism over time fell apart and recombined into " 'populism' and clerical anti-liberalism, 'populism' and nazism, 'populism' and trade unionist reformism, 'populism' and democratic anti-imperialism, and finally, 'populism' and socialism,"[79] each with distinct implications for the vision of the ideal social order and the distribution of power and wealth. The MNR spawned both the fascist Bolivian Socialist Falange and a number of radical left-wing alternatives. Ambitious projects for social and economic transformation, whether civilian or military sponsored, provoke mobilizations and opposition that eventually divide the government and lead finally to a redefinition reflecting the correlation of power among the contending national political forces and their international allies.

Finally, what about the military element as such? The fact that it was the military, with its particular institutional features, that acted as the vehicle of reform certainly lent unique characteristics to the Peruvian experiment. For example, policy implementation was uneven since political appointments to ministries and state agencies were dependent on the internal promotion patterns of the armed services.[80] Policy incoherence, discontinuity, and wars between government ministries and agencies, however, are not unique to Peru; they occurred in all the reformist regimes mentioned above. In fact, such conflicts are unavoidable if a regime's reforms are not rooted in powerfully organized class forces that provide the foundation for clear and coherent policy making. Similarly, the hierarchical law-and-order values and national security concerns of the military institution may heighten the rigidity of the evaluation of specific policies and the political mobilizational process in general. Yet, here again, it must be emphasized that the civilians writing first for *La Prensa* and *El Comercio,* and then for *Opinión Libre* and *El Tiempo,* often outdid the officers

[77] See Liisa North and David Raby, "The Dynamic of Revolution and Counterrevolution: Mexico under Cardenas, 1934–40," *LARU Studies,* vol. 2 no. 1 (Toronto, October 1977).

[78] See Rene Zavaleta Mercado, "Consideraciones Generales sobre la Historia de Bolivia (1932–1971)," in Pablo Gonzalez Casanova, ed., *Historia de America Latina* (Mexico: Siglo xxi, 1978).

[79] Laclau, *Politics and Ideology,* pp. 197–198.

[80] See, for example, Hector Béjar, *La Revolución en la Trampa* (Lima: Ediciones Socialismo y Participación, 1977), and Thorndike, *No. Mi General!*

in their expressions of alarm concerning subversion and mass militancy. The military institutional factors were important in defining the character of the regime upon its ascension to power as well as in the determination and conduct of policy. Neither the coup of 1968 nor the performance of the government, however, can be understood in isolation from the historical context, and social and political forces at play, and even contemporary economic theories concerning development and underdevelopment.

What is remarkable to date, however, is the survival of the basic unity of the military institution despite the severity of the internal conflicts.[81] The transitions within and between "phases" of the experiment were negotiated among the different branches, indicating that the ultimate loyalty of the officers was directed to the institution itself. In that respect, comparisons with Brazil 1964–1979, the Pinochet regime in Chile, and Videla in Argentina may be appropriate. The highly professional contemporary armed forces of Latin America have recently displayed a capacity for maintaining a degree of institutional loyalty not manifested in previous periods of the continent's history. This may be explained by the central function they have assumed (and been assigned by United States military strategists) in the wake of the Cuban Revolution—the repression of internal subversion.[82] Depending upon the extent to which they identified the achievement of mass welfare goals as the prerequisite for national military security, however, some Peruvian officers are hesitant partners in the increasingly repressive function they have been playing since August 1975.

[81] For a discussion of military institutional character per se of the regime, see Luis Pásara in Chapter 10 in this volume. The different tendencies described here developed simultaneously with the maintenance of an institutional cohesion that might be described as a contradictory unity.

[82] See Alfred Stepan, "The New Professionalism of Internal Warfare and Military Role Expansion," in Alfred Stepan, ed., *Authoritarian Brazil* (New Haven: Yale University Press, 1973).

9

Velasco, Officers, and Citizens:
The Politics of Stealth

Cynthia McClintock

When the government of Juan Velasco Alvarado came to power in 1968, few analysts expected it to carry through major reform initiatives.[1] The Velasco regime was of course a military government, and few Latin American military regimes had advanced significant reforms benefiting the popular classes. Moreover, in Peru the military had historically supported the positions of the nation's elites. Indeed, many top officers in Peru's military had participated only a few years before in the crushing of major peasant movements, and many had been trained at military schools with anticommunist principles.

Yet by 1975, the Velasco government had successfully advanced a significant number of reforms. Its agrarian reform was the most sweeping in Latin America, with the exception of Cuba. The government nationalized various large foreign enterprises and sought to regulate foreign investment, especially through measures in the Andean

Research for this article was partially funded by the Social Science Research Council and by the Inter-American Foundation, through a grant to the Woodrow Wilson Center. For helpful comments on an earlier version of the article, I am grateful to John Bailey, Susan Eckstein, Dennis Gilbert, Abraham F. Lowenthal, Kevin Middlebrook, Martin Scurrah, John Sheahan, and Fernando Trazegnies. I would also like to thank José María Caballero, Luis Pásara, Henry Pease García, Augusto Zimmerman, and especially Antonio Muñoz Najar and Diana Davis of Lima's Ford Foundation office for their help in facilitating interviews for me in Lima in July 1979.

[1] At about the time of the coup, the major Lima weekly *Caretas* dubbed Velasco a "Conservative nationalist"; see George D. E. Philip, *The Rise and Fall of the Peruvian Military Radicals, 1968–1976* (London: The Athlone Press, University of London, 1978), p. 76. In the first major book-length study of the government, Aníbal Quijano, *Nationalism and Capitalism in Peru: A Study in Neo-Imperialism* (New York: Monthly Review Press, 1971), Quijano argues that the goal of the military government was largely to restructure and "modernize" capitalism along lines favored by the United States. Few analysts expected much even of the agrarian reform; see Colin Harding, "Land Reform and Social Conflict," in Abraham F. Lowenthal, ed., *The Peruvian Experiment: Continuity and Change under Military Rule* (Princeton, N.J.: Princeton University Press, 1975), p. 235.

Pact. In both the agrarian and industrial sectors, the government developed creative programs for workers' control of enterprises. During a period when income was becoming more concentrated at the top in many Latin American nations, in Peru it was redistributed from the apex of the distribution profile within the first quartile, and the government's programs seemed likely to achieve further redistribution in the future. In Henry Pease García's phrase, the Velasco government achieved "the eclipse of oligarchical power"—a long-standing goal of most civilian political leaders and citizens, hitherto elusive.

Despite these achievements, the Velasco government failed to win significant support from popular groups.[2] Even the peasants who became members of the coastal agrarian cooperatives, who probably gained the most from Velasco's reforms, failed to give solid support to the government. The lack of popular support for Velasco was a key factor in the success of the *Putsch* by Morales Bermúdez in August 1975. Various other problems described in previous chapters in this volume—the impending economic crisis, the newly threatening geopolitical context after Allende's fall, and Velasco's increasingly serious illness—were perhaps of greater immediate importance to the military officers who sought a new "centrist" leadership, but Velasco's inability to legitimize his government over the course of almost seven years enabled the officers to oust Velasco easily, without fear of popular protest.[3]

This chapter has several purposes. The first is to understand why the Velasco government was so much more successful in its reform-mongering than in its support-gathering. To this end, the chapter examines the government's most important policy success: its agrarian reform. I suggest that both the government's success in reform-mongering and its failure in support-gathering may be attributed to the government's stealth. By sending out confusing and ambiguous signals about its intentions and then suddenly taking the initiative, the government deflected opposition to its reform measures until it was too late for the opposition to mount a concerted challenge. While

[2] For data on this question, see Cynthia McClintock, *Peasant Cooperatives and Political Change in Peru* (Princeton, N.J.: Princeton University Press, 1981), chapter 10.

[3] The economic and political difficulties before Velasco were of course to some extent interrelated. The post-1974 economic problems turned a cautious "wait-and-see" attitude among many groups in Peru into a skeptical one. Previously, citizens' lack of enthusiasm for the Velasco government had limited the feasibility of any attempt to finance investment programs internally, via taxation, and had thus been a factor in the government's decision to turn to international banks for investment funds.

confusing the potential opposition to reforms, however, the government also confused groups whose support it would eventually need.[4] These arguments are derived primarily from my intensive study of three agrarian cooperatives in two regions during the 1970s.

Were alternative strategies for reform-mongering and support-gathering available to the Velasco government? Would a more open process with greater civilian input have been more successful? This chapter examines two other areas of action by the Velasco government—industrial policy and participation policy—and suggests that the answer to these questions is no. The government's reforms in both of these areas must be judged failures, albeit original and creative ones, especially with respect to enterprise democracy. In industrial policy, the government moved too slowly, and industrialists successfully undermined the reform program. The government's participation policy illuminated the regime's most basic policy tensions. Overall, then, this chapter highlights serious problems inherent in reform-mongering: when a government hides what it wants to do in order to succeed, it confuses citizens; but when it openly proclaims its goals, it meets greater opposition, frequently fails, and then both disillusions and confuses citizens.

A third goal of this chapter is to illuminate the general nature of the Velasco government. As other chapters in this book and studies elsewhere point out, neat "conceptual boxes" are not available for a valid characterization of this "confounding," "ambiguous," "perplexing" regime.[5] It is hard to characterize because of the relative

---

[4] My analysis was stimulated by the work of Albert O. Hirschman, *Journeys Toward Progress* (New York: Anchor, 1965), pp. 327–384. I am especially indebted to his discussion of "shifting alliances" and of the "semantics of problem-solving." My conclusions about the viability of the proposed reform-mongering strategies, however, are less optimistic than Hirschman's. Somewhat similar strategies are suggested by Samuel P. Huntington, *Political Order in Changing Societies* (New Haven: Yale University Press, 1968), pp. 344–396.

[5] The ambiguity of the government's program was first emphasized by Abraham F. Lowenthal. See Abraham F. Lowenthal, "Peru's Ambiguous Revolution," in Lowenthal, ed., *The Peruvian Experiment*. Note too that the ambiguity of the government is related conceptually to its autonomy. As Cleaves and Pease García point out, under Velasco the military seemed to perceive itself as autonomous from socioeconomic classes in the nation. The military wanted to maintain a distance from all classes, to allow it to affect the interests of any class as it deemed appropriate. Such distance entails ambiguity, as policies by definition are not in line with the desires of any one class. Other useful discussions of the government's ambiguity include Evelyne Huber Stephens, *The Politics of Workers' Participation: The Peruvian Approach in Comparative Perspective* (New York: Academic Press, 1980), especially pp. 84–89; Rosemary Thorp and Geoffrey Bertram, *Peru*

shortage of information about the key officers. (My analysis draws heavily on informal interviews in July 1979 with some twenty military and civilian policy makers about the Velasco years, and on my study of the development of agrarian policy over time.)[6] It is also hard to characterize because of the variety of personal and ideological factions within the military leadership, and because the political perspectives of individual leaders changed during their time in office.

My analysis is based on the premise that the government can be best understood through what it did, through its specific policies. Yet, it is hard to separate what was from what might have been. The promise of uncharted new possibilities sensed in Peru in the early 1970s was ultimately not realized; but while the experiment lasted, it inspired some, and frightened many. It is also hard to separate what was in the "Phase One" of the military government from what was reversed under Morales Bermúdez. Indeed, as reforms of the early 1970s were rather easily dismantled in "Phase Two," it became clear how small was the group of military "progressives" and how long the odds had been against Velasco's reforms from the start.

The next section of this chapter introduces basic features of the Velasco government, in part to provide the necessary background for

1890–1977: Growth and Policy in an Open Economy (London: Macmillan and Co., 1978), especially pp. 302–303; Anthony Ferner, "A New Development Model for Peru? Anomalies and Readjustments," *Bulletin of the Society for Latin American Studies,* no. 28 (April 1978), pp. 42–63; and Pedro Ortiz Vergara, *"Los Caminos Equivocados y la Nueva Vía Política Persuana"* (manuscript, University of Venezuela at Alto Barinas, 1979).

[6] Virtually no scholars were able to inteview top officers systematically during their rule, to observe policy making "from the inside," or to review high-level correspondence or minutes from meetings. To my knowledge, the most rigorous attempt to analyze the perspectives of top officers is the chapter by Liisa North in this volume (Chapter 8), based on public statements and interviews, primarily to the press. In greater despair of the possibility for a "rigorous" analysis in the conventional social science sense, Luis Pásara, Peter Cleaves, Henry Pease García, and I have tried to construe the aims of the military leaders from informal interviews, a less systematic review of public documents, and our actual experiences "in the field." Perhaps for this reason our assessments of the government are, in some cases, quite different. Very useful works on the military include Henry Pease García, *El Ocaso del Poder Oligárquico: Lucha Política en la Escena Oficial, 1968–1975* (Lima: DESCO, 1977); Alfred Stepan, *The State and Society: Peru in Comparative Perspective* (Princeton: Princeton University Press, 1978); Peter S. Cleaves and Martin J. Scurrah, *Agriculture, Bureaucracy, and Military Government in Peru* (Ithaca: Cornell University Press, 1978); and Lowenthal, ed., *The Peruvian Experiment.*

the subsequent detailed discussion of policy formulation. This section aims both to summarize widely held views of the government and to suggest that a great deal about the regime remains unknown.

THE VELASCO GOVERNMENT AND ITS PLANS

Top military officers originally were not very clear about what they wanted to do: as one leader put it, "We had a series of concerns but they were not very precise."[7] The main concerns were to begin agrarian reform, to expropriate the International Petroleum Company, and to ensure that communism did not become an important force in Peru.

What were the reasons for these concerns? The desire for agrarian reform was motivated in part by the analytical perception that some "forty families" owned an astoundingly large percentage of Peru's productive land; such a skewed land tenure pattern had been widely criticized as a key reason for Peru's socioeconomic backwardness relative to other Latin American nations. Agrarian reform was also motivated by indignation that in the past these "forty families" had manipulated the military for their own purposes. Moreover, in the aftermath of guerrilla insurgencies during the 1960s, many officers apparently pinned their hopes on agrarian reform as a check against communism: to own land would be to have a real stake in Peru as a nation, to have "something to defend." The desire to expropriate IPC was widespread and intense among Peruvians. Effective regulation of IPC was one key promise made by Fernando Belaúnde in his victorious 1963 campaign; the popular perception that he did not fulfill this promise was a major reason for his downfall. Officers saw the privileges of IPC as an affront to Peru's national sovereignty. Years before, General Velasco had apparently confronted IPC over a question of transportation for a military unit in the La Brea and Pariñas area held by IPC, and the confrontation may have left Velasco especially sensitive to the unusual prerogatives of the company in Peru.[8] Anticommunism was a basic premise in military schools in most Latin American nations during the postwar period and Peru's military schools were no exception.[9] An intense, visceral anticommunist stance

---

[7] Confidential interview, July 27, 1980.

[8] The incident is described by Adalberto J. Pinelo in his *The Multinational Corporation as a Force in Latin American Politics: A Case Study of the International Petroleum Company in Peru* (New York: Praeger Publishers, 1973), pp. 146–147.

[9] See Victor Villaneuva, *El CAEM y la Revolución de la Fuerza Armada* (Lima: Instituto de Estudios Peruanos, 1972) and Stepan, *The State and Society*, pp. 117–157.

characterized even many officers who were later to be classified as progressive.

These concerns did not constitute a "plan" (despite Velasco's claims to the contrary in 1974).[10] Various critical policy areas, especially political participation issues, had been given virtually no advance consideration by the top officers.[11] Moreover, as high-ranking officers sat down to spell out policies, they found that policy preferences differed widely—even with respect to agrarian reform, an area where most officers thought that at least *something* should be done. Disagreements arose over the swathe to be cut by the agrarian refom and the industrial reform; over the extent of regulation of foreign investment; over the advantages of state enterprise versus worker-controlled enterprise; and over the character of citizen participation in government.

In his analysis of military leadership and policies during the Velasco era, Henry Pease García identifies three general "tendencies" within top military circles: the "bourgeois liberals," the "progressives," and "La Misión." Pease García emphasizes that these tendencies were no more than that—they were not ideologies, and not clearly factions. Adherents shifted in response to changes in the international context and internal political dynamics.

Yet, the tendencies and their major adherents must be identified if policy changes are to be understood. The bourgeois liberal tendency was perhaps dominant in the government in 1968. Its principal figures included General Ernesto Montagne and Admiral Luis Vargas Caballero and a considerable number of other ministers, most of whom were removed by 1971. The bourgeois liberal orientation favored private enterprise and saw reforms only as a means to promote efficiency and support private industrialists.

In contrast, the progressive orientation was sympathetic to socialist alternatives and was committed to the achievement of both equality and liberty. Progressive views underlay much of the "fully participatory social democracy" perspective. The years 1972 and 1973 marked the apex of the power of the progressives in general and Velasco in particular. By this time, Velasco had consolidated the political position of key officer allies, and the generals whose stars seemed to be shining brightest were particularly progressive: Leonidas Rodríguez

[10] On July 28, 1974, Velasco released the Plan Inca—a plan he claimed had been drawn up shortly before the 1968 coup by its principal plotters. Very few analysts of Peruvian politics believe the authenticity of the Plan Inca. See also the discussion of the government's plan in Chapter 10 of this volume by Luis Pásara.

[11] See Stepan, *The State and Society*, pp. 133–136. He emphasizes the relatively strong consensus on agrarian reform in contrast to political participation.

Figueroa and Jorge Fernández Maldonado. As in Velasco's case, the origins of these officers were humble—Rodríguez Figueroa was born in the Cuzco region and, reputedly, once worked in highland mines, while Fernández Maldonado was the son of a post office employee in Moquegua, a remote southern area. As Liisa North documents in Chapter 8 of this volume, however, the number of officers firmly committed to a progressive position was never great, and by 1974 their influence waned as economic and geopolitical problems loomed.

In 1974 and 1975, the political momentum was with "La Misión," led by Javier Tantaleán. Although "rightist" in a certain sense, the propensities of "La Misión" and its head, Tantaleán, were very different from those of the bourgeois liberals and their leaders, Montagne and Vargas Caballero (see Chapter 8). "La Misión" was intensely anticommunist, but in contrast to the bourgeois liberals, it sought to counter "communist subversion" by developing political organizations controlled by the state and enhancing the government's role in the economy. "La Misión" was widely accused of gangsterish tactics reminiscent of McCarthyism in the United States.

General Velasco was of course a key figure in the struggle among these political tendencies. By all accounts, his ability to lead—to persuade, to cajole, to badger—was crucial to the victory of the progressives over the bourgeois liberals in the first years of military rule. And, by all accounts, his movement away from the progressives and toward "La Misión" in 1974 and 1975 was crucial to the alienation of the progressives and their decision to ally with Morales Bermúdez in the 1975 coup. What, then, was Velasco's plan?

Information on Velasco's background is scant. His origins might be classified as "petty bourgeois" by some, as more humble by others. He was the son of a "medical helper"—a kind of pharmacist without a pharmacy—who may also have worked as a schoolteacher. The family lived not in Lima but on the outskirts of Piura, a small city in the far north. One of eleven children, Velasco had to struggle to finish secondary school. He joined the army as a private, in part to enable further education, and graduated from the Chorrillos Military School in Lima with honors. Of what we know about his adulthood prior to his rise to the presidency, nothing suggests a radical political perspective. Velasco married into an upper-middle-class family; maintained personal ties to some members of the elite Prado family; and "rose steadily but unspectacularly" within military ranks prior to 1968.[12]

---

[12] Philip, *The Rise and Fall*, p. 76. Other points in the paragraph are drawn from Cleaves and Scurrah, *Agriculture, Bureaucracy, and Military Government in Peru*, p. 16.

Velasco was not considered white, but rather a *cholo* (an individual of Indian origin adopting Spanish ways).

From my 1979 interviews with Velasco's colleagues and opponents—and also with one of his military school teachers—a certain image of the leader emerged. He was never described as an intellectual or even as particularly bright. Apparently he owed his professional achievement to good, solid military behavior and a fine feel for people's strengths, weaknesses, and sensitivities, a capacity that enabled him to unify diverse kinds of officers. Velasco was further described as daring and impetuous, but possessed of a strong moral fiber and characterized by good intentions. One officer commented that Velasco was "tough on the surface but tender at heart."

In February 1977, Velasco gave an interview to the Peruvian news weekly *Caretas*. Velasco was not many months from his death at the time, and his illness was decapacitating physically and mentally. Yet, Velasco's words suggest the characteristics attributed to him in the interviews—a spirited individual, not given to cautious reflection:[13]

> *Caretas:* Now how would you identify the objective [of your government]?
>
> Velasco: To make Peru an independent nation and to change structures so that Peru might develop as independent, as sovereign. Not a sold-out nation on its knees. What was it like here? Here the American ambassador governed! When I was President, the ambassador had to ask for a meeting and I kept him six feet away. I hassled them. I kicked out the American military mission Here there were 50 or 60 American "big cheese" and the Peruvian government had to pay their salaries, their travel, even for the cat the family would bring. And they were part of the CIA's information network. . . .
>
> *Caretas:* Many people consider you to be full of rancor. What do you think about this?
>
> Velasco: Rancor? Against whom? Against nobody! I didn't hit anyone, I haven't struck any blows. I led a revolution. It was a well-planned revolution. Because we began to act straightaway, to operate at high speed. We have done so many things at a frightening speed. I knew that at any moment they might

---

[13] *Caretas,* February 3, 1977 (no. 512), pp. 30–33. My translation. The first four questions and answers were the first four reported in the *Caretas* interview, except for a very brief opening question-and-answer; the last two questions-and-answers were given separately, a bit later in the interview.

kick me out. Because here in Peru, tragically, the oligarchy never dies. . . .

Caretas: Do you believe that?

Velasco: . . . Many have said that one of the things the Revolution did was to eliminate the oligarchy. Well, I think we haven't seen the end of the oligarchy. Remnants are still here, and those remnants are growing once again. . . .

Caretas: And why do you believe you were ousted?

Velasco: Political ambition, the desire for power. . . .

Caretas: Some groups always reproach you as a friend of the Communists, as one who was soft on them. . . .

Velasco: Not only that. They have said I made Communism official. This is a stupidity. . . . How am I going to emerge a Communist? I have been a military officer all my life. There were some people half reds in the government. . . . There was infiltration. . . .

Caretas: Did you feel any proximity to any political party?

Velasco: I had some sympathy for the Christian Democrats, at the beginning. The only party that had precise and concrete viewpoints was the Christian Democracy. The rest were pure blah-blah-blah.

Nationalism, an end to the oligarchy, and anticommunism thus emerged as the goals of Velasco and other reformist officers. These goals did not encompass middle-level strategies for their achievement, nor did they consider such critically important policy areas as capital-accumulation strategies, technologies appropriate for Peru, or political participation. Indeed, as Cleaves and Pease García point out, especially in the policy areas that were not of central concern to top officers, they relied heavily on civilian experts for specific proposals. For example, they sought little advice on agrarian reform policy, but quite a lot on industrial policy and participation policy. In interviews, analysts both sympathetic and hostile to Velasco emphasized the limited critical capacities of many top officers. Apparently, "often the military leaders would reject a civilian proposal out of hand on the grounds that it was communist; but, if exactly the same project were presented a second time to the officers and its 'noncommunist' principles emphasized, the project would be accepted."[14] A civilian expert who worked on the industrial reform commented: "there was almost no understanding of the meaning of the Industrial Commu-

[14] Confidential interview with a civilian scholar of Peru's military, July 22, 1979.

nity in the government. . . . They liked the idea of profit-sharing, but the concept of 'conciliation of classes' was way beyond their grasp."[15] This expert added: "The officers had the conceptual ability to win single battles, but not a war."

One final question must be asked in light of my introductory discussion: Did Velasco intend a strategy of stealth for his policies? Was the obfuscation that characterized the agrarian reform program deliberate? A definitive answer is difficult. On the one hand, Velasco and the progressives in his inner circle were vague about the specifics of their designs; if a leader is uncertain where he wants to go, it is hard to devise a devious plan for how to get there. Many of the regime's sudden attacks on elites—such as the expropriation of the fishmeal enterprises in 1973 and the takeover of the major news dailies in 1974—almost certainly were not seriously contemplated in advance by the Velasco government.

On the other hand, these leaders were military officers, schooled in strategy and tactics. A minority faction in the military, Velasco and the progressives had to have finely honed political skills to advance their reforms both within leadership ranks and within the society at large. Velasco was sensitive to his opposition and problems of timing.[16] A certain Machiavellianism emerges at several points in the development of agrarian policy, and also, although less often, in the development of industrial policy.

Reform-Mongering and Popular Support:
The Agrarian Sector[17]

Stealth was very important to the success of the agrarian reform measures. As almost simultaneous events in neighboring Chile

[15] Confidential interview with expert on the industrial sector, July 23, 1979. The comment is particularly interesting because the expert would have preferred a more radical law but did not blame military "ideology" for the rejection of such a law.

[16] Said Velasco, for example, on the discussion of the draft social property law: "We have not opened up the dialogue so that *they can make us lose time* by alleging the inconvenience of adopting this new sector." Quote is cited by Lowenthal, "Peru's Ambiguous Revolution," p. 11.

[17] My account of agrarian reform policy draws on my own interviews and observations in rural Peru as well as on secondary sources. I studied three agrarian cooperatives in depth; two were rather small crop enterprises on the coast near Trujillo and one was a large livestock enterprise in the highlands near Huancayo, which included as members several ex-haciendas and many peasant communities. In 1973-1974, I conducted a sample survey in these cooperatives as well as in control sites. I returned to these sites in 1975, 1977, and 1979. I have also

showed, an agrarian elite anticipating sweeping expropriations retaliates: for the most part, Chile's landowners sold every last tractor and chicken they could (often across the country's borders) and united to stop Allende's reforms, often violently.[18] In contrast, the gradual, unexpected intensification of Peru's agrarian reform calmed many smaller *hacendados* into acquiescence during the early years while the government was establishing its reform machinery. Moreover, via stealth, the government divided the landowners: it confronted, sequentially and separately, the largest landowners, next the rather large, finally the medium-size. The medium-size landowners did not come to the defense of the larger ones because they had believed only the oligarchy would be affected. Later, by the time the medium-size landowners were affected, the largest ones had been compelled to leave their enterprises and had no incentive to work on behalf of other landowners. But there was a Catch-22 in this strategy of stealth: it confused and disarmed not only *hacendados*, industrialists, and bourgeois liberal officers but also would-be allies of the government.

Disarming and Confusing the Opposition, 1968–1973

During the first nine months of Velasco's government, the proclamation of a strong agrarian reform law was in doubt. The minister of agriculture was General José Benavides, a bourgeois liberal with political clout: he was a wealthy landowner with close ties to other wealthy landowners, and he was a respected officer, the son of a former president of Peru. Benavides opposed drafts of the law then in preparation, and his opposition naturally seemed a serious obstacle to the establishment of a strong law. Benavides spoke frequently with members of the National Agrarian Society (SNA), the landowners' lobby group, discussing almost exclusively agricultural productivity,

---

briefly visited cooperatives in Puno, Cañete, and Chancay. With respect to secondary sources, particularly helpful studies include Pease García, *El Ocaso del Poder Oligárquico;* Henry Pease García, "La Reforma Agraria Peruana en la Crisis del Estado Oligárquico," in DESCO, ed., *Estado y Política Agraria* (Lima: DESCO 1977), pp. 13–136; Harding, "Land Reform and Social Conflict"; James R. Agut, "The 'Peruvian Revolution' and Catholic Corporatism: Armed Forces Rule since 1968" (Doctoral dissertation, University of Miami, 1975); Ortiz Vergara, *Los Caminos Equivocados;* and Kevin Jay Middlebrook and David Scott Palmer, *Military Government and Political Development: Lessons from Peru,* A Sage Professional Paper, (Beverly Hills, Calif., 1975).

[18] See especially Kyle Steenland, *Agrarian Reform under Allende: Peasant Revolt in the South* (Albuquerque: University of New Mexico Press, 1977); and Brian Loveman, *Struggle in the Countryside: Politics and Rural Labor in Chile, 1919–1973* (Bloomington: Indiana University Press, 1976).

not land tenure structure.[19] But in June 1969, Velasco forced Benavides' resignation, charging that the minister's public opposition to the law was tantamount to flagrant insubordination.[20]

The principal agrarian reform law was announced only twelve days later, but after further intense debate, despite the departure of Benavides. The meeting of the Council of Ministers the day before the proclamation lasted seven hours, the longest meeting on record since the coup.[21] The following day brought one of the boldest and most sudden acts of the Velasco regime: the military's occupation and expropriation of the agro-industrial base of Peru's oligarchical apex, the huge sugar complexes on the northern coast.

Despite the dramatic steps of June 1969, most observers still believed that the reform would not affect all haciendas.[22] The new minister of agriculture, General Jorge Barandiarán Pagador, waffled on policy issues—perhaps intentionally.[23] Velasco, Barandiarán, and other officials emphasized that the key goal of the reform was to increase agricultural productivity, stimulate private industry, and achieve social peace.[24] The reform would stimulate private industry by providing a larger internal market and by enticing ex-landowners to invest their agrarian bonds (the compensation for their haciendas) in industry.[25] Officers reminded both North American officials and the Peruvian elite that the Alliance for Progress had recommended agrarian reform as a recourse against revolution and suggested that they concurred with this principle.

Meanwhile, landowners plotted to undermine the law by subdi-

[19] Pease García, *El Ocaso del Poder Oligárquico,* pp. 67–68; and Agut, "The 'Peruvian Revolution,' " pp. 212–213.

[20] Agut, "The 'Peruvian Revolution,' " p. 211.

[21] Ibid., p. 213.

[22] On pp. 235–240 in "Land Reform and Social Conflict," Harding is emphatic on this point. He cites reports by USAID and FAO analysts, as well as speeches by officials in the Peruvian government.

[23] Pease García, "La Reforma Agraria Peruana," pp. 99–100; note also the footnotes on p. 100 and p. 105 suggesting possible "Machiavellianism."

[24] See particularly Velasco's speech announcing the reform and that of a few months later before a group of Peruvian executives (CADE), reprinted in *Velasco: La Voz de la Revolución,* vol. 1 (Lima: Ediciones Participación, Oficina Nacional de Difusión del Sinamos, 1972), pp. 48–55 and pp. 161–172. See also official communiqué published in *Expreso,* June 23, 1971 and cited by Harding, "Land Reform and Social Conflict," p. 241, and the excerpt from a speech by Barandiarán cited by Pease García, "La Reforma Agraria Peruana," p. 105.

[25] Specifically, if *hacendados* invested from their own funds an amount equal to the value of their agrarian bonds in a government-approved project, then these bonds would be converted into cash at their face value (revised to discounted face value in 1970). In fact, only a trivial percentage of the bonds was ever so converted.

viding their estates among various "purchasers," usually relatives or friends of the owners, so that each subdivision would fall under the legal landholding maximum. This strategy had been used by landowners challenged by reform in many Latin American nations, with considerable success—particularly in Chile during the Frei government.[26] In Peru, the practice was encouraged by minister of agriculture Barandiarán himself[27] and was widely used in 1969–1970. But, if the *hacendados* were busy subdividing, they were not thereby concentrating all their energies on decapitalizing their estates or fortifying their political organizations.

The subdivision strategy was very harmful to rural workers, whose employment was often threatened and whose unions were frequently destroyed by estate parcelling. Rural workers began to organize against subdivision and many Ministry of Agriculture officials supported them. In late 1970 and early 1971, strikes were organized in various coastal regions, and the National Agrarian Society became more active in its opposition to agrarian reform, but still in nonviolent ways—newspaper campaigns and legalistic arguments before commissions.[28] In February 1971, Velasco issued one of the most important decrees of the agrarian reform: the annulment, retroactive, of the subdivision of the lucrative coastal orange estate, Huando. Similar annulments followed throughout the country. For the first time, it was clear that the Velasco government would truly enforce the legal landholding limits (approximately 150 hectares for coastal, irrigated land and some 30 to 70 hectares in the highlands, depending on the province and on irrigation facilities).

In 1972 and 1973, expropriations accelerated. The antisubdivision decisions of 1971 had stirred medium-size landowners to much more vigorous protest through the SNA. But in May 1972, with no forewarning or precedent, the government summarily liquidated the SNA. Its offices and property were simply taken over. The sudden attack significantly weakened the ability of the medium-size landowners to resist expropriation.[29] The decision to liquidate the SNA was a crucial one that apparently reflected the new strength of the progressive tendency within the government. The progressive stronghold, SINAMOS (National System for the Support of Social Mobili-

---

[26] On the extent of subdivision in Chile and the inability of Allende to expropriate the new subdivisions, see the figures in Kyle Steenland, "Rural Strategy Under Allende," *Latin American Perspectives,* vol. 1, no. 2 (Summer 1974), pp. 129–146.

[27] Harding, "Land Reform and Social Conflict," p. 237.

[28] Pease García, "La Reforma Agraria Peruana," p. 93 and p. 106.

[29] Ibid., p. 111.

zation), had been established in name in July 1971 and then in fact in April 1972. In March 1971, Barandiarán had been replaced as minister of agriculture by Valdez Angulo.[30]

Yet, even by 1973, when it was obvious that the 1969 law would be implemented, many individual small and medium-size landowners could not be sure of the fate of their properties. Given the scarcity of land in Peru, the official limits for holdings seemed high. And gradually, the government began to apply other conditions for expropriation, such as illegal labor practices, which had been included in both Belaúnde's law and Velasco's but which few analysts thought would be activated. Application of these conditions was subjective—hence, the uncertainty even of landowners whose holdings were below the official maximums.[31] Ultimately, almost all holdings over 50 hectares on the coast and 30 in the highlands and upper jungle area were expropriated. Indeed, when these limits were made official in 1975, they were perceived as rather high because they had been *de facto* limits for some time[32]—but in 1973 most landowners did not believe the reform would be so sweeping.

What does the pattern of the agrarian reform between 1969 and 1973 reveal about the "plan" of the military nucleus discussed in the first section of this chapter? The trajectory of land expropriations suggests that the goal uppermost in the officers' minds was to "break the back" of the oligarchy, in the common Peruvian phrase, and not to check "communism" or foster "social peace." The priority reform targets of the military were the large, lucrative, primarily coastal es-

[30] The political perspective of neither Barandiarán nor Valdez Angulo is very clear. Barandiarán resigned from his post after he had lost an argument with Velasco. (In March 1971, angry workers at the Tumán agro-industrial sugar complex had held Barandiarán captive for several hours, and the minister wanted to retaliate by sending in troops. Velasco refused. For details, see Kevin Jay Middlebrook, "Land for the Tiller: Political Participation and the Peruvian Military's Agrarian Reform" [B.A. thesis, Harvard College, 1972], p. 78).

[31] The nature of this reform process is described by William Whyte: "I asked government officials 'How is it that so many hectares by law could be untouchable, but this area is gone and here and there smaller properties have been taken over?' They pointed out to me that there are about thirty-two other clauses in the law that give the government the possibility of intervening and some of these are very much judgmental sorts of things." See William F. Whyte, "Panel Discussion," in Leila A. Bradfield, ed., *Chile and Peru: Two Paths to Social Justice* (Kalamazoo, Mich.: Western Michigan University, Institute of International and Area Studies, 1974), p. 128.

[32] Exact landholding maximums were more complex for both the 1969 and 1975 laws, but these are reasonable approximations. The 1969 maximums were established in Decree Law 17716, and the 1975 maximums in Decree Law 21333. On the political context of this decree, see Pease García, "La Reforma Agraria Peruana," p. 118.

tates owned by oligarchical families. These estates were not the sites of guerrilla agitation. Just the contrary: the peasants on these estates comprised a relatively well-paid "peasant aristocracy" that, in comparison with other Latin American countries, was weakly unionized and, when unionized, was most often affiliated with APRA, a political party that was far from communist.[33] The areas of radical peasant protest were almost exclusively the poorer highlands regions, particularly Cuzco.[34] Yet, these areas were the last to be affected by the agrarian reform, generally not until 1974 and 1975; considerable pressure had been necessary from progressives in SINAMOS and other agencies to assure expropriations in these areas.[35] Various scholars suggest that sudden peasant protests stimulated reform policy at various junctures during Velasco's tenure.[36] The failure of the regime to attend quickly to areas of peasant unrest, however, suggests that these protests were not an intense concern of the progressive military circle, but rather convenient pretexts in their debate with the bourgeois liberals. Velasco was apparently voicing the principle "better reform than revolution" as a debating point.[37]

Worrying and Confusing Would-be Allies

By 1973, it was evident that the government's reforms had benefited primarily families in the upper two or three deciles of the income

[33] See Julio Cotler and Felipe Portocarrero, "Peru: Peasant Organizations," in Henry A. Landsberger, ed., *Latin American Peasant Movements* (Ithaca, N.Y.: Cornell University Press, 1969); and Oscar Delgado, "La Organización de los Campesinos y el Sistema Político," *Apuntes,* no. 25 (July 1972), pp. 84–106.

[34] See Cotler and Portocarrero, "Peru: Peasant Organizations"; Wesley W. Craig, Jr., "Peru: The Peasant Movement of La Convención," in Landsberger, ed., *Latin American Peasant Movements;* Howard Handelman, *Struggle in the Andes: Peasant Political Mobilization in Peru* (Austin: University of Texas Press, 1975); and Philip, *The Rise and Fall,* pp. 38–40.

[35] Through January 1974, the number of families benefiting from the reform in the most agitated and poorest regions—called "Mancha India" and incorporating Apurímac, Ayacucho, Cajamarca, Cuzco, Huancavelica, and Puno—was less than one third the number in Peru as a whole. Between January 1974 and January 1976, however, the number of family beneficiaries in "Mancha India" increased more than 100 percent, versus only about 65 percent in the nation as a whole. Data are from the *Reforma Agraria en Cifras,* a serial publication of the Ministry of Agriculture. The uncertainty of expropriations and the pressures from progressives are discussed in McClintock, *Peasant Cooperatives and Political Change,* chapter 2.

[36] See especially Agut, "The 'Peruvian Revolution,'" pp. 211–212; and Harding, "Land Reform and Social Conflict."

[37] It is interesting to note that just such a strategy has been advised by some reform-mongering scholars. See Hirschman, *Journeys Toward Progress.*

distribution.[38] Some of the families in these upper deciles were the new members of agrarian cooperatives, formerly hacienda workers, especially those on the larger coastal estates.[39] The reform had not significantly benefited poorer peasants—the families in remote highlands peasant communities,[40] called *comuneros,* or the families with little or no land that migrate for a season or longer to estates for work as day laborers, called *eventuales.* In 1973–1975, progressive groups within the government turned their attention to helping these disadvantaged peasant families, but without much success. The result was unfortunate for the government as a whole. As progressives tried to help more disadvantaged peasants, they alienated the better-off groups that had benefited from previous policies. The government was thus in the worst of both worlds: it never gained the support of the disadvantaged groups because it never delivered on its promises, and it weakened the support of those for whom it had delivered.

During this period, the progressive thrust in the government came largely from SINAMOS. This agency, examined in detail in a subsequent section of this chapter, grew rapidly in 1972 and 1973 and was very salient in the countryside, even more so than the Ministry of Agriculture. Many SINAMOS policy positions dovetailed with preferences of disadvantaged *comuneros* and *eventuales,* and as a result, cooperative members often perceived SINAMOS to be allied with the disadvantaged groups against the cooperative members.

A major responsibility of SINAMOS during 1973–1975 was to organize the National Agrarian Confederation (CNA).[41] The confederation included local Agrarian Leagues, regional-level Agrarian Federations, and the national-level CNA with a leadership board. SINAMOS was in charge of enlisting groups into the local leagues and monitoring the election of delegates to the higher level bodies. In carrying out these tasks, SINAMOS made a conscious decision to weight representation in the CNA toward peasant communities and

---

[38] Richard C. Webb, "Government Policy and the Distribution of Income in Peru, 1963–1973," in Lowenthal, ed., *The Peruvian Experiment.*

[39] Unfortunately, no study to date identifies the location of the "average" cooperative member, or different kinds of cooperative members, in the income distribution during the early 1970s. Data from Webb, "Government Policy and the Distribution of Income," and from the Organización Internacional del Trabajo, *Estudio Sobre Ingresos de los Trabajadores Rurales en el Peru* (Lima: 1975), suggest wide differences in rural incomes and relatively high incomes for coastal cooperative members.

[40] "Peasant community" is the term used in Peru for rural communities with a certain sense of historic group identity, often based on long-standing kinship ties.

[41] The responsibilities given SINAMOS for the CNA are stipulated in Decree Law 19400 establishing the CNA.

away from cooperatives.[42] Peasant communities constituted about 75 percent of the CNA's membership in 1975, in contrast to some 40 percent of the agricultural population and a smaller percentage of gross agricultural product; cooperatives constituted only about 20 percent of the membership.[43] Considerable attention was also given to the organization of leagues in disadvantaged highlands areas; thirteen leagues were organized in Cuzco, more than in any other region except Ancash.[44]

Not surprisingly, these CNA peasant representatives with their progressive SINAMOS allies called for sharp redistributive measures in Peru's countryside. They urged that the agrarian reform be accelerated and intensified, especially in the more remote areas, a step fully acceptable to previous reform beneficiaries. Other policies advanced by the CNA, however, troubled many cooperative members.[45] The CNA supported the principles of "social property," a new mode of enterprise organization that cooperative members interpreted as state farms that would usurp their new rights in the cooperatives. It called for "just" and "equal" treatment for "peasants without land" and urged that cooperatives incorporate as full members a large number of *eventuales,* the so-called seasonal workers, who were often not "seasonal" and who received few of the advantages provided by the cooperatives to members. The CNA also proposed sharper price increases for food produced primarily by peasant communities (e.g., potatoes) than for foods produced largely by larger cooperative enterprises (e.g., sugar or rice). Moreover, the CNA did *not* vigorously promote various measures that would have appealed to cooperative members, such as a moratorium on the agrarian debt and the institutionalization of systems for the popular election and recall of SINAMOS officials.

Of the various initiatives, probably the move to require the admission of more seasonal workers as enterprise members was most trou-

---

[42] On the consciousness of the SINAMOS decision, I am drawing on an interview with Dr. Victoriano Caceres-Roca of the Dirección General de Organizaciones Rurales of SINAMOS in Lima, June 4, 1975; and on an interview with Dr. Pedro Ortiz of CENCIRA in Lima, April 30, 1975.

[43] For the make-up of the CNA, see SINAMOS, *La Confederación Nacional Agraria: Información Básica* (Lima: Dirección General de Organizaciones Rurales, January 1975), p. 4.

[44] Ibid.

[45] See Confederación Nacional Agraria, *Congreso de Instalación de la Confederación Nacional Agraria* (Lima: CNA, 1974) and Confederación Nacional Agraria, *Plan de Trabajo de la Confederación Nacional Agraria* (Lima: CNA, 1975). The CNA's proposals are discussed in greater detail in McClintock, *Peasant Cooperatives and Political Change,* chapter 9.

bling to the cooperative members.[46] Jealous of their new prerogatives and wary of further structural change, cooperative members did not want to help the seasonal workers. Despite considerable pressure from SINAMOS, the CNA, and often the Ministry of Agriculture, pressure that included support for seasonal workers' unions, the cooperatives refused to bend on this issue. Cooperative leaders devised various strategies to counter the official pressure, and few new members were ever admitted.

When SINAMOS and the progressive forces in other agencies did not sow discontent among cooperative members, they often sowed confusion. Responsibility for this outcome lies not so much upon the progressive forces themselves as upon their gradual defeat by other groups within the government. When the progressives were sidelined, so of course were many of their programs, to the consternation of expectant peasants. One particularly important example was the proposal for "Central Cooperatives" (*Centrales*), or second-level cooperatives that join various local cooperatives in an area.[47]

In the vision of progressives in government agencies, the Central Cooperatives would play a large role in marketing and processing agro-industrial goods and in industrializing Peruvian agriculture.[48] They would husband the political and economic resources of the single cooperatives and enable more effective competition against private commercial intermediaries. Moreover, the *Centrales* would check the trend toward increasingly wide socioeconomic gaps among the cooperatives by provisions for pooling machinery and for redistributing some profits among members of cooperatives.

The *Central* was promoted by progressives in SINAMOS, the Ministry of Agriculture, CENCIRA (a training and research agency), and DESCO (an independent research and development institution with relatively close ties to official progressives in this period). By 1975, most cooperative members had heard about the *Central* plan. Mem-

---

[46] This issue is analyzed more fully in McClintock, *Peasant Cooperatives and Political Change*, chapter 9.

[47] This paragraph and the next are based largely on my interviews and observations in three agrarian cooperatives in two regions. Information on attitudes toward the *centrales* is based on eighty-eight interviews in four sites in 1975 and thirty-three interviews in two sites in 1977, not drawn from strict samples. See McClintock, *Peasant Cooperatives and Political Change*, chapter 9.

[48] This vision is well described in Mario Padrón Castillo and Henry Pease García, *Planificación Rural, Reforma Agraria y Organización Campesina* (Lima: DESCO, 1975), pp. 263–299; and in Douglas E. Horton, "Land Reform and Reform Enterprises in Peru," report submitted to the Land Tenure Center and the World Bank (1974) (mimeograph), pp. 59–60.

bers' attitudes toward *Centrales* tended to reflect the socioeconomic position of their cooperative. In economically ascendant enterprises, where members looked to a future of superiority and dominance in their area, peasants were opposed; in economically modest enterprises—the majority—peasants were generally in favor of *Centrales*. In one of the three major cooperatives in my study, the leaders of the enterprise were enthusiastic and took the initiative themselves to launch a *Central*.

But gradually the move toward *Centrales* stalled. Groups rising within the government apparently rejected the *Central* concept in favor of either enlarging the state's role in marketing and agro-industrialization or maintaining the present role of private capital in these spheres. By 1977, only about twenty-eight *Centrales* had been established, serving only some 200 cooperatives, and most of these *Centrales* were merely accounting centers without the ambitious marketing and agro-industrialization functions originally envisioned by progressives.[49] The *Central* enthusiastically initiated in the enterprise in my study was gradually undermined as government funds never materialized and a social property enterprise and the state took over functions that had previously been assumed to be the major tasks of the *Central*.

Thus, many cooperative members perceived uncertainty in the Velasco government and gradually came to feel uncertain about it themselves. Moreover, many members saw the regime threatening the very structures it had created, and gradually felt threatened themselves. In the areas of my study, peasant support for the government dipped between 1969 and 1974, more in sites that had become cooperatives than in a control site that had not.[50] The following two comments suggest the peasants' skepticism; in the second comment, note the peasant's criticism of the hiring of more "permanent workers" (i.e., admitting new cooperative members):

> The laws are too complicated, and by the time you have one law figured out, they've changed it to a new one. It's not worth the effort.[51]

[49] Data are from the Dirección de Apoyo a las Empresas Campesinas, Ministry of Agriculture, July 1977.

[50] The 1969 and 1974 surveys were based on careful samples and used exactly the same question. For details on survey methodology and sites and on responses to this item, see McClintock, *Peasant Cooperatives and Political Change*, chapters 4 and 10.

[51] Interview with *comunero* from a peasant community in my study, October 1973.

SINAMOS only created confusion, destroying what was left of the enterprise with the hacienda, and setting a bad example. They promised aid and *capacitación,* but they didn't come through. They broke down work discipline, and people didn't want to work. It was their fault too that land was invaded and divided among many people who now have the land. . . . And it was their fault too that many permanent workers were hired, allied to the former leaders, until there were almost 400 employees, when at the most 200 are necessary, and it became impossible to pay everyone. The workers didn't want to work and there was no respect. Also, they got four administrators named, one for each ex-hacienda in the SAIS, who didn't know anything about administration. When the situation had become impossible, some of the SINAMOS guys left, and we kicked out the others. Now we've begun to organize our own enterprise little by little, the people trust us, and we're all learning. . . .[52]

It might be asked if the negative assessments of the Velasco government were related to the cooperatives' economic difficulties or to perceived problems in Velasco's overall economic policies. Traditionally, agrarian reform is believed to bring about economic dislocation, at least in the short run. Moreover, some analysts suggested that the Velasco government hoped to transfer resources from the agrarian sector to the industrial. Others wondered how such different types of productive systems—the largely self-managed cooperatives, the small private farms, and larger marketing firms, some owned by the state, some by capitalists—could all operate together in the agricultural sector without fateful "contradictions" or catastrophe.

None of these fears were borne out. The Velasco government was economically supportive of the *cooperatives* (not necessarily agriculture as a whole). In comparison to the 1960s, government loans to agricultural enterprises had increased, and food prices had improved a bit during the last year or so of Velasco's government (in relation to nonfood prices).[53] The agrarian debt—the compensation owed to the state and the *hacendados* for the reform—at first constituted a gargantuan burden, but as inflation skyrocketed in the middle and later 1970s, it became a minor item in the budgets of most enterprises.[54]

[52] José María Caballero and Manuel A. Tello, "Problemas Post-Reforma Agraria en Cajamarca y La Libertad" (Lima: Centro Peruano de Estudios Sociales, 1976), p. 32.

[53] For further information on these data, see McClintock, *Peasant Cooperatives and Political Change,* chapter 10.

[54] See *The Andean Report* 3, no. 3 (March, 1977), p. 48. The debt obligation was officially cancelled in 1979.

According to official statistics, Peruvian agricultural product grew at an average annual rate slightly above 2.7 percent between 1970 and 1975, compared with falling at an average annual rate of −1.3 percent between 1965 and 1968.[55] Most agrarian cooperatives were performing as well or slightly better economically as cooperatives than they had as haciendas.[56] Moreover, although cooperative members were critical of the government in 1974, in most of the cooperative sites surveyed, substantial majorities reported that the cooperatives "helped a lot" or "helped some" and slimmer majorities reported that they were "better-off" in 1974 than in 1969.[57]

REFORM-MONGERING AND POPULAR SUPPORT:
THE INDUSTRIAL SECTOR[58]

In contrast to reform in the agrarian sector, reform in the industrial sector did not culminate in dramatic and enduring structural change. Although the industrial reforms were particularly creative, enriching analysts' understanding of workers' control programs, and although they were important in building political awareness among industrial workers, the reforms themselves did not really survive the fall of Velasco. In 1976 and 1977, the first key measure, the Industrial Community Law, was mutilated; and the second, the Social Property Law, affected a much smaller sector of the economy than originally anticipated.

Why was reform-mongering in the industrial sector relatively unsuccessful? Certainly, top military officers did not share the widespread feeling that *some* kind of reform *had* to be achieved (as they had for the agrarian sector). But the dynamics of the reform-mongering

[55] Figures vary somewhat. My calculations are based on the *Latin America Economic Report* 3, no. 14 (April 11, 1975), p. 54, for the six years between 1970 and 1974; and on *Informativo Político*, no. 40 (January, 1976), p. 23, for 1975. Slightly greater gains are reported by Hugo Cabieses and Carlos Otero, *Economía Peruana: Un Ensayo de Interpretación* (Lima: DESCO, 1977), p. 210. Figures for 1965–1968 are from Cabieses and Otero, *Economía Peruana*, p. 210.

[56] See McClintock, *Peasant Cooperatives and Political Change*, chapter 8. It is possible that the government's figures are optimistic.

[57] Ibid., chapter 10.

[58] The information in this section is based on my interviews in Lima in 1979 and on secondary sources. Particularly helpful studies include Peter T. Knight, "New Forms of Economic Organization in Peru: Toward Workers' Self-Management," in Lowenthal, ed., *The Peruvian Experiment;* Giorgio Alberti, Jorge Santistevan, and Luis Pásara, eds., *Estado y Clase: La Comunidad Industrial en el Peru* (Lima: Instituto de Estudios Peruanos, 1977); Stephens, *The Politics of Workers' Participation;* and Philip, *The Rise and Fall*, pp. 123–127, and 141–142.

process itself seem important, too. In contrast to the process in the agrarian sector, the government's bark was bigger than its bite. The development of reform policies was slower and more open, especially to civilian input—perhaps, more "democratic." In this way, the government sought greater legitimacy and support for its measures. But, forewarned, large and small industrialists united in opposition to the reforms.

The first major new policy for the industrial sector was the Industrial Community Law. As Cleaves and Pease García pointed out, this law did not originate solely from the President's Advisory Committee (COAP) as the Agrarian Reform Law had. Rather, it sprang from the responsible ministry with substantial input from civilians there and was circulated first for comment among ministries as a draft law in May 1970. The key framers of the actual law, Decree Law 18384 issued in September 1970, were the minister of industries, Admiral Jorge Dellepiane, and Dr. Virgilio Roel, a civilian who had taught at the CAEM.[59] The law called for workers in all manufacturing firms of more than five employees to form industrial communities that would receive 10 percent of the firm's book profits in cash every year and another 15 percent in new shares; the communities also had a right to representation on the firm's board of directors in proportion to the percentage of shares held. The devolution of shares and representation was to continue annually until the community attained a 50 percent position.

The law dismayed industrialists. Very possibly in an intentional effort to disarm industrialists,[60] Velasco insisted repeatedly in public that the law would only help industry.[61] In contrast to the reform-mongering process in the agrarian sector, however, Velasco's soothing

[59] The term "minister of industries" and subsequently "Ministry of Industries" is used only for the sake of convenience. During the first years of the Velasco government, the full name of the ministry was the "Ministry of Industries and Commerce"; it later became the "Ministry of Industries and Tourism." On the importance of Dr. Roel's role in the development of the law, see Stephens, *The Politics of Workers' Participation,* p. 110.

[60] According to a confidential interview on July 22, 1979, Velasco argued at this time in the COAP for outright nationalization of industry. In another interview with a scholar, a sub-head of COAP indicated concern about "alarming the reaction" by the social property scheme; see Knight, "New Forms of Economic Organization," p. 375.

[61] Giorgio Alberti, "Estado, Clase Empresarial, y Comunidad Industrial," in Alberti, Santistevan, and Pásara, *Estado y Clase.* Said Velasco, for example: "The industrialists haven't studied the law and haven't realized that it benefits them just as it benefits the principal group in the enterprise, the workers. . . ." Cited by Alberti, "Estado, Clase Empresarial, y Comunidad Industrial," p. 51.

words were not repeated by his minister, Dellepiane. One of the most radical officers in the government, Dellepiane was not reticent about his views. His 1969 interview in *Oiga* quoted by North presumably troubled industrialists. The reform proposals made to the COAP by Dellepiane and Roel went much further than the eventual law; in these defeated proposals, the industrial community was to gain a larger percentage of the firm's shares at its inception, and was not restricted to a 50 percent maximum.[62] These proposals were circulated among various ministries; Dellepiane's views could not have been a secret to industrialists. Moreover, about a month before the law's announcement, Dellepiane went on television to explain it and contended that the industrial community would indeed go beyond 50 percent; the "explanation" had to be publicly disavowed by Velasco. Finally, some six months later, it was charged that, in a seminar for promoters of the industrial communities, Ministry of Industries officials were propagating class struggle through the community. This was apparently the last straw, and Dellepiane and Roel were removed in April 1971. The new minister of industries was Admiral Alberto Jiménez de Lucio, who proved much more sympathetic to industrialists.

The calls for a more radical industrial policy continued, however, only outside the walls of the Ministry of Industries. The focus of attention was upon social property, a kind of production cooperative that aspired to mix the advantages of authentic workers' participation in worker-controlled enterprises with the advantages of economic equity for workers in state-run enterprises. Interest in social property originated from a group called the *libertarios*, who sought a form of socialism that incorporated individual liberties.[63] Among the *libertarios* were lay Catholic intellectuals, some of whom were leftist dissidents from the Christian Democratic party, and individuals of anarchist Marxist tendencies. Apparently, Velasco himself gradually became convinced of the validity of the social property idea from conversations with General Arturo Valdes Palacio, a head of COAP, as well as with Jaime Llosa, a *libertario* who had become a high SINAMOS official.[64]

In contrast to his reassuring words and sudden actions in other reform areas, Velasco proclaimed the "predominance" of social property in Peru's economy of the future long before the law had even

[62] This statement as well as the following ones in this paragraph are based on Stephens, *The Politics of Worker's Participation*, pp. 92–96.

[63] Knight, "New Forms of Economic Organization," pp. 375–379.

[64] Confidential interview, July 24, 1979.

been written. In his 1972 independence day speech to the nation, Velasco stressed the importance of social property:

> The development of a vigorous Social Property sector will be realized in the organization of a diversified but coherent mix of fully participating enterprises that constitute a profoundly Peruvian expression of a new revolutionary principle in the economic field. Such economic participation must be the sustenance of the participatory social democracy that our movement accepts as the model of social and political reorganization that orients the course of the Peruvian Revolution.[65]

Social property emerged yet more slowly, and with still greater civilian input, than the Industrial Community Law. Various commissions worked on a draft of the Social Property Law between August 1972 and August 1973; in August 1973, the draft law was presented to the public for comment and criticism; the revised law was finally issued in May 1974. Meanwhile, of course, industrialists fretted, fumed, and failed to invest.

Another source of concern to industrialists during the 1972–1974 period was the activity of the labor office within SINAMOS. This agency included former colleagues of Dellepiane and Roel as well as many young political activists with leftist proclivities. The office worked primarily with the industrial communities and frequently encouraged industrial community leaders to seek a radicalization of industrial policy. A key SINAMOS effort was support for the National Confederation of Industrial Communities (CONACI) and, in particular, its first national congress in March 1973. To the dismay of industrialists and the Ministry of Industries, the CONACI congress took various radical steps: it criticized the "conciliatory" aims of the Industrial Community Law and stressed the important role of unions in society; it asked that workers' organizations participate directly in government agencies to assure a transformation to socialism; and it requested an immediate increase in community representatives to 50 percent on all firms' boards of directors. None of these requests was ever to be granted by the government, but in 1973 and 1974 that was far from clear to industrialists.

Meanwhile, as Velasco and his progressive allies spoke of social property and a stronger industrial community system, industrialists organized to block these reforms. Whereas in the agrarian sector landowner groups had been confronted sequentially and separately, in the

---

[65] *Velasco: Voz de la Revolución,* vol. II, p. 337.

industrial sector large and small industrialists felt challenged simultaneously. Moreover, the Industrial Community Law did not deprive them of their economic political base—their companies—as the agrarian reform did landowners. Further, whereas the landowners' association (the SNA) was quickly abolished, the industrialists' association (the SNI) was not. Small industrialists, who were affected by the Industrial Community law if their firm employed six people, gradually became especially active in the SNI.[66]

The industrialists thus successfully undermined the government's reforms. They used various accounting ploys to reduce the net income of their firms and, thereby, the amount of profits and shares distributed to the industrial community. When the communities complained to the Ministry of Industries, the ministry merely returned letters to the owners urging compliance; it had neither the inclination nor the legal authority to do much more.[67] As a result, by the end of 1975, the industrial communities had gained only about 17 percent of the ownership shares in the sector.[68] Perhaps more important, as documented in chapters 3 and 4, the industrialists exploited import and tariff laws to their maximum advantage and withheld investment. These practices were a major factor in the deterioration of the economy after 1974. As the economy weakened, the social property program languished; the program required substantial government funds for the support of new enterprises, but these were no longer available. By August 1975, only one social property enterprise had been established; by May 1976, only three; about fifty were "in formation."[69] Social property was very far from "predominance."

The lack of popular support for the Velasco government in cities is thus easier to understand than the dearth of support in the countryside. The military had promised a great deal, stirred aspirations, and failed to deliver. Discontent was marked prior to the dip in workers' real wages that occurred in about June 1975.[70] Unfortunately, formal survey data on popular support for the government in urban areas in 1974–1975 are not available, but unrest was obvious. The number of

[66] Alberti, "Estado, Clase Empresarial, y Comunidad Industrial," p. 68.

[67] Stephens, *The Politics of Workers' Participation*, pp. 98–99.

[68] E.V.K. FitzGerald, *The Political Economy of Peru, 1956–1978* (Cambridge: Cambridge University Press, 1979), p. 125.

[69] Francisco Moncloa, *Perú: ¿Qué Pasó?* (Lima: Editorial Horizonte, 1977), pp. 133–134.

[70] FitzGerald, *The Political Economy of Peru*, p. 310, and Denis Sulmont, "Labour Conflicts and Popular Mobilisation: Peru 1968–76," paper presented in Seminar on Third World Strikes, Institute of Social Studies, The Hague, September 1977, p. 56.

strikes in Peru between 1973 and 1975 was almost double the number between 1966 and 1968, and the average duration of the strike and the percentage of the labor force involved more than doubled across the two periods; 1973–1975 strike activity was the highest ever in Peru and very high by Latin American standards generally.[71] Perhaps the most critical was the unrest of February 5, 1975. On February 3, the Guardia Civil declared a work stoppage; without any police vigilance in Lima, a large number of the city's poor sacked stores, and a smaller number, encouraged by political activists of various convictions, set fire to downtown government offices. The events spelled the end of the Velasco government not so much because some groups had agitated against it but because thereafter no groups came to defend it.[72]

POLITICAL PARTICIPATION IN THE VELASCO ERA[73]

Political participation is defined as the amount of citizen input into government decision making and as the character of the dialogue between citizen and official. As such, it is of course a central issue for most regimes, and certainly was for Velasco's. The Velasco government claimed that it was establishing a "fully participatory social democracy" and that SINAMOS was the key to its implementation:

The social and political process that Peru had been experiencing since October 1968 bases its revolutionary essence on its unflagging effort to substantively modify the traditional structure of power in Peruvian society. In the words of the President of the Republic, the revolutionary process in Peru is aimed at ". . . building in our nation a fully participatory social democracy. . . ." [And, in a later speech] "The social order that we are constructing must be based on the global concept of a participatory democracy, that is to say, a democracy in which the people, freely organized, take part in all aspects of decision and exercise, directly or with a minimum of in-

[71] Sulmont, "Labour Conflicts," p. 48, and Stephens, *The Politics of Worker's Participation*, p. 242.

[72] See Hector Béjar, *La Revolución en la Trampa* (Lima: Ediciones Socialismo y Participación, 1976), pp. 201–208.

[73] Particularly useful studies of the participation issue include David Scott Palmer, *"Revolution from Above": Military Government and Popular Participation in Peru, 1968–1972*, Latin American Dissertation Series, no. 47 (Ithaca, N.Y.: Cornell University, 1973); Sandra L. Woy-Hazelton, "Political Participation in a Non-Electoral System" (Paper presented at the 20th annual convention of the International Studies Association, March 21–24, 1979); Carlos Franco, *Peru: Participación Popular* (Lima: Centro de Estudios para el Desarrollo y la Participación, or CEDEP, 1979); Béjar, *La Revolución en la Trampa;* Stepan, *The State and Society;* and Agut, "The 'Peruvian Revolution.' "

termediation, all forms of power, in its economic, cultural, social and political dimensions."[74]

The claims for a fully participatory social democracy were fraught with contradictions. In these claims and in the actions of SINAMOS during 1972–1973, the progressives were taking the government's reform program to its limit. Yet this limit was very real and could not be transgressed. The progressives and their civilian allies either did not accept or did not admit these boundaries. Thus, in its policy toward participation, the government committed a fatal error: rhetoric far surpassed action. The government seemed unable to give up its ideological illusions and pretensions. At first, the government may only have confused citizens, but ultimately it became morally bankrupt in their eyes.

The regime's strategy for political participation emerged slowly, after at least eighteen months of skirting the issue,[75] and with a great deal of input from Carlos Delgado, a former affiliate of the APRA party and Cornell-trained social scientist.[76] The ultimate decision in mid-1971 was to establish a government agency, SINAMOS, for the "social mobilization" task. When the government opted for SINAMOS, it simultaneously repudiated political parties, including a Velasquista party (the so-called no-party thesis). Moreover, the government rejected spontaneous popular mobilization.

These decisions reflected various concerns of the leadership. Apparently, given the anticommunist ideological strain in the Peruvian military, many officers feared that spontaneous grassroots organizing by peasants and workers would be easily susceptible to communist influence. When Committees for the Defense of the Revolution did emerge from the grassroots in various regions in 1970, the government viewed them suspiciously; they had "erupted like measles," said Velasco.[77] Many officers were also skeptical of political parties. They reasoned that parties in Peru had performed poorly, serving only as the personal vehicles of their leaders. Moreover, many officers may still have felt the decades-old tension and rivalry between the military and APRA and hoped for a participation policy that would leave APRA behind in the dustbins of history.

---

[74] Citation is from the introduction to the organic Law of SINAMOS, Decree Law 19352 (my translation). See also *Velasco: La Voz de la Revolución;* and Carlos Delgado, *Testimonio de Lucha* (Lima: PEISA, 1973).

[75] Palmer, *"Revolution from Above,"* pp. 43–46.

[76] In my 1980 interviews, various military officers described Delgado's role as pivotal and his impact as catastrophic to the government.

[77] Velasco's phrase is cited by Palmer, *"Revolution from Above,"* p. 88.

Yet the overriding concerns of many officers seem to have been even more basic. They apparently hoped to maintain the principles of the military institution, particularly the military hierarchy with its traditional criteria for advancement and promotion, which would have been devastated by the establishment of a political party. They probably also hoped that the military itself would retain control over the participatory process. These desires fixed the ultimate parameters of the participatory process in Peru, parameters that the progressives and their civilian allies would not be able to expand.

SINAMOS: The "Progressive" Vision

The progressives in SINAMOS for the most part did not accept these parameters. The agency attracted many respected intellectuals and activists on the left, including Jaime Llosa, mentioned previously as a key participant in the development of the social property program; and Hector Béjar, a leader of the 1965 guerrilla activity in the highlands who was taken prisoner and jailed until Velasco's general pardon in 1970. SINAMOS officials of such political convictions often perceived themselves as "bureaucratic guerrillas" who could push the military to the left and, perhaps more important, use the agency as a base for advancing their own radical ideas among citizens.[78] Especially in 1971 and 1972, the bureaucratic guerrillas had some reason to believe their strategy might work. Rodríguez Figueroa, a firm progressive and close friend of Velasco, had been catapulted to power as the head of the agency, and his political star still seemed on the rise. There was official discussion of making SINAMOS a "super-ministry" that would coordinate the activities of all other ministries and their citizen participation policies.[79] When the contradictions of a government agency "supporting" popular mobilization were brought up, various officials would point out that SINAMOS was to be a transitional organization that would "wither away" after popular mobilization was achieved and that strategies for citizens' selection and recall of SINAMOS officials could be devised as well.[80]

[78] A full discussion of this conception is given in Jorge Santistevan, "Estado y Comuneros Industriales," in Alberti, Santistevan, and Pásara, Estado y Clase, p. 133.

[79] Agut, "The 'Peruvian Revolution,'" p. 453–460.

[80] On the transitional character of SINAMOS, see Palmer, "Revolution from Above," p. 105; and Woy-Hazelton, "Political Participation," p. 17, citing Carlos Franco in particular. On popular accountability for SINAMOS officials, see McClintock, Peasant Cooperatives and Political Change, p. 361.

Moreover, arguments could be made for the soundness of the SIN-AMOS idea.[81] SINAMOS would not be deflected from its broader goals by partisan politics and the rhetorical games of electoral competition. Without an elaborate ideology of its own, SINAMOS would not be absorbed in endless and divisive ideological debate—as in fact Peru's left was in 1980. As a government institution with a budget over $90 million in its first year, SINAMOS would enjoy an access to state agencies and a level of funding far beyond what most political parties could anticipate; these advantages would enable it to support popular mobilization more effectively. Whereas Peru's political parties had tended to concentrate their efforts in major coastal cities, SINAMOS was organized on a territorial hierarchy that required attention to all parts of the nation: 384 local planning offices were established in ninety-one zones under eleven regional offices.[82] Although the national office retained major prerogatives, regional autonomy was considerable. For example, I found the activities of the Huancayo SINAMOS very different from those of the Trujillo SIN-AMOS: the background and skills of field agents (*promotores*) also varied greatly.[83]

By progressive criteria, some SINAMOS activities were successful. Perhaps the organization's most important success was its work with the National Agrarian Confederation. Despite the unfortunate consequences of its structure and concerns for commitment to the Velasco government among established cooperative members, the CNA was the first organization in Peru to bring thousands of peasants into national politics. SINAMOS worked with the CNA, but did not co-opt it; indeed, as the CNA became increasingly radical and powerful, the only way the Morales Bermúdez government saw to deter the confederation was to decapitate it—which it did in June 1978.[84] In its work with CONACI, potentially the CNA's counterpart in the industrial sector, SINAMOS struggled against the Ministry of Industries to allow CONACI to voice clearly its desires for more radical industrial policies.[85] The first round was won by SINAMOS, but in 1974, many officials in the Labor Department of SINAMOS, including the de-

[81] A thoughtful discussion of the major principles of SINAMOS is provided by Woy-Hazelton, "Political Participation."

[82] Full description of the organization is given in Sandra L. Woy-Hazelton, "Political Participation in Peru: A Military Model of Mobilization" (Doctoral dissertation, University of Virginia, 1978), chapter 3.

[83] Ibid.

[84] For a full discussion, see McClintock, *Peasant Cooperatives and Political Change*, pp. 357–363.

[85] This statement and subsequent ones in the paragraph are based largely on Santistevan, "Estado y Comuneros Industriales."

partment's chief, were transferred out of the department on charges of "procommunism." Subsequently, SINAMOS did work to twist CONACI into a progovernment organization, and a strong and united labor confederation failed to emerge.

SINAMOS: Limits and Parameters

The progressive vision of SINAMOS was flawed. The hopes of the progressives were dashed against the military's refusal to surrender power, a refusal that undercut SINAMOS from the heady days of its inauguration to its retreat in 1975 and 1976.

SINAMOS preached a doctrine of participation that it did not itself practice. Neither its personnel nor its policies were chosen with civilian input. The agency remained closely tied to the military hierarchy. High-ranking military officers became directors of eight of the ten regional offices in 1972 and were placed in seven of the sixteen top positions in the agency's national office.[86] The commander of the Lima military region was also head of the tenth region of SINAMOS, responsible for Lima's "new towns" (migrant settlements).[87] In January 1974, Rodríguez Figueroa was replaced as head of the agency by General Rudecino Zavaleta, who was aligned with the "La Misión" tendency. The change triggered a dramatic shift in SINAMOS' policies and signalled the decline of the progressive tendency in the government—but it was a decision made exclusively by the inner officers' circle. Whatever the expectations of the progressives for the future, local *promotores* were recruited by and responsible to their superiors in the zonal and regional offices. Despite a measure of regional autonomy and efforts to select *promotores* from the area, familiar with its indigenous population and speaking the indigenous language of the area, most SINAMOS employees had relatively middle-class origins: as of 1974, about 70 percent of *promotores* had studied beyond the secondary level.[88]

The "nonpartisan" and "non-ideological" claims of SINAMOS were also flawed. The agency's criticisms of Peru's political parties as organizations run in top-down fashion by their leaders for personal goals and its charges that Peru's leftist parties were inclined to treat workers and peasants as "students" or even "children" who must be educated by an "enlightened vanguard," had a certain validity. Such

[86] Palmer, *"Revolution from Above,"* pp. 94–96.

[87] David Collier, *Squatters and Oligarchs: Authoritarian Rule and Policy Change in Peru* (Baltimore: Johns Hopkins University Press, 1976), p. 108.

[88] Woy-Hazelton, "Political Participation," p. 184.

attacks only exacerbated the traditional rivalry between civilian political leaders and the military, however. In practice, SINAMOS had many features of a political party, a military version of a party perhaps, and did in fact compete with political parties. In its denial of these aims and its claims to a "higher" legitimacy than parties, the military enraged many party leaders.

Moreover, although ideology may be divisive, SINAMOS' lack of a clear-cut ideology engendered other problems just as serious. As ideology was not a valid criterion in recruitment, citizens of all political perspectives, and often unknown political perspectives, were hired. Probably a majority were not committed to the "revolution." At the regional level, many top officials thought the government's reforms were going too far, whereas most *promotores,* often young people with social science backgrounds and loosely Marxist sympathies, thought the reforms were not going far enough.[89] Many *promotores* promised more than they could deliver. Gradually also, elements of the "La Misión" tendency entered SINAMOS and carried out co-optive efforts of the kind described in Chapter 10 by Luis Pásara, often without the knowledge of progressives. The upshot was conflict and confusion.[90]

Moreover, theoretically nonideological, SINAMOS did not give sufficient attention to its own principles. For example, the government said that SINAMOS should promote both "authentic participation" (i.e., respect the authentic political voice of a community) and "equal participation" (i.e., encourage equal access to participatory organizations and equality in general).[91] But in many situations, both principles could not be upheld simultaneously. In their assemblies, cooperative members would "authentically" vote to restrict the membership opportunities of *eventuales,* thereby violating the tenet of equal participation. What could the SINAMOS official do in such instances? No guidelines were ever established and officials often tried to advance equal access, even though thereby overruling community decisions.

Despite its relative success in the development of the CNA and even to some extent in the development of CONACI, the parameters

[89] This assessment is based on my own observation of the Trujillo and Huancayo SINAMOS, and on Sandra L. Woy-Hazelton, "SINAMOS, Infrastructure of Participation," in John Booth and Mitchell Seligson, eds., *Political Participation in Latin America* (New York: Holmes and Meier, 1978).

[90] See especially Franco, *Perú: Participación Popular.*

[91] See Decree Law 18896 and the pamphlets on SINAMOS published by the agency itself in 1972–1973.

of mobilization by SINAMOS were constant and strict. By 1973 and 1974, as the industrialists' campaign against social property and other reforms were gaining momentum and as government funds were short, it would seem that the only way to assure the advance of industrial reforms was to mobilize citizens behind them. SINAMOS would have had to rally industrial community workers, the migrants to Lima's "new towns," and others to pressure the government. But organizing in the "new towns" was sharply restricted by the policies of the housing ministry, headed by the liberal bourgeois Rear Admiral Vargas Caballero, and by policies of the Tenth Regional Office of SINAMOS, which was also opposed to popular mobilization. Villa El Salvador was the only major "new town" where SINAMOS was active, largely because Villa El Salvador, a very large and remote "new town," fell into a different SINAMOS zone, where the director was relatively sympathetic to popular mobilization.[92]

Overall, rather than resolving the contradictions in the military government's ideas and the conflicts between different tendencies among military leaders, SINAMOS embodied them. The goals and structure of the agency were confused, and citizens saw the confusion and feared what might emerge from it. To citizens' queries about what SINAMOS was, the agency usually could explain only what it was *not:* it was not a Peruvian FBI, it was not a corporatist trick. Other explanations were lyrical, but still uninformative:

> SINAMOS is you. We are all SINAMOS, the men and women of the coast, the highlands and the jungle, . . . those who want to construct a revolutionary nation. SINAMOS is you, me and all our brothers, who in the cooperatives, the SAIS, the labor communities, the universities, the neighborhood assemblies, the public administration . . . are working and learning, constructing a new society of participation in revolutionary Peru. So don't ask what SINAMOS is. SINAMOS is you.[93]

CONCLUSION

This paper has highlighted serious problems in the reform-mongering process of the Revolutionary Government of the Armed Forces. A re-

[92] Interviews at DESCO in July 1979 with scholars specializing in urban political economy, in particular with V. Raúl Guerrero de los Rios.

[93] "Movilización Social y SINAMOS" (Lima: SINAMOS, n.d.), back cover. See also the various other SINAMOS pamphlets, "8 Preguntas a la Revolución Peruana," "63 Preguntas y Respeustas," "De Quién y Para Qué?" all published in Lima without dates (probably in 1973).

formist course, precluding the mass popular mobilization of a revolution, emerges as hazardous—by and large more hazardous than various scholarly analyses have suggested.

Velasco's agrarian reform successfully undermined Peru's elite "forty families" and transferred much of Peru's best land to peasants. This success was predicated, however, upon strategies of defusing and confusing opposition to the reform and of taking sudden, unexpected action. Such strategies have been recommended by various scholars of reform-mongering, most prominently by Samuel Huntington; examining in detail the case of the reforms by Turkey's Mustafa Kemal in the 1920s and 1930s, Huntington argues that Kemal's success may be attributed to "concealing his aims, separating the reforms from each other, and pushing for only one change at a time," thus dividing the opposition, as well as to his "blitzkrieg tactics in handling each individual issue or set of issues."[94] In her analysis of the reform strategies of Egypt's Abdul Gamal Nasser and Peru's Velasco, Ellen Kay Trimberger also points to the advantages of deflecting opposition by "deliberate obfuscation."[95]

Neither Huntington nor Trimberger acknowledges the Achilles' heel of this strategy: ultimately, moral bankruptcy for the government. In the Peruvian case, the government's record of confusing signals to large and medium-size landowners followed by sudden action against them left the officers unable to reassure peasants of their intentions in the final years of the Velasco era. The Peruvian case thus bears out the admonitions of Hirschman about such a reform-mongering approach, which he terms the "majority through shifting alliances" alternative. Of the five alternatives identified by Hirschman, the "majority through shifting alliances" is the only one that he believes will usually result in "strong intellectual and moral disapproval."[96] Hirschman comments: "the price of [such] progress and reform is the betrayal of one's friends—for what else is this maneuver which we have blandly termed 'shifting of alliances?' "[97]

On the other hand, an open and honest approach to reform-mongering is also hazardous, as various scholars have pointed out.[98] The difficulties of such a strategy are well illustrated by the failure of

---

[94] Huntington, *Political Order in Changing Societies,* pp. 346, and 352.

[95] Ellen Kay Trimberger, *Revolution from Above: Military Bureaucrats and Development in Japan, Turkey, Egypt, and Peru* (New Brunswick: Transaction, 1978), p. 149.

[96] Hirschman, *Journeys Toward Progress,* p. 382.

[97] Ibid., p. 380.

[98] See especially Huntington, *Political Order in Changing Societies,* pp. 386–396; and Hirschman, *Journeys Toward Progress,* pp. 327–384.

the Velasco government's industrial reforms. In the case of these reforms, the government was much more direct in its intentions, working with civilians and allowing more time for the development of sound policies. But the result was a more concerted and successful effort by opponents to undermine the reforms. The government's promises went unfulfilled, the reforms were never fully implemented, and citizens were again disillusioned.

What could have been done? If the nature of Peru's military leadership in this period is taken as a given, the answer has to be, very little. In the context of this "given," mass mobilization along revolutionary lines was not an option.

Yet, at least for the optimist, there are "what if"s. After 1973, when the government had squeezed most of the benefits it could from a Machiavellian strategy, it might have been more direct and honest to citizens about its very real internal and external dilemmas. Expectations and fears might not have been raised so high. Today, SINAMOS is often made a scapegoat for all the problems of the Velasco period. But SINAMOS by and large reflected the problems of increasing political polarization within the military as well as the military's own reluctance to surrender its ultimate authority. If these parameters had been recognized and dealt with by SINAMOS officials and military leaders, perhaps citizens would have felt some understanding of the government and stood up behind it in the difficult months of 1975.

When the Military Dreams

Luis Pásara

The emergence of Peru's military regime was spectacular, but its collapse was simple. For these reasons, the regime's attempt to transform Peru demands explanation. In this chapter, I seek to contribute toward an explanation of this phenomenon by describing the regime's major characteristics. I consider the regime's origins, its mechanisms of political articulation, the role given civilian allies, and the legitimizing ideology contributed by these civilian allies. Finally, I examine the regime's weaknesses and limitations, using in-depth analysis of the reform of justice administration as a specific example. I have based much of my discussion in this chapter upon extensive informal interviews with military and civilian leaders who were active during the military government's tenure in power.

THE GOAL OF THE MILITARY'S PLAN

Until 1968, as indicated in Chapter 1 of this volume, by Julio Cotler, the dominant classes had not been able to resolve the national question. They had been unable to forge a class of political leaders. This failure was evident in the absence of a national design, and it had resulted in the nonpolitical integration of the popular classes into the system. The political regime, commonly termed "oligarchical," maintained itself by the systematic exclusion of broad sectors of the population, which meant that most Peruvians were only indirectly incorporated into the national market and had a miserable standard of living. This exclusion thus continued the system of precapitalist relations. It also signified that most Peruvians were blocked from participation in the political system through the restriction of suffrage to the literate and through the imposition of Spanish as an official language. The tensions created by this type of societal arrangement (and

Oscar Dancourt contributed to this work with several key comments after reading the draft. Cynthia McClintock's patience in revising and improving the translation should also be mentioned.

the state which made it possible) first became evident in the 1930s when the American Popular Revolutionary Alliance (APRA) arose with impressive force and presented a militant front composed of urban-based classes led by the petty bourgeoisie. Later, in the 1960s, the peasants were the protagonists of the social mobilization that upset the current regime, uniting in their desire to satisfy their claims to the land.

In both cases, the oligarchical state was able to avoid serious upheaval by granting minor concessions and exercising open repression. Between the crisis of the 1930s and the military revolt of October 3, 1968, for example, social security benefits were increased for the more organized and militant workers, women were given the vote, the parties of the bourgeoisie gained legal recognition, and a land reform was passed. But the basic national problem remained historically unresolved—these measures failed to transform Peruvian society and politically incorporate the masses. On the contrary, they were a way of avoiding radical change. This is to say, the oligarchical faction of the dominant class was unable to overcome its limitations and consequently remained identified as the social sector that had to be liquidated in order to accomplish, through the state, the urgent and long postponed national tasks. Thus, in the elections of 1963, practically all of the political parties agreed on certain basic reforms (agrarian reform especially) to be implemented as essential parts of the "development" that the country required. The civilian regime in power from 1963 until 1968, ideologically reformist and basically representative of the more advanced sector of the bourgeoisie, failed in its attempt at reform, however, because it was blocked by the resistance of the oligarchy; therefore, the problem remained unresolved.

It was within this framework that the military plan of 1968 arose.[1] Its political platform can be found in three central points, expressed not only in speeches and legal measures but also in a variety of coherent actions: (1) the eradication of the so-called oligarchy based on land ownership; (2) the implementation of a series of reforms aimed at "homogenizing" the country by reducing social distances or contrasts between classes, thus eliminating the focal points of social tension that in the view of the military ran contrary to the interests of national security; and (3) the development of a suitable international position affirming the national sovereignty against United States he-

[1] Books concerning the Peruvian military regime are abundant. The most complete bibliography, published in 1977, has been elaborated by Clemencia Galindo de Jaworski and is included as an appendix in Henry Pease García, *El Ocaso del Poder Oligárquico: Lucha Política en la Escena Oficial, 1968–1975* (Lima: DESCO, 1977).

gemony in an effort to gain a better basis for economic and political negotiation.

Within these proposals, the agrarian issue represented the central problem, the resolution of which constituted the chief axis of the military government's plan. In economic terms, the eradication of the latifundia would contribute to the expansion of the domestic market and provide a stronger basis for industrial growth. In political terms, uprooting the surviving feudalism would not only establish reliable bases for converting the majority of the population into citizens, but also, through this, allow the regime to take up the "Indian problem" and resolve the national question. This explains why, in the ten years of military government, the most advanced and successful of the reforms was the agrarian reform and the most effective of the many social organizations the government promoted was the National Agrarian Confederation (CNA), which achieved a mass representation, based, above all, on the beneficiaries of agrarian reform, and which permits its survival as an institution despite its legal dissolution by the government of Morales Bermúdez.

These points came to be the essential objectives of the military's plan but did not constitute a government program. Such a program was probably gradually defined through events, according to relations between social forces at different times, as well as by trends within the Peruvian armed forces. Therefore, we cannot speak in terms of a "model" when defining the characteristics of a political plan without a fixed content.

The recognition of a certain flexibility in the strategy and tactics of the military government has compelled some authors to eschew any definitions of the regime imposed on Peru in 1968.[2] In the analyses of these authors, the play of internal tendencies within the military leadership supercedes considerations of overall relations between the state and society and the specific role of the state in the development of the society. Thus they lose sight of the fact that the discrepancies and even the contradictions that exist to a greater or lesser extent within any government do not necessarily mean that the regime will in fact fail to arrive at a firm course in its actions. Such a result is readily apparent in the Peruvian military regime; a clear reformist aspiration

---

[2] The author whose work most reflects this interpretative trend is Henry Pease García, especially in "La Reforma Agraria Peruana en la Crisis del Estado Oligárquico," in *Estado y Política Agraria* (Lima: DESCO, 1977), pp. 15–136. In his latest work, however, he refers to the existence of "a model, although a contradictory one," which suggests that his interpretation has passed to the opposite pole. See *Los Caminos del Poder: Tres Años de Crisis en la Escena Política* (Lima: DESCO, 1979), p. 20.

colored its actions and, above all, marked its behavior in contrast to the rest of the social participants.

Thus, it seems justifiable to refer to *one* specific government program, led by General Juan Velasco Alvarado, that developed between 1968 and 1975, *one* basically coherent course. To be sure, this government sheltered within it differing views regarding certain state actions, but without a doubt, it managed to create harmony among conflicting viewpoints and to overcome them during seven years of a reformist regime institutionally representative of the armed forces. To refer to the nucleus of the experiment's plan, however, requires an examination of its origins in the petty bourgeoisie and its military character.

ORIGINS OF THE MILITARY'S PLAN: PETTY BOURGEOIS

The petty bourgeoisie—which makes up the basic and largest class in the armed forces, as shown in Chapter 8 of this volume, by Liisa North—provided the impetus for trying to reconcile classes in Peruvian society. The petty bourgeoisie, by virtue of its intermediate social position in capitalist society, "believe[d] itself to be above class antagonisms";[3] thus, when faced with sharp social tensions, its members tended to believe that it was possible and desirable to achieve a reasonable harmonization of interests. In Peru, attempts were made to reduce the societal differences stemming from the oligarchical regime's exclusionist policies by compensatory reforms, the most illustrative of which was the industrial community reform. This measure was to allow all employees—managers *and* workers—to collectively appropriate part of an enterprise's profits and thus share management and dividends with the shareholders. It was thought that this reform would progressively merge the interests of all the classes. Velasco defined the official provisions concerning the industrial community in the following manner:

> It is entirely logical that in substantially modifying the condition of absolute private ownership of the means of production, the total opposition to it would also accept substantial modifications. Therefore it seems inarguable that the alleged inability to reconcile class interests, which led to the theory of class struggle as an interpretative formulation of permanent and universal historical validity, should be questioned.

[3] Karl Marx, "El 18 de Brumario de Luis Bonaparte," in Karl Marx, Federico Engels, *Obras Escogidas* (Moscow: Progreso, 1969), p. 127.

Thus, we have grounds to examine, constructively, the possibility of finding a road for conciliation of conflicting social interests, which, for the above reasons, should not be conceived in terms of a rigid, absolute, and insurmountable antagonism.[4]

In order that one does not think this desired conciliation was just rhetoric, mention should be made of the way in which the industrial community was supposed to alter existing labor relations: it was to lessen the importance of the trade union and the burden of conflicts arising from wage negotiations. According to General Pedro Sala Orosco, the minister of labor of the military regime: "When the participation of the labor community in the ownership of the enterprise is significant, the conditions of work and remuneration will tend to be determined within the firm, in the hands of the board of directors, for the convenience of workers and employees *because the new situation that is being created will make it possible.*"[5]

In my view, it was the middle-class origins of the reform plan that permitted the illusion that the plan would, as stated by a civilian ideologist of the regime, "set up a political program and a model for development that had national dimensions and that could therefore count on the support of all Peruvians, independent of their partisan origins."[6] Differences among the social classes do not exist or can be overcome by conciliation, according to this perspective.

The aim of conciliation referred not only to classes but also to the interests of foreign capital, which the regime tried to subject to "conditions compatible with the national interests." Toward this goal, affirming a nationalist position, it took anti-imperialist measures (e.g., nationalizations) and urged cooperation among Third World nations: the Andean Pact and the Group of 77 saw in the Peruvian military government a protagonist of the first order. Both measures were to have placed the country on a better footing for negotiation once it had liquidated old foreign enclaves, broken the dependence of the military on United States technology (through the acquisition of Soviet arms), and improved the strength of the less developed nations through mutual support and united action.

Although the failure of the conciliation attempt with foreign capi-

[4] Juan Velasco Alvarado, *Velasco: La Voz de la Revolución* (Lima: Ediciones Participatión, Oficina Nacional de Difusión del Sinamos, 1972), 2:118–119.

[5] Pedro Sala Orosco, *La Política de la Revolución en el Sector Trabajo,* mimeographed (Lima: undated), p. 10. Italics added.

[6] Hector Béjar, *La Revolución en la Trampa* (Lima: Ediciones Socialismo y Participación, 1977), p. 157.

tal would be evident only over the long term, as the pattern and results of foreign investment were examined, the failure of the conciliation attempt with regard to Peruvian social classes was quickly evident. Specifically, in the industrial community, workers and owners each attempted to maximize their own interests through it. The growing opposition to the reforms by concerned sectors did not subsume the regime itself, however, due to the political inviability of the alternatives; or, as Aníbal Quijano correctly predicted, the utopia of conciliation could last as long as the principal social participants were not prepared for open confrontation.[7] In fact, if one takes strikes as any indication, class conflict grew significantly during the Velasco regime. The deterioration of the regime's program resulting from these conflicts gave rise to "phase two" of the military government, which was clearly regressive compared to the "phase one." But it must be noted that the attempts to conciliate interests in conflict forced both sectors further apart and in fact impeded the government's finding a coherent social base for its programs.

To point out the middle-class character of the military plan is not to maintain that the military government represented the petty bourgeoisie. The ideological character of the class cannot be identified with its representative. Although the plan arose from one sector of the petty bourgeoisie (and some of its members had acquired reformist tendencies, especially since the 1950s), the pretentiousness of the military, imposing reforms without consulting the will of social classes, alienated the professional and white-collar middle classes. As we shall see later, only the most radical faction of these sectors—which adhered to the reformist civilian parties and was disappointed by them in the 1950s—would respond to Velasco's proposal, which assigned them a subordinate position.

THE MILITARY CHARACTER OF THE GOVERNMENT PLAN

A second key feature of the plan's origin was its military character, entailing a subordinate role for civilians. Its military nature ensured that the petty bourgeoisie's aim of conciliating classes would be imposed authoritatively and bureaucratically. Various analyses of the Velasco regime have pointed this out. In brief, they note that the armed forces, like the Catholic Church, as one of the few efficient institutions in the social structure, were acutely aware of the oligarchical crisis and its effects in terms of social conflict. This conflict, which

[7] Aníbal Quijano, *Nacionalismo, Imperialismo, y Militarismo en el Perú* (Buenos Aires: Periferia, 1971), p. 126.

began in the 1950s, ran parallel to the development of a vision of the nation in certain portions of the dominant classes. Alfred Stepan has shown that officials were concerned about the existing tensions and sought ways to resolve them even before the appearance of guerrillas in 1965,[8] an event cited by many authors as the catalyst that "awakened" the military's social conscience. In fact, professional military analysis, derived from work by the military intelligence, had determined that the continuing inability of the dominant classes to resolve the nation's problems constituted a threat to national security. From this perspective sprang the military's identification of security with development, which became a fundamental part of the plan. It should be understood that the relationship between security and development not only initially motivated the regime but also contributed to the shape of the government's plans and programs. In 1974, for example, when the government risked a large investment in an oil pipeline to transfer a hypothetical petroleum reserve from the jungle to the coast, the regime sought not only to convert Peru into an oil exporter rapidly but also to occupy the Amazon for geopolitical considerations and to ensure Peru's petroleum self-sufficiency in the event of a possible international conflict after Chile's change of government in 1973.

This type of decision—based on strategic and geopolitical factors—gave the impression of an apparently contradictory direction in the economic as well as political areas. The decisions about the public debt, for example (apart from the arms purchases, which weighed heavily in the composition of the external debt) were justified by the need for rapid economic growth to sustain an armed conflict with Chile, which since 1973—when Pinochet took power—had seemed more and more likely. Velasco's government was also sensitive to the problems created by situations termed "subversive." This sensitivity was due not only to the professional education of the military but also to its markedly anticommunist indoctrination.

In addition, the military imposed a distinct political style on the administration of its programs. Military personnel filled a good portion of the high-level positions within the state apparatus, ensuring the effectiveness of command. The reforms were initiated from the state, and because their terms were defined as above class interests, that is to say, they did not correspond to specific demands from various classes nor resulted from a process of negotiation among them,

[8] Alfred Stepan, *The State and Society: Peru in Comparative Perspective* (Princeton: Princeton University Press, 1978), pp. 127–136.

they had to be imposed authoritatively, based on coercion rather than on acceptance. Consequently, in the state's denial of its social base, all social participants were seen as enemies of the reform plan, increasing in turn the necessity for authoritarianism and, eventually, for repression. This style of imposing authoritatively what the military command saw as the remedies for a society in crisis, was well expressed by a former chancellor of the military regime, who, in defending the need to decree a regionalization of the country without consultation, appealed to his listeners, "Is the sick man cured by the medicines that he chooses?"[9]

This military style not only implies that political consultation is unnecessary; the workings of a command system also assume that consultation is inconvenient. In narrating the military preparations for October 3, 1968, a retired general explained: "We did not know what it was for. That is the way work should be done: only the command—which has delegated portions of the task—knows the whole of the plan."[10] A civilian sympathetic to the reformist military scheme revealed the consequences of the work of the military command in terms of the precariousness of the regime: "While there were persons of a more progressive mentality in the more important ranks of the military, the rigidity of military discipline worked in favor of the social reforms, inasmuch as the officers and soldiers backed, due to discipline, the opinions and decisions of their superiors."[11] The support of the ambitious plan of social reforms through military discipline does not imply that its contents represented only the commands. As Pease points out, precisely because of the rigid hierarchy of the military command, the armed forces became the government;[12] significantly, the military commands were made to coincide with the highest positions in the government.

Understanding the military character of the entire plan allows one to perceive the government's frequently irrational authoritarianism, bureaucratism, and voluntarism. These elements rendered the regime socially and economically pervasive; the variety and scope of the reforms aimed to integrate a larger sector of the population than was ever achieved before. Yet, at the same time the regime was far from the populism previously experienced in Latin America (Perón in Argentina, Vargas in Brazil, etc.), since it absolutely excluded political

---

[9] Lecture given by General (ret.) Edgardo Mercado Jarrín in the Universidad del Pacífico, Lima, March 14, 1979.

[10] Interview with General (ret.) Arturo Valdés Palacio, Lima, August 14, 1976.

[11] Béjar, *La Revolución en la Trampa*, pp. 30–31.

[12] Pease García, *El Ocaso del Poder Oligárquico*, p. 140.

participation. This vertical style of government was suffered by the population while unsuccessful attempts were made to limit civilians to watching the course of the military action in government, as is done in war. That style, which characterized both purely military activities and also government behavior, was generated by the military institution itself. One of the generals who headed the National System of Support for Social Mobilization (SINAMOS) explained the military's participation in the government in the following terms:

> In the first year there was much dialogue with all the officers throughout the country; each minister informed and explained [government decisions] to all officers, including the noncommissioned ones. When now it is said that the army did not participate, this is not true. It had no reason to cast votes. Yet at the end of the explanations the officers always applauded.[13]

This view of the masses as the receiver of information and transmitter of applause is probably what led, in 1975, after other forms of political control had failed and the crisis of the regime had become evident, to the organization of the "dialogues with the people" in state capitals. One or two ministers would lecture and then dismiss the questions of the people, who were then counted as "participants" in a mechanism of political consultation.

It is almost unnecessary to add that the officers' ideology included a view of the masses. Pease suggests that "the common man, the laborer, a peasant, appear to be seen as the equivalent of the soldier in the military hierarchy."[14] This conception, deprecatory and at the same time fearful of popular action because of its connotations of disorder and lack of direction, casts the decreed reform as a concession and not a revindication. No matter how radical a position is, its content is in the nature of a mere gift made by the rulers to the masses. This is important because it highlights a limiting characteristic of the plan: the possibility of alliances with subordinate sectors is cancelled beforehand. There is no other incorporation possible except unconditional support; as the military's maxim orders: "with no question or grumbling."

None of the above presumes to disregard the differences among individual participants in the military government (Vargas Caballero, and Fernández Maldonado, for example, or Tantaleán and Leonidas

---

[13] Interview with General (ret.) Leonidas Rodríguez Figueroa, August 18, 1976.

[14] Pease García, *El Ocaso del Poder Oligárquico*, p. 140.

Rodríguez), who probably represented trends within the armed forces, which were expressed in the somewhat contradictory actions of the state apparatus. These trends undoubtedly led to tensions—at times rather severe—which were resolved in two ways. On the one hand, certain compromises were made on the scope and content of the reforms. For example, an urban reform was never approved, probably as a result of an internal bargain; such a step would have been perceived as "cubanization" of the Peruvian Revolution. In addition, administrative sectionalization institutionalized these decisions. The allocation of decisions to corresponding parts of the state apparatus permitted a certain amount of leeway to those in its charge and led to conflicts among governmental sectors controlled by officers who disagreed with one another. This was apparent in the problems between the SINAMOS and the Ministry of Industries over the "promoting" of the industrial communities.[15] And, on the other hand, divisions were also produced by certain critical issues that weakened the legitimacy of the regime within the armed forces. For example, it is clear that in 1974 Vice Admiral Vargas Caballero was forced to resign the command of the navy because of his resistance to the decision to expropriate the newspapers, thus giving rise to the crisis that would end Velasco's leadership.

But the recognition of these trends does not imply that the logic of the plan can be found solely in the results of its actions, like the mathematical median of a set of contradictory forces. On the contrary, the entire institution stood behind the objectives and essential features of the military plan. These remarks of Admiral Vargas Caballero, who was on the conservative extreme of the Velasco regime, illustrate what constitutes the justification for government intervention:

> The last days of the Belaúnde government gave the impression that there was no government, that we were headed towards chaos. Although I did not view with sympathy the military's entry into the government, ... (I) was faced with a *fait accompli,* because all the army did. ... This government should make the necessary transformations. For example, an agrarian reform well conceived and implemented, modification of parts of the constitution not being fulfilled, elimination of a series of injustices (widespread ignorance, illiteracy, great numbers of people who lack access to health and to everything). A military government could accomplish all these

---

[15] Jorge Santistevan, "El Estado y los Comuneros Industriales," in Giorgio Alberti, Jorge Santistevan, and Luis Pásara, *Estado y Clase: La Comunidad Industrial en el Perú* (Lima: Instituto de Estudios Peruanos, 1977), pp. 105–188.

transformations. . . . A country which needs to change rapidly, needs a dictatorship. The bad thing is that there is no good dictator. . . . Hitler and Mussolini, in the beginning, did much good for their countries because they took them out of crisis, but later they committed atrocities. Perhaps Franco is an exception to this rule.[16]

Thus, the essential motivation of the military plan was not alien to the more conservative sectors of the military. In other words, the high degree of correspondence between the character of the military institution and the character of the form and content of the Velasco regime indicate that the military's central actions were representative of the whole of the armed forces and not of only one group of officers, as some scholars would have us believe. Undoubtedly, within this framework, differences and contradictions arose that reflected the economically dominant as well as the popular classes' interests in reclaiming the military's plan for themselves. In the ensuing confrontations, officers compromised, or one sector managed to impose its will on another, without straying from the basic path of the government program, but contributing a certain definition to its evolution, until the dismantling of the program, which began in 1976. That is why the existence of trends does not permit us to confidently argue that they corresponded to different programs. Similarly, as we shall see later, the political collapse of the government's program is not explained by the domination of one trend over another, but by the social isolation of its conciliatory content and the hierarchical nature of its politics, both of which were essential elements of the regime.

It should be noted, however, that the dominance of one trend over another and the progressive definition of the regime according to its actions inevitably entailed repercussions within the armed forces itself. Since a fundamental part of the political game consisted in controlling the levels of decision making through promotions and retirements in the military hierarchy, designating military chiefs, and naming the ministers, these became key means of manipulation by the existing political tendencies within the regime. Gradually, the military regime distanced itself from institutional consensus as a source of legitimacy, concerning itself instead with the manipulation of military appointments, on which it based its survival to an ever greater extent. Moreover, the active participation of officers in the state apparatus inevitably politicized them. Both of these developments undermined the military regime and led in 1977, under the

[16] Interview with Admiral (ret.) Luis Vargas Caballero, Lima, September 7, 1976.

leadership of Morales Bermúdez, to the decision to retire from the government in order to preserve the institutional integrity of the armed forces.

CONCESSIONS AND REPRESSION

Although the essential part of the regime's program may be explained by institutional consensus, the course of governmental actions and decisions must be discussed in relation to the dynamics generated by the government's own initial measures and the response from social participants. The case of the agrarian reform is illustrative.[17] This law did not respond to immediate pressures from the peasant movement, which was, in fact, in a state of retreat; but once the law was passed and the expropriation of land made feasible by the government, mobilization began and soon overflowed the limits set by the governmental plan. The program then had to be modified to include new channeling mechanisms not anticipated when the reform was designed. As Eric Hobsbawm pointed out as early as 1971, the Peruvian officers managed to achieve the opposite of what they had sought.[18]

Consequently, one cannot find the terms of a political program in an archetypal political plan before October 3, 1968, or shortly thereafter. What we do have before 1968 is a methodology for the management of a social conflict. It emerged in 1962–1963 during the "first institutional coup"—the short-lived military government that opened the way for Belaúnde's reformist civilian regime—when the military implemented an agrarian reform in the Valley of La Convención (Cuzco) using a combination of social reform and selective repression. Such a combination was also characteristic of the Velasco government.

As pointed out earlier, the military intended not only to establish itself above the interests of the classes in conflict but also to impose its programs coercively. Consensus was only one element that accompanied and endorsed the regime's action, but it did not generate it. By failing to represent the expectations of any class, the plan competed with all the other political participants, and the military had to resort periodically to repression of all of them. The military perceived the dynamic that its reforms unleashed, however, and understood that to

[17] For an analysis of the peasant dynamic in relation to the agrarian reform, see Luis Pásara, *Reforma Agraria: Derecho y Conflicto* (Lima: Instituto de Estudios Peruanos, 1978), chapters 3 and 4.

[18] Eric Hobsbawm, "Perú: The Peculiar 'Revolution,'" *New York Review of Books*, December 16, 1971, pp. 29–36.

respond to political mobilization through repression was not enough. As a result, toward 1971, a framework was developed, subsequently institutionalized as SINAMOS, that had two aspects: (1) the interplay of mechanisms of concession and repression; and (2) the implementation of structures of co-optation to supplant existing social organizations. The specific character of the military's response varied according to the resources available, the aggressiveness of the popular movement's demands, and the specific political context of the moment.

One example is the government's strategy toward the teachers' movement, which has maintained its ability to fight and organize over the last decade. Breaking off in December 1971 from the General Confederation of Peruvian Workers (CGTP), which was oriented to the pro-Moscow Communist party and was an ally of the government, the teachers organized, beginning in May 1972, a powerful, national-level union under the influence of the extreme left. It periodically waged important fights to improve working conditions. In the face of their opposition, the government simultaneously or successively resorted to the use of threats, conceded to moderate wage increases, repressed leaders (who were jailed and/or deported), confused the issues in conflict by mounting public opinion campaigns, sought the understanding of teachers and asked the support of the heads of families against the opposition leaders, and, finally, undertook divisive actions to establish parallel unions controlled by the government. The actions taken in each confrontation with the teachers were affected by the government's evaluation of whether it could impose its will or whether it would be forced to concede. Thus, in facing demands of the teachers' union in 1974 when the government was preparing to expropriate the newspapers (perhaps its boldest reform and certainly one of its more controversial, especially to the bourgeoisie), Velasco's government tried to "open the dialogue" with the teachers' union, only to close it later when conditions allowed.

Another good example of the government's concession/repression tactics concerns peasant mobilization. Again, the government proceeded with flexibility, combining strategies and searching for accommodation according to circumstances. In July 1974 (the same period mentioned above), an important wave of land invasions was promoted by the Peasant Confederation of Peru (CCP) in the southern highlands in Andahuaylas.[19] Simultaneously, the government faced a

---

[19] For a peasant version concerning these events, see QUINTANILLA, Lino, *Testimonio de Andahuaylas*, mimeographed (Lima: CICIP, 1974).

sharp reaction from the wealthier quarters of Lima to the expropriation of the newspapers, which, as has been pointed out, had caused a split within the government that had almost resulted in a break with the navy. While it politically repressed the disturbances in the capital, the government sent delegates to the area of the land invasions and signed agreements with the peasants in which the regime virtually capitulated to the peasants, not only with respect to the land invasions already effected but also with respect to the application of its model of cooperative enterprise under state control. This is to say, the government agreed to legalize the effectuated land grab and permitted the acreage to be parceled out to individual families. Some weeks later, when the number of haciendas taken by the peasants had increased, the government went on the offensive, feeling that the problem with the newspapers had been overcome. It detained the leaders of the CCP, physically removed the peasants from the lands, created a governmental agrarian organization in the area, to whose members it transferred the land pending expropriation.

ENCLOSURE AND CO-OPTATION

In the previous examples, we have seen, in addition to the strategy of concession/repression, the appearance of organizations controlled by the government. As redistributive channels for specific social sectors, these organizations politically encapsulated the population, segmenting it into vertical structures that were controlled from above, connected to the state apparatus, and organized according to functions so as to avoid the "troublesome social classes."

The case of the *pueblos jóvenes* ("young towns," or slums) has been carefully analyzed by Stepan.[20] The goods redistributed were property titles. The control was exercised by the military's chiefs in the area. The election of leaders was carried out in steps in such a way that there was never a group larger than fifty persons participating. As a result, electoral criteria were narrowed, impeding debate of overall platforms relating to the more general social issues. The "support" given by the state included direct vigilance of the organization and removal of undesirable candidates who, government officials explained, "wouldn't be good interlocutors."

Equally important was the case of the National Agrarian Confederation (CNA), created to replace the National Agrarian Society, (founded by the oligarchy) and to compete with the CCP. It sought to

[20] Stepan, *The State and Society,* chapter 5.

embrace individual proprietors, cooperative farmers, and landless peasants, and it enjoyed the state's legal, political, and financial backing. Law 19400 established the CNA, and SINAMOS spread it throughout the country in less than eighteen months. Its development (until it fell into official disgrace in 1976, as the reform program was cancelled) was marked by a progressive linkage to the public administration at local decision making levels, particularly in regard to production issues concerning crops and livestock.

Of greater significance is the case of the *Central* of Workers of the Peruvian Revolution (CTRP). Intended as the only *Central,* it remained merely one of four, the others being the Communist, Aprista, and Christian Democrat. Dedicated to recruiting unions in the less organized sectors, it worked with officials hired by the state and supported the government in all its actions, including repression of popular mobilizations.

Cotler terms "corporative" control that which attempts to depoliticize the middle and lower classes by reducing politics to the events of daily life.[21] This was done through multiclass organizations representing the major sections of the economy, which divided the interests of classes by focusing upon specific problems, and which renounced participation in decisions regarding the whole of the society and the state. Through these institutions the state sought to gain the capacity to selectively channel the popular demands of the most organized sectors and grant them some improvements accompanied by political control. The evident purpose was to sidestep political consciousness and class organization, substituting for them the political loyalty of those who benefited from the reforms and who thus were co-opted by the encapsulating organizations. Cotler adds an economic motive to the political one: co-opting the popular sector, which was capable of exercising pressure regarding the distribution of income, would impede the political mobilization that would have exceeded the redistributive potential of the system and affected the accumulation of capital.

What kind of success could these forms of political co-optation achieve? It should be taken into account that at the level of the popular social organizations, the attempts of the government were fated to compete fundamentally with the left. The APRA maintained a position of tactical retreat, which it abandoned only in the second phase

[21] Julio Cotler, "The New Mode of Political Domination in Perú," in Abraham F. Lowenthal, ed., *The Peruvian Experiment: Continuity and Change under Military Rule* (Princeton: Princeton University Press, 1975), pp. 44–78.

of the military government to present itself as the successor to the military. The left wing grew during the first phase, in good part because of the expectations generated by the regime's reforms and its relative failures, but it was not capable of producing a truly political mobilization, only a track-union one.[22] It developed a capacity for political agitation that, although disturbing and resisting the government's plans of co-optation, did not manage to constitute an alternative.

Under these conditions, the government's success in political terms depended on its distributive capacity and on an efficient political incorporation. In a country like Peru, the redistribution should not have been limited to improving conditions for those already in the upper quarter of the income distribution profile, which, as Richard Webb and Adolfo Figueroa have shown, was just the result of the military's reforms.[23] Instead, it should have reached the more impoverished Peruvians, furnishing them employment and improving their living standards. Here, the government collided with the limits of its economic model, which, given the pattern of capitalist accumulation and the regime's unwillingness to transform the dependent structure of production, did not allow a massive incorporation of the population into the productive sphere and the bettering of living conditions.

The impossibility of sufficiently redistributing income was probably the first factor that affected the base of legitimacy that the plan sought. The second factor was the regime's inability to join even those who benefited from the reforms in a movement that would give them the authority of political decision. This inability stemmed from the nature of the military regime.

It makes sense to ask why the government, given its military character and authoritarianism, agitated ideologically for popular revindications and tried to establish these measures of enclosure instead of openly repressing demands from below and all other forms of participation. To respond requires consideration of the military's general perspective and its efforts to resolve the national question through a formula that included as much of the population as possible (as opposed to the former oligarchical regime, the inviability of which had been especially demonstrated by the aggressive peasant movement of the 1960s). The military plan attempted to gather the more urgent social demands, thus defusing their explosiveness and giving them direction. On a lower level, it could be considered the "infiltration"

[22] Felipe Portocarrero, in Mirko Lauer, ed., *El Reformismo Burgués (1968–1976)* (Lima: Mosca Azul, 1978), p. 226.

[23] Adolfo Figueroa and Richard C. Webb, *Distribución del Ingreso en el Perú* (Lima: Instituto de Estudios Peruanos, 1975).

work of officers who tried to tilt the regime to the left, making more room available to popular demands. In any case, the military plan had as an inherent limit the negation of political participation by the newest social participants—the peasant adjudicators of land, the industrial workers, and the inhabitants of *pueblos jóvenes*—who, in principle, were all included in the government's program.

It is clear that the government attempted to overcome its political limitations in other ways. One of these, mentioned by Cynthia McClintock in Chapter 9 of this book, was ambiguity, a search for ways to superficially satisfy the interests in conflict. The results were similar to those obtained by the bats in their dealings with the mice and the birds; legend tells of the tactics the bats used to pass themselves off as relatives of the mice and birds until a war between the two species made the bats enemies of both. The government also sought to resolve differences through control of the means of communication. In 1972, a government administration of broadcasting was created within the Ministry of the Interior and later became the National System of Information in charge of the newspapers nationalized in 1974, working along lines already established for television and radio. The aim of these expropriations was clearly expressed by a participant in the ministerial sessions who said, when the newspapers were taken over: "[the ministers] wanted more support for the government . . . it was expected from the newspapers a real support for the process.[24]

The different tendencies existing within the government were present in the design and construction of these forms of political control. Let us take the case of the development of the CTRP, which arose in 1972 as the regime's answer to the growing demands of the labor movement. One of its protagonists, a member of the SINAMOS leadership, related:

> The meetings to form a *Central* began in the National Intelligence Service. Here were the military and the civilians. Alternatives were thought of. The first possibility was to make a single *Central* with all the workers, the second possibility was to make a government *Central,* and the third was to join with the CNT [the *Central* of the Christian Democrats]. . . . the council [of ministers] deliberated and was inclined to the government *Central.* Graham stated that the single *Central* was a danger. They did not realize that it could be controlled from the government! . . .

[24] Interview with General (ret.) Arturo Valdés Palacio, Lima, September 8, 1976.

The CTRP arose from the debate over a union reform law that sought to "decapitate" all the managing groups. On "D-Day" all the organizations would have been beheaded and the law was to impose new requirements for electing leaders. The work previously done by us would ensure that our own apparatus would emerge, elected by the bases.

We stayed [working there for] four months, but when the people [from SINAMOS] saw that there were even PIP [police] involved, they fell back. Leonidas [Rodríguez] authorized us to withdraw.[25]

By this account, the different tendencies within the government—from those in charge of "promoting participation" to those responsible for repressing mobilization—shared the view of a need to mount a union structure that the government could control. A discrepancy was produced by the methods of establishing control, however: one sector believed it was possible to induce control, while the other sector imposed it violently. The difference is not inconsiderable; the National Confederation of Industrial Communities (CONACI), however, also created under the government banner by the less authoritarian group, was later divided by the actions of the opposing unit. The CNA faced similar problems stemming from this conflict of tendencies, which produced diverse styles and degrees in the control of the popular movement.

Beginning with the overall economic and political limits of the plan, these mechanisms of co-optation proceeded to waste themselves without reaching efficiency. They were incapable of substantially redistributing income and incorporating the population into the mechanisms of political decision. The structures of enclosure were deflated—as in the parallel case of the teachers' union, the SERP—or they would be emancipated from official tutelage when the government regressed—as in the case of the CNA. In other words, the political forms follow the fate of the plan.

It is necessary, however, to pause to consider the effect of the regime's enclosing actions. On one hand, they included a certain degree of political agitation—greater in the case of agrarian reform, but not inconsiderable in labor relations—and the promotion of popular organizations where none existed. In both cases, these government mechanisms not only failed to gain full and lasting support but the leaders and organizations went outside the political parameters established by the government. This is explained by revealing, through facts, the state's role as its presence extended throughout society.

[25] Interview with José Luis Alvarado, Bogotá, August 29, 1976.

Contrary to the government's intentions, the government's actions had a politicizing effect.

THE ROLE OF THE CIVILIANS

In light of the preceding analysis, it is clear that the government's plan had a limited resonance for the Peruvian people. One reason was Peru's political history. The APRA had already achieved an immense political mobilization via reformist proclamations. When the 1968 reform plan came by decree through the military route, the Peruvian people faced a political paradox: the Aprista and the military programs were very similar, but the party and the army in fact were enemies. The middle-class support that the government might have ganed was already militant in the APRA party and, as a consequence of APRA's historical confrontation with the army, stood in an antimilitarist position. So, the lack of popular support for the military's program can be explained not only by the military's inability to consider mass action, as discussed above, but also by historical factors, that is, APRA's preemption of a reformist program.

The only group that effectively rallied to the military's support in 1968 was a civilian sector composed primarily of intellectuals or professionals of the petty bourgeoisie who had been frustrated and disillusioned by the ineffectiveness of the 1960s' attempts at reform through democratic methods. In other words, the programs desired by the middle classes in the 1950s and 1960s had been electorally defeated, or had failed during Belaúnde's government.

Although many of these civilians shared similar experiences, often as members of the Social Progressive and Christian Democrat movements, they were recruited individually to personal advisory positions in the government. As one of these civilians related:

> On the 20th (October, 1968) I came across Juan José Vega on Tacna Avenue and he told me: "I was looking for you, the colonels need civilian advisers." He took me to the palace. I spoke for two hours with Fernández Maldonado, he explained what they wanted and took me to have coffee in the Sevillian patio and he told me, "I'm going to introduce you to my brother." He was Leonidas Rodríguez.[26]

For a civilian to incorporate himself into the government meant to remain subordinate to the authority of the armed forces and to the principle of their unity, which was bureaucratically (and not politi-

[26] Ibid.

cally) maintained.[27] It meant the demobilization of these civilian political agents, who thus remained within "a process held subject almost entirely to a strict, rigidly bureaucratic game," according to one of those involved.[28] Most serious, however, was that despite the civilians' intentions to radicalize the regime, they were also called upon to fulfill a demobilizing role from within the state apparatus, or through a political contribution that sought to tame the popular movement, or finally through the formulation of a depoliticizing ideology.

Outside of an important group of technocrats, who pragmatically suspended their Aprista or Belaúndista attachments and elaborated economic policies, we can distinguish two major groups among the civilian sectors of the military regime. One group consisted of men associated with the pro-Soviet Communist party or under its influence. The government delegated to them the control of the newspaper *Expreso* when it was expropriated in March of 1970 so that the regime could obtain some support in the media. This sector's support of the government was based on the fact that "the basic program of the Left was the program of the revolutionary military team," according to a revealing appraisal subsequently made by a leader of the Communist party.[29] The government did in fact consider the Communists allies. As a civilian close to President Velasco remarked: "The Communists were tactical allies; but we could not say so."[30] The usefulness of this alliance to the government was dubious. The Communists did act as a counterweight to opposition from conservative groups and APRA (which was feared but never really materialized). But the Communists gained many advantages through their tactic of "critical support," thanks to the fact that they had their own political organization and others under their control as well. Moreover, the Communists did not fight labor demands, but sparked them and channelled them; this group only tried to delegitimize demands when they could not contain them within the apparatus they could control. The Communist party thus profited politically, increasing its own ranks, in exchange for acting as a calming transmission belt and fighting the reactionary enemies of the government. Both roles, as a spark to political agitation and as aggressive enemy of the opposition, are emphasized by a general's remark: "The result of *Expreso* was positive. . . . All the ministers hated it. But Velasco said: "Who will chal-

[27] Portocarrero, in Lauer, ed., *El Reformismo Burgués*, p. 156.

[28] Béjar, *La Revolución en la Trampa*, pp. 199–200.

[29] Gustavo Espinoza, in Mirko Lauer, *El Reformismo Burgués*, p. 108.

[30] Interview with Augusto Zimmerman, Panamá, August 27, 1976.

lenge *El Comercio?" La Cronica* belonged to the state, but it was useless."[31]

The second civilian group emerged in July 1971, around the task of organizing SINAMOS. The most prominent figure in this group was the anthropologist Carlos Delgado, personal adviser to President Velasco. Delgado's group of intellectuals and professionals was known as "the steam roller," and its basic feature was fundamental opposition to the Communist party. The essential difference between the two civilian sectors was ideological: the first adhered to the Leninist party model, while the latter developed the "no-party thesis." The first responded mostly to the direction of a single political party and, therefore, were only allies, while the other depended entirely on the military government. Thus the military leadership granted the Delgado group greater confidence, which allowed them to develop the official ideology of the regime.

IDEOLOGY MADE TO MEASURE

The essential traits of the ideology developed by the civilians bear the curious virtue of completely satisfying the needs of the military avant-garde who led the regime. Above all, this ideology—like various other reform ideologies in the underdeveloped world—was neither capitalist nor communist, seeking a "third way"—with a certain Christian-Democratic, or at least, Catholic, ring to it—which coincided well with the military ideology: "On the one hand . . . lawlessness; on the other, repression. We [represented] the Aristotelian Mean: we wanted the law to be upheld—as it has to be—but with liberty."[32]

There are two relatively original proposals in this ideology. The first of these, the no-party thesis, was very practical. To establish a political party would have meant changing the military bureaucratic axis on which the political leadership rested; and the military bureaucratic orientation was reinforced through the process of promotions, which were decided politically but justified as if they were "institutional." The introduction of a political organization would have raised the question of the role of the military in it. Either some officers would join and would thus acquire greater weight than the rest, or none would join and the organization would have no real strength; or

[31] Interview with General (ret.) Arturo Valdés Palacio, Lima, September 8, 1976.

[32] Interview with General (ret.) Arturo Valdés Palacio, September 4, 1976.

finally, everyone would join and thus duplicate the military structure, incorporating civilians to compete for power or as aides-de-camp. The complementary problem of civilian participation was also raised. In any case, a party structure assumed that the civilians would not restrict themselves to their roles as "advisers" and would share decision making power. This principle was not acceptable in the military's framework of the political process. Faced with this impasse, the no-party thesis, advocated in rather anarchistic terms, was a piece of ideological salvation that was thought to solve the problem, leaving all decision making capacity to the military commands.

The civilian ideologues incorporated, as a second original proposal, the theory of "full participatory social democracy" to legitimize the regime and as a substitute for the alternative of political parties. If one had to summarize the thinking of the principal governmental ideologues, one would state: from the violent and furious criticism of the political party as an expression of political participation and class interests, the ideologues came to denounce mechanisms of "intermediation and manipulation" based on the assumption that such mechanisms make of the party a form of "expropriation of the popular will." The next step was to seek an alternative to the party. To this end, the function of "political participation" was assigned to first-level economic organizations. In principle, this function applied to the entities created by the military plan in the different sectors: workers' communities for the reformed private enterprises, agrarian cooperatives, "agricultural societies of social interest," peasant communities that benefited from the agrarian reform, and, moreover, the incipient enterprises of social property. All these enterprises had received "economic power" through plans implemented by the government; the ideologues said that these entities should also have political power. That is to say, when adequately organized, they should receive political decision making capacity.

On the grounds of this last principle, the ideologues explained, for example, the "transference" of the newspapers with national circulation to the organized sectors: a paper for the peasants, another for the workers' communities, etc. It should be noted, however, that such organization, supposedly necessary to "receive the transference," was not the same as that preceding the military government. Namely, the laborers were not to become presumed proprietors of a newspaper as members of their unions but rather as "members of a community," a distinction acquired only when the Velasco government created the Industrial Community. The same was true of the peasants. It was not their unions or their traditional peasant communities that qualified them to "receive the transference of power." This would be done for the agricultural workers through the newly created "base organizations," production cooperatives; and for the "community members," if they affiliated and structured themselves within the officially designated apparatus, i.e., the National Agrarian Confederation. It is important to note that the difference was not formal. The workers' community and the agrarian cooperative attempted to unite the workers around entrepreneurial interests instead of around the grievance interests that characterized the union.

If we follow the development of the regime's ideology, we find an additional element: the creation of new "organizations of participation" that did not correspond to enterprises awarded some benefit by the government's reforms. These were organizations with administrative responsibilities that brought people together in a functional manner and around interests that were not based upon class. An example was the communal educational center, which galvanized teachers and parents around instruction questions. Others were the groups without economic power, like the associations of *pueblos jóvenes* ("young towns") and the unions created by official initiative, which replaced already existing popular organizations. The official ideology justified these last actions by rejecting all forms of popular organization not directly created or promoted by the government as "oligarchical." It was maintained that the "manipulation of political groups or enfeebled leadership" occurred in these organizations just as in the parties and that intermediation impeded "participation."

The declaration of an official ideologue illustrates the argument we have synthesized:

> the Peruvian Revolution recognized from its beginning the need to create effective mechanisms for participation (production cooperatives, SAIS, workers' communities, social property enterprises, communal educational centers, press assigned to social sectors). The transference of economic and political power to the majorities could gradually be realized through their own and autonomous base organizations. . . . Thus we are experiencing the germination of a new power structure, of a structure of popular power. . . . Respecting the existence of the parties, but clearly considering them expressions of the traditional power structure, the [Peruvian] process orients its action towards the base organizations, supporting their consolidation and articulation. In this way genuine federations of workers and peasants appear—such as CONACI and in the future the CNA—that are truly representative.[33]

[33] Francisco Guerra-García, *El Peruano, un Proceso Abierto* (Lima: Libros de Contratiempo, 1975), p. 91.

Even after "Phase One," Héctor Béjar continued to justify the imposition of an organizing structure on the agrarian sector, using the improbable argument that the previous agricultural unions were fictitious entities, controlled by the landowners.[34] As we have seen, before this argument could be elaborated, the government had already created its own organizations aimed at replacing previous organizations and channeling the popular movement. The depoliticizing objective of these organizations was supported by the civilian ideologues, under the formula of "turning politics into issues of daily life"—i.e., apparently disconnecting politics from the executive power of the state and transferring it first to the economic organizations:

> If we observe present Peruvian circumstances, we would find that where collective self-managed property is affirmed (SAIS, communities, cooperatives) "political" conflict if progressively extinguished and the actions of the political parties lose significance. This does not mean the immediate or eventual disappearance of political behavior. It means simply its reappearance in daily habits. It begins to reinstate itself thus in the vital reflexes of the centers of production.[35]

In addition to the economic organizations, "politics" should operate in such organizations as the communal educational centers and "zonal basic planning unit" that "are superimposed on the basis of two state organizations (the Ministry of Education and the SINAMOS)."[36] It is important to note that those governmentally promoted organizations, unable to accede to overall political decisions, remained joined and subject to certain inferior and sectorial levels of the public administration.

This effort by the civilian ideologues to hide the real mechanisms of power in effect during the Velasco government bore no relation to real life. These new organizations were not mechanisms of political participation but of co-optation and subjection to the government's plans. Workers' control over the supposedly self-managed enterprises could not be exercised because it conflicted with the interventionist role of the state, a key feature of the economic model. Assuming that the workers could have exercised control over the enterprises, that power would still have had nothing to do with the control of the state

[34] Béjar, *La Revolución en la Trampa*, p. 119.
[35] Carlos Franco, *La Revolución Participatoria* (Lima: Mosca Azul, 1974), p. 139.
[36] Ibid.

structure, the only real area in which decisions were made concerning the direction of the society. The theory of "fully participatory social democracy" came only to mask the hierarchical military control—hierarchical, authoritarian, and excluding the masses from power. The military could not seek to institutionalize civilian power without threatening its own bases of support.

The social tensions that developed during the first six years of the military regime served to make clear the ideological character of these justifying doctrines (in the most deprecatory sense of the term "ideology"). Because not all the members of the regime shared these beliefs, some other solutions were attempted to deal with the government's political problem. Thus, in May 1972, at the inspiration of General Tantalén, the minister of fisheries, the Revolutionary Labor Movement (MLR) was begun. This movement subsequently extended its actions to other labor sectors, violently imposing union directives, eliminating leaders of the opposition, and intimidating assemblies.[37]

Subsequently, the struggle between the officers of the regime involved civilian sectors and gave rise to two more ideological claims: the distinction between supporters and militants in the "revolutionary" process, and the label "infiltrator" that participants of opposing political tendencies gave each other. These steps were clearly facilitated by the ideological ambiguity of the plan.

With regard to the status of the "militant," General Leonidas Rodríguez, then the chief of SINAMOS, said:

> It is not the same to support the ["revolutionary"] process as to be a militant in it. To support the process and not be an activist in it signifies that one does not subscribe to its theory, nor its strategy of development, nor its final model of society. To support the process but not be an activist signifies, therefore, that one has a theory, a strategy, and a model of society different from ours, that is to say, a position different from ours. . . . The revolution specifies an activist commitment, and to be a militant means to identify with the theory and practice . . . of this revolution,[38] . . . be with it for better or worse. . . . The organizations that merely express their support for the revolution are in fact outside it. . . . To be an activist means to have confidence in the men that lead the revolution.[39]

[37] For a fictionalized, but not unreal, version, concerning the actions of the MLR, see Guillermo Thorndike, *No, Mi General!* (Lima: Mosca Azul, 1976).

[38] *Expreso,* December 16, 1973.

[39] *La Prensa,* December 16, 1973.

The unconditional support demanded of the "activist" was evident, yet no participation in decision making or in the distribution of power was offered in return, making activism all the more improbable.

All the sectors within the regime accused other participants and public officials who did not participate of being infiltrators. Actually, in the ambiguous ideological framework, placed in a rigidly hierarchical structure, anyone except the chief could be an infiltrator. This recourse also tended to reinforce the authority of superiors in the hierarchy, but in a manner more superficial than real. Both these recourses were less useful in establishing political support for the government than in providing fuel for ideological debate, which became especially grueling after the transfer of the daily papers to distinct civilian groups in 1974.

In Lima, in February 1975, after a social explosion triggered by a police strike that showed the lack of organized support for the Velasco plan, a group of civilians created the Peruvian Revolution Movement. It was rapidly declared illegitimate by the government, which named the organizing committee of the Political Organization of the Peruvian Revolution as its replacement. Among the recommended tasks of this new organization, cited in a memorandum by Velasco himself, were: "to counteract attacks, infiltrations, confusionism . . . [and to provide] ideological and political defense for the revolution."[40] For these purposes it was necessary to "maintain coordination with the Commission of Ministers. Thus, they will be informed of the political fluctuations of the moment." Then the memorandum warns that "the government of the revolution conducts the PROCESS. It can take positions in defense of the revolution (measures of force) that may not appear 'humanistic.' IT IS IN [self-]DEFENSE." The new apparatus was never established; the Velasco regime fell a few weeks after the committee was installed. But it should be noted that this new apparatus was to be a mechanism only for articulating support. It did not provide for participation in the decisions of the government, which remained, from the beginning, in the hands of the military.

AND THE REFORMS?

The changes introduced by the military regime have shaken the organization of Peruvian society. The nature of the plan, however, has

[40] Copied in Béjar, *La Revolución en la Trampa,* pp. 251–252.

meant that the proposed goals of the reforms have been only partially attained, were short-lived, or have not been reached at all, depending on the particular case. We shall see this in an examination of the administration of justice.

In the context of the oligarchic state, the formally prevailing liberal republican law was generated by a transference of foreign jurisprudential principles that had little or nothing to do with the actual social economic reality, but, in fact, obscured it. As a result, legal regulation became a dead letter in the semifeudal relations expressed in the axis of local power: landholder-police-judge-subprefect. In spite of what was contained in the constitution and the laws, exploitation predominated in the rural areas, and secondarily, norms of communal tradition. The administration of justice, deeply tied to the traditional mechanisms of power, legalized domination; for instance, the *hacendados* that by *de facto* means took pieces of land that—until then—had been possessed by the peasant communities, found a legal formula that legitimized violently acquired property; a certain judicial process enabled the judge to award a title that the newly constituted owner lacked.

Under the Velasco regime, the official criticism was directed at the prevailing law on the one hand, criticizing it as a legitimizing element of the established order, and at the administration of justice as such on the other, blaming it for the prevailing traditional order. In 1970, President Velasco said: "One of the greatest fundamental wrongs in Peru was the slow and faulty administration of justice. The previous judicial power was truly the symbol of the decrepitude and the insensitivity of the whole established social order."[41] Velasco also maintained that "domination by the judicial system was one way of assuring that everything continued the same in Peru"[42] and charged that the administration of justice had always been "two-faced; one face austere and cruel for the humble and one tolerant and good for the powerful."[43] Going beyond questions of obsolete and inadequate laws, this appraisal emphasized an image of justice based on class, benefiting the dominant sectors to the detriment of the majority. This analysis had some basis. It related characteristics of the judiciary to characteristics of the society that it attempted to change and to which it served as a base of support. Furthermore, one does not find in the judiciary's official documents a conceptualization at this level of ab-

[41] Message to the Nation, July 28, 1970.
[42] Message to the Civil Police, August 30, 1970.
[43] Message on the third anniversary of the revolution, October 3, 1971.

straction. The judiciary rejected the government's criticism, conceding only that trials moved slowly, and blaming the delay on the lack of resources given by the state and on proceeding statutes that only the government could modify.[44]

With respect to actual measures adopted, the government began by providing courts that specialized in resolving conflicts arising from specific reform programs, such as the agrarian issue of labor community relations. Additionally, courts of this type were also to manage, under government control, labor and political conflicts—thus emerged an agrarian court and a labor communities court. The jurisdiction on labor was strengthened to better deal with the claims and collective negotiations, and the military courts were noticeably enlarged to handle political crimes.

With respect to the traditional judiciary, two measures were declared. One was a reform of the composition of the corps of magistrates. Members of the Supreme Court were removed in 1970; the new court was in charge of a special ratification of judges, and a law lowered the retirement age. The National Justice Council was created to name, promote, and dismiss the judges. This body, which was primarily appointed by the government, brought into the judicial career a certain number of private firm practitioners and lawyers working for the state who brought with them experiences and perspectives different from those prevalent in judicial apparatus. The council also established a rigid system of investigations and sanctions over judges.

Legal reforms with respect to civil issues were restricted to expediating and simplifying the decisions concerning alimony, the executory proceedings, and declaration of heirs. In criminal law, the reforms gave judges investigating a case power for sentencing in certain crimes, set up the one-member tribunal for other crimes, shortened the procedure, created a procedural route for *habeas corpus*, and expanded the statutes concerning press crimes. Moreover, conditional liberty was facilitated; but at the same time, penalties were strengthened, including the reimposition of the death penalty.

An evaluation of these measures must note that they are inconsistent with the official analysis of the deficiencies of the judicial system. If a new type of justice was sought, as was maintained in presidential speeches, it could not be achieved by simply replacing magistrates.

[44] For a detailed account of these criticisms and the responses of the judges, see Luis Pásara, "La Administración de Justicia, Según las Autoridades Políticas y Judiciales" in Corte Suprema de Justicia de la República/Consejo Latinoamericano de Derecho y Desarrollo, *Seminario sobre Derecho y Cambio Social,* mimeographed (Lima, 1977), pp. 229–265.

For the indebted and delinquent alike, the legal changes were essentially repressive and centered on expediency. Two serious contradictions were evident in the changes.

The first contradiction resulted perhaps from the search for a certain spectacularity in results. The legal changes brought about an increase in the more drastic penal sanctions, notably the death penalty, and swifter execution of judgments. These sanctions were applied by the very same bodies that had been accused of administering questionable justice. This type of drastic sanction or swift sentencing against the debtor was incompatible with social reforms that recognized the inheritance of an administration of justice that was "hard on the poor," inefficient, and uncertain in its methods and results.

The second contradiction is seen in the procedural reforms, which appeared to ignore the infrastructural limitations of the courts. The government did not allocate more resources to the courts; in 1976, the whole judicial structure received only .36 percent of the national budget. In passing new laws attempting to force improvement, the government overloaded the already congested judicial apparatus and obtained even poorer results.

The distance between the government's actual measures and its ambitious ideological formulation is explained by various factors. One was that the program of social reforms touched only certain specific areas, which were removed from the duties of the judiciary, and left unaltered the problems that the people took to the civil or criminal courts. Consequently, significant changes were not made to these bodies. A second factor was that the proposed new judicial system would clash with economic realities—the profound inequities that conditioned the economic, social, and cultural capacity of individuals to accede to the administration of justice. These conditions were not substantially altered by the regime's limited reforms. The official critique, then, sought to correspond to dissatisfaction with the judicial apparatus but did not represent a serious commitment to change it, nor a way of changing it. In conclusion, the judicial apparatus itself was the object of changes and measures of a bureaucratic nature. These were imposed from the outside, in clear hierarchical and authoritarian manner, in an attempt to gain adherents to the military's ideological program. But they were not part of an effort to allow the judges themselves to undertake reform of the state apparatus under their charge.

The result of this attempt to reform the judicial system, was rather limited. The majority of judges submitted to the government on two levels. At the level of ideological debate, the leading ranks of the judiciary, incapable of formulating a conceptual alternative for the administration of justice, ended up attempting to see the will of the government as the source of law. This capitulation replaced the creation of jurisprudence. The best example of this was given by the president of the Supreme Court who, in 1974, affirmed: "In the historical moment in which we are living, according to the Statute that governs us, no law can be incompatible with the high goals of the revolution. Even the constitution only remains in force when its propositions are compatible with and serve to support the achievement of these goals."[45] At the level of concrete decisions, this capitulation affected decisions by the judiciary in those areas especially sensitive to power. The evidence gathered in research on the behavior of the judges before the appeals of *habeas corpus* demonstrates this clearly.[46] Rationalizations of ill-disguised legal trials in judicial decisions served to justify failures to support individual rights that were being infringed.

Moreover, the judges were intimidated by the drastic sanctions they faced for any delay or negligence.[47] As a consequence, research conducted in 1976 found that half of the sampled judges were not disposed to support a hypothetical *habeas corpus* case posed by someone who had been deported "for disrupting order"; this result corresponds to the actual behavior of the tribunals. Eighty-five percent of the interviewed judges did not suggest changes in the repressive press law instituted by the military government, and two-thirds were inclined to use it repressively; half the judges also favored maintaining and applying the government's decree that left the constitution ambiguously suspended and replaced by the "objectives of the revolutionary government."[48] Perhaps most important is the fact that, fundamentally, Peruvian justice did not change. It continues to be expensive, inaccessible to the masses, profoundly discriminatory, and predominantly formalist. The changes brought about by the new courts tended to disappear in the political framework of the second phase of the military government. The only positive results were a

[45] José García Salazar, "Discurso-Memoria del Presidente de la Corte Suprema" in *El Peruano,* March 19, 1974.

[46] DESCO, *Cambios en la Administración de Justicia 1968–1975,* mimeographed (Lima, 1976), p. 64. This work sampled thirty-four cases at random; none of these resources to *habeas corpus*—more than half of which corresponded to the violation of rights of political leaders—were supported by judicial power.

[47] This conclusion arose from an empirical study on judges: Luis Pásara, "¿Pueden Cambiar los Jueces?" a work presented to a meeting on law and society organized by CLACSO, mimeographed (Buenos Aires, May 28–June 2, 1979).

[48] DESCO, *Formación y Conceptualización Jurídica de los Magistrados,* mimeographed (Lima, 1976), pp. 32, 36, 42, 44.

certain raising of the judges' social consciousness and a pluralization of the positions within the judiciary.

It is obvious that the characteristics of the military program are crucially important in explaining the lean results of the attempted judicial reform. The program's ambiguity, its bureaucratic and authoritarian character, and the limited social transformation being put into effect are elements that arose from the nature of the regime and that contaminated and thwarted the reform.

THE RETURN TO REALITY

The left has frequently classified the Velasco regime as "bourgeois reformism." A curious bourgeois reformism this one, rejected by the most qualified spokesmen of the bourgeoisie, who disagreed with the basic features of the program (the state as entrepreneur and controller, the collective participation of workers in the management of the enterprise, for example). These representatives of the bourgeoisie had no institutional or partisan representation in the government; as a result, they were left in a state of uncertainty. They could not make sure predictions, and prediction is essential to capital investors.

The military's program did reserve, or better yet, "assigned," an important place to the bourgeoisie, in spite of its "socialist" rhetoric—both in terms of profit and in terms of a policy of preferential protection to industry. Perhaps this policy could be identified with what is called "the historic interests" of the bourgeoisie; the bourgeoisie thought that the Velasco regime did not represent its interests but rather threatened them. Some factions of the bourgeoisie did join the program, however. Among the industrialists, for example, the Association of Exporters (ADEX) broke away from the industrialists' lobby association, the National Industrial Society (SNI), and proceeded to adopt the industrial policy of the regime and collaborate with it. The National Confederation of Retailers (CONACO) also supported the government's program. Similarly, in 1972, the newspaper *La Prensa*, under the control of the bourgeoisie, proposed an alliance with the military government:

> The revolution has reformed without violence a large part of that which could have been reformed. It has distanced the country from the *acriollado* capitalist pattern that reigned until 1968, and although while doing so it has undoubtedly managed to get us closer to the socialist world, it has tried at all times to maintain itself independent of communist ideology and schemes. . . . Certainly this

is a new path. It presents grave problems, but promises perhaps to solve the greater ills already present in our society and even in the developed world: the class struggle, the strikes, urban anarchy, rural guerrilla wars. . . . *La Prensa* proposes an economic alliance among all Peruvians, laying aside any political differences which may exist.[49]

This alliance did not crystallize. The industrial entrepreneurs and the businessmen substantially enriched themselves by taking advantage of the conditions created by the process of social change. They tried to influence and pressure the government through various methods that included the acceptance of important duties in public administration. But the government did not share power with them and continued to try to impose upon them a social program that did not correspond to their perceived interests. In response, the bourgeoisie sabotaged programs like the industrial community, as well as crippling the economy, at the macro level, through systematic capital flight.

The conflict between the bourgeoisie and the regime unfolded chiefly on the ideological plane, probably because on no other plane could power be disputed. For this reason, the expropriation of the newspapers was critical; the newspapers had been the forum for ideological conflict, as much for the government that took them over as for the bourgeoisie that protested actively against it. The bourgeoisie perceived the weakness of the government in its reliance on the armed forces for survival, and it attacked the government on this score. The bourgeoisie stated that the government was moving toward communism and that social agitation was originating from infiltrators within the state apparatus. These kinds of attacks helped to promote a new consensus within the armed forces about the overall failure of Velasco's program, resulting in the change from Phase One to Phase Two under Morales Bermúdez.

The government did stir social mobilization even though it later attempted to frame it and check it. The government's reforms opened new areas of social conflict, despite its efforts. The government's official ideology was provocative. For example, this slogan for the countryside—"Peasants, the patron will no longer grow fat from your poverty"—created expectations beyond what could be fulfilled by the Agrarian Reform Law. In contrast, the structures that arose to channel mobilization functioned briefly and only superficially.

[49] *La Prensa*, August 2, 1972.

One of the most important examples of the weakness of the agrarian reform was the case of Huando. This prosperous hacienda situated north of Lima was subdivided under the terms of the Agrarian Reform Law, although in violation of the procedures in some aspects. In October 1970, the workers began a strike that lasted five months; as a result, the original subdivision of Huando was annulled. The workers were supported by other peasant groups, union workers, and radical sectors of the government. Their views were expressed in the newspaper *Expreso*. When the network of agrarian organizations promoted by the government began to be established two years later, two principal leaders of the struggle in Huando were recruited as "promoters" in the payroll of the SINAMOS. Nevertheless, the production cooperative that worked the Huando land leaned toward the leftist CCP and not the official CNA.

The case illustrates the weakness of the mechanisms for enclosure, which sought to defend the regime but were infected by the regime's own precariousness. Placing the state over the classes alienated the government from one possible base of social support; this dilemma was too difficult to be solved by restructuring social organizations to make them supportive of the regime. Certainly, as Stepan observed, these state structures would have greater success when the previous institutional and ideological organization were weak.[50] To use his example, the state structures were more successfully established in the *pueblos jóvenes* than in the agrarian cooperatives. But in the long run, these structures could not give the government what it did not have. Class conflict left less and less room for a program that attempted to reshape class interests. The same fate befell the government as befell its political arm, SINAMOS; it was rejected by both sides in most conflicts.

The dynamic generated by the implementation of the military program is one of sharp social conflicts. As Giorgio Alberti notes, as the reforms met their limits, political and economic conflicts were intensified and the regime's inability to achieve hegemony was clear.[51] Conflicts within the government were thereby sharpened, leading to actions within the state apparatus that were more markedly contradictory, which in turn heightened social conflict. The autonomy from class interests sought by the government emerged as temporary and diminishing. Autonomy existed in inverse proportion to social con-

[50] Stepan, *The State and Society*, p. 226.
[51] Giorgio Alberti, "Estado, Clase Empresarial, y Comunidad Industrial," in Alberti, Santistevan, Pásara, *Estado y clase;* pp. 77–78.

flict, but the reforms were reappropriated by each of the confronted interests. The conflict of classes and groups toppled the supposed neutrality of the regime's program; and when it was put to run in society, it was left without any backing.

In the context of the regime's inherent weakness, the economic crisis accelerated its end. The expansion of imports for the domestic market precipitated a balance-of-payments crisis, which the government was in no condition to face due to its high level of external indebtedness. Under international financial pressure, the distributive capacity of the regime was narrowed and its political space cut. The exhaustion of the project has been well described by Alberti:

> given the sharpening of the economic crisis, the beginning of inflation, the problems arising from the political economy that has altered the structure of property and the traditional methods of accumulation without having greatly affected the structure of production. . . , and the sectoral and regional unbalances, the regime was facing a progressively more serious crisis at all levels of society. The crisis was evident principally in the high incidence of social conflict, such as strikes, shutdowns, and land invasions. The ideologies and the reforms that should have constructed social democracy and mass participation found no resonance in the political and social reality of the country.[52]

As the officially controlled social organizations became useless, repression accentuated. In the second phase of the military government, SINAMOS was replaced by a state of emergency that forbade strikes, limited the listing of demands by unions, and permitted the detention and deportation of opponents. As the government was corroded by corruption, the "transfer of power to the civilians" became a way out. This "transfer" was intended to keep the breakdown within the armed froces, but it could not prevent the total floundering of the program.

Utopian and conciliatory, authoritarian and arbitrary, this regime's program could not be taken by anyone as his own, although many individuals agreed with some of its measures. As the program proposed to redefine the role of all social groups at the same time, it was difficult for any group to be in agreement with the entire program. Certain beliefs of the regime found some acceptance, but the program as a whole did not attain the legitimacy that only the concrete and effective representation of the interests of one class or an al-

[52] Ibid., p. 82.

liance of classes can gain. The autonomy of the state, upon which was developed the military's attempt to reform the whole society from above, and which in fact gave the military great leeway for radicalizing its measures, was at the same time the major weakness of the whole program.

If the Peruvian experiment was able to endure so many years, it was thanks to the previous historical failure of Peru's dominant class, which gave great room for such an ambitious reformist illusion. After those years, we have returned to reality, a reality transformed in good part by measures implemented by Velasco's program, though not in the terms anticipated. Social frustrations appear to have been vented. As a politician from the right said, "the best is that the military has shaken the tree";[53] the traditional oligarchy has been liquidated, and the country has advanced in political awareness and organization. As the popular response to the recessive economic policy of phase two—including demonstrations and nation-wide strikes—demonstrated, all social sectors have been politicized, contrary to what the program intended.

[53] Interview with Celso Sotomarino, *Caretas,* October 2, 1978 (no. 547), p. 59.

IV

Overviews of the Peruvian
Experiment

Revolution and Redistribution in Latin America

Susan Eckstein

Whereas the other essays in this volume highlight the Velasco regime's attempts to use state power to transform the Peruvian socioeconomic structure and the internal and international class forces that severely dampened its efforts, this chapter compares—in terms of social and economic developments—Peru's revolutionary experience with that of Mexico, Bolivia, and Cuba. In all four nations, the revolutions displaced dominant classes obstructing capitalist expansion.[1] Political groups assumed control of the central state apparatus through extralegal means and, at least in the countryside, destroyed the economic and political power base of the previously dominant group in a fashion that restructured class relations.

There are important differences among the four revolutionary experiences, however, and this chapter explores how these different characteristics may have affected the outcomes of the revolutions. First, Peru's experience was a revolution "from above," whereas

Research for this essay was partially funded by the Tinker Foundation. Cynthia McClintock provided me with very helpful comments on an earlier version of the chapter.

[1] From a global perspective, the revolutions did not replace feudal with capitalist modes of production, for Latin America was incorporated into the world capitalist economy when conquered and colonized by the Spanish and Portuguese. In the Latin American context, revolutions have not involved a break with a precapitalist past. I shall use the terms capitalist and socialist to refer to dominant patterns of ownership: private and public, respectively. It should be kept in mind, however, that even the revolutionary governments that remained committed to private ownership nationalized key industries. And Cuba continues to be integrated into the world capitalist economy, despite collectivization of ownership. Capitalism and socialism in their ideal-typical forms exist in none of the countries under study. On Cuba's global capitalist relations, and their impact on the domestic economy, see Susan Eckstein, "Capitalist Constraints on Cuban Socialist Development," *Comparative Politics* (April 1980), pp. 253–274, and "The Socialist Transformation of Cuban Agriculture: Domestic and International Constraints," *Social Problems* (October 1981).

Mexico's, Bolivia's, and Cuba's were revolutions "from below."[2] Peru's revolution was "from above" because the takeover and initiation of the social transformation were organized and led by high-level state officials with little mass participation. To be sure, there had been unrest in cities and countryside earlier in the 1960s, but the Velasquistas had not been associated with any protest group before assuming power. By contrast, Mexico, Bolivia, and Cuba, experienced revolutions "from below," as workers and peasants in all three countries were more directly involved in the societal upheavals. In none of the countries, however, did "popular" groups alone transform the society.

Although both types of revolutions, by definition, involve class transformations, we might expect the results of the two to differ somewhat, according to the different class alliances that bring them about. Leaders of "elite revolutions" might use state power to advance interests of classes other than their own; but we would expect peasants and workers to share more in the fruits of victory when they actively participate in the insurrection. If the class base of upheavals affects subsequent societal development, peasants and workers in postrevolutionary Mexico, Bolivia, and Cuba should enjoy benefits unavailable to their Peruvian counterparts.

Studies of social change, however, suggest that the dominant pattern of ownership instituted after revolutions might have a greater impact on how resources are allocated than on the class alliances associated with the upheavals. Governments of societies based primarily on private ownership and those in which ownership is largely collective may be equally committed to development and distributive goals, but the former may be constrained in ways that the latter are not. When private ownership is the rule, governments must provide sufficient incentive to induce internal investments; therefore, they

[2] Revolutions from below are abrupt transformations of basic socioeconomic and political institutions that are accompanied and partly effectuated by the involvement of lower- and working-class groups in the destruction of the old regime. Revolutions from above or "elite revolutions" are abrupt transformations that occur without the participation of "popular" groups. On the distinction between the two types of revolutions, see Barrington Moore, Jr., *Social Origins of Dictatorship and Democracy* (Boston: Beacon Press, 1966); Ellen Kay Trimberger, *Revolution from Above: Military Bureaucrats and Development in Japan, Turkey, Egypt, and Peru* (New Brunswick, N.J.: Transaction Books, 1978); Theda Skocpol, *States and Social Revolutions in France, Russia, and China* (Cambridge: Cambridge University Press, 1979); Susan Eckstein and Peter Evans, "Revolution as Cataclysm and Coup: Political Transformation and Economic Development in Mexico and Brazil," *Comparative Studies in Sociology* 1 (1978): 129–155.

cannot readily implement policies that favor laboring classes at the expense of capital. Because socialist regimes assume direct responsibility for production, they are not faced with the same constraint. In principle, they are better able to award workers a larger share of the product of their labor than governments in capitalist societies. In practice, however, the workers' share is likely to depend on the priority the government assigns to consumption versus investment. Allocative policies, of course, will also hinge on the state's capacity to generate surplus. But if the main form of ownership has a greater bearing on the way state power is deployed after a revolution than the class alliances associated with the upheaval, then we would expect the most significant differences among the countries to be between Cuba on the one hand and Mexico, Bolivia, and Peru on the other.

Yet world economy theory would suggest that the status of countries and the way countries are integrated into the world economy play a more decisive role than either internal class alliances or property relations in shaping developmental patterns. According to Immanuel Wallerstein, there is a single world economy, it is capitalist, and production within it is oriented toward trade profit maximization.[3] Because Wallerstein claims that the contemporary world is not divided into two distinct blocs—one capitalist, the other socialist—he posits that production in all countries is largely determined by the same market and geopolitical forces. He argues that the main difference between countries hinges on their so-called core, semi-peripheral, or peripheral status within the world economy. Economically and politically, core countries are strongest, and peripheral countries are weakest, but semi-peripheral countries have considerable potential, especially during periods of economic downturn (including the current one), to increase their share of the world surplus. While Wallerstein does recognize that revolutions may help countries modify their role in the world economy, he views prospects for less developed countries as not very great, especially in the periphery.

If Wallerstein is correct, the main differences among the postrevolutionary societies will depend on the status of the countries within the world economy. The semi-peripheral countries should have a larger surplus than the peripheral countries to use for productive and distributive purposes. His criteria for classifying countries are not well defined, but Bolivia, with one of the poorest and least diversified

[3] See Immanuel Wallerstein, *The Capitalist World-Economy* (Cambridge: Cambridge University Press, 1979), especially chapters 1, 4, and 5.

TABLE 11.1
Economic Growth, Manufacturing, and Export Diversification in Selected Latin American Nations

	Bolivia	Peru	Cuba	Mexico	Brazil
	GNP PER CAPITA (IN CONSTANT DOLLARS OF 1970)				
1950	189	278	322[a]	362	187
1955	175	337	329	416	224
1960	151	364	463	467	268
1965	173	430	428	536	291
1970	201	446	492	656	364
1976	257	500	721	718	525
	MANUFACTURING SHARE OF GDP (PERCENTAGE)				
1950	15%	15%	n.a.[b]	21%	20%
1955	18	15	22	21	22
1960	14	18	45	19	18
1965	15	20	43	21	17
1970	13	21	48	23	25
1976	14	23	41	24	26
	MAIN EXPORT AS PERCENTAGE OF TOTAL EXPORTS				
1955	67%	25%	80%	29%	59%
1960	81	17	79	21	56
1965	85	23	86	19	44
1970	57	28	77	9	34
1975	39	23	89	16	15

Sources: James Wilkie, ed., *Statistical Abstract of Latin America* 20 (Los Angeles: University of California, Latin America Center, 1980): 239, 247, 248, 392; Claes Brundenius, *Measuring Economic Growth and Income Distribution in Revolutionary Cuba* (Sweden Research Policy Institute, University of Lund, July 1979), p. 14.

[a] Cuban data in 1950 are based on the gross domestic product; after 1960, the data are based on the gross material product (GMP). GMP is the total value of goods and productive services (excluding housing, health, education, sports and culture, defense, and public administration). GNP, by contrast, includes the total value of goods and services produced.

[b] Cuban data include mining, petroleum, and quarrying, which together account for about 1 percent of the national product.

economies and one of the most unstable governments in Latin America was, without question, peripheral when its *ancien régime* collapsed (see Table 11.1). Mexico had a growing industrial sector (largely foreign owned) and a strong, stable government at the eve of its revolution. Although it was one of the most economically developed Latin American countries at the time, it probably still constituted part of the periphery. By the time of the other revolutions, however, it had developed to the point of inclusion in the semi-periphery. Peru and Cuba are more difficult to categorize; they had both peripheral and semi-peripheral characteristics when their respective upheavals occurred, although neither had as large an economic base as Mexico. When Castro came to power, Cuba ranked seventh in GNP per capita in Latin America and its manufacturing sector accounted for as large a share of the national product as Mexico's then did. Yet its economy was exceptionally tied to the export of a single agricultural commodity, and much of its industrial production was sugar-related. Peru's export sector was more diversified than Cuba's, and its economy was more productive and developed than Bolivia's. The world economy thesis would thus lead us to expect qualitatively different patterns in Mexico and Bolivia by the time of the upheaval in the latter. It would also lead us to expect postrevolutionary development possibilities in Cuba and Peru to be similar in important respects, despite their contrasting dominant modes of economic organization.

The revolutions in each country began in different years: 1910 in Mexico, 1952 in Bolivia, 1959 in Cuba, and 1968 in Peru. Therefore, contrasts among the countries could reflect the various amounts of time elapsed since the respective upheavals or global political and economic conditions at the time of each revolution. Were the longevity factor important, the impact of revolution should be most apparent in Mexico and least so in Peru. Were the period in world history important, the results of the Mexican revolution should differ considerably from outcomes in the other countries. Because of limited data on the pre-World War II period, it is difficult to assess the early impact of Mexico's 1910 upheaval. To help correct for this problem, we will compare developments in Mexico with developments in Brazil. Brazil never experienced a political transformation comparable to Mexico's. If we find similar developments in Mexico and Brazil, conditions in Mexico might be attributable to the way the country was integrated historically into the world economy and not to its revolution and the time lapse since.

The Peruvian case also presents a methodological problem. If we find little change in Peru, the explanation might rest with the relative "youth" of the transformation or with the limits of revolutions from above. By contrasting changes in Peru with changes during comparable periods in the other postrevolutionary societies, the time factor will be "controlled for."

I will examine below the impact that the revolutions have had on aspects of social welfare, in particular on land and income distribution and on health care and nutrition. Although these measures do not exhaust the components of social welfare, they include the most important. Using available data, I will assess whether the class alliances associated with the revolutions, the dominant pattern of property ownership, status within the world economy, or timing/longevity best accounts for postrevolutionary cross-national social welfare patterns.[4]

LAND DISTRIBUTION

Land was inequitably distributed in the four countries on the eve of their upheavals. Mexico had the highest Gini index value of land concentration on the continent, even twenty years after the demise of its *ancien régime*. Bolivia had the second highest Gini index, and Peru scored only slightly lower. Ownership in Cuba was least concentrated; by regional standards, it was moderate.[5]

In 1910, less than 3 percent of Mexican landholders owned more than 90 percent of the productive land.[6] The proportion held by Mexican peasants had declined in the late nineteenth century after the Porfirio Díaz government encouraged large surveying companies and private businessmen to purchase or appropriate lands traditionally held by peasant communities. In Bolivia, 6 percent of the landowners held 92 percent of the land before the revolution; and on the eve of the Velasco coup, about .2 percent of the Peruvian farmowners held 69 percent of Peru's farmland. At the other extreme, 59 percent of the Bolivian landholders, with less than 5 hectares each, controlled only .2 percent of the farmland, while 83 percent of the Peruvian landholders, who also held no more than 5 hectares each, controlled 6 percent of the land in farms (see Table 11.2).

The situation in prerevolutionary Cuba was somewhat different. By regional standards, not only was land concentration moderate but also *minifundismo* was limited. Eight percent of the farm population controlled 71 percent of the land, and only 20 percent of all holdings were smaller than 5 hectares; that 20 percent accounted for 1 percent of the land. The Great Depression and competition from foreign-owned agrobusinesses had forced many peasants off the land before 1959.

---

[4] Other factors do complicate the analysis here. First, revolutionary change is a process. Revolutions are not events that terminate at a given point in time. Thus, revolutionary forces become less decisive in shaping societal developments as other counteracting tendencies assert themselves. While the revolutionary-linked factors considered here are believed to be among the most important, other factors, such as the nature of leadership and the extent to which the state operates autonomously of socioeconomic groups, are also likely to shape the outcomes of social transformation.

[5] World Bank, *Land Reform in Latin America: Bolivia, Chile, Mexico, Peru and Venezuela*, staff working paper, no. 275, April 1978, p. 2.

[6] Edmundo Flores, *Vieja Revolución, Nuevos Problemas* (Mexico City: Editorial Joaquin Mortiz, 1970), p. 155.

All four countries implemented land reforms that transformed rural class relations, encouraged efficient land use, and ushered in more equitable land distributions. The land reforms were announced in the countries shortly after the respective political upheavals. They served to reduce the number of large, privately owned farm units and the portion of the land area that they held. Between the latest pre-revolutionary and latest postrevolutionary years for which there are data, the land area in large farms dropped most in Cuba, least in Bolivia. The privately held land in independently owned farms of 1,000 or more hectares dropped from 92 to 65 percent in Bolivia, from 69 to 42 percent in Peru, and from 82 (in 1923, after the breakdown of the *ancien régime* but before widespread land distribution) to 32 percent in Mexico.[7] In Cuba, most holdings over 67 hectares were outlawed after 1963. In 1967, only about 5 percent of the privately owned land was in farms with over 67 hectares; in 1950, more than 71 percent of the farm area had been in holdings that large.

The land reforms in the three countries undergoing capitalist revolutions had their greatest impact on sectors of agriculture where crops were grown. Although postrevolutionary Bolivian governments have awarded settlers in the sparsely populated tropical lowlands large properties, especially but not exclusively for ranching, the share of *crop land* in estates over 1,000 hectares dropped from 79 to 10 percent within two years after the announcement of the country's reform law (see Table 11.3). The percentage of crop land in estates over 1,000 hectares dropped to similar levels in postrevolutionary Mexico and Peru, although in Mexico the property transformation took decades.

At the same time that large landholders in each country lost property, sharecroppers, tenant farmers, and some rural wage workers gained land rights. Frequently they acquired property rights to land that they had held in usufruct. Because usufruct rights differed before the respective upheavals, the size of postreform peasant holdings also vary. And because most sharecroppers and tenant farmers had access to little usufruct land under the old orders, the land reforms did not resolve the problem of *minifundismo*. Since the respective upheavals, the proportion of farm units with 5 hectares or less increased in Mexico and Cuba (though it decreased between 1950 and 1960 in Mexico); in Bolivia the proportion declined by less than 3 percent. No data are available on Peru. *Minifundismo* becomes especially problem-

---

[7] Some landholdings exceed the legal maximum because the governments have not always enforced the law and because individual family members at times have each legally claimed holdings even though they operated the land as a single unit.

TABLE 11.2
Agricultural Holdings in Selected Latin American Nations, 1923–1970

	Percentage of Farm Units					Percentage of Land Area				
Holdings[a]	1923	1950	1960	1967	1970	1923	1950	1960	1967	1970
Bolivia										
Less than 5		59.3%		56.6%	14.0[b]		.2			.2[b]
5–99.9		25.7		41.4	6.0		1.5			1.0
100–999.9		7.2		1.6	1.0		6.4			3.0
1,000		6.3		.4	1.0		91.9			65.0
Brazil										
Less than 10		34.4	44.8		51.4		1.3	2.4		3.1
10–99.9		51.0	44.7		39.0		15.3	19.0		20.1
100–999.9		13.0	9.4		8.5		32.5	34.4		37.2
1,000+		1.6	.9		.8		50.9	44.2		39.2
Cuba										
Less than 5		20.1[c]		47.4[d]			1.0[c]		14.9[d]	
5–99.9		71.9		51.7			28.7		80.0	
100–999.9		8.0		.9			71.0		5.1	
1,000+										

Mexico							
Less than 5	59.0	72.6	65.9	18.0[b]	.8	.9	.8	.7[b]
5–99.9	32.0	21.2	26.0	11.0	5.0	5.5	5.7	6.0
100–999.9	7.0	4.7	6.4	2.0	12.0	14.1	15.3	15.0
1,000+	2.0	1.5	1.6	.3	82.0	79.4	78.4	32.0
Peru							
Less than 5	83.4[c]			66.0[b]			5.8[c]	6.0[b]
5–99.9	15.3			12.0			10.3	10.0
100–999.9	1.1			.8			14.6	11.0
1,000+	.2			.1			69.2	42.0

Sources: Wilkie, ed., *Statistical Abstract of Latin America* 19: 50–53. Sergio Aranda, *La Revolución Agraria en Cuba* (Mexico City: Siglo xxi, 1968), pp. 138, 162; José Illan, *Cuba: Facts and Figures of an Economy in Ruin*, trans. George Wehby (Miami: Editorial ATP, 1964), p. 151. Bolivia, Ministerio de Asuntos Campesinos y Agropecuarios, *Diagnostico del Sector Agropecuario 1974*, La Paz, p. 459. World Bank, *Land Reform in Latin America: Bolivia, Chile, Mexico, Peru and Venezuela*, staff working paper, no. 275 (April 1978), pp. 21, 23, 30.

[a] In hectares.

[b] 1970 data refer exclusively to private sector. Land reform beneficiaries accounted for 78, 69, and 21 percent of the farm units and 31, 46, and 31 percent of the land in farms in Bolivia, Mexico and Peru, respectively. The Peruvian data are for 1973.

[c] Data for 1945.

[d] The 1967 data, which exclude Havana and Oriente provinces and refer only to the private sector, refer to farms of less than 6.7 hectares, 6.7 to 67 hectares, and over 67 hectares, respectively.

[e] Data for 1961.

TABLE 11.3

Importance of Estates over 1,000 Hectares in Selected Latin American Nations, before and after Revolution

	Percent of Total Crop Land in Estates over 1,000 Hectares	Percent of All Farm Families on Estates over 1,000 Hectares
	PREREFORM	
Mexico (1923)	70%	70%
Bolivia (1950)	79	79
Peru (1961)	22	26
	POSTREFORM	
Mexico (1960)	29	
(1970)[a]	12	
Bolivia (1955)	10	
Peru (1973)	10	

Source: World Bank, *Land Reform in Latin America*, p. 13.

[a] Decreases from 1960 to 1970 resulted largely from the shift in census coverage. In 1970, the definition of large estates is 400 hectares or more of crop land.

atic when successive generations of land reform beneficiaries subdivide the small allotments.

The four reforms do, however, differ somewhat. Moreover, the reforms have not been implemented uniformly within each country. There are regional variations, reflecting specific local economic exigencies and class dynamics.

In Mexico and Bolivia, the reforms institutionalized a dual economy in agriculture while outlawing *latifundismo*. The reforms permitted both capitalist and petty commodity production. In both countries to the advantage of peasants and small farmers, the accumulation and concentration of land, labor, and the "means of production" have been circumscribed in the peasant sector. Land allotted to peasants cannot be legally sold, mortgaged, or rented.[8] Although peasants have generally received only small parcels, the reforms have given them a sense of security and improved social standing. The reforms have also served to restructure social relations in the countryside in that they put an end to seigniorial prerogatives.

Prerevolutionary land relations and struggles shaped the nature of the reforms implemented in the two countries. Mexico reinstituted *ejidos,* land collectively owned by villages but generally farmed individually (by families). The reform was precapitalist and anticapitalist in inspiration: it was designed to *restore* land that had been confiscated

[8] Even though the reform laws at times are violated, especially in Mexico's wealthiest agricultural zones, the reforms do restrict the spread of capitalist market relations to the peasant sector.

TABLE 11.4
Percent of Farmland and Farm Families Affected
by Land Reform in Selected Latin American Nations

	Total Land Redistributed as Percentage of Total Land on Farms	Land Reform Beneficiaries as Percentage of Agricultural Families
Mexico		
1930	6%	25%
1940	22	54
1960	26	42
1970	43[a]	66
Bolivia		
1955	—	49
1970	30	34
Peru		
1973	50	14
1974	—	25
1976	—	24

Source: For Mexico and Bolivia, see World Bank, *Land Reform in Latin America,* pp. 11, 19.

For Peru, see E.V.K. FitzGerald, *The State and Economic Development: Peru since 1968* (Cambridge: Cambridge University Press, 1976), p. 32, and Cynthia McClintock, *Peasant Cooperatives and Political Change in Peru* (Princeton: Princeton University Press, 1981), p. 61.

[a] This percentage increased in part because the 1970 census decreased its coverage of lands by excluding wide areas of idle, mainly barren, lands on private farms.

from peasants in the nineteenth century and to give them, individually and collectively, greater control over production on their property. Individual ownership was prohibited at the insistence of Emilio Zapata and his followers. As a precondition for collaboration with the revolutionary leadership, Zapata insisted on a reform that would prevent a land-grab, as had occurred after the 1856 agrarian reform.[9]

In Mexico, extensive redistribution did not occur until more than twenty years after the fall of Porfirio Díaz. Although only 25 percent of the farm families received land by 1930, ten years later, over half of the farm families had acquired land; and during the decade, the proportion of farmland redistributed jumped from 6 to 22 percent (Table 11.4). Because the rural population subsequently expanded and the government cut back its redistribution program, the percentage of agricultural families benefiting from the reform dropped 12 percentage points by 1960. By 1970, however, the government once again stepped up its reform program and the agricultural labor force

[9] See John Womack, Jr., *Zapata and the Mexican Revolution* (New York: Vintage Books, 1969).

declined. As a consequence, the proportion of farm families with land rose to 66 percent.

Land was redistributed much more rapidly in Bolivia. The Bolivian revolutionary government promulgated a land reform law in 1953, and by 1955, 49 percent of farm families had land. Not until thirty years after the outbreak of the Mexican upheavals did as large a percentage of the agricultural families in Mexico receive land. As previously noted, however, after the initial pressure for redistribution, the Bolivian government began to allot large land tracts to settlers in the sparsely settled lowlands, to the point that land once again is highly inequitably distributed. Many of the new agrarian elite are former *latifundistas.*[10]

In both Mexico and Bolivia, peasants in the organized and rebellious areas were the most likely to receive land grants: in the Morelos region in Mexico and in the highlands and Cochabamba areas in Bolivia. The Mexican government redistributed property especially when peasant communities submitted petitions and when agricultural workers disrupted farm production. In 1936, for example, President Cárdenas redistributed land in the Laguna region after massive strikes on cotton estates. He then accelerated land redistribution throughout the country, granting more land titles than any other president.[11] At times, where production had been mechanized, such as on the cotton estates, he established agricultural collectives. He allocated land both to restore order in the countryside and to broaden his political base of support.[12] The Great Depression and abuse by "revolutionary" leaders who had confiscated large holdings for themselves had generated widespread discontent in the 1920s. The increase in land allocations in the 1960s also followed a period of turmoil in the countryside. But post-Cárdenas presidents rarely encouraged collective *ejidos.*

In Bolivia, land redistribution almost always depended on the balance between pressure from below and resistance from above. Soon after the new government took power in 1952, organized peasants in-

[10] Susan Eckstein, "The Transformation of a 'Revolution from Below': International Capital, the State, and the Domestic Bourgeoisie in Bolivia," *Comparative Studies in Society and History* 25 (1983).

[11] Pablo González Casanova, *Democracy in Mexico* (New York: Oxford University Press, 1970), p. 223.

[12] Wayne Cornelius, "Nation-Building, Participation, and Distribution: The Politics of Social Reform under Cárdenas," in Gabriel Almond, et al., ed., *Crisis, Choice, and Change: Historical Studies of Political Development* (Boston: Little, Brown, 1973).

vaded hacienda lands. The peasants drove owners off their holdings and redistributed the property among themselves. In addition, court rulings on land claims hinged more on the relative power of peasants and landlords than on the specifications of the reform law.[13] Because the government was weak, local class struggles largely determined the extent of land distribution.[14]

Thus, both in Mexico and in Bolivia, peasants benefited from their participation in the revolution. But during periods when they were quiescent and in regions where they were not concentrated, agrarian policies tended to favor large farmers. In Mexico in the 1940s and in Bolivia in the early 1970s, for example, the respective governments promoted large-scale farming.[15] But the large farmers gained favor not merely because they maximized profits from trade, as the world economy thesis would lead us to expect; they gained favor also because they had acquired considerable political clout by then. In Bolivia, many large-scale farming ventures proved to be unprofitable, and the government took over the producers' outstanding debts. The resource-poor state, in the process, was decapitalized.[16]

Cuba, by contrast, had two official agrarian reforms, in 1959 and 1963. Although the first allowed farmers to maintain up to 402 hectares, it also created a propertied small farmer class, as in Mexico and Bolivia, by awarding land titles to tenant farmers, sharecroppers, and some rural wage workers. Unlike Mexico's and Bolivia's reforms,

[13] World Bank, *Land Reform*, pp. 22, 124.

[14] While the *de facto* land distribution occurred within two or three years, the certification of land titles still has not been completed. By 1970 less than one third of the eligible farm population received titles. Ibid., p. 22.

[15] Raymond Vernon, *The Dilemma of Mexico's Development* (Cambridge: Harvard University Press, 1963); Eckstein, "The Transformation of a 'Revolution from Below' "; Clark Reynolds, *The Mexican Economy: Twentieth-Century Structure and Growth* (New Haven: Yale University Press, 1970); Ministerio de Asuntos Campesinos y Agropecuarios, *Diagnostico del Sector Agropecuario* (1974); and Javier Albó, "Desarrollo rural," *Presencia* 32 (edición de homenaje al sesquicentenario de Bolivia) (August 6, 1975): 748. In northern Mexico, the government has been generous in supplying not only land but also credit, marketing and technical services, and irrigation, and it has supplied such resources both to *ejidatarios* and to private farmers there because it recognizes the importance of the region for national growth and trade. World Bank, *Land Reform*, p. 84. Reflecting the shift in Bolivian government agrarian policies, between 1953 and 1973 the average size holding decreased from 5.9 to 3.1 hectares in the peasant areas in the highlands, the valleys, and the Yungas, while the average allotment size increased in the lowlands occupied by agrarian capitalists. Moreover, since the mid-1960s, the state agricultural development bank has allocated almost all its funds to large farmers in the lowlands.

[16] Eckstein, "The Transformation of a 'Revolution from Below.' "

however, the first reform in Cuba also transformed large capital-intensive holdings into state farms. The sugar plantations had initially been converted into cooperatives, but within a few years, the government transformed them into state farms. The second reform left only about 30 percent of the farmland—in parcels rarely exceeding 67 hectares—in private hands.

Thus, the island land reforms also institutionalized a dual economy in agriculture, but one combining a variant of petty commodity with a socialist mode of production. Government efforts to convince small farmers to turn their properties over to the state or to organize their production on a cooperative basis have thus far failed. In this respect, the dominant mode of production has not determined land ownership patterns throughout agriculture in Cuba, just as it has not in Mexico and Bolivia.

In implementing its different land policies, the Castro government responded to class pressures on the one hand and to constraints imposed by the organization of agriculture on the other hand. By socializing the large farms that produced for the export market and by regulating trade, the government could capture foreign-exchange revenues and regulate work conditions on the farms. But the Cuban reforms served political as well as economic functions. As in Mexico and Bolivia, land allocations to peasants in Cuba occurred mainly in the areas of greatest unrest. In Cuba alone, though, the government intervened to undermine the power of large-scale, market-oriented producers; Castro has used state power differently than heads of governments in the other two countries experiencing revolutions from below. In particular, when large-scale cultivators obstructed production in defiance of the regime, the government expropriated their properties.[17] Had the government been concerned with output maximization above all, it would have given in to the large farmers; productivity on already converted state farms had proved to be lower than on private holdings.[18]

To date, the Castro government has not expropriated the properties of the small farmers with whom it initially allied, in part, no doubt, to maintain their support. It has manipulated production on

[17] When large rangers, for example, suspended cattle purchases from small ranchers to protest the radicalization of the revolution, the government expropriated the properties of the large landholders.

[18] Andrés Bianchi, "Agriculture," in Dudley Seers, ed., *Cuba: The Economic and Social Revolution* (Chapel Hill: University of North Carolina Press, 1964); Donald Bray and Timothy Harding, "Cuba," in Ronald Chilcote and Joel Edelstein, eds., *Latin America: The Struggle with Dependency and Beyond* (New York: John Wiley, 1974), p. 635.

small farms over the years, however. When the government attempted to maximize sugar exports in the late 1960s, for example, it regulated what private farmers produced, pressured them to work part time on state farms and to collaborate with state plans, and discouraged them from hiring labor.[19] Although small farmers often produced more and better quality goods than workers on state farms,[20] they concentrated on crops that enhanced their own profits. Many of them did not produce sugar, which maximized the state's foreign exchange earnings. In the 1970s, the government once again permitted private sales, decontrolled prices of certain commodities, ceased pressuring farmers to join state plans, and allowed them to hire labor. The government adopted a more permissive stance toward the private sector when demand for labor in the state sector receded. State farms required less labor once sugar harvesting was mechanized. Thus, the Cuban as well as the Mexican and Bolivian governments responded to peasant and small farmer interests mainly when political considerations outweighed or did not conflict with major economic concerns.

Although the Velasco government did not initiate Peru's first agrarian reform, it implemented the most sweeping reform in the country's history. Because of peasant land seizures and politicization, especially in the highlands, all presidential candidates in both the 1956 and the 1963 elections had promised agrarian reform. The Belaúnde administration is alleged to have killed thousands of peasants involved in land takeovers,[21] but soon after assuming office it purchased *some* farms and transferred ownership to workers on the estates. In the Convención area, tenant farmers organized a general strike against *hacendados* and resisted working for the landlords until they were granted land rights.[22] Finally, in 1964, Belaúnde promulgated a general law that called for the redistribution of all estate

[19] Eckstein, "The Socialist Transformation of Cuban Agriculture."

[20] Lee Lockwood, *Castro's Cuba, Cuba's Fidel* (New York: Vintage Books, 1969), p. 100.

[21] Cynthia McClintock, *Peasant Cooperatives and Political Change in Peru* (Princeton: Princeton University Press, 1981), p. 71.

[22] On rural unrest in the 1960s, see Wesley Craig, "Peru: the Peasant Movement of La Convención," in Henry Landsberger, ed., *Latin American Peasant Movements* (Ithaca, N.Y.: Cornell University Press, 1969); World Bank, *Land Reform*, p. 27; Susan Bourque and David Scott Palmer, "Transforming the Rural Sector: Government Policy and Peasant Response," in Abraham F. Lowenthal, ed., *The Peruvian Experiment: Continuity and Change under Military Rule* (Princeton: Princeton University Press, 1975), pp. 183–185, 195; and Colin Harding, "Land Reform and Social Conflict in Peru," in Lowenthal, ed., *The Peruvian Experiment*, pp. 22–53.

lands exceeding 150 hectares and for the conversion of usufruct to property rights among hacienda peasants. The law exempted highly productive enterprises and foreign exchange producing farmers— that is, large farmers on the coast—from expropriation. Because highland *hacendados* tended to be less wealthy and powerful than their coastal counterparts, they failed in their efforts to block land reform measures. Nonetheless, even in the highlands, the law was never aggressively implemented (for the most part, it merely legalized *de facto* occupations of lands). By 1969, about 4 percent of the land had been redistributed among 1 percent of the rural families.[23]

Yet the Belaúnde law had aroused expectations throughout the country. Owners began to fear that their properties were in jeopardy. Their ability to enforce labor compliance was eroding, especially as peasant unions, often with the backing of political parties, agitated for land. They responded by selling off livestock and farm equipment, cutting back investments, and liquidating portions of their properties.[24] Concomitantly, urban investment opportunities became more attractive to them.

It was against this backdrop that Velasco issued his agrarian reform program. Although he assumed power without the backing of rural workers and peasants, he addressed the rural crisis with policies favoring them over the oligarchy. Leaving medium-sized commercial farms untouched, he expropriated and collectivized the largest and most economically important estates. Large estates and estates not managed directly by their owners were entirely expropriated, unlike in Mexico where landowners were entitled to maintain a portion of their holdings. By 1977, there were virtually no more haciendas in Peru.

Four years after its establishment, Velasco's agrarian reform had redistributed a smaller percentage of farmland than Castro's, but more than either Mexico's or Bolivia's (Tables 11.2 and 11.4). Moreover, the Peruvian land reform served to restructure agrarian ownership more in accord with the Cuban than the Mexican or Bolivian model. The Velasco government transferred ownership and management of estates to farm workers, in the form of cooperatives.[25] To date, however, Peru has no state farms, the cooperatives operate

---

[23] World Bank, *Land Reform*, p. 27.

[24] Ibid., pp. 50–51.

[25] Not only did the Velasco administration no longer exempt highly productive and export-oriented estates from expropriation; it also required that the estates be converted into cooperatives. Belaúnde had promoted cooperatives, but on a voluntary basis through local initiatives. See Bourque and Palmer, "Transforming the Rural Sector," p. 195.

within a wider economy premised on market principles, and the proportion of the farm population that has individual holdings is much higher in Peru than in Cuba.[26]

As in Cuba, though, the organization of production prior to the revolution influenced how property relations were restructured in Peru. Different agrarian reform policies were implemented in different sectors of agriculture. In both countries, the large, capital-intensive holdings that produced for the export market were not subdivided into small plots. Yet, the somewhat different land policies currently in effect in the sugar sectors in Peru and Cuba demonstrate that governments have certain discretionary powers. Technical and market considerations alone have not determined how property has been redistributed.

The experience of Peru suggests that land reform can be more sweeping in a capitalist country experiencing a revolution from above than in a comparable country experiencing a revolution from below. More and better quality farmland was redistributed in Peru in four years than in Mexico and Bolivia since their respective upheavals. Whereas in Mexico large landowners were able to retain fertile land, in Peru they could not. Furthermore, Peru's elite revolution left few large private holdings intact. As of 1970–1973, there were more than twice as many farms in the private sector with over 100 hectares in Mexico and Bolivia as in Peru (Table 11.2).

Although the poorest and most economically insecure sector in the Peruvian countryside benefited little from the agrarian reform, Peru's elite revolution was responsive to pressures from below. In a number of documented instances, the Velasco government modified its policies to appease rural laborers. For example, it conceded to peasant demands for land and allowed farm laborers to continue holding private livestock on cooperatives,[27] despite government intentions to eliminate private plots and private livestock ownership on cooperatives. Moreover, after 1973, it extended the agrarian reform to remote, disadvantaged areas, in part to accommodate discontent peasants there.[28]

---

[26] Although Peru does not have state farms, the government regulates cooperative activities in important ways. The government has determined the basic organizational structure of the cooperatives and how certain cooperative resources are to be allocated. To a certain extent, it also regulates cooperative production priorities and aspects of marketing. After the downfall of Velasco, state intervention in cooperative operations increased. McClintock, *Peasant Cooperatives and Political Change in Peru*, pp. 34–35.

[27] World Bank, *Land Reform*, pp. 50–51.

[28] In 1974, certain divisions of the government, especially SINAMOS and the National Agrarian Confederation (CNA), aggressively advanced the interests of

Yet land reform beneficiaries constitute a much smaller percentage of all agricultural families in Peru than in Mexico or Bolivia (Table 11.4). The Peruvian reform did nothing for landless temporary workers, and little for the 40 percent of the rural population living in peasant communities.[29] The difference among the three countries in the number of reform beneficiaries reflects the structure of agriculture prior to the upheavals, however, more than the limits of a revolution from above. Prior to the revolutions in Mexico and Bolivia, big estates occupied a larger percentage of the agricultural land, especially crop land, and families of large estate workers constituted a much greater percentage of all farm families than in Peru (Table 11.3). As previously noted, workers on such farms have been the main beneficiaries of the three land reform programs.

There are actually signs that the Peruvian agrarian revolution may be redirected, as the Mexican and Bolivian revolutions have been. Upon recapturing the presidency in 1980 (when the military relinquished power), Belaúnde made known his intention to parcel up the cooperatives and restore individual ownership.[30] Although the oligarchy would not thereby be resurrected, capitalist production relations would be reinstituted on the Velasco-created cooperatives. Accordingly, a new basis for land concentration and profit would be established. Members of the cooperatives will probably not prove to be sufficiently forceful to obstruct the changes, and some of them, no doubt, will see the agrarian reorganization as an opportunity for private gain.

In sum, no single factor accounts for land distribution policies after revolution. Land reforms were implemented in the countries that experienced revolutions both from below and above. The cross-national comparison demonstrates that peasant collaboration in the destruction of the old order is only one of several factors shaping subsequent land policies. Although the Bolivian, Cuban, and Peruvian revolutionary governments redistributed land to peasants and farm laborers within the first two years in power, in Mexico, the rural poor did not receive land grants on a massive scale until the 1930s. Peasants do not necessarily gain in the short-run when they partake in the destruction of the *ancien régime*.[31]

---

disadvantaged peasants. McClintock, *Peasant Cooperatives and Political Change in Peru*, pp. 263–264. That is, the Velasco administration responded not only to pressure from below but also to pressure from within the state apparatus.

[29] Ibid., pp. 63, 73.

[30] *New York Times*, January 25, 1981.

[31] The Mexican revolution officially occurred between 1910 and 1917. Official nomenclature should not, however, obfuscate social fact. Only after the imple-

The greater readiness of the Peruvian government (compared with the Mexican) to redistribute land may, in part, reflect the different timing of the two revolutions. Prior to Castro's assumption of power, Latin American governments tended to initiate widespread land reforms only when pressured by agrarian rebellions. Yet, even in Mexico, peasants received land not merely because of pressure from below. The followers of Zapata and Pancho Villa had fought for land for two decades before any significant land allocations took place. It was only when the Great Depression weakened the landed elite's ability to resist expropriation that widespread land redistribution occurred. By 1968, however, the international political climate had changed, as had global and national economic dynamics. In the aftermath of the Cuban socialist transformation, governments in the region began to promulgate land reforms to *avert* revolution.[32] Furthermore, as Latin American countries successfully promoted import-substitution industrialization after World War II, the power of landed oligarchs diminished; and as new investment opportunities arose, large landowners began to diversify their economic interests. Consequently, not only did their capacity to oppose agrarian reform diminish but also they had less to lose by an agrarian reform. This was true in Peru at the time of the Velasco coup.

Whereas different historical contexts may make certain reform outcomes more likely, land policies are affected by other forces as well. For one, the cross-national comparison suggests that land distribution patterns issued at roughly the same period of world history differ in certain respects in countries instituting different dominant modes of production. Bolivia and Peru reduced the number of big farms and the proportion of land area such farms controlled, but not nearly as much as did Cuba.

Yet all four countries implemented policies that prevent any one form of property ownership and mode of organizing production from dominating all of agriculture. Prerevolutionary sharecroppers and tenant farmers gained land rights in all four countries, even though in

mentation of the agrarian reform in the 1930s was the power of landed oligarchs undermined and the class structure transformed. For the first two decades following the destruction of the dictatorial regime of Porfirio Díaz, Mexico experienced civil war, not revolution.

[32] On Latin American land reforms, see James Wilkie, *Measuring Land Reform, Supplement to the Statistical Abstract of Latin America* (Los Angeles: University of California Latin American Center, 1974), p. 3. I have contrasted land reform programs in Latin American countries that have and have not had revolutions in "The Impact of Revolution on Social Welfare in Latin America," *Theory and Society* 11 (1982).

no country did petty commodity production become the dominant economic mode.

Furthermore, while all four postrevolutionary reforms did restructure agrarian relations to improve profit from trade, as the world economy perspective would lead us to expect, none of the allocative patterns can be understood merely in terms of global economic dynamics. In order to respond to constraints imposed by the world economy on the one hand, and to internal class pressures on the other, all four countries instituted different land policies in different sectors of agriculture and at different points in time. The revolutionary regimes gave primacy to peasant concerns mainly when they were in crisis and in the process of consolidating power.

INCOME DISTRIBUTION

The analysis of the effect of revolution on income distribution presents certain methodological problems. First, the statistics should be viewed merely as rough approximations of the real distribution of wealth, because earnings of the self-employed and of persons with private sources of income are apt to be underrepresented. Second, available data do not permit a full assessment of the impact of the four revolutions on the apportionment of income, for information on the prerevolutionary periods is not available for all the countries.

The information that is available, though, suggests that the extent to which and way in which income is redistributed after revolution depends, above all, on the main form of property ownership (see Table 11.5). Before 1959, Cuba's lowest income earners received the smallest share of the national income. Since then, they have come to earn a larger share and the wealthy a smaller share than in any of the other countries surveyed. Yet longitudinal data do indicate that the dominant mode of production is not the only factor shaping income allocations after revolution: distributive patterns have changed *within* each country since the respective upheavals. These patterns have changed as the economies have diversified and as international and internal class pressures have changed.

Although there is no data on income distribution among percentile groups before 1950, there is indirect evidence that the Mexican Revolution did serve to redistribute income to low income groups before World War II.[33] The relative earnings of low income groups im-

[33] Cynthia Hewitt de Alcántara, *Ensayo Sobre la Satisfacción de Necesidades Básicas del Pueblo Mexicano entre 1940 y 1970* (Mexico: El Colegio de México, Centro de Estudios Sociológicos, 1977), and the references therein.

proved when the depression weakened the then dominant economic elite's power to oppose Cárdenas' income distributing measures. Cárdenas' extensive land program, for example, served to increase peasant income earnings, at the expense of *latifundistas*. After World War II, however, the rural and urban poor began to bear the costs of the country's economic growth. Once the Depression subsided and the war opened up new economic opportunities, Mexican governments started to intervene increasingly in the interests of upper income groups (excluding the wealthiest 10 percent). The class base of the regime in the process shifted away from the groups that helped "make" the revolution. The state provided business with ever more infrastructure, capital assistance, and protection from import competition at the same time that it cut back support to *ejidatarios* and co-opted and repressed labor.

Consequently, as Mexico joined the economic vanguard of Latin America, the distribution of income worsened. Estimates of income distribution concur that between 1950 and the mid-1970s the share of the national pie accruing to the poor declined.[34] One study estimates that the richest 10 percent earned 15 times more than the poorest 10 percent in 1958, and 35 times more than two decades later.[35] The redistribution favored "middle-class" groups, above all the white collar stratum and organized workers. There is even some evidence suggesting that the absolute as well as the relative income of the poorest fraction of the population deteriorated in the post World War II period.[36]

As in Mexico, the revolution in Bolivia initially ushered in a more egalitarian society than the one it displaced, but in the absence of income data for the pre-1952 period, it is impossible to document the extent of the change. The agrarian reform that was implemented in response to pressure from below enabled peasants to appropriate the full product of their labor. The earnings of the newly propertied peasants who marketed their output accordingly improved. Moreover, industrial workers, and, above all, miners gained significant wage and fringe benefit increases, in return for their collaboration with the new regime.

[34] In addition to the source cited in Table 11.5, see Ifegenia de Navarrete, "La Distribución del Ingreso en México: Tendencias y Perspectivas," in David Ibarra, et al., *El Perfil de México en 1980* (Mexico City, Siglo xxi, 1970), p. 37; Reynolds, *The Mexican Economy*, p. 84; and Roger Hansen, *The Politics of Mexican Development* (Baltimore: The Johns Hopkins Press, 1971), pp. 8, 72, 74.

[35] Enrique Hernández Laos and Jorge Córdova Chávez, "Estructura de la Distribución del Ingreso en México," *Comercio Exterior* 29 (May 1979): 507.

[36] Hansen, *The Politics of Mexican Development*, pp. 8, 72, 74.

TABLE 11.5
Estimates of Share of National Income Held by Percentile Groups in Selected Latin American Nations

| | Poorest | | | | Richest | | |
	0–20	21–40	41–60	61–80	81–100	91–100	96–100
Bolivia							
1968 [H]	4	13.7	8.9	14.3	59.1	—	35.7
1975 [E]		13[a]	26		61.0	44.5	—
1975 [H]		14[b]	29		58.0	41.7	—
Brazil [E]							
1960	3.9	7.4	13.6	20.3	54.8	39.6	28.3
1970	3.4	6.6	10.9	17.2	61.9	46.7	34.1
1972	3.2	5.9	9.5	16.5	64.9	50.4	37.9
Mexico [H]							
1950	5.6	7.5	10.9	16.7	59.4	45.5	35.1
1958	5.5	9.0	13.5	19.0	52.9	35.7	25.5
1963	3.7	6.8	11.2	20.2	58.1	41.6	28.6
1968	3.4	7.3	11.5	19.7	58.1	42.0	27.1
1970	3.8	8.0	13.7	18.7	55.8	39.2	27.7
1975	1.7	6.0	11.5	20.0	60.2	43.4	—
1977	3.3	7.7	12.9	21.1	55.1	38.0	25.5

Percentile Groups

Peru							
1961 [E]	2.5	5.5	10.2	17.4	64.4	49.2	39.0
1972 [H]	1.9	5.1	11.0	21.0	61.0	42.9	—
Cuba [E]							
1953	2.1	4.1	11.0	22.8	60.0	38.5	28.0
1960	8.0	12.5	14.5	17.0	48.0	31.0	17.0
1962	6.2	11.0	16.3	25.1	41.4	23.0	12.7
1973	7.8	12.5	19.2	25.5	35.0	19.9	9.5

Sources: Irma Adelman and Cynthia Morris, "An Anatomy of Patterns of Income Distribution in Developing Countries." (Manuscript, AID, 1971); and Bolivia, Ministerio de Finanzas, Informe Musgrave, *Reforma Fiscal en Bolivia, I: El Marco Economico General* (La Paz, 1977), pp. 170–171. Sylvia Hewlett, *The Cruel Dilemmas of Development: Twentieth-Century Brazil* (Basic Books, 1980), Table 13. Enrique Hernández Laos and Jorge Córdova Chávez, "Estructura de la Distribución del Ingreso en México," *Comercio Exterior* 29 (May 1979): 507. World Bank, *World Development Report*, 1979, pp. 172–173; and Richard C. Webb, *Government Policy and the Distribution of Income in Peru, 1963–1973* (Cambridge: Harvard University Press, 1977), p. 91. Brundenius, "Measuring Income Distribution in Pre- and Post-Revolutionary Cuba," *Cuban Studies Estudios Cubanos* (July 1979), p. 43; 1960 figures are rough estimates. For the 1962 data, see Brundenius, "Development Strategies and Basic Needs in Revolutionary Cuba," in Brundenius and Mats Lundahl, eds., *Development Strategies and Basic Needs in Latin America: Some Challenges for the 1980s* (Boulder, Colo. Westview Press, 1982), p.154.

[a] Poorest 10 percent received 3 percent of the national income.

[b] Poorest 10 percent received 3.1 percent of the national income.

[E] Economically active population.

[H] Households.

There is evidence that in 1968 (the first year for which data is available for percentile groups) the poorest 40 percent received a larger portion of the national income in industrially underdeveloped Bolivia than in any of the other capitalist countries under study. The cross-national variance proves that there is a range of income dispersion possible under capitalism, and it suggests that the range may in part depend on the degree of industrialization. Not only in Mexico but also, as we shall see below, in Brazil and Peru, industrialization has had an adverse effect on the share of income accruing to the poorest income groups. Were there income data by quintile for Mexico before its post-World War II industrial boom, we probably would find an income dispersion more comparable to Bolivia's than in recent decades.

But the poorest 40 percent's share of the national income has deteriorated over the years in Bolivia, even in the absence of significant industrialization. It has deteriorated because the classes in whose interest the state has come to rule have shifted, and international policies toward Bolivia have changed. Nonetheless, the poorest 40 percent still enjoy a larger share of the national income in Bolivia than in the more industrial capitalist countries under examination.

The biggest change in postrevolutionary Bolivian income policy occurred in 1956. That year an International Monetary Fund (IMF) Stabilization program, enforced with United States military assistance, reduced labor's political power. The IMF and the United States made loans conditional on a wage freeze and a cutback of the benefits that labor had won in the revolution. The stabilization program also hurt the national industrial bourgeoisie, because the IMF insisted that the Bolivian government retract industrial tariff protection and end industrial subsidies.[37] International capital has confined the main industrial opportunities to the semi-periphery, and affected income distribution in the process.

While stabilization modified Bolivian class dynamics, peasants and labor formally remained part of the ruling coalition until the 1964 coup. Since then Bolivia has been governed, for the most part, by conservative military regimes. The drop in the income share to the poorest 40 percent of the population during a 1968–1975 period reflects the "purification" (a term used by the leader of the 1964 coup) of Bolivia's capitalist revolution. In accordance with the procapital

---

[37] Susan Eckstein, *The Impact of Revolution: A Comparative Analysis of Mexico and Bolivia* (SAGE Publications, Contemporary Political Sociology Series, 1976), p. 22.

bias of post-1964 governments, market-oriented producers in the lowlands received not only large land tracts but also extensive state-backed foreign loans. And peasant earnings have been constricted by official price ceilings for their products.

Income patterns in Brazil lend further credibility to the industrialization and world economy hypotheses.[38] As Brazil rapidly industrialized in the 1960s, income distribution deteriorated: the share of the national income accruing to the poorest 40 percent of the economically active population decreased while the share to the wealthiest 20 percent increased. The industrial expansion resulted largely from an influx of foreign capital after the military took power in 1964.

Yet the Brazilian-Mexican comparison reveals that political forces may indeed modify the impact of capitalist industrial dynamics. Although the share of the national income accruing to the poorest 40 percent deteriorated both in Mexico and Brazil in the 1960s, it deteriorated less in Mexico. Moreover, whereas the income share going to the top 5 percent declined during the 1960s in Mexico, it increased in Brazil. The Mexican social transformation, and the civilian regime to which it gave rise, appear to have helped the petty bourgeoisie and organized labor (who fall within the top 2-3 decile groups) appropriate a larger portion of the national income than their counterparts under Brazil's post-1964 repressive military rule. In essence, the more egalitarian trend in Mexico, compared with Brazil, suggests that internal class dynamics and not merely semi-peripheral status affect income distribution patterns.

The information on Peru suggests that Peru's elite-led revolution contributed to a "downward" redistribution of wealth, but not to the poorest 40 percent of the economically active population. While available data on the 1961-1972 period do not allow us to discern what change occurred before and after the Velasco takeover, there is evidence that income distribution deteriorated before 1968 and improved afterward: between 1950 and 1966, families in the top half of the income ladder, by and large, enjoyed a faster rate of income growth than the bottom half.[39]

It might appear from the cross-national comparison that low in-

---

[38] For a discussion of industrialization in Brazil and its effect on income distribution, see Peter Evans, *Dependent Development: The Alliance of Multinational, State, and Local Capital in Brazil* (Princeton: Princeton University Press, 1979); and Sylvia Hewlett, *The Cruel Dilemmas of Development: Twentieth-Century Brazil* (New York: Basic Books, 1980).

[39] Richard Charles Webb, "Government Policy and the Distribution of Income in Peru, 1963-1973," in Lowenthal, ed., *The Peruvian Experiment*, p. 89.

come groups fare better when they partake in the destruction of the old order than when they do not, for the lowest income earners have captured a smaller share of the national income in Peru since its elite revolution than in Mexico, Bolivia, and Cuba since their respective social upheavals. But the changes reflect how the Velasco administration responded to the organization of the economy in the prerevolutionary epoch and to constraints imposed by domestic and foreign groups with political and economic clout. Income benefits have been limited mainly to workers in the modern sector of the rural and urban economy, both because capital would resist financing more extensive distributive and redistributive measures and because modern sector workers have opposed attempts by government agencies to allow other workers to share their income gains.[40]

The "youth" of the Peruvian social transformation, by contrast, cannot in itself account for the limited redistribution to the very poor, for two reasons. First, the Cuban poor increased their income share significantly within four years after Castro assumed power. Second, since the downfall of Velasco, income—as detailed below—has become more concentrated.

The income distribution that has occurred in Peru may be attributable to the expropriation of large agricultural holdings and the initial distributive effect of the industrial reform legislation. Prior to the agrarian reform, many *hacendados* earned as much as one hundred times the income of their employees.[41] In the coastal area, the rich estate owners were displaced by a group of reform beneficiaries who have come to fall within the nation's upper-middle-income bracket.[42] Members of cooperatives have benefited from wage gains, from low interest government loans, and—in the 1970s—from improved prices for their products. To the extent that the surplus of cooperatives has increased, the earnings of cooperative members has collectively increased.[43] Accordingly, the basis of income distribution has changed with the reorganization of property relations on large farms. Moreover, cooperative members have been able to supplement their income with lucrative sales from private parcels and animals that they

[40] McClintock, *Peasant Cooperatives and Political Change in Peru*, p. 265.

[41] Ibid., p. 219.

[42] World Bank, *Land Reform*, pp. 70, 92–93.

[43] For information on profits in the cooperatives, see McClintock, *Peasant Cooperatives and Political Change in Peru*, pp. 224–225, 249. The larger, more prosperous cooperatives, with more capital and greater economies of scale, tended both to generate the most profits and to experience the largest wage gains.

have been able to retain.[44] Because cooperative members have received larger increases in earnings than have technicians and office and skilled workers they employ, income equalization has occurred even on individual farms.[45]

Yet it must be remembered that the cooperatives affect only a small portion of the farm population and that the income-generating effects of the agrarian reform have varied considerably regionally. The earning power of highland Indian communities did not improve as much as that of coastal cooperatives. Initially the Agrarian Reform Law even denied peasants in the highlands the right to seek employment and maintain plots outside their community of residence, thereby depriving them of an important former source of supplementary income; however, after peasants protested, the restrictions were relaxed.[46]

Moreover, nonresident farm workers have benefited little from the agrarian reform, partly because the more powerful resident workers have effectively monopolized income opportunities on the cooperatives.[47] Cooperative members have exploited nonmembers, to the extent that the income differences between permanent and temporary workers is estimated to be about 2:1.[48] Apparently the real income of temporary workers has not changed since the prereform period,[49] implying a widening income gap between the two groups of rural laborers.

The industrial reform explicitly called for a redistribution of wealth within Peruvian firms, though not to the same extent as did the agrarian reform. The Industrial Community Law specified that workers should gradually gain ownership shares in the firms where they were employed. While the reform affected only about 38 percent of the industrial labor force,[50] it required all firms with more than 5 employees to allocate immediately 25 percent of pre-tax profits (10 percent in cash, 15 percent in shares) to its employees and, over time,

[44] Ibid., pp. 226, 231.

[45] World Bank, *Land Reform*, p. 70. Greater wage equalization apparently occurred on the agrarian reform units in the highlands, however, than on the coast. McClintock, *Peasant Cooperatives and Political Change in Peru*, pp. 226–229.

[46] Bourque and Palmer, "Transforming the Rural Sector," pp. 190, 204.

[47] Unless women were permanent employees of the cooperatives, they, as well as day laborers, were excluded from membership.

[48] McClintock, *Peasant Cooperatives and Political Change in Peru*, p. 275.

[49] Ibid., p. 276.

[50] E.V.K. FitzGerald, *The State and Economic Development: Peru since 1968* (Cambridge: Cambridge University Press, 1976), p. 73.

up to 50 percent. In the early 1970s, a social property reform was also introduced, to reduce inequality *among enterprises,* through government regulation of firm wage and employment policies. As of May 1974, however, workers had captured only about 9 percent of company shares;[51] and after Velasco's fall, the government permitted capital to circumvent the reform legislation and major enterprises were offered back to private buyers. By 1977, it was generally agreed that the last traces of the original novel elements of Velasco's industrial program had disappeared.[52] They were terminated because hoped-for new investments—by foreign as well as domestic capital—did not follow the reform. Multinational corporations, for example, preferred investing in Brazil, where not only was the market larger but also their ownership and control over production and profits were not threatened. Thus, the response of the business community further supports the thesis that capitalist industrialization tends to be associated with income concentration.

There are no data on income distribution by percentile groups in Peru after 1972, but world economic pressures and the shift in the ruling coalition since then have limited the government's capacity and inclination to redistribute wealth downward. For example, the changes that the government had to make in the industrial reform program in order to better compete for scarce investment capital have undoubtedly had a negative effect on income distribution. Secondly, since the mid-1970s, the IMF and private international banks have made loans to Peru (as to Bolivia) contingent on wage restrictions. Information on real wages and salaries does not reveal that employee earnings fell drastically in the latter 1970s, or that unemployment increased.[53]

Calculations based on available data indicate that income distribution has improved most in postrevolutionary Cuba. The share of national income captured by the poorest 40 percent increased and that captured by the wealthiest 20 percent decreased markedly during the first year of Castro's rule.[54] Several factors contributed to the

[51] McClintock, *Peasant Cooperatives and Political Change in Peru,* p. 38.

[52] Rosemary Thorp, "Inflation, Stabilisation, and the Return to Democracy in Peru, 1975–1979," working paper no. 49 of the Latin American Program at the Wilson Center (Washington, D.C., 1979), p. 13.

[53] For a discussion of Peru's 1975–1979 financial stabilization program, and its effects, see ibid. According to official sources, which Thorp cites (p. 14), real wages and salaries in firms with ten or more employees were, in 1977, 79 and 65 percent, respectively, of what they were in 1973.

[54] According to Brundenius, much of the income redistribution noted in the 1953–1960 period occurred after the revolution. See Claes Brundenius, "Measur-

dramatic income redistribution: the first agrarian reform, which deprived larger farmers of and provided small farmers with income-generating land; the reduction of urban rents, which lowered earnings of the rentier class; the rise in the minimum wage; and the emigration of prerevolutionary elite.

Since 1960, income redistribution has continued to be most equitable in Cuba. The pace of redistribution has slowed down, however, and the main beneficiaries of redistribution in recent years have been middle income groups, including the 61–80 percentile group, which was initially hurt by the revolution. The shift occurred as the Castro regime became progressively concerned with productivity, especially among skilled workers, and progressively influenced by Soviet wage incentive schemes. Because post-1962 Cuban income data excluded the private sector, however, and because the earnings of some independent farmers are known to be high, island income was less equitably distributed in 1973 than the figures convey, and income statistics for Cuba and the other countries are not entirely comparable. In the mid-1960s, independent farmers were known to earn between 10,000 and 20,000 pesos a year; by contrast, cabinet ministers earned 8,400 pesos, and top technicians and specialists 10,000 pesos. Private farmers were among the richest Cubans.[55]

The significance of income statistics, as well as the data base, is distinctive in Cuba. Under Castro, non-wage policies have eroded much of the historical importance of earnings, to the extent that income is a much less adequate indicator of material living standards on the island than in the other countries. The Castro government, for example, is the only government under study that provides its poor with social security, free health care, and unemployment insurance. In addition, it has not allowed the price of basic foods and the cost of rent to rise since the early 1960s. Available information, however, does indicate that per capita consumption of a wide variety of material goods has improved little if at all since the mid-1960s.[56] But because basic foods are rationed, low income groups suffered much less than

ing Income Distribution in Pre- and Post-Revolutionary Cuba," *Cuban Studies/Estudios Cubanos* 9 (July 1979), pp. 30–32. His data, unfortunately, do not allow us to look at income trends in the late 1960s when the government reduced income opportunities for high-income groups.

[55] Leo Huberman and Paul Sweezy, *Socialism in Cuba* (New York: Monthly Review Press, 1969), p. 118.

[56] Susan Eckstein, "Income Distribution and Consumption on Post-Revolutionary Cuba: An Addendum to Brundenius," *Cuban Studies/Estudios Cubanos* 10 (January 1980), p. 96.

TABLE 11.6
Per Capita Income by Income Strata in Selected Latin American Nations

Quintiles	Brazil		Cuba		Peru	
	1960	1976	1953	1973	1961	1972
	ESTIMATES OF REAL INCOME PER CAPITA BY INCOME STRATA (1970 DOLLARS)					
0–20%	59	95	33	236	68	40
20–40%	135	183	66	374	159	189
40–60%	234	309	176	574	296	344
60–80%	342	607	365	763	489	548
80–100%	916	2,317	961	1,044	1,261	1,746
(Top 5%)	(1,869)	(5,475)	(1,792)	(1,136)	(2,365)	(3,234)
GDP/Capita	337	702	320	598	455	572
	RELATIVE INCOME LEVELS PER CAPITA BY INCOME STRATA (GDP/CAPITA = 100)					
0–20%	18	14	10	39	15	7
20–40%	40	26	21	63	35	33
40–60%	69	44	55	96	65	60
60–80%	101	86	114	128	107	96
80–100%	272	330	300	175	277	305
(Top 5%)	(555)	(780)	(560)	(190)	(520)	(565)
$\frac{\text{Top 20\%}}{\text{Bottom 20\%}}$	15.1	23.6	30.0	4.5	18.5	43.6
$\frac{\text{Top 5\%}}{\text{Bottom 20\%}}$	30.8	55.7	56.0	4.9	34.7	80.7

Source: Brundenius, "Development Strategies and Basic Needs in Revolutionary Cuba," p. 156.

they would have in a market economy.[57] Nonetheless, by the early 1970s, both wage and consumer policies (except concerning basic foods) were favoring middle and upper income groups.

Estimates of Brazilian, Peruvian, and Cuban real and relative per capita income of percentile groups further suggest that socialization of the economy has a more egalitarian effect on income distribution than private ownership. But it also suggests that most income groups may benefit more from a repressive, semi-peripheral regime than from a somewhat populist but economically weaker regime. As shown in Table 11.6, before Castro assumed power, the real and the relative per capita income of the poorest 3 quintiles was less; and the ratio between the earnings of the top and bottom 20 percent was greater in

[57] Although a black market has operated as long as rationing has been in effect, material consumption depends much less on market power in Castro's Cuba than in the other countries under study.

Cuba than in the other two countries. By the 1970s, however, the real and the relative per capita income of the three poorest quintiles was greater and the per capita income gap between the top and bottom 20 percent was much less in Cuba than in either Brazil or Peru.

Table 11.6 also shows that low income groups have benefited more from Brazil's so-called economic miracle than from Peru's revolution from above. The table shows, for example, that between 1960–1961 and 1972–1976 the real income per capita of all income groups improved in Brazil; in Peru, the real per capita income of the poorest 20 percent deteriorated, although that of all other income groups did improve. The table also shows that the real per capita earnings of all income groups was higher in Peru than in Brazil in 1960–1961, but that by 1972–1976 the poorest, as well as the two wealthiest quintiles, earned less in Peru than in Brazil. It also shows that during this sixteen-year period the relative income per capita of all but the richest 20 percent deteriorated both in Brazil and in Peru, but more so for the poorest 20 percent in Peru than in Brazil. Moreover, the table shows that during the period under consideration the gap between the per capita income of the top and bottom 20 percent widened more in Peru than in Brazil. The Brazilian foreign-financed growth oriented regime (1967–1974) has had some "trickle down" effect on the poor, which Peru's more nationalist and less dynamic economy has not. Nonetheless, it should be remembered that neither Brazil's nor Peru's development strategy has improved the relative per capita income standing of the very poor.

In sum, a cross-national comparison reveals that income distribution improves after revolution, especially when ownership of production is socialized. But the egalitarian effect of revolution diminishes with time. Low income groups benefit most from the class upheavals, including in Cuba, when the new regimes are consolidating power. In all countries surveyed, the share of income accruing to the poor diminished with the expansion of the economies. The cross-national comparison also reveals that the dynamics of the international economy have affected the industrial process in the countries surveyed. When capital intensive industrialization expands, with foreign assistance, income inequality increases. The Mexican-Brazilian comparison does demonstrate, though, that in the semi-periphery, where capital intensive industrial expansion has been concentrated, middle and low income groups may benefit somewhat more and the elite somewhat less when a postrevolutionary society institutionalizes a corporately organized civilian regime than when a regime excludes "popular" groups from power, formally as well as informally. Among countries equally situated in the world economy, revolutions, through the institutions to which they give rise, may have some positive effect on income distribution.

HEALTH CARE

The well-being and productive capacity of a population depends, in part, on health care. Good health requires a well-balanced and adequate diet. It also requires access to a medical system that provides quality care. Three indicators are used here to measure the scope of the system: the per capita supply of physicians, nurses, and hospital beds. In principle, doctors can, because of their training, provide better quality care than nurses and paraprofessionals, but nurses can provide an array of services for which doctors are unnecessary. In resource-poor countries with low health standards, there may be a positive trade-off between large staffs of less expensive paraprofessionals and a small cadre of costly physicians. Therefore, we will look at the supply of both doctors and nurses. Furthermore, although much health care does not require hospitalization, the supply of hospital beds does reflect the capability of a delivery system to provide whatever intensive in-patient care might be necessary.

A health care system must be measured not only in terms of the range of its facilities but also in terms of how effective it is in addressing the health needs of a population. Health needs would seem to be well met if a populace's life expectancy rate is high and if the people are relatively free of illness. Our analysis will focus specifically on infant life expectancy, that is, on the number of deaths of infants under one year old per 1,000 live births.

Since health welfare, including infant mortality, depends, in addition, on the adequacy of a populace's diet, as well as on the adequacy of the medical system, two measures of diet will be examined: per capita caloric and per capita protein intake. Protein intake is a better indicator of nutrition, but it accounts for only one source of nutrients. Since poverty is widespread in the Third World, and since poor people often consume insufficient calories, total caloric consumption will be assessed as well.

The Health Care Delivery System: The Supply of Doctors, Nurses, and Hosptial Beds

According to information on the countries surveyed, as long as the dominant mode of production remains capitalist, revolutions appear

TABLE 11.7
Health Care in Selected Latin American Nations

	Bolivia	Cuba	Brazil	Mexico	Peru
Population per physician					
1958	—	2,839	—	—	—
1960	3,700	1,200	2,170	1,800	2,200
1966	—	1,146	—	—	—
1970	2,300	1,400	1,950	1,440	1,920
1975	—	952	—	—	—
1976	2,120	1,100	1,650	—	1,580
Population per nursing population					
1958	—	8,262.0	—	—	—
1960	—	—	—	2,650	3,640
1966	—	786.5	—	—	—
1970	2,730	581.9	3,300	1,570	3,200
1975	—	443.8	—	—	—
1976	3,520	—	—	—	—
Population per hospital bed					
1958	—	239	—	—	—
1960	580	—	275	590	490
1970	490	215	260	930	470
1975	—	204	—	—	—
Infant Mortality (per 1,000 live births)					
1940–44	101.0	—	164.7	119.3	116.5
1945–49	123.1	38.9	117.5	104.5	108.6
1950–54	98.8	—	107.3	91.8	99.9
1955–59	81.8	32.4	107.6	77.9	98.8
1965	76.5	38.4	—	60.7	74.0
1970	—	38.4	110.0	68.5	65.1
1973	—	28.9	—	52.0	—
1976/1977	158.0	23.0	62.0	65.0	—

Sources: World Bank, *World Tables,* 1976, pp. 484, 506, 518, 520; World Bank, *World Development Report,* 1979, pp. 168–169; Dirección Central de Estadística, *Anuario Estadístico de Cuba,* 1975, pp. 26, 231–232; Domínguez, *Cuba: Order and Revolution* (Cambridge: The Belknap Press of Harvard University Press, 1978), p. 185; Wilkie, ed., *Statistical Abstract of Latin America,* 19:95.

not to have any predictable effect on the health care system (see Table 11.7). Per capita medical personnel and hospital facilities tend to increase in countries that have experienced a social transformation, but not consistently. Nor is per capita supply consistently greater in countries that have undergone revolution than in countries of roughly similar levels of development that have not had revolutions.

The main cross-national difference in medical facilities among the countries under study appears to be attributable to the capitalist or socialist organization of the economy. Cuba has the largest supply of doctors, nurses, and hospital beds per capital, and according to available data, the supply of each has tended to improve most in Cuba since the revolution; its per capita supply of medical personnel is much greater than Mexico's and Brazil's. Mexico, in fact, has the worst per capita supply of hospital beds of any of the countries under study. The level of development of societal productive resources is thus not a decisive factor accounting for cross-national differences in health care facilities.

The expansion and reorganization of the health care system in postrevolutionary Cuba has been so great and so different from the other countries' as to suggest that socialization of the economy provides options that private ownership does not. In light of the fact that one third to one half of the country's doctors emigrated in the first five years to Castro's rule,[58] Cuba's current supply of doctors is especially impressive. The Castro regime sponsored a massive campaign to attract students to medicine. With all graduates guaranteed jobs and with nearly all doctors government-employed, the expansion of the medical profession is a direct reflection of the state's commitment to upgrading health care. Cuba has expanded its supply of doctors to the point that it exports them; Cuban doctors now work in Angola, Ethiopia, and other foreign countries.[59]

The Castro government has modified its medical care priorities over the years, however. It initially invested in a costly and elitist medical cadre system; witness the extensive training of physicians during the first decade of the revolution. Once it replaced the physicians who emigrated, though, it invested in paramedical care, promoting new types of personnel, e.g., medical and dental assistants (against some initial opposition of the medical and dental professions), and upgrading others such as nurses.[60] The nurse-to-population ratio, which had been about two or three times lower in Cuba around the time of the revolution than in the capitalist countries for which we have information, was about 3.5 to 8 times higher by 1970.

The Castro regime has come to promote a less costly, less capital intensive health care system than the capitalist countries. Not only has it invested heavily in low-skilled medical cadres but it also has reoriented its health service system from the hospital to the community. It has built numerous health centers, and it has mobilized citizens for street cleaning, immunization, and disease control cam-

[58] V. Navarro, "Health, Health Services, and Health Planning in Cuba," *International Journal of Health Services* 2 (1972), p. 413.

[59] For a discussion of Cuba's medical and other civilian aid programs, and of the country's capacity to export human capital, see Eckstein, "The Material and Ideological Bases of Cuba's Foreign Aid Program," *Politics and Society* (1982).

[60] Navarro, "Health, Health Services, and Health Planning in Cuba," p. 414.

paigns, which seem to have contributed to a rapid reduction in infectious diseases.[61] Moreover, it has made medical care free to all citizens. Yet its outlays for in-patient hospital care have been unimpressive. In 1970, Cuba had more hospital beds per citizen than any of the capitalist countries, but its supply had already been larger before the revolution.

In sum, in comparison with the capitalist countries experiencing revolutions from above and below, the Cuban health care system is less oriented to profit making, capital intensive care and less class biased. The qualitative and quantitative changes that the Castro regime alone initiated suggest that governments in socialized economies are either better able or more inclined to invest in health welfare and that they allocate funds differently than governments in capitalist societies. Although state ownership of the "means of production" in itself provides no guarantee that medical outlays and health standards will improve, available evidence suggests that it creates possibilities that private ownership does not.

Infant Mortality

Infant mortality is the one welfare component under study that appears not to be affected by revolution. According to available data, infant mortality rates did decline after the respective upheavals (see Table 11.7). But the death rate dropped most in Brazil (at least between 1960 and 1970), even though that country has not had a revolution.

Infant mortality rates are much lower in Castro's Cuba than in any of the other postrevolutionary societies, but Cuba's rates were already much lower before 1959. Moreover, the data indicate that the death rate in Cuba during the 1970s dropped below the 1958 level, but that it rose in the 1960s. It may be that health care deteriorated under Castro until a new generation of doctors replaced the physicians who emigrated. But the increase undoubtedly also reflects an improvement in data collection—in 1969, 98 percent of all deaths were reported, whereas only 53 percent were reported in 1956.[62]

Interestingly, the level of overall economic development and the position of countries within the world economy has no consistent bearing on cross-national infant mortality rates. Through 1970, Brazil had the highest infant mortality rate of any of the countries under

[61] Ibid., pp. 424, 430
[62] Ibid.

TABLE 11.8

Nutrition in Selected Latin American Nations

	Bolivia	Cuba	Brazil	Mexico	Peru
Per capita caloric supply (percentage of requirements)					
1960	69%	—	102%	107%	97%
1970	77	—	109	110	98
1974	83	107	118	121	92
Per capita protein supply (total grams per day)					
1960	43	—	61	65	61
1970	46	64	64	65	62
1974	47	—	61	66	53

Sources: World Bank, *World Tables*, 1976, p. 519. Wilkie, ed., *Statistical Abstract of Latin America* 19:23. Vicente Navarro, "Health, Health Services, and Health Planning in Cuba," *International Journal of Health Services* 2 (1972): 404.

study, despite its large resource base and despite significant improvements in its rate in the 1960s.

Nutrition

Nutrition, by contrast, appears to depend more on the overall level of development of an economy than on the type of revolution a country undergoes (see Table 11.8). From 1960 to 1974, per capita caloric intake was lowest in Bolivia and highest in Mexico and Brazil. Protein consumption, however, varied much less by country.

Although nutritional standards seem, at least in the long-run, to depend more on societal aggregate economic resources than on class transformations, it may well be that the respective land reforms did help improve protein and caloric intake in the short-run, at least among low income groups in the countryside. Without information on the four pretransformation periods and on the early postrevolutionary period in Mexico, though, it is impossible to assess whether this indeed is true. Most likely, the agrarian reforms, as well as other social policies initiated when the new regimes consolidated power, helped raise nutritional standards of low income groups.

Peru is the only country where per capita protein and caloric consumption, according to available information, declined after the revolution. Possibly it declined because such a small portion of the rural population benefited from the land reform, because other agrarian policies (e.g., credit and pricing) did not favor most of the peasant sector,[63] and because the earning power of the country's poor, as pre-

[63] FitzGerald, *The State and Economic Development*, p. 32.

viously noted, had deteriorated. The 1978 agreement between Peru and the IMF to limit wages and salaries while allowing prices to rise with the inflation rate seems, from available information, to have contributed to the continued deterioration of nutritional standards. Since nationwide aggregate statistics are available for only the first few postrevolutionary years, it is difficult to assess conclusively the impact of the Peruvian Revolution. Data on Lima, however, give no basis for optimism.[64] According to one study of low income groups in the city, caloric intake dropped 22 percent between 1972 and 1978, from 1,934 to 1,512 calories. In the latter year, calorie consumption was 62 percent of the recommended level. Moreover, the calories that Lima's poor received came principally from non-protein sources. Protein consumption during the six year period fell from 52.7 to 41.2 grams, the minimum recommended level being 65.1 grams. Another study found that between 1977 and 1978 calorie consumption deteriorated not only in low but also in middle income groups in the city. For the average low income Lima family in the first quarter of 1978, calorie consumption was 62 percent of the Food and Agricultural Organization (FAO) requirements, compared with 78 percent a year earlier; for the average middle income family, the fall was from 96 to 66 percent.

The experience of Mexico suggests that postrevolutionary capital intensive development affects the nutritional standards of different groups unequally. Food consumption of low income groups, especially in the countryside, improved significantly under Cárdenas. Under Cárdenas, peasant consumption depended as much on subsistence agriculture and informal exchanges among neighborhoods as on goods purchased in the market. But as rural communities were progressively integrated into the money economy after World War II, peasant food consumption came to depend on market purchasing power. Consequently, whereas farm output has risen dramatically since 1940, most *ejidatarios* have not benefited from the gains. In the 1960s, Mexican upper- and middle-income group consumption of fruits, vegetables, and protein improved, while low income consumption deteriorated.[65] The earning power of Mexicans deteriorated to the point that by the end of the 1960s the income of 40 percent of all

[64] The following information draws on material cited in Henry Dietz, "The IMF from the Bottom Up: Social Impacts of Stabilization Policies in Lima, Peru" (Paper presented at the Latin American Studies Association Meeting, Bloomington, Indiana, October 1980), pp. 9–10; and Thorp, "Inflation, Stabilisation, and the Return of Democracy in Peru," p. 25, fn. 33.

[65] Hewitt de Alcántara, *Ensayo Sobre la Satisfacción de Necesidades Basicas del Pueblo Mexicano entre 1940 y 1970*, p. 40.

farm families and 26 percent of all nonagricultural families was believed to be less than the minimum needed to assure an adequate diet.[66] Although the government in the early 1970s implemented several programs to improve low income nutritional standards, the programs have thus far had little impact.

The situation in Cuba reveals that the islanders, as a whole, fare no better under socialism than people in the more economically developed capitalist countries. Low income groups may consume more calories and protein on the island than in the other countries, however, because the Castro government guarantees all Cubans a basic low-cost diet. The state in Cuba is more free than the state in the other countries to counter market tendencies, and it has used its power accordingly.

Thus, while policies of governments after revolution *may*, in the short-run, shape societal dietary patterns, nutritional standards appear to vary mainly with the overall level of development of the economy. At least in the capitalist countries, however, once the new regimes become institutionalized, nutrition varies by class.

In conclusion, this analysis suggests that only in socialized economies is the health care system likely to change markedly with revolution. Since the respective revolutions, Cuba's health care system has expanded most, and it has been organized along different lines than the systems in the other countries. Furthermore, both the health care system and the policies affecting nutrition appear to be least class biased in post-1959 Cuba. The reorganization of the Cuban health system, however, at least during the first decade of Castro's rule, did not have a positive effect on infant mortality.

CONCLUSION

The comparison of the impact of Peru's revolution from above and Mexico's, Bolivia's, and Cuba's revolutions from below reveals that both types of social transformations have ushered in societies more egalitarian than those they replaced. In all four countries, however, low income groups have tended to gain most when the new regimes consolidated power. Subsequently, the interests of the popular sectors were sacrificed to those of middle- and upper-income groups.

The rural masses benefited from revolution mainly in conjunction with agrarian reforms. Although all four land reforms have perpetuated *minifundismo*, recipients of land titles enjoy a modicum of secu-

[66] Ibid., p. 43.

rity and the opportunity to appropriate the full product of their labor, which rural wage workers and peasants dependent on usufruct arrangements do not.

Yet the analysis has shown that peasants and workers do not necessarily benefit most when they participate in the destruction of the old order. Peasants and rural farm laborers gained land where they were disruptive, but in Mexico only after a global depression weakened the ability of large landowners to resist expropriation. Moreover, the Peruvian experience has demonstrated that rural laborers may benefit even when they do not actively participate in the transformation of power, and that they can, under certain conditions, gain benefits sooner after revolutions from above than after revolutions from below.

The level of development of the economy and the way that the societies have been integrated into the world economy historically have shaped how the postrevolutionary societies have developed, quite independently of how the upheavals originated. The four revolutionary governments adapted land policies to property relations under the *ancien régimes* and they reorganized agriculture to profit from trade.

Global constraints have also been a factor restricting labor's ability to improve its earning power and influence over the organization of production. Labor did benefit from the revolutions, but as the postrevolutionary governments became concerned with attracting foreign investment and financial capital and with improving profits from trade, labor was marginalized. Nonetheless, the Mexican-Brazilian comparison reveals that revolutionary-linked forces may modify the income generating effect of capitalist industrial dynamics, even if not to the advantage of the lowest income earners.

The dominant mode of production instituted under the new order is the aspect of revolution that affects patterns of land and income distribution and health care most profoundly. To the extent that ownership of the economy is socialized, the state has direct access to the surplus generated. Although the Castro regime has not consistently allocated the resources it controls to low income groups, since it need not provide a favorable "climate" to induce domestic and foreign capital to invest, it can more readily redistribute income downward than can the capitalist regimes. For similar reasons, it also has been more free to redesign its health care system in accordance with societal needs rather than business interests and market power.

But the experiences of Mexico, Bolivia, Cuba, and Peru suggest that the distributive effects of both capitalist and socialist revolutions are limited. Although socialization of the economy in Cuba has allowed certain allocative options that capitalist dynamics have not, this analysis has shown that the capacity to improve the welfare of Third World people by any revolutionary means is constricted by the weak position of less developed nations within the global economy, by investment-consumption tradeoffs, and by internal political and economic pressures.

12

The Economics of the Peruvian Experiment in Comparative Perspective

John Sheahan

The structural reforms initiated in Peru from 1968 through 1973 deserve a special place in modern Latin American history because of their originality, their unexpected creation of new possibilities, and their concern for the underprivileged. But the long-term process needed to correct initial mistakes and to encourage wider participation by methods consistent with growth was choked off by serious failures of national economic policy with respect to exchange rates, relative prices, and the fundamental requirements of macroeconomic consistency.[1] What is particularly striking about these failures and the breakdown to which they inexorably led is their similarity to a basic pattern evident during the last thirty years in other countries that have tried to restructure their economic systems: it is almost as if

I would like to express particular thanks to Cynthia McClintock, Raúl Torres, and Maria Clara Uribe for their very helpful questions and suggestions.

[1] Details of the structural reforms in the first stage of the Velasco regime are thoroughly discussed in Abraham F. Lowenthal, ed., *The Peruvian Experiment: Continuity and Change under Military Rule* (Princeton: Princeton University Press, 1975). The country's economic history and main lines of development policy into the 1970s are presented in Rosemary Thorp and Geoffrey Bertram, *Peru 1890–1977: Growth and Policy in an Open Economy* (London: Macmillan & Co., 1978). Among the many useful discussions of the economic policies and events leading up to the breakdown of 1974–1978 are Roberto Abusada-Salah, "Políticas de Industrialización en el Perú, 1960–1976," *Economía* (December 1977), pp. 9–34; Carlos Amat y León, "La Economía de la Crisis Peruana," Fundación Friedrich Ebert, ILDIS, Working Paper Series, no. 16 (Lima: April 1978); César Huberto Cabrera, "Perú: La Crisis y la Política de Estabilzación," Fundación Friedrich Ebert, ILDIS, Working Paper Series, no. 17 (Lima: April 1978); E.V.K. FitzGerald, *The State and Economic Development: Peru since 1968* (Cambridge: Cambridge University Press, 1976), and *The Political Economy of Peru, 1956–1978* (Cambridge: Cambridge University Press, 1979); Jorge González, *Perú: Una Economia en Crisis, Interpretación y Bases para una Solución* (Lima: Universidad del Pacifico, 1978); and the chapters in the present volume by Daniel Schydlowsky and Juan Wicht (Chapter 4), FitzGerald (Chapter 3), Laura Guasti (Chapter 6), Barbara Stallings (Chapter 5), and Rosemary Thorp (Chapter 2).

Argentina under Perón, Chile under Allende, and Peru under Velasco had all been handed the same set of unworkable instructions.

If one were forced to choose between levels of policy—between serious attempts at structural reform in Latin America and on-going management of macroeconomic variables—it would be easy to agree that the first of these two is the more significant. But it is not sufficient to initiate promising reforms; it is also necessary not to ignore the problem of near-term survival. Peru will probably have another chance; maybe even Argentina and Chile will have other chances. But such opportunities for significant reform come only rarely, and that makes it an extremely costly matter to undermine the chance by poor economic management. Why then do so many of the reform regimes repeat the same mistakes? Is it natural impatience, aggravated by histories of extreme inequality and special privilege under regimes nominally using the market system? Does the very *conception* of economic consistency become identified with special privilege? Does structural reform come to mean or to require rejection of the kinds of discipline that would permit viable economic solutions?

The first section of this chapter summarizes central aspects of the common pattern of policy choice. The second considers some of the specific factors in the Peruvian case that are missing from this pattern and some disagreements about which aspects of economic policy were beneficial and which were harmful. The next section suggests alternative economic policies that might be more consistent with the combined goals of industrialization, increased autonomy, and wider participation in the growth process. The last section in the chapter speculates on the underlying pressures that repeatedly create similar choices and similar breakdowns.

THE COMMON PATTERN OF POLICY CHOICE AND VARIATIONS WITHIN IT

The main elements in the pattern may be grouped into three sets: (1) changes in the structures of production and trade; (2) policies concerning labor and wages, consumption, and aggregate demand; and (3) questions of the ownership of the means of production and the institutional framework that shape the distribution of income and power in the society.

Changes in the Structures of Production and Trade

A common theme of the countries that have attempted to promote modernization and increased autonomy in the postwar period has been the rejection of the ideas of free trade and comparative advantage in favor of policies intended to stimulate faster growth of the industrial sector. The mixture of methods has varied considerably, and such differences have had important consequences, but they have all aimed to raise the relative profitability of investment in the industrial sector through protection. Peru is distinctive mainly in that it started late, a generation after Argentina, Brazil, Chile, Colombia, and Mexico. Well after analyses of the results of this approach by Celso Furtado and others had led most economists to the conviction that it was so clearly unsuccessful as to be hardly worth debating, Peru repeated it.[2] That may demonstrate that each country has to learn from its own mistakes, but it also points to the tenacity of the problems creating pressures to make the attempt.

The decisions to break away from the pattern of relatively free trade were in part responses to market forces that kept the countries specialized in primary production while collective preferences for change were increasing. For Peru, as for all countries with originally good natural resources and limited industrial skills, market forces inhibit industrialization because primary exports provide earnings of foreign exchange that keep down the price of foreign currency and thereby make imports of industrial goods less costly than domestic production. Diversification should not be precluded forever; as nonrenewable natural resources are gradually used up and population pressures hold down the opportunity cost of labor, market forces should eventually foster the growth of labor-intensive industries. In Peru in the 1960s, the potential for expansion of primary production did begin to run into serious problems, including increasing costs and lower returns for further irrigation projects, overfishing that led to reduced supplies of fishmeal (the leading export of the decade), and decreasing potential for further output from the mining sector without heavy new capital investment.[3] These factors were acting to encourage a gradual shift away from primary production into industry, but at an exceedingly slow pace. If industrialization is seen as the key to modernization and autonomy, and if domestic business is not actively interested in pursuing it, the superficially evident solution is to speed things up through protection. The problem is not the goal but the failure to find a better way to move toward it.

[2] See the 1966 quotation from Furtado to this effect and the accompanying discussion in Albert Hirschman, *A Bias for Hope* (New Haven: Yale University Press, 1971), p. 88.

[3] Rosemary Thorp, "The Post-Import-Substitution Era: The Case of Peru," *World Development* (January-February 1977), pp. 125–136; Thorp and Bertram, *Peru 1890–1977*, especially chapters 11–12, pp. 205–256.

Much as Argentina and Brazil had done long before, Peru undertook at the end of the 1950s a series of increasingly strong measures to stimulate industrialization by restricting import competition. Successive tariff increases under Fernando Belaúnde Terry's government were followed by Velasco's 1970 measures that prohibited imports of any product placed on the national register of manufactures by any domestic producer.[4] In addition, the government granted generous tax incentives to industrial investors and special tariff-exemption privileges for low-cost imports of the capital equipment and inputs they chose to buy.[5] As everywhere, such policies encouraged investment in the least desirable form: they favored the purchase of foreign labor-saving machinery and the accentuation of an unnecessarily import-dependent structure of production.[6]

The microeconomic inefficiency of this process added to the standard set of macroeconomic problems with the balance of payments and inflation. Rising relative prices of industrial goods, by turning the domestic terms of trade against the primary sector, discouraged expansion of output and exports. Rising import requirements of an industrial sector unable to export, combined with disincentives to the primary sector, led straight toward increasing foreign exchange problems. In the high period of import substitution for most Latin American countries, from 1950 to 1970, it is striking to see how the region departed from all the rest of the world, industrialized or developing, market-oriented or centrally planned, in terms of decreasing shares of exports and falling ratios of exports to production.[7]

[4] In addition to the studies by Thorp, Pedro-Pablo Kuczynski reviews the Belaúnde period in *Peruvian Democracy Under Economic Stress: An Account of the Belaúnde Administration, 1963–1968* (Princeton: Princeton University Press, 1977), and Jorge Torres gives details on import restrictions in "Proteciones efectivas y sustitución de importaciones en Perú," CISEPA (December 1976).

[5] Amat y León, "La Economia de la Crisis Peruana," pp. 52–55.

[6] Abusada-Salah "Politicas de Industrialización." Thorp and Bertram, *Peru 1890–1977*, p. 315, make the surprising statement that industry "remained very import-dependent despite the efforts at re-structuring undertaken by the Military." Since the incentives actually used by the military government made imported capital equipment and materials cheaper relative to domestic inputs, "despite" seems to put the matter upside down.

[7] World Bank, *World Tables 1976* (Washington, D.C.: IBRD, 1976). Developing countries in the western hemisphere failed to keep up with the rate of growth of total exports for the world as a whole, for developing countries considered separately, or for centrally planned economic systems. Contrary to the experience of the rest of the world, exports fell relative to production for the region from 1950 to 1960, and from 1965 to 1970, though not between 1960 and 1965 (comparative tables 1 and 2, pp. 392 and 401).

Peru paid more attention to these issues than the other countries had. Major efforts were made to develop copper export capacity and to search for oil. The Certex scheme of tax incentives to stimulate nontraditional exports, which had been prepared by the Belaúnde government, was put into effect under Velasco. This might have helped considerably in the absence of inflationary increases in domestic costs, but as domestic inflation gathered strength, the Certex scheme was undercut by the policy of holding to a fixed exchange rate. The real return to exporters per dollar of foreign exchange earned was reduced every year from 1970 through 1975.[8]

Prices and Wages, Consumption, and Macroeconomic Balance

With respect to inflation, wage policies, and consumption, two major groups of countries can be distinguished: those in which protection to stimulate industrialization was part of a radical break from the previous political-social framework and those in which it was a matter of an alternative technique within an established system. The distinction might be considered as one between populist regimes oriented toward the interests of labor and conservative regimes greatly concerned with protection of property owners. Examples of the first group are Argentina under Perón, Chile during the Allende government, Castro's Cuba, and Peru under Velasco. Examples of the second are Brazil, Colombia, and in most respects, Mexico.

The basic context for all these countries included increased investment demand, higher industrial profits and improved bargaining positions for urban labor, increasing domestic prices generated both by protection and by the stimulus to final demand, increasing imports of materials and equipment, and increasing problems with exports. The responses differed among countries in two general ways: (1) whether or not they recognized and acted on the need to apply restraints on aggregate demand; and (2) what social groups were required to bear the burden of the restraints.

Argentina and Mexico may be considered as polar cases of the two groups of countries. The Perón government's strong measures to promote industrialization were part of an express policy that aimed to shift income from primary to urban producers and to raise real wages of urban workers. The rural sector had to bear the costs both of industrial investment and of higher real wages: the latter was part of the

[8] John Sheahan, "Peru: Economic Policies and Structural Change, 1968–1978," *Journal of Economic Studies*, vol. 7, no. 1 (1980).

target because the government's power base was the urban labor force. Wages did increase sharply, as did the rate of inflation and problems of foreign exchange.[9] To stimulate consumption and investment simultaneously is often possible, but the quantities are crucial. If aggregate demand grows faster than productive capacity, the foundations begin to cave in.

Mexico introduced protective measures more gradually, within a totally different political context. In straight economic terms, Mexico's greater restraint in the use of protection meant less inflationary pressure and less adverse effect on the primary sector. The institutional framework was also more favorable than in Argentina, in the sense that organized urban labor was incorporated into the governing party prior to the industrialization drive.[10] The government was committed to increasing real wages but had a strong base from which to control the rate of increase. Wages and consumption were allowed to rise but not so rapidly that problems of inflation and external balance got out of hand. Since the government could restrain increases in urban consumption, it could avoid putting extreme pressure on primary producers while continuing to provide incentives to industrialists. The Mexican transition process was certainly not free of strains, but it was far smoother than transition in Argentina.

In his explanation of this crucial ability to control the rate of wage increases, Robert Kaufman concluded that the Mexican experience shows "how little it really takes for most capitalist (or for that matter, socialist) systems to manipulate the workers and the poor."[11] He is right to imply that more egalitarian policies were possible. If the labor force had been able to exert pressure to achieve at least part of the needed restraint by using taxes to hold down consumption of higher income groups, real wages could have risen more rapidly. That was not Mexico's style. It should at least be recognized, however, that restraint had to be imposed somewhere. And it could hardly be said that Mexican workers have fared less well in the last thirty years than organized labor in Argentina.

Peru, like Chile in the brief Allende period, followed a path closer

---

[9] Carlos Díaz-Alejandro, *Essays on the Economic History of the Argentine Republic* (New Haven: Yale University Press, 1970); Richard Mallon and Juan Sourrouille, *Economic Policy Making in a Conflict Society, the Argentine Case* (Cambridge: Harvard University Press, 1975).

[10] Robert Kaufman, "Mexico and Latin America Authoritarianism," in José Luis Reyna and Richard Weinert, eds., *Authoritarianism in Mexico* (Philadelphia: Institute for the Study of Human Issue, 1977).

[11] Ibid., p. 228.

to the Argentine example. Neither government made a total commitment to union labor. Both made some efforts to restrain the rate of increase of wages, but they both ignored, or failed to act on, the need to restrain the growth of demand to fit the growth of productive capacity. Peru combined rapidly rising government spending with subsidized consumption of food and petroleum products and extraordinarily high tax privileges for private industry. The public sector deficit reached 5 percent of the gross national product by 1973, and 10 percent by 1975.[12] Any gains from the bitter fights to hold down increases of money wages were swept away by the failure to control aggregate demand. Inflation and external deficits do not arrive by one particular path: they come from *any* direction in which restraint is abandoned.

Cuba provides the one striking exception to the rule that reform governments seem unable to avoid excess demand. The rare combination of egalitarian change and avoidance of explosion might be attributed to the socialist model, but that arises the further question of what is it in socialism that allows such success. At least two factors seem of great importance. One is that concern for equality was not translated into rising urban real wages in any sustained way; the government focused instead on rising real income in the *rural* sector.[13] That is a distinctly more equalizing policy than rising urban wages, and it has the added advantage that it does not directly increase production costs in the industrial sector. The other special factor was that the government had the power to hold down the total output of consumer goods and used rationing to allocate this fixed total so that real urban consumption could not either spill over into excess imports or reduce resources available for investment.

In a sense, Cuba and Mexico achieved by different paths the same result: holding down the growth of consumption in order to raise investment rapidly. The differences in method are of great interest. Cuba achieved much more equalization because profits were eliminated and because relative incomes were raised for the poorest group, i.e., those in agriculture. Mexico, however, was able to provide more than Cuba in other ways. Urban labor incomes also could be raised

[12] Sheahan, "Peru," table 4.
[13] David Barkin, "The Redistribution of Consumption in Cuba," *Review of Radical Political Economics* 4, no. 5 (1972), pp. 1–23; Jorge Domínguez, *Cuba: Order and Revolution* (Cambridge: Harvard University Press, 1978); James Malloy, "Generalization of Political Support and Allocation of Costs," in Carmelo Mesa-Lago, ed., *Revolutionary Change in Cuba* (Pittsburgh: University of Pittsburgh Press, 1971), pp. 23–42.

and, although the total supply of consumer goods was controlled, supplies of specific goods were not. Workers, and everyone else, can choose what they want to buy; they can work for firms not owned by the government or for those that are. Mexicans have retained more choice, more growth of incomes, and more inequality.

Questions of the International Framework and Ownership of the Means of Production

If industrialization is to lead to increased autonomy, it must presumably be carried out in large measure by domestic producers, public or private. Goals of autonomy and efficiency both call for efforts to avoid industrial structures heavily dependent on foreign technology and in particular to avoid production methods that replace domestic labor by capital-intensive production techniques. Policies of protection systematically go the wrong way in all these respects. Protection acts as a magnet drawing foreign investment toward profitable production behind import barriers and it underwrites high-cost investment in foreign technology. The best solution is to use other promotional techniques instead of protection. If the latter is used, however, the damage might be reduced by use of direct screening techniques to control investment decisions or by public investment in those fields in which domestic private investment does not respond to new opportunities.

Peru tried both of these options within a context of extreme protection. Following Colombian policies initiated after the eye-opening research of Constantine Vaitsos there, Peru led the Andean Pact toward systematic measures to review foreign investment proposals, to limit permissible payments for foreign technology, to check on the prices paid for imports from associated firms, and to insist on eventual sale of equity to domestic investors.[14] But Peru failed to follow Colombia's lead in also adopting a policy of progressively increasing prices for foreign exchange. In Colombia, this helped to discourage unnecessary dependence on imported inputs and to encourage investment in possible exports.

Peru differed from Colombia, but not from the other major industrializing countries, in placing great emphasis on public investment. Brazil and Mexico did exactly the same, despite their more conserva-

[14] Shane Hunt, "Direct Foreign Investment in Peru: New Rules for an Old Game," in Lowenthal, ed., *The Peruvian Experiment*, pp. 302–349; Constantine Vaitsos, "Power, Knowledge, and Development Policy," in Gerald Helleiner, ed., *A World Divided, the Less Developed Countries, and the International Economy* (Cambridge: Cambridge University Press, 1976), pp. 113–146.

tive policy orientations. For all of them, it was a means to stave off entry by foreign firms—or to purchase control from existing foreign firms—and to implement investment projects left undeveloped by private firms. Besides, it gave the governments more power.

In Peru, two additional elements deserve special attention: (1) a somewhat mechanistic belief that public ownership would provide control of "the surplus," or of investment resources in general; and (2) a rare concern for worker participation through cooperatives and worker-managed firms.

Central control of investment through government ownership could in principle improve the allocation of investment, and experience in the Soviet Union has shown that it can be used to speed up industrialization. Every industrial conglomerate in the West presumably agrees that decisions guided or coordinated by central headquarters can improve investment allocation. In practice, however, central allocation does not always prove to be very productive. For Cuba it clearly did not, at least in the 1960s. And in most Latin American countries, the prior problem is that public firms rarely seem able to generate any surplus to use for any purpose at all. State-owned firms can become drains on the system rather than contributors to it. Ownership does not convey an automatic surplus; the surplus has to be earned. Nor does public ownership guarantee that the firm will avoid foreign technology, favor labor intensive techniques, and economize on imports. In the absence of controls on deficits of state firms, they may behave very nearly the same as private firms with protected markets. For allocation decisions, ownership may matter less than the incentives and controls that guide management from outside the firm.[15]

Beyond allocative efficiency is the question of the use of government ownership to constrain both economic and political choice. State ownership is not the same thing as social ownership, in the sense of the right of the people who constitute the society to determine goals and methods. East European critics of centralized state control of the means of production have done a great deal to clarify the difference between state ownership and participation in control by the society as a whole.[16]

---

[15] FitzGerald, *The Political Economy of Peru*, pp. 38, 127–128, and 190–199; John Sheahan, "Public Enterprise in Developing Countries," in William Shepherd and Associates, *Public Enterprise: Economic Analysis of Theory and Practice* (Lexington, Mass.: Lexington Books, 1976), pp. 205–233.

[16] Wlodzimierz Brus, *Socialist Ownership and Political Systems* (London: Routledge and Kegan Paul, 1975); Branko Horvat, *The Yugoslav Economic System* (White Plains, N.Y.: International Arts and Sciences Press, 1976); G. Konrád and I.

Peru is distinctive not for state ownership, nor for any remarkable ability to guide the state firms constructively, but rather for the variety of forms of ownership. In addition to the state firms, they included agricultural cooperatives, worker-managed industrial firms, and companies owned jointly by workers and private capitalists. As was surely to be expected, this heterogeneous collection of experiments led to enormous complications, both with respect to production and to issues of inequality within the labor force.[17] Major problems developed regarding discrimination against workers outside the participatory groups. The joint problems of work incentives and inequality might possibly have been corrected if time had allowed, but the industrial experiments were curtailed radically during the 1977 economic crisis. In agriculture, the collectives have so far not been seriously cut back, and Cynthia McClintock's field research suggests real progress in dealing with work incentives and inequality.[18]

Peru resembles Chile more than any other Latin American country in terms of the variety of forms of participation attempted. Some of the worker-run firms in Chile achieved better operating results, and these experiences may point to better ways to handle participation in the future.[19] Worker-run firms could conceivably become an important solution to at least some of the difficulties of insufficient employment opportunities in private and state-owned firms; in Chile, they have been of some help in this sense during the severe unemployment of the post-Allende years.[20]

Social reform in Peru should not be identified with changes in

---

Szelényi, "Social Conflicts of Underurbanization: The Hugarian Case," in Mark Field, ed., *Social Consequences of Modernization in Communist Countries* (Baltimore: Johns Hopkins University Press, 1976).

[17] Peter Knight, "Workers' Self-Management," in Lowenthal, ed., *The Peruvian Experiment*, pp. 350–401, and "Social Property in Peru: From Hegemony to Survival" (Paper presented at the Wilson Center Conference, Washington, November 1978); FitzGerald, *The Political Economy of Peru*, 124–126, 198–199.

[18] Cynthia McClintock, *Peasant Cooperatives and Political Change in Peru* (Princeton: Princeton University Press, 1981), chapter 8.

[19] Andrew Zimbalist and Juan Espinosa, *Economic Democracy: Workers' Participation in Chilean Industry, 1970–1973* (New York: Academic Press, 1978).

[20] Leopoldo Moraga Vega, "Formación du un Sector Autogestionado," and "Transformación de Empresas Tradicionales en Autogestionadas," Instituto de la Autogestión (Santiago: April 1978); Mario Livingtstone, "La Participación en la Empresa Autogestionada," *Sociedad y Autogestión* (April-June 1979), pp. 12–24; "El Sector Autogestionado Chileno," in *Sociedad y Autogestion* (April-June, 1979), pp. 25–31.

property ownership. It is possible for the state to take over the means of production but fail to contribute to national income because of poor choices with respect to investment or failure to control costs. It is also possible for welfare-oriented governments, as in Denmark and Sweden, to do a great deal to help the economically weak and to tax the rich without significant public ownership. Peruvian policies included an amazingly wide range of measures intended to improve access to education, the welfare of poor migrants to the cities, the conditions of labor, and the nutrition of the urban poor.[21] Some of these measures worked poorly, and public enterprise management under military officers did not leave a particularly brilliant record either. But the discussion preceding is meant to underline the proposition that they never had a chance: the failure of national policy to limit aggregate demand to productive capacity and the distortions induced by the combination of extreme protection and inappropriate exchange rates meant that the system was bound to break down no matter how well designed the social reforms or how well-run the public firms.

Conflicting Interpretations and Factors Omitted

The three main strands in the common pattern of policy choice leave out many of the specifics of the Peruvian experience and also leave out some fundamental questions of constraints on domestic policy choices. Which factors have to be regarded as fixed limitations and which may be considered instead as problems that could, at least in principle, be resolved by different responses of national policy?

The articles in this volume by Laura Guasti (Chapter 6) and Barbara Stallings (Chapter 5) and many of the points made by E.V.K. FitzGerald (Chapter 3) direct attention to factors outside the common pattern, particularly external opposition, adverse changes in world market conditions and the availability of Peru's natural resources, and the Peruvian industrialists' reluctance (or relative incapacity) to act. These issues might be divided in two groups. One set consists of important handicaps imposed upon Peru by external forces, which must be taken into account in any adequate explanation of the breakdown from 1974 through 1978. The other set consists of disagreements over the fundamental process of causation or the possible paths to more viable solutions.

[21] Lowenthal, ed., *The Peruvian Experiment*; Alfred Stepan, *The State and Society: Peru in Comparative Perspective* (Princeton: Princeton University Press, 1978).

External Factors

The external factors that made reforms more difficult for Peru include a steep rise in prices of imported food in the early 1970s, a sudden drop in the fish catch and fishmeal export volume, bad luck with the expensive search for oil, opposition by the United States to credit after nationalization of the International Petroleum Company, and resistance by foreign mining companies to make the major new investments required for increased production.

The increase in prices for imported food meant an inescapable loss of real income, an added foreign exchange problem, and a threat of greater inflation. Possible responses of conventional market policy might have been to allow domestic food price increases to drive down consumption and stimulate domestic output, while increasing the price of foreign exchange to help curb imports and favor exports. But the government, understandably, wished to avoid increasing food prices for the urban poor, who had very little margin of consumption to cut back. This might have been handled by using food stamps or other subsidies targeted at the poor, while allowing market prices to rise, both to encourage domestic food production and to discourage consumption by those who were not poor.[22] Instead, the policy adopted was to subsidize imported food for *all* consumers, to control domestic food prices despite the adverse impact on home production, and to borrow abroad to finance the subsidized imports. The cumulative result was to magnify greatly the initial damage.

With respect to the disappearing *anchoveta*, the drop in export earnings was $189 million, from the peak in 1970 to the lowest year, 1973.

---

[22] The alternative approach recommended here is exemplified by the policy change made in Sri Lanka in response to the same problem of increasing world food prices and resultant costs of domestic subsidy in 1973–1974. The basic ration of subsidized rice previously made available to everyone was replaced by a selective subsidized ration limited to the lower half of the income distribution. At the same time, the controlled price for rice outside the ration was removed so that the upper half of the income distribution had to pay the full market price. See Paul Isenman, "Basic Needs: the Case of Sri Lanka," *World Development* 8 (1980): 237–258. Isenman points out that the concentration of aid on the poorest people had two advantages. One is that it reduced the use of public financing to subsidize consumption of higher income groups. The other is that it helped answer the most serious problem of all in 1973–1974, which was that the aggregate shortage was so severe that rations meant to be available to the poor could not be supplied. Death rates for the poor went up partly because consumption of limited supplies by the non-poor, at subsidized prices, was too great. The new system should lessen the danger of inability to provide minimum supplies of rice to the poor. (Isenman, "Basic Needs," pp. 240–241.)

That hurt. The increase in import spending as excess demand grew from 1972 through 1975 was equal to $1.8 billion, roughly nine times the value of the loss on the export side.[23] Again, the specific problem was serious, but the main questions are the reasons for the surge in import demand and for keeping a fixed exchange rate in the face of export problems combined with accelerating imports.

No one can measure the value of the oil not discovered, or the copper that would have been produced if there had been no constraints on investment, or the generalized waste involved in allowing military officials of varying managerial competence to use their agencies and public firms without significant limits on either their budgets or their objectives. Military governments need not as a universal rule ignore questions of costs and economic efficiency, but the case of Peru should give pause to anyone who thinks that "strong governments" (in the sense of military regimes) can be counted on to reduce the inefficiency of politics-ridden civilian bureaucracies.

The resistance by foreign-owned mining companies to making new investments in Peruvian ventures and the opposition of the United States government to giving credit to Peru are both emphasized by Barbara Stallings (Chapter 5). She makes a good case; these handicaps must be regarded as systematic rather than accidental. In the context of a reform government determined to exercise control over natural resources and foreign trade, it would be amazing if foreign mining companies did anything other than try to get any movable assets out quickly or change the government if they thought they could. Laura Guasti (Chapter 6) points out that the situation was different in manufacturing: new firms came in and existing firms expanded through the Velasco period. The difference is partly in the risk. The needed investment in mining had to come in very large chunks, and income from it always depended on government decisions about ownership, exchange rates, and permission to export. Industrial investment demanded less capital, and income from it was related more to the domestic markets stimulated by government spending. Peru did not suffer anything resembling the relentless, generalized hostility that foreign firms and the United States government demonstrated toward Chile during the Allende period.

If there is any answer to such conflicts it must reckon with the near-certainty that reform governments will be handicapped by opposition from some foreign-owned firms. Reform governments probably will have little choice but to take over the assets of the more an-

[23] Banco Central de Reserva del Perú, *Memoria 1975*, pp. 105 and 112.

tagonistic firms and to accept the accompanying burden of financing investment. Since both sides lose when this happens, there should be some room for negotiation to avoid this outcome. But when such negotiations fail and the government decides to nationalize, then it must take responsibility for finding investment resources and must deal with difficult problems of selectivity. It must create coherent processes to decide which lines of investment to undertake and at what rate, given constraints on aggregate demand and on the external deficit that can be incurred without losing policy control to lending institutions. Without trying to second guess the Peruvian government on the skill of negotiations and the ability to manage the assets once nationalized, it is evident that too little thought was given to the necessity of careful selectivity in investment decisions and to desirable limits on spending and external borrowing.

For people who sympathize with the Velasco regime's intentions to aid the underprivileged, it is infuriating that the wealthier outside world did so much to make things more difficult. It may appear irrelevant or misleading to insist on the self-defeating character of many of the economic choices made by the Peruvian government. The problem is that this familiar set of choices would ensure destructive results even if the outside world blessed the whole attempt and all the ocean's fish leaped into Peruvian nets. The external world deserves all the blame it gets, but it remains terribly important for any future efforts at social reform to realize that the basic lines of Peruvian domestic policy were unworkable.

Conflicts of Interpretation Within the Basic Pattern

Of the three main strands in the common pattern of policy choice discussed above, practically everyone seems to agree on the importance of macroeconomic balance, if not on its feasibility; but interpretations of the other two elements are very much in dispute with respect to direction and to the process of causation. The feasibility of macroeconomic balance by raising taxes or by restraining government spending, when so many groups have such strong claims for attention, is very much open to doubt. Technically, it is easy to argue that a combination of sales or excise taxes on manufactured goods, with steep taxes on urban land values and some restraint on the tax privileges given to industrialists for investment, could have permitted substantial increases in government spending without explosion. The answer that the Peruvian government could not do these things because it did not have the political power is surprising for a government that eliminated the national legislature and all political parties, took over the press and many private firms, made strong efforts to limit wage increases, placed military officers in charge of all government institutions, and sent a fair number of people to jail or into exile for expressing opposition. It seems more plausible to suggest that the military rulers did not understand issues of economic balance and that the economic advisers who might .have clarified the question were either too circumspect to say much about it, were told to keep quiet, or—the main point below—did not believe in using market forces and monetary balance as a matter of principle.

The other two elements in the common policy making pattern— protection and structural reform—involve conflicts both of fundamental economic analysis and of social goals. At one extreme, Daniel Schydlowsky and Juan Wicht (Chapter 4) blame protection and the reforms for the economic breakdown. At the other extreme, Fitz-Gerald (Chapter 3) regards protection and public ownership as fundamental components of any successful development program.

To argue in favor of an even more closed and controlled economic system would be readily understandable if it were combined with a clear social preference for a subsistence-level economy that relied only minimally on income from industrial activities and placed little value on contact with the outside world. Gandhi would have approved, as would many of the most profound moral philosophers of human history. But it is almost surely self-defeating to close off a small economy if the goal is one of industrialization and modernization. The economics of self-sufficiency for a small economy insulated from competitive pressures would severely limit possibilities for any rise in per capita incomes. Apart from the food and clothing industries, the market that the Peruvian economy would constitute would preclude any reasonable level of efficiency in almost any modern industry. It is not just that industries would have high money costs and would need high prices to operate under such conditions: high costs mean essentially that the value of the income produced by inefficient industries is low; the income available to the country is correspondingly condemned to remain small.

Much of FitzGerald's argument for protection and control seems to be based on the belief that Peruvian industrialists are incapable of competing effectively with the outside world; industrialization in an open economy must mean acceptance of predominantly foreign investment. Rosemary Thorp states some of the same concerns. These issues need more empirical study, but it would be easy to agree that the present entrepreneurial capacities of Peruvian industrialists are in general more limited than those of, say, Japanese or Korean or Mexican industrialists. They may be behind even other small- and medium-sized countries such as Chile and Colombia, though that would be a difficult question to settle to everyone's satisfaction.

Rosemary Thorp shares the position that Peruvian industrialists are behind those of otherwise comparable developing countries, but she places more emphasis on historical factors, which may be subject to change. One important historical or cultural factor is surely the very poor record of access to educational opportunities in Peru. This weak area of the society was one of the key targets for reform under Velasco, although those efforts ran into particularly severe limitations. Failure to provide the most minimal educational opportunities to the non-rich has kept that country's entrepreneurial and leadership capacities far below what they could be, given all the other constraints operating on the society.

Nathaniel Leff has carried out some fascinating studies of entrepreneurship in developing countries which suggest several interacting ideas: (1) Small numbers of potent industrialists appear rapidly in all countries in which they are permitted to exist (usually groups of family-linked operators rather than public corporations), even when the local culture appears to have been highly adverse to entrepreneurship prior to national independence; (2) entrepreneurship grows in reaction to opportunities provided by a well-functioning economy because coherent risk-taking pays off in such an environment; and (3) the small number of active businessmen in the early stages of industrialization implies a high concentration of assets and political influence that may be employed to dominate economic policy and to block social programs.[24] The dual problem is to encourage economic activity by industrialists and to limit their political role. The issue is the ability to promote competing social groups and to maintain wide participation in the political process, while adopting policies that make the economy as a whole more functional; there is no permanent impasse to entrepreneurship embedded in a particular culture.

In Peru's case, industrialization began very late, even compared with Chile and Colombia, partly because the country's wealth of nat-

---

[24] This is a highly selective paraphrase of some of the points made in Nathaniel Leff, "Industrial Organization and Entrepreneurship in the Developing Countries: The Economic Groups," *Economic Development and Cultural Change* (July 1978), pp. 661–675; "Entrepreneurship and Economic Development: The Problem Revisited," *Journal of Economic Literature* (March 1979), pp. 46–64; " 'Monopoly Capitalism' and Public Policy in Developing Countries," *Kyklos* 32, fasc. 4 (1979), pp. 718–738.

ural resources maintained the economic and political strength of re-source owners, kept up the supply of foreign exchange (and thus kept down its cost), and made industrial imports cheaper than they would have been in the absence of the natural resource exports. All this has been changing. Peruvian natural resource constraints are becoming increasingly acute, and Peruvian capacities for industrial production are growing. The shift toward industry can be speeded up by keeping foreign exchange expensive in real terms or slowed down by the op-posite policy choice. If economic policies favor promotion of indus-trial exports and a combination of higher priced foreign exchange with decreased protection, relatively low-cost industries will thrive and those that are relatively high cost will be held back. The rate of expansion of Peru's industrial sector should be greater in the aggre-gate, with structural changes favorable to those firms and industries able to provide higher real income relative to the resources they use.

If instead the country were to move toward a more closed and con-trolled economy, it might still gradually develop its industrial sector, but that would inescapably consist of the kind of industry dependent upon shelter from external competition. Firms would be less aware of changes in technology, more closely tied to individually negotiated political support, more apt to be selected by criteria other than con-tribution to national income, less able to provide export earnings to pay for nonsubstitutable imports, and less able to obtain economies of scale. They could, on the other hand, be more exclusively Peruvian firms, more closely linked to the evolution of the Peruvian economy, and more secure in their investment decisions (provided that the economy is managed in ways that avoid contradictions and negative turns). The choices are radically different, with real problems and possibly high social costs either way. The argument here is that there is more room for aggregate growth of income and therefore more pos-sibly to improve well-being of the very poor on the export track. A strong preference for domestically managed political control of the economy, however, would argue for the opposite.

Finally, with respect to the role of the social reforms in the 1974–1978 breakdown, the criticisms of specific measures made by Schydlowsky and Wicht contain many valid points but do not in any way compel a conclusion that the reforms so aggravated the situation that they ensured a crisis. The land reform and experiments with worker control introduced elements of confusion and perverse incen-tives that made the situation more difficult than it would otherwise have been. But agricultural production increased at about the same slow pace as before and industrial production at a faster pace than before. That does not prove that the reforms were free of any negative effects on output. It should have been possible to speed up production growth in agriculture, given either individual ownership of the land formerly held in large estates or an effective system of planned change in land use. Merely handing control of the estates to worker cooperatives was an understandable option in social terms but not immediately helpful for the national supply of food. And some of the changes in labor legislation did more to protect those already employed, regardless of their production, than to create new employment opportunities for additional workers who could have contributed to total output. The reforms were shot through with confusion and missed opportunities, but the confusion need not have been fatal: it restricted real income growth but did not blow the lid off the economy. If policies concerning protection, exchange rates, total spending, and taxes had provided a functional economy, the reforms could have been adapted and corrected to preserve benefits for the weak without dragging down the whole economy. That is one of the main reasons to insist on the need for consistent macroeconomic policies.

ALTERNATIVE WAYS TO COMBINE GREATER EQUALITY WITH SUSTAINED INDUSTRIALIZATION

Considered as an abstract problem of economic analysis, any set of internally consistent objectives can be pursued in an almost infinite variety of ways. But every society operates with complex restrictions stemming from its own traditions and from the specific purposes of the current regime. The range of conceivably acceptable economic solutions is cut down greatly. For those governments that attempt social reform in combination with efforts to achieve faster industrialization and greater autonomy, the roads are few. Many good analysts have come to the conclusion that, at least within the boundaries of a market-oriented system, there are none. This negative view may be correct. Peru in the 1970s was yet one more example of failure. The failure, however, may have been due in part to excessively limited perceptions of what is possible. Alternative routes may be arbitrarily dismissed as politically impossible because they are not understood; they may not even be seen to exist as conceptual alternatives. We all have trouble seeing anything for which we are not looking.

Following are summary statements of three alternative strategies that might be followed by reform governments concerned with economic growth. Each raises many issues beyond the scope of this essay. They are simply intended to illustrate options that might permit reformist-populist governments to get past the obstacles that repeatedly stop them.

One alternative, placing the emphasis on industrialization and rate of growth of income, has been worked out in detail by Marcelo Diamand.[25] The essential economic component of the strategy is a departure from comparative advantage, achieved by fixing an exchange rate for industrial products that links their average domestic price to world market values. To simplify greatly a complex set of ideas, if the initial situation is one in which Peruvian industries have costs that range from 20 to 60 percent above external prices, the price of foreign exchange should be raised (relative to the domestic price level) by something on the order of 40 percent. One set of Peruvian industries, those whose prices were initially between 20 and 40 percent above external prices, would at this new exchange rate have prices below those of external competitors. They would no longer need protection to survive but could instead become exporters. The other set of Peruvian industries, those with prices initially more than 40 percent above external levels, would remain unable to compete. The structure of production and the orientation of new investment would be redirected toward the lower cost set of producers. The industrial sector as a whole could grow more rapidly and at lower cost by expansion into external markets, while the principle of selection according to comparative efficiency could be retained *among industries*.

A major objection to any such strategy of moving to a promotional exchange rate for industrial exports is that it could accelerate domestic inflation, and the latter could in turn undercut any stimulus to exports. This problem bears somewhat differently on prices of standardized primary products and on prices of manufactured goods. Primary product prices are very likely to move upward by the full amount of any devaluation because they are closely linked to world prices. For manufactured goods, prices are more often based on costs of production. Those which rely on imported inputs would necessarily rise in price, and not gain much stimulus, while those based on labor and other domestic inputs could gain significant competitive advantage. Given a combination of inflationary danger and need to promote industrial exports, the best solution might be to use a separate exchange rate for them, or to use some form of direct subsidy. On the one hand, it is easy to see that the process could explode if infla-

[25] Marcelo Diamand, *Doctrines Económicas, Desarrollo e Independencia* (Buenos Aires: Paidos, 1973), and "Towards a Change in the Economic Paradigm Through the Experience of Developing Countries," *Journal of Development Economics* (1978), pp. 19–53.

tion gained strength. On the other hand, it should be possible to succeed if domestic inflationary pressures are held back during the process of movement to the new set of relative prices. In fact, the Peruvian economy finally did accomplish something like this kind of necessary transition during the clean-up period from 1975 through 1978, at great cost in terms of reduced real wages but with no need to repeat the squeeze unless new inflationary pressures get out of control.

Diamand's approach breaks out of the limited way of thinking that identifies exports with primary products and therefore creates an unnecessary opposition between export promotion and industrialization. It is close in spirit to the proposals of Schydlowsky and Wicht. It is also close to the general idea of the Certex system in Peru and to the differential exchange rates for exports other than coffee that have been used in the past in Colombia. It could be regarded as a system of subsidizing industrial exports. But it has the virtue, as contrasted to import substitution, of concentrating the gains selectively on the activities that add most to national income.

What would this approach do for the poor? That depends on who they are, where they are, and how close the economy is to full employment. In some countries of the Far East, initially close to full employment, the expansion of industrial employment by promotion of industrial exports succeeded in creating labor shortages and driving up real wages very rapidly. In Argentina, where the poor are in the cities and the rural sector consists more of large landholders, Diamand's approach might also help equalize incomes. In Peru, where the extreme poverty is mostly in the rural sector and full employment (in any sense of generalized shortages of labor) is at best a distant possibility, the prospects are much worse. Primary reliance on this strategy could help urban labor but might well damage the rural poor.

If industrialization is a lower priority than equalization, then a second and more appropriate strategy would be to emphasize satisfaction of basic needs of the poor, especially in the rural sector. It could consist of nutritional programs, rural development aimed at increased productivity, guaranteed income or price support for rural producers at minimum subsistence levels, and concentration of investment on social overhead capital. This strategy would need to be constrained in degree to fit the productive limits of the economy; it could be strengthened only if productive capacity were raised. So it would again be necessary to devote resources to some industrial investment and to find ways to promote exports sufficient to pay for needed imports. That would require reduced growth of real wages and nonwage incomes in the urban sector to fit the total resources available for urban consumption. The approach need not exclude industrialization and growth, though the pace would probably be slower than with the first strategy. Its possible rate would depend mainly on the efficiency of the allocation and subsequent operation of the resources directed to investment.

The first of these two strategies could repair some of the gaping holes in the populist-reformist programs by providing through industrial exports the foreign exchange needed to finance the required growth of imports, and by shifting from a costly process of unselective industrial protection toward industrial growth concentrated in areas of highest contributions to national income. But it could worsen inequality by favoring urban incomes over rural and by concentrating the gains of national income in a relatively small group of export industries. The second strategy would do more to alleviate poverty, but it would not ensure ability to finance imports and it could leave domestic industry in a permanent backwater. If both industrialization and equality are strongly held goals, each approach needs the other.

Oscar Muñoz has recently begun a major study of alternative development strategies, basing his initial discussion to a considerable degree on problems encountered with the alternate extremes of the Allende and post-Allende periods in Chile.[26] His study poses many more questions than those discussed here, but it follows much the same line of thought: any set of policies intended to permit sustained modernization while helping the poor must combine industrial export promotion with some form of basic needs program going outside the market. He makes clear that this two-sided develement strategy would require strong constraints on urban consumption of industrial products, effective taxation of income and consumption of higher income urban groups, and restraints on both the rate of growth of urban industrial wages and government spending. It might include a policy to keep high tariffs on imports of consumer durable goods, but with the crucial addition of domestic consumption taxes equal to the import duties so that productive resources would not be pulled toward their production. Tariffs would then serve as constraints on consumption but not as distortions of the production structure.

[26] Óscar Muñoz, "Desarrollo, Distribución del Ingreso y Democratización," *Estudios Cieplan,* no. 32 (April 1979).

Political Reality and Questions of Possibility

Were these alternative strategies politically impossible in Peru in the 1970s? Are they now? Are they generally impossible in all reformist-populist regimes in Latin America?

If one considers the class base of the reformist regimes, which may to varying degrees be identified with urban labor and perhaps industrialists, then any whole-hearted adoption of the basic needs strategy seems most improbable. Urban labor usually identifies "poverty" with itself. The peasants and landless rural labor are out of sight. It is only when peasants become rich farmers that they carry much political weight. It would have to be an unusually generous and broadly conceived kind of populism that would hold back urban consumption of manufactured products to concentrate resources among the rural poor. The Velasco regime seemed to start out with the rural poor in mind, but when the squeeze became intense, these same poor dropped out of the policy picture.[27]

If a pure basic needs strategy appears unlikely to gain sustained support (and might in fact not work, if insufficient attention is paid to exports), a combination of this approach with industrial export promotion would seem to offer a sufficiently wide distribution of benefits—to urban workers, industrialists, and the poor—to have some chance of success in a nonauthoritarian system. The lack of attention to industrial exports in the Velasco period is not evidence that the possibility had to be forsaken because of fierce opposition; it was not tried. When Rosemary Thorp emphasizes the need to expand exports and lauds the Velasco government for trying to do that, her references are entirely to *primary* exports.[28] When Jürgen Schuldt and Guido Pennano conclude that the system had no possibility of survival, they argue that a policy of export promotion had to be rejected because it could work only "at the expense of the industrial production."[29] The vision of possibilities excluded an essential element of a solution.

Until the changes in Peruvian exports achieved by changed incentives beginning in 1977, evidence about the possibility was limited mainly to experiences of other developing countries. Between 1967

[27] Dennis Gilbert, "The End of the Peruvian Revolution: A Class Analysis" (Paper prepared for the national meeting of the Latin American Studies Association, Pittsburgh, April 1979).

[28] Thorp, "The Post-Import Substitution Era."

[29] Guideo Pennano and Jürgen Schuldt, "Premisas y Antecedentes para la Evaluación del Proyecto del Plan Tupac Amaru," *Apuntes,* no. 6 (1977), p. 57.

and 1975, the exports of manufactured goods by all developing countries combined increased at an annual rate of 16 percent (compared to 11 percent for similar exports by developed market economies and 6 percent for centrally planned economies). By 1975, industrial exports were equal to 22 percent of all exports of developing countries, and fully 49 percent for East and South Asia.[30] Within Latin America, both Colombia and Brazil adopted policies in 1967 of continual small increases in the price of foreign exchange to encourage nontraditional exports. Colombia raised the share of its industrial production sold in export markets from almost nothing in 1960 (0.7 percent) to 7.5 percent by 1973. Brazil went from 0.4 percent to 4.4 percent in the same period. The incremental ratios of added manufactured exports as shares of added industrial production were close to 15 percent in both cases.[31] That means that the national industrial sectors were beginning to cover a significant share of the added costs of imports necessary for domestic industrial production: industrial growth began to be freed of its dependence on primary export earnings.

Such arguments about possibility as demonstrated by other countries must be gaining acceptance in Peru. Nontraditional exports were $65 million in 1970 and $102 million five years later, aided by the Certex subsidy but constrained by the failure to adjust the exchange rate in line with domestic inflation.[32] The Certex scheme was broadened in the following years and the currency was radically devalued. By 1979, nontraditional exports (measured here as the "others" after taking out all the major primary products) reached $668 million, more than six times the 1975 level.[33] Traditional primary exports rose greatly in 1979, too, more because of steeply increased prices in world markets than because of national policies, but still the nontraditionals came to 19 percent of the total.

It remains possible that in the 1980s industrial exports will be afflicted by greatly increased protectionism in the industrialized countries. The industrialized countries are bound to have a difficult time competing, with the enormous gaps in real wages that now exist,

---

[30] Donald B. Keesing, "World Trade and Output of Manufactures: Structural Trends and Developing Countries Exports," World Bank staff working paper, no. 316 (January 1979).

[31] Bela Balassa, "Export Incentives and Export Performance in Developing Countries: A Comparative Analysis," *Weltwirtschaftliches Archiv* 114 (1978): 24–61, table 2 on p. 36.

[32] Sheahan, "Peru."

[33] *Perú Económico* (January 1980), p. 2.

against those developing countries that actively promote industrial exports. The industrialized nations could react by allowing competition and readjusting their production structures to meet it as well as they can, or they could gradually tighten protectionist ropes around their necks. If they compete openly, both they and the developing countries will gain. If they retreat to intensified protection, both they and the developing countries will lose. But those developing countries that have generated strong export industries would seem to be in far better shape to continue to thrive than those that have failed to try.

All of this is not to argue that industrial export promotion comes free. Laura Guasti in this volume and recent Peruvian discussion raise a number of serious objections.[34] These include the concern that it may be chiefly multinationals located in Peru rather than Peruvian firms that respond to export incentives; that the firms and industries that succeed may be the more modern and capital-intensive producers who do not generate many employment opportunities; that industrial exporters will gain a dominant political position and will try to repress domestic labor because their markets are external and higher wages mean only higher costs; that the spread of income from added export promotion will be limited to urban producers and will leave out the rural poor completely; that the exchange rates needed to encourage exports will make import costs of food increase to the detriment of the urban poor; that the economy will be just as dependent on external markets as with primary exports; and that, in general, an export-oriented policy either favors or requires policies identified with such regimes as those of Brazil or Chile.

Some of these concerns may be answered by empirical investigation: they are all plausible, or possible, but one would need a great deal of factual information to assess their reality. Donald Keesing has recently completed a book-length review of just such questions, and a study of my own, getting longer and less certain with each revision, brings together evidence and arguments on many of them.[35] In general, these studies underline the reality of the industrial expansion to

[34] Javier Iguíñiz Echeverria, "Reflexiones Polemicas Sobre Dos Alternatives a la Situación Económica Actual," Fundación Freidrich Ebert, ILDIS, Working Papers Series, no. 15 (Lima: April 1978); ECO, *Avances de Investigación,* special edition (November 1978), "La Exportación no Tradicional: Sus Limitaciones como Estrategia de Desarrollo."

[35] Donald B. Keesing, "Trade Policy for Developing Countries," World Bank staff working paper, no. 353 (August 1979); John Sheahan, "Exports of Manufactured Products by Developing Countries: A Key to Success or a New Trap?" (Paper presented for discussion at the meeting of the Eastern Economic Association, Boston, May 1979).

be expected from any serious program of stimulating industrial exports, and the near-certainty that this will improve urban employment conditions and urban labor incomes, but they leave open a great deal of room for further exploration of social effects and of the consequences for rural incomes. The possibility that the policy could aggravate inequalities should be recognized. Some of the defects of the approach, particularly with respect to the way it leaves out the rural poor, could be offset by an accompanying program of rural development to increase agricultural productivity and a basic needs program directed to the very poor. To push industrial exports without the balancing strategy in the present Peruvian context could be costly in social terms. To push a basic needs program without promoting industrial exports would leave the society with little scope for growth of income. Peru needs both.

WHERE ARE THE ROOTS OF THE ECONOMIC PROBLEMS?

Keynes was surely right that economists are best viewed as the plumbers for society. They should be asked to check systematically on emerging problems, or to make specific repairs, but not to design the house or tell people how to live in it.[36] At the level of the plumber's concerns, the breakdown of the Peruvian economy can best be explained as a case of grossly misleading price signals that bent the pipes out of shape, accompanied by a surge or excess demand that exceeded the capacity of the system. Peruvian economic policies, like those of all other Latin American populist-reformist governments, sent negative price signals to exporters, and positive price signals to industrialists encouraging them to build an import-intensive industrial structure. At the same time, the government launched its own long-term investment projects and increased military expenditures, while stimulating private investment demand and subsidizing private consumption. That was too much. It could not work. It will never work, under capitalism or socialism or anything else.

Peru could conceivably resume in the 1980s a path of growth with greater equality than in the past by holding down the consumption of the rich through taxation, by improving production incentives for the

---

[36] A friend with a better memory than mine has pointed out that Keynes' model for the economist was the dentist rather than the plumber. "If economists could manage to get themselves thought of as humble, competent people, on a level with dentists, that would be splendid." Keynes, "Economic Possibilities for Our Grandchildren," in *Essays in Persuasion* (New York: Harcourt Brace, 1932), p. 373. The plumber still seems to me the more appropriate image.

agricultural cooperatives and industrial peasant producers, by holding the growth of real wages up to (but not beyond) the rate of growth of productive capacity, by using both prices and taxes to discourage import dependence and capital-intensive investment, and by using exchange rates and direct incentives to orient the industrial structure toward exports. Whether preferences emphasize equality and current consumption or more growth is Peru's business. Either way is perfectly feasible, provided the claims add up consistently.

The repeated economic results of reformist-populist governments—runaway inflation, foreign exchange crises, deepening external debt, and loss of autonomy—all trace back to a failure to make the parts add up. The imbalances may be initiated or aggravated by all kinds of exogenous problems and by systematic resistance of social groups afraid to lose their positions. One might well conclude that external and domestic opposition were dominant in the Chilean tragedy and that they gravely hampered Peru, but it would not be accurate or helpful to suggest that such factors are *all* that was wrong. The imbalances and distortions of domestic policy created nonviable systems.

Many intellectual and political problems underlie the pattern of nonworkable policies established in successive populist-reformist regimes. The intellectual problems include a failure to realize that price signals can lead to behavior in unwanted directions; misinterpretation of the facts of idle capacity and unemployment as evidence that the economy has no outer limit of capacity; convictions that industrial exports are impossible or too small to be worth bothering about; a belief that import controls can take care of foreign exchange problems when the production system has become import dependent; preoccupation with holding down food prices or raising wages for urban workers, without realization or concern for what these policies do to rural incomes and production incentives. All these problems are complex and invite research and debate. They were all present in Peru. But there is something else beneath all this.

Alfred Stepan's analysis of the Peruvian experience in political and social terms, comparing such inclusionary corporatist regimes to more exclusionary systems, suggests that concern for economic efficiency is a "characteristic legitimacy principle" of the latter but not of the former.[37] Peru certainly fits his model; the government assigned high priority to economic nationalism and low to economic efficiency. Of the complex set of explanatory factors that he uses, one of the most

[37] Stepan, *The State and Society,* chapter 3, especially table 3.1.

powerful components is the intellectual and moral tradition of Catholic concerns for fairness, for "just prices" and "just wages" as opposed to price and wage determination through market forces. The moral tradition can easily be linked to Marxist thought, as it is in the writing of Gustavo Gutierrez.[38] But it need not be identified with Marxism any more than with Buddhism: all moral traditions give great weight to equity and to principles establishing just positions within the social order.

The conflict between moral principles and market forces is especially intense in Latin America, partly because ethical and religious questions retain so much of their historical importance and partly because the objective economic and social realities are so gruesomely unequal. High concentrations of property ownership and of access to education and information guarantee that the market forces implied by movement toward increased efficiency work systematically in favor of privileged groups.[39] If one believes that both equity and efficiency are desirable characteristics of an economic system, it is relatively easy to reconcile them in Northern Europe and in some Asian countries, but not in Latin America. Still, it remains possible to identify paths of growth that would allow for more nearly equal participation and greater efficiency than those followed.

Hypothesis: there would not be so much confusion, doubt, and inconsistency if the people making decisions in reformist regimes did not have somewhere in their preference systems a conviction that they *should* reject market criteria and economic constraints. Price and income constraints are seen as perverse, demeaning, and immoral. They are perceived, correctly, as emphasizing action in response to selfish material incentives. They allow everyone to go off in directions of individual choice without any necessary concern for social goals, in a context in which only a small majority has access to the knowledge and capital necessary to take advantage of incentives to invest, save, and export. Concepts of fairness, of the need to stimulate and to equip the poor who lack such capacity to respond to incentives, dominate concepts of efficiency and consistency.

Conceptions of fairness and underlying rejection of market forces shape perceptions of what is possible. The very real problems of implementing equitable and effective tax policies, or stimulating ex-

[38] Gustavo Gutierrez, *A Theory of Liberation* (Maryknoll, N.Y.: Orbis Books, 1973), especially chapter 6.

[39] John Sheahan, "Market-Oriented Economic Policies and Political Repression in Latin America," *Economic Development and Cultural Change* (January 1980), pp. 267–291.

port-oriented industrialization, are converted from issues requiring patient strategy into impossibilities best condemned or ignored. Professional analysis and empirical research may slowly reshape such perceptions of possibilities, but they are like throwing beanbags against the tanks of profound moral convictions.

If this hypothesis is to some degree correct, if the fundamental issues are really questions of moral conviction, what then? Then it probably should be recognized that egalitarian reformist governments will always have extreme difficulties in finding a viable path, even if all the rest of the world blesses the attempt. They might just possibly have a better chance if, while keeping foremost their concern for moral values, they treated market forces not as enemies to be crushed but as possible instruments of policy to lead workers and firms in socially desired directions.

13

The Peruvian Experiment Reconsidered

Abraham F. Lowenthal

This brief essay discusses the meaning and legacy of Peru's experiment. Its aim is to stress several central features of Peru's experience from 1968 to 1980. I hope in this personal "afterword" to highlight some of the points this volume makes, to clarify others, and to supplement and correct a few as well.

I have not been studying Peru systematically since 1974. Obviously, I cannot contribute new data on Peru, nor novel interpretations grounded in the contextually sensitive analysis this book features.[1] What I hope to contribute instead is a sense of perspective derived precisely from relative distance, and from a fairly detailed appreciation of Peru before 1968. That background leads me to advance two propositions, each of them somewhat contrary to the dominant thrust of this volume's chapters, but each amply supported by evidence in the book.

First, although most authors in this symposium stress the Peruvian experiment's shortfalls, I will argue that Peru's military rulers largely succeeded at what they set out to do when they took power in 1968. Second, although most authors in this collection argue that Peru since 1975 has been returning to the conditions and policies that preceded military rule and that the whole period (1968–1980) thus underlined fundamental continuities, I will emphasize that Peru has changed significantly during this period, both in ways the military sought and in ways they did not.

[1] Much of what I know about Peru since 1974 comes from the chapters in this volume, from the other papers presented at the workshop from which this book emerged, and from a brief trip to Lima in 1979, discussed in Abraham F. Lowenthal, "Dateline Peru: A Sagging Revolution," *Foreign Policy*, no. 38 (Spring 1980). Specific points derived from other sources are footnoted below.

For help preparing and improving this paper, I am very grateful to Cynthia McClintock and Richard Sholk. I am also indebted to Julio Cotler, Jane Jaquette, Hélan Jaworski, David Scott Palmer, Luis Pásara, and Javier Silva Ruete for their comments on my draft.

THE PERUVIAN EXPERIMENT AS A SUCCESS

Evaluations of Peru's experiment, in this volume and elsewhere, tend to contrast the military regime's professed goals—many very ambitious and some contradictory among themselves—with its actual record. Peru's military rulers claimed at various times that they would accelerate Peru's economic growth and radically improve its distribution; restructure society on the basis of equity and of new concepts of property and other social relationships; expand political participation; end class strife; transform national values and create a "new Peruvian man"; overcome external dependence; and make Peru a Third World leader.[2] Not surprisingly, the Peruvian experiment did not achieve these extravagant ambitions.

The regime's aim to spur Peru's economic growth clearly failed, as Daniel Schydlowsky and Juan Wicht emphasize and others confirm. The country's rate of growth per capita slowed and then declined during the military's years (although a recovery was underway in the regime's last year). Productivity fell in both agriculture and industry. Peru's balance of payments deteriorated sharply, and its external debt climbed to unprecedented levels.[3]

Having talked so ardently of social justice and economic redistribution, Peru's military rulers did not even improve the country's regressive tax system; indeed, it became somewhat more regressive.[4] Having proclaimed the need for fundamental structural reforms, the military presided over measures that left the lower half of the nation's

[2] Three convenient sources for information on the maximum program of Peru's revolutionary military are: Juan Velasco Alvarado, *La Voz de la Revolución*, 2 volumes (Lima: Oficina Nacional de Información, 1972); "Plan Inca," as published in all Lima daily newspapers on July 29, 1974; and Carlos Delgado, *Testimonio de Lucha* (Lima: Biblioteca Peruana, 1973). Descriptive and analytic reviews of the first phase of most of the specific reforms may be found in Abraham F. Lowenthal, ed., *The Peruvian Experiment: Continuity and Change under Military Rule* (Princeton: Princeton University Press, 1975).

[3] A convenient summary of Peru's economy after twelve years of military rule is to be found in the World Bank's report, *Peru: Major Development Policy Issues and Recommendations* (Washington, D.C.: International Bank for Reconstruction and Development, June 1981). Further data may be found most easily in successive issues of the very useful Peruvian monthly publication, *Perú Económico*.

[4] See Richard C. Webb, *Government Policy and the Distribution of Income in Peru, 1963–1973* (Cambridge: Harvard University Press, 1977), pp. 55–57. Webb cautions against drawing conclusions about overall distribution from the impact of any specific policy. Nevertheless, he makes the case that redistributive policies during the period of military rule reinforced the dualistic structure of the economy and did little for the rural/traditional sector (see pp. 88–89, 101).

income recipients virtually unaffected, and the lowest quarter worse off. On some indicators—caloric intake and health statistics, particularly—Peru's poor are actually poorer now than before, as Susan Eckstein points out and as the World Bank has documented.[5]

Except for some features of the agrarian reform, none of the regime's innovative social and economic experiments, announced with such breathlessness, has survived intact into the 1980s. SINAMOS, the social mobilization agency that was supposed to build new means to channel effective popular mobilization, has disappeared with hardly a trace. The much touted educational reform was largely eviscerated. The "social property" sector—once heralded as the eventually predominant part of the economy—now affects only a few marginal firms. What Schydlowsky and Wicht say about the industrial reform is harsh but accurate and broadly representative: "While the goal was to improve equity, expand industry, and police the undesirable actions of entrepreneurs, the result was to consolidate an aristocracy of workers, increase entrepreneurial efforts to find ways around the system, spark capital flight, and inhibit new job creation."

Having pronounced "full participation" a major goal, Peru's military leaders found themselves first dismantling participatory organizations and eventually being repudiated at the polls by a public that never embraced the experiment.[6] And having vowed to end class strife in Peru, the military left behind—as Julio Cotler and Luis Pásara suggest—a country affected more than ever by labor unrest.

Nor did the regime's talk of changing national values and creating a "new Peruvian man" make much of a dent. The "new man" is nowhere to be found, nor even talked about, in Peru today. The military regime will more likely be remembered in a generation for having ex-

[5] During the 1970s, real incomes of the lowest 25 percent of Peru's families dropped 18 percent. Per capita calorie consumption declined during the 1970s for low and middle income families in Peru, and the incidence of typhoid, malaria, dysentery, and other diseases associated with poverty increased. See World Bank, *Peru: Major Development Issues and Recommendations,* pp. 34–35.

[6] It is striking that the two candidates in the 1980 election who were identified with the military together polled less than 5 percent of the votes, while close to 90 percent were registered by the parties specifically repudiated by the armed forces in 1968: Acción Popular, APRA, and the parties of the left. The military's failure ever to build a sympathetic constituency, even among beneficiaries of its reforms, was highlighted as one of the Peruvian experiment's weak links in Abraham F. Lowenthal's "Peru's Ambiguous Revolution," in Lowenthal, ed., *The Peruvian Experiment,* pp. 3–43, especially pp. 6 and 43. The chapters in this volume by Cotler, Pásara, McClintock, and Cleaves/Pease García analyze the reasons for this crucial flaw.

panded Lima's middle class and legitimated its concerns than for profoundly reshaping national ideals.

Despite the regime's vigorous efforts to reduce external dependence, the nation found itself by 1980 still highly vulnerable to changes in international economic circumstances, as Rosemary Thorp emphasizes. Judged by the expenditure of foreign exchange in royalty payments, Peru's technological dependency may actually have increased under the military government.[7] Although the role of foreign corporations in Peru's extractive sector was sharply reduced, foreign private commercial banks vastly expanded their role.[8] Laura Guasti's observation that "rather than diminish the effects of international corporate dynamics in Peru, the government only changed which international corporate groups would have the most domestic impact" is pertinent (though overstated). And, as E.V.K. FitzGerald points out, Peru's only means for resolving the nation's economic problems remained, as for so long, to combine repressive wage policies at home with hope for rising world prices for its exports, still mainly primary products. In sum, Peru is still dependent, highly so.

Peru's aspirations to become a leader among Third World nations have fizzled. At the height of the Velasco regime, Peru was prominent in the Andean Pact, the OAS, the Group of 77, the Non-Aligned Movement, and the United Nations. No longer does Peru attract such attention or take a leadership role in regional or international fora. The country's international profile has by now receded to dimensions approximating Peru's weight in the world economy. (The selection of a Peruvian, Javier Pérez de Cuellar, as secretary general of the United Nations was a tribute to the individual diplomat, not primarily a recognition of Peru).[9]

The conclusion, then, is inescapable. If one defines Peru's revolution in terms of the maximum goals advanced by a small cadre of military officers and the civilian ideologues who counseled them (codi-

[7] See Dennis Gilbert, "The End of the Peruvian Revolution: A Class Analysis," *Studies in Comparative International Development* 15 (Spring 1980): 15–38.

[8] For a general survey of this trend, see Robert Devlin, "Los Bancos transnacionales, la deuda externa y el Perú," *Revista de la CEPAL,* no. 14 (August 1981). For discussion of internal political implications, see Barbara Stallings, "Peru and the U.S. Banks: Privatization of Financial Relations," in Richard R. Fagen, ed., *Capitalism and the State in U.S.-Latin American Relations* (Stanford: Stanford University Press, 1979).

[9] Indeed, Pérez de Cuellar gained this international post soon after being rejected in Lima for the post of ambassador to Brazil. See Michael Berlin, "With the World on Edge, the U.N. Turns to a Quiet Peruvian," *Los Angeles Times,* January 3, 1982.

fied in the post-hoc "Plan Inca" released in 1974), the experiment obviously failed. That point is amply demonstrated in this volume—although the number of structural, systemic, conjunctural, and accidental factors cited in these chapters to explain the failure suggests that caution should be exercised in deriving lessons from Peru's experience.

Judged by a different standard, however, Peru's military leaders largely succeeded. If one defines the Peruvian experiment as the core program of nationalist affirmation, economic modernization, antioligarchical reform, and systematic state-building supported institutionally by the armed forces in 1968, the agenda was implemented to an impressive degree.

When Peru's armed forces took power in October 1968, they sought to break an impasse that had prevented several overdue reforms from being adopted. Measures previously undertaken in many other Latin American countries had in Peru long been thwarted. Peru's traditional landed interests still had such a hold on the country's agriculture, finance, politics, and the press that reforms could be put off even when substantial national consensus had already been reached. By 1968, virtually all politically aware Peruvians not themselves directly dependent on perpetuating a preindustrial, land-based system of nearly feudal character agreed on the need for structural transformations. It was widely understood that Peru needed to redistribute land and other property; to extend more widely education, suffrage, and political participation; to create a stronger state and to undertake national planning; to establish controls in order to assure that foreign investment would better serve the country; and to reduce Peru's external vulnerability. But overwhelming agreement on these points among professionals, intellectuals, politicians, technocrats, labor leaders, and industrialists had not produced action.

The efforts to change one of the world's most inequitable patterns of land tenure illustrate how Peru's establishment first kept the issue from being debated, then vetoed reforms, and finally frustrated the implementation of those measures that were eventually adopted.[10] The power of a few families to keep agrarian reform from being undertaken, even after all major political parties had endorsed the con-

[10] This discussion draws from Lowenthal, "Peru's Ambiguous Revolution," in Lowenthal, ed., *The Peruvian Experiment*, pp. 26–30, and from the many sources cited there. For an analysis of the contradictions that plagued the military government's agrarian reform efforts, see José María Caballero, *From Belaúnde to Belaúnde: Peru's Military Experiment in Third-Roadism,* Working Paper Series, no. 36 (Cambridge, England: Center of Latin American Studies, 1981).

cept and in the face of mounting peasant violence in some parts of the country, contributed importantly to the Peruvian army's sense that its own intervention was needed. The military's successful, if limited, experience with an agrarian reform in the La Convención region during their temporary rule in 1962–1963 reinforced their perception that "reform from above" under military auspices could prevent the emergence of a national security threat from a mobilized peasantry.[11]

Proposals to strengthen Peru's state and to require foreign investment to serve national needs were also familiar but long put off. Almost every writer on Peru's problems in this century has emphasized the need to strengthen the nation's anemic public sphere, but Peru in the mid-1960s still allowed taxes to be collected by a private banking firm, which actually charged the government for the use of its own revenue. Peru's Central Bank in the 1960s was still directly responsive to narrow private interests. The Peruvian state's share of national investment in the 1960s was lower than that in any comparable South American nation. As for foreign investment, Peru's governments during the 1950s had conspicuously bucked the prevailing Latin American nationalist trend.[12] Peru in those years granted one concession after another to foreign investors in mining, petroleum, and manufacturing. President Belaúnde's inability to resolve the controversy over the International Petroleum Company—that is, to end IPC's anomalous exemptions from Peru's laws—symbolized the problem of external dependence.

Some headway was made on many of these long-standing issues during Belaúnde's period, but stalemate had developed on many fronts by 1968, and frustration was deepening.[13] One source of difficulty was the power of the congress to block change, and the disproportionate influence in the congress of traditional interests; the exceptional powers granted to Finance Minister Manuel Ulloa in the summer of 1968 were a belated attempt to overcome these obstacles. Another source was competitive jockeying for advantage among the political parties, each of them interested in an immediate electoral

[11] See Wesley Craig, "The Peasant Movement of La Convención," in Henry Landsberger, ed., *Latin American Peasant Movements* (Ithaca, N.Y.: Cornell University Press, 1969); and José Z. García, "Military Government in Peru, 1968–1971" (Doctoral dissertation, University of New Mexico, Albuquerque, 1973).

[12] See Shane Hunt, "Direct Foreign Investment in Peru: New Rules for an Old Game," in Lowenthal, ed., *The Peruvian Experiment*, pp. 302–349.

[13] The best discussion of this period is Jane S. Jaquette, "The Politics of Development in Peru," Dissertation Series, Latin American Studies Program (Ithaca, N.Y.: Cornell University, 1971).

edge. A third was perceived weakness and incompetence in the executive, illustrated in the IPC imbroglio, the final twist of which—the controversy over a supposed missing page in the IPC agreement—fatally weakened Belaúnde's regime.

Into this context of programmatic consensus and political impasse entered Peru's armed forces. Their core program—announced generally in the first manifesto on October 3 and further expanded in the provisional national planning document evolved during their first three months—comprised the reform agenda common to Belaúnde's Acción Popular, Haya de la Torre's APRA, and the Christian Democratic parties. What distinguished Peru's military rulers was not the originality of their program, but their capacity to put familiar ideas into effect.

Almost immediately, for instance, Peru's military rulers resolved the IPC imbroglio. Although negotiations dragged on for years (until some modest, disguised compensation was eventually paid), the political fact is that after IPC's installations were physically taken over and the company nationalized on October 9, the case ceased to be an issue. A problem which Peru's civilian politicians had been unable to tackle for a generation was removed by Peru's army within seven days.

The armed forces acted with similar decisiveness in other realms, albeit after some delay to build internal consensus.[14] In June 1969, they decreed and began at once to implement a sweeping agrarian reform, starting boldly with the rich sugar estates of the coast. During the course of the next five years, the agrarian reform was extended rapidly and extensively until it became one of the hemisphere's most thorough rural transformations.

Other reform measures followed in a flurry, some 4,000 laws in all. By 1973, the armed forces had gone well beyond its initial agenda and the underlying institutional consensus that had been established, and had begun to undertake steps that were increasingly radical in concept and tone.[15] By 1975, indeed, the Peruvian experiment had gone so far that some influential military leaders thought it threatened the interests of the armed forces as an institution. At that point,

[14] See David Scott Palmer, *Peru: The Authoritarian Tradition* (New York: Praeger Publishers, 1980), pp. 102–103.

[15] See Lowenthal, "Peru's Ambiguous Revolution," Lowenthal, ed., *The Peruvian Experiment*, especially pp. 18–20, for a discussion of the extension and radicalization of Peru's experiment. Important insights about this process may be found in this volume in the chapters by Cynthia McClintock and by Peter Cleaves and Henry Pease García.

some reverses occurred—both before and after General Velasco's ouster in August 1975—but the experiment did not end, nor were its first and fundamental reforms ever undone.

By the time Peru's armed forces relinquished power in 1980, much of its initial "core" program had been achieved, in fact. The country's land tenure system had been substantially and permanently altered. Although the state's growth had been more rapid than could be effectively managed, a significantly stronger public apparatus had been created. National planning had been institutionalized. The number of Peruvians actively participating in the national polity—as reflected in the growth of the potential and actual electorate between 1963 and 1980, for example—had vastly expanded, thanks in large measure to the military's decision to extend suffrage to the illiterate. So had the number and strength of the organizations through which Peruvians could pursue their interests—cooperatives, unions, and neighborhood organizations.

As for Peru's international relationships, Peru did not overcome dependence during this period, but it did gain national stature, dignity, and self-confidence previously notably absent.[16] The nation's relationships with foreign investors became considerably more symmetrical in fact and in perception, in large part because of the state's expanded role.[17] Peru gained military strength in comparison with its immediate neighbors, Chile and Ecuador, thus alleviating a long-standing national trauma (although perhaps at excessive financial cost). The country's international relationships became considerably more diverse and have remained so. And although Peru's general international stature has receded substantially since the early 1970s, its foreign policy remains considerably more assertive and independent (at least of the United States) than before 1968.[18]

In all these respects, Peru's military rulers contributed importantly

[16] I am indebted on this point to an extensive unpublished paper by Ricardo Luna, a member of Peru's diplomatic service. See also Stephen Gorman, "Peruvian Foreign Policy since 1975: External Political and Economic Initiatives," in Elizabeth G. Ferris and Jenny K. Lincoln, ed., *Latin American Foreign Policies: Global and Regional Dimensions* (Boulder, Colo.: Westview, 1981).

[17] Stanley F. Rose, *The Peruvian Revolution's Approach: Investment Policy and Climate 1968–1980* (Buffalo, N.Y.: William S. Hein, 1981).

[18] An analysis of Peru's voting record in the United Nations during the past fifteen years shows, for instance, that Peru, continued even after its return to civilian rule to take positions different from those of the United States much more often than before 1968. See Richard Sholk, "U.S.-Peruvian Foreign Policy Divergence in U.N. General Assembly Voting, 1963–79" (November 1981). An interesting question is whether Peru's foreign policy now is independent of other international sources, particularly the Non-Aligned Movement.

to overcoming the previous gap between the country's evolving socio-economic realities and its political institutions and public policies. During these years, Peru experienced, in accelerated form, changes of structure and policy that had occurred in countries like Chile and Brazil over several decades of populist politics. The country's modernization overwhelmed traditional patterns. In this fundamental sense, Peru's experiment succeeded.[19] The fact that early efforts by the Belaúnde regime to undo some of the military's reforms were resisted, and then even abandoned, is eloquent testimony to this success.[20]

PERU TRANSFORMED

President Belaúnde's return to Peru's National Palace in 1980—and his insistent reiteration of many elements of the program he had offered Peru's voters fully eighteen years earlier—gave many observers a sense of *déjà vu*. Some argued that Peru was going back fundamentally to things as they were before the twelve-year interlude of military rule, or even earlier. Other analysts who would not take this stance, including most of the authors in this volume, still emphasize continuity more than change as the main legacy of those years.

Obviously, there is much to support this view. Belaúnde himself has changed remarkably little. Many of his principal colleagues, including Ulloa, are back. The traditional political parties prominent in the 1960s dominate Congress once again, and Belaúnde's Acción Popular is not the only party sticking close to its earlier program; APRA and the Christian Democratic party are likewise adhering to earlier postulates. The Peruvian state is rapidly withdrawing from many sectors of the economy. Major efforts are underway again to attract foreign investment. Foreign borrowing remains high, as Peru continues to seek an external solution for its lack of internally generated capital. Debate in Peru has resurfaced between nationalist/protectionist and internationalist/export-oriented interest groups. So has frustration with congressional obstacles to new legislation, and even (in 1981) the use of a temporary period of "emergency powers" to break a legislative impasse (as in June 1968).

More fundamentally, Peru's continuity is evident in many ways.

[19] Compare the parallel but distinct discussions in Palmer, *Peru: The Authoritarian Tradition,* and Ernest H. Preeg, *The Evolution of a Revolution: Peru and Its Relations with the United States, 1968–1980* (Washington, D.C.: National Planning Association, 1981).

[20] Carlos Franco, "Una Mirada al futuro, 1968-1978," *Marka* (October 8, 1981), pp. 30–31.

Peru is still overwhelmingly poor. As one Peruvian intellectual pointed out after the devastating 1970 earthquake, many highland Peruvians live every day in conditions outsiders seem to notice only after a natural disaster: makeshift housing, inadequate food, no schools, no potable water, no access to medical care, and utter isolation.[21] The Peruvian experiment did not alter these grim realities.

Compounding its poverty, Peru is still unintegrated. It remains largely split ethnically, fractured geographically, and divided by class; income distribution is still badly skewed. Most rural Peruvians did not obtain land from the agrarian reform. Peru's urban poor did not fare appreciably better than before the military takeover. Many industrial workers did not become members of the "industrial communities" the military regime created because their firms were not large enough; most of those who did join such communities did not receive significant benefits. Relatively few have benefited from the extension of social security benefits, for only an aristocracy of workers qualifies for the system. Although year-round sugar workers gained handsomely from the agrarian reforms, thousands of seasonal workers on the sugar estates were unhelped, if not made even more marginal than before. Almost all the income redistribution effectuated by Peru's reforms has occurred within the wealthiest quarter of the population.[22]

[21] Augusto Salazar Bondy, "Peru: Un Antiguo Desastre," in Bondy, ed., *Entre Escila y Caribdis* (Lima: Instituto Nacional de Cultura, 1973), pp. 121–128.

[22] There are a number of works on the distributive implications of the Peruvian military government's reforms. For a general discussion of income distribution, see Webb, *Government Policy and the Distribution of Income in Peru, 1963–1973*; Adolfo Figueroa, "The Impact of Current Reforms on Income Distribution in Peru," in Alejandro Foxley, ed., *Income Distribution in Latin America* (London: Cambridge University Press, 1976); and Carlos Amat y León and Héctor León, *Distribución del Ingreso Familiar* (Lima: Universidad del Pacífico, 1981).

On agrarian reform, see José María Caballero, *Agricultura, Reforma Agraria y Pobreza Campesina* (Lima: Instituto de Estudios Peruanos, 1980); or *Agrarian Reform and the Transformation of the Peruvian Countryside*, Working Paper Series, no. 29 (Cambridge, England: Center of Latin American Studies, 1977).

On industrial reform, see Roberto Abusada-Salah, "Propiedad Social: Algunas Consideraciones Económicas," *Documentos de Trabajo CISEPA* (Lima: Pontífica Universidad Católica, October 1973); "Reformas Estructurales y Crisis Económica en el Sector Industrial Peruano," Latin American Program Working Paper, no. 29 (Washington, D.C.: The Wilson Center, 1978); and Giorgio Alberti, Jorge Santistevan, and Luis Pásara, *Estado y Clase: La Comunidad Industrial en el Perú* (Lima: Instituto de Estudios Peruanos, 1977).

For a discussion of the urban poor, see Henry A. Dietz, *Poverty and Problem-Solving under Military Rule: The Urban Poor in Lima, Peru* (Austin: University of Texas Press, 1980).

Many of the problems Peru faces in the 1980s are still the historic ones Peruvians have been talking about and trying to deal with for generations: lack of national integration, economic backwardness, badly exploited natural resources, and dependence. It is striking that many of the points made by Haya de la Torre and by José Carlos Mariátegui sixty years ago—and even by Manuel González Prada a century ago—are still centrally relevant in Peru today.[23]

All this is true. Historians a generation from now, therefore, will undoubtedly understand the twelve-year Peruvian experiment largely in terms of its essential continuity with the nation's past. But it is important to emphasize, more than most of the other essays in this volume do, how much Peru actually was transformed during the military years. Peru in the 1980s is *not* Peru as it was before 1968.

What has changed most in Peru is the structure and distribution of power. The traditional landed families and their financial institutions have lost most of their influence.[24] Most of Peru's former oligarchs have fallen from unquestioned authority to oblivion or even ignominy. The major newspapers—*La Prensa* and *El Comercio*—that for so long established the limits of debate in Peru have been severely weakened, and no comparably influential newspaper has yet emerged.[25] No publication successfully defines issues for discussion in Peru today (and the best candidates to assume this role—*El Observador* and *Caretas,* for example—are vulnerable in part because they are unconnected to the old power structure). The Catholic Church, once very prominent, is barely visible. The presence and influence of the United

---

Regarding the social security system, see Carmelo Mesa-Lago, *Social Security in Latin America: Pressure Groups, Stratification, and Inequality* (Pittsburgh: University of Pittsburgh Press, 1978), chapter 4.

On sugar workers, see Santiago Roca, *Las Cooperativas Azucareras del Perú: Distribución de Ingresos* (Lima: ESAN Campodónico, 1975). See also Cynthia McClintock, "Post-Revolutionary Agrarian Politics in Peru," in Stephen Gorman, ed., *Post-Revolutionary Politics in Peru* (Boulder, Colo.: Westview, 1982).

[23] See Julio Cotler, *Clase, Estado, y Nación en el Perú* (Lima: Instituto de Estudios Peruanos, 1978). Cf. John N. Plank, "Peru: A Study in the Problem of Nation-Forming" (Doctoral dissertation, Harvard University, 1958); and Manuel González Prada, *Horas de Lucha* (Callao: Tip. "Lux," 1924).

[24] Henry Pease García, *El Ocaso del Poder Oligárquico: Lucha Política en la Escena Oficial, 1968–1975* (Lima: DESCO, 1977). See also Dennis L. Gilbert, "The Oligarchy and the Old Regime in Peru," Latin American Dissertation Series, no. 69 (Ithaca, N.Y.: Cornell University, 1977).

[25] For a critical discussion of press reform under the military government, see David Booth, "The Reform of the Press in Peru: Myths and Realities," in David Booth and Bernardo Sorj, eds., *Military Reformism and Social Classes: Aspects of the Peruvian Experience, 1968–1980* (London: Macmillan & Co., forthcoming).

States—both of the American Embassy and of United States corporations and other institutions—are sharply reduced. The armed forces themselves are on the defensive: discredited, widely disdained, credibly accused of corruption and incompetence, wary about getting drawn back into the political vortex.

Where has all the power gone? In part, to new entrepreneurs who have made a great deal of money during the past decade, mainly in import substitution industries, in mining, and in real estate. New "first families"—nationally oriented, aggressive, and conspicuous— have begun to emerge in Lima. These families lack the social prestige and the political connections of the displaced upper class, but they are beginning to express themselves politically through the media and special interest associations. Less tied to foreign interests than previous elites, more oriented toward the production of consumer goods and less inclined to rely on interlocking financial networks to assure their wealth, these newly rich Peruvians could help change Peru in the years to come if they are able to provide the entrepreneurial dynamism the country has always lacked.

In part, power has also gravitated to the extensive technocracy that emerged as a result of the state's rapid expansion.[26] Even though the state's economic role has receded somewhat since 1975, the important influence of trained personnel—economists, engineers, agronomists, social scientists, administrators of all kinds—has become a fixture in Peru, in both the public and the private sector. A list of the most powerful persons in Peru today would undoubtedly include several government ministers and heads of public enterprises of middle class (or more humble) background with no source of influence beyond their own expertise.[27] The technocracy—expanding, reformist, committed to change—has not yet found a vehicle of its own for political expression, but its influence is growing nevertheless.

A third source of power—and also one of expanding significance—

[26] See David G. Becker, " 'Bonanza Development' and the 'New Bourgeoisie' in Peru under Military Rule," *Comparative Political Studies* (Fall 1982), for a discussion of the "new bourgeoisie," which rose to a position of dominance under military rule. Becker suggests that reform of the educational system and certain policies toward transnational corporations (TNCs) endowed the bourgeoisie with "knowledge capital" and a "managerial ideology," which allowed it to adapt successfully to late capitalism.

[27] *Caretas* (issue no. 658, August 3, 1981) reports that interviews with one hundred Peruvian opinion leaders revealed that the ten individuals perceived as most powerful included President Belaúnde and his wife, two major business figures, two leading political figures outside the government, and four cabinet officers, most of whom are more technocrats than political figures in their own right.

has been the increasingly mobilized populace. Trade unions, still heavily influenced by political parties, are far stronger than they were in the 1960s, despite recent efforts to weaken them. Many more Peruvians are union members than before, and they are increasingly militant, able to call and to implement national or regional general strikes and otherwise to demonstrate their force.[28] *Campesinos* lack a well-articulated structure following the military regime's disbanding of the Confederación Nacional Agraria, which it had created, but the military's urge to abort the CNA was itself something of a testimony to its significance and potential. The presence and influence of at least some peasants in the national political process—those in the cooperatives created by the military regime—is much greater than ever before in Peru's history.[29]

A significant share of Peru's expanded electorate is militantly anti-establishment, in ways that never previously happened in Peru. Five leftist parties won over 31 percent of the vote in the 1978 election for the Constituent Assembly, an astonishing gain over the 6 percent that leftist parties registered in 1962. The leftists garnered only 16 percent of the vote in 1980, but they still represent an unprecedentedly strong force for change in Peru. Indeed, it is possible that they may eventually bring to Peru some of the revolutionary transformations Peru's army vanguard promised but could not deliver.

Peru has been altered in other significant ways as well. The country's economic structure was substantially transformed during these years. The military government oversaw a major building of the nation's industrial infrastructure. Steel production multiplied from 80,000 metric tons in 1967 to 450,000 in 1974; cement production more than doubled—from 1 million metric tons in 1967 to 2.3 million in 1973. Both energy production and consumption rose steadily, faster than in any previous period. Industry's share of the national economy continued to rise from 22 percent of the national product in 1964 to over 26 percent in 1975. The share of exports accounted for by nontraditional sources (mainly industrial goods) multiplied from 3 percent in 1970 to 22 percent in 1980. For comparison, steel production rose more gradually in Colombia between 1967 and 1974, from

[28] Evelyn H. Stephens, "The Velasco Regime; Its Legacy, and the Return to Democratic Politics in Peru," manuscript (March 1981). See also Julian Laite, "Miners and National Politics in Peru, 1900–1974," *Journal of Latin American Studies* 12, no. 2 (November 1980), pp. 317–340, especially 335–340.

[29] See Howard Handelman, "Peasants, Landlords, and Bureaucrats: The Politics of Agrarian Reform in Peru," American Universities Field Staff, *Reports for South America*, no. 1 (1981).

207,000 metric tons to 244,000; Chile's steel production was unchanged, at 596,000 for both years. The share of manufacturing industry in Colombian GDP rose from 21 percent to 22 percent between 1963 and 1975; for Chile, the proportion fell from 24 to 21 percent in the same period.[30]

The country's public administration has been drastically altered. In the mid-1960s, Peru had one of the hemisphere's weakest and most chaotic bureaucracies. Now the Peruvian state—including its public enterprises—has emerged as one of the strongest in Latin America.[31] Public employees have tripled, and the national budget rose 246 percent between 1970 and 1976. The state's share of the national economy climbed from 24.7 percent in 1968 to 49.9 percent in 1977.[32] Its role in several crucial sectors—the economy's commanding heights, which used to be dominated by foreign investment—is even greater.[33] And the modes, practice, and even language of public administration have been sharply changed since 1968.

The role and influence of foreign private corporations, in turn, has been drastically curtailed. Some have been eliminated entirely: IPC, Grace, Marcona, and Cerro de Pasco, several fishmeal companies, and a few public utilities. Those that remain—Southern Peru Copper Corporation, Occidental Petroleum, and various manufacturing and

[30] On steel, cement, and energy, see *U.N. Statistical Yearbook* (New York: U.N. Statistical Office, various years). On industry's share of the Peruvian national economy, see E.V.K. FitzGerald, *The Political Economy of Perú, 1956–78: Economic Development and the Restructuring of Capital* (Cambridge: Cambridge University Press, 1979), p. 69. (For the other countries, see *U.N. Statistical Yearbook.*) On non-traditional exports, see DESCO, *Estrategias y Políticas de Industrialización* (Lima, 1981), p. 268.

[31] See Peter S. Cleaves and Martin J. Scurrah, *Agriculture, Bureaucracy, and Military Government in Peru* (Ithaca, N.Y.: Cornell University Press, 1980).

For a further discussion of Peru's underdeveloped state apparatus before 1968, see Shane Hunt, "Distribution, Growth and Government Economic Behavior in Peru," in Gustav Ranis, ed., *Government and Economic Development* (New Haven, Conn.: Yale University Press, 1971), pp. 375–428.

[32] Budget figures are final-consumption expenditures of the central government, based on purchase cost at current prices, calculated from Instituto Nacional de Estadística, Dirección General de Cuentas Nacionales, *Cuentas Nacionales del Perú, 1950–1978* (Lima, 1978), pp. 47–51. For state share of national economy, see Cleaves and Scurrah, *Agriculture, Bureaucracy and Military Government*, p. 72. This calculation of the public sector as percentage of GNP includes central government, social security, and state enterprises, based on Central Bank figures. I am indebted to Richard Sholk for research assistance on this point.

[33] Cf. the role played by United States corporations in Peru in the 1960s as reported by Charles T. Goodsell in *American Corporations and Peruvian Politics* (Cambridge: Harvard University Press, 1974.)

service companies—are more subject to the state's control than before. Control over foreign corporations has been reinforced by Peru's adherence to Decision 24 of the Andean Pact and solidarity with UNCTAD (United Nations Conference on Trade and Development) and SELA (Latin American Economic System) negotiating positions. The foreign share of the corporate sector in Peru's economy is now less than half what it was in 1968 in aggregate dollar terms, and it is even further reduced in terms of effective political and economic leverage.[34] Foreign (including United States) banks are certainly more exposed and involved in Peru than they used to be, but their profile is low and their political influence is limited, much less than that of the earlier mining corporations and utilities.

Finally, and interrelated with all these other trends, Peru's value structure has changed significantly, at least in part as a result of the military experiment.[35] This point is hard to document, but those familiar with Peru recognize the change: the kind of people who attend the Cine Pacífico in Miraflores; the looks exchanged between Peruvians of different classes; the attitudes felt and expressed toward foreigners and toward highland Indians; the assumptions about the possibility of social mobility in Peru; attitudes and practices in male-female relations; educational concepts and procedures; the recognition of Quechua as an official national language; and so on. These changes in values and expectations, though intangible, will have powerful consequences.

Not all the changes that occurred during these years were caused or even intended by Peru's armed forces. Trade union militancy and leftist mobilization, for example, occurred against the will of substantial sectors of the military, as Liisa North makes clear. The legitimation of middle-class aspirations ran counter to the aim of at least some military officers for a solidary, classless society. The emergence of stronger regional self-consciousness and assertiveness in parts of Peru contradicted the objective of fuller national integration. But all these shifts did occur, and they may fairly be attributed, at least in part, to the Peruvian experiment. Transformative trends which had been underway in Peru were reinforced and some considerably accelerated by the military rulers. The Peruvian experiment, then, was not a simple interlude, but an important transition in the country's history.

It is impossible to know, of course, what will happen to Peru next.

[34] FitzGerald, *The Political Economy of Perú*, pp. 119–21.

[35] Among members of peasant cooperatives, for instance, considerable changes in values and attitudes are documented by Cynthia McClintock in *Peasant Cooperatives and Political Change in Peru* (Princeton: Princeton University Press, 1981).

Will Belaúnde's new term usher in a period of strengthened participatory politics, or will it be a mere interval between military takeovers? Will the Peruvian "Unified Left" manage to coalesce, or will its potential to affect Peru's politics again be dissipated? Will APRA, Peru's oldest and largest party but increasingly a collection of old men and their memories, provide a ready constituency and apparatus for a new political movement, or will it frustrate the efforts of others to build popular support? Will the incipient terrorism of the early 1980s spread, will it be severely repressed, or will the nation's political institutions co-opt antisystem sentiment?

Will Peru's economic modernization continue and deepen, or will the nation's growth be stifled in an unfavorable international environment? Will Peru become an increasingly integrated nation, or will sharpening income disparities polarize it still further? How will the drug traffic affect Peru's society, economy, and politics? What role will be played in Peru's future by the expanded and experienced technocracy? by the mobilized peasantry? by the militant trade unions? by the politicized military?

Such questions cannot be answered now. Until they can be, however, the ultimate significance of Peru's experiment will not be clear.

Index

Abusada-Salah, Roberto, 125, 390n
Acción Popular, *see* AP
accumulation model, 23, 29, 65, 67–69, 73, 76, 77, 84, 88, 324
ADEX (Association of Exporters), 230, 339
administrative reform, 113–15, 221–26, 224, 225, 231–32, 242–43, 258, 273, 318, 334, 428
Agency for International Development, *see* AID
agrarian reform, 5, 95–96, 103–104, 105, 109, 114, 131, 239, 289, 341, 363n, 372–73, 419–20, 421; benefits of, 384–85; need for, 41, 249, 320; populism and, 284–95; progressives and, 290–95; SINAMOS and, 287–88, 289–92, 294; Velasco regime and, 229, 275–276, 279, 284–95. *See also* property
Agrarian Reform Law, 225, 238, 288n, 340, 341, 373
agricultural cooperatives, *see* cooperatives; and *Centrales*
agricultural societies of social interest, *see* SAISs
Agriculture, Ministry of, 223–24, 229, 287, 290, 292
AID (Agency of International Development), 161, 164
Alberti, Georgio, 341–42
Alianza Popular Revolucionaria Americana, *see* APRA
Alliance for Progress, 16, 88, 286
Amazon, 66, 76, 117, 191n–92n, 315
American Smelting and Refining Company, 189n, 191n
Anaconda Copper Company, 189n
Andean Pact, 22, 76, 152, 202, 260, 261, 275–76, 313, 394, 418, 429; Andean market, 76, 154, 156, 182,

192–93, 194, 196, 202; Andean oil pipeline, 21, 76, 155
AP (Acción Popular, Popular Action), 30, 31, 33, 99, 215, 219, 267–68, 421, 423
APRA (or Apra or Aprista Party; Alianza Popular Revolucionaria Americana, American Popular Revolutionary Alliance), 11, 14, 30, 99, 161, 214, 267–68, 289, 323–24, 423; Belaúde's government and, 16, 17, 237–38; capitalism and, 17–18, 20, 25; "Convivencia" and, 13–14, 16; Haya de la Torre and, 8–9, 30–31, 421; history of, 7, 8–9, 246–48, 249, 310; Odría's dictatorship and, 11, 13–14, 15, 16, 17, 250; oligarchy and, 7–10, 13–14, 15, 215, 238; reform program of, 15, 16, 327; RGAF and, 18, 30, 32, 33, 215, 246–47, 249, 310, 327
Aprista Party, *see* APRA
Argentina, 111, 118, 236, 273, 274, 387–414 passim
armed forces, *see* Revolutionary Government of the Armed Forces
arms purchases, 26, 27, 28, 118, 169, 171, 237, 315
Association of Exporters, *see* ADEX
August 1975 coup, 148–49, 202n, 240, 245, 276, 317. *See also* Velasco Alvarado, Juan, ouster of
autonomy of state, 29, 30, 44, 66, 68–69, 209–244 passim, 343

balance of payments, 17, 26, 43, 45, 47, 53, 55, 57, 60, 79, 80–82, 95n, 115, 120, 126, 107, 163n, 198; economic policies and, 132–33, 201; import substitution and, 112–13; Phase Two and, 122, 167–68

Library of Congress Cataloging in Publication Data

Main entry under title:
The Peruvian experiment reconsidered.

Includes index.
1. Peru—Politics and government—
1968–   —Addresses, essays, lectures.
2. Peru—Economic conditions—
1968–   —Addresses, essays, lectures.
I. McClintock, Cynthia.   II. Lowenthal, Abraham F.
F3448.2.P49   1983   320.985   82-61377
ISBN 0-691-07648-0 / ISBN 0-691-02214-3 (pbk.)

							0
							2 **He** Helium 4.00260

			III A	IV A	V A	VI A	VII A	
			5 **B** Boron 10.81	6 **C** Carbon 12.011	7 **N** Nitrogen 14.0067	8 **O** Oxygen 15.9994	9 **F** Fluorine 18.998403	10 **Ne** Neon 20.179

	I B	II B	13 **Al** Aluminum 26.98154	14 **Si** Silicon 28.0855	15 **P** Phosphorus 30.97376	16 **S** Sulfur 32.06	17 **Cl** Chlorine 35.453	18 **Ar** Argon 39.948
28 **Ni** Nickel 58.69	29 **Cu** Copper 63.546	30 **Zn** Zinc 65.38	31 **Ga** Gallium 69.72	32 **Ge** Germanium 72.59	33 **As** Arsenic 74.9216	34 **Se** Selenium 78.96	35 **Br** Bromine 79.904	36 **Kr** Krypton 83.80
46 **Pd** Palladium 106.42	47 **Ag** Silver 107.868	48 **Cd** Cadmium 112.41	49 **In** Indium 114.82	50 **Sn** Tin 118.69	51 **Sb** Antimony 121.75	52 **Te** Tellurium 127.60	53 **I** Iodine 126.9045	54 **Xe** Xenon 131.29
78 **Pt** Platinum 195.08	79 **Au** Gold 196.9665	80 **Hg** Mercury 200.59	81 **Tl** Thallium 204.383	82 **Pb** Lead 207.2	83 **Bi** Bismuth 208.9804	84 **Po** Polonium (209)[a]	85 **At** Astatine (210)[a]	86 **Rn** Radon (222)[a]

metals ← → nonmetals

63 **Eu** Europium 151.96	64 **Gd** Gadolinium 157.25	65 **Tb** Terbium 158.9254	66 **Dy** Dysprosium 162.50	67 **Ho** Holmium 164.9304	68 **Er** Erbium 167.26	69 **Tm** Thulium 168.9342	70 **Yb** Ytterbium 173.04	71 **Lu** Lutetium 174.967
95 **Am** Americium (243)[a]	96 **Cm** Curium (247)[a]	97 **Bk** Berkelium (247)[a]	98 **Cf** Californium (251)[a]	99 **Es** Einsteinium (252)[a]	100 **Fm** Fermium (257)[a]	101 **Md** Mendelevium (258)[a]	102 **No** Nobelium (259)[a]	103 **Lr** Lawrencium (260)[a]

C H E M I S T R Y Sixth Edition

Charles E. Mortimer

Muhlenberg College

Wadsworth Publishing Company • Belmont, California • A Division of Wadsworth, Inc.

To J.S.M. and C.E.M.$^{(II)}$

Chemistry Editor: Jack C. Carey
Production Editor: Harold Humphrey
Managing Designer: MaryEllen Podgorski
Cover and Text Designer: Adriane Bosworth
Cover Photographs: Hoar frost crystal by Stephen J. Krasemann, Peter Arnold, Inc.; sand dunes © David Muench, 1985.
Print Buyer: Karen Hunt
Art Supervision and Page Layout: Wendy Calmenson
Copy Editor: Gregory Gullickson
Technical Illustration: J & R Art Services; Victor Royer
Photo Research: Tobi Zausner; Roberta Spieckerman Associates
Editorial Assistant: Ruth Singer
Compositor: Syntax International

Printed in the United States of America

1 2 3 4 5 6 7 8 9 10——90 89 88 87 86

ISBN 0-534-05670-9

Library of Congress Cataloging in Publication Data

Mortimer, Charles E.
  Chemistry.

  Includes index.
  1. Chemistry,   I. Title.
QD31.2.M65   1986   540   85–11490
ISBN 0–534–05670–9

PREFACE

This text has now evolved through six editions. Throughout the years, the book has been modified not only because chemistry is a large and growing field, but also because the needs, interests, and abilities of the student audience are constantly changing. Nevertheless, the work has been rooted in a constant philosophy. It was written to explain chemistry, not just present chemical facts. As a result, each new concept is explained as fully as necessary for understanding, simplified where necessary, but never distorted.

In the present edition, the first chapter, with its overview of the history of chemistry, certain chemical terms, the metric system, significant figures, and calculation method, sets the scene for the remainder of the book. The method used to solve problems is presented using easily understood nonchemical examples.

Chapter 2, a new chapter, contains an introduction to *atomic theory*. Details of the electronic structure of atoms and of nuclear chemistry are left for later (Chapters 6 and 27), but enough material on atomic theory is presented to offer a firm base for the introduction of stoichiometry.

Stoichiometry is central to an understanding of all chemical concepts. The early introduction of stoichiometry not only permits it to be used throughout the entire course (which reinforces student skills) but also allows for the gradual enlargement of the topic. Furthermore, this early placement facilitates the design of a coordinated laboratory program (for which *solution stoichiometry* is included). Because stoichiometry is often difficult for beginning students, it has been developed more slowly. For ease in handling, it has been divided into two parts—one centering on *formulas* and *compounds* (Chapter 3), and the other focusing on the *chemical reaction* (Chapter 4).

Thermochemistry (Chapter 5) follows stoichiometry, underscoring the fact that chemistry is concerned with both energy and matter and that both are amenable to quantitative treatment. The early discussion of thermochemistry prepares the way for the use of energy concepts (such as ionization energy, lattice energy, and bond energy) in the development of later topics.

In the next seven chapters, the structure and physical properties of matter are covered in order of increasing complexity. The *electronic structure of atoms* (covered in Chapter 6) leads to the consideration of chemical bonding—the *ionic bond* (in Chapter 7), a basic presentation of the *covalent bond* and *resonance* (in Chapter 8) and *molecular geometry*, *hybridization*, and *molecular orbitals* (in Chapter 9). The states of matter are covered in Chapters 10 (*gases*) and 11 (*liquids* and *solids*). Chapter 12 consists of a discussion of the physical properties of *solutions*.

Reactions in Aqueous Solution, Chapter 13, introduced in the last edition, has been well received. This chapter is placed after the chapter on solutions, which it logically follows. The discussion of reactions of this type, which constitute a high proportion of all chemical reactions investigated, lays the groundwork for later discussions (notably ionic equilibria, acids and bases, electrochemistry, and descriptive chemistry). Furthermore, the chapter presents a vehicle for the introduction of oxidation-reduction reactions somewhat earlier than in the chapter on electrochemistry (Chapter 20).

This detailed study of the chemical reaction is continued in the next sequence of chapters. The rates of chemical reactions (*chemical kinetics*) is the topic of Chapter 14. The four chapters that follow (15 through 18) present *chemical equilibrium*, a large and important topic. *Chemical Thermodynamics* (Chapter 19) is written in a way that focuses on the chemical reaction and equilibrium systems.

Electrochemistry is postponed until after thermodynamics and equilibrium have been discussed so that principles of thermodynamics (particularly Gibbs free energy) and equilibrium (notably, expressions for equilibrium constants) can be used to develop electrochemical concepts (electromotive force, electrode potentials, the Nernst equation).

Descriptive chemistry occupies most of the remainder of the book: *nonmetals* (Chapters 21 through 24), *metals* and *complex compounds* (Chapters 25 and 26), *organic chemistry* (Chapter 28), and *biochemistry* (Chapter 29). *Nuclear Chemistry* (Chapter 27) has been completely reworked in this edition.

This organization of topics is not meant to be restrictive. The format of this book is intended to permit relatively wide latitude in course organization. Over the years, many chapters have been divided in an effort to make the text more flexible and to facilitate the preparation of a course outline (chapters on bonding, ionic equilibrium, and the descriptive chemistry of the nonmetals are examples). In this edition, both *Atomic Structure* and *Stoichiometry* have been divided.

A number of features appear in this book to help the student.

Examples, designed to illustrate how to solve chemical problems, are used extensively throughout the text.

Boxes are used to set off step by step directions for the solution of basic problems. Students find this boxed material useful for initial assignments and also for reference in later work.

Summaries, which are given at the end of each chapter, have been rewritten for this edition. They provide a succinct overview of the chapter, tie it together, and present it in a somewhat different light.

Key terms are listed (with section references) and defined at the end of each chapter. Students will find these lists useful as an aid in studying the material of the chapter and as a help in solving chapter-end problems. As a quick reference for later work, these key terms have been collected into a *Glossary* that appears in the *Appendix*. Important *new terms* continue to be set in boldface type at the point in the text where they are first introduced and defined.

Chapter-end problems are grouped according to type with the addition of a new category labeled as "unclassified." In each category except the unclassified group, the problems are paired into sets of similar problems. The answer to the odd-numbered problem (color-keyed) of each pair is given in the Appendix. Answers are not given for the even-numbered problem of the pair.

The *Appendix* has been expanded. It now includes a *Glossary of Key Terms, Answers to Color-Keyed Problems, Notes on Mathematical Operations*, plus an increased number of tables of constants and conversion factors. These extended lists of data now include: *Electrode Potentials, Equilibrium Constants, Thermodynamic Data* (standard enthalpies of formation, standard Gibbs free energies of formation, and standard absolute entropies), and *Average Bond Energies*.

For this edition we have a qualitative analysis version of the text. I am delighted that Larry Epstein of the University of Pittsburgh has updated the highly respected King and Caldwell qualitative analysis book and made it consistent with my text. So the student can more conveniently take the book to the laboratory, the material appears in paperback and is shrunk wrapped to the book (instead of being bound in the book), for those people who want a qualitative version.

The number of supplementary materials available for use with this text has been increased. The list includes: a new laboratory manual which has optional software for the last four experiments (by Lawrence Epstein), computer software keyed to the text (by Stan Smith of the University of Illinois and Elizabeth Kean of the University of Wisconsin), a study guide (by Donald and Louise Shive of Muhlenberg College), a test file (by Lawrence Epstein), a solutions manual (by the undersigned), an answer book, transparencies of selected key illustrations from the text, and the Wadsworth testing service available on IBM or Apple II e/c disks.

I sincerely thank the following persons for their comments and suggestions:

Craig Allen, Indiana University
Charles W. Armbruster, University of Missouri—St. Louis
James Bowser, State University of New York—College at Fredonia
Robert C. Brasted, University of Minnesota
Eugene R. Corey, University of Missouri—St. Louis
Lawrence M. Epstein, University of Pittsburgh
David T. Farrar, Cumberland College
James P. Friend, Drexel University
Milton E. Fuller, California State University—Hayward
John I. Gelder, Oklahoma State University
David Goldberg, Brooklyn College
Frank J. Gomba, U. S. Naval Academy
Robert Grimley, Purdue University
Charles G. Haas, Pennsylvania State University
Delwin Johnson, St. Louis Community College at Forest Park
Louis J. Kirschenbaum, University of Rhode Island
Doris Kolb, Illinois Central College
W. H. Nelson, University of Rhode Island
Gordon C. Parker, University of Toledo
Stephen B. W. Roeder, San Diego State University
Joe W. Vaughn, Northern Illinois University
Gordon H. Williams, Monterey Peninsula College
Stephen W. Yates, University of Kentucky

I also acknowledge, with thanks, the efforts of the Wadsworth staff in producing this book. Especial notice should be given to Jack Carey, Chemistry Editor; Harold Humphrey, Production Editor; and MaryEllen Podgorski, Managing Designer.

Suggestions for the improvement of this edition will be welcomed.

Charles E. Mortimer

BRIEF CONTENTS

DETAILED CONTENTS

INTRODUCTION

C H A P T E R

1

Chemistry may be defined as the science that is concerned with the characterization, composition, and transformations, of matter. This definition, however, is far from adequate. It fails to convey the spirit of chemistry, for it, like all science, is a vital, growing enterprise, not an accumulation of knowledge. The sciences are self-generating; the very nature of each new scientific concept stimulates fresh observation and experimentation that lead to progressive refinement as well as to the development of other concepts. Since the interests of scientific fields overlap, the boundaries between them are not distinct, and scientific concepts and methods find universal application. In the light of scientific growth, it is not surprising that a given scientific pursuit frequently crosses artificial, human-imposed boundaries.

Nevertheless, there is a common, if somewhat vague, understanding of the province of chemistry, and we must return to our preliminary definition. A fuller understanding will emerge as this book unfolds. Chemistry is concerned with the composition and the structure of substances and with the forces that hold these structures together. The physical properties of substances are studied, since they provide clues for structural determinations, serve as the basis for identification and classification, and indicate possible uses for specific materials. The *chemical reaction*, however, is the focus of chemistry. The interest of chemistry extends to every conceivable aspect of these transformations and includes such considerations as detailed descriptions of how and at what rates reactions proceed, the conditions required to bring about desired changes and to prevent undesired changes, the energy changes that accompany chemical reactions, the syntheses of substances that occur in nature and of those that have no natural counterparts, and the quantitative mass relations between the materials involved in chemical changes.

1.1 The Development of Modern Chemistry

Modern chemistry, which emerged late in the eighteenth century, took hundreds of years to develop. The story of its development can be divided roughly into five periods:

1. Practical arts (—— to 600 B.C.). The production of metals from ores, the manufacture of pottery, brewing, baking, and the preparation of dyes and of drugs are ancient arts. Archaeological evidence proves that the inhabitants of ancient Egypt and Mesopotamia were skilled in these crafts, but how and when the crafts first developed are not known.

These arts, which are chemical processes, became highly developed during this period. The development, however, was *empirical*, that is, based on practical experience alone without reference to underlying chemical principles. The Egyptian metalworkers knew how to obtain copper by heating malachite ore with charcoal. They did not know, nor did they seek to know, why the process worked and what actually occurred in the fire.

2. Greek theory (600 B.C. to 300 B.C.). The philosphical aspect (or theoretical aspect) of chemistry began in classical Greece about 600 B.C. The foundation of Greek science was the search for principles through which an understanding of nature could be obtained. Two theories of the Greeks became very important in the centuries that followed:

a. A concept that all substances found on earth are composed of four elements (earth, air, fire, and water) in various proportions originated with Greek philosophers of this period.

b. A theory that matter consists of separate and distinct units called **atoms** was proposed by Leucippus and extended by Democritus in the fifth century B.C.

Plato proposed that the atoms of one element differ in shape from the atoms of another. Furthermore, he believed that atoms of one element could be changed (or **transmuted**) into atoms of another by changing the shape of the atoms.

The concept of transmutation is also found in Aristotle's theories. Aristotle (who did not believe in the existence of atoms) proposed that the elements, and therefore all substances, are composed of the same primary matter and differ only in the forms that this matter assumes. To Aristotle, the form included not only the shape but also the qualities (such as color and hardness) that distinguish one substance from others. He proposed that changes in form constantly occur in nature and that all material things (animate and inanimate) grow and develop from immature forms to adult forms. (Throughout the Middle Ages, it was believed that minerals could grow and that mines would be replenished after minerals were removed from them.)

3. Alchemy (300 B.C. to 1650 A.D.). The philosophical tradition of ancient Greece and the craft tradition of ancient Egypt met in Alexandria, Egypt (the city founded by Alexander the Great in 331 B.C.), and **alchemy** was the result of the union. The early alchemists used Egyptian techniques for the handling of materials to investigate theories concerned with the nature of matter. Books written in Alexandria (the oldest known works on chemical topics) contain diagrams of chemical apparatus and descriptions of many laboratory operations (for example, distillation, crystallization, and sublimation).

The philosophical content of alchemy incorporated elements of astrology and mysticism into the theories of the earlier Greeks. A dominant interest of the alchemists was the transmutation of base metals, such as iron and lead, into the noble metal, gold. They believed that a metal could be changed by changing its qualities (particularly its color) and that such changes occur in nature—that metals strive for the perfection represented by gold. Furthermore, the alchemists believed that these changes could be brought about by means of a very small amount of a powerful transmuting agent (later called the *philosopher's stone*).

In the seventh century A.D., the Arabs conquered the centers of Hellenistic civilization (including Egypt in 640 A.D.), and alchemy passed into their hands. Greek texts were translated into Arabic and served as the foundation for the work of Arab alchemists. The Arabs called the philosopher's stone *aliksir* (which was later corrupted into *elixir*). Arab alchemists believed that this substance could

The Alchemist, painted by the Flemish artist David Teniers in 1648. *Fisher Scientific Company.*

not only ennoble metals by transmuting them into gold but could also ennoble life by curing all diseases. For centuries afterward, the two principal goals of alchemy were the transmutation of base metals into gold and the discovery of an *elixir of life* that could make humans immortal by preventing death.

In the twelfth and thirteenth centuries, alchemy was gradually introduced into Europe by translation of Arabic works into Latin. Most of the translations were made in Spain where, after the Islamic conquest in the eighth century, a rich Moorish culture was established and flourished.

A school of **iatrochemistry,** a branch of alchemy concerned with medicine, flourished in the sixteenth and seventeenth centuries. On the whole, however, European alchemists added little that was new to alchemical theory. Their work is important because they preserved the large body of chemical data that they had received from the past, added to it, and passed it on to later chemists.

Alchemy lasted until the seventeenth century. Gradually the theories and attitudes of the alchemists began to be questioned. The work of Robert Boyle, who published *The Sceptical Chymist* in 1661, is noteworthy. Although Boyle believed that the transmutation of base metals into gold might be possible, he severely criticized alchemical thought. Boyle emphasized that chemical theory should be derived from experimental evidence.

4. Phlogiston (1650 to 1790). Throughout most of the eighteenth century, the phlogiston theory dominated chemistry. This theory, which was later shown to be erroneous, was principally the work of Georg Ernst Stahl. **Phlogiston** (a "fire principle") was assumed to be a constituent of any substance that could undergo combustion.

Upon combustion, a substance was thought to lose its phlogiston and be reduced to simpler form. Air was believed to function in a combustion by carrying off the phlogiston as it was released. Whereas we would think of the combustion of wood in the following terms:

wood + oxygen gas (from air) ⟶ *ashes + oxygen-containing gases*

according to the phlogiston theory,

wood ⟶ *ashes + phlogiston* (removed by air)

Wood, therefore, was believed to be a compound composed of ashes and phlogiston. Readily combustible materials were thought to be rich in phlogiston.

The phlogiston theory interpreted **calcination** in a similar way. The formation of a metal oxide (called a calx) by heating a metal in air is called a calcination:

metal + oxygen gas (from air) ⟶ *calx* (a metal oxide)

According to the phlogiston theory, a metal is a compound composed of a calx and phlogiston. Calcination, therefore, was thought to be the loss of phlogiston by a metal:

metal ⟶ *calx + phlogiston* (removed by air)

The phlogiston theory was extended to explain many other chemical phenomena. Certain metals, for example, can be prepared by heating the metal oxide with carbon:

calx (a metal oxide) *+ carbon* ⟶ *metal + carbon monoxide gas*

In a process of this type, the carbon (supposedly rich in phlogiston) was thought to replace the phlogiston lost through calcination:

calx + phlogiston (from carbon) ⟶ *metal*

One difficulty inherent in the phlogiston theory was never adequately explained. When wood burns, it supposedly *loses* phlogiston and the resulting ashes weigh *less* than the original piece of wood. On the other hand, in calcination, the *loss* of phlogiston is accompanied by an increase in weight, since the calx (a metal oxide) weighs *more* than the original metal. The adherents of the phlogiston theory recognized this problem, but throughout most of the eighteenth century the importance of weighing and measuring was not realized.

5. Modern chemistry (1790⸺). The work of Antoine Lavoisier in the late eighteenth century is generally regarded as the beginning of modern chemistry. Lavoisier deliberately set out to overthrow the phlogiston theory and revolutionize chemistry. He relied on the results of quantitative experimentation (he used the chemical balance extensively) to arrive at his explanations of a number of chemical phenomena.

The **law of conservation of mass** states that there is no detectable change in mass during the course of a chemical reaction. In other words, the total mass of all materials entering into a chemical reaction equals the total mass of all products of the reaction. This law is implicit in earlier work, but Lavoisier stated it explicitly and used it as the cornerstone of his science. To Lavoisier, therefore, the phlogiston theory was impossible.

The role that gases play in reactions proved to be a stumbling block to the development of chemical theory. When the law of conservation of mass is applied to a combustion or calcination, the masses of the gases used or produced in these reactions must be taken into account. The correct interpretation of these processes, therefore, had to wait until chemists identified the gases involved and developed methods to handle and measure gases. Lavoisier drew upon the results of other scientists' work with gases to explain these reactions.

Antoine Lavoisier, 1743–1794.
Smithsonian Institution.

In interpreting chemical phenomena, Lavoisier used the modern definitions of *element* and *compound* (see Section 1.2). The phlogiston theory regarded a metal as a *compound* composed of a calx and phlogiston. Lavoisier showed that a metal is an *element* and that the corresponding calx is a *compound* composed of the metal and of oxygen from the air.

In his book *Traité Elémentaire de Chimie* (*Elementary Treatise on Chemistry*), published in 1789, Lavoisier used essentially modern terminology. The present-day language of chemistry is based on the system of nomenclature that Lavoisier helped to devise.

The achievements of scientists since the 1790s are described throughout this book. More has been learned about chemistry in the two centuries following Lavoisier than in the twenty centuries preceding him. Chemistry has gradually developed five principal branches (these divisions, however, are arbitrary and the classification is subject to criticism):

a. Organic chemistry. The chemistry of the compounds of carbon (except for few that are classified as inorganic compounds). The term *organic* is a holdover from the time when it was believed that these compounds could be derived only from plant or animal sources.

b. Inorganic chemistry The chemistry of all the elements except carbon. Some simple carbon compounds (for example, the carbonates and carbon dioxide) are traditionally classified as inorganic compounds, since they can be derived from mineral sources.

c. Analytical chemistry. The identification of the composition, both qualitative and quantitative, of substances.

d. Physical chemistry. The study of the physical principles that underlie the structure of matter and chemical transformations.

e. Biochemistry. The chemistry of living systems, both plant and animal.

1.2 Elements, Compounds, and Mixtures

Matter, the material of which the universe is composed, may be defined as anything that occupies space and has mass. Mass is a measure of quantity of matter. A body that is not being acted on by some external force has a tendency to remain at rest or, when it is in motion, to continue in uniform motion in the same direction. This property is known as inertia. The mass of a body is proportional to the inertia of the body.

The mass of a body is invariable; the weight of a body is not. Weight is the gravitational force of attraction exerted by the earth on a body; the weight of a given body varies with the distance of that body from the center of the earth. The weight of a body is directly proportional to its mass as well as to the earth's gravitational attraction. At any given place, therefore, two objects of equal mass have equal weight.

The ancient Greeks originated the concept that all matter is composed of a limited number of simple substances called **elements.** The Greeks assumed that all the matter found on earth is derived from four elements: *earth*, *air*, *fire*, and *water*. Since heavenly bodies were thought to be perfect and unchangeable, celestial matter was assumed to be composed of a different element, the *ether*, which later came to be known as *quintessence* (from Latin, meaning *fifth element*). This Greek theory dominated scientific thought for centuries.

In 1661, Robert Boyle proposed an essentially modern definition of an element in his book *The Sceptical Chymist:* "I now mean by Elements . . . certain Primitive and Simple, or perfectly unmingled bodies; which not being made of any other bodies, or of one another, are the Ingredients of which all those call'd perfectly mixt Bodies are immediately compounded, and into which they are ultimately resolved." Boyle made no attempt to identify specific substances as elements. He did, however, emphasize that the proof of the existence of elements, as well as their identification, rested on chemical experimentation.

Boyle's concept of a chemical element was firmly established by Antoine Lavoisier in the following century. Lavoisier accepted a substance as an element if it could not be decomposed into simpler substances. Furthermore, he showed that a compound is produced by the union of elements. Lavoisier correctly identified 23 elements (although he incorrectly included light, heat, and several simple compounds in his list).

At present, 108 elements are known. Of these, 85 have been isolated from natural sources; the remainder have been prepared by nuclear reactions (Section 27.7).

Each element is assigned a **chemical symbol** that has been decided upon by international agreement. Most of these symbols consist of one or two letters. Three-letter symbols are used, however, for the most recently discovered elements, which have been prepared by nuclear reactions. Whereas the name of an element may differ from one language to another, the symbol does not. Nitrogen, for example, is called *azoto* in Italian and *Stickstoff* in German, but the symbol for nitrogen is N in any language. These symbols are listed in the table of the elements that appears inside the back cover of this book.

Most of the symbols correspond closely to the English names of the elements. Some of them, however, do not. The symbols for some of the elements have been assigned on the basis of their Latin names; these elements are listed in Table 1.1. The symbol for tungsten, W, is derived from the German name for the element, *Wolfram.*

The 15 most abundant elements in the earth's crust, bodies of water, and atmosphere are listed in Table 1.2. This classification includes those parts of the universe from which we can obtain the elements. The earth consists of a core (which is probably composed of iron and nickel) surrounded successively by a mantle and a thin crust. The crust is 20 to 40 miles thick and constitutes only about 1% of the earth's mass.

If the entire earth were considered, a list different from that of Table 1.2 would result, and the most abundant element would be iron. On the other hand, the most abundant element in the universe as a whole is hydrogen, which is thought to constitute about 75% of the total mass of the universe.

Whether an element finds wide commercial use depends not only upon its abundance but also upon its accessibility. Some familiar elements (such as copper,

Table 1.1 Symbols of elements derived from Latin names

English Name	Latin Name	Symbol
antimony	stibium	Sb
copper	cuprum	Cu
gold	aurum	Au
iron	ferrum	Fe
lead	plumbum	Pb
mercury	hydrargyrum	Hg
potassium	kalium	K
silver	argentum	Ag
sodium	natrium	Na
tin	stannum	Sn

Table 1.2 Abundance of the elements (earth's crust, bodies of water, and atmosphere)

Rank	Element	Symbol	Percent by Mass
1	oxygen	O	49.2
2	silicon	Si	25.7
3	aluminum	Al	7.5
4	iron	Fe	4.7
5	calcium	Ca	3.4
6	sodium	Na	2.6
7	potassium	K	2.4
8	magnesium	Mg	1.9
9	hydrogen	H	0.9
10	titanium	Ti	0.6
11	chlorine	Cl	0.2
12	phosphorus	P	0.1
13	manganese	Mn	0.1
14	carbon	C	0.09
15	sulfur	S	0.05
—	all others	—	0.56

tin, and lead) are not particularly abundant but are found in nature in ore deposits, from which they can be obtained readily. Other elements that are more abundant (such as titanium, rubidium, and zirconium) are not widely used, either because their ores are widespread in nature or because the extraction of the elements from their ores is difficult or expensive.

Compounds are substances that are composed of two or more elements in fixed proportions. The **law of definite proportions** (first proposed by Joseph Proust in 1799) states that a pure compound always consists of the same elements combined in the same proportion by mass. The compound *water*, for example, is always formed from the elements *hydrogen* and *oxygen* in the proportion 11.19% hydrogen to 88.81% oxygen. Over twelve thousand inorganic compounds are known, and

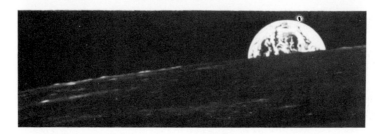

Earth rise over the Moon's horizon taken from the Apollo 10 lunar module. The most abundant element in the universe is hydrogen, in the entire earth is iron, and in the earth's crust, bodies of water, and atmosphere is oxygen. *NASA.*

over four million organic compounds have either been synthesized or isolated from natural sources. The properties of compounds are different from the properties of the elements of which they are composed.

An element or a compound is called a **pure substance.** All other kinds of matter are mixtures. **Mixtures** are prepared from two or more pure substances and have variable compositions. The properties of a mixture depend upon the composition of the mixture and the properties of the pure substances that form the mixture. There are two types of mixtures. A **heterogeneous mixture** is not uniform throughout but consists of parts that are physically distinct. A sample containing iron and sand, for example, is a heterogeneous mixture. A **homogeneous mixture** appears uniform throughout and is called a **solution.** Air, salt dissolved in water, and a silver-gold alloy are examples of a gaseous, a liquid, and a solid solution, respectively.

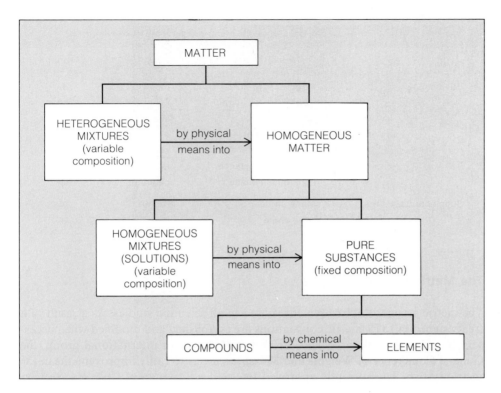

Figure 1.1 Classification of matter

The classification of matter is summarized in Figure 1.1. From the figure we can see that the only type of *heterogeneous matter* is the heterogeneous mixture. The classification *homogeneous matter*, however, includes homogeneous mixtures and pure substances (elements and compounds).

A physically distinct portion of matter that is uniform throughout in composition and properties is called a **phase.** Homogeneous materials consist of only one phase. Heterogeneous materials consist of more than one phase. The phases of heterogeneous mixtures have distinct boundaries and are usually easily discernible.

In the heterogeneous mixture *granite*, for example, it is possible to identify pink feldspar crystals, colorless quartz crystals, and shiny black mica crystals. When the number of phases in a sample is being determined, all portions of the same kind are counted as a single phase. Granite, therefore, is said to consist of three phases. The relative proportions of the three phases of granite may vary from sample to sample.

Figure 1.1 notes that both types of mixtures can be separated into their components by *physical means*, but that compounds can be separated into their constituent elements only by *chemical means*. Changes in state (such as the melting of a solid and the vaporization of a liquid), as well as changes in shape or state of subdivision, are examples of **physical changes**—changes that do not involve the production of new chemical species. Physical means (such as filtration and distillation) may be used to separate the components of a mixture, but a substance that was not present in the original mixture is never produced by these means. **Chemical changes,** on the other hand, are transformations in which substances are converted into other substances.

Photo of granite (magnified 10×) showing feldspar, quartz, and mica crystals. *Grant Heilman.*

	Measurement	Unit	Symbol
Table 1.3 Base units and supplementary units of the International System of Units			
Base units	length	meter	m
	mass	kilogram	kg
	time	second	s
	electric current	ampere	A
	temperature	kelvin	K
	amount of substance	mole	mol
	luminous intensity	candela	cd
Supplementary units	plane angle	radian	rad
	solid angle	steradian	sr

1.3 The Metric System

The metric system of measurement is used in all scientific studies. As a result of a treaty signed in 1875, metric conventions are established and modified when necessary by international agreement. From time to time, an international group, the General Conference of Weights and Measures, meets to ratify improvements in the metric system. The currently approved International System of Units (*Le Système International d'Unitès*, officially abbreviated SI) is a modernization and simplification of an old system that developed from one proposed by the French Academy of Science in 1790. Lavoisier was a member of the committee that formulated the original system.

The International System is founded on seven base units and two supplementary units (see Table 1.3 and the appendix). The selection of primary standards for the base units is arbitrary. For example, the primary standard of mass, the kilogram, is defined as the mass of a cylinder of platinum-irridium alloy that is kept at the International Bureau of Weights and Measures at Sèvres, France. Throughout the years, the primary standards for some base units have been changed when new standards appeared to be superior to old ones.

Multiples or fractions of base units are indicated by the use of prefixes (see Table 1.4). The base unit of length, the meter (m), is usually not used to record the distances between cities. A larger unit, the kilometer (km), is more convenient. The kilometer is equal to 1000 meters; its name is obtained by adding the prefix *kilo*- (which means 1000 ×) to the name of the base unit:

$$1 \text{ km} = 1000 \text{ m} \tag{1.1}$$

The centimeter (cm) is a smaller unit than the meter. The prefix *centi*- means 0.01 ×, and the centimeter is 0.01 meter:

$$1 \text{ cm} = 0.01 \text{ m} \tag{1.2}$$

Note that the name for the base unit for mass, the kilogram, contains a prefix. The names of other units of mass are obtained by substituting other prefixes for the prefix *kilo*-. The name of no other base unit contains a prefix.

Other SI units, called derived units, are obtained from the base units by algebraic combination. Examples are the SI unit for volume, which is the cubic meter

Table 1.4 Prefixes used to modify unit terms in the metric system		
Prefix	Abbreviation	Factor
tera-	T-	$1\ 000\ 000\ 000\ 000\ \times$ or 10^{12}
giga-	G-	$1\ 000\ 000\ 000\ \times$ or 10^{9}
mega-	M-	$1\ 000\ 000\ \times$ or 10^{6}
kilo-	k-	$1\ 000\ \times$ or 10^{3}
hecto-	h-	$100\ \times$ or 10^{2}
deka-	da-	$10\ \times$ or 10
deci-	d-	$0.1\ \times$ or 10^{-1}
centi-	c-	$0.01\ \times$ or 10^{-2}
milli-	m-	$0.001\ \times$ or 10^{-3}
micro-	μ-	$0.000\ 001\ \times$ or 10^{-6}
nano-	n-	$0.000\ 000\ 001\ \times$ or 10^{-9}
pico-	p-	$0.000\ 000\ 000\ 001\ \times$ or 10^{-12}
femto-	f-	$0.000\ 000\ 000\ 000\ 001\ \times$ or 10^{-15}
atto-	a-	$0.000\ 000\ 000\ 000\ 000\ 001\ \times$ or 10^{-18}

(abbreviated m^3), and the SI unit for velocity, which is the meter per second (abbreviated m/s or $m \cdot s^{-1}$).

Some derived units are given special names. The SI unit for force, for example, is the newton. This unit is derived from the base units for mass (the kilogram, kg), length (the meter, m), and time (the second, s). The **newton** is the force that gives a mass of 1 kg an acceleration of 1 m/s^2 (see Section 3.1):

$$1\ N = 1\ kg \cdot m/s^2 \tag{1.3}$$

The current terminology of the International System has been developed since 1960. Some units that were defined prior to this time do not conform to SI rules and are not SI units. The use of some of these units is, however, permitted. The liter, for example, which is defined as 1 cubic decimeter (and hence is 1000 cm^3), may be used in addition to the official SI unit of volume, the cubic meter. Certain other units that are not a part of SI are to be retained for a limited period of time. The standard atmosphere (atm, a unit of pressure) falls into this category. The use of still other units that are outside the International System is discouraged. For example, the International Committee of Weights and Measures considers it preferable to avoid the use of the calorie as an energy unit.

Not all scientists have adopted SI units, but use of the system appears to be growing. Strict adherence to the International System, however, poses a problem since it eliminates some units that previously have been used widely. Since much of the data found in the chemical literature have been recorded in units that are not SI units, one must be familiar with both the old and the new units.

1.4 Significant Figures

Every measurement is uncertain to some extent. Suppose, for example, that we wish to measure the mass of an object. If we use a platform balance, we can determine the mass to the nearest 0.1 g. An analytical balance, on the other hand,

Modern analytical balances capable of giving results to the nearest 0.1 mg. *Left:* A mechanical single-pan balance. *Right:* An electronic, digital readout balance that can be interfaced with other equipment. *Sauter Division of Mettler Instrument Corporation.*

is capable of giving results correct to the nearest 0.0001 g. The exactness, or precision, of the measurement depends upon the limitations of the measuring device and the skill with which it is used.

The precision of a measurement is indicated by the number of figures used to record it. The digits in a properly recorded measurement are **significant figures.** These figures include all those that are known with certainty plus one more, which is an estimate.

Suppose that a platform balance is used and the mass of an object is determined to be 12.3 g. The chances are slight that the actual mass of the object is exactly 12.3 g, no more nor less. We are sure of the first two figures (the 1 and the 2); we know that the mass is greater than 12 g. The third figure (the 3), however, is somewhat inexact. At best it tells us that the true mass lies closer to 12.3 g than to either 12.2 g or 12.4 g. If, for example, the actual mass were 12.28 . . . g or 12.33 . . . g, the value would be correctly recorded in either case as 12.3 g *to three significant figures.*

If, in our example, we were to arbitrarily add a zero to the measurement, we would indicate a value containing *four significant figures* (12.30 g), which would be incorrect and misleading. The value 12.30 g indicates that we believe the actual mass to be between 12.29 g and 12.31 g. We have, however, no idea of the magnitude of the integer in the second decimal place, since we have determined the value only to the nearest 0.1 g. The zero does not indicate that the second decimal place is unknown or undetermined. Rather, it should be interpreted in the same way that any other figure is (see, however, rule 1, which follows). Since the uncertainty in the measurement lies in the 3, this digit should be the last significant figure reported.

On the other hand, we have no right to drop a zero if it is significant. A value of 12.0 g that has been determined to the precision indicated should be recorded that way. It is incorrect to record 12 g for this measurement since 12 g indicates a precision of only *two* significant figures instead of the *three* significant figures of the measurement.

The following rules can be used to determine the proper number of significant figures to be recorded for a measurement.

1. *Zeros used only to locate the decimal point are not significant.* Suppose that the distance between two points is measured as 3 cm. This measurement could be expressed as 0.03 m since 1 cm is 0.01 m:

3 cm = 0.03 m

Both values, however, contain only *one* significant figure. The zeros in the second value, since they merely serve to locate the decimal point, are not significant. The precision of a measurement cannot be increased by changing units.

Zeros that arise as a part of a measurement are significant. The number 0.0005030 has four significant figures. The zeros after 5 are significant. Those preceding the numeral 5 are not significant since they have been added only to locate the decimal point.

Occasionally, it is difficult to determine the number of significant figures in a value that contains zeros, such as 600. Are the zeros significant, or do they merely serve to locate the decimal point? This type of problem can be avoided by using scientific notation (see Appendix C.2). The decimal is located by the power of 10 employed; the first part of the term contains only significant figures. The value 600, therefore, can be expressed in any of the following ways, depending upon how precisely the measurement has been made:

6.00×10^2 (three significant figures)

6.0×10^2 (two significant figures)

6×10^2 (one significant figure)

There is another convention for handling numbers with zeros before the decimal point. If a decimal point is indicated in a number such as 200., then all the figures preceding the decimal point are significant. If a decimal point is *not* used, then the zeros are *not* significant. Hence:

200.°C has three significant figures

200°C has one significant figure

250.°C has three signficant figures

250°C has two significant figures

275°C has three significant figures

Although this practice is not universally employed, we will use it later in this book because it is convenient in certain instances (particularly in recording temperatures).

2. *Certain values, such as those that arise from the definition of terms, are exact.* For example, by definition, there are *exactly* 1000 mL in one liter (1 L). The value 1000 may be considered to have an infinite number of significant figures (zeros) following the decimal point.

Values obtained by counting may also be exact. The H_2 molecule, for example, contains exactly 2 atoms, not 2.1 or 2.3. Other counts, however, are inexact. The population of the world, for example, is estimated and is not derived from an actual count.

3. *At times*, the answer to a calculation contains more figures than are significant. The following rules should be used to round off such a value to the correct number of digits.

a. If the figure following the last number to be retained is less than 5, all the unwanted figures are discarded and the last number is left unchanged:

3.6247 is 3.62 to three significant figures

b. If the figure following the last number to be retained is greater than 5, or is 5 with other digits following it, the last figure is increased by 1 and the unwanted figures are discarded:

7.5647 is 7.565 to four significant figures

6.2501 is 6.3 to two significant figures

c. If the figure following the last figure to be retained is 5 and there are no figures or only zeros following the 5, the 5 is discarded and the last figure increased by 1 if it is an odd number or left unchanged if it is an even number. In a case of this type, the last figure of the rounded-off value is always an even number. Zero is considered an even number:

3.250 is 3.2 to two significant figures

7.635 is 7.64 to three significant figures

8.105 is 8.10 to three significant figures

The idea behind this procedure, which is arbitrary, is that on the average as many values will be increased as are decreased.

The number of significant figures in the answer to a calculation depends upon the precision of the values used in the calculation. Consider the following problem. If we place 2.38 g of salt in a container that has a mass of 52.2 g, what will be the mass of the container plus salt? Simple addition gives 54.58 g. But we cannot know the mass of the two together any more precisely than we know the mass of one alone. The result must be rounded off to the nearest 0.1 g, which gives 54.6 g.

4. *The result of an* adddition *or* subtraction *should be reported to the same number of decimal places as that of the term with the least number of decimal places.* The answer for the addition

$$
\begin{array}{r}
161.032 \\
5.6 \\
\underline{32.4524} \\
199.0844
\end{array}
$$

should be reported as 199.1 since the number 5.6 has only one digit following the decimal point.

5. *The answer to a multiplication or division is rounded off to the same number of significant figures as is possessed by the least precise term used in the calculation.* The result of the multiplication

$$152.06 \times 0.24 = 36.4944$$

should be reported as 36 since the least precise term in the calculation is 0.24 (two significant figures).

1.5 Chemical Calculations

Units should be indicated as an integral part of all measurement. It makes little sense to say that the length of an object is 5.0. What does the value mean: 5.0 cm, 5.0 m, 5.0 ft? Careful use of units will simplify problem solving and reduce the probability of making errors.

The unit labels that are included in the terms employed in a calculation should undergo the same mathematical operations as the numbers. In any calculation, the units that appear in both numerator and denominator are canceled, and those remaining appear as a part of the answer. If the answer does not have the units sought, a mistake has been made in the way that the calculation has been set up.

Many problems may be solved by the use of one or more **conversion factors.** A factor of this type is derived from an equality and is design to convert a measurement from one unit into another. Suppose, for example, that we wish to calculate the number of centimeters in 5.00 inches (in). One inch, by definition, equals exactly 2.54 cm. The conversion factor that we need to solve the problem is derived from this relationship:

$$2.54 \text{ cm} = 1.00 \text{ in} \tag{1.4}$$

If we divide both sides of this equation by 1.00 in, we obtain

$$\frac{2.54 \text{ cm}}{1.00 \text{ in}} = 1 \tag{1.5}$$

The factor (2.54 cm/1.00 in) is equal to 1 since the numerator and the denominator are equivalent.

Our problem can be stated in the following way:

$$? \text{ cm} = 5.00 \text{ in}$$

Multiplication by the conversion factor that we derived solves the problem:

$$? \text{ cm} = 5.00 \text{ in} \left(\frac{2.54 \text{ cm}}{1.00 \text{ in}} \right) = 12.7 \text{ cm} \tag{1.6}$$

Since the factor is equal to 1, this operation does not change the value of the given quantity. Notice that the *inch* labels cancel, and the answer is left in the desired unit, *centimeters.*

A second conversion factor can be derived from the relation

$$2.54 \text{ cm} = 1.00 \text{ in} \tag{1.4}$$

by dividing both sides of the equation by 2.54 cm:

$$1 = \frac{1.00 \text{ in}}{2.54 \text{ cm}} \tag{1.7}$$

This factor, which is also equal to 1, is the reciprocal of the factor previously derived and can be used to convert centimeters to inches. For example, the number of inches that equals 20.0 cm can be found in the following way:

$$? \text{ in} = 20.0 \text{ cm} \left(\frac{1.00 \text{ in}}{2.54 \text{ cm}} \right) = 7.87 \text{ in} \tag{1.8}$$

A *single* equality that relates two units, therefore, can be used to derive *two* conversion factors. The factors are reciprocals of one another. In the solution to a problem, the correct factor to use is the one that will lead to the cancellation of the unit that is to be eliminated. Notice that here this unit is found in the denominator of the factor.

If an incorrect factor is used in the solution to a problem, the units of the answer will not be the units sought. If, for example, the factor used in the solution shown in Equation 1.8 were the inverse of the correct factor, the result would look like this:

$$? \text{ in} = 20.0 \text{ cm} \left(\frac{2.54 \text{ cm}}{1.00 \text{ in}} \right) = 50.8 \text{ cm}^2/\text{in} \tag{1.9}$$

This answer, although mathematically correct, is not particularly useful, nor does it answer the question. Since this answer does not have the desired units, it is immediately obvious that a mistake has been made.

The solution to some problems requires the use of several factors. If we wish to find the number of centimeters in 0.750 ft, we can state the problem in the following way:

$$? \text{ cm} = 0.750 \text{ ft}$$

Since 1.00 ft = 12.0 in, we derive the conversion factor (12.0 in/1.00 ft), which is of course equal to 1. Multiplication by this factor converts feet into inches but does not complete the solution:

$$? \text{ cm} = 0.750 \text{ ft} \left(\frac{12.0 \text{ in}}{1.00 \text{ ft}} \right)$$

The factor needed to convert inches into centimeters is (2.54 cm/1.00 in), and thus

$$? \text{ cm} = 0.750 \text{ ft} \left(\frac{12.0 \text{ in}}{1.00 \text{ ft}} \right) \left(\frac{2.54 \text{ cm}}{1.00 \text{ in}} \right) = 22.9 \text{ cm} \tag{1.10}$$

The relations between some units of the English system and metric units are given in Table 1.5.

Table 1.5 Relations between some English and metric units.		
Length		
1 inch = 2.54 centimeters (exact)		
0.62137 mile = 1 kilometer		
Volume		
1 quart (U.S. liquid) = 0.94633 liter		
61.024 cubic inches = 1 liter		
Mass		
1 pound (avdp.) = 453.59 grams		
2.2046 pounds (avdp.) = 1 kilogram		

Example 1.1

If Jules Verne had used SI units, what title would he have given his book *Twenty Thousand Leagues under the Sea*? Express the answer to three significant figures and in the SI unit that will give the smallest number that is greater than 1. One league is 3.45 miles; 1 mile is 1609 m.

Solution

First we convert leagues into meters. The conversion is accomplished by the use of two factors derived from the data given:

$$? \text{ m} = 20{,}000 \text{ league}\left(\frac{3.45 \text{ mile}}{1 \text{ league}}\right)\left(\frac{1609 \text{ m}}{1 \text{ mile}}\right) = 111{,}000{,}000 \text{ m} = 1.11 \times 10^8 \text{ m}$$

Notice that the factors successively convert leagues to miles and then miles to meters. Each factor converts the units in the *denominator* of the factor to the units in the *numerator* of the factor.

Next we change the units of the answer from the base unit *meter* to the SI unit that will satisfy the requirement stated in the problem. From Table 1.4 we note that a megameter (Mm) is 10^6 meters and a gigameter (Gm) is 10^9 meters. The magnitude of our answer (10^8 meters) is between the two. In order to get an answer that is greater than 1, we convert to megameters:

$$? \text{ Mm} = 1.11 \times 10^8 \text{ m}\left(\frac{1 \text{ Mm}}{10^6 \text{ m}}\right) = 1.11 \times 10^2 \text{Mm} = 111 \text{ Mm*}$$

or, *One Hundred and Eleven Megameters under the Sea*. Since the circumference of the earth is approximately 40.0 Mm, Captain Nemo's submarine could travel a distance equal to about two and three-quarters times the circumference of the earth without surfacing.

---

* Notice that the symbol m stands for the base unit meter. The abbreviations *m*- and *M*- represent the prefixes *milli*- and *mega*- respectively. Hence,

  m stands for *meter*

  mm stands for *millimeter*

  Mm stands for *megameter*

Percentages

Factors can be derived from percentages. Consider, for example, the percentages used to express the composition of the alloy used to make the American five-cent piece. The "nickel" is actually 75.0% copper and 25.0% nickel, by mass. Six factors, counting reciprocals, can be derived from these data.

Since a *percentage* is the number of parts *per hundred*, it is convenient to use exactly one hundred mass units of the alloy in the derivation of the factors. In 100.0 g of alloy there would be 75.0 g copper and 25.0 g of nickel. If we use the symbol ∞ to indicate "is equivalent to," we can indicate the following three relations that pertain to this copper-nickel alloy:

1. 100.0 g alloy ∞ 75.0 g Cu   (1.11)

2. 100.0 g alloy ∞ 25.0 g Ni   (1.12)

3. 75. 0 g Cu ∞ 25.0 g Ni   (1.13)

In the derivation of factors, the ∞ sign is treated in the same way as an equal sign. Hence, each of these relations will yield two factors—one the inverse of the other. The factor required for the solution of a problem can be derived from the relation that involves the pertinent units. We can, for example, derive the factors

$$\frac{100.0 \text{ g alloy}}{75.0 \text{ g Cu}} \quad \text{and} \quad \frac{75.0 \text{ g Cu}}{100.0 \text{ g alloy}}$$

from the first relation (Equation 1.11).

Example 1.2

How many grams of nickel must be added to 50.0 g of copper to make the coinage alloy previously described?

Solution

In order to find the grams of nickel required, we must multiply the term *50.0 g Cu* by a factor. We need a conversion factor that relates *g Ni* (in the numerator) to *g Cu* (in the denominaator). Relation 3, given previously, (Equation 1.13) can yield such a factor; it is (25.0 g Ni/75.0 g Cu). The solution is

$$? \text{ g Ni} = 50.0 \text{ g Cu} \left(\frac{25.0 \text{ g Ni}}{75.0 \text{ g Cu}} \right) = 16.7 \text{ g Ni}$$

Example 1.3

Sterling silver is an alloy consisting of 92.5% Ag and 7.5% Cu. How many kilograms of sterling silver can be made from 3.00 kg of pure silver?

Solution

We must use a conversion factor to modify the term *3.00 kg Ag*. It is clear that we need a factor to convert *kg Ag* into *kg sterling*. We can derive the desired factor from the percentage of silver in sterling silver. Since sterling silver is 92.5% Ag by mass,

100.0 kg sterling $\approx$ 92.5 kg Ag

The factor we need, therefore, is (100.0 kg sterling/92.5 kg Ag). Notice that the label *kg Ag* appears in the denominator of this factor and will cancel the unit of the given quantity:

$$? \text{ kg sterling} = 3.00 \cancel{\text{ kg Ag}}\left(\frac{100.0 \text{ kg sterling}}{92.5 \cancel{\text{ kg Ag}}}\right) = 3.24 \text{ kg sterling}$$

Rates

Frequently, information is given in the form of a ratio, or the answer to a problem is a ratio. The cost per unit item, the distance traveled per unit time, and the number of items per unit mass are examples. The word *per* implies division, and the number in the denominator is 1 (exactly) unless specified otherwise. A speed of 50 kilometers per hour is 50 km/1 hr.

The numerator and denominator of such a ratio are equivalent:

50 km $\approx$ 1 hr   (1.14)

These ratios may be used, therefore, as conversion factors—either in the form in which they are given (50 km/1 hr) or in the inverted form (1 hr/50 km).

At times, the answer to a problem is a ratio. To solve problems of this kind, we use the data given in the problem to set up a ratio of the type asked for (distance per time, for example). The units of this ratio are then modified by using conversion factors until the ratio is in the form desired.

Example 1.4

What is the speed of a car (in km/hr) if it travels 16 km in 13 min?

Solution

Since the ratio we desire is in terms of *distance per unit time*, we derive a ratio of this type from the data given. We are told that the car traveled 16 km in 13 min, so we can base our calculation on the ratio (16 km/13 min):

$$\frac{? \text{ km}}{1 \text{ hr}} = \left(\frac{16 \text{ km}}{13 \text{ min}}\right)$$

Note that we must change the units in the denominator of this factor from *minutes* to *hours*. The factor that we need can be derived from

$$60 \text{ min} = 1 \text{ hr}$$

and is (60 min/1 hr). The solution is

$$\frac{? \text{ km}}{1 \text{ hr}} = \left(\frac{16 \text{ km}}{13 \text{ min}}\right)\left(\frac{60 \text{ min}}{1 \text{ hr}}\right) = \left(\frac{74 \text{ km}}{1 \text{ hr}}\right) = 74 \text{ km/hr}$$

Density

Density is one type of ratio that is frequently used in chemistry. The **density** of a substance is the mass per unit volume of that substance:

$$density = \frac{mass}{volume} \tag{1.15}$$

Density may be expressed in grams per cubic centimeter (g/cm^3). The volume used here, the cubic centimeter (cm^3), is the volume of a cube that is one centimeter on a side. At other times, kilograms per cubic meter (kg/m^3) may be used. Here the volume indicated, the cubic meter (m^3), is the volume of a cube one meter on a side.

For liquids or liquid solutions, the unit usually employed is grams per milliliter (g/mL). The following relations involving the liter (L) are, by definition, exact:

$$1 \text{ L} = 1000. \text{ cm}^3$$

$$1 \text{ L} = 1000. \text{ mL}$$

Therefore,

$$1 \text{ mL} = 1 \text{ cm}^3 \text{ (exactly)}$$

and g/cm^3 equals g/mL.

For gases, densities are usually expressed in grams per liter (g/L). Some densities are recorded in Table 1.6.

Table 1.6 Densities of some solids and liquids in g/cm^3

copper	8.93
iron	7.86
gold	19.32
lead	11.34
silver	10.50
zinc	7.14
water	1.00
ethyl alcohol	0.791
milk	1.03
ice	0.917
limestone	2.70
diamond	3.51

Example 1.5

"Eureka," shouted Archimedes when he figured out how to determine whether King Hiero's crown was pure gold and not harm the crown. He submerged the crown in a vessel filled with water. The volume of water that overflowed the vessel equaled the volume of the crown. Then, by determining the mass of the crown, he could calculate its density. A crown made of pure gold has the same density as pure gold (see Table 1.6).

Suppose that a crown weighs 1325. g and has a volume of 124.0 cm^3. (a) What is the density of the crown? (b) Is the crown pure gold?

Solution

(a) We can find the density of the crown by using the equation

$$density = \frac{mass}{volume} \tag{1.15}$$

$$= \frac{1325.\,g}{124.0 cm^3}$$

$$= 10.69 \text{ g/cm}^3$$

(b) The density that we have calculated (10.69 g/cm^3) is much lower than the value for pure gold (19.32 g/cm^3; see Table 1.6). Obviously, the gold of the crown has been debased by the addition of other metals.

Example 1.6

The mass of the earth is 5.976×10^{24} kg and the volume of the earth is 1.083×10^{21} m^3. What is the mean density of the earth in grams per cubic centimeter?

Solution

We base the solution on the *mass per volume* ratio derived from the data given in the problem:

$$\frac{?\,g}{1 \text{ cm}^3} = \left(\frac{5.976 \times 10^{24} \text{ kg}}{1.083 \times 10^{21} \text{ m}^3} \right)$$

Since the volume is given in the problem in terms of m^3, we must derive a relation between cm^3 and m^3. By taking the third power of both sides of the equation

$$100 \text{ cm} = 1 \text{ m}$$

we get

$$(10^2 \text{ cm})^3 = (1 \text{ m})^3$$

$$10^6 \text{ cm}^3 = 1 \text{ m}^3$$

The factor that we derive from this relation is $(1 \text{ m}^3/10^6 \text{ cm}^3)$. To convert kg to g, we use the relation

$$10^3 \text{ g} = 1 \text{ kg}$$

and derive the factor (10^3 g/1 kg). The solution is

$$\frac{?\,g}{1 \text{ cm}^3} = \left(\frac{5.976 \times 10^{24}\,\cancel{kg}}{1.083 \times 10^{21}\,\cancel{m^3}} \right) \left(\frac{10^3 \text{ g}}{1\,\cancel{kg}} \right) \left(\frac{10^{-6}\,\cancel{m^3}}{1 \text{ cm}^3} \right) = \left(\frac{5.518 \text{ g}}{1 \text{ cm}^3} \right) = 5.518 \text{ g/cm}^3$$

The mean density of the earth is 5.518 g/cm^3. (In comparison, the density of water is 1.00 g/cm^3.)

The Conversion Factor Method of Problem Solving

If the value sought is *not a ratio:*

1. Write the unit in which the answer should be expressed, an equal sign, and that quantity given in the problem that will lead to a solution.

2. Derive a conversion factor in which the unit in the denominator is the same as the unit of the given quantity. The factors may be derived from information given in the problem or from the definition of a unit.

3. Write the conversion factor after the given quantity (written in step 1) to indicate multiplication. Cancel units. When this multiplication is performed, the answer will be expressed in the unit in the numerator of the factor.

4. If this is not the one sought, additional conversion factors must be employed. The unit in the denominator of each factor should cancel the unit in the numerator of the preceding factor.

5. Continue the process until the only uncanceled unit is the desired unit.

6. Perform the mathematical operations indicated and obtain the answer.

If the value sought *is a ratio:*

1. Write the units in which the answer should be expressed (they will be in the form of a ratio), an equal sign, and a ratio of the same general type as that desired (for example, *distance/time*), derived from the data given in the problem.

2. Derive one or more conversion factors that can be used to convert the units of the given ratio into the desired units.

3. Write the conversion factors after the given ratio. In some instances, the unit numerator of the factor will cancel the units in the denominator of the given quantity. In other instances, the units in the denominator of the factor will cancel those in the numerator of the given quantity.

4. Perform the mathematical operations indicated and obtain the answer, which should be in the units sought.

Example 1.7

The mean density of the moon is 3.341 g/cm³ and the mass of the moon is 7.350×10^{25} g. What is the volume of the moon?

Solution

Density relates mass and volume. We are given the mass of the moon and asked to find the volume. We multiply the mass (7.350×10^{25} g) by a conversion factor. The factor that we need to solve the problem is the reciprocal of the density ($1 \text{ cm}^3/3.341 \text{ g}$). In this way, the g units will cancel:

$$? \text{ cm}^3 = 7.350 \times 10^{25} \text{ g} \left(\frac{1 \text{ cm}^3}{3.341 \text{ g}} \right) = 2.200 \times 10^{25} \text{ cm}^3*$$

---

* Cancellation of units will not be indicated in future examples.

Summary

Chemistry is the science that is concerned with the *characterization, composition,* and *transformations* of matter. The modern science took centuries to develop from its roots in the *practical arts of ancient civilizations* and the *theories of the ancient Greeks* through *alchemy* and *phlogiston chemistry.* The modern period was ushered in by the work of Antoine Lavoisier, who based his work on the *law of conservation of mass.*

The classification of *matter* rests on the identification of *elements,* substances that cannot be decomposed into simpler substances and from which all other types of matter are made. Over 100 elements are known. Each element is assigned a one-, two-, or three-letter *chemical symbol. Compounds* are composed of two or more elements in fixed proportions. They are produced by chemical reactions and can be decomposed only by *chemical means.* Elements and compounds are called *pure substances.*

Mixtures are formed from two or more pure substances in variable proportions and may be separated into these components by *physical means.* Mixtures that appear uniform throughout are called *homogeneous;* those that are not uniform throughout are called *heterogeneous.*

The *metric system* of measurement (a decimal system) is used for all scientific studies. The currently approved *International System of Units* (abbreviated *SI*) is a modernization and simplification of an old system. The International System is based on seven *base units* and three *supplementary units.* Other SI units, called *derived units,* are obtained from the base units by algebraic combination. Multiples or fractions of base units or derived units are indicated by the addition of prefixes to the names of the units.

The precision of a measurement is indicated by using only *significant figures* to record it. Furthermore, the answer to a calculation should be reported to the correct number of significant figures (the number is based on the precision of the values used in the calculation). Many chemical calculations may be solved by the use of *conversion factors.*

Key Terms

Some of the more important terms introduced in this chapter are listed below. Definitions for terms not included in this list may be located in the text by use of the index.

Chemical symbol (Section 1.2) A one-, two-, or three-letter abbreviation assigned by international agreement to each element.

Chemistry (Introduction) The science that is concerned with the characterization, composition, and transformations of matter.

Compound (Section 1.2) A pure substance that is composed of two or more elements in fixed proportions and that can be chemically decomposed into these elements.

Conversion factor (Section 1.5) A ratio in which the numerator and denominator are equivalent quantities in different units. A conversion factor is used in calculations to convert the units of a measurement into other units.

Density (Section 1.5) Mass per unit volume.

Element (Section 1.2) A pure substance that cannot be decomposed into simpler substances.

Law of conservation of mass (Section 1.1) There is no detectable change in mass during the course of a chemical reaction.

Law of definite proportions (Section 1.2) A pure compound always consists of the same elements combined in the same proportions by mass.

Mass (Section 1.2) A measure of quantity of matter.

Matter (Section 1.2) Anything that occupies space and has mass.

Metric system (Section 1.3) A decimal system of measurement that is used in all scientific studies.

Mixture (Section 1.2) A sample of matter that consists of two or more pure substances, does not have a fixed composition, and may be separated into its components by physical means.

Phase (Section 1.2) A physically distinct portion of matter that is uniform throughout in composition and properties.

SI unit (Section 1.3) A unit that is used in the International System of Units (*Le Système International d' Unitès*).

Significant figures (Section 1.4) Digits in a measurement that indicate the precision of the measurement. These figures include all those that are known with certainty plus one more, which is an estimate.

Solution (Section 1.2) A mixture of two or more pure substances that is uniform throughout (homogeneous).

Substance (Section 1.2) An element or a compound. Substances have fixed compositions and properties.

Weight (Section 1.2) The gravitational force of attraction exerted by the earth on a body.

Problems*

1.1 Compare and contrast: **(a)** law of conservation of mass, law of definite proportions; **(b)** compound, element; **(c)** weight, mass; **(d)** organic chemistry, biochemistry; **(e)** a megameter, a millimeter.

1.2 Compare and contrast: **(a)** mixture, compound; **(b)** heterogeneous mixture, homogeneous mixture; **(c)** physical change, chemical change; **(d)** mass of an object, density of an object; **(e)** 1.000 L, 1000. cm^2

1.3 Give the names of the elements for which the symbols are **(a)** I, **(b)** Fe, **(c)** P, **(d)** K, **(e)** Cu, **(f)** Co.

1.4 Give the names of the elements for which the symbols are **(a)** Cl, **(b)** Cr, **(c)** Mg, **(d)** Mn, **(e)** Li, **(f)** Pb.

1.5 Give the symbols for the following elements: **(a)** aluminum, **(b)** antimony, **(c)** silver, **(d)** silicon, **(e)** sodium, **(f)** neon.

1.6 Give the symbols for the following elements: **(a)** mercury, **(b)** hydrogen, **(c)** helium, **(d)** strontium, **(e)** tin, **(f)** tungsten.

1.7 State the number of significant figures in each of the following: **(a)** 600, **(b)** 606, **(c)** 600., **(d)** 600.06, **(e)** 0.06.

1.8 State the number of significant figures in each of the following: **(a)** 0.1243, **(b)** 0.0400, **(c)** 250.03, **(d)** 1.320, **(e)** 10.000.

1.9 Perform the following calculations and report the answers to the proper numbers of significant figures: **(a)** 36.12/625.1, **(b)** 1.62×0.075, **(c)** 602.1 + 63.02 + 1.623, **(d)** 1.325 − 0.1, **(e)** $(13.273 \times 0.062)/372.0$.

1.10 Perform the following calculations and report the answers to the proper numbers of significant figures: **(a)** 14.5 + 0.023, **(b)** 13.265 − 2.065, **(c)** 607.1×3.20, **(d)** 0.062/327.5, **(e)** $(1.307 \times 625)/0.076$.

1.11 Perform the following calculations and report the answers to the proper numbers of significant figures: **(a)** $(1.25 \times 10^6) + (1.273 \times 10^5)$, **(b)** $(6.03 \times 10^{-2}) - (3.06 \times 10^{-3})$, **(c)** $(1.552 \times 10^{-2})/(1.6 \times 10^3)$, **(d)** $(5.5 \times 10^{-6})^2$, **(e)** $(7.613 \times 10^8)(1.0132 \times 10^{-2})$.

1.12 Perform the following calculations and report the answers to the proper numbers of significant figures: **(a)** $(1.333 \times 10^{-6})(1.5 \times 10^2)$, **(b)** $375.(6.0225 \times 10^{23})$, **(c)** $(6.50 \times 10^{-7}) - (9.325 \times 10^{-9})$, **(d)** $1.58/(3.2761 \times 10^{-5})$, **(e)** $(1.65 \times 10^9) + (6.72 \times 10^7)$.

1.13 **(a)** How many centimeters are in 1 kilometer **(b)** How many kilograms are in 1 milligram? **(c)** How many decimeters are in 1 dekameter? **(d)** How many nanoseconds are in 10 milliseconds? **(e)** How many terameters are in 100 micrometers?

1.14 **(a)** How many kilograms are in 1 gigagram? **(b)** How many attometers are in 100 picometers? **(c)** How many cubic dekameters are in 16 liters? **(d)** How many nanograms are in 1 hectogram? **(e)** How many millimeters are in 65 micrometers?

1.15 Express each of the following values in the SI unit that will give the smallest number that is greater than 1: **(a)** 0.020 g, **(b)** 150,000 g, **(c)** 1,500,000 m, **(d)** 1.2×10^{-10} m, **(e)** 3.7×10^{-4} g, **(f)** 630,000,000 kg, **(g)** 0.00006 mm.

1.16 Express each of the following values in the SI unit that will give the smallest number that is greater than 1: **(a)** 36,000 kg, **(b)** 3.0×10^{-5} m, **(c)** 6.0×10^7 m, **(d)** 0.003 kg, **(e)** 36,500 pm, **(f)** 0.00065 Mg, **(g)** 1.7×10^{-13} g.

1.17 The liter is defined as 1 cubic decimeter. **(a)** How many liters are in 1 cubic meter? **(b)** How many cubic meters are in 1 liter?

1.18 The ångstrom unit (Å), which is defined as 10^{-10} m, is not an SI unit. **(a)** How many nanometers are equal to 1 Å? **(b)** How many picometers are equal to 1 Å? **(c)** The radius of a chlorine atom is 0.99 Å. What is this distance in nanometers and in picometers?

1.19 The deepest part of the Pacific Ocean is 5968 fathoms deep. What is this depth in meters? One fathom is exactly 6 feet.

1.20 In apothecaries' measures, 1 scruple is 20 grains, 1 ounce is 480 grains, and 1 gram is 0.03215 ounce. What mass in grams equals the mass of 1 scruple?

1.21 One furlong is defined as one-eighth of a mile. How many kilometers are there in a six-furlong race? The following relations are exact: 1 mile = 5280 ft, 12 in = 1 ft, 1 in = 2.54 cm. Give answer to three significant figures.

1.22 A tun consists of four hogsheads, one hogshead is 0.500 butt, one butt is 126 gallons, one gallon is 3.785 L, and 1 L is 1.00 dm^3. How many cubic meters are equal to 1.00 tun?

1.23 A day on Mars is 8.864×10^4 seconds long and a year is 5.935×10^7 seconds long. **(a)** How many earth days are equivalent to 1 day on Mars? **(b)** How many earth days are equivalent to 1 year on Mars? **(c)** How many Mars days are in 1 Mars year?

1.24 A day on Jupiter is 3.543×10^4 seconds long and a year is 3.743×10^8 seconds long. **(a)** How many earth days are equivalent to 1 day on Jupiter? **(b)** How many earth days are equivalent to 1 year on Jupiter? **(c)** How many Jupiter days are in 1 Jupiter year?

1.25 The mean distance of the earth from the sun is 1.496×10^8 km, which is defined as one astronomical unit (au). The mean radius of the moon's orbit around the earth is 0.002570 au. The mean radius of the earth at the equator is 6378 km. The distance from the earth to the moon is the equivalent of how many trips around the circumference of the earth at the equator?

---

* The more difficult problems are marked with asterisks. The appendix contains answers to color-keyed problems.

1.26 If the metric system is adopted for everyday use, fabric will be sold in meters (not yards), milk in liters (not quarts), and meat in kilograms (not pounds). Given that 1 inch = 2.54 cm, 1 pint = 473.2 ml, and 1 pound = 453.6 g, what percentage increase does each of the following represent? **(a)** fabric: 1.00 meter instead of 1 yard, **(b)** milk: 1.00 liter instead of 1.00 quart, **(c)** meat: 1.00 kilogram instead of 2.00 pounds.

1.27 One cord of wood (a stack 4 ft high by 8 ft long by 4 ft deep) has a volume of 128 ft^3. What is the volume of 1 cord in m^3? One inch equals 2.54 cm exactly.

1.28 One gallon is 231 in^3. What is the volume of 1 gallon in cm^3? One inch equals 2.54 cm exactly.

1.29 Pure gold is 24 karat (abbreviated K). **(a)** A ring is made of 18 K gold. What percentage of the metal is gold? **(b)** A gold alloy contains 87.5% Au. How is this alloy rated in terms of karats of gold?

1.30 Pure gold is 24 karat (abbreviated K). **(a)** An alloy called blue gold is made from 36.0 g of Au and 12.0 g of Fe. How is this alloy rated in terms of karats of gold? **(b)** How much copper must be used with 350. g of Au in order to make a 14 K gold alloy?

1.31 How many grams of platinum must be used with 125 g of gold to make a type of white gold called platinum gold that is 60.0% Au and 40.0% Pt?

1.32 How many grams of zinc must be used with 2.35 kg of copper to make a type of brass that is 35.0% Zn and 65.0% Cu?

1.33 A type of bronze consists of 90.0% Cu and 10.0% Sn. **(a)** How many grams of Sn must be used to make 1.75 kg of alloy? **(b)** How many grams of the alloy can be made from 1.75 kg of Cu?

1.34 A type of silver solder consists of 63.0% Ag, 30.0% Cu, and 7.0% Zn. **(a)** How many grams of copper must be used to make 0.500 kg of solder? **(b)** How many grams of solder can be made from 0.635 kg of silver?

1.35 According to estimates, 1.0 g of seawater contains on the average 4.0 pg of Au. If the total mass of all the oceans is 1.6×10^{12} Tg, how many grams of gold are in the oceans of the earth?

1.36 The human body is 0.0040% iron. How many milligrams of iron does a 165-pound person contain? One pound is 453.6 g.

* **1.37** A white brass consists of 60.0% Cu, 25.0% Zn, and 15.0% Ni. **(a)** How many grams of the alloy can be made from 1.00 kg Cu, 350. g Zn, and 200. g Ni? **(b)** How many grams of each of the pure metals would be left over?

* **1.38** One kind of type metal consists of 82.0% Pb, 15.0% Sb, and 3.0% Sn. **(a)** How many grams of alloy can be made from 1.23 kg Pb, 250. g Sb, and 100. g Sn? **(b)** How many grams of each of the pure metals would be left over?

1.39 A swimmer completed a 1650. yard race in 14 minutes and 48 seconds. What was the swimmer's average speed **(a)** in miles per hour? **(b)** in meters per second?

1.40 A runner completed a marathon (26 miles and 385 yards) in 2 hours and 25 minutes. What was the runner's average speed **(a)** in miles per hour? **(b)** in meters per second?

1.41 The speed limit on the highway is 55 miles per hour. Convert this value to kilometers per hour. The following relations are exact: 1 mile = 5280 ft, 1 ft = 12 in, 1 in = 2.54 cm.

1.42 One knot is 1.1508 miles per hour. What is this speed in cm/s? The following relations are exact: 1 mile = 5280 ft, 1 ft = 12 in, 1 in = 2.54 cm.

1.43 Under certain conditions, a hydrogen molecule travels $0.131 \mu m$ between collisions with other molecules and undergoes 1.40×10^{10} collisions in one second. What is the mean speed of the hydrogen molecule under these conditions in m/s?

1.44 The light year is a unit used in measurement of astronomical distances and is defined as the distance that light travels in 1 year. The speed of light is 2.9979×10^8 m/s. How many km are equal to 1 light year?

1.45 (a) The radius of the earth at the equator is 6.378×10^3 km. It takes 24.00 hours for the earth to make a complete rotation on its axis. How fast is a spot on the equator rotating around the axis in meters per second and in miles per hour? **(b)** The mean radius of the earth's orbit around the sun (measured from the center of the sun) is 1.496×10^8 km. It takes 365.25 days (one year) for the earth to complete an orbit around the sun. How fast is the earth moving around the sun in miles per hour and in meters per second?

1.46 (a) The radius of Mercury at the equator is 2.436×10^3 km. Mercury takes 58.66 earth days to make a complete rotation on its axis. How fast is a spot on the equator rotating around the axis in miles per hour and in meters per second? **(b)** The mean radius of Mercury's orbit around the sun (measured from the center of the sun) is 5.796×10^7 km. Mercury takes 87.99 earth days (one Mercury year) to complete an orbit around the sun. How fast is Mercury moving around the sun in miles per hour and in meters per second?

1.47 A cube of sodium 15.0 cm on a side weighs 3.28 kg. What is the density of sodium in g/cm^3?

1.48 A cube of platinum 2.500 cm on a side weighs 0.3352 kg. What is the density of platinum in g/cm^3?

1.49 The density of diamond is 3.51 g/cm^3. What is the volume of a 1.00 carat diamond? One carat is 200 mg.

1.50 The density of diamond is 3.51 g/cm^3 and of graphite is 2.22 g/cm^3. Both substances are pure carbon. What volume would 10.0 g of carbon occupy **(a)** in the form of diamond? **(b)** in the form of graphite?

1.51 The mass of the sun is 1.991×10^{30} kg and the density of the sun is 1.410 g/cm^3. What is the volume of the sun in m^3?

1.52 The mass of the earth is 5.979×10^{24} kg and the density of the earth is 5.519 g/cm^3. What is the volume of the earth in m^3?

1.53 Under certain conditions, the density of dry air is 1.205 g/L. What is the mass of air in a room that is 3.658 m wide by 4.572 m long by 2.438 m high?

1.54 A swimming pool that is 3.05 m wide by 6.10 m long has an average depth of 2.75 m. The density of water is 1.00 g/cm^3. What is the mass of water in the pool when it is filled?

1.55 One barrel of crude oil weighs 0.136 metric tonnes. A metric tonne is exactly 1000 kg. A barrel has a volume equal to 158.98 L. What is the density of crude oil in g/mL?

1.56 The density of coconut oil is 57.7 pounds/ft^3. What is the value in g/cm^3? The following relations are exact: 1 ft = 12 in, 1 in = 2.54 cm, 1 pound = 453.6 g.

*$**1.57**$ The mass of Venus is 4.883 × 10^{15} Tg and the density of Venus is 5.256 g/cm^3. What is the radius of Venus? Express the answer in the SI unit that will give the smallest number that is greater than 1.

*$**1.58**$ Saturn's density is the lowest of all the planets (even lower than that of water) and is 0.1246 times the density of earth. The mass of Saturn, on the other hand, is 95.07 times the mass of earth. Use these data to compare the volume of Saturn to the volume of earth.

*$**1.59**$ A very long tube with a cross-sectional area of 1.00 cm^2 is filled with mercury to a height of 76.0 cm. At what height would water stand in this tube if the tube were filled with a mass of water equal to that of the mercury? The density of mercury is 13.60 g/cm^3 and of water is 1.00 g/cm^3.

*$**1.60**$ A cube containing small iron ball bearings closely packed together is filled with water. The contents of the assembly weigh 1091.80 g. When ethyl alcohol is substituted for the water, the contents weigh 1077.17 g. What is the length of a side of the cube? The relevant densities can be found in Table 1.6.

INTRODUCTION TO ATOMIC THEORY

The atomic theory is the foundation upon which modern chemistry has been built. An understanding of atomic structure and the ways in which atoms interact is central to an understanding of chemistry. In this chapter, we will have our first look at the atomic theory. This topic will be extended in Chapter 6 (*The Electronic Structure of Atoms*) and Chapter 27 (*Nuclear Chemistry*).

2.1 Dalton's Atomic Theory

Credit for the first atomic theory is usually given to the ancient Greeks, but the concept may have had its origins in even earlier civilizations. The atomic theory of Leucippus and Democritus (fifth century B.C.) held that the continued subdivision of matter would ultimately yield atoms, which could not be further divided. The word *atom* is derived from the Greek word *atomos*, which means "uncut" or "indivisible." Aristotle (fourth century B.C.) did not accept the atomic theory. He believed that matter could hypothetically be divided endlessly into smaller and smaller particles.

The theories of the ancient Greeks were based on abstract thought, not on planned experimentation. For approximately two thousand years the atomic theory remained mere speculation. The existence of atoms was accepted by Robert Boyle in his book *The Sceptical Chymist* (1661) and by Isaac Newton in his books *Principia* (1687) and *Opticks* (1704). John Dalton, however, proposed an atomic theory—which he developed in the years 1803 to 1808—that is a landmark in the history of chemistry.

John Dalton, 1766–1844. *Smithsonian Institution.*

Many scientists of the time believed that all matter consists of atoms, but Dalton went further. Dalton developed an atomic theory that explains the laws of chemical change. He also made the concept quantitative by assigning relative masses to the atoms of different elements. The principal postulates of Dalton's theory are

1. Elements are composed of extremely small particles called atoms. All atoms of the same element are alike, and atoms of different elements are different.

2. The separation of atoms and the union of atoms occur in chemical reactions. In these reactions, no atom is created or destroyed, and no atom of one element is converted into an atom of another element.

3. A chemical compound is the result of the combination of atoms of two or more elements. A given compound always contains the same kinds of atoms combined in the same proportions.

Dalton's theory in its broad outline is valid today, but his first postulate has had to be modified. Dalton believed that all atoms of a given element have equal atomic masses. Today we know that many elements consist of several types of atoms that differ in mass (see the discussion of isotopes in Section 2.8). We can say, however, that all atoms of the same element are chemically similar and that atoms of one element are chemically different from atoms of another. Furthermore, we can use an average mass for the atoms of each element. In most calculations, no mistake is made by proceeding as if an element consists of only one type of atom with an average mass.

Dalton derived the quantitative aspects of his theory from two laws of chemical change:

1. The law of conservation of mass states that there is no detectable change in mass during the course of a chemical reaction. In other words, the total mass of all substances entering into a chemical reaction equals the total mass of all the products of the reaction. The second postulate of Dalton's theory explains this law. Since chemical reactions consist of the separating and joining of atoms and since atoms are neither created nor destroyed in these processes, the total mass of all the atoms entering into a chemical reaction is constant no matter how the atoms are grouped together.

2. The law of definite proportions states that a pure compound always contains the same elements combined in the same proportions by mass. The third postulate of Dalton's theory explains this law. Since a given compound is the result of the combination of atoms of two or more elements in fixed proportions, the elements of the compound are present in fixed proportions by mass.

On the basis of his theory, Dalton proposed a third law of chemical combination, the law of multiple proportions. This law states that when two elements, A and B, form more than one compound, the amounts of A that are combined in these compounds with a fixed amount of B are in a small whole-number ratio. This law follows from Dalton's view that the atoms in a compound are combined in fixed proportions. For example, carbon and oxygen form two compounds: carbon dioxide and carbon monoxide. In carbon dioxide, *two* atoms of oxygen are combined with one atom of carbon, and in carbon monoxide, one atom of oxygen is combined with one atom of carbon. When the two compounds are compared, therefore, the masses of oxygen that combine with a fixed mass of carbon stand in the ratio 2:1. The experimental verification of the law of multiple proportions was strong support for Dalton's theory.

2.2 The Electron

In Dalton's theory and in the theories of the Greeks, atoms were regarded as the smallest posssible components of matter. Toward the end of the nineteenth century, it began to appear that the atom itself might be composed of even smaller particles. This change in viewpoint was brought about by experiments with electricity.

In 1807–1808, the English chemist Humphry Davy discovered five elements (potassium, sodium, calcium, strontium, and barium) by using electricity to decompose compounds. This work led Davy to propose that elements are held together in compounds by attractions that are electrical in nature.

In 1832–33, Michael Faraday ran an important series of experiments in chemical electrolysis, processes in which compounds are decomposed by electricity. Faraday studied the relationship between the amount of electricity used and the amount of compound decomposed, and he formulated the laws of chemical electrolysis (Section 20.4). On the basis of Faraday's work, George Johnstone Stoney proposed in 1874 that units of electrical charge are associated with atoms. In 1891, Stoney proposed that these units be called **electrons.**

Attempts to pass an electric current through a vacuum led to Julius Plücker's discovery of **cathode rays** in 1859. Two electrodes are sealed in a glass tube from which air is almost completely removed. When a high voltage is impressed across these electrodes, rays stream from the negative electrode, which is called the cathode. These rays are negatively charged, travel in straight lines, and cause the walls opposite the cathode to glow. The picture tubes used in television sets and computer monitors are modern cathode-ray tubes in which the rays are focused on screens that are coated with substances that give off flashes of light when struck by radiation.

In the latter part of the nineteenth century, cathode rays were extensively studied. The results of many scientists' experiments led to the conclusion that the rays are streams of fast-moving, negatively charged particles. The particles were eventually called electrons, as Stoney suggested. The electrons, which originate from the metal of which the cathode is composed, are the same no matter what metal is employed as the cathode.

Since unlike charges attract, the streams of electrons that constitute a cathode ray are attracted toward the positive plate when two oppositely charged plates are placed on either side of them (Figure 2.1c). The rays, therefore, are deflected from their usual straight-line path in an electric field. The degree of deflection is influenced by two factors:

1. It varies *directly* with the size of the charge of the particle, q. A particle with a high charge is deflected more than a particle with a low charge. The extent of the deflection, therefore, increases as q increases.

2. It varies *inversely* with the mass of the particle, m. A particle with a large mass is deflected less than one with a small mass. The degree of deviation from a straight-line path, therefore, is proportional to $1/m$.

The combination of these factors—the ratio of charge to mass, q/m—therefore determines the extent to which the electrons are deflected from a straight-line path in an electric field. Electrons are also deflected in a magnetic field. In this case, however, the deflection is at right angle to the applied field (Figure 2.1a). Notice that in the figure, the magnetic field is at right angles to the electric field, so that both electron paths occur in the same plane.

In 1897, Joseph J. Thomson determined the value of q/m for the electron by studying the deflections of cathode rays in electric and magnetic fields. He measured the radius of curvature of the deflection caused by a magnetic field of known field strength (Figure 2.1a). He then determined the strength of the electric field required to balance the magnetic field so that there was no net deflection (Figure

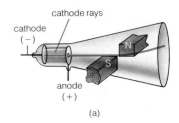

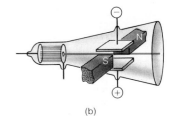

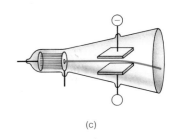

Figure 2.1 Deflections of cathode rays. (a) In a magnetic field. (b) With magnetic and electric fields balanced; no net deflection. (c) In an electric field.

Joseph J. Thomson, 1856–1940.
*Burndy Library, courtesy AIP
Niels Bohr Library.*

2.1b). From his measurements he calculated the value of q/m. The modern value is

$$q/m = -1.7588 \times 10^8 \text{ C/g}$$

The *coulomb* (C) is the SI unit of electric charge. One coulomb is the quantity of charge that passes a given point in an electric circuit in one second when the current is one ampere.

The Charge of the Electron

The first precise measurement of the charge of the electron was made by Robert A. Millikan in 1909. In Millikan's experiment (Figure 2.2), electrons are produced by the action of X rays on the molecules of which air is composed. Very small drops of oil pick up electrons and acquire electric charges. The oil drops are allowed to settle between two horizontal plates, and the mass of a particular drop is determined by measuring its rate of fall.

When the plates are charged, the rate of fall of the drop is altered because the negatively charged drop is attracted to the upper, positive plate. The amount of charge on the plates can be adjusted so that the drop will stop falling and remain suspended. The charge on the drop can be calculated from the mass of the drop and the charge on the plates after this adjustment has been made.

Since a given drop can pick up one or more electrons, the charges calculated in this way are not identical. They are, however, all simple multiples of the same value, which is assumed to be the charge on a single electron:

$$q = -e = -1.6022 \times 10^{-19} \text{ C}$$

The value e is called a **unit electrical charge.** The electron has a unit *negative*

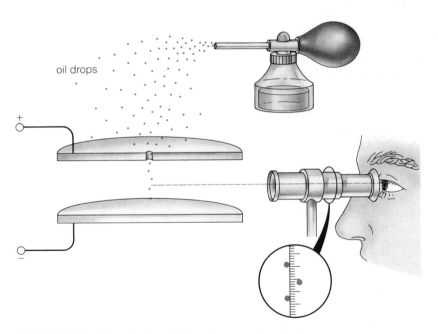

Figure 2.2 Milikan's determination of the charge on the electron

oil drops

charge, $-e$. The mass of the electron can be calculated from the value of q/m and the value of q:

$$m = \frac{q}{q/m} = \frac{-1.6022 \times 10^{-19} \text{ C}}{-1.7588 \times 10^8 \text{ C/g}} = 9.1096 \times 10^{-28} \text{ g}$$

2.3 The Proton

If one or more electrons are removed from a neutral atom or molecule, the residue has a positive charge equal to the sum of the negative charges of the electrons removed. If one electron is removed from a neon atom (symbol, Ne), a Ne^+ ion results; if two are removed, a Ne^{2+} ion results, and so forth. Positive particles of this type (positive ions) are formed in an electric discharge tube when cathode rays rip electrons from the atoms or molecules of the gas present in the tube. These positive ions move *toward* the negative electrode. If holes have been bored in this electrode, the positive ions pass through them (see Figure 2.3). The electrons of the cathode rays, since they are negatively charged, move in the opposite direction (toward the positive electrode).

These streams of positive ions, called **positive rays,** were first observed by Eugen Goldstein in 1886. The deflections of positive rays in electric and magnetic fields were studied by Wilhelm Wien (1898) and J. J. Thomson (1906). Values of q/m were determined for the positive ions by using essentially the same method employed in the study of cathode rays.

When different gases are used in the discharge tube, different types of positive ions are produced. When hydrogen gas is used, a positive particle results that has the smallest mass (and hence the largest q/m value) of any positive ion observed.

$$q/m = +9.5791 \times 10^4 \text{ C/g}$$

These particles, now called **protons,** are assumed to be a component of all atoms. The proton has a unit *positive* charge $(+e)$—a charge equal in magnitude to that of the electron but opposite in sign:

$$q = +e = +1.6022 \times 10^{-19} \text{ C}$$

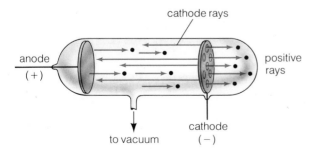

Figure 2.3 Positive rays

Table 2.1	Subatomic particles			
		Mass		
Particle	Grams	Unified Atomic Mass Units[a]	Charge[b]	
Electron	9.109535×10^{-28}	0.0005485803	1−	
Proton	1.672649×10^{-24}	1.007276	1+	
Neutron	1.674954×10^{-24}	1.008665	0	

[a] The unified atomic mass unit (u) is 1/12 the mass of a ^{12}C atom (Section 2.9).
[b] The unit charge is 1.60219×10^{-19} C.

The mass of the proton, which is 1836 times the mass of the electron, can be calculated from these data:

$$m = \frac{q}{q/m} = \frac{+1.6022 \times 10^{-19}\ \text{C}}{+9.5791 \times 10^{4}\ \text{C/g}} = 1.6726 \times 10^{-24}\ \text{g}$$

2.4 The Neutron

Since atoms are electrically neutral, a given atom must contain as many electrons as protons. To account for the total masses of atoms, Ernest Rutherford in 1920 postulated the existence of an uncharged particle. Since this particle is uncharged, it is difficult to detect and to characterize. In 1932, however, James Chadwick published the results of his work, which established the existence of the **neutron.** He was able to calculate the mass of the neutron from data on certain nuclear reactions (see Chapter 27) in which neutrons are produced. By taking into account the masses and energies of all particles used and produced in these reactions, Chadwick determined the mass of the neutron, which is very slightly larger than that of the proton. The proton has a mass of 1.6750×10^{-24} g, and the proton 1.6726×10^{-24} g.

The properties of the electron, proton, and neutron are summarized in Table 2.1. Other subatomic particles have been identified. For the study of chemistry, however, atomic structure is adequately explained on the basis of the electron, proton, and neutron.

2.5 The Nuclear Atom

Natural Radioactivity

Certain atoms are unstable combinations of the subatomic particles. These atoms spontaneously emit rays and in this way change into atoms with a different chemical identity. This process, called **radioactivity,** was discovered by Henri Becquerel in 1896. In subsequent years, Ernest Rutherford explained the nature of the three types of radiation emitted by radioactive substances that occur in nature (see Table

Table 2.2	Types of radioactive emissions		
Ray	Symbol	Composition	Charge of Component
Alpha	α	particles containing 2 protons and 2 neutrons	2+
Beta	β	electrons	1−
Gamma	γ	very short wavelength; electromagnetic radiation	0

2.2).* The three types are identified by the first three letters of the Greek alphabet: alpha (α), beta (β), and gamma (γ).

1. Alpha radiation consists of particles that carry a 2+ charge and have a mass approximately four times that of the proton. These α particles are ejected from the radioactive substance at speeds around 16,000 km/s (approximately 0.05 times the speed of light). When α particles were first studied, the neutron had not yet been discovered. We now know that an α particle consists of two protons and two neutrons.

2. Beta radiation consists of streams of electrons that travel at approximately 130,000 km/s (approximately 0.4 times the speed of light).

3. Gamma radiation is essentially a highly energetic form of light. Gamma rays are uncharged and are similar to X rays.

Rutherford's Atomic Model

In 1911, Rutherford reported the results of experiments in which α particles were used to investigate the structure of the atom. A beam of α particles was directed against a very thin (about 0.0004-cm thick) foil of gold, silver, or copper. The large majority of the α particles went directly through the foil. Some, however, were deflected from their straight-line path, and a few recoiled back toward their source (Figure 2.4).

Rutherford explained the results of these experiments by proposing that an atom consists of two parts.

1. A **nucleus** exists in the center of the atom. Most of the mass and all of the positive charge of the atom are concentrated in the nucleus. The nucleus is now believed to contain protons and neutrons, which together account for the mass of the nucleus. The protons in the nucleus are responsible for the positive charge of the nucleus.

2. Electrons, which occupy most of the total volume of the atom, are outside the nucleus (**extranuclear**) and move rapidly around it. Since an atom is electrically neutral, the total positive charge of the nucleus (from the protons it contains)

Ernest Rutherford, 1871–1937. *American Institute of Physics, Niels Bohr Library.*

---

* Other types of radiation have now been identified. These radiations, however, result from the disintegration of atoms that have been made by nuclear reactions and not from atoms that occur in nature.

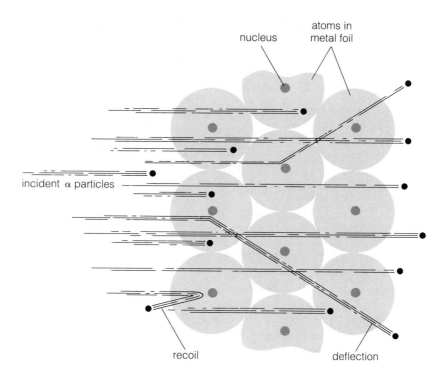

nucleus

atoms in
metal foil

incident α particles

recoil

deflection

Figure 2.4 Deflections and recoil of α particles by nuclei of metal foil in Rutherford's experiment. (Not to scale).

equals the total negative charge of all the electrons. The number of electrons, therefore, is equal to the number of protons.

It is important to grasp the scale of this model. If a nucleus of an atom were the size of a tennis ball, the atom would have a diameter of over one mile. Since most of the volume of an atom is empty space, most α particles pass directly through the target foils. The comparatively light electrons do not deflect the heavier, fast-moving α particles. A close approach of an α particle (which is positively charged) to a nucleus (which is also positively charged) results in the repulsion of the α particle and deflection from its straight-line path. In a very few instances, when an α particle scores a direct hit on a nucleus, the particle is reflected back toward its source. The composition and stability of the nucleus are discussed in Chapter 27.

2.6 Atomic Symbols

An atom is identified by two numbers, the atomic number and the mass number:

1. The **atomic number,** Z, is the number of unit positive charges on the nucleus. Since the proton has a $1+$ charge, the atomic number is equal to the number of protons in the nucleus of the atom:

number of protons $= Z$ (2.1)

An atom is electrically neutral. The atomic number, therefore, also indicates the number of extranuclear electrons in an uncombined atom.

2. The **mass number,** A, of an atom is the total number of protons and neutrons (collectively called **nucleons**) in the nucleus of the atom:

$$A = number\ of\ neutrons\ +\ number\ of\ protons \tag{2.2}$$

$$A = number\ of\ neutrons\ +\ Z$$

The number of neutrons can be calculated, therefore, by subtracting the atomic number (the number of protons) from the mass number (the number of protons and neutrons taken together):

$$number\ of\ neutrons = A - Z \tag{2.3}$$

The mass *number* is the total *number* of nucleons in a nucleus and not the mass of the nucleus. The mass number, however, is a whole-number approximation of the atomic mass in atomic mass units (u), since the mass of the proton and the mass of the neutron are each approximately equal to 1 u and the mass of the electron is negligible in comparison.

An atom of an element is designated by the chemical symbol for the element with the atomic number of the element placed at the lower left and the mass number placed at the upper left*:

$$^{A}_{Z}Symbol$$

The symbol $^{35}_{17}Cl$ designates an atom of chlorine that has 17 protons (Z) and 18 neutrons ($A - Z$) in the nucleus and 17 extranuclear electrons (Z). An atom of sodium with the symbol $^{23}_{11}Na$ has 11 protons and 12 neutrons in the nucleus and 11 electrons in motion around this nucleus.

Example 2.1

How many protons, neutrons, and electrons are in a $^{63}_{29}Cu$ atom?

Solution

The atomic number ($Z = 29$) indicates that there are 29 protons in the nucleus of the copper atom (symbol, Cu) and 29 electrons outside the nucleus. The number of neutrons can be calculated from the mass number ($A = 63$) and the atomic number ($Z = 29$):

$$number\ of\ neutrons = A - Z \tag{2.3}$$
$$= 63 - 29 = 34$$

---

* The other corners are reserved for other designations: the upper right for the charge if the atom has lost or gained electrons and become an ion, the lower right corner for the number of atoms present in a molecule or in a formula unit.

The nucleus of the copper atom, therefore, contains 29 protons and 34 neutrons. There are 29 electrons outside the nucleus.

Example 2.2

What is the symbol for an atom of potassium (symbol, K) that contains 19 protons, 22 neutrons, and 19 electrons?

Solution

Since the atom contains 19 protons and 19 electrons, the atomic number, Z, is 19. The mass number of the atom is equal to the sum of the number of protons and the number of neutrons:

$$A = \textit{number of protons} + \textit{number of neutrons} \tag{2.2}$$
$$= 19 + 22 = 41$$

The symbol for the atom is $^{41}_{19}\text{K}$.

A charged particle containing one or more atoms is called an **ion**. A **monatomic ion** is formed from a *single atom* by the loss or gain of one or more electrons. When a symbol is used to identify an ion, the charge of the ion is noted at the upper right of the symbol for the ion.

The following equations are useful in interpreting the charge of a monatomic ion:

$$\textit{charge of ion} = \textit{total positive charge} + \textit{total negative charge} \tag{2.4}$$

$$\textit{charge of ion} = \textit{total charge of protons} + \textit{total charge of electrons} \tag{2.5}$$

Since the proton has a charge of $1+$ and the electron has a charge of $1-$,

$$\textit{charge of ion} = \textit{number of protons} - \textit{number of electrons} \tag{2.6}$$

Remember that the number of protons is equal to the atomic number, Z.

Example 2.3

What is the composition of (a) a $^{27}_{13}\text{Al}^{3+}$ ion? (b) a $^{32}_{16}\text{S}^{2-}$ ion?

Solution

$$\text{(a)} \quad \textit{number of protons} = Z \tag{2.1}$$
$$= 13$$

$$\textit{number of neutrons} = A - Z \tag{2.3}$$
$$= 27 - 13 = 14$$

The number of electrons in a neutral atom is the same as the number of protons (in this case, 13). Since the ion has a *positive* charge of 3, however, the atom must have *lost* three electrons. Hence, the ion has 10 electrons. Note that

$$charge\ of\ ion = number\ of\ protons - number\ of\ electrons \qquad (2.6)$$

$$number\ of\ electrons = number\ of\ protons - charge\ of\ ion \qquad (2.7)$$

Thus,

$$number\ of\ electrons = 13 - (3+) = 10$$

The ion contains 13 protons and 14 neutrons in the nucleus and 10 electrons outside the nucleus.

(b) $number\ of\ protons = Z$ $\qquad (2.1)$
$$= 16$$

$number\ of\ neutrons = A - Z$ $\qquad (2.3)$
$$= 32 - 16 = 16$$

In this case, the ion has a *negative* charge of 2, which means that it must have *gained* two electrons. Since the neutral atom has 16 electrons (the same as the number of protons), the ion has 18 electrons. We can also find the number of electrons by using Equation 2.7:

$$number\ of\ electrons = number\ of\ protons - charge\ of\ ion \qquad (2.7)$$
$$= 16 - (2-) = 16 + 2 = 18$$

The ion contains 16 protons and 16 neutrons in the nucleus and 18 electrons outside the nucleus.

Example 2.4

What is the symbol for (a) an ion of fluorine (symbol, F) that contains 9 protons and 10 neutrons in the nucleus and 10 extranuclear electrons? (b) an ion of iron (symbol, Fe) that contains 26 protons and 30 neutrons in the nucleus and 24 extranuclear electrons?

Solution

(a) $Z = number\ of\ protons$ $\qquad (2.1)$
$$= 9$$

$A = number\ of\ protons + number\ of\ neutrons$ $\qquad (2.2)$
$$= 9 + 10 = 19$$

Since the ion has one more electron than protons (10 as compared to 9), the charge is $1-$. Or,

$$charge\ of\ ion = total\ charge\ of\ protons + total\ charge\ of\ electrons \qquad (2.5)$$
$$= (9+) + (10-) = 1-$$

The symbol for the ion is $^{19}_{9}F^{-}$.

Z = *number of protons*   (2.1)
    = 26

A = *number of protons + number of neutrons*   (2.2)
    = 26 + 30 = 56

The ion has 2 more protons than electrons (26 in comparison to 24). Its charge, therefore, is $2+$. Or,

charge of ion = total charge of protons + total charge of electrons   (2.5)
    = $(26+) + (24-) = 2+$

The symbol for the ion is $^{56}_{26}Fe^{2+}$

2.7 Atomic Number and the Periodic Table

The periodic table is a very useful device for correlating the properties of the elements. In later chapters we will consider the history, the theoretical basis, and many uses of the periodic table. In this section, prominent features of the table will be introduced so that you can begin to gain familiarity with it.

Certain groups of elements have very similar chemical and physical properties. One of these groups consists of helium (He), neon (Ne), argon (Ar), krypton (Kr), xenon (Xe), and radon (Rn), which are colorless gases of low reactivity. These elements, called the **noble gases,** have atomic numbers of 2, 10, 18, 36, 54, and 86.

Another group of elements consists of highly reactive, soft metals: lithium (Li), sodium (Na), potassium (K), rubidium (Rb), cesium (Cs), and francium (Fr). The atomic numbers of these elements, which are called the **alkali metals,** are 3, 11, 19, 37, 55, and 87.

Comparison of the atomic numbers of the elements in these two groups shows that in a list of the elements arranged by increasing atomic number, each noble gas is followed by an alkali metal. The study of other groups of elements in addition to these two reveals that, in general, the properties of the elements exhibit a repeating pattern when the elements are arranged by atomic number. The **periodic law** states that when the elements are studied in order of increasing atomic number, similarities in properties recur periodically.

The periodic table is based on this law. It is designed in such a way that similar elements are grouped together and the properties of the elements can be predicted from their positions in the table. Three features of the table, which is found inside the front cover of this book, are:

1. The elements found in a horizontal row in the table are collectively called a **period.** The first period consists of only two elements: hydrogen (H, $Z = 1$) and helium (He, $Z = 2$). The second period consists of eight elements and runs from lithium (Li, $Z = 3$) to neon (Ne, $Z = 10$). Subsequent periods contain 8, 18, 18, and 32 elements.

The elements that have atomic numbers from 58 to 71 and that appear at the bottom of the chart are called the **lanthanides** or **lanthanoids.** They belong in the sixth period (which consists of 32 elements), and they should actually appear in the body of the chart after lanthanum (La, $Z = 57$). The chart should be vertically cut, the sections separated, and the lanthanides inserted into their proper position. This arrangement is not used because it is inconvenient to reproduce.

The alkali metals react vigorously with water—the heavier members of the group react explosively! Here, sodium metal reacts with water to produce hydrogen gas and a solution of sodium hydroxide. *Russ Kinne, Photo Researchers, Inc.*

The same considerations pertain to the elements with atomic numbers from 90 to 103, which are called the **actinides** or **actinoids** and which appear below the lanthanides at the bottom of the periodic table. They belong in the seventh period and should be inserted after actinium (Ac, $Z = 89$).

With the exception of the first period, each period begins with an alkali metal and ends with a noble gas. The element before the noble gas in each complete period (except for the first period) is a **halogen,** a very reactive nonmetal. The halogens are fluorine (F), chlorine (Cl), bromine (Br), iodine (I), and astatine (At).

2. The elements that appear in a given vertical column in the table make up what is called a **group** or **family.** The elements of a group have similar chemical properties. Three groups that we have mentioned are the noble gases, the alkali metals, and the halogens. Each group is given a designation that usually consists of a Roman numeral followed by the letter A or B. Several systems for designating groups are in current use, however.

3. A **metal** is an element that in general has a characteristic luster, conducts heat and electricity well, and can be pounded into various shapes without breaking. A **nonmetal,** on the other hand, is an element that is not lustrous, is a poor conductor of heat and electricity, and is brittle in the solid state. The chemical properties of metals differ from those of the nonmetals.

About 80% of the known elements are metals. The stepped diagonal line in the periodic table marks the approximate division between the metals and the nonmetals. The nonmetals are found to the right of this line. The division, however, is not sharp. The elements close to this line, sometimes called **metalloids** or **semimetals,** have properties that are intermediate between those of metals and nonmetals.

Notice that a range of properties is exhibited in a period. Each period, with the exception of the first, begins with a highly reactive metal—an alkali metal. The properties change in going from element to element. The metallic properties fade and are replaced by nonmetallic properties. Each period beyond the first ends with a highly reactive nonmetal, a halogen, followed by a noble gas.

2.8 Isotopes

All atoms of a given element have the same atomic number. Some elements, however, consist of several types of atoms that differ from one another in mass number. Atoms that have the same atomic number but different mass numbers are called **isotopes.**

Two isotopes of chlorine occur in nature: $^{35}_{17}Cl$ and $^{37}_{17}Cl$. The atomic compositions of these isotopes are

$^{35}_{17}Cl$ 17 protons   18 neutrons   17 electrons

$^{37}_{17}Cl$ 17 protons   20 neutrons   17 electrons

Both these atoms have 17 protons and 17 electrons, but $^{35}_{17}Cl$ has 18 neutrons and $^{37}_{17}Cl$ has 20 neutrons. Isotopes, therefore, differ in the number of neutrons in the nucleus, and as a result, they differ in atomic mass.

The chemical properties of an atom depend principally upon the numbers of protons and electrons that the atom contains (given by the atomic number).

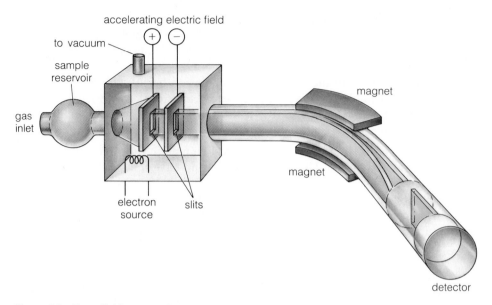

accelerating electric field

to vacuum

sample
reservoir

gas
inlet

magnet

magnet

electron
source

slits

detector

Figure 2.5 Essential features of a mass spectrometer

Isotopes of the same element, therefore, have very similar (in most cases, indistinguishable) chemical properties. Some elements exist in nature in only one isotopic form (for example, sodium, beryllium, and fluorine). Most elements, however, have more than one natural isotope—tin has 10.

The **mass spectrometer** is used to determine the types of isotopes present in an element, the exact masses of these isotopes, and the relative amount of each isotope present. The essential features of the instrument are shown in Figure 2.5. Positive ions are produced from vaporized material by bombardment with electrons. These ions are attracted toward a negatively charged slit. They are accelerated by the attraction and pass through the slit with a high velocity.

The beam of ions is then passed through a magnetic field. Charged particles are deflected from a straight-line path in a magnetic field and follow a circular path. As is the case with the electrons of cathode rays, the degree of deflection of any given particle depends upon the ratio of its charge to its mass, q/m (Section 2.2).

All the ions that pass through the final slit have the same value of q/m. Ions with other values of q/m can be made to pass through this slit by adjusting the magnetic field strength or the voltage used to accelerate the ions. Consequently, each type of ion present can be made to pass through the slit separately. The detector measures the intensity of each ion beam, which depends upon the relative amount of each isotope present in the sample.

Example 2.5

Write symbols for the two isotopes of silver (Ag, $Z = 47$), one of which has 60 neutrons and the other of which has 62 neutrons.

Solution

Both isotopes have 47 protons, since the atomic number is 47. The mass number of each of the isotopes is found by adding the number of protons and the number of neutrons:

$$A = \text{number of protons} + \text{number of neutrons} \qquad (2.2)$$
$$= 47 + 60 = 107$$
$$= 47 + 62 = 109$$

The symbols, therefore, are $^{107}_{47}\text{Ag}$ and $^{109}_{47}\text{Ag}$.

2.9 Atomic Weights

Atoms are extremely small particles that cannot be weighed individually. A very important aspect of Dalton's work is his attempt to determine the relative masses of atoms. Dalton based his system on the hydrogen atom, comparing the masses of all other atoms to the mass of the hydrogen atom. As an example, consider the way in which Dalton assigned a relative mass to the oxygen atom.

Water is a compound that consists of 88.8% oxygen and 11.2% hydrogen by mass. Dalton incorrectly assumed that in water one atom of oxygen is combined with one atom of hydrogen. On this basis, the mass of a single oxygen atom and the mass of a single hydrogen atom would stand in the ratio of 88.8 to 11.2, which is approximately 8 to 1. The arbitrary assignment of a mass of 1 to the hydrogen atom would give a relative mass of approximately 8 to the oxygen atom.*

The formulation that Dalton used for water is incorrect. Actually, one atom of oxygen is combined with *two* atoms of hydrogen. The mass of one oxygen atom, therefore, is approximately 8 times the mass of *two* hydrogen atoms. If one hydrogen atom is assigned a mass of 1, two hydrogen atoms would have a combined mass of 2. Thus, on this scale, one oxygen atom has a relative mass of approximately 8 times 2, or 16.

Even though Dalton made errors in assigning relative atomic masses, he must be given credit for introducing the concept and recognizing its importance. The relative masses of atoms are the basis for the solution of quantitative chemical problems. These values are called **atomic weights,** a term that is not literally correct (since it refers to masses, not weights) but a term that is sanctioned by long usage.

Any relative atomic mass scale must be based on the arbitrary assignment of a value to one atom that is chosen as a standard. Dalton used the hydrogen atom as his standard and assigned it a value of 1. In later years, chemists used naturally occurring oxygen as the standard and set its atomic weight equal to exactly 16. The standard used today is the $^{12}_{6}\text{C}$ atom. The **atomic mass unit** (for which the SI symbol is u) is defined as one-twelfth the mass of the $^{12}_{6}\text{C}$ atom. On this scale, therefore, the $^{12}_{6}\text{C}$ atom has a mass of exactly 12 u.

The masses of the proton, neutron, and electron based on the $^{12}_{6}\text{C}$ scale are

---

* Since the figures that Dalton used for the percent composition of water were very inaccurate, Dalton actually proposed a relative mass of 7 for the oxygen atom.

given in Table 2.1. The mass of an atom, however cannot be calculated from these values. With the exception of ^1_1H (the nucleus of which consists of a single proton), the sum of the masses of the particles that make up a nucleus is always larger than the actual mass of the nucleus.

Einstein showed that matter and energy are equivalent. These mass differences, in terms of energy, account for what is called the **binding energy** of the nucleus. If it were possible to pull a nucleus apart, the binding energy would be the energy required to do the job. The reverse process, the condensation of nucleons into a nucleus, would release the binding energy and there would be an attendant decrease in mass. (Binding energy is discussed in Section 27.8.)

Atomic masses are determined by use of the mass spectrometer. Most elements occur in nature as mixtures of isotopes. In these cases, the instrument can be used to determine the relative amount of each isotope present in the element as well as the atomic mass of each isotope. The data for chlorine show that the element consists of 75.77% $^{35}_{17}Cl$ atoms (mass, 34.969 u) and 24.23% $^{37}_{17}Cl$ atoms (mass, 36.966 u). Any sample of chlorine from a natural source consists of these two isotopes in this proportion.

The atomic weight of the element chlorine is the weighted average of the atomic masses of the natural isotopes. We *cannot* find the average by adding the masses of the isotopes and dividing by 2. The value obtained in this way would be correct only if the element consisted of equal numbers of atoms of the two isotopes. Instead, the *weighted* average is found by multiplying the atomic mass of each isotope by its fractional abundance and adding the values obtained. A fractional abundance is the decimal equivalent of the percent abundance:

$$
\begin{array}{lll}
 & \textit{(abundance)} \quad \textit{(mass)} & \\
^{35}_{17}Cl & (0.7577)(34.969 \text{ u}) = & 26.496 \text{ u} \\
^{37}_{17}Cl & (0.2423)(36.966 \text{ u}) = & \underline{8.957 \text{ u}} \\
 & & 35.453 \text{ u}
\end{array}
$$

The accepted value for chlorine is 35.453 ± 0.001 u.

No atom of chlorine has a mass of 35.453 u, but it is convenient to think in terms of such an atom. In most calculations, no mistake is made by assuming that a sample of an element consists of only one type of atom with the average mass, the atomic weight. This assumption is valid because there is a huge number of atoms in even a small sample of matter. There are, for example, more atoms in a drop of water than there are people on earth.

With very few exceptions, a mixture of this type has a constant composition. The atomic weight of such an element is an average value that takes into account the masses of the types of atoms and their relative abundance in nature (see Section 2.8).

Several types of carbon atoms occur in nature. The carbon-12 atom, which is employed as the standard for atomic weights, is the most abundant one. When the percentages and masses of all the types of carbon atoms are taken into account, the average relative mass for naturally occurring carbon is 12.011, which is the value recorded as the atomic weight of carbon. About three-quarters of the atomic weights of the elements are average values that take into account the several types of atoms that make up the element. The remainder give the relative mass of a single type of atom. In the periodic table that appears inside the front cover of this book, the *atomic number* of an element is found *above* the symbol of the element; the *atomic weight* appears *below* the name of the element. Atomic weights are also given in the alphabetically arranged table of elements that appears inside the back cover of this book.

Example 2.6

What is the atomic weight of magnesium to four significant figures? The element consists of 78.99% $^{24}_{12}Mg$ atoms (mass, 23.99 u), 10.00% $^{25}_{12}Mg$ atoms (mass, 24.99 u), and 11.01% $^{26}_{12}Mg$ atoms (mass, 25.98 u).

Solution

	(*abundance*) (*mass*)
$^{24}_{12}Mg$	$(0.7899)(23.99 \text{ u}) = 18.95 \text{ u}$
$^{25}_{12}Mg$	$(0.1000)(24.99 \text{ u}) = 2.50 \text{ u}$
$^{26}_{12}Mg$	$(0.1101)(25.98 \text{ u}) = \underline{2.86 \text{ u}}$
	24.31 u

Example 2.7

Carbon occurs in nature as a mixture of $^{12}_{6}C$ and $^{13}_{6}C$. The atomic mass of $^{12}_{6}C$ is exactly 12 u, by definition, and the atomic mass of $^{13}_{6}C$ is 13.003 u. The atomic weight of carbon is 12.011 u. What is the atom percent of $^{12}_{6}C$ in natural carbon?

Solution

The equation to determine the atomic weight of carbon is

$$(\text{abundance } ^{12}_{6}C)(\text{mass } ^{12}_{6}C) + (\text{abundance } ^{13}_{6}C)(\text{mass } ^{13}_{6}C) = \text{atomic weight C}$$

If we let x equal the abundance of $^{12}_{6}C$, then $(1 - x)$ is the abundance of $^{13}_{6}C$. Therefore,

$$(x)(12.000) + (1 - x)(13.003) = 12.011$$

$$12.000x + 13.003 - 13.003x = 12.011$$

$$-1.003x = -0.992$$

$$x = 0.989$$

Atoms of $^{12}_{6}C$ constitute 98.9% of the total number.

Very small amounts of $^{14}_{6}C$ also occur in nature. The amount is so small, however, that the isotope can be ignored in the calculation of the atomic weight of carbon.

Summary

Modern atomic theory stems from the work of John Dalton, who based his theory on the *law of conservation of mass* and the *law of definite proportions*. On the basis of his concept, Dalton proposed a third law of chemical combination: the *law of multiple proportions*.

An atom, which is the smallest particle of an element that can combine with the atoms of other elements to form compounds, is made up of subatomic particles. A number of classic experiments identified and described three fundamental subatomic particles—the electron, the proton, and the neutron—and their positions within the atom.

The *electron* has a negative charge, $-e$. The *proton* has a positive charge equal in magnitude to the charge of the electron but opposite in sign, $+e$. The *neutron* is uncharged. The mass of the electron is much smaller than the mass of the proton or the neutron.

Protons and neutrons are in the *nucleus*, which is found in the center of the atom. The nucleus is small in comparison to the overall size of the atom, contains most of the mass of the atom, and has a positive charge (from the protons it contains). Electrons, which occupy most of the volume of the atom, surround the nucleus. A neutral atom contains the same number of electrons as there are protons in the nucleus, so that the total negative charge equals the total positive charge. Monatomic ions (charged atoms) contain more electons than protons (*negative ions*) or fewer electrons than protons (*positive ions*).

The number of protons in the nucleus of an atom is given by the *atomic number*. All atoms of a given element have the same atomic number. Elements are classified by atomic number in the *periodic table*. The elements found in a horizontal row of the table are collectively called a *period*. The elements found in a given vertical column of the table have similar chemical properties and are collectively called a *group*. The periodic table also classifies elements as *metals*, *nonmetals*, or *metalloids*.

The *mass number* of an atom is the total number of protons and neutrons found in the nucleus of the atom. Atoms of a given element that have different mass numbers (and hence different numbers of neutrons in the nucleus) are called *isotopes*. The mass of an atom is expressed on a scale in which the mass of the $^{12}_{6}C$ atom is set at exactly 12 u. The *atomic weight* of an element takes into account the mass of each isotope of the element and its relative abundance in nature.

Key Terms

Actinides, actinoids (Section 2.7) The elements from atomic number 90 (thorium, Th) to 103 (lawrencium, Lr) that follow the element actinium (Ac, $Z = 89$) and that are customarily placed at the bottom of the periodic table.

Alkali metals (Section 2.7) A group of highly reactive, soft metals comprised of lithium (Li), sodium (Na), potassium (K), rubidium (Rb), cesium (Cs), and francium (Fr).

Alpha particle, α (Section 2.5) A particle that consists of two protons and two neutrons and is emitted by certain radioactive nuclei.

Atom (Section 2.1) The smallest particle of an element that can combine with the atoms of other elements to form compounds.

Atomic mass unit, u (Section 2.9) A unit of mass equal to one-twelfth the mass of a $^{12}_{6}C$ atom.

Atomic number, Z (Section 2.6) The number of protons in the nucleus of an atom of an element. In an uncharged atom, it is also equal to the number of electrons.

Atomic weight (Section 2.9) The average mass of atoms of an element relative to the mass of a $^{12}_{6}C$ atom taken as exactly 12 u.

Beta particle, β (Section 2.5) An electron emitted by certain radioactive nuclei.

Binding energy (Section 2.9) The energy required by a hypothetical process in which a nucleus is decomposed into nucleons; the energy equivalent of the difference between the sum of the masses of the nucleons of a nucleus and the actual mass of the nucleus.

Cathode rays (Section 2.2) Streams of electrons that are emitted by the cathode (negative electrode) when electricity is passed through a tube that contains a gas under very low pressure.

Electron (Section 2.2) A subatomic particle that has a mass approximately 0.00055 u, carries a one-unit negative charge, and is found outside the nucleus in an atom.

Gamma radiation, γ (Section 2.5) A highly energetic form of radiation that is similar to X rays and is emitted by certain radioactive nuclei.

Group, family (Section 2.7) A collection of elements that appear in the same vertical column in the periodic table.

Halogens (Section 2.7) A group of highly reactive, nonmetallic elements comprised of fluorine (F), chlorine (Cl), bromine (Br), iodine (I), and astatine (At).

Ion (Section 2.6) A particle made up of an atom or a group of atoms that bears an electric charge. An ion may have either a positive charge (because one or more electrons have been lost) or a negative charge (because one or more electrons have been gained).

Isotopes (Section 2.8) Atoms of the same element that have the same atomic number but different mass numbers; they differ in the number of neutrons in the nucleus.

Lanthanides, lanthanoids (Section 2.7) The elements from atomic number 58 (cerium, Ce) to 71 (lutetium, Lu) that follow lanthanum (La, $Z = 57$) and that are customarily placed at the bottom of the periodic table.

Law of conservation of mass (Section 2.1) There is no detectable change in mass during the course of a chemical reaction.

Law of definite proportions (Section 2.1) A pure compound always consists of the same elements in the same proportions by mass.

Law of multiple proportions (Section 2.1) When two elements, A and B, form more than one compound, the amounts of A that are combined in these compounds with a fixed amount of B stand in a small whole-number ratio.

Mass number, A (Section 2.6) The number of protons and neutrons, taken together, in the nucleus of an atom.

Mass spectrometer (Section 2.8) An instrument used to determine the types of isotopes present in an element, the exact masses of these isotopes, and the relative amount of each isotope present.

Metal (Section 2.7) An element that has a characteristic luster, conducts heat and electricity well, and deforms without breaking when pounded; found in the periodic table to the left of the stepped, diagonal line.

Metalloid, semimetal (Section 2.7) An element that is not clearly a metal or a nonmetal but has properties of both; found in the periodic table near the stepped, diagonal line.

Neutron (Section 2.4) A subatomic particle that has a mass of approximately 1.0087 u, is uncharged, and is found in the nucleus of an atom.

Noble gases (Section 2.7) A group of colorless, gaseous, nonmetallic elements that are not very reactive. It consists of: helium (He), neon (Ne), argon (Ar), krypton (Kr), xenon (Xe), and radon (Rn).

Nonmetal (Section 2.7) An element that is not lustrous, is a poor conductor of heat and electricity, and is brittle in the solid state; found in the periodic table to the right of the stepped, diagonal line.

Nucleon (Section 2.6) A proton or a neutron, both of which are found in the nucleus of an atom.

Nucleus (Section 2.5) The small, dense, positively charged center of an atom; it contains the protons and neutrons.

Period (Section 2.7) A collection of elements that are arranged in a single horizontal row of the periodic table.

Periodic law (Section 2.7) The chemical and physical properties of the elements are periodic functions of atomic number.

Positive rays (Section 2.3) Rays of positive ions; the ions are formed when cathode rays in a cathode ray tube remove electrons from atoms.

Proton (Section 2.3) A subatomic particle that has a mass of approximately 1.0073 u, carries a unit positive charge, and is found in the nucleus of the atom.

Radioactivity (Section 2.5) The spontaneous emission of radioactive rays by an unstable atomic nucleus, which in the process is transformed into a different nucleus; radioactive substances that occur in nature emit alpha, beta, and gamma rays.

Unit electrical charge, e (Section 2.2) 1.6022×10^{-9} C. The magnitude of the charge of the proton and electron; the proton has a unit *positive* charge and the electron a unit *negative* charge.

Problems*

Dalton's Theory, Laws of Chemical Combination

2.1 State the law of conservation of mass and the law of definite proportions. How do they differ? How does Dalton's theory account for them?

2.2 Compare and contrast the law of definite proportions and the law of multiple proportions. Use the compounds NO and NO_2 in your discussion.

2.3 In compound I, 50.0 g of sulfur is combined with 50.0 g of oxygen. In compound II, 50.0 g of sulfur is combined with 75.0 g of oxygen. Show how these data illustrate the law of multiple proportions. How does Dalton's theory account for these facts?

2.4 In methane, 15 g of hydrogen is combined with 45 g of carbon; in ethylene, 30 g of hydrogen is combined with 180. g of carbon. Show how these data illustrate the law of multiple proportions. How does Dalton's theory account for these facts?

2.5 Dalton believed that all atoms of a given element are alike in all respects. Why did this part of Dalton's theory have to be modified? How has it been changed?

2.6 Chlorine has two natural isotopes: $^{37}_{17}Cl$ and $^{35}_{17}Cl$. Hydrogen reacts with chlorine to form the compound hydrogen chloride, HCl. Wouldn't a given amount of hydrogen react with different masses of the two isotopes

---

* The more difficult problems are marked with asterisks. The appendix contains answers to color-keyed problems.

of chlorine? How, then, can you account for the validity of the law of definite proportions?

Subatomic Particles

2.7 Which positive ion is deflected more in an electric field? Why? **(a)** H^+ or Ne^+, **(b)** Ne^+ or Ne^{2+}.

2.8 J. J. Thomson determined the ratio of charge to mass of the electron (q/m). Why was the method he used unable to yield either value separately?

2.9 In the study of positive rays, the proton was found to have the largest q/m value of any positive ion observed. Calculate the value of q/m for each of the following positive ions: **(a)** $_1^1H^+$, which has a mass of 1.67×10^{-24} g; **(b)** $_2^4He^+$, which has a mass of 6.64×10^{-24} g; **(c)** $_{10}^{20}Ne^{2+}$, which has a mass of 3.32×10^{-23} g.

2.10 In a Millikan oil-drop experiment, the following values were obtained for the charges on three oil drops: -3.2×10^{-19} C, -4.8×-10^{-19} C, and -8.0×10^{-19} C. **(a)** Why are the values different from one another? **(b)** Show how the unit charge, e, could be derived from these three values.

The Nuclear Atom

2.11 Describe the three types of radiation emitted by radioactive substances that occur in nature.

2.12 Rutherford used several metal foils in his alpha particle scattering experiments. Compare the number of wide-angle deflections observed for a Cu foil with the number observed for a Au foil of the same thickness.

2.13 The approximate radius of a nucleus, r, is given by the formula $r = A^{1/3}(1.3 \times 10^{-13}$ cm$)$, where A is the mass number of the nucleus. What is the radius of the $_{13}^{27}Al$ nucleus? The atomic radius of the $_{13}^{27}Al$ atom is approximately 143 pm. If the diameter of this atom were 1.00 km (which is 0.621 mile), what would be the diameter of its nucleus (in cm)?

*__2.14__ Use the data given in problem 2.13 to calculate the percentage of the total volume of the aluminum atom that is occupied by the nucleus. The volume of a sphere, V, is given by the formula $V = \frac{4}{3}\pi r^3$, where r is the radius of the sphere.

Atomic Symbols

2.15 (a) Describe the composition of the $_{33}^{75}As$ atom. **(b)** Give the symbol that designates the atom that contains 80 protons and 122 neutrons.

2.16 (a) Describe the composition of the $_{47}^{107}Ag$ atom. **(b)** Give the symbol that designates the atom that contains 79 protons and 118 neutrons.

2.17 Complete the following table:

Symbol	Z	A	Protons	Neutrons	Electrons
Cs	55	133	—	—	—
Bi	—	209	—	—	—
—	56	138	—	—	56
Sn	—	—	—	70	50
Kr	—	84	—	48	—
Sc^{3+}	—	—	—	24	—
—	8	—	—	8	10

2.18 Complete the following table:

Symbol	Z	A	Protons	Neutrons	Electrons
Ca	20	40	—	—	—
Ge	—	74	—	—	—
—	24	52	—	—	24
Te	—	—	—	78	52
La	—	139	—	82	—
Zn^{2+}	—	—	—	34	—
—	7	—	—	7	10

2.19 (a) How many protons and electrons does the Ag^+ ion have? **(b)** the Se^{2-} ion?

2.20 (a) How many protons and electrons does the Ga^{3+} ion have? **(b)** the I^- ion?

Periodic Table

2.21 Compare the meanings of the terms *period* and *group*.

2.22 How many elements belong to the **(a)** third period, **(b)** fourth period?

2.23 Classify each of the following elements as a metal or a nonmetal: **(a)** Kr, **(b)** K, **(c)** P, **(d)** Pt.

2.24 Classify each of the following elements as a metal or a nonmetal: **(a)** B, **(b)** Ba, **(c)** Bi, **(d)** Br.

Isotopes, Atomic Weights

2.25 Silver occurs in nature as a mixture of two isotopes: $_{47}^{107}Ag$, which has an atomic mass of 106.906 u, and $_{47}^{109}Ag$, which has an atomic mass of 108.905 u. The atomic weight of silver is 107.868. What is the percent abundance of each of the two isotopes?

2.26 Rhenium occurs in nature as a mixture of two isotopes: $_{75}^{185}Re$, which has an atomic mass of 184.953 u, and $_{75}^{187}Re$, which has an atomic mass of 186.956 u. The atomic weight of rhenium is 186.207. What is the percent abundance of each of the two isotopes?

2.27 Vanadium occurs in nature as a mixture of two isotopes: $_{23}^{50}V$, which has an atomic mass of 49.9472 u, and $^{51}_{23}V$, which has an atomic mass of 50.9440 u. The atomic weight of vanadium is 50.9415. What is the percent abundance of each of the two isotopes?

2.28 Lithium occurs in nature as a mixture of two isotopes: ^6_3Li, which has an atomic mass of 6.015 u, and ^7_3Li, which has an atomic mass of 7.016 u. The atomic weight of lithium is 6.941. What is the percent abundance of each of the two isotopes?

2.29 An element consists of 60.10% of an isotope with an atomic mass of 68.926 u and 39.90% of an isotope with an atomic mass of 70.925 u. What is the atomic weight of the element?

2.30 An element consists of 90.51% of an isotope with an atomic mass of 19.992 u, 0.27% of an isotope with an atomic mass of 20.994 u, and 9.22% of an isotope with an atomic mass of 21.990 u. What is the atomic weight of the element?

Unclassified Problems

2.31 In the study of positive rays, the proton ($^1_1H^+$) was found to have the largest value of q/m of any positive ion observed. **(a)** What is the value of q/m for the proton? **(b)** What charge would the ^4_2He atom (approximate mass, 6.64×10^{-24} g) require to produce an ion that would have a q/m value equal to or larger than the q/m value of the proton? **(c)** Why is this charge impossible to obtain?

2.32 Copper consists of two isotopes: $^{63}_{29}Cu$, which has an atomic mass of 62.930 u, and $^{65}_{29}Cu$, which has an atomic mass of 64.928 u. The atomic weight of copper is 63.546. What is the percent abundance of each of the two isotopes?

2.33 Use the periodic table to determine **(a)** in what period Cu is found, **(b)** whether Cu is a metal or a nonmetal, **(c)** what two elements you would expect to be chemically similar to Cu.

2.34 (a) Describe the composition of the $^{63}_{29}Cu$ atom and the $^{65}_{29}Cu$ atom. **(b)** Copper forms two ions: Cu^+ and Cu^{2+}. How many electrons does each ion have?

2.35 The isotopes of neon were the first to be identified. The following values of q/m were obtained: 4.38×10^3 C/g, 4.59×10^3 C/g, 4.81×10^3 C/g, 8.76×10^3 C/g, and 9.64×10^3 C/g. The unit charge, e, is 1.60×10^{-19} C, and 1 u is 1.66×10^{-24} g. For each q/m measurement, calculate the mass in atomic mass units (u) that corresponds to one unit charge, e. What mass numbers and charges correspond to the q/m values?

CHAPTER 3

STOICHIOMETRY, PART I: CHEMICAL FORMULAS

Alfred North Whitehead, the philosopher and mathematician, wrote, "All science as it grows toward perfection becomes mathematical in its ideas." Modern chemistry began when Lavoisier and chemists of his time recognized the importance of careful measurement and began to ask questions that could be answered quantitatively. Stoichiometry (derived from the Greek *stoicheion*, meaning "element," and *metron* meaning "to measure") is the branch of chemistry that deals with the quantitative relationships between the elements in the formation of compounds and between the elements and compounds involved in chemical reactions. The atomic theory of matter is basic to this study.

3.1 Molecules and Ions

The noble gases (helium, neon, argon, krypton, xenon, and radon) are the only elements that occur in nature as isolated atoms. The other elements, as well as all compounds, occur in forms that are derived from atoms. Molecules and ions are two important types of particles derived from atoms. These chemical particles will be described in greater detail in later chapters (Chapter 7, *Properties of Atoms and the Ionic Bond;* Chapter 8, *The Covalent Bond;* and Chapter 9, *Molecular Geometry*).

Molecules

A molecule is a particle that is formed from two or more atoms that are bound tightly together. In chemical and physical processes, molecules behave as units. Some elements and many compounds exist as molecules. Examples are illustrated in Figure 3.1.

The atomic composition of a substance is indicated by a chemical formula. In a formula, chemical symbols are used to indicate the types of atoms present, and subscripts to indicate the relative number of atoms of each type. If a symbol carries no subscript, the number 1 is understood. In the case of a molecular substance, the formula describes the composition of a molecule and is sometimes called a molecular formula. The formula H_2O, for example, indicates that a molecule of water contains two atoms of hydrogen and one atom of oxygen.

In molecules of elements, all the atoms are the same. A number of elements occur in nature as diatomic molecules, which are molecules that contain two atoms joined together. The elements that exist as diatomic molecules are listed in Table

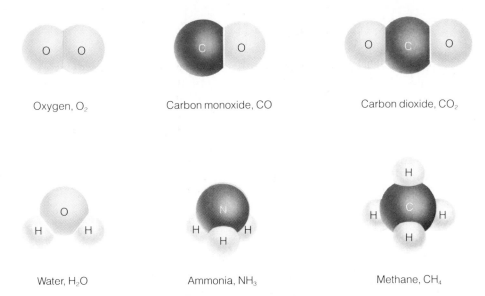

Oxygen, O_2

Carbon monoxide, CO

Carbon dioxide, CO_2

Water, H_2O

Ammonia, NH_3

Methane, CH_4

Figure 3.1 Models of some simple molecules.

3.1. It is important to remember that these elements occur in this form, since their chemical and physical properties reflect their molecular structure.

Some elements form molecules that contain more than two atoms. Sulfur molecules, for example, consist of eight atoms and have the molecular formula S_8. The molecular formula of a phosphorus molecule is P_4.

Molecules of compounds contain atoms of two or more elements. Some of these molecules are diatomic; HCl, CO, and NO are examples. Other molecules of compounds are more complex. The molecular formula of a compound tells only the number and type of atoms present in a molecule of the compound. It does not tell how these atoms are joined together. The formula NH_3, for example, indicates only that the ammonia molecule contains three hydrogen atoms and one nitrogen atom. A structural formula for the ammonia molecule indicates the way in which the atoms are joined:

$$H{-}N{-}H$$
$$|$$
$$H$$

In a **structural formula** a separate symbol is used to indicate each atom, and dashes are used to show how these atoms are joined. Notice that even a structural formula has a shortcoming. The arrangement in space of the atoms of a molecule is not shown. The ammonia molecule, for example, has a pyramidal arrangement, which is illustrated in Figure 3.1.

Ions

An **ion** is a particle that is made up of an atom or a group of atoms and that bears an electric charge. There are two types:

1. A **cation** has a positive charge (because one or more electrons have been lost).

2. An **anion** has a negative charge (because one or more electrons have been gained).

Table 3.1 Elements that occur in nature as diatomic molecules

Element	Formula
hydrogen	H_2
nitrogen	N_2
oxygen	O_2
fluorine	F_2
chlorine	Cl_2
bromine	Br_2
iodine	I_2

Cl⁻   Na⁺

Figure 3.2   Sodium chloride crystal structure

Monatomic ions (ions that are formed from a single atom) have been discussed in Section 2.6, and the Al^{3+}, S^{2-}, Fe^{2+}, and F^- ions were described in Examples 2.3 and 2.4. In general, monatomic cations are formed from atoms of metals, and monatomic anions are formed from atoms of nonmetals. **Polyatomic ions** are charged particles that contain more than one atom. Examples include the ammonium ion, NH_4^+, the sulfate ion, SO_4^{2-}, and the hydroxide ion, OH^-. Ions are described more fully in Chapter 7.

Ionic compounds are made up of cations and anions arranged in a geometric pattern to form a crystal. Sodium chloride, for example, is formed from sodium ions, Na^+, and chloride ions, Cl^-, which together form a crystal of sodium chloride (Figure 3.2). A sodium chloride crystal is made up of large numbers of these ions held together by plus-minus attractions.

In the crystal, there is *one* sodium ion, Na^+, for every *one* chloride ion, Cl^-. The formula of the compound is NaCl. The formula does not describe a molecule, nor does it indicate that the ions are paired, since no ion in the crystal can be considered as belonging exclusively to another. Rather, the formula indicates the *simplest* ratio of ions of each type required to produce the crystal.

The formulas of ionic compounds, therefore, are derived from the formulas of their ions. The formula of barium chloride, for example, is derived from the formula of the barium ion, Ba^{2+}, and the formula of the chloride ion, Cl^-. Since a crystal is electrically neutral, the total charge of all the positive ions must equal the total charge of all the negative ions. In barium chloride, therefore must be *two* chloride ions for every *one* barium ion. Thus,

Ba^{2+} and $2\,Cl^-$ form $BaCl_2$

In the formula of an ionic compound, the formula of the cation is written first. The arrangement of ions in a $BaCl_2$ crystal is different from that in the NaCl crystal. The $BaCl_2$ crystal must accommodate ions in a cation to anion ratio of 1 to 2. The cation to anion ratio in the NaCl crystal is 1 to 1.

Example 3.1

What are the formulas of the compounds that contain the O^{2-} ion with (a) the Na^+ ion? (b) the Ca^{2+} ion? (c) the Fe^{3+} ion?

Solution

(a) The total charge of the cations must equal the total charge of the anions. Consequently, there must be *two* Na^+ ions (total charge, 2^+) for every *one* O^{2-} ion (total charge, $2-$). The formula is Na_2O.

(b) Since the cation has a charge of 2^+ and the anion has a charge of $2-$, electrical neutrality is obtained by a cation to anion ratio of 1 to 1. The formula is CaO.

(c) The cation has a charge of $3+$, and the anion has a charge of $2-$. The lowest common multiple of 3 and 2 is 6. *Two* Fe^{3+} ions (total charge, $6+$) and *three* O^{2-} ions (total charge, $6-$) must be taken. The formula is Fe_2O_3.

Other Forms

Some elements and compounds exist in forms that are neither molecular nor ionic. In diamond, a large number of carbon atoms occur in a three-dimensional crystal pattern and are joined by a network of bonds similar to those found in molecules. In fact, the entire diamond crystal can be viewed as one giant molecule. Some compounds (silicon dioxide, SiO_2, for example) occur in similar forms. Metals have structures in which a large number of metal atoms are mutually bound together by what are called metallic bonds. These other forms are discussed in later chapters. The formulas used for them employ the simplest whole-number subscripts that give the correct ratio of atoms present in the substance.

3.2 Empirical Formulas

The molecular formula of hydrogen peroxide, H_2O_2, indicates that there are two atoms of hydrogen and two atoms of oxygen in a molecule of hydrogen peroxide. Notice that the ratio of hydrogen to oxygen atoms (2 to 2) is not the *simplest* whole-number ratio (which is 1 to 1). A formula that is written using the simplest whole-number ratio is called an **empirical formula** or a **simplest formula**. The *molecular* formula of hydrogen peroxide is H_2O_2; the *empirical* formula is HO.

The molecular formula gives the actual atomic composition of the molecule. The empirical formula gives only the simplest whole-number ratio of atoms in the compound. More data are required to derive the molecular formula of a molecular compound than are required to derive the empirical formula of the compound.

For some molecular compounds, the molecular and empirical formulas are identical; examples are

$$H_2O \qquad H_2SO_4 \qquad CO_2 \qquad NH_3$$

The subscripts in these formulas cannot be reduced to any simpler ratio. For many molecular compounds, however, the molecular and empirical formulas are different. The molecular formulas

$$N_2H_4 \qquad B_3N_3H_6 \qquad C_6H_6$$

correspond to the empirical formulas

$$NH_2 \qquad BNH_2 \qquad CH$$

Notice that the atomic ratio for an empirical formula can be obtained by reducing the atomic ratio of the molecular formula to the lowest possible set of whole numbers.

Example 3.2

Derive the empirical formulas of the following compounds for which molecular formulas are given: (a) ethane, C_2H_6, (b) glucose, $C_6H_{12}O_6$, (c) propane, C_3H_8, and (d) cyclobutane, C_4H_8.

Solution

For each of the molecular formulas, we look for the *largest* whole-number factor that can be divided into *each* subscript.

(a) For C_2H_6, the subscripts 2 and 6 are each divisible by 2. The empirical formula is CH_3.

(b) For $C_6H_{12}O_6$, the subscripts 6, 12, and 6 are each divisible by 6. The empirical formula is CH_2O.

(c) For C_3H_8, there is no common factor other than 1 that can be divided into each of the subscripts. The empirical formula is the same as the molecular formula, C_3H_8.

(d) For C_4H_8, the subscripts 4 and 8 are each divisible by 4. The empirical formula is CH_2.

The formula of an ionic compound (such as $BaCl_2$ or $NaCl$) gives the *simplest* ratio of ions of each type present in a crystal of the compound. The formulas of most ionic compounds, therefore, are *empirical formulas*.

A few ionic compounds, however, have formulas that can be reduced to simpler terms. Sodium peroxide is such a compound. In sodium peroxide, two sodium ions (Na^+) are present for every one peroxide ion (O_2^{2-}):

$$2\,Na^+ \qquad \text{and} \qquad O_2^{2-} \qquad \text{form} \qquad Na_2O_2$$

This formula can be reduced to NaO, which is the empirical formula of sodium peroxide. The problem encountered with the formula of sodium peroxide is not common. The formulas of most ionic compounds are empirical formulas, and the atomic ratios they indicate cannot be reduced.

3.3 Formula Weights, Molecular Weights

The **formula weight** of a substance is the sum of the atomic weights of all the atoms in the formula of the substance. The formula weight of H_2O, for example, can be calculated as follows:

$$
\begin{aligned}
2(\text{atomic weight H}) = 2(1.0) &= 2.0 \\
\text{atomic weight O} &= 16.0 \\
\hline
\text{formula weight } H_2O &= 18.0
\end{aligned}
$$

The formula weight of $BaCl_2$ is

$$
\begin{aligned}
\text{atomic weight Ba} &= 137.3 \\
2(\text{atomic weight Cl}) = 2(35.5) &= 71.0 \\
\hline
\text{formula weight } BaCl_2 &= 208.3
\end{aligned}
$$

If the formula in question pertains to a molecular substance and is a molecular formula, the corresponding formula weight may also be called a molecular weight. A **molecular weight** is the sum of the atomic weights of the atoms that constitute a *molecule*. The formula weight of H_2O is also the molecular weight of the substance, since the formula is a description of the composition of the water molecule. In the case of $BaCl_2$, however, the formula weight is *not* a molecular weight, since $BaCl_2$ is an ionic compound and molecules of $BaCl_2$ do not exist. How to distinguish between molecular and ionic substances will be discussed in later chapters.

Example 3.3

Calculate the formula weight of aluminum sulfate, $Al_2(SO_4)_3$. Use atomic weights to the first decimal place.

Solution

In a chemical formula, a subscript that follows a parenthesis modifies everything that appears between the parentheses. In the present case, the formula weight is

$$
\begin{aligned}
2(\text{atomic weight Al}) = 2(27.0) &= 54.0 \\
3(\text{atomic weight S}) = 3(32.1) &= 96.3 \\
12(\text{atomic weight O}) = 12(16.0) &= 192.0 \\
\hline
\text{formula weight } Al_2(SO_4)_3 &= 342.3
\end{aligned}
$$

An alternative way to solve the problem involves adding the formula weights of the ions found in the compound. The formula weight of an ion is calculated from the atomic weights of the atoms that make up the ion. Since the mass of the electron is extremely small (0.00055 u), no correction is made for electrons lost or gained. Furthermore, when a compound is considered, the number of electrons lost (by the cations) is equal to the number of electrons gained (by the anions).

In the present case, the formula weight of the Al^{3+} ion is merely the atomic weight of Al (27.0). The formula weight of the SO_4^{2-} ion is:

$$
\begin{array}{rl}
\text{atomic weight S} = & 32.1 \\
4(\text{atomic weight O}) = 4(16.0) = & 64.0 \\
\hline
\text{formula weight } SO_4^{2-} = & 96.1
\end{array}
$$

The formula weight of $Al_2(SO_4)_3$, therefore, is:

$$
\begin{array}{rl}
2(\text{formula weight } Al^{3+}) = 2(27.0) = & 54.0 \\
3(\text{formula weight } SO_4^{2-}) = 3(96.1) = & 288.3 \\
\hline
\text{formula weight } Al_2(SO_4)_3 = & 342.3
\end{array}
$$

3.4 The Mole

Since the atomic weight of fluorine is 19.0 and of hydrogen is 1.0, an atom of fluorine is 19 times heavier than an atom of hydrogen.* If we take 100 fluorine atoms and 100 hydrogen atoms, the mass of the collection of fluorine atoms will be 19 times the mass of the collection of hydrogen atoms. The masses of any two samples of fluorine and hydrogen that contain the same number of atoms will stand in the ratio of 19.0 to 1.0, which is the ratio of their atomic weights.

Now suppose that we take 19.0 g of fluorine and 1.0 g of hydrogen, which are values in grams numerically equal to the atomic weights of the elements. Since the masses of the samples stand in the ratio of 19.0 to 1.0, the samples must contain the same number of atoms. In fact, a sample of any element that has a mass in grams numerically equal to the atomic weight of the element will contain this same number of atoms.

This number is called **Avogadro's number,** named in honor of Amedeo Avogadro, who first interpreted the behavior of gases in chemical reactions in terms of the numbers of reacting molecules (Section 10.8). The value of Avogadro's number has been experimentally determined; to six significant figures it is

$$6.02205 \times 10^{23}$$

The amount of a substance that contains Avogadro's number of elementary units is called a **mole** (abbreviated *mol*), which is an SI base unit. The mole is defined as the amount of substance that contains as many elementary entities as there are atoms in exactly 12 g of $^{12}_{6}C$.

Thus, a sample of an element that has a mass in grams numerically equal to the atomic weight of the element is a mole of atoms of the element and contains Avogadro's number of atoms. The atomic weight of beryllium, for example, is 9.01218. Thus,

$$9.01218 \text{ g Be} = 1 \text{ mol Be} = 6.02205 \times 10^{23} \text{ Be atoms}$$

---

* In order to simplify the discussion, we have rounded off these atomic weights to the first figure following the decimal point.

A mole consists of Avogadro's number of entities. A mole of a molecular substance consists of Avogadro's number of molecules and has a mass in grams numerically equal to the molecular weight of the substance. The molecular weight of H_2O, for example, is 18.02. Thus,

$$18.02 \text{ g } H_2O = 1 \text{ mol } H_2O = 6.022 \times 10^{23} \text{ } H_2O \text{ molecules}$$

Since a molecule of water contains two H atoms and one O atom, a mole of H_2O contains two moles of H atoms and one mole of O atoms.

When the mole designation is used, the type of entity being measured *must* be specified. A mole of H *atoms* contains 6.02×10^{23} H atoms and to three significant figures has a mass of 1.01 g; a mole of H_2 *molecules* contains 6.02×10^{23} H_2 molecules and has a mass of 2.02 g. For fluorine,

$$1 \text{ mol } F = 6.02 \times 10^{23} \text{ F atoms} = 19.0 \text{ g fluorine}$$

$$1 \text{ mol } F_2 = 6.02 \times 10^{23} \text{ } F_2 \text{ molecules} = 38.0 \text{ g fluorine}$$

What about ionic substances? The designation "1 mol $BaCl_2$" means that the sample contains Avogadro's number of formula units—the entity specified. One mole of $BaCl_2$, therefore, has a mass of 208.3 g, the formula weight of $BaCl_2$. In reality, one mole of $BaCl_2$ contains

$$1 \text{ mol } Ba^{2+} = 6.02 \times 10^{23} \text{ } Ba^{2+} \text{ ions} = 137.3 \text{ g barium}$$

$$2 \text{ mol } Cl^- = 2(6.02 \times 10^{23}) \text{ } Cl^- \text{ ions} = 2(35.5) \text{ g } Cl^- = 71.0 \text{ g chlorine}$$

which together make up

$$1 \text{ mol } BaCl_2 = 6.02 \times 10^{23} \text{ } BaCl_2 \text{ units} = 208.3 \text{ g } BaCl_2$$

The atomic weights used to solve a problem should be expressed to the proper number of significant figures. The data given in the statement of a problem determine how precise the answer to the problem should be, and the atomic weights used in the solution should be expressed to the number of significant figures that reflects this precision.

Notice that an atomic weight (and by extension, a formula weight) may appear in three different ways.

1. An atomic weight can be expressed as a pure number, without any units. This is the way that atomic weights are given in periodic tables and lists of the elements. An atomic weight is, after all, a *ratio* of the mass of an average atom of an element to one-twelfth the mass of a $^{12}_{6}C$ atom. The atomic weight of sodium is 22.98977.

2. If the mass of the $^{12}_{6}C$ atom is assigned a mass of exactly 12 u, then the mass of an average atom of an element is the atomic weight in atomic mass units, u. The mass of an atom of sodium is the atomic weight of sodium in atomic mass units: 22.98977 u.

3. A mole of an element has a mass equal to the atomic weight of the element expressed in grams. The atomic weight of sodium in grams, therefore, is the mass of one mole of sodium: 22.98977 g/mol.

Example 3.4

What number of moles of aluminum is present in 125 g of Al?

Solution

Notice that the answer should be expressed to three significant figures. First, we state the problem in the following way:

? mol Al = 125 g Al

Next we derive a conversion factor to solve the problem. To three significant figures, the atomic weight of Al is 27.0; therefore,

1 mol Al = 27.0 g Al

We use the conversion factor that has the unit *g Al* in the denominator since that is the unit that must be eliminated:

$$? \text{ mol Al} = 125 \text{ g Al} \left(\frac{1 \text{ mol Al}}{27.0 \text{ g Al}} \right) = 4.63 \text{ mol Al}$$

Example 3.5

How many grams of sulfuric acid, H_2SO_4, must be taken in order to get 0.2500 mol of H_2SO_4?

Solution

The answer should be expressed to four significant figures. We state the problem:

? g H_2SO_4 = 0.2500 mol H_2SO_4

To four significant figures the formula weight of H_2SO_4 is 98.08; therefore,

1 mol H_2SO_4 = 98.08 g H_2SO_4

The unit that must be eliminated in this problem is *mol* H_2SO_4, and the conversion factor must have this unit in the denominator:

$$? \text{ g } H_2SO_4 = 0.2500 \text{ mol } H_2SO_4 \left(\frac{98.08 \text{ g } H_2SO_4}{1 \text{ mol } H_2SO_4} \right) = 24.52 \text{ g } H_2SO_4$$

Example 3.6

How many carbon atoms are there in a 1.000 carat diamond? Diamond is pure carbon and one carat is exactly 0.2 g.

Solution

Since the value 0.2 g, which arises from the definition of the carat, is exact, it does not limit the number of significant figures in the answer. The precision of the answer is limited by the value 1.000 carat (which has four significant figures). The problem is:

? atoms C = 0.2000 g C

We derive a conversion factor from the atomic weight of C (to four significant figures):

1 mol C = 12.01 g C

with the unit *g C* in the denominator so that this unit will cancel:

$$? \text{ atoms C} = 0.200 \text{ g C} \left(\frac{1 \text{ mol C}}{12.01 \text{ g C}} \right)$$

At this point, the calculation would give an answer expressed in mol C. Using Avogadro's number (to four significant figures), we derive a conversion factor from

1 mol C = 6.022 × 10²³ atoms C

with the unit *mol C* in the denominator so that it will cancel. Multiplication by this factor completes the solution:

$$? \text{ atoms C} = 0.2000 \text{ g C} \left(\frac{1 \text{ mol C}}{12.01 \text{ g C}} \right) \left(\frac{6.022 \times 10^{23} \text{ atoms C}}{1 \text{ mol C}} \right)$$

$$= 1.003 \times 10^{22} \text{ atoms C}$$

3.5 Percentage Composition of Compounds

The percentage composition of a compound is readily calculated from the formula of the compound. The subscripts of the formula give the number of moles of each element in a mole of the compound. From this information and from the atomic weights of the elements, we can obtain the number of grams of each element contained in a mole of the compound. The percentage of a given element is 100 times the mass of the element divided by the mass of a mole of the compound. The process is illustrated in Example 3.7.

Example 3.7

What is the percentage of Fe in Fe_2O_3 calculated to three significant figures?

Solution

One mole of Fe_2O_3 contains

$$2 \text{ mol Fe} = 2(55.8) \text{ g Fe} = 111.6 \text{ g Fe}$$
$$3 \text{ mol O} = 3(16.0) \text{ g O} = \underline{48.0 \text{ g O}}$$
$$159.6 \text{ g}$$

The sum of the masses, 159.6 g, is the mass of one mole of Fe_2O_3. The percentage of Fe in Fe_2O_3 is

$$\frac{111.6 \text{ g Fe}}{159.6 \text{ g Fe}_2O_3} \times 100\% = 69.92\% \text{ Fe in Fe}_2O_3$$

The percentage composition of a compound is frequently determined by chemical analysis. These data can then be used to find the empirical formula of the compound. Example 3.8 illustrates a method used for the analysis of organic compounds.

Example 3.8

Nicotine is a compound that contains carbon, hydrogen, and nitrogen. If a 2.50 g sample of nicotine is burned in oxygen, 6.78 g of CO_2, 1.94 g of H_2O, and 0.432 g of N_2 are the products of the combustion. What is the percentage composition of nicotine?

Solution

Note that we will work to three significant figures. We first calculate the quantity of each element present in the 2.50 g sample of nicotine. The carbon in the sample formed 6.78 g of CO_2. We ask, therefore,

$$? \text{ g C} = 6.78 \text{ g CO}_2$$

The conversion factor that we must use to solve this problem is the fraction that we would use to find the percentage of C in CO_2. Since 1 mol of CO_2 (44.0 g CO_2) contains 1 mol of C (12.0 g C),

$$12.0 \text{ g C} \approx 44.0 \text{ g CO}_2$$

We derive the conversion factor (12.0 g C/44.0 g CO_2):

$$? \text{ g C} = 6.78 \text{ g CO}_2\left(\frac{12.0 \text{ g C}}{44.0 \text{ g CO}_2}\right) = 1.85 \text{ g C}$$

The same procedure is used to find the number of grams of hydrogen in the nicotine sample. The hydrogen of the nicotine formed 1.94 g of H_2O. In 1 mol of H_2O (18.0 g) there are 2 mol of H atoms (2.02 g). Therefore,

$$? \text{ g H} = 1.94 \text{ g H}_2O\left(\frac{2.02 \text{ g H}}{18.0 \text{ g H}_2O}\right) = 0.218 \text{ g H}$$

In a combustion such as the one described, the nitrogen does not combine with oxygen but is evolved as N_2. Hence the sample contained 0.432 g N.

The quantity of each element present in the 2.50 g sample is used to determine the percentage composition of nicotine:

$$\frac{1.85 \text{ g C}}{2.50 \text{ g nicotine}} \times 100\% = 74.0\% \text{ C in nicotine}$$

$$\frac{0.218 \text{ g H}}{2.50 \text{ g nicotine}} \times 100\% = 8.72\% \text{ H in nicotine}$$

$$\frac{0.432 \text{ g N}}{2.50 \text{ g nicotine}} \times 100\% = 17.3\% \text{ N in nicotine}$$

Some simple stoichiometric problems can be solved by use of the proportions derived from formulas.

Example 3.9

Silver sulfide, Ag_2S, occurs in nature as the mineral argentite, which is an ore of silver. How many grams of silver are theoretically obtainable from 250.0 g of an impure ore that is 70.00% Ag_2S?

Solution

The problem can be stated as follows:

? g Ag = 250.0 g ore

If we take 100 g of the ore, we will get 70.00 g of Ag_2S, since the ore is 70.0% Ag_2S. Notice that the number 100 is exact (it arises from the definition of *percent*); the number 70.00 is not. Therefore,

70.00 g Ag_2S ⇔ 100 g ore

and the factor (70.00 g Ag_2S/100 g ore) can be derived:

$$? \text{ g Ag} = 250.0 \text{ g ore} \left(\frac{70.00 \text{ g Ag}_2\text{S}}{100 \text{ g ore}} \right)$$

The *g ore* labels cancel, and at this point we have an answer in *g Ag₂S*. The solution to the problem can be completed by use of the same factor as that used to find the percentage of Ag in Ag_2S. From the formula Ag_2S, we derive

2 mol Ag ⇔ 1 mol Ag_2S

2 (107.9) g Ag ⇔ 247.9 g Ag_2S

215.8 g Ag ⇔ 247.9 g Ag_2S

Therefore,

$$? \text{ g Ag} = 250.0 \text{ g ore} \left(\frac{70.00 \text{ g Ag}_2\text{S}}{100 \text{ g ore}} \right) \left(\frac{215.8 \text{ g Ag}}{247.9 \text{ g Ag}_2\text{S}} \right) = 152.3 \text{ g Ag}$$

3.6 Derivation of Formulas

Data from the chemical analysis of a compound are used to derive the empirical formula of the compound. The analysis gives the proportions by mass of the elements that make up the compound. The simplest or empirical formula indicates the atomic proportions of the compound—the relative numbers of atoms of various types that make up the compound.

Since a mole of atoms of one element contains the same number of atoms as a mole of atoms of any other element, the ratio by moles is the same as the ratio by atoms. The number of moles of each element present in a sample of the compound is readily obtained from the mass of each element present. The simplest whole-number ratio by moles (which is the same as the ratio by atoms) is used to write the empirical formula. The procedure is illustrated in the examples that follow.

Example 3.10

What is the empirical formula of a compound that contains 43.6% P and 56.4% O?

Solution

We assume, for convenience, that we have a sample with a mass of 100.0 g. On the basis of the percentage composition, this sample contains 43.6 g P and 56.4 g O.

Next, we use the method illustrated in Example 3.4 to find the number of moles of P atoms and O atoms in these quantities. To three significant figures, the atomic weight of P is 31.0 and of O is 16.0:

$$? \text{ mol P} = 43.6 \text{ g P}\left(\frac{1 \text{ mol P}}{31.0 \text{ g P}}\right) = 1.41 \text{ mol P}$$

$$? \text{ mol O} = 56.4 \text{ g O}\left(\frac{1 \text{ mol O}}{16.0 \text{ g O}}\right) = 3.53 \text{ mol O}$$

The ratio by atoms is the same as the ratio by moles of atoms. There are therefore 1.41 atoms of P for every 3.53 atoms of O in the compound. We need, however, the simplest *whole-number* ratio in order to write the formula. By dividing the two values by the smaller value, to get

$$\text{for P,} \frac{1.41}{1.41} = 1.00 \qquad \text{for O,} \frac{3.53}{1.41} = 2.50$$

We still do not have a whole-number ratio, but we can get one by multiplying each of these values by 2. Hence, the simplest whole-number ratio is 2 to 5, and the empirical formula is P_2O_5.

Example 3.11

Caffeine, which occurs in coffee, tea, and kola nuts, is a stimulant for the central nervous system. A 1.261 g sample of pure caffeine contains 0.624 g C, 0.065 g H, 0.364 g N, and 0.208 g O. What is the empirical formula of caffeine?

1. If the data are given in terms of percentage composition, base the calculation on a 100.0 g sample of the compound. In this instance, the number of grams of each element present in the sample will be numerically equal to the percentage of that element present in the compound. There is no need to find percentages if the data are given in terms of the number of grams of each element present in a sample of the compound.

2. Convert the number of grams of each element present in the sample to the number of moles of *atoms* of each element. The conversion factors needed are derived from the fact that 1 mol of *atoms* of an element (numerator) is an *atomic* weight in grams (denominator).

3. Divide each of the values obtained in step 2 by the smallest value. If every number obtained in this way is not a whole number, multiply *each number* by the same simple integer in such a way that whole numbers will result.

4. A ratio by moles of atoms is the same as a ratio by atoms. The whole numbers obtained in step 3 are the subscripts of the empirical formula.

Solution

The results of a chemical analysis are usually reported in terms of percentages. However, any mass ratio can be converted into a mole ratio and, in this form, used to derive an empirical formula. There is no need to convert the data given in this example into percentages. We calculate the number of moles of each element present in the sample:

$$? \text{ mol C} = 0.624 \text{ g C} \left(\frac{1 \text{ mol C}}{12.0 \text{ g C}} \right) = 0.0520 \text{ mol C}$$

$$? \text{ mol H} = 0.065 \text{ g H} \left(\frac{1 \text{ mol H}}{1.0 \text{ g H}} \right) = 0.065 \text{ mol H}$$

$$? \text{ mol N} = 0.364 \text{ g N} \left(\frac{1 \text{ mol N}}{14.0 \text{ g N}} \right) = 0.0260 \text{ mol N}$$

$$? \text{ mol O} = 0.208 \text{ g O} \left(\frac{1 \text{ mol O}}{16.0 \text{ g O}} \right) = 0.0130 \text{ mol O}$$

Division of each of these values by the smallest value (0.130) gives the ratio

4 mol C : 5 mol H : 2 mol N : 1 mol O

The empirical formula of caffeine, therefore, is $C_4H_5N_2O$.

The molecular formula of a compound can be derived from the empirical formula if the molecular weight of the compound is known.

Example 3.12

What is the molecular formula of the oxide of phosphorus that has the empirical formula P_2O_5 (derived in Example 3.10) if the molecular weight of this compound is 284?

Solution

The value obtained by adding the atomic weights indicated by the empirical formula P_2O_5 is 142. If we divide this formula weight into the actual molecular weight, we get

$$\frac{284}{142} = 2$$

There are, therefore, twice as many atoms of each kind present in a molecule as indicated by the empirical formula. The molecular formula is P_4O_{10}.

Example 3.13

The molecular weight of caffeine is 194 and the empirical formula of caffeine is $C_4H_5N_2O$. What is the molecular formula of caffeine?

Solution

The formula weight indicated by $C_4H_5N_2O$ is 97. Since the molecular weight is twice this value, the molecular formula of caffeine is $C_8H_{10}N_4O_2$.

Example 3.14

Glucose, a simple sugar, is a constituent of human blood and tissue fluids and is a principal source of energy for cells. The compound contains 40.0% C, 6.73% H, and 53.3% O and has a molecular weight of 180.2. What is the molecular formula of glucose?

Solution

The most convenient way to solve the problem is to calculate the number of moles of each element in a mole of glucose. We first determine the number of grams of each element in a mole of glucose (180.2 g). Since the compound contains 40.0% C, there are 40.0 g of C in 100 g of glucose, and we use the factor (40.0 g C/100 g glucose):

$$? \text{ g C} = 1 \text{ mol glucose}\left(\frac{180.2 \text{ g glucose}}{1 \text{ mol glucose}}\right)\left(\frac{40.0 \text{ g C}}{100 \text{ g glucose}}\right) = 72.1 \text{ g C}$$

In like manner, the number of grams of H and of O can be found:

$$? \text{ g H} = 1 \text{ mol glucose} \left(\frac{180.2 \text{ g glucose}}{1 \text{ mol glucose}} \right) \left(\frac{6.73 \text{ g H}}{100 \text{ g glucose}} \right) = 12.1 \text{ g H}$$

$$? \text{ g O} = 1 \text{ mol glucose} \left(\frac{180.2 \text{ glucose}}{1 \text{ mol glucose}} \right) \left(\frac{53.3 \text{ g O}}{100 \text{ g glucose}} \right) = 96.0 \text{ g O}$$

Next, we determine the number of moles of atoms that each of these values represents:

$$? \text{ mol C} = 72.1 \text{ g C} \left(\frac{1 \text{ mol C}}{12.0 \text{ g C}} \right) = 6.00 \text{ mol C}$$

$$? \text{ mol H} = 12.1 \text{ g H} \left(\frac{1 \text{ mol H}}{1.01 \text{ g H}} \right) = 12.0 \text{ mol H}$$

$$? \text{ mol O} = 96.0 \text{ g O} \left(\frac{1 \text{ mol O}}{16.0 \text{ g O}} \right) = 6.00 \text{ mol O}$$

These values are the number of moles of atoms of each element in a mole of glucose molecules. They are also the number of atoms of each type in a molecule of glucose. The molecular formula, therefore, is $C_6H_{12}O_6$.

The problem may also be solved by first determining the empirical formula from the analytical data (it is CH_2O) and then using the molecular weight to derive the molecular formula.

Summary

The stoichiometry of a chemical compound is based on the *chemical formula* of the compound. If the compound is made up of *molecules*, the *molecular formula* gives the exact number of each type of atom in a molecule. If the compound is made up of *ions*, the formula is written by using the simplest whole-number ratio of ions present in a crystal of the compound.

A *mole* of an element consists of *Avogadro's number* of atoms of the element and has a mass equal to the atomic weight of the element in grams. A mole of a compound contains Avogadro's number of formula units of the compound and has a mass equal to the *formula weight* (or *molecular weight* if the compound is molecular)

of the compound in grams. By interpreting the formulas of compounds in terms of moles, the percent composition of compounds can be derived and other simple stoichiometric problems can be solved.

If the percent composition of a compound has been determined by experiment, use of the mole concept enables one to derive the *empirical formula* of the compound. The empirical formula is a formula written with the simplest whole-number ratio of atoms. The molecular formula of a molecular compound can be derived from the empirical formula of the compound if the molecular weight of the compound is known.

Key Terms

Some of the more important terms introduced in this chapter are listed below. Definitions for terms not included in this list may be located in the text by use of the index.

Anion (Section 3.1)   An ion that has a negative charge.

Avogadro's number (Section 3.4)   The number of entities in one mole: 6.02205×10^{23}.

Cation (Section 3.1)   An ion that has a positive charge.

Chemical formula (Section 3.1)   A representation of a compound that uses chemical symbols to indicate the types and relative numbers of atoms present in the compound.

Diatomic molecule (Section 3.1) A molecule consisting of two atoms.

Empirical formula (Section 3.2) A chemical formula for a compound that is written using the simplest whole-number ratio of atoms present in the compound; also called the **simplest formula**.

Formula weight (Section 3.3) The sum of the atomic weights of the atoms in a formula.

Ion (Section 3.1) A particle that is made up of an atom or a group of atoms and that bears either a positive or a negative charge.

Mole (Section 3.4) The amount of substance that contains the same number of elementary entities as there are atoms in exactly 12 g of $^{12}_{6}C$; a collection of Avogadro's number of units.

Molecular formula (Section 3.1) A chemical formula for a molecular substance that gives the number and type of each atom in a molecule of the substance.

Molecular weight (Section 3.3) The sum of the atomic weights of the atoms that constitute a molecule.

Molecule (Section 3.1) A particle formed from two or more atoms that are bound tightly together.

Monatomic ion (Section 3.1) An ion formed from a single atom.

Polyatomic ion (Section 3.1) An ion formed from two or more atoms.

Stoichiometry (Introduction) The quantitative relationships between the elements that make up a compound and between the elements and compounds that are involved in a chemical reaction.

Structural formula (Section 3.1) A chemical formula for a molecule in which a separate symbol is used to indicate each atom and dashes are used to show how these atoms are joined.

Problems*

Formulas, Molecules, and Ions

3.1 Compare and contrast: **(a)** empirical formula, molecular formula; **(b)** molecular weight, formula weight; **(c)** molecular formula, structural formula.

3.2 Compare and contrast: **(a)** cation, anion; **(b)** monatomic ion, polyatomic ion; **(c)** SO_3, SO_3^{2-}.

3.3 How many atoms and how many ions are in one formula unit of each of the following: **(a)** Na_2O, **(b)** $CrCl_3$, **(c)** $CuSO_4$, **(d)** $Ba(OH)_2$?

3.4 How many atoms and how many ions are in one formula unit of each of the following: **(a)** $ZnCl_2$, **(b)** $Ca_3(PO_4)_2$, **(c)** Na_2CO_3, **(d)** KOH?

3.5 Give the formulas of the compounds formed by the magnesium ion, Mg^{2+}, with **(a)** the chloride ion, Cl^-, **(b)** the sulfate ion, SO_4^{2-}, **(c)** the nitride ion, N^{3-}.

3.6 Give the formulas of the compounds formed by the aluminum ion, Al^{3+}, with **(a)** the fluoride ion, F^-, **(b)** the oxide ion, O^{2-}, **(c)** the phosphate ion, PO_4^{3-}.

3.7 Give the formulas of the compounds formed by the carbonate ion, CO_3^{2-}, with **(a)** the potassium ion, K^+, **(b)** the calcium ion, Ca^{2+}, **(c)** the iron(III) ion, Fe^{3+}.

3.8 Give the formulas of the compounds formed by the sulfate ion, SO_4^{2-}, with **(a)** the silver ion, Ag^+, **(b)** the nickel(II) ion, Ni^{2+}, **(c)** the chromium(III) ion, Cr^{3+}.

3.9 Determine the empirical formula that corresponds to each of the following molecular formulas: **(a)** B_9H_{15}, **(b)** $C_{10}H_{18}$, **(c)** S_2F_{10}, **(d)** I_2O_5, **(e)** $H_4P_4O_{12}$.

3.10 Determine the empirical formula that corresponds to each of the following molecular formulas: **(a)** P_4S_{10}, **(b)** $Fe_3(CO)_{12}$, **(c)** $H_6P_4O_{13}$, **(d)** $B_{20}H_{16}$, **(e)** $P_3N_3Cl_6$.

The Mole, Avogadro's Number

3.11 How many moles and how many molecules are in 75.0 g of **(a)** H_2, **(b)** H_2O, **(c)** H_2SO_4?

3.12 How many moles and how many molecules are in 50.0 g of **(a)** Cl_2, **(b)** HCl, **(c)** CCl_4?

3.13 How many atoms are in each of the samples described in Problem 3.11?

3.14 How many atoms are in each of the samples described in Problem 3.12?

3.15 Determine the mass (in grams) of **(a)** 3.00×10^{20} O_2 molecules, **(b)** 3.00×10^{-3} mol of O_2.

3.16 Determine the mass (in grams) of **(a)** 5.00×10^{25} CO_2 molecules, **(b)** 5.00×10^{-2} mol of CO_2.

3.17 Only one isotope of cobalt occurs in nature. To four significant figures, determine the mass (in grams) of a single atom of this isotope of cobalt.

* The more difficult problems are marked with asterisks. The appendix contains answers to color-keyed problems.

3.18 Only one isotope of phosphorus occurs in nature. To four significant figures, determine the mass (in grams) of a single atom of this isotope of phosphorus.

3.19 Only one isotope of element X occurs in nature. One atom of this isotope has a mass of 2.107×10^{-22} g. What is the atomic weight of element X?

3.20 Only one isotope of element Y occurs in nature. One atom of this isotope has a mass of 9.123×10^{-23} g. What is the atomic weight of element Y?

3.21 The international prototype of the kilogram is a cylinder made from an alloy that is 90.000% platinum and 10.000% iridium. **(a)** How many moles of Pt and how many moles of Ir are in the cylinder? **(b)** How many atoms of each kind are present?

3.22 Sterling silver is 92.5% Ag and 7.5% Cu. How many Ag atoms are present in the alloy for every one atom of Cu?

3.23 **(a)** What is the mass (in grams) of one mole of $^{12}_{6}C$. **(b)** What is the mass (in grams) of a single atom of $^{12}_{6}C$? **(c)** To four significant figures, what is the gram equivalent of one atomic mass unit (1.000 u)?

3.24 The faraday (F), a quantity of charge equivalent to one mole of electrons, is equal to 96,485 C. Use this value to determine the charge (in coulombs) on one electron.

*__3.25__ The distance from the earth to the sun is 1.496×10^{8} km. Suppose that the atoms in 1.000 mole were enlarged into spheres 1.000 cm in diameter. If these spheres were arranged in a line so that they touched one another, would the line reach the sun?

*__3.26__ The continent of North America has an area of 2.440×10^{7} km^2. If the continent were divided into Avogadro's number of squares, what would be the length of a side of one of the squares? Express the answer in the SI unit that will give the smallest number greater than 1.

Percentage Composition of Compounds

3.27 Arrange the following formulas in order of increasing percentage of sulfur: **(a)** $CaSO_4$, **(b)** SO_2, **(c)** H_2S, **(d)** $Na_2S_2O_3$.

3.28 Arrange the following formulas in order of increasing percentage of nitrogen: **(a)** $NaNO_3$, **(b)** NH_3, **(c)** NO_2, **(d)** NH_4NO_3.

3.29 To four significant figures, what percentage of As_2S_5 is arsenic?

3.30 To four significant figures, what percentage of Ce_2O_3 is cerium?

3.31 To four significant figures, what percentage of $KClO_3$ is oxygen?

3.32 To four significant figures, what percentage of $BaCrO_4$ is chromium?

3.33 What mass of lead is theoretically obtained from 15.0 kg of galena ore that is 72.0% PbS?

3.34 What mass of manganese is theoretically obtainable from 25.0 kg of pyrolusite ore that is 65.0% MnO_2?

3.35 How many grams of phophorus and of oxygen are theoretically needed to make 6.000 g of P_4O_6?

3.36 How many grams of sulfur and of chlorine are theoretically needed to make 5.000 g of S_2Cl_2?

3.37 Cinnamaldehyde, a compound found in cinnamon oil, contains carbon, hydrogen, *and oxygen*. The combustion of a 6.50 g sample of the compound yields 19.49 g of CO_2 and 3.54 g of H_2O. What is the percentage composition of cinnamaldehyde?

3.38 A plastic derived from methyl methacrylate contains carbon, hydrogen, *and oxygen*. The combustion of a 12.62 g sample of the plastic yields 27.73 g of CO_2 and 9.09 g of H_2O. What is the percentage composition of the plastic?

*__3.39__ The mineral hematite is Fe_2O_3. Hematite ore contains unwanted material called gangue, in addition to Fe_2O_3. If 5.000 kg of ore contains 2.7845 kg of Fe, what percentage of the ore is Fe_2O_3?

*__3.40__ Sulfur-containing compounds are an undesirable component of some oils. The amount of sulfur in an oil can be determined by oxidizing the sulfur to SO_4^{2-} and precipitating the sulfate ion as $BaSO_4$, which can be collected, dried, and weighed. From a 6.300 g sample of an oil, 1.063 g of $BaSO_4$ was obtained. What is the percentage of sulfur in the oil?

Determination of Formulas

3.41 Determine the molecular formulas to which the following empirical formulas and formula weights pertain: **(a)** SNH, 188.32; **(b)** PF_2, 137.94; **(c)** CH_2, 70.15; **(d)** NO_2, 46.01; **(e)** C_2NH_2, 120.15.

3.42 Determine the molecular formulas to which the following empirical formulas and formula weights pertain: **(a)** $SOCl_2$, 118.96; **(b)** PN_3H_4, 231.12; **(c)** C_3H_2Cl, 147.00; **(d)** B_2H_3, 98.60; **(e)** HCO_2, 90.04.

3.43 A compound contains 31.29% calcium, 18.75% carbon, and 49.96% oxygen. What is the empirical formula of the compound?

3.44 A compound contains 22.85% sodium, 21.49% boron, and 55.66% oxygen. What is the empirical formula of the compound?

3.45 Myristic acid, obtained from coconut oil, is 73.61% carbon, 12.38% hydrogen, and 14.01% oxygen. What is the empirical formula of myristic acid?

3.46 Aspirin is 60.00% carbon, 4.48% hydrogen, and 35.52% oxygen. What is the empirical formula of aspirin?

3.47 Vanillin, the active flavoring agent of the vanilla bean, contains 63.14% carbon, 5.31% hydrogen, and 31.55% oxygen. What is the empirical formula of vanillin?

3.48 Ascorbic acid, vitamin C, contains 40.91% carbon, 4.59% hydrogen, and 54.50% oxygen. What is the empirical formula of ascorbic acid?

3.49 The barbiturates are derivatives of barbituric acid that are used as sedatives. Barbituric acid is 37.50% carbon, 3.15% hydrogen, 21.87% nitrogen, and 37.47% oxygen. What is the empirical formula of barbituric acid?

3.50 Ethylenediaminetetraacetic acid (EDTA) is 41.09% carbon, 5.53% hydrogen, 9.58% nitrogen, and 43.80% oxygen. What is the empirical formula of EDTA?

3.51 The molecular weight of saccharin is 183.18 and the compound is 45.90% carbon, 2.75% hydrogen, 26.20% oxygen, 17.50% sulfur, and 7.65% nitrogen. What is the molecular formula of saccharin?

3.52 The molecular weight of cholesterol is 386 and the compound contains 83.9% carbon, 12.0% hydrogen, and 4.1% oxygen. What is the molecular formula of cholesterol?

3.53 A sample of a compound that contains only carbon, hydrogen, and nitrogen was burned in oxygen and 7.922 g of CO_2, 4.325 g of H_2O, and 0.840 g of N_2 were obtained. **(a)** How many moles of C atoms, of H atoms, and of N atoms did the sample contain? **(b)** What is the empirical formula of the compound? **(c)** What was the mass of the sample that was burned?

3.54 A sample of a compound that contains only carbon, hydrogen, and sulfur was burned in oxygen and 9.682 g of CO_2, 4.956 g of H_2O, and 3.523 g of SO_2 were obtained. **(a)** How many moles of C atoms, of H atoms, and of S atoms did the sample contain? **(b)** What is the empirical formula of the compound? **(c)** What was the mass of the sample that was burned?

3.55 Blood hemoglobin contains 0.342% Fe. If each formula unit of hemoglobin contains four Fe^{2+} ions, what is the formula weight of hemoglobin?

3.56 Chlorophyll a, the green coloring matter of plants, contains 2.72% Mg. If each formula unit of chlorophyll a has one Mg^{2+} ion, what is the formula weight of chlorophyll a?

*3.57** When 6.65 g of the hydrate $NiSO_4 \cdot xH_2O$ was heated in a vacuum, the water was driven off and 3.67 g of anhydrous $NiSO_4$ remained. What is the value of x in the formula $NiSO_4 \cdot xH_2O$?

*3.58** When 7.50 g of the hydrate $BeSO_4 \cdot xH_2O$ was heated in a vacuum, the water was driven off and 4.45 g of anhydrous $BeSO_4$ remained. What is the value of x in the formula $BeSO_4 \cdot xH_2O$?

*3.59** In the analysis of an 8.61 g sample of a compound that contains chromium and chlorine, the chlorine in the sample is converted into AgCl. The process yields 20.08 g of AgCl. What is the empirical formula of the chloride of chromium?

*3.60** In the analysis of a 5.21 g sample of a compound that contains tin and chlorine, the chlorine in the sample is converted into AgCl. The process yields 11.47 g of AgCl. What is the empirical formula of the chloride of tin?

*3.61** An element, X, forms a compound with nitrogen for which the formula is X_3N. If 40.21% of the compound is nitrogen, what is the atomic weight of X?

*3.62** An element, X, forms a compound with carbon for which the formula is XC_2. If 37.48% of the compound is carbon, what is the atomic weight of X?

Unclassified Problems

3.63 List the names and formulas of the seven elements that occur in nature as diatomic molecules.

3.64 Potassium cyanide, KCN, is extremely poisonous. A lethal dose is approximately 5.00 mg for every kilogram of body weight. **(a)** How many milligrams of KCN constitutes a lethal quantity for a 70.0 kg person. **(b)** How many moles of KCN are in this amount of KCN? **(c)** How many formula units of KCN are present?

3.65 A sulfide of an element, A, contains three S atoms per formula unit and is 43.71% sulfur. What is the formula weight of the compound?

3.66 If the formula of the compound described in Problem 3.65 is A_xS_3, what is the atomic weight of A if x is **(a)** 1, **(b)** 2, **(c)** 3, **(d)** 4?

3.67 Muscone, the odor-bearing constituent of musk, has the molecular formula $C_{16}H_{30}O$. What is the percentage composition of muscone?

3.68 A 5.000 g sample of muscone (see Problem 3.67) is burned in oxygen. **(a)** If all of the carbon is converted into CO_2, what mass of CO_2 is obtained. **(b)** If all of the hydrogen is converted into H_2O, what mass of H_2O is obtained?

3.69 The empirical formula of a compound is either C_6H_6O or $C_6H_6O_2$. If the compound is 65.4% carbon, which of the two formulas is correct?

3.70 Methyl salicylate, found in wintergreen oil, is 63.14% carbon, 5.31% hydrogen, and 31.55% oxygen. What is the empirical formula of methyl salicylate?

3.71 One molecule of the hormone insulin has a mass of 9.5×10^{-21} g. What is the molecular weight of insulin?

STOICHIOMETRY, PART II: CHEMICAL EQUATIONS

4

In this chapter, the principles of stoichiometry are applied to chemical reactions. The quantitative relationships between substances involved in a reaction are derived from the chemical equation for the reaction. The stoichiometric interpretation of a chemical equation is based on the mole.

4.1 Chemical Equations

Chemical equations are representations of chemical reactions in terms of the symbols and formulas of the elements and compounds involved. The substances that enter into a reaction are called reactants, and the substances formed in a reaction are called products. In a chemical equation, the formulas of the reactants are indicated on the left and those of the products on the right. An arrow is used instead of the customary equal sign of the algebraic equation; it may be considered as an abbreviation for the word *yields*.

Consider the simple equation:

$$2\,H_2 + O_2 \longrightarrow 2\,H_2O$$

On a molecular level, this equation states that two hydrogen molecules, $2\,H_2$, and one oxygen molecule, O_2, react to form two water molecules, $2\,H_2O$ (see Figure 4.1). The numbers appearing before the formulas, called *coefficients*, indicate the number of molecules of each type involved in the reaction. If no coefficient appears before a given formula, the number 1 is understood.

According to the law of conservation of mass, the same number of atoms of each type must be indicated on both the left side and the right side of the equation. In the course of a reaction, atoms may move from molecule to molecule, but the numbers and types of atoms involved remain constant. In our equation:

$$2\,H_2 + O_2 \longrightarrow 2\,H_2O$$

there are four atoms of hydrogen and two atoms of oxygen on each side. We say that the equation is *balanced*. In writing a chemical equation, coefficients are used to balance the equation. The correct formulas for the reactants and products are used, and they are not changed when the equation is balanced.

Before we can write a chemical equation, we must know what is formed by the reaction and the formulas for all substances involved. Chemical equations

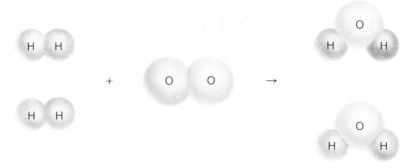

Figure 4.1 Representation of two hydrogen molecules reacting with two oxygen molecules to form two water molecules

report the results of experimentation. One of the goals of chemistry is the discovery and development of principles that make it possible to predict the products of chemical reactions. We will give careful attention to any generalization of this type. All too often, however, the products of a particular set of reactants must be memorized. Furthermore, any prediction is subject to modification if experiment dictates. What may appear reasonable on paper is not neccessarily what occurs in the laboratory.

There are two steps in writing a chemical equation:

1. The first step is to write the correct formulas for the reactants, an arrow, and then the correct formulas of the products. As an example, consider the reaction of carbon disulfide, CS_2, and chlorine, Cl_2, which produces carbon tetrachloride, CCl_4, and disulfur dichloride, S_2Cl_2. To represent this reaction, we write

$$CS_2 + Cl_2 \longrightarrow CCl_4 + S_2Cl_2$$

If the physical states of the substances involved are of interest, they may be indicated in parentheses after each formula. The common states encountered are:

(g) for *gas*

(l) for *liquid*

(s) for *solid*

(aq) for *in aqueous solution*

For our example:

$$CS_2(l) + Cl_2(g) \longrightarrow CCl_4(l) + S_2Cl_2(l)$$

2. The second step is to balance the equation. The same number of atoms of each element must be indicated on both the left side and the right side of the equation. In our example, the carbon atoms and sulfur atoms are balanced. One carbon atom and two sulfur atoms are indicated on both the left side and the right side of the equation. The chlorine atoms, however, are not balanced. There are *two* chlorine atoms (one Cl_2 molecule) on the left and *six* chlorine atoms on the right (four in the CCl_4 molecule and two in the S_2Cl_2 molecule). The equation can be balanced by indicating that three molecules of Cl_2 should be used for the reaction. Thus,

$$CS_2(l) + 3\,Cl_2(g) \longrightarrow CCl_4(l) + S_2Cl_2(l)$$

The simplest types of chemical equations are balanced by trial and error, as the following example illustrates. Notice that an equation is balanced by changing the coefficients of the formulas in the equation and not by changing the formulas themselves.

Example 4.1

When steam, $H_2O(g)$, is passed over hot iron, Fe(s), hydrogen gas, $H_2(g)$, and an oxide of iron that has the formula $Fe_3O_4(s)$ are produced. Write a balanced equation for this equation.

Solution

1. The unbalanced expression is:

$$Fe(s) + H_2O(g) \longrightarrow Fe_3O_4(s) + H_2(g)$$

2. We notice that one atom of Fe and one atom of O appear on the left, but three atoms of Fe and four atoms of O are shown on the right. It is tempting to substitute another oxide of iron, FeO, for Fe_3O_4, since this substitution would produce a balanced equation immediately. Such an equation, however, would be without value. Experiment indicates that Fe_3O_4, not FeO, is a product of the reaction. Balancing an equation is never accomplished by altering the formulas of the products of the reaction.

In the equation for the reaction of iron and steam, three atoms of Fe and four molecules of H_2O are needed to provide the iron and oxygen atoms required for the formation of Fe_3O_4:

$$3\,Fe(s) + 4\,H_2O(g) \longrightarrow Fe_3O_4(s) + H_2(g)$$

The equation is now balanced except for hydrogen, which may be balanced as follows:

$$3\,Fe(s) + 4\,H_2O(g) \longrightarrow Fe_3O_4(s) + 4\,H_2(g)$$

Combustions in Oxygen

In Chapter 3, data from the combustion of compounds in oxygen were used to derive percentage compositions and empirical formulas. We will use this type of reaction to provide practice in equation writing. The products of a *complete* combustion of a compound in oxygen $O_2(g)$, may be predicted on the basis of the elements that make up the compound. At 25°C, if the compound contains:

carbon—$CO_2(g)$ is produced

hydrogen—$H_2O(l)$ is produced

sulfur—$SO_2(g)$ is produced

nitrogen—$N_2(g)$ is produced

Example 4.2

Write a chemical equation for the complete combustion of ethane, $C_2H_6(g)$, in oxygen.

Solution

Since ethane contains carbon and hydrogen, the products of the reaction are $CO_2(g)$ and $H_2O(l)$.

1. $C_2H_6(g) + O_2(g) \longrightarrow CO_2(g) + H_2O(l)$

2. To balance the two carbon atoms of C_2H_6, the production of two molecules of CO_2 must be indicated. The six hydrogen atoms of C_2H_6 require that three molecules of H_2O be produced.

$$C_2H_6(g) + O_2(g) \longrightarrow 2\,CO_2(g) + 3\,H_2O(l)$$

Only the oxygen remains unbalanced. There are seven oxygen atoms on the right and only two on the left. In order to get seven oxygen atoms on the left, we would have to take $3\frac{1}{2}$, or $\frac{7}{2}$, molecules of O_2:

$$C_2H_6(g) + \tfrac{7}{2}O_2(g) \longrightarrow 2\,CO_2(g) + 3\,H_2O(l)$$

Customarily, equations are written with whole-number coefficients. By multiplying the entire equation by two, we get

$$2\,C_2H_6(g) + 7\,O_2(g) \longrightarrow 4\,CO_2(g) + 6\,H_2O(l)$$

4.2 Problems Based on Chemical Equations

A chemical equation can be interpreted in several different ways. Consider, for example, the equation:

$$2\,H_2 + O_2 \longrightarrow 2\,H_2O$$

On the simplest level, this equation shows that hydrogen reacts with oxygen to produce water. On the atomic-molecular level, it states that:

$$2 \text{ molecules } H_2 + 1 \text{ molecule } O_2 \longrightarrow 2 \text{ molecules } H_2O$$

If we consider $2N$ molecules of hydrogen, where N is Avogadro's number (6.02205×10^{23}), then

$$2N \text{ molecules } H_2 + N \text{ molecules } O_2 \longrightarrow 2N \text{ molecules } H_2O$$

Avogadro's number of molecules, however, is one mole of molecules. The equation can also be read, therefore, as

$$2 \text{ mol } H_2 + 1 \text{ mol } O_2 \longrightarrow 2 \text{ mol } H_2O$$

The last interpretation is the one that enables us to solve stoichiometric problems. The coefficients of the chemical equation give the ratios, by moles, in which the substances react and are produced. Since according to the equation

2 mol of H_2 *reacts with* 1 mol of O_2,

10 mol of H_2 *would require* 5 mol of O_2.

Furthermore, since the equation shows that

2 mol of H_2 *produces* 2 mol of H_2O,

10 mol of H_2 *would produce* 10 mol of H_2O.

Example 4.3

Determine the number of moles of $O_2(g)$ that are required to react with 5.00 mol of $C_2H_6(g)$ according to the equation:

$$2\,C_2H_6(g) + 7\,O_2(g) \longrightarrow 4\,CO_2(g) + 6\,H_2O(l)$$

Solution

We must derive the number of moles of O_2 from the value "5.00 mol C_2H_6":

$$? \text{ mol } O_2 = 5.00 \text{ mol } C_2H_6$$

The stoichiometric relationship derived from the coefficients of the chemical equation is

$$2 \text{ mol } C_2H_6 \rightleftharpoons 7 \text{ mol } O_2$$

From this relationship, we can derive the conversion factor that we need to solve the problem. Since this ratio must have the units *mol C_2H_6* in the denominator, it is (7 mol O_2/2 mol C_2H_6). The solution is:

$$? \text{ mol } O_2 = 5.00 \text{ mol } C_2H_6 \left(\frac{7 \text{ mol } O_2}{2 \text{ mol } C_2H_6} \right) = 17.5 \text{ mol } O_2$$

There are three steps in the solution to a problem in which the quantities of substances are expressed in grams instead of moles.

1. The amount of the substance given in the problem is converted from grams to moles by using the formula weight of the substance.

2. The stoichiometric ratio derived from the coefficients of the chemical equation (which is a mole ratio) is used to convert the moles of substance given into moles of substance sought.

3. The value for moles of substance sought is converted into grams of substance sought by using the formula weight of the substance sought.

Example 4.4

Chlorine can be prepared by the reaction:

$$MnO_2(s) + 4\,HCl(aq) \longrightarrow MnCl_2(aq) + Cl_2(g) + 2\,H_2O$$

(a) How many grams of HCl are required to react with 25.0 g of MnO_2? (b) How many grams of Cl_2 are produced by the reaction?

Solution

(a) The problem is begun by writing:

$$? \text{ g HCl} = 25.0 \text{ g } MnO_2$$

The stoichiometric ratio to be derived from the chemical equation will be expressed in moles. Therefore, we convert *g MnO_2* into *mol MnO_2*. The formula weight of MnO_2 is 86.9:

$$? \text{ g HCl} = 25.0 \text{ g } MnO_2 \left(\frac{1 \text{ mol } MnO_2}{86.9 \text{ g } MnO_2} \right)$$

The chemical equation gives the relation:

$$1 \text{ mol } MnO_2 \approx 4 \text{ mol HCl}$$

from which we derive the conversion factor (4 mol HCl/1 mol MnO_2):

$$? \text{ g HCl} = 25.0 \text{ g } MnO_2 \left(\frac{1 \text{ mol } MnO_2}{86.9 \text{ g } MnO_2} \right)\left(\frac{4 \text{ mol HCl}}{1 \text{ mol } MnO_2} \right)$$

At this point, the calculation would give the number of moles of HCl required. We must therefore convert *mol HCl* into *g HCl* to get our answer. The formula weight of HCl is 36.5:

$$? \text{ g HCl} = 25.0 \text{ g } MnO_2 \left(\frac{1 \text{ mol } MnO_2}{86.9 \text{ g } MnO_2} \right)\left(\frac{4 \text{ mol HCl}}{1 \text{ mol } MnO_2} \right)\left(\frac{36.5 \text{ g HCl}}{1 \text{ mol HCl}} \right)$$
$$= 42.0 \text{ g HCl}$$

(b) The same procedure is used to solve this problem. Grams of MnO_2 is converted into moles of MnO_2. The mole reaction from the chemical equation

$$1 \text{ mol } MnO_2 \approx 1 \text{ mol } Cl_2$$

is used to find the number of moles of Cl_2 produced. Finally, moles of Cl_2 is converted into grams of Cl_2:

$$? \text{ g } Cl_2 = 25.0 \text{ g } MnO_2 \left(\frac{1 \text{ mol } MnO_2}{86.9 \text{ g } MnO_2} \right)\left(\frac{1 \text{ mol } Cl_2}{1 \text{ mol } MnO_2} \right)\left(\frac{71.0 \text{ g } Cl_2}{1 \text{ mol } Cl_2} \right)$$
$$= 20.4 \text{ g } Cl_2$$

Example 4.5

The amount of carbon monoxide in a sample of a gas can be determined by the reaction

$$I_2O_5(s) + 5\,CO(g) \longrightarrow I_2(s) + 5\,CO_2(g)$$

If a gas sample liberates 0.192 g of I_2, how many grams of CO were present in the sample?

Solution

The relationship, by moles, between the two substances of interest is obtained from the chemical equation. It is

$$5 \text{ mol CO} \rightleftharpoons 1 \text{ mol } I_2$$

We also need to know:

$$1 \text{ mol } I_2 = 254 \text{ g } I_2$$

$$1 \text{ mol CO} = 28.0 \text{ g CO}$$

Conversion factors from these three relations are needed to solve the problem. The solution is:

$$? \text{ g CO} = 0.192 \text{ g } I_2 \left(\frac{1 \text{ mol } I_2}{254 \text{ g } I_2}\right)\left(\frac{5 \text{ mol CO}}{1 \text{ mol } I_2}\right)\left(\frac{28.0 \text{ g CO}}{1 \text{ mol CO}}\right) = 0.106 \text{ g CO}$$

4.3 Limiting Reactants

In some problems, quantities are given for two or more reactants. Suppose, for example, that we are asked how much H_2O can be prepared from 2 mol of H_2 and 2 mol of O_2. The chemical equation

$$2\,H_2 + O_2 \longrightarrow 2\,H_2O$$

states that 2 mol of H_2 will react with only 1 mol of O_2. In the problem, however, 2 mol of H_2 and 2 mol of O_2 are given. More O_2 has been supplied than can be used. When all the H_2 has been consumed, the reaction will stop. At this point, 1 mol of O_2 will have been used and 1 mol of O_2 will remain unreacted. The amount of H_2 supplied limits the reaction and determines how much H_2O will be formed. Hydrogen, therefore, is called the **limiting reactant.**

Whenever the quantities of two or more reactants are given in a problem, we must determine which one limits the reaction before the problem can be solved.

Example 4.6

How many moles of H_2 can theoretically be prepared from 4.00 mol of Fe and 5.00 mol of H_2O? The chemical equation for the reaction is:

$$3\,Fe(s) + 4\,H_2O(g) \longrightarrow Fe_3O_4(s) + 4\,H_2(g)$$

Solution

The first step is to determine which reactant limits the reaction. The chemical equation shows that:

$$3\text{ mol Fe} \rightleftharpoons 4\text{ mol }H_2O$$

We will compare the amount of reactants given in the problem with the amounts shown in this relationship. The amount of Fe given in the problem is 4.00 mol, which is:

$$\frac{4.00\text{ mol Fe}}{3\text{ mol Fe}} = 1.33$$

times the amount stated in the stoichiometric relationship derived from the chemical equation. The 5.00 mol of H_2O given in the problem is

$$\frac{5.00\text{ mol }H_2O}{4\text{ mol }H_2O} = 1.25$$

times the amount stated in the relationship derived from the chemical equation. The H_2O, therefore, limits the extent of the reaction, since a smaller *proportionate*

Calculations Based on Chemical Equations

1. State the problem. Indicate the *substance sought* (using grams as the desired unit), an equal sign, and the mass of the *substance given* (in grams).

2. Enter the factor that will convert the mass of the *substance given* into the moles of *substance given*. The conversion factor is derived from the fact that 1 mol of a substance (numerator) is a formula weight in grams (denominator).

3. Enter the conversion factor that is derived from the coefficients of the chemical equation and that relates the number of moles of *substance sought* (numerator) to the number of moles of *substance given* (denominator).

4. Enter the factor that will convert the number of moles of *substance sought* to grams of *substance sought*. The formula weight of the substance sought in grams (numerator) is 1 mol of the substance sought (denominator).

5. Carry out the mathematical operations indicated to obtain the answer. All units should cancel except grams of the *substance sought*.

If quantities are given for more than one reactant in the problem:

1. For each reactant, calculate the number of moles supplied from the amounts given in the problem (see preceding step 2).

2. Divide each of these values by the coefficient that, in the chemical equation for the reaction, precedes the formula of the reactant being considered.

3. The smallest number obtained in step 2 pertains to the reactant that limits the extent of the reaction. Use the quantity of this reactant to solve the problem in the way previously outlined.

amount has been supplied (1.25 is a smaller number than 1.33). Since 1.25 times the amount of H_2O stated in the relationship has been supplied, only 1.25 times the amount of Fe stated in the relationship can react. The remainder will be left over. The problem is solved on the basis of the H_2O supplied (the limiting reactant):

$$? \text{ mol } H_2 = 5.00 \text{ mol } H_2O \left(\frac{4 \text{ mol } H_2}{4 \text{ mol } H_2O} \right) = 5.00 \text{ mol } H_2$$

Example 4.7

How many grams of N_2F_4 can theoretically be prepared from 4.00 g of NH_3 and 14.0 g of F_2? The chemical equation for the reaction is

$$2 NH_3(g) + 5 F_2(g) \longrightarrow N_2F_4(g) + 6 HF(g)$$

Solution

The first step is to determine which reactant limits the reaction. We find the number of moles of each reactant present before reaction. The molecular weight of NH_3 is 17.0 and of F_2 is 38.0:

$$? \text{ mol } NH_3 = 4.00 \text{ g } NH_3 \left(\frac{1 \text{ mol } NH_3}{17.0 \text{ g } NH_3} \right) = 0.235 \text{ mol } NH_3$$

$$? \text{ mol } F_2 = 14.0 \text{ g } F_2 \left(\frac{1 \text{ mol } F_2}{38.0 \text{ g } F_2} \right) = 0.368 \text{ mol } F_2$$

The stoichiometric relationship derived from the chemical equation is

$$2 \text{ mol } NH_3 \approx 5 \text{ mol } F_2$$

We compare the number of moles supplied with these quantities. The problem specified 0.235 mol of NH_3, which is

$$\frac{0.235 \text{ mol } NH_3}{2 \text{ mol } NH_3} = 0.118$$

of the amount stated in the relationship derived from the chemical equation. The 0.368 mol F_2 is

$$\frac{0.368 \text{ mol } F_2}{5 \text{ mol } F_2} = 0.0736$$

of the amount given in the relationship from the chemical equation. The F_2, therefore, is the limiting reactant, since a smaller *proportionate* amount has been supplied (0.0736 is a smaller number than 0.118). The problem is solved on the basis of the amount of F_2 supplied:

$$? \text{ g } N_2F_4 = 0.368 \text{ mol } F_2$$

The relationship between the quantity of F_2 employed and the quantity of N_2F_4 produced is derived from the chemical equation. It is

$$5 \text{ mol } F_2 \approx 1 \text{ mol } N_2F_4$$

The molecular weight of N_2F_4 is 104:

$$1 \text{ mol } N_2F_4 = 104 \text{ g } N_2F_4$$

The solution to the problem is

$$? \text{ g } N_2F_4 = 0.368 \text{ mol } F_2 \left(\frac{1 \text{ mol } N_2F_4}{5 \text{ mol } F_2} \right) \left(\frac{104 \text{ g } N_2F_4}{1 \text{ mol } N_2F_4} \right) = 7.65 \text{ g } N_2F_4$$

4.4 Percent Yield

Frequently, the quantity of a product actually obtained from a reaction is less than the amount calculated. It may be that portions of the reactants do not react, or that portions of the reactants react in a way different from that desired (side reactions), or that not all of the product is recovered. The **percent yield** relates the amount of product that is actually obtained (the **actual yield**) to the amount of product that theory would predict (the **theoretical yield**):

$$\text{percent yield} = \frac{\text{actual yield}}{\text{theoretical yield}} \times 100\% \qquad (4.1)$$

Example 4.8

If 4.80 g of N_2F_4 is obtained from the experiment described in Example 4.7, what is the percent yield?

Solution

The theoretical yield is 7.65 g N_2F_4 (the result of the calculation described in Example 4.7). The actual yield is 4.80 g N_2F_4 (stated in this problem). The percent yield, therefore, is

$$\frac{4.80 \text{ g } N_2F_4}{7.65 \text{ g } N_2F_4} \times 100\% = 62.7\%$$

4.5 Molar Solutions

Many chemical reactions are carried out in solution. Stoichiometric calculations for reactions of this type are based on the volumes of the solutions employed and the concentrations of these solutions. The concentration of a solution is the amount of a substance (called a **solute**) dissolved in a given quantity of **solvent,** or the amount of solute present in a given quantity of solution.

Several methods are used to express solution concentrations (see Chapter 12).

Molarity is a method that is employed in the study of the stoichiometry of reactions that take place in solution. The **molarity**, M, of a solution is the number of moles of solute dissolved in one liter of solution.

A 1.0 M solution contains 1.0 mol of solute in 1 L of solution

A 1.5 M solution contains 1.5 mol of solute in 1 L of solution

A 3.0 M solution contains 3.0 mol of solute in 1 L of solution

Notice that the definition is based on *one liter* (1 L). The value stated as the molarity of a solution pertains to the amount of solute that would be present in exactly one liter of the solution. If a given sample of the solution is less (or more) than one liter, the number of moles of solute in the sample is proportionately less (or more) than the numerical value of the molarity. For a 3.0 M solution:

1000 mL, which is 1 L, contains 3.0 mol of solute

500 mL, which is 0.5 L, contains 1.5 mol of solute

2000 mL, which is 2 L, contains 6.0 mol of solute

Figure 4.2 Volumetric flask

All three of these samples are said to have a concentration of 3.0 M.

Notice also that the definition of molarity is based on one liter of *solution* and not on one liter of solvent (which is usually water). When a liquid solution is prepared, the volume of the solution rarely equals the sum of the volumes of the pure components. Usually the final volume of the solution is less or more than the total of the volumes of the substances used to prepare it. It is not practical, therefore, to try to predict the amount of solvent to be used to prepare a given solution. Volumetric flasks (Figure 4.2) are generally used in the preparation of molar solutions. In the preparation of a solution, the correct amount of solute is placed in the flask; the solvent is then added, with careful and constant mixing, until the solution fills the flask to the calibration mark on the neck of the flask.

Example 4.9

What mass of NaOH is required to prepare 0.250 L of a 0.300 M solution of NaOH?

Solution

The solution is 0.300 M, and therefore

0.300 mol NaOH $\backsim$ 1 L NaOH sol'n

We find the number of moles of NaOH needed to make 0.250 L of solution:

$$? \text{ mol NaOH} = 0.250 \text{ L NaOH sol'n} \left(\frac{0.300 \text{ mol NaOH}}{1 \text{ L NaOH sol'n}} \right) = 0.0750 \text{ mol NaOH}$$

The formula weight of NaOH to three significant figures is 40.0; therefore,

40.0 g NaOH $=$ 1 mol NaOH

The number of grams of NaOH needed is:

$$? \text{ g NaOH} = 0.075 \text{ mol NaOH} \left(\frac{40.0 \text{ g NaOH}}{1 \text{ mol NaOH}}\right) = 3.00 \text{ g NaOH}$$

The problem could have been solved in one step:

$$? \text{ g NaOH} = 0.250 \text{ L NaOH sol'n} \left(\frac{0.300 \text{ mol NaOH}}{1 \text{ L NaOH sol'n}}\right)\left(\frac{40.0 \text{ g NaOH}}{1 \text{ mol NaOH}}\right)$$
$$= 3.00 \text{ g NaOH}$$

Example 4.10

(a) Determine the number of moles of $AgNO_3$ in 25.0 mL of 0.600 M $AgNO_3$ solution. (b) What volume of this solution must be taken in order to get 0.0500 mol of $AgNO_3$?

Solution

(a) The problem is begun by writing:

$$? \text{ mol AgNO}_3 = 25.0 \text{ mL AgNO}_3 \text{ sol'n}$$

Since the concentration of $AgNO_3$ in the solution is 0.600 M,

$$0.600 \text{ mol AgNO}_3 \rightleftharpoons 1000 \text{ mL AgNO}_3 \text{ sol'n}$$

from which we derive a conversion factor to solve the problem:

$$? \text{ mol AgNO}_3 = 25.0 \text{ mL AgNO}_3 \text{ sol'n} \left(\frac{0.600 \text{ mol AgNO}_3}{1000 \text{ mL AgNO}_3 \text{ sol'n}}\right)$$
$$= 0.0150 \text{ mol AgNO}_3$$

(b) The same relationship (in inverse form) is used to solve this problem:

$$? \text{ mL AgNO}_3 \text{ sol'n} = 0.0500 \text{ mol AgNO}_3 \left(\frac{1000 \text{ mL AgNO}_3 \text{ sol'n}}{0.600 \text{ mol AgNO}_3}\right)$$
$$= 83.3 \text{ mL AgNO}_3 \text{ sol'n}$$

Often solutions must be prepared by diluting concentrated reagents. The molarities of some common concentrated reagents are listed in Table 4.1. These values can be used to determine the proportion of reagent and water required to prepare a solution of a desired concentration.

The number of moles of solute in a sample of a solution may be obtained by multiplying the volume of the sample (V_1, in liters) by the molarity of the solution (M_1, the number of moles of solute in 1 L of the solution):

number of moles of solute $= V_1 M_1$

If, for example, we take 0.500 L of a 6.00 M solution (which may also be written as 6.00 mol/L):

Table 4.1 Composition of some common concentrated reagents

Reagent	Formula	Formula Weight	Percent by Mass	Molarity
acetic acid	$HC_2H_3O_2$	60.05	100	17.5
hydrochloric acid	HCl	36.46	37	12.0
nitric acid	HNO_3	63.01	70	15.8
phosphoric acid	H_3PO_4	98.00	85	14.7
sulfuric acid	H_2SO_4	98.07	96	18.0
ammonia	NH_3	17.03	28	14.8

$$\textit{number of moles of solute} = V_1M_1$$

$$= (0.500 \text{ L})(6.00 \text{ mol/L})$$

$$= 3.00 \text{ mol}$$

When the solution is diluted to a new volume, V_2, *it still contains the same number of moles of solute.* The concentration has been decreased to M_2, but the product V_2M_2 equals the same number of moles. Therefore,

$$V_1M_1 = V_2M_2 \qquad (4.2)$$

If the 0.500 L sample of 6.00 M solution is diluted until the new volume (V_2) is 2.00 L, the new molarity (M_2) will be:

$$V_1M_1 = V_2M_2$$

$$(0.500 \text{ L})(6.00 \text{ } M) = (2.00 \text{ L})M_2$$

$$M_2 = 1.50 \text{ } M$$

Since a volume term is found on both sides of Equation 4.2, any volume unit can be used to express V_1 and V_2, provided the same unit is used for each. Note that this equation is used for dilution problems only.

Example 4.11

What volume of concentrated HCl should be used to prepare 500 mL of a 3.00 M HCl solution?

Solution

From Table 4.1 we note that concentrated HCl is 12.0 M:

$$V_1M_1 = V_2M_2$$

$$V_1(12.0 \text{ } M) = (500 \text{ mL})(3.00 \text{ } M)$$

$$V_1 = 125 \text{ mL}$$

The solution would be prepared by adding 125 mL of concentrated HCl to enough water to make the total volume 500 mL.

4.6 Stoichiometry of Reactions in Solution

Chemical equations are the basis for all calculations dealing with the stoichiometry of reactions. Whether a reaction occurs in solution or not, any calculation is based on a mole ratio derived from a chemical equation. *The first step in solving any problem, therefore, is to write the chemical equation.*

Reaction stoichiometry is interpreted in terms of moles. For pure substances, masses are converted into moles by using formula weights. For substances in solution, the number of moles is obtained from the volume of the sample and the molarity of the solution (the number of moles per liter).

Example 4.12

What volume of 0.750 M NaOH is required to react with 50.0 mL of 0.159 M H_2SO_4 according to the following equation?

$$H_2SO_4(aq) + 2\,NaOH(aq) \longrightarrow Na_2SO_4(aq) + 2\,H_2O$$

Solution

We find the number of moles of H_2SO_4 in the sample:

$$? \text{ mol } H_2SO_4 = 50.0 \text{ mL } H_2SO_4 \text{ sol'n} \left(\frac{0.150 \text{ mol } H_2SO_4}{1000 \text{ mL } H_2SO_4 \text{ sol'n}} \right)$$

$$= 0.00750 \text{ mol } H_2SO_4$$

From the equation, we see that

$$2 \text{ mol NaOH} \backsimeq 1 \text{ mol } H_2SO_4$$

Therefore,

$$? \text{ mol NaOH} = 0.00750 \text{ mol } H_2SO_4 \left(\frac{2 \text{ mol NaOH}}{1 \text{ mol } H_2SO_4} \right) = 0.0150 \text{ mol NaOH}$$

Finally, we find the volume of 0.750 M NaOH solution that contains 0.0150 mol of NaOH:

$$? \text{ mL NaOH sol'n} = 0.0150 \text{ mol NaOH} \left(\frac{1000 \text{ mL NaOH sol'n}}{0.750 \text{ mol NaOH}} \right)$$

$$= 20.0 \text{ mL NaOH sol'n}$$

The problem could be solved in one step:

$$? \text{mL NaOH sol'n} = 50.0 \text{ mL } H_2SO_4 \text{ sol'n} \left(\frac{0.150 \text{ mol } H_2SO_4}{1000 \text{ mL } H_2SO_4 \text{ sol'n}} \right)$$

$$\times \left(\frac{2 \text{ mol NaOH}}{1 \text{ mol } H_2SO_4} \right) \left(\frac{1000 \text{ mL NaOH sol'n}}{0.750 \text{ mol NaOH}} \right)$$

$$= 20.0 \text{ mL NaOH sol'n}$$

Example 4.13

A soda mint tablet contains $NaHCO_3$ as an antacid. One tablet requires 34.5 mL of 0.138 M HCl for complete reaction. Determine the number of grams of $NaHCO_3$ that one tablet contains. The chemical equation for the reaction is:

$$NaHCO_3(s) + HCl(aq) \longrightarrow NaCl\ (aq) + CO_2(g) + H_2O$$

Solution

$$? \text{ g NaHCO}_3 = 34.5 \text{ mL HCl sol'n} \left(\frac{0.138 \text{ mol HCl}}{1000 \text{ mL HCl sol'n}} \right) \left(\frac{1 \text{ mol NaHCO}_3}{1 \text{ mol HCl}} \right)$$

$$\times \left(\frac{84.0 \text{ g NaHCO}_3}{1 \text{ mol NaHCO}_3} \right) = 0.400 \text{ g NaHCO}_3$$

The first factor (derived from the molarity of the HCl solution) is used to find the number of moles of HCl in the sample of HCl solution. The second factor (derived from the coefficients of the chemical equation) converts this number of moles of HCl into the number of moles of $NaHCO_3$ that will react with it. The final factor (derived from the formula weight of $NaHCO_3$) converts *moles* of $NaHCO_3$ into *grams* of $NaHCO_3$.

Example 4.14

A 25.0 mL sample of a solution of $Ba(OH)_2$ requires 37.3 mL of a 0.150 M solution of HCl for complete reaction. What is the molarity of the $Ba(OH)_2$ solution? The equation for the reaction is

$$Ba(OH)_2(aq) + 2\,HCl(aq) \longrightarrow BaCl_2(aq) + 2\,H_2O$$

Solution

The molarity of the $Ba(OH)_2$ solution is the number of moles of $Ba(OH)_2$ dissolved in 1000 mL of solution. Thus,

$$? \text{ mol Ba(OH)}_2 = 1000 \text{ mL Ba(OH)}_2 \text{ sol'n} \left(\frac{37.3 \text{ mL HCl sol'n}}{25.0 \text{ mL Ba(OH)}_2 \text{ sol'n}} \right)$$

$$\times \left(\frac{0.150 \text{ mol HCl}}{1000 \text{ mL HCl sol'n}} \right) \left(\frac{1 \text{ mol Ba(OH)}_2}{2 \text{ mol HCl}} \right)$$

$$= 0.112 \text{ mol Ba(OH)}_2$$

The solution is 0.112 M $Ba(OH)_2$.

Additional discussion of solutions and examples that pertain to them are found in Section 12.6.

Summary

Chemical equations are representations of chemical reactions in which chemical symbols and formulas are used to represent the substances involved. An equation is written using the correct formulas for the *reactants* and *products* and is balanced by adding *coefficients* to indicate numbers of formula units. If no coefficient appears before a formula, the number 1 is understood.

The *coefficients* of a balanced chemical equation are used to derive *mole ratios* between any two substances that are indicated in the equation. These mole ratios are the basis of stoichiometric calculations. They can be used to calculate the theoretical quantity of a reactant needed for—or a product produced by—a given reaction.

Sometimess, quantities of two or more reactants are given in a problem. In these instances, the *limiting reactant* is the reactant that is supplied in the *smallest stoichiometric amount* and that therefore limits the amounts of products that can be obtained. A problem of this type is solved by identifying the limiting reactant and basing the calculation on the amount of this substance that has been provided.

The amount of product that a calculation indicates a given chemical reaction should produce is called the *theoretical yield*. This quantity is the maximum amount that can be obtained. At times, the amount of product that is actually obtained, called the *actual yield*, is smaller than the theoretical yield. The percentage of the theoretical yield that the actual yield represents is called the *percent yield*.

In calculations for reactions that take place in solution, the concentrations of the solutions used are important. The *molarity* of a solution is the number of moles of solute dissolved in one liter of solution. The number of moles of a reactant, therefore, is calculated from the molarity of the solution of the reactant and the volume of that solution used in the reaction.

Key Terms

Some of the more important terms introduced in this chapter are listed below. Definitions for terms not included in this list may be located in the text by use of the index.

Actual yield (Section 4.4) The amount of product actually obtained from a chemical reaction.

Chemical equation (Section 4.1) A representation of a chemical reaction in terms of the symbols and formulas of the elements and compounds involved.

Coefficient (Section 4.1) A number placed before a symbol or formula in a chemical equation.

Concentration (Section 4.5) The amount of a substance dissolved in a given quantity of solution or solvent.

Limiting reactant (Section 4.3) The reactant that, based on the chemical equation, is supplied in the smallest stoichiometric amount and hence limits the quantity of product that can be obtained from a chemical reaction.

Molarity (Section 4.5) The number of moles of a substance (called a solute) dissolved in one liter of solution.

Percent yield (Section 4.4) 100% times the actual yield divided by the theoretical yield.

Product (Section 4.1) A substance formed in a chemical reaction.

Reactant (Section 4.1) A substance consumed in a chemical reaction.

Solute (Section 4.5) A component of a solution that is present in an amount that is smaller than the amount of the solvent. The solute is said to be dissolved in the solvent.

Solvent (Section 4.5) The component of a solution that is present in the largest amount or that determines the physical state of the solution.

Theoretical yield (Section 4.4) The maximum amount of product that can be obtained from a chemical reaction, as calculated by use of stoichiometric theory on the basis of the chemical equation for the reaction.

Problems*

Chemical Equations

4.1 Balance the following chemical equations:

(a) $Al(s) + HCl(aq) \longrightarrow AlCl_3(aq) + H_2(g)$

(b) $Cu_2S(l) + Cu_2O(l) \longrightarrow Cu(l) + SO_2(g)$

(c) $WC(s) + O_2(g) \longrightarrow WO_3(s) + CO_2(g)$

(d) $Al_4C_3(s) + H_2O(l) \longrightarrow Al(OH)_3(s) + CH_4(g)$

---

* The more difficult problems are marked with asterisks. The appendix contains answers to color-keyed problems.

4.2 Balance the following chemical equations:
(a) $TiCl_4(l) + H_2O(l) \longrightarrow TiO_2(s) + HCl(g)$
(b) $NH_3(g) + O_2(g) \longrightarrow N_2(g) + H_2O(g)$
(c) $HBrO_3(aq) + HBr(aq) \longrightarrow Br_2(l) + H_2O(l)$
(d) $AuCl(s) \longrightarrow AuCl_3(aq) + Au$

4.3 Balance the following chemical equations:
(a) $Fe_2S_3(s) + HCl(aq) \longrightarrow FeCl_3(aq) + H_2S(g)$
(b) $KClO_3(s) \longrightarrow KCl(s) + O_2(g)$
(c) $I_4O_9(s) \longrightarrow I_2O_5(s) + I_2(s) + O_2(g)$
(d) $Ba_3N_2(s) + H_2O(l) \longrightarrow Ba(OH)_2(aq) + NH_3(g)$

4.4 Balance the following chemical equations:
(a) $HNO_3(l) + P_4O_{10}(s) \longrightarrow HPO_3(l) + N_2O_5(s)$
(b) $HNO_2(aq) \longrightarrow HNO_3(aq) + NO(g) + H_2O(l)$
(c) $Al(s) + NaOH(aq) + H_2O(l) \longrightarrow NaAl(OH)_4(aq) + H_2(g)$
(d) $B_2O_3(s) + C(s) + Cl_2(g) \longrightarrow BCl_3(g) + CO(g)$

4.5 Write an equation for the complete combustion of each of the following compounds in oxygen, $O_2(g)$:
(a) cyclohexane, $C_6H_{12}(l)$; **(b)** toluene, $C_7H_8(l)$; **(c)** octane, $C_8H_{18}(l)$.

4.6 Write an equation for the complete combustion of each of the following compounds in oxygen, $O_2(g)$:
(a) propane, $C_3H_8(g)$; **(b)** heptane, $C_7H_{16}(l)$; **(c)** benzene, $C_6H_6(l)$.

4.7 Write an equation for the complete combustion of each of the following compounds in oxygen, $O_2(g)$:
(a) butane, $C_4H_{10}(g)$; **(b)** thiophene, $C_4H_4S(l)$; **(c)** pyridene, $C_5H_5N(l)$.

4.8 Write equations for the complete combustion of each of the following compounds in oxygen, $O_2(g)$: **(a)** aniline, $C_6H_7N(l)$; **(b)** dimethyl sulfide, $C_2H_6S(l)$; **(c)** thiazole, $C_3H_3NS(l)$.

Problems Based on Chemical Equations

4.9 Upon heating, $NaN_3(s)$ decomposes to $Na(l)$ and $N_2(g)$. This reaction serves as a convenient laboratory preparation of pure nitrogen gas. **(a)** Write the chemical equation for the reaction. **(b)** What number of moles of $NaN_3(s)$ is required to prepare 1.00 mol of $N_2(g)$? **(c)** What mass of $N_2(g)$ is produced by the decomposition of 2.50 g of $NaN_3(s)$? **(d)** What mass of $Na(l)$ is produced when 1.75 g of $N_2(g)$ is prepared?

4.10 The reaction of $P_4O_{10}(s)$ and $PCl_5(s)$ yields $Cl_3PO(l)$ as the only product. **(a)** Write the chemical equation for the reaction. **(b)** How many moles of $Cl_3PO(l)$ can be prepared from 1.00 mol of $PCl_5(s)$? **(c)** What mass of $PCl_5(s)$ is required to prepare 12.0 g of $Cl_3PO(l)$? **(d)** What mass of $P_4O_{10}(s)$ is required to react with 7.50 g of $PCl_5(s)$?

4.11 Use the equation:

$$2\,NaNH_2(l) + N_2O(g) \longrightarrow NaN_3(s) + NaOH(s) + NH_3(g)$$

to determine the number of grams of $NaNH_2(l)$ and of

$N_2O(g)$ that are required to prepare 50.0 g of $NaN_3(s)$, assuming complete reaction.

4.12 Pure, dry $NO(g)$ can be made by the reaction:

$$3\,KNO_2(s) + KNO_3(s) + Cr_2O_3(s) \longrightarrow 4\,NO(g) + 2\,K_2CrO_4(s)$$

Determine the number of grams of each reactant required for the preparation of 6.00 g of $NO(g)$, assuming complete reaction.

4.13 Use the equation:

$$PI_3(s) + 3\,H_2O(l) \longrightarrow 3\,HI(g) + H_3PO_3(l)$$

to determine the number of grams of $HI(g)$ that will result from the reaction of 5.00 g of $PI_3(s)$, assuming complete reaction.

4.14 Use the equation:

$$P_4O_{10}(s) + 6\,H_2O(l) \longrightarrow 4\,H_3PO_4(l)$$

to determine the number of grams of $H_3PO_4(l)$ produced by the reaction of 6.00 g of $P_4O_{10}(s)$, assuming complete reaction.

4.15 What is the maximum number of grams of $NH_4SCN(s)$ that can be prepared from 9.00 g of $CS_2(l)$ and 3.00 g of $NH_3(g)$? The equation for the reaction is:

$$CS_2(l) + 2\,NH_3(g) \longrightarrow NH_4SCN(s) + H_2S(g)$$

4.16 What is the maximum number of grams of $OF_2(g)$ that can be prepared from 2.50 g of $F_2(g)$ and 2.50 g of NaOH? The equation for the reaction is:

$$2\,F_2(g) + 2\,NaOH(aq) \longrightarrow OF_2(g) + 2\,NaF(aq) + H_2O(l)$$

4.17 What is the maximum number of grams of $SF_4(g)$ that can be prepared from 6.00 g of $SCl_2(g)$ and 3.50 g of $NaF(s)$? The equation for the reaction is:

$$3\,SCl_2(g) + 4\,NaF(s) \longrightarrow SF_4(g) + S_2Cl_2(l) + 4\,NaCl(s)$$

4.18 What is the maximum number of grams of $B_2H_6(g)$ that can be prepared from 2.650 g of $NaBH_4(s)$ and 4.560 g of $BF_3(g)$? The equation for the reaction is:

$$3\,NaBH_4(s) + 4\,BF_3(g) \longrightarrow 3\,NaBF_4(s) + 2\,B_2H_6(g)$$

4.19 In an experiment, 5.00 g of $LiBH_4(s)$ was reacted with excess $NH_4Cl(s)$, and 2.16 g of $B_3N_3H_6(l)$ was isolated. The equation for the reaction is:

$$3\,LiBH_4(s) + 3\,NH_4Cl(s) \longrightarrow B_3N_3H_6(l) + 9\,H_2(g) + 3\,LiCl(s)$$

What was the percent yield of $B_3N_3H_6(l)$?

4.20 In an experiment, 6.00 g of $Ca_3P_2(s)$ was reacted with excess $H_2O(l)$, and 1.40 g of $PH_3(g)$ was obtained. The equation for the reaction is:

$$Ca_3P_2(s) + 6\,H_2O(l) \longrightarrow 3\,Ca(OH)_2(s) + 2\,PH_3(g)$$

What was the percent yield of $PH_3(g)$?

4.21 A 7.69 g sample of a mixture of $CaC_2(s)$ and $CaO(s)$ was reacted with excess water. The equations for the reactions are:

$$CaC_2(s) + 2\,H_2O(l) \longrightarrow Ca(OH)_2(aq) + C_2H_2(g)$$

$$CaO(s) + H_2O(l) \longrightarrow Ca(OH)_2(aq)$$

The $C_2H_6(g)$ produced by the experiment has a mass of 2.34 g. Assume complete reaction and calculate the percentage of the mixture that is $CaC_2(s)$.

4.22 A 10.00 g sample of a mixture of $CaCO_3(s)$ and $CaSO_4(s)$ was added to excess $HCl(aq)$. The $CaCO_3(g)$ reacted:

$$CaCO_3(s) + 2\,HCl(aq) \longrightarrow$$
$$CaCl_2(aq) + H_2O(l) + CO_2(g)$$

but the $CaSO_4(s)$ did not. The $CO_2(g)$ produced had a mass of 1.50 g. Assume complete reaction and calculate the percentage of the mixture that is $CaCO_3(s)$.

*4.23 A sample of a mixture of $C_2H_6(g)$ and $C_3H_8(g)$ was burned in $O_2(g)$, and 12.50 g of $CO_2(g)$ and 7.20 g of $H_2O(l)$ were obtained. What percentage of the mixture is $C_2H_6(g)$? The equations for the reactions are:

$$2\,C_2H_6(g) + 7\,O_2(g) \longrightarrow 4\,CO_2(g) + 6\,H_2O(l)$$

$$C_3H_8(g) + 5\,O_2(g) \longrightarrow 3\,CO_2(g) + 4\,H_2O(l)$$

*4.24 A sample of a mixture of $CaCO_3(s)$ and $NaHCO_3(s)$ was heated and the compounds decomposed:

$$CaCO_3(s) \longrightarrow CaO(s) + CO_2(g)$$

$$2\,NaHCO_3(s) \longrightarrow Na_2CO_3(s) + H_2O(l) + CO_2(g)$$

The decomposition of the sample yielded 17.6 g of $CO_2(g)$ and 2.70 g of $H_2O(l)$. What percentage of the original mixture is $CaCO_3(s)$?

Molarity

4.25 Calculate the molarity of each of the following solutions: **(a)** 4.00 g of NaOH in exactly 250 mL of solution, **(b)** 13.0 g of NaCl in 1.50 L of solution, **(c)** 10.0 g of $AgNO_3$ in exactly 350 mL of solution.

4.26 Calculate the molarity of each of the following solutions: **(a)** 94.5 g of HNO_3 in exactly 250 mL of solution, **(b)** 6.500 g of $KMnO_4$ in 2.000 L of solution, **(c)** 26.6 g of Na_2SO_4 in exactly 125 mL of solution.

4.27 Calculate the number of moles of solute in each of the following samples of solutions: **(a)** 1.20 L of 0.0500 M $Ba(OH)_2$, **(b)** 25.0 mL of 6.00 M H_2SO_4, **(c)** 0.250 L of 0.100 M NaCl.

4.28 Calculate the number of moles of solute in each of the following samples of solutions: **(a)** 2.50 L of 2.00 M HCl, **(b)** 50.0 mL of 0.250 M $AgNO_3$, **(c)** 0.125 L of 0.0400 M NaOH.

4.29 What mass of solute should be used to prepare each of the following solutions? **(a)** 500.0 mL of 0.02000 M

$KMnO_4$, **(b)** 2.000 L of 1.500 M KOH, **(c)** 25.00 mL of 0.2000 M $BaCl_2$.

4.30 What mass of solute should be used to prepare each of the following solutions? **(a)** 100.0 mL of 6.000 M NaOH, **(b)** 1.500 L of 0.6000 M KIO_3, **(c)** 250.0 mL of 0.1000 M $AgNO_3$.

4.31 How many milliliters of each concentrated reagent (see Table 4.1) should be used to prepare each of the following solutions? **(a)** 0.250 L of 3.50 M $HC_2H_3O_2$, **(b)** 1.50 L of 0.500 M HNO_3, **(c)** 75.0 mL of 0.600 M H_2SO_4.

4.32 How many milliliters of each concentrated reagent (see Table 4.1) should be used to prepare each of the following solutions? **(a)** 0.500 L of 0.600 M HCl, **(b)** 50.0 mL of 5.00 M H_3PO_4, **(c)** 0.750 L of 0.300 M NH_3.

Reactions in Solution

4.33 How many milliliters of 0.250 M KOH will react with 15.0 mL of 0.350 M H_2SO_4? The equation for the reaction is:

$$2\,KOH(aq) + H_2SO_4(aq) \longrightarrow$$
$$K_2SO_4(aq) + 2\,H_2O(l)$$

4.34 How many milliliters of 0.215 M HCl will react with 38.4 mL of 0.112 M $Ba(OH)_2$? The equation for the reaction is:

$$2\,HCl(aq) + Ba(OH)_2(aq) \longrightarrow BaCl_2(aq) + 2\,H_2O(l)$$

4.35 What is the molarity of a solution of $H_2C_2O_4$ if 25.0 mL of the solution requires 37.5 mL of 0.220 M NaOH for complete reaction? The equation for the reaction is:

$$H_2C_2O_4(aq) + 2\,NaOH(aq) \longrightarrow$$
$$NaC_2O_4(aq) + 2\,H_2O(l)$$

4.36 What is the molarity of a solution of $Ca(OH)_2$ if 50.0 mL of the solution requires 46.0 mL of 0.0250 M HCl for complete reaction? The equation for the reaction is:

$$Ca(OH)_2(aq) + 2\,HCl(aq) \longrightarrow$$
$$CaCl_2(aq) + 2\,H_2O(l)$$

4.37 What is the molarity of a solution of Na_2CrO_4 if 25.60 mL of the solution requires 43.01 mL of 0.150 M $AgNO_3$ solution for complete reaction?

$$2\,AgNO_3(aq) + Na_2CrO_4(aq) \longrightarrow$$
$$Ag_2CrO_4(s) + 2\,NaNO_3(aq)$$

4.38 What is the molarity of a solution of KNO_2 if 32.16 mL of the solution requires 22.78 mL of 0.1500 M $KMnO_4$ for complete reaction? The equation for the reaction is:

$$5\,KNO_2(aq) + 2\,KMnO_4(aq) + 3\,H_2SO_4(aq) \longrightarrow$$
$$5\,KNO_3(aq) + 2\,MnSO_4(aq) + K_2SO_4(aq) + 3\,H_2O(l)$$

4.39 When $H_3PO_4(aq)$ is added to 125 mL of a solution of $BaCl_2$, 3.26 g of $Ba_3(PO_4)_2(s)$ precipitates. What is the molarity of the $BaCl_2$ solution? The equation for the reaction is:

$$3\,BaCl_2(aq) + 2\,H_3PO_4(aq) \longrightarrow$$
$$Ba_3(PO_4)_2(s) + 6\,HCl(aq)$$

4.40 When $Na_2CrO_4(aq)$ is added to 145 mL of a solution of $AgNO_3$, 2.79 g of $Ag_2CrO_4(s)$ precipitates. What is the molarity of the $AgNO_3$ solution? The equation for the reaction is:

$$2\,AgNO_3(aq) + Na_2CrO_4(aq) \longrightarrow$$
$$Ag_2CrO_4(s) + 2\,NaNO_3(aq)$$

4.41 What volume of $0.3625\ M\ Na_2S_2O_3$ is required to react with 1.256 g of $I_2(s)$? The equation for the reaction is:

$$2\,Na_2S_2O_3(aq) + I_2(s) \longrightarrow$$
$$2\,NaI(aq) + Na_2S_4O_6(aq)$$

4.42 What volume of $1.350\ M\ KBrO_3$ is required to react with 2.500 g of $N_2H_4(l)$? The equation for the reaction is:

$$4\,KBrO_3(aq) + 6\,N_2H_4(l) \longrightarrow$$
$$6\,N_2(g) + 4\,KBr(aq) + 12\,H_2O(l)$$

4.43 When iron metal is added to a solution of a silver salt, the iron goes into solution and the silver precipitates out. For example,

$$Fe(s) + 2\,AgNO_3(aq) \longrightarrow 2\,Ag(s) + Fe(NO_3)_2(aq)$$

What mass of $Fe(s)$ is required to remove all of the silver from 2.00 L of $0.650\ M\ AgNO_3$?

4.44 When solid sulfur is added to a hot solution of Na_2SO_3, the $S(s)$ dissolves to form $Na_2S_2O_3$. The equation is:

$$Na_2SO_3(aq) + S(s) \longrightarrow Na_2S_2O_3(aq)$$

What mass of $S(s)$ will dissolve in 150.0 mL of $0.2500\ M$ Na_2SO_3?

4.45 A 2.50 g sample of a mixture of $NaCl(s)$ and $NaNO_3(s)$ is dissolved in water. The resulting solution requires 30.0 mL of $0.600\ M\ AgNO_3$ for complete reaction. What percentage of the mixture is $NaCl(s)$? The equation for the reaction is:

$$NaCl(aq) + AgNO_3(aq) \longrightarrow AgCl(s) + NaNO_3(aq)$$

4.46 A 0.4565 g sample of impure N_2H_4 requires 36.46 mL of $0.2156\ M\ KBrO_3$ for complete reaction. What percentage of the sample is N_2H_4? The equation for the reaction is:

$$4\,KBrO_3(aq) + 6\,N_2H_4(l) \longrightarrow$$
$$6\,N_2(g) + 4\,KBr(aq) + 12\,H_2O(l)$$

4.47 Balance the following equations:
(a) $N_2O_4(l) + KI(s) \longrightarrow KNO_3(s) + NO(g) + I_2(s)$
(b) $S_2Cl_2(l) + NH_4Cl(s) \longrightarrow S_4N_4(s) + S(s) + HCl(g)$
(c) $TiO_2(s) + C(s) + Cl_2(g) \longrightarrow TiCl_4(l) + COCl_2(g)$
(d) $AgClO_3(s) + Cl_2(g) \longrightarrow$
$$AgCl(s) + ClO_2(g) + O_2(g)$$

4.48 What is the molarity of **(a)** 25.0 mL of a $0.250\ M$ solution of NaOH diluted to exactly 100 mL? **(b)** 25.0 g of NaOH dissolved in 0.750 L of solution? **(c)** a solution of NaOH, 35.0 mL of which requires 28.2 mL of $0.150\ M$ H_2SO_4 for reaction? The equation for the reaction is:

$$2\,NaOH(aq) + H_2SO_4(aq) \longrightarrow$$
$$Na_2SO_4(aq) + 2\,H_2O(l)$$

4.49 What volume of a $0.600\ M$ solution of HCl should be taken **(a)** to get 0.125 mol of HCl? **(b)** to prepare 0.500 L of $0.100\ M$ HCl? **(c)** to react with 1.50 g of $CaCO_3(s)$? The equation for the reaction is:

$$CaCO_3(s) + 2\,HCl(aq) \longrightarrow$$
$$CaCl_2(aq) + CO_2(g) + H_2O(l)$$

4.50 What is the molarity of a solution of $FeCl_2$ if 22.62 mL of the solution requires 48.89 mL of $0.1262\ M$ $KMnO_4$ for complete reaction? The equation for the reaction is:

$$5\,FeCl_2(aq) + KMnO_4(aq) + 8\,HCl(aq) \longrightarrow$$
$$5\,FeCl_3(aq) + MnCl_2(aq) + KCl(aq) + 4\,H_2O(l)$$

***4.51** A sample of a mixture of Na_2SO_3 and $Na_2S_2O_3$ is dissolved in water and reacted with HCl(aq). The equations for the reactions of the compounds are:

$$Na_2SO_3(aq) + 2\,HCl(aq) \longrightarrow$$
$$2\,NaCl(aq) + SO_2(g) + H_2O(l)$$

$$Na_2S_2O_3(aq) + 2\,HCl(aq) \longrightarrow$$
$$2\,NaCl(aq) + SO_2(g) + S(s) + H_2O(l)$$

The reactions yield 6.59 g of $S(s)$ and 22.1 g of $SO_2(g)$. What percentage of the mixture is $Na_2S_2O_3$?

4.52 When 0.500 g of $Al(s)$ is added to 0.100 L of $0.350\ M$ solution of $Cu(NO_3)_2$, copper metal precipitates. The equation for the reaction is:

$$2\,Al(s) + 3\,Cu(NO_3)_2(aq) \longrightarrow$$
$$2\,Al(NO_3)_3(aq) + 3\,Cu(s)$$

(a) What is the limiting reactant? **(b)** What mass of $Cu(s)$ is obtained?

4.53 A chemist wishes to make 5.00 g of $CuCl(s)$ by the reaction:

$$2\,CuCl_2(aq) + Na_2SO_3(aq) + H_2O(l) \longrightarrow$$
$$2\,CuCl(s) + Na_2SO_4(aq) + 2\,HCl(aq)$$

How many grams of $CuCl_2$ and of Na_2SO_3 should be used if the method gives an 85.0% yield, $CuCl_2$ is to be the limiting reactant, and a 50.0% excess of Na_2SO_3 is to be used?

4.54 Suppose that a metal, X, forms a solid oxide with the formula XO_3, and the oxide reacts with $H_2(g)$ to form the free metal and $H_2O(l)$. **(a)** Write the chemical equation for the reaction. **(b)** A 3.31 g sample of $XO_3(s)$ reacts with $H_2(g)$ to yield 1.24 g of $H_2O(l)$. Use the chemical equation to calculate the formula weight of XO_3. **(c)** What is the atomic weight of X?

4.55 Chromyl chloride, CrO_2Cl_2, can be prepared by the reaction:

$$K_2Cr_2O_7(s) + 4\,KCl(s) + 3\,H_2SO_4(l) \longrightarrow$$
$$2\,CrO_2Cl_2(l) + 3\,K_2SO_4(s) + 3\,H_2O(l)$$

In one preparation, 20.0 g of $K_2Cr_2O_7(s)$ and 20.0 g of $KCl(s)$ were used and 15.08 g of CrO_2Cl_2 was isolated. What was the percent yield?

*4.56 A 32.4 g sample of an alloy of Mg and Al produces 1.66 mol of $H_2(g)$ when added to excess HCl(aq). What percentage of the alloy is Mg? The equations for the reactions are:

$$Mg(s) + 2\,HCl(aq) \longrightarrow MgCl_2(aq) + H_2(g)$$
$$2\,Al(s) + 6\,HCl(aq) \longrightarrow 2\,AlCl_3(aq) + 3\,H_2(g)$$

THERMOCHEMISTRY

In the course of a chemical reaction, energy is either liberated or absorbed. Calculations relating to these energy changes are as important as those concerned with the masses of reacting substances. **Thermochemistry** is the study of the heat released or absorbed by chemical and physical processes. In succeeding chapters, calculations involving these energy changes will be encountered frequently. In this chapter, this type of calculation will be introduced.

5.1 Energy Measurement

It is common to think of force as the application of physical strength—as pushing. In the absence of friction, a body in motion would remain in motion at a constant velocity, and a body at rest would stay at rest (its velocity would be zero). If these bodies are pushed, there will be a change in their velocities. The increase in velocity per unit time is called the **acceleration.**

Suppose, for example, that we have a body moving at a velocity of 1 m/s. Assume that this body is acted on by a constant force—that is, given a sustained push in the direction of its motion. The body will move faster and faster. At the end of one second it may be moving at the rate of 2 m/s. At the end of 2 s, its speed may be 3 m/s. If the body picks up speed at the rate of one meter per second in a second, its acceleration is said to be 1 m/s^2.

A force that gives a *one gram* body an acceleration of 1 m/s^2 is not so large as a force that gives a *one kilogram* body the same acceleration. The magnitude of a **force** (F), therefore, is proportional to the mass of the body (m) as well as to the acceleration (a) that the force produces:

$$F = ma \tag{5.1}$$

The SI unit of force is called the newton (symbol, N) and is derived from the base units of mass (the kilogram), length (the meter), and time (the second):

$$F = ma \tag{5.1}$$
$$1\ \text{N} = (1\ \text{kg})(1\ \text{m/s}^2)$$
$$= 1\ \text{kg·m/s}^2$$

Work (W) is defined as force times the distance through which the force acts (d):

$$W = Fd \tag{5.2}$$

In the International System, the unit of work is the joule (symbol, J). The joule is defined as the work done when a force of one newton acts through a distance of one meter:

$$W = Fd \qquad (5.2)$$
$$1 \text{ J} = (1 \text{ N})(1 \text{ m})$$
$$= 1 \text{ N} \cdot \text{m}$$
$$= 1 \text{ kg} \cdot \text{m}^2/\text{s}^2$$

Energy may be defined as the capacity to do work. There are many forms of energy, such as heat energy, electrical energy, and chemical energy. When one form of energy is converted into another form, energy is neither created nor destroyed. In the International System, the SI unit of work, the joule, is the unit used for all energy measurements, including heat measurements. The unit is named in honor of James Joule (1818–89), a student of John Dalton. Joule demonstrated that a definite quantity of heat is obtained when a given amount of work is converted to heat.

5.2 Temperature and Heat

Temperature is a measure of hotness or coldness. It is that property of matter that determines the direction in which heat flows spontaneously. When two objects at different temperatures are placed in contact, heat will flow from the object at the higher temperature to the object at the lower temperature until the two are at the same temperature. Indeed, heat may be defined as that form of energy that flows spontaneously from a body at a higher temperature to a body at a lower temperature.

Measurement of Temperature

Most liquids expand as the temperature increases. The mercury thermometer is designed to use the expansion of mercury to measure temperature. A thermometer of this type consists of a small bulb sealed to a tube that has a narrow bore (called a capillary tube). The bulb and part of the tube contain mercury, the space above the mercury is evacuated, and the upper end of the tube is sealed. When the temperature increases, the mercury expands and rises in the capillary tube.

The Celsius temperature scale, named for Anders Celsius, a Swedish astronomer, is employed in scientific studies and is a part of the International System. The scale is based upon the assignment of exactly 0°C to the normal freezing point of water and exactly 100°C to the normal boiling point of water*. When a thermometer is placed in a mixture of ice and water, the mercury will stand at a height that is marked on the tube as 0°C. When the thermometer is placed in boiling water under standard atmospheric pressure, the mercury will rise to a position that is marked 100°C. The tube is marked between these two fixed points to indicate 100 equal divisions, each of which represents one degree. The thermometer is calibrated below 0°C and above 100°C by marking off degrees of the same size. The Celsius scale

---

* The atmosphere exerts a pressure on the surface of the earth. The average pressure of the atmosphere at sea level and 0°C is called a *standard atmosphere* (symbol, *atm*) and is now defined in terms of SI units (see Section 10.1). Freezing points and boiling points determined under a pressure of 1 atm are called *normal* freezing points and *normal* boiling points.

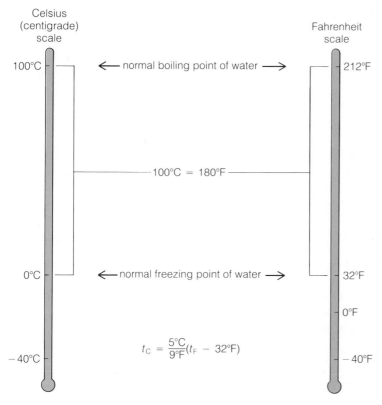

Figure 5.1 Comparison of the Celsius (centigrade) and Fahrenheit temperature scales

was formerly called the **centigrade scale,** derived from the Latin words *centum* (a hundred) and *gradus* (a degree).

On the **Fahrenheit temperature scale** (named for G. Daniel Fahrenheit, a German instrument maker) the normal freezing point of water is 32°F and the normal boiling point of water is 212°F. Since there are 100 Celsius degrees and 180 (212 minus 32) Fahrenheit degrees between these two fixed points, 5 Celsius degrees equal 9 Fahrenheit degrees.

The Fahrenheit temperature scale is not used in scientific work. Conversion of temperature from the Fahrenheit scale (t_F) to the Celsius scale (t_C) can be accomplished in the following way:

1. Subtract 32 from the Fahrenheit reading. The value obtained tells how many Fahrenheit degrees the temperature is above the freezing point of water.

2. Since 5 Celsius degrees equal 9 Fahrenheit degrees, 5/9 of the value obtained is the number of Celsius degrees above the freezing point of water, which is 0°C.

Hence,

$$t_C = \frac{5°C}{9°F}(t_F - 32°F) \tag{5.3}$$

In Figure 5.1, the two temperature scales are compared. The thermodynamic temperature scale, called the Kelvin scale, is described in Section 10.3.

Measurement of Heat

The joule is the SI unit that is used for all energy measurements, including heat measurements. In the past, however, chemists have customarily measured heat in calories. The specfic heat of a substance is defined as the amount of heat required to raise the temperature of 1 g of the substance by 1°C. The calorie was originally defined in terms of the specific heat of water. The one-degree temperature interval had to be specified, however, since the specific heat of water changes slightly as the temperature changes. For many years, the calorie was defined as the amount of heat required to raise the temperature of 1 g of water from 14.5°C to 15.5°C.

Very precise determinations of heat energy, in joules, can be made by electrical measurements. The calorie is now defined, therefore, in terms of its joule equivalent rather than in terms of the specific heat of water:

$$1 \text{ cal} = 4.184 \text{ J (exactly)}$$

Several points should be noted:

1. The joule and the calorie are relatively small units for measurement of thermochemical values. Such values are frequently reported in kilojoules (a kJ is 1000 J) and kilocalories (a kcal is 1000 cal).

2. The International Committee of Weights and Measures recommends that all energy measurements be based on the joule and that the calorie no longer be used. In the past, however, thermochemical values have customarily been recorded in calories and kilocalories.

    a. To convert a value given in *calories* to *joules*, multiply by (4.184 J/cal).

    b. To convert a value given in *kilocalories* to kilojoules, multiply by (4.184 kJ/kcal).

3. For our purposes, the specific heat of water can be considered to be a constant, 4.184 J/(g°C) or 1.000 cal/(g°C), over any temperature interval between the freezing point and the boiling point of water.

5.3 Calorimetry

The heat capacity (C) of a given mass of a substance is the amount of heat required to raise the temperature of the mass by 1°C. Specific heat is the heat capacity of *one gram* of a substance—the amount of heat required to raise the temperature of 1 g of the substance by 1°C. Therefore,

$$C = (\text{mass})(\text{specific heat}) \tag{5.4}$$

Since the specific heat of water is 4.184 J/(g°C), the heat capacity of 125 g of water is:

$$
\begin{aligned}
C &= (\text{mass})(\text{specific heat}) \\
&= [125 \text{ g}][4.184 \text{ J/(g°C)}] \\
&= 523 \text{ J/°C}
\end{aligned}
\tag{5.4}
$$

This sample absorbs 523 J of heat for each degree that the temperature increases. Twice this amount of heat would be required to raise the temperature by 2°C. In general,

$$q = C(t_2 - t_1) \tag{5.5}$$

where q is the heat absorbed by the sample, C is the heat capacity of the sample, t_2 is the final temperature, and t_1 is the initial temperature. The heat absorbed by a 125 g sample of water when it is heated from 20.0°C to 25.00°C can be calculated in the following way:

$$
\begin{aligned}
q &= C(t_2 - t_1) \tag{5.5}\\
&= (523 \text{ J/°C})(25.00°\text{C} - 20.00°\text{C})\\
&= (523 \text{ J/°C})(5.00°\text{C})\\
&= 2615 \text{ J} = 2.62 \text{ kJ*}
\end{aligned}
$$

Calorimeters are devices used to measure the heat changes that accompany chemical reactions. The type of reaction being studied determines what type of calorimeter is employed. A bomb calorimeter (Figure 5.2) is used to measure the heat evolved by a combustion. An experiment using a bomb calorimeter is run as follows:

1. A carefully weighed sample of the reactant is placed in a bomb, which is then filled with oxygen gas under pressure.

2. The bomb is submerged in a weighed quantity of water that has been placed in a well-insulated container. A stirrer is used to keep the water at a uniform temperature, that of the rest of the apparatus.

3. The initial temperature of the assembly (t_1) is taken.

4. The combustion reaction is initiated by electrically heating an ignition wire that has been placed within the bomb.

5. The heat evolved by the reaction is taken up by the calorimeter and its contents and causes the temperature of the assembly to increase. The final temperature (t_2) is taken.

6. Both the water and the calorimeter itself absorb heat. The total heat capacity of the calorimeter and its contents, C_{total}, is calculated:

$$C_{\text{total}} = C_{\text{H}_2\text{O}} + C_{\text{cal.}} \tag{5.6}$$

a. The heat capacity of the water in the calorimeter, $C_{\text{H}_2\text{O}}$, can be calculated from the mass of the water employed and the specific heat of water.

b. The heat capacity of the rest of the device, $C_{\text{cal.}}$, must be determined experimentally. The determination involves the measurement of the temperature increase of the calorimeter after a known amount of heat has been used to warm it. The heat used for this purpose is obtained either by running a reaction that

---

* Notice that if Equation 5.5 is used to analyze a process in which a substance cools, t_2 (the final temperature) will be a smaller value than t_1 (the initial temperature). The quantity ($t_2 - t_1$), therefore, will be a negative value, and q will be a negative value. Since q is defined as heat *absorbed* by the sample, a negative sign on a value of q means that heat is *evolved* by the substance.

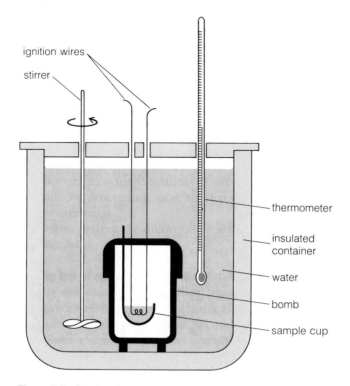

ignition wires
stirrer
thermometer
insulated container
water
bomb
sample cup

Figure 5.2 Bomb calorimeter

evolves a known amount of heat in the calorimeter or by using a measured amount of electrical energy to warm it.

7. The heat liberated in the experiment (q) is calculated from the total heat capacity, C_{total}, and the increase in temperature ($t_2 - t_1$):

$$q = C_{total}(t_2 - t_1) \qquad (5.5)$$

Example 5.1

A bomb calorimeter is used to measure the heat evolved by the combustion of glucose, $C_6H_{12}O_6$:

$$C_6H_{12}O_6(s) + 6\,O_2(g) \longrightarrow 6\,CO_2(g) + 6\,H_2O(l)$$

A 3.00 g sample of glucose is placed in the bomb, which is filled with oxygen gas under pressure. The bomb is placed in a well-insulated calorimeter vessel that is then filled with 1.20 kg of water. The initial temperature of the assembly is 19.00°C. The reaction mixture is ignited by the electrical heating of the wire within the bomb. The reaction causes the temperature of the calorimeter and its contents to increase to 25.50°C. The heat capacity of this calorimeter is 2.21 kJ/°C. The molecular weight of glucose is 180. How much heat is evolved by the combustion of 1 mol of glucose?

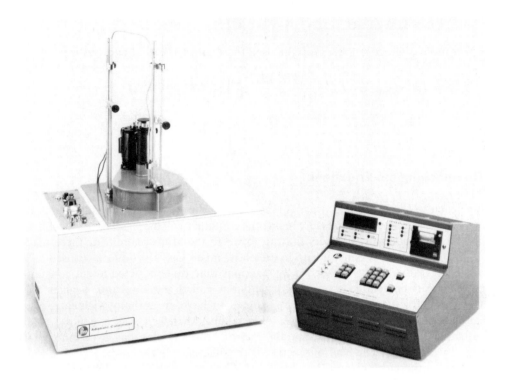

Bomb calorimeter. *Allied Corporation, Fisher Scientific.*

Solution

Since 1.20×10^3 g of water is employed and the specific heat of water is 4.18 J/(g°C), the heat capacity of the water in the calorimeter, C_{H_2O}, is:

$$C = (\text{mass})(\text{specific heat}) \tag{5.4}$$
$$C_{H_2O} = [1.20 \times 10^3 \text{ g}][4.18 \text{ J/(g°C)}]$$
$$= 5.02 \times 10^3 \text{ J/°C} = 5.02 \text{ kJ/°C}$$

The heat capacity of the calorimeter, $C_{cal.}$, is 2.21 kJ/°C. The total heat capacity, C_{total}, is:

$$C_{total} = C_{H_2O} + C_{cal.} \tag{5.6}$$
$$= 5.02 \text{ kJ/°C} + 2.21 \text{ kJ/°C}$$
$$= 7.23 \text{ kJ/°C}$$

Thus, 7.23 kJ of heat is needed to raise the temperature of the assembly by 1°C. The amount of heat *absorbed* by the calorimeter and the water is:

$$q = C_{total}(t_2 - t_1) \tag{5.5}$$
$$= (7.23 \text{ kJ/°C})(25.50°C - 19.00°C)$$
$$= (7.23 \text{ kJ/°C})(6.50°C)$$
$$= 47.0 \text{ kJ}$$

This quantity (47.0 kJ) is also the amount of heat *evolved* by the combustion of 3.00 g of glucose. Therefore,

$$47.0 \text{ kJ} \approx 3.00 \text{ g } C_6H_{12}O_6$$

For a mole of glucose (180. g of glucose), the quantity of heat evolved is:

$$? \text{ kJ} = 180. \text{ g } C_6H_{12}O_6 \left(\frac{47.0 \text{ kJ}}{3.00 \text{ g } C_6H_{12}O_6} \right) = 2.82 \times 10^3 \text{ kJ}$$

5.4 Thermochemical Equations

If a reaction that produces a gas (or produces more gas than it consumes) is run in a closed container, the pressure inside the container will increase. Most reactions, however, are run in containers that are open to the atmosphere. For these reactions, the pressure is constant no matter how much gas is produced or used.*

The heat liberated or absorbed by reactions that are conducted under constant pressure can be related to a property that is called **enthalpy** and is given the symbol H. Every pure substance is assumed to have an enthalpy (which is also called a *heat content*).[†] A given set of reactants, therefore, has a definite total enthalpy, $H_{reactants}$. The corresponding set of products also has a definite total enthalpy, $H_{products}$. The heat of reaction is the difference between these two enthalpies and is therefore given the symbol ΔH. The uppercase Greek delta, Δ, is used to indicate a difference:

$$\Delta H = H_{products} - H_{reactants} \tag{5.7}$$

1. Reactions that liberate heat are called **exothermic reactions.** For reactions of this type, the products have a lower enthalpy than the reactants; ΔH is a negative value. When the reaction occurs, the products replace the reactants in the system. The enthalpy of the reaction system decreases (ΔH is negative), and the difference is given off as heat (see Figure 5.3).

2. Reactions that absorb heat are called **endothermic reactions.** For reactions of this type, the enthalpy of the products is higher than the enthalpy of the reactants, and ΔH is positive. When the reaction occurs, heat must be supplied in order to raise the enthalpy of the system (see Figure 5.4).

---

* Reactions run in a calorimeter bomb may or may not cause the pressure inside the bomb to change appreciably. The equation for the reaction described in Example 5.1 is:

$$C_6H_{12}O_6(s) + 6\,O_2(g) \longrightarrow 6\,CO_2(g) + 6\,H_2O(l)$$

Notice that 6 mol of gas (O_2 gas) is consumed and 6 mol of gas (CO_2 gas) is produced. The pressure inside the bomb, therefore, does not change much when the reaction occurs.

If a reaction produces more moles of gas than it uses, the pressure inside a calorimeter bomb builds up. If such a reaction occurs in a container that is open to the atmosphere, the gases that are produced escape. The pressure in this case remains constant and equal to the pressure of the atmosphere. For such a reaction, the heat measured when the pressure is allowed to change is slightly different from the heat measured at constant pressure. In a case of this type, a correction is applied to the value obtained by use of a bomb calorimeter (see Section 19.2).

There are no appreciable pressure effects for many reactions, including those that do not involve gases (for example, reactions run in solution) and those in which the number of moles of gas used equals the number of moles of gas produced.

[†] Note that *heat content* (or *enthalpy*), H, is different from *heat capacity*, C (defined in Section 5.3). The similarity between the names makes it preferable to use the term *enthalpy* instead of *heat content*.

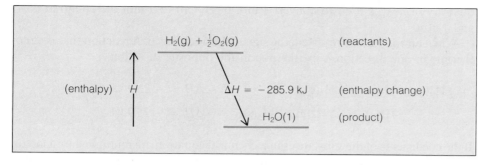

Figure 5.3 Enthalpy diagram for an exothermic reaction

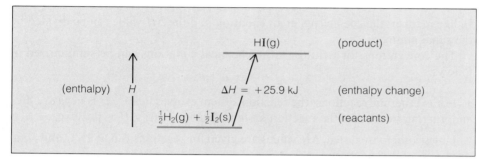

Figure 5.4 Enthalpy diagram for an endothermic reaction

The enthalpies of chemical substances depend upon temperature, pressure, and the physical state. By convention, ΔH values are usually reported for reactions run at 25°C and standard atmospheric pressure (Section 10.2). If any other conditions are employed, they are noted.

Thermochemical data may be given by writing a chemical equation for the reaction under consideration and noting beside it the ΔH value for the reaction *as it is written*. The appropriate value of ΔH is the one required when the equation is read in molar quantities. Contrary to usual practice, fractional coefficients may be used to balance the chemical equation. A fractional coefficient simply indicates a fraction of a mole of a substance. Thus,

$$H_2(g) + \tfrac{1}{2}O_2(g) \longrightarrow H_2O(l) \qquad \Delta H = -286 \text{ kJ}$$

When 1 mol of hydrogen gas reacts with $\tfrac{1}{2}$ mol of oxygen gas to produce 1 mol of liquid water, 286 kJ of heat is evolved.

The state of each substance in the reaction must be indicated in the equation. A designation such as (g) for gas, (s) for solid, (l) for liquid, or (aq) for "in aqueous solution" is placed after each formula. The need for this convention can be demonstrated by comparing the following equation with the preceding one:

$$H_2(g) + \tfrac{1}{2}O_2(g) \longrightarrow H_2O(g) \qquad \Delta H = -242 \text{ kJ}$$

Notice that 44 kJ less heat is liberated by the second reaction (in which gaseous H_2O is produced) than by the first reaction (in which liquid H_2O is produced). This quantity of heat is used to convert 1 mol of $H_2O(l)$ to 1 mol of $H_2O(g)$ at 25°C and 1 atm.

When an equation is reversed, the sign of ΔH is changed. A reaction that is endothermic in one direction is exothermic in the opposite direction:

$$\tfrac{1}{2}H_2(g) + \tfrac{1}{2}I_2(s) \longrightarrow HI(g) \qquad\qquad \Delta H = +25.9 \text{ kJ}$$

$$HI(g) \longrightarrow \tfrac{1}{2}H_2(g) + \tfrac{1}{2}I_2(s) \qquad \Delta H = -25.9 \text{ kJ}$$

If the coefficients of the substances in a chemical equation are multiplied by a factor, the ΔH value must be multiplied by the same factor. For example, if the last equation is multiplied through by 2, the ΔH value must also be multiplied by 2:

$$2\,HI(g) \longrightarrow H_2(g) + I_2(s) \qquad \Delta H = 2(-25.9 \text{ kJ}) = -51.8 \text{ kJ}$$

In like manner, the coefficients of an equation and the ΔH value can be divided by the same number.

The conventions for writing thermochemical equations can be summarized as follows:

1. For exothermic reactions (the reaction system evolves heat), ΔH is negative. For endothermic reactions (the reaction system absorbs heat), ΔH is positive.

2. Unless otherwise noted, ΔH values are given for reactions run at 25°C and standard atmospheric pressure.

3. Designations such as (g), (s), (l), and (aq) are placed behind the formulas in the equation to indicate the physical state of each substance.

4. The coefficients of the substances in the chemical equation indicate the number of moles of each substance involved in the reaction (fractions may be used), and the ΔH value corresponds to these quantities of materials.

5. If the coefficients in the chemical equation are multiplied or divided by a number, the ΔH value must be multiplied or divided by the same number.

6. When a chemical equation is reversed, the sign but not the magnitude of the ΔH value is changed.

Thermochemical problems are solved in much the same way that simple stoichiometric problems are solved.

Example 5.2

The thermite reaction is highly exothermic:

$$2\,Al(s) + Fe_2O_3(s) \longrightarrow 2\,Fe(s) + Al_2O_3(s) \qquad \Delta H = -848 \text{ kJ}$$

How much heat is liberated when 36.0 g of Al reacts with excess Fe_2O_3?

Solution

The equation and ΔH value show that:

$$-848 \text{ kJ} \approx 2 \text{ mol Al}$$

Since the atomic weight of Al is 27.0,

$$? \text{ kJ} = 36.0 \text{ g Al} \left(\frac{1 \text{ mol Al}}{27.0 \text{ g Al}} \right) \left(\frac{-848 \text{ kJ}}{2 \text{ mol Al}} \right) = -565 \text{ kJ}$$

5.5 The Law of Hess

The basis of many thermochemical calculations is the law of constant heat summation, which Germain H. Hess established experimentally in 1840. This law of Hess states that the change in enthalpy for any chemical reaction is constant, whether the reaction occurs in one step or in several steps. Thermochemical data, therefore, may be treated algebraically.

Consider, for example, the reaction of graphite with oxygen that produces carbon dioxide gas:

$$C(\text{graphite}) + O_2(g) \longrightarrow CO_2(g) \qquad \Delta H = -393.5 \text{ kJ}$$

This transformation can also occur in two steps: the reaction of graphite with O_2 that forms CO, followed by the reaction of CO with O_2 that forms CO_2. Addition of the equations for the steps gives a result that is identical with the equation for the direct reaction (see Figure 5.5).

$$
\begin{array}{ll}
C(\text{graphite}) + \tfrac{1}{2}O_2(g) \longrightarrow CO(g) & \Delta H = -110.5 \text{ kJ} \\
\underline{CO(g) + \tfrac{1}{2}O_2(g) \longrightarrow CO_2(g)} & \underline{\Delta H = -283.0 \text{ kJ}} \\
C(\text{graphite}) + O_2(g) \longrightarrow CO_2(g) & \Delta H = -393.5 \text{ kJ}
\end{array}
$$

Since thermochemical data can be treated algebraically, it is possible to derive an enthalpy of reaction from measurements made on other reactions. Suppose, for example, that the following thermochemical equations are given:

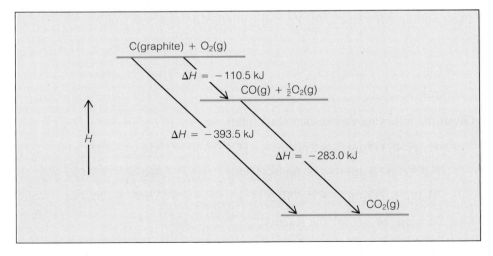

Figure 5.5 Enthalpy diagram to illustrate the law of Hess

$$C(graphite) + O_2(g) \longrightarrow CO_2(g) \qquad\qquad \Delta H = -393.5 \text{ kJ} \qquad (5.8)$$

$$H_2(g) + \tfrac{1}{2}O_2(g) \longrightarrow H_2O(l) \qquad\qquad \Delta H = -285.9 \text{ kJ} \qquad (5.9)$$

$$CH_4(g) + 2O_2(g) \longrightarrow CO_2(g) + 2H_2O(l) \qquad \Delta H = -890.4 \text{ kJ} \qquad (5.10)$$

These relations can be used to find the ΔH for the reaction in which methane, CH_4, is prepared from carbon and hydrogen. This enthalpy change cannot be measured directly:

$$C(graphite) + 2H_2(g) \longrightarrow CH_4(g) \qquad \Delta H = ?$$

Since 1 mol of C(graphite) appears on the left of Equation 5.8 and also on the left of the desired equation, Equation 5.8 is written as previously given:

$$C(graphite) + O_2(g) \longrightarrow CO_2(g) \qquad \Delta H = -393.5 \text{ kJ} \qquad (5.8)$$

Two moles of $H_2(g)$ appear on the left of the desired equation and only one mole of $H_2(g)$ appears on the left of Equation 5.9. Equation 5.9, therefore, is multiplied by 2, and the ΔH value is multiplied by 2:

$$2H_2(g) + O_2(g) \longrightarrow 2H_2O(l) \qquad \Delta H = -571.8 \text{ kJ} \qquad (5.11)$$

One mole of $CH_4(g)$ appears on the *right* side of the desired equation. Equation 5.10 is therefore reversed, and the sign of the ΔH value is changed:

$$CO_2(g) + 2H_2O(l) \longrightarrow CH_4(g) + 2O_2(g) \qquad \Delta H = +890.4 \text{ kJ} \qquad (5.12)$$

Equations 5.8, 5.11, and 5.12 are added. Terms common to both sides of the final equation ($2O_2$, CO_2, and $2H_2O$) are canceled:

$$C(graphite) + O_2(g) \longrightarrow CO_2(g) \qquad\qquad \Delta H = -393.5 \text{ kJ} \qquad (5.8)$$

$$2H_2(g) + O_2(g) \longrightarrow 2H_2O(l) \qquad\qquad \Delta H = -571.8 \text{ kJ} \qquad (5.11)$$

$$\underline{CO_2(g) + 2H_2O(l) \longrightarrow CH_4(g) + 2O_2(g) \qquad \Delta H = +890.4 \text{ kJ} \qquad (5.12)}$$

$$C(graphite) + 2H_2(g) \longrightarrow CH_4(g) \qquad\qquad \Delta H = -74.9 \text{ kJ}$$

The resulting ΔH value is the enthalpy of reaction that was sought.

Example 5.3

Given the following thermochemical equations:

$$4NH_3(g) + 3O_2(g) \longrightarrow 2N_2(g) + 6H_2O(l) \qquad \Delta H = -1531 \text{ kJ} \qquad (5.13)$$

$$N_2O(g) + H_2(g) \longrightarrow N_2(g) + H_2O(l) \qquad \Delta H = -367.4 \text{ kJ} \qquad (5.14)$$

$$H_2(g) + \tfrac{1}{2}O_2(g) \longrightarrow H_2O(l) \qquad\qquad \Delta H = -285.9 \text{ kJ} \qquad (5.15)$$

Find the value of ΔH for the reaction:

$$2NH_3(g) + 3N_2O(g) \longrightarrow 4N_2(g) + 3H_2O(l)$$

Solution

Since the desired equation has 2 mol of $NH_3(g)$ on the left, we divide Equation 5.13 by 2 and the ΔH value by 2. We multiply Equation 5.14 and the corresponding ΔH value by 3 so that the coefficient of $N_2O(g)$ in the final equation will be 3. To eliminate the $3\,H_2(g)$ added to the left in the last step, we reverse Equation 5.15 and multiply it by 3; the corresponding ΔH value is multiplied by 3 and its sign changed:

$$2\,NH_3(g) + \tfrac{3}{2}O_2(g) \longrightarrow N_2(g) + 3\,H_2O(l) \qquad \Delta H = -765.5 \text{ kJ}$$

$$3\,N_2O(g) + 3\,H_2(g) \longrightarrow 3\,N_2(g) + 3\,H_2O(l) \qquad \Delta H = -1102.2 \text{ kJ}$$

$$3\,H_2O(l) \longrightarrow 3\,H_2(g) + \tfrac{3}{2}O_2(g) \qquad \Delta H = +857.7 \text{ kJ}$$

The equations and ΔH values are added. Terms common to both sides of the final equation ($\tfrac{3}{2}O_2$, $2\,H_2$, and $3\,H_2O$) are canceled:

$$2\,NH_3(g) + 3\,N_2O(g) \longrightarrow 4\,N_2(g) + 3\,H_2O(l) \qquad \Delta H = -1010.0 \text{ kJ}$$

5.6 Enthalpies of Formation

A convenient method for calculating a ΔH for a reaction involves the use of recorded values that are called standard enthalpies of formation. We will first describe how these values are defined and then show how they are used.

A **standard enthalpy of formation** (given the symbol ΔH_f°) is the value of ΔH that corresponds to a reaction in which *one mole* of a substance at 1 atm and a particular reference temperature is prepared from its constituent elements in their most stable forms at 1 atm pressure and the reference temperature. Several parts of this definition should be explained.

1. This definition may be said to apply to reactions that involve compounds and elements in their standard states. The **standard state** of a liquid or solid is the pure liquid or pure solid under a pressure of 1 atm. The standard state of a gas is the gas at a pressure of 1 atm, assuming ideal behavior (see Sections 10.5 and 10.13). The symbol ΔH° is used to indicate standard enthalpy changes, which apply to reactions involving only substances in their standard states.*

2. The reference temperature that is usually selected is 25°C. Most tabulated ΔH_f° values (as well as the ΔH_f° values used in this book) pertain to reactions at a reference temperature of 25°C.

3. Some elements exist in more than one form. The form of the element used to derive a ΔH_f° value is the one that is most stable (lowest enthalpy) at 1 atm and the reference temperature. Carbon, for example, occurs as diamond and as graphite. The enthalpy of diamond is higher than the enthalpy of graphite:

$$C(\text{graphite}) \longrightarrow C(\text{diamond}) \qquad \Delta H^\circ = +1.9 \text{ kJ} \qquad (5.16)$$

---

* The ΔH values previously given in this chapter are in reality ΔH° values. Since the distinction was not important to the discussion, it was not noted.

Graphite, therefore, is the form that is most stable at 25°C and 1 atm, and is the form used to derive ΔH_f° values for the compounds of carbon.

Consider two reactions for the formation of $CO_2(g)$:

$$C(\text{graphite}) + O_2(g) \longrightarrow CO_2(g) \qquad \Delta H^\circ = -393.5 \text{ kJ} \qquad (5.17)$$

$$C(\text{diamond}) + O_2(g) \longrightarrow CO_2(g) \qquad \Delta H^\circ = -395.4 \text{ kJ} \qquad (5.18)$$

The standard enthalpy of formation of $CO_2(g)$ is given by Equation 5.17, the reaction that employs C(graphite).

Oxygen is another element that occurs in more than one form. The oxygen molecule, $O_2(g)$, has a lower enthalpy than the ozone molecule, $O_3(g)$:

$$\tfrac{3}{2}O_2(g) \longrightarrow O_3(g) \qquad \Delta H^\circ = +142 \text{ kJ} \qquad (5.19)$$

The stable form of oxygen at 1 atm and 25°C, therefore, is $O_2(g)$. This form is used to derive standard enthalpies of formation (such as that given in Equation 5.17). Note that for an element that occurs in nature as a diatomic molecule (H_2, N_2, O_2, F_2, Cl_2, Br_2, and I_2), the atomic form is one of very high enthalpy. The stable form of each of these elements is the diatomic molecule—$O_2(g)$ for oxygen, *not* $O(g)$.

By convention, the standard enthalpy of formation of the most stable form of an element at 1 atm and the reference temperature (the ΔH° for the reaction in which this form of the element is prepared from itself) *is equal to zero.* Note, however, that Equation 5.16 may be said to represent the standard enthalpy of formation of C(diamond), and Equation 5.19 may be said to represent the standard enthalpy of formation of $O_3(g)$.

Enthalpy of formation, therefore, is a specific type of enthalpy change. The ΔH values for the reactions shown in Figures 5.3 and 5.4 are in reality the ΔH_f° values of $H_2O(l)$ and $HI(g)$, respectively:

$$H_2(g) + \tfrac{1}{2}O_2(g) \longrightarrow H_2O(l) \qquad \Delta H_f^\circ = -285.9 \text{ kJ}$$

$$\tfrac{1}{2}H_2(g) + \tfrac{1}{2}O_2(g) \longrightarrow HI(g) \qquad \Delta H_f^\circ = +25.9 \text{ kJ}$$

Enthalpies of formation are either measured directly or calculated from other thermochemical data by applying the law of Hess. The result of the calculation given in Section 5.5:

$$C(\text{graphite}) + 2\,H_2(g) \longrightarrow CH_4(g) \qquad \Delta H_f^\circ = -74.9 \text{ kJ}$$

is the standard enthalpy of formation of $CH_4(g)$. Some standard enthalpies of formation are listed in Table 5.1.

The standard enthalpy change for a reaction can be calculated from the standard enthalpies of formation of the compounds involved in the reaction. For example, the standard enthalpy change for the reaction:

$$C_2H_4(g) + H_2(g) \longrightarrow C_2H_6(g) \qquad \Delta H^\circ = ?$$

can be calculated from the standard enthalpies of formation of ethylene, $C_2H_4(g)$, and ethane, $C_2H_6(g)$:

Table 5.1 Enthalpies of formation (kJ/mol) at 25°C and 1 atm

Compound	ΔH_f°	Compound	ΔH_f°
$AgCl(s)$	-127.0	$CS_2(l)$	$+87.86$
$Al_2O_3(s)$	-1669.8	$Fe_2O_3(s)$	-822.2
$BaCO_3(s)$	$-1218.$	$HBr(g)$	-36.2
$BaO(s)$	-588.1	$HCl(g)$	-92.30
$CaCO_3(s)$	-1206.9	$HCN(g)$	$+130.5$
$CaO(s)$	-635.5	$HF(g)$	$-269.$
$Ca(OH)_2(s)$	-986.59	$HgBr_2(s)$	$-169.$
$Ca_3P_2(s)$	-504.17	$HI(g)$	$+25.9$
$CF_4(g)$	-913.4	$HNO_3(l)$	-173.2
$CH_4(g)$	-74.85	$H_2O(g)$	-241.8
$C_2H_2(g)$	$+226.7$	$H_2O(l)$	-285.9
$C_2H_4(g)$	$+52.30$	$H_2S(g)$	-20.2
$C_2H_6(g)$	-84.68	$MgO(s)$	-601.83
$C_6H_6(l)$	$+49.04$	$NaCl(s)$	-411.0
$CH_3Cl(l)$	$-132.$	$NF_3(g)$	$-113.$
$CH_3NH_2(g)$	$-28.$	$NH_3(g)$	-46.19
$CH_3OH(g)$	-201.2	$NH_4NO_3(s)$	-365.1
$CH_3OH(l)$	-238.6	$NO(g)$	$+90.37$
$C_2H_5OH(l)$	-277.6	$NO_2(g)$	$+33.8$
$CO(g)$	-110.5	$PH_3(g)$	$+9.25$
$CO_2(g)$	-393.5	$SO_2(g)$	-296.9
$COCl_2(g)$	$-223.$	$ZnO(s)$	-348.0

$$2\,C(\text{graphite}) + 2\,H_2(g) \longrightarrow C_2H_4(g) \qquad \Delta H_f^\circ = +52.30 \text{ kJ} \qquad (5.20)$$

$$2\,C(\text{graphite}) + 3\,H_2(g) \longrightarrow C_2H_6(g) \qquad \Delta H_f^\circ = -84.68 \text{ kJ} \qquad (5.21)$$

Equation 5.20 is written in reverse form, which indicates a transformation in which $C_2H_4(g)$ breaks down into its elements. The appropriate value of the enthalpy change for the reverse reaction is $-\Delta H_f^\circ(C_2H_4)$ or -52.30 kJ. The elements from the decomposition of $C_2H_4(g)$ plus an additional mole of $H_2(g)$ can be imagined to form $C_2H_6(g)$. Equation 5.21, therefore, is written as shown. When these two equations are added, the desired thermochemical equation is obtained:

$$
\begin{array}{ll}
CH_4(g) \longrightarrow 2\,C(\text{graphite}) + 2\,H_2(g) & \Delta H_f^\circ = -52.30 \text{ kJ} \\
\underline{2\,(\text{graphite}) + 3\,H_2(g) \longrightarrow C_2H_6(g)} & \underline{\Delta H_f^\circ = -84.68 \text{ kJ}} \\
C_4H_4(g) + H_2(g) \longrightarrow C_2H_6(g) & \Delta H_f^\circ = -136.98 \text{ kJ}
\end{array}
$$

The ΔH° of the reaction is therefore $\Delta H_f^\circ(C_2H_6) - \Delta H_f^\circ(C_2H_4)$.

In general, a ΔH° value for a reaction may be obtained by subtracting the sum of the enthalpies of formation of the reactants from the sum of the enthalpies of formation of the products:

$$\Delta H^\circ = \sum \Delta H_f^\circ(\text{products}) - \sum \Delta H_f^\circ(\text{reactants}) \qquad (5.22)$$

Using Enthalpies of Formation to Derive ΔH Values.

1. Write the chemical equation for the reaction.
2. Substitute in the equation:

$$\Delta H^\circ = \sum \Delta H_f^\circ(\text{products}) - \sum \Delta H_f^\circ(\text{reactants})$$

a. The term $\Sigma \Delta H_f^\circ$(products) is the sum of the standard enthalpies of formation of the *compounds* that appear on the *right* side of the chemical equation.

b. The term $\Sigma \Delta H_f^\circ$(reactants) is the sum of the standard enthalpies of formation of the *compounds* that appear on the *left* side of the chemical equation.

To obtain either of these sums, multiply the standard enthalpy of formation of each compound by the number of moles of that compound involved in the reaction (given by the appropriate coefficient of the chemical equation). No enthalpy terms are introduced for *elements* that appear in the chemical equation in their stable forms at 1 atm pressure and the reference temperature (25°C).

The uppercase Greek sigma, Σ, indicates a sum. By reversing the sign of $\Sigma \Delta H_f^\circ$(reactants), we indicate a process in which the reactants are broken down into their constituent elements. The term $\Sigma \Delta H_f^\circ$(products) indicates the formation of the products from these elements.

Two things should be kept in mind when using this approach to determine ΔH° values:

1. Standard enthalpies of formation are given in kilojoules per *mole*. Each of the values listed in Table 5.1 pertains to the formation of only *one* mole of the compound. If more than one mole (or less than one mole) of the compound is involved in the reaction being studied, the ΔH_f° value must be multiplied by the number of moles involved.

2. The standard enthalpy of formation of an *element* in its most stable form at 1 atm and at the reference temperature is zero. No terms for elements are added into the sums $\Sigma \Delta H_f^\circ$(products) and $\Sigma \Delta H_f^\circ$(reactants)

Consider the reaction:

$$2\,NH_3(g) + 3\,Cl_2(g) \longrightarrow N_2(g) + 6\,HCl(g) \qquad \Delta H^\circ = ?$$

The enthalpy change can be calculated in the following way:

$$\begin{aligned}\Delta H^\circ &= \sum \Delta H_f^\circ(\text{products}) - \sum \Delta H_f^\circ(\text{reactants}) \qquad (5.22)\\ &= 6\Delta H_f^\circ(HCl) - 2\Delta H_f^\circ(NH_3)\\ &= (6\text{ mol})(-92.30\text{ kJ/mol}) - (2\text{ mol})(-46.19\text{ kJ/mol})\\ &= -553.80\text{ kJ} + 92.38\text{ kJ} = -461.42\text{ kJ}\end{aligned}$$

The calculation may be checked by the addition of the appropriate thermochemical equations.

1. Since the reaction produces 6 mol of HCl(g), the equation for the standard enthalpy of formation of one mole of HCl(g) is multiplied by 6 and the ΔH_f° of HCl(g) is multiplied by 6.

$$3\,H_2(g) + 3\,Cl_2(g) \longrightarrow 6\,HCl(g) \qquad \Delta H^\circ = 6\Delta H_f^\circ = -553.80\ kJ$$

2. The reaction *consumes* two moles of $NH_3(g)$. The equation for the *formation* of $NH_3(g)$ is multiplied by 2 and *reversed*. The value of ΔH_f° of $NH_3(g)$ is multiplied by 2 and the sign changed.

$$2\,NH_3(g) \longrightarrow H_2(g) + 3\,H_2(g) \qquad \Delta H^\circ = -2\Delta H_f^\circ = +92.38\ kJ$$

3. These two thermochemical expressions are added. No separate equation is introduced for the elements that are involved in the reaction (Cl_2 and N_2):

$$
\begin{array}{lll}
3\,H_2(g) + 3\,Cl_2(g) \longrightarrow 6\,HCl(g) & \Delta H^\circ = & 6\Delta H_f^\circ = -553.80\ kJ \\
\underline{2\,NH_3(g) \longrightarrow N_2(g) + 3\,H_2(g)} & \underline{\Delta H^\circ = -2\Delta H_f^\circ = +92.38\ kJ} \\
2\,NH_3(g) + 3\,Cl_2(g) \longrightarrow N_2(g) + 6\,HCl(g) & \Delta H^\circ = & -461.42\ kJ
\end{array}
$$

The terms "$3\,H_2(g)$" cancel in the addition. Notice that "$3\,Cl_2(g)$" and "$N_2(g)$" appear in the final equation even though no special provision was made for their introduction.

Example 5.4

Use enthalpies of formation to calculate the ΔH° of the reaction:

$$Fe_2O_3(s) + 3\,CO(g) \longrightarrow 2\,Fe(s) + 3\,CO_2(g)$$

Solution

The values needed can be found in Table 5.1.

$$
\begin{aligned}
\Delta H^\circ &= \sum \Delta H_f^\circ(\text{products}) - \sum \Delta H_f^\circ(\text{reactants}) && (5.22) \\
&= 3\Delta H_f^\circ(CO_2) - [\Delta H_f^\circ(Fe_2O_3) + 3\Delta H_f^\circ(CO)] \\
&= (3\ mol)(-393.5\ kJ/mol) - [(1\ mol)(-822.2\ kJ/mol) \\
&\qquad\qquad\qquad\qquad\qquad\qquad + (3\ mol)(-110.5\ kJ/mol)] \\
&= -1180.5\ kJ + 1153.7\ kJ = -26.8\ kJ
\end{aligned}
$$

Example 5.5

Given the following data:

$$B_2H_6(g) + 6\,H_2O(l) \longrightarrow 2\,H_3BO_3(s) + 6\,H_2(g) \qquad \Delta H^\circ = -493.4\ kJ$$

ΔH_f° of $H_3BO_3(s)$ is $-1088.7\ kJ/mol$, and ΔH_f° of $H_2O(l)$ is $-285.9\ kJ/mol$. Calculate the standard enthalpy of formation of B_2H_6.

Solution

In this case, the value of $\Delta H°$ for a reaction is known and a $\Delta H_f°$ value for one of the reactants is sought:

$$\Delta H° = \sum \Delta H_f°(\text{products}) - \sum \Delta H_f°(\text{reactants}) \qquad (5.22)$$

$$\Delta H° = 2\Delta H_f°(H_3BO_3) - [\Delta H_f°(B_2H_6) + 6\Delta H_f°(H_2O)]$$

$$-493.4 \text{ kJ} = (2 \text{ mol})(-1088.7 \text{ kJ/mol}) - [(1 \text{ mol})\Delta H_f°(B_2H_6)$$
$$+ (6 \text{ mol})(-285.9 \text{ kJ/mol})]$$

$$-493.4 \text{ kJ} = -2177.4 \text{ kJ} - [(1 \text{ mol})\Delta H_f°(B_2H_6) - 1715.4 \text{ kJ}]$$

$$-493.4 \text{ kJ} = -462.0 \text{ kJ} - (1 \text{ mol})\Delta H_f°(B_2H_6)$$

$$\Delta H_f°(B_2H_6) = +31.4 \text{ kJ/mol}$$

5.7 Bond Energies

Atoms are held together in molecules by chemical bonds (see Chapter 7). The energy required to *break* the bond that holds two atoms together in a diatomic molecule is called the **bond dissociation energy**. These values are reported in kilojoules per mole of bonds. In the following equations, which illustrate this process, dashes are used to represent the bonds between atoms; H_2, for example, appears as H—H:

$$\text{H—H(g)} \longrightarrow 2 \text{ H(g)} \qquad \Delta H = +435 \text{ kJ}$$

$$\text{Cl—Cl(g)} \longrightarrow 2 \text{ Cl(g)} \qquad \Delta H = +243 \text{ kJ}$$

$$\text{H—Cl(g)} \longrightarrow \text{H(g)} + \text{Cl(g)} \qquad \Delta H = +431 \text{ kJ}$$

Each of these ΔH values is *positive*, which indicates that energy is *absorbed* in each process. The bond in the H_2 molecule is the strongest of the three. It takes the most energy to pull the atoms of the H_2 molecule apart.

If one of these equations is reversed, the sign of the ΔH value must be changed:

$$\text{H(g)} + \text{Cl(g)} \longrightarrow \text{H—Cl(g)} \qquad \Delta H = -431 \text{ kJ}$$

When a bond forms, energy is *released*—the same amount that is *required* to break the bond.

Bond dissociation energies may be used to determine some ΔH values. Consider the reaction:

$$\text{H}_2(g) + \text{Cl}_2(g) \longrightarrow 2 \text{ HCl(g)} \qquad \Delta H = 2\Delta H_f° = -184.6 \text{ kJ}$$

The ΔH value for this reaction is twice the enthalpy of formation of HCl(g), since the equation indicates the formation of two moles of HCl(g). We can derive this ΔH value from bond dissociation energies in the following way. The enthalpy change is the sum of the ΔH values for the energy *required* to break 1 mol of H—H bonds, the energy *required* to break 1 mol of Cl—Cl bonds, and the energy *evolved* by the formation of 2 mol of H—Cl bonds:

$$H—H(g) \longrightarrow 2\,H(g) \qquad\qquad \Delta H = +435 \text{ kJ}$$

$$Cl—Cl(g) \longrightarrow 2\,Cl(g) \qquad\qquad \Delta H = +243 \text{ kJ}$$

$$2\,H(g) + 2\,Cl(g) \longrightarrow 2\,H—Cl(g) \qquad \Delta H = 2(-431 \text{ kJ}) = -862 \text{ kJ}$$

The sum of these equations is:

$$H—H(g) + Cl—Cl(g) \qquad 2\,H—Cl(g) \qquad \Delta H = -184 \text{ kJ}$$

In this example, the total energy evolved by bond formation ($\Delta H = -862$ kJ) exceeds the total energy required for bond breaking ($\Delta H = +435$ kJ $+ 243$ kJ $= + 678$ kJ). The reaction, therefore, is exothermic.

In endothermic reactions, the reverse is true. More energy is required to break bonds than is released when new bonds form. Consider the reactions:

$$N_2(g) + O_2(g) \longrightarrow 2\,NO(g) \qquad \Delta H = 2\Delta H_f^\circ = +180.74 \text{ kJ}$$

None of the bonds in these molecules is a single bond, and we will not use dashes to indicate them. The bond dissociation energies for the three diatomic molecules indicated in the equation, however, have been determined and can be used to find the ΔH for the reaction.

The total energy required to break the bonds in the $N_2(g)$ and $O_2(g)$ molecules is the sum of the bond dissociation energies of the two molecules:

$$N_2(g) \qquad 2\,N(g) \qquad \Delta H = \quad +941 \text{ kJ}$$
$$\underline{O_2(g) \longrightarrow 2\,O(g) \qquad \Delta H = \quad +494 \text{ kJ}}$$
$$\text{total energy to break bonds} = +1435 \text{ kJ}$$

The ΔH for the energy evolved by the formation of 2 mol of NO(g) is obtained by multiplying the bond dissociation energy of the NO(g) molecule by 2 and changing the sign:

$$\underline{2\,N(g) + 2\,O(g) \longrightarrow 2\,NO(g) \qquad \Delta H = 2(-627 \text{ kJ}) = -1254 \text{ kJ}}$$
$$\text{total energy to form bonds} = -1254 \text{ kJ}$$

The ΔH value for the reaction is derived by adding the ΔH values for the bonds broken and the bonds formed. Since more energy is required to break bonds than is released by bond formulation, the reaction is endothermic:

$$\Delta H = +1435 \text{ kJ} - 1254 \text{ kJ} = +181 \text{ kJ}$$

$$N_2(g) + O_2(g) \longrightarrow 2\,NO(g) \qquad \Delta H = +181 \text{ kJ}$$

This method would be extremely limited if we were restricted to the use of bond dissociation energies for diatomic molecules. Instead, the system is extended by deriving approximate bond energy values for the bonds found in other types of molecules.

A molecule that contains more than two atoms, such as H_2O, is called a **polyatomic molecule**. There are two H—O bonds in the H_2O molecule, and dissociation of the H_2O molecule into atoms involves breaking these two H—O bonds. The ΔH for the reaction:

$$H—O—H(g) \longrightarrow 2\,H(g) + O(g) \qquad \Delta H = +926 \text{ kJ}$$

Table 5.2 Average bond energies (kJ/mol)[a]

Bond	Average Bond Energy	Bond	Average Bond Energy
Br—Br	193	H—I	297
C—C	347	I—I	151
C=C	619	N—Cl	201
C≡C	812	N—H	389
C—Cl	326	N—N	159
C—F	485	N=N	418
C—H	414	N≡N	941
C—N	293	O—Cl	205
C=N	616	O—F	184
C≡N	879	O—H	463
C—O	335	O—O	138
C=O	707	$O_2^{[b]}$	494
Cl—Cl	243	P—Cl	326
F—F	155	P—H	318
H—Br	364	S—Cl	276
H—Cl	431	S—H	339
H—F	565	S—S	213
H—H	435		

[a] Reactants and products in gaseous state.

[b] Double bond of molecular oxygen.

refers to a process in which *two* moles of H—O bonds are broken. The **average bond energy** of the H—O bond, therefore, is $+926$ kJ/(2 mol), or $+463$ kJ/mol.

In the H_2O molecule, the H—O bonds are equivalent. If the bonds were broken one at a time, however, at the ΔH values would not be the same.

$$H—O—H(g) \longrightarrow H(g) + O—H(g) \qquad \Delta H = +501 \text{ kJ}$$

$$O—H(g) \longrightarrow O(g) + H(g) \qquad \Delta H = +425 \text{ kJ}$$

In general, the second bond of a molecule such as H_2O is easier to break than the first. The fragment remaining after one H has been removed (O—H) is not so stable as the original molecule (H—O—H). The ΔH values for the individual steps given above are not important to us. The average of the ΔH values for the steps is $+463$ kJ/mol, which is the average bond energy and the value used in calculations involving the H—O bond.

The strength of a bond in a molecule depends upon the structure of the entire molecule. Consequently, the bond energy of a given type of bond is not the same in all molecules containing that bond. For example, the H—O bond energy in the H—O—H molecule is different from the H—O bond energy in the H—O—Cl molecule. The values listed in Table 5.2 for diatomic molecules are bond dissociation energies. The other values listed are average bond energies, and each of these values is an average derived from a large number of cases. Since many bond energies are approximations, a ΔH value obtained by use of these values must be regarded as an estimate.

In some molecules, two atoms are bonded together by multiple bonds. Two nitrogen atoms, for example, can be joined by a single bond (N—N), a double bond

(N=N), or a triple bond (N≡N), depending on the molecule. Multiple bonds are indicated in Table 5.2. Notice that the bond energy increases in the order: single bond < double bond < triple bond in a series of this type:

N—N	+159 kJ/mol	C—C	+347 kJ/mol	C—N	+293 kJ/mol
N=N	+418 kJ/mol	C=C	+619 kJ/mol	C=N	+616 kJ/mol
N≡N	+941 kJ/mol	C≡C	+812 kJ/mol	C≡N	+879 kJ/mol

Three factors should be kept in mind when bond energies are used to determine a ΔH for a reaction.

1. *The method as presented should be used only for reactions in which all reactants and products are gases.** *

2. The results of calculations of this type should be regarded as estimates because the values for many bond energies are approximations.

3. At times, the bond energies for certain bonds that cannot be simply defined do not fit into the general pattern of average bond energies. We will avoid examples that involve this complication until this type of bond has been discussed (Section 8.4).

Example 5.6

Use average bond energies to calculate the value of ΔH for the reaction:

$$2\,H{-}\underset{\underset{\displaystyle H}{|}}{N}{-}H(g) + 3\,Cl{-}Cl(g) \longrightarrow N{\equiv}N(g) + 6\,H{-}Cl(g)$$

Solution

We can imagine the reaction to take place in a series of steps. Energy is absorbed (ΔH is positive) when a bond is broken, and energy is evolved (ΔH is negative) when a bond is formed. Six moles of N—H bonds are broken:

$$2\,H{-}\underset{\underset{\displaystyle H}{|}}{N}{-}H(g) \longrightarrow 2\,N(g) + 6\,H(g) \qquad \Delta H = 6(+389\ kJ) = +2334\ kJ$$

Three moles of Cl—Cl bonds are broken:

$$3\,Cl{-}Cl(g) \longrightarrow 6\,Cl(g) \qquad \Delta H = 3(+243\ kJ) = +729\ kJ$$

One mole of N≡N bonds is formed:

$$2\,N(g) \longrightarrow N{\equiv}N(g) \qquad \Delta H = -941\ kJ$$

---

* The ΔH values for other types of reactions can be calculated using bond energies, provided terms are introduced to account for changes in state of the reactants and products. This type of calculation will not be presented.

Six moles of H—Cl bonds are formed:

$$6\,H(g) + 6\,Cl(g) \longrightarrow 6\,H—Cl(g) \qquad \Delta H = 6(-431\ kJ) = -2586\ kJ$$

The sum of these steps is the answer to our problem:

$$2\,NH_3(g) + 3\,Cl_2(g) \longrightarrow N_2(g) + 6\,HCl(g) \qquad \Delta H = -464\ kJ$$

The solution to this problem can be indicated in a briefer manner. We list all of the bonds that are broken (ΔH values will be positive) and all of the bonds that are formed (ΔH values will be negative). The answer is the sum of the list. Thus,

Bonds broken:	ΔH:
6 mol of N—H bonds	6 mol($+389$ kJ/mol) $=$ $+2334$ kJ
3 mol of Cl—Cl bonds	3 mol($+243$ kJ/mol) $=$ $+729$ kJ
Bonds formed:	
1 mol of N≡N bonds	1 mol(-941 kJ/mol) $=$ -941 kJ
6 mol of H—Cl bonds	6 mol(-431 kJ/mol) $=$ -2586 kJ
Result:	-464 kJ

In Section 5.6, enthalpies of formation were used to calculate the value of ΔH for this reaction. The value obtained in this way (-461 kJ) is a more reliable value than the one derived from bond energies (-464 kJ).

Summary

Thermochemistry is the study of the heat liberated or absorbed by chemical and physical changes. The unit used for all energy measurements, including heat measurements, is the *joule*. The temperature scale used in scientific studies is the *Celsius scale.*

The *heat capacity* of a sample is the amount of heat required to increase the temperature of the sample by one Celsius degree. A heat change for a reaction is determined by running the reaction in a device called a *calorimeter* and measuring the temperature change of the calorimeter and its contents. The quantity of heat involved is calculated from this temperature change and the total heat capacity of the calorimeter and its contents.

The heat liberated or absorbed by a chemical reaction is related to a property called *enthalpy* (or heat content). If the products of a reaction have a higher enthalpy than the reactants, then heat is absorbed when the reaction occurs. A reaction of this type is said to be *endothermic*, and the change in enthalpy, ΔH, for the reaction is positive. If the products of a reaction have a lower enthalpy than the reactants, ΔH is negative and the reaction liberates heat. A reaction of this type is said to be *exothermic.*

A *thermochemical equation* consists of a chemical equation together with the ΔH value that corresponds to the equation when read in molar quantities. Stoichiometric problems that involve heat changes can be solved by using thermochemical equations. These equations may be multiplied by a factor (ΔH is multiplied by the same factor), divided by a factor (ΔH is divided by the same factor), or reversed (the sign of ΔH is changed).

Thermochemical equations can be written on the basis of the results of calorimetric experiments. Three additional methods have been given for deriving the equations from thermochemical data.

1. A number of thermochemical equations can be added to obtain a new thermochemical equation. The justification for this procedure is the *law of Hess*, which states that a ΔH for a given reaction is constant whether the reaction occurs in one step or in several steps.

2. *Standard enthalpies of formation* can be used to obtain the enthalpy change for a reaction by means of the equation:

$$\Delta H^{\circ} = \sum \Delta H_f^{\circ}(\text{products}) - \sum \Delta H_f^{\circ}(\text{reactants})$$

3. *Average bond energies* can be used. The ΔH for the reaction is the sum of the ΔH for the energy required to break the chemical bonds of the reactants and the ΔH for the energy released by the formation of the bonds of the products.

Key Terms

Some of the more important terms introduced in this chapter are listed below. Definitions for terms not included in this list may be located in the text by use of the index.

Bond energy (Section 5.7) The energy required to break a bond between two atoms in a molecule. This general term includes two types of measurements. A bond dissociation energy refers to the energy required to break a specific bond that holds two atoms together in a particular diatomic molecule. An average bond energy, however, pertains to the bonds found in polyatomic molecules and is an average value based on a number of cases.

calorie, cal (Section 5.2) The approximate quantity of heat required to raise the temperature of 1 g of water from $14.5°C$ to $15.5°C$; defined by the relationship: 1 cal = 4.184 J (exactly).

Calorimeter (Section 5.3) A device used to measure the heat transferred in chemical reactions and physical changes.

Celsius temperature scale (Section 5.2) A temperature scale based on the assignment of $0°C$ to the normal freezing point of water and $100°C$ to the normal boiling point of water.

Endothermic reaction (Section 5.4) A chemical reaction in which heat is absorbed.

Energy (Section 5.1) The capacity to do work.

Enthalpy, H (Section 5.4) The heat content of a sample of matter; for a reaction run at constant pressure, the change in enthalpy, ΔH, is the heat transferred (liberated or absorbed).

Enthalpy of formation (Section 5.6) For a given compound, the enthalpy change for a reaction in which 1 mol of the compound is prepared from the most stable forms of its elements. A standard enthalpy of formation, ΔH_f°, pertains to a formation reaction run at 1 atm pressure and at a designated reference temperature (usually $25°C$).

Exothermic reaction (Section 5.4) A chemical reaction in which heat is liberated.

Fahrenheit temperature scale (Section 5.2) A temperature scale on which the normal freezing point of water is $32°F$ and the normal boiling point of water is $212°F$.

Heat (Section 5.2) The form of energy that flows spontaneously from a body at a higher temperature to a body at a lower temperature.

Heat capacity (Section 5.3) The amount of heat required to raise the temperature of a given mass by $1°C$.

Joule, J (Section 5.1) The SI unit for all energy measurements; $1 \text{ kg m}^2/\text{s}^2$.

Law of Hess, law of constant heat summation (Section 5.5) The change in enthalpy for any chemical reaction is constant, whether the reaction occurs in one step or in several steps.

Polyatomic molecule (Section 5.7) A molecule that contains more than two atoms.

Specific heat (Section 5.2) The amount of heat required to raise the temperature of 1 g of a substance by $1°C$.

Temperature (Section 5.2) Degree of hotness or coldness; that property of matter that determines the direction in which heat flows spontaneously.

Thermochemistry (Introduction) Study of the energy changes that accompany chemical and physical changes.

Problems*

Heat Measurements, Calorimetry

5.1 Normal body temperature is $98.6°F$. What is normal body temperature in degrees Celsius?

5.2 What temperature in degrees Celsius corresponds to $0°F$?

5.3 What temperature in degrees Celsius corresponds to $-40°F$?

5.4 A thermostat is set at $68°F$. What is the setting in degrees Celsius?

5.5 What is the heat capacity of 325 g of water?

5.6 What mass of water has a heat capacity of $565 \text{ J}/°C$?

5.7 How many kilojoules of heat will raise the temperature of 1.50 kg of water from $22.00°C$ to $25.00°C$?

5.8 How many kilojoules of heat will raise the temperature of 1.75 kg of water from $23.00°C$ to $42.00°C$?

5.9 What is the specific heat of ethyl alcohol if 129 J of heat is required to raise the temperature of 15.0 g of ethyl alcohol from $22.70°C$ to $26.20°C$?

5.10 What is the specific heat of iron if 186 J of heat is required to raise the temperature of 165 g of iron from $23.20°C$ to $25.70°C$?

---

* The more difficult problems are marked with asterisks. The appendix contains answers to color-keyed problems.

5.11 The specific heat of lead is 0.129 J/(g°C). How many joules of heat is required to raise the temperature of 207 g of lead from 22.25°C to 27.65°C?

5.12 If 95.5 J of heat raises the temperature of a sample of gold from 21.50°C to 29.35°C, what is the mass of the sample? The specific heat of gold is 0.132 J/(g°C).

5.13 The specific heat of nickel is 0.444 J/(g°C). If 50.0 J of heat is added to a 32.3 g sample of nickel at 23.25°C, what is the final temperature of the sample?

5.14 The specific heat of diethyl ether is 2.33 J/(g°C). If 113 J of heat raises the temperature of a 12.5 g sample of diethyl ether to 27.35°C, what was the initial temperature of the sample?

5.15 A 1.45 g sample of acetic acid, $HC_2H_3O_2$, was burned in excess oxygen in a bomb calorimeter. The calorimeter, which alone had a heat capacity of 2.67 kJ/°C, contained 0.750 kg of water. The temperature of the calorimeter and its contents increased from 24.32°C to 27.95°C. What quantity of heat would be liberated by the combustion of 1.00 mol of acetic acid?

5.16 A 2.30 g sample of quinone, $C_6H_4O_2$, was burned in excess oxygen in a calorimeter. The calorimeter, which alone had a heat capacity of 3.27 kJ/°C, contained 1.00 kg of water. The temperature of the calorimeter and its contents increased from 19.22°C to 27.07°C. What quantity of heat would be liberated by the combustion of 1.00 mol of quinone?

5.17 The combustion of 1.00 mol of glucose, $C_6H_{12}O_6$, liberates 2.82×10^3 kJ of heat. If 1.25 g of glucose is burned in a calorimeter containing 0.950 kg of water, and the temperature of the assembly increases from 20.10°C to 23.25°C, what is the heat capacity of the calorimeter?

5.18 The combustion of 1.00 mol of sucrose, $C_{12}H_{22}O_{11}$, liberates 5.65×10^3 kJ of heat. A calorimeter that has a heat capacity of 1.23 kJ/°C contains 0.600 kg of water. How many grams of sucrose would be burned in the calorimeter to raise the temperature of the calorimeter and its contents from 23.00°C to 27.00°C?

Thermochemical Equations

5.19 Indicate whether each of the following reactions is *exothermic* or *endothermic:*

(a) $Br_2(l) + Cl_2(g) \longrightarrow 2\,BrCl(g)$ $\Delta H = +29.4$ kJ
(b) $NH_3(g) + HCl(g) \longrightarrow NH_4Cl(s)$ $\Delta H = -176$ kJ
(c) $N_2O_4(g) \longrightarrow 2\,NO_2(g)$ $\Delta H = +58.0$ kJ
(d) $CS_2(l) + 3\,Cl_2(g) \longrightarrow CCl_4(l) + S_2Cl_2(l)$
$$\Delta H = -112\text{ kJ}$$

5.20 Indicate whether each of the following reactions if *exothermic* or *endothermic*:

(a) $2\,NaN_3(s) \longrightarrow 2\,Na(s) + 3\,N_2(g)$ $\Delta H = +42.7$ kJ
(b) $2\,KClO_3(s) \longrightarrow 2\,KCl(s) + 3\,O_2(g)$
$$\Delta H = -89.4\text{ kJ}$$
(c) $SnCl_2(s) + Cl_2(g) \longrightarrow SnCl_4(l)$ $\Delta H = -195.4$ kJ
(d) $2\,HgO(s) \longrightarrow 2\,Hg(l) + O_2(g)$ $\Delta H = +181.4$ kJ

5.21 The combustion of 1.000 g of benzene, $C_6H_6(l)$, in $O_2(g)$ liberates 41.84 kJ of heat and yields $CO_2(g)$ and $H_2O(l)$. Write the thermochemical equation for the combustion of *one mole* of $C_6H_6(l)$.

5.22 The combustion of 1.000 g of ethyl alcohol, $C_2H_5OH(l)$, in $O_2(g)$ liberates 29.69 kJ of heat and yields $CO_2(g)$ and $H_2O(l)$. Write the thermochemical equation for the combustion of *one mole* of $C_2H_5OH(l)$.

5.23 Hydrazine, $N_2H_4(l)$, is used in rocket fuels. The thermochemical equation for the combustion of hydrazine is

$$N_2H_4(l) + O_2(g) \longrightarrow N_2(g) + 2\,H_2O(l)$$
$$\Delta H = -622.4\text{ kJ}$$

What quantity of heat is liberated by the combustion of 1.000 g of $N_2H_4(l)$?

5.24 Glucose, $C_6H_{12}O_6(s)$, is converted into ethyl alcohol, $C_2H_5OH(l)$, in the fermentation of fruit juice to produce wine:

$$C_6H_{12}O_6(s) \longrightarrow 2\,C_2H_5OH(l) + 2\,CO_2(g)$$
$$\Delta H = -67.0\text{ kJ}$$

What quantity of heat is liberated when a liter of wine containing 95.0 g of $C_2H_5OH(l)$ is produced?

5.25 Given the thermochemical equation:

$$2\,NaN_3(s) \longrightarrow 2\,Na(s) + 3\,N_2(g)\quad \Delta H = +42.7\text{ kJ}$$

(a) What is the value of ΔH for the preparation of 1.50 kg of $N_2(g)$? **(b)** How many grams of $NaN_3(s)$ would be decomposed by 125 kJ of heat?

5.26 Given the thermochemical equation:

$$2\,NH_3(g) + 3\,N_2O(g) \longrightarrow 4\,N_2(g) + 3\,H_2O(l)$$
$$\Delta H = -1010\text{ kJ}$$

(a) What quantity of heat is liberated by the reaction of 50.0 g of $N_2O(g)$ with excess $NH_3(g)$? **(b)** What quantity of heat is liberated by the reaction that produces 50.0 g of $N_2(g)$?

Law of Hess

5.27 Given:

(a) $H_2S(g) + \frac{3}{2}O_2(g) \longrightarrow H_2O(l) + SO_2(g)$
$$\Delta H = -562.6\text{ kJ}$$
(b) $CS_2(l) + 3\,O_2(g) \longrightarrow CO_2(g) + 2\,SO_2(g)$
$$\Delta H = -1075.2\text{ kJ}$$

Calculate the value of ΔH for the reaction:

$$CS_2(l) + 2\,H_2O(l) \longrightarrow CO_2(g) + 2\,H_2S(g)$$

5.28 Given:

(a) $2\,NH_3(g) + 3\,N_2O(g) \longrightarrow 4\,N_2(g) + 3\,H_2O(l)$
$$\Delta H = -1010\text{ kJ}$$
(b) $4\,NH_3(g) + 3\,O_2(g) \longrightarrow 2\,N_2(g) + 6\,H_2O(l)$
$$\Delta H = -1531\text{ kJ}$$

Calculate the value of ΔH for the reaction:

$$N_2(g) + \frac{1}{2}O_2(g) \longrightarrow N_2O(g)$$

5.29 Given:

(a) $2 NF_3(g) + 2 NO(g) \longrightarrow N_2F_4(g) + 2 ONF(g)$
$$\Delta H = -82.9 \text{ kJ}$$

(b) $NO(g) + \frac{1}{2} F_2(g) \longrightarrow ONF(g) \quad \Delta H = -156.9 \text{ kJ}$

(c) $Cu(s) + F_2(g) \longrightarrow CuF_2(s) \quad \Delta H = -531.0 \text{ kJ}$

Calculate the value of ΔH for the reaction:

$$2 NF_3(g) + Cu(s) \longrightarrow N_2F_4(g) + CuF_2(s)$$

5.30 Given:

(a) $FeO(s) + H_2(g) \longrightarrow Fe(s) + H_2O(g)$
$$\Delta H = +24.7 \text{ kJ}$$

(b) $3 FeO(s) + \frac{1}{2} O_2(g) \longrightarrow Fe_3O_4(s)$
$$\Delta H = -317.6 \text{ kJ}$$

(c) $H_2(g) + \frac{1}{2} O_2(g) \longrightarrow H_2O(g) \quad \Delta H = -241.8 \text{ kJ}$

Calculate the value of ΔH for the reaction:

$$3 Fe(s) + 4 H_2O(g) \longrightarrow Fe_3O_4(s) + 4 H_2(g)$$

5.31 Given:

(a) $BCl_3(g) + 3 H_2O(l) \longrightarrow H_3BO_3(s) + 3 HCl(g)$
$$\Delta H = -112.5 \text{ kJ}$$

(b) $B_2H_6(g) + 6 H_2O(l) \longrightarrow 2 H_3BO_3(s) + 6 H_2(g)$
$$\Delta H = -493.4 \text{ kJ}$$

(c) $\frac{1}{2} H_2(g) + \frac{1}{2} Cl_2(g) \longrightarrow HCl(g) \quad \Delta H = -92.3 \text{ kJ}$

Calculate the value of ΔH for the reaction:

$$B_2H_6(g) + 6 Cl_2(g) \longrightarrow 2 BCl_3(g) + 6 HCl(g)$$

5.32 Given:

(a) $OF_2(g) + H_2O(l) \longrightarrow O_2(g) + 2 HF(g)$
$$\Delta H = -276.6 \text{ kJ}$$

(b) $SF_4(g) + 2 H_2O(l) \longrightarrow SO_2(g) + 4 HF(g)$
$$\Delta H = -827.5 \text{ kJ}$$

(c) $S(s) + O_2(g) \longrightarrow SO_2(g) \quad \Delta H = -296.9 \text{ kJ}$

Calculate the value of ΔH for the reaction:

$$2 S(s) + 2 OF_2(g) \longrightarrow SO_2(g) + SF_4(g)$$

5.33 Given:

(a) $OSCl_2(l) + H_2O(l) \qquad SO_2(g) + 2 HCl(g)$
$$\Delta H = +10.3 \text{ kJ}$$

(b) $PCl_3(l) + \frac{1}{2} O_2(g) \longrightarrow OPCl_3(l) \quad \Delta H = -325.1 \text{ kJ}$

(c) $P(s) + \frac{3}{2} Cl_2(g) \longrightarrow PCl_3(l) \quad \Delta H = -306.7 \text{ kJ}$

(d) $4 HCl(g) + O_2(g) \longrightarrow 2 Cl_2(g) + 2 H_2O(l)$
$$\Delta H = -202.6 \text{ kJ}$$

Calculate the value of ΔH for the reaction:

$$2 P(s) + 2 SO_2(g) + 5 Cl_2(g) \longrightarrow$$
$$2 OSCl_2(l) + 2 OPCl_3(l)$$

5.34 Given:

(a) $2 ClF_3(g) + 2 NH_3(g) \longrightarrow$
$N_2(g) + 6 HF(g) + Cl_2(g) \quad \Delta H = -1195.6 \text{ kJ}$

(b) $N_2H_4(l) + O_2(g) \longrightarrow N_2(g) + 2 H_2O(l)$
$$\Delta H = -622.4 \text{ kJ}$$

(c) $4 NH_3(g) + 3 O_2(g) \longrightarrow 2 N_2(g) + 6 H_2O(l)$
$$\Delta H = -1530.6 \text{ kJ}$$

Calculate the value of ΔH for the reaction:

$$3 N_2H_4(l) + 4 ClF_3(g) \longrightarrow$$
$$3 N_2(g) + 12 HF(g) + 2 Cl_2(g)$$

*5.35 Given:

(a) $NH_3(g) + HNO_3(l) \longrightarrow NH_4NO_3(s)$
$$\Delta H = -145.7 \text{ kJ}$$

(b) $NH_4NO_3(s) \longrightarrow N_2O(g) + 2 H_2O(l)$
$$\Delta H = -125.2 \text{ kJ}$$

(c) $3 NO(g) \longrightarrow N_2(g) + NO_2(g) \quad \Delta H = -1169.2 \text{ kJ}$

(d) $4 NH_3(g) + 5 O_2(g) \longrightarrow 4 NO(g) + 6 H_2O(l)$
$$\Delta H = -1169.2 \text{ kJ}$$

(e) $NO(g) + \frac{1}{2} O_2(g) \longrightarrow NO_2(g) \quad \Delta H = -56.6 \text{ kJ}$

Calculate the values of ΔH for the reaction:

$$3 NO_2(g) + H_2O(l) \longrightarrow 2 HNO_3(l) + NO(g)$$

*5.36 Given:

(a) $2 NH_3(g) + 3 N_2O(g) \longrightarrow 4 N_2(g) + 3 H_2O(l)$
$$\Delta H = -1010. \text{ kJ}$$

(b) $N_2O(g) + 3 H_2(g) \longrightarrow N_2H_4(l) + H_2O(l)$
$$\Delta H = -317. \text{ kJ}$$

(c) $2 NH_3(g) + \frac{1}{2} O_2(g) \longrightarrow N_2H_4(l) + H_2O(l)$
$$\Delta H = -143 \text{ kJ}$$

(d) $H_2(g) + \frac{1}{2} O_2(g) \longrightarrow H_2O(l) \quad \Delta H = -286. \text{ kJ}$

Calculate the value of ΔH for the reaction:

$$N_2H_4(l) + O_2(g) \longrightarrow N_2(g) + 2 H_2O(l)$$

Enthalpies of Formation

5.37 Write thermochemical equations that correspond to the following standard enthalpies of formation:
(a) $AgCl(s)$, -127 kJ/mol; (b) $NO_2(g)$, $+33.8 \text{ kJ/mol}$;
(c) $CaCO_3(s)$, -1206.9 kJ/mol.

5.38 Write thermochemical equations that correspond to the following standard enthalpies of formation:
(a) $HCN(g)$, $+130.5 \text{ kJ/mol}$; (b) $CS_2(l)$, $+87.86 \text{ kJ/mol}$;
(c) $NH_4NO_3(s)$, -365.1 kJ/mol.

5.39 Use standard enthalpies of formation (Table 5.1) to calculate the value of $\Delta H°$ for the reaction:

$$2 H_2S(g) + 3 O_2(g) \longrightarrow 2 H_2O(l) + 2 SO_2(g)$$

5.40 Use standard enthalpies of formation (Table 5.1) to calculate the value of $\Delta H°$ for the reaction:

$$Fe_2O_3(s) + 3 H_2(g) \longrightarrow 3 Fe(s) + 3 H_2O(g)$$

5.41 Use standard enthalpies of formation (Table 5.1) to calculate the value of $\Delta H°$ for the reaction:

$$2 NH_3(g) + 2 CH_4(g) + 3 O_2(g) \longrightarrow$$
$$2 HCN(g) + 6 H_2O(l)$$

5.42 Use standard enthalpies of formation (Table 5.1) to calculate the value of $\Delta H°$ for the reaction:

$$NH_3(g) + 3 F_2(g) \longrightarrow NF_3(g) + 3 HF(g)$$

5.43 (a) Write the chemical equation for the combustion of one mole of methyl alcohol, $CH_3OH(l)$, in $O_2(g)$. The products of the reaction are $CO_2(g)$ and $H_2O(l)$. (b) Use standard enthalpies of formation (Table 5.1) to calculate the value of $\Delta H°$ for the reaction.

5.44 (a) Write the chemical equation for the combustion of one mole of benzene, $C_6H_6(l)$, in $O_2(g)$. The products of the reaction are $CO_2(g)$ and $H_2O(l)$. (b) Use standard enthalpies of formation (Table 5.1) to calculate the value of $\Delta H°$ for the reaction.

5.45 (a) Write the thermochemical equation for the combustion of one mole of hydrazine, $N_2H_4(l)$, in $O_2(g)$. The products of the reaction are $N_2(g)$ and $H_2O(l)$, and the value of $\Delta H°$ for the reaction is -622.4 kJ. (b) Use your answer together with values from Table 5.1 to calculate the standard enthalpy of formation of hydrazine.

5.46 (a) Write the thermochemical equation for the combustion of one mole of urea, $CO(NH_2)_2(s)$, in $O_2(g)$. The products of the reaction are $N_2(g)$, $CO_2(g)$, and $H_2O(l)$, and the value of $\Delta H°$ for the reaction is -632 kJ. (b) Use your answer together with values from Table 5.1 to calculate the standard enthalpy of formation of urea.

5.47 Use the thermochemical equation:

$$CaCO_3(s) + 2\,NH_3(g) \longrightarrow CaCN_2(s) + 3\,H_2O(l)$$
$$\Delta H° = +90.1 \text{ kJ}$$

together with values from Table 5.1 to calculate the standard enthalpy of formation of $CaCN_2(s)$.

5.48 Use the thermochemical equation:

$$CaC_2(s) + 2\,H_2O(l) \longrightarrow C_2H_2(g) + Ca(OH)_2(s)$$
$$\Delta H° = -125.3 \text{ kJ}$$

together with values from Table 5.1 to calculate the standard enthalpy of formation of $CaC_2(s)$.

Bond Energies

5.49 Use average bond energies (Table 5.2) to calculate the enthalpy of formation of $HF(g)$. Compare your answer to the value given in Table 5.1.

5.50 Use average bond energies (Table 5.2) to calculate the enthalpy of formation of $N_2H_4(g)$:

$$N{\equiv}N(g) + 2\,H{-}H(g) \longrightarrow H{-}N{-}N{-}H(g)$$
(with H substituents on each N)

5.51 Use the thermochemical equation:

$$XeF_2(g) + H_2(g) \longrightarrow 2\,HF(g) + Xe(g)$$
$$\Delta H = -430 \text{ kJ}$$

together with average bond energies (Table 5.2) to calculate the average bond energy of the Xe—F bond in $XeF_2(g)$.

5.52 The standard enthalpy of formation of $ClF_5(g)$ is -254.8 kJ/mol. Use this value together with average bond energies from Table 5.2 to calculate the average bond energy of the Cl—F bond in $ClF_5(g)$.

5.53 Use average bond energies (Table 5.2) to calculate ΔH for the reaction:

$$H{-}C{=}C{-}H(g) + H{-}H(g) \longrightarrow H{-}C{-}C{-}H(g)$$
(ethene + hydrogen → ethane)

5.54 Use average bond energies (Table 5.2) to calculate ΔH for the reaction:

$$H{-}C{-}O{-}H(g) + H{-}Cl(g) \longrightarrow$$
(methanol)

$$H{-}C{-}Cl(g) + H{-}O{-}H(g)$$

5.55 Use average bond energies (Table 5.2) to calculate ΔH for the reaction:

$$4\,H{-}Cl(g) + O_2(g) \longrightarrow$$
$$2\,H{-}O{-}H(g) + 2\,Cl{-}Cl(g)$$

5.56 Use average bond energies (Table 5.2) to calculate ΔH for the reaction:

$$F{-}O{-}F(g) + H{-}O{-}H(g) \longrightarrow$$
$$O_2(g) + 2\,H{-}F(g)$$

5.57 (a) Use average bond energies (Table 5.2) to calculate ΔH for the reaction:

$$H{-}C{\equiv}N(g) + 2\,H{-}H(g) \longrightarrow H{-}C{-}N(g)$$
(with H substituents)

(b) Use standard enthalpies of formation from Table 5.1 to calculate $\Delta H°$ for the reaction. How well do the values agree?

5.58 (a) Use average bond energies (Table 5.2) to calculate ΔH for the reaction:

$$H{-}C{-}H(g) + 4\,F{-}F(g) \longrightarrow F{-}C{-}F(g) + 4\,H{-}F(g)$$

(b) Use standard enthalpies of formation from Table 5.1 to calculate $\Delta H°$ for the reaction. How well do the values agree?

*5.59 Use average bond energies (Table 5.2) to calculate the enthalpy of formation of $HCN(g)$:

$$\tfrac{1}{2}H{-}H(g) + C(\text{graphite}) + \tfrac{1}{2}N{\equiv}N(g) \longrightarrow$$
$$H{-}C{\equiv}N(g)$$

Note that the values for the formation of the H—C and C≡N bonds assume that C(g) is used, and therefore:

$$C(\text{graphite}) \longrightarrow C(g) \quad \Delta H = +717 \text{ kJ}$$

must be added into the total energy required.

*5.60 Use average bond energies (Table 5.2) to calculate the enthalpy of formation of $CH_3OH(g)$:

$$C(\text{graphite}) + 2\,H\text{—}H(g) + \tfrac{1}{2}O_2(g) \longrightarrow H\text{—}\overset{\displaystyle H}{\underset{\displaystyle H}{\overset{|}{\underset{|}{C}}}}\text{—O—H}$$

Note that the values for the formation of the H—C and C—O bonds assume that C(g) is used, and therefore:

$$C(\text{graphite}) \longrightarrow C(g) \quad \Delta H = +717 \text{ kJ}$$

must be added into the total energy required.

Unclassified Problems

5.61 Given the thermochemical equation:

$$2\,ClF_3(g) + 2\,NH_3(g) \longrightarrow$$
$$N_2(g) + 6\,HF(g) + Cl_2(g) \quad \Delta H° = -1195.6 \text{ kJ}$$

Calculate the standard enthalpy of formation of $ClF_3(g)$.

5.62 According to the thermochemical equation given in Problem 5.61, how much heat is liberated by the complete reaction of 125 g of $ClF_3(g)$ with $NH_3(g)$?

5.63 Given:

(a) $P_4O_{10}(s) + 6\,H_2O(l) \longrightarrow 4\,H_3PO_4(s)$
$$\Delta H = -397 \text{ kJ}$$

(b) $PCl_5(s) + 4\,H_2O(l) \longrightarrow H_3PO_4(s) + 5\,HCl(g)$
$$\Delta H = -136 \text{ kJ}$$

(c) $OPCl_3(l) + 3\,H_2O(l) \longrightarrow H_3PO_4(s) + 3\,HCl(g)$
$$\Delta H = -68 \text{ kJ}$$

Find the value of ΔH for the reaction:

$$P_4O_{10}(s) + 6\,PCl_5(s) \longrightarrow 10\,OPCl_3(l)$$

5.64 A 1.50 g sample of glutaric acid, $H_2C_5H_6O_4(s)$, was burned in excess $O_2(g)$ in a bomb calorimeter. The calorimeter, which alone had a heat capacity of 2.20 kJ/°C, contained 1.25 kg of water. The temperature of the calorimeter and its contents increased from 22.00°C to 25.29°C. What quantity of heat would be liberated by the combustion of 1.00 mol of glutaric acid?

5.65 Use average bond energies to calculate the ΔH for the reaction:

$$4\,H\text{—N}\text{—}H(g) + 3\,O_2(g) \longrightarrow$$
$$\underset{\displaystyle H}{\overset{|}{}}$$
$$2\,N\equiv N(g) + 6\,H\text{—O—H}(g)$$

CHAPTER 6

THE ELECTRONIC STRUCTURE OF ATOMS

In this chapter, we continue the discussion of atomic structure that was begun in Chapter 2. Here, we are concerned principally with the number, arrangement, and energies of the electrons in an atom. In large measure, it is the electronic structure of an atom that determines the chemical properties of the atom.

Much of the theory of electronic structure has been derived from experiments that involve electromagnetic radiation. We must, therefore, first consider the nature of this type of energy.

6.1 Electromagnetic Radiation

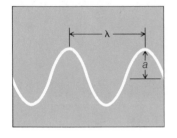

Figure 6.1 Wavelength, λ, and amplitude, a, of a wave

Radio waves, infrared waves, visible light, and X rays are types of electromagnetic radiation. Electromagnetic radiation travels through space in a wave motion (Figure 6.1). The following terms are used to describe these waves.

1. The **wavelength,** λ (lambda), is the distance between two similar points on two successive waves (such as the distance from crest to crest or trough to trough).

2. The **amplitude,** a, of a wave is the height of a crest (or the depth of a trough). The **intensity** (or brightness) of the radiation is proportional to the square of the amplitude, a^2.

3. In a vacuum, all electromagnetic waves, regardless of wavelength, travel at the same speed, 2.9979×10^8 m/s. This speed is called the **speed of light** and is given the symbol c.

4. The **frequency** of the radiation, v (nu), is the number of waves that pass a given spot in a second. For a given type of radiation, the wavelength times the number of waves per second (the frequency) equals the distance traveled per second (the speed of light):

$$\lambda v = c \tag{6.1}$$

and therefore,

$$v = \frac{c}{\lambda} \tag{6.2}$$

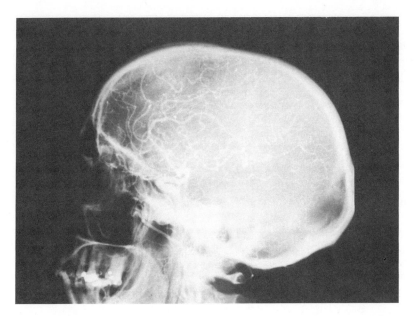

An x ray of a living head after an opaque substance has been injected into a vein. This photograph was made to determine whether a tumor or blood clot is obstructing a blood vessel. X rays are electromagnetic radiations with wavelengths shorter than visible light, in the range 10^{-12} m to 10^{-8}. *Manfred Kage, Peter Arnold, Inc.*

In this book, we will use the unit *per second* (1/s or s^{-1}) for frequency. Notice that expressing c in *meters per second* and λ in *meters* in Equation 6.2 will yield a value of v in *per second*.* The SI unit of frequency is the hertz (symbol, Hz) which is defined as:

$$1 \text{ Hz} = 1/s$$

A microwave oven. Microwaves are electromagnetic radiations with wavelengths longer than visible light, in the range 10^{-3} m to 10^{-1} m. *Sharp.*

The hertz was named for Heinrich Hertz, who in 1888 generated electromagnetic waves with wavelengths larger than those of visible light and who demonstrated that long-wavelength radiation exhibits the same phenomena as light does.

The electromagnetic spectrum is shown in Figure 6.2. Radio waves have very long wavelengths, infrared waves (radiant heat) have moderate wavelengths, and γ rays (from radioactive decay) have extremely short wavelengths. White light (visible light) consists of radiation with wavelengths in the approximate range of 4×10^{-7} m to 7.5×10^{-7} m (which is 400 nm to 750 nm).[†]

---

* At times the unit is recorded as *cycles per second* (cycle/s), since frequency is the number of cycles or waves that pass a given spot in a second. This usage requires that wavelength be recorded in such units as *meters per cycle* so that cancellation of units is possible.

† In the past, wavelengths have been measured in ångstrom units (Å), 10^{-10} *m*. This unit is not a part of the International System. The International Committee of Weights and Measures recommends that the nanometer (nm), 10^{-9} m, be used instead:

$1 \text{ Å} = 10^{-10}$ m $= 10^{-8}$ cm
$1 \text{ nm} = 10^{-9}$ m $= 10^{-7}$ cm

Therefore,

$1 \text{ Å} = 0.1$ nm $\qquad$ and $\qquad$ $1 \text{ nm} = 10$ Å

The range 400 nm to 750 nm corresponds to 4000 Å to 7500 Å.

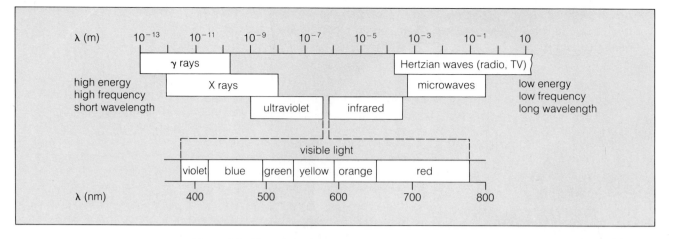

Figure 6.2 Electromagnetic radiation. (Note that the approximate ranges of electromagnetic radiations are plotted on a logarithmic scale in the upper part of the diagram. The spectrum of visible light is not plotted in this way.)

Example 6.1

What is the frequency of (a) red light with a wavelength of 700. nm, and (b) violet light with a wavelength of 400. nm?

Solution

(a) Equation 6.2 gives the relation of frequency to wavelength. Since c is given in units of *meters per second*, λ should be changed into *meters*. Thus:

$$? \text{ m} = 700. \text{ nm} \frac{10^{-9} \text{ m}}{1 \text{ nm}} = 7.00 \times 10^{-7} \text{ m}$$

Then, by use of Equation 6.2,

$$\nu = \frac{c}{\lambda} \tag{6.2}$$

$$= \frac{3.00 \times 10^8 \text{ m/s}}{7.00 \times 10^{-7} \text{ m}} = 4.29 \times 10^{14}/\text{s}$$

(b) The wavelength of this radiation is 4.00×10^{-7} m. Hence,

$$\nu = \frac{3.00 \times 10^8 \text{ m/s}}{4.00 \times 10^{-7} \text{ m}} = 7.50 \times 10^{14}/\text{s}$$

Notice that the light with the longer wavelength (red light) has the lower frequency. In other words, fewer long-wavelength waves pass a given spot in one second.

The wave theory successfully interprets many properties of electromagnetic radiation. Other properties, however, require that such radiation be considered as consisting of particles. In 1900, Max Planck proposed the quantum theory of radiant energy. Planck suggested that radiant energy could be absorbed or given off only in definite quantities, called quanta. The energy of a quantum, E, is proportional to the frequency of the radiation, v:

$$E = hv \tag{6.3}$$

The proportionality constant, h, is Planck's constant, 6.6262×10^{-34} J·s.

Since E and v are directly proportional, high-energy radiation has a high frequency. A high frequency means that a large number of waves pass a spot in one second. The wavelength of high-energy radiation, therefore, must be short. On the other hand, low-energy radiation has a low frequency and a long wavelength. In 1905, Albert Einstein proposed that Planck's quanta were discontinuous bits of energy, which were later named photons.

Example 6.2

What is the energy of a quantum of (a) red light with a frequency of 4.29×10^{14}/s, and (b) violet light with a frequency of 7.50×10^{14}/s?

Solution

We use Equation 6.3 to find the energy per quantum. Planck's constant is 6.63×10^{-34} J·s.

(a) $E = hv$ (6.3)
$= (6.63 \times 10^{-34} \text{ J·s})(4.29 \times 10^{14}/\text{s})$
$= 2.84 \times 10^{-19}$ J

(b) $E = (6.63 \times 10^{-34} \text{ J·s})(7.50 \times 10^{14}/\text{s})$
$= 4.97 \times 10^{-19}$ J

Notice that the radiation with the lower frequency (red light) has the lower energy per quantum (as well as the longer wavelength—see Example 6.1 and Figure 6.2).

6.2 Atomic Spectra

When a ray of light is passed through a prism, the ray is bent, or refracted. The amount that a wave is refracted depends upon its wavelength. A wave with a short wavelength is bent more than one with a long wavelength. Since ordinary white light consists of waves with all the wavelengths in the visible range, a ray of white light is spread out into a wide band called a continuous spectrum. The spectrum is a rainbow of colors with no blank spots—violet merges into blue, blue into green, and so on.

When gases or vapors of a chemical substance are heated in an electric arc or a Bunsen flame, light is emitted. If a ray of this light is passed through a prism, a line spectrum is produced (Figure 6.3). This spectrum consists of a limited

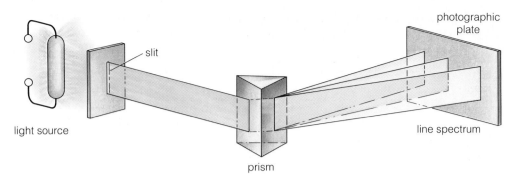

Figure 6.3 The spectroscope

number of colored lines, each of which corresponds to a different wavelength of light. The line spectrum of each element is unique.

The frequencies that correspond to the lines in the visible region of the hydrogen spectrum are given by the equation:

$$v = \frac{c}{\lambda} = (3.289 \times 10^{15}/\text{s})\left(\frac{1}{2^2} - \frac{1}{n^2}\right) \qquad n = 3, 4, 5\ldots \qquad (6.4)$$

where n is an integer equal to, or greater than, 3.

This relationship, proposed by J. J. Balmer in 1885, was derived from experimental observations and was not based on any theory of atomic structure. The series of spectral lines in the visible region that is described by the Balmer equation is called the Balmer series.

Bohr Theory

Niels Bohr, 1885–1962.
*American Institute of Physics,
Niels Bohr Library.*

In 1913, Niels Bohr proposed a theory for the electronic structure of the hydrogen atom that explained the line spectrum of this element. The hydrogen atom contains one electron and a nucleus that consists of a single proton. Bohr's theory includes the following points.

1. The electron of the hydrogen atom can exist only in certain circular orbits (which are also called energy levels or shells). These shells are arranged concentrically around the nucleus. Each shell is designated by a letter (K, L, M, N, O . . .) or a value of n (1, 2, 3, 4, 5 . . .).

2. The electron has a definite energy characteristic of the orbit in which it is moving. The K level ($n = 1$), the shell closest to the nucleus, has the smallest radius. An electron in the K level has the lowest possible energy since it is as close to the positive charge of the nucleus as is possible. With increasing distance from the nucleus (K, L, M, N, O; $n = 1, 2, 3, 4, 5$), the radius of the shell and the energy of an electron in the shell increase. Energy would have to be supplied to move the electron (which bears a negative charge) farther and farther away from the positive charge of the nucleus. No electron can have an energy that would place it between the permissible shells.

3. When the electrons of an atom are as close to the nucleus as possible (for hydrogen, one electron in the K shell), they are in the condition of lowest possible energy, called the ground state. When the atoms are heated in an electric arc or

Bunsen flame, electrons absorb energy and jump to outer levels, which are higher energy states. The atoms are said to be in excited states.

4. When an electron falls back to a lower level, it emits a definite amount of energy. The energy difference between the high-energy state and low-energy state is emitted in the form of a quantum of light. The light quantum has a characteristic frequency (and wavelength) and produces a characteristic spectral line. In spectral studies, many atoms are absorbing energy at the same time that many others are emitting it. Each spectral line corresponds to a different electron transition.

Bohr derived an equation for the energy that an electron would have in each orbit, E_{orbit}. This equation can be simplified to

$$E_{orbit} = -\frac{(2.179 \times 10^{-18} \text{ J})}{n^2} \qquad n = 1, 2, 3 \ldots \qquad (6.5)$$

We shall let the energy of the electron in an outer level (n_o) be indicated by E_o and the energy of the electron in an inner level (n_i) be indicated by E_i. When the electron falls from the outer level to the inner level, $(E_o - E_i)$ is given off as a photon of light. According to Planck's equation, the energy of a photon is equal to $h\nu$. Therefore,

$$h\nu = E_o - E_i \qquad \text{(for } E_o \rightarrow E_i) \qquad (6.6)$$

$$h\nu = \frac{(-2.179 \times 10^{-18} \text{ J})}{n_o^2} - \frac{(-2.179 \times 10^{-18} \text{ J})}{n_i^2}$$

$$h\nu = (2.179 \times 10^{-18} \text{ J})\left(\frac{1}{n_i^2} - \frac{1}{n_o^2}\right) \qquad (6.7)$$

Since $h = 6.626 \times 10^{-34} \text{ J}\cdot\text{s}$,

$$\nu = \left(\frac{2.179 \times 10^{-18} \text{ J}}{6.626 \times 10^{-34} \text{ J}\cdot\text{s}}\right)\left(\frac{1}{n_i^2} - \frac{1}{n_o^2}\right)$$

$$\nu = (3.289 \times 10^{15}/\text{s})\left(\frac{1}{n_i^2} - \frac{1}{n_o^2}\right) \qquad (6.8)$$

The lines produced by electron transitions to the $n = 2$ level from higher levels are described by the equation

$$\nu = (3.289 \times 10^{15}/\text{s})\left(\frac{1}{2^2} - \frac{1}{n_o^2}\right) \qquad n = 3, 4, 5 \ldots \qquad (6.4)$$

This equation is the same as the equation Balmer derived from experimental data.

The relationship between some of the electron transitions of the hydrogen atom and the spectral lines is illustrated in Figure 6.4. Since electron transitions to the $n = 1$ level (Lyman series) release more energy than those to the $n = 2$ level (Balmer series), the wavelengths of the lines of the Lyman series are *shorter* than those of the Balmer series. The lines of the Lyman series occur in the ultraviolet region. On the other hand, the lines of the Paschen series, which represent transitions to the $n = 3$ level, occur at wavelengths *longer* than the Balmer series. The Paschen lines appear in the infrared region.

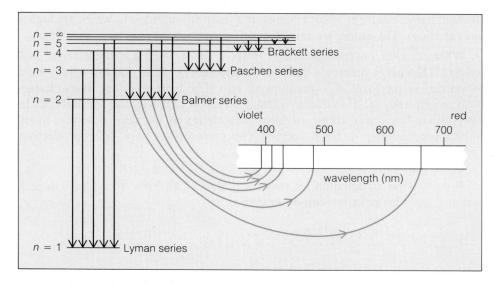

Figure 6.4 The relation between some electron transitions of the hydrogen atom and the spectral lines of the visible region

The Bohr theory is highly successful in interpreting the spectrum of hydrogen. It fails, however, to explain the spectra of atoms that contain more than one electron. Bohr's model of the atom, therefore, ultimately had to be modified (see Section 6.4).

Example 6.3

What are the frequency and wavelength of the line in the hydrogen spectrum that corresponds to an electron transition from the $n = 3$ level to the $n = 2$ level?

Solution

We use Equation 6.8 to find the frequency of the spectral line.

$$\nu = (3.289 \times 10^{15}/s)\left(\frac{1}{n_i^2} - \frac{1}{n_o^2}\right) \tag{6.8}$$

$$= (3.289 \times 10^{15}/s)\left(\frac{1}{2^2} - \frac{1}{3^2}\right)$$

$$= (3.289 \times 10^{15}/s)\left(\frac{1}{4} - \frac{1}{9}\right)$$

$$= 0.4568 \times 10^{15}/s = 4.568 \times 10^{14}/s$$

The wavelength may be derived by using Equation 6.2.

$$\lambda = \frac{c}{\nu} \tag{6.2}$$

$$= \frac{2.998 \times 10^8 \text{ m/s}}{4.568 \times 10^{14}/\text{s}}$$

$$= 6.563 \times 10^{-7} \text{ m} = 656.3 \text{ nm}$$

Note that the conversion from meters to nanometers can be accomplished in the following way:

$$? \text{ nm} = 6.563 \times 10^{-7} \text{ m}\left(\frac{1 \text{ nm}}{10^{-9} \text{ m}}\right) = 6.563 \times 10^2 \text{ nm} = 656.3 \text{ nm}$$

6.3 Atomic Number and the Periodic Law

Early in the nineteenth century, chemists became interested in the chemical and physical similarities between elements. In 1817 and 1829, Johann W. Döbereiner published articles in which he examined the properties of sets of elements that he called triads (Ca, Sr, Ba; Li, Na, K; Cl, Br, I; and S, Se, Te). The elements of each set have similar properties, and the atomic weight of the second element of a set is approximately equal to the average of the atomic weights of the other two elements of the set.

In following years, many chemists attempted to classify the elements into groups on the basis of similarities in properties. In the years 1863–66, John A. R. Newlands proposed and developed his "law of octaves." Newlands stated that when the elements are listed by increasing atomic weight, the eighth element is similar to the first, the ninth to the second, and so forth. He compared this relationship to octaves of muscial notes. Unfortunately, the actual relationship is not so simple as Newlands supposed. At the time he presented it, his work seemed forced and was not taken seriously by other chemists. Much later, however, Newlands was awarded the Davy Medal by the Royal Society for this work.

The modern periodic classification of the elements stems from the works of Julius Lothar Meyer (1869) and, in particular, Dmitri Mendeleev (1869). Mendeleev proposed a periodic law: when the elements are studied in order of increasing atomic weight, similarities in properties recur periodically. Mendeleev's table listed the elements in such a way that similar elements appeared in vertical columns, called groups (see Figure 6.5).

In order to make similar elements appear under one another, Mendeleev had to leave blanks for undiscovered elements in his table. On the basis of his system, he predicted the properties of three of the missing elements. The subsequent discovery of scandium, gallium, and germanium, each of which was found to have properties much like those predicted by Mendeleev, demonstrated the validity of the periodic system. The existence of the noble gases (He, Ne, Ar, Kr, Xe, and Rn) was unforeseen by Mendeleev. Nevertheless, after their discovery in the years 1892–98, these elements readily fitted into the periodic table.

The plan of the periodic table required that three elements (K, Ni, and I) be placed out of the order determined by increasing atomic weight. Iodine, for example, should be element number 52 on the basis of atomic weight. Instead, iodine was arbitrarily made element number 53 so that it would fall in a group of the table with chemically similar elements (F, Cl, and Br). Subsequent study of the periodic classification convinced many that some fundamental property other than atomic

Dmitri Mendeleev, 1834–1907. *Smithsonian Institution.*

Period	Group														
	I		II		III		IV		V		VI		VII		VIII	
	a	b	a	b	a	b	a	b	a	b	a	b	a	b	a	b (0)
1	H 1.0															He 4.0
2	Li 6.9		Be 9.0		B 10.8		C 12.0		N 14.0		O 16.0		F 19.0			Ne 20.2
3	Na 23.0		Mg 24.3		Al 27.0		Si 28.1		P 31.0		S 32.1		Cl 35.5			Ar 39.9
4	K 39.1		Ca 40.1		Sc 45.0		Ti 47.9		V 50.9		Cr 52.0		Mn 54.9		Fe 55.8 Co 58.9 Ni 58.7	
4		Cu 63.5		Zn 65.4		Ga 69.7		Ge 72.6		As 74.9		Se 79.0		Br 79.9		Kr 83.8
5	Rb 85.5		Sr 87.6		Y 88.9		Zr 91.2		Nb 92.9		Mo 95.9		Tc		Ru 101.1 Rh 102.9 Pd 106.4	
5		Ag 107.9		Cd 112.4		In 114.8		Sn 118.7		Sb 121.8		Te 127.6		I 126.9		Xe 131.3
6	Cs 132.9		Ba 137.3		La* 138.9		Hf 178.5		Ta 180.9		W 183.9		Re 186.2		Os 190.2 Ir 192.2 Pt 195.1	
6		Au 197.0		Hg 200.6		Tl 204.4		Pb 207.2		Bi 209.0		Po		At		Rn
7	Fr		Ra		Ac**											

*	Ce 140.1	Pr 140.9	Nd 144.2	Pm	Sm 150.4	Eu 152.0	Gd 157.3	Tb 158.9	Dy 162.5	Ho 164.9	Er 167.3	Tm 168.9	Yb 173.0	Lu 175.0
**	Th 232.0	Pa	U 238.0	Np	Pu	Am	Cm	Bk	Cf	Es	Fm	Md	No	Lr

Figure 6.5 Periodic table based on the Mendeleev table of 1871. (Elements that were not known in 1871 appear in the colored squares.)

weight is the cause of the observed periodicity. It was proposed that this fundamental property is in some way related to atomic number, which at that time was only a serial number derived from the periodic system.

The Periodic Law of Moseley

The work of Henry G. J. Moseley in the years 1913 and 1914 solved the problem. When high-energy cathode rays are focused on a target, X rays are produced (Figure 6.6). This X radiation can be resolved into its component wavelengths, and the line spectra thus obtained can be recorded photographically. Different X-ray spectra result when different elements are used as targets; each spectrum consists of only a few lines.

Moseley studied the X-ray spectra of 38 elements with atomic numbers between 13 (aluminum) and 79 (gold). Using a corresponding spectral line for each element, he found that there is a linear relationship between the square root of the frequency of the line and the atomic number of the element (Figure 6.7). In other words, the

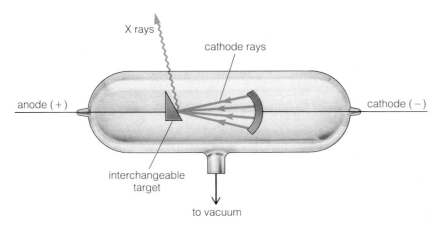

Figure 6.6 X-ray tube

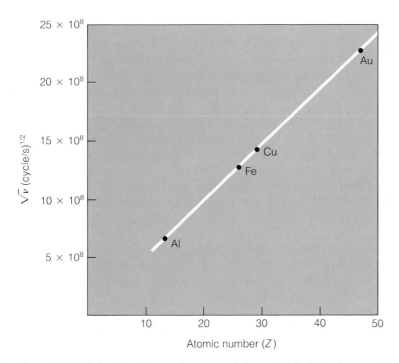

Figure 6.7 Relationship between frequency of characteristic X-ray lines and atomic number

square root of the frequency of the spectral line increases by a constant amount from element to element when the elements are arranged by increasing atomic number.

Moseley was able, therefore, to assign the correct atomic number to any element on the basis of its X-ray spectrum. In this way he settled the problem involving the classification of elements that have atomic weights out of line with those of their neighbors (K, Ni, and I). He also stated that there should be 14 elements in the series from $_{58}$Ce to $_{71}$Lu (found at the bottom of the chart in Figure 6.5), and he established that these elements should follow lanthanum in the periodic table. Moseley's diagrams indicated that at that time four elements before number 79 (gold) remained to be discovered (numbers 43, 61, 72, and 75). On the basis of Moseley's work, the periodic law was redefined: the chemical and physical properties of the elements are periodic functions of *atomic number*.

Moseley's atomic numbers agreed roughly with the nuclear charges that Rutherford had calculated on the basis of the α-particle scattering experiments. Moseley proposed, therefore, that the atomic number, Z, is the number of units of positive charge of the atomic nucleus. He said: "There is in the atom a fundamental quantity, which increases by regular steps as we pass from one element to the next. This quantity can only be the charge on the central positive nucleus."

X rays are electromagnetic radiations that have much shorter wavelengths (and consequently higher frequencies and energies) than those of visible light (Section 6.1). The X-ray spectrum of an element is believed to arise from certain electron transitions within the target atoms of the element (Section 6.1). In the X-ray tube, the cathode rays rip electrons from the inner shells of the target atoms. X rays are produced when outer electrons fall back into these vacancies. Since an electron transition to the K level of an atom from a higher level is one in which a relatively large amount of energy is released, the frequency of the resulting radiation is high. The corresponding wavelength, therefore, is short and is characteristic of X rays.

The frequency of the radiation released by an electron transition also depends upon the charge on the nucleus of the atom. The amount of energy released is directly proportional to the square of the nuclear charge (Z^2). The higher the charge, the more energy released and the shorter the wavelength of the radiation emitted. Moseley's observations reflect this relationship.

At the present time, the most popular form of the periodic table is the long form shown inside the front cover of this book. We discussed the periodic table in Section 2.7. Recall that periods consist of those elements that are arranged in horizontal rows in the table. Groups (or families) appear in vertical columns and consists of elements that have similar chemical and physical properties.

It is important to note that several methods of assigning the A or B designations to the group numbers are in current use. Three ways are illustrated in Figure 6.8.

1. The method shown at the top (a) is the one that is used in this book. Here, groups I A and II A are followed by III B, IV B, and so on. Group III A is found in the thirteenth column. In this system, the A and B designations denote certain classifications of elements—representative elements (the A groups) and transition elements (the B groups)—that we will discuss later (Section 6.9).

2. The method shown in the middle (b) is the oldest of the three. Here, groups I A and II A are followed by III A, IV A, and so on. The thirteenth column is group III B. Although Mendeleev did not assign A and B group designations, the system shown in (b) arose from the type of table that appears in Figure 6.5 and that is based on a chart devised by Mendeleev. Notice that the group designations that appear in (b) are similar to those shown in Figure 6.5.

3. The method shown at the bottom (c) is a new one that has been proposed to remove the ambiguities that exist in the group designations. This method has not yet been widely adopted.

6.4 Wave Mechanics

In the years 1900–1905, Max Planck and Albert Einstein developed the quantum theory of light. The revolutionary feature of this theory is that light can be assumed to be emitted in small particles, called photons. Prior to this time, the

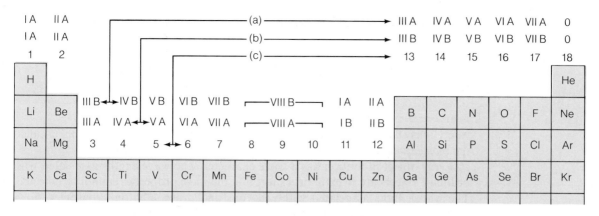

Figure 6.8 Methods for assigning group designations to the groups of the periodic table. See text for explanation.

properties of light were explained by assuming that light consists of waves of energy, and certain properties of light are still best explained by making such an assumption. At the present time, light is treated as waves of energy *and* as streams of photons. Each concept has the support of experimental observation. Which model is used for a given purpose depends upon which is more convenient.

In the same way that light has both a wave and a particle-like character, matter has a dual nature. This dualism, however, evolved in the reverse order. In the experiments that characterized the electron (such as the determination of the charge-to-mass ratio), the electron was considered solely as a charged particle. Later, the wave properties of the electron were investigated.

The de Broglie Relation

In 1924, Louis de Broglie proposed that electrons and other particles have wave properties. The energy of a photon of light, E, is equal to its frequency, v, times Planck's constant, h:

$$E = hv \tag{6.3}$$

Since $v = c/\lambda$, where c is the speed of light and λ is the wavelength (Section 6.1), we can substitute c/λ for v:

$$E = h\frac{c}{\lambda} \tag{6.9}$$

Using Einstein's equation, $E = mc^2$, where m is the effective mass of the photon, we substitute mc^2 for E:

$$mc^2 = h\frac{c}{\lambda} \tag{6.10}$$

This equation is solved for λ, the wavelength:

$$\lambda = \frac{h}{mc} \tag{6.11}$$

Louis de Broglie, 1892-.
American Institute of Physics, Niels Bohr Library.

According to de Broglie, a similar equation can be used to assign a wavelength to an electron:

$$\lambda = \frac{h}{mv} \tag{6.12}$$

where m is the mass of the electron and v is its velocity. The product mv is called the *momentum*.

Every object in motion has a wave character. The wavelengths associated with ordinary objects are so extremely short that the wave properties cannot be detected. The wavelengths associated with electrons and other subatomic particles, however, are a different story.

Example 6.4

(a) In baseball, a fast pitch has been timed at 44.1 m/s (98.6 miles/hour). Calculate the wavelength associated with a baseball (mass, 146 g) moving at 44.1 m/s. (b) According to the Bohr theory, the velocity of the electron in the hydrogen atom is 2.19×10^6 m/s. Calculate the wavelength associated with the electron (mass, 9.11×10^{-28} g) moving at this velocity.

Note that since $1 \text{ J} = 1 \text{ kg·m}^2/\text{s}^2$,

$$h = 6.63 \times 10^{-34} \text{ J·s} = 6.63 \times 10^{-34} \text{ kg·m}^2/\text{s}$$

Solution

(a) $\lambda = \dfrac{h}{mv}$ (6.12)

$$= \frac{6.63 \times 10^{-34} \text{ kg·m}^2/\text{s}}{(0.146 \text{ kg})(44.1 \text{ m/s})}$$

$$= 1.03 \times 10^{-34} \text{ m}$$

(b) $\lambda = \dfrac{h}{mv}$ (6.12)

$$= \frac{6.63 \times 10^{-34} \text{ kg·m}^2/\text{s}}{(9.11 \times 10^{-31} \text{ kg})(2.19 \times 10^6 \text{ m/s})}$$

$$= 3.32 \times 10^{-10} \text{ m} = 0.332 \text{ nm}$$

The wavelength associated with the baseball is so short that it cannot be detected by any known device. The wavelength associated with the electron, however, is in the X-ray region of the electromagnetic spectrum.

Shortly after de Broglie published his theory, Clinton Davisson and Lester Germer confirmed experimentally that electrons do indeed have wave properties. They showed that electrons are diffracted by a crystal in the same way that X rays are (see the Bragg equation in Section 11.13). Furthermore, the diffraction of the electron beam occurs at exactly the angle predicted on the basis of the de Broglie wavelength.

Heisenberg's Uncertainty Principle

Bohr's idea that an electron in an atom can possess only certain, definite quantities of energy was an important step in the development of atomic theory. The Bohr theory offered a satisfactory model for explaining the spectrum of the hydrogen atom. However, attempts to extend the theory to explain the spectra of atoms containing more than one electron were unsuccessful. The reason for this problem was soon discovered.

In the Bohr approach, the electron was regarded as a charged particle in motion. In order to predict the path of a moving body, we must know both its position and velocity at the same time. Werner Heisenberg's uncertainty principle (1926) states that it is impossible to determine simultaneously the exact *position* and exact *momentum* of a body as small as the electron. The more precisely we try to determine one of these values, the more uncertain we are of the other.

We see objects by noting their interception of the light rays used to illuminate them. Radiation with an extremely short wavelength would be needed to locate an object as small as the electron. Radiation that has a short wavelength has a high frequency and is very energetic (Section 6.1). When it strikes the electron, the impact causes the direction of motion and the speed of the electron to change. The attempt to locate the electron changes the momentum of the electron drastically.

Photons with longer wavelengths are less energetic and would have a smaller effect on the momentum of the electron. Because of their longer wavelength, however, such photons would not indicate the position of the electron very precisely. The two uncertainties are therefore related. According to Heisenberg, the uncertainty in the position of an object, Δx, times the uncertainty in the momentum of the object, Δmv, is equal to or greater than Planck's constant, h, divided by 4π:

$$\Delta x \Delta mv \geq h/4\pi \qquad (6.13)$$

The uncertainty in measurement is very important for objects as small as the electron, but it is not significant for objects of ordinary size.

Example 6.5

What is the uncertainty in the velocity of (a) a baseball (mass, 0.146 kg), and (b) an electron (mass, 9.11×10^{-31} kg) if the position of each object is located to within 1.00×10^{-11} m (0.0100 nm, which is about 10% of the radius of an average atom).

$$\Delta x \Delta mv \geq \frac{h}{4\pi} \tag{6.13}$$

$$\Delta v \geq \frac{h}{4\pi m \Delta x} \tag{6.14}$$

$$\geq \frac{5.28 \times 10^{-35} \text{ kg·m}^2/\text{s}}{m \Delta x}$$

(a) $\quad \Delta v \geq \dfrac{5.28 \times 10^{-35} \text{ kg·m}^2/\text{s}}{(0.146 \text{ kg})(1.00 \times 10^{-11} \text{ m})}$

$$\geq 3.62 \times 10^{-23} \text{ m/s}$$

The *uncertainty* in the velocity of the baseball works out to be equal to or greater than a rate that would cause a displacement of 1.14 nm in one million years.

(b) $\quad \Delta v \geq \dfrac{5.28 \times 10^{-35} \text{ kg·m}^2/\text{s}}{(9.11 \times 10^{-31} \text{ kg})(1.00 \times 10^{-11} \text{ m})}$

$$\geq 5.80 \times 10^6 \text{ m/s}$$

The *uncertainty* in the velocity of the electron is about 2% of the speed of light and more than twice as great as the velocity of the electron itself as calculated by Bohr (2.19×10^6 m/s).

In light of the Heisenberg uncertainty principle, any attempt to extend Bohr's approach is futile. A precise description of the path of an electron in an atom is impossible. Instead, Erwin Schrödinger used de Broglie's relation to develop an equation that describes the electron in terms of its wave character.

The Schrödinger Equation

The **Schrödinger equation** is the basis of **wave mechanics.** The equation is written in terms of a **wave function,** ψ (psi), for an electron. When the equation is solved for the electron in the hydrogen atom, a series of wave functions is obtained. Each wave function corresponds to a definite energy state for the electron and pertains to a region in which the electron may be found. The wave function of an electron describes what is called an **orbital** (so named to distinguish it from the orbit of Bohr).

The intensity of a wave is proportional to the square of its amplitude. The wave function, ψ, is an amplitude function. At any position in space, the value of ψ^2 for a very small volume is proportional to the electron charge density. The charge of the electron can be assumed to be spread out into a charge cloud by the rapid motion of the electron. The cloud is denser in some regions than other. The probability of finding the electron in a given region is proportional to the density of the charge cloud at that spot. The probability is high in a region where the cloud is dense. This interpretation does not attempt to describe the path of the electron; it merely predicts where an electron is likely to be found.

Erwin Schrödinger, 1887–1961.
California Institute of Technology Archives.

For an electron in the $n = 1$ state of the hydrogen atom, the charge cloud has the greatest density near the nucleus and becomes thinner as the distance from the nucleus increases (Figure 6.9). More information about this probability distribution can be obtained from the curves of Figure 6.10. In curve (a), ψ^2 is plotted against distance from the nucleus. The probability of finding the electron in a small volume segment is greatest near the nucleus and approaches zero as the distance from the nucleus increases.

Curve (b) is a radial probability curve. The *total* probability of finding the electron at a given distance from the nucleus is plotted against distance. Imagine a group of very thin spherical shells arranged one after the other with the center of each shell at the center of the nucleus. What is the probability of finding the electron in each of these shells? The probability of finding the electron in a small volume segment is greatest near the nucleus. A shell close to the nucleus, however, contains fewer of these volumes segments than one farther out. The radial probability takes both factors into account.

The curve shows a maximum at a distance a_0. The total probability of finding the electron at all points of distance r from the nucleus is greatest when r is equal to a_0. This value is the same as the value determined by the Bohr theory for the radius of the $n = 1$ shell. In the Bohr theory, a_0 is the distance at which the electron is *always* found in the $n = 1$ shell. In wave mechanics, a_0 is the distance at which the electron is likely to be found most often.

Since in principle an electron can be found at any finite distance from the nucleus, it is not possible to draw a shape that bounds a region in which the probability or finding the electron is 100%. A surface can be drawn, however, that connects points of equal probability and that encloses a volume in which the probability of finding the electron is high (for example, 90%). Such a representation, called a **boundary surface diagram,** is shown in Figure 6.11 for the electron in the $n = 1$ state of the hydrogen atom.

6.5 Quantum Numbers

In wave mechanics (or quantum mechanics), the electron distribution of an atom containing a number of electrons is divided into *shells*. The shells, in turn, are thought to consist of one or more *subshells*, and the subshells are assumed to be

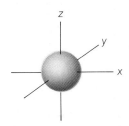

Figure 6.9 Cross section of the charge cloud of an electron in the $n = 1$ state of the hydrogen atom

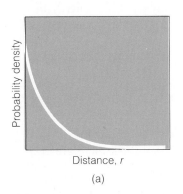

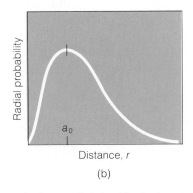

Figure 6.10 Probability curves for an electron in the $n = 1$ state of the hydrogen atom.
(a) Probability of finding the electron per unit volume versus distance from the nucleus.
(b) Probability of finding the electron at a given distance versus distance from the nucleus.

Figure 6.11 Boundary surface representation of an electron in the $n = 1$ state of the hydrogen atom. (Volume encloses 90% of the electron density. Nucleus is at the origin.)

composed of one or more *orbitals*, which the *electrons* occupy. Each electron of an atom is identified by a combination of four quantum numbers, which loosely indicate shell, subshell, orbital, and electron spin.

The **principal quantum number,** n, corresponds approximately to the n introduced by Bohr. It identifies the shell, or level, to which the electron belongs. These shells are regions where the probability of finding an electron is high. The value of n is a positive integer:

$$n = 1, 2, 3 \ldots$$

The larger the value of n, the farther the shell is from the nucleus and the higher the energy of the electron in that shell.

Each shell consists of one or more **subshells,** or **sublevels.** The number of subshells in a principal shell is equal to the value of n. There is only one subshell in the $n = 1$ shell, there are two in the $n = 2$ shell, three in the $n = 3$ shell, and so on. Each subshell in a shell is assigned a **subsidiary quantum number,** l. The values of l for the sublevels of a shell are determined by the shell's value of n. There is one value of l for each term in the series:

$$l = 0, 1, 2, 3 \ldots (n - 1) \tag{6.15}$$

When $n = 1$, the only value of l is 0, and there is only one subshell. When $n = 2$, there are two subshells that have l values of 0 and 1, respectively. When $n = 3$, the three subshells have l values of 0, 1, and 2.

Other symbols are used at times to denote subshells. A letter is used to represent each value of l in the following way:

$$l = \quad 0, \quad 1, \quad 2, \quad 3, \quad 4, \quad 5 \ldots$$
$$\text{notation} = \quad s, \quad p, \quad d, \quad f, \quad g, \quad h \ldots$$

The first four notations are the initial letters of adjectives formerly used to identify spectral lines: sharp, principal, diffuse, and fundamental. For l values higher than 3, the letters proceed alphabetically—g, h, i, and so on. Combining the principal quantum number with one of these letters gives a convenient way to designate a subshell. The subshell with $n = 2$ and $l = 0$ is called the $2s$ subshell. The subshell with $n = 2$ and $l = 1$ is called the $2p$ subshell. Table 6.1 contains a summary of subshell notation for the first four shells. Within any shell, the energy of the electrons increases with increasing value of l. Thus, for example, the energy of electrons in the $n = 3$ shell increases in the order $3s < 3p < 3d$.

Each subshell consists of one or more orbitals. The number of orbitals in a subshell is given by the equation

$$\text{number of orbitals} = 2l + 1 \tag{6.16}$$

In any $l = 0$ subshell, for example, there is $2(0) + 1 = 1$ orbital. In any $l = 1$ subshell, there are $2(1) + 1 = 3$ orbitals. In any $l = 2$ subshell, there are $2(2) + 1 = 5$ orbitals. In other words,

$$\text{notation} = \quad s, \quad p, \quad d, \quad f, \quad g \ldots$$
$$l = \quad 0, \quad 1, \quad 2, \quad 3, \quad 4 \ldots$$
$$\text{number of orbitals} = \quad 1, \quad 3, \quad 5, \quad 7, \quad 9 \ldots$$

Table 6.1 Subshell notations

n	l	Subshell Notation
1	0	$1s$
2	0	$2s$
2	1	$2p$
3	0	$3s$
3	1	$3p$
3	2	$3d$
4	0	$4s$
4	1	$4p$
4	2	$4d$
4	3	$4f$

Table 6.2   The orbitals of the first four shells

Shell n	Subshell l	Orbital m_l	Subshell Notation	Number of Orbitals per Subshell
1	0	0	1s	1
2	0	0	2s	1
	1	$+1, 0, -1$	2p	3
3	0	0	3s	1
	1	$+1, 0, -1$	3p	3
	2	$+2, +1, 0, -1, -2$	3d	5
4	0	0	4s	1
	1	$+1, 0, -1$	4p	3
	2	$+2, +1, 0, -1, -2$	4d	5
	3	$+3, +2, +1, 0, -1, -2, -3$	4f	7

An *s* subshell consists of one orbital, a *p* subshell consists of three orbitals, a *d* subshell consists of five orbitals, and so on.

Each orbital within a given subshell is identified by a **magnetic orbital quantum number,** m_i. For any subshell, the values of m_l are given by the terms in the series:

$$m_l = +l, +(l-1)\ldots 0 \ldots -(l-1), -l$$

Thus, for $l = 0$, the only permitted value of m_l is 0 (one *s* orbital). For $l = 1$, m_l can be $+1$, 0, and -1 (three *p* orbitals). For $l = 2$, m_l can be $+2$, $+1$, 0, -1, and -2 (five *d* orbitals). Notice that the values of m_l are derived from l, and that the values of l are derived from n.

Each orbital in an atom, therefore, is identified by a set of values for n, l, and m_l. An orbital described by the quantum numbers $n = 2$, $l = 1$, and $m_l = 0$, is an orbital in the *p* subshell of the second shell—a 2*p* orbital. The quantum numbers for the orbitals of the first four shells are given in Table 6.2.

In Section 6.4, the electron charge cloud of the 1*s* orbital was discussed (see Figures 6.9, 6.10, and 6.11). Each of the three parts of Figure 6.12 pertains to the charge cloud of the 2*s* orbital. Figure 6.12(a) is a radial probability curve for the 2*s* orbital. The curve shows two places where the probability of finding an electron is relatively high: one is close to the nucleus and the other is farther out. In the charge cloud of the 2*s* orbital, therefore, there are two regions where the electron density is relatively high. They appear in Figure 6.12(b), which is a cross section of the electron density of the orbital. The boundary surface diagram of the 2*s* orbital, however, appears the same as that for the 1*s* orbital, except for size. Compare Figure 6.12(c) with Figure 6.11. All *s* orbitals are spherical.

Boundary surface diagrams for the three 2*p* orbitals are shown in Figure 6.13. In these diagrams, the nucleus is at the origin. The electron density of a *p* orbital is not spherical. Instead, each *p* orbital consists of two sections, called lobes, that are on either side of a plane that passes through the nucleus. The shapes of the three orbitals are identical. They differ, however, in the way that the lobes are directed. Since the lobes may be considered to lie along the *x*, *y*, or *z* axis, they are given the designations $2p_x$, $2p_y$, and $2p_z$.

A magnetic field has no effect on the energy of an *s* electron, since an *s* orbital is spherical. No matter how we turn a sphere, it always looks the same with regard to a fixed frame of reference. A spherical orbital (an *s* orbital) in a magnetic field presents only one aspect toward the lines of force.

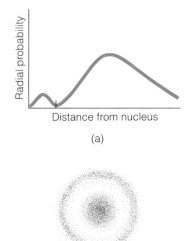

Distance from nucleus

(a)

(b)

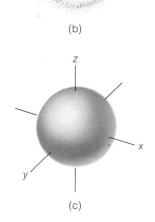

(c)

Figure 6.12 Diagrams for the 2*s* orbital. (a) Radial probability distribution. (b) Cross section of electron charge cloud. (c) Boundary surface diagram.

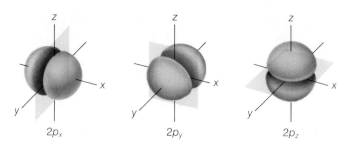

Figure 6.13 Boundary surface diagrams for the 2*p* orbitals

The *p* orbitals are not spherical. Each *p* sublevel consists of three orbitals that differ in their orientation. Each *p* orbital presents a different aspect toward the lines of force of a magnetic field. These *p* orbitals are identical in terms of energy. In the absence of the magnetic field, no distinction between electrons that occupy different *p* orbitals is noted. If spectral studies are run using a magnetic field, however, some of the lines of the spectrum are split into several lines. This effect, called the **Zeeman effect,** disappears when the magnetic field is removed. The m_l value of an orbital is associated with the orientation of the orbital in relation to a direction fixed by a magnetic field.

Boundary surface diagrams of the five 3*d* orbitals are shown in Figure 6.14. The shape of the d_{z^2} orbital is different from the others, but they are all equivalent in terms of energy.

The first three quantum numbers (n, l, and m_l) arise from solutions to the Schrödinger wave equation. A fourth quantum number, the **magnetic spin quantum number,** m_s, is necessary to describe an electron completely. An electron has magnetic properties like those of a charged particle that is spinning on an axis. A spinning charge generates a magnetic field and an electron has a magnetic field associated with it that can be described in terms of an apparent spin. The magnetic spin quantum number of an electron can have one of two values:

$$m_s = +\tfrac{1}{2} \text{ or } -\tfrac{1}{2}$$

Two electrons that have different m_s values (one $+\tfrac{1}{2}$ and the other $-\tfrac{1}{2}$) are said to have *opposed spins*. The spin magnetic moments of these two electrons cancel each other. Each orbital can hold two electrons with opposed spins.

The existence of electron spin was demostrated in an experiment reported by Otto Stern and Walther Gerlach in 1921 (see Figure 6.15). Silver was vaporized in a furnace and a beam of silver atoms produced. This beam was split in two by passing it through an inhomogeneous (nonuniform) magnetic field. The silver atom contains 47 electrons; 24 have a spin of one type and 23 have a spin of the opposite type. Hence, 46 of the 47 electrons form 23 pairs that have spins and no associated magnetic fields. The spin of the unpaired electron (the 47th) determines the direction of deflection of the silver atom in the magnetic field. The deflection is caused by the interaction between the magnetic field associated with the spin of the electron and the external magnetic field. In a collection of silver atoms, half will have an unpaired electron with $m_s = +\tfrac{1}{2}$ and half will have an unpaired electron with $m_s = -\tfrac{1}{2}$. Thus, the beam of silver atoms is split in half.

Each electron, therefore, may be described by a set of four quantum numbers:

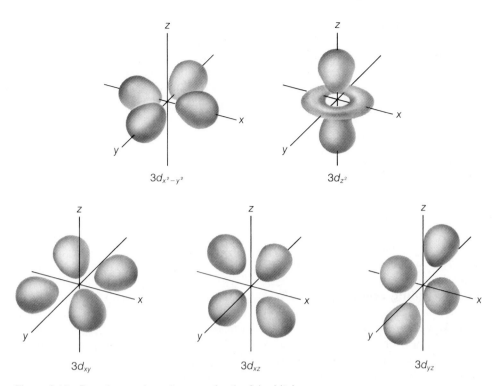

Figure 6.14 Boundary surface diagrams for the 3d orbitals

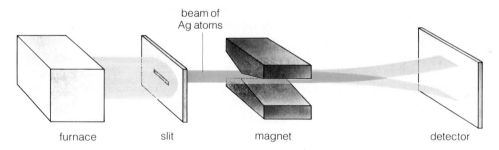

Figure 6.15 The Stern-Gerlach experiment

1. n gives the shell and the relative average distance of the electron from the nucleus.

2. l gives the subshell and the shape of the orbital for the electron. In the absence of a magnetic field, each orbital of a given subshell is equivalent in energy.

3. m_l designates the orientation of the orbital.

4. m_s refers to the spin of the electron.

Pauli's Exclusion Principle

The **exclusion principle** of Wolfgang Pauli states that no two electrons in the same atom may have identical sets of all four quantum numbers. Even if two electrons have the same values for n, l, and m_l they will differ in their m_s values. This situation indicates that two electrons are paired in a single orbital. Two electrons paired

Wolfgang Pauli, 1900–1958.
CERN, courtesy AIP Niels Bohr Library.

in a $1s$ orbital, for example, have (n, l, m_l, m_s) quantum sets of $(1, 0, 0, +\frac{1}{2})$ and $(1, 0, 0, -\frac{1}{2})$. According to the exclusion principle, therefore, an orbital may hold no more than two electrons.

Quantum numbers for the orbitals of the first four shells are given in Table 6.2. The quantum number sets for the electrons in these orbitals can be obtained by indicating an m_s value (either $+\frac{1}{2}$ or $-\frac{1}{2}$) with the set of n, l, m_l values that denote the orbital.

The maximum number of electrons that a shell can hold is given by $2n^2$. Each orbital can hold two electrons. The maximum number of electrons in a shell, therefore, is equal to twice the number of orbitals in the shell. The maximum number of electrons for a subshell can be calculated by multiplying the number of orbitals in the subshell by 2. The capacities of the shells and subshells from $n = 1$ to $n = 4$ are given in Table 6.3.

6.6 Orbital Filling and Hund's Rule

The way electrons are arranged in an atom is called the **electronic configuration** of the atom. For the first 18 elements, the ground-state electronic configurations can be derived by assuming that the electrons occupy the shells by increasing value of n, and within a shell by increasing value of l. The situation for elements with atomic numbers higher than 18 is slightly more complicated and is discussed in Section 6.7.

Two ways to indicate the electronic configuration of an atom are shown in Table 6.4. In the **orbital diagrams,** each orbital is indicated by a dash and an electron is represented by an arrow either pointing up, ↑, to represent one direction of electron spin, or pointing down, ↓, to represent the opposite direction (m_s can be either $+\frac{1}{2}$ or $-\frac{1}{2}$). In the **electronic notations,** the electronic configuration of an atom is summarized in a slightly different way. The symbols $1s$, $2s$, $2p$, and so on, are used to indicate *subshells*, and superscripts are added to indicate the number of electrons in each subshell.

The single electron of a hydrogen atom occupies a $1s$ orbital ($n = 1$, $l = 0$, $m_l = 0$). In the orbital diagram that appears in Table 6.4, one arrow is shown in the blank for the $1s$ orbital. The electronic notation for the H atom is $1s^1$.

The helium atom has two electrons with opposite spins in the $1s$ orbital, and two arrows, pointing in opposite directions, are shown in the blank for the $1s$ orbital in the orbital diagram. The electronic notation for the He atom is $1s^2$. Note that the $n = 1$ shell of the helium atom is filled.

The lithium atom has a pair of electrons in the $1s$ orbital plus one electron in the $2s$ orbital ($n = 2$, $l = 0$, $m_l = 0$). The electronic notation for the Li atom is $1s^2 2s^1$. The next atom, beryllium, has electron pairs in both the $1s$ and $2s$ orbitals; the electronic notation for the Be atom is $1s^2 2s^2$.

The boron atom has five electrons. Two electrons, with spins paired, occupy the $1s$ orbital; another pair of electrons occupies the $2s$ orbital, and the fifth electron is present in a $2p$ orbital. The $2p$ subshell ($n = 2$, $l = 1$) consists of three orbitals (with m_l values of $+1$, 0, and -1). Since the three $2p$ orbitals are of equal energy, the fifth electron of boron can occupy any one of the three. In the orbital diagram for boron that appears in Table 6.4, an arrow is shown in one of the $2p$ orbitals, but these orbitals are not identified by m_l values. The electronic notation for the B atom is $1s^2\ 2s^2\ 2p^1$.

Table 6.3 Maximum number of electrons for the subshells of the first four shells

Subshell Notation	Orbitals per Subshell $(2l + 1)$	Electrons per Subshell $2(2l + 1)$	Electrons per Shell $(2n^2)$
1s	1	2	2
2s	1	2	8
2p	3	6	
3s	1	2	18
3p	3	6	
3d	5	10	
4s	1	2	32
4p	3	6	
4d	5	10	
4f	7	14	

Table 6.4 Electronic configurations of the first ten elements

| | Orbital Diagram | | | | | |
	1s	2s		2p		Electronic Notation
$_1$H	↑					$1s^1$
$_2$He	↑↓					$1s^2$
$_3$Li	↑↓	↑				$1s^2\, 2s^1$
$_4$Be	↑↓	↑↓				$1s^2\, 2s^2$
$_5$B	↑↓	↑↓	↑			$1s^2\, 2s^2\, 2p^1$
$_6$C	↑↓	↑↓	↑	↑		$1s^2\, 2s^2\, 2p^2$
$_7$N	↑↓	↑↓	↑	↑	↑	$1s^2\, 2s^2\, 2p^3$
$_8$O	↑↓	↑↓	↑↓	↑	↑	$1s^2\, 2s^2\, 2p^4$
$_9$F	↑↓	↑↓	↑↓	↑↓	↑	$1s^2\, 2s^2\, 2p^5$
$_{10}$Ne	↑↓	↑↓	↑↓	↑↓	↑↓	$1s^2\, 2s^2\, 2p^6$

The electronic configuration of the sixth element, carbon, can be derived from the configuration of boron by indicating an additional electron. Questions arise, however, concerning the placement of this sixth electron of carbon. Does the sixth electron belong in the $2p$ orbital that already holds one electron, or does it belong in another orbital? What is the spin orientation of the sixth electron?

Hund's rule of maximum multiplicity provides the answers. Hund's rule states that the electrons are distributed among the orbitals of a subshell in a way that gives the maximum number of unpaired electrons with parallel spins. The term *parallel spins* means that all the unpaired electrons spin in the same direction—all the m_s values of these electrons have the same sign.

In carbon, therefore, each of the $2p$ electrons occupies a separate orbital, and these two electrons have the same spin orientation. These two unpaired electrons are clearly shown in the orbital diagram for carbon given in Table 6.4. The distinction, however, is not apparent in the electronic notation, $1s^2\, 2s^2\, 2p^2$.

Notice that all the superscripts in this notation are even numbers. Such a situation does *not* necessarily mean that all the electrons are paired in orbitals. Customarily, the electronic notation gives the electronic configuration by *subshells* (not by *orbitals*). The unpaired electrons can be shown, however, by using a separate designation for each orbital. The notation for carbon would be $1s^2\, 2s^2\, 2p_x^1\, 2p_y^1$.

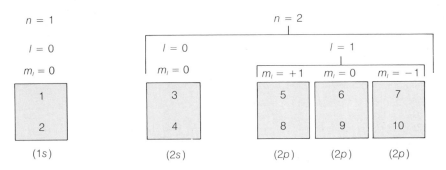

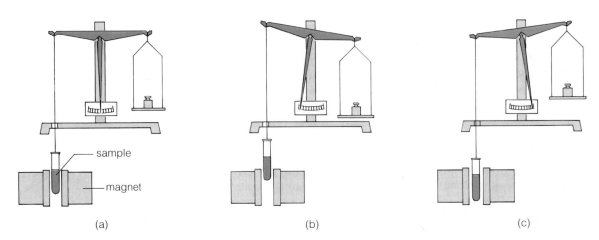

Figure 6.16 Order in which the orbitals of the $n = 1$ and $n = 2$ shells are filled

Figure 6.17 Determination of magnetic properties. (a) Sample weighed in the absence of a magnetic field (magnet turned off). (b) Diamagnetic sample is repelled by magnetic field. (c) Paramagnetic sample is attracted into magnetic field.

This device is not necessary if we remember that there are three $2p$ orbitals and that Hund's rule requires that the two electrons occupy separate orbitals.

Figure 6.16 illustrates Hund's rule. The orbitals are represented by squares. The order of filling is shown by numbers entered into these squares. Since electrons are negatively charged and repel each other, they spread out and occupy the $2p$ orbitals singly before they begin to pair. The electronic configurations for B, C, N, O, F, and Ne given in Table 6.4 illustrate Hund's rule. The five orbitals of a d subshell and the seven orbitals of an f subshell are filled in the same way— electrons successively occupy each orbital of the subshell singly, and only after each orbital holds one electron does electron pairing occur. Hund's rule has been confirmed by magnetic measurements.

The number of umpaired electrons in an atom, ion, or molecule can be determined by magnetic measurements. **Paramagnetic substances** are drawn into a magnetic field (Figure 6.17). Substances that contain unpaired electrons are paramagnetic. The magnetic moment depends upon the number of unpaired electrons present. Two effects contribute to the paramagnetism of an atom: the spin of the unpaired electrons and the orbital motion of these electrons. The effect of electron spin is the greater of the two, and in many cases, the effect of orbital motion is negligible.

I A							0
$_1$H	II A	III A	IV A	V A	VI A	VII A	$_2$He
$1s^1$							$1s^2$
$_3$Li	$_4$Be	$_5$B	$_6$C	$_7$N	$_8$O	$_9$F	$_{10}$Ne
$2s^1$	$2s^2$	$2s^22p^1$	$2s^22p^2$	$2s^22p^3$	$2s^22p^4$	$2s^22p^5$	$2s^22p^6$
$_{11}$Na	$_{12}$Mg	$_{13}$Al	$_{14}$Si	$_{15}$P	$_{16}$S	$_{17}$Cl	$_{18}$Ar
$3s^1$	$3s^2$	$3s^23p^1$	$3s^23p^2$	$3s^23p^3$	$3s^23p^4$	$3s^23p^5$	$3s^23p^6$

Table 6.5 Electronic configurations of the outer shells of the elements of the first three periods

Diamagnetic substances are weakly repelled by a magnetic field (Figure 6.17). A material is diamagnetic if all of its electrons are paired. Diamagnetism is a property of all matter, but it is obscured by the stronger paramagnetic effect if unpaired electrons are present.*

In Table 6.5, the electronic notations for the *outer shells* of atoms of the elements of the first three periods are shown. In each atom that contains electrons in inner shells, these shells are complete. Notice the similarity between the configurations of elements of the same group. All of the elements of group I A, for example, have one electron in an *s* orbital in the outer shell. The similarity in electronic configuration between elements of a given group accounts for their similarities in properties.

The outermost shells of these atoms are called valence shells, and electrons in them are called valence electrons. All the electrons in the valence shell, regardless of subshell, are counted as valence electrons. For what are called representative elements (members of A groups in the table we use), the number of valence electrons is the same as the group number. The noble gases (group 0) have eight electrons in their valence shells with the exception of helium, which has two.

6.7 Electronic Structures of the Elements

The data of Tables 6.4 and 6.5 indicate a way in which the electronic configurations of atoms can be derived. We start with the hydrogen atom, which has one electron in a 1s orbital. By adding one electron, we get the configuration of an atom of the next element, helium (which is $1s^2$). In this manner, we go from element to element until we derive the configuration of the atom that we desire. This method was first suggested by Wolfgang Pauli and is called the aufbau method (*aufbau* means "building up" in German).

In a few cases, the electronic configurations obtained by use of the aufbau method are in error. These errors, however, are small and usually involve only one misplaced electron. The correct electronic configurations of the elements are given later, in Table 6.6.

---

* Ferromagnetic substances, such as iron, are strongly attracted into a magnetic field. Ferromagnetism is a form of paramagnetism that is shown by only a few solid substances.

Table 6.6 Electronic configurations of the elements

Element	Z	1s	2s	2p	3s	3p	3d	4s	4p	4d	4f	5s	5p	5d	5f	6s	6p	6d	7s
H	1	1																	
He	2	2																	
Li	3	2	1																
Be	4	2	2																
B	5	2	2	1															
C	6	2	2	2															
N	7	2	2	3															
O	8	2	2	4															
F	9	2	2	5															
Ne	10	2	2	6															
Na	11	2	2	6	1														
Mg	12	2	2	6	2														
Al	13	2	2	6	2	1													
Si	14	2	2	6	2	2													
P	15	2	2	6	2	3													
S	16	2	2	6	2	4													
Cl	17	2	2	6	2	5													
Ar	18	2	2	6	2	6													
K	19	2	2	6	2	6		1											
Ca	20	2	2	6	2	6		2											
Sc	21	2	2	6	2	6	1	2											
Ti	22	2	2	6	2	6	2	2											
V	23	2	2	6	2	6	3	2											
Cr	24	2	2	6	2	6	5	1											
Mn	25	2	2	6	2	6	5	2											
Fe	26	2	2	6	2	6	6	2											
Co	27	2	2	6	2	6	7	2											
Ni	28	2	2	6	2	6	8	2											
Cu	29	2	2	6	2	6	10	1											
Zn	30	2	2	6	2	6	10	2											
Ga	31	2	2	6	2	6	10	2	1										
Ge	32	2	2	6	2	6	10	2	2										
As	33	2	2	6	2	6	10	2	3										
Se	34	2	2	6	2	6	10	2	4										
Br	35	2	2	6	2	6	10	2	5										
Kr	36	2	2	6	2	6	10	2	6										
Rb	37	2	2	6	2	6	10	2	6			1							
Sr	38	2	2	6	2	6	10	2	6			2							
Y	39	2	2	6	2	6	10	2	6	1		2							
Zr	40	2	2	6	2	6	10	2	6	2		2							
Nb	41	2	2	6	2	6	10	2	6	4		1							
Mo	42	2	2	6	2	6	10	2	6	5		1							
Tc	43	2	2	6	2	6	10	2	6	6		1							
Ru	44	2	2	6	2	6	10	2	6	7		1							
Rh	45	2	2	6	2	6	10	2	6	8		1							
Pd	46	2	2	6	2	6	10	2	6	10									
Ag	47	2	2	6	2	6	10	2	6	10		1							
Cd	48	2	2	6	2	6	10	2	6	10		2							
In	49	2	2	6	2	6	10	2	6	10		2	1						
Sn	50	2	2	6	2	6	10	2	6	10		2	2						
Sb	51	2	2	6	2	6	10	2	6	10		2	3						
Te	52	2	2	6	2	6	10	2	6	10		2	4						
I	53	2	2	6	2	6	10	2	6	10		2	5						
Xe	54	2	2	6	2	6	10	2	6	10		2	6						

Element	Z	1s	2s	2p	3s	3p	3d	4s	4p	4d	4f	5s	5p	5d	5f	6s	6p	6d	7s
Cs	55	2	2	6	2	6	10	2	6	10		2	6			1			
Ba	56	2	2	6	2	6	10	2	6	10		2	6			2			
La	57	2	2	6	2	6	10	2	6	10		2	6	1		2			
Ce	58	2	2	6	2	6	10	2	6	10	2	2	6			2			
Pr	59	2	2	6	2	6	10	2	6	10	3	2	6			2			
Nd	60	2	2	6	2	6	10	2	6	10	4	2	6			2			
Pm	61	2	2	6	2	6	10	2	6	10	5	2	6			2			
Sm	62	2	2	6	2	6	10	2	6	10	6	2	6			2			
Eu	63	2	2	6	2	6	10	2	6	10	7	2	6			2			
Gd	64	2	2	6	2	6	10	2	6	10	7	2	6	1		2			
Tb	65	2	2	6	2	6	10	2	6	10	9	2	6			2			
Dy	66	2	2	6	2	6	10	2	6	10	10	2	6			2			
Ho	67	2	2	6	2	6	10	2	6	10	11	2	6			2			
Er	68	2	2	6	2	6	10	2	6	10	12	2	6			2			
Tm	69	2	2	6	2	6	10	2	6	10	13	2	6			2			
Yb	70	2	2	6	2	6	10	2	6	10	14	2	6			2			
Lu	71	2	2	6	2	6	10	2	6	10	14	2	6	1		2			
Hf	72	2	2	6	2	6	10	2	6	10	14	2	6	2		2			
Ta	73	2	2	6	2	6	10	2	6	10	14	2	6	3		2			
W	74	2	2	6	2	6	10	2	6	10	14	2	6	4		2			
Re	75	2	2	6	2	6	10	2	6	10	14	2	6	5		2			
Os	76	2	2	6	2	6	10	2	6	10	14	2	6	6		2			
Ir	77	2	2	6	2	6	10	2	6	10	14	2	6	7		2			
Pt	78	2	2	6	2	6	10	2	6	10	14	2	6	9		1			
Au	79	2	2	6	2	6	10	2	6	10	14	2	6	10		1			
Hg	80	2	2	6	2	6	10	2	6	10	14	2	6	10		2			
Tl	81	2	2	6	2	6	10	2	6	10	14	2	6	10		2	1		
Pb	82	2	2	6	2	6	10	2	6	10	14	2	6	10		2	2		
Bi	83	2	2	6	2	6	10	2	6	10	14	2	6	10		2	3		
Po	84	2	2	6	2	6	10	2	6	10	14	2	6	10		2	4		
At	85	2	2	6	2	6	10	2	6	10	14	2	6	10		2	5		
Rn	86	2	2	6	2	6	10	2	6	10	14	2	6	10		2	6		
Fr	87	2	2	6	2	6	10	2	6	10	14	2	6	10		2	6		1
Ra	88	2	2	6	2	6	10	2	6	10	14	2	6	10		2	6		2
Ac	89	2	2	6	2	6	10	2	6	10	14	2	6	10		2	6	1	2
Th	90	2	2	6	2	6	10	2	6	10	14	2	6	10		2	6	2	2
Pa	91	2	2	6	2	6	10	2	6	10	14	2	6	10	2	2	6	1	2
U	92	2	2	6	2	6	10	2	6	10	14	2	6	10	3	2	6	1	2
Np	93	2	2	6	2	6	10	2	6	10	14	2	6	10	4	2	6	1	2
Pu	94	2	2	6	2	6	10	2	6	10	14	2	6	10	6	2	6		2
Am	95	2	2	6	2	6	10	2	6	10	14	2	6	10	7	2	6		2
Cm	96	2	2	6	2	6	10	2	6	10	14	2	6	10	7	2	6	1	2
Bk	97	2	2	6	2	6	10	2	6	10	14	2	6	10	8	2	6	1	2
Cf	98	2	2	6	2	6	10	2	6	10	14	2	6	10	10	2	6		2
Es	99	2	2	6	2	6	10	2	6	10	14	2	6	10	11	2	6		2
Fm	100	2	2	6	2	6	10	2	6	10	14	2	6	10	12	2	6		2
Md	101	2	2	6	2	6	10	2	6	10	14	2	6	10	13	2	6		2
No	102	2	2	6	2	6	10	2	6	10	14	2	6	10	14	2	6		2
Lr	103	2	2	6	2	6	10	2	6	10	14	2	6	10	14	2	6	1	2

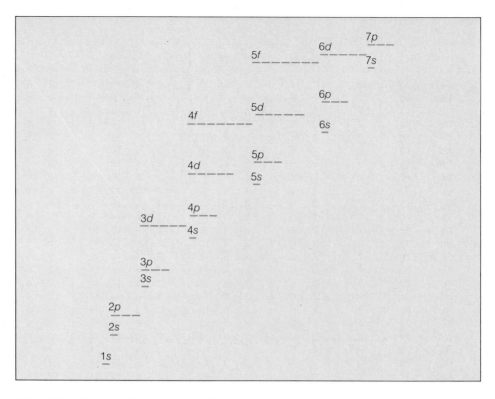

Figure 6.18 Aufbau order of atomic orbitals

The electron added in going from one element to the next in the aufbau procedure is called the **differentiating electron.** It makes the configuration of an atom different from that of the atom that precedes it. The differentiating electron is added in each step to the orbital of lowest energy available to it.

All the orbitals of a given subshell have equivalent energies. The energy of any one of the $3p$ orbitals, for example, is the same as the energy of either of the other two $3p$ orbitals. All five $3d$ orbitals are like in terms of energy. Orbitals that belong to different subshells of the same shell, however, have different energies. For a given value of n, the energies increase in the order $s < p < d < f$. In the $n = 3$ shell, for example, the $3s$ orbital has the lowest energy, a $3p$ orbital has an intermediate energy, and a $3d$ orbital has the highest energy. At times, the energies of orbitals from different shells overlap. In some atoms, for example, the $4s$ orbital has a lower energy than a $3d$ orbital.

There is no standard order of orbitals, based on energy, that pertains to all the elements. In the *hypothetical* aufbau process, the character of the atom changes as protons and neutrons are added to the nucleus and more and more electrons are introduced. Fortunately, the orbital energy order varies from element to element in a slow and regular manner. As a result, the aufbau order shown in Figure 6.18 can be derived.

This order pertains *only* to the orbital position that the differentiating electron takes in the aufbau process. Electronic configurations can be derived from the diagram shown in Figure 6.18 by successively filling the orbitals, starting at the bottom of the chart and proceeding upward. Remember that there are three orbitals in a p sublevel, five in a d, and seven in an f. A given sublevel is filled before electrons are added to the next sublevel.

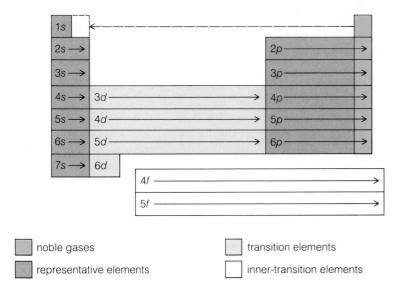

| noble gases | transition elements |
| representative elements | inner-transition elements |

Figure 6.19 Type of differentiating electron related to position of the element in the periodic table

The periodic table can be used to derive electronic configurations. In Figure 6.19, the type of differentiating electron is related to the position of the element in the periodic chart. Notice that the table can be divided into an "s block," a "p block," a "d block," and an "f block." The principal quantum number of the differentiating electron is equal to the period number for the "s block" and "p block" elements, the period number minus 1 for the "d block" elements, and the period number minus 2 for the "f block" elements. Use a periodic table (such as the one inside the front cover) to follow the discussion as we derive the electronic configurations of the elements.

The first period consists of only two elements—hydrogen and helium—both of which are "s block" elements. The configuration of hydrogen is $1s^1$, and that of helium is $1s^2$.

The second period begins with lithium ($1s^2 2s^1$) and beryllium ($1s^2 2s^2$), for which electrons are added to the $2s$ orbital. For the six elements that complete this period—boron ($1s^2 2s^2 2p^1$) to the noble gas neon ($1s^2 2s^2 2p^6$)—electrons are gradually added to the three $2p$ orbitals.

The pattern of the second period is repeated in the third. The two "s block" elements are sodium ($1s^2 2s^2 2p^6 3s^1$) and magnesium ($1s^2 2s^2 2p^6 3s^2$). The six "p block" elements go from aluminum ($1s^2 2s^2 2p^6 3s^2 3p^1$) to the noble gas argon ($1s^2 2s^2 2p^6 3s^2 3p^6$).

In the discussion of the configurations of the remaining elements, only the outer orbitals will be indicated. The first overlap of orbital energies is observed with potassium ($Z = 19$), the first element of the fourth period. The configuration of potassium is . . . $3s^2 3p^6 4s^1$, despite the fact that $3d$ orbitals are vacant. In like manner, calcium ($Z = 20$) has the configuration . . . $3s^2 3p^6 4s^2$. Notice that potassium and calcium are "s block" elements.

With the next element, scandium ($Z = 21$), the $3rd$ subshells comes into use (. . . $3s^2 3p^6 3d^1 4s^2$). In the series from scandium to zinc, the $3d$ subshell is gradually filled. The configuration of zinc ($Z = 30$) is . . . $3s^2 3p^6 3d^{10} 4s^2$. These "d

block" elements are called transition elements. They are said to exhibit inner building, since the last electron is added to the shell ($n = 3$) next to the outermost shell ($n = 4$). The elements from number 21 to 30, which belong to B families in the table that we use, are said to form the first transition series. With element 31, gallium ($\ldots 3s^2\, 3p^6\, 3d^{10}\, 4s^2\, 4p^1$), the $4p$ subshell begins to be filled. The fourth period ends with krypton ($Z = 36, \ldots 3s^2\, 3p^6\, 3d^{10}\, 4s^2\, 4p^6$).

The fifth period starts with rubidium ($Z = 37, \ldots 4s^2\, 4p^6\, 5s^1$) and strontium ($Z = 38, \ldots 4s^2\, 4p^6\, 5s^2$), with electrons being added to the $5s$ subshell even though both $4d$ and $4f$ orbitals are vacant. Notice that these two elements are "s block" elements. A second transition series follows, in which electrons are added to the $4d$ subshell. It starts with yttrium ($Z = 39, \ldots 4s^2\, 4p^6\, 4d^1\, 5s^2$) and ends with cadmium ($Z = 48, \ldots 4s^2\, 4p^6\, 4d^{10}\, 5s^2$). The fifth period ends with the series from indium to xenon, with electrons being added to the $5p$ subshell. Xenon ($Z = 54$) has the configuration $\ldots 4s^2\, 4p^6\, 4d^{10}\, 5s^2\, 5p^6$. The $4f$ subshell is still vacant at the end of this period.

The sixth period is far more complicated as far as orbital order is concerned. The first two elements, cesium ($Z = 55, \ldots 4d^{10}\, 5s^2\, 5p^6\, 6s^1$) and barium ($Z = 56, \ldots 4d^{10}\, 5s^2\, 5p^6\, 6s^2$) have electrons in the $6s$ subshell. Here, we come upon a complication of the aufbau procedure. The $4f$ and $5d$ subshells are close in energy. The next electron (for lanthanum, $Z = 57$) is added to the $5d$ subshell (thus lanthanum is a transition element), but the next electron (for cerium, $Z = 58$) is added to the $4f$ subshell, and the electron added for lanthanum falls back into the $4f$ subshell. For La, the configuration is $\ldots 4d^{10}\, 4f^0\, 5s^2\, 5p^6\, 5d^1\, 6s^2$. For Ce, the configuration is $\ldots 4d^{10}\, 4f^2\, 5s^2\, 5p^6\, 5d^0\, 6s^2$. For the elements 58 to 70 (cerium to ytterbium), electrons are added to the $4f$ subshell.

These elements are called inner-transition elements. For elements of this type, electron addition occurs in the third subshell ($4f$) from the outermost subshell ($6s$). After the $4f$ subshell has been filled, the next electron is added to the $5d$ subshell. Thus, for lutetium ($Z = 71$) the configuration is $\ldots 4d^{10}\, 4f^{14}\, 5s^2\, 5p^6\, 5d^1\, 6s^2$. This third transition series is completed and the $5d$ subshell filled with element 80, mercury ($\ldots 4d^{10}\, 4f^{14}\, 5s^2\, 5p^6\, 5d^{10}\, 6s^2$). The period ends with the filling of the $6p$ sublevel in elements 81 to 86.

The seventh period is incomplete and includes many elements that do not occur in nature but have been made by nuclear reactions. In general, this period follows the pattern established by the sixth period. Elements 87 and 88 have electrons added to the $7s$ sublevel, for element 89 and electron is added to the $6d$ sublevel, elements 90 to 103 constitute a second inner-transition series and exhibit an electron buildup of the $5f$ sublevel, and the transition elements 104, 105, and 106 have electrons added to the $6d$ sublevel. The actual electronic configurations of some seventh-period atoms deviate slightly from the configurations predicted by the aufbau method (Table 6.6).

To determine the electronic configuration of any element, we start with hydrogen, and on the basis of the periodic table account for every electron added until the desired element is reached. The method is illustrated by the following examples.

Example 6.6

Write the electronic notation for the electronic configuration of tin (Sn, $Z = 50$).

Solution

We trace our way through the periodic table, adding terms so as to account for the electron added to each element up to $Z = 50$ (tin). Check the method by using a periodic table:

first period: $1s^2$ (which takes us up to $_2$He)
second period: $2s^2\, 2p^6$ (which takes us up to $_{10}$Ne)
third period: $3s^2\, 3p^6$ (which takes us up to $_{18}$Ar)
fourth period: $4s^2\, 3d^{10}\, 4p^6$ (which takes us up to $_{36}$Kr)
fifth period: $5s^2\, 4d^{10}\, 5p^2$ (which takes us up to $_{50}$Sn)

The terms should be rearranged to give the notation in proper sequence:

$1s^2\, 2s^2\, 2p^6\, 3s^2\, 3p^6\, 3d^{10}\, 4s^2\, 4p^6\, 4d^{10}\, 5s^2\, 5p^2$

Example 6.7

Write the electronic notation for the electronic configuration of neodymium (Nd, $Z = 60$).

Solution

first period: $1s^2$
second period: $2s^2\, 2p^6$
third period: $3s^2\, 3p^6$
fourth period: $4s^2\, 3d^{10}\, 4p^6$
fifth period: $5s^2\, 4d^{10}\, 5p^6$
sixth period: $6s^2\, 4f^4$

Upon rearrangement, the notation is

$1s^2\, 2s^2\, 2p^6\, 3s^2\, 3p^6 3d^{10}\, 4s^2\, 4p^6\, 4d^{10}\, 4f^4\, 5s^2\, 5p^6\, 6s^2$

The notations for lanthanum ($Z = 57$) and the lanthanides ($Z = 58$ to 71) pose a problem. The notations for $_{57}$La ends ... $4f^0\, 5s^2\, 5p^6\, 5d^1\, 6s^2$. One might expect that the notation for the next element, $_{58}$Ce, would end ... $4f^1\, 5s^2\, 5p^6\, 5d^1\, 6s^2$. Instead, the differentiating $5d$ electron added for $_{57}$La falls back into the $4f$ sub-shell, so that the notation for $_{58}$Ce ends ... $4f^2\, 5s^2\, 5p^6\, 5d^0\, 6s^2$. Subsequent notations end ... $4f^3\, 5s^2\, 5p^6\, 5d^0\, 6s^2$ (for $_{59}$Pr), ... $4f^4\, 5s^2\, 5p^6\, 5d^0\, 6s^2$ (for $_{60}$Nd), and so on.

Example 6.8

Write the electronic notation for the electronic configuration of tungsten (W, $Z = 74$).

Solution

first period: $1s^2$
second period: $2s^2\, 2p^6$

third period: $3s^2\ 3p^6$
fourth period: $4s^2\ 3d^{10}\ 4p^6$
fifth period: $5s^2\ 4d^{10}\ 5p^6$
sixth period: $6s^2\ 4f^{14}\ 5d^4$

Upon rearrangement, the notation is

$$1s^2\ 2s^2\ 2p^6\ 3s^2\ 3p^6\ 3d^{10}\ 4s^2\ 4p^6\ 4d^{10}\ 4f^{14}\ 5s^2\ 5p^6\ 5d^4\ 6s^2$$

The aufbau order cannot be used to interpret processes that involve the loss of electrons (ionizations). The configuration of the iron atom, Fe, is $1s^2\ 2s^2\ 2p^6\ 3s^2$ $3p^6\ 3d^6\ 4s^2$, and that of the Fe^{2+} ion is $1s^2\ 2s^2\ 2p^6\ 3s^2\ 3p^6\ 3d^6$. Ionization, therefore results in the loss of the $4s$ electrons even though $3d$ electrons are the last added by the aufbau method. The Fe atom has 26 protons in the nucleus and 26 electrons. The Fe^{2+} ion has 26 protons in the nucleus but only 24 electrons. The order of orbital energies is different in the atom and in the ion. In general, the first electrons lost in an ionization are those with the highest values of n and l. Electronic notations, therefore, should be written by increasing value of n and not by the hypothetical order of filling.

Sometimes electronic notations are written in an abbreviated form in which the symbol for a noble gas, enclosed in brackets, is used to represent the configuration of an inner core of electrons. Thus, for example, the configuration of

$$_{53}I \qquad \text{is shown as} \qquad [Kr]\ 4d^{10}\ 5s^2\ 5p^5$$

Here, the symbol $[Kr]$ stands for the electronic configuration of Kr, which accounts for the first 36 electrons of I: $1s^2\ 2s^2\ 2p^6\ 3s^2\ 3p^6\ 3d^{10}\ 4s^2\ 4p^6$. In like manner:

$_3$Li	is shown as	$[He]\ 2s^1$	instead of	$1s^2\ 2s^1$
$_{12}$Mg	is shown as	$[Ne]\ 3s^2$	instead of	$1s^2\ 2s^2\ 2p^6\ 3s^2$
$_{26}$Fe	is shown as	$[Ar]\ 3d^6\ 4s^2$	instead of	$1s^2\ 2s^2\ 2p^6\ 3s^2\ 3p^6\ 3d^6\ 4s^2$

6.8 Half-filled and Filled Subshells

In Table 6.6 the correct electronic configurations of the elements are listed. The configurations predicted by the aufbau procedure are confirmed by spectral and magnetic studies for most elements. A few, however, exhibit slight variations from the standard pattern. In certain instances, it is possible to explain these variations on the basis of the stability of a filled or half-filled subshell.

The predicted configuration for the $3d$ and $4s$ subshells in the chromium atom $(Z, 24)$ is $3d^4\ 4s^2$, whereas the experimentally derived configuration is $3d^5\ 4s^1$. Presumably the stability gained by having one unpaired electron in each of the five $3d$ orbitals (a half-filled subshell) accounts for the fact that the $3d^5\ 4s^1$ config-uration is the one observed. The existence of a half-filled subshell also accounts for the fact that the configuration for the $4d$ and $5s$ subshells of molybdenum $(Z, 42)$, which is in the same group as chromium, is $4d^5\ 5s^1$ rather than the predicted $4d^4\ 5s^2$.

The stability of a half-filled $4f$ subshell is evident in the configuration of gadolinium (Z, 64). The configuration predicted by the aufbau method for this inner-transition elements ends ... $4f^8\ 5s^2\ 5p^6\ 5d^0\ 6s^2$. The accepted structure of gadolinium, however, ends ... $4f^7\ 5s^2\ 5p^6\ 5d^1\ 6s^2$, which contains a half-filled $4f$ subshell and one $5d$ electron.

For copper (Z, 29), the predicted configuration for the last two subshells is $3d^9\ 4s^2$, whereas the experimentally derived structure is $3d^{10}\ 4s^1$. The explanation for this deviation lies in the stability of the $3d^{10}\ 4s^1$ configuration that results from the completed $3d$ subshell. Silver (Z, 47) and gold (Z, 79), which are in the same group as copper, also have configurations with completely filled d subshells instead of the $(n-1)d^9\ ns^2$ configurations predicted. In the case of palladium (Z, 46) two electrons are involved—the only case with a difference of more than one electron. The predicted configuration for the last two subshells of palladium is $4d^8\ 5s^2$; the observed configuration is $4d^{10}\ 5s^0$.

Half-filled and filled subshells also contribute to the stability of atoms in cases where the aufbau order is followed. Several examples are noted in Sections 7.2 and 7.3. The stability of the noble gases, however, is the most important example. The noble gases have configurations in which all subshells are filled. That these arrangements are very stable is shown by the low order of chemical reactivity of these elements.

Other types of deviations are observed, particularly among elements with high atomic numbers. For our purposes these exceptions are not important. In general, the chemistry of the elements is satisfactorily explained on the basis of the predicted configurations.

6.9 Types of Elements

The elements may be classified according to their electron configurations:

1. The noble gases. In the periodic table the noble gases are found at the end of each period in group 0. They are colorless monatomic gases, which are chemically unreactive, and diamagnetic. With the exception of helium (which has the configuration $1s^2$), all the noble gases have outer configurations of $ns^2\ np^6$, a very stable arrangement.

2. The representative elements. These elements are found in the A families of the periodic table that we use and include metals and nonmetals. They exhibit a wide range of chemical behavior and physical characteristics. Some of the elements are diamagnetic and some are paramagnetic. The compounds of these elements, however, are generally diamagnetic and colorless. All of their electronic shells are either complete or stable ($ns^2\ np^6$) except the outer shell, to which the last electron may be considered as having been added. This outer shell is termed the valence shell: electrons in it are valence electrons. The number of valence electrons for each atom is the same as the group number. The chemistry of these elements depends upon these valence electrons.

3. The transition elements. These elements are found in the B families of the periodic table that we use. They are characterized by inner building—the differentiating electron added by the aufbau procedure is an inner d electron. Electrons from the two outermost shells are used in chemical reactions. All of these elements are metals and most of them are paramagnetic and form highly colored, paramagnetic compounds.

4. The inner-transition elements. These elements are found at the bottom of the periodic table, but they belong to the sixth and seventh periods after the elements of group III B. The sixth-period series of 14 elements that follows lanthanum is called the lanthanide series. The seventh-period series that follows actinium is known as the actinide series. The differentiating electron in each atom is an f electron. It is added to the shell that is two shells in from the outermost shell. The outer three shells, therefore, may be involved in the chemistry of these elements. All inner-transition elements are metals. They are paramgnetic and their compounds are paramagnetic and colored.

Summary

All types of *electromagnetic radiation* have wave characteristics, may be described in terms of *wavelength* (λ) and *frequency* (v), and proceed through space at the same speed (the *speed of light*, c). These three quantities are related: $v = c/\lambda$. Electromagnetic radiation has a dual character—particle as well as wave. It can be considered to be absorbed or emitted in *quanta* (also called *photons*), which are definite quantities of energy. The energy of a quantum, E, is proportional to the frequency of the radiation; $E = hv$, where h is *Planck's constant*.

Light is emitted by gases or vapors of chemical substances when they are heated in an electric arc. A *line spectrum* results when a ray of this light is passed through a prism. A spectrum of this type consists of a limited number of colored lines, each corresponding to a different wavelength of light. The line spectrum of each chemical element is unique.

The *Bohr theory* for the electronic structure of the hydrogen atom arose from the study of the line spectrum of that element. According to Bohr, the energy of the electron of the hydrogen atom is quantized and the electron can exist only in certain orbits or energy shells that surround the nucleus. Energy is radiated when the electron of an atom falls from one orbit to another of lower energy. The photon emitted (which is responsible for one line of the line spectrum) has an energy corresponding to the energy difference between the two orbits.

In the same way that light has both a wave and a particle character, the electron has a dual nature. Its wavelength (λ) is given by the *de Broglie relation*: $\lambda = h/mv$, where h is Planck's constant and mv is the *momentum* of the electron (mass times velocity).

Heisenberg's uncertainty principle states that it is impossible to determine simultaneously the exact position and the exact momentum of a body as small as the electron. In light of this principle, any attempt to extend Bohr's approach is futile. Instead, the *Schrödinger equation* is used to describe electronic configuration in terms of the wave character of electrons.

According to this model, electrons are described in terms of three-dimensional waves. These waves correspond to definite energy states (*orbitals*), regions where there is a high probability of finding the electrons. Each electron is described by four quantum numbers:

1. The *principal quantum number*, n, identifies the shell or level in which the electron is found. The value of n is a positive integer: 1, 2, 3. . . .

2. The *subsidiary quantum number*, l, identifies the subshell and the shape of the orbital for the electron. In a given shell (indicated by n), l may have all the integral values in the series 0, 1, 2, 3, . . . $(n-1)$. The designations s, p, d, f. . . are sometimes used for $l = 0, 1, 2, 3$ . . . respectively.

3. The *magnetic orbital quantum number*, m_l, identifies the orientation of the orbital within the subshell. For a given value of l, m_l may have all the integral values from $+l$ to $-l$ (including 0). The number of m_l values for each l value is the number of orbitals in that subshell.

4. The *magnetic spin quantum number*, m_s, refers to the relative spin that the electron may have ($+\frac{1}{2}$ or $-\frac{1}{2}$). Each orbital can hold two electrons (which are said to be paired) with opposed spins.

Pauli's exclusion principle states that no two electrons in the same atom may have identical sets of all four quantum numbers.

The electronic configuration of an atom may be derived by an *aufbau method*, in which electrons are successively added on the basis of orbital energies until the desired configuration is obtained. The distribution of electrons among the orbitals of a subshell follows *Hund's rule*, which states that the electrons are distributed in a way that gives the maximum number of unpaired electrons with parallel spins. Substances with unpaired electrons are *paramagnetic* (drawn into a magnetic field). Substances in which all electrons are paired are *diamagnetic* (repelled by a magnetic field).

By studying the X-ray spectra of elements, *Moseley* was able to establish the significance of atomic number. The modern periodic classification is based on this work. The periodic table can be used to derive electronic configurations of the elements, since the arrangement of the periodic table is based on the chemical properties of the elements, which in turn depend upon their electronic structures.

Key Terms

Some of the more important terms introduced in this chapter are listed below. Definitions for terms not included in this list may be located in the text by use of the index.

Aufbau method (Section 6.7) A method of deriving the electronic configurations of atoms in which electrons are successively added (on the basis of orbital energies) until the desired configuration is obtained.

Diamagnetic substance (Section 6.6) A substance that is repelled by a magnetic field. In such a substance all electrons are paired.

Electromagnetic radiation (Section 6.1) Radiant energy that travels at a characteristic speed (the speed of light, c) and that may be interpreted in terms of waves or quanta.

Electronic configuration (Section 6.6) The manner in which electrons are arranged in an atom; may be indicated by an orbital diagram or by an electronic notation (see Table 6.3)

Energy shell, energy level (Sections 6.2 and 6.5) A group of atomic orbitals that have the same value of n, the principal quantum number.

Excited state (Section 6.2) A state of an atom in which the electronic configuration gives the atom a higher energy than the ground state.

Exclusion principle of Pauli (Section 6.5) No two electrons in the same atom may have identical sets of all four quantum numbers.

Frequency, v (Section 6.1) The number of waves of electromagnetic radiation that pass a given spot in 1 s; $v = c/\lambda$.

Ground state (Section 6.2) The state of lowest possible energy of an atom in which all the electrons in the atom are as close to the nucleus as possible.

Hund's rule (Section 6.6) In the ground state of an atom, electrons are distributed among the orbitals of a subshell in a way that gives the maximum number of unpaired electrons with parallel spins.

Inner-transition element (Sections 6.7 and 6.9) The lanthanide and actinide elements found at the bottom of the periodic table. In atoms of these elements the differentiating electron added by the aufbau method is an f electron added to the shell that is two shells in from the outermost shell.

Magnetic orbital quantum number, m_l (Section 6.5) A quantum number that indicates the orientation of the orbital of the electron to which the value pertains. For a given value of l, m_l may have all the integral values from $+l$ to $-l$ (including 0). The number of m_l values for each l value is the number of orbitals in that subshell.

Magnetic spin quantum number, m_s (Section 6.5) A quantum number that refers to the relative spin of the electron to which the value pertains. Each orbital may hold two electrons of opposed spin ($+\frac{1}{2}$ and $-\frac{1}{2}$).

Orbit (Section 6.2) In the Bohr theory, an allowed state of an electron, characterized by a value of n.

Orbital (Section 6.4) An energy state for an electron characterized by three quantum numbers: n, l, and m_l. A given orbital may hold two electrons with opposed spin.

Paramagnetic substance (Section 6.6) A substance that is drawn into a magnetic field. Such a substance contains unpaired electrons.

Photon (Section 6.1) A quantum of radiant energy.

Principal quantum number, n (Section 6.5) The quantum number that indicates the energy shell of the electron to which the value pertains. The values of n are positive integers: 1, 2, 3. . . .

Quantum (Section 6.1) A small, definite quantity of radiant energy. Planck's theory assumes that radiant energy is absorbed or emitted in these quanta. The energy of a quantum, E, is directly proportional to the frequency of the radiation, v; and the proportionality constant, h, is Planck's constant (6.6262×10^{-34} J $\cdot$ s).

Representative element (Section 6.9) An element that belongs to an A group in the periodic table that we use (the one found inside the front cover of this book). For these elements, the differentiating electron added by the aufbau method is an s or a p electron added to the outermost shell.

Spectrum (Section 6.2) A pattern of light produced by the dispersal of a light beam into its component wavelengths. Since it consists of all wavelengths, white light produces a **continuous spectrum**. Light emitted by a substance in an excited state, however, produces a **line spectrum**, in which only certain wavelengths appear.

Speed of light, c (Section 6.1) The speed at which the waves of all electromagnetic radiation travel in a vacuum: 2.9979×10^8 m/s.

Subshell (Section 6.5) A division of an electron shell characterized by a particular value of l. An electron shell may hold one or more subshells, and a given subshell may hold one or more orbitals. For the subshells, the designations s, p, d, f . . . are used for $l = 0$, 1, 2, 3 . . . respectively.

Subsidiary quantum number, l (Section 6.5) A quantum number that indicates the type of subshell and the shape of the orbital of the electron to which the value pertains. In a given shell (indicated by n), l may have all the integral values in the series 0, 1, 2, 3 . . . $(n - 1)$.

Transition element (Sections 6.7 and 6.9) An element found in a B group of the periodic table that we use (the one found inside the front cover of this book). For these elements, the differentiating electron added by the aufbau method is a d electron added to the shell that is next to the outermost shell.

Uncertainty principle (Section 6.4) It is impossible to determine, simultaneously, the exact position and the exact momentum (mass times velocity, mv) of an electron.

Valence electrons (Section 6.6) The electrons found in the outermost shell in the ground state of an atom of a representative element.

Wave function, ψ (Section 6.4) A solution to the Schrödinger wave equation; it describes an orbital. The square of the wave function, ψ^2, at any point is proportional to the electron charge density or the probability of finding the electron at that point.

Wavelength, λ (Section 6.1) The distance between two similar points on two successive waves of electromagnetic radiation.

Problems*

Electromagnetic Radiation

6.1 Which radiation is more energetic: **(a)** infrared radiation or microwaves, **(b)** yellow light or blue light, **(c)** a radio wave or a microwave?

6.2 Compare and contrast: **(a)** wavelength, frequency; **(b)** wavelength, amplitude; **(c)** quantum of light, photon of light; **(d)** speed of light, frequency of light.

6.3 What is the frequency and energy per quantum (in joules) of **(a)** a gamma ray with a wavelength of 0.600 pm, **(b)** a microwave with a wavelength of 2.50 cm?

6.4 What is the frequency and energy per quantum (in joules) of **(a)** yellow light with a wavelength of 585 nm, **(b)** ultraviolet rays with a wavelength of 32.5 nm?

6.5 What is the wavelength and energy per quantum (in joules) of **(a)** an infrared ray with a frequency of 5.71×10^{12}/s, **(b)** green light with a frequency of 5.71×10^{14}/s? Express each wavelength in the SI unit that will give the smallest number greater than 1.

6.6 What is the wavelength and energy per quantum (in joules) of **(a)** an X ray with a frequency of 3.00×10^{19}/s, **(b)** a radio wave with a frequency of 8.66×10^5/s? Express each wavelength in the SI unit that will give the smallest number greater than 1.

*6.7 The photoelectric effect consists of the emission of electrons from the surface of a metal when the metal is irradiated by light. A photon with a minimum energy of 3.97×10^{-19} J is necessary to eject an electron from barium. **(a)** What frequency and wavelength (in nanometers) correspond to this value? **(b)** Will blue light with a wavelength of 450 nm work?

*6.8 The photoelectric effect consists of the emission of electrons from the surface of a metal when the metal is irradiated by light. A photon with a minimum energy of 5.90×10^{-19} J is necessary to eject an electron from magnesium. **(a)** What frequency and wavelength (in nanometers) correspond to this value? **(b)** Will violet light with a wavelength of 400 nm work?

*6.9 The photoelectric effect consists of the emission of electrons from the surface of a metal when the metal is irradiated by light. An electron is ejected from the surface of gold when the gold is irradiated by photons that have wavelengths of 258 nm or less. **(a)** What is the minimum energy (in joules) required to eject an electron from gold? **(b)** If the photon used has a higher energy than that required to release an electron, the excess energy is imparted to the electron in the form of kinetic energy (energy of motion). If a photon with a wavelength of 200 nm is used, what is the kinetic energy (in joules) of the ejected electron?

*6.10 The photoelectric effect consists of the emission of electrons from the surface of a metal when the metal is irradiated by light. An electron is ejected from the surface of mercury when the mercury is irradiated by photons that have wavelengths of 273 nm or less. **(a)** What is the minimum energy (in joules) required to eject an electron from mercury? **(b)** If the photon used has a higher energy than that required to release an electron, the excess energy is imparted to the electron in the form of kinetic energy (energy of motion). If a photon with a wavelength of 160 nm is used, what is the kinetic energy (in joules) of the ejected electron?

6.11 Voyager I sent back pictures from Saturn from a distance of 8.0×10^6 miles. How many seconds did it take a signal to reach the earth? One mile is 1.609 km.

6.12 The star Arcturus is 36 light years away from earth. A light year is the distance that light travels in one year. How many kilometers is Arcturus from the earth?

6.13 How many photons are in a 1.00×10^{-16} J signal of red light with a wavelength of 750 nm?

6.14 How many photons are in a 1.00×10^{-16} J signal of violet light with a wavelength of 400 nm?

Atomic Spectra

6.15 According to Bohr, what is the source of the light emitted by a substance in a spectroscope?

6.16 Compare and constrast: **(a)** line spectrum, continuous spectrum; **(b)** ground state, excited state; **(c)** Balmer series of spectral lines, Lyman series of spectral lines;

---

* The more difficult problems are marked with asterisks. The appendix contains answers to color-keyed problem.

(d) energy of an electron in the K shell, energy of an electron in the O shell.

6.17 What is the wavelength (in nanometers) of the spectral line that corresponds to an electron transition from the $n = 6$ level to the $n = 1$ level in the hydrogen atom?

6.18 What is the wavelength (in nanometers) of the spectral line that corresponds to an electron transition from the $n = 5$ level to the $n = 3$ level in the hydrogen atom?

6.19 The spectral lines of hydrogen in the visible region correspond to electron transitions to the $n = 2$ level from higher levels. What is the electron transition that corresponds to the 434.0 nm spectral line?

6.20 The spectral lines of hydrogen in the visible region correspond to electron transitions to the $n = 2$ level from higher levels. What is the electron transition that corresponds to the 379.0 nm spectral line?

*6.21 The Pfund series of lines in the hydrogen spectrum occurs at wavelengths of from 2.279 μm to 7.459 μm. What are the corresponding electron transition?

*6.22 The Brackett series of lines in the hydrogen spectrum occurs at wavelengths of from 1.458 μm to 4.051 μm. What are the corresponding electron transitions?

Periodic Law

6.23 Mendeleev and Moseley each in his own time stated that several elements remained to be discovered. On what basis did each make his prediction?

6.24 What change did Moseley make in Mendeleev's periodic law?

6.25 Moseley found that the frequency, v, of a characteristic line of the X-ray spectrum of an element is related to the atomic number, Z, of the element by the formula $\sqrt{v} = a(Z - b)$, where a is approximately $5.0 \times 10^7/\sqrt{s}$ and b is approximately 1.0. What is the atomic number of an element for which the corresponding line in the X-ray spectrum occurs at a wavelength of 0.83 nm? What is the element?

6.26 Moseley found that the frequency, v, of a characteristic line of the X-ray spectrum of an element is related to the atomic number, Z, of the element by the formula $\sqrt{v} = a(Z - b)$, where a is approximately $5.0 \times 10^7/\sqrt{s}$ and b is approximately 1.0. What is the atomic number of an element for which the corresponding line in the X-ray spectrum occurs at a wavelength of 0.15 nm? What is the element?

6.27 What is the wavelength of the line in the X-ray spectrum of $_{30}Zn$ that conforms to the formula given in Problem 6.25?

6.28 What is the wavelength of the line in the X-ray spectrum of $_{50}Sn$ that conforms to the formula given in Problem 6.26?

Quantum Numbers

6.29 What is the de Broglie wavelength (in nanometers) associated with a H_2 molecule (mass, 3.35×10^{-24} g) that has a velocity of 2.45×10^3 m/s?

6.30 Compare the de Broglie wavelengths (in nanometers) of **(a)** an electron (mass, 9.11×10^{-28} g) and **(b)** a proton (mass, 1.67×10^{-24} g), each moving at 1.00% the speed of light.

6.31 If the de Broglie wavelength of an electron (mass, 9.11×10^{-28} g) is 0.100 nm, at what velocity is the electron moving?

6.32 If the de Broglie wavelength of a neutron (mass, 1.67×10^{-24} g) is 0.100 nm, at what velocity is the neutron moving?

6.33 Use Equation 6.13 to find **(a)** the uncertainty in the velocity of a 1.00 g particle if the uncertainty in the position of particle is 0.0100 nm, and **(b)** the uncertainty in the position of a proton (mass, 1.67×10^{-24} g) if the uncertainty in the velocity of the proton is 1.00 m/s.

6.34 Use Equation 6.13 to find **(a)** the uncertainty in the velocity of a neutron (mass, 1.67×10^{-24} g) if the uncertainty in the position of the particle is 0.0100 nm, and **(b)** the uncertainty in the position of a rifle bullet (mass, 1.90 g) if the uncertainty in the velocity of the bullet is 1.00 m/s.

6.35 List the four quantum numbers, tell what each identifies, and state the values that each may assume.

6.36 Describe the $n = 4$ level in terms of subshells, orbitals, and electrons.

6.37 Give the values for all four quantum numbers for each electron in the ground state of the nitrogen atom. Use positive values of m_l and m_s first.

6.38 Give the values for all four quantum numbers for each electron in the ground state of the sodium atom. Use positive values of m_l and m_s first.

6.39 Each electron in an atom may be characterized by a set of four quantum numbers. For each of the following parts, tell how many different sets of quantum numbers are possible, such that each set contains all the values listed: **(a)** $n = 4$; **(b)** $n = 2$, $l = 2$; **(c)** $n = 2$, $l = 0$; **(d)** $n = 4$, $l = 2$, $m_l = +3$; **(e)** $n = 4$, $l = 3$, $m_l = -2$; **(f)** $n = 3$, $l = 1$, $m_l = 0$; **(g)** $n = 3$, $l = 1$.

6.40 Each electron in an atom may be characterized by a set of four quantum numbers. For each of the following parts, tell how many different sets of quantum numbers are possible, such that each set contains all the values listed: **(a)** $n = 3$; **(b)** $n = 4$, $l = 3$; **(c)** $n = 3$, $l = 4$; **(d)** $n = 4$, $l = 2$, $m_l = 0$; **(e)** $n = 1$, $l = 0$, **(f)** $n = 3$, $l = 0$, $m_l = +1$; **(g)** $n = 2$, $l = 1$, $m_l = -1$.

6.41 In the ground state of $_{33}As$: **(a)** how many electrons have $l = 1$ as one of their quantum numbers? **(b)** how many electrons have $m_l = 0$ as one of their quantum numbers? **(c)** how many electrons have $m_l = -1$ as one of their quantum numbers?

6.42 In the ground state of $_{56}Ba$: **(a)** how many electrons have $l = 0$ as one of their quantum numbers? **(b)** how many electrons have $m_l = +2$ as one of their quantum numbers? **(c)** how many electrons have $l = 2$ as one of their quantum numbers?

Electronic Configurations

6.43 Give the orbital diagram for the electronic configuration of $_{28}Ni$ and the corresponding electronic notation by subshells.

6.44 Give the orbital diagram for the electronic configuration of $_{34}Se$ and the corresponding electronic notation by subshells.

6.45 Identify the atoms that have the following ground-state electronic configurations in their outer shell or shells: **(a)** $3s^2\,3p^5$, **(b)** $3s^2\,3p^6 3d^5\,4s^1$, **(c)** $4s^2\,4p^6\,4d^{10}\,4f^5\,5s^2\,5p^6\,6s^2$, **(d)** $3s^2\,3p^6\,4s^1$, **(e)** $4s^2\,4p^6$.

6.46 Identify the atoms that have the following ground-state electronic configurations in their outer shell or shells: **(a)** $3s^2\,3p^6\,3d^3\,4s^2$, **(b)** $4s^2\,4p^3$, **(c)** $5s^2\,5p^6$, **(d)** $4s^2\,4p^6\,4d^{10}\,4f^6\,5s^2\,5p^6\,6s^2$, **(e)** $4s^2\,4p^6\,5s^2$.

6.47 State the number of unpaired electrons in each of the atoms given in Problem 6.45. Which atoms are paramagnetic?

6.48 State the number of unpaired electrons in each of the atoms given in Problem 6.46. Which atoms are paramagnetic?

6.49 Write the notations by subshells for the ground-state electronic configurations of the following atoms: **(a)** $_{56}Ba$, **(b)** $_{82}Pb$, **(c)** $_{39}Y$, **(d)** $_{54}Xe$, **(e)** $_{70}Yb$, **(f)** $_{52}Te$.

6.50 Write the notations by subshells for the ground-state electronic configurations of the following atoms: **(a)** $_{37}Rb$, **(b)** $_{51}Sb$, **(c)** $_{25}Mn$, **(d)** $_{60}Nd$, **(e)** $_{53}I$, **(f)** $_{79}Au$.

6.51 State the number of unpaired electrons in each of the atoms listed in Problem 6.49. Which atoms are paramagnetic?

6.52 State the number of unpaired electrons in each of the atoms listed in Problem 6.50. Which atoms are paramagnetic?

6.53 Classify each of the following elements as a noble gas, a representative element, a transition element, or an inner-transition element. Also state whether the element is a metal or a nonmetal: **(a)** potassium, **(b)** phosphorus, **(c)** promethium, **(d)** platinum, **(e)** krypton.

6.54 Classify each of the following elements as a noble gas, a representative element, a transition element, or an inner-transition element. Also state whether the element is a metal or a nonmetal: **(a)** argon, **(b)** barium **(c)** cobalt, **(d)** dysprosium, **(e)** einsteinium.

6.55 **(a)** List the elements that have half-filled $4p$ subshells. **(b)** List the metals in the fourth period that have no unpaired electrons. **(c)** List the nonmetals in the second period that have one unpaired electron. **(d)** List the elements in the fourth period that have half-filled s subshells.

6.56 **(a)** List the elements that have half-filled $3d$ subshells. **(b)** List the metals in the fourth period that have one unpaired electron. **(c)** List the nonmetals in the third period that have no unpaired electrons. **(d)** List the elements in the fifth period that have half-filled p subshells.

Unclassified Problems

6.57 The meter is defined as 1,650,763.73 wavelengths of the orange line in the spectrum of $_{36}^{86}Kr$. What is the wavelength (in nanometers) and frequency of this light?

6.58 A persistent line in the spectrum of neon occurs at a frequency of $4.683 \times 10^{14}/s$. What is the wavelength (in nanometers), energy per quantum (in joules), and color of this light?

6.59 A compound used in sunscreens, p-aminobenzoic acid (called PABA) absorbs ultraviolet radiation, with maximum absorption occurring at 265 nm. What is the corresponding frequency and energy per quantum (in joules)?

6.60 A speeding bullet has been timed at 320. m/s. **(a)** What wavelength (in meters) would be associated with a 200. pound man if he could move as fast as a speeding bullet? **(b)** If he could move faster than a speeding bullet, would his wavelength be longer or shorter than that calculated in the first part of this question? One pound is 453.6 g.

6.61 The diameter of the nucleus of the oxygen atom is approximately 6.6×10^{-15} m. The mass of a proton inside that nucleus is 1.7×10^{-27} kg. If the uncertainty in the position of the proton is equal to the diameter of the nucleus itself, what is the uncertainty in the velocity of the proton?

6.62 Moseley found that the frequency, v, of a characteristic line of the X-ray spectrum of an element is related to the atomic number, Z, of the element by the formula $\sqrt{v} = a(Z - b)$, where a is approximately $5.0 \times 10^7/\sqrt{s}$ and b is approximately 1.0. What is the atomic number of the element for which the corresponding line in the X-ray spectrum occurs at a wavelength of 0.18 nm? What is the element?

6.63 Examine the electronic configurations given in Table 6.5. List the elements of the first six periods that have configurations deviating from those predicted by the aufbau method. In which of these cases can the deviation be ascribed to the presence of a half-filled subshell? A filled subshell?

6.64 Compare the elements of a period and a group in terms of **(a)** electronic configuration, and **(b)** chemical properties.

6.65 Write the notations by subshells for the ground-state electronic configurations of **(a)** $_{18}Ar$, **(b)** $_{35}Br$, **(c)** $_{48}Cd$, **(d)** $_{66}Dy$, **(e)** $_{57}La$, **(f)** $_{37}Rb$.

*6.66 The amount of energy required to remove the most loosely held electron from an isolated atom in its ground state is called the first ionization energy of the element under consideration. **(a)** Calculate the frequency of the hydrogen spectral line that corresponds to an electron transition from $n = \infty$ to $n = 1$. **(b)** Calculate the energy of this transition (in joules). **(c)** What is the first ionization energy of hydrogen in kilojoules per mole?

PROPERTIES OF ATOMS AND THE IONIC BOND

Chemical bonds, which form when atoms combine, are the result of changes in electron distribution. There are three fundamental types of bonding:

1. Ionic bonding (Chapter 7) results when electrons are transferred from one type of atom to another. The atoms of one of the reacting elements lose electrons and become positively charged ions. The atoms of the other reactant gain electrons and become negatively charged ions. The electrostatic (plus-minus) attraction between the oppositely charged ions holds them together in a crystal structure.

2. In covalent bonding (Chapters 8 and 9) electrons are shared, not transferred. A single covalent bond consists of a pair of electrons shared by two atoms. Molecules are made up of atoms covalently bonded to each other.

3. Metallic bonding (Chapter 25) is found in metals and alloys. The metal atoms are arranged in a three-dimensional structure. The outer electrons of these atoms are free to move throughout the structure and are responsible for binding it together.

Ionic bonding is the principal topic of this chapter. The opening sections of the chapter are devoted to the consideration of several atomic properties that are important to the study of chemical bonding.

7.1 Atomic Sizes

How an atom reacts depends upon many factors. Nuclear charge and electron configuration are the most important. The effective size of the atom is also of importance. Determination of this size, however, is a problem. The wave theory predicts that beyond a region of high density, the electron cloud of an atom thins out gradually and ends only at infinity. We cannot isolate and measure a single atom.

It is possible, however, to measure in several ways the distance between the nuclei of two atoms that are bonded together. Atomic radii are derived from these bond distances.* The Cl—Cl bond distance in the Cl_2 molecule, for example, is 198 pm.[†] One-half of this value, 99 pm, is assumed to be the atomic radius of

---

* The bond distances of *single* covalent bonds are employed. See Section 8.1.

[†] Atomic dimensions were recorded in ångstrom units in the past (1 Å $= 10^{-10}$ m). In the International System, these dimensions are recorded in nanometers (1 nm $= 10^{-9}$ m) or picometers (1 pm $= 10^{-2}$ m). The Cl—Cl bond distance is

$$1.98 \text{ Å} = 0.198 \text{ nm} = 198 \text{ pm} = 1.98 \times 10^{-10} \text{ m}$$

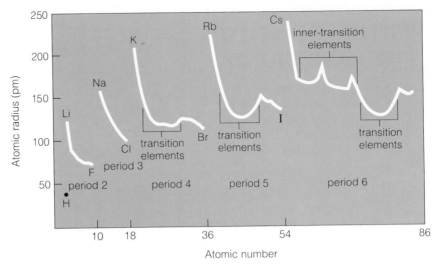

Figure 7.1 Atomic radii of the elements in picometers (1 pm = 10^{-12} m)

chlorine. In turn, the atomic radius of Cl (99 pm) can be substracted from the C—Cl bond distance (176 pm) to derive the atomic radius of C (77 pm). The effective size of an atom may vary slightly from bond to bond when the atom is bonded to other types of atoms. Such variations, however, are usually less than a few picometers. Data derived in this way, therefore, can be used in making comparisons.

Atomic radius is plotted against atomic number in Figure 7.1. Values for the noble gases are not available. Two trends should be noted:

1. Within a group of the periodic table, an increase in atomic radius is generally observed from top to bottom. Values for the group I A elements (Li, Na, K, Rb, and Cs) and the group VII A elements (F, Cl, Br, and I) are labeled in Figure 7.1. The increase in atomic radius within each group is clearly evident. As we move from one atom to the next down a group, an additional electron level is employed, and an increase in atomic size follows.

There is, however, also an increase in the number of protons in the nucleus. The resulting increase in nuclear charge is a factor that tends to decrease atomic size. The full nuclear charge, however, is shielded from the outer electrons by electrons that lie between them and the nucleus. The number of shielding electrons increases from atom to atom in a group along with the increase in nuclear charge. As a result, the effective nuclear charge that an outer electron experiences is not the full nuclear charge. The size, therefore, is largely determined by the value of the principal quantum number, *n*, of the outer electrons.

2. The atomic radii of the representative elements decrease across a period from left to right. Notice the portion of the curve in Figure 7.1 that pertains to the elements of the second period (from Li to F). As we move from one atom to the next, an electron is added to the *same level* (*n* = 2) and a proton is added to the nucleus. The increase in nuclear charge is not accompanied by an equivalent increase in shielding. The shielding of one electron in a level by another electron in the same level is not very effective. As a result, the effective nuclear charge experienced by an electron in the *n* = 2 level increases across the period, these electrons are drawn in toward the nucleus, and the atomic size decreases.

The transition elements and inner-transition elements show some variations from this general pattern. For the transition elements the differentiating electrons fill inner *d* orbitals. The effect of nuclear charge on outer, size-determining electrons is reduced by the shielding effect of inner electrons. For a transition series, therefore, the gradual buildup of electrons in inner *d* orbitals at first retards the rate of decrease in atomic radius and then, toward the end of the series when the inner *d* subshell nears completion, causes the radius to increase.

The general trends in atomic radii are summarized in Figure 7.2. As a rule, atoms of metals are larger than atoms of nonmetals. The atomic radii of most metals are larger than 120 pm. The atomic radii of most nonmetals are smaller than 120 pm.

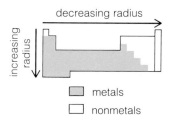

Figure 7.2 General trends in atomic radii in relation to the periodic classification

7.2 Ionization Energies

The amount of energy required to remove the most loosely held electron from an isolated atom in its ground state is called the **first ionization energy:**

$$A(g) \longrightarrow A^+(g) + e^-$$

The symbol A(g) stands for a gaseous atom of any element.

Recall the conventions regarding the assignment of signs to energy terms that were presented in Section 5.4:

1. When a system *absorbs* energy, the corresponding ΔH value is given a *positive* sign. A process of this type is called **endothermic.**

2. When a system *evolves* energy, the corresponding ΔH value is given a *negative* sign. A process of this type is called **exothermic.**

In the determination of ionization energies, energy is *used* to pull the electron away from the atom, where it is held by the attraction that the nucleus exerts. Since energy is absorbed, ionization energies have positive signs. The first ionization energy of sodium, for example, may be represented as follows:

$$Na(g) \longrightarrow Na^+(g) + e^- \quad \Delta H_{1st\ ion\ en} = +496\ kJ$$

Ionization energies are given in electron volts for individual electrons (eV/atom) or in kilojoules per mole (kJ/mol) for a mole of electrons.* An ionization energy expressed in kJ/mol refers to the energy required to remove 1 mol of electrons (6.022×10^{23} electrons) from 1 mol of atoms (6.022×10^{23} atoms). Ionization energy is plotted against atomic number in Figure 7.3. We can make the following generalizations:

1. In general, ionization energy *increases* across a period from left to right. Notice the portions of the curve that pertain to the second-period elements (from Li to

---

* One electron volt is the kinetic energy acquired by an electron in passing through a potential difference of 1 V in a vacuum:

$$1\ eV/atom = 1.6022 \times 10^{-19}\ J/atom = 96.487\ kJ/mol$$

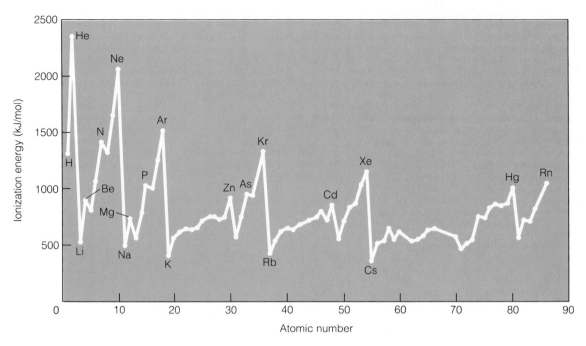

Figure 7.3 First ionization energies of the elements versus atomic number

Ne), the third-period elements (from Na to Ar), and so on. The ionization energy increases because the atoms become smaller and the effective nuclear charge increases. Removal of the electron becomes more and more difficult.

2. In general, ionization energy *decreases* within a group of representative elements from top to bottom. The elements of group I A (Li, Na, K, Rb, and Cs) and the elements of group 0 (He, Ne, Ar, Kr, Xe, and Rn) are labeled in Figure 7.3. As we go from atom to atom down a group, the nuclear charge increases, but the effect is largely canceled by the increase in the number of shielding electrons in the inner shells. The atoms become larger, and the electron that is removed comes from a higher and higher level. Removal of the electron becomes easier and ionization energy decreases.

The ionization energies of the transition elements do not increase across a period as rapidly as those of the representative elements. The ionization energies of the inner-transition elements remain almost constant. In these series, the differentiating electrons are being added to inner shells. The resulting increase in shielding accounts for the effects noted.

Atoms of metals tend to lose electrons and become positive ions in chemical reactions. Atoms of nonmetals do not usually behave in this way. Metals, therefore, are elements that have comparatively low ionization energies, and nonmetals are elements that have comparatively high ones. The ionization energies of most metals are below 1000 kJ/mol and of most nonmetals are above 1000 kJ/mol.

Several features of the curve in Figure 7.3 relate to certain electron configurations. Consider the points on the curve that pertain to

1. The noble gases (He, Ne, Ar, Kr, Xe and Rn), each of which has an $ns^2 \, np^6$ configuration in the outer shell (except for He, which has the configuration $1s^2$).

Table 7.1 Ionization energies of the third-period metals					
		Ionization Energies (kJ/mol)			
Metal	Group	First	Second	Third	Fourth
Na	I A	+496	+4,563	+6,913	+9,541
Mg	II A	+738	+1,450	+7,731	+10,545
Al	III A	+577	+1,816	+2,744	+11,575

2. The elements Be, Mg, Zn, Cd, and Hg, each of which has a *filled s subshell* in the outermost shell (ns^2).

3. The elements N, P, and As, each of which has a *half-filled p subshell* in the outermost shell ($ns^2\,np^3$).

The ionization energy of each of these elements (particularly the noble gases) is higher than the ionization energy of the element that follows it in the periodic table. These three types of electron configuration, therefore, may be said to be comparatively stable, since it is relatively difficult to remove an electron from each of them. In each case, it is easier to remove an electron from an atom of the next element.

We have so far discussed only *first* ionization energies. The **second ionization energy** of an element refers to the removal of *one* electron from a 1 + ion of the element:

$$A^+(g) \longrightarrow A^{2+}(g) + e^-$$

The second ionization energy of sodium, for example, may be represented as follows:

$$Na^+(g) \longrightarrow Na^{2+}(g) + e^- \quad \Delta H_{2nd\ ion\ en} = +4,563\ kJ$$

The *third* ionization energy pertains to the removal of *one* electron from a 2+ ion. Removing an electron, which has a negative charge, from an ion that has a positive charge becomes more and more difficult as the charge on the ion increases. Consequently, the ionization energies increase in the order: first < second < third, and so on. Since ionization energies above the third are extremely large for any element, ions with charges higher than 3 + seldom exist under ordinary conditions.

Ionization energies in kilojoules per mole for the first three elements of the third period are listed in Table 7.1. For each element, the ionization energies increase from the first to the fourth, as expected. Notice, however, that in each case there is a decided jump in the required energy after all the valence electrons have been removed. These points are marked in the table; the number of valence electrons equals the group number. After the valence electrons have been removed, it is necessary to break into the very stable $2s^2\,2p^6$ noble-gas arrangement of the shell beneath the valence shell to remove the next electron.

The trends in first ionization energy are summarized in Figure 7.4. Notice that the most reactive metals are found in the lower-left corner of the periodic table. This reactivity in terms of electron loss descrease as we move upward or to the right from this corner of the chart.

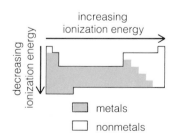

Figure 7.4 General trends in ionization energy in relation to the periodic classification

7.3 Electron Affinities

The energy change associated with the process in which an electron is added to a gaseous atom in its ground state is called a **first electron affinity**:

$$e^- + A(g) \longrightarrow A^-(g)$$

Notice that an electron affinity pertains to a process in which a *negative* ion is produced from a neutral atom (by electron *gain*). An ionization energy, on the other hand, pertains to a process in which a *positive* ion is produced from a neutral atom (by electron *loss*).

Some electron affinities listed in Table 7.2. Energy is usually (but not always) *evolved* by these processes. Most first electron affinities, therefore, have *negative* signs.* The first electron affinity of fluorine, for example, is -328 kJ/mol:

$$e^- + F(g) \longrightarrow F^-(g) \qquad \Delta H_{1\text{st elec af}} = -328 \text{ kJ}$$

Some of the values listed in Table 7.2 have positive signs. For example,

$$e^- + Ne(g) \longrightarrow Ne^-(g) \qquad \Delta H_{1\text{st elec af}} = +29 \text{ kJ}$$

A positive sign on an electron affinity value indicates that work must be done (energy absorbed) to force the atom under consideration to accept an additional electron. An electron approaching a neutral atom is attracted by the nucleus of the atom but repelled by the electrons of the atom. If the attraction is greater than the repulsion, energy is released when the negative ion forms. If the repulsion is greater than the attraction, energy is required to form the negative ion.

A small atom should have a greater tendency toward electron gain than a large atom. The added electron is, on the average, closer to the positively charged nucleus of a small atom. The atomic radii of the elements decrease and the effective nuclear charges increase across a period from left to right. We would expect the electron affinities of the corresponding elements to become larger and larger negative values. This trend is only roughly followed (see Table 7.2.).

Exceptions to this generalization should be noted. In the second period, for example, the value for beryllium (filled $2s$ subshell), nitrogen (half-filled $2p$ subshell), and neon (all subshells filled) are out of line. These elements have relatively stable electron configurations and do not accept additional electrons readily. Similar exceptions may be noted for corresponding elements of the other periods. In any period, the atom with the greatest tendency toward electron gain (largest negative value) is the group VII A element (F, Cl, Br, I, and At). The electron configuration of each of these elements is one electron short of a noble-gas configuration.

How do electron affinities vary from element to element within the same periodic group? No pattern that pertains to all the groups seems to exist. In the case of the group VII A elements, the electron affinity of fluorine appears to be out of line (see Table 7.2.). Based on atomic size, fluorine—the smallest atom of the

---

* In some sources, electron affinity is defined in terms of the *energy released* by these processes. In these sources, electron affinity values are given positive signs if they pertain to processes in which energy is liberated. This sign convention is the opposite of the one employed in this book. *Negative* signs are consistently used to indicated energy *released*, and *positive* signs are used to indicate energy *absorbed*.

Table 7.2 Electron affinities (kJ/mol)[a]

A. Addition of one electron

H −73									He (+21)
Li −60	Be (+240)		B −27	C −122	N 0	O −141	F −328		Ne (+29)
Na −53	Mg (+230)		Al −43	Si −134	P −72	S −200	Cl −349		Ar (+35)
K −48	Ca (+156)		Ga −29	Ge −116	As −77	Se −195	Br −325		Kr (+39)
Rb −47	Sr (+168)		In −29	Sn −121	Sb −101	Te −190	I −295		Xe (+41)
Cs −45	Ba (+52)		Tl −29	Pb −35	Bi −91	Po −183	At −270		Rn (+41)

B. Addition of two electrons

O	S
+704	+332

[a] Values in parentheses have been obtained by theoretical calculations. Other values are experimental measurements.

group—might be expected to liberate the most energy when an electron is added. In the case of a small atom, however, the added electron is not only strongly attracted by the nucleus, but it is also strongly repelled by the electrons already present in the atom. The electron charge of the valence electrons is more concentrated in a small shell than it is when the *same number* of electrons is placed in a larger shell. For fluorine, it is believed that this stronger repulsion offsets the stronger attraction brought about by small atomic size.

Some second electron affinities have been determined. These values refer to processes in which an electron is added to a negative ion. For example,

$$e^- + O^-(g) \longrightarrow O^{2-}(g) \qquad \Delta H_{\text{2nd elec af}} = +845 \text{ kJ}$$

Since a negative ion and an electron repel each other, energy is required, not released, by the process. All second electron affinities have positive signs.

Calculations for the production of a multicharged negative ion must take into consideration all pertinent electron affinities. The total effect for any such ion is always endothermic. In the formation of the O^{2-} ion from the O atom, for example, less energy is *released* by the first electron affinity,

$$e^- + O(g) \longrightarrow O^-(g) \qquad \Delta H_{\text{1st elec af}} = -141 \text{ kJ}$$

than is *required* by the second electron affinity,

$$e^- + O^-(g) \longrightarrow O^{2-}(g) \qquad \Delta H_{\text{2nd elec af}} = +845 \text{ kJ}$$

The overall process, therefore, is endothermic:

$$2e^- + O(g) \longrightarrow O^{2-}(g) \qquad \Delta H = +704 \text{ kJ}$$

The compound formed from Ca^{2+} and Cl^- ions, calcium chloride, has the formula $CaCl_2$. Two Cl^- ions are required for every Ca^{2+} ion. Calcium oxide, which is composed of Ca^{2+} and O^{2-} ions, has the formula CaO. The formula gives the *simplest* ratio of ions.

An atom of Al (a group III A metal) attains a noble-gas configuration by the loss of three electrons. The oxide of aluminum consists of Al^{3+} and O^{2-} ions. In order to balance the charge, two Al^{3+} ions (total charge, 6+) and three O^{2-} ions (total charge, 6−) must be indicated in the formula for the compound, Al_2O_3.

7.5 Lattice Energies

Ionic crystals, sodium chloride (NaCl) magnified × 17.
Runk/Schoenberger from Grant Heilman.

The enthalpy change associated with the condensation of gaseous positive and negative ions into a crystal is called a lattice energy. The lattice energy of sodium chloride, for example, is −788 kJ/mol:

$$Na^+(g) + Cl^-(g) \longrightarrow NaCl(s) \qquad \Delta H = -788 \text{ kJ}$$

Since energy is always *evolved* in these processes, all lattice energies have *negative* signs. The lattice energy (with the sign changed) of a given crystal may also be viewed as the amount of energy required to separate the ions of that crystal:

$$NaCl(s) \longrightarrow Na^+(g) + Cl^-(g) \qquad \Delta H = +788 \text{ kJ}$$

The importance of the lattice energy may be seen by using a method of analysis developed independently by Max Born and Fritz Haber in 1916. The Born-Haber cycle for the preparation of sodium chloride will serve as an example (see Figure 7.7).

The Born-Haber analysis is based on the law of Hess (Section 5.5), which states that the change in enthalpy for any chemical reaction is a constant, no matter whether the reaction is brought about in one step or in several steps. The enthalpy change for the preparation of *one mole* of NaCl(s) *in one step* from Na(s) and $Cl_2(g)$ is the enthalpy of formation of the compound (Section 5.6):

$$Na(s) + \tfrac{1}{2}Cl_2(g) \longrightarrow NaCl(s) \qquad \Delta H_f^\circ = -411 \text{ kJ} \qquad (7.1)$$

We can also *imagine* one mole of NaCl(s) to be prepared from Na(s) and $Cl_2(g)$ by a series of steps. The sum of the ΔH values for these steps must equal, according to the law of Hess, the enthalpy of formation of NaCl(s), which is the ΔH value for the single-step preparation. A list of this series of steps follows.

1. Crystalline sodium metal is sublimed into gaseous sodium atoms: 108 kJ of energy is *absorbed* per mole of Na (the enthalpy of sublimation):

$$Na(s) \longrightarrow Na(g) \qquad \Delta H_{subl} = +108 \text{ kJ} \qquad (7.2)$$

2. *One-half mole* of gaseous Cl_2 molecules is dissociated into *one mole* of gaseous Cl atoms; 122 kJ of energy is *absorbed* in the process. The enthalpy of dissociation of $Cl_2(g)$, also called the bond energy of the Cl—Cl bond (Section 5.7), is +243 kJ per mole of Cl_2. Since the dissociation of one mole of Cl_2 produces two moles of Cl atoms, and since only one mole of Cl atoms is needed to form one mole of NaCl, only one-half the dissociation energy is needed:

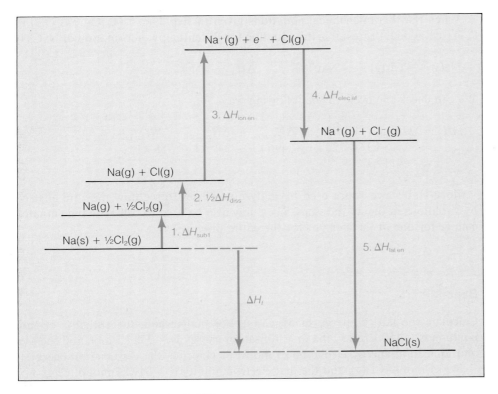

Figure 7.7 Born-Haber cycle for NaCl(s)

$$\tfrac{1}{2}Cl_2(g) \longrightarrow Cl(g) \qquad \tfrac{1}{2}\Delta H_{diss} = \tfrac{1}{2}(+243 \text{ kJ}) = +122 \text{ kJ} \qquad (7.3)$$

3. The gaseous sodium atoms are ionized into gaseous sodium ions. The amount of energy *required* is the first ionization energy of sodium (Section 7.2):

$$Na(g) \longrightarrow Na^+(g) + e^- \qquad \Delta H_{ion\ en} = +496 \text{ kJ} \qquad (7.4)$$

4. Electrons are added to the gaseous chlorine atoms to produce gaseous chloride ions. The enthaply change per mole of Cl(g) is the first electron affinity of chlorine (Section 7.3). Energy is *liberated:*

$$Cl(g) + e^- \longrightarrow Cl^-(g) \qquad \Delta H_{elec\ af} = -349 \text{ kJ} \qquad (7.5)$$

This is the first step in which energy is liberated. Even so, the amount liberated is not sufficient to make up for the total amount absorbed in the preceding steps.

5. In this final step, the gaseous ions condense into one mole of crystalline sodium chloride. The corresponding enthalpy change, the lattice energy of NaCl(s), is -788 kJ/mol, which represents energy *liberated:*

$$Na^+(g) + Cl^-(g) \longrightarrow NaCl(s) \qquad \Delta H_{lat\ en} = -788 \text{ kJ} \qquad (7.6)$$

It is clear that most of the energy liberated by the overall reaction comes from this step. It is this step that makes the whole process energetically favorable.

When the thermochemical equations given in step 1 to 5 [Equations (7.2) to (7.6)] are added, the result is the equation for the enthalpy of formation of NaCl(s):

$$\text{Na(s)} + \tfrac{1}{2}\text{Cl}_2\text{(g)} \longrightarrow \text{NaCl(s)} \qquad \Delta H_f^{\circ} = 411 \text{ kJ} \qquad (7.1)$$

We can check the cycle in the following way:

$$\begin{aligned}
\Delta H_f^{\circ} &= \Delta H_{\text{subl}} + \tfrac{1}{2}\Delta H_{\text{diss}} + \Delta H_{\text{ion en}} + \Delta H_{\text{elec af}} + \Delta H_{\text{lat en}} \\
&= +108 \text{ kJ} + 122 \text{ kJ} + 496 \text{ kJ} - 349 \text{ kJ} - 788 \text{ kJ} \\
&= -411 \text{ kJ}
\end{aligned}$$

Born-Haber cycles are used to analyze processes to see how they are affected by variations in one of the steps. They may also be used to calculate the enthalpy change for one of the steps or for the entire process.

Example 7.1

Calculate the lattice energy of $\text{MgCl}_2\text{(s)}$. For magnesium, the enthalpy of sublimation is $+150$ kJ/mol, the first ionization energy is $+738$ kJ/mol, and the second ionization energy is $+1450$ kJ/mol. For chlorine, the dissociation energy is $+243$ kJ/mol of $\text{Cl}_2\text{(g)}$, and the first electron affinity is -349 kJ/mol of Cl(g). For $\text{MgCl}_2\text{(s)}$, the enthalpy of formation is -642 kJ/mol.

Solution

The thermochemical equations for the steps of the cycle must add up to the thermochemical equation for the enthalpy of formation of one mole of $\text{MgCl}_2\text{(s)}$:

$$\text{Mg(s)} + \text{Cl}_2\text{(g)} \longrightarrow \text{MgCl}_2\text{(s)} \qquad \Delta H_f^{\circ} = -642 \text{ kJ}$$

Notice that in this case the positive ion has a $2+$ charge, and hence the first and second ionization energies of the metal must be used. In addition, since one mole of MgCl_2 is formed from two moles of Cl atoms, we must employ the dissociation energy of one mole of Cl_2 molecules as well as two times the electron affinity of one mole of Cl atoms. The steps are:

step	chemical equation	ΔH
sublimation of Mg	$\text{Mg(s)} \longrightarrow \text{Mg(g)}$	$+150$ kJ
first ionization energy of Mg	$\text{Mg(g)} \longrightarrow \text{Mg}^+\text{(g)} + e^-$	$+738$ kJ
second ionization energy of Mg	$\text{Mg}^+\text{(g)} \longrightarrow \text{Mg}^{2+}\text{(g)} + e^-$	$+1450$ kJ
dissociation of Cl_2	$\text{Cl}_2\text{(g)} \longrightarrow 2\,\text{Cl(g)}$	$+243$ kJ
first electron affinity for 2 mol of Cl atoms	$2\,\text{Cl(g)} + 2e^- \longrightarrow 2\,\text{Cl}^-\text{(g)}$	$2(-349 \text{ kJ}) = -698$ kJ
lattice energy	$\text{Mg}^{2+}\text{(g)} + 2\,\text{Cl}^-\text{(g)} \longrightarrow \text{MgCl}_2\text{(s)}$	$\Delta H_{\text{lat en}}$
total	$\text{Mg(s)} + \text{Cl}_2\text{(g)} \longrightarrow \text{MgCl}_2\text{(s)}$	$+1883 \text{ kJ} + \Delta H_{\text{lat en}}$

The total value of ΔH, however, must equal the enthalpy of formation of $\text{MgCl}_2\text{(s)}$; therefore,

$$+1883 \text{ kJ} + \Delta H_{\text{lat en}} = -642 \text{ kJ}$$

$$\Delta H_{\text{lat en}} = -2525 \text{ kJ}$$

The lattice energy of $MgCl_2(s)$ is -2525 kJ/mol.

The difference between the lattice energy of $MgCl_2$ (-2525 kJ/mol) and the lattice energy of NaCl (-788 kJ/mol) is caused largely by the difference in the charges of the cations of these two compounds. The attraction between a Mg^{2+} ion (with a 2+ charge) and a Cl^- ion is stronger than the attraction between a Na^+ ion (with only a 1+ charge) and a Cl^- ion.

In general, the magnitude of the lattice energy depends upon two factors:

1. Charges of the ions. *More energy* is liberated by the formation of crystals that contain ions with *charges higher than 1+ and 1−* than is liberated by the formation of crystals that contain only 1+ and 1− ions. Ions with high charges attract oppositely charged ions more strongly than do ions with only a 1+ or a 1− charge. The values given in Table 7.3 reflect this fact.

2. Sizes of the ions. The closer two charges of opposite sign can approach each other, the stronger the resulting force of attraction. Hence, *more energy* is liberated when *small ions* form a crystal than when large ions form a crystal, provided the ionic charges of the compounds are similar. Since the Na^+ ion (radius, 95 pm) is smaller than the Cs^+ ion (radius, 169 pm), the difference between the lattice energy of NaCl (-788 kJ/mol) and the lattice energy of CsCl (-669 kJ/mol) is not surprising. Compare also the lattice energies of Na_2O and Cs_2O, given in Table 7.3.

Table 7.3 Some lattice energies				
Type of Compound[a]	Compound	Component Ions	Sum of Ionic Radii (pm)[b]	Lattice Energy (kJ/mol)
1+, 1−	NaCl	Na^+, Cl^-	95 + 181 = 276	−788
	CsCl	Cs^+, Cl^-	169 + 181 = 350	−669
1+, 2−	Na_2O	$2 Na^+$, O^{2-}	95 + 140 = 235	−2570
	Cs_2O	$2 Cs^+$, O^{2-}	169 + 140 = 309	−2090
2+, 1−	$MgCl_2$	Mg^{2+}, $2 Cl^-$	65 + 181 = 246	−2525
2+, 2−	MgO	Mg^{2+}, O^{2-}	65 + 140 = 205	−3890

[a] The charge on the cation and anion, respectively.
[b] Given in order of the radius of the cation followed by the radius of the anion.

7.6 Types of Ions

The driving force of an ionic reaction is the electrostatic attraction of the ions for one another. This attraction results in the liberation of the lattice energy.

Lattice energy is an important factor in determining the charges the atoms assume in the formation of an ionic crystal:*

---

* The correct thermodynamic function to use to check reaction spontaneity is the change in Gibbs free energy, ΔG, not the change in enthalpy, ΔH (see Section 19.4). The approach used here is valid, however, for the formation of an ionic crystal.

1. *Why doesn't Na lose two electrons and become "Na²⁺"?* The energy required for this process is the sum of the first and second ionization energies of Na (Table 7.1):

$$+496 \text{ kJ/mol} + 4563 \text{ kJ/mol} = +5059 \text{ kJ/mol}$$

The lattice energy of an imaginary "NaCl₂" would be far too small to compensate for the energy required by this ionization. The lattice energy of "NaCl₂" would probably be approximately the same as that of $MgCl_2$, -2525 kJ/mol (Table 7.3). The removal of an electron beyond the noble-gas configuration requires too much energy.

2. *Since Na cannot lose two electrons in ion formation, how is Mg able to lose two electrons to become Mg^{2+}?* The Mg atom attains a noble-gas configuration through this loss. The sum of the first second ionization energies of Mg (Table 7.1) is much less than the sum for Na:

$$+738 \text{ kJ/mol} + 1450 \text{ kJ/mol} = +2188 \text{ kJ/mol}$$

The lattice energy of $MgCl_2$, -2525 kJ/mol (Table 7.3) is more than enough to supply the energy required for this ionization.

3. *Since less energy is required to remove one electron than is required to remove two, why doesn't Mg form a "Mg^{+}" ion?* In this case, the energy required to form "Mg^{+}" would be only $+738$ kJ/mol (the first ionization energy of Mg, Table 7.1). On the other hand, the lattice energy of the imaginary "MgCl" would be only on the order of the lattice energy of NaCl (-788 kJ/mol). The larger lattice energy of $MgCl_2$ (-2525 kJ/mol, brought about by the higher charge on Mg^{2+}) favors the formation of $MgCl_2$.

We can see, therefore, why so many metals form cations with s^2p^6 (noble-gas) configurations. More than three electrons are never lost or gained in ion formation. The energy required to bring about a gain or loss or more than three electrons is not available. Compounds with formulas such as $TiCl_4$, $SnBr_4$, SF_6, PCl_5, and SiO_2 are not ionic.

Energy considerations also favor the formation of negative ions with noble-gas electron configurations. All monatomic anions are noble-gas ions. Atoms of nonmetals add electrons until the noble-gas configuration is reached, and the attainment of this limit is favored:

1. *According to the electron affinity data in Table 7.2, the formation of O^- releases energy (-141 kJ/mol) and the formation of O^{2-} requires energy ($+704$ kJ/mol). Why doesn't the O atom form the "O^-" ion rather than the O^{2-} ion?* The lattice energy of an imaginary "NaO" would probably be only on the order of the lattice energy of NaCl (which is -788 kJ/mol). The lattice energy of Na_2O (which contains the O^{2-} ion) is -2570 kJ/mol. On balance, the formation of the noble-gas ion, O^{2-}, is favored.

2. *Why doesn't the Cl atom form a "Cl^{2-}" ion instead of the Cl^- ion?* More energy would be liberated by the formation of the crystal lattice of an imaginary "Na_2Cl" (probably, about -2200 kJ/mol) than is liberated by the formation of the NaCl lattice (-788 kJ/mol). The production of the "Cl^{2-}" ion, however, would require the input of an extremely large amount of energy—more than any lattice energy could supply. The electron added to Cl^- to produce "Cl^{2-}" would be added be-

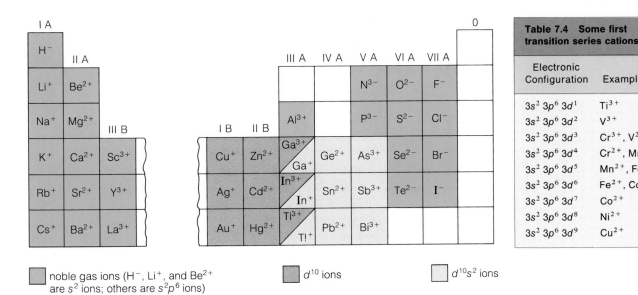

Figure 7.8 Types of ions and their relations to the periodic table

Table 7.4 Some first transition series cations

Electronic Configuration	Example
$3s^2\,3p^6\,3d^1$	Ti^{3+}
$3s^2\,3p^6\,3d^2$	V^{3+}
$3s^2\,3p^6\,3d^3$	$Cr^{3+},\,V^{2+}$
$3s^2\,3p^6\,3d^4$	$Cr^{2+},\,Mn^{3+}$
$3s^2\,3p^6\,3d^5$	$Mn^{2+},\,Fe^{3+}$
$3s^2\,3p^6\,3d^6$	$Fe^{2+},\,Co^{3+}$
$3s^2\,3p^6\,3d^7$	Co^{2+}
$3s^2\,3p^6\,3d^8$	Ni^{2+}
$3s^2\,3p^6\,3d^9$	Cu^{2+}

noble gas ions (H^-, Li^+, and Be^{2+} are s^2 ions; others are s^2p^6 ions) $\quad$ d^{10} ions $\quad$ $d^{10}s^2$ ions

yond an s^2p^6 configuration. It would be added to the next higher quantum level, screened from the nuclear charge by a closed s^2p^6 shell, and repelled by the electrons already present in the negatively charged Cl^- ion. The addition would require a large amount of energy. Such additions—beyond a noble-gas configuration—are never observed.

We can identify several types of ions, classified by electronic configuraion (see Figure 7.8 and Table 7.4):

1. Noble-gas ions. These ions are isoelectronic with noble gases (see Section 7.4). All monatomic anions belong to this classification. There are two types of noble-gas ions:

a. s^2 ions. These ions are isoelectronic with helium (electronic configuration, $1s^2$). There are only three s^2 ions: H^-, Li^+, and Be^{2+}.

b. s^2p^6 ions. Most noble-gas ions are s^2p^6 ions, which have eight electrons in the valence shell (see Figure 7.8).

2. d^{10} ions. Certain metals undergo ionic reactions even though they cannot possibly produce s^2p^6 cations. Zinc, for example, would have to lose 12 electrons to get a noble-gas configuration. In its reactions, zinc forms the Zn^{2+} ion by the loss of two electrons:

$$Zn(\ldots 3s^2\,3p^6\,3d^{10}\,4s^2) \longrightarrow Zn^{2+}(\ldots 3s^2\,3p^6\,3d^{10}) + 2e^-$$

The ionization energies of Zn and the lattice energies of Zn^{2+} compounds favor the formation of this ion. The electron configuration of the Zn^{2+} ion is a stable one. All of the subshells in the outer shell of the Zn^{2+} ion are filled. Other atoms form ions with $ns^2\,np^6\,nd^{10}$ configurations similar to that of Zn^{2+}. They are called d^{10} ions and are listed in Figure 7.8.

3. $d^{10}s^2$ ions. Tin forms a cation, Sn^{2+}, that will serve as an example of another type of ion:

$$Sn(\ldots 4s^2\, 4p^6\, 4d^{10}\, 5s^2\, 5p^2) \longrightarrow Sn^{2+}(\ldots 4s^2\, 4p^6\, 4d^{10}\, 5s^2) + 2e^-$$

This configuration is also a stable one; all of the electronic subshells that are occupied are filled. Ions with similar $(n-1)s^2\, (n-1)p^6\, (n-1)d^{10}\, ns^2$ configurations are called $d^{10}s^2$ ions. Note that the configuration of a d^{10} ion is overlayed by two electrons in an s orbital. Nine $d^{10}s^2$ ions are listed in Figure 7.8. The larger elements of group III A can form both $d^{10}s^2$ ions and d^{10} ions.

4. Other types. In the reactions of the transition metals, inner d electrons may be lost as well as the outer s electrons. The outer s electrons, however, are lost first. Most transition elements cannot form ions with any of the regular configurations (s^2, s^2p^6, d^{10}, or $d^{10}s^2$). A list of some of these from the first transition series is given in Table 7.4. The configuration listed in the table is that of the outer shell of the ion.

Many transition metals form more than one type of cation. Examples are Cu^+ and Cu^{2+}, Cr^{2+} and Cr^{3+}, and Fe^{2+} and Fe^{3+}. More energy is required to produce the Fe^{3+} ion than is required to produce the Fe^{2+} ion. The lattice energies of Fe^{3+} compounds, however, are larger than those of Fe^{2+} compounds. These factors balance to the point that is possible to prepare compounds of both ions.

7.7 Ionic Radius

The distance between the centers of two adjacent ions in a crystal can be determined by X-ray diffraction (Section 11.13). For most crystals, this distance is the sum of the radius of a cation and the radius of an anion. Dividing such a distance to obtain the two radii is a problem.

One solution to the problem is to study a crystal composed of very small cations and large anions, such as lithium iodide (Figure 7.9a). In the LiI crystal, I^- ions are assumed to touch each other. The distance between two I^- ions (d in Figure 7.9a) is divided in half to get the radius of the I^- ion:

$$\text{radius } I^- = 432 \text{ pm}/2 = 216 \text{ pm}$$

In most crystals, the anions do not touch each other. The distance d in Figure 7.9b could not be used in a similar way.

Once the radius of the I^- ion has been found, other ionic radii can be calculated. If the distance between the center of a K^+ ion and an I^- ion is determined (d' in Figure 7.9b), the radius of the K^+ ion can be found by subtracting the I^- radius from the K^+ to I^- distance:

$$d' = \text{radius } K^+ + \text{radius } I^-$$
$$349 \text{ pm} = \text{radius } K^+ + 216 \text{ pm}$$
$$\text{radius } K^+ = 133 \text{ pm}$$

A positive ion is always smaller than the atom from which it is derived (Figure 7.10). The radius of K is 203 pm, and the radius of K^+ is 133 pm. In the

Chapter 7   Properties of Atoms and the Ionic Bond

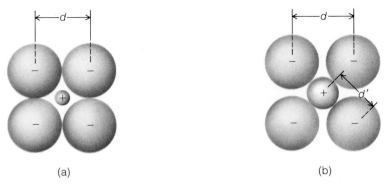

(a)   (b)

Figure 7.9 Determination of ionic radii. (See text for further discussion.)

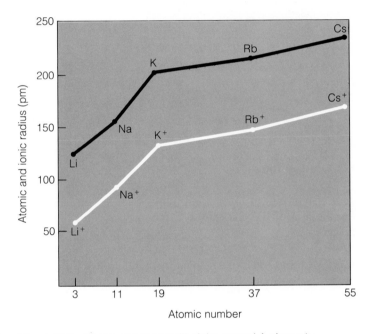

Figure 7.10 Atomic and ionic radii of the group I A elements

formation of the K^+ ion, the loss of an electron represents the loss of the entire $n = 4$ level of the K atom. Furthermore, the protons outnumber the electrons in the positive ion. The electrons of the ion are drawn in closer to the nucleus. For similar reasons, a 2^+ ion is larger than a $3+$ ion. For example,

   radius Fe $= 117$ pm   radius $Fe^{2+} = 75$ pm   radius $Fe^{3+} = 60$ pm

A negative ion is always larger than the atom from which it is derived (Figure 7.11). The radius of the Cl atom is 99 pm, and the radius of the Cl^- ion is 181 pm. In the formation of the Cl^- ion, the addition of an electron causes an increase in the extent to which the valence electrons repel one another, and the valence level expands.

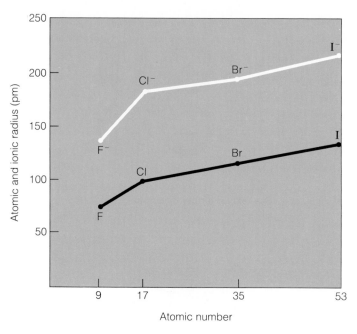

Figure 7.11 Atomic and ionic radii of the group VII A elements

7.8 Nomenclature of Ionic Compounds

The nomenclature (system of naming) of ionic compounds is based on a number of rules. The cation (positive ion) of the compound is named first, and the anion (negative ion) is named second.

1. Cations. Most cations are monatomic ions formed by metal atoms. If the metal forms only one type of cation, the name of the ion is the same as the name of the metal:

Na^+ is the sodium ion
Mg^{2+} is the magnesium ion
Al^{3+} is the aluminum ion

Some metals form more than one type of cation. In these cases, the distinction between the cations may be made by indicating the charge of the cation in its name. The charge is indicated by a Roman numeral in parentheses added to the *English* name of the metal:

Cu^+ is the copper(I) ion and Cu^{2+} is the copper(II) ion
Fe^{2+} is the iron(II) ion and Fe^{3+} is the iron(III) ion

In an older method used to distinguish between two types of ions formed by a metal, the ending of the name of the metal is changed. The *Latin* name of the metal is employed when the symbol for the metal is derived from the Latin. The ending *-ous* is used in the name of that ion of the pair that has the lower charge, and the ending *-ic* is used to name the ion that has the higher charge:

Table 7.5 Some common ions

Cations		Anions	
ammonium	NH_4^+	acetate	$C_2H_3O_2^-$
copper(I) or cuprous	Cu^+	bromide	Br^-
lithium	Li^+	chlorate	ClO_3^-
potassium	K^+	chloride	Cl^-
silver	Ag^+	chlorite	ClO_2^-
sodium	Na^+	cyanide	CN^-
		fluoride	F^-
barium	Ba^{2+}	hydroxide	OH^-
cadmium	Cd^{2+}	hypochlorite	ClO^-
calcium	Ca^{2+}	iodide	I^-
chromium(II) or chromous	Cr^{2+}	nitrate	NO_3^-
cobalt(II) or cobaltous	Co^{2+}	nitrite	NO_2^-
copper(II) or cupric	Cu^{2+}	perchlorate	ClO_4^-
iron(II) or ferrous	Fe^{2+}	permanganate	MnO_4^-
lead(II) or plumbous	Pb^{2+}		
magnesium	Mg^{2+}	carbonate	CO_3^{2-}
manganese(II) or manganous	Mn^{2+}	chromate	CrO_4^{2-}
mercury(I) or mercurous*	Hg_2^{2+}	dichromate	$Cr_2O_7^{2-}$
mercury(II) or mercuric	Hg^{2+}	oxide	O^{2-}
nickel(II) or nickelous	Ni^{2+}	peroxide	O_2^{2-}
tin(II) or stannous	Sn^{2+}	sulfate	SO_4^{2-}
zinc	Zn^{2+}	sulfide	S^{2-}
		sulfite	SO_3^{2-}
aluminum	Al^{3+}		
chromium (III) or chromic	Cr^{3+}	arsenate	AsO_4^{3-}
iron(III) or ferric	Fe^{3+}	nitride	N^{3-}
		phosphate	PO_4^{3-}

* A diatomic ion that is given the name mercury(I) because it can be thought of as consisting of two Hg^+ ions.

Cu^+ is the cuprous ion and Cu^{2+} is the cupric ion
Fe^{2+} is the ferrous ion and Fe^{3+} is the ferric ion

Notice that the charge is not explicitly given and that the method cannot be used if the metal forms more than two different cations.

A **polyatomic ion** is one that is formed from several atoms held together by covalent bonds (see Chapter 8). There are not many polyatomic cations; two common ones are:

NH_4^+ the ammonium ion
Hg_2^{2+} the mercury(I) or mercurous ion

The Hg_2^{2+} ion is given the name mercury(I) because it may be considered to be made up of two Hg^+ ions. A list of common cations is given in Table 7.5.

2. Anions. Monatomic anions are formed by atoms of nonmetals. Their names are derived by replacing the usual ending of the name of the nonmetal with the ending *-ide:*

Cl$^-$ is the chloride ion
O^{2-} is the oxide ion
N^{3-} is nitride ion

All ions that have names that end with *-ide* are not monatomic, however. A few polyatomic anions have this ending; for example,

CN$^-$ is the cyanide ion
OH$^-$ is the hydroxide ion
O$_2^{2-}$ is the peroxide ion

Many polyatomic anions are known. Common ones are included in the list of anions given in Table 7.5, a list that should be mastered at this point. The system used for naming these anions is discussed in Section 13.6.

The name of an ionic compound consists of the name of the cation followed by the name of the anion (as a separate word):

Fe$_2$O$_3$ is iron(III) oxide or ferric oxide
PbCO$_3$ is lead(II) carbonate or plumbous carbonate
Ag$_3$PO$_4$ is silver phosphate
(NH$_4$)$_2$S is ammonium sulfide
Cu(CN)$_2$ is copper(II) cyanide or cupric cyanide
Mg(NO$_3$)$_2$ is magnesium nitrate

Summary

The *radius of an atom*, its *ionization energy*, and its *electron affinity* are *periodic properties* and depend upon the structure of the atom. An understanding of these properties helps us to understand how and why atoms react to form ionic compounds.

In an ionic reaction, atoms of *metals lose* electrons (and form *positive ions*) and atoms of *nonmetals gain* electrons (and form *negative* ions). Atoms of metals are in general relatively large and lose electrons more easily than atoms of nonmetals. Atoms of nonmetals, on the other hand, are in general relatively small and gain electrons more readily than atoms of metals.

The driving force of the ionic reaction is the electrostatic attraction of the positive and negative ions for one another, which results in the formation of an *ionic crystal* and the liberation of the *lattice energy*. A lattice energy may be calculated by use of the *Born-Haber cycle*, a mathematical treatment of the enthalpy changes that are involved in the formation of ionic crystals. The cycle is also a means of studying the importance of the various energy considerations that are involved in the formation of ionic crystals.

Since most of the steps of the Born-Haber cycle are endothermic, the lattice energy (a highly exothermic step) plays a dominant role in the determination of the way in which atoms react to form an ionic compound. In the reaction, the *types of ions* produced (which may be classified according to electronic configuration) depend largely upon the correlation of *ionization potential*, *electron affinity*, and *lattice energy*.

In ionic crystals, the anions are usually larger than the cations. *Anions* are *larger* and *cations* are *smaller* than the atoms from which they are derived.

In the naming of an ionic compound, the *cation* is named *first* and the *anion* is named *second*. The name of the cation is the same as the name of the metal from which the cation is derived. When a metal forms more than one cation, the charge of the ion may be indicated by a Roman numeral enclosed in parentheses after the English name of the metal. The name of a monatomic anion is derived by replacing the usual ending of the name of the nonmetal with the ending, *-ide*. The names of polyatomic anions may be obtained from Table 7.5.

Key Terms

Some of the more important terms introduced in this chapter are listed below. Definitions for terms not included in this list may be located in the text by use of the index.

Anion (Section 7.4)   A negatively charged ion; an atom or a group of atoms that has gained one or more electrons.

Atomic radius (Section 7.1)   An approximation of the radius of an atom, based on the division of bond distances.

Bond distance (Section 7.1)   The distance between the nuclei of two atoms that are bonded together.

Born-Haber cycle (Section 7.5)   A method of analysis of the enthalpy change of a process. The ΔH for the entire process is set equal to the sum of the ΔH values for a series of steps that produces the same change.

Cation (Section 7.4)   A positively charged ion; an atom or a group of atoms that has lost one or more electrons.

d^{10} ion (Section 7.6)   A cation that has an $ns^2\, np^6\, nd^{10}$ electronic configuration in its outer shell (where n is the principal quantum number of this shell).

$d^{10}s^2$ ion (Section 7.6)   A cation that has an $(n-1)s^2$ $(n-1)p^6\,(n-1)d^{10}\,ns^2$ electronic configuration, which is a d^{10} electronic configuration plus an additional shell that contains two electrons in an s orbital.

Effective nuclear charge (Section 7.1)   The positive charge experienced by an outer electron in an atom after the charge of the nucleus has been effectively decreased by the shielding effect of inner electrons.

Electron affinity (Section 7.3)   A first electron affinity is the energy change associated with the process in which an electron is added to a gaseous atom in its ground state. Second and higher electron affinities pertain to processes in which electrons are added to negative ions.

Enthalpy of sublimation (Section 7.5)   The enthalpy change associated with a process in which a solid is converted directly into a gas.

Ion (Sections 7.4 and 7.6)   A particle that is made up of an atom or a group of atoms and that bears either a positive or negative charge. A **monatomic ion** is formed from a single atom, and a **polyatomic ion** is formed from two or more atoms.

Ionic bonding (Section 7.4)   The attraction that exists between positive and negative ions and that holds them together in a crystal structure. It results from the transfer of electrons.

Ionic compound (Section 7.4)   A compound consisting of cations and anions held together by electrostatic attraction into a crystal structure, which is a repeating geometric pattern.

Ionic radius (Section 7.7)   An approximation of the radius of an ion, based on the division of the distances between the nuclei of adjacent ions in an ionic crystal.

Ionic reaction (Section 7.4)   A reaction in which electrons are transferred, with the attendant formation of cations and anions.

Ionization energy (Section 7.2)   The amount of energy required to remove the most loosely held electron from an isolated atom in its ground state is a first ionization energy. Second and higher ionization energies pertain to processes in which electrons are removed from positive ions.

Isoelectronic (Section 7.4)   The same in electronic configuration.

Lattice energy (Section 7.5)   The enthalpy change associated with the condensation of gaseous ions into an ionic crystal.

Noble-gas ion (Section 7.4 and 7.6)   A cation or an anion that is isoelectronic with a noble gas; an s^2 or an s^2p^6 ion.

s^2 ion (Sections 7.4 and 7.6)   A noble-gas cation or anion that has two electrons in an s orbital as the electronic configuration of its outer shell; these ions are isoelectronic with helium.

s^2p^6 ion (Sections 7.4 and 7.6)   A noble-gas cation or anion that has two electrons in an s orbital and six electrons in three p orbitals as the electronic configuration of its outer shell.

Shielding (Section 7.1)   The effect brought about by inner electrons in diminishing the nuclear charge experienced by outer electrons.

Problems*

Properties of Atoms

7.1 Describe the way that the atomic radii of the representative elements of a period vary and explain the observed trend.

7.2 Describe the way that the atomic radii of the elements of an A family of the periodic table vary and explain the observed trend.

7.3 Which member of each of the following pairs would you predict to be the larger? **(a)** P, Cl; **(b)** P, Sb; **(c)** Ga, P; **(d)** Si, P; **(e)** Na, P; **(f)** Al, P.

7.4 Which member of each of the following pairs would you predict to be the larger? **(a)** Ba, B; **(b)** Cs, Cd; **(c)** Ga, Ge; **(d)** In, Se; **(e)** Ba, Br; **(f)** Ga, Tl.

7.5 Given the following bond distances: N—Cl, 174 pm; Cl—F, 170 pm; F—F, 142 pm. Based on these data, what is the atomic radius of N?

7.6 Given the following bond distances: As—I, 255 pm; I—Br, 247 pm; Br—Br, 228 pm. Based on these data, what is the As—Br bond distance?

7.7 Which member of each of the following pairs would you expect to have the higher first ionization energy? **(a)** S, Ar; **(b)** Ar, Kr; **(c)** S, As; **(d)** Ba, Sr; **(e)** Cs, Ba; **(f)** Sn, As.

7.8 Which member of each of the following pairs would you expect to have the higher first ionization energy? **(a)** Cl, I; **(b)** I, Xe; **(c)** Se, Cl; **(d)** K, Mg; **(e)** Rb, Cs; **(f)** Sb, Se.

7.9 (a) Why is the second ionization energy of an element always larger than the first ionization energy? **(b)** For K, the second ionization energy is about *seven times* the first ionization energy (3051 kJ/mol compared to 419 kJ/mol). For Ca, the second ionization energy is about *two times* the first ionization energy (1145 kJ/mol compared to 590 kJ/mol). Why is the difference larger for K than it is for Ca?

7.10 Why are second electron affinities always positive values?

7.11 Why is the electron affinity of fluorine smaller than would be expected on the basis of the electron affinities of the other halogens?

7.12 Why are the electron affinities of beryllium, nitrogen, and neon out of line in comparison to the values for the elements of the second period?

7.13 The first electron affinity of sulfur is -200 kJ/mol. The energy required for the addition of two electrons to the sulfur atom is $+322$ kJ/mol. What is the second electron affinity of sulfur?

7.14 The addition of one electron to the selenium atom liberates 195 kJ/mol. The addition of two electrons to the selenium atom requires 225 kJ/mol. What are the first and second electron affinities of selenium?

Lattice Energy, Born-Haber Cycle

7.15 Use the following data to calculate the lattice energy of CsCl. The enthalpy of formation of CsCl is -443 kJ/mol. The enthalpy of sublimation of Cs is $+78$ kJ/mol, and the first ionization energy of Cs is $+375$ kJ/mol. The dissociation energy of Cl_2 is $+243$ kJ/mol *of Cl_2 molecules* and the first electron affinity of Cl is -349 kJ/mol *of Cl atoms*.

7.16 Use the following data to calculate the lattice energy of KBr. The enthalpy of formation of KBr is -392 kJ/mol. The enthalpy of sublimation of K is $+89$ kJ/mol, and the first ionization energy of K is $+418$ kJ/mol. The enthalpy change for the transformation $Br_2(l) \rightarrow 2Br(g)$ is $+224$ kJ/mol *of Br_2 molecules*, and the first electron affinity of Br is -325 kJ/mol *of Br atoms*.

7.17 Use the following data to calculate the lattice energy of CaO. The enthalpy of formation of CaO is -636 kJ/mol. The enthalpy of sublimation of Ca is $+192$ kJ/mol, the first ionization energy of Ca is $+590$ kJ/mol, and the second ionization energy of Ca is $+1145$ kJ/mol. The enthalpy of dissociation of O_2 is $+494$ kJ/mol *of O_2 molecules*, the first electron affinity of O is -141 kJ/mol *of O atoms*, and the second electron affinity of O is $+845$ kJ/mol *of O^- ions*.

7.18 Use the following data to calculate the lattice energy of BaO. The enthalpy of formation of BaO is -558 kJ/mol. The enthalpy of sublimation of Ba is $+176$ kJ/mol, the first ionization energy of Ba is $+503$ kJ/mol, and the second ionization energy of Ba is $+965$ kJ/mol. The enthalpy of dissociation of O_2 is $+494$ kJ/mol *of O_2 molecules*, the first electron affinity of O is -141 kJ/mol *of O atoms*, and the second electron affinity of O is $+845$ KJ/mol *of O^- ions*.

7.19 Use the following data to calculate the enthalpy of formation of Rb_2O. The enthalpy of sublimation of Rb is $+82$ kJ/mol, and the first ionization energy of Rb is $+403$ kJ/mol. The enthalpy of dissociation of O_2 is $+494$ kJ/mol *of O_2 molecules*, the first electron affinity of O is -141 kJ/mol *of O atoms*, and the second electron affinity of O is $+845$ kJ/mol *of O^- ions*. The lattice energy of Rb_2O is -2250 kJ/mol.

7.20 Use the following data to calculate the enthalpy of formation of $SrCl_2$. The enthalpy of sublimation of Sr is $+164$ kJ/mol, the first ionization energy of Sr is $+549$ kJ/mol, and the second ionization energy of Sr is $+1064$ kJ/mol. The enthalpy of dissociation of Cl_2 is $+243$ kJ/mol *of Cl_2 molecules*, and the first electron affinity of Cl is -349 kJ/mol *of Cl atoms*. The lattice energy of $SrCl_2$ is -2150 kJ/mol.

7.21 Given the following ionic radii: Ca^{2+}, 99 pm; Rb^+, 148 pm; Cs^+, 169 pm; F^-, 136 pm; O^{2-}, 140 pm; S^{2-}, 185 pm; I^-, 216 pm. From each of the following pairs, identify that compound for which more energy is liberated by the formation of the crystal from gaseous ions. **(a)** CaS or RbF, **(b)** RbF or RbI, **(c)** CsI or CaO.

---

* The more difficult problems are marked with asterisks. The appendix contains answers to color-keyed problems.

7.22 Given the following ionic radii: Mg^{2+}, 65 pm; Na^+, 95 pm; Sr^{2+}, 113 pm; Ba^{2+}, 135 pm; O^{2-}, 140 pm; Se^{2-}, 198 pm; I^-, 216 pm. From each of the following pairs, identify that compound for which more energy is liberated by the formation of the crystal from gaseous ions. **(a)** NaI or SrSe, **(b)** BaSe or SrSe, **(c)** MgI_2 or Na_2O.

7.23 Consider the lattice energies of NaBr, Na_2S, and MgS. List the compounds in the order of increasing quantity of energy liberated. Why did you select the order that you used?

7.24 Consider the lattice energies of $FeCl_2$, $FeCl_3$, FeO, and Fe_2O_3. List the compounds in the order of increasing quantity of energy liberated. Why did you select the order that you used?

The Ionic Bond, Types of Ions

7.25 Write the notations by subshells for the electronic configurations of the following ions: **(a)** Cu^+, **(b)** Cr^{3+}, **(c)** Cl^-, **(d)** Cs^+, **(e)** Cd^{2+}, **(f)** Co^{2+}.

7.26 Write the notations by subshells for the electronic configurations of the following ions: **(a)** K^+, **(b)** S^{2-}, **(c)** Ag^+, **(d)** Fe^{3+}, **(e)** La^{3+}, **(f)** Sr^{2+}.

7.27 (a) State the number of unpaired electrons in each of the ions listed in Problem 7.25. **(b)** Which of these ions would you expect to be diamagnetic and which paramagnetic?

7.28 (a) State the number of unpaired electrons in each of the ions listed in Problem 7.26. **(b)** Which of these ions would you expect to be diamagnetic and which paramagnetic?

7.29 For each of the following parts, give the formulas of two ions (cations or anions) that are isoelectronic with the atom or ion: **(a)** He, **(b)** Br^-, **(c)** Hg, **(d)** Au^+, **(e)** K^+.

7.30 For each of the following parts, give the formulas of two ions (cations or anions) that are isoelectronic with the atom or ion: **(a)** Ar, **(b)** F^-, **(c)** Ba^{2+}, **(d)** Cd^{2+}, **(e)** Cd.

7.31 Identify the s^2, s^2p^6, d^{10}, and $d^{10}s^2$ ions that are included in the following list: Ag^+, Al^{3+}, As^{3+}, Au^+, Ba^{2+}, Be^{2+}, Bi^{3+}, Br^-.

7.32 Identify the s^2, s^2p^6, d^{10}, and $d^{10}s^2$ ions that are included in the following list: Ca^{2+}, Cd^{2+}, Cl^-, Cs^+, Cu^+, Ga^+, Ga^{3+}, Ge^{2+}.

7.33 Give the formulas for the chlorides, oxides, and nitrides of sodium, magnesium, and aluminum.

7.34 Give the formulas for the compounds that contain the potassium, calcium, and iron(III) ions with the nitrate (NO_3^-), sulfate (SO_4^{2-}), and phosphate (PO_4^{3-}) ions.

Ionic Radii

7.35 Why is a cation smaller than the atom from which it is derived? How does the size vary with the number of electrons removed in the formation of the cation?

7.36 Why is an anion larger than the atom from which it is derived? How does the size vary with the number of electrons added in the formation of the anion?

7.37 Which member of each of the following pairs would you predict to be larger? **(a)** Cu or Cu^{2+}, **(b)** Se^{2-} or Te^{2-}, **(c)** Tl^+ or Sn^{2+}, **(d)** Tl^+ or Tl^{3+}, **(e)** N^{3-} or O^{2-}.

7.38 Which member of each of the following pairs would

you predict to be larger? **(a)** Sn^{2+} or Pb^{2+}, **(b)** Ag^+ or Cd^{2+}, **(c)** Ba^{2+} or Ba, **(d)** Te^{2-} or I^-, **(e)** Cr^{2+} or Cr^{3+}.

7.39 Which member of each of the following pairs would you predict to be larger? **(a)** Mg^{2+} or Al^{3+}, **(b)** Zn^{2+} or Cd^{2+}, **(c)** O^{2-} or F, **(d)** Sc^{3+} or Sr^{2+}, **(e)** Mg or Mg^{2+}.

7.40 Which member of each of the following pairs would you predict to be larger? **(a)** K^+ or Ca^{2+}, **(b)** N or N^{3-}, **(c)** Pb^{2+} or Bi^{3+}, **(d)** Cl^- or I^-, **(e)** Cu^+ or Cu^{2+}.

Nomenclature of Ionic Compounds

7.41 Give formulas for: **(a)** ammonium acetate, **(b)** aluminum sulfate, **(c)** cobalt(III) sulfide, **(d)** barium carbonate, **(e)** potassium arsenate.

7.42 Give formulas for: **(a)** sodium peroxide, **(b)** nickel(II) phosphate, **(c)** copper(I) chloride, **(d)** lead(II) nitrate, **(e)** mercury(I) sulfate.

7.43 Give formulas for: **(a)** iron(III) carbonate, **(b)** manganese(II) nitrate, **(c)** calcium phosphate, **(d)** lithium oxide, **(e)** silver nitrite.

7.44 Give formulas for: **(a)** zinc chloride, **(b)** calcium chlorate, **(c)** lead(II) sulfate, **(d)** potassium nitride, **(e)** aluminum oxide.

7.45 Name the following: **(a)** $CaSO_3$, **(b)** $AgClO_3$, **(c)** $Sn(NO_3)_2$, **(d)** CdI_2, **(e)** $Cr(IO_3)_3$.

7.46 Name the following: **(a)** Al_2O_3, **(b)** HgO, **(c)** Na_2CrO_4, **(d)** $KMnO_4$, **(e)** NH_4NO_3.

7.47 Name the following: **(a)** $Mg(OH)_2$, **(b)** $PbCrO_4$, **(c)** $Fe_2(SO_4)_3$, **(d)** $K_2Cr_2O_7$, **(e)** Li_2SO_3.

7.48 Name the following: **(a)** $Ni(CN)_2$, **(b)** $ZnCO_3$, **(c)** SnF_2, **(d)** Na_2O_2, **(e)** $NaClO_3$.

Unclassified Problems

7.49 Of all the steps of the Born-Haber cycle, why is the lattice energy so important to the success of the preparation of an ionic compound?

7.50 Compare the nonmetals and metals as to: **(a)** atomic radius, **(b)** ionization potential.

7.51 Given the following bond distances: P—P, 220 pm; P—I, 243 pm; C—I, 210 pm. Based on these data, what is the C—P bond distance?

7.52 Of all the elements in the third period (Na through Ar): **(a)** which has the largest atomic radius? **(b)** which has the highest first ionization energy? **(c)** which liberates the most energy per mole upon the addition of electrons to form the $1-$ anion? **(d)** which is the most reactive metal? **(e)** which is the most reactive nonmetal? **(f)** which is the least reactive element? **(g)** how many are metals?

7.53 Using arguments based on energy changes involved in the formation of ionic compounds, explain why Cu forms both the Cu^+ and Cu^{2+} ions, but Na forms only the Na^+ ion and not the Na^{2+} ion.

7.54 Use the following data to calculate the enthalpy of formation of sodium sulfide. The enthalpy of sublimation of Na is $+108$ kJ/mol, and the first ionization energy of Na is $+496$ kJ/mol. The enthalpy changes for the transformation $S(s) \rightarrow S(g)$ is $+279$ kJ/mol. The first electron affinity of S is -200 kJ/mol of S atoms, and the second electron affinity of S is $+532$ kJ/mol of S^- ions. The lattice energy of Na_2S is -2192 kJ/mol.

CHAPTER

8

THE COVALENT BOND

In the last chapter, we discussed the formation and some properties of ionic compounds. In this chapter, the covalent bond (in which electrons are shared by the bonded atoms) will be introduced. In addition, we will consider bonds that have a character intermediate between the purely ionic and the purely covalent.

8.1 Covalent Bonding

In the reactions of metals with nonmetals, atoms of metals have a tendency to lose electrons and atoms of nonmetals have a tendency to gain electrons. As a result, electrons are transferred in these reactions and ionic compounds are formed.

When atoms of nonmetals interact, electron transfer does not occur, because the atoms are similar in their attraction for electrons (identical when two atoms of the same element are concerned). Instead of the transfer of electrons, electrons are shared and molecules are formed.

The atoms of molecules are held together by **covalent bonding,** in which electron pairs are shared between atoms. A **single covalent bond** consists of a pair of electrons (with opposite spins) that is assumed to occupy orbitals of both atoms involved in the bond.

As an example, consider the bond formed by two hydrogen atoms. An individual hydrogen atom has a single electron that is symmetrically distributed around the nucleus in a 1s orbital. When two hydrogen atoms form a covalent bond, the atomic orbitals overlap in such a way that the electron clouds reinforce each other in the region between the nuclei, and there is an increased probability of finding an electron in this region. According to the Pauli exclusion principle, the two electrons of the bond must have opposite spins. The strength of the bond comes from the attraction of the positively charged nuclei for the negative cloud of the bond (see Figure 8.1).

The hydrogen molecule can be represented by the symbol H:H or H—H. In the first structure, the dots stand for the shared electron pair; in the second structure, a dash represents the electron pair of the bond. Although the electrons belong to the molecule as a whole, each hydrogen atom can be considered to have the noble-gas configuration of helium (two electrons in the $n = 1$ level). This consideration is based upon the premise that both shared electrons contribute to the stable configuration of each hydrogen atom. In other words, the electrons of the bond are counted twice—once for each of the bonded atoms.

The formula of hydrogen, H_2, describes a discrete unit—a molecule— and hydrogen gas consists of a collection of such molecules. There are no molecules in

Figure 8.1 Representation of the electron distribution in a hydrogen molecule

strictly ionic substances. The formula for sodium chloride is NaCl, which indicates the *simplest ratio of ions* in a crystal of sodium chloride (1 to 1). Formulas such as Na_2Cl_2 or Na_3Cl_3 are incorrect because there are no such molecules present in crystalline sodium chloride, and these formulas do not give the simplest ratio of ions. For covalent substances, however, a formula such as H_2O_2 can be correct. This formula describes a molecule that contains two hydrogen atoms and two oxygen atoms.

Molecular structures are often drawn by using symbols of the elements along with dots to represent valence electrons (see Figure 7.5). These electron-dot formulas are called **valence-bond structures** or **Lewis structures,** named after Gilbert N. Lewis, who proposed this theory of covalent bonding in 1916. (More recent theories of covalent bonding are discussed in Chapter 9.) The Lewis theory emphasizes the attainment of a noble-gas electronic configuration on the part of atoms in covalent molecules. For most atoms this means the attainment of an octet. For hydrogen, however, the two-electron configuration of helium is stable.

The hydrogen molecule is diatomic (contains two atoms). Certain other elements also exist as diatomic molecules (see Table 3.1). An atom of any halogen (group VII A element) has seven valence electrons. By the formation of a single covalent bond between two of these atoms, each atom attains an octet electronic configuration characteristic of a noble gas. In the case of fluorine, for example,

$$:\!\ddot{F}\!\cdot\ +\ \cdot\ddot{F}\!: \longrightarrow\ :\!\ddot{F}\!:\!\ddot{F}\!: \qquad (\text{or } :\!\ddot{F}\!-\!\ddot{F}\!:)$$

Only the electron pair between the two atoms is shared and forms a part of the covalent bond. Notice that in accounting for the octet on each atom, the electrons of the bond are counted twice—once for each atom.

The number of electron-pair bonds that an atom forms in a molecule can often be predicted from the number of electrons required by the atom to fill its valence level. Since for the nonmetals the number of valence electrons is the same as the group number, one might predict that VII A elements, such as Cl (with seven valence electrons), would from one covalent bond to attain a stable octet; VI A elements, such as O and S (with six valence electrons), two covalent bonds; V A elements, such as N and P (with five valence electrons), three covalent bonds; and IV elements, such as C (with four valence electrons), four covalent bonds. These predictions are borne out in many compounds. Consider the following hydrides:

Gilbert N. Lewis, 1875–1946.
Photographer Johan Hagemeyer: Bancroft Library, courtesy AIP Neils Bohr Library.

$$H\cdot\ +\ \cdot\ddot{C}l\!: \longrightarrow\ H\!:\!\ddot{C}l\!: \qquad (\text{or } H\!-\!\ddot{C}l\!:)$$

hydrogen chloride

$$2\,H\cdot\ +\ \cdot\ddot{O}\!: \longrightarrow\ \overset{\textstyle H}{H\!:\!\ddot{O}\!:} \qquad (\text{or } \overset{\textstyle H}{H\!-\!\ddot{O}\!:})$$

water

$$3\,H\cdot\ +\ \cdot\ddot{N}\!\cdot \longrightarrow\ \overset{\textstyle H}{H\!:\!\ddot{N}\!:\!H} \qquad (\text{or } \overset{\textstyle H}{H\!-\!\underset{\displaystyle\cdot\cdot}{N}\!-\!H})$$

ammonia

$$4\,H\cdot\ +\ \cdot\dot{C}\cdot \longrightarrow\ \overset{\textstyle H}{\underset{\textstyle H}{H\!:\!C\!:\!H}} \qquad (\text{or } \overset{\textstyle H}{\underset{\textstyle H}{H\!-\!C\!-\!H}})$$

methane

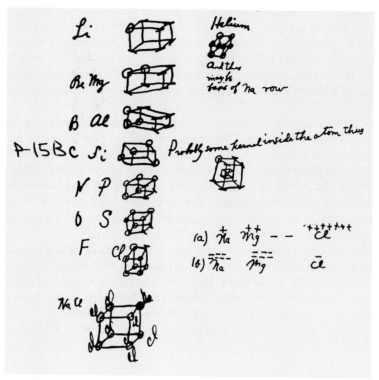

Lewis's original notes on the electronic structures of the atoms. He used the cube (which has eight corners) and showed helium (mistakenly, he meant neon) with all corners filled (an octet). He states '' and this may be the basis of Na row.'' From this start, Lewis developed the octet rule for covalent bonding. *From G. N. Lewis,* Valence, *Dover Publications, Inc., New York, 1966.*

Notice that in these molecules, each hydrogen atom can be considered to have a complete $n = 1$ shell and the other atoms to have noble-gas octets.

More than one electron pair may be shared by two atoms. In these instances, the atoms are said to be joined by **multiple bonds.** Two shared electron pairs are called a **double bond;** three shared electron pairs are called a **triple bond.** Consider, for example, the N_2 molecule. Nitrogen is in group V A, and a nitrogen atom has five valence electrons. The formation of the N_2 molecule may be represented as follows:

$$:\dot{N}\cdot + \cdot\dot{N}: \longrightarrow :N::N: \qquad (\text{or} :N\equiv N:)$$

Three electron pairs are shared by the two atoms, which are said to be joined by a *triple bond.* Notice that as a result of this formulation, each nitrogen atom may be considered to have an octet of electrons.

Other examples of molecules that contain double and triple bonds are:

$$:\ddot{O}: + :C: + :\ddot{O}: \longrightarrow :\ddot{O}::C::\ddot{O}: \qquad (\text{or} :\ddot{O}=C=\ddot{O}:)$$

carbon dioxide

$$2\,H\cdot \; + \; \cdot \overset{\displaystyle \cdot}{C}\!: \; + \; :\overset{\displaystyle \cdot}{C}\cdot \; + \; 2\,H\cdot \;\longrightarrow\; H\!:\!\overset{\displaystyle \cdot\cdot}{\underset{}{C}}\!:\!:\!\overset{\displaystyle \cdot\cdot}{\underset{}{C}}\!:\!H$$

ethylene (or H—C=C—H) with H H above the carbons

$$H\cdot \; + \; \cdot \overset{\displaystyle \cdot}{C}\!: \; + \; :\overset{\displaystyle \cdot}{C}\cdot \; + \; \cdot H \;\longrightarrow\; H\!:\!C\!:\!\!:\!\!:\!C\!:\!H$$

acetylene (or H—C≡C—H)

A method for drawing Lewis structures is given in Section 8.5. Before it is presented, we must introduce some other concepts upon which the method depends.

8.2 Transition between Ionic and Covalent Bonding

The bonding in most compounds is intermediate between purely ionic and purely covalent.

The best examples of ionic bonding are found in compounds formed by a metal with a very low ionization energy (for example, Cs) and a nonmetal that has a strong tendency toward electron gain (for example, F). In a compound such as CsF, the ions exist as separate units in the crystal.

A purely covalent bond is found only in molecules formed from two *identical* atoms, such as Cl_2. One Cl atom attracts electrons to the same extent as any other. The electron cloud of the bond is distributed symmetrically around the two nuclei. In other words, the bonding electrons are shared equally by the two identical atoms.

The bonding in most compounds is somewhere between these two extremes. One approach to the study of these bonds of intermediate character is based on **ion distortion.** The character of the bonding in a compound that contains a metal and a nonmetal can be interpreted in terms of the interactions between the ions. The positively charged ion is believed to attract and deform the electron cloud of the anion. The electron cloud of the negative ion is drawn toward the cation. In extreme cases, ion deformation can lead to compounds that are more covalent than ionic (see the sequence of drawings in Figure 8.2). The degree of covalent character that a compound has can be considered to correspond to the extent that the anion is distorted.

1. Anions. How easily an anion can be distorted depends upon its size and charge. A *large anion*, in which the outer electrons are far away from the nucleus, is easily deformed. The iodide ion (I^-, ionic radius of 216 pm) is more easily distorted than the fluoride ion (F^-, ionic radius of 136 pm). If an anion has a *high negative charge*, so much the better. In a highly charged anion the electrons outnumber the protons to a greater extent than in an anion with a lower charge. The electron cloud of a highly charged anion is easily distorted. The S^{2-} ion, for example, is more easily distorted than the Cl^- ion.

2. Cations. The ability of a cation to distort the electron cloud of a neighboring anion also depends upon size and charge. *A small cation with a high positive charge* is the most effective in bringing about anion distortion. A cation of this type has a high concentration of positive charge.

In any group of metals in the periodic table, the member that forms the smallest cation (for example, Li in group I A) has the greatest tendency toward the formation of compounds with a high degree of covalent character. All compounds of

ionic bond

distorted ions

polarized
covalent bond

covalent bond

Figure 8.2 Transition between ionic and covalent bonding

beryllium (Be^{2+} is the smallest cation of any group II A element) are significantly covalent. Boron (the smallest member of group III A) forms only covalent compounds. The hypothetical B^{3+} ion would have a comparatively high charge combined with a very small size, which would cause extensive anion distortion leading to covalent bonding.

The first four metals of the fourth period from chlorides in which each of the "cations" is isoelectronic with Ar. In this series—KCl, $CaCl_2$, $ScCl_3$, and $TiCl_4$—the covalent character increases with increasing charge and decreasing size of the "cation." KCl is strongly ionic, and $TiCl_4$, a liquid, is definitely covalent. Truly ionic compounds that contains cations with a charge of $3+$ or higher are rare. Such compounds as $SnCl_4$, $PbCl_4$, $SbCl_5$, and BiF_5 are covalent.

A second approach to bonds of intermediate character considers the **polarization of covalent bonds**. A purely covalent bond results only when two *identical* atoms are bonded. Whenever two *different* atoms are joined by a covalent bond, the electron density of the bond is not symmetrically distributed around the two nuclei. The electrons of the bond are not shared equally. No matter how similar the atoms may be, there will be a difference in their ability to attract electrons.

Chlorine has a greater attraction for electrons than bromine has. In the BrCl molecule the electrons of the covalent bond are more strongly attracted by the chlorine atom than by the bromine atom. The electron cloud of the bond is denser in the vicinity of the chlorine atom. The chlorine end of the bond, therefore, has a partial negative charge. Since the molecule as a whole is electrically neutral, the bromine end is left with a partial positive charge of equal magnitude. Such a bond, with positive and negative poles, is called a **polar covalent bond**. The partial charges of the bond are indicated by the symbols δ^+ and δ^- to distinguish them from full ionic charges.

The greater the difference between the electron-attracting ability of two atoms joined by a covalent bond, the more polar the bond, and the larger the magnitude of the partial charges. If the unequal sharing of electrons were carried to an extreme, one of the bonded atoms would have all of the bonding electrons, and separate ions would result (look at the drawings in Figure 8.2 in the reverse order from that shown).

A polar covalent molecule tends to turn in an electric field between charged plates in such a way that the negative end of the molecule is toward the positive plate and the positive end is toward the negative plate (Figure 8.3). Polar molecules arranged in this way affect the amount of charge that a pair of electrically charged plates can hold. As a result, measurements can be made that allow the calculation of a value called the dipole moment.

If two equal charges with opposite signs are separated by a known distance, the **dipole moment** is

$$dipole\ moment\ =\ (charge)(distance) \tag{8.1}$$

The dipole moments of nonpolar molecules, such as H_2, Cl_2, and Br_2, are zero. The dipole moment of polar diatomic molecules increases as the polarity of the molecule increases.

Linus Pauling has used dipole moment to calculate the **partial ionic character** of a covalent bond. If HCl were completely ionic, the H^+ ion and the Cl^- ion would each have a unit charge (1.60×10^{-19} C). The bond distance in the HCl molecule is 127 pm (which is 1.27×10^{-10} m). The dipole moment of the imaginary H^+Cl^- would be

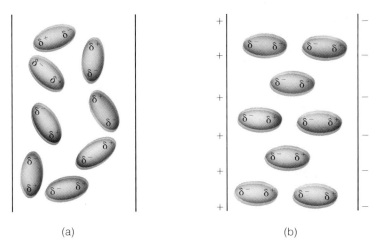

(a)   (b)

Figure 8.3 Effect of an electrostatic field on the orientation of polar molecules. (a) With plates uncharged, (b) with plates charged.

$$dipole\ moment = (charge)(distance)$$
$$= (1.60 \times 10^{-19}\ \text{C})(1.27 \times 10^{-10}\ \text{m})$$
$$= 2.03 \times 10^{-29}\ \text{C·m} = 6.08\ \text{D}$$

The debye unit, D, is 3.34×10^{-30} C·m.

The experimentally determined dipole moment of HCl is 1.03 D. If we compare the observed dipole moment to the dipole moment calculated for H^+Cl^-, we get:

$$1.03\ \text{D}/6.08\ \text{D} = 0.169$$

Thus, the HCl bond appears to be about 16.9% ionic.

8.3 Electronegativity

Electronegativity is a measure of the relative ability of an atom in a molecule to attract electrons to itself. The polarity of the HCl bond may be said to arise from the difference between the electronegativity of the Cl atom and that of the H atom. Since the Cl atom is more electronegative than the H atom, the Cl end of the bond bears a partial negative charge, δ^-, and the H end of the bond bears a partial positive charge, δ^+.

The concept of electronegativity is useful but inexact. Electronegativity values are given on an arbitrary scale—they are *relative* values, useful only in making qualitative comparisons between elements. There is no simple, direct way to measure electronegativities, and several methods of calculating them have been proposed.

The relative electronegativity scale of Linus Pauling is based on bond energies. A bond formed between two atoms that have different electronegativities is a polar bond. A polar covalent bond is always stronger than would be expected on the basis of equal electron sharing. The difference represents the amount of energy needed to overcome the δ^+, δ^- partial charges of the polar bond that have been produced by unequal electron sharing. The size of the difference in bond energy, therefore, is related to the size of the difference between the electronegativities of

Table 8.1 Relative electronegativities

H 2.2							He —
Li 1.0	Be 1.6	B 2.0	C 2.6	N 3.0	O 3.4	F 4.0	Ne —
Na 0.9	Mg 1.3	Al 1.6	Si 1.9	P 2.2	S 2.6	Cl 3.2	Ar —
K 0.8	Ca 1.0	Ga 1.8	Ge 2.0	As 2.2	Se 2.6	Br 3.0	Kr —
Rb 0.8	Sr 0.9	In 1.8	Sn 2.0	Sb 2.1	Te 2.1	I 2.7	Xe —
Cs 0.8	Ba 0.9	Tl 2.0	Pb 2.3	Bi 2.0	Po 2.0	At 2.2	Rn —

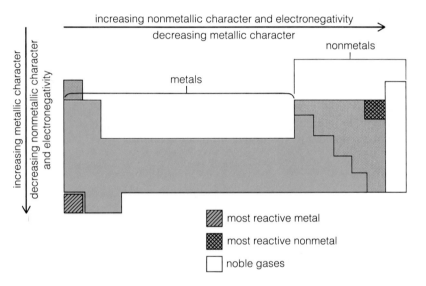

Figure 8.4 The relation between position in the periodic classification and metallic or nonmetallic reactivity

the bonded atoms. The scale was developed by the arbitrary assignment of a value of 4.0 to the F atom (the most electronegative atom).

Some relative electronegativities are given in Table 8.1. In general, electronegativity increases from left to right across any period (with increasing number of valence electrons) and from bottom to top in any group (with decreasing size). The most highly electronegative elements are found in the upper right-hand corner of the periodic table (ignoring the noble gases). The least electronegative elements are found in the lower-left corner of the chart.

Metals are elements that have small attractions for valence electrons (low electronegativities). Nonmetals, except for the noble gases, have large attractions (high electronegativities). Electronegativities, therefore, can be used to rate the reactivities of metals and nonmetals. The positions of the elements in the periodic table are helpful in making predictions concerning chemical reactivity (see Figure 8.4).

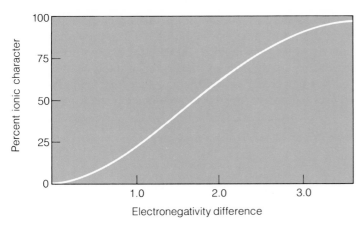

Figure 8.5 Percent ionic character of a bond plotted against the difference in the electronegativities of the two bonded atoms

Table 8.2	Some properties of the hydrogen halides			
Hydrogen Halide	Dipole Moment (D)	Bond Energy (kJ/mol)	Electronegativity of Halogen	Electronegativity Difference between Hydrogen and Halogen
HF	1.91	565	F = 4.0	1.8
HCl	1.03	431	Cl = 3.2	1.0
HBr	0.78	364	Br = 3.0	0.8
HI	0.38	297	I = 2.7	0.5

Electronegativities can be used to predict the nature of the bonding that a compound will have. The larger the difference between the electronegativities of two atoms, the more polar the bond between these atoms will be. In Figure 8.5, the percent ionic character of a bond is plotted against the electronegativity difference of the two bonded atoms. An electronegativity difference of about 1.7 corresponds to a partial ionic character of about 50%.

According to the curve, the electronegativity difference of 3.2 for CsF indicates a partial ionic character of 92%; a difference of 2.3 for NaCl indicates a partial ionic character of 73%; and a difference of 2.1 for MgO indicates a partial ionic character of 67%. All three of these compounds are principally ionic.

Usually the electronegativity difference between two nonmetals is not very large. In these cases the bonds are predominantly covalent, and the electronegativity difference gives the degree of polarity of the covalent bond. If the electronegativity difference is zero or very small (as in the case of the C-to-S bond, for example) an essentially nonpolar bond can be assumed. The larger the electronegativity difference, the more polar the covalent bond is. The atom that has the negative partial charge of the polar bond is the one with the higher electronegativity. By using electronegativities, we can predict that HF is the most polar and has the highest bond energy of any of the hydrogen halides (see Table 8.2). The partial ionic character of the H—F bond is about 45%, even though the electronegativity difference between H and F (1.8) might lead one to expect a higher value.

The concept of electronegativity is inexact. Since this property depends not only upon the structure of the atom under consideration but also upon the number and nature of the atoms to which it is bonded, the electronegativity of an atom is not constant. The electronegativity of phosphorus, for example, is different in PCl_3 than it is in PF_5. Electronegativity values, therefore, are approximations, and electronegativity differences cannot be treated in a completely rigorous manner.

Example 8.1

Which bond is the more polar: (a) N—O or C—O, (b) S—F or O—F?

Solution

(a) The electronegativity differences are:

for the N—O bond: electroneg.$_O$ − electroneg.$_N$ = 3.4 − 3.0 = 0.4
for the C—O bond: electroneg.$_O$ − electroneg.$_C$ = 3.4 − 2.6 = 0.8

The C—O bond is the more polar. In each case the O atom has the δ^- charge.
    The same conclusion can be derived from the periodic table alone. Electronegativity increases in a period from left to right. Consequently, the electronegativity values of the atoms fall in the order C < N < O. The C—O bond combines the atom with the lowest electronegativity (C) and the atom with the highest electronegativity (O), and therefore is the more polar bond.

(b) The electronegativity differences are

for the S—F bond: electroneg.$_F$ − electroneg.$_S$ = 4.0 − 2.6 = 1.4
for the O—F bond: electroneg.$_F$ − electroneg.$_O$ = 4.0 − 3.4 = 0.6

The S—F bond is the more polar of the two. In both bonds the F atom has the δ^- charge.
    The F atom is the more electronegative atom of each bond, since it is the atom closest to the top right. Since S is below O in group VI A, S is *less* electronegative than O. The S—F bond, therefore, is the more polar of the two, since it is the combination of the atom with the lowest electronegativity (S) with the atom with the highest electronegativity (F).

8.4 Formal Charge

In the formation of certain covalent bonds, *both* of the shared electrons are furnished by *one* of the bonded atoms. For example, in the reaction of ammonia with a proton (a hydrogen atom stripped of its electron), the unshared electron pair of the nitrogen atom of NH_3 is used to form a new covalent bond:

$$H:\overset{\displaystyle ..}{\underset{\displaystyle \overset{..}{H}}{N}}:H + H^+ \longrightarrow \left[H:\overset{\displaystyle H}{\underset{\displaystyle \overset{..}{H}}{\overset{..}{N}}}:H \right]^+$$

ammonia   *ammonium ion*

A bond formed in this way is frequently called a "coordinate covalent" bond but it is probably unwise to do so. Labeling a specific bond as a "coordinate covalent" bond implies that it is different from other covalent bonds, and there is little justification for this notion. All electrons are alike no matter what their source. All the bonds in NH_4^+ are identical. It is impossible to distinguish between them.

Notice, however, that the number of electron-pair bonds on the N atom of NH_4^+ does not agree with the number that one would predict. Since a nitrogen atom has five valence electrons (N is in group V A), it would be expected to satisfy the octet principle by sharing three electron pairs. This prediction is correct for NH_3; it is not correct for NH_4^+.

An explanation for this observation may be obtained by calculating the formal charges of the atoms in NH_4^+. A **formal charge** is calculated by apportioning the bonding electrons equally between the bonded atoms, one electron to each atom for each covalent bond, and then comparing the number of electrons that a given atom has in the structure with the number of valence electrons that this atom would have when electrically neutral.

In NH_4^+, the N atom may be considered to have four valence electrons—one from the division of each of the four covalent bonds. Since a neutral N atom has five valence electrons, the N atom in the NH_4^+ is assigned a formal charge of $1+$. Each H atom of the NH_4^+ has the same number of electrons in the structure that it has as a neutral atom, and hence carries no formal charge.

We can derive a formula for calculating formal charge in the following way. If all the valence electrons were removed from an atom (a number equal to the group number for the A family elements), the resulting ion would have a *positive* charge equal to:

$$+(num.\ valence\ e^-)$$

This would be the charge on the atom if it had no valence electrons associated with it. In a molecule, however, the atom has valence electrons associated with it—shared (as covalent bonds) and, in some cases, unshared. If the electron pairs of the covalent bonds are divided equally between the two atoms that are bonded together, the atom in question will get one electron for each shared pair of electrons (a $1-$ charge for each shared *pair*). In addition, the atom will have a $1-$ charge for each unshared *electron* that it has in the molecule. The total *negative* charge from these sources is:

$$-[\tfrac{1}{2}(num.\ shared\ e^-) + (num.\ unshared\ e^-)]$$

The formal charge of the bonded atom, therefore, is given by the formula:

$$formal\ charge\ =\ +(num.\ valence\ e^-) - \tfrac{1}{2}(num.\ shared\ e^-) - (num.\ unshared\ e^-)$$
$$(8.2)$$

Since the N atom (a group V A atom) in NH_4^+ shares four electron pairs and has no unshared electrons, its formal charge is:

$$formal\ charge\ =\ +5 - 4 - 0 = 1+$$

Each H atom in NH_4^+ has a formal charge of zero:

$$formal\ charge\ =\ +1 - 1 - 0 = 0$$

The formal charge of the N atom in NH_4^+ is indicated in the following way:

$$
\begin{array}{c}
\text{H} \\
| \\
\text{H}-\overset{\oplus}{\text{N}}-\text{H} \\
| \\
\text{H}
\end{array}
$$

We can now explain the difference between the predicted and actual number of bonds on the N atom in NH_4^+. A hypothetical N^+ would have four valence electrons and be able to form four covalent bonds. An uncharged N atom, on the other hand, has five valence electrons and can form only three covalent bonds.

A formal charge is, as the name implies, only a formality. In the assignment of formal charges, the assumption is made that the electron pair of any covalent bond is shared equally by the bonded atoms. Such an assumption is usually not true, and formal charges must be interpreted carefully. The electron density on the N atom in NH_4^+ is less than that on the N atom in NH_3, but the actual charge is not a full positive charge since the bonding electrons are not equally shared.

As another example of the way in which formal charges are calculated, consider the $POCl_3$ molecule:

$$
\begin{array}{ccc}
 & :\!\overset{..}{\text{O}}\!: & \\
 & | & \\
:\!\overset{..}{\underset{..}{\text{Cl}}}\!- & \!\!\text{P}\!\!- & :\!\overset{..}{\underset{..}{\text{Cl}}}\!: \\
 & | & \\
 & :\!\overset{..}{\underset{..}{\text{Cl}}}\!: &
\end{array}
$$

The formal charge of the O atom is:

$$
\textit{formal charge} = +(\textit{num. valence } e^-) - \tfrac{1}{2}(\textit{num. shared } e^-) - (\textit{num. unshared } e^-)
$$
$$
= +6 - 1 - 6 = 1-
$$

The formal charge of the P atom is:

$$
\textit{formal charge} = +5 - 4 - 0 = 1+
$$

The formal charge of each Cl atom is:

$$
\textit{formal charge} = +7 - 1 - 6 = 0
$$

The structure of the molecule is

$$
\begin{array}{ccc}
 & :\!\overset{..}{\text{O}}\!\overset{\ominus}{:} & \\
 & | & \\
:\!\overset{..}{\underset{..}{\text{Cl}}}\!- & \!\!\overset{\oplus}{\text{P}}\!\!- & :\!\overset{..}{\underset{..}{\text{Cl}}}\!: \\
 & | & \\
 & :\!\overset{..}{\underset{..}{\text{Cl}}}\!: &
\end{array}
$$

Notice that the sum of the formal charges in the $POCl_3$ structure is zero. The formal charges of any molecule add up to zero. The sum of the formal charges of the atoms in an ion equals the charge of the ion.

An atom in a Lewis structure that has the number of bonds expected on the basis of its group number has no formal charge. If possible, a Lewis structure should be drawn so that each atom has the number of bonds expected on the basis of its group number. Frequently, however, it is not possible.

Atoms that are bonded to each other in a structure should not have formal charges with the same sign. The repulsion between the charges would tend to break the bond between the atoms. A Lewis structure in which this **adjacent charge rule** is violated is usually not an accurate representation of the molecule or ion (see Example 8.4 in Section 8.5).

8.5 Lewis Structures

The following examples illustrate how to draw Lewis structures. The steps in the method are described in the first example.

Example 8.2

Diagram the Lewis structure of the chlorate ion, ClO_3^-. In the ion, the Cl atom is the central atom to which the three O atoms are bonded.

Solution

1. Find the total number of valence electrons supplied by all the atoms in the structure. The number supplied by each A family element is the same as the group number of the element. For a negative ion, increase the number by the charge of the ion. For a positive ion, decrease the number by the charge of the ion. The total number of valence electrons in ClO_3^- is

$$
\begin{array}{rl}
7 & \text{(from the Cl atom)} \\
18 & \text{(from the three O atoms)} \\
\underline{1} & \text{(from the ionic charge)} \\
26 &
\end{array}
$$

2. Determine the number of electrons that would be required to give two electrons to each H atom individually and eight electrons to each of the other atoms individually. Since there are no H atoms in the ClO_3^- ion,

$$
\begin{aligned}
\textit{num. } e^- \textit{ for individual atoms} &= 2(\textit{num. H atoms}) + 8(\textit{num. other atoms}) \\
&= 2(0) + 8(4) = 32
\end{aligned}
$$

3. The number obtained in step 2 minus the number obtained in step 1 is the number of electrons that must be shared in the final structure:

$$
\begin{aligned}
\textit{num. bonding } e^- &= (\textit{num. } e^- \textit{ for individual atoms}) - (\textit{total num. } e^-) \\
&= 32 - 26 = 6
\end{aligned}
$$

4. One-half the number of bonding electrons (from step 3) is the number of electron pairs used in the bonding of the final structure:

$$
\begin{aligned}
\textit{num. } e^- \textit{ pair bonds} &= (\textit{num. bonding } e^-)/2 \\
&= 6/2 = 3
\end{aligned}
$$

5. Write the symbols for the atoms present in the structure, arranging them in the way that they are found in the structure. Indicate covalent electron-pair bonds by dashes written between the symbols. Indicate one electron-pair bond between each pair of symbols, and then use any remaining from the number calculated in step 4 to make multiple bonds (note that if the structure contains H atoms, each H atom is limited to one bond):

$$
\begin{array}{c}
O \\
| \\
Cl\!-\!O \\
| \\
O
\end{array}
$$

6. The total number of electrons (step 1) minus the number of bonding electrons (step 3) is the number of unshared electrons. Complete the electron octet of each atom (other than the H atoms) by adding dots to represent unshared electrons:

$$
\begin{aligned}
\textit{num. unshared } e^- &= (\textit{total num. } e^-) - (\textit{num. bonding } e^-) \\
&= 26 - 6 = 20
\end{aligned}
$$

$$
\begin{array}{c}
:\!\ddot{O}\!: \\
| \\
:\!Cl\!-\!\ddot{O}\!: \\
| \\
:\!\ddot{O}\!:
\end{array}
$$

7. Indicate the formal charges of the atoms where appropriate. The formal charge of the Cl atom is

$$
\begin{aligned}
\textit{formal charges} &= (\textit{num. valence } e^-) - \tfrac{1}{2}(\textit{num. shared } e^-) - (\textit{num. unshared } e^-) \\
&= +7 - 3 - 2 = 2+
\end{aligned}
$$

The formal charge of each O atom is

$$formal\ charge = +6 - 1 - 6 = 1-$$

The structure is

$$
\begin{array}{c}
: \overset{..}{\underset{}{O}} : {}^{\ominus} \\
| \\
: \overset{..}{Cl} \overset{2+}{—} \overset{..}{\underset{..}{O}} : {}^{\ominus} \\
| \\
: \overset{}{\underset{..}{O}} : {}^{\ominus}
\end{array}
$$

Notice that the formal charges add up to the charge of the ion, which is $1-$.

Example 8.3

Diagram the Lewis structure of the SO_2 molecule. The molecule is angular and the two O atoms are bonded to a central S atom.

Solution

1. The total number of valence electrons in the molecule is

$$
\begin{array}{ll}
6 & \text{(from the S atom)} \\
\underline{12} & \text{(from the two O atoms)} \\
18 &
\end{array}
$$

2. $num.\ e^-$ for individual atoms $= 2(num.\ H\ atoms) + 8(num.\ other\ atoms)$
$$= 2(0) + 8(3) = 24$$

3. $num.\ bonding\ e^- = (num.\ e^-\ for\ individual\ atoms) - (total\ num.\ e^-)$
$$= 24 - 18 = 6$$

4. $num.\ e^-\ pair\ bonds = (num.\ bonding\ e^-)/2$
$$= 6/2 = 3$$

5.
$$O \overset{}{=} \underset{}{S} \overset{}{=} O$$

6. $num.\ unshared\ e^- = (total\ num.\ e^-) - (num.\ bonding\ e^-)$
$$= 18 - 6 = 12$$

$$: \overset{..}{O} : \overset{}{=} \overset{..}{S} \overset{}{=} : \overset{..}{O} :$$

7. $formal\ charge = +(num.\ valence\ e^-) - \frac{1}{2}(num.\ shared\ e^-) - (num.\ unshared\ e^-)$

For the S atom,

$$formal\ charge = +6 - 3 - 2 = 1+$$

For the left-hand O atom,

$$formal\ charge = +6 - 2 - 4 = 0$$

For the right-hand O atom,

formal charge $= +6 - 1 - 6 = 1-$

The structure is

Notice that an equivalent structure can be drawn, one in which the double bond connects the right-hand O atom to the S atom.

Example 8.4

Diagram the Lewis structure of nitric acid, HNO_3. The N atom is the central atom to which the three O atoms are bonded. The H atom is bonded to one of the O atoms.

Solution

1. The total number of valence electrons in the molecule is

1	(from the H atom)
5	(from the N atom)
18	(from the three O atoms)
24	

2. *num. e^- for individual atoms* $= 2(num.\ H\ atoms) + 8(num.\ other\ atoms)$
$$= 2(1) + 8(4) = 34$$

3. *num. bonding e^-* $= (num.\ e^-\ for\ individual\ atoms) - (total\ num.\ e^-)$
$$= 34 - 24 = 10$$

4. *num. e^- pair bonds* $= (num.\ bonding\ e^-)/2$
$$= 10/2 = 5$$

5. The molecule contains five bonds. If we indicate one bond between each pair of atoms, we use four of the five and have one left over with which to make a double bond. There are three possibilities, which we label (a), (b), and (c).

Since the H atom is limited to one bond, a structure with a double bond between H and O is not possible.

6. *num. unshared e^-* $= (total\ num.\ e^-) - (num.\ bonding\ e^-)$
$$= 24 - 10 = 14$$

Chapter 8   The Covalent Bond

7. The addition of formal charges to the three structures gives

(a)   (b)   (c)

Structure (c) must be discarded because adjacent atoms in the molecule carry formula charges with the same sign. Both structures (a) and (b), which are equivalent, are valid Lewis structures. In the next section we will see how the bonding in the nitric acid molecule is based on *both* of these structures.

8.6 Resonance

In some cases the properties of a molecule or ion are not adequately represented by a single Lewis structure. The structure for SO_2 that was derived in Example 8.3, for example,

is unsatisfactory in two respects. The structure depicts the S atom as bonded to one O atom by a double bond and to the other O atom by a single bond. Double bonds are shorter than single bonds, yet experimental evidence shows that both S to O linkages are the same length. The structure also shows one of the O atoms to be more negative than the other. It is known, however, that both of the O atoms are the same in this respect.

In a case of this type, two or more valence-bond structures can be used in combination to depict the molecule. The molecule is said to be a **resonance hybrid** of the structures, which are called **resonance forms.** For SO_2,

The actual structure does not correspond to either resonance form alone. Instead, the true structure is intermediate between the two forms. Each of the S to O bonds is neither the single bond shown in one of the resonance forms nor the double bond shown in the other form. It is intermediate between the two. Both bonds, therefore, are identical. Each O atom may be considered to have a formal charge of $\frac{1}{2}-$, since in one form it has a formal charge of 1 − and in the other it has a formal charge of zero. The oxygens, therefore, are equally negative.

There is only one type of SO_2 molecule and only one structure. The electrons of the molecule do *not* flip back and forth so that the molecule is in one form at one moment and in the other form at the next. The molecule always has the same structure. The problem arises because the Lewis theory is limited—not because the SO_2 molecule is unusual.

The two equivalent Lewis structures for the nitric acid molecule that were derived in Example 8.4 are resonance forms for the molecule:

How to Diagram Lewis Structures

1. Find the total number of valence electrons supplied by all the atoms in the structure. The number supplied by each A family element is the same as the group number of the element:

   a. For a negative ion, increase the number by the charge of the ion.

   b. For a positive ion, decrease the number by the charge of the ion.

2. Determine the number of electrons that would be required to give two electrons to each H atom individually and eight electrons to each of the other atoms individually:

num. e^- for individual atoms = 2(num. H atoms) + 8(num. other atoms)

3. The number obtained in step 2 minus the number obtained in step 1 is the number of electrons that must be shared in the final structure:

num. bonding e^- = (num. e^- for individual atoms) − (total num. e^-)

4. One-half the number of bonding electrons (step 3) is the number of covalent bonds in the final structure:

num. e^- pair bonds = (num. bonding e^-)/2

5. Write the symbols for the atoms present in the structure, arranging them in the way that they are found in the structure.

6. Indicate electron-pair bonds by dashes written between the symbols. Indicate one bond between each pair of symbols, and then use any remaining from the total calculated in step 4 to make multiple bonds. Note that each H atom is limited to one bond.

7. The total number of electrons (step 1) minus the number of bonding *electrons* (step 3) is the number of unshared electrons:

num. unshared e^- = (total num. e^-) − (num. bonding e^-)

Complete the electron octet of each atom (other than the H atoms) by adding dots to represent unshared electrons.

8. Indicate the formal charges of the atoms where appropriate, and evaluate the structure.

The actual structure of the molecule is intermediate between the two forms. The two right-hand N to O bonds have the same bond distance (121 pm), and each of these bonds is shown as a double bond in one resonance form and as a single bond in the other form. The left-hand N to O bond (shown as a single bond in *both* resonance forms) is longer than the others (141 pm).

The delocalization of charge in an ion is illustrated by the resonance of the carbonate ion, CO_3^{2-}. This ion is planar, all bonds are equivalent (between single and double bonds), and all oxygen atoms are equally negative. The formal charges add up to the charge on the ion:

As depicted by resonance, the charge is delocalized; it is impossible to locate the exact position of the "extra" two electrons that give the ion its negative charge.

The resonance forms are equivalent for each of the species that we have so far discussed: SO_2, $HONO_2$, and CO_3^{2-}. In cases such as this, each resonance form contributes equally to the resonance hybrid. For this reason, each C to O bond in the CO_3^{2-}, ion, for example, is equivalent to the others and may be considered a $1\frac{1}{3}$ bond. In some resonance hybrids, however, not all of the resonance forms are equivalent. Some forms may be of lower energy than others and hence make major contributions to the hydrid. Other forms may be of such a high energy that they contribute little, if anything, to the hybrid. We must therefore evaluate the resonance forms to determine which forms are important. The following considerations pertain to resonance forms:

1. *All resonance forms for a given molecule or ion must have the same configuration of nuclei. The resonance forms of a given species differ in the arrangement of electrons and not in the arrangement of nuclei.*

The correct arrangement of atoms in the cyanate ion, for example, is OCN^-. A structure in which the arrangement of atoms is either NOC^- or CNO^- could not be a resonance form for the cyanate ion.

2. *Two atoms that are bonded together should not have formal charges with the same sign. Resonance forms in which this adjacent charge rule is violated usually do not contribute significantly to the resonance hybrid.*

For the compound FNO_2:

resonance form (c) is discarded because it violates the adjacent charge rule—the F and N atoms each bear positive formal charges.

3. *The most important resonance forms of a given resonance hybrid have the smallest number of formal charges and the lowest values for these charges. The best forms have no formal charges at all.*

Of the possible resonance forms for the cyanate ion:

resonance form (c) is not an important contributor to the resonance hybrid, since (c) has higher formal charges than the other forms.

Notice that resonance form (c) for the FNO_2 molecule, given under rule 2, is poorer than (a) and (b) not only because it violates the adjacent charge rule but also because of the larger number of formal charges that (c) contains.

4. *Usually all the resonance forms of a given resonance hybrid have the same number of shared electrons, the largest number possible.*

A resonance form:

$$^\ominus\!:\ddot{\text{O}}\!-\!\overset{\oplus}{\text{C}}\!=\!\ddot{\text{N}}\!:^\ominus$$

for the cyanate ion will not be an important contributor, because only three electron pairs are shared in this structure, whereas in the forms shown under rule 3, four electron pairs are shared. Notice also that the C atom in this structure does not have an electron octet and that the structure has a comparatively large number of formal charges.

5. *In the most important resonance forms of a given resonance hybrid, the distribution of positive and negative formal charges should be in agreement with the electronegativities of the atoms. The most electronegative atom in the structure, for example, should not carry a positive formal charge.*

For the FNO molecule:

(a)   (b)

both forms probably contribute to a resonance hybrid. Resonance form (b), however, is not as important a contributor as form (a) is, because in form (b) the highly electronegative fluorine atom is assigned a positive formal charge. In addition, form (a) is better than form (b) because form (a) has a smaller number of formal charges (rule 3).

Notice that form (c) for FNO_2, shown under rule 2, is unimportant not only because of rules 2 and 3, but also because the F atom, the most electronegative atom, has a positive formal charge in form (c).

Notice also that form (c) for the CNO^- ion, shown under rule 3, is not an important resonance form not only because rule 3 is violated, but also because in form (c) a positive formal charge is impressed upon the O atom, the most electronegative atom of the structure.

Example 8.5

Diagram the resonance forms of the N_2O molecule. Dinitrogen oxide is a linear molecule and the atoms are arranged NNO.

Solution

We follow the rules given in Example 8.2 for drawing Lewis structures:

1. The total number of valence electrons in the molecules is

$$
\begin{array}{ll}
10 & \text{(from the two N atoms)} \\
\underline{6} & \text{(from the O atom)} \\
16 &
\end{array}
$$

2. *num. e^- for individual atoms* $= 2(num.\ H\ atoms) + 8(num.\ other\ atoms)$
$$= 2(0) + 8(3) = 24$$

3. *num. bonding e^-* $= (num.\ e^-\ for\ individual\ atoms) - (total\ num.\ e^-)$
$$= 24 - 16 = 8$$

4. *num. e^- pair bonds* $= (num.\ bonding\ e^-)/2$
$$= 8/2 = 4$$

5. We can imagine three ways to arrange the four electron-pair bonds in the molecule:

$$
\begin{array}{ccc}
\text{N}=\text{N}=\text{O} & \text{N}\equiv\text{N}-\text{O} & \text{N}-\text{N}\equiv\text{O} \\
(a) & (b) & (c)
\end{array}
$$

6. *num. unshared e^-* $= (total\ num.\ e^-) - (num.\ bonding\ e^-)$
$$= 16 - 8 = 8$$

$$
\begin{array}{ccc}
:\ddot{\text{N}}=\text{N}=\ddot{\text{O}}: & :\text{N}\equiv\text{N}-\ddot{\ddot{\text{O}}}: & :\ddot{\ddot{\text{N}}}-\text{N}\equiv\text{O}: \\
(a) & (b) & (c)
\end{array}
$$

7. The addition of formal charges gives

$$
\begin{array}{ccc}
{}^{\ominus}:\ddot{\text{N}}=\overset{\oplus}{\text{N}}=\ddot{\text{O}}: & :\text{N}\equiv\overset{\oplus}{\text{N}}-\ddot{\ddot{\text{O}}}:^{\ominus} & {}^{(2-)}:\ddot{\ddot{\text{N}}}-\overset{\oplus}{\text{N}}\equiv\text{O}:^{\oplus} \\
(a) & (b) & (c)
\end{array}
$$

Structure (c) must be discarded, since it violates the adjacent charge rule (both the central N atom and the O atom carry positive formal charges). The resonance forms of the N_2O molecule are

$$
{}^{\ominus}:\ddot{\text{N}}=\overset{\oplus}{\text{N}}=\ddot{\text{O}}: \longleftrightarrow :\text{N}\equiv\overset{\oplus}{\text{N}}-\ddot{\ddot{\text{O}}}:^{\ominus}
$$

8.7 Nomenclature of Covalent Binary Compounds

A **binary compound** is a compound formed from only two elements. The nomenclature of ionic binary compounds is discussed in Section 7.8. Covalent binary compounds are formed from two nonmetals. Most of the covalent binary compounds of carbon are classified as organic compounds, and their nomenclature is discussed in Chapter 28.

The name of an inorganic covalent binary compound is derived from the names of the two elements that form it, with the *less* electronegative element named first. The *more* electronegative element is named second, and the ending *-ide* is substituted for the usual ending of the name of that element. Greek prefixes (see Table 8.3) are added to the names of the elements to indicate the numbers of atoms of each type that are found in the molecule. The prefix *mono-* is usually omitted. The oxides of nitrogen serve as examples:

Table 8.3 Greek prefixes used in naming covalent binary compounds

Prefix	Value
mono-	1
di-	2
tri-	3
tetra-	4
penta-	5
hexa-	6
hepta-	7
octa-	8
nona-	9
deca-	10

N_2O is dinitrogen oxide
NO is nitrogen oxide
N_2O_3 dinitrogen trioxide
NO_2 is nitrogen dioxide
N_2O_4 is dinitrogen tetroxide
N_2O_5 is dinitrogen pentoxide

Certain binary compounds have acquired nonsystematic names by which they are known exclusively. The list of such substances includes water (H_2O), ammonia (NH_3), hydrazine (N_2H_4), and phosphine (PH_3). Notice that the formulas of the last three compounds are customarily written in inverted form. According to the rules, the symbol H should appear first in each of these formulas, since in each case hydrogen is the less electronegative element.

Summary

Atoms of nonmetals interact to form *molecules*, which are held together by *covalent bonds*. In a *single* covalent bond, *one* electron pair is shared between two atoms. In a *double* covalent bond, *two* electron pairs are shared, and in a *triple* covalent bond, *three* electron pairs are shared. Atoms of many nonmetals attain *noble-gas electronic configurations* (*two* electrons in the valence shell for *hydrogen*, *eight* electrons for *other nonmetals*) by forming covalent bonds during the formation of molecules or ions. When counting the electrons of the atoms of the covalent structure, the shared electrons are counted twice—once for each of the bonded atoms.

The bonding in most compounds is intermediate between the purely ionic and the purely covalent. One approach to the study of *bonds of intermediate character* is based on *ion distortion*. The positively charged cation is believed to attract and deform the negative electron cloud of the anion. This deformation leads to enhanced covalence, and in extreme cases can result in compounds that are predominantly covalent. The *degree of ion distortion increases* as the *cation* gets *smaller*, the *anion* gets *larger*, and the *charges* on the ions *increase*.

A second approach to bonds of intermediate character involves the *polarization of covalent bonds*. A covalent bond formed between dissimilar atoms is polar—one end is more negative than the other. The atom that has a greater attraction for electrons is more negative than the other atom. If there is a large difference between the electron-attracting abilities of the atoms, a predominantly ionic bond results. By measurement of the *dipole moment* and *bond distance* of a diatomic molecule, it is possible to calculate the *partial ionic character* of the bond in the molecule.

Electronegativity is a measure of the relative ability of an atom in a molecule to attract electrons to itself. These values can be used to rate the reactivities of metals and nonmetals and to make predictions concerning the nature of the bonding in a compound.

A method was introduced for drawing *Lewis structures* for covalent species. In these structures, *dots* are used to represent *valence electrons*, and each atom of the structure may be considered to have an octet of electrons associated with it (except for the H atom, which has only two electrons). *Covalent bonding* is represented by *pairs of dots* or by *dashes*. The evaluation of the results of the method depends upon the distribution of *formal charges* in the covalent species. A formal charge is a charge that is arbitrarily assigned to the atoms of a structure on the assumption that the bonding electrons are shared equally between the bonded atoms.

In some cases, the properties of a covalent molecule or ion are not adequately represented by a single Lewis structure. In a case of this type, two or more valence-bond structures, called *resonance forms*, can be used in combination to depict the molecule, which is called a *resonance hybrid*. The rules for drawing resonance forms were given; they refer principally to favorable and unfavorable distributions of formal charges in the resonance forms.

A method for naming covalent binary compounds uses the suffix *-ide* and prefixes to denote the number of atoms of each type present in a molecule of the compound.

Key Terms

Some of the more important terms introduced in this chapter are listed below. Definitions for terms not included in this list may be located in the text by use of the index.

Adjacent charge rule (Section 8.5)   In a Lewis structure, atoms that are bonded together should not have formal charges with the same sign.

Binary compound (Section 8.7)   A compound formed from two elements.

Covalent bond (Section 8.1)   A bond formed between two atoms by electron sharing. In a **single bond,** one electron pair is shared. Double and triple covalent bonds are called **multiple bonds.** In a **double bond,** two electron pairs are shared, and in a **triple bond,** three electron pairs are shared.

Dipole moment (Section 8.2)   A value calculated by multiplying the distance separating two equal charges with opposite signs by the magnitude of the charge.

Electronegativity (Section 8.3)   A measure of the relative ability of an atom in a molecule to attract electrons to itself.

Formal charge (Section 8.4)   A charge arbitrarily assigned to an atom in a covalent structure by apportioning the bonding electrons equally between the bonded atoms. These charges are useful in interpreting the properties and structures of covalent species, but the concept is merely a convention.

Lewis structure (Sections 8.1 and 8.5)   A representation of a covalent molecule or ion in which only the valence levels of the atoms are shown, a dash is used to represent a covalent bond (a pair of electrons), and dots are used to represent unshared electrons.

Partial ionic character (Sections 8.2 and 8.3)   A value (given as a percentage) that relates the polarity of a covalent bond to the polarity that would exist if the atoms were joined by an ionic bond.

Polar covalent bond (Section 8.2)   A covalent bond that has partial charges (δ^+ and δ^-) as a result of unequal sharing of bonding electrons.

Resonance (Section 8.6)   A concept in which two or more Lewis structures are used to describe the structure of a covalent molecule or ion. The actual structure of the covalent species is said to be a **hybrid** of the Lewis structures, which are called **resonance forms.**

Problems*

Transition between Ionic and Covalent Bonding

8.1 List all the nonmetallic elements that occur as diatomic molecules.

8.2 The formula P_2Br_4 is correct but the formula Ba_2Br_4 is not. Why?

8.3 How do the structures of NaCl and HCl differ?

8.4 What are multiple covalent bonds? Give examples.

8.5 On the basis of anion distortion, predict which member of each of the following pairs is the more covalent.
(a) HgF_2 or HgI_2, **(b)** FeO or Fe_2O_3, **(c)** CdS or CdSe, **(d)** CuI or CuI_2, **(e)** $SbBr_3$ or $BiBr_3$, **(f)** BeO or MgO, **(g)** MgS or MgO, **(h)** KCl or $ScCl_3$, **(i)** $PbCl_2$ or $BiCl_3$.

8.6 On the basis of anion distortion, predict which member of each of the following pairs is the more covalent.
(a) Tl_2O or Tl_2O_3, **(b)** BeO or BeS, **(c)** $SnCl_2$ or $SnCl_4$, **(d)** NaCl or Na_2Se, **(e)** CaS or BaS, **(f)** MgO or Al_2O_3, **(g)** InI or TlI, **(h)** SnI_2 or $PbCl_2$, **(i)** Na_3N or NaF.

8.7 The bond distance in the HBr molecule is 143 pm, and the dipole moment of HBr is 0.78 D. Calculate the percent partial ionic character of the H—Br bond. The unit charge, e, is 1.60×10^{-19} C, and 1.00 D is 3.34×10^{-30} C·m.

8.8 The bond distance in the HI molecule is 162 pm, and the dipole moment of HI is 0.38 D. Calculate the percent partial ionic character of the H—I bond. The unit charge, e, is 1.60×10^{-19} C, and 1.00 D is 3.34×10^{-30} C·m.

8.9 The bond distance in the BrCl molecule is 214 pm, and the dipole moment of BrCl is 0.57 D. Calculate the percent partial ionic character of the Br—Cl bond. The unit charge, e, is 1.60×10^{-19} C, and 1.00 D is 3.34×10^{-30} C·m.

8.10 The bond distance in the ClF molecule is 163 pm, and the dipole molecule of ClF is 0.88 D. Calculate the percent partial ionic character of the Cl—F bond. The unit charge, e, is 1.60×10^{-19} C, and 1.00 D is 3.34×10^{-30} C·m.

Electronegativity

8.11 Explain how electronegativity varies with position in the periodic chart and how that position can be used to rate the reactivity of an element.

---

* The more difficult problems are marked with asterisks. The appendix contains answers to color-keyed problems.

8.12 Define and discuss the difference in meaning between the terms *electron affinity* and *electronegativity*.

8.13 Use electronegativity differences to predict whether the bonds formed between the following pairs of elements would be *ionic* (roughly, a difference of 1.7 or more) or covalent. If *covalent* (roughly a difference of less than 1.7), estimate the polarity of the bond (a difference of 0, effectively nonpolar; 0.1 − 0.5, low polarity; 0.6 − 1.0 moderate polarity; 1.1 − 1.6, high polarity). **(a)** B, Br; **(b)** Ba, Br; **(c)** Rb, Br; **(d)** C, S; **(e)** C, O; **(f)** Al, Cl; **(g)** C, H; **(h)** C, I; **(i)** C, N; **(j)** Ca, N.

8.14 Use electronegativity differences to predict whether the bonds formed between the following pairs of elements would be *ionic* (roughly, a difference of 1.7 or more) or covalent. If covalent (roughly, a difference of less than 1.7), estimate the polarity of the bond (a difference of 0, effectively nonpolar; 0.1 − 0.5, low polarity; 0.6 − 1.0, moderate polarity; 1.1 − 1.6, high polarity). **(a)** N, Cl; **(b)** Na, Cl; **(c)** C, F; **(d)** Ca, F; **(e)** O, F; **(f)** O, Cl; **(g)** S, H; **(h)** P, H; **(i)** P, Cl; **(j)** P, O.

8.15 Use electronegativities to arrange the bonds listed in each part in the order of increasing ionic character. **(a)** Cs—O, Ca—O, C—O, Cl—O; **(b)** Cs—I, Ca—I, C—I, Cl—I; **(c)** Cs—H, Ca—H, C—H, Cl—H.

8.16 Use electronegativities to arrange the bonds listed in each part in the order of increasing ionic character. **(a)** O—F, I—F, In—F, N—F; **(b)** O—H, O—F, N—H, N—F; **(c)** N—S, N—O, N—Cl, S—Cl.

8.17 For each of the following pairs, use electronegativities to determine which bond is more polar. In each case, tell which end of the bond has the partial negative charge. **(a)** N—I, P—I; **(b)** N—H, P—H; **(c)** N—H, N—F; **(d)** N—H, N—Cl; **(e)** N—S, P—S; **(f)** N—O, P—O.

8.18 For each of the following pairs, use electronegativities to determine which bond is more polar. In each case, tell which end of the bond has the partial negative charge. **(a)** H—O, H—S; **(b)** H—C, H—Si; **(c)** C—O, C—S; **(d)** C—O, Si—O; **(e)** O—Cl, S—Cl; **(f)** H—Te, H—Se; **(g)** Te—I, Se—I.

Lewis Structures

8.19 Draw Lewis structures for the following molecules (include formal charges): **(a)** PH_4^+, **(b)** BH_4^-, **(c)** CH_4, **(d)** SiH_4, **(e)** SCS. When a subscript is added to a symbol in a formula, the atoms denoted are directly and separately bonded to the atom immediately following or immediately preceding in the formula.

8.20 Draw Lewis structures for the following molecules (include formal charges): **(a)** $HCCl_3$, **(b)** H_3COH, **(c)** SeO_2, **(d)** CO_2, **(e)** HCN. When a subscript is added to a symbol in a formula, the atoms denoted are directly and separately bonded to the atom immediately following or immediately preceding in the formula.

8.21 Draw Lewis structures for the following molecules (include formal charges): **(a)** $OSCl_2$, **(b)** $OCCl_2$, **(c)** $OPCl_3$, **(d)** ClSSCl. When a subscript is added to a symbol in a formula, the atoms denoted are directly and

separately bonded to the atom immediately following or immediately preceding in the formula.

8.22 Draw Lewis structures for the following molecules (include formal charges): **(a)** ClOCl, **(b)** H_2NOH, **(c)** NCCN, **(d)** $[O_3SSSO_3]^{2-}$. When a subscript is added to a symbol in a formula, the atoms denoted are directly, and separately bonded to the atom immediately following or immediately preceding in the formula.

8.23 Draw Lewis structures for the following ions (include formal charges): **(a)** SO_4^{2-}, **(b)** ClO_2^-, **(c)** CN^-, **(d)** AsO_3^{3-}. When a subscript is added to a symbol in a formula, the atoms denoted are directly and separately bonded to the atom immediately following or immediately preceding in the formula.

8.24 Draw Lewis structures for the following ions (include formal charges): **(a)** $CH_3CO_2^-$, **(b)** PO_4^{3-}, **(c)** SO_3^{2-}, **(d)** $H_2PO_2^-$. When a subscript is added to a symbol in a formula, the atoms denoted are directly and separately bonded to the atom immediately following or immediately preceding in the formula.

8.25 Draw Lewis structures for the following molecules (include formal charges): **(a)** F_2NNF_2, **(b)** HNNH, **(c)** HCCH, **(d)** HOOH. When a subscript is added to a symbol in a formula, the atoms denoted are directly and separately bonded to the atom immediately following or immediately preceding in the formula.

8.26 Draw Lewis structures for the following molecules (include formal charges): **(a)** I_2PPI_2, **(b)** H_2CCH_2, **(c)** PF_3, **(d)** H_3O^+. When a subscript is added to a symbol in a formula, the atoms denoted are directly and separately bonded to the atom immediately following or immediately preceding in the formula.

Resonance

8.27 Complete the following Lewis structures for the hyponitrite ion, $N_2O_2^{2-}$, by adding dots for unshared valence electrons and indicating formal charges. Evaluate the importance of each structure as a contributor to a resonance hybrid.

$$O—N=N—O, \quad O=N—N—O$$

8.28 Complete the following Lewis structures for the N_2F_2 molecule by adding dots for unshared valence electrons and indicating formal charges. Evaluate the importance of each structure as a contributor to a resonance hybrid.

$$F—N=N—F, \quad F=N—N—F$$

8.29 Complete the following Lewis structures for the ketene molecule, H_2C_2O, by adding dots for unshared valence electrons and indicating formal charges. Evaluate the importance of each structure as a contributor to a resonance hybrid.

$$\begin{array}{cc} H—C=C=O, & H—C—C\equiv O \\ | & | \\ H & H \end{array}$$

8.30 Complete the following Lewis structures for the HONS molecule by adding dots for unshared valence electrons and indicating formal charges. Evaluate the importance of each structure as a contributor to a resonance hybrid.

$$H-O-N=S, \quad H-O=N-S$$

8.31 Complete the following Lewis structures for the ClCN molecule by adding dots for unshared valence electrons and indicating formal charges. Evaluate the importance of each structure as a contributor to a resonance hybrid.

$$Cl-C\equiv N, \quad Cl\equiv C-N, \quad Cl=C=N$$

8.32 Complete the following Lewis structures for the $ClONO_2$ molecule by adding dots for unshared valence electrons and indicating formal charges. Evaluate the importance of each structure as a contributor to a resonance hybrid.

$$\overset{\displaystyle O}{\underset{\displaystyle |}{Cl-O-N}}=O, \quad \overset{\displaystyle O}{\underset{\displaystyle |}{Cl-O}}=N-O, \quad \overset{\displaystyle O}{\underset{\displaystyle |}{Cl}}=O-N-O$$

8.33 Compare the N to O bond distance found in the NO_2^- ion to that found in the NO_2^+ ion.

8.34 Compare the C to O bond distance found in the H_2CO molecule to that found in the HCO_2^- ion. In both H_2CO and HCO_2^-, the C atom is the central atom to which all of the other atoms are bonded.

8.35 Diagram the resonance forms of the HNSO molecule.

8.36 Diagram the resonance forms of the HNPN molecule.

8.37 Diagram the resonance forms of the FNNN molecule.

8.38 Diagram the resonance forms of the OPN molecule.

8.39 Diagram the resonance forms of the acetamide molecule, $HC(O)NH_2$ (in which one H atom, one O atom and one NH_2 group are bonded to the carbon atom).

8.40 Diagram the resonance forms of the nitramide molecule, H_2NNO_2.

8.41 Diagram the resonance forms of the F_2NNO molecule.

8.42 In the S_2N_2 molecule, the four atoms are arranged in a ring with alternating S and N atoms. Diagram the resonance forms of the S_2N_2 molecule.

8.43 Diagram the resonance forms of the oxalate ion, $O_2CCO_2^{2-}$.

8.44 Diagram the resonance forms of the $ONNO_2$ molecule.

Nomenclature of Covalent Binary Compounds

8.45 Give formulas for: **(a)** diiodine pentoxide, **(b)** dichlorine hexoxide, **(c)** disulfur dinitride, **(d)** tetraphosphorus octoxide, **(e)** sulfur tetrachloride, **(f)** xenon trioxide.

8.46 Give formulas for: **(a)** tetrasulfur tetranitride, **(b)** tetraphosphorus pentasulfide, **(c)** iodine heptoxide, **(d)** diselenium dibromide, **(e)** oxygen difluoride, **(f)** arsenic pentafluoride.

8.47 Name the following: **(a)** S_2F_2, **(b)** P_4S_7, **(c)** IF_5, **(d)** $SeBr_4$, **(e)** NF_3, **(f)** XeF_4.

8.48 Name the following: **(a)** P_2Cl_4, **(b)** N_2F_2, **(c)** P_4S_3, **(d)** S_2F_{10}, **(e)** ClF_3, **(f)** XeF_6.

Unclassified Problems

8.49 The electronegativity difference between I and Cl is 0.5, which corresponds to a partial ionic character of about 6.0% for the I—Cl bond. The bond distance of I—Cl is 232 pm. What would you predict the dipole moment of the ICl molecule to be? The unit charge, e, is 1.60×10^{-19} C and 1.00 D is 3.34×10^{-30} C·m.

8.50 The following species are isoelectronic: CO, NO^+, CN^-, and N_2. **(a)** Draw Lewis structures for each and include formal charges. **(b)** Each of the four reacts with metal atoms or metal cations to form complexes. When a complex is prepared, we can assume that an electron pair from one of the four forms a covalent bond by occupying an empty orbital of the metal atom or metal cation. For each heteronuclear species, tell which atom is bonded to the metal.

8.51 When is the concept of resonance applied? What is the difference in meaning between the terms *resonance hybrid* and *resonance form*? Why are H—C≡N: and H—N≡C: not resonance forms of the same molecule? Summarize the criteria used to evaluate the importance of a given resonance form in contributing to a resonance hybrid.

8.52 Draw Lewis structures for the following. If the species is a resonance hybrid, draw all the important resonance forms. **(a)** ONF, **(b)** O_2NF, **(c)** NSF_3, **(d)** NF_3, **(e)** ONF_3, **(f)** ONF_2^+.

8.53 Complete the following Lewis structures by adding dots for unshared valence electrons and indicating formal charges. Evaluate each structure as to its importance as a contributor to a resonance hybrid.

(a) $H-\underset{\underset{\displaystyle H}{\displaystyle |}}{N}-C\equiv N, \quad H-\underset{\underset{\displaystyle H}{\displaystyle |}}{N}=C=N$

(b) $H-\underset{\underset{\displaystyle H}{\displaystyle |}}{C}=N=N, \quad H-\underset{\underset{\displaystyle H}{\displaystyle |}}{C}-N\equiv N$

(c) $N=S-F, \quad N-S=F$

8.54 Complete the following Lewis structures by adding dots for unshared valence electrons and indicating formal charges. Evaluate each structure as to its importance as a contributor to a resonance hybrid.

(a) For FCN: $F-C\equiv N, \quad F=C=N, \quad F\equiv C-N$

(b) For N_3^-: $N-N\equiv N, \quad N=N=N, \quad N\equiv N-N$

(c) For SCN^-: $S-C\equiv N, \quad S=C=N, \quad S\equiv C-N$

(d) For CN_2^{2-}: $N-C\equiv N, \quad N=C=N, \quad N\equiv C-N$

CHAPTER 9

MOLECULAR GEOMETRY, MOLECULAR ORBITALS

The simple theory of covalent bonding that was presented in the last chapter has some shortcomings. Lewis structures, based on the octet rule, cannot be drawn for some molecules or for some covalently bonded polyatomic ions. The theory presented thus far fails to account for another important aspect of the subject—the shapes (or molecular geometry) of covalent species. In this chapter, the discussion of covalent bonding is extended and the theory of molecular orbitals (bonding orbitals that extend over whole molecules) is presented.

9.1 Exceptions to the Octet Rule

We have seen that certain ions do not have noble-gas configurations and that some of these ions are relatively stable. Some molecules also have atoms with configurations other than those that the octet principle would lead us to expect.

A few molecules (such as NO and NO_2) have an odd number of valence electrons. The NO molecule has a total of eleven valence electrons (five from the N atom and six from the O atom). The NO_2 molecule contains seventeen valence electrons (five from the N atom and twelve from the two O atoms). It is impossible to divide an odd number of electrons so that each atom of the molecule has a configuration of eight electrons (an even number). There are not many stable odd-electron molecules. Odd-electron species are usually very reactive and consequently short-lived.

More common are the molecules that have an even number of valence electrons but contain atoms with valence shells of less than, or more than, eight electrons. In the BF_3 molecule, the B atom has six valence electrons around it:

In the PCl_5 molecule, the P atom is bonded to five Cl atoms, and consequently the P atom has ten electrons in its valence shell. The S atom in SF_6 has twelve valence electrons around it, since the S atom forms single covalent bonds with six F atoms.

For the elements of the second period, only four bonding orbitals are available ($2s$ and $2p$). The number of covalent bonds on atoms of these elements is therefore limited to a maximum of four. The elements of the third and subsequent periods, however, have more orbitals available in their outer electron shells. In some compounds these elements form four, five, six, or (infrequently) an even higher number of covalent bonds. In valence-bond structures representing compounds containing elements of the third and subsequent periods, therefore, the octet principle is frequently violated. Apparently, the criteria for covalent bond formation should be centered on the electron pair rather than on the attainment of an octet.

9.2 Electron-Pair Repulsions and Molecular Geometry

The geometric arrangement of atoms in molecules and ions may be predicted by means of the **valence-shell electron-pair repulsion (VSEPR) theory:**

1. In the following discussion, we will consider molecules and ions in which a *central atom* is bonded to two or more atoms.

2. Because electron pairs repel one another, the electron pairs in the *valence shell of the central atom* are assumed to take positions as far apart as possible. The shape of the molecule or ion is a consequence of these electron-pair repulsions.

3. All the valence-shell electron pairs of the *central atom* are considered—both the pairs that form covalent bonds (called **bonding pairs**) and the pairs that are unshared (called **nonbonding pairs** or **lone pairs**).

4. The nonbonding pairs help to determine the positions of the atoms in the molecule or ion. The shape of the molecule or ion, however, is described in terms of the positions of the nuclei and not in terms of the positions of the electron pairs.

Some examples will make these points clear. In the diagrams that follow, only the electron pairs in the valence shell of the central atom are shown. Bonding pairs are indicated by dashes, and nonbonding pairs are indicated by dots. The central atom in many of these examples does not obey the octet rule.

1. Two pairs of electrons. A mercury atom has two electrons in its valence shell $(6s^2)$. Each of these electrons is used to form a covalent bond with an electron of a chlorine atom in the $HgCl_2$ molecule. The molecule is **linear:**

$$Cl—Hg—Cl$$

The $HgCl_2$ molecule adopts a shape in which the two electron-pair bonds are as far apart as possible. Molecules in which the central atom has two bonding electron pairs (but no nonbonding electron pairs) in its valence shell are always linear. Beryllium, zinc, cadmium, and mercury form molecules of this type.

2. Three pairs of electrons. A boron atom has three valence electrons (B is a member of group III A). In the BF_3 molecule, each fluorine atom (group VII A) supplies one electron for the formation of a single bond with an electron of the B atom. The boron trifluoride molecule is **triangular** and **planar:**

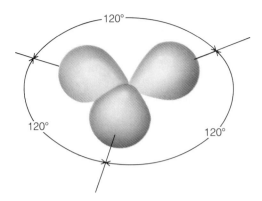

Figure 9.1 Triangular planar arrangement of three pairs of electrons

The angle formed by any two bonds in the molecule (the so-called F—B—F bond angle) is 120°. This arrangement provides the greatest possible separation between the three electron pairs (see Figure 9.1).

Tin(II) chloride vapor, $SnCl_2$, consists of **angular** molecules:

$$
\underset{Cl}{\overset{\ddot{S}n}{\diagup}}\underset{Cl}{\diagdown}
$$

A tin atom has four electrons in its valence shell (Sn is a member of group IV A), and each chlorine atom supplies one electron to form a bond. These six electrons constitute three electron pairs (two bonding and one nonbonding). The pairs assume a triangular planar configuration because of electron-pair repulsion. The shape of the molecule, however, is described in terms of the positions of its atoms, not the positions of its electrons. Tin (II) chloride molecules are therefore described as angular.

The Cl—Sn—Cl bond angle in $SnCl_2$, however, is less than 120° (about 95°). The nonbonding electron pair, which is under the influence of only one positive center, spreads out over a larger volume than a bonding pair, which is under the influence of two nuclei. As a result, the two bonds of the $SnCl_2$ molecule are forced closer together than is normal for a triangular planar arrangement. Nonbonding pairs repel bonding pairs more than bonding pairs repel other bonding pairs.

3. Four pairs of electrons. In the methane molecule, CH_4, the carbon atom has four bonding pairs of electrons in its valence shell. The Lewis structure for the molecule is

$$
\begin{array}{c}
H \\
| \\
H-C-H \\
| \\
H
\end{array}
$$

The bond pairs repel each other least when the bonds are directed toward the corners of a regular tetrahedron (see Figures 9.2 and 9.3). All the bonds in this arrangement are equidistant from one another, and all H—C—H bond angles are 109° 28′. The **tetrahedral** configuration is a common and important one. Many molecules and ions (for example, ClO_4^-, SO_4^{2-}, and PO_4^{3-}) are tetrahedral. The structure of ammonia, NH_3,

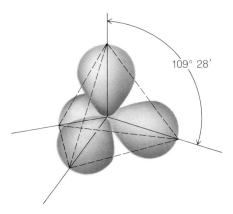

Figure 9.2 Tetrahedral arrangement of four pairs of electrons

$$H-\overset{\cdot\cdot}{N}-H$$
$$\overset{|}{H}$$

can also be related to the tetrahedron (Figure 9.3). The N atom has three bonding electron pairs and one nonbonding electron pair in its valence shell. The four pairs assume a tetrahedral configuration which causes the *atoms* of the molecule to have a **trigonal pyramidal** arrangement with the N atom at the apex of the pyramid. The nonbonding electron pair of the molecule squeezes the bonding pairs together so that each H—N—H bond angle is 107° rather than the tetrahedral angle of 109° 28′.

The valence shell of the O atom in the water molecule has two bonding pairs and two nonbonding pairs:

$$:\overset{\cdot\cdot}{O}-H$$
$$\overset{|}{H}$$

The four electron pairs are arranged in an approximately tetrahedral manner (Figure 9.3) so that the *atoms* of the molecule have a **V-shaped (angular)** configuration. Since there are two nonbonding pairs in the molecule, the bonding pairs are forced together even more than those in the NH_3 molecule. Hence, the H—O—H bond angle in H_2O (105°) is less than the H—N—H bond angle in NH_3 (107°).

4. Five pairs of electrons. In the PCl_5 molecule, the five valence electrons of the phosphorus atom (P is a member of group V A) form five bonding pairs with electrons from five chlorine atoms:

$$\begin{array}{c} & Cl \\ & | \\ Cl \diagdown & \\ & P-Cl \\ Cl \diagup & | \\ & Cl \end{array}$$

The shape that minimizes electron-pair repulsion is the **trigonal bipyramid** (Figure 9.4a). The five bonds in the structure, however, are not equivalent.

The positions that lie around the "equator" (numbers 2, 4, and 5 in the figure) are called **equatorial positions.** The positions at the "north pole" and "south pole"

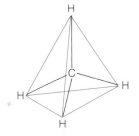

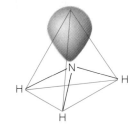

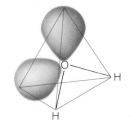

Figure 9.3 Geometries of methane (CH_4), ammonia (NH_3), and water (H_2O) molecules. (Bonding pairs shown as lines.)

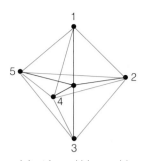

(a)   trigonal bipyramid

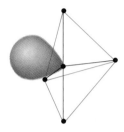

(b)   irregular tetrahedron

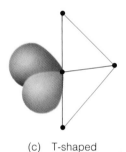

(c)   T-shaped

Figure 9.4   Geometries of molecules in which the central atom has five pairs of electrons. (Bonding pairs shown as lines.)

(numbers 1 and 3 in the figure) are called **axial positions**. Equatorial atoms lie in the same plane. Any bond angle formed by two equatorial atoms and the central atom is 120°. The axial atoms are on an axis that is at right angles to the equatorial plane. Any bond angle formed by an axial atom, the central atom, and an equatorial atom is 90°. In addition, the P—Cl axial bond length (219 pm) is slightly longer than the equatorial bond length (204 pm).

When one or more nonbonding electron pairs are present in a molecule of this type, the *nonbonding pairs occupy equatorial positions.* An equatorial position offers the nonbonding pair more room than an axial position. Consider the sulfur tetrafluoride molecule as an example. In SF_4, four of the six valence electrons of the sulfur atom (S is a group VI A element) are used to form bonding pairs, and the remaining two constitute a nonbonding pair:

$$\begin{array}{c} F \\ | \\ \overset{\cdot\cdot}{S}-F \\ \diagup | \\ F \quad F \end{array}$$

The five electron pairs are arranged in approximately the form of a trigonal bipyramid, with the nonbonding pair occupying an equatorial position (Figure 9.4b). The atoms of the molecule form what is described as an **irregular tetrahedron.**

The nonbonding electron pair affects the bond angles in the SF_4 molecule. The bonding pairs appear to be swept back, away from the nonbonding pair, so that the bond angles are less than those observed in the PCl_5 molecule. The two axial bonds form an angle of 173° with each other (instead of 180°). The two equatorial bonds form an angle of 102° with each other (instead of 120°).

In chlorine trifluoride, ClF_3, three of the seven valence electrons of the chlorine atom (a group VII A element) form bonding pairs, and the remaining four electrons make up two nonbonding pairs:

$$\begin{array}{c} F \\ | \\ \overset{\cdot\cdot}{\underset{\cdot\cdot}{Cl}}-F \\ | \\ F \end{array}$$

Placement of the two nonbonding pairs in equatorial positions produces a **T-shaped** molecule (Figure 9.4c). The distortion introduced by the nonbonding electron pairs causes the F—Cl—F bond angle, formed by an axial bond and the equatorial bond, to be 87° 30′ (rather than 90°).

The xenon atom of the xenon difluoride molecule, XeF_2, has three nonbonding pairs and two bonding pairs in its valence shell, since six of the eight valence electrons of Xe (group O) remain unshared after two bonds have formed:

$$\begin{array}{c} F \\ | \\ \overset{\cdot\cdot}{\underset{\cdot\cdot}{Xe}}: \\ | \\ F \end{array}$$

All three nonbonding electron pairs occupy equatorial positions. Xenon difluoride is a **linear** molecule (compare Figures 9.4 and 24.11).

Chapter 9   Molecular Geometry, Molecular Orbitals

5. Six pairs of electrons. In the sulfur hexafluoride molecule, SF_6, the sulfur atom (group VI A) has six bonding pairs in its valence shell:

$$
\begin{array}{c}
F \quad F \\
F \diagdown \mid \diagup F \\
S \\
F \diagup \mid \diagdown F \\
F
\end{array}
$$

(a)   octahedron

The form that minimizes electron-pair repulsion is the regular *octahedron* (Figure 9.5a). All the positions are equivalent, all the bond distances are equal, and all the angles formed by any adjacent bonds are 90°.

The bromine atom of the bromine pentafluoride molecule, BrF_5, has five bonding pairs and one nonbonding pair in its valence shell:

$$
\begin{array}{c}
F \\
F \diagdown \mid \diagup F \\
Br \\
F \diagup \raisebox{-2pt}{$\cdot\cdot$} \diagdown F
\end{array}
$$

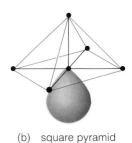

(b)   square pyramid

A Br atom has seven valence electrons (group VII A). In BrF_5, five of these electrons are engaged in bonding five fluorine atoms, and the other two constitute a nonbonding pair. The electron pairs are directed to the corners of an octahedron. The atoms of the molecule form a **square pyramid** (Figure 9.5b).

The nonbonding electron pair causes some distortion in BrF_5. Four of the bonds in the molecule (the ones that bond the atoms of the base of the pyramid to the central atom) are swept back—away from the nonbonding pair. As a result, an angle formed by the F atom at the apex of the pyramid, the Br atom, and a F atom as the base of the pyramid (see Figure 9.5b) is 85° rather than 90°.

The iodine atom of the IF_4^- ion has four bonding pairs and two nonbonding pairs in its valence shell:

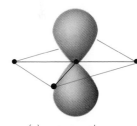

(c)   square planar

Figure 9.5 Geometries of molecules and ions in which the central atom has six pairs of electrons. (Bonding pairs shown as lines.)

$$
\begin{array}{c}
F \diagdown \raisebox{2pt}{$\cdot\cdot$} \diagup F^- \\
I \\
F \diagup \raisebox{-2pt}{$\cdot\cdot$} \diagdown F
\end{array}
$$

To account for the charge on the ion, we can consider that the central I atom gains an electron and becomes an I^- ion with eight valence electrons. Four of these electrons are used to form bonding pairs, and the other four electrons constitute two nonbonding pairs. Since the total number of electron pairs is six, the electron pairs of this ion assume octahedral positions. The nonbonding pairs take positions opposite one another, which minimizes electron-pair repulsion (Figure 9.5c). The ion, therefore, has a **square planar** geometry. The relationships between molecular shape and valence-shell electron pairs are summarized in Table 9.1

The concept of electron-pair repulsions can be extended to molecules and ions that contain multiple bonds. A multiple bond is counted as a unit for the purpose of applying the concept. Carbon dioxide (CO_2) and hydrogen cyanide (HCN), for example, are *linear* molecules like species that have two bonding pairs in the valence shell of the central atom:

$$
O{=}C{=}O \qquad H{-}C{\equiv}N
$$

Table 9.1 **Number of electron pairs in the valence shell of the central atom; and shape of molecule or ion**

Number of Electron Pairs				
Total	Bonding	Nonbonding	Shape of Molecule or Ion	Examples
2	2	0	linear	$HgCl_2$, $CuCl_2^-$
3	3	0	triangular planar	BF_3, $HgCl_3^-$
3	2	1	angular	$SnCl_2$, NO_2^-
4	4	0	tetrahedral	CH_4, BF_4^-
4	3	1	trigonal pyramidal	NH_3, PF_3
4	2	2	angular	H_2O, ICl_2^+
5	5	0	trigonal bipyramidal	PCl_5, $SnCl_5^-$
5	4	1	irregular tetrahedral	$TeCl_4$, IF_4^+
5	3	2	T-shaped	ClF_3, BrF_3
5	2	3	linear	XeF_2, ICl_2^-
6	6	0	octahedral	SF_6, PF_6^-
6	5	1	square pyramidal	IF_5, SbF_5^{2-}
6	4	2	square planar	BrF_4^-, XeF_4

The carbonyl chloride molecule, $OCCl_2$, has a *triangular planar* structure similar to that of BF_3:

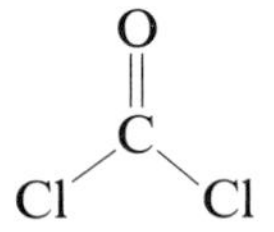

A double bond, however, takes up more room than a single bond. In $OCCl_2$, the double bond forces the C—Cl bonds closer together than is normal for the triangular planar arrangement. The Cl—C—Cl bond angle, therefore, is 111° rather than 120°.

The theory can also be applied to resonance structures. Dinitrogen oxide, N_2O, is a *linear* molecule (similar to $HgCl_2$):

The nitrite ion, NO_2^-, has an *angular* structure similar to that of $SnCl_2$:

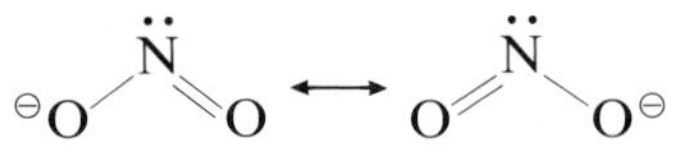

The bond angle of this molecule is 115° (rather than 120°) because of the effect of the nonbonding pair.

The nitrate ion, NO_3^-, is triangular planar (similar to BF_3):

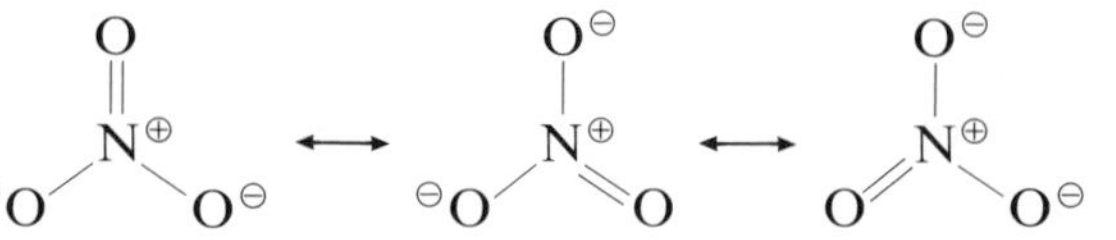

In this ion all of the O—N—O bond angles are 120°, since neither a nonbonding pair nor a multiple bond introduces distortion. The resonance forms tell us that all of the N—O linkages are identical.

Example 9.1

Use VSEPR theory to predict the shapes of the following ions. All the bonds in these structures are single bonds. Assume that each halogen atom contributes one electron to the valence shell of the central atom for bond formation: (a) $TlCl_2^+$, (b) AsF_2^+, (c) IBr_2^-, (d) $SnCl_3^-$, (e) ClF_4^-.

Solution

The number of valence electrons of the central atom (A), plus one electron for each substituent halogen atom (X), and an adjustment for the charge of the ion (chg), give the total number of electrons in the valence shell of the central atom. One-half of this number is the total number of electron pairs. Since each halogen atom is bonded by a single bond pair, the number of halogen atoms is also the number of bonding electron pairs. The number of nonbonding electron pairs is obtained by subtraction:

	Electrons A + X + chg = total	Electron pairs total	bdg	nonbdg	Shape
(a) $TlCl_2^+$	$3 + 2 - 1 = 4$	2	2	0	linear
(b) AsF_2^+	$5 + 2 - 1 = 6$	3	2	1	angular
(c) IBr_2^-	$7 + 2 + 1 = 10$	5	2	3	linear
(d) $SnCl_3^-$	$4 + 3 + 1 = 8$	4	3	1	trigonal pyramidal
(e) ClF_4^-	$7 + 4 + 1 = 12$	6	4	2	square planar

Example 9.2

Draw Lewis structures for the following and predict their shape: (a) ONF (b) SO_4^{2-}, (c) SO_3^{2-}, (d) CO_3^{2-}.

Solution

angular	tetrahedral	trigonal pyramidal	(a resonance hybrid) triangular planar
(a)	(b)	(c)	(d)

9.3 Hybrid Orbitals

With very few exceptions, the predictions based on VSEPR theory have been shown to be correct. The theory predicts, for example, that the methane molecule (CH_4) is tetrahedral, since the central C atom has four bonding pairs of electrons

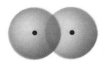

Figure 9.6 Overlap of the 1s orbitals of two hydrogen atoms

in its valence shell (Figures 9.2 and 9.3). This prediction has been confirmed by a variety of experimental evidence. It is known, with a high degree of certainty, that all four bonds of the CH_4 molecule are equivalent in length and strength and that all H—C—H bond angles are the tetrahedral angle, 109° 28′.

According to the valence-bond theory, a covalent bond consists of a pair of electrons (with spins paired) that is shared by two atoms. The formation of a co-valent bond (Figure 9.6) may be *imagined* to occur when an orbital of one atom (containing an unpaired electron) overlaps an orbital of another atom (containing an unpaired electron). If we work within the framework of this theory, how can we account for the tetrahedral bonding of CH_4?

The ground-state electron configuration of carbon ($1s^2 2s^2 2p^1 2p^1$) shows only two unpaired electrons. One might incorrectly expect that the C atom would form only two covalent bonds with H atoms. If a $2s$ electron were promoted to the vacant $2p$ orbital, however, the resulting excited state of the C atom ($1s^2 2s^1 2p^1 2p^1 2p^1$) would provide four unpaired electrons for bond formation.* How can we construct a model of the bonding in CH_4 based on this excited state of the C atom?

We assume that each bonding orbital of the molecule can be described as the product of the overlap of an atomic orbital of the C atom with a $1s$ orbital of a H atom. Since the four tetrahedral bonding orbitals are equivalent, the four atomic orbitals of the C atom used in making them must be exactly alike, with their axes directed at angles of 109° 28′ from one another. A $2s$ orbital of C and a $2p$ orbital of C, however, are not equivalent and are not oriented in the manner described (see Figures 6.12 and 6.13). We cannot, therefore, picture the bonds being formed from them in this simple way.

This problem has been traditionally handled by using an alternative description of the excited C atom. Imagine that the *total* electron distribution of the valence shell of the excited C atom—consisting of one unpaired electron in the $2s$ orbital plus three unpaired electrons in the three $2p$ orbitals—is divided into four equal portions that have identical shapes and are arranged in a tetrahedral manner. Since the total electron distribution involves four electrons, the electron density of each of the four equal portions corresponds to one electron. We can say that each por-tion represents one electron in an atomic orbital of a new type—an sp^3 **hybrid orbital.**

The wave functions that describe the $2s$ and $2p$ orbitals can be mathematically combined to give wave functions for the four equivalent sp^3 hybrid orbitals. The designation sp^3 indicates the number and type of orbitals used in the mathematical combination. The superscripts in notations of this type do not pertain to numbers of electrons. Each sp^3 hybrid orbital has one-quarter s character and three-quarters p character.

It is equally valid to describe the valence shell of the excited C atom in terms of four electrons separately occupying a $2s$ orbital and three $2p$ orbitals, or in terms of four electrons separately occupying four equivalent sp^3 hybrid orbitals. The total electron distribution represented by either description is the same. Each solu-tion reflects an equally satisfactory solution of the Schrödinger equation. The

---

* Energy is required to unpair and promote one of the $2s$ electrons. This energy, however, is more than recovered in our hypothetical process by the formation of the four covalent bonds of the CH_4 molecule. Energy is required to pull a covalent bond apart (Section 5.7). The reverse process, the formation of a covalent bond, releases energy. Although the formation of CH_2 would not require that energy be used for electron promotion, less energy would be released by the formation of only *two* covalent bonds than would be released by the formation of *four*. On balance, the formation of CH_4 is favored.

sp linear

sp² triangular planar

Table 9.2 Hybrid orbitals

Simple Atomic Orbitals	Hybrid Type	Geometry	Example
s, p_x	sp	linear	$HgCl_2$
s, p_x, p_y	sp^2	triangular planar	BF_3
s, p_x, p_y, p_z	sp^3	tetrahedral	CH_4
$d_{x^2-y^2}, s, p_x, p_y$	dsp^2	square planar	$PtCl_4^{2-}$
$d_{z^2}, s, p_x, p_y, p_z$	dsp^3 or sp^3d	trigonal bipyramidal	PF_5
$d_{z^2}, d_{x^2-y^2}, s, p_x, p_y, p_z$	d^2sp^3 or sp^3d^2	octahedral	SF_6

bonding in CH_4, therefore, can be described in terms of the overlap of the $1s$ orbitals of four H atoms with sp^3 hybrid orbitals of C.

Other types of hybrid orbitals are used to describe the bonding in other molecules. These sets need not involve all the atomic orbitals of the valence shell of the central atom. Wave functions for three equivalent sp^2 **hybrid orbitals,** for example, can be obtained by mathematically combining the wave functions for one s and two p orbitals. One of the three p orbitals is not included in this scheme. The axes of the three sp^2 hybrid orbitals lie in a plane and are directed at angles. 120° apart. The set is used to account for the bonding of a *triangular planar* molecule in which the central atom has three bonding pairs of electrons (like BF_3).

A set of sp **hybrid orbitals** (derived from one s orbital and one p orbital of the central atom) may be used to describe the bonding of *linear* molecules in which the central atom has two bonding pairs of electrons (like $HgCl_2$ or $BeCl_2$). Notice that the number of hybrid orbitals of a given type equals the number of simple atomic orbitals used in the mathematical combination that yields the type.

Common types of hybrid orbitals are listed in Table 9.2, and their directional characteristics are illustrated in Figure 9.7. Two of the sets described employ d orbitals of specified types (see Table 9.2 and Figure 6.14). The d orbitals used in a given set may be from the outer shell of the central atom or from the inner shell next to the outer shell. The octahedral hybrid orbitals, for example, may therefore be called d^2sp^3, or sp^3d^2 orbitals. Note that the hybrid orbitals of a dsp^3 (or sp^3d) set are not equivalent (see the discussion of trigonal bipyramidal molecules in Section 9.2).

The concept of hybrid orbitals may also be used to give an approximate description of molecules that contain one or more nonbonding electron pairs in the valence shell of the central atom. In NH_3, for example, we can assume that the central N atom employs sp^3 hybrid orbitals and that one of these orbitals contains a nonbonding electron pair, while the others are used to form bonds with H atoms. The H—N—H bond angles in NH_3 (107°) are close to the tetrahedral angle of the sp^3 hybrid orbitals (109° 28′)—the deviation can be ascribed to the influence of the nonbonding electron pair.

sp³ tetrahedral

dsp³ or
sp³d trigonal bipyramidal

9.4 Molecular Orbitals

The theories of molecular structure that we have discussed so far describe the bonding in molecules in terms of *atomic* orbitals. The **method of molecular orbitals** is a different approach in which orbitals are associated with the molecule as a

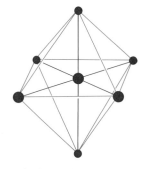

d²sp³ or *sp³d²* octahedral

Figure 9.7 Directional characteristics of hybrid orbitals

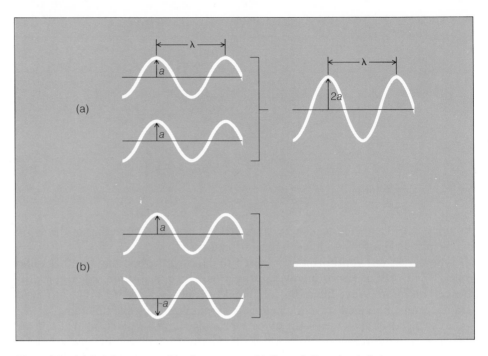

Figure 9.8 (a) Reinforcement of in-phase waves. (b) Cancellation of out-of-phase waves.

whole. The electronic structure of a molecule is derived by adding electrons to these molecular orbitals in an aufbau order. Corresponding to the practice of indicating atomic orbitals by the letters *s*, *p*, and so on, molecular orbitals are assigned the Greek letter designations σ (sigma), π (pi), and so on.

If two waves of the same wavelength (λ) and amplitude (a) are combined and are in phase, they reinforce each other (Figure 9.8a). The wavelength of the resultant wave remains the same, but the amplitude of the resultant wave is $a + a = 2a$. Two waves that are completely out of phase, however, cancel each other (Figure 9.8b); the "amplitude" of the resultant is $a + (-a) = 0$. The combination of waves can be *additive* or *subtractive*.

The molecular orbitals of the H_2 molecule can be imagined to result from the overlap of the 1*s* orbitals of two H atoms (Figure 9.6). If the overlap results in wave reinforcement (the additive combination), the electron density in the region between the nuclei is high. The attraction of the nuclei for this extra electronic charge holds the molecule together. The molecular orbital is called a **sigma bonding orbital** and is given the symbol σ (Figure 9.9).

In the combination, two atomic orbitals are used, and therefore two molecular orbitals must be produced. The other molecular orbital is the result of the out-of-phase combination of waves (the subtractive combination). The electron density in the region between the nuclei is low. In this case, the nuclei repel each other, since the low charge density between the nuclei does little to counteract this repulsion. This orbital is called a **sigma antibonding orbital** (given the symbol σ^*), since its net effect is disruptive (Figure 9.9). Sigma orbitals (both σ and σ^*) are cylindrically symmetrical about a line joining the two nuclei. Rotation of the molecule about this axis causes no observable change in orbital shape.

An energy-level diagram for the formation of $\sigma 1s$ and $\sigma^* 1s$ molecular orbitals from the 1*s* atomic orbitals of two atoms is shown in Figure 9.10. The energy of

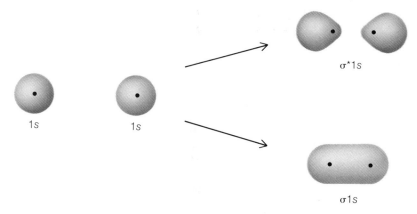

Figure 9.9 Formation of σ and σ^* molecular orbitals from 1s atomic orbitals

the σ bonding orbital is lower than that of either atomic orbital from which it is derived, whereas the energy of the σ^* antibonding orbitals is higher. When two atomic orbitals are combined, the resulting bonding molecular orbital represents a decrease in energy, and the antibonding molecular orbital represents an increase in energy.

Any orbital (atomic or molecular) can hold two electrons of opposed spin. In the hydrogen molecule, two electrons (with spins paired) occupy the $\sigma 1s$ orbital, the molecular orbital of lowest energy available to them. The σ^*1s orbital is unoccupied. One-half the difference between the number of bonding electrons and the number of antibonding electrons gives the number of bonds in the molecule (the **bond order**):

$$\text{bond order} = \tfrac{1}{2}[(\textit{num. bonding } e^-) - (\textit{num. antibonding } e^-)]$$

For H_2,

$$\text{bond order} = \tfrac{1}{2}(2 - 0) = 1$$

If an attempt is made to combine two helium atoms, a total of four electrons must be placed in the two molecular orbitals. Since the $\sigma 1s$ orbital is filled with two electrons, the other two must be placed in the higher σ^*1s orbital. The bond order in He_2 then would be

$$\text{bond order} = \tfrac{1}{2}(2 - 2) = 0$$

He_2 does not exist. The disruptive effect of the antibonding electrons cancels the bonding effect of the bonding electrons.

There is evidence that the hydrogen molecule ion, H_2^+, and the helium molecule ion, He_2^+, exist under proper conditions. The hydrogen molecule ion consists of two protons (H nuclei) and a single electron in the $\sigma 1s$ orbital. The bond order of H_2^+, therefore, is $\tfrac{1}{2}(1 - 0) = \tfrac{1}{2}$. The helium molecule ion consists of two helium nuclei and three electrons. Two of the three electrons, with spins paired, are placed in the $\sigma 1s$ orbital and the other electron is placed in the σ^*1s orbital. The bond order of He_2^+, therefore, is $\tfrac{1}{2}(2 - 1) = \tfrac{1}{2}$.

The combination of two 2s orbitals produces σ and σ^* molecular orbitals similar to those formed from 1s orbitals. The molecular orbitals derived from 2p

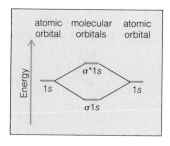

Figure 9.10 Energy-level diagram for the formation of σ and σ^* molecular orbitals from the 1s orbitals of two atoms

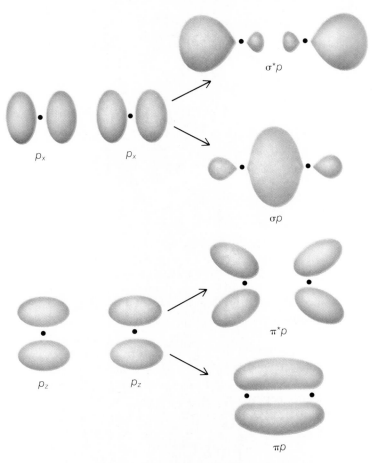

p_x p_x

σ^*p

σp

p_z p_z

π^*p

πp

Figure 9.11 Formation of molecular orbitals from p atomic orbitals

atomic orbitals, however, are slightly more complicated. The three $2p$ orbitals of an atom are directed along the x, y, and z coordinates. If we consider that a diatomic molecule is formed by the atoms approaching each other along the x axis, the p_x atomic orbitals approach each other head-on and overlap to produce $\sigma 2p$ bonding and σ^*2p antibonding molecular orbitals (Figure 9.11). All sigma orbitals are completely symmetrical about the internuclear axis.

In the formation of a diatomic molecule (Figure 9.11), the p_z atomic orbitals approach each other side-to-side and produce a **pi bonding molecular orbital** (symbol, π) and a **pi antibonding molecular orbital** (symbol, π^*). Pi orbitals are not cylindrically symmetrical about the internuclear axis. Instead, the side-to-side approach of the p orbitals leads to a π orbital consisting of two regions of charge density that lie above and below the internuclear axis (see Figure 9.11). The net effect of the π orbital, however, is to hold the molecule together. The π^* orbital has a low electron density in the region between the nuclei (see Figure 9.11). The net effect of the π^* orbital is disruptive.

The p_y orbitals, which are not shown in Figure 9.11, also approach each other sideways. They produce another set of π and π^* orbitals, which lies at right angles to the first set. The two $\pi 2p$ orbitals are degenerate (have equal energies) and the two π^*2p orbitals are degenerate. Six molecular orbitals, therefore, arise from the two sets of $2p$ atomic orbitals—one $\sigma 2p$, one σ^*2p, two $\pi 2p$, and two π^*2p. These

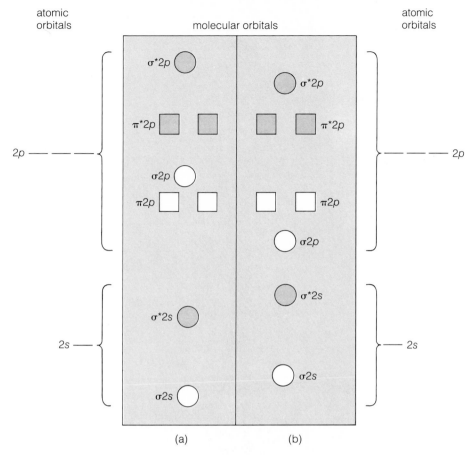

Figure 9.12 Aufbau orders for the homonuclear diatomic molecules of elements of the second period. (a) Li_2 to N_2. (b) O_2 and F_2.

six, together with the two derived from the $2s$ atomic orbitals, make a total of eight molecular orbitals obtained from the $n = 2$ atomic orbitals of two atoms.

To illustrate the aufbau process for these molecular orbitals, we will consider the homonuclear diatomic molecules of the second-period elements (molecules formed from two atoms of the same second-period element). There are two aufbau orders for these molecules (Figure 9.12). The first order (a) pertains to the molecules Li_2 to N_2; the second order (b) is the order for O_2 and F_2.

The second order (b) is the easier of the two to understand. An aufbau order is based on orbital energies. The energy of a molecular orbital depends upon the energies of the atomic orbitals used in its derivation and upon the degree and type of overlap between these atomic orbitals. Since $2s$ orbitals are lower in energy than $2p$ orbitals, the molecular orbitals derived from $2s$ orbitals are lower in energy than any molecular orbital derived from $2p$ orbitals. Because the overlap of the $2p$ orbitals that form the $\sigma 2p$ orbital is greater than the overlap of $2p$ orbitals that form $\pi 2p$ orbitals, the $\sigma 2p$ orbital is lower in energy than the degenerate $\pi 2p$ molecular orbitals. The antibonding orbitals of each type represent an increase in energy that is approximately equal to the decrease in energy represented by the bonding orbitals of that type. This aufbau order, however, is believed to be followed only by O_2 and F_2.

In the development of the order shown in (b), it is assumed that the $2s$ orbitals

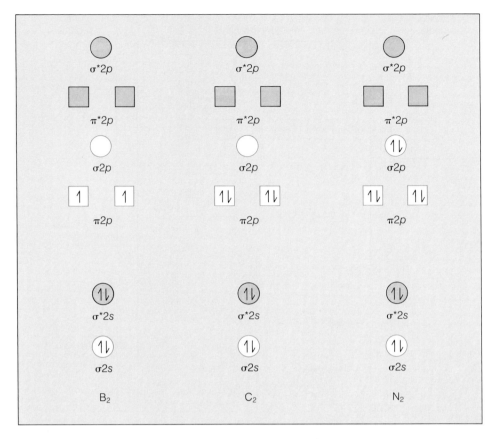

Figure 9.13 Molecular orbital energy-level diagrams for B_2, C_2, and N_2

interact only with each other and that the $2p$ orbitals used in the derivation of σ and σ^* orbitals interact only with each other. This assumption is approximately valid if the energies of the $2s$ and $2p$ orbitals are widely separated (as they are in O and F). If the energies of the $2s$ and $2p$ orbitals are close in energy, s-p interaction also occurs. The result of this additional interaction is that the σ and σ^* molecular orbitals derived from the $2s$ orbitals become more stable (of lower energy), and the σ and σ^* molecular orbitals derived from $2p$ orbitals become less stable (of higher energy). This effect produces the aufbau order shown in Figure 9.12a. The important difference between Figures 9.12b and 9.12a is that in (a) the $\sigma 2p$ orbital has been switched from below the two degenerate $\pi 2p$ orbitals to above these two orbitals. The order shown in (a) is followed by the molecules from Li_2 to N_2.

Lithium is a member of group I A, and each Li atom has one valence electron. The Li_2 molecule, therefore, has two electrons with opposed spins in the molecular orbital of lowest energy, the $\sigma 2s$ orbital. The bond order of Li_2 is $\frac{1}{2}(2 - 0) = 1$.

If we attempt to make a Be_2 molecule, four electrons must be accommodated, since each Be atom has two $2s$ electrons. The $\sigma 2s$ orbital is filled when two electrons are entered. The other two electrons are placed in the $\sigma^* 2s$ orbital. The net effect of two bonding electrons and two antibonding electrons is no bond. The bond order is $\frac{1}{2}(2 - 2) = 0$. Be_2 does not exist.

Molecular orbital energy-level diagrams for the molecules B_2, C_2, and N_2 are shown in Figure 9.13. The orbitals are arranged from bottom to top in the pertinent aufbau order (a). Each diagram is obtained by placing the correct number of

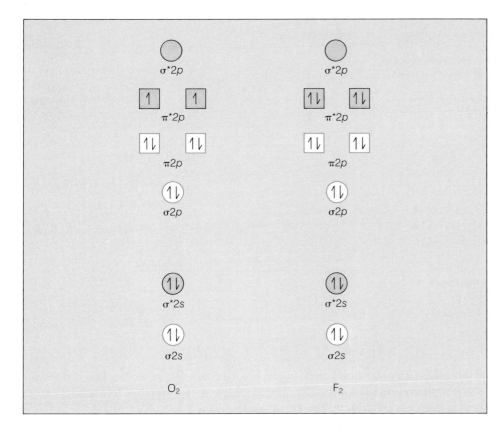

Figure 9.14 Molecular orbital energy-level diagrams for O_2 and F_2

electrons one after the other into the lowest molecular orbital available. Hund's rule is followed in the filling. The two $\pi 2p$ orbitals have equal energies, and an electron enters each separately before electron pairing is begun.

In the case of B_2, the molecule has six valence electrons (three from each B atom, since B is a member of group III A). The first two electrons are placed in the $\sigma 2s$ orbital, and the second two are placed in the σ^*2s orbital. The last two electrons are placed in separate $\pi 2p$ orbitals. As a result, the B_2 molecule has two unpaired electrons and is paramagnetic. The paramagnetism of the B_2 molecule offers confirmation that aufbau order (a) is followed. If order (b) were followed, the last two electrons, with spins paired, would be placed in the $\sigma 2p$ orbital and the molecule would be diamagnetic. The bond order of the B_2 molecule is $\frac{1}{2}(4 - 2) = 1$.

The diagrams for C_2 and N_2 are obtained by adding eight and ten electrons, respectively. Notice that C_2 has a bond order of 2 and N_2 has a bond order of 3. Neither molecule contains unpaired electrons.

Molecular orbital diagrams for O_2 and F_2 are given in Figure 9.14; aufbau order (b) is used. The diagram for O_2 is obtained by placing twelve electrons (six from each O atom) into the molecular orbitals. The last two electrons are placed in π^*2p orbitals separately. The O_2 molecule, therefore, has two unpaired electrons and is paramagnetic. The bond order of O_2 is $\frac{1}{2}(8 - 4) = 2$. The Lewis structure for O_2,

Table 9.3 Properties of diatomic molecules of the elements of the second period

Molecule	σ2s	σ*2s	π2p	σ2p	π*2p	σ*2p	Bond Order	Bond Length (pm)	Bond Energy (kJ/mol)	Unpaired Electrons
[a]Li$_2$	2						1	267	106	0
[b]Be$_2$	2	2					0	—	—	0
[a]B$_2$	2	2	2				1	159	289	2
[a]C$_2$	2	2	4				2	131	627	0
N$_2$	2	2	4	2			3	110	941	0
	σ2s	σ*2s	σ2p	π2p	π*2p	σ*2p				
O$_2$	2	2	2	4	2		2	121	494	2
F$_2$	2	2	2	4	4		1	142	155	0
[b]Ne$_2$	2	2	2	4	4	2	0	—	—	0

[a] Exists only in the vapor state at elevated temperatures.
[b] Does not exist.

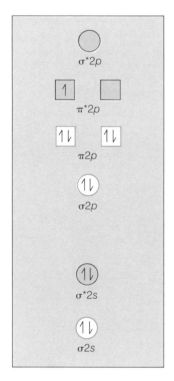

Figure 9.15 Molecular orbital energy-level diagram for NO

is unsatisfactory. It shows the double bond of the O$_2$ molecule, but it does not show the two unpaired electrons. The diagram for F$_2$ employs fourteen electrons (seven from each F atom). The F$_2$ molecule has a bond order of 1.

A summary of the homonuclear diatomic molecules of the second-period elements is given in Table 9.3. As the number of bonds increases, the bond distance shortens and the bonding becomes stronger. The molecule bonded most strongly is N$_2$, which is held together by a triple bond. Molecules for which the method assigns a bond order of zero (Be$_2$ and Ne$_2$) do not exist.

Molecular orbital diagrams can also be drawn for diatomic ions. Diagrams for the N$_2^+$ and O$_2^+$ *cations* can be obtained by *removing* one electron from the N$_2$ and O$_2$ diagrams, respectively. Diagrams for the O$_2^-$ (superoxide) and O$_2^{2-}$ (peroxide) *anions* can be obtained by *adding* one and two electrons, respectively, to the O$_2$ diagram. A diagram for the acetylide ion, C$_2^{2-}$, results when two electrons are added to the C$_2$ diagram.

For molecules such as CO and NO, the same types of molecular orbitals, although slightly distorted, are formed. Either aufbau order may be used in most cases, with the same qualitative results. The actual order, however, is uncertain.

Since CO is isoelectronic with N$_2$ (each molecule has ten valence electrons), the molecular orbital energy-level diagram for CO is similar to that for N$_2$ (Figure 9.13). Carbon monoxide, therefore, has a bond order of 3. The dissociation energy of the CO molecule is about the same as that of the N$_2$ molecule.

We have said that it is impossible to diagram a Lewis structure for a molecule with an odd number of valence electrons. Nitrogen oxide, NO, is such a molecule. Since five valence electrons are contributed by the N atom and six valence electrons by the O atom, the total number of valence electrons is eleven. An energy-level diagram for the molecular orbitals of NO is given in Figure 9.15. Since there are eight bonding electrons and three antibonding electrons shown in the diagram, a bond order of $\frac{1}{2}(8 - 3)$, or $2\frac{1}{2}$, is indicated. Nitrogen oxide is paramagnetic. The NO molecule has one unpaired electron in a π*2p orbital.

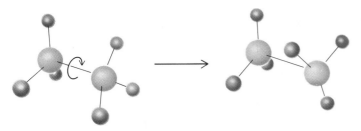

Figure 9.16 Rotation about the C—C bond in ethane

9.5 Molecular Orbitals in Polyatomic Species

Molecular orbitals can be derived for molecules that contain more than two atoms, such as H_2O and NH_3. In each case the number of molecular orbitals derived equals the number of atomic orbitals used, and the molecular orbitals encompass the whole molecule. For many purposes, however, it is convenient to think in terms of molecular orbitals that are localized between adjacent atoms. Consider the series

$$
\begin{array}{ccc}
\begin{array}{c}\text{H}\;\;\text{H}\\ | \quad | \\ \text{H}-\text{C}-\text{C}-\text{H}\\ | \quad | \\ \text{H}\;\;\text{H}\end{array}
&
\begin{array}{c}\text{H} \qquad \text{H}\\ \diagdown\quad\diagup \\ \text{C}=\text{C}\\ \diagup\quad\diagdown \\ \text{H} \qquad \text{H}\end{array}
&
\text{H}-\text{C}\equiv\text{C}-\text{H}
\\
\textit{ethane} & \textit{ethylene} & \textit{acetylene}
\end{array}
$$

Each C atom in ethane may be considered to use sp^3 hybrid orbitals in the formation of σ bonds with the other C atom and the three H atoms (Figure 9.16). Thus, all bond angles are 109° 28′, the tetrahedral angle. Since σ bonding orbitals are symmetrical about the internuclear axis, free rotation about each bond is possible. Rotation about the C—C bond causes a changing atomic configuration (Figure 9.16).

A model for the bonding in a molecule that contains one or more multiple bonds may be derived from a σ bonding skeleton of the molecule (a framework of atoms held together by single bonds). The σ bonding skeleton of ethylene is

$$
\begin{array}{c}
\text{H} \qquad\qquad \text{H}\\ \diagdown\qquad\qquad\diagup \\ \text{C}-\text{C}\\ \diagup\qquad\qquad\diagdown \\ \text{H} \qquad\qquad \text{H}
\end{array}
$$

The ethylene molecule is planar, and the σ bonds around each C atom are arranged in a triangular planar manner (the pattern predicted by VSEPR theory). The H—C—H bond angles are 118° and the H—C—C bond angles ae 121°, values that are close to the triangular planar angle of 120° (Figure 9.17).

We can account for the geometry of this molecule by assuming that each C atom uses sp^2 hybrid orbitals to form the σ bonding skeleton. One of the three $2p$ orbitals of each carbon is not involved in the formation of the sp^2 hybrid orbitals. These $2p$ orbitals are directed at right angles to the plane of the molecule and overlap to form a π bonding orbital (Figure 9.17). The electron density of the

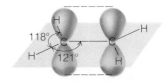

Figure 9.17 Geometric configuration of ethylene. (Shapes of the p orbitals that overlap to form a π bond are simplified; σ bonds are shown as lines.)

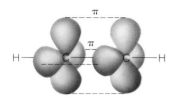

Figure 9.18 Formation of the π bonds of acetylene. (Orbital shapes are simplified; σ bonds are shown as solid lines.)

π bond is above and below the plane of the molecule. Free rotation about the C—C linkage is impossible without breaking this π bond.

The σ bonding skeleton of acetylene is

$$H—C—C—H$$

The molecule is linear (as would be predicted by VSEPR theory). Each C atom may be assumed to use sp (linear) hybrid orbitals to form two σ bonds. Two $2p$ orbitals of each C atom are not involved in the formation of the sp^2 hybrid orbitals. These $2p$ orbitals overlap to form two π bonding molecular orbitals (Figure 9.18). Note that each π bond has two centers of charge density—on either side of the axis of the σ bonding skeleton.

The multiple bonds of ethylene and acetylene are localized between two nuclei. In some molecules and ions **multicenter** (or **delocalized**) **bonding** exists in which some bonding electrons bond more than two atoms. The description of these species by the valence-bond approach requires the use of resonance structures.

An example of delocalized bonding is found in the carbonate ion (Figure 9.19). The ion is triangular planar, and each O—C—O bond angle is 120°. The C atom may be assume to use sp^2 hybrid orbitals to form the σ bonding skeleton. One $2p$ orbital is not used in the sp^2 hybrid set. This $2p$ orbital projects at right angles to the plane of the ion and overlaps similar $2p$ orbitals of the O atoms (Figure 9.19). If we imagine the overlap of these $2p$ orbitals two at a time, we derive the resonance forms of the ion. The $2p$ orbital of C, however, can simultaneously overlap all three of the $2p$ orbitals of the three O atoms. The result is a system of π molecular orbitals that extends over all the atoms in the ion. The structures of sulfur trioxide, SO_3, and the nitrate ion, NO_3^-, are similar.

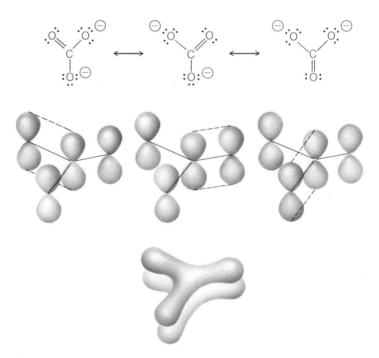

Figure 9.19 Multicenter π bonding system of the carbonate ion and the relationship to resonance structures

9.6 $p\pi$-$d\pi$ Bonding

The Lewis structure for phosphoric acid (H_3PO_4) is

$$
\begin{array}{c}
\overset{\ominus}{:\!\ddot{O}\!:} \\
| \\
H-\overset{..}{\underset{..}{O}}-\overset{\oplus}{P}-\overset{..}{\underset{..}{O}}-H \\
| \\
:\!O\!: \\
| \\
H
\end{array}
$$

All the atoms in this structure conform to the octet rule. In many compounds of phosphorus, however, the P atom forms more than four covalent bonds (for example, PF_5). Since the P atom has $3d$ orbitals available in its valence shell, the octet limit of four covalent bonds does not apply to P.

If we introduce a double bond into the structure

$$
\begin{array}{c}
:\!O\!: \\
\| \\
H-\overset{..}{\underset{..}{O}}-P-\overset{..}{\underset{..}{O}}-H \\
| \\
:\!O\!: \\
| \\
H
\end{array}
$$

the P atom no longer conforms to the octet rule (the structure shows five bonds on the P atom), and the formal charges are eliminated. In past examples, a π bond has been the result of the overlap of two p orbitals. Here, the π bond is formed by the overlap of a filled $2p$ orbital of the O atom with an empty $3d$ orbital of the P atom. As such, it is an example of what is sometimes called **$p\pi$-$d\pi$ bonding**.

There is evidence to support the structure that contains the double bond. The P—O bond distance shown in the structure as a double bond is 152 pm, which is shorter than the bond distance for the three remaining P—O bonds (shown as single bonds), 157 pm.

Based on atomic radii, however, the bond distance calculated for a P—O single bond is 176 pm. It appears, therefore, that even those bonds shown in the structure as single bonds are shorter than expected. This shortening may be explained by postulating that $p\pi$-$d\pi$ interaction, also called **back bonding**, occurs to some extent (less than a bond order of 1) in all the P—O bonds. The phosphate ion is sometimes shown as

$$
\left[
\begin{array}{c}
O \\
\vdots \\
O\!-\!-\!-\!P\!-\!-\!-\!O \\
\vdots \\
O
\end{array}
\right]^{3-}
$$

with the broken lines indicating $p\pi$-$d\pi$ interactions. All the bond distances in the structure are 154 pm.

In compounds in which a third-period nonmetal (Si, P, S, or Cl) is bonded to O, N, or F, $p\pi$-$d\pi$ bonding is particularly important. Since the second-period non-metals have no d orbitals in their valence shells, $p\pi$-$d\pi$ bonding does not occur in compounds in which the central atom is a second-period element. Such compounds (for example, $HONO_2$) can contain double bonds, but these bonds are formed by the use of s or p orbitals.

The Lewis structure and the double-bond structure for sulfuric acid, H_2SO_4, are

The S—O bond distances in the molecule are 154 pm (for the bonds shown as single bonds) and 142 pm (for the bonds shown as double bonds). The calculated S—O single-bond distance (170 pm), however, is longer than either of the measured bond distances, and $p\pi$-$d\pi$ interactions are postulated for all the S—O bonds.

In the sulfate ion

all the S—O bonds are equivalent, and the bond distance of 149 pm indicates some $p\pi$-$d\pi$ character in each.

For perchloric acid, $HClO_4$, the Lewis structure and the double-bond structure are

Three of the Cl—O bonds (those shown as double bonds) have bond distances of 141 pm; the bond distance of the Cl—O bond shown as a single bond is 164 pm. The Cl—O bond distance in the perchlorate ion (ClO_4^-) is 146 pm. Since the calculated Cl—O single-bond distance is 165 pm, $p\pi$-$d\pi$ interaction appears to be a characteristic of all the Cl—O bonds, in the ion as well as in the molecule.

Either a Lewis structure or a double-bond representation may be used to describe any one of these acids. In the case of a Lewis structure, the observed shortening of a bond represented in the other structure as a double bond may be ascribed to the effect of the attraction of plus and minus formal charges. No matter which representation is used, $p\pi$-$d\pi$ interactions must be used for even the single bonds to account for the shortness of the measured bond distances.

Summary

Some molecules exist in which atoms have electronic configurations other than those the octet principle would lead us to expect. Some molecules have an *odd number of valence electrons;* one atom, therefore, must have an unpaired electron. In other molecules, atoms have valence shells of *less than* or *more than eight electrons.* The valence-bond structures for these molecules, therefore, do not follow Lewis's octet principle.

The geometric arrangement of atoms in molecules and ions may be predicted by means of the *valence-shell-*

electron-pair repulsion theory. In covalent species in which there is a *central atom*, the *electron pairs* in the valence shell of this central atom are assumed to take *positions as far apart as possible* in order to minimize the effect of the repulsions between electron pairs. The shape of the molecule or ions, therefore, is a consequence of these electron-pair repulsions. In a determination of the geometric arrangement of a molecule or ion, both *bonding* and *nonbonding electron pairs of the central atom* are considered. The method can be extended to more complicated molecules and to resonance hybrids.

The shapes of covalent molecules and ions are readily explained on the basis of valence-shell-electron-pair repulsion theory. These geometries, however, are difficult to explain on the basis of the shapes of atomic orbitals and the valence-bond theory. A rationalization of the geometries of covalent species based on the overlap of atomic orbitals can be derived by using the *method of hybrid orbitals.* In this procedure, the wave functions of pertinent atomic orbitals of a central atom are mathematically combined (or *hybridized*) to produce wave functions of a set of *hybrid orbitals.* Through the use of these hybrid orbitals, the bonding and geometry of these species can be explained in terms of orbital overlap.

The bonding of covalent molecules and ions can also be described in terms of the *method of molecular orbitals.* In this method, the bonding in molecules is *not* described in terms of *orbitals* localized on the *atoms* of the structure. *Molecular orbitals* are associated with the *molecule* as a whole. The electronic structure of the molecule is obtained by adding electrons to the molecular orbitals in an aufbau order. There are several types of molecular orbitals (*sigma* and *pi orbitals* were described), and for each type, *bonding* and *antibonding* orbitals exist. The *bond order* of a diatomic molecule is equal to one-half the number of bonding electrons minus one-half the number of antibonding electrons.

In compounds of elements found in the third and higher periods, atoms of these elements may engage in $p\pi$-$d\pi$ *bonding.* A π bond is formed by the overlap of a d orbital of this type of atom with a p orbital of another atom. In phosphoric acid, for example, the P atom may use a $3d$ orbital to form a π bond with an O atom, which uses a $2p$ orbital. In the resulting structure, the P atom has five electron-pair bonds and does not, therefore, follow the octet rule. The structure with the $p\pi$-$d\pi$ bond, however, has no formal charges. As such, it is more energetically favorable than the Lewis structure in which there are formal charges.

Key Terms

Some of the more important terms introduced in this chapter are listed below. Definitions for terms not included in this list may be located in the text by use of the index.

Antibonding molecular orbital (Section 9.4)   A molecular orbital in which electron density is low in the internuclear region. The two electrons in an antibonding molecular orbital have higher energies than they would if they were in the atomic orbitals from which the antibonding molecular orbital was derived.

Bonding molecular orbital (Section 9.4)   A molecular orbital in which electron density is high in the internuclear region. The two electrons in a bonding molecular orbital have lower energies than they would if they were in the atomic orbitals from which the bonding molecular orbital was derived.

Bonding pair of electrons (Section 9.2)   A pair of electrons used to form a covalent bond between two atoms.

Bond order (Section 9.4)   In a diatomic molecule, one-half the number of bonding electrons minus one-half the number of antibonding electrons.

Hybridization (Section 9.3)   A concept used in valence-bond theory in which the wave functions of pertinent atomic orbitals of an atom are mathematically combined to produce the wave functions of a new set of equivalent hybrid orbitals. By the use of these hybrid orbitals, the bonding in certain covalent species can be described in terms of orbital overlap.

Molecular orbital (Section 9.4)   An orbital associated with a molecule rather than an atom.

Nonbonding pair of electrons, lone pair of electrons (Section 9.2)   On an atom in a covalent molecule or ion, a pair of electrons that is not involved in bonding.

$p\pi$-$d\pi$ bond (Section 9.6)   A π bond formed by the overlap of a p orbital with a d orbital.

Pi bond (Section 9.4)   A covalent bond in which electron density is concentrated in two regions above and below an axis joining the two bonded nuclei.

Sigma bond (Section 9.4)   A covalent bond that has high electron density in the region between the two nuclei and is symmetrical about an axis joining the two bonded nuclei.

Valence-bond theory (Section 9.3)   A theory that assumes that a covalent bond is formed by the overlap of two atomic orbitals, each of which contains an unpaired electron.

Valence-shell-electron-pair repulsion theory (Section 9.2)   A theory that permits the prediction of the shape of a covalent molecule or ion on the basis of repulsions between the bonding and nonbonding electron pairs in the valence shell of the central atom.

Problems*

VSEPR Theory; Hybrid Orbitals

9.1 Neither the bonding in NO nor in PCl_5 follows the octet rule. How do they deviate? Why is the type of deviation found in PCl_5 never found in molecules in which N is the central atom?

9.2 Why is it necessary to postulate the hybridization of the orbitals of C in order to explain the bonding in CH_4 by the overlap of atomic orbitals?

9.3 Let A represent a central atom, B represent an atom bonded by an electron-pair bond to A, and E represent an unshared electron pair on A. What shapes are predicted by VSEPR theory for AB_2, AB_3, AB_2E, AB_4, AB_3E, AB_2E_2, AB_5, AB_4E, AB_3E_2, AB_2E_3, AB_6, AB_5E, and AB_4E_2?

9.4 Let A represent a central atom, B represent an atom bonded by an electron-pair bond to A. What are the bond angles in the molecules: AB_2, AB_3, AB_4, AB_5, and AB_6. Assume that there are no unshared electron pairs on A in any of these molecules.

9.5 Use VSEPR theory to predict the geometric shapes of the following molecules and ions. All the bonds in the structures are single bonds. Assume that each halogen contributes one electron to the valence shell of the central atom for bond formation. (a) AsF_5, (b) TeF_5^-, (c) SnH_4, (d) $CdBr_2$, (e) IF_4^-, (f) AsF_4^-, (g) IBr_2^-, (h) AsF_2^+, (i) $AsCl_4^+$, (j) GeF_3^-.

9.6 Use VSEPR theory to predict the geometric shapes of the following molecules and ions. All the bonds in the structures are single bonds. Assume that each halogen contributes one electron to the valence shell of the central atom for bond formation. (a) TeF_4, (b) ClF_4^-, (c) $CuCl_2^-$, (d) ICl_2^-, (e) SCl_2, (f) GaI_3, (g) BrF_3, (h) SeF_3^+, (i) XeF_5^+, (j) $SbCl_6^-$.

9.7 Use VSEPR theory to predict the geometric shapes of the following molecules and ions. All the bonds in the structures are single bonds. Assume that each halogen contributes one electron to the valence shell of the central atom for bond formation. (a) $BeCl_2$, (b) BeF_3^-, (c) BF_4^-, (d) SF_4, (e) XeF_4, (f) AsH_3, (g) XeF_3^+, (h) SiF_6^{2-}, (i) SeF_5^-, (j) ClF_2^+.

9.8 Use VSEPR theory to predict the geometric shapes of the following molecules and ions. All the bonds in the structures are single bonds. Assume that each halogen contributes one electron to the valence shell of the central atom for bond formation. (a) $AgCl_2^-$, (b) GeF_2, (c) $SeBr_2$, (d) ClF_2^-, (e) BrF_5, (f) SiF_5^-, (g) ICl_3, (h) ICl_4^-, (i) $SbCl_5$, (j) BiI_4^-.

9.9 What type of hybrid orbital is employed by the central atom of each of the species listed in Problem 9.5?

9.10 What type of hybrid orbital is employed by the central atom of each of the species listed in Problem 9.6?

9.11 What type of hybrid orbital is employed by the central atom of each of the species listed in Problem 9.7?

9.12 What type of hybrid orbital is employed by the central atom of each of the species listed in Problem 9.8?

9.13 Draw Lewis structures for the following and use VSEPR theory to predict their geometric shapes: (a) H_2CO, (b) O_3, (c) HCN, (d) XeO_3, (e) $H_2PO_2^-$.

9.14 Draw Lewis structures for the following and use VSEPR theory to predict their geometric shapes: (a) ClOCl, (b) $OClO^-$, (c) ClO_3^-, (d) N_3^-, (e) CO_3^{2-}.

9.15 Draw Lewis structures for the following and use VSEPR theory to predict their geometric shapes: (a) $OSCl_2$, (b) $OPCl_3$, (c) SeO_2, (d) SF_2, (e) OSbCl.

9.16 Draw Lewis structures for the following and use VSEPR theory to predict their geometric shapes: (a) ONCl, (b) O_2NCl, (c) OCN^-, (d) O_2SCl_2, (e) H_3O^+.

9.17 Draw Lewis structures for the following and use VSEPR theory to predict their geometric shapes: (a) NO_2^-, (b) NO_2^+, (c) NH_2^-, (d) NH_4^+, (e) NO_3^-.

9.18 Draw Lewis structures for the following and use VSEPR theory to predict their geometric shapes: (a) SO_2, (b) SO_3, (c) SO_3^{2-}, (d) SO_4^{2-}, (e) SCl_2.

*9.19 Draw Lewis structures for the following molecules and predict their geometric shapes: (a) HNNN, (b) HONO, (c) FNNF, (d) $ONNO_2$, (e) H_2CNN.

*9.20 Draw Lewis structures for the following molecules and ions and predict their geometric shapes: (a) $O_3ClOClO_3$, (b) $(O_3SOOSO_3)^{2-}$, (c) ClSSCl, (d) $HOOSO_3^-$, (e) H_2NOH.

9.21 Draw dot structures for the following molecules and ions in which the central atom does not obey the octet rule (although the other atoms do). Predict the geometric shape of each: (a) $OXeF_4$, (b) $(HO)_5IO$, (c) XeO_6^{4-}, (d) $O_2ClF_4^-$, (e) $O_2IF_2^-$.

9.22 Draw dot structures for the following molecules and ion in which the central atom does not obey the octet rule (although the other atoms do). Predict the geometric shape of each: (a) $FOSF_5$, (b) OSF_4, (c) $(HO)_4XeO_2$, (d) O_2ClF_3, (e) $OClF_4^-$.

*9.23 The effective volume of a bond pair is assumed to decrease with increasing electronegativity of the atom bonded to the central atom. In the light of this generalization, would you expect the Cl atoms of the trigonal bipyramidal PCl_2F_3 to occupy axial or equatorial positions?

*9.24 In view of the opening statement of Problem 9.23, predict which of the PX_3 molecules (where X is F, Cl, Br, or I) would have the smallest X—P—X bond angles.

---

* The more difficult problems are marked with asterisks. The appendix contains answers to color-keyed problems.

9.25 Arrange the following in decreasing order of bond angle: **(a)** Cl_2O, **(b)** CCl_4, **(c)** NCl_3.

9.26 Describe the bond angles in the following as accurately as possible: **(a)** SF_2, **(b)** SF_4, **(c)** SF_6.

9.27 State the bond angles and the type of hybrid orbitals employed for bonding by the central atom in each of the following: **(a)** BeF_2, **(b)** BeF_3^-, **(c)** BF_4^-, **(d)** PF_5, **(e)** IF_6^+.

9.28 State the bond angles and the type of hybrid orbitals employed for bonding by the central atom in each of the following: **(a)** BF_3, **(b)** CF_4, **(c)** SiF_5^-, **(d)** PF_6^-, **(e)** NH_4^+.

Molecular Orbitals, $p\pi$-$d\pi$ Bonding

9.29 Compare the valence bond description of N_2 with the molecular orbital description of this molecule.

9.30 What is the difference between a bonding and an antibonding molecular orbital in terms of electron distribution and energy?

9.31 Draw a molecular-orbital energy-level diagram and state the bond order for each of the following: **(a)** H_2, **(b)** H_2^+, **(c)** HHe, **(d)** He_2, **(e)** He_2^+.

9.32 By means of molecular-orbital energy-level diagrams, describe the bonding of the homonuclear diatomic molecules of the second period elements. State the bond order in each molecule and whether the molecule should be paramagnetic or diamagnetic.

9.33 The anion of calcium carbide, CaC_2, should properly be called the acetylide ion, C_2^{2-}. **(a)** Draw molecular-orbital energy level diagrams for C_2 and C_2^{2-}. **(b)** State the bond order in C_2 and C_2^{2-}. **(c)** With what neutral molecule is C_2^{2-} isoelectronic?

9.34 Oxygen forms compounds containing the dioxygenyl ion, O_2^+ (for example, O_2PtF_6), the superoxide ion, O_2^- (for example, KO_2), and the peroxide ion, O_2^{2-} (for example Na_2O_2). **(a)** Draw molecular-orbital energy-level diagrams for O_2^+, O_2, O_2^-, and O_2^{2-}. **(b)** State the bond order for each species. **(c)** Which of the four are paramagnetic? State the number of unpaired electrons in each of the species that is paramagnetic.

9.35 The bond distance in N_2 is 109 pm, in N_2^+ is 112 pm, in O_2 is 121 pm, and in O_2^+ is 112 pm. Draw molecular-

orbital energy-level diagrams for these four species and explain why the bond distances vary in the way described.

9.36 (a) Draw molecular-orbital energy-level diagrams for CO and NO. **(b)** Use your diagrams to determine the bond order of CO, CO^+, CO^-, NO, NO^+, and NO^-. **(c)** Which of these species are paramagnetic? State the number of unpaired electrons in each of the species that is paramagnetic.

9.37 In the SiO_4^{4-} ion, the Si—O bond distance is 163 pm. The Si—O bond distance calculated from atomic radii is 176 pm. Explain the difference.

9.38 The atomic radius of H is 32 pm, of F is 64 pm, and of P is 110 pm. In PH_3, the P—H bond distance is 142 pm, and in PF_3, the P—F bond distance is 155 pm. Compare the bond distances in PH_3 and in PF_3 with those expected on the basis of atomic radii. What reason can you give for any discrepancy?

Unclassified Problems

9.39 Use the VSEPR theory to predict the geometric shape of the following molecules and ions. All the bonds in the structures are single bonds. **(a)** IF_2^+, **(b)** IF_2^-, **(c)** IF_3, **(d)** ClF_4^+, **(e)** ClF_4^-, **(f)** ClF_5.

9.40 What type of hybrid orbitals is employed by the central atom of each of the species listed in Problem 9.39?

9.41 Draw Lewis structures for the following molecules and ions and predict their geometric shapes: **(a)** H_3CCH_3, **(b)** H_2CCH_2, **(c)** H_2NNH_2, **(d)** HCCH, **(e)** NCCN, **(f)** ClO_2^+, **(g)** $FClO_3$, **(h)** F_2ClO^+, **(i)** XeF_4.

9.42 Discuss the structure of NO_2^- in terms of resonance and in terms of delocalized π bonding.

9.43 Draw the resonance forms for the ozone molecule, O_3, and for the sulfur dioxide molecule, SO_2. The O—O bond distance in O_3 is 127 pm, which is between the O—O single bond distance of 148 pm and the double bond distance of 110 pm. On the other hand, the S—O bond distance in SO_2 is 143 pm, which is shorter than either the S—O single bond distance of 170 pm or the double bond distance of 148 pm. Explain.

9.44 Refer to Table 9.3 and list: **(a)** the bond order of every molecule given in the table, **(b)** the bond order of each species when one electron is removed from each, and **(c)** the bond order of each species when one electron is added to each (omit Ne_2).

CHAPTER 10 GASES

Gases are believed to consist of widely separated molecules in rapid motion. Any two (or more) gases can be mixed in any proportion to prepare a perfectly uniform mixture; no such generalization can be made for liquids. Since the molecules of a gas are separated by comparatively large distances, the molecules of one gas can easily fit between the molecules of another gas. This molecular model can also be used to explain the fact that gases are readily compressed. Compression consists of forcing gas molecules closer together.

A gas expands to fill any container into which it is introduced. When a gas that has an odor is released into a room, it can soon be detected in all parts of the room. Gases diffuse because the gas molecules are in constant, rapid motion. Furthermore, in the course of their random motion, gas molecules strike the walls of the container. These impacts explain the fact that gases exert pressure.

10.1 Pressure

Pressure is defined as force per unit area. The pressure of a gas is equal to the force that the gas exerts on the walls of the container divided by the surface area of the container:

$$\text{pressure} = \frac{\text{force}}{\text{area}}$$

The SI unit of pressure is the pascal (abbreviated Pa), which is defined as the pressure equivalent to a force of one newton ($1 \text{ N} = 1 \text{ kg·m/s}^2$) acting on one square meter:

$$1 \text{ Pa} = \frac{1 \text{ N}}{1 \text{ m}^2}$$

$$= \frac{1 \text{ kg·m/s}^2}{1 \text{ m}^2} = 1 \text{ kg/m·s}^2$$

The chemist, however, usually measures gas pressures by relating them to the pressure of the atmosphere.

A barometer is used to measure the pressure that the atmosphere exerts. This instrument was devised in the seventeenth century by Evangelista Torricelli, a pupil

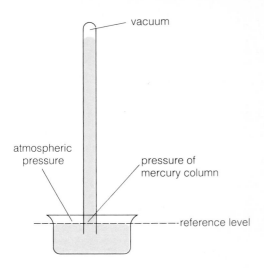

Figure 10.1 Barometer

of Galileo. A tube, approximately 850 mm in length and sealed at one end, is filled with mercury and inverted in an open container of mercury (Figure 10.1). The mercury falls in the tube but does not completely run out. The pressure of the atmosphere on the surface of the mercury in the dish supports the column of mercury in the tube.

The space above the mercury inside the tube is a nearly perfect vacuum. Since mercury is not very volatile at room temperature, only a negligible amount of mercury vapor occupies this space. Therefore, practically no pressure is exerted on the upper surface of the mercury in the column. The pressure inside the tube at the reference level shown in Figure 10.1 results from the weight of the mercury column alone. This pressure is equal to the atmospheric pressure outside the tube at the reference level.

The height of mercury in the tube serves as a measure of the atmospheric pressure. When the atmospheric pressure rises, it pushes the mercury higher in the tube. Remember that pressure is force *per unit area*. Whether the tube has a relatively large or small cross-sectional area, a given atmospheric pressure will support the mercury in the tube to the same height.

The pressure of the atmosphere changes from day to day and from place to place. The average pressure at sea level and 0°C supports a column of mercury to a height of 760 mm; this value is called 1 atmosphere (abbreviated atm). The definition of the standard atmosphere, however, is given in terms of the pascal:

$$1 \text{ atm} = 101{,}325 \text{ Pa} = 101.325 \text{ kPa}$$

The pressure equivalent to a height of 1 mm of mercury is called 1 torr (named for Torricelli); therefore,

$$1 \text{ atm} = 760 \text{ torr}$$

The International Committee of Weights and Measures recommends that pressures not be recorded in torrs. The preceding relationship can be used to convert readings made in terms of the height of a mercury column (in torrs) into atmospheres.

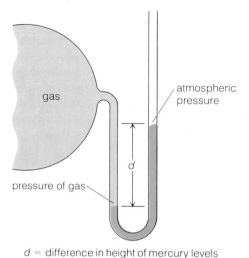

d = difference in height of mercury levels

Figure 10.2 A type of manometer

A **manometer,** a device that is used to measure the pressure of a sample of a gas, is patterned after the barometer. The type of manometer shown in Figure 10.2 consists of a U tube containing mercury. One arm of the U tube is open to the atmosphere; atmospheric pressure is exerted on the mercury in this arm. The other arm is connected to a container of a gas in such a way that the gas exerts pressure on the mercury in this arm.

If the gas sample were under a pressure *equal* to atmospheric pressure, the mercury would stand at the same level in both arms of the U tube. In the experiment illustrated in Figure 10.2, the gas pressure is *greater* than atmospheric pressure. The difference in height between the two mercury levels (in mm of mercury) must be added to the barometric pressure (in mm of mercury or in torr) to obtain the pressure of the gas (in mm of mercury or in torr). If the pressure of the gas were *less* than atmospheric, the mercury in the left arm of the manometer shown in Figure 10.2 would stand at a higher level than the mercury in the right arm, and the difference in height would have to be subtracted from atmospheric pressure.

10.2 Boyle's Law

The relationship between the volume and the pressure of a sample of a gas was studied by Robert Boyle in 1662. Boyle found that increasing the pressure on a sample of a gas causes the volume of the gas to decrease proportionately. If the pressure is doubled, the volume is cut in half. If the pressure is increased threefold, the volume is decreased to one-third its original value. **Boyle's law** states that at constant temperature the volume of a sample of gas varies inversely with the pressure:

$$V \propto \frac{1}{P}$$

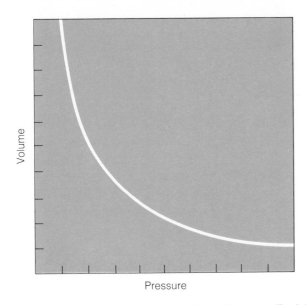

Robert Boyle, 1627–1691.
*American Institute of Physics,
Niels Bohr Library.*

Figure 10.3 Pressure-volume curve for an ideal gas (Boyle's law)

The proportionality can be changed into an equality by the introduction of a constant, k:

$$V = \frac{k}{P} \qquad \text{or} \qquad PV = k \tag{10.1}$$

The value of the constant depends upon the size of the sample and the temperature. Pressure-volume data for an ideal gas (see Section 10.5) are plotted in Figure 10.3.

The volume of a gas is customarily measured in liters. The liter is defined as 1 cubic decimeter ($1\ dm^3 = 1000\ cm^3$). Since there are 1000 mL in 1 L, 1 mL is $1\ cm^3$.

Example 10.1

A sample of a gas occupies 360 mL under a pressure of 0.750 atm. If the temperature is held constant, what volume will the sample occupy under a pressure of 1.000 atm?

Solution

First, we tabulate the data given in the problem:

Initial conditions: $V_i = 360.\ \text{mL}$ $P_i = 0.750\ \text{atm}$
Final conditions: $V_f = ?\ \text{mL}$ $P_f = 1.000\ \text{atm}$

The final volume can be obtained by correcting the intial volume for the change in pressure. The units sought are the same as the units of the quantity given:

$? \text{ mL} = (360.\ \text{mL}) \text{ (pressure correction)}$

Correction factors are *not* the same as *conversion* factors. A correction factor is not equal to 1. We can derive two pressure-correction factors from the data given:

(1.000 atm/0.750 atm)   (0.750 atm/1.000 atm)

Which one should be used?

Since the pressure *increases* from 0.750 atm to 1.000 atm, the volume must *decrease*. The correction factor must be a fraction less than 1. Hence,

$$? \, mL = 360. \, mL \left(\frac{0.750 \, atm}{1.000 \, atm} \right) = 270. \, mL$$

This problem can also be solved by using Equation 10.1. For a given sample of gas at a constant temperature, the product PV remains constant. Hence,

$$P_f V_f = P_i V_i \tag{10.2}$$

where the subscripts, f and i, identify final and initial states. If we solve the equation for the final volume, we get:

$$V_f = V_i \left(\frac{P_i}{P_f} \right) = 360. \, mL \left(\frac{0.750 \, atm}{1.000 \, atm} \right) = 270. \, mL$$

Example 10.2

At 0°C and 5.00 atm, a given sample of a gas occupies 75.0 L. The gas is compressed to a final volume of 30.0 L at 0°C. What is the final pressure?

Solution

Initial conditions: $V_i = 75.0 \, L$ $P_i = 5.00 \, atm$ $t = 0°C$
Final conditions: $V_f = 30.0 \, L$ $P_f = ? \, atm$ $t = 0°C$

The initial pressure must be corrected for the volume change. The temperature is constant, so no temperature correction is necessary:

$? \, atm = (5.00 \, atm) \, (volume \, correction)$

Volume and pressure are inversely related. Since the volume decreases, the pressure must increase. The volume-correction factor must be a fraction greater than 1. We put the larger volume measurement in the numerator of the factor:

$$? \, atm = 5.00 \, atm \left(\frac{75.0 \, L}{30.0 \, L} \right) = 12.5 \, atm$$

An alternative method of solving the problem involves the use of Equation 10.2. Here, we solve the equation for the final pressure:

$$P_f = P_i \left(\frac{V_i}{V_f} \right) = 5.00 \, atm \left(\frac{75.0 \, L}{30.0 \, L} \right) = 12.5 \, atm$$

A gas expands when it is heated. Hot-air balloons racing. *Taurus Photos.*

0.3 Charles' Law

The relationship between the volume and the temperature of a gas sample was studied by Jacques Charles in 1787. His work was considerably extended by Joseph Gay-Lussac in 1802.

A gas expands when it is heated at constant pressure. Experimental data show that for each Celsius degree rise in temperature, the volume of a gas increases 1/273 of its value at 0°C if the pressure is held constant. A sample of a gas that has a volume of 273 mL at 0°C would expand 1/273 of 273 mL, or 1 mL, for each degree rise in temperature. At 1°C, the volume of the sample would be 274 mL. At 10°C, the volume would have increased by 10 mL to a value of 283 mL. At 273°C, the sample would have expanded 273 mL to a volume of 546 mL, which is double the original volume. These data are recorded in Table 10.1.

Although the volume increases in a regular manner with increase in temperature, the volume is *not* directly proportional to the Celsius temperature. An increase in temperature from 1°C to 10°C, for example, does not increase the volume tenfold, but only from 274 mL to 283 mL. An absolute temperature scale, with temperatures measured in kelvins, is defined in such a way the volume *is* directly proportional to kelvin temperature.

A **kelvin reading** (denoted by T) is obtained by adding 273 to the Celsius temperature (denoted by t).

$$T = t + 273$$

Table 10.1 Variation of the volume of a sample of gas with temperature

Volume (mL)	Temperature (°C)	(K)
273	0	273
274	1	274
283	10	283
546	273	546

Note that absolute temperatures are given in kelvins (abbreviated K), not degrees kelvin, and that the degree sign is not used in the abbreviation. Absolute temperatures are listed in the last column in Table 10.1.

The fact that volume is directly proportional to absolute temperature is readily recognized from the data in Table 10.1, since the volume was selected to point up this relationship. For example, when the absolute temperature is doubled (273 K to 546 K), the volume doubles (273 mL to 546 mL). The volume of any sample of a gas varies directly with *absolute* temperature if the pressure is held constant. This generalization is known as **Charles' law:**

$$V \propto T$$
$$V = k'T \tag{10.3}$$

The numerical value of the proportionality constant k' depends upon the pressure and the size of the gas sample.

The absolute temperature scale was first proposed by William Thomson, Lord Kelvin, in 1848; the unit is named in his honor. Any absolute measurement scale must be based on a zero point that represents the complete absence of the property being measured. On scales of this type, negative values are impossible. A length given in centimeters is an absolute measurement, since 0 cm represents the complete absence of length. One can say that 10 cm is twice 5 cm because these are absolute measurements.

The Celsius temperature scale is not an absolute scale. The zero point, 0°C, is the freezing point of water, not the lowest possible temperature. Negative Celsius temperatures are possible, and doubling the Celsius temperature of a sample of a gas does not double the volume of the gas. On the other hand, the kelvin scale is absolute: 0 K is the lowest possible temperature, and negative kelvin temperatures are as impossible as negative lengths or negative volumes. Doubling the kelvin temperature of a sample of gas doubles the volume.

If volume versus temperature is plotted for a sample of a gas, a straight line results (see Figure 10.4). Since volume is directly proportional to absolute temperature, the volume of the gas *theoretically* should be zero at absolute zero. Upon cooling, gases liquefy and then solidify before temperatures this low are reached. No substance exists as a gas at a temperature near absolute zero. The straight-line temperature-volume curve, however, can be extended to a volume of zero.

The temperature that corresponds to zero volume is −273.15°C. The kelvin is the same size as the Celsius degree, but the zero point of the kelvin scale is moved to −273.15°C. Exact conversion of a Celsius temperature into kelvins can be accomplished, therefore, by adding 273.15 to the Celsius reading:

$$T = t + 273.15 \tag{10.4}$$

For most problems, this value can be rounded off to 273 without introducing significant error.

William Thomson, Lord Kelvin (1824–1907). *The Bettmann Archive, Inc.*

Example 10.3

A sample of a gas has a volume of 79.5 mL at 45°C. What volume will the sample occupy at 0°C when the pressure is held constant?

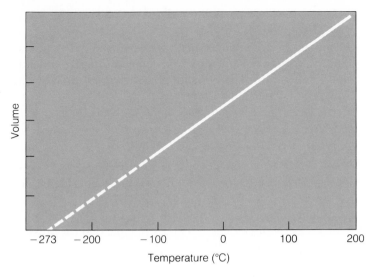

Figure 10.4 Temperature-volume curve for an ideal gas (Charles' law)

Solution

We tabulate the data given in the problem. The Celsius temperatures (t) are converted into absolute temperatures (T): $T = t + 273$,

Initial conditions:	$V_i = 79.5$ mL	$t_i = 45°C$	$T_i = 318$ K
Final conditions:	$V_f = ?$ mL	$t_f = 0°C$	$T_f = 273$ K

Therefore,

$$? \text{ mL} = (79.5 \text{ mL}) (\text{temperature correction})$$

Since the temperature decreases from 318 K to 273 K, the volume must decrease. A correction factor with a value less than 1 must be used:

$$? \text{ mL} = 79.5 \text{ mL} \left(\frac{273 \text{ K}}{318 \text{ K}}\right) = 68.2 \text{ mL}$$

We can also solve this problem by using Equation 10.3. Since $V/T = k'$, $V_f/T_f = k'$ and $V_i/T_i = k'$. Hence:

$$\frac{V_f}{T_f} = \frac{V_i}{T_i} \tag{10.5}$$

If we solve the equation for the final volume, we get:

$$V_f = V_i \left(\frac{T_f}{T_i}\right) = 79.5 \text{ mL} \left(\frac{273 \text{ K}}{318 \text{ K}}\right) = 68.2 \text{ mL}$$

10.4 Amontons' Law

The pressure of a gas confined in a container increases when the gas is heated. The mathematical relationship between pressure and temperature is similar to that between volume and temperature. The pressure of a gas varies directly with *absolute* temperature when the volume is constant:

$$P \propto T$$

$$P = k''T \tag{10.6}$$

In this instance the value of k'' depends upon the amount of gas considered and its volume.

This generalization is sometimes called **Amontons' law.** In 1703, Guillaume Amontons constructed an air thermometer based on the principle that the pressure of a gas is a measure of the temperature of the gas.

Example 10.4

A 10.0-L container is filled with a gas to a pressure of 2.00 atm at 0°C. At what temperature will the pressure inside the container be 2.50 atm?

Solution

Initital conditions:	$V_i = 10.0$ L	$P_i = 2.00$ atm	$T_i = 273$ K
Final conditions:	$V_f = 10.0$ L	$P_f = 2.50$ atm	$T_f = ?$ K

No volume correction is needed since the volume is constant. All temperatures must be expressed in kelvins in any gas problem. Therefore,

$$? \text{ K} = (273 \text{ K}) \,(\text{pressure correction})$$

Pressure varies directly with absolute temperature. The temperature must increase to produce the increase in pressure observed. A factor greater than 1 must be used:

$$? \text{ K} = 273 \text{ K} \left(\frac{2.50 \text{ atm}}{2.00 \text{ atm}} \right) = 341 \text{ K}$$

The answer can then be converted to the Celsius scale:

$$t = T - 273$$
$$= 341 \text{ K} - 273 \text{ K} = 68°\text{C}$$

We can also solve this problem by using Equation 10.6. Since $P/T = k''$, $P_f/T_f = k''$ and $P_i/T_i = k''$. Therefore,

$$\frac{P_f}{T_f} = \frac{P_i}{T_i} \tag{10.7}$$

If we solve Equation 10.7 for T_f, we get:

$$T_f = T_i \left(\frac{P_f}{P_i} \right) = 273 \text{ K} \left(\frac{2.50 \text{ atm}}{2.00 \text{ atm}} \right) = 341 \text{ K}$$

0.5 Ideal Gas Law

The volume of a gas, at fixed temperature and pressure, varies directly with the number of moles of gas considered. Obviously, 1 mol of gas (a gram molecular weight) occupies half the volume that 2 mol occupies when the temperature and pressure of both samples are the same. Furthermore, the volume of 1 mol of a given gas is the same as the volume of 1 mol of any other gas if the volumes are measured at the same temperature and pressure (Avogadro's principle, described in Section 10.8). If n is the number of moles of gas,

$$V \propto n$$

or

$$V = k'''n \tag{10.8}$$

The numerical value of the proportionality constant, k''', depends upon the temperature and pressure of the gas.

The relationship can be combined with expressions for Boyle's law and Charles' law to give a general equation relating volume, temperature, pressure, and number of moles. Volume is inversely proportional to pressure and directly proportional to absolute temperature and to number of moles:

$$V \propto \frac{1}{P} \qquad V \propto T \qquad V \propto n$$

Therefore,

$$V \propto \left(\frac{1}{P}\right)(T)(n)$$

The proportionality can be changed into an equality by the use of a constant. In this case, the constant is given the designation R:

$$V = R\left(\frac{1}{P}\right)(T)(n)$$

Rearrangement gives:

$$PV = nRT \tag{10.9}$$

Under ordinary conditions of temperature and pressure, most gases conform well to the behavior described by this equation. Deviations occur, however, under extreme conditions (low temperature and high pressure; Section 10.13). A hypothetical gas that follows the behavior described by the equation exactly, under all conditions, is called an **ideal gas.** The equation is known, therefore, as the **equation of state for an ideal gas.**

By convention, **standard temperature and pressure (STP)** are defined as 0°C (which is 273.15 K) and exactly 1 atm pressure. The volume of 1 mol of an ideal gas at STP, derived from experimental measurements, is 22.4136 L. These data can be used to evaluate the ideal gas constant, R. Solution of the equation of state for R yields:

$$R = \frac{PV}{nT}$$

Substitution of the data for the STP molar volume of an ideal gas gives:

$$R = \frac{(1 \text{ atm})(22.4136 \text{ L})}{(1 \text{ mol})(273.15 \text{ K})} = 0.082056 \text{ L·atm/(K·mol)}$$

When this value of R is employed, volume must be expressed in liters, pressure in atmospheres, and temperature in kelvins. Values of R in other units appear in Table 10.2.

The number of moles of gas in a sample, n, is equal to the mass of the sample, g, divided by the molecular weight of the gas, M:

$$n = \frac{g}{M}$$

Substitution of (g/M) for n in $PV = nRT$ gives

$$PV = \left(\frac{g}{M}\right)RT \tag{10.10}$$

Many problems can be solved by use of this form of the equation of state.

Example 10.5

The volume of a sample of a gas is 462 mL at 35°C and 1.15 atm. Calculate the volume of the sample at STP.

Solution

Initial conditions:	$V_i = 462 \text{ mL}$	$T_i = 308 \text{ K}$	$P_i = 1.15 \text{ atm}$
Final conditions:	$V_f = ? \text{ mL}$	$T_f = 273 \text{ K}$	$P_f = 1.00 \text{ atm}$

The correction-factor approach can be used to solve the problem:

$$? \text{ mL} = (462 \text{ mL})(\text{temperature correction})(\text{pressure correction})$$

Each of these corrections is considered separately. First, the decrease in temperature, from 308 K to 273 K, causes the volume to decrease by a factor of (273 K/308 K). Second, the decrease in pressure, from 1.15 atm to 1.00 atm, causes the volume to increase by a factor of (1.15 atm/1.00 atm), since pressure and volume are inversely related:

$$? \text{ mL} = 462 \text{ mL}\left(\frac{273 \text{ K}}{308 \text{ K}}\right)\left(\frac{1.15 \text{ atm}}{1.00 \text{ atm}}\right) = 471 \text{ mL}$$

Table 10.2 Values of the ideal gas constant, R, in various units	
R	Units
8.2056×10^{-2}	$L \cdot atm/(K \cdot mol)$
8.3143×10^3	$L \cdot Pa/(K \cdot mol)$
8.3143×10^3	$g \cdot m^2/(s^2 \cdot K \cdot mol)$
8.3143	$J/(K \cdot mol)$
8.3143	$m^3 \cdot Pa/(K \cdot mol)$
8.3143	$kg \cdot m^2/(s^2 \cdot K \cdot mol)^2$

We can also solve this problem by noting that $PV = nRT$, and therefore $PV/T = nR$. Since n is a constant for a given sample of a gas, and since R is also a constant,

$$\frac{P_f V_f}{T_f} = \frac{P_i V_i}{T_i} \tag{10.11}$$

If we solve Equation 10.11 for V_f, we get:

$$V_f = V_i \left(\frac{P_i}{P_f}\right)\left(\frac{T_f}{T_i}\right) = 462 \text{ mL} \left(\frac{1.15 \text{ atm}}{1.00 \text{ atm}}\right)\left(\frac{273 \text{ K}}{308 \text{ K}}\right) = 471 \text{ mL}$$

Example 10.6

At what pressure will 0.250 mol of $N_2(g)$ occupy 10.0 L at 100.°C?

Solution

$$P = ? \text{ atm} \qquad V = 10.0 \text{ L} \qquad n = 0.250 \text{ mol} \qquad T = 373 \text{ K}$$

Problems in which only one set of conditions is stated are readily solved by substitution in the equation of state:

$$PV = nRT \tag{10.9}$$

$$P(10.0 \text{ L}) = (0.250 \text{ mol})[0.0821 \text{ L} \cdot atm/(K \cdot mol)](373 \text{ K})$$

$$P = 0.766 \text{ atm}$$

Example 10.7

How many moles of CO are present in a 500. mL sample of CO(g) collected at 50.°C and 1.50 atm?

Solution

The units of the values substituted into $PV = nRT$ must correspond to the units in which R is expressed. Therefore, we express the volume in liters and the temperature in kelvins:

$$PV = nRT \qquad (10.9)$$

$$(1.50 \text{ atm})(0.500 \text{ L}) = n[0.0821 \text{ L·atm}/(\text{K·mol})](323 \text{ K})$$

$$n = 0.0283 \text{ mol}$$

Example 10.8

What volume will 10.0 g of $CO_2(g)$ occupy at 27°C and 2.00 atm?

Solution

The problem can be solved in one step if (g/M) is substituted for n in the equation of state. The molecular weight of CO_2 is 44.0 g/mol:

$$PV = \left(\frac{g}{M}\right)RT \qquad (10.10)$$

$$(2.00 \text{ atm})V = \left(\frac{10.0 \text{ g}}{44.0 \text{ g/mol}}\right)[0.0821 \text{ L·atm}/(\text{K·mol})](300. \text{ K})$$

$$V = 2.80 \text{ L}$$

Example 10.9

What is the density of $NH_3(g)$ at 100.°C and 1.15 atm?

Solution

We rearrange:

$$PV = \left(\frac{q}{M}\right)RT \qquad (10.10)$$

so as to find the density, g/V:

$$\frac{g}{V} = \frac{PM}{RT} \qquad (10.12)$$

The molecular weight of NH_3 is 17.0 g/mol. Hence:

$$\frac{g}{M} = \frac{(1.15 \text{ atm})(17.0 \text{ g/mol})}{[0.0821 \text{ L·atm}/(\text{K·mol})](373 \text{ K})}$$

$$= 0.638 \text{ g/L}$$

1. Tabulate the data given in the problem. List the *initial conditions* (V_i, P_i, and t_i) and the *final conditions* (V_f, P_f, and t_f).

2. Convert the temperature readings that are given in degrees Celsius (t) into kelvins (T). $T = t + 273.15$. For most problem work, 273 is acceptable.

A. Conversion Factor Method

3. The solution consists of finding the *final* value of one of the three variables (V, P or T) by correcting the *initial* value of this variable. Multiply the initial value by correction factors to correct for changes in the other two variables.

4. Consider each correction separately. A correction factor consists of a fraction derived from the initial and final values of the same variable (V, P, or T). One of these values is placed in the numerator of the factor, the other in the denominator. Two fractions, therefore, can be derived—one numerically greater than 1, the other less than 1. Decide whether the change being considered should result in an increase or a decrease in the value being corrected. On this basis, select the fraction to be employed as the correction factor.

5. Since the units in the numerator and denominator of a correction factor are the same, they cancel. The answer has the same units as the value being corrected.

6. If a temperature is sought, it will be obtained in kelvins. The Celsius equivalent may be found at the end of the process: $t = T - 273.15$.

B. Formula Method

3. From $PV = nRT$, we derive $PV/T = nR$. For a given gas sample, n is a constant as well as R. Since $P_f V_f / T_f = nR$, and $P_i V_i / T_i = nR$,

$$\frac{P_f V_f}{T_f} = \frac{P_i V_i}{T_i}$$

We substitute the values from steps 1 and 2 into this equation and solve for the unknown.

4. If a temperature is sought, it will be obtained in kelvins. The Celsius equivalent may be found at the end of the process: $t = T - 273.15$.

Example 10.10

(a) Cyclopropane is a gas that is used as a general anesthetic. The gas has a density of 1.50 g/L at 50.°C and 0.948 atm. What is the molecular weight of cyclopropane?
(b) The empirical formula of cyclopropane is CH_2. What is the molecular formula of the compound?

Solution

(a) Since the density of 1.50 g/L, 1.50 g of the gas will occupy 1.00 L under the conditions specified:

$$PV = \left(\frac{g}{M}\right)RT \tag{10.10}$$

$$(0.948 \text{ atm})(1.00 \text{ L}) = \left(\frac{1.50 \text{ g}}{M}\right)[0.0821 \text{ L} \cdot \text{atm}/(\text{K} \cdot \text{mol})](323 \text{ K})$$

$$M = 42.0 \text{ g/mol}$$

(b) The formula weight of the empirical formula, CH_2, is 14.0. If we divide this formula weight into the molecular weight, we get $(42.0/14.0) = 3$. There are therefore three times as many atoms in the molecule as are indicated by the empirical formula. The molecular formula of cyclopropane is C_3H_6.

10.6 Kinetic Theory of Gases

The kinetic theory of gases provides a model to explain the regularity that is observed in the behavior of all gases. In 1738, Daniel Bernoulli explained Boyle's law by assuming that the pressure of a gas results from the collisions of gas molecules with the walls of the container. Bernoulli's explanation constitutes an early and simple expression of key aspects of the kinetic theory. The theory was enlarged and developed in the middle of the nineteenth century by many scientists, notably Krönig, Clausius, Maxwell, and Boltzmann.

The kinetic theory of gases includes the following postulates:

1. Gases consist of molecules widely separated in space. The actual volume of the individual molecules is negligible in comparison to the total volume of the gas as a whole. The word *molecule* is used here to designate the smallest particle of any gas; some gases (for example, the noble gases) consist of uncombined atoms.

2. Gas molecules are in constant, rapid, straight-line motion; they collide with each other and with the walls of the container. Although energy may be transferred from one molecule to another in these collisions, no kinetic energy (energy of motion) is lost.

3. The average kinetic energy of the molecules of a gas depends upon the temperatures; it increases as the temperature increases. At a given temperature, the molecules of all gases have the same average kinetic energy.

4. The attractive forces between gas molecules are negligible.

The gas laws can be explained by the kinetic theory. Consider *Boyle's law*. According to the theory, gas pressure is caused by molecular collisions with the walls of the container. If the number of molecules per unit volume (the molecular concentration) is increased, a higher pressure will result because of the larger number of collisions per unit time. Reducing the volume of a gas crowds the molecules into a smaller space, which produces a higher molecular concentration and a proportionally higher pressure.

Charles' law and *Amontons' law* relate the properties of gases to changes in temperature. The average kinetic energy of the molecules of a gas is proportional to the absolute temperature. At absolute zero, the kinetic energy of the molecules is theoretically zero; the molecules are at rest. Since the volume of the molecules of an ideal gas is negligible, the volume of an ideal gas at absolute zero is theoretically zero.

As the temperature is increased, the molecules move at increasing speeds. The collisions of the gas molecules with the walls of the container become increasingly more vigorous and more frequent. As a result, the pressure increases in the manner described by Amontons' law.

The pressure of a gas that is being heated can be held constant if the gas is allowed to expand. The increasing volume keeps the pressure constant by reducing the number of collisions that the molecules make with the container walls in a given time. In this way, the decreasing frequency of the collisions compensates for the increasing intensity of the collisions. Charles' law describes this situation.

0.7 Derivation of the Ideal Gas Law from the Kinetic Theory

The equation of state for an ideal gas may be derived as follows. Consider a gas sample that contains N molecules, each having a mass of m. If this sample is enclosed in a cube a cm on a side, the total volume of the gas is:

$$V = a^3 \text{ cm}^3$$

Although the molecules are moving in every possible direction, the derivation is simplified if we assume that one-third of the molecules ($\frac{1}{3} N$) are moving in the direction of the x axis, one-third in the y direction, and one-third in the z direction. For a very large number of molecules, this assumption is valid. The velocity of a single molecule may be divided into x, y, and z components. For a very large number of molecules, the averages of these components are equal. The result, therefore, is equivalent to one-third of the molecules moving in each of the x, y, and z directions.

The pressure of the gas on any wall is due to the impacts of the molecules on that wall. The force of each impact can be calculated from the change in momentum per unit time. Consider the shaded wall in Figure 10.5 and take into account only those molecules moving in the direction of the x axis. A molecule moving in this direction will strike this wall every $2 \times a$ cm of its path, since after an impact it must go to the opposite wall (a distance of a cm) and return (a distance of a cm) before the next impact. If the molecule is moving with a velocity of u cm/s, in one second it will have gone u cm and have made $u/2a$ collisions with the wall under consideration.

Momentum is mass times velocity. Before an impact, the momentum of the molecule is mu; after an impact, the momentum is $-mu$ (the sign is changed because the direction is changed—velocity takes into account speed and direction). Therefore, the *change* in momentum equals $2 mu$.

In one second a molecule makes $u/2a$ collisions, and the change in momentum per collision is $2mu$. Therefore, in one second the total change in momentum per molecule is

$$\left(\frac{u}{2a}\right) 2mu = \frac{mu^2}{a}$$

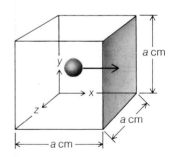

Figure 10.5 Derivation of the ideal gas law

The total change in momentum (force) for all of the molecules striking the wall in one second is

$$\frac{N}{3} \times \frac{mu^2}{a}$$

In this expression, u^2 is the average of the squares of all the molecular velocities.

Pressure is force per unit area. The area of the shaded wall is a^2 cm^2. The pressure on the wall under consideration, therefore, is:

$$\text{pressure} = \frac{force}{area}$$

$$P = \frac{\dfrac{Nmu^2}{3a}}{a^2} = \frac{Nmu^2}{3a^3}$$

Since the volume of the cube is a^3 cm^3, $V = a^3$, and:

$$P = \frac{Nmu^2}{3V} \qquad \text{or} \qquad PV = \frac{1}{3}Nmu^2 \tag{10.13}$$

This equation can be written:

$$PV = (\tfrac{2}{3}N)(\tfrac{1}{2}mu^2) \tag{10.14}$$

The kinetic energy of any body is one-half the product of its mass times the square of its speed. The average molecular kinetic energy, therefore, is:

$$KE = \tfrac{1}{2}mu^2 \tag{10.15}$$

By substitution of Equation 10.15 into Equation 10.14:

$$PV = \tfrac{2}{3}N(KE) \tag{10.16}$$

The average molecular kinetic energy, KE, is directly proportional to the absolute temperature, T, or $KE \propto T$. The number of molecules is directly proportional to the number of moles, n, or $N \propto n$. Hence:

$$N(KE) \propto nT$$

The substitution of this expression into Equation 10.14 requires that a constant be included, since the expression is a proportionality, not an equality. The required constant can be combined with the $\tfrac{2}{3}$ (which is also a constant). The combined constant equals the gas constant, R. Thus,

$$PV = nRT \tag{10.9}$$

0.8 Gay Lussac's Law of Combining Volumes and Avogadro's Principle

In 1808, Joseph Gay-Lussac reported the results of his experiments with reacting gases. When measured at constant temperature and pressure, the volume of gases that are used or produced in a chemical reaction can be expressed in ratios of small whole numbers. This statement is called **Gay-Lussac's law of combining volumes.**

One of the reactions Gay-Lussac studied is the reaction in which hydrogen chloride *gas* is produced from hydrogen *gas* and chlorine *gas*. If the volumes of all the gases are measured at the same temperature and pressure,

1 volume hydrogen + 1 volume chlorine $\longrightarrow$ 2 volumes hydrogen chloride

For example,

10 L hydrogen + 10 L chlorine $\longrightarrow$ 20 L hydrogen chloride

Joseph Gay-Lussac, 1778–1850. *Nuclear Regulatory Commission.*

Gay-Lussac did not know the formulas for these substances and did not write chemical equations. The volume ratio, however, is given by the coefficients of the gases in the chemical equation:

$$H_2(g) + Cl_2(g) \longrightarrow 2\,HCl(g)$$

The law is applicable only to gases. The volumes of solids and liquids cannot be treated in this way.

The explanation for the law of combining volumes was proposed in 1811 by Amedeo Avogadro. **Avogadro's principle** states that equal volumes of all gases at the same temperature and pressure contain the same number of molecules.

Gay-Lussac's data show that equal volumes of $H_2(g)$ and $Cl_2(g)$ react. Since the reaction requires equal numbers of H_2 and Cl_2 molecules, a given volume of either gas must contain the same number of molecules. According to Gay-Lussac, the volume of $HCl(g)$ produced is twice the volume of $H_2(g)$ used. The equation shows that the number of HCl molecules produced is twice the number of H_2 molecules used. We conclude that the number of HCl molecules in a "volume" is the same as the number of H_2 molecules in a "volume." The same comparison can be made between HCl and Cl_2.

The total volume of the reacting gases need not equal the volume of the gases produced. This fact is illustrated by another of Gay-Lussac's examples:

$$2\,CO(g) + O_2(g) \longrightarrow 2\,CO_2(g)$$

Amedeo Avogadro, 1776–1856. *California Institute of Technology Archives.*

The volume ratio for this reaction is:

2 volumes $CO(g)$ + 1 volume $O_2(g)$ $\longrightarrow$ 2 volumes $CO_2(g)$

The relative numbers of molecules involved in the reaction are given by the chemical equation. If we take $2x$ CO molecules, then:

$2x$ molecules $CO(g)$ + x molecules $O_2(g)$ $\longrightarrow$ $2x$ molecules $CO_2(g)$

By comparing these two statements, we see that one "volume" of any of the gases contains the same number of molecules, x.

Example 10.11

(a) According to the following equation, what volume of oxygen is required for the complete combustion of 15.0 L of ethane, $C_2H_6(g)$, if all gases are measured at the same temperature and pressure:

$$2\,C_2H_6(g) + 7\,O_2(g) \longrightarrow 4\,CO_2(g) + 6\,H_2O(g)$$

(b) What volume of carbon dioxide gas is produced?

Solution

(a) The relationship between the volume of $C_2H_6(g)$ and the volume of $O_2(g)$ is given by the coefficients of the chemical equation

$$2\text{ L } C_2H_6 \doteqdot 7\text{ L } O_2$$

This relationship is used to derive a conversion factor:

$$?\text{ L } O_2 = 15.0\text{ L } C_2H_6\left(\frac{7\text{ L } O_2}{2\text{ L } C_2H_6}\right) = 52.5\text{ L } O_2$$

(b) In this case, the relationship is

$$2\text{ L } C_2H_6 \doteqdot 4\text{ L } CO_2$$

Therefore,

$$?\text{ L } CO_2 = 15.0\text{ L } C_2H_6\left(\frac{4\text{ L } CO_2}{2\text{ L } C_2H_6}\right) = 30.0\text{ L } CO_2$$

According to Avogadro's principle, equal volumes of any two gases at the same temperature and pressure contain the same number of molecules. Conversely, equal numbers of molecules of any two gases under the same conditions of temperature and pressure will occupy equal volumes. A mole of a substance contains 6.022×10^{23} molecules (Avogadro's number). A mole of a gas, therefore, should occupy the same volume as a mole of any other gas if they are both measured under the same conditions of temperature and pressure. At STP this volume, called the STP molar volume of a gas, is 22.414 L. The molecular weight of a gas, therefore, is the mass, in grams, of 22.4 L of the gas at STP. For most gases, the deviation from this ideal is less than 1%.

The STP molar volume of a gas can be used to solve some problems. All such calculations, however, can also be made by using the equation of state, $PV = nRT$.

Example 10.12

What is the density of fluorine gas, $F_2(g)$, at STP?

Solution

The molecular weight of F_2 is 38.0 g/mol:

$$1 \text{ mol } F_2 = 38.0 \text{ g } F_2$$

At STP the volume of a mole of any gas is 22.4 L:

$$1 \text{ mol } F_2 = 22.4 \text{ L } F_2$$

Therefore,

$$? \text{ g } F_2 = 1 \text{ L } F_2 \left(\frac{1 \text{ mol } F_2}{22.4 \text{ L } F_2} \right) \left(\frac{38.0 \text{ g } F_2}{1 \text{ mol } F_2} \right) = 1.70 \text{ g } F_2$$

The density is 1.70 g/L.

Example 10.13

What is the molecular weight of a gas that has a density of 1.34 g/L at STP?

Solution

$$? \text{ g} = 1 \text{ mol} \left(\frac{22.4 \text{ L}}{1 \text{ mol}} \right) \left(\frac{1.34 \text{ g}}{1 \text{ L}} \right) = 30.0 \text{ g}$$

The molecular weight of the gas is 30.0 g/mol.

10.9 Stoichiometry and Gas Volumes

Stoichiometric problems may be based on the volumes of gases that are involved in a chemical reaction. Gay-Lussac's law of combining volumes is used to solve problems that deal with the volumes of two gases (see Section 10.8). Some problems concern the relationship between the *volume* of a gas and the *mass* of another substance. Examples of this type of problem follow. The clue to their solution is, as usual, the mole.

Example 10.14

A 0.400 g sample of sodium azide, $NaN_3(s)$, is heated and decomposes:

$$2NaN_3(s) \longrightarrow 2 \text{ Na(s)} + 3 N_2(g)$$

What volume of $N_2(g)$, measured at 25°C and 0.980 atm, is obtained?

Solution

We find the number of moles of NaN_3 in the sample. Since

    1 mol NaN_3 = 65.0 g NaN_3

    ? mol NaN_3 = 0.400 g $NaN_3 \left(\dfrac{1 \text{ mol } NaN_3}{65.0 \text{ g } NaN_3} \right)$ = 0.00615 mol NaN_3

From the chemical equation, we derive

    2 mol NaN_3 $\approx$ 3 mol N_2

Therefore,

    ? mol N_2 = 0.00615 mol $NaN_3 \left(\dfrac{3 \text{ mol } N_2}{2 \text{ mol } NaN_3} \right)$ = 0.00923 mol N_2

We find the volume of $N_2(g)$ by using the equation of state:

$$PV = nRT$$

$$(0.980 \text{ atm}) \, V = (0.00923 \text{ mol})[0.0821 \text{ L} \cdot \text{atm}/(K \cdot \text{mol})](298 \text{ K})$$

$$V = 0.230 \text{ L}$$

Example 10.15

How many liters of $CO(g)$, measured at STP, are needed to reduce 1.00 kg of $Fe_2O_3(s)$? The chemical equation is

    $Fe_2O_3(s) + 3\,CO(g) \longrightarrow 2\,Fe(s) + 3\,CO_2(g)$

Solution

We first find the number of moles of Fe_2O_3 in 1.00×10^3 g of Fe_2O_3. Since:

    1 mol Fe_2O_3 = 159.6 g Fe_2O_3

    ? mol Fe_2O_3 = 1.00×10^3 g $Fe_2O_3 \left(\dfrac{1 \text{ mol } Fe_2O_3}{159.6 \text{ g } Fe_2O_3} \right)$ = 6.27 mol Fe_2O_3

From the equation, we see that:

    1 mol Fe_2O_3 $\approx$ 3 mol CO

Therefore,

    ? mol CO = 6.27 mol $Fe_2O_3 \left(\dfrac{3 \text{ mol } CO}{1 \text{ mol } Fe_2O_3} \right)$ = 18.8 mol CO

At STP,

    1 mol CO = 22.4 L CO

Calculations Based on Chemical Equations and Involving Gas Volumes

The following types of problems may be encountered:

1. A *volume* of gas A is given and the *volume* of gas B is sought.

a. *The volumes of both gases are measured under the same conditions of temperature and pressure.* Use Gay-Lussac's law of combining volumes. (See Example 10.11)

b. *The volumes of the two gases are measured under different conditions.* Use Gay-Lussac's law of combining volumes to find the volume of gas B under the conditions given for gas A. Use correction factors to correct this volume of gas B so that it conforms to the final conditions given in the problem.

2. A *mass* of substance A is given and the *volume* of gas B is sought.

a. Find the number of moles of A.

b. Use this number of moles of A to find the number of moles of B. The mole relationship of B to A is given by the chemical equation.

c. Find the volume of gas B by substituting in $PV = nRT$; n is the number of moles found in step (b); P and T are the conditions under which the volume of B is measured. (See Examples 10.14 and 10.15)

3. A *volume* of gas A is given and the *mass* of substance B is sought.

a. Determine the number of moles of gas A by using $PV = nRT$.

b. Use this number of moles of A to find the number of moles of B. The mole relationship of B to A is given by the chemical equation.

c. Find the mass of B from the number of moles of B determined in step (b). One mole of B is the molecular weight of B in grams. (See Example 10.16.)

Solutions to problems of types 2 and 3 may be simplified if the gas volumes are measured at STP. The volume of 1 mol of any gas at STP is 22.4 L. This relationship can be used in steps 2(c) and 3(a) in place of $PV = nRT$. (See Examples 10.15 and 10.16.)

Therefore,

$$? \text{ L CO} = 18.8 \text{ mol CO} \left(\frac{22.4 \text{ L CO}}{1 \text{ mol CO}} \right) = 421 \text{ L CO}$$

The last step could have been solved by using the equation of state:

$$PV = nRT$$

$$(1 \text{ atm}) V = (18.8 \text{ mol})[0.0821 \text{ L} \cdot \text{atm}/(\text{K} \cdot \text{mole})](273 \text{ K})$$

$$V = 421 \text{ L}$$

Example 10.16

How many grams of Fe is needed to produce 100. L of $H_2(g)$, measured at STP? The equation is

$$3\,Fe(s) + 4\,H_2O \longrightarrow Fe_3O_4(s) + 4\,H_2(g)$$

Solution

First, the number of moles of H_2 is found. At STP

$$1\ mol\ H_2 = 22.4\ L\ H_2$$

$$?\ mol\ H_2 = 100.\ L\ H_2 \left(\frac{1\ mol\ H_2}{22.4\ L\ H_2}\right) = 4.46\ mol\ H_2$$

(The last step could also be accomplished by substituting in $PV = nRT$.) From the equation,

$$3\ mol\ Fe \Leftrightarrow 4\ mol\ H_2$$

we find,

$$?\ mol\ Fe = 4.46\ H_2 \left(\frac{3\ mol\ Fe}{4\ mol\ H_2}\right) = 3.35\ mol\ Fe$$

The atomic weight of Fe is 55.8; therefore,

$$?\ g\ Fe = 3.35\ mol\ Fe \left(\frac{55.8\ g\ Fe}{1\ mol\ Fe}\right) = 187\ g\ Fe$$

10.10 Dalton's Law of Partial Pressures

The behavior of a mixture of gases that do not react with one another is frequently of interest. The pressure that a component of such a mixture would exert if it were the only gas present in the volume under consideration is the **partial pressure** of the component. **Dalton's law of partial pressures** (1801) states that the total pressure of a mixture of gases that do not react is equal to the sum of the partial pressures of all the gases present. If the total pressure is P_{total} and the partial pressures are $p_A, p_B, p_C, \cdots$

$$P_{total} = p_A + p_B + p_C + \cdots \tag{10.17}$$

Suppose that 1 L of gas A at 0.2 atm pressure and 1 L of gas B at 0.4 atm pressure are mixed. If the *final volume is 1 L* and the temperature is constant, the pressure of the mixture will be 0.6 atm.

According to the kinetic theory, the molecules of gas A have the same average kinetic energy as the molecules of gas B, since the two gases are at the same temperature. Furthermore, the kinetic theory assumes that the gas molecules do not attract one another if the gases do not react chemically. Consequently, the act of mixing two or more gases does not change the average kinetic energy of any of the gases. Each gas exerts the same pressure that it would exert if it were the only gas present in the container.

If n_A mol of gas A and n_B mol of gas B are mixed, the total number of moles of gas in the mixture is $(n_A + n_B)$. The ratio of the number of moles of A to the total number of moles present is called the mole fraction of A, X_A:

$$X_A = \frac{n_A}{n_A + n_B} = \frac{n_A}{n_{total}} \tag{10.18}$$

The fraction of the total pressure that is due to gas A is given by the mole fraction of A. The partial pressure of A, therefore, is

$$p_A = \left(\frac{n_A}{n_A + n_B}\right)P_{total} = X_A P_{total} \tag{10.19}$$

The partial pressure of B is equal to the mole fraction of B times the total pressure:

$$p_B = \left(\frac{n_B}{n_A + n_B}\right)P_{total} = X_B P_{total} \tag{10.20}$$

Notice that the sum of the mole fraction is 1:

$$X_A + X_B = 1$$

$$\frac{n_A}{n_A + n_B} + \frac{n_B}{n_A + n_B} = \frac{n_A + n_B}{n_A + n_B} = 1$$

Suppose that a mixture contains 1 mol of A and 4 mol of B. Then the total number of moles is five, the mole fraction of A is one-fifth, and the mole fraction of B is four-fifths. The partial pressure of A, therefore, is one-fifth of the total pressure, and the partial pressure of B is fourth-fifths of the total pressure.

If it is not very soluble in water, a gas evolved in the course of a laboratory experiment is frequently collected over water. The gas is conducted into an inverted bottle that has been filled with water. The gas displaces the water, and the collected gas is mixed with water vapor. The total pressure of the mixture is the sum of the partial pressure of the gas and the partial pressure of the water vapor. In Figure 10.6, the total pressure is equal to the barometric pressure, since the water stands at the same level inside the bottle as outside it. The pressure of the dry gas is found by subtracting the vapor pressure of water at the temperature of the experiment (Table 10.3) from the barometric pressure.

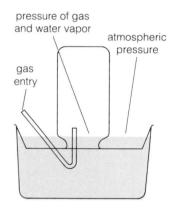

Figure 10.6 Schematic diagram of the collection of gas over water

---

Example 10.17

A 370. mL sample of oxygen is collected over water at 23°C and a barometric pressure of 0.992 atm. What volume would this sample occupy dry and at STP?

Table 10.3 Vapor pressure of water

Temperature (°C)	Pressure (atm)	(torr)	Temperature (°C)	Pressure (atm)	(torr)
0	0.0060	4.6	25	0.0313	23.8
1	0.0065	4.9	26	0.0332	25.2
2	0.0070	5.3	27	0.0352	26.7
3	0.0075	5.7	28	0.0373	28.3
4	0.0080	6.1	29	0.0395	30.0
5	0.0086	6.5	30	0.0419	31.8
6	0.0092	7.0	31	0.0443	33.7
7	0.0099	7.5	32	0.0470	35.7
8	0.0106	8.0	33	0.0496	37.7
9	0.0113	8.6	34	0.0525	39.9
10	0.0121	9.2	35	0.0555	42.2
11	0.0130	9.8	40	0.0728	55.3
12	0.0138	10.5	45	0.0946	71.9
13	0.0148	11.2	50	0.122	92.5
14	0.0158	12.0	55	0.155	118.0
15	0.0168	12.8	60	0.197	149.4
16	0.0179	13.6	65	0.247	187.5
17	0.0191	14.5	70	0.308	233.7
18	0.0204	15.5	75	0.380	289.1
19	0.0217	16.5	80	0.467	355.1
20	0.0231	17.5	85	0.571	433.6
21	0.0245	18.7	90	0.692	525.8
22	0.0261	19.8	95	0.834	633.9
23	0.0277	21.1	100	1.000	760.0
24	0.0294	22.4	105	1.192	906.1

Solution

The vapor pressure of water at 23°C is 0.0277 atm. Consequently, the initial pressure of the oxygen is

$$0.992 \text{ atm} - 0.028 \text{ atm} = 0.964 \text{ atm}$$

Therefore,

Initial conditions: $V_i = 370. \text{ mL}$ $O_i = 0.964 \text{ atm}$ $T_i = 296 \text{ K}$
Final conditions: $V_f = ? \text{ mL}$ $P_f = 1.000 \text{ atm}$ $T_f = 273 \text{ K}$

$$? \text{ mL} = 370. \text{ mL} \left(\frac{0.964 \text{ atm}}{1.000 \text{ atm}}\right)\left(\frac{273 \text{ K}}{296 \text{ K}}\right) = 329 \text{ mL}$$

The problem could also be solved by using Equation 10.11:

$$V_f = V_i\left(\frac{P_i}{P_f}\right)\left(\frac{T_f}{T_i}\right) = 370. \text{ mL}\left(\frac{0.964 \text{ atm}}{1.000 \text{ atm}}\right)\left(\frac{273 \text{ K}}{296 \text{ K}}\right) = 329 \text{ mL}$$

Example 10.18

A mixture of 40.0 g of oxygen and 40.0 g of helium has a total pressure of 0.900 atm. What is the partial pressure of oxygen?

Solution

The molecular weight of O_2 is 32.0. Forty grams of O_2 is 40.0/32.0, or 1.25 mol of O_2. Helium is a monatomic gas with an atomic weight of 4.00. Thus 40.0/4.0, or 10.0, mol of He is present in the mixture. Therefore,

$$X_{O_2} = \frac{n_{O_2}}{n_{O_2} + n_{He}}$$

$$X_{O_2} = \frac{1.25 \text{ mol}}{(1.25 + 10.0) \text{ mol}} = \frac{1.25 \text{ mol}}{11.2 \text{ mol}} = 0.112$$

The partial pressure of O_2 is

$$\begin{aligned} P_{O_2} &= X_{O_2} P_{total} \\ &= (0.112)(0.900 \text{ atm}) \\ &= 0.101 \text{ atm} \end{aligned}$$

The partial pressure of He is:

$$\begin{aligned} p_{He} &= p_{total} - p_{O_2} \\ &= 0.900 \text{ atm} - 0.101 \text{ atm} = 0.799 \text{ atm} \end{aligned}$$

11 Molecular Speeds

In Section 10.7 we derived the expression

$$PV = \tfrac{1}{3}Nmu^2 \tag{10.13}$$

For one mole of a gas, the number of molecules, N, is Avogadro's number; and N times the mass of a single molecule, m, is the molecular weight, M:

$$PV = \tfrac{1}{3}Mu^2 \tag{10.21}$$

Also for one mole, $PV = RT$; thus,

$$RT = \tfrac{1}{3}Mu^2 \tag{10.22}$$

Rearranging and solving for the molecular speed, we obtain

$$u = \sqrt{\frac{3RT}{M}} \tag{10.23}$$

The speed, u, in this equation, as in previous equations, is the root-mean-square speed. The **root-mean-square speed** is the speed of a molecule that has the average kinetic energy of a collection of molecules at the temperature under consideration. The kinetic energy of a molecule is:

$$KE = \tfrac{1}{2}mu^2$$

where m is the mass of the molecule and u is its speed. The average kinetic energy (or mean kinetic energy) of a collection of molecules is obtained by averaging the $\tfrac{1}{2}mu^2$ values for the molecules. We may find a value for u by taking this mean kinetic energy (which is equal to $\tfrac{1}{2}mu^2$), solving for u^2, and then taking the square root of u^2. The value for u obtained in this way is called a root-mean-square speed because it is obtained by taking the square *root* of a u^2 value that is derived from a *mean* of terms that contain the *squares* of speeds.

In order to use the equation for the root-mean-square speed, Equation 10.23, R must be expressed in appropriate units (see Table 10.2). If u is to be obtained in m/s and M is expressed in g/mol, the appropriate value of R is 8.3143×10^3 g·m²/(s²·K·mol).

Example 10.19

Calculate to three significant figures the root-mean-square speed of a H_2 molecule at (a) 0°C and (b) 100.°C.

Solution

(a) $u = \sqrt{\dfrac{3RT}{M}}$ (10.23)

$$= \sqrt{\dfrac{3[8.314 \times 10^3 \text{ g·m}^2/(\text{s}^2 \cdot \text{K} \cdot \text{mol})](273 \text{ K})}{2.016 \text{ g/mol}}}$$

$$= 1.84 \times 10^3 \text{ m/s}$$

(b) $$= \sqrt{\dfrac{3[8.314 \times 10^3 \text{ g·m}^2/(\text{s}^2 \cdot \text{K} \cdot \text{mol})](373 \text{ K})}{2.016 \text{ g/mol}}}$$

$$= 2.15 \times 10^3 \text{ m/s}$$

These root-mean-square speeds of the hydrogen molecule are high—4.12×10^3 mile/hr at 0°C and 4.81×10^3 mile/hr at 100°C. The diffusion of one gas through another gas, however, does not occur this rapidly. Although a given molecule travels at a high speed, its direction is continually being changed through collisions with other molecules. At 1 atm pressure and 0°C a hydrogen molecule, on the average, undergoes about 1.4×10^{10} collisions in one second. The average distance traveled between collisions is only 1.3×10^{-5} cm; this value is called the mean free path of hydrogen.

Not all of the molecules of a gas have the same kinetic energy and travel at the same speed. Since energy can be exchanged in these collisions, the speed as

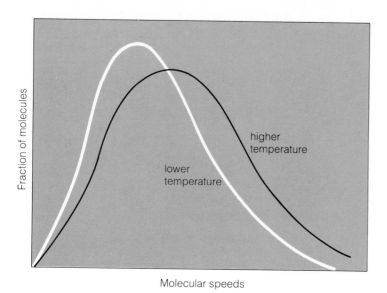

Figure 10.7 Distribution of molecular speeds

well as the direction of a molecule changes continually. In any sample of a gas, however, there is a large number of molecules, so that the molecular speeds are distributed over a range in a definite manner.

Distributions of the molecular speeds of a gas, called **Maxwell-Boltzmann distributions,** at two temperatures are shown in Figure 10.7. The fraction of the total number of molecules that has a particular speed is plotted against molecular speed. Each curve has a maximum, and the speed corresponding to the maximum is the most probable speed for that distribution. In other words, more molecules move at this speed than at any other. Comparatively few molcules possess very high or very low speeds.

When the temperature of a gas is increased, the curve broadens and shifts toward higher speeds. Fewer molecules than previously move at the lower speeds, and more molecules move at the higher speeds. The addition of heat has caused the molecules, on the average, to move faster. Recall that the speed of a hydrogen molecule that has the average kinetic energy at 0°C is 1.84×10^3 m/s, and at 100°C is 2.15×10^3 m/s.

According to Equation 10.14:

$$PV = \tfrac{2}{3}N(KE) \tag{10.14}$$

Hence,

$$KE = \frac{3\,PV}{2\,N}$$

For one mole of gas, $PV = RT$ and N is Avogadro's number:

$$KE = \frac{3\,RT}{2\,N} \tag{10.24}$$

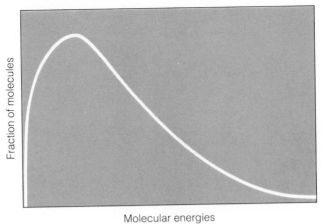

Figure 10.8 Distribution of molecular energies

The average molecular kinetic energy can be found by means of this equation. The appropriate value of R to use is 8.3143 J/(K·mol).

Example 10.20

Calculate to three significant figures the average kinetic energy of a H_2 molecule at 0°C.

$$KE = \frac{3RT}{2N} \tag{10.24}$$

$$= \frac{3[8.314 \text{ J/(K·mol)}](273 \text{ K})}{2(6.022 \times 10^{23} \text{ molecule/mol})}$$

$$= 5.65 \times 10^{-21} \text{ J/molecule}$$

Notice that the molecular weight of the gas does not enter into the calculation, and the answer is the average kinetic energy for *any* gas molecule at 0°C.

A typical curve for the distribution of molecular energies is shown in Figure 10.8. Distribution curves of this type can be drawn for liquids and solids as well as gases.

10.12 Graham's Law of Effusion

Suppose that samples of two gases, A and B, are confined separately in identical containers under the same conditions of temperature and pressure. The kinetic theory of gases states that gases at the same temperature have the same average

kinetic energy. The average kinetic energy of the molecules of gas A (KE_A), therefore, is the same as the average kinetic energy of the molecules of gas B (KE_B):

$$KE_A = KE_B$$

The kinetic energy of a body with a mass m moving at a speed u is:

$$KE = \tfrac{1}{2}mu^2$$

Therefore,

$$KE_A = \tfrac{1}{2}m_A u_A^2 \qquad \text{and} \qquad KE_B = \tfrac{1}{2}m_B u_B^2$$

The molecules of gas A (or gas B) do not all move at the same speed. The symbol u_A (as well as u_B) stands for the speed of a molecule that has the average kinetic energy. Since:

$$KE_A = KE_B$$
$$\tfrac{1}{2}m_A u_A^2 = \tfrac{1}{2}m_B u_B^2$$

or

$$m_A u_A^2 = m_B u_B^2$$

By rearranging the equation, we get

$$\frac{u_A^2}{u_B^2} = \frac{m_B}{m_A}$$

Extracting the square root of both sides of the equation give us

$$\frac{u_A}{u_B} = \sqrt{\frac{m_B}{m_A}}$$

The ratio of the molecular masses, m_B/m_A, is the same as the ratio of the molecular weights, M_B/M_A. Therefore,

$$\frac{u_A}{u_B} = \sqrt{\frac{M_B}{M_A}}$$

Now let us suppose that each container has an identical, extremely small opening (called an orifice) in it. Gas molecules will escape through these orifices; the process is called molecular effusion. The rate of effusion, r, is equal to the rate at which molecules strike the orifice, which in turn is proportional to molecular speed, u. Molecules that move rapidly will effuse at a faster rate than slower-moving molecules. The ratio u_A/u_B, therefore, is the same as the ratio of the effusion rates, r_A/r_B:

$$\frac{r_A}{r_B} = \sqrt{\frac{M_B}{M_A}} \qquad\qquad (10.25)$$

Thomas Graham, 1805–1869.
*National Portrait Gallery,
Smithsonian Institution.*

This equation is an expressin of **Graham's law of effusion,** which Thomas Graham experimentally derived during the period 1828 to 1833.

The relationship may also be expressed in terms of *gas densities*. Since the density of a gas, d, is proportional to the molecular weight of the gas, M, Graham's law may also be written

$$\frac{r_A}{r_B} = \sqrt{\frac{d_B}{d_A}} \tag{10.26}$$

It is not surprising that the lighter of two molecules with the same kinetic energy will effuse more rapidly than the heavier one. (Notice the *inverse* relationship.) The molecular weight of O_2 is 32, and the molecular weight of H_2 is 2. Since

$$\frac{r_{H_2}}{r_{O_2}} = \sqrt{\frac{M_{O_2}}{M_{H_2}}}$$

$$\frac{r_{H_2}}{r_{O_2}} = \sqrt{\frac{32}{2}} = \sqrt{16} = 4$$

Hydrogen will effuse four times more rapidly than oxygen.

This principle has been used for the separation of isotopes. Uranium occurs in nature as 0.72% $^{235}_{92}U$ and 99.28% $^{238}_{92}U$. Of the two isotopes, only ^{235}U will undergo nuclear fission. In the development of the atomic bomb, it was necessary to separate ^{235}U from ^{238}U. The separation was accomplished by converting natural uranium into uranium hexafluoride, which boils at 56°C. The uranium hexafluoride actually is a mixture of $^{235}UF_6$ and $^{238}UF_6$. This mixture as a gas and at low pressure was allowed to effuse through a porous barrier. The lighter $^{235}UF_6$ effuses 1.004 times faster than the heavier $^{238}UF_6$. Hence the emerging gas has a higher $^{235}UF_6$ content than the original mixture. This effusion procedure must be repeated thousands of times to effect a significant separation.

Example 10.21

What is the molecular weight of gas X if it effuses 0.876 times as rapidly as $N_2(g)$?

Solution

The ratio of the rate of effusion of gas X to the rate of effusion of $N_2(g)$ is

$$\frac{r_X}{r_{N_2}} = 0.876$$

The molecular weight of N_2 is 28.0. Therefore,

$$\sqrt{\frac{M_{N_2}}{M_X}} = \frac{r_X}{r_{N_2}}$$

$$\sqrt{\frac{28.0}{M_X}} = 0.876$$

We square both sides of the equation and solve for M_X:

$$\frac{28.0}{M_X} = 0.767$$

$$M_X = \frac{28.0}{0.767} = 36.5$$

0.13 Real Gases

The gas laws describe the behavior of an ideal or perfect gas—a gas defined by the kinetic theory. Under ordinary conditions of temperature and pressure, real gases follow the ideal gas laws fairly closely. At low temperatures and/or high pressures, however, they do not.

For an ideal gas, $PV = nRT$, and hence:

$$\frac{PV}{RT} = n \tag{10.27}$$

If we consider one mole of an ideal gas, $n = 1$, and $PV/RT = 1$. In Figure 10.9 PV/RT (the so-called **compressibility factor**) is plotted against pressure for several gases at constant temperature. The curves for the real gases deviate significantly from that for an ideal gas (a straight line at $PV/RT = 1$). There are two reasons for the deviations.

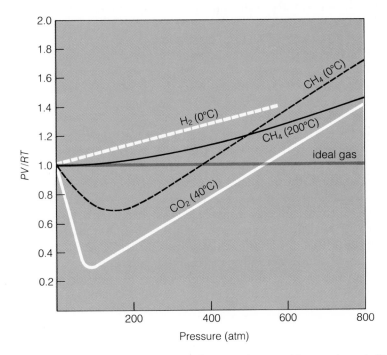

Figure 10.9 *PV/RT* versus pressure for several gases at temperatures indicated

1. Intermolecular forces of attraction. The kinetic theory assumes that there are no attractive forces between gas molecules. Such attractions must exist, however, because all gases can be liquefied. Intermolecular attractions hold the molecules together in the liquid state.

If we assume that P in the expression PV/RT is the applied pressure, a deviation from ideality would be apparent in the measured volume, V. Intermolecular forces of attraction *reduce* the volume by pulling the gas molecules together. In this respect, they augment the applied pressure. Furthermore, the higher the applied pressure, the more the effect of intermolecular attractions will be felt, since gas molecules are closer together at higher pressures. This factor tends to cause the value PV/RT to be *less* than 1.

2. Molecular volume. The kinetic theory assumes that gas molecules are points in space and that the actual volume of the molecules is not significant. At absolute zero, the temperature at which molecular motion stops, the volume of an ideal gas is therefore zero. Real gases, of course, do not have zero molecular volumes. When the applied pressure is increased, the space between the molecules is reduced, but the molecules themselves cannot be compressed. The result is that the measured volume is *larger* than the volume calculated for an ideal gas, where the molecular volume is neglected. Again, the deviation is more pronounced at higher pressures. The molecules are closer together at higher pressures and the molecular volume is a larger fraction of the total volume. This factor tends to cause the value PV/RT to be *greater* than 1.

These two factors operate at the same time and against one another. Which factor predominates depends upon the experimental conditions. In Figure 10.9 those portions of the curves that are *below* the $PV/RT = 1$ line correspond to conditions under which the effect of intermolecular attractive forces is predominant. For those portions that are *above* this line, molecular volume is the predominant effect.

Examine the curves for H_2 (at 0°C), CH_4 (at 0°C), and CO_2 (at 40°C). The curve for CO_2 falls farther below the $PV/RT = 1$ line than the curve for any other gas. We conclude that the attractions between CO_2 molecules are greater than those between the molecules of the other gases. Indeed, since the curve for H_2 lies entirely above this line, the forces of attraction between H_2 molecules must be so weak that at 0°C they cause little deviation from ideality.

Compare the curve for CH_4 at 0°C to that for the same gas at 200°C. As a result of intermolecular attractions, part of the curve for CH_4 at 0°C lies below the $PV/RT = 1$ line. The curve for the gas at the higher temperature lies entirely above this line. At high temperatures, gas molecules have high kinetic energies and move so rapidly that the attractive forces between the molecules have little effect. At low temperatures, however, the molecules move more slowly. The attractive forces pull the molecules together so that the observed volume is less than that predicted by the gas law. The curves of Figure 10.9 show, therefore, that real gases follow the ideal gas laws most closely at low pressures and high temperatures.

Johannes van der Waals in 1873 modified the equation of state for an ideal gas to take into account these two effects. The **van der Waals equation** is

$$\left(P + \frac{n^2a}{V^2}\right)(V - nb) = nRT \tag{10.28}$$

Table 10.4	van der Waals constants	
	a (L^2 atm/mol^2)	b (L/mol)
H_2	0.244	0.0266
He	0.0341	0.0237
N_2	1.39	0.0391
O_2	1.36	0.0318
Cl_2	6.49	0.0562
NH_3	4.17	0.0371
CO	1.49	0.0399
CO_2	3.59	0.0427

The numerical values of the constants a and b for each gas are determined by experiment. Typical values are listed in Table 10.4.

The term $n^2 a/V^2$ is added to the measured pressure, P, to correct for the intermolecular attractive forces. Pressure is caused by the collisions of the gas molecules with the walls of the container. The effect of a given collision would be greater if the molecule were not held back by the attraction of other molecules. Consequently, the pressure that is measured is *less* than it would be if these attractive forces did not exist. The term $n^2 a/V^2$ is added to P so that $(P + n^2 a/V^2)$ represents the pressure of an ideal gas, one in which there are no molecular forces.

The term (n/V) represents a concentration (mol/L). If x molecules are confined in a liter, there are $(x - 1)$ ways for a given molecule to collide or interact with another molecule, since it cannot collide with itself. This factor applies to all the molecules; therefore, a total of $\frac{1}{2}x(x - 1)$ possible interactions exists for the entire collection of molecules. The fraction $\frac{1}{2}$ is added so that a given interaction is not counted twice—once for each of the molecules entering into it. If a large number of molecules are present, $(x - 1)$ is approximately equal to x, and the proportionality is $\frac{1}{2}x^2$ to a good approximation. Hence the number of interactions between gas molecules is proportional to the *square* of the concentration. The van der Waals constant a may be regarded as a proportionality constant (incorporating the $\frac{1}{2}$), and the correction term is $n^2 a/V^2$.

The constant b, multiplied by n, is subtracted from the total volume of the gas to correct for the portion of the volume that is not compressible because of the intrinsic volume of the gas molecules. A given gas molecule cannot move through the entire volume of the container since other molecules are present. The volume through which they can move can be obtained by subtracting an amount called the excluded volume from the total volume.

If the molecules are assumed to be spherical and have a radius r, the excluded volume per molecule is not merely the volume of the molecule, $\frac{4}{3}\pi r^3$. Since the closest approach of *two* molecules is $2r$ (Figure 10.10), the excluded volume for *two* molecules is $\frac{4}{3}\pi(2r)^3$, which is $8(\frac{4}{3}\pi r^3)$. For one molecule this volume is $4(\frac{4}{3}\pi r^3)$, which is four times the molecular volume. Hence, for a mole of molecules, N molecules,

$$b = 4N(\tfrac{4}{3}\pi r^3) \tag{10.29}$$

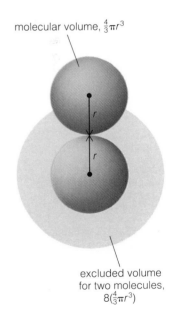

molecular volume, $\frac{4}{3}\pi r^3$

excluded volume for two molecules, $8(\frac{4}{3}\pi r^3)$

Figure 10.10 van der Waals correction, b, for excluded volume

10.14 Liquefaction of Gases

Boiling liquid hydrogen, *Photo Researchers, Inc.*

Liquefaction of a gas occurs under conditions that permit the intermolecular attractive forces to bind the gas molecules together in the liquid form. If the pressure is high, the molecules are close together, and the effect of the attractive forces is appreciable. The attractive forces are opposed by the motion of the gas molecules; thus, liquefaction is favored by low temperatures, where the average kinetic energy of the molecules is low. The behavior of a gas deviates more and more from ideality as the temperature is lowered and the pressure is raised. At extremes of these conditions, gases liquefy.

The higher the temperature of a gas, the more difficult it is to liquefy and the higher the pressure that must be employed (Table 10.5). For each gas there is a temperature above which it is impossible to liquefy the gas no matter how high the applied pressure. This temperature is called the critical temperature of the gas under consideration. The critical pressure is the minimum pressure needed to liquefy a gas at its critical temperature. The critical constants of some common gases are listed in Table 10.6.

The critical temperature of a gas gives an indication of the strength of the intermolecular attractive forces of that gas. A substance with weak attractive forces would have a low critical temperature; above this temperature, the molecular motion is too violent to permit the relatively weak forces to hold the molecules in the liquid state. The substances of Table 10.6 are listed in order of increasing critical temperature; the magnitude of the intermolecular attractive forces (related to the a of Table 10.4) increases in this same order. Helium, which has weak attractive forces, can exist as a liquid only below 5.3 K; the strong attractive forces of water permit it to be liquefied up to a temperature of 647.2 K. The critical constants have been used to evaluate the constants of the van der Waals equation.

The data of Table 10.6 show that it is necessary to cool many gases below room temperature (about 295 K) before these substances can be liquefied. Commercial liquefaction procedures make use of the Joule-Thomson effect to cool gases. When most compressed gases are allowed to expand to a lower pressure, they cool. In the expansion, work is done against the intermolecular attractive forces. The energy used in performing this work must be taken from the kinetic energy of the gas molecules themselves; hence, the temperature of the gas decreases. This effect was studied by James Joule and William Thomson (Lord Kelvin) during the years

Table 10.5 Pressures needed to liquefy carbon dioxide. (Vapor pressures of liquid CO_2.)

Temperature (°C)	Pressure (atm)
−50	6.7
−30	14.1
−10	26.1
10	44.4
20	56.5
30	71.2
31	72.8

Table 10.6 Critical point data

Gas	Critical Temperature (K)	Critical Pressure (atm)
He	5.3	2.26
H_2	33.3	12.8
N_2	126.1	33.5
CO	134.0	35.0
O_2	154.4	49.7
CH_4	190.2	45.6
CO_2	304.2	72.8
NH_3	405.6	111.5
H_2O	647.2	217.7

1852–62. The liquefaction of air is accomplished by first allowing cooled, compressed air to expand. The temperature of the air falls to a lower level. This cooled air is used to precool entering compressed air, and the expansion of this compressed air results in the attainment of even lower temperatures. The cooled, expanded air is recycled through the compression chamber. Eventually the cooling and compression produce liquid air.

Summary

The four variables needed to define the state of a gas sample are volume, pressure, temperature, and amount. *Volume* (V) is usually expressed in *liters* (L). *Pressure* (P) may be expressed in *pascals* (Pa, the SI unit of pressure), in *torrs* (torr, equal to 1 mm of mercury), or *standard atmospheres* (atm, 1 atm = 760 torr = 101,325 Pa). *Temperature* must be expressed in *kelvins* (K, which is obtained by adding 273.15 to the Celsius temperature). The *amount* of gas in the sample is expressed in *moles* (mol, the SI unit for amount of substance).

The simple gas laws describe the relationships between two of the four variables when the other variables are held constant. According to *Boyle's law*, P varies *inversely* with V when T and n are constant. *Charles' law* states that V and T vary *directly* with one another when P and n are constant. *Amontons' law* states that P varies *directly* with T when V and n are constant. The *equation of state for an ideal gas* ($PV = nRT$) gives the relationship between all four variables. The constant in this equation, R, is called the *ideal gas constant*.

By substituting g/M (where g is the mass of the gas sample and M is the molecular weight of the gas) for n in the ideal gas equation, a useful form of this equation is obtained. By means of this equation, problems involving *gas densities* (g/V) and problems involving *molecular weights* can be solved.

For chemical reactions that involve gases, the ideal gas law can be used to solve stoichiometric problems in which gas volumes are given or sought. *Gay-Lussac's law of combining volumes* describes the relationship between the volumes of two gases involved in a chemical reaction, and *Avogadro's principle* provides an explanation for Gay-Lussac's law. *Dalton's law of partial pressures* states that the total pressure of a mixture of gases is equal to the sum of the partial pressures of the component gases. The *partial pressure* of a gas in a mixture is equal to the pressure the gas would exert if it occupied the container alone under the same conditions.

The *kinetic theory of gases* explains the behavior of gases in terms of a model. According to the theory, gases consist of *molecules* that are widely separated in space, have *volumes* that are *negligible* in comparison to the volume of the gas as a whole, have *negligible attractive forces* operating between molecules, and are in constant *motion*. The *kinetic energies* of the molecules depend upon the *temperature*.

Both the speeds and the kinetic energies of the molecules of a gas sample are distributed over ranges of values (*Maxwell-Boltzmann distributions*). The kinetic theory can be used to derive equations to find the *root-mean-square speed* of the molecules in a gas sample and the *average kinetic energy* per molecule. *Graham's law* compares the rates of effusion of two gases.

The behavior of a real gas deviates from that described by the ideal gas law because real gas molecules have *finite volumes* and exert *attractive forces* on one another. The *van der Waals equation*, which is a modification of the equation of state for an ideal gas, takes these two sources of deviation into account. The deviation from ideality that a real gas exhibits is most pronounced at *high pressures* and *low temperatures*. Under these conditions the gas molecules are close together and have low kinetic energies. At extremes of these conditions, gases liquefy.

Key Terms

Some of the more important terms introduced in this chapter are listed below. Definitions for terms not included in this list may be located in the text by use of the index.

Amontons' law (Section 10.4) At constant volume, the pressure of a sample of gas varies directly with the absolute temperature.

Atmosphere, atm (Section 10.1) A unit of pressure that is defined as 101,325 Pa; 1 atm = 760 torr.

Avogadro's principle (Section 10.8) Equal volumes of all gases at the same temperature and pressure contain the same number of molecules.

Barometer (Section 10.1) A device for measuring the pressure that the atmosphere exerts on the surface of the earth.

Boyle's law (Section 10.2) At constant temperature, the volume of a gas varies inversely with the pressure.

Charles' law (Section 10.3) At constant pressure, the volume of a gas varies directly with the absolute temperature.

Compressibility factor (Section 10.13) PV/RT where P is the pressure of a gas, V is the volume, R is the ideal gas constant, and T is the absolute temperature. For 1 mole of an ideal gas, the compressibility factor is always equal to 1.

Critical pressure (Section 10.14) The pressure required to liquefy a gas at its critical temperature.

Critical temperature (Section 10.14) The temperature above which it is impossible to liquefy the gas under study, no matter how high the applied pressure.

Dalton's law of partial pressures (Section 10.10) The total pressure of a mixture of gases that do not react is equal to the sum of the partial pressures of all the gases present.

Gay-Lussac's law of combining volumes (Section 10.8) At constant temperature and pressure, the volumes of gases used or produced in a chemical reaction stand in ratios of small whole numbers.

Graham's law of effusion (Section 10.12) The rate of effusion of a gas is inversely proportional to the square root of its density or the square root of its molecular weight.

Ideal gas constant, R (Section 10.5) The proportionality constant in the equation of state for an ideal gas; 0.082056 L·atm/(K·mol). See Table 10.2 for other values.

Ideal gas law (Section 10.5) The product of the pressure, P, and the volume, V, of a sample of a gas is equal to the number of moles of gas, n, times the ideal gas constant, R, times the absolute temperature, T; $PV = nRT$.

Kelvin temperature scale (Section 10.3) An absolute temperature scale on which a reading is obtained by adding 273.15 to the value in degrees Celsius.

Kinetic theory of gases (Sections 10.6, 10.7, and 10.11) A model on the molecular level that can be used to explain the gas laws and from which the ideal gas equation can be derived.

Maxwell-Boltzmann distribution (Section 10.11) The way in which kinetic energy or molecular speed is distributed among the molecules of a gas.

Mean free path (Section 10.11) The average distance that a molecule travels between collisions with other gas molecules.

Mole fraction, X (Section 10.10) The ratio of the number of moles of a component in a mixture to the total number of moles in the mixture.

Partial pressure (Section 10.10) The pressure that a component of a mixture of gases would exert if it were the only gas in the volume under consideration.

Pascal (Section 10.1) The SI unit of pressure; equal to a force of one newton (which is 1 kg·m/s^2) acting on a square meter.

Pressure (Section 10.1) Force per unit area.

Root-mean-square speed (Section 10.11) The square root of the average of the squares of the molecular speeds.

Standard temperature and pressure, STP (Section 10.5) 0°C (which is 273.15 K) and 1 atm pressure.

STP molar volume (Section 10.8) The volume of one mole of a gas at standard temperature and pressure; 22.414 L.

torr (Section 10.1) A unit of pressure equivalent to the pressure that will support a column of mercury to a height of 1 mm, 1/760th of an atmosphere.

van der Waals equation (Section 10.13) An equation of state for gases; a modification of the ideal gas equation that takes into account intermolecular attractions and the volumes that gas molecules occupy.

Problems*

Simple Gas Laws

10.1 State: **(a)** Boyle's law, **(b)** Charles' law, **(c)** Amonton's law.

10.2 For each of the following pairs of variables, which correspond to measurements made on an ideal gas, draw a rough graph to show how one quantity varies with the other: **(a)** P vs. V, with T constant; **(b)** T vs. V, with P constant; **(c)** P vs. T, with V constant; **(d)** PV vs. V, with T constant.

10.3 The volume of a sample of gas is 650. mL at a pressure of 1.60 atm. Assume that the temperature is held constant. **(a)** What is the volume of the sample at a pressure of 2.00 atm? **(b)** What is the pressure of the sample when the volume is 1000. mL? **(c)** What is the pressure of the sample when the volume is 500. mL?

10.4 The volume of a sample of gas is 1.65 L at a pressure of 0.650 atm. Assume that the temperature is held constant. **(a)** What is the volume of the sample at a pressure of 0.500 atm? **(b)** What is the pressure of the sample when the volume is 1.00 L? **(c)** What is the pressure of the sample when the volume is 2.75 L?

---

* The more difficult problems are marked with asterisks. The appendix contains answers to color-keyed problems.

10.5 The volume of a sample of gas at 50.°C is 2.50 L. Assume that the pressure is held constant. **(a)** What is the volume of the gas at −10.°C? **(b)** At what temperature (in °C) would the volume be 1.25 L? **(c)** At what temperature (in °C) would the volume be 2.75 L?

10.6 The volume of a sample of gas at 0°C is 136. mL. Assume that the pressure is held constant. **(a)** What is the volume of the gas at 25.°C? **(b)** At what temperature (in °C) would the volume be 100. mL? **(c)** At what temperature (in °C) would the volume be 250. mL?

10.7 A container is filled with a gas to a pressure of 1.50 atm at 20.°C. **(a)** What pressure will develop within the sealed container if it is heated to 60°C? **(b)** At what temperature (in °C) would the pressure be 30.0 atm? **(c)** At what temperature (in °C) would the pressure be 1.00 atm?

10.8 A container is filled with a gas to a pressure of 50.0 atm at 0.°C. **(a)** What pressure will develop within the sealed container if it is heated to 20°C? **(b)** At what temperature (in °C) would the pressure be 100. atm? **(c)** At what temperature (in °C) would the pressure be 46.0 atm?

10.9 A gas thermometer contains 250.00 mL of gas at 0°C and 1.00 atm pressure. If the pressure remains at 1.00 atm, how many milliliters will the volume increase for every one Celsius degree that the temperature rises?

10.10 A McLeod gauge is an instrument used to measure extremely low pressures. Assume that a 250. mL sample of gas from a low pressure system is compressed in a McLeod gauge to a volume of 0.0525 mL, where the pressure of the sample is 0.0355 atm. What is the pressure of the gas in the system?

Ideal Gas Law

10.11 Complete the following table which pertains to samples of an ideal gas.

Pressure	Volume	Moles	Temperature
P	V	n	T
2.00 atm	_____	1.50 mol	100.°C
0.600 atm	1.00 L	_____	100. K
4.45 atm	50.0 mL	0.0105 mol	
_____	1.25 L	2.60 mol	75.°C

10.12 Complete the following table which pertains to samples of an ideal gas.

Pressure	Volume	Moles	Temperature
P	V	n	T
0.500 atm	_____	0.600 mol	120.°C
1.50 atm	352. mL	_____	60.°C
_____	40.1 L	3.75 mol	20.°C
26.3 atm	2.26 L	2.56 mol	_____

10.13 A sample of gas occupies 650. mL at STP. What volume will the sample occupy at 100.°C and 5.00 atm?

10.14 A sample of gas occupies 2.50 L at 25°C and 0.575 atm. What volume will the sample occupy at STP?

10.15 The volume of a sample of gas is 750. mL at 75°C and 0.750 atm. At what temperature (in °C) will the sample occupy 1.000 L under a pressure of 1.000 atm?

10.16 A 1.00 L sample of a gas is collected at 25°C and 1.25 atm. What is the pressure of the gas at 200.°C if the volume is 4.00 L?

10.17 What volume will 5.00 g of N_2O gas occupy at 50.°C and 12.0 atm?

10.18 What volume will 16.0 g of O_2 gas occupy at 10.°C and 0.500 atm?

10.19 What is the mass of 250. mL of Cl_2 gas at 25°C and 0.350 atm?

10.20 What is the mass of 6.50 L of N_2 gas at 250.°C and 12.5 atm?

10.21 What is the density of CH_4 gas at 25°C and 1.50 atm?

10.22 What is the density of SO_2 gas at 100.°C and 0.750 atm?

10.23 If the temperature is held constant at −10.°C, at what pressure will the density of Ar gas be 1.00 g/L?

10.24 If the pressure is held constant at 0.650 atm, at what temperature (in °C) will the density of H_2S gas be 0.650 g/L?

10.25 A gas has a density of 0.645 g/L at 65°C and 0.886 atm. What is the molecular weight of the gas?

10.26 A gas has a density of 1.59 g/L at 37°C and 1.35 atm. What is the molecular weight of the gas.

Gay-Lussac's Law of Combining Volumes and Avogadro's Principle

10.27 Hydrogen cyanide, HCN(g), a highly poisonous compound, is commercially prepared by the following reaction run at a high temperature and in the presence of a catalyst:

$$2\,CH_4(g) + 3\,O_2(g) + 2\,NH_3(g) \longrightarrow 2\,HCN(g) + 6\,H_2O(g)$$

How many liters of $CH_4(g)$, $O_2(g)$, and $NH_3(g)$ are required and how many liters of $H_2O(g)$ produced in the preparation of 15.0 L of HCN(g)? Assume that all gas volumes are measured under the same conditions of temperature and pressure.

10.28 Consider the preparation of HCN(g) by the procedure outlined in Problem 10.27. If 7.00 L of $CH_4(g)$ is reacted, how many liters of $O_2(g)$ and $NH_3(g)$ are required for the reaction and how many liters of HCN(g) and $H_2O(g)$ are produced by the reaction? Assume that all gas volumes are measured under the same conditions of temperature and pressure.

10.29 Ammonia, $NH_3(g)$, reacts with oxygen gas in the presence of a Pt catalyst to yield NO(g) and $H_2O(g)$. **(a)** Write a chemical equation for the reaction. **(b)** What volume of NO(g) can be obtained from 16.0 L of $NH_3(g)$ and 16.0 L of $O_2(g)$? The volumes of all gases are measured under the same conditions.

10.30 In the absence of a catalyst, ammonia, $NH_3(g)$, reacts with oxygen gas to yield nitrogen gas and $H_2O(g)$. **(a)** Write a chemical equation for the reaction. **(b)** What volume of $N_2(g)$ can be obtained from 9.00 L of $NH_3(g)$ and 9.00 L of $O_2(g)$? The volumes of all gases are measured under the same conditions.

10.31 A mixture is prepared from 0.900 L of $NH_3(g)$ and 1.200 L of $Cl_2(g)$. These substances react according to the equation:

$$2\,NH_3(g) + 3\,Cl_2(g) \longrightarrow N_2(g) + 6\,HCl(g)$$

If the volumes of all the gases are measured at the same temperature and pressure, list the volumes of all the substances present at the conclusion of the reaction.

10.32 A gaseous mixture is prepared from 130. mL of $NF_3(g)$ and 200. mL of $H_2O(g)$. When the gas mixture is ignited by a spark, a reaction occurs:

$$2\,NF_3(g) + 3\,H_2O(g) \longrightarrow 6\,HF(g) + NO(g) + NO_2(g)$$

If the volumes of all the gases are measured at the same temperature and pressure, list the volumes of all the substances present at the conclusion of the reaction.

10.33 The reaction of $NH_3(g)$ and $F_2(g)$ in the presence of a copper catalyst yields $NF_3(g)$ and $NH_4F(s)$. **(a)** Write the chemical equation for the reaction. **(b)** How many milliliters of $NH_3(g)$ and of $F_2(g)$ are required to make 50.0 mL of $NF_3(g)$ if a 65.0% yield is obtained? Assume that all gases are measured under the same conditions of temperature and pressure.

10.34 The reaction of $SF_6(g)$ and $SO_3(g)$ at 300°C produces $SO_2F_2(g)$. **(a)** Write the chemical equation for the reaction. **(b)** How many milliliters of $SF_6(g)$ and of $SO_3(g)$ are required to make 75.0 mL of $SO_2F_2(g)$ if a 42.5% yield is obtained? Assume that all gases are measured under the same conditions of temperature and pressure.

10.35 Use Avogadro's principle to determine the density of $N_2O(g)$ at STP.

10.36 Use Avogadro's principle to determine the density of $SF_6(g)$ at STP.

10.37 Use Avogadro's principle to determine the molecular weight of a gas that has a density of 5.710 g/L at STP.

10.38 Use Avogadro's principle to determine the molecular weight of a gas that has a density of 0.901 g/L at STP.

10.39 Federal standards limit the amount of $SO_2(g)$ in the air to a maximum of 80. $\mu g/m^3$. One cubic meter is 1.00×10^3 L. **(a)** How many grams of $SO_2(g)$ is this? **(b)** How many moles of SO_2? **(c)** What is the partial pressure of SO_2 in air at STP that contains 80. $\mu g/m^3$ of $SO_2(g)$? **(d)** What percentage of the total number of molecules in this air sample are $SO_2(g)$ molecules?

10.40 Federal standards limit the amount of $CO(g)$ in the air to a maximum of 10,000 $\mu g/m^3$. One cubic meter is 1.00×10^3 L. **(a)** What is the maximum partial pressure of $CO(g)$ in air at STP that meets this standard? **(b)** How many molecules of CO would be present in 1.00 L of this air? **(c)** What percentage of the total number of molecules are CO molecules?

Stoichiometry and Gas Volumes

10.41 Calcium hydride, $CaH_2(s)$, reacts with water to yield $H_2(g)$ and $Ca(OH)_2(s)$. **(a)** Write the chemical equation for this reaction. **(b)** How many grams of $CaH_2(s)$ is required to prepare 3.00 L of $H_2(g)$ at STP?

10.42 Calcium metal, $Ca(s)$, reacts with water to yield $H_2(g)$ and $Ca(OH)_2(s)$. **(a)** Write the chemical equation for this reaction. **(b)** How many grams of $Ca(s)$ is required to prepare 3.00 L of $H_2(g)$ at STP? Compare your answer to that of Problem 10.41.

10.43 Aluminum carbide, $Al_4C_3(s)$, reacts with water to yield methane gas, $CH_4(g)$, and $Al(OH)_3(g)$. **(a)** Write the chemical equation for this reaction. **(b)** What volume of CH_4 (measured at 35°C and 0.775 atm) would be obtained by the reaction of 0.250 g of $Al_4C_3(s)$?

10.44 Lanthanum carbide, $La_2(C_2)_3(s)$, reacts with water to yield acetylene gas, $C_2H_2(g)$, and $La(OH)_3(s)$. **(a)** Write the chemical equation for this reaction. **(b)** What volume of C_2H_2 (measured at 20.°C and 0.250 atm) would be obtained by the reaction of 0.650 g of $La_2(C_2)_3$?

10.45 The reaction of $NH_3(g)$ and $F_2(g)$ in the presence of a copper catalyst yields $NF_3(g)$ and $NH_4F(s)$. **(a)** Write the chemical equation for the reaction. **(b)** What is the theoretical yield of NF_3 (in grams) from a preparation that employs 350. mL of $NH_3(g)$ and 250. mL of $F_2(g)$? Assume that all gases are measured at STP.

10.46 Cyanogen, $C_2N_2(g)$, is a flammable, highly poisonous gas. It can be prepared by a catalyzed gas-phase reaction between $HCN(g)$ and $NO_2(g)$. The products of the reaction are $C_2N_2(g)$, $NO(g)$, and $H_2O(g)$. **(a)** Write the chemical equation for the reaction. **(b)** What is the theoretical yield of C_2N_2 (in grams) for a preparation that employs 175 mL of $HCN(g)$ and 130. mL of $NO_2(g)$? Assume that all gases are measured at STP.

10.47 The combustion of 120. mL of a gaseous compound that contains only C and H requires 900. mL of $O_2(g)$ and produces 600. mL of $CO_2(g)$ and 0.483 g of $H_2O(l)$. All gas measurements are made at STP. **(a)** Calculate the number of moles of each substance involved in the reaction. **(b)** Use your answers from part (a) to derive whole-number coefficients for the chemical equation for the reaction. **(c)** Determine the formula for the hydrocarbon and write the equation for the reaction.

10.48 The combustion of 135 mL of a gaseous compound that contains only C and H requires 675 mL of $O_2(g)$ and produces 405 mL of $CO_2(g)$ and 0.434 g of $H_2O(l)$. All gas measurements are made at STP. **(a)** Calculate the number of moles of each susbstance involved in the reaction. **(b)** Use your answers from part (a) to derive whole-number coefficients for the chemical equation for the reaction. **(c)** Determine the formula for the hydrocarbon and write the equation for the reaction.

*10.49 Magnesium and aluminum react with aqueous acids to give hydrogen gas:

$$Mg(s) + 2\,H^+(aq) \longrightarrow H_2(g) + Mg^{2+}(aq)$$

$$2\,Al(s) + 6\,H^+(aq) \longrightarrow 3\,H_2(g) + 2\,Al^{3+}(aq)$$

A 12.50 g sample of an alloy of Mg and Al produces 14.34 L of H_2 gas (measured at STP) when reacted with an acid. What percentage of the alloy is Al?

*10.50 Zinc and aluminum react with aqueous acids to give hydrogen gas:

$$Zn(s) + 2\,H^+(aq) \longrightarrow H_2(g) + Zn^{2+}(aq)$$

$$2\,Al(s) + 6\,H^+(aq) \longrightarrow 3\,H_2(g) + 2\,Al^{3+}(aq)$$

A 30.00 g sample of an alloy of Zn and Al produces 34.90 L of H_2 gas (measured at STP) when reacted with an acid. What percentage of the alloy is Zn?

Dalton's Law of Partial Pressures

10.51 A mixture of 0.560 g of $O_2(g)$ and 0.560 g of $N_2(g)$ exerts a pressure of 0.600 atm. What is the partial pressure of each gas?

10.52 A mixture of 0.924 g of $N_2O(g)$ and 0.825 g of $NO(g)$ exerts a pressure of 1.32 atm. What is the partial pressure of each gas?

10.53 The partial pressure of $CH_4(g)$ is 0.225 atm and of $C_2H_6(g)$ is 0.165 atm in a mixture of the two gases. (a) What is the mole fraction of each gas in the mixture? (b) If the mixture occupies 9.73 L at 35°C, what is the total number of moles of gas in the mixture? (c) How many grams of each gas is present in the mixture?

10.54 The partial pressure of $Ne(g)$ is 0.225 atm and of $Ar(g)$ is 0.750 atm in a mixture of the two gases. (a) What is the mole fraction of each gas in the mixture? (b) If the mixture occupies 5.10 L at 100.°C, what is the total number of moles of gas in the mixture? (c) How many grams of each gas is present in the mixture?

10.55 A 500. mL sample of a gas is collected over water at 30.°C and a barometric pressure of 1.010 atm. What volume would the gas occupy if dry and at 100.°C and a pressure of 1.000 atm?

10.56 A 625 mL sample of a gas is collected over water at 70.°C and a barometric pressure of 0.983 atm. If the gas is dried and placed in a 750. mL container at 27°C, what pressure will it exert?

*10.57 A sample of a gas, collected over water at 50.°C, occupies a volume of 1.000 L. The wet gas exerts a pressure of 1.000 atm. When dried, the sample occupies 1.000 L and exerts a pressure of 1.000 atm at 95°C. What is the vapor pressure of water at 50.°C?

*10.58 A sample of a gas, collected over water at 75°C, occupies a volume of 1.500 L. The wet gas exerts a pressure of 1.000 atm. When dried, the sample occupies 560. mL and exerts a pressure of 1.500 atm at 41°C. What is the vapor pressure of water at 75°C?

Kinetic Theory of Gases, Graham's Law

10.59 What is the root-mean-square speed of the $N_2(g)$ molecule at 100. K and at 500. K?

10.60 What is the root-mean-square speed of the $CO_2(g)$ molecule at 125 K and at 650. K?

10.61 At what temperature would the root-mean-square speed of the $N_2O(g)$ molecule equal the root-mean-square speed of the $N_2(g)$ molecule at 300. K?

10.62 At what temperature would the root-mean-square speed of the $F_2(g)$ molecule equal the root-mean-square speed of the $Cl_2(g)$ molecule at 400. K?

10.63 Compare the rate of effusion of $N_2O(g)$ with that of $N_2(g)$ under the same conditions.

10.64 Compare the rate of effusion of $F_2(g)$ with that of $Cl_2(g)$ under the same conditions.

10.65 A gas, X, effuses 0.629 times as fast as $O_2(g)$ under the same conditions. What is the molecular weight of gas X?

10.66 A gas, Y, effuses 1.05 times faster than $SO_2(g)$ under the same conditions. What is the molecular weight of gas Y?

10.67 At 25°C and 0.500 atm, the density of $N_2(g)$ is 0.572 g/L. The rate of effusion of $N_2(g)$ through an apparatus is 9.50 mL/s. (a) What is the density of a sample of a gas that effuses at a rate of 6.28 mL/s through the same apparatus under the same conditions (b) What is the molecular weight of the gas?

10.68 At 0.456 atm and 55°C, the density of gas X is 1.25 g/L. A volume of 15.0 mL of gas X effuses through an apparatus in 1.00 s. The rate of effusion of gas Y through the same apparatus and under the same conditions is 20.4 mL/s. (a) Calculate the density of gas Y under the experimental conditions. (b) What is the molecular weight of gas Y?

10.69 Calculate the density of a gas at STP if a given volume of the gas effuses through an apparatus in 5.00 min and the same volume of oxygen, at the same temperature and pressure, effuses through this apparatus in 6.30 min.

10.70 Use Graham's law to calculate the molecular weight of a gas if a given volume of the gas effuses through an apparatus in 300 s and the same volume of $CH_4(g)$, under the same conditions of temperature and pressure, effuses through the same apparatus in 219 s.

Real Gases

10.71 Which gas of those listed in Table 10.4 would you expect to: (a) have the highest critical temperature? (b) follow the ideal gas law most closely? (c) have the lowest critical temperature? (d) have the largest molecular volume? (e) have the weakest intermolecular forces?

10.72 Which member of each of the following pairs would follow the ideal gas law more closely (a) H_2 (molecular weight, 2.0) or HI (molecular weight, 127.9); (b) a gas at 100°C or the same gas at 100 K; (c) a gas under a pressure of 1.0 atm or the same gas under a pressure of 10.0 atm; **(d)** a gas with a critical temperature of 100 K or a gas with a critical temperature of 300 K. Give reasons for your predictions.

10.73 Calculate the pressure exerted by 1.000 mol of $O_2(g)$ confined to a volume of 1.000 L at 0.°C by **(a)** the ideal gas law, and **(b)** the van der Waals equation. **(c)** Compare the results.

10.74 Calculate the pressure exerted by 1.000 mol of $NH_3(g)$ confined to a volume of 1.000 L at 0.°C by **(a)** the ideal gas law, and **(b)** the van der Waals equation. **(c)** Compare the results.

10.75 Calculate the pressure exerted by 1.000 mol of $O_2(g)$ confined to a volume of 10.000 L at 0.°C by **(a)** the ideal gas law, and **(b)** the van der Waals equation. **(c)** Compare the results to each other and to those of Problem 10.73.

10.76 Calculate the pressure exerted by 1.000 mol of $O_2(g)$ confined to a volume of 1.000 L at 127.°C by **(a)** the ideal gas law, and **(b)** the van der Waals equation. **(c)** Compare the results to each other and to those of Problem 10.73.

10.77 (a) Use the value of the van der Waals constant b for CO_2 (0.0427 L/mol) to calculate the volume of a CO_2 molecule (in liters). **(b)** At STP, what percentage of the total volume of CO_2 gas is molecular volume?

10.78 The value of the van der Waals constant b for $Kr(g)$ is 0.0398 L/mol. Use this value to calculate the radius of a krypton atom.

Unclassified Problems

*   **10.79** A 10.0-L tank of helium is filled to a pressure of 150 atm. How many 1.50 L toy balloons can be inflated to a pressure of 1.00 atm from the tank? Assume no change in temperature. Note that the tank cannot be emptied below a pressure of 1.00 atm.

10.80 At temperature above 50°C, nitrogen oxide, $NO(g)$, decomposes to yield dinitrogen oxide, $N_2O(g)$ and nitrogen dioxide, $NO_2(g)$. **(a)** Write the chemical equation for this reaction. **(b)** What total volume of gases would result from the decomposition of 35.0 mL of $NO(g)$

at 200.°C and 0.986 atm? Assume that all gases are measured under the same conditions. **(c)** What are the partial pressures of $N_2O(g)$ and $NO_2(g)$ in this gas mixture?

10.81 The complete combustion of octane yields carbon dioxide and water:

$$2\,C_8H_{18}(g) + 25\,O_2(g) \longrightarrow 16\,CO_2(g) + 18\,H_2O(g)$$

What volume of gas is produced from the complete combustion of 0.650 g of $C_8H_{18}(g)$ at a temperature of 450°C and a pressure of 12.5 atm?

*   **10.82** The complete combustion of 0.430 g of a compound that contains only C and H produced 672 mL of CO_2 gas (measured at STP) and 0.630 g of H_2O. The 0.430 gas sample occupied 156 mL at 50.°C and 0.850 atm. What is the molecular formula of the compound?

*   **10.83** One mole of $N_2O_4(g)$ was placed in a container and allowed to dissociate:

$$N_2O_4(g) \longrightarrow 2\,NO_2(g)$$

The mixture resulting from the dissociation (N_2O_4 and NO_2) occupied 45.17 L at a total pressure of 1.000 atm and 65.°C. **(a)** Use the equation of state to find the total number of moles of gas present. **(b)** Allow x to equal the number of moles of $N_2O_4(g)$ that dissociates. In terms of x, how many moles of $NO_2(g)$ are produced by the dissociation? Use the value obtained in (a) to find the number of moles of $N_2O_4(g)$ and $NO_2(g)$. **(c)** What are the mole fractions of $N_2O_4(g)$ and $NO_2(g)$ in the mixture? **(d)** What are the partial pressures of $N_2O_4(g)$ and $NO_2(g)$?

10.84 Draw rough graphs to show for a collection of molecules **(a)** the distribution of molecular speeds for two different temperatures, **(b)** the distribution of molecular energies.

10.85 (a) List the postulates of the kinetic theory of gases. **(b)** What are the reasons that real gases deviate from ideal behavior?

10.86 Consider 1.00 mol of $CO(g)$ at 25°C. At 75.0 atm, the volume of the sample is 0.324 L. At 800 atm, the volume of the sample is 0.0533 L. **(a)** What should the volumes be according to the ideal gas law? **(b)** Account for the deviations. **(c)** What are the values of PV/RT for the two pressures?

LIQUIDS AND SOLIDS

C H A P T E R

11

The kinetic energies of gas molecules decrease when the temperature is lowered. Consequently, the intermolecular attractive forces cause the gas molecules to condense into a liquid when the gas has been cooled sufficiently. The molecules are closer together and the attractive forces exert a greater influence in a liquid than in a gas. Molecular motion, therefore, is more restricted in the liquid state than in the gaseous state.

Additional cooling causes the kinetic energies of the molecules to decrease further and ultimately produces a solid. In a crystalline solid the molecules assume positions in a crystal lattice, and the motion of the molecules is restricted to vibration about these fixed points.

The kinetic energies of the molecules of a gas are *high* enough to cause the intermolecular attractive forces to assume a role that can be minimized in the development of a satisfactory theory of gases. The kinetic energies of molecules (or ions) in crystals are *low* enough to be easily overcome by the attractive forces so as to produce highly ordered, crystalline structures that have been well characterized by diffraction techniques. Our understanding of the intermediate state, the liquid state, however, is not so complete as that of the other two states.

1.1 Intermolecular Forces of Attraction

Atoms are held together in molecules by covalent bonds, but what forces attract molecules to each other in the liquid and solid states? Several types of attractive forces hold molecules together; taken as a group, they are called intermolecular attractive forces. Two types are discussed in this section, and a third is presented in the next section.

Dipole-dipole forces occur between polar molecules. Molecules of this type have dipoles and line up in an electric field (see Section 8.2). Dipole-dipole forces are caused by the attractions of the positive and negative poles of the molecules for one another. In a crystal of a polar molecular substance, the molecules are lined up in a way that reflects the dipole-dipole forces (Figure 11.1).

Figure 11.1 Orientation of polar molecules in a crystal

Electronegativity differences between atoms can be used to predict the degree of polarity of a diatomic molecule as well as the positions of the positive and negative poles. A prediction concerning the polarity of a molecule that contains more than two atoms, however, must be based upon a knowledge of the geometry of the molecule, the polarities of the bonds, *and* the arrangement of nonbonding electron pairs.

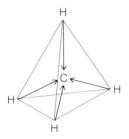

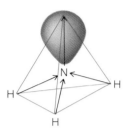

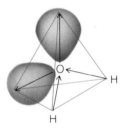

Figure 11.2 Analysis of the polarities of the methane (CH$_4$), ammonia (NH$_3$), and water (H$_2$O) molecules. (Arrows point toward the negative ends of the individual dipoles that compose the dipole moment of the molecule.)

Consider the three molecules (CH$_4$, NH$_3$, and H$_2$O) represented in Figure 11.2 The dipole moment of a molecule is the result of the individual bond dipoles and the nonbonding electron pairs of the molecule. In each of the molecules under consideration, the central atom is more electronegative than the H atoms bonded to it. The negative end of each *bond* dipole, therefore, points toward the central atom. In CH$_4$, the tetrahedral arrangement of the four polar C — H bonds produces a molecule that is not polar; CH$_4$ has no dipole moment. The center of positive charge of the *molecule* (derived by considering all four bonds) falls in the center of the C atom and coincides with the center of negative charge for the molecule.

On the other hand, the trigonal pyramidal NH$_3$ molecule is polar (its dipole moment is 1.49 D). The three polar bonds and the nonbonding electron pair are arranged so that the molecule has a dipole with the negative end directed toward the top of the trigonal pyramid and the positive end toward the bottom. Similarly, the angular H$_2$O molecule is polar (its dipole moment is 1.85 D). The polar bonds and the nonbonding electron pairs contribute to a dipole with the negative end directed toward the O atom and the positive end directed toward a point halfway between the two H atoms.

The influence that a nonbonding pair of electrons has on the dipole moment of a molecule is seen in the case of NF$_3$. The NF$_3$ molecule has a structure similar to that of NH$_3$ (Figure 11.3), but the direction of the polarity of the bonds is the reverse of that in NH$_3$ since F is more electronegative than N. Nitrogen trifluoride has a dipole moment of 0.24 D, a surprisingly low value in view of the highly polar nature of the N—F bonds. The N—F bond dipoles combine to give the molecule a dipole with the negative end in the direction of the base pyramid, but the contribution of the nonbonding electron pair works in the opposite direction and reduces the total polarity of the molecule.

What intermolecular forces attract *nonpolar* molecules to each other in the liquid and solid states? Such molecules do not have permanent dipoles, but nevertheless, they can be liquefied. Some type of intermolecular force, therefore, must exist in addition to the dipole-dipole force.

The existence of **London forces (dispersion forces)** is postulated.* These forces are thought to arise from the motion of electrons. At one instant, the electron cloud of a molecule may be distorted so that a dipole is produced in which one part of the molecule is slightly more negative than the rest. At the next instant, the positions of the negative and positive poles of the dipole will be different because the electrons have moved. Over a period of time (a very short period of time—electrons move rapidly), the effects of these **instantaneous dipoles** cancel so that a nonpolar molecule has no permanent dipole moment.

The instantaneous, fluctuating dipole of a molecule, however, induces matching dipoles in neighboring molecules (lined up in the same way that permanent dipoles are aligned). The motion of the electrons of neighboring molecules is synchronized (see Figure 11.4). The force of attraction between these instantaneous dipoles constitutes the London force. *The strongest London forces occur between large, complex molecules, which have large electron clouds that are easily distorted, or polarized.*

Since all molecules contain electrons, London forces also exist between polar

---

* Johannes van der Waals postulated the existence of intermolecular attractive forces between gas molecules in 1873 (Section 10.13). The explanation of the origin of the type of intermolecular force discussed here was proposed by Fritz London in 1930. Although there is a lack of uniformity in the use of terms, currrent usage appears to favor calling these specific forces *London forces* and intermolecular forces in general *van der Waals forces.*

molecules. In the case of nonpolar molecular substances, London forces are the *only* intermolecular forces that exist. The values listed in Table 11.1 illustrate the fact that London forces are the principal intermolecular forces for most molecular substances. The hydrogen bond, a special type of dipole-dipole interaction that is discussed in the next section, is responsible for the magnitude of the dipole-dipole energy listed for H_2O, NH_3, and (to a lesser extent) HCl.

The dipole moments of the molecules listed in Table 11.1 increase in the order given, and the dipole-dipole energies increase in the same order. The London energies, however, depend upon the sizes of the molecules. The largest molecule listed is HI, and it has the strongest London forces. HCl is a more polar molecule than HI; the electronegativity of Cl is 3.2, and the electronegativity of I is 2.7. The dipole-dipole energy of HCl is higher than that of HI. The London energy of HI, however, is so much higher than the London energy of HCl, that the *total* effect is that the molecules of HI are more strongly attracted to one another than the molecules of HCl are. The boiling point of HI is 238 K, which is higher than the boiling point of HCl (188 K).

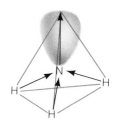

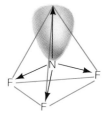

Figure 11.3 Comparison of the polarity of ammonia (NH_3) with nitrogen trifluoride (NF_3). (Arrows point toward the negative ends of the individual dipoles that compose the dipole moment of the molecule.)

Table 11.1 Intermolecular attractive energies in some simple molecular crystals

Molecule	Dipole Moment (D)	Attractive Energies (kJ/mol)		Melting Point (K)	Boiling Point (K)
		Dipole-Dipole	London		
CO	0.12	0.0004	8.74	74	82
HI	0.38	0.025	27.9	222	238
HBr	0.78	0.69	21.9	185	206
HCl	1.03	3.31*	16.8	158	188
NH_3	1.49	13.3*	14.7	195	240
H_2O	1.84	36.4*	9.0	273	373

* Caused by hydrogen bonding (see Section 11.2)

Figure 11.4 Instantaneous dipoles

11.2 The Hydrogen Bond

The intermolecular attractions of certain hydrogen-containing compounds are unusually strong. These attractions occur in compounds in which hydrogen is covalently bonded to highly electronegative elements of small atomic size. In these compounds the atom of the electronegative element exerts such a strong attraction on the bonding electrons that the hydrogen atom is left with a significant δ^+ charge. In fact, the hydrogen atom is almost an exposed proton since it has no shielding electrons.

The hydrogen atom of one molecule and a pair of unshared electrons on the electronegative atom of another molecule are mutually attracted and form what is called a **hydrogen bond.** Because of its small size, each hydrogen atom is capable of forming only one hydrogen bond. The association of HF, H_2O and NH_3 by hydrogen bonds (indicated by dotted lines) can be roughly diagrammed as follows:

$$H-F \cdots H-F \cdots \qquad H-\overset{\displaystyle \cdot\cdot}{\underset{\displaystyle H}{O}} \cdots H-\overset{\displaystyle \cdot\cdot}{\underset{\displaystyle H}{O}} \cdots \qquad H-\overset{\displaystyle H}{\underset{\displaystyle H}{N}} \cdots H-\overset{\displaystyle H}{\underset{\displaystyle H}{N}} \cdots$$

Unusual properties are characteristic of compounds in which hydrogen bonding occurs. In Figure 11.5 the normal boiling points of the hydrogen compounds of the elements of groups IV A, V A, VI A, and VII A are plotted. The series CH_4, SiH_4, GeH_4, and SnH_4 illustrates the expected trend in boiling point for compounds in which the only intermolecular forces are London forces; the boiling point increases as the molecular size increases. The hydrogen compounds of the IV A elements are nonpolar molecules; the central atom of each molecule has no unshared electron pair.

In each compound of the other three series of Figure 11.5, however, London forces are aided by dipole-dipole forces in holding the molecules together. Nevertheless, the boiling point of the first member of each series (HF, H_2O, and NH_3) is unusually high in comparison to those of the other members of the series. In each of these three compounds, hydrogen bonding increases the difficulty of separating the molecules from the liquid state. Extensive hydrogen bonding is not found in any of the other compounds for which a boiling point is plotted in Figure 11.5. In addition to high boiling points, compounds that are associated by hydrogen bonding have abnormally high melting points, enthalpies of vaporization, enthalpies of fusion, and viscosities. We will discuss these properties later in this chapter.

Hydrogen bonding occurs not only between the identical molecules of some pure compounds but also between the different molecules that make up certain solutions. There are two requirements for strong hydrogen bonding:

1. The polarity of the molecule that supplies the proton for the formation of the hydrogen bond (the *proton donor*) must be such that the hydrogen atom has a relatively high δ^+ charge. The increasing strength of the hydrogen bonds N—H $\cdots$ N < O—H $\cdots$ O < F—H $\cdots$ F parallels the increasing electronegativity of the atom bonded to hydrogen, N < O < F. The high positive charge on the hydrogen atom attracts the electron pair from another molecule strongly, and the small size of the hydrogen atom permits the second molecule to approach closely.

2. The atom (of the *proton acceptor*) that supplies the electron pair for the hydrogen bond must be relatively small. Really effective hydrogen bonds are formed only by fluorine, oxygen, and nitrogen compounds. Chlorine compounds form weak hydrogen bonds, as evidenced by the slight displacement of the boiling point of HCl (Figure 11.5). Chlorine has approximately the same electronegativity as nitrogen. A chlorine atom, however, is larger than a nitrogen atom, and the electron cloud of the chlorine atom is, therefore, more diffuse than that of the nitrogen atom.

An examination of Figure 11.5 will show that hydrogen bonding has a greater effect on the boiling point of water than on the boiling point of hydrogen fluoride.

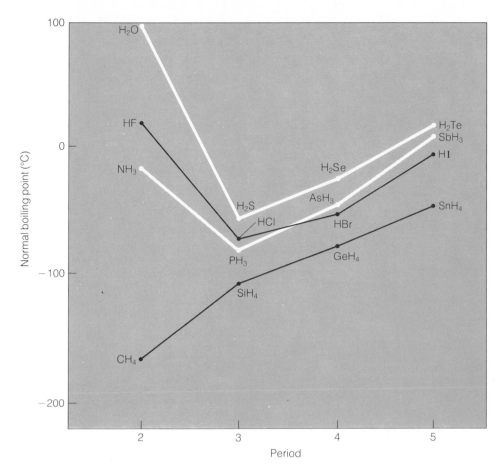

Figure 11.5 Normal boiling points of the hydrogen compounds of the elements of groups IV A, V A, VI A, and VII A

This effect is observed even though the O—H $\cdots$ O bond is only about two-thirds as strong as F—H $\cdots$ F bond. There are, *on the average,* twice as many hydrogen bonds *per molecule* in H_2O as there are *per molecule* in HF. The oxygen atom of each water molecule has two hydrogen atoms and two unshared electron pairs. The fluorine atom of the hydrogen fluoride molecule has three electron pairs that can bond with hydrogen atoms but only one hydrogen atom with which it can form a hydrogen bond.

Other properties of water are affected to an unusual degree by hydrogen bonding. The tetrahedral arrangement of the hydrogen atoms and the unshared electron pairs of oxygen in water cause the hydrogen bonds of the ice crystal to be arranged in this manner and lead to the open structure of the ice crystal (see Figure 11.6). Ice, therefore, has a comparatively low density. In water at the freezing point, the molecules are arranged more closely together; water, therefore, has a higher density than ice—an unusual situation. It should be noted that H_2O molecules are associated by hydrogen bonds in the liquid state but not to the same extent, nor in the rigid manner, that they are associated in ice.

Hydrogen bonding also accounts for the unexpectedly high solubilities of some compounds containing oxygen, nitrogen, and fluorine in certain hydrogen-containing solvents, notably water. Thus, ammonia (NH_3) and methanol (CH_3OH) dissolve in water through the formation of hydrogen bonds:

Figure 11.6 Arrangement of H_2O molecules in ice. Note the open structure, which is held together by hydrogen bonding.

$$
\begin{array}{cc}
\text{H} & \text{H} \\
| & | \\
\text{H}-\text{N}\cdots\text{H}-\text{O} & \text{H}-\text{C}-\text{O}\cdots\text{H}-\text{O} \\
| & \quad | \quad\quad | \\
\text{H} \quad\quad \text{H} & \text{H} \quad \text{H} \quad\quad \text{H}
\end{array}
$$

In addition, certain oxygen-containing anions (for example, the sulfate ion, SO_4^{2-}) dissolve in water through hydrogen-bond formation.

Hydrogen bonding plays a vital role in determining the structures and properties of molecules of living systems. The alpha helix of proteins (see Figure 29.3 in Section 29.1) and the double helix of DNA (see Figure 29.6 in Section 29.4) are each held together by hydrogen bonding. The making and breaking of hydrogen bonds is of central importance in cell division and in the synthesis of proteins by cells (see Section 29.4).

11.3 The Liquid State

In gases, the molecules move rapidly in a completely random manner. In most solids, the molecules are held together in the orderly arrangements typical of crystals. The liquid state is intermediate between the gaseous state and the solid state.

In liquids, the molecules move slowly enough for the intermolecular attractive forces to be able to hold them together into a definite volume. The molecular motion, however, is too rapid for the attractive forces to fix the molecules into definite positions in a crystal structure. A liquid, consequently, retains its volume but not its shape. Liquids flow and assume the shapes of their containers.

Iceberg, Glacier Bay, Alaska. Ice floats because it is less dense than liquid water.
Keith Gunnar, Photo Researchers, Inc.

A change in pressure has almost no effect on the volume of a liquid since there is little free space between the molecules. An increase in temperature, however, increases the volume of most liquids slightly and, consequently, decreases the liquid density. When the temperature of a liquid is increased, the average kinetic energy of the molecules increases, and this increased molecular motion works against the attractive forces. The expansion, however, is much less than that observed for gases, in which the effect of attractive forces is negligible.

Two liquids that are soluble in one another will diffuse into each other when placed together. If one liquid is carefully poured on top of another more dense liquid, the boundary between the two liquids will be sharp and easily seen. This boundary will gradually become less distinct and, in time, will disappear as the molecules of the two liquids diffuse into each other.

The diffusion of liquids is a much slower process than the diffusion of gases. Since the molecules of liquids are relatively close together, a molecule undergoes a tremendous number of collisions in a given time period. The average distance it travels between collisions, the mean free path, is much shorter for a molecule of a liquid than it is for a molecule of a gas. Gases, therefore, diffuse much more rapidly than liquids.

All liquids exhibit resistance to flow, a property known as **viscosity.** One way of determining the viscosity of a liquid is to measure the time that it takes for a definite amount of the liquid to pass through a tube of small diameter under a given pressure. Resistance to flow is largely due to the attractions between molecules, and the measurement of the viscosity of a liquid gives a simple estimate of the strength of these attractions. In general, as the temperature of a liquid is increased, the cohesive forces are less able to cope with increasing molecular motion,

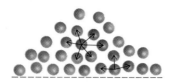

Figure 11.7 Schematic diagram indicating the unbalanced intermolecular forces on the surface molecules of a liquid as compared to the balanced intermolecular forces on the interior molecules

and the viscosity decreases. On the other hand, increasing the pressure generally increases the viscosity of a given liquid.

Surface tension is another property of liquids caused by the intermolecular attractive forces. A molecule in the center of a liquid is attracted equally in all directions by surrounding molecules. Molecules on the surface of a liquid, however, are attracted only toward the interior of the liquid (Figure 11.7). The surface molecules, therefore, are pulled inward, and the surface area of a liquid tends to be minimized. This behavior accounts for the spherical shape of liquid drops. Surface tension is a measure of this inward force on the surface of a liquid, the force that must be overcome to expand the surface area. The surface tension of a liquid decreases with increasing temperature since the increased molecular motion tends to decrease the effect of the intermolecular attractive forces.

11.4 Evaporation

The kinetic energies of the molecules of a liquid follow a Maxwell-Boltzmann distribution similar to the distribution of kinetic energy among gas molecules (Figure 11.8). The kinetic energy of a given molecule of a liquid is continually changing as the molecule collides with other molecules. At any given instant, however, some of the molecules of the total collection have relatively high energies and some have relatively low energies. The molecules with kinetic energies high enough to overcome the attractive forces of surrounding molecules can escape from the liquid and enter the gas phase if they are close to the surface and are moving in the right direction. They use part of their energy to work against the attractive forces when they escape.

In time, the loss of a number of high-energy molecules causes the average kinetic energy of the molecules remaining in the liquid to decrease, and the temperature of the liquid falls. When liquids evaporate from an open container, heat flows into the liquid from the surroundings to maintain the temperature of the liquid. In this way the supply of high-energy molecules is replenished, and the process continues until all of the liquid has evaporated. The total quantity of heat required to vaporize a mole of liquid at a given temperature is called the molar enthalpy of vaporization of that liquid. At 25°C, for example,

$$H_2O(l) \longrightarrow H_2O(g) \qquad \Delta H_v = +43.8 \text{ kJ}$$

The absorption of heat by an evaporating liquid explains why swimmers emerging from the water become chilled as the water evaporates from their skin. Likewise, the regulation of body temperature is, in part, accomplished by the evaporation of perspiration from the skin. Various cooling devices have made use of this principle. A water cooler of the Middle East consists of a jar of unglazed pottery filled with water. The water saturates the clay of the pottery and evaporates from the outer surface of the jar, thus cooling the water remaining in the jar.

The rate of evaporation increases as the temperature of a liquid is raised. When the temperature is increased, the average kinetic energy of the molecules increases, and the number of molecules with energies high enough for them to escape into the vapor phase increases (Figure 11.8).

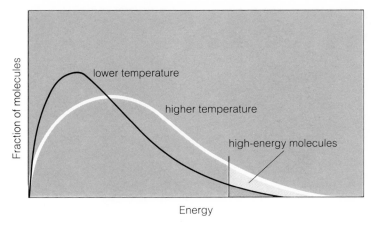

Fraction of molecules

lower temperature

higher temperature

high-energy molecules

Energy

Figure 11.8 Distribution of kinetic energy among molecules of a liquid

.5 Vapor Pressure

When a liquid in a closed container evaporates, the vapor molecules cannot escape from the vicinity of the liquid. In the course of their random motion, some of the vapor molecules return to the liquid. We can represent the process for water by using a double arrow:

$$H_2O(l) \rightleftharpoons H_2O(g)$$

The rate of return of the vapor molecules to the liquid depends upon the concentration of the molecules in the vapor. The more molecules that there are in a given volume of vapor, the greater the number that will strike the liquid and be recaptured.

At the start, the rate of return of molecules from the vapor to the liquid is low since there are few molecules in the vapor. The continued vaporization, however, causes the concentration of the molecules in the vapor to increase. The rate of condensation, therefore, also increases. Eventually the system reaches a point at which the rate of condensation equals the rate of vaporization.

This condition, in which the rates of two opposite tendencies are equal, is called a state of equilibrium. At equilibrium, the concentration of molecules in the vapor state is constant because molecules leave the vapor through condensation at the same rate that molecules add to the vapor through vaporization. Similarly, the quantity of liquid is a constant because molecules are returning to the liquid at the same rate that they are leaving it.

It is important to note that a condition of equilibrium does not imply that nothing is going on. In any system, the numbers of molecules present in the liquid and in the vapor are constant because the two opposing changes are taking place at the same rates and *not* because vaporization and condensation have stopped.

Since the concentration of the molecules in the vapor is a constant at equilibrium, the pressure that the vapor exerts is a constant too. The pressure of vapor in equilibrium with a liquid at a given temperature is called the equilibrium vapor pressure of the liquid. The vapor pressure of a given liquid is determined by the temperature and increases when the temperature is increased.

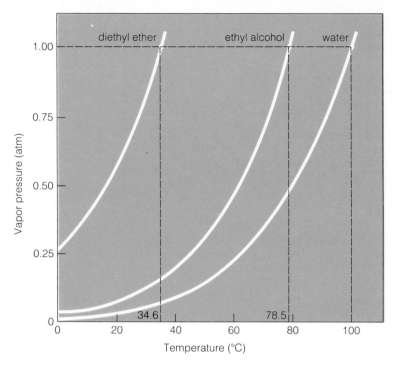

Figure 11.9 Vapor-pressure curves for diethyl ether, ethyl alcohol, and water

Figure 11.9 shows the temperature-vapor pressure curves for diethyl ether, ethyl alcohol, and water. The curves show the increase in vapor pressure that accompanies an increase in temperature. The curve for each substance could be extended to the critical temperature of that substance. At the critical temperature, the vapor pressure equals the critical pressure, and the curves end at this point. Above the critical temperature only one phase can exist—the gas and liquid phases are not distinguishable from one another.

The magnitude of the vapor pressure of a liquid gives an indication of the strength of the intermolecular attractive forces of that liquid. Liquids that have strong attractive forces have low vapor pressures. At 20°C, the vapor pressure of water is 0.023 atm, of ethyl alcohol is 0.058 atm, and of diethyl ether is 0.582 atm. The forces of attraction are strongest in water and weakest in diethyl ether. A list of the vapor pressure of water at various temperatures is given in Table 9.3.

11.6 Boiling Point

The temperature at which the vapor pressure of a liquid equals the external pressure is called the **boiling point** of the liquid. At this temperature, vapor produced in the interior of a liquid results in the bubble formation and turbulence that is characteristic of boiling. Bubble formation is impossible at temperatures below the boiling point. The atmospheric pressure on the surface of the liquid prevents the formation of bubbles with internal pressures that are less than the pressure of the atmosphere.

The temperature of a boiling liquid remains constant until all the liquid has been vaporized. In an open container the maximum vapor pressure that can be attained by any liquid is the atmospheric pressure. This vapor pressure is attained at the boiling point. Heat must be added to a boiling liquid to maintain the temperature because in the boiling process, the high-energy molecules are lost by the liquid. The higher the rate at which heat is added to a boiling liquid, the faster the liquid boils. The temperature of the liquid, however, does not rise.

The boiling point of a liquid changes with changes in external pressure. Water, for example, will boil at 98.6°C at a pressure of 0.950 atm and at 101.4°C at a pressure of 1.05 atm. Only at a pressure of 1.00 atm will water boil at 100°C. The normal boiling point of a liquid is defined as the temperature at which the vapor pressure of the liquid equals 1 atm. Boiling points given in reference books are understood to be normal boiling points, and when the term *boiling point* is used without qualification, normal boiling point should be assumed.

The normal boiling points of diethyl ether (34.6°C), ethyl alcohol (78.5°C), and water are indicated on the vapor-pressure curves of Figure 11.9. The boiling point of a liquid can be read from its vapor-pressure curve by finding the temperature at which the vapor pressure of the liquid equals the prevailing pressure.

The changes in atmospheric pressure at any one geographic location cause a maximum variation of about 2°C in the boiling point of water. The variations from place to place, however, can be greater than this. The average barometric pressure at sea level is approximately 1 atm. At higher elevations, average barometric pressures are less. At an elevation of 1524 m (which is 5,000 feet) above sea level, for example, the average barometric pressure is 0.836 atm; at this pressure, water boils at 95.1°C. Water boils at 90.1°C at 0.695 atm, which is the average atmospheric pressure at 3048 m (which is 10,000 feet) above sea level.

If a liquid has a high normal boiling point or decomposes when heated, it can be made to boil at lower temperatures by reducing the pressure. This procedure is followed in vacuum distillation. Water can be made to boil at 10°C, which is considerably below room temperature, by adjusting the pressure to 0.0121 atm (see Table 10.3). Unwanted water is removed from many food products by boiling it away under reduced pressure. In these procedures, the product is not subjected to temperatures that bring about decomposition or discoloration.

1.7 Enthalpy of Vaporization

The quantity of heat that must be supplied to vaporize a mole of a liquid at a specified temperature is called the molar enthalpy of vaporization, ΔH_v. Enthalpies of vaporization are usually recorded at the normal boiling point in kilojoules per mole (see Table 11.2).

The magnitude of the molar enthalpy of vaporization gives an indication of the strength of the intermolecular attractive forces. A high enthalpy of vaporization indicates that these forces are strong. The enthalpy of vaporization of a liquid, however, includes both the energy required to overcome the intermolecular attractive forces and the energy needed to expand the vapor. The volume of a gas is considerably larger than the volume of the liquid from which it is derived. A volume of about 1700 mL of steam, for example, is produced by the vaporization of 1 mL of of water at 100°C. Energy must be supplied to do the work of pushing back the atmosphere to make room for the vapor.

When a mole of vapor is condensed into a liquid, energy is released, not absorbed. This enthalpy change is called the molar enthalpy of condensation. It has

Table 11.2 Enthalpies of vaporization of liquids at their normal boiling points

Liquid	Formula	t_b Normal Boiling Point (°C)	ΔH_v Enthalpy of Vaporization (kJ/mol)
water	H_2O	100.0	40.7
benzene	C_6H_6	80.1	30.8
ethyl alcohol	C_2H_5OH	78.5	38.6
carbon tetrachloride	CCl_4	76.7	30.0
chloroform	$CHCl_3$	61.3	29.4
diethyl ether	$(C_2H_5)_2O$	34.6	26.0

a negative sign, but it is numerically equal to the molar enthalpy of vaporization at the same temperature.

The enthalpy of vaporization of a liquid decreases as the temperature increases, and it equals zero at the critical temperature of the substance.

The Clausius-Clapeyron Equation

Over a relatively narrow temperature range, the enthalpy of vaporization can be considered to be constant. Under such conditions, the vapor pressure of a liquid, p (in atm), is related to the temperature at which it is measured, T (in K), by the equation:

$$\log p = -\frac{\Delta H_v}{2.303RT} + C \tag{11.1}$$

where ΔH_v is the molar enthalpy of vaporization (in J/mol), R is the ideal gas constant [8.3143 J/(K·mol)], and C is a constant that is characteristic of the liquid under study. Points for the vapor-pressure curves shown in Figure 11.9 may be obtained by substituting appropriate values into Equation 11.1.

If we wish to compare the vapor pressure of a liquid, p_1, at one temperature, T_1, to the vapor pressure of the same liquid, p_2, at a second temperature, T_2, we can derive a very useful equation in the following way:

$$\text{At } T_2: \quad \log p_2 = -\frac{\Delta H_v}{2.303R}\left(\frac{1}{T_2}\right) + C \tag{11.2}$$

$$\text{At } T_1: \quad \log p_1 = -\frac{\Delta H_v}{2.303R}\left(\frac{1}{T_1}\right) + C \tag{11.3}$$

By subtracting Equation 11.3 from Equation 11.2, we get:

$$\log p_2 - \log p_1 = -\frac{\Delta H_v}{2.303R}\left(\frac{1}{T_2} - \frac{1}{T_1}\right) \tag{11.4}$$

which can be rearranged to:

$$\log\left(\frac{p_2}{p_1}\right) = \left(\frac{\Delta H_v}{2.303R}\right)\left(\frac{T_2 - T_1}{T_1 T_2}\right) \tag{11.5}$$

This equation, known as the **Clausius-Clapeyron equation,** was first proposed by Benoît Clapeyron in 1834 and later derived from thermodynamic theory by Rudolf Clausius.

Example 11.1

The normal boiling point of chloroform, $CHCl_3$, is 334 K. At 328 K, the vapor pressure of chloroform is 0.824 atm. What is the enthalpy of vaporization of chloroform for this temperature range?

Solution

If we set $T_2 = 334$ K, then $p_2 = 1.000$ atm, $T_1 = 328$ K, and $p_1 = 0.824$ atm.

$$\log\left(\frac{p_2}{p_1}\right) = \left(\frac{\Delta H_v}{2.303\ R}\right)\left(\frac{T_2 - T_1}{T_1 T_2}\right) \tag{11.5}$$

$$\log\left(\frac{1.000\ \text{atm}}{0.824\ \text{atm}}\right) = \left(\frac{\Delta H_v}{(2.303)[8.314\ \text{J/(K}\cdot\text{mol)}]}\right)\left[\frac{334\ \text{K} - 328\ \text{K}}{(328\ \text{K})(334\ \text{K})}\right]$$

$$\Delta H_v = 29{,}390\ \text{J/mol}$$
$$= 29.4\ \text{kJ/mol}$$

Example 11.2

The vapor pressure of carbon disulfide, CS_2, is 0.526 at 301 K. What is the vapor pressure of CS_2 at 273 K? The enthalpy of vaporization of CS_2 over this temperature range is 27.6 kJ/mol.

Solution

We set $T_2 = 301$ K, $p_2 = 0.526$ atm, $T_1 = 273$ K, and $\Delta H_v = 2.76 \times 10^4$ J/mol. Hence,

$$\log\left(\frac{p_2}{p_1}\right) = \left(\frac{\Delta H_v}{2.303R}\right)\left(\frac{T_2 - T_1}{T_1 T_2}\right) \tag{11.5}$$

$$\log\left(\frac{0.526\ \text{atm}}{p_1}\right) = \left(\frac{2.76 \times 10^4\ \text{J/mol}}{(2.303)[8.314\ \text{J/(K}\cdot\text{mol)}]}\right)\left(\frac{301\ \text{K} - 273\ \text{K}}{(273\ \text{K})(301\ \text{K})}\right)$$

$$= 0.491$$

$$\left(\frac{0.526\ \text{atm}}{p_1}\right) = 31.0$$

$$p_1 = 0.170\ \text{atm}$$

Example 11.3

What is the boiling point of water at a pressure of 0.695 atm? The enthalpy of vaporization of water may be taken as 40.7 kJ/mol.

Solution

At the normal boiling point of water, 373 K, the vapor pressure of water is 1.000 atm. Therefore, p_1 = 1.000 atm, T_1 = 373 K, p_2 = 0.695 atm, and ΔH_v = 4.07 $\times$ 10^4 J/mol. Hence,

$$\log\left(\frac{p_2}{p_1}\right) = \left(\frac{\Delta H_v}{2.303R}\right)\left(\frac{T_2 - T_1}{T_1 T_2}\right) \tag{11.5}$$

$$\log\left(\frac{1.000 \text{ atm}}{0.695 \text{ atm}}\right) = \left(\frac{4.07 \times 10^4 \text{ J/mol}}{(2.303)[8.314 \text{ J/(K·mol)}]}\right)\left(\frac{373 \text{ K} - T_2}{(373 \text{ K})T_2}\right)$$

$$0.1580 = 2126\left(\frac{373 \text{ K} - T_2}{(373 \text{ K})T_2}\right)$$

$$1.028 T_2 = 373 \text{ K}$$

$$T_2 = 363 \text{ K}$$

The boiling point of water at a pressure of 0.695 atm is 363 − 273 = 90.°C.

11.8 The Freezing Point

When a liquid is cooled, the molecules move more and more slowly. Eventually a temperature is reached at which some of the molecules have kinetic energies that are low enough to allow the intermolecular attractions to hold them in crystal structure. The substance then starts to freeze. Gradually the low-energy molecules assume positions in the crystal pattern. The molecules remaining in the liquid have a higher temperature because of the loss of these low-energy molecules. Heat must be removed from the liquid to maintain the temperature.

The normal freezing point of a liquid is the temperature at which solid and liquid are in equlibrium under a total pressure of 1 atm. At the freezing point, the temperature of the solid-liquid system remains constant until all of the liquid is frozen. The quantity of heat that must be removed to freeze a mole of a substance at the freezing point is called the molar enthalpy of crystallization. This quantity represents the difference between the enthalpies of the liquid and the solid.

At times the molecules of a liquid, as they are cooled, continue the random motion characteristic of the liquid state at temperatures below the freezing point. Such liquids are referred to as undercooled or supercooled liquids. These systems can usually be caused to revert to the freezing temperature and the stable solid-liquid equilibrium by scratching the interior walls of the container with a stirring rod or by adding a seed crystal around which crystallization can occur. The crystallization process supplies heat, and the temperature is brought back to the freezing point until normal crystallization is complete.

Table 11.3 Enthalpies of fusion of solids at their melting points

Solid	Formula	t_f Melting Point (°C)	ΔH_f Enthalpy of Fusion (kJ/mol)
water	H_2O	0.0	6.02
benzene	C_6H_6	5.5	9.83
ethyl alcohol	C_2H_5OH	−117.2	4.60
carbon tetrachloride	CCl_4	−22.9	2.51
chloroform	$CHCl_3$	−63.5	9.20
diethyl ether	$(C_2H_5)_2O$	−116.3	7.26

Some supercooled liquids can exist for long periods, or even permanently, in this state. When these liquids are cooled, molecules solidify in a random arrangement typical of the liquid state rather than in an orderly geometric pattern of a crystal. Substances of this type have complex molecular forms for which crystallization is difficult. They are frequently called **amorphous solids, vitreous materials,** or **glasses;** examples include glass, tar, and certain plastics. Amorphous solids have no definite freezing or melting points. These transitions take place over a temperature range. The solids break into fragments that have curved, shell-like surfaces. Crystalline materials break into fragments with planar surfaces at characteristic angles.

When a crystalline substance is heated, the temperature at which solid-liquid equilibrium is attained under air at 1 atm pressure is called the **melting point.** It is, of course, the same temperature as the freezing point of the substance. The quantity of heat that must be *added* to melt a mole of the material at the melting point is called the **molar enthalpy of fusion,** ΔH_f, and is numerically equal to the enthalpy of crystallization but opposite in sign (Table 11.3).

11.9 Vapor Pressure of a Solid

Molecules in crystals vibrate about their positions in the crystal structure. A distribution of kinetic energies exists among these molecules similar to the distribution for liquids and gases. Energy is transmitted from molecule to molecule within a crystal; the energy of any one molecule, therefore, is not constant. High-energy molecules on the surface of the crystal can overcome the attractive forces of the crystal and escape into the vapor phase. If the crystal is in a closed container, an equilibrium is eventually reached in which the rate of the molecules leaving the solid equals the rate at which the vapor molecules return to the crystal. The vapor pressure of a solid at a given temperature is a measure of the number of molecules in a given volume of the vapor at equilibrium.

Every solid has a vapor pressure, although some pressures are very low. Vapor pressure is inversely proportional to the strength of the attractive forces. Ionic crystals, therefore, have very low vapor pressures.

Since the ability of molecules to overcome the intermolecular forces of attraction depends upon their kinetic energies, the vapor pressure of a solid increases as the temperature increases. The temperature-vapor pressure curve for ice is illustrated in Figure 11.10. This curve intersects the vapor-pressure curve for water at the

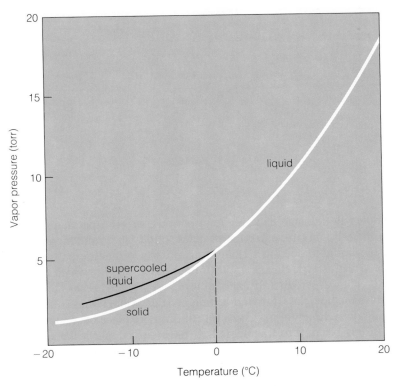

Figure 11.10 Vapor-pressure curves for ice and water near the freezing point. (Vapor pressures are partial pressures of H_2O under air at a total pressure of 1.00 atm.)

freezing point. At the freezing point, the vapor pressures of solid and liquid are equal.

In the absence of air, the normal freezing point of water (1 atm total pressure) is 0.0025°C (see Section 11.10 and Figure 11.11). *In air*, however, and under a total pressure of 1 atm, the freezing point of water is 0.0000°C, which is the commonly reported value. The difference in freezing point is caused by the presence of dissolved air in the water (Section 12.8). The vapor pressures plotted in Figure 11.10 are the partial pressures of H_2O in air with the total pressure equal to 1 atm. Freezing points are usually determined in air. In any event, however, any change in freezing point of a given substance caused by the presence of air is generally very small.

11.10 Phase Diagrams

The temperature-pressure phase diagram for water conveniently illustrates the conditions under which water can exist as solid, liquid, or vapor, as well as the conditions that bring about changes in the state of water. Figure 11.11 is a schematic representation of the water system. It is not drawn to scale, and some of its features are exaggerated so that important details can be easily seen. Every substance has its own phase diagram, which is derived from experimental observations.

The diagram of Figure 11.11 relates to what is called a one-component system; that is, it pertains to the behavior of water in the absence of any other substance. No part of the total pressure of any system described by the diagram is due to

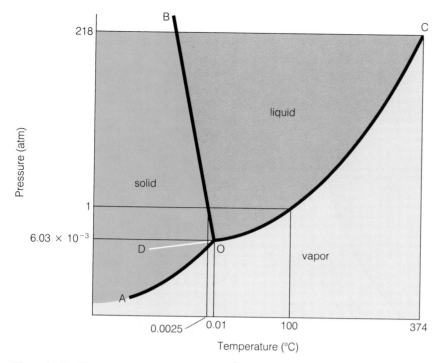

Figure 11.11 Phase diagram for water. (Not drawn to scale.)

the pressure of a gas other than water vapor. The vapor-pressure curves plotted in Figure 11.10 (measured in air under a constant total pressure of 1 atm) therefore deviate slightly, but only very slightly, from the vapor-pressure curves of Figure 11.11 (for which the vapor pressure of water is the *total* pressure). The easiest way to interpret the phase diagram for water is to visualize the total pressure acting on a system in mechanical terms—for example, as a piston acting on the material of the system contained in a cylinder.

In Figure 11.11, curve OC is a vapor-pressure curve for liquid and terminates at the critical point, C. Any point on this line describes a set of temperature and pressure conditions under which liquid and vapor can exist in equilibrium. The extension DO is the curve for supercooled liquid; systems between liquid and vapor described by points on this line are metastable. (The term *metastable* is applied to systems that are not in the most stable state possible at the temperature in question.) Curve AO is a vapor-pressure curve for solid and represents a set of points that describe the possible temperature and pressure conditions for solid-vapor equilibria. The line BO, the melting-point curve, represents conditions for equilibria between solid and liquid.

These three curves intersect at point O, a triple point. Solid, liquid, and vapor can exist together in equilibrium under the conditions represented by this point: 0.01°C (which is 273.16 K) and a pressure of 0.00603 atm (or 4.58 torr).

The phases (solid, liquid, and vapor) that exist in equilibrium under a set of temperature and pressure conditions can be read from the phase diagram. The temperature and pressure define a point on the diagram. The phases can be read from the position of the point. If the point falls

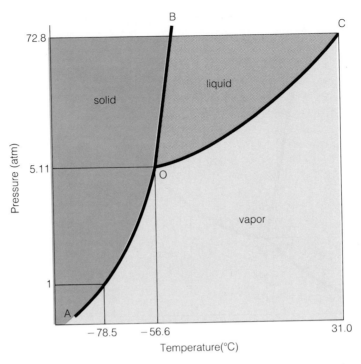

Figure 11.12 Phase diagram for carbon dioxide. (Not drawn to scale.)

1. *In a region* labeled solid, liquid, or vapor, only *one phase* exists—the phase noted on the diagram

2. *On a line, two phases* exist; the phases are those that are marked in the regions on both sides of the line

3. *On a point,* all *three phases* exist; there is only one such point in the phase diagram given for water—the triple point

The slope of the melting-point (or freezing-point) curve, BO, shows that the freezing point decreases as the pressure is increased. A slope of this type is observed for only a few substances, such as gallium, bismuth, and water. It indicates an unusual situation in which the liquid expands upon freezing. At 0°C a mole of water occupies 18.00 cm^3, and a mole of ice occupies 19.63 cm^3. The system expands, therefore, when one mole of liquid water freezes into ice. An increase in pressure on the system would oppose this expansion and the freezing process. Hence, the freezing point of water is lowered when the total pressure is increased. In Figure 11.11 the slope of the line BO is exaggerated.

Phase changes brought about by temperature changes at constant pressure may be read from a phase diagram by interpreting a horizontal line drawn at the reference pressure (like the line drawn at 1.00 atm in Figure 11.11). The point where this line intersects curve BO indicates the normal melting point (or freezing point), and the point where the 1.00 atm line intersects curve CO represents the normal boiling point. Beyond this point, only vapor exists.

Phase changes brought about by pressure changes at constant temperature may be read from a vertical line drawn at the reference temperature. If the pressure is increased, for example, at 0.0025°C (Figure 11.11), the point where the vertical line crosses AO is the pressure where vapor changes to solid, and the point where the vertical line crosses BO represents the pressure where solid changes to liquid. Above this point, only liquid exists.

For materials that contract upon freezing (that is, the solid phase is more dense than the liquid phase), the freezing-point curve slants in the opposite direction, and the freezing point increases as the pressure is increased. This behavior is characteristic of most substances. The freezing-point curves of most phase diagrams slant to the right, as is seen in the phase diagram for carbon dioxide in Figure 11.12.

The process in which a solid goes directly into a vapor without going through the liquid state is known as **sublimation;** this process is reversible. The phase diagram for carbon dioxide is typical for substances that sublime at ordinary pressures rather than melt and then boil. The triple point of the carbon dioxide system is $-55.6°C$ at a pressure of 5.11 atm. Liquid carbon dioxide exists only at pressures greater than 5.11 atm. When solid carbon dioxide (dry ice) is heated at 1 atm pressure, it is converted directly into gas at $-78.5°C$. This relationship is shown in Figure 11.12. The **molar enthalpy of sublimation** is the heat that must be added to a mole of solid to convert it directly into a gas.

11.11 Types of Crystalline Solids

Crystals are formed by atoms, ions, or molecules. We can classify crystals into four types according to the kind of particles that make up the crystal and the forces that hold them together:

1. Ionic crystals. Positive and negative ions are held in the crystal arrangement by electrostatic attraction. Because these forces are strong, ionic substances have high melting points. Ionic crystals are hard and brittle. Figure 11.13 shows what happens if an attempt is made to deform an ionic crystal. Because of the movement of one plane of ions over another, ions with the same charge are brought next to one another. The crystal breaks into fragments. Ionic compounds are good conductors of electricity when molten or in solution but not in the crystalline state, where the ions are not free to move.

An ionic crystal, fluorite, CaF_2.
© *George Roos, Peter Arnold, Inc.*

2. Molecular crystals. Molecules occupy positions in crystals of covalent compounds. The intermolecular forces that hold the molecules in the crystal structure are not nearly so strong as the electrostatic forces that hold ionic crystals together. Molecular crystals, therefore, are soft and have low melting points, usually below 300°C.

London forces hold nonpolar molecules in the structure. In crystals of polar molecules, dipole-dipole forces as well as London forces occur. Polar compounds, therefore, generally melt at slightly higher temperatures than nonpolar compounds of *comparable molecular size and shape.*

In general, molecular substances do not conduct electricity in the solid or liquid states. A few molecular compounds, such as water, dissociate to a very slight extent and produce low concentrations of ions; these liquids are poor electrical conductors.

3. Network crystal. In these crystals, atoms occupy positions and they are joined by a network of covalent bonds. The entire crystal can be looked at as one giant molecule. In diamond, an example of this type of crystal, carbon atoms are bonded

A molecular crystal, a snowflake (H_2O). *Carl Zeiss, Photo Researchers, Inc.*

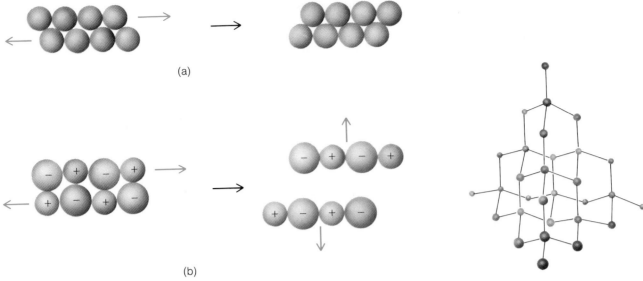

Figure 11.13 Effect of deformation on (a) a metallic crystal and (b) an ionic crystal

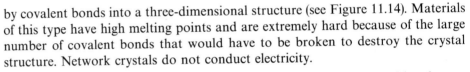

Figure 11.14 Arrangement of atoms in a diamond crystal

Network crystals, quartz (silicon dioxide, SiO_2). *Barry L. Runk from Grant Heilman.*

Metallic crystals, surface of a piece of zinc, showing crystalline structure. *Berenice Abbott, Photo Researchers, Inc.*

by covalent bonds into a three-dimensional structure (see Figure 11.14). Materials of this type have high melting points and are extremely hard because of the large number of covalent bonds that would have to be broken to destroy the crystal structure. Network crystals do not conduct electricity.

4. Metallic crystals. The outer electrons of metal atoms are loosely held and move freely throughout a metallic crystal. The remainder of the metal atoms, positive ions, occupy fixed positions in the crystal. The negative cloud of the freely moving electrons, sometimes called an electron gas or a sea of electrons, binds the crystal together. This binding force, called a metallic bond, is described more fully in Section 25.1.

The metallic bond is strong. Most metals have high melting points, high densities and structures in which the positive ions are packed together closely (called closest-packed arrangements). Unlike with ionic crystals, the positions of the positive ions can be altered without destroying the crystal because of the uniform cloud of negative charge provided by the freely moving electrons (see Figure 11.13). Most metallic crystals, therefore, are easily deformed, and most metals are malleable (capable of being beaten into shape) and ductile (capable of being drawn into wire). The freely moving electrons are also responsible for the fact that most metals are good conductors of electricity.

The properties of the four types of crystals are summarized in Table 11.4.

11.12 Crystals

A crystal structure is a symmetrical array of atoms, ions, or molecules arranged in a repeating, three-dimensional pattern. The symmetry of a crystal can be described in terms of a crystal lattice. A lattice is a three-dimensional arrangement

Table 11.4 Types of crystalline solids

Crystal	Particles	Attractive Forces	Properties	Examples
ionic	positive and negative ions	electrostatic attractions	high m.p. hard, brittle good electrical conductor in molten state	NaCl, BaO, KNO$_3$
molecular	polar molecules	London and dipole-dipole	low m.p. soft nonconductor or extremely poor conductor of electricity in liquid state	H$_2$O, NH$_3$, SO$_2$
	nonpolar molecules	London		H$_2$, Cl$_2$, CH$_4$
network	atoms	covalent bonds	very high m.p. very hard nonconductor of electricity	C (diamond) SiC, AlN, SiO$_2$
metallic	positive ions and mobile electrons	metallic bonds	fairly high m.p. hard or soft malleable and ductile good electrical conductor	Ag, Cu, Na, Fe, K

of points that represent sites with identical surroundings in the same orientation. If one starts with *any* lattice point and goes a definite distance in a set direction, a second lattice point will be encountered. The points are identical and have identical surroundings. A simple cubic lattice is shown in Figure 11.15.

A crystal lattice can usually be derived from a crystal structure by replacing the centers of the material units (atoms, for example) with lattice points. Notice, however, that the definition of a crystal lattice requires that the lattice points and their surroundings be *identical*. A lattice of an ionic crystal, therefore, can be defined with the points centering on the cations, *or* on the anions, *or* on some sites between the two.

A crystal lattice can be divided into identical parts called unit cells (see Figure 11.15). In theory, a lattice can be reproduced by stacking its unit cells in three dimensions. The idea of a unit cell can also be applied to a crystal structure. These units cells are considered to consist of all the material units of which the crystal is composed (*both* cations and anions of an ionic crystal) rather than just lattice points. Keep in mind that the unit cell of a crystal structure has all the components of the crystal in the correct ratios. Repeating the unit cell of a crystal structure in three dimensions generates the structure itself.

The simplest types of unit cells are the cubic unit cells (Figure 11.16). Notice that it is possible to have points at positions other than the corners of the unit cells. In the body-centered cubic unit cell, a point occurs in the center of the cell. In the face-centered cubic unit cell, a point occurs in the center of each face of the cell.

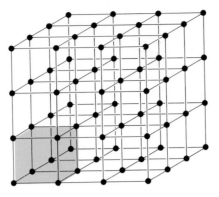

Figure 11.15 Simple cubic space lattice.
(A unit cell is shown in color.)

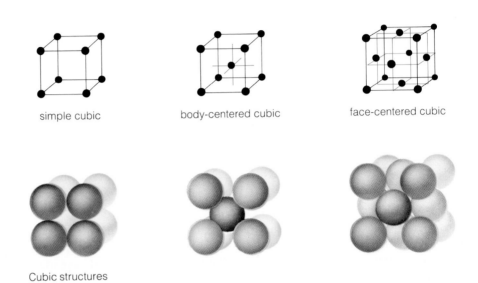

simple cubic body-centered cubic face-centered cubic

Cubic structures

Figure 11.16 Cubic structures

In crystals of metals, we may assume that atoms occupy lattice positions (even though the outer electrons of the metal atoms move freely throughout the structure). In counting the number of atoms per unit cell, one must keep in mind that atoms on corners or faces are shared by adjoining cells. Eight unit cells share each corner atom, and two unit cells share each face-centered atom (see Figure 11.17). A body-centered atom is not shared between unit cells and belongs exclusively to the unit cell in which it is found.

1. The simple cubic unit cell contains the equivalent of only one atom (eight corners at one-eighth atom each).

2. The body-centered cubic unit cell contains two atoms (eight corners at one-eighth atom each and one unshared atom in the center).

3. The face-centered cubic unit cell contains the equivalent of four atoms (eight corners at one-eighth atom each and six face-centered atoms at one-half atom each).

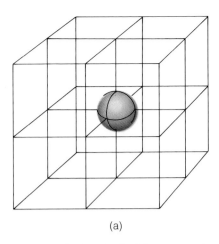

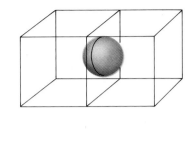

(a)   (b)

Figure 11.17 In crystals, (a) a corner atom is shared by eight unit cells, and (b) a face-centered atom is shared by two cells

Example 11.4

Nickel crystallizes in a face-centered cubic crystal. The edge of a unit cell is 352 pm. The atomic weight of nickel is 58.7, and its density is 8.94 g/cm^3. Calculate Avogadro's number from these data.

Solution

Since 1 pm = 10^{-10} cm,

$$352 \text{ pm} = 3.52 \times 10^{-8} \text{ cm}$$

The volume of one unit cell is $(3.52 \times 10^{-8} \text{ cm})^3$, or 4.36×10^{-23} cm^3. Since the unit cell is face-centered, it contains four atoms. Therefore,

$$4 \text{ atoms} \approx 4.36 \times 10^{-23} \text{ cm}^3$$

We derive from the density,

$$1 \text{ cm}^3 \approx 8.94 \text{ g Ni}$$

The number of atoms in 58.7 g of Ni is Avogadro's number:

$$? \text{ atoms} = 58.7 \text{ g Ni}\left(\frac{1 \text{ cm}^3}{8.94 \text{ g Ni}}\right)\left(\frac{4 \text{ atoms}}{4.36 \times 10^{-23} \text{ cm}^3}\right) = 6.02 \times 10^{23} \text{ atoms}$$

Example 11.5

Sodium crystallizes in a cubic structure, and the edge of a unit cell is 430 pm. The density of sodium is 0.963 g/cm^3, and the atomic weight of sodium is 23.0. How many atoms of sodium are contained in one unit cell? What type of cubic unit cell does sodium form?

Solution

The edge of the unit is 4.30×10^{-8} cm. The volume of the unit cell, therefore, is $(4.30 \times 10^{-8}$ cm$)^3$, or 7.95×10^{-23} cm^3. We must find the number of Na atoms in this volume.

We derive our conversion factors from the density of Na:

$$0.963 \text{ g Na} \approxeq 1 \text{ cm}^3$$

and the fact that 1 mol of Na (which is 23.0 g of Na) contains Avogadro's number of Na atoms:

$$6.02 \times 10^{23} \text{ atoms Na} = 23.0 \text{ g Na}$$

The solution is

$$? \text{ atoms Na} = 7.95 \times 10^{-23} \text{ cm}^3 \left(\frac{0.963 \text{ g Na}}{1 \text{ cm}^3} \right) \left(\frac{6.02 \times 10^{23} \text{ atoms Na}}{23.0 \text{ g Na}} \right)$$

$$= 2.00 \text{ atoms Na}$$

Sodium crystallizes in a body-centered cell since the body-centered cubic unit cell is the only cubic unit cell that contains two atoms.

Crystal data can be used to calculate atomic radii:

1. In the case of a simple cubic unit cell, the atomic radius, r, is one-half the length of the edge of the cell, a (see Figure 11.16):

$$r = a/2 \tag{11.6}$$

2. In a face-centered cubic unit cell, the atoms that lie along an edge do not touch. We must calculate the length of the face diagonal (see Figure 11.18a). From the Pythagorean theorem for right triangles,

$$\text{hypotenuse}^2 = \text{side}^2 + \text{side}^2$$
$$(\text{face diagonal})^2 = a^2 + a^2$$
$$= 2a^2$$
$$\text{face diagonal} = a\sqrt{2} \tag{11.7}$$

This diagonal is equal to four radii:

$$4r = a\sqrt{2}$$
$$r = a\sqrt{8} \tag{11.8}$$

3. We must determine the length of a cube diagonal to find the atomic radius of an atom that forms a body-centered cubic unit cell (see Figure 11.18b). From the figure, we see that the diagonal of a cube is the diagonal of a rectangle formed by the edge of the cube, a, and the diagonal of a face, $a\sqrt{2}$. Therefore,

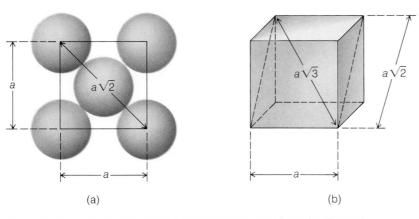

(a)　　　　　　　　　　　　(b)

Figure 11.18 Determination of (a) a face diagonal and (b) a cube diagonal

$$(\text{cube diagonal})^2 = a^2 + (a\sqrt{2})^2$$
$$= 3a^2$$
$$\text{cube diagonal} = a\sqrt{3} \tag{11.9}$$

This diagonal is equal to four atomic radii:

$$4r = a\sqrt{3}$$
$$r = \frac{a\sqrt{3}}{4} \tag{11.10}$$

Example 11.6

Sodium crystallizes in a body-centered cubic unit cell with the length of the edge equal to 430 pm. What is the atomic radius of Na?

Solution

The cube diagonal of the unit cell is

$$\text{cube diagonal} = a\sqrt{3}$$
$$= (430\ \text{pm})\sqrt{3}$$
$$= 745\ \text{pm}$$

This length is four atomic radii:

$$4r = 745\ \text{pm}$$
$$r = 186\ \text{pm}$$

11.13 Crystal Structure by X-ray Diffraction

Much of what is known about the internal structure of crystals has been learned from X-ray diffraction experiments. When two X-rays that have the same wavelength are in phase, they reinforce each other and produce a wave that is stronger

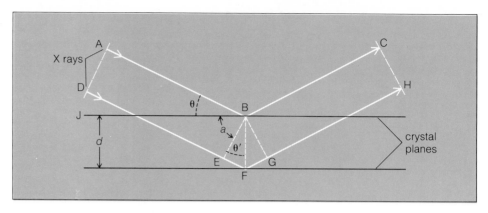

Figure 11.19 Derivation of the Bragg equation

than either of the original waves. Two waves that are completely out of phase cancel each other (see Figure 9.8).

Figure 11.19 illustrates the way the crystal spacings can be determined by use of X-rays of a single wavelength, λ. The rays strike the parallel planes of the crystal (which are separated by a distance, d) at an angle θ. Some of the rays are reflected from the upper plane, some from the second plane, and some from the lower planes. A strong reflected beam will result only if all the reflected rays are in phase.

In Figure 11.19 the distance that the lower ray travels (DFH) is farther than the distance that the upper ray travels (ABC) by an amount equal to EF + FG. The rays will be in phase at BG only if the difference is equal to a whole number of wavelengths:

$$EF + FG = n\lambda$$

where n is a simple integer.

Since angle ABE is a right angle,

$$\theta + a = 90°$$

Angle JBF is also a right angle, and

$$\theta' + a = 90°$$

The angle θ' is therefore equal to θ. The sine of angle θ' is equal to EF/BF (the ratio of the side opposite the angle to the hypotenuse). Since line BF is equal to d,

$$\sin \theta = \frac{EF}{d}$$

or

$$EF = d \sin \theta$$

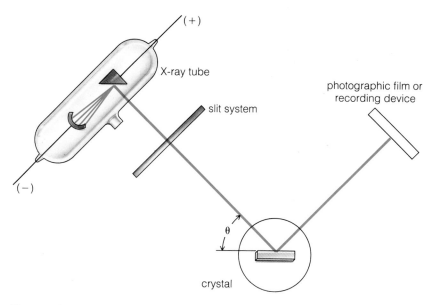

Figure 11.20 X-ray diffraction of crystals. (Schematic.)

The expression

$$FG = d \sin \theta$$

can be derived in the same way. Therefore,

$$EF + FG = 2d \sin \theta$$

Since $EF + FG$ is equal to $n\lambda$,

$$n\lambda = 2d \sin \theta \tag{11.11}$$

This equation, derived by William Henry Bragg and his son William Lawrence Bragg in 1913, is called the **Bragg equation.**

With X rays of a definite wavelength, reflection at various angles will be observed for a given set of planes separated by a given distance, d. These reflections correspond to $n = 1, 2, 3$, and so on, and are spoken of as first order, second order, third order, and so on. With each successive order, the angle θ increases and the intensity of the reflected beam weakens.

Figure 11.20 is a schematic representation of an X-ray spectrometer. An X-ray beam defined by a slit system impinges upon a crystal that is mounted on a turntable. A detector (photographic plate, ionization chamber, or Geiger counter) is positioned as shown in the figure. As the crystal is rotated, strong signals flash out as angles are passed that satisfy the Bragg equation. Any set of regularly positioned planes that contain atoms can give rise to reflections—not only those that form the faces of the unit cells. Thus, the value of d is not necessarily the edge of the unit cell, although the two are always mathematically related.

Example 11.7

The diffraction of a crystal of barium with X radiation of wavelength 229 pm gives a first-order reflection at $27° 8'$. What is the distance between the crystal planes?

Solution

Substitution into the Bragg equation gives

$$n\lambda = 2d \sin \theta$$

$$1(229 \text{ pm}) = 2d(0.456)$$

$$d = 251 \text{ pm}$$

11.14 Crystal Structure of Metals

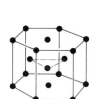

Figure 11.21 Hexagonal closest-packed structure

In the large majority of cases, metal crystals belong to one of three classifications: body-centered cubic (Figure 11.16), face-centered cubic (Figure 11.16), and hexagonal closest-packed (Figure 11.21). The geometric arrangement of atoms in the face-centered cubic and the hexagonal closest-packed crystals is such that each atom has a coordination number of 12 (each is surrounded by 12 other atoms at equal distances). If the atoms are viewed as spheres, there is a minimum of empty space in these two types of crystals (about 26%), and both of the crystal lattices are called **closest-packed structures.** The body-centered cubic arrangement is slightly more open than either of the closest-packed arrangements (about 32% empty space); each atom of a body-centered cubic crystal has a coordination number of 8.

The difference between the two closest-packed structures may be derived from a consideration of Figure 11.22. The shaded circles of the diagram represent the first layer of spheres, which are placed as close together as possible. The second layer of spheres (open circles of Figure 11.22) are placed in the hollows formed by adjacent spheres of the first layer. The first two layers (a and b) of both the face-centered cubic and the hexagonal closest-packed arrangements are the same. The difference arises in the placement of the third and subsequent layers.

In the hexagonal closest-packed arrangement, the spheres of the third layer are placed so that they are directly over those of the first layer. The sequence of layers may be represented as *ababab.* . . . In the face-centered cubic structure, however, the spheres of the third layer (c) are placed over the holes (marked x in Figure 11.22) formed by the arrangements of the first two layers. The spheres of the fourth layer of the face-centered cubic structure are placed so that they are directly over those of the first layer, and the sequence of layers is *abcabc.* . . .

The crystal structures of metals are summarized in Table 11.5. Equal numbers of metals crystallize in each of the three structures (hexagonal closest-packed, face-centered cubic, and body-centered cubic). The closest packing of most metallic crystals helps to explain the relatively high densities of metals. The structures of a few metals (for example, manganese and mercury) do not fall into any of the three categories, and the symbols for these metals do not appear in the table. Some

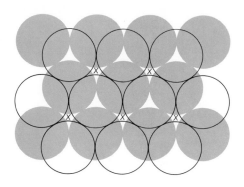

Figure 11.22 Schematic representation of the first two layers of the closest-packed arrangements

Table 11.5   Crystal structures of metals

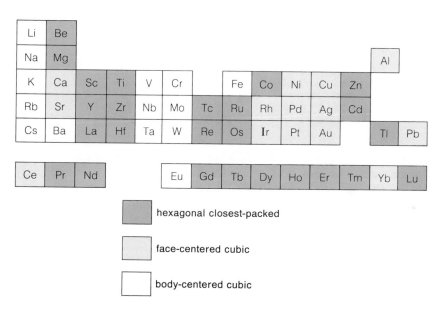

metals exhibit **crystal allotropy;** that is, different crystal forms of the same metal are stable under different conditions. For example, a modification of calcium exists in each of the three structures. The crystal structure of each metal that is indicated in Table 11.5 is the one that is stable under ordinary conditions. In addition to many metals, the noble gases (except for He) also crystallize in the face-centered cubic lattice.

1.15 Ionic Crystals

The structures of ionic crystals are more complicated than those of metallic crystals. An ionic crystal must accommodate ions of opposite charge and different size in the proper stoichiometric ratio and in such a way that electrostatic attractions outweigh electrostatic repulsions.

cesium chloride
CsCl

sodium chloride
NaCl

zinc blende
ZnS

Figure 11.23 Crystal structures of ionic compounds of the MX type. (Colored spheres represent cations.)

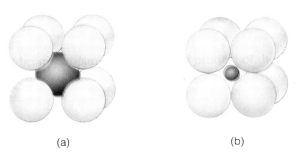

(a)

(b)

Figure 11.24 The cesium chloride structure
(a) with cation-anion contact and (b) without cation-anion contact.
(The colored spheres represent the cation.)

The potential energy of interaction (*PE*) between two ions is directly proportional to the product of the charges between the two ions (q_1 and q_2) and inversely proportional to the distance between the centers of the two ions (*d*):

$$PE = \frac{kq_1q_2}{d} \tag{11.12}$$

where *k* is equal to 8.988×10^9 J·m/C² if q_1 and q_2 are expressed in coulombs (C) and *d* is expressed in meters. If the charges have the same sign (both positive or both negative), they will repel each other and the potential energy will be a *positive* value (energy is *required* to push the ions together). On the other hand, if the charges have unlike signs, they will attract each other and the potential energy will be a *negative* value (energy is *released* when the ions come together). The most stable structure for a given compound, therefore, is one in which the largest possible number of cation-anion attractions exist and one in which the positive and negative ions are as close together as possible (small value of *d*).

The three most common crystal types for ionic compounds of formula MX are shown in Figure 11.23. In each diagram, there are as many cations per unit cell as there are anions (one each in CsCl and four each in NaCl and ZnS, taking into account sharing by adjacent cells). A 1:1 stoichiometric ratio is represented, therefore, in each case.

In the cesium chloride (CsCl) structure, the Cs^+ ion (the central ion in the CsCl structure shown in Figure 11.23) has eight Cl^- ions as nearest neighbors (the Cs^+ ion is said to have a coordination number of 8). In the sodium chloride (NaCl) crystal, a Na^+ ion has six Cl^- ions as nearest neighbors (a coordination number of 6). In the zinc blende (ZnS) structure, each Zn^{2+} ion has four S^{2-} ions as

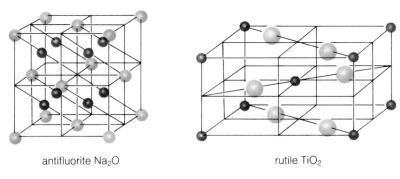

antifluorite Na$_2$O   rutile TiO$_2$

Figure 11.25 Crystal structures of ionic compounds of the MX$_2$ type. (Colored spheres represent anions.)

Table 11.6	Crystal structures of some ionic compounds
Structure	Examples
cesium chloride	CsCl, CsBr, CsI, TlCl, TlBr, TlI, NH$_4$Cl, NH$_4$Br
sodium chloride	halides of Li$^+$, Na$^+$, K$^+$, Rb$^+$ oxides and sulfides of Mg^{2+}, Ca^{2+}, Sr^{2+}, Ba^{2+}, Mn^{2+}, Ni^{2+} AgF, AgCl, AgBr, NH$_4$I
zinc blende	sulfides of Be^{2+}, Zn^{2+}, Cd^{2+}, Hg^{2+} CuCl, CuBr, CuI, AgI
fluorite	fluorides of Ca^{2+}, Sr^{2+}, Ba^{2+}, Cd^{2+}, Pb^{2+} BaCl$_2$, SrCl$_2$, ZrO$_2$, ThO$_2$, UO$_2$
antifluorite	oxides and sulfides of Li$^+$, Na$^+$, K$^+$, Rb$^+$
rutile	fluorides of Mg^{2+}, Ni^{2+}, Mn^{2+}, Zn^{2+}, Fe^{2+} oxides of Ti^{4+}, Mn^{4+}, Sn^{4+}, Te^{4+}

nearest neighbors (a coordination number of 4). In terms of crystal stability brought about by plus-minus attractions, the CsCl crystal, in which each Cs$^+$ ion has a coordination number of 8, would appear to be best.

There is, however, another factor to take into consideration: the distance between the cation and the anion, d, which becomes a matter of the comparison of the size of the cation to the size of the anion. In the CsCl structure, the Cs$^+$ ion in the center is assumed to touch each of the Cl$^-$ ions at the corners (see Figure 11.24a). Consider a compound in which the cation is much smaller than the anion. A small cation could not touch the anions that surround it (see Figure 11.24b) since electrostatic repulsions between the anions would prevent the anions from being squeezed together. As a result, the size of the plus-minus attraction would be comparatively low (d would be larger than necessary). In such an event, the compound would crystallize in a pattern with a lower coordination number for the cation but one that would permit closer cation-anion contact.

Two structures for ionic compounds of formula MX$_2$ or M$_2$X are shown in Figure 11.25. A third structure, the fluorite structure (named for the mineral fluorite, CaF$_2$), is similar to the antifluorite structure shown in Figure 11.25 except that cation and anion positions are exchanged. Examples of ionic compounds that crystallize in the types of crystal structures we have mentioned are listed in Table 11.6.

porization (in J/mol), and R is the ideal gas constant [8.3143 J/(K·mol)].

Closest-packed crystal(Sections 11.11 and 11.14) A crystal structure in which the atoms are so efficiently packed that a maximum number are included in a given volume, a face-centered cubic or hexagonal closest-packed crystal.

Coordination number in a crystal (Sections 11.14 and 11.15) The number of nearest neighbors that an atom or an ion has in a crystal structure.

Crystal(Sections 11.11 and 11.12) A solid composed of a symmetrical array of atoms, ions, or molecules arranged in a repeating three-dimensional pattern.

Crystal allotropes(Section 11.14) Two or more different crystal forms of the same substance that are stable under different conditions.

Crystal defect (Section 11.16) A crystal imperfection caused by a dislocation, missing ions, misplaced ions, or the presence of impurities.

Crystal lattice (Section 11.12) A three-dimensional, symmetrical pattern of points that defines a crystal; the points represent sites that have identical environments in the same orientation.

Dipole-dipole force (Section 11.1) An intermolecular force caused by the mutual attraction of oppositely charged poles of neighboring polar molecules.

Dislocations (Section 11.16) Crystal defects in which planes of atoms are misaligned.

Enthalpy of condensation (Section 11.7) The enthalpy change associated with the condensation of a given quantity of vapor (usually one mole or one gram) into a liquid at a specified temperature.

Enthalpy of crystallization (Section 11.8) The enthalpy change associated with the conversion of a given quantity of a liquid (usually one mole or one gram) into a solid at a specified temperature.

Enthalpy of fusion (Section 11.8) The energy required to melt a given quantity of a solid (usually one mole or one gram) at a specified temperature.

Enthalpy of vaporization (Sections 11.4 and 11.7) The energy required to vaporize a given quantity of a liquid (usually one mole or one gram) at a specified temperature.

Equilibrium (Section 11.5) A condition in which the rates of two opposing tendencies are equal.

Evaporation, vaporization(Section 11.4) The process in which a liquid is converted into a gas.

Face-centered cubic unit cell(Section 11.12) A unit cell of a crystal that consists of a cube with identical constituent particles located at each corner and at the center of each face.

Freezing point(Section 11.8) The temperature at which solid and liquid phases are in equilibrium. If the total pressure is 1 atm, the value is called the **normal freezing point.**

Hydrogen bond(Section 11.2) An intermolecular attraction that occurs between a hydrogen atom of one molecule and a pair of electrons on an atom in another molecule. The polarity of the molecule that supplies the hydrogen atom must be such that the hydrogen has a relatively high δ^+ charge, and the electron pair must be supplied by a small, highly electronegative atom (principally N, O, and F).

Instantaneous dipole (Section 11.1) A fluctuating temporary dipole induced in molecules by the motion of electrons; the cause of London (dispersion) forces.

Intermolecular forces(Section 11.1) Forces of attraction between molecules; these forces hold molecules together in condensed states (liquids and solids).

Interstitial position (Section 11.16) A position between the regular positions of a crystal structure.

London forces, dispersion forces(Section 11.1) Intermolecular forces brought about by attractions between instantaneous dipoles, which in turn are caused by the motion of electrons in the molecules.

Melting point (Section 11.8) See **freezing point.**

Nonstoichiometry(Section 11.16) A condition in which the composition of a crystal of a compound does not conform to the formula of the compound.

Phase diagram (Section 11.10) A diagram that graphically presents the number and type of phases in which a chemical system exists under a given set of temperature and pressure conditions.

Simple cubic unit cell (Section 11.12) A unit cell of a crystal that consists of a cube with identical constituent particles located at the corners.

Sublimation(Section 11.10) The process in which a solid goes directly into a gas without going through the liquid state.

Surface tension(Section 11.3) A measure of the inward force on the surface of a liquid caused by intermolecular attractive forces.

Triple point(Section 11.10) The temperature and pressure at which a substance can exist simultaneously as a solid, a liquid, and a gas in equilibrium with each other.

Unit cell(Section 11.12) The smallest part of a crystal that will reproduce the crystal when repeated in three dimensions.

Vapor pressure (Section 11.5) The pressure of vapor in equilibrium with a pure liquid or a pure solid at a given temperature.

Viscosity(Section 11.3) A property of liquids; resistance to flow.

X-ray diffraction (Section 11.13) A method of determining the structure of a crystal by directing X rays at the crystal and measuring the angles at which the rays are scattered (or reflected).

Problems*

Intermolecular Attractive Forces

11.1 Give an explanation for the following. **(a)** The dipole moment of OF_2 is 0.30 D but the dipole moment of BeF_2 is zero. **(b)** The dipole moment of PF_3 is 1.03 D but the dipole moment of BF_3 is zero. **(c)** The dipole moment of SF_4 is 0.63 D but the dipole moment of SnF_4 is zero.

11.2 Describe the difference between London forces and dipole-dipole forces. In what types of molecular substances do each exist? Which type is stronger in *most* molecular substances where both exist?

11.3 Which molecules (not ions) given as examples in Table 9.1 in Chapter 9 would you expect to have dipole moments of zero?

11.4 How could the measurement of the dipole moment of the trigonal bipyramidal molecule PCl_2F_3 help to determine whether the Cl atoms occupy axial or equatorial positions?

11.5 Explain why the dipole moment of SCO is 0.72 D, whereas the dipole moment of CO_2 is zero. Would CS_2 have a dipole moment?

11.6 In Table 8.1, the electronegativity of C is given as 2.6 and that of O is given as 3.4. On the other hand, the dipole moment of CO is only 0.12 D, which means that the dipole-dipole forces of CO are very small. Draw the Lewis structure of CO and offer an explanation for the low dipole moment of CO.

11.7 The dipole moment of PF_3 is 1.03 D, whereas the dipole moment of PF_5 is zero. Explain.

11.8 The dipole moment of NH_3 (1.49 D) is greater than that of NF_3 (0.24 D). On the other hand, the dipole moment of PH_3 (0.55 D) is less than PF_3 (1.03 D). Explain these results.

11.9 Explain why the following melting points fall in the order given: F_2 ($-233°C$), Cl_2 ($-103°C$), Br_2 ($-7°C$), I_2 ($113.5°C$).

11.10 Consider the following molecules, each of which is tetrahedral with the C atom as the central atom: CH_4, CH_3Cl, CH_2Cl_2, $CHCl_3$, CCl_4. In which of these compounds would dipole-dipole forces exist in the liquid state? In what order would you expect the boiling points of the compounds to fall?

The Hydrogen Bond

11.11 The compound KHF_2 can be prepared by the reaction of KF and HF in water solution. Explain the structure of the HF_2^- ion.

11.12 Although the $H \cdots F$ hydrogen bond is the strongest hydrogen bond known, the effect of hydrogen bonding on the properties of the following hydrides falls in the order: $H_2O > HF > NH_3$. Explain this observation.

11.13 Although there are exceptions, most acid salts (such as $NaHSO_4$) are more soluble in water than the corresponding normal salts (Na_2SO_4). Offer an explanation for this generalization.

11.14 Diagram the structures of the following molecules and explain how the water solubility of each compound is enhanced by hydrogen bonding. **(a)** NH_3, **(b)** H_2NOH, **(c)** H_3COH, **(d)** H_2CO.

11.15 The normal boiling point of the compound ethylene diamine, $H_2NCH_2CH_2NH_2$ is 117°C and that of propyl amine, $CH_3CH_2CH_2NH_2$ is 49°C. The molecules, however, are similar in size and molecular weight. What reason can you give for the difference in boiling point?

11.16 Offer an explanation as to why chloroform, $CHCl_3$, and acetone,

$$CH_3-\overset{\overset{\textstyle O}{\|}}{C}-CH_3$$

mixtures have higher boiling points than either pure component.

The Liquid State

11.17 Briefly explain how and why each of the following gives an indication of the strength of the intermolecular forces of attraction of a substance: **(a)** critical temperature, **(b)** surface tension, **(c)** viscosity, **(d)** vapor pressure, **(e)** enthalpy of vaporization, **(f)** normal boiling point.

11.18 Explain, using a Maxwell-Boltzmann distribution curve, why an evaporating liquid becomes cool. Describe the condition that exists when an evaporating liquid is placed in a closed container.

11.19 **(a)** Why does the boiling point of a liquid vary with pressure? **(b)** What is the normal boiling point? **(c)** Use the curves of Figure 11.9 to estimate the boiling point of diethyl ether, ethyl alcohol, and water at 0.50 atm.

11.20 Use the data of Table 10.3 to estimate the boiling point of water at **(a)** 0.010 atm, and **(b)** 0.025 atm.

---

* The more difficult problems are marked with asterisks. The appendix contains answers to color-keyed problems.

11.21 The vapor pressure of nitrobenzene is 0.0136 atm at 85°C and 0.0510 atm at 115°C. What is the molar enthalpy of vaporization of nitrobenzene for this temperature range?

11.22 The vapor pressure of carbon tetrachloride is 0.417 atm at 50°C and 0.593 atm at 60°C. What is the molar enthalpy of vaporization of carbon tetrachloride for this temperature range?

11.23 The vapor pressure of methyl alcohol at 50°C is 0.530 atm. The molar enthalpy of vaporization of the compound is 37.6 kJ/mol. What is the normal boiling point of methyl alcohol?

11.24 The vapor pressure of cyclohexane at 25°C is 0.130 atm. The molar enthalpy of vaporization of the compound is 31.8 kJ/mol. What is the normal boiling point of cyclohexane?

11.25 The vapor pressure of toluene at 90°C is 0.532 atm. The molar enthalpy of vaporization of the compound is 35.9 kJ/mol. What is the vapor pressure of toluene at 100°C?

11.26 The vapor pressure of cyclohexane at 61°C is 0.527 atm. The molar enthalpy of vaporization of the compound is 31.8 kJ/mol. What is the vapor pressure of cyclohexane at 50°C?

11.27 The normal boiling point of water is 100.°C and the molar enthalpy of vaporization of water is 40.7 kJ/mol. What is the boiling point of water under a pressure of 0.500 atm?

11.28 The normal boiling point of chlorobenzene is 132°C and the molar enthalpy of vaporization of chlorobenzene is 36.5 kJ/mol. What is the boiling point of chlorobenzene under a pressure of 0.100 atm?

Phase Diagrams

11.29 Use the following data to draw a rough phase diagram for hydrogen: normal melting point, 14.01 K; normal boiling point, 20.38 K; triple point, 13.95 K, 7×10^{-2} atm; critical point, 33.3 K, 12.8 atm; vapor pressure of solid at 10 K, 1×10^{-3} atm.

11.30 Use the following data to draw a rough phase diagram for krypton: normal boiling point, -152°C; normal melting point, -157°C; triple point, -169°C, 0.175 atm; critical point, -63°C, 54.2 atm; vapor pressure of solid at -199°C, 1.3×10^{-3} atm. Which has the higher density at a pressure of one atmosphere, solid Kr or liquid Kr?

11.31 Figure 11.11 is the phase diagram for water. Describe the phase changes that occur, and the approximate pressures at which they occur, when the pressure on the H_2O system is gradually increased **(a)** at a constant temperature of -1°C, **(b)** at a constant temperature of 50°C, **(c)** at a constant temperature of -50°C.

11.32 Figure 11.12 is the phase diagram for carbon dioxide. Describe the phase changes that occur, and the approximate pressures at which they occur, when the pressure on the CO_2 system is gradually increased **(a)** at a constant temperature of -60°C, **(b)** at a constant temperature of 55°C, **(c)** at a constant temperature of 0°C.

11.33 Refer to Figure 11.11 and describe the phase changes that occur and the approximate temperatures at which they occur, when water is heated from -30°C to 110°C **(c)** under a pressure of 1×10^{-3} atm, **(b)** under a pressure of 0.5 atm, **(c)** under a pressure of 1.1 atm.

11.34 Refer to Figure 11.12 and describe the phase changes that occur and the approximate temperatures at which they occur, when carbon dioxide is heated from -80°C to 20°C **(a)** under a pressure of 1 atm, **(b)** under a pressure of 5.5 atm, **(c)** under a pressure of 70 atm.

11.35 Sublimation is sometimes used to purify solids. The impure material is heated, and the pure crystalline product condenses on a cold surface. Is it possible to purify ice by sublimation? What conditions would have to be employed?

11.36 Briefly explain how and why the slope of the melting-point curve of a phase diagram for a substance depends upon the relative densities of the solid and liquid forms of the substance.

Types of Crystalline Solids

11.37 What types of forces must be overcome in order to melt crystals of the following: **(a)** Si, **(b)** Ba, **(c)** F_2, **(d)** BaF_2, **(e)** BF_3, **(f)** PF_3?

11.38 What types of forces must be overcome in order to melt crystals of the following: **(a)** O_2, **(b)** Cl_2, **(c)** Cl_2O, **(d)** Ca, **(e)** $CaCl_2$, **(f)** CaO?

11.39 Which substance of each of the following pairs would you expect to have the higher melting point: **(a)** ClF or BrF, **(b)** BrCl or Cl_2, **(c)** CsBr or BrCl, **(d)** Cs or Br_2, **(e)** C(diamond) or Cl_2? Why?

11.40 Which substance of each of the following pairs would you expect to have the higher melting point: **(a)** Sr or Cl_2, **(b)** $SrCl_2$ or $SiCl_4$, **(c)** $SiCl_4$ or $SiBr_4$, **(d)** $SiCl_4$ or SCl_4, **(e)** SiC(carborundum) or $SiCl_4$? Why?

Crystals

11.41 Xenon crystallizes in the face-centered cubic system, and the edge of a unit cell is 620 pm. What is the density of crystalline xenon?

11.42 Vanadium crystallizes in the body-centered system, and the edge of a unit cell is 305 pm. What is the density of vanadium?

11.43 Silver crystallizes in a cubic system, and the edge of the unit cell is 408 pm. The density of silver is 10.6 g/cm³. How many atoms of Ag are contained in a unit cell? What type of unit cell does Ag form?

11.44 Tantalum crystallizes in a cubic system, and the edge of the unit cell is 330 pm. The density of tantalum is 16.6 g/cm³. How many atoms of Ta are contained in one unit cell? What type of unit cell does Ta form?

11.45 An element crystallizes in the body-centered cubic system, and the edge of a unit cell is 286 pm. The density of the element is 7.92 g/cm^3. Find the atomic weight of the element.

11.46 An element crystallizes in the face-centered cubic system, and the edge of a unit cell is 392 pm. The density of the element is 21.5 g/cm^3. Find the atomic weight of the element.

11.47 Calcium crystallizes in the face-centered cubic system. The density of calcium is 1.55 g/cm^3. What is the length of an edge of the unit cell?

11.48 Copper crystallizes in a face-centered cubic lattice. The density of copper is 8.93 g/cm^3. What is the length of an edge of the unit cell?

11.49 Palladium crystallizes in the face-centered cubic system, and the edge of a unit cell is 389 pm. Calculate the dimensions of a cube that would contain one mole of Pd (106 g).

11.50 Sodium crystallizes in the body-centered cubic system, and the edge of a unit cell is 430 pm. Calculate the dimensions of a cube that would contain one mole of Na (23.0 g).

11.51 Aluminum crystallizes in the face-centered cubic system, and the edge of a unit cell is 405 pm. Calculate the atomic radius of Al.

11.52 Chromium crystallizes in the body-centered cubic system, and the edge of a unit cell is 287.5 pm. Calculate the atomic radius of Cr.

*11.53 Indium crystallizes in the face-centered *tetragonal* system. In the crystal, the base of the unit cell is a square 458 pm on a side, and the height of the unit cell is 494 pm. What is the density of In?

*11.54 Xenon difluoride, XeF$_2$, *molecules* crystallize in the body-centered *tetragonal* system. In the crystal, the base of the unit cell is a square 432 pm on a side, and height of the unit cell is 699 pm. Assume that *molecules* occupy positions in the unit cell. What is the density of XeF$_2$?

Crystal Structure by X-Ray Diffraction

11.55 In the X-ray study of a crystal using X rays with a wavelength of 71.0 pm, a first-order reflection was obtained at an angle of 12.0°. What is the distance between the planes responsible for this reflection? The sine of 12.0° is 0.208.

11.56 In the X-ray study of a gold crystal using X rays with a wavelength of 154 pm, a first-order reflection was obtained at an angle of 22.17°. What is the distance between the planes responsible for this reflection? The sine of 22.17° is 0.377.

11.57 In the X-ray study of a crystal, a set of crystal planes for which *d* is 180 pm is responsible for a first-order reflection at an angle of 22.0°. What is the wavelength of the X rays that were employed? The sine of 22.0° is 0.375.

11.58 In the X-ray study of a crystal, a set of crystal planes for which *d* is 248 pm is responsible for a first-order reflection at an angle of 8.21°. What is the wavelength

of the X rays that were employed? The sine of 8.21° is 0.1428.

11.59 In the X-ray study of a crystal using X rays with a wavelength of 154 pm, a first-order reflection is obtained at an angle of 11.0°. What is the wavelength of X rays that show this same reflection at an angle of 13.92°? The sine of 11.0° is 0.191 and the sine of 13.92° is 0.241.

11.60 In the X-ray study of a crystal using X rays with a wavelength of 154 pm, a first-order reflection is obtained at an angle of 16.0°. What is the wavelength of X rays that show this same reflection at an angle of 20.33°? The sine of 16.0° is 0.276 and the sine of 20.33° is 0.347.

11.61 At what angle would a first-order reflection be observed in the X-ray study of a set of crystal planes for which *d* is 204 pm if the X rays used have a wavelength of 154 pm? At what angle would a second-order reflection be observed?

11.62 At what angle would a first-order reflection be observed in the X-ray study of a set of crystal planes for which *d* is 303 pm if the X rays used have a wavelength of 71.0 pm? At what angle would a second-order reflection be observed?

Ionic Crystals

11.63 **(a)** How many ions of each type are shown in the unit cell of the sodium chloride crystal depicted in Figure 11.23? **(b)** The density of silver chloride, which crystallizes in the sodium chloride crystal structure, is 5.57 g/cm^3. What is the length of the edge of the AgCl unit cell similar to the one for NaCl shown in Figure 11.23? **(c)** Use equations given in Section 11.12 to determine the shortest distance between a Ag$^+$ ion and a Cl$^-$ ion.

11.64 **(a)** How many ions of each type are shown in the unit cell of the sodium chloride crystal depicted in Figure 11.23? **(b)** The density of potassium fluoride, which crystallizes in the sodium chloride crystal structure, is 2.468 g/cm^3. What is the length of the edge of the KF unit cell similar to the one for NaCl shown in Figure 11.23? **(c)** Use equations given in Section 11.12 to determine the shortest distance between a K$^+$ ion and a F$^-$ ion.

11.65 **(a)** How many ions of each type are shown in the unit cell of the cesium chloride crystal depicted in Figure 11.23? **(b)** The density of cesium chloride is 3.99 g/cm^3. What is the length of the edge of the CsCl unit cell as shown in Figure 11.23? **(c)** Use equations given in Section 11.12 to determine the shortest distance between a Cs$^+$ ion and a Cl$^-$ ion.

11.66 **(a)** How many ions of each type are shown in the unit cell of the zinc sulfide crystal depicted in Figure 11.23? **(b)** The density of copper(I) chloride, which crystallizes in the zinc sulfide crystal structure, is 4.14 g/cm^3. What is the length of the edge of the CuCl unit cell similar to the one for ZnS shown in Figure 11.23? **(c)** Use equations given in Section 11.12 to determine the shortest distance between a Cu$^+$ ion and a Cl$^-$ ion.

11.67 **(a)** Lead(II) sulfide crystallizes in the sodium chloride structure. The shortest distance between a Pb^{2+} ion and a S^{2-} ion is 297 pm. What is the length of the edge of a unit cell of PbS similar to the one for NaCl shown in Figure 11.23? **(b)** What is the density, in g/cm³, of PbS?

11.68 (a) Potassium chloride crystallizes in the sodium chloride structure. The shortest distance between a K^+ ion and a Cl^- ion is 314 pm. What is the length of the edge of a unit cell of KCl similar to the one for NaCl shown in Figure 11.23? **(b)** What is the density, in g/cm³, of KCl?

11.69 (a) Thallium(I) chloride crystallizes in the cesium chloride structure. The shortest distance between a Tl^+ ion and a Cl^- ion is 333 pm. What is the length of the edge of a unit cell of TlCl similar to the one for CsCl shown in Figure 11.23? **(b)** What is the density, in g/cm³, of TlCl?

11.70 Cadmium sulfide crystallizes in the zinc sulfide crystal structure. The shortest distance between a Cd^{2+} ion and a S^{2-} ion is 253 pm. What is the length of the edge of a unit cell of CdS similar to the one for ZnS shown in Figure 11.23? **(b)** What is the density, in g/cm³, of CdS?

11.71 In a given crystal, the distance between the centers of a cation and a neighboring anion is approximately equal to the sum of the ionic radii of the two ions. Some ionic radii are: Na^+, 95 pm; K^+, 133 pm; Ca^{2+}, 99 pm; Ba^{2+}, 135 pm; Ni^{2+}, 69 pm; Ag^+, 126 pm; Cl^-, 181 pm; Br^-, 195 pm; O^{2-}, 140 pm; S^{2-}, 184 pm. Refer to Equation 11.12 in Section 11.15 and arrange the following (each of which crystallizes in the sodium chloride system) in decreasing order of lattice energy (most negative value first): AgCl, BaO, CaS, KCl, NaBr, and NiS.

11.72 In a given crystal, the distance between the centers of a cation and a neighboring anion is approximately equal to the sum of the ionic radii of the two ions. Some ionic radii are: Na^+, 95 pm; K^+, 133 pm; Ag^+, 126 pm; Mg^{2+}, 65 pm; Sr^{2+}, 113 pm; Mn^{2+}, 80 pm; F^-, 136 pm; I^-, 216 pm; O^{2-}, 140 pm; S^{2-}, 184 pm. Refer to Equation 11.12 in Section 11.15 and arrange the following (each of which crystallizes in the sodium chloride system) in decreasing order of lattice energy (most negative value first): AgF, KF, MgO, NaI, MgS, and MnO.

Defect Structures

11.73 Cadmium oxide, CdO, crystallizes in the sodium chloride system, with four Cd^{2+} and for O^{2-} ions per unit cell (see Figure 11.23). The compound, however, usually is nonstoichiometric, with a formula that approximates $CdO_{0.995}$. The defect occurs because some cation positions in the crystal are occupied by Cd *atoms* instead of Cd^{2+} *ions* and an equivalent number of anion positions are vacant. **(a)** What percent of the anion sites are vacant? **(b)** If the edge of the unit cell is 469.5 pm, what would be the density of a perfect crystal? **(c)** What is the density of the nonstoichiometric crystal? Use 112.40 for the atomic weight of Cd and 16.00 for the atomic weight of O.

*11.74 **(a)** The edge of the NaCl unit cell shown in Figure 11.23 is 563.8 pm and the density of NaCl is 2.165 g/cm³. Use these data to calculate the apparent molecular weight of NaCl to four significant figures. **(b)** The difference between the value calculated from crystal data and the actual molecular weight of NaCl (58.44) is ascribed to a type of crystal defect in which Na *atoms* replace a number of Na^+ *ions* in the crystal and an equal number of Cl^- ions is missing from crystal positions. On the basis of your answer for part (a), calculate the percentage of anion sites that are vacant.

Unclassified Problems

11.75 Which substance of each of the following pairs would you expect to have the higher melting point: **(a)** Li or H_2, **(b)** LiH or H_2, **(c)** Li or LiH, **(d)** H_2 or Cl_2, **(e)** H_2 or HCl, **(f)** H_2O or H_2S, **(g)** CH_4 or SiH_4? Why?

11.76 The vapor pressure of heptane at 90.°C is 0.775 atm and at 60.°C is 0.275 atm. Calculate a value for the molar enthalpy of vaporization. What is the normal boiling point of heptane?

11.77 Lithium crystallizes in the body-centered cubic system, and the length of the edge of a unit cell is 350 pm. The atomic weight of Li is 6.94, and the density of Li is 0.534 g/cm³. Use these data to calculate Avogadro's number.

11.78 Molybdenum has an atomic radius of 136 pm and crystallizes in a body-centered cubic system. What is the length of an edge of a unit cell? What is the density of Mo?

11.79 In the X-ray study of a crystal using X rays with a wavelength of 194 pm, a first-order reflection was obtained at an angle of 25.9°. What is the distance, d, between the planes responsible for this reflection? The sine of 25.9° is 0.4368.

*11.80 Assume that hard-sphere atoms with a radius of r make up a face-centered cubic unit cell. Use the equations in Section 11.12 to calculate the following in terms of r: **(a)** the length of the edge of a unit cell, **(b)** the volume of one unit cell, **(c)** the total volume of the atoms that make up one unit cell, **(d)** the percentage of the volume of a unit cell that is empty space.

*11.81 Assume that hard-sphere atoms with a radius of r make up a body-centered cubic unit cell. Use the equations in Section 11.12 to calculate the following in terms of r: **(a)** the length of the edge of a unit cell **(b)** the volume of one unit cell, **(c)** the total volume of the atoms that make up one unit cell, **(d)** the percentage of the volume of a unit cell that is empty space. Compare your answer for this problem to the answer for Problem 11.80. Which of the two unit cells, face-centered or body-centered, is more closely packed?

11.82 Describe the crystal defects that alter the stoichiometry of a crystal and those that do not.

*11.83 Iron(II) oxide crystallizes in the NaCl structure, with four cations and four anions per unit cell (see Figure 11.23). The crystals, however, are always deficient in iron. Some cation sites are vacant and some contain Fe^{3+} ions instead of Fe^{2+} ions, but the combination is such that the structure is electrically neutral. The formula approximates $Fe_{0.95}O$. (a) What is the ratio of Fe^{2+} ions to Fe^{3+} ions in the crystal? (b) What percentage of the cation sites are vacant? Hint: consider a crystal that contains 100. O^{2-} ions.

CHAPTER SOLUTIONS
12

Solutions are homogeneous mixtures. They are usually classified according to their physical state; gaseous, liquid, and solid solutions can be prepared. Dalton's law of partial pressures describes the behavior of gaseous solutions, of which air is the most common example. Certain alloys are solid solutions; coinage silver is copper dissolved in silver, and brass is a solid solution of zinc in copper. Not all alloys are solid solutions, however. Some are heterogeneous mixtures, and some are intermetallic compounds. Liquid solutions are the most common and are probably the most used by chemists in chemical investigations.

12.1 Nature of Solutions

The component of a solution that is present in greatest quantity is usually called the solvent, and all other components are called solutes. This terminology is loose and arbitrary. It is sometimes convenient to designate a component as the solvent even though it is present in only small amounts. At other times, the assignment of the terms *solute* and *solvent* has little significance (for example, in describing gaseous solutions).

Certain pairs of substances will dissolve in each other in all proportions. Complete miscibility is characteristic of the components of all gaseous solutions and of some pairs of components of liquid and solid solutions. For most materials, however, there is a limit to the amount of the substance that will dissolve in a given solvent. The solubility of a substance in a particular solvent at a specified temperature is the maximum amount of the solute that will dissolve in a definite amount of the solvent and produce a stable system.

For a given solution, the amount of solute dissolved in a given amount of solvent or dissolved in a given amount of solution is the concentration of the solute. Solutions containing a relatively low concentration of solute are called dilute solutions; those of relatively high concentrations are called concentrated solutions.

If an excess of solute (more than will normally dissolve) is added to a quantity of a liquid solvent, an equilibrium is established between the undissolved solute and the dissolved solute:

$$\text{solute}_{\text{undissolved}} \rightleftharpoons \text{solute}_{\text{dissolved}}$$

The undissolved solute may be a solid, liquid, or gas. At equilibrium in such a system, the rate at which the pure solute dissolves equals the rate at which the dissolved solute comes out of solution. The concentration of the dissolved solute, therefore, is a constant. A solution of this type is called a **saturated solution,** and its concentration is the *solubility* of the solute in question.

That such dynamic equilibria exist has been shown experimentally. If small crystals of a solid solute are placed in contact with a saturated solution of the solute, the crystals are observed to change in size and shape. Throughout this experiment, however, the concentration of the saturated solution does not change, nor does the quantity of excess solute decrease or increase.

An **unsaturated solution** has a lower concentration of solute than a saturated solution. On the other hand, it is sometimes possible to use a solid solute to prepare a **supersaturated solution,** one in which the concentration of solute is higher than that of a saturated solution. A supersaturated solution, however, is metastable, and if a very small amount of pure solute is added to it, the amount of solute that is in excess of that needed to saturate the solution will precipitate.

2.2 The Solution Process

London forces are the only intermolecular forces between nonpolar covalent molecules. On the other hand, the intermolecular attractions between polar covalent molecules are due to dipole-dipole forces as well as to London forces. In substances in which there is hydrogen bonding, the intermolecular forces are unusually strong.

Nonpolar substances and polar substances are generally insoluble in one another. Carbon tetrachloride (a nonpolar substance) is insoluble in water (a polar substance). The attraction of one water molecule for another water molecule is much greater than an attraction between a carbon tetrachloride molecule and a water molecule. Hence, carbon tetrachloride molecules are "squeezed out," and these two substances form a two-liquid-layer system.

Iodine, a nonpolar material, is soluble in carbon tetrachloride. The attractions between I_2 molecules in solid iodine are approximately of the same type and magnitude as those between CCl_4 molecules in pure carbon tetrachloride. Hence, significant iodine-carbon tetrachloride attractions are possible, and iodine molecules can mix with carbon tetrachloride molecules. The resulting solution is a random molecular mixture.

Methyl alcohol, CH_3OH, like water, consists of polar molecules that are highly associated. In both pure liquids the molecules are attracted to one another through hydrogen bonding:

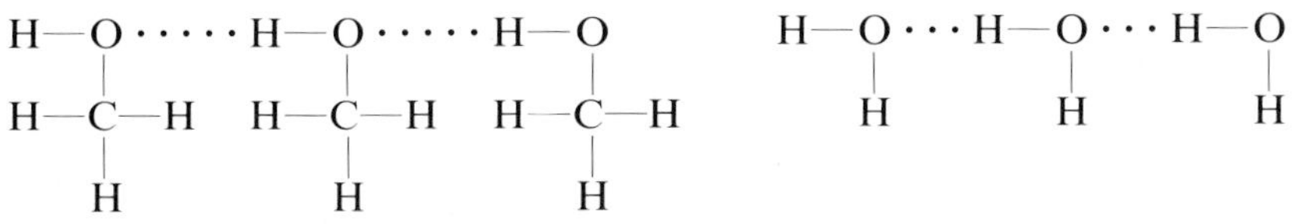

Methyl alcohol and water are miscible in all proportions. In solutions of methyl alcohol in water, CH_3OH and H_2O molecules are associated through hydrogen bonding:

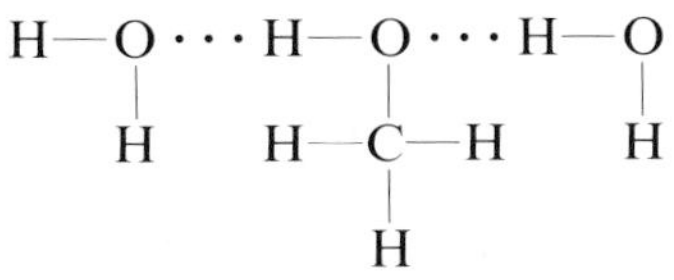

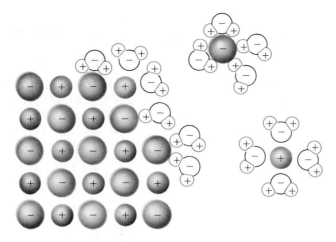

Figure 12.1 Solution of an ionic crystal in water

Methyl alcohol does not dissolve in nonpolar solvents. The strong intermolecular attractions of pure methyl alcohol are not overcome unless the solvent molecules can form attractions of equal, or almost equal, strength with the methyl alcohol molecules.

In general, polar materials dissolve only in polar solvents, and nonpolar substances are soluble in nonpolar solvents. This is the first rule of solubility: "like dissolves like." Network crystals (the diamond, for example), in which the atoms that make up the crystal are held together by covalent bonds, are insoluble in all liquids. This crystalline structure is far too stable to be broken down by a solution process. Any potential solute-solvent attractions cannot approach the strength of the covalent bonding in this type of crystal.

Polar liquids (water, in particular) can function as solvents for many ionic compounds. The ions of the solute are electrostatically attracted by the polar solvent molecules—negative ions by the positive poles of the solvent molecules, positive ions by the negative poles of the solvent molecules. These ion-dipole attractions can be relatively strong.

Figure 12.1 diagrams the solution of an ionic crystal in water. The ions in the center of the crystal are attracted equally in all directions by the oppositely charged ions of the crystal. The electrostatic attractions on the ions of the surface of the cyrstal, however, are unbalanced. Water molecules are attracted to these surface ions, the positive ends of the water molecules to the anions, and the negative ends of the water molecules to the cations. The ion-dipole attractions formed in this way allow the ions to escape from the crystal and drift into the liquid phase. The dissolved ions are **hydrated** and move through the solution surrounded by a sheath of water molecules. All ions are hydrated in water solution.

12.3 Hydrated Ions

Negative ions are hydrated in water solution by means of attractions between the ion and the hydrogen atoms of the water molecule. In some cases (the sulfate ion, for example) these attractions may be one or more hydrogen bonds:

$$\begin{bmatrix} \begin{array}{ccccc} \mathrm{H} & & & & \mathrm{H} \\ | & & & & | \\ \mathrm{O-H}\cdots\mathrm{O} & & \mathrm{O}\cdots\mathrm{H-O} \\ & & \mathrm{S} & & \\ \mathrm{O-H}\cdots\mathrm{O} & & \mathrm{O}\cdots\mathrm{H-O} \\ | & & & & | \\ \mathrm{H} & & & & \mathrm{H} \end{array} \end{bmatrix}^{2-}$$

Positive ions are hydrated by means of attractions between the ion and the unshared electron pairs of the oxygen atom of the water molecule. These attractions are strong. In many cases, each cation is hydrated by a definite number of H_2O molecules:

$$\begin{bmatrix} \begin{array}{cccc} \mathrm{H} & & \mathrm{H} \\ | & & | \\ \mathrm{H-O} & & \mathrm{O-H} \\ & \mathrm{Be} & \\ \mathrm{H-O} & & \mathrm{O-H} \\ | & & | \\ \mathrm{H} & & \mathrm{H} \end{array} \end{bmatrix}^{2+}$$

Additional water molecules form hydrogen bonds with those molecules that are bonded to the cation or anion. These outer layers of water molecules, however, are more loosely held.

What factors lead to the formation of strong interactions between the ion and the water molecules?

1. Ions with *high charges* strongly attract the H or O atoms of H_2O molecules.

2. *Small ions* are more effective than large ones because the charge is more highly concentrated in small ions.

A number of *covalent* compounds of metals produce hydrated *ions* in water solution. The compounds of beryllium, for example, are covalent when pure. The same factor that is largely responsible for the covalent character of the compounds of beryllium (a high ratio of ionic charge to ion size) also leads to the formation of very stable hydrated ions:

$$\mathrm{BeCl_2(s) + 4\,H_2O \longrightarrow Be(H_2O)_4^{2+}(aq) + 2\,Cl^-(aq)}$$

The formation of a bond always liberates energy, and the breaking of a bond always requires energy. The energy *released* by a hypothetical process in which hydrated ions are formed from gaseous ions is called the **enthalpy of hydration** of the ions. For example,

$$\mathrm{K^+(g) + Cl^-(g) \longrightarrow K^+(aq) + Cl^-(aq)} \qquad \Delta H = -684.1 \text{ kJ}$$

The size of the enthalpy of hydration depends upon the concentration of the final solution. If no distinction is made (as in the example previously given), it is assumed that the enthalpy change pertains to a process in which the ions are hydrated to the greatest possible extent. This high degree of hydration would occur only if the solution were *very dilute*. The corresponding ΔH values are called enthalpies of hydration at **infinite dilution.**

The value of an enthalpy of hydration gives an indication of the strength of the attractions between the ions and the water molecules that hydrate them. A large negative value (which indicates a large quantity of energy evolved) shows that the ions are strongly hydrated.

Frequently, hydrated ions remain in the crystalline solids that are obtained by the evaporation of aqueous solutions of salts. Thus,

$FeCl_3 \cdot 6H_2O$ consists of $Fe(H_2O)_6^{3+}$ and Cl^- ions
$BeCl_2 \cdot 4H_2O$ consists of $Be(H_2O)_4^{2+}$ and Cl^- ions
$ZnSO_4 \cdot 7H_2O$ consists of $Zn(H_2O)_6^{2+}$ and $SO_4(H_2O)^{2-}$ ions
$CuSO_4 \cdot 5H_2O$ consists of $Cu(H_2O)_4^{2+}$ and $SO_4(H_2O)^{2-}$ ions

Water molecules can also occur in crystalline hydrates by taking positions in the crystal structure without associating with any specific ion ($BaCl_2 \cdot 2H_2O$ is an example) or by occupying interstices (holes) of a crystal structure (the hydrous silicates called zeolites are examples).

12.4 Enthalpy of Solution

The enthalpy change associated with the process in which a solute dissolves in a solvent is called the **enthalpy of solution.** The value of an enthalpy of solution (given in kJ/mol of solute) depends upon the concentration of the final solution in the same way that an enthalpy of hydration does. Unless otherwise noted, an enthalpy of solution is considered to apply to the preparation of a solution that is infinitely dilute. The enthalpy of solution is almost constant for any dilute solution of a given solute-solvent pair.

The enthalpy change observed when a solution is prepared is the net result of the energy *required* to break apart certain chemical bonds or attractions (solute-solute and solvent-solvent) and the energy *released* by the formation of new ones (solute-solvent). The enthalpy of solution for the preparation of a solution of KCl in water, for example, can be considered to be the sum of two enthalpy changes:

1. The energy required to break apart the KCl crystal structure and form gaseous ions (the *lattice energy* with sign changed):

$$KCl(s) \longrightarrow K^+(g) + Cl^-(g) \qquad \Delta H = +701.2 \text{ kJ}$$

2. The *enthalpy of hydration* of KCl, which is the energy released when the gaseous ions are hydrated:

$$K^+(g) + Cl^-(g) \longrightarrow K^+(aq) + Cl^-(aq) \qquad \Delta H = -684.1 \text{ kJ}$$

This *enthalpy of hydration* is actually the sum of two enthalpy changes: the energy required to break the hydrogen bonds between some of the water molecules and the energy released when these water molecules hydrate the ions. It is, however, difficult to investigate these two effects separately.

In this example, the overall process is endothermic. The enthalpy of solution is positive because more energy is required in step 1 than is released in step 2:

$$KCl(s) \longrightarrow K^+(aq) + Cl^-(aq) \qquad \Delta H = +17.1 \text{ kJ}$$

Some enthalpies of solution are negative because more energy is liberated by the hydration of the ions of the solute (step 2) than is required to break apart the crystal structure (step 1):

1.	$AgF(s) \longrightarrow Ag^+(g) + F^-(g)$	$\Delta H = +910.9$ kJ
2.	$Ag^+(g) + F^-(g) \longrightarrow Ag^+(aq) + F^-(aq)$	$\Delta H = -931.4$ kJ
	$AgF(s) \longrightarrow Ag^+(aq) + F^-(aq)$	$\Delta H = -20.5$ kJ

The factors that lead to a large positive value for step 1 (high ionic charges and small ions—see Section 12.3) also lead to a large negative value for step 2. Consequently, the values for the steps (ignoring signs) are usually numerically close, and the enthalpy of solution itself is a much smaller value than either of the values that goes into it. A relatively small error in the lattice energy or the enthalpy of hydration can therefore lead to a proportionately large error in the enthalpy of solution. As an example, consider the preceding calculation, in which the enthalpy of solution for AgF was found. An error of 10 kJ in either of the first two values (which is about a 1% error in either case) would cause the final result to be in error by 10 kJ, which in the case of the enthalpy of solution is an error of almost 50%!

If a solvent other than water is employed in the preparation of a solution, the same type of analysis can be made. The values for the second step are called **enthalpies of solvation.**

Similar considerations apply to the solution of nonionic materials. The lattice energies of molecular crystals are not so large as those of ionic crystals since the forces holding molecular crystals together are not so strong as those holding ionic crystals together. Solvation energies for these nonionic materials, however, are also low. For molecular substances that dissolve in nonpolar solvents without ionization and without appreciable solute-solvent interaction, the enthalpy of solution is endothermic and has about the same magnitude as the enthalpy of fusion of the solute.

Gases generally dissolve in liquids with the evolution of heat. Since no energy is required to separate the molecules of a gas, the predominant enthalpy change of such a solution process is the solvation of the gas molecules; the process, therefore, is exothermic. There are exceptions to this generalization, however, particularly if the gas (solute) reacts with the liquid (solvent).

2.5 Effect of Temperature and Pressure on Solubility

The effect of a temperature change on the solubility of a substance depends upon whether heat is absorbed or evolved *when a saturated solution is prepared*. Suppose that a small quantity of solute dissolves in a nearly saturated solution with the absorption of heat. We can represent the equilibrium between excess solid solute and solute dissolved in a saturated solution as:

energy + solute (s) $\rightleftharpoons$ solute (dissolved)

The effect of a temperature change on this system can be predicted by means of a principle proposed by Henri Le Chatelier in 1884. **Le Chatelier's principle** states that a system in equilibrium reacts to a stress in a way that counteracts the stress and establishes a new equilibrium state.

Suppose that we have a beaker containing a saturated solution of the type previously described together with some excess solid solute in equilibrium with it. What will be the effect if we raise the temperature? According to Le Chatelier's principle, the system will react in a way that lowers the temperature. It can do that if it shifts to the direction in which heat is absorbed (to the right in the equation given previously). The shift means that more solute will dissolve. We conclude that *raising the temperature increases the solubility* of this particular solute.

What will happen if we lower the temperature? Le Chatelier's principle predicts that the system will react in a way that raises the temperature—a way that liberates energy. The reaction will shift to the left; solute will precipitate out of solution. We conclude that *lowering the temperature decreases the solubility* of this particular solute. Our two conclusions are actually the same. If a solute undergoes an *endothermic solution process*, therefore, *the solubility of the solute increases* with *increasing temperature*. Most ionic solutes behave in this way.*

Consider the case of a substance that dissolves in a nearly saturated solution with the evolution of heat:

solute (s) $\rightleftharpoons$ solute (dissolved) + energy

Le Chatelier's principle predicts that if the temperature were raised, this system would shift to the left (the direction in which heat is absorbed) and that solute would precipitate out of solution. If a solute undergoes an *exothermic solution process*, therefore, *the solubility of the solute decreases with increasing temperature*. A few ionic compounds (such as Li_2CO_3 and Na_2SO_4) behave in this fashion. In addition, the solubility of all gases decreases as the temperature is raised. Warming a soft drink causes bubbles of carbon dioxide gas to come out of solution.

How much the solubility changes when the temperature changes depends upon the magnitude of the enthalpy of solution. The solubilities of substances with small enthalpies of solution do not change much with changes in temperature.

Changes in pressure ordinarily have little effect upon the solubilities of solid and liquid solutes. However, increasing or decreasing the pressure on a solution that contains a dissolved gas has a definite effect. William Henry in 1803 discovered that the amount of a gas that dissolves in a given quantity of a liquid at constant temperature is directly proportional to the partial pressure of the gas above the solution. Henry's law is closely followed only by dilute solutions at relatively low pressures. Gases that are extremely soluble generally react chemically with the solvent (for example, hydrogen chloride gas in water reacts to produce hydrochloric acid); these solutions do not follow Henry's law.

The blood of deep-sea divers becomes saturated with air under the comparatively high pressures characteristic of the depths at which such divers work. If this

---

* The amount of heat absorbed or evolved when one mole of solute dissolves in a solvent varies with the amount of solvent used. The ΔH values considered here pertain to the preparation of *saturated solutions* from nearly saturated solutions. The ΔH values recorded as enthalpies of solution, however, usually pertain to the preparation of *dilute solutions*. For a given solute, the numerical values for these two ΔH terms are different. At times, the ΔH value for the preparation of a *concentrated* solution is a *positive* value and the ΔH value for the preparation of a *dilute* solution is a *negative* value. The ions are hydrated more completely in a dilute solution than they are in a concentrated solution. Hence, more energy is liberated by ion hydration in the preparation of a dilute solution than in the preparation of a concentrated solution.

pressure is relieved too rapidly, as by too rapid an ascent to the surface, the air comes out of solution rapidly and forms bubbles in the circulatory system of the afflicted diver. This condition, known as the "bends," affects nerve impulses as well as blood circulation and may be fatal. A solution to the problem involves the use of an artificial atmosphere of helium and oxygen in place of air (which is largely nitrogen and oxygen). Helium is much less soluble in blood and body fluids than is nitrogen.

12.6 Concentrations of Solutions

The concentration of a solute in a solution can be expressed in several different ways. We have discussed some of these in previous sections, and we will now review the common ways to express solution concentrations:

1. The percentage by mass of a solute in a solution is 100 times the mass of the solute divided by the *total mass* of the solution. A 10% aqueous solution of sodium chloride contains 10 g of NaCl and 90 g of H_2O. Volume percentages are seldom used in chemistry. Figures recorded as percentages should be understood to be based on mass unless a specific notation to the contrary is made.

2. The mole fraction, X, of a component of a solution is the ratio of the number of moles of that component to the *total number* of moles of all the substances present in the solution (see Section 10.10):

$$X_A = \frac{n_A}{n_A + n_B + n_C + \ldots} \tag{12.1}$$

where X_A is the mole fraction of A, and n_A, n_B, n_C ... are the number of moles of A, B, C .... The sum of the mole fractions of all the components present in the solution must equal 1.

$$X_A + X_B + X_C + \ldots = 1$$

Example 12.1

A gaseous solution contains 2.00 g of He and 4.00 g of O_2. What are the mole fractions of He and O_2 in the solution?

Solution

We first find the number of moles of each component present in the solution:

$$? \text{ mol He} = 2.00 \text{ g He} \left(\frac{1 \text{ mol He}}{4.00 \text{ g He}} \right) = 0.500 \text{ mol He}$$

$$? \text{ mol O}_2 = 4.00 \text{ g O}_2 \left(\frac{1 \text{ mol O}_2}{32.0 \text{ g O}_2} \right) = 0.125 \text{ mol O}_2$$

We use these values to find the mole fractions:

$$X_{He} = \frac{n_{He}}{n_{He} + n_{O_2}}$$

$$= \frac{0.500 \text{ mol}}{0.500 \text{ mol} + 0.125 \text{ mol}} = \frac{0.500 \text{ mol}}{0.625 \text{ mol}} = 0.800$$

$$X_{O_2} = \frac{n_{O_2}}{n_{He} + n_{O_2}}$$

$$= \frac{0.125 \text{ mol}}{0.625 \text{ mol}} = 0.200$$

Notice that the sum of the mole fractions is equal to 1.

3. The **molarity**, M, of a solution is the number of moles of solute per liter of *solution:*

$$molarity = \frac{num. \text{ moles solute}}{num. \text{ liters solution}} \tag{12.2}$$

The use of molarity as a unit of concentration has been discussed in Section 4.5 and illustrated in Example 4.9, 4.10, and 4.11. Two additional examples are presented here.

Example 12.2

(a) How many grams of concentrated nitric acid solution should be used to prepare 250. mL of 2.00 M HNO$_3$? The concentrated acid is 70.0% HNO$_3$.
(b) If the density of the concentrated nitric acid solution is 1.42 g/mL, what volume should be used?

Solution

(a) The factors used to solve the problem are derived from the following facts (in order):

1. Since the desired solution is 2.00 M, there must be 2.00 mol HNO$_3$ in 1.00 L.
2. The molecular weight of HNO$_3$ is 63.0.
3. In 100. g of concentrated nitric acid (70.0% HNO$_3$) there are 70.0 g of HNO$_3$:

$$? \text{ g conc HNO}_3 = 0.250 \text{ L sol'n} \left(\frac{2 \text{ mol HNO}_3}{1.00 \text{ L sol'n}}\right)\left(\frac{63.0 \text{ g HNO}_3}{1 \text{ mol HNO}_3}\right)\left(\frac{100. \text{ g conc HNO}_3}{70.0 \text{ g HNO}_3}\right)$$

$$= 45.0 \text{ g conc HNO}_3$$

(b) The density of the concentrated acid is used to convert the answer to part (a) into mL of concentrated HNO_3:

$$? \text{ mL conc } HNO_3 = 45.0 \text{ g conc } HNO_3 \left(\frac{1.00 \text{ mL conc } HNO_3}{1.42 \text{ g conc } HNO_3} \right)$$

$$= 31.7 \text{ mL conc } HNO_3$$

Example 12.3

What is the molarity of concentrated HCl if the solution contains 37.0% HCl by mass and if the density of the solution is 1.18 g/mL?

Solution

In order to find the molarity of the solution, we must determine the number of moles of HCl in 1 L of solution. The problem can be solved by using factors derived in the following way:

1. The mass of 1 L of the solution is found by means of the density.

2. The mass of pure HCl in this quantity of solution is obtained by use of the percent composition.

3. The molecular weight of HCl (36.5) is used to convert the mass of HCl into moles of HCl:

$$? \text{ mol HCl} = 1.00 \times 10^3 \text{ mL sol'n} \left(\frac{1.18 \text{ g sol'n}}{1 \text{ mL g sol'n}} \right) \left(\frac{37.0 \text{ g HCl}}{100. \text{ g sol'n}} \right) \left(\frac{1 \text{ mol HCl}}{36.5 \text{ g HCl}} \right)$$

$$= 12.0 \text{ mol HCl}$$

Since 1 L of the solution contains 12.0 mol HCl, the solution is 12.0 M.

There is a disadvantage to basing a unit of concentration on the volume of solution. When the temperature changes, the volume of a solution expands or contracts and, therefore, a concentration based on that volume changes. For exact work, a solution should be prepared and have its molarity determined at the temperature at which the solution is to be used.

4. The molality, m, of a solution is defined as the number of moles of solute dissolved in a kilogram of solvent:

$$molality = \frac{num. \ moles \ solute}{num. \ kilograms \ solvent} \tag{12.3}$$

A 1.000 m solution of urea, $CO(NH_2)_2$, is made by dissolving 1.000 mol of urea (60.06 g) in 1000. g of water. Notice that the volume is *not* based on the total volume of solution. The final volume is of no importance. One molal solutions of different solutes, each containing 1000. g of water, will have different volumes. All these solutions, however, will have the same mole fractions of solute and solvent (see Example 12.5).

Example 12.4

What is the molality of a 12.5% solution of glucose, $C_6H_{12}O_6$, in water? The molecular weight of glucose is 180.0.

Solution

The molality of the solution equals the number of moles of glucose dissolved in one kilogram of water. The factors used are derived from the following facts:

1. In a 12.5% solution, 12.5 g of $C_6H_{12}O_6$ is dissolved in $(100.0 \text{ g} - 12.5 \text{ g}) = 87.5 \text{ g } H_2O$.

2. The molecular weight of $C_6H_{12}O_6$ is 180.0.

$$? \text{ mol } C_6H_{12}O_6 = 1000. \text{ g } H_2O \left(\frac{12.5 \text{ g } C_6H_{12}O_6}{87.5 \text{ g } H_2O} \right) \left(\frac{1 \text{ mol } C_6H_{12}O_6}{180.0 \text{ g } C_6H_{12}O_6} \right)$$

$$= 0.794 \text{ mol } C_6H_{12}O_6$$

The solution is 0.794 m in $C_6H_{12}O_6$.

Example 12.5

What are the mole fractions of solute and solvent in a 1.00 m aqueous solution?

Solution

The molecular weight of H_2O is 18.0. We find the number of moles of water in 1000 g of H_2O:

$$? \text{ mol } H_2O = 1000. \text{ g } H_2O \left(\frac{1 \text{ mol } H_2O}{18.0 \text{ g } H_2O} \right) = 55.6 \text{ mol } H_2O$$

A 1.00 m aqueous solution contains

$$\frac{\begin{aligned} n_{solute} &= 1.0 \text{ mol} \\ n_{H_2O} &= 55.6 \text{ mol} \end{aligned}}{n_{total} = 56.6 \text{ mol}}$$

The mole fractions are

$$X_{solute} = \frac{n_{solute}}{n_{total}} = \frac{1.0 \text{ mol}}{56.6 \text{ mol}} = 0.018$$

$$X_{H_2O} = \frac{n_{H_2O}}{n_{total}} = \frac{55.6 \text{ mol}}{56.6 \text{ mol}} = 0.982$$

These mole fractions pertain to all 1.00 m aqueous solutions.

Example 12.6

What is the molality of a 0.5000 M solution of sucrose, $C_{12}H_{22}O_{11}$, in water? The density of the solution is 1.064 g/mL, and the molecular weight of $C_{12}H_{22}O_{11}$ is 342.3.

Solution

1. We first use the density of the solution to find the mass of one liter of the solution.

$$? \text{ g sol'n} = 1000. \text{ mL sol'n}\left(\frac{1.064 \text{ g sol'n}}{1.000 \text{ mL sol'n}}\right) = 1064 \text{ g sol'n}$$

2. Since the solution is 0.5000 M, one liter of solution contains 0.5000 mol of $C_{12}H_{22}O_{11}$. The mass of $C_{12}H_{22}O_{11}$ in one liter of solution is:

$$? \text{ g } C_{12}H_{22}O_{11} = 0.5000 \text{ mol } C_{12}H_{22}O_{11}\left(\frac{342.3 \text{ g } C_{12}H_{22}O_{11}}{1 \text{ mol } C_{12}H_{22}O_{11}}\right)$$

$$= 171.2 \text{ g } C_{12}H_{22}O_{11}$$

3. The mass of one liter of solution (from 1) *minus* the mass of solute in one liter of solution (from 2) *equals* the mass of water in one liter of solution.

$$1064 \text{ g} - 171 \text{ g} = 893 \text{ g } H_2O$$

4. The molality of the solution is the number of moles of $C_{12}H_{22}O_{11}$ dissolved in 1000. g of water.

$$? \text{ mol } C_{12}H_{22}O_{11} = 1000. \text{ g } H_2O\left(\frac{0.5000 \text{ mol } C_{12}H_{22}O_{11}}{893 \text{ g } H_2O}\right)$$

$$= 0.560 \text{ mol } C_{12}H_{22}O_{11}$$

The solution is 0.560 m in $C_{12}H_{22}O_{11}$.

Molality is often used to express the concentration of solutions that employ solvents other than water. In each case, all the 1 m solutions that employ the same solvent have the same mole fractions of solute and solvent. The mole fraction of solute in any 1 m carbon tetrachloride solution is 0.133; the mole fraction of solvent is 0.867. These numbers differ from those in Example 12.5 because the molecular weight of carbon tetrachloride is different from that of water. A kilogram of CCl_4, therefore, is a different number of moles than a kilogram of H_2O.

The molality of a given solution does not vary with temperature since the solution is prepared on the basis of the masses of the components; mass does not vary with temperature changes. The *molality* of a *very dilute* aqueous solution is approximately the same as the *molarity* of the solution since 100 g of water occupies approximately 100 mL.

5. The normality of a solution, N, is the number of *equivalent weights* per liter of solution. Equivalent weights and normality are discussed in Section 13.8. We note here, however, that normal concentrations, like molar concentrations, are based on

Volumetric flask

the *total volume* of solution. Consequently, volumetric flasks are used in the preparation of solutions of a given normality, and the normality of a solution, like the molarity, varies slightly with temperature.

12.7 Vapor Pressure of Solutions

Consider a solution prepared from two components, A and B. The vapor pressure of the solution (P_{total}) is equal to the sum of the partial pressure of A (p_A) and the partial pressure of B (p_B):

$$P_{total} = p_A + p_B \tag{12.4}$$

The partial pressures in this equation may be found by means of a relationship known as **Raoult's law,** which pertains to what are called *ideal solutions*. The partial pressure of A, for example, is given by the equation:

$$p_A = X_A P_A^\circ \tag{12.5}$$

where X_A is the mole fraction of A in the solution and P_A° is the vapor pressure of *pure* A at the temperature of the experiment.

An **ideal solution** is one in which the intermolecular forces between A and B molecules, A and A molecules, and B and B molecules are all essentially the same. In such a situation, the tendency of an A molecule to escape into the vapor is the same whether it is surrounded by A molecules in pure A or surrounded by a mixture of A and B molecules in the solution. The partial pressure of A for the solution, therefore, is equal to the vapor pressure of pure A reduced in proportion to the number of molecules of A present out of the total number of molecules in the solution.

Suppose that we prepare a solution from 4 mol of A and 1 mol of B. Since the total number of moles in the solution is 5, the mole fraction of A is 4/5. Only 4 out of every 5 molecules in the solution are A molecules. The partial pressure of A, therefore, is 4/5 the vapor pressure of pure A (where 5 out of 5 molecules in the liquid are A molecules).

The partial pressure of B can be found by use of a similar equation:

$$p_B = X_B P_B^\circ \tag{12.6}$$

where X_B is the mole fraction of B in the solution and P_B° is the vapor pressure of *pure* B at the temperature of the experiment. In our hypothetical solution, the mole fraction of B is 1/5 since 1 mol is B out of a total of 5 mol. The partial pressure of B, therefore, is 1/5 the vapor pressure of pure B.

According to Equation 12.4, the vapor pressure of the solution is equal to the sum of the two partial pressures (Equations 12.5 and 12.6):

$$P_{total} = X_A P_A^\circ + X_B P_B^\circ \tag{12.7}$$

The vapor pressure of an *ideal solution*, therefore, can be derived from the vapor pressure of the pure components by taking into account the proportion of the components (by moles) present in the solution.

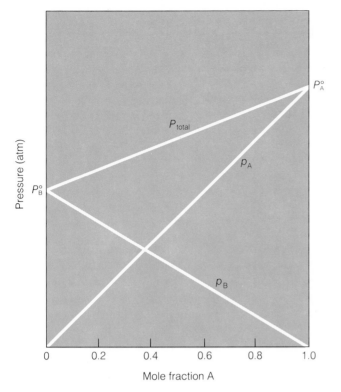

Figure 12.2 Typical total and partial pressure curves for solutions that follow Raoult's law

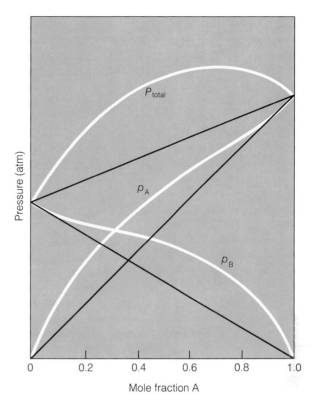

Figure 12.3 Typical total and partial vapor-pressure curves for solutions that show positive deviations from Raoult's law. (Black lines are based on Raoult's law.)

In Figure 12.2, the partial pressures of A and B as well as the total vapor pressures of solutions of A and B are plotted against solution concentration. The total vapor-pressure curve is the sum of the two partial-pressure curves. In the figure, pressures are plotted against mole fraction of A. Since the mole fractions of A and B for a given solution must add up to 1, the mole fraction of B for a given point is easily derived from the scale of the x axis. When X_A is 0.2, for example, X_B is 0.8.

Few solutions are ideal. Frequently, the A to B, A to A, and B to B intermolecular attractive forces differ in strength and the solution, therefore, is not ideal. Two types of deviations from Raoult's law are observed:

1. Positive deviations. The partial pressures of A and B and the total vapor pressure are *higher* than predicted (Figure 12.3). This type of deviation is observed when the attractive forces between A and B molecules are *weaker* than those between two A molecules or two B molecules. In such a situation, A molecules find it easier to escape from the liquid, and the partial pressure of A is higher than predicted. The behavior of B molecules is similar.

2. Negative deviations. The partial pressures of A and B and the total vapor pressure are *lower* than predicted (Figure 12.4). The A-B attractions are *stronger* than A-A or B-B attractions. The A molecules find it more difficult to leave the liquid, and the partial pressure of A is lower than predicted. The behavior of B molecules is similar.

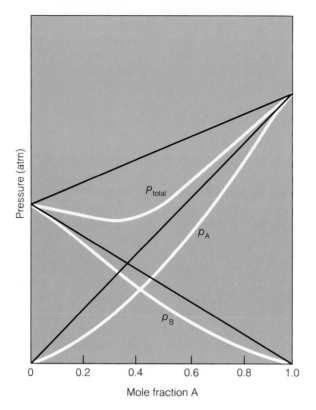

Figure 12.4 Typical total and partial vapor-pressure curves for solutions that show negative deviations from Raoult's law. (Black lines are based on Raoult's law.)

Example 12.7

Heptane (C_7H_{16}) and octane (C_8H_{18}) form ideal solutions. What is the vapor pressure at 40°C of a solution that contains 3.00 mol of heptane and 5.00 mol of octane? At 40°C, the vapor pressure of heptane is 0.121 atm and the vapor pressure of octane is 0.041 atm.

Solution

The total number of moles is 8.00. Therefore,

$$X_{\text{heptane}} = \frac{3.00 \text{ mol}}{8.00 \text{ mol}} = 0.375$$

$$X_{\text{octane}} = \frac{5.00 \text{ mol}}{8.00 \text{ mol}} = 0.625$$

The vapor pressure is

$$\begin{aligned}
P_{\text{total}} &= X_{\text{heptane}} P^\circ_{\text{heptane}} + X_{\text{octane}} P^\circ_{\text{octane}} \\
&= 0.375(0.121 \text{ atm}) + 0.625(0.041 \text{ atm}) \\
&= 0.045 \text{ atm} + 0.026 \text{ atm} \\
&= 0.071 \text{ atm}
\end{aligned}$$

Consider a *dilute* solution prepared from a solute (which we will designate as B) that is *nonvolatile* ($P_B^\circ = 0$, for all practical purposes) and that does not dissociate in solution. The vapor pressure of the solution is caused by solvent molecules alone (A molecules). Such solutions usually follow Raoult's law:

$$P_{total} = X_A P_A^\circ \qquad (12.8)$$

Since $X_A + X_B = 1$, $X_A = 1 - X_B$. Therefore,

$$P_{total} = (1 - X_B)P_A^\circ \qquad (12.9)$$

or

$$P_{total} = P_A^\circ - X_B P_A^\circ \qquad (12.10)$$

which means that the vapor pressure of pure A, P_A°, is lowered by an amount equal to $X_B P_A^\circ$.

The vapor pressure of a solution prepared from 1 mol of a nonvolatile, nondissociating solute and 99 mol of solvent is 99% of the vapor pressure of the pure solvent at the same temperature. The escape of the solvent molecules to the vapor is reduced because only 99% of the molecules in the solution are solvent molecules. The other 1% of the molecules in the solution are not volatile. The vapor pressure of the solvent is reduced by an amount that is proportional to the mole fraction of nonvolatile solute present.

Example 12.8

Assuming ideality, calculate the vapor pressure of a 1.00 *m* solution of a nonvolatile, nondissociating solute in water at 50°C. The vapor pressure of water at 50°C is 0.122 atm.

Solution

The mole fraction of water in a 1.00 *m* solution is 0.982 (from Example 12.5). The vapor pressure of a 1.00 *m* solution of this type at 50°C is

$$
\begin{aligned}
P_{total} &= X_{H_2O} P_{H_2O}^\circ \\
&= (0.982)(0.122 \text{ atm}) \\
&= 0.120 \text{ atm}
\end{aligned}
$$

12.8 Boiling Point and Freezing Point of Solutions

The lowering of the vapor pressure in solutions of nonvolatile solutes affects the boiling points and freezing points of these solutions.

The boiling point of a liquid is defined as the temperature at which the vapor pressure of the liquid is equal to the prevailing atmospheric pressure. Boiling points measured under 1 atm pressure are called normal boiling points. Since the addition

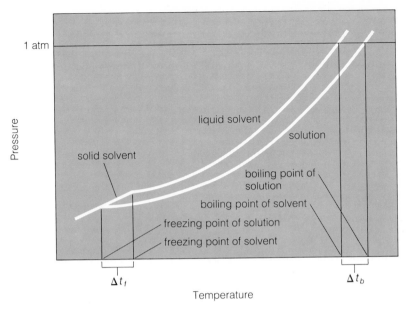

Figure 12.5 Vapor-pressure curves of a pure solvent and a solution of a nonvolatile solute under a total pressure of 1 atm. (Not drawn to scale.)

of a nonvolatile solute decreases the vapor pressure of a liquid, a solution will not boil at the normal boiling point of the solvent at 1 atm pressure. It is necessary to increase the temperature above this point in order to attain a vapor pressure over the solution of 1 atm. The boiling point of a solution containing a nonvolatile molecular solute, therefore, is higher than that of the pure solvent. The elevation is proportional to the concentration of solute in the solution.

This effect is illustrated by the vapor-pressure curves plotted in Figure 12.5. The extent to which the vapor-pressure curve of the solution lies below the vapor-pressure curve of the solvent is proportional to the mole fraction of solute in the solution. The elevation of the boiling point, Δt_b, reflects this displacement of the vapor-pressure curve. For a given solvent the elevation is the same for all solutions of the same concentration.

Concentrations are customarily expressed in molalities, rather than mole fractions, for problems involving boiling-point elevations. The boiling point of a 1 m aqueous solution, for example, is 0.512°C higher than the boiling point of water. Table 12.1 lists molal boiling-point elevation constants for several solvents.

The boiling point of a 0.5 m solution would be expected to be elevated by an amount equal to half the molal constant. Thus, the boiling-point elevation, Δt_b, of a solution can be calculated by multiplying the molal boiling-point elevation constant of the solvent, k_b, by the molality of the solution, m:

$$\Delta t_b = m k_b \tag{12.11}$$

In reality, this relationship is only approximate. A more exact statement would require that the concentration be expressed in mole fraction of solute, not in molality. However, molalities of *dilute* solutions are proportional (at least with sufficient accuracy) to mole fractions of solute. And since Raoult's law only describes the behavior of most real solutions satisfactorily if they are dilute, the use of molalities in these calculations is justified.

Solvent	Boiling Point (°C)	k_b (°C/m)	Freezing Point (°C)	k_f (°C/m)
acetic acid	118.1	+3.07	16.6	−3.90
benzene	80.1	+2.53	5.5	−5.12
camphor	—	—	179.	−39.7
carbon tetrachloride	76.8	+5.02	−22.8	−29.8
chloroform	61.2	+3.63	−63.5	−4.68
ethyl alcohol	78.4	+1.22	−114.6	−1.99
naphthalene	—	—	80.2	−6.80
water	100.0	+0.512	0.0	−1.86

At the freezing point the vapor pressure of solid and liquid are equal. In Figure 12.5 the vapor-pressure curves of the liquid solvent and the solid solvent intersect at the freezing point of the solvent. At this temperature, however, the vapor pressure of the solution is lower than the equilibrium vapor pressure of the pure solvent. The vapor-pressure curve of the solution intersects the vapor-pressure curve of the solid solvent at a lower temperature. The freezing point of the solution, therefore, is lower than that of the pure solvent. As in the case of boiling-point elevations, freezing-point depressions depend upon the concentration of the solution and the solvent employed. Molal freezing-point depression constants for some solvents are listed in Table 12.1. The freezing-point depression, Δt_f, of a solution can be calculated from the molality of the solution and the constant for the solvent, k_f:

$$\Delta t_f = m k_f \qquad (12.12)$$

This statement assumes that the solute does not form a solid solution with the solvent. If a solid solution forms, the relationship is not valid.

Example 12.9

What are the boiling point and freezing point of a solution prepared by dissolving 2.40 g of biphenyl ($C_{12}H_{10}$) in 75.0 g of benzene? The molecular weight of biphenyl is 154.

Solution

The molality of the solution is the number of moles of biphenyl dissolved in 1000. g of benzene:

$$? \text{ mol } C_{12}H_{10} = 1000 \text{ g benzene} \left(\frac{2.40 \text{ g } C_{12}H_{10}}{75.0 \text{ g benzene}} \right) \left(\frac{1 \text{ mol } C_{12}H_{10}}{154 \text{ g } C_{12}H_{10}} \right)$$

$$= 0.208 \text{ mol } C_{12}H_{10}$$

The molal boiling-point elevation constant for benzene solutions is $+2.53°C/m$ (Table 12.1):

$$\Delta t_b = mk_b \tag{12.11}$$
$$= (0.208\ m)(+2.53°C/m)$$
$$= +0.526°C$$

The normal boiling point of benzene is 80.1°C (Table 12.1). The boiling point of the solution, therefore, is

$$80.1°C + 0.5°C = 80.6°C$$

The molal freezing-point depression constant for benzene solutions is $-5.12°C/m$ (Table 12.1):

$$\Delta t_f = mk_f \tag{12.12}$$
$$= (0.208\ m)(-5.12°C/m)$$
$$= -1.06°C$$

The normal freezing point of benzene is 5.5°C (Table 12.1). The freezing point of the solution, therefore, is

$$5.5°C - 1.1°C = 4.4°C$$

Example 12.10

A solution prepared by dissolving 0.300 g of an unknown nonvolatile solute in 30.0 g of carbon tetrachloride has a boiling point that is 0.392°C higher than that of pure CCl_4. What is the molecular weight of the solute?

Solution

For CCl_4 solutions, k_b is $+5.02°C/m$ (Table 12.1). We find the molality of the solution from the boiling-point elevation:

$$\Delta t_b = mk_b \tag{12.11}$$
$$+0.392°C = m(+5.02°C/m)$$
$$m = 0.0781\ m$$

Next, we find the number of grams of solute dissolved in 1000 g of CCl_4:

$$?\ \text{g solute} = 1000\ \text{g}\ CCl_4 \left(\frac{0.300\ \text{g solute}}{30.0\ \text{g}\ CCl_4}\right) = 10.0\ \text{g solute}$$

Since the solution is 0.0781 m, 10.0 g of solute is 0.0781 mole of solute:

$$?\ \text{g solute} = 1\ \text{mol solute}\left(\frac{10.0\ \text{g solute}}{0.0781\ \text{mol solute}}\right) = 128\ \text{g solute}$$

The molecular weight of the solute is 128.

Chapter 12   Solutions

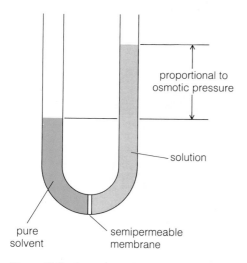

proportional to
osmotic pressure

solution

pure
solvent

semipermeable
membrane

Figure 12.6 Osmosis

12.9 Osmosis

The properties of solutions that depend principally upon the concentration of dissolved particles, rather than upon the nature of these particles, are called colligative properties. For solutions of nonvolatile solutes, these properties include vapor-pressure lowering, freezing-point depression, boiling-point elevation, and osmotic pressure. The last of these, osmotic pressure, is the topic of this section.

A membrane, such as cellophane or parchment, that permits some molecules or ions, but not all, to pass through it is called a semipermeable membrane. Figure 12.6 shows a membrane that is permeable to water but not to sucrose (cane sugar) placed between pure water and a sugar solution. At the start of the experiment, the water in the left arm of the U tube stands at the same height as the sugar solution in the right arm. Water molecules, but not sugar molecules, can go through the membrane in either direction. However, there are more water molecules per unit volume on the left side (the side containing pure water) than on the right. The rate of passage through the membrane from left to right, therefore, exceeds the rate in the opposite direction.

As a result, the number of water molecules on the right increases, the sugar solution becomes more dilute, and the height of the solution in the right arm of the U tube increases. This process is called osmosis. The difference in height between the levels of the liquids in the two arms of the U tube is a measure of the osmotic pressure.

The increased hydrostatic pressure on the right (caused by an increase in the amount of solution in the right arm) tends to force water molecules through the membrane from right to left, so that ultimately the rate of passage to the left equals the rate of passage to the right. The final condition, therefore, is an equilibrium state with equal rates of passage of water molecules through the membrane in both directions. If a pressure that is higher than the equilibrium pressure is applied to the solution in the right arm, water is forced in a direction contrary to that normally observed. This process, called reverse osmosis, is used to secure pure water from salt water.

Similarities exist between the behavior of water molecules in osmosis and the behavior of gas molecules in diffusion. In both processes molecules diffuse from

Purification of tap water for laboratory use by reverse osmosis. *Millipore Corporation.*

Desalinization plant. *George Daniell, Photo Researchers, Inc.*

regions of high concentrations to regions of low concentration. In 1887 Jacobus van't Hoff discovered the relation:

$$\pi V = nRT \tag{12.13}$$

where π is the osmotic pressure (in atm), n is the number of moles of solute dissolved in volume V (in liters), T is absolute temperature, and R is the gas constant [0.08206 L·atm/(K·mol)]. The similarity between this equation and the equation of state for an ideal gas is striking. The equation may be written in the form

$$\pi = \left(\frac{n}{V}\right) RT \tag{12.14}$$

$$\pi = MRT \tag{12.15}$$

where M is the molarity of the solution. Osmosis plays an important role in plant and animal physiological processes; the passage of substances through the semipermeable walls of a living cell, the action of the kidneys, and the rising of sap in trees are prime examples.

The membranes of red blood cells are semipermeable. If red blood cells are placed in pure water, the net effect of the flow of water through the cell walls is that water will move into the cells to dilute the cell fluid. As a result, the cells will swell and, in time, rupture. If red blood cells are placed in a concentrated sugar solution, the net effect is that water will move through the cell membranes and leave the cells to dilute the surrounding solution. As a result, the cells will shrivel. To prevent either of these events from occurring in intravenous feeding, the solutions used must be *isotonic* with blood (that is, they must have the same osmotic pressure as blood).

Example 12.11

Find the osmotic pressure of blood at normal body temperature (37°C) if the blood behaves as if it were a 0.296 *M* solution of a nonionizing solute.

Solution

$$\pi = MRT \qquad (12.15)$$
$$= (0.296 \text{ mol/L})[0.0821 \text{ L} \cdot \text{atm/(K} \cdot \text{mol})](310 \text{ K})$$
$$= 7.53 \text{ atm}$$

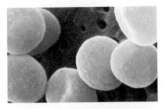

Example 12.12

An aqueous solution contains 30.0 g of a protein in 1.00 L. The osmotic pressure of the solution is 0.0167 atm at 25°C. What is the approximate molecular weight of the protein?

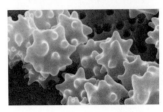

(Top) Normal red blood cells in an isotonic solution. (Middle) In pure water, cells swell up and in time will rupture. (Bottom) In a concentrated sugar solution, the cells shrivel. *Micrographs from M. Sheetz, R. Painter, and S. Singer*, J. Cell Biology, 1976. 70:193.

Solution

We use the van't Hoff equation to find the number of moles of protein present in the solution:

$$\pi = \left(\frac{n}{V}\right) RT \qquad (12.14)$$

$$0.0167 \text{ atm} = \left(\frac{n}{1.00 \text{ L}}\right)[0.0821 \text{ L} \cdot \text{atm/(K} \cdot \text{mol})](298 \text{ K})$$

$$n = 6.83 \times 10^{-4} \text{ mol}$$

Since there are 30.0 g of protein in the solution,

$$? \text{ g protein} = 1 \text{ mol protein} \left(\frac{30.0 \text{ g protein}}{6.83 \times 10^{-4} \text{ mol protein}}\right)$$

$$= 4.39 \times 10^4 \text{ g protein}$$

The molecular weight of the protein is approximately 43,900.

Since proteins have high molecular weights, the molal and molar concentrations of saturated solutions of proteins are very low. For the solution described in this example, the following effects can be calculated:

vapor-pressure lowering	0.000000385 atm
boiling-point elevation	0.000350°C
freezing-point depression	−0.00127°C
osmotic pressure	0.0167 atm

Clearly, the first three are too small for accurate measurement. The osmotic pressure of this solution, however, would make the difference in the height of the two columns shown in Figure 12.6 approximately 17 cm, an amount that is easily measured.*

12.10 Distillation

A solution of a nonvolatile solute can be separated into its components by simple distillation. This procedure consists of boiling away the volatile solvent from the solute. The solvent is collected by condensing the vapor. The solute is the residue that remains after the distillation.

A solution of two volatile components that follows Raoult's law (Figure 12.2) can be separated into its components by a process known as fractional distillation. According to Raoult's law, each component contributes to the vapor pressure of the solution in proportion to its mole fraction times its vapor pressure in the pure state (P_A° and P_B°):

$$P_{total} = X_A P_A^\circ + X_B P_B^\circ \qquad (12.7)$$

Let us consider a two-component solution in which the mole fraction of A is 0.75 and the mole fraction of B is 0.25. Assume that, at the temperature of the experiment, the vapor pressure of pure A is 1.20 atm and the vapor pressure of pure B is 0.40 atm. Then,

$$
\begin{aligned}
P_{total} &= X_A P_A^\circ + X_B P_B^\circ \qquad (12.7)\\
&= 0.75(1.20 \text{ atm}) + 0.25(0.40 \text{ atm})\\
&= 0.90 \text{ atm} + 0.10 \text{ atm}\\
&= 1.00 \text{ atm}
\end{aligned}
$$

Since the total pressure is 1.00 atm, the temperature of the experiment is the normal boiling point of the solution. The partial pressures of A and B are 0.90 atm and 0.10 atm.

The composition of the *vapor* in equilibrium with this solution can be calculated by comparing the partial pressure of each component with the total vapor pressure of the solution. In the vapor, therefore,

$$X_{A, vapor} = \frac{0.90 \text{ atm}}{1.00 \text{ atm}} = 0.90 \qquad X_{B, vapor} = \frac{0.10 \text{ atm}}{1.00 \text{ atm}} = 0.10$$

The solution, in which $X_A = 0.75$, is in equilibrium with vapor in which $X_{A, vapor} = 0.90$. For ideal solutions, the vapor is always richer than the liquid in the more volatile component (which in this instance is A—it has the higher vapor pressure).

---

* The osmotic pressure of 0.0167 atm can be converted into 0.0167 atm(760 torr/atm) = 12.7 torr, which is 12.7 mm of mercury or 1.27 cm of mercury. Since the density of mercury is 13.6 g/cm³, which is 13.6 times the density of water, it takes a column of water 13.6(1.27 cm) = 17.3 cm high to match the height of the mercury column.

In a distillation of the solution of A and B, the vapor that comes off and condenses is richer in A than the liquid remaining behind. The actual compositions of vapor and liquid change as the distillation proceeds, but at any given time this generalization is true. By collecting the condensed vapor in several fractions and subjecting these fractions to repeated distillation, the components of the original mixture can eventually be obtained in substantially pure form.

For systems that deviate from Raoult's law, the situation is somewhat different. A positive deviation may lead to a maximum in the total vapor-pressure curve (Figure 12.3). The maximum corresponds to a solution, of definite composition, that has a vapor pressure higher than either pure component. A solution of this type, called a minimum boiling azeotrope, will boil at a *lower* temperature than either of the two pure components. Ethyl alcohol and water form a minimum boiling azeotrope that contains 4.0% water and has a normal boiling point of 78.17°C. Ethyl alcohol and water boil at 78.3°C and 100°C, respectively.

If a system shows a negative deviation from Raoult's law (Figure 12.4), there may be a minimum in the P_{total} curve. The solution that has a concentration corresponding to this minimum will have a vapor pressure, at any given temperature, lower than either pure component. A solution of this type boils at a temperature *higher* than either pure component and is called a maximum boiling azeotrope. Hydrochloric acid and water form such an azeotrope containing 20.22% HCl and boiling at 108.6°C. Pure HCl has a boiling point of -80°C.

The vapor in equilibrium with a maximum or minimum boiling azeotrope has the same concentration as the liquid. Azeotropes, therefore, like pure substances, distill without change. Fractional distillation of a solution containing two components that form an azeotrope will eventually produce one pure component and the azeotrope, but not both pure components.

11 Solutions of Electrolytes

If an aqueous solution contains ions, it will conduct electricity. Pure water itself is slightly ionized and is a poor conductor:

$$2\,H_2O \rightleftharpoons H_3O^+(aq) + OH^-(aq)$$

The solute of an aqueous solution that is a better electric conductor than pure water alone is called an electrolyte. An electrolyte is wholly or partly ionized in water soluton. Covalent solutes that are exclusively molecular in solution and therefore do nothing to enhance the conductivity of the solvent are called nonelectrolytes; sucrose (cane sugar) is an example.

Electrolytes can be further divided into two groups:

1. Strong electrolytes are virtually completely ionic in water solution.

2. Weak electrolytes are polar covalent substances that are incompletely dissociated in water solution. The conductivity of a 1 m soluton of a weak electrolyte is lower than the conductivity of a 1 m solution of a strong electrolyte.

The boiling-point elevations and freezing-point depressions of dilute solutions of electrolytes are different from those of solutions of nonelectrolytes with the same

Table 12.2 Observed freezing-point depressions for some aqueous solutions compared to calculated depressions[a]

Solute	Concentration of Solution		
	0.001 m	0.01 m	0.1 m
calculated for nonelectrolyte	0.00186°C	0.0186°C	0.186°C
sucrose	0.00186	0.0186	0.188
calculated for 2 ions/formula	0.00372	0.0372	0.372
NaCl	0.00366	0.0360	0.348
calculated for 3 ions/formula	0.00558	0.0558	0.558
K_2SO_4	0.00528	0.0501	0.432
calculated for 4 ions/formula	0.00744	0.0744	0.744
$K_3[Fe(CN)_6]$	0.00710	0.0626	0.530

[a] Calculated on the assumptions that k_f for water is $-1.86°C$/molal over the entire range of concentrations, the salts are 100% ionic in solution, and the ions act independently of one another in their effect on the freezing point of the solution.

Svante Arrhenius, 1859–1927.
Smithsonian Institution.

concentrations. Since 1 mol of NaCl contains 2 mol of ions (1 mol of Na^+ and 1 mol of Cl^-) and since colligative properties depend upon the number of dissolved particles and not their nature, we would expect the freezing-point depression of a 1 m solution of NaCl to be twice that of a 1 m solution of a nonelectrolyte. We would also expect the freezing-point depression of a solution of K_2SO_4 (which contains 3 mol of ions per mole of K_2SO_4) to be three times that of a solution having the same concentration and containing a solute that does not dissociate into ions.

The observed freezing-point depressions listed in Table 12.2 agree approximately with these predictions. The observed values agree best with the calculated values when the solutions are most dilute. Data such as these, together with data from electrical conductivity experiments, led Svante Arrhenius to propose his "chemical theory of electrolytes" in 1887. The boiling-point elevations of solutions of electrolytes are proportionately higher than the boiling-point elevations of solutions of nonelectrolytes with the same concentrations.

12.12 Interionic Attractions in Solution

The **van't Hoff factor,** i, is defined as the ratio of an observed measurement of a colligative property for a solute in a solution to the value expected for a solute that does not dissociate. In the case of freezing-point depression, for example,

$$i = \frac{\Delta t_f}{mk_f} \tag{12.16}$$

The preceding equation can be rearranged to

$$\Delta t_f = imk_f \tag{12.17}$$

When dissociation of a solute occurs, it is necessary to correct the molality of the solution for calculations involving colligative properties. The i factor will do

Table 12.3 van't Hoff factor, i, for various strong electrolytes in solution[a]

Electrolyte	Concentration of Solution		
	0.001 m	0.01 m	0.1 m
NaCl	1.97	1.94	1.87
$MgSO_4$	1.82	1.53	1.21
K_2SO_4	2.84	2.69	2.32
$K_3[Fe(CN)_6]$	3.82	3.36	2.85

[a] From freezing-point determinations.

Table 12.4 Characteristics of solutes

Solute	Form of Solute in 1 m Solution	van't Hoff Factor for Δt_f; Dilute Solutions of Molality, m $\Delta t_f = ik_f m$	Examples
nonelectrolytes	molecules	$i = 1$	$C_{12}H_{22}O_{11}$ (sucrose) CON_2H_4 (urea) $C_3H_5(OH)_3$ (glycerol)
strong electrolytes	ions	$i \approx n$[a]	NaCl KOH
weak electrolytes	molecules and ions	$1 < i < n$[a]	$HC_2H_3O_2$ NH_3 $HgCl_2$

[a] n = number of moles of ions per mole of solute.

just that. Since 1 mol of NaCl dissociates into 2 mol of ions in solution (1 mol of Na^+ and 1 mol of Cl^-), the i factor for a solution of NaCl is theoretically 2. If we assume that each ion acts independently, the effective concentration of a 0.001 m solution of NaCl would be 0.002 m. In other words, $i = 2$, $m = 0.001$ m, and

$$\Delta t_f = 2(0.001 \ m)k_f$$

Inspection of the i values recorded in Table 12.3 reveals that the i factors do not exactly equal the number of ions per formula unit for each of the strong electrolytes listed. Thus, for 0.001 m solutions, the i factor for NaCl is 1.97 (not 2), for K_2SO_4 is 2.84 (not 3), and for $K_3[Fe(CN)_6]$ is 3.28 (not 4). Furthermore, the i value changes with concentration of the solution and approaches the value expected for complete dissociation as the solution becomes more dilute.

Interionic attractions occur in solutions of electrolytes, and the ions are not completely independent of one another in the way that uncharged solute molecules are. The electrical forces that operate between oppositely charged ions reduce the effectiveness of these ions. As a solution is diluted, the ions spread farther and farther apart, their influence on one another diminishes, and the i factor approaches its limiting value. Notice that the interionic attractions in solutions of $MgSO_4$ produce a stronger effect than those in solutions of NaCl, even though both solutes contain two moles of ions per mole of compound. For 0.001 m MgSO$_4$, $i = 1.82$, whereas for 0.001 m NaCl, $i = 1.97$. Both the ions of MgSO$_4$ are doubly charged (Mg^{2+}, SO$_4^{2-}$), whereas the ions of NaCl are singly charged (Na$^+$, Cl$^-$). The interionic attractions are stronger in solutions of magnesium sulfate.

Some characteristics of solutes are summarized in Table 12.4. Formulas in which the van't Hoff factor, i, appears are used in calculations of freezing-point depression, boiling-point elevation, and osmotic pressure when the solute is an electrolyte:

$$\Delta t_f = imk_f \tag{12.17}$$

$$\Delta t_b = imk_b \tag{12.18}$$

$$\pi = iMRT \tag{12.19}$$

Summary

Solutions are *homogeneous mixtures*. The component present in the greatest quantity is usually called the *solvent* and all other components are called *solutes*. The amount of solute dissolved in a given amount of solvent or dissolved in a given amount of solution is called the *concentration* of the solution. *Dilute solutions* have relatively low concentrations; *concentrated solutions* have relatively high concentrations. A solution that contains as much solute as can be dissolved is called a *saturated solution;* solutions with lower concentrations are called *unsaturated solutions.*

The nature and strength of the attractive forces between solute-solute, solvent-solvent, and solute-solvent particles determine, in large measure, the extent of the solubility of a solute in a given solvent. The highest solubility is observed when these forces are similar; "like dissolves like."

The *enthalpy of solution*, the ΔH value that pertains to the preparation of a solution, is the net result of the *energy required* to break apart certain bonds or attractions (solute-solute and solvent-solvent) and the *energy released* by the formation of new ones (solute-solvent). If the solvent is water, the process in which solute-solvent attractions form is called *hydration*, and the energy released is called the *enthalpy of hydration.*

Le Chatelier's principle can be used to predict the effect of a change in temperature on the solubility of a solute. If the solution process is *endothermic*, the solubility *increases* with *increasing temperature*. If the solution process is *exothermic*, the solubility *decreases* with *increasing temperature*. Changes in pressure ordinarily have little effect on the solubilities of solid and liquid solutes. The solubility of a *gas* in a *liquid solution*, however, is proportional to the *partial pressure* of the gas above the solution (*Henry's law*).

The *concentrations* of *solutions* are expressed in terms of *mass percent, mole fraction* (X), *molarity* (M), *molality* (M), and *normality* (N).

The *vapor pressure* of a solution is equal to the *sum* of the *partial pressures* of the components of the solution. For a volatile component of an ideal solution, *Raoult's law* states that the *partial pressure* is equal to the *mole fraction of the component* in the solution *times the vapor pressure of the pure component.*

For *dilute solutions* of a *nonvolatile solute* in a volatile solvent, the *vapor pressure* of the solution is equal to the *partial pressure* of the *solvent*, as given by Raoult's law. As a consequence, the *vapor pressure* and the *freezing point* of the solution are *lower* and the *boiling point higher* than the values for the pure solvent.

Colligative properties depend upon the *concentration* of solute in a solution and not upon the *nature* of the solute. These properties include *vapor-pressure lowering, freezing-point depression, boiling-point elevation,* and *osmotic pressure.* The *osmotic pressure* of a solution is the pressure that develops in the process in which there is a net movement of solvent molecules through a *semipermeable membrane* that separates two solutions, the movement occurring in the direction of the more concentrated solution.

Electrolytes are solutes that are *ionic* (to a greater or lesser degree) in water solution. Solutions of electrolytes, therefore, conduct electricity better than pure water does. *Strong electrolytes* are virtually *completely ionic,* and *weak electrolytes* are *not completely ionized.* Because a mole of an electrolyte produces more than a mole of particles when it is dissolved in water (taking ions into account), the colligative properties of solutions of electrolytes differ from those of solutions of molecular substances.

Key Terms

Some of the more important terms introduced in this chapter are listed below. Definitions for terms not included in this list may be located in the text by use of the index.

Azeotrope (Section 12.10)   A solution that has a higher or lower vapor pressure than any of the pure components of which it is composed. If the vapor pressure is higher, the solution is a minimum-boiling azeotrope; if lower, a maximum boiling azeotrope.

Colligative property (Section 12.9)   A property of a solution that depends principally upon the concentration of dissolved particles rather than on the nature of those particles; vapor-pressure lowering, freezing-point depression, boiling-point elevation, and osmotic pressure.

Distillation (Section 12.10)   The separation of a liquid solution into its components by vaporization and condensation.

Electrolyte (Section 12.11)   A solute that dissolves in water to produce a solution that is a better conductor of electricity than pure water alone. The electrical conductivity of the solution is caused by the ionization of the solute by water.

Enthalpy of hydration (Sections 12.3 and 12.4)   The enthalpy change associated with the process in which gaseous ions of a given quantity of solute (usually one mole) are hydrated.

Enthalpy of solution (Section 12.4)   The enthalpy change associated with the process in which a given quantity of a solute (usually one mole) dissolves in a solvent. The value depends upon the concentration of the final solution and the temperature.

Henry's law (Section 12.5)   When gas dissolves in a liquid without reaction, the amount of a gas that dissolves in a given quantity of the liquid is directly proportional to the partial pressure of the gas above the solution.

Hydration (Sections 12.3 and 12.4)   The process in which water molecules are attracted to and surround solute particles.

Ideal solution (Section 12.7)   A solution that obeys Raoult's law; for a solution of two components, A and B, an ideal solution is one in which the intermolecular forces between A and B, A and A, and B and B are essentially the same.

Le Chatelier's principle (Section 12.5)   When the conditions are changed, a system in equilibrium reacts in a way that tends to counteract the change.

Molal boiling-point elevation constant, k_b (Section 12.8)   The elevation of the boiling point of a solvent brought about by dissolving one mole of a nonvolatile, nondissociating solute in 1000 g of the solvent (a 1 m solution); the value of k_b is specific to the solvent considered.

Molal freezing-point depression constant, k_f (Section 12.8)   The depression of the freezing point of a solvent brought about by dissolving one mole of a nonvolatile, nondissociating solute in 1000 g of the solvent (a 1 m solution); the value of k_f is specific to the solvent considered.

Molality, m (Section 10.6)   A solution concentration; the number of moles of solute per one kilogram of solvent.

Osmosis (Section 12.9)   The process in which there is a net movement of solvent molecules through a semipermeable membrane separating two solutions; movement occurs in the direction of the more concentrated solution.

Raoult's law (Section 12.7)   The partial pressure of a component in the vapor of an ideal solution is equal to the mole fraction of the component in the solution times the vapor pressure of the pure component.

van't Hoff factor, i (Section 12.12)   The ratio of a measured colligative property for a solution (boiling-point elevation, freezing-point depression, or osmotic pressure) to the value calculated for that property on the assumption that the solute is a nonelectrolyte.

Problems*

The Solution Process

12.1 The enthalpy of solution of I_2 in CCl_4 is about the same size as the enthalpy of fusion of pure I_2. Why cannot a similar statement be made about the dissolution of an ionic substance in water?

12.2 Why is Br_2 more soluble in CCl_4 than I_2 is?

12.3 What factors cause an ionic solute to have a high enthalpy of hydration?

12.4 Describe three ways in which water occurs in crystalline hydrates.

12.5 Which member of each of the following pairs would you expect to be the more soluble in water? **(a)** CH_3OH or CH_3CH_3, **(b)** CCl_4 or $NaCl$, **(c)** CH_3F or CH_3Cl.

12.6 Which member of each of the following pairs would you expect to be the more soluble in water? **(a)** NF_3 or NaF, **(b)** N_2O or N_2, **(c)** NH_3 or CH_4.

---

* The more difficult problems are marked with asterisks. The appendix contains answers to color-keyed problems.

12.7 Which member of each of the following pairs would you expect to be the more strongly hydrated? **(a)** Li^+ or Na^+, **(b)** Fe^{2+} or Fe^{3+}, **(c)** K^+ or Ca^{2+}, **(d)** F^- or Br^-, **(e)** Be^{2+} or Ba^{2+}.

12.8 Which member of each of the following pairs would you expect to be the more strongly hydrated? **(a)** Li^+ or Be^{2+}, **(b)** O^{2-} or S^{2-}, **(c)** Sn^{2+} or Pb^{2+}, **(d)** Mg^{2+} or Al^{3+}, **(e)** Co^{2+} or Co^{3+}.

12.9 Which value indicates the liberation of more energy: the enthalpy of hydration for the preparation of a *dilute* aqueous solution of an ionic solute or the enthalpy of hydration for the preparation of a *concentrated* aqueous solution of an ionic solute? Why?

12.10 Why is the enthalpy of hydration so important to the process in which an ionic solute dissolves in water?

12.11 The lattice energy of $SrCl_2$ is $-2150.$ kJ/mol. The enthalpy of hydration of $SrCl_2$ (infinite dilution) at 298 K is -2202 kJ/mol. What is the enthalpy of solution of $SrCl_2$ for the preparation of very dilute solutions at 298 K?

12.12 The lattice energy of $MgCl_2$ is -2525 kJ/mol. The enthalpy of hydration of $MgCl_2$ (infinite dilution) at 298 K is $-2680.$ kJ/mol. What is the enthalpy of solution of $MgCl_2$ for the preparation of very dilute solutions at 298 K?

12.13 The enthalpy of solution of KF at 298 K for the preparation of very dilute solutions is -18 kJ/mol. The lattice energy of KF is -812 kJ/mol. What is the enthalpy of hydration of this compound at 298 K? Describe the processes to which this value pertains.

12.14 The enthalpy of solution of KI at 298 K for the preparation of very dilute solutions is $+20.$ kJ/mol. The lattice energy of KI is -647 kJ/mol. What is the enthalpy of hydration of this compound at 298 K? Describe the processes to which this value pertains.

12.15 Henry's law may be stated as $p = KX$, where p is the partial pressure of a gas over a saturated solution, X is the mole fraction of the dissolved gas in the solution, and K is a constant. For aqueous solutions of $N_2O(g)$ at 0.°C, K is 9.74×10^2 atm. How many moles of $N_2O(g)$ will dissolve in 270. g of H_2O at 0.°C if the partial pressure of $N_2O(g)$ over the solution is 1.50 atm? How many grams of $N_2O(g)$?

12.16 Henry's law may be stated as $p = KX$, where p is the partial pressure of a gas over a saturated solution, X is the mole fraction of the dissolved gas in the solution, and K is a constant. For aqueous solutions of $CO_2(g)$ at 0.°C, K is 7.30×10^2 atm. How many moles of $CO_2(g)$ will dissolve in 225 g of H_2O at 0.°C if the partial pressure of $CO_2(g)$ over the solution is 2.50 atm? How many grams of $CO_2(g)$?

Concentrations of Solutions

12.17 What is the mole fraction of ethyl alcohol (C_2H_5OH) in an aqueous solution of ethyl alcohol that is 39.0% ethyl alcohol by mass?

12.18 A solution of phenol (C_6H_5OH) in ethyl alcohol (C_2H_5OH) is 20.3% phenol by mass. What is the mole fraction of phenol in the solution?

12.19 In a solution of naphthalene $(C_{10}H_8)$ in toluene (C_7H_8), the mole fraction of naphthalene is 0.200. What is the percent by mass of naphthalene in the solution?

12.20 In an aqueous solution of urea (CON_2H_4), the mole fraction of urea is 0.130. What is the percent by mass of urea in the solution?

12.21 How many grams of $AgNO_3$ should be used to prepare 250 mL of 0.600 M $AgNO_3$ solution?

12.22 How many grams of $KMnO_4$ should be used to prepare 2.50 L of 0.120 M $KMnO_4$ solution?

12.23 Concentrated HBr is 48.0% HBr by mass and has a density of 1.50 g/mL. **(a)** How many grams of concentrated HBr should be used to prepare 750. mL of 1.50 M HBr solution? **(b)** How many milliliters of concentrated HBr should be used to prepare this solution?

12.24 Concentrated HI is 47.0% HI by mass and has a density of 1.50 g/mL. **(a)** How many grams of concentrated HI should be used to prepare 1.50 L of 0.600 M HI solution? **(b)** How many milliliters of concentrated HI should be used to prepare this solution?

12.25 (a) What is the molarity of concentrated HF if the solution is 48.0% HF by mass and has a density of 1.17 g/mL? **(b)** What is the molality of this solution?

12.26 (a) What is the molarity of a solution of $AgNO_3$ if the solution is 10.0% $AgNO_3$ by mass and has a density of 1.09 g/mL? **(b)** What is the molality of this solution?

12.27 A concentrated solution of NaOH is 50.0% NaOH by mass and has a density of 1.54 g/mL. If 25.0 mL of this solution is diluted to a final volume of 750. mL, what is the molarity of the resulting solution?

12.28 A concentrated solution of KOH is 45.0% KOH by mass and a density of 1.46 g/mL. If 125 mL of this solution is diluted to a final volume of 1.50 L, what is the molarity of the resulting solution?

12.29 A solution of formic acid, $HCHO_2$, is 23.6 M and has a density of 1.20 g/mL. What is the concentration of the solution in terms of percent $HCHO_2$ by mass?

12.30 A solution of perchloric acid, $HClO_4$, is 11.7 M and has a density of 1.67 g/mL. What is the concentration of the solution in terms of percent $HClO_4$ by mass?

12.31 What volume of concentrated acetic acid should be used to prepare 250. mL of 6.00 M $HC_2H_3O_2$ solution? See Table 4.1.

12.32 What volume of concentrated nitric acid should be used to prepare 3.50 L of 0.150 M HNO_3 solution? See Table 4.1.

12.33 A 35.0 mL sample of concentrated H_3PO_4 is diluted to a final volume of 250. mL. What is the molarity of the resulting solution? See Table 4.1.

12.34 A 150. mL sample of concentrated NH_3 is diluted to a final volume of 500. mL. What is the molarity of the resulting solution? See Table 4.1.

*12.35 A quantity of sodium was added to water and 50.4 mL of hydrogen gas (measured dry and at STP) together with 175 mL of a solution of NaOH were produced. (a) Write the chemical equation for the reaction. (b) What is the molarity of the NaOH solution?

*12.36 A quantity of sodium peroxide, Na_2O_2, was added to water and 84.0 mL of oxygen gas (measured dry and at STP) together with 125 mL of a solution of NaOH were produced. (a) Write the chemical equation for the reaction. (b) What is the molarity of the NaOH solution?

12.37 What is the mole fraction of solute in a 1.00 m solution in which toluene (C_7C_8) is the solvent?

12.38 What is the mole fraction of solute in a 1.00 m solution in which cyclohexane (C_6H_{12}) is the solvent?

12.39 What is the molality of an aqueous solution of sucrose ($C_{12}H_{22}O_{11}$) that is 12.5% $C_{12}H_{22}O_{11}$ by mass?

12.40 What is the molality of an aqueous solution of urea (CON_2H_4) that is 10.0% CON_2H_4 by mass?

Vapor Pressure, Freezing Point, Boiling Point of Solutions

12.41 Methyl alcohol, CH_3OH, and ethyl alcohol, C_2H_5OH, form ideal solutions. At 50.°C, the vapor pressure of pure methyl alcohol is 0.529 atm, and the vapor pressure of pure ethyl alcohol is 0.292 atm. What is the vapor pressure at 50.°C of a solution containing 24.00 g of methyl alcohol and 5.76 g of ethyl alcohol?

12.42 Heptane, C_7H_{16}, and octane, C_8H_{18}, form ideal solutions. At 80.°C, the vapor pressure of pure heptane is 0.561 atm, and the vapor pressure of pure octane is 0.230 atm. What is the vapor pressure at 80.°C of a solution containing 20.0 g of heptane and 98.0 g of octane?

12.43 Use the data given in Problem 12.41 to find the mole fraction of methyl alcohol in a solution containing methyl alcohol and ethyl alcohol if the solution has a vapor pressure of 0.400 atm at 50.°C.

12.44 Use the data given in Problem 12.42 to find the mole fraction of octane in a solution containing heptane and octane if the solution has a vapor pressure of 0.500 atm at 80.°C.

12.45 Benzene, C_6H_6, and toluene, C_7H_8, form ideal solutions. At 90.°C, the vapor pressure of pure benzene is 1.326 atm, and the vapor pressure of pure toluene is 0.532 atm. What is the mole fraction of toluene in a solution that boils at 90.°C and 1.000 atm pressure?

12.46 Chloroform, $CHCl_3$, and carbon tetrachloride, CCl_4, form ideal solutions. At 70.°C, the vapor pressure of pure chloroform is 1.341 atm, and the vapor pressure of pure carbon tetrachloride is 0.819 atm. What is the mole fraction of chloroform in a solution that boils at 70.°C and 1.000 atm pressure?

12.47 A solution containing 1.00 mol of acetone and 1.50 mol of chloroform has a vapor pressure of 0.329 atm at 35°C. At this temperature, the vapor pressure of pure acetone is 0.453 atm, and the vapor pressure of pure chloroform is 0.388 atm. (a) What would the vapor pres-

sure of this solution be if the components formed ideal solutions? (b) Does the vapor pressure of the solution show a positive or a negative deviation from that predicted by Raoult's law? (c) Is heat evolved or absorbed when this solution is prepared? (d) Do acetone and chloroform form a minimum- or maximum-boiling azeotrope?

12.48 A solution containing 0.250 mol of ethyl alcohol and 0.375 mol of chloroform has a vapor pressure of 0.328 atm at 35°C. At this temperature, the vapor pressure of pure ethyl alcohol is 0.136 atm, and the vapor pressure of pure chloroform is 0.388 atm. (a) What would the vapor pressure of this solution be if the components formed ideal solutions? (b) Does the vapor pressure of the solution show a positive or a negative deviation from that predicted by Raoult's law? (c) Is heat evolved or absorbed when this solution is prepared? (d) Do ethyl alcohol and chloroform form a minimum- or a maximum-boiling azeotrope?

12.49 A solution prepared from 96.0 g of a nonvolatile, nondissociating solute in 5.25 mole of toluene has a vapor pressure of 0.161 atm at 60.°C. What is the molecular weight of the solute? The vapor pressure of pure toluene at 60.°C is 0.184 atm.

12.50 A solution prepared from 196 g of a nonvolatile, nondissociating solute in 5.00 mole of water has a vapor pressure of 0.312 atm at 75°C. What is the molecular weight of the solute? The vapor pressure of pure water at 75°C is 0.380 atm.

12.51 The antifreeze commonly used in car radiators is ethylene glycol, $C_2H_4(OH)_2$. How many grams of ethylene glycol should be added to 1.00 kg of water to produce a solution that freezes at $-15.0°C$?

12.52 How many grams of glucose, $C_6H_{12}O_6$, should be added to 250. g of water to produce a solution that freezes at $-2.50°C$?

12.53 A solution that contains 4.32 g of naphthalene, $C_{10}H_8$, in 150. g of ethylene dibromide freezes at 7.13°C. The normal freezing point of ethylene dibromide is 9.79°C. What is the freezing point constant, k_f, for ethylene dibromide?

12.54 A solution that contains 14.8 g of naphthalene, $C_{10}H_8$, in 300. g of nitrobenzene freezes at 3.00°C. The normal freezing point of nitrobenzene is 5.70°C. What is the freezing point constant, k_f, for nitrobenzene?

12.55 What is the freezing point of a solution that contains 64.3 g of sucrose, $C_{12}H_{22}O_{11}$, in 200. g of water?

12.56 What is the freezing point of a solution that contains 6.10 g of benzoic acid, $HC_7H_5O_2$, in 125 g of camphor?

12.57 A solution that contains 13.2 g of solute in 250. g of CCl_4 freezes at $-33.0°C$. What is the molecular weight of the solute?

12.58 A solution that contains 22.0 g of ascorbic acid (vitamin C) in 100. g of water freezes at $-2.33°C$. What is the molecular weight of ascorbic acid?

12.59 What is the boiling point of a solution that contains 40.5 g of glycerol, $C_3H_5(OH)_3$, in 100. g of water?

12.60 What is the boiling point of a solution that contains 12.5 g of biphenyl, $C_{12}H_{10}$, in 100. g of bromobenzene? The normal boiling point of bromobenzene is 156.0°C, and k_b for bromobenzene is +6.26°C/m.

12.61 A solution that contains 3.86 g of X in 150. g of ethyl acetate boils at 78.21°C. What is the molecular weight of X? The normal boiling point of ethyl acetate is 77.06°C, and k_b for ethyl acetate is +2.77°C/m.

12.62 Lauryl alcohol is obtained from coconut oil and is used to make detergents. A solution of 5.00 g of lauryl alcohol in 100. g of benzene boils at 80.78°C. What is the molecular weight of lauryl alcohol?

Osmotic Pressure

12.63 What is the osmotic pressure of an aqueous solution that contains 2.00 g of glucose ($C_6H_{12}O_6$) in 250. mL of solution at 25°C?

12.64 What is the osmotic pressure of an aqueous solution that contains 6.00 g of urea (CON_2H_4) in 400. mL of solution at 20°C?

12.65 A solution that contains 9.30 g hemoglobin per 200. mL of solution has an osmotic pressure of 0.0171 atm at 27°C. What is the molecular weight of hemoglobin?

12.66 An aqueous solution that contains 0.157 g of penicillin G in 100. mL of solution has an osmotic pressure of 0.115 atm at 25°C. What is the molecular weight of penicillin G?

12.67 An aqueous solution containing 1.00 g/L of the ethoxylate of lauryl alcohol has an osmotic pressure of 0.0448 atm at 20°C. What is the molecular weight of this solute?

12.68 An aqueous solution containing 4.50 g of a protein in 100. mL of solution has an osmotic pressure of 0.0157 atm at 25°C. What is the molecular weight of the protein?

12.69 A protein has a molecular weight of 3000. The osmotic pressure of a saturated solution of this protein in water is 0.274 atm at 25°C. **(a)** How many grams of the protein are dissolved in one liter of the saturated solution? **(b)** What is the molarity of the solution?

12.70 The molecular weight of codeine is 317. The osmotic pressure of a saturated solution of codeine in water is 0.641 atm at 25°C. **(a)** How many grams of codeine are dissolved in one liter of the saturated solution? **(b)** What is the molarity of the solution?

Solutions of Electrolytes

12.71 A solution containing 2.00 g of $CaCl_2$ in 98.00 g of water freezes at −0.880°C. What is the van't Hoff factor, i, for the freezing point of this solution?

12.72 A solution containing 0.200 g of $NiSO_4$ in 19.800 g of water freezes at −0.150°C. What is the van't Hoff factor, i, for the freezing point of this solution?

12.73 A solution is prepared from 3.00 g of NaOH and 75.00 g of water. If the van't Hoff factor, i, for the freezing point of this solution is 1.83, at what temperature will the solution freeze?

12.74 A solution is prepared from 3.81 g of $MgCl_2$ in a volume of 400. mL. The van't Hoff factor, i, for the osmotic pressure of this solution at 25°C is 2.61. What is the osmotic pressure of the solution at 25°C?

12.75 What is the freezing point of a 0.125 m aqueous solution of a weak acid, HX, if the acid is 4.00% ionized? Ignore interionic attractions.

12.76 A 0.0200 m solution of a weak acid, HY, in water freezes at −0.0385°C. Ignore interionic attractions and calculate the percentage ionization of the weak acid.

Unclassified Problems

12.77 How does the sign of an enthalpy of solution determine the effect of a temperature change on the solubility of a solute?

12.78 The lattice energy of LiF is −1049.0 kJ/mol and of LiCl is −862.0 kJ/mol. The enthalpy of hydration at 298 K for the preparation of a dilute solution for LiF is −1044.3 kJ/mol and for LiCl is −899.0 kJ/mol. Calculate the enthalpy of solution for the preparation of a dilute solution of each of these compounds at 298 K. Compare the values for the three energy measurements for LiF to those for LiCl. Why do they vary in the way observed?

12.79 The volume of a solution changes as the temperature changes. Thus, a concentration of a given solution determined at one temperature may not be correct for the same solution at another temperature. Which methods of expressing concentrations yield results that are temperature-independent and which yield results that are temperature-dependent?

*12.80 A given aqueous solution has a density of x g/mL and is $y\%$ solute by mass. Derive a mathematical equation relating the molarity of the solution, M, to the molality of the solution, m.

12.81 Liquids A and B form ideal solutions. The vapor pressure of pure A is 0.700 atm at the normal boiling point of a solution prepared from 0.250 mol of B and 0.650 mol of A. What is the vapor pressure of pure B at this temperature?

*12.82 A solution containing 20.0 g of a nonvolatile solute in exactly 1.00 mol of a volatile solvent has a vapor pressure of 0.500 atm at 20.°C. A second mole of solvent is added to the mixture, and the resulting solution has a vapor pressure of 0.550 atm at 20.°C **(a)** What is the molecular weight of the solute? **(b)** What is the vapor pressure of the pure solvent at 20.°C?

*12.83 Air is approximately 80.0% N_2 and 20.0% O_2 by volume. **(a)** What are the partial pressures of N_2 and O_2 in air if the total pressure is 1.000 atm? **(b)** Henry's law may be stated as $p = KX$, where p is the partial pressure of the gas over a saturated solution, X is the mole fraction of the dissolved gas, and K is a constant. At $0.°C$, the values of K for N_2 and O_2 are 5.38×10^4 atm and 2.51×10^4 atm, respectively. What are the mole fractions of N_2 and O_2 in a saturated aqueous solution at $0°C$ under a pressure of 1.000 atm? **(b)** What is the freezing point of the solution?

12.84 A solution that contains a certain quantity of X dissolved in 75.0 g of acetic acid freezes at $14.40°C$. A solution that contains this same quantity of X dissolved in 75.0 g of cyclohexane boils at $82.32°C$. The normal freezing point of acetic acid is $16.60°C$ and k_f for acetic acid is $-3.90°$ C/m. The normal boiling point of cyclohexane is $80.74°C$. What is the boiling point constant, k_b for cyclohexane?

12.85 A solution that contains 4.20 g of X in $200.$ g of chloroform boils at $62.29°C$. What is the molecular weight of X?

12.86 (a) Insulin has an approximate molecular weight of 5700, but in water solution it forms a dimer with a molecular weight of $11,400$. What is the osmotic pressure of an aqueous solution that contains 0.250 g of insulin in 50.0 mL of solution at $20°C$? **(b)** Assuming that the density of the insulin solution is 1.00 g/cm^3, what is the difference in height between the two arms of an apparatus similar to that shown in Figure 12.6? Since mercury has a density of 13.6 g/cm^3 and water has a density of 1.00 g/cm^3, in the measurement of pressure, the height of a column of water is 13.6 times the height of a column of mercury.

12.87 A solution prepared by adding a given mass of a solute to 20.0 g of benzene freezes at a temperature $0.384°C$ below the freezing point of pure benzene. The freezing point of a solution prepared from the same mass of the solute and 20.0 g of water freezes at $-0.4185°C$. Assume that the solute is undissociated in benzene solution but is completely dissociated into ions in water solution. How many ions result from the ionization of one molecule in water solution?

CHAPTER 13   REACTIONS IN AQUEOUS SOLUTION

Reactions that are run in aqueous solution are usually rapid for several reasons. The reactants are in a small state of subdivision (solutes exist as molecules or ions rather than as aggregates of these). The attractions between the particles of pure solute (molecules or ions) are at least partially overcome when the solution is prepared. These particles are free to move about through the solution, and a proportion of the ensuing collisions between solute particles results in reaction. In this chapter, we will discuss several types of reactions that take place in aqueous solution.

13.1 Metathesis Reactions

A methathesis reaction has the general form

$$AB + CD \longrightarrow AD + CB$$

In the reaction, the cations and anions of the substances involved exchange partners. This type of reaction is a common one, particularly in aqueous solution.

A specific example of a metathesis reaction is

$$AgNO_3(aq) + NaCl(aq) \longrightarrow AgCl(s) + NaNO_3(aq)$$

Since we are talking about reactions in aqueous solution, the symbol (aq) will be omitted from future examples. The symbols (g) for gaseous and (s) for solid, however, will be used.

The preceding equation is written using *complete formulas* for the compounds involved. These substances, however, are ionic. A solution of a soluble ionic substance in water contains hydrated ions. The equation can be written using *ionic formulas* for the compounds involved—although the complete formula for the insoluble AgCl(s) is used:

$$Ag^+ + NO_3^- + Na^+ + Cl^- \longrightarrow AgCl(s) + Na^+ + NO_3^-$$

Why did the reaction occur? Collisions of the Ag^+ and Cl^- ions result in the formation of AgCl, which is insoluble and falls out of solution. An insoluble substance formed in this way is called a **precipitate,** and the process is called a **precipitation.** Sodium nitrate ($NaNO_3$), the other product of the reaction, is soluble in water and remains in solution in the form of hydrated ions.

Settling ponds in which magnesium hydroxide is precipitated from seawater. The $Mg(OH)_2$ is produced by a metathesis reaction between the Mg ions of seawater and OH^- ions from $Ca(OH)_2$, which is added. The $Mg(OH)_2$ is used in a process for the production of Mg metal (see Section 25.5). *Dow Chemical U.S.A.*

If we eliminate the spectator ions (ions that appear on both sides of the equation and hence do not enter into the reaction), we get the *net ionic form* of the equation:

$$Ag^+ + Cl^- \longrightarrow AgCl(s)$$

This is the most general form of the equation. It tells us that a solution of any soluble Ag^+ salt and a solution of any soluble Cl^- salt will produce insoluble AgCl when mixed.

Suppose that we mix solutions of NaCl and NH_4NO_3. The ionic equation for the "reaction" is

$$Na^+ + Cl^- + NH_4^+ + NO_3^- \longrightarrow Na^+ + NO_3^- + NH_4^+ \rightarrow Cl^-$$

All of the compounds involved in the "reaction" are soluble in water. If we eliminate spectator ions from the equation, nothing is left. There is, therefore, no reaction, which is usually indicated in the following way:

$$Na^+ + Cl^- + NH_4^+ + NO_3^- \longrightarrow N.R.$$

There are other reasons for a metathesis reaction to occur in addition to the formation of an insoluble solid. Consider the reaction that occurs when a hydrochloric acid solution and a solution of sodium sulfide are mixed:

complete formulas for compounds:
$$2\,HCl + Na_2S \longrightarrow H_2S(g) + 2\,NaCl$$

ionic formulas:
$$2\,H^+ + 2\,Cl^- + 2\,Na^+ + S^{2-} \longrightarrow H_2S(g) + 2\,Na^+ + 2\,Cl^-$$

net ionic equation:
$$2\,H^+ + S^{2-} \longrightarrow H_2S(g)$$

In this reaction, collisions of the H^+ and S^{2-} ions have formed a gas, H_2S, which is only slightly soluble and which escapes from the solution.

In a third type of metathesis reaction, a weak electrolyte is produced. Soluble weak electrolytes do not dissociate completely into ions in aqueous solution. They exist principally in the form of molecules. An acid-base neutralization reaction (see Section 13.4) is a metathesis reaction of this type:

complete formulas for compounds: $HCl + NaOH \longrightarrow H_2O + NaCl$

ionic formulas: $H^+ + Cl^- + Na^+ + OH^- \longrightarrow H_2O + Na^+ + Cl^-$

net ionic equation: $H^+ + OH^- \longrightarrow H_2O$

The reaction occurs because the H^+ and OH^- ions form H_2O molecules, and water is a weak electrolyte.

Metathesis reactions, then, occur when a precipitate, an insoluble gas, or a weak electrolyte is formed. In ionic equations for these reactions,

1. A *soluble salt* is indicated by the formulas of the ions that make up the compound.

2. An *insoluble* or *slightly soluble compound* is indicated by the complete formula of the compound followed by the symbol (s).

3. An *insoluble* or *slightly soluble gas* is indicated by the molecular formula of the gas followed by the symbol (g).

4. A *weak electrolyte* is indicated by the molecular formula of the compound. Weak electrolytes are partly dissociated into ions in aqueous solution, but they exist principally in molecular form.

In order to write equations for metathesis reactions, we need to identify these types of compounds. The following rules are designed for this purpose:

1. Solubility rules.   The classification of ionic substances according to their solubility in water is difficult. Nothing is completely "insoluble" in water. The degree of solubility varies greatly from one "soluble" substance to another. Nevertheless, a solubility classification scheme is useful even though it must be regarded as approximate. The rules given in Table 13.1 apply to compounds of the following cations:

   a. *1 + cations.* Li^+, Na^+, K^+, Rb^+, Cs^+, NH_4^+, Ag^+

   b. *2 + cations.* Mg^{2+}, Ca^{2+}, Sr^{2+}, Ba^{2+}, Mn^{2+}, Fe^{2+}, Co^{2+}, Ni^{2+}, Cu^{2+}, Zn^{2+}, Cd^{2+}, Hg^{2+}, Hg_2^{2+}, Sn^{2+}, Pb^{2+}

   c. *3 + cations.* Fe^{3+}, Al^{3+}, Cr^{3+}

Compounds that dissolve to the extent of at least 10 g/L at 25°C are listed as *soluble*. Those that fail to dissolve to the extent of 1 g/L are classed as *insoluble*. Compounds with solubilities that are intermediate between these limits are listed as *slightly soluble* (and marked with a star in the table). These standards are common but arbitrary. The common inorganic acids are soluble in water. These compounds dissolve in water to produce H^+(aq) ions (see Section 13.4).

2. Gases.   Common gases formed in metathesis reactions are listed in Table 13.2. Reactions in which three of the gases (CO_2, SO_2, and NH_3) are produced may be viewed as involving the initial formation of a substance that then breaks down

Table 13.1	Solubilities of some ionic compounds in water[a]
	Mainly Water-Soluble
NO_3^-	All nitrates are soluble.
$C_2H_3O_2^-$	All acetates are soluble.
ClO_3^-	All chlorates are soluble.
Cl^-	All chlorides are soluble except $AgCl$, Hg_2Cl_2, and $PbCl_2^*$.
Br^-	All bromides are soluble except $AgBr$, Hg_2Br_2, $PbBr_2^*$, and $HgBr_2^*$.
I^-	All iodides are soluble except AgI, Hg_2I_2, PbI_2, and HgI_2.
SO_4^{2-}	All sulfates are soluble except $CaSO_4^*$, $SrSO_4$, $BaSO_4$, $PbSO_4$, Hg_2SO_4, and $Ag_2SO_4^*$.
	Mainly Water-Insoluble
S^{2-}	All sulfides are insoluble except those of the I A and II A elements and $(NH_4)_2S$.
CO_3^{2-}	All carbonates are insoluble except those of the I A elements and $(NH_4)_2CO_3$.
SO_3^{2-}	All sulfites are insoluble except those of the I A elements and $(NH_4)_2SO_3$.
PO_4^{3-}	All phosphates are insoluble except those of the I A elements and $(NH_4)_3PO_4$.
OH^-	All hydroxides are insoluble except those of the I A elements, $Ba(OH)_2$, $Sr(OH)_2^*$, and $Ca(OH)_2^*$.

[a] The following cations are considered: those of the I A and II A families, NH_4^+, Ag^+, Al^{3+}, Cd^{2+}, Co^{2+}, Cr^{3+}, Cu^{2+}, Fe^{2+}, Fe^{3+}, Hg_2^{2+}, Hg^{2+}, Mn^{2+}, Ni^{2+}, Pb^{2+}, Sn^{2+}, and Zn^{2+}.

* Soluble compounds dissolve to the extent of at least 10 g/L at $25°C$. Slightly soluble compounds (marked with an *) dissolve to the extent of from 1 g/L to 10 g/L at $25°C$.

Table 13.2	Rules for the formation of some common gases by metathesis reactions
	Gas
H_2S	Any sulfide (salt of S^{2-}) and any acid form $H_2S(g)$ and a salt.
CO_2	Any carbonate (salt of CO_3^{2-}) and any acid form $CO_2(g)$, H_2O, and a salt.
SO_2	Any sulfite (salt of SO_3^{2-}) and any acid form $SO_2(g)$, H_2O, and a salt.
NH_3	Any ammonium salt (salt of NH_4^+) and any soluble strong hydroxide react upon heating to form $NH_3(g)$, H_2O, and a salt.

to give the gas and H_2O. The reaction of Na_2SO_3 and HCl, for example, produces H_2SO_3:

$$2\,Na^+ + SO_3^{2-} + 2\,H^+ + 2\,Cl^- \longrightarrow H_2SO_3 + 2\,Na^+ + 2\,Cl^-$$

The H_2SO_3 is unstable and decomposes to give H_2O and SO_2:

$$H_2SO_3 \longrightarrow H_2O + SO_2(g)$$

The ionic equation for the complete reaction, therefore, is:

$$2\,Na^+ + SO_3^{2-} + 2\,H^+ + 2\,Cl^- \longrightarrow H_2O + SO_2(g) + 2\,Na^+ + 2\,Cl^-$$

The net ionic equation for the reaction is:

$$SO_3^{2-} + 2H^+ \longrightarrow H_2O + SO_2(g)$$

A typical reaction of a carbonate and an acid is:

$$2K^+ + CO_3^{2-} + 2H^+ + 2NO_3^- \longrightarrow H_2O + CO_2(g) + 2K^+ + 2NO_3^-$$

The net ionic equation for this reaction is:

$$CO_3^{2-} + 2H^+ \longrightarrow H_2O + CO_2(g)$$

Ammonium salts and soluble strong bases react in the following way (particularly when the solution is warmed):

$$NH_4^+ + Cl^- + Na^+ + OH^- \longrightarrow H_2O + NH_3(g) + Na^+ + Cl^-$$

The net ionic equation for the reaction of an ammonium salt and a strong base is:

$$NH_4^+ + OH^- \longrightarrow NH_3(g) + H_2O$$

3. **Weak electrolytes.** A simplified list of rules follows (see Section 13.4):

a. Acids. The common strong acids are $HClO_4$, $HClO_3$, HCl, HBr, HI, HNO_3, and H_2SO_4 (first ionization only). Other common acids are weak electrolytes ($HC_2H_3O_2$, H_3PO_4, and HNO_2 are examples of weak acids).

b. Bases. The soluble hydroxides (those of the I A elements and Ba^{2+}) and the slightly soluble hydroxides (those of Ca^{2+} and Sr^{2+}) are strong electrolytes. Most other hydroxides (those of Ca^{2+} and Sr^{2+}) are strong electrolytes. Most other hydroxides are insoluble.

c. Salts. Most common salts are strong electrolytes.

d. Water. Water is a weak electrolyte.

Example 13.1

Write balanced ionic equations for the reactions that occur when aqueous solutions of the following pairs of compounds are mixed. Show all substances (both reactants and products) in proper form:

(a) $FeCl_3$ and $(NH_4)_3PO_4$
(b) Na_2SO_4 and $CuCl_2$
(c) $ZnSO_4$ and $Ba(OH)_2$
(d) $CaCO_3$ and HNO_3

Solution

(a) $Fe^{3+} + 3Cl^- + 3NH_4^+ + PO_4^{3-} \longrightarrow FePO_4(s) + 3NH_4^+ + 3Cl^-$
(b) $2Na^+ + SO_4^{2-} + Cu^{2+} + 2Cl^- \longrightarrow$ N.R.

(c) $Zn^{2+} + SO_4^{2-} + Ba^{2+} + 2\,OH^- \longrightarrow Zn(OH)_2(s) + BaSO_4(s)$

(d) $CaCO_3(s) + 2\,H^+ + 2\,NO_3^- \longrightarrow H_2O + CO_2(g) + Ca^{2+} + 2\,NO_3^-$

Metathesis reactions are reversible to some extent. Aqueous equilibrium systems of this type are discussed in Chapters 17 and 18.

Metathesis reactions also occur in the absence of water. Examples are:

$$CaF_2(s) + H_2SO_4(l) \longrightarrow CaSO_4(s) + 2\,HF(g)$$
$$2\,NaNO_3(s) + H_2SO_4(l) \longrightarrow Na_2SO_4(s) + 2\,HNO_3(g)$$

The reactants in these reactions are heated, and the acids (HF and HNO_3, which are soluble in water) are driven off as gases.

13.2 Oxidation Numbers

An important type of reaction that occurs in aqueous solution, the oxidation-reduction reaction, is discussed in the next section. Before this type of reaction is considered, however, we must discuss the concept of oxidation numbers, an arbitary but useful convention.

Oxidation numbers are charges (fictitious charges in the case of covalent species) assigned to the atoms of a compound according to some arbitrary rules. The oxidation numbers of monatomic ions are the same as the charges on the ions. In NaCl, for example, the oxidation number of sodium in Na^+ is $1+$ and the oxidation number of chlorine in Cl^- is $1-$.

The oxidation numbers of the atoms in a covalent molecule can be derived by assigning the electrons of each bond to the more electronegative of the bonded atoms. For the molecule

$$H\!:\!\ddot{C}\!l\!:$$

both electrons of the covalent bond are assigned to the chlorine atom since chlorine is more electronegative than hydrogen. The chlorine atom is said to have an oxidation number of $1-$ since the assignment has given it one more electron than it has as a neutral atom. The hydrogen atom is said to have an oxidation number of $1+$ because its only valence electron has been assigned to the chlorine atom.

In the case of a nonpolar bond between identical atoms, in which there is no electronegativity difference, the bonding electrons are divided equally between the bonded atoms in deriving oxidation numbers. Thus, the oxidation numbers of both chlorine atoms are zero in the molecule

$$:\!\ddot{C}\!l\!:\!\ddot{C}\!l\!:$$

The following rules, based on these ideas, can be used to assign oxidation numbers:

1. Any uncombined atom or any atom in a molecule of an element is assigned an oxidation number of zero.

2. The sum of the oxidation numbers of the atoms in a compound is zero, since compounds are electrically neutral.

3. The oxidation number of a monatomic ion is the same as the charge on the ion. In their compounds, group I A metals (Li, Na, K, Rb, and Cs) always have oxidation numbers of $1+$, group II A elements (Be, Mg, Ca, Sr, and Ba) always have oxidation numbers of $2+$.

4. The sum of the oxidation numbers of the atoms that constitute a polyatomic ion equals the charge on the ion.

5. The oxidation number of fluorine, the most electronegative element, is $1-$ in all fluorine-containing compounds.

6. In most oxygen-containing compounds, the oxidation number of oxygen is $2-$. There are, however, a few exceptions:

    a. In peroxides each oxygen has an oxidation number of $1-$. The two O atoms of the peroxide ion, O_2^{2-}, are equivalent. Each must be assigned an oxidation number of $1-$ so that the sum equals the charge on the ion.

    b. In the superoxide ion, O_2^-, each oxygen has an oxidation number of $\frac{1}{2}-$.

    c. In OF_2 the oxygen has an oxidation number of $2+$ (see rule 5).

7. The oxidation number of hydrogen is $1+$ in all its compounds except the metallic hydrides (CaH_2 and NaH are examples), in which hydrogen is in the $1-$ oxidation state.

8. In a combination of two nonmetals (either a molecule or a polyatomic ion) the oxidation number of the more electronegative element is negative and equal to the charge on the common monatomic ion of that element. In PCl_3, for example, the oxidation number of Cl is $1-$, and of P is $3+$. In CS_2, the oxidation number of S is $2-$, and of C is $4+$.

Example 13.2

What is the oxidation number of the P atom in H_3PO_4?

Solution

The oxidation numbers of the molecule must add up to zero. Therefore,

$$3(ox. \ no. \ H) + (ox. \ no. \ P) + 4(ox. \ no. \ O) = 0$$

Let x equal the oxidation number of P. Each H is assigned an oxidation number of $1+$ (see rule 7), and each O is assigned an oxidation number of $2-$ (see rule 6):

$$3(1+) + x + 4(2-) = 0$$
$$x = 5+$$

Example 13.3

What is the oxidation number of Cr in the dichromate ion, $Cr_2O_7^{2-}$?

Solution

Let x equal the oxidation number of Cr. The sum of the oxidation numbers must equal the charge of the ion, $2-$. The oxidation number of O is $2-$ (see rule 6):

$$2(ox.\ no.\ Cr) + 7(ox.\ no.\ O) = 2-$$
$$2x + 7(2-) = 2-$$
$$2x = 12+$$
$$x = 6+$$

Notice that oxidation state of an element is reported on the basis of a single atom. It would be misleading to say that oxygen has an oxidation number of $2-$ in H_2O and $4-$ in SO_2. In both compounds, the O atom has an oxidation number of $2-$.

Example 13.4

What is the oxidation number of Cl in calcium perchlorate, $Ca(ClO_4)_2$?

Solution

$$(ox.\ no.\ Ca) + 2(ox.\ no.\ Cl) + 8(ox.\ no.\ O) = 0$$

Let x equal the oxidation number of Cl. Since Ca is a member of group II A, its oxidation number is $2+$, which is the charge on a Ca^{2+} ion. The oxidation number of O is $2-$. Therefore,

$$(2+) + 2x + 8(2-) = 0$$
$$2x = 14+$$
$$x = 7+$$

There is another way to solve problems of this type. Since the charge on the Ca^{2+} ion is $2+$, and since there are two perchlorate ions for every one Ca^{2+} ion in the compound, the charge on the perchlorate ion must be $1-$. The ion has the formula ClO_4^-. Therefore,

$$(ox.\ no.\ Cl) + 4(ox.\ no.\ O) = 1-$$
$$x + 4(2-) = 1-$$
$$x = 7+$$

These values should be interpreted with care. The ionic charges have physical significance; the oxidation numbers of O and Cl are merely conventions, although useful ones.

Frequently an element exhibits a range of oxidation numbers in its compounds. Nitrogen, for example, exhibits oxidation numbers from $3-$ (as in NH_3) to $5+$ (as in HNO_3).

1. The highest oxidation number of an A family element is the same as its group number. The number of valence electrons that an A family element has is equal to its group number. It is not logical to expect an atom to lose more valence electrons than it has. The highest possible charge—even a hypothetical one, therefore—is the same as the group number.

2. The lowest oxidation number of an A family element in a compound containing the element is the same as the charge of a monatomic ion of the element.

The highest oxidation number of sulfur (a member of group VI A) is $6+$ (in H_2SO_4, for example). The lowest oxidation number of sulfur is $2-$ (as in Na_2S and H_2S). In its compounds, the highest oxidation number of sodium (found in group I A) is the same as the lowest oxidation number, $1+$. The oxidation number of uncombined sodium is, of course, zero. There are, however, exceptions to these generalizations (fluorine and oxygen, for example).

Oxidation numbers are not the same as formal charges. In the assignment of formal charges to the atoms of a covalent molecule, the bonding electrons are divided equally between the bonded atoms, and any bond polarity caused by the unequal sharing of electrons is ignored. In the assignment of oxidation numbers, the bonding electrons are assigned to the more electronegative atom. Both concepts are merely conventions. Formal charges are useful in interpreting the structure and some of the properties of covalent molecules. Oxidation numbers are useful in many ways. They can be used to help in writing formulas, in systematizing the chemistry of the elements, in recognizing and organizing oxidation-reduction phenomena, and in balancing oxidation-reduction equations.

13.3 Oxidation-Reduction Reactions

The term *oxidation* was originally applied to reactions in which substances combined with oxygen, and *reduction* was defined as the removal of oxygen from an oxygen-containing compound. The meanings of the terms have gradually been broadened. Today *oxidation* and *reduction* are defined on the basis of change in oxidation number.

Oxidation is the process in which an atom undergoes an algebraic increase in oxidation number, and **reduction** is the process in which an atom undergoes an algebraic decrease in oxidation number. On this basis, oxidation-reduction is involved in the reaction

$$\underset{0}{S} + \underset{0}{O_2} \longrightarrow \underset{4+\ 2-}{S\ O_2}$$

The oxidation number of each type of atom is written below its symbol. Since the oxidation number of the S atom *increases* from 0 to $4+$, sulfur is said to be *oxidized*. The oxidation number of the O atom *decreases* from 0 to $2-$, and oxygen is said to be *reduced*. Oxidation-reduction is not involved in the reaction

$$S\ O_2 + H_2\ O \longrightarrow H_2\ S\ O_3$$
$$4+\ 2-1+\ 2-1+4+2-$$

since no atom undergoes a change in oxidation number.

It is apparent, from the way in which oxidation numbers are assigned, that *neither oxidation nor reduction can occur by itself.* Furthermore, *the total increase in oxidation number must equal the total decrease in oxidation number.* In the reaction of sulfur and oxygen, the sulfur undergoes an increase of 4. Each oxygen atom undergoes a decrease of 2. Since two O atoms appear in the equation, the total decrease is 4.

Since one substance cannot be reduced unless another is simultaneously oxidized, the substance that is reduced is responsible for the oxidation. This substance is called, therefore, the **oxidizing agent** or **oxidant.** Because of the interdependence of the two processes, the opposite is also true. The material that is itself oxidized is called the **reducing agent** or **reductant.** Therefore,

$$\underset{\substack{0\\ \textit{oxidized}\\ \textit{reducing agent}}}{S} + \underset{\substack{0\\ \textit{reduced}\\ \textit{oxidizing agent}}}{O_2} \longrightarrow \underset{\substack{4+\ 2-}}{S\ O_2}$$

Equations for oxidation-reduction reactions, which are commonly called redox reactions, are usually more difficult to balance than those for reactions that do not entail oxidation and reduction. Two methods are commonly used to balance oxidation-reduction equations: the ion-electron method and the oxidation-number method. Either of these methods may be used, and both will be discussed. For clarity, the physical state of the reactants and products will not be indicated in the examples that follow. In addition, the symbol H^+, instead of H_3O^+ or $H^+(aq)$, will be used.

The Ion-Electron Method for Balancing Redox Equations

Reactions in which electrons are transferred are clearly examples of oxidation-reduction reactions. In the reaction of sodium and chlorine, a sodium atom loses its valence electron to a chlorine atom:

$$\underset{0}{2\,Na} + \underset{0}{Cl_2} \longrightarrow \underset{1+}{2\,Na^+} + \underset{1-}{2\,Cl^-}$$

For simple ions the oxidation number is the same as the charge on the ion. It follows, then, that electron loss represents a type of oxidation, and electron gain represents a type of reduction. This equation can be divided into two **partial equations** that represent **half reactions:**

Oxidation: $\qquad 2\,Na \longrightarrow 2\,Na^+ + 2e^-$

Reduction: $\quad 2e^- + Cl_2 \longrightarrow 2\,Cl^-$

The **ion-electron method** of balancing oxidation-reduction equations employs partial equations. One partial equation is used for the oxidation (in which electrons are lost), and another partial equation is used for the reduction (in which electrons are gained). The final equation is obtained by combining the partial equations in such a way that the number of electrons lost equals the number of electrons gained.

Two slightly different procedures are employed to balance equations by the ion-electron method. One is used for reactions that take place in acid solution, the other for reactions that occur in alkaline solution. We will give examples of both procedures.

An example of a reaction that occurs in *acid solution* is

$$Cr_2O_7^{2-} + Cl^- \longrightarrow Cr^{3+} + Cl_2$$

In this unbalanced expression, H_2O and H^+ are not shown. The proper numbers of H_2O molecules and H^+ ions, as well as their positions in the final equation (whether on the left or the right), are determined in the course of the balancing:

1. Two skeleton partial equations for the half reactions are written. The central elements of the partial equations (Cr and Cl) are balanced:

$$Cr_2O_7^{2-} \longrightarrow 2\,Cr^{3+}$$

$$2\,Cl^- \longrightarrow Cl_2$$

2. Now the H and O atoms are balanced. Since the reaction occurs in acid solution, H_2O and H^+ can be added where needed. For each O atom that is needed, one H_2O is added to the side that is deficient. The hydrogen is then brought into balance by the addition of H^+.

Seven O atoms are needed on the right side of the first partial equation; therefore, $7H_2O$ are added to this side. The H atoms of the first partial equation are then balanced by the addition of $14H^+$ to the left side. The second partial equation is already in material balance:

$$14H^+ + Cr_2O_7^{2-} \longrightarrow 2Cr^{3+} + 7H_2O$$
$$2Cl^- \longrightarrow Cl_2$$

3. The next step is to balance the partial equations electrically. In the first partial equation, the net charge is $12+$ on the left side of the equation ($14+$ and $2-$) and $6+$ on the right. Six electrons must be added to the left. In this way, the net charge on both sides of the equation will be $6+$. The second partial equation is balanced electrically by the addition of two electrons to the right:

$$6e^- + 14H^+ + Cr_2O_7^{2-} \longrightarrow 2Cr^{3+} + 7H_2O$$
$$2Cl^- \longrightarrow Cl_2 + 2e^-$$

4. The number of electrons gained must equal the number of electrons lost. The second partial equation, therefore, is multiplied through by 3:

$$6e^- + 14H^+ + Cr_2O_7^{2-} \longrightarrow 2Cr^{3+} + 7H_2O$$
$$6Cl^- \longrightarrow 3Cl_2 + 6e^-$$

5. Addition of the two partial equations gives the final equation. In the addition, the electrons cancel:

$$14H^+ + Cr_2O_7^{2-} + 6Cl^- \longrightarrow 2Cr^{3+} + 3Cl_2 + 7H_2O$$

As a second example, consider the reaction

$$MnO_4^- + As_4O_6 \longrightarrow Mn^{2+} + H_3AsO_4$$

which also occurs in *acid solution*. The same steps are followed:

1. The equation is divided into two skeleton partial equations. The As atoms in the second partial equation are balanced:

$$MnO_4^- \longrightarrow Mn^{2+}$$
$$As_4O_6 \longrightarrow 4H_3AsO_4$$

2. The first partial equation can be brought into material balance by the addition of $4H_2O$ to the right side and $8H^+$ to the left side. In the second partial equation, $10H_2O$ must be added to the left side to make up the needed 10 oxygens. If we stopped at this point, there would be 20 hydrogen atoms on the left and 12 on the right. Therefore, $8H^+$ must be added to the right:

$$8H^+ + MnO_4^- \longrightarrow Mn^{2+} + 4H_2O$$
$$10H_2O + As_4O_6 \longrightarrow 4H_3AsO_4 + 8H^+$$

3. To balance the net charges, electrons are added:

$$5e^- + 8\,H^+ + MnO_4^- \longrightarrow Mn^{2+} + 4\,H_2O$$

$$10\,H_2O + As_4O_6 \longrightarrow 4\,H_3AsO_4 + 8\,H^+ + 8e^-$$

4. The first partial equation must be multiplied through by 8 and the second by 5 so that the same number of electrons are lost in the oxidation partial equation as are gained in the reduction partial equation:

$$40e^- + 64\,H^+ + 8\,MnO_4^- \longrightarrow 8\,Mn^{2+} + 32\,H_2O$$

$$50\,H_2O + 5\,As_4O_6 \longrightarrow 20\,H_3AsO_4 + 40\,H^+ + 40e^-$$

5. When these two partial equations are added, water molecules and hydrogen ions must be canceled as well as electrons. It is poor form to leave an equation with $64\,H^+$ on the left and $40\,H^+$ on the right:

$$24\,H^+ + 18\,H_2O + 5\,As_4O_6 + 8\,MnO_4^- \longrightarrow 20\,H_3AsO_4 + 8\,Mn^{2+}$$

Equations for reactions that take place in *alkaline solution* are balanced in a manner slightly different from those that occur in acidic solution. All the steps are the same except the second one; H^+ cannot be used to balance equations for reactions that occur in alkaline solution. As an example, consider the reaction

$$MnO_4^- + N_2H_4 \longrightarrow MnO_2 + N_2$$

that takes place in alkaline solution:

1. The equation is divided into two partial equations:

$$MnO_4^- \longrightarrow MnO_2$$

$$N_2H_4 \longrightarrow N_2$$

2. For reactions occurring in alkaline solution, OH^- and H_2O are used to balance oxygen and hydrogen. For each oxygen that is needed, one H_2O molecule is added to the side of the partial equation that is deficient. The hydrogen is balanced next. For each hydrogen that is needed, one H_2O molecule is added to the side that is deficient and one OH^- ion is added to the opposite side.

In the first partial equation, the right side is deficient by two oxygen atoms. We add, therefore, $2\,H_2O$ to the right side:

$$MnO_4^- \longrightarrow MnO_2 + 2\,H_2O$$

The partial equation is now deficient by four hydrogen atoms on the left side. To make up these four hydrogen atoms, we add $4\,H_2O$ to the left side and $4\,OH^-$ to the right:

$$4\,H_2O + MnO_4^- \longrightarrow MnO_2 + 2\,H_2O + 4\,OH^-$$

Elimination $2\,H_2O$ from both sides of the partial equation, we get:

$$2\,H_2O \longrightarrow MnO_4^- \longrightarrow MnO_2 + 4\,OH^-$$

In order to bring the second partial equation into material balance, we must add four hydrogen atoms to the right side. For *each* hydrogen atom needed, we add one H_2O to the side deficient in hydrogen and one OH^- to the opposite side. In the present case we add $4\,H_2O$ to the right side and $4\,OH^-$ to the left to make up the four hydrogen atoms needed on the right:

$$4\,OH^- + N_2H_4 \longrightarrow N_2 + 4\,H_2O$$

3. Electrons are added to effect charge balances:

$$3e^- + 2\,H_2O + MnO_4^- \longrightarrow MnO_2 + 4\,OH^-$$
$$4\,OH^- + N_2H_4 \longrightarrow N_2 + 4\,H_2O + 4e^-$$

4. The lowest common multiple of 3 and 4 is 12. Therefore, the first partial equation is multiplied through by 4 and the second by 3 so that the number of electrons gained equals the number lost:

$$12e^- + 8\,H_2O + 4\,MnO_4^- \longrightarrow 4\,MnO_2 + 16\,OH^-$$
$$12\,OH^- + 3\,N_2H_4 \longrightarrow 3\,N_2 + 12\,H_2O + 12e^-$$

5. Addition of these partial equations, with cancellation of OH^- ions and H_2O molecules as well as electrons, gives the final equation:

$$4\,MnO_4^- + 3\,N_2H_4 \longrightarrow 4\,MnO_2 + 3\,N_2 + 4\,H_2O + 4\,OH^-$$

As a final example, consider the following skeleton equation for a reaction in *alkaline solution:*

$$Br_2 \longrightarrow BrO_3^- + Br^-$$

In this reaction the same substance, Br_2, is both oxidized and reduced. Such reactions are called **disproportionations** or **auto-oxidation-reduction reactions:**

1.
$$Br_2 \longrightarrow 2\,BrO_3^-$$
$$Br_2 \longrightarrow 2\,Br^-$$

2.
$$12\,OH^- + Br_2 \longrightarrow 2\,BrO_3^- + 6\,H_2O$$
$$Br_2 \longrightarrow 2\,Br^-$$

3.
$$12\,OH^- + Br_2 \longrightarrow 2\,BrO_3^- + 6\,H_2O + 10e^-$$
$$2e^- + Br_2 \longrightarrow 2\,Br^-$$

4.
$$12\,OH^- + Br_2 \longrightarrow 2\,BrO_3^- + 6\,H_2O + 10e^-$$
$$10e^- + 5\,Br_2 \longrightarrow 10\,Br^-$$

5. $12\,OH^- + 6\,Br_2 \longrightarrow 2\,BrO_3^- + 10\,Br^- + 6\,H_2O$

When the ion-electron method is applied to a disproportional reaction, the coefficients of the resulting equation usually are divisible by some common number, since one reactant was used in both partial equations. The coefficients of this equation are all divisible by 2 and should be reduced to the lowest possible terms:

$$6\,OH^- + 3\,Br_2 \longrightarrow BrO_3^- + 5\,Br^- + 3\,H_2O$$

Most oxidation-reduction equations may be balanced by the ion-electron method, which is especially convenient for electrochemical reactions and reactions of ions in water solution. However, several misconceptions that can arise must be pointed out. Half reactions cannot occur alone, and partial equations do not represent complete chemical changes. Even in electrochemical cells, where the two half reactions take place at different electrodes, the two half reactions always occur simultaneously.

Whereas the partial equations probably represent an overall, if not detailed, view of the way an oxidation-reduction reaction occurs in an electrochemical cell, the same reaction in a beaker may not take place in this way at all. The method should *not* be interpreted as necessarily giving the correct mechanism by which a reaction occurs. It is, at times, difficult to recognize whether a given reaction is a legitimate example of an electron-exchange reaction. The reaction

$$\underset{4+}{SO_3^{2-}} + \underset{5+}{ClO_3^-} \longrightarrow \underset{6+}{SO_4^{2-}} + \underset{3+}{ClO_2^-}$$

looks like an electron-exchange reaction, can be made to take place in an electrochemical cell, and can be balanced by the ion-electron method. However, this reaction has been shown to proceed by direct oxygen exchange (from ClO_3^- to SO_3^{2-}) and *not* by electron exchange.

The Oxidation-Number Method for Balancing Redox Equations

There are three steps in the oxidation-number method for balancing oxidation-reduction equations. We will use the equation for the reaction of nitric acid and hydrogen sulfide to illustrate this method. The unbalanced expression for the reaction is

$$HNO_3 + H_2S \longrightarrow NO + S + H_2O$$

1. The oxidation numbers of the atoms in the equation are determined in order to identify atoms undergoing oxidation or reduction. Thus,

$$\underset{5+}{HNO_3} + \underset{2-}{H_2S} \longrightarrow \underset{2+}{NO} + \underset{0}{S} + H_2O$$

Nitrogen is reduced (from $5+$ to $2+$, a decrease of 3), and sulfur is oxidized (from $2-$ to 0, an increase of 2).

2. Coefficients are added so that the total decrease and the total increase in oxidation number will be equal. We have a decrease of 3 and an increase of 2 indicated in the unbalanced expression. The lowest common multiple of 3 and 2 is 6. We therefore indicate $2\,HNO_3$ and $2\,NO$ (for a total decrease of 6) and $3\,H_2S$ and $3\,S$ (for a total increase of 6):

$$2\,HNO_3 + 3\,H_2S \longrightarrow 2\,NO + 3\,S + H_2O$$

3. Balancing is completed by inspection. This method takes care of only those substances that are directly involved in oxidation-number change. In this example, the method does not assign a coefficient to H_2O. We note, however, that there are now eight H atoms on the left of the equation. We can indicate the same number of H atoms on the right by showing $4\,H_2O$:

Chapter 13   Reactions in Aqueous Solution

$$2\,HNO_3 + 3\,H_2S \longrightarrow 2\,NO + 3\,S + 4\,H_2O$$

The final, balanced equation should be checked to ensure that there are as many atoms of each element on the right as there are on the left.

The oxidation-number method can also be used to balance net ionic equations, in which only those ions and molecules that take part in the reaction are shown. Consider the reaction between $KClO_3$ and I_2:

$$H_2O + I_2 + ClO_3^- \longrightarrow IO_3^- + Cl^- + H^+$$

The K^+ ion does not take part in the reaction and is not shown in the equation. The steps in balancing the equation follow:

1. $H_2O + \underset{0}{I_2} + \underset{5+}{ClO_3^-} \longrightarrow \underset{5+}{IO_3^-} + \underset{1-}{Cl^-} + H^+$

2. *Each* iodine atom undergoes an increase of 5 (from 0 to 5+), but there are *two* iodine atoms in I_2. The increase in oxidation number is therefore 10. Chlorine undergoes a decrease of 6 (from 5+ to 1−). The lowest common multiple of 6 and 10 is 30. Therefore, $3\,I_2$ molecules must be indicated (a total increase of 30) and $5\,ClO_3^-$ ions are needed (a total decrease of 30). The coefficients of the products, IO_3^- and Cl^-, follow from this assignment:

$$H_2O + 3\,I_2 + 5\,ClO_3^- \longrightarrow 6\,IO_3^- + 5\,Cl^- + H^+$$

3. If H_2O is ignored, there are now 15 oxygen atoms on the left and 18 oxygen atoms on the right. To make up three oxygen atoms on the left, we must indicate $3\,H_2O$ molecules. It then follows that the coefficient of H^+ must be 6 to balance the hydrogens of the H_2O molecules:

$$3\,H_2O + 3\,I_2 + 5\,ClO_3^- \longrightarrow 6\,IO_3^- + 5\,Cl^- + 6\,H^+$$

An ionic equation must indicate charge balance as well as mass balance. Since the algebraic sum of the charges on the left (5−) equals that on the right (5−), the equation is balanced.

3.4 Arrhenius Acids and Bases

The several concepts of acids and bases that are in current use are the topic of Chapter 16. The Arrhenius concept of acids and bases, the oldest of these, is presented in this section.

An **acid** is defined as a substance that dissociates in water to produce H_3O^+ ions, which are sometimes shown as $H^+(aq)$ ions. For example,

$$H-\overset{\cdot\cdot}{\underset{\underset{H}{|}}{O}}: + H-\overset{\cdot\cdot}{\underset{\cdot\cdot}{Cl}}:(g) \longrightarrow \left[H-\overset{\cdot\cdot}{\underset{\underset{H}{|}}{O}}-H\right]^+ (aq) + :\overset{\cdot\cdot}{\underset{\cdot\cdot}{Cl}}:^- (aq)$$

Pure HCl gas consists of covalent molecules. In water, the H^+ (which is nothing more than a proton) of the HCl molecule is strongly attracted by an electron pair of the O atom of a H_2O molecule. The transfer of the proton to the H_2O molecule produces what is called a **hydronium ion** (H_3O^+) and leaves behind a Cl^- ion.

Every ion is hydrated in water solution, which is indicated by the symbol (aq) placed behind the formula of the ion. This symbolism does not give the number of water molecules associated with each ion. The number in most cases is not known and in many cases is variable. The H^+ ion, however, is a special case. The positive charge of the H^+ ion (the proton) is not shielded by any electrons, and in comparison to other ions, the H^+ ion is extremely small. The H^+ ion, therefore, is strongly attracted to an electron pair of a H_2O molecule.

There is, however, evidence that the H_3O^+ ion has three additional water molecules associated with it in an ion that has the formula $H_9O_4^+$. Other evidence supports the idea that several types of hydrated ions exist simultaneously in water solution. Some chemists, therefore, prefer to represent the hydrated proton as $H^+(aq)$. The process in which HCl molecules dissolve in water would be indicated:

$$HCl(g) \longrightarrow H^+(aq) + Cl^-(aq)$$

In the Arrhenius system, a **base** is a substance that contains hydroxide ions, OH^-, or dissolves in water to produce hydrated hydroxide ions, $OH^-(aq)$:

$$NaOH(s) \longrightarrow Na^+(aq) + OH^-(aq)$$

$$Ca(OH)_2(s) \longrightarrow Ca^{2+}(aq) + 2\,OH^-(aq)$$

The only soluble metal hydroxides are those of the group I A elements and $Ba(OH)_2$, $Sr(OH)_2$, and $Ca(OH)_2$ of group II A. Insoluble hydroxides, however, react as bases with acids.

The reaction of an acid and a base is called a **neutralization.** Ionic equations for two neutralization reactions are:

$$Ba^{2+}(aq) + 2\,OH^-(aq) + 2\,H^+(aq) + 2\,Cl^-(aq) \longrightarrow$$
$$Ba^{2+}(aq) + 2\,Cl^-(aq) + 2\,H_2O$$

$$Fe(OH)_3(s) + 3\,H^+(aq) + 3\,NO_3^-(aq) \longrightarrow Fe^{3+}(aq) + 3\,NO_3^-(aq) + 3\,H_2O$$

The barium chloride $(BaCl_2)$ and iron(III) nitrate $[Fe(NO_3)_3]$ produced by these reactions are called **salts,** which are ionic compounds with cations derived from bases and anions derived from acids.

The net ionic equation for both of the preceding neutralization reactions is:

$$H_3O^+(aq) + OH^-(aq) \longrightarrow 2\,H_2O$$

which may also be written:

$$H^+(aq) + OH^-(aq) \longrightarrow H_2O$$

Acids are classified as strong or weak depending upon the extent of their dissociation in water (see Table 13.3). A **strong acid** is 100% dissociated in dilute water solution. The common strong acids are HCl, HBr, HI, HNO_3, H_2SO_4 (first H^+ dissociation only), $HClO_4$, and $HClO_3$. Other common acids are **weak acids,** which are less than 100% dissociated in dilute water solution. Acetic acid $(HC_2H_3O_2)$, for example, is a weak acid:

Table 13.3	Some common acids		

ACIDS
Binary Compounds

Monoprotic Acids		Polyprotic Acids	
HF*	hydrofluoric acid	H_2S*	hydrosulfuric acid
HCl	hydrochloric acid		
HBr	hydrobromic acid		
HI	hydroiodic acid		

Ternary Compounds

Monoprotic Acids		Polyprotic Acids	
HNO_3	nitric acid	H_2SO_4**	sulfuric acid
HNO_2*	nitrous acid	H_2SO_3*	sulfurous acid
$HClO_4$	perchloric acid	H_3PO_4*	phosphoric acid
$HClO_3$	chloric acid		
$HClO_2$*	chlorous acid	H_2CO_3*	carbonic acid
$HOCl$*	hypochlorous acid	H_3BO_3*	boric acid
$HC_2H_3O_2$*	acetic acid		

* Weak acid.
** The second dissociation is weak.

$$H_2O + HC_2H_3O_2(aq) \rightleftharpoons H_3O^+(aq) + C_2H_3O_2^-(aq)$$

The reversible arrow ($\rightleftharpoons$) is used in this equation to show that reactions occur in both directions. In a 1 M solution of acetic acid, a balance is achieved with 0.4% of the $HC_2H_3O_2$ dissociated into ions.

All soluble metal hydroxides are strong bases. After all, these substances are 100% ionic when pure. There are a few molecular weak bases, the most common being an aqueous solution of ammonia, NH_3:

$$NH_3(aq) + H_2O \rightleftharpoons NH_4^+(aq) + OH^-(aq)$$

In this reaction, the ammonia molecule accepts a proton from the water molecule to form the ammonium ion and the hydroxide ion. The reaction, however, is reversible to about the same extent as that for the ionization of acetic acid.

Acids that can lose only one proton per molecule (such as HCl, $HC_2H_3O_2$, and HNO_3) are called **monoprotic acids.** Some acids can lose more than one proton per molecule; they are called **polyprotic acids.** A molecule of sulfuric acid, for example, can lose two protons:

$$H_2SO_4(l) + H_2O \longrightarrow H_3O^+(aq) + HSO_4^-(aq)$$

$$HSO_4^-(aq) + H_2O \rightleftharpoons H_3O^+(aq) + SO_4^{2-}(aq)$$

Only one proton is neutralized if 1 mol of H_2SO_4 is reacted with 1 mol of NaOH:

$$H_2SO_4(aq) + NaOH(aq) \longrightarrow NaHSO_4(aq) + H_2O$$

The salt obtained, $NaHSO_4$, is called an **acid salt** because it contains an acid hydrogen. If 1 mol of H_2SO_4 is reacted with 2 mol of $NaOH$, both acid hydrogens are neutralized. The **normal salt,** Na_2SO_4, is obtained:

$$H_2SO_4(aq) + 2\,NaOH(aq) \longrightarrow Na_2SO_4(aq) + 2\,H_2O$$

The acid salt can be reacted with $NaOH$ to produce the normal salt:

$$NaHSO_4(aq) + NaOH(aq) \longrightarrow Na_2SO_4(aq) + H_2O$$

The products of the neutralization of a polyprotic acid, therefore, depend upon the quantities of acid and base employed.

Phosphoric acid, H_3PO_4, has three acid hydrogens, and three salts (two acid salts as well as the normal salt) can be obtained from it:

$$NaH_2PO_4 \qquad Na_2HPO_4 \qquad Na_3PO_4$$

13.5 Acidic and Basic Oxides

The oxides of metals are called **basic oxides.** The oxides of the group I A metals and those of Ca, Sr, and Ba dissolve in water to produce hydroxides. All these oxides are ionic. When one of them dissolves in water, it is the oxide ion that reacts with the water:

$$O^{2-}(aq) + H_2O \longrightarrow 2\,OH^-(aq)$$

The oxides (as well as the hydroxides) of other metals are insoluble in water.

Nevertheless, metal oxides and hydroxides are chemically related. When heated, most hydroxides (with the notable exception of the hydroxides of the I A metals) are converted into oxides:

$$Mg(OH)_2(s) \longrightarrow MgO(s) + H_2O(g)$$

Metal oxides, as well as hydroxides, can be neutralized by acids:

$$MgO(s) + 2\,H^+(aq) \longrightarrow Mg^{2+}(aq) + H_2O$$

$$Mg(OH)_2(s) + 2\,H^+(aq) \longrightarrow Mg^{2+}(aq) + 2\,H_2O$$

The insoluble Fe_2O_3 (like many other insoluble oxides) will react with acids, even though it will not react with water to produce a hydroxide:

$$Fe_2O_3(s) + 6\,H^+(aq) \longrightarrow 2\,Fe^{3+}(aq) + 3\,H_2O$$

Most of the oxides of the nonmetals are **acidic oxides.** Many of them react with water to produce oxyacids:

$$Cl_2O + H_2O \longrightarrow 2\,HOCl$$

$$Cl_2O_7 + H_2O \longrightarrow 2\,HClO_4$$

Stalactites (from the top) and stalagmites (from the bottom) are icicle-shaped structures composed of calcium carbonate, $CaCO_3$, that occur in caves. They are formed by the evaporation of dripping water containing calcium hydrogen carbonate, $Ca(HCO_3)_2$:

$$Ca^{2+}(ag) + 2\,HCO_3^-(ag) \longrightarrow CaCO_3(s) + H_2O + CO_2(g)$$

Runk/Schoenberger from Grant Heilman.

$$N_2O_5 + H_2O \longrightarrow 2\,HNO_3$$

$$P_4O_{10} + 6\,H_2O \longrightarrow 4\,H_3PO_4$$

$$SO_3 + H_2O \longrightarrow H_2SO_4$$

$$SO_2 + H_2O \rightleftharpoons H_2SO_3$$

$$CO_2 + H_2O \rightleftharpoons H_2CO_3$$

In the last two cases, both the oxides [$SO_2(g)$ and $CO_2(g)$] and the acids [$H_2SO_3(aq)$ and $H_2CO_3(aq)$] exist in the solutions. For some nonmetal oxides (N_2O and CO are examples), there are no corresponding acids.

Oxides of nonmetals will neutralize bases. The same products are obtained from the reaction of an acidic oxide as are obtained from the reaction of the corresponding acid:

$$H_2SO_3(aq) + 2\,OH^-(aq) \longrightarrow SO_3^{2-}(aq) + 2\,H_2O$$

$$SO_2(g) + 2\,OH^-(aq) \longrightarrow SO_3^{2-}(aq) + H_2O$$

Mortar consists of lime [$Ca(OH)_2$], sand [SiO_2], and water. The initial hardening of mortar occurs when the mortar dries out. Over a long period of time, however, the mortar sets by absorbing $CO_2(g)$ from the air and forming insoluble $CaCO_3$:

$$Ca(OH)_2(s) + CO_2(g) \longrightarrow CaCO_3(s) + H_2O$$

Some oxides have both basic and acidic properties (Al_2O_3 and ZnO are examples). They are called amphoteric oxides and are formed principally by the elements in the center of the periodic table, near the border line between the metals and the nonmetals:

$$Al_2O_3(s) + 6\,H^+(aq) \longrightarrow 2\,Al^{3+}(aq) + 3\,H_2O$$

$$Al_2O_3(s) + 2\,OH^-(aq) + 3\,H_2O \longrightarrow 2\,Al(OH)_4^-(aq)$$
$$aluminate\ ion$$

$$ZnO(s) + 2\,H^+(aq) \longrightarrow Zn^{2+}(aq) + H_2O$$

$$ZnO(s) + 2\,OH^-(aq) + H_2O \longrightarrow Zn(OH)_4^{2-}(aq)$$
$$zincate\ ion$$

Acidic and basic oxides react directly, and many of these reactions are of industrial significance. In the manufacture of pig iron (see Section 25.6), $CaCO_3$ (limestone) is used as a flux. The $CaCO_3$ decomposes into CaCO and CO_2 at the high temperatures of the blast furnance. The CaO, a basic oxide, reacts with SiO_2, an acidic oxide present in the iron ore, to form slag ($CaSiO_3$) and thereby remove the unwanted SiO_2:

$$CaCO_3(s) + SiO_2(s) \longrightarrow CaSiO_3(l) + CO_2(g)$$

In the open-hearth process for the manufacture of steel from pig iron, the hearth is often lined with CaO or MgO (basic oxides) to remove the oxides of silicon, phosphorus, and sulfur (acidic oxides) that are present in the pig iron as impurities.

Glass is made from various combinations of acidic and basic oxides. Ordinary soft glass is made from lime ($CaCO_3$), soda (Na_2CO_3), and silica (SiO_2). The corresponding basic oxides are CaO and Na_2O, the acidic oxide is SiO_2, and the product is a mixture of sodium and calcium silicates.

Substitutions are sometimes made for these oxides. If boric oxide, an acidic oxide, is substituted for a part of the SiO_2, a borosilicate (Pyrex) glass is produced. The use of PbO as a part of the basic-oxide component produces flint glass (used for lenses). The use of some basic oxides produces colored glasses; examples are FeO (light green), Cr_2O_3 (dark green), and CoO (blue).

13.6 Nomenclature of Acids, Hydroxides, and Salts

Some common acids are listed in Table 13.3. Rules for naming these compounds and the salts derived from them follow.

1. Aqueous solutions of *binary compounds that function as acids* are named by modifying the root of the name of the element that is combined with hydrogen. The prefix *hydro-* and the suffix *-ic* are used, followed by the word *acid:*

HCl forms hydrochloric acid
H_2S forms hydrosulfuric acid

2. *Metal hydroxides* are named in the manner described in Section 7.8:

$Mg(OH)_2$ is magnesium hydroxide

$Fe(OH)_2$ is iron(II) hydroxide or ferrous hydroxide

3. The names of *salts of binary acids* are given the ending *-ide*. They are named according to the rules given in Section 7.8.

4. *Ternary acids* are composed of three elements. When oxygen is the third element, the compound is called an *oxyacid*.

a. If an element forms only one oxyacid, the acid is named by changing the ending of the name of the element to *-ic* and adding the word *acid:*

H_3BO_3 is boric acid

b. If there are two common oxyacids of the same element, the ending *-ous* is used in naming the oxyacid of the element in its lower oxidation state; the ending *-ic* is used to denote the higher oxidation state (see Table 13.3):

HNO_2 is nitrous acid

HNO_3 is nitric acid

c. There are a few series of oxyacids for which two names are not enough. See the names of the oxyacids of chlorine in Table 13.3. The prefix *hypo-* is added to the name of an *-ous* acid to indicate an oxidation state of the central element lower than that of the *-ous* acid:

$HClO_2$ is chlorous acid (Cl has an oxidation number of $3+$)

$HOCl$ is hypochlorous acid (Cl has an oxidation number of $1+$)

The prefix *per-* is added to the name of an *-ic* acid to indicate an oxidation state of the central atom that is higher than that of the *-ic* acid:

$HClO_3$ is chloric acid (Cl has an oxidation number of $5+$)

$HClO_4$ is perchloric acid (Cl has an oxidation number of $7+$)

5. The names of the *anions of normal salts* are derived from the names of the acids from which the salts are obtained. The *-ic* ending is changed to *-ate*, and the *-ous* ending is changed to *-ite*. Prefixes, if any, are retained:

SO_4^{2-} (from sulfuric acid) is the sulfate ion

OCl^- (from hypochlorous acid) is the hypochlorite ion

The name of the salt itself is obtained by combining the name of the cation with the name of the anion:

$NaNO_2$ is sodium nitrite

$Fe(ClO_4)_3$ is iron(III) perchlorate or ferric perchlorate

6. In naming the *anion of an acid salt*, the number of acid hydrogens retained by the anion must be indicated. The prefix *mono-* is usually omitted:

$H_2PO_4^-$ is the dihydrogen phosphate ion

HPO_4^{2-} is the hydrogen phosphate ion

PO_4^{3-} (the anion of the normal salt) is the phosphate ion

In an older system, the prefix *bi-* was used in place of the word *hydrogen* in the name of the anion of an acid salt derived from a diprotic acid:

HCO_3^- is the hydrogen carbonate ion or the bicarbonate ion
HSO_3^- is the hydrogen sulfite ion or the bisulfite ion

13.7 Volumetric Analysis

A volumetric analysis is one that relies on the precise measurement of the volume of a solution. A procedure called a titration is employed (see Figure 13.1). In one type of titration, a solution of known concentration, called a standard solution, is added to a measured volume of an unknown solution until the reaction is complete. The standard solution is placed in a graduated tube called a buret. The buret is fitted with a stopcock at the lower end to permit the solution to be withdrawn in controlled amounts. A measured volume of the unknown solution, or a weighed mass of a solid unknown dissolved in water, is placed in a flask together with a few drops of a substance known as an indicator. The standard solution from the buret is slowly added to the flask until the indicator changes color. Throughout the addition, the contents of the flask are kept well mixed by swirling. At the equivalence point, as shown by the color change of the indicator, equivalent amounts of the two reactants have been used. The volume of standard solution employed is read from the buret. In some titrations, a measured volume of a standard solution or a measured mass of a substance of known purity dissolved in water is placed in a flask. The unknown solution is then added to the flask from a buret until the equivalence point is reached.

Three types of volumetric analyses are in common use. They are based on precipitation reactions, acid-base neutralizations, and oxidation-reduction reactions. These three types are illustrated in the examples that follow.

Example 13.5

An effluent from a manufacturing process is analyzed for Cl^- content. A 10.00 g sample of the waste water, some additional water, and a few drops of a dilute K_2CrO_4 solution (as an indicator) are placed in a flask. A 0.1050 M solution of $AgNO_3$ is added from the buret. The reaction is:

$$Cl^-(aq) + AgNO_3(aq) \longrightarrow AgCl(s) + NO_3^-(aq)$$

After the Cl^- has been substantially used up by the formation of AgCl (a white precipitate), the next small amount of Ag^+ added forms the red precipitate Ag_2CrO_4:

$$2\,Ag^+(aq) + CrO_4^{2-} \longrightarrow Ag_2CrO_4(s)$$

The appearance of the red color signals the end of the titration, which occurs when 30.20 mL of the 0.1050 M AgNO$_3$ solution has been added. What is the percent Cl^- in the waste water?

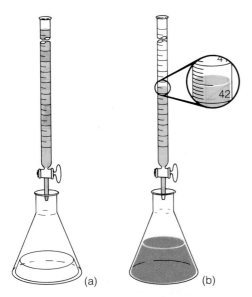

Figure 13.1 An acid-base titration. (a) The buret contains the standard solution. The unknown solution and indicator are placed in the flask. (b) Solution is added from the buret to the flask. Equivalence point is reached when the indicator changes color.

Solution

First we find the number of moles of $AgNO_3$ that have been used:

$$? \text{ mol } AgNO_3 = 30.20 \text{ mL sol'n} \left(\frac{0.1050 \text{ mol } AgNO_3}{1000. \text{ mL sol'n}} \right)$$

$$= 3.171 \times 10^{-3} \text{ mol } AgNO_3$$

From the chemical equation, we see that

$$1 \text{ mol } Cl^- \rightleftharpoons 1 \text{ mol } AgNO_3$$

and since the atomic weight of Cl is 35.45, we can find the mass of Cl^- in the sample in the following way:

$$? \text{ g } Cl^- = 3.171 \times 10^{-3} \text{ mol } AgNO_3 \left(\frac{1 \text{ mol } Cl^-}{1 \text{ mol } AgNO_3} \right) \left(\frac{34.45 \text{ g } Cl^-}{1 \text{ mol } Cl^-} \right)$$

$$= 0.1124 \text{ g } Cl^-$$

The mass percent of Cl^- in the sample is

$$\left(\frac{0.1124 \text{ g } Cl^-}{10.00 \text{ g sample}} \right) 100\% = 1.124\% \text{ } Cl^-$$

Example 13.6

A 25.00 g sample of vinegar, which contains acetic acid ($HC_2H_3O_2$), is placed in a flask together with a few drops of a phenolphthalein solution (to serve as an indicator). The phenolphthalein is colorless in acidic solution. A 0.4600 M solution of NaOH is added from a buret, and the reaction is:

$$NaOH(aq) + HC_2H_3O_2(aq) \longrightarrow NaC_2H_3O_2(aq) + H_2O$$

When 37.50 mL of the 0.4600 M NaOH solution has been added, the phenolphthalein changes to a pink color, which indicates the end of the titration. What is the mass percent of acetic acid in the sample of vinegar?

Solution

The number of moles of NaOH employed can be found in the following way:

$$? \text{ mol NaOH} = 37.50 \text{ mL sol'n} \left(\frac{0.4600 \text{ mol NaOH}}{1000. \text{ mL sol'n}} \right)$$

$$= 1.725 \times 10^{-2} \text{ mol NaOH}$$

Since the equation shows

$$1 \text{ mol } HC_2H_3O_2 \rightleftharpoons 1 \text{ mol NaOH}$$

and since the molecular weight of $HC_2H_3O_2$ is 60.05,

$$? \text{ g } HC_2H_3O_2 = 1.725 \times 10^{-2} \text{ mol NaOH} \left(\frac{1 \text{ mol } HC_2H_3O_2}{1 \text{ mol NaOH}} \right) \left(\frac{60.05 \text{ g } HC_2H_3O_2}{1 \text{ mol } HC_2H_3O_2} \right)$$

$$= 1.036 \text{ g } HC_2H_3O_2$$

The mass percent of $HC_2H_3O_2$ in the vinegar sample is

$$\left(\frac{1.036 \text{ g } HC_2H_3O_2}{25.00 \text{ g vinegar}} \right) 100\% = 4.144\% \ HC_2H_3O_2 \text{ in vinegar}$$

Example 13.7

A 0.4308 g sample of iron ore is dissolved in acid and the iron converted into the Fe^{2+} state. This solution is titrated with a 0.02496 M solution of potassium permanganate, $KMnO_4$, which is dark purple in color. The following reaction occurs during the addition of the $KMnO_4$ solution:

$$8 H^+ + 5 Fe^{2+} + MnO_4^- \longrightarrow 5 Fe^{3+} + Mn^{2+} + 4 H_2O$$

The products of this reaction are not highly colored and the solution is a faint yellow. Once all of the Fe^{2+} has reacted, however, the solution is turned pink by the addition of an extra drop of the $KMnO_4$ solution. In this way, the $KMnO_4$ serves as its own indicator. The titration requires 27.35 mL of the 0.02496 M $KMnO_4$ solution. What is the mass percent of iron in the ore?

Solution

First we find the number of moles of $KMnO_4$ consumed in the reaction:

$$? \text{ mol } KMnO_4 = 27.35 \text{ mL sol'n} \left(\frac{0.02496 \text{ mol } KMnO_4}{1000. \text{ mL sol'n}} \right)$$

$$= 6.827 \times 10^{-4} \text{ mol } KMnO_4$$

Since the equation shows

$$5 \text{ mol } Fe^{2+} \rightleftharpoons 1 \text{ mol } KMnO_4$$

and since the atomic weight of iron is 55.85,

$$? \text{ g Fe} = 6.827 \times 10^{-4} \text{ mol } KMnO_4 \left(\frac{5 \text{ mol Fe}}{1 \text{ mol } KMnO_4} \right) \left(\frac{55.85 \text{ g Fe}}{1 \text{ mol Fe}} \right)$$

$$= 0.1906 \text{ g Fe}$$

This is the quantity of iron found in the 0.4308 g sample of ore. Therefore,

$$\left(\frac{0.1906 \text{ g Fe}}{0.4308 \text{ g ore}} \right) 100\% = 44.24\% \text{ Fe in ore}$$

13.8 Equivalent Weights and Normality

All volumetric analysis problems can be solved in the way that was used in the last section, on the basis of the mole and using molarity to express solution concentrations. There is, however, another method, one based on what are called *equivalents* and using *normality* to express solution concentrations. The definition of an equivalent, which is an amount of a reactant, depends upon the type of reaction being considered, but it is always framed so that one equivalent of a given reactant will react with exactly one equivalent of another.

Two types of reactions for which equivalents are defined are neutralization reactions and oxidation-reduction reactions. The mass of one equivalent of a compound is called an **equivalent weight.** In general:

$$equivalent\ weight = \frac{formula\ weight}{a} \tag{13.1}$$

where the value of a depends upon the type of reaction considered.

1. For *neutralization reactions*, equivalent weights are based on the fact that one $H^+(aq)$ ion reacts with one $OH^-(aq)$ ion:

$$H^+(aq) + OH^-(aq) \longrightarrow H_2O$$

One equivalent weight of an acid is the amount of the acid that supplies one mole of $H^+(aq)$ ions, and one equivalent weight of a base is the amount of the base that supplies one mole of $OH^-(aq)$ ions. The value of a in Equation 13.1, therefore, is the number of moles of $H^+(aq)$ supplied by one mole of the acid or the number of moles of $OH^-(aq)$ supplied by one mole of the base for the reaction being considered.

2. For *oxidation-reduction* reactions, equivalent weights are based either on the number of moles of electrons exchanged *or* on oxidation-number changes. The number of moles of electrons lost by an oxidation (or the increase in oxidation number) must equal the number of moles of electrons gained by the reduction (or the decrease in oxidation number). Hence, a in Equation 13.1 is the number of moles of electrons lost or gained by a mole of the reactant. The value of a can also be defined as the total change in oxidation number (either up or down) that the atoms in a formula unit undergo. For the half reaction:

$$5e^- + 8\,H^+ + \underset{7+}{MnO_4^-} \longrightarrow \underset{2+}{Mn^{2+}} + 4\,H_2O$$

a is 5, and the equivalent weight of $KMnO_4$ is the formula weight of this compound divided by 5. For the half reaction:

$$6e^- + 14\,H^+ + \underset{6+}{Cr_2O_7^{2-}} \longrightarrow 2\,\underset{3+}{Cr^{3+}} + 7\,H_2O$$

a is 6, and the equivalent weight of $K_2Cr_2O_7$ is the formula weight of this compound divided by 6. Notice that the change in oxidation number for *each* Cr atom is 3, which makes a total change of 6 for the compound $K_2Cr_2O_7$ (the same as the number of moles of electrons indicated as gained in the partial equation).

The *normality*, N, of a solution is the number of gram equivalent weights of solute dissolved in one liter of solution. The normality of a solution and its molarity (M) are related:

$$N = aM \tag{13.2}$$

The number of equivalents of A in a sample of a solution of A, e_A, can be obtained by multiplying the volume of the sample, V_A (in liters), by the normality of the solution, N_A (which is the number of equivalents of A in one liter of solution):

$$e_A = V_A N_A \qquad (V_A \text{ in liters}) \tag{13.3}$$

By design, $e_A = e_B$, and therefore

$$V_A N_A = V_B N_B \tag{13.4}$$

Since a volume term appears on both sides of Equation 13.4, any volume unit can be used to express V_A and V_B provided that both volumes are expressed in the same unit.

Example 13.8

(a) What is the normality of a solution of H_2SO_4 if 50.00 mL of the solution requires 37.52 mL of 0.1492 N NaOH for complete neutralization?
(b) What is the molarity of the solution?

Solution

(a)
$$V_A N_A = V_B N_B$$
$$(50.00 \text{ mL})N_A = (37.52 \text{ mL})(0.1492 \text{ N})$$
$$N_A = 0.1120 \text{ N}$$

(b) Since 1 mol of H_2SO_4 is 2 equivalents, $a = 2$. Therefore

$$N = aM$$
$$0.1120 \text{ equiv/L} = (2 \text{ equiv/mol})M$$
$$M = 0.05600 \text{ mol/L}$$

Example 13.9

A 0.4308 g sample of iron ore is dissolved in acid and the iron converted to the Fe^{2+} state. The solution is reacted with a solution of potassium permanganate. The reaction, in which Fe^{2+} is oxidized to Fe^{3+}, requires 27.35 mL of 0.1248 N $KMnO_4$. What is the mass percent of iron in the ore?

Solution

This problem is the same as that given in Example 13.7. Here, however, we will solve it by using equivalents and normality. We find the number of equivalents of $KMnO_4$ used:

$$e_A = V_A N_A$$
$$= (0.02735 \text{ L})(0.1248 \text{ equiv/L})$$
$$= 3.413 \times 10^{-3} \text{ equiv}$$

The number of equivalents of $KMnO_4$ used is the same as the number of equivalents of iron in the ore sample.

In the reaction, the oxidation number of the iron increases by one unit (from $2+$ to $3+$). The equivalent weight of iron, therefore, is the same as the atomic weight, 55.85:

$$? \text{ g Fe} = 3.413 \times 10^{-3} \text{ equiv Fe} \left(\frac{55.85 \text{ g Fe}}{1 \text{ equiv Fe}} \right) = 0.1906 \text{ g Fe}$$

The mass percent of Fe in the ore sample, therefore, is

$$\left(\frac{0.1906 \text{ g Fe}}{0.4308 \text{ g ore}} \right) 100\% = 44.24\% \text{ Fe in ore}$$

Summary

Aqueous *metathesis reactions*, which have the general form:

$$AB + CD \longrightarrow AD + CB$$

occur because of the formation of a *precipitate, gas*, or a *weak electrolyte*. The products of many of these reactions can be predicted by using solubility rules, some simple generalizations concerning the formation of certain gases, and guidelines for the identification of weak and strong electrolytes.

By using some arbitrary rules, *oxidation numbers* can be assigned to atoms, both free and combined. *Oxidation-reduction reactions* (or *redox reactions*) constitute a second type of reaction that takes place in aqueous solution. *Oxidation* is that half of the reaction in which electrons are lost (with an atom undergoing an algebraic *increase* in *oxidation number*). The other half of the reaction, in which electrons are gained (with an atom undergoing an algebraic *decrease* in *oxidation number*) is called a *reduction*. Chemical equations for redox reactions can be balanced by the *ion-electron method*, which involves half reactions, or by the *oxidation-number method*.

In the Arrhenius concept, an *acid* is a substance that dissolves in water to produce H_3O^+ ions [also indicated as $H^+(aq)$ ions], and a *base* is a substance that contains OH^- ions or dissolves in water to produce OH^- ions. The reaction of an acid and a base, in which water and a salt is produced, is called a *neutralization*. The *oxides of metals* are *basic oxides*. They react with *acids* to form *salts*, and some of them react with *water* to form soluble *hydroxides*. Many of the *oxides of nonmetals* are *acidic oxides*; they react with *water* to form *oxyacids* and with *bases* to produce *salts*. The nomenclature of acids, hydroxides, and salts was reviewed.

Reactions that occur in aqueous solution can be used as the basis of analytical procedures. Three common types of *volumetric analyses* (titrations) are based on *precipitation* reactions, *redox* reactions, and *neutralization reactions*. *Volumetric analysis problems can be solved by using molarity as the unit for solution concentration and the *mole* for amount of reactant *or* by using *normality* as the unit for solution concentration and the *equivalent* for amount of reactant.

Key Terms

Some of the more important terms introduced in this chapter are listed below. Definitions for terms not included in this list may be located in the text by use of the index.

Acid (Section 13.4)   A covalent compound of hydrogen that dissociates in water to produce $H^+(aq)$ ions (or H_3O^+ ions).

Acidic oxide (Section 13.5)   An oxide of a nonmetal that reacts with water to form an acid.

Acid salt (Section 13.4)   A salt formed by the incomplete neutralization of a polyprotic acid. The anions of these salts retain one or more ionizable hydrogen atoms of the parent acid.

Amphoteric oxide (Section 13.5)   An oxide that has both acidic and basic properties and that will react with both acids and bases to form salts.

Base (Section 13.4)   In the Arrhenius system, a compound that dissociates in water to produce $OH^-(aq)$ ions.

Basic oxide (Section 13.5)   An oxide of a metal that reacts with water to form a base.

Disproportionation (Section 13.3)   A reaction in which a substance is both oxidized and reduced; an auto-oxidation-reduction reaction.

Equivalence point (Section 13.7)   That point in a titration where stoichiometrically equivalent amounts of reactants have been added.

Equivalent weight (Section 13.8)   A quantity defined on the basis of the reaction being considered in such a way that one equivalent weight of one reactant will react with exactly one equivalent weight of another. For an acid-base neutralization, the mass of acid or base that will supply one mole of $H^+(aq)$ or one mole of $OH^-(aq)$. For an oxidation-reduction reaction, the formula weight of the oxidant or reductant divided by either the number of moles of electrons lost or gained by a mole of the reactant *or* the total change in oxidation number for that reactant.

Half reaction (Section 13.3)   Half of an oxidation-reduction reaction; an oxidation or a reduction.

Hydronium ion (Section 13.4)   An ion formed from a proton and a water molecule; H_3O^+.

Indicator (Section 13.7)   A substance that signals the end of a titration by changing color.

Metathesis reaction (Section 13.1)   A reaction between two compounds in which cations and anions exchange partners.

Monoprotic acid (Sections 13.4 and 13.6)   An acid that can lose only one proton per molecule.

Net ionic equation (Section 13.1) A chemical equation that does not show spectator ions but includes only those species that are involved in the reaction.

Neutralization (Section 13.4) A reaction between an acid and a base or their oxides.

Normality (Section 13.8) A solution concentration; the number of equivalents of solute per liter of solution.

Normal salt (Section 13.4) A salt of a polyprotic acid formed by the loss of all ionizable protons by the acid.

Oxidation (Section 13.3) That part of an oxidation-reduction reaction characterized by electron loss or by an algebraic increase in oxidation number.

Oxidation number (Section 13.2) A positive or negative number (or zero) that is assigned to an atom in a compound according to arbitrary rules that take into account bond polarity. The concept is merely a convention.

Oxidizing agent (Section 13.3) A substance that is reduced in a chemical reaction, thereby causing the oxidation of another substance.

Oxyacid (Section 13.6) An acid composed of three elements, with oxygen as one of the three.

Partial equation (Section 13.3) A chemical equation for a half reaction written to show electron loss or electron gain.

Polyprotic acid (Sections 13.4 and 13.6) An acid that can lose more than one proton per molecule.

Precipitation (Section 13.1) The formation of an insoluble substance (called a **precipitate**) in an aqueous reaction.

Reducing agent (Section 13.3) A substance that is oxidized in a chemical reaction, thereby causing the reduction of another substance.

Reduction (Section 13.3) That part of an oxidation-reduction reaction characterized by electron gain or by an algebraic decrease in oxidation number.

Salt (Section 13.4) A compound derived from the reaction of an acid and a base; it contains a cation from the base and an anion from the acid.

Spectator ion (Section 13.1) An ion that is present during the course of an aqueous reaction but does not take part in the reaction.

Standard solution (Section 13.7) A solution that has a known concentration of solute.

Strong acids and bases (Section 13.4) Acids and bases that are completely ionized in dilute aqueous solution.

Titration (Section 13.7) A process in which a standard solution is reacted with a solution of unknown concentration in order to determine the unknown concentration.

Volumetric analysis (Section 13.7) A chemical analysis that is based on the measurement of the volume of a solution.

Weak acids and bases (Section 13.4) Acids and bases that are only partly dissociated in water solution.

Problems*

Metathesis Reactions

13.1 Write balanced complete ionic equations and net ionic equations for the reactions that occur between (a) $Fe(OH)_3$ and H_3PO_4, (b) Hg_2CO_3 and HCl, (c) Na_3PO_4 and $BaCl_2$, (d) BaS and $ZnSO_4$, (e) $Pb(NO_3)_2$ and H_2S.

13.2 Write balanced complete ionic equations and net ionic equations for the reactions that occur between (a) $Mg(OH)_2$ and HNO_3, (b) $Sr(OH)_2$ and $NiSO_4$, (c) $LiClO_3$ and $AlCl_3$, (d) $ZnSO_3$ and HCl, (e) $AgNO_3$ and CdI_2.

13.3 Write balanced complete ionic equations and net ionic equations for the reactions that occur between (a) Na_3PO_4 and HBr, (b) $Mg(NO_3)_2$ and $Ba(OH)_2$, (c) $SnCl_2$ and $(NH_4)_2SO_4$, (d) Na_2CO_3 and $Sr(C_2H_3O_2)_2$, (e) ZnS and HCl.

13.4 Write balanced complete ionic equations and net ionic equations for the reactions that occur between (a) Na_2SO_3 and HCl, (b) Na_2SO_3 and $CaCl_2$, (c) Na_2SO_4 and HCl, (d) $PbCO_3$ and HI, (e) Na_2SO_4 and $Ba(OH)_2$.

13.5 Write balanced complete ionic equations and net ionic equations for the reactions that occur between (a) $Pb(NO_3)_2$ and $MgSO_4$, (b) $Fe_2(CO_3)_3$ and HNO_3, (c) $Cd(ClO_3)_2$ and K_2S, (d) $MnCl_2$ and $CoSO_4$, (e) $(NH_4)_2SO_4$ and $Ca(OH)_2$.

13.6 Write balanced complete ionic equations and net ionic equations for the reactions that occur between (a) Ag_2S and HCl, (b) $PbSO_3$ and HNO_3, (c) $NH_4C_2H_3O_2$ and HCl, (d) $CaBr_2$ and $Hg_2(C_2H_3O_2)_2$, (e) $ZnSO_4$ and K_2S.

Oxidation Numbers

13.7 State the oxidation number of (a) U in U_2Cl_{10}, (b) Bi in BiO^+, (c) V in $Na_6V_{10}O_{28}$, (d) Sn in K_2SnO_3, (e) Ta in $Ta_6O_{19}^{8-}$, (f) Ti in $K_2Ti_2O_5$, (g) B in $Mg(BF_4)_2$.

13.8 State the oxidation number of (a) Te in Cs_2TeF_8, (b) Nb in K_3NbOF_6, (c) W in $K_2W_4O_{13}$, (d) U in $Li_2U_2O_7$, (e) Mo in $Mo_8O_{26}^{4-}$, (f) Zr in $K_2Zr_2O_5$, (g) Ta in Na_3TaF_8.

13.9 State the oxidation number of (a) N in N_2H_4, (b) N in NH_2OH, (c) S in $S_2O_5Cl_2$, (d) U in Mg_3UO_6, (e) P in $Na_3P_3O_9$, (f) N in CaN_2O_2, (g) V in Ca_2VO_4.

---

* The more difficult problems are marked with asterisks. The appendix contains answers to color-keyed problems.

13.10 State the oxidation number of **(a)** Cl in Cl_2O_4, **(b)** Sb in $Sb(OH)_2^+$ **(c)** Xe in $CsXeF_7$, **(d)** U in $Li_2U_2O_7$, **(e)** Br in BrF_6^-, **(f)** Bi in $Bi_6O_6^{6+}$.

13.11 State the oxidation number of **(a)** Xe in XeO_6^{4-}, **(b)** Ta in $TaOCl_3$, **(c)** U in UO_2^{2+}, **(d)** Sb in $Ca_2Sb_2O_7$, **(e)** Mo in $K_2Mo_4O_{13}$, **(f)** B in B_2Cl_4.

13.12 State the oxidation number of **(a)** B in $Ca_2B_2O_4$, **(b)** V in VO^{2+}, **(c)** S in SO_3F_2, **(d)** Te in H_6TeO_6, **(e)** P in P_4O_8, **(f)** P in OPF_3.

Oxidation-Reduction Reactions

13.13 For each of the following reactions, identify the substance oxidized, the substance reduced, the oxidizing agent, and the reducing agent:

(a) $Zn + Cl_2 \longrightarrow ZnCl_2$
(b) $2\,ReCl_5 + SbCl_3 \longrightarrow 2\,ReCl_4 + SbCl_5$
(c) $Mg + CuCl_2 \longrightarrow MgCl_2 + Cu$
(d) $2\,NO + O_2 \longrightarrow 2\,NO_2$
(e) $WO_3 + 3\,H_2 \longrightarrow W + 3\,H_2O$

13.14 For each of the following reactions, identify the substance oxidized, the substance reduced, the oxidizing agent and the reducing agent:

(a) $Cl_2 + 2\,NaBr \longrightarrow 2\,NaCl + Br_2$
(b) $Zn + 2\,HCl \longrightarrow ZnCl_2 + H_2$
(c) $Fe_2O_3 + 2\,Al \longrightarrow Al_2O_3 + 2\,Fe$
(d) $OF_2 + H_2O \longrightarrow O_2 + 2\,HF$
(e) $2\,HgO \longrightarrow 2\,Hg + O_2$

13.15 Balance the following by the change-in-oxidation-number method:

(a) $H_2O + MnO_4^- + ClO_2^- \longrightarrow$
$\qquad\qquad MnO_2 + ClO_4^- + OH^-$
(b) $H^+ + CrO_7^{2-} + H_2S \longrightarrow Cr^{3+} + S + H_2O$
(c) $H_2O + P_4 + HOCl \longrightarrow H_3PO_4 + Cl^- + H^+$
(d) $Cu + H^+ + NO_3^- \longrightarrow Cu^{2+} + NO + H_2O$
(e) $PbO_2 + HI \longrightarrow PbI_2 + I_2 + H_2O$

13.16 Balance the following by the change-in-oxidation-number method:

(a) $Fe^{2+} + H^+ + ClO_3^- \longrightarrow Fe^{3+} + Cl^- + H_2O$
(b) $Pt + H^+ + NO_3^- + Cl^- \longrightarrow$
$\qquad\qquad PtCl_6^{2-} + NO + H_2O$
(c) $Cu + H^+ + SO_4^{2-} \longrightarrow Cu^{2+} + SO_2 + H_2O$
(d) $Pb + PbO_2 + H^+ + SO_4^{2-} \longrightarrow PbSO_4 + H_2O$
(e) $MnO_2 + HI \longrightarrow MnI_2 + I_2 + H_2O$

13.17 Complete and balance the following equations by the ion-electron method. All reactions occur in acid solution.

(a) $ClO_3^- + I^- \longrightarrow Cl^- + I_2$
(b) $Zn + NO_3^- \longrightarrow Zn^{2+} + NH_4^+$
(c) $H_3AsO_3 + BrO_3^- \longrightarrow H_3AsO_4 + Br^-$
(d) $H_2SeO_3 + H_2S \longrightarrow Se + HSO_4^-$
(e) $ReO_2 + Cl_2 \longrightarrow HReO_4 + Cl^-$

13.18 Complete and balance the following equations by the ion-electron method. All reactions occur in acid solution.

(a) $Fe^{2+} + Cr_2O_7^{2-} \longrightarrow Fe^{3+} + Cr^{3+}$
(b) $HNO_2 + MnO_4^- \longrightarrow NO_3^- + Mn^{2+}$
(c) $As_2S_3 + ClO_3^- \longrightarrow H_3AsO_4 + S + Cl^-$
(d) $IO_3^- + N_2H_4 \longrightarrow I^- + N_2$
(e) $Cu + NO_3^- \longrightarrow Cu^{2+} + NO$

13.19 Complete and balance the following equations by the ion-electron method. All reactions occur in acid solution.

(a) $AsH_3 + Ag^+ \longrightarrow As_4O_6 + Ag$
(b) $Mn^{2+} + BiO_3^- \longrightarrow MnO_4^- + Bi^{3+}$
(c) $NO + NO_3^- \longrightarrow N_2O_4$
(d) $MnO_4^- + HCN + I^- \longrightarrow Mn^{2+} + ICN$
(e) $Zn + H_2MoO_4 \longrightarrow Zn^{2+} + Mo^{3+}$

13.20 Complete and balance the following equations by the ion-electron method. All reactions occur in acid solution.

(a) $S_2O_3^{2-} + IO_3^- + Cl^- \longrightarrow SO_4^{2-} + ICl_2^-$
(b) $Se + BrO_3^- \longrightarrow H_2SeO_3 + Br^-$
(c) $H_3AsO_3 + MnO_4^- \longrightarrow H_3AsO_4 + Mn^{2+}$
(d) $H_5IO_6 + I^- \longrightarrow I_2$
(e) $Pb_3O_4 \longrightarrow Pb^{2+} + PbO_2$

13.21 Complete and balance the following equations by the ion-electron method. All reactions occur in alkaline solution.

(a) $HClO_2 \longrightarrow ClO_2 + Cl^-$
(b) $MnO_4^- + I^- \longrightarrow MnO_4^{2-} + IO_4^-$
(c) $P_4 \longrightarrow HPO_3^{2-} + PH_3$
(d) $SbH_3 + H_2O \longrightarrow Sb(OH)_4^- + H_2$
(e) $CO(NH_2)_2 + OBr^- \longrightarrow CO_3^{2-} + N_2 + Br^-$

13.22 Complete and balance the following equations by the ion-electron method. All reactions occur in alkaline solution.

(a) $Mn(OH)_2 + O_2 \longrightarrow Mn(OH)_3$
(b) $Cl_2 \longrightarrow ClO_3^- + Cl^-$
(c) $HXeO_4^- \longrightarrow XeO_6^{4-} + Xe + O_2$
(d) $As + OH^- \longrightarrow AsO_3^{3-} + H_2$
(e) $S_2O_4^{2-} + O_2 \longrightarrow SO_3^{2-} + OH^-$

13.23 Complete and balance the following equations by the ion-electron method. All reactions occur in alkaline solution.

(a) $S^{2-} + I_2 \longrightarrow SO_4^{2-} + I^-$
(b) $CN^- + MnO_4^- \longrightarrow CNO^- + MnO_2$
(c) $Au + CN^- + O_2 \longrightarrow Au(CN)_2^- + OH^-$
(d) $Si + OH^- \longrightarrow SiO_3^{2-} + H_2$
(e) $Cr(OH)_3 + BrO^- \longrightarrow CrO_4^{2-} + Br^-$

13.24 Complete and balance the following equations by the ion-electron method. All reactions occur in alkaline solution.

(a) $Al + H_2O \longrightarrow Al(OH)_4^- + H_2$
(b) $S_2O_3^{2-} + OCl^- \longrightarrow SO_4^{2-} + Cl^-$
(c) $I_2 + Cl_2 \longrightarrow H_3IO_6^{2-} + Cl^-$

(d) $Bi(OH)_3 + Sn(OH)_4^{2-} \longrightarrow Bi + Sn(OH)_6^{2-}$

(e) $NiO_2 + Fe \longrightarrow Ni(OH)_2 + Fe(OH)_3$

13.25 Complete and balance the following equations by the ion-electron method. All reactions occur in acid solution.

(a) $P_4 + HOCl \longrightarrow H_3PO_4 + Cl^-$

(b) $XeO_3 + I^- \longrightarrow Xe + I_3^-$

(c) $UO^{2+} + Cr_2O_7^{2-} \longrightarrow UO_2^{2+} + Cr^{3+}$

(d) $H_2C_2O_4 + BrO_3^- \longrightarrow CO_2 + Br^-$

(e) $Te + NO_3^- \longrightarrow TeO_2 + NO$

13.26 Complete and balance the following equations by the ion-electron method. All reactions occur in alkaline solution.

(a) $Al + NO_3^- \longrightarrow Al(OH)_4^- + NH_3$

(b) $Ni^{2+} + Br_2 \longrightarrow NiO(OH) + Br^-$

(c) $S \longrightarrow SO_3^{2-} + S^{2-}$

(d) $S_2O_3^{2-} + I_2 \longrightarrow SO_4^{2-} + I^-$

(e) $S^{2-} + HO_2^- \longrightarrow SO_4^{2-} + OH^-$

Acids and Bases; Acidic and Basic Oxides

13.27 What is an amphoteric oxide? Give the formulas of the ions formed by ZnO in acidic solution and in alkaline solution.

13.28 Give examples of monoprotic acids and polyprotic acids, normal salts and acid salts.

13.29 Write chemical equations for the reactions of HNO_3 with (a) KOH, (b) $Ca(OH)_2$, (c) $Al(OH)_3$. Assume complete neutralization.

13.30 Write equations for the reactions of NaOH with (a) $HClO_3$, (b) H_2SO_4, (c) H_3PO_4. Assume complete neutralization.

13.31 Write the chemical equations for the reactions of KOH and H_3PO_4 that produce (a) KH_2PO_4, (b) K_2HPO_4, (c) K_3PO_4.

13.32 Write chemical equations for the reactions of NaOH with (a) $NaHSO_4$, (b) NaH_2PO_4, (c) H_3AsO_4. Assume that an excess of NaOH is employed.

13.33 Write equations for the reactions of the following with water: (a) Cl_2O, (b) Cs_2O, (c) N_2O_5, (d) CO_2, (e) CaO.

13.34 Write equations for the reactions of the following with water: (a) SO_3, (b) BaO, (c) P_4O_{10}, (d) Na_2O, (e) Cl_2O_3.

13.35 Give the formulas of the anhydrides of the following: (a) $HClO_4$, (b) HNO_2, (c) H_2SO_3, (d) H_3BO_3, (e) $Al(OH)_3$.

13.36 Give the formulas of the anhydrides of the following: (a) $Zn(OH)_2$, (b) KOH, (c) HIO_3, (d) $Fe(OH)_3$, (e) H_2SeO_4.

13.37 Give names for: (a) $HBrO_3$, (b) HNO_3, (c) H_2SO_3, (d) $KHSO_3$, (e) K_2SO_4, (f) $Cu(ClO_3)_2$.

13.38 Give names for: (a) $NaBrO_3$, (b) NaBr, (c) HBr(aq), (d) $NaNO_2$, (e) $NaHCO_3$, (f) H_3BO_3.

13.39 Give formulas for: (a) iron(III) phosphate,

(b) magnesium perchlorate, (c) potassium dihydrogen phosphate, (d) lead(II) sulfate, (e) iron(II) nitrite, (f) nickel(II) nitrate.

13.40 Give formulas for: (a) hypoiodous acid, (b) iodic acid, (c) hydroiodic acid, (d) magnesium hydrogen carbonate, (e) calcium phosphate, (f) iron(III) nitrate.

Volumetric Analysis

13.41 What is the molarity of a solution of H_2SO_4 if 25.00 mL of this solution requires 32.15 mL of a 0.6000 M solution of NaOH for complete neutralization?

13.42 What is the molarity of a solution of $Ba(OH)_2$ if 25.00 mL of this solution requires 15.27 mL of a 0.1000 M solution of HCl for complete neutralization?

13.43 A 1.250 g sample of impure $Mg(OH)_2$ requires 29.50 mL of 0.6000 M HCl for neutralization. If the impurity is $MgCl_2$, what is the mass percent of $Mg(OH)_2$ in the impure sample?

13.44 A 0.300 g sample of impure oxalic acid ($H_2C_2O_4$) is completely neutralized by 27.0 mL of a 0.179 M solution of NaOH. What is the mass percent of $H_2C_2O_4$ in the sample?

13.45 Potassium hydrogen phthalate, $KHC_8H_4O_4$, functions as a monoprotic acid. If a 1.46 g sample of impure $KHC_8H_4O_4$ requires 34.3 mL of 0.145 M NaOH for neutralization, what percentage of $KHC_8H_4O_4$ is in the material?

13.46 Potassium hydrogen phthalate, $KHC_8H_4O_4$, functions as a monoprotic acid. A 0.625 g sample of pure $KHC_8H_4O_4$ requires 27.8 mL of a solution of NaOH for neutralization. What is the molarity of the NaOH solution?

13.47 A 5.00 g sample of $NaNO_3$ contains NaCl as an impurity. The sample requires 15.3 mL of a 0.0500 M solution of $AgNO_3$ to precipitate all of the chloride as AgCl. (a) What mass of NaCl was present in the sample? (b) What is the mass percent of NaCl in the material?

13.48 A 1.00 g sample that contains Fe^{2+} is dissolved in 30.0 mL of water and the solution titrated against 0.0200 M $KMnO_4$. In the reaction, Fe^{2+} is oxidized to Fe^{3+} and MnO_4^- is reduced to Mn^{2+}. It takes 35.8 mL of the $KMnO_4$ solution to reach the equivalence point. (a) Write the chemical equation for the reaction. (b) What is the mass percent of Fe in the sample?

13.49 Hydrazine, N_2H_4, reacts with BrO_3^- in acid solution to produce N_2 and Br^-. (a) Write the chemical equation for the reaction. (b) A 0.132 g sample of impure hydrazine requires 38.3 mL of 0.0172 M $KBrO_3$ for complete reaction. What is the mass percent of hydrazine in the sample?

13.50 A 5.00 g sample of hemoglobin is treated in such a way as to produce small water-soluble molecules and ions by destroying the hemoglobin molecule. The iron in the aqueous solution that results from this procedure is reduced to Fe^{2+} and titrated against standard $KMnO_4$. In the titration, Fe^{2+} is oxidized to Fe^{3+} and MnO_4^- is reduced to Mn^{2+}. The sample requires 30.5 mL of 0.00200 M $KMnO_4$. What is the mass percent of iron in hemoglobin?

13.51 What fraction of a mole is one equivalent weight of each of the following: **(a)** N_2H_4 for a reaction in which N_2 is produced, **(b)** $KBrO_3$ for a reaction in which Br^- is produced, **(c)** $KBrO_3$ for a reaction in which Br_2 is produced, **(d)** $K_2Cr_2O_7$ for a reaction in which Cr^{3+} is produced, **(e)** H_3PO_4 for a reaction in which HPO_4^{2-} is produced, **(f)** $Ca(OCl)_2$ for a reaction in which Cl^- is produced?

13.52 What fraction of a mole is one equivalent weight of each of the following? **(a)** As_4O_6 for a reaction in which H_3AsO_4 is produced, **(b)** Se for a reaction in which H_2SeO_3 is produced, **(c)** H_2SO_4 for a reaction in which $NaHSO_4$ is produced, **(d)** HIO_3 for a reaction in which H_5IO_6 is produced, **(e)** HIO_3 for a reaction in which KIO_3 is produced, **(f)** KIO_3 for a reaction in which I^- is produced.

13.53 What are the normalities of $6.00\ M$ HCl, $6.00\ M$ H_2SO_4, and $6.00\ M$ H_3PO_4? Assume complete neutralization of the acids.

13.54 What are the molarities of $6.00\ N$ HCl, $6.00\ N$ H_2SO_4, and $6.00\ N$ H_3PO_4? Assume complete neutralization of the acids.

13.55 How many milliliters of $0.300\ N$ H_2SO_4 would be required to neutralize 38.0 mL of $0.450\ N$ NaOH?

13.56 How many milliliters of a $0.600\ N$ NaOH solution would be required to neutralize 35.0 mL of $0.520\ N$ H_2SO_4?

13.57 A 25.0 mL sample of a solution of an acid requires 43.5 mL of $0.235\ N$ NaOH for neutralization. What is the normality of the acid?

13.58 A 10.0 mL sample of a solution of a base requires 37.2 mL of $0.125\ N$ H_2SO_4 for neutralization. What is the normality of the base?

13.59 Lactic acid, the acid in sour milk, has the molecular formula $C_3H_6O_3$. A 0.612 g sample of pure lactic acid requires 39.3 mL of $0.173\ N$ NaOH for complete neutralization. **(a)** What is the equivalent weight of lactic acid? **(b)** How many acidic hydrogens per molecule does lactic acid have?

13.60 Citric acid, which may be obtained from lemon juice, has the molecular formula $C_6H_8O_7$. A 0.571 g sample of citric acid requires 42.5 mL of $0.210\ N$ NaOH for complete neutralization. **(a)** What is the equivalent weight of citric acid? **(b)** How many acidic hydrogens per molecule does citric acid have?

13.61 A sample of a Fe^{2+} solution requires 26.0 mL of a $0.0200\ M$ $K_2Cr_2O_7$ solution for a reaction in which Fe^{2+} is oxidized to Fe^{3+} and $Cr_2O_7^{2-}$ is reduced to Cr^{3+}. An identical sample of the same Fe^{2+} solution requires 41.6 mL of $KMnO_4$ solution for a reaction in which Fe^{2+} is oxidized to Fe^{3+} and MnO_4^- is reduced to Mn^{2+}. **(a)** What is the normality of the $K_2Cr_2O_7$ solution? **(b)** What is the normality of the $KMnO_4$ solution? **(c)** What is the molarity of the $KMnO_4$ solution?

13.62 A 0.6324 g sample of an iron ore is dissolved in an acid solution and the iron converted into the Fe^{2+} state.

The resulting solution requires 32.37 mL of a $0.2024\ N$ solution of $K_2Cr_2O_7$ for reaction. In the reaction, the Fe^{2+} is oxidized to Fe^{3+} and the $Cr_2O_7^{2-}$ is reduced to Cr^{3+}. What is the mass percent of iron in the ore?

Unclassified Problems

13.63 State the oxidation number of the atom other than O in each of the oxy-anions found in Table 7.5.

13.64 State the oxidation number of **(a)** Mo in $Na_3Mo_2Br_9$, **(b)** U in $U(OH)^{3+}$, **(c)** W in $W_2Cl_9^{3-}$, **(d)** N in NO_2^+ **(e)** Xe in $XeOF_4$, **(f)** Ge in $Ge_3O_9^{6-}$.

13.65 Write chemical equations for the reactions of the following in water (assume complete neutralization): **(a)** $Ca(OH)_2$ and CO_2, **(b)** CO_2 and OH^-, **(c)** ZnO and H^+, **(d)** BaO and SO_2, **(e)** FeO and H^+, **(f)** Al_2O_3, OH^-, and H_2O, **(g)** SO_2 and OH^-.

13.66 Balance the following by the change-in-oxidation-number method:

(a) $Sb + H^+ + NO_3^- \longrightarrow Sb_4O_6 + NO + H_2O$
(b) $NaI + H_2SO_4 \longrightarrow H_2S + I_2 + Na_2SO_4 + H_2O$
(c) $IO_3^- + H_2O + SO_2 \longrightarrow I_2 + SO_4^{2-} + H^+$
(d) $NF_3 + AlCl_3 \longrightarrow N_2 + Cl_2 + AlF_3$
(e) $As_4O_6 + Cl_2 + H_2O \longrightarrow H_3AsO_4 + HCl$

13.67 Complete and balance the following equations by the ion-electron method. All reactions occur in acid solution.

(a) $Hg_5(IO_6)_2 + I^- \longrightarrow HgI_4^{2-} + I_2$
(b) $MnO_4^- + Mn^{2+} + H_2P_2O_7^{2-} \longrightarrow$
$$Mn(H_2P_2O_7)_3^{3-}$$
(c) $CS(NH_2)_2 + BrO_3^- \longrightarrow CO(NH_2)_2 + SO_4^{2-} + Br^-$
(d) $Co(NO_2)_6^{3-} + MnO_4^- \longrightarrow Co^{2+} + NO_3^- + Mn^{2+}$
(e) $CNS^- + IO_3^- + Cl^- \longrightarrow CN^- + SO_4^{2-} + ICl_2^-$
(f) $CrI_3 + Cl_2 \longrightarrow CrO_4^{2-} + IO_3^- + Cl^-$

13.68 Iodine, I_2, reacts with the thiosulfate ion, $S_2O_3^{2-}$, to form the iodide ion, I^-, and the tetrathionate ion, $S_4O_6^{2-}$. **(a)** Write the chemical equation for this reaction. **(b)** How many grams of I_2 will react with 25.00 mL of a $0.0500\ M$ solution of $Na_2S_2O_3$?

13.69 Because the oxygen of H_2O_2 can be either oxidized (to O_2) or reduced (to H_2O), hydrogen peroxide can function as a reducing agent or as an oxidizing agent. Write and balance equations (by the ion-electron method) to show the following reactions of H_2O_2: **(a)** the oxidization of PbS to $PbSO_4$ in acid solution, **(b)** the oxidation of $Cr(OH)_3$ to CrO_4^{2-} in alkaline solution, **(c)** the reduction of MnO_4^- to Mn^{2+} in acid solution, **(d)** the reduction of Ag_2O to Ag in alkaline solution.

13.70 A 1.24 g sample of impure BaO_2 is dissolved in water containing $H^+(aq)$ and H_2O_2 (aq) is produced. The H_2O_2 is titrated with $0.0650\ M$ $KMnO_4$ solution. In the titration, MnO_4^- is reduced to Mn^{2+} and H_2O_2 is oxidized to $O_2(g)$. The sample requires 33.3 mL of the $0.0650\ M$ $KMnO_4$ solution for complete reaction. What percentage of the sample is BaO_2?

CHEMICAL KINETICS

Chemical kinetics is the study of the speeds, or rates, of chemical reactions. A small number of factors control how fast a reaction will occur. Investigation of these factors provides clues to the ways in which reactants are transformed into products in chemical reactions. The detailed description of the way a reaction occurs, based on the behavior of atoms, molecules, and ions , is called a reaction mechanism. Most chemical changes take place by mechanisms that consist of several steps. We can never be sure that a proposed mechanism represents reality—mechanisms are only educated guesses based on kinetic studies.

4.1 Reaction Rates

Consider a hypothetical reaction:

$$A_2(g) + B_2(g) \longrightarrow 2\,AB(g)$$

Throughout the time that the reaction is occurring, A_2 and B_2 are being gradually used up. The concentrations of these two substances, which are usually expressed in moles per liter, are decreasing. Since AB is being produced at the same time, the concentration of AB is increasing. The rate of the reaction is a measure of how fast these changes are taking place.

The symbol for the concentration of a substance consists of the formula of the substance enclosed in brackets. The symbol [AB], for example, stands for the concentration of AB. The symbol Δ[AB], therefore, stands for a change in the concentration of AB.

The rate of the reaction between A_2 and B_2 could be expressed in terms of Δ[AB], the increase in the concentration of AB that occurs in a given time interval, Δt:

$$\text{rate of appearance of AB} = \frac{\Delta[AB]}{\Delta t}$$

If the concentration of AB is expressed in mol/L and time in seconds, the rate would have the units

$$\frac{\text{mol/L}}{\text{s}} = \text{mol/(L·s)}$$

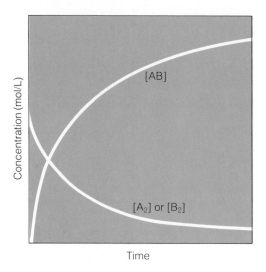

Figure 14.1 Curves showing changes in concentrations of substances with time for the reaction $A_2 + B_2 \rightarrow 2\,AB$

The rate of the reaction could also be expressed in terms of the decrease in the concentration of A_2 or B_2 that takes place in a time interval. The rate based on the concentration of A_2, for example, would be

$$\text{rate of disappearance of } A_2 = \frac{-\Delta[A_2]}{\Delta t}$$

Since the concentration of A_2 is becoming smaller, $\Delta[A_2]$ is a negative value. The minus sign is included in this expression so that the rate will be a positive value.

The rate based on the concentration of AB is not numerically the same as the rate based on the concentration of A_2 or B_2. Suppose that at a given instant the concentration of A_2 is decreasing by 0.02 mol/L in one second. The rate of decrease in the concentration of A_2, therefore, is 0.02 mol/(L·s).

The chemical equation:

$$A_2(g) + B_2(g) \longrightarrow 2\,AB(g)$$

shows two moles of AB produced for every one mole of A_2 used. In the same time interval that the concentration of A_2 decreases by 0.02 mol/L, the concentration of AB must increase by 0.04 mol/L. The rate of increase in the concentration of AB, therefore, is 0.04 mol/(L·s). These two values—the rate of disappearance of A_2, 0.02 mol/(L·s), and the rate of appearance of AB, 0.04 mol/(L·s)—describe the rate of the same reaction at the same instant. The rate of a reaction may be described in terms of the rate of appearance of a product or the rate of disappearance of a reactant, but *the basis of the rate measurement must be specified.*

The rate of a reaction usually changes as the reaction proceeds. In Figure 14.1, the concentrations of AB and A_2 are plotted against time. If the initial concentration of B_2 is the same as the initial concentration of A_2, then a curve for $[B_2]$ against time is the same as the one shown for $[A_2]$ against time.

In the figure, the concentration of the product, AB, starts at zero and rises rapidly at the beginning of the reaction. During this period, the concentration of

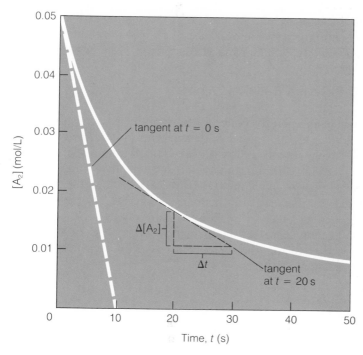

Figure 14.2 Determination of reaction rate by drawing tangents to the curve for [A₂] against time

the reactant, A_2, drops rapidly. The curves show, however, that the concentrations change more slowly as the reaction goes on. The rates of most chemical reactions depend upon the concentrations of the reactants. As these substances are used up, the reactions slow down. The rate at the start of the reaction is called the **initial rate.**

The rate of decrease in the concentration of A_2 at a given time can be obtained from the slope of a tangent drawn to the $[A_2]$ curve at the point that corresponds to the time of interest. In Figure 14.2, a tangent is drawn to the curve at $t = 0$ s. The tangent is extended so that it may be clearly seen that $[A_2]$ is changing by -0.05 mol/L $(\Delta[A_2])$ for a 10 s time interval (Δt):

$$\text{rate of disappearance of } A_2 = \frac{-\Delta[A_2]}{\Delta t}$$

$$= \frac{-(-0.05 \text{ mol/L})}{10 \text{ s}} = 0.005 \text{ mol/(L·s)}$$

This value is the initial rate of the reaction in terms of the disappearance of A_2.

At $t = 20$ s, the rate has decreased. Notice that the tangent to the curve at $t = 20$ s declines by -0.006 mol/L for a 10 s interval:

$$\text{rate of disappearance of } A_2 = \frac{-(-0.006 \text{ mol/L})}{10 \text{ s}} = 0.0006 \text{ mol/(L·s)}$$

Obtaining the data for a concentration curve is often difficult. The concentrations must be determined at definite times throughout the course of the reaction without disturbing the reaction. The best methods for such determinations are based on the continuous measurement of a property that changes as the reaction occurs. Changes in pressure, color (the appearance or disappearance of a colored substance), acidity, conductivity, volume, and viscosity have been used.

14.2 Concentrations and Reaction Rates

Reaction rates usually depend upon the concentrations of the reacting substances. For most reactions, the rates are highest when the concentrations of reactants are high. This effect can be explained on the basis of the collision theory of reaction rates (see Section 14.3). The high concentrations mean that a relatively large number of molecules are crowded into a given volume. Under these conditions, the collisions between reacting molecules that convert them into molecules of product are relatively frequent, and consequently the reaction is more rapid.

For each chemical reaction there is a mathematical expression, called a **rate equation** or a **rate law,** that relates the concentrations of the reactants to the reaction rate. For the reaction

$$2\,N_2O_5(g) \longrightarrow 4\,NO_2(g) + O_2(g)$$

the rate equation is

$$\text{rate} = k[N_2O_5]$$

The expression tells us that the rate is directly proportional to the concentration of N_2O_5. If the concentration is doubled, the rate is doubled. If the concentration is tripled, the rate is tripled. The proportionality constant, k, is called the **rate constant.** *The form of the rate equation and the value of k must be determined by experiment.* The numerical value of k depends upon the temperature and the terms in which the rate is expressed.

The rate of the reaction

$$NO_2(g) + 2\,HCl(g) \longrightarrow NO(g) + H_2O(g) + Cl_2(g)$$

is proportional to the concentration of NO_2 times the concentration of HCl:

$$\text{rate} = k[NO_2][HCl]$$

Doubling the concentration of NO_2 would double the reaction rate. Doubling the concentration of HCl would also double the reaction rate. If the concentrations of both reactants were doubled at the same time, the reaction rate would increase fourfold.

For the reaction

$$2\,NO(g) + 2\,H_2(g) \longrightarrow N_2(g) + 2\,H_2O(g)$$

the rate equation is

$$\text{rate} = k[NO]^2[H_2]$$

The rate of the reaction is directly proportional to the *square* of the concentration of NO times the concentration of H_2. When the concentration of NO is increased by a factor of *two*, the rate increases by a factor of *four* (since 2^2 is 4). When the concentration of H_2 is increased by a factor of *two*, the rate increases by the factor of *two*. If the concentrations of both NO and H_2 were doubled, the rate would increase eightfold (since $2^2 \times 2 = 8$).

The **order** of a reaction is given by the *sum of the exponents* of the concentration terms in the rate equation. The decomposition of N_2O_5 is said to be first order, since the exponent of $[N_2O_5]$ in the rate equation is 1:

$$\text{rate} = k[N_2O_5]$$

The reaction between NO_2 and HCl is said to be first order in NO_2, first order in HCl, and second order overall:

$$\text{rate} = k[NO_2][HCl]$$

The reaction between NO and H_2 is second order in NO, first order in H_2, and third order overall:

$$\text{rate} = k[NO]^2[H_2]$$

The rate equation for a reaction, and consequently the order of a reaction, must be determined experimentally. They cannot be derived from the chemical equation for the reaction. The order of a reaction need not be a whole number. Reactions of a fractional order, as well as zero order, are known. For the decomposition of acetaldehyde (CH_3CHO),

$$CH_3CHO(g) \longrightarrow CH_4(g) + CO(g)$$

at 450°C, the rate equation is

$$\text{rate} = k[CH_3CHO]^{3/2}$$

The reaction, therefore, is three-halves order.

The decomposition of $N_2O(g)$ on gold surfaces at relatively high pressures of N_2O is zero order:

$$2\,N_2O(g) \xrightarrow{\text{Au}} 2\,N_2(g) + O_2(g) \qquad \text{rate} = k$$

When the pressure of N_2O is high, the decomposition proceeds at a steady rate that does not depend upon the concentration of N_2O.

Chemically similar reactions do not necessarily have the same type of rate equation. Consider the following two reactions:

$$H_2(g) + I_2(g) \longrightarrow 2\,HI(g) \qquad \text{rate} = k[H_2][I_2]$$

$$H_2(g) + Br_2(g) \longrightarrow 2\,HBr(g) \qquad \text{rate} = \frac{k[H_2][Br_2]^{1/2}}{k' + [HBr]/[Br_2]}$$

The last example shows that some reactions do not correspond to any simple order. Note also that this rate equation includes a term for the concentration of a product (HBr).

Example 14.1

The data given in the following table pertain to the reaction

$$2\,NO(g) + O_2(g) \longrightarrow 2\,NO_2(g)$$

run at 25°C. Determine the form of the rate equation and the value of the rate constant, k.

| | Initial concentration | | Initial rate |
Experiment	NO mol/L	O_2 mol/L	Appearance of NO_2 mol/(L·s)
A	1×10^{-3}	1×10^{-3}	7×10^{-6}
B	1×10^{-3}	2×10^{-3}	14×10^{-6}
C	1×10^{-3}	3×10^{-3}	21×10^{-6}
D	2×10^{-3}	3×10^{-3}	84×10^{-6}
E	3×10^{-3}	3×10^{-3}	189×10^{-6}

Solution

The rate equation is in the form

$$\text{rate of appearance of } NO_2 = k[NO]^x[O_2]^y$$

Data from the table are used to find the values of the exponents x and y.

In the first three experiments (A, B, and C), the concentration of NO is held constant and the concentration of O_2 is changed. Any change in the rate observed in this series of experiments, therefore, is caused by the change in the concentration of O_2. The concentration of O_2 in experiment B is double that in experiment A, and the rate observed in experiment B is twice the rate in experiment A. Comparison of the data from experiment C with the data from experiment A shows that when the concentration of O_2 is increased threefold, the rate increases threefold. The value of y, therefore, is 1. The rate is directly proportional to the first power of $[O_2]$.

In the last three experiments (C, D, and E), the concentration of O_2 is held constant (at 3×10^{-3} mol/L) and the concentration of NO is changed. The increase in rate that is observed in this series of experiments is caused by the increase in the concentration of NO. The concentration of NO in experiment D is *two* times the concentration of NO in experiment C. The rate observed in experiment D, however, is *four* times the rate observed in experiment C. It appears that the square of $[NO]$ must appear in the rate equation since 2^2 is 4.

We can check this conclusion by comparing the data from experiment E to the data from experiment C. The concentration of NO increases by a factor of 3:

$$\frac{3 \times 10^{-3} \text{ mol/L}}{1 \times 10^{-3} \text{ mol/L}} = 3$$

The rate increases by a factor of 9:

$$\frac{189 \times 10^{-6} \text{ mol/(L·s)}}{21 \times 10^{-6} \text{ mol/(L·s)}} = 9$$

Since 3^2 is 9, the exponent x must be 2; the term for the concentration of NO is squared. The rate equation is rate of the appearance of $NO_2 = k[NO]^2[O_2]$

The value of k can be obtained by using the data from any of the experiments. The same value should be obtained in each case. The data from experiment A are used in the following way:

$$\text{rate of appearance of } NO_2 = k[NO]^2[O_2]$$

$$7 \times 10^{-6} \, mol/(L \cdot s) = k(1 \times 10^{-3} \, mol/L)^2(1 \times 10^{-3} \, mol/L)$$

$$7 \times 10^{-6} \, mol/(L \cdot s) = k(1 \times 10^{-9} \, mol^3/L^3)$$

$$k = \frac{7 \times 10^{-6} \, mol/(L \cdot s)}{1 \times 10^{-9} \, mol^3/L^3}$$

$$k = 7 \times 10^3 \, L^2/(mol^2 \cdot s)$$

14.3 Concentrations and Time

The rate equation (or rate law) for a chemical reaction is a mathematical expression that relates the *rate* of the reaction to the *concentrations* of the reactants. A rate equation of this type can be converted by means of the calculus into an expression that gives the relation between the *concentrations* of the reactants and the elapsed *time*. In this section, we discuss the use of the latter type of equation for three simple kinds of reactions.

First-Order Reactions

The decomposition of N_2O_5:

$$2 \, N_2O_5(g) \longrightarrow 4 \, NO_2(g) + O_2(g)$$

is an example of a first-order reaction. The rate equation for the reaction is:

$$\text{rate} = k[N_2O_5]$$

We can write a general expression for the rate equation for a first-order reaction by representing the concentration of the reactant by the symbol $[A]$. Then:

$$\text{rate} = k[A]$$

This rate equation can be expressed in terms of the rate of decrease in the concentration of A:

$$-\frac{\Delta[A]}{t} = k[A] \tag{14.1}$$

Rearrangement gives:

$$-\frac{\Delta[A]}{[A]} = k \, \Delta t \tag{14.2}$$

which may be written in its differential form:

$$-\frac{d[A]}{[A]} = k\,dt \qquad (14.3)$$

By means of the calculus, Equation 14.3 may be integrated to give:

$$\log\left(\frac{[A]_0}{[A]}\right) = \frac{kt}{2.303} \qquad (14.4)$$

where $[A]_0$ is the original concentration of A (the concentration at time 0), $[A]$ is the concentration of A at time t, and k is the rate constant.

Since:

$$\log(a/b) = \log a - \log b$$

the first term in Equation 14.4 can be transformed in the following way:

$$\log([A]_0/[A]) = \log[A]_0 - \log[A]$$

Equation 14.4, therefore, may be written in the form:

$$\log[A] = -\frac{kt}{2.303} + \log[A]_0 \qquad (14.5)$$

Equation 14.5 is in the form of an equation for a straight line:

$$y = mx + b$$

with $\log[A] = y$, $t = x$, $-k/2.303 = m$, and $\log[A]_0 = b$. Consequently, if $\log[A]$ is plotted against t, a straight line results with a slope (which is m) equal to $-k/2.303$ and an intercept (which is b) of $\log[A]_0$.

Typical curves for first-order reactions are shown in Figures 14.3 and 14.4. In Figure 14.3, the concentration of the reactant is plotted against time ($[A]$ against t). In Figure 14.4, $\log[A]$ is plotted against t for the same reaction. Notice that the latter figure is a straight line with a slope of $-k/2.303$.

If, for a given reaction, a straight line results when the logarithm of the concentration of the reactant is plotted against time, the reaction is first order. Furthermore, the value of the rate constant, k, can be obtained from the slope of the straight line.

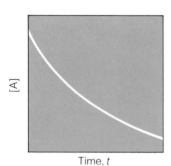

Figure 14.3 A plot of concentration of reactant, [A], *versus* time, *t*, for a first-order reaction for which rate = k[A]

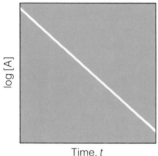

Figure 14.4 A plot of the logarithm of reactant, log[A], *versus* time, *t*, for a first-order reaction. For any first-order reaction, a plot of this type is a straight line with a slope equal to $-k/2.303$.

Example 14.2

For the reaction:

$$2\,N_2O_5(g) \longrightarrow 4\,NO_2(g) + O_2(g)$$

a straight line results when $\log[N_2O_5]$ is plotted against t. The slope of the line derived from data for a reaction run at 35°C is $-5.86 \times 10^{-5}/s$. Find the value of the rate constant, k, for this first-order reaction.

Chapter 14   Chemical Kinetics

Solution

According to Equation 14.5, the slope of the line is:

Slope $= -k/2.303$

Therefore,

$$-k/2.303 = -5.86 \times 10^{-5}/\text{s}$$
$$k = 1.35 \times 10^{-4}/\text{s}$$

Example 14.3

In an investigation of the decomposition of $N_2O_5(g)$ at 35°C, an initial concentration of $N_2O_5(g)$, $[N_2O_5]_0$, of 0.0300 mol/L was used. Use the rate constant derived in Example 14.2. (a) What will the concentration of $N_2O_5(g)$ be after 30.0 minutes? (b) How many minutes will it take for the concentration of $N_2O_5(g)$ to drop to 0.0200 mol/L? (c) How many minutes will it take for 90.0% of the $N_2O_5(g)$ to decompose?

Solution

Since the questions are asked in terms of minutes, not seconds, it is convenient to convert the value of k derived in Example 14.2 into units of "/min" from "/s".

$$k = \left(\frac{1.35 \times 10^{-4}}{1 \text{ s}}\right)\left(\frac{60 \text{ s}}{1 \text{ min}}\right) = 8.10 \times 10^{-3} \text{ min}$$

(a) Equation 14.4 is used:

$$\log\left(\frac{[N_2O_5]_0}{[N_2O_5]}\right) = \frac{kt}{2.303}$$

$$\log\left(\frac{0.0300 \text{ mol/L}}{[N_2O_5]}\right) = \frac{(8.10 \times 10^{-3}/\text{min})(30.0 \text{ min})}{2.303}$$

$$= 0.1055$$

$$\frac{0.0300 \text{ mol/L}}{[N_2O_5]} = \text{antilog } 0.1055$$

$$= 1.275$$

$$[N_2O_5] = \frac{0.0300 \text{ mol/L}}{1.275}$$

$$= 0.0235 \text{ mol/L}$$

(b) Equation 14.4 is again used:

$$\log\left(\frac{0.0300 \text{ mol/L}}{0.0200 \text{ mol/L}}\right) = \frac{(8.10 \times 10^{-3}/\text{min})t}{2.303}$$

$$2.303 \log 1.50 = (8.10 \times 10^{-3}/\text{min})t$$

$$t = \frac{2.303 \log 1.50}{8.10 \times 10^{-3}/\text{min}}$$

$$= \frac{2.303(0.176)}{8.10 \times 10^{-3}/\text{min}}$$

$$= 50.0 \text{ min}$$

(c) This type of problem can be solved by the method used in part (b). Since 90.0% of the N_2O_5 has decomposed, $[N_2O_5]$ is equal to 10.0% of the original concentration, $[N_2O_5]_0$:

$$[N_2O_5] = 0.100[N_2O_5]_0$$
$$= 0.100(0.0300 \text{ mol/L})$$
$$= 0.00300 \text{ mol/L}$$

This value is then substituted in Equation 14.4 in the manner employed in part (b). Another way to solve the problem is to note that since

$$[N_2O_5] = 0.100[N_2O_5]_0$$

$$\frac{[N_2O_5]_0}{[N_2O_5]} = \frac{[N_2O_5]_0}{0.100[N_2O_5]_0}$$

$$= 10.0$$

We use Equation 14.4 again:

$$\log\left(\frac{[N_2O_5]_0}{[N_2O_5]}\right) = \frac{kt}{2.303} \tag{14.4}$$

$$\log 10 = \frac{(8.10 \times 10^{-3}/\text{min})t}{2.303}$$

$$t = \frac{2.303(\log 10)}{8.10 \times 10^{-3}/\text{min}}$$

$$= 284 \text{ min}$$

The time required for half the reactant to react is known as the **half-life** of the reaction, $t_{1/2}$. If one-half of the original concentration of reactant has disappeared,

$$[A] = \tfrac{1}{2}[A]_0 \tag{14.6}$$

We substitute Equation 14.6 into Equation 14.4:

$$\log\left(\frac{[A]_0}{[A]}\right) = \frac{kt}{2.303} \tag{14.4}$$

$$\log\left(\frac{[A]_0}{\tfrac{1}{2}[A]_0}\right) = \frac{kt_{1/2}}{2.303}$$

$$\log 2 = \frac{kt_{1/2}}{2.303}$$

$$t_{1/2} = \frac{2.303(\log 2)}{k}$$

$$t_{1/2} = \frac{0.693}{k} \tag{14.7}$$

Notice that the half-life of any given first-order reaction is a constant that is independent of the concentration of reactant.

Example 14.4

What is the half-life for the decomposition of $N_2O_5(g)$ at 35°C? The rate constant for this reaction run at this temperature is 8.10×10^{-3}/min.

Solution

We solve the problem by substituting into Equation 14.7:

$$t_{1/2} = \frac{0.693}{k} \tag{14.7}$$

$$= \frac{0.693}{8.10 \times 10^{-3}/\text{min}}$$

$$= 85.6 \text{ min}$$

Example 14.5

The half-life for the decomposition of $N_2O_5(g)$ at 65°C is 2.38 min. What is the value of the rate constant, k, for the reaction at this temperature?

Solution

From Equation 14.7,

$$k = \frac{0.693}{t_{1/2}}$$

$$= \frac{0.693}{2.38 \text{ min}}$$

$$= 0.291/\text{min}$$

The curve shown in Figure 14.5, a plot of $[A]$ against t for a first-order reaction, is similar to that shown in Figure 14.3. In Figure 14.5, however, the half-life of the reaction is featured.

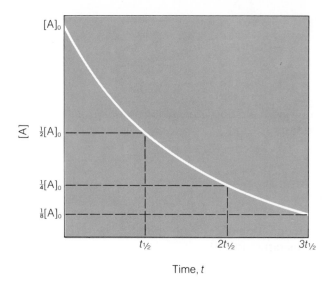

Figure 14.5 A plot of concentration of reactant, [A], *versus* time, *t*, for a first-order reaction. Three half-life periods and the corresponding concentrations are marked on the curve.

At the start of the reaction ($t = 0$), the concentration of A is $[A]_0$, which is indicated in Figure 14.5. After a single half-life period has elapsed, the concentration of A has decreased to one-half the original concentration, $\frac{1}{2}[A]_0$. After a second half-life period has elapsed, $t = 2t_{1/2}$ in Figure 14.5, the concentration of A has decreased by another factor of one-half, to $\frac{1}{4}[A]_0$. This regular decrease is typical of first-order reactions.

Second-Order Reactions

The following are examples of second-order reactions. The corresponding rate equations are shown beside the chemical equations for the reactions.

1. $\quad 2\,NO_2(g) \longrightarrow 2\,NO(g) + O_2(g) \qquad$ rate $= k[NO_2]^2 \qquad$ (14.8)

2. $NO(g) + O_3(g) \longrightarrow NO_2(g) + O_2(g) \qquad$ rate $= k[NO][O_3] \qquad$ (14.9)

We can see, therefore, that two general expressions can be written for rate equations for second-order reactions:

$$\text{rate} = k[A]^2 \tag{14.10}$$

$$\text{rate} = k[A][B] \tag{14.11}$$

We will discuss only the first type of rate equation (Equation 14.10), which is the simpler of the two to handle mathematically. It can be used to describe rate equations for second-order reactions in which there is only a single reactant (such as the reaction shown in Equation 14.8). It can also be used to handle cases in which there are two different reactants (such as that shown in Equation 14.9), but both reactants are present in the same concentration.

Chapter 14 Chemical Kinetics

The differential form of the rate equation (Equation 14.10) is:

$$-\frac{d[A]}{[A]^2} = k\,dt \tag{14.12}$$

By use of calculus, this equation can be converted into:

$$\frac{1}{[A]} - \frac{1}{[A]_0} = kt \tag{14.13}$$

where $[A]_0$ is the initial concentration of A (the concentration of A at time = 0), $[A]$ is the concentration of A at time = t, and k is the rate constant. Equation 14.13 can be rearranged to:

$$\frac{1}{[A]} = kt + \frac{1}{[A]_0} \tag{14.14}$$

Comparison of Equation 14.14 to the general equation for a straight line:

$$y = mx + b$$

reveals that the curve that results when $\frac{1}{[A]}$ is plotted against t is a straight line with a slope equal to k and an intercept of $\frac{1}{[A]_0}$ (see Figure 14.6).

We can find an expression for the half-life of a second-order reaction of this type in the following way. Since half of the original quantity of A has been used at $t_{1/2}$:

$$[A] = \frac{[A]_0}{2} \tag{14.15}$$

Hence, from Equation 14.13:

$$\frac{1}{[A]_0/2} - \frac{1}{[A]_0} = kt_{1/2}$$

$$\frac{2}{[A]_0} - \frac{1}{[A]_0} = kt_{1/2}$$

$$\frac{1}{[A]_0} = kt_{1/2}$$

$$t_{1/2} = \frac{1}{k[A]_0} \tag{14.16}$$

Notice that the half-life of this type of reaction is not independent of the concentration of reactant. The half-life of a specific first-order reactant is the same no matter what initial concentration of reaction is used. The half-life of a specific second-order reaction, however, is variable and depends upon the initial concentration of reactant.

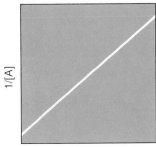

Figure 14.6 A plot of 1/[A] *versus* time, t, for a second-order reaction for which rate = $k[A]^2$. For any second-order reaction of this type, a plot of 1/[A] vs. t is a straight line.

Example 14.6

The decomposition of HI(g):

$$2\,HI(g) \longrightarrow H_2(g) + I_2(g)$$

is a second-order reaction, and the rate constant for the reaction run at 410°C is 5.1×10^{-4} L/(mol·s). In an experiment at 410°C, the initial concentration of HI(g) was 0.36 mol/L. (a) What is the concentration of HI(g) after 12 minutes have elapsed? (b) How many minutes will it take for the concentration of HI to drop to 0.25 mol/L? (c) What is the half-life of this sytem?

Solution

As in our previous examples, it is more convenient to work with minutes rather than seconds as our time unit. We convert the value of k from units of "L/(mol·s)" to units of "L/(mol·min)."

$$k = \left(\frac{5.1 \times 10^{-4}}{1 \ (mol·s)}\right)\left(\frac{60 \ s}{1 \ min}\right) = 3.06 \times 10^{-2} \ L/(mol·min)$$

(a) We use Equation 14.14:

$$\frac{1}{[HI]} = kt + \frac{1}{[HI]_0}$$

$$\frac{1}{[HI]} = [3.06 \times 10^{-2} \ L/(mol·min)][12 \ min] + \frac{1}{0.36 \ mol/L}$$

$$= 0.367 \ L/mol + 2.78 \ L/mol$$

$$= 3.15 \ L/mol$$

$$[HI] = 0.32 \ mol/L$$

(b) We can use Equation 14.13:

$$kt = \frac{1}{[HI]} - \frac{1}{[HI]_0}$$

$$[3.06 \times 10^{-2} \ L/(mol·min)]t = \frac{1}{0.25 \ mol/L} - \frac{1}{0.36 \ mol/L}$$

$$= 4.00 \ L/mol - 2.78 \ L/mol$$

$$= 1.22 \ L/mol$$

$$t = 40 \ min$$

(c) The half-life can be found by using Equation 14.16:

$$t_{1/2} = \frac{1}{k[HI]_0}$$

$$= \frac{1}{[3.06 \times 10^{-2} \ L/(mol·min)][0.36 \ mol/L]}$$

$$= 91 \ min$$

Notice that this half-life period applies only if the initial concentration of HI is 0.36 mol/L. For any other value of $[HI]_0$, $t_{1/2}$ would be different.

Zero-Order Reactions

The rate of a zero-order reaction is independent of the concentration of reactant. In general,

$$\text{rate} = k[A]^0 \tag{14.17}$$

and since $[A]^0 = 1$,

$$\text{rate} = k \tag{14.18}$$

The decompositions of certain gases on the surfaces of solid catalysts are examples of zero-order reactions. The catalyst is written over the arrow in the chemical equation:

$$2\,N_2O(g) \xrightarrow{Au} 2\,N_2(g) + O_2(g)$$

$$2\,HI(g) \xrightarrow{Au} H_2(g) + I_2(g)$$

$$2\,NH_3(g) \xrightarrow{W} N_2(g) + 3\,H_2(g)$$

The differential form of the rate equation for a zero-order reaction is:

$$-\frac{d[A]}{dt} = k \tag{14.19}$$

which can be converted into:

$$[A]_0 - [A] = kt \tag{14.20}$$

or,

$$[A] = -kt + [A]_0 \tag{14.21}$$

Comparison of Equation 14.21 with the equation for a straight line:

$$y = mx + b$$

shows that a plot of $[A]$ against t for a zero-order reaction is a straight line with a slope of $-k$ and an intercept of $[A]_0$ (see Figure 14.7).

An equation for the half-life of a zero-order reaction can be derived from Equation 14.20 by noting that at $t_{1/2}$, $[A]$ is $\frac{1}{2}[A]_0$. Hence:

$$kt_{1/2} = [A]_0 - \tfrac{1}{2}[A]_0 \tag{14.22}$$

$$t_{1/2} = \frac{[A]_0}{2k}$$

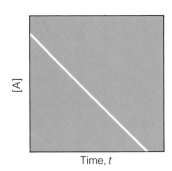

Figure 14.7 A plot of the concentration of reactant, [A], *versus* time, t, for a zero-order reaction for which rate $= k$. For any zero-order reaction, a graph of this type is a straight line.

Table 14.1 Characteristics of some reactions

Order	Rate Equation	Concentration-Time Relationship	Straight-line Plot	Half-life
Zero	rate = k	$[A]_0 - [A] = kt$	$[A]$ vs. t	$[A]_0/2k$
First	rate = $k[A]$	$\log\left(\dfrac{[A]_0}{[A]}\right) = \dfrac{kt}{2.303}$	$\log[A]$ vs. t	$0.693/k$
Second	rate = $k[A]^2$	$\dfrac{1}{[A]} - \dfrac{1}{[A]_0} = kt$	$\dfrac{1}{[A]}$ vs. t	$1/k[A]_0$

Table 14.1 summarizes the characteristics of the zero-order, first-order, and second-order reactions that we have discussed.

Example 14.7

A study of the decomposition of NOCl(g) at 200°C:

$$2\,NOCl(g) \longrightarrow 2\,NO(g) + Cl_2(g)$$

produced the following data:

time (s)	[NOCl](mol/L)
0	0.0250
200	0.0202
400	0.0169
700	0.0136
900	0.0120

Is this reaction zero, first, or second order in NOCl?

Solution

We construct the following table:

t (s)	[NOCl] (mol/L)	log [NOCl]	1/[NOCl] (L/mol)
0	0.0250	−1.60	40.0
200	0.0202	−1.69	49.5
400	0.0169	−1.77	59.2
700	0.0136	−1.87	73.5
900	0.0120	−1.92	83.3

The data in this table are used to prepare three plots: [NOCl] against t, log [NOCl] against t, and 1/[NOCl] against t. In Figure 14.8, we see that the plot of 1/[NOCl] against t is linear. Hence, the reaction is second order in NOCl (see Table 14.1).

$$\text{rate} = k[\text{NOCl}]^2$$

4.4 Single-Step Reactions

The chemical equation for a reaction gives the stoichiometric relationships between the initial reactants and the final products. Usually, however, a reaction occurs by way of a mechanism that consists of several steps. A product of the step may be a reactant in the next step.

Consider the formation of nitrosyl fluoride (ONF) as an example:

$$2\,\text{NO(g)} + \text{F}_2(\text{g}) \longrightarrow 2\,\text{ONF(g)}$$

This reaction is believed to follow a two-step mechanism:

1. $\text{NO(g)} + \text{F}_2(\text{g}) \longrightarrow \text{ONF(g)} + \text{F(g)}$

2. $\text{NO(g)} + \text{F(g)} \longrightarrow \text{ONF(g)}$

Notice that the equations for the steps of the mechanism add up to the chemical equation for the overall reaction. The F atoms that are produced in the first step are used in the second step and therefore cancel in the addition. The F atoms are **reaction intermediates**—substances that are produced and used in the course of a reaction and are therefore neither reactants nor products of the reaction.

Some reactions, however, are believed to occur by a single step. The reaction between methyl bromide (CH_3Br) and sodium hydroxide in aqueous ethyl alcohol as a solvent,

$$\text{CH}_3\text{Br} + \text{OH}^- \longrightarrow \text{CH}_3\text{OH} + \text{Br}^-$$

and the gas-phase reaction

$$\text{CO(g)} + \text{NO}_2(\text{g}) \longrightarrow \text{CO}_2(\text{g}) + \text{NO(g)}$$

are examples. In this section we will consider how reactions of this type occur. Our discussion also applies to the manner in which a single step of a multistep mechanism takes place.

The Collision Theory

The **collision theory of reaction rates** describes reactions in terms of collisions between reacting molecules. Assume that the hypothetical gas-phase reaction:

$$\text{A}_2(\text{g}) + \text{B}_2(\text{g}) \longrightarrow 2\,\text{AB(g)}$$

takes place through collisions between A_2 and B_2 molecules, as shown in Figure 14.9. An A_2 and a B_2 molecule strike one another. The old A—A and B—B bonds

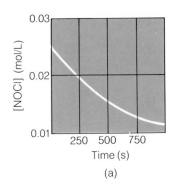
(a)

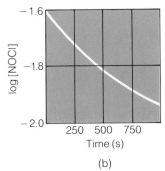
(b)

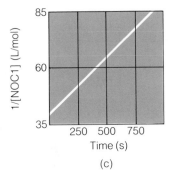
(c)

Figure 14.8 Plots of kinetic data from a study of the reaction $2\,\text{NOCl(g)} \rightarrow 2\,\text{NO(g)} + \text{Cl}_2(\text{g})$ at 200°C. (a) [NOCl] *versus* t, (b) log [NOCl] *versus* t, (c) 1/[NOCl] *versus* t. Since the plot of part (c) is linear, the reaction is second order (see Table 14.1).

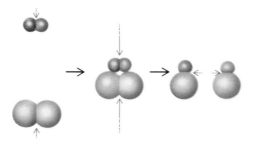

Figure 14.9 Collision between an A_2 molecule and a B_2 molecule resulting in a reaction

break while simultaneously two new A—B bonds form, and two AB molecules leave the scene of the collision. The rate of the reaction is proportional to the number of these collisions that occur in a given time interval.

Calculations show, however, that the number of molecular collisions per unit time in a situation such as this is extremely large. At room temperature and 1 atm pressure, about 10^{31} collisions/L occur in 1 s. If each collision between an A_2 and B_2 molecule resulted in a reaction, the process would be over in a fraction of a second. Most reactions are not this rapid.

Not every A_2-B_2 collision, therefore, can lead to a reaction. Usually the number of collisions that produce reactions, called **effective collisions,** is a very small fraction of the total number of collisions between A_2 and B_2 molecules.

There are two reasons why a collision may not be effective. First, the molecules may be improperly aligned (see Figure 14.10). Second, the collision may be so gentle that the molecules rebound unchanged. The electron cloud of a molecule is, of course, negatively charged. When two slow-moving molecules approach one another closely, they rebound because of the repulsion due to the charges of their electron clouds. Faster-moving molecules, however, are not deterred by this repulsion; the impact of the collision causes the reaction to occur. For an effective collision, the sum of the energies of the colliding molecules must equal or exceed some minimum value.

The effect of temperature on reaction rates reinforces this view. The rates of almost all chemical reactions increase when the temperature is raised. The effect is observed for endothermic as well as exothermic reactions. An increase of 10°C in the temperature, at temperatures near room temperature, is often found to increase the reaction rate from 100% to 300%. The more rapid molecular motion that results from an increase in temperature brings about a larger number of molecular collisions per unit time. This factor alone, however, cannot account for the increase in speed. Raising the temperature from 25°C to 35°C causes an increase in the total number of molecular collisions of only about 2%. Obviously, increasing the temperature must increase the fraction of molecular collisions that are effective, and this factor must be the more important of the two.

By an examination of Figure 14.11, we can understand why proportionately more molecular collisions result in reactions at a higher temperature than at a lower temperature. Two molecular energy distribution curves are shown—one for a temperature, t_1, and another for a higher temperature, t_2. The minimum energy required for reaction is indicated on Figure 14.11. The number of molecules at t_1 with energies equal to or greater than this minimum energy is proportional to the area, a, under the curve for t_1.

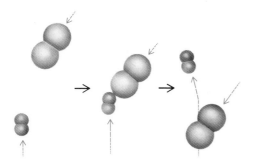

Figure 14.10 Collision between an A_2 molecule and a B_2 molecule producing no reaction

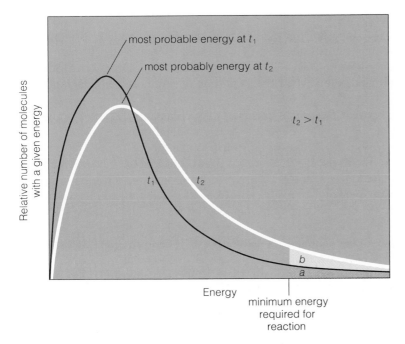

Figure 14.11 Molecular energy distributions at temperatures t_1 and t_2

The curve for temperature t_2 is shifted only slightly in the direction of higher energy. At t_2, however, the number of molecules possessing sufficient energy to react successfully upon collision is greatly increased and is proportional to the area $a + b$. An increase in temperature, therefore, produces an increase in reaction rate principally because the proportion of effective collisions is increased. The increase in the total number of collisions per unit time is only a minor factor. The influence of temperature on reaction rates is analyzed mathematically in Section 14.7.

The Transition State Theory

The energy requirements for a successful collision are described in a slightly different way by the **transition state theory.** Let us again consider the reaction between A_2 and B_2. In a gentle collision, the A_2 and B_2 molecules are repelled by the charges of their electron clouds and never get close enough for A—B bonds to

Flashbulb before and after firing. The bulb contains magnesium wire in an atmosphere of pure oxygen. Passing a small electric current through the Mg wire heats it and provides the activation energy for the reaction, which rapidly produces magnesium oxide, heat, and light. *Fundamental Photographs.*

form. In a successful collision, however, high-energy A_2 and B_2 molecules are assumed to form a short-lived **activated complex,** A_2B_2. The A_2B_2 complex may split to form two AB molecules or may split to re-form A_2 and B_2 molecules:

$$A_2 + B_2 \rightleftharpoons \begin{bmatrix} A ---- A \\ | \quad\quad | \\ | \quad\quad | \\ B ---- B \end{bmatrix} \longrightarrow 2\,AB$$

An activated complex, usually shown between brackets, is not a molecule that can be isolated or detected. Instead, it is an unstable arrangement of atoms that exists only for a moment. It is sometimes called a **transition state.** In the activated complex, the A—A and B—B bonds are weakened and partly broken, and the A—B bonds are only partly formed. The activated complex is a state of relatively high potential energy.

A potential-energy diagram for the reaction between A_2 and B_2 is shown in Figure 14.12. The figure illustrates how the potential energy of the substances involved in the reaction changes in the course of the reaction. Distances along the reaction coordinate indicate how far the formation of products from reactants has progressed.

The difference between the potential energy of the reactants, A_2 and B_2, and the potential energy of the activated complex, A_2B_2, is called the **energy of activation** and is given the symbol $E_{a,f}$. In any collision between an A_2 and a B_2 molecule, the total energy of the molecules remains constant, but kinetic energy (energy of motion) and potential energy may be converted from one form into the other. In a successful collision, part of the kinetic energy of fast-moving A_2 and B_2 molecules is used to provide the energy of activation and produce the high-energy activated complex.

The activated complex can split in two ways. If it re-forms the reactants, A_2 and B_2, the energy of activation, $E_{a,f}$, is released in the form of kinetic energy to the A_2 and B_2 molecules. In this case, there is no net reaction. If the complex splits into the product, two AB molecules, the energy indicated as $E_{a,r}$ on Figure 14.12 is released as kinetic energy to the AB molecules. The difference between the energy absorbed, $E_{a,f}$, and the energy evolved, $E_{a,r}$, is the enthalpy change, ΔH, for the reaction:

$$\Delta H = E_{a,f} - E_{a,r}$$

Since $E_{a,r}$ is larger than $E_{a,f}$ in this example, ΔH is negative and the reaction is exothermic.

The energy of activation is a potential-energy barrier between the reactants and products. Even though the energy of the reactant molecules is higher than the energy of the product molecules, the system must climb a potential-energy hill before it can coast down to a state of lower energy. When A_2 and B_2 molecules that have relatively low kinetic energies approach each other, they do not have enough energy between them to produce the activated complex. The repulsion between their electron clouds prevents them from approaching each other closely enough to form the complex. In this case the molecules have only enough energy to get partway up the hill. Then, repelling each other, they coast back down the hill and fly apart unchanged.

Suppose that the reaction diagrammed in Figure 14.12 were reversible. The reverse reaction can be interpreted by reading the figure from right to left. The energy

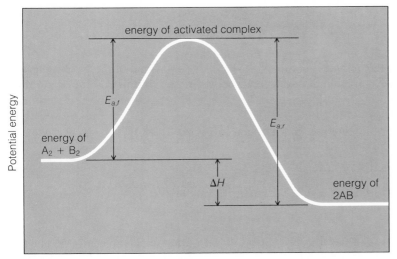

Figure 14.12 Potential-energy diagram for the hypothetical reaction $A_2 + B_2 \rightleftharpoons A_2B_2 \rightleftharpoons 2\,AB$

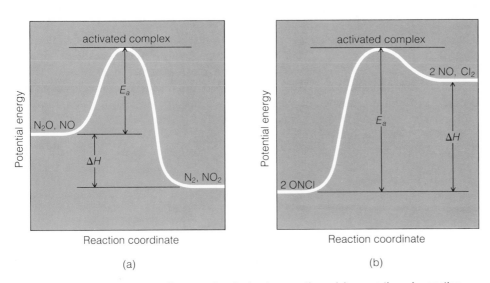

Figure 14.13 Potential-energy diagrams for single-step reactions: (a) an exothermic reaction, and (b) an endothermic reaction

of activation for the reverse reaction is $E_{a,r}$, and the energy released by the formation of the products (in this case A_2 and B_2) from the activated complex is $E_{a,f}$. The enthalpy change for the reverse reaction is

$$\Delta H = E_{a,r} - E_{a,f}$$

The enthalpy change is positive, since $E_{a,r}$ is larger than $E_{a,f}$. The reverse reaction is endothermic.

Two potential-energy diagrams are shown in Figure 14.13—one for an exothermic single-step reaction and one for an endothermic single-step reaction. The exothermic reaction, between N_2O and NO, can be represented as follows:

$$N\equiv N{-}O + N{=}O \rightleftharpoons \left[N\equiv N\cdots O\cdots N\overset{\displaystyle O}{\diagup\diagdown}\right] \longrightarrow N\equiv N + O{-}N\overset{\displaystyle O}{\diagup\diagdown}$$

The diagram of the activated complex shows the N—O bond of the N_2O molecule stretched and weakened and a new bond, between the O atom and the N atom of the NO molecule, partially formed. The energy of activation for the reaction is 209 kJ/mol; ΔH is -138 kJ/mol.

The endothermic reaction diagrammed in Figure 14.13 is

$$O{=}N\diagdown{}_{Cl} + {}_{Cl}\diagup{}N{=}O \rightleftharpoons \left[O{=}N{\overset{\cdot}{\underset{Cl}{}}} \quad {\underset{Cl}{\overset{\cdot}{}}}N{=}O\right] \longrightarrow$$

$$O{=}N + Cl{-}Cl + N{=}O$$

In the activated complex the N—Cl bonds of both ONCl molecules are in the process of breaking and a new Cl—Cl bond is starting to form. The energy of activation for the reaction is 98 kJ/mol; ΔH is $+76$ kJ/mol.

14.5 Rate Equations for Single-Step Reactions

The molecularity of a single step in a reaction refers to the number of molecules that participate in the step. Thus, a step of a mechanism may be called unimolecular, bimolecular, or termolecular depending upon whether one, two, or three molecules react in the step. Most reactions do not occur in a single step, but proceed through a sequence of steps. Each step may be described in terms of its molecularity, but *such a description is not applied to a reaction as a whole when it consists of more than one step.*

The molecularity of a single-step reaction determines its reaction order. The coefficients in the chemical equation for the step appear as exponents in the rate equation. For example,

$$2\,A + B \longrightarrow \text{products} \qquad \text{rate} = k[A]^2[B]$$

the coefficient (2) of A in the chemical equation is the exponent of $[A]$ in the rate equation; the coefficient of B is the exponent of $[B]$. Since the reaction involves three molecules, it is termolecular and the rate equation is third order overall. This method for deriving rate equations cannot be applied routinely to all chemical equations; *it is used only if the chemical equation pertains to a reaction that occurs in one step.* The following types of steps are encountered.

1. Unimolecular steps. A unimolecular reaction is first order:

$$A \longrightarrow \text{products} \qquad \text{rate} = k[A]$$

A reaction of this type occurs when a high-energy A molecule breaks into smaller molecules or rearranges into a new molecular structure. The rate of the reaction is proportional to the concentration of A molecules present.

2. Bimolecular steps. There are two types of bimolecular steps. The first one is

$$A + B \longrightarrow \text{products} \qquad \text{rate} = k[A][B]$$

The reaction occurs by collisions between A and B molecules. The rate of the reaction is proportional to the number A-B collisions per second. If we double the concentration of A, the rate would double since there would be twice as many A molecules in a given volume and twice as many A-B collisions per second. If we tripled the concentration of A, the number of collisions per second would increase by a factor of 3. Whatever we do to the concentration of A is reflected in the rate. The rate, therefore, is proportional to the first power of $[A]$.

In like manner, changes in the concentration of B produce similar changes in the number of A-B collisions per second. The rate is also proportional to the first power of $[B]$. The reaction, therefore, is first order in A, first order in B, and second order overall, as shown by the rate equation given previously.

The second type of bimolecular step is

$$2\,A \longrightarrow \text{products} \qquad \text{rate} = k[A]^2$$

The step occurs by collisions between two A molecules. Suppose that there are n molecules of A in a container. The number of collisions per second for a *single* A molecule is proportional to the number of other A molecules present, $n - 1$. The *total* number of collisions per second for all n molecules might incorrectly be expected to be proportional to n times $(n - 1)$. It is, however, proportional to $\frac{1}{2}n(n - 1)$. The factor $\frac{1}{2}$ is included so that a given collision is not counted twice— once for a collision in which molecule 1 hits molecule 2 and again for a collision in which molecule 2 hits molecule 1.

Since n is a very large number, $(n - 1)$ is equal to n for all practical purposes. We can say that the total number of collisions per second is proportional to $\frac{1}{2}n^2$. Since the rate of the reaction is proportional to the total number of collisions per second,

$$\text{rate} \propto \tfrac{1}{2}n^2$$

The number of molecules in the container, n, determine the concentration of A; n^2, therefore, is proportional to $[A]^2$. The constant $\frac{1}{2}$ can be incorporated into the proportionality constant, k. Thus,

$$\text{rate} = k[A]^2$$

The collision theory, therefore, can be used to justify the fact that the molecularity of a step determines the reaction order.

3. Termolecular steps. There are, in theory, three types of termolecular reactions:

$$A + B + C \longrightarrow \text{products} \qquad \text{rate} = k[A][B][C]$$
$$2\,A + B \longrightarrow \text{products} \qquad \text{rate} = k[A]^2[B]$$
$$3\,A \longrightarrow \text{products} \qquad \text{rate} = k[A]^3$$

Termolecular steps are encountered in reaction mechanisms. They are, however, not common since they involve three-body collisions. Such collisions in which three bodies must come together simultaneously are rare.

The steps in the preceding list are the only types that are thought to occur in reaction mechanisms. Mechanism steps that involve a molecularity higher than three are never postulated. The chance that an effective four-body collision will occur with any regularity is so slight that such collisions are never proposed as a part of a reaction mechanism.

14.6 Reaction Mechanisms

The rate equation for a reaction must be determined by experimentation. A mechanism for the reaction is proposed on the basis of this rate equation and any other available evidence—such as the detection of a reaction intermediate. A mechanism, therefore, is only a hypothesis.

The following rate equation for the formation of nitrosyl fluoride was obtained experimentally:

$$2\,NO + F_2 \longrightarrow 2\,ONF \qquad \text{rate} = k[NO][F_2]$$

The suggested mechanism and the corresponding bimolecular rate equations are

1. $NO + F_2 \longrightarrow ONF + F \qquad \text{rate}_1 = k_1[NO][F_2]$

2. $NO + F \longrightarrow ONF \qquad \text{rate}_2 = k_2[NO][F]$

The two steps add up to the overall reaction, with the F atoms as a reaction intermediate. The first step is assumed to be much slower than the second step. Step 1 produces F atoms slowly. As soon as they are produced, they are rapidly used by step 2. Step 1, therefore, is the bottleneck of the reaction; the overall reaction cannot be faster than this step. Since step 1 controls the overall rate, it is called the **rate-determining step.** For this reason, the rate equation for step 1 is the rate equation for the overall change, with $k = k_1$.

There is no way to tell from a chemical equation whether the reaction it describes proceeds by one step or several. Consider two chemically similar reactions. The reaction of methyl bromide, CH_3Br, and OH^- ion is second order:

$$OH^- + CH_3Br \longrightarrow CH_3OH + Br^- \qquad \text{rate} = k[CH_3Br][OH^-]$$

A single-step mechanism is consistent with this rate equation. The reaction is believed to proceed through a transition state in which the OH^- ion approaches the C atom on the opposite side from the Br atom:

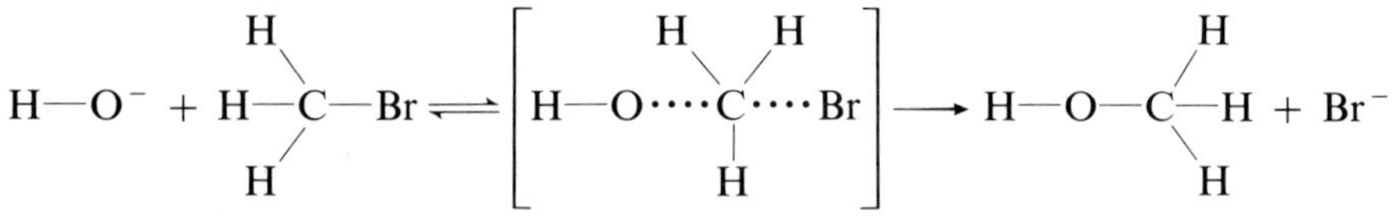

The reaction between tertiary butyl bromide, $(CH_3)_3CBr$, and OH^- ion is chemically similar, but it is first order:

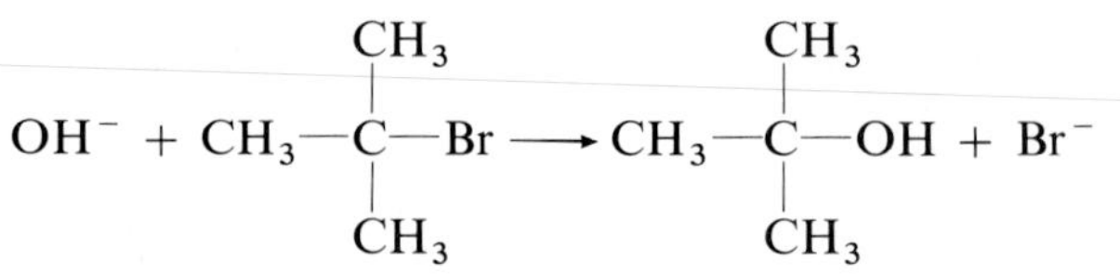

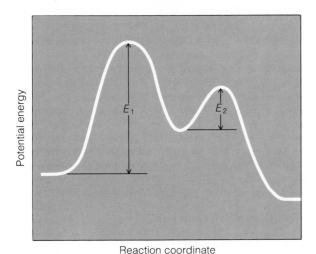

Figure 14.14 Potential-energy diagram for a two-step mechanism in which the first step is rate-determining

The approach of the OH^- ion to the central C atom is blocked by the CH_3-groups, and this reaction follows a different mechanism from that of the reaction between CH_3Br and OH^-. It is thought to occur by two steps:

1. $\qquad (CH_3)_3CBr \longrightarrow (CH_3)_3C^+ + Br^- \qquad$ rate$_1 = k_1[(CH_3)_3CBr]$

2. $(CH_3)_3C^+ + OH^- \longrightarrow (CH_3)_3COH \qquad$ rate$_2 = k_2[(CH_3)_3C^+][OH^-]$

The first step, a unimolecular step in which the $(CH_3)_3CBr$ molecule ionizes, is thought to be the rate-determining step. The overall rate equation, therefore, corresponds to the unimolecular rate equation of step 1.

Each step of a multistep mechanism has a transition state and an activation energy. A two-step mechanism in which the first step is rate-determining, such as the last one or the one for the reaction of NO and F_2, would have a reaction profile similar to that shown in Figure 14.14. The energy of activation for the first step, E_1 on the diagram, is higher than the energy of activation for the second step, E_2. The overall rate, therefore, depends upon the rate at which reacting molecules get over the first potential-energy barrier.

What about a multistep mechanism in which the first step is not rate-determining? Consider the reaction

$$CH_3OH + H^+ + Br^- \longrightarrow CH_3Br + H_2O \qquad \text{rate} = k[CH_3OH][H^+][Br^-]$$

The exponents of the experimentally derived rate equation are the same as the coefficients in the chemical equation. A termolecular single-step mechanism would be consistent with this rate equation. The reaction, however, is believed to occur by a series of steps, none of which is a three-body collision. The third step is thought to be the slowest:

1. $\qquad CH_3OH + H^+ \longrightarrow CH_3OH_2^+ \qquad\qquad$ rate$_1 = k_1[CH_3OH][H^+]$

2. $\qquad\qquad CH_3OH_2^+ \longrightarrow CH_3OH + H^+ \qquad\qquad$ rate$_2 = k_2[CH_3OH_2^+]$

3. $Br^- + CH_3OH_2^+ \longrightarrow CH_3Br + H_2O \qquad$ rate$_3 = k_3[CH_3OH_2^+][Br^-]$

In the first step, the reaction intermediate $CH_3OH_2^+$ is formed. This intermediate can decompose back into CH_3OH and H^+ (step 2) or react with Br^- to form the products (step 3).

Since the third step is the rate-determining step, the overall rate depends upon it:

$$rate = rate_3 = k_3[CH_3OH_2^+][Br^-]$$

This expression, however, contains a term for the concentration of the reaction intermediate, $[CH_3OH_2^+]$. To eliminate this term, we assume that the concentration of the reaction intermediate $CH_3OH_2^+$ becomes constant after the reaction has been going on for a while. That is to say, the intermediate is used as fast as it produced. The intermediate is produced in step 1:

$$\text{rate of appearance of } CH_3OH_2^+ = k_1[CH_3OH][H^+]$$

It is used in steps 2 and 3:

$$\text{rate of disappearance of } CH_3OH_2^+ = k_2[CH_3OH_2^+] + k_3[CH_3OH_2^+][Br^-]$$

Since the third step is *much* slower than the second, k_3 is *much* smaller than k_2. We can, therefore, neglect the term $k_3[CH_3OH_2^+][Br^-]$ since it is much smaller than the term $k_2[CH_3OH_2^+]$:

$$\text{rate of appearance of } CH_3OH_2^+ = \text{rate of disappearance of } CH_3OH_2^+$$

$$k_1[CH_3OH][H^+] = k_2[CH_3OH_2^+]$$

Therefore,

$$[CH_3OH_2^+] = \frac{k_1[CH_3OH][H^+]}{k_2}$$

If we substitute this value into the rate equation for the third step, we get

$$rate = rate_3 = k_3[CH_3OH_2^+][Br^-]$$

$$rate = k_3 \left(\frac{k_1[CH_3OH][H^+]}{k_2} \right)[Br^-]$$

$$rate = \frac{k_1 k_3}{k_2}[CH_3OH][H^+][Br^-]$$

The constants can be combined into a single constant to give

$$rate = k[CH_3OH][H^+][Br^-]$$

which is the experimentally determined rate equation. Note that

$$k = \frac{k_1 k_3}{k_2}$$

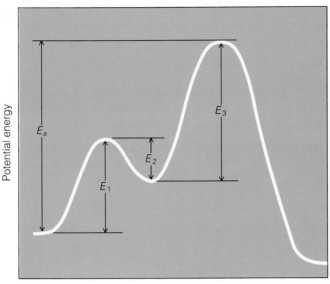

Figure 14.15 Potential-energy diagram for a three-step mechanism in which the third step is rate-determining

A reaction profile for a three-step mechanism such as the preceding one might look something like that shown in Figure 14.15. The activation energies for the steps (E_1, E_2, and E_3) are indicated on the diagram. Remember that step 2 is the reverse of step 1.

The reaction between H_2 gas and Br_2 vapor at temperatures around 200°C provides an example of an important type of reaction mechanism called a chain mechanism:

$$H_2 + Br_2 \longrightarrow 2\,HBr$$

The mechanism for the reaction can be described in four parts:

1. Chain initiation. Some Br_2 molecules dissociate into atoms:

$$Br_2 \longrightarrow 2\,Br$$

2. Chain propagation. The Br atoms are reactive intermediates called chain carriers. A Br atom reacts with a H_2 molecule:

$$Br + H_2 \longrightarrow H\,Br + H$$

The reaction produces a molecule of product, HBr, and a second chain carrier, an H atom. The H atom reacts with a Br_2 molecule:

$$H + Br_2 \longrightarrow HBr + Br$$

producing another molecule of HBr and the original chain carrier, a Br atom. The Br atom reacts with another H_2 molecule, and the cycle starts again. These two steps are repeated over and over again.

3. Chain inhibition. If a H atom collides with a HBr molecule, the reaction that results is said to inhibit the overall reaction:

$$H + HBr \longrightarrow H_2 + Br$$

Since a molecule of product is used (HBr) and a molecule of reactant is produced (H_2), this step slows down the overall reaction. It does not, however, break the chain or stop the reaction since a chain carrier (Br) is also produced.

4. Chain termination. Two chains are terminated when two chain carriers come together:

$$2\,Br \longrightarrow Br_2$$
$$2\,H \longrightarrow H_2$$
$$H + Br \longrightarrow HBr$$

The reaction of $H_2(g)$ and $Cl_2(g)$ is believed to follow a similar mechanism. A mixture of these two gases at room temperature can be kept for a long period of time *in the dark* without reacting. If the mixture is exposed to light, a violently rapid reaction occurs. Light is believed to start the chain reaction by dissociating some Cl_2 molecules into atoms. The reaction of H_2 and Br_2 is also light sensitive, but the reaction at room temperature is slower.

Many reactions are thought to occur by a chain mechanism. Chain reactions are usually very rapid; some of them are explosive.

14.7 Rate Equations and Temperature

The rate constant, k, varies with temperature in a manner described by the following equation:

$$k = Ae^{-E_a/RT} \tag{14.23}$$

where A is a constant that is characteristic of the reaction being studied, e is the base of natural logarithms (2.718 . . .), E_a is the energy of activation for the reaction (in J/mol), R is the molar gas constant [8.3143 J/(K·mol)], and T is the absolute temperature. The equation was first proposed by Svante Arrhenius in 1889 and is known as the **Arrhenius equation.**

For a single-step reaction, the factor $e^{-E_a/RT}$ represents the fraction of molecules that has the energy of activation needed for a successful reaction (see Figure 14.11 in Section 14.4). The constant A, called the **frequency factor,** incorporates other factors that influence reaction rate, such as the frequency of molecular collisions and the geometric requirements for the alignment of colliding molecules that react. The Arrhenius equation is only approximate, but in most cases the approximation is a good one.

The Arrhenius equation also applies to multistep reactions. For a reaction that follows a mechanism such as that to which Figure 14.14 applies, the Arrhenius parameters A and E_a are those for the first step (A_1 and E_1), since the first step is the rate-determining step. In most multistep reactions, however, A and E_a are composites of the values for the individual steps.

In the three-step reaction that was discussed in the last section and in which the third step was rate-determining (see Figure 14.15),

$$k = \frac{k_1 k_3}{k_2}$$

The rate constant for each step may be expressed in terms of the Arrhenius equation (see Equation 14.23). Therefore,

$$k = \frac{A_1 e^{-E_1/RT} A_3 e^{-E_3/RT}}{A_2 e^{-E_2/RT}}$$

or

$$k = \frac{A_1 A_3}{A_2} e^{-(E_1 + E_3 - E_2)/RT}$$

Hence the Arrhenius parameters for the overall rate constant are

$$A = \frac{A_1 A_3}{A_2}$$

and

$$E_a = E_1 + E_3 - E_2$$

If we trace these energy terms in Figure 14.15—E_1 minus E_2 plus E_3—we can see that the overall energy of activation in this case (indicated as E_a in the figure) is equal to the height of the potential-energy barrier of the third step above the potential energy of the initial reactants.

If we take the natural logarithm of the Arrhenius equation, we get

$$\ln k = \ln A - \frac{E_a}{RT} \tag{14.24}$$

which may be transformed into

$$2.303 \log k = 2.303 \log A - \frac{E_a}{RT} \tag{14.25}$$

or

$$\log k = \log A - \frac{E_a}{2.303RT} \tag{14.26}$$

For a given reaction, there are two variables in this equation, k and T. If we rearrange it into

$$\log k = -\frac{E_a}{2.303R} \left(\frac{1}{T}\right) + \log A \tag{14.27}$$

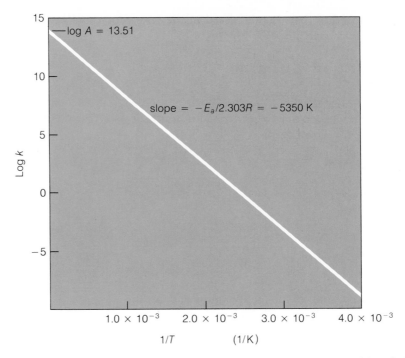

Figure 14.16 Plot of $\log k$ versus $1/T$ for the reaction $2\,N_2O_5(g) \rightarrow 4\,NO_2(g) + O_2(g)$

we can see that the equation is in the form of an equation for a straight line ($y = mx + b$). A plot of $\log k$ against ($1/T$) is a straight line with a slope of $-E_a/2.303R$ and a y-intercept of $\log A$ (Figure 14.16). If values of k are determined at several temperatures and the data plotted in this manner, E_a for the reaction can be calculated from the slope of the curve and A can be obtained by taking the antilogarithm of the y-intercept.

The curve shown in Figure 14.16 pertains to the first-order reaction:

$$2\,N_2O_5(g) \longrightarrow 4\,NO_2(g) + O_2(g)$$

The slope of the curve is -5350 K, from which we obtain

$$-\frac{E_a}{2.30R} = -5350 \text{ K}$$

$$\begin{aligned} E_a &= (5350 \text{ K})(2.30)[8.31 \text{ J/(K}\cdot\text{mol)}] \\ &= 102{,}000 \text{ J/mol} = 102 \text{ kJ/mol} \end{aligned}$$

The y-intercept is 13.51, and therefore

$$\log A = 13.51$$

$$A = 3.2 \times 10^{13}/\text{s}$$

The values of E_a and A for a reaction can also be found from the rate constants for two different temperatures. If the rate constant at T_1 is k_1 and at T_2 is k_2, then

$$\log k_2 = \log A - \frac{E_a}{2.303RT_2} \tag{14.28}$$

and

$$\log k_1 = \log A - \frac{E_a}{2.303RT_1} \tag{14.29}$$

Subtraction of Equation 14.29 from Equation 14.28 gives:

$$\log k_2 - \log k_1 = -\frac{E_a}{2.303RT_2} + \frac{E_a}{2.303RT_1} \tag{14.30}$$

Since $\log x - \log y$ is $\log (x/y)$,

$$\log \left(\frac{k_2}{k_1}\right) = \frac{E_a}{2.303R} \left(\frac{1}{T_1} - \frac{1}{T_2}\right) \tag{14.31}$$

or

$$\log \left(\frac{k_2}{k_1}\right) = \frac{E_a}{2.303R} \left(\frac{T_2 - T_1}{T_1 T_2}\right) \tag{14.32}$$

If this equation is solved for the energy of activation, E_a, the following relationship is obtained:

$$E_a = 2.303R \left(\frac{T_1 T_2}{T_2 - T_1}\right) \log \left(\frac{k_2}{k_1}\right) \tag{14.33}$$

The uses of the last two equations are illustrated in the following examples.

Example 14.8

For the reaction

$$2\,NOCl(g) \longrightarrow 2\,NO(g) + Cl_2(g)$$

the rate equation is

rate of production of $Cl_2 = k[NOCl]^2$

The rate constant, k, is 2.6×10^{-8} L/(mol·s) at 300. K and 4.9×10^{-4} L/(mol·s) at 400. K. What is the energy of activation, E_a, for the reaction?

Solution

Let

$$T_1 = 300.\ K$$
$$T_2 = 400.\ K$$

$$k_1 = 2.6 \times 10^{-8} \text{ L/(mol} \cdot \text{s)}$$

$$k_2 = 4.9 \times 10^{-4} \text{ L/(mol} \cdot \text{s)}$$

R is 8.31 J/(K·mol), and substitution into Equation 14.33 gives

$$E_a = 2.30R \left(\frac{T_1 T_2}{T_2 - T_1} \right) \log \left(\frac{k_2}{k_1} \right) \tag{14.33}$$

$$= 2.30[8.31 \text{ J/(K} \cdot \text{mol})] \left(\frac{(300. \text{ K})(400. \text{ K})}{400. \text{ K} - 300. \text{ K})} \right) \log \left(\frac{4.9 \times 10^{-4} \text{ L/(mol} \cdot \text{s)}}{2.6 \times 10^{-8} \text{ L/(mol} \cdot \text{s)}} \right)$$

$$= [19.1 \text{ J/(K} \cdot \text{mol})](1200 \text{ K}) \log (1.88 \times 10^4)$$
$$= (22{,}900 \text{ J/mol})(4.28)$$
$$= 98{,}000 \text{ J/mol} = 98.0 \text{ kJ/mol}$$

Example 14.9

Given the data found in Example 14.8, find the value of k at 500. K.

Solution

Let

$$T_1 = 400. \text{ K}$$

$$T_2 = 500. \text{ K}$$

$$k_1 = 4.9 \times 10^{-4} \text{ L/(mol} \cdot \text{s)}$$

$$k_2 = \text{unknown}$$

$$E_a = 9.8 \times 10^4 \text{ J/mol}$$

We use Equation 14.32:

$$\log \left(\frac{k_2}{k_1} \right) = \frac{E_a}{2.30R} \left(\frac{T_2 - T_1}{T_1 T_2} \right)$$

$$= \frac{9.8 \times 10^4 \text{ J/mol}}{2.30[8.31 \text{ J/(K} \cdot \text{mol})]} \left(\frac{500. \text{ K} - 400. \text{ K}}{(400. \text{ K})(500. \text{ K})} \right)$$

$$= (5.13 \times 10^3 \text{ K})(5.00 \times 10^{-4} \text{ K})$$

$$= 2.57$$

Therefore,

$$\frac{k_2}{k_1} = \text{antilog } 2.57 = 3.7 \times 10^2$$

or

$$k_2 = (3.7 \times 10^2)k_1$$
$$= (3.7 \times 10^2)[4.9 \times 10^{-4} \text{ L/(mol} \cdot \text{s)}]$$
$$= 0.18 \text{ L/(mol} \cdot \text{s)}$$

Since the relation between k and T is exponential, a small change in T causes a relatively large change in k. Any change in the rate constant is, of course, reflected in the rate of the reaction. For the reaction considered in Examples 14.8 and 14.9, a $100°$ increase in the temperature causes the following effects:

300 K to 400 K   rate increases 18,800 times
400 K to 500 K   rate increases 367 times

The marked effect of a temperature increase is obvious. Notice, however, that the reaction rate is affected more at low temperatures than at high temperatures.

The energies of activation of many reactions range from 60 kJ/mol to 250 kJ/mol, values that are on the same scale as bond energies. For a $10°$ rise is temperature, from 300 K to 310 K, the rate of reaction varies with the energy of activation in the following way:

$E_a = 60$ kJ/mol   rate increases about 2 times

$E_a = 250$ kJ/mol   rate increases about 25 times

1.8 Catalysts

A catalyst is a substance that increases the rate of a chemical reaction without being used up in the reaction. A catalyst may be recovered unchanged at the end of the reaction. Oxygen can be prepared by heating potassium chlorate ($KClO_3$) by itself. Or, a small amount of manganese dioxide (MnO_2) can be used as a catalyst for this reaction. When MnO_2 is present, the reaction is much more rapid and the decomposition of $KClO_3$ takes place at a satisfactory rate at a lower temperature:

$$2\,KClO_3(s) \xrightarrow[\text{heat}]{MnO_2} 2\,KCl(l) + 3\,O_2(g)$$

The catalyst is written over the arrow in the chemical equation since a catalyst does not affect the overall stoichiometry of the reaction. The MnO_2 may be recovered unchanged at the conclusion of the reaction.

The mere *presence* of a catalyst does not cause the effect on the reaction rate. A catalyzed reaction takes place by a pathway, or mechanism, that is different from the one that the uncatalyzed reaction follows. Suppose, for example, that an uncatalyzed reaction occurs by collisions between X and Y molecules:

X + Y $\longrightarrow$ XY

The catalyzed reaction might follow a two-step mechanism consisting of

1. X + C $\longrightarrow$ XC
2. XC + Y $\longrightarrow$ XY + C

where C is the catalyst. Notice that the catalyst is used in the first step and regenerated in the second. It is, therefore, used over and over again. Consequently, only a small amount of a catalyst is needed to do the job.

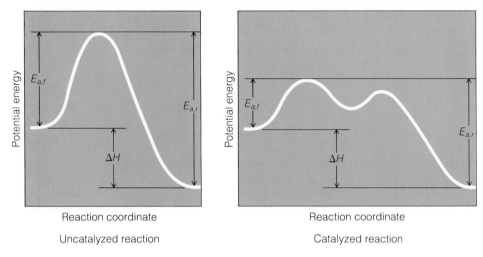

Figure 14.17 Potential-energy diagrams for a reaction in the absence and presence of a catalyst

A catalyst, therefore, works by opening a new path by which the reaction can take place. The catalyzed path has a lower overall energy of activation than the uncatalyzed path does (see Figure 14.17); this accounts for the more rapid reaction rate. Two additional points can be derived from Figure 14.17:

1. The enthalpy change, ΔH, for the catalyzed reaction is the same as the ΔH for the uncatalyzed reaction.

2. For reversible reactions, the catalyst has the same effect on the reverse reaction that it has on the forward reaction. The energy of activation for the reverse reaction, $E_{a,r}$ is lowered by the catalyst to the same extent that energy of activation for the forward reaction, $E_{a,f}$, is lowered.

A **homogeneous catalyst** is present in the same phase as the reactants. An example of homogeneous catalysis in the gas phase is the effect of chlorine gas on the decomposition of dinitrogen oxide gas. Dinitrogen oxide, N_2O, is relatively unreactive at room temperature, but at temperatures near 600°C it decomposes according to the equation

$$2\,N_2O(g) \longrightarrow 2\,N_2(g) + O_2(g)$$

The uncatalyzed reaction is thought to occur by means of a complex mechanism that includes the following steps:

1. Through collisions between N_2O molecules, some N_2O molecules gain enough energy to split apart:

$$N_2O(g) \longrightarrow N_2(g) + O(g)$$

2. The oxygen atoms are very reactive. They readily react with other N_2O molecules:

$$O(g) + N_2O(g) \longrightarrow N_2(g) + O_2(g)$$

The final products of the reaction are N_2 and O_2. The O atom is a reaction intermediate and not a final product. The energy of activation for the uncatalyzed reaction is about 240 kJ/mol.

The reaction is catalyzed by a trace of chlorine gas. The path that has been proposed for the catalyzed reaction consists of the following steps:

1. At the temperature of the decomposition, and particularly in the presence of light, some chlorine molecules dissociate into chlorine atoms:

$$Cl_2(g) \longrightarrow 2\,Cl(g)$$

2. The chlorine atoms readily react with N_2O molecules:

$$N_2O(g) + Cl(g) \longrightarrow N_2(g) + ClO(g)$$

3. The decomposition of the unstable ClO molecules follows:

$$2\,ClO(g) \longrightarrow Cl_2(g) + O_2(g)$$

Notice that the catalyst (Cl_2) is returned to its original state in the last step. The final products of the catalyzed reaction ($2\,N_2$ and O_2) are the same as those of the uncatalyzed reaction. Cl and ClO are not products because they are used in steps that follow the ones in which they are produced. The energy of activiation for the reaction catalyzed by chlorine is about 140 kJ/mol, which is considerably lower than E_a for the uncatalyzed reaction (240 kJ/mol).

In **heterogeneous catalysis** the reactants and catalyst are present in different phases. Reactant molecules are *adsorbed* on the surface of the catalyst in these processes, and the reaction takes place on that surface. **Adsorption** is a process in which molecules adhere to the surface of a solid. Charcoal, for example, is used in gas masks as an adsorbent for noxious gases. In ordinary **physical adsorption,** the molecules are held to the surface by London forces.

Heterogeneous catalysis, however, usually takes place through **chemical adsorption (or chemisorption),** in which the adsorbed molecules are held to the surface by bonds that are similar in strength to those in chemical compounds. When these bonds form, the chemisorbed molecules undergo changes in the arrangement of their electrons. Some bonds of the molecules may be stretched and weakened, and in some cases even broken. Hydrogen molecules, for example, are believed to be adsorbed as hydrogen atoms on the surface of platinum, palladium, nickel, and other metals. The chemisorbed layer of molecules or atoms, therefore, functions as a reaction intermediate in a surface-catalyzed reaction.

The decomposition of N_2O is catalyzed by gold. A proposed mechanism for the gold-catalyzed decomposition is diagrammed in Figure 14.18. The steps are

1. Molecules of $N_2O(g)$ are chemisorbed on the surface of the gold:

$$N_2O(g) \longrightarrow N_2O(\text{on Au})$$

2. The bond between the O atom and the adjacent N atom of a N_2O molecule is weakened when the O atom bonds to the gold. This N—O bond breaks and an N_2 molecule leaves:

$$N_2O(\text{on Au}) \longrightarrow N_2(g) + O(\text{on Au})$$

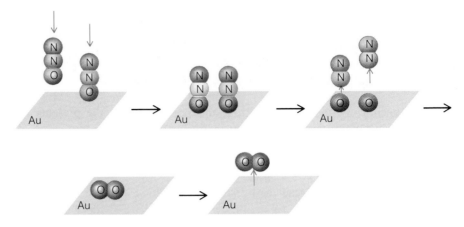

Figure 14.18 Proposed mode of decomposition of N_2O on Au

3. Two O atoms on the surface of the gold combine to form an O_2 molecule that enters the gas phase:

$$O(\text{on Au}) + O(\text{on Au}) \longrightarrow O_2(g)$$

The energy of activation for the gold-catalyzed decomposition is about 120 kJ/mol, which is lower than E_a for either the uncatalyzed decomposition (240 kJ/mol) or the chlorine-catalyzed decomposition (140 kJ/mol).

The second step of the mechanism of the gold-catalyzed decomposition is believed to be the rate-determining step. The rate of this step is proportional to the fraction of the gold surface that holds chemisorbed N_2O molecules. If one-half the surface is covered, step 2 is faster than if only one-quarter of the surface is occupied. This fraction, however, is directly proportional to the pressure of $N_2O(g)$. If the pressure is low, the fraction of surface covered will be low. The rate of the reaction, therefore, is proportional to the concentration of $N_2O(g)$, and the decomposition is first order:

$$\text{rate} = k[N_2O]$$

At high pressures of N_2O, the surface of the gold becomes completely covered; the fraction is equal to 1. Under these conditions, the reaction becomes zero order; that is, the rate is unaffected by changes in the concentration of $N_2O(g)$:

$$\text{rate} = k$$

The gold surface is holding all the N_2O molecules that it can, and the pressure of $N_2O(g)$ is high enough to keep the surface saturated. Small changes in the pressure of $N_2O(g)$ do not cause the chemisorbed N_2O molecules to decompose any more slowly or rapidly.

The electronic structure and arrangement of atoms on the surface of a catalyst determine its activity. Lattice defects and irregularities are thought to be active sites for catalysis. The surfaces of some catalysts can be changed by the addition of substances called **promoters,** which enhance the catalytic activity. In the synthesis of ammonia,

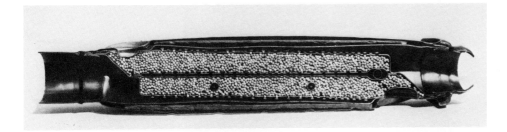

A cross-sectional view of a catalytic converter used in automobiles. Engine exhaust, which enters on the right, is conducted to the top of the converter and forced to pass through dual beds of catalytic beads before exiting at the bottom and to the left. Air is inducted into the chamber between the catalytic beds. The beads contain Pt, Pd, and Rh and are designed to catalyze the oxidation of CO and hydrocarbons to CO_2 and the transformation of the oxides of nitrogen into N_2 and O_2. *General Motors Corporation.*

$$N_2(g) + 3\,H_2(g) \xrightarrow{\text{Fe}} 2\,NH_3(g)$$

an iron catalyst is made more effective when traces of potassium or vanadium are added to it.

Catalytic **poisons** are substances that inhibit the activity of catalysts. For example, small amounts of arsenic destroy the power of platinum to catalyze the preparation of sulfur trioxide from sulfur dioxide:

$$2\,SO_2(g) + O_2(g) \xrightarrow{\text{Pt}} 2\,SO_3(g)$$

Presumably, platinum arsenide forms on the surface of the platinum and destroys its catalytic activity.

Catalysts are generally highly specific in their activity. In some cases a given substance will catalyze the synthesis of one set of products from certain reagents, whereas another substance will catalyze the synthesis of completely different products from the same reactants. In these cases, both reactions are possible and the products obtained are those that are produced most rapidly. Carbon monoxide and hydrogen can be made to yield a wide variety of products, depending upon the catalyst employed and the conditions of the reaction.

If a cobalt or nickel catalyst is used, CO and H_2 produce mixtures of hydrocarbons. One hydrocarbon produced, for example, is methane, CH_4:

$$CO(g) + 3\,H_2(g) \xrightarrow{\text{Ni}} CH_4(g) + H_2O(g)$$

On the other hand, methanol is the product of the reaction of CO and H_2 when a mixture of zinc and chromic oxides is employed as a catalyst:

$$CO(g) + 2\,H_2(g) \xrightarrow{\text{ZnO/Cr}_2\text{O}_3} CH_3OH(g)$$

The catalytic converter installed on car mufflers is a recent application of surface catalysis. Carbon monoxide and hydrocarbons from unburned fuel are present in automobile engine exhaust and are serious air pollutants. In the converter, the exhaust gases and additional air are passed over a catalyst that consists of metal oxides. The CO and hydrocarbons are converted into CO_2 and H_2O, which are re-

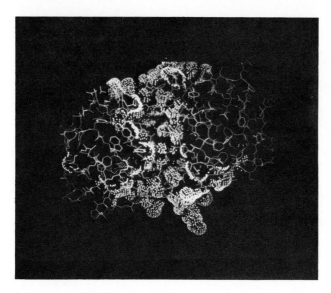

Model of an enzyme. *T. L. Blundell.*

latively harmless and are released to the atmosphere. Since the catalyst is poisoned by lead, unleaded gasoline must be used in automobiles equipped with catalytic converters.

Many industrial processes depend upon catalytic procedures, but the natural catalysts known as enzymes are even more important to man. These extremely complicated substances catalyze life processes such as digestion, respiration, and cell synthesis. The large number of complex chemical reactions that occur in the body, and that are necessary for life, can occur at the relatively low temperature of the body because of the action of enzymes. Thousands of enzymes are known, and each serves a specific function. Research into the structure and action of enzymes may lead to a better understanding of the causes of disease and the mechanism of growth.

Summary

The *rate* of a reaction can be expressed in terms of the *decrease* in concentration of a *reactant* per unit time or the *increase* in concentration of a *product* per unit time. The reaction rate is usually directly proportional to the concentrations of reactants raised to various powers (including zero). The mathematical statement that relates reaction rate to the concentrations of reactants is called a *rate equation* or a *rate law*. The proportionality constant in the rate equation, k, is called the *rate constant*. The *order* of a reaction is equal to the *sum of the exponents* of the concentration terms in the rate equation. The form of a rate equation can be determined by measuring the *initial rates* of a series of reactions in which the *initial concentrations* of the reactants are varied.

Rate equations (which relate reaction *rates* to *concentrations*) can be converted into mathematical expressions that relate *concentrations* to *elapsed time*. These expressions can be used to find a concentration at a given time or to identify the order of a reaction (see Table 14.1).

The *half-life* of a reaction is the time that it takes for half of a reactant to be converted into products. For *first-order reactions*, the half-life is *independent* of the initial *concentrations* of reactants. For other reaction orders, the half-life varies with initial concentrations.

The *collision theory* accounts for the rate of a chemical reaction on the basis of *collisions* between *reacting molecules*. For an *effective collision* (one that results in a reaction), a *minimum energy* is required and the colliding molecules must be *aligned properly*.

The *transition state theory* describes a step in a chemical reaction in terms of the attainment of a transition state (or an *activated complex*). A *potential-energy diagram* can be used to show the potential energies of reactants, activated complex, and products. The *energy of activation*, the difference between the potential energy of the reactants and the potential energy of the activated complex, is a *potential-energy barrier* between reactants products. The *lower* the energy of activation, the *faster* the reaction will be.

Reaction mechanisms, which may consist of one step or several, describe the way in which reactions occur on an atomic, molecular, or ionic level. The *molecularity* of a single *step* of a reaction mechanism determines its reaction *order*. The rate equations for the steps of a proposed mechanism must fit together in such a way as to produce the experimentally determined rate equation for the reaction.

An *increase in temperature increases* the *fraction* of molecules with energies *higher* than the energy of activation. As a result, the *rate* of the reaction *increases*. The *Arrhenius equation* relates the rate constant, k (which increases as the temperature increases), the energy of activation, E_a, and the absolute temperature, T.

Reaction rates are also increased by the addition of *catalysts*. The mechanism of a catalyzed reaction is different from the mechanism of the uncatalyzed reaction. The catalyzed path has a *lower energy of activation*, which accounts for the *more rapid* reaction rate.

Key Terms

Some of the more important terms introduced in this chapter are listed below. Definitions for terms not included in this list may be located in the text by use of the index.

Activated complex (Section 14.4) An unstable arrangement of atoms that exists for only a moment in the course of a chemical reaction; also called a **transition state.**

Arrhenius equation (Section 14.7) An equation that describes how the rate constant for a chemical reaction varies with temperature and with energy of activation.

Catalyst (Section 14.8) A substance that increases the rate of a chemical reaction without being used up in the reaction.

Chain mechanism (Section 14.6) A multistep mechanism for a reaction in which, after an initiation step, two steps are repeated over and over again. A product of the first of these steps is a reactant in the second, and a product of the second of these steps is a reactant in the first.

Chemical adsorption (Section 14.8) A process through which solid, heterogeneous catalysts work. The adsorbed reactant molecules are held to the surface of the catalyst by bonds that are similar in strength to chemical bonds, and in the process the adsorbed molecules become activated.

Chemical kinetics (Introduction) The study of the rates and mechanisms of chemical reactions.

Collision theory (Section 14.4) A theory that describes reactions in terms of collisions between reacting particles (atoms, molecules, or ions).

Effective collision (Section 14.4) A collision between two particles (atoms, molecules, or ions) that results in a reaction.

Energy of activation (Section 14.4) The difference in energy between the potential energy of the reactants and the potential energy of the activated complex in a reaction.

Enzyme (Section 14.8) A natural catalyst that is effective in a biochemical process (such as digestion, respiration, or cell synthesis).

First-order reaction (Sections 14.2 and 14.3) A reaction for which the sum of the exponents of the concentration terms in the rate equation is 1; the rate equation has the form $rate = k[A]$.

Half-life (Section 14.3)   The time required for half of a reactant to react. For first-order reactions, the half-life is independent of the original concentrations of reactants; for reactions of other orders, the half-life depends upon the original concentrations of reactants.

Heterogeneous catalyst (Section 14.8)   A catalyst that is present in a different phase from that of the reactants.

Homogeneous catalyst (Section 14.8)   A catalyst that is present in the same phase as the reactants.

Molecularity (Section 14.5)   The number of reacting particles (atoms, molecules, or ions) that participate in a single step of a reaction mechanism. A step may be **unimolecular, bimolecular, or termolecular,** depending upon whether *one, two,* or *three* particles react in it.

Order of a chemical reaction (Section 14.2)   The sum of the exponents of the concentration terms in the rate equation for a reaction.

Rate constant (Section 14.2)   The proportionality constant in a rate equation.

Rate-determining step (Section 14.5)   The slowest step in a multistep reaction mechanism; the one that determines how fast the overall reaction proceeds.

Rate equation (Section 14.2)   A mathematical equation that relates the rate of a chemical reaction to the concentration of reactants.

Reaction intermediate (Section 14.4)   A substance that is produced and used in the course of a chemical reaction and is therefore neither a reactant nor a product of the reaction.

Reaction mechanism (Section 14.5)   The detailed description of the way a reaction occurs based on the behavior of atoms, molecules, or ions; may include more than one step.

Reaction rate (Section 14.1)   The rate at which a reaction proceeds, expressed in terms of the increase in the concentration of a product per unit time or the decrease in the concentration of a reactant per unit time; the value changes during the course of the reaction.

Second-order reaction (Sections 14.2 and 14.3)   A reaction for which the sum of the exponents of the concentration terms in the rate equation is 2; the rate equation has the form $rate = k[A]^2$ or $rate = k[A][B]$.

Third-order reaction (Section 14.2)   A reaction for which the sum of the exponents of the concentration terms in the rate equation is 3; the rate equation has the form $rate = k[A]^3$, $rate = k[A]^2[B]$, or $rate = k[A][B][C]$.

Transition state theory (Section 14.4)   A theory that proposes reacting particles must assume a specific arrangement, called a transition state, before they can form the products of the reaction.

Zero-order reaction (Sections 14.2 and 14.3)   A reaction for which the rate is a constant value that is independent of concentration; the rate equation for a zero-order reaction contains no concentration term (the concentration term would be raised to the zero power) and has the form $rate = k$.

Problems*

Reaction Rates, Rate Equations

14.1 For a reaction in which A and B form C, the following data were obtained from three experiments:

[A] (mol/L)	[B] (mol/L)	Rate of Formation of C (mol/L·s)
0.30	0.15	7.0×10^{-4}
0.60	0.30	2.8×10^{-3}
0.30	0.30	1.4×10^{-3}

(a) What is the rate equation for the reaction? **(b)** What is the numerical value of the rate constant, k?

14.2 For a reaction in which A and B form C, the following data were obtained from three experiments:

[A] (mol/L)	[B] (mol/L)	Rate of Formation of C (mol/L·s)
0.030	0.030	0.30×10^{-4}
0.060	0.060	1.20×10^{-4}
0.060	0.090	2.70×10^{-4}

(a) What is the rate equation for the reaction? **(b)** What is the numerical value of the rate constant, k?

14.3 The rate equation for the reaction $A \rightarrow B + C$ is expressed in the form

rate of disappearance of $A = k[A]^x$

The value of the rate constant, k, is 0.100 (units unspecified) and $[A] = 0.050$ mol/L. What are the units of k and the rate of the reaction in mol/(L·s) if the reaction is: **(a)** zero order in A, **(b)** first order in A, **(c)** second order in A?

14.4 The rate equation for the reaction $A \rightarrow B + C$ is expressed in terms of the concentration of A only. The rate of disappearance of A is 0.0080 mol/(L·s) when $[A] = 0.20$ mol/L. Calculate the value of k if the reaction is **(a)** zero order in A, **(b)** first order in A, **(c)** second order in A.

14.5 The reaction:

$$2 NO(g) + Cl_2(g) \longrightarrow 2 ONCl(g)$$

is second order in NO(g), first order in $Cl_2(g)$, and third order overall. Compare the initial rate of reaction of a mixture of 0.02 mol of NO(g) and 0.02 mol of $Cl_2(g)$ in a one-liter container with **(a)** the rate of the reaction when half of the NO(g) has been consumed, **(b)** the rate of the reaction when half of the $Cl_2(g)$ has been consumed, **(c)** the rate of the reaction when two-thirds of the NO(g) has been consumed, **(d)** the initial rate of a mixture of 0.04 mol of NO(g) and 0.02 mol of $Cl_2(g)$ in a one-liter container, **(e)** the initial rate of a mixture of 0.02 mol of NO(g) and 0.02 mol of $Cl_2(g)$ in a 0.5-L container.

14.6 The single-step reaction:

$$NO_2Cl(g) + NO(g) \longrightarrow NO_2(g) + ONCl(g)$$

is reversible; $E_{a,f}$ is 28.9 kJ and $E_{a,r}$ is 41.8 kJ. Draw a potential energy diagram for the reaction. Indicate $E_{a,f}$, $E_{a,r}$, and ΔH on the diagram.

14.7 Why are some collisions between molecules of reactants not effective?

14.8 A common and serious mistake is to assume that the rate equation for a reaction can be derived from the balanced chemical equation for the reaction by using the coefficients of the chemical equation as exponents in the rate equation. Why cannot rate equations be derived in this way?

Concentrations and Time

14.9 The reaction

$$C_2H_5Cl(g) \longrightarrow C_2H_4(g) + HCl(g)$$

is first order in C_2H_5Cl. The rate constant is 1.60×10^{-6}/s for the reaction conducted at 650. K. In an investigation of the decomposition of $C_2H_5Cl(g)$, an initial concentration of 0.165 mol/L was used. **(a)** What will the concentration of $C_2H_5Cl(g)$ be after 125 hours? **(b)** How many hours will it take for the concentration of C_2H_5Cl to drop to 0.100 mol/L? **(c)** How many hours will it take for 75.0% of the C_2H_5Cl to decompose?

14.10 The reaction

$$S_2F_{10}(g) \longrightarrow SF_6(g) + SF_4(g)$$

is first order in $S_2F_{10}(g)$. The rate constant is 4.94×10^{-6}/s for the reaction conducted at 448 K. In an investigation of the decomposition of $S_2F_{10}(g)$, an initial concentration of 0.235 mol/L was used. **(a)** What will the concentration of $S_2F_{10}(g)$ be after 32.5 hours? **(b)** How many hours will it take for the concentration of $S_2F_{10}(g)$ to drop to 0.230 mol/L? **(c)** How many hours will it take for 35.0% of the S_2F_{10} to decompose?

---

* The more difficult problems are marked with asterisks. The appendix contains answers to color-keyed problems.

14.11 Use the data given in problem 14.9 to determine the half-life (in hours) for the decomposition of $C_2H_5Cl(g)$ at 650. K.

14.12 Use the data given in problem 14.10 to determine the half-life (in hours) for the decomposition of $S_2F_{10}(g)$ at 448 K.

14.13 The decomposition of $NO_2(g)$:

$$2\,NO_2(g) \longrightarrow 2\,NO(g) + O_2(g)$$

is a second order reaction, and the rate constant is 0.755 L/(mol·s) for the reaction conducted at 603 K. In an experiment at 603 K, the initial concentration of $NO_2(g)$ was 0.00650 mol/L. **(a)** What is the concentration of $NO_2(g)$ after 125 s have elapsed? **(b)** How many seconds will it take for the concentration of $NO_2(g)$ to drop to 0.00100 mol/L?

14.14 The decomposition of $NOCl(g)$:

$$2\,NOCl(g) \longrightarrow 2\,NO(g) + Cl_2(g)$$

is a second order reaction and the rate constant is 0.0480 L/(mol·s) for the reaction conducted at 200°C. In an experiment at 200°C, the initial concentration of $NOCl(g)$ was 0.400 mol/L. **(a)** What is the concentration of $NOCl(g)$ after 15.0 min have elapsed? **(b)** How many minutes will it take for the concentration of $NOCl(g)$ to drop to 0.150 mol/L?

14.15 Determine the half-life for the decomposition of $NO_2(g)$ described in problem 14.13.

14.16 Determine the half-life for the decomposition of $NOCl(g)$ described in problem 14.14.

14.17 The decomposition of $N_2O_5(g)$:

$$2\,N_2O_5(g) \longrightarrow 4\,NO_2(g) + O_2(g)$$

is first order. The half-life for this reaction at 45°C is 21.8 min. What is the rate constant (in /s) for the reaction at this temperature?

14.18 The decomposition of cyclobutane, $C_4H_8(g)$:

$$C_4H_8(g) \longrightarrow 2\,C_2H_4(g)$$

is first order. The half-life for this reaction at 700. K is 1.57 hour. What is the rate constant (in /s) for this reaction at this temperature?

14.19 A study of the decomposition of $SO_2Cl_2(g)$ at 320.°C:

$$SO_2Cl_2(g) \longrightarrow SO_2(g) + Cl_2(g)$$

produced the following data:

time (min)	$[SO_2Cl_2]$ (mol/L)
0	0.0450
100.	0.0394
200.	0.0345
300.	0.0302
500.	0.0233
700.	0.0179

Use these data to determine graphically whether the reaction is zero, first, or second order in SO_2Cl_2.

14.20 A study of the decomposition of $Cl_2O_7(g)$ at 100.°C:

$$2\,Cl_2O_7(g) \longrightarrow 2\,Cl_2(g) + 7\,O_2(g)$$

produced the following data:

time (min)	$[Cl_2O_7]$ (mol/L)
0	0.0600
15.5	0.0482
25.0	0.0421
50.0	0.0295
60.0	0.0256
72.5	0.0214

Use these data to determine graphically whether the reaction is zero, first, or second order in Cl_2O_7.

Reaction Mechanisms, Catalysts

14.21 The reaction:

$$2\,ICl(g) + H_2(g) \longrightarrow I_2(g) + 2\,HCl(g)$$

at temperatures above 200.°C is first order in $ICl(g)$ and first order in $H_2(g)$. Suggest a mechanism of two steps with the first step rate-determining to account for the rate equation.

14.22 The reaction:

$$2\,NO_2Cl \longrightarrow 2\,NO_2(g) + Cl_2(g)$$

is first order in $NO_2Cl(g)$. Suggest a mechanism of two steps with the first step rate-determining to account for the rate equation.

*14.23 According to the collision theory, a first-order decomposition (A → products) proceeds by the following steps:

$$A + A \xrightarrow{k_1} A^* + A$$
$$A^* + A \xrightarrow{k_2} A + A$$
$$A^* \xrightarrow{k_3} \text{products}$$

In step 1, two A molecules collide, energy is transferred, and one molecule (marked A*) attains a high-energy state. A subsequent collision of A* can cause the process to reverse (step 2). Some A* molecules, however, decompose to form the products in the rate determining step. Derive a rate equation from this mechanism by assuming that [A*] becomes constant after the reaction has been going on for a while (that is, A* is used as fast as it is being produced). Remember that since step 3 is slow, k_3 is much smaller than k_2.

*14.24 For the reaction:

$$N_2O_5(g) + NO(g) \longrightarrow 3\,NO_2(g)$$

the rate equation is

$$\text{rate of disappearance of } N_2O_5 = \frac{k_1 k_3 [N_2O_5][NO]}{k_2[NO_2] + k_3[NO]}$$

The suggested mechanism is:

$$N_2O_5 \xrightarrow{k_1} NO_2 + NO_3$$
$$NO_2 + NO_3 \xrightarrow{k_2} N_2O_5$$
$$NO + NO_3 \xrightarrow{k_3} 2\,NO_2$$

Assume that [NO_3] becomes constant after the reaction has been going on for a while (that is, NO_3 is used as fast as it is produced). Show that the mechanism leads to the observed rate equation.

*14.25 The rate equation for the reaction:

$$2\,NO(g) + O_2(g) \longrightarrow 2\,NO_2(g)$$

is second order in NO(g) and first order in $O_2(g)$. The following mechanism has been suggested:

$$NO + O_2 \xrightarrow{k_1} NO_3$$
$$NO_3 \xrightarrow{k_2} NO + O_2$$
$$NO_3 + NO \xrightarrow{k_3} 2\,NO_2$$

The third step in the mechanism is the rate-determining

step. Assume that [NO_3] becomes constant after the reaction has been going on for a while (that is, NO_3 is used as fast as it is produced). Show that this mechanism leads to the observed rate equation. Remember that k_3 is much smaller than either k_1 or k_2.

*14.26 The rate equation for the reaction:

$$2\,O_3(g) \longrightarrow 3\,O_2(g)$$

has been determined experimentally to be:

$$\text{rate of disappearance of } O_3 = k\,\frac{[O_3]^2}{[O_2]}$$

The following mechanism has been postulated for the decomposition of ozone:

$$O_3 \xrightarrow{k_1} O_2 + O$$
$$O_2 + O \xrightarrow{k_2} O_3$$
$$O + O_3 \xrightarrow{k_3} 2\,O_2$$

The third step of the mechanism is the rate-determining step. Assume that [O] becomes constant after the reaction has been going on for a while (that is, O is used as fast as it is produced). Show that this mechanism leads to the observed rate equation. Remember that k_3 is much smaller than either k_1 or k_2.

14.27 Use potential energy diagrams to explain how a catalyst functions. Does a catalyst affect the value of ΔH for the reaction? Can a catalyst slow a reaction down? Can a catalyst be found that affects only the forward reaction of a reversible reaction? Explain each of your answers.

14.28 For the mechanism for the decomposition of ozone outlined in problem 14.26, the proposed activation energies for the three steps are 100. kJ, 4 kJ, and 24 kJ. The value of ΔH for the overall reaction is -285 kJ. Draw a potential energy diagram for the reaction.

Rate Equations and Temperature

14.29 For the reaction:

$$NO_2Cl(g) + NO(g) \longrightarrow NO_2(g) + ONCl(g)$$

A is 8.3×10^8 and E_a is 28.9 kJ/mol. The rate equation is first order in NO_2Cl and first order in NO. What is the rate constant, k, for the reaction at 500. K?

14.30 For the reaction:

$$NO(g) + N_2O(g) \longrightarrow NO_2(g) + N_2(g)$$

A is 2.5×10^{11} and E_a is 209 kJ/mol. The rate equation is first order in NO and first order in N_2O. What is the rate constant, k, for the reaction at 1000. K?

14.31 The reaction:

$$2\,NO(g) \longrightarrow N_2(g) + O_2(g)$$

is second order in NO(g). The rate constant is 0.143 L/(mol·s) for the reaction at 1400. K and 0.659 L/(mol·s) for the reaction at 1500. K. What is the energy of activation for the reaction?

14.32 The reaction:

$$HI(g) + CH_3I(g) \longrightarrow CH_4(g) + I_2(g)$$

is first order in each of the reactants and second order overall. The rate constant is 1.7×10^{-5} L/(mol·s) for the reaction at 430. K and 9.6×10^{-5} L/(mol·s) for the reaction at 450. K. What is the energy of activation for the reaction?

14.33 The reaction:

$$C_2H_4(g) + H_2(g) \longrightarrow C_2H_6(g)$$

is first order in C_2H_4, first order in H_2, and second order overall. The energy of activation for the reaction is 181 kJ/mol and k is 1.3×10^{-3} L/(mol·s) for the reaction at 700. K. What is the value of k for the reaction conducted at 730. K?

14.34 The reaction:

$$NO(g) + N_2O(g) \longrightarrow NO_2(g) + N_2(g)$$

is first order in each of the reactants and second order overall. The energy of activation of the reaction is 209 kJ/mol and k is 0.77 L/(mol·s) for the reaction at 950. K. What is the value of k for the reaction conducted at 1000. K?

14.35 The reaction:

$$C_2H_5Br(g) \longrightarrow C_2H_4(g) + HBr(g)$$

is first order in C_2H_5Br. The rate constant, k, is 2.0×10^{-5}/s at 650. K, and the energy of activation, E_a, is 226 kJ/mol. At what temperature is the rate constant 6.0×10^{-5}/s?

14.36 The reaction:

$$2\,N_2O_5(g) \longrightarrow 4\,NO_2(g) + O_2(g)$$

is first order in C_2H_5Br. The rate constant, k, is 2.0×10^{-5}/s at 650. K, and the energy of activation, E_a, is 226 kJ/mol. At what temperature is the rate constant 6.0×10^{-5}/s?

14.37 At 400. K, a certain reaction is 50.0% complete in 1.50 min. At 430. K, the same reaction is 50.0% complete in 0.50 min. Calculate the energy of activation of the reaction.

14.38 What is the energy of activation of a reaction that increases ten-fold in rate when the temperature is increased from 300. K to 310. K?

Unclassified Problems

14.39 The rate equation for the reaction:

$$2\,NO(g) + 2\,H_2(g) \longrightarrow N_2(g) + 2\,H_2(g)$$

is second order in NO(g) and first order in $H_2(g)$. **(a)** Write an equation for the rate of appearance of $N_2(g)$. **(b)** If concentrations are expressed in mol/L, what units would the rate constant, k, have? **(c)** Write an equation for the rate of disappearance of NO(g). Would k in this equation have the same numerical value as k in the equation of part a?

14.40 The reaction:

$$C_2H_5Cl(g) \longrightarrow C_2H_4(g) + HCl(g)$$

is first order in C_2H_5Cl. The rate constant for the reaction conducted at 600. K is 3.5×10^{-8}/s and for the reaction at 650. K is 1.6×10^{-6}/s. What is the energy of activation for the reaction?

14.41 Use the data given in problem 14.40 to calculate the half-life for the decomposition of C_2H_5Cl **(a)** at 600. K, **(b)** at 650. K.

14.42 The reaction:

$$CH_4(g) + Cl_2(g) \longrightarrow CH_3Cl(g) + HCl(g)$$

proceeds by a chain mechanism. The chain propagators are Cl· atoms and CH_3· radicals, and it is believed that free H· atoms are not involved. Write a series of equations showing the mechanism and identify the chain-initiating, chain-sustaining, and chain-terminating steps.

14.43 What is the difference between a heterogeneous and homogeneous catalyst? Describe the way in which each type of catalyst functions.

14.44 The synthesis of perbromates has only recently been accomplished. The best preparation involves the oxidation of bromates in alkaline solution by fluorine. What reasons can you give to account for the difficulty encountered in the synthesis of perbromates? How well would you expect perbromates to function as oxidizing agents?

C H A P T E R CHEMICAL EQUILIBRIUM

15

Under suitable conditions, nitrogen and hydrogen react to form ammonia:

$$N_2(g) + 3H_2(g) \longrightarrow 2NH_3(g)$$

On the other hand, ammonia decomposes at high temperatures to yield nitrogen and hydrogen:

$$2NH_3(g) \longrightarrow N_2(g) + 3H_2(g)$$

The reaction is reversible, and the equation for the reaction can be written

$$N_2(g) + 3H_2(g) \rightleftharpoons 2NH_3(g)$$

The double arrow ($\rightleftharpoons$) indicates that the equation can be read in either direction.

All reversible processes tend to attain a state of equilibrium. For a reversible chemical reaction, an equilibrium state is attained when the rate at which a chemical reaction is proceeding equals the rate at which the reverse reaction is proceeding. Equilibrium systems that involve reversible chemical reactions are the topic of this chapter.

15.1 Reversible Reactions and Chemical Equilibrium

Consider a hypothetical reversible reaction

$$A_2(g) + B_2(g) \rightleftharpoons 2AB(g)$$

This equation may be *read either forward or backward*. If A_2 and B_2 are mixed, they will react to produce AB. A sample of pure AB, on the other hand, will decompose to form A_2 and B_2.

Suppose that we place a mixture of A_2 and B_2 in a container. They will react to produce AB, and their concentrations will gradually decrease as the forward reaction occurs (see Figure 15.1). Since the concentrations of A_2 and B_2 decrease, the rate of the forward reaction decreases.

At the start of the experiment, the reverse reaction cannot occur since there is no AB present. As soon as the forward reaction produces some AB, however,

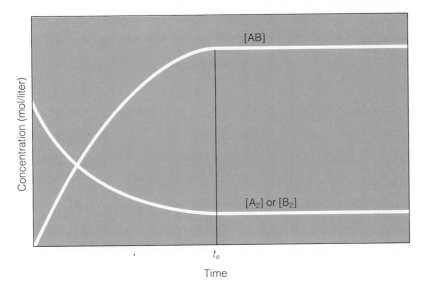

Figure 15.1 Curves showing changes in concentrations of materials with time for the reaction $A_2 + B_2 \rightleftharpoons 2\,AB$. Equilibrium is attained at time t_e.

the reverse reaction begins. The reverse reaction starts slowly (since the concentration of AB is low) and gradually picks up speed.

As time passes, the rate of the forward reaction decreases and the rate of the reverse reaction increases until the two rates are equal. At this point, **chemical equilibrium** is established. An equilibrium condition is a dynamic one in which two opposing changes are occurring at equal rates.

At equilibrium, the concentrations of all the substances are constant. The concentration of AB is constant, since AB is produced by the forward reaction at the same rate that it is used by the reverse reaction. In like manner, A_2 and B_2 are being made (by the reverse reaction) at the same rate that they are being used (by the forward reaction). It is important to note that the concentrations are constant because the rates of the opposing reactions are equal and *not* because all activity has stopped. Data for the experiment are plotted in Figure 15.1. Equilibrium is attained at time t_e.

If we assume that the forward and reverse reactions occur by simple one-step mechanisms, the rate of the forward reaction is

$$\text{rate}_f = k_f[A_2][B_2]$$

and the rate of the reverse reaction is

$$\text{rate}_r = k_r[AB]^2$$

At equilibrium, these two rates are equal, and therefore

$$\text{rate}_f = \text{rate}_r$$
$$k_f[A_2][B_2] = k_r[AB]^2$$

This equation can be rearranged to

$$\frac{k_f}{k_r} = \frac{[AB]^2}{[A_2][B_2]}$$

The rate constant of the forward reaction, k_f, divided by the rate constant of the reverse reaction, k_r, is equal to a third constant, which is called the **equilibrium constant**, K:

$$\frac{k_f}{k_r} = K \tag{15.1}$$

Therefore,

$$K = \frac{[AB]^2}{[A_2][B_2]}$$

The numerical value of K varies with temperature. There are an unlimited number of combinations of concentrations that pertain to equilibrium systems for this reaction. The concentrations, however, of A_2, B_2, and AB for *any* system in equilibrium at a given temperature will, when expressed in the preceding manner, equal the same value of K.

In general, for any reversible reaction

$$w\text{W} + x\text{X} \rightleftharpoons y\text{Y} + z\text{Z} \tag{15.2}$$

at equilibrium,

$$K = \frac{[Y]^y[Z]^z}{[W]^w[X]^x} \tag{15.3}$$

By convention, the concentration terms for the substances on the *right* of the chemical equation are written in the *numerator* of the expression for the equilibrium constant.

As an example, consider the reversible reaction,

$$4\,\text{HCl(g)} + \text{O}_2\text{(g)} \rightleftharpoons 2\,\text{H}_2\text{O(g)} + 2\,\text{Cl}_2\text{(g)} \tag{15.4}$$

The expression for the equilibrium constant that corresponds to this chemical equation is:

$$K = \frac{[\text{H}_2\text{O}]^2[\text{Cl}_2]^2}{[\text{HCl}]^4[\text{O}_2]} \tag{15.5}$$

If the general equation (Equation 15.2) were written in reverse form:

$$y\text{Y} + z\text{Z} \rightleftharpoons w\text{W} + x\text{X} \tag{15.6}$$

the expression for the equilibrium constant (which we will indicate as K') would be:

$$K' = \frac{[W]^w[X]^x}{[Y]^y[Z]^z} \tag{15.7}$$

Notice that K' (in Equation 15.7) is the reciprocal of K (in Equation 15.3):

$$K' = \frac{1}{K} \tag{15.8}$$

For our example (Equation 15.4), the chemical equation in reverse form is:

$$2\,H_2O(g) + 2\,Cl_2(g) \rightleftharpoons 4\,HCl(g) + O_2(g) \qquad (15.9)$$

and the expression for the corresponding equilibrium constant is:

$$K = \frac{[HCl]^4[O_2]}{[H_2O]^2[Cl_2]^2} \qquad (15.10)$$

In our derivation, we assumed that the forward and reverse reactions occurred by mechanisms each consisting of a single step. Does the law of chemical equilibrium hold for reactions that occur by mechanisms of more than one step? It does. Consider the reaction

$$2\,NO_2Cl(g) \rightleftharpoons 2\,NO_2(g) + Cl_2(g)$$

for which the expression for the equilibrium constant is

$$K = \frac{[NO_2]^2[Cl_2]}{[NO_2Cl]^2} \qquad (15.11)$$

The reaction is believed to occur by means of a mechanism consisting of two steps:

1. $\qquad NO_2Cl \underset{k_1'}{\overset{k_1}{\rightleftharpoons}} NO_2 + Cl$

2. $NO_2Cl + Cl \underset{k_2'}{\overset{k_2}{\rightleftharpoons}} NO_2 + Cl_2$

Symbols for the rate constants appear above and below the arrows in these equations. The symbol k is used for the rate constant of the forward reaction, and k' is used for the reverse reaction. The subscripts of these symbols designate the steps.

Since the overall reaction is reversible, each step of the mechanism must also be reversible. When equilibrium is established for the overall reaction, each step of the mechanism must be in equilibrium. Therefore,

$$K_1 = \frac{k_1}{k_1'} = \frac{[NO_2][Cl]}{[NO_2Cl]} \qquad (15.12)$$

and

$$K_2 = \frac{k_2}{k_2'} = \frac{[NO_2][Cl_2]}{[NO_2Cl][Cl]} \qquad (15.13)$$

The product of these expressions (Equation 15.12 times Equation 15.13) is

$$K_1K_2 = \frac{k_1k_2}{k_1'k_2'} = \frac{[NO_2][Cl]}{[NO_2Cl]}\frac{[NO_2][Cl_2]}{[NO_2Cl][Cl]} = \frac{[NO_2]^2[Cl_2]}{[NO_2Cl]^2}$$

which is the same as the expression for the equilibrium constant that we derived directly from the equation for the overall change (Equation 15.11). In this case, the equilibrium constant for the overall change is the product of the equilibrium constants of each of the steps:

$$K = K_1 K_2$$

15.2 The Equilibrium Constant K_c

An equilibrium constant in which the concentrations of substances are expressed in moles per liter is sometimes given the designation K_c.* For the reaction:

$$H_2(g) = I_2(g) \rightleftharpoons 2\,HI(g)$$

the value of K_c for equilibrium systems at 425°C is:

$$K_c = \frac{[HI]^2}{[H_2][I_2]} = 54.5$$

The numerical value of an equilibrium constant must be determined experimentally. If the concentrations (in mol/L) of the substances present in any equilibrium mixture at 425°C are substituted into the expression for K_c, the result will equal 54.5 (see Table 15.1).

An equilibrium mixture may be prepared from the substances that appear on the right in the corresponding chemical equation, from those on the left, or from

Table 15.1   Equilibrium systems for the reaction:
$H_2(g) + I_2(g) \rightleftharpoons 2\,HI(g)$ at 425°C

	Initial Concentrations (mol/L)			Equilibrium Concentrations (mol/L)			Equilibrium Constant $K_c = \dfrac{[HI]^2}{[H_2][I_2]}$
	$[H_2]$	$[I_2]$	$[HI]$	$[H_2]$	$[I_2]$	$[HI]$	
1.	—	—	0.0150	0.00160	0.00160	0.0118	54.4
2.	0.00932	0.00805	—	0.00257	0.00130	0.0135	54.5
3.	0.00104	—	0.0145	0.00224	0.00120	0.0121	54.5
4.	0.00375	0.00375	0.00375	0.00120	0.00120	0.00886	54.5

---

* For exact work, equilibrium constants that have been derived from thermodynamic measurements should be used (Section 19.7). These thermodynamic equilibrium constants are written in terms of activities rather than concentrations (in mol/L for a K_c; Section 15.2) or pressures (in atm for a K_p; Section 15.3). At low concentrations and pressures up to a few atmospheres, however, concentrations and partial pressures may be used with reasonable accuracy.

A full discussion of activities is beyond the scope of this book. We note, however, that an activity *does not have units* since it is a *ratio* of an actual concentration or pressure to the concentration or pressure of the substance in the standard state. As a result, thermodynamic equilibrium constants are *quantities without units*. For this reason, equilibrium constants of all types are frequently expressed without units. As an introduction to the topic of chemical equilibrium, however, we shall use units for K_c and K_p in this chapter. In some instances (the HI equilibrium, for example), K_c has no units because they cancel.

a combination of substances. In the experiments listed in Table 15.1, equilibrium mixtures for the reaction:

$$H_2(g) + I_2(g) = 2\,HI(g)$$

were obtained by allowing pure HI to dissociate (experiment 1), mixing H_2 and I_2 (experiment 2), mixing H_2 and HI (experiment 3), and mixing all three substances (experiment 4). In terms of concentrations, none of the equilibrium mixtures listed in the table is like any other; but the concentrations for each of them, when substituted into the expression for K_c, give an essentially constant value for K_c.

Example 15.1

For the reaction

$$N_2O_4(g) \rightleftharpoons 2\,NO_2(g)$$

the concentrations of the substances present in an equilibrium mixture at 25°C are

$$[N_2O_4] = 4.27 \times 10^{-2}\ mol/L$$
$$[NO_2] = 1.41 \times 10^{-2}\ mol/L$$

What is the value of K_c for this temperature?

Solution

$$K = \frac{[NO_2]^2}{[N_2O_4]}$$
$$= \frac{(1.41 \times 10^{-2}\ mol/L)^2}{(4.27 \times 10^{-2}\ mol/L)}$$
$$= 4.66 \times 10^{-3}\ mol/L$$

Example 15.2

At 500 K, 1.00 mol of ONCl(g) is introduced into a one-liter container. At equilibrium, the ONCl(g) is 9.0% dissociated:

$$2\,ONCl(g) \rightleftharpoons 2\,NO(g) + Cl_2(g)$$

Calculate the value of K_c for the equilibrium at 500 K.

Solution

By considering exactly one liter, we simplify the problem, since the number of moles of a gas is the same as the concentration of the gas (in mol/L).

Since the ONCl is 9.0% dissociated,

number of moles dissociated = 0.090(1.00 mol) = 0.090 mol ONCl

We must subtract this quantity from the number of moles of ONCl present initially. The concentration of ONCl at equilibrium, therefore, is

$$[ONCl] = 1.00 \text{ mol/L} - 0.090 \text{ mol/L} = 0.91 \text{ mol/L}$$

The ONCl that dissociates produces NO and Cl_2. We can derive the amounts of these substances produced from the coefficients of the chemical equation:

$$2\,ONCl \rightleftharpoons 2\,NO + Cl_2$$
$$ 0.090 \text{ mol} \quad 0.045 \text{ mol}$$

Since 2 mole of ONCl produces 2 mol of NO, 0.090 mol of ONCl will produce 0.090 mol of NO. The equation shows that 2 mol of ONCl produces only 1 mol of Cl_2; therefore, 0.090 mol of ONCl will produce 0.045 mol of Cl_2. The equilibrium concentrations are

$$[ONCl] = 0.91 \text{ mol/L}$$
$$[NO] = 0.090 \text{ mol/L}$$
$$[Cl_2] = 0.045 \text{ mol/L}$$

A technique for developing data of this type consists of the preparation of a table showing the initial concentrations, the changes in these values, and finally the equilibrium concentrations. The stoichiometry of the reaction enters into the derivation of the values for the second row (under *change*).

	2 ONCl	$\rightleftharpoons$	2 NO	+	Cl_2
at start:	1.00 mol/L		—		—
change:	−0.090 mol/L		+ 0.090 mol/L		+ 0.045 mol/L
at equilibrium:	0.91 mol/L		0.090 mol/L		0.045 mol/L

Therefore,

$$K = \frac{[NO]^2[Cl_2]}{[ONCl]^2}$$

$$= \frac{(0.090 \text{ mol/L})^2(0.045 \text{ mol/L})}{(0.91 \text{ mol/L})^2}$$

$$= 4.4 \times 10^{-4} \text{ mol/L}$$

K_c and Position of Equilibrium

The magnitude of the value of the equilibrium constant gives an indication of the position of equilibrium. Recall that the concentration terms of substances on the right of the equation are written in the numerator of the expression for the equilbrium constant. For the reaction

$$CO(g) + Cl_2(g) \rightleftharpoons COCl_2(g)$$

at 100°C,

$$K_c = \frac{[COCl_2]}{[CO][Cl_2]} = 4.57 \times 10^9 \text{ L/mol}$$

From this relatively large value of K_c, we conclude that equilibrium concentrations at 100°C of CO and Cl_2 are small and that the synthesis of $COCl_2$ is virtually complete. In other words, the reaction to the right is fairly complete at equilibrium.

For the reaction

$$N_2(g) + O_2(g) \rightleftharpoons 2\,NO(g)$$

at 1700°C,

$$K_c = \frac{[NO]^2}{[N_2][O_2]} = 3.52 \times 10^{-4}$$

We conclude from this small value of K_c that at 1700°C NO is largely dissociated into N_2 and O_2 at equilibrium. The reaction to the left is fairly complete.

Predicting the Direction of a Reaction

For the reaction

$$PCl_5(g) \rightleftharpoons PCl_3(g) + Cl_2(g)$$

at 250°C,

$$K_c = \frac{[PCl_3][Cl_2]}{[PCl_5]} = 0.0415 \text{ mol/L}$$

Suppose that a mixture of 0.100 mol of $PCl_5(g)$, 0.0500 mol of $PCl_3(g)$, and 0.0300 mol of $Cl_2(g)$ is placed in a 1.00 L container. Is this an equilibrium system, or will a net reaction occur in one direction or the other?

If the mixture is an equilibrium mixture, the concentrations of the three substances, when substituted into the expression for K_c, will equal K_c. A value obtained by substituting initial concentrations into the expression for the equilibrium constant is called a reaction quotient and is given the symbol Q. For the example at hand,

$$Q = \frac{[PCl_3][Cl_2]}{[PCl_5]}$$

$$= \frac{(0.0500 \text{ mol/L})(0.0300 \text{ mol/L})}{(0.100 \text{ mol/L})} = 0.0150 \text{ mol/L}$$

In this case, Q (0.0150 mol/L) is smaller than K_c (0.0415 mol/L). The system is not in equilibrium. The reaction will proceed from *left to right*. The concentrations of those substances that appear in the numerator of Q (right side of the chemical equation) will increase, and the concentrations of those substances that appear in the denominator of Q (left side of the chemical equation) will decrease. The value of Q, therefore, will increase until Q becomes equal to K_c. At that point, equilibrium is established.

In general, the values of a Q and the corresponding K_c may be related in one of three ways:

1. $Q < K_c$ In this instance, the reaction will move from left to right (the forward direction) to approach equilibrium. In this way, Q will increase until it equals K_c.

2. $Q = K_c$ The system is in equilibrium.

3. $Q > K_c$ In this instance, the reaction will move from right to left (the reverse direction) to approach equilibrium. In this way, Q will decrease until it equals K_c.

Example 15.3

For the reaction

$$2\,SO_2(g) + O_2(g) \rightleftharpoons 2\,SO_3(g)$$

at 827°C, K_c is 36.9 L/mol. If 0.0500 mol of $SO_2(g)$, 0.0300 mol of $O_2(g)$, and 0.125 mol of $SO_3(g)$ are mixed in a 1.00 L container at 827°C, in what direction will the reaction proceed?

Solution

$$Q = \frac{[SO_3]^2}{[SO_2]^2[O_2]}$$

$$= \frac{(0.125 \text{ mol/L})^2}{(0.0500 \text{ mol/L})^2(0.0300 \text{ mol/L})} = 208 \text{ L/mol}$$

Since Q (208 L/mol) is larger than K_c (36.9 L/mol), the reaction will proceed from *right to left* (SO_3 will dissociate).

Heterogeneous Equilibria

Equilibria between substances in two or more phases are called **heterogeneous equilibria.** The concentration of a pure solid or a pure liquid is constant when the temperature and pressure are constant. For any heterogeneous equilibrium, therefore, the values of the concentrations of solids or liquids involved are included in the value of K_c, and concentration terms for these substances do not appear explicitly in the expression for the equilibrium constant.

For example, for the reaction

$$CaCO_3(s) \rightleftharpoons CaO(s) + CO_2(g)$$

the values for the concentrations of CaO and $CaCO_3$ are included in the value of K_c, and the expression for the equilibrium constant is

$$K_c = [CO_2]$$

Hence, at any fixed temperature the equilibrium concentration of CO_2 over a mixture of the solids is a definite value. The equilibrium constant for the reaction

$$3\,Fe(s) + 4\,H_2O(g) \rightleftharpoons Fe_3O_4(s) + 4\,H_2(g)$$

is expressed in the following terms:

$$K_c = \frac{[H_2]^4}{[H_2O]^4}$$

Some facts dealing with expressions for equilibrium constants may be summarized as follows:

1. The concentration terms for substances that appear on the *right side* of the chemical equation are written in the *numerator* of the expression for K_c. The concentration terms for substances that appear on the *left side* are written in the *denominator*.

2. No concentration terms are included for pure solids or pure liquids. The value of K_c includes these terms.

3. The value of K_c for a given equilibrium is constant if the equilibrium temperature does not change. At a different temperature, the value of K_c is different.

4. The magnitude of K_c for a given equilibrium indicates the position of equilibrium. A *large* value of K_c indicates that the reaction to the right is fairly complete. A *small* value of K_c indicates that the reaction to the *left* is fairly complete. A value of K_c that is neither very large nor very small indicates an intermediate situation.

Equilibrium Concentrations Using K_c

The following examples illustrate how K_c expressions may be used to find equilibrium concentrations.

Example 15.4

K_c for the HI equilibrium at 425°C is 54.5:

$$H_2(g) + I_2(g) \rightleftharpoons 2\,HI(g)$$

A quantity of HI(g) is placed in a 1.00 L container and allowed to come to equilibrium at 425°C. What are the concentrations of $H_2(g)$ and $I_2(g)$ in equilibrium with 0.50 mol/L of HI(g)?

Solution

The concentrations of $H_2(g)$ and $I_2(g)$ must be equal since they are produced in equal amounts by the decomposition of HI(g). Therefore, let

$$[H_2] = [I_2] = x$$

We are told that the equilibrium concentration of HI is

$$[HI] = 0.50 \text{ mol/L}$$

We substitute these values into the equation for the equilibrium constant and solve for x:

$$K_c = \frac{[HI]^2}{[H_2][I_2]} = 54.5$$

$$\frac{(0.50 \text{ mol/L})^2}{x^2} = 54.5$$

$$54.5x^2 = 0.25 \text{ mol}^2/\text{L}^2$$

$$x^2 = 0.00456 \text{ mol}^2/\text{L}^2$$

$$x = 0.068 \text{ mol/L}$$

The equilibrium concentrations are

$$[\text{HI}] = 0.50 \text{ mol/L}$$

$$[\text{H}_2] = [\text{I}_2] = 0.068 \text{ mol/L}$$

Example 15.5

For the reaction

$$\text{H}_2(g) + \text{CO}_2(g) \rightleftharpoons \text{H}_2\text{O}(g) + \text{CO}(g)$$

K_c is 0.771 at 750°C. If 0.0100 mol of H_2 and 0.0100 mol of CO_2 are mixed in a one-liter container at 750°C, what are the concentrations of all substances present at equilibrium?

Solution

Since the container has a volume of one liter, the numerical values of the concentrations (in mol/L) are the same as the numbers of moles used. If x mol of H_2 reacts with x mol of CO_2 out of the total amounts supplied, x mol of H_2O and x mol of CO will be produced. Hence,

	$\text{H}_2(g)$	$+$	$\text{CO}_2(g)$	$\rightleftharpoons$ $\text{H}_2\text{O}(g) +$	CO(g)
at start:	0.0100 mol/L		0.0100 mol/L	—	—
change:	$-x$		$-x$	$+x$	$+x$
at equilibrium:	(0.0100 mol/L $- x$)		(0.0100 mol/L $- x$)	x	x

$$K_c = \frac{[\text{H}_2\text{O}][\text{CO}]}{[\text{H}_2][\text{CO}_2]} = 0.771$$

$$= \frac{x^2}{(0.0100 \text{ mol/L} - x)^2} = 0.771$$

If we extract the square root of both sides of this equation, we get

$$\frac{x}{(0.0100 \text{ mol/L} - x)} = 0.878$$

$$x = 0.0878 \text{ mol/L} - 0.878x$$

$$x = 0.00468 \text{ mol/L}$$

At equilibrium, therefore,

$$[\text{H}_2] = [\text{CO}_2] = 0.0100 \text{ mol/L} - 0.00468 \text{ mol/L}$$
$$= 0.0053 \text{ mol/L}$$

$$[\text{H}_2\text{O}] = [\text{CO}] = 0.00468 \text{ mol/L}$$

5.3 The Equilibrium Constant K_p

The partial pressure of a gas is a measure of its concentration. Equilibrium constants for reactions involving gases, therefore, may be written in terms of the partial pressures of the reacting gases. An equilibrium constant of this type is given the designation K_p.

For the calcium carbonate equilibrium

$$CaCO_3(s) \rightleftharpoons CaO(s) + CO_2(g)$$

the equilibrium constant in terms of partial pressures is

$$K_p = p_{CO_2}$$

For the equilibrium

$$N_2(g) + 3H_2(g) \rightleftharpoons 2NH_3(g)$$

the K_p is

$$K_p = \frac{(p_{NH_3})^2}{(p_{N_2})(p_{H_2})^3}$$

There is a simple relation between the K_p for a reaction and the equilibrium constant derived from concentrations. Consider the reaction

$$wW + xX \rightleftharpoons yY + zZ \tag{15.14}$$

If *all* these materials are *gases*,

$$K_p = \frac{(p_Y)^y(p_Z)^z}{(p_W)^w(p_X)^x} \tag{15.15}$$

Assume that each of the gases follows the ideal gas law

$$PV = nRT$$

Then the partial pressure of any gas, p, is

$$p = \frac{n}{V}RT$$

The concentration of a gas in mol/L is equal to n/V. Therefore, for gas W

$$p_W = [W]RT \tag{15.16}$$
$$(p_W)^w = [W]^w(RT)^w \tag{15.17}$$

If we substitute expressions such as Equation 15.17 for the partial-pressure terms in the expression for K_p (Equation 15.15), we get

$$K_p = \frac{[Y]^y(RT)^y[Z]^z(RT)^z}{[W]^w(RT)^w[X]^x(RT)^x} \tag{15.18}$$

$$= \frac{[Y]^y[Z]^z}{[W]^w[X]^x}(RT)^{+y+z-w-x}$$

The fractional term in the last equation is equal to K_c:

$$K_p = K_c(RT)^{+y+z-w-x} \tag{15.19}$$

If we read the chemical equation for the reaction

$$w\text{W} + x\text{X} \rightleftharpoons y\text{Y} + z\text{Z} \tag{15.14}$$

in molar quantities,

$y + z$ = number of moles of gases on the right

$w + x$ = number of moles of gases on the left

We let Δn equal the change in the number of moles of gases when the equation is read from left to right:

$$\Delta n = (y + z) - (w + x) = +y + z - w - x \tag{15.20}$$

Therefore,

$$K_p = K_c(RT)^{\Delta n} \tag{15.21}$$

Partial pressures are expressed in atmospheres, concentrations are expressed in moles per liter, R is 0.08206 L·atm/(K·mol), and T is the absolute temperature in K.

For the reaction

$$\text{PCl}_5(g) \rightleftharpoons \text{PCl}_3(g) + \text{Cl}_2(g)$$

Δn is $+1$. Therefore,

$$K_p = K_c(RT)^{+1}$$

For the reaction

$$\text{CO}(g) + \text{Cl}_2(g) \rightleftharpoons \text{COCl}_2(g)$$

$\Delta n = -1$. Therefore,

$$K_p = K_c(RT)^{-1} \qquad \text{or} \qquad K_p = \frac{K_c}{(RT)}$$

For the reaction

$$\text{H}_2(g) + \text{I}_2(g) \rightleftharpoons 2\,\text{HI}(g)$$

$\Delta n = 0$. Therefore,

$$K_p = K_c(RT)^0 \qquad \text{or} \qquad K_p = K_c$$

Example 15.6

For the reaction

$$2\,SO_3(g) \rightleftharpoons 2\,SO_2(g) + O_2(g)$$

at 1100 K, K_c is 0.0271 mol/L. What is K_p at this temperature?

Solution

Two moles of $SO_3(g)$ produce a total of 3 mol of gases. Therefore,

$$\Delta n = +1$$
$$K_p = K_c(RT)^{+1}$$
$$= (0.0271 \text{ mol/L})\{[0.0821 \text{ L} \cdot \text{atm}/(\text{K} \cdot \text{mol})](1100 \text{ K})\}$$
$$= 2.45 \text{ atm}$$

Example 15.7

What is K_c for the reaction

$$N_2(g) + 3\,H_2(g) \rightleftharpoons 2\,NH_3(g)$$

at 500°C if K_p is $1.50 \times 10^{-5}/\text{atm}^2$ at this temperature?

Solution

There are 4 mol of gases indicated on the left of the chemical equation and 2 mol of gases indicated on the right. Therefore,

$$\Delta n = -2$$

The temperature is 500°C, which is

$$T = 773 \text{ K}$$

Therefore,

$$K_p = K_c(RT)^{\Delta n}$$
$$(1.50 \times 10^{-5}/\text{atm}^2) = K_c\{[0.0821 \text{ L} \cdot \text{atm}/(\text{K} \cdot \text{mol})](773 \text{ K})\}^{-2}$$
$$(1.50 \times 10^{-5}/\text{atm}^2) = \frac{K_c}{(63.5 \text{ L} \cdot \text{atm/mol})^2}$$
$$K_c = (1.50 \times 10^{-5}/\text{atm}^2)(4.03 \times 10^3 \text{ L}^2 \cdot \text{atm}^2/\text{mol}^2)$$
$$= 6.04 \times 10^{-2} \text{ L}^2/\text{mol}^2$$

Example 15.8

For the reaction

$$C(s) + CO_2(g) \rightleftharpoons 2\,CO(g)$$

K_p is 167.5 atm at 1000°C. What is the partial pressure of CO(g) in an equilibrium system in which the partial pressure of $CO_2(g)$ is 0.100 atm?

Solution

$$K_p = \frac{(p_{CO})^2}{p_{CO_2}} = 167.5 \text{ atm}$$

$$\frac{(p_{CO})^2}{0.100 \text{ atm}} = 167.5 \text{ atm}$$

$$(p_{CO})^2 = 16.8 \text{ atm}^2$$

$$p_{CO} = 4.10 \text{ atm}$$

Example 15.9

K_p for the equilibrium

$$FeO(s) + CO(g) \rightleftharpoons Fe(s) + CO_2(g)$$

at 1000°C is 0.403. If CO(g), at a pressure of 1.000 atm, and excess FeO(s) are placed in a container at 1000°C, what are the pressures of CO(g) and $CO_2(g)$ when equilibrium is attained?

Solution

Let x equal the partial pressure of CO_2 when equilibrium is attained. Since 1 mol of CO_2 is produced for every 1 mol of CO used, the partial pressure of CO_2 is equal to the decrease in the pressure of CO:

	FeO(s) +	CO(g)	$\rightleftharpoons$ Fe(s) +	$CO_2(g)$
at start:		1.000 atm		—
change:		$-x$		$+x$
at equilibrium:		1.000 atm $-x$		x

$$K_p = \frac{p_{CO_2}}{p_{CO}} = 0.403$$

$$\frac{x \text{ atm}}{1.000 \text{ atm} - x} = 0.403$$

$$x = p_{CO_2} = 0.287 \text{ atm}$$

$$1.000 - x = p_{CO} = 0.713 \text{ atm}$$

5.4 Le Chatelier's Principle

What happens to an equilibrium system if an experimental condition (such as temperature or pressure) is changed? The effects of such changes were summarized in 1884 by Henri Le Chatelier. Le Chatelier's principle states that a system in equilibrium reacts to a stress in a way that counteracts the stress and establishes a new equilibrium state. This important generalization is very simple to apply:

1. Concentration changes. If the concentration of substance is *increased*, the equilibrium will shift in a way that will *decrease* the concentration of the substance that was added. Suppose that we have a system in equilibrium

$$H_2(g) + I_2(g) \rightleftharpoons 2\,HI(g)$$

Henri Le Chatelier, 1850–1936. *Smithsonian Institution.*

and we *increase* the concentration of H_2 by adding more H_2 to the system. The equilibrium is upset, and the system will react in a way that will *decrease* the concentration of H_2. It can do that by using up some of the H_2 (and some I_2 as well) to form more HI. When equilibrium is established again, the concentration of HI will be higher than it was initially. The position of equilibrium is said to have shifted to the right.

If the concentration of HI is increased by adding HI to the system, the position of equilibrium will shift to the left. In this way some HI will be used up. When equilibrium is established again, the concentrations of H_2 and I_2 will be higher than they were initially.

Removal of one of the substances from an equilibrium system will also cause the position of equilibrium to shift. If, for example, HI could be removed, the position of equilibrium would shift to the right. Additional HI would be produced and the concentrations of H_2 and I_2 would decrease.

By the continuous removal of a product it is possible to drive some reversible reactions "to completion." At a relatively high temperature, complete conversion of $CaCO_3(s)$ into $CaO(s)$:

$$CaCO_3(s) \rightleftharpoons CaO(s) + CO_2(g)$$

can be accomplished by removing the CO_2 gas as fast as it is produced.

2. Pressure changes. Le Chatelier's principle may also be used to make qualitative predictions of the effect of pressure changes on systems in equilibrium. Consider the effect of a pressure increase on an equilibrium mixture of SO_2, O_2, and SO_3:

$$2\,SO_2(g) + O_2(g) \rightleftharpoons 2\,SO_3(g)$$

In the forward reaction two gas molecules ($2\,SO_3$) are produced by the disappearance of three gas molecules ($2\,SO_2 + O_2$). Two gas molecules do not exert as high a pressure as three gas molecules. When the pressure on an equilibrium mixture is increased (or the volume of the system decreased), the position of equilibrium shifts to the right. In this way the system counteracts the change. Alternatively, decreasing the pressure (or increasing the volume) causes the position of this equilibrium to shift to the left.

For reactions in which $\Delta n = 0$, pressure changes have no effect on the position of equilibria. Equilibria involving the systems

The manufacture of ammonia is an important industrial process. One use of the compound, as a fertilizer, is shown here. *Farmland Industries*.

$$H_2(g) + I_2(g) \rightleftharpoons 2\,HI(g)$$

$$N_2(g) + O_2(g) \rightleftharpoons 2\,NO(g)$$

$$H_2(g) + CO_2(g) \rightleftharpoons H_2O(g) + CO(g)$$

are not influenced by changing the pressure since there is no difference in the total volume in either the forward or reverse direction for any one of these reactions.

For a system that involves only liquids and solids, the effect of pressure on the position of equilibrium is slight and may usually be ignored for ordinary changes in pressure. Large pressure changes, however, can significantly alter such equilibria; and at times, even slight changes in such equilibria are of interest. For example, the position of equilibrium

$$H_2O(s) \rightleftharpoons H_2O(l)$$

is forced to the right by an increase in pressure because a given quantity of water occupies a smaller volume in the liquid state than in the solid state (its density is higher in the liquid state).

Pressure changes affect equilibria involving gases to a much greater degree. For example, a high pressure would favor the production of a high yield of ammonia from the equilibrium

$$N_2(g) + 3\,H_2(g) \rightleftharpoons 2\,NH_3(g)$$

Hence, Le Chatelier's principle is of practical importance as an aid in determining favorable reaction conditions for the production of a desired substance.

For heterogeneous equilibria the effect of pressure is predicted by counting the number of moles of *gas* indicated on each side of the equation. For example, the position of equilibrium

$$3\,Fe(s) + 4\,H_2O(g) \rightleftharpoons Fe_3O_4(s) + 4\,H_2(g)$$

is virtually unaffected by pressure because there are four moles of gas indicated on each side of the equation.

3. Temperature changes. In order to predict the effect of a temperature change on a system in equilibrium, the nature of the heat effect that accompanies the reaction must be known. At 25°C, the thermochemical equation for the synthesis of ammonia is

$$N_2(g) + 3\,H_2(g) \rightleftharpoons 2\,NH_3(g) \qquad \Delta H = -92.4\ kJ$$

Since ΔH is negative, the reaction to the right evolves heat. We can write the equation to indicate heat as a product:

$$N_2(g) + 3\,H_2(g) \rightleftharpoons 2\,NH_3(g) + 92.4\ kJ$$

The forward reaction is *exothermic,* and the reverse reaction is *endothermic.* In other words, the forward reaction produces heat, and the reverse reaction uses heat. If heat is added (the temperature of the system is raised), the position of equilibrium will shift to the left—the direction in which heat is absorbed. If the mixture is cooled, the position of equilibrium will shift to the right—the direction in which heat is evolved. The highest yields of NH_3 will be obtained at the lowest temperatures. Unfortunately, if the temperature is too low, the reaction will be extremely slow. High pressures and temperatures around 500°C are employed in the commercial process.

Consider the reaction

$$CO_2(g) + H_2(g) \rightleftharpoons CO(g) + H_2(g) \qquad \Delta H = +41.2\ kJ$$

Since ΔH is positive, the forward reaction is endothermic. We write the equation

$$41.2\ kJ + CO_2(g) + H_2(g) \rightleftharpoons CO(g) + H_2O(g)$$

Increasing the temperature *always* favors the endothermic change, and decreasing the temperature *always* favors the exothermic change. In this case, the reaction is forced to the right by an increase in temperature. A decrease in temperature causes the position of equilibrium to shift to the left.

The numerical value of the equilibrium constant changes when the temperature is changed. Data for two equilibria are given in Table 15.2. The reaction between N_2 and H_2 to form NH_3 is exothermic in the forward direction and is shifted to the left by an increase in temperature. As a result, the concentrations of the substances on the left ($[N_2]$ and $[H_2]$, which appear in the *denominator* of K_c) are *increased.* The concentration of the substance on the right ($[NH_3]$, which appears in the *numerator* of K_c) is *decreased.* With an increase in temperature, therefore, the value of K_c decreases.

The reaction between CO_2 and H_2 is endothermic in the forward direction and is shifted to the right by a temperature increase. The concentrations of the sub-

Table 15.2 Variation of equilibrium constants with temperature	
Forward Reaction, Exothermic $N_2(g) + 3H_2(g) \rightleftharpoons 2NH_3(g)$ $\Delta H° = -92.4\,kJ$	
Temperature (°C)	$K_c(L^2/mol^2)$
300	9.6
400	0.50
500	0.060
600	0.014
Forward Reaction, Endothermic $CO_2(g) + H_2(g) \rightleftharpoons CO(g) + H_2O(g)$ $\Delta H° = +41.2\,kJ$	
Temperature (°C)	$K_c = K_p$
700	0.63
800	0.93
900	1.29
1000	1.66

stances on the right increase (numerator of K_c), the concentrations of the substances on the left decrease (denominator of K_c), and the value of K_c increases.

4. Addition of a catalyst. The presence of a catalyst has no effect on the position of a chemical equilibrium, since a catalyst affects the rates of the forward and reverse reactions equally (see Section 14.7). A catalyst will, however, cause a system to attain equilibrium more rapidly than it otherwise would.

Summary

If the substances that take part in a reversible reaction are mixed in a container, they will react in a way that establishes a *dynamic equilibrium state*. At equilibrium, the *forward* reaction is occuring at the *same rate* as the *reverse* reaction. The *concentrations* of all the substances involved are therefore *constant*. These concentrations may be used to derive a fraction called an *equilibrium constant*, K. For the general reaction:

$$wW + xX \rightleftharpoons yY + zZ$$

$$K = \frac{[Y]^y[Z]^z}{[W]^w[X]^x}$$

The numerical value of K varies with *temperature*. It does *not vary* with changes in the *amounts of substances* used to establish the equilibrium, changes in *pressure*, or the presence of a *catalyst*.

An equilibrium constant in which the concentrations are expressed in *moles per liter* is given the designation K_c. If K_c is a *large* number, the *forward* reaction is fairly complete. If K_c is a *small* number, the *reverse* reaction is fairly complete.

A *reaction quotient*, Q, has the same form as K_c but is used to decide how a set of substances will react to establish equilibrium. If Q is *less* than K_c, the reversible reaction will proceed to the *right* to establish equilibrium. If Q is *greater* than K_c, the reaction will move to the *left*.

Equilibria between substances in *two or more phases* are called *heterogeneous equilibria*. In the expression for K_c for a system of this type, terms for pure solids or pure liquids do not appear.

Equilibrium constants for reactions involving gases may be written in terms of the *partial pressures* of the gases (in *atmospheres*) and are given the designation K_p. The two constants K_c and K_p are related: $K_p = K_c(RT)^{\Delta n}$. The term Δn is the change in the number of moles of gases when the equation is read from left to right. Both constants, K_c and K_p, may be used to find equilibrium concentrations.

Le Chatelier's principle predicts how a system in equilibrium will respond to changes in experimental conditions. An *increase in the concentration* of a gas will cause the equilibrium to shift in the direction that will decrease the concentration of the gas. The *removal of a substance* will cause the equilibrium to shift in the direction in which that substance is produced. Increasing the *pressure* causes a shift in the direction that will decrease the number of moles of gas. Increasing the *temperature* causes a shift in the direction of the endothermic change and results in a change in the numerical values of K_c and K_p. The addition of a *catalyst* causes a system to achieve equilibrium faster but does not alter the position of equilibrium.

Key Terms

Some of the more important terms introduced in this chapter are listed below. Definitions for terms not included in this list may be located in the text by use of the index.

Chemical equilibrium (Section 15.1) A state in which the rate of a reversible reaction in the forward direction equals the rate in the reverse direction.

Equilibrium constant, K (Sections 15.1, 15.2, and 15.3) A constant for an equilibrium system equal to a fraction in which the numerator is the product of the concentrations of the substances on the right of the chemical equation, each raised to a power corresponding to its coefficient in the chemical equation, and the denominator is the product of the concentrations of the substances on the left of the chemical equation, each raised to a power corresponding to its coefficient in the chemical equation. A value obtained by expressing the concentrations in moles per liter is given the symbol K_c (Section

15.2); one written in terms of partial pressures (in atmospheres) is given the symbol K_p (Section 15.3).

Heterogeneous equilibrium (Section 15.2) An equilibrium state between substances in more than one phase, such as that between solids and gases.

Homogeneous equilibrium (Section 15.2) An equilibrium state between substances that are all present in the same phase.

Le Chatelier's principle (Section 15.4) A system in equilibrium reacts to a change in conditions in a way that counteracts the applied change and establishes a new equilibrium state.

Reaction quotient, Q (Section 15.2) A value obtained by substituting concentrations into the expression for an equilibrium constant, K_c. If $Q = K_c$, the system is in equilibrium. If $Q < K_c$, the reaction will proceed to the right. If $Q > K_c$, the reaction will proceed to the left.

Problems*

Chemical Equilibrium, Le Chatelier's Principle

15.1 For each of the following reactions, write an expression for the equilibrium constant K_c:
(a) $2\,H_2S(g) + CH_4(g) \rightleftharpoons CS_2(g) + 4\,H_2(g)$
(b) $2\,NO_2(g) \rightleftharpoons N_2O_4(g)$
(c) $2\,Pb_3O_4(s) \rightleftharpoons 6\,PbO(s) + O_2(g)$
(d) $C(s) + CO_2(g) \rightleftharpoons 2\,CO(g)$
(e) $2\,NO(g) \rightleftharpoons N_2(g) + O_2(g)$

15.2 For each of the following reactions, write an expression for the equilibrium constant K_c:
(a) $Ni(s) + 4\,CO(g) \rightleftharpoons Ni(CO)_4(g)$
(b) $CO(g) + H_2O(g) \rightleftharpoons CO_2(g) + H_2(g)$
(c) $2\,CO_2(g) \rightleftharpoons 2\,CO(g) + O_2(g)$
(d) $2\,Ag_2O(s) \rightleftharpoons 4\,Ag(s) + O_2(g)$
(e) $4\,NH_3(g) + 5\,O_2(g) \rightleftharpoons 4\,NO(g) + 6\,H_2O(g)$

15.3 Indicate in which direction each of the equilibria given in problem 15.1 will shift with an increase in pressure.

15.4 Indicate in which direction each of the equilibria given in problem 15.2 will shift with an increase in pressure.

15.5 For each of the reactions given in problem 15.1, write the expression for the equilibrium constant K_p. In each case, also give the equation that relates K_c to K_p.

15.6 For each of the reactions given in problem 15.2, write the expression for the equilibrium constant K_p. In each case, also give the equation that relates K_c to K_p.

15.7 For the equilibrium:

$$N_2(g) + O_2(g) \rightleftharpoons 2\,NO(g)$$

K_c is 4.08×10^{-4} at 2000. K and 3.60×10^{-3} at 2500. K. Is the reaction as written exothermic or endothermic?

15.8 For the equilibrium:

$$NiO(s) + CO(g) \rightleftharpoons Ni(s) + CO_2(g)$$

K_c is 4.54×10^3 at 936 K and 1.58×10^3 at 1125 K. Is the reaction as written exothermic or endothermic?

15.9 The reaction:

$$CH_4(g) + 2\,H_2S(g) \rightleftharpoons CS_2(g) + 4\,H_2(g)$$

is endothermic from left to right. How would each of the following changes, when applied to a system in equilibrium, affect the position of equilibrium? **(a)** increase the temperature, **(b)** add $H_2S(g)$, **(c)** remove $CS_2(g)$, **(d)** increase the pressure, **(e)** add a catalyst.

15.10 The reaction:

$$4\,HCl(g) + O_2(g) \rightleftharpoons 2\,Cl_2(g) + 2\,H_2O(g)$$

is exothermic from left to right. How would each of the following changes, when applied to a system in equilibrium, affect the position of equilibrium? **(a)** increase the temperature, **(b)** decrease the pressure, **(c)** add $H_2O(g)$, **(d)** remove $HCl(g)$, **(e)** add a catalyst.

15.11 The reaction:

$$NiO(s) + CO(g) \rightleftharpoons Ni(s) + CO_2(g)$$

is exothermic from left to right. How would each of the following changes, when applied to a system in equilibrium, affect the position of equilibrium? **(a)** decrease the temperature, **(b)** decrease the pressure, **(c)** add $NiO(s)$, **(d)** add $CO(g)$, **(e)** remove $CO_2(g)$.

15.12 The reaction:

$$C(s) + CO_2(g) \rightleftharpoons 2\,CO(g)$$

is endothermic from left to right. How would each of the following changes, when applied to a system in equilibrium, affect the position of equilibrium? **(a)** add $CO_2(g)$, **(b)** remove $C(s)$, **(c)** increase the temperature, **(d)** decrease the pressure, **(e)** remove $CO(g)$.

15.13 For the equilibrium:

$$4\,HCl(g) + O_2(g) \rightleftharpoons 2\,Cl_2(g) + 2\,H_2O(g)$$

at 480.°C, K_c is 889 L/mol. If 0.030 mol of $HCl(g)$, 0.020 mol of $O_2(g)$, 0.080 mol of Cl_2, and 0.070 mol of $H_2O(g)$ are mixed in a one-liter container, in what direction will the reaction proceed?

15.14 For the equilibrium:

$$CH_4(g) + H_2O(g) \rightleftharpoons CO(g) + 3\,H_2(g)$$

at 1500.°C, K_c is 5.67 mol²/L². If 0.020 mol of $CH_4(g)$, 0.060 mol $H_2O(g)$, 0.030 mol of $CO(g)$, and 0.500 mol of $H_2(g)$ are mixed in a one-liter container, in what direction will the reaction proceed?

15.15 For the equilibrium:

$$N_2(g) + O_2(g) \rightleftharpoons 2\,NO(g)$$

at 1800. K, K_c is 1.20×10^{-4}. If 0.060 mol of $N_2(g)$, 0.075 mol of $O_2(g)$, and 0.00025 mol of $NO(g)$ are mixed in a one-liter container at 1800. K, in what direction will the reaction proceed?

---

* The more difficult problems are marked with asterisks. The appendix contains answers to color-keyed problems.

15.16 For the equilibrium:

$$NH_4HS(s) \rightleftharpoons NH_3(g) + H_2S(g)$$

at 24°C, K_c is 1.58×10^{-4} mol²/L². If 0.0205 mol of $NH_3(g)$, 0.00750 mol of H_2S, and excess solid NH_4HS are mixed in a one-liter container at 24°C, in what direction will the reaction proceed?

The Equilibrium Constant K_c

15.17 Calculate the value of K_c for the equilibrium system:

$$H_2(g) + I_2(g) \rightleftharpoons 2\,HI(g)$$

at 395°C from the following concentrations of an equilibrium mixture: $[H_2] = 0.0064$ mol/L, $[I_2] = 0.0016$ mol/L, and $[HI] = 0.0250$ mol/L.

15.18 At a certain temperature, 0.0740 mol of $PCl_5(g)$ was introduced into a one-liter container. Equilibrium was established:

$$PCl_5(g) \rightleftharpoons PCl_3(g) + Cl_2(g)$$

At equilibrium, the concentration of $PCl_3(g)$ was 0.0500 mol/L. **(a)** What were the equilibrium concentrations of $Cl_2(g)$ and $PCl_5(g)$? **(b)** What is the value of K_c at the temperature of the experiment?

15.19 If 0.0600 mol of $SO_3(g)$ is placed in a one-liter container at 1000. K, 36.7% of the $SO_3(g)$ is dissociated when equilibrium is established:

$$2\,SO_3(g) \rightleftharpoons 2\,SO_2(g) + O_2(g)$$

(a) What are the equilibrium concentrations of $SO_3(g)$, $SO_2(g)$, and $O_2(g)$? **(b)** What is the value of K_c for the equilibrium at 1000. K?

15.20 If 0.200 mol of $NO(g)$ is placed in a one-liter container at 2600. K, 22.0% of the $NO(g)$ is dissociated when equilibrium is established:

$$2\,NO(g) \rightleftharpoons N_2(g) + O_2(g)$$

(a) What are the equilibrium concentrations of $NO(g)$, $N_2(g)$, and $O_2(g)$? **(b)** What is the value of K_c for the equilibrium at 2600. K?

15.21 For the equilibrium:

$$CO(g) + 2\,H_2(g) \rightleftharpoons CH_3OH(g)$$

at 225°C, K_c is 10.2 L²/mol². What is the concentration of $CH_3OH(g)$ in equilibrium with $CO(g)$ at a concentration of 0.075 mol/L and $H_2(g)$ at a concentration of 0.060 mol/L?

15.22 For the equilibrium:

$$2\,NO(g) \rightleftharpoons N_2(g) + O_2(g)$$

at 1800. K, K_c is 8.36×10^3. What concentration of $NO(g)$ is in equilibrium with $N_2(g)$ at a concentration of 0.0560 mol/L and $O_2(g)$ at a concentration of 0.0745 mol/L?

15.23 For the equilibrium:

$$H_2O(g) + CO(g) \rightleftharpoons H_2(g) + CO_2(g)$$

at 750°C, K_c is 1.30. If 0.600 mol of $H_2O(g)$ and 0.600 mol of $CO(g)$ are mixed in a one-liter container at 750°C, what are the concentrations of all four substances when equilibrium is established?

15.24 For the equilibrium:

$$2\,IBr(g) \rightleftharpoons I_2(g) + Br_2(g)$$

at 150.°C, K_c is 8.5×10^{-3}. If 0.0600 mol of $IBr(g)$ is placed in a one-liter container at 150.°C, what are the concentrations of all three substances when equilibrium is established?

15.25 For the equilibrium:

$$H_2(g) + I_2(g) \rightleftharpoons 2\,HI(g)$$

at 425°C, K_c is 54.8. If 1.000 mol of $H_2(g)$, 1.000 mol of $I_2(g)$, and 1.000 mol of $HI(g)$ are placed in a one-liter container at 425°C, what are the concentrations of all three gases when equilibrium is established?

15.26 For the equilibrium:

$$Br_2(g) + Cl_2(g) \rightleftharpoons 2\,BrCl(g)$$

at 400. K, K_c is 7.0. If 0.045 mol of $Br_2(g)$, 0.045 mol of $Cl_2(g)$, and 0.045 mol of $BrCl(g)$ are placed in a one-liter container at 400. K, what are the concentrations of all three gases when equilibrium is established?

*15.27 For the equilibrium:

$$FeO(s) + CO(g) \rightleftharpoons Fe(s) + CO_2(g)$$

at 1000.°C, K_c is 0.403. **(a)** If 0.0500 mol of $CO(g)$ and excess solid FeO are confined in a one-liter container at 1000.°C, what are the concentrations of $CO(g)$ and $CO_2(g)$ when equilibrium is attained? **(b)** What mass of Fe(s) is present when the system reaches equilibrium?

*15.28 For the equilibrium:

$$3\,Fe(s) + 4\,H_2O(g) \rightleftharpoons Fe_3O_4(s) + 4\,H_2(g)$$

at 900.°C, K_c is 5.1. **(a)** If 0.050 mol of $H_2O(g)$ and excess solid Fe are placed in a one-liter container at 900.°C, what are the concentrations of $H_2O(g)$ and $H_2(g)$ when equilibrium is established? **(b)** What mass of $Fe_3O_4(s)$ is present when the system reaches equilibrium?

The Equilibrium Constant K_p

15.29 At 1000.°C, solid carbon was introduced into a container filled with $H_2(g)$ at 1.000 atm pressure. When equilibrium was established:

$$C(s) + 2\,H_2(g) \rightleftharpoons CH_4(g)$$

the partial pressure of $CH_4(g)$ in the equilibrium mixture was 0.138 atm. **(a)** What was the partial pressure of $H_2(g)$

in the equilibrium mixture? **(b)** What is the value of K_p for the equilibrium at 1000.°C?

15.30 At 400.°C, $COCl_2(g)$ at a pressure of 0.60 atm was introduced into a container. When equilibrium was established:

$$COCl_2(g) \rightleftharpoons CO(g) + Cl_2(g)$$

the partial pressure of $CO(g)$ in the equilibrium mixture was 0.14 atm. **(a)** What were the partial pressures of $COCl_2(g)$ and $Cl_2(g)$ in the equilibrium mixture? **(b)** What is the value of K_p for the equilibrium at 400.°C?

15.31 Solid NH_4HS was introduced into an evacuated container at 24°C. When equilibrium was established:

$$NH_4HS(s) \rightleftharpoons NH_3(g) + H_2S(g)$$

the total pressure (of the gases NH_3 and H_2S taken together) was 0.614 atm. What is the value of K_p for the equilibrium at 24°C?

15.32 Solid HgO was introduced into an evacuated container at 450.°C. When equilibrium was established:

$$2\,HgO(s) \rightleftharpoons 2\,Hg(g) + O_2(g)$$

the total pressure (of the gases Hg and O_2 taken together) was 1.07 atm. What is the value of K_p for the equilibrium at 450.°C?

15.33 A mixture consisting of 1.000 mol of $CO(g)$ and 1.000 mol of $H_2O(g)$ is placed in a 10.00-L container at 800. K. At equilibrium, 0.665 mol of $CO_2(g)$ and 0.665 mol of $H_2(g)$ are present:

$$CO(g) + H_2O(g) \rightleftharpoons CO_2(g) + H_2(g)$$

(a) What are the equilibrium concentrations of all four gases? **(b)** What is the value of K_c for the equilibrium at 800. K? **(c)** What is the value of K_p for the equilibrium at 800. K?

15.34 At 585 K and a total pressure of 1.000 atm, $ONCl(g)$ is 56.4% dissociated:

$$2\,ONCl(g) \rightleftharpoons 2\,NO(g) + Cl_2(g)$$

Assume that 1.000 mol of $ONCl(g)$ was present before dissociation. **(a)** How many moles of $ONCl(g)$, $NO(g)$, and $Cl_2(g)$ are present at equilibrium? **(b)** What is the total

number of moles of gas present at equilibrium? **(c)** What are the equilibrium partial pressures of the three gases? **(d)** What is the numerical value of K_p for the equilibrium at 585 K?

15.35 At 250.°C, $PCl_5(g)$ was introduced into an evacuated container until the pressure was 1.000 atm. When equilibrium was established:

$$PCl_5(g) \rightleftharpoons PCl_3(g) + Cl_2(g)$$

the pressure inside the container was 1.714 atm. **(a)** What were the partial pressures of $PCl_5(g)$, $PCl_3(g)$, and $Cl_2(g)$ in the equilibrium mixture? **(b)** What is the value of K_p for the equilibrium at 250.°C?

15.36 At 55°C, $N_2O_4(g)$ was introduced into an evacuated container until the pressure was 0.650 atm. When equilibrium was established:

$$N_2O_4(g) \rightleftharpoons 2\,NO_2(g)$$

the pressure inside the container was 0.980 atm. **(a)** What are the partial pressures of $N_2O_4(g)$ and $NO_2(g)$ in the equilibrium mixture? **(b)** What is the value of K_p for the equilibrium at 55°C?

15.37 For the equilibrium:

$$4\,HCl(g) + O_2(g) \rightleftharpoons 2\,Cl_2(g) + 2\,H_2O(g)$$

at 480.°C, K_c is 889 L/mol. What is K_p for the equilibrium at 480.°C?

15.38 For the equilibrium:

$$CH_4(g) + H_2O(g) \rightleftharpoons CO(g) + 3\,H_2(g)$$

at 1500.°C, K_c is 5.67 mol²/L². What is K_p for the equilibrium at 1500.°C?

15.39 Use the data in problem 15.37 to determine K_c and K_p for the equilibrium:

$$2\,Cl_2(g) + 2\,H_2O(g) \rightleftharpoons 4\,HCl(g) + O_2(g)$$

at 480.°C.

15.40 Use the data in problem 15.38 to determine K_c and K_p for the equilibrium:

$$CO(g) + 3\,H_2(g) \rightleftharpoons CH_4(g) + H_2O(g)$$

at 1500.°C.

15.41 For the equilibrium:

$$CH_3OH(g) \rightleftharpoons CO(g) + 2H_2(g)$$

at 275°C, K_p is 1.14×10^3 atm². What is K_c for the equilibrium at 275°C?

15.42 For the equilibrium:

$$CO(g) + Cl_2(g) \rightleftharpoons COCl_2(g)$$

at 100.°C, K_p is 1.49×10^8/atm. What is K_c for the equilibrium at 100.°C?

15.43 Use that data in problem 15.41 to determine K_c and K_p for the equilibrium:

$$CO(g) + 2H_2(g) \rightleftharpoons CH_3OH(g)$$

at 275°C.

15.44 Use that data in problem 15.42 to determine K_c and K_p for the equilibrium:

$$COCl_2(g) \rightleftharpoons CO(g) + Cl_2(g)$$

at 100.°C.

15.45 For the equilibrium:

$$N_2(g) + O_2(g) \rightleftharpoons 2NO(g)$$

at 2400. K, K_p is 2.5×10^{-3}. The partial pressure of $N_2(g)$ is 0.50 atm, and the partial pressure of $O_2(g)$ is 0.50 atm in a mixture of the two gases. What is the partial pressure of NO(g) when equilibrium is established at 2400. K?

15.46 For the equilibrium:

$$N_2(g) + 3H_2(g) \rightleftharpoons 2NH_3(g)$$

at 350.°C, K_p is 7.73×10^{-4}/atm². **(a)** If the partial pressure of $N_2(g)$ is 9.4 atm and the partial pressure of $H_2(g)$ is 28.0 atm in an equilibrium mixture at 350.°C, what is the partial pressure of $NH_3(g)$? **(b)** What is the total pressure? **(c)** What is the mole fraction of $NH_3(g)$ present?

Unclassified Problems

15.47 Consider an equilibrium system described by a chemical equation in which $\Delta n = 0$. **(a)** What are the units of K_c? **(b)** What is the change in the position of equilibrium brought about by an increase in pressure? **(c)** What is the relationship between K_c and K_p for the equilibrium?

15.48 The reaction $A(g) + B(g) \rightleftharpoons C(g)$ is exothermic as written. Assume that an equilibrium system is established. How would the concentration of C(g) change with **(a)** an increase in temperature, **(b)** an increase in pressure, **(c)** the addition of A(g), **(d)** the addition of a catalyst, **(e)** the removal of B(g)? How would the numerical value of K_c change with **(f)** an increase in temperature, **(g)** an increase in pressure, **(h)** the addition of a catalyst, **(i)** the addition of A(g)?

15.49 A quantity of solid $CaCO_3$ was introduced into an evacuated container at 800. K. Equilibrium was established:

$$CaCO_3(s) \rightleftharpoons CaO(s) + CO_2(g)$$

The equilibrium pressure of $CO_2(g)$ was 0.220 atm. What is the value of K_c for the equilibrium at 800. K?

15.50 At 425°C, K_c is 1.82×10^{-2} for the equilibrium:

$$2HI(g) \rightleftharpoons H_2(g) + I_2(g)$$

Assume that equilibrium is established at 425°C by adding only HI(g) to the reaction flask. **(a)** What are the concentrations of $H_2(g)$ and $I_2(g)$ in equilibrium with 0.0100 mol/L of HI(g)? **(b)** What was the initial concentration of HI(g) before equilibrium was established? **(c)** What percent of the HI(g) added is dissociated at equilibrium?

15.51 For the equilibrium system:

$$4HCl(g) + O_2(g) + 2C_2H_4(g) \rightleftharpoons 2C_2H_4Cl_2(g) + 2H_2O(g)$$

what is the equation that relates K_c and K_p?

15.52 For the equilibrium:

$$PCl_5(g) \rightleftharpoons PCl_3(g) + Cl_2(g)$$

at a given temperature, K_p is 2.25 atm. A quantity of $PCl_5(g)$ is introduced into an evacuated flask at the reference temperature. When equilibrium is established, the partial pressure of $PCl_5(g)$ is 0.25 atm. **(a)** What are the equilibrium partial pressures of $PCl_3(g)$ and $Cl_2(g)$? **(b)** What was the initial pressure of $PCl_5(g)$ before any of it has dissociated into $PCl_3(g)$ and $Cl_2(g)$? **(c)** What mole percent of $PCl_5(g)$ had dissociated in this system at equilibrium?

*15.53 At a certain temperature, an equilibrium was established:

$$N_2O_4(g) \rightleftharpoons 2\,NO_2(g)$$

In the equilibrium mixture, the partial pressure of $N_2O_4(g)$ was 0.50 atm and the partial pressure of $NO_2(g)$ was 0.50 atm. **(a)** What is the value of K_p at this temperature? **(b)** If the total pressure is increased from 1.00 atm to 2.00 atm and the temperature is held constant, what are the partial pressures of the components of an equilibrium mixture? Note that the quadratic formula must be used to solve this problem.

THEORIES OF
ACIDS AND BASES

C H A P T E R

16

Throughout the history of chemistry various acid-base concepts have been proposed and used. In this chapter four concepts in current use are reviewed. Each of the definitions can be applied with advantage in appropriate circumstances. In a given situation the chemist uses the concept that best suits the purpose.

The earliest criteria for the characterization of acids and bases were the experimentally observed properties of aqueous solutions. An acid was defined as a substance that in water solution tastes sour, turns litmus red, neutralizes bases, and so on. A substance was a base if its aqueous solution tastes bitter, turns litmus blue, neutralizes acids, and so on. Concurrent with the development of generalizations concerning the structure of matter, scientists searched for a correlation between acidic and basic properties and the structure of compounds that exhibit these properties.

16.1 The Arrhenius Concept

When Svante Arrhenius published a "chemical theory of electrolytes" in 1887, he proposed that an electrolyte dissociates into ions in water solution. On this basis, an *acid* came to be defined as a compound that produces $H^+(aq)$ ions in water solution and a *base* a compound that produces $OH^-(aq)$ ions in water solution. The strength of an acid or a base is determined by the extent that the compound dissociates in water. A strong acid or base is one that dissociates completely. Note that the Arrhenius concept is based on the ions of water. The net ionic equation for a *neutralization* is

$$H^+(aq) + OH^-(aq) \longrightarrow H_2O$$

The Arrhenius concept is presented in Section 13.4.

Oxides may be incorporated into the Arrhenius scheme (see Section 13.5). The oxides of many nonmetals react with water to form acids and are therefore called *acidic oxides* or *acid anhydrides*. For example,

$$N_2O_5(s) + H_2O \longrightarrow 2H^+(aq) + 2NO_3^-(aq)$$

Many oxides of metals dissolve in water to form hydroxides. Metal oxides are called *basic oxides* or *base anhydrides*:

$$Na_2O(s) + H_2O \longrightarrow 2Na^+(aq) + 2OH^-(aq)$$

Acidic oxides and basic oxides may react in the absence of water to produce salts. It must be noted, however, that not all acids and bases can be derived from oxides (HCl and NH_3 are examples of compounds that cannot be).

The Arrhenius concept is severely limited by its emphasis on water and reactions in aqueous solution. Later definitions are more general, serve to correlate more reactions, and are applicable to reactions in nonaqueous media.

16.2 The Brønsted-Lowry Concept

In 1923 Johannes Brønsted and Thomas Lowry independently proposed a broader concept of acids and bases. According to the Brønsted-Lowry definitions, an acid is a substance that can donate a proton and a base is a substance that can accept a proton. In these terms, the reaction of an acid with a base is the transfer of a proton from the acid to the base; this is the only type of reaction formally treated by this theory. Acids and bases may be either molecules or ions.

In the reaction

$$HC_2H_3O_2(aq) + H_2O(aq) \rightleftharpoons H_3O^+(aq) + C_2H_3O_2^-(aq)$$

the acetic acid molecule, $HC_2H_3O_2$, functions as an *acid* and releases a proton to the H_2O molecule, which functions as a *base*. This reaction is reversible (as shown by the double arrow) and the system exists in equilibrium.

Now, consider the reverse reaction (from right to left). In this reaction, the H_3O^+ ion donates a proton to the acetate ion, $C_2H_3O_2^-$. The H_3O^+ ion, therefore, functions as an *acid* and the $C_2H_3O_2^-$ ion, because it accepts a proton from this acid, functions as a *base*. It follows, then, that two acids ($HC_2H_3O_2$ and H_3O^+) and two bases (H_2O and $C_2H_3O_2^-$) are involved in this reversible reaction, which is actually a competition between two bases for a proton.

In the forward direction, the base H_2O gains a proton and becomes the acid H_3O^+, and in the reverse direction, the acid H_3O^+ loses a proton and becomes the base H_2O. Such an acid-base pair, which is related through the loss or gain of a proton, is called a conjugate pair:

H_2O is the conjugate base of H_3O^+
H_3O^+ is the conjugate acid of H_2O

In like manner, $HC_2H_3O_2$ and $C_2H_3O_2^-$ are related and form a second conjugate acid-base pair in this reversible system. We can indicate conjugate relationships by the use of subscripts in the following manner:

$$\underset{Acid_1}{HC_2H_3O_2(aq)} + \underset{Base_2}{H_2O} \rightleftharpoons \underset{Acid_2}{H_3O^+(aq)} + \underset{Base_1}{C_2H_3O_2^-(aq)}$$

There are many molecules and ions that can functions as acids in certain reactions and as bases in other reactions. Water, for example, acts as a base in the preceding reaction; but when it reacts with ammonia, NH_3, it functions as an acid:

$$\underset{Acid_1}{H_2O} + \underset{Base_2}{NH_3(aq)} \rightleftharpoons \underset{Acid_2}{NH_4^+(aq)} + \underset{Base_1}{OH^-(aq)}$$

Table 16.1 Some amphiprotic substances		
	Conjugate Pair	
Amphiprotic Substance	Acid	Base
H_2O	H_2O H_3O^+	OH^- H_2O
NH_3	NH_3 NH_4^+	NH_2^- NH_3
HSO_4^-	HSO_4^- H_2SO_4	SO_4^{2-} HSO_4^-
HPO_4^{2-}	HPO_4^{2-} $H_2PO_4^-$	PO_4^{3-} HPO_4^{2-}

In this reaction, the conjugate *base* of H_2O is the OH^- ion. In like manner, NH_3 functions as a base in the preceding reaction with H_2O. In the reaction with the hydride ion, H^-, in liquid ammonia, NH_3 acts as an acid:

$$\underset{Acid_1}{NH_3} + \underset{Base_2}{H^-} \rightleftharpoons \underset{Acid_2}{H_2} + \underset{Base_1}{NH_2^-}$$

Substances that can function as acids or bases are called *amphiprotic;* several amphiprotic substances are listed in Table 16.1.

The neutralization reaction of the Arrhenius system, therefore, may be interpreted in terms of the Brønsted definitions. Such a reaction is merely the acid-base reaction between the conjugate acid and the conjugate base of the amphiprotic solvent, water:

$$\underset{Acid_1}{H_3O^+(aq)} + \underset{Base_2}{OH^-(aq)} \rightleftharpoons \underset{Acid_2}{H_2O} + \underset{Base_1}{H_2O}$$

16.3 Strength of Brønsted Acids and Bases

In Brønsted terms the strength of an acid is determined by its tendency to donate protons, and the strength of a base is dependent upon its tendency to receive protons. The reaction

$$\underset{Acid_1}{HCl(aq)} + \underset{Base_2}{H_2O} \rightleftharpoons \underset{Acid_2}{H_3O^+(aq)} + \underset{Base_1}{Cl^-(aq)}$$

proceeds virtually to completion (from left to right). We must conclude, therefore, that HCl is a stronger acid than H_3O^+, since it has the stronger tendency to lose protons and the equilibrium is displaced far to the right. In addition, it is apparent that H_2O is a stronger base than Cl^- since, in the competition for protons, water molecules succeed in holding practically all of them. The strong acid, HCl, has a weak conjugate base, Cl^-.

A strong acid, which has a great tendency to lose protons, is necessarily conjugate to a weak base, which has a small tendency to gain and hold protons.

Hence, *the stronger the acid, the weaker its conjugate base.* In like manner, a strong base attracts protons strongly and is necessarily conjugate to a weak acid. one that does not readily lose protons. *The stronger the base, the weaker its conjugate acid.*

Acetic acid in 1.0 M solution is 0.42% ionized at 25°C (see Section 17.1). The equilibrium

$$\underset{\text{Acid}_1}{HC_2H_3O_2(aq)} + \underset{\text{Base}_2}{H_2O} \rightleftharpoons \underset{\text{Acid}_2}{H_3O^+(aq)} + \underset{\text{Base}_1}{C_2H_3O_2^-(aq)}$$

is displaced to the left. This equation may be said to represent a competition between bases (acetate ions and water molecules), for protons. The position of the equilibrium shows that the $C_2H_3O_2^-$ ion is a stronger base than H_2O; at equilibrium more protons form $HC_2H_3O_2$ molecules than form H_3O^+ ions. We may also conclude that H_3O^+ is a stronger acid than $HC_2H_3O_2$; at equilibrium more H_3O^+ ions than $HC_2H_3O_2$ molecules have lost protons. In the preceding example we note again that the stronger acid, H_3O^+, is conjugate to the weaker base, H_2O, and the stronger base, $C_2H_3O_2^-$, is conjugate to the weaker acid, $HC_2H_3O_2$.

One further conclusion should be stated. In a given reaction, *the position of equilibrium favors the formation of the weaker acid and the weaker base.* Thus, in the reaction of HCl and H_2O, the equilibrium concentrations of H_3O^+ and Cl^- (the *weaker* acid and base, respectively) are *high*, whereas in the solution of acetic acid, the equilibrium concentrations of H_3O^+ and $C_2H_3O_2^-$ (the *stronger* acid and base, respectively) are *low*.

In Table 16.2, some acids are listed in decreasing order of acid strength (the ability to donate protons). A second column in the table lists the conjugate bases of these acids. Perchloric acid, $HClO_4$, is the strongest acid listed, and its conjugate base, the perchlorate ion, ClO_4^-, is the weakest base. Hydride ion, H^- is the strongest base in the table, and its conjugate acid, H_2, is the weakest acid. The inverse relation between the acid and base strengths of a conjugate pair is evident.

The strength of an acid is determined by the ability of the acid to donate a proton. The reactions of water and the first three acids listed in Table 16.2 go virtually to completion:

$$HClO_4(aq) + H_2O \longrightarrow H_3O^+(aq) + ClO_4^-(aq)$$

$$HCl(aq) + H_2O \longrightarrow H_3O^+(aq) + Cl^-(aq)$$

$$HNO_3(aq) + H_2O \longrightarrow H_3O^+(aq) + NO_3^-(aq)$$

Each of these acids is a stronger acid than H_3O^+, and in a Brønsted acid-base reaction, the weaker acid is formed predominantly.

Aqueous solutions of $HClO_4$, HCl, and HNO_3 of the same concentration appear to be of the same acid strength. The acid properties of the solutions are due to the H_3O^+ ion, which the compounds produce to an equivalent extent in their reactions with water. Water is said to have a leveling effect on acids stronger than H_3O^+. The strongest acid that can exist in water solution is the conjugate acid of water, H_3O^+. Acids that are weaker than H_3O^+ are not leveled by water. Thus, $HC_2H_3O_2$, H_3PO_4, H_2S, and other weak acids show a wide variation in their degree of ionization—the extent to which they form H_3O^+ in their reactions with water (see Section 17.1).

Water also levels bases. The strongest base capable of existing in water solution

Table 16.2 Relative strengths of some conjugate acid-base pairs

Acid		Base
$HClO_4$	$\xrightarrow{\text{100\% in H}_2\text{O}}$	ClO_4^-
HCl	$\xrightarrow{\text{100\% in H}_2\text{O}}$	Cl^-
HNO_3	$\xrightarrow{\text{100\% in H}_2\text{O}}$	NO_3^-
H_3O^+		H_2O
H_3PO_4		$H_2PO_4^-$
$HC_2H_3O_2$		$C_2H_3O_2^-$
H_2CO_3		HCO_3^-
H_2S		HS^-
NH_4^+		NH_3
HCN		CN^-
HCO_3^-		CO_3^{2-}
HS^-		S^{2-}
H_2O		OH^-
NH_3	$\xleftarrow{\text{100\% in H}_2\text{O}}$	NH_2^-
H_2	$\xleftarrow{\text{100\% in H}_2\text{O}}$	H^-

Increasing Acid Strength (upward arrow, left column)

Increasing Base Strength (downward arrow, right column)

is the conjugate base of water, OH^-. Many substances, such as NH_2^- and H^-, are stronger bases than OH^-. In water solution, however, these strongly basic substances accept protons to form OH^- ions; these reactions are essentially complete. The apparent basicity of strongly basic materials in water is reduced to the level of the OH^- ion:

$$H_2O + NH_2^-(aq) \longrightarrow NH_3(aq) + OH^-(aq)$$

$$H_2O + H^-(aq) \longrightarrow H_2(g) + OH^-(aq)$$

Substances, such as ammonia, that are less basic than OH^- are not leveled by water and show varying degrees of ionization in aqueous solution (see Section 17.1).

The leveling effect is observed for solvents other than water. The strongest acid in liquid ammonia solutions is the conjugate acid of ammonia, the ammonium ion, NH_4^+. Acetic acid (which is incompletely ionized in water) is completely ionized in liquid ammonia, since $HC_2H_3O_2$ is stronger acid than NH_4^+:

$$HC_2H_3O_2 + NH_3 \longrightarrow NH_4^+ + C_2H_3O_2^-$$

The strongest base that can exist in liquid ammonia is the conjugate base of ammonia, the amide ion, NH_2^-. In liquid ammonia, the hydride ion, H^-, reacts completely and rapidly to form hydrogen and the amide ion:

$$NH_3 + H^- \longrightarrow H_2 + NH_2^-$$

The hydride ion, therefore, is a stronger base than the amide ion. Liquid ammonia reduces H^- to the level of the conjugate base of ammonia, NH_2^-. Notice that this reaction establishes the order of base strength for H^- and NH_2^- (see Table 16.2).

16.4 Acid Strength and Molecular Structure

In order to analyze the relationships between molecular structure and acid strength, we will divide acids into two types: covalent hydrides and oxyacids. Each of these types will be considered in turn.

1. Hydrides. Some covalent binary compounds of hydrogen (such as H_2S and HCl) are acidic. Two factors influence the acid strength of the hydride of an element: the electronegativity of the element and the atomic size of the element. The first of these factors is best understood by comparing the hydrides of the elements of a period. The second is important when group comparisons are made.

a. Hydrides of the elements of a period. The acid strengths of the hydrides of the elements of a period increase from left to right across the period in the same order that the electronegativities of the elements increase. We would expect a highly electronegative element to withdraw electrons from the hydrogen and facilitate its release as a proton.

Consider the hydrides of nitrogen, oxygen, and fluorine of the second period. The electronegativity of these elements increases in the order

$$N < O < F$$

and acid strength of the hydrides increases in the same order:

$$NH_3 < H_2O < HF$$

A water solution of ammonia (NH_3) is basic:

$$NH_3(g) + H_2O \rightleftharpoons NH_4^+(aq) + OH^-(aq)$$

Water dissociates to a very small extent and forms extremely low concentrations of both $H_3O^+(aq)$ and OH^- (aq):

$$H_2O + H_2O \rightleftharpoons H_3O^+(aq) + OH^-(aq)$$

A water solution of hydrogen fluoride is acidic:

$$HF(g) + H_2O \rightleftharpoons H_3O^+(aq) + F^-(aq)$$

The electronegativities of the following third-period elements fall in the order

$$P < S < Cl$$

The acid strengths of the hydrides of these elements increase in the same order; PH_3 does not react with water, H_2S is a weak acid, and HCl is a strong acid:

$$PH_3 < H_2S < HCl$$

b. Hydrides of the elements of a group. The acidity of the hydrides of the elements of a group increases with increasing size of the central atom. Consider the hydrides of the group VI A and group VII A elements:

$$H_2O < H_2S < H_2Se < H_2Te$$
$$HF < HCl < HBr < HI*$$

This order is the reverse of that expected on the basis of electronegativity. The first hydride of each series (H_2O and HF) is the weakest acid of the series and is formed by the element with the highest electronegativity.

The two factors that influence acid strength are the electronegativity of the central atom and the size of the central atom. When these factors work against each other, the effect of atomic size outweighs the electronegativity effect. A proton is more easily removed from a hydride in which the central atom is large and its electron cloud therefore diffuse than from one in which the central atom is small.

When the hydrogen compounds of the elements of a period are compared, the small differences in the sizes of the central atom are unimportant. The size of the central atom, however, becomes very important when the hydrides of the elements of a group are compared. The atomic radii of the members of a group increase markedly from the lightest to the heaviest members. Fluorine has an atomic radius of 71 pm, and iodine has an atomic radius of 133 pm; HF is a weak acid, and HI is a strong acid.

Consider the hydrides of carbon, sulfur, and iodine. The electronegativities of C, S, and I, elements that belong to different groups, are about. the same (2.5). The atomic radius of C is 77 pm, of S is 103 pm, and of I is 133 pm. There is a marked increase in the acidity of the hydride with the increase in the size of the central atom. Methane, CH_4, does not dissociate in water, H_2S is a weak acid, and HI is a strong acid.

2. Oxyacids. The oxyacids are compounds that are derived from the structure

$$\overset{a\qquad b}{H-O-Z}$$

In each of these compounds, the acidic hydrogen is bonded to an O atom, and the variation in the size of this atom is very small. The key to the acidity of these oxyacids, therefore, lies with the electronegativity of the atom Z.

If Z is an atom of a metal with a low electronegativity, the electron pair that is marked b will belong completely to the O atom, which has a high electronegativity. The compound will be an ionic hydroxide—a base. Sodium hydroxide (HO^-Na^+, usually written Na^+OH^-) falls into this category.

If Z is an atom of a nonmetal with a high electronegativity, the situation is different. The bond marked b will be a strong covalent bond, not an ionic bond. Instead of adding to the electron density around the O atom, Z will tend to reduce the electron density, even though oxygen is itself highly electronegative. The effect will be felt in bond a. The O atom will draw the electron density of this H—O bond away from the H atom, which will allow the proton to dissociate and make the compound acidic. Hypochlorous acid, HOCl, is an acid of this type.

The higher the electronegativity of Z, the more the electrons of the H—O

---

* In dilute aqueous solution, HCl, HBr, and HI are virtually completely dissociated.

bond are drawn away from the H atom and the more readily the proton is lost. In the series

HOI < HOBr < HOCl

the electronegativity of Z increases (I < Br < Cl), and the acid strength increases in the same order.

In some molecules, additional O atoms are bonded to Z. For example,

$$
\begin{array}{c}
\text{O} \\
| \\
\text{H—O—Z—O}
\end{array}
$$

These O atoms draw electrons away from the Z atom and make it more positive. The Z atom, therefore, becomes more effective in withdrawing electron density away from the O atom that is bonded to H. In turn, the electrons of the H—O bond are drawn more strongly away from the H atom. The net effect makes it easier for the proton to dissociate and increases the acidity of the compound.

The more O atoms bonded to Z, the stronger the acid is. This effect is illustrated by the following series of acids, which are arranged by increasing order of acid strength:

$$
\text{H—}\overset{..}{\underset{..}{\text{O}}}\text{—}\overset{..}{\underset{..}{\text{Cl}}}\text{:} \ < \ \text{H—}\overset{..}{\underset{..}{\text{O}}}\text{—}\overset{\oplus}{\underset{..}{\text{Cl}}}\text{—}\overset{..}{\underset{..}{\text{O}}}\text{:}^{\ominus} \ < \ \text{H—}\overset{..}{\underset{..}{\text{O}}}\text{—}\overset{:\overset{..}{\text{O}}\text{:}^{\ominus}}{\underset{..}{\text{Cl}}}^{2+}\overset{..}{\underset{..}{\text{O}}}\text{:}^{\ominus} \ < \ \text{H—}\overset{..}{\underset{..}{\text{O}}}\text{—}\overset{:\overset{..}{\text{O}}\text{:}^{\ominus}}{\underset{:\overset{}{\text{O}}\text{:}^{\ominus}}{\text{Cl}}}^{3+}\overset{..}{\underset{..}{\text{O}}}\text{:}^{\ominus}
$$

Notice that the formal charge on the central atom increases in this series. As the formal charge on the Cl increases, the electron density of the H—O bond shifts away from the H atom. As a result, the acidity increases.

Chemists frequently correlate the acid strength of a series of oxyacids such as this with the oxidation number of the central atom rather than with the formal charge of the central atom as we have done. In the series of the oxyacids of chlorine, formal charge and oxidation number increase in the same order so that it may appear that either could be used:

	HOCl	HOClO	HOClO$_2$	HOClO$_3$
formal charge of Cl	0	1+	2+	3+
oxidation number of Cl	1+	3+	5+	7+

In some cases, however, oxidation number is not a reliable indicator—formal charge must be used. The oxyacids of phosphorus, for example, are all weak acids—about of equal strength:

$$
\begin{array}{ccc}
\text{H—}\overset{..}{\underset{..}{\text{O}}}\text{—}\overset{:\overset{..}{\text{O}}\text{:}^{\ominus}}{\underset{\text{H}}{\overset{\oplus}{\text{P}}}}\text{—H} &
\text{H—}\overset{..}{\underset{..}{\text{O}}}\text{—}\overset{:\overset{..}{\text{O}}\text{:}^{\ominus}}{\underset{\text{H}}{\overset{\oplus}{\text{P}}}}\text{—}\overset{..}{\underset{..}{\text{O}}}\text{—H} &
\text{H—}\overset{..}{\underset{..}{\text{O}}}\text{—}\overset{:\overset{..}{\text{O}}\text{:}^{\ominus}}{\underset{:\overset{}{\text{O}}\text{:}}{\overset{\oplus}{\text{P}}}}\text{—}\overset{..}{\underset{..}{\text{O}}}\text{—H} \\
& & \\
& & \text{H}
\end{array}
$$

formal charge of P	1+	1+	1+
oxidation number of P	1+	3+	5+

Any prediction based on oxidation number is incorrect; there is practically no difference in acid strength between any of these compounds. This conclusion, however, could be reached by noting the formal charge of P in the structures.

We can rate the acid strength of compounds of this type of counting the number of O atoms bonded to Z but *not bonded to H atoms:*

$$H-\ddot{O}-\overset{\oplus}{N}\!\!=\!\!\ddot{O}\quad\text{(with }:\!\ddot{O}\!:^{\ominus}\text{ above N)}$$

is a stronger acid than

$$H-\ddot{O}-N\!\!=\!\!\ddot{O}$$

nitric acid
(a resonance hybrid)

nitrous acid

$$H-\ddot{O}-\overset{(2+)}{S}-\ddot{O}-H\quad\text{(with }:\!\ddot{O}\!:^{\ominus}\text{ above and }:\!\ddot{O}\!:^{\ominus}\text{ below S)}$$

is a stronger acid than

$$H-\ddot{O}-\overset{\oplus}{S}-\ddot{O}-H\quad\text{(with }:\!\ddot{O}\!:^{\ominus}\text{ above S)}$$

sulfuric acid

sulfurous acid

In general, the strengths of acids that have the general formula

$$(HO)_m ZO_n$$

can be related to the value of n:

a. If $n = 0$, the acid is *very weak:* $HOCl$, $(HO)_3B$

b. If $n = 1$, the acid is *weak:* $HOClO$, $HONO$, $(HO)_2SO$, $(HO)_3PO$

c. If $n = 2$, the acid is *strong:* $HOClO_2$, $HONO_2$, $(HO)_2SO_2$

d. If $n = 3$, the acid is *very strong:* $HOClO_3$, $HOIO_3$

The first proton of each acid that belongs to the last two categories ($n = 2$ and $n = 3$) is virtually completely dissociated in water. The distinction between the two groups applies to dissociations in solvents other than water.

The effect of electron-withdrawing groups is also seen in organic acids. None of the H atoms of ethanol:

$$H-O-\overset{\displaystyle H}{\underset{\displaystyle H}{C}}-\overset{\displaystyle H}{\underset{\displaystyle H}{C}}-H$$

dissociates as a proton in water solution. The introduction of another O atom into the molecule:

$$H-O-\overset{\displaystyle O}{C}-\overset{\displaystyle H}{\underset{\displaystyle H}{C}}-H$$

produces the compound called acetic acid (which we have previously written $HC_2H_3O_2$). Acetic acid is a weak monoprotic acid: only the H of the H—O group is acidic. There are a large number of organic acids that contain the

$$\underset{\text{O}}{\overset{\text{O}}{\underset{\|}{\text{H}-\text{O}-\text{C}-}}}$$

group, which is called the carboxyl group. Most carboxylic acids are weak acids and may be considered to belong to the (b) category of our previous classification ($n = 1$).

The carboxylic acids may be assigned the general formula

$$\underset{}{\overset{\text{O}}{\underset{\|}{\text{H}-\text{O}-\text{C}-\text{R}}}}$$

Modifications in the R group can bring about enhanced acidity. If one or more of the H atoms that are bonded to C in acetic acid are replaced by highly electronegative atoms (such as Cl), the acidity is increased. Trichloroacetic acid, for example,

$$\text{H}-\text{O}-\overset{\text{O}}{\overset{\|}{\text{C}}}-\overset{\text{Cl}}{\underset{\text{Cl}}{\text{C}}}-\text{Cl}$$

is a much stronger acid than acetic acid.

Trends in base strength are readily derived from conjugate relationships. A strong acid is conjugate to a weak base. We can, for example, predict that S^{2-} is a weaker base than O^{2-} since H_2S is a stronger acid than H_2O.

16.5 The Lewis Concept

In reality, the Brønsted concept enlarges the definition of a base much more than it does that of an acid. In the Brønsted system a base is a molecule or ion that has an unshared electron pair with which it can attract and hold a proton, and an acid is a substance that can supply a proton to a base. If a molecule or ion can share an electron pair with a proton, it can do the same thing with other substances as well.

Gilbert N. Lewis proposed a broader concept of acids and bases which liberated acid-base phenomena from the proton. Although Lewis first proposed his system in 1923, he did little to develop it until 1938. Lewis defined a **base** as a substance that has an unshared electron pair with which it can form a covalent bond with an atom, molecule, or ion. An **acid** is a substance that can form a covalent bond by accepting an electron pair from a base. The emphasis has been shifted by the Lewis concept from the proton to the electron pair and covalent-bond formation.

An example of an acid-base reaction that is not treated as such by any other acid-base concept is

$$\underset{acid}{\overset{:\ddot{\text{F}}:}{\underset{:\ddot{\text{F}}:}{:\ddot{\text{F}}-\text{B}}}} + \underset{base}{\overset{\text{H}}{\underset{\text{H}}{:\text{N}-\text{H}}}} \longrightarrow \overset{:\ddot{\text{F}}: \ \text{H}}{\underset{:\ddot{\text{F}}: \ \text{H}}{:\ddot{\text{F}}-\text{B}-\text{N}-\text{H}}}$$

Chapter 16   Theories of Acids and Bases

Many Lewis acids and bases of this type can be titrated against one another by the use of suitable indicators in the same way that traditional acids and bases can be titrated.

Substances that are bases in the Brønsted system are also bases according to the Lewis concept. However, the Lewis definition of an acid considerably expands the number of substances that are classified as acids. A Lewis acid must have an empty orbital capable of receiving the electron pair of the base; the proton is but a single example of a Lewis acid.

Chemical species that can function as Lewis acids include the following:

1. Molecules or atoms that have incomplete octets:

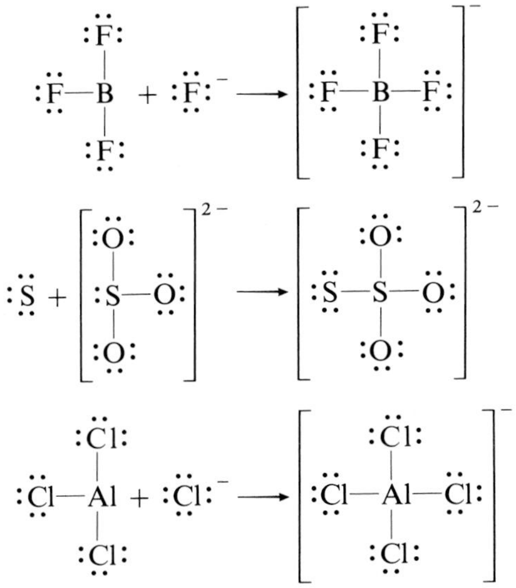

$$:\ddot{F}-B \;+\; :\ddot{F}:^{-} \longrightarrow \left[:\ddot{F}-\overset{:\ddot{F}:}{\underset{:\ddot{F}:}{B}}-\ddot{F}: \right]^{-}$$

$$:\ddot{S} \;+\; \left[:\overset{:\ddot{O}:}{\underset{:\ddot{O}:}{S}}-\ddot{O}: \right]^{2-} \longrightarrow \left[:\overset{:\ddot{O}:}{\underset{:\ddot{O}:}{S}}-S-\ddot{O}: \right]^{2-}$$

$$:\ddot{C}l-Al \;+\; :\ddot{C}l:^{-} \longrightarrow \left[:\ddot{C}l-\overset{:\ddot{C}l:}{\underset{:\ddot{C}l:}{Al}}-\ddot{C}l: \right]^{-}$$

Aluminum chloride, although it reacts as $AlCl_3$, is actually a dimer—Al_2Cl_6. The formation of the dimer from the monomer may be regarded as a Lewis acid-base reaction in itself since a chlorine atom in each $AlCl_3$ unit supplies an electron pair to the aluminum atom of the other $AlCl_3$ unit to complete the octet of the aluminum atom; these bonds are indicated by $\cdots$ in the diagram

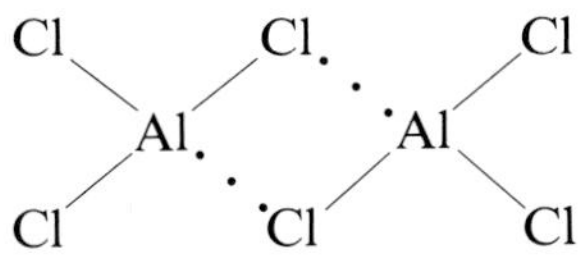

2. Many simple cations can function as Lewis acids—for example,

$$Cu^{2+} + 4:NH_3 \longrightarrow Cu(:NH_3)_4^{2+}$$

$$Fe^{3+} + 6:C\equiv N:^{-} \longrightarrow Fe(:C\equiv N:)_6^{3-}$$

3. Some metal atoms can function as acids in the formation of compounds such as the carbonyls, which are produced by the reaction of the metal with carbon monoxide:

$$Ni + 4:C\equiv O: \longrightarrow Ni(:C\equiv O:)_4$$

4. Compounds that have central atoms capable of expanding their valence shells are Lewis acids in reactions in which this expansion occurs. Examples are

$$SnCl_4 + 2\,Cl^- \longrightarrow SnCl_6^{2-}$$

$$SiF_4 + 2\,F^- \longrightarrow SiF_6^{2-}$$

$$PF_5 + F^- \longrightarrow PF_6^-$$

In each of the first two reactions, the valence shell of the central atom (Sn and Si) is expanded from 8 to 12 electrons, and in the third reaction the valence shell of P goes from 10 to 12 electrons.

5. Some compounds have an acidic site because of one or more multiple bonds in the molecule. Examples are

The reactions of silica, SiO_2, with metal oxides are analogous to the reaction of carbon dioxide with the oxide ion, although both silica and the silicate products (compounds of SiO_3^{2-}) form network solids held together in large aggregates by Si—O bonds. This reaction is important in high-temperature metallurgical processes in which a basic oxide is added to an ore to remove silica in the form of silicates (slag). Many of the processes used in the manufacture of glass, cement, and ceramics involve the reaction of the base O^{2-} (from metal oxides, carbonates, and so forth) with acid oxides (such as SiO_2, Al_2O_3, and B_2O_3).

Arrhenius and Brønsted acid-base reactions may be interpreted in Lewis terms by focusing attention on the proton as a Lewis acid:

$$H^+(aq) + OH^-(aq) \longrightarrow H_2O$$

in which case the Brønsted acid is termed a secondary Lewis acid since it serves to provide the primary Lewis acid, the proton. Probably a better interpretation is that which classifies Brønsted acid-base reactions as Lewis base displacements. The Brønsted acid is interpreted as a complex in which the Lewis acid (proton) is already combined with a base; the reaction is viewed as a displacement of this base by another, stronger base:

$$H_3O^+ + OH^- \longrightarrow H_2O + H_2O$$

In this reaction the base OH^- displaces the weaker base H_2O from its combination with the acid, the proton.

All Brønsted acid-base reactions are Lewis base displacements. In the reaction

$$HCl + H_2O \longrightarrow H_3O^+ + Cl^-$$

the base H_2O displaces the weaker base, Cl^-. A base supplies an electron pair to a nucleus and is therefore called nucleophilic (from Greek, meaning "nucleus loving"). Base displacements are nucleophilic displacements.

Nucleophilic displacements may be identified among reactions that are not Brønsted acid-base reactions. The formation of $Cu(NH_3)_4^{2+}$ has been previously used as an illustration of a Lewis acid-base reaction. Since the reaction occurs in water, the formation of this complex is more accurately interpreted as the displacement of the base H_2O from the complex $Cu(H_2O)_4^{2+}$ by the stronger base NH_3:

$$Cu(H_2O)_4^{2+} + 4\,NH_3 \longrightarrow Cu(NH_3)_4^{2+} + 4\,H_2O$$

Lewis acids accept an electron pair in a reaction with a base; they are electrophilic (from Greek, meaning "electron loving"). Acid displacements, or electrophilic displacements, are not so common as base displacements, but this type of reaction is known. For example, if $COCl_2$ is viewed as a combination of $COCl^+$ (an acid) with Cl^- (a base), the reaction

$$COCl_2 + AlCl_3 \longrightarrow COCl^+ + AlCl_4^-$$

is an electrophilic displacement in which the acid $AlCl_3$ displaces the weaker acid $COCl^+$ from its complex with the base Cl^- (Table 16.3). The reaction

$$SeOCl_2 + BCl_2 \longrightarrow SeOCl^+ + BCl_4^-$$

may be similarly interpreted.

Lewis theory is frequently used to interpret reaction mechanisms. Examples of such interpretations are found in Sections 28.5 and 28.6.

16.6 Solvent Systems

The principles of the Arrhenius water concept can be used to devise acid-base schemes for many solvents. In a solvent system an acid is a substance that gives the cation characteristic of the solvent, and a base is a substance that yields the anion characteristic of the solvent. Thus, the reaction of an acid and a base, a neutralization, yields the solvent as one of its products. Many solvent systems of acids and bases have been developed (Table 16.3); the water concept is but a single example of a solvent system.

The ammonia system has been investigated more extensively than any other, with the exception of the water system. The properties of liquid ammonia (boiling point, $-33.4°C$) are strikingly similar to those of water. Liquid ammonia is associated through hydrogen bonding, and the NH_3 molecule is polar. Hence, liquid ammonia is an excellent solvent for ionic and polar compounds, and it functions as an ionizing solvent for electrolytes. Many compounds form ammoniates, which are analogous to hydrates ($BaBr_2 \cdot 8\,NH_3$ and $CaCl_2 \cdot 6\,NH_3$ are examples), and ions are solvated in liquid ammonia solutions [$Ag(NH_3)_2^+$ and $Cr(NH_3)_6^{3+}$ are examples]. Whereas solutions of electrolytes in ammonia are good conductors of electricity, pure liquid ammonia, like water, has a relatively low conductance.

The autoionization of ammonia:

$$2\,NH_2 \rightleftharpoons NH_4^+ + NH_2^-$$

Table 16.3 Some solvent systems

Solvent	Acid Ion	Base Ion	Typical Acid	Typical Base
H_2O	H_3O^+ $(H^+ \cdot H_2O)$	OH^-	HCl	NaOH
NH_3	NH_4^+ $(H^+ \cdot NH_3)$	NH_2^-	NH_4Cl	$NaNH_2$
NH_2OH	NH_3OH^+ $(H^+ \cdot NH_2OH)$	$NHOH^-$	$NH_2OH \cdot HCl$ (NH_3OH^+, Cl^-)	$K(NHOH)$
$HC_2H_3O_2$	$H_2C_2H_3O_2^+$ $(H^+ \cdot HC_2H_3O_2)$	$C_2H_3O_2^-$	HCl	$NaC_2H_3O_2$
SO_2	SO^{2+}	SO_3^{2-}	$SOCl_2$	Cs_2SO_3
N_2O_4	NO^+	NO_3^-	NOCl	$AgNO_3$
$COCl_2$	$COCl^+$	Cl^-	$(COCl)AlCl_4$	$CaCl_2$

which occurs only to a low degree, is responsible for the electrical conductivity of pure solvent, just as the autoionization of water:

$$2\,H_2O \rightleftharpoons H_3O^+ + OH^-$$

is responsible for the electrical properties of this compound.

Any compound that produces ammonium ion, NH_4^+, in liquid ammonia solution is an acid, and any compound that yields amide ion, NH_2^-, is a base. Thus, the neutralization reaction is the reverse of the autoionization reaction:

$$NH_4^+ + NH_2^- \longrightarrow 2\,NH_3$$

Indicators may be used to follow an acid-base reaction in liquid ammonia. For example, phenolphthalein is red in a liquid ammonia solution of potassium amide, KNH_2, and becomes colorless after a stoichiometrically equivalent amount of ammonium chloride has been added.

In addition to the neutralization reaction, the ammonium ion in liquid ammonia undergoes other reactions analogous to the reactions of the hydronium ion in water. For example, metals such as sodium react with the ammonium ion to liberate hydrogen:

$$2\,Na(s) + 2\,NH_4^+ \longrightarrow 2\,Na^+ + H_2(g) + 2\,NH_3(l)$$

The reactions of the amide ion are analogous to those of the hydroxide ion:

$$Zn(OH)_2(s) + 2\,OH^- \longrightarrow Zn(OH)_4^{2-} \qquad \text{(in water solution)}$$

$$Zn(NH_2)_2(s) + 2\,NH_2^- \longrightarrow Zn(NH_2)_4^{2-} \qquad \text{(in ammonia solution)}$$

$$Hg^{2+} + 2\,OH^- \longrightarrow HgO(s) + H_2O \qquad \text{(in water solution)}$$

$$3\,Hg^{2+} + 6\,NH_2^- \longrightarrow Hg_3N_2(s) + 4\,NH_3 \quad \text{(in ammonia solution)}$$

Many properties and reactions of compounds belonging to the ammonia system have been predicted and correlated by comparison to the better-known chemistry of the compounds of the water system. In fact, the study of various solvent systems has been responsible for greatly increasing our knowledge of the reactions that occur in solvents other than water.

Summary

According to the *Arrhenius theory*, an *acid* produces $H^+(aq)$ in aqueous solution and a *base* produces $OH^-(aq)$ in aqueous solution. The reaction between an acid and a base, in which water is produced, is called a *neutralization*.

The *Brønsted-Lowry concept* defines acids and bases (which may be molecules or ions) in terms of the exchange of a proton. In an acid-base reaction, an *acid donates a proton* to a *base*, which *accepts it*. In losing a proton, $acid_1$ becomes $base_1$ (the *conjugate base* of $acid_1$); and in gaining a proton, the original $base_2$ becomes $acid_2$ (the *conjugate acid* of $base_2$).

$$acid_1 + base_2 \rightleftharpoons acid_2 + base_1$$

The strengths of acids and bases are based on their tendencies to lose or gain protons. The stronger the acid (or base), the weaker is the conjugate base (or acid). An acid-base reaction always proceeds *from the stronger* acid and base *to the weaker* acid and base.

In terms of *molecular structure*, two factors influence the *acid strength* of the covalent *hydrides* of the elements: the *electronegativity* of the element and the *atomic size* of the element. When the hydrides of the elements of a *period* are compared, the *strongest acid* is found to be formed by the *most electronegative* element. When the hydrides of the elements of a *group* are compared, the *strongest acid* is found to be formed by the *largest atom*. The strength of an *oxyacid*, H—O—Z, increases with increasing *electronegativity of Z*. In oxyacids where additional O atoms are bonded to Z, $(HO)_m ZO_n$, acid strength *increases* with *increasing value of n*.

In the *Lewis concept*, the formation of a *covalent bond* is the criterion for defining acid-base reactions. A *base* (a *nucleophilic* substance) *supplies* an unshared *electron pair* for the formation of a covalent bond with an *acid* (an *electrophilic* substance). The Lewis theory is also used to interpret reaction mechanisms, such as *nucleophilic* and *electrophilic displacements*.

The principles of the Arrhenius acid-base concept, which centers on water, can be used to develop *acid-base schemes* for other *solvents*. An *acid* is a substance that gives the *cation* characteristic of the solvent and a *base* is a substance that gives the *anion* characteristic of the solvent. The solvent is, therefore, a product of the reaction of an acid and a base, a *neutralization*.

Key Terms

Some of the more important terms introduced in this chapter are listed below. Definitions for terms not included in this list may be located in the text by use of the index.

Amphiprotic substance (Section 16.2) A substance that can function as a Brønsted acid (through proton loss) and as a Brønsted base (through proton gain).

Arrhenius acid (Sections 13.4 and 16.1) A compound that dissociates in water to produce $H^+(aq)$ ions (or H_3O^+ ions).

Arrhenius base (Sections 13.4 and 16.1) A compound that dissolves in water to produce $OH^-(aq)$ ions.

Arrhenius neutralization (Sections 13.4 and 16.1) A reaction in which $H^+(aq)$ from an acid and $OH^-(aq)$ from a base react to form water.

Brønsted acid (Section 16.2) A molecule or ion that can donate protons.

Brønsted base (Section 16.2) A molecule or ion that can accept protons.

Conjugate pair (Section 16.2) A Brønsted acid-base pair that is related through the loss or gain of a proton; for example, NH_4^+ (a Brønsted acid) and NH_3 (a Brønsted base) form a conjugate pair.

Electrophilic displacement (Section 16.5) A reaction in which a Lewis acid displaces a second, weaker Lewis acid from an acid-base complex; a Lewis acid displacement.

Leveling effect (Section 16.3) An effect of a solvent on the strength of a Brønsted acid or a Brønsted base. An acid in solution can be no stronger than the conjugate acid of the solvent; a base in solution can be no stronger than the conjugate base of the solvent. Stronger acids or bases react with the solvent to produce the acid or base that is conjugate to the solvent.

Lewis acid (Section 16.5) A substance that can form a covalent bond by sharing an electron pair that is donated by a Lewis base; an electrophilic substance.

Lewis base (Section 16.5) A substance that can form a covalent bond with a Lewis acid by donating an electron pair toward the formation of the bond; a nucleophilic substance.

Nucleophilic displacement (Section 16.5) A reaction in which a Lewis base displaces a second, weaker Lewis base from an acid-base complex; a Lewis base displacement.

Solvent-system acid (Section 16.6) A substance that yields the cation characteristic of the solvent.

Solvent-system base (Section 16.6) A substance that yields the anion characteristic of the solvent.

Solvent-system neutralization (Section 16.6) A reaction between an acid and a base that yields the solvent as one of the products.

Problems*

Acid-Base Concepts

16.1 Ammonium chloride (NH_4Cl) reacts with sodium amide ($NaNH_2$) in liquid ammonia to produce sodium chloride and ammonia. Interpret the reaction in terms of the Brønsted, the Lewis, and the solvent theories of acids and bases. State clearly what acid(s) and base(s) are involved in each case.

16.2 Give one sentence definitions of an *acid*, a *base*, and a *neutralization reaction* based on **(a)** the Arrhenius concept, **(b)** the Brønsted-Lowry concept, **(c)** the Lewis concept, and **(d)** the solvent-system concept.

16.3 Briefly discuss, using chemical equations, how the compound H_2O is classified according to **(a)** the Arrhenius concept, **(b)** the Brønsted-Lowry concept, and **(c)** the Lewis concept.

16.4 Briefly discuss the role of the proton in defining an acid and a base in **(a)** the Arrhenius concept, **(b)** the Brønsted-Lowry concept, **(c)** the Lewis concept, **(d)** the solvent-system concept.

Brønsted-Lowry Concept

16.5 Give the conjugate base of: **(a)** H_3PO_4, **(b)** $H_2PO_4^-$, **(c)** NH_3, **(d)** HS^-, **(e)** H_2SO_4.

16.6 Give the conjugate base of: **(a)** $HOCl$, **(b)** H_3O^+, **(c)** NH_4^+, **(d)** HCO_3^-, **(e)** HPO_4^{2-}.

16.7 Give the conjugate acid of: **(a)** H^-, **(b)** H_2O, **(c)** HS^-, **(d)** NH_3, **(e)** $H_2AsO_4^-$.

16.8 Give the conjugate acid of: **(a)** F^-, **(b)** OH^-, **(c)** PO_4^{3-}, **(d)** PH_3, **(e)** NO_2^-.

16.9 Identify all the Brønsted acids and bases in the following equations:
(a) $NH_3 + HCl \rightleftharpoons NH_4^+ + Cl^-$
(b) $HSO_4^- + CN^- \rightleftharpoons HCN + SO_4^{2-}$
(c) $H_2PO_4^- + CO_3^{2-} \rightleftharpoons HPO_4^{2-} + HCO_3^-$
(d) $H_3O^+ + HS^- \rightleftharpoons H_2S + H_2O$
(e) $HS^- + OH^- \rightleftharpoons H_2O + S^{2-}$

16.10 Identify all the Brønsted acids and bases in the following equations:
(a) $H_2O + O^{2-} \rightleftharpoons OH^- + OH^-$
(b) $NH_4^+ + OH^- \rightleftharpoons NH_3 + H_2O$
(c) $N_2H_4 + HSO_4^- \rightleftharpoons N_2H_5^+ + SO_4^{2-}$
(d) $H_2PO_4^- + CN^- \rightleftharpoons HCN + HPO_4^{2-}$
(e) $H_2O + NH_2^- \rightleftharpoons NH_3 + OH^-$

16.11 Write chemical equations to illustrate the behavior of the following as Brønsted acids: **(a)** H_2O, **(b)** HF, **(c)** HSO_3^-, **(d)** NH_4^+ **(e)** NH_3.

16.12 Write chemical equations to illustrate the behavior of the following as Brønsted acids: **(a)** $HOCl$, **(b)** HPO_4^{2-}, **(c)** HS^-, **(d)** H_2S, **(e)** H_3O^+.

16.13 Write chemical equations to illustrate the behavior of the following as Brønsted bases: **(a)** H^-, **(b)** OH^-, **(c)** N^{3-}, **(d)** H_2O, **(e)** HSO_4^-.

16.14 Write chemical equations to illustrate the behavior of the following as Brønsted bases: **(a)** HCO_3^-, **(b)** NH_2^-, **(c)** NH_3, **(d)** O^{2-}, **(d)** SO_4^{2-}.

16.15 Each of the following reactions is displaced to the right. Make a list of all the Brønsted acids that appear in these equations with these acids arranged according to decreasing acid strength. Make a similar list for Brønsted bases.
(a) $H_3O^+ + H_2PO_4^- \rightleftharpoons H_3PO_4 + H_2O$
(b) $HCN + OH^- \rightleftharpoons H_2O + CN^-$
(c) $H_3PO_4 + CN^- \rightleftharpoons HCN + H_2PO_4^-$
(d) $H_2O + NH_2^- \rightleftharpoons NH_3 + OH^-$

16.16 Each of the following reactions is displaced to the right. Make a list of all the Brønsted acids that appear in these equations with these acids arranged according to decreasing acid strength. Make a similar list for Brønsted bases.
(a) $HCO_3^- + OH^- \rightleftharpoons H_2O + CO_3^{2-}$
(b) $HC_2H_3O_2 + HS^- \rightleftharpoons H_2S + C_2H_3O_2^-$
(c) $H_2S + CO_3^{2-} \rightleftharpoons HCO_3^- + HS^-$
(d) $HSO_4^- + C_2H_3O_2^- \rightleftharpoons HC_2H_3O_2 + SO_4^{2-}$

16.17 On the basis of your lists from problem 16.15 would you expect an appreciable reaction (over 50%) between the species listed in each of the following parts?
(a) $H_3O^+ + CN^- \longrightarrow$
(b) $NH_3 + CN^- \longrightarrow$
(c) $HCN + H_2PO_4^- \longrightarrow$
(d) $H_3PO_4 + NH_2^- \longrightarrow$

16.18 On the basis of your lists from problem 16.16 would you expect an appreciable reaction (over 50%) between the species listed in each of the following parts?
(a) $HCO_3^- + C_2H_3O_2^- \longrightarrow$
(b) $HSO_4^- + HS^- \longrightarrow$
(c) $HC_2H_3O_2 + CO_3^{2-} \longrightarrow$
(d) $H_2S + C_2H_3O_2^- \longrightarrow$

---

* The appendix contains answers to color-keyed problems.

16.19 Compare the acidity of AsH_3, H_2Se, and HBr. How does acid strength vary among the hydrides of the elements of a period?

16.20 Compare the acidity of H_2S, H_2Se, and H_2Te. How does acid strength vary among the hydrides of the elements of a group?

16.21 Which compound of each of the following pairs is the stronger acid?

(a) H_3PO_4 or H_3AsO_4

(b) H_3AsO_3 or H_3AsO_4

(c) H_2SO_4 or H_2SO_3

(d) H_3BO_3 or H_2CO_3

(e) H_2Se or HBr

16.22 Which compound of each of the following pairs is the stronger acid?

(a) H_2SO_4 or H_2SeO_4

(b) H_2Te or HI

(c) HNO_3 or HNO_2

(d) H_2SO_3 or $HClO_3$

(e) $HClO_3$ or HIO_3

16.23 Which compound of each of the following pairs is the stronger base?

(a) P^{3-} or S^{2-}

(b) PH_3 or NH_3

(c) SiO_3^{2-} or SO_3^{2-}

(d) NO_2^- or NO_3^-

(e) Br^- or F^-

16.24 Which compound of each of the following pairs is the stronger base?

(a) HSO_3^- or HSO_4^-

(b) O^{2-} or S^{2-}

(c) BrO_3^- or IO_3^-

(d) SO_4^{2-} or PO_4^{3-}

(e) ClO_3^- or ClO_2^-

16.25 Draw Lewis structures (include formal charges) for selinic acid, H_2SeO_4, and telluric acid, H_6TeO_6. Which is the stronger acid? Note that six HO— groups are bonded to the Te atom in teluric acid.

16.26 Perchloric acid, $HClO_4$, is a stronger acid than chloric acid, $HClO_3$. On the other hand, periodic acid, H_5IO_6, is a weaker acid than iodic acid, HIO_3. Draw Lewis structures for the four compounds (include formal charges). Note that six O atoms are bonded to a central I atom in periodic acid and that five of the O atoms have H atoms bonded to them.

16.27 Interpret the following reactions in terms of Lewis theory:

(a) $AuCN + CN^- \longrightarrow Au(CN)_2^-$

(b) $F^- + HF \longrightarrow HF_2^-$

(c) $S + S^{2-} \longrightarrow S_2^{2-}$

(d) $S{=}C{=}S + SH^- \longrightarrow S_2CSH^-$

(e) $Fe + 5\,CO \longrightarrow Fe(CO)_5$

16.28 Interpret the following reactions in terms of Lewis theory:

(a) $AlF_3 + F^- \longrightarrow AlF_4^-$

(b) $H^- + H_2C{=}O \longrightarrow H_3CO^-$

(c) $Ag^+ + 2\,NH_3 \longrightarrow Ag(NH_3)_2^+$

(d) $SeF_4 + F^- \longrightarrow SeF_5^-$

(e) $Zn(OH)_2 + 2\,OH^- \longrightarrow Zn(OH)_4^{2-}$

16.29 Interpret the following as Lewis displacement reactions. For each, state the type of displacement, what is displaced, and the agent for the displacement.

(a) $CH_3I + OH^- \longrightarrow CH_3OH + I^-$

(b) $S^{2-} + H_2O \longrightarrow HS^- + OH^-$

(c) $Br_2 + FeBr_3 \longrightarrow Br^+ + FeBr_4^-$

(d) $NH_4^+ + OH^- \longrightarrow NH_3 + H_2O$

(e) $HONO_2 + H^+ \longrightarrow NO_2^+ + H_2O$

16.30 Interpret the following as Lewis displacement reactions. For each, state the type of displacement, what is displaced, and the agent for the displacement.

(a) $Ge + GeS_2 \longrightarrow 2\,GeS$

(b) $CH_3Cl + AlCl_3 \longrightarrow CH_3^+ + AlCl_4^-$

(c) $O^{2-} + H_2O \longrightarrow 2\,OH^-$

(d) $NH_3 + H^- \longrightarrow H_2 + NH_2^-$

(e) $NO^+ + H_2O \longrightarrow H^+ + HNO_2$

Unclassified Problems

16.31 What is the leveling effect of a solvent? Use chemical equations in your answer, and describe the leveling of both acids and bases.

16.32 (a) What is an amphiprotic substance? (b) Give four examples of amphiprotic substances. Select both molecules and ions as your examples. (c) Write chemical equations to illustrate the behavior of the substances that you selected as examples.

16.33 (a) What is the difference in meaning between the terms amphiprotic and amphoteric? (b) Is H_2O amphoteric? amphiprotic?

16.34 Sulfur dioxide is a significant contributor to atmospheric pollution. The sulfurous acid produced by the reaction of SO_2 and atmospheric moisture adversely affects the eyes, skin, and respiratory systems of humans, destroys plant life, and causes the corrosion of metals and the deterioration of other materials. The reaction of SO_2 with water can be roughly indicated as:

$$H_2O + SO_2 \longrightarrow H_2OSO_2 \longrightarrow (HO)_2SO$$

(a) Draw Lewis structures (complete with formal charges) for the compounds given. **(b)** Interpret the two steps of the sequence in terms of the Lewis acid-base theory.

(c) Why does the proton migration of the second step occur?

16.35 Write equations analogous to the following but employing compounds of the water system instead of compounds of the ammonia system:

(a) $KNH_2 + NH_4NO_3 \longrightarrow KNO_3 + 2\,NH_3$

(b) $Ca_3N_2 + 4\,NH_3 \longrightarrow 3\,Ca(NH_2)_2$

(c) $Cl_2 + 2\,NH_3 \longrightarrow NH_4Cl + H_2NCl$

(d) $2\,Na + 2\,NH_3 \longrightarrow 2\,NaNH_2 + H_2$

(e) $Zn(NH_2)_2 + 2\,NaNH_2 \longrightarrow Na_2[Zn(NH_2)_4]$

IONIC EQUILIBRIUM, PART I

C H A P T E R

17

The principles of chemical equilibrium can be applied to equilibrium systems that involve molecules and ions in water solution. In pure water, H_3O^+ and OH^- ions exist in equilibrium with H_2O molecules from which they are derived. Weak electrolytes are partially ionized in water solution and exist in equilibrium with their ions. An understanding of these systems is important to the study of analytical chemistry.

7.1 Weak Electrolytes

Strong electrolytes are completely ionized in water solution. A 0.01 M solution of $CaCl_2$, for example, contains Ca^{2+} ions (at a concentration of 0.01 M), Cl^- ions (at a concentration of 0.02 M), and no $CaCl_2$ molecules at all. Weak electrolytes, however, are *incompletely* ionized in water solution. Dissolved molecules exist in equilibrium with their ions in such solutions. The following chemical equation represents the dissociation of acetic acid in water:

$$HC_2H_3O_2 + H_2O \rightleftharpoons H_3O^+ + C_2H_3O_2^-$$

The equilibrium constant for this reaction as written is

$$\frac{[H_3O^+][C_2H_3O_2^-]}{[HC_2H_3O_2][H_2O]} = K_a'$$

In dilute solutions, the concentration of water may be considered to be a constant. The number of moles of water used in forming H_3O^+ (which is about 0.001 mol in 1 L of a 0.1 M solution of acetic acid) is very small in comparison to the large number of moles of water present (which is about 55.5 mol in 1 L of the solution). If we combine $[H_2O]$ with K_a', we get

$$\frac{[H_3O^+][C_2H_3O_2^-]}{[HC_2H_3O_2]} = K_a'[H_2O] = K_a$$

We shall follow the practice of representing the concentration of hydronium ion, $[H_3O^+]$, by the symbol $[H^+]$. The simplied expression for the equilibrium constant K_a, sometimes called an acid dissociation constant, and the corresponding simplied chemical equation are

$$HC_2H_3O_2 \rightleftharpoons H^+ + C_2H_3O_2^-$$

$$\frac{[H^+][C_2H_3O_2^-]}{[HC_2H_3O_2]} = K_a$$

By convention, the *ions* are written on the *right* of the chemical equation for a reversible ionization. Consequently, the terms for the concentrations of the *ions* appear in the *numerator* of the expression for K_a.

The degree of dissociation, α, of a weak electrolyte in water solution is the fraction of the total concentration of the electrolyte that is in ionic form at equilibrium. These values are frequently given in terms of percent ionized, which is 100α.

Example 17.1

At 25°C, a 0.1000 M solution of acetic acid ($HC_2H_3O_2$) is 1.34% ionized. What is the ionization constant, K_a, for acetic acid?

Solution

Let us assume that we have exactly one liter of solution. Since the acid is 1.34% ionized, the number of moles of $HC_2H_3O_2$ in *ionic form* is

$$(0.0134)(0.1000 \text{ mol } HC_2H_3O_2) = 0.00134 \text{ mol } HC_2H_3O_2$$

We subtract this number from the total number of moles of $HC_2H_3O_2$ to get the number of moles of acid in *molecular form:*

$$(0.1000 \text{ mol } HC_2H_3O_2) - (0.00134 \text{ mol } HC_2H_3O_2) = 0.0987 \text{ mol } HC_2H_3O_2$$

According to the chemical equation for the ionization, 1 mol of H^+ and 1 mol of $C_2H_3O_2^-$ are produced for every 1 mol of $HC_2H_3O_2$ that ionizes. Therefore, the concentrations at equilibrium are

$$HC_2H_3O_2 \rightleftharpoons H^+ + C_2H_3O_2^-$$
$$0.0987 \ M \qquad 0.00134 \ M \qquad 0.00134 \ M$$

These concentrations may be used to find the numerical value of the equilibrium constant:

$$K_a = \frac{[H^+][C_2H_3O_2^-]}{[HC_2H_3O_2]}$$

$$= \frac{(0.00134)(0.00134)}{(0.0987)}$$

$$= 1.82 \times 10^{-5}$$

In future problem work, we shall express equilibrium constants to two significant figures. Higher accuracy is usually not warranted.*

---

* Equilibrium concentrations should be written in terms of activities, not concentrations. The activity of an ion is a theoretical concentration that takes into account interionic attractions (see Section 12.12). The concentrations of ions in dilute solutions of weak electrolytes are so small, however, that interionic attractions are negligible. Under these conditions molar concentrations may be used rather than activities. Resonably accurate results are obtained from this practice.

Example 17.2

What are the concentrations of all species present in 1.00 M acetic acid at 25°C? For $HC_2H_3O_2$, K_a is 1.8×10^{-5}.

Solution

If we let x equal the number of moles of $HC_2H_3O_2$ in ionic form in one liter of solution, the equilibrium concentrations are

$$HC_2H_3O_2 \rightleftharpoons H^+ + C_2H_3O_2^-$$
$$(1.00 - x)\,M \qquad x\,M \qquad x\,M$$

We substitute these values into the expression for K_a:

$$K_a = \frac{[H^+][C_2H_3O_2^-]}{[HC_2H_3O_2]}$$

$$1.8 \times 10^{-5} = \frac{x^2}{(1.00 - x)}$$

The result can be rearranged to

$$x^2 + (1.8 \times 10^{-5})x - 1.8 \times 10^{-5} = 0$$

An equation in the form

$$ax^2 + bx + c = 0$$

is called a quadratic equation (see the appendix). Solutions to a quadratic equation can be found by substitution in the quadratic formula:

$$x = \frac{-b \pm \sqrt{b^2 - 4ac}}{2a}$$

In the present problem, $a = 1$, $b = 1.8 \times 10^{-5}$, and $c = -1.8 \times 10^{-5}$. If we substitute these values into the quadratic formula, we get

$$x = 4.2 \times 10^{-3}\,M*$$

Therefore,

$$[H^+] = [C_2H_3O_2^-] = x = 4.2 \times 10^{-3}\,M$$
$$[HC_2H_3O_2] = (1.00 - x)\,M$$
$$= (1.00 - 0.0042)\,M$$
$$= 0.9958\,M$$

---

* There are always two solutions to a quadratic equation. One of them must be discarded because it represents a physical impossibility. The two solutions obtained in the present case are

$$x = 4.2 \times 10^{-3}\,M \quad \text{and} \quad x = -4.2 \times 10^{-3}\,M$$

The second solution is impossible. The concentration of $HC_2H_3O_2$ is $(1.00 - x)$. Substitution of the second value (which is a negative number) for x gives a final $HC_2H_3O_2$ concentration that would require more $HC_2H_3O_2$ than was supplied, and would lead to negative concentrations of H^+ and $C_2H_3O_2^-$.

Notice that the value of K_a that we employed has two significant figures. Our answer, therefore, cannot be given to more than two significant figures. The concentration of $HC_2H_3O_2$ must be rounded off:

$$[HC_2H_3O_2] = 1.0 \ M$$

This value is the same as the initial concentration of $HC_2H_3O_2$.

The use of the quadratic formula in problem solving may often be avoided by making an approximation that is frequently employed in calculations involving aqueous equilibria. The subtraction of a very small number from a large number does not significantly change the value of the large number and may be neglected.

In the preceding example such a small amount of acetic acid is ionized (x) that the quantity $(1.00 - x)$, which is the concentration of acetic acid molecules, is for all practical purposes equal to 1.00 (as previously noted). By using 1.00 instead of $(1.00 - x)$ for the concentration of $HC_2H_3O_2$, we find

$$1.8 \times 10^{-5} = \frac{[H^+][C_2H_3O_2^-]}{[HC_2H_3O_2]}$$

$$= \frac{x^2}{1.00}$$

$$x = 4.2 \times 10^{-3} \ M$$

which is the same as the result obtained through the use of the quadratic formula.

The subtraction of a *small* number from another *small* number may *not* be neglected. Consequently, the quadratic formula *must* be used to solve some problems. A good procedure to determine when the simplified method is justified is the following:

1. Set up the problem in the same way as that used in Example 17.2. That is,

$$[HC_2H_3O_2] = (1.00 - x) \ M$$

$$[H^+] = x \ M$$

$$[C_2H_3O_2^-] = x \ M$$

2. Solve the problem using the simplified method. In the example, substitute 1.00 M for $[HC_2H_3O_2]$ instead of $(1.00 - x) \ M$, on the assumption that x is small in comparison to 1.00 M.

3. Check the answer obtained by the simplified method against the assumption made. In the case at hand, since $x = 4.2 \times 10^{-3} \ M$,

$$(1.00 - x) = (1.00 - 0.0042) = 0.9958 \ M$$

which to two significant figures is 1.0 M. Our assumption was justified.

4. The values of ionization constants are given to two significant figures, and we will solve problems to this limit of accuracy. If the subtraction in step 3 changes the value (when it is recorded to two significant figures), then the assumption was not justified. The problem must be solved again, and this time the quadratic formula must be used.

Example 17.3

What are the concentrations of all species present in a 0.10 M solution of HNO_2 at 25°C? For HNO_2, K_a is 4.5×10^{-4}.

Solution

If we let x equal the number of moles of HNO_2 in ionic form in one liter of solution, the equilibrium concentrations are

$$\underset{(0.10 - x)\,M}{HNO_2} \;\rightleftharpoons\; \underset{x\,M}{H^+} + \underset{x\,M}{NO_2^-}$$

We attempt the simplified method and substitute 0.10 M for $[HNO_2]$ instead of $(0.10 - x)\,M$:

$$4.5 \times 10^{-4} = \frac{[H^+][NO_2^-]}{[HNO_2]}$$

$$= \frac{x^2}{0.10}$$

$$x = 6.7 \times 10^{-3}\,M$$

On this basis,

$$\begin{aligned}[HNO_2] &= (0.10 - x)\,M \\ &= (0.10 - 0.0067)\,M \\ &= 0.093\,M\end{aligned}$$

We can see that the use of the simplified method was not justified; x is not negligible in comparison to 0.10 M, since the subtraction changes the value (when it is recorded to two significant figures) from 0.10 M to 0.093 M. We must solve the problem again and this time use the quadratic formula:

$$4.5 \times 10^{-4} = \frac{x^2}{(0.10 - x)}$$

$$x^2 + (4.5 \times 10^{-4})x - 4.5 \times 10^{-6} = 0$$

By use of the quadratic formula:

$$x = [H^+] = [NO_2^-] = 6.5 \times 10^{-3}\,M$$

$$(0.10 - x) = [HNO_2] = 0.094\,M$$

The percent ionization of a weak electrolyte is found by dividing the number of moles of solute in the ionic form by the total number of moles of solute and

Table 17.1 Ion concentrations and percent ionization of solutions of acetic acid at 25°C

Concentration of Solution (M)	$[H^+]$ or $[C_2H_3O_2^-]$ (M)	Percent Ionization
1.00	0.00426	0.426
0.100	0.00134	1.34
0.0100	0.000418	4.18
0.00100	0.000126	12.6

multiplying the fraction obtained by 100. The percent ionization of the acetic acid solution described in Example 17.2 is

$$\frac{4.2 \times 10^{-3}\ M}{1.00\ M} \times 100 = 0.42\%$$

The ion concentration and percent ionization of solutions of acetic acid of various concentrations are listed in Table 17.1. The percent ionization increases with dilution, which is consistent with Le Chatelier's principle. Addition of water to an equilibrium system of a weak electrolyte:

$$HC_2H_3O_2 + H_2O \rightleftharpoons H_2O^+ + C_2H_3O_2^-$$

shifts the equilibrium to the right. Proportionately more of the solute is found in the ionic form.

An equilibrium system of a weak electrolyte can be prepared from compounds that supply the ions of the weak electrolyte. The following example is an illustration of this procedure.

Example 17.4

What are the concentrations of all species present in a solution made by diluting 0.10 mol of HCl and 0.50 mol of $NaC_2H_3O_2$ to 1.0 L?

Solution

Hydrochloric acid and sodium acetate are strong electrolytes. We may assume, therefore, that before equilibrium is attained, the concentration of H^+ is 0.10 M and the concentration of $C_2H_3O_2^-$ is 0.50 M. If we let x equal the number of moles per liter of acetic acid at equilibrium, the equilibrium concentrations are

$$HC_2H_3O_2 \rightleftharpoons H^+ + C_2H_3O_2^-$$
$$(x)\ M \quad (0.10 - x)\ M \quad (0.50 - x)\ M$$

Substitution of these terms into the expression for K_a gives

$$1.8 \times 10^{-5} = \frac{(0.10 - x)(0.50 - x)}{x}$$

We note that x must be a comparatively large value, since x appears in the denominator of the expression and K_a (which is 1.8×10^{-5}) is a relatively small number. This equation, therefore, must be solved by means of the quadratic formula, since x is not negligible in comparison with 0.10 or 0.50.

A simpler way to solve the problem is to assume that the reaction goes as far to the left as is possible and that then a portion of the acetic acid that has been formed dissociates into ions. In the *reverse* reaction, 0.10 mol of H^+ will react with 0.10 mol of $C_2H_3O_2^-$ to form 0.10 mol of $HC_2H_3O_2$. Therefore, all the H^+ will be used, 0.40 mol of $C_2H_3O_2^-$ will be left of the original 0.50 mol supplied, and 0.10 mol of $HC_2H_3O_2$ will be formed. After we have interpreted the system in terms of complete reaction to the left, we assume that y mol of $HC_2H_3O_2$ dissociates into ions:

$$HC_2H_3O_2 \rightleftharpoons H^+ + C_2H_3O_2^-$$

	$HC_2H_3O_2$	H^+	$C_2H_3O_2^-$
after mixing:	—	0.10 M	0.50 M
reaction to left:	0.10 M	—	0.40 M
equilibrium:	$(0.10 - y)$ M	(y) M	$(0.40 + y)$ M

Now, y is indeed negligible in comparison with both 0.10 and 0.40, and we may simplify the problem by neglecting y in the terms for the concentrations of acetic acid and acetate ion. Thus,

$$1.8 \times 10^{-5} = \frac{[H^+][C_2H_3O_2^-]}{[HC_2H_3O_2]}$$

$$= \frac{y(0.40)}{(0.10)}$$

$$y = 4.5 \times 10^{-6} \ M$$

We can see from the value obtained for y that the approximations applied to $[C_2H_3O_2^-]$ and $[HC_2H_3O_2]$ are justified. To two significant figures, the equilibrium concentrations are

$$[H^+] = 4.5 \times 10^{-6} \ M$$

$$[C_2H_3O_2^-] = 0.40 \ M$$

$$[HC_2H_3O_2] = 0.10 \ M$$

The hydroxides of most metals are either strong electrolytes or slightly soluble compounds. There are some water-soluble compounds, however, that produce alkaline solutions in which equilibria exist between molecules and ions. The most important such compound is ammonia, NH_3, and the chemical equation for the reversible reaction is

$$H_2O + NH_3 \rightleftharpoons NH_4^+ + OH^-$$

The expression for the equilibrium constant (a base dissociation constant) for this reaction,

$$K_b' = \frac{[NH_4^+][OH^-]}{[NH_3][H_2O]}$$

Table 17.2 Ionization constants at 25°C

	Weak Acids	K_a
acetic	$HC_2H_3O_2 \rightleftharpoons H^+ + C_2H_3O_2^-$	1.8×10^{-5}
benzoic	$HC_7H_5O_2 \rightleftharpoons H^+ + C_7H_5O_2^-$	6.0×10^{-5}
chlorous	$HClO_2 \rightleftharpoons H^+ + ClO_2^-$	1.1×10^{-2}
cyanic	$HOCN \rightleftharpoons H^+ + OCN^-$	1.2×10^{-4}
formic	$HCHO_2 \rightleftharpoons H^+ + CHO_2^-$	1.8×10^{-4}
hydrazoic	$HN_3 \rightleftharpoons H^+ + N_3^-$	1.9×10^{-5}
hydrocyanic	$HCN \rightleftharpoons H^+ + CN^-$	4.0×10^{-10}
hydrofluoric	$HF \rightleftharpoons H^+ + F^-$	6.7×10^{-4}
hypobromous	$HOBr \rightleftharpoons H^+ + BrO^-$	2.1×10^{-9}
hypochlorous	$HOCl \rightleftharpoons H^+ + ClO^-$	3.2×10^{-8}
nitrous	$HNO_2 \rightleftharpoons H^+ + NO_2^-$	4.5×10^{-4}

	Weak Bases	K_b
ammonia	$NH_3 + H_2O \rightleftharpoons NH_4^+ + OH^-$	1.8×10^{-5}
aniline	$C_6H_5NH_2 + H_2O \rightleftharpoons C_6H_5NH_3^+ + OH^-$	4.6×10^{-10}
dimethylamine	$(CH_3)_2NH + H_2O \rightleftharpoons (CH_3)_2NH_2^+ + OH^-$	7.4×10^{-4}
hydrazine	$N_2H_4 + H_2O \rightleftharpoons N_2H_5^+ + OH^-$	9.8×10^{-7}
methylamine	$CH_3NH_2 + H_2O \rightleftharpoons CH_3NH_3^+ + OH^-$	5.0×10^{-4}
pyridine	$C_5H_5N + H_2O \rightleftharpoons C_5H_5NH^+ + OH^-$	1.5×10^{-9}
trimethylamine	$(CH_3)_3N + H_2O \rightleftharpoons (CH_3)_3NH^+ + OH^-$	7.4×10^{-5}

simplifies to the following if the concentration of water is assumed to be a constant:

$$K_b = K_b'[H_2O] = \frac{[NH_4^+][OH^-]}{[NH_3]}$$

Table 17.2 lists the ionization constants for some compounds that function as weak acids and some that function as weak bases. Certain ions also can function as weak acids and others as weak bases. These systems are discussed in later sections of this chapter.

The values of ionization constants change with temperature. At 25°C, K_a for acetic acid is 1.8×10^{-5}; at 100°C, K_a for this weak acid is 1.1×10^{-5}. Ionization constants are usually reported for equilibrium systems at 25°C.

17.2 The Ionization of Water

Pure water is itself a very weak electrolyte and ionizes according to the equation

$$H_2O + H_2O \rightleftharpoons H_3O^+ + OH^-$$

In simplified form this equation is

$$H_2O \rightleftharpoons H^+ + OH^-$$

The expression for the ionization constant derived from the simplified equation is

$$K = \frac{[H^+][OH^-]}{[H_2O]}$$

In dilute solutions the concentration of water is virtually a constant, and we may combine $[H_2O]$ with the constant K. Thus,

$$K[H_2O] = [H^+][OH^-]$$

This constant, $K[H_2O]$, is called the ion product of water, or the **water dissociation constant**, and is given the symbol K_w. At 25°C,

$$K_w = 1.0 \times 10^{-14} = [H^+][OH^-] \qquad (17.1)$$

In pure water,

$$[H^+] = [OH^-] = x$$
$$[H^+][OH^-] = 1.0 \times 10^{-14}$$
$$x^2 = 1.0 \times 10^{-14}$$
$$x = 1.0 \times 10^{-7} \, M$$

The concentrations of both of the ions of water are equal to $1.0 \times 10^{-7} \, M$ in pure water or in any neutral solution at 25°C. In 1 L, only 10^{-7} mol of water is in ionic form out of a total of approximately 55.5 mol.

Both $H^+(aq)$ and $OH^-(aq)$ exist in any aqueous solution. In an acid solution the concentration of $H^+(aq)$ is larger than $1.0 \times 10^{-7} \, M$ and larger than the $OH^-(aq)$ concentration. In an alkaline solution the $OH^-(aq)$ concentration is larger than $10 \times 10^{-7} \, M$ and larger than the $H^+(aq)$ concentration.

Example 17.5

What are $[H^+]$ and $[OH^-]$ in a 0.020 M solution of HCl?

Solution

The quantity of $H^+(aq)$ ion obtained from the ionization of water is negligible compared to that derived from the hydrochloric acid. Since HCl is a strong electrolyte, $[H^+] = 0.020 \, M$:

$$[H^+][OH^-] = 1.0 \times 10^{-14}$$
$$(2.0 \times 10^{-2})[OH^-] = 1.0 \times 10^{-14}$$
$$[OH^-] = \frac{1.0 \times 10^{-14}}{2.0 \times 10^{-2}}$$
$$[OH^-] = 5.0 \times 10^{-13} \, M$$

Notice that $[OH^-]$ is extremely small. In this solution there would be one OH^- ion for every 40 billion H^+ ions.

Example 17.6

What are $[H^+]$ and $[OH^-]$ in a 0.0050 M solution of NaOH?

Solution

Sodium hydroxide is a strong electrolyte, and therefore $[OH^-] = 5.0 \times 10^{-3}$ M:

$$[H^+][OH^-] = 1.0 \times 10^{-14}$$

$$[H^+](5.0 \times 10^{-3}) = 1.0 \times 10^{-14}$$

$$[H^+] = \frac{1.0 \times 10^{-14}}{5.0 \times 10^{-3}}$$

$$[H^+] = 2.0 \times 10^{-12}\ M$$

17.3 pH

Vinegar has a pH of from 2.4 to 3.4.

The pH of oranges is from 3.0 to 4.0. *Photo Researchers, Inc.*

The concentration of $H^+(aq)$ in a solution may be expressed in terms of the pH scale. The pH of a solution is defined as

$$pH = \log \frac{1}{[H^+]} = -\log [H^+] \tag{17.2}$$

The common logarithm of a number is the power to which 10 must be raised in order to get the number (see the appendix). If

$$a = 10^n$$

then

$$\log a = n$$

Therefore, if

$$a = 10^{-3}$$

then

$$\log a = -3$$

The pH is the *negative* logarithm of the hydrogen ion concentration. Therefore, if

$$[H^+] = 10^{-3}\ M$$

$$\log [H^+] = -3$$

$$pH = -\log [H^+] = 3$$

For a neutral solution, therefore,

$$[H^+] = 10^{-7} \, M$$
$$pH = -\log(10^{-7}) = -(-7)$$
$$pH = 7$$

The *pOH* of a solution is defined in the same terms:

$$pOH = -\log[OH^-] \tag{17.3}$$

The relationship between *pH* and *pOH* can be derived from the water constant:

$$[H^+][OH^-] = 10^{-14}$$

We take the logarithm of each term:

$$\log[H^+] + \log[OH^-] = \log(10^{-14})$$

and multiply through by -1

$$-\log[H^+] - \log[OH^-] = -\log(10^{-14})$$

or

$$pH + pOH = 14 \tag{17.4}$$

For a 0.01 *M* solution of NaOH, which is a strong base,

$$[OH^-] = 10^{-2} \, M$$
$$pOH = -\log[OH^-] = 2$$

Since the sum of the *pH* and *pOH* of a solution at 25°C equals 14,

$$pH = 12$$

Example 17.7

What is the *pH* of a solution that is 0.050 *M* in H^+?

Solution

$$[H^+] = 5.0 \times 10^{-2} \, M$$
$$\log[H^+] = \log 5.0 + \log 10^{-2}$$

The logarithm of 5.0 can be found in the logarithm table that appears in the appendix:

$$\log[H^+] = 0.70 - 2.00 = -1.30$$
$$pH = 1.30$$

Example 17.8

What is the pH of a solution for which $[OH^-] = 0.030\ M$?

Solution

$$[OH^-] = 3.0 \times 10^{-2}$$
$$\log[OH^-] = \log 3.0 + \log 10^{-2}$$
$$= 0.48 - 2.00 = -1.52$$
$$p\text{OH} = 1.52$$
$$p\text{H} = 14.00 - p\text{OH}$$
$$= 14.00 - 1.52 = 12.48$$

An alternative solution is

$$[H^+][OH^-] = 1.0 \times 10^{-14}$$
$$[H^+] = \frac{1.0 \times 10^{-14}}{3.0 \times 10^{-2}} = 3.3 \times 10^{-13}$$
$$\log[H^+] = \log 3.3 + \log 10^{-13}$$
$$= 0.52 - 13.00 = -12.48$$
$$p\text{H} = 12.48$$

Example 17.9

What is the $[H^+]$ of a solution with a pH of 10.60?

Solution

Since

$$p\text{H} = \log[H^+]$$
$$\log[H^+] = -p\text{H}$$

In the present example, $p\text{H} = 10.60$, and therefore

$$\log[H^+] = -10.60$$
$$[H^+] = 10^{-10.60} = 2.5 \times 10^{-11}\ M$$

If a logarithm table is used, the value of $\log[H^+]$ must be divided into two parts: a decimal portion (which is called a mantissa and which *must* be positive) and a negative whole number (which is called a characteristic). Thus,

$$\log[H^+] = -10.60 = 0.40 - 11.00$$
$$[H^+] = \text{antilog}\,0.40 \times \text{antilog}(-11)$$

The antilogarithm of 0.40 is obtained by finding the number that corresponds to

Table 17.3   The pH scale

pH	$[H^+]$	$[OH^-]$	
14	10^{-14}	10^0	
13	10^{-13}	10^{-1}	
12	10^{-12}	10^{-2}	
11	10^{-11}	10^{-3}	increasing alkalinity
10	10^{-10}	10^{-4}	
9	10^{-9}	10^{-5}	
8	10^{-8}	10^{-6}	
7	10^{-7}	10^{-7}	neutrality
6	10^{-6}	10^{-8}	
5	10^{-5}	10^{-9}	
4	10^{-4}	10^{-10}	
3	10^{-3}	10^{-11}	increasing acidity
2	10^{-2}	10^{-12}	
1	10^{-1}	10^{-13}	
0	10^0	10^{-14}	

this logarithm in the logarithm table (it is 2.5). The antilogarithm of -11 is 10^{-11}. Therefore,

$$[H^+] = 2.5 \times 10^{-11}\ M$$

The preceding example illustrates an important attribute of logarithms. The only significant figures in a logarithmic term, such as a pH, are found in the decimal portion. In Example 17.9, the mantissa (0.40) has two significant figures, and its antilogarithm (2.5) has two significant figures. The characteristic (-11) serves only to locate the decimal point in the final antilogarithm (10^{-11}). Hence, the pH values 1.30, 10.60, and 14.00 all have only *two* significant figures.

It should be kept in mind that pH relates to a power of 10. Hence, a solution of pH $= 1$ has a H^+(aq) concentration 100 times that of a solution of pH $= 3$ (not three times). Furthermore, since the pH is related to a *negative* exponent, the lower the pH value, the larger the concentration of H^+(aq). At pH $= 7$, a solution is neutral. Solutions with pH's below 7 are acidic. Those with pH's above 7 are alkaline. These relationships are summarized in Table 17.3.

The ionization constant of a weak acid or a weak base can be determined by measuring the pH of a solution of known concentration of the weak electrolyte.

Example 17.10

The pH of a 0.10 M solution of a weak acid HX is 3.30. What is the ionization constant of HX?

Solution

$$HX \rightleftharpoons H^+ + X^-$$

$$pH = 3.30$$

$$\log[H^+] = -3.30$$

$$[H^+] = 10^{-3.30} = 5.0 \times 10^{-4} \ M$$

Since the solution was prepared from HX alone,

$$[H^+] = [X^-] = 5.0 \times 10^{-4} \ M$$

The concentration of HX in the solution is for all practical purposes equal to 0.10 M. The small quantity of HX that dissociated need not be considered. The equilibrium concentrations, therefore, are

$$
\begin{array}{ccccc}
HX & \rightleftharpoons & H^+ & + & X^- \\
0.10\ M & & 5.0 \times 10^{-4}\ M & & 5.0 \times 10^{-4}\ M
\end{array}
$$

The value of the ionization constant is

$$K_a = \frac{[H^+][X^-]}{[HX]}$$

$$= \frac{(5.0 \times 10^{-4})^2}{1.0 \times 10^{-1}} = \frac{25 \times 10^{-8}}{1.0 \times 10^{-1}}$$

$$K_a = 2.5 \times 10^{-6}$$

17.4 Indicators

A modern digital pH meter. The electrodes that are placed into a sample solution form an electrochemical cell. The potential that the cell develops depends upon the concentration of H^+ in the solution. The device is calibrated in pH units, rather than volts. See Section 20.9, Example 20.13. *Corning Medical and Scientific Instruments.*

Indicators are organic compounds of complex structure that change color in solution as the pH changes. Methyl orange, for example, is red in solutions of pH below 3.1 and yellow in solutions of pH above 4.5. The color of this indicator is a varying mixture of yellow and red in the pH range between 3.1 and 4.5. Many indicators have been described and used. A few are listed in Table 17.4.

The pH of a solution is usually determined by use of a pH meter, but indicators may also be used for this purpose. If thymol blue is yellow in a test solution and methyl orange is red in another sample of the same solution, the pH of the solution is between 2.8 and 3.1. Reference to Table 17.4 shows that thymol blue is yellow only in solutions of pH greater than 2.8, and methyl orange is red only in solutions of pH less than 3.1. If enough indicators are employed, it is possible to determine pH values that are accurate to the first decimal place.

Indicators are weak acids or weak bases. Since they are intensely colored, only a few drops of a dilute solution of an indicator need be employed in any determination. Hence, the acidity of the solution in question is not significantly altered by the addition of the indicator.

If we let the symbol HIn stand for the litmus molecule (which is red) and the symbol In$^-$ stand for the anion (which is blue) derived from the weak acid, the equation for the litmus equilibrium may be written

Table 17.4 Some indicators			
Indicator	Acid Color	pH Range of Color Change	Alkaline Color
thymol blue	red	1.2–2.8	yellow
methyl orange	red	3.1–4.5	yellow
bromcresol green	yellow	3.8–5.5	blue
methyl red	red	4.2–6.3	yellow
litmus	red	5.0–8.0	blue
bromthymol blue	yellow	6.0–7.6	blue
thymol blue	yellow	8.0–9.6	blue
phenolphthalein	colorless	8.3–10.0	red
alizarin yellow	yellow	10.0–12.1	lavender

$$HIn \rightleftharpoons H^+ + In^-$$
red   *blue*

According to the principle of Le Chatelier, increasing the concentration of H^+ shifts the equilibrium to the left, and the red (or acid) color of HIn is observed. On the other hand, addition of OH^- decreases the concentration of H^+. The equilibrium shifts to the right, and the blue (or alkaline) color of In^- is observed.

The ionization constant for litmus is approximately equal to 10^{-7}:

$$10^{-7} = \frac{[H^+][In^-]}{[HIn]}$$

We may rearrange this expression in the following manner:

$$\frac{10^{-7}}{[H^+]} = \frac{[In^-]}{[HIn]}$$

At a pH of 5 or below, the red color of litmus is observed. If we substitute $[H^+] = 10^{-5}$, which corresponds to pH $= 5$, into the preceding expression, we get

$$\frac{10^{-7}}{10^{-5}} = \frac{1}{100} = \frac{[In^-]}{[HIn]} \begin{matrix} \longleftarrow \text{blue} \\ \longleftarrow \text{red} \end{matrix}$$

Thus, the mixture appears red to the eye when the concentration of the red HIn is 100 times (or more) that of the blue In^-.

The blue color of litmus is observed in solutions of pH $= 8$ or higher. If $[H^+] = 10^{-8}$,

$$\frac{10^{-7}}{10^{-8}} = \frac{10}{1} = \frac{[In^-]}{[HIn]} \begin{matrix} \longleftarrow \text{blue} \\ \longleftarrow \text{red} \end{matrix}$$

When the concentration of the blue In^- ion is 10 times that of the red HIn, or approximately 91% of the indicator is in ionic form, the blue color of the In^- ions

$$3.50 = 3.92 + \log \frac{[OCN^-]}{[HOCN]}$$

$$\log \frac{[OCN^-]}{[HOCN]} = -0.42$$

$$\frac{[OCN^-]}{[HOCN]} = 0.38$$

Example 17.15

What is the *pH* of a solution made by mixing 100. mL of 0.15 *M* HCl and 200. mL of 0.20 *M* aniline ($C_6H_5NH_2$)? Assume that the volume of the final solution is 300. mL.

Solution

The number of moles of HCl used and the number of moles of aniline used are

$$? \text{ mol HCl} = 100. \text{ mL sol'n} \left(\frac{0.15 \text{ mol HCl}}{1000 \text{ mL sol'n}} \right)$$

$$= 0.015 \text{ mol HCl}$$

$$? \text{ mol aniline} = 200. \text{ mL sol'n} \left(\frac{0.20 \text{ mol aniline}}{1000 \text{ mL sol'n}} \right)$$

$$= 0.040 \text{ mol aniline}$$

One mole of aniline reacts with one mole of H^+. Thus,

$$C_6H_5NH_2 + \quad H^+ \quad \longrightarrow C_6H_5NH_3^+$$

before reaction:	0.040 mol	0.015 mol	—
after reaction:	0.025 mol	—	0.015 mol

The number of moles in one liter of the final solution is

$$? \text{ mol } C_6H_5NH_3^+ = 1000 \text{ mL sol'n} \left(\frac{0.015 \text{ mol } C_6H_5NH_3^+}{300. \text{ mL sol'n}} \right)$$

$$= 0.050 \text{ mol } C_6H_5NH_3^+$$

$$? \text{ mol } C_6H_5NH_2 = 1000 \text{ mL sol'n} \left(\frac{0.025 \text{ mol } C_6H_5NH_2}{300. \text{ mL sol'n}} \right)$$

$$= 0.083 \text{ mol } C_6H_5NH_2$$

Therefore, the concentrations in the solution are

$$C_6H_5NH_2 + H_2O \rightleftharpoons C_6H_5NH_3^+ + OH^-$$
$$0.083 \ M \qquad\qquad\qquad 0.050 \ M$$

$$\frac{[C_6H_5NH_3^+][OH^-]}{[C_6H_5NH_2]} = 4.6 \times 10^{-10}$$

Culture media (agar) must be buffered to a pH that will enable bacteria to grow. Here, a paper disc saturated with an antibiotic is placed in the center of an agar plate in which six streaks of different bacteria are placed. The effectiveness of the antibiotic against some of the bacteria is apparent. *Pfizer Inc.*

$$\frac{(0.050)[OH^-]}{(0.083)} = 4.6 \times 10^{-10}$$

$$[OH^-] = 7.6 \times 10^{-10} \, M$$

$$[H^+] = 1.3 \times 10^{-5} \, M$$

$$p\mathrm{H} = 4.89$$

The use of buffers is an important part of many industrial processes. Examples are electroplating and the manufacture of leather, photographic materials, and dyes. In bacteriological research, culture media are generally buffered to maintain the pH required for the growth of the bacteria being studied. Buffers are used extensively in analytical chemistry and are used to calibrate pH meters. Human blood is buffered to a pH of 7.4 by means of bicarbonate, phosphate, and complex protein systems.

17.7 Polyprotic Acids

Polyprotic acids are acids that contain more than one acid hydrogen per molecule. Examples include sulfuric acid (H_2SO_4), oxalic acid ($H_2C_2O_4$), phosphoric acid (H_3PO_4), and arsenic acid (H_3AsO_4). Polyprotic acids ionize in a stepwise manner, and there is an ionization constant for each step. Numbers are added to the subscripts of the symbol K_a in order to specify the step to which the constant applies.

Phosphoric acid is triprotic and ionizes in three steps:

$$H_3PO_4 \rightleftharpoons H^+ + H_2PO_4^- \qquad \frac{[H^+][H_2PO_4^-]}{[H_3PO_4]} = K_{a1} = 7.5 \times 10^{-3}$$

$$H_2PO_4^- \rightleftharpoons H^+ + HPO_4^{2-} \qquad \frac{[H^+][HPO_4^{2-}]}{[H_2PO_4^-]} = K_{a2} = 6.2 \times 10^{-8}$$

$$HPO_4^{2-} \rightleftharpoons H^+ + PO_4^{3-} \qquad \frac{[H^+][PO_4^{3-}]}{[HPO_4^{2-}]} = K_{a3} = 1 \times 10^{-12}$$

Thus, in an aqueous solution of phosphoric acid three equilibria occur together with the water equilibrium.

The ionization of phosphoric acid is typical of all polyprotic acids in that the primary ionization is stronger than the secondary, and the secondary ionization is stronger than the tertiary. This trend in the value of the ionization constant is consistent with the nature of the particle that releases a proton in each step. One would predict that a proton would be released more readily by an uncharged molecule than by the corresponding uninegative ion and more readily by a uninegative ion than by the corresponding binegative ion.

No polyprotic acid is known for which all ionizations are complete. The primary ionization of sulfuric acid is essentially complete:

$$H_2SO_4 \longrightarrow H^+ + HSO_4^-$$

but the secondary ionization is not:

$$HSO_4^- \rightleftharpoons H^+ + SO_4^{2-} \qquad \frac{[H^+][SO_4^{2-}]}{[HSO_4^-]} = K_{a2} = 1.3 \times 10^{-2}$$

Solutions of carbon dioxide are acidic. Carbon dioxide reacts with water to form carbonic acid, H_2CO_3. The reaction, however, is not complete—most of the carbon dioxide exists in solution as CO_2 molecules. Therefore, we shall indicate the primary ionizations as

$$CO_2 + H_2O \rightleftharpoons H^+ + HCO_3^- \qquad \frac{[H^+][HCO_3^-]}{[CO_2]} = K_{a1} = 4.2 \times 10^{-7}$$

where the symbol $[CO_2]$ is used to represent the total concentration of $CO_2(aq)$ and H_2CO_3. The second ionization step is

$$HCO_3^- \rightleftharpoons H^+ + CO_3^{2-} \qquad \frac{[H^+][CO_3^{2-}]}{[HCO_3^-]} = K_{a2} = 4.8 \times 10^{-11}$$

An analogous situation exists for solutions for sulfur dioxide in water. The acidity of aqueous SO_2 has been attributed to the ionization of sulfurous acid, H_2SO_3. However, H_2SO_3 has never been isolated in pure form. In solution it apparently exists in equilibrium with $SO_2(aq)$:

$$SO_2(aq) + H_2O \rightleftharpoons H_2SO_3(aq)$$

Table 17.5 Ionization constants of some polyprotic acids

arsenic	H_3AsO_4	$\rightleftharpoons H^+ + H_2AsO_4^-$	$K_{a1} = 2.5 \times 10^{-4}$
	$H_2AsO_4^-$	$\rightleftharpoons H^+ + HAsO_4^{2-}$	$K_{a2} = 5.6 \times 10^{-8}$
	$HAsO_4^{2-}$	$\rightleftharpoons H^+ + AsO_4^{3-}$	$K_{a3} = 3 \times 10^{-13}$
carbonic	$CO_2 + H_2O$	$\rightleftharpoons H^+ + HCO_3^-$	$K_{a1} = 4.2 \times 10^{-7}$
	HCO_3^-	$\rightleftharpoons H^+ + CO_3^{2-}$	$K_{a2} = 4.8 \times 10^{-11}$
hydrosulfuric	H_2S	$\rightleftharpoons H^+ + HS^-$	$K_{a1} = 1.1 \times 10^{-7}$
	HS^-	$\rightleftharpoons H^+ + S^{2-}$	$K_{a2} = 1.0 \times 10^{-14}$
oxalic	$H_2C_2O_4$	$\rightleftharpoons H^+ + HC_2O_4^-$	$K_{a1} = 5.9 \times 10^{-2}$
	$HC_2O_4^-$	$\rightleftharpoons H^+ + C_2O_4^{2-}$	$K_{a2} = 6.4 \times 10^{-5}$
phosphoric	H_3PO_4	$\rightleftharpoons H^+ + H_2PO_4^-$	$K_{a1} = 7.5 \times 10^{-3}$
	$H_2PO_4^-$	$\rightleftharpoons H^+ + HPO_4^{2-}$	$K_{a2} = 6.2 \times 10^{-8}$
	HPO_4^{2-}	$\rightleftharpoons H^+ + PO_4^{3-}$	$K_{a3} = 1 \times 10^{-12}$
phosphorous (diprotic)	H_3PO_3	$\rightleftharpoons H^+ + H_2PO_3^-$	$K_{a1} = 1.6 \times 10^{-2}$
	$H_2PO_3^-$	$\rightleftharpoons H^+ + HPO_3^{2-}$	$K_{a2} = 7 \times 10^{-7}$
sulfuric	H_2SO_4	$\rightleftharpoons H^+ + HSO_4^-$	strong
	HSO_4^-	$\rightleftharpoons H^+ + SO_4^{2-}$	$K_{a2} = 1.3 \times 10^{-2}$
sulfurous	$SO_2 + H_2O$	$\rightleftharpoons H^+ + HSO_3^-$	$K_{a1} = 1.3 \times 10^{-2}$
	HSO_3^-	$\rightleftharpoons H^+ + SO_3^{2-}$	$K_{a2} = 5.6 \times 10^{-8}$

We shall represent the primary ionization of sulfurous acid as

$$SO_2 + H_2O \rightleftharpoons H^+ + HSO_3^-$$

The ionization constants of some polyprotic acids are listed in Table 17.5.

Polyprotic acids form more than one salt. Depending upon the stoichiometric ratio of reactants, the reaction of NaOH and H_2SO_4 yields either the normal salt Na_2SO_4 (sodium sulfate) or the acid salt $NaHSO_4$ (sodium hydrogen sulfate or sodium bisulfate). Three salts may be derived from phosphoric acid: NaH_2PO_4 (sodium dihydrogen phosphate), Na_2HPO_4 (sodium hydrogen phosphate), and Na_3PO_4 (sodium phosphate).

Example 17.16

Calculate $[H^+]$, $[H_2PO_4^-]$, $[HPO_4^{2-}]$, $[PO_4^{3-}]$, and $[H_3PO_4]$ in a 0.10 M solution of phosphoric acid.

Solution

The principal source of H^+ is the primary ionization. The H^+ produced by the other ionizations, as well as that from the ionization of water, is negligible in comparison. Furthermore, the concentration of $H_2PO_4^-$ derived from the primary ionization is not significantly diminished by the secondary ionization. Thus, we write

$$H_3PO_4 \rightleftharpoons H^+ + H_2PO_4^-$$
$$(0.10 - x)\ M \qquad (x)\ M \qquad (x)\ M$$

The problem must be solved by means of the quadratic formula since x is not negligible in comparison to 0.10 M:

$$\frac{[H^+][H_2PO_4^-]}{[H_3PO_4]} = 7.5 \times 10^{-3}$$

$$\frac{x^2}{(0.10 - x)} = 7.5 \times 10^{-3}$$

$$x = [H^+] = [H_2PO_4^-] = 2.4 \times 10^{-2} \, M$$

$$(0.10 - x) = [H_3PO_4] = 7.6 \times 10^{-2} \, M$$

The $[H^+]$ and $[H_2PO_4^-]$ apply to the secondary ionization. Therefore,

$$\begin{array}{ccc} H_2PO_4^- & \rightleftharpoons & H^+ & + \ HPO_4^{2-} \\ 2.4 \times 10^{-2} \, M & & 2.4 \times 10^{-2} \, M \end{array}$$

$$\frac{[H^+][HPO_4^{2-}]}{[H_2PO_4^-]} = 6.2 \times 10^{-8}$$

$$\frac{(2.4 \times 10^{-2})[HPO_4^{2-}]}{(2.4 \times 10^{-2})} = 6.2 \times 10^{-8}$$

$$[HPO_4^{2-}] = 6.2 \times 10^{-8} \, M$$

In any solution of H_3PO_4 that does not contain ions derived from another electrolyte, the concentration of the secondary ion is equal to K_{a2}.

For the tertiary ionization,

$$\begin{array}{ccc} HPO_4^{2-} & \rightleftharpoons & H^+ & + \ PO_4^{3-} \\ 6.2 \times 10^{-8} \, M & & 2.4 \times 10^{-2} \, M \end{array}$$

$$\frac{[H^+][PO_4^{3-}]}{[HPO_4^{2-}]} = 1 \times 10^{-12}$$

$$\frac{(2.4 \times 10^{-2})[PO_4^{3-}]}{(6.2 \times 10^{-8})} = 1 \times 10^{-12}$$

$$[PO_4^{3-}] = 3 \times 10^{-18} \, M$$

Example 17.17

What are $[H^+]$, $[HS^-]$, $[S^{2-}]$, and $[H_2S]$ in a 0.10 M solution of H_2S?

Solution

K_{a1} for H_2S is 1.1×10^{-7}. Therefore, the small amount of H_2S that ionizes is negligible in comparison with the original concentration of H_2S. In addition, the concentrations of H^+ and HS^- are not significantly altered by the secondary ionization ($K_{a2} = 1.0 \times 10^{-14}$). Thus:

$$\begin{array}{ccc} H_2S & \rightleftharpoons & H^+ & + \ HS^- \\ 0.10 \, M & & (x) \, M & (x) \, M \end{array}$$

$$\frac{[H^+][HS^-]}{[H_2S]} = 1.1 \times 10^{-7}$$

$$\frac{x^2}{0.10} = 1.1 \times 10^{-7}$$

$$x = [H^+] = [HS^-] = 1.0 \times 10^{-4} \, M$$

These concentrations also apply to the secondary ionization:

$$\begin{array}{cccc} HS^- & \rightleftharpoons & H^+ & + \; S^{2-} \\ 1.0 \times 10^{-4} \, M & & 1.0 \times 10^{-4} \, M & ? \end{array}$$

$$\frac{[H^+][S^{2-}]}{[HS^-]} = 1.0 \times 10^{-14}$$

$$\frac{(1.0 \times 10^{-4})[S^{2-}]}{(1.0 \times 10^{-4})} = 1.0 \times 10^{-14} \, M$$

$$[S^{2-}] = 1.0 \times 10^{-14} \, M$$

The concentration of the secondary ion is equal to K_{a2} in any solution of H_2S that does not contain ions derived from another electrolyte.

The product of the expressions for the two ionizations of H_2S is

$$\left(\frac{[H^+][HS^-]}{[H_2S]}\right)\left(\frac{[H^+][S^{2-}]}{[HS^-]}\right) = K_{a1}K_{a2}$$

$$\frac{[H^+]^2[S^{2-}]}{[H_2S]} = (1.1 \times 10^{-7})(1.0 \times 10^{-14})$$

$$= 1.1 \times 10^{-21}$$

This very convenient relationship can be misleading. Superficially it looks as though it applies to a process in which one sulfide ion is produced for every two H^+ ions. However, the ionization of H_2S does not proceed in this manner. In any solution of H_2S, the concentration of $H^+(aq)$ is much larger than the concentration of sulfide ion (see Example 17.17). The majority of the H_2S molecules that ionize do so only to the HS^- stage, and S^{2-} ions result only from the small ionization of the secondary ion.

At 25°C a saturated solution of H_2S is 0.10 M. For a *saturated solution*, therefore,

$$\frac{[H^+]^2[S^{2-}]}{(0.10)} = 1.1 \times 10^{-21}$$

$$[H^+]^2[S^{2-}] = 1.1 \times 10^{-22}$$

This relation can be used to calculate the sulfide ion concentration of a solution of known pH that has been saturated with H_2S.

Example 17.18

What is the sulfide ion concentration of a dilute HCl solution that has been saturated with H_2S if the solution is buffered to a pH of 3.00?

Solution

Since the $pH = 3.00$,

$$[H^+] = 1.0 \times 10^{-3} \, M$$

Therefore,

$$[H^+]^2[S^{2-}] = 1.1 \times 10^{-22}$$
$$(1.0 \times 10^{-3})^2[S^{2-}] = 1.1 \times 10^{-22}$$
$$[S^{2-}] = 1.1 \times 10^{-16} \, M$$

In a saturated solution of pure H_2S (see Example 17.17), $[S^{2-}] = 1.0 \times 10^{-14}$ M. In the H_2S solution described in this problem, the common ion, H^+, has repressed the ionization of H_2S. In addition, since the solution contains H^+ ions from a source other than H_2S, $[H^+]$ does not equal $[HS^-]$, and consequently $[S^{2-}]$ does not equal K_{a2}.

17.8 Ions That Function as Acids and Bases

That the anions of polyprotic acids (such as $H_2PO_4^-$ and HS^-) have acidic properties is not surprising. What is perhaps unexpected, however, is that certain ions derived from normal salts (such as $C_2H_3O_2^-$, NO_2^-, NH_4^+, and Fe^{3+}) form acidic or basic solutions:

1. Anions derived from weak acids (such as $C_2H_3O_2^-$ and NO_2^-) form basic solutions.

2. Cations derived from weak bases (such as NH_4^+ and Fe^{3+}) form acidic solutions.

We will consider the anions of weak acids first. In water solution, the acetate ion reacts with water to increase the concentration of OH^- ions:

$$C_2H_3O_2^- + H_2O \rightleftharpoons HC_2H_3O_2 + OH^-$$

This reaction of the acetate ion is similar to that of any other weak base, such as NH_3, with water:

$$NH_3 + H_2O \rightleftharpoons NH_4^+ + OH^-$$

The fact that the acetate ion has a charge and the ammonia molecule does not is unimportant. Both species are bases, and both equilibria have corresponding K_b values. The reaction of an ion with water, however, is sometimes called a **hydrolysis reaction.**

According to the Brønsted theory (see Section 16.3), the acetate ion is the conjugate base of acetic acid. The chemical equations for the two equilibria and corresponding expressions for the equilibrium constants are

$$HC_2H_3O_2 \rightleftharpoons H^+ + C_2H_3O_2^- \qquad K_a = \frac{[H^+][C_2H_3O_2^-]}{[HC_2H_3O_2]}$$

$$C_2H_3O_2^- + H_2O \rightleftharpoons HC_2H_3O_2 + OH^- \qquad K_b = \frac{[HC_2H_3O_2][OH^-]}{[C_2H_3O_2^-]}$$

The two constants are related in the following way. The product of K_a and K_b is

$$K_aK_b = \left(\frac{[H^+][C_2H_3O_2^-]}{[HC_2H_3O_2]}\right)\left(\frac{[HC_2H_3O_2][OH^-]}{[C_2H_3O_2^-]}\right)$$

$$K_aK_b = [H^+][OH^-]$$

Since $[H^+][OH^-]$ is equal to the water dissociation constant, K_w,

$$K_aK_b = K_w \qquad (17.7)$$

This relation provides a convenient way to obtain the value of K_b for the anion derived from a weak acid:

$$K_b = K_w/K_a \qquad (17.8)$$

In the case of the K_b for the hydrolysis of the acetate ion,

$$K_b = (1.0 \times 10^{-14})/(1.8 \times 10^{-5}) = 5.6 \times 10^{-10}$$

Anions derived from *strong* acids (such as Cl^- from HCl) and cations derived from *strong* bases (such as Na^+ from NaOH) do not react with water to affect the pH. An equilibrium of this type (a hydrolysis equilibrium) results only when the ion can form a molecule or ion that is a *weak electrolyte* in the reaction with water. Strong acids and bases do not exist as molecules in water solution.

Example 17.19

What is the pH of a 0.10 M solution of $NaC_2H_3O_2$?

Solution

The salt $NaC_2H_3O_2$ completely dissociates into Na^+ and $C_2H_3O_2^-$ ions in water solution. The Na^+ ion does not react with H_2O. Let x equal the equilibrium concentration of $HC_2H_3O_2$ that results from the hydrolysis of $C_2H_3O_2^-$ ions:

$$C_2H_3O_2^- + H_2O \rightleftharpoons HC_2H_3O_2 + OH^-$$
$$\text{0.10 } M \qquad\qquad (x)\ M \qquad (x)\ M$$

Since the value of K_b is very small (5.6×10^{-10}), x is small and $[C_2H_3O_2^-]$ may be assumed to be equal to 0.10 M rather than $(0.10 - x)$ M:

$$\frac{[HC_2H_3O_2][OH^-]}{[C_2H_3O_2^-]} = K_b$$

$$\frac{x^2}{0.10} = 5.6 \times 10^{-10}$$

$$x^2 = 5.6 \times 10^{-11}$$

$$x = [HC_2H_3O_2] = [OH^-] = 7.5 \times 10^{-6} \, M$$

$$pOH = -\log(7.5 \times 10^{-6}) = 5.12$$

$$pH = 14.00 - 5.12 = 8.88$$

The weaker the electrolyte from which an ion is derived, the more extensive is its reaction with water. A 0.1 M solution of sodium acetate has a pH of 8.9, and the pH of a 0.1 M solution of sodium cyanide is 11.2. In each case it is the hydrolysis of the anion that causes the solution to be alkaline. The sodium ion does not undergo hydrolysis:

$$C_2H_3O_2^- + H_2O \rightleftharpoons HC_2H_3O_2 + OH^-$$

$$CN^- + H_2O \rightleftharpoons HCN + OH^-$$

Since HCN ($K_a = 4.0 \times 10^{-10}$) is a weaker electrolyte than $HC_2H_3O_2$ ($K_a = 1.8 \times 10^{-5}$), HCN does a better job of tying up protons than $HC_2H_3O_2$ does. Therefore, the hydrolysis of CN^- is more complete than that of $C_2H_3O_2^-$, and the concentration of OH^- is higher in the NaCN solution than in the $NaC_2H_3O_2$ solution. Note, however, that in both of these systems the position of equilibrium is such that the reverse reaction, which may be regarded as a neutralization, proceeds to a greater extent than the forward reaction since H_2O is a weaker electrolyte than either HCN or $HC_2H_3O_2$.

A cation derived from a weak base reacts with water to form an acidic solution. Consider the reaction of the ammonium ion:

$$NH_4^+ + H_2O \rightleftharpoons NH_3 + H_3O^+$$

This reaction of NH_4^+ is similar to the ionization of any other weak acid such as $HC_2H_3O_2$. If we represent the acid dissociation of the NH_4^+ ion in our customary way, we get

$$NH_4^+ \rightleftharpoons H^+ + NH_3$$

The equilibrium constant for this system, a K_a, can be derived by using the K_b for the base dissociation of NH_3, which is the conjugate base of NH_4^+:

$$NH_3 + H_2O \rightleftharpoons NH_4^+ + OH^-$$

According to the relation

$$K_a K_b = K_w$$

the acid dissociation constant may be found by substitution into

$$K_a = K_w/K_b \tag{17.9}$$

For the NH_4^+/NH_3 system,

$$K_a = (1.0 \times 10^{-14})/(1.8 \times 10^{-5}) = 5.6 \times 10^{-10}$$

Example 17.20

What is the pH of a 0.30 M solution of NH_4Cl?

Solution

In water solution, NH_4Cl completely dissociates into NH_4^+ and Cl^- ions. The Cl^- ion, since it is derived from a strong acid, does not react with water. Let x equal the equilibrium concentration of NH_3 from the hydrolysis of NH_4^+:

$$NH_4^+ \rightleftharpoons H^+ + NH_3$$
$$0.30\ M \qquad (x)\ M \quad (x)\ M$$

$$\frac{[H^+][NH_3]}{[NH_4^+]} = 5.6 \times 10^{-10}$$

$$\frac{x^2}{0.30} = 5.6 \times 10^{-10}$$

$$x^2 = 1.7 \times 10^{-10}$$

$$x = [H^+] = [NH_3] = 1.3 \times 10^{-5}\ M$$

$$pH = -\log(1.3 \times 10^{-5}) = 4.89$$

The cations of the I A metals, as well as Ca^{2+}, Sr^{2+}, and Ba^{2+}, do not react with H_2O, since they are derived from strong bases. Most other metal cations, however, do hydrolyze. In the hydrolysis of a metal cation a coordinated water molecule of the hydrated cation donates a proton to a free water molecule:

$$Fe(H_2O)_6^{3+}(aq) + H_2O \rightleftharpoons Fe(OH)(H_2O)_5^{2+}(aq) + H_3O^+(aq)$$

Such equations are sometimes written without indicating the coordinated water:

$$Fe^{3+}(aq) + H_2O \rightleftharpoons Fe(OH)^{2+}(aq) + H^+(aq)$$

Additional steps in the hydrolysis of the ion produce $Fe(OH)_2^+$, $[Fe_2(OH)_2(H_2O)_8]^{4+}$, polynuclear ions of a higher order, and ultimately a precipitate of hydrous Fe_2O_3.

Mathematical analysis of the hydrolysis of metal cations is complicated by several factors. As in the hydrolysis of the Fe^{3+} ion, more than one hydrolytic product usually exists, and many of these are polynuclear. For many systems reliable values for the equilibrium constants are not available, and in many instances not all of the equilibria have been identified. Occasionally, reaction proceeds to the point where the metal hydroxide or the hydrous metal oxide precipitates.

The hydrolysis of an anion derived from a weak polyprotic acid proceeds in several steps. The acid dissociation constants for H_2S are

$$H_2S \rightleftharpoons H^+ + HS^- \qquad K_{a1} = 1.1 \times 10^{-7}$$

$$HS^- \rightleftharpoons H^+ + S^{2-} \qquad K_{a2} = 1.0 \times 10^{-14}$$

Therefore, the base dissociation constants for the ions are

$$S^{2-} + H_2O \rightleftharpoons HS^- + OH^- \qquad K_{b1} = \frac{K_w}{K_{a2}} = 1.0$$

$$HS^- + H_2O \rightleftharpoons H_2S + OH^- \qquad K_{b2} = \frac{K_w}{K_{a1}} = 9.1 \times 10^{-8}$$

Notice that the *first* base dissociation constant is obtained by dividing the water constant by the *second* acid dissociation constant of H_2S.

In solutions of a soluble sulfide, the first step of the hydrolysis of the sulfide ion is so nearly complete that it far overshadows the second, and the pH of the solution may be calculated by neglecting the hydrolysis of the HS^- ion.

Example 17.21

What is the pH of a 0.10 M solution of Na_2S?

Solution

$$S^{2-} \quad + H_2O \rightleftharpoons HS^- + OH^-$$
$$(0.10 - x)\, M \qquad\qquad (x)\, M \quad (x)\, M$$

$$\frac{[HS^-][OH^-]}{[S^{2-}]} = 1.0$$

$$\frac{x^2}{(0.10 - x)} = 1.0$$

$$x^2 + x - 0.10 = 0$$

This equation is solved by using the quadratic formula:

$$x = \frac{-1.00 + \sqrt{1.00 + 0.40}}{2.00}$$

$$x = [OH^-] = 9.2 \times 10^{-2}\, M$$

$$pOH = 1.04$$

$$pH = 12.96$$

The pH of a solution of a normal salt can be predicted on the basis of the strengths of the acid and base from which the salt is derived:

1. Salt of a strong base and a strong acid. Examples are: $NaCl$, KNO_3, and $Ba(ClO_3)_2$. Neither cation nor anion hydrolyzes. The solution has a pH of 7.

2. Salt of a strong base and a weak acid. Examples are: KNO_2, $Ca(C_2H_3O_2)_2$, and $NaCN$. The anion hydrolyzes to produce OH^- ions. The solution has a pH that is higher than 7.

3. Salt of a weak base and a strong acid. Examples are: NH_4NO_3, $FeBr_2$, and $AlCl_3$. The cation hydrolyzes to produce H_3O^+ ions. The pH of the solution is below 7.

4. Salt of a weak base and a weak acid. Examples are: $NH_4C_2H_3O_2$, NH_4CN, and $Cu(NO_2)_2$. Both cation and anion hydrolyze. The pH of the solution depends upon the extent to which each ion hydrolyzes. The pH of a solution of $NH_4C_2H_3O_2$ is 7 since NH_3 ($K_b = 1.8 \times 10^{-5}$) and $HC_2H_3O_2$ ($K_a = 1.8 \times 10^{-5}$) are equally weak. The pH of a solution of NH_4CN, on the other hand, is above 7 because HCN ($K_a = 4.0 \times 10^{-10}$) is a weaker acid than NH_3($K_b = 1.8 \times 10^{-5}$) is a base. As a consequence, the CN^- hydrolyzes to a greater extent (producing OH^-) than the NH_4^+ does (producing H_3O^+).

The pH of a solution of an acid salt (such as $NaHS$, NaH_2PO_4, Na_2HPO_4, and $NaHCO_3$) is affected not only by the hydrolysis of the anion but also by the acid dissociation of the anion. Solutions of these salts may be acidic or alkaline. The two important equilibria in solutions of NaH_2PO_4, for example, are the acid dissociation of the $H_2PO_4^-$ ion:

$$H_2PO_4^- \rightleftharpoons H^+ + HPO_4^{2-} \qquad K_{a2} = 6.2 \times 10^{-8}$$

and the hydrolysis of the $H_2PO_4^-$ ion:

$$H_2PO_4^- + H_2O \rightleftharpoons H_3PO_4 + OH^-$$

$$K_{b3} = \frac{K_w}{K_{a1}} = \frac{1.0 \times 10^{-14}}{7.5 \times 10^{-3}} = 1.3 \times 10^{-12}$$

Since the equilibrium constant for the dissociation (which produces H^+) is larger than the equilibrium constant for the hydrolysis (which produces OH^-), a solution of NaH_2PO_4 is acidic.

On the other hand, a solution of Na_2HPO_4 is alkaline. The two pertinent equilibria are

$$HPO_4^{2-} \rightleftharpoons H^+ + PO_4^{3-} \qquad K_{a3} = 1 \times 10^{-12}$$

$$HPO_4^{2-} + H_2O \rightleftharpoons H_2PO_4^- + OH^- \qquad K_{b2} = \frac{K_w}{K_{a2}} = \frac{1.0 \times 10^{-14}}{6.2 \times 10^{-8}}$$

$$= 1.6 \times 10^{-7}$$

The base dissociation occurs to a greater extent than the acid dissociation, and the pH of the solution is higher than 7.

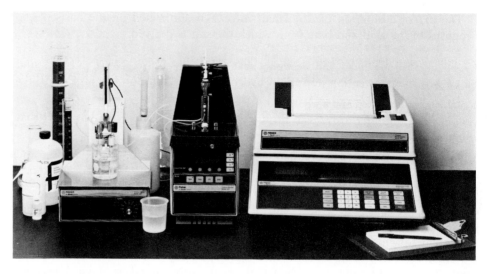

Automatic titration. *Allied Corporation, Fisher Scientific.*

17.9 Acid-Base Titrations

We are now in a position to study acid-base titrations in some detail. Let us consider the titration of a 50.0 mL sample of 0.100 M HCl with a 0.100 M NaOH solution. Since both HCl and NaOH are strong electrolytes, the only equilibrium to be considered is the water equilibrium.

The concentration of $H^+(aq)$ in the original 50.0 mL sample of acid in the titration flask is 0.100 M (or 10^{-1} M). The pH, therefore, is 1.00.

After the addition of 10.0 mL of 0.100 M NaOH from the buret, the equivalent of 40.0 mL of 0.100 M HCl remains unneutralized. The number of moles of $H^+(aq)$ in the titration flask, therefore, is

$$? \text{ mol } H^+ = 40.0 \text{ mL}\left(\frac{0.100 \text{ mol } H^+}{1000 \text{ mL}}\right) = 4.00 \times 10^{-3} \text{ mol } H^+$$

The total volume of the solution after the addition is 60.0 mL (which is 6.00×10^{-2} L), and therefore,

$$[H^+] = \frac{4.00 \times 10^{-3} \text{ mol } H^+}{6.00 \times 10^{-2} \text{ L}} = 6.67 \times 10^{-2} \text{ } M$$

$$pH = 1.18$$

When 50.0 mL of 0.100 M NaOH has been added from the buret, the equivalence point is reached. All the acid is neutralized, and the pH is 7.00.

As NaOH solution is added beyond the equivalence point, the solution in the titration flask becomes increasingly alkaline. When 60.0 mL of 0.100 M NaOH has been added, for example, the solution contains the equivalent of 10.0 mL of 0.100 M NaOH:

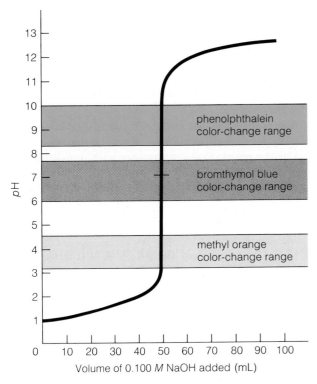

Figure 17.1 Titration of 50.0 mL of 0.100 M HCl with 0.100 M NaOH

Table 17.6 Titration of 50.0 mL of 0.100 M HCl with 0.100 M NaOH	
Volume of 0.100 M NaOH Added (mL)	pH
0.0	1.00
10.0	1.18
20.0	1.37
30.0	1.60
40.0	1.96
49.0	3.00
49.9	4.00
50.0	7.00
50.1	10.00
51.0	11.00
60.0	11.96
70.0	12.22
80.0	12.36
90.0	12.46
100.0	12.52

$$? \text{ mol OH}^- = 10.0 \text{ mL}\left(\frac{0.100 \text{ mol OH}^-}{1000 \text{ mL}}\right) = 1.00 \times 10^{-3} \text{ mol OH}^-$$

The total volume of the solution at this point is 110.0 mL (which is 1.10×10^{-1} L), and, therefore,

$$[\text{OH}^-] = \frac{1.00 \times 10^{-3} \text{ mol OH}^-}{1.10 \times 10^{-1} \text{ L}} = 9.09 \times 10^{-3} \ M$$

$$p\text{OH} = 2.04$$

$$p\text{H} = 11.96$$

The values in Table 17.6 were obtained from calculations such as these. The data of Table 17.6 are plotted in Figure 17.1. Notice that the curve rises sharply in the section around the equivalence point. Whereas the first 49.9 mL of NaOH solution added causes the pH to change by three units, the next 0.2 mL added causes a change of *six* units in the pH.

The color-change ranges of three indicators are shown in Figure 17.1. Each indicator exhibits its acid color at pH's below its range and its alkaline color at pH's above its range. In the course of the titration, the pH of the solution changes along the curve from left to right. The end point of the titration is signaled when the indicator changes to its alkaline color.

Any of the three indicators would be satisfactory to use for this titration. The color-change ranges of all three indicators fall in the straight portion of the pH curve where one drop of NaOH solution causes a sharp increase in the pH.

Let us now consider the titration of 50.0 mL of 0.100 M acetic acid—a weak acid—with 0.100 M sodium hydroxide. The concentration of H^+ in the original 50.0 mL sample of acid may be calculated by using the equilibrium constant of acetic acid (see Example 17.2). From Table 17.1 we see that $[H^+] = 1.34 \times 10^{-3}$ M. The pH of the solution is therefore 2.87.

The solution resulting from the addition of 10.0 mL of 0.100 M NaOH to the 50.0 mL sample of 0.100 M $HC_2H_3O_2$ is, in effect, a buffer since it contains a mixture of $C_2H_3O_2^-$ ions, produced by the neutralization, together with unneutralized $HC_2H_3O_2$. The pH of a buffer is conveniently calculated by the use of the relation

$$pH = pK_a + \log\left(\frac{[A^-]}{[HA]}\right) \tag{17.6}$$

which was derived in Section 17.6. For acetic acid the pK_a is 4.74 (the negative logarithm of 1.8×10^{-5}). The ratio $[C_2H_3O_2^-]/[HC_2H_3O_2]$ is easily calculated. After 10.0 mL of NaOH is added, 10/50 of the acid of the original 50.0 mL sample has been neutralized; it has, in effect, been converted into the salt sodium acetate. Since 40/50 of the acid remains unneutralized, the ratio is 1 to 4. Thus,

$$pH = pK_a + \log\left(\frac{[C_2H_3O_2^-]}{[HC_2H_3O_2]}\right)$$
$$= 4.74 + \log(1/4)$$
$$= 4.14$$

At the equivalence point all of the acid has been neutralized, and the solution (100. mL) is effectively 0.0500 M in sodium acetate. The calculation of the pH of this solution must take into account the hydrolysis of the $C_2H_3O_2^-$ ion (see Example 17.19):

$$C_2H_3O_2^- + H_2O \rightleftharpoons HC_2H_3O_2 + OH^-$$
$$ 0.0500\ M (x)\ M (x)\ M$$

$$\frac{[HC_2H_3O_2][OH^-]}{[C_2H_3O_2^-]} = 5.6 \times 10^{-10}$$

$$\frac{x^2}{5.00 \times 10^{-2}} = 5.6 \times 10^{-10}$$

$$x = [OH^-] = 5.3 \times 10^{-6}$$

$$pOH = 5.28$$

$$pH = 8.72$$

Notice that the equivalence point in this titration does not occur at a pH of 7.

After the equivalence point, the addition of NaOH causes the solution to become increasingly alkaline. The added OH^- shifts the hydrolysis equilibrium to the left. The effect of the hydrolysis on the pH is negligible. Thus, the calculations from this point on are identical to those for the HCl-NaOH titration.

Data for a $HC_2H_3O_2$-NaOH titration are summarized in Table 17.7 and plotted

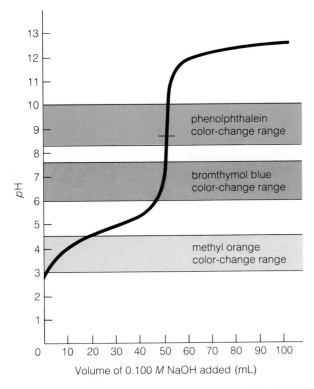

Table 17.7 Titration of 50.0 mL of 0.100 M $HC_2H_3O_2$ with 0.100 M NaOH	
Volume of 0.100 M NaOH Added (mL)	pH
0.0	2.87
10.0	4.14
20.0	4.56
30.0	4.92
40.0	5.34
49.0	6.44
49.9	7.45
50.0	8.72
50.1	10.00
51.0	11.00
60.0	11.96
70.0	12.22
80.0	12.36
90.0	12.46
100.0	12.52

Figure 17.2   Titration of 50.0 mL of 0.100 M $HC_2H_3O_2$ with 0.100 M NaOH

in Figure 17.2. The equivalence point of this titration occurs at a higher pH than that of the preceding titration, and all pH values on the acid side of the equivalence point are higher. Consequently, the rapidly ascending portion of the curve around the equivalence point is reduced in length. From the curve of Figure 17.2 we can see that methyl orange is not a suitable indicator for this titration. Neither is bromthymol blue suitable, since its color change would start after 47.34 mL of NaOH had been added and continue until 49.97 mL had been added; this would hardly constitute a sharp end point for a titration. Phenolphthalein, however, would be a satisfactory indicator to employ.

Other titration curves may be drawn following the general line of approach outlined here. Figure 17.3 represents the titration curve for the titration of 50.0 mL of 0.100 M NH_3 with 0.100 M HCl. In this instance methyl orange could be used as the indicator. Figure 17.4 is the titration curve for the titration of 50.0 mL of 0.100 M $HC_2H_3O_2$ with 0.100 M NH_3; both solutes are weak electrolytes. No indicator can be found that would function satisfactorily for this titration, and such titrations—between weak electrolytes—are not usually run.

Titrations may be conducted potentiometrically. For example, a titration may be performed with the electrodes of a pH meter immersed in the solution being analyzed. The pH of the solution is determined after successive additions of reagent. The equivalence point of the titration is indicated by an abrupt change in the pH, but additions and readings are continued beyond this point. The equivalence point may be determined by graphing the data and estimating the volume corresponding to the midpoint of the steeply rising portion of the titration curve.

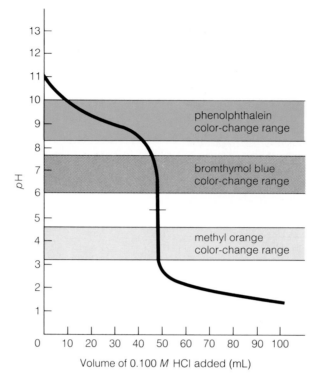

Figure 17.3 Titration of 50.0 mL of 0.100 M NH$_3$ with 0.100 M HCl

The potentiometric titration of a weak electrolyte serves as an important method of determining the dissociation constant of the electrolyte. Since

$$pH = pK_a + \log([A^-]/[HA]) \tag{17.6}$$

the pK_a of the electrolyte is equal to the pH of the solution at half neutralization (where $[A^-] = [HA]$); but the pK_a, and hence the K_a itself, may be determined from any point on the titration curve.

Example 17.22

The equivalence point in the titration of 40.00 mL of a solution of a weak monoprotic acid occurs when 35.00 mL of a 0.100 M NaOH solution has been added. The pH of the solution is 5.75 after 20.00 mL of the NaOH solution has been added. What is the dissociation constant of the acid?·

Solution

Since 35.00 mL of NaOH solution is required for complete neutralization, the acid is 20/35 neutralized after 20.00 mL of NaOH has been added. In other words, 15/35 of the acid is in the form HA, and 20/35 is in the form A$^-$. The ratio $[A^-]/[HA]$ is therefore 20 to 15, or 1.33:

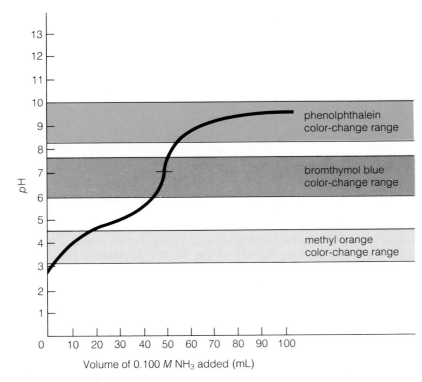

Figure 17.4 Titration of 50.0 mL of 0.100 M HC$_2$H$_3$O$_2$ with 0.100 M NH$_3$

$$pH = pK_a + \log\left(\frac{[A^-]}{[HA]}\right)$$

$$5.75 = pK_a + \log(1.33)$$

$$pK_a = 5.63$$

$$K_a = 2.4 \times 10^{-6}$$

Summary

Aqueous solutions of soluble *weak electrolytes* contain dissolved *molecules* in *equilibrium* with the constituent *ions*. In the expressions for the equilibrium constants for such systems, the *concentrations* of the *ions* are written in the *numerator* and the *concentrations* of the *molecules* appear in the *denominator*. Constants for weak acids are called *acid dissociation constants* (K_a); constants for weak bases are called *base dissociation constants* (K_b). The *degree of dissociation* of a weak electrolyte can be used to determine the value of the equilibrium constant. An equilibrium system may be prepared by dissolving *molecules* of the weak electrolyte in water, by dissolving compounds that supply the *ions* of the weak electrolyte in water, or by dissolving a mixture of *both* in water. The equilibrium constant may be used to determine equilibrium concentrations.

Pure *water* is a *weak electrolyte* and ionizes to produce the H$^+$(aq) ion (or H$_3$O$^+$ ion) and the OH$^-$(aq) ion. The ionization constant, K_w, is called the *water dissociation constant*, and is equal to 1.0×10^{-14} at 25°C: $K_w = [\text{H}^+][\text{OH}^-] = 1.0 \times 10^{-14}$. In pure water or in dilute solutions, the *concentration of* H$_2$O is virtually a *constant*. Hence, the concentration of H$_2$O is included in the values of the equilibrium constants and the term [H$_2$O] does not explicitly appear in equilibrium constant expressions.

The concentration of H^+(aq) in a solution may be expressed in terms of pH. An *acid solution* has a pH that is *less than 7*; the pH of an *alkaline solution* is *greater than 7*.

Indicators are compounds that *change color* in solution as the pH *of the solution changes*. They may be used to determine the pH of a solution and to locate the *end point* of a titration.

The *common-ion effect* is used to *repress* the *ionization* of weak electrolytes. The extent of the dissociation of a weak acid or a weak base in a solution is reduced if a compound that contains an ion in common with the weak electrolyte is added to the solution.

A *buffer* is a solution that contains relatively high concentrations of a *weak acid* and a *salt* of the acid or a *weak base* and a *salt* of the base. A solution of this type is capable of *maintaining a constant pH* even when small amounts of acids or bases are added. The *Henderson-Hasselbalch equation*, $pH = pK_a + \log([A^-]/[HA])$, can be used to calculate the concentrations of substances required to produce a buffer with a desired pH.

Polyprotic acids, which contain more than one ionizable hydrogen per molecule, ionize in steps. For each step, there is an equilibrium constant, $K_{a1}, K_{a2}\ldots$. A useful equation that pertains to a *saturated solution of H_2S* (a weak diprotic acid) at 25°C, $[H^+]^2[S^{2-}] = 1.1 \times 10^{-22}$, can be derived from the two ionization constants for H_2S and the fact that a saturated solution of H_2S at 25°C is 0.10 *M*.

Certain *ions* can *react with water* (in what are sometimes called *hydrolysis reactions*) to change the pH. The *anion* of a weak *acid* is the *conjugate base* of the acid (and produces OH^- ions in reactions with water). The *cation* derived from a weak *base* is the *conjugate acid* of the base (and produces H^+ ions in reactions with water). The product of the constants K_a and K_b for a given conjugate pair equals K_w: $K_a K_b = K_w$. The pH of solutions of salts that contain ions that hydrolyze are *not* usually *equal to 7* (unless both cation and anion hydrolyze to the same extent).

When a solution of an acid (or base) is gradually added to a solution of a sample in the course of a titration, the pH of the solution continually changes. A *titration curve* consists of a plot of the pH of the solution *against* the *volume of acid* (or *base*) added. These curves help determine the correct indicator to use for a titration, and they are useful in interpreting the results of potentiometric titrations.

Key Terms

Some of the more important terms introduced in this chapter are listed below. Definitions for terms not included in this list may be located in the text by use of the index.

Acid-base indicator (Section 17.4)   A compound that changes color in solution as the pH of the solution changes.

Acid dissociation constant, K_a (Section 17.1)   A equilibrium constant that pertains to an equilibrium involving a weak acid and the ions derived from it in water solution.

Base dissociation constant, K_b (Section 17.1)   An equilibrium constant that pertains to an equilibrium involving a weak base and the ions derived from it in water solution.

Buffer (Section 17.6)   A solution capable of maintaining its pH at a fairly constant value even when small amounts of acids or bases are added.

Common-ion effect (Section 17.5)   The effect on an equilibrium system caused by the addition of a compound that has an ion in common with a compound present in the system.

Degree of dissociation, α (Section 17.1)   The fraction of the total concentration of a weak electrolyte that is in ionic form in water solution at equilibrium.

End point (Section 17.9)   That point in a titration when the indicator changes color.

Equivalence point (Section 17.9)   That point in a titration

when an equivalent amount of base or acid has been added to the sample of acid or base being titrated.

Henderson-Hasselbalch equation (Section 17.6)   An equation that permits the calculation of the pH of a buffer; $pH = pK_a + \log([A^-]/[HA])$, where pK_a is the negative logarithm of the acid dissociation constant of the weak acid used to prepare the buffer, $[A^-]$ is the concentration of anions, and $[HA]$ is the concentration of molecules of the weak acid.

Hydrolysis (Section 17.8)   A reaction of a cation or an anion with water that affects the pH.

pH (Section 17.3)   The negative logarithm (base 10) of the concentration of H^+(aq) ions in an aqueous solution; $pH = -\log[H^+]$.

pK (Section 17.6)   The negative logarithm (base 10) of an equilibrium constant; $pK = -\log K$

pOH (Section 17.3)   The negative logarithm (base 10) of the concentration of OH^-(aq) ions in an aqueous solution; $pOH = -\log[OH^-]$

Titration curve (Section 17.9)   A graph that shows how the pH of a solution changes during the course of a titration; the pH is plotted against the volume of base or acid added.

Water dissociation constant (Section 17.2)   The product of the concentration of H^+(aq) and the concentration of OH^-(aq) in any aqueous system; at 25°C, $K_w = [H^+][OH^-] = 1.0 \times 10^{-14}$.

Problems*

Weak Electrolytes

17.1 Propanoic acid ($HC_3H_5O_2$, a weak monoprotic acid) is 0.72% ionized in 0.25 M solution. What is the ionization constant for this acid?

17.2 A 0.20 M solution of dichloroacetic acid (HO_2CCHCl_2, a weak monoprotic acid) is 33% ionized. What is the ionization constant of this acid?

17.3 In a 0.25 M solution of benzyl amine, $C_7H_7NH_2$, the concentration of $OH^-(aq)$ is 2.4×10^{-3} M.

$$C_7H_7NH_2 + H_2O \rightleftharpoons C_7H_7NH_3^+ + OH^-$$

What is the value of K_b for the aqueous ionization of benzyl amine?

17.4 In a 0.25 M solution of strychnine ($C_{21}H_{22}N_2O_2$, which is indicated St in the following equation), the concentration of $OH^-(aq)$ is 6.7×10^{-4} M.

$$St + H_2O \rightleftharpoons StH^+ + OH^-$$

What is the value of K_b for the aqueous ionization of strychnine?

17.5 In a 0.300 M solution of cyanoacetic acid, $H(O_2CCH_2CN)$, the concentration of $H^+(aq)$ is 0.032 M. What is the value of K_a for the aqueous ionization of cyanoacetic acid?

17.6 In a 0.36 M solution of anisic acid, $HC_8H_7O_3$, the concentration of $H^+(aq)$ is 3.5×10^{-3} M. What is the value of K_a for the aqueous ionization of anisic acid?

17.7 The ionization constant of lactic acid, $HC_3H_5O_3$, is 1.5×10^{-4}. **(a)** What is the concentration of $H^+(aq)$ in a 0.16 M solution of lactic acid? **(b)** What is the percent ionization of $HC_3H_5O_3$ in this solution?

17.8 (a) What is the concentration of $H^+(aq)$ in a 0.25 M solution of benzoic acid? **(b)** What is the percent ionization of $HC_7H_5O_2$ in this solution?

17.9 What are the concentrations of $N_2H_5^+(aq)$, $OH^-(aq)$, and $N_2H_4(aq)$ in a 0.15 M solution of hydrazine (N_2H_4)?

17.10 What are the concentrations of $C_6H_5NH_2(aq)$, $OH^-(aq)$, and $C_6H_5NH_3^+(aq)$ in a 0.40 M solution of aniline?

17.11 A weak acid, HX, is 1.2% ionized in 0.15 M solution. What percent of HX is ionized in a 0.030 M solution?

17.12 A weak acid, HY, is 0.10% ionized in 0.15 M solution. At what concentration is the acid 1.0% ionized?

17.13 (a) What concentration of $HClO_2$ molecules is in equilibrium with 0.030 M $H^+(aq)$ in a solution prepared from pure chlorous acid? **(b)** How many moles of $HClO_2$ should be used to prepare 1.0 L of this solution?

17.14 For the aqueous ionization of chloroacetic acid:

$$H(O_2CCH_2Cl)(aq) \rightleftharpoons H^+(aq) + ClCH_2CO_2^-(aq)$$

K_a is 1.4×10^{-3}. **(a)** What concentration of chloroacetic acid molecules is in equilibrium with 0.025 M $H^+(aq)$ in a solution prepared from pure chloroacetic acid? **(b)** How many moles of chloroacetic acid should be used to prepare 1.0 L of this solution?

17.15 In an aqueous solution of NH_3, the concentration of $OH^-(aq)$ is 1.8×10^{-3} M. What is the concentration of $NH_3(aq)$?

17.16 In an aqueous solution of trimethylamine, $(CH_3)_3N$, the concentration of OH^- is 6.0×10^{-3} M. What is the concentration of trimethylamine?

17.17 What are the concentrations of $H^+(aq)$, $N_3^-(aq)$, and $HN_3(aq)$ in a solution prepared from 0.23 mol of sodium azide (NaN_3) and 0.10 mol of HCl in a total volume of 1.0 L?

17.18 What are the concentrations of $H^+(aq)$, $CHO_2^-(aq)$, and $HCHO_2(aq)$ in a solution prepared from 0.22 mole of sodium formate ($NaCHO_2$) and 0.15 mole of HCl in a total volume of 1.0 L?

17.19 For the aqueous ionization of hydroxylamine:

$$HONH_2(aq) + H_2O \rightleftharpoons HONH_3^+(aq) + OH^-(aq)$$

the value of K_b is 1.1×10^{-8}. What are the concentrations of $OH^-(aq)$, $HONH_3^+(aq)$, and $HONH_2(aq)$ in a solution prepared from 0.20 mol of $HONH_3^+Cl^-$ and 0.35 mol of NaOH in a total volume of 1.0 L?

17.20 What are the concentrations of $OH^-(aq)$, $N_2H_5^+(aq)$, and $N_2H_4(aq)$ in a solution prepared from 0.45 mol of $N_2H_5^+Cl^-$ and 0.32 mol of NaOH in a total volume of 1.0 L?

17.21 What are the concentrations of $NH_3(aq)$, $NH_4^+(aq)$, and $OH^-(aq)$ in a solution prepared by adding 150 mL of 0.45 M NH_4Cl to 300 mL of 0.30 M NaOH? Assume that the total volume of the solution is 450 mL.

17.22 What are the concentrations of $H^+(aq)$, $C_7H_5O_2^-(aq)$, and $HC_7H_5O_2(aq)$ in a solution prepared by adding 10 mL of 0.30 M sodium benzoate, $NaC_7H_5O_2$, to 15 mL of 0.20 M HCl? Assume that the total volume of the solution is 25 mL.

*17.23 What are the concentrations of $H^+(aq)$, $ClO_2^-(aq)$, and $HClO_2(aq)$ in a 0.26 M solution of chlorous acid?

*17.24 What are the concentrations of $OH^-(aq)$, $(CH_3)_2NH_2^+(aq)$, and $(CH_3)_2NH$ in a 0.45 M solution of dimethylamine?

---

* The more difficult problems are marked with asterisks. The appendix contains answers to color-keyed problems.

17.25 What are the concentrations of $H^+(aq)$ and $OH^-(aq)$ in **(a)** a 0.015 M solution of HNO_3, and **(b)** a 0.0025 M solution of $Ba(OH)_2$?

17.26 What are the concentrations of $H^+(aq)$ and $OH^-(aq)$ in **(a)** 0.00030 M solution of HCl, and **(b)** a 0.016 M solution of $Ca(OH)_2$?

17.27 What pH corresponds to each of the following? **(a)** $[H^+] = 7.3 \times 10^{-5}\ M$, **(b)** $[H^+] = 0.084\ M$, **(c)** $[OH^-] = 3.3 \times 10^{-4}\ M$, **(d)** $[OH^-] = 0.042\ M$.

17.28 What pH corresponds to each of the following? **(a)** $[H^+] = 0.0056\ M$, **(b)** $[H^+] = 3.9 \times 10^{-8}\ M$, **(c)** $[OH^-] = 6.9 \times 10^{-9}\ M$, **(d)** $[OH^-] = 0.00077\ M$.

17.29 What concentration of $H^+(aq)$ corresponds to each of the following? **(a)** $pH = 1.23$, **(b)** $pH = 10.92$, **(c)** $pOH = 4.32$, **(d)** $pOH = 12.34$.

17.30 What concentration of $H^+(aq)$ corresponds to each of the following? **(a)** $pH = 5.66$, **(b)** $pH = 9.65$, **(c)** $pOH = 2.45$, **(d)** $pOH = 8.16$.

17.31 What concentration of $OH^-(aq)$ corresponds to each of the following? **(a)** $pH = 3.33$, **(b)** $pH = 7.99$, **(c)** $pOH = 0.16$, **(d)** $pOH = 10.22$.

17.32 What concentration of $OH^-(aq)$ corresponds to each of the following? **(a)** $pH = 0.22$, **(b)** $pH = 12.13$, **(c)** $pOH = 4.66$, **(d)** $pOH = 10.01$.

17.33 A 0.26 M solution of a weak acid, HX, has a pH of 2.86. What is the ionization constant, K_a, of the acid?

$$HX \rightleftharpoons H^+ + X^-$$

17.34 A 0.44 M solution of a weak base, B, has a pH of 11.12. What is the ionization constant, K_b, of the base?

$$B + H_2O \rightleftharpoons BH^+ + OH^-$$

17.35 What is the pH of a 0.30 M NH_3 solution?

17.36 What is the pH of a 0.12 M HOCN solution?

17.37 How many moles of chlorous acid, $HClO_2$, must be used to prepare 1.00 L of a solution that has a pH of 2.60?

17.38 How many moles of benzoic acid, $HC_7H_5O_2$, must be used to prepare 500. mL of a solution that has a pH of 2.44?

17.39 An indicator, HIn, has an ionization constant of 9.0×10^{-9}. The acid color of the indicator is yellow, and the alkaline color is red. The yellow color is visible when the ratio of yellow form to red form is 30 to 1, and the red form is predominant when the ratio of red form to yellow form is 2 to 1. What is the pH range of the color change of the indicator?

17.40 In each of the following parts, a given solution affects the indicators in the way shown. Refer to Table 17.4, and describe the pH of each solution as completely as possible. **(a)** Thymol blue turns blue and alizarin yellow turns yellow, **(b)** bromcresol green turns blue and bromthymol blue turns yellow, **(c)** methyl orange turns yellow and litmus turns red.

17.41 A solution is prepared by dissolving 0.010 mol of sodium nitrite, $NaNO_2$, in 100. mL of 0.035 M nitrous acid, HNO_2. Assume that the volume of the resulting solution is 100. mL. Calculate **(a)** the pH of the solution and **(b)** the percent ionization of HNO_2.

17.42 A solution is prepared by dissolving 0.010 mol of sodium formate, $Na(CHO_2)$, in 100. mL of 0.025 M formic acid, $HCHO_2$. Assume that the volume of the resulting solution is 100. mL. Calculate **(a)** the pH of the solution and **(b)** the percent ionization of $HCHO_2$.

17.43 A solution prepared from 0.028 mol of a weak acid, HX, and 0.0070 mol of NaX diluted to 200. mL has a pH of 3.66. What is the ionization constant, K_a, of HX?

17.44 A solution is prepared from 3.0×10^{-3} mol of a weak acid, HX, and 6.0×10^{-4} mol of NaX diluted to 200. mL. The solution has a pH of 4.80. What is the ionization constant, K_a, of HX?

17.45 A 0.10 M solution of hydrazine, N_2H_4, containing an unknown concentration of hydrazine hydrochloride, $N_2H_5^+Cl^-$, has a pH of 7.15. What is the concentration of hydrazine hydrochloride in the solution?

17.46 A 0.24 M solution of dimethylamine, $(CH_3)_2NH$, containing an unknown concentration of dimethylamine hydrochloride, $(CH_3)_2NH_2^+Cl^-$, has a pH of 10.40. What is the concentration of dimethylamine hydrochloride?

17.47 A solution prepared from 0.060 mol of a weak acid, HX, diluted to 250 mL has a pH of 2.89. What is the pH of the solution after 0.030 mol of solid NaX has been dissolved in it? Assume that no significant volume change occurs when the NaX is dissolved in the solution.

17.48 A 0.049 M solution of a weak acid, HX, has a pH of 3.55. What is the pH of 500. mL of the solution after 0.010 mol of solid NaX has been dissolved in it? Assume that no significant volume change occurs when the NaX is dissolved in the solution.

17.49 What concentrations should be used to prepare an ammonia-ammonium ion buffer with a pH of 9.50?

17.50 What concentrations should be used to prepare a benzoic acid-benzoate ion buffer with a pH of 5.00?

17.51 **(a)** What are the concentrations of $H^+(aq)$, HCO_3^- (aq), $CO_3^{2-}(aq)$, and $CO_2(aq)$ in a saturated solution of carbonic acid (0.034 M in CO_2)? **(b)** What is the pH of the solution?

17.52 Calculate the concentrations of $H^+(aq)$, $H_2AsO_4^-$ (aq), $HAsO_4^{2-}(aq)$, $AsO_4^{3-}(aq)$, and $H_3AsO_4(aq)$ in a 0.30 M solution of arsenic acid.

17.53 A 0.15 M solution of HCl is saturated with H_2S. **(a)** What is the concentration of S^{2-}? **(b)** What is the concentration of $HS^-(aq)$?

17.54 A solution with a pH of 3.30 is saturated with H_2S. What is the concentration of $S^{2-}(aq)$?

17.55 What should the concentration of $H^+(aq)$ be in order to have a sulfide ion concentration of $3.0 \times 10^{-17} M$ when the solution is saturated with H_2S?

17.56 What should the concentration of $H^+(aq)$ be in order to have a sulfide ion concentration of $2.0 \times 10^{-19} M$ when the solution is saturated with H_2S?

Ions That Function as Acids and Bases

17.57 What is the pH of a 0.15 M solution of sodium nitrite ($NaNO_2$)?

17.58 What is the pH of a 0.10 M solution of sodium benzoate ($NaC_7H_5O_2$)?

17.59 What is the pH of a 0.20 M solution of aniline hydrochloride ($C_6H_5NH_3^+Cl^-$)?

17.60 What is the pH of a 0.13 M solution of hydrazine hydrochloride ($N_2H_5^+Cl^-$)?

17.61 A solution of sodium benzoate has a pH of 9.00. What is the concentration of sodium benzoate?

17.62 What concentration of ammonium chloride, NH_4Cl, will produce a solution with a pH of 5.20?

17.63 The pH of a 0.15 M solution of NaX is 9.77. What is the value of K_a of the weak acid HX?

17.64 The pH of a 0.30 M solution of NaX is 9.50. What is the value of K_a of the weak acid HX?

*17.65 The $Zn(OH)^+$ ion is believed to be the only zinc-containing ion resulting from the reaction of the $Zn^{2+}(aq)$ ion with water. What is the pH of a 0.010 M solution of $Zn(NO_3)_2$? The K_{inst} of $Zn(OH)^+$ is 4.1×10^{-5}.

*17.66 The $Cd(OH)^+$ ion is believed to be the only cadmium-containing ion resulting from the reaction of the $Cd^{2+}(aq)$ ion with water. What is the concentration of $Cd^{2+}(aq)$ in a solution of $Cd(ClO_4)_2$ that has a pH of 5.48? The K_{inst} of $Cd(OH)^+$ is 6.9×10^{-5}.

Acid-Base Titrations

17.67 Determine pH values for a titration curve pertaining to the titration of 30.00 mL of 0.100 M benzoic acid, $HC_7H_5O_2$, with 0.100 M NaOH: **(a)** after 10.00 mL of the NaOH solution has been added, **(b)** after 30.00 mL of the NaOH solution has been added, **(c)** after 40.00 mL of the NaOH solution has been added.

17.68 Determine pH values for a titration curve pertaining to the titration of 25.00 mL of 0.100 M NH_3 with a 0.100 M solution of HCl: **(a)** after 10.00 mL of the HCl solution has been added, **(b)** after 25.00 mL of the HCl solution has been added, **(c)** after 35.00 mL of the HCl solution has been added.

17.69 In the titration of 25.00 mL of a solution of a weak acid HX with 0.250 M NaOH, the pH of the solution is 4.50 after 5.00 mL of the NaOH solution has been added. The equivalence point in the titration occurs when 30.40 mL of the NaOH solution has been added. What is the ionization constant, K_a, for the weak acid HX?

17.70 The equivalence point in the titration of 50.00 mL of a solution of acetic acid occurs when 33.00 mL of 0.200 M NaOH has been added. How many mL of the NaOH solution should be added to 50.00 mL of the acetic acid solution to produce a solution with a pH of 5.04?

Unclassified Problems

17.71 Morphine is a weak base, and the aqueous ionization can be indicated as:

$$M(aq) + H_2O \rightleftharpoons MH^+(aq) + OH^-(aq)$$

In a 0.0050 M solution of morphine, the ratio of $OH^-(aq)$ ions to morphine molecules is 1.0/83. What is the value of K_b for the aqueous ionization of morphine?

*17.72 What are the concentrations of $NH_3(aq)$, $NH_4^+(aq)$, and $OH^-(aq)$ in a solution prepared from 0.15 mol of $(NH_4)_2SO_4$ and 0.10 mol of NaOH dissolved in a total volume of 750 mL?

17.73 (a) An indicator, HIn, exhibits its acid color at pH's below 5.49. At a pH of 5.49, the ratio of $[HIn]$ to $[In^-]$ is 2.0 to 1.0. What is the ionization constant, K_a, of the indicator? **(b)** What is the pH at the other end of the pH change range if the ratio of $[HIn]$ to $[In^-]$ at that point is 1.0 to 2.0?

17.74 Cocaine is a weak base. The aqueous ionization of cocaine can be indicated as:

$$C(aq) + H_2O \rightleftharpoons CH^+(aq) + OH^-(aq)$$

A $5.0 \times 10^{-3} M$ solution of cocaine has a pH of 10.04. What is the ionization constant, K_b, of this substance?

17.75 A 0.050 M solution of formic acid, $HCHO_2$, containing an unknown concentration of formate ion, CHO_2^-, derived from sodium formate, has a pH of 3.70. What is the concentration of formate ion in the solution?

17.76 How many moles of sodium hypochlorite, NaOCl, should be added to 200. mL of 0.22 M hypochlorous acid, HOCl, to produce a buffer with a pH of 6.75? Assume that no volume change occurs when the NaOCl is added to the solution.

*17.77 What are the concentrations of $H^+(aq)$, $HSO_4^-(aq)$, $SO_4^{2-}(aq)$, and $H_2SO_4(aq)$ in a 0.20 M solution of H_2SO_4?

17.78 What is the difference between the end point and the equivalence point in a titration?

C H A P T E R
18
IONIC EQUILIBRIUM, PART II

Homogeneous, aqueous equilibrium systems involving weak acids and bases were discussed in Chapter 17. This chapter begins with a study of heterogeneous systems in which slightly soluble solids are in equilibrium with their constituent ions in solution. Equilibrium principles apply to the precipitation of such solids in the qualitative or quantitative determinations of dissolved ions. Several additional types of homogeneous systems are also considered, including the equilibria that occur in the formation of complex ions in solution and equilibria associated with amphoteric substances.

18.1 The Solubility Product

Most substances are soluble in water to at least some slight extent. If an "insoluble" or "slightly soluble" material is placed in water, an equilibrium is established when the rate of dissolution of ions from the solid equals the rate of precipitation of ions from the *saturated solution.* Thus, an equilibrium exists between solid silver chloride and a saturated solution of silver chloride:

$$AgCl(s) \rightleftharpoons Ag^+(aq) + Cl^-(aq)$$

The equilibrium constant is

$$K' = \frac{[Ag^+][Cl^-]}{[AgCl]}$$

Since the concentration of a pure solid is a constant, $[AgCl]$ may be combined with K' to give

$$K_{SP} = K'[AgCl] = [Ag^+][Cl^-]$$

The constant K_{SP} is called a **solubility product.** The ionic concentrations of the expression are those for a saturated solution at the reference temperature. Since the solubility of a salt usually varies widely with temperature, the numerical value for K_{SP} for a salt changes with temperature. A table of solubility products at 25°C is given in the appendix.

The numerical value of K_{SP} for a salt may be found from the molar solubility of the salt.

Example 18.1

At 25°C, 0.00188 g of AgCl dissolves in one liter of water. What is the K_{SP} of AgCl?

Solution

The number of moles of AgCl (formula weight, 143) dissolved in one liter is:

$$? \text{ mol AgCl} = 0.00188 \text{ g AgCl} \left(\frac{1 \text{ mol AgCl}}{143 \text{ g AgCl}} \right)$$

$$= 1.31 \times 10^{-5} \text{ mol AgCl}$$

For each mole of AgCl dissolving, 1 mol of Ag^+ and 1 mol of Cl^- are formed:

$$AgCl(s) \rightleftharpoons \underset{1.31 \times 10^{-5} M}{Ag^+} + \underset{1.31 \times 10^{-5} M}{Cl^-}$$

$$K_{SP} = [Ag^+][Cl^-]$$
$$= (1.31 \times 10^{-5})^2$$
$$= 1.7 \times 10^{-10}$$

For salts that have more than two ions per formula unit, the ion concentrations must be raised to the powers indicated by the coefficients of the balanced chemical equation:

$$Mg(OH)_2(s) \rightleftharpoons Mg^{2+} + 2\,OH^- \qquad K_{SP} = [Mg^{2+}][OH^-]^2$$
$$Bi_2S_3(s) \rightleftharpoons 2\,Bi^{3+} + 3\,S^{2-} \qquad K_{SP} = [Bi^{3+}]^2[S^{2-}]^3$$
$$Hg_2Cl_2(s) \rightleftharpoons Hg_2^{2+} + 2\,Cl^- \qquad K_{SP} = [Hg_2^{2+}][Cl^-]^2$$

For a salt of this type the calculation of the K_{SP} from the molar solubility requires that the chemical equation representing the dissociation process be carefully interpreted.

Example 18.2

At 25°C, 7.8×10^{-5} mol of silver chromate dissolves in one liter of water. What is the K_{SP} of Ag_2CrO_4?

Solution

For each mole of Ag_2CrO_4 that dissolves, 2 mol of Ag^+ and 1 mol of CrO_4^{2-} are formed. Therefore,

$$Ag_2CrO_4(s) \rightleftharpoons \underset{2(7.8 \times 10^{-5}) M}{2\,Ag^+} + \underset{7.8 \times 10^{-5} M}{CrO_4^{2-}}$$

$$K_{SP} = [Ag^+]^2[CrO_4^{2-}]$$
$$= (1.56 \times 10^{-4})^2(7.8 \times 10^{-5})$$
$$= 1.9 \times 10^{-12}$$

Example 18.3

The K_{SP} of CaF_2 is 3.9×10^{-11} at 25°C. What is the concentration of Ca^{2+} and of F^- in the saturated solution? How many grams of calcium fluoride will dissolve in 100. mL of water at 25°C?

Solution

Let x equal the molar solubility of CaF_2:

$$CaF_2(s) \rightleftharpoons Ca^{2+} + 2F^-$$
$$ x \qquad 2x$$

$$K_{SP} = [Ca^{2+}][F^-]^2 = 3.9 \times 10^{-11}$$
$$x(2x)^2 = 3.9 \times 10^{-11}$$
$$4x^3 = 3.9 \times 10^{-11}$$
$$x = 2.1 \times 10^{-4}\ M$$

Therefore,

$$[Ca^{2+}] = x = 2.1 \times 10^{-4}\ M$$
$$[F^-] = 2x = 4.2 \times 10^{-4}\ M$$

$$?\ g\ CaF_2 = 100.\ mL\ H_2O \left(\frac{2.1 \times 10^{-4}\ mol\ CaF_2}{1000\ mL\ H_2O}\right)\left(\frac{78\ g\ CaF_2}{1\ mol\ CaF_2}\right)$$
$$= 1.6 \times 10^{-3}\ g\ CaF_2$$

The solubilities of some salts in water are higher than those predicted by calculations based on the K_{SP} values. Consider the barium carbonate system

$$BaCO_3(s) \rightleftharpoons Ba^{2+}(aq) + CO_3^{2-}(aq)$$

The carbonate ion in this solution undergoes hydrolysis, since it is a weak base (see Section 17.8):

$$H_2O + CO_3^{2-}(aq) \rightleftharpoons HCO_3^-(aq) + OH^-(aq)$$

The concentration of the CO_3^{2-} ion is reduced by this reaction with water, the $BaCO_3$ equilibrium is forced to the right, and more $BaCO_3$ dissolves than would otherwise be the case. A calculation of molar solubility based on the K_{SP} for $BaCO_3$ would give the concentration of CO_3^{2-} that must be present in the solution at equilibrium. More than the corresponding amount of $BaCO_3$ must dissolve, however, in order to provide not only this concentration of CO_3^{2-} but also the CO_3^{2-} that is converted into HCO_3^- by hydrolysis. In the solutions of some salts (PbS, for example) both cation and anion hydrolyze.

Theoretically, the solubility of CaF_2 (see Example 18.3) is very slightly increased by the hydrolysis of the F^- ion. The degree of hydrolysis is so low, however, that this hydrolysis may be neglected in this solubility calculation. The value for the solubility of CaF_2 listed in the handbook corresponds to the value calculated in Example 18.3.

The salt effect is another factor that may cause a calculated solubility to be in error. The solubility of a salt is increased by the addition of another electrolyte to the solution. Silver chloride, for example, is about 20% more soluble in 0.02 M KNO_3 solutions than it is in pure water:

$$AgCl(s) \rightleftharpoons Ag^+(aq) + Cl^-(aq)$$

The K^+ and NO_3^- ions help create an ionic atmosphere in the solution so that Ag^+ and Cl^- ions are surrounded by ions of opposite charges. As a result, the Ag^+ and Cl^- ions are held in solution more firmly and are less apt to recombine to form $AgCl(s)$. The net effect is that the solubility equilibrium shifts to the right.

18.2 Precipitation and the Solubility Product

The numerical value of the K_{SP} of a salt is a quantitative statement of the limit of solubility of the salt. When the values for the concentrations of the ions of a salt solution are substituted into an expression similar to that for the K_{SP} of the salt, the result is called the ion product of the solution. The K_{SP} is the ion product of a saturated solution.

We can calculate an ion product for a test solution and compare the result to the K_{SP} for the salt under consideration. Three types of comparisons are possible:

1. The ion product is less than the K_{SP}. This solution is unsaturated. Additional solid can be dissolved in it—up to the limit described by the K_{SP}.

2. The ion product is greater than the K_{SP}. The solution is momentarily supersaturated. Precipitation will occur until the ion product equals the K_{SP}.

3. The ion product equals the K_{SP}. This solution is saturated.

The following examples illustrate the application of this method.

Example 18.4

Will a precipitate form if 10. mL of 0.010 M $AgNO_3$ and 10. mL of 0.00010 M NaCl are mixed? Assume that the final volume of the solution is 20. mL. For AgCl, $K_{SP} = 1.7 \times 10^{-10}$.

Solution

Diluting a solution to twice its original volume reduces the concentrations of ions in the solution to half their original value. If there were no reaction, the ion concentrations would be

$$[Ag^+] = 5.0 \times 10^{-3} \, M$$
$$[Cl^-] = 5.0 \times 10^{-5} \, M$$

The ion product is

$$[Ag^+][Cl^-] = ?$$
$$(5.0 \times 10^{-3})(5.0 \times 10^{-5}) = 2.5 \times 10^{-7}$$

Since the ion product is larger than the K_{SP} (1.7×10^{-10}), precipitation of AgCl should occur.

Example 18.5

Will a precipitate of $Mg(OH)_2$ form in a 0.0010 M solution of $Mg(NO_3)_2$ if the pH of the solution is adjusted to 9.0? The K_{SP} of $Mg(OH)_2$ is 8.9×10^{-12}.

Solution

If the $pH = 9.0$, the $pOH = 5.0$:

$$[OH^-] = 1.0 \times 10^{-5} \, M$$

Since $[Mg^{2+}] = 1.0 \times 10^{-3} \, M$, the ion product is

$$[Mg^{2+}][OH^-]^2 = ?$$
$$(1.0 \times 10^{-3})(1.0 \times 10^{-5})^2 = 1.0 \times 10^{-13}$$

Since the ion product is less than 8.9×10^{-12}, no precipitate will form.

The common-ion effect influences solubility equilibria. As an example, consider the system

$$BaSO_4(s) \rightleftharpoons Ba^{2+}(aq) + SO_4^{2-}(aq)$$

The addition of sulfate ion, from sodium sulfate, to a saturated solution of barium sulfate will cause the equilibrium to shift to the left; the concentration of Ba^{2+} will decrease, and $BaSO_4$ will precipitate. Since the product $[Ba^{2+}][SO_4^{2-}]$ is a constant, increasing $[SO_4^{2-}]$ will cause $[Ba^{2+}]$ to decrease.

The amount of barium ion in a solution may be determined by precipitating the Ba^{2+} as $BaSO_4$. The precipitate is then removed by filtration and is dried and weighed. The concentration of Ba^{2+} left in solution after the precipitation may be reduced to a very low value if excess sulfate ion is employed in the precipitation. As a general rule, however, too large an excess of the common ion should be avoided. At high ionic concentrations the salt effect increases the solubility of a salt, and for certain precipitates the formation of a complex ion may lead to enhanced solubility.

Example 18.6

The K_{SP} of $BaSO_4$ is 1.5×10^{-9}. What is the solubility of $BaSO_4$ in $0.050 M$ Na_2SO_4? (At 25°C a saturated solution of $BaSO_4$ is $3.9 \times 10^{-5} M$.)

Solution

The SO_4^{2-} derived from the $BaSO_4$ is negligible in comparison to the $[SO_4^{2-}]$ already present in the solution ($5.0 \times 10^{-2} M$):

$$[Ba^{2+}][SO_4^{2-}] = K_{SP}$$
$$[Ba^{2+}][SO_4^{2-}] = 1.5 \times 10^{-9}$$
$$[Ba^{2+}](5.0 \times 10^{-2}) = 1.5 \times 10^{-9}$$
$$[Ba^{2+}] = 3.0 \times 10^{-8} M$$

The solubility of $BaSO_4$ has been reduced from $3.9 \times 10^{-5} M$ to $3.0 \times 10^{-8} M$ by the common-ion effect.

At times, the common-ion effect is used to *prevent* the formation of a precipitate. Consider the precipitation of magnesium hydroxide from a solution that contains Mg^{2+} ions:

$$Mg(OH)_2(s) \rightleftharpoons Mg^{2+}(aq) + 2OH^-(aq)$$

The precipitation can be prevented by holding the concentration of OH^- to a low value. If the hydroxide ion is supplied by the weak base ammonia

$$NH_3 + H_2O \rightleftharpoons NH_4^+ + OH^-$$

the concentration of OH^- can be controlled by the addition of NH_4^+. When the common ion NH_4^+ is added, the ammonia equilibrium shifts to the left, which reduces the concentration of OH^-. In this way, the concentration of OH^- can be held to a level that will not cause $Mg(OH)_2$ to precipitate.

Example 18.7

What concentration of NH_4^+, derived from NH_4Cl, is necessary to prevent the formation of an $Mg(OH)_2$ precipitate in a solution that is $0.050 M$ in Mg^{2+} and $0.050 M$ in NH_3? The K_{SP} of $Mg(OH)_2$ is 8.9×10^{-12}, K_b for NH_3 is 1.8×10^{-5}.

We first calculate the maximum concentration of hydroxide ion that can be present in the solution without causing $Mg(OH)_2$ to precipitate:

$$[Mg^{2+}][OH^-]^2 = 8.9 \times 10^{-12}$$
$$(5.0 \times 10^{-2})[OH^-]^2 = 8.9 \times 10^{-12}$$
$$[OH^-]^2 = 1.8 \times 10^{-10}$$
$$[OH^-] = 1.3 \times 10^{-5} \ M$$

The concentration of OH^-, therefore, can be no higher than $1.3 \times 10^{-5} \ M$. From the expression for the ionization constant for NH_3, we can derive the concentration of NH_4^+ that will maintain the concentration of OH^- at this level:

$$\frac{[NH_4^+][OH^-]}{[NH_3]} = 1.8 \times 10^{-5}$$

$$\frac{[NH_4^+](1.3 \times 10^{-5})}{(5.0 \times 10^{-2})} = 1.8 \times 10^{-5}$$

$$[NH_4^+] = 6.9 \times 10^{-2} \ M$$

Thus, the *minimum* concentration of NH_4^+ that must be present is 0.069 *M*.

Frequently, a solution contains more than one ion capable of forming a precipitate with another ion that is to be added to the solution. For example, a solution might contain both Cl^- and CrO_4^{2-} ions, both of which form insoluble salts with Ag^+. When Ag^+ is added to the solution, the less soluble silver salt will precipitate first. If the addition is continued, eventually a point will be reached where the more soluble salt will begin to precipitate along with the less soluble.

Example 18.8

A solution is 0.10 *M* in Cl^- and 0.10 *M* in CrO_4^{2-}. If solid $AgNO_3$ is gradually added to this solution, which will precipitate first, AgCl or Ag_2CrO_4? Assume that the addition causes no change in volume. For AgCl, $K_{SP} = 1.7 \times 10^{-10}$; for Ag_2CrO_4, $K_{SP} = 1.9 \times 10^{-12}$.

Solution

When a precipitate *begins* to form, the pertinent ion product *just* exceeds the K_{SP} of the solid. Therefore, we calculate the concentrations of Ag^+ needed to precipitate AgCl and Ag_2CrO_4:

$$AgCl(s) \rightleftharpoons Ag^+ + Cl^- \qquad\qquad Ag_2CrO_4(s) \rightleftharpoons 2\,Ag^+ + CrO_4^{2-}$$
$$\quad\ \ ? \quad\ \ 0.10 \ M \qquad\qquad\qquad\qquad\qquad ? \qquad 0.10 \ M$$

$$[Ag^+][Cl^-] = 1.7 \times 10^{-10} \qquad\qquad [Ag^+]^2[CrO_4^{2-}] = 1.9 \times 10^{-12}$$

$$[Ag^+](0.10) = 1.7 \times 10^{-10}$$
$$[Ag^+] = 1.7 \times 10^{-9} \; M$$

$$[Ag^+]^2(0.10) = 1.9 \times 10^{-12}$$
$$[Ag^+]^2 = 1.9 \times 10^{-11}$$
$$[Ag^+] = 4.4 \times 10^{-6} \; M$$

Therefore, AgCl will precipitate first.

Example 18.9

(a) In the experiment described in Example 18.8, what will be the concentration of the Cl^- ion when Ag_2CrO_4 begins to precipitate? (b) At this point, what percent of the chloride ion originally present remains in solution?

Solution

(a) From the preceding example, we see that $[Ag^+] = 4.4 \times 10^{-6} \; M$ when Ag_2CrO_4 starts to precipitate. At this point, the concentration of chloride ion will be

$$[Ag^+][Cl^-] = 1.7 \times 10^{-10}$$
$$(4.4 \times 10^{-6})[Cl^-] = 1.7 \times 10^{-10}$$
$$[Cl^-] = \frac{1.7 \times 10^{-10}}{4.4 \times 10^{-6}} = 3.9 \times 10^{-5} \; M$$

Thus, until the $[Cl^-]$ is reduced to $3.9 \times 10^{-5} \; M$, no Ag_2CrO_4 will form. (b) Since the original concentration of chloride was $0.10 \; M$, the percent of Cl^- remaining in solution when Ag_2CrO_4 starts to precipitate is

$$\frac{3.9 \times 10^{-5}}{1.0 \times 10^{-1}} \times 100 = 0.039\%$$

Chromate ion is used as a precipitation indicator for Cl^- ion. The concentration of chloride ion in a solution can be determined by titrating a sample of the solution against a standard $AgNO_3$ solution in the buret, using a few drops of K_2CrO_4 as an indicator. In the course of the titration white AgCl precipitates. The appearance of red Ag_2CrO_4 indicates that the precipitation of chloride ion is essentially complete. In a quantitative procedure of this type, the concentration of CrO_4^{2-} used is much less than employed in the preceding problem. Hence, a higher concentration of Ag^+ is required to start the precipitation of Ag_2CrO_4, and a lower concentration of Cl^- will be present in the solution when the Ag_2CrO_4 begins to precipitate.

8.3 Precipitation of Sulfides

The sulfide ion concentration in an acid solution that has been saturated with H_2S is extremely low. In 10 mL of a saturated H_2S solution that has been made $0.3 \; M$ in H^+, there are approximately seven S^{2-} ions. Nevertheless, when Pb^{2+} ions are added to such a solution, PbS precipitates immediately. It seems unlikely that the precipitate forms as a result of the reaction of Pb^{2+} ions with S^{2-} ions.

There is evidence that in this and in similar sulfide precipitations, a hydrosulfide forms initially and then decomposes to give the normal sulfide:

$$Pb(HS)_2(s) \rightleftharpoons PbS(s) + H_2S(aq)$$

The hydroxides of many metals are known to produce oxides in a parallel manner. In fact, what is known as lead hydroxide, $Pb(OH)_2$, is in reality hydrous lead oxide, $PbO \cdot xH_2O$. The hydrosulfide of lead could form as a result of the reaction of Pb^{2+} ions with either H_2S molecules or HS^- ions. The concentrations of H_2S and HS^- are much higher than the concentration of S^{2-}.

An equilibrium constant does not depend upon the reaction mechanism by which the equilibrium is attained (see Section 15.1). Provided the system is in equilibrium, the relationship expressed by the solubility product principle is valid no matter what series of reactions produces the precipitate. We may therefore use K_{SP} to calculate favorable reaction conditions for the formation of a desired precipitate or reaction conditions that will prevent the formation of a precipitate.

Example 18.10

A solution that is 0.30 M in H^+, 0.050 M in Pb^{2+}, and 0.050 M in Fe^{2+} is saturated with H_2S. Should PbS and/or FeS precipitate? The K_{SP} of PbS is 7×10^{-29}, and the K_{SP} of FeS is 4×10^{-19}.

Solution

In Section 17.7, we derived the following equation for any saturated solution of H_2S at 25°C:

$$[H^+]^2[S^{2-}] = 1.1 \times 10^{-22}$$

Since this solution is 0.30 M in H^+,

$$(3.0 \times 10^{-1})^2[S^{2-}] = 1.1 \times 10^{-22}$$
$$[S^{2-}] = 1.2 \times 10^{-21} \ M$$

Both Pb^{2+} and Fe^{2+} are 2+ ions, and the form of the ion product is

$$[M^{2+}][S^{2-}]$$

where M^{2+} stands for either metal ion. Since both are present in concentrations of 0.050 M,

$$[M^{2+}][S^{2-}]$$
$$(5.0 \times 10^{-2})(1.2 \times 10^{-21}) = 6.0 \times 10^{-23}$$

This ion product is greater than the K_{SP} of PbS; therefore, PbS will precipitate. The ion product, however, is less than the K_{SP} of FeS. The solubility of FeS has not been exceeded. No FeS will form.

Example 18.11

What must be the H^+ concentration of a solution that is $0.050\ M$ in Ni^{2+} to prevent the precipitation of NiS when the solution is saturated with H_2S? The K_{SP} of NiS is 3×10^{-21}.

Solution

$$[Ni^{2+}][S^{2-}] = 3 \times 10^{-21}$$
$$(0.050)[S^{2-}] = 3 \times 10^{-21}$$
$$[S^{2-}] = 6 \times 10^{-20}\ M$$

Therefore, the $[S^{2-}]$ must be less than $6 \times 10^{-20}\ M$ if NiS is not to precipitate. For a solution saturated with H_2S,

$$[H^+]^2[S^{2-}] = 1.1 \times 10^{-22}$$
$$[H^+]^2(6 \times 10^{-20}) = 1.1 \times 10^{-22}$$
$$[H^+] = 0.04\ M$$

The $[H^+]$ must be greater than $0.04\ M$ to prevent the precipitation of NiS.

The preceding examples illustrate an important analytical technique. In the usual qualitative analysis scheme, certain cations are separated into groups on the basis of whether their sulfides precipitate in acidic solution. In a solution that has an H^+ concentration of $0.3\ M$, the sulfides of Hg^{2+}, Pb^{2+}, Cu^{2+}, Bi^{3+}, Cd^{2+}, and Sn^{2+} are insoluble, whereas the sulfides of Fe^{2+}, Co^{2+}, Ni^{2+}, Mn^{2+}, and Zn^{2+} are soluble.

In considering systems that involve sulfide precipitation, one must note that the H^+ concentration of a solution increases when a sulfide precipitates from the solution.

Example 18.12

A solution that is $0.050\ M$ in Cd^{2+} and $0.10\ M$ in H^+ is saturated with H_2S. What concentration of Cd^{2+} remains in solution after CdS has precipitated? The K_{SP} of CdS is 1.0×10^{-28}.

Solution

For each Cd^{2+} ion precipitated, two H^+ ions are added to the solution:

$$Cd^{2+}(aq) + H_2S(aq) \rightleftharpoons CdS(s) + 2\,H^+(aq)$$

We shall assume that virtually all the Cd^{2+} precipitates as CdS. Hence, the precipitation introduces 0.10 mol of H^+ per liter of solution, and the final $[H^+]$ is $0.20\ M$. Therefore,

$$[H^+]^2[S^{2-}] = 1.1 \times 10^{-22}$$

$$(0.20)^2[S^{2-}] = 1.1 \times 10^{-22}$$

$$[S^{2-}] = 2.8 \times 10^{-21}$$

The concentration of Cd^{2+} after the CdS has precipitated may be derived from the K_{SP} of CdS:

$$[Cd^{2+}][S^{2-}] = 1.0 \times 10^{-28}$$

$$[Cd^{2+}](2.8 \times 10^{-21}) = 1.0 \times 10^{-28}$$

$$[Cd^{2+}] = 3.6 \times 10^{-8} \ M$$

From our answer we can see that our assumption was justified. The value of $[H^+]$ that we used was well within our limits of accuracy.

18.4 Equilibria Involving Complex Ions

Complex ions are discussed in Chapter 26. These ions, however, take part in some aqueous equilibria that should be discussed in this chapter. A **complex ion** is an aggregate consisting of a central metal cation (usually a transition-metal ion) surrounded by a number of ligands. The **ligands** of a complex may be anions, molecules, or a combination of the two.

A ligand must have an unshared pair of electrons with which it can bond to the central ion. Thus, the ammonia molecule, NH_3, functions as a ligand in the formation of complex ions—the ammonium ion, NH_4^+, does not:

In addition to ammonia, the requirement is met by many molecules and anions:

The charge of a complex ion can be found by adding the charges of all the particles of which it is composed. The charge of the $Fe(CN)_6^{4-}$ ion, for example, equals the sum of the charges of one Fe^{2+} ion and six CN^- ions:

$$Fe^{2+} + 6\,CN^- \longrightarrow Fe(CN)_6^{4-}$$

Examples of complex ions are: $Ag(NH_3)_2^+$, $Cd(NH_3)_4^{2+}$, $Cu(NH_3)_4^{2+}$, $Fe(CN)_6^{3-}$, $Fe(CN)_6^{4-}$, $CdCl_4^{2-}$, $Ag(S_2O_3)_3^{5-}$, $Cu(H_2O)_4^{2+}$, and $Zn(OH)_4^{2-}$.

All ions are hydrated in water solution. Most hydrated metal ions should be regarded as complex ions since each metal ion has a definite number of water molecules tightly bonded to it. This number is difficult to determine and is not known with certainty for some species. Nevertheless, in water solution, complexes probably form by the replacement of water ligands by other ligands. For example,

$$Cu(H_2O)_6^{2+} + NH_3 \rightleftharpoons Cu(H_2O)_5(NH_3)^{2+} + H_2O$$

For simplicity, however, the coordinated water molecules are usually not shown:

$$Cu^{2+} + NH_3 \rightleftharpoons Cu(NH_3)^{2+}$$

The dissociation, as well as the formation, of a complex ion occurs in steps. Thus, the $Ag(NH_3)_2^+$ ion dissociates as follows:

$$Ag(NH_3)_2^+ \rightleftharpoons Ag(NH_3)^+ + NH_3 \qquad K_{d1} = \frac{[Ag(NH_3)^+][NH_3]}{[Ag(NH_3)_2^+]}$$

$$= 1.4 \times 10^{-4}$$

$$Ag(NH_3)^+ \rightleftharpoons Ag^+ + NH_3 \qquad K_{d2} = \frac{[Ag^+][NH_3]}{[Ag(NH_3)^+]}$$

$$= 4.3 \times 10^{-4}$$

The product of the two dissociation constants is called the **instability constant** of the $Ag(NH_3)_2^+$ ion. This instability constant corresponds to the overall dissociation of the ion:

$$Ag(NH_3)_2^+ \rightleftharpoons Ag^+ + 2 NH_3$$

$$\left(\frac{[Ag(NH_3)^+][NH_3]}{[Ag(NH_3)_2^+]} \right) \left(\frac{[Ag^+][NH_3]}{[Ag(NH_3)^+]} \right) = \frac{[Ag^+][NH_3]^2}{[Ag(NH_3)_2^+]}$$

$$K_{inst} = K_{d1} K_{d2} = (1.4 \times 10^{-4})(4.3 \times 10^{-4}) = 6.0 \times 10^{-8}$$

The reciprocals of dissociation constants pertain to equilibrium reactions written in reverse form and are called **formation constants** or **stability constants.**

For many complexes the values of the equilibrium constants for the individual steps of the dissociation are not known, although the value for the overall dissociation may have been determined. Note, however, that an overall instability constant for a complex ion must be cautiously interpreted since the chemical equation to which it applies does not take into consideration any intermediate species. Some instability constants are given in the appendix.

Example 18.13

A 0.010 M solution of $AgNO_3$ is made 0.50 M in NH_3 and the $Ag(NH_3)_2^+$ complex forms. (a) What is the concentration of $Ag^+(aq)$ in the solution? (b) What percentage of the total concentration of silver is in the form $Ag^+(aq)$?

18.5 Amphoterism

The hydroxides of certain metals, called amphoteric hydroxides, can function as acids or bases. These water-insoluble compounds dissolve in solutions of low pH or high pH. Zinc hydroxide, for example, dissolves in hydrochloric acid to produce solutions of zinc chloride, $ZnCl_2$:

$$Zn(OH)_2(s) + 2H^+(aq) \longrightarrow Zn^{2+}(aq) + 2H_2O$$

Zinc hydroxide will also dissolve in sodium hydroxide solutions:

$$Zn(OH)_2(s) + 2OH^-(aq) \longrightarrow Zn(OH)_4^{2-}(aq)$$

The $Zn(OH)_4^{2-}$ complex ion is called the zincate ion. The oxide corresponding to an amphoteric hydroxide reacts in the same way. For example,

$$ZnO(s) + 2H^+(aq) \longrightarrow Zn^{2+}(aq) + H_2O$$
$$ZnO(s) + 2OH^-(aq) + H_2O \longrightarrow Zn(OH)_4^{2-}(aq)$$

Other examples of amphoteric compounds are $Al(OH)_3$, $Sn(OH)_2$, $Cr(OH)_3$, $Be(OH)_2$, Sb_2O_3, and As_2O_3. Many other compounds, including $Cu(OH)_2$ and Ag_2O, exhibit this property to a lesser degree.

The following series of equations can be used to describe the reactions that occur when the OH^- concentration of a $Zn^{2+}(aq)$ solution is gradually increased:

$$Zn^{2+}(aq) + OH^-(aq) \rightleftharpoons Zn(OH)^+(aq)$$
$$Zn(OH)^+(aq) + OH^-(aq) \rightleftharpoons Zn(OH)_2(s)$$
$$Zn(OH)_2(s) + OH^-(aq) \rightleftharpoons Zn(OH)_3^-(aq)$$
$$Zn(OH)_3^-(aq) + OH^-(aq) \rightleftharpoons Zn(OH)_4^{2-}(aq)$$

The precipitation of $Zn(OH)_2$ is observed when the proper pH is reached, and upon further increase in pH, the precipitate dissolves. The formulas of the amphoterate anions used here are based upon the fact that $NaZn(OH)_3$ and $Na_2Zn(OH)_4$ have been isolated from such solutions.

The process can be reversed. Acidification of solutions of the zincate ion results in the stepwise removal of OH^-. For example,

$$Zn(OH)_4^{2-}(aq) + H^+(aq) \rightleftharpoons Zn(OH)_3^-(aq) + H_2O$$

The cation of an amphoteric hydroxide has the ability to form complex ions with H_2O and OH^-. Equations for the preceding reactions can be written showing coordinated water molecules. For example,

$$Zn(H_2O)_6^{2+}(aq) + OH^-(aq) \rightleftharpoons Zn(OH)(H_2O)_5^+(aq) + H_2O$$

The reactions can be interpreted, therefore, as replacements of the ligands of the zinc-complex ion. In the Brønsted interpretation of this reaction, the $Zn(H_2O)_6^{2+}$ ion is an acid that releases a proton to the OH^- ion, a base.

In general, amphoteric systems are very complicated and much remains to be learned about them. The equilibrium constants are of doubtful validity. Indeed, there is evidence that not all the ions and equilibria in systems of this type have been identified. Probably the reactions of most systems are much more complicated than we have depicted them.

We have considered only mononuclear complexes (complexes with but a single coordinated metal ion). Polynuclear complexes, however, appear to be common; $Sn_2(OH)_2^{2+}$ and $Sn_3(OH)_4^{2+}$ as well as $SnOH^+$ have been identified in Sn^{2+} solutions. The formula of the aluminate ion is usually written as $Al(OH)_4^-$, and such a tetrahedral ion has been identified in 0.1 M to 1.5 M aluminate solutions in which the pH is 13 or higher. Under other conditions, however, polynuclear complexes of aluminum are thought to occur.

Advantage is taken of the amphoteric nature of some hydroxides in analytical chemistry and in some commercial processes. For example, Mg^{2+} and Zn^{2+} may be separated from a solution containing the two ions by making the solution alkaline:

$$Mg^{2+} + 2\,OH^- \rightleftharpoons Mg(OH)_2(s)$$

$$Zn^{2+} + 4\,OH^- \rightleftharpoons Zn(OH)_4^{2-}$$

The insoluble magnesium hydroxide, which is not amphoteric, may be removed by filtration from the solution containing the zincate ion.

In the production of aluminum metal from bauxite (impure hydrated Al_2O_3), the ore is purified prior to its reduction to aluminum metal. This purification is accomplished by dissolving the aluminum oxide in a solution of sodium hydroxide and removing the insoluble impurities by filtration:

$$Al_2O_3(s) + 2\,OH^- + 3\,H_2O \longrightarrow 2\,Al(OH)_4^-$$

When the filtered solution is acidified, pure aluminum hydroxide precipitates and is recovered.

Summary

An *equilibrium* between a *slightly soluble compound* and a saturated aqueous solution of its *ions* is described by a type of equilibrium constant called a *solubility product*, K_{SP}. The numerical value of a K_{SP} can be found from the molar solubility of the compound in question. In turn, a K_{SP} can be used to calculate the solubility of the corresponding salt.

The numerical *value of the* K_{SP} of a salt is a quantitative statement of the *limit of solubility* of the salt. An *ion product* is a value obtained by substituting proposed ionic concentrations into an expression similar to that of the K_{SP}. If the ion product is *less* than the K_{SP}, the solution is *unsaturated*. If the ion product is *greater* than the K_{SP}, a *precipitate* will form. If the ion product is *equal* to the K_{SP}, the solution is *saturated* and the system is in equilibrium, but *no precipitate* will form.

The *common-ion effect* influences solubility equilibria. The *addition of a common ion* causes virtually *complete precipitation*. The common-ion effect can also be used to *prevent* the formation of a precipitate. The concentration of OH^- from the dissociation of NH_3 can be held to a low level by the addition of the common ion NH_4^+, and in this way the precipitation of a hydroxide can be prevented.

The *precipitation of sulfides* can be controlled by adjusting the acidity of the solution. The higher the concentration of H^+ in a saturated H_2S solution, the lower the concentration of S^{2-}; at 25°C: $[H^+]^2[S^{2-}] = 1.1 \times 10^{-22}$. Hence, *certain sulfides can be precipitated in solutions that are 0.30 M in H^+, other sulfides cannot* be.

Complex ions exist in aqueous solution in equilibrium with their components. The dissociation, as well as the formation, of a complex ion occurs in steps. The product of the stepwise equilibrium constants is called the *instability constant* for the complex ion. The reciprocals of these constants are called *formation constants*. Slightly soluble substances can often be dissolved through the formation of complex ions.

Certain hydroxides, called *amphoteric hydroxides*, can function as *acids* or *bases*. These hydroxides dissolve in solutions of low or high *p*H. Zinc hydroxide, $Zn(OH)_2$, for example, dissolves in $H^+(aq)$ to form the $Zn^{2+}(aq)$ ion, and in $OH^-(aq)$ to form the $Zn(OH)_4^{2-}(aq)$ ion. Separation of a metal hydroxide that is amphoteric from one that is not can be accomplished by using an *alkaline solution*; the *amphoteric hydroxide will dissolve*, the other will not.

Key Terms

Some of the more important terms introduced in this chapter are listed below. Definitions for terms not included in this list may be located in the text by use of the index.

Amphoterism (Section 18.5) A property of the hydroxides of certain metals that permits them to function as acids or bases; amphoteric substances are water-insoluble and dissolve in solutions of low *p*H or high *p*H.

Complex ion (Section 18.4) An aggregate consisting of a central metal cation surrounded by a number of ligands.

Instability constant (Section 18.4) An equilibrium constant for the overall dissociation of a complex ion into a metal cation and ligands; the reciprocal is called a **formation constant**.

Ion product (Section 18.2) A value obtained by substituting proposed concentrations into an expression simi-

lar to that of the solubility product. The value of the ion product is compared to the value of the K_{SP} to determine whether a precipitate will form when the ion concentrations are adjusted to the proposed values. If the ion product is larger than the K_{SP}, a precipitate will form.

Ligand (Section 18.4) An anion or a molecule that has an unshared pair of electrons with which it can bond to a metal cation in the formation of a complex ion.

Salt effect (Section 18.1) The increase in solubility of a slightly soluble substance observed following the addition of another electrolyte to the solution.

Solubility product, K_{SP} (Section 18.1) The equilibrium constant for a system involving a slightly soluble substance in equilibrium with a saturated solution of its ions. The constant is the product of the ion concentrations, with the concentrations raised to the powers indicated by the coefficients of the balanced chemical equation.

Problems*

The Solubility Product

18.1 Write the expression for the K_{SP} for each of the following compounds: **(a)** Bi_2S_3, **(b)** $PbCrO_4$, **(c)** $Ag_2C_2O_4$, **(d)** $AgIO_3$.

18.2 Write an expression for the K_{SP} for each of the following compounds: **(a)** PbI_2, **(b)** $Cr(OH)_3$, **(c)** $Ba_3(PO_4)_2$, **(d)** Hg_2Cl_2.

18.3 At 25°C, 1.7×10^{-5} mol of $Cd(OH)_2$ is dissolved in 1.0 L of saturated solution. Calculate the K_{SP} of $Cd(OH)_2$.

18.4 At 25°C, 5.2×10^{-6} mol of $Ce(OH)_3$ is dissolved in 1.0 L of saturated solution. Calculate the K_{sp} of $Ce(OH)_3$.

18.5 At 25°C, the concentration of IO_3^- ion in a saturated $Ba(IO_3)_2$ solution is 5.5×10^{-4} *M*. What is the K_{SP} of $Ba(IO_3)_2$?

18.6 At 25°C, the concentration of Pb^{2+} ion in a saturated

$Pb(IO_3)_2$ solution is 4.0×10^{-5} *M*. What is the K_{SP} of $Pb(IO_3)_2$?

18.7 Use K_{SP} values to determine whether Ag_2CO_3 or $CuCO_3$ has the lower molar solubility.

18.8 Use K_{SP} values to determine whether Ag_2S or CuS has the lower molar solubility.

18.9 Use the K_{SP} value to determine the molar solubility of SrF_2.

18.10 Use the K_{SP} value to determine the molar solubility of $Ag_2C_2O_4$.

18.11 How many moles of $Ni(OH)_2$ will dissolve in 1.0 L of a solution of NaOH with a *p*H of 12.34?

18.12 How many moles of $Cu(OH)_2$ will dissolve in 1.0 L of a solution of NaOH with a *p*H of 8.23?

18.13 How many moles of BaF_2 will dissolve in 250. mL of a 0.12 *M* NaF solution?

18.14 How many moles of $PbBr_2$ will dissolve in 150. mL of a 0.25 *M* NaBr solution?

---

* The appendix contains answers to color-keyed problems.

Precipitation and K_{SP}

18.15 Calculate the final concentrations of $Na^+(aq)$, $C_2O_4^{2-}(aq)$, $Ba^{2+}(aq)$, and $Cl^-(aq)$ in a solution prepared by adding 100. mL of 0.20 M $Na_2C_2O_4$ to 150. mL of 0.25 M $BaCl_2$.

18.16 Calculate the final concentrations of $Sr^{2+}(aq)$, $NO_3^-(aq)$, $Na^+(aq)$, and $F^-(aq)$ in a solution prepared by adding 50. mL of 0.30 M $Sr(NO_3)_2$ to 150. mL of 0.12 M NaF.

18.17 What concentration of F^- is necessary to start the precipitation of SrF_2 from a saturated solution of $SrSO_4$?

18.18 What concentration of SO_4^{2-} is necessary to start the precipitation of $BaSO_4$ from a saturated solution of BaF_2?

18.19 What minimum concentration of NH_4^+ is necessary to prevent the formation of a $Fe(OH)_2$ precipitate from a solution that is 0.020 M in Fe^{2+} and 0.020 M in NH_3?

18.20 What minimum concentration of NH_4^+ is necessary to prevent the formation of a $Mn(OH)_2$ precipitate from a solution that is 0.030 M in Mn^{2+} and 0.030 M in NH_3?

18.21 A solution is 0.090 M in Mg^{2+} and 0.33 M in NH_4^+. What minimum concentration of NH_3 will cause $Mg(OH)_2$ to precipitate?

18.22 A solution is 0.030 M in Mn^{2+} and 0.025 M in NH_4^+. What minimum concentration of NH_3 will cause $Mn(OH)_2$ to precipitate?

18.23 If 20. mL of a 0.015 M $Pb(NO_3)_2$ solution and 50. mL of a 0.020 M solution of $NaCl$ are mixed, will $PbCl_2$ precipitate?

18.24 If 30. mL of a 0.040 M $Mg(NO_3)_2$ solution and 70. mL of a 0.020 M solution of NaF are mixed, will MgF_2 precipitate?

18.25 If 25 mL of a 0.050 M $CaCl_2$ solution and 50. mL of a 0.020 M Na_2SO_4 solution are mixed, will $CaSO_4$ precipitate?

18.26 If 5.0 mL of a 0.30 M $AgNO_3$ solution and 7.5 mL of a 0.015 M Na_2SO_4 solution are mixed, will Ag_2SO_4 precipitate?

18.27 A solution is 0.15 M in Pb^{2+} and 0.20 M in Ag^+. **(a)** If solid Na_2SO_4 is very slowly added to this solution, which will precipitate first, $PbSO_4$ or Ag_2SO_4? Neglect volume changes. **(b)** The addition of Na_2SO_4 is continued until the second cation just starts to precipitate as the sulfate. What is the concentration of the first cation at this point?

18.28 A solution is 0.10 M in CrO_4^{2-} and 0.15 M in SO_4^{2-}. **(a)** If solid $Ba(NO_3)_2$ is very slowly added to this solution, which will precipitate first, $BaCrO_4$ or $BaSO_4$? Neglect volume changes. **(b)** The addition of $Ba(NO_3)_2$ is continued until the second anion just starts to precipitate as the barium salt. What is the concentration of the first anion at this point?

Precipitation of Sulfides

18.29 A solution that is 0.30 M in $H^+(aq)$ and 0.15 M in Ni^{2+} is saturated with H_2S. Will NiS precipitate?

18.30 A solution that is 0.25 M in $H^+(aq)$ and 0.10 M in Co^{2+} is saturated with H_2S. Will CoS precipitate?

18.31 What is the lowest concentration of $H^+(aq)$ that must be present in a 0.25 M solution of Mn^{2+} to prevent the precipitation of MnS when the solution is saturated with H_2S?

18.32 What is the lowest concentration of $H^+(aq)$ that must be present in a 0.50 M solution of Zn^{2+} to prevent the precipitation of ZnS when the solution is saturated with H_2S?

18.33 What concentration of $H^+(aq)$ should be present in a solution that is 0.20 M in Ni^{2+} and 0.20 M in Cd^{2+} so that when the solution is saturated with H_2S the maximum possible amount of CdS will precipitate but no NiS will precipitate at any stage?

18.34 What concentration of $H^+(aq)$ should be present in a solution that is 0.20 M in Pb^{2+} and 0.20 M in Zn^{2+} so that when the solution is saturated with H_2S the maximum possible amount of PbS will precipitate but no ZnS will precipitate at any stage?

18.35 A solution that is 0.20 M in $H^+(aq)$ and 0.20 M in $Pb^{2+}(aq)$ is saturated with H_2S. What concentration of $Pb^{2+}(aq)$ remains in solution after PbS has precipitated? Note that it is necessary to take into account the increase in acidity caused by the precipitation. Use 7.0×10^{-29} as the K_{SP} for PbS.

18.36 A solution that is 0.010 M in $H^+(aq)$ and 0.025 M in $Sn^{2+}(aq)$ is saturated with H_2S. What concentration of $Sn^{2+}(aq)$ remains in solution after SnS has precipitated? Note that it is necessary to take into account the increase in acidity caused by the precipitation. Use 1.0×10^{-26} as the K_{SP} for SnS.

Complex Ions

18.37 Compare the molar solubilities of **(a)** $AgCl$, **(b)** $AgBr$, and **(c)** AgI in 0.50 M NH_3 solution.

18.38 A 0.010 M solution of $AgNO_3$ is made 0.50 M in NH_3, thus forming the $Ag(NH_3)_2^+$ complex ion. Will $AgCl$ precipitate if sufficient $NaCl$ is added to make the solution 0.010 M in Cl^-?

Unclassified Problems

18.39 How many moles of Ag_2CO_3 will dissolve in 150. mL of a 0.15 M solution of Na_2CO_3 solution?

18.40 A saturated solution of a slightly soluble hydroxide, $M(OH)_2$, has a pH of 9.53. What is the K_{SP} of $M(OH)_2$?

18.41 A solution is prepared by mixing 10. mL of 0.50 M $CaCl_2$ with 10. mL of a solution that is 0.50 M in NH_3 and 0.050 M in NH_4^+. Will $Ca(OH)_2$ precipitate?

18.42 A solution that is 0.50 M in $H^+(aq)$ and 0.030 M in Cd^{2+} is saturated with H_2S. Will CdS precipitate?

18.43 A solution that is 0.10 M in $H^+(aq)$, 0.30 M in $Cu^{2+}(aq)$, and 0.30 M in $Fe^{2+}(aq)$ is saturated with H_2S.

Calculate the concentrations of $H^+(aq)$, $S^{2-}(aq)$, $Cu^{2+}(aq)$, and $Fe^{2+}(aq)$. Note that it is necessary to take into account any increase in acidity caused by the precipitation of a sulfide. Use 8.0×10^{-37} as the K_{SP} for CuS and 4.0×10^{-19} as the K_{SP} for FeS.

ELEMENTS OF CHEMICAL THERMODYNAMICS

CHAPTER 19

Thermodynamics is the study of the energy changes that accompany physical and chemical changes. An important aspect of the laws of chemical thermodynamics is that they enable us to predict whether a particular chemical reaction is theoretically possible under a given set of conditions. A reaction that has a natural tendency to occur of its own accord is said to be spontaneous. Thermodynamic principles can also be used to determine the extent of a spontaneous reaction— the position of equilibrium.

Thermodynamics, however, has nothing to say about the rate or mechanism of a spontaneous reaction. These questions are the concern of chemical kinetics (see Chapter 14). Some spontaneous changes occur extremely slowly. The stable form of carbon under ordinary conditions is graphite, not diamond. The change from diamond to graphite, therefore, is thermodynamically spontaneous. This change, however, is so extremely slow that it is not observed at ordinary temperatures and pressures.

9.1 First Law of Thermodynamics

Many scientists of the late-eighteenth and early-nineteenth centuries studied the relationship between work and heat. Thermodynamics had its origins in these studies. By the 1840s it became clear that

1. Work and heat are both forms of a larger classification called energy.

2. One form of energy can be converted into another form.

3. Energy cannot be created or destroyed.

The first law of thermodynamics is the law of conservation of energy: energy can be converted from one form into another but it cannot be created or destroyed. In other words, the total energy of the universe is a constant.

In applying thermodynamic concepts, we frequently confine our attention to the changes that occur within definite boundaries. The portion of nature that is included within these boundaries is called a system. The remainder is called the surroundings. A mixture of chemical compounds, for example, can constitute a system. The container and everything else around the system make up what is called the surroundings.

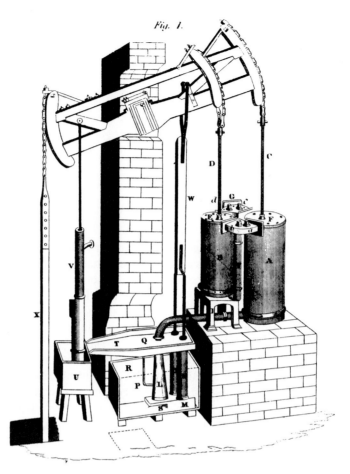

Thermodynamics began with the study of steam engines.
The steam engine shown here is of the earliest type—
invented by Newcomen. *The Bettman Archive*.

A system is assumed to have an internal energy, *E*, which includes all possible forms of energy attributable to the system. Important contributions to the internal energy of a system include the attractions and repulsions between the atoms, molecules, ions, and subatomic particles that make up the system, and the kinetic energies of all of its parts.

According to the first law of thermodynamics, the internal energy of an *isolated* system is constant. The actual value of *E* for any system is not known and cannot be calculated. Thermodynamics, however, is concerned only with *changes* in internal energy, and these changes can be measured.

The state of a system can be defined by specifying the values of properties such as temperature, pressure, and composition. The internal energy of a system depends upon the state of the system and not upon how the system arrived at that state. Internal energy is therefore called a state function. Consider a sample of an ideal gas that occupies a volume of 1 L at 100 K and 1 atm pressure (state A). At 200 K and 0.5 atm (state B), the sample occupies a volume of 4 L. According to the first law, the internal energy of the system in state A, E_A, is a constant, as is the internal energy of the system in state B, E_B.

It follows that the difference in the internal energies of the two states, ΔE, is also a constant and is independent of the path taken between state A and state B.

It makes no difference whether the gas is heated before the pressure change, whether the heating is done after the pressure change, or, indeed, whether the total change is brought about in several steps:

$$\Delta E = E_B - E_A$$

Suppose that we have a system in an *initial* state and that the internal energy of the system is E_i. If the system absorbs heat from the surroundings, q, the internal energy of the system will now be

$$E_i + q$$

If the system now uses some of its internal energy to do work on the surroundings, w, the internal energy of the system in the *final* state, E_f, will be

$$E_f = E_i + q - w$$
$$E_f - E_i = q - w$$
$$\Delta E = q - w \tag{19.1}$$

It is important to keep in mind the conventions regarding the signs of these quantities:

q, positive = heat *absorbed* by the system

q, negative = heat *evolved* by the system

w, positive = work done *by* the system

w, negative = work done *on* the system

The values of q and w involved in changing a system from an initial state to a final state depend upon the way in which the change is carried out. The value of $(q - w)$, however, is a constant, equal to ΔE, for the change no matter how it is brought about. If a system undergoes a change in which the internal energy of the system remains constant, the work done by the system equals the heat absorbed by the system.

9.2 Enthalpy

For ordinary chemical reactions, the work term generally arises as a consequence of pressure-volume changes. The work done against the pressure of the atmosphere if the system expands in the course of the reaction (because gases are produced) is an example of pressure-volume work. The term PV has the dimensions of work. Pressure, which is force per unit area, may be expressed in newtons per square meter (N/m^2). If volume is expressed in cubic meters (m^3), the product PV is

$$PV = (N/m^2)(m^3) = N \cdot m$$

The newton·meter (which is a joule) is a unit of work, since work is defined as force (the newton) times distance (the meter). In like manner, liter·atmospheres are units of work. If the pressure is held constant, the work done in expansion from V_A to V_B is

$$w = P(V_B - V_A) = P\Delta V \tag{19.2}$$

No pressure-volume work can be done by a process carried out at constant volume, and $w = 0$. Thus, at *constant volume* the equation

$$\Delta E = q - w$$

becomes

$$\Delta E = q_v \tag{19.3}$$

where q_v is the heat absorbed by the system at constant volume.

Processes carried out at constant pressure are far more common in chemistry than those conducted at constant volume. If we restrict our attention to pressure-volume work, the work done in constant pressure processes is $P\Delta V$. Thus, at *constant pressure* the equation

$$\Delta E = q - w$$

becomes

$$\Delta E = q_P - P\Delta V$$

Or, by rearranging,

$$q_P = \Delta E + P\Delta V \tag{19.4}$$

where q_P is the heat absorbed by the system at constant pressure.

The thermodynamic function enthalpy, H, is defined by the equation

$$H = E + PV \tag{19.5}$$

Therefore,

$$q_P = \Delta H \tag{19.6}$$

The heat absorbed by a reaction conducted at constant pressure is equal to the change in enthalpy. Enthalpy, like internal energy, is a function of the state of the system and is independent of the manner in which the state was achieved. The validity of the law of Hess rests on this fact (see Section 5.5).

When a bomb calorimeter is used to make a calorimetric determination (see Section 5.3), the heat effect is measured at constant volume. Ordinarily, reactions are run at constant pressure. The relationship between change in enthalpy and change in internal energy is used to convert heats of reaction at constant volume ($q_V = \Delta E$) to heats of reaction at constant pressure ($q_P = \Delta H$). The conversion is made by considering the change in volume of the products. The changes in the volumes of liquids and solids are so small that they are neglected.

For reactions involving gases, however, volume changes may be significant. Let us say that V_A is the total volume of gaseous reactants, V_B is the total volume of gaseous products, n_A is the number of moles of gaseous reactants, n_B is the number of moles of gaseous products, and the pressure and temperature are constant:

$$PV_A = n_A RT \text{ and } PV_B = n_B RT$$

Thus,

$$\begin{aligned} P\,\Delta V &= PV_B - PV_A \\ &= n_B RT - n_A RT \\ &= (n_B - n_A)RT \\ &= (\Delta n)RT \end{aligned} \tag{19.7}$$

Since

$$\Delta H = \Delta E + P\,\Delta V \tag{19.8}$$

then,

$$\Delta H = \Delta E + (\Delta n)RT \tag{19.9}$$

where Δn is the number of moles of gaseous products minus the number of moles of gaseous reactants.

In order to solve problems using this equation, we must express the value of R in appropriate units. We have noted that liter·atmospheres are units of energy. The value of R, 0.082057 L·atm/(K·mol), may be converted to J/(K·mol) by use of factors derived from the relations

$$1 \text{ atm} = 1.01325 \times 10^5 \text{ N/m}^2$$

$$1 \text{ L} = 1 \times 10^{-3} \text{ m}^3$$

$$1 \text{ J} = 1 \text{ N·m}$$

Thus,

$$8.2057 \times 10^{-2} \frac{\text{L·atm}}{\text{K·mol}} \left(\frac{1.01325 \times 10^5 \text{ N/m}^2}{1 \text{ atm}} \right) \left(\frac{10^{-3} \text{ m}^3}{1 \text{ L}} \right) \left(\frac{1 \text{ J}}{1 \text{ N·m}} \right)$$

$$= 8.3144 \text{ J/(K·mol)}$$

Various types of calculations involving enthalpy changes are a topic of Chapter 5. A list of standard enthalpies of formation is found in Table 5.1.

Example 19.1

The heat of combustion at constant volume of $CH_4(g)$ is measured in a bomb calorimeter at 25°C and is found to be -885.4 kJ/mol. What is ΔH?

Solution

For the reaction

$$CH_4(g) + 2\,O_2(g) \longrightarrow CO_2(g) + 2\,H_2O(l) \qquad \Delta E = -885.4 \text{ kJ}$$

$$\Delta n = \text{(moles gaseous products)} - \text{(moles gaseous reactants)}$$
$$= (1 \text{ mol}) - (1 \text{ mol} + 2 \text{ mol}) = -2 \text{ mol}$$

Therefore,

$$\Delta H = \Delta E + (\Delta n)RT$$
$$= -885.4 \text{ kJ} + (-2 \text{ mol})[8.314 \text{ J/(K·mol)}](298.2 \text{ K})$$
$$= -885.4 \text{ kJ} - 4958 \text{ J}$$
$$= -885.4 \text{ kJ} - 5.0 \text{ kJ} = -890.4 \text{ kJ}$$

Example 19.2

Calculate $\Delta H°$ and $\Delta E°$ for the reaction

$$OF_2(g) + H_2O(g) \longrightarrow O_2(g) + 2\,HF(g)$$

The standard enthalpies of formation are $OF_2(g)$, $+23.0$ kJ/mol; $H_2O(g)$, -241.8 kJ/mol; and $HF(g)$, -268.6 kJ/mol.

Solution

The standard enthalpies of formation are used to calculate $\Delta H°$ for the reaction (see Section 5.6):

$$\Delta H° = 2\Delta H_f°(HF) - [\Delta H_f°(OF_2) + \Delta H_f°(H_2O)]$$
$$= 2(-268.6 \text{ kJ}) - [(+23.0 \text{ kJ}) + (-241.8 \text{ kJ})]$$
$$= -537.2 \text{ kJ} + 218.8 \text{ kJ} = -318.4 \text{ kJ}$$

This value of $\Delta H°$ is used to find $\Delta E°$. For the reaction $\Delta n = +1$ mol,

$$\Delta E° = \Delta H° - (\Delta n)RT$$
$$= -318.4 \text{ kJ} - (1 \text{ mol})[(8.314 \text{ J/(K·mol)}](298.2 \text{ K})$$
$$= -318.4 \text{ kJ} - 2479 \text{ J}$$
$$= -318.4 \text{ kJ} - 2.5 \text{ kJ} = -320.9 \text{ kJ}$$

Example 19.3

For the reaction

$$B_2H_6(g) + 3\,O_2(g) \longrightarrow B_2O_3(s) + 3\,H_2O(l)$$

$\Delta E°$ is -2143.2 kJ. (a) Calculate $\Delta H°$ for the reaction. (b) Determine the value of the standard enthalpy of formation of $B_2H_6(g)$. For $B_2O_3(s)$, $\Delta H_f° = -1264.0$ kJ/mol and for $H_2O(l)$, $\Delta H_f° = -285.9$ kJ/mol.

Solution

(a) $\Delta n = -4$. Therefore,

$$\Delta H° = \Delta E° + (\Delta n)RT$$
$$= -2143.2 \text{ kJ} + (-4 \text{ mol})[8.31 \times 10^{-3} \text{ kJ/(K·mol)}](298 \text{ K})$$
$$= -2143.2 \text{ kJ} - 9.91 \text{ kJ}$$
$$= -2153.1 \text{ kJ}$$

(b) $\quad \Delta H° = \Delta H_f°(B_2O_3) + 3\,\Delta H_f°(H_2O) - \Delta H_f°(B_2H_6)$

$-2153.1 \text{ kJ} = (-1264.0 \text{ kJ}) + 3(-285.9 \text{ kJ}) - \Delta H_f°(B_2H_6)$

$\Delta H_f°(B_2H_6) = +31.4 \text{ kJ}$

.3 Second Law of Thermodynamics

The first law of thermodynamics puts only one restriction on chemical or physical changes—energy must be conserved. The first law, however, provides no basis for determining whether a proposed change will be spontaneous. The second law of thermodynamics establishes criteria for making this important prediction.

The thermodynamic function *entropy*, S, is central to the second law. Entropy may be interpreted as a measure of the randomness, or disorder, of a system. A highly disordered system is said to have a high entropy. Since a disordered condition is more probable than an ordered one, entropy may be regarded as a probability function. One statement of the *second law of thermodynamics* is: every spontaneous change is accompanied by an increase in entropy.

As an example of a spontaneous change, consider the mixing of two ideal gases. The two gases, which are under the same pressure, are placed in bulbs that are joined by a stopcock (see Figure 19.1). When the stopcock is opened, the gases spontaneously mix until each is evenly distributed throughout the entire apparatus. Why did this spontaneous change occur? The first law cannot help us answer this question. Throughout the mixing, the volume, total pressure, and temperature remain constant. Since the gases are ideal, no intermolecular forces exist, and neither the internal energy nor the enthalpy of the system is affected.

This change represents an increase in entropy. The final state is more random and hence more probable than the initial state. The random motion of the gas molecules has produced a more disordered condition. The fact that the gases mix spontaneously is not surprising; one would have predicted it from experience. Indeed, it would be surprising if the reverse were to be observed—a gaseous mixture spontaneously separating into two pure gases, each occupying one of the bulbs.

For a given substance the solid, crystalline state is the state of lowest entropy (most ordered); the gaseous state is the state of highest entropy (most random); and the liquid state is intermediate between the other two. Hence, when a substance either melts or vaporizes, its entropy increases. The reverse changes crystallization and condensation, are changes in which the entropy of the substance decreases. Why, then, should a substance spontaneously freeze at temperatures below its melting point, since this change represents a decrease in the entropy of the substance?

All the entropy effects that result from the proposed change must be considered. When two ideal gases mix by the process previously described, there is no exchange of matter or energy between the isolated system in which the change occurs and its surroundings. The only entropy effect is an increase in the entropy of the isolated system itself. Usually, however, a chemical reaction or a physical change is conducted in such a way that the system is not isolated from its surroundings. The total change in entropy is equal to the sum of the change in the entropy of the system (ΔS_{system}) and the change in entropy of the surroundings ($\Delta S_{surroundings}$):

$$\Delta S_{total} = \Delta S_{system} + \Delta S_{surroundings} \qquad (19.10)$$

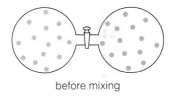

before mixing

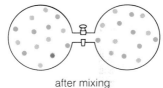

after mixing

Figure 19.1 Spontaneous mixing of two gases

Table 19.1 Entropy changes for the transformation $H_2O(l) \rightarrow H_2O(s)$ at 1 atm			
Temperature (°C)	ΔS_{system} [J/(K·mol)]	$\Delta S_{surroundings}$ (J/(K·mol))	ΔS_{total} [J/(K·mol)]
+1	−22.13	+22.05	−0.08
0	−21.99	+21.99	0
−1	−21.85	+21.93	+0.08

When a liquid freezes, the enthalpy of fusion is evolved by the liquid and absorbed by the surroundings. This energy increases the random motion of the surrounding molecules and therefore increases the entropy of the surroundings. The spontaneous freezing of a liquid at a temperature below the melting point occurs, therefore, because the decrease in entropy of the liquid (ΔS_{system}) is more than offset by the increase in entropy of the surroundings ($\Delta S_{surroundings}$), so that there is a net increase in entropy.

The *total* change in entropy should always be considered to determine spontaneity. When a substance melts, the entropy increases, but this effect alone does not determine whether or not the transformation is spontaneous. The entropy of the surroundings must also be considered, and spontaneity is indicated only if the total entropy of system and surroundings taken together increases.

The data of Table 19.1 pertain to the freezing of water. The meaning of the units of ΔS values will be discussed in later sections. For the moment, let us be concerned only with the numerical values listed in the table. At $-1°C$ the change is spontaneous; ΔS_{total} is positive. At $+1°C$, however, ΔS_{total} is negative, and freezing is not a spontaneous change. On the other hand, the reverse change, melting, is spontaneous at $+1°C$ (the signs of all ΔS values would be reversed).

At $0°C$, the melting point, ΔS_{total} is zero, which means that neither freezing nor melting is spontaneous. At this temperature a water-ice system would be in equilibrium, and no *net* change would be observed. Note, however, that freezing or melting can be made to occur at $0°C$ by removing or adding heat, but neither change will occur spontaneously.

Thus, the ΔS_{total} of a postulated change may be used as a criterion for whether the change will occur spontaneously. The entropy of the universe is steadily increasing as spontaneous changes occur. Rudolf Clausius summarized the first and second laws of thermodynamics as: "*The energy of the universe is constant; the entropy of the universe tends toward a maximum.*"

Entropy, like internal energy and enthalpy, is a state function. The entropy, or randomness, of a system in a given state is a definite value, and hence, ΔS for a change from one state to another is a definite value depending only on the initial and final states and not on the path between them.

It must be emphasized that, whereas thermodynamic concepts can be used to determine what changes are possible, thermodynamics has nothing to say about the rapidity of change. Some thermodynamically favored changes occur very slowly. Although reactions between carbon and oxygen, as well as between hydrogen and oxygen, at 25°C and 1 atm pressure are definitely predicted by theory, mixtures of carbon and oxygen and mixtures of hydrogen and oxygen can be kept for prolonged periods without significant reaction; such reactions are generally initiated by suitable means. Thermodynamics can authoritatively indicate postulated changes that will *not* occur and need not be attempted, and it can tell us how to alter the conditions of a presumably unfavored reaction in such a manner that the reaction will be thermodynamically possible.

19.4 Gibbs Free Energy

The type of change of primary interest to the chemist is, of course, the chemical reaction. The $\Delta S_{surroundings}$ for a reaction conducted at constant temperature and pressure may be calculated by means of the equation

$$\Delta S_{surroundings} = -\frac{\Delta H}{T} \tag{19.11}$$

where ΔH is the enthalpy change of the reaction and T is the absolute temperature. The change in the entropy of the surroundings is brought about by the heat transferred into or out of the surroundings because of the enthalpy change of the reaction. Since heat *evolved* by the reaction is *absorbed* by the surroundings (and *vice versa*), the sign of ΔH must be reversed. Hence, the larger the value of $-\Delta H$, the more disorder created in the surroundings and the larger the value of $\Delta S_{surroundings}$.

On the other hand, the change in the entropy of the surroundings is *inversely* proportional to the absolute temperature at which the change takes place. A given quantity of heat added to the surroundings at a low temperature (where the randomness is relatively low initially) will create a larger *difference* in the disorder of the surroundings than the same quantity of heat added at a high temperature (where the randomness is relatively high to begin with). Entropy is therefore measured in units of J/K.

In the last section we noted that

$$\Delta S_{total} = \Delta S_{system} + \Delta S_{surroundings} \tag{19.10}$$

If $-\Delta H/T$ is substituted for $\Delta S_{surrounding}$ and if the symbol ΔS (without a subscript) is used to indicate the entropy change of the system, the following equation is obtained:

$$\Delta S_{total} = \Delta S - \frac{\Delta H}{T} \tag{19.12}$$

Multiplication by T gives

$$T\Delta S_{total} = T\Delta S - \Delta H \tag{19.13}$$

By reversing the signs of the terms of this equation, we get

$$-T\Delta S_{total} = \Delta H - T\Delta S \tag{19.14}$$

We can use this equation to show how a function called the Gibbs free energy determines reaction spontaneity.

Gibbs free energy, G, is defined by the equation

$$G = H - TS \tag{19.15}$$

For a chemical reaction conducted at constant temperature and pressure,

$$\Delta G = \Delta H - T\Delta S \tag{19.16}$$

If we compare Equation 19.16 to Equation 19.14

$$-T\Delta S_{\text{total}} = \Delta H - T\Delta S \tag{19.14}$$

we see that

$$\Delta G = -T\Delta S_{\text{total}} \tag{19.17}$$

On the basis of this result, we note that

1. If ΔG is negative, the reaction is spontaneous. Since ΔS_{total} is greater than zero for a spontaneous change, $T\Delta S_{\text{total}}$ must also be greater than zero and $-T\Delta S_{\text{total}}$ must be less than zero. Therefore, for a spontaneous change at constant temperature and pressure,

$$\Delta G < 0$$

and when a spontaneous change occurs, the free energy of the system decreases.

The negative value of $T\Delta S_{\text{total}}$ is used in Equations 19.14 and 19.17 so that the signs of ΔG values will be like the signs of other energy terms. A *negative* value indicates that energy is *liberated* by the system.

2. If ΔG is zero, the system is in equilibrium. For a system in equilibrium, ΔS_{total} is zero and, therefore,

$$\Delta G = 0$$

3. If ΔG is positive, the reaction is not spontaneous. The reverse of the reaction, however, will be spontaneous.

Notice that all the terms in the very important equation

$$\Delta G = \Delta H - T\Delta S$$

pertain to changes in the properties of the *system*. The use of free-energy values, therefore, removes the need to consider changes in the surroundings. Notice also that each term in the equation is an energy term. Since ΔS is measured in J/K, the term $T\Delta S$ is expressed in J; ΔH and ΔG are also expressed in J.

Gibbs free energy is named for J. Willard Gibbs, who developed the application of thermodynamic concepts to chemistry. The change in Gibbs free energy, ΔG, combines two factors that influence reaction spontaneity:

$$\Delta G = \Delta H - T\Delta S$$

1. Reactions tend to seek a minimum in energy. Spontaneity is favored if the ΔH value is negative (the system liberates energy). A negative value of ΔH helps to make the ΔG value negative, which indicates a spontaneous reaction.

J. Willard Gibbs, 1839–1903.
*American Institute of Physics,
Niels Bohr Library.*

Table 19.2 Thermodynamic values for some chemical reactions at 25°C and 1 atm (kJ)			
Reaction	ΔH	$- \quad (T \Delta S)$	$= \quad \Delta G$
(a) $H_2(g) + Br_2(l) \longrightarrow 2\,HBr(g)$	-72.47	$- \; (+34.02)$	$= \; -106.49$
(b) $2\,H_2(g) + O_2(g) \longrightarrow 2\,H_2O(l)$	-571.70	$- \; (-97.28)$	$= \; -474.42$
(c) $Br_2(l) + Cl_2(g) \longrightarrow 2\,BrCl(g)$	$+29.37$	$- \; (+31.17)$	$= \; -1.80$
(d) $2\,Ag_2O(s) \longrightarrow 4\,Ag(s) + O_2(g)$	$+61.17$	$- \; (+39.50)$	$= \; +21.67$

2. Reactions tend to seek a maximum in randomness. Spontaneity is favored if the value of ΔS is positive (randomness increases). Since ΔS appears in the term $-T\Delta S$, a positive value of ΔS helps to make the value of ΔG negative, which indicates a spontaneous reaction.

The most favorable circumstance for a negative value of ΔG, which indicates a spontaneous reaction, is a negative value of ΔH together with a positive value of ΔS [see reaction (a) in Table 19.2]. It is possible, however, for a large negative value of ΔH to outweigh an unfavorable entropy change, resulting in a negative value of ΔG [see reaction (b) in Table 19.2]. In addition, a large positive value of $T\Delta S$ can overshadow an unfavorable enthalpy change, giving rise to a negative value of ΔG [see reaction (c) in Table 19.2]. For most chemical reactions at 25°C and 1 atm, the absolute value of ΔH is much larger than the value of $T\Delta S$. Under these conditions exothermic reactions are usually spontaneous no matter how the entropy changes.

With increasing temperature, however, the value of $T\Delta S$ increases and the influence of the entropy effect on ΔG increases. Usually, neither ΔH nor ΔS changes greatly with increasing temperature. The term $T\Delta S$, however, includes the temperature itself so that at high temperatures $T\Delta S$ can be sufficiently large to be the dominant influence on ΔG. For example, consider reaction (d) in Table 19.2 (a typical decomposition reaction) for which both ΔH and ΔS are positive. At 25°C, ΔH is larger than $T\Delta S$ and therefore ΔG is positive. If we assume that ΔS does not change with increasing temperature (the actual change is small), at 300°C the value of $T\Delta S$ would be $+75.95$ kJ because of the increase in the value of T. Consequently, $T\Delta S$ would be larger than ΔH (which also does not change greatly with increasing temperature), and ΔG would be negative.

The values in Table 19.2 pertain to the differences between the free energy of the products and the free energy of the reactants at 25°C and 1 atm. However, in some cases [notably reaction (c)] the reaction goes to an intermediate, equilibrium state rather than to completion because the free energy of the equilibrium state is lower than the free energy of the state at which the reaction is complete. Until equilibrium is discussed (see Section 19.7), we should refrain from drawing conclusions as to *the degree of completion* of a reaction from such data.

Table 19.3 is a summary of how the signs of ΔH and ΔS for a given reaction determine reaction spontaneity. For a reaction to be spontaneous, ΔG must be negative, and the sign of ΔG depends upon the signs of ΔH and ΔS:

$$\Delta G = \Delta H - T\Delta S$$

At low temperatures, the sign of ΔG is determined by the sign of ΔH. At high

Table 19.3 Effect of the signs of ΔH and ΔS on reaction spontaneity

ΔH	ΔS	$\Delta G = \Delta H - T\Delta S$	Remarks
−	+	−	Reaction spontaneous at all temperatures
+	−	+	Reaction nonspontaneous at all temperatures
−	−	− (at low T) + (at high T)	Reaction spontaneous at low temperatures Reaction nonspontaneous at high temperatures
+	+	+ (at low T) − (at high T)	Reaction nonspontaneous at low temperatures Reaction spontaneous at high temperatures

temperatures, since T appears in the term $-T\Delta S$, this term becomes the dominant factor in the calculation.

Gibbs free energy, like the other thermodynamic functions we have discussed, is a state function. The value of ΔG for a process depends only upon the final and initial states of the system and not upon the path taken between those states. When a spontaneous reaction occurs, the free energy of the system declines.

19.5 Standard Free Energies

A standard free energy change, which is given the symbol ΔG°, is the free-energy change for a process at 1 atm in which the reactants in their standard states are converted to the products in their standard states. The value of ΔG° for a reaction can be derived from standard free energies of formation in the same way that ΔH° values can be calculated from standard enthalpies of formation. Tabulated data usually consists of values measured at 25°C.

The standard free energy of formation of a compound, ΔG_f°, is defined as the change in standard free energies when 1 mol of the compound is formed from its constituent elements in their standard states. According to this definition, the standard free energy of formation of any element in its standard state is zero. The value of ΔG° for a reaction is equal to the sum of the standard free energies of formation of the products minus the sum of the standard free energies of formation of the reactants. Some standard free energies of formation are given in Table 19.4.

Example 19.4

Use ΔG_f° values from Table 19.4 to calculate ΔG° for the transformation

$$2\,NO(g) + O_2(g) \longrightarrow 2\,NO_2(g)$$

Solution

$$\begin{aligned}
\Delta G^\circ &= 2\Delta G_f^\circ(NO_2) - 2\Delta G_f^\circ(NO) \\
&= 2(+51.84\text{ kJ}) - 2(+86.69\text{ kJ}) \\
&= -69.70\text{ kJ}
\end{aligned}$$

Table 19.4   Gibbs free energy of formation (kJ/mol) at 25°C and 1 atm

Compound	ΔG_f°	Compound	ΔG_f°
$AgCl(s)$	−109.70	Fe_2O_3	−741.0
$Al_2O_3(s)$	−1576.41	$HBr(g)$	−53.22
$BaCO_3(s)$	−1138.9	$HCl(g)$	−95.27
$BaO(s)$	−528.4	$HF(g)$	−270.7
$CaCO_3(s)$	−1128.76	$HI(g)$	+1.30
$CaO(s)$	−604.2	$H_2O(g)$	−228.61
$Ca(OH)_2(s)$	−896.76	$H_2O(l)$	−237.19
$CH_4(g)$	−50.79	$H_2S(g)$	−33.0
$C_2H_2(g)$	+209.20	$NaCl(s)$	−384.05
$C_2H_4(g)$	+68.12	$NH_3(g)$	−16.7
$C_2H_6(g)$	−32.89	$NO(g)$	+86.69
$C_6H_6(l)$	+129.66	$NO_2(g)$	+51.84
$CO(g)$	−137.28	$SO_2(g)$	−300.37
$CO_2(g)$	−394.38	$ZnO(s)$	−318.19

19.6 Absolute Entropies

The addition of heat to a substance results in an increase in molecular randomness. Hence, the entropy of a substance increases as the temperature increases. Conversely, cooling a substance makes it more ordered and decreases its entropy. At absolute zero the entropy of a perfect crystalline substance may be taken as zero. This statement is sometimes called the **third law of thermodynamics** and was first formulated by Walther Nernst in 1906. The entropy of an imperfect crystal, a glass, or a solid solution is not zero at 0 K.

On the basis of the third law, absolute entropies can be calculated from heat capacity data. The **standard absolute entropy** of a substance, S°, is the entropy of the substance in its standard state at 1 atm. Some S° values at 25°C are given in Table 19.5. The ΔS° value for a reaction is equal to the sum of the absolute entropies of the products minus the sum of the absolute entropies of the reactants. Note that the absolute entropy of an element is *not* equal to zero and that the absolute entropy of a compound is *not* the entropy change when the compound is formed from its constituent elements.

Example 19.5

(a) Use absolute entropies from Table 19.5 to calculate the standard entropy change, ΔS°, for the formation of one mole of HgO(s) from its elements. (b) The standard enthalpy of formation, ΔH_f°, of HgO(s) is −90.7 kJ/mol. Calculate the standard free energy of formation, ΔG_f°, of HgO(s).

Solution

(a) $Hg(l) + \frac{1}{2}O_2(g) \longrightarrow HgO(s)$

$\Delta S^\circ = S^\circ(HgO) - [S^\circ(Hg) + \frac{1}{2}S^\circ(O_2)]$

Table 19.5		Absolute entropy [J/K·mol)] at 25°C and 1 atm	
Substance	$S°$	Substance	$S°$
Ag(s)	42.72	HCl(g)	186.7
AgCl(s)	96.11	HF(g)	173.5
Al(s)	28.3	Hg(l)	77.4
$Al_2O_3(s)$	51.00	HgO(s)	72.0
$Br_2(l)$	152.3	HI(g)	206.3
C(graphite)	5.69	$H_2O(g)$	188.7
Ca(s)	41.6	$H_2O(l)$	69.96
$CaCO_3(s)$	92.9	$H_2S(g)$	205.6
CaO(s)	39.8	$I_2(s)$	116.7
$Ca(OH)_2(s)$	76.1	La(s)	57.3
$CH_4(g)$	186.2	Li(s)	28.0
$C_2H_2(g)$	200.8	$N_2(g)$	191.5
$C_2H_4(g)$	219.5	Na(s)	51.0
$C_2H_6(g)$	229.5	NaCl(s)	72.38
$Cl_2(g)$	223.0	$NH_3(g)$	192.5
CO(g)	197.9	NO(g)	210.6
$CO_2(g)$	213.6	$NO_2(g)$	240.5
$F_2(g)$	203.3	$O_2(g)$	205.03
Fe(s)	27.2	S(rhombic)	31.9
$Fe_2O_3(s)$	90.0	$SO_2(g)$	248.5
$H_2(g)$	130.6	Zn(s)	41.6
HBr(g)	198.5	ZnO(s)	43.9

$$= (72.0 \text{ J/K}) - [(77.4 \text{ J/K}) + \tfrac{1}{2}(205.0 \text{ J/K})]$$
$$= -107.9 \text{ J/K}.$$

(b) $\Delta G° = \Delta H° - T\Delta S°$
$$= -90.7 \text{ kJ} - (298.2 \text{ K})(-0.1079 \text{ kJ/K})$$
$$= -90.7 \text{ kJ} + 32.2 \text{ kJ}$$
$$= -58.5 \text{ kJ}$$

Many problems can be solved by use of $\Delta S°$ values (calculated from $S°$ values; see Table 19.5), $\Delta H_f°$ values (see Table 5.1), and $\Delta G_f°$ values (see Table 19.4). Approximate solutions for several types of problems can be found by making the assumption that the values of ΔH and ΔS do not change with a change in temperature. The assumption is usually a good one since observed changes in these values are comparatively small.

Example 19.6

For the reaction

$$NH_4Cl(s) \longrightarrow NH_3(g) + HCl(g)$$

$\Delta S° = +285$ J/K, $\Delta H° = +177$ kJ, and $\Delta G° = +91.9$ kJ at 25°C. (a) Is the reaction spontaneous at 25°C? (b) Assume that ΔH and ΔS do not change with an increase in temperature and calculate the value of $\Delta G°$ at 500°C (which is 773 K). Is the reaction spontaneous at this temperature?

Solution

(a) Since $\Delta G°$ is a positive value at 25°C ($+91.9$ kJ), the reaction is not spontaneous at this temperature. The reverse reaction

$$NH_3(g) + HCl(g) \longrightarrow NH_4Cl(s)$$

for which $\Delta G°$ is -91.9 kJ would be spontaneous at 25°C.

(b) For the reaction as given in the problem,

$$NH_4Cl(s) \longrightarrow NH_3(g) + HCl(g)$$

$$\begin{aligned}
\Delta G° &= \Delta H° - T\Delta S° \\
&= +177 \text{ kJ} - (773 \text{ K})(+0.285 \text{ kJ/K}) \\
&= +177 \text{ kJ} - 220 \text{ kJ} = -43 \text{ kJ}
\end{aligned}$$

Notice that we express $\Delta S°$ in kJ/K so that the term $T\Delta S°$ will have the same units (kJ) as $\Delta H°$. Since $\Delta G°$ is a negative value at 500°C, the reaction is spontaneous at this temperature. This result is typical of decomposition reactions, which are endothermic and proceed to a greater and greater extent as the temperature is increased.

Example 19.7

For the vaporization of methyl alcohol,

$$CH_3OH(l) \rightleftharpoons CH_3OH(g)$$

$\Delta H° = +37.4$ kJ and $\Delta S°$ is $+111$ J/K at 25°C and 1 atm. Assume that these values do not change with an increase in temperature. When $\Delta G° = 0$, the transformation is spontaneous in neither direction, the system is in equilibrium, and the temperature is the normal boiling point of methyl alcohol. Calculate the normal boiling point of CH_3OH.

Solution

$$\Delta G° = \Delta H° - T\Delta S°$$

$$0 = +37.4 \text{ kJ} - T(+0.111 \text{ kJ/K})$$

$$T = \frac{+37.4 \text{ kJ}}{+0.111 \text{ kJ/K}} = 337 \text{ K}$$

The normal boiling point according to this calculation, therefore, is $337 - 273 = 64°C$. The handbook lists the normal boiling point of methyl alcohol as 64.96°C. Since $\Delta H°$ and $\Delta S°$ do change slightly with temperature, our calculated value is in error by a small amount.

There are other ways to obtain $\Delta G°$ values besides calculations using $\Delta H°$ and $S°$ values. Two additional types of data from which $\Delta G°$ values may be derived are equilibrium constants (Section 19.7) and electrochemical measurements (Section 20.8). The results obtained from calorimetric, equilibrium, and electrochemical data are in complete agreement.

19.7 Gibbs Free Energy and Equilibrium

Since ΔG is zero for a system in equilibrium, free-energy changes can be used to evaluate the equilibrium state of a chemical reaction. The free energy of a substance in a state other than its standard state, G, is related to its standard free energy, $G°$, by the equation

$$G = G° + RT \ln a \tag{19.18}$$

where R is the ideal gas constant, 8.3144 J/(K·mol), T is the absolute temperature, and ln a is the natural logarithm of the activity of the substance.

The activity of a substance is its effective concentration. The activity of a substance in its standard state is equal to 1. Notice that since the natural logarithm of 1 is zero, the equation states that $G = G°$ when the substance is in its standard state. The standard state of an ideal gas is the gas at a pressure of 1 atm. If the partial pressure of the gas is 0.5 atm, the gas is said to have an activity of 0.5. The standard state of a solute in a solution is a 1 M concentration of the solute, neglecting corrections for nonideal behavior. Thus, the activity of a solute approximates the solute's concentration in molarity, particularly when the solution is dilute. The standard state of a liquid or a solid is the pure liquid or pure solid at 1 atm.

Equation 19.18 can be used to derive an expression for the free-energy change that accompanies a chemical reaction. The free-energy change of the general equation

$$w\text{W} + x\text{X} \rightleftharpoons y\text{Y} + z\text{Z}$$

is given by the equation

$$\Delta G = \Delta G° + RT \ln \left(\frac{(a_Y)^y (a_Z)^z}{(a_W)^w (a_X)^x} \right) \tag{19.19}$$

The fraction contains the activities of the substances participating in the reaction, with each activity raised to a power equal to the coefficient in the balanced chemical equation. The logarithmic term of the equation corrects $\Delta G°$ to the more general condition in which the activities of the substances are not each equal to 1.

At equilibrium, $\Delta G = 0$ and, therefore,

$$0 = \Delta G° + RT \ln \frac{(a_Y)^y (a_Z)^z}{(a_W)^w (a_X)^z} \tag{19.20}$$

Since the system is in equilibrium, the activities that appear in this equation are equilibrium activities, and the fraction is the thermodynamic equilibrium constant, K. Therefore,

$$\Delta G^{\circ} = -RT \ln K \tag{19.21}$$

or

$$\Delta G^{\circ} = -2.303RT \log K \tag{19.22}$$

The ideal gas constant, R, is 8.3144 J/(K·mol). For an equilibrium system at 25°C (which is 298.15 K), therefore,

$$\begin{aligned}
\Delta G^{\circ} &= -2.303RT \log K \\
&= -2.303[8.3144 \text{ J/(K·mol)}](298.15 \text{ K}) \log K \\
&= -(5709 \text{ J/mol}) \log K \\
&= -(5.709 \text{ kJ/mol}) \log K
\end{aligned}$$

Example 19.8

Calculate K_p for the following reaction at 25°C:

$$2\,SO_2(g) + O_2(g) \rightleftharpoons 2\,SO_3(g)$$

For $SO_2(g)$, ΔG_f° is -300.4 kJ/mol. For $SO_3(g)$, ΔG_f° is -370.4 kJ/mol.

Solution

The standard free energy change for the reaction is

$$\begin{aligned}
\Delta G^{\circ} &= 2\Delta G_f^{\circ}(SO_3) - 2\Delta G_f^{\circ}(SO_2) \\
&= 2 \text{ mol}(-370.4 \text{ kJ/mol}) - 2 \text{ mol}(-300.4 \text{ kJ/mol}) \\
&= -140.0 \text{ kJ}
\end{aligned}$$

We use this value to find K_p. Since

$$\begin{aligned}
\Delta G^{\circ} &= -(5.709 \text{ kJ/mol}) \log K \\
\log K &= \frac{\Delta G^{\circ}}{-5.709 \text{ kJ/mol}} \\
&= \frac{-140.0 \text{ kJ/mol}}{-5.709 \text{ kJ/mol}} = 24.52
\end{aligned}$$

Therefore,

$$K = \text{antilog } 24.52 = 3.3 \times 10^{24}$$

The type of K obtained by this method depends upon the definition of the standard states used in the determination of ΔG° values. For the reactions of gases, K_p's are obtained since the standard state of a gas is defined as the gas at a partial pressure of 1 atm.

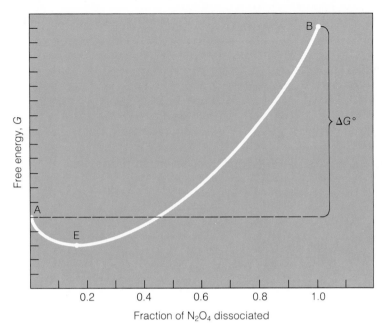

Figure 19.2 Free energy of a system that contains the equivalent of 1 mol of N_2O_4 as the reaction $N_2O_4(g) \rightleftharpoons NO_2(g)$ occurs (25°C and 1 atm)

For the reaction at 25°C:

$$N_2O_4(g) \rightleftharpoons 2\,NO_2(g)$$
$$\Delta G° = +5.40 \text{ kJ}$$

Since $\Delta G°$ is positive, we might predict that N_2O_4 in its standard state at 25°C and 1 atm would not dissociate into NO_2 at all and that the reverse reaction (the formation of N_2O_4 from NO_2) would go to completion. Both these predictions are incorrect.

If we use the value of $\Delta G°$ to calculate the equilibrium constant for this system at 25°C, we find

$$K_p = 0.113$$

At equilibrium, therefore, some of the N_2O_4 is dissociated.

The free energy of a system in which this reaction occurs at 25°C and 1 atm is plotted against the fraction of N_2O_4 dissociated in Figure 19.2. Point A represents the standard free energy of 1 mol of N_2O_4, point B represents the standard free energy of 2 mol of NO_2, and the intervening points on this curve represent the free energies of mixtures of N_2O_4 and NO_2. Absolute values of free energies are not known, and no scale is indicated on the vertical axis of the diagram. Differences in free energies, however, can be calculated so that shape of the curve is accurately represented.

The free energy curve exhibits a minimum at the equilibrium point, E, where 16.6% of the N_2O_4 is dissociated. The difference between the standard free energy of 2 mol of NO_2 (point B) and the standard free energy of 1 mol of N_2O_4 (point A) is $\Delta G°$ for the reaction (+5.40 kJ) and is indicated on the figure. However, ΔG

for the preparation of the equilibrium mixture (point E) from 1 mol of N_2O_4 (point A) is -0.84 kJ, which indicates that N_2O_4 will spontaneously dissociate until equilibrium is reached.

The figure shows that equilibrium can be approached from either direction. Thus, $\Delta G = -6.23$ kJ for the preparation of the equilibrium mixture (point E) from 2 mol of pure NO_2 (point B). The negative values of ΔG for both changes (from A to E and from B to E) indicate that both changes are spontaneous.

We must be careful, therefore, when we interpret the meaning of $\Delta G°$ values in relation to reaction spontaneity. Values of K corresponding to various $\Delta G°$ values are listed in Table 19.6. A large *negative* value of $\Delta G°$ means that K for the reaction is a large *positive* value, and therefore the reaction from left to right will go virtually to completion. On the other hand, if $\Delta G°$ is a large positive value, K will be extremely small, thus indicating that the reverse reaction, from right to left, will go virtually to completion. Only if the value of $\Delta G°$ is neither very large nor very small (see Table 19.6) will the value of K indicate a situation in which the reaction will not go essentially to completion in one direction or the other.

Table 19.6 Values of K corresponding to $\Delta G°$ values according to the equation $\Delta G° = -2.303RT \log K$

$\Delta G°$ (kJ)	K
-200	1.1×10^{35}
-100	3.3×10^{17}
-50	5.7×10^{8}
-25	2.4×10^{4}
-5	7.5
0	1.0
$+5$	0.13
$+25$	4.2×10^{-5}
$+50$	1.7×10^{-9}
$+100$	3.0×10^{-18}
$+200$	9.3×10^{-36}

9.8 Equilibrium Constants and Temperature

We can use the relationship between the change in Gibbs free energy and the equilibrium constant to develop an equation that relates the equilibrium constant and temperature. We assume that $\Delta H°$ and $\Delta S°$ do not change with changes in temperature. Then, at temperature T_1 the value of $\Delta G_1°$ is

$$\Delta G_1° = \Delta H° - T_1 \Delta S° \tag{19.23}$$

The equilibrium constant K_1 that corresponds to temperature T_1, is given by the equation:

$$\Delta G_1° = -RT_1 \ln K_1 \tag{19.24}$$

Since the right sides of Equations 19.23 and 19.24 are each equal to $\Delta G_1°$, they are equal to each other:

$$\Delta H° - T_1 \Delta S° = -RT_1 \ln K_1 \tag{19.25}$$

or,

$$T_1 \Delta S° = RT_1 \ln K_1 + \Delta H° \tag{19.26}$$

By dividing through by T_1, we get

$$\Delta S° = R \ln K_1 + \frac{\Delta H°}{T_1} \tag{19.27}$$

Using the same method, we can derive an equation that pertains to a different temperature, T_2, for which the equilibrium constant is K_2:

$$\Delta S° = R \ln K_2 + \frac{\Delta H°}{T_2} \tag{19.28}$$

Here, the right sides of Equations 19.27 and 19.28 are each equal to $\Delta S°$, and therefore they are equal to each other:

$$R \ln K_2 + \frac{\Delta H°}{T_2} = R \ln K_1 + \frac{\Delta H°}{T_1} \tag{19.29}$$

$$R \ln K_2 - R \ln K_1 = \frac{\Delta H°}{T_1} - \frac{\Delta H°}{T_2} \tag{19.30}$$

$$R \ln \left(\frac{K_2}{K_1}\right) = \Delta H° \left(\frac{1}{T_1} - \frac{1}{T_2}\right) \tag{19.31}$$

$$2.303 R \log \left(\frac{K_2}{K_1}\right) = \Delta H° \left(\frac{T_2 - T_1}{T_1 T_2}\right) \tag{19.32}$$

$$\log \left(\frac{K_2}{K_1}\right) = \frac{\Delta H°}{2.303 R} \left(\frac{T_2 - T_1}{T_1 T_2}\right) \tag{19.33}$$

In problems involving this equation, the value of R that should be used is 8.314 J/(K·mol). Since $\Delta H°$ varies with temperature, Equation 19.33 is only approximate. Over a narrow temperature range, however, a value of $\Delta H°$ that is an average for the pertinent temperature range may be used with good results.

Notice the similarity between Equation 19.33 and the Clausius-Clapeyron equation (Section 11.7). The Clausius-Clapeyron equation relates vapor pressure and temperature. The vapor pressure of a substance is a type of K_p since it pertains to an equilibrium between a substance and its vapor.

Example 19.9

For the reaction

$$CO_2(g) + H_2(g) \rightleftharpoons CO(g) + H_2O(g)$$

K_p is 0.63 at 700°C and 1.66 at 1000°C. (a) What is the value of $\Delta H°$ for the temperature range considered? (b) What is the value of K_p at 800°C?

Solution

(a) Let $T_1 = 700°C = 973$ K, $K_1 = 0.63$, $T_2 = 1000°C = 1273$ K, and $K_2 = 1.66$.

$$\log \left(\frac{K^2}{K_1}\right) = \frac{\Delta H°}{2.303 R} \left(\frac{T_2 - T_1}{T_1 T_2}\right) \tag{19.33}$$

$$\log \left(\frac{1.66}{0.63}\right) = \frac{\Delta H°}{2.303[8.314 \text{ J/(K·mol)}]} \left(\frac{1273 \text{ K} - 973 \text{ K}}{(973 \text{ K})(1273 \text{ K})}\right)$$

$$0.421 = \frac{\Delta H°}{19.15 \text{ J/(K·mol)}} \left(\frac{300 \text{ K}}{1.239 \times 10^6 \text{ K}^2}\right)$$

$$\Delta H° = 3.33 \times 10^4 \text{ J/mol}$$

(b) Let $T_1 = 700°C = 973$ K, $K_1 = 0.63$, $T_2 = 800°C = 1073$ K, and $K_2 =$ unknown.

$$\log\left(\frac{K_2}{0.63}\right) = \frac{3.33 \times 10^4 \text{ J/mol}}{2.303[8.314 \text{ J/(K·mol)}]} \left(\frac{1073 \text{ K} - 973 \text{ K}}{(973 \text{ K})(1073 \text{ K})}\right)$$

$$\log\left(\frac{K_2}{0.63}\right) = 0.167$$

$$\left(\frac{K_2}{0.63}\right) = 1.47$$

$$K_2 = 0.93$$

Summary

According to the *first law of thermodynamics*, which is the law of conservation of energy, when a system changes from an initial state to a final state, the *change in internal energy* of the system, ΔE, is equal to the *heat absorbed* by the system, q, *minus* the *work done* by the system, w: $\Delta E = q - w$. For an ordinary chemical reaction, the work term generally arises as a consequence of *pressure-volume work*. Thus, at *constant volume*, no pressure-volume work can be done and $\Delta E = q_V$. The quantity of heat measured in a bomb calorimeter is a heat of reaction at constant volume, q_V or ΔE.

At *constant pressure*, $w = P\Delta V$, and therefore, $\Delta E = q_P - P\Delta V$. The thermodynamic function *enthalpy*, H, is defined by the equation $H = E + PV$. Hence, $\Delta H = \Delta E + P\Delta V$, $\Delta E = \Delta H - P\Delta V$, and $q_P = \Delta H$. A heat of reaction at constant pressure is a ΔH. The two values ΔH and ΔE are related by the equation: $\Delta H = \Delta E + (\Delta n)RT$.

According to the *second law of thermodynamics*, every spontaneous change is accompanied by an *increase in entropy*. The thermodynamic function entropy, S, may be considered to be a measure of *disorder*, or *randomness*. The *total change* in entropy (the change in the *surroundings* as well as in the *system*) must be considered to determine spontaneity.

Gibbs free energy, G, provides a criterion for spontaneity that centers on the system alone. This thermodynamic function is defined by the equation: $G = H - TS$. For a reaction at constant temperature and pressure: $\Delta G = \Delta H - T\Delta S$, and a *negative value* of ΔG indicates that the reaction is *spontaneous*. If the system is in *equilibrium*, $\Delta G = 0$. A standard free energy change for a reaction, $\Delta G°$, can be calculated from tabulated standard free energies of formation, $\Delta G_f°$.

The *third law of thermodynamics* states that at 0 K, the entropy of a perfect crystalline substance is zero. On the basis of this law, *standard absolute entropies*, $S°$, are calculated from heat capacity data. These $S°$ values are tabulated. A *standard change in entropy*, $\Delta S°$, can be calculated from the tabulated $S°$ values. In turn, $\Delta G°$ values can be found from tabulated $\Delta H_f°$ values and $\Delta S°$ values.

Standard free energy change and the equilibrium constant are related: $\Delta G° = -RT \ln K$. The value of a $\Delta G°$, therefore, can be used to predict the degree of completion of the corresponding reaction and the position of equilibrium. By use of equations involving $\Delta G°$, an equation can be derived that relates the equilibrium constant and temperature:

$$\log(K_2/K_1) = (\Delta H°/2.303RT)[(T_2 - T_1)/T_1 T_2].$$

Key Terms

Some of the more important terms introduced in this chapter are listed below. Definitions for terms not included in this list may be located in the text by use of the index.

Enthalpy, H (Section 19.2) A thermodynamic function defined by the equation $H = E + PV$, where E is the internal energy of the system, P is the pressure, and V is the volume. For a reaction run at constant pressure, the change in enthalpy, ΔH, is the heat transferred, q_P.

Entropy, S (Section 19.3) A measure of the randomness, or disorder, of a system; used as a criterion of reaction spontaneity; expressed in J/(K·mol).

First law of thermodynamics (Section 19.1) Energy can be converted from one form into another but it cannot be created or destroyed.

Gibbs free energy, G (Section 19.4) The thermodynamic function that takes into account both the enthalpy, H, and entropy, S, of a system; $G = H - TS$. For a reaction at constant temperature and pressure, $\Delta G = \Delta H - T\Delta S$.

Internal Energy, E (Section 19.1) The energy content of a system; it includes all possible forms of energy attributable to the system. The change in the internal energy of a system, ΔE, is defined as the difference between the heat absorbed by the system, q, and the work done by the system, w: $\Delta E = q - w$.

Second law of thermodynamics (Section 19.3) Every spontaneous change is accompanied by an increase in entropy.

Spontaneous change (Section 19.4) A change that has a natural tendency to occur without heat being added or work being done on the system. Some spontaneous changes are very slow, however.

Standard absolute entropy, $S°$ (Section 19.6) The entropy of a substance in its standard state; calculated on the basis of the third law of thermodynamics; expressed in J/(K·mol).

Standard free energy of formation, $\Delta G_f°$ (Section 19.5) The free-energy change for the process in which 1 mol of a compound in its standard state is made from its constituent elements in their standard states.

State function (Section 19.1) A function that depends upon the state of a system (defined by specifying properties such as temperature, pressure, and composition) and not on how the system arrived at that state; E, H, S, and G are state functions, q and w are not.

Surroundings (Section 19.1) That part of nature not included within the boundaries of the system under consideration.

System (Section 19.1) That part of nature that is under consideration.

Thermodynamics (Introduction) The study of the energy changes that accompany chemical and physical changes.

Third law of thermodynamics (Section 19.6) At 0 K, the entropy of a perfect crystalline substance is zero.

Problems*

The First Law, Internal Energy, Enthalpy

19.1 What is the first law of thermodynamics? What is the difference between internal energy, E, and enthalpy, H?

19.2 What is a state function? List the state functions that are described in this chapter. In the equation $\Delta E = q - w$, are q and w state functions?

19.3 The combustion of 1.000 g of ethyl alcohol, $C_2H_5OH(l)$, in a bomb calorimeter (at constant volume) evolves 29.62 kJ of heat at 25°C. The products of the combustion are $CO_2(g)$ and $H_2O(l)$. The molecular weight of ethyl alcohol is 46.06. **(a)** What is $\Delta E°$ for the combustion of 1.000 mol of ethyl alcohol? **(b)** Write the chemical equation for the reaction. What is $\Delta H°$ for the combustion of 1.000 mol of ethyl alcohol? **(c)** Use values from Table 5.1 to calculate the enthalpy of formation of ethyl alcohol.

19.4 The combustion of 1.000 g of thiourea, $CS(NH_2)_2(s)$, in a bomb calorimeter (at constant volume) evolves 15.37 kJ of heat at 25°C. The products of the combustion are $CO_2(g)$, $SO_2(g)$, $N_2(g)$, and $H_2O(l)$. The molecular weight of thiourea is 76.12. **(a)** What is $\Delta E°$ for the combustion of 1.000 mol of thiourea? **(b)** Write the chemical equation for the reaction. What is $\Delta H°$ for the combustion of 1.000 mol of thiourea? **(c)** Use values from Table 5.1 to calculate the enthalpy of formation of thiourea.

19.5 Calculate $\Delta E°$ for the combustion of octane, $C_8H_{18}(l)$, to $CO_2(g)$ and $H_2O(l)$ at 25°C. The value of $\Delta H°$ for this reaction is -5470.71 kJ/mol of octane.

19.6 Calculate $\Delta E°$ for the combustion of ethylene $C_2H_4(g)$ to $CO_2(g)$ and $H_2O(l)$ at 25°C. The value of $\Delta H°$ for this reaction is -1410.8 kJ/mol of ethylene.

19.7 For the reaction:

$$3\,NO_2(g) + H_2O(l) \longrightarrow 2\,HNO_3(l) + NO(g)$$

$\Delta H°$ is -71.53 kJ. What is $\Delta E°$?

19.8 For the reaction:

$$Ca_3P_2(s) + 6\,H_2O(l) \longrightarrow 3\,Ca(OH)_2(s) + 2\,PH_3(g)$$

$\Delta H°$ is -721.70 kJ. What is $\Delta E°$?

19.9 For the reaction:

$$CaNCN(s) + 3\,H_2O(l) \longrightarrow CaCO_3(s) + 2\,NH_3(g)$$

$\Delta E°$ is -261.75 kJ. Use values from Table 5.1 to calculate the enthalpy of formation of $CaNCN(s)$.

19.10 For the reaction:

$$NH_4NO_3(s) \longrightarrow N_2O(g) + 2\,H_2O(l)$$

$\Delta E°$ is -127.49 kJ. Use values from Table 5.1 to calculate the enthalpy of formation of $N_2O(g)$.

---

* The appendix contains answers to color-keyed problems.

19.11 How can entropy and Gibbs free energy be used as criteria for reaction spontaniety?

19.12 The standard enthalpy of formation of an element, ΔH_f°, is zero and the standard free energy of formation of an element, ΔG_f° is zero, but the standard absolute entropy of an element, S°, is not zero. Explain.

19.13 Use the data given in Table 19.4 to calculate ΔG° for the following proposed reactions:

$$SO_2(g) + H_2(g) \longrightarrow H_2S(g) + O_2(g)$$

$$SO_2(g) + 3 H_2(g) \longrightarrow H_2S(g) + 2 H_2O(l)$$

What would you predict the products of the reaction of $SO_2(g)$ and $H_2(g)$ at 25°C to be?

19.14 A chemist claims that the following reaction occurs at 25°C:

$$SF_6(g) + 8 HI(g) \longrightarrow H_2S(g) + 6 HF(g) + 4 I_2(g)$$

Is it theoretically possible? Use values from Table 19.4 plus the fact that ΔG_f° for $SF_6(g)$ is -992 kJ/mol to calculate ΔG° for the reaction.

19.15 Will both $BF_3(g)$ and $BCl_3(l)$ hydrolyze at 25°C according to the following equation (where X is F or Cl):

$$BX_3 + 3 H_2O(l) \longrightarrow H_3BO_3(aq) + 3 HX(aq)$$

The pertinent ΔG_f° values are: $H_3BO_3(aq)$, -963.32 kJ/mol; HF(aq), -276.48 kJ/mol; HCl(aq), -131.17 kJ/mol; $H_2O(l)$, -237.19 kJ/mol; $BF_3(g)$, -1093.28 kJ/mol; $BCl_3(l)$, -379.07 kJ/mol.

19.16 For oxygen difluoride, $OF_2(g)$, ΔG_f° is $+40.6$ kJ/mol. **(a)** Is the preparation of $OF_2(g)$ from its elements at 25°C a spontaneous reaction? **(b)** For ozone, $O_3(g)$, ΔG_f° is $+163.43$ kJ/mol. Is it theoretically possible to prepare $OF_2(g)$ at 25°C by the reaction:

$$3 F_2(g) + O_3(g) \longrightarrow 3 OF_2(g)$$

19.17 For the reaction:

$$HCOOH(l) \longrightarrow CO(g) + H_2O(l)$$

ΔH° is $+15.79$ kJ and ΔS° is $+215.27$ J/K. Calculate ΔG°. Is the decomposition of formic acid, HCOOH(l), spontaneous at 25°C?

19.18 For the reaction:

$$2 CHCl_3(l) + O_2(g) \longrightarrow 2 COCl_2(g) + 2 HCl(g)$$

ΔH° is -366 kJ and ΔS° is $+340.$ J/K. Calculate ΔG°. Is the formation of the poisonous gas phosgene, $COCl_2$, from chloroform, $CHCl_3$, and oxygen a spontaneous reaction at 25°C?

19.19 For the reaction:

$$C_2H_4(g) + H_2(g) \longrightarrow C_2H_6(g)$$

ΔH° is -136.98 kJ. **(a)** Use values from Table 19.4 to calculate ΔG° for the reaction. **(b)** Use ΔG° and ΔH° to

calculate ΔS° for the reaction. **(c)** Calculate the value of ΔS° for the reaction by using S° values from Table 19.5.

19.20 For the reaction:

$$CO(g) + 2 H_2(g) \longrightarrow CH_3OH(l)$$

(a) calculate ΔH° using values from Table 5.1. **(b)** The absolute entropy, S°, of $CH_3OH(l)$ is 126.78 J/(K·mol). Use this fact and values from Table 19.5 to calculate ΔS° for the reaction. **(c)** Use ΔH° and ΔS° to calculate ΔG° for the reaction. **(d)** Use the value of ΔG° for the reaction and the value of ΔG_f° for CO(g) from Table 19.4 to calculate the standard free energy of formation of $CH_3OH(l)$.

19.21 What is the standard free energy of formation, ΔG_f° of $PH_3(g)$? For $PH_3(g)$: ΔH_f° is $+9.25$ kJ/mol and S° is 210.0 J/(K·mol). For the standard state of $P_4(s)$, S° is 177.6 J/(K·mol) and for $H_2(g)$, S° is 130.5 J/(K·mol).

19.22 The standard enthalpy of formation, ΔH_f°, of $CS_2(l)$ is $+87.9$ kJ/mol. The absolute entropy, S°, is of C(graphite) is 5.69 J/(K·mol), of S(rhombic) is 31.9 J/(K·mol), and of $CS_2(l)$ is 151.0 J/(K·mol). Calculate the standard free energy of formation, ΔG_f°, of $CS_2(l)$.

19.23 For the reaction:

$$PCl_5(g) \longrightarrow PCl_3(g) + Cl_2(g)$$

at 25°C, ΔH° is $+92.5$ kJ and ΔS° is $+182$ J/K. **(a)** Calculate the value of ΔG° for 25°C. Is the reaction spontaneous at this temperature? **(b)** Assume that ΔH and ΔS are constant with changes in temperature and calculate the value of ΔG for the reaction at 300.°C. Is the reaction spontaneous at this temperature?

19.24 For the reaction:

$$CaCO_3(s) \longrightarrow CaO(s) + CO_2(g)$$

at 25°C, ΔH° is $+178$ kJ and ΔS° is $+160.$ J/K. **(a)** Calculate the value of ΔG° for the reaction at 25°C. Is the reaction spontaneous at this temperature? **(b)** Assume that ΔH and ΔS are constant with changes in temperature and calculate the value of ΔG° for the reaction at 1000.°C. Is the reaction spontaneous at this temperature?

19.25 Calculate the normal boiling point of ammonia, $NH_3(l)$, given that ΔH is $+23.3$ kJ/mol and ΔS is $+97.2$ J/(K·mol) for the vaporization.

19.26 Calculate the normal boiling point of n-hexane, $C_6H_{14}(l)$, given that ΔH is $+29.6$ kJ/mol and ΔS is $+86.5$ J/(K·mol) for the vaporization.

19.27 Use the reaction:

$$SO_2(g) + Cl_2(g) \longrightarrow SO_2Cl_2(l)$$

to find the absolute entropy, S°, of $SO_2Cl_2(l)$. For $SO_2Cl_2(l)$, ΔH_f° is -389.1 kJ/mol and ΔG_f° is -313.8 kJ/mol. Thermodynamic values for $SO_2(g)$ and $Cl_2(g)$ are found in Tables 5.1, 19.4, and 19.5.

19.28 For $HgBr_2(s)$, ΔH_f° is -169.5 kJ/mol and ΔG_f° is -162.3 kJ/mol. The absolute entropies of Hg(l) and $Br_2(l)$ are given in Table 19.5. What is S° for $HgBr_2(s)$?

19.29 The combustion of cyanogen, $C_2N_2(g)$, in oxygen forms $CO_2(g)$ and $N_2(g)$ and produces an extremely hot flame. For $C_2N_2(g)$, ΔG_f° is $+296.27$ kJ/mol and S° is 242.09 J/(K·mol). Use these data and values from Tables 19.4 and 19.5 to calculate ΔH° for the reaction at 25°C.

19.30 For the vaporization of bromine:

$$Br_2(l) \rightleftharpoons Br_2(g)$$

at 25°C, ΔG° is $+3.14$ kJ. The absolute entropies at 25°C, S°, are 245.3 J/(K·mol) for $Br_2(g)$, and 152.3 J/(K·mol) for $Br_2(l)$. Calculate the value for the enthalpy of vaporization of bromine at 25°C.

Gibbs Free Energy and Equilibrium

19.31 Use the values given in Problem 19.30 to calculate the value of K_p for the vaporization of bromine at 25°C. What is the vapor pressure of bromine at 25°C?

19.32 For the vaporization of water:

$$H_2O(l) \rightleftharpoons H_2O(g)$$

at 25°C, ΔG° is 8.58 kJ. Calculate the value of K_p for the vaporization of water at 25°C. What is the vapor pressure of water at 25°C?

19.33 The value of ΔG_f° for $ZnCO_3(s)$ is -731.36 kJ/mol. Use this fact and values from Table 19.4 to determine K_p for the reaction

$$ZnCO_3(s) \rightleftharpoons ZnO(s) + CO_2(g).$$

19.34 For $SO_3(g)$, ΔG_f° is -370.37 kJ/mol. Use this fact and values from Table 19.4 to determine K_p for the reaction

$$SO_2(g) + NO_2(g) \rightleftharpoons SO_3(g) + NO(g)$$

19.35 For urea, $CO(NH_2)_2(s)$, ΔG_f° is -197.15 kJ/mol. Use this fact and values from Table 19.4 to determine K_p for the reaction:

$$CO_2(g) + 2 NH_3(g) \rightleftharpoons H_2O(g) + CO(NH_2)_2(s)$$

19.36 For the reaction:

$$Br_2(l) + Cl_2(g) \rightleftharpoons 2 BrCl(g)$$

ΔG° is -1.80 kJ. What is K_p for the reaction?

19.37 For the reaction:

$$PCl_5(g) \rightleftharpoons PCl_3(g) + Cl_2(g)$$

at 25°C, K_p is 1.8×10^{-7} atm. What is ΔG° for the reaction?

19.38 At 25°C, K_p is 0.108 atm for the reaction:

$$NH_4HS(s) \rightleftharpoons NH_3(g) + H_2S(g)$$

Use this fact and values from Table 19.4 to calculate the value of ΔG_f° for $NH_4HS(s)$.

19.39 For the equilibrium:

$$HC_2H_3O_2(aq) \rightleftharpoons H^+(aq) + C_2H_3O_2^-(aq)$$

K_a is 1.8×10^{-5} at 25°C. What is ΔG° for this reaction at 25°C?

19.40 For the reaction:

$$H^+(aq) + OH^-(aq) \rightleftharpoons H_2O$$

ΔH° is -55.9 kJ and ΔS° is $+80.4$ J/K at 25°C. Calculate the value of ΔG° and the value of K_w at 25°C for the reaction:

$$H_2O \rightleftharpoons H^+(aq) + OH^-(aq)$$

19.41 For the reaction:

$$N_2(g) + O_2(g) \rightleftharpoons 2 NO(g)$$

at 2000. K, K_p is 4.08×10^{-4}, and for the reaction at 2500. K, K_p is 3.60×10^{-3}. **(a)** What is ΔH° for the temperature range considered? **(b)** What is the value of K_p for the reaction at 2250. K?

19.42 For the reaction:

$$NiO(s) + CO(g) \rightleftharpoons Ni(s) + CO_2(g)$$

at 936 K, K_p is 4.54×10^{-4}, and for the reaction at 1125 K, K_p is 1.58×10^{-3}. **(a)** What is ΔH° for the temperature range considered? **(b)** What is the value of K_p for the reaction at 1050. K?

19.43 For the reaction:

$$N_2(g) + 3 H_2(g) \rightleftharpoons 2 NH_3(g)$$

at 400.°C, K_p is 1.6×10^{-4}, and ΔH° is -32.6 kJ for the reaction run at temperatures around 400.°C. What is K_p for the reaction at 450.°C?

19.44 For the reaction:

$$H_2(g) + I_2(g) \rightleftharpoons 2 HI(g)$$

at 425°C, K_p is 54.5, and ΔH° is -14.5 kJ for the reaction run at temperatures from 300°C to 400°C. What is K_p for the reaction at 350.°C?

Unclassified Problems

19.45 The combustion of 1.000 g of cyclohexane, $C_6H_{12}(l)$, in a bomb calorimeter (at constant volume) evolves 46.48 kJ of heat at 25°C. The products of the combustion are $CO_2(g)$ and $H_2O(l)$. The molecular weight of cyclohexane is 84.16. **(a)** What is ΔE° for the combustion of 1.000 mol of cyclohexane? **(b)** Write the chemical equation for the reaction. What is ΔH° for the combustion? **(c)** Use values from Table 5.1 to calculate the enthalpy of formation of cyclohexane.

19.46 The signs of the standard free energies of formation of all the oxides of nitrogen are positive. What implications does this fact have regarding **(a)** the preparation of these oxides from nitrogen and oxygen at 25°C, and **(b)** the products of the combustion of a nitrogen-containing compound in oxygen?

19.47 For the reaction:

$$2\,Li(s) + H_2(g) \longrightarrow 2\,LiH(s)$$

at 25°C, $\Delta H°$ is -180.8 kJ and $\Delta S°$ is -137.3 J/K. **(a)** Calculate the value of $\Delta G°$ for the reaction at 25°C. Is the reaction spontaneous at this temperature? **(b)** Assume that ΔH and ΔS are constant with changes in temperature and calculate the value of ΔG for the reaction at 1200.°C. Is the reaction spontaneous at this temperature?

19.48 Graphite is the standard state of carbon, and $S°$ for graphite is 5.694 J/(K·mol). For diamond, $\Delta H_f°$ is $+1.895$ kJ/mol, and $\Delta G_f°$ is $+2.866$ kJ/mol. What is the absolute entropy, $S°$, of diamond? Which form of carbon is more ordered?

19.49 For the reaction:

$$2\,Ag_2O(s) \rightleftharpoons 4\,Ag(s) + O_2(g)$$

at 25°C, $\Delta H°$ is $+61.18$ kJ. The standard absolute entropies of the reactants at 25°C are: $Ag_2O(s)$, 121.71 J/(K·mol); $Ag(s)$ 42.72 J/(K·mol); $O_2(g)$, 205.03 J/(K·mol). **(a)** Calculate the value of $\Delta G°$ for the reaction at 25°C. **(b)** Calculate the value of K_p for the decomposition at 25°C.

19.50 For the reaction:

$$2\,ONCl(g) \rightleftharpoons 2\,NO(g) + Cl_2(g)$$

at 500. K, K_p is 1.8×10^{-2} atm, and for the reaction at 585 K, K_p is 0.37 atm. **(a)** What is $\Delta H°$ for the reaction at the temperature range considered? **(b)** What is the value of K_p for the reaction at 550. K?

C H A P T E R **ELECTROCHEMISTRY**
20

All chemical reactions are fundamentally electrical in nature since electrons are involved (in various ways) in all types of chemical bonding. Electrochemistry, however, is primarily the study of oxidation-reduction phenomena.

The relations between chemical change and electrical energy have theoretical as well as practical importance. Chemical reactions can be used to produce electrical energy (in cells that are called either voltaic or galvanic cells). Electrical energy can be used to bring about chemical transformations (in electrolytic cells). In addition, the study of electrochemical processes leads to an understanding, as well as to the systemization, of oxidation-reduction phenomena that take place outside cells.

20.1 Metallic Conduction

An electric current is the flow of electric charge. In metals this charge is carried by electrons, and electrical conduction of this type is called metallic conduction. The current results from the application of an electric force supplied by a battery or some other source of electrical energy. A complete circuit is necessary to produce a current.

Metallic crystals may be described in terms of mobile electron clouds permeating relatively fixed structures of positive metal ions (see Section 25.1). When electrons are forced into one end of a metal wire, the impressed electrons displace other electrons of the cloud at the point of entry. The displaced electrons, in turn, assume new positions by pushing neighboring electrons ahead, and this effect is transmitted down the length of the wire until electrons are forced out of the wire at the opposite end. The current source may be regarded as an electron pump, for it serves to force electrons into one end of the circuit and drain them off from the other end. At any position in the wire, electrical neutrality is preserved, since the rate of electrons in equals the rate of electrons out.

The analogy between the flow of electricity and the flow of a liquid is an old one. In earlier times electricity was described in terms of a current of "electric fluid." Conventions of long standing, which may be traced back to Benjamin Franklin (1747) and which were adopted before the electron was identified, ascribe a positive charge to this current. We shall interpret electrical circuits in terms of the movement of electrons. Remember, however, that by convention electric current is arbitrarily described as positive and as flowing in the opposite direction.

Electric current is measured in amperes (A). Quantity of electric charge is measured in coulombs (C); the coulomb is defined as the quantity of electricity carried past a point in one second by a current of one ampere. Therefore,

$$1 \text{ A} = 1 \text{ C/s}$$

and

$$1 \text{ C} = 1 \text{ A} \cdot \text{s}$$

The current is forced through the circuit by an electrical potential difference, which is measured in volts (V). It takes one joule of work to move one coulomb from a lower to a higher potential when the potential difference is one volt. One volt, therefore, equals one joule/coulomb, and one volt·coulomb is a unit of energy and equals one joule:

$$1 \text{ V} = 1 \text{ J/C}$$
$$1 \text{ V} \cdot \text{C} = 1 \text{ J}$$

The higher the potential difference between two points in a given wire, the more current the wire will carry between those two points. George Ohm in 1826 expressed the quantitative relation between potential difference, $\mathscr{E}$, in volts, and current, I, in amperes, as

$$I = \mathscr{E}/R \quad \text{or} \quad \mathscr{E} = IR$$

where the proportionality constant, R, of Ohm's law is called the resistance. Resistance is measured in ohms (Ω). One volt is required to force a current of one ampere through a resistance of one ohm.

Resistance to the flow of electricity in metals is probably caused by the vibration of the metal ions about their lattice positions. These vibrations interfere with the motion of the electrons and retard the current. As the temperature is increased, the thermal motion of the metal ions is increased. Hence, the resistance of metals increases and the metals become poorer conductors.

20.2 Electrolytic Conduction

Electrolytic conduction, in which the charge is carried by ions, will not occur unless the ions of the electrolyte are free to move. Electrolytic conduction, therefore, is exhibited principally by molten salts and by aqueous solutions of electrolytes. Furthermore, a sustained current through an electrolytic conductor requires that chemical change accompany the movement of ions.

These principles of electrolytic conduction are best illustrated by reference to

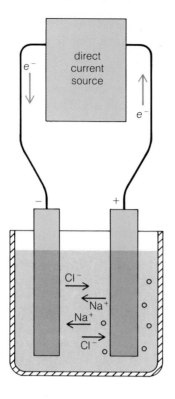

cathode   anode   **Figure 20.1** Electrolysis of molten

$Na^+ + e^- \rightarrow Na$ $2\,Cl^- \rightarrow Cl_2 + 2e^-$ sodium chloride

an electrolytic cell such as the one diagrammed in Figure 20.1 for the electrolysis of molten NaCl between inert electrodes.* The current source pumps electrons into the left-hand electrode, which therefore may be considered to be negatively charged. Electrons are drained from the right-hand, positive electrode. In the electric field thus produced, sodium ions (cations) are attracted toward the negative pole (cathode), and chloride ions (anions) are attracted toward the positive pole (anode). Electric charge in electrolytic conduction is carried by cations moving toward the **cathode** and anions moving in the opposite direction, toward the **anode.**

For a complete circuit, electrode reactions must accompany the movement of ions. *At the cathode some chemical species* (not necessarily the charge carrier) *must accept electrons and be reduced. At the anode, electrons must be removed from some chemical species, which as a consequence is oxidized.* The conventions relating to the terms anode and cathode are summarized in Table 20.1.

In the diagrammed cell, sodium ions are *reduced* at the *cathode:*

$$Na^+ + e^- \longrightarrow Na$$

and chloride ions are *oxidized* at the *anode:*

$$2\,Cl^- \longrightarrow Cl_2 + 2e^-$$

---

* Inert electrodes are not involved in electrode reactions.

Table 20.1   Electrode conventions

	Cathode	Anode
ions attracted	cations	anions
direction of electron movement	into cell	out of cell
half-reaction	reduction	oxidation
polarity		
electrolysis cell	negative	positive
galvanic cell	positive	negative

Proper addition of these two partial equations gives the reaction for the entire cell:

$$2\,NaCl(l) \xrightarrow{\;electrolysis\;} 2\,Na(l) + Cl_2(g)$$

In the actual operation of the commercial cell used to produce metallic sodium, calcium chloride is added to lower the melting point of sodium chloride, and the cell is operated at a temperature of approximately 600°C. At this temperature, sodium metal is a liquid.

We can trace the flow of negative charge through the circuit of Figure 20.1 as follows. Electrons leave the current source and are pumped into the cathode where they are picked up by and reduce sodium ions that have been attracted to this negative electrode. Chloride ions move away from the cathode toward the anode and thus carry negative charge in this direction. At the anode, electrons are removed from the chloride ions, thus oxidizing them to chlorine gas. These electrons are pumped out of the cell by the current source. In this manner the circuit is completed.

Electrolytic conduction, then, rests on the mobility of ions, and anything that inhibits the motion of these ions causes resistance to the current. Factors that influence the electrical conductivity of solutions of electrolytes include interionic attractions, solvation of ions, and viscosity of the solvent. These factors rest on solute-solute attractions, solute-solvent attractions, and solvent-solvent attractions, respectively. The average kinetic energy of the solute ions increases as the temperature is raised, and therefore, the resistance of electrolytic conductors generally decreases as the temperature is raised (that is, conduction increases). Furthermore, the effect of each of the three previously mentioned factors decreases as the temperature is increased.

At all times the solution is electrically neutral. The total positive charge of all of the cations equals the total negative charge of all of the anions.

20.3 Electrolysis

The electrolysis of molten sodium chloride serves as a commercial source of sodium metal and chlorine gas. Analogous procedures are used to prepare other very active metals (such as potassium and calcium). When certain aqueous solutions are electrolyzed, however, water is involved in the electrode reactions rather than the ions derived from the solute. Hence, the current-carrying ions are not necessarily discharged at the electrodes.

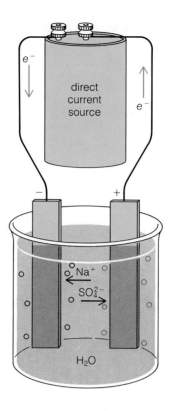

cathode	anode
$2e^- + 2H_2O \rightarrow H_2(g) + 2OH^-$	$2H_2O \rightarrow O_2(g) + 4H^+ + 4e^-$

Figure 20.2 Electrolysis of aqueous sodium sulfate

In the electrolysis of aqueous sodium sulfate, sodium ions move toward the cathode and sulfate ions move toward the anode (see Figure 20.2). Both these ions are difficult to discharge. When this electrolysis is conducted between inert electrodes, hydrogen gas is evolved at the cathode, and the solution surrounding the electrode becomes alkaline. Reduction occurs at the cathode; but rather than the reduction of the sodium ion:

$$e^- + Na^+ \longrightarrow Na$$

the *net change* that occurs is the reduction of water:

$$2e^- + 2H_2O \longrightarrow H_2(g) + 2OH^-$$

Water is an extremely weak electrolyte. Pure water is approximately $2 \times 10^{-7}\%$ ionized at 25°C:

$$2H_2O \rightleftharpoons H_3O^+ + OH^-$$

or, more briefly,

$$H_2O \rightleftharpoons H^+ + OH^-$$

The exact mechanism of the cathode reaction in the electrolysis of aqueous Na_2SO_4 is not known. It may be that the hydrogen ions from water are discharged and that the reaction proceeds as follows:

$$H_2O \rightleftharpoons H^+ + OH^-$$
$$2e^- + 2H^+ \longrightarrow H_2(g)$$

Multiplication of the first equation by 2 followed by addition of the two equations gives the net change for the reduction:

$$2e^- + 2H_2O \longrightarrow H_2(g) + 2OH^-$$

In general, water is reduced at the cathode (producing hydrogen gas and hydroxide ions) whenever the cation of the solute is difficult to reduce.

Oxidation occurs at the anode, and in the electrolysis of aqueous Na_2SO_4, the anions (SO_4^{2-}) that migrate toward the anode are difficult to oxidize:

$$2SO_4^{2-} \longrightarrow S_2O_8^{2-} + 2e^-$$

Therefore, the oxidation of water occurs preferentially. The mode of this reaction may be

$$H_2O \rightleftharpoons H^+ + OH^-$$
$$4OH^- \longrightarrow O_2(g) + 2H_2O + 4e^-$$

Multiplying the first equation by 4 and adding the equations, we get the net change for the oxidation:

$$2H_2O \longrightarrow O_2(g) + 4H^+ + 4e^-$$

At the anode the evolution of oxygen gas is observed, and the solution surrounding the pole becomes acidic. In general, water is oxidized at the anode (producing oxygen gas and hydrogen ions) whenever the anion of the solute is difficult to oxidize.

The complete reaction for the electrolysis of aqueous Na_2SO_4 may be obtained by adding the cathode and anode reactions:

$$2[2e^- + 2H_2O \longrightarrow H_2(g) + 2OH^-]$$
$$\underline{2H_2O \longrightarrow O_2(g) + 4H^+ + 4e^-}$$
$$6H_2O \longrightarrow 2H_2(g) + O_2(g) + 4H^+ + 4OH^-$$

If the solution is mixed, the hydrogen ions and hydroxide ions that are produced neutralize one another, and the net change for the cell:

$$2H_2O \xrightarrow{electrolysis} 2H_2(g) + O_2(g)$$

is merely the electrolysis of water. In the course of the electrolysis, the hydrogen ions migrate away from the anode, where they are produced, toward the cathode. In like manner, the hydroxide ions move toward the anode. These ions neutralize one another in the solution between the two electrodes.

Evaporators used to secure sodium hydroxide from the solution left after the electrolysis of aqueous sodium chloride. *Hooker Chemical Company.*

The electrolysis of an aqueous solution of NaCl between inert electrodes serves as an example of a process in which the anion of the electrolyte is discharged, but the cation is not:

$$
\begin{aligned}
\text{anode:} && 2\,Cl^- &\longrightarrow Cl_2(g) + 2e^- \\
\text{cathode:} && 2e^- + 2\,H_2O &\longrightarrow H_2(g) + 2\,OH^- \\
\hline
&& 2\,H_2O + 2\,Cl^- &\longrightarrow H_2(g) + Cl_2(g) + 2\,OH^-
\end{aligned}
$$

Since the sodium ion remains unchanged in the solution, the reaction may be indicated

$$
2\,H_2O + 2\,Na^+ + 2\,Cl^- \xrightarrow{\ electrolysis\ } H_2(g) + Cl_2(g) + 2\,Na^+ + 2\,OH^-
$$

This process is a commercial source of hydrogen gas, chlorine gas, and, by evaporation of the solution left after electrolysis, sodium hydroxide.

In the electrolysis of a solution of $CuSO_4$ between inert electrodes (see right portion of Figure 20.4, given subsequently), the current is carried by the Cu^{2+} and SO_4^{2-} ions. The current-carrying cations are discharged, but the anions are not:

$$
\begin{aligned}
\text{anode:} && 2\,H_2O &\longrightarrow O_2(g) + 4\,H^+ + 4e^- \\
\text{cathode:} && 2[2e^- + Cu^{2+} &\longrightarrow Cu(s)] \\
\hline
&& 2\,Cu^{2+} + 2\,H_2O &\longrightarrow O_2(g) + 2\,Cu(s) + 4\,H^+
\end{aligned}
$$

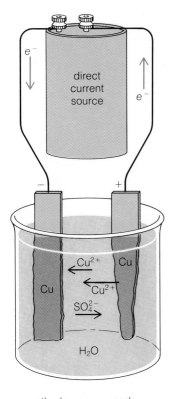

cathode   anode
$2e^- + Cu^{2+} \rightarrow Cu(s)$ $Cu(s) \rightarrow Cu^{2+} + 2e^-$

Figure 20.3 Electrolysis of aqueous cupric sulfate between copper electrodes

It is, of course, possible to have both ions of the solute discharged during the electrolysis of an aqueous solution. An example is the electrolysis of $CuCl_2$ between inert electrodes:

anode: $2\,Cl^- \longrightarrow Cl_2(g) + 2e^-$
cathode: $2e^- + Cu^{2+} \longrightarrow Cu(s)$
$$\overline{Cu^{2+} + 2\,Cl^- \longrightarrow Cu(s) + Cl_2(g)}$$

It is also possible to have the electrode itself enter into an electrode reaction. If aqueous $CuSO_4$ is electrolyzed between copper electrodes (see Figure 20.3), Cu^{2+} ions are reduced at the cathode:

$$2e^- + Cu^{2+} \longrightarrow Cu$$

but of the *three* possible anode oxidations:

$$2\,SO_4^{2-} \longrightarrow 2\,S_2O_8^{2-} + 2e^-$$

$$2\,H_2O \longrightarrow O_2(g) + 4\,H^+ + 4e^-$$

$$Cu(s) \longrightarrow Cu^{2+} + 2e^-$$

(*Top*) About 90% of U.S. primary copper is produced from open-pit mines (such as shown here) in Arizona, Utah, New Mexico, Montana, and Nevada. The balance of U.S. primary copper comes from underground mines, chiefly in Arizona and Michigan. *Copper Development Association, Inc.*

(*Bottom*) Cathodes of 99.98% pure copper are lifted from an electrolytic refining tank. *The Anaconda Minerals Company.*

the oxidation of the copper metal of the electrode is observed to occur. Hence, at the anode, copper from the electrode goes into solution as Cu^{2+} ions, and at the cathode, Cu^{2+} ions plate out as $Cu(s)$ on the electrode. This process is used to refine copper. Impure copper is used as the anode of an electrolytic cell, and a solution of $CuSO_4$ is electrolyzed. Pure copper plates out on the cathode. Active electrodes are also used in electroplating processes. In silver plating, silver anodes are employed.

20.4 Stoichiometry of Electrolysis

The quantitative relationships between electricity and chemical change were first described by Michael Faraday in 1832 and 1833. Faraday's work is best understood by reference to the half-reactions that occur during electrolysis. The change at the cathode in the electrolysis of molten sodium chloride:

$$Na^+ + e^- \longrightarrow Na$$

shows that one electron is required to produce one sodium atom. One mole of electrons (Avogadro's number of electrons) is required to produce one mole of sodium metal (22.9898 g Na). The quantity of charge equivalent to one mole of electrons is called the **faraday** (F) and has been found to equal 96,485 coulombs (C), which for ordinary problem work is customarily rounded off to 96,500 C:

$$1 F = 96,500 C$$

Michael Faraday, 1791–1867.
Argonne National Laboratory.

If 2 F of electricity were used, 2 mol of Na would be produced.

In the same time that electrons equivalent to 1 F of electricity are added to the cathode, that same number of electrons is removed from the anode:

$$2 Cl^- \longrightarrow Cl_2(g) + 2e^-$$

The removal of 1 mol of electrons (1 F) from the anode would result in the discharge of 1 mol of Cl^- ions and the production of 0.5 mol of chlorine gas. If 2 F of electricity flow through the cell, 2 mol of Cl^- ions are discharged and 1 mol of Cl_2 gas is liberated.

Electrode reactions, therefore, may be interpreted in terms of moles and faradays. The anode oxidation of the hydroxide ion, for example,

$$4 OH^- \longrightarrow O_2(g) + 2 H_2O + 4e^-$$

may be read as stating that 4 mol of OH^- ion produce 1 mol of O_2 gas and 2 mol of H_2O when 4 F of electricity is passed through the cell.

The relationships between moles of substances and faradays of electricity are the basis of stoichiometric calculations that involve electrolysis. Remember that one ampere (1 A) is equal to a current rate of one coulomb (1 C) per second:

$$1 A = 1 C/s$$

Example 20.1

The charge on a single electron is 1.6022×10^{-19} C. Calculate Avogadro's number from the fact that 1 F = 96,485 C.

Solution

$$? \text{ electrons} = 9.6485 \times 10^4 \text{ C} \left(\frac{1 \text{ electron}}{1.6022 \times 10^{-19} \text{ C}} \right)$$

$$= 6.0220 \times 10^{23} \text{ electrons}$$

Example 20.2

In the electrolysis of $CuSO_4$, how much copper is plated out on the cathode by a current of 0.750 A in 10.0 min?

Solution

The number of faradays used may be calculated as follows:

$$? \text{ F} = 10.0 \text{ min} \left(\frac{60 \text{ s}}{1 \text{ min}} \right) \left(\frac{0.750 \text{ C}}{1 \text{ s}} \right) \left(\frac{1 \text{ F}}{96,500 \text{ C}} \right)$$

$$= 0.00466 \text{ F}$$

The cathode reaction is $Cu^{2+} + 2e^- \rightarrow Cu(s)$, and therefore 2 F plates out one mole (63.5 g) of $Cu(s)$:

$$? \text{ g Cu} = 0.00466 \text{ F} \left(\frac{63.5 \text{ g Cu(s)}}{2 \text{ F}} \right) = 0.148 \text{ g Cu(s)}$$

Example 20.3

(a) What volume of $O_2(g)$ at STP is liberated at the anode in the electrolysis of $CuSO_4$ described in Example 20.2? (b) If 100 ml of 1.00 M $CuSO_4$ is employed in the cell, what is the H^+ (aq) concentration at the end of the electrolysis? Assume that there is no volume change for the solution during the experiment and that the anode reaction is

$$2 H_2O \longrightarrow 4 H^+(aq) + O_2(g) + 4e^-.$$

Solution

(a) Four faradays produce one mole of $O_2(g)$, 22.4 L at STP:

$$? \text{ liter } O_2(g) = 0.00466 \text{ F} \left(\frac{22.4 \text{ L } O_2(g)}{4 \text{ F}} \right)$$

$$= 0.0261 \text{ L } O_2(g)$$

(b) Four faradays also produce 4 mol of H^+(aq):

$$? \text{ mol } H^+(\text{aq}) = 0.00466 \text{ F} \left(\frac{1 \text{ mol } H^+(\text{aq})}{1 \text{ F}} \right)$$

$$= 0.00466 \text{ mol } H^+(\text{aq})$$

The small contribution of H^+(aq) from the ionization of water may be ignored, and we may assume that there are 0.00466 mol H^+(aq) in 100. mL of solution:

$$? \text{ mol } H^+(\text{aq}) = 1000. \text{ mL solution} \left(\frac{0.00466 \text{ mol } H^+(\text{aq})}{100. \text{ mL solution}} \right)$$

$$= 0.0466 \text{ mol } H^+(\text{aq})$$

The solution is therefore 0.0466 M in hydrogen ion.

In Figure 20.4, two electrolytic cells are set up in series. Electricity passes through one cell first and then through the other before returning to the current source. If silver nitrate is electrolyzed in one of the cells, the cathode reaction is

$$Ag^+ + e^- \longrightarrow Ag(s)$$

and metallic silver is plated out on the electrode used. By weighing this electrode before and after the electrolysis, one can determine the quantity of silver plated out and hence the number of coulombs that have passed through the cell. One faraday would plate out 107.868 g of silver. One coulomb, therefore, is equivalent to

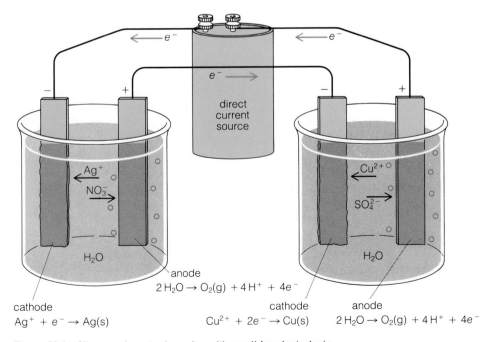

Figure 20.4 Silver coulometer in series with a cell for electrolysis

$$(107.868 \text{ g Ag})/(96{,}485 \text{ C}) = 1.1180 \times 10^{-3} \text{ g Ag/C}$$

The same number of coulombs pass through both cells in a given time when these cells are arranged in series. The number of coulombs used in an electrolysis, therefore, can be determined by the addition, in series, of this **silver coulometer** to the circuit of the experimental cell.

Example 20.4

(a) What mass of copper is plated out in the electrolysis of $CuSO_4$ in the same time that it takes to deposit 1.00 g of Ag in a silver coulometer that is arranged in series with the $CuSO_4$ cell? (b) If a current of 1.00 A is used, how many minutes is required to plate out this quantity of copper?

Solution

(a) From the electrode reactions we see that 2 F deposits 63.5 g Cu and 1 F deposits 107.9 g Ag:

$$? \text{ g Cu} = 1.00 \text{ g Ag} \left(\frac{1 \text{ F}}{107.9 \text{ g Ag}} \right) \left(\frac{63.5 \text{ g Cu}}{2 \text{ F}} \right) = 0.294 \text{ g Cu}$$

(b) $? \text{ min} = 1.00 \text{ g Ag} \left(\dfrac{96{,}500 \text{ C}}{107.9 \text{ g Ag}} \right) \left(\dfrac{1 \text{ s}}{1 \text{ C}} \right) \left(\dfrac{1 \text{ min}}{60 \text{ s}} \right)$

$\qquad = 14.9 \text{ min}$

20.5 Voltaic Cells

A cell that is used as a source of electrical energy is called a voltaic cell or a galvanic cell after Alessandro Volta (1800) or Luigi Galvani (1780), who first experimented with the conversion of chemical energy into electrical energy.

The reaction between metallic zinc and copper(II) ions in solution is illustrative of a spontaneous change in which electrons are transferred:

$$\text{Zn(s)} + \text{Cu}^{2+}(\text{aq}) \longrightarrow \text{Zn}^{2+}(\text{aq}) + \text{Cu(s)}$$

The exact mechanism by which electron transfer occurs is not known. We may, however, represent the above reaction as a combination of two half-reactions:

$$\text{Zn(s)} \longrightarrow \text{Zn}^{2+}(\text{aq}) + 2e^-$$
$$2e^- + \text{Cu}^{2+}(\text{aq}) \longrightarrow \text{Cu(s)}$$

In a voltaic cell these half-reactions are made to occur at different electrodes so that the transfer of electrons takes place through the external electrical circuit rather than directly between zinc metal and copper(II) ions.

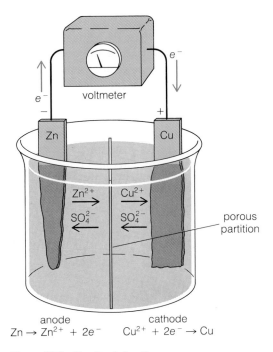

anode   cathode
$Zn \rightarrow Zn^{2+} + 2e^-$ $Cu^{2+} + 2e^- \rightarrow Cu$

Figure 20.5 The Daniell cell

The cell diagrammed in Figure 20.5 is designed to make use of this reaction to produce an electric current. The half-cell on the left contains a zinc metal electrode and $ZnSO_4$ solution. The half-cell on the right consists of a copper metal electrode in a solution of $CuSO_4$. The half-cells are separated by a porous partition that prevents the mechanical mixing of the solutions but permits the passage of ions under the influence of the flow of electricity. A cell of this type is called a **Daniell cell.**

When the zinc and copper electrodes are joined by a wire, electrons flow from the zinc electrode to the copper electrode. At the zinc electrode the zinc metal is *oxidized* to zinc ions. This electrode is the anode, and the electrons that are the product of the oxidation *leave* the cell from this pole (see Table 20.1). The electrons travel the external circuit to the copper electrode where they are used in the reduction of copper(II) ions to metallic copper. The copper thus produced plates out on the electrode. The copper electrode is the cathode. Here, the electrons *enter* the cell and *reduction* occurs.

Since electrons are produced at the zinc electrode, this anode is designated as the negative pole. Electrons travel from the negative pole to the positive pole in the external circuit of any voltaic cell when the cell is operating. The cathode, where electrons are used in the electrode reaction, is therefore the positive pole. Within the cell the movement of ions completes the electric circuit. At first glance, it is surprising that anions, which are negatively charged, should travel toward an anode that is the negative electrode. Conversely, cations, which carry a positive charge, travel toward the cathode, which is the positive pole.

Careful consideration of the electrode reactions provides the answer to this problem. At the anode, zinc ions are being produced and electrons left behind in the metal. At all times the electrical neutrality of the solution is maintained. In the solution surrounding the electrode there must be as much negative charge from anions as there is positive charge from cations. Hence, SO_4^{2-} ions move toward the anode to neutralize the effect of the Zn^{2+} ions that are being produced. At the same time, zinc ions move away from the anode toward the cathode. At the cathode, electrons are being used to reduce Cu^{2+} ions to copper metal. While the Cu^{2+} ions are being discharged, more Cu^{2+} ions move into the region surrounding the cathode to take the place of the ions being removed. If this did not occur, a surplus of SO_4^{2-} ions would build up around the cathode.

The porous partition is added to prevent mechanical mixing of the solutions of the half-cells. If Cu^{2+} ions came into contact with the zinc metal electrode, electrons would be transferred directly rather than through the circuit. In the normal operation of the cell, this "short circuit" does not occur because the Cu^{2+} ions move in a direction away from the zinc electrode.

Actually this cell would work if a solution of an electrolyte other than $ZnSO_4$ were used in the anode compartment, and if a metal other than copper were used for the cathode. The substitutes, however, must be chosen so that the electrolyte in the anode compartment does not react with the zinc electrode and the cathode does not react with Cu^{2+} ions.

20.6 Electromotive Force

If $1\ M$ $ZnSO_4$ and $1\ M$ $CuSO_4$ solutions are employed in the Daniell cell, the cell may be represented by the notation

$$Zn(s)|Zn^{2+}(1\ M)|Cu^{2+}(1\ M)|Cu(s)$$

in which the vertical lines represent phase boundaries. By convention, the substance forming the anode is listed first. The other materials of the cell are then listed in the order that one would encounter them leading from the anode to the cathode. The composition of the cathode is given last.

Electric current is produced by a voltaic cell as a result of the **electromotive force** (emf) of the cell, which is measured in volts. The greater the tendency for the cell reaction to occur, the higher the emf of the cell. The emf of a given cell, however, also depends upon the concentrations of the substances used to make the cell and the temperature.

A **standard emf**, $\mathscr{E}°$, pertains to the electromotive force of a cell, in which all reactants and products are present in their standard states. Values of $\mathscr{E}°$ are usually given for measurements made at $25°C$. The standard state of a solid or a liquid is, of course, the pure solid or pure liquid itself. The standard state of a gas or a substance in solution is a defined state of *ideal unit activity*—that is, corrections are applied for deviations from ideality caused by intermolecular and interionic attractions. For our discussion we shall make the assumption that the activity of ions may be represented by their molar concentrations and the activity of gases by their pressures in atmospheres. Hence, according to this approximation, a standard cell would contain ions at $1\ M$ concentrations and gases (if any) at 1 atm pressures. In the cell notations that follow, concentrations will be indicated only if they deviate from standard.

If the emf of a cell is to be used as a reliable measure of the tendency for the cell reaction to occur, the voltage must be the maximum value obtainable for the particular cell under consideration. If there is an appreciable flow of electricity during measurement, the voltage measured, $\mathscr{E}$, will be reduced because of the internal resistance of the cell. In addition, when the cell delivers current, the electrode reactions produce concentration changes that reduce the voltage.

The emf of a cell, therefore, must be measured with no appreciable flow of electricity through the cell. This measurement is accomplished by the use of a potentiometer. The circuit of a potentiometer includes a source of variable voltage and a means of measuring this voltage. The cell being studied is connected to the potentiometer circuit in such a way that the emf of the cell is opposed by the emf of the potentiometer.

If the emf of the cell is larger than that of the potentiometer, electrons will flow in the normal direction for a spontaneously discharging cell of that type. On the other hand, if the emf of the potentiometer current source is larger than that of the cell, electrons will flow in the opposite direction, thus causing the cell reaction to be reversed. When the two emf's are exactly balanced, no electrons flow. This voltage is the *reversible emf* of the cell. The emf of a standard Daniell cell is 1.10 V.

Faraday's laws apply to the cell reactions of voltaic, as well as electrolytic, cells. One precaution must be observed, however. Electricity is generated by the simultaneous oxidation and reduction half-reactions that occur at the anode and cathode, respectively. Both must occur if the cell is to deliver current. Two faradays of electricity will be produced, therefore, by the oxidation of 1 mol of zinc at the anode *together with* the reduction of 1 mol of Cu^{2+} ions at the cathode. The partial equations

$$\text{anode:} \qquad Zn \longrightarrow Zn^{2+} + 2e^-$$

$$\text{cathode:} \quad 2e^- + Cu^{2+} \longrightarrow Cu$$

when read in terms of moles, represent the flow of two times Avogadro's number of electrons or the production of 2 F of electricity.

The quantity of electrical energy, in joules, produced by a cell is the product of the quantity of electricity delivered, in coulombs, and the emf of the cell, in volts (see Section 20.1). The electrical energy *produced* by the reaction between 1 mol of zinc metal and 1 mol of copper(II) ions may be calculated as follows:

$$2(96,500 \text{ C})(1.10 \text{ V}) = 212,000 \text{ J} = 212 \text{ kJ}$$

One volt·coulomb is a joule.

The emf used in the preceding calculation is the reversible emf ($\mathscr{E}°$) of the standard Daniell cell and hence the maximum voltage for this cell. Therefore, the value secured (212 kJ) is the maximum work that can be obtained from the operation of this type of cell. The maximum *net* work* that can be obtained from a chemical reaction conducted at a constant temperature and pressure is a measure of the *decrease* in the Gibbs free energy (see Section 19.4) of the system. For the standard Daniell cell, ΔG is -212 kJ. Hence,

$$\Delta G = -nF\mathscr{E} \qquad (20.1)$$

---

* Some reactions proceed with an increase in volume, and the system must do work to expand against the atmosphere in order to maintain a constant pressure. The energy for this pressure-volume work is not available for any other purpose; it must be expended in this way if the reaction is to occur at constant pressure. Pressure-volume work is not included in the potentiometric measurement of the electrical work of any cell. Net work (or available work) is work other than pressure-volume work.

where n is the number of moles of electrons transferred in the reaction (or the number of faradays produced), F is the value of the faraday in appropriate units, and $\mathscr{E}$ is the emf in volts. If F is expressed as 96,485 C, ΔG is obtained in joules. A change in free energy derived from a standard emf, $\mathscr{E}°$, is given the symbol $\Delta G°$.

The free energy change of a reaction is a measure of the tendency of the reaction to occur. If work must be done on a system to bring about a change, the change is not spontaneous. At constant temperature and pressure a spontaneous change is one from which net work can be obtained. Hence, for any spontaneous reaction the free energy of the system decreases; ΔG is negative. Since $\Delta G = -nF\mathscr{E}$, only if $\mathscr{E}$ is positive will the cell reaction be spontaneous and serve as a source of electrical energy.

20.7 Electrode Potentials

In the same way that a cell reaction may be regarded as the sum of two half-reactions, the emf of a cell may be thought of as the sum of two half-cell potentials. However, it is impossible to determine the absolute value of the potential of a single half-cell. A relative scale has been established by assigning a value of zero to the voltage of a standard reference half-cell and expressing all half-cell potentials relative to this reference electrode.

The reference half-cell used is the standard hydrogen electrode, which consists of hydrogen gas, at 1 atm pressure, bubbling over a platinum electrode (coated with finely divided platinum to increase its surface) that is immersed in an acid solution containing $H^+(aq)$ at unit activity. In Figure 20.6 a standard hydrogen electrode is shown connected by means of a salt bridge to a standard Cu^{2+}/Cu electrode. A salt bridge is a tube filled with a concentrated solution of a salt (usually KCl), which conducts the current between the half-cells but prevents the mixing of the solutions of the half-cells. The cell of Figure 20.6 may be diagrammed as

$$Pt|H_2|H^+||Cu^{2+}|Cu$$

A double bar indicates a salt bridge. The hydrogen electrode is the anode, the copper electrode is the cathode, the emf of the cell is 0.34 V.

The cell emf is considered to be the sum of the half-cell potential for the oxidation half reaction (which we shall give the symbol $\mathscr{E}°_{ox}$) and the half-cell potential for the reduction half reaction (which we shall indicate as $\mathscr{E}°_{red}$). For the cell of Figure 20.6,

$$\text{anode:} \qquad H_2 \longrightarrow 2H^+ + 2e^- \qquad \mathscr{E}°_{ox} = \quad 0.00\text{ V}$$

$$\text{cathode:} \quad 2e^- + Cu^{2+} \longrightarrow Cu \qquad \mathscr{E}°_{red} = +0.34\text{ V}$$

Since the hydrogen electrode is arbitrarily assigned a potential of zero, the entire cell emf is ascribed to the standard Cu^{2+}/Cu electrode. The value $+0.34$ V is called the standard electrode potential of the Cu^{2+}/Cu electrode. Notice that *electrode potentials are given for reduction half-reactions.* If the symbol $\mathscr{E}°$ (without a subscript) is used for an electrode potential, $\mathscr{E}°_{red}$ is understood.

If a cell is constructed from a standard hydrogen electrode and a standard Zn^{2+}/Zn electrode, the zinc electrode is the anode, and the emf of the cell is 0.76 V. Thus,

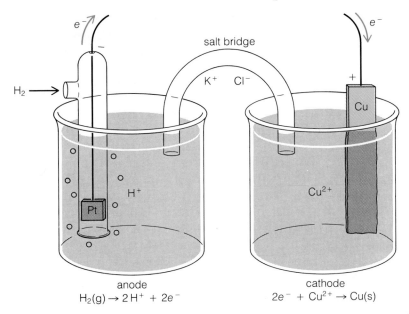

anode

$H_2(g) \rightarrow 2H^+ + 2e^-$

cathode

$2e^- + Cu^{2+} \rightarrow Cu(s)$

Figure 20.6 Standard hydrogen electrode and a Cu^{2+}/Cu electrode

anode: $\qquad Zn \longrightarrow Zn^{2+} + 2e^- \qquad \mathscr{E}^\circ_{ox} = +0.76 \text{ V}$

cathode: $\quad 2e^- + 2H^+ \longrightarrow H_2 \qquad \mathscr{E}^\circ_{red} = \quad 0.00 \text{ V}$

The value $+0.76$ V is sometimes called an **oxidation potential,** since it corresponds to an oxidation half-reaction. An electrode potential, however, is a **reduction potential.** To obtain the electrode potential of the Zn^{2+}/Zn couple, we must change the sign of the oxidation potential so that the potential corresponds to the reverse half-reaction, a reduction:

$$2e^- + Zn^{2+} \longrightarrow Zn \qquad \mathscr{E}^\circ_{red} = -0.76 \text{ V}$$

It is not necessary to use a cell containing a standard hydrogen electrode to obtain a standard electrode potential. For example, the standard potential of the Ni^{2+}/Ni electrode may be determined from the cell

$$Ni|Ni^{2+}||Cu^{2+}|Cu$$

The emf of this cell is 0.59 V, and the nickel electrode functions as the anode:

$$Ni + Cu^{2+} \longrightarrow Ni^{2+} + Cu \qquad \mathscr{E}^\circ_{cell} = +0.59 \text{ V}$$

The standard electrode potential of the Cu^{2+}/Cu electrode has been determined:

$$2e^- + Cu^{2+} \longrightarrow Cu \qquad \mathscr{E}^\circ_{red} = +0.34 \text{ V}$$

If we subtract the Cu^{2+}/Cu half-reaction from the cell reaction and subtract the half-cell potential from the cell emf, we obtain

$$Ni \longrightarrow Ni^{2+} + 2e^- \qquad \mathscr{E}^\circ_{ox} = +0.25 \text{ V}$$

Table 20.2 Standard electrode potentials at 25°C[a]

Half-Reaction	$\mathscr{E}°$ (Volts)
$Li^+ + e^- \rightleftharpoons Li$	-3.045
$K^+ + e^- \rightleftharpoons K$	-2.925
$Ba^{2+} + 2e^- \rightleftharpoons Ba$	-2.906
$Ca^{2+} + 2e^- \rightleftharpoons Ca$	-2.866
$Na^+ + e^- \rightleftharpoons Na$	-2.714
$Mg^{2+} + 2e^- \rightleftharpoons Mg$	-2.363
$Al^{3+} + 3e^- \rightleftharpoons Al$	-1.662
$2H_2O + 2e^- \rightleftharpoons H_2 + 2OH^-$	-0.82806
$Zn^{2+} + 2e^- \rightleftharpoons Zn$	-0.7628
$Cr^{3+} + 3e^- \rightleftharpoons Cr$	-0.744
$Fe^{2+} + 2e^- \rightleftharpoons Fe$	-0.4402
$Cd^{2+} + 2e^- \rightleftharpoons Cd$	-0.4029
$Ni^{2+} + 2e^- \rightleftharpoons Ni$	-0.250
$Sn^{2+} + 2e^- \rightleftharpoons Sn$	-0.136
$Pb^{2+} + 2e^- \rightleftharpoons Pb$	-0.126
$2H^+ + 2e^- \rightleftharpoons H_2$	0
$Cu^{2+} + 2e^- \rightleftharpoons Cu$	$+0.337$
$Cu^+ + e^- \rightleftharpoons Cu$	$+0.521$
$I_2 + 2e^- \rightleftharpoons 2I^-$	$+0.5355$
$Fe^{3+} + e^- \rightleftharpoons Fe^{2+}$	$+0.771$
$Ag^+ + e^- \rightleftharpoons Ag$	$+0.7991$
$Br_2 + 2e^- \rightleftharpoons 2Br^-$	$+1.0652$
$O_2 + 4H^+ + 4e^- \rightleftharpoons 2H_2O$	$+1.229$
$Cr_2O_7^{2-} + 14H^+ + 6e^- \rightleftharpoons 2Cr^{3+} + 7H_2O$	$+1.33$
$Cl_2 + 2e^- \rightleftharpoons 2Cl^-$	$+1.3595$
$MnO_4^- + 8H^+ + 5e^- \rightleftharpoons Mn^{2+} + 4H_2O$	$+1.51$
$F_2 + 2e^- \rightleftharpoons 2F^-$	$+2.87$

[a] Data from A. J. de Bethune and N. A. Swendeman Loud, "Table of Electrode Potentials and Temperature Coefficients," pp. 414–424 in *Encyclopedia of Electrochemistry* (C. A. Hampel, editor), Van Nostrand Reinhold, New York, 1964, and from A. J. de Bethune and N. A. Swendeman Loud, *Standard Aqueous Electrode Potentials and Temperature Coefficients,* 19 pp., C. A. Hampel, publisher, Skokie, Illinois, 1964.

The electrode potential is therefore

$$2e^- + Ni^{2+} \longrightarrow Ni \qquad \mathscr{E}°_{red} = -0.25 \text{ V}$$

Standard electrode potentials are listed in Table 20.2, and a more complete list is found in the appendix. The table is constructed with the most positive electrode potential (greatest tendency for reduction) at the bottom. Hence, if a pair of electrodes is combined to make a voltaic cell, the reduction half-reaction (cathode) of the cell will be that listed for the electrode that stands lower in the table, and the oxidation half-reaction (anode) will be the *reverse* of that shown for the electrode that stands higher in the table.

For example, consider a cell constructed from standard Ni^{2+}/Ni and Ag^+/Ag electrodes. The table entries for these electrodes are

$$Ni^{2+} + 2e^- \rightleftharpoons Ni \qquad \mathscr{E}°_{red} = -0.250 \text{ V}$$

$$Ag^+ + e^- \rightleftharpoons Ag \qquad \mathscr{E}°_{red} = +0.799 \text{ V}$$

Of the two ions, the Ag^+ ion shows the greater tendency for reduction. The Ag^+/Ag electrode is therefore the cathode, and the Ni^{2+}/Ni electrode is the anode. The half-reaction that takes place at an anode is an oxidation, and the half-cell potential is an oxidation potential. The sign of the table entry for the Ni^{2+}/Ni half-cell, therefore, must be reversed to give an $\mathscr{E}^\circ_{ox}$:

anode: $Ni \longrightarrow Ni^{2+} + 2e^-$ $\mathscr{E}^\circ_{ox} = +0.250$ V

cathode: $2e^- + 2Ag^+ \longrightarrow 2Ag$ $\mathscr{E}^\circ_{red} = +0.799$ V

The cell reaction and cell emf may be obtained by addition:

$Ni + 2Ag^+ \longrightarrow Ni^{2+} + 2Ag$ $\mathscr{E}^\circ_{cell} = +1.049$ V

Notice that the half-reaction for the reduction of Ag^+ must be multiplied by 2 before the addition so that the electrons lost and gained in the half-reactions will cancel. The $\mathscr{E}^\circ$ for the Ag^+/Ag electrode, however, is *not* multiplied by 2. The magnitude of an electrode potential depends upon the temperature and the concentrations of materials used in the construction of the half-cell. These variables are fixed for *standard* electrode potentials. Indication of the stoichiometry of the cell reaction does not imply that a concentration change has been made.

Actually the reactions implied by the half-cell potentials are

$$2H^+ + Ni \longrightarrow H_2 + Ni^{2+}$$
$$\underline{H_2 + 2Ag^+ \longrightarrow 2H^+ + 2Ag}$$
$$Ni + 2Ag^+ \longrightarrow Ni^{2+} + 2Ag$$

Notice, however, that in the addition of these reactions, the H_2 molecules and H^+ ions cancel.

Electrode potentials are also useful for the evaluation of oxidation-reduction reactions that take place outside of electrochemical cells. An *oxidizing agent* is a substance that brings about an oxidation and in the process is itself reduced. A strong *oxidizing* agent, therefore, has a high positive *reduction* potential, $\mathscr{E}^\circ_{red}$. The strongest oxidizing agent given in Table 20.2 is $F_2(g)$ since the highest $\mathscr{E}^\circ_{red}$ given in the table is

$F_2(g) + 2e^- \longrightarrow 2F^-(aq)$ $\mathscr{E}^\circ_{red} = +2.87$ V

The best oxidizing agents listed in the table are F_2, MnO_4^- in acid, Cl_2, and $Cr_2O_7^{2-}$ in acid.

A *reducing agent* is itself oxidized in bringing about a reduction. A strong *reducing* agent, therefore, has a high, positive *oxidation* potential. Remember that $\mathscr{E}^\circ_{ox}$ values are obtained by changing the signs of the table values; the corresponding oxidation half-reactions are derived by reversing the partial equations shown. The strongest reducing agent given in Table 20.2 is Li metal since the highest $\mathscr{E}^\circ_{ox}$ derived from the table values is

$Li(s) \longrightarrow Li^+(aq) + e^-$ $\mathscr{E}^\circ_{ox} = +3.045$ V

The best reducing agents given in the table are the active metals Li, K, Ba, Ca, and Na.

Whether or not a proposed reaction will be spontaneous *with all substances present at unit activity* can be determined by use of electrode potentials. A spontaneous reaction is indicated only if the emf of the reaction is positive.

Example 20.5

Use electrode potentials to determine whether the following proposed reactions are spontaneous with all substances present at unit activity:

(a) $Cl_2(g) + 2 I^-(aq) \longrightarrow 2 Cl^-(aq) + I_2(s)$

(b) $2 Ag(s) + 2 H^+(aq) \longrightarrow 2 Ag^+(aq) + H_2(g)$

Solution

(a) In the proposed reaction, the Cl_2 is reduced to Cl^- (and we need an $\mathscr{E}^\circ_{red}$ for this half-reaction) and the I^- is oxidized to I_2 (and we need an $\mathscr{E}^\circ_{ox}$ for this half-reaction):

$$
\begin{array}{lr}
2e^- + Cl_2(g) \longrightarrow 2 Cl^-(aq) & \mathscr{E}^\circ_{red} = +1.360 \text{ V} \\
2 I^-(aq) \longrightarrow I_2(s) + 2e^- & \mathscr{E}^\circ_{ox} = -0.536 \text{ V} \\
\hline
Cl_2(g) + 2 I^-(aq) \longrightarrow 2 Cl^-(aq) + I_2(s) & \text{emf} = +0.824 \text{ V}
\end{array}
$$

Since the overall emf is positive, the reaction is spontaneous.

(b) In this reaction, Ag is oxidized ($\mathscr{E}^\circ_{ox}$ needed) and H^+ is reduced ($\mathscr{E}^\circ_{red}$ needed):

$$
\begin{array}{lr}
2 Ag(s) \longrightarrow 2 Ag^+(aq) + 2e^- & \mathscr{E}^\circ_{ox} = -0.799 \text{ V} \\
2 H^+(aq) + 2e^- \longrightarrow H_2(g) & \mathscr{E}^\circ_{red} = 0.000 \text{ V} \\
\hline
2 Ag(s) + 2 H^+(aq) \longrightarrow 2 Ag^+(aq) + H_2(g) & \text{emf} = -0.799 \text{ V}
\end{array}
$$

The reaction is *not* spontaneous as written. The reverse reaction (between Ag^+ and H_2) would be spontaneous (emf $= +0.799$ V).

There are several factors that must be kept in mind when using a table of electrode potentials to predict the course of a chemical reaction. Because $\mathscr{E}$ changes with changes in concentration, many presumably unfavored reactions can be made to occur by altering the concentrations of the reacting species. In addition, some theoretically favored reactions proceed at such a slow rate that they are of no practical consequence.

Correct use of the table also demands that all pertinent half-reactions of a given element be considered before making a prediction. On the basis of the half-reactions

$$3e^- + Fe^{3+} \rightleftharpoons Fe \qquad \mathscr{E}^\circ_{red} = -0.036 \text{ V}$$

$$2e^- + 2 H^+ \rightleftharpoons H_2 \qquad \mathscr{E}^\circ_{red} = 0.000 \text{ V}$$

one might predict that the products of the reaction of iron with H^+ would be hydrogen gas and Fe^{3+} ions (emf for the complete reaction, $+0.036$ V). The oxidation state iron(II), however, lies between metallic iron and the oxidation state iron(III). Once an iron atom has lost two electrons and becomes an Fe^{2+} ion, further oxidation is opposed, as may be seen from the reverse of the following:

$$e^- + Fe^{3+} \rightleftharpoons Fe^{2+} \qquad \mathscr{E}^\circ_{red} = +0.771 \text{ V}$$

Thus, the reaction yields Fe^{2+} ions only. This fact could have been predicted by an examination of the half-reaction

$$2e^- + Fe^{2+} \rightleftharpoons Fe \qquad \mathscr{E}^\circ_{red} = -0.440 \text{ V}$$

The $\mathscr{E}_{ox}$ for the production of Fe^{2+} ions from the reaction of iron metal and H^+ ions ($+0.440$ V) is greater than that for the production of Fe^{3+} ions ($+0.036$ V), and hence the former is favored.

We may summarize the electrode potentials for iron and its ions as follows:

$$Fe^{3+} \xrightarrow{+0.771 \text{ V}} Fe^{2+} \xrightarrow{-0.440 \text{ V}} Fe$$
$$\underset{-0.036 \text{ V}}{\underline{\qquad\qquad\qquad\qquad\qquad}}$$

The preceding predictions are immediately evident from this diagram, if we remember that oxidation is the reverse of the relation corresponding to an electrode potential.

Occasionally an oxidation state of an element is unstable toward disproportionation (auto oxidation-reduction, see Section 13.3). The electrode potentials for copper and its ions may be summarized as follows:

$$Cu^{2+} \xrightarrow{+0.153 \text{ V}} Cu^+ \xrightarrow{+0.521 \text{ V}} Cu$$
$$\underset{+0.337 \text{ V}}{\underline{\qquad\qquad\qquad\qquad\qquad}}$$

From this we see that the Cu^+ ion is not a very stable one. In water, Cu^+ ions disproportionate to copper metal and Cu^{2+} ions:

$$2\,Cu^+(aq) \longrightarrow Cu(s) + Cu^{2+}(aq)$$

The emf for this reaction is $+0.521 - 0.153 = +0.368$ V. Species unstable toward disproportionation may be readily recognized. The electrode potential for a reduction of the species is more positive than the electrode potential for a reduction in which the species is produced. An inspection of the diagram for iron and its ions shows that the Fe^{2+} ion is stable toward such disproportionation.

20.8 Gibbs Free Energy Change and Electromotive Force

The reversible emf of a cell, $\mathscr{E}^\circ_{cell}$, is a measure of the decrease in Gibbs free energy for the cell reaction:

$$\Delta G^\circ = -nF\mathscr{E}^\circ \qquad\qquad (20.1)$$

We can, therefore, use standard electrode potentials to calculate ΔG° values.

Example 20.6

Use electrochemical data given in the appendix to calculate the value of $\Delta G°$ for the reaction

$$2\,Ag(s) + Cl_2(g) \longrightarrow 2\,AgCl(s)$$

Solution

We use the standard electrode potentials to calculate the standard potential for the reaction:

$2\,Ag(s) + 2\,Cl^-(aq) \longrightarrow 2\,AgCl(s) + 2e^-$	$\mathscr{E}°_{ox} = -0.222$ V
$2e^- + Cl_2(g) \longrightarrow 2\,Cl^-(aq)$	$\mathscr{E}°_{red} = +1.359$ V
$2\,Ag(s) + Cl_2(g) \longrightarrow 2\,AgCl(s)$	$\mathscr{E}°_{cell} = +1.137$ V

Since $n = 2$ (which means that 2 mol of electrons are transferred),

$$\begin{aligned}
\Delta G° &= -nF\mathscr{E}° \\
&= -2(96{,}500\text{ C})(+1.137\text{ V}) \\
&= -219{,}400\text{ J} = -219.4\text{ kJ}
\end{aligned}$$

Note that $1\text{ J} = 1\text{ V}\cdot\text{C}$.

The $\Delta G°$ values obtained in this way can be used, together with standard enthalpy changes ($\Delta H°$ values), to calculate standard changes in entropy ($\Delta S°$ values).

Example 20.7

Calculate the value of $\Delta S°$ for the reaction

$$2\,Ag(s) + Cl_2(g) \longrightarrow 2\,AgCl(s) \qquad \Delta H° = -254.0\text{ kJ}$$

Solution

We are given $\Delta H°$ for the reaction and we note from Example 20.6 that $\Delta G° = -219.4$ kJ. Therefore,

$$\Delta G° = \Delta H° - T\Delta S°$$

$$-219.4\text{ kJ} = -254.0\text{ kJ} - T\,\Delta S°$$

$$T\,\Delta S° = -34.6\text{ kJ}$$

Since $T = 298$ K,

$$\begin{aligned}
\Delta S° &= \frac{T\Delta S°}{T} \\
&= \frac{-(34{,}600\text{ J})}{298\text{ K}} \\
&= -116\text{ J/K}
\end{aligned}$$

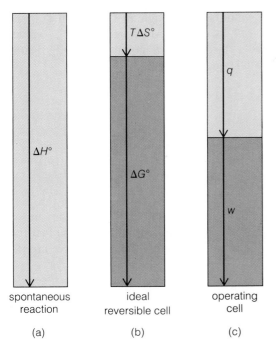

Figure 20.7 Relations between thermodynamic functions for the reaction $2\,Ag(s) + Cl_2(g) \longrightarrow 2\,AgCl(s)$ at 25°C and 1 atm

The fact that $\Delta S°$ is negative means that the system becomes more ordered (less random) as the reaction proceeds. Notice that a mole of gas is consumed during the course of the reaction; the decrease in the entropy of the system is therefore not surprising.

The results of Examples 20.6 and 20.7 are summarized in Figure 20.7. If the reaction is conducted outside the cell (a), heat equivalent to $\Delta H°$ is evolved. In the case of the ideal, reversible cell (b), the maximum amount of useful work is obtained ($\Delta G°$) and heat equivalent to $T\Delta S°$ is evolved. Since $\Delta G° = \Delta H° - T\Delta S°$,

$$\Delta H° = \Delta G° + T\Delta S°$$

as the figure illustrates. The ideal, reversible cell is an abstraction, not an operating device. When the reversible emf of a cell is measured, the emf of the cell is balanced against an external emf in such a way that no current flows. In this way the maximum voltage that the cell is capable of producing is measured. In an operating cell (c), less than the maximum amount of work is done (w) and an amount of heat greater than $T\Delta S°$ is evolved (q).

The relationship between $\Delta G°$ and emf is useful in several other ways. An $\mathscr{E}°_{cell}$, for example, can be calculated from a $\Delta G°$ value for a cell reaction. In addition, free energy changes provide an answer to the problem of combining two $\mathscr{E}^\circ_{red}$ values to obtain a third $\mathscr{E}^\circ_{red}$ value. Even though an $\mathscr{E}^\circ_{ox}$ and an $\mathscr{E}^\circ_{red}$ may be combined to give an emf of a *cell*, two electrode potentials ($\mathscr{E}^\circ_{red}$ values) may *not* be combined directly to give a third *electrode* potential (an $\mathscr{E}^\circ_{red}$ value). For example, the sum of the two partial equations

$$2e^- + Fe^{2+} \longrightarrow Fe \qquad \mathscr{E}^\circ_{red} = -0.440 \text{ V}$$

$$e^- + Fe^{3+} \longrightarrow Fe^{2+} \qquad \mathscr{E}^\circ_{red} = +0.771 \text{ V}$$

is the partial equation

$$3e^- + Fe^{3+} \longrightarrow Fe$$

The electrode potential for the final half-reaction, however, is *not* the sum of the other two $\mathscr{E}^\circ_{red}$ values. A solution to the problem is provided by the fact that free energy changes are additive in the same way that enthalpy changes are (the law of Hess).

Example 20.8

Use $\mathscr{E}^\circ_{red}$ values to find the $\mathscr{E}^\circ_{red}$ for the half-reaction

$$3e^- + Fe^{3+} \longrightarrow Fe$$

Solution

Whereas two $\mathscr{E}^\circ_{red}$ values may not be added to give a third, the ΔG° values for two half-reactions may be added to give a ΔG° value for a third half-reaction:

$$
\begin{array}{lccl}
 & \mathscr{E}^\circ_{red} & \Delta G^\circ = -nF\mathscr{E}^\circ & \\
2e^- + Fe^{2+} \longrightarrow Fe & -0.440 \text{ V} & = -2(-0.440)F = & +0.880F \\
e^- + Fe^{3+} \longrightarrow Fe^{2+} & +0.771 \text{ V} & = -1(+0.771)F = & -0.771F \\
\hline
3e^- + Fe^{3+} \longrightarrow Fe & & & +0.109F
\end{array}
$$

Notice that we make no attempt to multiply $+0.109$ V by the value of the faraday. The $\mathscr{E}^\circ_{red}$ for the third half-reaction is found from the ΔG° value ($+0.109F$). Since three electrons are gained, $n = 3$:

$$\Delta G^\circ = -nF\mathscr{E}^\circ_{red}$$

$$+0.109F = -3F\mathscr{E}^\circ_{red}$$

$$\mathscr{E}^\circ_{red} = \frac{+0.109F}{-3F} = -0.036 \text{ V}$$

Electrode potentials may also be used to determine equilibrium constants. In Section 19.7, we noted that

$$\Delta G^\circ = -2.303RT \log K \qquad (20.2)$$

Since

$$\Delta G^{\circ} = -nF\mathscr{E}^{\circ}$$

$$nF\mathscr{E}^{\circ} = 2.303RT \log K$$

$$\mathscr{E}^{\circ} = \frac{2.303RT}{nF} \log K \tag{20.3}$$

When $T = 298.15$ K (25°C), substitution for R, F, and T gives

$$\mathscr{E}^{\circ} = \frac{0.05916 \text{ V}}{n} \log K \tag{20.4}$$

Example 20.9

Use electrochemical data to calculate the equilibrium constant K for the reaction at 25°C:

$$Fe^{2+}(aq) + Ag^{+}(aq) \rightleftharpoons Fe^{3+}(aq) + Ag(s)$$

$$K = [Fe^{3+}]/[Fe^{2+}][Ag^{+}]$$

Solution

The half-reactions are

$$Fe^{2+} \longrightarrow Fe^{3+} + e^{-} \qquad \mathscr{E}^{\circ}_{ox} = -0.771 \text{ V}$$

$$e^{-} + Ag^{+} \longrightarrow Ag(s) \qquad \mathscr{E}^{\circ}_{red} = +0.799 \text{ V}$$

The $\mathscr{E}^{\circ}$ value for the reaction, therefore, is $+0.028$ V and $n = 1$:

$$\mathscr{E}^{\circ} = \frac{0.0592 \text{ V}}{n} \log K$$

$$+0.028 \text{ V} = \frac{0.0592 \text{ V}}{1} \log K$$

$$\log K = 0.47$$

$$K = 3.0$$

20.9 Effect of Concentration on Cell Potentials

In Section 19.7, we considered the relationship

$$\Delta G = \Delta G^{\circ} + 2.303RT \log Q \tag{20.5}$$

where ΔG is the free energy change for a chemical reaction, ΔG° is the *standard* free energy change for that reaction, R is 8.3143 J/(K·mol), T is the absolute temperature, and Q is the reaction quotient, a fraction derived from the activities of the substances involved in the reaction. For the hypothetical reaction

$$w\text{W} + x\text{X} \longrightarrow y\text{Y} + z\text{Z}$$

where the lower-case letters represent the coefficients of the balanced chemical equation

$$Q = \frac{(a_\text{Y})^y (a_\text{Z})^z}{(a_\text{W})^w (a_\text{X})^x} \tag{20.6}$$

the activity of each substance is raised to a power equal to the coefficient of that substance in the balanced chemical equation. The *numerator* of Q is the product of the activity terms for the substances on the *right* of the chemical equation. The *denominator* of Q is the product of the activity terms for the substances on the *left* of the chemical equation. Since the activity of a pure solid is assumed to be unity at all times, the activity term for a solid is always equal to 1. For our work, we will assume that the activity of a substance in solution is given by the molar concentration of the substance and the activity of a gas is equal to the partial pressure of the gas in atmospheres.

Since $\Delta G = -nF\mathscr{E}$ and $\Delta G^\circ = -nF\mathscr{E}^\circ$,

$$\Delta G = \Delta G^\circ + 2.303RT \log Q$$

$$-nF\mathscr{E} = -nF\mathscr{E}^\circ + 2.303RT \log Q$$

$$\mathscr{E} = \mathscr{E}^\circ - \frac{2.303RT}{nF} \log Q \tag{20.7}$$

If we substitute 298.15 K for T (which is 25°C), 8.3144 J/(K·mol) for R, 96,485 C/mol for F, we get

$$\mathscr{E} = \mathscr{E}^\circ - \frac{0.05916\ \text{V}}{n} \log Q \tag{20.8}$$

which is called the Nernst equation, named for Walther Nernst, who developed it in 1889. When the activities of all substances are unity (standard states), $\log Q = 0$ and $\mathscr{E} = \mathscr{E}^\circ$. The Nernst equation may be used to determine the emf of a cell constructed from nonstandard electrodes or to calculate the electrode potential of a half-cell in which all species are not present at unit activity.

Example 20.10

What is the electrode potential of a Zn^{2+}/Zn electrode in which the concentration of Zn^{2+} ions is $0.1M$?

Solution

The partial equation

$$2e^- + \text{Zn}^{2+} \longrightarrow \text{Zn}$$

Walther Nernst, 1864–1941.
*American Institute of Physics,
Niels Bohr Library, Sawyer
Collection.*

shows 2 electrons gained. If the symbol $[Zn^{2+}]$ is used to designate the molar concentration of Zn^{2+} ions:

$$\mathscr{E} = \mathscr{E}^\circ - \frac{0.0592}{2} \log\left(\frac{1}{[Zn^{2+}]}\right)$$

$\mathscr{E}^\circ_{red}$ for the Zn^{2+}/Zn electrode is -0.76 V:

$$\mathscr{E} = -0.76 - \frac{0.0592}{2} \log\left(\frac{1}{0.1}\right)$$

$$\mathscr{E} = -0.76 - 0.0296(1) = -0.79 \text{ V}$$

Example 20.11

What is the potential for the cell

$$\text{Ni}|\text{Ni}^{2+}(0.01\ M)\|\text{Cl}^-(0.2\ M)|\text{Cl}_2(1\ \text{atm})|\text{Pt}$$

Solution

Oxidation occurs at the Ni^{2+}/Ni electrode since it is the anode of the cell. The two half-reactions of the cell are

$$\text{Ni} \longrightarrow \text{Ni}^{2+} + 2e^- \qquad \mathscr{E}^\circ_{ox} = +0.25 \text{ V}$$

$$2e^- + \text{Cl}_2 \longrightarrow 2\,\text{Cl}^- \qquad \mathscr{E}^\circ_{red} = +1.36 \text{ V}$$

The cell reaction and $\mathscr{E}^\circ$ for the cell, therefore, are

$$\text{Ni} + \text{Cl}_2 \longrightarrow \text{Ni}^{2+} + 2\,\text{Cl}^- \qquad \mathscr{E}^\circ = +1.61 \text{ V}$$

Since $n = 2$,

$$\mathscr{E} = \mathscr{E}^\circ - \frac{0.0592}{2} \log\left(\frac{[\text{Cl}^-]^2[\text{Ni}^{2+}]}{p_{\text{Cl}_2}}\right)$$

$$\mathscr{E} = +1.61 - \frac{0.0592}{2} \log\left(\frac{(0.2)^2(0.01)}{(1)}\right)$$

$$\mathscr{E} = +1.61 - 0.0296 \log(0.0004)$$

$$\mathscr{E} = +1.61 + 0.10 = +1.71 \text{ V}$$

Example 20.12

What is the $\mathscr{E}$ of the cell

$$\text{Sn}|\text{Sn}^{2+}(1.0\ M)\|\text{Pb}^{2+}(0.0010\ M)|\text{Pb}$$

Solution

The following may be obtained from a table of standard electrode potentials:

20.11 Electrode Potentials and Electrolysis

An emf of a cell calculated from electrode potentials is the maximum voltage that the cell can develop. For the reverse process, an electrolysis, the emf is the minimum voltage required to bring about the electrolysis. In theory, we should be able to use $\mathscr{E}°$ values to determine what electrode reaction will occur in an electrolysis when a choice of several is possible.

Consider the electrolysis of an aqueous solution of $CuCl_2$. There are two possible cathode reactions:

$$2e^- + Cu^{2+}(aq) \longrightarrow Cu(s) \qquad \mathscr{E}°_{red} = +0.34 \text{ V}$$

$$2e^- + 2 H_2O \longrightarrow H_2(g) + 2 OH^-(aq) \qquad \mathscr{E}_{red} = -0.414 \text{ V}$$

The electrode potential for the reduction of water has been adjusted by use of the Nernst equation for the fact that in neutral aqueous solutions $[OH^-] = 10^{-7} M$, not $1.0 M$. Clearly, the reduction of Cu^{2+} is easier to bring about than the reduction of water, and the reduction of Cu^{2+} occurs at the cathode.

Two possible anode reactions should be considered:

$$2 Cl^-(aq) \longrightarrow Cl_2(g) + 2e^- \qquad \mathscr{E}°_{ox} = -1.36 \text{ V}$$

$$2 H_2O \longrightarrow O_2(g) + 4 H^+(aq) + 4e^- \qquad \mathscr{E}_{ox} = -0.82 \text{ V}$$

The electrode potential for the oxidation of water has been adjusted by use of the Nernst equation for the fact that in neutral aqueous solutions $[H^+] = 10^{-7} M$, not $1.0 M$. From these values it would seem that the oxidation of water would occur. In fact, the oxidation of Cl^- is the half-reaction that is observed.

Frequently, the voltage required for an electrolysis is higher than the value calculated by use of electrode potentials by an amount called the *overvoltage*. Overvoltage is thought to be caused by a slow rate of reaction at the electrodes. Excess applied voltage is required to make the electrolysis proceed at an appreciable rate. Overvoltages for the deposition of metals are low, but those required for the liberation of hydrogen gas or oxygen gas are usually appreciable. In the electrolysis of an aqueous solution of $CuCl_2$ the overvoltage of chlorine is less than the overvoltage of oxygen so that Cl_2 is liberated at the anode, not O_2.

The minimum voltage required for the electrolysis, therefore, is

$$\mathscr{E} = \mathscr{E}°_{red} + \mathscr{E}°_{ox}$$
$$= +0.34 \text{ V} - 1.36 \text{ V} = -1.02 \text{ V}$$

The value has a negative sign since it represents voltage *required*. A higher voltage than this would have to be used to take care of the overvoltage as well as to overcome the internal resistance of the cell.

The products of an electrolysis vary with the concentrations of ions in solution since the half-cell emf's are dependent upon concentrations. For example, the electrolysis of *dilute* aqueous solutions of chlorides yields oxygen gas at the anode rather than chlorine. Furthermore, after the primary electrode reactions occur, in which electrons are transferred, secondary reactions may occur. If chlorine is liberated in an alkaline solution, for example, ClO^- or ClO_3^- may be formed by the reaction of Cl_2 with OH^- ions.

12 The Corrosion of Iron

The corrosion of iron has serious economic consequences. The annual world-wide cost of replacing rusted iron objects runs to billions of dollars. The process itself is electrochemical in nature.

The corrosion of iron, rusting, occurs only in the presence of oxygen and water. At one place on the surface of the iron object, *oxidation* of the iron takes place:

$$\text{anode:} \quad \text{Fe(s)} \longrightarrow \text{Fe}^{2+}\text{(aq)} + 2e^-$$

At another spot on the surface, a reduction occurs, which involves $O_2(g)$ and H_2O:

$$\text{cathode:} \quad 4e^- + O_2(g) + 2\,H_2O \longrightarrow 4\,OH^-\text{(aq)}$$

In effect, therefore, a miniature voltaic cell is set up. The electrons produced at the anodic region move through the iron toward the cathodic region.

The *cations*, Fe^{2+} ions, produced at the anode, move through the water on the surface of the object toward the *cathode*. The *anions*, OH^- ions, produced at the cathode, move toward the *anode*. Somewhere between these two regions, the ions meet and form $Fe(OH)_2$. Iron(II) hydroxide, however, is not stable in the presence of moisture and oxygen. The hydroxide is oxidized to iron(III) hydroxide, which in reality is hydrated iron(III) oxide, $Fe_2O_3 \cdot x\,H_2O$, or rust.

The places where a rusted iron object becomes pitted are the anodic regions where iron goes into solution as Fe^{2+} ions. The cathodic regions are those that are most open to moisture and air, since $O_2(g)$ and H_2O are involved in the cathode reaction. The rust always forms at spots somewhat removed from those places where pitting occurs (between the anodic and cathodic regions).

When a painted iron object rusts, for example, the cathodic regions are spots where the paint has been broken away and bare iron metal is exposed to moisture and oxygen. The anodic regions, where the iron becomes pitted, are spots beneath the painted surface. The pitting causes more paint to flake off, which accelerates the rusting. The rust itself forms at spots between these two regions, usually closer to the cathodic region than to the anodic region—the transformation of $Fe(OH)_2$ to rust requires $O_2(g)$ and H_2O.

Salt water accelerates rusting because the ions present in the water help to carry the current in the miniature voltaic cells that are set up on the surface of the iron. Some ions, Cl^- for example, appear to catalyze the electrode reactions.

Impurities in the iron also enhance rusting. Very pure iron does not rust rapidly. Some types of impurities, strains, and crystal defects present in the iron attract electrons away from regions in the iron that become, therefore, anodic sites.

Iron or steel objects can be prevented from rusting by applying protective coatings (such as grease, paint, or other metals) which keep air and moisture away from the iron. Metal coatings are applied by electrolysis (Cr, Ni, and Cd are examples) or by dipping the object into molten metal (Zn and Sn are examples).

Galvanized iron is iron that has been coated with zinc. The iron is protected from rusting even if the zinc coating is broken. In such a case, the zinc, rather than the iron, serves as the anode and is oxidized since zinc is a more reactive metal than iron. For tin coatings, such as are used in "tin cans," the reverse is

Twin ribbons of zinc wire (about $\frac{1}{2}$ inch in diameter) are buried as sacrificial anodes alongside a section of the trans-Alaska pipeline to prevent electrochemical corrosion of the pipe. The ribbons are connected to the pipe at 500 or 1000-foot intervals. *The Alyeska Pipeline Service Company.*

true. If a tin coating is broken, the corrosion of the iron beneath is enhanced since iron is a more reactive metal than tin.

Metals that are more reactive than iron can be used as sacrificial anodes. To protect an underground iron tank, pipeline, or cable from rusting, pieces of reactive metals (such as Mg or Zn) are buried beside the iron object and connected to it by wires. By this means, the iron is not oxidized; it becomes the cathode and the more reactive metal becomes the anode. The reactive metal anodes are sacrificed to protect the iron. They oxidize away rapidly and must be replaced from time to time.

20.13 Some Commercial Voltaic Cells

Several voltaic cells are of commercial importance. The **dry cell** (see Figure 20.8) consists of a zinc metal container (which serves as the anode) that is filled

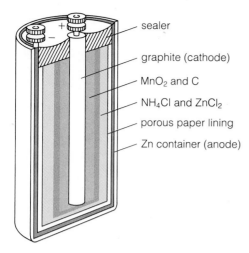

Figure 20.8 The dry cell

with a moist paste of ammonium chloride and zinc chloride and contains a graphite electrode (the cathode) surrounded by manganese dioxide. The electrode reactions are complex, but they may be approximately represented by

anode: $$Zn \longrightarrow Zn^{2+} + 2e^-$$

cathode: $$2e^- + 2\,MnO_2 + 2\,NH_4^+ \longrightarrow Mn_2O_3 \cdot H_2O + 2\,NH_3$$

The dry cell generates a voltage of approximately 1.25 to 1.50 V.

A newer type of dry cell which has found use in small electrical devices (such as hearing aids) consists of a zinc container as the anode, a carbon rod as the cathode, and moist mercury(II) oxide mixed with potassium hydroxide as the electrolyte. A lining of porous paper keeps the HgO separated from the zinc anode. The cell has a potential of approximately 1.35 V:

anode: $$Zn + 2\,OH^- \longrightarrow Zn(OH)_2 + 2e^-$$

cathode: $$2e^- + HgO + H_2O \longrightarrow Hg + 2\,OH^-$$

The **lead storage cell** consists of a lead anode and a grid of lead packed with lead dioxide as the cathode. The electrolyte is sulfuric acid, and the half-cell reactions are

anode: $$Pb(s) + SO_4^{2-} \longrightarrow PbSO_4(s) + 2e^-$$

cathode: $$2e^- + PbO_2(s) + SO_4^{2-} + 4\,H^+ \longrightarrow PbSO_4(s) + 2\,H_2O$$

In practice, the current obtainable from a lead storage cell is increased by constructing the cell from a number of cathode plates joined together and arranged alternately with a number of anode plates, which are also joined together. The potential difference of one cell is approximately 2 V. A storage battery consists of three or six such cells joined in series to produce a 6- or a 12-volt battery.

The electrode reactions of the storage battery can be reversed by the application of an external current source and in this manner the battery can be recharged. Since sulfuric acid is consumed as the storage battery delivers current, the state of charge of the battery can be determined by measuring the density of the battery electrolyte.

The **nickel-cadmium storage cell** has a longer life than the lead storage cell but is more expensive to manufacture:

anode: $$Cd(s) + 2\,OH^- \longrightarrow Cd(OH)_2(s) + 2e^-$$

cathode: $$2e^- + NiO_2(s) + 2\,H_2O \longrightarrow Ni(OH)_2(s) + 2\,OH^-$$

The potential of each cell of a nickel-cadmium battery is approximately 1.4 V, and the battery is rechargeable.

20.14 Fuel Cells

In the generation of electrical energy, heat from the combustion of a fuel (coal, oil, or natural gas) is used to convert water into steam. The steam is used to run a turbine which in turn drives a generator and produces electric current. At every step in the process, energy is lost in the form of heat. As a result, only about 30% to 40% of the energy obtained from the combustion of the fuel ends up as electrical energy.

Electrical cells that are designed to convert the energy from the combustion of fuels such as hydrogen, carbon monoxide, or methane directly into electrical energy are called fuel cells. Since in theory 100% of the free energy released by a combustion (ΔG) should be obtainable from an efficient fuel cell, extensive research into their development is currently being undertaken. Although approximately only 60% to 70% efficiency has been realized as yet, present fuel cells are about twice as efficient as processes in which the heat of combustion is used to generate electricity by mechanical means.

In a typical fuel cell, hydrogen and oxygen are bubbled through porous carbon electrodes into concentrated aqueous sodium hydroxide or potassium hydroxide. Catalysts are incorporated in the electrodes:

$$C|H_2(g)|OH^-|O_2(g)|C$$

The gaseous materials are consumed and are continuously supplied. The electrode reactions are

anode: $$2\,H_2(g) + 4\,OH^- \longrightarrow 4\,H_2O + 4e^-$$

cathode: $$4e^- + O_2(g) + 2\,H_2O \longrightarrow 4\,OH^-$$

The complete cell reaction is

$$2\,H_2(g) + O_2(g) \longrightarrow 2\,H_2O(l)$$

The cell is maintained at an elevated temperature, and the water produced by the cell reaction evaporates as it is formed.

Although hydrogen-oxygen fuel cells have been used to supply electricity in spacecraft, existing fuel cells are expensive and not commercially practical at the present time. Problems in their design include the development of electrode

Demonstration fuel cell designed to generate electrical power by the air oxidation of hydrogen-enriched hydrocarbon fuel. *U.S. Department of Energy.*

catalysts that will cause the electrode reactions to occur more rapidly, the design of cells that will function at lower temperatures than those that must be used currently, and the improvement of methods used to handle corrosive liquids (such as the KOH electrolyte) and gases under pressure.

Summary

An *electric current* is the flow of *electric charge*. In *metallic conduction*, the charge is carried by *electrons*. In *electrolytic conduction*, the charge is carried by *ions* moving through *molten salts* or *solutions*, and the motion of the ions is always accompanied by *chemical change*. In an *electrochemical cell*, *cations* move toward the *cathode* (the electrode at which *reduction* occurs), and *anions* move toward the *anode* (the electrode at which *oxidation* occurs).

Electricity is used to bring about desired chemical changes in *electrolysis*. The extent of chemical change depends upon the quantity of electricity that passes through the *electrolytic cell*. The quantity of charge equal to that carried by *one mole of electrons* is *one faraday* (F) and equals 96,485 C. The *stoichiometry* of electrochemistry rests on interpreting cell reactions in terms of *moles* of chemical substances and *faradays* (which represent moles of electrons).

In a *voltaic cell*, an oxidation-reduction reaction is used to *generate electricity*. The oxidation half reaction and the reduction half reaction occur at different electrodes so that the transfer of electrons takes place through the external electrical circuit. Electric current is produced as the result of the *electromotive force* (*emf*, $\mathscr{E}$) of the cell, which is measured in volts. The emf of a cell is a measure of the tendency for the cell reaction to occur and is related to the *change in Gibbs free energy*: $\Delta G° = -nF\mathscr{E}°$.

The emf of a cell ($\mathscr{E}°_{cell}$) may be regarded as the sum of two half-cell potentials: one for the *oxidation* at the *anode* ($\mathscr{E}°_{ox}$) and one for the *reduction* at the *cathode* ($\mathscr{E}°_{red}$). Half-cell potentials are expressed on a scale in which a value of *zero* is assigned to the *standard hydrogen electrode*. The *standard electrode potentials* that are recorded are given for *reduction half-reactions* and are, therefore, $\mathscr{E}_{red}^{\circ}$ values. An $\mathscr{E}_{ox}^{\circ}$ value for an oxidation half-reaction is numerically the same, but with the *opposite sign*, as the $\mathscr{E}_{red}^{\circ}$ for the corresponding reduction half-reaction (the oxidation written in the reverse order). Standard electrode potentials are used to calculate the *voltage* of a standard *cell*, evaluate the *strengths* of *oxidizing agents and reducing agents*, predict whether a proposed chemical reaction will be *spontaneous*, calculate ΔG° values (since $\Delta G^{\circ} = -nF\mathscr{E}^{\circ}$), and calculate *equilibrium constants* [since $\mathscr{E}^{\circ} = (2.303RT/nF)\log K$].

The emf of a cell varies with *temperature* and the *concentrations* of the substances used to make the cell. The *Nernst equation* is used to determine the emf of a cell constructed from nonstandard electrodes or to calculate the electrode potential of a nonstandard half-cell: $\mathscr{E} = \mathscr{E}^{\circ} - (2.303RT/nF)\log Q$. Because the electrode potential depends upon the concentrations of the ions used in the electrode, a cell (called a *concentration cell*) may be constructed from two half-cells of the same type that differ only in the concentrations of ions.

Provided *overvoltage* is taken into account, standard electrode potentials can be used to predict which electrode reactions will occur in an *electrolysis*. In theory, the emf calculated from electrode potentials should be the *minimum voltage* required to bring about the electrolysis.

The *corrosion of iron* is an *electrochemical* process. At one place on the surface of an iron object (the *anodic region*), iron is *oxidized* and at another spot (the *cathodic region*), a *reduction* that involves $O_2(g)$ and H_2O occurs. Recognition of the electrochemical nature of rusting leads to the design of measures (such as the use of *sacrificial anodes*) to counteract the process.

Commercial voltaic cells include the *dry cell*, a *Zn/HgO alkaline cell*, the *lead storage cell*, and the *nickel-cadmium storage cell*. *Fuel cells* are designed to convert the energy from the combustion of a fuel directly into electrical energy.

Key Terms

Some of the more important terms introduced in this chapter are listed below. Definitions for terms not included in this list may be located in the text by use of the index.

Ampere, A (Section 20.1)   The SI base unit for electric current; a current of one coulomb per second.

Anode (Section 20.2)   An electrode at which oxidation occurs.

Cathode (Section 20.2)   An electrode at which reduction occurs.

Concentration cell (Section 20.10)   A voltaic cell constructed from two half-cells that are composed of the same substances but that differ in the concentrations of the substances that make up the half cell.

Coulomb, C (Section 20.1)   A unit of electrical charge; the quantity of electricity carried past a given point in one second by a current of one ampere.

Daniell cell (Section 20.5)   A voltaic cell in which Zn metal is oxidized to Zn^{2+} ions at the anode and Cu^{2+} ions are reduced to Cu metal at the cathode.

Electrode (Section 20.2)   An anode or a cathode.

Electrolysis (Section 20.3)   The use of electric current to bring about chemical changes.

Electrolytic conduction (Section 20.2)   The conduction of electricity by the movement of ions through a solution or a molten salt. A sustained current requires that chemical changes at the electrodes also occur.

Electromotive force, emf (Section 20.6)   The potential difference between two electrodes of a voltaic cell, measured in volts; a measure of the tendency for an oxidation-reduction reaction to occur.

Faraday, F (Section 20.4)   The total charge of one mole of electrons; 9.64846×10^4 C.

Faraday's laws (Section 20.4)   The laws developed by Michael Faraday that describe the quantitative relationships between amount of electricity used and chemical change in an electrolysis.

Fuel cell (Section 20.14)   A voltaic cell is designed to convert the energy obtained from the combustion of a fuel directly into electrical energy.

Gibbs free energy change, ΔG (Sections 20.6 and 20.8)   For a voltaic cell, a measure of the maximum work that can be obtained from the cell; $\Delta G = -nF\mathscr{E}$.

Half-cell (Sections 20.5 and 20.7)   Half of a voltaic cell in which either an oxidation *or* a reduction occurs.

Metallic conduction (Section 20.1)   The conduction of electricity through a metal by electron displacement.

Nernst equation (Section 20.9)   The equation used to determine the emf of a cell in which the constituents are present in concentrations other than standard.

Overvoltage (Section 20.11)   An excess voltage (over that theoretically calculated as necessary) that must be applied in certain electrolyses so that they proceed at appreciable rates.

Oxidation potential, $\mathscr{E}_{ox}$ (Section 20.7)   A potential that corresponds to an oxidation half-reaction; an $\mathscr{E}_{ox}$ is numerically the same, but with the opposite sign, as the $\mathscr{E}_{red}$ for the corresponding reduction (the oxidation written in reverse order).

Reduction potential, $\mathscr{E}_{red}$ (Section 20.7)   A potential that corresponds to a reduction half-reaction. If the half-reaction were reversed (written as an oxidation), the corresponding oxidation potential ($\mathscr{E}_{ox}$) would be numerically the same as the $\mathscr{E}_{red}$ but with the sign changed.

Salt bridge (Section 20.7)   A tube filled with a concentrated solution of an electrolyte and connecting two half-cells of a voltaic cell; it conducts electric current between the half-cells while preventing their contents from mixing.

Silver coulometer (Section 20.4)   An electrolytic cell in which silver is plated out on a cathode placed in an electrical circuit to determine the number of coulombs that have passed through the circuit (by weighing the deposited silver).

Standard electrode potential, $\mathscr{E}°$ (Section 20.7)   A half-cell potential (measured in volts) for a *reduction* relative to a standard hydrogen electrode, which is assigned a potential of zero; measured with all substances present in their standard states. Values are customarily listed for potentials measured at 25°C.

Standard emf (Section 20.6)   The emf of a voltaic cell in which all reactants and products are in their standard states; the standard state for an ion is approximately a 1 M concentration and for a gas is approximately 1 atm pressure, and for a solid or liquid is the pure solid or liquid.

Standard hydrogen electrode (Section 20.7)   A reference electrode in which hydrogen gas, at 1 atm pressure, is bubbled over a Pt electrode that is immersed in an acid solution containing H^+(aq) ions at unit activity.

Voltaic cell (Section 20.5)   A cell that uses a chemical reaction to produce electrical energy; also called a galvanic cell.

Problems*

Conduction

20.1 Describe the mechanisms of metallic conduction and electrolytic conduction.

20.2 What is the effect of an increase in temperature on the conductivity of metals and on the conductivity of a solution of an electrolyte? Discuss the causes of resistance to the flow of electricity in these two types of conductors.

20.3 In an electrolytic cell: **(a)** What type of ions move toward the anode? **(b)** What type of half-reaction occurs at the anode? **(c)** What is the sign of the anode? **(d)** Do electrons enter the cell or leave the cell at the anode?

20.4 In a voltaic cell: **(a)** What type of ions move toward the anode? **(b)** What type of half-reaction occurs at the anode? **(c)** What is the sign of the anode? **(d)** Do electrons enter the cell or leave the cell at the anode?

Electrolytic Cells, Quantitative Relationships

20.5 Write the partial equations for the electrode reactions that occur in the electrolysis of the following aqueous solutions between inert electrodes: **(a)** Na_2SO_4 (aq), **(b)** NaCl(aq), **(c)** $CuCl_2$(aq), **(d)** $CuSO_4$(aq).

20.6 Write partial equations for the electrode reactions that occur in the electrolysis of the following aqueous solutions: **(a)** $CuSO_4$(aq) between inert electrodes, **(b)** $CuSO_4$(aq) between Cu electrodes, **(c)** $AgNO_3$(aq) between inert electrodes, **(d)** $AgNO_3$(aq) between Ag electrodes.

20.7 A Ni^{2+} solution is electrolyzed using a current of 1.25 A. What mass of Ni plates out in 30.0 min?

20.8 An acidic solution containing the BiO^+ ion is electrolyzed using a current of 2.50 A. Write the equation for the reaction at the cathode. What mass of Bi plates out in 45.0 min?

20.9 An acidic solution containing Pb^{2+} ions is electrolyzed and PbO_2(s) plated out on the *anode*. **(a)** Write the chemical equation for the anode reaction. **(b)** If a current of 0.750 A is used for 25.0 min, what mass of PbO_2(s) plates out? **(c)** If a solution contains 2.50 g of Pb^{2+}, how many minutes will it take to plate out all of the lead, as PbO_2(s) using a current of 0.750 amp?

20.10 A Ag^+ solution is electrolyzed using a current of 3.75 A. What mass of Ag plates out in 125. min?

20.11 How many minutes will it take to plate out 6.00 g of Cd from a Cd^{2+} solution using a current of 6.00 A?

20.12 How many minutes will it take to plate out 5.00 g of indium from a In^{3+} solution using a current of 1.50 A?

20.13 **(a)** If 0.872 g of Ag is deposited on the cathode of a silver coulometer, how many coulombs have passed through the circuit? **(b)** If the process takes 15.0 min, what was the current in A?

20.14 **(a)** What mass of Ni is deposited in the electrolysis of a solution of $NiSO_4$ in the same time that it takes to deposit 0.575 g of Ag in a silver coulometer that is arranged in series with the $NiSO_4$ cell? **(b)** If a current of 2.00 A is used, how many minutes does the process require?

20.15 In the electrolysis of molten $MgCl_2$, what volume of Cl_2 gas (measured at STP) is produced in the same time that it takes to plate out 6.50 g of Mg?

20.16 In the electrolysis of $AgNO_3$ solution, what mass of Ag is plated out at the cathode in the same time that it takes to liberate 6.00 L of O_2 gas (measured at STP) at the anode?

20.17 In the electrolysis of a NaCl solution, what volume of Cl_2(g) is produced at the same time that it takes to liberate 6.00 L of H_2(g)? Assume that both gases are measured at STP.

---

* The appendix contains answers to color-keyed problems.

20.18 In the electrolysis of a $CuSO_4$ solution, what mass of Cu is plated out on the cathode in the time that it takes to liberate 6.00 L of O_2 gas (measured at STP) at the anode?

20.19 The volume of the solution used in the electrolysis described in Problem 20.17 is 500 mL. Assume that this volume does not change. What is the molarity of OH^- ions after the process?

20.20 The volume of the solution used in the electrolysis described in Problem 20.18 is 750 mL. Assume that this volume does not change. What is the molarity of H^+ ions after the process?

20.21 If 125 mL of 0.750 M $CuCl_2$ solution is electrolyzed using a current of 3.50 A for 45.0 min, what are the final concentrations of Cu^{2+} and Cl^- ions? Assume that the volume of the solution does not change during the course of the electrolysis.

20.22 If 250. mL of a 0.150 M solution of $AgNO_3$ solution is electrolyzed using a current of 4.50 A for 12.5 min, what are the final concentrations of $Ag^+(aq)$, $NO_3^-(aq)$, and $H^+(aq)$ ions? Assume that the volume of the solution does not change during the course of the electrolysis.

Voltaic Cells, Electrode Potentials

20.23 (a) What is $\mathscr{E}°$ for the cell:

$$Mg|Mg^{2+}||Sn^{2+}|Sn$$

(b) Write the chemical equation for the cell reaction. **(c)** Which electrode is positive?

20.24 (a) What is $\mathscr{E}°$ for the cell:

$$Ni|Ni^{2+}||Cu^{2+}|Cu$$

(b) Write the chemical equation for the cell reaction. **(c)** Which electrode is positive?

20.25 (a) Give the notation for the cell that utilizes the reaction:

$$Cl_2(g) + 2I^-(aq) \longrightarrow 2Cl^-(aq) + I_2(s)$$

(b) What is $\mathscr{E}°$ for the cell? **(c)** Which electrode is the cathode?

20.26 (a) Give the notation for the cell that utilizes the reaction:

$$H_2(g) + Br_2(l) \longrightarrow 2H^+(aq) + 2Br^-(aq)$$

(b) What is $\mathscr{E}°$ for the cell? **(c)** Which electrode is the anode?

20.27 For the cell:

$$U|U^{3+}||Ag^+|Ag$$

$\mathscr{E}°$ is +2.588 V. Use the emf of the cell and $\mathscr{E}°$ for the Ag^+/Ag couple to calculate $\mathscr{E}°$ for the U^{3+}/U half-reaction.

20.28 For the cell:

$$Cu|Cu^{2+}||Pd^{2+}|Pd$$

$\mathscr{E}°$ is +0.650 V. Use the emf of the cell and $\mathscr{E}°$ for the Cu^{2+}/Cu couple to calculate $\mathscr{E}°$ for the Pd^{2+}/Pd half-reaction.

20.29 From the table of electrode potentials (acid solutions) that appears in the appendix, select a suitable substance for each of the following transformations. Assume that all soluble substances are present in 1 M concentrations. **(a)** an oxidizing agent capable of oxidizing Fe to Fe^{2+} but not Tl to Tl^+, **(b)** an oxidizing agent capable of oxidizing Mn^{2+} to MnO_4^- but not MnO_2 to MnO_4^-, **(c)** a reducing agent capable of reducing Fe^{2+} to Fe but not Mn^{2+} to Mn, **(d)** a reducing agent capable of reducing PbO_2 to Pb^{2+} but not MnO_2 to Mn^{2+}.

20.30 From the table of electrode potentials (acid solutions) that appears in the appendix, select a suitable substance for each of the following transformations. Assume that all soluble substances are present in 1 M concentrations. **(a)** an oxidizing agent capable of oxidizing Hg to Hg_2^{2+} but not Hg to Hg^{2+}, **(b)** an oxidizing agent capable of oxidizing Mn^{2+} to MnO_2 but not Cr^{3+} to $Cr_2O_7^{2-}$, **(c)** a reducing agent capable of reducing Sn^{4+} to Sn^{2+} but not Sn^{2+} to Sn, **(d)** a reducing agent capable of reducing I_2 to I^- but not Cu^{2+} to Cu.

20.31 Use $\mathscr{E}°$ values to predict whether each of the following skeleton equations represents a reaction that will occur in acid solution with all soluble substances present in 1 M concentrations. Complete and balance the equation for each reaction that is predicted to occur.

(a) $H_2O_2 + Cu^{2+} \longrightarrow Cu + O_2$
(b) $H_2O_2 + Ag^+ \longrightarrow Ag + O_2$
(c) $Ag^+ + Fe^{2+} \longrightarrow Ag + Fe^{3+}$
(d) $Au + Cl_2 \longrightarrow Au^{3+} + Cl^-$

20.32 Use $\mathscr{E}°$ values to predict whether each of the following skeleton equations represents a reaction that will occur in acid solution with all soluble substances present in 1 M concentrations. Complete and balance the equation for each reaction that is predicted to occur.

(a) $PbO_2 + Cl^- \longrightarrow Pb^{2+} + Cl_2$
(b) $Co + Cd^{2+} \longrightarrow Co^{2+} + Cd$
(c) $I^- + NO_3^- \longrightarrow I_2 + NO$
(d) $Mn^{2+} + Cr_2O_7^{2-} \longrightarrow MnO_4^- + Cr^{3+}$

20.33 Use $\mathscr{E}°$ values to predict whether each of the following skeleton equations represents a reaction that will occur in acid solution with all soluble substances present in 1 M concentrations. Complete and balance the equation for each reaction that is predicted to occur.

(a) $H_2SO_3 + H_2S \longrightarrow S$
(b) $MnO_4^- + Mn^{2+} \longrightarrow MnO_2$
(c) $Hg + Hg^{2+} \longrightarrow Hg_2^{2+}$
(d) $Mn^{2+} \longrightarrow MnO_2 + Mn$

20.34 Use $\mathscr{E}°$ values to predict whether each of the following skeleton equations represents a reaction that will occur in acid solution with all soluble substances present in 1 M concentrations. Complete and balance the equation for each reaction that is predicted to occur.

(a) $Co^{3+} + Co \longrightarrow Co^{2+}$
(b) $SO_4^{2-} + S \longrightarrow H_2SO_3$

(c) $Mn^{3+} + Mn \longrightarrow Mn^{2+}$

(d) $Sn^{4+} + Sn \longrightarrow Sn^{2+}$

20.35 Given the following standard electrode potential diagram (acid solution):

$$In^{3+} \xrightarrow{-0.434} In^+ \xrightarrow{-0.147\ V} In$$
$$\underset{-0.338\ V}{\underbrace{\hphantom{In^{3+} \xrightarrow{-0.434} In^+ \xrightarrow{-0.147\ V} In}}}$$

(a) Is the In^+ ion stable toward disproportionation in water solution? (b) Which ion is produced when In metal reacts with $H^+(aq)$? (c) The $\mathscr{E}°$ for Cl_2/Cl^- is $+1.36$ V. Will In react with Cl_2? What is the product? (d) Write balanced chemical equations for all reactions.

20.36 Given the following standard electrode potential diagram (acid solution):

$$Tl^{3+} \xrightarrow{+1.25\ V} Tl^+ \xrightarrow{-0.34\ V} Tl$$
$$\underset{+0.72\ V}{\underbrace{\hphantom{Tl^{3+} \xrightarrow{+1.25\ V} Tl^+ \xrightarrow{-0.34\ V} Tl}}}$$

(a) Is the Tl^+ ion stable toward diproportionation in water solution?
(b) Which ion is produced when Tl metal reacts with $H^+(aq)$? (c) The $\mathscr{E}°$ for Cl_2/Cl^- is $+1.36$ V. Will Tl react with Cl_2? What is the product? (d) Write balanced chemical equations for all reactions.

20.37 (a) Given:

$$Ti^{3+} + e^- \longrightarrow Ti^{2+} \qquad \mathscr{E}° = -0.369\ V$$
$$Ti^{2+} + 2e^- \longrightarrow Ti \qquad \mathscr{E}° = -1.628\ V$$

calculate $\mathscr{E}°$ for the half-reaction:

$$Ti^{3+} + 3e^- \longrightarrow Ti$$

(b) Will the Ti^{2+} ion disproportionate in aqueous solution? (c) Will Ti metal react with $H^+(aq)$? If so, which ion is produced?

20.38 (a) Given:

$$Co^{2+} + 2e^- \longrightarrow Co \qquad \mathscr{E}° = -0.277\ V$$
$$Co^{3+} + 3e^- \longrightarrow Co \qquad \mathscr{E}° = +1.113\ V$$

calculate $\mathscr{E}°$ for the half-reaction:

$$Co^{3+} + e^- \longrightarrow Co^{2+}$$

(b) Will the Co^{2+} ion disproportionate in aqueous solution? (c) Will Co metal react with $H^+(aq)$? If so, which ion is produced?

20.39 (a) Given:

$$Au^+ + e^- \longrightarrow Au \qquad \mathscr{E}° = +1.691\ V$$
$$Au^{3+} + 3e^- \longrightarrow Au \qquad \mathscr{E}° = +1.495\ V$$

calculate $\mathscr{E}°$ for the half-reaction:

$$Au^{3+} + 2e^- \longrightarrow Au^+$$

(b) Will the Au^+ ion disproportionate in aqueous solution? (c) Will Au metal react with $H^+(aq)$? If so, which ion is produced?

20.40 (a) Given:

$$Eu^{3+} + 3e^- \longrightarrow Eu \qquad \mathscr{E}° = -2.407\ V$$
$$Eu^{3+} + e^- \longrightarrow Eu^{2+} \qquad \mathscr{E}° = -0.429\ V$$

calculate $\mathscr{E}°$ for the half-reaction:

$$Eu^{2+} + 2e^- \longrightarrow Eu$$

(b) Will the Eu^{2+} ion disproportionate in aqueous solution? (c) Will Eu^{3+} and Eu react to give Eu^{2+}? (d) Will Eu metal react with $H^+(aq)$? If so, which ion is produced?

Gibbs Free Energy and Emf

20.41 Given the following:

$$PbSO_4 + 2e^- \rightleftharpoons Pb + SO_4^{2-} \qquad \mathscr{E}° = -0.359\ V$$
$$Pb^{2+} + 2e^- \rightleftharpoons Pb \qquad \mathscr{E}° = -0.126\ V$$

(a) Write the notation for a cell that uses these half-reactions. (b) Write the equation for the cell reaction. (c) Calculate $\mathscr{E}°$ for the cell. (d) Determine $\Delta G°$ for the cell reaction.

20.42 Given the following:

$$AgI + e^- \rightleftharpoons Ag + I^- \qquad \mathscr{E}° = -0.152\ V$$
$$Ag^+ + e^- \rightleftharpoons Ag \qquad \mathscr{E}° = +0.799\ V$$

(a) Write the notation for a cell that uses these half-reactions. (b) Write the equation for the cell reaction. (c) Calculate $\mathscr{E}°$ for the cell. (d) Determine $\Delta G°$ for the cell reaction.

20.43 (a) Diagram a cell for which the cell reaction is:

$$H^+ + OH^- \longrightarrow H_2O$$

(b) Calculate $\mathscr{E}°$ for the cell and $\Delta G°$ for the reaction.

20.44 (a) Diagram a cell for which the cell reaction (in acid solution) is:

$$2\,H_2 + O_2 \longrightarrow 2\,H_2O$$

(b) Calculate $\mathscr{E}°$ for the cell and $\Delta G°$ for the reaction.

20.45 (a) Use electrode potentials (see appendix) to calculate the emf of a standard cell that uses the reaction:

$$Cl_2(g) + 2\,Br^-(aq) \longrightarrow 2\,Cl^-(aq) + Br_2(l)$$

(b) What is $\Delta G°$ for the reaction? (c) If $\Delta H°$ for the reaction is -93.09 kJ, what is $\Delta S°$?

20.46 (a) Use electrode potentials (see appendix) to calculate the emf of a standard cell that uses the reaction:

$$2\,H_2O_2(aq) \longrightarrow O_2(g) + 2\,H_2O$$

(b) What is $\Delta G°$ for the reaction? (c) If $\Delta H°$ for the reaction is -189.44 kJ, what is $\Delta S°$?

20.47 For the half-reaction:

$$XeF_2(aq) + 2H^+(aq) + 2e^- \longrightarrow Xe(g) + 2HF(aq)$$

$\mathscr{E}°$ has been reported to equal $+2.64$ V. **(a)** Calculate $\Delta G°$ for the reaction:

$$XeF_2(aq) + H_2(g) \longrightarrow Xe(g) + 2HF(aq)$$

(b) The standard free energy of formation, $\Delta G_f°$, of HF(aq) is -276.48 kJ/mol. What is $\Delta G_f°$ of $XeF_2(aq)$?

20.48 Given the following electrode potentials:

$$H_3BO_3(s) + 3H^+(aq) + 3e^- \longrightarrow B(s) + 3H_2O$$
$$\mathscr{E}° = -0.869 \text{ V}$$

$$4H^+(aq) + O_2(g) + 4e^- \longrightarrow 2H_2O$$
$$\mathscr{E}° = +1.229 \text{ V}$$

calculate the value of $\Delta G_f°$ for $H_3BO_3(s)$. For $H_2O(l)$, $\Delta G_f°$ is -237.19 kJ/mol.

20.49 Use standard electrode potentials (see appendix) to calculate the equilibrium constant for the reaction (at 25°C):

$$Ni(s) + Sn^{2+}(aq) \rightleftharpoons Ni^{2+}(aq) + Sn(s)$$

20.50 Use standard electrode potentials (see appendix) to calculate the equilibrium constant for the reaction (at 25°C):

$$Cl_2(g) + H_2O \rightleftharpoons H^+(aq) + Cl^-(aq) + HOCl(aq)$$

20.51 Given the following:

$$2H_2O + 2e^- \rightleftharpoons H_2(g) + 2OH^-(aq)$$
$$\mathscr{E}° = -0.828 \text{ V}$$

calculate the value of the water constant, K_w, for 25°C:

$$H_2O \rightleftharpoons H^+(aq) + OH^-(aq)$$

20.52 Use standard electrode potentials (see appendix) to calculate the equilibrium constant for the reaction (at 25°C):

$$4H^+(aq) + 4Br^-(aq) + O_2(g) \rightleftharpoons 2Br_2(l) + 2H_2O$$

The Nernst Equation

20.53 (a) Calculate the emf of a cell formed from a $Mg^{2+}/$ Mg half-cell in which $[Mg^{2+}]$ is 0.0500 M and a Ni^{2+}/Ni half-cell in which $[Ni^{2+}]$ is 1.50 M. **(b)** Write the equation for the cell reaction. **(c)** Which electrode is positive?

20.54 (a) Calculate the emf of a cell formed from a Cd^{2+}/Cd half-cell in which $[Cd^{2+}]$ is 0.0600 M and a Ag^+/Ag half-cell in which $[Ag^+]$ is 2.50 M. **(b)** Write the equation for the cell reaction. **(c)** Which electrode is positive?

20.55 (a) Calculate the emf of a cell formed from a $Zn^{2+}/$ Zn half-cell in which $[Zn^{2+}]$ is 0.0500 M and a Cl_2/Cl^- half-cell in which $[Cl^-]$ is 0.0500 M and the pressure of $Cl_2(g)$ is 1.25 atm. **(b)** Write the equation for the cell reaction. **(c)** Which electrode is negative?

20.56 (a) Calculate the emf of a cell formed from a Pb^{2+}/Pb half-cell in which $[Pb^{2+}]$ is 6.00 M and a $H^+/$ H_2 half-cell in which $[H^+]$ is 0.0200 M and the pressure of $H_2(g)$ is 2.00 atm. **(b)** Write the equation for the cell reaction. **(c)** Which electrode is positive?

20.57 What is the concentration of Cd^{2+} in the cell:

$$Zn|Zn^{2+}(0.0900 \ M)||Cd^{2+}(? \ M)|Cd$$

if the emf of the cell is 0.4000 V?

20.58 What is the concentration of Ag^+ in the cell:

$$Cu|Cu^{2+}(3.50 \ M)||Ag^+(? \ M)|Ag$$

if the emf of the cell is 0.350 V?

20.59 (a) According to the $\mathscr{E}°$ value, should the following reaction proceed spontaneously at 25°C with all soluble substances present at 1.00 M concentration?

$$MnO_2(s) + 4H^+(aq) + 2Cl^-(aq) \longrightarrow$$
$$Mn^{2+}(aq) + 2H_2O + Cl_2(g)$$

(b) Would the reaction be spontaneous if the concentrations of $H^+(aq)$ and $Cl^-(aq)$ were each increased to 10.0 M?

20.60 For the half-reaction:

$$Cr_2O_7^{2-} + 14H^+ + 6e^- \longrightarrow 2Cr^{3+} + 7H_2O$$

$\mathscr{E}°$ is $+1.33$ V. What would the potential be if the concentration of $H^+(aq)$ were reduced to 0.100 M?

20.61 For a half-reaction of the form:

$$M^{2+} + 2e^- \rightleftharpoons M$$

what would be the effect on the electrode potential if **(a)** the concentration of M^{2+} were doubled? **(b)** the concentration of M^{2+} were cut in half?

20.62 Consider the following standard cell:

$$Sn|Sn^{2+}||Pb^{2+}|Pb$$

(a) Calculate the value of $\mathscr{E}°$ for the cell. **(b)** When the cell operates, the concentration of Sn^{2+} increases and the concentration of Pb^{2+} decreases. What are the concentrations of the ions when the emf of the cell is zero? Assume that the same volume of solution is used in each electrode compartment.

20.63 (a) Determine the emf of a cell prepared from two H^+/H_2 half-cells, one in which $[H^+]$ is 0.0250 M and the other in which $[H^+]$ is 5.00 M. The pressure of $H_2(g)$ in both half-cells is 1.00 atm. **(b)** Write an equation for the "cell reaction." **(c)** Determine the emf of the cell if the pressure of $H_2(g)$ is changed to 2.00 atm in the anode half-cell and to 0.100 atm in the cathode half-cell.

20.64 (a) Determine the emf of a cell prepared from two Ga^{3+}/Ga half-cells, one in which $[Ga^{3+}]$ is 2.00 M and the other in which $[Ga^{3+}]$ is 0.300 M. **(b)** Write an equation for the "cell reaction." **(c)** Which electrode is negative?

20.65 Sketch a cell for the electrolysis of molten $MgCl_2$ between inert electrodes. On the sketch indicate: **(a)** the signs of the electrodes, **(b)** the cathode and the anode, **(c)** the directions that the ions move, **(d)** the direction in which the electrons move, **(e)** the electrode reactions.

20.66 Sketch a cell for the electrolysis of a $CuSO_4$ solution between Cu electrodes. On the sketch indicate: **(a)** the signs of the electrodes, **(b)** the cathode and the anode, **(c)** the directions that the ions move, **(d)** the direction in which the electrons move, **(e)** the electrode reactions.

20.67 Sketch a voltaic cell in which the cell reaction is:

$$Mg(s) + 2Ag^+(aq) \longrightarrow Mg^{2+}(aq) + 2Ag(s)$$

On the sketch indicate: **(a)** the signs of the electrodes, **(b)** the cathode and the anode, **(c)** the directions that the ions move, **(d)** the direction in which the electrons move, **(e)** the electrode reactions, **(f)** the cell voltage.

20.68 Sketch a voltaic cell in which the cell reaction is:

$$Cd(s) + Cl_2(g) \longrightarrow Cd^{2+}(aq) + 2Cl^-(aq)$$

On the sketch indicate: **(a)** the signs of the electrodes, **(b)** the cathode and the anode, **(c)** the directions that the ions move, **(d)** the direction in which the electrons move, **(e)** the electrode reactions, **(f)** the cell voltage.

20.69 In the Hall process, aluminum is produced by the electrolysis of molten Al_2O_3. The electrode reactions are:

anode: $\quad C + 2O^{2-} \longrightarrow CO_2 + 4e^-$

cathode: $\quad 3e^- + Al^{3+} \longrightarrow Al$

In the process, the carbon of which the anode is composed is gradually consumed by the anode reaction. What mass of carbon is lost from the anode in the time that it takes to plate out 1.00 kg of Al?

20.70 How long would it take to produce enough aluminum by the Hall process (see Problem 20.69) to make a case of soft-drink cans (24 cans) if each can uses 5.00 g of Al, a current of 50,000 A is employed, and the efficiency of the cell is 90.0%?

20.71 How many hours will it take to plate out all the Ni in 200 mL of a 0.350 M Ni^{2+} solution using a current of 0.650 A?

20.72 For the cell:

$$Sn|Sn^{2+}||H^+, BiO^+|Bi$$

$\mathscr{E}°$ is $+0.456$ V. Use the emf of the cell and $\mathscr{E}°$ for the Sn^{2+}/Sn couple to calculate $\mathscr{E}°$ for the BiO^+/Bi half-reaction.

20.73 The following reactions occur at 25°C with all soluble substances present in 1 M concentrations:

$$Zn + Pb^{2+} \longrightarrow Zn^{2+} + Pb$$

$$Ti + Zn^{2+} \longrightarrow Ti^{2+} + Zn$$

$$2Lu + 3Ti^{2+} \longrightarrow 2Lu^{3+} + 3Ti$$

From this information alone, predict whether the following reactions will occur under similar conditions:
(a) $Pb + Ti^{2+} \longrightarrow Pb^{2+} + Ti$
(b) $2Lu + 3Pb^{2+} \longrightarrow 2Lu^{3+} + 3Pb$
(c) $2Lu^{3+} + 3Zn \longrightarrow 3Zn^{2+} + 2Lu$

20.74 (a) Use standard electrode potentials (see appendix) to calculate the emf of a standard cell based on the cell reaction:

$$I_2(s) + H_2S(aq) \longrightarrow$$
$$S(rhombic) + 2H^+(aq) + 2I^-(aq)$$

(b) What is $\Delta G°$ for the reaction? **(c)** If $\Delta S°$ for the reaction is $+11.7$ kJ/K, what is $\Delta H°$?

20.75 Calculate $\mathscr{E}°$ for the half-reaction:

$$PbBr_2(s) + 2e^- \longrightarrow Pb(s) + 2Br^-(aq)$$

from the following data:

$PbBr_2(s) \rightleftharpoons Pb^{2+}(aq) + 2Br^-(aq)$
$K_{SP} = 4.60 \times 10^{-6}$

$Pb^{2+}(aq) + 2e^- \longrightarrow Pb(s)$
$\mathscr{E}° = -0.126$ V

20.76 Suggest ways to increase the emf of a cell that is based on the reaction:

$$Fe(s) + 2H^+(aq) \longrightarrow Fe^{2+}(aq) + H_2(g)$$

20.77 Why does measurement of the density of the electrolyte in a lead storage battery give an indication of the state of charge of the battery?

21

THE NONMETALS, PART I: HYDROGEN AND THE HALOGENS

Within a period of the periodic table, metallic character *decreases* from left to right; within a group, metallic character *increases* from top to bottom. The stepped diagonal line shown in the periodic table is the approximate division between the metals (on the left) and the nonmetals (on the right). The first element, hydrogen, is also classified as a nonmetal. In this chapter, the chemistry of hydrogen and of the halogens (group VII A) is discussed.

HYDROGEN

Hydrogen does not fit well into any group of the periodic table. The hydrogen atom has only one valence electron and in this regard is like the atoms of group I A. The group I A elements, however, are metals and hydrogen is a nonmental. The hydrogen atom is one electron short of a noble-gas configuration like the atoms of the group VII A elements. Hydrogen, however, is less electronegative than the group VII A elements and its chemical properties deviate in important ways from the properties of those elements. The reason for the unique character of hydrogen is found in its very small atomic radius.

21.1 Occurrence and Properties of Hydrogen

Hydrogen atoms constitute about 15% of all the atoms present in the crust, bodies of water, and atmosphere of the earth. On the basis of mass, however, the percentage drops to less than 1% since hydrogen has a very low atomic mass. The most important compound of hydrogen found in nature is water, which is the principal source of the element. Hydrogen is also found in combined form in the hydrocarbons (compounds of carbon and hydrogen found in coal, natural gas, and petroleum), a few minerals (such as clay and certain hydrates), and the organic compounds that constitute the principal part of all plant and animal matter (see Chapters 28 and 29). Free hydrogen occurs in nature only in negligible amounts (for example, in volcanic gases).

Hydrogen is a colorless, odorless, tasteless gas. It has the lowest density of any chemical substance; at STP one liter of hydrogen weighs 0.0899 g. The two atoms of hydrogen of the H_2 molecule are joined by a single covalent bond, giving each atom a stable helium electronic configuration. The molecule is nonpolar; the weak nature of the intermolecular forces of attraction is indicated by the low normal boiling point $(-252.7°C)$, the normal melting point $(-259.1°C)$ and the critical temperature $(-240°C$ at a critical pressure of 12.8 atm). Hydrogen is virtually insoluble in water; approximately 2 ml of hydrogen will dissolve in 1 liter of water at room temperature and 1 atm pressure.

There are three isotopes of hydrogen. The most abundant isotope $_1^1H$, constitutes 99.985% of naturally occurring hydrogen; deuterium $_1^2H$ (also indicated as $_1^2D$) constitutes 0.015%; and the radioactive tritium, $_1^3H$ (also indicated as $_1^3T$) occurs only in trace amounts.

21.2 Industrial Production of Hydrogen

Large quantities of hydrogen are used by the chemical industry. The principal industrial sources are

1. Steam reformer process. This process is the one most widely used for the production of hydrogen in large quantities. A hydrocarbon, such as methane (CH_4), and steam are passed over a nickel catalyst at 900°C. The reactions that occur are

$$CH_4(g) + 2H_2O(g) \longrightarrow CO_2(g) + 4H_2(g)$$
$$CH_4(g) + H_2O(g) \longrightarrow CO(g) + 3H_2(g)$$

The gas emerging from the reformer furnace consists of H_2, CO, CO_2, and excess steam. This gas mixture is passed into a *shift converter* at 450°C, in which the CO is converted into CO_2:

$$CO(g) + H_2O(g) \longrightarrow CO_2(g) + H_2(g)$$

The CO_2 is removed from the resulting mixture of CO_2 and H_2 by passing the mixture through cold water under pressure or through a solution of an amine (a basic compound with which CO_2 reacts). In each case, the CO_2 dissolves but the H_2 does not.

2. Water gas. Coke is impure carbon that has been obtained from coal by heating it in the absence of air to drive off volatile components. Coke and steam react at high temperatures (1000°C) to produce a gaseous mixture known as water gas:

$$C(s) + H_2O(g) \longrightarrow CO(g) + H_2(g)$$

Since both CO and H_2 will burn, the mixture is used as a fuel as well as a source for H_2.

Hydrogen is obtained from water gas by liquefying the CO (high pressure, low temperature) and separating the gaseous H_2 from the liquid CO. As an alternative, the water gas can be passed into a shift converter, the CO converted into CO_2, and the CO_2 removed as described for the steam reformer process.

3. Iron and steam. Iron and steam react at temperatures of 650°C or higher:

$$3Fe(s) + 4H_2O(g) \longrightarrow Fe_3O_4(s) + 4H_2(g)$$

A catalytic cracking unit. *Mobil Oil Corporation.*

4. Cracking. Hydrogen is obtained by the catalytic decomposition of hydro-carbons at high temperatures. In petroleum refining, high molecular weight hydrocarbons are "cracked" into lower molecular weight compounds that are more valuable. Hydrogen is a by-product.

5. Electrolysis of sodium chloride brine. Hydrogen is a by-product (as is chlorine) in the industrial preparation of sodium hydroxide by the electrolysis of con-centrated solutions of sodium chloride:

$$2\,Na^+(aq) + 2\,Cl^-(aq) + 2\,H_2O \xrightarrow{\textit{electrolysis}}$$
$$2\,Na^+(aq) + 2\,OH^-(aq) + H_2(g) + Cl_2(g)$$

6. Electrolysis of water. Very pure but relatively expensive hydrogen is obtained by the electrolysis of water that contains a small amount of sulfuric acid or sodium hydroxide:

$$2\,H_2O \xrightarrow{\textit{electrolysis}} 2\,H_2(g) + O_2(g)$$

21.3 Hydrogen from Displacement Reactions

Reactions in which one element (or a group of elements) displaces another element (or a group of elements) from a compound are called **displacement reactions.** Hydrogen is a product of several types of displacement reactions:

1. The very reactive elements (Ca, Sr, Ba, and the group I A metals) react vigorously with water at room temperature to produce hydrogen and solutions of hydroxides. For example,

$$2\,Na(s) + 2\,H_2O \longrightarrow 2\,Na^+(aq) + 2\,OH^-(aq) + H_2(g)$$

$$Ca(s) + 2\,H_2O \longrightarrow Ca^{2+}(aq) + 2\,OH^-(aq) + H_2(g)$$

These reactions may be dangerous.

2. A long list of metals react with aqueous solutions of acids to produce hydrogen. For example,

$$Zn(s) + 2\,H^+(aq) \longrightarrow Zn^{2+}(aq) + H_2(g)$$

$$Fe(s) + 2\,H^+(aq) \longrightarrow Fe^{2+}(aq) + H_2(g)$$

$$2\,Al(s) + 6\,H^+(aq) \longrightarrow 2\,Al^{3+}(aq) + 3\,H_2(g)$$

By convention, the standard electrode potential of the H^+/H_2 electrode is zero:

$$2e^- + 2\,H^+(aq) \rightleftharpoons H_2(g) \qquad \mathscr{E}^\circ = 0.000 \text{ V}$$

Any metal that has a $\mathscr{E}^\circ_{ox}$ that is a positive value (the corresponding $\mathscr{E}^\circ_{red}$ would be a negative value) should, therefore, be capable of displacing hydrogen from an aqueous solution of an acid. The very reactive metals (Ca, Sr, Ba, and the group I A metals) react violently and such reactions are not run. Other metals (Pb, for example) react very slowly. A common laboratory preparation of hydrogen involves the reaction of zinc (a metal with a satisfactory order of reactivity) with hydrochloric acid.

3. Certain metals and nonmetals displace hydrogen from alkaline solutions. Examples are

$$Zn(s) + 2\,OH^-(aq) + 2\,H_2O \longrightarrow H_2(g) + Zn(OH)_4^{2-}(aq)$$
$$\text{\textit{zincate ion}}$$

$$2\,Al(s) + 2\,OH^-(aq) + 6\,H_2O \longrightarrow 3\,H_2(g) + 2\,Al(OH)_4^-(aq)$$
$$\text{\textit{aluminate ion}}$$

$$Si(s) + 2\,OH^-(aq) + H_2O \longrightarrow 2\,H_2(g) + SiO_3^{2-}(aq)$$
$$\text{\textit{silicate ion}}$$

Hydrogen is also conveniently prepared in the laboratory by means of the reactions of the metal hydrides with water. These reactions are discussed in the next section.

1.4 Reactions of Hydrogen

The bond energy of the H—H bond is 431 kJ/mol. In the course of most reactions this bond must be broken so that the H atoms can form new bonds with other atoms. Since this bond energy is relatively high, most reactions of hydrogen take place at elevated temperatures.

Hydrogen reacts with the metals of group I A and the heavier metals of group II A (Ba, Sr, and Ca) to form saltlike hydrides. The hydride ion (H^-) of these compounds is isoelectronic with helium and achieves this stable configuration by the addition of an electron from the metal. Since the electron affinity of hydrogen is low (-73 kJ/mol), hydrogen reacts in this manner only with the most reactive metals:

$$2 \text{Na(s)} + \text{H}_2\text{(g)} \longrightarrow 2 \text{NaH(s)}$$

$$\text{Ca(s)} + \text{H}_2\text{(g)} \longrightarrow \text{CaH}_2\text{(s)}$$

The saltlike hydrides react with water to form hydrogen:

$$\text{H}^- + \text{H}_2\text{O} \longrightarrow \text{H}_2\text{(g)} + \text{OH}^-\text{(aq)}$$

With certain other metals, such as platinum, palladium, and nickel, hydrogen forms **interstitial hydrides.** Many of these hydrides are nonstoichiometric; their apparent formulas depend upon the conditions under which they are prepared. Palladium can absorb up to 900 times its own volume of hydrogen. The interstitial hydrides resemble the metals from which they are derived. The crystal structures of the metals do not change (or change only slightly) as hydrogen is added. Whether these substances should be regarded as compounds is debatable. The name, interstitial hydrides, arises from the view that the hydrogen is only absorbed into the interstices of the metallic crystal.

Magnetic studies, however, indicate that electron pairing of some sort is involved in the formation of these hydrides. Many of the metals have unpaired electrons and, hence, are paramagnetic. A gradual loss of paramagnetism is observed as the hydrides form from the metal. Since the electrons of molecular hydrogen are paired, these studies imply that the hydrogen is incorporated into the crystal in atomic form, which would account for the catalytic activity of Pt, Pd, Ni, and other metals for many reactions of hydrogen. If the H—H bond is broken or even only weakened, the absorbed hydrogen should be much more reactive than ordinary H_2 gas.

Complex hydrides of boron and aluminum are important and useful compounds for chemical syntheses. Important examples are sodium borohydride and lithium aluminum hydride:

$$\text{Na}^+ \left[\begin{array}{c} \text{H} \\ \text{H:B:H} \\ \text{H} \end{array} \right]^- \qquad \text{Li}^+ \left[\begin{array}{c} \text{H} \\ \text{H:Al:H} \\ \text{H} \end{array} \right]^-$$

Since these compounds, as well as the saltlike hydrides, react with water to liberate hydrogen, they are prepared by reactions in ether:

$$4 \text{LiH} + \text{AlCl}_3 \longrightarrow \text{Li[AlH}_4\text{]} + 3 \text{LiCl}$$

Hydrogen forms covalent compounds with most of the nonmetals. It reacts with the halogens to form colorless, polar covalent gases:

$$\text{H}_2\text{(g)} + \text{Cl}_2\text{(g)} \longrightarrow 2 \text{HCl(g)}$$

Reactions with fluorine or chlorine will take place at room temperature or below, but the reactions with the less reactive bromine or iodine require higher temperatures ($400°\text{C}$ to $600°\text{C}$).

The reaction of hydrogen and oxygen in which H_2O is formed is highly exothermic and is the basis of the high temperature (ca. $2800°\text{C}$) produced by the oxyhydrogen torch. The reaction of hydrogen with sulfur is more difficult and requires high temperatures:

$$H_2(g) + S(g) \longrightarrow H_2S(g)$$

Hydrogen reacts with nitrogen at high pressures (300 to 1000 atm), at high temperatures (400°C to 600°C), and in the presence of a catalyst to produce ammonia (Haber process):

$$3\,H_2(g) + N_2(g) \rightleftharpoons 2\,NH_3(g)$$

Hydrogen does not react readily with carbon, but at high temperatures, hydrogen can be made catalytically to react with finely divided carbon (Bergius process); hydrocarbons are produced in these reactions:

$$2\,H_2(g) + C(s) \longrightarrow CH_4(g)$$

The ionization potential of hydrogen is relatively high (1312 kJ/mol). In none of the compounds formed between hydrogen and the nonmetals does hydrogen exist as positive ions; the bonding in all these compounds is polar covalent. Because of its large charge-to-radius ratio, the unassociated proton (H^+) does not exist in ordinary chemical systems. In pure acids the hydrogen atom is covalently bonded to the rest of the molecule, and in aqueous solutions the proton is hydrated.

Hydrogen reacts with many metal oxides to produce water and the free metal:

$$CuO(s) + H_2(g) \longrightarrow Cu(s) + H_2O(g)$$

$$WO_3(s) + 3\,H_2(g) \longrightarrow W(s) + 3\,H_2O(g)$$

$$FeO(s) + H_2(g) \longrightarrow Fe(s) + H_2O(g)$$

Some metals (W, for example) are commercially produced by the hydrogen reduction of oxide ores. The method is expensive, however, and is not used if an alternative, less-expensive method is available.

Carbon monoxide and hydrogen react at high temperatures and high pressures in the presence of a catalyst to produce methyl alcohol, CH_3OH:

$$CO(g) + 2\,H_2(g) \longrightarrow CH_3OH(g)$$

1.5 Industrial Uses of Hydrogen

The principal industrial uses of hydrogen are

1. Production of ammonia from N_2 and H_2 by the Haber process.

2. Production of hydrogen chloride from Cl_2 and H_2.

3. Synthesis of methyl alcohol from CO and H_2.

4. Refining of petroleum.

5. Hydrogenation of edible oils (corn, cotton seed, soy bean, peanut, and others) to produce shortenings and other foods (see Section 29.3).

6. Reduction of oxide ores to produce certain metals.

7. As a rocket fuel.

8. As a fuel in oxyhydrogen welding, atomic hydrogen welding, annealing furnaces, and electronic component fabrication.

THE HALOGENS

The elements of group VII A—fluorine, chlorine, bromine, iodine, and astatine—are called the halogens. The name "halogen" is derived from Greek and means "salt former." These elements, with the exception of astatine, occur extensively in nature in the form of halide salts. Astatine probably occurs in nature, in extremely small amounts, as a short-lived intermediate of natural radioactive decay processes. Most of our meager information about the chemistry of astatine, however, comes from the study of the small amounts of a radioactive isotope of this element prepared by nuclear reactions.

21.6 Properties of the Halogens

The electronic configurations of the halogens are listed in Table 21.1. Each halogen atom has one electron less than the noble gas that follows it in the periodic classification. There is, therefore, a marked tendency on the part of a halogen atom to attain a noble-gas configuration by the formation of a uninegative ion or a single covalent bond. Positive oxidation states exist for all the elements except fluorine.

Some properties of the halogens are summarized in Table 21.2; the symbol X stands for any halogen. Notice the following:

1. Physical state. Under ordinary conditions, the halogens exist as diatomic molecules with a single covalent bond joining the atoms of a molecule. The molecules are held together in the solid and liquid states by London forces. Of all the halogen molecules, I_2 is the largest, has the most electrons, and is the most polarizable. It is not surprising, therefore, that the intermolecular attractions between I_2 molecules are the strongest and that I_2 has the highest melting point and boiling point. At ordinary temperatures and pressures, I_2 is a solid, Br_2 is a liquid, and Cl_2 and F_2 are gases.

Table 21.1		Electronic configurations of the halogens															
Element	Z	1s	2s	2p	3s	3p	3d	4s	4p	4d	4f	5s	5p	5d	6s	6p
F	9	2	2	5												
Cl	17	2	2	6	2	5										
Br	35	2	2	6	2	6	10	2	5							
I	53	2	2	6	2	6	10	2	6	10		2	5			
At	85	2	2	6	2	6	10	2	6	10	14	2	6	10	2	5

2. First ionization energy. Within the *group*, ionization energy decreases with increasing atomic radius in the expected manner. The first ionization energy of fluorine is the highest of the group and of iodine is the lowest of the group. The halogen of each *period* has a relatively high ionization energy, second only to that of the noble gas of the period. There is, therefore, little tendency for a halogen atom to form a positive ion (although such ions as I_2^+, Br_2^+, Cl_2^+, and I_3^+ have been identified).

3. Electronegativity. Each halogen is the most reactive nonmetal of its period, and fluorine is the most reactive of all the nonmetals. Fluorine has the highest electronegativity of any element and F_2 is one of the strongest oxidizing agents known. The electronegativity of the halogens decreases in the order $F > Cl > Br > I$, and the oxidizing power of the halogens decreases in the same order.

4. Bond energy. Bond energy decreases from Cl_2 to Br_2 to I_2 since the increasing size of the halogen atom makes it easier and easier to break the bond between the atoms of the X_2 molecule. The bond dissociation energy of the F_2 molecule is, however, unusually low and out of line in comparison to the other values. The reason for this relatively low value is not completely understood but is ascribed to the effect of the nonbonding electrons in the F_2 molecule. A repulsion between the highly dense electron clouds of the small fluorine atoms is believed to weaken the bond and lower the energy required to break it.

The bond formed between fluorine and an element other than itself is always stronger than the bonds formed by any of the other halogens with the same element. The bond energies of the hydrogen halides, for example, are HF, 565 kJ/mol; HCl, 431 kJ/mol; HBr, 364 kJ/mol; and HI, 297 kJ/mol. The high order of chemical reactivity of F_2 in reactions with other nonmetals is the result, therefore, of the low bond energy of the F_2 molecule (less energy *required*), coupled with the high bond energies of the new bonds (more energy *released*).

5. Electrode potentials. The values for the X_2/X^- electrode potentials fall in the same order as the electronegativity values. Fluorine is the most reactive halogen—iodine the least. Since electrode potentials refer to processes that occur in aqueous solution and since fluorine reacts with water, the F_2/F^- electrode potential is obtained by calculation rather than by direct measurement.

Table 21.2 Some properties of the halogens

Property	F_2	Cl_2	Br_2	I_2
color	pale yellow	yellow-green	red-brown	violet-black
melting point (°C)	-223	-102	-7	$+114$
boiling point (°C)	-188	-34	$+59$	$+185$
atomic radius (pm)	72	99	114	133
ionic radius, X^- (pm)	136	181	195	216
first ionization energy (kJ/mol)	1.68×10^3	1.25×10^3	1.14×10^3	1.00×10^3
electronegativity	4.0	3.2	3.0	2.7
bond energy (kJ/mol)	155	243	193	151
standard electrode potential (V) $2e^- + X_2 \rightleftharpoons 2X^-$	$+2.87$	$+1.36$	$+1.07$	$+0.54$

The relative oxidizing ability of the halogens may be observed in displacement reactions. Thus, fluorine can displace chlorine, bromine, and iodine from their salts; chlorine can displace bromine and iodine from their salts; and bromine can displace iodine from iodides:

$$F_2(g) + 2\,NaCl(s) \longrightarrow 2\,NaF(s) + Cl_2(g)$$

$$Cl_2(g) + 2\,Br^-(aq) \longrightarrow 2\,Cl^-(aq) + Br_2(l)$$

$$Br_2(l) + 2\,I^-(aq) \longrightarrow 2\,Br^-(aq) + I_2(s)$$

Since fluorine actively oxidizes water (producing O_2), displacement reactions involving F_2 cannot be run in water solution.

21.7 Occurrence and Industrial Preparation of the Halogens

The principal natural sources of the halogens are listed in Table 21.3. The halogens are too reactive to occur in elemental form. The most common state in which they occur is as halide ions.

The halogens are produced commercially in the following ways:

1. Fluorine. Fluorine must be prepared by an electrochemical process because no suitable chemical agent is sufficiently powerful to oxidize fluoride ion to fluorine. Furthermore, since the oxidation of water is easier to accomplish than the oxidation of the fluoride ion, the electrolysis must be carried out under anhydrous conditions. In actual practice, a solution of potassium fluoride in anhydrous hydrogen fluoride is electrolyzed. Pure HF does not conduct electric current; the KF reacts with HF to produce ions (K^+ and HF_2^-) that can act as charge carriers. The HF_2^- ion is formed from a F^- ion hydrogen-bonded to a HF molecule ($F{-}H\cdots F^-$); this hydrogen bond is so strong that the H atom is exactly midway between the two F atoms. The hydrogen fluoride used in the electrolysis is commercially derived from fluorospar, CaF_2 (see Section 21.10):

$$2\,KHF_2(l) \xrightarrow[\text{heat}]{\textit{electrolysis}} H_2(g) + F_2(g) + 2\,KF(l)$$

Table 21.3 Occurrence of the halogens		
Element	Percent of Earth's Crust	Occurrence
fluorine	6.5×10^{-2}	CaF_2 (fluorospar), Na_3AlF_6 (cryolite), $Ca_5(PO_4)_3F$ (fluorapatite)
chlorine	5.5×10^{-2}	Cl^- (sea water and underground brines) $NaCl$ (rock salt)
bromine	1.6×10^{-4}	Br^- (sea water, underground brines, solid salt beds)
iodine	3.0×10^{-5}	I^- (oil-well brines, sea water)
		$NaIO_3$, $NaIO_4$ (impurities in Chilean saltpeter, $NaNO_3$)

Cells used for the electrolysis of sodium chloride brine. *Hooker Chemical Company*.

2. Chlorine. The principal industrial source of chlorine is the electrolysis of aqueous sodium chloride, from which sodium hydroxide and hydrogen are also products:

$$2\,Na^+(aq) + 2\,Cl^-(aq) + 2\,H_2O \xrightarrow{\ electrolysis\ }$$
$$H_2(g) + Cl_2(g) + 2\,Na^+(aq) + 2\,OH^-(aq)$$

Chlorine is also obtained, as a by-product, from the industrial processes in which the reactive metals Na, Ca, and Mg are prepared. In each of these processes an anhydrous molten chloride is electrolyzed and Cl_2 gas is produced at the anode. For example,

$$2\,NaCl(l) \xrightarrow{\ electrolysis\ } 2\,Na(l) + Cl_2(g)$$

3. Bromine. Bromine is commercially prepared by the oxidation of the bromide ion of salt brines or sea water with chlorine as the oxidizing agent:

$$Cl_2(g) + 2\,Br^-(aq) \longrightarrow 2\,Cl^-(aq) + Br_2(l)$$

The liberated Br_2 is removed from the solution by a stream of air and, in subsequent steps, collected from the air and purified.

4. Iodine. In the United States the principal source of iodine is the iodide ion found in oil-well brines. Free iodine is obtained by displacement using chlorine:

$$Cl_2(g) + 2I^-(aq) \longrightarrow 2Cl^-(aq) + I_2(s)$$

In addition, iodine is commercially obtained from the iodate impurity found in Chilean nitrates. Sodium bisulfite is used to reduce the iodate ion:

$$2IO_3^-(aq) + 5HSO_3^-(aq) \longrightarrow I_2(s) + 5SO_4^{2-}(aq) + 3H^+(aq) + H_2O$$

21.8 Laboratory Preparation of the Halogens

With the exception of fluorine (which must be prepared electrochemically), the free halogens are usually prepared in the laboratory by the action of oxidizing agents on aqueous solutions of the hydrogen halides or on solutions containing the sodium halides and sulfuric acid.

From a table of standard electrode potentials we can get an approximate idea of what oxidizing agents will satisfactorily oxidize a given halide ion. Thus, any couple with a standard electrode potential more positive than $+1.36$ V should oxidize the chloride ion ($\mathscr{E}^\circ_{red} = +1.36$ V) as well as the bromide ion ($\mathscr{E}^\circ_{red} = +1.07$ V) and the iodide ion ($\mathscr{E}^\circ_{red} = +0.54$ V). Recall, however, that standard electrode potentials are listed for half-reactions at 25°C with all materials in their standard states. Thus, even though the standard electrode potential of $MnO_2 \rightarrow Mn^{2+}$ is only $+1.23$ V, MnO_2 is capable of oxidizing the chloride ion if concentrated HCl is used (rather than HCl at unit activity) and if the reaction is heated. In actual practice, $KMnO_4$, $K_2Cr_2O_7$, PbO_2, and MnO_2 are frequently used to prepare the free halogens from halide ions:

$$MnO_2(s) + 4H^+(aq) + 2Cl^-(aq) \longrightarrow Mn^{2+}(aq) + Cl_2(g) + 2H_2O$$
$$2MnO_4^-(aq) + 16H^+(aq) + 10Br^-(aq) \longrightarrow 2Mn^{2+}(aq) + 5Br_2(l) + 8H_2O$$
$$Cr_2O_7^{2-}(aq) + 14H^+(aq) + 6I^-(aq) \longrightarrow 2Cr^{3+}(aq) + 3I_2(s) + 7H_2O.$$

21.9 The Interhalogen Compounds

Some of the reactions of the halogens are summarized in Table 21.4. The halogens react with each other to produce a number of interhalogen compounds. All the compounds with the formula XX' (such as $BrCl$) are known except IF. Four XX'_3 compounds have been prepared (ClF_3, BrF_3, ICl_3, and IF_3), and three XX'_5 compounds are known (ClF_5, BrF_5, and IF_5). The only XX'_7 compound that has been made is IF_7.

With the exception of ICl_3, all the molecules for which n of the formula XX'_n is greater than 1 are halogen fluorides in which fluorine atoms (the smallest and most electronegative of all the halogen atoms) surround a Cl, Br, or I atom. The stability of these compounds increases as the size of the central atom increases.

General Reaction	Remarks
$nX_2 + 2M \longrightarrow 2MX_n$	F_2, Cl_2 with practically all metals; Br_2, I_2 with all except noble metals
$X_2 + H_2 \longrightarrow 2HX$	
$3X_2 + 2P \longrightarrow 2PX_3$	with excess P; similar reactions with As, Sb, and Bi
$5X_2 + 2P \longrightarrow 2PX_5$	with excess X_2, but not with I_2; SbF_5, $SbCl_5$, AsF_5, $AsCl_5$, and BiF_5 may be similarly prepared
$X_2 + 2S \longrightarrow S_2X_2$	with Cl_2, Br_2
$X_2 + H_2O \longrightarrow H^+ + X^- + HOX$	not with F_2
$2X_2 + 2H_2O \longrightarrow 4H^+ + 4X^- + O_2$	F_2 rapidly; Cl_2, Br_2 slowly in sunlight
$X_2 + H_2S \longrightarrow 2HX + S$	
$X_2 + CO \longrightarrow COX_2$	Cl_2, Br_2
$X_2 + SO_2 \longrightarrow SO_2X_2$	F_2, Cl_2
$X_2 + 2X' \longrightarrow X_2' + 2X^-$	$F_2 > Cl_2 > Br_2 > I_2$
$X_2 + X_2' \longrightarrow 2XX'$	formation of the interhalogen compounds (all except IF)

Hence, neither BrF_7 nor ClF_7 has been prepared, although IF_7 is known; ClF_5 readily decomposes into ClF_3 and F_2, whereas BrF_5 and IF_5 are stable even at temperatures above 400°C.

The structures of the higher interhalogen compounds have received considerable attention because the bonding of the central atom in each of these molecules violates the octet principle (see Figure 21.1). The central atom of each XX_3' molecule has three bonding pairs and two nonbonding pairs of electrons in its valence shell, and the molecules, therefore, are T-shaped. The XX_5' molecules are square pyramidal since each of the central atoms has five bonding pairs and one nonbonding pair of electrons in its valence shell. The nonbonding electron pairs of the central atoms of these two types of molecules introduce some distortion. The I atom of the IF_7 molecule has seven bonding pairs of electrons in its valence shell. The IF_7 molecule is pentagonal bipyramidal.

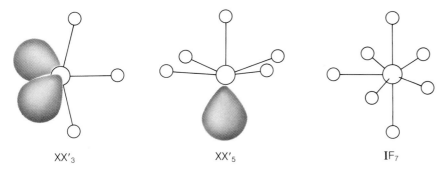

XX'$_3$ XX'$_5$ IF$_7$

Figure 21.1 Structures of XX_3', XX_5', and IF_7. (The unshared pairs in XX_3' and XX_5' molecules are responsible for some distortion from the regular T-shaped and square pyramidal structures.)

21.10 The Hydrogen Halides

Each of the hydrogen halides may be prepared by the direct reaction of hydrogen with the corresponding free halogen:

$$H_2 + X_2 \longrightarrow 2\,HX$$

The vigor of the reaction decreases markedly from fluorine to iodine. The reactions serve as important industrial sources of HCl, HBr, and HI.

Both HF and HCl can be prepared by the action of warm concentrated sulfuric acid on the corresponding natural halide, CaF_2 and NaCl. Both reactions serve as important industrial sources of the gases:

$$CaF_2(s) + H_2SO_4(l) \longrightarrow CaSO_4(s) + 2\,HF(g)$$

$$NaCl(s) + H_2SO_4(l) \longrightarrow NaHSO_4(s) + HCl(g)$$

All hydrogen halides are colorless gases at room temperature; sulfuric acid, on the other hand, is a high-boiling liquid. Thus, the foregoing reactions are examples of a general method for the preparation of a volatile acid from its salts by means of a nonvolatile acid. At higher temperatures (about 500°C), further reaction occurs between $NaHSO_4$ and NaCl:

$$NaCl(s) + NaHSO_4(l) \longrightarrow HCl(g) + Na_2SO_4(s)$$

Hydrogen bromide and hydrogen iodide cannot be made by the action of concentrated sulfuric acid on bromides and iodides because hot, concentrated sulfuric acid oxidizes these anions to the free halogens. The bromide and iodide ions are easier to oxidize than the fluoride and chloride ions:

$$2\,NaBr(s) + 2\,H_2SO_4(l) \longrightarrow Br_2(g) + SO_2(g) + Na_2SO_4(s) + 2\,H_2O(g)$$

Since the iodide ion is a stronger reducing agent (more easily oxidized) than the bromide ion, S and H_2S, as well as SO_2, are obtained as reduction products from the reaction of NaI with hot concentrated sulfuric acid.

Pure HBr or HI can be obtained by the action of phosphoric acid on NaBr or NaI; phosphoric acid is an essentially nonvolatile acid and is a poor oxidizing agent:

$$NaBr(s) + H_3PO_4(l) \longrightarrow HBr(g) + NaH_2PO_4(s)$$

$$NaI(s) + H_3PO_4(l) \longrightarrow HI(g) + NaH_2PO_4(s)$$

The hydrogen halides may be prepared by the reaction of water on the appropriate phosphorus trihalide:

$$PX_3 + 3\,H_2O \longrightarrow 3\,HX(g) + H_3PO_3(aq)$$

Convenient laboratory preparations of HBr and HI have been developed in which red phosphorus, bromine or iodine, and a limited amount of water are employed and in which no attempt is made to isolate the phosphorus trihalide intermediate.

Hydrogen fluoride molecules associate with each other through hydrogen bonding. The vapor consists of aggregates up to $(HF)_6$ at temperatures near the boiling point (19.4°C) but is less highly associated at higher temperatures. Gaseous HCl, HBr, and HI consist of single molecules. Liquid HF and solid HF are more highly hydrogen bonded than gaseous HF, and the boiling point and melting point of HF are abnormally high in comparison with those of the other hydrogen halides.

All hydrogen halides are very soluble in water; water solutions are called hydrohalic acids. Aqueous HI, for example, is called hydroiodic acid. The H—F bond is stronger than any other H—X bond; HF is a weak acid in water solution, whereas HCl, HBr, and HI are completely dissociated:

$$HF(aq) \rightleftharpoons H^+(aq) + F^-(aq)$$

The F^- ions from this dissociation are largely associated with HF molecules:

$$F^-(aq) + HF(aq) \rightleftharpoons HF_2^-(aq)$$

Concentrated HF solutions are more strongly ionic than dilute solutions and contain high concentrations of ions of the type HF_2^-, $H_2F_3^-$, and higher.

Hydrofluoric acid reacts with silica, SiO_2, and glass, which is made from silica:

$$SiO_2(s) + 6\,HF(aq) \longrightarrow 2\,H^+(aq) + SiF_6^{2-}(aq) + 2\,H_2O$$

When warmed, the reaction is

$$SiO_2(g) + 4\,HF(aq) \longrightarrow SiF_4(g) + 2\,H_2O(g)$$

For this reason, hydrofluoric acid must be stored in wax or plastic containers instead of glass bottles.

The fluorosilicate ion, SiF_6^{2-}, is an example of a large group of complex ions formed by the halide ions. Halo complexes are formed by most metals (with the notable exceptions of the group I A, group II A, and lanthanide metals) and with some nonmetals (for example, BF_4^-). The formulas of these complex ions are most commonly of the types $(MX_4)^{(4-)+n}$ and $(MX_6)^{(6-)+n}$, where n is the oxidation number of the central atom of the complex.

11 The Metal Halides

Metal halides can be prepared by direct interaction of the elements, by the reactions of the hydrogen halides with hydroxides or oxides, and by the reactions of the hydrogen halides with carbonates:

$$K_2CO_3(s) + 2\,HF(l) \longrightarrow 2\,KF(s) + CO_2(g) + H_2O$$

The character of the bonding in metal halides varies widely as do the physical properties of these compounds. A metal that has a low ionization energy generally forms halides that are highly ionic and consequently have high melting and boiling points. On the other hand, metals that have comparatively high ionization energies react, particularly with bromine and iodine, to form halides in which the bonding has a high degree of covalent character. These compounds have comparatively low melting points and boiling points.

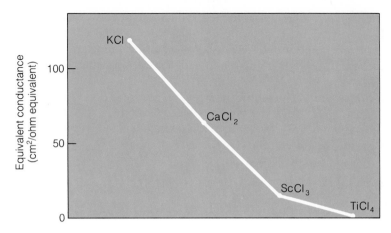

Figure 21.2 Equivalent conductances of some molten chlorides near the melting point

In general, the halides of the I A metals, the II A metals (with the exception of Be), and most of the inner-transition metals are largely ionic; halides of the remaining metals are covalent to a varying degree. Within a series of halides of metals of the same period, ionic character decreases from compound to compound as the oxidation number of the metal increases and the size of the cation undergoes a concomitant decrease. The ionic character of a compound is reflected in its ability to conduct electric current as measured by its conductance. The equivalent conductances of the molten chlorides of some fourth-period metals are plotted in Figure 21.2. The "cations" of the compounds (K^+, Ca^{2+}, Sc^{3+}, and Ti^{4+}) are isoelectronic. Potassium chloride is a completely ionic solid, and molten KCl has the highest conductance of the four compounds. Titanium(IV) chloride, $TiCl_4$, is a covalent liquid and is nonconducting.

If a metal exhibits more than one oxidation state, the halides of the highest oxidation state are the most covalent. Thus, the second member of each of the following pairs is a highly covalent, volatile liquid (melting points are given in parentheses): $SnCl_2$ (246°C), $SnCl_4$ (−33°C); $PbCl_2$ (501°C), $PbCl_4$ (−15°C); $SbCl_3$ (73.4°C), $SbCl_5$ (2.8°C).

Since fluorine is the most electronegative halogen, fluorides are the most ionic of the halides; ionic character decreases in the order: fluoride > chloride > bromide > iodide. The halides of aluminum are an excellent example of the relationship between ionic or covalent character and the size of the halide ion. Aluminum fluoride is an ionic substance. Aluminum chloride is semicovalent and crystallizes in a layer lattice in which electrically neutral layers are held together by London forces. Aluminum bromide and aluminum iodide are essentially covalent; the crystals consist of Al_2Br_6 and Al_2I_6 molecules, respectively.

The water solubility of fluorides is considerably different from that of the chlorides, bromides, and iodides. The fluorides of lithium, the group II A metals, and the lanthanides are only slightly soluble, whereas the other halides of these metals are relatively soluble.

Most chlorides, bromides, and iodides are soluble in water. The cations that form slightly soluble compounds with these halide ions include silver(I), mercury(I), lead(II), copper(I), and thallium(I).

The insolubility of the silver salts of Cl^-, Br^-, and I^- is the basis of a common test for these halide ions; AgCl is white, AgBr is cream, and AgI is yellow. The

Table 21.5 Oxyhalogen acids

Oxidation State of Cl, Br, and I	Formula of Acid				Name of Acid	Name of Anion Derived from Acid
1+	HOF	HOCl	HOBr	HOI	hypohalous acid	hypohalite ion
3+	–	HClO$_2$	–	–	halous acid	halite ion
5+	–	HClO$_3^a$	HBrO$_3^a$	HIO$_3^a$	halic acid	halate ion
7+	–	HClO$_4^a$	HBrO$_4^a$	$\begin{cases} HIO_4 \\ H_4I_2O_9 \\ H_5IO_6 \end{cases}$	perhalic acid	perhalate ion

^{a} Strong acids.

silver halide precipitates may be formed by the addition of a solution of silver nitrate to a solution containing the appropriate halide ion. Silver iodide is insoluble in excess ammonia; however, AgCl readily dissolves to form the $Ag(NH_3)_2^+$ complex ion and AgBr dissolves with difficulty. Silver fluoride is soluble in water. Precipitates of MgF_2 or CaF_2 are usually used to confirm the presence of the fluoride ion in a solution.

If the iodide ion in an aqueous solution is oxidized to iodine (the usual procedure employs chlorine), the I_2 can be extracted by cyclohexane, which forms a two-liquid-layer system with water. The solution of I_2 in cyclohexane is violet colored. In the corresponding test for the bromide ion, the Br_2-cyclohexane solution is brown.

.12 Oxyacids of the Halogens

The oxyacids of the halogens are listed in Table 21.5. The only oxyacid of fluorine that has been prepared is hypofluorous acid, HOF, a thermally unstable compound. The acids of chlorine and their salts are the most important of these compounds.

Lewis formulas for the oxychlorine acids are shown in Figure 21.3; removal of H^+ from each of these structures gives the electronic formula of the corresponding anion. However, Lewis structures, in which each Cl and O atom has a valence-electron octet, do not show that the Cl—O bonds in these compounds can have a considerable amount of double-bond character due to $p\pi$-$d\pi$ bonding (see Section 9.6).

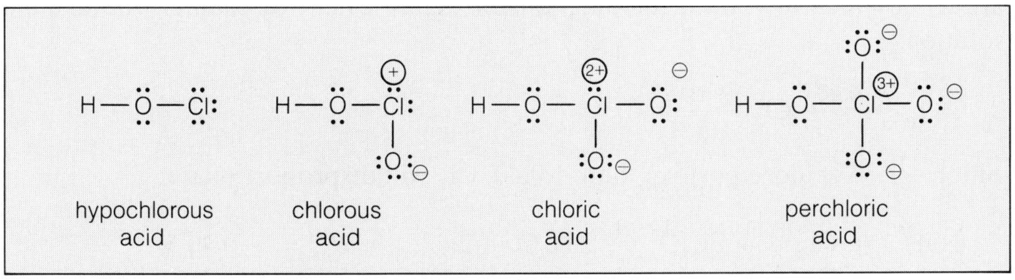

Figure 21.3 Lewis formulas for the oxychlorine acids

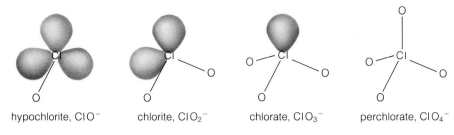

hypochlorite, ClO^- chlorite, ClO_2^- chlorate, ClO_3^- perchlorate, ClO_4^-

Figure 21.4 Structures of the oxychlorine anions

The oxybromine and oxyiodine anions have configurations similar to the analogous oxychlorine anions shown in Figure 21.4. The H_5IO_6 molecule is octahedral with five OH groups and one O atom in the six positions surrounding the central I atom.

The standard electrode potentials for Cl_2, Br_2, I_2, and the compounds of these elements in acidic and alkaline solution are summarized in Figure 21.5. The number shown over each arrow is the $\mathscr{E}_{red}^{\circ}$, in volts, for the reduction of the species on the left to that on the right. An oxidation potential for a transformation from right to left may, of course, be obtained by changing the sign of $\mathscr{E}_{red}^{\circ}$.

Perchloric acid ($HClO_4$), perbromic acid ($HBrO_4$), and the halic acids ($HClO_3$, $HBrO_3$, and HIO_3) are strong acids, but the remaining oxyacids are incompletely dissociated in water solution and exist in solution largely in molecular form. Hence, molecular formulas are shown in Figure 21.5 for the weak acids in acidic solution. In general, acid strength increases with increasing oxygen content.

Much of the chemistry of these compounds is effectively correlated by means of these electrode potential diagrams. Remember, however, that the recorded $\mathscr{E}^{\circ}$ values refer to reductions that take place at 25°C with all substances present in their standard states. Concentration changes and temperature changes alter $\mathscr{E}^{\circ}$ values. Furthermore, a cell emf tells nothing about the speed of the transformation to which it applies; some reactions for which the cell emfs are positive occur so slowly that they are of no practical importance. According to $\mathscr{E}_{red}^{\circ}$ values, the oxidation of water (in acid) and of the OH^- ion (in base) should be readily accomplished by many oxyhalogen compounds. These reactions, however, occur so slowly that it is possible to observe all the oxyhalogen compounds in solution.

One of the outstanding characteristics of the oxyhalogen compounds is their ability to function as oxidizing agents; all the $\mathscr{E}_{red}^{\circ}$ values are positive. The $\mathscr{E}_{red}^{\circ}$ values also show that, in general, these compounds are stronger oxidizing agents in acidic solution than in alkaline solution.

Many of these species are unstable toward disproportionation. Such substances are readily identified from the diagrams of Figure 21.5. For example, in alkaline solution:

$$ClO^- \xrightarrow{+0.40} Cl_2 \xrightarrow{+1.36} Cl^-$$

Since $+1.36$ is more positive than $+0.40$, Cl_2 will disproportionate:

$$
\begin{array}{ll}
4\,OH^- + Cl_2 \longrightarrow 2\,ClO^- + 2\,H_2O + 2e^- & \mathscr{E}_{ox}^{\circ} = -0.40 \text{ V} \\
\underline{2e^- + Cl_2 \longrightarrow 2\,Cl^-} & \underline{\mathscr{E}_{red}^{\circ} = +1.36 \text{ V}} \\
2\,OH^- + Cl_2 \longrightarrow ClO^- + Cl^- + H_2O & \mathscr{E}_{emf} = +0.96 \text{ V}
\end{array}
$$

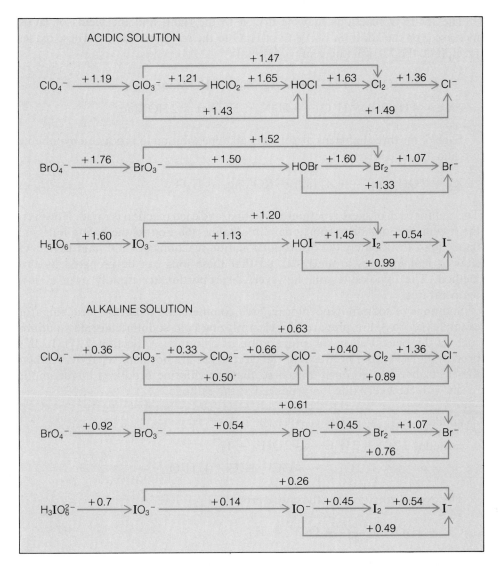

Figure 21.5 Standard electrode potential diagrams for chlorine, bromine, iodine, and their compounds

The $\mathscr{E}^{\circ}_{red}$ values indicate that HOCl, HOBr, HOI, HClO$_2$, and ClO$_3^-$ should disproportionate in acidic solution. In alkaline solution all species should disproportionate except the halide ions, ClO$_4^-$, BrO$_4^-$, BrO$_3^-$, H$_3$IO$_6^{2-}$, and IO$_3^-$.

1. Hypohalous acids and hypohalites. The hypohalous acids (HOX) are the weakest halogen oxyacids. They exist in solution but cannot be prepared in pure form. Each of the three halogens is slightly soluble in water and reacts to produce a low concentration of the corresponding hypohalous acid:

$$X_2 + H_2O \rightleftharpoons H^+(aq) + X^-(aq) + HOX(aq)$$

All standard potentials for these reactions are negative, and the reactions proceed to a very limited extent. Thus, at 25°C saturated solutions of the halogens contain the following HOX concentrations: HOCl, 3×10^{-2} M; HOBr, 1×10^{-3} M; HOI, 6×10^{-6} M.

The X_2-H_2O reactions may be driven to the right, and the yields of HOX increased, by the addition of Ag_2O or HgO to the reaction mixture. These oxides precipitate the X^- ion and remove $H^+(aq)$:

$$2\,X_2 + Ag_2O(s) + H_2O \longrightarrow 2\,AgX(s) + 2\,HOX(aq)$$

$$2\,X_2 + 4\,HgO(s) + H_2O \longrightarrow HgX_2 \cdot 3\,HgO(s) + 2\,HOX(aq)$$

Each of the three halogens dissolves in alkaline solution to produce a hypohalite ion and a halide ion:

$$X_2 + 2\,OH^-(aq) \longrightarrow X^-(aq) + XO^-(aq) + H_2O$$

The emf for each of these reactions is positive, and each reaction is rapid. However, the hypohalite ions disproportionate in alkaline solution to the halate ions and halide ions. Fortunately the disproportionation reactions of ClO^- and BrO^- are slow at temperatures around $0°C$, so that these ions can be prepared by this method. The hypoiodite ion, however, disproportionates rapidly even at low temperatures.

Solutions of sodium hypochlorite, used commercially in cotton bleaching (for example, Clorox), are prepared by electrolyzing cold sodium chloride solutions such as the ones used in the preparation of chlorine (see Section 21.7). In this process, however, the products of the electrolysis are not kept separate. Rather, the electrolyte is vigorously mixed so that the chlorine produced at the anode reacts with the hydroxide ion produced at the cathode:

anode: $\qquad\qquad 2\,Cl^- \longrightarrow Cl_2 + 2e^-$

cathode: $\quad 2e^- + 2\,H_2O \longrightarrow 2\,OH^- + H_2$

$$Cl_2 + 2\,OH^- \longrightarrow OCl^- + Cl^- + H_2O$$

The overall equation for the entire process is

$$Cl^- + H_2O \xrightarrow[cold]{electrolysis} OCl^- + H_2$$

The hypohalous acids and hypohalites are good oxidizing agents, particularly in acidic solution. The compounds decompose not only by disproportionation but also by the liberation of O_2 from the solutions. The reactions in which O_2 is liberated are slow, however, and are catalyzed by metal salts.

2. Halous acids and halites. The only known halous acid is chlorous acid ($HClO_2$). This compound cannot be isolated in pure form, and even in aqueous solution it decomposes rapidly. Chlorous acid is weak acid, but it is stronger than hypochlorous acid. The disproportionation of $HOCl$ in acidic solution does not yield $HClO_2$. The electrode potentials indicate, however, that it should be possible to make the chlorite ion by the disproportionation of ClO^- in alkaline solution. The disproportionation of ClO^- into ClO_3^- and Cl^-, however, is more favorable, and ClO_2^- cannot be made from ClO^-.

Chlorites are comparatively stable in alkaline solution and may be prepared from ClO_2 gas. Chlorine dioxide, a very reactive odd-electron molecule, is prepared by the reduction of chlorates in aqueous solution using sulfur dioxide gas as the reducing agent:

$$2\,ClO_3^-(aq) + SO_2(g) \longrightarrow ClO_2(g) + SO_4^{2-}(aq)$$

The chlorite ion is prepared by the reaction of ClO_2 gas with an alkaline solution of sodium peroxide (which forms the hydroperoxide ion HO_2^- in alkaline solution):

$$2\,ClO_2(g) + HO_2^-(aq) + OH^-(aq) \longrightarrow 2\,ClO_2^-(aq) + O_2(g) + H_2O$$

Solid chlorites are dangerous chemicals. They detonate when heated and are explosive in contact with combustible material.

3. Halic acids and halates. We have mentioned the disproportionation reactions of the hypohalite ions:

$$3\,XO^- \longrightarrow XO_3^- + 2\,X^-$$

Thus if a free halogen is added to a *hot*, concentrated solution of alkali, the corresponding halide and halate ions are produced rather than the halide and hypohalite ions:

$$3\,X_2 + 6\,OH^-(aq) \longrightarrow 5\,X^-(aq) + XO_3^-(aq) + 3\,H_2O$$

The chlorates are commercially prepared by the electrolysis of hot, concentrated solutions of chlorides (instead of the cold solutions used for the electrochemical preparation of the hypochlorites). The electrolyte is stirred vigorously so that the chlorine produced at the anode reacts with the hydroxide ion that is a product of the reduction at the cathode:

anode: $\qquad\qquad 2\,Cl^- \longrightarrow Cl_2 + 2\,e^-$

cathode: $\quad 2\,e^- + 2\,H_2O \longrightarrow 2\,OH^- + H_2$

$$3\,Cl_2 + 6\,OH^- \longrightarrow 5\,Cl^- + ClO_3^- + 3\,H_2O$$

If the three foregoing equations are added after the first two equations have each been multiplied through by 3, the equation for the overall process is obtained:

$$Cl^- + 3\,H_2O \xrightarrow[\text{hot}]{\text{electrolysis}} ClO_3^- + 3\,H_2$$

The chlorate crystallizes from the concentrated solution employed as the electrolyte of the cell. Although chlorates are generally water soluble, they are much less soluble than the corresponding chlorides.

Solutions of a halic acid can be prepared by adding sulfuric acid to a solution of the barium salt of the acid:

$$Ba^{2+}(aq) + 2\,XO_3^-(aq) + 2\,H^+(aq) + SO_4^{2-}(aq) \longrightarrow$$
$$BaSO_4(s) + 2\,H^+(aq) + 2\,XO_3^-(aq)$$

Pure $HBrO_3$ or $HClO_3$ cannot be isolated from aqueous solutions because of decomposition. Iodic acid, HIO_3, however, can be obtained as a white solid; this acid is generally prepared by oxidizing iodine with concentrated nitric acid. All halic acids are strong. The halates, as well as the halic acids, are strong oxidizing agents. The reactions of chlorates with easily oxidized materials may be explosive.

Chlorates decompose upon heating in a variety of ways. At high temperatures, and particularly in the presence of a catalyst, chlorates decompose into chlorides and oxygen:

$$2\,KClO_3(s) \xrightarrow[MnO_2]{heat} 2\,KCl(s) + 3\,O_2(g)$$

At more moderate temperatures, in the absence of a catalyst, the decomposition yields perchlorates and chlorides:

$$4\ KClO_3(s) \xrightarrow{heat} 3\,KClO_4(s) + KCl(s)$$

4. Perhalic acids and perhalates. Perchlorate salts are made by the controlled thermal decomposition of a chlorate or by the electrolysis of a cold solution of a chlorate. The free acid, a clear liquid, may be prepared by distilling a mixture of a perchlorate salt with concentrated sulfuric acid. A number of crystalline hydrates of perchloric acid are known. The compound $HClO_4 \cdot H_2O$ is of interest; the lattice positions of the crystal are occupied by H_3O^+ and ClO_4^- ions, and the solid is isomorphous (of the same crystalline structure) with NH_4ClO_4. Perchloric acid is a strong acid and a strong oxidizing agent. Concentrated $HClO_4$ may react violently when heated with organic substances; the reactions are frequently explosive.

Perbromates are prepared by the oxidation of bromates in alkaline solution using F_2 as the oxidizing agent. Several periodic acids have been prepared; the most common one is H_5IO_6. Periodates are made by the oxidation of iodates, usually by means of Cl_2 in alkaline solution. Salts of the anions IO_4^-, $I_2O_9^{4-}$, IO_6^{5-}, and IO_5^{3-} have been obtained.

21.13 Industrial Uses of the Halogens

The most important industrial uses of the halogens and halogen compounds are:

1. Fluorine. The most important fluorides produced commercially are synthetic cryolite and the fluorocarbons. Cryolite, Na_3AlF_6, is used as a supporting electrolyte in the electrolysis of molten Al_2O_3 for the production of aluminum (Hall process). The fluorocarbons are noted for their chemical inertness. The Freons (for example, CCl_2F_2) are used as refrigerants and aerosol propellants. Polytetrafluoroethylene (polymerized $F_2C{=}CF_2$, Teflon) is a solid fluorocarbon polymer that is highly resistant to chemical attack. Liquid fluorocarbons are used as chemically resistant lubricants.

The principal use of elemental fluorine is in the separation of ^{235}U (the isotope of uranium that undergoes atomic fission) from natural uranium (which is mostly ^{238}U). Uranium metal (which contains both isotopes) is converted into UF_6 (which sublimes at $56°C$). Since $^{235}UF_6$ has a lower molecular weight than $^{238}UF_6$, the $^{235}UF_6$ vapor effuses through a porous barrier slightly more rapidly than the $^{238}UF_6$ does and a separation of the two isotopes is effected by repeating an effusion process thousands of times.

Minor but well publicized uses of fluorides (principally NaF), are their addition to water supplies and toothpaste to prevent tooth decay.

2. Chlorine. A large number of chlorine-containing compounds are produced commercially. Most of these compounds are organic compounds that are made by use of chlorine or hydrogen chloride. They are used, for example, as plastics, solvents, pesticides, herbicides, pharmaceuticals, refrigerants, and dyes. Large quantities of HCl are produced to be used not only in the synthesis of organic products, but also in petroleum technology, metallurgy, metal cleaning (to remove metal oxides from metals), food processing, and in the manufacture of inorganic chlorides. Chlorine is used in the manufacture of paper, rayon, hydrogen chloride, bromine, iodine, sodium hypochlorite, and metal chlorides, in the disinfection of water, and in the bleaching of textiles.

3. Bromine. The principal use of bromine, at present, is in the manufacture of ethylene dibromide (CH_2BrCH_2Br) which is used with the anti-knock agent tetraethyl lead in leaded gasolines. Ethylene dibromide supplies bromine to convert the lead into $PbBr_2$ which is volatile at cylinder combustion temperatures and is swept out of the engine in the exhaust. The importance of this use of bromine is declining since antipollution laws forbid the use of leaded gasoline in new cars.

Bromine-containing organic compounds are used as intermediates in industrial syntheses, dyes, pharmaceuticals, fumigants, and fire-proofing agents. Inorganic bromides are used in medicine, in bleaching, and in photography ($AgBr$).

4. Iodine. Iodine and its compounds are not used as extensively as the other halogens and halides. Significant uses include the production of pharmaceuticals, dyes, and silver iodide (for photography).

Summary

Hydrogen is produced industrially from the reaction of CH_4 and steam (*steam reformer process*), from coke and steam (*water gas process*), from *iron and steam*, by *cracking* hydrocarbons (breaking down high molecular weight hydrocarbons into lower molecular weight compounds), and by *electrolysis* (of a NaCl brine, or of water itself). In the laboratory, hydrogen is most conveniently prepared by *displacement reactions* (a highly reactive metal with cold water, certain other metals with acids, and amphoteric elements with alkaline solutions).

Most reactions of hydrogen require *elevated temperatures* since the H—H bond must be broken in the course of the reaction and the *H—H bond energy is comparatively high*. Hydrogen forms several types of hydrides: *saltlike hydrides* (with very reactive metals), *interstitial hydrides* (with certain transition metals), and *complex hydrides* (which contain anions made up of boron or aluminum and hydrogen, such as BH_4^- and AlH_4^-). Hydrogen forms *covalent compounds* with most nonmetals. With the *halogens*, hydrogen forms colorless, covalent gases that have the general formula, HX, where X is an atom of a halogen. Hydrogen forms H_2O with oxygen, H_2S with sulfur, NH_3 with nitrogen (*Haber process*), and hydrocarbons with carbon (*Bergius process*). Hydrogen reduces many oxides of metals to give the free metal and water. With CO(g), hydrogen reacts (high temperatures and pressures, presence of a catalyst) to form methanol (CH_3OH). The industrial uses of hydrogen were reviewed.

The halogens exist as *diatomic molecules:* F_2 and Cl_2 are gases, Br_2 is a liquid, and I_2 is a solid. Each halogen is the *most reactive nonmetal* of its period and F_2 is the most reactive of all the nonmetals. The relative *oxidizing ability* of the halogens *decreases* with *increasing atomic size* of the halogens. Thus, F_2 can displace chlorine, bromine, and iodine from their salts, Cl_2 can displace bromine and iodine from their salts, and Br_2 can displace iodine from iodides.

The industrial preparations of the halogens are: *fluorine* by electrolysis of a solution of KF in liquid HF, *chlorine* by the electrolysis of aqueous NaCl or molten NaCl, *bromine* by the oxidation by Cl_2 of the Br^- ion of salt brines from sea water, and *iodine* by the displacement by Cl_2 of the I^- ion found in oil-well brines. With the exception of F_2 (which must be prepared electrochemically), the halogens are prepared in the laboratory by the action of oxidizing agents on aqueous solutions of the hydrogen halides or on solutions containing the sodium halides and H_2SO_4.

Compounds (called *interhalogen compounds*) formed between two different halogens are known. The *hydrogen halides* can be made by the direct reaction of hydrogen with the appropriate halogen. In addition, HF and HCl can be prepared by the action of warm, concentrated H_2SO_4 on CaF_2 and NaCl; and HBr and HI can be prepared by the action of H_3PO_4 on NaBr and NaI. The hydrogen halides can also be prepared by the reaction of *water* on the *appropriate phosphorus trihalide*. In aqueous solution, HCl, HBr, and HI are *strong acids*, and HF is a *weak acid*.

Metal halides can be prepared by the *direct interaction* of the elements, or by the reactions of the *hydrogen halides* with *hydroxides*, *oxides*, or *carbonates*. The character of the bonding in these compounds varies from strongly ionic to largely covalent. The chemistry of the *oxyacids of the halogens* and the salts of these acids is effectively correlated by *electrode potential diagrams*. The industrial uses of the halogens were reviewed.

Key Terms

Some of the more important terms introduced in this chapter are listed below. Definitions for terms not included in this list may be located in the text by use of the index.

Bergius process (Section 21.4) A process, carried out at high temperatures and in the presence of catalysts, in which hydrogen and finely divided carbon react to form hydrocarbons.

Cracking (Section 21.2) A process in which high molecular weight hydrocarbons are broken down into lower molecular weight compounds; used in petroleum refining.

Displacement reaction (Section 21.3) A reaction in which one element (or group of elements) displaces another element (or group of elements) from a compound

Haber process (Section 21.4) A process, run at high pressures (300 to 1000 atm), at high temperatures (400°C to 600°C), and in the presence of a catalyst, in which hydrogen and nitrogen react to produce ammonia.

Halogen (Section 21.6) A group VII A element: fluorine, chlorine, bromine, iodine, or astatine.

Interhalogen compound (Section 21.9) A compound that is composed of two or more different halogens.

Steam reformer process (Section 21.2) An industrial process used to prepare hydrogen by the reaction of steam with a hydrocarbon.

Water gas (Section 21.2) A mixture of carbon monoxide and hydrogen produced industrially by the reaction of steam and coke.

Problems*

Hydrogen

21.1 What are the principal ways in which hydrogen occurs in nature?

21.2 Discuss four methods by which hydrogen is prepared from water industrially.

21.3 Write chemical equations for the reactions of hydrogen with: **(a)** Na(s), **(b)** Ca(s), **(c)** $Cl_2(g)$, **(d)** $N_2(g)$, **(e)** $Cu_2O(s)$, **(f)** CO(g), **(g)** $WO_3(s)$.

21.4 Write chemical equations for the reactions by which hydrogen is prepared from: **(a)** Na(s) and H_2O, **(b)** Fe(s) and steam, **(c)** Zn(s) and H^+(aq), **(d)** Zn(s) and OH^-(aq), **(e)** C(s) and steam, **(f)** $CH_4(g)$ and steam, **(g)** $CaH_2(s)$ and H_2O.

21.5 How do the physical properties of hydrogen reflect the nature of the London forces between H_2 molecules?

21.6 Describe the properties and structure of the **(a)** salt-like hydrides, **(b)** interstitial hydrides, **(c)** complex hydrides, **(d)** covalent hydrides.

21.7 Compare the physical properties and the reactions with water of the two hydrides CaH_2 and HCl.

21.8 What is believed to account for the catalytic activity of Pd, Pt, and Ni in many reactions that involve hydrogen?

21.9 Calculate the mass of **(a)** Al, **(b)** Zn, and **(c)** Sn required to liberate 1.000 g of $H_2(g)$ from excess acid.

21.10 Calculate the mass of hydrogen that can be obtained by the reaction of **(a)** 6.00 g of Na(s) with excess water, **(b)** 6.00 g of NaH(s) with excess water, and **(c)** 6.00 g of $LiAlH_4$ with excess water (in which H_2, $Al(OH)_3$, and LiOH are produced).

21.11 **(a)** What mass of hydrogen would theoretically be required to reduce 1.00 kg of $WO_3(s)$ to yield W(s)? **(b)** What volume would this mass of $H_2(g)$ occupy at STP?

21.12 **(a)** What is the mass of 22.4 L of $H_2(g)$ at STP? **(b)** Assume that air is *by volume* 78.1% $N_2(g)$, 20.9% $O_2(g)$, and 1.0% Ar(g). Calculate the mass of 22.4 L of air at STP. **(c)** If a 22.4-L balloon were filled with $H_2(g)$ at STP, the difference between the mass of 22.4 L of air and 22.4 L of $H_2(g)$ would be the approximate value of the lifting power of the hydrogen. Calculate this value. Approximately how many times its own mass can a sample of hydrogen lift?

The Halogens

21.13 What are the principal natural sources of the halogens?

21.14 Describe the important industrial uses of the halogens.

21.15 Write chemical equations to show how to prepare the following: **(a)** F_2 from CaF_2, **(b)** Cl_2 from NaCl, **(c)** Br_2 from sea water, **(d)** I_2 from $NaIO_3$, **(e)** HBr from PBr_3.

21.16 Write chemical equations to show how $Cl_2(g)$ may be prepared from Cl^-(aq) by use of: **(a)** $MnO_2(s)$, **(b)** $PbO_2(s)$, **(c)** MnO_4^-(aq), **(d)** $Cr_2O_7^{2-}$(aq). **(e)** Can analogous reactions be used to prepare $F_2(g)$, $Br_2(l)$, or $I_2(s)$? Justify your answer.

21.17 Write chemical equations for the reactions of HF with **(a)** SiO_2, **(b)** Na_2CO_3, **(c)** KF, **(d)** CaO.

21.18 Write chemical equations for the reactions of $Cl_2(g)$ with **(a)** $H_2(g)$, **(b)** Zn(s), **(c)** P(s), **(d)** S(s), **(e)** $H_2S(g)$, **(f)** CO(g), **(g)** $SO_2(g)$, **(h)** I^-(aq), **(i)** cold H_2O.

21.19 Write chemical equations to show why concentrated HF(aq) is more strongly ionic than dilute HF(aq).

21.20 Since HCl(g) can be prepared from NaCl and H_2SO_4, why is it that the reaction of NaI and H_2SO_4 cannot be used to prepare HI(g)?

21.21 Which is larger: **(a)** the acid strength of HF or of HCl, **(b)** electronegativity of fluorine or of chlorine, **(c)** bond energy of Cl_2 or of I_2, **(d)** bond energy of Cl_2 or of F_2, **(e)** water solubility of AgCl or of AgF.

21.22 Which is larger: **(a)** intermolecular forces between I_2 molecules or those between F_2 molecules, **(b)** first ionization energy of fluorine or of iodine, **(c)** the melting point of F_2 or of Cl_2, **(d)** the boiling point of HCl or of HF, **(e)** oxidizing ability of Br_2 or I_2, **(f)** solubility in aqueous ammonia of AgI or of AgCl.

21.23 Which compound of each of the following pairs is the more strongly ionic? **(a)** BeF_2 or $BeBr_2$, **(b)** $FeCl_2$ or $FeCl_3$, **(c)** MgI_2 or SrI_2, **(d)** RbCl or $SrCl_2$. Explain the reason for your prediction in each case.

21.24 Which compound of each of the following pairs is the more strongly ionic? **(a)** $CaBr_2$ or $BaBr_2$, **(b)** TlBr or $TlBr_3$, **(c)** $CdBr_2$ or CdI_2, **(d)** $SrCl_2$ or YCl_3. Explain the reason for your prediction in each case.

21.25 Discuss the geometry of the anions of the oxyacids of chlorine.

---

* The more difficult problems are marked with asterisks. The appendix contains answers to color-keyed problems.

21.26 Discuss the molecular geometry of the interhalogen compounds XX'_3, XX'_5, and XX'_7.

21.27 Write chemical equations for the electrolysis of **(a)** dry, molten NaCl, **(b)** cold, aqueous solution of NaCl, **(c)** cold, aqueous solution of NaCl with the electrolyte stirred, **(d)** hot, concentrated aqueous solution of NaCl with the electrolyte stirred, **(e)** cold, aqueous solution of $NaClO_3$.

21.28 Write chemical equations for the reactions that are used to identify the halide ions in aqueous solution.

21.29 How many grams of $Cl_2(g)$ is produced in one hour by the electrolysis of an aqueous solution of NaCl if current of 1000 A is used?

21.30 How many grams of $Cl_2(g)$ is produced in the same time that it takes to prepare 1.000 kg of NaOH by the electrolysis of an aqueous solution of NaCl?

Unclassified Problems

21.31 Use the following data to calculate the lattice energy of NaH(s): The enthalpy of formation of NaH(s) is -57.3 kJ/mol. The enthalpy of sublimation of Na(s) is $+108$ kJ/mol, and the first ionization energy of Na(g) is $+496$ kJ/mol. The bond energy of $H_2(g)$ is $+435$ kJ/mol, and the first electron affinity of H(g) is -73 kJ/mol. Compare the value that you get with the lattice energy of NaCl(s), which is -788 kJ.

21.32 Use the bond energies found in Table 5.2 to calculate the standard enthalpy of formation of **(a)** HF(g), **(b)** $H_2O(g)$, and **(c)** $NH_3(g)$. **(d)** Compare your values with those found in Table 5.1.

*__21.33__ A quantity of $CaH_2(s)$ was added to water and $H_2(g)$ and a solution of $Ca(OH)_2(aq)$ were obtained. If the volume of the solution was 500. mL and the pH of the solution was 11.700, what volume of H_2 gas (measured at STP) was obtained?

21.34 **(a)** How many faradays of electricity is required to produce 1.000 kg of $Cl_2(g)$ by the electrolysis of molten NaCl? **(b)** How many liters of Cl_2 gas (measured at STP) is produced at the same time?

21.35 Perbromates have only recently been prepared. For the half-reaction:

$$2\,BrO_4^-(aq) + 16\,H^+(aq) + 14e^- \longrightarrow Br_2(l) + 8\,H_2O$$

$\mathscr{E}°$ is reported to be $+1.59$ V. **(a)** For $H_2O(l)$, $\Delta G_f°$ is -237.19 kJ/mol, and for $H^+(aq)$, $\Delta G_f°$ is 0.00. Calculate $\Delta G_f°$ for $BrO_4^-(aq)$. **(b)** Calculate $\mathscr{E}°$ for the half-reaction:

$$BrO_4^-(aq) + 2\,H^+(aq) + 2e^- \longrightarrow BrO_3^-(aq) + H_2O$$

The value of $\Delta G_f°$ for $BrO_3^-(aq)$ is $+21.71$ kJ/mol. **(c)** What oxidizing agent in the table in the appendix *should* be capable of oxidizing $BrO_3^-(aq)$ to $BrO_4^-(aq)$?

21.36 Write balanced chemical equations for the following disproportionations: **(a)** $ClO_3^-(aq)$ by the electrolysis of a cold, acidic solution (to ClO_4^- and Cl^-), **(b)** $Cl_2(g)$ by dissolution in an alkaline solution (to OCl^- and Cl^-), **(c)** $ClO^-(aq)$ by reacting in alkaline solution (to ClO_3^- and Cl^-).

THE NONMETALS, PART II: THE GROUP VI A ELEMENTS

C H A P T E R

22

Group VI A includes oxygen, sulfur, selenium, tellurium, and polonium. Oxygen is the most important and abundant of the group. Since the chemistry of oxygen is different from that of the other members, oxygen is considered separately before the others. Polonium is the product of the radioactive disintegration of radium. The most abundant isotope of polonium, ^{210}Po, has a half-life of only 138.7 days.

22.1 Properties of the Group VI A Elements

The electronic configurations of the group VI A elements are listed in Table 22.1. Each element is two electrons short of a noble-gas structure. Hence, these elements attain a noble-gas electronic configuration in the formation of ionic compounds by accepting two electrons per atom:

$$2\,Na^+ \qquad :\overset{..}{\underset{..}{S}}:^{2-}$$

The elements can also acquire noble-gas configurations through covalent-bond formation:

$$H:\overset{..}{Se}:\\ \overset{..}{H}$$

Certain properties of the group VI A elements are summarized in Table 22.2. Each member of the group is a less active nonmetal than the halogen of its period. The electronegatives of the elements decrease, in the expected manner, with increasing atomic number. Oxygen is the second most electronegative element

Table 22.2 Electronic configurations of the group VI A elements

Elements	Z	1s	2s	2p	3s	3p	3d	4s	4p	4d	4f	5s	5p	5d	6s	6p
O	8	2	2	4												
S	16	2	2	6	2	4										
Se	34	2	2	6	2	6	10	2	4							
Te	52	2	2	6	2	6	10	2	6	10		2	4			
Po	84	2	2	6	2	6	10	2	6	10	14	2	6	10	2	4

Table 22.2 Some properties of the group VI A elements

Property	Oxygen	Sulfur	Selenium	Tellurium
color	colorless	yellow	red to black	silver-white
molecular formula	O_2	S_8 rings	Se_8 rings Se_n chains	Te_n chains
melting point (°C)	−218.4	119	217	452
boiling point (°C)	−182.9	444.6	688	1390
atomic radius (pm)	74	104	117	137
ionic radius (2− ion) (pm)	140	184	198	221
first ionization energy (kJ/mol)	1312	1004	946	870
electronegativity	3.4	2.6	2.6	2.1
bond energy (single bonds) (kJ/mol)	138	213	184	138
$\mathscr{E}°$ for reduction of element to H_2X in acid solution (V)	+1.23	+0.14	−0.40	−0.72

in the periodic table (fluorine is first); sulfur is about as electronegative as iodine. Thus, the oxides of most metals are ionic, whereas the sulfides, selenides, and tellurides of only the most active metals (such as the I A and II A metals) are truly ionic compounds.

The group VI A elements are predominantly nonmetallic in chemical behavior; however, metallic characteristics appear in the heavier members of the group. The trend in increasing metallic character parallels, as expected, increasing atomic number, increasing atomic radius, and decreasing ionization potential. Polonium is the most metallic member of the group; it appears to be capable of forming cations that exist in aqueous solution, and the 2− state of polonium (in H_2Po, for example) is unstable. Whereas tellurium is essentially nonmetallic in character, unstable salts of tellurium with anions of strong acids have been reported. The ordinary form of elemental tellurium is metallic. Selenium exists in both metallic and nonmetallic crystalline modifications.

Sulfur, selenium, and tellurium exist in positive oxidation states in compounds in which they are combined with more electronegative elements (such as oxygen and the halogens). Oxygen is considered to have a positive oxidation number only in the few compounds that it forms with fluorine. For sulfur, selenium, and tellurium, the oxidation states of 4+ and 6+ are particularly important.

The electrode potentials listed in Table 22.2 give an idea of the strength of the group VI A elements as oxidizing agents. Oxygen is a strong oxidizing agent, but there is a striking decrease in this property from oxygen to tellurium. In fact, H_2Te and H_2Se are better *reducing* agents than hydrogen. Compare the $\mathscr{E}°$ values listed in Table 22.2 with those given for the halogens in Table 21.2.

22.2 Occurrence and Industrial Production of Oxygen

Oxygen is the most abundant element on earth (see Table 1.2). Free oxygen makes up about 21.0% by volume or 23.2% by mass of the atmosphere. Most minerals

Table 22.3	Composition of dry air		
Substance	Percent by Volume	Substance	Percent by Volume
N_2	78.00	CH_4	2×10^{-4}
O_2	20.95	Kr	1×10^{-4}
Ar	0.93	N_2O	5×10^{-5}
CO_2	0.03	H_2	5×10^{-5}
Ne	0.0018	Xe	8×10^{-6}
He	0.0005	O_3	1×10^{-6}

contain combined oxygen. Silica, SiO_2, is a common ingredient of many minerals and the chief constituent of sand. Silicon is second to oxygen in the order of natural abundance because of the widespread occurrence of silica. Other oxygen-containing minerals are oxides, sulfates, and carbonates. Oxygen is a constituent of the compounds that make up plant and animal matter. The human body is more than 60% oxygen.

Three isotopes of oxygen occur in nature: ^{16}O (99.759%), ^{18}O (0.204%), and ^{17}O (0.037%). The isotopes ^{14}O, ^{15}O, ^{19}O, and ^{20}O are artificial and unstable.

The principal commercial source of oxygen is the atmosphere. Air is a mixture. The composition of air varies with altitude and to a lesser extent with location. The analysis of air is made after water and solid particles (such as dust and spores) have been removed. Some of the components of air are listed in Table 22.3. The percentages given (by volume) are for clean, dry air at sea level.

Over 99% of the oxygen produced industrially is obtained from the liquefaction and fractional distillation of air. In the process, filtered, dry air from which the CO_2 has been removed is liquefied by compression and cooling. When the air is allowed to warm, nitrogen (boiling point, $-196°C$) boils away from the oxygen (boiling point, $-183°C$). The noble gases are obtained from the nitrogen and oxygen fractions by repeated distillations and other separation techniques.

A small amount of very pure but relatively expensive oxygen is produced commercially by the electrolysis of water:

$$2\,H_2O \xrightarrow{\text{electrolysis}} 2\,H_2(g) + O_2(g)$$

22.3 Laboratory Preparation of Oxygen

Oxygen is usually prepared in the laboratory by the thermal decomposition of certain oxygen-containing compounds. The following are used:

1. Oxides of metals of low reactivity. The oxides of silver (Ag_2O), mercury (HgO), and gold (Au_2O_3) decompose on heating to give oxygen gas and the free metal:

$$2\,HgO(s) \longrightarrow 2\,Hg(l) + O_2(g)$$

2. Peroxides. Oxygen and the oxide ion are produced when the peroxide ion, O_2^{2-}, is heated:

$$2\left[:\overset{..}{O}:\overset{..}{O}:\right]^{2-} \longrightarrow 2\left[:\overset{..}{O}:\right]^{2-} + O_2$$

Thus,

$$2\,Na_2O_2(s) \longrightarrow 2\,Na_2O(s) + O_2(g)$$
$$2\,BaO_2(s) \longrightarrow 2\,BaO(s) + O_2(g)$$

Oxygen can be obtained from the reaction of sodium peroxide and water at room temperature. The other product is an aqueous solution of sodium hydroxide:

$$2\,O_2^{2-}(aq) + 2\,H_2O \longrightarrow 4\,OH^-(aq) + O_2(g)$$

3. Nitrates and chlorates. Certain other compounds release all or part of their oxygen upon heating. Nitrates of the I A metals form nitrites:

$$2\,NaNO_3(l) \longrightarrow 2\,NaNO_2(l) + O_2(g)$$

Potassium chlorate loses all its oxygen; a catalyst (MnO_2) is generally used to lower the temperature required for this decomposition:

$$2\,KClO_3(s) \longrightarrow 2\,KCl(s) + 3\,O_2(g)$$

22.4 Reactions of Oxygen

The reactions of oxygen are often more sluggish than would be predicted from the fact that oxygen has a high electronegativity (3.4), second in this property only to fluorine (4.0). The reason for this slowness is that the bond energy of oxygen is high (494 kJ/mol); therefore, reactions that require the oxygen-to-oxygen bond to be broken occur only at high temperatures. Many of these reactions are relatively highly exothermic and produce sufficient heat to sustain themselves after having once been initiated by external heating. Whether self-sustaining or not, most oxygen reactions occur at temperatures considerably higher than room temperature.

Oxygen forms four different anions: the superoxide, peroxide, oxide, and ozonide ions. Molecular orbital diagrams for oxygen, the superoxide ion, and the peroxide ion are given in Figure 22.1. The **superoxide ion,** O_2^-, can be considered to arise from the addition of one electron to a π^*2p orbital of the O_2 molecule, which reduces the number of unpaired electrons to 1 and the bond order to $1\frac{1}{2}$. The **peroxide ion,** O_2^{2-}, contains two more electrons (in the π^*2p orbitals) than the O_2 molecule; hence, the bond order is reduced to 1, and the ion is diamagnetic. The **oxide ion,** O^{2-}, is isoelectronic with neon and is diamagnetic. The **ozonide ion,** O_3^-, is paramagnetic with one unpaired electron and is produced by reactions of ozone $(O_3$, see Section 22.6), with hydroxides of K, Rb, and Cs.

All metals except the less-reactive metals (for example, Ag and Au) react with oxygen. Oxides of all metals are known but some must be made indirectly. The most reactive metals of group I A (and those with largest atomic radii)—Cs, Rb, and K—react with oxygen at atmospheric pressure to produce superoxides. For example,

$$Cs(s) + O_2(g) \longrightarrow CsO_2(s)$$

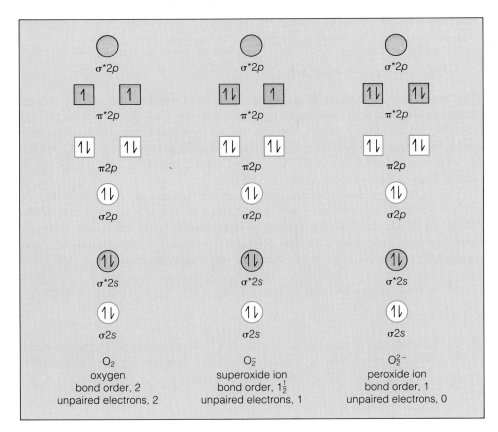

Figure 22.1 Molecular orbital energy-level diagrams for oxygen, the superoxide ion, and the peroxide ion

Sodium peroxide is produced by the reaction of sodium with oxygen:

$$2\,Na(s) + O_2(g) \longrightarrow Na_2O_2(s)$$

Lithium metal forms an ordinary oxide with O_2 rather than a peroxide or a superoxide because the small Li^+ ion cannot form a stable lattice with the larger O_2^{2-} or O_2^- ions:

$$4\,Li(s) + O_2(g) \longrightarrow 2\,Li_2O(s)$$

Generally, oxides form at much higher temperatures than either peroxides or superoxides. The ordinary oxides of Na, K, Rb, and Cs can be obtained by heating oxygen with an excess of the metal.

With the exception of barium (which reacts with oxygen to yield barium peroxide), the remaining metals generally produce normal oxides in their reactions with oxygen:

$$2\,Mg(s) + O_2(g) \longrightarrow 2\,MgO(s)$$

$$4\,Al(s) + 3\,O_2(g) \longrightarrow 2\,Al_2O_3(s)$$

Analogous reactions can be written for the preparation of CaO, CuO, ZnO, PbO, and other oxides. The reaction of mercury and oxygen is reversible:

$$2\,Hg(l) + O_2(g) \rightleftharpoons 2\,HgO(s)$$

For metals that have more than one electrovalence number, the oxide produced generally depends upon the quantity of oxygen, the quantity of the metal, and the reaction conditions. Thus, the reaction of iron and oxygen can be made to yield FeO (low pressure of oxygen, temperature above $600°C$), Fe_3O_4 (finely divided iron, heated in air at $500°C$), or Fe_2O_3 (iron heated in air at temperatures above $500°C$). Hydrated Fe_2O_3 is iron rust.

Except for the noble gases and the group VII A elements, all nonmetals react with oxygen. Oxides of the halogens and those of the heavier members of the noble-gas family have been prepared by indirect means. The reaction of oxygen with hydrogen produces water. The product of the reaction of carbon with oxygen depends upon the proportion of carbon to oxygen employed:

$$2\,C(s) + O_2(g) \longrightarrow 2\,CO(g)$$
$$C(s) + O_2(g) \longrightarrow CO_2(g)$$

In like manner, the product of the reaction of phosphorus and oxygen depends upon whether phosphorus is reacted in a limited oxygen supply (P_4O_6) or in excess oxygen (P_4O_{10}). Sulfur reacts to produce SO_2:

$$S(s) + O_2(g) \longrightarrow SO_2(g)$$

The reaction of nitrogen with oxygen requires extremely high temperatures. The following reaction occurs in a high-energy electric arc:

$$N_2(g) + O_2(g) \longrightarrow 2\,NO(g)$$

Additional oxides of sulfur (for example, SO_3) and nitrogen (for example, NO_2 and N_2O_5) are prepared by means other than the direct combination of the elements. Lower oxides can be reacted with oxygen to produce higher oxides. For example,

$$2\,Cu_2O(s) + O_2(g) \longrightarrow 4\,CuO(s)$$
$$2\,CO(g) + O_2(g) \longrightarrow 2\,CO_2(g)$$

Most reactions of compounds with oxygen yield the same products that would be obtained if the individual elements that make up the compounds were reacted directly. Thus,

$$2\,H_2S(g) + 3\,O_2(g) \longrightarrow 2\,H_2O(g) + 2\,SO_2(g)$$
$$CS_2(l) + 3\,O_2(g) \longrightarrow CO_2(g) + 2\,SO_2(g)$$
$$2\,C_2H_2(g) + 5\,O_2(g) \longrightarrow 4\,CO_2(g) + 2\,H_2O(g)$$
$$C_2H_6O(l) + 3\,O_2(g) \longrightarrow 2\,CO_2(g) + 3\,H_2O(g)$$

The reaction of zinc sulfide with oxygen illustrates a metallurgical process known as roasting. Many sulfide ores are subjected to this procedure (see Section 25.5):

$$2\,ZnS(s) + 3\,O_2(g) \longrightarrow 2\,ZnO(s) + 2\,SO_2(g)$$

The products of the reaction of a hydrocarbon with oxygen depend upon the amount of oxygen supplied. Thus, when natural gas (methane, CH_4) is burned in air, $H_2O(g)$, $C(s)$, $CO(g)$, and $CO_2(g)$ are produced by the oxidation.

In addition to water, hydrogen and oxygen form a compound called hydrogen peroxide, H_2O_2, which is colorless liquid that boils at $150.2°C$ and freezes at $-0.41°C$. Hydrogen peroxide can be made by treating peroxides with acids:

$$BaO_2(s) + 2\,H^+(aq) + SO_4^{2-}(aq) \longrightarrow H_2O_2(aq) + BaSO_4(s)$$

In this preparation the barium sulfate, which is insoluble, can be removed by filtration.

The peroxide linkage ($-O-O-$) exists in covalent compounds and ions in addition to H_2O_2 and the O_2^{2-} ion. For example, the peroxydisulfate ion, written $S_2O_8^{2-}$ or $[O_3SOOSO_3]^{2-}$, contains this linkage (see Section 22.12). The $S_2O_8^{2-}$ ion is produced by the electrolysis of sulfuric acid under suitable conditions; the reaction of this ion with water serves as a commercial preparation of hydrogen peroxide:

$$S_2O_8^{2-}(aq) + 2\,H_2O \longrightarrow H_2O_2(aq) + 2\,HSO_4^-(aq)$$

Hydrogen peroxide is a weak, diprotic acid in water solution. One or two hydrogens can be neutralized by sodium hydroxide to produce either sodium hydroperoxide ($NaHO_2$) or sodium peroxide (Na_2O_2). In the laboratory, H_2O_2 is used as an oxidizing or reducing agent.

22.5 Industrial Uses of Oxygen

Most of the commercial uses of oxygen stem from its ability to support combustion and sustain life. In many applications, the use of oxygen or oxygen-enriched air in place of atmospheric air increases the intensity and speed of reaction and thereby lowers costs and improves yields. The principal uses of oxygen are:

1. Production of steel

2. Processing and fabrication of metals

3. Production of oxygen-containing compounds such as sodium peroxide and organic compounds

4. Oxidizer for rocket fuels

5. The oxyacetylene torch

6. Biological treatment of waste water

7. Life support systems in medicine, in air and space travel, and in submarines

22.6 Ozone

The existence of an element in more than one form in the same physical state is called **allotropy,** and the forms are called **allotropes.** A number of elements

The fuel used to propel this Delta space vehicle was oxidized by liquid oxygen. *NASA.*

exhibit allotropy, for example, carbon, sulfur, and phosphorus. Oxygen exists in a triatomic form, ozone, in addition to the common diatomic modification.

The ozone molecule is diamagnetic and has an angular structure. Both oxygen-to-oxygen bonds have the same length (128 pm), which is intermediate between the double-bond distance (110 pm) and the single-bond distance (148 pm). The molecule may be represented as a resonance hybrid:

Ozone is a pale blue gas with a characteristic odor; predictably, its density is $1\frac{1}{2}$ times that of O_2. The normal boiling point of ozone is $-112°C$, and the normal melting point is $-193°C$. It is slightly more soluble in water than is O_2.

Ozone is produced by passing a silent electric discharge through oxygen gas. The reaction proceeds through the dissociation of an O_2 molecule into oxygen atoms and the combination of an O atom with a second O_2 molecule:

$$\tfrac{1}{2}O_2(g) \longrightarrow O(g) \qquad \Delta H = +247 \text{ kJ}$$

$$O(g) + O_2(g) \longrightarrow O_3(g) \qquad \Delta H = -105 \text{ kJ}$$

The energy released in the second step, in which a new bond is formed, is not sufficient to compensate for the energy required by the first step, in which a bond is broken. Hence, the overall reaction for the preparation of ozone is endothermic:

$$\tfrac{3}{2}O_2(g) \longrightarrow O_3(g) \qquad \Delta H^\circ_f = +142 \text{ kJ}$$

Ozone is highly reactive; it is explosive at temperatures above 300°C or in the presence of substances that catalyze its decomposition. Ozone will react with many substances at temperatures that are not high enough to produce reaction with O_2. The higher reactivity of O_3 in comparison to O_2 is consistent with the higher energy content of O_3.

22.7 Air Pollution

Several oxides, found in air in variable amounts, are air pollutants. Modern technological civilization is introducing foreign substances into the atmosphere at an ever-increasing rate. The principal air pollutants in terms of quantities present are the following:

1. *Carbon monoxide* is produced by the incomplete combustion of fuels. The automobile's internal-combustion engine is the principal source of this pollutant. The mass of CO produced by this source is about equal to half the mass of gasoline consumed.

Carbon monoxide is toxic because it combines with the hemoglobin of the blood and prevents the hemoglobin from carrying oxygen to the body tissues (see Section 26.1). In other ways, however, CO is not very reactive. Reaction with O_2 of the air to form CO_2 does occur, but very slowly.

2. *Oxides of sulfur* (SO_2 and SO_3) result from the combustion of coal, metallurgical processes, and petroleum combustion and refining. The major source is the

combustion of coal (which contains from 0.5% to 3.0% S) in the generation of electricity. The roasting of sulfide ores (see Section 25.5) is also a significant source of SO_2 pollution:

$$2 \text{ PbS(s)} + 3 \text{ O}_2(\text{g}) \longrightarrow 2 \text{ PbO(s)} + 2 \text{ SO}_2(\text{g})$$

Sulfur dioxide from these sources is slowly oxidized to SO_3 by O_2 in the air. The SO_3 forms sulfuric acid with atmospheric water, and SO_2 forms sulfurous acid. These substances are, of course, extremely corrosive, and are the principal acids in acid rain.

The oxides of sulfur are in some ways the most serious air pollutants. They are toxic, cause respiratory ailments, and are a serious health threat. They damage plant life, corrode metals, and erode marble and limestone. Ancient monuments (such as the Parthenon in Athens) which have stood for centuries are crumbling because of the pollution of modern civilization.

3. *Oxides of nitrogen* (NO and NO_2) are produced from the N_2 and O_2 of the air at the high temperatures characteristic of some combustions and in lightning storms. Significant amounts of NO are formed in the combustions carried out in automobile engines and in electric generating plants. Nitrogen dioxide is formed in the air by the oxidation of NO.

Small amounts of NO and NO_2 ordinarily occur in air and form a minor part of the nitrogen cycle. Nitrogen dioxide is considerably more toxic than NO. The gases, however, usually occur at relatively low concentrations so that the *direct* effect of these pollutants is not serious. The significance of these oxides lies in the role that they play in the formation of other, more serious pollutants (see *Hydrocarbons*, which follows).

4. *Hydrocarbons* are compounds that contain carbon and hydrogen. They are found in petroleum, natural gas, and coal. The compounds are released into the atmosphere by evaporation, petroleum refining, and incomplete combustion of fuels. The unburned hydrocarbons in automobile exhaust constitute a major source of this type of contamination.

A few hydrocarbons are carcinogenic (cancer-producing). The principal danger associated with hydrocarbon pollution, however, lies in the pollutants that are produced from hydrocarbons in the air. Nitrogen dioxide decomposes in sunlight to give O atoms:

$$\text{NO}_2(\text{g}) \longrightarrow \text{NO(g)} + \text{O(g)}$$

These O atoms react with O_2 to produce ozone, O_3:

$$\text{O(g)} + \text{O}_2(\text{g}) \longrightarrow \text{O}_3(\text{g})$$

Ozone is highly reactive and reacts with some hydrocarbons to produce oxygen-containing organic compounds. Since the process is initiated by sunlight, the products are sometimes called **photochemical pollutants.**

These substances are toxic and very irritating to the eyes, skin, and respiratory tract. They cause extensive crop damage and the deterioration of materials. They constitute what is called photochemical smog.

5. *Small particles* suspended in air are another important contributor to air pollution. The particles may consist of liquids or solids and vary in diameter from about 0.01 μm to 100 μm (the micrometer, μm, previously called the micron,

Pediment of the Parthenon in Athens, Greece, showing deterioration from air pollution. *Wide World Photos*.

is 10^{-4} cm). A principal source is the smoke from the combustion of coal. Industrial processes (for example, the manufacture of cement) also introduce particulate matter into the air. Automobile exhaust contains suspended particles.

Particles reduce visibility and pose a threat to health. They cause lung damage and may be toxic. Carcinogenic substances may be contained in soot particles. Particles in exhaust from older automobiles contain lead, a toxic substance which comes from the lead compounds that were added to gasoline to improve engine performance.

22.8 Allotropic Modifications of S, Se, and Te

All members of this group exist in more than one allotropic modification. For a given element the difference may be in molecular complexity (O_2 and O_3 for oxygen, see Section 22.6), in crystalline form, or in both.

The most important solid modifications of sulfur belong to the rhombic and monoclinic crystal systems (see Figure 22.2). The crystals of both allotropes are built from S_8 molecules. These molecules are in the form of puckered, eight-membered rings of S atoms in which the S atoms are bonded to each other by single covalent bonds and the S—S—S bond angle is about $105°$ (see Figure 22.3). In chemical equations, therefore, elementary sulfur should be indicated by the formula S_8. The usual practice, however, is to designate sulfur by the symbol S. This practice leads to less complicated equations that are nevertheless stoichiometrically valid.

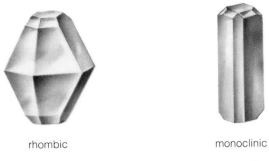

rhombic   monoclinic

Figure 22.2   Rhombic and monoclinic crystals of sulfur

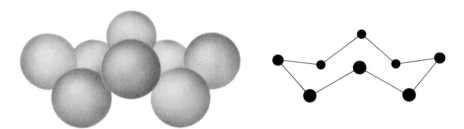

Figure 22.3   Structure of the S_8 molecule

Liquid sulfur undergoes a series of changes as its temperature is increased. At the melting point liquid sulfur is a light yellow, mobile liquid consisting principally of S_8 molecules. Upon continued heating the sulfur changes into a red-brown, highly viscous material. The viscosity reaches a maximum between 160°C and 200°C; upon further heating (up to the boiling point at 444.6°C), the viscosity of the liquid decreases. It is believed that the viscosity effect is caused by the dissociation of the S_8 rings and the formation of long chains of S atoms; at temperatures approaching the boiling point, it appears that these chains break into fragments. If sulfur is heated to approximately 200°C and then poured into cold water, a red-brown rubbery mass called plastic sulfur is obtained. It is assumed that plastic sulfur consists mainly of long chains of sulfur atoms; X-ray analysis of plastic sulfur has shown that it has the molecular structure characteristic of fibers. At room temperature, plastic sulfur, which is a supercooled liquid, slowly crystallizes and the S_8 rings re-form. Sulfur vapor has been shown to consist of S_8, S_6, S_4, and S_2 molecules; S_2 is paramagnetic, like O_2.

The stable modification of selenium at room temperature is a gray, metallic, hexagonal form, the crystals of which are constructed of zigzag chains of selenium atoms. It is this form that is used in photoelectric cells; the normally low electrical conductivity of hexagonal selenium is increased about 1000 times by exposure of the element to light. There are two monoclinic forms of selenium, both red; one of these has been shown to be made up of Se_8 rings that are similar to S_8 rings. In addition, amorphous forms of selenium have been described.

The common form of tellurium consists of silver-white, metallic hexagonal crystals built from zigzag chains of tellurium atoms. A black, amorphous form of tellurium exists.

The two modifications of polonium that have been reported belong to the cubic and rhombohedral systems.

22.9 Occurrence and Industrial Preparation of S, Se, and Te

The principal forms in which sulfur, selenium, and tellurium occur in nature are listed in Table 22.4. Sulfur is obtained from large underground beds of the free element by the **Frasch process** (see Figure 22.4). The sulfur is melted under-

Table 22.4 Occurrence of sulfur, selenium, and tellurium

Element	Percent of Earth's Crust	Occurrence
sulfur	0.05	native FeS_2 (pyrite), PbS (galena), HgS (cinnabar), ZnS (sphalerite), Cu_2S (chalcocite), $CuFeS_2$ (chalcopyrite) $CaSO_4 \cdot 2H_2O$ (gypsum), $BaSO_4$ (barite), $MgSO_4 \cdot 7H_2O$ (epsomite)
selenium	9×10^{-6}	small amounts of Se in some S deposits rare minerals: Cu_2Se, PbSe, Ag_2Se low concentrations in sulfide ores of Cu, Fe, Pb, Ni
tellurium	2×10^{-7}	small amounts of Te in some S deposits rare minerals: $AuTe_2$, PbTe, Ag_2Te, Au_2Te, Cu_2Te low concentrations in sulfide ores of Cu, Fe

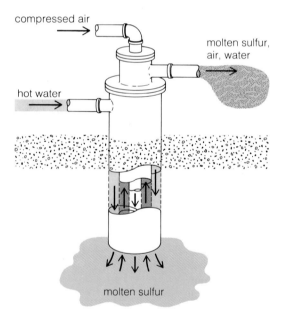

compressed air

molten sulfur, air, water

hot water

molten sulfur

Figure 22.4 The Frasch process

Sulfur, in liquid form from the Frasch process, is sprayed into pools to solidify. *Freeport-McMoRan Inc.*

ground by water that is heated to approximately 170°C under pressure and forced down to the deposits. A froth of sulfur, air, and water is forced to the surface by hot, compressed air. The sulfur thus obtained is about 99.5% pure.

The principal commercial source of both selenium and tellurium is the anode sludge obtained from the electrolytic refining of copper (see Section 25.7).

.10 Hydrogen Compounds of S, Se, and Te

Some reactions of sulfur, selenium, and tellurium are summarized in Table 22.5. The hydrogen compounds of sulfur, selenium, and tellurium can be prepared by the direct combination of the elements at elevated temperatures. Direct combination, however, is not a satisfactory source of the compounds. In addition to the inconvenience of the method, H_2S, H_2Se, and H_2Te are unstable at high temperatures, and the products are contaminated by starting materials.

The hydrogen compounds are readily obtained by the action of dilute acid on sulfides, selenides, and tellurides. For example,

$$FeS(s) + 2H^+(aq) \longrightarrow Fe^{2+}(aq) + H_2S(g)$$

Rhomic crystals of sulfur. *Fundamental Photographs, New York.*

Table 22.5 Some reactions of sulfur, selenium, and tellurium

Reaction of Sulfur	Remarks
$nS + mM \longrightarrow M_mS_n$	Se, Te react similarly with many metals (not noble metals)
$nS + S^{2-} \longrightarrow S_{n+1}^{2-}$	for S and Te, $n = 1$ to 5; for Se, $n = 1$ to 4
$S + H_2 \longrightarrow H_2S$	$S > Se > Te$; elevated temperatures; compounds are better prepared by actions of dilute HCl on sulfides, selenides, or tellurides
$S + O_2 \longrightarrow SO_2$	$S > Se > Te$; dioxides of Se and Te are easier to prepare with a mixture of $O_2 + NO_2$
$S + 3F_2 \longrightarrow SF_6$	S, Se, Te with excess F_2
$S + 2F_2 \longrightarrow SF_4$	S, Se; TeF_4 is made indirectly (TeF_6 + Te)
$2S + X_2 \longrightarrow S_2X_2$	S, Se; $X_2 = Cl_2$ or Br_2
$S + 2X_2 \longrightarrow SX_4$	S, Se, Te with excess Cl_2; Se, Te with excess Br_2; Te with excess I_2
$S_2Cl_2 + Cl_2 \longrightarrow 2SCl_2$	SCl_2 only, SBr_2 unknown; $SeCl_2$, $SeBr_2$ (only in vapor state); $TeCl_2$, $TeBr_2$ are made by thermal decomposition of higher halides
$S + 4HNO_3 \longrightarrow SO_2 + 4NO_2 + 2H_2O$	hot, concentrated nitric acid; S yields mixtures of SO_2 and SO_4^{2-}; Se yields H_2SeO_3 ($SeO_2 \cdot H_2O$); Te yields $2TeO_2 \cdot HNO_3$

The reaction of thioacetamide with water is a convenient laboratory source of H_2S:

$$\underset{\text{thioacetamide}}{\text{H}-\overset{\overset{\text{H}}{|}}{\underset{\underset{\text{H}}{|}}{\text{C}}}-\overset{\overset{\text{S}}{\|}}{\underset{\underset{\text{H}}{|}}{\underset{\text{N}}{\text{C}}}-\text{H}}\text{(aq)} + \text{H}_2\text{O} \longrightarrow \underset{\text{acetamide}}{\text{H}-\overset{\overset{\text{H}}{|}}{\underset{\underset{\text{H}}{|}}{\text{C}}}-\overset{\overset{\text{O}}{\|}}{\underset{\underset{\text{H}}{|}}{\underset{\text{N}}{\text{C}}}-\text{H}}\text{(aq)} + \text{H}_2\text{S(g)}$$

Hydrogen sulfide, hydrogen selenide, and hydrogen telluride are colorless, unpleasant-smelling, highly poisonous gases. They are composed of angular molecules, similar to the water molecule.

Hydrogen sulfide reacts with oxygen to yield water and either SO_2 or free S depending upon the amount of oxygen employed. The combustion of H_2Se or H_2Te in oxygen produces water and Se or Te.

The compounds H_2S, H_2Se, and H_2Te are all moderately soluble in water and are weak acids in aqueous solution. The trend in acid strength parallels that of the hydrogen halides—the elements of highest atomic number form the strongest acids. Thus, H_2Te is the strongest acid, and H_2S is the weakest acid of the group. The acids are diprotic and ionize in two steps:

$$H_2S(aq) \rightleftharpoons H^+(aq) + HS^-(aq)$$
$$HS^-(aq) \rightleftharpoons H^+(aq) + S^{2-}(aq)$$

The aqueous hydrogen sulfide system is discussed in Section 17.7.

The sulfides of the group I A and group II A metals are water soluble. The sulfides of the remaining metals are either insoluble or decompose in the presence of water to form insoluble hydroxides:

$$Al_2S_3(s) + 6 H_2O \longrightarrow 2 Al(OH)_3(s) + 3 H_2S(g)$$

Precipitation of the insoluble sulfides, under varying conditions, is extensively used in analytical procedures for the separation and identification of cations in solution (see Section 18.3). An analytical test for the sulfide ion consists of generating H_2S gas by adding acid to the sulfide and then identifying the H_2S by the insoluble, black PbS that forms on a filter paper wet with a solution of a soluble Pb^{2+} salt that is held in the gas:

$$Pb^{2+}(aq) + H_2S(g) \longrightarrow PbS(s) + 2 H^+(aq)$$

Sulfur dissolves in solutions of soluble sulfides and forms a mixture of polysulfide anions:

$$S^{2-}(aq) + nS(s) \longrightarrow S_{n+1}^{2-}(aq)$$

Polyselenide and polytelluride ions can be prepared by analogous reactions. For sulfur, ions varying in complexity from S_2^{2-} to S_6^{2-} have been prepared; Se_5^{2-} and Te_6^{2-} are the highest polyselenides and polytellurides known. The atoms of a polysulfide ion are joined into chains by single covalent bonds:

$$\left[\ddot{:S} \quad \ddot{S}. \atop .\ddot{S}. \quad .\ddot{S}: \right]^{2-}$$

The structure of the disulfide ion, S_2^{2-}, is similar to that of the peroxide ion (see Section 22.4). The mineral pyrite, FeS_2, is iron(II) disulfide.

At room temperature, polysulfides decompose in acid solution to yield mainly H_2S and free S; however, careful treatment of a polysulfide solution with concentrated HCl at $-15°C$ yields H_2S_2, H_2S_3, and small quantities of higher homologs. The hydrogen polysulfides are unstable, yellow oils.

22.11 The 4+ Oxidation State of S, Se, and Te

The important compounds in which sulfur appears in a 4+ oxidation state are sulfur dioxide (SO_2), sulfurous acid (H_2SO_3), and the salts of sulfurous acid— the sulfites. Both selenium and tellurium form compounds analogous to those of sulfur.

Sulfur dioxide is commercially obtained by burning sulfur:

$$S(s) + O_2(g) \longrightarrow SO_2(g)$$

or by roasting sulfide ores (such as ZnS, PbS, Cu_2S, and FeS_2) in air (see Section 25.5):

$$2\,ZnS(s) + 3\,O_2(g) \longrightarrow 2\,ZnO(s) + 2\,SO_2(g)$$

Sulfur dioxide is a colorless gas. It has a sharp, irritating odor and is poisonous. The molecules of SO_2 are angular, and the structure of the compound may be represented as a resonance hybrid:

The S—O bonds have additional double-bond character from $p\pi$-$d\pi$ bonding.

The polar nature of the SO_2 molecule is reflected in the ease with which sulfur dioxide may be liquefied. Sulfur dioxide liquefies at $-10°C$ (the normal boiling point) under a pressure of 1 atm, and at 20°C a pressure of about 3 atm will liquefy the gas. It is this property of SO_2 that makes the compound useful as a refrigerant.

Sulfur dioxide is moderately soluble in water, producing solutions of sulfurous acid, H_2SO_3. The acid is not very stable, and pure H_2SO_3 cannot be isolated. The extent of the reaction between dissolved SO_2 molecules and water is not known. Probably both H_2SO_3 and SO_2 molecules exist in the solution in equilibrium:

$$SO_2(aq) + H_2O \rightleftharpoons H_2SO_3(aq)$$

Sulfurous acid is a weak, diprotic acid. The first dissociation is

$$H_2SO_3(aq) \rightleftharpoons H^+(aq) + HSO_3^-(aq)$$

which is sometimes written as

$$SO_2(aq) + H_2O \rightleftharpoons H^+(aq) + HSO_3^-(aq)$$

The second dissociation is

$$HSO_3^-(aq) \rightleftharpoons H^+(aq) + SO_3^{2-}(aq)$$

Sulfurous acid, therefore, forms two series of salts: normal salts (for example, Na_2SO_3, sodium sulfite) and acid salts (for example, $NaHSO_3$, sodium bisulfite or sodium hydrogen sulfite).

Sulfites are often prepared by bubbling SO_2 gas through a solution of a hydroxide:

$$2\,OH^- + SO_2(g) \longrightarrow SO_3^{2-}(aq) + H_2O$$

If the addition is continued, acid sulfites are produced:

$$H_2O + SO_3^{2-}(aq) + SO_2(g) \longrightarrow 2\,HSO_3^-(aq)$$

The salts of sulfurous acid can be isolated from solution.

Since sulfurous acid is unstable, the addition of an acid to a sulfite or to an acid sulfite liberates SO_2 gas, which is a convenient way to prepare the gas in the laboratory:

$$SO_3^{2-}(aq) + 2\,H^+(aq) \longrightarrow SO_2(g) + H_2O$$

Sulfur dioxide, sulfurous acid, and sulfites can function as mild oxidizing agents, but reactions in which these compounds react as reducing agents (and are oxidized to the sulfate ion, SO_4^{2-}) are more numerous and more important. Many substances (such as potassium permanganate, potassium dichromate, chlorine, and bromine) oxidize sulfite to sulfate. In fact, sulfites are usually contaminated by traces of sulfates because of oxidation by the oxygen of the air:

$$2\,SO_3^{2-} + O_2(g) \longrightarrow 2\,SO_4^{2-}$$

Sulfites may be identified by the production of SO_2 gas upon acidification and by oxidation to the sulfate ion,

$$6\,H^+(aq) + 5\,SO_3^{2-}(aq) + 2\,MnO_4^-(aq) \longrightarrow$$
$$5\,SO_4^{2-}(aq) + 2\,Mn^{2+}(aq) + 3\,H_2O$$

followed by the precipitation of the sulfate as the insoluble barium salt:

$$Ba^{2+}(aq) + SO_4^{2-}(aq) \longrightarrow BaSO_4(s)$$

The dioxides of selenium and tellurium may be prepared by direct combination of the elements with oxygen; however, SeO_2 and TeO_2 are usually made by heating the product obtained from the oxidation of selenium or tellurium by concentrated nitric acid (see Table 22.5). Both SeO_2 and TeO_2 are white solids.

Selenous acid, H_2SeO_3, is formed when the very soluble SeO_2 is dissolved in water; it is a weak, diprotic acid and may be obtained in pure form by the evaporation of a solution of SeO_2. Tellurium dioxide is only slightly soluble in water, and pure H_2TeO_3 has never been prepared. Consequently, only very dilute solutions of tellurous acid have been studied.

Tellurium dioxide and selenium dioxide will dissolve in aqueous solutions of hydroxides to produce tellurites and selenites. If an excess of the dioxide is employed, the corresponding acid salt is obtained.

The selenium and tellurium compounds of the 4+ oxidation state are better oxidizing agents and poorer reducing agents than the corresponding sulfur compounds. Selenium dioxide, SeO_2, is a good oxidizing agent and is employed in certain organic syntheses.

.12 The 6+ Oxidation State of S, Se, and Te

Sulfur trioxide is produced when sulfur dioxide reacts with atmospheric oxygen. Since the reaction is very slow at ordinary temperatures, the commercial preparation is conducted at elevated temperatures (400 to 700°C) and in the presence of a catalyst (such as divanadium pentoxide or spongy platinum):

$$2\,SO_2(g) + O_2(g) \longrightarrow 2\,SO_3(g)$$

Sulfur trioxide is a volatile material (boiling point, 44.8°C). In the gas phase it consists of single molecules that are triangular planar in form with O—S—O bond angles of 120°. The electronic structure of the molecule may be represented as a resonance hybrid:

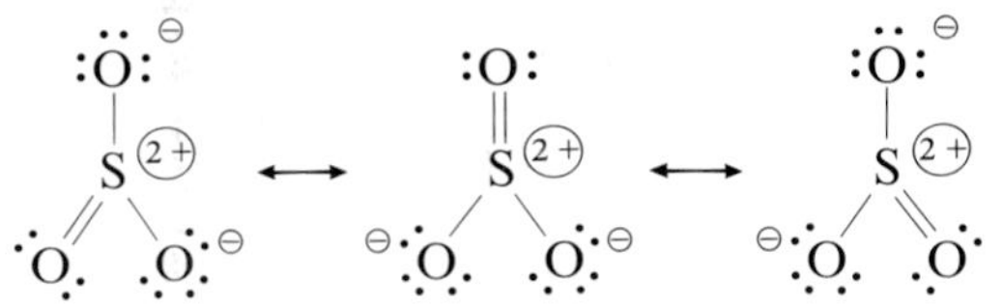

Additional double bonding, in excess of that represented by the resonance forms, arises from $p\pi$-$d\pi$ bonding. The compound exists in at least three solid modifications that are formed by the condensation of SO_3 units into larger molecules called polymers.

Sulfur trioxide is an extremely reactive substance and a strong oxidizing agent. It is the anhydride of sulfuric acid, H_2SO_4, and reacts vigorously with water to produce the acid and with metallic oxides to produce sulfates (see Section 13.5).

Sulfuric acid, an important industrial chemical, is made by the contact process in which SO_2 is catalytically oxidized to SO_3 in the manner previously described. The SO_3 vapor is bubbled through H_2SO_4 and pyrosulfuric acid ($H_2S_2O_7$) is formed:

$$SO_3(g) + H_2SO_4(l) \longrightarrow H_2S_2O_7(l)$$

Water is then added to the pyrosulfuric acid to make sulfuric acid of the desired concentration:

$$H_2S_2O_7(l) + H_2O \longrightarrow 2\,H_2SO_4(l)$$

This procedure, in which pyrosulfuric acid is formed, is easier to control than the direct reaction of SO_3 with water.

A sulfuric acid plant. *Texasgulf, Inc.*

Sulfuric acid is a colorless, oily liquid that freezes at 10.4°C and begins to boil at approximately 290°C with decomposition into water and sulfur trioxide. The electronic structure of sulfuric acid may be represented as

$$\text{H}-\overset{\displaystyle :\!\overset{\cdot\cdot}{\text{O}}:^{\ominus}}{\underset{\displaystyle :\!\overset{\cdot\cdot}{\text{O}}:_{\ominus}}{\overset{\cdot\cdot}{\text{O}}\!-\!\overset{(2+)}{\text{S}}\!-\!\overset{\cdot\cdot}{\text{O}}}}-\text{H}$$

However, the S—O bonds have a considerable degree of double-bond character from $p\pi$-$d\pi$ bonding, and the electronic formula

$$\text{H}-\overset{\displaystyle :\text{O}:}{\underset{\displaystyle :\text{O}:}{\overset{\cdot\cdot}{\text{O}}\!=\!\text{S}\!=\!\overset{\cdot\cdot}{\text{O}}}}-\text{H}$$

is sometimes used. The H_2SO_4 molecule, as well as the SO_4^{2-} ion, is tetrahedral.

When concentrated sulfuric acid is added to water, a large amount of heat is evolved. Sulfuric acid has a strong affinity for water and forms a series of hydrates (such as $H_2SO_4 \cdot H_2O$, $H_2SO_4 \cdot 2H_2O$, and $H_2SO_4 \cdot 4H_2O$). Sulfuric acid, therefore, is used as a drying agent. Gases that do not react with H_2SO_4 may be dried by being bubbled through the acid. The dehydrating power of concentrated sulfuric acid is also seen in the charring action of the acid on carbohydrates:

$$C_{12}H_{22}O_{11}(s) \xrightarrow{H_2SO_4} 12\,C(s) + 11\,H_2O(g)$$
$$\textit{sucrose}$$

Table 22.6 Standard electrode potentials of sulfuric, selenic, and telluric acids	
Reaction	Standard Electrode Potential
$2e^- + 4H^+ + SO_4^{2-} \rightleftharpoons H_2SO_3 + H_2O$	$\mathscr{E}° = +0.17$ V
$2e^- + 4H^+ + SeO_4^{2-} \rightleftharpoons H_2SeO_3 + H_2O$	$\mathscr{E}° = +1.15$ V
$2e^- + 2H^+ + H_6TeO_6 \rightleftharpoons TeO_2 + 4H_2O$	$\mathscr{E}° = +1.02$ V

In aqueous solution, sulfuric acid ionizes in two steps:

$$H_2SO_4 \longrightarrow H^+(aq) + HSO_4^-(aq)$$
$$HSO_4^-(aq) \rightleftharpoons H^+(aq) + SO_4^{2-}(aq)$$

Sulfuric acid is a strong electrolyte as far as the first dissociation is concerned. The second dissociation, however, is not complete. The acid forms two series of salts: normal salts (such as sodium sulfate, Na_2SO_4) and acid salts (such as sodium bisulfate, $NaHSO_4$). Most sulfates are soluble in water. However, barium sulfate ($BaSO_4$), strontium sulfate ($SrSO_4$), lead sulfate ($PbSO_4$), and mercury(I) sulfate (Hg_2SO_4) are practically insoluble; calcium sulfate ($CaSO_4$) and silver sulfate (Ag_2SO_4) are but slightly soluble. The formation of white, insoluble barium sulfate, the least soluble of the substances listed, is commonly used as a laboratory test for the sulfate ion.

Since sulfuric acid has a relatively high boiling point (or decomposition temperature), it is used to secure more volatile acids from their salts. This use is illustrated by the preparations of HF and HCl (see Section 21.10), as well as by the preparation of HNO_3 (see Section 23.7).

Sulfuric acid at unit concentration and 25°C is not a particularly good oxidizing agent (note the relatively low standard electrode potential in Table 22.6). Hot, concentrated sulfuric acid, however, is a moderately effective oxidizing agent. The oxidizing ability of hot, concentrated H_2SO_4 on bromides and iodides has already been noted (see Section 21.10). This reagent will also oxidize many nonmetals:

$$C(s) + 2H_2SO_4(l) \longrightarrow CO_2(g) + 2SO_2(g) + 2H_2O(g)$$

Most metals are oxidized by hot, concentrated sulfuric acid, including those metals of relatively low reactivity that are not oxidized by hydronium ion. For example, copper will not displace hydrogen from aqueous acids. Copper metal is, however, oxidized by hot, concentrated sulfuric acid, although hydrogen gas is not a product of the reaction:

$$Cu(s) + 2H_2SO_4(l) \longrightarrow CuSO_4(s) + SO_2(g) + 2H_2O(g)$$

Selenic acid, H_2SeO_4, is prepared by the oxidization of selenous acid, H_2SeO_3. Selenates may be prepared by the oxidation of the corresponding selenites. Selenium trioxide, the acid anhydride of selenic acid, is not very stable and decomposes to SeO_2 and O_2 on warming. Low yields of SeO_3 mixed with SeO_2 are produced when an electric discharge is passed through selenium vapor and oxygen. The trioxide may also be prepared by the reaction of potassium selenate, K_2SeO_4, and SO_3.

Selenic acid is very similar to sulfuric acid. In aqueous solution the first dissociation of H_2SeO_4 is strong and the second dissociation is weak. The acid forms normal and acid salts. Like the sulfate ion, the selenate ion is tetrahedral.

Telluric acid is prepared by the action of vigorous oxidizing agents on elemental tellurium. Unlike H_2SO_4 and H_2SeO_4, the formula of telluric acid is H_6TeO_6, which may be regarded as a hydrated form of the nonexistent H_2TeO_4. No compound of formula H_2TeO_4 has ever been prepared, although salts of an acid corresponding to this formula exist. Tellurium, like iodine, is a large atom and can accommodate six oxygen atoms, and telluric acid, like IO_6^{5-}, is octahedral. Telluric acid is not very similar to sulfuric acid, and H_6TeO_6 functions in aqueous solution as a very weak diprotic acid. If H_6TeO_6 is heated to approximately $350°C$, water is driven off and solid tellurium trioxide results. This compound is not very water soluble but reacts with alkalies to produce tellurates.

Both selenic and telluric acids are stronger oxidizing agents than sulfuric acid (see Table 22.6), although the reactions of H_2SeO_4 and H_6TeO_6 often proceed slowly.

There are other acids of sulfur in which S is in a 6+ oxidation state. Pyrosulfuric acid ($H_2S_2O_7$, also called disulfuric acid):

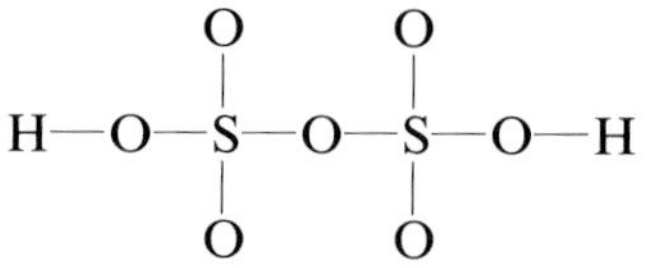

has been mentioned as the product of the reaction of SO_3 with H_2SO_4 in a 1:1 molar ratio. The pyrosulfate ion has been shown to have a structure in which two SO_4 tetrahedra are joined by an O atom common to both tetrahedra: $[O_3SOSO_3]^{2-}$. Pyrosulfuric acid is a stronger oxidizing agent and a stronger dehydrating agent than sulfuric acid.

A peroxy acid is an acid that contains a peroxide group (—O—O—) somewhere in the molecule. Two peroxy acids of sulfur exist: peroxymonosulfuric acid (H_2SO_5) and peroxydisulfuric acid ($H_2S_2O_8$):

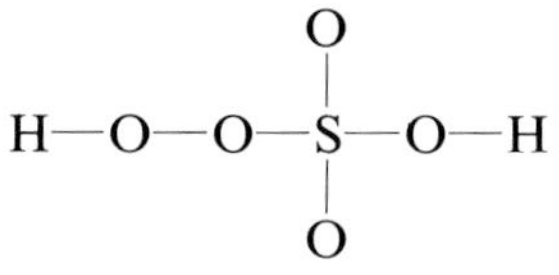

peroxymonosulfuric acid 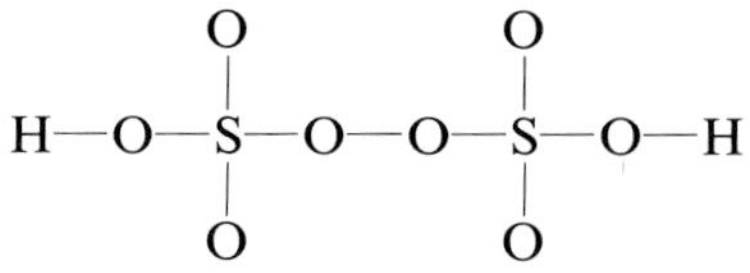   *peroxydisulfuric acid*

The structure of the peroxydisulfate ion consists of two complete SO_4 tetrahedra joined by an O—O bond.

Peroxydisulfuric acid is prepared by the electrolysis of moderately concentrated solutions of sulfuric acid (50 to 70%) at temperatures below room temperature (5 to 10°C). Potassium and ammonium salts of this acid are prepared by the electrolysis of the corresponding acid sulfates. The anode reaction in these electrolyses may be represented by the partial equation:

$$2\,HSO_4^- \longrightarrow S_2O_8^{2-} + 2\,H^+ + 2e^-$$

The reaction of peroxydisulfuric acid with water yields peroxymonosulfuric acid:

$$H_2S_2O_8 + H_2O \longrightarrow H_2SO_5 + H_2SO_4$$

Upon further hydrolysis, H_2SO_5 is decomposed into hydrogen peroxide and H_2SO_4:

$$H_2SO_5 + H_2O \longrightarrow H_2SO_4 + H_2O_2$$

Both peroxymonosulfuric acid and peroxydisulfuric acid are low melting solids. The first ionization of peroxydisulfuric acid is strong. The peroxydisulfate ion is one of the strongest oxidizing agents known:

$$2e^- + S_2O_8^{2-} \rightleftharpoons 2\,SO_4^{2-} \qquad \mathscr{E}^{\circ}_{red} = +2.01 \text{ V}$$

The oxidations, however, are slow and are usually catalyzed by Ag^+ ions. In both peroxy acids, sulfur is assumed to be in its highest oxidation state (6+). The oxygen atoms of the peroxide grouping, however, are each assigned an oxidation number of $1-$. In the course of an oxidation, it is the peroxide oxygens that change oxidation state (from $1-$ to $2-$).

There is another significant group of sulfur-containing anions. The most important representative of the group is the thiosulfate ion, $S_2O_3^{2-}$:

$$\begin{bmatrix} & O & \\ & | & \\ O - & S & - O \\ & | & \\ & S & \end{bmatrix}^{2-}$$

This tetrahedral ion may be regarded as a sulfate ion in which one oxygen atom has been replaced by a sulfur atom. In fact, the prefix "thio-" is used to name any species that may be considered to be derived from another compound by replacing an oxygen atom by a sulfur atom; the prefix is placed before the base name of the oxygen-containing compound. Thus, OCN^- is the cyanate ion and SCN^- is the thiocyanate ion; $CO(NH_2)_2$ is urea and $CS(NH_2)_2$ is thiourea.

Thiosulfates may be prepared by the reaction of sulfur with sulfites in aqueous solution:

$$SO_3^{2-}(aq) + S(s) \longrightarrow S_2O_3^{2-}(aq)$$

The corresponding acid does not exist. Upon acidification, thiosulfates decompose to elementary sulfur and SO_2 gas:

$$S_2O_3^{2-}(aq) + 2\,H^+(aq) \longrightarrow S(s) + SO_2(g) + H_2O$$

The two sulfur atoms of the thiosulfate ion are not equivalent. This has been shown by the reactions of a compound derived from a sulfite and radioactive sulfur, $^{35}_{16}S$. When a compound thus prepared is decomposed by acidification, all the activity ends in the elementary sulfur:

$$SO_3^{2-}(aq) + {}^{35}S(s) \longrightarrow {}^{35}SSO_3^{2-}(aq)$$

$$^{35}SSO_3^{2-}(aq) + 2\,H^+(aq) \longrightarrow {}^{35}S(s) + SO_2(g) + H_2O$$

Hence, the central sulfur atom is generally assigned an oxidation number of $6+$ (as in the sulfate ion), and the coordinated sulfur is usually assigned an oxidation number of $2-$ (corresponding to the oxidation number of the oxygen it replaces). The average oxidation state of sulfur in the ion is $2+$.

The thiosulfate ion is readily oxidized to the tetrathionate ion, $S_4O_6^{2-}$. The tetrathionate ion may be regarded as an analog of the peroxydisulfate ion, $S_2O_8^{2-}$, in which the peroxide group (—O—O—) is replaced by a disulfide group (—S—S—). Other thionate ions exist—for example, the dithionate ion, $S_2O_6^{2-}$, and the trithionate ion, $S_3O_6^{2-}$; the latter is structurally similar to the pyrosulfate ion, $S_2O_7^{2-}$, with a sulfur atom replacing the central oxygen atom.

22.13 Electrode Potential Diagrams for S

Electrode potential diagrams for sulfur and its compounds appear in Figure 22.5. On the basis of the $\mathscr{E}_{red}^{\circ}$ values, several substances shown in the diagrams should be able to disproportionate. In alkaline solution (but not in acid), sulfur itself forms S^{2-} and $S_2O_3^{2-}$. The thiosulfate ion is stable in alkaline solution but disproportionates to S and SO_2 in acid. The electrode potentials also show that both SO_2, in acid, and SO_3^{2-}, in base, are unstable toward disproportionation. The latter two reactions, however, are slow under ordinary conditions.

At standard concentrations and in acidic solution, the oxysulfur compounds shown in the diagram are only moderately strong oxidizing agents. In alkaline solution the oxysulfur compounds are poor oxidants. In fact, all the ions with the exception of SO_4^{2-} are easily oxidized in base and can function as reducing agents. The thiosulfate ion is easily oxidized to the tetrathionate ion $S_4O_6^{2-}$; $\mathscr{E}_{ox}^{\circ}$ for this transformation is only -0.08 V.

22.14 Industrial Uses of S, Se, and Te

The commercial uses of sulfur, selenium, and tellurium include the following:

1. Sulfur. Over 80% of the sulfur mined is used in the manufacture of sulfuric acid. The industrial importance of H_2SO_4 is reflected in the significance that is attached to figures for the annual consumption of the acid. These figures are used to rate the state of industrialization, standard of living, and economic well-being of a country.

Sulfuric acid is used in many industrial processes: in the production of other chemicals, fertilizers, pigments, iron, steel, and in petroleum refining. It is the electrolyte used in lead storage batteries. Elemental sulfur is used in the vulcanization of rubber, in the production of pigments, paints, paper, fungicides, insecticides, and in pharmaceuticals.

2. Selenium. Selenium has been used in photocells, devices which transmit electric current in proportion to the intensity of incident light. The electrical response to light of gray selenium also accounts for its use in xerography, the dry photocopying process. Selenium is also used in the production of colored glass, ceramics, pigments, alloys, steel, oxidation inhibitors for lubricating oils, and in the vulcanization of rubber.

3. Tellurium. Tellurium finds fewer uses than the other elements of this group.

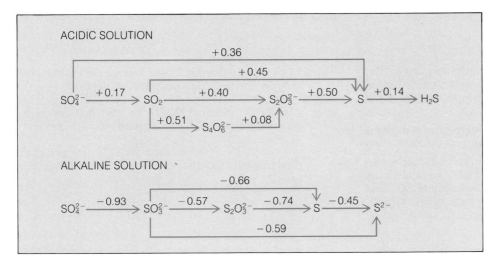

Figure 22.5 Electrode potential diagrams for sulfur and its compounds ($\mathscr{E}^{\circ}_{red}$ values given in volts)

Like selenium, tellurium is used in the vulcanization of rubber and in the manufacture of glass, ceramics, alloys, and enamel pigments.

Summary

Oxygen, the *most abundant element* on earth, is produced industrially principally by the *liquefaction and fractionation of air*. A small amount is produced by the *electrolysis of water*. In the laboratory, oxygen is prepared by the *thermal decomposition* of certain oxygen-containing compounds (oxides of metals of low reactivity, peroxides, nitrates, and chlorates).

Oxygen forms four different anions: the *oxide ion* (O^{2-}), the *superoxide ion* (O_2^-), the *peroxide ion* (O_2^{2-}), and the *ozonide ion* (O_3^-). All *metals* except the less-reactive ones (such as Ag and Au) react with oxygen. Except for the nobel gases and the halogens, all *nonmetals* react with oxygen directly. Most reactions of *compounds* with oxygen yield the same products that would be obtained if the individual elements that make up the compounds were reacted directly. The element *oxygen* exists in *two allotropic modifications:* O_3 (ozone) and O_2. Several oxides found in air in variable amounts are *air pollutants*. The commercial uses of oxygen were reviewed.

All members of group VI A exist in more than one allotropic form. *Sulfur* is obtained from underground beds of the free element by the *Frasch process*. Selenium and tellurium are obtained from the *anode sludge* that is produced in the *electrolytic refining of copper*. The hydrogen compounds H_2S, H_2Se, and H_2Te are *weak acids* and may be prepared by the action of acids on sulfides, selenides, and tellurides.

In addition to the 2- oxidation state found in the S^{2-}, Se^{2-}, and Te^{2-} ions, the 4+ and 6+ oxidation states of these elements are also important. The most important *4+ compounds* of sulfur are *sulfur dioxide* (SO_2), *sulfurous acid* (H_2SO_3), and the *sulfites* (salts of sulfurous acid). Comparable compounds of selenium and tellurium exist (although pure tellurous acid has never been isolated).

The most important 6+ compounds of sulfur are *sulfur trioxide* (SO_3), *sulfuric acid* (H_2SO_4), and the *sulfates*. Sulfuric acid, made industrially by the *contact process*, has many important uses. Selenium and tellurium also form trioxides and 6+ oxyacids. Other acids in which sulfur is in a 6+ oxidation state include *pyrosulfuric acid* and several *peroxyacids*. The *thiosulfates* are another significant group of sulfur-containing compounds. The industrial uses of S, Se, and Te were reviewed.

Key Terms

Some of the more important terms introduced in this chapter are listed below. Definitions for terms not included in this list may be located in the text by use of the index.

Allotropes (Section 22.6)   Two or more forms of the same element in the same physical state.

Contact process (Section 22.12)   A process for the manufacture of sulfuric acid in which SO_2 is catalytically oxidized to SO_3, the SO_3 vapor dissolved in H_2SO_4, and the resulting $H_2S_2O_7$ diluted with water to give H_2SO_4.

Frasch process (Section 22.9)   A process in which molten sulfur is obtained from underground deposits.

Peroxy acid (Section 22.12)   An acid that contains a peroxide group ($-O-O-$) somewhere in the molecule.

Photochemical pollutants (Section 22.7)   Air pollutants produced by a sequence of reactions that is initiated by sunlight.

Problems*

Oxygen

22.1 List the forms in which oxygen occurs in nature. How is oxygen produced industrially?

22.2 Write chemical equations for the preparation of oxygen from: **(a)** HgO(s), **(b)** Na_2O_2(s) and H_2O, **(c)** $NaNO_3$, **(d)** $KClO_3$(s), **(e)** H_2O.

22.3 Write chemical equations for the reactions of oxygen with: **(a)** K(s), **(b)** Na(s), **(c)** Li(s), **(d)** Mg(s), **(e)** Hg(l), **(f)** Ba(s).

22.4 Write chemical equations for the reactions of oxygen with: **(a)** C(s), **(b)** S(s), **(c)** P(s), **(d)** Cu_2O(s), **(e)** N_2(g), **(f)** H_2(g).

22.5 Write chemical equations for the complete combustion in oxygen of: **(a)** C_2H_5OH(l), **(b)** C_3H_6(g), **(c)** $C_4H_{10}S$(l), **(d)** PbS(s), **(e)** CuS(s).

22.6 Write chemical equations for the complete combustion in oxygen of: **(a)** ZnS(s), **(b)** $C_4H_8S_2$(l), **(c)** C_5H_{12}(l), **(d)** $C_4H_{10}O$(l), **(e)** C_6H_6(l).

22.7 **(a)** Compounds that contain the dioxygenyl ion, O_2^+, are known. Draw molecular-orbital energy-level diagrams for the dioxygenyl ion, O_2^+, and the superoxide ion, O_2^-. Compare the two ions as to **(b)** bond order, and **(c)** number of unpaired electrons.

22.8 Draw molecular-orbital energy-level diagrams for **(a)** O_2, **(b)** O_2^-, **(c)** O_2^{2-}. State the number of unpaired electrons and the bond order of each.

22.9 The products of the combustion of a hydrocarbon in oxygen depend upon the amount of oxygen supplied. Write chemical equations for the reactions of methane, CH_4(g), with oxygen that yield **(a)** C(s), **(b)** CO(g), **(c)** CO_2(g).

22.10 Compare the oxides of the I A elements (for example, Na_2O) with the oxides of the VI A elements (for example, SO_2) in regard to **(a)** physical state, **(b)** melting point, **(c)** nature of the bonding, **(d)** products of the reactions with water.

22.11 The standard enthalpy of formation of H_2O(l) is -285.9 kJ/mol and of O_3(g) is $+142.3$ kJ/mol. What is the enthalpy change when one mole of H_2O(l) is prepared from **(a)** H_2(g) and O_2(g), **(b)** H_2(g) and O_3(g)? In general, how do enthalpy changes for the reactions of ozone compare to those of oxygen?

***22.12** The standard enthalpy of formation of ozone, O_3(g), is $+142$ kJ/mol. The bond dissociation energy of O_2(g) is $+494$ kJ/mol. What is the *average* bond energy of the bonds in ozone?

Sulfur, Selenium, and Tellurium

22.13 Describe the Frasch process for mining elementary sulfur.

22.14 Describe the changes in sulfur that occur as the temperature is increased.

22.15 Write chemical equations for the reactions of sulfur with: **(a)** O_2(g), **(b)** S^{2-}(aq), **(c)** SO_3^{2-}(aq), **(d)** Fe(s), **(e)** F_2(g), **(f)** Cl_2(g), **(g)** HNO_3(l).

22.16 Write chemical equations for the reactions of H_2SO_4 with: **(a)** $C_{12}H_{22}O_{11}$(s), **(b)** $NaNO_3$(s), **(c)** Cu(s), **(d)** Zn(s), **(e)** ZnS(s), **(f)** Fe_2O_3(s).

---

* The more difficult problems are marked with asterisks. The appendix contains answers to color-keyed problems.

22.17 Write chemical equations for the reaction of water with:
(a) $CH_3C(NH_2)S(s)$, **(b)** $SO_2(g)$, **(c)** $SO_3(g)$, **(d)** $Al_2S_3(s)$, **(e)** $SeO_2(s)$, **(f)** $TeO_3(s)$, **(g)** $H_2SO_5(l)$, **(h)** $H_2S_2O_7(l)$.

22.18 Write chemical equations for the reactions of $SO_2(g)$ with: **(a)** O_2 (Pt catalyst), **(b)** $Cl_2(g)$, **(c)** H_2O, **(d)** $ClO_3^-(aq)$, **(e)** $OH^-(aq)$, **(f)** $SO_3^{2-}(aq)$ and H_2O.

22.19 Draw Lewis structures for and describe the geometric shape of: **(a)** H_2S, **(b)** SO_2, **(c)** SO_3, **(d)** SO_3^{2-}, **(e)** SO_4^{2-}.

22.20 Draw Lewis structures and describe the geometric shape of **(a)** S_3^{2-}, **(b)** $S_2O_3^{2-}$, **(c)** $S_4O_6^{2-}$, **(d)** $H_2S_2O_7$, **(e)** $H_2S_2O_8$.

22.21 Write chemical equations for the reactions of $HCl(aq)$ with: **(a)** $Na_2SO_3(s)$, **(b)** $Na_2S(s)$, **(c)** $Na_2S_2O_3(s)$.

22.22 Write chemical equations for the reactions of $O_2(g)$ with: **(a)** $S(s)$, **(b)** $H_2S(g)$, **(c)** $H_2Te(g)$, **(d)** $SO_3^{2-}(aq)$.

22.23 Explain why SF_4 can be prepared but OF_4 cannot be.

22.24 What is the difference in meaning between the prefixes *per-* and *peroxy-* as applied to the naming of acids?

22.25 Write balanced chemical equations for the disproportionation reaction of **(a)** S (to S^{2-} and $S_2O_3^{2-}$) in alkaline solution, **(b)** $S_2O_3^{2-}$ (to S and SO_2) in acid solution.

22.26 Chlorosulfonic acid, $HOSO_2Cl$ is the product of the reaction of SO_3 and HCl. The peroxydisulfuric acids (H_2SO_5 and $H_2S_2O_8$) can be prepared by the reaction of one mole of hydrogen peroxide, H_2O_2, with either one or two moles of chlorosulfonic acid. Write chemical equations for the reactions.

Unclassified Problems

22.27 Because the oxygen of H_2O_2 can be either oxidized (to O_2) or reduced (to H_2O), hydrogen peroxide can function as a reducing agent or as an oxidizing agent. Using the ion-electron method, write balanced chemical equations for the following reactions of H_2O_2: **(a)** the oxidation of Pb to $PbSO_4$ in acid solution, **(b)** the oxidation of $Cr(OH)_3$ to CrO_4^{2-} in alkaline solution, **(c)** the reduction of MnO_4^- to Mn^{2+} in acid solution, **(d)** the reduction of Ag_2O to Ag in alkaline solution.

22.28 Draw the resonance forms of the ozone molecule, O_3. What is the bond order? What is the shape of the molecule?

22.29 For each of the following compounds, write a sequence of chemical equations that starts with elemental sulfur and leads to the preparation of the compound given. **(a)** H_2S (not by direct union of the elements), **(b)** H_2SO_3, **(c)** $Na_2S_2O_3$, **(d)** $NaHSO_4$, **(e)** $H_2S_2O_7$.

22.30 Describe the geometric shapes of **(a)** SF_4, **(b)** SF_6, **(c)** H_6TeO_6.

22.31 Explain why **(a)** H_2Te is a stronger acid than H_2S, **(b)** H_2SO_4 is a stronger acid than H_6TeO_6.

22.32 Describe laboratory tests for: **(a)** $S^{2-}(aq)$, **(b)** SO_3^{2-}, **(c)** SO_4^{2-}, **(d)** $S_2O_3^{2-}$.

*22.33 According to standard electrode potentials, both SO_2 (in acid solution) and SO_3^{2-} (in alkaline solution) should disproportionate. These reactions, however, are slow. What products should be obtained in each of these disproportionation reactions? Note that it is necessary to take all possibilities given in Figure 22.5 into account.

CHAPTER 23

THE NONMETALS, PART III: THE GROUP V A ELEMENTS

Group V A includes nitrogen, phosphorus, arsenic, antimony, and bismuth. Collectively, these elements show a wider range of properties than is exhibited by either the group VI A elements or the group VII A elements.

23.1 Properties of the Group V A Elements

Within any A family of the periodic classification, metallic character increases (and nonmetallic character decreases) with increasing atomic number, atomic weight, and atomic size. This trend is particularly striking in group V A. The first ionization energies of the elements in the group, which are listed in Table 23.1, decrease from values typical of a nonmetal (N) to those characteristic of a metal (Bi). Nitrogen and phosphorus are generally regarded as nonmetals, arsenic and antimony as semimetals or metalloids, and bismuth as a metal.

The electronic configurations of the elements are listed in Table 23.2. Each element has three electrons less than the noble gas of its period, and the formation of trinegative ions might be expected. Nitrogen forms the nitride ion, N^{3-}, in combination with certain reactive metals, and phosphorus forms the phosphide ion, P^{3-}, less readily. The remaining elements of the group (As, Sb, and Bi), however, are more metallic than N and P and have no tendency to form comparable anions.

The loss of electrons and consequent formation of cations, which is characteristic of metals, is observed for the heavier members of the group. High ionization energies prohibit the loss of all five valence electrons by any element. Consequently, 5+ ions do not exist, and the 5+ oxidation state is attained only through covalent bonding. In addition, most of the compounds in which the group V A elements appear in the 3+ oxidation state are covalent. Antimony and bismuth, however, can form $d^{10}s^2$ ions, Sb^{3+} and Bi^{3+}, through loss of the p electrons of their valence levels. The compounds $Sb_2(SO_4)_3$, BiF_3, and $Bi(ClO_4)_3 \cdot 5H_2O$ are ionic. The 3+ ions of antimony and bismuth react with water to form antimonyl and bismuthyl ions (SbO^+ and BiO^+), as well as hydrated forms of these ions (for example, $Bi(OH)_2^+$):

$$Bi^{3+}(aq) + H_2O \rightleftharpoons BiO^+(aq) + 2H^+(aq)$$

Nitrogen, phosphorus, and arsenic do not form simple cations.

The oxides of the group V A elements become less acidic and more basic as the metallic character of the element increases. Thus N_2O_3, P_4O_6, and As_4O_6

Table 23.1 Some properties of the group V A elements

Property	Nitrogen	Phosphorus	Arsenic	Antimony	Bismuth
color	colorless	white, red, black	gray metallic, yellow	gray metallic, yellow	gray metallic
molecular formula	N_2	P_4 (white) P_n (black)	As_n (metallic) As_4 (yellow)	Sb_n (metallic) Sb_4 (yellow)	Bi_n
melting point (°C)	−210	44.1 (white)	814 (36 atm) (metallic)	630.5 (metallic)	271
boiling point (°C)	−195.8	280	633 (sublimes)	1325	1560
atomic radius (pm)	74	110	121	141	152
ionic radius (pm)	140 (N^{3-})	185 (P^{3-})		92 (Sb^{3+})	108 (Bi^{3+})
first ionization energy (kJ/mol)	1399	1061	965	830	772
electronegativity	3.0	2.2	2.2	2.1	2.0

Table 23.2 Electronic configurations of the group V A elements

ELEMENT	Z	1s	2s	2p	3s	3p	3d	4s	4p	4d	4f	5s	5p	5d	6s	6p
N	7	2	2	3												
P	15	2	2	6	2	3										
As	33	2	2	6	2	6	10	2	3							
Sb	51	2	2	6	2	6	10	2	6	10		2	3			
Bi	83	2	2	6	2	6	10	2	6	10	14	2	6	10	2	3

are acidic oxides; they dissolve in water to form acids, and they dissolve in solutions of alkalies to form salts of these acids. The compound Sb_4O_6 is amphoteric; it will dissolve in hydrochloric acid as well as in sodium hydroxide. The comparable oxide of bismuth is strictly basic; Bi_2O_3 is not soluble in alkalies, but the compound will dissolve in acids to produce bismuth salts.

All the oxides in which the elements exhibit a 5+ oxidation state are acidic, but the acidity declines markedly from N_2O_5 to Bi_2O_5. In addition, the stability of the 5+ oxidation state decreases with increasing atomic number; Bi_2O_5 is extremely unstable and has never been prepared in a pure state.

Many of the properties of nitrogen are anomalous in comparison to those of the other V A elements. This departure is characteristic of the first members of the groups of the periodic classification. Free nitrogen is surprisingly unreactive, partly because of the great strength of the bonding in the N_2 molecule:

$$:N\equiv N:$$

According to the molecular orbital theory, two π bonds and one σ bond join the atoms of a N_2 molecule, and the bond order is 3. The energy required to dissociate molecular N_2 into atoms is very high (941 kJ/mol).

Since nitrogen has no d orbitals in its valence level ($n = 2$), the maximum number of covalent bonds formed by nitrogen is four (for example, in NH_4^+). In

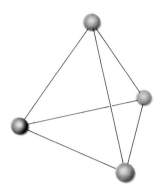

Figure 23.1 Structure of the P₄ molecule

the valence levels of the other V A elements, there are empty d orbitals which may be utilized in covalent bond formation. Hence, P, As, Sb, and Bi form as many as six covalent bonds in such species as PCl_5, PCl_6^-, AsF_5, $SbCl_6^-$, and $BiCl_5^{2-}$.

For the group as a whole, the $3-$, $3+$, and $5+$ oxidation states are most common. The importance and stability of the $5+$ and $3-$ states decline from the lighter to the heavier elements. Nitrogen, however, appears in every oxidation state from $3-$ to $5+$. Nitrogen also has a tendency toward the formation of multiple bonds (for example, in the cyanide ion, $C\equiv N^-$). The other V A elements do not form π bonds with p orbitals, but some multiple bond character can arise in the compounds of these elements (particularly those of P) from $p\pi$-$d\pi$ bonding.

Phosphorus, arsenic, and antimony occur in allotropic modifications. There are three important forms of phosphorus: white, red, and black. White phosphorus, a waxy solid, is obtained by condensing phosphorus vapor. Crystals of white phosphorus are formed from P_4 molecules (see Figure 23.1) in which each phosphorus atom has an unshared pair of electrons and completes its octet by forming single covalent bonds with the other three phosphorus atoms of the molecule. The substance is highly toxic.

White phosphorus is soluble in a number of nonpolar solvents (for example, benzene and carbon disulfide). In such solutions, in liquid white phosphorus, and in phosphorus vapor, the element exists as P_4 molecules. At temperatures above 800°C a slight dissociation of the P_4 molecules of the vapor into P_2 molecules is observed; these latter molecules are assumed to have a structure similar to that of the N_2 molecule. White phosphorus is the most reactive form of the element and is stored under water to protect it from atmospheric oxygen with which it spontaneously reacts.

Red phosphorus may be prepared by heating white phosphorus to about 250°C in the absence of air. It is a polymeric material in which many phosphorus atoms are joined in a network, but the details of the structure of red phosphorus are not known. Red phosphorus is not soluble in common solvents and is considerably less reactive than the white variety. It does not react with oxygen at room temperature.

Black phosphorus, a less common allotrope, is made by subjecting the element to very high pressures or by a slow crystallization of liquid white phosphorus in the presence of mercury as a catalyst and a seed of black phosphorus. Crystalline black phosphorus consists of layers of phosphorus atoms covalently joined into a network (see Figure 23.2). The distance between P atoms of adjacent layers is much greater than the distance between P atoms of the same layer since the

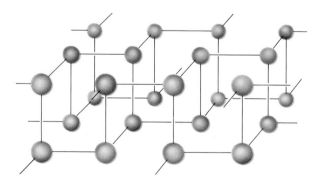

Figure 23.2 Structure of a layer of the black phosphorus crystal

Chapter 23   The Nonmetals, Part III: The Group V A Elements

P atoms of a given layer are covalently bonded to one another and the layers are held together by comparatively weak London forces. Hence, black phosphorus is a flaky material much like graphite (which also has a layer-type crystal, see Section 24.2), and like graphite, black phosphorus is an electrical conductor. Black phosphorus is the least soluble and least reactive form of the element.

Arsenic and antimony exist in soft, yellow, nonmetallic modifications which are thought to be formed from tetrahedral As_4 and Sb_4 molecules analogous to the P_4 molecules of white phosphorus. These yellow forms may be obtained by the rapid condensation of vapors and are soluble in carbon disulfide. They are unstable and are readily converted into stable, gray, metallic modifications.

Bismuth commonly occurs as a light gray metal with a reddish cast; the element does not exist in other modifications. The metallic modifications of arsenic, antimony, and bismuth are comparatively soft and brittle and have a metallic luster. Their crystalline structures are similar to the structure of black phosphorus, and they are electrical conductors.

23.2 The Nitrogen Cycle

In nature, nitrogen is constantly being removed from the atmosphere and returned to the atmosphere by several natural and artificial processes. These processes, taken together, constitute what is called the **nitrogen cycle.**

Nitrogen is a constituent element of all plant and animal protein. Since nitrogen is a comparatively unreactive element, the cells of living systems cannot directly assimilate the nitrogen of the air to use in the synthesis of proteins. The nitrogen of the air, however, is converted by several **nitrogen-fixation processes** into compounds that can be used by plants. These nitrogen-fixation processes constitute the first part of the nitrogen cycle.

During storms, lightning flashes cause some nitrogen and oxygen of the air to form nitrogen oxide:

$$N_2(g) + O_2(g) \longrightarrow 2\,NO(g)$$

Nitrogen dioxide is produced by the reaction of NO with additional O_2 from the air:

$$2\,NO(g) + O_2(g) \longrightarrow 2\,NO_2(g)$$

The NO_2 reacts with water to form nitric acid:

$$3\,NO_2(g) + H_2O(l) \longrightarrow 2\,HNO_3(l) + NO(g)$$

The nitric acid is washed to the earth where it forms nitrates in the soil, which can be used by plants as nutrients.

Certain soil bacteria, as well as nitrogen-fixing bacteria in the root nodules of leguminous plants (such as peas, beans, and alfalfa) fix atmospheric nitrogen into compounds that plants can assimilate. Fertilizers are used to augment the fixed nitrogen in the soil. Nitrogen-containing fertilizers are made from ammonia, which is itself produced commercially by a nitrogen-fixation process, the **Haber process:**

$$N_2(g) + 3\,H_2(g) \rightleftharpoons 2\,NH_3(g)$$

In the second stage of the nitrogen cycle, plants use the fixed nitrogen in the soil to make plant protein. The plant protein is in turn eaten by animals and used to make animal protein. Indeed, humans obtain their fixed nitrogen from the ingestion of both plant and animal protein.

In the third part of the nitrogen cycle, the cycle is completed. The decay of the waste products of animal metabolism and the death and decay of plants and animals liberates nitrogen as an end product. The N_2, therefore, is returned to the air.

23.3 Occurrence and Preparation of the Group V A Elements

The principal natural sources of the group V A elements are listed in Table 23.3. Nitrogen, like oxygen (see Section 22.2) and the noble gases (see Section 24.9), is produced commercially by the fractionation of liquid air. Nitrogen from this source, in cylinders, is usually employed when the gas is needed in the laboratory. On occasion, however, small amounts for laboratory use may be obtained by heating an aqueous solution saturated with ammonium chloride and sodium nitrite,

$$NH_4^+(aq) + NO_2^-(aq) \longrightarrow N_2(g) + 2\,H_2O$$

or by heating either sodium azide or barium azide,

$$2\,NaN_3(s) \longrightarrow 2\,Na(l) + 3\,N_2(g)$$

Phosphorus is the only member of group V A that does not occur in nature as an uncombined element. It is prepared industrially by heating a mixture of phosphate rock, sand, and coke in an electric furnace:

Table 23.3 Occurrence of the group V A elements		
Element	Percent of Earth's crust	Occurrence
nitrogen	0.0046 (0.03 including atmosphere)	N_2 (atmosphere) $NaNO_3$ (Chilean saltpeter)
phosphorus	0.12	$Ca_3(PO_4)_2$ (phosphate rock), $Ca_5(PO_4)_3F$ and $Ca_5(PO_4)_3Cl$ (apatite)
arsenic	5×10^{-4}	$FeAsS$(arsenopyrite), As_4S_4 (realgar), As_2S_3 (orpiment), As_4O_6 (arsenolite); native As; in ores of Cu, Pb, Co, Ni, Zn, Sn, Ag, and Au
antimony	5×10^{-5}	Sb_2S_3 (stibnite), Sb_4O_6 (senarmontite); native Sb; in ores of Cu, Pb, Ag, and Hg
bismuth	1×10^{-5}	Bi_2S_3 (bismuthinite), Bi_2O_3 (bismite); native Bi; in ores of Cu, Pb, Sn, Co, Ni, Ag, and Au

Mining phosphate rock. *W. R. Grace & Co.*

$$2\,Ca_3(PO_4)_2(s) + 6\,SiO_2(s) \longrightarrow 6\,CaSiO_3(l) + P_4O_{10}(g)$$

$$P_4O_{10}(g) + 10\,C(s) \longrightarrow P_4(g) + 10\,CO(g)$$

The calcium silicate is withdrawn as a molten slag from the bottom of the furnace, and the product gases are passed through water, which condenses the phosphorus vapor into a white solid.

Arsenic, antimony, and bismuth are obtained by carbon reduction of their oxides at elevated temperatures:

$$As_4O_6(s) + 6\,C(s) \longrightarrow As_4(g) + 6\,CO(g)$$

An important industrial source of the oxides is the flue dust obtained from the processes used in the production of certain metals, notably copper and lead. In addition, the oxides are obtained by roasting the sulfide ores of the elements in air; for example,

$$2\,Sb_2S_3(s) + 9\,O_2(g) \longrightarrow Sb_4O_6(g) + 6\,SO_2(g)$$

Although arsenic, antimony, and bismuth all occur as native ores, only the deposits of native bismuth are sufficiently large to be of commercial importance.

23.4 Nitrides and Phosphides

Elementary nitrogen reacts with a number of metals at high temperatures to form **ionic nitrides,** high-melting, white, crystalline solids that contain the N^{3-} ion. The group II A metals, cadmium, and zinc form ionic nitrides with the formula

M_3N_2 (where M is Be, Mg, Ca, Sr, Ba, Cd, or Zn) and lithium forms Li_3N. Ionic nitrides react with water to yield ammonia and hydroxides:

$$Ca_3N_2(s) + 6H_2O \longrightarrow 3Ca^{2+}(aq) + 6OH^-(aq) + 2NH_3(g)$$

Interstitial nitrides are made at elevated temperatures from many transition metals, in powdered form, and nitrogen or ammonia. A crystal of an interstitial nitride (VN, Fe_4N, W_2N, and TiN are examples) consists of metal atoms arranged in a lattice with nitrogen atoms occupying lattice holes (the interstices). These substances, therefore, frequently deviate from exact stoichiometry. They resemble metals and are hard, extremely high melting, good electrical conductors, and chemically unreactive.

Covalent nitrides include such compounds as S_4N_4, P_3N_5, Si_3N_4, Sn_3N_4, BN, and AlN. Some of these compounds are molecular in form. Others, such as BN and AlN, are substances in which a large number of atoms of the two elements are covalently bonded together into a network crystal. Both BN and AlN are made by reacting the elements at high temperatures. Two C atoms taken together have the same number of valence electrons (8) as one B atom (3 valence electrons) plus one N atom (5 valence electrons) combined. The compound BN, therefore, may be considered to be isoelectronic with carbon. Indeed, BN is known in two crystalline modifications, one resembling graphite and another extremely hard form resembling diamond.

Many metals react with white phosphorus to form phosphides. The group II A elements form phosphides with the formula M_3P_2 (where M is Be, Mg, Ca, Sr, or Ba), lithium forms Li_3P and sodium forms Na_3P. These compounds readily react with water to form phosphine (PH_3). For example,

$$Ca_3P_2(s) + 6H_2O \longrightarrow 3Ca^{2+}(aq) + 6OH^-(aq) + PH_3(g)$$

The phosphides of the group III A elements (such as BP, AlP, and GaP) form covalent network crystals similar to silicon, and like silicon these substances are semiconductors. Many phosphides of the transition metals are known (FeP, Fe_2P, Co_2P, RuP, and OsP_2 are examples). These substances are gray-black, semimetallic crystals that are electrical conductors.

The reactions of metals with arsenic, antimony, and, to a lesser extent, bismuth yield arsenides, stibnides, and bismuthides. These compounds become progressively more difficult to prepare as the atomic number of the group V A element increases.

23.5 Hydrogen Compounds

The group V A elements all form hydrogen compounds, the most important of which is ammonia, NH_3. Large quantities of ammonia are commercially prepared by the direct union of the elements (Haber process):

$$N_2(g) + 3H_2(g) \rightleftharpoons 2NH_3(g)$$

Ammonia is the only hydrogen compound of the V A elements that can be prepared directly. The reaction is conducted under high pressures (from 100 to 1000 atm), at 400° to 550°C, and in the presence of a catalyst. One catalyst, so employed, consists of finely divided iron and Fe_3O_4 containing small amounts of K_2O and Al_2O_3.

Smaller quantities of ammonia are produced as a by-product in the manufacture of coke by the destructive distillation of coal. Ammonia was formerly produced commercially by the reaction of calcium cyanamide, CaNCN, with steam under pressure:

$$CaNCN(s) + 3\,H_2O(g) \longrightarrow CaCO_3(s) + 2\,NH_3(g)$$

However, the Haber process has largely displaced this method as a commercial source of ammonia, and calcium cyanamide is produced chiefly as a fertilizer and as a raw material in the manufacture of certain nitrogen-containing organic compounds. Calcium cyanamide is produced in a two-step process. Calcium carbide, CaC_2, is made by the reaction of CaO and coke in an electric furnace:

$$CaO(s) + 3\,C(s) \longrightarrow CaC_2(s) + CO(g)$$

and the calcium carbide is reacted with relatively pure nitrogen at approximately 1000°C to produce calcium cyanamide:

$$CaC_2(s) + N_2(g) \longrightarrow CaNCN(s) + C(s)$$

In the laboratory, ammonia is conveniently prepared by the hydrolysis of nitrides (see Section 23.4) or by heating an ammonium salt with a strong alkali, such as NaOH or $Ca(OH)_2$, either dry or in solution:

$$NH_4^+(aq) + OH^-(aq) \longrightarrow NH_3(g) + H_2O$$

The ammonia molecule,

$$H-\overset{\cdot\cdot}{\underset{|}{N}}-H$$
$$H$$

is trigonal pyramidal with the nitrogen atom at the apex; this compound is associated through hydrogen bonding in the liquid and solid states.

Aqueous solutions of ammonia are alkaline:

$$NH_3(aq) + H_2O \rightleftharpoons NH_4^+(aq) + OH^-(aq)$$

In solution or as a dry gas, ammonia reacts with acids to produce ammonium salts:

$$NH_3(g) + HCl(g) \longrightarrow NH_4Cl(s)$$

The ammonium ion is tetrahedral.

Nitrogen is formed when ammonia is burned in pure oxygen:

$$4\,NH_3(g) + 3\,O_2(g) \longrightarrow 2\,N_2(g) + 6\,H_2O(g)$$

However, when a mixture of ammonia and air is passed over platinum gauze at 1000°C, nitric oxide, NO, is produced:

$$4\,NH_3(g) + 5\,O_2(g) \longrightarrow 4\,NO(g) + 6\,H_2O(g)$$

This catalyzed oxidation of NH_3 is a part of the Ostwald process for the manufacture of nitric acid (see Section 23.7).

Hydrazine, N_2H_4, may be considered to be derived from NH_3 by the replacement of a H atom by a —NH_2 group:

$$H-\overset{..}{N}-\overset{..}{N}-H$$
$$\quad\ \ |\quad\ \ |$$
$$\quad\ \ H\quad\ H$$

The compound, which is a liquid, may be prepared by oxidizing NH_3 with NaOCl. Hydrazine is less basic than NH_3 but does form cations in which one proton or two protons are bonded to the free electron pairs of the molecule. For example,

$$\left[\begin{array}{c} H \\ | \\ H-\overset{..}{N}-N-H \\ | \quad\ | \\ H \quad\ H \end{array}\right]^{+} Cl^{-} \qquad \left[\begin{array}{c} H \quad\ H \\ | \quad\ | \\ H-N-N-H \\ | \quad\ | \\ H \quad\ H \end{array}\right]^{2+} 2\,Cl^{-}$$

Hydrazine is a strong reducing agent and has found some use in rocket fuels.

Hydroxylamine, NH_2OH, is another compound which, like hydrazine, may be considered to be derived from the NH_3 molecule:

$$H-\overset{..}{N}-O-H$$
$$\quad\ \ |$$
$$\quad\ \ H$$

Like hydrazine, hydroxylamine is a weaker base than NH_3, but salts containing the $[NH_3OH]^{+}$ ion may be prepared.

Hydrazoic acid, HN_3, is another hydrogen compound of nitrogen. The structure of hydrazoic acid may be represented as a resonance hybrid:

$$H-\overset{..}{N}=\overset{\oplus}{N}=\overset{..}{\underset{\ominus}{N}}: \longleftrightarrow H-\overset{..}{\underset{..}{N}}-\overset{\ominus}{N}\equiv\overset{\oplus}{N}:$$

The two N—N bond distances of the molecule are not the same; the distance from the central N to the N bearing the H atom (124 pm) is longer than the other (113 pm). Hydrazoic acid may be made by reacting hydrazine (which forms the $[N_2H_5]^{+}$ ion in acidic solution) with nitrous acid (HNO_2):

$$N_2H_5^{+}(aq) + HNO_2(aq) \longrightarrow HN_3(aq) + H^{+}(aq) + 2\,H_2O$$

The free acid, a low-boiling liquid, may be obtained by distillation of the water solution. Hydrazoic acid is a weak acid. The heavy metal salts of the acid, such as lead azide, $Pb(N_3)_2$, explode upon being struck and are used in detonation caps.

Phosphine (PH_3) is a very poisonous, colorless gas that is prepared by the hydrolysis of phosphides or by the reaction of white phosphorus with concentrated solutions of alkalies:

$$P_4(s) + 3\,OH^{-}(aq) + 3\,H_2O \longrightarrow PH_3(g) + \quad 3\,H_2PO_2^{-}(aq)$$
$$\qquad\qquad\qquad\qquad\qquad\qquad\qquad\qquad\qquad \textit{hypophosphite ion}$$

The PH_3 molecule is pyramidal, similar to the NH_3 molecule. Unlike NH_3, however, the compound is not associated by hydrogen bonding in the liquid state.

Phosphine is much less basic than ammonia. Phosphonium compounds, such as $PH_4I(s)$ which can be made from dry $PH_3(g)$ and $HI(g)$, are unstable. They decompose at relatively low temperatures, or in aqueous solution, to yield the component gases.

Arsine (AsH_3), stibine (SbH_3), and bismuthine (BiH_3) are extremely poisonous gases that may be produced by the hydrolysis of arsenides, stibnides, and bismuthides (for example, Na_3As, Zn_3Sb_2, and Mg_3Bi_2). The yields of the hydrogen compounds become poorer with increasing molecular weight. Very poor yields of bismuthine are obtained by this method. The stability of the hydrogen compounds declines in the series from NH_3 to BiH_3. Bismuthine is very unstable and decomposes to the elements at room temperature. Arsine and stibine may be similarly decomposed by warming.

Arsine, stibine, and bismuthine have no basic properties and do not form salts with acids.

3.6 Halogen Compounds

The most important halides of the V A elements are the trihalides (for example, NF_3) and the pentahalides (for example, PF_5). All four binary trihalides of each of the V A elements have been made, but the tribromide and triiodide of nitrogen can be isolated only in the form of ammoniates ($NBr_3 \cdot 6\,NH_3$ and $NI_3 \cdot x\,NH_3$). The nitrogen trihalides are prepared by the halogenation of ammonia gas (NF_3, NBr_3), of an ammonium salt in acidic solution (NCl_3, NBr_3), or of concentrated aqueous ammonia (NI_3). Each of the trihalides of P, As, Sb, and Bi is prepared by direct halogenation of the V A element using a stoichiometric excess of the V A element to prevent pentahalide formation.

Bismuth trifluoride is an ionic compound, but the other trihalides are covalent. In the gaseous state the covalent trihalides exist as trigonal pyramidal molecules (see Figure 23.3). This molecular form persists in the liquid state and in all of the solids except AsI_3, SbI_3, and BiI_3, which crystallize in covalent layer lattices.

Nitrogen trifluoride is a very stable colorless gas, whereas the other trihalides of nitrogen are explosively unstable. The trihalides undergo hydrolysis:

$$NCl_3(l) + 3\,H_2O \longrightarrow NH_3(g) + 3\,HOCl(aq)$$

$$PCl_3(l) + 3\,H_2O \longrightarrow H_3PO_3(aq) + 3\,H^+(aq) + 3\,Cl^-(aq)$$

$$AsCl_3(l) + 3\,H_2O \longrightarrow H_3AsO_3(aq) + 3\,H^+(aq) + 3\,Cl^-(aq)$$

$$SbCl_3(s) + H_2O \longrightarrow SbOCl(s) + 2\,H^+(aq) + 2\,Cl^-(aq)$$

$$BiCl_3(s) + H_2O \longrightarrow BiOCl(s) + 2\,H^+(aq) + 2\,Cl^-(aq)$$

Nitrogen is more electronegative than Cl, and in the hydrolysis of NCl_3, N and Cl appear in $3-$ and $1+$ oxidation states, respectively. In each of the other hydrolysis reactions, the V A element appears in a $3+$ oxidation state and Cl in a $1-$ state. The metallic character of the V A elements increases with increasing atomic number, and Sb and Bi occur as oxo cations (SbO^+ and BiO^+) in the hydrolysis products of $SbCl_3$ and $BiCl_3$.

The pentahalide series is not so complete as the trihalide series. Since N has no d orbitals in its valence level, N can form no more than four covalent bonds.

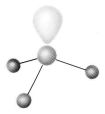

Figure 23.3 Molecular structure of the covalent trihalides of group V A elements

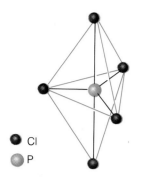

Cl

P

Figure 23.4 Structure of the gaseous PCl$_5$ molecule

Pentahalides of N, therefore, do not exist. All pentahalides of phosphorus are known with the exception of the pentaiodide; presumably there is not sufficient room around a phosphorus atom to accommodate five large iodine atoms. In addition, AsF$_5$, SbF$_5$, BiF$_5$, and SbCl$_5$ have been prepared.

The pentahalides may be prepared by direct reaction of the elements using an excess of the halogen and by the reaction of the halogen with the trihalide:

$$PCl_3(l) + Cl_2(g) \rightleftharpoons PCl_5(s)$$

The preceding reaction is reversible. In the gas phase the pentahalides dissociate to varying degrees.

The pentahalides are trigonal bipyramidal molecules in the gaseous and liquid state (see Figure 23.4). The crystal lattice of SbCl$_5$ consists of such molecules. Solid PCl$_5$ and PBr$_5$, however, form ionic lattices composed of PCl$_4^+$ and PCl$_6^-$ and PBr$_4^+$ and Br$^-$, respectively. Apparently it is impossible to pack six bromine atoms around a phosphorus atom since PBr$_6^-$ does not form. The cations are tetrahedral and the PCl$_6^-$ ion is octahedral (see Figure 23.5).

The phosphorus pentahalides undergo hydrolysis in two steps. For example,

$$PCl_5(s) + H_2O \longrightarrow POCl_3(l) + 2H^+(aq) + 2Cl^-(aq)$$

$$POCl_3(l) + 3H_2O \longrightarrow H_3PO_4(aq) + 3H^+(aq) + 3Cl^-(aq)$$

The phosphoryl halides, POX$_3$ (X = F, Cl, or Br) can be prepared by the hydrolysis of the appropriate pentahalide in a limited amount of water or by the reaction of the trihalide with oxygen:

$$2PCl_3(l) + O_2(g) \longrightarrow 2POCl_3(l)$$

Molecules of the phosphoryl halides have a PX$_3$ grouping arranged as a trigonal pyramid (see Figure 23.3) with an oxygen atom bonded to the phosphorus atom, thus forming a distorted tetrahedron.

A number of mixed trihalides (for example, NF$_2$Cl, PFBr$_2$, and SbBrI$_2$) and mixed pentahalides (for example, PCl$_2$F$_3$, PClF$_4$, and SbCl$_3$F$_2$) have been prepared. In addition, halides are known that conform to the general formula E$_2$X$_4$: N$_2$F$_4$, P$_2$Cl$_4$, P$_2$I$_4$, and As$_2$I$_4$. These compounds have molecular structures similar to the structure of hydrazine, N$_2$H$_4$.

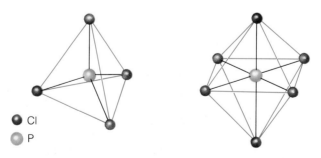

Cl

P

Figure 23.5 Structures of PCl$_4^+$ and PCl$_6^-$

Chapter 23 The Nonmetals, Part III: The Group V A Elements

Isomers are substances that have the same molecular formula but differ in the way the constituent atoms are arranged into molecules. Dinitrogen difluoride exists in two isomeric forms:

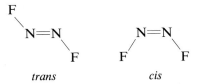

trans   *cis*

The double bond, composed of a σ bond and a π bond, between the two nitrogen atoms prevents free rotation about the nitrogen-nitrogen axis. In the *cis* isomer both fluorine atoms are on the same side of the double-bonded nitrogen atoms, whereas in the *trans* isomer the fluorine atoms are on opposite sides. Both molecules are planar.

3.7 Oxides and Oxyacids of Nitrogen

Oxides are known for every oxidation state of nitrogen from $1+$ to $5+$:

1. The $1+$ oxidation state. Dinitrogen oxide (also called nitrous oxide), N_2O, is prepared by gently heating molten ammonium nitrate:

$$NH_4NO_3(l) \longrightarrow N_2O(g) + 2\,H_2O(g)$$

It is a colorless gas and is relatively unreactive. At temperatures around $500°C$, however, dinitrogen oxide decomposes to nitrogen and oxygen; hence, N_2O supports combustion. Molecules of N_2O are linear, and the electronic structure of the compound may be represented as a resonance hybrid:

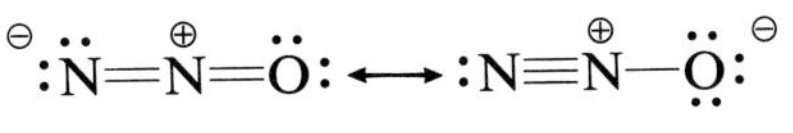

$$\overset{\ominus}{:}\ddot{N}=\overset{\oplus}{N}=\ddot{O}: \longleftrightarrow :N\equiv\overset{\oplus}{N}-\overset{\ominus}{\ddot{O}:}$$

Dinitrogen oxide is commonly called "laughing gas" because of the effect it produces when breathed in small amounts. The gas is used as a general anesthetic, and because of its solubility in cream, it is the gas used to charge whipped cream aerosol cans.

2. The $2+$ oxidation state. Nitrogen oxide (also called nitric oxide), NO, may be prepared by the direct reaction of the elements at high temperatures:

$$N_2(g) + O_2(g) \longrightarrow 2\,NO(g)$$

The reaction is endothermic ($\Delta H = +90.4 \text{ kJ/mol}$), but even at $3000°C$ the yield of NO is only approximately 4%. In a successful preparation the hot gases from the reaction must be rapidly cooled to prevent the decomposition of NO back into nitrogen and oxygen. By this reaction, atmospheric nitrogen is fixed during lightning storms. This reaction also serves as the basis of the **arc process** of nitrogen fixation in which an electric arc is used to provide the high temperatures necessary for the direct combination of nitrogen and oxygen. As a commercial source of NO, the arc process has been supplanted by the catalytic oxidation of ammonia from the Haber process (see Section 23.5).

The NO molecule contains an odd number of electrons, which means that at least one electron must be unpaired; for this reason, NO is paramagnetic. The electronic structure of the molecule may be represented by the resonance forms:

$$\ddot{\cdot}\ddot{N}{=}\ddot{O}\!: \longleftrightarrow \overset{\ominus}{\ddot{\cdot}\ddot{N}}{=}\overset{\oplus}{\dot{O}}\!:$$

The structure, however, is best described by molecular orbital theory, which assigns a bond order of $2\frac{1}{2}$ to the molecule and indicates that the odd electron is in a π^* orbital. The loss of an electron from NO produces the nitrosonium ion, NO^+. Since the electron is lost from an antibonding orbital, the NO^+ ion has a bond order of 3, and the bond distance in NO^+ (106 pm) is shorter than the bond distance in the NO molecule (114 pm). Ionic compounds of NO^+ are known (for example, $NO^+ HSO_4^-$, $NO^+ ClO_4^-$, and $NO^+ BF_4^-$).

Whereas odd-electron molecules are generally very reactive and highly colored, nitric oxide is only moderately reactive and is a colorless gas (condensing to a blue liquid and blue solid at low temperatures). In addition, NO shows little tendency to associate into N_2O_2 molecules by electron pairing. Nitrogen oxide reacts instantly with oxygen at room temperature to form nitrogen dioxide:

$$2\,NO(g) + O_2(g) \longrightarrow 2\,NO_2(g)$$

3. The 3+ oxidation state. Dinitrogen trioxide, N_2O_3, forms as a blue liquid when an equimolar mixture of nitric oxide and nitrogen dioxide is cooled to $-20°C$:

$$NO(g) + NO_2(g) \longrightarrow N_2O_3(l)$$

The compound is unstable under ordinary conditions and decomposes into NO and NO_2. Both NO and NO_2 are odd-electron molecules; N_2O_3 is formed by electron pairing, and the N_2O_3 molecule is thought to contain a N—N bond. Dinitrogen trioxide is the anhydride of nitrous acid, HNO_2, and dissolves in aqueous alkali to produce the nitrite ion, NO_2^-.

4. The 4+ oxidation state. Nitrogen dioxide, NO_2, and dinitrogen tetroxide, N_2O_4, exist in equilibrium:

$$2\,NO_2 \rightleftharpoons N_2O_4$$

Nitrogen dioxide consists of odd-electron molecules, is paramagnetic, and is brown in color. The dimer, in which the electrons are paired, is diamagnetic and colorless. In the solid state the oxide is colorless and consists of pure N_2O_4. The liquid is yellow in color and consists of a dilute solution of NO_2 in N_2O_4. As the temperature is raised, the gas contains more and more NO_2 and becomes deeper and deeper brown in color. At 135°C approximately 99% of the mixture is NO_2.

Nitrogen dioxide molecules are angular:

$$
\overset{\dot{}\ \overset{\oplus}{N}}{\underset{\ominus\ :\ddot{O}\cdot\quad\ddot{O}\!:}{\diagup\ \diagdown}}
\longleftrightarrow
\overset{\dot{}\ \overset{\oplus}{N}}{\underset{\cdot\ddot{O}\cdot\quad\ddot{O}\!:\ominus}{\diagup\ \diagdown}}
\longleftrightarrow
\overset{\ddot{}\ \ddot{N}}{\underset{\cdot\ddot{O}\cdot\quad\ddot{O}\cdot}{\diagup\ \diagdown}}
\longleftrightarrow
\overset{\ddot{}\ \ddot{N}}{\underset{:\ddot{O}\cdot\quad\ddot{O}\cdot}{\diagup\ \diagdown}}
$$

The structure of N_2O_4 is thought to be planar with two NO_2 units joined by a N—N bond.

Nitrogen dioxide is produced by the reaction of nitric oxide with oxygen. In the laboratory the compound is conveniently prepared by heating lead nitrate:

$$2\,Pb(NO_3)_2(s) \longrightarrow 2\,PbO(s) + 4\,NO_2(g) + O_2(g)$$

5. The 5+ oxidation state. Dinitrogen pentoxide, N_2O_5, is the acid anhydride of nitric acid; N_2O_5 may be prepared from this acid by dehydration using phosphorus (V) oxide:

$$4\,HNO_3(g) + P_4O_{10}(s) \longrightarrow 4\,HPO_3(s) + 2\,N_2O_5(g)$$

The compound is a colorless, crystalline material that sublimes at 32.5°C. The vapor consists of N_2O_5 molecules which are thought to be planar with the two nitrogen atoms joined through an oxygen atom (O_2NONO_2).

The electronic structure of the molecule may be represented as a resonance hybrid of

and other equivalent structures that have different arrangements of the double bonds. The compound is unstable in the vapor state and decomposes according to the equation

$$2\,N_2O_5(g) \longrightarrow 4\,NO_2(g) + O_2(g)$$

Crystals of N_2O_5 are composed of nitronium, NO_2^+, and nitrate, NO_3^-, ions. The compound is dissociated into these two ions in solutions in anhydrous sulfuric acid, nitric acid, and phosphoric acid. The nitrate ion is triangular planar. The nitronium ion is linear; it is isoelectronic with CO_2 and may be considered as a nitrogen dioxide molecule minus the odd electron. The ion is probably a reaction intermediate in certain reactions of nitric acid in the presence of sulfuric acid (nitrations). Ionic nitronium compounds have been prepared (for example, $NO_2^+ClO_4^-$, $NO_2^+BF_4^-$, $NO_2^+PF_6^-$).

The most important oxyacid of nitrogen is nitric acid, HNO_3, in which nitrogen exhibits an oxidation number of 5+. Commercially, nitric acid is produced by the **Ostwald process.** Nitric oxide from the catalytic oxidation of ammonia is reacted with oxygen to form nitrogen dioxide. This gas, together with excess oxygen, is passed into a tower where it reacts with warm water:

$$3\,NO_2(g) + H_2O \longrightarrow 2\,H^+(aq) + 2\,NO_3^-(aq) + NO(g)$$

The excess oxygen converts the NO into NO_2; this NO_2 then reacts with water as before. In this cyclic manner the nitric oxide is eventually completely converted into nitric acid. The product of the Ostwald process is about 70% HNO_3 and is known as concentrated nitric acid; more concentrated solutions may be prepared from it by distillation.

Pure nitric acid is a colorless liquid that boils at 83°C. It may be prepared in the laboratory by heating sodium nitrate with concentrated sulfuric acid:

$$NaNO_3(s) + H_2SO_4(l) \longrightarrow NaHSO_4(s) + HNO_3(g)$$

This preparation (from Chilean saltpeter) is a minor commercial source of the acid.

The HNO_3 molecule is planar and may be represented as a resonance hybrid:

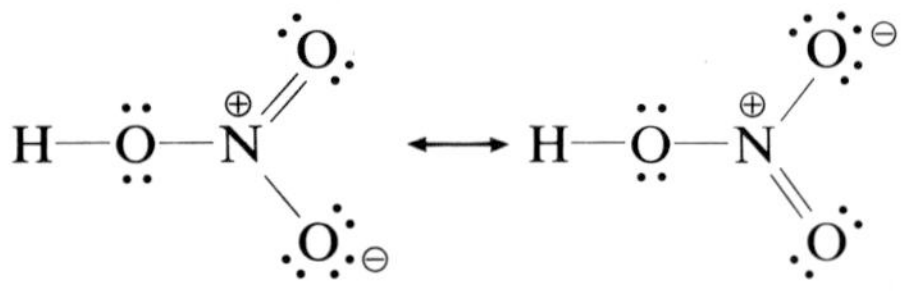

Nitric acid is a strong acid and is almost completely dissociated in aqueous solution. Most salts of nitric acid, which are called nitrates, are very soluble in water. The nitrate ion is triangular planar:

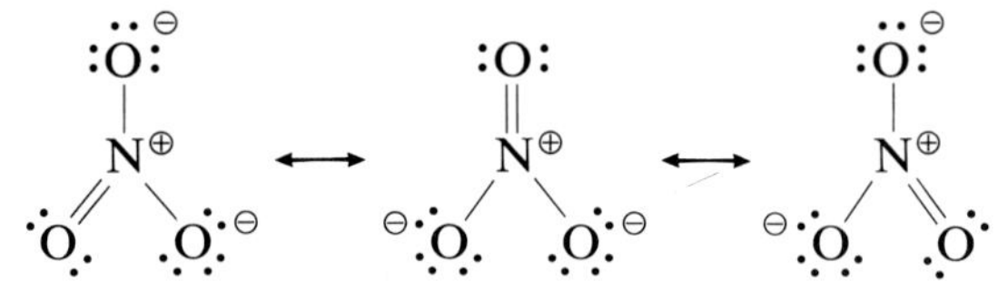

Nitric acid is a powerful oxidizing agent; it oxidizes most nonmetals (generally to oxides or oxyacids of their highest oxidation state) and all metals with the exception of a few of the noble metals. Many unreactive metals, such as silver and copper, that do not react to yield hydrogen with nonoxidizing acids, such as HCl, dissolve in nitric acid.

In nitric acid oxidations, hydrogen is almost never obtained; instead, a variety of nitrogen-containing compounds, in which nitrogen is in a lower oxidation state, is produced (see Table 23.4). The product to which HNO_3 is reduced depends upon the concentration of the acid, the temperature, and the nature of the material being oxidized. A mixture of products is usually obtained, but the principal product in many cases is NO when dilute HNO_3 is employed and the nitrogen(IV) oxides when concentrated HNO_3 is used.

Dilute:

$$3\,Cu(s) + 8\,H^+(aq) + 2\,NO_3^-(aq) \longrightarrow 3\,Cu^{2+}(aq) + 2\,NO(g) + 4\,H_2O$$

Concentrated:

$$Cu(s) + 4\,H^+(aq) + 2\,NO_3^-(aq) \longrightarrow Cu^{2+}(aq) + 2\,NO_2(g) + 2\,H_2O$$

Table 23.4 Standard electrode potentials for reductions of the nitrate ion	
Half Reaction	Standard Electrode Potential ($\mathscr{E}^{\circ}_{red}$)
$e^- + 2\,H^+ + NO_3^- \rightleftharpoons NO_2 + H_2O$	+0.80 V
$8e^- + 10\,H^+ + NO_3^- \rightleftharpoons NH_4^+ + 3\,H_2O$	+0.88 V
$2e^- + 3\,H^+ + NO_3^- \rightleftharpoons HNO_2 + H_2O$	+0.94 V
$3e^- + 4\,H^+ + NO_3^- \rightleftharpoons NO + 2\,H_2O$	+0.96 V
$8e^- + 10\,H^+ + 2\,NO_3^- \rightleftharpoons N_2O + 5\,H_2O$	+1.12 V
$10e^- + 6\,H^+ + 2\,NO_3^- \rightleftharpoons N_2 + 6\,H_2O$	+1.25 V

In some instances, however, strong reducing agents are known to produce almost pure compounds of nitrogen in lower oxidation states. (For example, the reaction of zinc and dilute nitric acid yields NH_3 as the reduction product of HNO_3.)

The half-reactions for the reduction of the nitrate ion in acid solution (see Table 23.4) show the $\mathscr{E}^\circ_{red}$ values to be strongly dependent upon the $H^+(aq)$ concentration. This concentration dependence is experimentally observed— below a concentration of $2\,M$, nitric acid has little more oxidizing power than solutions of HCl of corresponding concentration.

The oxyacid of nitrogen in which nitrogen has an oxidation number of $3+$ is nitrous acid, HNO_2. The compound is unstable toward disproportionation (particularly when warmed):

$$3\,HNO_2(aq) \longrightarrow H^+(aq) + NO_3^-(aq) + 2\,NO(g) + H_2O$$

As a result, pure HNO_2 has never been prepared. Instead, aqueous solutions of the acid are usually prepared by adding a strong acid (such as HCl) to a *cold* aqueous solution of a nitrite (such as $NaNO_2$):

$$H^+(aq) + NO_2^-(aq) \longrightarrow HNO_2(aq)$$

Such solutions are used directly, without attempting to isolate HNO_2, in laboratory procedures that require HNO_2. Aqueous solutions of HNO_2 may also be prepared by adding an equimolar mixture of $NO(g)$ and $NO_2(g)$ to water:

$$NO(g) + NO_2(g) + H_2O \rightleftharpoons 2\,HNO_2(aq)$$

The reaction is exothermic and reversible. Note that the acid anhydride of nitrous acid, N_2O_3, is prepared by the reaction of $NO(g)$ and $NO_2(g)$ at $-20°C$.

The acid is weak and may function as an oxidizing agent or a reducing agent. The electronic structure may be represented as:

Nitrites are prepared by adding $NO(g)$ and $NO_2(g)$ to solutions of alkalies:

$$NO(g) + NO_2(g) + 2\,OH^-(aq) \longrightarrow 2\,NO_2^-(aq) + H_2O$$

The nitrites of the I A metals are formed when the nitrates are heated. They may also be prepared by heating the nitrate with a reducing agent, such as lead, iron or coke:

$$NaNO_3(l) + C(s) \longrightarrow NaNO_2(l) + CO(g)$$

The nitrite ion is angular:

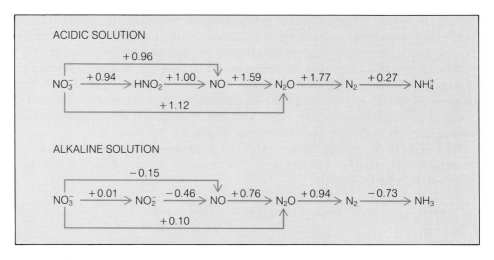

Figure 23.6 Electrode potential diagrams for nitrogen and some of its compounds (values given in volts)

Electrode potential diagrams for N_2 and some of its compounds appear in Figure 23.6. The compounds of nitrogen shown in the diagrams are much stronger oxidizing agents in acidic solution than in alkaline solution. In fact, the NO_3^- ion is a very weak oxidant in alkaline solution. Conversely, a given compound of nitrogen is easier to oxidize in alkaline solution than in acidic solution with the exception of NO_3^- which cannot be oxidized. The potentials also indicate that HNO_2 is unstable toward disproportionation to NO and NO_3^- in acid, whereas in alkaline solution the NO_2^- ion is stable toward such disproportionation.

23.8 Oxides and Oxyacids of Phosphorus

The two important oxides of phosphorus contain phosphorus in oxidation states of $3+$ (P_4O_6) and $5+$ (P_4O_{10}). Phosphorus(III) oxide, P_4O_6, is frequently called phosphorus trioxide, a name which dates from a time when only the empirical formula of the compound, P_2O_3, was known. The compound is a colorless substance that melts at 23.9°C and is the principal product when white phosphorus is burned in a limited supply of air. The structure of the P_4O_6 molecule (shown in Figure 23.7) is based on a P_4 tetrahedron (see Figure 23.1) and has an O atom inserted in each of the six edges of the tetrahedron.

Phosphorus(V) oxide, P_4O_{10}, is often called phosphorus pentoxide (based on the empirical formula, P_2O_5). The oxide is the product of the combustion of white phosphorus in an excess of oxygen. It is a white powder that sublimes at 360°C. The molecular structure of P_4O_{10} (see Figure 23.7) can be derived from the structure of P_4O_6 by adding an extra O atom to each P atom.

Phosphorus(V) oxide has a great affinity for water and is a very effective drying agent. Many different phosphoric acids may be prepared by the addition of water to P_4O_{10}. The most important acid of phosphorus in the $5+$ state, orthophosphoric acid (usually called phosphoric acid) results from the complete hydration of the oxide:

$$P_4O_{10} + 6 H_2O \longrightarrow 4 H_3PO_4$$

Phosphoric acid is obtained commercially by this means or by treating phosphate rock with sulfuric acid:

$$Ca_3(PO_4)_2(s) + 3 H_2SO_4(l) \longrightarrow 2 H_3PO_4(l) + 3 CaSO_4(s)$$

The compound is a colorless solid but is generally sold as an 85% solution. The electronic structure of H_3PO_4 may be represented as

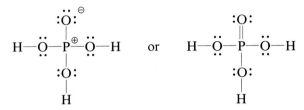

since the P—O bond has double-bond character from $p\pi$-$d\pi$ bonding. The H_3PO_4 molecule and the ions derived from it are tetrahedral (Figure 23.8).

Phosphoric acid is a weak, triprotic acid without effective oxidizing power:

$$H_3PO_4(aq) \rightleftharpoons H^+(aq) + H_2PO_4^-(aq)$$

$$H_2PO_4^-(aq) \rightleftharpoons H^+(aq) + HPO_4^{2-}(aq)$$

$$HPO_4^{2-}(aq) \rightleftharpoons H^+(aq) + PO_4^{3-}(aq)$$

Three series of salts may be derived from H_3PO_4 (the sodium salts, for example, are: NaH_2PO_4, Na_2HPO_4, and Na_3PO_4). The product of a given neutralization depends upon the stoichiometric ratio of H_3PO_4 to alkali.

Phosphates are important ingredients of commercial fertilizers. Phosphate rock is too insoluble in water to be used directly for this purpose. The more soluble calcium dihydrogen phosphate is a satisfactory fertilizer ingredient, however, and may be obtained by treatment of phosphate rock with an acid:

$$Ca_3(PO_4)_2(s) + 2 H_2SO_4(l) \longrightarrow Ca(H_2PO_4)_2(s) + 2 CaSO_4(s)$$

The mixture of $Ca(H_2PO_4)_2$ and $CaSO_4$ is called **superphosphate fertilizer.** A higher yield of the dihydrogen phosphate is obtained if phosphoric acid is employed in the reaction instead of sulfuric acid:

$$Ca_3(PO_4)_2(s) + 4 H_3PO_4(l) \longrightarrow 3 Ca(H_2PO_4)_2(s)$$

Since nitrates are also important constituents of fertilizers, the mixture obtained by treatment of phosphate rock with nitric acid is a highly effective fertilizer:

$$Ca_3(PO_4)_2(s) + 4 HNO_3(l) \longrightarrow Ca(H_2PO_4)_2(s) + 2 Ca(NO_3)_2(s)$$

Condensed phosphoric acids have more than one P atom per molecule. The members of one group of condensed phosphoric acids, the **polyphosphoric acids,** conform to the general formula $H_{n+2}P_nO_{3n+1}$ where n is 2 to 10. Examples are

P_4O_6

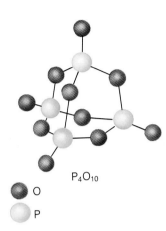

P_4O_{10}

- ● O
- ○ P

Figure 23.7 Structures of P_4O_6 and P_4O_{10}

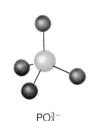

PO_4^{3-}

$P_2O_7^{4-}$

- ● O
- ○ P

Figure 23.8 Structures of PO_4^{3-} and $P_2O_7^{4-}$

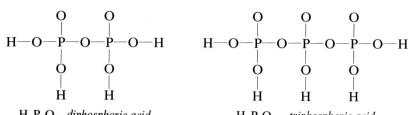

H₄P₂O₇, *diphosphoric acid*   H₅P₃O₁₀, *triphosphoric acid*

The polyphosphoric acids and polyphosphates have chain structures based on PO_4 tetrahedra which are joined through O atoms that are common to adjacent tetrahedra (Figure 21.8).

The metaphosphoric acids constitute another group of condensed phosphoric acids. These compounds have the general formula $H_nP_nO_{3n}$ where n is 3 to 7. Some of the metaphosphoric acids are cyclic. For example:

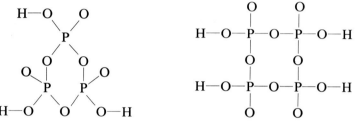

H₃P₃O₉, *trimetaphosphoric acid*   H₄P₄O₁₂, *tetrametaphosphoric acid*

In addition, there are high-molecular-weight, long-chain metaphosphoric acids which are always obtained as complex mixtures that are assigned the formula $(HPO_3)_n$. The molecules of these mixtures are based on long chains of

$$-\underset{\underset{OH}{|}}{\overset{\overset{O}{||}}{P}}-O-$$

units joined in such a way that each P atom is tetrahedrally bonded to four O atoms, but the complete structures are very complicated and involve phosphorus-oxygen units that link two chains together.

The condensed phosphoric acids may be obtained by the controlled addition of water to P_4O_{10}. For example,

$$P_4O_{10}(s) + 4\,H_2O \longrightarrow 2\,H_4P_2O_7(s)$$
diphosphoric acid

$$P_4O_{10}(s) + 2\,H_2O \xrightarrow{0°C} H_4P_4O_{12}(s)$$
tetrametaphosphoric acid

The dehydration of H_3PO_4 by heating also yields condensed acids. For example,

$$2\,H_3PO_4(l) \xrightarrow{215°C} H_4P_2O_7(l) + H_2O(g)$$
diphosphoric acid

$$n\,H_3PO_4(l) \xrightarrow{325°C} (HPO_3)_n(l) + n\,H_2O(g)$$
metaphosphoric acid mixture

On standing in water, all condensed phosphoric acids revert to H_3PO_4.

The oxyacid in which phosphorus has an oxidation number of $3+$ is phosphorous acid, H_3PO_3. Note that the -*ous* ending of the name of the acid differs from the -*us* ending of the name of the element. Phosphorous acid can be made by adding P_4O_6 to cold water,

$$P_4O_6(s) + 6 H_2O \longrightarrow 4 H_3PO_3(aq)$$

Condensed phosphorous acids also exist. Even though the H_3PO_3 molecule contains three hydrogen atoms, phosphorous acid is a weak, *diprotic* acid and is probably better formulated as $H_2(HPO_3)$:

$$H_2(HPO_3)(aq) \rightleftharpoons H^+(aq) + H(HPO_3)^-(aq)$$

$$H(HPO_3)^-(aq) \rightleftharpoons H^+(aq) + HPO_3^{2-}(aq)$$

The sodium salts NaH_2PO_3 and Na_2HPO_3 are known, but it is impossible to prepare Na_3PO_3.

Phosphorus has an oxidation number of $1+$ in hypophosphorous acid, H_3PO_2. Solutions of salts of the acid may be prepared by boiling white phosphorus with solutions of alkalies:

$$P_4(s) + 3 OH^-(aq) + 3 H_2O \longrightarrow PH_3(g) + 3 H_2PO_2^-(aq)$$

The acid, which is a colorless crystalline material, may be obtained by treating a solution of barium hypophosphite with sulfuric acid:

$$Ba^{2+}(aq) + 2 H_2PO_2^-(aq) + 2 H^+(aq) + SO_4^{2-}(aq) \longrightarrow$$
$$BaSO_4(s) + 2 H_3PO_2(aq)$$

removing the precipitated $BaSO_4$ by filtration, and evaporating the solution. Hypophosphorous acid is a weak monoprotic acid. The formula of the compound, therefore, is sometimes written $H(H_2PO_2)$:

$$H(H_2PO_2)(aq) \rightleftharpoons H^+(aq) + H_2PO_2^-(aq)$$

The number of protons released by phosphoric (three), phosphorous (two), and hypophosphorous (one) acids may be explained on the basis of the molecular structures of these compounds:

phosphoric acid

phosphorous acid

hypophosphorous acid

Only the hydrogen atoms bonded to oxygen atoms are acidic; those bonded to phosphorus atoms do not dissociate as $H^+(aq)$ in water. In each of these molecules the P—O bonds have $p\pi$-$d\pi$ double-bond character.

Electrode potential diagrams for phosphorus and some of its compounds appear in Figure 23.9. The most striking feature of the diagrams is that all the

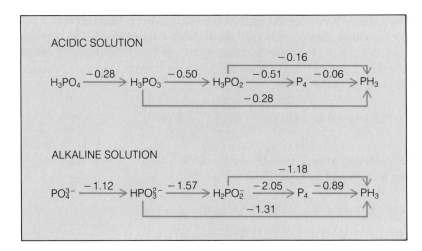

Figure 23.9 Electrode potential diagrams for phosphorus and some of its compounds

potentials are negative—in contrast to the potentials of the nitrogen diagram. Thus none of the substances is a good oxidizing agent, particularly in alkaline solution. Rather, H_3PO_3, H_3PO_2, and the salts of these acids have strong reducing properties; the acids are readily oxidized to H_3PO_4 and the anions are readily oxidized to PO_4^{3-}. With the exception of HPO_3^{2-} in alkaline solution, all species of intermediate oxidation state disproportionate; PH_3 is one of the products of each disproportionation.

23.9 Oxides and Oxyacids of As, Sb, and Bi

When arsenic, antimony, or bismuth is heated in air, a 3+ oxide is formed: As_4O_6, Sb_4O_6, or Bi_2O_3. These oxides serve as an excellent example of the change in metallic character that is observed within a group of elements of the periodic table. The lightest element of a group is the most nonmetallic, and its oxide, therefore, is the most acidic. The heaviest member of a group is the most metallic, and its oxide, therefore, is the most basic.

1. The oxide of the lightest element of the three, As_4O_6, is the most acidic of the three. Aqueous solutions of As_4O_6 are acidic and thought to contain arsenious acid, H_3AsO_3. When As_4O_6 dissolves in aqueous alkalies, arsenites (salts of AsO_3^{3-} and other forms of this anion) form. The oxide is exclusively acidic and will not dissolve in aqueous acids.

2. The oxide of the intermediate element of the three, Sb_4O_6, is amphoteric (it has both acidic and basic properties). The oxide will not dissolve in water, but it will dissolve in alkaline solutions (to give antimonites, salts of SbO_2^-) and also in acidic solutions (to give salts of SbO^+ or Sb^{3+}).

3. The oxide of the heaviest element of the three, Bi_2O_3, is exclusively basic. It will not dissolve in water or in aqueous alkalies, but it will dissolve in acids (to give salts of BiO^+ or Bi^{3+}). Bismuth(III) hydroxide, $Bi(OH)_3$, is the only true hydroxide of the group V A elements. When $OH^-(aq)$ is added to a solution of a Bi^{3+} salt, $Bi(OH)_3$ precipitates.

The molecular structures of the 5+ oxides of arsenic and antimony are not accurately known, and empirical formulas (As_2O_5 and Sb_2O_5) are employed. These oxides are prepared by the action of concentrated HNO_3 on the elements or the 3+ oxides, followed by the dehydration of the products of these reactions ($2 H_3AsO_4 \cdot H_2O$ and $Sb_2O_5 \cdot x H_2O$). The 5+ oxides are exclusively acidic. Orthoarsenic acid (H_3AsO_4, a triprotic acid) forms when As_2O_5 is dissolved in water. Arsenates (salts containing the AsO_4^{3-} ion) or antimonates (salts containing the $Sb(OH)_6^-$ ion) can be prepared by dissolving As_2O_5 or Sb_2O_5 in aqueous alkalies. Sodium antimonate, $NaSb(OH)_6$, is one of the least soluble sodium salts, and its formation is often used as a test for Na^+.

Bismuth(V) oxide has never been prepared in the pure state; it is unstable and readily loses oxygen. The red-brown product obtained by the action of strong oxidizing agents (such as Cl_2, OCl^-, and $S_2O_8^{2-}$) on a suspension of Bi_2O_3 in an alkaline solution is thought to be impure Bi_2O_5.

.10 Industrial Uses of the Group V A Elements

The most important industrial uses of the group V A elements and their compounds are:

1. Nitrogen. The manufacture of ammonia constitutes the principal use of elemental nitrogen. Smaller amounts of N_2 are used in the production of calcium cyanamid ($CaCN_2$). Because N_2 is relatively unreactive, gaseous nitrogen is used as an inert atmosphere in place of air for chemical and metallurgical processes that must be run in the absence of oxygen. The gas is used in food processing and packaging (coffee, for example) to prevent the spoilage and deterioration that is brought about by exposure to atmospheric oxygen. Liquid nitrogen has replaced liquid air in cryogenic work (low-temperature work) to avoid the danger associated with contact between the oxygen of the air and combustible materials. Liquid nitrogen is used for the preparation and transportation of frozen food as well as the transportation of perishable food.

The metal nitrides are high-melting, very hard, chemically unreactive, and electrical conductors, and their uses reflect these properties. They are used in the fabrication of refractory materials (heat-resistant materials), abrasives, grinding and cutting tools, and semiconductors.

The major industrial use of ammonia is the manufacture of nitric acid. Large amounts of ammonia are converted into various ammonium salts, used principally as fertilizers, and ammonia itself is used directly as a fertilizer. The compound is used to make hydrazine (H_2NNH_2, a component of rocket fuels) and urea (H_2NCONH_2, a fertilizer and an ingredient in the manufacture of plastic resins). Ammonia is employed in the Solvay process (for the manufacture of sodium carbonate), in petroleum, paper, rubber, and textile technology, and in the manufacture of dyes, drugs, and explosives.

The major use of nitric acid is in the production of nitrates, which are principally used in fertilizers and explosives. The reactions of nitric acid with certain organic compounds produce a number of commercial explosives (nitroglycerine, nitrocellulose, and trinitrotoluene are examples). Nitric acid has a large number of minor applications; all the nitrogen compounds of commerce are produced from nitric acid and/or ammonia.

2. Phosphorus. Most elemental phosphorus is used to make phosphorus(V) oxide, phosphoric acids, and the salts of these acids. Some phosphorus is used to make matches, warfare agents, and rodent poisons. Metal phosphides, and phosphorus itself, are used as alloying ingredients in the metallurgy of steel and copper. Some phosphides (GaP, BP, AlP, and InP) are semiconductors.

Phosphorus(V) oxide is used to make phosphoric acids, phosphates, and flame-retardant materials. The oxide functions as a catalyst for some reactions, is a desiccant (drying agent), and is used as a dehydrating agent in some organic reactions.

Phosphoric acid is used in the manufacture of fertilizers as well as directly as a fertilizer. The acid is used in phosphatizing, a process that produces a corrosion-resistant coating on iron objects and is applied prior to painting the objects. Phosphoric acid is used in polishing aluminum objects, in electropolishing steel articles, and in several ways in food technology.

Phosphates are used as fertilizers and in food processing, drugs, detergents, scouring powders, and toothpastes. Ammonium phosphate functions as a flame retardant and is used in textile technology.

3. Arsenic, Antimony, and Bismuth. These elements are not used in the amounts nor to the extent that nitrogen and phosphorus are. Arsenic, antimony, and bismuth are used in the production of a wide range of alloys. Either antimony or bismuth is a usual component of the alloys used as type metal. Molten type-metal alloys expand upon freezing. When they are used to make type for printing, the casts obtained have sharp edges. Low-melting alloys of antimony and bismuth are used to make safety plugs for boilers, fire sprinklers, solders, and electrical fuses. Arsenic is used in lead and copper alloys as a hardener and arsenic compounds find use as insecticides, rodent poisons, and weed killers. An important use of all three elements is the fabrication of semiconductors.

Summary

Collectively the group V A elements show a *wide range of properties. Nitrogen* and *phosphorus are nonmetals, arsenic* and *antimony* are *semimetals,* and *bismuth* is a *metal.* In nature, nitrogen is constantly being removed from the atmosphere and returned to it in the *nitrogen cycle.*

The principal industrial preparation of *nitrogen* is the *liquefaction* and *fractionation* of air. *Phosphorus* is obtained commercially by heating a mixture of *phosphate rock, sand,* and *coke* in an *electric furnace. Arsenic, antimony,* and *bismuth* are obtained by the *carbon reduction* of their *oxides* at elevated temperatures.

Nitrogen forms several types of nitrides: *ionic nitrides* (which contain the N^{3-} ion), *interstitial nitrides* (which have N atoms incorporated into the holes of a crystal of a metal), and *covalent nitrides* (in which N atoms are covalently bonded to other atoms to form molecules or network crystals). Phosphorus forms analogous types of *phosphides.*

Large amounts of *ammonia* are commercially prepared by direct reaction of nitrogen and hydrogen (*Haber*

process). Other important hydrides of nitrogen include *hydrazine* (H_2NNH_2) and *hydrazoic acid* (HN_3). *Phosphine* (PH_3) is prepared by the *hydrolysis of phosphides.*

All of the group V A elements form *trihalides* (such as NF_3), and many *pentahalides* (such as PF_5) are known. The *phosphoryl halides* have the general formula POX_3, where X is F, Cl, or Br.

Oxides of nitrogen are known for every oxidation state of nitrogen from $1+$ to $5+$. The most important oxyacid of nitrogen is *nitric acid,* HNO_3, which is prepared commercially from ammonia by the *Ostwald process.* Nitric acid is an important industrial chemical. *Nitrous acid* (HNO_2), which is *unstable toward disproportionation,* is prepared by adding a strong *acid* to a cold aqueous solution of a *nitrite.*

The two important oxides of phosphorus contain phosphorus in an oxidation state of $3+$ (P_4O_6) and $5+$ (P_4O_{10}). *Phosphorus(V) oxide* is the acid anhydride of *phosphoric acid,* H_3PO_4, which is a *weak, triprotic acid.* Phosphates are important ingredients of fertilizers. *Condensed phosphoric acids* have more than one P atom per molecule and include the *polyphosphoric acids* and the *metaphosphoric acids*. *Phosphorus(III) oxide* is the acid anhydride of *phosphorous acid*, H_3PO_3, which is a *weak, diprotic acid*. Phosphorus has an oxidation number of $1+$ in *hypophosphorous acid*, H_3PO_2, which is a *weak,* *monoprotic acid*. Arsenic, antimony, and bismuth form $3+$ *oxides* (As_4O_6, Sb_4O_6, and Bi_2O_3) and $5+$ *oxides* (As_2O_5, Sb_2O_5, and Bi_2O_5). The industrial uses of the group V A elements were reviewed.

Key Terms

Some of the more important terms introduced in this chapter are listed below. Definitions for terms not found in this list may be located in the text by use of the index.

Arc process (Section 23.7)   A nitrogen-fixation process in which nitrogen oxide, NO, is produced by the reaction of nitrogen and oxygen in an electric arc.

Condensed phosphoric acids (Section 23.8)   Acids that have more than one P atom per molecule. The classification includes the **polyphosphoric acids,** which conform to the general formula $H_{n+2}P_nO_{3n+1}$, where n is 2 to 10; and the **metaphosphoric acids,** $H_nP_nO_{3n}$, where n is 3 to 7.

Cyanamid process (Section 23.5)   A nitrogen-fixation in which calcium cyanamid, CaNCN, is prepared from calcium carbide, CaC_2, and nitrogen.

Haber process (Sections 23.2 and 23.5)   A nitrogen-fixation process for the preparation of ammonia from nitrogen and hydrogen.

Isomers (Section 23.6)   Substances that have the same molecular formula but differ in the way the constituent atoms are arranged into a molecule.

Nitrogen cycle (Section 23.2)   A group of natural and artificial processes by which nitrogen is constantly being removed from the atmosphere and returned to it.

Nitrogen fixation (Section 23.2)   A process in which elemental nitrogen is converted into a nitrogen-containing compound.

Ostwald process (Section 23.7)   A commercial process for the manufacture of nitric acid; ammonia is catalytically oxidized to NO, the NO is reacted with O_2 to form NO_2, and the NO_2 is reacted with water to form HNO_3.

Superphosphate fertilizer (Section 23.8)   A mixture of $Ca(H_2PO_4)_2$ and $CaSO_4$ used as a fertilizer and produced by the reaction of sulfuric acid and phosphate rock.

Problems*

Nitrogen

23.1 What is nitrogen fixation? Why is it important?

23.2 Write all the equations that you can for the reactions of elemental nitrogen. Explain the low order of chemical reactivity of N_2.

23.3 The normal boiling point of ethylene diamine, $H_2NCH_2CH_2NH_2$, is $117°C$ and the normal boiling point of propyl amine, $CH_3CH_2CH_2NH_2$, is $49°C$. The molecules, however, are similar in size and in molecular weight. What reason can you give for the difference in boiling point?

23.4 Discuss the preparation, structure, and properties of ammonia. Why is the normal boiling point of NH_3 high in comparison to the normal boiling points of PH_3, AsH_3, and SbH_3?

23.5 Write a chemical equation for the reaction of HNO_3 with **(a)** Cu, **(b)** Zn, **(c)** P_4O_{10}, **(d)** NH_3, **(e)** $Ca(OH)_2$.

23.6 Write chemical equations for the following reactions of ammonia: **(a)** $NH_3(g) + Ag^+(aq)$, **(b)** $NH_3(aq) + H^+(aq)$, **(c)** $NH_3(aq) + H_2O + CO_2(aq)$, **(d)** $NH_3(g) +$ $O_2(g)$, heated, **(e)** $NH_3(g) + O_2(g)$, heated with a Pt catalyst,   **(f)** $NH_3(g) + HCl(g)$,   **(g)** $NH_3(g) + V(s)$, heated, **(h)** $NH_3(l) + Na(s)$.

23.7 Write chemical equations for the thermal decompositions of: **(a)** NH_4NO_3, **(b)** a mixture of NH_4Cl and $NaNO_2$, **(c)** $NaNO_3$, **(d)** $Pb(NO_3)_2$, **(e)** NaN_3.

23.8 Write a chemical equation for the reaction of each of the following with water: **(a)** Li_3N, **(b)** AlN, **(c)** CaNCN, **(d)** NCl_3, **(e)** NO_2, **(f)** N_2O_5.

23.9 Write chemical equations for the reactions of HCl with: **(a)** H_2NNH_2, **(b)** H_2NOH, **(c)** $NaNO_2$, **(d)** NH_3, **(e)** $(NH_4)_2CO_3$.

23.10 Write a series of chemical equations for the preparation of nitric acid starting with N_2 as the source of nitrogen.

23.11 Write balanced chemical equations for the following oxidation-reduction reactions: **(a)** the reaction of NH_3 with OCl^- that produces N_2H_4 and Cl^-, **(b)** the reaction of NO_2 with H_2 in HCl solution that produces $[HONH_3]^+Cl^-$, **(c)** the electrolysis of NH_4F in anhydrous HF(l) that produces NF_3 and H_2.

---

* The appendix contains answers to color-keyed problems.

23.12 List the oxides of nitrogen and write a chemical equation for the preparation of each of them.

23.13 What are the characteristics of the three types of nitrides?

23.14 Boron nitride, BN, exists in two crystalline modifications—one resembling diamond and the other graphite. Describe, using drawings, the structures of these substances.

23.15 Draw Lewis structures (resonance forms if applicable) and describe the geometric shapes of the following: **(a)** NO_2^-, **(b)** NH_3, **(c)** NH_2^-, **(d)** cis-N_2F_2, **(e)** $trans$-N_2F_2.

23.16 Draw Lewis structures (resonance forms if applicable) and describe the geometric shapes of the following: **(a)** NO, **(b)** NO_2, **(c)** HNO_3, **(d)** NO_3^-, **(e)** HN_3.

Phosphorus, Group V A Elements in General

23.17 Discuss how the properties of the elements of group V A and the properties of the compounds derived from them change with increasing atomic number of the V A element.

23.18 Discuss the comparative reactivities, solubilities, and electrical conductivities of the three allotropic forms of phosphorus in terms of molecular structure.

23.19 Write a chemical equation for the reaction of each of the following with water: **(a)** PCl_3, **(b)** PCl_5, **(c)** Ca_3P_2, **(d)** $H_4P_2O_7$, **(e)** P_4O_6, **(f)** P_4O_{10}.

23.20 Write equations for the reactions of water with **(a)** Na_3As, **(b)** As_2O_5, **(c)** Mg_3Bi_2, **(d)** As_4O_6, **(e)** $SbCl_3$, **(f)** PH_4I.

23.21 Draw Lewis structures of orthophosphoric, phosphorous, and hypophosphorous acids. Tell how these structures explain the number of acidic protons per molecule.

23.22 Describe the geometric shapes of: **(a)** PCl_4^+, **(b)** PCl_6^-, **(c)** $SbCl_5$, **(d)** $Sb(OH)_6^-$, **(e)** P_4, **(f)** $POCl_3$, **(g)** P_4O_6, **(h)** P_4O_{10}.

23.23 What is the acid anhydride of **(a)** $H_4P_2O_7$, **(b)** H_3PO_3, **(c)** H_3AsO_4, **(d)** H_3AsO_3.

23.24 Write chemical equations for the preparations of the following acids by the reactions of P_4O_{10} and H_2O. **(a)** H_3PO_4, **(b)** $H_4P_2O_7$, **(c)** $H_5P_3O_{10}$, **(d)** $H_3P_3O_9$, **(e)** $H_4P_4O_{12}$.

23.25 Write chemical equations for the separate reactions of each of the following with H_2O, with aqueous NaOH, and with aqueous HCl: **(a)** P_4O_6, **(b)** Sb_4O_6, **(c)** Bi_2O_3.

23.26 Write chemical equations for the reactions of O_2 with **(a)** As, **(b)** P_4, **(c)** PCl_3, **(d)** NO, **(e)** Sb_2S_3.

Unclassified Problems

23.27 In 1892, Lord Rayleigh observed that the density of nitrogen prepared from air (by removal of H_2, O_2, and CO_2) was different from the density of nitrogen prepared from NH_4Cl and $NaNO_2$. On the basis of this observation, Rayleigh and William Ramsey isolated argon in 1894. Assume that air is 1.00% Ar, 78.00% N_2, and 21.00% O_2 (by volume). How should the densities of the two "nitrogen" samples compare?

23.28 What is the acid anhydride of each of the following? **(a)** $H_2N_2O_2$, **(b)** HNO_2, **(c)** HNO_3.

23.29 Describe the commercial processes used in the manufacture of **(a)** P_4, **(b)** NH_3, **(c)** H_3PO_4, **(d)** HNO_3, **(e)** superphosphate fertilizer, **(f)** As_4.

23.30 Write chemical equations for the reactions of aqueous NaOH with: **(a)** NH_4Cl, **(b)** P_4, **(c)** As_4O_6, **(d)** Sb_2O_5.

THE NONMETALS, PART IV: CARBON, SILICON, BORON, AND THE NOBLE GASES

CHAPTER 24

In this chapter, the nonmetals of group IV A (carbon and silicon), group III A (boron alone), and group 0 (the noble gases) are considered. These discussions complete the survey of the nonmetals that was begun in Chapter 21.

CARBON AND SILICON

Carbon, silicon, germanium, tin, and lead make up group IV A. The compounds of carbon are more numerous than the compounds of any other element with the possible exception of hydrogen. In fact, approximately ten compounds that contain carbon are known for every compound that does not. The chemistry of the compounds of carbon (most of which also contain hydrogen) is the subject of organic chemistry (see Chapter 28).

4.1 Properties of the Group IV A Elements

The transition from nonmetallic character to metallic character with increasing atomic number that is exhibited by the elements of group V A is also evident in the chemistry of the IV A elements. Carbon is strictly a nonmetal (although graphite is an electrical conductor). Silicon is essentially a nonmetal in its chemical behavior, but its electrical and physical properties are those of a semimetal. Germanium is a semimetal; its properties are more metallic than nonmetallic. Tin and lead are truly metallic, although some vestiges of nonmetallic character remain (the oxides and hydroxides of tin and lead, for example, are amphoteric).

Carbon exists in network crystals with the atoms of the crystal held together by covalent bonds (see Section 24.2). A large amount of energy is required to rupture some or all of these bonds in fusion or vaporization. Carbon, therefore, has the highest melting point and boiling point of the family (see Table 24.1). The heaviest member of the family, lead, exists in a typical metallic crystal. The crystalline forms of the intervening members show a transition between the two extremes displayed by carbon and lead, which accounts for the trend in melting points and boiling points of the elements (see Table 24.1).

The crystalline forms of silicon and germanium are similar to that of diamond. The bonds are not so strong as those in diamond, however, and silicon and

Table 24.1 Some properties of the group IV A elements

Property	Carbon[a]	Silicon	Germanium	Tin	Lead
melting point (°C)	3570	1420	959	232	327
boiling point (°C)	4827	2355	2700	2360	1755
atomic radius (pm)	77	117	122	141	154
ionization energy (kJ/mol)					
first	1090	782	782	704	714
second	2350	1570	1530	1400	1450
third	4620	3230	3290	2940	3090
fourth	6220	4350	4390	3800	4060
electronegativity	2.6	1.9	2.0	2.0	2.3

[a] Diamond

germanium are semiconductors (diamond is not). Silicon and germanium may be used to prepare impurity semiconductors (see Section 25.2) which are employed in transistors. Although one modification of tin has a diamond-type structure, the principal form of tin is metallic.

The electronic configurations of the elements are listed in Table 24.2. With the possible exception of carbon, the assumption of a noble-gas configuration through the formation of a $4-$ ion by electron gain is not observed. The electronegativities of the group IV A elements are generally low (see Table 24.1).

The ionization energies of the elements (see Table 24.1) show that the energy required for the removal of all four valence electrons from any given element is extremely high. Consequently, simple $4+$ ions of group IV A elements are unknown. Germanium, tin, and lead appear to be able to form $d^{10}s^2$ ions by the loss of two electrons. Of these $2+$ ions, however, only some of the compounds of Pb^{2+} (such as PbF_2 and $PbCl_2$) are ionic, the compounds of Ge^{2+} and Sn^{2+} are predominantly covalent, and those of Ge^{2+} are relatively unstable toward disproportionation to the $4+$ and 0 states.

In the majority of their compounds, the IV A elements are covalently bonded. Through the formation of four covalent bonds per atom, a IV A element attains the electronic configuration of the noble gas of its period. Compounds of the type AB_4 are tetrahedral. All the IV A elements can form such compounds, but only a few compounds of this type are known for lead (PbF_4, $PbCl_4$, and PbH_4) and they, with the exception of PbF_4, are thermally unstable.

In the case of carbon, the formation of four covalent bonds saturates the valence level. However, the other members of the group have empty d orbitals available in their valence levels and can form species in which the atom of the IV A element exhibits a covalence greater than four. The ions SiF_6^{2-}, $GeCl_6^{2-}$, $SnBr_6^{2-}$, $Sn(OH)_6^{2-}$, $Pb(OH)_6^{2-}$, and $PbCl_6^{2-}$ are octahedral.

The most important way in which carbon differs from the remaining elements of group IV A (as well as from all other elements) is the pronounced ability of carbon to form compounds in which many carbon atoms are bonded to each other in chains or rings. This property, called **catenation,** is exhibited by other elements near carbon in the periodic classification (such as boron, nitrogen, phosphorus, sulfur, oxygen, silicon, germanium, and tin) but to a much lesser extent than carbon; this property of carbon accounts for the large number of organic compounds.

Table 24.2 Electronic configurations of the group IV A elements

Element	Z	1s	2s	2p	3s	3p	3d	4s	4p	4d	4f	5s	5p	5d	6s	6p
C	6	2	2	2												
Si	14	2	2	6	2	2										
Ge	32	2	2	6	2	6	10	2	2							
Sn	50	2	2	6	2	6	10	2	6	10		2	2			
Pb	82	2	2	6	2	6	10	2	6	10	14	2	6	10	2	2

In group IV A the tendency for self-linkage diminishes markedly with increasing atomic number. The hydrides, which have the general formula E_nH_{2n+2} (where E is a group IV A element), illustrate this trend. There appears to be no limit to the number of carbon atoms that can bond together to form chains, and a very large number of hydrocarbons are known. For the other IV A elements, the most complex hydrides that have been prepared are Si_6H_{14}, Ge_9H_{20}, Sn_2H_6, and PbH_4. The carbon-carbon single bond energy (347 kJ/mol) is much greater than that of the silicon-silicon bond (226 kJ/mol), the germanium-germanium bond (188 kJ/mol), or the tin-tin bond (151 kJ/mol).

In addition, the C—C bond is about as strong as any bond that carbon forms with any other element. Typical bond energies for carbon bonds are: C—C, 347 kJ/mol; C—O, 335 kJ/mol; C—H, 414 kJ/mol; and C—Cl, 326 kJ/mol. In comparison, the Si—Si bond is much weaker than the bonds that silicon forms with other elements. Some bond energies for silicon bonds are: Si—Si, 226 kJ/mol; Si—O, 368 kJ/mol; Si—H, 328 kJ/mol; and Si—Cl, 391 kJ/mol. Silicon, therefore, has more of a tendency to bond to other elements than to bond to itself.

Another characteristic of carbon is its pronounced ability to form multiple bonds with itself and with other nonmetals. Groupings such as

$$\text{C}=\text{C} \qquad -\text{C}\equiv\text{C}- \qquad -\text{C}\equiv\text{N} \qquad \text{C}=\text{O} \qquad \text{and} \qquad \text{C}=\text{S}$$

are frequently encountered. No other IV A element uses p orbitals to form π bonds.

Only the truly nonmetallic members of the family, carbon and silicon, are treated in the sections that follow.

.2 Occurrence and Preparation of Carbon and Silicon

Carbon constitutes approximately 0.03% of the earth's crust. In addition, the atmosphere contains 0.03% CO_2 by volume and carbon is also an important constituent of all plant and animal matter. The allotropes of carbon, diamond and graphite, as well as impure forms of the element such as coal occur in nature. In combined form the element occurs in compounds with hydrogen (which are called **hydrocarbons** and are found in natural gas and petroleum), in the atmosphere as CO_2, and in carbonate minerals such as limestone ($CaCO_3$), dolomite ($CaCO_3 \cdot MgCO_3$), siderite ($FeCO_3$) witherite ($BaCO_3$), and malachite ($CuCO_3 \cdot Cu(OH)_2$).

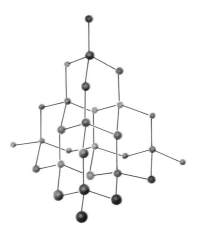

Figure 24.1 Arrangement of atoms in a diamond crystal

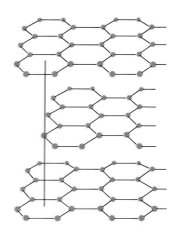

Figure 24.2 Arrangement of atoms in a graphite crystal

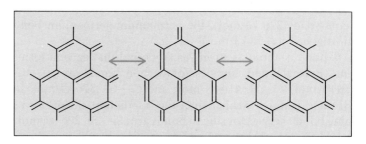

Figure 24.3 Resonance forms for a fragment of a graphite layer

In diamond each carbon atom is bonded through sp^3 hybrid orbitals to four other carbon atoms arranged tetrahedrally (see Figure 24.1). Strong bonds hold this network crystal together. Furthermore, all valence electrons of each carbon atom are paired in bonding orbitals—the valence level of each carbon atom can hold no more than eight electrons. Thus the diamond is extremely hard, high melting, stable, and a nonconductor of electricity.

Whereas the diamond is a colorless, transparent material with a high refractivity, graphite is a soft, black solid with a slight metallic luster. The graphite crystal is composed of layers formed from hexagonal rings of carbon atoms (see Figure 24.2). The layers are held together by relatively weak London forces; the distance from carbon atom to carbon atom in adjacent planes is 335 pm as compared with a distance of 141.5 pm between bonded carbon atoms of a plane. Since it is easy for the layers to slide over one another, graphite is soft and has a slippery feel. It is less dense than diamond.

The nature of the bonding in the layers of the graphite crystal accounts for some of the properties of this substance. Each carbon atom is bonded to three other carbon atoms, and all the bonds are perfectly equivalent. The C—C bond distance in graphite (141.5 pm) compared with that in the diamond (154 pm) suggests that a degree of multiple bonding exists in the former. Graphite may be represented as a resonance hybrid (see Figure 24.3) in which each bond is a $1\frac{1}{3}$ bond.

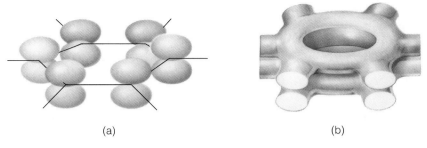

(a)   (b)

Figure 24.4 Schematic representation of the formation of the multicenter bonding system of a graphite fragment (σ bonds are shown as solid lines)

Each C atom in graphite forms σ bonds with three other C atoms through the use of sp^2 hybrid orbitals. The structure, therefore, is planar with the three σ bonds of each atom directed to the corners of an equilateral triangle. This bonding accounts for three of the four valence electrons of each C atom; the fourth, a p electron, is not involved in σ bond formation (see Figure 24.4a).

If only two adjacent atoms in a molecule had this electron arrangement, the additional p electrons would pair to form a localized π bond, and thus the atoms would be joined by a double bond. However, in graphite *each* C atom has an additional p electron, and the resonance forms depict the possibility of forming conventional double bonds in three ways. Since each p orbital overlaps with more than one other p orbital, an extended π bonding system that encompasses the entire structure forms (see Figure 24.4b). The electrons in this π bonding system are not localized between two atoms but are free to move throughout the entire layer. Hence, graphite has a metallic luster and is an electrical conductor. The conductivity is fairly large in a direction parallel to the layers but is small in a direction perpendicular to the planes of the crystal.

Silicon, which constitutes approximately 28% of the earth's crust, is the second most abundant element (oxygen is first). The element does not occur free in nature; rather, it is found as silicon dioxide (sometimes called silica) and in an enormous variety of silicate minerals.

Silicon is prepared by the reduction of silicon dioxide by coke at high temperatures in an electric furnace:

$$SiO_2(l) + 2\,C(s) \longrightarrow Si(l) + 2\,CO(g)$$

If a larger quantity of carbon is employed, silicon carbide (SiC, which is called "carborundum") is produced rather than silicon.

The only known modification of silicon has a structure similar to diamond. Crystalline silicon is a gray, lustrous solid that is a semiconductor. The bonds in silicon are not so strong as those in diamond, and the bonding electrons are not so firmly localized. Evidently, in silicon, electrons may be thermally excited to a conductance band that is energetically close to the valence band (see Section 25.2).

Very pure silicon, which is used in transistors, is prepared by a series of steps. First, impure silicon is reacted with chlorine to produce $SiCl_4$. The tetrachloride, a volatile liquid, is purified by fractional distillation and then reduced by hydrogen to elementary silicon. This product is further purified by zone refining (see Figure 25.10). In this process a short section of one end of a silicon rod is melted, and this melted zone is caused to move slowly along the rod to the other end by the movement of the heater. Pure silicon crystallizes from the melt, and the impurities are swept along in the melted zone to one end of the rod which is subsequently sawed off and discarded.

24.3 Carbides and Silicides

A large number of carbides are known. These compounds may be made by heating the appropriate metal or its oxide with carbon, carbon monoxide, or a hydrocarbon.

The saltlike carbides are made up of metal cations together with anions that contain carbon alone. The I A and II A metals, as well as Cu^+, Ag^+, Au^+, Zn^{2+}, and Cd^{2+}, form carbides that are sometimes called *acetylides* because they contain the *acetylide* ion, C_2^{2-}, which has the structure

$$[:C\equiv C:]^{2-}$$

Upon hydrolysis, acetylides yield acetylene, C_2H_2:

$$H-C\equiv C-H$$

For example,

$$CaC_2(s) + 2\,H_2O \longrightarrow Ca(OH)_2(s) + C_2H_2(g)$$

Calcium carbide is used in the commercial production of calcium cyanamid, CaNCN (see Section 23.5).

Beryllium carbide, Be_2C, and aluminum carbide, Al_4C_3, contain the *methanide* ion, C^{4-}, which upon hydrolysis yields methane, CH_4:

$$H-\overset{\displaystyle H}{\underset{\displaystyle H}{C}}-H$$

For example,

$$Al_4C_3(s) + 12\,H_2O \longrightarrow 4\,Al(OH)_3(s) + 3\,CH_4(g)$$

Interstitial carbides are formed by the transition metals and consist of metallic crystals with carbon atoms in the holes between the metal atoms of the crystal structure (the interstices). Examples of this type of carbide include TiC, TaC, W_2C, VC, and Mo_2C. Because interstitial carbides are very hard, high-melting, and chemically unreactive, they are used in the fabrication of cutting tools. They resemble metals in appearance and electrical conductivity.

The bonding in the covalent carbides SiC and Be_4C is completely covalent. These compounds are very hard, chemically unreactive, and do not melt even at high temperatures. Because of these properties, they are used as abrasives (in the place of industrial diamonds). Silicon carbide (carborundum) is produced by the reaction of SiO_2 and C in an electric furnace. The SiC crystal consists of a diamond-like tetrahedral network formed from alternating Si and C atoms. Boron carbide, B_4C, which is harder than SiC, is made by the reduction of B_2O_3 by carbon in an electric furnace.

Silicon dissolves in almost all molten metals, and in many of these instances, definite compounds called silicides are produced (Mg_2Si, $CaSi_2$, Li_3Si, and $FeSi$ are examples). Although probably none of the silicides is truly ionic, some of them react with water to produce hydrogen-silicon compounds that are called *silicon hydrides* or *silanes*.

The silanes are compounds that conform to the general formula Si_nH_{2n+2}; compounds in which n equals 1 to 6 are known. They resemble structurally the hydrocarbons that conform to the general formula C_nH_{2n+2} and are called the alkanes (see Figure 24.5). Although there is presumably no limit to the number of C atoms that can join together to form alkanes, the number of Si atoms that can bond together to form silanes appears to be limited because of the comparative weakness of the Si—Si bond (see Section 24.1). In addition, the alkanes are much less reactive than the silanes, which are spontaneously flammable in air:

$$2\,Si_2H_6(g) + 7\,O_2(g) \longrightarrow 4\,SiO_2(s) + 6\,H_2O(g)$$

The C—C bonds in the alkanes are all single bonds, but there are hydrocarbons (acetylene for example) which contain multiple bonds between C atoms. Silicon hydrides that contain multiple Si to Si bonds are unknown. The hydrocarbons are discussed in Chapter 28.

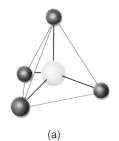

(a)

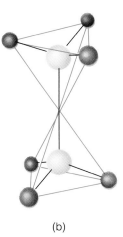

(b)

Figure 24.5 Arrangement of atoms in (a) CH_4 and SiH_4 and (b) C_2H_6 and Si_2H_6. (Larger spheres, C or Si, smaller spheres, H.)

24.4 Oxides and Oxyacids of C and Si

Carbon monoxide is formed by the combustion of carbon in a limited supply of oxygen at high temperatures (approximately $1000°C$):

$$2\,C(s) + O_2(g) \longrightarrow 2\,CO(g)$$

It is also produced by the reaction of CO_2 and C at high temperatures and is a constituent of water gas (see Section 21.2). Carbon monoxide is isoelectronic with nitrogen:

$$^{\ominus}:C\equiv O:^{\oplus}$$

and has two π bonds and one σ bond joining the atoms.

Carbon monoxide burns in air:

$$2\,CO(g) + O_2(g) \longrightarrow 2\,CO_2(g) \qquad \Delta H = -283\ kJ$$

Since this reaction is highly exothermic, carbon monoxide can be used as a fuel. The compound reacts with the halogens in sunlight to produce the carbonyl halides (OCX_2) and with sulfur vapor at high temperatures to form carbonyl sulfide (OCS).

Carbon monoxide is used as a reducing agent in metallurgical processes. At high temperatures, it reacts with many metal oxides to yield the free metal and CO_2:

$$FeO(s) + CO(g) \longrightarrow Fe(l) + CO_2(g)$$

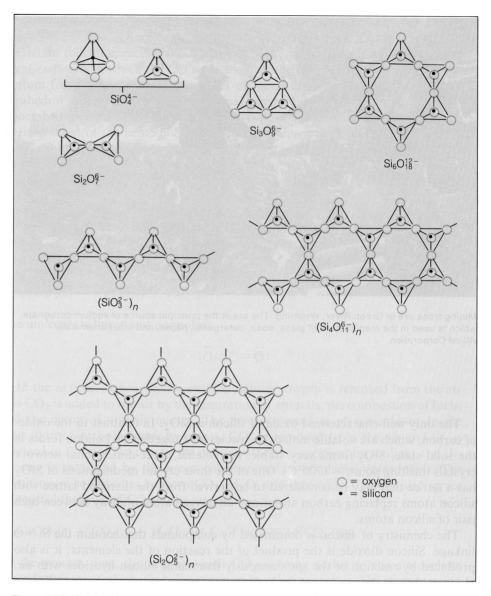

Figure 24.6 Schematic representation of the arrangement of atoms in the silicate ions

The four bond pairs of the Si atom are arranged in a tetrahedral manner.

The other silicate anions contain more than one SiO_4 tetrahedron joined together by bridge oxygen atoms (that is, oxygen atoms that are shared by two tetrahedra). The mineral thortveitite ($Sc_2Si_2O_7$) contains the $Si_2O_7^{6-}$ ion, which is formed by two SiO_4 tetrahedra joined by a single bridge oxygen atom (see Figure 24.6).

$$\left[\ddot{O} - Si - \ddot{O} - Si - \ddot{O} \right]^{6-}$$

Cyclic silicate anions are known in which tetrahedra are joined in a circle with each tetrahedron sharing two bridge oxygen atoms. The $Si_3O_9^{6-}$ anion in bentonite ($BaTiSi_3O_9$) consists of three SiO_4 tetrahedra joined in a circle, and in the $Si_6O_{18}^{12-}$ ion found in beryl ($Be_3Al_2Si_6O_{18}$) there are six (see Figure 24.6).

If three oxygen atoms of each SiO_4 tetrahedron are used as bridge atoms, a sheetlike anion results. The anion $(Si_2O_5^{2-})_n$ occurs in talc, $Mg_3(Si_4O_{10})(OH)_2$. Because of the layer structure, this material feels slippery. Occasionally, aluminum atoms take the places of some of the silicon atoms in certain anions. The hypothetical AlO_4 tetrahedron would have a 5− charge; consequently, such substitutions increase the negative charge of the anion. Muscovite, $KAl_3Si_3O_{10}(OH)_2$ contains a sheetlike alumino-silicate anion with one-fourth of the silicon atoms of the $(Si_2O_5^{2-})_n$ structure replaced by aluminum atoms.

If all four oxygen atoms of each SiO_4 tetrahedron are used as bridge atoms, the three-dimensional, diamond-like network crystal of SiO_2 results. If some of the Si atoms of this SiO_2 structure are replaced with Al atoms, an aluminosilicate anion is produced. Since Si atoms (each with four valence electrons) are replaced by aluminum atoms (each with three valence electrons), additional electrons (which provide the charge on the anion) are required to satisfy the bonding requirements of the structure. Framework aluminosilicates, such as the feldspars and zeolites, are of this type.

Glass is a mixture of silicates made by fusing SiO_2 with metal oxides and carbonates. Common soda-lime glass is made from Na_2CO_3, $CaCO_3$, and SiO_2. Special glasses may be made by the addition of other acidic and basic oxides (such as Al_2O_3, B_2O_3, PbO, and K_2O). Cement is a complex aluminosilicate mixture made from limestone ($CaCO_3$) and clay ($H_4Al_2Si_2O_9$).

24.5 Sulfur, Halogen, and Nitrogen Compounds of Carbon

Carbon disulfide, CS_2, is a volatile liquid prepared commercially by heating carbon and sulfur together in an electric furnace. The structure of the molecule is similar to that of CO_2:

$$:\overset{..}{S}=C=\overset{..}{S}:$$

The compound is a good solvent for nonpolar substances such as waxes and grease. Its use, however, is limited by its toxicity and flammability. It is used commercially in the manufacture of rayon and in the production of carbon tetrachloride.

Carbon tetrachloride is made commercially by heating carbon disulfide with chlorine:

$$CS_2(g) + 3\,Cl_2(g) \longrightarrow CCl_4(g) + S_2Cl_2(g)$$

Carbon tetrachloride, which is a liquid under ordinary conditions, is not flammable and is a good solvent for many nonpolar materials. It was formerly used in fire extinguishers and in dry cleaning, but these uses are now illegal because of the toxicity of the compound.

Carbon tetrafluroride, CF_4, which can be obtained by the fluorination of almost any carbon-containing compound, is a very stable gas. Mixed chlorine-fluorine compounds of carbon (in particular CCl_2F_2) are called the "freons." They are very stable, odorless, nontoxic gases that are used principally as refrigerants.

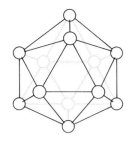

Figure 24.7 Arrangement of atoms in a B_{12} icosahedron

ulexite ($NaCaB_5O_9 \cdot 8H_2O$). Pure, crystalline boron may be obtained by reducing BBr_3 by hydrogen on a hot tungsten filament (at approximately 1500°C):

$$2\,BBr_3(g)\ +\ 3\,H_2(g) \longrightarrow 2\,B(s)\ +\ 6\,HBr(g)$$

The crystals, which condense on the filament, are black with a metallic luster.

The structures of three types of boron crystals have been determined, and at least one other allotrope is known to exist. Groups of 12 B atoms arranged in regular icosahedra (solid figures, each with 20 equilateral-triangular faces) occur in each of these crystalline modifications (see Figure 24.7). In the α-rhombohedral form, each B atom participates not only in the bonding of its icosahedron but also in bonding that icosahedron to others. Ordinary electron-pair bonds cannot account for the large number of boron-boron interactions of the structure since a boron atom has only three electrons and four orbitals in its valence level.

In metallic crystals there are too few valence electrons to form covalent bonds between neighboring metal atoms of the crystal lattice; the electrons belong to the crystal as a whole and serve to bind many nuclei together. Boron, however, is a nonmetal, and the properties of crystalline boron (low electrical conductivity, extreme hardness, brittleness, and high melting point) are more typical of a covalent, network type of crystal than of a metallic crystal.

The bonding in elementary boron has been interpreted as involving **three-center bonds** as well as the more common two-center bonds. In a three-center bond, three atoms are held together by an electron pair in a single molecular orbital. The molecular orbital is assumed to arise from the overlap of three atomic orbitals, one from each of the three bonded atoms. Several types of three-center bonds have been postulated, including the **BBB** bond found in crystalline boron (see Figure 24.8) and a **BHB** bond found in the boron hydrides (see Section 24.8).

24.8 Compounds of Boron

At very high temperatures (about 2000°C) boron reacts with many metals to form borides. These substances are very hard, are chemically stable, and have metallic conductivity. In the crystals of some metallic borides, the boron atoms are interstitial; in others, chains, octahedra, or layers of boron atoms are present. Magnesium boride, MgB_2, unlike the other borides, is readily hydrolyzed to produce a mixture of boron hydrides.

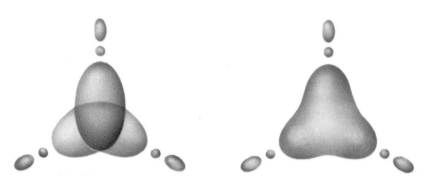

Figure 24.8 Formation of a three-center B—B—B bond

Boron reacts with ammonia or nitrogen at elevated temperatures to produce boron nitride, BN. This material is isoelectronic with carbon and has a crystal structure similar to graphite but with alternating boron and nitrogen atoms. At very high temperatures and pressures this modification of BN is converted to another form that has a diamond-type lattice and is almost as hard as diamond.

At high temperatures, boron reacts with the halogens to yield the trihalides. BF_3 and BCl_3 are gases, BBr_3 is a liquid, and BI_3 is a solid. The molecules of the trihalides are triangular planar:

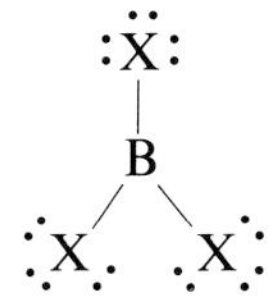

$$:\ddot{X}:$$
$$|$$
$$B$$
$$\diagup \qquad \diagdown$$
$$:\ddot{X}. \qquad .\ddot{X}:$$

Since the boron atom does not have an octet of electrons in each of these molecules, the trihalides react as electron acceptors (Lewis acids):

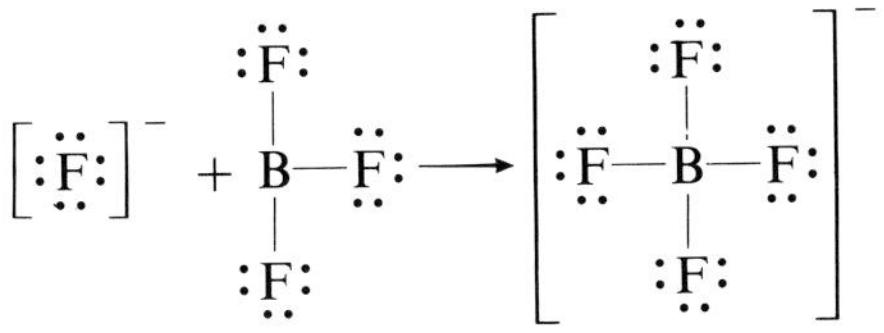

$$\left[:\ddot{F}:\right]^- + \begin{matrix} :\ddot{F}: \\ | \\ B-\ddot{F}: \\ | \\ :\ddot{F}: \end{matrix} \longrightarrow \left[\begin{matrix} :\ddot{F}: \\ | \\ :\ddot{F}-B-\ddot{F}: \\ | \\ :\ddot{F}: \end{matrix}\right]^-$$

$$NH_3 + BF_3 \longrightarrow H_3N{:}BF_3$$

$$H_2O + BF_3 \longrightarrow H_2O{:}BF_3$$

The fluoborate ion, BF_4^-, is tetrahedral.

Many borates occur in nature. Some may be prepared by fusion of metallic oxides with B_2O_3 or boric acid. Hydrated borates may be obtained by crystallization of the solution resulting from the neutralization of boric acid with aqueous alkali. The borate anions may be considered to be built up from triangular BO_3 units, with or without BO_4 tetrahedra, by the sharing of oxygen atoms between units in much the same way as the silicates are constructed. Borax, $Na_2B_4O_5(OH)_4 \cdot 8H_2O$, which can be prepared by neutralizing boric acid with NaOH in aqueous solution, contains the $B_4O_5(OH)_4^{2-}$ ion.

The acidification of an aqueous solution of any borate precipitates orthoboric acid (also called boric acid), H_3BO_3 or $B(OH)_3$, as soft, white crystals. This acid, which may also be prepared by the complete hydration of B_2O_3, has a layer-type crystal lattice in which there is extensive hydrogen bonding between $B(OH)_3$ molecules (see Figure 24.9). The crystal structure of the material accounts for its cleavage into sheets and its slippery feel. Boric acid and the borates are toxic.

Boric acid is a very weak, *monobasic* acid in solution. Its ionization in fairly dilute solution may be represented as

$$B(OH)_3(aq) + H_2O \rightleftharpoons H^+(aq) + B(OH)_4^-(aq)$$

or

$$(H_2O)B(OH)_3(aq) \rightleftharpoons H^+(aq) + B(OH)_4^-(aq)$$

The $B(OH)_4^-$ ion is tetrahedral. In more concentrated solutions, polymeric anions, such as $B_3O_3(OH)_4^-$, exist.

24.9 Properties of the Noble Gases

The properties of the noble gases reflect their very stable electronic configurations. The atoms have no tendency to combine with each other to form molecules; each element occurs as a colorless, monatomic gas. Each noble gas has the highest first ionization potential of any element in its period (see Table 24.5). The low melting points and boiling points of these elements are evidence of the weak nature of the London forces of attraction that operate between the atoms.

With increasing atomic number, the atomic size increases, and the outer electrons become slightly less tightly held. Therefore, the ionization potential decreases regularly from helium to radon. The increasing size of the electron cloud also accounts for the increasing strength of London forces and consequently the increasing boiling point and melting point from helium to radon.

All the noble gases occur in the atmosphere (see Table 24.5), and Ne, Ar, Kr, and Xe are by-products of the fractionation of liquid air. Certain natural gas deposits (located principally in Kansas, Oklahoma, and Texas) contain a higher percentage of helium than is found in air; these deposits constitute the major commercial source of helium. Isotopes of radon are produced in nature by the decay of certain radioactive elements. All the isotopes of radon are themselves radioactive; $^{222}_{86}Rn$ is produced by the radioactive decay of $^{226}_{88}Ra$ and has a half-life of 3.82 days, the longest of any radon isotope.*

Argon is used to fill electric light bulbs. The gas does not react with the hot filament but conducts heat away from it, thus prolonging its life. Argon is also used as an inert atmosphere in welding and high-temperature metallurgical processes. The gas protects the hot metals from air oxidation. Helium is used in lighter-than-air craft (its density is about 14% of the density of air) and in low-temperature work (it has the lowest boiling point of any known substance). Neon signs are made from discharge tubes containing neon gas at a low pressure. Radon has been used as a source of α particles in cancer therapy.

The first chemical reaction of a noble gas to be observed, the reaction of xenon with platinum hexafluoride (PtF_6), was reported by Neil Bartlett in 1962.

Table 24.5	Some properties of the noble gases			
Gas	Melting Point (°C)	Boiling Point (°C)	Ionization Energy (kJ/mol)	Abundance in Atmosphere (Volume %)[a]
He	—[b]	−268.9	2.37×10^3	5×10^{-4}
Ne	−248.6	−245.9	2.08×10^3	2×10^{-3}
Ar	−189.3	−185.8	1.52×10^3	0.93
Kr	−157	−152.9	1.35×10^3	1×10^{-4}
Xe	−112	−107.1	1.17×10^3	8×10^{-6}
Rn	−71	−61.8	1.04×10^3	trace

[a] Dry air at sea level.
[b] −272.2°C at 26 atm pressure.

---

* The half-life of a radioactive isotope is the time that it takes for half of a sample of the isotope to disapppear. See Chapter 27.

A jet of argon being used to stir molten steel. *American Iron and Steel Institute.*

Platinum hexafluoride is a powerful oxidizing agent; it reacts with oxygen to give $[O_2^+][PtF_6^-]$. Since the first ionization energy of *molecular* oxygen,

$$O_2 \longrightarrow O_2^+ + e^- \qquad \Delta H = +1180 \text{ kJ}$$

is close to the first ionization energy of xenon,

$$Xe \longrightarrow Xe^+ + e^- \qquad \Delta H = +1170 \text{ kJ}$$

Bartlett reasoned that xenon should react with PtF_6. Experiment verified this prediction, and a yellow-orange crystalline solid, originally reported as $[Xe]^+ [PtF_6]^-$ and now thought to be $[XeF]^+ [Pt_2 F_{11}]^-$, is produced by the reaction.

The best characterized noble-gas compounds are the xenon fluorides: XeF_2, XeF_4, and XeF_6. Each of these compounds may be prepared by direct reaction of Xe and F_2. The choice of reaction conditions, particularly the proportion of Xe to F_2 used, determines which fluoride is obtained. The xenon fluorides are colorless, crystalline solids (see Table 24.6).

Table 24.6	Properties of some compounds of xenon		
Oxidation State	Compound	Form	Melting Point (°C)
2+	XeF_2	colorless crystals	129
4+	XeF_4	colorless crystals	117
6+	XeF_6	colorless crystals	50
	$XeOF_4$	colorless liquid	−46
	XeO_3	colorless crystals	–
8+	XeO_4	colorless gas	–
	$Na_4XeO_6 \cdot 8H_2O$	colorless crystals	–

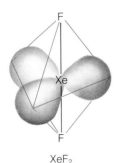

XeF$_2$

Figure 24.11 Structure of XeF$_2$

Oxygen-containing compounds of xenon are produced by reactions of the xenon fluorides with water. Partial hydrolysis of XeF$_6$ yields XeOF$_4$, a colorless liquid:

$$XeF_6(s) + H_2O \longrightarrow XeOF_4(l) + 2\,HF(g)$$

Complete hydrolysis of XeF$_6$ or hydrolysis of XeOF$_4$ produces a solution that yields solid XeO$_3$ upon evaporation:

$$XeF_6(s) + 3\,H_2O \longrightarrow XeO_3(aq) + 6\,HF(aq)$$

$$XeOF_4(l) + 2\,H_2O \longrightarrow XeO_3(aq) + 4\,HF(aq)$$

The compounds of xenon in its highest oxidation state, 8+, include XeO$_4$ and the perxenates (compounds of the XeO$_6^{4-}$ ion). Pure perxenic acid, H$_4$XeO$_6$, has never been prepared. Salts of this acid may be made by passing ozone gas through alkaline solutions of XeO$_3$:

$$12\,OH^-(aq) + 3\,XeO_3(aq) + O_3(g) \longrightarrow 3\,XeO_6^{4-}(aq) + 6\,H_2O$$

The acid anhydride of perxenic acid, XeO$_4$, is made by reacting barium perxenate, Ba$_2$XeO$_6$, with concentrated sulfuric acid at $-5°C$:

$$Ba_2XeO_6(s) + H_2SO_4(l) \longrightarrow 2\,BaSO_4(s) + XeO_4(g) + 2\,H_2O$$

The order of the group 0 elements according to decreasing reactivity (increasing ionization energy; see Table 24.5) should be: Rn > Xe > Kr > Ar > Ne > He. Thus, radon should be the most reactive noble gas. There is evidence that Rn reacts with fluorine. The radioactive disintegration of Rn isotopes, however, makes the chemistry of Rn difficult to assess. Krypton is not so reactive as Xe, but a few compounds of Kr have been prepared. The most important of these compounds is KrF$_2$, which is made by subjecting a mixture of Kr and F$_2$ to an electric discharge. No compounds of He, Ne, or Ar have been prepared as yet.

The structures of most xenon compounds have been determined and may be interpreted by a valence bond approach (see Figures 24.11 and 24.12).

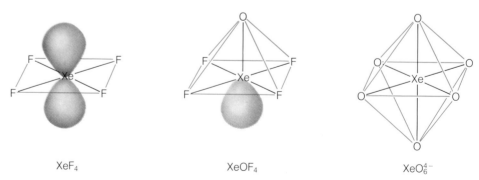

XeF$_4$ XeOF$_4$ XeO$_6^{4-}$

Figure 24.12 Structures of XeF$_4$, XeOF$_4$, and XeO$_6^{4-}$

Summary

Of all the elements of group IV A, *carbon* and *silicon* alone are *nonmetals* (although the *physical properties* of silicon are more like those of a *semimetal*). *Carbon* forms an unusually *large number of compounds* because of the ability of carbon to *catenate* as well as to *form multiple bonds*. The crystal structures of *diamond* and *graphite* account for the properties of these *allotropes of carbon*. The only known modification of elemental *silicon* has a *structure similar to* that of *diamond*.

A large number of *carbides* and *silicides* are known. *Silanes* (general formula Si_nH_{2n+2}) structurally resemble the lower members of the group of hydrocarbons called *alkanes* (general formula, C_nH_{2n+2}).

The two most important oxides of carbon are *carbon dioxide* (the acid anhydride of *carbonic acid*) and *carbon monoxide*. Whereas CO_2 and CO are volatile molecular species, the only well-characterized oxide of silicon, *silicon dioxide*, exists in the form of a *three-dimensional network crystal*. The chemistry of silicon is dominated by compounds that contain the *Si-O linkage*. A large number of *silicates* of various types occur in nature. Other important inorganic compounds of carbon include *carbon disulfide*, the *carbon halides, cyanides*, and *cyanates*.

Boron is the only group III A element that is a *nonmetal*. Boron forms borides with many metals, BN with nitrogen, and boron trihalides with the halogens. Many borates occur in nature. The oxide B_2O_3 is the acid anhydride of orthoboric acid, H_3BO_3, which is a very weak, monobasic acid in aqueous solution. Heating orthoboric acid yields metaboric acid, HBO_2. Boron forms several types of hydrides, called boranes. The structures of the boranes, as well as elemental boron itself, involve three-center bonds.

The noble gases have a very low order of chemical reactivity, reflecting the stability of their electronic structures. The best characterized noble-gas compounds are the xenon fluorides (XeF_2, XeF_4, and XeF_6), the xenon oxides (XeO_3 and XeO_4), xenon oxyfluoride ($XeOF_4$), and the perxenates (compounds containing the XeO_6^{4-} ion). Whereas a few compounds of krypton have been prepared (KrF_2, for example), no compounds of He, Ne, or Ar have been prepared as yet.

Key Terms

Some of the more important terms introduced in this chapter are listed below. Definitions for terms not included in this list may be located in the text by use of the index.

Boranes (Section 24.8) Compounds that contain only boron and hydrogen.

Carbonyl (Section 24.4) A compound that contains a carbonyl group (CO) such as carbonyl sulfide (COS), the carbonyl halides (COX_2), and the metal carbonyls.

Catenation (Section 24.1) The formation of chains or rings by atoms of the same element bonded to each other.

Noble gases (Section 24.9) The elements of group 0: He, Ne, Ar, Kr, Xe, and Rn.

Organic chemistry (Section 24.1) The chemistry of the hydrocarbons (compounds of carbon and hydrogen) and their derivatives.

Oxygen–carbon-dioxide cycle (Section 24.4) A group of natural and artificial processes by which O_2 and CO_2 are constantly being removed from the atmosphere and returned to it.

Photosynthesis (Section 24.4) The process by which plants make carbohydrates; CO_2 is removed from the air and O_2 is returned to it; the energy for the process is supplied by sunlight.

Silanes (Section 24.3) Compounds that contain only silicon and hydrogen.

Three-center bond (Section 24.7) A bond in which three atoms are bonded together by an electron pair in a single molecular orbital; found in boron and the hydrides of boron.

Problems*

Carbon and Silicon

24.1 Discuss the ways in which the chemistry of carbon differs from the chemistry of the other elements of group IV A.

24.2 What explanations may be offered for the fact that carbon has a greater tendency toward catenation than any other element?

24.3 Describe the three types of carbides.

---

* The appendix contains answers to color-keyed problems.

24.4 Describe the crystal structure of **(a)** diamond, **(b)** graphite, **(c)** SiC.

24.5 Name the following: **(a)** HCN(g), **(b)** HCN(aq), **(c)** KCN, **(d)** KOCN, **(e)** KSCN, **(f)** $Fe(CO)_5$, **(g)** $NaHCO_3$, **(h)** Na_2CO_3.

24.6 Draw Lewis structures for: **(a)** N_2, **(b)** CO, **(c)** CN^-, **(d)** OCN^-, **(e)** CS_2, **(f)** C_2H_2, **(g)** CCl_4, **(h)** CO_3^{2-}.

24.7 Write chemical equations for the reactions of CO(g) with: **(a)** Cl_2, **(b)** S, **(c)** O_2, **(d)** FeO, **(e)** Ni.

24.8 Write chemical equations for the reactions of H_2O with: **(a)** CaC_2, **(b)** Al_4C_3, **(c)** CO_2, **(d)** $CaCO_3$ and CO_2.

24.9 In alkaline solution, $\mathscr{E}°$ for the reduction of OCN^- to CN^- is -0.970 V and $\mathscr{E}°$ for the reduction of PbO to Pb is -0.580 V. Write partial equations for these half-reactions. Will PbO oxidize CN^- to OCN^-? If so, write the chemical equation for the reaction.

24.10 Write chemical equations for the following reactions: **(a)** $CaCO_3$(s) and SiO_2(s) (heated), **(b)** $CaCO_3$(s) (heated), **(c)** $CaCO_3$(s) and H^+(aq).

Boron

24.11 Describe the structure of B_2H_6.

24.12 Write equations to show how orthoboric acid ionizes in aqueous solution.

24.13 Write chemical equations for the following reactions: **(a)** B_2O_3 and Mg (heated), **(b)** BBr_3 and H_2 (heated), **(c)** B and N_2 (heated), **(d)** B and Mg (heated), **(e)** BF_3 and F^-.

24.14 Write chemical equations for the following reactions: **(a)** B_2O_3 and H_2O, **(b)** $B(OH)_3$ and OH^-(aq), **(c)** $B(OH)_3$ (mild heating), **(d)** $B(OH)_3$ (strong heating), **(e)** LiH and B_2H_6.

24.15 What is a three-center bond?

24.16 Describe the crystal structure of orthoboric acid. How does this crystal structure account for some of the properties of the substance?

24.17 A boron hydride is 81.2% boron. The mass of a 25.0 mL sample of the gas (measured at STP) is 0.0594 g. What is the molecular formula of the compound?

24.18 A gaseous compound consists of 22.2% B and 77.8% F. The mass of a 280. mL sample of the gas (measured at STP) is 1.22 g. What is the molecular formula of the compound?

The Noble Gases

24.19 Write equations showing how to prepare: **(a)** XeF_2, **(b)** XeF_4, **(c)** XeF_6, **(d)** $XeOF_4$, **(e)** XeO_3.

24.20 Draw Lewis structures for the following and predict the geometric configuration of each: **(a)** XeF_2, **(b)** XeF_4, **(c)** XeO_3, **(d)** $XeOF_4$, **(e)** XeO_4, **(f)** XeO_6^{4-}.

24.21 Argon is used to fill electric light bulbs and to provide an atmosphere under which high-temperature welding is carried out. Justify these uses.

24.22 What reasons can you give for the fact that the only binary noble gas compounds known are the fluorides and oxides of Kr, Xe, and Rn.

24.23 **(a)** Use the ion-electron method to write a chemical equation for the oxidation, in acid solution, of Mn^{2+}(aq) to MnO_4^-(aq) by XeO_3(aq), which is reduced to Xe(g). **(b)** In a reaction between XeO_3 and Mn^{2+} which occurs in 200 mL of solution, the Xe(g) produced occupied a volume of 448 mL (measured at STP). What is the molarity of the MnO_4^- solution resulting from the reaction? **(c)** What mass of XeO_3 was consumed by the reaction?

24.24 **(a)** Use the ion-electron method to write a chemical equation for the oxidation, in acid solution, of Cr^{3+}(aq) to $Cr_2O_7^{2-}$ by XeF_2(aq), which is converted into Xe(g) and F^-(aq). **(b)** In a reaction between XeF_2 and Cr^{3+} which occurs in 125 mL of solution, the Xe(g) produced occupied a volume of 504 mL (measured at STP). What is the molarity of the $Cr_2O_7^{2-}$ solution resulting from the reaction? **(c)** What mass of XeF_2 was consumed by the reaction?

24.25 Under the same conditions of temperature and pressure, a given volume of helium has a mass that is 1.986 times the mass of the same volume of hydrogen. Yet, the lifting power of a balloon filled with He(g) is approximately 92% of the lifting power of the balloon when filled with H_2(g). Explain this observation. The average molecular weight of air is 28.94.

24.26 What reason can you give for the fact that the boiling point of helium is lower than the boiling point of hydrogen?

Unclassified Problems

24.27 Compare the physical and chemical properties of CO_2, SiO_2, B_2O_3, and XeO_3.

24.28 Compare the compounds CF_4, SiF_4, and BF_3 with regard to their physical state, and reactivity toward H_2O and toward F^-. What reason can you give for the difference in reactivity?

24.29 Interpret the reactions between SiF_4 and F^- and between BF_3 and F^- in terms of the Lewis theory.

24.30 Magnesium forms two carbides: MgC_2 and Mg_2C_3. Upon treatment with H_2O, MgC_2(s) yields $Mg(OH)_2$(s) and C_2H_2(g), and Mg_2C_3(s) yields $Mg(OH)_2$(s) and C_3H_4(g). The gaseous product of the first reaction is acetylene, which has the structure $H—C\equiv C—H$; the gaseous product of the second reaction is propyne, which has the structure $CH_3—C\equiv C—H$. **(a)** Write chemical equations for the hydrolysis of the two carbides of magnesium. **(b)** The hydrolysis of a 0.973 g sample of a magnesium carbide yields 282 mL of a gaseous hydrocarbon at 25°C and 1.000 atm. What is the formula of the carbide that has been hydrolyzed?

METALS AND METALLURGY

CHAPTER 25

Several physical and chemical properties that are typical of metals are used to define this classification of elements—although the extent of each of these properties varies widely from metal to metal. Metals have superior electrical and thermal conductivities, characteristic luster, and the ability to be deformed under stress without cleaving. The tendency of these elements toward the formation of cations through electron loss and their formation of basic oxides are among the chemical characteristics of metals.

More than three-quarters of all known elements are metals. The stepped line that appears in the periodic table marks an approximate division between metals and nonmetals—the nonmetals appear in the upper right corner of the table. The division, however, is slightly arbitrary; elements that appear close to the line have intermediate properties.

25.1 The Metallic Bond

Metals have comparatively low ionization energies and electronegativities. Consequently, the outer electrons of metal atoms are relatively loosely held. In a metallic crystal, positive ions (which consist of metal atoms minus the outer electrons) occupy positions in the crystal structure. The outer electrons move freely throughout this structure and bond the crystal together.

The **band theory** describes this bonding in terms of molecular orbitals that extend over the entire crystal. A general idea of the band model for the lithium crystal can be developed in the following way. In the Li_2 molecule, the $2s$ orbital of one Li atom overlaps the $2s$ orbital of another, and $\sigma 2s$ and $\sigma^* 2s$ molecular orbitals are formed (see Section 9.4 and Table 9.3). In the ground state of the Li_2 molecule, only the $\sigma 2s$ molecular orbital is occupied by electrons. Nevertheless, the combination of *two* atomic orbitals produces *two* molecular orbitals even if one of them is unoccupied.

The $2s$ orbitals of two separate Li atoms have the same orbital energy and are said to be **degenerate.** When two Li atoms are brought together to form the Li_2 molecule, the degeneracy is split. The $\sigma 2s$ molecular orbital has a lower orbital energy than the $\sigma^* 2s$ has.

Now consider that a number of Li atoms are brought together into the arrangement of the Li crystal. The $2s$ orbitals of these Li atoms overlap and produce delocalized molecular orbitals that extend throughout the entire structure. *The number of molecular orbitals produced equals the number of atomic orbitals used to produce them.*

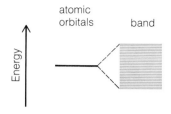

Figure 25.1 Formation of a band by the interaction of the 2s orbitals of lithium

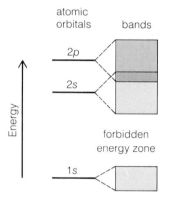

Figure 25.2 Overlap of the 2s and 2p-bands in metallic lithium

In even a very small sample of Li metal there is an extremely large number of atoms. Since each Li atom contributes one 2s orbital toward the formation of the delocalized molecular orbitals, an extremely large number of molecular orbitals are formed. The 2s atomic orbitals of the isolated Li atoms are degenerate, but the molecular orbitals of the Li crystal are not (see Figure 25.1). The molecular orbitals, taken together, make up what is called a **band**; each orbital constitutes an **energy level** within the band. These levels are very closely spaced in terms of energy and for all practical purposes form a continuous energy band. Even at low temperatures, electrons have enough energy to move from level to level within a band.

The 2s electron in a Li atom (electron configuration, $1s^2\ 2s^1$) is a valence electron, and the 2s-band of Li (see Figure 25.1) is sometimes called the **valence band.** Each Li atom has *one* electron in *one* 2s orbital. If N Li atoms formed a 2s-band, the band would contain N electrons and consist of N molecular orbitals. A molecular orbital, like any orbital, can hold *two* electrons with opposed spins. The 2s-band, therefore, can hold a maximum of $2N$ electrons. Since it contains only N electrons, the valence band of the Li crystal is one-half occupied. The band derived from the 2p orbitals of Li must also be considered, however.

In an isolated Li atom, there are three empty 2p orbitals that are close in energy to the 2s orbital. In metallic Li, a 2p-band, derived from these 2p orbitals, overlaps the 2s-band (see Figure 25.2). A 2p-band formed by N Li atoms would consist of $3N$ energy levels (since each Li atom has three 2p orbitals) and would be empty. This 2p-band is sometimes called the **conduction band** since electrons can move freely throughout it and thereby conduct electricity. In the case of the Li crystal, the 2s- and 2p-bands overlap so that the two bands can be considered to form one.

The shading in Figure 25.2 is designed to show band overlap, not electron occupancy. In fact, the combined bands formed by N Li atoms would consist of $4N$ energy levels (with a maximum capacity of $8N$ electrons) and would contain N electrons. The combined band, therefore, would be one-eighth filled.

If band overlap did not occur, beryllium would not conduct electricity. The electron configuration of Be is $1s^2\ 2s^2$, and consequently the 2s-band (the valence band) of Be is filled. The 2s-band of Be, however, is overlapped by an empty 2p-band (a conduction band). Beryllium is a metallic conductor because the combined band, resulting from the overlap of the 2s- and 2p-bands, is only one-quarter filled.

Figure 25.2 also shows a narrow band produced by the interaction of the 1s orbitals of Li. Since the 1s orbital is filled in the Li atom, the 1s-band is filled. These electrons do not appreciably affect the bonding. They are closely held by the Li nuclei and form a part of the positive ions that make up the crystal structure. The 1s-band is not overlapped by another band in the Li crystal. Instead, it is separated from the 2s-2p-band by a **forbidden energy zone.** No electron in Li has an energy that would place it in this forbidden zone. Electrons in the filled 1s-band do not have energies high enough to traverse the forbidden energy zone and enter the 2s-2p-band where they could contribute to the bonding and conductivity of Li.

In a metallic crystal, therefore, the valence electrons are held by all the atoms of the crystal and are highly mobile. The valence band, which may be only partially filled, is overlapped by an unfilled conduction band. Transference of an electron to a higher level within a band requires the addition of very little energy since the levels are close together. Thus the valence electrons of a metal can move to higher levels by absorbing light of a wide range of wavelengths. When these electrons fall to lower energy levels, light is radiated. The lustrous appearance of metals is caused by these electron transitions.

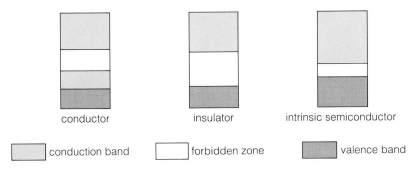

conductor   insulator   intrinsic semiconductor

▨ conduction band   ☐ forbidden zone   ▩ valence band

Figure 25.3   Energy-level band diagrams for three types of solids

The freely moving electrons of metallic crystals account for the high thermal and electrical conductivities of metals. Valence electrons of a metal absorb heat as kinetic energy and transfer it rapidly to all parts of the metal since their motion is relatively unrestricted.

Energy-level diagrams for conductors, insulators, and intrinsic semiconductors are shown in Figure 25.3. In the diagram for a conductor (such as Li), the valence band (from the 2s orbitals) is overlapped by an empty conduction band (from the 2p orbitals). These two bands are separated from an empty, upper conduction band (derived from orbitals of the third shell) by a forbidden energy zone. Electrical conduction takes place by means of the motion of electrons within the lower conduction band. There is no need to supply the energy required to bridge the forbidden zone and use the upper conduction band.

The diagram for the insulator, however, shows a completely filled valence band that is widely separated from a conduction band by a forbidden energy zone. Electron motion, and hence electrical conductivity, is possible only if energy is provided to promote electrons across the comparatively large forbidden zone to the conduction band. Normally such promotion does not occur, and hence the conductivities of insulators are extremely low.

An intrinsic semiconductor is a material that has a low electrical conductivity that is intermediate between that of a conductor and an insulator. This conductivity increases markedly with increasing temperature. For a semiconductor, the forbidden zone is sufficiently narrow that electrons can be promoted from the valence band to the conduction band by heat (see Figure 25.3). The vacancies left by the removal of electrons from the valence band permit the electrons remaining in the valence band to move under the influence of an electric field. Conduction takes place through the motion of electrons in the valence band as well as in the conduction band.

The electrical conductivity of a metal is not dependent upon thermal excitation of electrons. Whereas the conductivity of an intrinsic semiconductor increases with increasing temperature, the electrical conductivity of a metal decreases with increasing temperature. Presumably the increased temperature causes increased vibration of the metal ions of the crystal lattice which, in turn, impedes the flow of conduction electrons.

25.2 Semiconductors

Pure silicon and germanium function as intrinsic semiconductors. Both these elements crystallize in the diamond-type network structure in which each atom

A semiconductor chip of silicon compared to drops of water. *Intel Corporation.*

is bonded to four other atoms (see Figure 11.12). At room temperature the conductivity of either silicon or germanium is extremely low, since the electrons are fixed by the bonding of the crystal. At higher temperatures, however, the crystal bonding begins to break down; electrons are freed and are able to move through the structure, thereby causing the conductivity to increase.

The addition of small traces of certain impurities to either silicon or germanium enhances the conductivity of these materials and produces what are called **extrinsic** (or **impurity**) **semiconductors.** For example, if boron is added to pure silicon at the rate of one B atom per million Si atoms, the conductivity is increased by a factor of approximately one hundred thousand (from $4 \times 10^{-6}/(\Omega \cdot cm)$ to $0.8/(\Omega \cdot cm)$ at room temperature). Each Si atom has four valence electrons that are used in the bonding of the network lattice. A boron atom, however, has only three valence electrons. Hence, a B atom that assumes a position of a Si atom in the crystal can form only three of the four bonds required for a perfect lattice, and an electron vacancy (or hole) is introduced. An electron from a nearby bond can move into this vacancy, thus completing the four bonds on the B atom but, at the same time, leaving a vacancy at the original site of the electron. In this way electrons move through the structure, and the holes move in a direction opposite to that of the conduction electrons.

This type of extrinsic semiconductor, in which holes enable electron motion, is called a *p*-type semiconductor; the *p* stands for positive. The term is somewhat misleading, however, since the crystal, which is formed entirely from neutral atoms, is electrically neutral. The structure is electron deficient only with regard to the covalent bonding requirements of the lattice; it never has an excess of positive charge.

In addition to boron, other III A elements (Al, Ga, or In) can be added in small amounts to pure silicon or germanium to produce *p*-type semiconductors.

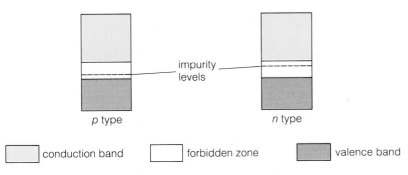

Figure 25.4 Energy-level band diagrams for extrinsic semiconductors

Impurities that owe their effect to their ability to accept electrons by means of the holes they produce in the crystal lattice are known as **acceptor impurities.**

The energy-level band diagram for *p*-type semiconductors is shown in Figure 25.4. Electron vacancies are responsible for the addition of *empty* impurity levels, just above the filled valence band, to a diagram that otherwise would be characteristic of an intrinsic semiconductor. Promotion of electrons from the valence band to the unoccupied impurity levels requires the addition of comparatively little energy, and conduction takes place in this manner.

Traces of group V A elements (P, As, Sb, or Bi) when added to silicon or germanium produce a second type of extrinsic semiconductor known as an *n*-type semiconductor; the *n* stands for negative. In this instance, each impurity atom has five valence electrons—one more than required by the bonding of the host crystal. The extra electron can move through the structure and function as a conduction electron. Impurities of this type are known as **donor impurities,** since they provide conduction electrons. The *n*-type semiconductor is negative only in the peculiar sense that more electrons are present than are required by the bonding scheme of the crystal; the substance is electrically neutral.

The energy-level diagram for the *n*-type semiconductor is shown in Figure 25.4. *Filled* impurity levels are introduced just below the empty conduction band by the addition of donor impurities. The electrons from these levels are easily excited into the conduction band by heating, and conduction occurs by this means. Semiconductors find use in photocells and transistors.

5.3 Physical Properties of Metals

The densities of metals show a wide variation. Of all the *solid* elements, lithium has the lowest density and osmium has the highest. The majority of metals, however, have relatively high densities in comparison with the densities of the solid nonmetals. The metals of groups I A and II A, which are called the *light metals*, are notable exceptions to this generalization. The close-packed arrangement of the atoms of most metallic crystals helps to explain the relatively high densities of most metals.

In Figure 25.5, the densities of the metals of the fourth, fifth, and sixth periods are plotted against group number. Each curve reaches a maximum approximately at group VIII (Fe, Ru, and Os). This trend reflects the trend in atomic radius.

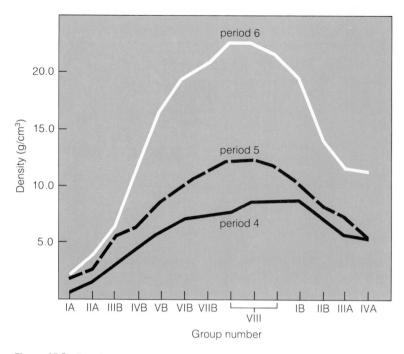

Figure 25.5 Densities of the metals of the fourth, fifth, and sixth periods

The atomic radii of the metals of each period reach a *minimum* at this point and the densities reach a maximum. The I A metals have the largest atomic radii and the smallest atomic masses of their periods; these factors coupled with their crystal structure give them comparatively low densities.

The melting points and the boiling points of the nonmetals show extreme variation—from the very low values of the gaseous elements (such as hydrogen and helium) to the extremely high values of the elements that crystallize in covalent network structures (such as the diamond and boron). There is considerable variation in the melting and boiling points of the metals, but, of course, the low values typical of the gaseous nonmetals are not observed. In general, most metals have comparatively high melting and boiling points.

In Figure 25.6, the melting points of the metals of the fourth, fifth, and sixth periods are plotted against group number. The striking feature of the curves is the maximum that appears at approximately the center of each one. Curves for the boiling point, enthalpy of fusion, enthalpy of vaporization, and hardness have approximately the same appearance. For a given period, the strength of the metallic bonding must therefore reach a maximum around the center of the transition series.

The strength of the metallic bonding is, of course, related to the number of delocalized electrons per atom used in the bonding. If we count only the ns, np, and *unpaired* $(n - 1)d$ electrons of a metal as bonding electrons, we get an order that approximates that of the properties we are considering. This analysis is a decided oversimplification. Other factors, such as atomic radius, nuclear charge, and crystal form, are involved.

The deformability, luster, thermal conductivity, and electrical conductivity are the properties most characteristic of metallic bonding and the metallic state. High electrical conductivity, which is measured in units of $1/(\Omega \cdot \text{cm})$, is character-

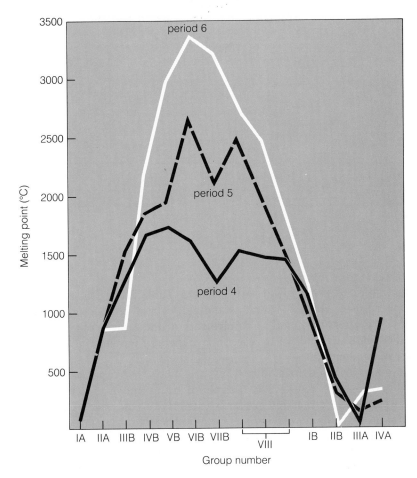

Figure 25.6 Melting points of the metals of the fourth, fifth, and sixth periods

istic of metals.* The following ranges of electrical conductivities, measured at 25°C, are observed:

1. *Metals:* 10^4 to $10^6/(\Omega \cdot cm)$
2. *Semiconductors:* 10^{-5} to $10/(\Omega \cdot cm)$
3. *Insulators:* 10^{-12} to $10^{-10}/(\Omega \cdot cm)$

---

* According to Ohm's law, $\mathscr{E} = IR$, where $\mathscr{E}$ is the potential difference in volts (V), I is the current in amperes (A), and R is the resistance in ohms (Ω). Hence, $I = \mathscr{E}/R$, and when the potential difference is 1 V, the electrical current is equal to $1/R$, a value called the conductance.

$$conductance = 1/R$$

The conductance of a metal wire varies *directly* with the cross-sectional area of the wire, a (at a constant voltage, more electricity will flow through a thick wire than a thin one) and *inversely* with the length of the wire, l:

$$conductance = ka/l$$

where k is a proportionality constant called the *conductivity* and is equal to the conductance of a 1 cm³ cube of the metal (1 cm² in cross-section and 1 cm long). Thus:

$$conductance = 1/R = ka/l$$
$$k = l/Ra$$

If l is measured in cm and a in cm², k has the units of $1/(\Omega \cdot cm)$.

Table 25.1 Electrical conductivities of the metals at 0°C in units of $10^4/(\text{ohm} \cdot \text{cm})$

Li 11.8	Be 18													
Na 23	Mg 25											Al 40		
K 15.9	Ca 23	Sc	Ti 1.2	V 0.6	Cr 6.5	Mn 20	Fe 11.2	Co 16	Ni 16	Cu 65	Zn 18	Ga 2.2		
Rb 8.6	Sr 3.3	Y	Zr 2.4	Nb 4.4	Mo 23	Tc	Ru 8.5	Rh 22	Pd 10	Ag 66	Cd 15	In 12	Sn 10	Sb 2.8
Cs 5.6	Ba 1.7	La 1.7	Hf 3.4	Ta 7.2	W 20	Re 5.3	Os 11	Ir 20	Pt 10	Au 49	Hg 4.4	Tl 7.1	Pb 5.2	Bi 1

The conductivities of some metals are listed in Table 25.1. The metals of group I B (copper, silver, and gold) are outstanding electrical conductors. Except for similarities in the relative standing of elements of the same group within a period, periodic trends are difficult to discern. In general, thermal conductivities parallel electrical conductivities.

Most metals are highly deformable. They are malleable, capable of being pounded into new shapes, and ductile, capable of being drawn into wire. The nondirectional character of metallic bonding accounts for the ease with which planes of metal atoms slide across one another under stress and thus explains why a metal crystal may be deformed without shattering. When the planes of an ionic crystal are displaced (see Figure 11.11), the new alignment brings ions of the same charge into proximity and results in the cleavage of the crystal. Covalent network crystals are deformed only by breaking the covalent bonds of the crystal, a process which also results in the fragmentation of the crystal.

25.4 Natural Occurrence of Metals

An ore is a naturally occurring material from which one or more metals can be profitably extracted. The principal types of ores and examples of each are listed in Table 25.2. A few of the less reactive metals occur in nature in elemental form; for many of these metals, these native ores constitute the most important source. The greatest tonnage of metals is derived from oxides—either oxide ores or metal oxides that are produced by the roasting of carbonate or sulfide ores.

Silicate minerals are abundant in nature. However, the extraction of metals from silicates is difficult, and the cost of such processes may be prohibitive. Consequently, only the less common metals are commercially derived from silicate ores. Phosphate minerals are, in general, rare and occur in low concentrations.

A number of metals occur as impurities in the ores of other metals so that both metals are derived from the same commercial operation. For example, cadmium metal is obtained as a by-product in the production of zinc.

Ores, as mined, generally contain variable amounts of unwanted materials (such as silica, clay, and granite), which are called gangue. The concentration of

Table 25.2 Occurrence of metals

Type of Ore	Examples
native metals	Cu, Ag, Au, As, Sb, Bi, Pd, Pt
oxides	Al_2O_3, Fe_2O_3, Fe_3O_4, SnO_2, MnO_2, TiO_2, $FeO \cdot Cr_2O_3$, $FeO \cdot WO_3$, Cu_2O, ZnO
carbonates	$CaCO_3$, $CaCO_3 \cdot MgCO_3$, $MgCO_3$, $FeCO_3$, $PbCO_3$, $BaCO_3$, $SrCO_3$, $ZnCO_3$, $MnCO_3$, $CuCO_3 \cdot Cu(OH)_2$, $2\,CuCO_3 \cdot Cu(OH)_2$
sulfides	Ag_2S, Cu_2S, CuS, PbS, ZnS, HgS, $FeS \cdot CuS$, FeS_2, Sb_2S_3, Bi_2S_3, MoS_2, NiS, CdS
halides	NaCl, KCl, AgCl, $KCl \cdot MgCl_2 \cdot 6H_2O$, NaCl and $MgCl_2$ in sea water
sulfates	$BaSO_4$, $SrSO_4$, $PbSO_4$, $CaSO_4 \cdot 2H_2O$, $CuSO_4 \cdot 2Cu(OH)_2$
silicates	$Be_3AlSi_6O_{18}$, $ZrSiO_4$, $Sc_2Si_2O_7$, $(NiSiO_3, MgSiO_3)^a$
phosphates	$[CePO_4, LaPO_4, NdPO_4, PrPO_4, Th_3(PO_4)_4]^a$, $LiF \cdot AlPO_4$

^{a} Occur in a single mineral but not in fixed proportions.

the desired metal must be sufficiently high to make its extraction chemically feasible and economically competitive. Ores of low concentration are worked only if they can be processed comparatively easily and inexpensively or if the metal product is scarce and valuable. The required concentration varies greatly from metal to metal. For aluminum or iron it should be 30% or more; for copper it may be 1% or less.

25.5 Metallurgy: Preliminary Treatment of Ores

Metallurgy is the science of extracting metals from their ores and preparing them for use. Metallurgical processes may be conveniently divided into three principal operations: (1) preliminary treatment, in which the desired component of the ore is concentrated, specific impurities removed, and/or the mineral is put into a suitable form for subsequent treatment; (2) reduction, in which the metal compound is reduced to the free metal; and (3) refining, in which the metal is purified and, in some cases, substances added to give desired properties to the final product. Since the problems encountered in each step vary from metal to metal, many different metallurgical procedures exist.

The processing of many ores requires, as a first step, that most of the gangue be removed. Such concentration procedures, which are usually carried out on ores that have been crushed and ground, may be based on physical or chemical properties. Physical separations are based on differences between the physical properties of the mineral and the gangue. Thus, through washing with water the particles of rocky impurities may often be separated from the heavier mineral particles. This separation may be accomplished by shaking the crushed ore in a stream of water on an inclined table; the heavier mineral particles settle to the bottom and are collected. Adaptations of this process exist.

Flotation is a method of concentration applied to many ores, especially those of copper, lead, and zinc. The finely crushed ore is mixed with a suitable oil

Froth flotation used to
concentrate a copper ore.
Freeport-McMoRan Inc.

and water in large tanks. The mineral particles are wetted by the oil, whereas the gangue particles are wetted by the water. Agitation of the mixture with air produces a froth which contains the oil and mineral particles. This froth floats on the top of the water and is skimmed off.

Magnetic separation is employed to separate Fe_3O_4 (the mineral magnetite) from gangue. The ore is crushed, and electromagnets are used to attract the particles of Fe_3O_4, which is ferromagnetic.

The removal of free metals from native ores may be considered to be a type of concentration. Certain ores, such as native bismuth and native copper, are heated to a temperature just above the melting point of the metal, and the liquid metal is poured away from the gangue. The process is called **liquation.**

Mercury will dissolve silver and gold to form what are called **amalgams.** Hence, the native ores of silver and gold are treated with mercury, the resulting liquid amalgam collected, and the free silver or gold recovered from the amalgam by distilling the mercury away.

The chemical properties of minerals are the basis of **chemical separations.** An important example is the **Bayer method** of obtaining pure aluminum oxide from the ore bauxite. Since aluminum hydroxide is amphoteric, the aluminum oxide is dissolved away from the ore impurities (principally ferric oxide and silicates) by treatment of the crushed ore with hot sodium hydroxide solution:

$$Al_2O_3(s) + 2 OH^-(aq) + 3 H_2O \longrightarrow 2 Al(OH)_4^-(aq)$$

The solution of sodium aluminate is filtered and cooled; its pH is adjusted downward by dilution and/or neutralization with carbon dioxide so that aluminum hydroxide precipitates. Pure aluminum oxide, ready for reduction, is obtained by heating the aluminum hydroxide:

$$2 Al(OH)_3(s) \longrightarrow Al_2O_3(s) + 3 H_2O(g)$$

The first step in the extraction of magnesium from sea water is a chemical concentration. The Mg^{2+} in sea water (approximately 0.13%) is precipitated as magnesium hydroxide by treatment of the sea water with a slurry of calcium hydroxide. The calcium hydroxide is obtained from CaO that is produced by roasting oyster shells ($CaCO_3$):

$$CaCO_3(s) \xrightarrow{heat} CaO(s) + CO_2(g)$$
$$CaO(s) + H_2O \longrightarrow Ca(OH)_2(s)$$
$$Mg^{2+}(aq) + Ca(OH)_2(s) \longrightarrow Mg(OH)_2(s) + Ca^{2+}(aq)$$

The magnesium hydroxide is converted to magnesium chloride by reaction with hydrochloric acid, and the magnesium chloride solution is evaporated to produce the dry $MgCl_2$ necessary for electrolytic reduction.

The metal component of some ores may be obtained by leaching. Thus, low-grade carbonate and oxide ores of copper may be leached with dilute sulfuric acid:

$$CuO(s) + 2 H^+(aq) \longrightarrow Cu^{2+}(aq) + H_2O$$
$$CuCO_3(s) + 2 H^+(aq) \longrightarrow Cu^{2+}(aq) + CO_2(g) + H_2O$$

and the resulting copper sulfate solutions may be directly subjected to electrolysis.

Silver and gold ores are leached with solutions of sodium cyanide in the presence of air since these metals form very stable complex ions with the cyanide ion. For native silver, argenitite (Ag_2S), and cerargyrite (AgCl), the reactions are

$$4 Ag(s) + 8 CN^-(aq) + O_2(g) + 2 H_2O \longrightarrow 4 Ag(CN)_2^-(aq) + 4 OH^-(aq)$$
$$Ag_2S(s) + 4 CN^-(aq) \longrightarrow 2 Ag(CN)_2^-(aq) + S^{2-}(aq)$$
$$AgCl(s) + 2 CN^-(aq) \longrightarrow Ag(CN)_2^-(aq) + Cl^-(aq)$$

After concentration many ores are roasted in air. The sulfide ores of the less reactive metals are directly reduced to the free metal by heating (see Section 25.6). However, the majority of the sulfide ores, as well as the carbonate ores, are converted into oxides by roasting:

$$2 ZnS(s) + 3 O_2(g) \longrightarrow 2 ZnO(s) + 2 SO_2(g)$$
$$PbCO_3(s) \longrightarrow PbO(s) + CO_2(g)$$

The free metals are more readily obtained from oxides than from sulfides or carbonates.

25.6 Metallurgy: Reduction

By far the largest quantity of metals, as well as the largest number of metals, are produced by smelting operations—high-temperature reduction processes in which the metal is usually secured in a molten state. In most of these processes a flux (such as limestone, $CaCO_3$) is used to remove the gangue that remains after ore concentration. The flux forms a slag with silicon dioxide and silicate impurities; for limestone and silicon dioxide the simplified equations are

$$CaCO_3(s) \longrightarrow CaO(s) + CO_2(g)$$

$$CaO(s) + SiO_2(s) \longrightarrow CaSiO_3(l)$$

The slag, which is a liquid at the smelting temperatures, generally floats on top of the molten metal and is readily separated from the metal.

The reducing agent employed for a given smelting operation is the least expensive material that is capable of yielding a product of the required purity. For the ores of the metals of low reactivity—for example, the sulfide ores of mercury, copper, and lead—no chemical agent is required. Mercury is produced by roasting cinnabar, HgS, in air:

$$HgS(s) + O_2(g) \longrightarrow Hg(g) + SO_2(g)$$

The mercury vapor is condensed in a receiver and requires no further purification.

Copper sulfide ores, after concentration by flotation, are smelted to a material called matte, which is essentially cuprous sulfide, Cu_2S. The matte is then reduced by blowing air through the molten material:

$$Cu_2S(l) + O_2(g) \longrightarrow 2\,Cu(l) + SO_2(g)$$

Any cuprous oxide that forms in this process is reduced by stirring the molten metal with poles of green wood. The copper produced by this method (blister copper) is about 99% pure and is refined by electrolysis.

Lead sulfide ores (galena) are subjected to a roasting operation in which a portion of the PbS is converted into lead oxide and lead sulfate:

$$2\,PbS(s) + 3\,O_2(g) \longrightarrow 2\,PbO(s) + 2\,SO_2(g)$$

$$PbS(s) + 2\,O_2(g) \longrightarrow PbSO_4(s)$$

The resulting PbS, PbO, and $PbSO_4$ mixture, together with fluxes, is smelted in the absence of air. The reactions, in which sulfur is oxidized and lead is reduced, are

$$PbS(s) + 2\,PbO(s) \longrightarrow 3\,Pb(l) + SO_2(g)$$

$$PbS(s) + PbSO_4(s) \longrightarrow 2\,Pb(l) + 2\,SO_2(g)$$

Some lead is also produced by smelting PbO with coke. The lead oxide is obtained by roasting the sulfide ore in an excess of air so that virtually complete conversion to the oxide results.

Iron, zinc, tin, cadmium, antimony, nickel, cobalt, molybdenum, lead, and other metals are produced by **carbon reduction** of oxides, which are obtained as ores or as the products of roasting operations.

The reactions that occur in a high-temperature carbon reduction are complex. In most cases the reduction is effected principally by carbon monoxide, not carbon. Since both the mineral and coke are solids that are not readily fusible, contact between them is poor and direct reaction slow:

$$MO(s) + C(s) \longrightarrow M(l) + CO(g)$$

(M stands for a metal.) However, a gas and a solid make better contact and react more readily:

$$2\,C(s) + O_2(g) \longrightarrow 2\,CO(g)$$
$$MO(s) + CO(g) \longrightarrow M(l) + CO_2(g)$$

The carbon dioxide that is produced is converted into carbon monoxide by reaction with coke:

$$C(s) + CO_2(g) \longrightarrow 2\,CO(g)$$

The most important commercial metal, iron, is produced by carbon reduction in a **blast furnace** designed to operate continuously (see Figure 25.7). The ore, coke, and a limestone flux are charged into the top of the furnace, and heated air, which is sometimes enriched with oxygen, is blown in at the bottom. The incoming air reacts with carbon to form carbon monoxide and to liberate considerable amounts of heat; at this point the temperature of the furnace is the highest (approximately 1500°C).

The iron ore (usually Fe_2O_3) is reduced in stages depending upon the temperature. Near the top of the furnace, where the temperature is lowest, Fe_3O_4 is the reduction product:

$$3\,Fe_2O_3(s) + CO(g) \longrightarrow 2\,Fe_3O_4(s) + CO_2(g)$$

The descending Fe_3O_4 is reduced to FeO in a lower, hotter zone:

$$Fe_3O_4(s) + CO(g) \longrightarrow 3\,FeO(s) + CO_2(g)$$

In the hottest zone, reduction to metallic iron occurs:

$$FeO(s) + CO(g) \longrightarrow Fe(l) + CO_2(g)$$

The molten iron collects in the bottom of the furnace. Molten slag, principally calcium silicate produced by the ultimate action of the flux on the gangue, also collects on the bottom. The slag floats on top of the molten iron, thus protecting the metal from being oxidized by the incoming air. The slag and iron are periodically drawn off. The hot exhaust gases are used to heat incoming air.

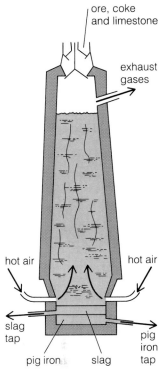

Figure 25.7 Diagram of a blast furnace (schematic)

The impure iron produced by the blast furnace (**pig iron**) contains up to 4% carbon, up to 2% silicon, some phosphorus, and a trace of sulfur. In the manufacture of steel (see Section 25.7), these impurities are removed or their concentrations are adjusted; in addition, certain metallic ingredients are added. The presence of some carbon in steel is desirable, and the amount of carbon in the final product is readily controlled in the refining process.

The carbon reduction of some oxides (for example, those of chromium, manganese, and tungsten) yields products that contain an appreciable quantity of carbon. If these metals are to be used in the manufacture of steel, the carbon content does not matter. However, since carbon impurities are difficult to remove from many metals, carbon reduction is not a satisfactory method for preparing these metals in a pure form. In such instances, as well as those in which carbon is incapable of effecting a reduction, reactive metals (such as Na, Mg, and Al) may be used as reducing agents. Processes that use metals as reducing agents are more expensive than those that employ carbon because the cost of the production of the metal used as a reducing agent must be taken into account.

The reduction of an oxide by aluminum is called a **Goldschmidt process** or a **thermite process**:

$$Cr_2O_3(s) + 2\,Al(s) \longrightarrow 2\,Cr(l) + Al_2O_3(l)$$

$$3\,MnO_2(s) + 4\,Al(s) \longrightarrow 3\,Mn(l) + 2\,Al_2O_3(l)$$

$$3\,BaO(s) + 2\,Al(s) \longrightarrow 3\,Ba(l) + Al_2O_3(l)$$

The reactions are highly exothermic, and molten metals are produced. The reaction of Fe_2O_3 and aluminum is used at times for the production of molten iron in welding operations and as the basis of incendiary (thermite) bombs. Other oxides commercially reduced by metals include: UO_3 (by Al or Ca), V_2O_5 (by Al), Ta_2O_5 (by Na), MoO_3 (by Al), ThO_2 (by Ca), and WO_3 (by Al).

The **Kroll process** involves the reduction of metal halides (such as $TiCl_4$, $ZrCl_4$, UF_4, and $LaCl_3$) by magnesium, sodium, or calcium. In the production of titanium, titanium tetrachloride is prepared by the reaction of titanium dioxide, carbon, and chlorine. The chloride is a liquid and is readily purified by distillation. Purified $TiCl_4$ is passed into molten magnesium or sodium at approximately 700°C under an atmosphere of argon or helium (which prevents oxidation of the product):

$$TiCl_4(g) + 2\,Mg(l) \longrightarrow Ti(s) + 2\,MgCl_2(l)$$

A **metal displacement** reaction employing zinc is used to obtain silver and gold from the solutions obtained from cyanide leaching operations:

$$2\,Ag(CN)_2^-(aq) + Zn(s) \longrightarrow 2\,Ag(s) + Zn(CN)_4^{2-}(aq)$$

Hydrogen reduction is used for the preparation of some metals (at high temperatures) when carbon reduction yields an unsatisfactory product. Examples are

$$GeO_2(s) + 2\,H_2(g) \longrightarrow Ge(s) + 2\,H_2O(g)$$

$$WO_3(s) + 3\,H_2(g) \longrightarrow W(s) + 3\,H_2O(g)$$

$$MoO_3(s) + 3\,H_2(g) \longrightarrow Mo(s) + 3\,H_2O(g)$$

Cells used for the production of magnesium metal by the electrolysis of molten $MgCl_2$. The cells operate at 700°C and greater than 100,000 A of direct current. The heavy copper busbars are required to deliver electrical power to the cells and the large black graphite rods are anodes. *Dow Chemical U.S.A.*

The metals are produced as powders by this method. Germanium is melted and cast into ingots, but tungsten (wolfram) and molybdenum have high melting points. They are heated and pounded into compact form. Hydrogen cannot be used to reduce the oxides of some metals because of the formation of undesirable hydrides.

The most reactive metals are prepared by **electrolytic reduction** of molten compounds. Sodium and magnesium (as well as the other I A and II A metals) are prepared by electrolysis of the fused chlorides. Sodium chloride is electrolyzed in a **Downs cell** (see Figure 25.8), which is designed to keep the products separate from one another so that they do not react:

anode: $\quad\quad 2\,Cl^- \longrightarrow Cl_2(g) + 2e^-$

cathode: $\quad e^- + Na^+ \longrightarrow Na(l)$

Purified Al_2O_3 is electrolyzed in the **Hall process** for the production of aluminum (see Figure 25.9). Aluminum oxide dissolved in molten cryolite, Na_3AlF_6, conducts electric current. The carbon lining of the cell serves as the cathode, and carbon anodes are used. The primary reaction at the anode may be considered to be the discharge of oxygen from oxide ions. However, the oxygen reacts with the carbon anodes so that the cell reactions are

anode: $\quad C(s) + 2\,O^{2-} \longrightarrow CO_2(g) + 4e^-$

cathode: $\quad 3e^- + Al^{3+} \longrightarrow Al(l)$

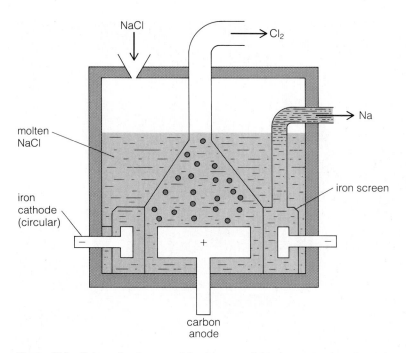

Figure 25.8 Schematic diagram of the Downs cell for the production of sodium and chlorine.

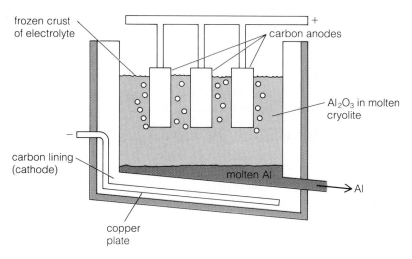

Figure 25.9 Schematic diagram of an electrolytic cell for the production of aluminum

The molten aluminum collects at the bottom of the cell and is periodically withdrawn.

Some metals are prepared by the electrolysis of aqueous solutions of their salts. Very pure zinc is produced by the electrolysis of zinc sulfate solutions. The zinc sulfate is obtained by treating zinc oxide (obtained from zinc sulfide ores by roasting) with sulfuric acid. The sulfuric acid for the process is made from the sulfur dioxide derived from the roasting of the sulfide ore:

Aluminum production by electrolytic reduction: A craneman is manipulating a giant crucible into position to tap one of the electrolytic cells containing molten aluminum. *Aluminum Company of America.*

anode: $$2\,H_2O \longrightarrow O_2(g) + 4\,H^+(aq) + 4e^-$$

cathode: $$2e^- + Zn^{2+}(aq) \longrightarrow Zn(s)$$

Aqueous solutions of salts of copper, cadmium, chromium, cobalt, gallium, indium, manganese, and thorium are electrolyzed to produce the corresponding metals. Electrolytically prepared metals generally require no further refining.

25.7 Metallurgy: Refining

Most of the metals obtained from reduction operations require refining to rid them of objectionable impurities. Refining processes vary widely from metal to metal, and for a given metal the method employed may vary with the proposed use of the final product. Along with the removal of materials that impart undesirable properties to the metal, the refining step may include the addition of substances to give the product desired characteristics. Some refining processes are designed to recover valuable metal impurities, such as gold, silver, and platinum.

Crude tin, lead, and bismuth are purified by liquation. In this process, ingots of the impure metals are placed at the top of a sloping hearth that is maintained at a temperature slightly above the melting point of the metal. The metal melts and flows down the inclined hearth into a well, leaving behind the solid impurities. Some low-boiling metals, such as zinc and mercury, are purified by distillation.

The Parkes process for refining lead, which also is a concentration method for silver, relies upon the selective dissolution of silver in molten zinc. A small amount of zinc (1 to 2%) is added to molten lead that contains silver as an impurity. Silver is much more soluble in zinc than in lead; lead and zinc are insoluble in each other. Hence, most of the silver concentrates in the zinc, which comes to the top of the molten lead. The zinc layer solidifies first upon cooling and is removed. The silver is obtained by remelting the zinc layer and distilling away the zinc, which is collected and used over again.

The Van Arkel process is based upon the thermal decomposition of a metal compound. The method, which is used for the purification of titanium, hafnium, and zirconium, involves the decomposition of a metal iodide on a hot metal filament. For example, impure zirconium is heated with a limited amount of iodine in an evacuated glass apparatus:

$$Zr(s) + 2 I_2(g) \longrightarrow ZrI_4(g)$$

The gaseous zirconium tetraiodide decomposes upon contact with a hot filament, and pure zirconium metal is deposited upon the filament:

$$ZrI_4(g) \longrightarrow Zr(s) + 2 I_2(g)$$

The regenerated iodine reacts with more zirconium. The process is very expensive and is employed for the preparation of limited amounts of very pure metals for special uses.

Another process capable of producing metals of very high purity is zone refining. A circular heater is fitted around a rod of an impure metal, such as germanium (see Figure 25.10). The heater, which is slowly moved down the rod, melts a band of the metal. As the heater moves along, pure metal recrystallizes out of the melt, and impurities are swept along in the molten zone to one end of the rod, which is subsequently discarded. More than one pass of the heater may be made on the same rod.

Electrolytic refining is an important and widely used method of purification. Many metals, including copper, tin, lead, gold, zinc, chromium, and nickel, are refined electrolytically. Plates of the impure metal are used as anodes, and the electrolyte is a solution of a salt of the metal. The pure metal plates out on the cathode. For copper, copper sulfate is employed as the electrolyte, and the electrode reactions are

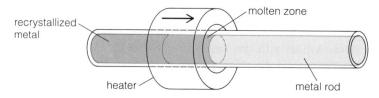

Figure 25.10 Schematic diagram of zone refining

anode: $\qquad$ $Cu(s) \longrightarrow Cu^{2+}(aq) + 2e^-$

cathode: $\quad 2e^- + Cu^{2+}(aq) \longrightarrow Cu(s)$

The more reactive metals in the crude copper anode, such as iron, are oxidized and pass into solution where they remain; they are not reduced at the cathode. The less reactive metals, such as silver, gold, and platinum, are not oxidized. As the copper anode dissolves away, they fall to the bottom of the cell from where they are recovered as a valuable "anode sludge."

There are two important ways in which pig iron is refined into steel. The principal impurities in pig iron are carbon (from the coke added in the reduction of the iron ore) as well as silicon, phosphorus, and sulfur (from the ore itself). In a refining process, these impurities are oxidized. The $CO(g)$ and $CO_2(g)$ produced from the C escape and the oxides of Si, P, and S (which are acidic oxides) are removed **by** slag formation with calcium oxide or other basic oxides:

Molten iron from a blast furnace being poured into a basic oxygen furnace. *American Iron and Steel Institute.*

$$CaO(s) + SiO_2(s) \longrightarrow CaSiO_3(l)$$

Calcium oxide is formed by the decomposition of limestone, $CaCO_3$, which is added in the refining process.

In the **open hearth process,** pig iron, scrap iron, Fe_2O_3, and limestone are heated in a shallow hearth lined with CaO or MgO. A blast of hot air and burning fuel is directed on the molten charge. The impurities are oxidized by the iron oxide and the hot air. Since it takes about 8 to 10 hours to produce a batch of steel, the quality of the product is easily controlled. Alloying metals (such as Mn, Cr, Ni, W, Mo, and V) may be added before the charge is poured.

Most of the steel produced today is made by the **basic oxygen process.** Molten pig iron, scrap iron, and powdered $CaCO_3$ are placed in a converter that is lined with basic oxides. The impurities are oxidized by pure oxygen under a pressure of 10 to 12 atm, which is blown onto the surface of the molten charge through a lance. The stream of oxygen and the escape of gaseous oxidation products keeps the charge mixed. The reactions are rapid and highly exothermic so that no external heat is required to keep the mass molten. The process is complete in about 20 to 50 minutes and gives a high-quality product.

25.8 The Group I A Metals

The I A metals, also called the **alkali metals,** constitute the most reactive group of metals. None of these elements is found free in nature, and all may be prepared by the electrolysis of dry, molten salts. The element francium, $Z = 87$, is formed in certain natural radioactive processes. All the isotopes of francium are radioactive with short half-lives, and the element is extremely rare.

The group I A elements are silvery metals; cesium has a slight golden yellow cast. The elements are comparatively soft (they can be cut by a knife) and have low melting points and boiling points (see Table 25.3). Melting point, boiling point, and hardness decrease with increasing atomic number. The metals are good conductors of heat and electricity. They have very low densities. Compare the densities given in Table 25.3 with the densities of the metals of the first transition series, which range from 2.5 g/cm^3 for $_{21}Sc$ to 8.9 g/cm^3 for $_{30}Cu$.

The alkali metals emit electrons when irradiated (the photoelectric effect). Cesium, which ejects electrons most readily, is used in the manufacture of photo-

Table 25.3 Some properties of the I A metals

	Lithium	Sodium	Potassium	Rubidium	Cesium
outer electronic configuration	$2s^1$	$3s^1$	$4s^1$	$5s^1$	$6s^1$
melting point (°C)	179	97.5	63.7	39.0	28.5
boiling point (°C)	1336	880	760	700	670
density (g/cm³)	0.53	0.97	0.86	1.53	1.90
atomic radius (pm)	123	157	203	216	235
ionic radius, M^+ (pm)	60	95	133	148	169
ionization energy (kJ/mol)					
first	520	496	419	403	376
second	7296	4563	3069	2640	2258
electrode potential, $\mathscr{E}^\circ_{red}$, (M^+/M) (V)	−3.05	−2.71	−2.93	−2.93	−2.92

cells (employed in light meters and electric eyes), which convert light signals into electric signals.

The electronic configuration of each of the alkali metals is that of the preceding noble gas (a noble gas core) plus a single s valence electron in the outer shell. These valence electrons are easily lost to give $1+$ ions that are isoelectronic with noble gases. Thus, an element of group I A has the lowest first ionization energy of any element of its period. The ease with which these elements lose electrons makes them extremely strong reducing agents.

The second ionization energies of the I A metals are so much higher than the first ionization energies that the $1+$ oxidation state is the only one observed for these metals. With few exceptions, alkali metal compounds are ionic.

In general, the reactivity of the elements increases with increasing atomic number—paralleling a decrease in first ionization potential. Thus, in most cases cesium is the most reactive element of the group and lithium is the least reactive. This order of reactivity is expected since a large atom holds its valence electron less tightly than a small atom; in a large atom the electron is farther from the nucleus and is screened from the positive nuclear charge by a large number of underlying electron shells.

Each I A element has the largest atomic radius and largest ionic radius of any element of its period. This comparatively large size combined with the low charge of the I A ions leads to species that have little polarizing ability (and hence form strongly ionic compounds) and that do not readily form complex ions.

All the hydroxides of the alkali metals are strong electrolytes. Alkali metal compounds are generally very soluble in water. However, the hydroxide, carbonate, phosphate, and fluoride of lithium are much less soluble than the corresponding salts of the other I A metals. Sodium ion may be precipitated from solution as sodium zinc uranyl acetate, $NaZn(UO_2)_3(C_2H_3O_2)_9 \cdot 6H_2O$. The perchlorate ion, ClO_4^-, the hexachloroplatinate ion, $[PtCl_6]^{2-}$, and the cobaltinitrite ion, $[Co(NO_2)_6]^{3-}$, may be used to precipitate K^+, Rb^+, and Cs^+.

The unipositive ammonium ion has a radius that lies between those of K^+ and Rb^+, and ammonium salts have solubilities that resemble those of the alkali metal salts. The ionic radius of the thallous ion, Tl^+, is similar to that of the rubidium ion. Not only do thallous compounds resemble rubidium compounds in solubility, but TlOH is also a strong electrolyte.

Table 25.4 Reaction of the I A metals[a]

Reaction	Remarks
$2\,M + X_2 \longrightarrow 2\,MX$	$X_2 =$ all halogens
$4\,Li + O_2 \longrightarrow 2\,Li_2O$	excess oxygen
$2\,Na + O_2 \longrightarrow Na_2O_2$	
$M + O_2 \longrightarrow MO_2$	$M =$ K, Rb, Cs
$2\,M + S \longrightarrow M_2S$	also with Se and Te
$6\,Li + N_2 \longrightarrow 2\,Li_3N$	Li only
$12\,M + P_4 \longrightarrow 4\,M_3P$	also with As, Sb
$2\,M + 2\,C \longrightarrow M_2C_2$	$M =$ Li and Na; other I A metals give non-stoichiometric interstitial compounds
$2\,M + H_2 \longrightarrow 2\,MH$	
$2\,M + 2\,H_2O \longrightarrow 2\,MOH + H_2$	room temperature
$2\,M + 2\,H^+ \longrightarrow 2\,M^+ + H_2$	violent reaction
$2\,M + 2\,NH_3 \longrightarrow 2\,MNH_2 + H_2$	liquid NH_3 presence of catalysts such as Fe; gaseous NH_3, heated

[a] $M =$ any I A metal, except where noted.

Some of the reactions of the I A metals are summarized in Table 25.4. Whereas the properties of lithium are similar in most respects to those of the other members of group I A, there are some dissimilarities which may be traced to the comparatively small size of Li and Li^+. The first members of the groups of the periodic table often deviate slightly in character from the remaining members of their groups. In addition, similarities may be observed between these first members and elements that adjoin them diagonally in the periodic table (diagonal relationships):

$$\begin{array}{cccc} Li & Be & B & C \\ Na & Mg & Al & Si \end{array}$$

Thus, lithium resembles magnesium in some of its properties. The magnesium ion has a slightly larger ionic radius (65 pm) than the lithium ion (60 pm), but the charge on the magnesium ion is $2+$.

Lithium resembles magnesium and differs from its congeners in the following ways. The carbonate, phosphate, and fluoride of lithium are only slightly soluble in water. Lithium forms an ordinary oxide rather than a peroxide or a superoxide upon burning in oxygen. Lithium ions are more strongly hydrated than those of any other I A element. Lithium reacts directly with nitrogen to give a nitride. Lithium hydroxide may be decomposed to Li_2O and water upon heating, and lithium carbonate decomposes to Li_2O and CO_2 upon ignition. Lithium nitrate decomposes upon heating:

$$4\,LiNO_3(s) \longrightarrow 2\,Li_2O(s) + 4\,NO_2(g) + O_2(g)$$

The nitrates of the other alkali metals form nitrites upon heating:

$$2\,MNO_3(s) \longrightarrow 2\,MNO_2(s) + O_2(g)$$

and the hydroxides and carbonates of Na, K, Rb, and Cs are thermally stable.

25.9 The Group II A Metals

The group II A metals, called the alkaline earth metals, are highly electropositive and constitute the second most reactive group of metals. They are not found free in nature and are commonly produced by the electrolysis of molten chlorides. Radium is a comparatively scarce element and all its isotopes are radioactive.

Because of its larger nuclear charge, each II A metal has a smaller atomic radius than that of the I A metal of its period. Since atoms of the II A metals are smaller and have two valence electrons instead of one, the II A metals have higher melting and boiling points and higher densities than the I A metals (see Table 25.5). In addition, the alkaline earth metals are harder than the alkali metals. Beryllium is hard enough to scratch glass and has a tendency toward brittleness; the degree of hardness declines with increasing atomic number. The alkaline earth metals are white metals with a silvery luster. They are good conductors of electricity.

Each of the II A metals has an electronic configuration consisting of a noble gas core plus two s electrons in the outer, valence level. The loss of the two valence electrons produces an ion that is isoelectronic not only with a noble gas but also with the I A metal ion of the same period. However, the alkaline earth metal ions have a larger nuclear charge than the alkali metal ions and are therefore considerably smaller. The beryllium ion is an exceptionally small cation.

Compared with the I A metal ions, the II A metal ions have considerably higher ratios of ionic charge to ionic radius. There are several important consequences of this fact. The hydration energy of a given alkaline earth ion is about five times that of the alkali metal ion of the same period. Furthermore, the compounds of the smaller members of the group, magnesium and beryllium, have appreciable covalent character because the cations of these metals have a strong polarizing effect on anions. This tendency for covalent bond formation is particularly pronounced for beryllium. All compounds of this metal, even those with the most electronegative elements such as oxygen and fluorine, have significant covalent character. Beryllium has the greatest tendency of the group toward the formation of complex ions; examples are $[Be(H_2O)_4]^{2+}$, $[Be(NH_3)_4]^{2+}$, BeF_4^{2-}, and $[Be(OH)_4]^{2-}$. Beryllium hydroxide is the only amphoteric hydroxide formed by a group II A metal.

Table 25.5   Some properties of the II A metals

	Beryllium	Magnesium	Calcium	Strontium	Barium
outer electronic configuration	$2s^2$	$3s^2$	$4s^2$	$5s^2$	$6s^2$
melting point (°C)	1280	651	851	800	850
boiling point (°C)	1500	1107	1440	1366	1537
density (g/cm³)	1.86	1.75	1.55	2.6	3.59
atomic radius (pm)	89	136	174	191	198
ionic radius, M^{2+} (pm)	31	65	99	113	135
ionization energy (kJ/mol)					
first	899	738	590	540	503
second	1757	1450	1145	1059	960
electrode potential, $\mathscr{E}^\circ_{red}$, (M^{2+}/M) (V)	−1.85	−2.36	−2.87	−2.89	−2.91

The covalent nature of beryllium halides is indicated by the poor electrolytic conduction of the anhydrous molten compounds; NaCl is generally added to anhydrous molten $BeCl_2$ in the electrolytic preparation of beryllium. Gaseous $BeCl_2$ molecules are linear and presumably of the *sp* hybrid type. In most solid compounds beryllium is tetrahedrally bonded through sp^3 hybrid orbitals. This configuration is observed in the complex ions of beryllium. Beryllium chloride is polymeric; each beryllium atom is joined to four chlorine atoms:

The BeO crystal may be considered to be composed of BeO_4 tetrahedra.

The ionization potentials of the II A metals are higher than those of the I A metals because of differences in atomic size and nuclear charge. The hydration energies of the II A cations, however, are also larger than those of the I A cations because of the smaller size and higher charge of the II A cations. Consequently, the electrode potentials of the II A metals are, in general, similar in magnitude to those of the I A metals.

The hydration energy is largest for Be^{2+} and smallest for Ba^{2+}, but the electrode potentials fall in the same order as the ionization potentials; Ba is the strongest reducing agent of the group and Be is the weakest. This order of reactivity is illustrated by the reactions of the alkaline earth metals with water. Beryllium fails to react even at red heat. Magnesium will react with boiling water or steam. Calcium, strontium, and barium react vigorously with cold water. Some chemical reactions of the group II A metals are summarized in Table 25.6.

Table 25.6 Reactions of the II A metals[a]	
Reaction	Remarks
$M + X_2 \longrightarrow MX_2$	X_2 = all halogens
$2M + O_2 \longrightarrow 2MO$	Ba also gives BaO_2
$M + S \longrightarrow MS$	also with Se and Te
$3M + N_2 \longrightarrow M_3N_2$	at high temperatures
$6M + P_4 \longrightarrow 2M_3P_2$	at high temperatures
$M + 2C \longrightarrow MC_2$	all except Be which forms Be_2C; high temperatures
$M + H_2 \longrightarrow MH_2$	M = Ca, Sr, Ba; high temperatures; Mg with H_2 under pressure
$M + 2H_2O \longrightarrow M(OH)_2 + H_2$	M = Ca, Sr, Ba; room temperature
$Mg + H_2O \longrightarrow MgO + H_2$	steam; Be does not react at red heat
$M + 2H^+ \longrightarrow M^{2+} + H_2$	
$Be + 2OH^- + 2H_2O \longrightarrow Be(OH)_4^{2-} + H_2$	Be only
$M + 2NH_3 \longrightarrow M(NH_2)_2 + H_2$	M = Ca, Sr, Ba; liquid ammonia in presence of catalysts
$3M + 2NH_3 \longrightarrow M_3N_2 + 3H_2$	gaseous NH_3; high temperatures

[a] M = any II A metal, except where noted.

Table 25.7 Solubility product constants of some II A metal salts

	OH^-	SO_4^{2-}	CO_3^{2-}	$C_2O_4^{2-}$	F^-	CrO_4^{2-}
Be^{2+}	1.6×10^{-26}	—	—	—	—	—
Mg^{2+}	8.9×10^{-12}	—	10^{-5}	8.6×10^{-5}	8×10^{-8}	—
Ca^{2+}	1.3×10^{-6}	2.4×10^{-5}	4.7×10^{-9}	1.3×10^{-9}	1.7×10^{-10}	7.1×10^{-4}
Sr^{2+}	3.2×10^{-4}	7.6×10^{-7}	7×10^{-10}	5.6×10^{-8}	7.9×10^{-10}	3.6×10^{-5}
Ba^{2+}	5.0×10^{-3}	1.5×10^{-9}	1.6×10^{-9}	1.5×10^{-8}	2.4×10^{-5}	8.5×10^{-11}

Almost all the salts of the I A metals are very soluble in water. In contrast, a number of II A metal compounds are not appreciably water soluble; the solubility products of some of these insoluble compounds are listed in Table 25.7.

The solubility of a salt depends upon the lattice energy of the salt (energy absorbed in the solution process):

$$MA(s) \longrightarrow M^{2+}(g) + A^{2-}(g)$$

and the hydration energies of the ions (energy evolved):

$$M^{2+}(g) \longrightarrow M^{2+}(aq)$$
$$A^{2-}(g) \longrightarrow A^{2-}(aq)$$

When the solubilities of salts containing the same anion are compared, the hydration energy of the anion may be neglected and solubility differences may be attributed to the combination of the other two factors.

The solubility of the alkaline earth sulfates decreases with increasing cation size; $BeSO_4$ is very soluble, and $BaSO_4$ is very insoluble. The lattice energies of the sulfates do not change greatly in the sequence from $BeSO_4$ to $BaSO_4$, presumably because the anion is so much larger than any II A cation. The trend in the solubility of the sulfates therefore parallels the trend in hydration energies of the ions. The hydration of the small Be^{2+} ion is by far the most exothermic of any ion of the group, and $BeSO_4$ is by far the most soluble sulfate formed by any ion of the group.

The trend in the solubility of hydroxides is the reverse of that of the sulfates; $Be(OH)_2$ is the least soluble alkaline earth hydroxide, and the solubility increases down the group. For hydroxides the lattice energy is dependent upon cation size. The strength of the crystal forces decreases with increasing cation size; $Be(OH)_2$ has the largest lattice energy of any alkaline earth hydroxide. Apparently the trend in lattice energy (energy required) overshadows the trend in hydration energy (energy released).

Solubility data cannot always be so simply interpreted. In the preceding solubility considerations we have ignored entropy effects. In addition, even though the lattice energies and hydration energies of a group of salts may vary regularly, the sum of the two energy effects and hence the solubilities of the salts may vary in an irregular manner.

The lattice energies of the oxides of the II A metals decrease regularly from BeO to BaO, and the effect of this trend is seen in the series of reactions of the alkaline earth oxides with water. Beryllium oxide is insoluble in and unreactive toward water. Magnesium oxide reacts very slowly with water; MgO that has been ignited at high temperatures, however, is practically inert. The oxides of calcium, strontium, and barium readily react with water to form hydroxides:

$$MO + H_2O \longrightarrow M(OH)_2$$

The carbonates of the alkaline earth metals decompose upon heating:

$$MCO_3(s) \longrightarrow MO(s) + CO_2(g)$$

The thermal stability of the carbonates varies directly with the size of the cation. Beryllium carbonate is very unstable and can be prepared only in an atmosphere of carbon dioxide presumably because of the enhanced stability of BeO over $BeCO_3$.

The tendency of the II A metal ions toward hydration causes a number of the compounds of these ions to hydrate with ease; $Mg(ClO_4)_2$, $CaCl_2$, $CaSO_4$, and $Ba(ClO_4)_2$ are used as desiccants.

The beryllium ion hydrolyzes in solution:

$$[Be(H_2O)_4]^{2+} + H_2O \rightleftharpoons [Be(H_2O)_3(OH)]^+ + H_3O^+$$

but the other cations do not. The hydroxides of beryllium and magnesium may be regarded as insoluble (see Table 25.7). Even though the hydroxides of calcium, strontium, and barium are limitedly soluble in water, these compounds are completely dissociated in aqueous solution.

The sulfides of the group are water soluble, and solutions of these compounds are alkaline due to the hydrolysis of the sulfide ion. In quantitative determinations barium ion is usually precipitated as barium sulfate; strontium ion, as strontium sulfate or strontium oxalate; and calcium ion, as calcium oxalate. Magnesium ion is precipitated as $Mg(NH_4)PO_4 \cdot 6H_2O$ by the HPO_4^{2-} ion in the presence of ammonia. Beryllium may be determined as the hydroxide.

Because of the extremely small size of Be and Be^{2+}, beryllium is even more exceptional with regard to the other members of group II A than lithium is with regard to the other members of group I A. The diagonal relationship between beryllium and aluminum is particularly striking. Although Al^{3+} is larger than Be^{2+}, the two ions have similar electric fields because of the higher charge of Al^{3+}.

Both elements have a strong tendency toward the formation of covalent compounds. The halides are largely covalent in nature, are soluble in organic solvents, and are strong Lewis acids. Both aluminum hydroxide and beryllium hydroxide are amphoteric, and both metals dissolve in solutions of hydroxides to give hydrogen. The standard electrode potential of beryllium is similar in magnitude to that of aluminum but much smaller than those of the other II A metals.

The carbides of beryllium and aluminum yield methane, CH_4, on hydrolysis:

$$Be_2C(s) + 4H_2O \longrightarrow 2Be(OH)_2(s) + CH_4(g)$$
$$Al_4C_3(s) + 12H_2O \longrightarrow 4Al(OH)_3(s) + 3CH_4(g)$$

The hydrolysis of the other II A metal carbides yields acetylene, C_2H_2.

Aluminum and beryllium (as well as magnesium) have thin protective oxide coatings, which make them resistant to attack by dilute nitric acid. Beryllium oxide and aluminum oxide are hard, extremely high melting, insoluble solids. Beryllium and aluminum form the stable fluoro complex anions BeF_4^{2-} and AlF_6^{3-}. The other II A metals do not form fluoro complexes that are stable in

Table 25.13 Some properties of the lanthanides

	Z	Postulated Electronic Configurations of Valence Subshells	Oxidation States	Atomic Radius, pm	Ionic Radius, M^{3+}, pm	$\mathscr{E}^\circ_{red}$ $3e^- + M^{3+} \rightarrow M$ (volts)
La	57	$5d^1\,6s^2$	3+	169	106	−2.52
Ce	58	$4f^2\,6s^2$	3+, 4+	165	103	−2.48
Pr	59	$4f^3\,6s^2$	3+, 4+	165	101	−2.46
Nd	60	$4f^4\,6s^2$	2+, 3+, 4+	164	100	−2.43
Pm	61	$4f^5\,6s^2$	3+	−	98	−2.42
Sm	62	$4f^6\,6s^2$	2+, 3+	166	96	−2.41
Eu	63	$4f^7\,6s^2$	2+, 3+	185	95	−2.41
Gd	64	$4f^7\,5d^1 6s^2$	3+	161	94	−2.40
Tb	65	$4f^9\,6s^2$	3+, 4+	159	92	−2.39
Dy	66	$4f^{10}\,6s^2$	3+, 4+	159	91	−2.35
Ho	67	$4f^{11}\,6s^2$	3+	158	89	−2.32
Er	68	$4f^{12}\,6s^2$	3+	157	88	−2.30
Tm	69	$4f^{13}\,6s^2$	2+, 3+	156	87	−2.28
Yb	70	$4f^{14}\,6s^2$	2+, 3+	170	86	−2.27
Lu	71	$4f^{14}\,5d^1 6s^2$	3+	156	85	−2.26

Table 25.14 Reactions of the lanthanides[a]

Reaction	Remarks
$2M + 3X_2 \longrightarrow 2MX_3$	X_2 = all halogens; Ce gives CeF_4 with F_2
$4M + 3O_2 \longrightarrow 2M_2O_3$	Ce gives CeO_2
$2M + 3S \longrightarrow M_2S_3$	not Eu; reactions with Se similar
$2M + N_2 \longrightarrow 2MN$	high temperatures; reactions with P_4, As, Sb, and Bi similar
$2M + 6H^+ \longrightarrow 2M^{3+} + 3H_2$	
$2M + 6H_2O \longrightarrow 2M(OH)_3 + 3H_2$	slow with cold water

[a] M = any lanthanide, except where noted.

ment of the d electrons of the transition elements are significant, whereas the number and arrangement of the f electrons of the inner-transition elements cause only minor variations in properties.

All lanthanides form ions in the characteristic group III B oxidation state, 3+ (see Table 25.14). For some of the elements other oxidation states are known, but these are less stable. The 3+ ions are formed through the loss of the two $6s$ electrons and one $4f$ electron (or one $5d$ electron, if available).

There is some evidence that f^0, f^7 (half-filled), and f^{14} (filled) ions have stable configurations. Thus, La^{3+} (f^0), Gd^{3+} (f^7), and Lu^{3+} (f^{14}) are the only ions that these elements form. The most stable 2+ and 4+ ions are Eu^{2+} (f^7), Yb^{2+} (f^{14}), Ce^{4+} (f^0), and Tb^{4+} (f^7). The ceric ion, Ce^{4+}, is a good oxidizing agent.

The elements occur together in nature because of their great chemical similarity. Promethium, which is radioactive and probably occurs only in trace amounts, is

Table 25.15 Reactions of aluminum, gallium, indium, and thallium

Reaction	Remarks
$2M + 3X_2 \longrightarrow 2MX_3$	X_2 = all halogens; Tl also gives TlX; no iodide of Tl^{3+}
$4M + 3O_2 \longrightarrow 2M_2O_3$	high temperatures; Tl also gives Tl_2O
$2M + 3S \longrightarrow M_2S_3$	high temperatures; Tl also gives Tl_2S; also with Se and Te
$2Al + N_2 \longrightarrow 2AlN$	Al only; GaN and InN may be prepared indirectly
$2M + 6H^+ \longrightarrow 2M^{3+} + 3H_2$	M = Al, Ga, and In; Tl gives Tl^+
$2M + 2OH^- + 6H_2O \longrightarrow 2M(OH)_4^- + 3H_2$	M = Al and Ga

M = Al, Ga, In, and Tl, except where noted.

an exception. The elements are extremely difficult to separate; repeated fractional crystallization and ion-exchange techniques have been employed to effect separations.

All the lanthanides are silvery white, very reactive metals. The electrode potentials for the reduction of the 3+ ions are strikingly similar (see Table 25.13). Some reactions of the lanthanides are given in Table 25.14; a number of the metals are also known to react with carbon to produce saltlike carbides and with hydrogen to give saltlike hydrides. The M_2O_3 oxides react with water to form insoluble hydroxides, $M(OH)_3$, that are not amphoteric. Insoluble carbonates, $M_2(CO_3)_3$, may be produced by the reactions of carbon dioxide with the oxides or hydroxides. The halides (with the exception of fluorides), nitrates, chlorates, acetates, and sulfates of the 3+ ions are water soluble; the phosphates, fluorides, oxalates, hydroxides, and carbonates are insoluble. The precipitation of the elements as oxalates serves as the basis of an analytical determination. In general, the compounds are paramagnetic and highly colored.

5.12 The Metals of Group III A

The characteristics of the group III A elements have been discussed in Section 24.6, and some of the properties of the metals are listed in Table 24.4.

Aluminum, the most abundant metal of the earth's crust (approximately 8%), is obtained by the electrolysis of molten Al_2O_3 (the Hall process, see Section 25.6). Gallium, indium, and thallium are widely distributed in nature but occur only in trace amounts; they may be prepared by the electrolysis of aqueous solutions of salts of the metals. They are soft, white metals with relatively low melting points (see Figure 25.6). Gallium has an unusually low melting point (30°C). Since its boiling point is not abnormally low (2070°C), gallium has an exceptional liquid range and has found use as a thermometer fluid.

The metals are fairly reactive (see Table 25.15). Aluminum, gallium, and indium (but not thallium) have protective oxide coatings and are passive toward nitric acid. However, all the metals react with nonoxidizing acids to liberate hydrogen. As expected from their $ns^2\,np^1$ electronic configurations, the most important oxidation state is $3+$. Most of the compounds of the metals in the $3+$ oxidation state are covalent. In water, however, the M^{3+} ions are stabilized through hydration, and the enthalpies of hydration are high.

The sulfates, nitrates, and halides are water soluble, but the M^{3+} ions hydrolyze readily:

$$M(H_2O)_6^{3+} + H_2O \longrightarrow M(H_2O)_5(OH)^{2+} + H_3O^+$$

For this reason, salts of weak acids (such as acetates, carbonates, sulfides, and cyanides) do not exist in water solution. Such salts are completely hydrolyzed:

$$M(H_2O)_6^{3+} + 3\,C_2H_3O_2^- \longrightarrow M(OH)_3(s) + 3\,H_2O + 3\,HC_2H_3O_2$$

In addition, complexes with ammonia do not exist in water:

$$M(H_2O)_6^{3+} + NH_3 \longrightarrow M(H_2O)_5(OH)^{2+} + NH_4^+$$

The hydroxides, $M(OH)_3$, are insoluble in water. Aluminum hydroxide and gallium hydroxide are amphoteric:

$$Al(OH)_3 + OH^- \longrightarrow Al(OH)_4^-$$
$$Ga(OH)_3 + OH^- \longrightarrow Ga(OH)_4^-$$

Aluminum sulfate forms an important series of double salts called alums, $MAl(SO_4)_2 \cdot 12\,H_2O$ (or $M_2SO_4 \cdot Al_2(SO_4)_3 \cdot 24\,H_2O$), where M may be almost any univalent cation (Na^+, K^+, Rb^+, Cs^+, NH_4^+, Ag^+, and Tl^+) except Li^+ (which is too small). In addition to Al^{3+}, other M^{3+} species form series of such double sulfates: Fe^{3+}, Cr^{3+}, Mn^{3+}, Ti^{3+}, Co^{3+}, Ga^{3+}, In^{3+}, Rh^{3+}, and Ir^{3+}.

Hydrides analogous to those of boron are not formed by aluminum, gallium, indium, and thallium. However, MH_4^- ions, which are analogous to the borohydride ion, are formed.

Among the heavier members of the group, compounds with the metal in a $1+$ oxidation state are known. The np^1 electron is more readily removed than the ns^2 electrons, which are sometimes called an inert pair. This effect is also seen for the M^{2+} ions of group IV A. The low reactivity of mercury has been ascribed to the $6s^2$ inert pair of its valence level.

Unlike the transition elements, however, the $1+$ state of the III A elements (their lowest state) is most stable among the heavier members of the group. No $1+$ compounds of aluminum are known. Gallium and indium form a few compounds (such as Ga_2S, Ga_2O at high temperatures, $InCl$, $InBr$, and In_2O). The Ga^+ and In^+ ions are not stable in water solution.

For thallium, however, the $1+$ state is important and stable. In fact, Tl^+ is more stable in water than Tl^{3+} (which is a strong oxidizing agent):

$$2e^- + Tl^{3+} \rightleftharpoons Tl^+ \qquad \mathscr{E}^\circ_{red} = +1.25 \text{ V}$$

The oxide Tl_2O dissolves in water to form the soluble hydroxide $TlOH$. Whereas the Tl^{3+} ion is extensively hydrolyzed in aqueous solution, the Tl^+ ion is not. A wide variety of Tl^+ compounds are known. The sulfate, nitrate, acetate, and fluoride are water soluble; the chloride, bromide, iodide, sulfide, and chromate are insoluble.

13 The Metals of Group IV A

Of the elements of group IV A, germanium, tin, and lead are classified as metals. The characteristics of the group as a whole are discussed in Section 24.1, and some of the properties of the metals are listed in Table 24.1. The metals are not abundant in nature; germanium is a rare element.

Germanium is a semiconductor and is used in the manufacture of transistors. It is a hard, brittle, white metal and has the highest melting point of the metals of the group. Tin and lead have relatively low melting points and low tensile strengths. Lead is especially soft and malleable.

The metals are fairly reactive (see Table 25.16). Lead frequently appears less reactive than the electrode potential,

$$2e^- + Pb^{2+} \rightleftharpoons Pb \qquad \mathscr{E}^\circ_{red} = -0.13 \text{ V}$$

would indicate because of the formation of surface coatings. Thus, the reaction of lead with sulfuric acid or hydrochloric acid is impeded by the formation of insoluble lead sulfate or lead chloride on the surface of the metal.

Since the elements have $ns^2\, np^2$ valence shell configurations, two oxidation states are observed: 4+ and 2+ (inert pair species). The 4+ state declines in importance and the 2+ state becomes increasingly important down the series: Ge, Sn, Pb. Thus, only a few 2+ germanium compounds are important (GeO, GeS, $GeCl_2$, $GeBr_2$, and GeI_2), and only a few 4+ lead compounds are important [PbO_2, $Pb(C_2H_3O_2)_4$, PbF_4, and $PbCl_4$]. The Sn^{2+} [stannous, or tin(II) ion] and Pb^{2+} [plumbous, or lead(II) ion] are the only cationic species of the group that exist in water; 4+ ions probably do not exist. Most of the pure 2+ and 4+ compounds are covalent, although PbF_2 is known to be ionic.

All the metals form dioxides; GeO_2 and SnO_2 are the products of the reactions of the metals with oxygen. Lead dioxide may be prepared by the oxidation of PbO or Pb^{2+} salts in alkaline solution:

$$Pb(OH)_3^-(aq) + OCl^-(aq) \longrightarrow PbO_2(s) + Cl^-(aq) + OH^-(aq) + H_2O$$

Table 25.16 Reactions of germanium, tin, and lead[a]	
Reaction	Remarks
$M + 2X_2 \longrightarrow MX_4$	X_2 = any halogen; M = Ge and Sn; Pb yields PbX_2
$M + O_2 \longrightarrow MO_2$	M = Ge and Sn; high temperatures; Pb yields PbO or Pb_3O_4
$M + 2S \longrightarrow MS_2$	M = Ge and Sn; high temperatures; Pb yields PbS
$M + 2H^+ \longrightarrow M^{2+} + H_2$	M = Sn and Pb
$3M + 4H^+ + 4NO_3^- \longrightarrow 3MO_2 + 4NO + 2H_2O$	M = Ge and Sn
$3Pb + 8H^+ + 2NO_3^- \longrightarrow 3Pb^{2+} + 2NO + 4H_2O$	
$M + OH^- + 2H_2O \longrightarrow M(OH)_3^- + H_2$	M = Sn and Pb; slow
$Ge + 2OH^- + 4H_2O \longrightarrow Ge(OH)_6^{2-} + 2H_2$	

[a] M = Ge, Sn, and Pb, except where noted.

Lead dioxide is a strong oxidizing agent:

$$2e^- + 4H^+ + PbO_2 \longrightarrow Pb^{2+} + 2H_2O \qquad \mathscr{E}^\circ_{red} = +1.46 \text{ V}$$

In acid solution PbO_2 oxidizes Mn^{2+} to MnO_4^- and Cl^- to Cl_2. In contrast to GeO_2 and SnO_2, PbO_2 is thermally unstable. Upon gentle heating PbO_2 decomposes to Pb_3O_4 (red lead); stronger heating gives PbO (litharge). The compound Pb_3O_4 contains lead in two oxidation states and may be represented as $Pb_2^{II}Pb^{IV}O_4$ like the compounds Fe_3O_4 and Co_3O_4, both of which conform to the formula $M^{II}(M^{III}O_2)_2$.

Germanates, stannates, and plumbates may be derived from the dioxides by reactions with aqueous alkali or in the case of PbO_2 by fusion with alkali metal oxides or alkaline earth oxides. The stannates and plumbates form trihydrates in which the anion is an octahedral hydroxy complex: $[M(OH)_6]^{2-}$; a few germanates of similar structure are known (for example, $Fe[Ge(OH)_6]$). There are no hydroxides of formula $M(OH)_4$, but hydrous MO_2 oxides may be prepared.

Treatment of the Sn^{2+} and Pb^{2+} ions in water solution with OH^- ion gives hydrous-oxide precipitates that are commonly assigned the formulas $Sn(OH)_2$ and $Pb(OH)_2$. By heating these products, SnO and PbO can be prepared; PbO is also the product of the reaction of lead and oxygen as well as of the decompositions of Pb_3O_4 and PbO_2. The compound GeO may be prepared by the hydrolysis of $GeCl_2$.

All the monoxides, as well as the hydrous oxides (or hydroxides), are amphoteric and dissolve in either acid or alkaline solution. In excess alkali, germanites, stannites, and plumbites are produced. For example:

$$PbO(s) + OH^-(aq) + H_2O \longrightarrow Pb(OH)_3^-(aq)$$

The stannite ion is a strong reducing agent:

$$2e^- + Sn(OH)_6^{2-} \longrightarrow Sn(OH)_3^- + 3OH^- \qquad \mathscr{E}^\circ_{red} = -0.93 \text{ V}$$

All the metals form monosulfides, MS, but only germanium and tin form disulfides, MS_2. The disulfides of germanium and tin may be prepared by the reactions of the metals and sulfur and may be precipitated from solutions of Ge^{IV} or Sn^{IV} compounds by H_2S. The disulfides, like the dioxides, are amphoteric. In solutions of alkali metal sulfides or ammonium sulfide, GeS_2 and SnS_2 dissolve to form thioanions; compounds of the SnS_3^{2-} and SnS_4^{4-} ions have been isolated from such solutions, but thiogermanates have not been obtained in pure form:

$$SnS_2(s) + S^{2-}(aq) \longrightarrow SnS_3^{2-}(aq)$$

Insoluble PbS and SnS may be precipitated from solutions by means of H_2S. Lead(II) sulfide is also the product of the direct union of the elements; SnS may be prepared by the thermal decomposition of SnS_2. Germanium(II) sulfide may be derived from the disulfide of germanium by the reaction

$$GeS_2 + Ge \longrightarrow 2GeS$$

None of the monosulfides are soluble in sulfide solutions.

Complete series of the tetrahalides of germanium, tin, and lead are known except for $PbBr_4$ and PbI_4. Lead in a 4+ state has strong oxidizing power and cannot exist in a compound with bromine and iodine in 1− states (which have reducing abilities). Lead(IV) chloride readily decomposes at 100°C:

$$PbCl_4(l) \longrightarrow PbCl_2(s) + Cl_2(g)$$

The tetrahalides, in general, are volatile covalent substances. They react readily with water to produce hydrous dioxides.

All the dihalides of germanium, tin, and lead are known. Germanium(II) halides, as well as tin(II) halides, may be prepared by the reaction of the appropriate tetrahalide and metal:

$$GeCl_4 + Ge \longrightarrow 2\,GeCl_2$$

The reactions of tin and the hydrohalic acids yield tin(II) halides. Lead(II) halides may be produced by the direct reaction of the elements. Since all PbX_2 compounds are insoluble in water, they may be precipitated from solutions containing Pb^{2+} by the addition of halide ions.

The dihalides are much less volatile than the tetrahalides, a fact which indicates an increased degree of ionic character; PbF_2, $PbCl_2$, and $PbBr_2$ are ionic in the solid state. The dihalides of germanium are not particularly stable. Complex anions, such as $GeCl_3^-$, $SnCl_4^{2-}$, $PbCl_3^-$, $PbCl_4^{2-}$, and $PbCl_6^{4-}$, are known. Both Sn^{2+} and Pb^{2+} form such ions in aqueous solution in the presence of halide ions; in general, the ions MX^+ and MX_3^- are most important. Insoluble lead(II) halides dissolve in solutions containing excess halide ions because of the formation of such complexes.

All three metals form covalent, volatile hydrides: GeH_4, germane; SnH_4, stannane; and PbH_4, plumbane. The hydride of lead is thermally unstable and decomposes to the elements at 0°C; SnH_4 decomposes at approximately 150°C. Continuing the trend established by carbon and silicon, germanium forms catenated hydrides of formula Ge_nH_{2n+2}, where n is any number from 2 to 8. Tin or lead form only the simple hydrides SnH_4 and PbH_4.

The Sn^{2+} and Pb^{2+} ions are hydrolyzed in water:

$$[Sn(H_2O)_6]^{2+} + H_2O \rightleftharpoons [Sn(H_2O)_5(OH)]^+ + H_3O^+ \qquad K_a \cong 10^{-2}$$

$$[Pb(H_2O)_6]^{2+} + H_2O \rightleftharpoons [Pb(H_2O)_5(OH)]^+ + H_3O^+ \qquad K_a \cong 10^{-8}$$

The reaction with water is particularly pronounced in the case of tin(II) compounds; excess acid is generally added to aqueous solutions of such compounds to inhibit this reaction and prevent the precipitation of basic salts, such as $Sn(OH)Cl$.

Lead(II) nitrate and lead(II) acetate are soluble in water; the acetate is only slightly dissociated. The sulfate, chromate, carbonate, sulfide, and all of the halides of Pb^{2+} are only slightly soluble in water.

Summary

The *band theory* describes the bonding in metals in terms of *molecular orbitals* that extend over the entire metallic structure. This band theory can be used to explain the *electrical conductivities* of *conductors, insulators,* and *semiconductors.* Pure substances (such as Si or Ge) that function as semiconductors are called *intrinsic semiconductors.* The addition of small traces of certain *impurities* to either Si or Ge enhances its conductivity and produces what is called an *extrinsic semiconductor.* The use of an *acceptor impurity* (such as B, Al, Ga, or In) produces a *p-type semiconductor,* whereas a *donor impurity* (such as P, As, Sb, or Bi) produces an *n-type semiconductor. Deformability, luster, thermal conductivity,* and *electrical conductivity* are the properties most characteristic of metals.

A number of types of *ores* of *metals* occur in nature (examples include oxides, carbonates, sulfides, halides, sulfates, silicates, phosphates, and native ores). *Metallurgy* is the science of extracting metals from their ores and preparing them for use. Metallurgical processes may be divided into three types of operations: *preliminary treatment, reduction,* and *refining.*

In *preliminary treatment,* the desired component of the ore is *concentrated* by certain *physical separations, flotation, magnetic separation, liquation, amalgamation, chemical separations* (for example, the *Bayer process*), or *leaching.* As a preliminary treatment the mineral may be put in a suitable form for subsequent treatment (as, for example, in the *roasting* of carbonate or sulfide ores).

In a *reduction,* the free metal is obtained from the metal compound. The largest number of metals are produced by *smelting* operations. In most of these processes, a *flux* is used to remove the *gangue* by the formation of a *slag.* Some metal ores (such as ores of Hg, Cu, or Pb) can be reduced by *heat alone. Carbon reduction* is used to produce many metals (examples are Fe, Zn, Sn, Cd, Sb, Ni, and Co). The most important commercial metal, *iron,* is produced by carbon reduction in a *blast furnace.* Reactive metals (such as Na, Mg, and Al) are used to reduce the oxides of some metals. In the *Goldschmidt process,* Al is used to reduce a metal oxide; in the *Kroll process,* either Mg, Na, or Ca is used to reduce a metal halide. *Hydrogen reduction* is used to reduce the oxides of some metal (such as Ge, W, and Mo) when carbon reduction yields an unsatisfactory product. *Electrolytic reduction* is also employed (particularly in the production of I A and II A metals in a *Downs cell* and of Al in the *Hall process*).

Most of the metals obtained from reductions require purification in a *refining process.* In such processes, substances may be added to give the product desired characteristics. Refining operations include: *liquation, distillation,* the *Parkes process,* the *Van Arkel process, zone refining,* and *electrolytic refining. Pig iron* from the blast furnace is refined into *steel* by the *open hearth process* or the *basic oxygen process.*

The *group I A elements,* called the *alkali metals,* are characterized by their low densities, softness, low melting points, low boiling points, and high degree of chemical reactivity. The *group II A elements,* called the *alkaline earth metals,* also have a high degree of chemical reactivity although their densities, melting points, and boiling points are higher than those of the I A metals.

The *transition elements* exhibit a wide variation in chemical properties. Both ns and $(n-1)d$ electrons are involved in compound formation. Most of the transition metals exist in *more than one oxidation state* in their compounds and many of these elements exist in a comparatively large number of positive oxidation states. The *chemical reactivity* of the transition elements varies from that exhibited by the metals that react with dilute acids (as well as with water or steam) to that exhibited by the unreactive, noble metals.

The outstanding feature of the chemistry of the *lanthanides,* which are inner-transition elements, is their *similarity.* They are all silvery white, *very reactive metals.* For each of them, the *most important oxidation state* is $3+$.

The *group III A metals* are soft, white metals with relatively low melting points. The metals are *fairly reactive* and for each of them the *most important oxidation state* is $3+$. The $1+$ state is also important for the heavier members of the group. Many of the $3+$ compounds of the metals are *covalent.*

Of the elements of group IV A, only Ge, Sn, and Pb are classified as metals. Germanium is a *semiconductor.* The important oxidation states of these metals are $2+$ and $4+$.

Key Terms

Some of the more important terms introduced in this chapter are listed below. Definitions for terms not included in this list may be located in the text by use of the index.

Alkali metal (Section 25.8) An element of group I A: Li, Na, K, Rb, or Cs.

Alkaline earth metal (Section 25.9) An element of group II A: Be, Mg, Ca, Sr, or Ba.

Band theory (Section 25.1) A theory that explains the bonding in metals in terms of molecular orbitals that extend over the entire crystal of the metal and that together make up what are called bands.

Basic oxygen process (Section 25.7) A process in which pig iron is refined into steel. The impurities in the pig iron are oxidized by a blast of pure oxygen.

Bayer process (Section 25.5) A process for obtaining pure aluminum oxide (for use in the production of aluminum metal) from the ore bauxite. Advantage is taken of the amphoteric nature of aluminum oxide to dissolve it away from ore impurities by use of a hot solution of NaOH.

Blast furnace (Section 25.6) A furnace for the carbon reduction of iron ore; pig iron, an impure form of iron, is produced.

Concentration of ores (Section 25.5) Processes in which the desired components of ores are separated from gangue.

Conduction band (Section 25.1) An empty band in a metallic crystal through which electrons are free to move and thereby conduct electricity.

Conductor (Section 25.1) A metal in which an empty conduction band overlaps the valence band and the valence electrons are free to conduct electricity.

Downs cell (Section 25.6) An electrolytic cell in which a reactive metal is produced by the electrolysis of the molten chloride of the metal.

Electrical conductivity (Section 25.3) A measure of the ability of a substance to conduct electricity; measured in units of $1.0/(ohm \cdot cm)$.

Extrinsic (or impurity) semiconductor (Section 25.2) A crystalline semiconductor to which impurities have been added to enhance its conductivity.

Flotation (Section 25.5) A method of ore concentration; the finely crushed ore is mixed with a suitable oil and water in a large tank. Agitation of the mixture with air produces a froth which contains the mineral particles and which is skimmed off.

Flux (Section 25.6) A substance (usually limestone, $CaCO_3$) used to form a slag in a smelting operation and thus remove the gangue.

Forbidden energy zone (Section 25.1) A zone in an energy diagram for the bands of a crystal; no electron can have an energy that would place it in this zone.

Gangue (Section 25.4) Unwanted material included with ores as mined.

Hall process (Section 25.6) The process by which aluminum is produced by the electrolysis of a solution of aluminum oxide in molten cryolite, Na_3AlF_6.

Insulator (Section 25.1) A substance in which a completely filled valence band is widely separated from a conduction band by a forbidden energy zone so that the valence electrons are normally not able to conduct electricity.

Intrinsic semiconductor (Sections 25.1 and 25.2) A pure, crystalline substance that functions as a semiconductor.

Kroll process (Section 25.6) The reduction of a metal halide by Mg, Na, or Ca.

Lanthanides (Section 25.11) The 14 inner-transition elements (with atomic numbers from 58 to 71) that follow lanthanum in the periodic table.

Leaching (Section 25.5) The removal of the metal component of an ore by use of a solution that contains a substance with which the desired component reacts to form a soluble species.

Matte (Section 25.6) Impure cuprous sulfide, Cu_2S, obtained by smelting copper sulfide ores.

Metallurgy (Section 25.5) The science of extracting metals from their ores and preparing these metals for use.

Native ore (Section 25.4) An ore in which a metal or a nonmetal (for example, Ag, Au, Bi, and S) occurs in elemental form.

n-type semiconductor (Section 25.2) An extrinsic semiconductor produced by the addition of a donor impurity (which has a larger number of valence electrons than the atoms of the host crystal) to an intrinsic semiconductor.

Open hearth process (Section 25.7) A process in which pig iron is refined into steel. The oxidation of the impurities in the pig iron is accomplished by reaction with iron oxide and air.

Ore (Section 25.4) A naturally occurring material from which one or more metals (or other chemical substances) can be profitably extracted.

Parkes process (Section 25.7) A process for removing silver from impure lead; the silver is selectively dissolved in molten zinc.

Pig iron (Section 25.6) An impure form of iron produced by the blast furnace.

p-type semiconductor (Section 25.2) An extrinsic semiconductor produced by adding an acceptor impurity (which has fewer valence electrons than the atoms of the host crystal) to an intrinsic semiconductor.

Reduction of an ore (Sections 25.5 and 25.6) A process in which a free metal is obtained from a metal compound found in an ore.

Refining (Sections 25.5 and 25.7) A process in which an impure metal is purified; in some cases, substances are added to give desired properties to the final product.

Roasting of ores (Section 25.5)   The process in which an ore is heated in air; used to convert sulfides and carbonates to oxides, which are more readily reduced to the free metals.

Semiconductor (Sections 25.1 and 25.2)   A material with a low electrical conductivity that increases markedly with increasing temperature. In crystals of semiconductors, the forbidden energy zone is sufficiently narrow so that electrons can be promoted from the valence band to the conduction band by heat.

Slag (Section 25.6)   A material that is formed from a flux and gangue in a smelting operation and therefore serves to remove the gangue.

Thermite process (Section 25.6)   The reduction of an oxide of a metal by aluminum; also called the **Goldschmidt process.**

Valence band (Section 25.1)   A band in a metallic crystal that contains the valence electrons of the metal.

Van Arkel process (Section 25.7)   A method for the purification of certain metals by the formation and subsequent thermal decomposition of an iodide of the metal.

Zone refining (Section 25.7)   A process used to purify certain metals in which a heated zone is caused to move along a rod of the impure metal. The impurities are swept along in the molten zone to one end of the rod.

Problems*

The Metallic Bond

25.1 How does the band theory of metallic bonding explain the luster, thermal conductivity, and electrical conductivity of metals?

25.2 Explain why the electrical conductivity of a metal *decreases* when the temperature is increased and the electrical conductivity of a semiconductor *increases* when the temperature is increased.

25.3 Use energy-level diagrams to explain the difference between conductors, insulators, and semiconductors.

25.4 Explain clearly the origin of the bands in a metallic crystal. What is a forbidden energy zone?

Physical Properties, Occurrence of Metals

25.5 What properties distinguish metals from nonmetals?

25.6 What are the principal types of ores of metals? Give an example of each type.

25.7 What diameter of iron wire must be used so that a given length will have an electrical conductivity equal to that of the same length of copper wire that is 1.0 cm in diameter? Electrical conductivities are listed in Table 25.1.

25.8 Explain why it is not surprising that the following ores are found in nature: **(a)** native ores of platinum, gold, and silver, **(b)** sulfate ores of barium, strontium, and lead, **(c)** Na^+ and Mg^{2+} in sea water, **(d)** sulfide ores of lead, bismuth, and nickel.

Metallurgy

25.9 What types of ores are roasted? Write a chemical equation for the roasting of an ore of each type. Why is the procedure used?

25.10 Describe the following metallurgical processes: **(a)** froth flotation, **(b)** Parkes process, **(c)** Van Arkel process, **(d)** Kroll process, **(e)** liquation, **(f)** zone refining, **(g)** thermite process.

25.11 Give the chemical equations for the reactions that occur in the blast furnace for the production of pig iron.

25.12 Describe the processes that are used to refine pig iron into steel.

25.13 Why is carbon reduction not used to obtain certain metals from their ores? What are used for the reductions in these cases?

25.14 Identify the following: **(a)** ore, **(b)** gangue, **(c)** alum, **(d)** amalgam, **(e)** flux, **(f)** slag, **(g)** smelting.

25.15 Use chemical equations to show how magnesium is obtained from sea water.

25.16 Describe, with chemical equations, the steps in the production of aluminum metal from bauxite.

25.17 Write chemical equations for the thermite reduction of: **(a)** UO_3 (by Al), **(b)** V_2O_5 (by Al), **(c)** Ta_2O_5 (by Na), **(d)** ThO_2 (by Ca), **(e)** WO_3 (by Al).

25.18 What metals are produced commercially by the electrolysis of molten salts? by the electrolysis of aqueous salt solutions?

25.19 Compare the metallurgical processes used to obtain copper from **(a)** low-grade $CuCO_3$ ores, **(b)** CuS ores.

25.20 Explain, using chemical equations, how impure copper is refined electrolytically. What is "anode sludge?"

25.21 Use chemical equations to compare the processes used to obtain lead from **(a)** $PbCO_3$ by roasting and carbon reduction, **(b)** PbS by incomplete roasting and smelting in the absence of air.

25.22 Explain, using chemical equations, how silver is obtained from low-grade ores of native silver.

The Representative Metals

25.23 Write chemical equations for the reactions that occur between Na and; **(a)** H_2, **(b)** N_2, **(c)** O_2, **(d)** Cl_2, **(e)** S, **(f)** P_4, **(g)** C, **(h)** H_2O, **(i)** NH_3.

25.24 According to first ionization potentials, the most reactive I A metal is cesium. According to standard electrode potentials, the most reactive I A metal is lithium. Reconcile these two observations.

25.25 Discuss the ways that the chemistry of lithium and its compounds differs from the chemistry of sodium and its compounds.

25.26 Explain why the compounds of beryllium are far more covalent than those of any other II A metal.

25.27 Write a chemical equation for the reaction that occurs between Ca and: **(a)** H_2, **(b)** N_2, **(c)** O_2, **(d)** Cl_2, **(e)** S, **(f)** P_4, **(g)** C, **(h)** H_2O, **(i)** NH_3.

25.28 The second ionization potential of the II A metals are larger than the first ionization potentials. Why do these elements not form 1+ ions instead of 2+ ions in their reactions?

25.29 Write a chemical equation for the reaction that occurs between Al and: **(a)** Cl_2, **(b)** O_2, **(c)** S, **(d)** N_2, **(e)** OH^-(aq), **(f)** H^+(aq).

25.30 Why do Al and Pb appear to be less reactive than electrode potentials would indicate?

25.31 Why is it impossible to precipitate Al_2S_3 from aqueous solutions containing Al^{3+}(aq) ions?

25.32 A "diagonal relationship" exists between Al and Be. Explain the atomic-ionic properties that cause such a relationship, and cite evidence for its existence.

---

* The more difficult problems are marked with asterisks. The appendix contains answers to color-keyed problems.

25.33 Write a chemical equation for the reaction that occurs between Sn and: **(a)** Cl_2, **(b)** O_2, **(c)** S, **(d)** $H^+(aq)$, **(e)** $OH^-(aq)$, **(f)** HNO_3.

25.34 Complete and balance the following chemical equations:

(a) $PbO_2(s) + H_2O + OH^-(aq) \longrightarrow$

(b) $PbO_2(s) \longrightarrow$ (mild heating)

(c) $PbO_2(s) \longrightarrow$ (strong heating)

(d) $PbO(s) + H_2O + OH^-(aq) \longrightarrow$

(e) $SnS(s) + S^{2-}(aq) \longrightarrow$

(f) $SnS_2(s) + S^{2-}(aq) \longrightarrow$

(g) $PbCl_2(s) + Cl^-(aq) \longrightarrow$

(h) $SnF_4(s) + F^-(aq) \longrightarrow$

The Transition Metals and Inner-transition Metals

25.35 Write chemical equations to compare the reactions of Fe, Cr, and Zn with: **(a)** Cl_2, **(b)** O_2, **(c)** S, **(d)** N_2, **(e)** H_2O, **(f)** $H^+(aq)$, **(g)** $OH^-(aq)$.

25.36 In what ways do the properties of the transition elements differ from those of the A family metals?

25.37 Write chemical equations for the reactions of CrO, Cr_2O_3, and CrO_3 with $H^+(aq)$ and with $OH^-(aq)$.

25.38 Group IV B consists of Ti, Zr, and Hf. Why do Zr and Hf resemble each other chemically much more than either of them resembles Ti?

*__25.39__ The standard electrode potential, $\mathscr{E}^\circ_{red}$, for the Hg_2^{2+}/Hg half-reaction is $+0.788$ V. For the cell:

$$Pt|Hg|Hg_2^{2+}(10^{-3}\ M)||Hg_2^{2+}(10^{-2}\ M)|Hg|Pt$$

$\mathscr{E}$ equals $+0.0296$ V. **(a)** What would be the emf of this concentration cell if the mercurous ion had the formula Hg^+? Notice that the concentrations given in the diagram for the cell correspond to the formula Hg_2^{2+}. **(b)** What would the standard electrode potential of the mercurous ion/mercury couple be if the formula of the mercurous ion were Hg^+? Notice that one liter of a 1 M Hg^+ solution would contain one-half the mass of "mercurous" ion that one liter of a 1 M solution of Hg_2^{2+} would contain. **(c)** Explain why measurement of the emf of the concentration cell proves that the formula of the mercurous ion is Hg_2^{2+}, whereas measurement of the $\mathscr{E}^\circ_{red}$ for the mercurous ion/mercury couple does *not* establish the formula of the ion.

25.40 What reasons can you give to explain the low order of reactivity of the noble metals?

25.41 Write an equation for each reaction that occurs between La and: **(a)** Cl_2, **(b)** O_2, **(c)** S, **(d)** N_2, **(e)** H_2O, **(f)** $H^+(aq)$.

25.42 The chemical properties of the transition metals vary widely from element to element. In contrast, the inner-transition metals markedly resemble each other chemically. Explain why this difference exists.

Unclassified Problems

25.42 What evidence supports the belief that the strength of the metallic bonding of the metals of the fourth and subsequent periods reaches a maximum around the center of the transition series? How can this trend be explained?

25.43 In what positions in the periodic table are the following types of metals found? **(a)** the most reactive, **(b)** the least reactive, **(c)** the softest, **(d)** amphoteric metals.

25.44 Give the products of the reactions of oxygen with: **(a)** K, **(b)** Na, **(c)** Li, **(d)** La, **(e)** Ba, **(f)** Ca, **(g)** Sn, **(h)** Sc, **(i)** Mn, **(j)** Al, **(k)** Zn.

25.45 Give the products of the reactions of nitrogen with: **(a)** Li, **(b)** La, **(c)** Mg, **(d)** Ca, **(e)** Sc, **(f)** Ti, **(g)** Al.

25.46 Give the products of the reactions of the following with $H^+(aq)$: **(a)** Fe, **(b)** Sc, **(c)** Ni, **(d)** Ce, **(e)** Al, **(f)** Sn, **(g)** Be.

25.47 Give the products of the reactions of the following with $OH^-(aq)$: **(a)** Be, **(b)** Cr, **(c)** Zn, **(d)** Al, **(e)** Ga, **(f)** Sn, **(g)** Ge.

COMPLEX COMPOUNDS

C H A P T E R

26

Chemists of the late-nineteenth century had difficulty in understanding how "molecular compounds" or "compounds of higher order" are bonded. The formation of a compound such as $CoCl_3 \cdot 6\,NH_3$ was baffling—particularly in this case since simple $CoCl_3$ does not exist. In 1893 Alfred Werner proposed a theory to account for compounds of this type. Werner wrote the formula of the cobalt compound as $[Co(NH_3)_6]Cl_3$. He assumed that the six ammonia molecules are symmetrically "coordinated" to the central cobalt atom by "subsidiary valencies" of cobalt while the "principal valencies" of cobalt are satisfied by the chloride ions. Werner spent over twenty years preparing and studying coordination compounds and perfecting and proving his theory. Although modern work has amplified his theory, it has required little modification.

Many practical applications have been derived from the study of complex compounds. Advances have resulted in such fields as metallurgy, analytical chemistry, biochemistry, water purification, textile dyeing, electrochemistry, and bacteriology. In addition, the study of these compounds has enlarged our understanding of chemical bonding, certain physical properties (for example, spectral and magnetic properties), minerals (many minerals are complex compounds), and metabolic processes (both heme of blood and chlorophyll of plants are complex compounds).

Alfred Werner, 1866–1919.
Edgar Fahs Smith Collection.

26.1 Structure

A complex ion or complex compound consists of a central metal cation to which several anions and/or molecules (called **ligands**) are bonded. With few exceptions, *free* ligands have at least one electron pair that is not engaged in bonding:

$$:\!\ddot{\underset{\cdot\cdot}{Cl}}\!:^{-} \qquad :C\equiv N\!:^{-} \qquad H\!-\!\ddot{\underset{|}{O}}\!: \qquad H\!-\!\underset{|}{\overset{\cdot\cdot}{N}}\!-\!H$$
$$\qquad\qquad\qquad\qquad\qquad\qquad H \qquad\qquad H$$

These electron pairs may be considered to be donated to the electron-deficient metal ions in the formation of complexes. Ligands, therefore, are substances that are capable of acting as Lewis bases. The bonding of complexes, however, shows a wide variation in character—from strongly covalent to predominantly ionic (see Section 26.5).

The ligands are said to be coordinated around the central cation in a **first coordination sphere.** In the formulas of complex compounds, such as

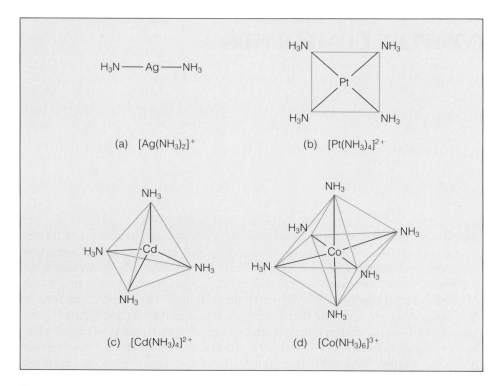

Figure 26.1 Common configurations of complex ions: (a) linear, (b) square-planar, (c) tetrahedral, (d) octahedral

$K_3[Fe(CN)_6]$ and $[Cu(NH_3)_4]Cl_2$, the first coordination sphere is indicated by square brackets. The ligands are arranged about the central ion in a regular geometric manner (see Figure 26.1). The number of atoms *directly* bonded to the central metal ion, or the number of coordination positions, is called the **coordination number** of the central ion.

The charge of a complex is the sum of the charges of the constituent parts. Complexes may be cations, anions, or neutral molecules. In each of the complexes of platinum(IV)—$[Pt(NH_3)_5Cl]^{3+}$, $[Pt(NH_3)_2Cl_4]^0$, and $[PtCl_6]^{2-}$—the platinum contributes $4+$, each chlorine contributes $1-$, and the coordinated ammonia molecules do not contribute to the charge of the complex.

An interesting series of platinum (IV) complexes appears in Table 26.1. The list is headed by the chloride of the $[Pt(NH_3)_6]^{4+}$ ion, and in each subsequent entry an ammonia molecule of the coordination sphere is replaced by a chloride ion. The *coordinated* ammonia molecules and chloride ions are tightly held and do not dissociate in water solution. Those chloride ions of the compound that are *not coordinated* to the platinum are ionizable. Aqueous solutions of the last three compounds of the table do not precipitate silver chloride upon the addition of silver nitrate, whereas solutions of the first four precipitate AgCl in amounts proportional to 4/4, 3/4, 2/4, and 1/4, respectively, of their total chlorine content. In each case, the total number of ions per formula unit derived from conductance data agrees with the formula listed in Table 26.1.

In general, the most stable complexes are formed by metal ions that have a high positive charge and a small ionic radius. The transition elements and the metals immediately following (notably the III A and IV A metals) have a marked tendency to form complexes. Few complexes are known for the lanthanides and

Table 26.1 Some platinum (IV) complex compounds

	Molar Conductance 0.001 M Solution[a] (25°C)	Number of Ions per Formula Unit	Number of Cl^- Ions per Formula Unit
$[Pt(NH_3)_6]Cl_4$	523	5	4
$[Pt(NH_3)_5Cl]Cl_3$	404	4	3
$[Pt(NH_3)_4Cl_2]Cl_2$	228	3	2
$[Pt(NH_3)_3Cl_3]Cl$	97	2	1
$[Pt(NH_3)_2Cl_4]$	0	0	0
$K[Pt(NH_3)Cl_5]$	108	2	0
$K_2[PtCl_6]$	256	3	0

[a] $cm^2/(\Omega \cdot mol)$

the I A and II A metals (with the exception of beryllium). The bonding of transition-metal complexes involves the d orbitals of the central metal atom.

Complexes containing metal ions with coordination numbers ranging from two to twelve are known. The majority of complexes, however, are two-, four-, and six-coordinate (see Figure 26.1), and the coordination number six is by far the most common.

Six-coordinate complexes are octahedral. The regular octahedral arrangement of atoms is frequently represented:

This representation is a convenient way to create a three-dimensional illusion. No difference between the bonds of the vertical axis and the other bonds should be inferred from this drawing. *All* the bonds are equivalent. Tetragonal geometry is a distorted form of the octahedral in which the bond distances along one of the axes are longer or shorter than the remaining bonds:

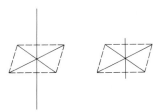

Four-coordinate complexes are known in tetrahedral and square-planar configurations. The square-planar configuration is the usual one for Pt^{II}, Pd^{II}, and Au^{III} and is assumed by many complexes of Ni^{II} and Cu^{II}. Examples include $[Pt(NH_3)_4]^{2+}$, $[PdCl_4]^{2-}$, $[AuCl_4]^-$, $[Ni(CN)_4]^{2-}$, and $[Cu(NH_3)_4]^{2+}$. In some instances there is evidence that square complexes may be tetragonal forms with two groups, along a vertical axis, located at greater distances from the

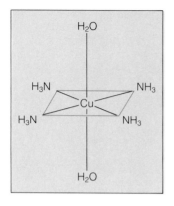

Figure 26.2 Configuration of $[Cu(NH_3)_4(H_2O)_2]^{2+}$

central ion than the ligands of the plane. Thus, $[Cu(NH_3)_4]^{2+}$ in water solution may have two water molecules coordinated in the manner shown in Figure 26.2. Hence, square-planar and octahedral geometries may be considered to merge.

For four-coordinate complexes the tetrahedral configuration is encountered more frequently than the square-planar and is particularly common for complexes of the nontransition elements. Certain complexes of Cu^I, Ag^I, Au^I, Be^{II}, Zn^{II}, Cd^{II}, Hg^{II}, Al^{III}, Ga^{III}, In^{III}, Fe^{III}, Co^{II}, and Ni^0 are tetrahedral. Examples include $[Cu(CN)_4]^{3-}$, $[BeF_4]^{2-}$, $[AlF_4]^-$, $[FeCl_4]^-$, $[Cd(CN)_4]^{2-}$, $[ZnCl_4]^{2-}$, and $[Ni(CO)_4]^0$. The oxyanions of certain transition metals (such as VO_4^{3-}, CrO_4^{2-}, FeO_4^{2-}, and MnO_4^-) are tetrahedral, resembling the tetrahedral oxyanions of nonmetals (such as SiO_4^{4-}, PO_4^{3-}, AsO_4^{3-}, SO_4^{2-}, and ClO_4^-). Although a number of tetrahedral complexes of transition elements are known, the majority of complexes of these elements are octahedral.

Linear, two-coordinate complexes are not so common as the other forms previously mentioned. However, well-characterized complexes of this type are known for Cu^I, Ag^I, and Hg^{II}; examples are $[CuCl_2]^-$, $[Ag(NH_3)_2]^+$, $[Au(CN)_2]^-$, $[Hg(NH_3)_2]^{2+}$, and $[Hg(CN)_2]^0$.

In general, each metal exhibits more than one coordination number and geometry in its complexes. Although all known complexes of Co^{III} are octahedral, most cations form more than one type of complex. For example, Al^{III} forms tetrahedral and octahedral complexes, Cu^I forms linear and tetrahedral complexes, and Ni^{II} forms square-planar, tetrahedral, and octahedral complexes.

Complexes of the transition elements are frequently highly colored. Examples of complexes that exhibit a wide range of colors are $[Co(NH_3)_6]^{3+}$ (yellow), $[Co(NH_3)_5(H_2O)]^{3+}$ (pink), $[Co(NH_3)_5Cl]^{2+}$ (violet), $[Co(H_2O)_6]^{3+}$ (purple), and $[Co(NH_3)_4Cl_2]^+$ (a violet form and a green form—see Section 26.4).

The ligands we have discussed thus far have been capable of forming only one bond with the central ion. They are referred to as **unidentate** (from Latin, meaning *one-toothed*) ligands. Certain ligands are capable of occupying more than one coordination position of a metal ion. Ligands that coordinate through two bonds from different parts of the molecule or anion are called **bidentate**. Examples are

carbonate ion   *oxalate ion*   *ethylenediamine*

The carbonate and oxalate ions each coordinate through two oxygen atoms. The ethylenediamine molecule (abbreviated *en*) coordinates through both nitrogen atoms. These positions are marked with arrows. Bidentate ligands form rings with the central metal ions:

$$CH_2—CH_2$$
$$NH_2 \qquad NH_2$$
$$M$$

The resulting metal complexes are called **chelates** (from Greek, meaning *claw*). The formation of five- or six-membered rings is generally favored.

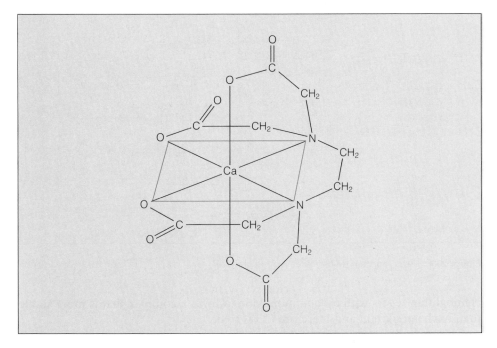

Figure 26.3 Ethylenediaminetetraacetate complex of Ca^{2+} ($[Ca(EDTA)]^{2-}$)

Multidentate ligands have been prepared that can coordinate at 2, 3, 4, 5, or 6 positions. In general, chelates are more stable than complexes containing only unidentate ligands. Thus, the sexadentate complexing agent ethylenediaminetetraacetate ion (EDTA),

$$^-O_2C-CH_2 \qquad\qquad CH_2-CO_2^-$$
$$N-CH_2-CH_2-N$$
$$^-O_2C-CH_2 \qquad\qquad CH_2-CO_2^-$$

is capable of forming a very stable complex with the calcium ion—an ion with one of the least tendencies toward the formation of complexes (see Figure 26.3).

Heme of hemoglobin is a chelate of Fe^{2+}, and chlorophyll is a chelate of Mg^{2+}. In both these substances the metal ion is coordinated to a quadridentate ligand, which may be considered to be derived from a porphin structure (see Figure 26.4) by the substitution of various groups for the H atoms of the porphin. The substituted porphins are called **porphyrins.**

Coordination around the iron atom of heme is octahedral. Four of the coordination positions are utilized in the formation of the heme (which is essentially planar), the fifth is used to bond the heme to a protein molecule (globin), and the sixth is used to coordinate either H_2O (hemoglobin) or O_2 (oxyhemoglobin). Coordination about this sixth position is reversible:

$$\text{hemoglobin} + O_2 \rightleftharpoons \text{oxyhemoglobin} + H_2O$$

and dependent upon the pressure of O_2. Hemoglobin picks up O_2 in the lungs and releases it in the body tissues, where it is used for the oxidation of food.

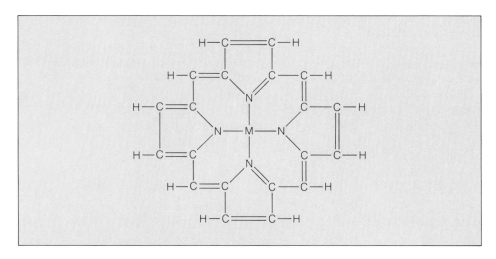

Figure 26.4 Metal porphin (M indicates a metal cation)

Hemoglobin reacts with carbon monoxide to form a complex that is more stable than oxyhemoglobin, and therefore CO is toxic.

Chlorophyll, a porphyrin of Mg^{2+}, the green pigment of plants, serves as a catalyst for the process of photosynthesis in which CO_2 and H_2O are converted into a carbohydrate (glucose) and O_2. The energy for photosynthesis comes from sunlight, and the chlorophyll molecule initiates this process by absorbing a quantum of light.

26.2 Labile and Inert Complexes

Certain complexes (which are called labile) rapidly undergo reactions in which ligands are replaced; other complexes (nonlabile, or inert, complexes) do not undergo these substitution reactions or do so slowly. This distinction applies to the *rate* of attainment of equilibrium and has no bearing on the position of equilibrium. With the exception of the complexes of Cr^{III} and Co^{III}, most octahedral complexes of the fourth period transition elements are very labile; exchange reactions come to equilibrium almost as fast as the reagents are mixed. The reason that the complexes of Co^{III} have been studied more than any other group of complexes is that these substances undergo ligand exchange reactions at a slower, more convenient rate.

The inertness of a complex should not be confused with its thermodynamic stability. Although $[Co(NH_3)_6]^{3+}$ is stable in aqueous solution:

$$[Co(NH_3)_6]^{3+} + 6\,H_2O \rightleftharpoons [Co(H_2O)_6]^{3+} + 6\,NH_3 \qquad K \cong 10^{-34}$$

the complex is unstable in aqueous acid:

$$[Co(NH_3)_6]^{3+} + 6\,H_3O^+ \rightleftharpoons [Co(H_2O)_6]^{3+} + 6\,NH_4^+ \qquad K \cong 10^{22}$$

Nevertheless, the $[Co(NH_3)_6]^{3+}$ ion can exist in dilute acid for weeks; the latter reaction must have a high activation energy. Thus, the complex is thermodynamically unstable and at the same time inert.

Examples of the reverse situation are also known. The stable complex

$[FeCl_6]^{3-}$ is very labile and undergoes rapid exchange with radioactive chloride in aqueous solution.

In many cases complex formation results in the stabilization of metal ions toward oxidation or reduction. Electrode potentials for Zn^{2+} and some complexes of this ion are

$$2e^- + Zn^{2+}(aq) \rightleftharpoons Zn(s) \qquad \mathscr{E}^\circ_{red} = -0.763 \text{ V}$$

$$2e^- + [Zn(NH_3)_4]^{2+} \rightleftharpoons Zn(s) + 4NH_3 \qquad \mathscr{E}^\circ_{red} = -1.04 \text{ V}$$

$$2e^- + [Zn(CN)_4]^{2-} \rightleftharpoons Zn(s) + 4CN^- \qquad \mathscr{E}^\circ_{red} = -1.26 \text{ V}$$

The increasing stability toward reduction observed in this series parallels increasing stability of the complexes toward dissociation in aqueous solution. The instability constant of $[Zn(NH_3)_4]^{2+}$ is approximately 10^{-10} and that of the $[Zn(CN)_4]^{2-}$ ion is about 10^{-18}.

In many instances complex formation results in the stabilization of a metal in a rare or otherwise unknown oxidation state. A classic example is afforded by the complexes of Co^{III}. Simple compounds containing cobalt in an oxidation state of $3+$ are rare. The electrode potential

$$e^- + [Co(H_2O)_6]^{3+} \rightleftharpoons [Co(H_2O)_6]^{2+} \qquad \mathscr{E}^\circ_{red} = +1.81 \text{ V}$$

indicates that the hydrated Co^{3+} ion is a strong oxidizing agent which is capable of oxidizing water to oxygen and hence incapable of prolonged existence in water.

In the presence of many complexing agents, such as NH_3, the $3+$ oxidation state of cobalt is much more stable toward reduction:

$$e^- + [Co(NH_3)_6]^{3+} \rightleftharpoons [Co(NH_3)_6]^{2+} \qquad \mathscr{E}^\circ_{red} = +0.11 \text{ V}$$

The $[Co(NH_3)_6]^{3+}$ ion can exist in aqueous solution. It does not oxidize water to oxygen, and, in fact, the reverse reaction—the oxidation of Co^{II} complexes by a stream of air—is used to prepare Co^{III} complexes. The ammonia complex of Co^{III}, which has an instability constant of about 10^{-34}, is much more stable toward dissociation than the ammonia complex of Co^{II}, which has an instability constant of approximately 10^{-5}.

The formation of a complex can prevent a metal cation from disproportionating. The copper(I) ion, for example, is unstable in water solution:

$$2Cu^+(aq) \longrightarrow Cu^{2+}(aq) + Cu(s)$$

The ammonia complex of this ion, $[Cu(NH_3)_2]^+$ is stable toward disproportionation. A similar situation is observed for the ions of gold: Au^+ is theoretically unstable toward disproportionation into Au^{3+} and Au metal. In addition, both gold ions are strong oxidizing agents and are capable of oxidizing water. However, stable complexes of both Au^I and Au^{III} are known.

26.3 Nomenclature

Since thousands of complexes are known and the number is constantly expanding, a system of nomenclature has been adopted for these compounds. The following list summarizes the important rules of the system. They are adequate for naming the simple and frequently encountered complexes.

1. If the complex is a salt, the cation is named first whether or not it is a complex ion.

2. The ligands of the complex are named first and the central metal atom is named last. The ligands are named in alphabetical order. The number of ligands of a particular type is indicated by a prefix: di (for two), tri (for three), tetra (for four), penta (for five), and hexa (for six). These prefixes are not considered in alphabetizing; the term *dichloro* (which indicates that two chloride ions function as ligands) is alphabetized under *c*, not *d*. When prefixes form a part of the name of the ligand, they *are* used in the alphabetizing; dimethylamine, $(CH_3)_2NH$, for example, is alphabetized under *d*. For complicated ligands (such as ethylenediamine in which the prefix *di* appears) the prefixes bis-, tris-, tetrakis, pentakis, and hexakis- (which indicate from two to six ligands) are employed with parentheses around the name of the ligand.

3. Anionic ligands are given -*o* endings. Examples are: OH^-, hydroxo; O^{2-}, oxo; S^{2-}, thio; F^-, fluoro; Cl^-, chloro; Br^-, bromo; I^-, iodo; CO_3^{2-}, carbonato; CN^-, cyano; CNO^-, cyanato; $C_2O_4^{2-}$, oxalato; NO_3^-, nitrato; NO_2^-, nitro; SO_4^{2-}, sulfato; and $S_2O_3^{2-}$, thiosulfato.

4. The names of neutral ligands are usually not changed. Important exceptions to this rule are: H_2O, aqua; NH_3, ammine; CO, carbonyl; and NO, nitrosyl.

5. If the complex is an anion, the ending -*ate* is employed, and if the symbol of the metal is derived from a Latin name, the Latin name of the metal is used as the root name. If the complex is a cation or a neutral molecule, the English name of the metal is always employed and no suffix is added.

6. The oxidation number of the central ion may be indicated by a Roman numeral, which is set off by parentheses and placed after the name of the complex (*Stock number*) *or* the charge of the complex may be indicated by an Arabic numeral followed by + or − and set off by parentheses (*Ewens-Bassett number*). The Arabic zero is used in the Stock system (to indicate an oxidation number of zero), but zero is not used in the Ewens-Bassett system (the absence of a number after the name of a complex indicates that it is uncharged).

Examples of these rules of nomenclature are:

$[Ag(NH_3)_2]Cl$	diamminesilver(I) chloride diamminesilver(1+) chloride	$[Cu(en)_2]SO_4$	bis(ethylenediamine)copper(II) sulfate bis(ethylenediamine)copper(2+) sulfate
$[Co(NH_3)_3Cl_3]$	triamminetrichlorocobalt(III) triamminetrichlorocobalt	$[Pt(NH_3)][PtCl_6]$	tetraammineplatinum(II) hexachloroplatinate(IV) tetraammineplatinum(2+) hexachloroplatinate(2−)
$K_4[Fe(CN)_6]$	potassium hexacyanoferrate(II) potassium hexacyanoferrate(4−)	$[CoCl(NH_3)_4(H_2O)]Cl_2$	tetraammineaquachlorocobalt(III) chloride tetraammineaquachlorocobalt(2+) chloride
$[Ni(CO)_4]$	tetracarbonylnickel(0) tetracarbonylnickel		

Common names are frequently employed when they are clearly more convenient than the systematic names (for example, ferrocyanide rather than hexacyanoferrate(II) for $[Fe(CN)_6]^{4-}$) or when the structure of the complex is not certain (for example, the aluminate ion).

26.4 Isomerism

Two compounds with the same molecular formula but different arrangements of atoms are called isomers. Such compounds differ in their chemical and physical properties. **Structural isomerism** is displayed by compounds that have different ligands within their coordination spheres. Several types of structural isomers may be identified.

The following pair of compounds of Co^{III} serve as an example of **ionization isomers**:

(a) $[Co(NH_3)_5(SO_4)]Br$ (b) $[Co(NH_3)_5Br]SO_4$

    red   *violet*

Conductance data show that both compounds dissociate into two ions in aqueous solution. In the first compound, the SO_4^{2-} ion is a part of the coordination sphere, and the Br^- ion is ionizable. An aqueous solution of compound (a) gives an immediate precipitate of AgBr upon the addition of $AgNO_3$, but since the SO_4^{2-} ion is not free, no precipitate forms upon the addition of $BaCl_2$. For compound (b), the reverse is true. An aqueous solution of this compound gives a precipitate of $BaSO_4$ but not AgBr since the SO_4^{2-} is ionizable and the Br^- is coordinated. Note that SO_4^{2-} functions as a unidentate ligand and that the charge on the complex ion of compound (a) is $1+$ and that of compound (b) is $2+$. There are numerous additional examples of ionization isomers, such as

$[Pt(NH_3)_4Cl_2]Br_2$ $[Pt(NH_3)_4Br_2]Cl_2$

Hydrate isomerism is analogous to ionization isomerism and is probably best illustrated by the following series of compounds that have the formula $CrCl_3 \cdot 6 H_2O$:

(a) $[Cr(H_2O)_6]Cl_3$ (b) $[Cr(H_2O)_5Cl]Cl_2 \cdot H_2O$ (c) $[Cr(H_2O)_4Cl_2]Cl \cdot 2 H_2O$

    violet   *green*   *green*

In a mole of each of these compounds there are six moles of water. However, in compound (a), six water molecules are coordinated; in compound (b), five; and in compound (c), four. The uncoordinated water molecules occupy separate positions in the crystals and are readily lost when compounds (b) and (c) are exposed to desiccants. The coordinated water, however, is not so easily removed. Further evidence for the structures of the compounds is afforded by conductance data (the compounds are composed of four, three, and two ions, respectively) and the quantity of AgCl precipitated (the compounds have three, two, and one ionizable chloride ions, respectively).

Another example of hydrate isomerism is given by the following pair of compounds:

$[Co(NH_3)_4(H_2O)Cl]Cl_2$ $[Co(NH_3)_4Cl_2]Cl \cdot H_2O$

Coordination isomers may exist in compounds that have two or more centers of coordination. Isomers arise through the exchange of ligands between these coordination centers. In simple examples, which involve only two complex ions per compound, the coordinated metal ions may be the same:

$[Cr(NH_3)_6][Cr(NCS)_6]$ $[Cr(NH_3)_4(NCS)_2][Cr(NH_3)_2(NCS)_4]$

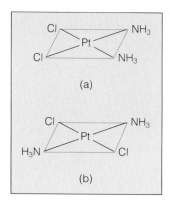

Figure 26.5 (a) *Cis* and (b) *trans* isomers of diamminedichloroplatinum(II)

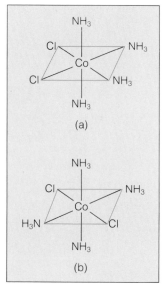

Figure 26.6 (a) *Cis* and (b) *trans* isomers of the tetraamminedichlorocobalt(III) ion

or different:

$$[Cu(NH_3)_4][PtCl_4] \qquad [Pt(NH_3)_4][CuCl_4]$$

and the oxidation state of the metals may vary:

$$[Pt(NH_3)_4][PtCl_6] \qquad\qquad [Pt(NH_3)_4Cl_2][PtCl_4]$$
tetraammineplatinum(II)   *tetraamminedichloroplatinum(IV)*
hexachloroplatinate(IV)   *tetrachloroplatinate(II)*

Linkage isomerism arises when ligands are capable of coordinating in two ways. The nitrite ion, NO_2^-, for example, can coordinate through an oxygen atom (—ONO, nitrito compounds) or through the nitrogen atom (—NO_2, nitro compounds):

$$[Co(NH_3)_5(NO_2)]Cl_2 \qquad\qquad [Co(NH_3)_5(ONO)]Cl_2$$
(yellow)   *(red)*
pentaamminenitrocobalt(III)   *pentaamminenitritocobalt(III)*
chloride   *chloride*

Some other ligands that are capable of forming linkage isomers are: CN^- which can coordinate either through the C atom or the N atom; SCN^-, through N or S; and CO, through C or O.

Stereoisomerism is a second general class of isomers. Compounds are stereoisomers when they both contain the same ligands in their coordination spheres but differ in the way that these ligands are arranged in space. One type of stereoisomerism is geometric, or *cis-trans*, isomerism.

An example of geometric isomerism is afforded by the *cis* and *trans* isomers of the square-planar diamminedichloroplatinum(II); see Figure 26.5. In the *cis* isomer the chlorine atoms are situated on adjacent corners of the square (along an edge), whereas in the *trans* isomer they occupy opposite corners (along the diagonal).

Since all the ligands of a tetrahedral complex have the same relationship to one another, *cis-trans* isomerism does not exist for this geometry. Many geometric isomers are known for octahedral complexes, however. There are two isomers of the tetraamminedichlorocobalt(III) ion; a violet *cis* form and a green *trans* form (see Figure 26.6).

A second type of stereoisomerism is **optical isomerism**. Some molecules and ions can exist in two forms that are not superimposable and that bear the same relationship that a right hand bears to a left hand. That the hands are not superimposable is readily demonstrated by attempting to put a left-handed glove on a right hand. Such molecules and ions are spoken of as being **chiral** or **dissymmetric,** and the forms are called **enantiomorphs** (from Greek, meaning *opposite forms*) or **mirror images** (since the one may be considered to be a mirror reflection of the other).

Enantiomorphs have identical physical properties except for their effects on plane-polarized light. Light that has been passed through a polarizer consists of waves that vibrate in a single plane. One enantiomorph (the **dextro** form), whether pure or in solution, will rotate the plane of the plane-polarized light of the right (clockwise); the other (the **levo** form) will rotate the plane an equal extent to the left (counterclockwise). The process is illustrated in Figure 26.7.

For this reason enantiomorphs are called optical isomers or **optical antipodes.** An equimolar mixture of enantiomorphs, called a **racemic modification,** has no

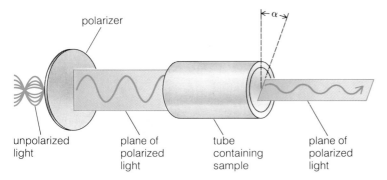

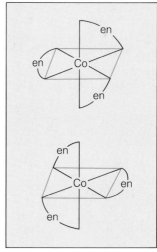

Figure 26.7 Rotation of the plane-polarized light. The plane is rotated by an angle after the light passes through a solution of an optically active isomer. In this case, rotation is to the right (clockwise) and the isomer is said to be dextrorotatory.

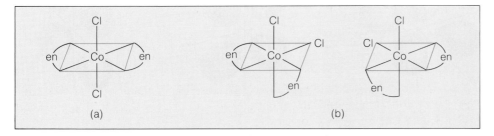

(a)   (b)

Figure 26.8 Dextro and levo forms of the tris(ethylenediamine)cobalt(III) ion

Figure 26.9 Isomers of the dichlorobis(ethylenediamine)cobalt(III) ion: (a) *trans* isomer, (b) optical isomers of the *cis* form

effect on plane-polarized light since it contains an equal number of *dextro*rotatory and *levo*rotatory forms.

The tris(ethylenediamine)cobalt(III) ion exists in enantiomorphic forms. Examination of the diagrams of Figure 26.8 confirms that the enantiomorphs are not superimposable and that the ions are chiral. Note that bidentate chelating agents can span only *cis* positions.

Both types of stereoisomerism—geometric and optical—are illustrated by the isomers of the dichlorobis(ethylenediamine)cobalt(III) ion (see Figure 26.9). The *trans* configuration of this ion is optically inactive, and a mirror image would be identical to the original. The *cis* arrangement, however, is chiral and exists in *dextro* and *levo* forms. The *trans* modification is said to be a *diastereoisomer* of either the *dextro* or *levo cis* modification.

26.5 The Bonding in Complexes

The first theory used to explain the bonding in complexes assumed quite simply that the ligands donate electron pairs to form covalent bonds with the central metal ions. Bonds formed in this way were called coordinate covalent bonds. During the years that followed, the **valence bond theory** grew out of this simple concept. The central metal ion is assumed to supply empty hybrid orbitals toward the formation of the complex (for example, $d^2 sp^3$ hybrid orbitals for the formation of an octahedral complex), and the ligands supply electron pairs to fill these orbitals and form covalent bonds. The valence bond theory fits many experimental observations well, but it fails to explain others in a satisfactory manner (notably,

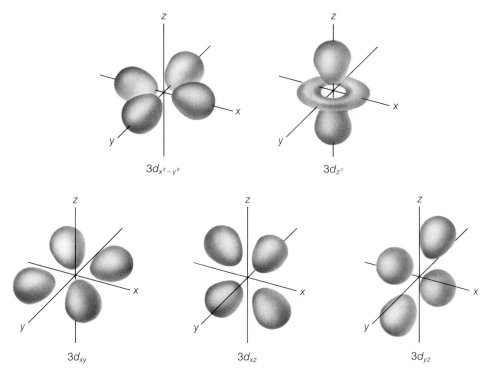

Figure 26.10 Boundary surface diagrams for the d orbitals

the numbers of unpaired electrons in certain complexes), and it has nothing at all to say about still other observations (notably, the colors of complexes).

Modern theories of the bonding in complexes are derived from the **crystal field theory.** In its simplest form, this theory explains the bonding in terms of electrostatic attractions between the positive charge of the central metal cation and the negative charges of the electron pairs of the ligands. An important aspect of this theory is the effect that the electrostatic field of the ligands has on the d orbitals of the central metal cation.

The outer electrons of transition-metal ions are d electrons (see Table 7.4). In a free transition-metal ion, all five of the d orbitals have equal orbital energies; they are degenerate. Not all of the d orbitals are energy equivalent, however, when they are surrounded by the negative field created by the ligands.

Consider the relation of the d orbitals (see Figure 26.10) to the arrangement of the ligands of an octahedral complex (see Figure 26.11a). The d_{z^2} and $d_{x^2-y^2}$ orbitals have lobes that point toward ligands, whereas the lobes of the d_{xy}, d_{xz}, and d_{yz} orbitals lie between ligands. Thus, in the complex two sets of d orbitals exist. The d_{xy}, d_{xz}, and d_{yz} orbitals (or t_{2g} **orbitals**) are equivalent to each other, and the d_{z^2} and $d_{x^2-y^2}$ orbitals (or e_g **orbitals**) are equivalent to each other and different from the first three. The symbols t_{2g} and e_g are applied to threefold degenerate and twofold degenerate sets of orbitals, respectively.

It is not immediately obvious that the d_{z^2} orbital is perfectly equivalent to the $d_{x^2-y^2}$ orbital. The d_{z^2} orbital may be regarded as a combination, in equal parts, of two hypothetical orbitals, $d_{z^2-y^2}$ and $d_{z^2-x^2}$, which have shapes exactly like that of the $d_{x^2-y^2}$ orbital (see Figure 26.12). Since the number of d orbitals is limited to five, the $d_{z^2-y^2}$ and $d_{z^2-x^2}$ orbitals have no independent existence.

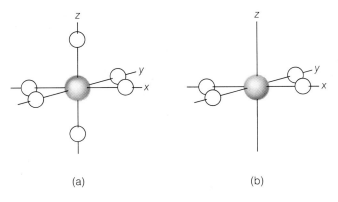

(a)   (b)

Figure 26.11   Arrangement of ligands of (a) octahedral and
(b) square-planar complexes in relation to sets of Cartesian
coordinates. Colored spheres are central metal ions; open
circles represent coordinating atoms of ligands

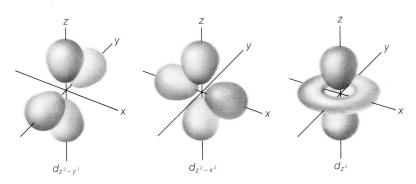

$d_{z^2-y^2}$ $d_{z^2-x^2}$ d_{z^2}

Figure 26.12   Diagram showing that the d_{z^2} orbitals may be considered to be
a combination of the $d_{z^2-y^2}$ and $d_{z^2-x^2}$ orbitals

In the crystal field theory the assumption is made that an electrostatic field
surrounding the central metal ion is produced by the negative ends of the dipolar
molecules or by the anions that function as ligands. A metal-ion electron in a d
orbital that has lobes directed toward ligands has a higher energy (owing to
electrostatic repulsion) than an electron in an orbital with lobes that point between
ligands. In octahedral complexes the orbitals of the e_g group, therefore, have
higher orbital energies than those of the t_{2g} group. The difference between the
orbital energies of the t_{2g} and e_g orbitals in an octahedral complex is given the
symbol Δ_o.

In a square-planar complex (see Figure 26.11b), the d orbitals exhibit four
different relationships. The lobes of the $d_{x^2-y^2}$ orbital point toward ligands, and
this orbital has the highest orbital energy. The lobes of the d_{xy} orbital lie between
orbitals but are coplanar with them, and hence this orbital is next highest in
orbital energy. The lobes of the d_{z^2} orbital point out of the plane of the complex,
but the belt around the center of the orbital (which contains about a third of the
electron density) lies in the plane. The d_{z^2} orbital, therefore, is next highest in
orbital energy. The d_{xz} and d_{yz} orbitals, which are degenerate, are least affected
by the electrostatic field of the ligands since their lobes point out of the plane of
the complex. These orbitals are lowest in orbital energy.

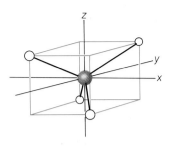

Figure 26.13 The relation of tetrahedrally arranged ligands to a set of Cartesian coordinates. Colored sphere is central metal ion; open circles, coordinating atoms of ligands.

The order of splitting of the d orbitals in a tetrahedral complex may be derived from an examination of Figure 26.13, which shows the relation of tetrahedrally arranged ligands to a system of Cartesian coordinates and a hypothetical cube. The lobes of the d_{xy}, d_{xz}, and d_{yz} orbitals point toward cube edges, and the lobes of the d_{z^2} and $d_{x^2-y^2}$ orbitals point toward the centers of cube faces. Notice that the distance from the center of a cube face to a ligand is farther than the distance from the center of a cube edge to a ligand. The order of orbital energies, therefore, is the reverse of that for octahedral coordination, and the threefold degenerate set, t_{2g}, is of higher energy than the twofold degenerate set, e_g. The difference in energy is given the symbol Δ_t.

The splitting of d-orbital energies in tetrahedral, octahedral, and square-planar complexes is summarized in Figure 26.14. A defect of the crystal field theory is that is centers on the ionic aspects of the bonding and fails to take into account the covalent character of the bonding. The **molecular orbital theory** is at the opposite extreme; it describes the bonding in terms of the formation of bonding and antibonding molecular orbitals. From either point of view, however, the same conclusions are reached regarding the distribution of electrons in the d orbitals of the central metal ion. The orders of d-orbital splitting are those shown in Figure 26.14. The importance of these splitting diagrams is discussed later in this section.

In an octahedral complex, the $3d_{z^2}$ and $3d_{x^2-y^2}$ orbitals along with the $4s$ and three $4p$ orbitals are assumed to overlap six orbitals from the ligands with the attendant formation of six bonding molecular orbitals and six antibonding molecular orbitals. The d_{xy}, d_{xz}, and d_{yz} orbitals (the t_{2g} set), which do not overlap the σ orbitals of the ligands, are essentially nonbonding. (The t_{2g} set can be used in π bonding, however.)

A bonding molecular orbital concentrates electron density between the atoms and is of relatively low energy in comparison with an antibonding molecular

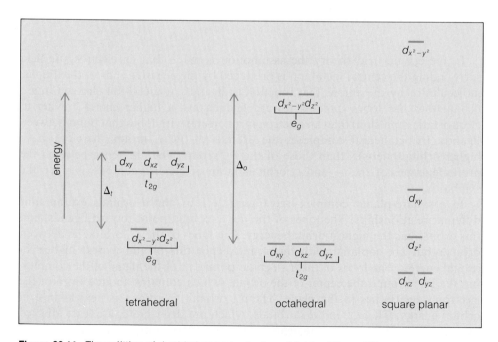

Figure 26.14 The splitting of d-orbital energies by ligand fields of three different geometries

Chapter 26 Complex Compounds

orbital, which has a low electron density between the atoms and acts as a disruptive force. A molecular orbital energy-level diagram for an octahedral complex with no π bonding is given in Figure 26.15.

Whenever two atomic orbitals of different energies combine, the character of the resulting bonding molecular orbital is predominantly that of the atomic orbital of lower energy, and the antibonding molecular orbital has mainly the character of the higher energy atomic orbital. In an octahedral complex the bonding orbitals have predominantly the character of ligand orbitals. The antibonding orbitals resemble metal orbitals more than ligand orbitals. The t_{2g} set, which are nonbonding, may be considered as purely metal orbitals.

In an octahedral complex, the six electron pairs from the ligands completely occupy the bonding molecular orbitals. The d electrons of the central metal ion are accommodated in the t_{2g} nonbonding orbitals and the $(e_g)_a$ antibonding orbitals. The difference between the energies of these sets is Δ_o. The four remaining antibonding orbitals are never occupied in the ground states of any known complex.

The conclusion reached by this treatment is much the same as that postulated by the crystal field theory. In an octahedral complex the degeneracy of the metal d orbitals may be considered to be split into a threefold degenerate set, t_{2g}, and a higher energy, metal-like, twofold degenerate set, which may be labeled $(e_g)_a$ or simply e_g.

The molecular orbital treatment may be applied to tetrahedral and square-planar complexes, but the applications are more complicated. The conclusions reached are in essential agreement with the splittings diagrammed in Figure 26.14.

For the octahedral complexes of a given metal ion, the magnitude of Δ_o is different for each set of ligands, and the electronic configurations of many complexes depend upon the size of Δ_o.

For complexes of transition-element ions with one, two, or three d electrons (which are referred to as d^1, d^2, or d^3 ions), the orbital occupancy is certain and

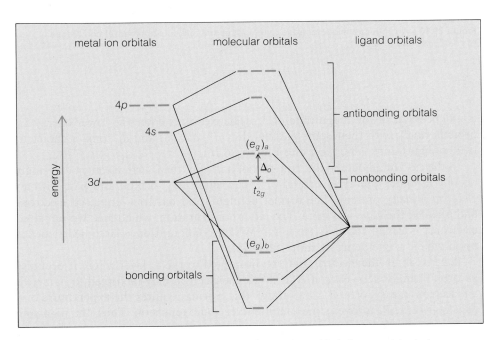

Figure 26.15 Diagram indicating the formation of molecular orbitals for an octahedral complex with no π bonding

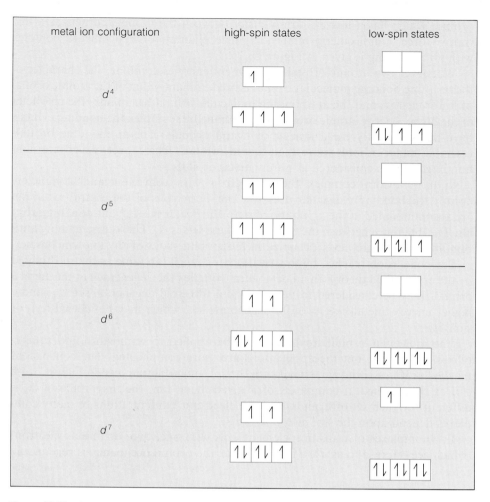

| metal ion configuration | high-spin states | low-spin states |

Figure 26.16 Arrangements of electrons in high-spin and low-spin octahedral complexes of d^4, d^5, d^6, and d^7 ions

is independent of the magnitude of Δ_o. The electrons enter the lower energy t_{2g} orbitals singly with their spins parallel. For d^4, d^5, d^6, and d^7 ions, a choice of two configurations is possible (see Figure 26.16).

In the case of an octahedral complex of a d^4 ion, the fourth electron can singly occupy a higher energy e_g orbital or it can enter a t_{2g} orbital and pair with an electron already present. The former configuration has four unpaired electrons and is called the **high-spin state.** The latter configuration, which has two unpaired electrons, is called the **low-spin state.** Which configuration is assumed depends upon which is energetically more favorable.

If Δ_o is small, the electron may be promoted to the e_g level where it occupies an orbital singly. However, if Δ_o is large, the electron may be forced to pair with an electron in a t_{2g} orbital even though this pairing requires the expenditure of a **pairing energy, P,** to overcome the inter-electronic repulsion. Thus, the high-spin configuration results when

$$\Delta_o < P$$

and the low-spin configuration results when

$$\Delta_o > P$$

The value of P depends upon the metal ion; Δ_o is different for each complex.

This conclusion is also valid for complexes of d^5, d^6, and d^7 ions. For a complex of a d^8 ion there is only one possible configuration: six electrons paired in the t_{2g} orbitals and two unpaired electrons in the e_g orbitals. Likewise, complexes of d^9 and d^{10} ions exist in only one configuration.

Values of Δ_o can be obtained from studies of the absorption spectra of complexes. In the complex $[Ti(H_2O)_6]^{3+}$, there is only one electron to be accommodated in either the t_{2g} or e_g orbitals. In the ground state this electron occupies a t_{2g} orbital. Excitation of the electron to an e_g orbital is possible when the energy required for this transition, Δ_o, is supplied. The absorption of light by the complex can bring about such excitations. The wavelength of light absorbed most strongly by the $[Ti(H_2O)_6]^{3+}$ ion is approximately 490 nm, which corresponds to a Δ_o of about 243 kJ/mol. The single absorption band of this complex spreads out over a considerable portion of the visible spectrum. Most of the red and violet light, however, is not absorbed, which causes the red-violet color of the complex.

The interpretation of the absorption spectra of complexes with more than one d electron is considerably more complicated, since more than two arrangements of d electrons are then possible. In general, for a given metal ion the replacement of one set of ligands by another causes a change in the energy difference between the t_{2g} and e_g orbitals, Δ_o, which gives rise to different light-absorption properties. In many instances a striking color change is observed when the ligands of a complex are replaced by other ligands.

Ligands may be arranged in a **spectrochemical series** according to the magnitude of Δ_o they bring about. From the experimental study of the spectra of many complexes, it has been found that the order is generally the same for the complexes of all of the transition elements in their common oxidation states with only occasional inversions of order between ligands that stand near to one another on the list. The order of some common ligands is

$$I^- < Br^- < Cl^- < F^- < OH^- < C_2O_4^{2-} < H_2O < NH_3$$
$$< en < NO_2^- < CN^-$$

The values of Δ_o induced by the halide ions are generally low, and complexes of these ligands usually have high-spin configurations. The cyanide ion, which stands at the opposite end of the series from the halide ions, induces the largest d-orbital splittings of any ligand listed. Cyano complexes generally have low-spin configurations.

A given ligand, however, does not always produce complexes of the same spin type. Thus, the hexaammine complex of Fe^{II} has a high-spin configuration, whereas the hexaammine complex of Co^{III} (which is isoelectronic with Fe^{II}) has a low-spin configuration.

For each metal ion there is a point in the series that corresponds to the change from ligands that produce high-spin complexes to ligands that form low-spin complexes. For example, Co^{II} forms high-spin complexes with NH_3 and ethylenediamine, but the NO_2^- and CN^- complexes of Co^{II} have low-spin configurations. The actual position in the series at which this change from high- to low-spin complex formation occurs depends upon the electron-pairing energy, P, for the metal ion, as well as the values of Δ_o for the complexes under consideration.

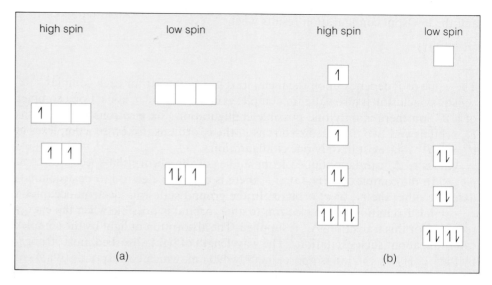

Figure 26.17 Arrangements of d electrons in high-spin and low-spin states in (a) a tetrahedral complex of a d^3 ion, and (b) a square-planar complex of a d^8 ion

In the case of tetrahedral complexes, the two orbitals of the e_g set have lower orbital energies than the three orbitals of the t_{2g} set (see Figure 26.14). Only one spin configuration is possible for a d^1 or a d^2 ion, each with electrons entered singly into the e_g orbitals. In theory, however, a high-spin state and a low-spin state should be possible for a d^3 ion (see Figure 26.17a), as well as for a d^4, d^5, or d^6 ion. No low-spin tetrahedral complexes are known, however.

In a typical tetrahedral complex, the energy difference between the t_{2g} and e_g sets, Δ_t, is low, about one-half of a typical Δ_o value. For all tetrahedral complexes:

$$\Delta_t < P$$

Consequently, after two electrons have been introduced singly into the two orbitals of the e_g set, it is easier to place the third electron singly into an orbital of the t_{2g} set than it is to supply the pairing energy, P, and pair this third electron with one already present in an orbital of the e_g set. This conclusion is also valid for the tetrahedral complexes of d^4, d^5, and d^6 ions. Consequently, all known tetrahedral complexes are high-spin complexes. Only one spin configuration is theoretically possible for the tetrahedral complexes of d^7, d^8, d^9, and d^{10} ions.

Square-planar complexes are sometimes formed by d^8 ions. In theory, a high-spin state and a low-spin state should be possible for the square-planar complexes of a d^8 ion (see Figure 26.17b). Actually, all known d^8 square-planar complexes have low-spin configurations (and are diamagnetic since all electrons are paired). The energy separation between the highest and next highest orbitals is so large that a high-spin state cannot be attained. For the square-planar complexes of d^7 ions, the configuration is similar to that of the low-spin state shown in Figure 26.17b with the exception that only one electron (instead of two) is present in the highest orbital occupied.

Summary

A *complex ion* (or a *complex compound*) is formed from a *central metal ion* and several anions and/or molecules (called *ligands*). A free ligand has an *electron pair* that is donated to the metal cation in the formation of the complex. The *coordination number* of the central metal ion is the number of atoms directly bonded to it or the number of coordination positions around it. Complexes with coordination numbers of from 2 to 12 are known, but the majority of complexes are two-, four- and six-coordinate. Complexes have definite shapes—six-coordinate, *octahedral;* four-coordinate, *tetrahedral* or *square-planar;* two-coordinate, *linear. Chelates* are formed by ligands that are capable of occupying more than one coordination position (*multidentate ligands*, or *chelating agents*).

Labile complexes rapidly undergo reactions in which ligands are replaced; *inert complexes* do not undergo these reactions or do so only slowly. Complex formation can result in the *stabilization* of metal ions toward oxidation or reduction. Important rules of a *system of nomenclature* for complex compounds were reviewed.

Isomers are compounds that have the same molecular formula but differ in the arrangement of atoms. Such compounds differ in their physical and chemical properties. *Structural isomerism* includes the following types: *ionization isomerism, hydrate isomerism, coordination isomerism,* and *linkage isomerism. Stereoisomerism* includes: *geometric isomerism* (or *cis-trans isomerism*) and *optical isomerism.*

Modern theories of the bonding in complexes are derived from the *crystal field theory.* This theory explains the bonding in terms of the *electrostatic attractions* between the *positive charge* of the *central metal cation* and the *negative charges* of the electron pairs of the *ligands.* The ligands, therefore, produce an electrostatic field around the central metal ion, which causes a *splitting* in the *energies of the d orbitals* of the metal ion.

The *molecular orbital* theory explains the bonding in terms of the formation of *bonding, antibonding,* and *nonbonding* molecular orbitals. For either the crystal field theory or the molecular orbital theory, the same conclusions are reached regarding the distributions of electrons in the *d* orbitals of the central metal ion.

In octahedral complexes, two *d* orbitals have higher energies than the other three *d* orbitals. This splitting of orbital energies makes it possible to have *low-spin* and *high-spin* complexes, which differ in the *number of unpaired electrons.* In high-spin complexes, the splitting energy is *low,* so that less energy is required to place electrons singly in the higher energy *d* orbitals than to supply the pairing energy required to pair them in the lower energy *d* orbitals. In low-spin complexes, the splitting energy is *high* so that it is energetically favorable for electrons to pair up in the *d* orbitals of lower energy. Ligands may be arranged in a *spectrochemical series* according to the magnitude of the splitting of *d* orbitals that they bring about.

Key Terms

Some of the more important terms introduced in this chapter are listed below. Definitions for terms not included in this list may be located in the text by use of the index.

Ammine ligand (Sections 26.1 and 26.3)   The ammonia molecule, NH_3.

Chelate (26.1)   A metal complex that contains coordinated, multidentate ligands.

Chelating agent (Section 26.1)   A ligand capable of occupying more than one coordination position on a central metal ion in a complex; a multidentate ligand.

Chiral molecule or ion (Section 26.4)   A molecule or an ion that can exist in two forms that are nonsuperimposable mirror images.

Cis-trans isomerism (Section 26.4)   A type of *stereoisomerism* (*geometric isomerism*) in which the isomers differ in the geometric arrangement of ligands around the central metal ion. In the cis isomer, two like ligands are as close together as possible. In the trans isomer, these two like ligands are as far apart as possible.

Coordination isomerism (Section 26.4)   A type of isomerism in which two complex compounds, each with more than one coordination center, vary in the way that the same set of ligands is distributed between the coordination centers.

Coordination number (Section 26.1)   The number of atoms directly bonded to the central metal cation of a complex.

Coordination sphere (Section 26.1)   The group of anions or molecules that are directly coordinated to the central metal ion of a complex.

Crystal field theory (Section 26.5)   A theory that explains the bonding of the central metal ion to the ligands of a complex in terms of electrostatic attractions between the positive charge of the metal ion and the negative charge of the electron pairs of the ligands.

Dextrorotatory compound (Section 26.4)   An optically active compound that rotates the plane of polarized light to the right (clockwise).

e_g orbitals (Section 26.5)   A degenerate set of two *d* orbitals of the central metal ion of a complex.

Enantiomorphs (Section 26.4)   Two different compounds that are mirror images of one another; one may be considered to be the mirror reflection of the other. The dextro form rotates the plane of polarized light to the right; the levo form, to the left.

Geometric isomerism (Section 26.4)   A type of isomerism in which the isomers differ in the geometric arrangement of the ligands around the central metal ion.

High-spin state (Section 26.5)   A state in which the electron configuration of the *d* orbitals of the central metal ion of a complex has a maximum number of unpaired electrons.

Hydrate isomerism (Section 26.4)   A type of isomerism in which two complex compounds differ as to whether water molecules are coordinated or occupy separate positions in the crystal structure of the compound.

Inert complex (Section 26.2)   A complex that does not undergo reactions in which its ligands are replaced, or does so only slowly.

Ionization isomerism (Section 26.4)   A type of isomerism in which two complexes differ as to whether a given anion is inside or outside the coordination sphere of the complex.

Isomers (Section 26.4)   Compounds that have the same molecular formula but different structures. Isomers have different chemical and physical properties.

Labile complex (Section 26.2)   A complex that rapidly undergoes reactions in which its ligands are replaced.

Levorotatory compound (Section 26.4)   An optically active compound that rotates the plane of polarized light to the left (counterclockwise).

Ligand (Section 26.1)   An anion or a molecule that uses an electron pair to coordinate to a central metal ion and form a complex.

Linkage isomerism (Section 26.4)   A type of isomerism in which two complexes differ as to the way a given ligand (that is present in both) coordinates to the central metal ion.

Low-spin state (Section 26.5)   A state in which the electron configuration of the *d* orbitals of the central metal ion of a complex has a minimum number of unpaired electrons.

Optical isomerism (Section 26.4)   A type of isomerism in which the two isomers are mirror images that are not superimposable.

Pairing energy (Section 26.5)   Energy required to pair two electrons in the same orbital.

Porphyrins (Section 26.1)   Chelates derived from a quadridentate ligand that is a derivative of the porphin structure (see Figure 26.4); examples include hemoglobin and chlorophyll.

Spectrochemical series (Section 26.5)   A series of ligands arranged in increasing order of the size of the splitting of *d* orbital energies, Δ_o, that they bring about.

Stereoisomers (Section 26.4)   Compounds that have the same molecular formula and are bonded in the same way but that differ in the way the constituent atoms are arranged in space.

Structural isomers (Section 26.4)   Compounds that have the same molecular formula but differ in the way the atoms are bonded together.

t_{2g} orbitals (Section 26.5)   A degenerate set of three *d* orbitals of the central metal ion of a complex.

Problems*

Structure of Complexes

26.1 State the oxidation number of the central atom in each of the following complexes: **(a)** $[Co(NO_2)_6]^{3-}$, **(b)** $[Au(CN)_4]^-$, **(c)** $[V(CO)_6]$ **(d)** $[Co(NH_3)_4Br_2]^+$, **(e)** $[Co(en)Cl_4]^{2-}$.

26.2 State the oxidation number of the central atom in each of the following complexes: **(a)** $[Ni(CO)_4]$, **(b)** $[Fe(H_2O)_2Cl_4]^-$, **(c)** $[Al(OH)_4]^-$, **(d)** $[Co(NH_3)_4Cl_2]^+$, **(e)** $[PdCl_6]^{2-}$.

26.3 What is the charge on the complex ion formed from: **(a)** Ag^+ and $2\,NH_3$, **(b)** Co^{2+} and $3\,C_2O_4^{2-}$, **(c)** Au^+ and $2\,CN^-$, **(d)** Pt^{4+}, $3\,H_2O$, and $3\,Br^-$, **(e)** Hg^{2+} and $4\,Cl^-$.

26.4 What is the charge on the complex ion formed from: **(a)** Ni^{2+} and $4\,CN^-$, **(b)** Ni^0 and $4\,CO$, **(c)** Co^{3+}, $4\,NH_3$, and $2\,Cl^-$, **(d)** Fe^{2+} and $6\,CN^-$, **(e)** Co^{3+}, $4\,H_2O$, and $2\,SO_4^{2-}$.

26.5 Write formulas for:

(a) zinc hexachloroplatinate(IV)

(b) potassium tetracyanonickelate(0)

(c) tetraamminechloronitrocobalt(III) sulfate

(d) potassium hexabromoaurate(III)

(e) sodium tetracyanodioxorhenate(V)

(f) tetraammineplatinum(II) amminetrichloroplatinate(II)

(g) tetraamminedithiocyanatochromium(III) diamminetetrathiocyanatochromate(III)

(h) potassium hexacyanonickelate(II)

26.6 Write formulas for:

(a) sodium dithiosulfatoargentate(I)

(b) diamminetetrachloroplatinum(IV)

(c) potassium aquapentachlororhodate(III)

(d) diamminebis(ethylenediamine)cobalt(II) chloride

(e) hexamminenickel(II) hexanitrocobaltate(III)

(f) hexacarbonylvanadium (0)

(g) tetraamminecopper(II) hexachlorochromate(III)

26.7 Convert the names that are given in Problem 26.5 (and which use Stock numbers) into names that employ Ewens-Bassett numbers.

26.8 Convert the names that are given in Problem 26.6 (and which use Stock numbers) into names that employ Ewens-Bassett numbers.

26.9 Name the following compounds. Use the Stock system.

(a) $K_4[Ni(CN)_4]$

(b) $K_2[Ni(CN)_4]$

(c) $(NH_4)_2[Fe(H_2O)Cl_5]$

(d) $[Cu(NH_3)_4][PtCl_4]$

(e) $[Ir(NH_3)_5(ONO)]Cl_2$

(f) $[Co(NH_3)_6]_2[Ni(CN)_4]_3$

26.10 Name the following compounds. Use the Stock system.

(a) $[Co(NO)(CO)_3]$

(b) $[Pt(NH_3)_2Cl_4]$

(c) $K_4[Pt(CN)_4]$

(d) $[Co(NH_3)_6]_4[Co(NO_2)_6]_3$

(e) $Na[Au(CN)_2]$

(f) $[Co(en)_2(SCN)Cl]Cl$

26.11 Name the compounds listed in Problem 26.9 by the Ewens-Basset system.

26.12 Name the compounds listed in Problem 26.10 by the Ewens-Basset system.

26.13 Given the following data, calculate the instability constant, K_{inst}, for the $Al(OH)_4^-$ ion:

$$3e^- + Al(OH)_4^- \rightleftharpoons Al + 4\,OH^-$$
$$\mathscr{E}°_{red} = -2.330\ V$$

$$3e^- + Al^{3+} \rightleftharpoons Al \qquad \mathscr{E}°_{red} = -1.662\ V$$

26.14 Given the following data, calculate the instability constant, K_{inst}, for the $AuBr_4^-$ ion:

$$3e^2 + AuBr_4^- \rightleftharpoons Au + 4\,Br^-$$
$$\mathscr{E}°_{red} = +0.870\ V$$

$$3e^- + Au^{3+} \rightleftharpoons Au \qquad \mathscr{E}°_{red} = +1.498\ V$$

Isomers of Complexes

26.15 Addition of a solution of potassium hexacyanoferrate(II) to Fe^{3+}(aq) yields a precipitate called Prussian blue. Addition of a solution of potassium hexacyanoferrate(III) to Fe^{2+}(aq) also yields a blue precipitate (Turnbull's blue). The blue precipitates are now known to be identical and are called potassium iron(III) hexacyanoferrate(II). Write the formula for **(a)** Prussian blue, **(b)** iron(III) hexacyanoferrate(III), a brown precipitate, **(c)** copper(II) hexacyanoferrate(II), a purple precipitate, **(d)** potassium iron(II) hexacyanoferrate(II), a white precipitate.

---

* The more difficult problems are marked with asterisks. The appendix contains answers to color-keyed problems.

26.16 Two compounds have the same empirical formula: $Co(NH_3)_3(H_2O)_2ClBr_2$. One mole of compound A readily loses one mole of water in a desiccator, whereas compound B does not lose water under the same conditions. An aqueous solution of A has a conductivity equivalent to that of a compound with two ions per formula unit. The conductivity of an aqueous solution of B corresponds to that of a compound with three ions per formula unit. When an aqueous solution of $AgNO_3$ is added to a solution of compound A, one mole of AgBr is precipitated per mole of A. A solution of compound B yields two moles of AgBr per mole of B. **(a)** Write formulas of A and B. **(b)** What type of isomers are A and B?

26.17 Write a formula for an example of **(a)** an ionization isomer of $[Co(NH_3)_5(NO_3)]SO_4$, **(b)** a linkage isomer of $[Mn(CO)_5(SCN)]$ that involves the SCN^- ion, **(c)** a coordination isomer of $[Pt(NH_3)_4][PtCl_4]$, **(d)** a hydrate isomer of $[Co(en)_2(H_2O)_2]Br_3$.

26.18 Write a formula for an example of **(a)** an ionization isomer of $[Pt(NH_3)_4(OH)_2]SO_4$, **(b)** a linkage isomer of $[Pd(dipy)(SCN)_2]$ (dipy is a bidentate ligand: 2,2'-dipyridine), **(c)** a hydrate isomer of $[Co(NH_3)_4(H_2O)Cl]Cl_2$, **(d)** a coordination isomer of $[Cr(NH_3)_4(C_2O_4)][Cr(NH_3)_2(C_2O_4)_2]$.

26.19 Identify all the possible isomers (stereoisomers as well as coordination isomers) of the compound $[Pt(NH_3)_4][PtCl_6]$.

26.20 Diagram the four stereoisomers of $[Pt(en)(NO_2)_2Cl_2]$.

26.21 Diagram all the stereoismers of each of the following molecules. In the formulas, py stands for pyridene, C_5H_5N, a unidentate ligand.

(a) $[Pt(NH_3)(py)ClBr]$ (square planar),

(b) $[Pt(NH_3)(py)Cl_2]$ (square planar),

(c) $[Pt(py)_2Cl_2]$ (square planar),

(d) $[Co(py)_2Cl_2]$ (tetrahedral).

26.22 Diagram the structures of all the steroisomers of the following octahedral complexes. Classify the structures as geometric or optical isomers.

(a) $[Cr(NH_3)_2(NCS)_4]^-$

(b) $[Co(NH_3)_3(NO_2)_3]$

(c) $[Co(en)(NH_3)_2Cl_2]^+$

(d) $[Co(en)Cl_4]^-$

(e) $[Co(en)_2ClBr]^+$

(f) $[Cr(NH_3)_2(C_2O_4)_2]^-$

(g) $[Cr(C_2O_4)_3]^{3-}$

Bonding in Complexes

26.23 The complex $[Ni(CN)_4]^{2-}$ is square planar and the complex $[NiCl_4]^{2-}$ is tetrahedral. Refer to Figure 26.17 and the text and predict the number of unpaired electrons in each complex.

26.24 The octahedral complexes $[Fe(CN)_6]^{3-}$ and $[FeF_6]^{3-}$ have one and five unpaired electrons, respectively. Offer an explanation for these observations.

26.25 For $[Mn(H_2O)_6]^{3+}$, which is a high-spin complex, Δ_o is approximately 250 kJ/mol. For $[Mn(CN)_6]^{3-}$, which is a low-spin complex, Δ_o is approximately 460 kJ/mol. **(a)** What conclusion can you reach in regard to the size of the electron-pairing energy, P, for Mn^{3+}? **(b)** Would you expect the complex $[Mn(C_2O_4)_3]^{3-}$ to be a high-spin or a low-spin complex?

26.26 For Fe^{2+}, the electron-pairing energy, P, is approximately 210 kJ/mol. Approximate values of Δ_o for the complexes $[Fe(H_2O)_6]^{2+}$ and $[Fe(CN)_6]^{4-}$ are 120 kJ/mol and 390 kJ/mol respectively. **(a)** Do these complexes have high-spin or low-spin configurations? **(b)** Draw a d-orbital splitting diagram for each.

26.27 Draw d-orbital splitting diagrams for the high-spin and low-spin octahedral complexes of **(a)** Zn^{2+}, **(b)** Cr^{2+}, **(c)** Cr^{3+}, **(d)** Fe^{2+}, **(e)** Fe^{3+}, **(f)** Ni^{2+}.

26.28 Draw d-orbital splitting diagrams for the high-spin and low-spin octahedral complexes of **(a)** Cu^+, **(b)** Cu^{2+}, **(c)** Co^{2+}, **(d)** Co^{3+}, **(e)** Mn^{2+}, **(f)** Mn^{3+}.

26.29 Draw d-orbital splitting diagrams for $[Co(NH_3)_6]^{2+}$ and $[Co(NH_3)_6]^{3+}$. The Δ_o values for these two complexes are approximately 120 kJ/mol and 270 kJ/mol, respectively. The pairing energy of Co^{2+} is approximately 270 kJ/mol and of Co^{3+} is approximately 210 kJ/mol.

26.30 Draw d-orbital splitting diagrams for **(a)** the square-planar complexes of Co^{2+} (all of which have one unpaired electron), **(b)** the square-planar complexes of Ni^{2+} (all of which are diamagnetic), **(c)** the tetrahedral complexes of Co^{2+}, **(d)** the octahedral complexes of Ru^{2+} (all of which are diamagnetic), **(e)** the octahedral complexes of Ir^{4+} (all of which have one unpaired electron).

26.31 Define the following terms: **(a)** coordination number **(b)** ligand, **(c)** chelate, **(d)** enantiomorph, **(e)** inert complex, **(f)** low-spin state.

26.32 What types of metal ions form complexes most readily? What configurations of complexes are most common?

26.33 Interpret the formation of $Ag(NH_3)_2^+$ from Ag^+ and NH_3 in terms of the Lewis theory.

26.34 How can dipole-moment measurement distinguish between the *cis-* and *trans-* isomers of the square planar $[Pt(NH_3)_2Cl_2]$?

26.35 The $Ti(H_2O)_6]^{3+}$ complex is red-violet. What change in color would be expected if the ligands of this complex were replaced by ligands that induce a larger Δ_o? Note that the color of the complex corresponds to light transmitted, not absorbed.

CHAPTER 27 NUCLEAR CHEMISTRY

Ordinary chemical reactions occur through changes in the electronic structures of atoms, molecules, and ions. In these reactions, the atomic nucleus is important only insofar as it influences the electrons. Matter, however, does undergo some transformations that involve the nucleus directly. These transformations are the subject of nuclear chemistry.

When Wilhelm Röntgen discovered X rays in 1895, he noticed that these invisible rays expose photographic plates and cause certain salts to glow. Henri Becquerel in 1896 investigated salts of this type and found that they emit invisible radiation in the absence of any external stimulus. Becquerel found that a double sulfate of potassium and uranium emits radiation capable of exposing a photographic plate that is well protected from light. He subsequently identified uranium as the source of the radiation. Following Becquerel's discovery, other radioactive elements were identified and isolated (notably by Marie and Pierre Curie), and the nature of the radiation was elucidated (principally by Ernest Rutherford). The radiation emitted by radioactive substances originates from transformations that take place in the nucleus.

27.1 The Nucleus

The symbolism used to identify atoms was discussed in Section 2.6. Each specific atom, called a **nuclide,** is characterized by an atomic number, Z, and a mass number, A. The composition of the nucleus of the nuclide can be derived from these numbers. The nucleus is thought to contain protons and neutrons, particles that are collectively called **nucleons.**

The number of protons in a specific nucleus corresponds to the atomic number (or nuclear charge), Z, of the nuclide. The total number of nucleons in the nucleus is given by the mass number, A. Thus,

number of nucleons $= A$

number of protons $= Z$

number of neutrons $= A - Z$

This information is indicated on the chemical symbol of a given nuclide. The mass number is placed at the upper left of the symbol and the atomic number is placed at the lower left. The symbols for the two lithium nuclides that occur in nature are:

$${}^{6}_{3}\text{Li} \text{ and } {}^{7}_{3}\text{Li}$$

All atoms of a given element have the same atomic number (and hence the same number of protons). Atoms of a given element, however, may have different mass numbers. Nuclides that have the same atomic number but different mass numbers are called isotopes. The symbols previously given represent two isotopes of the element lithium. Both isotopes have three protons in the nucleus ($Z = 3$), but ${}^{6}_{3}\text{Li}$ has three neutrons ($A - Z = 3$) and ${}^{7}_{3}\text{Li}$ has four neutrons ($A - Z = 4$).

Determination of the radii of a large number of atomic nuclei shows that the radius of a given nucleus, r, is directly related to the cube root of the mass number of the nucleus:

$$r = r_0 A^{1/3} \tag{27.1}$$

where r_0 is a constant.* The values of r_0 reported, which depend upon the experimental method used to determine them, range from 1.2×10^{-13} cm to 1.5×10^{-13} cm.

Assume that the nucleus is spherical. The volume of a sphere is $\frac{4}{3}\pi r^3$. Since the radius of a nucleus is proportional to $A^{1/3}$, the volume of the nucleus is proportional to A. The volume of a nucleus, therefore, is approximately proportional to the mass of the nucleus. As a result, nuclear density (mass per unit volume) is approximately constant for all nuclei. This density is about 10^{14} g/cm^3, an amazingly high value. One cubic centimeter of nuclear matter would weigh about 100 million metric tons. This high density does *not* mean, however, that the nucleons are tightly packed within a nucleus. A shell model for the nucleus (which is described later) depends upon the belief that the nucleons are not densely packed.

The nature of the forces that hold the nucleons into a nucleus is not completely understood. It is clear, however, that powerful cohesive forces between nucleons exist and that they effectively overcome the forces of repulsion caused by the charges of the nuclear protons.

In Figure 27.1, the number of neutrons is plotted against the number of protons for the naturally occurring, nonradioactive nuclei. The points, which represent stable combinations of protons and neutrons, lie in what may be called a zone of stability. Nuclei that have compositions represented by points that lie outside this zone spontaneously undergo radioactive transformations that tend to bring their compositions into, or closer to, this zone (see Section 27.3).

The stable nuclei of the lighter elements contain approximately equal numbers of neutrons and protons—a neutron/proton ratio of 1. The stable heavier nuclei, however, contain more neutrons than protons. With increasing atomic number, more and more protons are placed into the nucleus. A larger and larger excess of neutrons is required to overcome the effect of the forces of repulsion that operate between protons. As a result, the neutron/proton ratio increases with increasing

---

* The nuclear model of the atom was first proposed by Ernest Rutherford in 1911 on the basis of the scattering of alpha particles observed when these particles are directed against metal foils (Section 2.5). The radii of atomic nuclei have been derived from scattering experiments involving not only alpha particles but also electrons, protons, and neutrons. In addition, calculations based on certain nuclear properties [such as rate of radioactive decay (Section 27.5) and binding energy (Section 27.8)] have been used to derive nuclear radii.

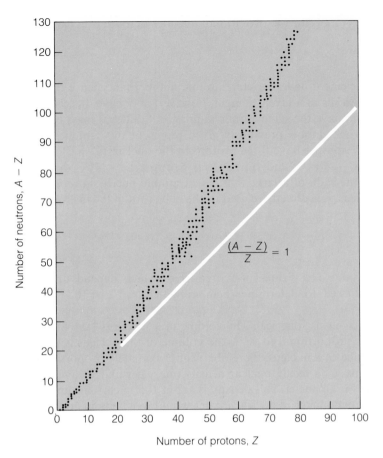

Figure 27.1 Neutron/proton ratio

atomic number until the ratio is approximately 1.5 at the end of the curve in Figure 27.1.

There appears, however, to be a limit to the number of protons that can be put into a nucleus, no matter how many neutrons are present. The largest stable nucleus is $^{209}_{83}Bi$. Nuclei that are larger than this exist, but all of them are radioactive.

Most naturally occurring, stable nuclides have an even number of protons and an even number of neutrons. Only five ($^{2}_{1}H$, $^{6}_{3}Li$, $^{10}_{5}B$, $^{14}_{7}N$, and $^{180}_{73}Ta$) have an odd number of protons and an odd number of neutrons (see Table 27.1). For each odd atomic number there are never more than two stable nuclides, whereas for an even atomic number as many as 10 stable nuclides may occur. The two elements of atomic number less than 83 that have never been proved to occur in nature ($_{43}Tc$ and $_{61}Pm$) have odd atomic numbers. Observations such as these suggest that there is a periodicity in nuclear structure similar to the periodicity of atomic structure. A nuclear shell model has been suggested.

It appears that unusual nuclear stability is associated with nuclides having a number or protons or neutrons equal to what is called a magic number: 2, 8, 20, 28, 50, 82, and 126. Magic numbers seem to indicate closed nuclear shells in the same way that the atomic numbers of the noble gases, 2, 10, 18, 36, 54, and 86, indicate stable electronic configurations. A high degree of nuclear stability is indicated by a high binding energy (see Section 27.8), a poor ability to capture neutrons

Table 27.1 Distribution of naturally occurring stable nuclides		
Protons	Neutrons	Number of Nuclides
even even	even odd	157 52 } 209
odd odd	even odd	50 5 } 55

(see Section 27.7), and a comparatively high natural abundance. In general, elements that have an atomic number equal to a magic number have a larger number of stable isotopes than neighboring elements do. The nuclides that have a magic number of protons as well as a magic number of neutrons, ^4_2He, $^{16}_8\text{O}$, $^{40}_{20}\text{Ca}$, and $^{208}_{82}\text{Pb}$, have notably high stabilities.

27.2 Nuclear Reactions

Several types of processes that involve nuclear transformations are discussed in this chapter:

1. Radioactive decay (Section 27.3), a process in which an unstable nucleus (called a radioactive nucleus) is changed by the emission of radiation.

2. Transmutation (Section 27.7), a process in which one nucleus is transformed into another through bombardment by various subatomic particles or ions.

3. Nuclear fission (Section 27.8), a process in which a heavy nucleus is split into lighter ones.

4. Nuclear fusion (Section 27.9), a process in which light nuclei are fused into a heavier one.

The equations that are used to summarize these nuclear reactions are designed to show the changes that occur in the nuclei involved. They are, therefore, different from ordinary chemical equations, which are designed to indicate the breaking and formation of chemical bonds. In an equation for a nuclear reaction, the nuclei are represented by atomic symbols (complete with mass numbers and atomic numbers).

Consider, for example, the process by which James Chadwick first characterized the neutron:

$$^9_4\text{Be} + {}^4_2\text{He} \longrightarrow {}^{12}_6\text{C} + {}^1_0\text{n}$$

The equation shows that the bombardment of a ^9_4Be nucleus with an α particle produces a $^{12}_6\text{C}$ nucleus and a neutron. The α particle, a product of a type of radioactive decay, consists of two protons and two neutrons and may be considered to be a ^4_2He nucleus. The neutron, indicated by the symbol ^1_0n, has a mass number (the total number of nucleons in the particle) of 1 and an atomic number (the charge of the particle) of 0.

A nuclear equation must be balanced in two ways:

1. The sum of the *superscripts* (which are *mass numbers*) of the species on the left side of the equation must equal the sum of the superscripts of the species on the right side. In the example previously given, this sum is 13 for each side of the equation.

2. The sum of the *subscripts* (which are *atomic numbers* or *charges*) of the species on the left side of the equation must equal the sum of the subscripts of the species on the right side. In the example, this sum is 6 for each side of the equation.

Example 27.1

The first transmutation reaction to be described was reported by Ernest Rutherford in 1919. The action of an α particle (^4_2He) on the $^{14}_7\text{N}$ nucleus produces a proton (^1_1H) and a new nucleus:

$$^4_2\text{He} + {}^{14}_7\text{N} \longrightarrow {}^1_1\text{H} + {}^x_y?$$

What is the nucleus that is produced in this way?

Solution

The sum of the mass numbers on the left must equal the sum of the mass numbers on the right:

$$4 + 14 = 1 + x$$
$$x = 17$$

The sum of the atomic numbers on the left must equal the sum of the atomic numbers on the right:

$$2 + 7 = 1 + y$$
$$y = 8$$

The element that has an atomic number of 8 is oxygen. The nucleus is $^{17}_8\text{O}$ and the complete equation is:

$$^4_2\text{He} + {}^{14}_7\text{N} \longrightarrow {}^{17}_8\text{O} + {}^1_1\text{H}$$

The energy changes associated with nuclear reactions are on a considerably higher level than those associated with ordinary chemical reactions. The energy released by the nuclear reaction described in Example 27.1, for example, is about 400,000 times the amount released when hydrogen and oxygen react to form water.

In any spontaneous nuclear reaction, the combined mass of the products is less than the combined mass of the reactants. The amount of energy released (ΔE) is equivalent to this difference in mass (Δm), and the energy equivalent can be calculated by means of Einstein's equation:

$$\Delta E = (\Delta m)c^2$$

The energy equivalent of one atomic mass unit (1 u) can be found in the following way. Since 1 u (Δm) is 1.660566×10^{-27} kg and the speed of light (c) is 2.997925×10^8 m/s, the energy equivalent (ΔE) of 1 u is:

$$\begin{aligned}
\Delta E &= (\Delta m)c^2 \\
&= (1.66057 \times 10^{-27} \text{ kg})(2.99792 \times 10^8 \text{ m/s})^2 \\
&= 1.49244 \times 10^{-10} \text{ kg m}^2/\text{s}^2
\end{aligned}$$

Since $1 \text{ kg m}^2/\text{s}^2 = 1 \text{ J}$,

$$\Delta E = 1.49244 \times 10^{-10} \text{ J}$$

This value is the energy equivalent of 1 u in joules.

The energy unit customarily employed by nuclear scientists is the MeV (a mega-electron volt, which is 10^6 electron volts). An electron volt is the energy acquired by an electron when it is accelerated through a potential difference of 1 V:

$$\begin{aligned}
1 \text{ eV} &= (\text{charge of electron})(1 \text{ V}) \\
&= (1.60219 \times 10^{-19} \text{ C})(1 \text{ V})
\end{aligned}$$

Since $1 \text{ V·C} = 1 \text{ J}$,

$$1 \text{ eV} = 1.60219 \times 10^{-19} \text{ J}$$

$$1 \text{ MeV} = 1.60219 \times 10^{-13} \text{ J}$$

The energy equivalent of 1 u in MeV, therefore, is

$$\frac{1.49244 \times 10^{-10} \text{ J/u}}{1.60219 \times 10^{-13} \text{ J/MeV}} = 931.500 \text{ MeV/u}$$

27.3 Radioactivity

Unstable nuclei spontaneously undergo certain changes that result in the attainment of more stable nuclear compositions. Some unstable nuclei are naturally occurring, others are produced synthetically. The three types of radiation (alpha, α; beta, β^-; and gamma, γ) emitted by radioactive substances that occur in nature were discussed in Section 2.5. Certain synthetic radioactive nuclides undergo other types of radioactive decay that have not been observed for any naturally occurring, unstable nuclide. In this section we will review the principal types of radioactive decay for both natural and synthetic radioactive nuclides.

Alpha Decay

Alpha emission consists of the ejection of α particles, which are made up of two protons and two neutrons and may be considered to be $^4_2$He nuclei. Both synthetic and natural nuclides may undergo α decay, which is common only for nuclides of mass number greater than 209 and atomic number greater than 82. Nuclides of this type have too many protons for stability. Points indicating the composition of these nuclides fall to the upper right in a neutron/proton plot, beyond the zone of stability (see Figure 27.1). The emission of an α particle reduces the number of protons by two and the number of neutrons by two and adjusts the composition downward at a slope of 45°, closer to the stability zone.

An example of α decay is

$$^{210}_{84}\text{Po} \longrightarrow ^{206}_{82}\text{Pb} + ^{4}_{2}\text{He}$$

Notice that this equation indicates the conservation of mass numbers (superscripts) and atomic numbers (subscripts). Equations such as these are written to indicate nuclear changes only. The electrons are customarily ignored. An α particle is emitted as a $^{4}_{2}\text{He}$ nucleus without electrons and with a 2+ charge. Subsequent to its emission, however, the α particle attracts electrons from other atoms (which become cations), and the α particle becomes a neutral atom of $^{4}_{2}\text{He}$. The $^{206}_{82}\text{Pb}$ is left, therefore, with a surplus of two electrons and with a 2- charge. The excess electrons are rapidly lost to surrounding cations.

Example 27.2

Determine the amount of energy released by the α-decay process:

$$^{210}_{84}\text{Po} \longrightarrow ^{206}_{82}\text{Pb} + ^{4}_{2}\text{He}$$

The following atomic masses are given: $^{210}_{84}\text{Po}$, 209.9829 u; $^{206}_{82}\text{Pb}$, 205.9745 u; and $^{4}_{2}\text{He}$, 4.0026 u.

Solution

The energy released by the process is equivalent to the difference in mass between the reactant nucleus ($^{210}_{84}\text{Po}$) and the products of the transformation (the product nucleus, $^{206}_{82}\text{Pb}$, and an α particle). The masses of neutral atoms, rather than the masses of *nuclei*, are generally recorded in tables of nuclides, but this causes no trouble in the calculation.

For the reactant, the mass of the $^{210}_{84}\text{Po}$ atom includes the mass of 84 electrons. For the products, the mass of the $^{206}_{82}\text{Pb}$ atom includes the mass of 82 electrons, and the mass of the $^{4}_{2}\text{He}$ atom includes the mass of two electrons, so that the mass of 84 electrons is included in the total. Thus, the masses of the electrons cancel when atomic masses are employed in the calculation:

$$\Delta m = (\text{mass } ^{210}_{84}\text{Po}) - (\text{mass } ^{206}_{82}\text{Pb} + \text{mass } ^{4}_{2}\text{He})$$
$$= 209.9829 \text{ u} - (205.9745 \text{ u} + 4.0026 \text{ u})$$
$$= 0.0058 \text{ u}$$

The energy released by the α decay of $^{210}_{84}\text{Pb}$ is:

$$0.0058 \text{ u} \times 931.5 \text{ MeV/u} = 5.4 \text{ MeV}$$

In an α-decay process, the α particle is emitted with a high kinetic energy. The nucleus that is left behind recoils with a lower kinetic energy. When the sum of the kinetic energies of the α particle and the recoiling product nucleus equals the decay energy, the product nucleus is left in the ground state. When the sum of the kinetic energies of these two particles is less than the decay energy, the product nucleus is left in an excited state (a higher energy state than the ground state). A nucleus in an excited state subsequently emits energy in the form of γ radiation to reach the ground state.

Gamma Radiation

Gamma radiation is electromagnetic radiation of very short wavelength. Its emission is caused by energy changes within the nucleus. Its emission alone does not cause changes in the mass number or in the atomic number of the nucleus. At times, nuclear transformations produce nuclei in excited states, and these nuclei then revert to their ground states by the emission of the excess energy in the form of γ radiation:

$$[^{125}_{52}\text{Te}]^* \longrightarrow ^{125}_{52}\text{Te} + \gamma$$
$$\textit{excited state} \qquad \textit{ground state}$$

The γ rays emitted by a specific nucleus have definite energy values because they correspond to transitions between energy levels of the nucleus. Thus, an emission spectrum of γ radiation is produced that is analogous to the line spectrum resulting from transitions of electrons between energy levels in an excited atom.

Gamma radiation frequently accompanies all other types of radioactive decay. The following α-decay process is an example:

$$^{228}_{90}\text{Th} \longrightarrow [^{224}_{88}\text{Ra}]^* + ^4_2\text{He}$$
$$[^{224}_{88}\text{Ra}]^* \longrightarrow ^{224}_{88}\text{Ra} + \gamma$$

The energies of the α particles and γ rays emitted in this α-decay process can be used to deduce the energy levels of the product nucleus. The α particles emitted have energies of 5.423 MeV, 5.341 MeV, 5.211 MeV, and other values. The γ radiation has energies of 0.084 MeV, 0.216 MeV, 0.132 MeV, and other values. It is assumed that the emission of the 5.423 MeV α particle results in the direct production of the $^{224}_{88}\text{Ra}$ nucleus in the ground state. No γ radiation accompanies these α particles. The emission of any of the other α particles (which have lower kinetic energies) leaves the product nucleus in an excited state (with a higher energy than it would have if it were in the ground state). A product nucleus in an excited state drops to a lower state and emits the energy difference in the form of a γ ray. The energies of the γ rays, therefore, can be used to derive a picture of the energy states of the $^{224}_{88}\text{Ra}$ nucleus (see Figure 27.2). Notice that for each α particle, the sum of the energy of the α particle, the energy of the γ radiation, and *the recoil energy of the product nucleus* equals the decay energy (which is 5.520 MeV for this example).

Electron Emission, β^- Decay

A radioactive process is classified as a beta decay if the atomic number of the radioactive nuclide, Z, changes but the mass number, A, does not change. Electron emission is the first of three beta-decay processes that we will discuss. Discussion of the other two—positron emission and electron capture—will follow.

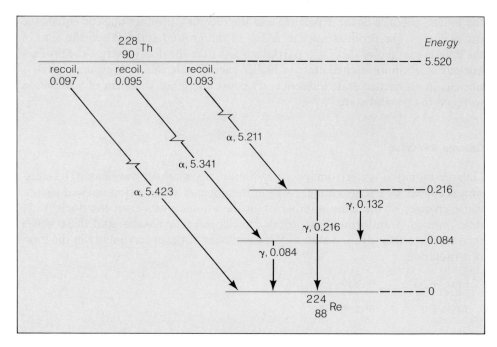

Figure 27.2 Energy-level diagram for the emission of α and γ radiation from $^{228}_{90}$Th. Energies are given in MeV. Energy levels of the product nucleus, $^{224}_{88}$Ra, are shown.

This type of beta decay is characterized by the emission of β^- particles, which are electrons and are given the symbol $_{-1}^0 e$. The superscript of the symbol is zero, since the β^- particle contains no nucleons. The subscript of the symbol is -1, which indicates the charge of the electron.

Electrons as such do not exist in the nucleus. When a β^- particle is emitted, a neutron of the nucleus is converted into a proton:

$$_0^1 n \longrightarrow {}_1^1 p + {}_{-1}^0 e$$

The symbol $_1^1 p$ is used to indicate a *nuclear* proton. We will later use the symbol $_1^1 H$ to indicate a *free* proton.

The net effect of β^- emission is that the number of neutrons is decreased by 1, the number of protons is increased by 1, and the total number of nucleons, therefore, does not change. Hence, the mass number does not change, but the atomic number is increased by 1. For example,

$$_4^{10} Be \longrightarrow {}_5^{10} B + {}_{-1}^0 e$$

Notice that in β^- decay, the neutron/proton ratio *decreases*, since the number of neutrons decreases and the number of protons increases. Nuclides that have too high a neutron/proton ratio for stability, therefore, decay by β^- emission. Points representing nuclides of this type lie to the left of the zone of stability in a plot of the neutron/proton ratio (see Figure 27.1). The decrease in the neutron/proton brought about by β^- emission brings such points closer to the zone of stability.

Beta decay is a common mode of radioactive disintegration and is observed for both natural and synthetic nuclides. Examples include:

$$^{186}_{73}\text{Ta} \longrightarrow {}^{186}_{74}\text{W} + {}^{0}_{-1}e$$

$$^{82}_{35}\text{Br} \longrightarrow {}^{82}_{36}\text{Kr} + {}^{0}_{-1}e$$

$$^{27}_{12}\text{Mg} \longrightarrow {}^{27}_{13}\text{Al} + {}^{0}_{-1}e$$

$$^{14}_{6}\text{C} \longrightarrow {}^{14}_{7}\text{N} + {}^{0}_{-1}e$$

Example 27.3

Calculate the energy released by the β^- decay of $^{14}_{6}\text{C}$ that is described by the equation:

$$^{14}_{6}\text{C} \longrightarrow {}^{14}_{7}\text{N} + {}^{0}_{-1}e$$

The atomic mass of $^{14}_{6}\text{C}$ is 14.00324 u, and of $^{14}_{7}\text{N}$ is 14.00307 u.

Solution

The energy released by this process can be calculated by using atomic masses instead of nuclear masses. If we add six orbital electrons to each side of the equation we get:

$$^{14}_{6}\text{C} + 6\,{}^{0}_{-1}e \longrightarrow {}^{14}_{7}\text{N} + {}^{0}_{-1}e + 6\,{}^{0}_{-1}e$$

We now have the equivalent of the mass of the $^{14}_{6}\text{C}$ *atom* on the left and the equivalent of the mass of the $^{14}_{7}\text{N}$ *atom* on the right. Thus,

$$\Delta m = (\text{mass } {}^{14}_{6}\text{C}) - (\text{mass } {}^{14}_{7}\text{N})$$
$$= 14.00324 \text{ u} - 14.00307 \text{ u}$$
$$= 0.00017 \text{ u}$$

The energy released is

$$0.00017 \text{ u} \times 931.5 \text{ MeV/u} = 0.16 \text{ MeV}$$

In β^- decay, the recoil energy of the product nucleus is negligible, since the ejected electron has a small mass. One might expect that the decay energy would be taken up by the kinetic energy of the β^- particle and that all β^- particles would have energies corresponding to this value. Instead, a continuous spectrum of β^--particle energies is observed, with the highest energy almost equal to the decay energy. It is postulated that when a β^- particle of less than maximum energy is ejected, an **antineutrino**, $\bar{\nu}$, that carries off the excess energy, is emitted at the same time:

$$^{14}_{6}\text{C} \longrightarrow {}^{14}_{7}\text{N} + {}^{0}_{-1}e + \bar{\nu}$$

The antineutrino is assumed to be an uncharged particle with a vanishingly small mass.

Unstable nuclides that have neutron/proton ratios below those required for stability (points that fall to the right of and below the zone of stability; see Figure 27.1) do not occur in nature. Many such nuclides have been made, however. Positron emission is one type of radioactive decay that increases the neutron/proton ratio of this type of nuclide.

Positron emission, or β^+ emission, consists of the ejection of a positron from the nucleus. The positron has the same mass as an electron but an opposite charge. It is indicated by the symbol ^0_1e. The ejection of a positron from the nucleus has the effect of converting a proton to a neutron.

$$^1_1p \longrightarrow {}^1_0n + {}^0_1e$$

Positron emission, therefore, results in an increase of 1 in the number of neutrons and a decrease of 1 in the number of protons. The neutron/proton ratio, therefore, is increased. Notice that in β^+ emission, the mass number does not change, but the atomic number *decreases* by 1.

Examples of this mode of radioactive decay include:

$$^{122}_{53}I \longrightarrow {}^{122}_{52}Te + {}^0_1e$$

$$^{38}_{19}K \longrightarrow {}^{38}_{18}Ar + {}^0_1e$$

$$^{23}_{12}Mg \longrightarrow {}^{23}_{11}Na + {}^0_1e$$

$$^{15}_8O \longrightarrow {}^{15}_7N + {}^0_1e$$

Example 27.4

Calculate the energy released by the β^+ process:

$$^{15}_8O \longrightarrow {}^{15}_7N + {}^0_1e$$

The atomic mass of $^{15}_8O$ is 15.00308 u, and of $^{15}_7N$ is 15.00011 u. The mass of an electron is 0.00055 u.

Solution

Since atomic masses are usually listed (instead of nuclear masses), we must use them to find the energy released by the process. If we add eight orbital electrons to each side of the equation we get:

$$^{15}_8O + 8\,{}^0_{-1}e \longrightarrow {}^{15}_7N + {}^0_1e + 8\,{}^0_{-1}e$$

We now have the equivalent of the mass of the $^{15}_8O$ *atom* (with eight electrons) on the left. On the right, we have the equivalent of the mass of the $^{15}_7N$ *atom* (with seven electrons), plus the mass of one orbital electron (making up the eight added), plus the mass of the ejected positron.

$$\Delta m = (\text{mass } {}^{15}_8O) - (\text{mass } {}^{15}_7N + \text{mass } {}^0_{-1}e + \text{mass } {}^0_1e)$$

Since the mass of the positron is identical to the mass of the electron:

$$\Delta m = (\text{mass } {}^{15}_{8}O) - [\text{mass } {}^{15}_{7}N + 2(\text{mass } {}^{0}_{-1}e)]$$
$$= 15.00308 \text{ u} - [15.00011 \text{ u} + 2(0.00055 \text{ u})]$$
$$= 15.00308 \text{ u} - 15.00121 \text{ u}$$
$$= 0.00187 \text{ u}$$

The energy released is:

$$0.00187 \text{ u} \times 931.5 \text{ MeV/u} = 1.74 \text{ MeV}$$

Notice that for spontaneous positron emission to occur, the atomic mass of the reactant nuclide must exceed the atomic mass of the product nuclide by at least 0.00110 u, the mass of two electrons.

In positron emission, a spectrum of β^{+} energies similar to that for β^{-} emission is observed. It is assumed that neutrinos, v, are ejected simultaneously and that these particles carry off some of the decay energy.

$$^{15}_{8}O \longrightarrow {}^{15}_{7}N + {}^{0}_{1}e + v$$

The positron was the first antiparticle to be observed. It has the same mass as an electron but differs in charge. When a positron and an electron collide, they annihilate each other, and γ radiation equivalent to the masses of the two particles is released:

$$^{0}_{1}e + {}^{0}_{-1}e \longrightarrow 2\gamma$$

Other types of antiparticles are thought to exist. The neutrino ejected in β^{+} emission and the antineutrino ejected in β^{-} emission constitute another pair.

Electron Capture

Electron capture (ec), like positron emission, is a process through which the neutron/proton ratio of an unstable, proton-rich nuclide may be increased (see Figure 27.1). Unlike positron emission, however, electron capture can occur when the mass difference between the reactant and product nuclides does not exceed 0.00110 u.

In this process, the nucleus captures an orbital electron from an inner electron-energy level. The captured electron converts a nuclear proton into a neutron. The transformation results in a product nucleus with one less proton and one more neutron. Consequently, the atomic number is decreased by 1 and the mass number does not change. The effect, therefore, is similar to the effect of β^{+} emission. Examples of electron capture are:

$$^{0}_{-1}e + {}^{197}_{80}Hg \xrightarrow{\ \text{ec}\ } {}^{197}_{79}Au$$

$$^{0}_{-1}e + {}^{106}_{47}Ag \xrightarrow{\ \text{ec}\ } {}^{106}_{46}Pd$$

$$^{0}_{-1}e + {}^{37}_{18}Ar \xrightarrow{\ \text{ec}\ } {}^{37}_{17}Cl$$

$$^{0}_{-1}e + {}^{7}_{4}Be \xrightarrow{\ \text{ec}\ } {}^{7}_{3}Li$$

$$^{0}_{-1}e + {}^{55}_{26}Fe \xrightarrow{\ \text{ec}\ } {}^{55}_{25}Mn$$

Example 27.5

Calculate the energy released by the electron-capture reaction:

$$_{-1}^{0}e + {}_{26}^{55}\text{Fe} \xrightarrow{\text{ec}} {}_{25}^{55}\text{Mn}$$

The atomic mass of ${}_{26}^{55}\text{Fe}$ is 54.93830 u and of ${}_{25}^{55}\text{Mn}$ is 54.93805 u.

Solution

If we add 25 electrons to each side of the equation as given, we get:

$$_{-1}^{0}e + {}_{26}^{55}\text{Fe} + 25\,_{-1}^{0}e \longrightarrow {}_{25}^{55}\text{Mn} + 25\,_{-1}^{0}e$$

The equation now indicates the *atomic* mass of ${}_{26}^{55}\text{Fe}$ (which includes the mass of 26 electrons) on the left and the atomic mass of ${}_{25}^{55}\text{Mn}$ (which includes the mass of 25 electrons) on the right. Thus,

$$\begin{aligned}
\Delta m &= (\text{mass } {}_{26}^{55}\text{Fe}) - (\text{mass } {}_{25}^{55}\text{Mn}) \\
&= 54.93830 \text{ u} - 54.93805 \text{ u} \\
&= 0.00025 \text{ u}
\end{aligned}$$

The energy equivalent to this Δm value is:

$$0.00025 \text{ u} \times 931.5 \text{ MeV/u} = 0.23 \text{ MeV}$$

In electron capture, the recoil energy of the product nucleus is negligible. If the product nucleus is left in the ground state, the decay energy is largely carried away by a neutrino that is ejected in the process. In addition, electron capture is accompanied by the production of X rays. The capture of an electron from the $n = 1$ or $n = 2$ energy level leaves a vacancy in that level. When an outer electron falls into this vacancy, X-ray emission follows.

Spontaneous Fission

Spontaneous fission (sf) is a process in which a heavy nucleus splits up into two lighter nuclei and several neutrons. Nearly all nuclides that have mass numbers higher than 230 undergo spontaneous fission, but the process is not observed for nuclides that have mass numbers lower than this value. It is believed that spontaneous fission is the result of the forces of repulsion between the large number of protons in these heavy nuclei. An example of a spontaneous fission is:

$$_{98}^{252}\text{Cf} \longrightarrow {}_{56}^{142}\text{Ba} + {}_{42}^{106}\text{Mo} + 4\,_{0}^{1}\text{n}$$

For any spontaneous fission reaction the sum of the masses of the products is less than the mass of the reactant nucleus, and energy equivalent to the difference in mass is released. The decay energy of a spontaneous fission reaction is large (on the order of 200 MeV) and is largely taken up by the kinetic energies of the products. Induced nuclear fission is discussed in Section 27.8.

7.4 Biological Effects of Radiation

The biological effects of radiation are caused by cellular changes that the radiation brings about. Matter may be changed in several ways when radiation passes through it. By absorbing energy from the radiation, electrons may be promoted to higher energy levels within atoms or molecules. These excited species revert to the ground state by releasing the excess energy in the form of electromagnetic radiations.

If electrons absorb enough energy from the radiation, they may be completely removed from the atoms or molecules, and as a result, positive ions may be formed. The electrons may leave the atoms or molecules with such high energies that they themselves can cause excitations or ionizations. Eventually, however, the ejected electrons lose enough energy so that they move slowly enough to be absorbed by atoms or molecules and form negative ions.

Consider the effect of radiation on the water molecule (an important ingredient of all biological systems). The primary reaction is the ejection of an electron and the formation of a positive ion:

$$H-\overset{..}{\underset{H}{O}}: \longrightarrow \left[H-\overset{..}{\underset{H}{O}}\cdot\right]^{+} + e^{-}$$

A negative ion is formed when an electron is absorbed by a water molecule:

$$H-\overset{..}{\underset{H}{O}}: + e^{-} \longrightarrow \left[H-\overset{..}{\underset{\overset{..}{H}}{O}}:\right]^{-}$$

These H_2O^{+} and H_2O^{-} ions break apart to form free radicals, which are molecules that have unpaired electrons in their valence levels.

$$\left[H-\overset{..}{\underset{H}{O}}\cdot\right]^{+} \longrightarrow H-\overset{..}{\underset{..}{O}}\cdot + H^{+}$$

$$\left[H-\overset{..}{\underset{\overset{..}{H}}{O}}:\right]^{-} \longrightarrow H-\overset{..}{\underset{..}{O}}:^{-} + H\cdot$$

Free radicals are short-lived and highly reactive. They attack and rupture the chemical bonds of the organic molecules within the cells.

This cellular damage causes a range of short-term and long-term effects. Among these effects are: blood disorders including leukemia, cataracts, gastrointestinal troubles, damage to the central nervous system, impaired fertility, and cancer. Exposure to radiation can also cause genetic damage. Radiation-induced changes in chromosomes can produce mutations that affect future generations.

The damage that external radiation does depends upon its ability to penetrate the body. The most dangerous type of external radiation, therefore, is gamma radiation, which is the most penetrating type. Gamma rays, like X rays, are able to pass through tissue. Alpha and beta radiation are far less penetrating than gamma radiation. The most energetic beta radiation is able to penetrate into tissue only a little more than one centimeter deep. Alpha radiation, the least penetrating type, can be stopped by a sheet of paper or by clothing.

Internal radiation is much more dangerous than external radiation. Internal radiation arises from a radioactive source that has entered the body (by inhalation, by ingestion, or through a wound). Alpha and beta radiation from internal sources cause much more damage than that from external sources.

27.5 Rate of Radioactive Decay

Detection of Radiation

Many techniques are employed to study the emissions of radioactive substances. Radiations from these materials affect photographic film in the same way that ordinary light does. Photographic techniques for the qualitative and quantitative detection of radiation are employed, but they are not very accurate, nor are they suitable for rapid analysis.

The energy of emissions from radioactive sources is absorbed by some substances (for example, zinc sulfide) and transformed into light. The zinc sulfide is said to fluoresce, and a little flash of light may be observed from the impact of each particle from the radioactive source. The image of a television tube is produced by this effect. This property has been put to use in an instrument known as a scintillation counter. The window of a sensitive photoelectric tube is coated with ZnS, and the flashes of light emitted by the ZnS when it is struck by radioactive emissions cause pulses of electric current to pass through the photoelectric tube. These signals are amplified and made to operate various kinds of counting devices.

The Wilson cloud chamber enables the paths of radiation arising from radioactive decay to be seen. When ionizing radiation passes through air, ions are produced along the path of the radiation. The chamber contains air that is saturated with the vapor of a liquid, such as water or alcohol. By the movement of a piston, the air in the chamber is suddenly expanded and cooled. In this way, the air becomes supersaturated with the vapor of the liquid. Droplets of the liquid condense on the ions that are formed by the particles as they move through the chamber, which makes the paths of these particles visible. Photographs of the cloud tracks may be made and studied. Such photographs provide information on the lengths of the paths, collisions undergone by the particles, the speed of the particles, and the effect of external forces on the behavior of the particles.

The essential features of a Geiger-Müller counter are diagrammed in Figure 27.3. The radiation enters the tube through a thin window. As a particle or a γ ray traverses the tube, which contains argon gas, it knocks electrons off the argon atoms in its path and forms Ar^+ ions. A potential of about 1000 to 1200 V is applied between the walls of the tube and a central wire. The walls of the tube function as the negative electrode and attract Ar^+ ions. The central wire functions as the positive electrode and attracts the electrons. The electrons moving under the influence of the high voltage acquire enough energy to ionize other argon atoms. A cascade of ions results that produces a pulse of electric current. The pulse is amplified to cause a clicker to sound or an automatic counting device to operate.

The Rate Law

The rates of decay of all radioactive substances have been found to be first-order (see Section 14.3) and to be independent of temperature. This lack of temperature

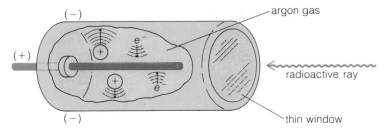

argon gas

(−)

(+)

e⁻

(+)

(−)

radioactive ray

thin window

Figure 27.3 Essential features of a Geiger-Müller counter tube

dependence implies that the activation energy of any radioactive decay is zero. The rate of decay, therefore, depends only upon the amount of radioactive substance present.

If we let N equal the number of atoms of radioactive substance, ΔN is the number of atoms that disintegrate in a time interval, Δt:

$$-\frac{\Delta N}{\Delta t} = kN \tag{27.2}$$

where k is the rate constant. The rate expression is negative because it represents the disappearance of the radioactive substance.

Rearrangement of the rate expression gives

$$-\frac{\Delta N}{N} = k\,\Delta t \tag{27.3}$$

which states that the fraction lost $(-\Delta N/N)$ in a given time interval (Δt) is directly proportional to the length of the time interval. The time required for half the sample to decay is a time interval defined as the **half-life**, $t_{1/2}$, which is a constant for each radioactive nuclide.

The curve of Figure 27.4, which shows the number of radioactive atoms versus time, is typical of first-order processes. Let N_0 equal the number of radioactive atoms present at the start. After a single half-life period has elapsed, one-half of the original number of atoms remain $(\frac{1}{2}N_0)$. This number is reduced by half (to $\frac{1}{4}N_0$) by the time another half-life has passed. Each radioactive nuclide has a characteristic half-life, and these vary widely. For example, ^5_3Li has a half-life estimated to be 10^{-21} s, and $^{238}_{92}\text{U}$ has a half-life of 4.51×10^9 years.

The rate equation may be written in its differential form:

$$-\frac{dN}{N} = kN \tag{27.4}$$

and by means of the calculus this equation may be integrated:

$$-2.303 \log\left(\frac{N}{N_0}\right) = kt \tag{27.5}$$

where N_0 is the amount present initially (at time zero) and N is the amount present at time t. Equation 27.5 may be rearranged to give:

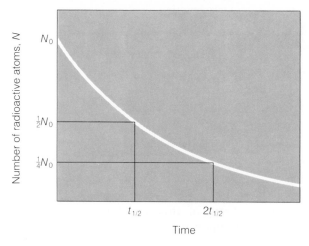

Figure 27.4 Curve showing the rate of a radioactive decay

$$\log\left(\frac{N_0}{N}\right) = \frac{kt}{2.303} \tag{27.6}$$

After a half-life period has elapsed, $t = t_{1/2}$, and the number of radioactive atoms left is equal to $\frac{1}{2}N_0$:

$$N = \tfrac{1}{2}N_0$$

Therefore

$$\frac{N_0}{N} = 2$$

Substitution into Equation 27.6 gives:

$$\log\left(\frac{N_0}{N}\right) = \frac{kt}{2.303} \tag{27.6}$$

$$\log 2 = \frac{kt_{1/2}}{2.303}$$

$$t_{1/2} = \frac{2.303 \log 2}{k}$$

$$t_{1/2} = \frac{0.693}{k} \tag{27.7}$$

Notice that N_0 and N in Equation 27.6 can be expressed in terms of *atoms*, *moles*, or *any mass unit* provided that they are both expressed in the same units. Since these variables appear in a *ratio* (N_0/N), the units cancel, and the numerical value of the ratio is the same no matter what units are used to derive it.

Example 27.6

The radioactive nuclide $^{60}_{27}\text{Co}$ has a half-life of 5.27 years. Calculate the mass of $^{60}_{27}\text{Co}$ that remains from a 0.0100 g sample of the nuclide after 1.00 year has elapsed.

Solution

We first find the rate constant for this disintegration. Equation 27.7 is rearranged and solved:

$$k = \frac{0.693}{t_{1/2}}$$

$$k = \frac{0.693}{5.27 \text{ year}} = 0.132/\text{year}$$

The mass of $^{60}_{27}\text{Co}$ remaining at the end of 1.00 year may be found by using Equation 27.6:

$$\log\left(\frac{N_0}{N}\right) = \frac{kt}{2.30} \tag{27.6}$$

$$= \frac{(0.132/\text{year})(1.00 \text{ year})}{2.30} = 0.0574$$

$$\frac{N_0}{N} = \text{antilog } 0.0574 = 1.14$$

$$\frac{0.0100 \text{ g}}{N} = 1.14$$

$$N = 0.00877 \text{ g}$$

Notice that N/N_0 (which is the inverse of the term N_0/N that appears in Equation 27.6) is the fraction of the original sample that remains. Here,

$$\frac{N}{N_0} = \frac{1}{(N_0/N)} = \frac{1}{1.14} = 0.877$$

Activity

The amount of radiation emanating from a source per unit time is called the **activity** of the source:

$$activity = -\frac{dN}{dt} = kN \tag{27.8}$$

Activities are expressed in terms of the number of disintegrations that occur in a given time interval (for example, a second or a minute). The curie (Ci) is a unit that is frequently used. According to the definition of the curie:

$$1 \text{ curie} = 1 \text{ Ci} = 3.70 \times 10^{10} \text{ disintegrations/s}$$

$$1 \text{ millicurie} = 1 \text{ mCi} = 3.70 \times 10^{7} \text{ disintegrations/s}$$

$$1 \text{ microcurie} = 1 \text{ } \mu\text{Ci} = 3.70 \times 10^{4} \text{ disintegrations/s}$$

Notice that the activity of a sample of a radioactive nuclide is proportional to the number of atoms present. Hence the ratio N_0/N is equal to the ratio of the activity of the sample at time $= 0$ to the activity of the sample at time $= t$:

$$\frac{N_0}{N} = \frac{(activity)_0}{(activity)} \tag{27.9}$$

Example 27.7

A sample of $^{35}_{16}\text{S}$, a β^- emitter, has an activity of 0.100 μCi. In 20.0 days, the activity of the sample has declined to 0.0853 μCi. What is the half-life of $^{35}_{16}\text{S}$?

Solution

We use Equation 27.6 to find the value of the rate constant, k:

$$\log\left(\frac{N_0}{N}\right) = \frac{kt}{2.303} \tag{27.6}$$

$$\log\frac{0.100 \text{ } \mu\text{Ci}}{0.0853 \text{ } \mu\text{Ci}} = \frac{k(20.0 \text{ day})}{2.303}$$

$$k = 7.95 \times 10^{-3}/\text{day}$$

The half-life can be derived from the value of k by using Equation 27.7:

$$t_{1/2} = \frac{0.693}{k}$$

$$= \frac{0.693}{7.95 \times 10^{-3}/\text{day}} = 87.2 \text{ days}$$

Example 27.8

The half-life of $^{100}_{43}\text{Tc}$, a β^- emitter, is 15.8 s. (a) How many atoms of $^{100}_{43}\text{Tc}$ are present in a sample with an activity of 0.200 μCi. (b) What is the mass of the sample?

Solution

(a) We use the half-life, $t_{1/2}$, find the rate constant, k:

$$k = \frac{0.693}{t_{1/2}}$$

$$= \frac{0.693}{15.8 \text{ s}} = 0.0439/\text{s}$$

Next, we find the activity of the sample in terms of the number of atoms that disintegrate per second:

$$? \text{ atoms/s} = 0.200 \ \mu\text{Ci}\left(\frac{3.70 \times 10^4 \text{ atoms/s}}{1.00 \ \mu\text{Ci}}\right) = 7.40 \times 10^3 \text{ atoms/s}$$

We substitute the value of k and the value of the *activity* in Equation 27.8 to find the number of atoms present, N:

$$activity = kN$$

$$(7.40 \times 10^3 \text{ atoms/s}) = (4.39 \times 10^{-2}/\text{s})N$$

$$N = 1.69 \times 10^5 \text{ atoms}$$

(b) The mass of the sample can be derived from the fact that the atomic weight of $^{100}_{43}\text{Tc}$ to three significant figures is 100. Thus,

$$? \text{ g } ^{100}\text{Tc} = 1.69 \times 10^5 \text{ atoms } ^{100}\text{Tc}\left(\frac{100 \text{ g } ^{100}\text{Tc}}{6.02 \times 10^{23} \text{ atoms } ^{100}\text{Tc}}\right)$$

$$= 2.81 \times 10^{-17} \text{ g } ^{100}\text{Tc}$$

Radiocarbon Dating

The radioactive nuclide $^{14}_{6}\text{C}$ is produced in the atmosphere by the action of cosmic-ray neutrons on $^{14}_{7}\text{N}$:

$$^{14}_{7}\text{N} + ^1_0\text{n} \longrightarrow ^{14}_{6}\text{C} + ^1_1\text{H}$$

In the atmosphere, the $^{14}_{6}\text{C}$ is oxidized to $CO_2(g)$, and this radioactive CO_2 mixes with nonradioactive CO_2. At the same time that $^{14}_{6}\text{C}$ is being produced, it is also disappearing through β^- decay:

$$^{14}_{6}\text{C} \longrightarrow ^{14}_{7}\text{N} + _{-1}^{0}e$$

The steady state is attained when the rate at which $^{14}_{6}\text{C}$ is being made equals the rate at which it is disappearing. At the steady state, the amount of $^{14}_{6}\text{C}$ *per one gram* of carbon (which consists principally of the stable nuclides $^{12}_{6}\text{C}$ and $^{13}_{6}\text{C}$) accounts for an activity of approximately 15 disintegrations per minute.

The CO_2 from the atmosphere is assimilated by plants through the process of photosynthesis. In turn, the plants are eaten by animals. In this way, $^{14}_{6}\text{C}$ becomes incorporated into plants and animals. In any living plant or animal, the amount of $^{14}_{6}\text{C}$ per gram of carbon is the same as the amount per gram in the atmosphere. When an organism dies, however, the amount of $^{14}_{6}\text{C}$ decreases through radioactive decay and is no longer replenished by the assimilation of carbon-containing compounds. The activity of the object, therefore, decreases. An indication of the age of a bone, a fragment of cloth, or a piece of wood can be obtained from the radiocarbon activity of the object, the radiocarbon activity of living organisms, and the half-life of $^{14}_{6}\text{C}$ (5730 years).

Geological Dating

Several methods of geological dating are based on the natural disintegration series. Consider, for example, the $^{238}_{92}U$ series, which ends with the stable nuclide $^{206}_{82}Pb$. The half-life for the α decay of $^{238}_{92}U$, the first step in the series, is 4.468×10^9 years. This half-life is much longer than any other half-life encountered in the series. As a result, the first step may be considered to be rate-determining and to govern the entire process.

We can find the age of a uranium mineral by measuring the ratio of $^{238}_{92}U$ atoms to $^{206}_{82}Pb$ atoms in a specimen of the mineral. We assume that when the rock formed, a closed system developed—that except for changes brought about by radioactive decay there has been no loss or gain of either nuclide since the rock solidified. In addition, we must take into account in our calculation any $^{206}_{82}Pb$ that was present when the rock was formed and that therefore did not result from the radioactive decay series.

Example 27.10

A rock is found to contain the following nuclides in the ratios indicated:

3920 atoms of ^{238}U *to* 915 atoms of ^{206}Pb *to* 1.00 atom of ^{204}Pb

The following ratio exists in pure lead ores (both nuclides are stable):

1.70 atoms of ^{206}Pb *to* 1.00 atom of ^{204}Pb

The rate constant, k, for the α decay of $^{238}_{92}U$ is 1.551×10^{-10}/year, and the decay ultimately yields one atom of ^{206}Pb for every atom of ^{238}U disintegrated. Determine the age of the rock.

Solution

Consider a system containing 3920 atoms of ^{238}U, 915 atoms of ^{206}Pb, and 1.00 atom of ^{204}Pb. From the ratio of ^{206}Pb atoms to ^{204}Pb atoms in pure lead ores (17.0 to 1.00) and the fact that our system contains 1.00 atom of ^{204}Pb, we deduce that 17.0 atoms of ^{206}Pb were present when the rock was formed. The number of ^{206}Pb atoms produced by the radioactive decay, therefore, is

915 atoms ^{206}Pb − 17 atoms ^{206}Pb = 898 atoms ^{206}Pb

Since one atom of ^{206}Pb is produced by every one atom of ^{238}U that decays, the number of ^{238}U atoms at $t = 0$ is

N_0 = 3920 atoms ^{238}U + 898 atoms ^{238}U = 4818 atoms ^{238}U

The number of atoms at the present time is

N = 3920 atoms ^{238}U

Therefore,

$$t = \frac{2.303}{k} \log\left(\frac{N_0}{N}\right)$$

$$= \frac{2.303}{1.551 \times 10^{-10}/\text{year}} \log\left(\frac{4818 \text{ atoms}}{3920 \text{ atoms}}\right)$$

$$= 1.330 \times 10^9 \text{ year}$$

Other radioactive-decay processes have been used as a basis for dating methods. The results of studies of this type have placed the age of the oldest terrestrial rocks at 3.7 billion years, whereas the ages of lunar rocks and meteorites have been measured as 4.6 billion years. The solar system (including the earth) is believed to be 4.6 billion years old.

7.7 Nuclear Bombardment Reactions

In 1919, Ernest Rutherford reported that the following transformation occurs when α particles (from the radioactive decay of $^{214}_{84}\text{Po}$) are passed through nitrogen:

$$^{14}_{7}\text{N} + ^{4}_{2}\text{He} \longrightarrow ^{17}_{8}\text{O} + ^{1}_{1}\text{H}$$

This was the first artificial transmutation of one element into another element to be reported. In the years following, thousands of such nuclear transmutations have been studied. It is assumed that the projectile (in this case, an α particle) forms a compound nucleus with the target ($^{14}_{7}\text{N}$), and that the compound nucleus very rapidly ejects a subsidiary particle ($^{1}_{1}\text{H}$) to form the product nucleus ($^{17}_{8}\text{O}$). Other projectiles, such as neutrons, deuterons ($^{2}_{1}\text{H}$), protons, and ions, are used in addition to α particles.

These reactions, called particle-particle reactions, are usually classified according to the type of projectile employed and the subsidiary particle ejected. Thus, the preceding reaction is called an (α, p) reaction, since an α particle was used as the projectile and a proton ($^{1}_{1}\text{H}$) was ejected. The complete transformation is indicated by the notation $^{14}_{7}\text{N}(\alpha, \text{p})^{17}_{8}\text{O}$. Examples of the more common type of particle-particle reactions are listed in Table 27.2.

	Table 27.2 Examples of nuclear reactions	
Type	Reaction	Radioactivity of Product Nuclide
(α, n)	$^{75}_{33}\text{As} + ^{4}_{2}\text{He} \longrightarrow ^{78}_{35}\text{Br} + ^{1}_{0}\text{n}$	β^+
(α, p)	$^{106}_{46}\text{Pd} + ^{4}_{2}\text{He} \longrightarrow ^{109}_{47}\text{Ag} + ^{1}_{1}\text{H}$	stable
(p, n)	$^{7}_{3}\text{Li} + ^{1}_{1}\text{H} \longrightarrow ^{7}_{4}\text{Be} + ^{1}_{0}\text{n}$	ec
(p, γ)	$^{14}_{7}\text{N} + ^{1}_{1}\text{H} \longrightarrow ^{15}_{8}\text{O} + \gamma$	β^+
(p, α)	$^{9}_{4}\text{Be} + ^{1}_{1}\text{H} \longrightarrow ^{6}_{3}\text{Li} + ^{4}_{2}\text{He}$	stable
(d, p)	$^{31}_{15}\text{P} + ^{2}_{1}\text{H} \longrightarrow ^{32}_{15}\text{P} + ^{1}_{1}\text{H}$	β^-
(d, n)	$^{209}_{83}\text{Bi} + ^{2}_{1}\text{H} \longrightarrow ^{210}_{84}\text{Po} + ^{1}_{0}\text{n}$	α
(n, γ)	$^{59}_{27}\text{Co} + ^{1}_{0}\text{n} \longrightarrow ^{60}_{27}\text{Co} + \gamma$	β^-
(n, p)	$^{45}_{21}\text{Sc} + ^{1}_{0}\text{n} \longrightarrow ^{45}_{20}\text{Ca} + ^{1}_{1}\text{H}$	β^-
(n, α)	$^{27}_{13}\text{Al} + ^{1}_{0}\text{n} \longrightarrow ^{24}_{11}\text{Na} + ^{4}_{2}\text{He}$	β^-

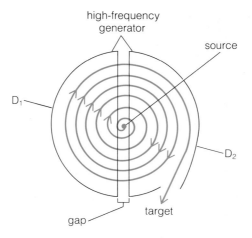

Figure 27.6 Path of a particle in a cyclotron

The first artificial, radioactive nuclide was produced by the (α, n) reaction:

$$^{27}_{13}\text{Al} + {}^{4}_{2}\text{He} \longrightarrow {}^{30}_{15}\text{P} + {}^{1}_{0}\text{n}$$

The product, $^{30}_{15}\text{P}$, decays by positron emission:

$$^{30}_{15}\text{P} \longrightarrow {}^{30}_{14}\text{Si} + {}^{0}_{1}e$$

Except for the nature of the product, there is no difference between nuclear reactions that produce stable nuclides and those that produce radioactive nuclides.

Particle Accelerators

Projectile particles that bear a positive charge are repelled by target nuclei. The repulsion is particularly strong for the heavier target nuclei, which have high positive charges. Consequently, only a small number of nuclear transformations can be brought about by the positive particles emitted by radioactive sources. Various particle accelerators are used to give protons, deuterons, α particles, and other cationic projectiles sufficiently high kinetic energies to overcome the electrostatic repulsions of the target nuclei. The cyclotron (see Figure 27.6) is one such instrument.

The ion source is located between two hollow D-shaped plates (D_1 and D_2), called dees, that are separated by a gap. The dees are enclosed in an evacuated chamber located between the poles of a powerful electromagnet (not shown in the figure). A high-frequency generator keeps the dees oppositely charged. Under the influence of the magnetic and electric fields, the ions move from the source in a circular path. Each time they reach the gap between the dees, the polarity of the dees is reversed. Thus, the positively charged particles are pushed out of a positive dee and attracted into a negative dee. Each time they traverse the gap, therefore, they are accelerated. Because of this, the particles travel an ever-increasing spiral path. Eventually, they penetrate a window in the instrument and, moving at extremely high speed, strike a target.

The linear accelerator (see Figure 27.7) operates in much the same way except that no magnetic field is employed. The particles are accelerated through a series

An overview of the Super-HILAC (Heavy Ion Linear Accelerator) at the Lawrence Berkeley Laboratory. This instrument will accelerate ions of all the elements in the periodic chart. *University of California, Lawrence Berkeley Laboratory.*

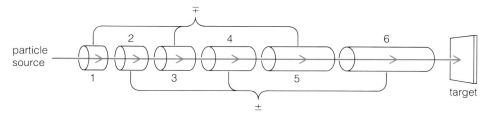

Figure 27.7   Schematic representation of a linear accelerator

of tubes enclosed in an evacuated chamber. A positive ion from the source is attracted into tube 1, which is negatively charged. At this time, the odd-numbered tubes have negative charges and the even-numbered tubes have positive charges. When the particle emerges from tube 1, the charges of the tubes are reversed, so that the even-numbered tubes are now negatively charged. The particle is repelled out of tube 1 (now positive) and attracted into tube 2 (now negative). As a result, it is accelerated.

Each time the particle leaves one tube to enter another, the charges of the tubes are reversed. Since the polarity of the tubes is reversed at a constant time interval, and since the speed of the particle increases constantly, each tube must be longer than the preceding one. The accelerated particles leave the last tube at high speed and strike the target.

Neutrons as Projectiles

Neutrons are particularly important projectiles because they bear no positive charge and therefore are not repelled by the positive charge of the target nuclei. A mixture of beryllium and an α emitter (such as $^{226}_{88}\text{Ra}$) is a convenient neutron source:

$$^{9}_{4}\text{Be} + ^{4}_{2}\text{He} \longrightarrow ^{12}_{6}\text{C} + ^{1}_{0}\text{n}$$

This reaction is the one James Chadwick used in his experiments that characterized the neutron (1932). The bombardment of beryllium by accelerated deuterons from a cyclotron is a more intense source of neutrons:

$$^{9}_{4}\text{Be} + ^{2}_{1}\text{H} \longrightarrow ^{10}_{5}\text{B} + ^{1}_{0}\text{n}$$

The atomic reactor is a very important source of neutrons (see Section 27.7).

Neutrons from nuclear reactions are known as **fast neutrons,** since they have very high kinetic energies. Fast neutrons cause nuclear reactions in which a subsidiary particle is ejected, such as (n, α) and (n, p) reactions. **Slow neutrons,** or **thermal neutrons,** are produced when the neutrons derived from a nuclear reaction are passed through a **moderator** (such as graphite, paraffin, water, hydrogen, or deuterium). Through collisions of neutrons with the nuclei of the moderator, the kinetic energies of the neutrons are decreased to values approximating those of ordinary gas molecules. Bombardments using slow neutrons bring about (n, γ) reactions which are also called **neutron-capture reactions,** since no subsidiary particle is ejected:

$$^{34}_{16}\text{S} + ^{1}_{0}\text{n} \longrightarrow ^{35}_{16}\text{S} + \gamma$$

Isotopes of practically every element have been prepared by this type of reaction.

Artificial Nuclides, Transuranium Elements

Nuclear reactions have been used to prepare isotopes of elements that do not exist in nature or that exist in extremely minute concentrations. Thus, isotopes of technetium, astatine, and francium have been prepared by the reactions:

$$^{96}_{42}\text{Mo} + ^{2}_{1}\text{H} \longrightarrow ^{97}_{43}\text{Tc} + ^{1}_{0}\text{n}$$

$$^{209}_{83}\text{Bi} + ^{4}_{2}\text{He} \longrightarrow ^{211}_{85}\text{At} + 2^{1}_{0}\text{n}$$

$$^{230}_{90}\text{Th} + ^{1}_{1}\text{H} \longrightarrow ^{223}_{87}\text{Fr} + 2^{4}_{2}\text{He}$$

The elements following uranium in the periodic table are called the **transuranium elements.** Since none of these elements occurs in nature, all of the ones listed have been made by nuclear reactions. Some of these reactions use artificial nuclides as targets. In these cases, the final products are therefore the result of preparations consisting of several steps. Examples of these preparations are:

$$^{238}_{92}\text{U} + ^{1}_{0}\text{n} \longrightarrow ^{239}_{92}\text{U} + \gamma$$

$$^{239}_{92}\text{U} \longrightarrow ^{239}_{93}\text{Np} + _{-1}^{0}e \qquad \text{neptunium}$$

$$^{239}_{93}\text{Np} \longrightarrow ^{239}_{94}\text{Pu} + _{-1}^{0}e \qquad \text{plutonium}$$

$$^{239}_{94}Pu + ^{2}_{1}H \longrightarrow ^{240}_{95}Am + ^{1}_{0}n \qquad \text{americium}$$

$$^{239}_{94}Pu + ^{4}_{2}He \longrightarrow ^{242}_{96}Cm + ^{1}_{0}n \qquad \text{curium}$$

$$^{238}_{92}U + ^{12}_{6}C \longrightarrow ^{244}_{98}Cf + 6^{1}_{0}n \qquad \text{californium}$$

$$^{238}_{92}U + ^{14}_{7}N \longrightarrow ^{246}_{99}Es + 6^{1}_{0}n \qquad \text{einsteinium}$$

$$^{238}_{92}U + ^{16}_{8}O \longrightarrow ^{250}_{100}Fm + 4^{1}_{0}n \qquad \text{fermium}$$

$$^{252}_{98}Cf + ^{10}_{5}B \longrightarrow ^{257}_{103}Lr + 5^{1}_{0}n \qquad \text{lawrencium}$$

$$^{249}_{98}Cf + ^{18}_{8}O \longrightarrow ^{263}_{106}Unh + 4^{1}_{0}n \qquad \text{unnilhexium}$$

The International Union of Pure and Applied Chemistry has recommended a system for assigning names and symbols to all elements with atomic numbers higher than 103. A name is composed of roots (see Table 27.3) derived from the digits that make up the atomic number of the element, and the ending *-ium* is added. Element 106, therefore, is:

un (for 1) + *nil* (for 0) + *hex* (for 6) + *ium* = *unnilhexium*

The symbols for these elements (the only symbols to consist of three letters) are made up of the first letter of each root of the name. The symbol for unnilhexium is *Unh*.

A 3×10^{-7} g sample of californium oxychloride, the first pure californium compound to be isolated in the laboratory (magnified 170 times). The compound gives off its own light as a result of radioactive decay. *University of California, Lawrence Berkeley Laboratory.*

7.8 Nuclear Fission

Binding Energy

For every atom except $^{1}_{1}H$ (the nucleus of which consists of a single proton), the sum of the masses of the component protons, neutrons, and electrons is larger than the actual mass of the atom. Consider, for example, the $^{35}_{17}Cl$ atom, which consists of 17 protons, 18 neutrons, and 17 electrons. The sum of the masses of these particles is:

mass of 17 protons + mass of 18 neutrons + mass of 17 electrons
$$17(1.007276 \text{ u}) + 18(1.008665 \text{ u}) + 17(0.000549 \text{ u}) = 35.288995 \text{ u}$$

The mass of the $^{35}_{17}Cl$ atom has been measured as 34.968853 u. The difference in mass, Δm, is:

$$\Delta m = 35.288995 \text{ u} - 34.968853 \text{ u} = 0.320142 \text{ u}$$

This difference expressed in its energy equivalent is called the binding energy of the nuclide in question:

$$0.320142 \text{ u} \times 931.502 \text{ MeV/u} = 298.213 \text{ MeV}$$

The binding energy of a nuclide is interpreted in terms of the nucleus of the nuclide. The binding energy may be considered to be the energy *required* to pull the nucleons of a nucleus apart or the energy *released* by a hypothetical process in which a group of nucleons combine to form a nucleus.

Table 27.3 Roots used to derive names and symbols for the elements with atomic numbers higher than 103

Digit of Z	Root
0	nil
1	un
2	bi
3	tri
4	quad
5	pent
6	hex
7	sept
8	oct
9	enn

The removal and addition of electrons also involve energy changes which, of course, have mass equivalents. These mass equivalents, however, are extremely small and may be neglected. The mass of the $_1^1$H atom, therefore, is indeed equal to the sum of the mass of a proton and the mass of an electron, since no nuclear binding energy is involved (the nucleus consists of a single proton).

We could find the binding energy of a nuclide by working with the mass of the *nucleus* alone. The mass values usually given in references, however, are *atomic* masses, and so atomic masses are used to calculate binding energies. In any nuclide, the number of protons is the same as the number of electrons (and each number is equal to the atomic number). It is convenient, therefore, to use the mass of the $_1^1$H atom for the calculation, which is illustrated in the example that follows.

Example 27.11

(a) Calculate the binding energy of the $_{26}^{56}$Fe nucleus in MeV. (b) What is the value in terms of MeV/nucleon? The mass of the neutron is 1.00866 u, of the $_1^1$H atom is 1.00783 u, and of the $_{26}^{56}$Fe atom is 55.93494 u.

Solution

(a) The $_{26}^{56}$Fe atom contains 26 protons and 26 electrons (which taken together equal 26 $_1^1$H atoms) plus 30 neutrons. The *calculated* mass of the $_{26}^{56}$Fe *atom is:*

mass of 26 $_1^1$H atoms + mass of 30 neutrons

26(1.00783 u) + 30(1.00866 u) = 56.46338 u

The mass difference, Δm, between the *calculated* mass and the *actual* mass is:

Δm = 56.46338 u − 55.93494 u = 0.52844 u

The binding energy, therefore, is:

0.52844 u × 931.50 MeV/u = 492.24 MeV

(b) The mass number of the nuclide indicates that there are 56 nucleons in the nucleus. Thus,

492.24 MeV/56 nucleons = 8.7900 MeV/nucleon

The binding energies of the nuclides are more readily compared in terms of **binding energy per nucleon,** which is obtained by dividing the binding energy of a nucleus by the number of nucleons in that nucleus. Since $_{17}^{35}$Cl contains 35 nucleons (17 protons and 18 neutrons) the binding energy per nucleon for this nuclide is:

$$\frac{298.213 \text{ MeV}}{35 \text{ nucleons}} = 8.52037 \text{ MeV/nucleon}$$

In Figure 27.8, binding energy per nucleon is plotted against mass number for the nuclides. At the beginning of the curve, the binding energy per nucleon rises

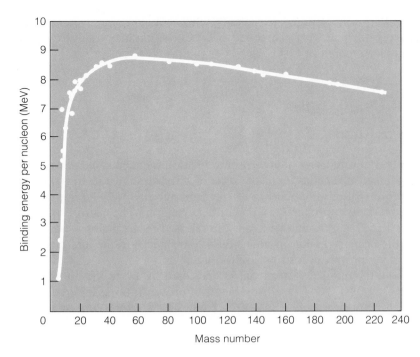

Figure 27.8　Binding energy per nucleon versus mass number

rapidly. An increase in the number of nucleons causes them to be held together more strongly. The curve reaches a maximum around iron, cobalt, and nickel. These nuclei are the most stable of all. After the maximum is reached, the curve drops off gradually, showing that the heavier nuclei are not so stable as those of intermediate mass.

Two types of processes can be interpreted by reference to the curve of Figure 27.8:

1. Nuclear fusion (discussed in Section 27.9) is a process in which two very light nuclei are fused into a heavier nucleus.

2. Nuclear fission is a process in which a heavy nucleus is split into two nuclei of intermediate mass (into those nearer the maximum of the curve).

In both of these processes, the nuclei produced have higher binding-energy-per-nucleon values than the nuclei that react. Each of these processes, therefore, results in the production of more stable nuclei and the liberation of large amounts of energy.

Nuclear Fission

In Section 27.3, we noted that nuclei with mass numbers larger than 230 undergo a form of radioactive decay known as spontaneous fission. In this type of process, a heavy (and unstable) nucleus splits into two lighter (but more stable) nuclei and several neutrons.

Fission can also be *induced* by projectiles. The most important of the induced fissions are those brought about by neutrons, but fissions can also be induced by protons ($^{1}_{1}H$), deuterons ($^{2}_{1}H$), and α particles ($^{4}_{2}He$). The fission of a given nuclide may occur in many different ways. Three sets of products that may result from the slow-neutron-induced fission of $^{235}_{92}U$ are:

$$^{235}_{92}U + ^{1}_{0}n \longrightarrow ^{95}_{39}Y + ^{138}_{53}I + 3\,^{1}_{0}n$$

$$^{235}_{92}U + ^{1}_{0}n \longrightarrow ^{90}_{36}Kr + ^{144}_{56}Ba + 2\,^{1}_{0}n$$

$$^{235}_{92}U + ^{1}_{0}n \longrightarrow ^{92}_{37}Rb + ^{140}_{55}Cs + 4\,^{1}_{0}n$$

All the nuclides indicated as products (primary-fission fragments) in these equations are β^- radioactive. The nuclei in the zone of stability shown in Figure 27.1 have neutron/proton ratios ranging from 1.0 (for light nuclei) to 1.2–1.3 (for nuclei of intermediate mass) to approximately 1.5 (for heavy nuclei). The neutron/proton ratio of $^{235}_{92}U$ is 1.55. Even though neutrons are released in the fissions shown in the equations, the primary-fission products (which are nuclei in the intermediate range) have neutron/proton ratios that are too high.

In β^- emission, the number of neutrons is decreased by 1 and the number of protons is increased by 1. As a result, the neutron/proton ratio is lowered. For example, in the β^- emission

$$^{95}_{39}Y \longrightarrow ^{95}_{40}Zr + \,_{-1}^{0}e$$

the neutron/proton ratio is lowered from 1.44 (for $^{95}_{39}Y$) to 1.38 (for $^{95}_{40}Zr$). For each primary-fission product, more than one step is usually necessary to reach a stable nucleus. For the fission:

$$^{235}_{92}U + ^{1}_{0}n \longrightarrow ^{95}_{39}Y + ^{138}_{53}I + 3\,^{1}_{0}n$$

the decay chains produced by the primary-fission fragments are:

$$^{235}_{92}U \text{ fission} \begin{cases} ^{95}_{39}Y \xrightarrow{\beta^-} ^{95}_{40}Zr \xrightarrow{\beta^-} ^{95}_{41}Nb \xrightarrow{\beta^-} ^{95}_{42}Mo \text{ (stable)} \\ ^{138}_{53}I \xrightarrow{\beta^-} ^{138}_{54}Xe \xrightarrow{\beta^-} ^{138}_{55}Cs \xrightarrow{\beta^-} ^{138}_{56}Ba \text{ (stable)} \end{cases}$$

Several hundred nuclides have been identified as products of $^{235}_{92}U$ fission. Approximately 90 decay chains have been characterized, each chain consisting of three or four steps. The radioactive nuclides produced in large number by nuclear fission are responsible for the hazards associated with nuclear reactors and with nuclear fallout.

The fission of each $^{235}_{92}U$ nucleus is induced by a single neutron and produces from two to four neutrons (as shown in the equations). In an overall fission process, an average of approximately 2.5 neutrons are produced per fission. If each neutron produced causes the fission of another $^{235}_{92}U$ nucleus, an explosively rapid chain reaction ensues.

If, for simplicity, we assume that two neutrons are produced per fission (a reproduction factor of 2), the first fission would produce two neutrons and cause two first-generation fissions. Each of these would cause two fissions—a total of four second-generation fissions. In succeeding generations there would be 8, 16, 32, 64, . . . fissions. In the nth generation, 2^n fissions would occur. Since each fission is extremely rapid, an explosion results. Since each fission releases about 200 MeV, a tremendous amount of energy is liberated.

In a small amount of $^{235}_{92}U$ undergoing fission, many of the neutrons produced are lost from the surface of the mass before they can bring about nuclear reactions.

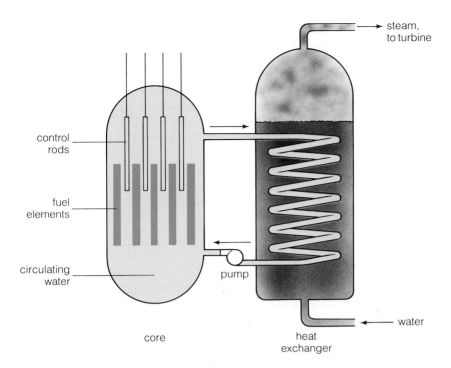

Figure 27.9 Essential features of a nuclear reactor

If the size of the fissionable material exceeds a certain critical mass, however, the neutrons are captured before they can leave the mass and an explosive chain reaction ensues. An atomic bomb is detonated by bringing pieces of fissionable material, each of subcritical size, together into one piece of supercritical size. The reaction is started by a stray neutron.

A number of nuclei, such as $^{238}_{92}U$, $^{231}_{91}Pa$, $^{237}_{93}Np$, and $^{232}_{90}Th$, undergo fission with fast, but not with slow, neutrons. Slow neutrons, however, can induce fission in $^{233}_{92}U$, $^{235}_{92}U$, and $^{239}_{94}Pu$. The nuclide $^{235}_{92}U$, which constitutes only about 0.7% of natural uranium, was employed in the contruction of the first atomic bomb. The separation of $^{235}_{92}U$ from the principal uranium isotope, $^{238}_{92}U$, was carried out in many ways. The most successful method was the separation of gaseous $^{235}UF_6$ by thermal diffusion through porous barriers. Advantage is taken of the fact that the lighter molecule effuses more rapidly (see the discussion of Graham's law in Section 10.12).

Nuclear Reactors

The controlled fission of nuclear fuels in a nuclear reactor serves as a source of energy, a source of propulsion (for nuclear ships and submarines), or as a source of neutrons and γ radiation for scientific research and the production of artificial nuclides. At present, approximately 14% of the electrical energy used in the United States is produced by nuclear reactors. Several types of nuclear reactors are used for the generation of electrical power. Features of the most common type are diagrammed in Figure 27.9.

Natural uranium, natural uranium enriched with $^{235}_{92}U$, $^{239}_{94}Pu$, or $^{233}_{92}U$, or a mixture of these may be employed as the fuel. The most commonly used fuel is natural uranium enriched with $^{235}_{92}U$. The fuel elements consists of pellets of UO_2

clad in either stainless steel or a zirconium alloy. The fuel elements are surrounded by a **moderator,** which is usually water, heavy water ($_1^2H_2O$), or graphite. The moderator serves to slow down the neutrons produced by fission, thus increasing the possibility of their capture.

The neutron-reproduction factor must be maintained close to a value of 1. That is, each fission (which is initiated by one neutron) must on the average produce one neutron in order to maintain the chain. If the reproduction factor falls below 1, the process will eventually stop. If it increases much above this level, the process may become dangerously rapid, leading to a meltdown of the core.

The process is controlled by using **control rods** that are inserted to any desired depth between the fuel elements of the core. The rods are made of cadmium, boron steel, or other materials that have the ability to capture excess neutrons:

$$_{48}^{113}Cd + _0^1n \longrightarrow _{48}^{114}Cd + \gamma$$

$$_5^{10}B + _0^1n \longrightarrow _5^{11}B + \gamma$$

By moving the control rods, the rate of the process can be adjusted.

The fission of the fuel in a nuclear reactor produces a large amount of heat. A cooling system is employed to remove this heat from the core to the outside, where it is used to produce steam that generates electricity by means of a steam turbine. In Figure 27.9, water (which also functions as the moderator) is used as the coolant. The water is circulated under pressure through a closed loop. Other types of nuclear reactors employ other coolants (air, helium, CO_2, liquid sodium, and heavy water, for examples).

Example 27.12

In a fission process, the products undergo successive β^- decay until stable nuclides are produced. If the equations for the fission and the β^- decays are added, the following equation is obtained (masses of the particles are indicated):

$$\underset{235.0439 \text{ u}}{_{92}^{235}U} \longrightarrow \underset{94.9058 \text{ u}}{_{42}^{95}Mo} + \underset{137.9052 \text{ u}}{_{56}^{138}Ba} + \underset{2(1.0087) \text{ u}}{2\,_0^1n} + \underset{6(0.00055) \text{ u}}{6\,_{-1}^0e}$$

Calculate the energy released in (a) MeV per fission, (b) kJ per gram of fuel.

Solution

(a) We first calculate the mass loss for the process.

$$\begin{aligned}
\Delta m &= 235.0439 \text{ u} - 94.9058 \text{ u} - 137.9052 \text{ u} - 2(1.0087) \text{ u} - 6(0.00055) \text{ u} \\
&= 235.0439 \text{ u} - 94.9058 \text{ u} - 137.9052 \text{ u} - 2.0174 \text{ u} - 0.0033 \text{ u} \\
&= 0.2122 \text{ u}
\end{aligned}$$

Since 1 u = 931.5 MeV,

$$(0.2122 \text{ u})(931.5 \text{ MeV/u}) = 197.7 \text{ MeV}$$

(b) If the equation is read in terms of moles, the mass loss (Δm) represented is 0.2122 g = 2.122×10^{-4} kg. We can calculate the energy released (ΔE) from the Einstein equation (where c is the speed of light, 2.998×10^8 m/s):

$$\Delta E = (\Delta m)c^2$$
$$= (2.122 \times 10^{-4} \text{ kg})(2.998 \times 10^8 \text{ m/s})^2$$
$$= 1.907 \times 10^{13} \text{ J} = 1.907 \times 10^{10} \text{ kJ}$$

Since this quantity of energy was released by 235.0 g of $^{235}_{92}$U, the energy released per gram of fuel is:

$$(1.907 \times 10^{10} \text{ kJ})/(235.0 \text{ g}) = 8.115 \times 10^7 \text{ kJ/g}$$

Breeder Reactor

It has been estimated that at the present rate of use, the supply of $^{235}_{92}$U in nature will last only 40 more years. Not only is the supply of this nuclide severely limited, but the isolation of the nuclide is extremely expensive. The other two nuclides that undergo fission with slow neutrons, $^{239}_{94}$Pu and $^{233}_{92}$U, do not occur in nature. The plutonium nuclide is obtained from $^{238}_{92}$U by the reactions:

$$^{238}_{92}\text{U} + ^1_0\text{n} \longrightarrow {}^{239}_{92}\text{U} + \gamma$$
$$^{239}_{92}\text{U} \longrightarrow {}^{239}_{93}\text{Np} + {}^0_{-1}e$$
$$^{239}_{93}\text{Np} \longrightarrow {}^{239}_{94}\text{Pu} + {}^0_{-1}e$$

The $^{233}_{92}$U nuclide is obtained by the reactions:

$$^{232}_{90}\text{Th} + ^1_0\text{n} \longrightarrow {}^{233}_{90}\text{Th} + \gamma$$
$$^{233}_{90}\text{Th} \longrightarrow {}^{233}_{91}\text{Pa} + {}^0_{-1}e$$
$$^{233}_{91}\text{Pa} \longrightarrow {}^{233}_{92}\text{U} + {}^0_{-1}e$$

Breeder reactors have been designed that produce more fissionable material than they use. Suppose that the fuel employed in the reactor is natural uranium enriched with $^{235}_{92}$U. The design of the reactor is such that one neutron from a $^{235}_{92}$U fission is used to sustain the fission chain. The other neutrons from the fission are used to react with $^{238}_{92}$U (the principal isotope present in natural uranium) to produce the fissionable $^{239}_{94}$Pu. If $^{232}_{90}$Th is incorporated into the fuel, the fissionable nuclide $^{233}_{92}$U can be produced. In this way, provision is made for the maintenance of a supply of nuclear fuel.

7.9 Nuclear Fusion

In nuclear fusions, very light nuclei combine to form heavier nuclei. The binding-energy curve given in Figure 27.8 shows that more energy per nucleon should be liberated by fusions than is liberated by fissions. The energy of the sun is believed to be derived from the conversion of hydrogen nuclei into helium nuclei by nuclear fusion. Reactions such as the following are postulated:

$$^1_1\text{H} + ^1_1\text{H} \longrightarrow {}^2_1\text{H} + {}^0_1e$$
$$^2_1\text{H} + ^1_1\text{H} \longrightarrow {}^3_2\text{He} + \gamma$$
$$^3_2\text{He} + ^3_2\text{He} \longrightarrow {}^4_2\text{He} + 2{}^1_1\text{H}$$

Picture of the sun taken by the solar telescope of Skylab. *NASA.*

Nuclei undergoing fusion repel each other strongly because of the positive charges that they bear. In order for these nuclei to get close enough together to combine, they must be given very high energies to overcome the forces of repulsion. For this reason, very high temperatures (on the order of 10^8 K) are required for fusion reactions, which are sometimes called thermonuclear reactions. In the hydrogen bomb, which is based on nuclear fusion, the high temperatures required for fusion to occur are supplied by a fission bomb.

At the high temperatures of fusion reactions, all molecules are dissociated into atoms, and the atoms are ionized into cations and electrons. This state of matter—a highly dense, extremely hot gas consisting of cations and electrons—is called plasma.

Design of a nuclear-fusion reactor requires that ways be found to confine the hot plasma as well as to achieve the high temperatures required. Extensive experimentation has been undertaken to study the confinement of hot plasma by strong magnetic fields, since no known material can be used for this purpose at the temperatures concerned. In laser fusion, high-powered, pulsed laser beams are used to heat and compress small pellets of fuel.

The fusion reaction:

$$\,^2_1\mathrm{H} + \,^3_1\mathrm{H} \longrightarrow \,^4_2\mathrm{He} + \,^1_0\mathrm{n}$$

appears promising for use in fusion reactors, since it has a relatively low ignition temperature and produces a relatively large amount of energy. The reaction uses deuterium, $\,^2_1\mathrm{H}$ (readily available from natural sources), and tritium, $\,^3_1\mathrm{H}$ (which,

The world's largest superconductivity magnets to be used in atomic fusion research. The strong magnetic field produced by these magnets (150,000 times that of the earth) will be used to confine the superhot fusion fuel. The magnets are constructed of superconducting niobium-titanium cable cooled by liquid helium to about 4 K. They consume less than 0.003% of the electric power that conventional water-cooled copper magnets of this size would consume. *University of California, Lawrence Livermore National Laboratory.*

however, is not very abundant in nature). A lithium blanket could be included in a fusion reactor to generate the required tritium by the reactions:

$$_0^1n + {}_3^6Li \longrightarrow {}_1^3H + {}_2^4He$$

$$_0^1n + {}_3^7Li \longrightarrow {}_1^3H + {}_2^4He + {}_0^1n$$

As an energy source, controlled fusion offers several advantages over nuclear fission. The fuel for nuclear fusion is readily available from nature in almost unlimited quantities. Although there are environmental hazards associated with handling neutrons and tritium (which is β^- radioactive with a half-life of 12.33 years), nuclear fusion is in general a cleaner process than fission. Fusion, unlike fission, does not produce large amounts of radioactive wastes (which include some nuclides that have very long half-lives). The costs of energy production by fusion should be lower than by fission.

Example 27.13

Consider the following fusion reaction (masses given below the symbols):

$$\begin{array}{ccccc} {}_1^2H & + & {}_1^3H & \longrightarrow & {}_2^4He & + & {}_0^1n \\ 2.01410\ u & & 3.01605\ u & & 4.00260\ u & & 1.00866\ u \end{array}$$

Calculate the energy released: (a) in MeV per fusion, (b) in kJ per gram of fuel.

Solution

(a) We calculate the loss in mass for the reaction:

$$\Delta m = 2.01410 \text{ u} + 3.01605 \text{ u} - 4.00260 \text{ u} - 1.00866 \text{ u}$$
$$= 0.01889 \text{ u}$$

Since 1 u = 931.5 MeV, the energy released is:

$$(0.01889 \text{ u})(931.5 \text{ MeV/u}) = 17.60 \text{ MeV}$$

(b) If the equation is read in terms of moles, the mass loss is 0.01889 g, or 1.889×10^{-5} kg.

$$\Delta E = (\Delta m)c^2$$
$$= (1.889 \times 10^{-5} \text{ kg})(2.998 \times 10^8 \text{ m/s})^2$$
$$= 1.698 \times 10^{12} \text{ J} = 1.698 \times 10^9 \text{ kJ}$$

The number of grams of fuel used in the reaction is:

$$2.01410 \text{ g} + 3.01605 \text{ g} = 5.03015 \text{ g}$$

Hence, the energy released in kJ/g is:

$$(1.698 \times 10^9 \text{ kJ})/(5.03015 \text{ g}) = 3.376 \times 10^8 \text{ kJ/g}$$

In Example 27.12, a typical fission reaction was found to release 8.115×10^7 kJ/g. The fusion described in this example releases more than four times as much energy per gram of fuel. Compare both results with the value for the complete combustion of carbon, which is approximately 33 kJ/g.

27.10 Uses of Radioactive Nuclides

Many uses have been developed for the nuclides that are the products of the processes run in nuclear reactors. Thickness gauges have been developed in which a radioactive source is placed on one side of the material to be tested (for example, a metal plate) and a counting device on the other side. The amount of radiation reaching the counter is a measure of the thickness of the material.

The effectiveness of lubricating oils is measured in an engine constructed from metal into which radioactive nuclides have been incorporated. After the engine has been run for a fixed time period, the oil is withdrawn and tested for the presence of radioactive particles accumulated through engine wear.

When a single pipeline is used to transfer more that one petroleum derivative (one after the other), a small amount of a radioactive nuclide is placed in the last portion of one substance to signal its end and the start of the other. The radiation may be used to activate an automatic valve system so that the liquids are diverted into different tanks.

Radiation is also used to preserve foods. It can be used to prevent potatoes from sprouting, to eliminate insects from grains, and to destroy bacteria that cause food spoilage.

We have discussed how to determine the age of materials of plant and animal origin by measuring the amount of $^{14}_{6}C$ present in them. This radioactive isotope of carbon has also been used to study photosynthesis. In this natural process through which plants grow, carbon dioxide is removed from the air by plants and is used to form carbon-containing compounds. The energy for photosynthesis is supplied by sunlight and the process is catalyzed by the green coloring matter of plants, chlorophyll. For example,

$$6\,CO_2(g) + 6\,H_2O(l) \longrightarrow C_6H_{12}O_6(s) + 6\,CO_2(g)$$

When CO_2 that contains $^{14}_{6}C$ is used, the carbon can be traced from simple compounds to more and more complex compounds as the reactions that make up the overall process occur.

Radioactive nuclides have found many uses in medical research, diagnosis, and therapy. The radiations from $^{60}_{27}Co$, a β^- and γ emitter, are used in cancer therapy. The nuclide $^{131}_{53}I$ is used in the diagnosis and treatment of thyroid disorders, since this gland concentrates ingested iodine. The patient consumes a low dose of $^{131}_{53}I$ in the form of NaI. The absorption of the radioactive iodine by the thyroid gland is followed by counting the γ activity. In this way, it can be determined whether the thyroid is functioning normally, is overactive, or is underactive.

The radioactive nuclide $^{131}_{53}I$ is also used to locate brain tumors. The nuclide is incorporated into a dye that, upon injection into the body, is preferentially adsorbed by cancerous cells. The locations of the dye, and hence the location of the tumor, is ascertained by scanning the skull.

The radioactive nuclide $^{24}_{11}Na$ is used to follow the circulation of blood in a patient, locate blood clots, and identify circulation disorders. The nuclide, in the form of a solution of NaCl, is injected intravenously and followed by use of a counting device.

The amount of blood in a patient (normally five to six liters) can be determined by using a method of analysis known as isotope dilution. A small quantity of blood is withdrawn and labeled with $^{24}_{11}Na$ (in the form of NaCl). The activity of the labeled blood is measured and the sample is injected back into the patient. Time is allowed for the labeled sample to mix with the rest of the blood in the patient. A second sample of blood is then withdrawn and the activity of this sample determined. This measurement is much lower than that for the first sample, since the radioactive nuclide has been diluted. Comparison of the activity of the second sample to the activity of the first sample gives a measure of the extent of the dilution, which can be used to calculate the total original volume.

Radioactive tracers have found wide use in chemical studies. The following structure of the thiosulfate ion,

is indicated as correct by studies using $^{35}_{16}S$. The thiosulfate ion is prepared by heating a sulfite with the radioactive sulfur:

$$^{35}S(s) + SO_3^{2-}(aq) \longrightarrow [^{35}SSO_3]^{2-}(aq)$$

Upon acidification of this thiosulfate solution, the radioactive sulfur is quantitatively precipitated. None of the radioactive sulfur is found in the SO_2 gas:

$$[^{35}SSO_3]^{2-}(aq) + 2\,H^+(aq) \longrightarrow {}^{35}S(s) + SO_2(g) + H_2O$$

In addition, upon decomposition of the silver thiosulfate derived from this ion, all of the radioactive sulfur ends in the silver sulfide:

$$Ag_2[^{35}SSO_3](s) + H_2O \xrightarrow{heat} Ag_2{}^{35}S(s) + SO_4^{2-}(aq) + 2\,H^+(aq)$$

These results indicate that the two sulfur atoms of the thiosulfate ion are not equivalent and that the proposed structure is probably the correct one.

Radioactive nuclides have been used to study reaction rates and mechanisms as well as the action of catalysts. By using radioactive tracers, it becomes possible to follow the progress of tagged molecules and atoms through a chemical reaction.

For example, the mechanism of the reaction between the sulfite ion and the chlorate ion:

$$SO_3^{2-} + ClO_3^- \longrightarrow SO_4^{2-} + ClO_2^-$$

has been shown to proceed by the exchange of an oxygen atom. The SO_3^{2-} ion used in the study contained ordinary oxygen atoms, but the ClO_3^- ion was prepared with $^{18}_8O$ atoms, which are not radioactive but which may be detected by use of a mass spectrograph. The SO_4^{2-} ion produced by the reaction contained $^{18}_8O$ in an amount that would indicated that one $^{18}_8O$ atom had been added to each SO_3^{2-} ion.

The mechanism proposed, therefore, is a Lewis nucleophilic displacement of ClO_2^- by SO_3^{2-} on one of the oxygen atoms of the ClO_3^- ion. The $^{18}_8O$ atoms are marked with asterisks:

Activation analysis is the determination of the quantity of an element in a sample by bombarding the sample with suitable nuclear projectiles and measuring the intensity of the radioactivity induced in the element being investigated. The induced activity is not influenced by the chemical bonding of the element. Neutrons are the most frequently employed projectiles. Techniques have been developed for the determination of more than 50 elements. This method is particularly valuable for the determination of elements present in extremely low concentrations.

Determinations of very low vapor pressures and very low solubilities may be made conveniently by using tagged materials. In order to measure the solubility of a slightly soluble compound, the substance is prepared in such a way that a radioactive nuclide is incorporated into it. The activity of a carefully measured sample of a saturated solution of this labeled compound is compared with the activity of the solid, labeled compound. The solubility of the compound is calculated from these activities. Examples of compounds for which the solubilities have been measured in this way include $BaSO_4$ (labeled with $^{35}_{16}S$), PbI_2 (labeled with $^{131}_{53}I$), and $MgNH_4PO_4 \cdot 6\,H_2O$ (labeled with $^{32}_{15}P$).

Summary

Each specific atom, called a *nuclide*, is characterized by an *atomic number* (Z, the nuclear charge or the number of protons in the nucleus) and a *mass number* (A, the number of nucleons in the nucleus). Only certain combinations of *nucleons* (protons and neutrons, collectively) are stable (nonradioactive). Points that represent these combinations fall in a *zone of stability* in a plot of number of neutrons against number of protons.

Unstable nuclides undergo *radioactive decay*.

1. In an *alpha-decay* process, α particles ($^4_2$He nuclei) are emitted from the nucleus.

2. *Gamma radiation* consists of electromagnetic radiation of very short wavelength. It is emitted when a nucleus in an excited state reverts to its ground state, and it frequently accompanies all other types of radioactive decay.

3. In β^- *decay*, electrons are emitted from the radioactive nucleus and in the process a nuclear neutron is converted into a nuclear proton.

4, In β^+ *decay*, positrons (positive electrons) are emitted, and in the process a nuclear proton is converted into a nuclear neutron.

5. *Electron capture* is a process in which an orbital electron is captured by the nucleus. The electron converts a nuclear proton into a nuclear neutron. X rays are produced when an outer electron falls into the position left by the captured electron.

6. In *spontaneous fission*, a heavy, unstable nucleus splits into two lighter nuclei and several neutrons.

In any of these radioactive processes (indeed in any spontaneous nuclear reaction), the combined mass of the products is less than the combined mass of the reactants. The difference in mass is equivalent to the energy released. The energy changes associated with nuclear reactions are on a considerably higher level than those associated with ordinary chemical reactions.

Among the instruments used to detect and study the emissions of radioactive substances are *scintillation counters*, *cloud chambers*, and *Geiger-Müller counters*. The rate of decay of all radioactive nuclides has been found to be *first-order*. The *half-life*, which is the time required for half of the sample to decay, is a constant for each radioactive nuclide. Knowledge of the half-life of radiocarbon permits the dating of carbon-containing objects. The *activity* of a radioactive source is the amount of radiation emanating from the source per unit time (the number of disintegrations that occur in a given time interval).

Frequently the nucleus produced in a radioactive decay is itself radioactive. The repetition of this situation results in a *chain*, or *series*, *of disintegration processes*. Three such chains occur in nature, and many more are known that involve artificial nuclides. Several methods of *geological dating* are based on the natural disintegration series.

Nuclear *transmutations* may be brought about by bombardment of a nucleus with projectiles (such as protons, neutrons, deuterons, α particles, and ions). Charged projectiles may be accelerated in a *particle accelerator* (such as a *cyclotron* or a *linear accelerator*). Many artificial nuclides of natural elements as well as a number of nuclides of the *transuranium elements* have been made by these bombardment reactions.

The sum of the masses of the components of any atom is larger than the mass of the atom itself. The difference expressed in its energy equivalent is called the *binding energy* of the nuclide (the amount of energy required to pull the nucleons of a nucleus apart). The binding energies of the nuclides show that energy is released when heavy nuclei split into lighter nuclei (*nuclear fission*) and when very light nuclei fuse into heavier nuclei (*nuclear fusion*).

Nuclear fission is induced by projectiles, usually neutrons. A *critical mass* of fissionable matter is required to produce a self-sustaining *chain reaction*. The controlled fission of nuclear fuels is used in *nuclear reactors* as a source of energy. Extremely high temperatures are required to bring about nuclear fusion. The combining nuclei must be given very high energies to overcome the forces of repulsion that operate between nuclei. The confinement of the hot fuel poses a difficult problem in the design of fusion reactors.

Radioactive nuclides have found numerous uses in industry, medicine, chemistry, geology, and biology. Since these nuclides emit radiation that can readily be detected, radioactive nuclides are used as *tracers*.

Key Terms

Some of the more important terms introduced in this chapter are listed below. Definitions for terms not included in this list may be located in the text by use of the index.

Activity (Section 27.5) The amount of radiation emanating from a source per unit time.

Alpha decay (Section 27.3) A type of radioactivity in which alpha particles (α) are ejected; an alpha particle consists of two neutrons and two protons and is given the symbol ^4_2He.

Antiparticle (Section 27.3) One part of a particle-antiparticle pair; the two parts destroy each other when they come into contact and are converted into a form of energy. The antiparticle of a charged particle has the same mass as the particle but a charge with the opposite sign (for example, the electron, $_{-1}^0e$, and the positron, ^0_1e). Some particle-antiparticle pairs are uncharged (for example, the neutrino and the antineutrino).

Beta decay (Section 27.3) A radioactive process in which the atomic number, Z, of the radioactive nuclide changes but the mass number, A, does not change. In electron emission, Z increases. In positron emission or in electron capture, Z decreases.

Binding energy (Section 27.8) The energy equivalent of the difference between the sum of the masses of the nucleons of a nucleus and the actual mass of the nucleus; interpreted as the energy required to decompose a nucleus into its component nucleons.

Breeder reactor (Section 27.8) A type of nuclear reactor that manufactures more nuclear fuel than it uses.

Control rods (Section 27.8) Rods made of substances that have the ability to capture neutrons. These rods are inserted between the fuel elements of a nuclear reactor core; they may be inserted to any desired depth, and they serve to control the nuclear reaction by capturing excess neutrons.

Critical mass (Section 27.8) The amount of a fissionable material required to sustain a nuclear chain reaction.

Curie (Section 27.5) A unit used in the measurement of the activity of a radioactive source (the number of disintegrations per unit time). One curie is 3.70×10^{10} disintegrations per second.

Cyclotron (Section 27.7) An instrument in which a charged particle is accelerated along a spiral path under the influence of magnetic and electric fields and caused to strike a target nucleus.

Electron capture (Section 27.3) A radioactive decay process exhibited by some artificial nuclides; a nucleus captures an electron from an inner shell, and the captured electron converts a proton into a neutron.

Electron emission, β^- **decay** (Section 27.3) A type of radioactivity in which an electron (symbol $_{-1}^0e$) is ejected from a nucleus, and in the process a neutron is converted into a proton.

Fast neutron (Section 27.7) A fast-moving neutron produced by a nuclear reaction.

Gamma radiation (Section 27.3) Electromagnetic radiation of very short wavelength and hence highly energetic.

Geiger-Müller counter (Section 27.5) A device used for the quantitative detection of radioactive emissions; it functions by counting the electrical impulses caused by the ionization of a gas in a chamber through which the emissions pass.

Geological dating (Section 27.6) A method of dating mineral specimens based on the natural radioactive disintegration series.

Half-life (Section 27.5) The time that it takes for one-half of a sample of a radioactive nuclide to decay.

Linear accelerator (Section 27.7) An instrument in which a charged particle is accelerated along a linear path and caused to strike a target nucleus.

Moderator (Sections 27.7 and 27.8) A substance that serves to slow down neutrons produced by nuclear reactions when these fast neutrons pass through it.

Neutrino (Section 27.3) An unchanged particle of vanishingly small mass that is ejected in the course of some radioactive processes from which it carries off energy.

Neutron-capture reaction (Section 27.7) A nuclear reaction in which a target nucleus is bombarded with slow neutrons. No subsidiary particle is ejected, and the net result is that the target nucleus captures an additional neutron.

Nuclear fission (Section 27.8) A process in which heavy nuclei are split into lighter nuclei.

Nuclear fusion (Section 27.9) A process in which very light nuclei are fused into heavier nuclei.

Nuclear reactor (Section 27.8) A reactor in which the controlled fission of a nuclear fuel serves as a source of energy.

Nucleon (Section 27.1) A proton or a neutron, both of which are found in the atomic nucleus.

Nuclide (Section 27.1) A term used to refer to a species of atom characterized by its atomic number and mass number; the term *isotope* refers to one species of atom out of two or more that are of the same element and that have the same atomic number but different mass numbers.

Particle-particle reaction (Section 27.7) A nuclear reaction in which a target nucleus and a projectile particle form a compound nucleus that rapidly ejects a subsidiary particle and forms a product nucleus. Reactions are indicated as follows: target nucleus (projectile, ejected particle) product nucleus; for example, $^{14}_7\text{Na}(\alpha, \text{p})^{17}_8\text{O}$.

Positron emission, β^+ decay (Section 27.3)   A type of radioactivity exhibited by some artificial nuclides in which a positron (a positive electron, given the symbol $_1^0e$) is ejected from a nucleus, and in the process a proton is converted into a neutron.

Radioactive decay series (Section 27.6)   A series of radioactive disintegrations that successively produce new radioactive nuclides until a nonradioactive nuclide is obtained.

Radiocarbon dating (Section 27.5)   A method of dating a carbon-containing object by counting the number of radioactive disintegrations of the $_6^{14}C$ present in a sample and calculating, by means of the half-life of this nuclide, the length of time for the object to achieve its present condition.

Scintillation counter (Section 27.5)   A device that is used for the quantitative detection of radioactive emissions and that functions by counting the flashes of light given off by a fluorescent substance struck by these emissions.

Slow neutron (Section 27.7)   A neutron, derived from a nuclear reaction, that has been slowed down by passage through a moderator; also called a **thermal neutron.**

Spontaneous fission (Section 27.3)   A process in which a heavy nucleus spontaneously splits up into two light nuclei and several neutrons; observed for nearly all nuclides that have mass numbers higher than 230.

Thermonuclear reaction (Section 27.8)   A nuclear fusion reaction; so called because of the high temperatures it requires.

Transuranium elements (Section 27.7)   The elements following uranium (atomic number, 92) in the periodic table.

Wilson cloud chamber (Section 27.5)   A device that enables the path of ionizing radiation to be seen as a cloud track formed by condensation of water vapor on the ions.

Zone of stability (Section 27.1)   A zone in a graph of number of neutrons *versus* number of protons in which points that represent stable nuclides fall.

Problems*

27.1 Write equations for the following examples of nuclear decay: **(a)** α emission by $^{193}_{83}Bi$, **(b)** β^- emission by $^{27}_{12}Mg$, **(c)** β^+ emission by $^{68}_{34}Se$, **(d)** electron capture by $^{71}_{32}Ge$.

27.2 Write equations for the following examples of radioactive decay: **(a)** α emission by $^{230}_{92}U$, **(b)** β^- emission by $^{24}_{10}Ne$, **(c)** β^+ emission by $^{22}_{11}Na$, **(d)** electron capture by $^{75}_{34}Se$.

27.3 Write equations for the following examples of nuclear decay: **(a)** α emission by $^{212}_{86}Rn$, **(b)** β^- emission by $^{60}_{27}Co$, **(c)** β^+ emission by $^{60}_{30}Zn$, **(d)** electron capture by $^{110}_{49}In$.

27.4 Write equations for the following examples of nuclear decay: **(a)** α emission by $^{210}_{84}Po$, **(b)** β^- emission by $^{83}_{35}Br$, **(c)** β^+ emission by $^{44}_{21}Sc$, **(d)** electron capture by $^{119}_{51}Sb$.

27.5 Write an equation for the spontaneous fission of $^{250}_{96}Cm$. Assume that the process produces two nuclei that are identical to one another and four neutrons.

27.6 Write an equation for the spontaneous fission of $^{256}_{100}Fm$. Assume that the process produces two nuclei that are identical to one another and four neutrons.

27.7 The nuclide $^{230}_{90}Th$ decays to $^{226}_{88}Ra$ by α emission. The mass of $^{230}_{90}Th$ is 230.033131 u, of $^{226}_{88}Ra$ is 226.025406 u, and of ^4_2He is 4.002603 u. Calculate the energy released in this process.

27.8 The nuclide $^{223}_{89}Ac$ decays to $^{219}_{87}Fr$ by α emission. The mass of $^{223}_{89}Ac$ is 223.01914 u, of $^{219}_{87}Fr$ is 219.00925 u, and of ^4_2He is 4.00260 u. Calculate the energy released in this process.

27.9 When $^{226}_{88}Ra$ decays by α emission, 4.785 MeV α particles (recoil energy of the product nucleus, 0.086 MeV) and 4.602 MeV α particles (recoil energy of the product nucleus, 0.083 MeV) are produced. **(a)** Write the equation for this nuclear transformation. **(b)** What is the energy of the γ radiation that accompanies the α emission? **(c)** What is the source of the γ radiation?

27.10 When $^{212}_{83}Bi$ decays by α emission, 6.090 MeV α particles (recoil energy of the product nucleus, 0.117 MeV) and 6.051 MeV α particles (recoil energy of the product nucleus 0.116 MeV) are produced. **(a)** Write the equation for this nuclear transformation. **(b)** What is the energy of the γ radiation that accompanies the α emission? **(c)** What is the source of the γ radiation?

27.11 Calculate the disintegration energy released by the β- decay of $^{25}_{11}Na$ (atomic mass, 24.98995 u). The atomic mass of the product nuclide, $^{25}_{12}Mg$, is 24.98584 u.

27.12 Calculate the disintegration energy released by the

β^- decay of $^{28}_{13}Al$ (atomic mass, 27.9819 u). The atomic mass of the product nuclide, $^{28}_{14}Si$, is 27.9769 u.

27.13 The nuclide $^{18}_8O$ (atomic mass, 17.99916 u) is produced by the β^+ decay of $^{18}_9F$ (atomic mass 18.00094 u). What is the decay energy?

27.14 The nuclide $^{13}_6C$ (atomic mass, 13.003355 u) is produced by the β^+ decay of $^{13}_7N$ (atomic mass, 13.005739 u). What is the decay energy?

27.15 What is the decay energy when $^{41}_{20}Ca$ (atomic mass, 40.962278 u) undergoes electron capture? The atomic mass of the product nuclide, $^{41}_{19}K$, is 40.961825 u.

27.16 What is the decay energy when $^{123}_{53}I$ (atomic mass, 122.90556 u) undergoes electron capture? The atomic mass of the product nuclide, $^{123}_{52}Te$, is 122.904278 u.

27.17 The nuclide $^{42}_{22}Ti$ (atomic mass, 42.9597 u) decays to $^{44}_{21}Sc$ (atomic mass, 43.9594 u). Is it energetically possible for the process to occur by positron emission, or must it occur by electron capture?

27.18 The nuclide $^{109}_{48}Cd$ (atomic mass, 108.904949 u) decays to $^{109}_{47}Ag$ (atomic mass, 108.904754 u). Is it energetically possible for the process to occur by positron emission, or must it occur by electron capture?

27.19 A nuclide decays to $^{140}_{58}Ce$ (atomic mass, 139.9054 u) by α emission. The atomic mass of ^4_2He is 4.0026 u. The decay energy of the process is 1.956 MeV. **(a)** What is the original nuclide? **(b)** What is the atomic mass of this nuclide?

27.20 A nuclide decays to $^{232}_{92}U$ (atomic mass 232.0371 u) by α emission. The atomic mass of ^4_2He is 4.0026 u. The decay energy of the process is 5.867 MeV. **(a)** What is the original nuclide? **(b)** What is the atomic mass of this nuclide?

27.21 The disintegration energy is 3.44 MeV for the β^- decay of $^{39}_{17}Cl$ to $^{39}_{18}Ar$ (atomic mass, 38.96432 u). What is the atomic mass of $^{39}_{17}Cl$?

27.22 The disintegration energy is 0.249 MeV for the β^- decay of $^{33}_{15}P$ to $^{33}_{16}S$ (atomic mass, 32.97146 u). What is the atomic mass of $^{33}_{15}P$?

27.23 The disintegration energy is 3.22 MeV for the β^+ decay of $^{104}_{47}Ag$ to $^{104}_{46}Pd$ (atomic mass, 103.90403 u). What is the atomic mass of $^{104}_{47}Ag$?

27.24 The disintegration energy is 2.97 MeV for the β^+ decay of $^{26}_{13}Al$ to $^{26}_{12}Mg$ (atomic mass, 25.98260 u). What is the atomic mass of $^{26}_{13}Al$?

27.25 When $^{41}_{20}Ca$ (atomic mass, 40.962278 u) decays by electron capture, the disintegration energy is 0.422 MeV. **(a)** Identify the nuclide produced. **(b)** What is the atomic mass of this nuclide?

---

* The more difficult problems are marked with asterisks. The appendix contains answers to color-keyed problems.

27.26 When $^{51}_{24}Cr$ (atomic mass, 50.944769 u) decays by electron capture, the disintegration energy is 0.751 MeV. **(a)** Identify the nuclide produced. **(b)** What is the atomic mass of this nuclide?

Rate of Radioactive Decay

27.27 The radioactive nuclide $^{55}_{27}Co$ has a half-life of 17.5 hours. What mass of $^{55}_{27}Co$ remains from a 0.0100 g sample after 24.0 hours have elapsed?

27.28 The radioactive nuclide $^{194}_{79}Au$ has a half-life of 39.5 hours. What mass of $^{194}_{79}Au$ remains from a 0.0100 g sample after 24.0 hours have elapsed?

27.29 The half-life of $^{59}_{26}Fe$ is 44.6 days. How long will it take for 95.0% of a sample of this nuclide to decay.

27.30 The half-life of $^{65}_{30}Zn$ is 243.8 days. How long will it take for 10.0% of a sample of this nuclide to decay?

27.31 The rate of decay of $^{195}_{79}Au$ is such that 79.8% of a sample of this nuclide remains as $^{195}_{79}Au$ after 60.0 days have elasped. **(a)** What is the rate constant for this radioactive disintegration? **(b)** What is the half-life of $^{195}_{79}Au$?

27.32 The rate of decay of $^{208}_{84}Po$ is such that 78.7% of a sample of this nuclide remains as $^{208}_{84}Po$ after 1.00 year has elapsed. **(a)** What is the rate constant for this radioactive disintegration? **(b)** What is the half-life of $^{208}_{84}Po$?

27.33 A sample of $^{45}_{20}Ca$, a β^- emitter, has an activity of 0.1000 μCi. In 60.0 days, the activity of the sample has declined to 0.0775 μCi. What is the half-life of $^{45}_{20}Ca$?

27.34 A sample of $^{48}_{21}Sc$, a β^- emitter, has an activity of 0.0500 μCi. After 30.0 hours, the activity of the sample has declined to 0.0310 μCi. What is the half-life of $^{48}_{21}Sc$?

27.35 The half-life of $^{134}_{53}I$, a β^- emitter, is 52.6 minutes. **(a)** How many atoms of $^{134}_{53}I$ are present in a sample that has activity of 0.150 μCi? **(b)** What is the mass of this sample?

27.36 The half-life of $^{32}_{15}P$, a β^- emitter, is 14.28 days. **(a)** How many atoms are present in a sample that has an activity of 1.00 mCi? A millicurie is 0.001 Ci. **(b)** What is the mass of this sample?

27.37 The half-life of $^{24}_{11}Na$ is 15.02 hours. What is the activity in curies of a 1.00×10^{-4} g sample of $^{24}_{11}Na$? The atomic mass of this nuclide is 23.99 u.

27.38 The half-life of $^{31}_{14}Si$ is 2.62 hours. What is the activity of a 5.00 mg sample of $^{31}_{14}Si$? The atomic mass of this nuclide is 30.98 u.

27.39 The carbon from the heartwood of a giant sequoia tree gives 11 $^{14}_{6}C$ counts per minute per gram of carbon, whereas the wood from the outer portion of the tree gives 15 $^{14}_{6}C$ counts per minute per gram of carbon. How old is the tree? The half-life of $^{14}_{6}C$ is 5730 years.

27.40 A sample of a wooden artifact gives 8.0 $^{14}_{6}C$ disintegrations per minute per gram of carbon. What is the approximate age of the artifact? The half-life of $^{14}_{6}C$ is 5730 years, and the radiocarbon activity of wood recently cut down is 15 disintegrations per minute per gram of carbon.

Disintegration Series

27.41 One of the decay series that occur in nature is that of the nuclide $^{232}_{90}Th$. The types of decay that occur successively in one route of the chain are: α, β^-, β^-, α, α, α, α, β^-, β^-, and α. Determine in order the members of the chain.

27.42 One of the decay series that occur in nature is that of the nuclide $^{235}_{92}U$. The types of decay that occur successively in one route of the chain are: α, β^-, α, β^-, α, α, α, α, β^-, α, and β^-. Determine in order the members of the chain.

27.43 Starting with $^{150}_{66}Dy$, the types of decay that occur successively in an artificial decay chain are: ec, β^+, α, and α. What are the members of the chain?

27.44 Starting with $^{215}_{89}Ac$, the types of decay that occur successively in an artificial decay chain are: α, α, ec, β^+, and ec. What are the members of the chain?

Nuclear Reactions

27.45 Write equations for the following induced nuclear reactions: **(a)** $^{35}_{17}Cl$ (n, α), **(b)** $^{9}_{4}Be$ (p, n), **(c)** $^{75}_{33}As$ (d, 2n), **(d)** $^{24}_{12}Mg$ (d, α), **(e)** $^{133}_{55}Cs$ (α, 4n), **(f)** $^{209}_{83}Bi$ (p, 8n), **(g)** $^{65}_{29}Cu$ ($^{12}_{6}C$, 3n), **(h)** $^{7}_{3}Li$ ($^{3}_{1}H$, α).

27.46 Write equations for the following induced nuclear reactions: **(a)** $^{203}_{81}Tl$ (n, α), **(b)** $^{18}_{8}O$ (p, n), **(c)** $^{57}_{26}Fe$ (d, n), **(d)** $^{31}_{15}P$ (d, $^{1}_{1}H$), **(e)** $^{109}_{47}Ag$ (α, n), **(f)** $^{79}_{35}Br$ (n 2n), **(g)** $^{115}_{49}In$ ($^{14}_{7}N$, 3n), **(h)** $^{32}_{16}S$ ($^{3}_{1}H$, n).

27.47 Given the following products of induced nuclear reactions and the types of reactions used to prepare them, what nuclide was used as the starting material? **(a)** (α, n) $^{13}_{7}N$, **(b)** (n, α) $^{3}_{1}H$, **(c)** (d, n) $^{8}_{4}Be$, **(d)** (p, γ) $^{13}_{7}N$, **(e)** (p, n) $^{96}_{43}Tc$, **(f)** (d, p) $^{76}_{33}As$, **(g)** (α, p) $^{48}_{22}Ti$.

27.48 Given the following products of induced nuclear reactions and the types of reactions used to prepare them, what nuclide was used as the starting material? **(a)** (n, γ) $^{83}_{35}Br$, **(b)** (n, α) $^{7}_{3}Li$, **(c)** (n, p) $^{35}_{16}S$, **(d)** (p, n) $^{7}_{4}Be$, **(e)** (d, 2n) $^{130}_{53}I$, **(f)** (α, p) $^{46}_{21}Sc$, **(g)** (d, 2n) $^{51}_{24}Cr$.

27.49 Some transuranium nuclides and the types of nuclear reactions that have been used to prepare them are listed following. In each case, what nuclide was used as the starting material? **(a)** ($^{13}_{6}C$, 4n) $^{257}_{104}Unq$, **(b)** ($^{15}_{7}N$, 4n) $^{260}_{105}Unp$, **(c)** (d, n) $^{239}_{93}Np$, **(d)** (α, 2n) $^{241}_{96}Cm$, **(e)** (α, p) $^{247}_{97}Bk$, **(f)** ($^{9}_{4}Be$, α3n) $^{252}_{100}Fm$.

27.50 Some transuranium nuclides and the types of nuclear reactions that have been used to prepare them are listed following. In each case, what nuclide was used as the starting material? **(a)** ($^{18}_{8}O$, 4n) $^{263}_{106}Unh$, **(b)** ($^{20}_{10}Ne$, 4n) $^{261}_{104}Unq$, **(c)** (d, 2n) $^{238}_{94}Pu$, **(d)** (α, n) $^{240}_{95}Am$, **(e)** ($^{14}_{7}N$, p3n) $^{248}_{98}Cf$, **(f)** ($^{12}_{6}C$, 4n) $^{245}_{99}Es$.

Nuclear Fission and Fusion

27.51 **(a)** Calculate the binding energy of the $^{64}_{30}Zn$ nucleus in MeV. The mass of the neutron is 1.00866 u, of the $^{1}_{1}H$ atom is 1.00783 u, and of the $^{64}_{30}Zn$ atom is 63.92914 u. **(b)** What is the value of the binding energy per nucleon?

27.52 (a) Calculate the binding energy of the $^{130}_{56}$Ba nucleus in MeV. The mass of the neutron is 1.00866 u, of the $^1_1$H atom is 1.00783 u, and of the $^{130}_{56}$Ba atom is 129.90628 u. **(b)** What is the value of the binding energy per nucleon?

27.53 The binding energy of $^{41}_{19}$K is 8.57584 MeV/nucleon. The mass of the neutron is 1.00866 u, and of the $^1_1$H atom is 1.00783 u. One atomic mass unit (1 u) is 931.502 MeV. What is the atomic mass (in u) of $^{41}_{19}$K?

27.54 The binding energy of $^{107}_{47}$Ag is 8.55341 u MeV/nucleon. The mass of the neutron is 1.00866 u, and of the $^1_1$H atom is 1.00783 u. One atomic mass unit (1 u) is 931.502 MeV. What is the atomic mass (in u) of $^{107}_{47}$Ag?

27.55 In a fission process, the products undergo β^- decay successively until stable nuclides are produced. If the equation for a particular fission and the equations for the β^- decays of the nuclides it produces are added, the following equation is obtained (the masses of the particles are indicated):

$$^{235}_{92}\text{U} \longrightarrow {}^{94}_{40}\text{Zr} + {}^{140}_{58}\text{Ce}$$
$$235.0439 \text{ u} \qquad 93.9063 \text{ u} \quad 139.9054 \text{ u}$$

$$+ \quad {}^1_0\text{N} \quad + \quad 6\,{}^{\,0}_{-1}e$$
$$1.0087 \text{ u} \qquad 6(0.00055 \text{ u})$$

Calculate the energy released in **(a)** MeV per fission, **(b)** kJ per gram of fuel.

27.56 In a fission process, the products undergo β^- decay successively until stable nuclides are produced. If the equation for a particular fission and the equations for the β^- decays of the nuclides it produces are added, the following equation is obtained (the masses of the particles are indicated):

$$^{235}_{92}\text{U} \longrightarrow {}^{99}_{44}\text{Ru} + {}^{133}_{55}\text{Cs}$$
$$235.0439 \text{ u} \qquad 98.9059 \text{ u} \quad 132.9054 \text{ u}$$

$$+ \quad 3\,{}^1_0\text{n} \quad + \quad 7\,{}^{\,0}_{-1}e$$
$$3(1.0087 \text{ u}) \qquad 7(0.00055 \text{ u})$$

Calculate the energy released in **(a)** MeV per fission, **(b)** kJ per gram of fuel.

27.57 Consider the following fusion reaction (masses given below the symbols):

$$^2_1\text{H} \quad + \quad {}^1_1\text{H} \longrightarrow {}^3_2\text{He}$$
$$2.01410 \text{ u} \qquad 1.00783 \text{ u} \qquad 3.01603 \text{ u}$$

Calculate the energy released: **(a)** in MeV per fusion, **(b)** in kJ per gram of fuel.

27.58 Consider the following fusion reaction (masses given below the symbols):

$$2\,{}^3_2\text{He} \longrightarrow {}^4_2\text{He} \quad + \quad 2\,{}^1_1\text{H}$$
$$2(3.01603 \text{ u}) \qquad 4.00260 \text{ u} \qquad 2(1.00783 \text{ u})$$

Calculate the energy released: **(a)** in MeV per fusion, **(b)** in kJ per gram of fuel.

27.59 Each of the following nuclides represents one of the products of a neutron-induced fission of $^{235}_{92}$U. In each case another nuclide and three neutrons are also produced. Identify the other nuclide. **(a)** $^{148}_{58}$Ce, **(b)** $^{121}_{47}$Ag, **(c)** $^{138}_{55}$Cs.

27.60 Each of the following nuclides represents one of the products of a neutron-induced fission of $^{235}_{92}$U. In each case another nuclide and three neutrons are also produced. Identify the other nuclide. **(a)** $^{96}_{40}$Zr, **(b)** $^{139}_{57}$La, **(c)** $^{90}_{36}$Kr.

Unclassified Problems

27.61 Define the following terms: **(a)** nuclide, **(b)** nucleon, **(c)** isotope, **(d)** critical mass, **(e)** thermal neutron, **(f)** fission, **(g)** fusion, **(h)** transuranium element.

27.62 Why is electron capture accompanied by the production of X rays.

27.63 The half-life of $^{237}_{93}$Np is 2.1×10^6 years, and the age of the earth is approximately 4.5×10^9 years. Assuming that none of this nuclide has been produced artificially, what fraction of the quantity of $^{237}_{93}$Np that was formed when the earth was created is now present?

27.64 It is believed that a $^{237}_{93}$Np disintegration series existed in nature at one time. The members of the series (with the exception of the stable nuclide that ends the series), however, have virtually disappeared through radioactive decay in the time since the earth was created. The particles emitted successively in the $^{237}_{93}$Np series are: α, β^-, α, α, β^-, α, α, α, β^-, α, and β^-. Determine in order the members of the series.

* **27.65** The half-life of $^3_1$H is 12.33 years. What is the activity, in curies, of 1.000 ml of $^3_1$H$_2$(g) at STP.

ORGANIC CHEMISTRY

The name organic chemistry derives from the early concept that substances of plant or animal origin (organic substances) were different from those of mineral origin (inorganic substances). In the middle of the nineteenth century, however, the idea that organic substances could only be synthesized by living organisms was gradually discounted. Not only has a large number of natural products been synthesized in the laboratory, but also countless related materials have been made that do not occur in nature. All these compounds contain carbon. Over a million carbon compounds are known.

Because it represents a convenient division of chemistry, the term organic chemistry is retained, but it is now commonly defined as the chemistry of carbon and its compounds. However, since some carbon compounds (such as carbonates, carbides, and cyanides) are traditionally classed as inorganic compounds, organic chemistry is probably better defined as the chemistry of the hydrocarbons (compounds containing only carbon and hydrogen) and their derivatives.

Carbon forms an unusually large number of compounds because of its exceptional ability to catenate (see Section 24.1). In addition, the carbon atom can form four very stable, single-covalent bonds; it also has the ability to form multiple bonds with other carbon atoms or with atoms of other elements.

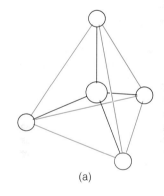

(a)

28.1 The Alkanes

In the first four sections of this chapter various types of hydrocarbons are characterized. The reactions of the hydrocarbons is the topic of Section 28.5. The simplest hydrocarbon is methane, CH_4. This molecule contains four equivalent carbon-hydrogen bonds arranged tetrahedrally (see Figure 28.1). The bonding may be considered to arise through the use of sp^3 hybrid orbitals of the carbon atom. Each of the bonds of methane is of the same length (109.5 pm), and each of the H—C—H bond angles is 109° 28′ (the so-called tetrahedral angle). The commonly employed structural formula of methane:

$$
\begin{array}{c}
\text{H} \\
| \\
\text{H}—\text{C}—\text{H} \\
| \\
\text{H}
\end{array}
$$

does not accurately represent the tetrahedral arrangement of the molecule.

(b)

Figure 28.1 Representations of the structure of methane, CH_4. (The bonds in (a) are of exaggerated length in comparison with the atomic sizes.)

The **alkanes** are hydrocarbons in which all the carbon-carbon bonds are single bonds; they may be considered to be derived from methane by the successive addition of —CH_2— units. Such a series of compounds is said to be **homologous** and the compounds are said to be **homologs.** Thus, the formula of the second member of the family, ethane:

$$
\begin{array}{c}
\quad\ \ H\ \ H \\
\quad\ \ | \quad\ | \\
H-C-C-H \\
\quad\ \ | \quad\ | \\
\quad\ \ H\ \ H
\end{array}
$$

may be formally derived by the introduction of a —CH_2— unit between the carbon and a hydrogen of methane. This molecule is also represented by the formula CH_3—CH_3.

The alkanes conform to the general formula C_nH_{2n+2}, where n is the number of carbon atoms in the compound. A few subsequent members of the family, and their names, are

$$
\begin{array}{c}
\quad H\ \ H\ \ H \\
\quad |\quad |\quad | \\
H-C-C-C-H \\
\quad |\quad |\quad | \\
\quad H\ \ H\ \ H
\end{array}
\qquad\qquad
\begin{array}{c}
\quad H\ \ H\ \ H\ \ H \\
\quad |\quad |\quad |\quad | \\
H-C-C-C-C-H \\
\quad |\quad |\quad |\quad | \\
\quad H\ \ H\ \ H\ \ H
\end{array}
$$

$$CH_3CH_2CH_3 \qquad\qquad CH_3CH_2CH_2CH_3$$
propane $\qquad\qquad\qquad$ *butane*

$$
\begin{array}{c}
\quad H\ \ H\ \ H\ \ H\ \ H \\
\quad |\quad |\quad |\quad |\quad | \\
H-C-C-C-C-C-H \\
\quad |\quad |\quad |\quad |\quad | \\
\quad H\ \ H\ \ H\ \ H\ \ H
\end{array}
$$

$$CH_3CH_2CH_2CH_2CH_3$$
pentane

These compounds are spoken of as **straight-chain** compounds even though the carbon chains are far from linear (see Figure 28.2); all the bond angles are approximately tetrahedral, and axial rotation of any carbon atom around a single bond of the chain is possible.

There is only one compound for each of the formulas CH_4, C_2H_6, and C_3H_8. However, there are two compounds with the formula C_4H_{10}: the compound with a straight chain (butane) and one with a **branched chain**:

$$
\begin{array}{c}
CH_3CHCH_3 \\
\quad | \\
\quad CH_3
\end{array}
$$

methylpropane

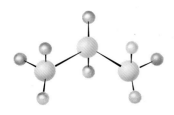

Figure 28.2 Representation of the structure of propane, $CH_3CH_2CH_3$

The two compounds of formula C_4H_{10} are **structural isomers** (compounds with the same molecular formula but different structural formulas); they have different properties.

There are three structural isomers of C_5H_{12}: pentane (the straight-chain compound),

Table 28.1 Simple alkyl radicals	
Formula	Name
CH_3-	methyl
CH_3CH_2-	ethyl
$CH_3CH_2CH_2-$	*normal*-propyl or *n*-propyl
CH_3CH- $\quad\ \ \|$ $\quad\ CH_3$	isopropyl
$CH_3CH_2CH_2CH_2-$	*normal*-butyl or *n*-butyl
CH_3CHCH_2- $\quad\ \|$ $\quad CH_3$	isobutyl
CH_3CH_2CH- $\qquad\ \|$ $\qquad CH_3$	*secondary*-butyl or *sec*-butyl
$\quad CH_3$ $\quad\ \|$ CH_3C- $\quad\ \|$ $\quad CH_3$	*tertiary*-butyl or *tert*-butyl

$$CH_3CH_2CHCH_3 \qquad \text{and} \qquad CH_3-\overset{\overset{\displaystyle CH_3}{\displaystyle |}}{\underset{\underset{\displaystyle CH_3}{\displaystyle |}}{C}}-CH_3$$
$$\qquad\ |$$
$$\quad\ CH_3$$

methylbutane   *dimethylpropane*

In the alkane series the number of possible structural isomers increases rapidly: there are five structural isomers for C_6H_{14}, nine for C_7H_{16}, and 75 for $C_{10}H_{22}$. It has been calculated that more than 4×10^9 isomers are possible for $C_{30}H_{62}$.

A branched-chain compound may be named in terms of the longest straight chain in the molecule. The side chains are named as alkyl radicals, and their positions on the straight chain are usually indicated by a numbering system. Alkyl radicals are fragments of alkane molecules from which a hydrogen atom has been removed; their names are derived from the name of the parent alkane with the ending changed to -*yl*. A list of common alkyl radicals appears in Table 28.1.

For example, the longest straight chain in the molecule:

$$CH_3\overset{\overset{\displaystyle CH_3}{\displaystyle |}}{C}-\overset{}{\underset{\underset{\displaystyle CH_2}{\displaystyle |}}{C}}HCH_2CH_3$$

consists of five carbon atoms, and the compound is named as a derivative of pentane. The pentane chain is numbered starting at the end that will give the side chains the lowest numbers:

Table 28.2 Physical properties of some straight-chain alkanes			
Compound	Formula	Melting Point (°C)	Boiling Point (°C)
methane	CH_4	-183	-162
ethane	C_2H_6	-172	-88
propane	C_3H_8	-187	-42
butane	C_4H_{10}	-135	1
pentane	C_5H_{12}	-131	36
hexane	C_6H_{14}	-94	69
heptane	C_7H_{16}	-91	99
octane	C_8H_{18}	-57	126
nonane	C_9H_{20}	-54	151
decane	$C_{10}H_{22}$	-30	174
hexadecane	$C_{16}H_{34}$	20	288
heptadecane	$C_{17}H_{36}$	23	303

$$\begin{array}{c} \overset{\displaystyle CH_3}{\underset{12345}{}} \\ CH_3C\!\!-\!\!-\!\!CHCH_2CH_3 \\ \underset{\displaystyle CH_3}{|}\;\;\underset{\displaystyle CH_2}{|} \\ CH_3 \end{array}$$

In the name a number is used to indicate the position of each substituent radical. Thus, the name of the compound is

2,2-dimethyl-3-ethylpentane

No numbers appear in the names of our earlier examples of structural isomers. The name methylpropane requires no number to indicate the position of the methyl radical with regard to the propane chain since there is only one possible position for the methyl group (number 2). If the methyl group were placed on either terminal carbon atom (number 1 or number 3), the compound would be the straight-chain isomer, butane. In like manner, the names methylbutane and dimethylpropane do not require the use of numbers; there is only one possible structure corresponding to each name.

Names for some of the higher straight-chain homologs may be obtained from Table 28.2, which lists the melting points and boiling points of some of the straight-chain alkanes. The melting point and boiling point increase as the length of the chain (and hence the molecular weight) of the hydrocarbon increases. The first four compounds are gases under ordinary conditions; higher homologs are liquids (C_5H_{12} to $C_{15}H_{32}$) and solids (from $C_{16}H_{34}$ on).

In addition to open-chain hydrocarbons, **cyclic hydrocarbons** are known. The **cycloalkanes** are ring structures that contain only single carbon-carbon bonds; they have the general formula C_nH_{2n}. Examples are

Table 28.3   Petroleum fractions

Fraction	Boiling Range (°C)	Carbon Content of Compounds	Use
gas	below 20	C_1–C_4	fuel
petroleum ether	20–90	C_5–C_7	solvent
gasoline	35–220	C_5–C_{12}	motor fuel
kerosene	200–315	C_{12}–C_{16}	jet fuel
fuel oil	250–375	C_{15}–C_{18}	diesel fuel
lubricating oils, greases	350 up	C_{16}–C_{20}	lubrication
paraffin wax	50–60 (m.p.)	C_{20}–C_{30}	candles
asphalt	viscous liquid		paving
residue	solid		fuel

cyclopropane   *cyclohexane*

The cyclohexane ring is not planar but is puckered in such a way that the C—C—C bond angles are 109° 28′, the tetrahedral angle. Three- and four-membered rings are strained because the C—C—C bond angles deviate significantly from the tetrahedral angle. The strain is greatest in cyclopropane, in which the C atoms form an equilateral triangle and the C—C—C bond angles are 60°. Thus, the cyclopropane ring is readily broken by H_2 (Ni catalyst) to give propane. Cyclobutane reacts with H_2 in an analogous manner (to give butane), but a higher temperature is required.

Petroleum is the principal source of alkanes and cycloalkanes. In the refining of petroleum the crude oil is first separated into fractions by distillation (see Table 28.3). Some higher-boiling fractions are subjected to **cracking processes** in which large molecules are broken down into smaller molecules, thus increasing the yield of the most valuable fraction, gasoline. In addition, small molecules are converted into large ones in what are called **alkylation processes.** Gases that are by-products of these processes, together with other substances that are obtained from the petroleum fractions, are important starting materials for the manufacture of many chemical products. More than 2000 such products (such as rubber, detergents, plastics, and textiles) are derived from the substances obtained from petroleum and natural gas.

28.2 The Alkenes

The alkenes, which are also called **olefins,** are hydrocarbons that have a carbon-carbon double bond somewhere in their molecular structure. The first member of the series is ethene (also called ethylene):

Night view of a fractional distillation column at a modern oil refinery. *American Petroleum Institute.*

$$\text{H}\diagdown\underset{\text{H}}{\overset{}{\text{C}}}=\underset{\text{H}}{\overset{}{\text{C}}}\diagup\text{H}$$

Each carbon atom of ethene uses sp^2 hybrid orbitals to form three sigma bonds: one with the other C atom and two with H atoms. Thus, all six atoms lie in the same plane, and all bond angles are approximately 120°. In addition, each carbon atom has an electron in a p orbital that is not engaged in the formation of sp^2 σ bonds. These two p orbitals are coplanar and perpendicular to the plane of the molecule; they overlap to form a π bonding orbital with regions of charge density above and below the plane of the molecule (see Section 9.5, Figure 9.17).

The p orbitals can overlap and form a π bonding orbital only when they lie in the same plane. Consequently, free rotation around the carbon-carbon double bond is not possible without breaking the π bond. The carbon-carbon bond distance in ethene (133 pm) is shorter than that in ethane (154 pm) because of the double bond. The π bond is not so strong as the σ bond; the carbon-carbon bond energy in ethane is approximately 340 kJ/mol, and the bond energy of the carbon-carbon double bond in ethene is about 610 kJ/mol.

Alkanes are called saturated hydrocarbons because all the valence electrons of the carbon atoms are engaged in single bond formation, and no more hydrogen atoms or atoms of other elements can be accommodated by the carbon atoms of the chain. Unsaturated hydrocarbons have one or more carbon-carbon multiple bonds and can undergo addition reactions (see Section 28.5) because of the availability of the π electrons of the multiple bond. In one such reaction hydrogen adds to ethene in the presence of a catalyst to form ethane:

$$\text{CH}_2{=}\text{CH}_2 + \text{H}_2 \xrightarrow{\text{Ni}} \text{CH}_3{-}\text{CH}_3$$

Alkenes conform to the general formula C_nH_{2n}. The name of an alkene is derived from the name of the corresponding alkane by changing the ending from -*ane* to -*ene*; a number is used, when necessary, to indicate the position of the double bond. The second member of the series is propene:

$$\text{CH}_2{=}\text{CH}{-}\text{CH}_3$$

New types of isomerism arise in the alkene series. The type of structural isomerism displayed by the alkanes (for example, butane and methylpropane) is known as chain isomerism. In addition to chain isomerism, position isomerism occurs in the olefin series. There is only one straight-chain butane. There are, however, two straight-chain butenes, and they differ in the position of the double bond:

$$\text{CH}_2{=}\text{CH}{-}\text{CH}_2{-}\text{CH}_3 \qquad \text{CH}_3{-}\text{CH}{=}\text{CH}{-}\text{CH}_3$$
1-butene   2-butene

In the first compound the double bond is located between carbon atoms number 1 and number 2, and the lower number (1) is used to indicate its position. In like manner, the lower number is used to indicate the position of the double bond (which occurs between carbon atoms number 2 and number 3) in the name of the second compound. In each case the chain is numbered from the end that gives the lowest possible number for the name. The name of a branched-chain alkene is derived from that of the longest straight chain that contains the double bond.

The alkenes also exhibit **geometric** (or **cis-trans**) **isomerism,** which is a type of **stereoisomerism.** Stereoisomers have the same structural formula but differ in the arrangement of the atoms in space. An example is provided by the isomers of 2-butene. Because of the restricted rotation around the double bond, one isomer exists with both methyl groups on the same side of the double bond (the *cis* isomer), and another isomer exists with the methyl groups on opposite sides of the double bond (the *trans* isomer). All carbon atoms of the molecule lie in the same plane:

cis-2-*butene*
boiling point, 1°C

trans-2-*butene*
boiling point, 2.5°C

The properties of the 2-butenes do not differ greatly. Other *cis-trans* isomers exhibit wide variation in their physical properties:

cis-1,2-*dichloroethene*
boiling point, 60.1°C

trans-1,2-*dichloroethene*
boiling point, 48.4°C

The physical properties of the alkenes are very similar to those of the alkanes. The C_2H_4, C_3H_6, and C_4H_8 compounds are gases under ordinary conditions; the C_5H_{10} to $C_{18}H_{36}$ compounds are liquids; and the higher alkenes are solids. All the compounds are only slightly soluble in water.

Molecules can contain more than one double bond—for example:

$$CH_2{=}CH{-}CH{=}CH_2$$
1,3-*butadiene*

an **alkadiene,** which is used to produce a type of synthetic rubber (see Section 26.10). **Cycloalkenes** are known—for example:

cyclohexene

28.3 The Alkynes

Molecules that contain carbon-carbon triple bonds are known as alkynes. These unsaturated hydrocarbons have the general formula C_nH_{2n-2} and constitute the **alkyne,** or **acetylene, series.** The first member of the series is ethyne, or acetylene:

$$H{-}C{\equiv}C{-}H$$

In acetylene each carbon atom uses *sp* hybrid orbitals to form a σ bond with a hydrogen atom and a σ bond with the other carbon atom. Consequently, the four atoms of the molecule lie in a straight line. In addition to the carbon-carbon σ bond, two π bonds are formed between the carbon atoms by the overlap of p orbitals (see Section 9.5, Figure 9.18). The resultant carbon-carbon bond distance (121 pm) is shorter than the carbon-carbon double-bond distance (133 pm). The π bonds are weaker than the C—C σ bond; the bond energy of the triple bond is approximately 830 kJ/mol (compared with the single bond energy of 340 kJ/mol). Alkynes readily undergo addition reactions across the triple bond because of the availability of the four electrons of the π bonds.

Alkynes are named in a manner analogous to that employed in naming alkenes; the ending -*yne* is used in place of -*ene*. Their physical properties are similar to those of the alkanes and alkenes. Both chain and position isomerism occur in the alkyne series, but *cis-trans* isomerism is not possible because of the linear geometry of the group X—C≡C—X, where X is a carbon atom or an atom of another element.

Notice that a branched-chain isomer of C_4H_6 is impossible; only two isomers of C_4H_6 exist:

$$HC\equiv CCH_2CH_3 \qquad CH_3C\equiv CCH_3$$
1-*butyne*   2-*butyne*

Both branched-chain and straight-chain isomers of C_5H_8 are known:

$$HC\equiv CCH_2CH_2CH_3 \qquad CH_3C\equiv CCH_2CH_3 \qquad HC\equiv CCHCH_3$$
$$CH_3$$

1-*pentyne*   2-*pentyne*   methyl-1-*butyne*

28.4 Aromatic Hydrocarbons

Aromatic hydrocarbons are compounds that have molecular structures based on that of benzene, C_6H_6. The six carbon atoms of benzene are arranged in a ring from which the hydrogen atoms are radially bonded (see Figure 28.3). The entire structure is planar, and all of the bond angles are 120°. The carbon-carbon bond distance is 139 pm, which is between the single-bond distance of 154 pm and the double-bond distance of 133 pm.

The electronic structure of benzene may be represented as a resonance hybrid:

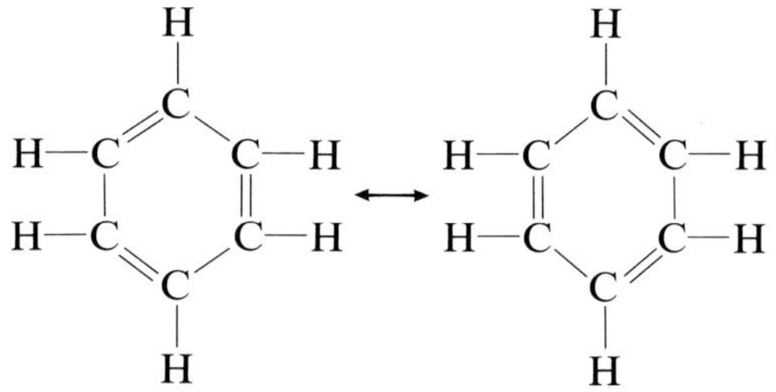

This representation correctly shows that all of the carbon-carbon bonds are equivalent and that each one is intermediate between a single bond and a double bond.

Each carbon atom of the ring uses sp^2 hybrid orbitals to form σ bonds with two adjacent carbon atoms and with a hydrogen atom. Therefore, the resulting framework of the molecule is planar with bond angles of 120° (see Figure 28.3).

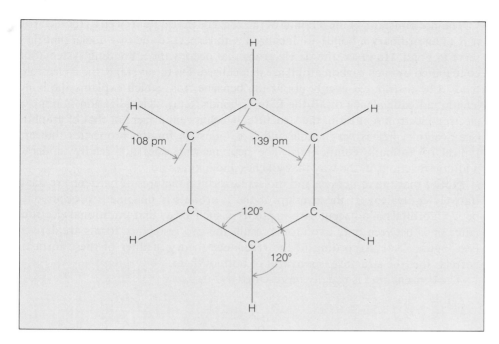

Figure 28.3 Geometry of the benzene molecule

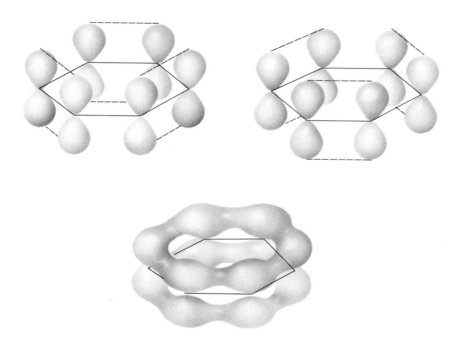

Figure 28.4 The π bonding system of benzene; σ bonds are indicated by the solid lines

A $2p$ electron of each carbon atom is not employed in the formation of the sp^2 hybrid σ bonds. The axes of these p orbitals are perpendicular to the plane of the molecule, and each p orbital can overlap two adjacent p orbitals. The result is the formation of a system of π orbitals with regions of charge density above and below the plane of the ring (see Figure 28.4).

The electron pairs of the σ bonds of the benzene molecule (as well as the electron pair of an ordinary π bond) are localized with respect to the two nuclei that they serve to bond. However, the six electrons that occupy the π bonding system (one contributed by each carbon atom) are delocalized. On the average, the π electrons tend to be distributed evenly about the benzene ring, which explains the bond length and equivalence of all the C to C bonds. Since delocalization minimizes electron-electron repulsion, the structure, which is reminiscent of that of graphite (see Section 24.2), is very stable and is responsible for the properties that are typical of aromatic compounds. The benzene ring does not readily undergo addition reactions in the way that alkenes and alkynes do.

Notice that the resonance and molecular-orbital pictures of benzene are qualitatively equivalent. If the overlap of the *p* orbitals is imagined to occur only between orbitals of adjacent carbon atoms in such a way that traditional electron-pair bonds between only two atoms result, the two resonance forms are derived (see Figure 28.4). According to the resonance theory, neither of these forms is correct; the true structure is a hybrid of both of them.

The benzene ring is usually represented as

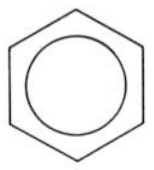

The carbon and hydrogen atoms of the ring are not shown. In formulas for benzene derivatives, such as

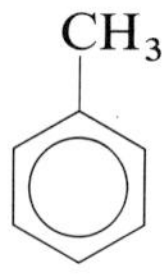

toluene or methylbenzene

and

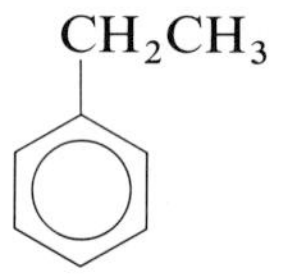

ethylbenzene

it is understood that the substituents replace hydrogen atoms of the ring. The radical formed from benzene by the removal of a hydrogen atom:

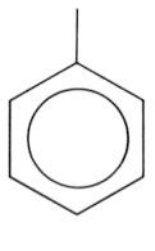

is called a **phenyl radical.** The phenyl radical is an example of an **aryl radical,** a group that is produced by the removal of a hydrogen atom from a carbon of the benzene ring of an aromatic compound.

There are three position isomers of any disubstituted benzene derivative, for example:

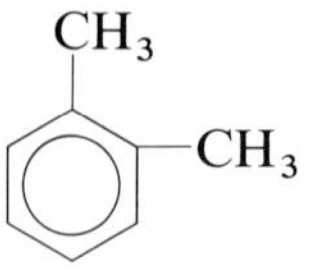

o-xylene

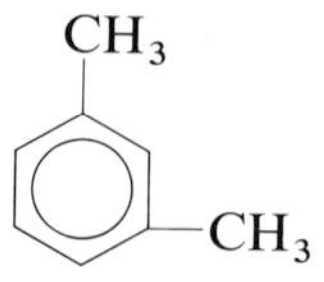

m-xylene

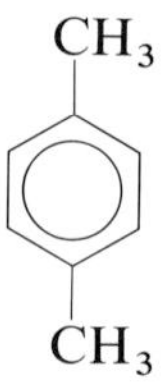

p-xylene

The prefixes *ortho-* (*o-*), *meta-* (*m-*), and *para-* (*p-*) are used to designate the positions of the two substituent groups. Numbers are used when more than two substituents are present on the ring:

1,3,5-*trinitrobenzene*

Compounds are known in which several rings are fused together. For example, napthalene, $C_{10}H_8$, is a planar molecule that is a resonance hybrid:

There are no hydrogen atoms bonded to the carbon atoms through which the rings are fused.

Aromatic compounds are obtained from processes that utilize the alkanes and cycloalkanes derived from petroleum. Coal is also a source of aromatic compounds. In the preparation of coke for industrial use (principally for the reduction of iron ore), bituminous coal is heated out of contact with air in retorts. Coal tar, a by-product of this process, is a black, viscous material from which various aromatic compounds may be separated.

28.5 Reactions of the Hydrocarbons

Combustion of any hydrocarbon in excess oxygen yields carbon dioxide and water:

$$CH_4(g) + 2 O_2(g) \longrightarrow CO_2(g) + 2 H_2O(g)$$

The reactions are highly exothermic, a fact that accounts for the use of hydrocarbons as fuels. Carbon compounds exist in oxidation states intermediate between the hydrocarbons and carbon dioxide. These compounds are discussed in sections that follow; they are not generally prepared by direct reaction with elementary oxygen.

The replacement of a hydrogen atom of a hydrocarbon molecule by another atom or group of atoms is called a **substitution reaction.** The alkanes react with chlorine or bromine in the presence of sunlight or ultraviolet light by means of a free-radical chain mechanism (see Section 14.5). The chain is initiated by the light-induced dissociation of a chlorine molecule into atoms:

$$Cl_2 \longrightarrow 2 Cl\cdot$$

Propagation of the chain occurs by the reactions

$$Cl\cdot + CH_4 \longrightarrow CH_3\cdot + HCl$$
$$CH_3\cdot + Cl_2 \longrightarrow CH_3Cl + Cl\cdot$$

The chain is terminated by the reactions

$$CH_3\cdot + Cl\cdot \longrightarrow CH_3Cl$$

$$Cl\cdot + Cl\cdot \longrightarrow Cl_2$$

$$CH_3\cdot + CH_3\cdot \longrightarrow CH_3CH_3$$

The reactions that terminate the chain occur at the walls of the container. The energy liberated by the formation of the new bond is transferred to the walls of the container. In a collision between radicals in the gas phase, the united fragments fly apart almost immediately because a third body is not present to carry away the energy released by bond formation. Hence, chain-terminating reactions do not occur with great frequency, and the initial reactants are rapidly consumed.

The overall reaction for the preceding mechanism is

$$CH_4 + Cl_2 \longrightarrow CH_3Cl + HCl$$

In addition to chloromethane, CH_3Cl, the reaction produces dichloromethane, CH_2Cl_2, trichloromethane (chloroform), $CHCl_3$, and tetrachloromethane (carbon tetrachloride), CCl_4. In terms of the chain mechanism, these compounds arise through collisions of chlorine atoms with already chlorinated methane molecules, for example:

$$Cl\cdot + CH_3Cl \longrightarrow CH_2Cl\cdot + HCl$$

$$CH_2Cl\cdot + Cl_2 \longrightarrow CH_2Cl_2 + Cl\cdot$$

Complex mixtures of mono- and poly-substituted isomers are obtained as products of the chlorination of higher alkanes.

Addition reactions are characteristic of unsaturated hydrocarbons. Numerous reagents add to the multiple bonds of alkenes and alkynes. In the addition of Br_2 to ethene, for example, each of the Br atoms of the Br_2 molecule bonds to a C atom of the double bond of ethene, which leaves a single bond between the C atoms:

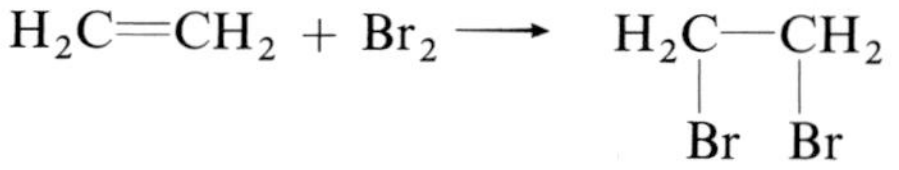

$$H_2C{=}CH_2 + Br_2 \longrightarrow \underset{\underset{Br\ \ \ Br}{|\ \ \ \ |}}{H_2C{-}CH_2}$$

1,2-*dibromoethane*

The Cl_2, Br_2, and H_2 molecules are called **symmetrical reagents**. In an addition reaction involving any one of these reagents, the same type of atom adds to both sides of the multiple bond:

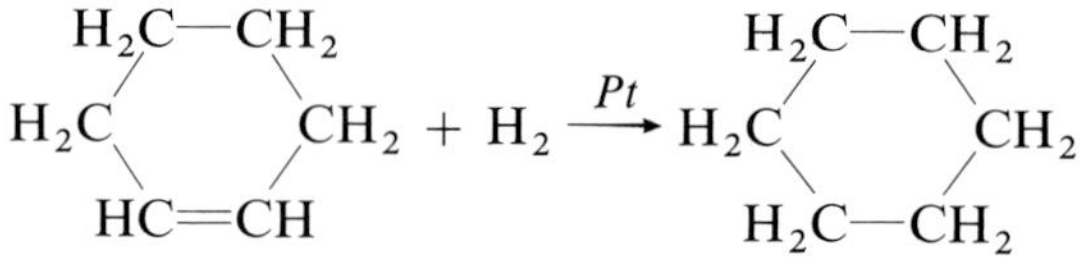

cyclohexane

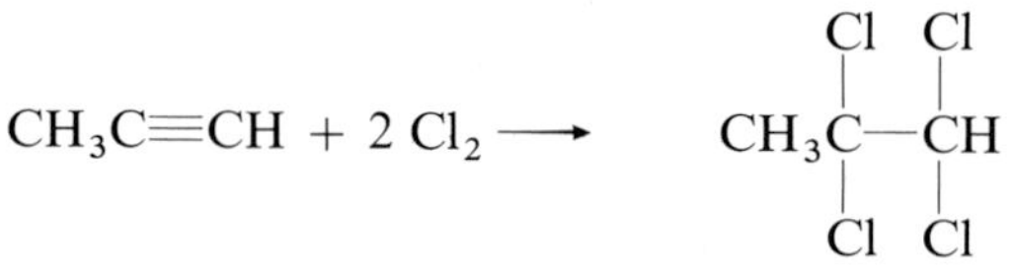

$$CH_3C{\equiv}CH + 2\,Cl_2 \longrightarrow \underset{\underset{Cl\ \ \ Cl}{|\ \ \ \ |}}{\overset{\overset{Cl\ \ \ Cl}{|\ \ \ \ |}}{CH_3C{-}CH}}$$

1,1,2,2-*tetrachloropropane*

The molecules of an **unsymmetrical reagent** (such as HBr, HCl, and HOH) consist of two different parts. When HCl, for example, adds to a multiple bond, H adds to one side and Cl adds to the other:

$$HC\equiv CH + HCl \longrightarrow CH_2\!=\!CHCl$$
chloroethene

$$CH_2\!=\!CHCl + HCl \longrightarrow CH_3\!-\!CHCl_2$$
1,1-dichloroethane

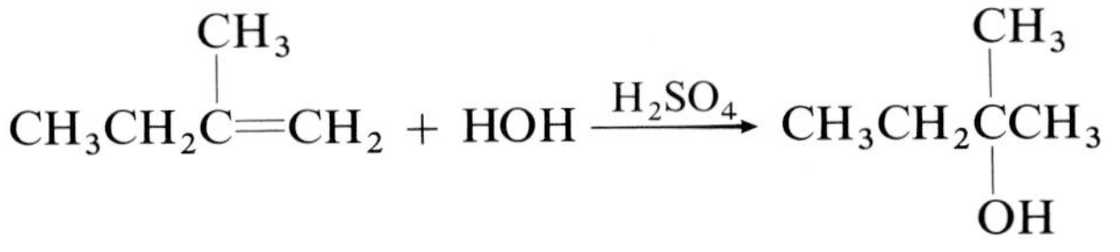

$$CH_3CH_2\overset{\displaystyle CH_3}{\underset{}{C}}\!=\!CH_2 + HOH \xrightarrow{\ H_2SO_4\ } CH_3CH_2\underset{\displaystyle OH}{\overset{\displaystyle CH_3}{C}}CH_3$$
2-methyl-2-butanol

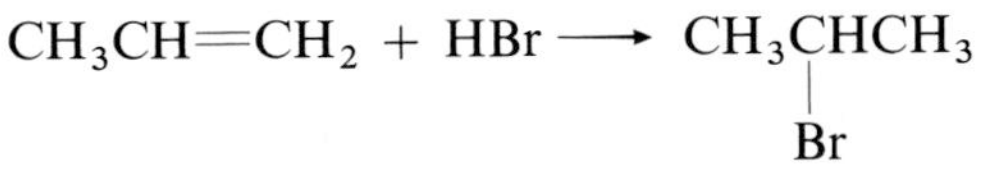

$$CH_3CH\!=\!CH_2 + HBr \longrightarrow CH_3\underset{\displaystyle Br}{CH}CH_3$$
2-bromopropane

When unsymmetrical molecules (such as HBr) add to the double bond of an olefin, two isomeric compounds are sometimes produced. Thus, in the last reaction of the previous series, two compounds are obtained:

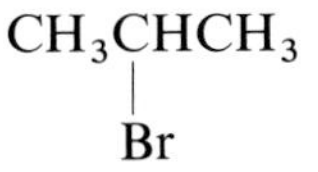

$$CH_3\underset{\displaystyle Br}{CH}CH_3 \qquad CH_3CH_2CH_2Br$$
2-bromopropane 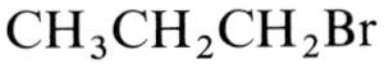   *1-bromopropane*

Over 90% of the product, however, is the 2-bromo-isomer. The principal product of such an addition is that in which the more positive part of the addend (a hydrogen atom in these cases) is bonded to the carbon that originally had the larger number of hydrogen atoms (**Markovnikov's rule**).

The initial step of the mechanism of the addition of HBr is thought to be an electrophilic attack by a proton (a Lewis acid) on the π electrons of the double bond (a Lewis base). The product of this step is a positive ion called a **carbocation**; for propene two such ions are possible:

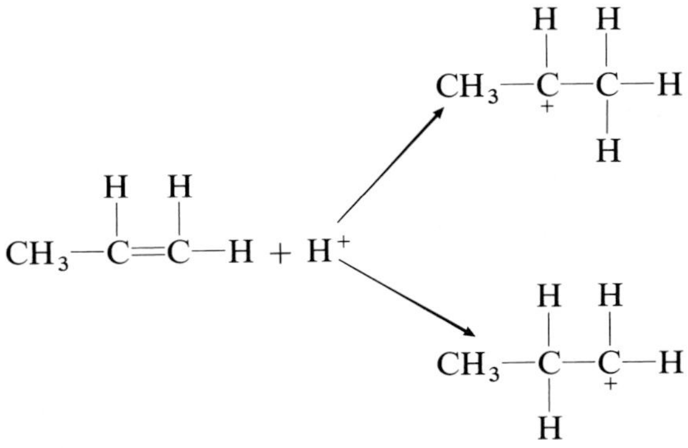

The π electrons are used to bond the incoming proton to one of the carbon atoms of the double bond which leaves the other carbon atom with a positive charge. The stability of carbocations is known to decrease in the order

$$\underset{R-\overset{\overset{\displaystyle R}{|}}{\underset{+}{C}}-R}{} > \underset{R-\overset{\overset{\displaystyle H}{|}}{\underset{+}{C}}-R}{} > \underset{R-\overset{\overset{\displaystyle H}{|}}{\underset{+}{C}}-H}{}$$

where R is an alkyl radical. Consequently, in the reaction of propene with HBr, the carbocation produced in larger quantity is the one shown on top.

Carbocations are highly reactive Lewis acids; they exist only transiently and rapidly combine with bromide ion (a Lewis base):

$$CH_3\overset{+}{C}HCH_3 + Br^- \longrightarrow \underset{\underset{Br}{|}}{CH_3CHCH_3}$$

$$CH_3CH_2CH_2^+ + Br^- \longrightarrow CH_3CH_2CH_2Br$$

Thus, the relative stabilities of the carbocations are responsible for the fact that 2-bromopropane is the principal product of the reaction.

In contrast to unsaturated open-chain hydrocarbons, the principal reactions of benzene are substitutions, not additions:

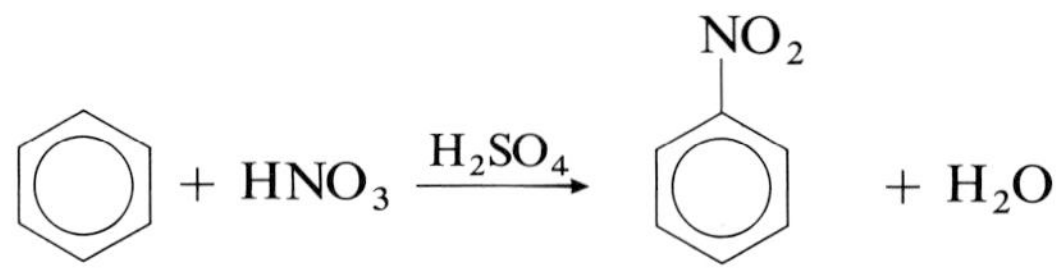

nitrobenzene

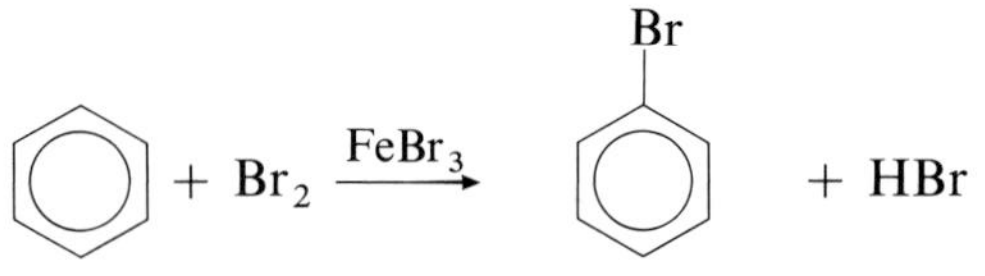

bromobenzene

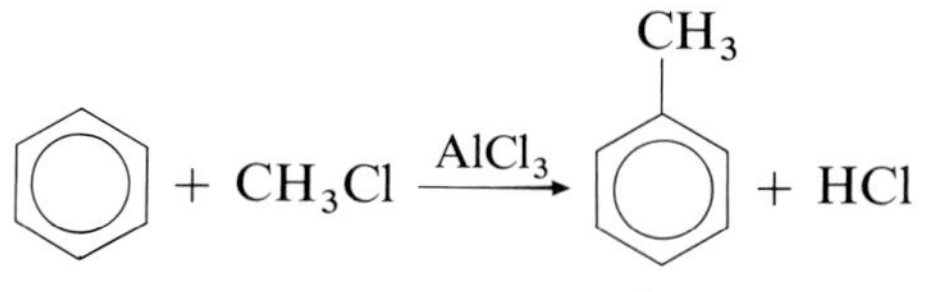

toluene

The last reaction is the Friedel-Crafts synthesis for the preparation of aromatic hydrocarbons.

The catalysts, which are indicated over the arrows in the preceding equations, produce powerful Lewis acids (NO_2^+, Br^+, and CH_3^+) as follows:

$$HNO_3 + 2\,H_2SO_4 \longrightarrow NO_2^+ + H_3O^+ + 2\,HSO_4^-$$

$$Br_2 + FeBr_3 \longrightarrow Br^+ + FeBr_4^-$$

$$CH_3Cl + AlCl_3 \longrightarrow CH_3^+ + AlCl_4^-$$

These cationic Lewis acids, which are short-lived reaction intermediates, are electrophilic, and we shall indicate them as E^+ in the mechanism that follows.

The benzene ring is attacked by the electrophilic group, E^+, which bonds to a carbon atom by means of a pair of π electrons and creates an activated complex with a positive charge:

Chapter 28 Organic Chemistry

Notice that the carbon atom to which E is bonded holds two groups in the complex; the remaining five carbon atoms hold only their customary hydrogen atoms. The complex is a resonance hybrid, and the charge is delocalized, thus providing a degree of stability. The π bonding system of benzene is more stable, however, and is restored by the loss of a proton:

The proton is lost to the anion produced in the reaction that generated the cationic electrophile:

$$H^+ + HSO_4^- \longrightarrow H_2SO_4$$

$$H^+ + FeBr_4^- \longrightarrow HBr + FeBr_3$$

$$H^+ + AlCl_4^- \longrightarrow HCl + AlCl_3$$

When a benzene ring holds two groups, three orientations are possible: *ortho* (*o*-), *meta* (*m*-), and *para* (*p*-):

o-chloronitrobenzene   m-chloronitrobenzene   p-chloronitrobenzene

In a reaction in which a second group is introduced into a benzene ring, the orientation that the entering group assumes is directed by the group already present. The chloro group, for example, directs an entering group into the *ortho* and *para* positions. A mixture of *ortho* and *para* isomers is obtained and practically none of the *meta* isomer:

Table 28.4 Directing influence of some functional groups on aromatic substitutions

ortho-para directing:

$$-F, \ -Cl, \ -Br, \ -I, \ -R, \ -OH, \ -OR, \ -NH_2$$

meta directing:

$$-NO_2, \ -SO_2OH, \ -C\equiv N, \ \overset{\overset{O}{\|}}{-C}-OH, \ \overset{\overset{O}{\|}}{-C}-OR, \ \overset{\overset{O}{\|}}{-C}-R, \ \overset{\overset{O}{\|}}{-C}-NH_2$$

In contrast, the nitro group is a *meta* director. Chlorination of nitrobenzene yields the *meta* isomer almost exclusively:

Groups are either *ortho-para* directing or *meta* directing. A list is given in Table 28.4.

In an aromatic substitution, the attack by the electrophilic group, E^+, occurs at a place on the benzene ring where the electron density is high. The directing influence of a group is believed to result from its effect on the distribution of the electron density of the ring. An *ortho-para* director is believed to build up electron density in these positions. A *meta* director, on the other hand, is believed to drain electron density from the *ortho* and *para* positions, leaving the *meta* position relatively negative.

28.6 Alcohols and Ethers

The alcohols may be considered as derivatives of hydrocarbons in which a hydroxyl group, OH, replaces a hydrogen. The hydroxyl group is one of a number of **functional groups,** which are groups of atoms that give organic compounds bearing them characteristic chemical and physical properties.

The alcohols are named as derivatives of a hydrocarbon consisting of the longest straight chain that contains the OH group. The ending of the parent hydrocarbon is changed from *-ane* to *-anol*, and numbers are used to indicate the positions of substituents, the lowest possible number being assigned to the OH group. Alcohols may be classified as *primary*, *secondary*, or *tertiary*, according to the number of alkyl radicals on the carbon atom holding the OH. Thus,

$$CH_3CH_2CH_2CH_2OH \qquad\qquad CH_3-\overset{\overset{\displaystyle CH_3}{|}}{CH}-\underset{\underset{\displaystyle OH}{|}}{CH}CH_3 \qquad\qquad CH_3\overset{\overset{\displaystyle CH_3}{|}}{\underset{\underset{\displaystyle OH}{|}}{C}}CH_2CH_3$$

1-butanol   *3-methyl-2-butanol*   *2-methyl-2-butanol*
a primary alcohol   *a secondary alcohol*   *a tertiary alcohol*

Table 28.5 Physical properties of some alcohols

Name	Formula	Melting Point (°C)	Boiling Point (°C)	Solubility in Water (g/100 g H_2O, 20°C)
methanol	CH_3OH	−98	65	miscible
ethanol	CH_3CH_2OH	−115	78	miscible
1-propanol	$CH_3(CH_2)_2OH$	−127	97	miscible
1-butanol	$CH_3(CH_2)_3OH$	−90	117	7.9
1-pentanol	$CH_3(CH_2)_4OH$	−79	138	2.4
1-hexanol	$CH_3(CH_2)_5OH$	−52	157	0.6

Alcohols associate through hydrogen bonding:

$$\underset{\displaystyle O-H\cdots O-H\cdots O-H}{\overset{\displaystyle R \qquad\quad R \qquad\quad R}{\big|\qquad\quad\big|\qquad\quad\big|}}$$

For this reason, the melting points and boiling points of the alcohols are higher than those of alkanes of corresponding molecular weight (see Table 28.5). The lower alcohols are miscible with water in all proportions because of intermolecular hydrogen bonding:

$$\underset{\displaystyle O-H\cdots O-H\cdots O-H}{\overset{\displaystyle H \qquad\quad R \qquad\quad H}{\big|\qquad\quad\big|\qquad\quad\big|}}$$

However, as the size of the alkyl radical increases, the alcohols become more like alkanes in their physical properties, and the higher alcohols are only slightly soluble in water.

Alcohols, like water, are amphiprotic substances. They can act as Brønsted bases (proton acceptors) with very strong acids:

$$H_2SO_4 + ROH \rightleftharpoons ROH_2^+ + HSO_4^-$$

With very strong bases they are Brønsted acids (proton donors):

$$ROH + H^- \longrightarrow OR^- + H_2$$

Alcohols, however, are more weakly acidic and basic than water; consequently, the conjugate acids (ROH_2^+) and conjugate bases (OR^-) are stronger than H_3O^+ and OH^-. The anion OR^-, known as an alkoxide ion, results from the reaction of an alcohol with a reactive metal (compare the reaction of water with sodium):

$$2\,CH_3CH_2OH + 2\,Na \longrightarrow 2\,CH_3CH_2ONa + H_2$$

The first member of the series, methanol (or methyl alcohol), is known as wood alcohol because it can be obtained by the destructive distillation of wood. The principal commercial source of this alcohol is the catalytic hydrogenation of carbon monoxide:

$$CO + 2H_2 \longrightarrow CH_3OH$$

The alcohol of alcoholic beverages is ethanol, or ethyl alcohol. It is prepared by the fermentation of starches or sugars. Ethanol is also commercially prepared from ethene. The indirect addition of water to olefins by means of sulfuric acid is a general method of preparing alcohols. The synthesis of ethanol proceeds by the following steps:

$$CH_2{=}CH_2 + H_2SO_4 \longrightarrow CH_3CH_2OSO_2OH$$

$$CH_3CH_2OSO_2OH + H_2O \longrightarrow CH_3CH_2OH + H_2SO_4$$

Alcohols can be prepared from alkyl halides by **displacement,** or **nucleophilic substitution, reactions:**

$$RX + OH^- \longrightarrow ROH + X^-$$

This is an important class of organic reactions. It includes the reactions of the alkyl halides, as well as the alcohols themselves, with a wide variety of nucleophilic substances. The reactions are usually reversible and are run under conditions that favor the formation of the desired compound; an excess of the nucleophilic reagent may be employed or the product may be removed from the reaction mixture as it forms (for example, by distillation).

A mechanism proposed to account for the reactions of primary and secondary halides or alcohols is the S_N2 mechanism, which can be illustrated by the reaction of hydroxide ion with methyl bromide. The hydroxide ion, a Lewis base, attacks the carbon atom and displaces the bromide ion (also a Lewis base), which takes along the electron pair with which it had been bonded:

activated complex

The attack of the OH^- ion takes place on the side of the carbon atom that is opposite the bromine atom. As the OH^- ion approaches, it begins to form a covalent bond, and the bromide ion begins to break away. The activated complex of the reaction is the form in which both nucleophilic groups are partially bonded to the carbon atom. The reaction causes inversion of the geometric arrangement of the groups attached to the carbon atom, a process that is customarily compared to the inversion of an umbrella in a high wind. The mechanism is given the designation S_N2 because it is the substitution of one nucleophilic group for another, and the rate-determining step (the formation of the activated complex) is bimolecular. The nucleophilic substitution reaction of HBr with CH_3OH proceeds through the formation of $CH_3OH_2^+$ and the displacement of H_2O from this ion by Br^-.

In the case of tertiary alkyl halides, the three alkyl groups bonded to the carbon atom bearing the halogen inhibit the rearward approach of the OH^- ion, and it is thought that tertiary alkyl halides undergo displacement reactions by a different mechanism. The rate-determining step is thought to be the formation of a carbocation:

$$CH_3-\underset{\underset{\displaystyle CH_3}{|}}{\overset{\overset{\displaystyle CH_3}{|}}{C}}-Br \longrightarrow CH_3\underset{\underset{\displaystyle CH_3}{|}}{\overset{\overset{\displaystyle CH_3}{|}}{C^+}} + Br^-$$

The carbocation is a powerful Lewis acid and rapidly reacts with water, which functions as a Lewis base:

$$CH_3-\underset{\underset{\displaystyle CH_3}{|}}{\overset{\overset{\displaystyle CH_3}{|}}{C^+}} + OH_2 \longrightarrow CH_3-\underset{\underset{\displaystyle CH_3}{|}}{\overset{\overset{\displaystyle CH_3}{|}}{C}}-OH_2^+$$

This ionic intermediate rapidly loses a proton to become the tertiary alcohol:

$$CH_3-\underset{\underset{\displaystyle CH_3}{|}}{\overset{\overset{\displaystyle CH_3}{|}}{C}}-OH_2^+ + OH^- \longrightarrow CH_3-\underset{\underset{\displaystyle CH_3}{|}}{\overset{\overset{\displaystyle CH_3}{|}}{C}}-OH + H_2O$$

This mechanism is given the designation S_N1 because it is a nucleophilic substitution in which the rate-determining step is unimolecular. The S_N1 mechanism is favored when the reaction is run in polar solvents (such as water), which aid the first-step ionization of the halide.

Tertiary alcohols also undergo S_N1 reactions. The steps of a typical substitution involving HBr are

$$(CH_3)_3COH + H^+ \rightleftharpoons (CH_3)_3COH_2^+ \qquad \text{(rapid, equilibrium)}$$
$$(CH_3)_3COH_2^+ \longrightarrow (CH_3)_3C^+ + H_2O \qquad \text{(rate determining)}$$
$$(CH_3)_3C^+ + Br^- \longrightarrow (CH_3)_3CBr$$

In all these nucleophilic substitution reactions, appreciable quantities of olefins are formed along with the substitution products; this is particularly true of the reactions of the tertiary compounds. Olefin formation is thought to proceed by the elimination of a proton by a carbocation:

$$H-\underset{\underset{\displaystyle H}{|}}{\overset{\overset{\displaystyle H}{|}}{C}}-\underset{\underset{\displaystyle CH_3}{|}}{\overset{\overset{\displaystyle CH_3}{|}}{C^+}} \longrightarrow H^+ + \underset{\underset{\displaystyle H}{|}}{\overset{\overset{\displaystyle H}{|}}{C}}=\underset{\underset{\displaystyle CH_3}{|}}{\overset{\overset{\displaystyle CH_3}{|}}{C}}$$

Tertiary carbocations are formed more readily than any other type (see Section 28.5). Elimination reactions of primary and secondary alcohols are thought to occur by a mechanism that does not involve the formation of carbocations.

The elimination of one water molecule from one molecule of an alcohol produces an olefin:

$$CH_3CH_2OH \xrightarrow[\textit{above 150°C}]{H_2SO_4} CH_2{=}CH_2 + H_2O$$

Under milder conditions only one molecule of water is removed from two molecules of alcohol, and an ether is produced:

$$CH_3CH_2OH + HOCH_2CH_3 \xrightarrow[130-140°C]{H_2SO_4} CH_3CH_2OCH_2CH_3 + H_2O$$

diethyl ether

Ethers, ROR, may be regarded as derivatives of water, HOH, in which both hydrogen atoms are replaced by alkyl groups, R. The alkyl groups may be alike or different. Ethers are also produced by nucleophilic substitution reactions involving alkoxide ions and alkyl halides:

$$CH_3CH_2O^- + CH_3CH_2CH_2Br \longrightarrow CH_3CH_2OCH_2CH_2CH_3 + Br^-$$

ethyl propyl ether

Unlike alcohols, ethers do not associate by hydrogen bonding. Therefore, the boiling points of ethers are much lower than those of alcohols of corresponding molecular weight:

$$CH_3CH_2OH \qquad\qquad CH_3OCH_3$$

ethanol   *dimethyl ether*
boiling point, 78°C   *boiling point, −24°C*

Notice that ethanol and dimethyl ether are isomeric; the type of isomerism displayed by this pair of compounds is known as **functional group isomerism**. The ethers are less reactive than the alcohols.

Polyhydroxy alcohols contain more than one OH group. Examples include 1,2-ethanediol (also called ethylene glycol):

$$\begin{array}{cc} CH_2 & CH_2 \\ | & | \\ OH & OH \end{array}$$

and 1,2,3-propanetriol (also called glycerol), which is derived from fats:

$$\begin{array}{ccc} CH_2 & CH & CH_2 \\ | & | & | \\ OH & OH & OH \end{array}$$

Unlike aliphatic alcohols, which do not dissociate in water solution, the aromatic alcohols are weak acids in water:

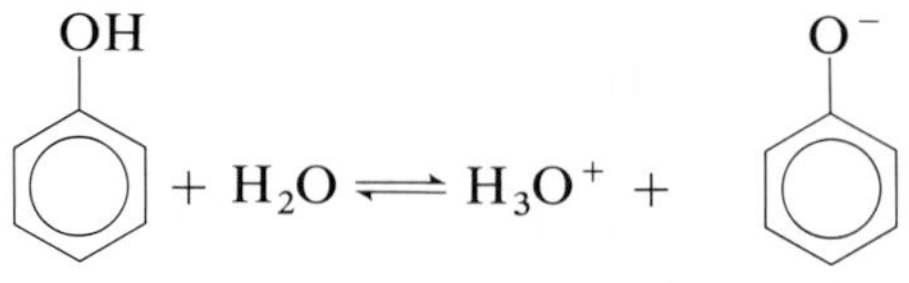

phenol   *phenoxide ion*

The acidity of phenol (carbolic acid) is attributed to the stability of the phenoxide ion in which the charge is delocalized by the π bonding system of the aromatic ring:

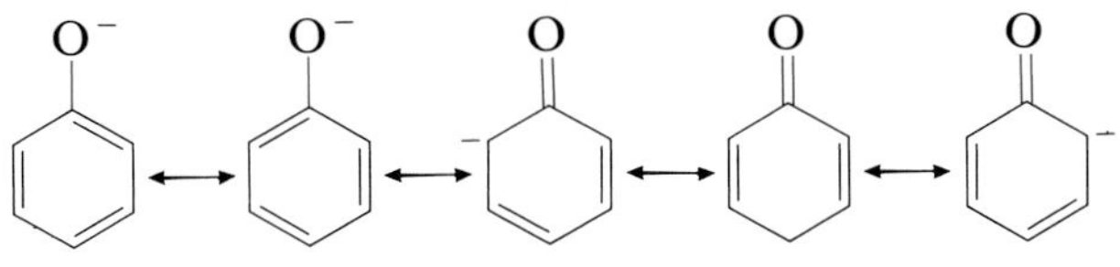

Aromatic halides do not readily undergo displacement reactions. Sodium phenoxide is commercially obtained from chlorobenzene by reaction with NaOH at elevated temperatures and under high pressure:

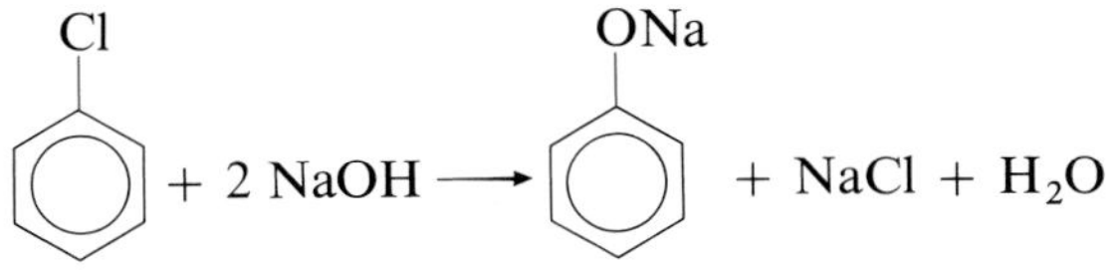

Phenol is derived by acidification of the phenoxide.

28.7 Carbonyl Compounds

A carbon atom can form a double bond with an oxygen atom to produce what is called a **carbonyl group**:

The double bond, like the carbon-carbon double bond, consists of a σ bond and a π bond between the bonded atoms. The carbon atom of the carbonyl group and the atoms bonded to it are coplanar and form bond angles of 120°, a geometry that is typical of sp^2 hybridized species. The carbonyl double bond differs from the olefinic double bond in that it is markedly polar (oxygen is more electronegative than carbon).

If the carbonyl group is bonded to one hydrogen or to two hydrogens, the compound is an **aldehyde**:

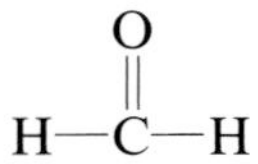

formaldehyde or methanal   *acetaldehyde or ethanal*   *3-methylbutanal*

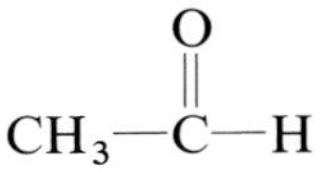

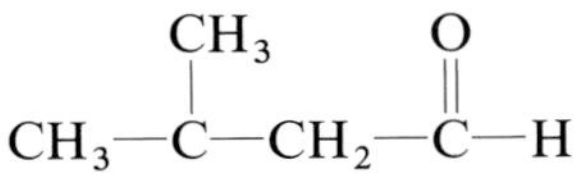

Systematic nomenclature of aldehydes employs the ending *-al*; substituent groups are given numbers based on the assignment of the number 1 (understood) to the carbonyl carbon.

In a **ketone** the carbonyl group is bonded to two alkyl or aryl groups, which may be alike or different:

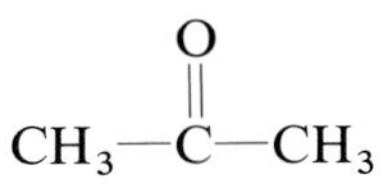

acetone or propanone   *methyl ethyl ketone or butanone*   *5-methyl-3-hexanone*

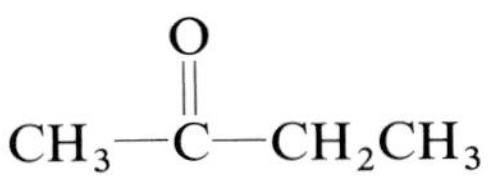

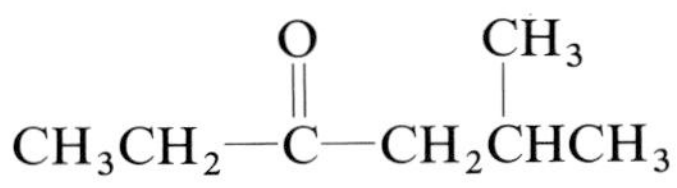

The ending -one is used to designate a ketone. Numbers are employed to indicate the positions of substituents on the longest continuous chain containing the carbonyl group, which is assigned the lowest possible number.

Aldehydes may be prepared by the mild oxidation of primary alcohols. An oxidizing agent such as potassium dichromate in dilute sulfuric acid may be used:

$$3\ RCH_2OH + Cr_2O_7^{2-} + 8\ H^+ \longrightarrow 3\ RC\overset{\displaystyle O}{\overset{\|}{}}H + 2\ Cr^{3+} + 7\ H_2O$$

Equations for a reaction such as this are usually written with the oxidizing agent indicated over the arrow and only the organic reactant and product shown. Thus,

$$CH_3CH_2OH \xrightarrow{Cr_2O_7^{2-}/H^+} CH_3C\overset{\displaystyle O}{\overset{\|}{}}H$$

When an aldehyde is prepared by the oxidation of a primary alcohol, provision must be made to prevent the aldehyde from being destroyed by further oxidation, since aldehydes are easily oxidized to carboxylic acids (see Section 28.8). Many aldehydes may be distilled out of the reaction mixture as they are formed.

Some aldehydes are made commercially by reacting alcohol vapors with air over a copper catalyst at elevated temperatures:

$$2\ CH_3OH + O_2 \xrightarrow{Cu} 2\ H\!-\!\overset{\displaystyle O}{\overset{\|}{C}}\!-\!H + 2\ H_2O$$

The oxidation of alcohols may also be conducted by passing the hot alcohol vapor over a heated copper catalyst in the absence of oxygen. This process results in the removal of a molecule of hydrogen from an alcohol molecule and is called a dehydrogenation; it avoids the danger of secondary oxidation of the aldehyde product:

$$CH_3CH_2CH_2OH \xrightarrow{Cu} CH_3CH_2\overset{\displaystyle O}{\overset{\|}{C}}\!-\!H + H_2$$

The oxidation of secondary alcohols produces ketones:

$$CH_3CH_2\overset{\displaystyle OH}{\overset{|}{C}}HCH_3 \xrightarrow{Cr_2O_7^{2-}/H^+} CH_3CH_2\overset{\displaystyle O}{\overset{\|}{C}}CH_3$$

Acetone (propanone) may be prepared by the oxidation of 2-propanol with oxygen or by the dehydrogenation of the alcohol:

$$CH_3\overset{\displaystyle OH}{\overset{|}{C}}HCH_3 \xrightarrow{Cu} CH_3\overset{\displaystyle O}{\overset{\|}{C}}CH_3 + H_2$$

The oxidation of tertiary alcohols results in the destruction of the carbon skeleton of the molecule.

The double bond of the carbonyl group readily undergoes many addition reactions. Reduction of aldehydes or ketones with hydrogen in the presence of a nickel or platinum catalyst yields primary or secondary alcohols:

$$\underset{\text{R}-\overset{\overset{\text{O}}{\|}}{\text{C}}-\text{H} + \text{H}_2}{} \longrightarrow \underset{\text{R}-\overset{\overset{\text{OH}}{|}}{\text{C}}\text{H}_2}{}$$

$$\underset{\text{R}-\overset{\overset{\text{O}}{\|}}{\text{C}}-\text{R} + \text{H}_2}{} \longrightarrow \underset{\text{R}-\overset{\overset{\text{OH}}{|}}{\text{C}}\text{H}-\text{R}}{}$$

When an unsymmetrical reagent (such as HCN) adds to the double bond, the more positive part of the addend (the hydrogen) adds to the oxygen, and the more negative part of the addend (the cyanide group) bonds to the carbon. This mode of addition reflects the polarity of a carbonyl double bond; the oxygen is negative with respect to the carbon:

$$\underset{\text{R}-\overset{\overset{\text{O}}{\|}}{\text{C}}-\text{R} + \text{H}-\text{C}\equiv\text{N}}{} \longrightarrow \text{R}-\overset{\overset{\text{OH}}{|}}{\underset{\underset{\text{C}\equiv\text{N}}{|}}{\text{C}}}-\text{R}$$

a cyanohydrin

The proposed mechanism for additions of this type consists of the electrophilic attack of the anionic Lewis base:

$$\underset{\text{R}-\overset{\overset{\text{O}}{\|}}{\text{C}}-\text{R} + \text{CN}^-}{} \longrightarrow \text{R}-\overset{\overset{\text{O}^-}{|}}{\underset{\underset{\text{CN}}{|}}{\text{C}}}-\text{R}$$

followed by combination with a proton:

$$\text{R}-\overset{\overset{\text{O}^-}{|}}{\underset{\underset{\text{CN}}{|}}{\text{C}}}-\text{R} + \text{H}^+ \longrightarrow \text{R}-\overset{\overset{\text{OH}}{|}}{\underset{\underset{\text{CN}}{|}}{\text{C}}}-\text{R}$$

An important addition reaction involves organomagnesium compounds known as **Grignard reagents.** Alkyl halides react with magnesium metal in dry diethyl ether:

$$\text{R}-\text{X} + \text{Mg} \longrightarrow \text{R}-\text{Mg}-\text{X}$$

These reagents are usually given the formula RMgX. The materials, however, possess a high degree of ionic character and may be mixtures of magnesium dialkyls (MgR_2) and magnesium halides (MgX_2). Water must be excluded from a Grignard reaction because these reagents are easily hydrolyzed:

$$\text{R}-\text{Mg}-\text{X} + \text{HOH} \longrightarrow \text{R}-\text{H} + \text{Mg(OH)X}$$

Victor Grignard, 1871–1934.
Burndy Library.

The formula Mg(OH)X stands for an equimolar mixture of magnesium hydroxide and magnesium halide.

A Grignard reagent adds to an aldehyde as follows:

$$R'-\overset{\overset{\textstyle O}{\|}}{C}-H \;+\; R-Mg-X \;\longrightarrow\; R'-\overset{\overset{\textstyle OMgX}{|}}{\underset{\underset{\textstyle R}{|}}{C}}-H$$

where the alkyl groups R and R′ may be alike or different. The addition compound is readily decomposed by water or by dilute acid.

$$R'-\overset{\overset{\textstyle OMgX}{|}}{\underset{\underset{\textstyle R}{|}}{C}}-H \;+\; HX \;\longrightarrow\; R'-\overset{\overset{\textstyle OH}{|}}{\underset{\underset{\textstyle R}{|}}{C}}-H \;+\; MgX_2$$

Thus, the ultimate product of the reaction of a Grignard reagent and an aldehyde is a secondary alcohol.

Hydrolysis of an addition compound formed by a Grignard reagent and a ketone yields a tertiary alcohol:

$$R'-\overset{\overset{\textstyle O}{\|}}{C}-R'' \;+\; RMgX \;\longrightarrow\; R'-\overset{\overset{\textstyle OMgX}{|}}{\underset{\underset{\textstyle R}{|}}{C}}-R''$$

$$R'-\overset{\overset{\textstyle OMgX}{|}}{\underset{\underset{\textstyle R}{|}}{C}}-R'' \;+\; HX \;\longrightarrow\; R'-\overset{\overset{\textstyle OH}{|}}{\underset{\underset{\textstyle R}{|}}{C}}-R'' \;+\; MgX_2$$

The alkyl groups may be alike or different.

In these reactions of Grignard reagents, new carbon-carbon bonds are formed, and the reactions are frequently useful as steps in organic syntheses. The alcohols produced may be oxidized to carbonyl compounds, subjected to displacement reactions, or dehydrated to olefins. Thus, a series of reactions may be employed to synthesize a desired compound from compounds of lower molecular weight.

28.8 Carboxylic Acids and Esters

Oxidation of the aldehyde group yields a carboxyl group:

$$-\overset{\overset{\textstyle O}{\|}}{C}-H \;\longrightarrow\; -\overset{\overset{\textstyle O}{\|}}{C}-OH$$

Compounds containing the —COOH group are weak acids (carboxylic acids); ionization constants for some of these acids are listed in Table 28.6:

Table 28.6 Properties of some carboxylic acids

Acid	Formula	Melting Point (°C)	Boiling Point (°C)	Ionization Constant at 25°C
methanoic (formic)	$HCOOH$	8	101	1.8×10^{-4}
ethanoic (acetic)	CH_3COOH	17	118	1.8×10^{-5}
propanoic (propionic)	CH_3CH_2COOH	-22	141	1.4×10^{-5}
butanoic (butyric)	$CH_3(CH_2)_2COOH$	-8	164	1.5×10^{-5}
pentanoic (valeric)	$CH_3(CH_2)_3COOH$	-35	187	1.6×10^{-5}
benzoic	C_6H_5COOH	122	249	6.0×10^{-5}

$$R-\overset{\overset{\displaystyle O}{\|}}{C}-OH + H_2O \rightleftharpoons R-\overset{\overset{\displaystyle O}{\|}}{C}-O^- + H_3O^+$$

The charge of the carboxylate anion is delocalized:

$$R-\overset{\overset{\displaystyle O}{\|}}{C}-O^- \longleftrightarrow R-\overset{\overset{\displaystyle O^-}{|}}{C}=O$$

The acids are associated through hydrogen bonding. Lower members of the series form dimers in the vapor state:

$$\begin{matrix} & O\text{---}H-O & \\ R-C & & C-R \\ & O-H\text{---}O & \end{matrix}$$

According to systematic nomenclature, the name of a carboxylic acid is derived from the parent hydrocarbon by elision of the final -*e*, addition of the ending -*oic*, and addition of the separate word *acid*. The numbers used to designate the positions of substituents on the carbon chain are derived by numbering the chain starting with the carbon of the carboxyl group:

$$CH_3CH_2\overset{\overset{\displaystyle O}{\|}}{C}-OH \qquad CH_3\overset{\overset{\displaystyle CH_3}{|}}{C}HCH_2\overset{\overset{\displaystyle O}{\|}}{C}-OH$$

propanoic acid   *3-methylbutanoic acid*

Carboxylic acids may be prepared by the oxidation of primary alcohols or aldehydes. Potassium dichromate or potassium permanganate is frequently employed as the oxidizing agent:

$$CH_3CH_2CH_2CH_2OH \xrightarrow{Cr_2O_7^{2-}/H^+} CH_3CH_2CH_2\overset{\overset{\displaystyle O}{\|}}{C}-OH$$

Acetic acid is commercially prepared by the air oxidation of acetaldehyde:

$$2\ CH_3\overset{\displaystyle O}{\overset{\displaystyle \|}{C}}\!-\!H + O_2 \xrightarrow{\ Mn(C_2H_3O_2)_2\ } 2\ CH_3\overset{\displaystyle O}{\overset{\displaystyle \|}{C}}\!-\!OH$$

Vigorous oxidation of an alkyl-substituted aromatic compound converts the side chain to a carboxyl group and thus yields benzoic acid:

toluene　　　　　*benzoic acid*

These oxidations do not touch the aromatic ring, an illustration of the stability of this structure.

The oxidation of an unsaturated hydrocarbon yields a variety of products, including carboxylic acids, depending upon conditions. Dilute aqueous permanganate at room temperature oxidizes olefins to glycols:

$$R\!-\!CH\!=\!CH\!-\!R \xrightarrow{\ MnO_4^-\ } R\!-\!\underset{\underset{\displaystyle OH}{|}}{CH}\!-\!\underset{\underset{\displaystyle OH}{|}}{CH}\!-\!R$$

Under more vigorous conditions (more concentrated solutions and heating), the carbon chain is cleaved at the double bond and carboxylic acids are produced:

$$R\!-\!CH\!=\!CH\!-\!R \xrightarrow{\ MnO_4^-\ } R\!-\!\overset{\displaystyle O}{\overset{\displaystyle \|}{C}}\!-\!OH + HO\!-\!\overset{\displaystyle O}{\overset{\displaystyle \|}{C}}\!-\!R$$

Alkynes also may be cleaved to yield acids:

$$R\!-\!C\!\equiv\!C\!-\!R \xrightarrow{\ MnO_4^-\ } R\!-\!\overset{\displaystyle O}{\overset{\displaystyle \|}{C}}\!-\!OH + HO\!-\!\overset{\displaystyle O}{\overset{\displaystyle \|}{C}}\!-\!R$$

Oxidation of some olefins yields ketones:

$$R\!-\!\underset{\underset{\displaystyle R}{|}}{C}\!=\!\underset{\underset{\displaystyle R}{|}}{C}\!-\!R \xrightarrow{\ MnO_4^-\ } R\!-\!\underset{\underset{\displaystyle R}{|}}{C}\!=\!O + O\!=\!\underset{\underset{\displaystyle R}{|}}{C}\!-\!R$$

Salts of carboxylic acids may be produced by the alkaline hydrolysis of alkyl cyanides; the cyanides are the product of nucleophilic substitution reactions of the CN^- ion with alkyl halides:

$$CH_3CH_2Br + CN^- \longrightarrow CH_3CH_2CN + Br^-$$

$$CH_3CH_2CN + OH^- + H_2O \longrightarrow CH_3CH_2\overset{\displaystyle O}{\overset{\displaystyle \|}{C}}\!-\!O^- + NH_3$$

Some compounds contain more than one carboxyl group. Examples include

$$
\begin{array}{ccc}
\begin{array}{c}
\text{COOH} \\
| \\
\text{COOH}
\end{array}
& \text{and} &
\begin{array}{c}
\text{CH}_2\text{COOH} \\
| \\
\text{HO}-\text{C}-\text{COOH} \\
| \\
\text{CH}_2\text{COOH}
\end{array} \\
\textit{oxalic acid} & & \textit{citric acid}
\end{array}
$$

Carboxylic acids react with alcohols to produce compounds known as **esters**:

$$
\underset{}{\overset{\text{O}}{\underset{\|}{\text{CH}_3\text{C}}}}-\text{OH} + \text{CH}_3\text{CH}_2\text{OH} \rightleftharpoons \left[\begin{array}{c} \text{OH} \\ | \\ \text{CH}_3\text{C}-\text{OH} \\ | \\ \text{OCH}_2\text{CH}_3 \end{array} \right] \rightleftharpoons
$$

$$
\underset{\textit{ethyl acetate}}{\overset{\text{O}}{\underset{\|}{\text{CH}_3\text{C}}}}-\text{OCH}_2\text{CH}_3 + \text{H}_2\text{O}
$$

Esterification reactions are reversible and proceed to equilibrium; they may be forced in either direction by the appropriate choice of conditions. The name of an ester reflects the alcohol and acid from which it is derived, the ending *-ate* being employed with the base of the name of the acid to give the second portion of the name of the ester. The lower molecular weight esters have pleasant, fruity odors.

The alkaline hydrolysis of an ester produces an alcohol and a salt of a carboxylic acid:

$$
\underset{}{\overset{\text{O}}{\underset{\|}{\text{RCOR}'}}} + \text{OH}^- \longrightarrow \text{R}-\overset{\text{O}}{\underset{\|}{\text{C}}}-\text{O}^- + \text{R}'\text{OH}
$$

28.9 Amines and Amides

The **amines** may be considered as derivatives of ammonia with one, two, or three hydrogen atoms replaced by alkyl or aryl groups:

$$
\begin{array}{ccc}
\begin{array}{c}
\text{H} \\
| \\
\text{CH}_3-\text{N}-\text{H}
\end{array}
&
\begin{array}{c}
\text{CH}_3 \\
| \\
\text{CH}_3-\text{N}-\text{H}
\end{array}
&
\begin{array}{c}
\text{CH}_3 \\
| \\
\text{CH}_3-\text{N}-\text{CH}_3
\end{array} \\
\textit{methylamine} & \textit{dimethylamine} & \textit{trimethylamine} \\
\textit{a primary amine} & \textit{a secondary amine} & \textit{a tertiary amine}
\end{array}
$$

The amines resemble ammonia in that they are weak bases:

$$
\text{CH}_3\text{NH}_2 + \text{H}_2\text{O} \rightleftharpoons \text{CH}_3\text{NH}_3^+ + \text{OH}^-
$$

$$
(\text{CH}_3)_2\text{NH} + \text{H}_2\text{O} \rightleftharpoons (\text{CH}_3)_2\text{NH}_2^+ + \text{OH}^-
$$

$$
(\text{CH}_3)_3\text{N} + \text{H}_2\text{O} \rightleftharpoons (\text{CH}_3)_3\text{NH}^+ + \text{OH}^-
$$

Table 28.7 Properties of some amines

Amine	Formula	Melting Point (°C)	Boiling Point (°C)	Ionization Constant at 25°C
methylamine	CH_3NH_2	−93	−7	5×10^{-4}
dimethylamine	$(CH_3)_2NH$	−96	7	7.4×10^{-4}
trimethylamine	$(CH_3)_3N$	−124	4	7.4×10^{-5}
ethylamine	$CH_3CH_2NH_2$	−81	17	5.6×10^{-4}
propylamine	$CH_3CH_2CH_2NH_2$	−83	49	4.7×10^{-4}
aniline	$C_6H_5NH_2$	−6	184	4.6×10^{-10}

Ionization constants for some amines are listed in Table 28.7. The amines form ionic salts with acids:

$$CH_3NH_2 + HCl \longrightarrow CH_3NH_3^+ + Cl^-$$

which may be decomposed by hydroxides:

$$CH_3NH_3^+ + OH^- \longrightarrow CH_3NH_2 + H_2O$$

The last reaction is the reverse of the ionization of methylamine in water; it is forced to yield the free amine by employment of an excess of OH^- or by warming.

Amines may be prepared by reacting alkyl halides with ammonia. These reactions are nucleophilic substitutions:

$$NH_3 + CH_3CH_2Br \longrightarrow CH_3CH_2NH_3^+ + Br^-$$

Treatment of the amine salt with hydroxide ion yields the free amine. Mixtures of primary, secondary, and tertiary amines are produced by this type of reaction.

Primary amines may be produced by the catalytic hydrogenation of alkyl cyanides:

$$CH_3CH_2C{\equiv}N + 2H_2 \longrightarrow CH_3CH_2CH_2{-}NH_2$$

Aniline is produced by the reduction of nitrobenzene. Hydrogen from iron and steam (with a trace of hydrochloric acid) serves as the reducing agent:

nitrobenzene   *aniline*

Some compounds that contain more than one amino group are important. Ethylenediamine (1,2-diaminoethane, $H_2N{-}CH_2{-}CH_2{-}NH_2$) is a useful chelating agent (see Section 26.1), and hexamethylenediamine (1,6-diaminohexane, $H_2N(CH_2)_6NH_2$) is used in the manufacture of nylon.

Amides may be produced from ammonia and carboxylic acids. The preparation proceeds through the formation of ammonium salts which eliminate water upon heating:

$$CH_3\overset{\overset{O}{\|}}{C}-OH + NH_3 \longrightarrow CH_3\overset{\overset{O}{\|}}{C}-O^-NH_4^+$$

$$\underset{\text{ammonium acetate}}{CH_3\overset{\overset{O}{\|}}{C}-O^-NH_4^+} \longrightarrow \underset{\text{acetamide}}{CH_3\overset{\overset{O}{\|}}{C}-NH_2} + H_2O$$

Amides may also be prepared by the nucleophilic substitution reaction of ammonia on an ester:

$$NH_3 + CH_3\overset{\overset{O}{\|}}{C}-OCH_2CH_3 \longrightarrow CH_3\overset{\overset{O}{\|}}{C}-NH_2 + CH_3CH_2OH$$

Primary and secondary amines react with acids in a similar manner to produce substituted amides, compounds in which alkyl or aryl radicals replace hydrogen atoms of the $-NH_2$ group.

8.10 Polymers

Starch, cellulose, and proteins are examples of natural **polymers**—molecules of high molecular weight that are formed from simpler molecules, called **monomers.** Important polymers, or **macromolecules,** that do not occur in nature have been synthesized; most of these are linear, or chain-type, structures although some are cross-linked.

Many polymers are formed from compounds that contain carbon-carbon double bonds by a process that is called **addition polymerization.** For example, ethene (ethylene) polymerizes upon heating (100°C–400°C) under high pressure (1000 atm); the product is called polyethylene:

$$\underset{\underset{H}{|}}{\overset{\overset{H}{|}}{C}}=\underset{\underset{H}{|}}{\overset{\overset{H}{|}}{C}} + \underset{\underset{H}{|}}{\overset{\overset{H}{|}}{C}}=\underset{\underset{H}{|}}{\overset{\overset{H}{|}}{C}} \longrightarrow -\underset{\underset{H}{|}}{\overset{\overset{H}{|}}{C}}-\underset{\underset{H}{|}}{\overset{\overset{H}{|}}{C}}-\underset{\underset{H}{|}}{\overset{\overset{H}{|}}{C}}-\underset{\underset{H}{|}}{\overset{\overset{H}{|}}{C}}-$$

The preceding equation shows the combination of only two molecules of ethene; the actual polymerization process continues by successive additions of $CH_2{=}CH_2$ molecules until chains of hundreds or thousands of $-CH_2-CH_2-$ units are produced. The product, polyethylene, is a tough, waxy solid.

An addition polymerization is thought to proceed by either a free radical or a carbocation chain mechanism. The free radical type may be initiated by small amounts of hydrogen peroxide or organic peroxides, which are readily split into free radicals (indicated by $Z\cdot$ in the equations that follow):

$$Z_2 \longrightarrow 2Z\cdot$$

A free radical from an initiator combines with one of the π electrons of a molecule of the monomer to form a new free radical:

$$Z\cdot + CH_2{=}CH_2 \longrightarrow Z{-}CH_2{-}CH_2\cdot$$

Chain propagation occurs by the combination of this free radical with another molecule of the monomer:

$$Z{-}CH_2{-}CH_2\cdot + CH_2{=}CH_2 \longrightarrow Z{-}CH_2{-}CH_2{-}CH_2{-}CH_2\cdot$$

and the molecule grows by repeated additions. Chain termination is caused by the combination of two free radicals or by other means, such as the elimination of a hydrogen atom.

A carbocation chain polymerization is initiated by a Lewis acid, such as $AlCl_3$ or BF_3. In the equations that follow, the proton is used to indicate the Lewis acid, or electrophilic, initiator although stronger Lewis acids are more frequently employed. Combination of the initiator with a molecule of the monomer produces a carbocation:

$$H^+ + CH_2{=}CH_2 \longrightarrow CH_3{-}CH_2^+$$

Chain propagation occurs through the combination of the carbocation with both π electrons of a molecule of the monomer:

$$CH_3{-}CH_2^+ + CH_2{=}CH_2 \longrightarrow CH_3{-}CH_2{-}CH_2{-}CH_2^+$$

Chain termination may occur by the elimination of a proton from a long-chain carbocation:

$$CH_3{-}CH_2(CH_2{-}CH_2)_nCH_2{-}CH_2^+ \longrightarrow$$
$$CH_3{-}CH_2(CH_2{-}CH_2)_nCH{=}CH_2 + H^+$$

Important polymers have been made from ethene derivatives. Orlon and acrilan are polymers of acrylonitrile, $CH_2{=}CH{-}C{\equiv}N$; the polymers have the structure

$$-CH_2{-}\underset{\displaystyle CN}{CH}{-}\left(CH_2{-}\underset{\displaystyle CN}{CH}\right)_n CH_2{-}\underset{\displaystyle CN}{CH}{-}$$

Teflon is a polymer of tetrafluoroethene, $CF_2{=}CF_2$. Vinyl chloride, $CH_2{=}CHCl$, and vinyl acetate:

$$CH_2{=}CH{-}O{-}\overset{\displaystyle O}{\overset{\displaystyle \|}{C}}{-}CH_3$$

are important monomers in the preparation of vinyl plastics. Lucite, or Plexiglas, is a polymer of methyl methacrylate, $CH_2{=}C(CH_3)COOCH_3$.

Natural rubber is a polymer of the diolefin 2-methyl-1,3-butadiene, or isoprene:

$$CH_2{=}\underset{\displaystyle CH_3}{C}{-}CH{=}CH_2$$

Such a system of alternating double and single bonds is called a **conjugated system**. Rubber consists of thousands of these units joined in a chain:

$$-CH_2-\underset{\underset{CH_3}{|}}{C}=CH-CH_2\left(CH_2-\underset{\underset{CH_3}{|}}{C}=CH-CH_2\right)_n CH_2-\underset{\underset{CH_3}{|}}{C}=CH-CH_2-$$

Notice that the polymer contains double bonds. Crude rubber is vulcanized by heating with sulfur. It is thought that the sulfur atoms add to some of the double bonds, thereby linking adjacent chains into a complex network. This process adds strength to the final product.

A number of types of synthetic rubber have been made utilizing such monomers as 1,3-butadiene (CH_2=CH—CH=CH_2), 2-chloro-1,3-butadiene (chloroprene, CH_2=C(Cl)—CH=CH_2), and 2,3-dimethyl-1,3-butadiene (CH_2=C(CH_3)—C(CH_3)=CH_2) alone or in combination. The product formed by the polymerization of two different monomers is called a **copolymer**; the molecular structures and properties of such materials depend upon the proportions of the two monomers employed. Buna S rubber is a copolymer of 1,3-butadiene and styrene (C_6H_5CH=CH_2). A section of the chain of this material has the structure

$$-CH_2-CH=CH-CH_2-\underset{\underset{\bigcirc}{|}}{CH}-CH_2-$$

Condensation polymerization occurs between molecules of monomers by the elimination of a small molecule, usually water. Proteins and polysaccharides are condensation polymers. Nylon, like the proteins, is a polyamide. It is formed by the condensation of a diamine [such as hexamethylenediamine, $H_2N(CH_2)_6NH_2$] and a dicarboxylic acid [such as adipic acid, $HOOC(CH_2)_4COOH$]. The polymerization occurs through the elimination of water molecules. The production of a small section of the chain can be illustrated as follows:

$$\cdots-\underset{\underset{H}{|}}{N}-H + H-O-\underset{\underset{}{||}}{\overset{O}{C}}-(CH_2)_4-\overset{O}{\underset{}{C}}-O-H + H-\underset{\underset{H}{|}}{N}-(CH_2)_6-\underset{\underset{H}{|}}{N}-H + H-O-\overset{O}{\underset{}{C}}-\cdots \longrightarrow$$

$$\cdots-\underset{\underset{H}{|}}{N}-\overset{O}{\underset{}{C}}-(CH_2)_4-\overset{O}{\underset{}{C}}-\underset{\underset{H}{|}}{N}-(CH_2)_6-\underset{\underset{H}{|}}{N}-\overset{O}{\underset{}{C}}-\cdots + 3\,H_2O$$

Dacron is a polyester formed by the elimination of water between ethylene glycol ($HOCH_2CH_2OH$) and a dicarboxylic acid (such as terephthalic acid, p-$HOOCC_6H_4COOH$):

$$\cdots-\overset{O}{\underset{}{C}}-O-H + H-O-CH_2-CH_2-O-H + H-O-\overset{O}{\underset{}{C}}-\bigcirc-\overset{O}{\underset{}{C}}-O-H + H-O-\cdots \longrightarrow$$

$$\cdots-\overset{O}{\underset{}{C}}-O-CH_2-CH_2-O-\overset{O}{\underset{}{C}}-\bigcirc-\overset{O}{\underset{}{C}}-O-\cdots + 3\,H_2O$$

Bakelite is a cross-linked polymer formed from phenol (C_6H_5OH) and formaldehyde ($H_2C=O$) by the elimination of water. Notice that the formaldehyde units condense in the *ortho* and *para* positions of phenol:

Chapter 28   Organic Chemistry

Summary

Hydrocarbons are compounds that contain *only carbon and hydrogen*. In the *alkanes* all the carbon-carbon bonds are *single bonds*. An open-chain alkane conforms to the general formula C_nH_{2n+2}, and an alkane with a ring structure (called a *cycloalkane*) conforms to the general formula C_nH_{2n}. An *alkene* (also called an *olefin*) has a carbon-carbon *double bond* somewhere in the molecule. The open-chain alkenes conform to the general formula C_nH_{2n}, and the *cycloalkenes* conform to the general formula C_nH_{2n-2}. An *alkyne* (which has the general formula C_nH_{2n-2}), has one carbon-carbon *triple bond* and an open-chain structure. The *aromatic hydrocarbons* are compounds that have molecular structures based on that of benzene, C_6H_6, which has a ring structure of six C atoms joined by σ bonds overlayed by a delocalized π bonding system.

The principal source of *alkanes* is *petroleum*. Aromatic hydrocarbons are obtained from *coal* as well as *processes* that utilize the alkanes and cycloalkanes derived from *petroleum*.

The replacement of hydrogen atom of a hydrocarbon by another atom or group of atoms is called a *substitution reaction*. *Addition reactions* are characteristic of *unsaturated hydrocarbons* (compounds with one or more multiple bonds). *Markovnikov's rule* may be used to predict the principal product when an *unsymmetrical reagent* adds to a multiple bond of an unsaturated hydrocarbon. The principal reactions of *aromatic hydrocarbons* are *substitutions, not additions*.

An *alcohol* is a derivative of an *alkane* in which a *hydroxyl group, OH,* replaces a hydrogen atom. Alcohols are prepared from alkyl halides by *displacement reactions*. This important class of organic reactions (which includes S_N1 and S_N2 reactions) includes the reactions of the alcohols themselves. *Ethers*, which have the general formula ROR (where the R groups are alkyl or aryl radicals that are alike or different), may be prepared from alcohols or from the reactions of alkoxide ions with alkyl halides. An *aromatic compound* that has an *OH group* bonded to a carbon atom of the ring is a weak acid called a *phenol*.

There are two types of *carbonyl compounds*: *aldehydes* (R—C(=O)—H, where R may be an alkyl radical, an aryl radical, or a hydrogen atom) and *ketones* (R—C(=O)—R, where the R groups may be alkyl radicals or aryl radicals that are alike or different). An aldehyde or a ketone may be prepared by the *oxidation* of the appropriate *alcohol*. The double bond of the carbonyl group readily undergoes *addition reactions* (with such substances as hydrogen, hydrogen cyanide, and *Grignard reagents*).

Carboxylic acids, R—C(=O)—OH (where R is an alkyl or aryl radical), may be prepared by the *oxidation of aldehydes, primary alcohols, alkenes,* or *alkynes*. Vigorous oxidation of an alkyl substituted aromatic compound converts the side chain into a carboxyl group. Carboxylic acids react with alcohols to produce compounds known as *esters*, R—C(=O)—OR (where the R groups are alkyl or aryl radicals that may be alike or different).

Amines are derivatives of ammonia with one, two, or three hydrogens replaced by alkyl or aryl groups. They are *weak bases* and form ionic salts with acids. They may be prepared by reacting alkyl halides with ammonia or by reducing cyanides. *Amides*, R—C(=O)—NH₂ (in which the R group is an alkyl or aryl radical) are prepared by the reactions of carboxylic acids or esters with ammonia or amines.

Structural isomers are compounds that have the same molecular formula but differ in the way that the atoms are bonded together. *Chain isomers, functional group isomers* and *position isomers* are types of structural isomers. In *stereoisomers*, the same atoms are bonded together in the same order, but the arrangement of the atoms in space is different. *Geometric isomers* and *optical isomers* are types of sterioisomers.

Polymers (or *macromolecules*) are high molecular-weight molecules that are formed from simpler molecules called *monomers*. Many polymers are formed by *addition polymerization* from compounds that contain double bonds. Addition polymers include: polyethylene, Orlon, Acrilan, Teflon, Lucite, and the vinyl plastics. *Natural rubber* is an addition polymer of 2-methyl-1,3-butadiene. Several types of synthetic rubber are made from 1,3-butadiene and derivatives of it. *Condensation polymerization* occurs between molecules of monomers by the *elimination of a small molecule*, usually water. Nylon, Dacron, and Bakelite are examples of condensation polymers.

Key Terms

Some of the more important terms introduced in this chapter are listed below. Definitions for terms not included in this list may be located in the text by the use of the index.

Addition reaction (Sections 28.2 and 28.5)   A reaction in which two parts of a reagent add to a multiple bond, one part to each side of the bond.

Addition polymerization (Section 28.10)   The formation of a polymer by the successive addition of molecules of the monomer, which is an alkene or a conjugated alkadiene.

Alcohol (Section 28.6)   A derivative of an alkane in which the hydroxyl group, OH, replaces a hydrogen atom. They are classified according to the number of alkyl groups bonded to the carbon atom that holds the OH group as a **primary alcohol** (one R group), a **secondary alcohol** (two R groups), or a **tertiary alcohol** (three R groups).

Aldehyde (Section 28.7)   A compound that has the general formula

$$\begin{array}{c} O \\ \parallel \\ R-C-H \end{array}$$

where R can be a hydrogen, an alkyl group, or an aryl group.

Alkadiene (Section 28.2)   An open-chain hydrocarbon that contains *two* carbon-carbon double bonds; the alkadienes conform to the general formula C_nH_{2n-2}.

Alkane (Section 28.1)   An open-chain hydrocarbon in which all carbon-carbon bonds are single bonds; the alkanes conform to the general formula C_nH_{2n+2}.

Alkene (Section 28.2)   An open-chain hydrocarbon that contains a carbon-carbon double bond; the alkenes conform to the general formula C_nH_{2n}.

Alkyl halide (Section 28.6)   A compound formed from an alkyl radical (R) and a halogen atom (X), RX.

Alkyl radical (Section 28.1)   A fragment of an alkane molecule from which a hydrogen atom has been removed (R).

Alkyne (Section 28.3)   An open-chain hydrocarbon that contains a carbon-carbon triple bond; the alkynes conform to the general formula C_nH_{2n-2}.

Amide (Section 28.9)   A compound with the general formula

$$\begin{array}{c} O \\ \parallel \\ R-C-NR_2 \end{array}$$

in which R may be a hydrogen atom, an alkyl radical, or an aryl radical, and the three R groups may be alike or different.

Amine (Section 28.9)   An organic base that can be con-sidered to be a derivative of ammonia (NH_3) with one hydrogen replaced (RNH_2, a **primary amine**), two hydrogens replaced (R_2NH, a **secondary amine**), or three hydrogens replaced (R_3N, a **tertiary amine**). The R groups may be either alkyl radicals or aryl radicals and in a given amine may be alike or different.

Aromatic compound (Section 28.4)   Benzene or a derivative of benzene.

Aryl radical (Section 28.4)   A radical formed by the removal of a hydrogen atom from a carbon of the benzene ring of an aromatic compound.

Carbocation (Section 28.5)   A positive ion formed by a group of atoms that contains a carbon atom that has only six valence electrons.

Carbonyl compound (Section 28.7)   A compound that contains a carbonyl group,

$$\begin{array}{c} O \\ \parallel \\ -C- \end{array}$$

Carboxylic acid (Section 28.8)   An organic acid that has the general formula

$$\begin{array}{c} O \\ \parallel \\ R-C-OH \end{array}$$

where R can be a hydrogen, alkyl radical, or aryl radical.

Condensation polymerization (Section 28.10)   A polymerization in which the monomer molecules combine with the elimination of a small molecule, usually water.

Conjugated double-bond system (Section 28.10)   A compound with a carbon chain containing alternating double and single bonds.

Copolymer (Section 28.10)   A polymer formed by the polymerization of two different monomers.

Cracking (Section 28.1)   An industrial process in which large molecules are broken down into smaller ones.

Cycloalkane (Section 28.1)   A hydrocarbon that has a ring arrangement of carbon atoms in which all the carbon-carbon bonds are single bonds; the cycloalkanes conform to the general formula C_nH_{2n}.

Cycloalkene (Section 28.2)   A hydrocarbon that has a ring arrangement of carbon atoms and contains a carbon-carbon double bond; the cycloalkenes conform to the general formula C_nH_{2n-2}.

Dehydrogenation (Section 28.7)   A reaction in which two hydrogen atoms are removed from a molecule to form a double bond.

Displacement reaction (Section 28.6)   A reaction in which one group displaces another from an organic molecule. It is also called a **nucleophilic substitution reaction** since it involves the substitution of one nucleophilic substance (a Lewis base) for another. If the rate-determining step is unimolecular, the reaction is called an S_N1 reaction; if bimolecular, an S_N2 reaction.

Ester of a carboxylic acid (Section 28.8) The product of the reaction of a carboxylic acid

$$\begin{matrix} & O \\ & \| \\ R\!-\!\!&C\!-\!OH \end{matrix}$$

(where R is a hydrogen atom, an alkyl radical, or an aryl radical) and an alcohol or phenol, R′OH (where R′ is an alkyl radical or an aryl radical);

$$\begin{matrix} & O \\ & \| \\ R\!-\!\!&C\!-\!OR' \end{matrix}$$

where R and R′ may be alike or different.

Ether (Section 28.6) A compound that has the general formula ROR, where the R groups may be alkyl or aryl radicals that are alike or different.

Friedel-Crafts synthesis (Section 28.5) A reaction of an aromatic compound with an alkyl halide in which HCl is eliminated and a new side chain introduced into the benzene ring of the aromatic compound.

Functional group (Section 28.6) An atom or a group of atoms that gives organic compounds bearing them characteristic physical and chemical properties.

Grignard reagent (Section 28.7) An organomagnesium compound, RMgX, where R can be an alkyl or an aryl radical and X is a halogen atom.

Homologous series (Section 28.1) A series of compounds that may be considered to be derived from the first member by the successive addition of a $-CH_2-$ unit. The members of a homologous series are called homologs and all of them conform to the same general formula.

Ketone (Section 28.7) A carbonyl compound that has the general formula

$$\begin{matrix} & O \\ & \| \\ R\!-\!\!&C\!-\!R \end{matrix}$$

where the R groups may be alkyl or aryl radicals that are alike or different.

Macromolecule (Section 28.10) A large, high molecular-weight molecule.

Markovnikov's rule (Section 28.5) The principal product of the addition of an unsymmetrical molecule to the double bond of an alkene is the compound in which the more positive part of the molecule bonds to the carbon atom of the double bond that originally had the larger number of hydrogen atoms.

Olefin (Section 28.2) An alkene.

Ortho, meta, and para isomers (Section 28.5) The three isomers of a disubstituted derivative of benzene. In the *ortho* isomer, the two substituents are on carbon atoms 1 and 2 of the benzene ring; in the *meta* isomer, 1 and 3; and in the *para* isomer, 1 and 4.

Polymers (Section 28.10) Macromolecules that are formed from simpler molecules called monomers.

Saturated hydrocarbon (Section 28.2) A hydrocarbon in which all the carbon-carbon bonds are single bonds; an alkane or a cycloalkane.

Stereoisomers (Section 28.2) Compounds that have the same molecular formula and are bonded in the same way but differ in the way the constituent atoms are arranged in space. Geometric isomers (Section 28.2), in organic chemistry, are compounds that owe their existence to the restricted rotation about a double bond. Optical isomers (discussed in Chapter 26, Section 26.4, and Chapter 29, Section 29.1) are compounds that are mirror images and that are not superimposable.

Structural isomers (Section 28.1) Compounds that have the same molecular formula but differ in the way the atoms are bonded together. Several types exist: chain isomers (Section 28.2) are compounds that differ in the arrangement of their carbon chains, functional-group isomers (Section 28.6) are compounds that differ in their functional groups (for example, an alcohol and an ether), and position isomers (Section 28.2) are compounds that have the same carbon chains but differ in the position of a substituent (or a multiple bond) in that chain.

Substitution reaction (Section 28.5) A reaction in which an atom or a group of atoms is substituted for another atom or group of atoms in a molecule.

Unsaturated hydrocarbon (Sections 28.2 and 28.3) A hydrocarbon that contains one or more carbon-carbon multiple bonds.

Problems*

Hydrocarbons

28.1 Write structural formulas for:
(a) 2,3-dimethylpentane
(b) 3-ethyl-3-methyl-1-pentene
(c) 2,5-dimethyl-3-hexyne
(d) 1,2,4-tribromobenzene
(e) *p*-dinitrobenzene
(f) cyclohexene
(g) cyclohexane

28.2 Write structural formulas for:
(a) *trans*-2-hexene
(b) 2,4-dimethyl-3-ethylpentane
(c) 2,4-dimethyl-1,4-pentadiene
(d) 3-isopropyl-1-hexyne
(e) 2,2,3-trichlorobutane
(f) *p*-xylene
(g) 2,3,6-trinitrotoluene

28.3 What is incorrect about each of the following names?
(a) 3-pentene
(b) 1,2-dimethylpropane
(c) 2-methyl-2-butyne
(d) 2-methyl-3-butyne
(e) 3,3-dimethyl-2-butene

28.4 What is incorrect about each of the following names?
(a) 2-ethylpentane
(b) 1,2,6-trichlorobenzene
(c) 4-methyl-3-pentene
(d) 2-methyl-2-pentyne
(e) 3,4-dibromobutane

28.5 Write structural formulas for all the mono-, di-, and tri-substituted chloro- derivatives of propane.

28.6 Write structural formulas for all the isomers that have the formula C_4H_8.

28.7 Write structural formulas for all the isomers that have the formula $C_4H_8Cl_2$.

28.8 Write structural formulas for all the isomers of **(a)** bromophenol, **(b)** dibromophenol, **(c)** tribromobenzene.

28.9 *Ortho*-, *meta*-, and *para*-isomers can be identified by determining the number of compounds that can be derived from each isomer when a third substituent is introduced into the ring (Körner's method). If one nitro group is introduced into the benzene ring of each of the following compounds, how many isomeric compounds would be secured from each? **(a)** *o*-dibromobenzene, **(b)** *m*-dibromobenzene, **(c)** *p*-dibromobenzene.

28.10 Write structural formulas for the ten dichloro substitution isomers of naphthalene.

28.11 For which of the following compounds are *cis*- and *trans*-isomers possible? **(a)** 2,3-dimethyl-2-butene, **(b)** 3-methyl-2-pentene, **(c)** 2-methyl-2-pentene, **(d)** CH(COOH)=CH(COOH)

28.12 *Cis*- and *trans*-isomers are known for certain alkenes. Why do the alkynes not display this type of isomerism?

28.13 What is (are) the product(s) of the reaction of bromine with each of the following? **(a)** methane, **(b)** 2-butene, **(c)** 2-butyne, **(d)** benzene (in the presence of $FeBr_3$).

28.14 Write equations for the reactions of **(a)** H_2 with *cis*-2-pentene, **(b)** H_2 with 2-pentyne, **(c)** HBr with $(CH_3CH_2)_2C$=CH_2, **(d)** HBr with CH_3C≡CH.

28.15 What product would be expected from the following? **(a)** nitration of phenol, **(b)** bromination of phenol, **(c)** nitration of nitrobenzene, **(d)** bromination of nitrobenzene, **(e)** nitration of benzoic acid, **(f)** nitration of bromobenzene, **(g)** nitration of toluene, **(h)** reaction of CH_3Cl with toluene in the presence of $AlCl_3$.

28.16 Write equations to show how the following can be made by means of addition reactions: **(a)** 1,2-dibromo-ethane from ethene, **(b)** 1,1-dibromoethane from ethyne, **(c)** cyclohexanol from cyclohexene.

28.17 **(a)** What is Markovnikov's rule? **(b)** How does the mechanism of the addition of HBr to an alkene explain why such an addition follows Markovnikov's rule?

28.18 Compare and contrast the mechanism of a substitution reaction of an alkane with the mechanism of a substitution reaction of an aromatic hydrocarbon.

Alcohols, Ethers, Carbonyl Compounds, Carboxylic Acids, Esters

28.19 Write structural formulas for: **(a)** butanal, **(b)** 2-butanone, **(c)** methyl ethyl ketone, **(d)** methyl ethyl ether, **(e)** methyl ethanoate, **(f)** benzaldehyde, **(g)** *m*-nitrobenzoic acid.

28.20 Write structural formulas for: **(a)** sodium benzoate, **(b)** phenol, **(c)** 3-methylhexanoic acid, **(d)** 3-methyl-2-hexanone, **(e)** *o*-bromophenol, **(f)** 2-methylpentanal, **(g)** ethyl acetate.

28.21 Name each of the following compounds:

(a) CH_3—$\underset{\underset{\displaystyle CH_3}{|}}{CH}$—$CH_2$—$CH_2$—$CH_2$—$OH$

(b) CH_3—$\underset{\underset{\displaystyle CH_3}{|}}{CH}$—$CH_2$—$\underset{\underset{\displaystyle OH}{|}}{CH}$—$CH_3$

---

* The more difficult problems are marked with asterisks. The appendix contains answers to color-keyed problems.

(c)

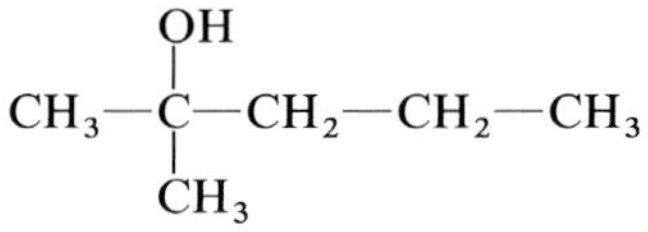

$$CH_3-\underset{\underset{CH_3}{|}}{\overset{\overset{OH}{|}}{C}}-CH_2-CH_2-CH_3$$

(d)

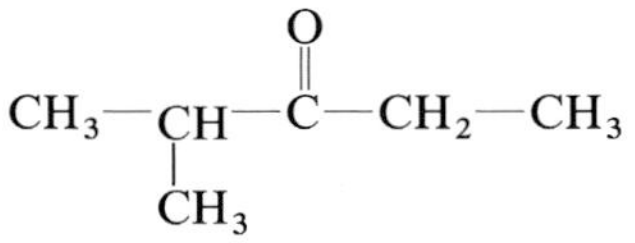

$$CH_3-\underset{\underset{CH_3}{|}}{CH}-\overset{\overset{O}{\|}}{C}-CH_2-CH_3$$

(e) $CH_3-\underset{\underset{CH_3}{|}}{CH}-O-CH_2-CH_3$

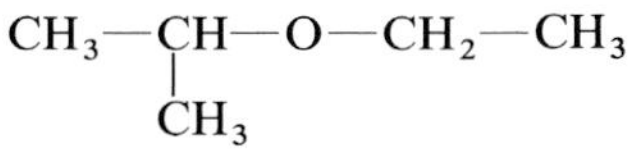

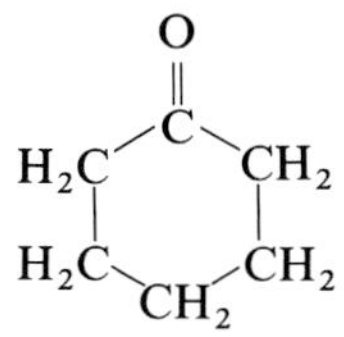

(f)

$$CH_3-\underset{\underset{CH_3}{|}}{CH}-CH_2-CH_2-\overset{\overset{O}{\|}}{C}-H$$

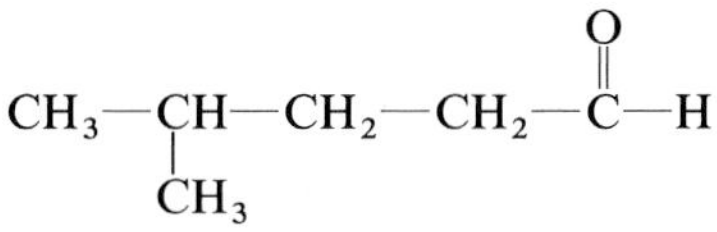

28.22 Name each of the following compounds:

(a)

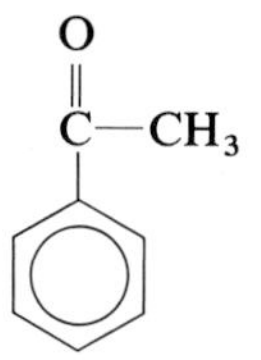

$$\overset{\overset{O}{\|}}{C}-CH_3$$

(b)

$$\overset{\overset{O}{\|}}{C}$$
$H_2C \quad CH_2$
$H_2C \quad CH_2$
CH_2

(c)

$$\overset{\overset{O}{\|}}{C}-O-CH_3$$

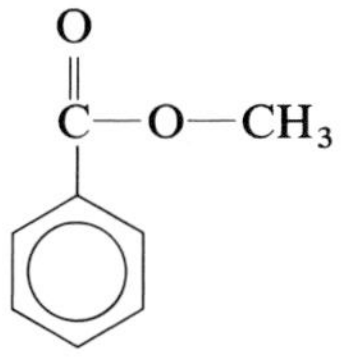

(d)

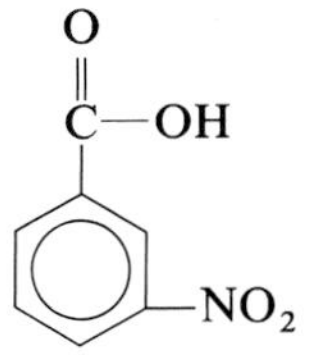

$$\overset{\overset{O}{\|}}{C}-OH$$
$-NO_2$

(e) CH_3
O

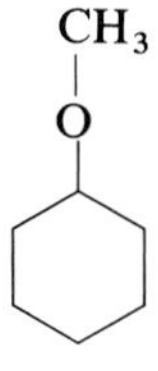

28.23 Write structural formulas for all the isomers that have the formula $C_4H_{10}O$.

28.24 Give an example of an isomer of each of the following: **(a)** ethyl acetate, **(b)** diethyl ether, **(c)** acetone, **(d)** butanal, **(e)** 1-pentanol, **(f)** butanoic acid.

28.25 What is the product of the reaction of 1-bromobutane with each of the following? **(a)** Mg, **(b)** NaCN, **(c)** OH^-(aq), **(d)** $NaOCH_2CH_3$.

28.26 What is the product of the reaction of 2-propanol with each of the following? **(a)** Na, **(b)** H_2SO_4 (high temperature), **(c)** H_2SO_4 (moderate temperature), **(d)** propanoic acid, **(e)** $K_2Cr_2O_7$ in acid solution.

28.27 What are the products when the following compounds are oxidized using vigorous conditions? **(a)** 2-hexene, **(b)** 2-methyl-2-butene, **(c)** 3-hexyne, **(d)** 1-propanol, **(e)** 2-propanol, **(f)** propanal, **(g)** p-nitrotoluene. What are the products when the following compounds are oxidized using mild conditions? **(h)** 2-hexene, **(i)** 1-propanol.

28.28 What are the products when the following compounds are reacted with H_2(g) in the presence of a suitable catalyst? **(a)** pentanal, **(b)** 2-pentanone, **(c)** 2-pentene, **(d)** 2-pentyne.

28.29 State the formulas of all products formed by the reaction of HBr with each of the following. **(a)** CH_3CH_2OH, **(b)** $CH_3CH_2CH_2MgBr$, **(c)** $CH_3CH_2COO^-Na^+$.

28.30 State the compound formed when each of the following is treated with aqueous NaOH: **(a)** $(CH_3)_2CHCOOH$, **(b)** $(CH_3)_2CHBr$, **(c)** $CH_3CH_2CH_2CN$, **(d)** $CH_3CH_2CH_2COOCH_2CH_3$.

28.31 What is the final product (obtained by hydrolysis of the initial product) of the reaction of ethyl magnesium bromide with each of the following? **(a)** methanal, **(b)** butanal, **(c)** butanone.

28.32 What Grignard reagent and what carbonyl compound should be used to prepare each of the following alcohols? **(a)** 3-methyl-2-butanol, **(b)** 2-methyl-2-butanol, **(c)** 2-methyl-1-butanol.

****28.33** Using 1-propanol and 2-propanol as the only organic starting materials, write a series of equations to show how to prepare each of the following. Use a Grignard reagent as one of the steps in each preparation. **(a)** 3-hexanol, **(b)** 2,3-dimethyl-2-butanol, **(c)** 2-methyl-2-pentanol, **(d)** 2-methyl-3-pentanol.

****28.34** Write equations to show how ethanol may be converted into the following substances (more than one step may be required for a given preparation). **(a)** ethene, **(b)** ethanal, **(c)** diethyl ether, **(d)** ethane, **(e)** acetic acid, **(f)** bromoethane, **(g)** ethyl cyanide, **(h)** 2-hydroxypropanoic acid.

Amines, Amides

28.35 Draw structural formulas for: **(a)** diphenylamine, **(b)** methyl ethyl amine, **(c)** 1,6-diaminohexane, **(d)** benzamide, **(e)** p-nitroaniline.

28.36 Draw structural formulas for: **(a)** trimethyl amine, **(b)** acetamide, **(c)** dimethyl propyl amine, **(d)** dimethyl phenylamine, **(e)** 2,6-dimethylaniline.

28.37 Write structural formulas for all the isomers that have the formula $C_4H_{11}N$. Name the compounds.

28.38 Give an example of an isomer of: **(a)** trimethylamine, **(b)** aminoacetic acid, **(c)** propionamide.

28.39 What are the products of the following reactions? **(a)** H_2 and CH_3CN, **(b)** H_2 and p-nitrotoluene, **(c)** 1-bromobutane and methylamine, **(d)** $CH_3COO^-NH_4^+$ heated, **(e)** HBr and $CH_3CH_2COO^-NH_4^+$, **(f)** HBr and $(CH_3CH_2)_2NH$, **(g)** OH^-(aq) and CH_3CH_2CN, **(h)** OH^-(aq) and $CH_3CH_2NH_3^+Cl^-$.

28.40 Write chemical equations to show the reactions of NH_3 with **(a)** 2-bromopropane, **(b)** propanoic acid, **(c)** methyl propanoate.

28.41 Arrange the following compounds in decreasing order of strength as Brønsted bases: CH_3CH_2OH, $CH_3CH_2O^-$, OH^-, CH_3COO^-, $CH_3CH_2NH_2$.

28.42 Arrange the following compounds in decreasing order of strength as Brønsted acids: CH_3CH_2OH, $CH_3CH_2OH_2^+$, H_2O, H_3O^+, CH_3COOH, $CH_3CH_2NH_2$.

Polymers

28.43 Describe with examples: **(a)** addition polymers, **(b)** copolymers, **(c)** condensation polymers.

28.44 Compare the function of $AlCl_3$ in a Friedel-Crafts reaction and in a polymerization.

28.45 What monomers are used to make: **(a)** polyethylene, **(b)** Teflon, **(c)** polystyrene, **(d)** Orlon, **(e)** Nylon, **(f)** rubber, **(g)** Bakelite, **(g)** Dacron.

28.46 Draw the structure of a section of each of the polymers listed in Problem 28.45.

Unclassified Problems

28.47 The general formula for the alkanes is C_nH_{2n+2}. What are the general formulas for the **(a)** alkenes, **(b)** alkynes, **(c)** alkadienes, **(d)** cycloalkanes?

28.48 Define the following: **(a)** olefin, **(b)** homologous series, **(c)** cracking, **(d)** conjugated system, **(e)** addition reaction, **(f)** substitution reaction.

28.49 Draw the resonance forms of **(a)** benzene, **(b)** naphthalene.

28.50. Why do alcohols have higher boiling points than hydrocarbons of corresponding molecular weight?

*28.51 Show by a series of reactions how to convert 1-propanol into 2-propanol.

28.52 Interpret the following in terms of the Lewis theory. **(a)** an S_N1 reaction of an alkyl halide, **(b)** an S_N2 reaction of an alcohol, **(c)** the addition of HCN to a ketone.

28.53 When the terms *primary*, *secondary*, and *tertiary* are applied to amines, their meanings are not the same as when they are applied to alcohols. Explain the distinction.

28.54 (a) Why is phenol a stronger acid than methanol? **(b)** Why is aniline a weaker base than methylamine?

BIOCHEMISTRY

29

Biochemistry is the science that is concerned with the composition and structure of substances that occur in living systems and the chemical reactions that take place in these systems. Impressive progress has been made in this branch of chemistry over the last thirty years. It is currently an area of intense research activity. In this chapter, we will survey some aspects of the field.

The principal component of living material is *water*. It constitutes from about 60% to 90% of all plants and animals. The quantity of inorganic substances present is comparatively small—usually less than 4%; the amount is largest in organisms that have skeletons. The remainder consists of organic compounds, most of which have complicated structures.

The four most abundant elements of the compounds found in living material are oxygen, carbon, hydrogen, and nitrogen. These four elements account for approximately 96% of the mass of the human body.

29.1 Proteins

Proteins are macromolecules that have molecular weights ranging from about 6000 to over 1,000,000. They are formed from simpler compounds called **α-amino acids.** An α-amino acid is a carboxylic acid that has an amino group, $-NH_2$, bonded to the C atom next to the carboxyl group, $-COOH$. The designation α (alpha) denotes the position of the amino group. The C atom adjacent to the carboxyl group is called the α-carbon atom. The general formula of these compounds is

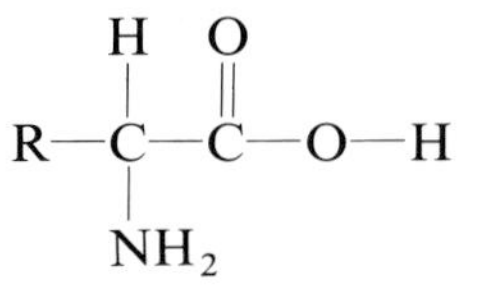

$$
\begin{array}{c}
\quad\;\; H \quad\; O \\
\quad\;\; | \quad\quad \| \\
R-C-C-O-H \\
\quad\;\; | \\
\quad\; NH_2
\end{array}
$$

The $-NH_2$ group is basic and will react with acids to form $-NH_3^+$. At a low pH, therefore, an amino acid exists as a cation, which will move toward the negative pole in an electric field:

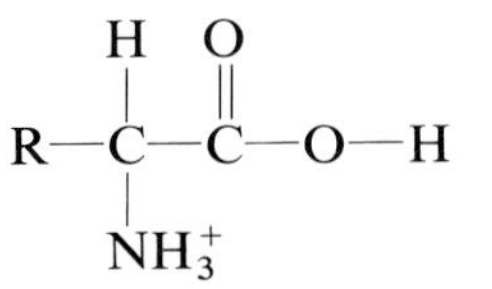

$$
\begin{array}{c}
\quad\;\; H \quad\; O \\
\quad\;\; | \quad\quad \| \\
R-C-C-O-H \\
\quad\;\; | \\
\quad\; NH_3^+
\end{array}
$$

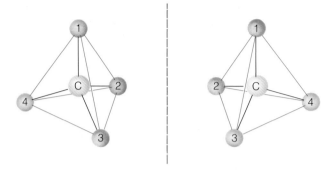

Figure 29.1 Optical isomers of a compound containing a chiral carbon atom (dashes represent reflection plane)

The —COOH group is acidic and forms —COO$^-$ with bases. At a high pH, therefore, amino acids are anions and move toward the positive pole in an electric field:

$$
\begin{array}{c}
\quad\;\; H \quad O \\
\quad\;\; | \quad\;\; \| \\
R-C-C-O^- \\
\quad\;\; | \\
\quad\; NH_2
\end{array}
$$

Internal neutralization, in which the proton from the —COOH group moves to the —NH$_2$ group, produces a **zwitterion**:

$$
\begin{array}{c}
\quad\;\; H \quad O \\
\quad\;\; | \quad\;\; \| \\
R-C-C-O^- \\
\quad\;\; | \\
\quad\; NH_3^+
\end{array}
$$

The amino acids provide examples of a type of stereoisomerism called **optical isomerism** (see Section 26.4). The simplest optical isomers are compounds that contain chiral carbon atoms—carbon atoms to which four different kinds of groups are bonded (see Figure 29.1). The mirror image (called an **enantiomorph**) of a molecule of this type is not superimposable on the original molecule.

The structures shown in Figure 29.1 are mirror reflections of one another. The dashed line represents the reflection plane. Start with any group (1, 2, 3, or 4) of the structure on the left and trace the shortest distance to the reflection plane. Continue to the right of the reflection plane for the same distance, and the same group will be found in the structure on the right.

A study of this figure reveals that the two structures cannot be superimposed. If groups 1 and 3 of the structures are superimposed, group 4 of one structure coincides with group 2 (not 4) of the other. No matter how the two structures are turned, it is impossible to make all four groups of one structure coincide with the same four groups, respectively, of the other structure. The two structures are isomers.

The physical properties of optical isomers are identical except for their effects on plane-polarized light (see Figure 26.7). The isomers are said to be optically active because they rotate the plane of plane-polarized light in either a clockwise or a counterclockwise direction. The isomer that rotates the plane to the right (clockwise) is said to be *dextro*rotatory, (+) or *d*. The other isomer rotates the plane an equal amount to the left and is said to be *levo*rotatory, (−) or *l*.

With the exception of glycine (for which R equals H), the α-carbon atoms of all α-amino acids have four different kinds of groups bonded to them and are, therefore, chiral. Consequently, optical isomers exist for the α-amino acids. The structures of the isomers are usually diagrammed

$$
\begin{array}{cc}
\underset{\text{L-}\textit{amino acid}}{\overset{\displaystyle \overset{\text{O}}{\underset{\parallel}{\text{C}}}-\text{OH}}{\underset{\displaystyle \text{R}}{\text{H}_2\text{N}-\text{C}-\text{H}}}}
&
\underset{\text{D-}\textit{amino acid}}{\overset{\displaystyle \overset{\text{O}}{\underset{\parallel}{\text{C}}}-\text{OH}}{\underset{\displaystyle \text{R}}{\text{H}-\text{C}-\text{NH}_2}}}
\end{array}
$$

The diagrams represent structures in which the chiral carbon atoms are in the plane of the paper, the —COOH and —R groups are behind the plane of the paper, and the —H and —NH$_2$ groups are in front of the plane of the paper. With such an arrangement of groups, the L-form is the one in which the amino group is to the left of the chain, and the D-form is the one in which the amino group is to the right. The structures can be related to the diagrams of Figure 29.1. The L-form is the one on the left in the figure if group 1 = —COOH, 2 = —R, 3 = —H, and 4 = —NH$_2$.

All the amino acids derived from proteins are L-amino acids. Only the L-forms can be utilized in the metabolic processes of the body. The sign of rotation should not be confused with the symbols D- or L- that are used to designate the configuration of the chiral carbon atom. Thus, the L-isomer of alanine (2-aminopropanoic acid) is *dextro*rotatory (+):

$$
\underset{\text{L-}(+)\text{-}\textit{alanine}}{\overset{\displaystyle \overset{\text{O}}{\underset{\parallel}{\text{C}}}-\text{OH}}{\underset{\displaystyle \text{CH}_3}{\text{H}_2\text{N}-\text{C}-\text{H}}}}
$$

In protein molecules, many amino acid units are linked together to form long chains. When two amino acids combine, the amino group of one molecule joins, with the elimination of water, to the carboxyl group of the second molecule. A **peptide linkage,**

$$
-\overset{\displaystyle \overset{\text{O}}{\parallel}}{\text{C}}-\underset{\displaystyle \text{H}}{\text{N}}-
$$

is formed:

$$H-N-C-C:O-H: + :H:N-C-C-O-H \longrightarrow$$

$$H-N-C-C-N-C-C-O-H + H_2O$$

The product, called a **dipeptide,** has a free amino group at one end and a free carboxyl group at the other. It can condense with other amino acids to form long chains called **polypeptides.** Proteins are polypeptides. The hydrolysis of a polypeptide is the reverse of the condensation process and produces amino acids.

The radicals, R, in the preceding formulas vary considerably in their structures. Some of them are simple hydrocarbons, some contain rings (including aromatic rings), some contain additional —NH$_2$ or —COOH groups, and some incorporate —SH or —OH groups in their structures. Twenty different α-amino acids are regularly found in proteins. A few others are occasionally found as minor constituents.

Proteins contain from about 50 to over 10,000 amino acid residues in a chain. The average molecular weight of an amino acid residue is about 110 to 120. A protein with a molecular weight of 300,000, therefore, contains roughly 300,000/120 or 2500 amino acid residues.

The amino acids in a given protein occur in a definite order. The same type of amino acid may be used many times in the polypeptide chain. Since a protein may contain hundreds or thousands of amino acid residues, a tremendous number of arrangements is possible even though only about 20 different amino acids are used.

The sequence of amino acid residues in a protein is called its **primary structure.** The primary structure of bovine insulin was determined in 1945–52 by Frederick Sanger. A fragment of the structure is shown in Figure 29.2. The complete structure contains 51 amino acid residues in two connected chains—one of 21 amino acid residues and the other of 30.

The spatial arrangement of the polypeptide chain of a protein is called the **secondary structure** of the protein. The most important arrangement is the **alpha helix.** In an α-helix, the chain is coiled in a form that resembles a spring (see Figure 29.3). There are about 3.6 amino acid residues in each turn. The helix is held together by hydrogen bonds between the loops of the coil. The hydrogen bonds are formed by the H atom of the N—H of one peptide group with the O atom of the C=O group of another peptide group (see Figure 29.3). Each peptide group is joined, by hydrogen bonding, to the third peptide group before it and the third peptide group following it.

Another type of secondary structure is the **pleated sheet** arrangement. Chains are held together in the form of pleated sheets by hydrogen bonds between adjacent chains. This arrangement is not so common as the α-helix arrangement.

The **tertiary structure** of a protein is the arrangement of the secondary structures brought about by interactions between the R groups of the amino acid residues.

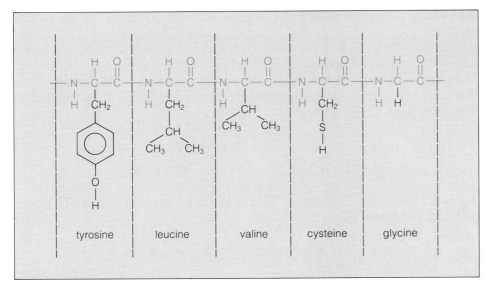

Figure 29.2 Fragment of bovine insulin protein chain. (The polypeptide chain is shown in color. The R radicals are shown in black. The names of the amino acids that make up the chains appear at the bottom.)

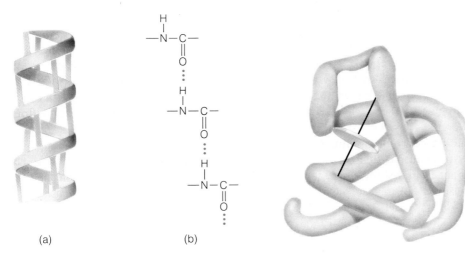

Figure 29.3 (a) Schematic representation for an α-helix. (The colored lines are hydrogen bonds.) (b) Hydrogen bonds between coils of an α-helix.

Figure 29.4 Tertiary structure of a globular protein. (The colored disc is an iron-containing heme group.)

The structure of a globular protein (so called because these proteins are usually approximately spherical in shape) is shown schematically in Figure 29.4.

The interactions that hold the coiled segments of the chain into a compact tertiary form do not involve the peptide linkages of the chain. Instead, these interactions take place between substituents of the R groups of the amino acid residues:

1. Some R radicals contain a —COOH group over and above the one involved in peptide formation. Other R radicals contain a second —NH$_2$ group. These two functional groups—one attached to one segment of the coil, the other attached to another segment—can react:

$$\underset{\substack{\displaystyle \| \\ O}}{-C}-O-H + H_2N- \longrightarrow \underset{\substack{\displaystyle \| \\ O}}{-C}-O^- + {}^+H_3N-$$

2. By mild oxidation, a disulfide linkage can form between two —SH groups attached to different places on the coil:

$$-S-H + H-S- \longrightarrow -S-S- + 2\,H^+ + 2e^-$$

3. Substituent groups can hydrogen-bond to one another:

$$\begin{array}{c} O- \\ | \\ -O\cdots H \\ | \\ H \end{array}$$

These interactions occur in places where the coils overlap.

The primary, secondary, and tertiary structures describe the arrangement of a single polypeptide chain. Some proteins contain more than one chain. The number of chains and the way in which they are arranged in the complete protein make up what is called the **quaternary structure** of the protein. For example, hemoglobin, the oxygen carrier in blood, is formed from four chains of two different types. Two of the chains each contain 140 amino acid residues. Each of the other two contains 146 amino acid residues. Each of the four chains has an iron-containing heme group (see Section 26.1) and has a tertiary structure similar to that shown in Figure 29.4.

29.2 Carbohydrates

Sugars, starches, and cellulose belong to a group of organic compounds called carbohydrates. The name was derived from the fact that most (but not all) compounds of this type have the general formula $C_x(H_2O)_y$, and might, therefore, appear to be hydrates of carbon. Carbohydrates, however, do not contain water. They are hydroxy aldehydes, hydroxy ketones, or substances derived from them. Carbohydrates are the principal substances of which plants are composed. They are an important food for animals—they serve as a source of energy and provide carbon chains for compounds that are synthesized by living organisms.

The simplest carbohydrates are the monosaccharides, or simple sugars. The most important monosaccharide is *glucose*. It is the most abundant sugar found in nature, and in animals it is a normal constituent of blood. The two optical isomers of glucose are

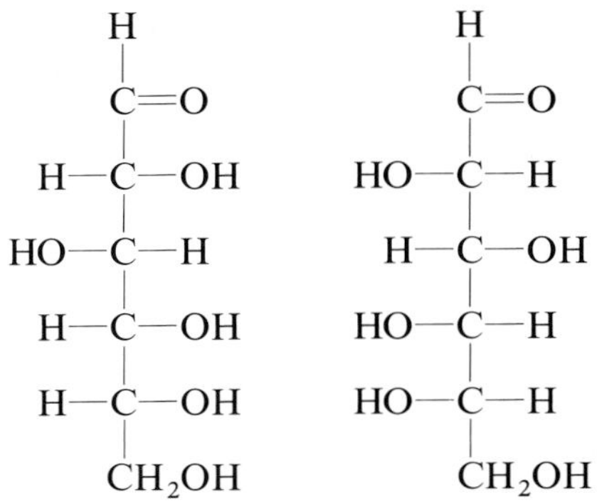

$$
\begin{array}{ccc}
& H & \\
& | & \\
& C{=}O & \\
H{-}C{-}OH & & HO{-}C{-}H \\
HO{-}C{-}H & & H{-}C{-}OH \\
H{-}C{-}OH & & HO{-}C{-}H \\
H{-}C{-}OH & & HO{-}C{-}H \\
& CH_2OH & CH_2OH
\end{array}
$$

D-(+)-*glucose*   L-(−)-*glucose*

There are four chiral carbon atoms in the molecule. The carbon atoms at each end of the molecule do not hold four different groups and are not chiral. Sixteen optical isomers (eight D,L pairs) of this formula exist. Only the preceding pair are called glucose.

D-glucose forms a cyclic molecule by an addition reaction involving the carbonyl group and a hydroxy group:

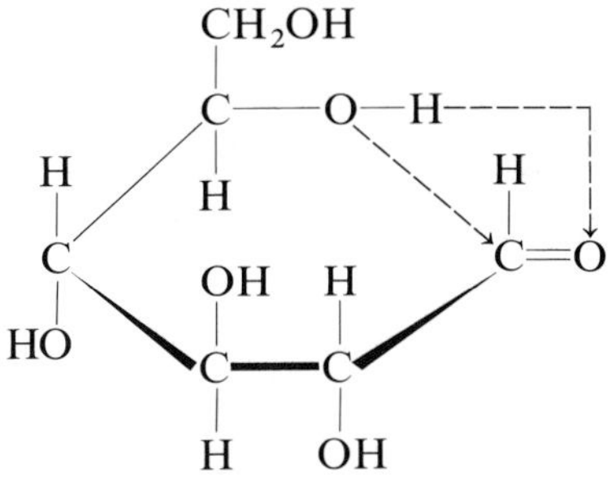

$$
\begin{array}{c}
CH_2OH \\
| \\
C{-}O{-}H{-}\cdots \\
H \\
C \quad\quad C{=}O \\
HO \quad OH \quad H \\
C{-}C \\
H \quad OH
\end{array}
$$

Ring formation produces a new chiral center, and two isomers of D-glucose exist which differ in the orientation of the new OH group:

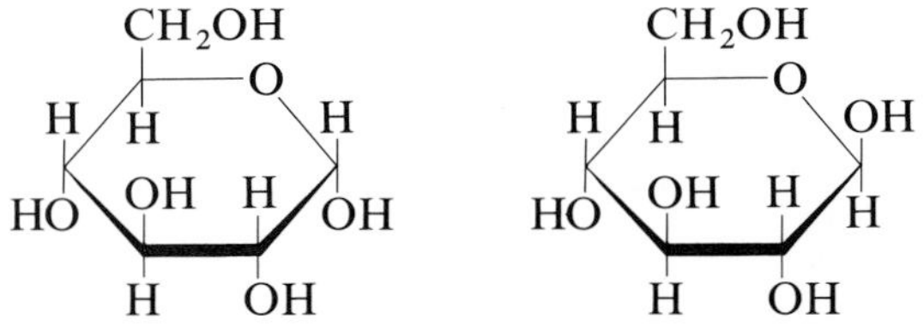

α-D-*glucose*   β-D-*glucose*

In these diagrams the carbon atoms of the ring are not shown. The rings are actually puckered, not planar. Notice that in the α form the OH group of the extreme right-hand carbon atom is on the same side of the ring as the OH group of the adjacent carbon atom. These OH groups may be said to be *cis* to each other. In aqueous solution, α and β forms of D-glucose exist in equilibrium, together with a low concentration of the open-chain form.

Fructose is a hydroxy ketone:

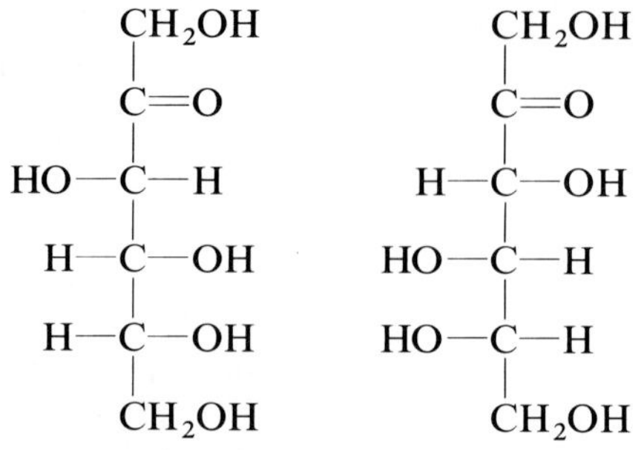

$$
\begin{array}{cc}
\mathrm{CH_2OH} & \mathrm{CH_2OH} \\
\mathrm{C}{=}\mathrm{O} & \mathrm{C}{=}\mathrm{O} \\
\mathrm{HO}{-}\mathrm{C}{-}\mathrm{H} & \mathrm{H}{-}\mathrm{C}{-}\mathrm{OH} \\
\mathrm{H}{-}\mathrm{C}{-}\mathrm{OH} & \mathrm{HO}{-}\mathrm{C}{-}\mathrm{H} \\
\mathrm{H}{-}\mathrm{C}{-}\mathrm{OH} & \mathrm{HO}{-}\mathrm{C}{-}\mathrm{H} \\
\mathrm{CH_2OH} & \mathrm{CH_2OH} \\
\text{D-(−)-\textit{fructose}} & \text{L-(+)-\textit{fructose}}
\end{array}
$$

There are three chiral carbon atoms in this molecule and eight stereoisomers (or four D,L pairs) of this formula are known. Cyclic forms of D-fructose are known with five- or six-membered rings.

Disaccharides are composed of two monosaccharide units. *Sucrose*, which is cane sugar, is a disaccharide. Acid hydrolysis of sucrose yields the two simple sugars D-glucose and D-fructose. In the sucrose molecule an α D-glucose unit and the β five-membered ring form of a D-fructose unit are joined through two OH groups by the elimination of a molecule of water:

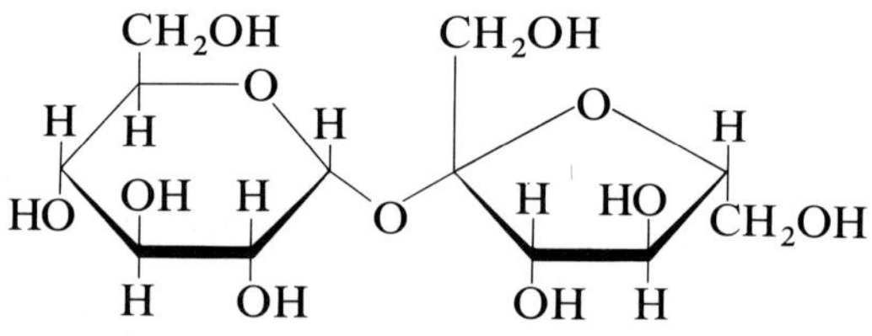

D-*glucose unit*   D-*fructose unit*

Cellulose and the substances that make up starch are polysaccharides (carbohydrates that contain many monosaccharide units) and they yield only D-glucose upon hydrolysis. It is estimated that the number of D-glucose units in the molecular structures of these substances may be as high as several thousand. The D-glucose units of cellulose are linked in long chains in β combination:

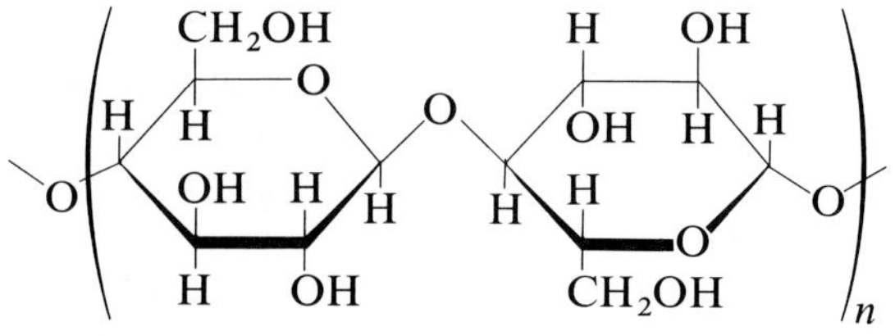

In starch, the D-glucose units are linked in a different manner; there are occasional cross links between long chains of D-glucose units arranged in α combination:

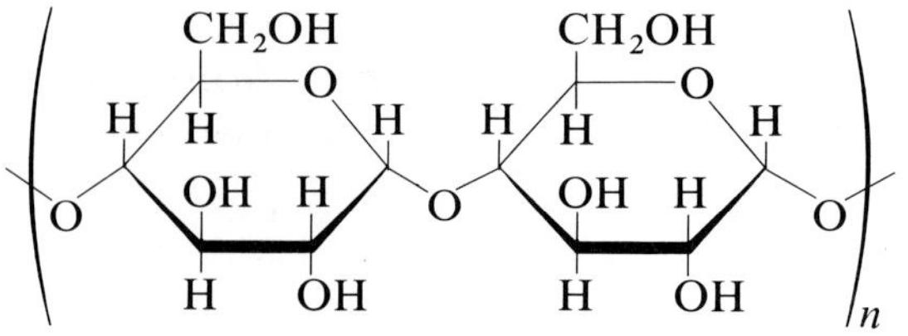

Starch is an important food material, but cellulose cannot be digested by man—an important distinction brought about by the difference in the way that the D-glucose units are linked together.

29.3 Fats and Oils

Fats and oils belong to a larger classification called lipids. Lipids are substances that can be dissolved away from biological material by solvents that are nonpolar or slightly polar (such as hydrocarbons, carbon tetrachloride, and diethyl ether). Since the classification is based on solubility, not structure, a wide variety of compounds are lipids. Fats, oils, some vitamins and hormones, and certain constituents of the cell walls are examples of some of the substances classified as lipids.

Fats and oils are esters of fatty acids and glycerol. The fatty acids are long straight-chain carboxylic acids (see Table 29.1). Some of them are saturated and some contain one or more carbon-carbon double bonds. Almost all the fatty acids isolated from natural sources contain an even number of carbon atoms.

Glycerol is a trihydroxy alcohol, 1,2,3-propanetriol:

$$H-O-CH_2$$
$$H-O-CH$$
$$H-O-CH_2$$

The esters formed from 1 mol of glycerol and 3 mol of fatty acid:

$$\overset{O}{\overset{\|}{R-C-O-H}}$$

Table 29.1 Some common fatty acids		
Saturated Acids		
Acid	Formula	Occurrence
lauric	$CH_3(CH_2)_{10}COOH$	coconut oil, palm oil, animal fat
myristic	$CH_3(CH_2)_{12}COOH$	coconut oil, palm oil, animal fat
palmitic	$CH_3(CH_2)_{14}COOH$	animal fat, cottonseed oil, palm oil
stearic	$CH_3(CH_2)_{16}COOH$	animal fat
Unsaturated Acids		
Acid	Formula	Positions of Double Bonds[a]	Occurrence
oleic	$C_{17}H_{33}COOH$	9	corn oil, cottonseed oil, olive oil
linoleic	$C_{17}H_{31}COOH$	9, 12	cottonseed oil, corn oil, linseed oil
linolenic	$C_{17}H_{29}COOH$	9, 12, 15	linseed oil
arachidonic	$C_{19}H_{31}COOH$	5, 8, 11, 14	sardine oil, corn oil, animal fat

[a] All these acids have straight chains. The carbon atom of the COOH group is number 1. The number given in the table indicates the first carbon of the double bond. Number 9, for example, indicates a double bond between carbon atoms 9 and 10.

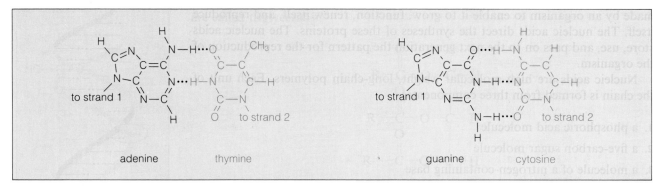

Figure 29.7 The four base radicals found in DNA. (The formulas are drawn in complementary pairs.)

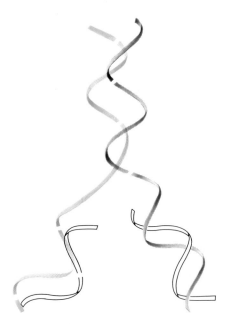

Figure 29.8 Replication of DNA double helix. (The strands unwind and each serves as a template for the synthesis of a new complementary strand.)

Consequently, they hold the two chains of the double helix a uniform distance apart.

When a cell divides, the two chains of a DNA double helix come apart. Each chain serves as a template, or pattern, for the synthesis of a new, complementary chain. Two identical double helices result from the process—each one containing one of the chains of the original double helix (see Figure 29.8).

Nucleotides from the surrounding solution form the new chains. The base of a nucleotide pairs with the complementary base of the DNA chain through the formation of hydrogen bonds. The nucleotides line up, therefore, in a way that is dictated by the order in which the bases occur in the DNA chain. The new chains formed from the nucleotides are complementary to the original DNA chains.

The order in which the bases occur in a DNA molecule constitutes the information used for the synthesis of proteins. Two types of RNA are used for these processes: messenger RNA and transfer RNA. RNA employs the same bases that DNA does with the exception of thymine. In RNA, uracil (U) is used in place of thymine (T). The structure of uracil is the same as that of thymine except that a H atom replaces the —CH₃ group. U, therefore, complements A in the same way that T does (see Figure 29.7).

An RNA chain is synthesized from nucleotides in the nucleus of the cell in such a way that the order of bases in the RNA chain complements the order of a section of the DNA chain. The DNA chain, therefore, acts as a template. Suppose, for example, that the order of bases of a small portion of the DNA chain is

C—C—A—A—C—G

The order of bases in the RNA chain that is made by using this part of the DNA chain as a pattern is

G—G—U—U—G—C

since G complements C and U complements A.

The chain formed in this way is called messenger RNA. A messenger RNA chain may contain about 500 bases in an order dictated by a *section* of a DNA chain, which contains altogether more than 100 million bases. The information in the section of the DNA chain (the order of bases) is said to be transcribed by the messenger RNA. This information is the message that the messenger carries from the cell nucleus to the ribosomes, where the protein is made.

The order of bases directs the order in which different amino acids are assembled in the formation of the protein. Each amino acid of the protein is specified by a set of three base groups (a base triplet) of the messenger RNA chain. The sequence

G—G—U—U—G—C

pertains to two amino acids. The code G—G—U specifies the amino acid glycine. The code U—G—C specifies the amino acid cysteine. The portion of the messenger RNA chain that contains the three bases of a code is called a codon. The preceding sequence described two codons.

A second type of RNA, called transfer RNA, is used to decipher the code and build the protein. Transfer RNA chains are the smallest nucleic acid chains. They consist of approximately 80 nucleotides and may contain a few bases other than the customary four.

A particular transfer RNA molecule bonds with a specific amino acid and carries it to the messenger RNA where it is inserted into the protein being made at the position directed by the code of the messenger RNA. The transfer RNA is said to translate the code. Each transfer RNA contains a base triplet (called an anticodon) that complements the triplet of a codon of messenger RNA. The anticodon of a particular transfer RNA corresponds to the specific amino acid that it carries.

Suppose, for example, that the codon of messenger RNA specifies the code GGU. The anticodon CCA that corresponds to this codon is found on transfer RNA that carries the amino acid glycine.

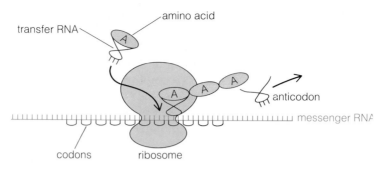

Figure 29.9 Synthesis of a protein by transfer RNA on messenger RNA.

The synthesis of a protein is thought to occur in steps (see Figure 29.9). Transfer RNA carrying an amino acid becomes attached to the messenger RNA by codon-anticodon pairing. A second transfer RNA becomes attached to the next codon of the messenger RNA chain. A peptide linkage is formed between the two amino acids of the two transfer RNA's. The first transfer RNA is then released and leaves behind its amino acid now bound into a dipeptide. A third transfer RNA, of a type specified by the next codon, becomes attached to the messenger RNA. As soon as a peptide bond connects the dipeptide to the amino acid of the third transfer RNA, the second transfer RNA is released. The process stops when a codon that does not correspond to any amino acid is encountered. The synthesis of more than one protein is directed by a single messenger RNA.

Specific enzymes catalyze every step of the entire process including the formation of the messenger RNA and the bonding of an amino acid to the transfer RNA. Formation of the polypeptides is rapid. It is estimated that hundreds of peptide bonds are formed in 1 min.

Any change in the DNA of the cell will result in a change in the messenger RNA produced from it and, consequently, an alteration in the resulting protein. Such changes are called **mutations.** The changes may prove to be beneficial, harmful, or trivial. They are passed on from generation to generation. Mutations are responsible for genetic diseases, such as Tay-Sachs disease, sickle-cell anemia, hemophilia, and Huntington's chorea.

29.5 Enzymes

Enzymes are biological catalysts. The term is derived from a Greek word that means *in leaven* since the action of yeast in fermentation was the first enzymatic action identified. Enzymes are involved in every reaction that occurs in a cell.

A cell contains over 1000 enzymes. A large number is required because enzymes are **specific** in their action. Some are so specific that they catalyze only one reaction of one particular compound. Enzymes are known that will hydrolyze only one definite type of peptide bond—one that involves a particular kind of amino acid residue. The enzymes that are least specific are probably those that hydrolyze most ester linkages.

Some enzymes are **stereochemically specific.** Such an enzyme might act on only the L form of an amino acid and not the D form, or an enzyme might be active only toward β linkages between glucose units of a carbohydrate and not α linkages.

Enzymes are amazingly efficient. The turnover number of an enzyme is the number of moles of reactant transformed in 1 min by the action of one mole of the enzyme. Turnover numbers vary from about 10,000 mol/min to 5,000,000 mol/min. Since these values are so high, only a small amount of each enzyme is required by a cell.

The action of enzymes permits the cell reactions to occur rapidly at the relatively low temperature of the body and at a pH near 7. When comparable reactions are run in the laboratory without the aid of enzymes, they require higher temperatures and the addition of acids or bases.

The substrate of an enzyme is the compound upon which it acts. If E is used to designate the enzyme, S the substrate, and P the product of the reaction, the overall process can be indicated as follows:

$$E + S \rightleftharpoons ES \longrightarrow E + P$$

ES, formed from the enzyme and the substrate, may be considered to be the activated complex for the reaction. The catalytic effect is brought about by a significant lowering of the energy of activation for the reaction (see Section 14.7).

Enzymes are surface catalysts. They are globular proteins and are much larger than the substrate upon which they act. Reaction occurs at an active site on the surface of the enzyme. The substrate is held to the active site by hydrogen bonding, ionic attraction, or some other type of chemical interaction.

The contour of an active site fits the shape of the substrate exactly, or more probably, the active site changes its conformation to fit the substrate molecule after it is attached. In the process, bonds within the substrate are stretched and weakened. In this way, the reaction is facilitated. After the products of the reaction leave, the active site is free to bind another substrate molecule.

Enzymes are specific in their action because they function by means of active sites that are tailored to fit a specific substrate or type of substrate. The stereochemical specificity of some enzymes is a result of the conformation of their active sites—the L form of a molecule might fit and the D form might not.

Even though the reaction occurs on a relatively small part of the surface—the active site—the rest of the enzyme molecule is important. It probably helps to form the active site into the required conformation and to hold it that way until after the reaction has occurred.

Most enzymes are conjugated proteins, that is, they contain nonprotein parts together with protein parts. If the nonprotein part is not easily removed, it is called a prosthetic group. If it is easily removed, it is called a coenzyme. Neither the coenzyme nor the protein part from which it is removed is active when the two are separated. Prosthetic groups and coenzymes are important because they help to form the active sites of enzymes. Many coenzymes are vitamins or compounds derived from vitamins. Some enzymes require the presence of metal ions (such as Co^{2+}, Fe^{2+}, Zn^{2+}, Cu^{2+}, and Mg^{2+}) to function.

The action of enzymes can be inhibited, or retarded, in several ways. An inhibitor is a substance that combines with an enzyme at the active site and prevents the enzyme from functioning. In competitive inhibition, the enzyme, E, and the inhibitor, I, combine reversibly:

$$E + I \rightleftharpoons EI$$

The combination of the enzyme and substrate is also reversible:

$$E + S \rightleftharpoons ES$$

The concentrations of S and I determine the amounts of ES and EI formed. Since the desired reaction depends upon the formation of ES, the reaction can be slowed down or stopped altogether if the concentration of I is relatively high.

The product of a reaction may serve as an inhibitor. **Product inhibition** is important since it serves to control the extent of reactions that occur in a cell. As the concentration of the product of some reactions increases, product inhibition gradually slows the reaction down and prevents an undesirable accumulation of product in the cell.

If a process occurs in a series of steps:

$$A \longrightarrow B \longrightarrow C \longrightarrow D$$

control of the entire sequence can be achieved if a product of the last step (D) inhibits a previous step (say, A → B). Such inhibition is called **feedback inhibition.** It too controls the amounts of materials produced in a cell.

If an inhibitor combines with an enzyme in an irreversible manner, the effect is called **noncompetitive inhibition**:

$$E + I \longrightarrow EI$$

The substrate cannot displace this type of inhibitor from the active site. Many poisons work by inhibiting enzyme reactions that are necessary for life processes.

Some drugs are competitive inhibitors. Antibiotics probably work by inhibiting enzyme reactions that are required by microorganisms. Sulfanilamide is believed to act as an inhibitor of an enzyme for which the substrate is *p*-aminobenzoic acid:

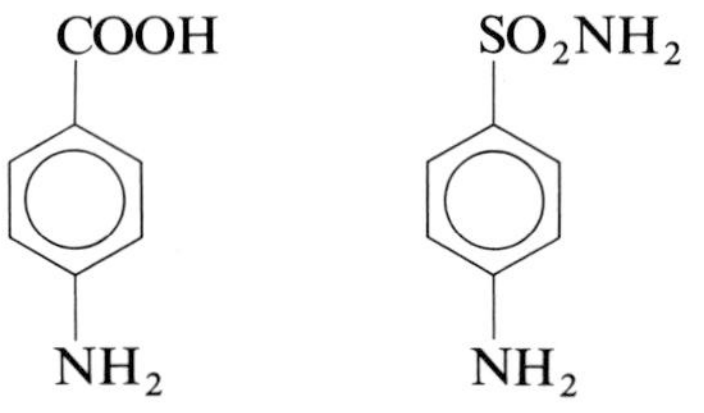

p-aminobenzoic acid   *sulfanilamide*

Notice the similarity between the structures of the two compounds, which compete for the active site. Certain microorganisms utilize the enzymatic reaction of *p*-aminobenzoic acid. Inhibition of the reaction by sulfanilamide causes the death of these microorganisms.

Many insecticides and herbicides are effective because they are enzymatic inhibitors.

29.6 Metabolism

Metabolism is a general term that refers to all the reactions that occur in a living organism. Metabolic reactions are divided into two groups:

1. Catabolic processes are those in which substances are broken down into simpler substances. These reactions provide the energy required by the organism. They also produce simple compounds from which larger ones are made.

2. Anabolic processes are those in which large molecules are synthesized from smaller ones. These processes require energy and produce substances needed for the reproduction and survival of the organism.

The primary source of energy for all life is the light from the sun. In photosynthesis, the chlorophyll of plants absorbs sunlight, which is used as a source of energy to bring about the manufacture of carbohydrates from CO_2 and H_2O. In this way, energy of the sun is stored as chemical energy in the plants. Humans obtain the energy required to sustain life from their food, which comes from plants or from animals that have been fed on plants.

A large amount of energy is liberated by the oxidation of glucose and other substances derived from food. If 1 mol of glucose is oxidized to CO_2 and H_2O, about 2870 kJ of energy is liberated. In the body, the oxidation is conducted gradually, in a controlled manner, through a sequence of many steps. Each step is catalyzed by an enzyme and involves a comparatively small energy effect. Enzymes cannot function at temperatures much higher than body temperature.

A part of the energy from the oxidation of glucose is dissipated as heat, which maintains body temperature. About 44% of the total energy available, however, is captured and stored. The energy is stored in high-energy molecules. The most important molecule of this type is adenosine triphosphate, or ATP:

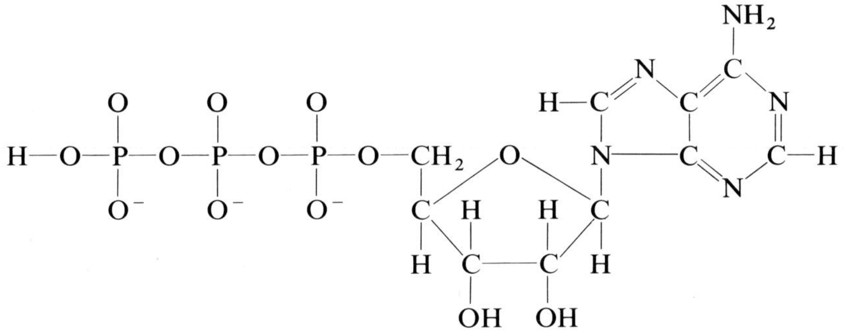

ATP is prepared from adenosine diphosphate, ADP. The structures of the two compounds are the same except that ATP has three phosphate groups and ADP has two:

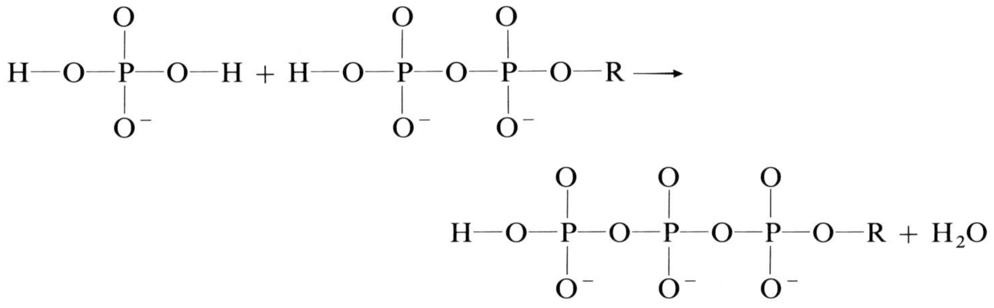

In this equation, R is used to indicate the organic part of the molecules.

The free energy change for the preparation of ATP from ADP is about $+33$ kJ/mol—which means that energy is required and the reaction will not occur by itself. In the cell, the reaction is coupled with another reaction that liberates more energy than the preparation of ATP requires. The overall change in free energy for the coupled reactions is negative. The following figures are typical:

such a way that the mantissa is positive. Thus,

$$\text{antilog}\,(-3.158) = \text{antilog}\,(0.842 - 4)$$
$$= 6.95 \times 10^{-4}$$

or

$$-3.158 = \log\,(6.95 \times 10^{-4})$$

Since logarithms are exponents, mathematical operations involving logarithms follow the rules for the use of exponents. When each of the following operations is performed, the logarithms of the values involved are found, the logarithms are treated as indicated, and the antilogarithm of the result is secured as the final answer.

1. *Multiplication.* $\qquad\qquad \log\,(ab) = \log a + \log b$

2. *Division.* $\qquad\qquad\quad \log\,(a/b) = \log a - \log b$

3. *Extraction of a root.* $\quad \log\,(a^{1/n}) = \dfrac{1}{n}\log a$

4. *Raising to a power.* $\quad\; \log\,(a^n) = n \log a$

Logarithms that employ the base 10 are called common logarithms. Natural logarithms (abbreviated 1n) employ the base e, where

$$e = 2.71828 \ldots$$

The relation between natural logarithms and common logarithms is

$$\ln a = 2.303 \log a$$

Thus, to find the natural logarithm of 6.040, we multiply the common logarithm of 6.040 by 2.303:

$$\ln 6.040 = 2.303 \log 6.040$$
$$= 2.303(0.7810)$$
$$= 1.7986$$

Logarithms can be used to evaluate an expression of the type e^n, where e is the base of natural logarithms. Since

$$\ln a = 2.303 \log a$$
$$\log a = \frac{\ln a}{2.303}$$

and since

$$\ln e^n = n$$
$$\log e^n = \frac{n}{2.303}$$

Therefore,

$$e^n = \text{antilog} \frac{n}{2.303}$$

For example, the value of $e^{2.209}$ can be found in the following way:

$$e^{2.209} = \text{antilog} \frac{2.209}{2.303} = \text{antilog } 0.9590$$

$$= 9.100$$

C.4 Quadratic Equations

An algebraic equation in the form

$$ax^2 + bx + c = 0$$

is called a **quadratic equation** in one variable. An equation of this type has two solutions given by the **quadratic formula**

$$x = \frac{-b \pm \sqrt{b^2 - 4ac}}{2a}$$

When the quadratic formula is used to find the answer to a chemical problem, two solutions are obtained. One of them, however, must be discarded because it represents a physical impossibility.

Assume that x in the equation

$$x^2 + 0.50\, x - 0.15 = 0$$

is the number of moles of a gas that dissociate under a given set of conditions. The values of the coefficients are: $a = 1$, $b = 0.50$, and $c = -0.15$; and

$$x = \frac{-0.50 \pm \sqrt{(0.50)^2 - 4(1)(-0.15)}}{2(1)}$$

$$x = \frac{-0.50 \pm 0.92}{2}$$

$$x = +0.21,\ -0.71$$

The value -0.71 is discarded because a negative amount of a substance is physically impossible.

	0	1	2	3	4	5	6	7	8	9
10	0000	0043	0086	0128	0170	0212	0253	0294	0334	0374
11	0414	0453	0492	0531	0569	0607	0645	0682	0719	0755
12	0792	0828	0864	0899	0934	0969	1004	1038	1072	1106
13	1139	1173	1206	1239	1271	1303	1335	1367	1399	1430
14	1461	1492	1523	1553	1584	1614	1644	1673	1703	1732
15	1761	1790	1818	1847	1875	1903	1931	1959	1987	2014
16	2041	2068	2095	2122	2148	2175	2201	2227	2253	2279
17	2304	2330	2355	2380	2405	2430	2455	2480	2504	2529
18	2553	2577	2601	2625	2648	2672	2695	2718	2742	2765
19	2788	2810	2833	2856	2878	2900	2923	2945	2967	2989
20	3010	3032	3054	3075	3096	3118	3139	3160	3181	3201
21	3222	3243	3263	3284	3304	3324	3345	3365	3385	3404
22	3424	3444	3464	3483	3502	3522	3541	3560	3579	3598
23	3617	3636	3655	3674	3692	3711	3729	3747	3766	3784
24	3802	3820	3838	3856	3874	3892	3909	3927	3945	3962
25	3979	3997	4014	4031	4048	4065	4082	4099	4116	4133
26	4150	4166	4183	4200	4216	4232	4249	4265	4281	4298
27	4314	4330	4346	4362	4378	4393	4409	4425	4440	4456
28	4472	4487	4502	4518	4533	4548	4564	4579	4594	4609
29	4624	4639	4654	4669	4683	4698	4713	4728	4742	4757
30	4771	4786	4800	4814	4829	4843	4857	4871	4886	4900
31	4914	4928	4942	4955	4969	4983	4997	5011	5024	5038
32	5051	5065	5079	5092	5105	5119	5132	5145	5159	5172
33	5185	5198	5211	5224	5237	5250	5263	5276	5289	5302
34	5315	5328	5340	5353	5366	5378	5391	5403	5416	5428
35	5441	5453	5465	5478	5490	5502	5514	5527	5539	5551
36	5563	5575	5587	5599	5611	5623	5635	5647	5658	5670
37	5682	5694	5705	5717	5729	5740	5752	5763	5775	5786
38	5798	5809	5821	5832	5843	5855	5866	5877	5888	5899
39	5911	5922	5933	5944	5955	5966	5977	5988	5999	6010
40	6021	6031	6042	6053	6064	6075	6085	6096	6107	6117
41	6128	6138	6149	6160	6170	6180	6191	6201	6212	6222
42	6232	6243	6253	6263	6274	6284	6294	6304	6314	6325
43	6335	6345	6355	6365	6375	6385	6395	6405	6415	6425
44	6435	6444	6454	6464	6474	6484	6493	6503	6513	6522
45	6532	6542	6551	6561	6571	6580	6590	6599	6609	6618
46	6628	6637	6646	6656	6665	6675	6684	6693	6702	6712
47	6721	6730	6739	6749	6758	6767	6776	6785	6794	6803
48	6812	6821	6830	6839	6848	6857	6866	6875	6884	6893
49	6902	6911	6920	6928	6937	6946	6955	6964	6972	6981

	0	1	2	3	4	5	6	7	8	9
50	6990	6998	7007	7016	7024	7033	7042	7050	7059	7067
51	7076	7084	7093	7101	7110	7118	7126	7135	7143	7152
52	7160	7168	7177	7185	7193	7202	7210	7218	7226	7235
53	7243	7251	7259	7267	7275	7284	7292	7300	7308	7316
54	7324	7332	7340	7348	7356	7364	7372	7380	7388	7396
55	7404	7412	7419	7427	7435	7443	7451	7459	7466	7474
56	7482	7490	7497	7505	7513	7520	7528	7536	7543	7551
57	7559	7566	7574	7582	7589	7597	7604	7612	7619	7627
58	7634	7642	7649	7657	7664	7672	7679	7686	7694	7701
59	7709	7716	7723	7731	7738	7745	7752	7760	7767	7774
60	7782	7789	7796	7803	7810	7818	7825	7832	7839	7846
61	7853	7860	7868	7875	7882	7889	7896	7903	7910	7917
62	7924	7931	7938	7945	7952	7959	7966	7973	7980	7987
63	7993	8000	8007	8014	8021	8028	8035	8041	8048	8055
64	8062	8069	8075	8082	8089	8096	8102	8109	8116	8122
65	8129	8136	8142	8149	8156	8162	8169	8176	8182	8189
66	8195	8202	8209	8215	8222	8228	8235	8241	8248	8254
67	8261	8267	8274	8280	8287	8293	8299	8306	8312	8319
68	8325	8331	8338	8344	8351	8357	8363	8370	8376	8382
69	8388	8395	8401	8407	8414	8420	8426	8432	8439	8445
70	8451	8457	8463	8470	8476	8482	8488	8494	8500	8506
71	8513	8519	8525	8531	8537	8543	8549	8555	8561	8567
72	8573	8579	8585	8591	8597	8603	8609	8615	8621	8627
73	8633	8639	8645	8651	8657	8663	8669	8675	8681	8686
74	8692	8698	8704	8710	8716	8722	8727	8733	8739	8745
75	8751	8756	8762	8768	8774	8779	8785	8791	8797	8802
76	8808	8814	8820	8825	8831	8837	8842	8848	8854	8859
77	8865	8871	8876	8882	8887	8893	8899	8904	8910	8915
78	8921	8927	8932	8938	8943	8949	8954	8960	8965	8971
79	8976	8982	8987	8993	8998	9004	9009	9015	9020	9025
80	9031	9036	9042	9047	9053	9058	9063	9069	9074	9079
81	9085	9090	9096	9101	9106	9112	9117	9122	9128	9133
82	9138	9143	9149	9154	9159	9165	9170	9175	9180	9186
83	9191	9196	9201	9206	9212	9217	9222	9227	9232	9238
84	9243	9248	9253	9258	9263	9269	9274	9279	9284	9289
85	9294	9299	9304	9309	9315	9320	9325	9330	9335	9340
86	9345	9350	9355	9360	9365	9370	9375	9380	9385	9390
87	9395	9400	9405	9410	9415	9420	9425	9430	9435	9440
88	9445	9450	9455	9460	9465	9469	9474	9479	9484	9489
89	9494	9499	9504	9509	9513	9518	9523	9528	9533	9538
90	9542	9547	9552	9557	9562	9566	9571	9576	9581	9586
91	9590	9595	9600	9605	9609	9614	9619	9624	9628	9633
92	9638	9643	9647	9652	9657	9661	9666	9671	9675	9680
93	9685	9689	9694	9699	9703	9708	9713	9717	9722	9727
94	9731	9736	9741	9745	9750	9754	9759	9763	9768	9773
95	9777	9782	9786	9791	9795	9800	9805	9809	9814	9818
96	9823	9827	9832	9836	9841	9845	9850	9854	9859	9863
97	9868	9872	9877	9881	9886	9890	9894	9899	9903	9908
98	9912	9917	9921	9926	9930	9934	9939	9943	9948	9952
99	9956	9961	9965	9969	9974	9978	9983	9987	9991	9996

APPENDIX E

STANDARD ELECTRODE POTENTIALS AT 25°C

Acid Solution	
Half Reaction	$\mathscr{E}°$ **(volts)**
$Li^+ + e^- \rightleftharpoons Li$	−3.045
$K^+ + e^- \rightleftharpoons K$	−2.925
$Rb^+ + e^- \rightleftharpoons Rb$	−2.925
$Cs^+ + e^- \rightleftharpoons Cs$	−2.923
$Ra^{2+} + 2e^- \rightleftharpoons Ra$	−2.916
$Ba^{2+} + 2e^- \rightleftharpoons Ba$	−2.906
$Sr^{2+} + 2e^- \rightleftharpoons Sr$	−2.888
$Ca^{2+} + 2e^- \rightleftharpoons Ca$	−2.866
$Na^+ + e^- \rightleftharpoons Na$	−2.714
$Ce^{3+} + 3e^- \rightleftharpoons Ce$	−2.483
$Mg^{2+} + 2e^- \rightleftharpoons Mg$	−2.363
$Be^{2+} + 2e^- \rightleftharpoons Be$	−1.847
$Al^{3+} + 3e^- \rightleftharpoons Al$	−1.662
$Mn^{2+} + 2e^- \rightleftharpoons Mn$	−1.180
$Zn^{2+} + 2e^- \rightleftharpoons Zn$	−0.7628
$Cr^{3+} + 3e^- \rightleftharpoons Cr$	−0.744
$Ga^{3+} + 3e^- \rightleftharpoons Ga$	−0.529
$Fe^{2+} + 2e^- \rightleftharpoons Fe$	−0.4402
$Cr^{3+} + e^- \rightleftharpoons Cr^{2+}$	−0.408
$Cd^{2+} + 2e^- \rightleftharpoons Cd$	−0.4029
$PbSO_4 + 2e^- \rightleftharpoons Pb + SO_4^{2-}$	−0.3588
$Tl^+ + e^- \rightleftharpoons Tl$	−0.3363
$Co^{2+} + 2e^- \rightleftharpoons Co$	−0.277
$H_3PO_4 + 2H^+ + 2e^- \rightleftharpoons H_3PO_3 + H_2O$	−0.276
$Ni^{2+} + 2e^- \rightleftharpoons Ni$	−0.250
$Sn^{2+} + 2e^- \rightleftharpoons Sn$	−0.136
$Pb^{2+} + 2e^- \rightleftharpoons Pb$	−0.126
$2H^+ + 2e^- \rightleftharpoons H_2$	0.0000
$S + 2H^+ + 2e^- \rightleftharpoons H_2S$	+0.142
$Sn^{4+} + 2e^- \rightleftharpoons Sn^{2+}$	+0.15
$SO_4^{2-} + 4H^+ + 2e^- \rightleftharpoons H_2SO_3 + H_2O$	+0.172
$AgCl + e^- \rightleftharpoons Ag + Cl^-$	+0.2222
$Cu^{2+} + 2e^- \rightleftharpoons Cu$	+0.337
$H_2SO_3 + 4H^+ + 4e^- \rightleftharpoons S + 3H_2O$	+0.450
$Cu^+ + e^- \rightleftharpoons Cu$	+0.521
$I_2 + 2e^- \rightleftharpoons 2I^-$	+0.5355
$MnO_4^- + e^- \rightleftharpoons MnO_4^{2-}$	+0.564
$O_2 + 2H^+ + 2e^- \rightleftharpoons H_2O_2$	+0.6824
$Fe^{3+} + e^- \rightleftharpoons Fe^{2+}$	+0.771

(continued)

Half Reaction	$\mathscr{E}°$ (volts)
$Hg_2^{2+} + 2e^- \rightleftharpoons 2\,Hg$	$+0.788$
$Ag^+ + e^- \rightleftharpoons Ag$	$+0.7991$
$2\,NO_3^- + 4\,H^+ + 2e^- \rightleftharpoons N_2O_4 + 2\,H_2O$	$+0.803$
$Hg^{2+} + 2e^- \rightleftharpoons Hg$	$+0.854$
$2\,Hg^{2+} + 2e^- \rightleftharpoons Hg_2^{2+}$	$+0.920$
$NO_3^- + 4\,H^+ + 3e^- \rightleftharpoons NO + 2\,H_2O$	$+0.96$
$Br_2 + 2e^- \rightleftharpoons 2\,Br^-$	$+1.0652$
$O_2 + 4\,H^+ + 4e^- \rightleftharpoons 2\,H_2O$	$+1.229$
$MnO_2 + 4\,H^+ + 2e^- \rightleftharpoons Mn^{2+} + 2\,H_2O$	$+1.23$
$Tl^{3+} + 2e^- \rightleftharpoons Tl^+$	$+1.25$
$Cr_2O_7^{2-} + 14\,H^+ + 6e^- \rightleftharpoons 2\,Cr^{3+} + 7\,H_2O$	$+1.33$
$Cl_2 + 2e^- \rightleftharpoons 2\,Cl^-$	$+1.3595$
$Au^{3+} + 2e^- \rightleftharpoons Au^+$	$+1.402$
$PbO_2 + 4\,H^+ + 2e^- \rightleftharpoons Pb^{2+} + 2\,H_2O$	$+1.455$
$Au^{3+} + 3e^- \rightleftharpoons Au$	$+1.498$
$Mn^{3+} + e^- \rightleftharpoons Mn^{2+}$	$+1.51$
$MnO_4^- + 8\,H^+ + 5e^- \rightleftharpoons Mn^{2+} + 4\,H_2O$	$+1.51$
$Ce^{4+} + e^- \rightleftharpoons Ce^{3+}$	$+1.61$
$2\,HOCl + 2\,H^+ + 2e^- \rightleftharpoons Cl_2 + 2\,H_2O$	$+1.63$
$PbO_2 + SO_4^{2-} + 4\,H^+ + 2e^- \rightleftharpoons PbSO_4 + 2\,H_2O$	$+1.682$
$Au^+ + e^- \rightleftharpoons Au$	$+1.691$
$MnO_4^- + 4\,H^+ + 3e^- \rightleftharpoons MnO_2 + 2\,H_2O$	$+1.695$
$H_2O_2 + 2\,H^+ + 2e^- \rightleftharpoons 2\,H_2O$	$+1.776$
$Co^{3+} + e^- \rightleftharpoons Co^{2+}$	$+1.808$
$S_2O_8^{2-} + 2e^- \rightleftharpoons 2\,SO_4^{2-}$	$+2.01$
$O_3 + 2\,H^+ + 2e^- \rightleftharpoons O_2 + H_2O$	$+2.07$
$F_2 + 2e^- \rightleftharpoons 2\,F^-$	$+2.87$

Alkaline Solution

Half Reaction	$\mathscr{E}°$ (volts)
$Al(OH)_4^- + 3e^- \rightleftharpoons Al + 4\,OH^-$	-2.33
$Zn(OH)_4^{2-} + 2e^- \rightleftharpoons Zn + 4\,OH^-$	-1.215
$Fe(OH)_2 + 2e^- \rightleftharpoons Fe + 2\,OH^-$	-0.877
$2\,H_2O + 2e^- \rightleftharpoons H_2 + 2\,OH^-$	-0.82806
$Cd(OH)_2 + 2e^- \rightleftharpoons Cd + 2\,OH^-$	-0.809
$S + 2e^- \rightleftharpoons S^{2-}$	-0.447
$CrO_4^{2-} + 4\,H_2O + 3e^- \rightleftharpoons Cr(OH)_3 + 5\,OH^-$	-0.13
$NO_3^- + H_2O + 2e^- \rightleftharpoons NO_2^- + 2\,OH^-$	$+0.01$
$O_2 + 2\,H_2O + 4e^- \rightleftharpoons 4\,OH^-$	$+0.401$
$NiO_2 + 2\,H_2O + 2e^- \rightleftharpoons Ni(OH)_2 + 2\,OH^-$	$+0.490$
$HO_2^- + H_2O + 2e^- \rightleftharpoons 3\,OH^-$	$+0.878$

Data from A. J. de Bethune and N. A. Swendeman Loud, "Table of Electrode Potentials and Temperature Coefficients," pp. 414–424 in *Encyclopedia of Electrochemistry* (C. A. Hampel, editor), Van Nostrand Reinhold, New York, 1964, and from A. J. de Bethune and N. A. Swendeman Loud, *Standard Aqueous Electrode Potentials and Temperature Coefficients*, 19 pp., C. A. Hampel, publisher, Skokie, Illinois, 1964.

F.1 Ionization Constants

	Monoprotic Acids	K_a
acetic	$HC_2H_3O_2 \rightleftharpoons H^+ + C_2H_3O_2^-$	1.8×10^{-5}
benzoic	$HC_7H_5O_2 \rightleftharpoons H^+ + C_7H_5O_2^-$	6.0×10^{-5}
chlorous	$HClO_2 \rightleftharpoons H^+ + ClO_2^-$	1.1×10^{-2}
cyanic	$HOCN \rightleftharpoons H^+ + OCN^-$	1.2×10^{-4}
formic	$HCHO_2 \rightleftharpoons H^+ + CHO_2^-$	1.8×10^{-4}
hydrazoic	$HN_3 \rightleftharpoons H^+ + N_3^-$	1.9×10^{-5}
hydrocyanic	$HCN \rightleftharpoons H^+ + CN^-$	4.0×10^{-10}
hydrofluoric	$HF \rightleftharpoons H^+ + F^-$	6.7×10^{-4}
hypobromous	$HOBr \rightleftharpoons H^+ + OBr^-$	2.1×10^{-9}
hypochlorous	$HOCl \rightleftharpoons H^+ + OCl^-$	3.2×10^{-8}
nitrous	$HNO_2 \rightleftharpoons H^+ + NO_2^-$	4.5×10^{-4}

	Polyprotic Acids	
arsenic	$H_3AsO_4 \rightleftharpoons H^+ + H_2AsO_4^-$	$K_{a1} = 2.5 \times 10^{-4}$
	$H_2AsO_4^- \rightleftharpoons H^+ + HAsO_4^{2-}$	$K_{a2} = 5.6 \times 10^{-8}$
	$HAsO_4^{2-} \rightleftharpoons H^+ + AsO_4^{3-}$	$K_{a3} = 3 \times 10^{-13}$
carbonic	$CO_2 + H_2O \rightleftharpoons H^+ + HCO_3^-$	$K_{a1} = 4.2 \times 10^{-7}$
	$HCO_3^- \rightleftharpoons H^+ + CO_3^{2-}$	$K_{a2} = 4.8 \times 10^{-11}$
hydrosulfuric	$H_2S \rightleftharpoons H^+ + HS^-$	$K_{a1} = 1.1 \times 10^{-7}$
	$HS^- \rightleftharpoons H^+ + S^{2-}$	$K_{a2} = 1.0 \times 10^{-14}$
oxalic	$H_2C_2O_4 \rightleftharpoons H^+ + HC_2O_4^-$	$K_{a1} = 5.9 \times 10^{-2}$
	$HC_2O_4^- \rightleftharpoons H^+ + C_2O_4^{2-}$	$K_{a2} = 6.4 \times 10^{-5}$
phosphoric	$H_3PO_4 \rightleftharpoons H^+ + H_2PO_4^-$	$K_{a1} = 7.5 \times 10^{-3}$
	$H_2PO_4^- \rightleftharpoons H^+ + HPO_4^{2-}$	$K_{a2} = 6.2 \times 10^{-8}$
	$HPO_4^{2-} \rightleftharpoons H^+ + PO_4^{3-}$	$K_{a3} = 1 \times 10^{-12}$
phosphorous (diprotic)	$H_3PO_3 \rightleftharpoons H^+ + H_2PO_3^-$	$K_{a1} = 1.6 \times 10^{-2}$
	$H_2PO_3^- \rightleftharpoons H^+ + H_2PO_3^{2-}$	$K_{a2} = 7 \times 10^{-7}$
sulfuric	$H_2SO_4 \rightleftharpoons H^+ + HSO_4^-$	strong
	$HSO_4^- \rightleftharpoons H^+ + SO_4^{2-}$	$K_{a2} = 1.3 \times 10^{-2}$
sulfurous	$SO_2 + H_2O \rightleftharpoons H^+ + HSO_3^-$	$K_{a1} = 1.3 \times 10^{-2}$
	$HSO_3^- \rightleftharpoons H^+ + SO_3^{2-}$	$K_{a2} = 5.6 \times 10^{-8}$

	Bases	K_b
ammonia	$NH_3 + H_2O \rightleftharpoons NH_4^+ + OH^-$	1.8×10^{-5}
aniline	$C_6H_5NH_2 + H_2O \rightleftharpoons C_6H_5NH_3^+ + OH^-$	4.6×10^{-10}
dimethylamine	$(CH_3)_2NH + H_2O \rightleftharpoons (CH_3)_2NH_2^+ + OH^-$	7.4×10^{-4}
hydrazine	$N_2H_4 + H_2O \rightleftharpoons N_2H_5^+ + OH^-$	9.8×10^{-7}
methylamine	$CH_3NH_2 + H_2O \rightleftharpoons CH_3NH_3^+ + OH^-$	5.0×10^{-4}
pyridine	$C_5H_5N + H_2O \rightleftharpoons C_5H_5NH^+ + OH^-$	1.5×10^{-9}
trimethylamine	$(CH_3)_3N + H_2O \rightleftharpoons (CH_3)_3NH^+ + OH^-$	7.4×10^{-5}

F.2 Solubility Products

Bromides

$PbBr_2$	4.6×10^{-6}
Hg_2Br_2	1.3×10^{-22}
$AgBr$	5.0×10^{-13}

Carbonates

$BaCO_3$	1.6×10^{-9}
$CdCO_3$	5.2×10^{-12}
$CaCO_3$	4.7×10^{-9}
$CuCO_3$	2.5×10^{-10}
$FeCO_3$	2.1×10^{-11}
$PbCO_3$	1.5×10^{-15}
$MgCO_3$	1×10^{-5}
$MnCO_3$	8.8×10^{-11}
Hg_2CO_3	9.0×10^{-17}
$NiCO_3$	1.4×10^{-7}
Ag_2CO_3	8.2×10^{-12}
$SrCO_3$	7×10^{-10}
$ZnCO_3$	2×10^{-10}

Chlorides

$PbCl_2$	1.6×10^{-5}
Hg_2Cl_2	1.1×10^{-18}
$AgCl$	1.7×10^{-10}

Chromates

$BaCrO_4$	8.5×10^{-11}
$PbCrO_4$	2×10^{-16}
Hg_2CrO_4	2×10^{-9}
Ag_2CrO_4	1.9×10^{-12}
$SrCrO_4$	3.6×10^{-5}

Fluorides

BaF_2	2.4×10^{-5}
CaF_2	3.9×10^{-11}
PbF_2	4×10^{-8}
MgF_2	8×10^{-8}
SrF_2	7.9×10^{-10}

Hydroxides

$Al(OH)_3$	5×10^{-33}
$Ba(OH)_2$	5.0×10^{-3}
$Cd(OH)_2$	2.0×10^{-14}
$Ca(OH)_2$	1.3×10^{-6}
$Cr(OH)_3$	6.7×10^{-31}
$Co(OH)_2$	2.5×10^{-16}
$Co(OH)_3$	2.5×10^{-43}
$Cu(OH)_2$	1.6×10^{-19}

Hydroxides (continued)

$Fe(OH)_2$	1.8×10^{-15}
$Fe(OH)_3$	6×10^{-38}
$Pb(OH)_2$	4.2×10^{-15}
$Mg(OH)_2$	8.9×10^{-12}
$Mn(OH)_2$	2×10^{-13}
$Hg(OH)_2$ (HgO)	3×10^{-26}
$Ni(OH)_2$	1.6×10^{-16}
$AgOH$ (Ag_2O)	2.0×10^{-8}
$Sr(OH)_2$	3.2×10^{-4}
$Sn(OH)_2$	3×10^{-27}
$Zn(OH)_2$	4.5×10^{-17}

Iodides

PbI_2	8.3×10^{-9}
Hg_2I_2	4.5×10^{-29}
AgI	8.5×10^{-17}

Oxalates

BaC_2O_4	1.5×10^{-8}
CaC_2O_4	1.3×10^{-9}
PbC_2O_4	8.3×10^{-12}
MgC_2O_4	8.6×10^{-5}
$Ag_2C_2O_4$	1.1×10^{-11}
SrC_2O_4	5.6×10^{-8}

Phosphates

$Ba_3(PO_4)_2$	6×10^{-39}
$Ca_3(PO_4)_2$	1.3×10^{-32}
$Pb_3(PO_4)_2$	1×10^{-54}
Ag_3PO_4	1.8×10^{-18}
$Sr_3(PO_4)_2$	1×10^{-31}

Sulfates

$BaSO_4$	1.5×10^{-9}
$CaSO_4$	2.4×10^{-5}
$PbSO_4$	1.3×10^{-8}
Ag_2SO_4	1.2×10^{-5}
$SrSO_4$	7.6×10^{-7}

Sulfides

Bi_2S_3	1.6×10^{-72}
CdS	1.0×10^{-28}
CoS	5×10^{-22}
CuS	8×10^{-37}
FeS	4×10^{-19}
PbS	7×10^{-29}
MnS	7×10^{-16}

Sulfides (continued)

HgS	1.6×10^{-54}
NiS	3×10^{-21}
Ag_2S	5.5×10^{-51}
SnS	1×10^{-26}
ZnS	2.5×10^{-22}

Miscellaneous

$NaHCO_3$	1.2×10^{-3}
$KClO_4$	8.9×10^{-3}
$K_2[PtCl_6]$	1.4×10^{-6}
$AgC_2H_3O_2$	2.3×10^{-3}
$AgCN$	1.6×10^{-14}
$AgCNS$	1.0×10^{-12}

F.3 Instability Constants

AlF_6^{3-}	1.4×10^{-20}
$Al(OH)_4^-$	1.3×10^{-34}
$Al(OH)^{2+}$	7.1×10^{-10}
$Cd(NH_3)_4^{2+}$	7.5×10^{-8}
$Cd(CN)_4^{2-}$	1.4×10^{-19}
$Cr(OH)^{2+}$	5×10^{-11}
$Co(NH_3)_6^{2+}$	1.3×10^{-5}
$Co(NH_3)_6^{3+}$	2.2×10^{-34}
$Cu(NH_3)_2^+$	1.4×10^{-11}
$Cu(NH_3)_4^{2+}$	4.7×10^{-15}
$Cu(CN)_2^-$	1×10^{-16}
$Cu(OH)^+$	1×10^{-8}
$Fe(CN)_6^{4-}$	1×10^{-35}
$Fe(CN)_6^{3-}$	1×10^{-42}
$Pb(OH)^+$	1.5×10^{-8}
$HgBr_4^{2-}$	2.3×10^{-22}
$HgCl_4^{2-}$	1.1×10^{-16}
$Hg(CN)_4^{2-}$	4×10^{-42}
HgI_4^{2-}	5.3×10^{-31}
$Ni(NH_3)_4^{2+}$	1×10^{-8}
$Ni(NH_3)_6^{2+}$	1.8×10^{-9}
$Ag(NH_3)_2^+$	6.0×10^{-8}
$Ag(CN)_2^-$	1.8×10^{-19}
$Ag(S_2O_3)_2^{3-}$	5×10^{-14}
$Ag(S_2O_3)_3^{5-}$	9.9×10^{-15}
$Zn(NH_3)_4^{2+}$	3.4×10^{-10}
$Zn(CN)_4^{2+}$	1.2×10^{-18}
$Zn(OH)_4^{2-}$	3.6×10^{-16}
$Zn(OH)^+$	4.1×10^{-5}

APPENDIX G
THERMODYNAMIC DATA (25°C)

Substance	ΔH_f° (kJ/mol)	ΔG_f° (kJ/mol)	S° (J/K mol)
Ag(s)	0.0	0.0	42.72
AgBr(s)	−99.50	−93.68	10.71
AgCl(s)	−127.0	−109.70	96.11
AgI(s)	−62.38	−66.32	114.2
Ag$_2$O	−30.6	−10.8	121.7
Al(s)	0.0	0.0	28.3
Al$_2$O$_3$(s)	−1669.8	−1576.4	51.00
Ba(s)	0.0	0.0	67.
BaCl$_2$(s)	−860.06	−810.9	126.
BaCO$_3$(s)	−1218.8	−1138.9	112.
BaO(s)	−588.1	−528.4	70.3
BaSO$_4$(s)	−1465.2	−1353.1	132.2
Br$_2$(l)	0.0	0.0	152.3
C(diamond)	+1.88	+2.89	2.43
C(graphite)	0.0	0.0	5.69
CCl$_4$(l)	−139.3	−68.6	214.4
CF$_4$(g)	−679.9	−635.1	262.3
CH$_4$(g)	−74.85	−59.79	186.2
C$_2$H$_2$(g)	+226.7	+209.20	200.8
C$_2$H$_4$(g)	+52.3	+68.12	219.5
C$_2$H$_6$(g)	−84.68	−32.89	229.5
C$_6$H$_6$(l)	+49.04	+129.66	159.8
CH$_3$COOH(l)	−487.0	−392.5	159.8
CH$_3$Cl(g)	−82.0	−58.6	234.2
CHCl$_3$(l)	−132.0	−71.5	202.9
CH$_3$NH$_2$(g)	−28.0	−27.6	241.5
CH$_3$OH(g)	−201.2	−161.9	237.7
CH$_3$OH(l)	−238.6	−166.2	126.8
C$_2$H$_5$OH(l)	−277.63	−174.77	160.7
CO(g)	−110.5	−137.28	197.9
CO$_2$(g)	−393.5	−394.39	213.6
COCl$_2$(g)	−223.0	−210.5	289.2
CS$_2$(l)	+87.86	+63.6	151.0
Ca(s)	0.0	0.0	41.6
CaCl$_2$(s)	−795.0	−750.2	113.8
CaCO$_3$(s)	−1206.9	−1128.76	92.9

Substance	ΔH_f° (kJ/mol)	ΔG_f° (kJ/mol)	S° (J/K mol)
CaO(s)	−635.5	−604.2	39.8
Ca(OH)$_2$(s)	−986.59	−896.76	76.1
CaSO$_4$(s)	−1432.7	−1320.3	106.7
Cl$_2$(g)	0.0	0.0	223.0
Co(s)	0.0	0.0	28.5
Cr(s)	0.0	0.0	23.8
Cr$_2$O$_3$(s)	−1128.4	−1046.8	81.2
Cu(s)	0.0	0.0	33.3
CuO(s)	−155.2	−127.2	43.5
Cu$_2$O(s)	−166.7	−146.4	100.8
CuS(s)	−48.5	−49.0	66.5
CuSO$_4$(s)	−769.9	−661.9	113.4
F$_2$(g)	0.0	0.0	203.3
Fe(s)	0.0	0.0	27.2
FeO(s)	−271.9	−255.2	60.75
Fe$_2$O$_3$(s)	−822.2	−741.0	90.0
Fe$_3$O$_4$(s)	−1117.1	−1014.2	146.4
H$_2$(g)	0.0	0.0	130.6
HBr(g)	−36.2	−53.22	198.5
HCl(g)	+92.30	−95.27	186.7
HCN(g)	+130.5	+120.1	201.79
HF(g)	−269.	−270.7	173.5
HI(g)	+25.9	+1.30	206.3
HNO$_3$(l)	−173.2	−79.91	155.6
H$_2$O(g)	−241.8	−228.61	188.7
H$_2$O(l)	−285.9	−237.19	69.96
H$_2$S(g)	−20.2	−33.0	205.6
H$_2$SO$_4$(l)	−811.32	−687.5	156.9
Hg(l)	0.0	0.0	77.4
HgO(s)	−90.7	−58.5	72.0
HgS(s)	−58.16	−48.82	77.8
I$_2$(s)	0.0	0.0	116.7
K(s)	0.0	0.0	63.6
KBr(s)	−392.2	−379.2	96.44
KCl(s)	−435.89	−408.32	82.68
KClO$_3$(s)	−391.2	−289.9	142.96
KF(s)	−562.6	−533.1	66.57
KNO$_3$(s)	−492.7	−393.1	132.93
La(s)	0.0	0.0	57.3
Li(s)	0.0	0.0	28.0
Li$_2$CO$_3$(s)	−1215.6	−1132.4	90.37
LiOH(s)	−487.2	−443.9	50.
Mg(s)	0.0	0.0	32.51
MgCl$_2$(s)	−641.8	−592.33	89.54
MgCO$_3$(s)	−1113.	−1029.	65.69
MgO(s)	−601.8	−569.6	26.8
Mg(OH)$_2$(s)	−924.7	−833.7	63.14
Mn(s)	0.0	0.0	31.8

(continued)

Substance	ΔH_f° (kJ/mol)	ΔG_f° (kJ/mol)	S° (J/K mol)
MnO(s)	−384.9	−363.2	60.2
MnO$_2$(s)	+520.9	−466.1	53.1
N$_2$(g)	0.0	0.0	191.5
NH$_3$(g)	−46.19	−16.7	192.5
NH$_4$Cl(s)	−315.4	−203.9	94.6
NO(g)	+90.36	+86.69	210.6
NO$_2$(g)	+33.8	+51.84	240.5
N$_2$O(g)	+81.55	+103.60	220.0
N$_2$O$_4$(g)	+9.67	+99.28	304.3
NOCl(g)	+52.59	+66.36	263.6
Na(s)	0.0	0.0	51.0
NaCl(s)	−411.0	−384.05	72.38
Na$_2$CO$_3$(s)	−1130.9	−1047.7	136.0
NaF(s)	−569.0	−541.0	58.6
NaHCO$_3$(s)	−947.7	−851.9	102.1
NaNO$_3$(s)	−424.8	−365.9	116.3
NaOH(s)	−426.7	−377.1	52.3
Ni(s)	0.0	0.0	30.1
NiO(s)	−244.3	−216.3	38.6
O$_2$(g)	0.0	0.0	205.03
P$_4$(s, white)	0.0	0.0	44.4
PCl$_3$(g)	−306.4	−286.3	311.7
PCl$_5$(g)	−398.9	−324.6	352.7
PH$_3$(g)	+9.25	+18.24	210.0
POCl$_3$(l)	−592.0	−545.2	324.6
Pb(s)	0.0	0.0	64.9
PbBr$_2$(s)	−277.0	−260.4	161.5
PbCl$_2$(s)	−359.2	−314.0	136.4
PbCO$_3$(s)	−700.0	−626.3	131.0
PbO(s)	−217.9	−188.5	69.5
PbO$_2$(s)	−276.6	−219.0	76.6
Pb$_3$O$_4$(s)	−734.7	−617.6	211.3
PbSO$_4$(s)	−918.4	−811.2	147.3
S(rhombic)	0.0	0.0	31.9
SO$_2$(g)	−296.9	−300.37	248.5
SO$_3$(g)	−395.2	−370.4	256.2
Si(s)	0.0	0.0	18.7
SiCl$_4$(g)	−640.2	−572.8	239.3
SiF$_4$(g)	−1548.	−1506.	284.5
SiO$_2$(s, quartz)	−859.4	−805.0	41.8
Sn(s)	0.0	0.0	51.5
SnCl$_4$(l)	−545.2	−474.0	258.6
SnO(s)	−286.2	−257.3	56.5
SnO$_2$(s)	−580.7	−519.7	52.3
Zn(s)	0.0	0.0	41.6
ZnO(s)	−348.0	−318.19	43.9
ZnS(s)	−202.9	−198.3	57.7
ZnSO$_4$(s)	−978.6	−871.6	124.7

AVERAGE BOND ENERGIES (kJ/mol)[a]

Bond	Average Bond Energy	Bond	Average Bond Energy
Br—Br	193	I—I	151
Br—Cl	216	N—Br	243
Br—F	249	N—Cl	201
Br—I	175	N—F	283
C—Br	285	N—H	389
C—C	347	N—N	159
C=C	619	N=N	418
C≡C	812	N≡N	941
C—Cl	326	N—O	201
C—F	485	N=O	607
C—H	414	O—Br	201
C—I	213	O—Cl	205
C—N	293	O—F	184
C=N	616	O—H	463
C≡N	879	O—I	201
C—O	335	O—O	138
C=O	707	O_2[b]	494
C≡O	1072	P—Cl	326
C—S	272	P—H	318
C=S	573	S—Br	217
Cl—Cl	243	S—Cl	276
Cl—F	249	S—F	285
Cl—I	208	S—H	339
F—F	155	S—S	213
H—Br	364	Si—Cl	301
H—Cl	431	Si—C	381
H—F	565	Si—F	565
H—H	435	Si—H	323
H—I	297	Si—O	368
I—F	278	Si—Si	226

[a] Reactants and products in gaseous state.

[b] Double bond of molecular oxygen.

APPENDIX I ANSWERS TO COLOR-KEYED PROBLEMS

Chapter 1 Introduction

1.1 (a) The *law of conservation of mass* states that there is no detectable change in mass during the course of a chemical reaction. The *law of definite proportions* states that a pure compound always consists of the same elements combined in the same proportions by mass. **(b)** A *compound* is a pure substance that is composed of two or more elements in fixed proportions. An *element* is a pure substance that cannot be decomposed into simpler substances. **(c)** *Weight* is the gravitational force of attraction exerted by the earth on a body. *Mass* is a measure of quantity of matter. **(d)** *Organic chemistry* is the study of the compounds of carbon (except for a few that are classified as inorganic compounds). *Biochemistry* is the chemistry of living systems, both plant and animal. **(e)** A *megameter* is 10^6 meters (1,000,000 m). A *millimeter* is 10^{-3} meters (0.001 m).

1.3 (a) iodine, **(b)** iron, **(c)** phosphorus, **(d)** potassium, **(e)** copper, **(f)** cobalt.

1.5 (a) Al, **(b)** Sb, **(c)** Ag, **(d)** Si, **(e)** Na, **(f)** Ne.

1.7 (a) 1, **(b)** 3, **(c)** 3, **(d)** 5, **(e)** 1.

1.9 (a) 0.05778, **(b)** 0.12, **(c)** 666.7, **(d)** 1.2, **(e)** 0.0022.

1.11 (a) 1.38×10^6, **(b)** 5.72×10^{-2}, **(c)** 9.7×10^{-6}, **(d)** 3.0×10^{-11}, **(e)** 7.714×10^6.

1.13 (a) 1×10^5, **(b)** 1×10^{-6}, **(c)** 1×10^2, **(d)** 1×10^7, **(e)** 1×10^{-16}.

1.15 (a) 2.0 cg, **(b)** 1.5×10^2 kg, **(c)** 1.5 Mm, **(d)** 1.2×10^2 pm, **(e)** 3.7×10^2 μg, **(f)** 6.3×10^2 Gg, **(g)** 6×10 nm.

1.17 (a) 1000 L (or 10^3 L), **(b)** 0.001 m³ (or 10^{-3} m³).

1.19 1.091×10^4 m

1.21 1.21 km

1.23 (a) 1.026 earth days/Mars day, **(b)** 686.9 earth days/Mars year, **(c)** 669.6 Mars days/Mars year.

1.25 9.594 trips

1.27 3.62 m³

1.29 (a) 75%, **(b)** 21 K.

1.31 83.3 g Pt

1.33 (a) 175 g Sn, **(b)** 1.94×10^3 g alloy

1.35 6.4×10^{12} g Au

1.37 (a) 1.33×10^3 g alloy, **(b)** 200 g Cu and 17 g Zn left over.

1.39 (a) 3.80 mile/hr, **(b)** 1.70 m/s.

1.41 89 km/hr

1.43 1.83×10^3 m/s.

1.45 (a) 463.8 m/s or 1038 mile/hr, **(b)** 2.979×10^4 m/s or 6.663×10^4 mile/hr.

1.47 0.972 g/cm³

1.49 0.0570 cm³

1.51 1.412×10^{27} m³

1.53 4.913×10^4 g

1.55 0.856 g/mL

1.57 6.053 Mm

1.59 1.03×10^3 cm

Chapter 2 Introduction to Atomic Theory

2.1 Dalton's explanation of the *law of conservation of mass:* since chemical reactions consist of the separating and joining of atoms, and since atoms are neither created nor destroyed in these processes, the total mass of all atoms entering into a chemical reaction is constant no matter how the atoms are grouped together. Dalton's explanation of the *law of definite proportions:* since a given compound is the result of the combination of atoms of two or more elements in fixed proportions, the elements of the compound are present in fixed proportions by mass.

2.3 Let 50.0 g of oxygen and 75.0 g of oxygen represent the masses of element A that are combined with a fixed mass of element B (50.0 g of sulfur). Then these two masses of oxygen (50.0 g and 75.0 g) stand in the whole-number ratio of 2 to 3. In the first compound, *two* atoms of oxygen are combined with one atom of sulfur (in SO_2); in the second compound, *three* atoms of oxygen are combined with one atom of sulfur (in SO_3).

2.5 Many elements consist of several types of atoms (isotopes) that differ in mass (have different numbers of neutrons in the nucleus). All atoms of the same element are chemically similar since they have the same numbers of protons in the nucleus and electrons surrounding the nucleus. Furthermore, the average mass of the atoms of each element can be used to solve problems with, in most cases, no error.

2.7 (a) The H^+ ion is deflected more because it has a lighter mass than Ne^+, **(b)** the Ne^{2+} ion is deflected more because it has a higher charge than Ne^+.

2.9 (a) 9.58×10^4 C/g, **(b)** 2.41×10^4 C/g, **(c)** 9.64×10^3 C/g.

2.11 See Table 2.2.

2.13 The radius of the $^{27}_{13}$Al nucleus is 3.9×10^{-13} cm. The diameter of the nucleus of an atom with a diameter of 1.00 km would be 2.7 cm (which is a little more than 1 inch).

2.15 (a) 33 protons and 42 neutrons in the nucleus and 33 electrons outside it, **(b)** $^{202}_{80}$Hg.

2.19 (a) 47 protons and 46 electrons, **(b)** 34 protons and 36 electrons.

2.21 A *period* consists of those elements found in a horizontal row in the table. A *group* consists of the elements that are found in a given vertical column in the table. The elements of a group have similar chemical properties, whereas the elements of a period exhibit a range of chemical properties.

2.23 (a) Kr, nonmetal, **(b)** K, metal, **(c)** P, nonmetal, **(d)** Pt, metal.

2.25 51.88% $^{107}_{47}Ag$ and 48.12% $^{109}_{47}Ag$.

2.27 99.75% $^{51}_{23}V$ and 0.25% $^{50}_{23}V$.

2.29 The atomic weight of the element is 69.72 (the element is Ga).

Chapter 3   Stoichiometry, Part I: Chemical Formulas

3.1 (a) An *empirical formula* is one that is written using the simplest whole-number ratio of atoms in the compound. A *molecular formula* gives the actual numbers of atoms of each kind in a molecule of the compound. **(b)** The *formula weight* of a substance is the sum of the atomic weights of all the atoms in a formula of the substance. A *molecular weight* is the sum of the atomic weights of the atoms that make up a molecule of a substance. **(c)** A *molecular formula* describes the atomic composition of a molecule; it gives the numbers of each kind of atoms present in the molecule. A *structural formula* shows how the atoms that make up a molecule are arranged in the molecule; a separate symbol is used to indicate each atom and dashes are used to show how these atoms are joined.

3.3 (a) Na_2O: 3 atoms and 2 ions ($2\,Na^+$ and O^{2-}), **(b)** $CrCl_3$: 4 atoms and 4 ions (Cr^{3+} and $3\,Cl^-$), **(c)** $CuSO_4$: 6 atoms and 2 ions (Cu^{2+} and SO_4^{2-}), **(d)** $Ba(OH)_2$: 5 atoms and 3 ions (Ba^{2+} and $2\,OH^-$)

3.5 (a) $MgCl_2$, **(b)** $MgSO_4$, **(c)** Mg_3N_2

3.7 (a) K_2CO_3, **(b)** $CaSO_4$, **(c)** $Fe_2(CO_3)_3$

3.9 (a) B_3H_5, **(b)** C_5H_9, **(c)** SF_5, **(d)** I_2O_5, **(e)** HPO_3

3.11 (a) 37.1 mol H_2, 2.23×10^{25} molecules H_2; **(b)** 4.17 mol H_2O, 2.51×10^{24} molecules H_2O; **(c)** 0.765 mol H_2SO_4, 4.61×10^{23} molecules H_2SO_4

3.13 (a) 4.48×10^{25} atoms, **(b)** 7.53×10^{24} atoms, **(c)** 3.23×10^{24} atoms

3.15 (a) 0.0159 g O_2, **(b)** 0.0960 g O_2

3.17 9.786×10^{-23} g/atom Co

3.19 The atomic weight of the element is 126.9 (the element is I).

3.21 (a) 4.6135 mol Pt and 0.52024 mol Ir, **(b)** 2.7783×10^{24} atoms Pt and 3.1329×10^{23} atoms Ir.

3.23 (a) One mole of $^{12}_6C$ is exactly 12. g **(b)** 1.9927×10^{-23} g/atom $^{12}_6C$, **(c)** 1.661×10^{-24} g/u.

*3.25 They would extend 6.0221×10^{18} km, which is over 4×10^{10} times the distance.

3.27 $CaSO_4$ (23.6% S) < $Na_2S_2O_3$ (40.6% S) < SO_2 (50.1% S) < H_2S (94.1% S)

3.29 48.31% As

3.31 39.17% O

3.33 9.35 kg Pb

3.35 3.380 g P and 2.620 g O

3.37 81.8% C, 6.11% H, and 12.1% O.

*3.39 79.62% Fe_2O_3

3.41 (a) $S_4N_4H_4$, **(b)** P_2F_4, **(c)** C_5H_{10}, **(d)** NO_2, **(e)** $C_6N_3H_6$

3.43 CaC_2O_4

3.45 $C_7H_{14}O$

3.47 $C_8H_8O_3$

3.49 $C_4H_4N_2O_3$

3.51 $C_7H_5O_3SN$

3.53 (a) 0.1800 mol C atoms, 0.4800 mol H atoms, and 0.0600 mol N atoms, **(b)** C_3H_8N, **(c)** 3.487 g

3.55 The formula weight of hemoglobin is 6.53×10^4

3.57 $x = 7$, the formula is $NiSO_4 \cdot 7\,H_2O$

*3.59 $CrCl_2$

*3.61 The atomic weight of X is 6.944.

Chapter 4   Stoichiometry, Part II: Chemical Equations

4.1 (a) $2\,Al(s) + 6\,HCl(aq) \longrightarrow 2\,AlCl_3(aq) + 3\,H_2(g)$
(b) $Cu_2S(l) + 2\,Cu_2O(l) \longrightarrow 6\,Cu(l) + SO_2(g)$
(c) $2\,WC(s) + 5\,O_2(g) \longrightarrow 2\,WO_3(s) + 2\,CO_2(g)$
(d) $Al_4C_3(s) + 12\,H_2O(l) \longrightarrow 4\,Al(OH)_3(s) + 3\,CH_4(g)$

4.3 (a) $Fe_2S_3(s) + 6\,HCl(aq) \longrightarrow 2\,FeCl_3(aq) + 3\,H_2S(g)$
(b) $2\,KClO_3(s) \longrightarrow 2\,KCl(s) + 3\,O_2(g)$
(c) $I_4O_9(s) \longrightarrow I_2O_5(s) + I_2(s) + 2\,O_2(g)$
(d) $Ba_3N_2(s) + 6\,H_2O(l) \longrightarrow 3\,Ba(OH)_2(s) + 2\,NH_3(g)$

4.5 (a) $C_6H_{12}(l) + 9\,O_2(g) \longrightarrow 6\,CO_2(g) + 6\,H_2O(l)$
(b) $C_7H_8(l) + 9\,O_2(g) \longrightarrow 7\,CO_2(g) + 4\,H_2O(l)$
(c) $2\,C_8H_{18}(l) + 25\,O_2(g) \longrightarrow 16\,CO_2(g) + 18\,H_2O(l)$

4.7 (a) $2\,C_4H_{10}(g) + 13\,O_2(g) \longrightarrow 8\,CO_2(g) + 10\,H_2O(l)$
(b) $C_4H_4S(l) + 6\,O_2(g) \longrightarrow 4\,CO_2(g) + 2\,H_2O(l) + SO_2(g)$
(c) $4\,C_5H_5N(l) + 25\,O_2(g) \longrightarrow 20\,CO_2(g) + 10\,H_2O(l) + 2\,N_2(g)$

4.9 (a) $2\,NaN_3(s) \longrightarrow 2\,Na(l) + 3\,N_2(g)$, **(b)** 0.667 mol $NaN_3(s)$, **(c)** 1.62 g N_2, **(d)** 0.958 g Na

4.11 60.0 g $NaNH_2(l)$ and 33.8 g $N_2O(g)$ are required

4.13 4.66 g $HI(g)$

4.15 6.71 g $NH_4SCN(s)$

4.17 2.10 g $SF_4(g)$

4.19 35.1% yield

4.21 75.0% $CaC_2(s)$

*4.23 45.6% $C_2H_6(g)$

4.25 (a) 0.400 M, **(b)** 0.148 M, **(c)** 0.168 M

4.27 (a) 0.0600 mol $Ba(OH)_2$, **(b)** 0.150 mol H_2SO_4, **(c)** 0.0250 mol NaCl

4.29 (a) 1.580 g $KMnO_4$, **(b)** 168.3 g KOH, **(c)** 1.041 g $BaCl_2$

4.31 (a) 50.0 mL of glacial $HC_2H_3O_2$, **(b)** 47.5 mL of concentrated HNO_3, **(c)** 2.50 mL of concentrated H_2SO_4

4.33 42.0 mL KOH solution

4.35 0.165 M $H_2C_2O_4$ solution

4.37 0.1260 M Na_2CrO_4

4.39 0.130 M $BaCl_2$

4.41 27.30 mL $Na_2S_2O_3$ solution

4.43 36.3 g $Fe(s)$

4.45 42.0% NaCl

Chapter 5   Thermochemistry

5.1 37.0°C

5.3 −40°C

5.5 1.36 kJ/°C

5.7 18.8 kJ

5.9 2.46 J/(g°C)

5.11 144 J

5.13 26.74°C

5.15 873 kJ

5.17 2.25 kJ/°C

5.19 (a) endothermic, (b) exothermic, (c) endothermic, (d) exothermic

5.21 $C_6H_6(l) + \frac{15}{2}O_2(g) \longrightarrow 6\,CO_2(g) + 3\,H_2O(l)$
$$\Delta H = -3268 \text{ kJ}$$

5.23 19.42 kJ

5.25 (a) $\Delta H = +763$ kJ, (b) 381 g $NaN_3(s)$

5.27 $\Delta H = +50.0$ kJ

5.29 $\Delta H = -300.1$ kJ

5.31 $\Delta H = -1376.0$ kJ

5.33 $\Delta H = -1081.6$ kJ

5.35 $\Delta H = -71.4$ kJ

5.37 (a) $Ag(s) + \frac{1}{2}Cl_2(g) \longrightarrow AgCl(s)$ $\Delta H_f^\circ = -127$ kJ
(b) $\frac{1}{2}N_2(g) + O_2(g) \longrightarrow NO_2(g)$ $\Delta H_f^\circ = +33.8$ kJ
(c) $Ca(s) + C(graphite) + \frac{3}{2}O_2(g) \longrightarrow CaCO_3(s)$ $\Delta H_f^\circ = -1206.9$ kJ

5.39 $\Delta H^\circ = -1125.2$ kJ

5.41 $\Delta H^\circ = -1212.3$ kJ

5.43 (a) $CH_3OH(l) + \frac{3}{2}O_2(g) \longrightarrow CO_2(g) + 2\,H_2O(l)$
(b) $\Delta H^\circ = -764.1$ kJ

5.45 (a) $N_2H_4(l) + O_2(g) \longrightarrow N_2(g) + 2H_2O(l)$
(b) $\Delta H^\circ = +50.6$ kJ

5.47 $\Delta H_f^\circ = -351.5$ kJ/mol

5.49 $\Delta H_f^\circ = -270$ kJ/mol (from bond energies), Table 5.1 gives −269 kJ/mol.

5.51 +132 kJ/mol

5.53 $\Delta H = -121$ kJ

5.55 $\Delta H = -120$ kJ

5.57 (a) $\Delta H = -150$ kJ, (b) $\Delta H^\circ = -159$ kJ

5.59 +112 kJ/mol

Chapter 6   The Electronic Structure of Atoms

6.1 (a) infrared radiation, (b) blue light, (c) microwave

6.3 (a) 5.00×10^{20}/s, 3.31×10^{-13} J;
(b) 1.20×10^{10}/s, 7.95×10^{-24} J

6.5 (a) 5.25×10^{-5} m (52.5 μm), 3.78×10^{-21} J;
(b) 5.25×10^{-7} m (525 nm), 3.78×10^{-19} J

*6.7 (a) 5.99×10^{14}/s, 500 nm; (b) yes

*6.9 (a) 7.70×10^{-19} J, (b) 2.24×10^{-19} J

6.11 43 s

6.13 377 photons

6.15 When an electron in an excited state of an atom falls back to a lower level, energy is emitted. The energy difference between the high energy state and the low energy state is emitted in the form of a quantum of light.

6.17 93.75 nm

6.19 from $n = 5$ to $n = 2$

*6.21 from $n = \infty$ to $n = 5$ and from $n = 6$ to $n = 5$

6.23 In order to make similar elements appear under one another in the periodic table, Mendeleev had to leave blanks for undiscovered elements in his table. Moseley studied the X-ray spectra of 38 elements. He found that the square root of the frequency of a corresponding spectral line increases by a constant amount from element to element when the elements are arranged by atomic number. Moseley's graphs indicated that at that time four elements before number 79 remained to be discovered.

6.25 $Z = 13$, Al

6.27 0.14 nm

6.29 0.0807 nm

6.31 7.28×10^6 m/s

6.33 (a) 5.28×10^{-21} m/s, (b) 31.6 nm

6.35 The principal quantum number, n, gives the shell and the relative average distance of the electron from the nucleus $[n = 1, 2, 3, \ldots]$. The subsidiary quantum number, l, gives the subshell and the shape of the orbital for the electron $[l = 0, 1, 2, 3, \ldots, (n-1)]$. The magnetic orbital quantum number, m_l, designates the orientation of the orbital $[m_l = +l, +(l-1), \ldots, 0, \ldots, -(l-1), -l]$. The magnetic spin quantum number, m_s, refers to the spin of the electron $[m_s = +1/2$ or $-1/2]$.

6.37

Electron	n	l	m_l	m_s
1	1	0	0	+1/2
2	1	0	0	−1/2
3	2	0	0	+1/2
4	2	0	0	−1/2
5	2	1	+1	+1/2
6	2	1	0	+1/2
7	2	1	−1	+1/2

6.39 (a) 32, (b) impossible, (c) 2, (d) impossible, (e) 2, (f) 2, (g) 6

6.41 (a) 15 electrons have $l = 1$ as one of their quantum numbers, (b) 15 electrons have $m_l = 0$ as one of their quantum numbers, (c) 7 electrons have $m_l = -1$ as one of their quantum numbers

6.43

	1s	2s	2p	3s	3p	3d	4s
$_{28}$Ni	⇅	⇅	⇅ ⇅ ⇅	⇅	⇅ ⇅ ⇅	⇅ ⇅ ⇅ ↑ ↑	⇅

$1s^2 2s^2 2p^6 3s^2 3p^6 3d^8 4s^2$

6.45 (a) $_{17}$Cl, (b) $_{24}$Cr, (c) $_{61}$Pm, (d) $_{19}$K, (e) $_{36}$Kr

6.47 (a) 1, paramagnetic; (b) 6, paramagnetic; (c) 5, paramagnetic; (d) 1, paramagnetic; (e) 0, diamagnetic

6.49 (a) $_{56}$Ba, $1s^2\,2s^2\,2p^6\,3s^2\,3p^6\,3d^{10}\,4s^2\,4p^6\,4d^{10}\,5s^2\,5p^6\,6s^2$
(b) $_{82}$Pb, $1s^2\,2s^2\,2p^6\,3s^2\,3p^6\,3d^{10}\,4s^2\,4p^6\,4d^{10}\,4f^{14}\,5s^2\,5p^6\,5d^{10}\,6s^2\,6p^2$
(c) $_{39}$Y, $1s^2\,2s^2\,2p^6\,3s^2\,3p^6\,3d^{10}\,4s^2\,4p^6\,4d^1\,5s^2$
(d) $_{54}$Xe, $1s^2\,2s^2\,2p^6\,3s^2\,3p^6\,3d^{10}\,4s^2\,4p^6\,4d^{10}\,5s^2\,5p^6$
(e) $_{70}$Yb, $1s^2\,2s^2\,2p^6\,3s^2\,3p^6\,3d^{10}\,4s^2\,4p^6\,4d^{10}\,4f^{14}\,5s^2\,5p^6\,6s^2$
(f) $_{52}$Te, $1s^2\,2s^2\,2p^6\,3s^2\,3p^6\,3d^{10}\,4s^2\,4p^6\,4d^{10}\,5s^2\,5p^4$

6.51 (a) 0, diamagnetic; (b) 2, paramagnetic; (c) 1, paramagnetic; (d) 0, diamagnetic; (e) 0, diamagnetic; (f) 2, paramagnetic

6.53 (a) representative metal, (b) representative nonmetal, (c) inner-transition metal, (d) transition metal, (e) noble-gas nonmetal

6.55 (a) As, (b) Ca, Zn; (c) B, F; (d) K, Cr, Cu.

Chapter 7 Properties of Atoms and the Ionic Bond

7.1 The atomic radius decreases from left to right across a period. Electrons are added to the *same level* and the nuclear charge increases (without an equivalent increase in shielding).

7.3 (a) P, (b) Sb, (c) Ga, (d) Si, (e) Na, (f) Al.

7.5 The atomic radius of N is 75 pm.

7.7 (a) Ar, (b) Ar, (c) S, (d) Sr, (e) Ba, (f) As.

7.9 (a) Since an electron has a negative charge, it is more difficult to remove an electron from a $1+$ ion than from a neutral atom. Furthermore, a $1+$ ion is smaller than the atom from which it is derived and the electrons are held more tightly because they are closer to the nucleus. (b) The outer subshells of the electronic configurations of the two atoms are: for K, ... $3s^2 3p^6 4s^1$; for Ca, ... $3s^2 3p^6 4s^2$. The effect noted can be explained on the basis of the origin of the electrons removed. For Ca, both the first and the second electrons are removed from a $4s$ orbital (of the valence level). For K, the first electron is removed from a $4s$ orbital (of the valence level), but the second electron is removed from a $3p$ orbital of a very stable $s^2 p^6$ noble-gas arrangement of an *inner* level.

7.11 Fluorine is a small atom and the electronic charge density of the valence shell is high. The energy liberated by the addition of an electron to fluorine is lower than would otherwise be the case because of the repulsion between the seven electrons in the valence shell and the added electron.

7.13 The second electron affinity of sulfur is $+522$ kJ/mol.

7.15 The lattice energy of CsCl is -669 kJ/mol.

7.17 The lattice energy of CaO is -3514 kJ/mol.

7.19 The enthalpy of formation of Rb_2O is -329 kJ/mol.

7.21 (a) CaS, (b) RbF, (c) CaO.

7.23 $NaBr < Na_2S < MgS$. More energy is released by Na_2S than by NaBr because S^{2-} is more highly charged and smaller than Br^-. More energy is released by MgS than by Na_2S because Mg^{2+} is more highly charged and smaller than Na^+.

7.25 (a) Cu^+ $1s^2 2s^2 2p^6 3s^2 3p^6 3d^{10}$, (b) Cr^{3+} $1s^2 2s^2 2p^6 3s^2 3p^6 3d^3$, (c) Cl^- $1s^2 2s^2 2p^6 3s^2 3p^6$, (d) Cs^+ $1s^2 2s^2 2p^6 3s^2 3p^6 3d^{10} 4s^2 4p^6 4d^{10} 5s^2 5p^6$, (e) Cd^{2+} $1s^2 2s^2 2p^6 3s^2 3p^6 3d^{10} 4s^2 4p^6 4d^{10}$, (f) Co^{2+} $1s^2 2s^2 2p^6 3s^2 3p^6 3d^7$.

7.27 (a) 0, 3, 0, 0, 0, 3. (b) diamagnetic: Cu^+, Cl^-, Cs^+, Cd^{2+}; paramagnetic: Cr^{3+}, Co^{2+}.

7.29 (a) H^-, Li^+, Be^{2+} (b) Se^{2-}, Rb^+, Sr^{2+}, Y^{3+} (c) Tl^+, Pb^{2+}, Bi^{3+} (d) Hg^{2+}, Tl^{3+} (e) Ca^{2+}, Sc^{3+}, Cl^-, S^{2-}, P^{3-}.

7.31 s^2: Be^{2+}; $s^2 p^6$: Al^{3+}, Ba^{2+}, Br^-; d^{10}: Ag^+, Au^+; $d^{10} s^2$: As^{3+}, Bi^{3+}.

7.33 NaCl, $MgCl_2$, $AlCl_3$; Na_2O, MgO, Al_2O_3; Na_3N, Mg_3N_2, AlN.

7.35 In the formation of cations, the outermost electrons are lost. The size decreases as the number of electrons lost increases.

7.37 (a) Cu, (b) Te^{2-}, (c) Tl^+, (d) Tl^+, (e) N^{3-}.

7.39 (a) Mg^{2+}, (b) Cd^{2+}, (c) O^{2-}, (d) Sr^{2+}, (e) Mg.

7.41 (a) $NH_4C_2H_3O_2$, (b) $Al_2(SO_4)_3$, (c) Co_2S_3, (d) $BaCO_3$, (e) K_3AsO_4.

7.43 (a) $Fe_2(CO_3)_3$, (b) $Mn(NO_3)_2$, (c) $Ca_3(PO_4)_2$, (d) Li_2O, (e) $AgNO_2$.

7.45 (a) calcium sulfite, (b) silver chlorate, (c) tin(II) nitrate, (d) cadmium iodide, (e) chromium(III) iodate.

7.47 (a) magnesium hydroxide, (b) lead chromate, (c) iron(III) sulfate, (d) potassium dichromate, (e) lithium sulfite.

Chapter 8 The Covalent Bond

8.1 H_2, F_2, Cl_2, Br_2, I_2, At_2, O_2, N_2

8.3 NaCl consists of Na^+ and Cl^- ions in a crystal structure; HCl exists as a collection of covalently bonded molecules.

8.5 (a) HgI_2, (b) Fe_2O_3, (c) CdSe, (d) CuI_2, (e) $SbBr_3$, (f) BeO, (g) MgS, (h) $ScCl_3$, (i) $BiCl_3$.

8.7 11% ionic character in the H—Br bond

8.9 5.5% ionic character in the Br—Cl bond

8.11 Neglecting the noble gases, electronegativity increases from left to right across a period and from bottom to top up a group. The most reactive nonmetal (F) is found in the upper-right corner and the most reactive metal (Cs) is found in the lower-left corner.

8.13 Electronegativity differences are given in parentheses. *covalent nonpolar:* C, S (0) *covalent low polarity:* C, H (0.4); C, I (0.1); C, N (0.4) *covalent moderate polarity:* B, Br (1.0); C, O (0.8) *covalent high polarity:* Al, Cl (1.6) *ionic:* Ba, Br (2.1); Rb, Br (2.2); Ca, N (2.0)

8.15 Electronegativity differences are given in parentheses. (a) Cl—O (0.2), C—O (0.8), Ca—O (2.4), Cs—O (2.6); (b) C—I (0.1), Cl—I (0.5), Ca—I (1.7), Cs—I (1.9); (c) C—H (0.4), Cl—H (1.0), Ca—H (1.2), Cs—H (1.4)

8.17 The information given in parentheses consists of the electronegativity difference followed by the atom of the bond that has the partial negative charge. (a) P—I (0.5, I) > N—I (0.3, N); (b) N—H (0.8, N) > P—H (0, same); (c) N—F (1.0, F) > N—H (0.8, N); (d) N—H (0.8, N) > N—Cl (0.2, Cl); (e) N—S (0.4, N) = P—S (0.4, S); (f) P—O (1.2, 0) > N—O (0.4, 0)

8.19

8.21

8.23

8.25 (a) $\ddot{\text{F}}$—N—N—$\ddot{\text{F}}$ **(b)** H—$\ddot{\text{N}}$=$\ddot{\text{N}}$—H **(c)** H—C≡C—H
with :F: :F: below

(d) H—$\ddot{\text{O}}$—$\ddot{\text{O}}$—H

8.27 (a) $^{\ominus}$:$\ddot{\text{O}}$—N=N—$\ddot{\text{O}}$:$^{\ominus}$ **(b)** :$\ddot{\text{O}}$=N—$\ddot{\text{N}}$—$\ddot{\text{O}}$:$^{\ominus}$

(a) is the only important contributor, (b) violates the adjacent charge rule.

8.29 (a) H—C=C=$\ddot{\text{O}}$: **(b)** H—$\overset{\ominus}{\text{C}}$—C≡$\overset{\oplus}{\text{O}}$:
with H below each

(a) is the more important contributor (no formal charges), (b) is less important because in (b) a positive formal charge is impressed on the more electronegative atom.

8.31 (a) :$\ddot{\text{Cl}}$—C≡N: **(b)** :$\overset{(2+)}{\ddot{\text{Cl}}}$=C—$\ddot{\text{N}}$:$^{(2-)}$ **(c)** :$\ddot{\text{Cl}}$=C=$\overset{\ominus}{\ddot{\text{N}}}$:

(a) is the most important contributor (no formal charges), (b) is the least important (most highly charged), in both (b) and (c) the most electronegative atom has a positive formal charge.

8.33 :$\overset{\text{O}:^{\ominus}}{\text{N}}$=O ⟷ :N—$\overset{\text{O}}{\text{O}}$:$^{\ominus}$ O=$\overset{\oplus}{\text{N}}$=O

The bond distance is shorter in the nitronium ion, NO_2^+, (115 pm) than in the nitrite ion, NO_2^-, (124 pm). In NO_2^+, the N to O bonds are double bonds; NO_2^- is a resonance hybrid with N to O bonds that are approximately 1.5 bonds.

8.35 H—$\overset{\ominus}{\text{N}}$—$\overset{\oplus}{\text{S}}$=O ⟷ H—N=$\overset{\oplus}{\text{S}}$—$\ddot{\text{O}}$:$^{\ominus}$

8.37 :$\ddot{\text{F}}$—$\overset{\oplus}{\text{N}}$=N=$\ddot{\text{N}}$: ⟷ :$\ddot{\text{F}}$—$\overset{\ominus}{\text{N}}$—N≡N:

8.39 H—C—$\ddot{\text{N}}$—H ⟷ H—C=$\overset{\oplus}{\text{N}}$—H
(with :O: and H above) (with $^{\ominus}$:O: and H above)

8.41 :$\ddot{\text{F}}$—N—N=O ⟷ :$\ddot{\text{F}}$—$\overset{\oplus}{\text{N}}$=N—$\ddot{\text{O}}$:$^{\ominus}$
(with :F: below) (with :F: below)

8.43 structures of C—C with O groups ⟷ ⟷

8.45 (a) I_2O_5, **(b)** Cl_2O_6, **(c)** S_2N_2, **(d)** P_4O_8, **(e)** SF_4, **(f)** XeO_3

8.47 (a) disulfur difluoride, **(b)** tetraphosphorus heptasulfide, **(c)** iodine pentafluoride, **(d)** selenium tetrabromide, **(e)** nitrogen trifluoride, **(f)** xenon tetrafluoride

Chapter 9 Molecular Geometry; Molecular Orbitals

9.1 The NO molecule has an odd number of valence electrons (11 electrons). In the PCl_5 molecule, the P atom has 10 electrons in the valence level (and forms bonds with 5 Cl atoms). The N atom has only 4 orbitals in the valence level ($2s$ and $2p$) and therefore can form a maximum of 4 bonds. The P atom, on the other hand, has 9 orbitals in the valence level ($3s$, $3p$, and $3d$).

9.3 AB_2, linear; AB_3, triangular planar; AB_2E, angular; AB_4, tetrahedral; AB_3E, trigonal pyramidal; AB_2E_2, angular; AB_5, trigonal bipyramidal; AB_4E, irregular tetrahedral; AB_3E_2,

T-shaped; AB_2E_3, linear; AB_6, octahedral; AB_5E, square pyramidal; AB_4E_2, square planar.

9.5 (a) AsF_5: AB_5, trigonal bipyramidal;
(b) TeF_5^-: AB_5E, square pyramidal; **(c)** SnH_4, AB_4, tetrahedral;
(d) $CdBr_2$: AB_2, linear; **(e)** IF_4^-: AB_4E_2, square planar;
(f) AsF_4^-: AB_4E, irregular tetrahedral; **(g)** IBr_2^-: AB_2E_3, linear;
(h) AsF_2^+: AB_2E, angular; **(i)** $AsCl_4^+$: AB_4, tetrahedral;
(j) GeF_3^-: AB_3E, trigonal pyramidal.

9.7 (a) $BeCl_2$: AB_2, linear; **(b)** BeF_3^-: AB_3, triangular planar;
(c) BF_4^-: AB_4, tetrahedral; **(d)** SF_4: AB_4E, irregular tetrahedral;
(e) XeF_4: AB_4E_2, square planar;
(f) AsH_3: AB_3E, trigonal pyramidal;
(g) XeF_3^+: AB_3E_2, T-shaped; **(h)** SiF_6^{2-}: AB_6, octahedral;
(i) SeF_5^-: AB_5E, square pyramidal; **(j)** ClF_2^+: AB_2E_2, angular.

9.9 (a) dsp^3, **(b)** d^2sp^3, **(c)** sp^3, **(d)** sp, **(e)** d^2sp^3, **(f)** dsp^3, **(g)** dsp^3, **(h)** sp^2, **(i)** sp^3, **(j)** sp^3.

9.11 (a) sp, **(b)** sp^2, **(c)** sp^3, **(d)** dsp^3, **(e)** d^2sp^3, **(f)** sp^3, **(g)** dsp^3, **(h)** d^2sp^3, **(i)** d^2sp^3, **(j)** sp^3.

9.13 (a) triangular planar,
(b) angular,
(c) H—C≡N: linear,
(d) trigonal pyramidal,
(e) tetrahedral

9.15 (a) trigonal pyramidal,
(b) tetrahedral
(c) angular,
(d) angular,
(e) angular

9.17 (a) angular,
(b) O=$\overset{\oplus}{\text{N}}$=O linear,
(c) angular, **(d)** tetrahedral,

(e)

$:O:^\ominus$ 　　　　　 $:O:$

$^\ominus:O:$ — $N^\oplus$ — $O:$ 　⟷　 $^\ominus:O:$ — $N^\oplus$ = $O:$ — ⟷ —

$:O:^\ominus$

$^\ominus:O:$ — $N^\oplus$ — $O:^\ominus$ 　　triangular planar

9.19 (a)

$\underset{H}{}\;N=N=N:$ 　⟷　 $\underset{H}{}\;:N—N≡N:$

(b)

$\underset{H}{}\;:O—N:$ 　⟷　 $\underset{H}{}\;:O=N:$ 　$:O:$

(c)

$N=N$ and $N=N$ 　two compounds

(cis) 　　　(trans)

(d)

$N—N^\oplus$ ⟷ 　 $N—N^\oplus$ 　free rotation around the N—N bond

(e)

$\underset{H}{\overset{H}{C}}=N^\oplus=N:^\ominus$

9.21 (a)

$Xe^\oplus$ with F, F, F, F and $:O:^\ominus$ 　square pyramidal,

(b)

$I^\oplus$ with O—H groups 　octahedral,

(c)

$Xe\;(2+)$ 　octahedral, **(d)** $Cl^\oplus$ 　octahedral,

(e)

$I:^\oplus$ 　irregular tetrahedral

9.23 The bond pair for the P—F bond occupies a smaller volume than the bond pair for the P—Cl bond. The Cl atoms, therefore, occupy equatorial positions. For a bond pair in an equatorial position, *two* other bond pairs occur at an angle of 90°. For a bond pair in an axial position, *three* other bond pairs occur at an angle of 90°. The prediction has been confirmed by experiment.

9.25 The angle in CCl_4 is 109° 28′ (the tetrahedral angle). The effect of *one* lone pair in NCl_3 (a trigonal pyramidal molecule) reduces the angle from the tetrahedral angle and the effect of

two lone pairs in Cl_2O (an angular molecule) reduces the angle still more.

9.27 (a) 180°, *sp*; **(b)** 120°, *sp²*; **(c)** 109° 28′, *sp³*, **(d)** 90° and 120°, *dsp³*; **(e)** 90°, *d²sp³*.

9.29 The Lewis structure shows a triple bond ($:N≡N:$). The molecular-orbital energy level diagram for N_2 (following) shows a bond order of three. The bonding consists of one σ bond and two π bonds.

σ^*2p	——	
π^*2p	—— ——	
$\sigma\,2p$	⇅	
$\pi\,2p$	⇅ ⇅	
σ^*2s	⇅	
$\sigma 2s$	⇅	

9.31

	(a) H_2	(b) H_2^+	(c) HHe	(d) He_2	(e) He_2^+
σ^*1s	——	——	↑	⇅	↑
$\sigma 1s$	⇅	↑	⇅	⇅	⇅
Bond Order:	1	0.5	0.5	0	0.5

9.33 (a)

	C_2	C_2^{2-}
σ^*2p	——	——
π^*2p	—— ——	—— ——
$\sigma 2p$	——	⇅
$\pi 2p$	⇅ ⇅	⇅ ⇅
σ^*2s	⇅	⇅
$\sigma 2s$	⇅	⇅

(b) Bond order for C_2 is 2 and for C_2^{2-} is 3, **(c)** C_2^{2-} is isoelectronic with N_2.

9.35

	N_2	N_2^+
σ^*2p	——	——
π^*2p	—— ——	—— ——
$\sigma 2p$	⇅	↑
$\pi 2p$	⇅ ⇅	⇅ ⇅
σ^*2s	⇅	⇅
$\sigma 2s$	⇅	⇅
bond order:	3	2.5

	O_2	O_2^+
σ^*2p	——	——
π^*2p	↑ ↑	↑
$\pi 2p$	⇅ ⇅	⇅ ⇅
$\sigma 2p$	⇅	⇅
σ^*2s	⇅	⇅
$\sigma 2s$	⇅	⇅
bond order:	2	2.5

The bond order of N_2^+ (2.5) is less than that of N_2 (3) since a *bonding* electron is removed in the formation of the ion. The bond distance of N_2^+ (112 pm), therefore, is longer than that of N_2 (109 pm), the bond energy of N_2^+ (841 kJ/mol) is lower than that of N_2 (941 kJ/mol). The bond order of O_2^+ (2.5) is greater than that of O_2 (2) since an *antibonding* electron is removed in the formation of the ion. The bond distance of O_2^+ (112 pm), therefore, is shorter than that of O_2 (121 pm), and the bond energy of O_2^+ (623 kJ/mol) is higher than that of O_2 (490 kJ/mol).

9.37 In the SiO_4^{4-} ion, $p\pi$-$d\pi$ interaction results from the overlap of filled $2p$ orbitals of the O atoms with empty $3d$ orbitals of the Si atom.

10.1 **(a)** At constant temperature, the volume of a gas sample varies inversely with the pressure. **(b)** At constant pressure, the volume of a gas sample varies directly with the absolute temperature. **(c)** At constant volume, the pressure of a gas sample varies directly with the absolute temperature.

10.3 **(a)** 520. mL, **(b)** 1.04 atm, **(c)** 2.08 atm

10.5 **(a)** 2.04 L, **(b)** $-111°C$, **(c)** 82°C

10.7 **(a)** 1.70 atm, **(b)** $5.59 \times 10^3°C$, **(c)** $-78°C$

10.9 **(a)** 0.92 mL

10.11

P	V	n	T
2.00 atm	23.0 L	1.50 mol	100.°C
0.600 atm	1.00 L	0.0731 mol	100. K
4.45 atm	50.0 mL	0.0105 mol	$-15.°C$
59.4 atm	1.25 L	2.60 mol	75.°C

10.13 178 mL

10.15 346°C

10.17 0.251 L

10.19 0.254 g

10.21 0.981 g/L

10.23 0.541 atm

10.25 20.2 g/mol (the gas is Ne)

10.27 15.0 L $CH_4(g)$, 22.5 L $O_2(g)$, 15.0 L $NH_3(g)$ required; 45.0 L $H_2O(g)$ produced

10.29 **(a)** $4\,NH_3(g) + 5\,O_2(g) \longrightarrow 4\,NO(g) + 6\,H_2O(g)$ **(b)** 12.8 L NO(g)

10.31 0.100 L of $NH_3(g)$, 0.400 L of $N_2(g)$, 2.400 L of HCl(g)

10.33 **(a)** $4\,NH_3(g) + 3\,F_2(g) \longrightarrow NF_3(g) + 3\,NH_4F(s)$, **(b)** 307.6 mL of $NH_3(g)$ and 230.7 mL of $F_2(g)$.

10.35 1.96 g/L

10.37 128.0 g/mol

10.39 **(a)** 8.0×10^{-5} g SO_2, **(b)** 1.2×10^{-6} mol SO_2, **(c)** 2.8×10^{-8} atm, **(d)** 2.8×10^{-6}% SO_2 molecules

10.41 **(a)** $CaH_2(s) + 2\,H_2O(l) \longrightarrow Ca(OH)_2(s) + H_2(g)$, **(b)** 2.82 g $CaH_2(s)$

10.43 **(a)** $Al_4C_3(s) + 12\,H_2O(l) \longrightarrow 3\,CH_4(g) + 4\,Al(OH)_3(s)$, **(b)** 0.170 L

10.45 **(a)** $4\,NH_3(g) + 3\,F_2(g) \longrightarrow NF_3(g) + 3\,NH_4F(s)$, **(b)** 0.264 g $NF_3(g)$

10.47 **(a)** 0.00536 mol unknown, 0.0402 mol O_2, 0.0268 mol CO_2, and 0.0268 mol H_2O; **(b)** dividing each value by the smallest gives: 1:7.5:5:5, which in terms of whole numbers is 2:15:10:10, **(c)** $2\,C_5H_{10}(g) + 15\,O_2(g) \longrightarrow 10\,CO_2(g) + 10\,H_2O(l)$

*10.49 69.5% Al

10.51 $p_{O_2} = 0.280$ atm, $p_{N_2} = 0.320$ atm

10.53 **(a)** $X_{CH_4} = 0.577$, $X_{C_2H_6} = 0.423$; **(c)** 0.150 mol, **(c)** 1.39 g CH_4 and 1.90 g C_2H_6

10.55 596 mL

*10.57 0.122 atm

10.59 298 m/s at 100 K, 667 m/s at 500 K

10.61 471 K

10.63 the rate of effusion of N_2O is 0.798 times that of N_2

10.65 80.9 g/mol (the gas is HBr)

10.67 **(a)** 1.31 g/L, **(b)** 64.1 g/mol (the gas is SO_2)

10.69 0.900 g/L

10.71 **(a)** Cl_2, **(b)** He, **(c)** He, **(d)** Cl_2, **(e)** He

10.73 **(a)** 22.41 atm, **(b)** 21.79 atm, **(c)** The pressure calculated by the van der Waals equation is less than that calculated by the ideal gas law. The difference is caused principally by the failure of the ideal gas law to take the forces of attraction between O_2 molecules into consideration.

10.75 **(a)** 2.241 atm, **(b)** 2.235 atm, **(c)** the pressure calculated by the van der Waals equation is again less than that calculated by the ideal gas law. The difference, however, is less than the difference found in Problem 10.73. Since the volume is larger in this problem, the effect of the intermolecular attractive forces is lower and the gas behavior is more ideal.

10.77 **(a)** 1.77×10^{-26} L/molecule, **(b)** 0.0478% of the total volume is CO_2 gas is molecular volume

Chapter 11   Liquids and Solids

11.1 **(a)** OF_2 is an angular molecule, BeF_2 is a linear molecule; **(b)** PF_3 is a trigonal pyramidal molecule, BF_3 is triangular planar; **(c)** SF_4 is an irregular tetrahedral molecule, SnF_4 is a tetrahedral molecule.

11.3 $HgCl_2$, BF_3, CH_4, PCl_5 XeF_2, SF_6, XeF_4

11.5 Each molecule is linear. In O=C=O, the effect of the C=O bond dipoles cancel since the polarities are equal and opposite in direction. In S=C=O, however, the polarities of the C=S and C=O bonds are *not* equal and therefore cannot completely cancel. In S=C=S, the linear arrangement of two identical C=S bonds creates a molecule with a zero dipole moment.

11.7 The PF_5 molecule is trigonal bipyramidal and the effects of the P—F bond polarities cancel. The PF_3 molecule is trigonal pyramidal with a nonbonding pair of electrons on P, at the apex of the pyramid.

11.9 The melting points increase with increasing size of the molecules. An increase in size means that the electron clouds are larger, farther from the nucleus, and more easily distorted. Hence, the London forces are stronger in the larger molecules.

11.11 The ion consists of a F^- ion hydrogen bonded to a H-F molecule: $F \cdots H—F^-$

11.13 The anion of an acid salt (HSO_4^-) has a lower charge than the anion of the normal salt (SO_4^{2-}). Consequently, the lattice energies of acid salts are lower than those of normal salts. When a salt dissolves in water, the lattice energy represents energy *required* by the solution process. In addition, the anions of acid salts can hydrogen bond more extensively with H_2O molecules than the anions of normal salts can. The electrons on the O atoms of either the anion of the acid salt or the anion of the normal salt enable both types of ions to function as proton acceptors in the formation of H bonds with the H_2O molecules of the solution. In the case of the anion of the acid salt, however, the presence of the highly positive H atom permits such anions to act also as proton donors in the formation of hydrogen bonds.

11.15 Since the molecules are similar in size and shape, the London forces of each are similar. The H atoms and electron pairs of the $-NH_2$ groups, however, can enter into hydrogen bonding. Since $H_2NCH_2CH_2NH_2$ has *two* $-NH_2$ groups, hydrogen bonding is more extensive in this compound.

11.17 **(a)** A substance with strong intermolecular forces of attraction would have a high critical temperature since strong forces are capable of holding the molecules together into the liquid state even at high temperatures where the kinetic energies of the molecules are relatively high. **(b)** The molecules in the center of a liquid are attracted equally in all directions by surrounding molecules. The molecules at the surface of a liquid are attracted only toward the interior of the liquid. Strong intermolecular attractive forces lead to high surface tensions. (c) Strong intermolecular attractive forces means that molecules will *not* move past one another easily, the viscosity will be high. (d) A molecule can escape from the liquid phase into the gaseous phase only if it has enough energy to overcome the attractive forces of its neighbors. Strong intermolecular forces of attraction mean that fewer molecules will have enough energy to escape from the liquid phase to the vapor phase; low vapor pressures result. (e) A high enthalpy of vaporization means that a large quantity of energy is required to overcome the intermolecular forces of attraction, which therefore must be strong. (f) The normal boiling point of a liquid is that temperature at which the vapor pressure of the liquid is one atmosphere. Strong intermolecular forces mean that the vapor pressure at a given temperature is low. In order for the vapor pressure to equal one atmosphere, the temperature must be relatively high.

11.19 (a) The boiling point of a liquid is the temperature at which the vapor pressure of the liquid equals the pressure of the surroundings. If the pressure of the surroundings is increased, the temperature of the liquid must be increased until the vapor pressure of the liquid equals the pressure of the surroundings. **(b)** The normal boiling point of a liquid is the temperature at which the vapor pressure of the liquid equals one atmosphere. **(c)** At 0.50 atm, the boiling points are: diethyl ether, 15°C; ethyl alcohol, 60°C; water, 80.3°C

11.21 50.9 kJ/mol

11.23 65°C (338 K)

11.25 0.732 atm

11.27 81°C (354 K)

11.29 The phase diagram for H_2 has an overall appearance similar to that for CO_2 (see Figure 11.10). The scales of the axes must be changed.

11.31 (a) At -1°C: initially vapor; at 5.55×10^{-3} atm, vapor condenses to solid; at 133 atm, solid melts to liquid; **(b)** At 50°C: initially vapor; at 0.122 atm, vapor condenses to liquid; **(c)** At -50°C: initially vapor; at 3.89×10^{-5} atm vapor condenses to solid. It is impossible to get values as accurate as the ones that are given here by reading from the phase diagram in Figure 11.11.

11.33 (a) When water is heated at 1×10^{-3} atm, the only phase transition that occurs is at -20.2°C, where solid sublimes into vapor; **(b)** At 0.5 atm: solid initially; at 0.0625°C, the solid melts to liquid; at 81.6°C, the liquid vaporizes; **(c)** At 1.1 atm: solid initially; at 0.00175°C, solid melts into liquid; at 102.7°C, the liquid vaporizes. It is impossible to get values as accurate as the ones that are given here by reading from the phase diagram in Figure 11.11.

11.35 Ice can be purified by sublimation. The pressure would have to be less than the pressure at the triple point (0.00603 atm or 4.58 torr). If the pressure used is located on a vapor pressure curve for ice, the corresponding temperature would be a maximum for the condensing surface.

11.37 (a) covalent bonds (Si forms a network crystal), **(b)** metallic bonds, **(c)** London forces, **(d)** ionic bonds, **(e)** London forces, **(f)** London forces and dipole-dipole forces.

11.39 (a) BrF, greater electronegativity difference between Br and F creates higher dipole in molecule, **(b)** BrCl, molecule has a dipole since bonded atoms differ in electronegativity, **(c)** CsBr, an ionic compound, **(d)** Cs, metals have higher melting points than nonmetals, **(e)** C(diamond) forms a network crystal.

11.41 3.66 g/cm^3

11.43 4 atoms Ag/unit cell, face-centered cubic

11.45 55.8 g/mol (the element is Fe)

11.47 556 pm

11.49 a cube 2.07 cm on an edge

11.51 143 pm

*11.53 7.36 g/cm^3

11.55 171 pm

11.57 135 pm

11.59 194 pm

11.61 22.2°, 49.0°

11.63 (a) $4Na^+$ ions, $4Cl^-$ ions; **(b)** 555 pm; **(c)** 278 pm

11.65 (a) One Cs^+ ion, one Cl^- ion; **(b)** 412 pm; **(c)** 357 pm

11.67 (a) 594 pm, **(b)** 7.59 g/cm^3

11.69 (a) 358 pm, **(b)** 6.98 g/cm^3

11.71 NiS, BaO, CaS, NaBr, AgCl, KCl

11.73 (a) 0.5% O^{2-} vacancies, **(b)** 8.241 g/cm^3, **(c)** 8.236 g/cm^3

Chapter 12   Solutions

12.1 Whether $I_2(s)$ is melted or dissolved in CCl_4, energy must be added to overcome the attractive forces between I_2 molecules in the solid. The forces between I_2 molecules in liquid I_2 and the forces between I_2 and CCl_4 molecules in the solution are similar in strength and nature. When an ionic substance dissolves in water, the comparatively large energy required to melt the crystal (the lattice energy) is partly or completely offset by the energy released by the hydration of the ions. When an ionic crystal is melted, there is no energy effect comparable to the hydration energy.

12.3 Small ions and highly charged ions

12.5 (a) CH_3OH, **(b)** NaCl, **(c)** CH_3F

12.7 (a) Li^+, **(b)** Fe^{3+}, **(c)** Ca^{2+}, **(d)** F^-, **(e)** Be^{2+}

12.9 When an ionic solute dissolves in a nearly saturated solution, the enthalpy of hydration is less than when it dissolves in a very dilute solution. An ion is hydrated by fewer water molecules in a concentrated solution than in a dilute solution.

12.11 -52 kJ/mol

12.13 -830 kJ/mol The enthalpy of hydration is the energy released when the gaseous ions of the solute are hydrated. This enthalpy change is actually the sum of two enthalpy changes: the energy required to break some hydrogen bonds between some water molecules and the energy released when these water molecules hydrate the ions.

12.15 0.0231 mol N_2O, 1.02 g N_2O

12.17 0.200

12.19 25.8% $C_{10}H_8$

12.21 25.5 g $AgNO_3$

12.23 (a) 189.6 g concentrated HBr, **(b)** 126.4 mL concentrated HBr

12.25 (a) 28.1 M HF, **(b)** 46.2 m HF

12.27 0.642 M NaOH

12.29 90.5% $HCHO_2$

12.31 85.7 mL concentrated $HC_2H_3O_2$

12.33 2.06 M H_3PO_4

*12.35 (a) $2 Na(s) + 2 H_2O \longrightarrow 2 NaOH(aq) + H_2(g)$, **(b)** 0.0257 M NaOH

12.37 0.0842

12.39 0.418 m $C_{12}H_{22}O_{11}$

12.41 0.495 atm

12.43 0.456

12.45 0.411

12.47 (a) 0.414 atm, (b) negative, (c) evolved,
(d) maximum-boiling azeotrope

12.49 128 g/mol

12.51 500. g $C_2H_4(OH)_2$

12.53 $-11.8°C/m$

12.55 $-1.75°C$

12.57 154 g/mol

12.59 102.25°C

12.61 62.0 g/mol

12.63 1.09 atm

12.65 6.70×10^4 g/mol

12.67 537 g/mol

12.69 (a) 33.6 g/L, (b) 0.112 M

12.71 $i = 2.57$

12.73 $-3.40°C$

12.75 $-0.242°C$

Chapter 13 Reactions in Aqueous Solution

13.1 (a) $Fe(OH)_3(s) + H_3PO_4 \longrightarrow FePO_4(s) + 3H_2O$
(b) $Hg_2CO_3(s) + 2H^+ + 2Cl^- \longrightarrow Hg_2Cl_2(s) + H_2O + CO_2(g)$
(c) $3Na^+ + PO_4^{3-} + Ba^{2+} + 2Cl^- \longrightarrow$ N.R.
(d) $Ba^{2+} + S^{2-} + Zn^{2+} + SO_4^{2-} \longrightarrow BaSO_4(s) + ZnS(s)$
(e) $Pb^{2+} + 2NO_3^- + H_2S \longrightarrow PbS(s) + 2H^+ + NO_3^-$
net: $Pb^{2+} + H_2S \longrightarrow PbS(s) + 2H^+$

13.3 (a) $3Na^+ + PO_4^{3-} + 3H^+ + 3Br^- \longrightarrow H_3PO_4 + 3Na^+ + 3Br^-$
net: $3H^+ + PO_4^{3-} \longrightarrow H_3PO_4$
(b) $Mg^{2+} + 2NO_3^- + Ba^{2+} + 2OH^- \longrightarrow Mg(OH)_2(s) + Ba^{2+} + 2NO_3^-$
net: $Mg^{2+} + 2OH^- \longrightarrow Mg(OH)_2(s)$
(c) $Sn^{2+} + 2Cl^- + 2NH_4^+ + SO_4^{2-} \longrightarrow$ N.R.
(d) $2Na^+ + CO_3^{2-} + Sr^{2+} + 2C_2H_3O_2^- \longrightarrow SrCO_3(s) + 2Na^+ + 2C_2H_3O_2^-$
net: $Sr^{2+} + CO_3^{2-} \longrightarrow SrCO_3(s)$
(e) $ZnS(s) + 2H^+ + 2Cl^- \longrightarrow Zn^{2+} + 2Cl^- + H_2S(g)$
net: $ZnS(s) + 2H^+ \longrightarrow Zn^{2+} + H_2S(g)$

13.5 (a) $Pb^{2+} + 2NO_3^- + Mg^{2+} + SO_4^{2-} \longrightarrow PbSO_4(s) + Mg^{2+} + NO_3^-$
net: $Pb^{2+} + SO_4^{2-} \longrightarrow PbSO_4(s)$
(b) $Fe_2(CO_3)_3(s) + 6H^+ + 6NO_3^- \longrightarrow 2Fe^{3+} + 6NO_3^- + 3CO_2(g) + 3H_2O$
net: $Fe_2(CO_3)_3(s) + 6H^+ \longrightarrow 2Fe^{3+} + 3CO_2(g) + 3H_2O$
(c) $Cd^{2+} + 2ClO_3^- + 2K^+ + S^{2-} \longrightarrow CdS(s) + 2K^+ + 2ClO_3^-$
net: $Cd^{2+} + S^{2-} \longrightarrow CdS(s)$
(d) $Mn^{2+} + 2Cl^- + Co^{2+} + SO_4^{2-} \longrightarrow$ N.R.
(e) $2NH_4^+ + SO_4^{2-} + Ca^{2+} + 2OH^- \longrightarrow CaSO_4(s) + 2NH_3(g) + 2H_2O$

13.7 (a) 5+, (b) 3+, (c) 5+, (d) 4+, (e) 5+, (f) 4+, (g) 3+

13.9 (a) 2−, (b) 1−, (c) 6+, (d) 6+, (e) 5+, (f) 1+, (g) 4+

13.11 (a) 8+, (b) 5+, (c) 6+, (d) 5+, (e) 6+, (f) 2+

13.13 Oxidized (reducing agent): (a) Zn, (b) $SbCl_3$, (c) Mg,
(d) NO, (e) H_2. Reduced (oxidizing agent): (a) Cl_2, (b) $ReCl_5$,
(c) $CuCl_2$, (d) O_2, (e) WO_3.

13.15 (a) $4H_2O + 4MnO_4^- + 3ClO_2^- \longrightarrow 4MnO_2 + 3ClO_4^- + 4OH^-$
(b) $8H^+ + Cr_2O_7^{2-} + 3H_2S \longrightarrow 2Cr^{3+} + 3S + 7H_2O$

(c) $6H_2O + P_4 + 10HOCl \longrightarrow 4H_3PO_4 + 10Cl^- + 10H^+$
(d) $3Cu + 8H^+ + 2NO_3^- \longrightarrow 3Cu^{2+} + 2NO + 4H_2O$
(e) $PbO_2 + 4HI \longrightarrow PbI_2 + I_2 + 2H_2O$

13.17 (a) $6H^+ + ClO_3^- + 6I^- \longrightarrow Cl^- + 3I_2 + 3H_2O$
(b) $10H^+ + 4Zn + NO_3^- \longrightarrow 4Zn^{2+} + NH_4^+ + 3H_2O$
(c) $3H_3AsO_3 + BrO_3^- \longrightarrow 3H_3AsO_4 + Br^-$
(d) $2H_2SeO_3 + H_2S \longrightarrow 2Se + HSO_4^- + H^+ + 2H_2O$
(e) $4H_2O + 2ReO_2 + 3Cl_2 \longrightarrow 2HReO_4 + 6Cl^- + 6H^+$

13.19 (a) $6H_2O + 4AsH_3 + 24Ag^+ \longrightarrow As_4O_6 + 24Ag + 24H^+$
(b) $14H^+ + 2Mn^{2+} + 5BiO_3^- \longrightarrow 2MnO_4^- + 5Bi^{3+} + 7H_2O$
(c) $4H^+ + 2NO + 4NO_3^- \longrightarrow 3N_2O_4 + 2H_2O$
(d) $11H^+ + 2MnO_4^- + 5HCN + 5I^- \longrightarrow 2Mn^{2+} + 5ICN + 8H_2O$
(e) $12H^+ + 3Zn + 2H_2MoO_4 \longrightarrow 3Zn^{2+} + 2Mo^{3+} + 8H_2O$

13.21 (a) $OH^- + 5HClO_2 \longrightarrow 4ClO_2 + Cl^- + 3H_2O$
(b) $8OH^- + 8MnO_4^- + I^- \longrightarrow 8MnO_4^{2-} + IO_4^- + 4H_2O$
(c) $4OH^- + 2H_2O + P_4 \longrightarrow 2HPO_3^{2-} + 2PH_3$
(d) $OH^- + SbH_3 + 3H_2O \longrightarrow Sb(OH)_4^- + 3H_2$
(e) $CO(NH_2)_2 + 3OBr^- \longrightarrow CO_2 + N_2 + 3Br^- + 2H_2O$

13.23 (a) $8OH^- + S^{2-} + 4I_2 \longrightarrow SO_4^{2-} + 4H_2O + 8I^-$
(b) $H_2O + 3CN^- + 2MnO_4^- \longrightarrow 3CNO^- + 2MnO_2 + 2OH^-$
(c) $2H_2O + 4Au + 8CN^- + O_2 \longrightarrow 4Au(CN)_2^- + 4OH^-$
(d) $H_2O + Si + 2OH^- \longrightarrow SiO_3^{2-} + 2H_2$
(e) $4OH^- + 2Cr(OH)_3 + 3BrO^- \longrightarrow 2CrO_4^{2-} + 3Br^- + 5H_2O$

13.25 (a) $6H_2O + P_4 + 10HOCl \longrightarrow 4H_3PO_4 + 10Cl^- + 10H^+$
(b) $6H^+ + XeO_3 + 9I^- \longrightarrow Xe + 3I_3^- + 3H_2O$
(c) $8H^+ + 3UO^{2+} + Cr_2O_7^{2-} \longrightarrow 3UO_2^{2+} + 2Cr^{3+} + 4H_2O$
(d) $3H_2C_2O_4 + BrO_3^- \longrightarrow 6CO_2 + Br^- + 3H_2O$
(e) $4H^+ + 3Te + 4NO_3^- \longrightarrow 3TeO_2 + 4NO + 2H_2O$

13.27 Amphoteric oxides have both acidic and basic properties.
ZnO forms Zn^{2+} in acidic solution and $Zn(OH)_4^{2-}$ in alkaline
solution.

13.29 (a) $KOH + HNO_3 \longrightarrow KNO_3 + H_2O$
(b) $Ca(OH)_2 + 2HNO_3 \longrightarrow Ca(NO_3)_2 + 2H_2O$
(c) $Al(OH)_3 + 3HNO_3 \longrightarrow Al(NO_3)_3 + 3H_2O$

13.31 (a) $KOH + H_3PO_4 \longrightarrow KH_2PO_4 + H_2O$
(b) $2KOH + H_3PO_4 \longrightarrow K_2HPO_4 + 2H_2O$
(c) $3KOH + H_3PO_4 \longrightarrow K_3PO_4 + 3H_2O$

13.33 (a) $Cl_2O + H_2O \longrightarrow HOCl$
(b) $Cs_2O + H_2O \longrightarrow 2CsOH$
(c) $N_2O_5 + H_2O \longrightarrow 2HNO_3$
(d) $CO_2 + H_2O \longrightarrow H_2CO_3$
(e) $CaO + H_2O \longrightarrow Ca(OH)_2$

13.35 (a) Cl_2O_7, (b) N_2O_3, (c) SO_2, (d) B_2O_3, (e) Al_2O_3

13.37 (a) bromic acid, (b) nitric acid, (c) sulfurous acid, (d) potassium hydrogen sulfite, (e) potassium sulfate, (f) copper(II) chlorate

13.39 (a) $FePO_4$, (b) $Mg(ClO_4)_2$, (c) KH_2PO_4, (d) $PbSO_4$,
(e) $Fe(NO_2)_2$, (g) $Ni(NO_3)_2$

13.41 0.3858 M

13.43 41.29% $Mg(OH)_2$

13.45 69.6% $KHC_8H_4O_4$

13.47 (a) 0.0447 g NaCl, (b) 0.894% NaCl

13.49 (a) $3N_2H_4 + 2BrO_3^- \longrightarrow 3N_2 + 2Br^- + 6H_2O$,
(b) 24.0% N_2H_4

13.51 (a) 1/4, (b) 1/6, (c) 1/5, (d) 1/6, (e) 1/2, (f) 1/4

13.53 6.00 N HCl, 12.0 N H_2SO_4, 18.00 N H_3PO_4

13.55 57.0 mL

13.57 0.409 N

13.59 (a) 90.0 g/equivalent, (b) one

13.61 (a) 0.1200 N $K_2Cr_2O_7$, (b) 0.0750 N $KMnO_4$, (c) 0.0150 M $KMnO_4$

Chapter 14 Chemical Kinetics

14.1 (a) rate of formation of C = $k[A][B]$, (b) 0.016 L/(mol·s)

14.3 (a) k = 0.100 mol/(L·s),   rate = 0.100 mol/(L·s); (b) k = 0.100/s,
rate = 0.0050 mol/(L·s); (c) k = 0.100 L/(mol·s), rate = 0.00025 mol/(L·s)

14.5 (a) 3/16 of the original rate, (b) zero, (c) 2/27 of the original rate, (d) 4 times the original rate, (e) 8 times the original rate

14.7 The reactant molecules may be improperly aligned or the collision may be so gentle that the molecules rebound unchanged.

14.9 (a) 0.0803 mol/L, (b) 87.0 hr, (c) 241 hr

14.11 120 hr

14.13 (a) 0.00403 mol/L, (b) 1.12 × 10³ s

14.15 204 s

14.17 5.30 × 10⁻⁴/s

14.19 The plot of log [SO_2Cl_2] *versus* t is a straight line; the reaction is first order in SO_2Cl_2.

14.21 step 1: ICl + H₂ ⟶ HCl + HI;
step 2: HI + ICl ⟶ HCl + I₂

14.23 [A] = (k_1/k_2)[A]; therefore, rate = (k_1k_3/k_2)[A]

*14.25 *rate of appearance of NO_3 = rate of disappearance of NO_3*
$$k_1[NO][O_2] = k_2[NO_3] + k_3[NO_3][NO]$$
The last term $(k_3[NO_3][NO])$ may be neglected since k_3 is small.
$$[NO_3] = (k_1/k_2)[NO][O_2]$$
Since step 3 is rate-determining:
$$\text{rate} = k_3[NO_3][NO]$$
substitute the expression for the concentration of NO_3 into this rate equation:
$$\text{rate} = (k_1k_3/k_2)[NO]^2[O_2]$$

14.27 See Figure 14.17. A catalyst provides a new pathway for the reaction. This mechanism has a lower energy of activation so that a higher fraction of collisions are effective and the reaction is faster. The value of ΔH is not changed by a catalyst. The change in enthalpy is not affected by the height of E_a between the reactants and products but depends only upon the energy levels of the reactants and products. Since the uncatalyzed path is presumably always available, a catalyst cannot slow a reaction down by forcing it to take a path with a higher E_a. Both $E_{a,f}$ and $E_{a,r}$ are decreased by the same amount of energy by the catalyst so that the forward and reverse reactions are affected to the same degree.

14.29 7.9 × 10⁵ L/(mol·s)

14.31 267 kJ/mol

14.33 4.7 × 10⁻³ L/(mol·s)

14.35 667 K (or 395°C)

14.37 52.3 kJ/mol

Chapter 15 Chemical Equilibrium

15.1 (a) $\dfrac{[CS_2][H_2]^4}{[H_2S]^2[CH_4]} = K_c$ (b) $\dfrac{[N_2O_4]}{[NO_2]^2} = K_c$

(c) $[O_2] = K_c$ **(d)** $\dfrac{[CO]^2}{[CO_2]} = K_c$ **(e)** $\dfrac{[N_2][O_2]}{[NO]^2} = K_c$

15.3 (a) left, (b) right, (c) left, (d) left (e) no change

15.5 (a) $\dfrac{(p_{CS_2})(p_{H_2})^4}{(p_{H_2S})^2(p_{CH_4})} = K_p$, $K_p = K_c(RT)^{+2}$

(b) $\dfrac{(p_{N_2O_4})}{(p_{NO_2})^2} = K_p$, $K_p = K_c(RT)^{-1}$

(c) $p_{O_2} = K_p$, $K_p = K_c(RT)^{+1}$ **(d)** $\dfrac{(p_{CO})^2}{(p_{CO_2})} = K_p$, $K_p = K_c(RT)^{+1}$

(e) $\dfrac{(p_{N_2})(p_{O_2})}{(p_{NO})^2} = K_p$, $K_p = K_c$

15.7 endothermic

15.9 (a) right, (b) right, (c) right, (d) left, (e) no change

15.11 (a) right, (b) no change, (c) no change, (d) right, (e) right

15.13 left

15.15 right

15.17 61

15.19 (a) [SO_3] = 0.0380 mol/L, [SO_2] = 0.0220 mol/L, [O_2] = 0.0110 mol/L; (b) 3.69 × 10⁻³ mol/L

15.21 0.0028 mol/L

15.23 [H_2O] = [CO] = 0.280 mol/L, [H_2] = [CO_2] = 0.320 mol/L

15.25 [H_2] = [I_2] = 0.319 mol/L, [HI] = 2.362 mol/L

15.27 (a) [CO] = 0.0356 mol/L, [CO_2] = 0.0144 mol/L; (b) 0.804 g Fe

15.29 (a) 0.724 atm, (b) 0.263/atm

15.31 0.0942 atm²

15.33 (a) [CO] = [H_2O] = 0.0335 mol/L, [CO_2] = [H_2] = 0.0665 mol/L; (b) K_c = 3.94; (c) K_p = K_c = 3.94

15.35 (a) p_{PCl_5} = 0.286 atm, p_{PCl_3} = p_{Cl_2} = 0.714 atm; (b) K_p = 1.78 atm

15.37 14.4/atm

15.39 K_p = 0.0694 atm, K_c = 1.12 × 10⁻³ mol/L

15.41 0.563 mol²/L²

15.43 K_p = 8.77 × 10⁻⁴/atm², K_c = 1.78 L²/mol²

15.45 0.024 atm

Chapter 16 Theories of Acids and Bases

16.1 Brønsted: acid₁ (NH_4^+) reacts with base₂ (NH_2^-) to form conjugate base₁ (NH_3) and conjugate acid₂ (NH_3). According to this theory, NH_3 is amphiprotic; Lewis: a nucleophilic displacement of NH_3 by NH_2^- on NH_4^+. Solvent system: acid (NH_4Cl) reacts with base ($NaNH_2$) to form solvent ($2NH_3$) and a salt ($NaCl$).

16.3 (a) Arrhenius concept: H_2O is neither an acid nor a base. (b) Brønsted-Lowry concept: H_2O (which is amphiprotic) can function as an acid: $H_2O + NH_2^- \rightleftharpoons NH_3 + OH^-$ or base: $NH_3 + H_2O \rightleftharpoons H_3O^+ + NH_4^+$ (c) Lewis concept: H_2O can supply a pair of electrons for the formation of a covalent bond and as such is a nucleophilic substance (a base):

$$H^+ + :\overset{\displaystyle ..}{\underset{\displaystyle |}{O}}-H \longrightarrow H-\overset{\displaystyle ..}{\underset{\displaystyle |}{O}}-H^+$$
$$\qquad\quad H \qquad\qquad\qquad H$$

16.5 (a) $H_2PO_4^-$, (b) HPO_4^{2-}, (c) NH_2^-, (d) S^{2-}, (e) HSO_4^-

16.7 (a) H_2, (b) H_3O^+, (c) H_2S, (d) NH_4^+, (e) H_3AsO_4

16.9 　Acid$_1$　　Base$_2$　　Acid$_2$　　Base$_1$
(a) HCl 　+ NH_3 　$\rightleftharpoons$ 　NH_4^+ 　+ Cl^-
(b) HSO_4^- + CN^- 　$\rightleftharpoons$ 　HCN + SO_4^{2-}
(c) $H_2PO_4^-$ + CO_3^{2-} $\rightleftharpoons$ HCO_3^- + HPO_4^{2-}
(d) H_3O^+ + HS^- 　$\rightleftharpoons$ 　H_2S + H_2O
(e) HS^- 　+ OH^- 　$\rightleftharpoons$ 　H_2O 　+ S^{2-}

16.11 (a) $H_2O + NH_2^- \rightleftharpoons NH_3 + OH^-$
(b) $HF + OH^- \rightleftharpoons H_2O + F^-$
(c) $HSO_3^- + H_2O \rightleftharpoons H_3O^+ + SO_3^{2-}$
(d) $NH_4^+ + OH^- \rightleftharpoons H_2O + NH_3$
(e) $NH_3 + H^- \rightleftharpoons H_2 + NH_2^-$

16.13 (a) $H_2O + H^- \rightleftharpoons H_2 + OH^-$
(b) $H_3O^+ + OH^- \rightleftharpoons H_2O + H_2O$
(c) $NH_3 + N^{3-} \rightleftharpoons NH^{2-} + NH_2^-$
(d) $HCN + H_2O \rightleftharpoons H_3O^+ + CN^-$
(e) $HSO_4^- + HClO_4 \rightleftharpoons ClO_4^- + H_2SO_4$

16.15 Acids (strength decreasing): H_3O^+, H_3PO_4, HCN, H_2O, NH_3 Bases (strength decreasing): NH_2^-, OH^-, CN^-, $H_2PO_4^-$, H_2O

16.17 (a) yes, **(b)** no, **(c)** no, **(d)** yes

16.19 HBr is a strong acid, H_2Se is a weak acid, and AsH_3 is not acidic. The acid strengths of the hydrides of the elements of a period increase from left to right across the period in the same order that the electronegativities of the elements increase.

16.21 (a) H_3PO_4, **(b)** H_3AsO_4, **(c)** H_2SO_4, **(d)** H_2CO_3, **(e)** HBr

16.23 (a) P^{3-}, **(b)** NH_3, **(c)** SiO_3^{2-}, **(d)** NO_2^-, **(e)** F^-

16.25

H_2SeO_4 is a stronger acid than H_6TeO_6.

16.27 (a) acid: $AuCN$, base: CN^-; **(b)** acid: HF, base: F^-; **(c)** acid: S, base: S^{2-}; **(d)** acid: CS_2, base: SH^-; **(e)** acid: Fe, base: CO.

16.29 (a) nucleophilic, I^- displaced by OH^-; **(b)** nucleophilic, OH^- displaced by S^{2-}; **(c)** electrophilic, Br^+ displaced by $FeBr_3$, **(d)** nucleophilic, NH_3 displaced by OH^-; **(e)** electrophilic, NO_2^+ displaced by H^+

Chapter 17　Ionic Equilibria, Part I

17.1 1.3×10^{-5}

17.3 2.3×10^{-5}

17.5 3.8×10^{-3}

17.7 (a) $4.9 \times 10^{-3} M$, **(b)** 3.1%

17.9 $[N_2H_5^+] = [OH^-] = 3.8 \times 10^{-4} M$, $[N_2H_4] = 0.15 M$

17.11 2.7% ionized

17.13 (a) $0.082 M$, **(b)** 0.112 mol $HClO_2$

17.15 $0.18 M$

17.17 $[H^+] = 1.5 \times 10^{-5} M$, $[N_3^-] = 0.13 M$, $[HN_3] = 0.10 M$

17.19 $[OH^-] = 0.15 M$, $[HONH_3^+] = 1.5 \times 10^{-8} M$, $[HONH_2] = 0.20 M$

17.21 $[NH_3] = 0.15 M$, $[OH^-] = 0.05 M$, $[NH_4^+] = 5.4 \times 10^{-5} M$

*17.23 $[H^+] = 0.048 M$, $[ClO_2^-] = 0.048 M$, $[HClO_2] = 0.21 M$

17.25 (a) $[H^+] = 0.015 M$, $[OH^-] = 6.7 \times 10^{-13} M$; **(b)** $[H^+] = 2.0 \times 10^{-12} M$, $[OH^-] = 0.0050 M$

17.27 (a) 4.14, **(b)** 1.08, **(c)** 10.52, **(d)** 12.62

17.29 (a) $0.059 M$, **(b)** $1.2 \times 10^{-11} M$, **(c)** $2.1 \times 10^{-10} M$, **(d)** $0.022 M$

17.31 (a) $2.1 \times 10^{-11} M$, **(b)** $9.8 \times 10^{-7} M$, **(c)** $0.69 M$, **(d)** $6.0 \times 10^{-11} M$

17.33 7.3×10^{-6}

17.35 11.37

17.37 0.0031 mol $HClO_2$

17.39 $6.57 - 8.35$

17.41 (a) 3.80, **(b)** 0.46%

17.43 5.5×10^{-5}

17.45 $0.70 M$

17.47 4.85

17.49 $[NH_4^+]/[NH_3] = 0.56$

17.51 (a) $[H^+] = [HCO_3^-] = 1.2 \times 10^{-4} M$, $[CO_3^{2-}] = 4.8 \times 10^{-11} M$, $[CO_2] = 0.034 M$, **(b)** 3.92

17.53 (a) $4.9 \times 10^{-21} M$, **(b)** $7.4 \times 10^{-8} M$

17.55 $1.9 \times 10^{-3} M$

17.57 8.26

17.59 2.68

17.61 $0.60 M$

17.63 4.3×10^{-7}

*17.65 5.82

17.67 (a) 3.92, **(b)** 8.46, **(c)** 12.16

17.69 6.2×10^{-6}

Chapter 18　Ionic Equilibrium, Part II

18.1 (a) $[Bi^{3+}]^2[S^{2-}]^3 = K_{SP}$, **(b)** $[Pb^{2+}][CrO_4^{2-}] = K_{SP}$, **(c)** $[Ag^+]^2[C_2O_4^{2-}] = K_{SP}$, **(d)** $[Ag^+][IO_3^-] = K_{SP}$

18.3 2.0×10^{-14}

18.5 8.3×10^{-11}

18.7 molar solubility of $CuCO_3$ (1.6×10^{-5} mol $CuCO_3$/L) lower than that of Ag_2CO_3 (1.3×10^{-4} mol Ag_2CO_3/L)

18.9 5.8×10^{-4} mol SrF_2/L

18.11 3.3×10^{-13} mol $Ni(OH)_2$

18.13 4.2×10^{-4} mol BaF_2

18.15 $[Na^+] = 0.16 M$, $[Cl^-] = 0.30 M$, $[Ba^{2+}] = 0.070 M$, $[C_2O_4^{2-}] = 2.1 \times 10^{-7} M$

18.17 $9.5 \times 10^{-4} M$ F^-

18.19 $1.2 M$ NH_4^+

18.21 $0.18 M$ NH_3

18.23 $PbCl_2$ will not precipitate, ion product $= 8.4 \times 10^{-7}$, $K_{SP} = 1.6 \times 10^{-5}$

18.25 $CaSO_4$ will precipitate, ion product $= 2.2 \times 10^{-4}$, $K_{SP} = 2.4 \times 10^{-5}$

18.27 (a) $PbSO_4$ will precipitate first, **(b)** $[Pb^{2+}] = 4.3 \times 10^{-5} M$

18.29 NiS will not precipitate, ion product $= 1.8 \times 10^{-22}$, $K_{SP} = 3.0 \times 10^{-21}$

18.31 $2.0 \times 10^{-4} M$

18.33 $0.086 M$ H^+ (minimum)

18.35 $2.3 \times 10^{-7} M$ Pb^{2+}

18.37 (a) 2.4×10^{-2} mol AgCl/L, **(b)** 1.4×10^{-3} mol AgBr/L, **(c)** 1.9×10^{-5} mol AgI/L

Chapter 19 Elements of Chemical Thermodynamics

19.1 The first law states that energy can be converted from one form into another but it cannot be created or destroyed. Enthalpy, H, is related to internal energy, E, of a system by the equation: $H = E + PV$, where P is the pressure and V is the volume of the system.

19.3 (a) -1364.3 kJ/mol, **(b)** -1366.8 kJ, **(c)** -277.9 kJ/mol

19.5 -5459.55 kJ

19.7 -66.58 kJ

19.9 -184.79 kJ/mol

19.11 A reaction is spontaneous if it results in an increase in the total entropy of the system and its surroundings. If the system alone is considered, a spontaneous change is indicated if the Gibbs free energy of the system decreases.

19.13 $+267.4$ kJ, -207.0 kJ, $H_2S(g)$ and $H_2O(l)$

19.15 For BF_3: $\Delta G^\circ = +12.09$ kJ; for BCl_3: $\Delta G^\circ = -266.19$ kJ; BCl_3 will hydrolyze at 25°C, but BF_3 will not.

19.17 $\Delta G^\circ = -48.39$ kJ; HCOOH will decompose spontaneously

19.19 (a) -101.01 kJ, **(b)** -120.6 J/K, **(c)** -120.6 J/K

19.21 $+18.25$ kJ/mol

19.23 (a) $+38.3$ kJ, no; **(b)** -11.8 kJ, yes

19.25 239.7 K (or -33.4°C)

19.27 208 J/(K·mol)

19.29 -1095.00 kJ

19.31 $K_p = 0.282$, 0.282 atm

19.33 5.12×10^{-4}

19.35 $K_p = 0.443$

19.37 $+38.5$ kJ

19.39 $+27$ kJ

19.41 (a) $+181$ kJ, **(b)** 1.37×10^{-3}

19.43 1.1×10^{-4}

Chapter 20 Electrochemistry

20.1 In metallic conduction, electrons moving through a metallic crystal carry the charge. In electrolytic conduction, ions moving through the molten salt or the solution carry the charge. Electrolytic conduction also involves electrode reactions (oxidation at the anode and reduction at the cathode).

20.3 (a) anions, **(b)** oxidations, **(c)** positive, **(d)** electrons leave the cell from the anode.

20.5 (a) cathode: $2 H_2O + 2e^- \longrightarrow H_2 + 2OH^-$,
   anode: $2 H_2O \longrightarrow 4 H^+ + O_2 + 4e^-$
(b) cathode: $2 H_2O + 2e^- \longrightarrow H_2 + 2 OH^-$,
   anode: $2 Cl^- \longrightarrow Cl_2 + 2e^-$
(c) cathode: $Cu^{2+} + 2e^- \longrightarrow Cu$, anode: $2Cl^- \longrightarrow Cl_2 + 2e^-$
(d) cathode: $Cu^{2+} + 2e^- \longrightarrow Cu$,
   anode: $2 H_2O \longrightarrow 4 H^+ + O_2 + 4e^-$

20.7 0.684 g Ni

20.9 (a) $Pb^{2+} + 2 H_2O \longrightarrow PbO_2(s) + 4 H^+ + 2e^-$,
(b) 1.39 g PbO_2, **(c)** 51.7 min

20.11 28.6 min.

20.13 (a) 780 C, **(b)** 0.867 A

20.15 5.99 L $Cl_2(g)$

20.17 6.00 L $Cl_2(g)$

20.19 1.07 M OH^-

20.21 $[Cu^{2+}] = 0.358$ M, $[Cl^-] = 0.717$ M

20.23 (a) $+2.227$ V, **(b)** $Mg + Sn^{2+} \longrightarrow Mg^{2+} + Sn$, **(c)** the Sn^{2+}/Sn electrode

20.25 (a) $Pt(s)|I_2(s)|I^-(aq)||Cl^-(aq)|Cl_2(g)|Pt(s)$,
(b) $+0.8240$ V, **(c)** the Cl_2/Cl^- electrode is the cathode

20.27 -1.789 V

20.29 (a) $PbSO_4$; Cd^{2+}; Cr^{3+};
(b) Au^+; PbO_2, SO_4^{2-}, and H^+; HOCl and H^+; Ce^{4+};
(c) Ga; Cr; Zn; **(d)** Au^+; Cl^-; Cr^{3+}; Tl^+

20.31 (a) no, **(b)** $H_2O_2 + 2 Ag^+ \longrightarrow 2 Ag + O_2 + 2 H^+$,
(c) $Ag^+ + Fe^{2+} \longrightarrow Ag + Fe^{3+}$, **(d)** no

20.33 (a) $H_2SO_3 + 2H_2S \longrightarrow 3 S + 3 H_2O$.
(b) $2 MnO_4^- + 3 Mn^{2+} + 2 H_2O \longrightarrow 5 MnO_2 + 4 H^+$,
(c) $Hg + Hg^{2+} \longrightarrow Hg_2^{2+}$, **(d)** no

20.35 (a) In^+ will disproportionate, **(b)** In^{3+},
(c) In will react with Cl_2, In^{3+} will be produced,
(d) $3 In^+ \longrightarrow 2 In + In^{3+}$, $2 In + 6 H^+ \longrightarrow 2 In^{3+} + 3 H_2$,
$2 In + 3 Cl_2 \longrightarrow 2 In^{3+} + 6 Cl^-$

20.37 (a) -1.208 V, **(b)** Ti^{2+} will not disproportionate,
(c) Ti will react with H^+(aq), Ti^{2+} is produced.

20.39 (a) $+1.397$ V, **(b)** Au^+ will disproportionate,
(c) Au will not react with H^+(aq).

20.41 (a) $Pb(s)|PbSO_4(s)|SO_4^{2-}(aq)||Pb^{2+}(aq)|Pb(s)$,
(b) $Pb^{2+} + SO_4^{2-} \longrightarrow PbSO_4$, **(c)** $+0.233$ V, **(d)** -45.0 kJ

20.43 (a) $Pt(s)|H_2(g)|OH^-(aq)||H^+(aq)|H_2(g)|Pt(s)$,
(b) $+0.828$ V, -79.9 kJ

20.45 (a) $+0.2943$ V, **(b)** -56.79 kJ, **(c)** -121.7 J/K

20.47 (a) -509.5 kJ, **(b)** -43.5 kJ/mol

20.49 7.1×10^3

20.51 1.0×10^{-4}

20.53 (a) $+2.157$ V, **(b)** $Mg + Ni^{2+} \longrightarrow Mg^{2+} + Ni$,
(c) the Ni^{2+}/Ni electrode is positive

20.55 (a) $+2.2406$ V, **(b)** $Zn + Cl_2 \longrightarrow Zn^{2+} + 2Cl^-$,
(c) the Zn^{2+}/Zn electrode is negative

20.57 $[Cd^{2+}] = 2.04$ M

20.59 (a) $\mathscr{E}^\circ = -0.13$ V, no, **(b)** $\mathscr{E} = +0.05$ V, yes

20.61 (a) increased by 0.00891 V, **(b)** decreased by 0.00891 V

20.63 (a) $+0.136$ V,
(b) $H_2 + 2 H^+(5.00\ M) \longrightarrow H_2 + 2 H^+(0.0250\ M)$,
(c) $+0.175$ V

Chapter 21 The Nonmetals, Part I: Hydrogen and the Halogens

21.1 Hydrogen occurs in water, hydrocarbons (found in coal, petroleum, and natural gas), a few minerals (such as clay and hydrates), and the organic compounds that constitute the principal part of all plant and animal matter.

21.3 (a) $Na(s) + H_2(g) \longrightarrow 2 NaH(s)$,
(b) $Ca(s) + H_2(g) \longrightarrow CaH_2(s)$,
(c) $Cl_2(g) + H_2(g) \longrightarrow 2 HCl(g)$,
(d) $N_2(g) + 3 H_2(g) \rightleftharpoons 2 NH_3(g)$,
(e) $Cu_2O(s) + H_2(g) \longrightarrow 2 Cu(s) + H_2O(g)$,
(f) $CO(g) + H_2(g) \longrightarrow CH_3OH(l)$,
(g) $WO_3(s) + 3 H_2(g) \longrightarrow W(s) + 3 H_2O(g)$

21.5 The low melting point, low boiling point, and low critical temperature reflect the weak nature of the London forces between H_2 molecules. The forces are relatively weak because the electron cloud of the molecule is relatively small.

21.7 CaH_2 is an ionic, crystalline solid. It reacts with water to produce $H_2(g)$ and $Ca(OH)_2$. HCl is a covalent gas. It ionizes in water to produce hydrochloric acid, $H^+(aq)$ and $Cl^-(aq)$.

21.9 (a) 8.922 g Al, **(b)** 32.43 g Zn, **(c)** 58.87 g Sn

21.11 (a) 26.1 g H_2, **(b)** 289 L

21.13 The halogens occur most commonly as halide ions. Fluorospar, CaF_2, cryolite, Na_3AlF_6, and fluroapatite, $Ca_5(PO_4)_3F$, are important sources of fluorine. Chlorine, bromine, and iodine occur in sea water as halide ions. Rock salt, NaCl, is an important source of chlorine. Oil-well brines, sodium iodate ($NaIO_3$), and sodium periodate ($NaIO_4$) are sources of iodine.

21.15 (a) $CaF_2(s) + H_2SO_4(l) \longrightarrow 2 HF(g) + CaSO_4(s)$
$HF(l) + KF(s) \longrightarrow KHF_2(s)$
electrolysis, heat: $2 KHF_2(l) \longrightarrow H_2(g) + F_2(g) + 2 KF(l)$
(b) electrolysis, heat: $2 NaCl(l) \longrightarrow 2 Na(l) + Cl_2(g)$
(c) $2 Br^-$ (aq, sea water) $+ Cl_2(g) \longrightarrow Br_2(l) + 2 Cl^-(aq)$
(d) $2 IO_3^-(aq) + 5 HSO_3^-(aq) \longrightarrow I_2(s) + 5 SO_4^{2-}(aq) + 3 H^+(aq) + H_2O$
(e) $PBr_3(l) + 3 H_2O \longrightarrow 3 HBr(g) + H_3PO_3(aq)$

21.17 (a) $6 HF(aq) + SiO_2(s) \longrightarrow 2 H^+(aq) + SiF_6^{2-}(aq) + 2 H_2O$
$4 HF(aq) + SiO_2(s) \longrightarrow SiF_4(g) + 2 H_2O$
(b) $2 HF(aq) + CO_3^{2-}(aq) \longrightarrow 2 F^-(aq) + CO_2(g) + H_2O$
(c) $HF(l) + KF(s) \longrightarrow KHF_2(l)$
$HF(aq) + F^-(aq) \longrightarrow HF_2^-(aq)$
(d) $2 HF(aq) + CaO(s) \longrightarrow CaF_2(s) + H_2O$

21.19 HF is a weak acid: $HF \rightleftharpoons H^+ + F^-$. In concentrated solutions, however, the F^- ion becomes associated with HF molecules: $F^- + HF \longrightarrow HF_2^-$. This reaction decreases $[F^-]$ in the solution and drives the HF ionization reaction to the right causing an increase in $[H^+]$.

21.21 (a) acid strength of HCl, **(b)** electronegativity of fluorine, **(c)** bond energy of Cl_2, **(d)** bond energy of Cl_2, **(e)** water solubility of AgF

21.23 (a) BeF_2, fluorine more electronegative than chlorine; **(b)** $FeCl_2$, compounds of the lower oxidation state of iron are more ionic; **(c)** MgI_2, Sr has a lower first ionization energy than Mg; **(d)** RbCl, oxidation number of Sr^{2+} is larger than that of Rb^+ and size of Sr^{2+} is smaller than that of Rb^+.

21.25 See Figure 21.4: ClO^-, linear; ClO_2^-, angular; ClO_3^-, trigonal pyramidal; ClO_4^-, tetrahedral

21.27 (a) $2 NaCl(l) \longrightarrow 2 Na(l) + Cl_2(g)$
(b) $2 Cl^-(aq) + 2 H_2O \longrightarrow H_2(g) + Cl_2(g) + 2 OH^-(aq)$
(c) $Cl^-(aq) + H_2O \longrightarrow OCl^-(aq) + H_2(g)$
(d) $Cl^-(aq) + 3 H_2O \longrightarrow ClO_3^-(aq) + 3 H_2(g)$
(e) $ClO_3^-(aq) + H_2O \longrightarrow ClO_4^-(aq) + H_2(g)$

21.29 1324 g $Cl_2(g)$

Chapter 22 The Nonmetals, Part II: The Group VI A Elements

22.1 Free O_2 in air. Combined oxygen in: SiO_2; oxide, carbonate, sulfate, and silicate minerals; water; compounds found in plants and animals. Most O_2 is obtained commercially by the liquefaction and fractionation of air. Small amounts are prepared industrially by the electrolysis of water.

22.3 (a) $O_2(g) + K(s) \longrightarrow KO_2(s)$
(b) $O_2(g) + 2 Na(s) \longrightarrow Na_2O_2(s)$
(c) $O_2(g) + 4 Li(s) \longrightarrow 2 Li_2O(s)$
(d) $O_2(g) + 2 Mg(s) \longrightarrow 2 MgO(s)$

(e) $O_2(g) + 2 Hg(l) \longrightarrow 2 HgO(s)$
(f) $O_2(g) + Ba(s) \longrightarrow BaO_2(s)$

22.5 (a) $C_2H_5OH(l) + 3 O_2(g) \longrightarrow 2 CO_2(g) + 3 H_2O$
(b) $2 C_3H_6(g) + 9 O_2(g) \longrightarrow 6 CO_2(g) + 6 H_2O(l)$
(c) $2 C_4H_{10}S(l) + 15 O_2(g) \longrightarrow$
$8 CO_2(g) + 10 H_2O(l) + 2 SO_2(g)$
(d) $2 PbS(s) + 3 O_2(g) \longrightarrow 2 PbO(s) + 2 SO_2(g)$
(e) $2 CuS(s) + 3 O_2(g) \longrightarrow 2 CuO(s) + 2 SO_2(g)$

22.7 (a)

	O_2^+	O_2^-
σ^*2p	⎯⎯	⎯⎯
π^*2p	↑ ⎯	↑↓ ↑
$\pi 2p$	↑↓ ↑↓	↑↓ ↑↓
$\sigma 2p$	↑↓	↑↓
σ^*2s	↑↓	↑↓
$\sigma 2s$	↑↓	↑↓

(b) bond order: 2.5   1.5
(c) unpaired electrons: 1   1

22.9 (a) $CH_4(g) + 2 O_2(g) \longrightarrow C(s) + 2 H_2O(l)$
(b) $2 CH_4(g) + 3 O_2(g) \longrightarrow 2 CO(g) + 4 H_2O(l)$
(c) $CH_4(g) + 2 O_2(g) \longrightarrow CO_2(g) + 2 H_2O(l)$

22.11 (a) -285.9 kJ, **(b)** -333.3 kJ, the reactions of O_3 are more exothermic than those of O_2

22.13 See Section 22.9. The sulfur is melted underground by water that is heated to approximately $170°C$ under pressure and forced down to the deposits. A froth of sulfur, air, and water is forced to the surface by hot, compressed air.

22.15 (a) $S(s) + O_2(g) \longrightarrow SO_2(g)$
(b) $S(s) + S^{2-}(aq) \longrightarrow S_2^{2-}(aq)$
(c) $S(s) + SO_3^{2-}(aq) \longrightarrow S_2O_3^{2-}(aq)$
(d) $S(s) + Fe(s) \longrightarrow FeS(s)$
(e) $S(s) + 3 F_2(g) \longrightarrow SF_6(g)$
$S(s) + 2 F_2(g) \longrightarrow SF_4(g)$
(f) $2 S(s) + Cl_2(g) \longrightarrow S_2Cl_2(l)$
(g) $S(s) + 4 HNO_3(l) \longrightarrow SO_2(g) + 4 NO_2(g) + 2 H_2O$

22.17 (a) $H_2O + CH_3CS(NH_2)(s) \longrightarrow$
$H_2S(g) + CH_3CO(NH_2)(aq)$
(b) $H_2O + SO_2(g) \longrightarrow H_2SO_3(aq)$
(c) $H_2O + SO_3(g) \longrightarrow H_2SO_4(aq)$
(d) $3 H_2O + Al_2S_3(s) \longrightarrow 3 H_2S(g) + Al(OH)_3(s)$
(e) $H_2O + SeO_2(s) \longrightarrow H_2SeO_3(aq)$
(f) $H_2O + TeO_2(s) \longrightarrow H_2TeO_3(aq)$
(g) $H_2O + H_2SO_5(l) \longrightarrow H_2SO_4(l) + H_2O_2(l)$
(h) $H_2O + H_2S_2O_7(l) \longrightarrow 2 H_2SO_4(l)$

22.19 (a) $H\!-\!\overset{..}{\underset{|}{S}}\!:$ angular, **(b)** angular, (a resonance hybrid)

(c) triangular planar, (a resonance hybrid)

(d) trigonal pyramidal,

(e) tetrahedral

22.21 (a) $2 H^+(aq) + Na_2SO_3(s) \longrightarrow SO_2(g) + H_2O + 2 Na^+(aq)$

(b) $2 H^+(aq) + Na_2S(s) \longrightarrow H_2S(g) + 2 Na^+(aq)$
(c) $2 H^+(aq) + Na_2S_2O_3(s) \longrightarrow$
$SO_2(g) + H_2O + S(s) + 2 Na^+(aq)$

22.23 In SF_4, four of the six valence electrons of the S atom are used to form bonding electron pairs and the remaining two valence electrons constitute a nonbonding pair. Thus the valence shell of the S atom has 5 pairs of electrons. The O atom cannot have this number of electrons in its valence level—it is restricted to four pairs since it has only four orbitals in its valence level.

22.25 (a) $6 OH^- + 4 S \longrightarrow 2 S^{2-} + S_2O_3^{2-} + 3 H_2O$
(b) $2 H^+ + S_2O_3^{2-} \longrightarrow S + SO_2 + H_2O$

Chapter 23 The Nonmetals, Part III: The Group V A Elements

23.1 A nitrogen fixation process is one in which nitrogen from the air is converted into compounds. Nitrogen is a comparatively unreactive element, the cells of living systems cannot directly assimilate the nitrogen of the air to use in the synthesis of proteins.

23.3 Since the molecules are similar in size and shape, the London forces of each are similar. The H atoms and electron pairs of the $-NH_2$ groups, however, can enter into hydrogen bonding. Since $H_2NCH_2CH_2NH_2$ has *two* $-NH_2$ groups, hydrogen bonding is more extensive in this compound and as a consequence its boiling point is higher.

23.5 (a) dilute: $3 Cu(s) + 8 H^+(aq) + 2 NO_3^-(aq) \longrightarrow$
$3 Cu^{2+}(aq) + 2 NO(g) + 4 H_2O$ concentrated: $Cu(s) + 4 H^+(aq) + 2 NO_3^-(aq) \longrightarrow Cu^{2+}(aq) + 2 NO_2(g) + 2 H_2O$
(b) $Zn(s) + 10 H^+(aq) + NO_3^-(aq) \longrightarrow 4 Zn^{2+}(aq) + NH_4^+(aq) + 3 H_2O$ **(c)** $P_4O_{10}(s) + 4 HNO_3(l) \longrightarrow 4 HPO_3(s) + 2 N_2O_5(s)$ **(d)** $NH_3(g) + H^+(aq) \longrightarrow NH_4^+(aq)$
(e) $Ca(OH)_2(s) + 2 H^+(aq) \longrightarrow Ca^{2+}(aq) + H_2O$

23.7 (a) $NH_4NO_3(s) \longrightarrow N_2O(g) + 2 H_2O(g)$
(b) $NH_4Cl(s) + NaNO_2(s) \longrightarrow N_2(g) + 2 H_2O(g) + NaCl(s)$
(c) $2 NaNO_3(s) \longrightarrow 2 NaNO_2(s) + O_2(g)$
(d) $2 Pb(NO_3)_2(s) \longrightarrow 2 PbO(s) + 4 NO_2(g) + O_2(g)$
(e) $2 NaN_3(s) \longrightarrow 2 Na(l) + 3 N_2(g)$

23.9 (a) $H_2NNH_2(l) + H^+(aq) \longrightarrow H_2NNH_3^+(aq)$
(b) $H_2NOH(s) + H^+(aq) \longrightarrow HONH_3^+(aq)$ **(c)** $NO_2^-(aq) + H^+(aq) \longrightarrow HNO_2(aq)$ **(d)** $NH_3(aq) + H^+(aq) \longrightarrow NH_4^+(aq)$
(e) $(NH_4)_2CO_3(s) + 2 H^+(aq) \longrightarrow 2 NH_4^+(aq) + CO_2(g) + H_2O$

23.11 (a) $2 NH_3(aq) + OCl^-(aq) \longrightarrow N_2H_4(l) + Cl^-(aq) + H_2O$ **(b)** $2 NO_2(g) + 5 H_2(g) + 2 H^+(aq) \longrightarrow 2 HONH_3^+(aq) + 2 H_2O$ **(c)** $NH_4F + 2 HF(l) \longrightarrow NF_3(g) + 3 H_2(g)$

23.13 *Ionic nitrides* are high-melting, white, crystalline solids that contain the N^{3-} ion. Crystals of *interstitial nitrides* contain nitrogen atoms in the holes (interstices) formed by the metal atoms of the crystal structure; they are hard, extremely high melting, good electrical conductors, and chemically unreactive. The category *covalent nitrides* includes compounds that are molecular in form (such as S_4N_4, P_3N_5, and Si_3N_4) and others that form network crystals (such as AlN and BN); their properties, therefore, vary widely—from gases to hard, crystalline solids.

23.15 (a) angular

(b) $H-\overset{\cdot\cdot}{N}-H$ trigonal pyramidal **(c)** $H-\overset{\cdot\cdot}{N}:^{\ominus}$ angular
$\quad\quad\quad |$
$\quad\quad\quad H$ $\quad\quad\quad\quad\quad\quad\quad\quad\quad H$

(d) $\overset{H}{\underset{H}{}}N=\overset{\cdot\cdot}{N}$ planar **(e)** $N=N$ planar

23.17 With increasing atomic number, the metallic character of the elements increases. The first ionization energy decreases and it becomes easier to produce cations and less easy to make anions. The oxides of the elements become more basic, less acidic. The higher oxidation states become less stable.

23.19 (a) $3 H_2O + PCl_3(l) \longrightarrow H_3PO_3(aq) + 3 H^+(aq) + 3 Cl^-(aq)$ **(b)** $H_2O + PCl_5(s) \longrightarrow POCl_3(l) + 2 H^+(aq) + 2 Cl^-(aq)$ $4 H_2O + PCl_5(s) \longrightarrow H_3PO_4(aq) + 5 H^+(aq) + 5 Cl^-(aq)$ **(c)** $6 H_2O + Ca_3P_2(s) \longrightarrow 3 Ca^{2+}(aq) + 6 OH^-(aq) + 2 PH_3(g)$
(d) $H_2O + H_4P_2O_7(l) \longrightarrow 2 H_3PO_4(aq)$
(e) $6 H_2O + P_4O_6(s) \longrightarrow 4 H_3PO_3(aq)$
(f) $6 H_2O + P_4O_{10}(s) \longrightarrow 4 H_3PO_4(aq)$

23.21

phosphoric acid   phosphorous acid

hypophosphorous acid

23.23 (a) P_4O_{10}, **(b)** P_4O_6, **(c)** As_2O_5, **(d)** As_4O_6

23.25 (a) $P_4O_6(s) + 6 H_2O \longrightarrow 4 H_3PO_3(aq)$
$P_4O_6(s) + 8 OH^-(aq) \longrightarrow 4 HPO_3^{2-}(aq) + 2 H_2O$
$P_4O_6(s) + 4 OH^-(aq) + 2 H_2O \longrightarrow 4 H_2PO_3^-(aq)$
$P_4O_6(s) + H^+(aq) \longrightarrow N.R.$
(b) $Sb_4O_6(s) + H_2O \longrightarrow N.R.$
$Sb_4O_6(s) + 4 OH^- \longrightarrow 4 SbO_2^-(aq) + 2 H_2O$
$Sb_4O_6(s) + 4 H^+(aq) + 4 Cl^-(aq) \longrightarrow 4 SbOCl(s) + 2 H_2O$
(c) $Bi_2O_3(s) + H_2O \longrightarrow N.R.$
$Bi_2O_3(s) + OH^-(aq) \longrightarrow N.R.$
$Bi_2O_3(s) + 6 H^+(aq) \longrightarrow 2 Bi^{3+}(aq) + 3 H_2O$

Chapter 24 The Nonmetals, Part IV: Carbon, Silicon, Boron, and the Noble Gases

24.1 Carbon has a pronounced ability to form compounds in which many carbon atoms are bonded to each other in chains or rings (catenation). Carbon to carbon bonds are about as strong as those that carbon forms to any other atom. Carbon has a pronounced ability to form multiple bonds with itself and with other nonmetals. For these reasons, carbon forms an extremely large number of compounds.

24.3 *Saltlike carbides* are made up of metal cations and anions that contain carbon alone (C_2^{2-} and C^{4-} are examples). *Interstitial carbides* are formed by transition metals and consist of metallic crystals with carbon atoms in the holes between the metal atoms of the crystal structure (the interstices). *Covalent carbides* are held together by covalent bonds; SiC and Be_4C form network crystals that are hard, are chemically unreactive, and do not melt even at high temperatures.

24.5 (a) hydrogen cyanide, **(b)** hydrocyanic acid, **(c)** potassium cyanide, **(d)** potassium cyanate, **(e)** potassium thiocyanate, **(f)** pentacarbonyl iron(0), **(g)** sodium hydrogen carbonate, **(h)** sodium carbonate

24.7 (a) $CO(g) + Cl_2(g) \longrightarrow COCl_2(g)$
(b) $CO(g) + S(s) \longrightarrow COS(g)$
(c) $2 CO(g) + O_2(g) \longrightarrow 2 CO_2(g)$
(d) $CO(g) + FeO(s) \longrightarrow Fe(l) + CO_2(g)$
(e) $4 CO(g) + Ni(s) \longrightarrow Ni(CO)_4(g)$

24.9 $2 e^- + H_2O + OCN^- \longrightarrow CN^- + 2 OH^-$
$2 e^- + H_2O + PbO \longrightarrow Pb + OCN^-$
$PbO + CN^- \longrightarrow Pb + OCN^-$

24.11 Each B atom has two H atoms (called terminal H atoms) bonded to it by conventional covalent bonds. The resulting BH_2 fragments are joined together by two hydrogen bridges—three center B—H—B bonds. The two B atoms and four terminal H atoms lie in a plane and the bridge H atoms lie above and below this plane.

24.13 (a) $B_2O_3(s) + 3\,Mg(s) \longrightarrow 2\,B(s) + 3\,MgO(s)$
(b) $2\,BBr_3(g) + 3\,H_2(g) \longrightarrow 2\,B(s) + 6\,HBr(g)$
(c) $2\,B(s) + N_2(g) \longrightarrow 2\,BN(s)$
(d) $2\,B(s) + Mg(s) \longrightarrow MgB_2(s)$
(e) $BF_3(g) + F^-(aq) \longrightarrow BF_4^-(aq)$

24.15 A bond in which three atoms are bonded together by an electron pair in a single molecular orbital; found in boron and the hydrides of boron.

24.17 B_4H_{10}

24.19 (a) $Xe(g) + F_2(g) \longrightarrow XeF_2(s)$
(b) $Xe(g) + 2\,F_2(g) \longrightarrow XeF_4(s)$
(c) $Xe(g) + 3\,F_2(g) \longrightarrow XeF_6(s)$
(d) $XeF_6(s) + H_2O \longrightarrow XeOF_4(l) + 2\,HF(g)$
(e) $XeF_6(s) + 3\,H_2O \longrightarrow XeO_3(aq) + 6\,HF(aq)$

24.21 Argon is used to fill electric light bulbs since the gas does not react with the hot filament but conducts heat away from it thus prolonging its life. The gas is used as an inert atmosphere in high-temperature metallurgical processes and thus protects the hot metal from air oxidation.

24.23 (a) $5\,XeO_3 + 6\,Mn^{2+} + 9\,H_2O \longrightarrow$
$5\,Xe + 6\,MnO_4^- + 18\,H^+$
(b) $0.120\,M\ MnO_4^-$ **(c)** $3.59\,g\ XeO_3$

24.25 If we consider 22.41 L of each gas at STP,

He has a mass of 4.003 g
H_2 has a mass of 2.016 g

The volume of He, therefore, has a mass that is $4.003/2.016 = 1.986$ times that of the volume of H_2. The lifting power of a gas, however, is the difference between the mass of a volume of air minus the mass of the same volume of the gas. Again considering 22.41 L of each gas at STP

He has a lifting power $= 28.94\,g - 4.00\,g = 24.94\,g$
H_2 has a lifting power $= 28.94\,g - 2.02\,g = 26.92\,g$

The lifting power of He, therefore, is $(24.94\,g)/(26.92\,g) = 0.9264$ times that of H_2 (or 92.64%).

Chapter 25   Metals and Metallurgy

25.1 The transference of an electron to a higher level within a band requires the addition of very little energy since the levels are close together. Thus the valence electrons of a metal can move to higher levels by absorbing light of a wide range of wavelengths. When the electrons fall to lower levels, light is radiated. The lustrous appearance of metals is caused by these electron transitions. The freely moving electrons of metallic crystals account for the high thermal and electrical conductivities of metals. Valence electrons absorb heat as kinetic energy and transfer it rapidly to all parts of the metal since their motion is relatively unrestricted.

25.3 See Figure 25.3. In conductors the valence band is overlapped by an empty conduction band so that conduction can occur by the movement of electrons throughout the conduction band. Insulators and semiconductors have empty conduction bands that are separated from filled valence bands by forbidden energy zones. In semiconductors, the forbidden zone is sufficiently narrow that electrons can be promoted from the valence band to the conduction band by heat. Thermal promotion does not occur in insulators since the forbidden energy zone is comparatively wide.

25.5 Metals have superior electrical and thermal conductivities, characteristic luster, and the ability to be deformed under stress without cleaving. They are usually hard, high melting, and high boiling. Chemically, metals have a tendency to form cations through electron loss, form basic oxides, and are usually good reducing agents.

25.7 2.4 cm

25.9 The sulfides of less reactive metals are directly reduced to the free metal by heating in air:

$$HgS(s) + O_2(g) \longrightarrow Hg(l) + SO_2(g)$$

The majority of sulfide and carbonate ores are converted into oxides by roasting:

$$2\,ZnS(s) + 3\,O_2(g) \longrightarrow 2\,ZnO(s) + 2\,SO_2(g)$$
$$PbCO_3(s) \longrightarrow PbO(s) + CO_2(g)$$

The free metals are more readily obtained from oxides than from sulfides or carbonates.

25.11 $3\,Fe_2O_3(s) + CO(g) \longrightarrow 2\,Fe_3O_4(s) + CO_2(g)$
$Fe_3O_4(s) + CO(g) \longrightarrow 3\,FeO(s) + CO_2(g)$
$FeO(s) + CO(g) \longrightarrow Fe(l) + CO_2(g)$
$CaCO_3(s) \longrightarrow CaO(s) + CO_2(g)$
$CaO(s) + SiO_2(s) \longrightarrow CaSiO_3(l)$
$C(s) + CO_2(g) \longrightarrow 2\,CO(g)$

25.13 In some cases, the metals produced contain appreciable quantities of carbon (an impurity that is difficult to remove). In other cases, the carbon is incapable of effecting a reduction. Reductions may be carried out by means of electrolysis, or using reactive metals (such as Na, Mg, and Al) or hydrogen as reducing agents.

25.15 by heating: $CaCO_3(s) \longrightarrow CaO(s) + CO_2(g)$
$CaO(s) + H_2O \longrightarrow Ca^{2+}(aq) + 2\,OH^-(aq)$
$Mg^{2+}(aq) + 2\,OH^-(aq) \longrightarrow Mg(OH)_2(s)$
$Mg(OH)_2(s) + 2\,H^+(aq) + 2\,Cl^-(aq) \longrightarrow$
$Mg^{2+}(aq) + 2\,Cl^-(aq) + 2\,H_2O$
electrolysis, dry, molten salt: $MgCl_2(l) \longrightarrow Mg(l) + Cl_2(g)$

25.17 (a) $UO_3 + 2\,Al \longrightarrow U + Al_2O_3$
(b) $3\,V_2O_5 + 10\,Al \longrightarrow 6\,V + 5\,Al_2O_3$
(c) $Ta_2O_5 + 10\,Na \longrightarrow 2\,Ta + 5\,Na_2O$
(d) $ThO_2 + 2\,Ca \longrightarrow Th + 2\,CaO$
(e) $WO_3 + 2\,Al \longrightarrow W + Al_2O_3$

25.19 (a) Leaching of the carbonate ore by dilute sulfuric acid gives a solution of $CuSO_4$, from which the Cu is obtained by electrolysis. **(b)** The CuS ore is concentrated by flotation and smelted to Cu_2S (matte). The Cu_2S is reduced by blowing air through the molten material and impure, blister Cu is obtained. This impure Cu is refined by electrolysis. The impure Cu is made the anode of the cell and pure Cu plates out on the cathode.

25.21 (a) $PbCO_3(s) \longrightarrow PbO(s) + CO_2(g)$
$PbO(s) + C(s) \longrightarrow Pb(l) + CO(g)$
(b) $2\,PbS(s) + 3\,O_2(g) \longrightarrow 2\,PbO(s) + 2\,SO_2(g)$
$PbS(s) + 2\,O_2(g) \longrightarrow PbSO_4(s)$
$PbS(s) + 2\,PbO(s) \longrightarrow 3\,Pb(l) + SO_2(g)$
$PbS(s) + PbSO_4(s) \longrightarrow 2\,Pb(l) + 2\,SO_2(g)$

25.23 (a) $2\,Na(s) + H_2(g) \longrightarrow 2\,NaH(s)$
(b) $Na(s) + N_2(g) \longrightarrow$ N.R.
(c) $2\,Na(s) + O_2(g) \longrightarrow Na_2O_2(s)$
(d) $2\,Na(s) + Cl_2(g) \longrightarrow 2\,NaCl(s)$
(e) $2\,Na(s) + S(s) \longrightarrow Na_2S(s)$
(f) $12\,Na(s) + P_4(s) \longrightarrow 4\,Na_3P(s)$
(g) $2\,Na(s) + 2\,C(s) \longrightarrow Na_2C_2(s)$
(h) $2\,Na(s) + 2\,H_2O \longrightarrow 2\,Na^+(aq) + 2\,OH^-(aq) + H_2(g)$
(i) $2\,Na(s) + 2\,NH_3(l) \longrightarrow 2\,NaNH_2(s) + H_2(g)$

25.25 The small sizes of Li and Li^+ account for the difference in properties between Li and the other group I A metals. The carbonate, phosphate, and fluoride of Li^+ are only slightly soluble in water; the corresponding salts of Na^+ are water soluble.

Li forms an ordinary oxide (Li_2O) rather than a peroxide or superoxide upon burning in oxygen; Na forms a peroxide. Li^+ ions are more strongly hydrated than those of any other I A element. Lithium reacts directly with N_2 to form a nitride; Na does not react with N_2. Upon heating, LiOH decomposes to Li_2O and H_2O and Li_2CO_3 decomposes to Li_2O and CO_2; NaOH and Na_2CO_3 are thermally stable. $LiNO_3$ decomposes to Li_2O, NO_2 and O_2 upon heating, but $NaNO_3$ forms $NaNO_2$ and O_2 when heated.

25.27 (a) $Ca(s) + H_2(g) \longrightarrow CaH_2(s)$
(b) $3\,Ca(s) + N_2(g) \longrightarrow Ca_3N_2(s)$
(c) $2\,Ca(s) + O_2(g) \longrightarrow 2\,CaO(s)$
(d) $Ca(s) + Cl_2(g) \longrightarrow CaCl_2(s)$
(e) $Ca(s) + S(s) \longrightarrow CaS(s)$
(f) $6\,Ca(s) + P_4(s) \longrightarrow 2\,Ca_3P_2$
(g) $Ca(s) + 2\,C(s) \longrightarrow CaC_2(s)$
(h) $Ca(s) + 2\,H_2O \longrightarrow Ca(OH)_2(s) + H_2(g)$
(i) $Ca(s) + 2\,NH_3(l) \longrightarrow Ca(NH_2)_2(s) + H_2(g)$

25.29 (a) $2\,Al(s) + 3\,Cl_2(g) \longrightarrow 2\,AlCl_3(s)$
(b) $4\,Al(s) + 3\,O_2(g) \longrightarrow 2\,Al_2O_3(s)$
(c) $2\,Al(s) + 3\,S(s) \longrightarrow Al_2S_3(s)$
(d) $2\,Al(s) + N_2(g) \longrightarrow 2\,AlN(s)$
(e) $2\,Al(s) + 2\,OH^-(aq) + 6\,H_2O \longrightarrow$
$2\,Al(OH)_4^-(aq) + 3\,H_2(g)$
(f) $2\,Al(s) + 6\,H^+(aq) \longrightarrow 2\,Al^{3+}(aq) + 3\,H_2(g)$

25.31 The Al^{3+} ion has a high charge and hydrolyzes extensively. The S^{2-} ion also hydrolyzes. The compound Al_2S_3 is completely hydrolyzed in water:

$$2\,Al^{3+}(aq) + 3\,S^{2-}(aq) + 6\,H_2O \longrightarrow 2\,Al(OH)_3(s) + 3\,H_2S(g)$$

25.33 (a) $Sn(s) + 2\,Cl_2(g) \longrightarrow SnCl_4(l)$
(b) $Sn(s) + O_2(g) \longrightarrow SnO_2(s)$
(c) $Sn(s) + 2\,S(s) \longrightarrow SnS_2(s)$
(d) $Sn(s) + 2\,H^+(aq) \longrightarrow Sn^{2+}(aq) + H_2(g)$
(e) $Sn(s) + OH^-(aq) + 2\,H_2O \longrightarrow Sn(OH)_3^-(aq) + H_2(g)$
(f) $3\,Sn(s) + 4\,H^+(aq) + 4\,NO_3^-(aq) \longrightarrow$
$3\,SnO_2(s) + 4\,NO(g) + 2\,H_2O$

25.35 (a) $2\,Fe(s) + 3\,Cl_2(g) \longrightarrow 2\,FeCl_3(s)$
$2\,Cr(s) + 3\,Cl_2(g) \longrightarrow 2\,CrCl_3(s)$
$Zn(s) + Cl_2(g) \longrightarrow ZnCl_2(s)$
(b) $3\,Fe(s) + 2\,O_2(g) \longrightarrow Fe_3O_4(s)$
$4\,Cr(s) + 3\,O_2(g) \longrightarrow 2\,Cr_2O_3(s)$
$2\,Zn(s) + O_2(g) \longrightarrow 2\,ZnO(s)$
(c) $Fe(s) + S(s) \longrightarrow FeS(s)$
$Cr(s) + S(s) \longrightarrow CrS(s)$
$Zn(s) + S(s) \longrightarrow ZnS(s)$
(d) $Fe(s) + N_2(g) \longrightarrow$ N.R.
$2\,Cr(s) + N_2(g) \longrightarrow 2\,CrN(s)$
$Zn(s) + N_2(g)$ N.R.
(e) $3\,Fe(s) + 4\,H_2O(g) \longrightarrow Fe_3O_4(s) + 4\,H_2(g)$
$2\,Cr(s) + 3\,H_2O(g) \longrightarrow Cr_2O_3(s) + 3\,H_2(g)$
$Zn(s) + H_2O(g) \longrightarrow ZnO(s) + H_2(g)$
(f) $Fe(s) + 2\,H^+(aq) \longrightarrow Fe^{2+}(aq) + H_2(g)$
$Cr(s) + 2\,H^+(aq) \longrightarrow Cr^{2+}(aq) + H_2(g)$
$Zn(s) + 2\,H^+(aq) \longrightarrow Zn^{2+}(aq) + H_2(g)$
(g) $Fe(s) + OH^-(aq) \longrightarrow$ N.R.
$2\,Cr(s) + 6\,OH^-(aq) + 6\,H_2O \longrightarrow 2\,Cr(OH)_6^{3-}(aq) + 3\,H_2(g)$
$Zn(s) + 2\,OH^-(aq) + 2\,H_2O \longrightarrow Zn(OH)_4^{2-}(aq) + H_2(g)$

25.37 $CrO(s) + 2\,H^+(aq) \longrightarrow Cr^{2+}(aq) + H_2O$
$CrO(s) + OH^-(aq) \longrightarrow$ N.R.
$Cr_2O_3(s) + 6\,H^+(aq) \longrightarrow 2\,Cr^{3+}(aq) + 3\,H_2O$
$Cr_2O_3(s) + 2\,OH^-(aq) + 3\,H_2O \longrightarrow 2\,Cr(OH)_4^-(aq)$
$CrO_3(s) + H_2O \longrightarrow H_2CrO_4(aq)$
$CrO_3(s) + 2\,OH^-(aq) \longrightarrow CrO_4^{2-}(aq) + H_2O$

***25.39 (a)** $+0.0592$ V, **(b)** $+0.770$ V, **(c)** There would be no way to know that $+0.788$ V is the correct standard electrode potential. The use of "Hg^+" at "1.0 $\dot{M}$" would give a result that would be regarded as the correct standard electrode potential. For

concentration cells, however, standard electrode potentials are not involved. A calculation for the cell described in part (a) and based on a "1.0 M" concentration of "Hg^+" with one electron exchanged would give $+0.0592$ V as the result, but the actual measurement would be $+0.0296$ V.

25.41 (a) $2\,La(s) + 3\,Cl_2(g) \longrightarrow 2\,LaCl_3(s)$
(b) $4\,La(s) + 3\,O_2(g) \longrightarrow 2\,La_2O_3(s)$
(c) $2\,La(s) + 3\,S(s) \longrightarrow La_2S_3(s)$
(d) $2\,La(s) + N_2(g) \longrightarrow 2\,LaN(s)$
(e) $2\,La(s) + 6\,H_2O \longrightarrow 2\,La(OH)_3(s) + 3\,H_2(g)$
(f) $2\,La(s) + 6\,H^+(aq) \longrightarrow 2\,La^{3+}(aq) + 3\,H_2(g)$

Chapter 26   Complex Compounds

26.1 (a) $3+$, **(b)** $3+$, **(c)** 0, **(d)** $3+$, **(e)** $2+$

26.3 (a) $+$, **(b)** $4-$, **(c)** $-$, **(d)** $+$, **(e)** $2-$

26.5 (a) $Zn[PtCl_6]$, **(b)** $K_4[Ni(CN)_4]$,
(c) $[Co(NH_3)_4Cl(NO_2)]_2SO_4$,
(d) $K_3[AuBr_6]$, **(e)** $Na_3[Re(CN)_4O_2]$,
(f) $[Pt(NH_3)_4][Pt(NH_3)Cl_3]_2$,
(g) $[Cr(NH_3)_4(SCN)_2][Cr(NH_3)_2(SCN)_4]$, **(h)** $K_4[Ni(CN)_6]$

26.7 (a) zinc hexachloroplatinate($2-$),
(b) potassium tetracyanonickelate,
(c) tetraamminechloronitrocobalt($1+$) sulfate,
(d) potassium hexabromoaurate($3-$),
(e) sodium tetracyanodioxorhenate($3-$),
(f) tetraammineplatinum($2+$) amminetrichloroplatinate($1-$),
(g) tetraamminedithiocyanatochromium($1+$) diamminetetrathiocyanatochromate($1-$),
(h) potassium hexacyanonickelate($4-$)

26.9 (a) potassium tetracyanonickelate(0),
(b) potassium tetracyanonickelate(II),
(c) ammonium aquapentachloroferrate(III),
(d) tetraamminecopper(II) tetrachloroplatinate(II),
(e) pentaamminenitritoiridium(III) chloride,
(f) hexaamminecobalt(III) tetracyanonickelate(II)

26.11 (a) potassium tetracyanonickelate($4-$),
(b) potassium tetracyanonickelate($2-$),
(c) ammonium aquapentachloroferrate($2-$),
(d) tetraamminecopper($2+$) tetrachloroplatinate($2-$),
(e) pentaamminenitritoiridium($2+$) chloride,
(f) hexaamminecobalt($3+$) tetracyanonickelate($2-$)

26.13 1.34×10^{-34}

26.15 (a) $KFe[Fe(CN)_6]$, **(b)** $Fe[Fe(CN)_6]$, **(c)** $Cu_2[Fe(CN)_6]$,
(d) $K_2Fe[Fe(CN)_6]$

26.17 (a) $[Co(NH_3)_5(SO_4)]NO_3$, **(b)** $[Mn(CO)_5(NCS)]$,
(c) $[Pt(NH_3)_3Cl][Pt(NH_3)Cl_3]$, **(d)** $[Co(en)_2(H_2O)Br]Br_2H_2O$

26.19 Let a = NH_3. $[Pta_4][PtCl_6]$, one compound; $[Pta_3Cl][PtCl_5]$, one compound; $[Pta_4Cl_2][PtCl_4]$, two compounds—one with the Cl^- ligands of the octahedral cation *cis* to one another and the other with the Cl^- ligands of the octahedral cation *trans* to one another; $[Pta_3Cl_3][PtaCl_3]$, two compounds—one in which any one of the three Cl^- ligands of the octahedral cation is *cis* to both of the other Cl^- ligands, and another compound in which two of the three Cl^- ligands of the octahedral cations are *trans* to one another and the other Cl^- ligand *cis* to each of the original two.

26.21 Let a = NH_3, and py = pyridene,

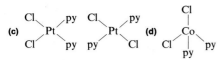

(c) Cl—Pt—py / Cl—Pt—py structures, **(d)** Cl—Co—py structure

26.23 $[Ni(CN)_4]^{2-}$ has no unpaired electrons, $[NiCl_4]^{2-}$ has two unpaired electrons. From the position of CN^- on the spectrochemical series, $[Ni(CN)_4]^{2-}$ would be predicted to be a low spin complex. Ni^{2+} is a d^8 ion.

26.25 **(a)** The pairing energy must be greater than 250 kL/mol and less than 460 kJ/mol. Actually, P is 335 kJ/mol. **(b)** Since $C_2O_4^{2-}$ induces a smaller Δ_0 than H_2O (see the spectrochemical series), $[Mn(C_2O_4)_3]^{3-}$ should be a high-spin complex.

26.27 **(a)** Zn_2^+, a d^{10} ion

low spin   **high spin**

(b) Cr^{2+}, a d^4 ion

low spin   **high spin**

(c) Cr^{3+}, a d^3 ion

low spin   **high spin**

(d) Fe^{2+}, a d^6 ion

low spin   **high spin**

(e) Fe^{3+}, a d^5 ion

low spin   **high spin**

(f) Ni^{2+}, a d^8 ion

low spin   **high spin**

26.29 $[Co(NH_3)_6]^{2+}$ is a d^7 high-spin octahedral complex. $[Co(MH_3)_6]^{3+}$ is a d^6 low-spin octahedral complex. See Figure 26.16 for splitting diagrams.

Chapter 27   Nuclear Chemistry

27.1 **(a)** $^{193}_{83}Bi \longrightarrow ^{189}_{81}Tl + ^{4}_{2}He$, **(b)** $^{27}_{12}Mg \longrightarrow ^{27}_{13}Al + ^{0}_{-1}e$, **(c)** $^{68}_{34}Se \longrightarrow ^{68}_{33}As + ^{0}_{1}e$, **(d)** $^{71}_{12}Ge + ^{0}_{-1}e \longrightarrow ^{71}_{31}Ga$

27.3 **(a)** $^{212}_{86}Rn \longrightarrow ^{208}_{84}Po + ^{4}_{2}He$, **(b)** $^{60}_{27}Co \longrightarrow ^{60}_{28}Ni + ^{0}_{-1}e$, **(c)** $^{60}_{30}Zn \longrightarrow ^{60}_{29}Cu + ^{0}_{1}e$, **(d)** $^{110}_{49}In + ^{0}_{-1}e \longrightarrow ^{110}_{48}Cd$

27.5 $^{250}_{96}Cm \longrightarrow 4^{1}_{0}n + 2^{123}_{48}Cd$

27.7 4.771 MeV

27.9 **(a)** $^{226}_{88}Ra \longrightarrow ^{222}_{86}Rn + ^{4}_{2}He$, **(b)** 0.186 MeV, **(c)** Some α particle emissions leave the product nuclei in excited states.

When a product nucleus drops to a lower energy state, the energy difference is emitted in the form of γ radiation.

27.11 3.83 MeV

27.13 0.63 MeV

27.15 0.422 MeV

27.17 The process must occur by electron capture.

27.19 **(a)** $^{144}_{60}Nd$, **(b)** 143.9101 u

27.21 38.96801 u

27.23 103.90856 u

27.25 **(a)** $^{41}_{19}K$, **(b)** 40.961825 u

27.27 0.00387 g

27.29 193 days

27.31 **(a)** 0.00376/day, **(b)** 184 days

27.33 163 days

27.35 **(a)** 2.53×10^7 atoms, **(b)** 5.63×10^{-15} g

27.37 868 Ci

27.39 2.56×10^3 years

27.41 $^{232}_{90}Th$, $^{228}_{88}Ra$, $^{228}_{89}Ac$, $^{228}_{90}Th$, $^{224}_{88}Ra$, $^{220}_{86}Rn$, $^{216}_{84}Po$, $^{212}_{82}Pb$, $^{212}_{83}Bi$, $^{212}_{84}Po$, $^{208}_{82}Pb$

27.43 $^{150}_{66}Dy$, $^{150}_{65}Tb$, $^{150}_{64}Gd$, $^{146}_{62}Sm$, $^{142}_{60}Nd$

27.45 **(a)** $^{35}_{17}Cl + ^{1}_{0}n \longrightarrow ^{32}_{15}P + ^{4}_{2}He$

(b) $^{9}_{4}Be + ^{1}_{1}H \longrightarrow ^{9}_{5}B + ^{1}_{0}n$
(c) $^{75}_{33}As + ^{2}_{1}H \longrightarrow ^{75}_{34}Se + 2^{1}_{0}n$
(d) $^{24}_{12}Mg + ^{2}_{1}H \longrightarrow ^{22}_{11}Na + ^{4}_{2}He$
(e) $^{133}_{55}Cs + ^{4}_{2}He \longrightarrow ^{133}_{57}La + 4^{1}_{0}n$
(f) $^{209}_{83}Bi + ^{1}_{1}H \longrightarrow ^{202}_{84}Po + 8^{1}_{0}n$
(g) $^{65}_{29}Cu + ^{12}_{6}C \longrightarrow ^{74}_{35}Br + 3^{1}_{0}n$
(h) $^{7}_{3}Li + ^{3}_{1}H \longrightarrow ^{6}_{2}He + ^{4}_{2}He$

27.47 **(a)** $^{10}_{5}B$, **(b)** $^{6}_{3}Li$, **(c)** $^{7}_{3}Li$, **(d)** $^{12}_{6}C$, **(e)** $^{96}_{42}Mo$, **(f)** $^{75}_{33}As$, **(g)** $^{45}_{21}Sc$

27.49 **(a)** $^{248}_{98}Cf$, **(b)** $^{249}_{98}Cf$, **(c)** $^{238}_{92}U$, **(d)** $^{239}_{94}Pu$, **(e)** $^{244}_{96}Cm$, **(f)** $^{250}_{98}Cf$

27.51 **(a)** 559.09 MeV, **(b)** 8.7358 MeV/nucleon

27.53 40.96182 u

27.55 **(a)** 205.1 MeV/fission, **(b)** 8.421×10^7 kJ/g

27.57 **(a)** 5.50 MeV/fusion, **(b)** 1.76×10^8 kJ/g

27.59 **(a)** $^{85}_{34}Se$, **(b)** $^{112}_{45}Rh$, **(c)** $^{95}_{37}Rb$

Chapter 28   Organic Chemistry

28.1 **(a)** CH_3—CH—CH—CH_2—CH_3, with CH_3 and CH_3 branches

(b) CH_2=CH—C—CH_2—CH_3 with CH_3 and CH_2—CH_3 branches

(c) CH_3—CH—C≡C—CH—CH_3 with CH_3 and CH_3 branches

(d) dibromobenzene structure, **(e)** dinitrobenzene structure, **(f)** cyclic structure with CH_2, H_2C, CH, H_2C, CH_2, CH

(g)

28.3 (a) The lowest possible number should be used, name should be 2-pentene; **(b)** The longest chain consists of 4 atoms, name should be 2-methylbutane; **(c)** Compound does not exist, C atom number 2 is pentavalent; **(d)** The lowest possible numbers should be used, name should be 3-methyl-1-butyne; **(e)** Compound does not exist, C atom number 3 is pentavalent.

28.5 *monosubstituted:* 1- and 2-chloropropane. *disubstituted:* 1,1-; 2,2-; 1,2-; and 1,3-dichloropropane. *trisubstituted:* 1,1,1-; 1,1,2-; 1,1,3-; 1,2,2-; and 1,2,3-trichloropropane.

28.7 *dichlorobutanes:* 1,1-; 2,2-; 1,2- (*d, l* pair); 1,3- (*d, l* pair); 1,4-; 2,3- (*d, l* pair and an optically inactive form). *dichloro-2-methylpropanes:* 1,1-; 1,2-; 1,3-

28.9 (a) two (2,3- and 3,4-dibromonitrobenzene), **(b)** three (2,6-; 2,4-; and 3,5-dibromonitrobenzene), **(c)** one (2,5-dibromonitrobenzene)

28.11 (b) and **(d)**

28.13 (a) bromomethane, dibromomethane, tribromomethane, tetrabromomethane, **(b)** 2,3-dibromobutane, **(c)** 2,2,3,3-tetrabromobutane, **(d)** bromobenzene

28.15 (a) *o-* and *p-*nitrophenol, **(b)** *o-* and *p-*bromophenol, **(c)** *m-*dinitrobenzene, **(d)** *m-*bromonitrobenzene, **(e)** *m-*nitrobenzoic acid, **(f)** *o-* and *p-*bromonitrobenzene, **(g)** *o-* and *p-*nitrotoluene, **(h)** *o-* and *p-*xylene

28.17 (a) When unsymmetrical molecules (such as HBr) add to a carbon-carbon double bond, the positive part of the molecule (the H atom in the case of HBr) is bonded to the C atom of the double bond that originally had the larger number of H atoms bonded to it. **(b)** In the first step of the mechanism, the H^+ from the HBr adds to the olefin to form a carbocation. The more stable carbocation is the one in which the H^+ adds to the C atom that already has the larger number of H atoms bonded to it. The addition of the H^+ to one C atom of the double bond, leaves the other C atom with a positive charge.

28.19

(a) CH$_3$—CH$_2$—CH$_2$—C$\overset{\text{O}}{\|}$—H,

(b) CH$_3$—C$\overset{\text{O}}{\|}$—CH$_2$—CH$_3$,

(c) same as (b), **(d)** CH$_3$—O—CH$_2$—CH$_3$,

(e) CH$_3$—C$\overset{\text{O}}{\|}$—OCH$_3$

(f) **(g)**

28.21 (a) 4-methyl-1-pentanol, **(b)** 4-methyl-2-pentanol, **(c)** 2-methyl-2-pentanol, **(d)** 2-methyl-3-pentanone, **(e)** ethyl isopropyl ether, **(f)** 4-methylpentanal

28.23 1-butanol; 2-butanol (*d, l* pair); 2-methyl-1-propanol; methyl *n*-propyl ether; methyl isopropyl ether; diethyl ether

28.25 (a) *n*-butyl magnesium bromide, **(b)** *n*-butyl cyanide, **(c)** 1-butanol, **(d)** ethyl *n*-butyl ether

28.27 (a) acetic acid and butanoic acid, **(b)** acetic acid and acetone, **(c)** propanoic acid,

(d) propanoic acid, **(e)** propanoic acid, **(f)** acetone, **(g)** *p*-nitrobenzoic acid, **(h)** 2,3-hexanediol, **(i)** propanal

28.29 (a) CH$_3$CH$_2$Br and H$_2$O, **(b)** CH$_3$CH$_2$CH$_3$ and MgBr, **(c)** CH$_3$CH$_2$COOH and NaBr

28.31 (a) 1-propanol, **(b)** 3-hexanol, **(c)** 3-methyl-3-pentanol

***28.33** 1. Two Grignard reagents should be prepared [CH$_3$CH$_2$CH$_2$MgBr and (CH$_3$)$_2$CHMgBr] by converting the alcohols into bromo compounds and then reacting these bromo compounds with Mg in dry ether. 2. Propanal may be obtained by the mild oxidation of 1-propanol and acetone may be obtained by the oxidation of 2-propanol. 3. The desired products are obtained by hydrolysis of the products of the reactions of: **(a)** CH$_3$CH$_2$CH$_2$MgBr and CH$_3$CH$_2$CHO, **(b)** (CH$_3$)$_2$CHMgBr and (CH$_3$)$_2$CO, **(c)** CH$_3$CH$_2$CH$_2$MgBr and (CH$_3$)$_2$CO, **(d)** (CH$_3$)$_2$CHMgBr and CH$_3$CH$_2$CHO

28.35 (a) **(b)** CH$_3$—N—CH$_2$—CH3 (with H below N)

(c) H$_2$N—CH$_2$—CH$_2$—CH$_2$—CH$_2$—CH$_2$—CH$_2$—NH$_2$

(d) **(e)**

28.37 1-aminobutane, 2-aminobutane, 2-methyl-1-aminopropane, 2-methyl-2-aminopropane, methyl *n*-propyl amine, methyl isopropyl amine, diethyl amine, dimethyl ethyl amine

28.39 (a) ethyl amine, **(b)** *p*-methylaniline, **(c)** methyl *n*-butyl amine, **(d)** acetamide, **(e)** propanoic acid, **(f)** diethylammonium bromide, **(g)** propanoic acid, **(h)** ethyl amine

28.41 CH$_3$CH$_2$O$^-$, OH$^-$, CH$_3$CH$_2$NH$_2$, CH$_3$COO$^-$, CH$_3$CH$_2$OH

28.43 (a) Addition polymers are formed by the successive addition of molecules of the monomer, which is an alkene or a conjugated alkadiene. Polyethylene, Orlon, acrilan, Teflon, the vinyl plastics, Lucite, rubber and polystyrene are addition polymers. **(b)** Copolymers are formed by the polymerization of two different monomers. Buna S rubber is a copolymer. **(c)** Condensation polymers are formed by the combination of the monomer molecules with the elimination of a small molecule, usually water. Nylon, Dacron, and Bakelite are condensation polymers.

28.45 (a) CH$_2$=CH$_2$, **(b)** CF$_2$=CF$_2$, **(c)** C$_6$H$_5$CH=CH$_2$, **(d)** CH$_2$=CHCN, **(e)** H$_2$N(CH$_2$)$_6$NH$_2$ and HOOC(CH$_2$)$_4$COOH, **(f)** CH$_2$=C(CH$_3$)CH=CH$_2$, **(g)** C$_6$H$_5$OH and HCHO, **(h)** HOCH$_2$CH$_2$OH and *p*-HOOCC$_6$H$_4$COOH

Chapter 29   Biochemistry

29.1 (a), **(d)**, and **(e)**

29.3 H$_2$N—CH—C$\overset{\text{O}}{\|}$—NH—CH—C$\overset{\text{O}}{\|}$—NH—CH—C$\overset{\text{O}}{\|}$—OH (with CH$_3$ below each CH)

29.5 Hydrogen bonding is responsible for holding the polypeptide chains of a protein into a secondary structure (alpha helix and pleated sheets are examples). The secondary structures of the proteins are arranged into tertiary structures by interactions between the R groups of the amino acid residues of the polypeptide chains. Types of interactions include: salt formation, disulfide linkages, and hydrogen bonding.

29.7 Since neither C atom in glycine is chiral, optical isomers of glycine do not exist.

29.9 A carbohydrate is a hydroxy aldehyde, a hydroxy ketone, or a substance derived from them.

29.11 $CH_2(OH)CH(OH)CHO$, C atom number 2 is chiral, two optical isomers (a d, l pair) exist

29.13

$$CH_3CH_2CH{=}CHCH_2CH{=}CHCH_2CH{=}CH(CH_2)_7COOCH_2$$
$$|$$
$$CH_3CH_2CH{=}CHCH_2CH{=}CHCH_2CH{=}CH(CH_2)_7COOCH + 9H_2 \longrightarrow$$
$$|$$
$$CH_3CH_2CH{=}CHCH_2CH{=}CHCH_2CH{=}CH(CH_2)_7COOCH_2$$

$$CH_3(CH_2)_{16}COOCH_2$$
$$|$$
$$CH_3(CH_2)_{16}COOCH$$
$$|$$
$$CH_3(CH_2)_{16}COOCH_2$$

29.15

$$RCOOCH_2 \qquad\qquad HOCH_2$$
$$| \qquad\qquad\qquad\qquad |$$
$$RCOOCH + 3\,OH^- \longrightarrow 3\,RCOO^- + HOCH$$
$$| \qquad\qquad\qquad\qquad |$$
$$RCOOCH_2 \qquad\qquad HOCH_2$$

29.17 An alpha helix is a secondary structure of a protein; a single polypeptide chain held into the shape of a helix by hydrogen bonding. A double helix is the secondary structure of DNA; a coil made up of two chains of DNA and held together by hydrogen bonding between the bases of the nucleotides.

29.19 7.65×10^5

29.21 The number of moles of reactant transformed per unit time by the action of an enzyme.

29.23 A competitive inhibitor combines reversibly with the active site of an enzyme and hence competes with the substrate. A noncompetitive inhibitor combines irreversibly with the active site of an enzyme. The substrate cannot displace a noncompetitive inhibitor.

29.25 A catabolic process is a biological process in which substances are broken down into simpler substances. An anabolic process is a biological process in which large molecules are synthesized from smaller ones.

GLOSSARY

A

Acid (Section 13.4) According to the Arrhenius definition, a covalent compound of hydrogen that dissociates in water to produce $H^+(aq)$ ions (or H_3O^+ ions). *See also,* **Arrhenius acid, Brønsted acid, Lewis acid,** and **solvent-system acid.**

Acid-base indicator (Section 17.4) A compound that changes color in solution as the pH of the solution changes.

Acid dissociation constant, K_a (Section 17.1) An equilibrium constant that pertains to an equilibrium involving a weak acid and the ions derived from it in water solution.

Acidic oxide (Section 13.5) An oxide of a nonmetal that reacts with water to form an acid.

Acid salt (Section 13.4) A salt formed by the incomplete neutralization of a polyprotic acid. The anions of these salts retain one or more ionizable hydrogen atoms of the parent acid.

Actinides, actinoids (Section 2.7) The elements from atomic number 90 (thorium, Th) to 103 (lawrencium, Lr) that follow the element actinium (Ac, $Z = 89$) and that are customarily placed at the bottom of the periodic table.

Activated complex (Section 14.4) An unstable arrangement of atoms that exists for only a moment in the course of a chemical reaction, also called a **transition state.**

Active site (Section 29.5) The position on the surface of an enzyme at which a reaction occurs.

Activity (Section 27.5) The amount of radiation eminating from a radioactive source per unit time.

Actual yield (Section 4.4) The amount of product actually obtained from a chemical reaction. *See also,* **percent yield** and **theoretical yield.**

Addition polymerization (Section 28.10) The formation of a polymer by the successive addition of molecules of the monomer, which is an alkene or a conjugated alkadiene.

Addition reaction (Sections 28.2 and 28.5) A reaction in which two parts of a reagent add to a multiple bond, one part to each side of the bond.

Adjacent charge rule (Section 8.6) Atoms that are bonded together in a Lewis structure should not have formal charges with the same sign.

Alcohol (Section 28.6) A derivative of an alkane in which the hydroxyl group, OH, replaces a hydrogen atom. They are classified according to the number of alkyl groups bonded to the carbon atom that holds the OH group as a **primary alcohol** (one R group), **secondary alcohol** (two R groups), or a **tertiary alcohol** (three R groups).

Aldehyde (Section 28.7) A compound that has the general formula

where R can be a hydrogen atom, an alkyl group, or an aryl group.

Alkadiene (Section 28.2) An open-chain hydrocarbon that contains *two* carbon-carbon double bonds; the alkadienes conform to the general formula C_nH_{2n-2}.

Alkali metal (Sections 2.7 and 25.8) An element of group I A: Li, Na, K, Rb, Cs, and Fr.

Alkaline earth metal (Section 25.9) An element of group II A: Be, Mg, Ca, Sr, or Ba.

Alkane (Section 28.1) An open-chain hydrocarbon in which all carbon-carbon bonds are single bonds; the alkanes conform to the general formula C_nH_{2n+2}.

Alkene (Section 28.2) An open-chain hydrocarbon that contains a carbon-carbon double bond; the alkenes conform to the general formula C_nH_{2n}.

Alkyl halide (Section 28.6) A compound formed from an alkyl radical (R) and a halogen atom (X), RX.

Alkyl radical (Section 28.1) A fragment of an alkane molecule from which a hydrogen atom has been removed (R).

Alkyne (Section 28.3) An open-chain hydrocarbon that contains a carbon-carbon triple bond; the alkynes conform to the general formula C_nH_{2n-2}.

Allotropes (Section 22.6) Two or more forms of the same element in the same physical state.

Alpha-amino acid (Section 29.1) A carboxylic acid with an amino group ($-NH_2$) on the alpha carbon, which is the carbon atom next to the carboxyl group.

Alpha decay (Section 27.3) A type of radioactivity in which alpha particles are ejected; an alpha particle consists of two neutrons and two protons and is given the symbol ^4_2He.

Alpha particle, α (Section 2.5) A particle that consists of two protons and two neutrons and that is emitted by certain radioactive nuclei.

Amide (Section 28.9) A compound with the general formula

$$R-\overset{\overset{\displaystyle O}{\|}}{C}-NR_2$$

in which R may be a hydrogen atom, an alkyl radical, or an aryl radical, and the three R groups may be alike or different.

Amine (Section 28.9) An organic base that can be considered to be a derivative of ammonia (NH_3) with one hydrogen replaced (RNH_2, a **primary amine**), two hydrogens replaced (R_2NH, a **secondary amine**), or three hydrogens replaced (R_3N, a **tertiary amine**). The R groups may be either alkyl radicals or aryl radicals and in a given amine may be alike or different.

Ammine ligand (Sections 26.1 and 26.3) The ammonia molecule, NH_3.

Amonton's law (Section 10.4) At constant volume, the pressure of a sample of gas varies directly with the absolute temperature.

Amorphous solids (Section 11.8) Solids in which the component molecules are not arranged in an orderly, geometric pattern typical of crystals; these solids have no definite melting or freezing points.

Ampere, A (Section 20.1) The SI base unit for electric current; a current of one coulomb per second.

Amphiprotic substance (Section 16.2) A substance that can function as a Brønsted acid (through proton loss) and as a Brønsted base (through proton gain).

Amphoteric oxide (Section 13.5) An oxide that has both acidic and basic properties and that will react with both acids and bases to form salts.

Amphoterism (Section 18.5) A property of the hydroxides of certain metals that permits them to function as acids or bases; amphoteric substances are water-insoluble and dissolve in solutions of low *p*H or high *p*H.

Anabolic process (Section 29.6) A biological process in which large molecules are synthesized from smaller ones.

Anion (Sections 3.1 and 7.4) A negatively charged ion; an atom or a group of atoms that has gained one or more electrons.

Anode (Section 20.2) The electrode of an electrochemical cell at which oxidation occurs.

Antibonding molecular orbital (Section 9.4) A molecular orbital in which electron density is low in the internuclear region. The two electrons in an antibonding molecular orbital have higher energies than they would if they were in the atomic orbitals from which the antibonding molecular orbital was derived.

Anticodon (Section 29.4) The portion of a transfer RNA chain that contains a sequence of three bases that compliment the base triplet of a messenger RNA codon. A given anticodon corresponds to a specific amino acid that a particular transfer RNA carries.

Antiparticle (Section 27.3) One part of a particle-antiparticle pair. A pair of particles of this type destroy each other when they come into contact and they are converted into a form of energy. The antiparticle of a charged particle has the same mass as the particle but a charge with the opposite sign (for example, the electron, $_{-1}^{0}e$, and the positron, $_{1}^{0}e$). Some particle-antiparticle pairs are uncharged (for example, the neutrino and the antineutrino).

Arc process (Section 23.7) A nitrogen-fixation process in which nitrogen oxide, NO, is produced by the reaction of nitrogen and oxygen in an electric arc.

Aromatic compound (Section 28.4) Benzene or a derivative of benzene.

Arrhenius acid (Sections 13.4 and 16.1) A compound that dissociates in water to produce H^+(aq) (or H_3O^+ ions).

Arrhenius base (Sections 13.4 and 16.1) A compound that dissolves in water to produce OH^-(aq) ions.

Arrhenius equation (Section 14.7) An equation that describes how the rate constant for a chemical reaction varies with temperature and energy of activation.

Arrhenius neutralization (Sections 13.4 and 16.1) A reaction in which H^+(aq) from an acid and OH^-(aq) from a base react to form water.

Aryl radical (Section 28.4) A radical formed by the removal of a hydrogen atom from a carbon of a benzene ring of an aromatic compound.

Atmosphere, atm (Section 10.1) A unit of pressure that is defined as 101,325 Pa; 1 atm = 760 torr.

Atom (Section 2.1) The smallest particle of an element that can combine with the atoms of other elements to form compounds.

Atomic mass unit, u (Section 2.9) A unit of mass equal to one-twelfth the mass of a $_6^{12}C$ atom.

Atomic number, Z (Section 2.6) The number of protons in the nucleus of an atom of an element. In an uncharged atom, it is also equal to the number of electrons.

Atomic radius (Section 7.1) An approximation of the radius of an atom based on the division of bond distances.

Atomic weight (Section 2.9) The average mass of atoms of an element relative to the mass of a $_6^{12}C$ atom taken as exactly 12 u.

Aufbau method (Section 6.7) A method of deriving the electronic configurations of atoms in which electrons are successively added (on the basis of orbital energies) until the desired configuration is obtained.

Avogadro's number (Section 3.4) The number of entities in one mole; 6.02205×10^{23}.

Avogadro's principle (Section 10.8) Equal volumes of all gases at the same temperature and pressure contain the same number of molecules.

Azeotrope (Section 12.10) a solution that has a higher or lower vapor pressure than any of the pure components of which it is composed. If the vapor pressure is higher, the solution is a **minimum-boiling azeotrope**; if lower, a **maximum boiling azeotrope**.

B

Band theory (Section 25.1) A theory that explains the bonding in metals in terms of molecular orbitals that extend over the entire crystal of the metal and that together make up what are called bands.

Barometer (Section 10.1) A device for measuring the pressure that the atmosphere exerts on the surface of the earth.

Base (Section 13.4) In the Arrhenius system, a compound that dissociates in water to produce OH^-(aq) ions. *See also*, **Arrhenius base, Brønsted base, Lewis base**, and **solvent system base**.

Base dissociation constant, K_b (Section 17.1) An equilibrium constant that pertains to an equilibrium involving a weak base and the ions derived from it in water solution.

Basic oxide (Section 13.5) An oxide of a metal that reacts with water to form a base.

Basic oxygen process (Section 25.7) A process in which pig iron is refined into steel. The impurities in the pig iron are oxidized by a blast of pure oxygen.

Bayer process (Section 25.5) A process for obtaining pure aluminum oxide (for use in the production of aluminum metal) from the ore bauxite. Advantage is taken of the amphoteric nature of aluminum oxide to dissolve it away from ore impurities by use of a hot solution of NaOH.

Bergius process (Section 21.4) A process, carried out at high temperatures and in the presence of catalysts, in which hydrogen and finely divided carbon react to form hydrocarbons.

Bertholide (Section 11.16) A nonstoichiometric substance.

Beta decay (Section 27.3) A radioactive process in which the atomic number, Z, of the radioactive nuclide changes but the mass number, A, does not change. In electron emission, Z increases. In positron emission or in electron capture, Z decreases.

Beta particle, β (Section 2.5) An electron emitted by certain radioactive nuclei.

Binary compound (Section 8.7) A compound formed from two elements.

Binding energy (Sections 2.9 and 27.8) The energy equivalent of the difference between the sum of the masses of the nucleons of a nucleus and the actual mass of the nucleus; interpreted as the energy required to decompose a nucleus into its component nucleons.

Blast furnace (Section 25.6) A furnace for the carbon reduction of iron ore; pig iron, an impure form of iron, is produced.

Body-centered cubic unit cell (Section 11.12) A unit cell of a crystal that is a cube with identical constituent particles located at the corners and at the center of the structure.

Boiling point (Section 11.6) The temperature at which the vapor pressure of a liquid equals the external pressure is the boiling point of that liquid. The **normal boiling point** of a liquid is the temperature at which the vapor pressure of the liquid equals 1 atm.

Bond distance (Section 7.1) The distance between the nuclei of two atoms that are bonded together.

Bond energy (Section 5.7) The energy required to break a bond between two atoms in a molecule. This general term includes two types. A **bond dissociation energy** refers to the energy required to break a specific bond that holds two atoms together in a particular diatomic molecule. An **average bond energy,** however, pertains to the bonds found in polyatomic molecules and is an average value based on a number of cases.

Bonding molecular orbital (Section 9.4) A molecular orbital in which electron density is high in the internuclear region. The two electrons in a bonding molecular orbital have lower energies than they would if they were in the atomic orbitals from which the bonding molecular orbital was derived.

Bonding pair of electrons (Section 9.2) A pair of electrons used to form a covalent bond between two atoms.

Bond order (Section 9.4) In a diatomic molecule, one-half the number of bonding electrons minus one-half the number of antibonding electrons.

Boranes (Section 24.8) Compounds that contain only boron and hydrogen.

Born-Haber cycle (Section 7.5) A method of analysis of the enthalpy change of a process in which the ΔH for the entire process is set equal to the sum of the ΔH values for a series of steps that produce the same change.

Boyle's law (Section 10.2) At constant temperature, the volume of a gas varies inversely with the pressure.

Bragg equation (Section 11.13) An equation that relates the distance between crystal planes with the angles at which an X ray with a known wavelength is reflected from those planes: $n\lambda = 2d \sin \theta$ where n is the order of the reflection (a simple integer), λ is the wavelength of the X rays used, d is the distance between the crystal planes, and θ is the angle at which the X rays are reflected.

Breeder reactor (Section 27.8) A type of nuclear reactor that manufactures more nuclear fuel than it uses.

Brønsted acid (Section 16.2) A molecule or ion that can donate protons.

Brønsted base (Section 16.2) A molecule or ion that can accept protons.

Buffer (Section 17.6) A solution capable of maintaining its pH at a fairly constant value even when small amounts of acids or bases are added.

C

calorie, cal (Section 5.2) The approximate quantity of heat required to raise the temperature of 1 g of water from 14.5°C to 15.5°C; defined by the relationship: 1 cal = 4.184 J (exactly).

Calorimeter (Section 5.3) A device used to measure the heat transferred in chemical reactions and physical changes.

Carbocation (Section 28.5) An unstable positive ion formed by a group of atoms that contains a carbon atom that has only six valence electrons.

Carbohydrate (Section 29.2) A hydroxy aldehyde, a hydroxy ketone, or a substance derived from them.

Carbonyl compound (Sections 24.4 and 28.7) A compound that contains a carbonyl group,

such as an aldehyde, a ketone, carbonyl sulfide (OCS), the carbonyl halides (OCX_2), and the metal carbonyls.

Carboxylic acid (Section 28.8) An organic acid that has the general formula

$$R—\overset{\overset{\displaystyle O}{\|}}{C}—OH$$

where R can be an alkyl radical or an aryl radical.

Catabolic process (Section 29.6) A biological process in which substances are broken down into simpler substances.

Catalyst (Section 14.8) A substance that increases the rate of a chemical reaction without being used up in the reaction.

Catenation (Section 24.1) The formation of chains or rings by atoms of the same element bonded to each other.

Cathode (Section 20.2) The electrode of an electrochemical cell at which reduction occurs.

Cathode ray (Section 2.2) Streams of electrons that are emitted by the cathode (negative electrode) when electricity is passed through a tube that contains a gas under a very low pressure.

Cation (Sections 3.1 and 7.4) A positively charged ion; an atom or a group of atoms that has lost one or more electrons.

Celsius temperature scale (Section 5.2) A temperature scale based on the assignment of 0°C to the normal freezing point of water and 100°C to the normal boiling point of water.

Chain mechanism (Section 14.6) A multistep mechanism for a reaction in which, after an initiation step, two steps are repeated over and over again. A product of the first of these steps is a reactant in the second, and a product of the second of these steps is a reactant in the first.

Charles' law (Section 10.3) At constant pressure, the volume of a gas varies directly with the absolute temperature.

Chelate (Section 26.1) A metal complex that contains coordinated multidentate ligands.

Chelating agent (Section 26.1) A ligand capable of occupying more than one coordination position on a central metal ion in a complex; a **multidentate ligand.**

Chemical adsorption (14.8) A process through which solid, heterogeneous catalysts work. The adsorbed reactant molecules are held to the surface of the catalyst by bonds that are similar in strength to chemical bonds, and in the process the adsorbed molecules become activated.

Chemical equation (Section 4.1) A representation of a chemical reaction in terms of the symbols and formulas of the elements and compounds involved.

Chemical equilibrium (Section 15.1) A state in which the rate of a reversible reaction in the forward direction equals the rate in the reverse direction.

Chemical formula (Section 3.1) A representation of a compound that uses chemical symbols to indicate the types and relative numbers of atoms present in the compound.

Chemical kinetics (Introduction to Chapter 14) The study of the rates and mechanisms of chemical reactions.

Chemical symbol (Section 1.2) A one-, two-, or three-letter abbreviation assigned by international agreement to each element.

Chemistry (Introduction to Chapter 1) The science that is concerned with the characterization, composition, and transformations of matter.

Chiral carbon atom (Section 29.1) A carbon atom that has four different groups bonded to it. Molecules that have a carbon atom of this type are **chiral** (their mirror images are not superimposable on them).

Chiral molecule or ion (Section 26.4) A molecule or an ion that can exist in two forms that are nonsuperimposable mirror images.

Cis-trans **isomerism** (Section 26.4) A type of *stereoisomerism* (*geometric isomerism*) in which the isomers differ in the geometric arrangement of ligands around the central metal ion. In the *cis* isomer, two like ligands are as close together as possible. In the *trans* isomer, these two like ligands are as far apart as possible.

Clausius-Clapeyron equation (Section 11.7) An equation that relates the vapor pressures of a liquid at two temperatures to each other and to the enthalpy of vaporization of the liquid:

$$\log \left| \frac{p_2}{p_1} \right| = \frac{\Delta H_v}{2.303\,R} \left| \frac{T_2 - T_1}{T_1 T_2} \right|$$

where p_1 is the vapor pressure at T_1 (in K), p_2 is the vapor pressure at T_2 (in K), ΔH_v is the enthalpy of vaporization (in J/mol), and R is the ideal gas constant [8.3143 J/(Kmol)].

Closest-packed crystal (Sections 11.11 and 11.14) A crystal structure in which the atoms are so efficiently packed that a maximum number are included in a given volume: a face-centered cubic or hexagonal closest-packed crystal.

Codon (Section 29.4) A portion of a messenger RNA chain that contains a sequence of three bases that constitutes a code.

Coefficient (Section 4.1) A number placed before a symbol or formula in a chemical equation.

Colligative property (Section 12.9) A property of a solution that depends principally upon the concentration of dissolved particles rather than the nature of those particles; vapor-pressure lowering, freezing-point depression, boiling-point elevation, and osmotic pressure.

Collision theory (Section 14.4) A theory that describes reactions in terms of collisions between reacting particles (atoms, molecules, or ions).

Common-ion effect (Section 17.5) The effect on an equilibrium system caused by the addition of a compound that has an ion in common with one present in the system.

Complex ion (Section 18.4) An aggregate consisting of a central metal cation surrounded by a number of ligands.

Compound (Section 1.2) A pure substance that is composed of two or more elements in fixed proportions and that can be chemically decomposed into these elements.

Compressibility factor (Section 10.13) PV/RT where P is the pressure of a gas; V, the volume; R, the ideal gas constant; and T, the absolute temperature. For 1 mol of an ideal gas, the compressibility factor is always equal to 1.

Concentration (Section 4.5) The amount of a substance dissolved in a given quantity of solution or solvent.

Concentration Cell (Section 20.10) A voltaic cell constructed from two half-cells that are composed of the same substances but that differ in the concentrations of the substances that make up the half-cells.

Concentration of ores (Section 25.5) Processes in which the desired components of ores are separated from gangue.

Condensation polymerization (Section 28.10) A polymerization in which the monomer molecules combine with the elimination of a small molecule, usually water.

Condensed phosphoric acids (Section 23.8) Acids that have more than one P atom per molecule. The classification includes the **polyphosphoric acids,** which conform to the general formula $H_{n+2}P_nO_{3n+1}$, where n is 2 to 10; and the **metaphosphoric acids,** $H_nP_nO_{3n}$, where n is 3 to 7.

Conduction band (Section 25.1) An empty band in a metallic crystal through which electrons are free to move and thereby conduct electricity.

Conductor (Section 25.1) A substance in which the valence electrons are free to move throughout an empty conduction band that overlaps the valence band; in this way, the valence electrons are able to conduct electricity.

Conjugated double-bond system (Section 28.10) A compound with a carbon chain containing alternating double and single bonds.

Conjugate pair (Section 16.2) A Brønsted acid-base pair that is related through the loss or gain of a proton; for example, NH_4^+ (a Brønsted acid) and NH_3 (a Brønsted base) form a conjugate pair.

Contact process (Section 22.12) A process for the manufacture of sulfuric acid in which SO_2 is catalytically oxidized to SO_3, the SO_3 vapor dissolved in H_2SO_4, and the resulting $H_2S_2O_7$ diluted with water to give H_2SO_4.

Control rods (Section 27.8) Rods made of substances that have the ability to capture neutrons; these rods are placed between the fuel elements of a nuclear reactor core where they may be inserted to any desired depth and serve to control the nuclear reaction by capturing excess neutrons.

Conversion factor (Section 1.5) A ratio in which the numerator and denominator are equivalent quantities expressed in different units. A conversion factor is used in calculations to convert the units of a measurement into other units.

Coordination isomerism (Section 26.4) A type of isomerism in which two complex compounds, each with more than one coordination center, vary in the way that the same set of ligands is distributed between the coordination centers.

Coordination number in a complex (Section 26.1) The number of atoms directly bonded to the central metal cation of a complex.

Coordination number in a crystal (Sections 11.14 and 11.15) The number of nearest neighbors that an atom or an ion has in a crystal structure.

Coordination sphere (Section 26.1) The group of anions or molecules that are directly coordinated to the central metal ion of a complex.

Copolymer (Section 28.10) A polymer formed by the polymerization of two different monomers.

Coulomb, C (Section 20.1) A unit of electrical charge; the quantity of electricity carried past a given spot in one second by a current of one ampere.

Coupled reaction (Section 29.4) A pair of biological reactions such that one drives the other since the first reaction liberates more energy that the second requires.

Covalent bond (Section 8.1) A bond formed between two atoms by electron sharing. In a **single bond,** one electron pair is shared. Double and triple covalent bonds are called **multiple bonds.** In a **double bond,** two electron pairs are shared, and in a **triple bond,** three electron pairs are shared.

Cracking (Sections 21.2 and 28.1) A process in which high molecular weight hydrocarbons are broken down into lower molecular weight compounds; used in petroleum refining.

Critical mass (Section 27.8) The amount of a fissionable material required to sustain a nuclear chain reaction.

Critical pressure (Section 10.14) The pressure required to liquefy a gas at its critical temperature.

Critical temperature (Section 10.14) The temperature above which it is impossible to liquefy the gas under study no matter how high the applied pressure.

Crystal (Sections 11.11 and 11.12) A solid composed of a symmetrical array of atoms, ions, or molecules arranged in a repeating three-dimensional pattern.

Crystal allotropes (Section 11.14) Two or more different crystal forms of the same substance that are stable under different conditions.

Crystal defect (Section 11.16) A crystal imperfection caused by a dislocation, missing ions, misplaced ions, or the presence of impurities.

Crystal field theory (Section 26.5) A theory that explains the bonding of the central metal ion to the ligands of a complex in terms of electrostatic attractions between the positive charge of the metal ion and the negative charge of electron pairs of the ligands.

Crystal lattice (Section 11.12) A three-dimensional, symmetrical pattern of points that defines a crystal in which the points represent sites that have identical environments in the same orientation.

Curie (Section 27.5) A unit used in the measurement of the activity of a radioactive source (the number of disintegrations per unit time). One curie is 3.70×10^{10} disintegrations per second.

Cyanamid process (Section 23.5) A nitrogen-fixation process in which calcium cyanamid, $CaNCN$, is prepared from calcium carbide, CaC_2, and nitrogen.

Cycloalkane (Section 28.1) A hydrocarbon that has a ring arrangement of carbon atoms in which all the carbon-carbon bonds are single bond; the cycloalkanes conform to the general formula C_nH_{2n}.

Cycloalkene (Section 28.2) A hydrocarbon that has a ring arrangement of carbon atoms and contains a carbon-carbon double bond; the cycloalkenes conform to the general formula C_nH_{2n-2}.

Cyclotron (Section 27.7) An instrument in which a charged particle is accelerated along a spiral path under the influence of magnetic and electric fields and caused to strike a target nucleus.

D

Dalton's law of partial pressures (Section 10.10) The total pressure of a mixture of gases that do not react is equal to the sum of the partial pressures of all the gases present.

Daniell cell (Section 20.5) A voltaic cell in which Zn metal is

oxidized to Zn^{2+} ions at the anode and Cu^{2+} ions are reduced to Cu metal at the cathode.

Degree of dissociation, (Section 17.1) The fraction of the total concentration of a weak electrolyte that is in ionic form in water solution at equilibrium.

Dehydrogenation (Section 28.7) A reaction in which two hydrogen atoms are removed from a molecule to form a double bond.

Density (Section 1.5) Mass per unit volume.

Deoxyribonucleic acid, DNA (Section 29.4) A nucleic acid composed of nucleotides that contain deoxyribose units as the sugar component.

Dextrorotatory compound (Section 26.4) An optically active compound that rotates the plane of polarized light to the right (clockwise).

Diamagnetic substance (Section 6.6) A substance that is repelled by a magnetic field, behavior exhibited by substances in which all electrons are paired.

Diatomic molecule (Section 3.1) A molecule consisting of two atoms.

Dipole-dipole force (Section 11.1) An intermolecular force caused by the mutual attraction of oppositely charged poles of neighboring polar molecules.

d^{10} **ion** (Section 7.6) A cation that has an $ns^2\,np^6\,nd^{10}$ electronic configuration in its outer shell (where n is the principal quantum number of this shell).

Dipole moment (Section 8.2) A value calculated by multiplying the distance separating two equal charges with opposite signs times the magnitude of the charge.

Disaccharide (Section 29.2) A carbohydrate molecule that is composed of two monosaccharide units.

Dislocations (Section 11.16) Crystal defects in which planes of atoms are misaligned.

Displacement reaction (Section 21.3) A reaction in which one element (or group of elements) displaces another element (or group of elements) from a compound.

Displacement reaction (Section 28.6) A reaction in which one group displaces another from an organic molecule; also called a **nucleophilic substitution reaction** since it involves the substitution of one nucleophilic substance (a Lewis base) for another. If the rate-determining step is unimolecular, the reaction is called an S_N1 reaction; if bimolecular, an S_N2 **reaction.**

Disproportionation (Section 13.3) A reaction in which a substance is both oxidized and reduced; an auto-oxidation-reduction.

Distillation (Section 12.10) The separation of a liquid solution into its components by vaporization and condensation.

Double helix (Section 29.4) The secondary structure of DNA, a coil made from two chains of DNA.

Downs cell (Section 25.6) An electrolytic cell in which a reactive metal is produced by the electrolysis of the molten chloride of the metal.

$d^{10}s^2$ **ion** (Section 7.6) A cation that has an $(n-1)s^2\,(n-1)p^6$ $(n-1)d^{10}\,ns^2$ electronic configuration, which is a d^{10} electronic configuration plus an additional shell that contains two electrons in an s orbital.

E

Effective collision (Section 14.4) A collision between two particles (atoms, molecules, or ions) that results in a reaction.

Effective nuclear charge (Section 7.1) The positive charge experienced by an outer electron in an atom after the charge of the nucleus has been effectively decreased by the shielding effect of inner electrons.

e_g orbitals (Section 26.5) A degenerate set of two d orbitals of the central metal ion of a complex.

Electrical conductivity (Section 25.3) A measure of the ability of a substance to conduct electricity; measured in units of $1/(\Omega \cdot cm)$.

Electrode (Section 20.2) An anode or a cathode in an electrochemical cell.

Electrolysis (Section 20.3) The use of electric current to bring about chemical changes.

Electrolyte (Section 12.11) A solute that dissolves in water to produce a solution that is a better conductor of electricity than pure water alone; the electrical conductivity of the solution is caused by the ionization of the solute by water.

Electrolytic conduction (Section 20.2) The conduction of electricity by the movement of ions through a solution or a molten salt. A sustained current requires that chemical changes at the electrodes also occur.

Electromagnetic radiation (Section 6.1) Radiant energy that travels at a characteristic speed (the speed of light, c) and that may be interpreted in terms of waves or quanta.

Electromotive force, emf (Section 20.6) The potential difference between two electrodes of a voltaic cell, measured in volts; a measure of the tendency for an oxidation-reduction reaction to occur.

Electron (Section 2.2) A subatomic particle that has a mass of approximately 0.00055 u, carries a one-unit negative charge, and is found outside the nucleus in an atom.

Electron affinity (Section 7.3) The energy change associated with the process in which an electron is added to a gaseous atom in its ground state is a first electron affinity. Second and higher electron affinities pertain to processes in which electrons are added to negative ions.

Electron capture, β^- decay (Section 27.3) A type of radioactivity exhibited by some artificial nuclides in which a nucleus captures an electron from an inner shell and the captured electron converts a proton into a neutron.

Electronegativity (Section 8.3) A measure of the relative ability of an atom in a molecule to attract electrons to itself.

Electron emission, β^- decay (Section 27.3) A type of radioactivity in which an electron (symbol $_{-1}^{0}e$) is ejected from a nucleus and in the process a neutron is converted into a proton.

Electronic configuration (Section 6.6) The manner in which electrons are arranged in an atom; may be indicated by orbital diagram or by electronic notation (see Table 6.3).

Electrophilic displacement (Section 16.5) A reaction in which a Lewis acid displaces a second, weaker, Lewis acid from an acid-base complex; a Lewis **acid displacement.**

Element (Section 1.2) A pure substance that cannot be decomposed into simpler substances.

Empirical formula (Section 3.2) A chemical formula for a compound that is written using the simplest whole-number ratio of atoms present in the compound; also called the **simplest formula.**

Enantiomorphs (Section 26.4) Two different compounds that are mirror images of one another; one may be considered to be the mirror reflection of the other. The **dextro** form rotates the plane of polarized light to the right; the **levo** form, to the left.

Endothermic reaction (Section 5.4) A chemical reaction in which heat is absorbed.

End point (Section 17.9) That point in a titration when the indicator changes color.

Energy (Section 5.1) The capacity to do work.

Energy of activation (Section 14.4) The difference in energy between the potential energy of the reactants and the potential energy of the activated complex of a reaction.

Energy shell, energy level (Sections 6.2 and 6.5) A group of orbitals in an atom that have the same value of n, the principal quantum number.

Enthalpy, H (Sections 5.4 and 19.2) A thermodynamic function defined by the equation $H = E + PV$, where E is the internal energy of the system, P is the pressure, and V is the volume. For a reaction run at constant pressure, the change in enthalpy, ΔH, is the heat transferred, q_p.

Enthalpy of condensation (Section 11.7) The enthalpy change associated with the condensation of a given quantity of vapor (usually one mole or one gram) into a liquid at a specified temperature.

Enthalpy of crystallization (Section 11.8) The enthalpy change associated with the conversion of a given quantity of a liquid (usually one mole or one gram) into a solid at a specified temperature.

Enthalpy of formation (Section 5.6) For a given compound, the enthalpy change for a reaction in which 1 mol of the compound is prepared from the most stable forms of its elements. A **standard enthalpy of formation,** ΔH_f°, pertains to a formation reaction run at 1 atm pressure and a designated reference temperature (usually 25°C).

Enthalpy of fusion (Section 11.8) The energy required to melt a given quantity of a solid (usually one mole or one gram) at a specified temperature.

Enthalpy of hydration (Sections 12.3 and 12.4) The enthalpy change associated with the process in which gaseous ions of a given quantity of solute (usually one mole) are hydrated.

Enthalpy of solution (Section 12.4) The enthalpy change associated with the process in which a given quantity of a solute (usually one mole) dissolves in a solvent. The value depends upon the concentration of the final solution and the temperature.

Enthalpy of sublimation (Section 7.5) The enthalpy change associated with a process in which a solid is converted directly into a gas.

Enthalpy of vaporization (Sections 11.4 and 11.7) The energy required to vaporize a given quantity of a liquid (usually one mole or one gram) at a specified temperature.

Entropy, S (Section 19.3) A measure of the randomness, or disorder, of a system; used a criterion of reaction spontaneity; expressed in $J/(K \cdot mol)$.

Enzyme (Sections 14.8 and 29.5) A natural catalyst that is effective in a biochemical process (such as digestion, respiration, and cell synthesis).

Enzyme inhibition (Section 29.5) A process in which the action of an enzyme is prevented or retarded. In **competitive inhibition,** an inhibitor combines reversibly with the active site and hence competes with the substrate. In **noncompetitive inhibition,** an inhibitor combines in an irreversible manner with the active site. In **product inhibition,** a product of the enzyme-catalyzed reaction acts as an inhibitor and controls the reaction rate.

Equilibrium (Section 11.5) A condition in which the rates of two opposing tendencies are equal.

Equilibrium constant, K (Sections 15.1, 15.2, and 15.3) A constant for an equilibrium system equal to a fraction in which the numerator is the product of the concentrations of the substances on the right of the chemical equation, each raised to a power corresponding to its coefficient in the chemical equation, and the denominator is the product of the concentrations of the substances on the left of the chemical equation, each raised to a power corresponding to its coefficient in the chemical equation. A value obtained by expressing the concentrations in moles per liter is given the symbol K_c (Section 15.2); one written in terms of partial pressures (in atmospheres) is given the symbol K_p (Section 15.3).

Equivalence point (Sections 13.7 and 17.9) That point in a titration where stoichiometrically equivalent amounts of reactants have been added.

Equivalent weight (Section 13.8) A quantity defined on the basis of the reaction being considered in such a way that one equivalent weight of one reactant will react with exactly one equivalent weight of another. For an acid-base neutralization, the mass of acid or base that will supply one mole of $H^+(aq)$ or one mole of $OH^-(aq)$. For an oxidation-reduction reaction, the formula weight of the oxidant or reductant divided by the number of moles of electrons lost or gained by a mole of the reactant *or* the total change in oxidation number for that reactant.

Ester of a carboxylic acid (Section 28.8) The product of the reaction of a carboxylic acid and an alcohol or phenol

$$R-\overset{\overset{\textstyle O}{\|}}{C}-OR$$

where the R groups may be alkyl or aryl radicals that are alike or different.

Ether (Section 28.6) A compound that has the general formula ROR, where the R groups may be alkyl or aryl radicals that are alike or different.

Evaporation; vaporization (Section 11.4) The process in which a liquid is converted into a gas.

Excited state (Section 6.2) A state of an atom in which the electronic configuration gives the atom a higher energy than the ground state.

Exclusion principle of Pauli (Section 6.5) No two electrons in the same atom may have identical sets of all four quantum numbers.

Exothermic reaction (Section 5.4) A chemical reaction in which heat is liberated.

Extrinsic (or impurity) semiconductor (Section 25.2) A crystalline semiconductor to which impurities have been added to enhance its conductivity.

F

Face-centered cubic unit cell (Section 11.12) A unit cell of a crystal that consists of a cube with identical constituent particles located at each corner and at the center of each face.

Fahrenheit temperature scale (Section 5.2) A temperature scale on which the normal freezing point of water is 32°F and the normal boiling point of water is 212°F.

Faraday, F (Section 20.4) The total charge of one mole of electrons; 9.64846×10^4 C.

Faraday's laws (Section 20.4) The laws developed by Michael Faraday that describe the quantitative relationships between the amount of electricity used and the chemical change in an electrolysis.

Fast neutron (Section 27.7) A fast-moving neutron produced by a nuclear reaction.

Fats and oils (Section 29.3) Mixtures of esters of fatty acids and glycerol (which is 1,2,3-propanetriol). Fats are solids at room temperature; oils are liquids.

Fatty acids (Section 29.3) Long, straight-chain carboxylic acids; some are saturated and some contain one or more carbon-carbon double bonds.

First law of thermodynamics (Section 19.1) Energy can be converted from one form into another but it cannot be created or destroyed.

First-order reaction (Sections 14.2 and 14.3) A reaction for which the sum of the exponents of the concentration terms in the rate equation is 1; the rate equation has the form: $rate = k[A]$.

Flotation (Section 25.5) A method of ore concentration in which the finely crushed ore is mixed with a suitable oil and water in a large tank. Agitation of the mixture with air produces a froth which contains the mineral particles and which is skimmed off.

Flux (Section 25.6) A substance (usually limestone, $CaCO_3$) used to form a slag in a smelting operation and thus remove the gangue.

Forbidden energy zone (Section 25.1) A zone in an energy diagram for the bands of a crystal; no electron can have an energy that would place it in this zone.

Formal charge (Section 8.4) A charge arbitrarily assigned to an atom in a covalent structure by apportioning the bonding electrons equally between the bonded atoms. These charges are useful in interpreting the properties and structures of covalent species, but the concept is merely a convention.

Formula weight (Section 3.3) The sum of the atomic weights of the atoms in a formula.

Frasch process (Section 22.9) A process in which molten sulfur is obtained from underground deposits.

Freezing point (Section 11.8) The temperature at which solid and liquid phases are in equilibrium. If the total pressure is 1 atm, the value is called the **normal freezing point.**

Frequency, (Section 6.1) The number of waves of electromagnetic radiation that pass a given spot in 1 s; $\nu = c/\lambda$.

Friedel-Crafts synthesis (Section 28.5) A reaction of an aromatic compound with an alkyl halide in which HCl is eliminated and a new side chain is introduced into the benzene ring of the aromatic compound.

Fuel cell (Section 20.4) A voltaic cell that is designed to convert the energy obtained from the combustion of a fuel directly into electrical energy.

Functional group (Section 28.6) An atom or a group of atoms that gives organic compounds bearing them characteristic physical and chemical properties.

G

Gamma radiation (Section 2.5 and 27.3) Highly energetic, electromagnetic radiation of very short wavelength that is emitted by certain radioactive nuclei.

Gangue (Section 25.4) Unwanted material included with ores as mined.

Gay-Lussac's law of combining volumes (Section 10.8) At constant temperature and constant pressure, the volumes of gases used or produced in a chemical reaction stand in ratios of small, whole numbers.

Geiger-Müller counter (Section 27.5) A device used for the quantitative detection of radioactive emissions and that functions by counting the electrical impulses caused by the ionization of a gas in a chamber through which the emissions pass.

Geological dating (Section 27.6) A method of dating mineral specimens based on the natural radioactive disintegration series.

Geometric isomerism (Section 26.4) A type of isomerism in which the isomers differ in the geometric arrangement of the ligands around the central metal ion.

Levorotatory compound (Section 26.4) An optically active compound that rotates the plane of polarized light to the left (counterclockwise).

Lewis acid (Section 16.5) A substance that can form a covalent bond by sharing an electron pair that is donated by a Lewis base; an **electrophilic substance.**

Lewis base (Section 16.5) A substance that can form a covalent bond with a Lewis acid by donating an electron pair toward the formation of the bond; a **nucleophilic substance.**

Lewis structure (Sections 8.1 and 8.5) A representation of a covalent molecule or ion in which only the valence levels of the atoms are shown, a dash is used to represent a covalent bond (a pair of electrons), and dots are used to represent unshared electrons.

Ligand (Sections 18.4 and 26.1) An anion or a molecule that has an unshared pair of electrons with which it can bond to a metal cation in the formation of a complex ion.

Limiting reactant (Section 4.3) The reactant that, based on the chemical equation, is supplied in the smallest stoichiometric amount and hence limits the quantity of product that can be obtained from a chemical reaction.

Linear accelerator (Section 27.7) An instrument in which a charged particle is accelerated along a linear path and caused to strike a target nucleus.

Linkage isomerism (Section 26.4) A type of isomerism in which two complexes differ as to the way a given ligand (that is present in both) coordinates to the central metal ion.

Lipids (Section 29.3) Substances that can be dissolved away from biological material by solvents that are nonpolar or slightly polar. The class is large and includes fats, oils, some vitamins and hormones, and certain constituents of the walls of cells.

London forces, dispersion forces (Section 11.1) Intermolecular forces brought about by attractions between instantaneous dipoles, which in turn are caused by the motion of electrons in the molecules.

Low-spin state (Section 26.5) A state in which the electron configuration of the d orbitals of the central metal ion of a complex has the minimum number of unpaired electrons.

M

Macromolecule (Section 28.10) A large, high molecular-weight molecule.

Magnetic orbital quantum number, m_l (Section 6.5) A quantum number that indicates the orientation of the orbital of the electron to which the value pertains. For a given value of l, m_l may have all the integral values from $+l$ to $-l$ (including 0). The number of m_l values for each l value is the number of orbitals in that subshell.

Magnetic spin quantum number, m_s (Section 6.5) A quantum number that refers to the relative spin of the electron to which the value pertains. Each orbital may hold two electrons of opposed spin ($+\frac{1}{2}$ and $-\frac{1}{2}$).

Markovnikov's rule (Section 28.5) The principal product of the addition of an unsymmetrical molecule to the double bond of an alkene is the compound in which the more positive part of the molecule bonds to the carbon atom of the double bond that originally had the larger number of hydrogen atoms.

Mass (Section 1.2) A measure of quantity of matter.

Mass number, A (Section 2.6) The number of protons and neutrons, taken together, in the nucleus of an atom.

Mass spectrometer (Section 2.8) An instrument used to determine the types of isotopes present in an element, the exact masses of these isotopes, and the relative amount of each isotope present.

Matte (Section 25.6) Impure cuprous sulfide, Cu_2S, obtained by smelting copper sulfide ores.

Matter (Section 1.2) Anything that occupies space and has mass.

Maxwell-Boltzmann distribution (Section 10.11) The way in which kinetic energy or molecular speed is distributed among the molecules of a gas.

Mean free path (Section 10.11) The average distance that a molecule travels between collisions with other gas molecules.

Melting point (Section 11.8) See freezing point.

Messenger RNA (Section 29.4) An RNA chain synthesized in the nucleus of a cell in such a way that the order of bases complements the order in a section of the DNA chain. Messenger RNA moves from the cell nucleus to the ribosomes where it directs, through its sequence of codons, the synthesis of a protein from amino acids.

Metabolism (Section 29.5) All the reactions that occur in a living organism.

Metal (Section 2.7) An element that has a characteristic luster, conducts heat and electricity well, and deforms without breaking when pounded; found in the periodic table to the left of the stepped, diagonal line.

Metallic conduction (Section 20.1) The conduction of electricity through a metal by electron displacement.

Metalloid, semimetal (Section 2.7) An element that is not clearly a metal or a nonmetal but that has properties of both; found in the periodic table near to the stepped, diagonal line.

Metallurgy (Section 25.5) The science of extracting metals from their ores and preparing these metals for use.

Metathesis reaction (Section 13.1) A reaction between two compounds in which cations and anions exchange partners.

Metric system (Section 1.3) A decimal system of measurement that is used in all scientific studies.

Mixture (Section 1.2) A sample of matter that consists of two or more pure substances, does not have a fixed composition, and may be separated into its components by physical means.

Moderator (Sections 27.7 and 27.8) A substance that serves to slow down neutrons produced by nuclear reactions when these fast neutrons are passed through it.

Molal boiling-point elevation constant, k_b (Section 12.8) The elevation of the boiling point of a solvent brought about by dissolving one mole of a nonvolatile, nondissociating solute in 1000 g of the solvent (a 1 m solution); the value of k_b is specific to the solvent considered.

Molal freezing-point depression constant, k_f (Section 12.8) The depression of the freezing point of a solvent brought about by dissolving one mole of a nonvolatile, nondissociating solute in 1000 g of the solvent (a 1 m solution); the value of k_f is specific to the solvent considered.

Molality, m (Section 10.6) A solution concentration; the number of moles of solute per one kilogram of solvent.

Molarity (Section 4.5) The number of moles of a substance (called a solute) dissolved in one liter of solution.

Mole (Section 3.4) The amount of substance that contains the same number of elementary entities as there are atoms in exactly 12 g of $^{12}_{6}C$; a collection of Avogadro's number of units.

Molecular formula (Section 3.1) A chemical formula for a molecular substance that gives the number and type of each atom present in a molecule of the substance.

Molecularity (Section 14.5) The number of reacting particles (atoms, molecules, or ions) that participate in a single step of a reaction mechanism. A step may be **unimolecular, bimolecular, or termolecular** depending on whether *one, two,* or *three* particles react in it.

Molecular orbital (Section 9.4) An orbital associated with a molecule rather than an atom.

Molecular weight (Section 3.3) The sum of the atomic weights of the atoms that constitute a molecule.

Molecule (Section 3.1) A particle formed from two or more atoms that are bound tightly together.

Mole fraction, *X* (Section 10.10) The ratio of the number of moles of a component in a mixture to the total number of moles present in the mixture.

Monatomic ion (Section 3.1) An ion that is formed from a single atom.

Monoprotic acid (Sections 13.4 and 13.6) An acid that can lose only one proton per molecule.

Monosaccharide (Section 29.2) A simple sugar; a molecule obtained from the hydrolysis of a polymeric carbohydrate.

Mutation (Section 29.4) A change in the DNA of a cell that ultimately results in an alteration of the proteins synthesized by that cell.

N

Native ore (Section 25.4) An ore in which a metal or a nonmetal occurs in elemental form (examples include: Ag, Au, Bi, and S).

Nernst equation (Section 20.9) The equation used to determine the emf of a cell in which the constituents are present in concentrations other than standard.

Net-ionic reaction (Section 13.1) A chemical equation that does not show spectator ions but includes only those species that are involved in the reaction.

Neutralization (Section 13.4) A reaction between an acid and a base or their oxides.

Neutrino (Section 27.3) An uncharged particle of vanishingly small mass that is ejected in the course of some radioactive processes from which it carries off energy.

Neutron (Section 2.4) A subatomic particle that has a mass of approximately 1.0087 u, is uncharged, and is found in the nucleus of an atom.

Neutron-capture reaction (Section 27.7) A nuclear reaction in which a target nucleus is bombarded with slow neutrons. No subsidiary particle is ejected and the net result is that the target nucleus captures an additional neutron.

Nitrogen cycle (Section 23.2) A group of natural and artificial processes by which nitrogen is constantly being removed from the atmosphere and returned to it.

Nitrogen fixation (Section 23.2) A process in which elemental nitrogen is converted into a nitrogen-containing compound.

Noble gases (Sections 2.7 and 24.9) The elements of group 0: helium, neon, argon, krypton, xenon, and radon.

Noble-gas ion (Sections 7.4 and 7.6) A cation or an anion that is isoelectronic with a noble gas; an s^2 or an s^2p^6 ion.

Nonbonding pair of electrons, lone pair of electrons (Section 9.2)

A pair of electrons on an atom in a covalent molecule or ion that is not involved in bonding.

Nonmetal (Section 2.7) An element that is not lustrous, is a poor conductor of heat and electricity, and is brittle in the solid state; found in the periodic table to the right of the stepped, diagonal line.

Nonstoichiometry (Section 11.16) A condition in which the composition of a crystal of a compound does not conform to the formula of the compound; for example, in crystals of FeO (which should contain one Fe^{2+} ion for every one O^{2-} ion according to the formula) there are more O^{2-} ions than Fe^{2+} ions.

Normality (Section 13.8) A solution concentration: the number of equivalents of solute per liter of solution.

Normal salt (Section 13.4) A salt of a polyprotic acid formed by the loss of all ionizable protons by the acid.

n-type semiconductor (Section 25.2) An extrinsic semiconductor produced by the addition of a donor impurity (which has a larger number of valence electrons than the atoms of the host crystal) to an intrinsic semiconductor.

Nuclear fission (Section 27.8) A process in which heavy nuclei are split into lighter nuclei.

Nuclear fusion (Section 27.9) A process in which very light nuclei are fused into heavier nuclei.

Nuclear reactor (Section 27.8) A reactor in which the controlled fission of a nuclear fuel serves as a source of energy.

Nucleic acid (Section 29.4) A high molecular-weight, long-chain polymer formed from nucleotides.

Nucleon (Sections 2.6 and 27.1) A proton or a neutron, both of which are found in the atomic nucleus.

Nucleophilic displacement (Section 16.5) A reaction in which a Lewis base displaces a second, weaker, Lewis base from an acid-base complex; a Lewis **base displacement.**

Nucleotide (Section 29.4) A unit of a nucleic acid formed from a phosphoric acid molecule, a five-carbon sugar molecule, and a molecule of a nitrogen-containing base.

Nucleus (Section 2.5) The small, dense, positively charged center of an atom that contains the protons and neutrons.

Nuclide (Section 27.1) A term used to refer to a species of atom characterized by its atomic number and mass number; the term **isotope** refers to one species of atom out of two or more that are of the same element and that have the same atomic number but different mass numbers.

O

Olefin (Section 28.2) An alkene.

Open hearth process (Section 25.7) A process in which pig iron is refined into steel. The oxidation of the impurities in the pig iron is accomplished by reaction with iron oxide and air.

Optical isomerism (Section 26.4) A type of isomerism in which the two isomers are mirror images that are not superimposable.

Orbit (Section 6.2) In the Bohr theory, an allowed state of an electron, characterized by a value of *n*.

Orbital (Section 6.4) An energy state for an electron characterized by three quantum numbers: *n, l,* and m_l. A given orbital may hold two electrons with opposed spin.

Order of a chemical reaction (Section 14.2) The sum of the exponents of the concentration terms in the rate equation for a reaction.

Ore (Section 25.4) A naturally occurring material from which one or more metals (or other chemical substances) can be profitably extracted.

Organic chemistry (Section 24.1) The chemistry of the hydrocarbons (compounds of carbon and hydrogen) and their derivatives.

Ortho, meta, and para isomers (Section 28.5) The three isomers of a disubstituted derivative of benzene. In the *ortho* isomer, the two substituents are on carbon atoms 1 and 2; in the *meta* isomer, 1 and 3; in the *para* isomer, 1 and 4.

Osmosis (Section 12.9) The process in which there is a net movement of solvent molecules through a semipermeable membrane separating two solutions in the direction of the more concentrated solution.

Ostwald process (Section 23.7) A commercial process for the manufacture of nitric acid; ammonia is catalytically oxidized to NO, the NO is reacted with O_2 to form NO_2, and the NO_2 is reacted with water to form HNO_3.

Overvoltage (Section 20.11) An excess voltage (over that theoretically calculated as necessary) that must be applied in certain electrolyses so that they proceed at appreciable rates.

Oxidation (Section 13.3) That part of an oxidation-reduction reaction characterized by electron loss or by an algebraic increase in oxidation number.

Oxidation number (Section 13.2) A positive or negative number (or zero) that is assigned to an atom in a compound according to arbitrary rules that take into account bond polarity. The concept is merely a convention.

Oxidation potential, $\mathscr{E}_{ox}$ (Section 20.7) A potential that corresponds to an oxidation half-reaction; an $\mathscr{E}_{ox}$ is numerically the same, but with the opposite sign, as the $\mathscr{E}_{red}$ for the corresponding reduction (the oxidation written in reverse order).

Oxidizing agent (Section 13.3) A substance that is reduced in a chemical reaction and that thereby causes the oxidation of another substance.

Oxyacid (Section 13.6) An acid composed of three elements with oxygen as one of the three.

Oxygen-carbon-dioxide cycle (Section 24.4) A group of natural and artificial processes by which O_2 and CO_2 are constantly being removed from the atmosphere and returned to it.

P

Pairing energy (Section 26.5) Energy required to pair two electrons in the same orbital.

Paramagnetic substance (Section 6.6) A substance that is drawn into a magnetic field, behavior that is characteristic of substances that contain unpaired electrons.

Parkes process (Section 25.7) A process for removing silver from impure lead; the silver is selectively dissolved in molten zinc.

Partial equation (Section 13.3) A chemical equation for a half reaction written to show electron loss or electron gain.

Partial ionic character (Section 8.2) A value (given as a percentage) that relates the polarity of a covalent bond to the polarity that would exist if the atoms were joined by an ionic bond.

Partial pressure (Section 10.10) The pressure that a component of a mixture of gases would exert if it were the only gas present in the volume under consideration.

Particle-particle reaction (Section 27.7) A nuclear reaction in which a target nucleus and a projectile particle form a compound nucleus that rapidly ejects a subsidiary particle and forms a product nucleus. Reactions are indicated: target nucleus (projectile, ejected particle) product nucleus; for example, $^{14}_{7}Na(\alpha, p)^{17}_{8}O$.

Pascal (Section 10.1) The SI unit of pressure; equal to the force of one newton (which is $1\ kg \cdot m/s^2$) acting on a square meter.

Peptide linkage (Section 29.1) The —C(O)NH— linkage formed when two amino acids combine. The amino group of one molecule joins, with the elimination of water, to the carboxyl group of another molecule.

Percent yield (Section 4.4) 100% times the actual yield divided by the theoretical yield.

Period (Section 2.7) A collection of elements that are arranged in a single horizontal row of the periodic table.

Periodic law (Section 2.7) The chemical and physical properties of the elements are periodic functions of increasing atomic number.

Peroxy acid (Section 22.12) An acid that contains a peroxide group (—O—O—) somewhere in the molecule.

pH (Section 17.3) The negative logarithm (base 10) of the concentration of $H^+(aq)$ ions in an aqueous solution; $pH = -\log[H^+]$.

Phase (Section 1.2) A physically distinct portion of matter that is uniform throughout in composition and properties.

Phase diagram (Section 11.10) A diagram that graphically presents the number and type of phases in which a chemical system exists under a given set of conditions of temperature and pressure.

Photochemical pollutants (Section 22.7) Air pollutants produced by a sequence of reactions that is initiated by sunlight.

Photon (Section 6.1) A quantum of radiant energy.

Photosynthesis (Section 24.4) The process by which plants make carbohydrates; CO_2 is removed from the air and O_2 is returned to it; the energy for the process is supplied by sunlight.

Pi bond (Section 9.4) A covalent bond in which electron density is concentrated in two regions above and below an axis joining the two bonded nuclei.

Pig iron (Section 25.6) An impure form of iron produced by the blast furnace.

pK (Section 17.6) The negative logarithm (base 10) of an equilibrium constant; $pK = -\log K$

pOH (Section 17.3) The negative logarithm (base 10) of the concentration of $OH^-(aq)$ ions in an aqueous solution; $pOH = -\log[OH^-]$

Polar covalent bond (Section 8.2) A covalent bond that has partial charges (δ^+ and δ^-) as a result of unequal sharing of bonding electrons.

Polyatomic ion (Section 3.1) An ion that is formed from two or more atoms.

Polyatomic molecule (Section 5.7) A molecule that contains more than two atoms.

Polymers (Section 28.10) Macromolecules that are formed from simpler molecules called **monomers.**

Polypeptide (Section 29.1) A protein; a macromolecule formed by the condensation of many amino acid molecules.

Polyprotic acid (Sections 13.4 and 13.6) An acid that can lose more than one proton per molecule.

Polysaccharide (Section 29.2) A carbohydrate molecule that contains many monosaccharide units; examples are starch and cellulose, both of which yield D-glucose upon hydrolysis.

Porphyrins (Section 26.1) Chelates derived from a quadridentate ligand that is a derivative of the porphin structure (see Figure 26.4); examples include hemoglobin and chlorophyll.

Positive rays (Section 2.3) Rays that consist of positive ions formed by the removal of electrons from atoms through the action of cathode rays in a cathode ray tube.

Positron emission, β^+ **decay** (Section 27.3) A type of radioactivity exhibited by some artificial nuclides in which a positron (a positive electron, given the symbol $_1^0e$) is ejected from a nucleus and in the process a proton is converted into a neutron.

$p\pi$-$d\pi$ bond (Section 9.6) A π bond formed by the overlap of a p orbital with a d orbital.

Precipitation (Section 13.1) The formation of an insoluble or a slightly soluble substance (called a **precipitate**) in an aqueous reaction.

Pressure (Section 10.1) Force per unit area.

Primary structure of a protein (Section 29.1) The sequence of amino acids in the protein chain.

Principal quantum number, n (Section 6.5) The quantum number that indicates the energy shell of the electron to which the value pertains. The values of n are positive integers: 1, 2, 3, . . .

Product (Section 4.1) A substance formed in a chemical reaction.

Protein (Section 29.1) A macromolecule formed from amino acids; a polypeptide.

Proton (Section 2.3) A subatomic particle that has a mass of approximately 1.0073 u, carries a unit positive charge, and is found in the nucleus of the atom.

p-type semiconductor (Section 25.2) An extrinsic semiconductor produced by adding an acceptor impurity (which has fewer valence electrons than the atoms of the host crystal) to an intrinsic semiconductor.

Q

Quantum (Section 6.1) A small, definite quantity of radiant energy. Planck's theory assumes that radiant energy is absorbed or emitted in these quanta. The energy of a quantum, E, is directly proportional to the frequency of the radiation, v, and the proportionality constant, h, is Planck's constant (6.6262 × 10^{-34} J·s).

Quaternary structure of a protein (Section 29.1) The number of protein chains and the way their tertiary structures are arranged in a complete protein.

R

Radioactive decay series (Section 27.6) A series of radioactive disintegrations that successively produce new radioactive nuclides until a nonradioactive nuclide is obtained.

Radioactivity (Section 2.5) The spontaneous emission of radioactive rays by an unstable atomic nucleus, which in the process is transformed into a different nucleus; radioactive substances that occur in nature emit alpha, beta, and gamma rays.

Radiocarbon dating (Section 27.5) A method of dating a carbon-containing object by counting the number of radioactive disintegrations of the $_6^{14}C$ present in a sample and calculating, by means of the half-life of this nuclide, the length of time for the object to achieve its present condition.

Raoult's law (Section 12.7) The partial pressure of vapor of a component of an ideal solution is equal to the mole fraction of the component in the solution times the vapor pressure of the pure component.

Rate constant (Section 14.2) The proportionality constant in a rate equation.

Rate-determining step (Section 14.5) The slowest step in a multistep reaction mechanism; the one that determines how fast the overall reaction proceeds.

Rate equation (Section 14.2) A mathematical equation that relates the rate of a chemical reaction to the concentrations of reactants.

Reactant (Section 4.1) A substance consumed in a chemical reaction.

Reaction intermediate (Section 14.4) A substance that is produced and used in the course of a chemical reaction and is, therefore, neither a reactant nor a product of the reaction.

Reaction mechanism (Section 14.5) The detailed description of the way a reaction occurs based on the behavior of atoms, molecules, or ions; may include more than one step.

Reaction quotient, Q (Section 15.2) A value, Q, obtained from the concentrations of the substances in a system capable of reaching an equilibrium state. The value is obtained by substituting the concentrations into an expression similar to that for the equilibrium constant, K_c. If Q is equal to K_c, the system is in equilibrium. If Q is smaller than K_c, the reaction will proceed to the right. If Q is greater than K_c, the reaction will proceed to the left.

Reaction rate (Section 14.1) The rate at which a reaction proceeds, expressed in terms of the increase in the concentration of a product per unit time or the decrease in the concentration of a reactant per unit time; value changes during the course of the reaction.

Reducing agent (Section 13.3) A substance that is oxidized in a chemical reaction and thereby causes the reduction of another substance.

Reduction (Section 13.3) That part of an oxidation-reduction reaction characterized by electron gain or by an algebraic decrease in oxidation number.

Reduction of an ore (Sections 25.5 and 25.6) A process in which a free metal is obtained from a metal compound found in an ore.

Reduction potential, $\mathscr{E}_{red}$ (Section 20.7) A potential that corresponds to a reduction half-reaction. If the half-reaction were reversed (written as an oxidation), the corresponding oxidation potential ($\mathscr{E}_{ox}$) would be numerically the same as the $\mathscr{E}_{red}$ but with the sign changed.

Refining (Sections 25.5 and 25.7) A process in which an impure metal is purified; in some cases, substances are added to give desired properties to the final product.

Representative element (Section 6.9) An element that belongs to an A group in the periodic table that we use (the one found inside the front cover of this book). For these elements, the differentiating electron added by the aufbau method is an s or a p electron added to the outermost shell.

Resonance (Section 8.6) A concept in which two or more Lewis structures are used to describe the structure of a covalent molecule or ion. The actual structure of the covalent species is said to be a **hybrid** of the Lewis structures, which are called **resonance forms.**

Ribonucleic acid, RNA (Section 29.4) A nucleic acid composed of nucleotides that contain ribose units as the sugar component.

Roasting of ores (Section 25.5) The process in which an ore is heated in air; used to convert sulfides and carbonates to oxides, which are more readily reduced to the free metal.

Root-mean-square speed (Section 10.11) The square root of the average of the squares of molecular speeds.

S

Salt (Section 13.4) A compound derived from the reaction of an acid and a base; it contains a cation from the base and an anion from the acid.

Salt bridge (Section 20.7) A tube filled with a concentrated solution of an electrolyte and connecting two half-cells of a voltaic cell; it conducts electric current between the half-cells while preventing their contents from mixing.

Salt effect (Section 18.1) The increase in solubility of a slightly soluble substance observed following the addition of another electrolyte to the solution.

Saponification (Section 29.3) The process in which a triglyceride or a mixture of triglycerides is heated with an aqueous solution of a base to yield glycerol and the salts of fatty acids (**soaps**).

Saturated hydrocarbon (Section 28.2) A hydrocarbon in which all the carbon-carbon bonds are single bonds; an alkane or a cycloalkane.

Scintillation counter (Section 27.5) A device that is used for the quantitative detection of radioactive emissions and that functions by counting the flashes of light given off by a fluorescent substance struck by these emissions.

Secondary structure of a protein (Section 29.1) The spatial arrangement of a protein chain, which includes the α-helix (a coiled arrangement similar to that of a spring) and the pleated sheet.

Second law of thermodynamics (Section 19.3) Every spontaneous change is accompanied by an increase in entropy.

Second-order reaction (Sections 14.2 and 14.3) A reaction for which the sum of the exponents of the concentration terms in the rate equation is 2; the rate equation has the form: $rate = k[A]^2$ or $rate = k[A][B]$.

Semiconductor (Sections 25.1 and 25.2) A material with a low electrical conductivity that increases markedly with increasing temperature (but still remains well below the level of the conductivities of conductors). In crystals of semiconductors, the forbidden energy zone is sufficiently narrow that electrons can be promoted from the valence band to the conduction band by heat.

Shielding (Section 7.1) The effect brought about by inner electrons in diminishing the nuclear charge experienced by outer electrons.

Sigma bond (Section 9.4) A covalent bond in which electron density is high in the region between the two nuclei and which is symmetrical about an axis joining the two bonded nuclei.

Significant figures (Section 1.4) Digits in a measurement that indicate the precision of the measurement. These figures include all those that are known with certainty plus one more, which is an estimate.

Silanes (Section 24.3) Compounds that contain only silicon and hydrogen.

Silver coulometer (Section 20.4) An electrolytic cell in which silver is plated out on a cathode placed in an electrical circuit to determine the number of coulombs that have passed through the circuit (by weighing the deposited silver).

Simple cubic unit cell (Section 11.12) A unit cell of a crystal that consists of a cube with identical constituent particles located at the corners.

s^2 ion (Sections 7.4 and 7.6) A noble-gas cation or an anion that has two electrons in an s orbital as the electronic configuration of its outer shell; these ions are isoelectronic with helium.

SI unit (Section 1.3) A unit that is used in the International System of Units. (*Le Système International d' Unitès*).

Slag (Section 25.6) A material that is formed from a flux and gangue in a smelting operation and therefore serves to remove the gangue.

Slow neutron (Section 27.7) A neutron, derived from a nuclear reaction, that has been slowed down by passage through a moderator; also called a **thermal neutron.**

Smelting (Section 25.6) A high-temperature reduction process in which a free metal is secured from its concentrated and purified ore.

Solubility product, K_{SP} (Section 18.1) The equilibrium constant for a system involving a slightly soluble substance in equilibrium with a saturated solution of its ions. The constant is the product of the ion concentrations with the concentrations raised to the powers indicated by the coefficients of the balanced chemical equation.

Solute (Section 4.5) A component of a solution that is present in an amount that is smaller than the amount of the solvent. The solute is said to be dissolved in the solvent.

Solution (Section 1.2) A mixture of two or more pure substances that is uniform throughout (homogeneous).

Solvent (Section 4.5) The component of a solution that is present in the largest amount or that determines the physical state of the solution.

Solvent-system acid (Section 16.6) A substance that yields the cation characteristic of the solvent.

Solvent-system base (Section 16.6) A substance that yields the anion characteristic of the solvent.

Solvent-system neutralization (Section 16.6) A reaction between an acid and a base that yields the solvent as one of the products.

Specific heat (Section 5.2) The amount of heat required to raise the temperature of 1 g of a substance by 1°C.

Spectator ion (Section 13.1) An ion that is present during the course of an aqueous reaction but one that does not take part in the reaction.

Spectrochemical series (Section 26.5) A series of ligands arranged in increasing order of the size of the splitting of d orbital energies, Δ_o, that they bring about.

Spectrum (Section 6.2) A pattern of light produced by the dispersal of a light beam into its component wavelengths. Since it consists of all wavelengths, white light produces a **continuous spectrum.** Light emitted by a substance in an excited state, however, produces a **line spectrum** in which only certain wavelengths appear.

Speed of light, c (Section 6.1) The speed at which the waves of all electromagnetic radiation travel in a vacuum; 2.9979×10^8 m/s.

$s^2 p^6$ ion (Section 7.4 and 7.6) A noble-gas cation or anion that has two electrons in an s orbital and six electrons in three p orbitals as the electronic configuration of its outer shell.

Spontaneous change (Section 19.4) A change that has a natural tendency of its own to occur without work being done on the system. Some spontaneous changes are very slow, however.

Spontaneous fission (Section 27.3) A process in which a heavy nucleus spontaneously splits up into two lighter nuclei and several neutrons; observed for nearly all nuclides that have mass numbers higher than 230.

Standard absolute entropy, $S°$ (Section 19.6) The entropy of a substance in its standard state; calculated on the basis of the third law of thermodynamics; expressed in J/(K·mol).

Standard electrode potential, $\mathscr{E}°$ (Secion 20.7) A half-cell potential (measured in volts) for a *reduction* relative to a standard hydrogen electrode, which is assigned a potential of zero; measured with all substances present in their standard states. Values are customarily listed for potentials measured at 25°C.

Standard emf (Section 20.6) The emf of a voltaic cell in which all reactants and products are present in their standard states; the standard state for an ion is approximately 1 M, for a gas is approximately 1 atm pressure, and for a solid or liquid is the pure solid or liquid.

Standard free energy of formation, $\Delta G_f°$ (Section 19.5) The free energy change for the process in which 1 mol of a compound in its standard state is made from its constituent elements in their standard states.

Standard hydrogen electrode (Section 20.7) A reference electrode in which hydrogen gas, at 1 atm pressure, is bubbled over a Pt electrode that is immersed in an acid solution containing $H^+(aq)$ ions at unit activity.

Standard solution (Section 13.7) A solution that has a known concentration of solute.

Standard temperature and pressure, STP (Section 10.5) 0°C (which is 273.15 K) and 1 atm pressure.

State function (Section 19.1) A function that depends upon the state of a system (defined by specifying properties such as temperature, pressure, and composition) and not on how that system arrived at that state; E, H, S, and G are state functions, q and w are not.

Steam reformer process (Section 21.2) An industrial process used to prepare hydrogen by the reaction of steam with a hydrocarbon.

Stereoisomers (Sections 26.4 and 28.2) Compounds that have the same molecular formula and are bonded in the same way but differ in the way that the constituent atoms are arranged in space. Two types exist. **Geometric isomers** (Section 28.2) in organic chemistry, are compounds that owe their existence to restricted rotation about a double bond. **Optical isomers** (discussed in Chapter 26, Section 26.4 and in Chapter 29, Section 29.1) are compounds that are mirror images and that are not superimposable.

Stoichiometry (Introduction to Chapter 3) The quantitative relationships between the elements that make up a compound and between the elements and compounds that are involved in a chemical reaction.

STP molar volume (Section 10.8) The volume of one mole of a gas at standard temperature and pressure; 22.414 L.

Strong acids and bases (Section 13.4) Acids and bases that are completely ionized in dilute aqueous solution.

Structural formula (Section 3.1) A chemical formula for a molecule in which a separate symbol is used to indicate each atom and dashes are used to show how these atoms are joined together.

Structural isomers (Sections 26.4 and 28.1) Compounds that have the same molecular formula but differ in the way the atoms are bonded together. Several types exist: **chain isomers** (Section 28.2) are compounds that differ in the arrangement of their carbon chains, **functional group isomers** (Section 28.6) are compounds that differ in their functional groups (for example, an alcohol and an ether), and **position isomers** (Section 28.2) are compounds that have the same carbon chains but differ in the position of a substituent (or a multiple bond) in that chain.

Sublimation (Section 11.10) The process in which a solid goes directly into a gas without going through the liquid state.

Subshell (Section 6.5) A division of an electron shell characterized by a particular value of l. An electron shell may hold one or more subshells and a given subshell may hold one or more orbitals. For the subshells, the designations $s, p, d, f, \ldots$ are used for $l = 0, 1, 2, 3, \ldots$ respectively.

Subsidiary quantum number, l (Section 6.5) A quantum number that indicates the type of subshell and the shape of the orbital of the electron to which the value pertains. In a given shell (indicated by n), l may have all the integral values in the series: 0, 1, 2, 3, $\ldots (n - 1)$.

Substance (Section 1.2) An element or a compound. Substances have fixed compositions and properties.

Substitution reaction (Section 28.5) A reaction in which an atom

or a group of atoms is substituted for another atom or group of atoms in a molecule.

Substrate (Section 29.5) A substance that undergoes reaction at the active site of an enzyme.

Superphosphate fertilizer (Section 23.8) A mixture of $Ca(H_2PO_4)_2$ and $CaSO_4$ used as a fertilizer and produced by the reaction of sulfuric acid and phosphate rock.

Surface tension (Section 11.3) A measure of the inward force on the surface of a liquid caused by intermolecular attractive forces.

Surroundings (Section 19.1) That part of nature not included within the boundaries of the system under consideration.

System (Section 19.1) That part of nature that is under consideration.

T

Temperature (Section 5.2) Degree of hotness or coldness; that property of matter that determines the direction in which heat flows spontaneously.

Tertiary structure of a protein (Section 29.1) The arrangement of secondary structures of proteins brought about by interactions between groups (other than the peptide linkage) in the protein chain.

t_{2g} orbitals (Section 26.5) A degenerate set of three d orbitals of the central metal ion of a complex.

Theoretical yield (Section 4.4) The maximum amount of product that can be obtained from a chemical reaction, as calculated by use of stoichiometric theory on the basis of the chemical equation for the reaction.

Thermite process (Section 25.6) The reduction of an oxide of a metal by aluminum; also called the **Goldschmidt process**.

Thermochemistry (Introduction to Chapter 5) Study of the energy changes that accompany chemical and physical changes.

Thermodynamics (Introduction to Chapter 19) The study of the energy changes that accompany chemical and physical changes.

Thermonuclear reaction (Section 27.8) A nuclear fusion reaction, so called because of the high temperatures required by this type of process.

Third law of thermodynamics (Section 19.6) At 0 K, the entropy of a perfect crystalline substance is zero.

Third-order reaction (Section 14.2) A reaction for which the sum of the exponents of the concentration terms in the rate equation is 3; the rate equation has the form: $rate = k[A]^3$, $rate = k[A]^2[B]$, or $rate = k[A][B][C]$.

Three-center bond (Section 24.7) A bond in which three atoms are bonded together by an electron pair in a single molecular orbital; found in boron and the hydrides of boron.

Titration (Section 13.7) A process in which a standard solution is reacted with a solution of unknown concentration in order to determine the unknown concentration.

Titration curve (Section 17.9) A graph that shows how the pH of a solution changes during the course of a titration; the pH is plotted against the volume of base or acid added.

torr (Section 10.1) A unit of pressure equivalent to the pressure that will support a column of mercury to a height of 1 mm; 1/760th of an atmosphere.

Transfer RNA (Section 29.4) The smallest type of nucleic acid found in the cell. A particular transfer RNA carries a specific amino acid and has an anticodon that corresponds to this amino acid.

Transition element (Sections 6.7 and 6.9) An element that is found in a B group of the periodic table that we use (the one found inside the front cover of this book). For these elements, the differentiating electron added by the aufbau method is a *d* electron added to the shell that is next to the outermost shell.

Transition state theory (Section 14.4) A theory that assumes that reacting particles must assume a specific arrangement, called a transition state, before they can form the products of the reaction.

Transuranium element (Section 27.7) The elements following uranium (atomic number, 92) in the periodic table.

Triglyceride (Section 29.3) A fat or an oil; an ester formed from 1 mol of glycerol and 3 mol of fatty acids (which may be alike or different).

Triple point (Section 11.10) The temperature and pressure at which a substance can exist simultaneously as a solid, a liquid, and a gas in equilibrium with each other.

Turnover number (Section 29.5) The number of moles of reactant transformed per unit time by the action of 1 mol of an enzyme.

U

Uncertainty principle (Section 6.4) It is impossible to determine, simultaneously, the exact position and the exact momentum (mass times velocity, *mv*) of an electron.

Unit cell (Section 11.12) The smallest part of a crystal that will reproduce the crystal when repeated in three dimensions.

Unit electrical charge, *e* (Section 2.2) 1.6022×10^{-19} C. The magnitude of the charge of the proton and electron; the proton has a unit *positive* charge and the electron has a unit *negative* charge.

Unsaturated hydrocarbon (Section 28.2 and 28.3) A hydrocarbon that contains one or more carbon-carbon multiple bonds.

V

Valence band (Section 25.1) A band in a metallic crystal that contains the valence electrons of the metal.

Valence-bond theory (Section 9.3) A theory that assumes that a covalent bond is formed by the overlap of two atomic orbitals each of which contains an unpaired electron.

Valence electrons (Section 6.6) The electrons found in the outermost shell in the ground state of an atom of a representative element.

Valence-shell electron-pair repulsion theory (Section 9.2) A theory that permits the prediction of the shape of a covalent molecule or ion on the basis of repulsions between the bonding and nonbonding electron pairs in the valence shell of the central atom.

Van Arkel process (Section 25.7) A method for the purification of certain metals by the formation and subsequent thermal decomposition of an iodide of the metal.

van der Waals equation (Section 10.13) An equation of state for gases; a modification of the ideal gas equation that takes into account intermolecular attractions and the volumes that gas molecules occupy.

van't Hoff factor, *i* (Section 12.12) The ratio of a measured colligative property for a solution (boiling-point elevation, freezing-point depression, or osmotic pressure) to the value calculated for that property on the assumption that the solute is a nonelectrolyte.

Vapor pressure (Section 11.5) The pressure of vapor in equilibrium with a pure liquid or a pure solid at a given temperature.

Viscosity (Section 11.3) A property of liquids; resistance to flow.

Voltaic cell (Section 20.5) A cell that uses a chemical reaction to produce electrical energy; also called a **galvanic cell**.

Volumetric analysis (Section 13.7) A chemical analysis that is based on the measurement of the volume of a solution.

W

Water dissociation constant (Section 17.2) The product of the concentration of $H^+(aq)$ and the concentration of $OH^-(aq)$ in any aqueous system; at 25°C, $K_w = [H^+][OH^-] = 1.0 \times 10^{-14}$.

Water gas (Section 21.2) A mixture of carbon monoxide and hydrogen produced industrially by the reaction of steam and coke.

Wave function, (Section 6.4) A solution to the Schrödinger wave equation; it describes an orbital. The square of the wave function, ψ^2, at any point is proportional to the electron charge density or the probability of finding the electron at that point.

Wavelength (Section 6.1) The distance between two similar points on two successive waves of electromagnetic radiation.

Weak acids and bases (Section 13.4) Acids and bases that are only partly dissociated in water solution.

Weight (Section 1.2) The gravitational force of attraction exerted by the earth on a body.

Wilson cloud chamber (Section 27.5) A device that enables the path of ionizing radiation to be seen as a cloud track formed by condensation of water vapor on the ions.

X

X-ray diffraction (Section 11.13) A method of determining the structure of a crystal by directing X rays at the crystal and measuring the angles at which the rays are scattered (or reflected).

Z

Zero-order reaction (Sections 14.2 and 14.3) A reaction for which the rate is a constant value that is independent of concentration; the rate equation for a zero-order reaction contains no concentration term (the concentration term would be raised to the zero power) and has the form: *rate = k*.

Zone of stability (Section 27.1) A zone in a graph of number of neutrons *versus* number of protons in which points that represent stable nuclides fall.

Zone refining (Section 25.7) A process used to purify certain metals in which a heated zone is caused to move along a rod of the impure metal. The impurities are swept along in the molten zone to one end of the rod.

Zwitterion (Section 29.1) A form of an amino acid brought about by internal neutralization; the proton of the —COOH group moves to the —NH₂ group so that —COO⁻ and —NH₃⁺ form.

INDEX

A reference to an *illustration* is marked with an *i* following the page number, one to a *definition* is marked with a *d*, and one to a table is marked with a *t*.

A reference to an *illustration* is marked with an *i* following the page number, one to a *definition* is marked with a *d*, and one to a table is marked with a *t*.

A reference to an *illustration* is marked with an *i* following the page number, one to a *definition* is marked with a *d*, and one to a table is marked with a *t*.

A reference to an *illustration* is marked with an *i* following the page number, one to a *definition* is marked with a *d*, and one to a table is marked with a *t*.